W9-CSF-716

CHILTON'S ELECTRONIC ENGINE CONTROLS CODE MANUAL

Vice President & General Manager John P. Kushnerick
Editor-In-Chief Kerry A. Freeman, S.A.E.
Managing Editor Dean F. Morgantini, S.A.E. □ **Managing Editor** David H. Lee, A.S.E., S.A.E.
Senior Editor Richard J. Rivele, S.A.E. □ **Senior Editor** Nick D'Andrea **Senior Editor** Ron Webb
Project Manager Peter M. Conti, Jr. □ **Project Manager** Ken Grabowski, A.S.E.
Project Manager Richard T. Smith
Service Editors Lawrence C. Braun, S.A.E., A.S.C., Thomas B. Dallett, Robert E. Doughten,
Thomas G. Gaeta, Michael L. Grady, Martin J. Gunther, Steve Horner, Neil Leonard, A.S.E.,
Robert McAnally, Steven Morgan, Michael J. Randazzo, James B. Steele,
Larry E. Stiles, Jim Taylor, Anthony Tortorici, A.S.E., S.A.E.
Editorial Consultants Edward K. Shea, S.A.E., Stan Stephenson

Production Manager W. Calvin Settle, Jr., S.A.E
Assistant Production Manager Andrea Steiger
Mechanical Artist Lorraine Martinelli
Special Projects Peter Kaprielyan

Sales Director Albert M. Kushnerick □ **Assistant** Jacquelyn T. Powers
Regional Sales Managers Joseph Andrews, Jr., David Flaherty, Larry W. Marshall

OFFICERS
President Gary R. Ingersoll
Senior Vice President, Book Publishing & Research Ronald A. Hoxter

CHILTON BOOK COMPANY

ONE OF THE **ABC PUBLISHING COMPANIES**,
A PART OF **CAPITAL CITIES/ABC, INC.**
Manufactured in USA   ©1990 Chilton Book Company ● Chilton Way, Radnor, Pa. 19089
ISBN 0-8019-8051-8   1234567890   0987654321

SAFETY NOTICE

Proper service and repair procedures are vital to the safe, reliable operation of all motor vehicles, as well as the personal safety of those performing repairs. This manual outlines procedures for servicing and repairing vehicles using safe, effective methods. The procedures contain many NOTES, CAUTIONS and WARNINGS which should be followed along with standard safety procedures to eliminate the possibilty of personal injury or improper service which could damage the vehicle or compromise its safety.

It is important to note that the repair procedures and techniques, tools and parts for servicng motor vehicles, as well as the skill and experience of the individual performing the work vary widely. It is not possible to anticipate all of the conceivable ways or conditions under which vehicles may be serviced, or to provide cautions as to all of the possible hazards that may result. Standard and accepted safety precautions and equipment should be used when handling toxic or flammable fluids, and safety goggles or other protection should be used during cutting, grinding, chiseling, prying, or any other process that can cause material removal or projectiles.

Some procedures require the use of tools specially designed for a specific purpose. Before substituting another tool or procedure, you must be completely satisfied that neither your personal safety, nor the performance of the vehicle will be endangered

Troubleshooting and Diagnosis

INDEX

TROUBLESHOOTING AND DIAGNOSIS

Diagnostic Equipment and Special Tools

While we may think that with no moving parts, electronic components should never wear out, in the real world malfunctions do occur. The problem is that any computer-based system is extremely sensitive to electrical voltages and cannot tolerate careless or haphazard testing or service procedures. An inexperienced individual can literally do major damage looking for a minor problem by using the wrong kind of test equipment or connecting test leads or connectors with the ignition switch ON. Therefore, when selecting test equipment, make sure the manufacturers instructions state that the tester is compatible with whatever type of electronic control system is being serviced. Read all instructions carefully and double check all test points before installing probes or making any connections.

The following section outlines basic diagnosis techniques for dealing with computerized engine control systems. Along with a general explanation of the various types of test equipment available to aid in servicing modern electronic automotive systems, basic repair techniques for wiring harnesses and connectors is given. Read the basic information before attempting any repairs or testing on any computerized system, to provide the background of information necessary to avoid the most common and obvious mistakes that can cost both time and money. Likewise, the individual system sections for engine controls, fuel injection and feedback carburetors should be read from the beginning to the end before any repairs or diagnosis is attempted. Although the replacement and testing procedures are simple in themselves, the systems are not, and unless one has a thorough understanding of all components and their function within a particular fuel injection system (for example), the logical test sequence these systems demand cannot be followed. Minor malfunctions can make a big difference, so it is important to know how each component affects the operation of the overall electronic system to find the ultimate cause of a problem without replacing good components unnecessarily. It is not enough to use the correct test equipment; the test equipment must be used correctly.

Safety Precautions

CAUTION
Whenever working on or around any computer-based microprocessor control system, always observe these general precautions to prevent the possibility of personal injury or damage to electronic components:

• Never install or remove battery cables with the key ON or the engine running. Jumper cables should be connected with the key OFF to avoid power surges that can damage electronic control units. Engines equipped with computer controlled systems should avoid both giving and getting jump starts due to the possibility of serious damage to components from arcing in the engine compartment when connections are made with the ignition ON.

• Always remove the battery cables before charging the battery. Never use a high-output charger on an installed battery or attempt to use any type of "hot shot" (24 volt) starting aid.

• Exercise care when inserting test probes into connectors to insure good connections without damaging the connector or spreading the pins. Always probe connectors from the rear (wire) side, NOT the pin side, to avoid accidental shorting of terminals during test procedures.

• Never remove or attach wiring harness connectors with the ignition switch ON, especially to an electronic control unit.

• Do not drop any components during service procedures and never apply 12 volts directly to any component (like a solenoid or relay) unless instructed specifically to do so. Some component electrical windings are designed to safely handle only 4 or 5 volts and can be destroyed in seconds if 12 volts are applied directly to the connector.

• Remove the electronic control unit if the vehicle is to be placed in an environment where temperatures exceed approximately 176°F (80°C), such as a paint spray booth or when arc- or gas-welding near the control unit location in the car.

Organized Troubleshooting

When diagnosing a specific problem, organized troubleshooting is a must. The complexity of a modern automobile demands that you approach any problem in a logical, organized manner. There are certain troubleshooting techniques that are standard:

1. Establish when the problem occurs. Does the problem appear only under certain conditions? Were there any noises, odors, or other unusual symptoms? Make notes on any symptoms found, including warning lights and trouble codes, if applicable.

2. Isolate the problem area. To do this, make some simple tests and observations; then eliminate the systems that are working properly. Check for obvious problems such as broken wires or split or disconnected vacuum hoses. Always check the obvious before assuming something complicated is the cause.

3. Test for problems systematically to determine the cause once the problem area is isolated. Are all the components functioning properly? Is there power going to electrical switches and motors? Is there vacuum at vacuum switches and/or actuators? Is there a mechanical problem such as bent linkage or loose mounting screws? Doing careful, systematic checks will often turn up most causes on the first inspection without wasting time checking components that have little or no relationship to the problem.

4. Test all repairs after the work is done to make sure that the problem is fixed. Some causes can be traced to more than one component, so a careful verification of repair work is important to pick up additional malfunctions that may cause a problem to reappear or a different problem to arise. A blown fuse, for example, is a simple problem that may require more than just replacing a fuse. If you don't look for a problem that caused a fuse to blow, a shorted wire may go undetected.

The diagnostic tree charts are designed to help solve problems by leading the user through closely defined conditions and tests so that only the most likely components, vacuum and electrical circuits are checked for proper operation when troubleshooting a particular malfunction. By using the trouble trees to eliminate those systems and components which normally will not cause the condition described, a problem can be isolated within one or more systems or circuits without wasting time on unnecessary testing. Experience has shown that most problems tend to be the result of a fairly simple and obvious cause, such as loose or corroded connectors or air leaks in the intake system. A careful inspection of components during testing is essential to quick and accurate troubleshooting. Frequent references to special test equipment will be found in the text and in the diagnosis charts. These devices or compatible equivalents are necessary to perform some of the more complicated test procedures listed, but many components can be functionally tested with the quick checks outlined in the "On-Car Service" procedures. Aftermarket testers are available from a variety of sources, as well as from the vehicle manufacturer, but care should be taken that any test equipment being used is designed to diagnose that particular system accurately without damaging the control unit (ECU) or components being tested.

NOTE: Pinpointing the exact cause of trouble in an electrical system can sometimes only be done using special test equipment. The following describes commonly used test equipment and explains how to put it to best use in diagnosis. In addition to the information covered below, the manufacturer's instructions booklet provided with the tester should be read and clearly understood before attempting any test procedures.

Jumper Wires

Jumper wires are simple, yet extremely valuable pieces of test equipment. Jumper wires are merely wires that are used to bypass sections of a circuit. The simplest type of jumper wire is merely a length of multistrand wire with an alligator clip at each end. Jumper wires are usually fabricated from lengths of standard automotive wire and whatever type of connector (alligator clip, spade connector or pin connector) that is required for the particular vehicle being tested. The well-equipped tool box will have several different styles of jumper wires in several different lengths. Some jumper wires are made with three or more terminals coming from a common splice for special-purpose testing. In cramped, hard-to-reach areas it is advisable to have insulated boots over the jumper wire terminals in order to prevent accidental grounding, sparks, and possible fire, especially when testing fuel system components.

Jumper wires are used primarily to locate open electrical circuits, on either the ground (–) side of the circuit or on the hot (+) side. If an electrical component fails to operate, connect the jumper wire between the component and a good ground. If the component operates only with the jumper installed, the ground circuit is open. If the ground circuit is good, but the component does not operate, the circuit between the power feed and component is open. You can sometimes connect the jumper wire directly from the battery to the hot terminal of the component, but first make sure the component uses 12 volts in operation. Some electrical components, such as fuel injectors, are designed to operate on about 4 volts and running 12 volts directly to the injector terminals can burn out the wiring. By inserting an in-line fuseholder between a set of test leads, a fused jumper wire can be used for bypassing open circuits. Use a 5 amp fuse to provide protection against voltage spikes. When in doubt, use a voltmeter to check the voltage input to the component and measure how much voltage is being applied normally. By moving the jumper wire successively back from the lamp toward the power source, you can isolate the area of the circuit where the open is located. When the component stops functioning, or the power is cut off, the open is in the segment of wire between the jumper and the point previously tested.

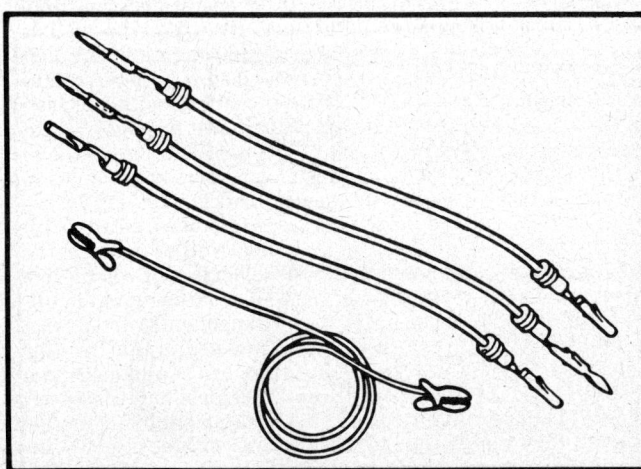

Typical jumper wires with various terminal ends

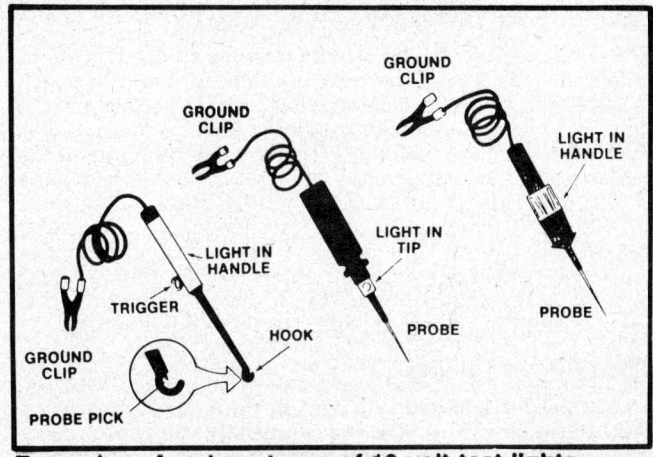

Examples of various types of 12 volt test lights

CAUTION

Never use jumpers made from wire that is of lighter gauge than used in the circuit under test. If the jumper wire is of too small gauge, it may overheat and possibly melt. Never use jumpers to bypass high-resistance loads (such as motors) in a circuit. Bypassing resistances, in effect, creates a short circuit which may, in turn, cause damage and fire. Never use a jumper for anything other than temporary bypassing of components in a circuit.

---

12 Volt Test Light

The 12 volt test light is used to check circuits and components while electrical current is flowing through them. It is used for voltage and ground tests. Twelve volt test lights come in different styles but all have three main parts; a ground clip, a probe, and a light. The most commonly used 12 volt test lights have pick-type probes. To use a 12 volt test light, connect the ground clip to a good ground and probe wherever necessary with the pick. The pick should be sharp so that it can penetrate wire insulation to make contact with the wire, without making a large hole in the insulation. The wrap-around light is handy in hard to reach areas or where it is difficult to support a wire to push a probe pick into it. To use the wrap around light, hook the wire to be probed with the hook and pull the trigger. A small pick will be forced through the wire insulation into the wire core.

CAUTION

Do not use a test light to probe electronic ignition spark plug or coil wires. Never use a pick-type test light to probe wiring on computer controlled systems unless specifically instructed to do so.

Like the jumper wire, the 12 volt test light is used to isolate opens in circuits. But, whereas the jumper wire is used to bypass the open to operate the load, the 12 volt test light is used to locate the presence of voltage in a circuit. If the test light glows, you know that there is power up to that point; if the 12 volt test light does not glow when its probe is inserted into the wire or connector, you know that there is an open circuit (no power). Move the test light in successive steps back toward the power source until the light in the handle does glow. When it does glow, the open is between the probe and point previously probed.

NOTE: The test light does not detect that 12 volts (or any particular amount of voltage) is present; it only detects that some voltage is present. It is advisable before using the test light to touch its terminals across the battery posts to make sure the light is operating properly.

Self-Powered Test Light

The self-powered test light usually contains a 1.5 volt penlight battery. One type of self-powered test light is similar in design to the 12 volt test light. This type has both the battery and the light in the handle and pick-type probe tip. The second type has the light toward the open tip, so that the light illuminates the contact point. The self-powered test light is dual-purpose piece of test equipment. It can be used to test for either open or short circuits when power is isolated from the circuit (continuity test). A powered test light should not be used on any computer controlled system or component unless specifically instructed to do so. Many engine sensors can be destroyed by even this small amount of voltage applied directly to the terminals.

Open Circuit Testing

To use the self-powered test light to check for open circuits, first isolate the circuit from the vehicle's 12 volt power source by disconnecting the battery or wiring harness connector. Connect the test light ground clip to a good ground and probe sections of the circuit sequentially with the test light. (start from either end of the circuit). If the light is out, the open is between the probe and the circuit ground. If the light is on, the open is between the probe and end of the circuit toward the power source.

Short Circuit Testing

By isolating the circuit both from power and from ground, and using a self-powered test light, you can check for shorts to ground in the circuit. Isolate the circuit from power and ground. Connect the test light ground clip to a good ground and probe any easy-to-reach test point in the circuit. If the light comes on, there is a short somewhere in the circuit. To isolate the short, probe a test point at either end of the isolated circuit (the light should be on). Leave the test light probe connected and open connectors, switches, remove parts, etc., sequentially, until the light goes out. When the light goes out, the short is between the last circuit component opened and the previous circuit opened.

NOTE: The 1.5 volt battery in the test light does not provide much current. A weak battery may not provide enough power to illuminate the test light even when a complete circuit is made (especially if there are high resistances in the circuit). Always make sure that the test battery is strong. To check the battery, briefly touch the ground clip to the probe; if the light glows brightly the battery is strong enough for testing. Never use a self-powered test light to perform checks for opens or shorts when power is applied to the electrical system under test. The 12-volt vehicle power will quickly burn out the 1.5 volt light bulb in the test light.

Voltmeter

A voltmeter is used to measure voltage at any point in a circuit, or to measure the voltage drop across any part of a circuit. It can also be used to check continuity in a wire or circuit by indicating current flow from one end to the other. Voltmeters usually have various scales on the meter dial and a selector switch to allow the selection of different voltages. The voltmeter has a positive and a negative lead. To avoid damage to the meter, always connect the negative lead to the negative (–) side of circuit (to ground or nearest the ground side of the circuit) and connect the positive lead to the positive (+) side of the circuit (to the power source or the nearest power source). Note that the negative voltmeter lead will always be black and that the positive voltmeter will always be some color other than black (usually red). Depending on how the voltmeter is connected into the circuit, it has several uses.

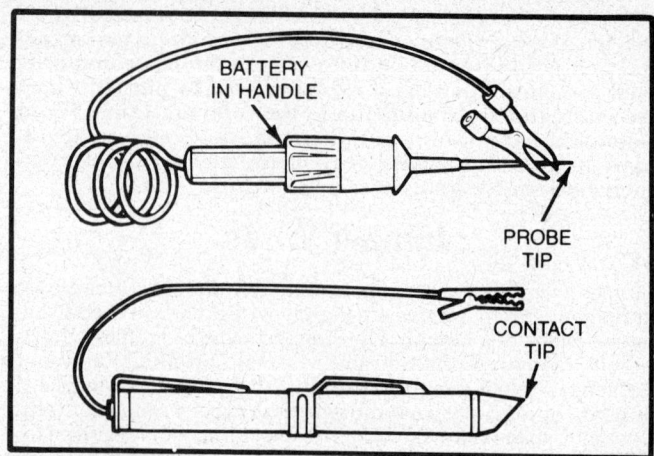

Two types of self-powered test lights

A voltmeter can be connected either in parallel or in series with a circuit and it has a very high resistance to current flow. When connected in parallel, only a small amount of current will flow through the voltmeter current path; the rest will flow through the normal circuit current path and the circuit will work normally. When the voltmeter is connected in series with a circuit, only a small amount of current can flow through the circuit. The circuit will not work properly, but the voltmeter reading will show if the circuit is complete or not.

Available Voltage Measurement

Set the voltmeter selector switch to the 20V position and connect the meter negative lead to the negative post of the battery. Connect the positive meter lead to the positive post of the battery and turn the ignition switch ON to provide a load. Read the voltage on the meter or digital display. A well-charged battery should register over 12 volts. If the meter reads below 11.5 volts, the battery power may be insufficient to operate the electrical system properly. This test determines voltage available from the battery and should be the first step in any electrical trouble diagnosis procedure. Many electrical problems, especially on computer controlled systems, can be caused by a low state of charge in the battery. Excessive corrosion at the battery cable terminals can cause a poor contact that will prevent proper charging and full battery current flow.

Normal battery voltage is 12 volts when fully charged. When the battery is supplying current to one or more circuits it is said to be "under load". When everything is off the electrical system is under a "no-load" condition. A fully charged battery

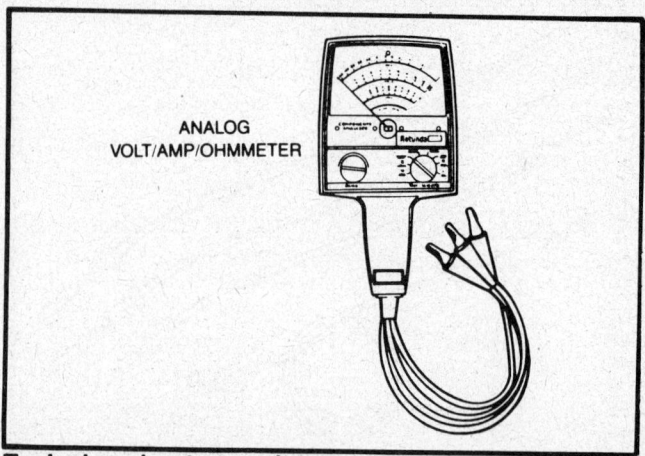

Typical analog-type voltmeter

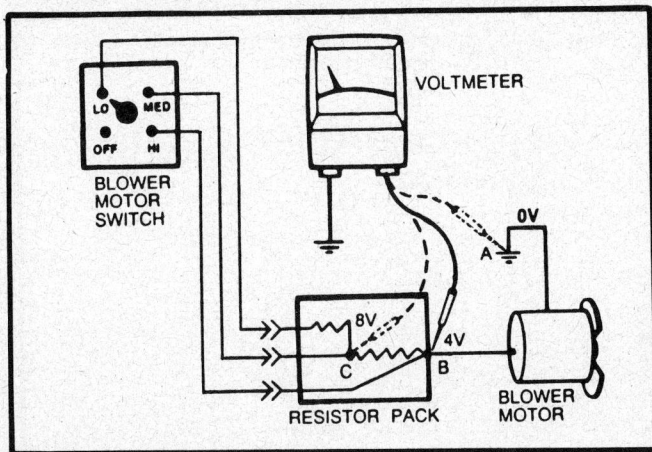

Measuring available voltage in a blower circuit

may show about 12.5 volts at no load; will drop to 12 volts under medium load; and will drop even lower under heavy load. If the battery is partially discharged the voltage decrease under heavy load may be excessive, even though the battery shows 12 volts or more at no load. When allowed to discharge further, the battery's available voltage under load will decrease more severely. For this reason, it is important that the battery be fully charged during all testing procedures to avoid errors in diagnosis and incorrect test results.

VOLTAGE DROP

When current flows through a resistance, the voltage beyond the resistance is reduced (the larger the current, the greater the reduction in voltage). When no current is flowing, there is no voltage drop because there is no current flow. All points in the circuit which are connected to the power source are at the same voltage as the power source. The total voltage drop always equals the total source voltage. In a long circuit with many connectors, a series of small, unwanted voltage drops due to corrosion at the connectors can add up to a total loss of voltage which impairs the operation of the normal loads in the circuit.

Indirect Computation of Voltage Drops

1. Set the voltmeter selector switch to the 20 volt position.
2. Connect the meter negative lead to a good ground.
3. Probe all resistances in the circuit with the positive meter lead.
4. Operate the circuit in all modes and observe the voltage readings.

Direct Measurement of Voltage Drops

1. Set the voltmeter switch to the 20 volt position.
2. Connect the voltmeter negative lead to the ground side of the resistance load to be measured.
3. Connect the positive lead to the positive side of the resistance or load to be measured.
4. Read the voltage drop directly on the 20 volt scale.

Too high a voltage indicates too high a resistance. If, for example, a blower motor runs too slowly, you can determine if there is too high a resistance in the resistor pack. By taking voltage drop readings in all parts of the circuit, you can isolate the problem. Too low a voltage drop indicates too low a resistance. If, for example, a blower motor runs too fast in the MED and/or LOW position, the problem can be isolated in the resistor pack by taking voltage drop readings in all parts of the circuit to locate a possibly shorted resistor. The maximum allowable voltage drop under load is critical, especially if there is

more than one high resistance problem in a circuit because all voltage drops are cumulative. A small drop is normal due to the resistance of the conductors.

High Resistance Testing

1. Set the voltmeter selector switch to the 4 volt position.
2. Connect the voltmeter positive lead to the positive post of the battery.
3. Turn on the headlights and heater blower to provide a load.
4. Probe various points in the circuit with the negative voltmeter lead.
5. Read the voltage drop on the 4 volt scale. Some average maximum allowable voltage drops are:
   FUSE PANEL – 7 volts
   IGNITION SWITCH – 5 volts
   HEADLIGHT SWITCH – 7 volts
   IGNITION COIL (+) – 5 volts
   ANY OTHER LOAD – 1.3 volts

NOTE: Voltage drops are all measured while a load is operating; without current flow, there will be no voltage drop.

Ohmmeter

The ohmmeter is designed to read resistance (ohms) in a circuit or component. Although there are several different styles of ohmmeters, all will usually have a selector switch which permits the measurement of different ranges of resistance (usually the selector switch allows the multiplication of the meter reading by 10, 100, 1000, and 10,000). A calibration knob al-

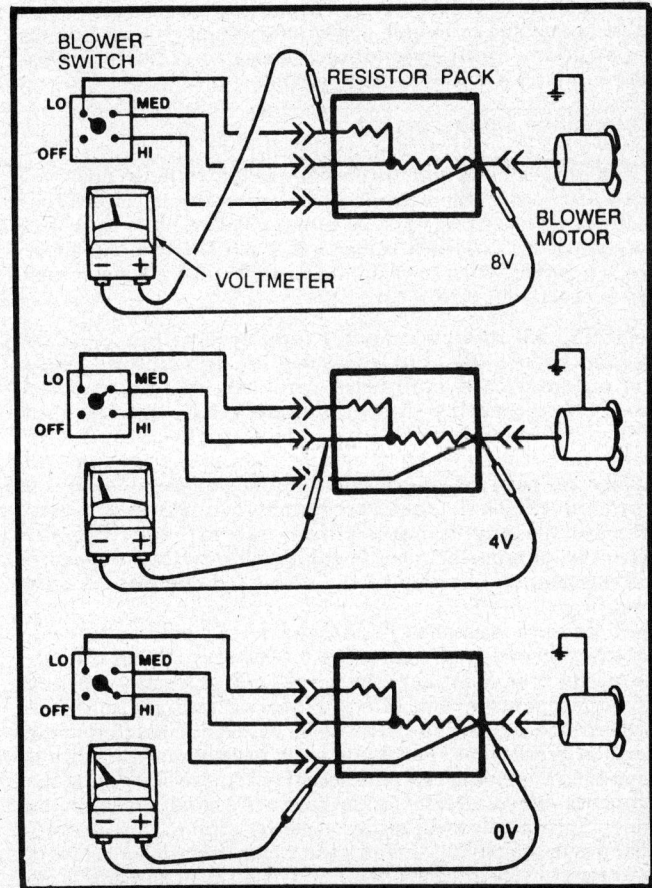

Direct measurement of voltage drops in a circuit

lows the meter to be set at zero for accurate measurement. Since all ohmmeters are powered by an internal battery (usually 9 volts), the ohmmeter can be used as a self-powered test light. When the ohmmeter is connected, current from the ohmmeter flows through the circuit or component being tested. Since the ohmmeter's internal resistance and voltage are known values, the amount of current flow through the meter depends on the resistance of the circuit or component being tested.

The ohmmeter can be used to perform continuity test for opens or shorts (either by observation of the meter needle or as a self-powered test light), and to read actual resistance in a circuit. It should be noted that the ohmmeter is used to check the resistance of a component or wire while there is no voltage applied to the circuit. Current flow from an outside voltage source (such as the vehicle battery) can damage the ohmmeter, so the circuit or component should be isolated from the vehicle electrical system before any testing is done. Since the ohmmeter uses its own voltage source, either lead can be connected to any test point.

NOTE: When checking diodes or other solid state components, the ohmmeter leads can only be connected one way in order to measure current flow in a single direction. Make sure the positive (+) and negative (-) terminal connections are as described in the test procedures to verify the one-way diode operation.

In using the meter for making continuity checks, do not be concerned with the actual resistance readings. Zero resistance, or any resistance readings, indicate continuity in the circuit. Infinite resistance indicates an open in the circuit. A high resistance reading where there should be none indicates a problem in the circuit. Checks for short circuits are made in the same manner as checks for open circuits except that the circuit must be isolated from both power and normal ground. Infinite resistance indicates no continuity to ground, while zero resistance indicates a dead short to ground.

Resistance Measurement

The batteries in an ohmmeter will weaken with age and temperature, so the ohmmeter must be calibrated or "zeroed" before taking measurements. To zero the meter, place the selector switch in its lowest range and touch the two ohmmeter leads together. Turn the calibration knob until the meter needle is exactly on zero.

NOTE: All analog (needle) type ohmmeters must be zeroed before use, but some digital ohmmeter models are automatically calibrated when the switch is turned on. Self-calibrating digital ohmmeters do not have an adjusting knob, but it's a good idea to check for a zero readout before use by touching the leads together. All computer controlled systems require the use of a digital ohmmeter with at least 10 megohms impedance for testing. Before any test procedures are attempted, make sure the ohmmeter used is compatible with the electrical system, or damage to the on-board computer could result.

To measure resistance, first isolate the circuit from the vehicle power source by disconnecting the battery cables or the harness connector. Make sure the key is OFF when disconnecting any components or the battery. Where necessary, also isolate at least one side of the circuit to be checked to avoid reading parallel resistances. Parallel circuit resistances will always give a lower reading than the actual resistance of either of the branches. When measuring the resistance of parallel circuits, the total resistance will always be lower than the smallest resistance in the circuit. Connect the meter leads to both sides of the circuit (wire or component) and read the actual measured ohms on the meter scale. Make sure the selector switch is set to

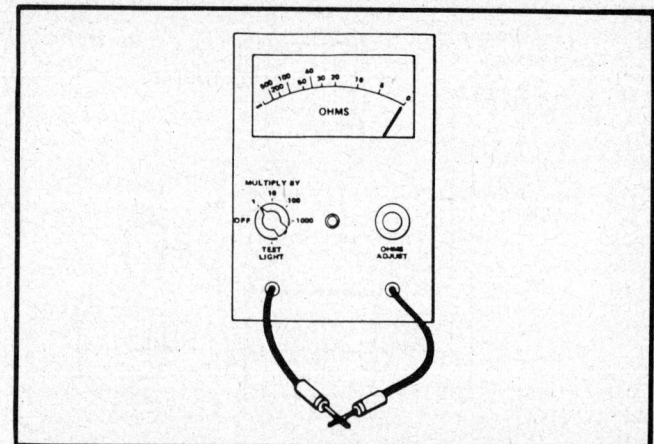

Analog ohmmeters must be calibrated before use by touching the probes together and adjusting the knob

the proper ohm scale for the circuit being tested to avoid misreading the ohmmeter test value.

CAUTION

Never use an ohmmeter with power applied to the circuit. Like the self-powered test light, the ohmmeter is designed to operate on its own power supply. The normal 12 volt automotive electrical system current could damage the meter.

Ammeters

An ammeter measures the amount of current flowing through a circuit in units called amperes or amps. Amperes are units of electron flow which indicate how fast the electrons are flowing through the circuit. Since Ohm's Law dictates that current flow in a circuit is equal to the circuit voltage divided by the total circuit resistance, increasing voltage also increases the current level (amps). Likewise, any decrease in resistance will increase the amount of amps in a circuit. At normal operating voltage, most circuits have a characteristic amount of amperes, called "current draw" which can be measured using an ammeter. By referring to a specified current draw rating, measuring the amperes, and comparing the two values, one can determine what is happening within the circuit to aid in diagnosis. An open circuit, for example, will not allow any current to flow so the ammeter reading will be zero. More current flows through a heavily loaded circuit or when the charging system is operating.

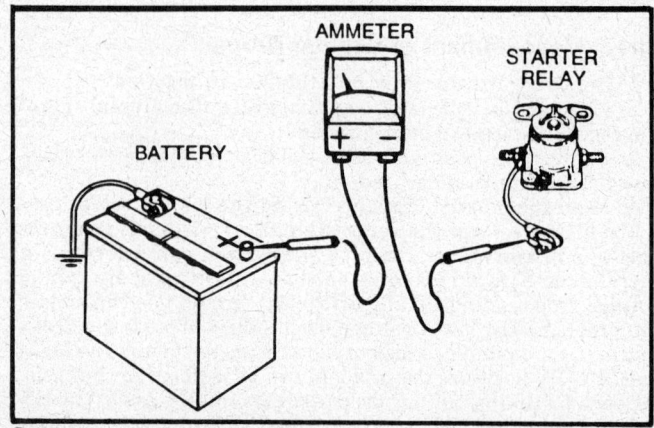

Battery current drain test

An ammeter is always connected in series with the circuit being tested. All of the current that normally flows through the circuit must also flow through the ammeter; if there is any other path for the current to follow, the ammeter reading will not be accurate. The ammeter itself has very little resistance to current flow and therefore will not affect the circuit, but it will measure current draw only when the circuit is closed and electricity is flowing. Excessive current draw can blow fuses and drain the battery, while a reduced current draw can cause motors to run slowly, lights to dim and other components not to operate properly. The ammeter can help diagnose these conditions by locating the cause of the high or low reading.

Multimeters

Different combinations of test meters can be built into a single unit designed for specific tests. Some of the more common combination test devices are known as Volt-Amp testers, Tach-Dwell meters, or Digital Multimeters. The Volt-Amp tester is used for charging system, starting system or battery tests and consists of a voltmeter, an ammeter and a variable resistance carbon pile. The voltmeter will usually have at least two ranges for use with 6, 12 and 24 volt systems. The ammeter also has more than one range for testing various levels of battery loads and starter current draw and the carbon pile can be adjusted to offer different amounts of resistance. The Volt-Amp tester has heavy leads to carry large amounts of current and many later models have an inductive ammeter pickup that clamps around the wire to simplify test connections. On some models, the ammeter also has a zero-center scale to allow test-

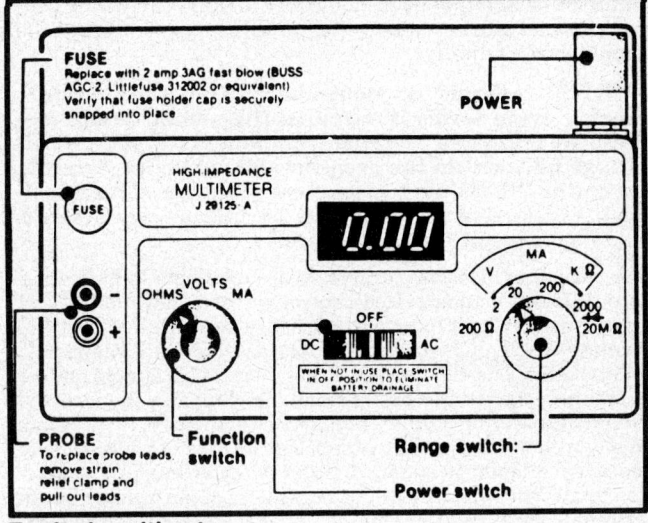

Typical multimeter

ing of charging and starting systems without switching leads or polarity. A digital multimeter is a voltmeter, ammeter and ohmmeter combined in an instrument which gives a digital readout. These are often used when testing solid state circuits because of their high input impedence (usually 10 megohms or more).

The tach-dwell meter combines a tachometer and a dwell (cam angle) meter and is a specialized kind of voltmeter. The tachometer scale is marked to show engine speed in rpm and the dwell scale is marked to show degrees of distributor shaft rotation. In most electronic ignition systems, dwell is determined by the control unit, but the dwell meter can also be used to check the duty cycle (operation) of some electronic engine control systems. Some tach-dwell meters are powered by an internal battery, while others take their power from the car battery in use. The battery powered testers usually require calibration much like an ohmmeter before testing.

Special Test Equipment

A variety of diagnostic tools are available to help troubleshoot and repair computerized engine control systems. The most sophisticated of these devices are the console-type engine analyzers that usually occupy a garage service bay, but there are several types of aftermarket electronic testers available that will allow quick circuit tests of the engine control system by plugging directly into a special connector located in the engine compartment or under the dashboard. Several tool and equipment manufacturers offer simple, hand-held testers that measure various circuit voltage levels on command to check all system components for proper operation. Although these testers usually cost about $300–500, consider that the average computer control unit (or ECM) can cost just as much and the money saved by not replacing perfectly good sensors or components in an attempt to correct a problem could justify the purchase price of a special diagnostic tester the first time it's used.

These computerized testers can allow quick and easy test measurements while the engine is operating or while the car is being driven. In addition, the on-board computer memory can be read to access any stored trouble codes; in effect allowing the computer to tell you where it hurts and aid trouble diagnosis by pinpointing exactly which circuit or component is malfunctioning. In the same manner, repairs can be tested to make sure the problem has been corrected. The biggest advantage these special testers have is their relatively easy hookups that

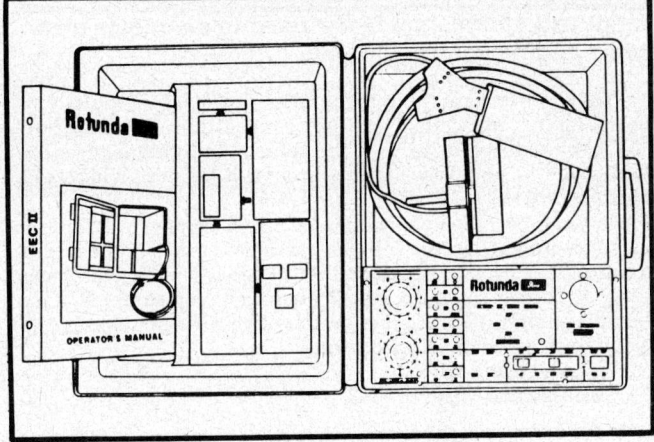

Typical electronic engine control tester

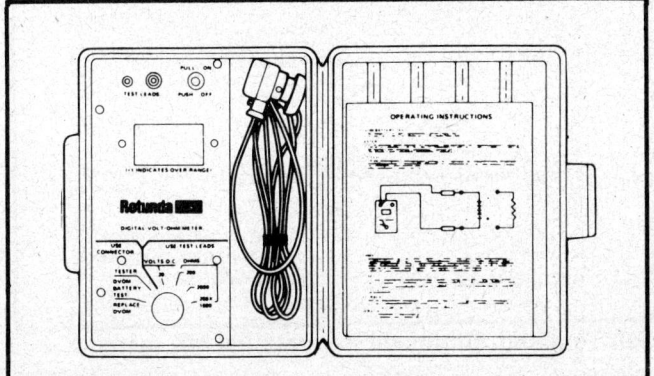

Digital volt-ohmmeter

minimize or eliminate the chances of making the wrong connections and getting false voltage readings or damaging the computer accidentally.

NOTE: It should be remembered that these testers check voltage levels in circuits; they don't detect mechanical problems or failed components if the circuit voltage falls within the preprogrammed limits stored in the tester PROM unit. Also, most of the hand-held testers are designed to work only on one or two systems made by a specific manufacturer.

A variety of aftermarket testers are available to help diagnose different computerized control systems. Owatonna Tool Company (OTC), for example, markets a device called the OTC Monitor which plugs directly into the assembly line diagnostic link (ALDL). The OTC tester makes diagnosis a simple matter of pressing the correct buttons and, by changing the internal PROM or inserting a different diagnosis cartridge, it will work on any model from full size to subcompact, over a wide range of years. An adapter is supplied with the tester to allow connection to all types of ALDL links, regardless of the number of pin terminals used. By inserting an updated PROM into the OTC tester, it can be easily updated to diagnose any new modifications of computerized control systems.

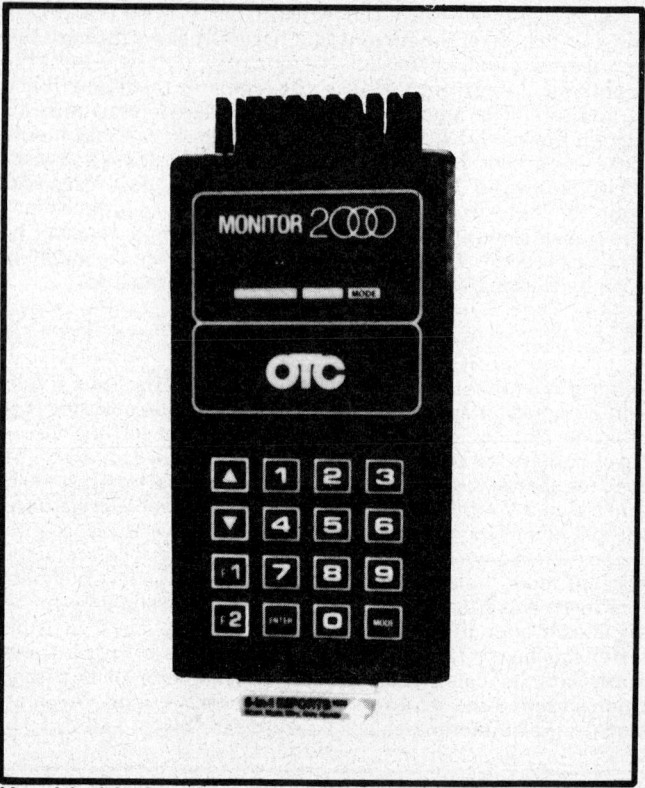

Hand-held aftermarket tester used to diagnosis electronic engine control systems

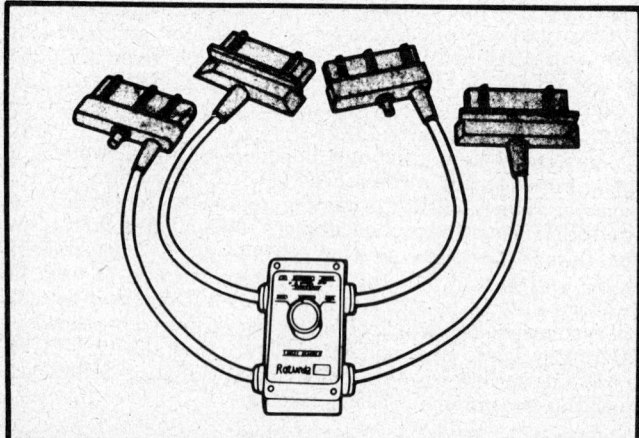

Typical adapter wiring harness for connecting tester to diagnostic terminal

Wiring Diagrams

The average automobile contains about ½ mile of wiring, with hundreds of individual connections. To protect the many wires from damage and to keep them from becoming a confusing tangle, they are organized into bundles, enclosed in plastic or taped together and called wire harnesses. Different wiring harnesses serve different parts of the vehicle. Individual wires are color-coded to help trace them through a harness where sections are hidden from view.

A loose or corroded connection or a replacement wire that is too small for the circuit will add extra resistance and an additional voltage drop to the circuit. A 10 percent voltage drop can result in slow or erratic motor operation, for example, even though the circuit is complete. Automotive wiring or circuit conductors can be in any 1 of 3 forms:

1. Single strand wire
2. Multistrand wire

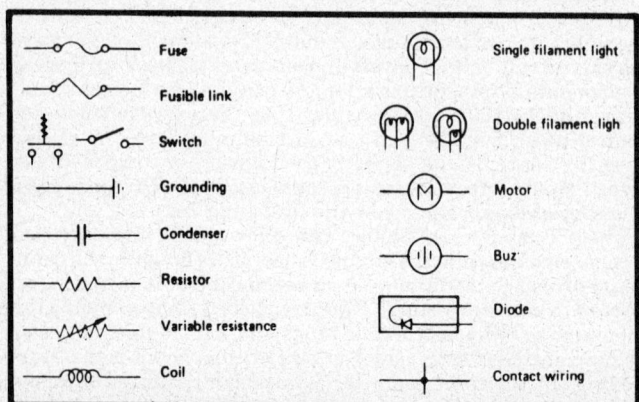

Fuse
Fusible link
Switch
Grounding
Condenser
Resistor
Variable resistance
Coil

Single filament light
Double filament ligh
Motor
Buz
Diode
Contact wiring

Typical electrical symbols found on wiring diagrams

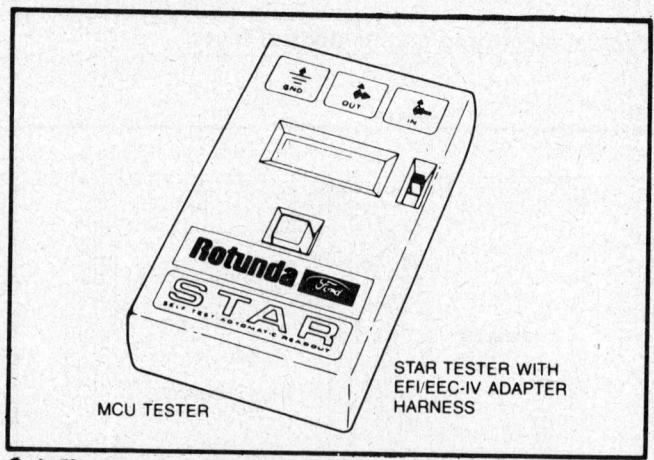

MCU TESTER

STAR TESTER WITH EFI/EEC-IV ADAPTER HARNESS

Self-Test and Automatic Readout (STAR) tester

3. Printed circuitry

Single strand wire has a solid metal core and is usually used inside such components as alternators, motors, relays and other devices. Multistrand wire has a core made of many small strands of wire twisted together into a single conductor. Most of the wiring in an automotive electrical system is made up of multistrand wire, either as a single conductor or grouped together in a harness. All wiring is color-coded on the insulator, either as a solid color or as a colored wire with an identification stripe. A printed circuit is a thin film of copper or other conductor that is printed on an insulator backing. Occasionally, a printed circuit is sandwiched between two sheets of plastic for more protection and flexibility. A complete printed circuit, consisting of conductors, insulating material and connectors for lamps or other components is called a printed circuit board. Printed circuitry is used in place of individual wires or harnesses in places where space is limited, such as behind instrument panels.

Wire Gauge

Since computer-controlled automotive electrical systems are very sensitive to changes in resistance, the selection of properly sized wires is critical when systems are repaired. The wire gauge number is an expression of the cross section area of the conductor. The most common system for expressing wire size is the American Wire Gauge (AWG) system.

Wire cross section area is measured in circular mils. A mil is one-thousandth of an inch (0.001); a circular mil is the area of a circle one mil in diameter. For example, a conductor $\frac{1}{4}$ inch in diameter is 0.250 in. or 250 mils. The circular mil cross section area of the wire is 250 squared or 62,500 circular mils. Imported car models usually use metric wire gauge designations, which is simply the cross section area of the conductor in square millimeters (mm^2).

Gauge numbers are assigned to conductors of various cross section areas. As gauge number increases, area decreases and the conductor becomes smaller. A 5 gauge conductor is smaller than a 1 gauge conductor and a 10 gauge is smaller than a 5 gauge. As the cross section area of a conductor decreases, resistance increases and so does the gauge number. A conductor with a higher gauge number will carry less current than a conductor with a lower gauge number.

NOTE: Gauge wire size refers to the size of the conductor, not the size of the complete wire. It is possible to have two wires of the same gauge with different diameters because one may have thicker insulation than the other.

12 volt automotive electrical systems generally use 10, 12, 14, 16 and 18 gauge wire. Main power distribution circuits and larger accessories usually use 10 and 12 gauge wire. Battery cables are usually 4 or 6 gauge, although 1 and 2 gauge wires are occasionally used. Wire length must also be considered when making repairs to a circuit. As conductor length increases, so does resistance. An 18 gauge wire, for example, can carry a 10 amp load for 10 feet without excessive voltage drop; however if a 15 foot wire is required for the same 10 amp load, a 16 gauge wire must be used.

An electrical schematic shows the electrical current paths when a circuit is operating properly. It is essential to understand how a circuit works before trying to figure out why it doesn't. Schematics break the entire electrical system down into individual circuits and show only one particular circuit. In a schematic, no attempt is made to represent wiring and components as they physically appear on the vehicle; switches and other components are shown as simply as possible. Face views of harness connectors show the cavity or terminal locations in all multi-pin connectors to help locate test points.

If you need to backprobe a connector while it is on the component, the order of the terminals must be mentally reversed. The wire color code can help in this situation, as well as a keyway, lock tab or other reference mark.

Wiring Repairs

Soldering is a quick, efficient method of joining metals permanently. Everyone who has to make wiring repairs should know how to solder. Electrical connections that are soldered are far less likely to come apart and will conduct electricity much better than connections that are only "pig-tailed" together. The most popular (and preferred) method of soldering is with an electrical soldering gun. Soldering irons are available in many sizes and wattage ratings. Irons with higher wattage ratings deliver higher temperatures and recover lost heat faster. A small soldering iron rated for no more than 50 watts is recommended, especially on electrical systems where excess heat can damage the components being soldered.

There are three ingredients necessary for successful soldering; proper flux, good solder and sufficient heat. A soldering flux is necessary to clean the metal of tarnish, prepare it for soldering and to enable the solder to spread into tiny crevices. When soldering, always use a resin flux or resin core solder which is non-corrosive and will not attract moisture once the job is finished. Other types of flux (acid core) will leave a residue tht will attract moisture and cause the wires to corrode. Tin is a unique metal with a low melting point. In a molten state, it dissolves and alloys easily with many metals. Solder is made by mixing tin with lead. The most common proportions are 40/60, 50/50 and 60/40, with the percentage of tin listed first. Low priced solders usually contain less tin, making them very difficult for a beginner to use because more heat is required to melt the solder. A common solder is 40/60 which is well suited for general use, but 60/40 melts easier, has more tin for a better joint and is preferred for electrical work.

Soldering Techniques

Successful soldering requires that the metals to be joined be heated to a temperature that will melt the solder (usually 360–

COMMON SYMBOLS FOR AUTOMOTIVE COMPONENTS USED IN SCHEMATIC DIAGRAMS

Chilton service manuals use schematic diagrams to show how electrical and other types of components work and how such components are connected to make circuits. The following components that are shown whole are represented in full lines in a rectangular shape and are identified by name. When only a part of a component is shown in a schematic diagram, the rectangular shape is outlined with a dashed line.

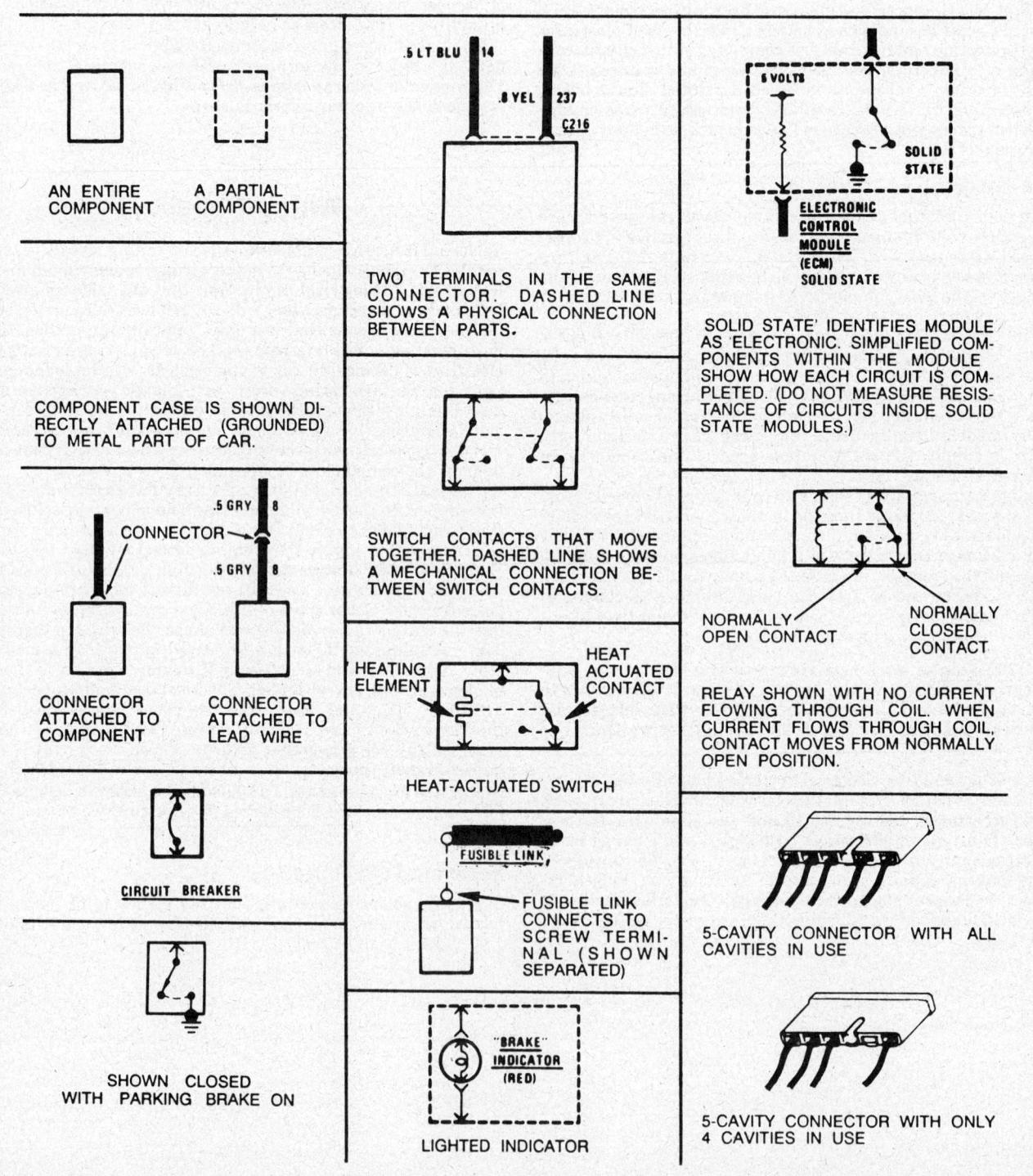

AN ENTIRE COMPONENT

A PARTIAL COMPONENT

TWO TERMINALS IN THE SAME CONNECTOR. DASHED LINE SHOWS A PHYSICAL CONNECTION BETWEEN PARTS.

ELECTRONIC CONTROL MODULE (ECM) SOLID STATE

'SOLID STATE' IDENTIFIES MODULE AS 'ELECTRONIC. SIMPLIFIED COMPONENTS WITHIN THE MODULE SHOW HOW EACH CIRCUIT IS COMPLETED. (DO NOT MEASURE RESISTANCE OF CIRCUITS INSIDE SOLID STATE MODULES.)

COMPONENT CASE IS SHOWN DIRECTLY ATTACHED (GROUNDED) TO METAL PART OF CAR.

SWITCH CONTACTS THAT MOVE TOGETHER. DASHED LINE SHOWS A MECHANICAL CONNECTION BETWEEN SWITCH CONTACTS.

NORMALLY OPEN CONTACT

NORMALLY CLOSED CONTACT

RELAY SHOWN WITH NO CURRENT FLOWING THROUGH COIL. WHEN CURRENT FLOWS THROUGH COIL, CONTACT MOVES FROM NORMALLY OPEN POSITION.

CONNECTOR

CONNECTOR ATTACHED TO COMPONENT

CONNECTOR ATTACHED TO LEAD WIRE

HEATING ELEMENT

HEAT ACTUATED CONTACT

HEAT-ACTUATED SWITCH

CIRCUIT BREAKER

FUSIBLE LINK

FUSIBLE LINK CONNECTS TO SCREW TERMINAL (SHOWN SEPARATED)

5-CAVITY CONNECTOR WITH ALL CAVITIES IN USE

SHOWN CLOSED WITH PARKING BRAKE ON

"BRAKE" INDICATOR (RED)

LIGHTED INDICATOR

5-CAVITY CONNECTOR WITH ONLY 4 CAVITIES IN USE

WIRE IS GROUNDED, AND GROUND IS NUMBERED FOR REFERENCE ON COMPONENT LOCATION TABLE.

WIRE IS INDIRECTLY CONNECTED TO GROUND. (WIRE MAY HAVE ONE OR MORE SPLICES BEFORE IT IS GROUNDED.)

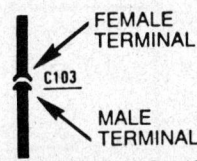

CONNECTOR REFERENCE NO. IS LISTED IN COMPONENT LOCATION TABLE, WHICH ALSO SHOWS TOTAL NO. OF TERMINALS POSSIBLE: C103 (6 CAVITIES).

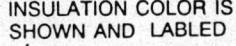
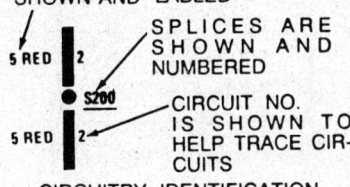

CIRCUITRY IDENTIFICATION

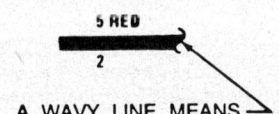

A WAVY LINE MEANS WIRE IS TO BE CONTINUED

WIRE INSULATION IS ONE COLOR, WITH ANOTHER COLOR STRIPE (EXAMPLE: RED COLOR, WITH YELLOW STRIPE).

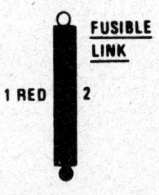

FUSIBLE LINK SHOWS WIRE SIZE AND INSULATION COLOR.

CURRENT PATH IS CONTINUED AS LABLED. THE ARROW SHOWS THE DIRECTION OF CURRENT FLOW, AND IS REPEATED WHERE CURRENT PATH CONTINUES.

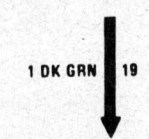

A WIRE IS SHOWN WHICH CONNECTS TO ANOTHER CIRCUIT. THE WIRE IS SHOWN AGAIN ON THAT CIRCUIT.

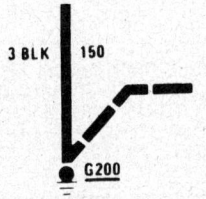

THE DASHED LINE INDICATES THAT THE CIRCUITRY IS NOT SHOWN IN COMPLETE DETAIL BUT IS COMPLETE ON THE INDICATED PAGE.

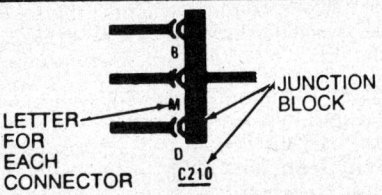
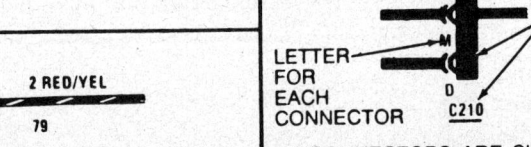

3 CONNECTORS ARE SHOWN CONNECTED TOGETHER AT A JUNCTION BLOCK. FOURTH WIRE IS SOLDERED TO COMMON CONNECTION ON BLOCK.

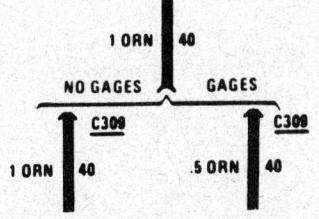

WIRE CHOICES FOR OPTIONS OR DIFFERENT MODELS ARE SHOWN AND LABLED.

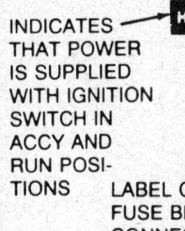

INDICATES THAT POWER IS SUPPLIED WITH IGNITION SWITCH IN ACCY AND RUN POSITIONS

CURRENT CAN FLOW ONLY IN THE DIRECTION OF THE ARROW

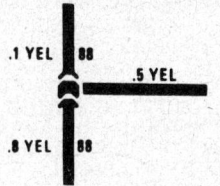

3 WIRES ARE SHOWN CONNECTED TOGETHER WITH A PIGGYBACK CONNECTOR

HOSE COLORS ARE SHOWN AT A VACUUM JUNCTION.

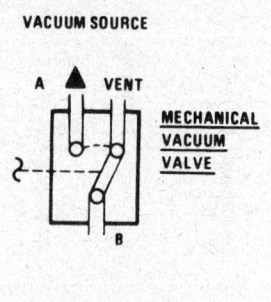

VACUUM SOURCE

A VENT

MECHANICAL VACUUM VALVE

B

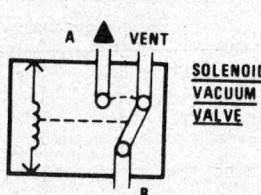

VACUUM SOURCE

A VENT

SOLENOID VACUUM VALVE

B

2-POSITION VACUUM MOTORS

IN THE 'AT REST' POSITION SHOWN, THE VALVE SEALS PORT 'A' AND VENTS PORT 'B' TO THE ATMOSPHERE. WHEN THE VALVE IS MOVED TO THE 'OPERATED' POSITION, VACUUM FROM PORT 'A' IS CONNECTED TO PORT 'B'. THE SOLENOID VACUUM VALVE USES THE SOLENOID TO MOVE THE VALVE.

VACUUM MOTORS OPERATE LIKE ELECTRICAL SOLENOIDS, MECHANICALLY PUSHING OR PULLING A SHAFT BETWEEN TWO FIXED POSITIONS. WHEN VACUUM IS APPLIED, THE SHAFT IS PULLED IN. WHEN NO VACUUM IS APPLIED, THE SHAFT IS PUSHED ALL THE WAY OUT BY A SPRING.

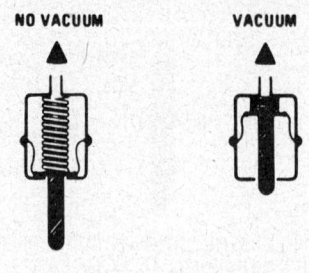

NO VACUUM   VACUUM

SINGLE-DIAPHRAGM MOTOR

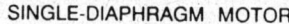

EASY FLOW DIRECTION

NO FLOW DIRECTION

VACUUM CHECK VALVE

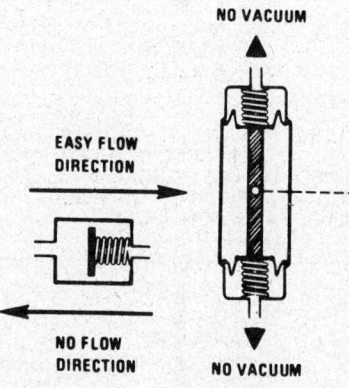

NO VACUUM

NO VACUUM

DOUBLE DIAPHRAGM MOTOR

DOUBLE-DIAPHRAGM MOTORS CAN BE OPERATED BY VACUUM IN TWO DIRECTIONS. WHEN THERE IS NO VACUUM, THE MOTOR IS IN THE CENTER 'AT REST' POSITION.

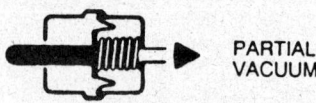

PARTIAL VACUUM

SERVO MOTOR

SOME VACUUM MOTORS, SUCH AS THE SERVO MOTOR IN THE CRUISE CONTROL, CAN POSITION THE ACTUATING ARM AT ANY POSITION BETWEEN FULLY EXTENDED AND FULLY RETRACTED. THE SERVO IS OPERATED BY A CONTROL VALVE THAT APPLIES VARYING AMOUNTS OF VACUUM TO THE MOTOR. THE HIGHER THE VACUUM LEVEL, THE GREATER THE RETRACTION OF THE MOTOR ARM. SERVO MOTORS WORK LIKE THE TWO-POSITION MOTORS; THE ONLY DIFFERENCE IS IN THE WAY THE VACUUM IS APPLIED. SERVO MOTORS ARE GENERALLY LARGER AND PROVIDE A CALIBRATED CONTROL.

METRIC SIZE	AWG SIZES
.22	24
.35	22
.5	20
.8	18
1.0	16
2.0	14
3.0	12
5.0	10
8.0	8
13.0	6
19.0	4
32.0	2

Wire Size Conversion Table

Typical wiring diagram schematic symbols

460°F). Contrary to popular belief, the purpose of the soldering iron is not to melt the solder itself, but to heat the parts being soldered to a temperature high enough to melt the solder when it touches the work. Melting flux-cored solder on the soldering iron will usually destroy the effectiveness of the flux.

NOTE: Soldering tips are made of copper for good heat conductivity, but must be "tinned" regularly for quick transfer of heat to the project and to prevent the solder from sticking to the iron. To "tin" the iron, simply heat it and touch the flux-cored solder to the tip; the solder will flow over the hot tip. Wipe the excess off with a clean rag, but be careful as the iron will be hot.

After some use, the tip may become pitted. If so, simply dress the tip smooth with a smooth file and "tin" the tip again. An old saying holds that "metals well cleaned are half soldered." Flux-cored solder will remove oxides but rust, bits of insulation and oil or grease must be removed with a wire brush or emery cloth.

For maximum strength in soldered parts, the joint must start off clean and tight. Weak joints will result if there are gaps too wide for the solder to bridge.

If a separate soldering flux is used, it should be brushed or swabbed only on areas that are to be soldered. Most solders

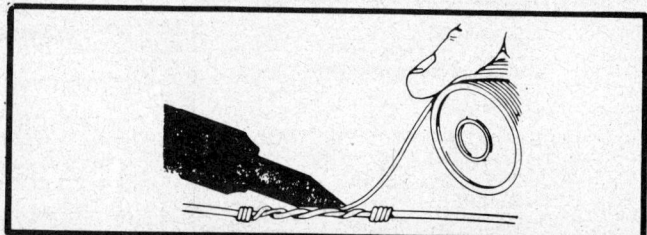

Proper soldering method. Allow the soldering iron to heat the wire first, then apply the solder as shown

contain a core of flux and separate fluxing is unnecessary. Hold the work to be soldered firmly. It is best to solder on a wooden board, because a metal vise will only rob the piece to be soldered of heat and make it difficult to melt the solder. Hold the soldering tip with the broadest face against the work to be soldered. Apply solder under the tip close to the work, using enough solder to give a heavy film between the iron and the piece being soldered, while moving slowly and making sure the solder melts properly. Keep the work level or the solder will run to the lowest part and favor the thicker parts, because these require more heat to melt the solder. If the soldering tip overheats (the solder coating on the face of the tip burns up), it should be retinned. Once the soldering is completed, let the soldered joint stand until cool. Tape and seal all soldered wire splices after the repair has cooled.

Wire Harness and Connectors

The on-board computer (ECM) wire harness electrically connects the control unit to the various solenoids, switches and sensors used by the control system. Most connectors in the engine compartment or otherwise exposed to the elements are protected against moisture and dirt which could create oxidation and deposits on the terminals. This protection is important because of the very low voltage and current levels used by the computer and sensors. All connectors have a lock which secures the male and female terminals together, with a secondary lock holding the seal and terminal into the connector. Both terminal locks must be released when disconnecting ECM connectors.

These special connectors are weather-proof and all repairs

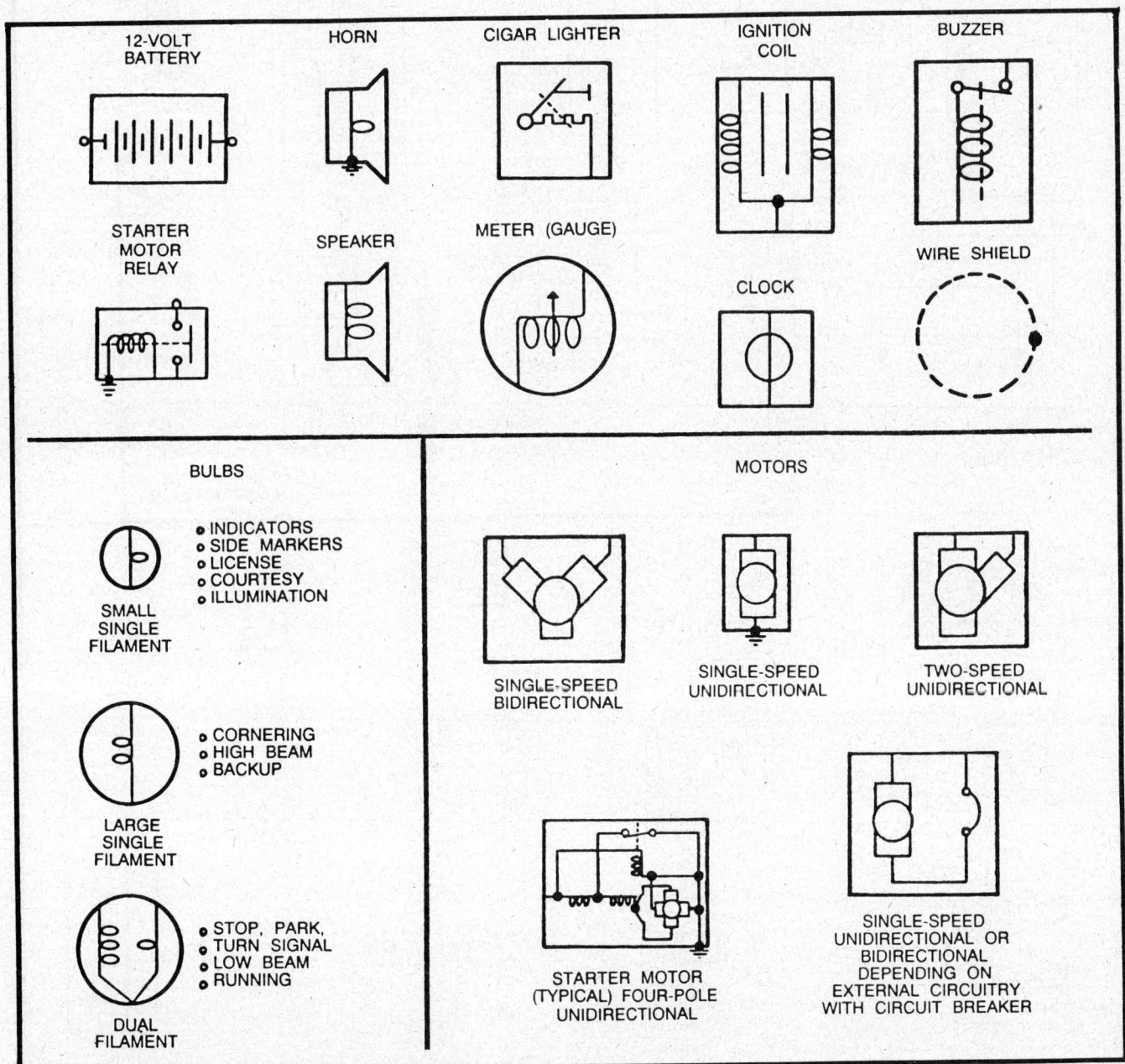

Typical wiring diagram schematic symbols

require the use of a special terminal and the tool required to service it. This tool is used to remove the pin and sleeve terminals. If removal is attempted with an ordinary pick, there is a good chance that the terminal will be bent or deformed. Unlike standard blade type terminals, these terminals cannot be straightened once they are bent. Make certain that the connectors are properly seated and all of the sealing rings in place when connecting leads. On some models, a hinge-type flap provides a backup or secondary locking feature for the terminals. Most secondary locks are used to improve the connector reliability by retaining the terminals if the small terminal lock tangs are not positioned properly.

Tinning the soldering iron before use

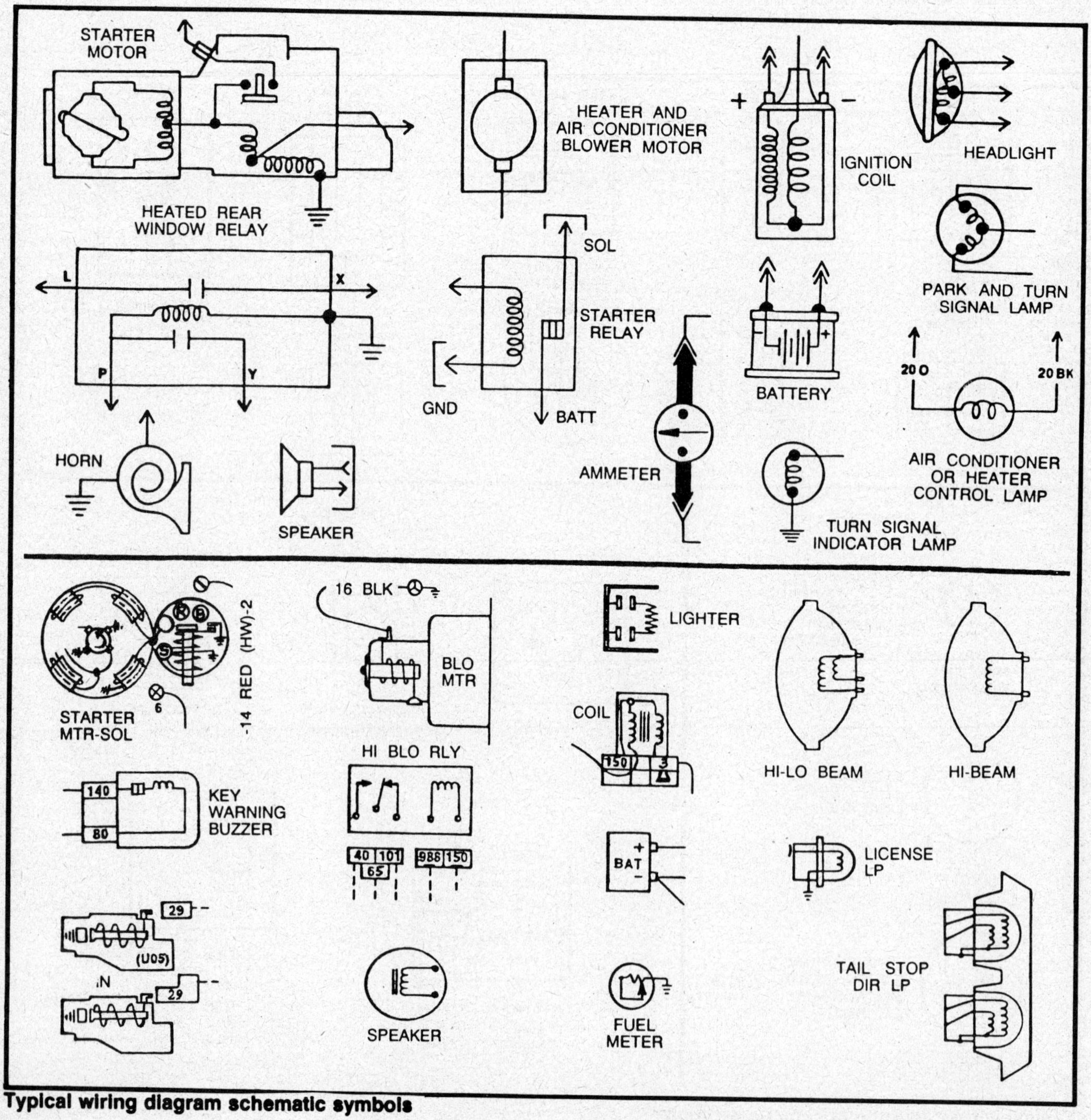

STARTER MOTOR

HEATED REAR WINDOW RELAY

HEATER AND AIR CONDITIONER BLOWER MOTOR

IGNITION COIL

HEADLIGHT

L

X

P

Y

SOL

STARTER RELAY

GND

BATT

PARK AND TURN SIGNAL LAMP

BATTERY

20 O

20 BK

AMMETER

HORN

SPEAKER

TURN SIGNAL INDICATOR LAMP

AIR CONDITIONER OR HEATER CONTROL LAMP

STARTER MTR-SOL

-14 RED (HW)-2

16 BLK

BLO MTR

LIGHTER

COIL

150

3

HI-LO BEAM

HI-BEAM

HI BLO RLY

KEY WARNING BUZZER

140

80

40 | 101

65

988 | 150

(U05)

29

N

29

SPEAKER

BAT

FUEL METER

LICENSE LP

TAIL STOP DIR LP

Typical wiring diagram schematic symbols

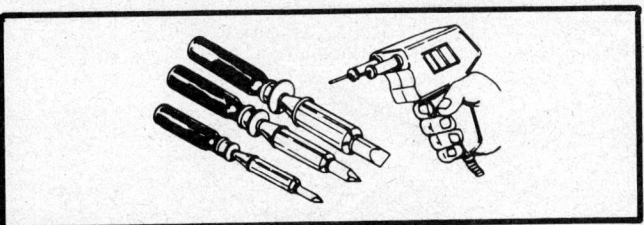

Various types of soldering guns

Molded-on connectors require complete replacement of the connection. This means splicing a new connector assembly into the harness. All splices in on-board computer systems should be soldered to insure proper contact. Use care when probing the connections or replacing terminals in them as it is possible to short between opposite terminals. If this happens to the wrong terminal pair, it is possible to damage certain components. Always use jumper wires between connectors for circuit checking and never probe through weatherproof seals.

Open circuits are often difficult to locate by sight because corrosion or terminal misalignment are hidden by the connectors. Merely wiggling a connector on a sensor or in the wiring harness may correct the open circuit condition. This should always be considered when an open circuit or a failed sensor is indicated. Intermittent problems may also be caused by oxidized or loose connections. When using a circuit tester for diagnosis, always probe connections from the wire side. Be careful not to damage sealed connectors with test probes.

All wiring harnesses should be replaced with identical parts, using the same gauge wire and connectors. When signal wires are spliced into a harness, use wire with high temperature insulation only. With the low voltage and current levels found in the system, it is important that the best possible connection at all wire splices be made by soldering the splices together. It is seldom necessary to replace a complete harness. If replacement is necessary, pay close attention to insure proper harness rout-

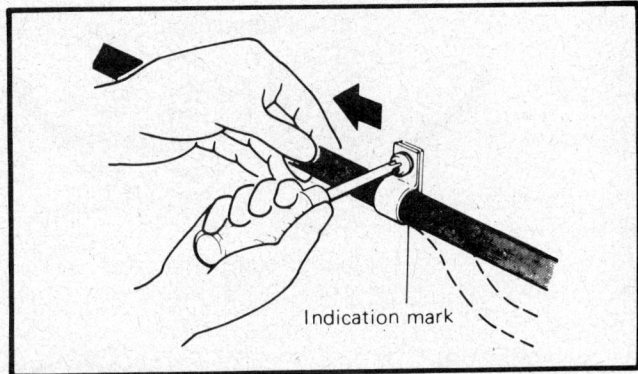

Indication mark

Secure the wiring harness at the indication marks, if used, to prevent vibrations from causing wear and a possible short

WIRE HARNESS REPAIR PROCEDURES

Condition	Location	Correction
Non-continuity	Using the electric wiring diagram and the wiring harness diagram as a guideline, check the continuity of the circuit in question by using a tester, and check for breaks, loose connector couplings, or loose terminal crimp contacts.	**Breaks**—Reconnect the point of the break by using solder. If the wire is too short and the connection is impossible, extend it by using a wire of the same or larger size. Solder Be careful concerning the size of wire used for the extension **Loose couplings**—Hold the connector securely, and insert it until there is a definite joining of the coupling. If the connector is equipped with a locking mechanism, insert the connector until it is locked securely. Crimp by using pliers — Solder **Loose terminal crimp contacts**—Remove approximately 2 in. (5mm) of the insulation covering from the end of the wire, crimp the terminal contact by using a pair of pliers, and then, in addition, complete the repair by soldering.
Short-circuit	Using the electric wiring diagram and the wiring harness diagram as a guideline, check the entire circuit for pinched wires.	Remove the pinched portion, and then repair any breaks in the insulation covering with tape. Repair breaks of the wire by soldering.
Loose terminal	Pull the wiring lightly from the connector. A special terminal removal tool may be necessary for complete removal.	Raise the terminal catch pin, and then insert it until a definite clicking sound is heard. Catch pin

Note: There is the chance of short circuits being caused by insulation damage at soldered points. To avoid this possibility, wrap all splices with electrical tape and use a layer of silicone to seal the connection against moisture. Incorrect repairs can cause malfunctions by creating excessive resistance in a circuit.

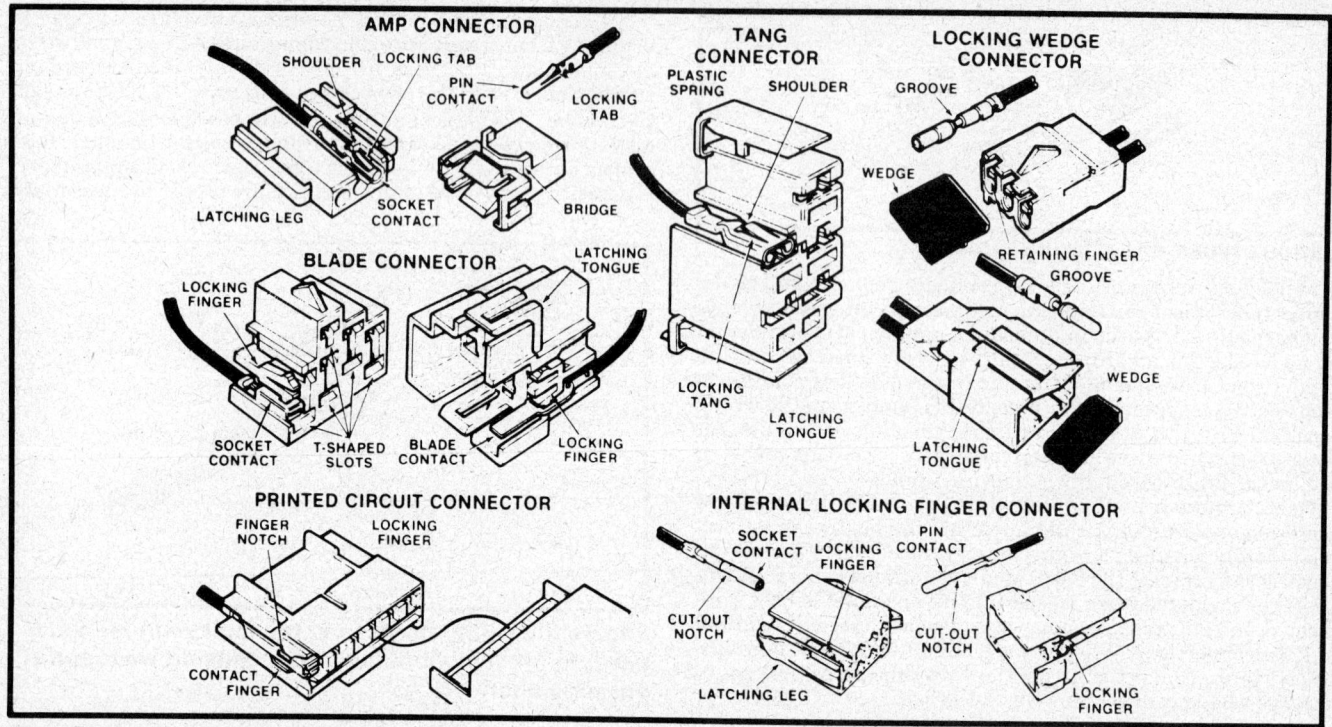

Various types of electrical connectors

ing. Secure the harness with suitable plastic wire clamps to prevent vibrations from causing the harness to wear in spots or contact any hot components.

NOTE: Weatherproof connectors cannot be replaced with standard connectors. Instructions are provided with replacement connector and terminal packages.

Some wire harnesses have mounting indicators (usually pieces of colored tape) to mark where the harness is to be secured.

In making wiring repairs, it's important that you always replace damaged wires with wires that are the same gauge as the wire being replaced. The heavier the wire, the smaller the

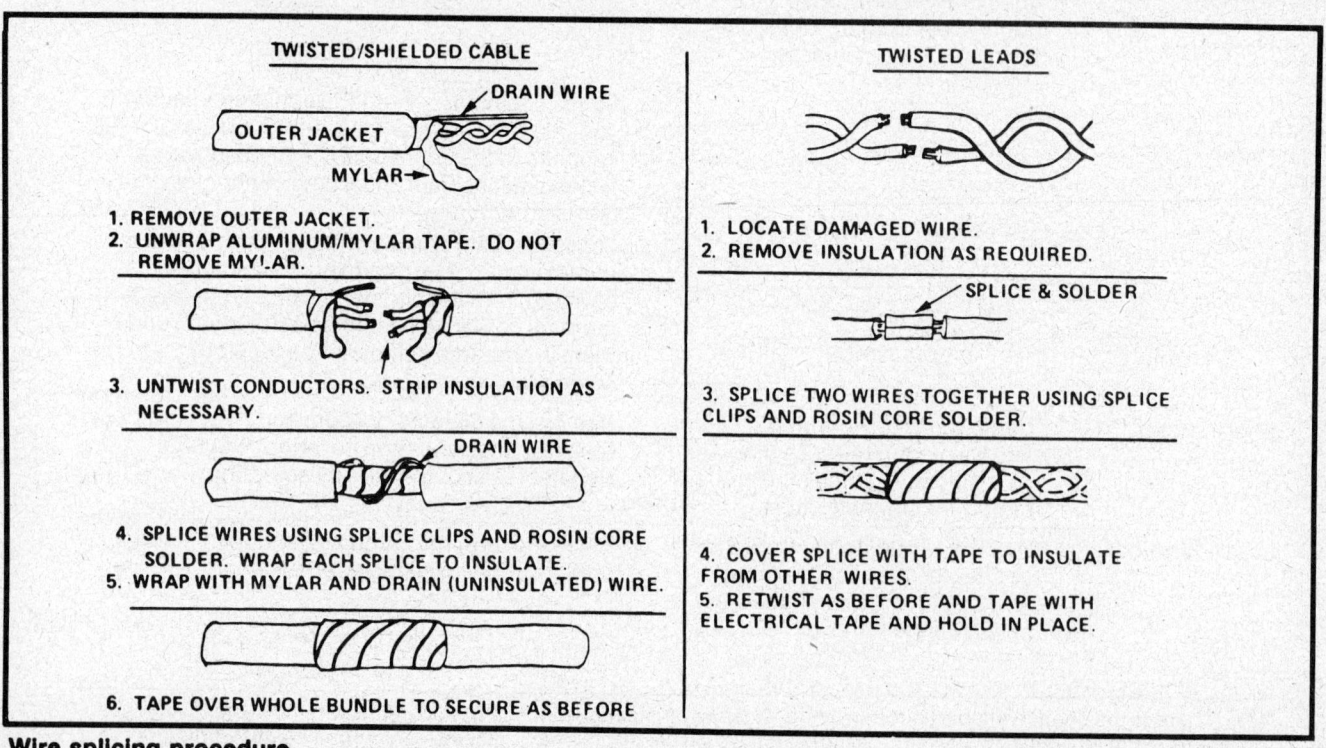

Wire splicing procedure

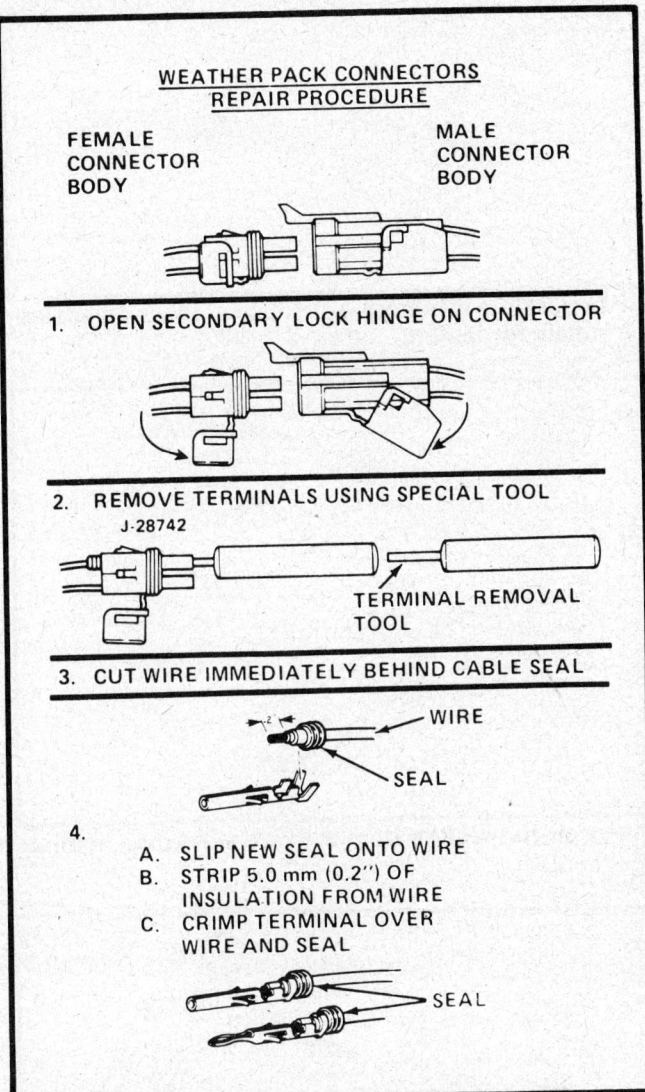

Repairing Weatherpak connectors. Note special terminal removal tools

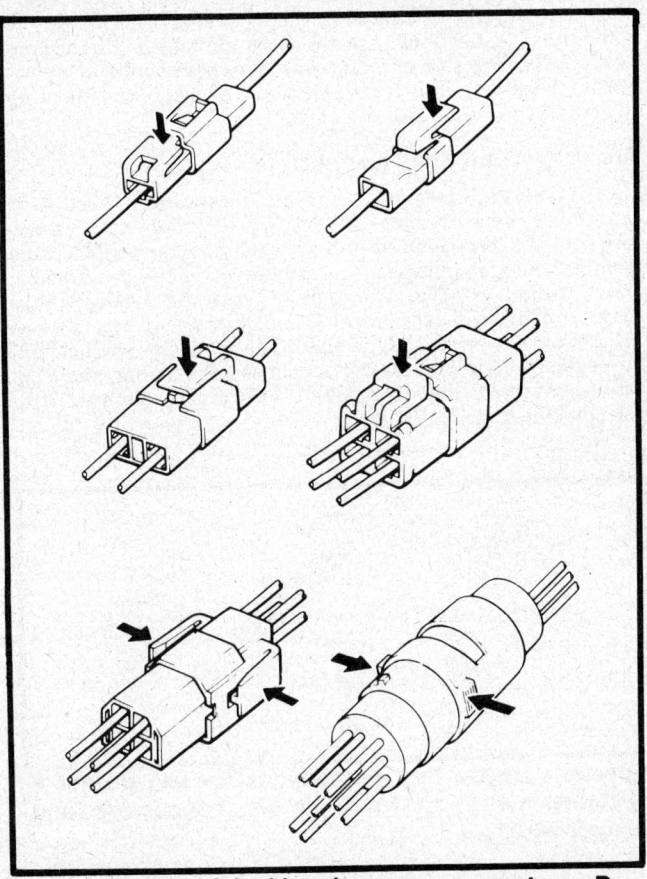

Various types of locking harness connectors. Depress the locks at the arrows to separate the connectors

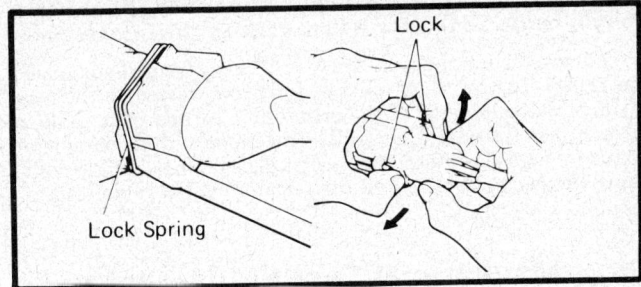

Some electrical connectors use a lock spring instead of the molded locking tabs

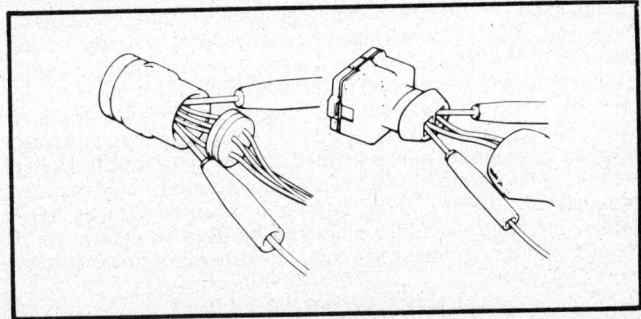

Correct method of testing weatherproof connectors. Do not pierce connector seals with test probes

gauge number. Wires are color-coded to aid in identification and whenever possible the same color coded wire should be used for replacement. A wire stripping and crimping tool is necessary to install solderless terminal connectors. Test all crimps by pulling on the wires; it should not be possible to pull the wires out of a good crimp.

Wires which are open, exposed or otherwise damaged are repaired by simple splicing. Where possible, if the wiring harness is accessible and the damaged place in the wire can be located, it is best to open the harness and check for all possible damage. In an inaccessible harness, the wire must be bypassed with a new insert, usually taped to the outside of the old harness.

When replacing fusible links, be sure to use fusible link wire, NOT ordinary automotive wire. Make sure the fusible segment is of the same gauge and construction as the one being replaced and double the stripped end when crimping the terminal connector for a good contact. The melted (open) fusible link segment of the wiring harness should be cut off as close to the harness as possible, then a new segment spliced in as described. In the case of a damaged fusible link that feeds two harness wires, the harness connections should be replaced with two fusible link wires so that each circuit will have its own separate protection.

Most of the problems caused in the wiring harness are due to bad ground connections. Always check all vehicle ground connections for corrosion or looseness before performing any power feed checks to eliminate the chance of a bad ground affecting the circuit.

Repairing Hard Shell Connectors

Unlike molded connectors, the terminal contacts in hard shell connectors can be replaced. Weatherproof hard-shell connectors with the leads molded into the shell have non-replaceable terminal ends. Replacement usually involves the use of a special terminal removal tool that depress the locking tangs (barbs) on the connector terminal and allow the connector to be removed from the rear of the shell. The connector shell should be replaced if it shows any evidence of burning, melting, cracks, or breaks. Replace individual terminals that are burnt, corroded, distorted or loose.

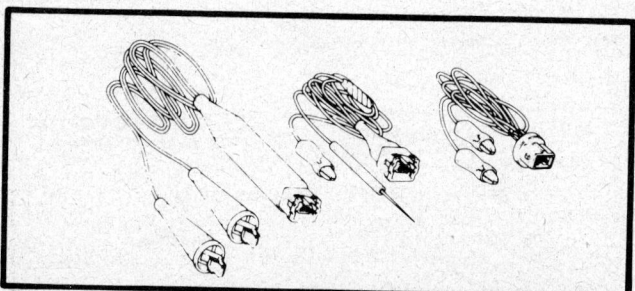

Special purpose test connections for use on some systems made up from factory connectors and jumper wires

NOTE: The insulation crimp must be tight to prevent the insulation from sliding back on the wire when the wire is pulled. The insulation must be visibly compressed under the crimp tabs, and the ends of the crimp should be turned in for a firm grip on the insulation.

The wire crimp must be made with all wire strands inside the crimp. The terminal must be fully compressed on the wire strands with the ends of the crimp tabs turned in to make a firm grip on the wire. Check all connections with an ohmmeter to insure a good contact. There should be no measurable resistance between the wire and the terminal when connected.

Mechanical Test Equipment
VACUUM GAUGE

Most gauges are graduated in inches of mercury (in. Hg), although a device called a manometer reads vacuum in inches of water (in. H₂O). The normal vacuum reading usually varies between 18 and 22 in. Hg at sea level. To test engine vacuum, the vacuum gauge must be connected to a source of manifold vacuum. Many engines have a plug in the intake manifold which can be removed and replaced with an adapter fitting. Connect the vacuum gauge to the fitting with a suitable rubber hose or, if no manifold plug is available, connect the vacuum gauge to any device using manifold vacuum, such as EGR valves, etc. The vacuum gauge can be used to determine if enough vacuum is reaching a component to allow its actuation.

HAND VACUUM PUMP

Small, hand-held vacuum pumps come in a variety of designs.

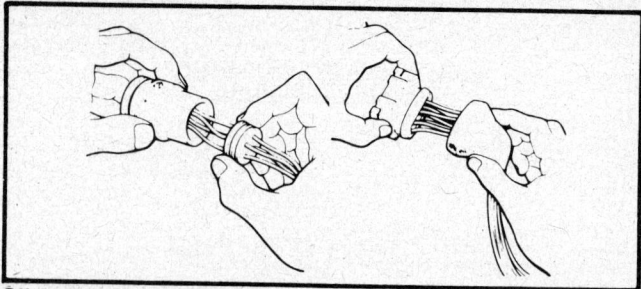

Slide back the weatherproof seals or boots on sealed terminals for testing

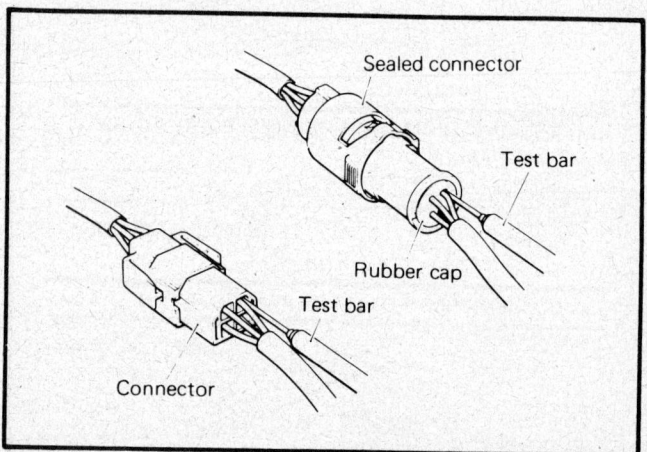

Probe all connectors from the wire side when testing

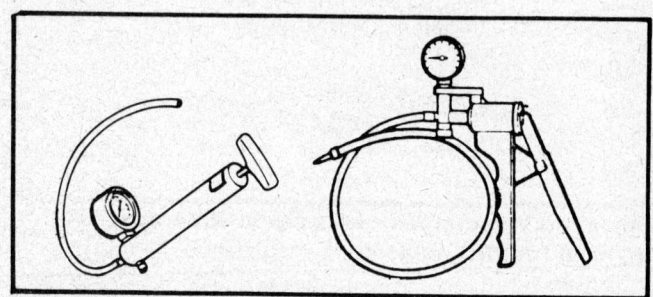

Typical hand vacuum pumps

Most have a built-in vacuum gauge and allow the component be tested without removing it from the vehicle. Operate the pump lever or plunger to apply the correct amount of vacuum required for the test specified in the diagnosis routines. The level of vacuum in inches of Mercury (in. Hg) is indicated on the pump gauge. For some testing, an additional vacuum gauge may be necessary.

Intake manifold vacuum is used to operate various systems and devices on late model cars. To correctly diagnose and solve problems in vacuum control systems, a vacuum source is necessary for testing. In some cases, vacuum can be taken from the intake manifold when the engine is running, but vacuum is normally provided by a hand vacuum pump. These hand vacuum pumps have a built-in vacuum gauge that allow testing while the device is still attached to the car. For some tests, an additional vacuum gauge may be necessary.

American Motors Corporation/Jeep

INDEX

AMERICAN MOTORS CORPORATION/JEEP

C4 System

NOTE: The following information pretains to certain 1980–82, 4 cyl models.

SELF-DIAGNOSTIC SYSTEM

Description

The C4 system should be considered as a possible source of trouble for engine performance, fuel economy and exhaust emission complaints only after normal tests and inspections that would apply to a vehicle without the C4 system have been performed. An integral self-diagnostic system detects the problems that are most likely to occur.

Entering Diagnostic Mode

From under the dash, locate the pigtail wire test connector. Using a test bulb, connect one lead to the test connector and the other to a ground.

As a routine system check, the test bulb will turn **ON** when the ignition switch is first turned **ON** and the engine not started. If the test lead is grounded, the system will flash a code 12, which indicates that the diagnostic system is functioning normal (i.e., no rpm voltage to ECM). This consists of 1 flash followed by a pause and then 2 flashes. After a longer pause, the code will be repeated 2 more times. The cycle will repeat itself until the engine is either or the ignition switch turned **OFF**. When the engine is started, the bulb will remain illuminated for a few seconds.

If the test lead is grounded, with the engine operating, and a fault has been detected by the system, the trouble code will be flashed 3 times. If more than 1 fault has been detected, the 2nd trouble code will be flashed 3 times after the 1st code is flashed; the series of code flashes will then be repeated.

Operation

A trouble code indicates a problem within a specific circuit, for example, Code 14 indicates a problem in the coolant temperature sensor circuit. This includes the coolant temperature sensor, wire harness and/or Electronic Control Module (ECM).

Because the self-diagnostic subsystem does not detect all possible faults, the absence of a flashed code does not always indicate that there is no problem with the system. To determine this, a system operational test is necessary. This test should be performed when the test bulb does not indicate a problem but the C4 system is suspected because no other reason can be found for a specific complaint. In addition to the test bulb, a dwell meter, test lamp, digital volt-ohmmeter, tachometer, vacuum gauge and jumper wires are required to diagnose system problems. A test lamp rather than a voltmeter should be used when so instructed. Although most dwell meters should be acceptable, if one causes a change in engine operation, when it is connected to the mixture control (MC) solenoid dwell lead, it should not be used. The following models of older Sun tach/dwell units should not be used: G, GA, TDT1, 2, 5, 216, and 216-1.

The dwell meter, set for the V6 engine scale and connected to a lead from the mixture control (MC) solenoid in the carburetor, is used to determine the air/fuel mixture dwell. When the dwell meter is connected, do not allow the terminal to contact ground. This includes hoses because they may be conductive. On a normally operating engine, the dwell at both idle and partial throttle will be vary between 10–50 degrees. Varying means the pointer continually moves back and forth across the scale. The amount it varies is not important, only the fact that it does vary.

This indicates Closed Loop operation, meaning the mixture is being varied according to the input voltage to the ECM from the Oxygen Sensor. With the Wide Open Throttle (WOT) or cold engine operation, the mixture will be a fixed value and the pointer will not vary. This is Open Loop operation, meaning the oxygen sensor output has no effect on the mixture. If there is a question whether or not the system is in Closed Loop operation, richening or leaning the mixture will cause the dwell to vary if the system is in Closed Loop operation.

NOTE: Normally, system tests should be performed on a warm engine (upper radiator hose hot).

TROUBLE CODE MEMORY

When a fault is detected in the system, the test bulb will be illuminated and a trouble code will be set in the memory of the ECM. However, if the fault is intermittent, the test bulb will be extinguished when the fault no longer exists, but the trouble code will remain in the ECM memory.

LONG TERM MEMORY

The ECM, with most C4 Systems, has a long term memory. With this provision, trouble codes are not lost when the ignition switch is turned **OFF**. Certain troubles may not appear until the engine has been operated 5–18 minutes at partial throttle. For this reason, and for intermittent troubles, a long term memory is desirable.

Clearing Diagnostic Memory

To clear the long term memory, disconnect and connect the battery negative cable.

NOTE: Long term memory causes approximately a 13ma battery drain with the ignition switch OFF.

C3 System

NOTE: The following information pretains to certain 1985, V6 models.

SELF-DIAGNOSTIC SYSTEM

Description

The self-diagnostic system detects the troubles most likely to occur. The diagnostic system illuminates the "Check Engine" light on the instrument panel when a trouble is detected.

When a trouble develops in the feedback system, the "Check Engine" light will illuminate and a trouble code will be stored in the ECM memory. If the fault is intermittent, the "Check Engine" light will be turned **OFF** after 10 seconds when the trouble ceases. However, the trouble code will be retained in the ECM memory until it is erased.

Entering Diagnostic Mode

1. Using a jumper wire, connect it between the trouble code test terminals 6 and 7, of the 15-terminal diagnostic connector (D-2), which is located at the left rear side of the engine compartment.
2. Turn the ignition switch ON.

NOTE: For a bulb and system check, the "CHECK ENGINE" light will illuminate when the ignition switch is ON and the engine not started. If the TEST terminals are grounded, the light will flash a code 12 which consists of 1 flash followed by a short pause, then 2 flashes in quick succession. After a long pause, the code will repeat 2 more times.

3. Start the engine; the "Check Engine" light will remain **ON** momentarily and turn **OFF**. If the "Check Engine" light remains **ON**, the self-diagnostic system has detected a trouble. The trouble code will be flashed 3 times. If more than 1 problem has been detected, each trouble code will be flashed 3 times.

NOTE: The trouble codes will flash in numeric order (lowest number code first). The trouble code series will repeat as long as the TEST terminals are grounded.

Because the self-diagnostic system does not detect all possible troubles, the absence of a code does not mean there are no troubles in the system. To determine if there is a system trouble, a System Performance Test is necessary. This test is made when the "Check Engine" light and self-diagnostic system do not indicate a trouble but the system is suspected because no other reason can be found for the complaint.

Clearing Diagnostic Memory

To clear the long term memory, disconnect the negative battery cable, for at least 10 seconds and reconnect it.

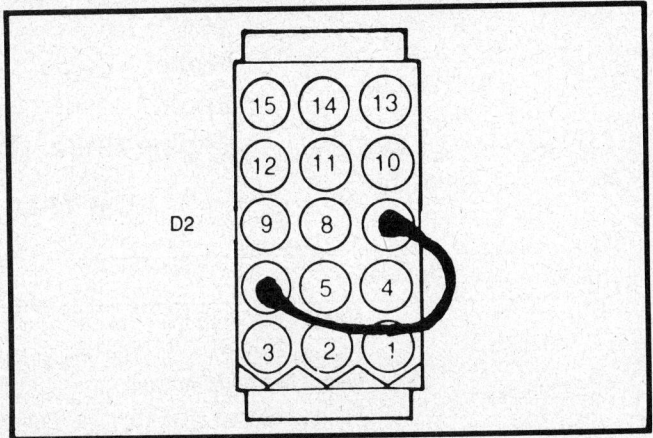

View of a jumper wire installed on the diagnostic connector—1985 models

AMERICAN MOTOR CORPORATION

Year—1980
Model—Spirit
Engine—2.5L (151 cid) 2 bbl 4 cyl
Engine Code—VIN B

ECM TROUBLE CODES

Code	Explanation
12	No tach signal to the ECM
13	Oxygen sensor circuit. The engine has to operate for approximately 5 minutes at partial throttle before this code will appear
14	Shorted coolant sensor circuit. The engine has to operate 2 minutes before this code will appear
15	Open coolant sensor circuit. The engine has to operate for appoximately 5 minutes at partial throttle before this code will appear
21 & 22	(At same time)—Grounded Wide Open Throttle (WOT) switch circuit
22	Grounded adaptive or Wide Open Throttle (WOT) switch circuit
23	Open or grounded carburetor MD solenoid circuit
44	Lean oxygen sensor. The engine has to operate for about 5 minutes in closed loop and partial throttle with a load before this code will appear
44 & 45	(At same time)—Faulty oxygen sensor
45	Rich oxygen sensor indication. The engine has to operate for about 5 minutes in closed loop and partial throttle with a load before this code will appear
51	Faulty calibration unit (PROM) or installation
52 & 53	Display OFF, intermittent ECM problem. Display light ON, faulty ECM
54	Faulty MC solenoid and/or ECM
55	Faulty oxygen sensor or ECM

Year – 1980
Model – Eagle
Engine – 2.5L (151 cid) 2 bbl 4 cyl
Engine Code – VIN B

ECM TROUBLE CODES

Code	Explanation
12	No tach signal to the ECM
13	Oxygen sensor circuit. The engine has to operate for approximately 5 minutes at partial throttle before this code will appear
14	Shorted coolant sensor circuit. The engine has to operate 2 minutes before this code will appear
15	Open coolant sensor circuit. The engine has to operate for appoximately 5 minutes at partial throttle before this code will appear
21 & 22	(At same time) – Grounded Wide Open Throttle (WOT) switch circuit
22	Grounded adaptive or Wide Open Throttle (WOT) switch circuit
23	Open or grounded carburetor MD solenoid circuit
44	Lean oxygen sensor. The engine has to operate for about 5 minutes in closed loop and partial throttle with a load before this code will appear
44 & 45	(At same time) – Faulty oxygen sensor
45	Rich oxygen sensor indication. The engine has to operate for about 5 minutes in closed loop and partial throttle with a load before this code will appear
51	Faulty calibration unit (PROM) or installation
52 & 53	Display OFF, intermittent ECM problem. Display light ON, faulty ECM
54	Faulty MC solenoid and/or ECM
55	Faulty oxygen sensor or ECM

Year — 1980
Model — Concord
Engine — 2.5L (151 cid) 2 bbl 4 cyl
Engine Code — VIN B

ECM TROUBLE CODES

Code	Explanation
12	No tach signal to the ECM
13	Oxygen sensor circuit. The engine has to operate for approximately 5 minutes at partial throttle before this code will appear
14	Shorted coolant sensor circuit. The engine has to operate 2 minutes before this code will appear
15	Open coolant sensor circuit. The engine has to operate for appoximately 5 minutes at partial throttle before this code will appear
21 & 22	(At same time) — Grounded Wide Open Throttle (WOT) switch circuit
22	Grounded adaptive or Wide Open Throttle (WOT) switch circuit
23	Open or grounded carburetor MD solenoid circuit
44	Lean oxygen sensor. The engine has to operate for about 5 minutes in closed loop and partial throttle with a load before this code will appear
44 & 45	(At same time) — Faulty oxygen sensor
45	Rich oxygen sensor indication. The engine has to operate for about 5 minutes in closed loop and partial throttle with a load before this code will appear
51	Faulty calibration unit (PROM) or installation
52 & 53	Display OFF, intermittent ECM problem. Display light ON, faulty ECM
54	Faulty MC solenoid and/or ECM
55	Faulty oxygen sensor or ECM

Year – 1981
Model – Spirit
Engine – 2.5L (151 cid) 2 bbl 4 cyl
Engine Code – VIN B

ECM TROUBLE CODES

Code	Explanation
12	No tach signal to the ECM
13	Oxygen sensor circuit. The engine has to operate for approximately 5 minutes at partial throttle before this code will appear
14	Shorted coolant sensor circuit. The engine has to operate 2 minutes before this code will appear
15	Open coolant sensor circuit. The engine has to operate for appoximately 5 minutes at partial throttle before this code will appear
21 & 22	(At same time) – Grounded Wide Open Throttle (WOT) switch circuit
22	Grounded adaptive or Wide Open Throttle (WOT) switch circuit
23	Open or grounded carburetor MD solenoid circuit
44	Lean oxygen sensor. The engine has to operate for about 5 minutes in closed loop and partial throttle with a load before this code will appear
44 & 45	(At same time) – Faulty oxygen sensor
45	Rich oxygen sensor indication. The engine has to operate for about 5 minutes in closed loop and partial throttle with a load before this code will appear
51	Faulty calibration unit (PROM) or installation
52 & 53	Display OFF, intermittent ECM problem. Display light ON, faulty ECM
54	Faulty MC solenoid and/or ECM
55	Faulty oxygen sensor or ECM

Year – 1981
Model – Concord
Engine – 2.5L (151 cid) 2 bbl 4 cyl
Engine Code – VIN B

ECM TROUBLE CODES

Code	Explanation
12	No tach signal to the ECM
13	Oxygen sensor circuit. The engine has to operate for approximately 5 minutes at partial throttle before this code will appear
14	Shorted coolant sensor circuit. The engine has to operate 2 minutes before this code will appear
15	Open coolant sensor circuit. The engine has to operate for appoximately 5 minutes at partial throttle before this code will appear
21 & 22	(At same time) – Grounded Wide Open Throttle (WOT) switch circuit
22	Grounded adaptive or Wide Open Throttle (WOT) switch circuit
23	Open or grounded carburetor MD solenoid circuit
44	Lean oxygen sensor. The engine has to operate for about 5 minutes in closed loop and partial throttle with a load before this code will appear
44 & 45	(At same time) – Faulty oxygen sensor
45	Rich oxygen sensor indication. The engine has to operate for about 5 minutes in closed loop and partial throttle with a load before this code will appear
51	Faulty calibration unit (PROM) or installation
52 & 53	Display OFF, intermittent ECM problem. Display light ON, faulty ECM
54	Faulty MC solenoid and/or ECM
55	Faulty oxygen sensor or ECM

Year—1981
Model—Eagle
Engine—2.5L (151 cid) 2 bbl 4 cyl
Engine Code—VIN B

ECM TROUBLE CODES

Code	Explanation
12	No tach signal to the ECM
13	Oxygen sensor circuit. The engine has to operate for approximately 5 minutes at partial throttle before this code will appear
14	Shorted coolant sensor circuit. The engine has to operate 2 minutes before this code will appear
15	Open coolant sensor circuit. The engine has to operate for appoximately 5 minutes at partial throttle before this code will appear
21 & 22	(At same time)—Grounded Wide Open Throttle (WOT) switch circuit
22	Grounded adaptive or Wide Open Throttle (WOT) switch circuit
23	Open or grounded carburetor MD solenoid circuit
44	Lean oxygen sensor. The engine has to operate for about 5 minutes in closed loop and partial throttle with a load before this code will appear
44 & 45	(At same time)—Faulty oxygen sensor
45	Rich oxygen sensor indication. The engine has to operate for about 5 minutes in closed loop and partial throttle with a load before this code will appear
51	Faulty calibration unit (PROM) or installation
52 & 53	Display OFF, intermittent ECM problem. Display light ON, faulty ECM
54	Faulty MC solenoid and/or ECM
55	Faulty oxygen sensor or ECM

Year — 1982
Model — Spirit
Engine — 2.5L (151 cid) 2 bbl 4 cyl
Engine Code — VIN B

ECM TROUBLE CODES

Code	Explanation
12	No tach signal to the ECM
13	Oxygen sensor circuit. The engine has to operate for approximately 5 minutes at partial throttle before this code will appear
14	Shorted coolant sensor circuit. The engine has to operate 2 minutes before this code will appear
15	Open coolant sensor circuit. The engine has to operate for appoximately 5 minutes at partial throttle before this code will appear
21 & 22	(At same time) — Grounded Wide Open Throttle (WOT) switch circuit
22	Grounded adaptive or Wide Open Throttle (WOT) switch circuit
23	Open or grounded carburetor MD solenoid circuit
44	Lean oxygen sensor. The engine has to operate for about 5 minutes in closed loop and partial throttle with a load before this code will appear
44 & 45	(At same time) — Faulty oxygen sensor
45	Rich oxygen sensor indication. The engine has to operate for about 5 minutes in closed loop and partial throttle with a load before this code will appear
51	Faulty calibration unit (PROM) or installation
52 & 53	Display OFF, intermittent ECM problem. Display light ON, faulty ECM
54	Faulty MC solenoid and/or ECM
55	Faulty oxygen sensor or ECM

Year – 1982
Model – Concord
Engine – 2.5L (151 cid) 2 bbl 4 cyl
Engine Code – VIN B

ECM TROUBLE CODES

Code	Explanation
12	No tach signal to the ECM
13	Oxygen sensor circuit. The engine has to operate for approximately 5 minutes at partial throttle before this code will appear
14	Shorted coolant sensor circuit. The engine has to operate 2 minutes before this code will appear
15	Open coolant sensor circuit. The engine has to operate for appoximately 5 minutes at partial throttle before this code will appear
21 & 22	(At same time) – Grounded Wide Open Throttle (WOT) switch circuit
22	Grounded adaptive or Wide Open Throttle (WOT) switch circuit
23	Open or grounded carburetor MD solenoid circuit
44	Lean oxygen sensor. The engine has to operate for about 5 minutes in closed loop and partial throttle with a load before this code will appear
44 & 45	(At same time) – Faulty oxygen sensor
45	Rich oxygen sensor indication. The engine has to operate for about 5 minutes in closed loop and partial throttle with a load before this code will appear
51	Faulty calibration unit (PROM) or installation
52 & 53	Display OFF, intermittent ECM problem. Display light ON, faulty ECM
54	Faulty MC solenoid and/or ECM
55	Faulty oxygen sensor or ECM

Year — 1982
Model — Eagle
Engine — 2.5L (151 cid) 2 bbl 4 cyl
Engine Code — VIN B

ECM TROUBLE CODES

Code	Explanation
12	No tach signal to the ECM
13	Oxygen sensor circuit. The engine has to operate for approximately 5 minutes at partial throttle before this code will appear
14	Shorted coolant sensor circuit. The engine has to operate 2 minutes before this code will appear
15	Open coolant sensor circuit. The engine has to operate for appoximately 5 minutes at partial throttle before this code will appear
21 & 22	(At same time) — Grounded Wide Open Throttle (WOT) switch circuit
22	Grounded adaptive or Wide Open Throttle (WOT) switch circuit
23	Open or grounded carburetor MD solenoid circuit
44	Lean oxygen sensor. The engine has to operate for about 5 minutes in closed loop and partial throttle with a load before this code will appear
44 & 45	(At same time) — Faulty oxygen sensor
45	Rich oxygen sensor indication. The engine has to operate for about 5 minutes in closed loop and partial throttle with a load before this code will appear
51	Faulty calibration unit (PROM) or installation
52 & 53	Display OFF, intermittent ECM problem. Display light ON, faulty ECM
54	Faulty MC solenoid and/or ECM
55	Faulty oxygen sensor or ECM

Year — 1985
Model — Wagoneer (California Only)
Engine — 2.8L (173 cid) V6
Engine Code — VIN W

ECM TROUBLE CODES

Code	Explanation
12	No distributor reference pulses to the ECM. This code is not stored in memory and will only flash while the trouble exists. This is a normal code with the ignition ON and the engine not operating
13	Oxygen sensor circuit. The engine must operate up to 5 minutes at part throttle, under road load, before this code will appear
14	Coolant sensor circuit has short circuit. The engine must operate up to 5 minutes before this code will appear
15	Coolant sensor circuit has open circuit. The engine must operate up to 5 minutes before the code will appear
21	Throttle position sensor circuit. The engine must operate up to 25 seconds, at the specified curb idle speed, before this code will appear
23	MC solenoid circuit has short circuit to ground or an open circuit
34	Vacuum sensor. The engine must operate up to 5 minutes at the specified curb idle speed before this code will appear
41	No distributor reference pulses to the ECM at the specified engine manifold vacuum — this code will be stored in memory
42	Electronic Spark Timing (EST) bypass circuit or EST circuit has short circuit to ground or an open circuit
44	Lean exhaust indication. The engine must operate up to 5 minutes, be in closed loop operation and at part throttle before this code will appear
44 & 45	(At the same time) Faulty oxygen sensor circuit
45	Rich exhaust indication. The engine must operate up to 5 minutes, be in closed loop and at part throttle before this code will appear
51	Faulty calibration unit (PROM) or installation. It requires up to 30 seconds before this code will appear
54	MC solenoid circuit has short circuit and or a faulty ECM
55	Voltage reference has short circuit to ground (terminal 21), a faulty oxygen sensor or ECM

Year — 1985
Model — Cherokee (California Only)
Engine — 2.8L (173 cid) V6
Engine Code — VIN W

ECM TROUBLE CODES

Code	Explanation
12	No distributor reference pulses to the ECM. This code is not stored in memory and will only flash while the trouble exists. This is a normal code with the ignition ON and the engine not operating
13	Oxygen sensor circuit. The engine must operate up to 5 minutes at part throttle, under road load, before this code will appear
14	Coolant sensor circuit has short circuit. The engine must operate up to 5 minutes before this code will appear
15	Coolant sensor circuit has open circuit. The engine must operate up to 5 minutes before the code will appear
21	Throttle position sensor circuit. The engine must operate up to 25 seconds at the specified curb idle speed before this code will appear
23	MC solenoid circuit has short circuit to ground or an open circuit
34	Vacuum sensor. The engine must operate up to 5 minutes at the specified curb idle speed before this code will appear
41	No distributor reference pulses to the ECM at the specified engine manifold vacuum. This code will be stored in memory
42	Electronic Spark Timing (EST) bypass circuit or EST circuit has short circuit to ground or an open circuit
44	Lean exhaust indication. The engine must operate up to 5 minutes, be in closed loop operation and at part throttle before this code will appear
44 & 45	(At the same time) Faulty oxygen sensor circuit
45	Rich exhaust indication. The engine must operate up to 5 minutes, be in closed loop and at part throttle before this code will appear
51	Faulty calibration unit (PROM) or installation. It requires up to 30 seconds before this code will appear
54	MC solenoid circuit has short circuit and or a faulty ECM
55	Voltage reference has short circuit to ground (terminal 21), a faulty oxygen sensor or ECM

Year — 1985
Model — Comanche (California Only)
Engine — 2.8L (173 cid) V6
Engine Code — VIN W

ECM TROUBLE CODES

Code	Explanation
12	No distributor reference pulses to the ECM. This code is not stored in memory and will only flash while the trouble exists. This is a normal code with the ignition ON and the engine not operating
13	Oxygen sensor circuit. The engine must operate up to 5 minutes at part throttle, under road load, before this code will appear
14	Coolant sensor circuit has short circuit. The engine must operate up to 5 minutes before this code will appear
15	Coolant sensor circuit has open circuit. The engine must operate up to 5 minutes before the code will appear
21	Throttle position sensor circuit. The engine must operate up to 25 seconds at the specified curb idle speed before this code will appear
23	MC solenoid circuit has short circuit to ground or an open circuit
34	Vacuum sensor. The engine must operate up to 5 minutes at the specified curb idle speed before this code will appear
41	No distributor reference pulses to the ECM at the specified engine manifold vacuum. This code will be stored in memory
42	Electronic Spark Timing (EST) bypass circuit or EST circuit has short circuit to ground or an open circuit
44	Lean exhaust indication. The engine must operate up to 5 minutes, be in closed loop operation and at part throttle before this code will appear
44 & 45	(At the same time) Faulty oxygen sensor circuit
45	Rich exhaust indication. The engine must operate up to 5 minutes, be in closed loop and at part throttle before this code will appear
51	Faulty calibration unit (PROM) or installation. It requires up to 30 seconds before this code will appear
54	MC solenoid circuit has short circuit and or a faulty ECM
55	Voltage reference has short circuit to ground (terminal 21), a faulty oxygen sensor or ECM

INDEX

CHRYSLER CORPORATION/JEEP-EAGLE

Chrysler's Electronic Fuel Injection Systems

SELF-DIAGNOSTIC SYSTEM

Description

The Electronic Fuel Injection (EFI) system is a computer regulated single point fuel injection system that provides precise air/fuel ratio for all driving conditions.

The Turbocharged Multi-Point Fuel Injection (MPFI) system combines an electronic fuel and spark advance control system with a turbocharged intake system.

At the center of these systems is a pre-programmed computer known as a Single Module Engine Controller (SMEC) that regulates ignition timing, air-fuel ratio, emission control devices, cooling fan, charging system, and idle speed. This component can adapt its requirement to meet changing operating conditions.

Various sensors provide the input necessary for the Logic Module (1984–87) or the Single Module Engine Controller (SMEC) (1988–89) to correctly regulate the fuel flow at the fuel injector. These include the Manifold Absolute Pressure, Throttle Position, Oxygen Sensor, Coolant Temperature, Throttle Body Temperature, and Vehicle Distance sensors. In addition to the sensors, various switches and relays that provide important information and system control. These include the Neutral-Safety Switch, Air-Conditioning Clutch Relay and Auto Shut Down Relay.

All inputs to the Logic Module (1984–87) or Single Module Engine Controller (1988–89) are converted into signals which are sent to the Power Module (1984–87) or used by the computer (1988–89). Based on these inputs, air-fuel ratio, Ignition Timing or other controlled outputs are adjusted accordingly.

On the 1984–87 models, the Logic Module tests many of its own input and output circuits. If a fault is found in a major system, this information is stored in the Logic Module. Information on this fault can be displayed to a technician by means of the instrument panel power loss lamp or by connecting a diagnostic read out and reading a numbered display code which directly relates to a general fault. If the problem is repaired or ceases to exist, the Logic Module cancels the fault code after 20-40 vehicle starts.

On the 1988–89 models, the Single Module Engine Controller (SMEC) tests many of its own input and output circuits. If a fault is found in a major system, this information is stored in the Memory. Information on this fault can be displayed to a technician by means of the instrument panel "Check Engine" lamp or by connecting the Diagnostic Readout Box II (DRB-II) and read descriptions of any faults which have been stored. If the problem is repaired or ceases to exist, the SMEC cancels the Fault Code after 50–100 vehicle key on/off cycles.

Entering Diagnostic Mode

1. Connect the Diagnostic Readout Box tool No. C-4805 or equivalent, to the diagnostic connector located in the engine compartment near the passenger side strut tower.

2. Start the engine if possible, cycle the transmission selector and the air conditioning switch, if applicable. Turn OFF the engine.

3. Turn the ignition switch ON, OFF, ON, OFF, ON. Within 5 seconds record all the diagnostic codes shown on the diagnostic readout box tool, observe the power loss lamp on the instrument panel the lamp should light for 2 seconds on 1984–85 models and 3 seconds on 1986–88 models, then, go out (bulb check).

Operation

After all codes have been shown and has indicated Code 55 end of message, actuate the following component switches. The digital display must change its numbers when the following switches are activated and released:
   a. Brake pedal.
   b. Gear shift selector **P, R, P**.
   c. Air conditioning switch (if applicable).
   d. Electric backlite switch (if applicable).

Clearing Diagnostic Memory

Turn the ignition switch OFF; the test mode system should turn OFF and be exited. With a Diagnostic Readout Box attached to the system and the ATM control button not pressed, the computer will continue to cycle the selected circuits for 5 minutes and automatically shut the system down.

Jeep-Eagle Electronic Control System

SELF-DIAGNOSTIC SYSTEM

Description

The Jeep-Eagle Multi-Port Fuel Injection (MPFI) system is a simultaneous double fire type. All of the injectors fire simultaneously once every engine revolution, delivering half of the fuel needed for combustion. The system is controlled by an Electronic Control Unit (ECU). The ECU constantly adjusts the amount of fuel injected to meet the changing operating conditions by controlling the injector pulse width. The ECU also adjusts the ignition timing by controlling the ignition coil operation through the ignition module. The ECU determines these factors by inputs from various sensors that monitor engine operating conditions. The ECU monitors and analyzes its various inputs, computes engine fuel and ignition timing requirements, then adjusts them accordingly.

The ECU, the various sensors and switches that provide the ECU inputs and outputs comprise the engine control system.

Entering Diagnostic Mode

Entering the Jeep-Eagle self-diagnostic system requires the use of a special adapter that connects with the Diagnostic Readout Box II (DRB-II). These systems require the adapter because all of the system diagnosis is done off-board instead of on-board like most vehicles. The adapter, which is a computer module itself, measures signals at the diagnostic connector and converts the signals into a form which the DRB-II can use to perform tests.

CONNECTING DIAGNOSTIC READOUT BOX

The DRB-II is connected to the Jeep-Eagle adapter by a 6 pin and 15 pin connectors. The Jeep-Eagle adapter is connected to the engine diagnostic connector, located in the engine compartment. The connections can be made in any order.

When the diagnostic readout box is operating properly and the adapter connected properly, all positions on the display should be briefly illuminated and the copyright message should appear. The copyright message should stay on for 3 seconds and then the main menu should appear. If the main menu does not appear, or the display does not light, check all of the connections for proper contact. Make sure the DRB cartridge is installed snugly.

OBTAINING FAULT CODES

1. Connect the readout box to the adapter. Then connect the

adapter to diagnostic connector located in the engine compartment.

2. Start the engine, if possible, cycle the transmission selector and the air conditioning switch. Turn **OFF** the engine.

3. Turn the ignition switch **ON** to access the read fault code data. Record all the fault code messages displayed on the read-out box.

Sustem Displays
MAIN MENU

The "Main Menu" presents all of the diagnostic features available through the DRB-II for the vehicle. The menu displays 3 functions, they are: system tests, state displays and adjustments.

SYSTEM TESTS

The system test is an interactive, functional test of certain systems. During the test, the display provides instructions to the technician such as, "TURN ON KEY", "SHIFT TO PARK", "TURN ON A/C", etc. It then monitors the signal through the diagnostic connector to make sure the requested action occurs. If the display continues to display the action and the action has been performed, press the ENTER button to indicate the action has been performed. This will set the fault code. If all instructions are performed and all components test correctly the system will display a "VEHICLE PASSES ELECTRICAL TEST" message.

STATE DISPLAYS

The state display function enables the technician to view conditions as they exist at the signal level. There are 2 types of data that are monitored for diagnostic purposes: analog and digital. Analog signals are monitored at those pins corresponding to the vehicle harness splices (fuel pump relay, battery voltage, etc.). Digital signals correspond to the data transmitted by the system controllers. The data is displayed in common units (temperature, pressure, etc.) and is not analyzed according to diagnostic intent. The technician must scroll through the display screen to view all of the functions.

ADJUSTMENTS

When selected from the main menu, this option provides a means to adjust the Throttle Position Sensor (TPS). It also allows erasure of the stored trouble codes.

Clearing Diagnostic Memory

To clear the trouble codes stored in the system, select "ADJUSTMENTS" from the main menu display. Then select select the option to erase the codes. The option may vary depending on the vehicle type selected.

Turn the ignition switch **OFF**; the test mode system should be exited. With a Diagnostic Readout Box attached to the system and the Actuator Test Mode (ATM) control button not pressed, the computer will continue to cycle the selected circuits for 5 minutes and automatically turn the system **OFF**.

As a final method of clearing codes, the battery can be disconnected. This should be used only as last resort as other vehicle memory functions could be effected.

CHRYSLER CORPORATION

Year – 1984
Model – Daytona
Engine – 2.2L (135 cid) EFI 4 cyl
Engine Code – VIN D

ECM TROUBLE CODES

Code	Explanation
88	Start of test
11	Engine not cranked since battery was disconnected
12	Memory standby power lost
13	Manifold Absolute Pressure (MAP) sensor pneumatic circuit – power loss/limited lamp is ON
14	Manifold Absolute Pressure (MAP) sensor electrical system – power loss/limited lamp is ON
15	Vehicle Speed Sensor (VSS) circuit
16	Lose of battery voltage sense – power loss/limited lamp is ON
21	Oxygen (O_2) sensor circuit
22	Coolant Temperature Sensor (CTS) circuit – power loss/limited lamp is ON
24	Throttle Position Sensor (TPS) circuit – power loss/limited lamp is ON
25	Automatic Idle Speed (AIS) control circuit
26	Peak injector current has not been replaced
27	Fuel interface circuit (internal fuel circuit problem of logic module)
31	Canister purge solenoid circuit
32	Power loss lamp circuit
34	Problem in the Exhaust Gas Recirculation (EGR) solenoid circuit
35	Fan control relay circuit
37	Shift indicator lamp circuit – manual transmissions only
41	Charging system excess or no field circuit
42	Automatic Shut Down (ASD) relay circuit
43	Spark interface (internal) circuits
44	Logic module failure
46	Battery voltage too high – power loss/limited lamp is ON
47	Battery voltage too low
51	Closed loop fuel system problem – oxygen signal either too lean or too rich
52	Logic module problem or failure
53	Logic module problem or failure
54	Logic module problem or failure
55	End of message
88	Start of message – this code only appears on the diagnostic readout Tool C-4805 or equivalent, and means start of message.

Year – 1984
Model – Laser
Engine – 2.2L (135 cid) EFI 4 cyl
Engine Code – VIN D

ECM TROUBLE CODES

Code	Explanation
88	Start of test
11	Engine not cranked since battery was disconnected
12	Memory standby power lost
13	Manifold Absolute Pressure (MAP) sensor pneumatic circuit – power loss/limited lamp is ON
14	Manifold Absolute Pressure (MAP) sensor electrical system – power loss/limited lamp is ON
15	Vehicle Speed Sensor (VSS) circuit
16	Lose of battery voltage sense – power loss/limited lamp is ON
21	Oxygen (O_2) sensor circuit
22	Coolant Temperature Sensor (CTS) circuit – power loss/limited lamp is ON
24	Throttle Position Sensor (TPS) circuit – power loss/limited lamp is ON
25	Automatic Idle Speed (AIS) control circuit
26	Peak injector current has not been replaced
27	Fuel interface circuit (internal fuel circuit problem of logic module)
31	Canister purge solenoid circuit
32	Power loss lamp circuit
34	Problem in the Exhaust Gas Recirculation (EGR) solenoid circuit
35	Fan control relay circuit
37	Shift indicator lamp circuit – manual transmissions only
41	Charging system excess or no field circuit
42	Automatic Shut Down (ASD) relay circuit
43	Spark interface (internal) circuits
44	Logic module failure
46	Battery voltage too high – power loss/limited lamp is ON
47	Battery voltage too low
51	Closed loop fuel system problem – oxygen signal either too lean or too rich
52	Logic module problem or failure
53	Logic module problem or failure
54	Logic module problem or failure
55	End of message
88	Start of message – this code only appears on the diagnostic readout Tool C-4805 or equivalent, and means start of message.

Year – 1984
Model – Daytona
Engine – 2.2L (135 cid) Turbo 4 cyl
Engine Code – VIN E

ECM TROUBLE CODES

Code	Explanation
88	Start of test
11	Logic module has not recognized distributor signal since battery was reconnected
12	Memory standby power lost
13	Manifold Absolute Pressure (MAP) sensor pneumatic circuit – power loss/limited lamp is ON
14	Manifold Absolute Pressure (MAP) sensor electrical system – power loss/limited lamp is ON
15	Vehicle Speed Sensor (VSS) circuit
21	Oxygen (O$_2$) sensor circuit
22	Coolant Temperature Sensor (CTS) circuit – power loss/limited lamp is ON
24	Throttle Position Sensor (TPS) circuit – power loss/limited lamp is ON
25	Automatic Idle Speed (AIS) control circuit
31	Canister purge solenoid circuit
32	Power loss lamp circuit
33	A/C wide cut out relay circuit
34	Problem in the Exhaust Gas Recirculation (EGR) solenoid circuit
35	Fan control relay circuit
41	Charging system excess or no field circuit
42	Automatic Shut Down (ASD) relay driver circuit
43	Spark interface (internal) circuits
44	Logic module failure
45	Overboost shut-off circuit – power loss/limited lamp is ON
46	Battery voltage too high – power loss/limited lamp is ON
47	Battery voltage too low
51	Closed loop fuel system problem – oxygen sensor signal either too lean or too rich
52	Logic module problem or failure
53	Logic module problem or failure
54	Distributor sync pick-up circuit
55	End of message

Year – 1984
Model – Laser
Engine – 2.2L (135 cid) Turbo 4 cyl
Engine Code – VIN E

ECM TROUBLE CODES

Code	Explanation
88	Start of test
11	Logic module has not recognized distributor signal since battery was reconnected
12	Memory standby power lost
13	Manifold Absolute Pressure (MAP) sensor pneumatic circuit – power loss/limited lamp is ON
14	Manifold Absolute Pressure (MAP) sensor electrical system – power loss/limited lamp is ON
15	Vehicle Speed Sensor (VSS) circuit
21	Oxygen (O_2) sensor circuit
22	Coolant Temperature Sensor (CTS) circuit – power loss/limited lamp is ON
24	Throttle Position Sensor (TPS) circuit – power loss/limited lamp is ON
25	Automatic Idle Speed (AIS) control circuit
31	Canister purge solenoid circuit
32	Power loss lamp circuit
33	A/C wide cut out relay circuit
34	Problem in the Exhaust Gas Recirculation (EGR) solenoid circuit
35	Fan control relay circuit
41	Charging system excess or no field circuit
42	Automatic Shut Down (ASD) relay driver circuit
43	Spark interface (internal) circuits
44	Logic module failure
45	Overboost shut-off circuit – power loss/limited lamp is ON
46	Battery voltage too high – power loss/limited lamp is ON
47	Battery voltage too low
51	Closed loop fuel system problem – oxygen sensor signal either too lean or too rich
52	Logic module problem or failure
53	Logic module problem or failure
54	Distributor sync pick-up circuit
55	End of message

Year — 1984
Model — Dodge 600
Engine — 2.2L (135 cid) EFI 4 cyl
Engine Code — VIN D

ECM TROUBLE CODES

Code	Explanation
88	Start of test
11	Engine not cranked since battery was disconnected
12	Memory standby power lost
13	Manifold Absolute Pressure (MAP) sensor pneumatic circuit — power loss/limited lamp is ON
14	Manifold Absolute Pressure (MAP) sensor electrical system — power loss/limited lamp is ON
15	Vehicle Speed Sensor (VSS) circuit
16	Lose of battery voltage sense — power loss/limited lamp is ON
21	Oxygen (O$_2$) sensor circuit
22	Coolant Temperature Sensor (CTS) circuit — power loss/limited lamp is ON
24	Throttle Position Sensor (TPS) circuit — power loss/limited lamp is ON
25	Automatic Idle Speed (AIS) control circuit
26	Peak injector current has not been replaced
27	Fuel interface circuit — internal fuel circuit problem of logic module
31	Canister purge solenoid circuit
32	Power loss lamp circuit
33	Air conditioning Wide Open Throttle (WOT) cut out relay circuit
34	Problem in the Exhaust Gas Recirculation (EGR) solenoid circuit
35	Fan control relay circuit
37	Shift indicator lamp circuit — manual transmissions only
41	Charging system excess or no field circuit
42	Automatic Shut Down (ASD) relay circuit
43	Spark interface (internal) circuits
44	Logic module failure
46	Battery voltage too high — power loss/limited lamp is ON
47	Battery voltage too low
51	Closed loop fuel system problem — oxygen sensor signal either too lean or too rich
52	Logic module problem or failure
53	Logic module problem or failure
54	Logic module problem or failure
55	End of message
88	Start of message — this code only appears on the diagnostic readout Tool C-4805 or equivalent, and means start of message

Year — 1984
Model — Caravelle
Engine — 2.2L (135 cid) EFI 4 cyl
Engine Code — VIN D

ECM TROUBLE CODES

Code	Explanation
88	Start of test
11	Engine not cranked since battery was disconnected
12	Memory standby power lost
13	Manifold Absolute Pressure (MAP) sensor pneumatic circuit — power loss/limited lamp is ON
14	Manifold Absolute Pressure (MAP) sensor electrical system — power loss/limited lamp is ON
15	Vehicle Speed Sensor (VSS) circuit
16	Lose of battery voltage sense — power loss/limited lamp is ON
21	Oxygen (O$_2$) sensor circuit
22	Coolant Temperature Sensor (CTS) circuit — power loss/limited lamp is ON
24	Throttle Position Sensor (TPS) circuit — power loss/limited lamp is ON
25	Automatic Idle Speed (AIS) control circuit
26	Peak injector current has not been replaced
27	Fuel interface circuit — internal fuel circuit problem of logic module
31	Canister purge solenoid circuit
32	Power loss lamp circuit
33	Air conditioning Wide Open Throttle (WOT) cut out relay circuit
34	Problem in the Exhaust Gas Recirculation (EGR) solenoid circuit
35	Fan control relay circuit
37	Shift indicator lamp circuit — manual transmissions only
41	Charging system excess or no field circuit
42	Automatic Shut Down (ASD) relay circuit
43	Spark interface (internal) circuits
44	Logic module failure
46	Battery voltage too high — power loss/limited lamp is ON
47	Battery voltage too low
51	Closed loop fuel system problem — oxygen sensor signal either too lean or too rich
52	Logic module problem or failure
53	Logic module problem or failure
54	Logic module problem or failure
55	End of message
88	Start of message — this code only appears on the diagnostic readout Tool C-4805 or equivalent, and means start of message

Year – 1984
Model – Dodge 600
Engine – 2.2L (135 cid) Turbo 4 cyl
Engine Code – VIN E

ECM TROUBLE CODES

Code	Explanation
88	Start of test
11	Logic module has not recognized distributor signal since battery was reconnected
12	Memory standby power lost
13	Manifold Absolute Pressure (MAP) sensor pneumatic circuit – power loss/limited lamp is ON
14	Manifold Absolute Pressure (MAP) sensor electrical system – power loss/limited lamp is ON
15	Vehicle Speed Sensor (VSS) circuit
21	Oxygen (O₂) sensor circuit
22	Coolant Temperature Sensor (CTS) circuit – power loss/limited lamp is ON
24	Throttle Position Sensor (TPS) circuit – power loss/limited lamp is ON
25	Automatic Idle Speed (AIS) control circuit
31	Canister purge solenoid circuit
32	Power loss lamp circuit
33	A/C wide cut out relay circuit
34	Problem in the Exhaust Gas Recirculation (EGR) solenoid circuit
35	Fan control relay circuit
41	Charging system excess or no field circuit
42	Automatic Shut Down (ASD) relay driver circuit
43	Spark interface (internal) circuits
44	Logic module failure
45	Overboost shut-off circuit – power loss/limited lamp is ON
46	Battery voltage too high – power loss/limited lamp is ON
47	Battery voltage too low
51	Closed loop fuel system problem – oxygen sensor signal either too lean or too rich
52	Logic module problem or failure
53	Logic module problem or failure
54	Distributor sync pick-up circuit
55	End of message

Year — 1984
Model — Caravelle
Engine — 2.2L (135 cid) Turbo 4 cyl
Engine Code — VIN E

ECM TROUBLE CODES

Code	Explanation
88	Start of test
11	Logic module has not recognized distributor signal since battery was reconnected
12	Memory standby power lost
13	Manifold Absolute Pressure (MAP) sensor pneumatic circuit — power loss/limited lamp is ON
14	Manifold Absolute Pressure (MAP) sensor electrical system — power loss/limited lamp is ON
15	Vehicle Speed Sensor (VSS) circuit
21	Oxygen (O$_2$) sensor circuit
22	Coolant Temperature Sensor (CTS) circuit — power loss/limited lamp is ON
24	Throttle Position Sensor (TPS) circuit — power loss/limited lamp is ON
25	Automatic Idle Speed (AIS) control circuit
31	Canister purge solenoid circuit
32	Power loss lamp circuit
33	A/C wide cut out relay circuit
34	Problem in the Exhaust Gas Recirculation (EGR) solenoid circuit
35	Fan control relay circuit
41	Charging system excess or no field circuit
42	Automatic Shut Down (ASD) relay driver circuit
43	Spark interface (internal) circuits
44	Logic module failure
45	Overboost shut-off circuit — power loss/limited lamp is ON
46	Battery voltage too high — power loss/limited lamp is ON
47	Battery voltage too low
51	Closed loop fuel system problem — oxygen sensor signal either too lean or too rich
52	Logic module problem or failure
53	Logic module problem or failure
54	Distributor sync pick-up circuit
55	End of message

Year — 1984
Model — E-Class
Engine — 2.2L (135 cid) EFI 4 cyl
Engine Code — VIN D

ECM TROUBLE CODES

Code	Explanation
88	Start of test
11	Engine not cranked since battery was disconnected
12	Memory standby power lost
13	Manifold Absolute Pressure (MAP) sensor pneumatic circuit — power loss/limited lamp is ON
14	Manifold Absolute Pressure (MAP) sensor electrical system — power loss/limited lamp is ON
15	Vehicle Speed Sensor (VSS) circuit
16	Lose of battery voltage sense — power loss/limited lamp is ON
21	Oxygen (O_2) sensor circuit
22	Coolant Temperature Sensor (CTS) circuit — power loss/limited lamp is ON
24	Throttle Position Sensor (TPS) circuit — power loss/limited lamp is ON
25	Automatic Idle Speed (AIS) control circuit
26	Peak injector current has not been replaced
27	Fuel interface circuit — internal fuel circuit problem of logic module
31	Canister purge solenoid circuit
32	Power loss lamp circuit
33	Air conditioning Wide Open Throttle (WOT) cut out relay circuit
34	Problem in the Exhaust Gas Recirculation (EGR) solenoid circuit
35	Fan control relay circuit
37	Shift indicator lamp circuit — manual transmissions only
41	Charging system excess or no field circuit
42	Automatic Shut Down (ASD) relay circuit
43	Spark interface (internal) circuits
44	Logic module failure
46	Battery voltage too high — power loss/limited lamp is ON
47	Battery voltage too low
51	Closed loop fuel system problem. Oxygen sensor signal either too lean or too rich
52	Logic module problem or failure
53	Logic module problem or failure
54	Logic module problem or failure
55	End of message
88	Start of message — this code only appears on the diagnostic readout Tool C-4805 or equivalent, and means start of message

Year – 1984
Model – E-Class
Engine – 2.2L (135 cid) Turbo 4 cyl
Engine Code – VIN E

ECM TROUBLE CODES

Code	Explanation
88	Start of test
11	Logic module has not recognized distributor signal since battery was reconnected
12	Memory standby power lost
13	Manifold Absolute Pressure (MAP) sensor pneumatic circuit – power loss/limited lamp is ON
14	Manifold Absolute Pressure (MAP) sensor electrical system – power loss/limited lamp is ON
15	Vehicle Speed Sensor (VSS) circuit
21	Oxygen (O_2) sensor circuit
22	Coolant Temperature Sensor (CTS) circuit – power loss/limited lamp is ON
24	Throttle Position Sensor (TPS) circuit – power loss/limited lamp is ON
25	Automatic Idle Speed (AIS) control circuit
31	Canister purge solenoid circuit
32	Power loss lamp circuit
33	A/C wide cut out relay circuit
34	Problem in the Exhaust Gas Recirculation (EGR) solenoid circuit
35	Fan control relay circuit
41	Charging system excess or no field circuit
42	Automatic Shut Down (ASD) relay driver circuit
43	Spark interface (internal) circuits
44	Logic module failure
45	Overboost shut-off circuit – power loss/limited lamp is ON
46	Battery voltage too high – power loss/limited lamp is ON
47	Battery voltage too low
51	Closed loop fuel system problem – oxygen sensor signal either too lean or too rich.
52	Logic module problem or failure
53	Logic module problem or failure
54	Distributor sync pick-up circuit
55	End of message

Year — 1984
Model — New Yorker
Engine — 2.2L (135 cid) Turbo 4 cyl
Engine Code — VIN E

ECM TROUBLE CODES

Code	Explanation
88	Start of test
11	Logic module has not recognized distributor signal since battery was reconnected
12	Memory standby power lost
13	Manifold Absolute Pressure (MAP) sensor pneumatic circuit—power loss/limited lamp is ON
14	Manifold Absolute Pressure (MAP) sensor electrical system—power loss/limited lamp is ON
15	Vehicle Speed Sensor (VSS) circuit
21	Oxygen (O$_2$) sensor circuit
22	Coolant Temperature Sensor (CTS) circuit—power loss/limited lamp is ON
24	Throttle Position Sensor (TPS) circuit—power loss/limited lamp is ON
25	Automatic Idle Speed (AIS) control circuit
31	Canister purge solenoid circuit
32	Power loss lamp circuit
33	A/C wide cut out relay circuit
34	Problem in the Exhaust Gas Recirculation (EGR) solenoid circuit
35	Fan control relay circuit
41	Charging system excess or no field circuit
42	Automatic Shut Down (ASD) relay driver circuit
43	Spark interface (internal) circuits
44	Logic module failure
45	Overboost shut-off circuit—power loss/limited lamp is ON
46	Battery voltage too high—power loss/limited lamp is ON
47	Battery voltage too low
51	Closed loop fuel system problem—oxygen sensor signal either too lean or too rich.
52	Logic module problem or failure
53	Logic module problem or failure
54	Distributor sync pick-up circuit
55	End of message

Year – 1984
Model – LeBaron
Engine – 2.2L (135 cid) EFI 4 cyl
Engine Code – VIN D

ECM TROUBLE CODES

Code	Explanation
88	Start of test
11	Engine not cranked since battery was disconnected
12	Memory standby power lost
13	Manifold Absolute Pressure (MAP) sensor pneumatic circuit – power loss/limited lamp is ON
14	Manifold Absolute Pressure (MAP) sensor electrical system – power loss/limited lamp is ON
15	Vehicle Speed Sensor (VSS) circuit
16	Lose of battery voltage sense – power loss/limited lamp is ON
21	Oxygen (O_2) sensor circuit
22	Coolant Temperature Sensor (CTS) circuit – power loss/limited lamp is ON
24	Throttle Position Sensor (TPS) circuit – power loss/limited lamp is ON
25	Automatic Idle Speed (AIS) control circuit
26	Peak injector current has not been replaced
27	Fuel interface circuit – internal fuel circuit problem of logic module
31	Canister purge solenoid circuit
32	Power loss lamp circuit
33	Air conditioning Wide Open Throttle (WOT) cut out relay circuit
34	Problem in the Exhaust Gas Recirculation (EGR) solenoid circuit
35	Fan control relay circuit
37	Shift indicator lamp circuit – manual transmissions only
41	Charging system excess or no field circuit
42	Automatic Shut Down (ASD) relay circuit
43	Spark interface (internal) circuits
44	Logic module failure
46	Battery voltage too high – power loss/limited lamp is ON
47	Battery voltage too low
51	Closed loop fuel system problem – oxygen sensor signal either too lean or too rich
52	Logic module problem or failure
53	Logic module problem or failure
54	Logic module problem or failure
55	End of message
88	Start of message – this code only appears on the diagnostic readout Tool C-4805 or equivalent, and means start of message

Year — 1984
Model — LeBaron
Engine — 2.2L (135 cid) Turbo 4 cyl
Engine Code — VIN E

ECM TROUBLE CODES

Code	Explanation
88	Start of test
11	Logic module has not recognized distributor signal since battery was reconnected
12	Memory standby power lost
13	Manifold Absolute Pressure (MAP) sensor pneumatic circuit — power loss/limited lamp is ON
14	Manifold Absolute Pressure (MAP) sensor electrical system — power loss/limited lamp is ON
15	Vehicle Speed Sensor (VSS) circuit
21	Oxygen (O_2) sensor circuit
22	Coolant Temperature Sensor (CTS) circuit — power loss/limited lamp is ON
24	Throttle Position Sensor (TPS) circuit — power loss/limited lamp is ON
25	Automatic Idle Speed (AIS) control circuit
31	Canister purge solenoid circuit
32	Power loss lamp circuit
33	A/C wide cut out relay circuit
34	Problem in the Exhaust Gas Recirculation (EGR) solenoid circuit
35	Fan control relay circuit
41	Charging system excess or no field circuit
42	Automatic Shut Down (ASD) relay driver circuit
43	Spark interface (internal) circuits
44	Logic module failure
45	Overboost shut-off circuit — power loss/limited lamp is ON
46	Battery voltage too high — power loss/limited lamp is ON
47	Battery voltage too low
51	Closed loop fuel system problem — oxygen sensor signal either too lean or too rich
52	Logic module problem or failure
53	Logic module problem or failure
54	Distributor sync pick-up circuit
55	End of message

Year — 1985
Model — Daytona
Engine — 2.2L (135 cid) Turbo 4 cyl
Engine Code — VIN E

ECM TROUBLE CODES

Code	Explanation
88	Start of test
11	Engine not cranked since battery was disconnected
12	Memory standby power lost
13	Manifold Absolute Pressure (MAP) sensor pneumatic circuit — power loss/limited lamp is ON
14	Manifold Absolute Pressure (MAP) sensor electrical system — power loss/limited lamp is ON
15	Vehicle Speed Sensor (VSS) circuit
16	Lose of battery voltage sense — power loss/limited lamp is ON
21	Oxygen (O_2) sensor circuit
22	Coolant Temperature Sensor (CTS) circuit — power loss/limited lamp is ON
23	Throttle body temperature sensor circuit
24	Throttle Position Sensor (TPS) circuit — power loss/limited lamp is ON
25	Automatic Idle Speed (AIS) control circuit
26	Number 1 injector circuit
27	Number 2 injector circuit
31	Canister purge solenoid circuit
32	Power loss lamp circuit
33	A/C wide cut out relay circuit
34	Problem in the Exhaust Gas Recirculation (EGR) solenoid circuit
35	Fan control relay circuit
36	Wastegate solenoid circuit — power loss/limited lamp is ON
37	Barometric read solenoid circuit
41	Charging system excess or no field circuit
42	Automatic Shut Down (ASD) relay driver circuit
43	Spark interface (internal) circuits
44	Battery temperature is out of range
45	Overboost shut-off circuit — power loss/limited lamp is ON
46	Battery voltage too high — power loss/limited lamp is ON
47	Battery voltage too low
51	Closed loop fuel system problem — oxygen sensor signal stuck at the lean position
52	Oxygen sensor signal stuck at the rich position
53	Logic module problem or failure
54	Distributor sync pick-up circuit
55	End of message

CHRYSLER CORPORATION
DIAGNOSTIC CODE DATA

Year – 1985
Model – Laser
Engine – 2.2L (135 cid) Turbo 4 cyl
Engine Code – VIN E

ECM TROUBLE CODES

Code	Explanation
88	Start of test
11	Engine not cranked since battery was disconnected
12	Memory standby power lost
13	Manifold Absolute Pressure (MAP) sensor pneumatic circuit – power loss/limited lamp is ON
14	Manifold Absolute Pressure (MAP) sensor electrical system – power loss/limited lamp is ON
15	Vehicle Speed Sensor (VSS) circuit
16	Lose of battery voltage sense – power loss/limited lamp is ON
21	Oxygen (O$_2$) sensor circuit
22	Coolant Temperature Sensor (CTS) circuit – power loss/limited lamp is ON
23	Throttle body temperature sensor circuit
24	Throttle Position Sensor (TPS) circuit – power loss/limited lamp is ON
25	Automatic Idle Speed (AIS) control circuit
26	Number 1 injector circuit
27	Number 2 injector circuit
31	Canister purge solenoid circuit
32	Power loss lamp circuit
33	A/C wide cut out relay circuit
34	Problem in the Exhaust Gas Recirculation (EGR) solenoid circuit
35	Fan control relay circuit
36	Wastegate solenoid circuit – power loss/limited lamp is ON
37	Barometric read solenoid circuit
41	Charging system excess or no field circuit
42	Automatic Shut Down (ASD) relay driver circuit
43	Spark interface (internal) circuits
44	Battery temperature is out of range
45	Overboost shut-off circuit – power loss/limited lamp is ON
46	Battery voltage too high – power loss/limited lamp is ON
47	Battery voltage too low
51	Closed loop fuel system problem – oxygen sensor signal stuck at the lean position
52	Oxygen sensor signal stuck at the rich position
53	Logic module problem or failure
54	Distributor sync pick-up circuit
55	End of message

Year – 1985
Model – Dodge Daytona
Engine – 2.2L (135 cid) EFI 4 cyl
Engine Code – VIN D

ECM TROUBLE CODES

Code	Explanation
88	Start of test
11	Engine not cranked since battery was disconnected
12	Memory standby power lost
13	Manifold Absolute Pressure (MAP) sensor pneumatic circuit – power loss/limited lamp is ON
14	Manifold Absolute Pressure (MAP) sensor electrical system – power loss/limited lamp is ON
15	Vehicle Speed Sensor (VSS) circuit
16	Lose of battery voltage sense – power loss/limited lamp is ON
21	Oxygen (O₂) sensor circuit
22	Coolant Temperature Sensor (CTS) circuit – power loss/limited lamp is ON
23	Throttle body temperature sensor circuit
24	Throttle Position Sensor (TPS) circuit – power loss/limited lamp is ON
25	Automatic Idle Speed (AIS) control circuit
26	Peak injector current has not been replaced
27	Fuel interface circuit – internal fuel circuit problem of logic module
31	Canister purge solenoid circuit
32	Power loss lamp circuit
33	Air conditioning Wide Open Throttle (WOT) cut out relay circuit
34	Problem in spare driver circuit
35	Fan control relay circuit
36	Problem in spare driver circuit
37	Shift indicator lamp circuit – manual transmissions only
41	Charging system excess or no field circuit
42	Automatic Shut Down (ASD) relay circuit
43	Spark interface (internal) circuits
44	Battery temperature is out of range
46	Battery voltage too high – power loss/limited lamp is ON
47	Battery voltage too low
51	Closed loop fuel system problem – oxygen sensor signal stuck at the lean position
52	Oxygen sensor signal stuck at the rich position
53	Logic module problem or failure
55	End of message
88	Start of message – this code only appears on the diagnostic readout Tool C-4805 or equivalent, and means start of message

Year — 1985
Model — Laser
Engine — 2.2L (135 cid) EFI 4 cyl
Engine Code — VIN D

ECM TROUBLE CODES

Code	Explanation
88	Start of test
11	Engine not cranked since battery was disconnected
12	Memory standby power lost
13	Manifold Absolute Pressure (MAP) sensor pneumatic circuit — power loss/limited lamp is ON
14	Manifold Absolute Pressure (MAP) sensor electrical system — power loss/limited lamp is ON
15	Vehicle Speed Sensor (VSS) circuit
16	Lose of battery voltage sense — power loss/limited lamp is ON
21	Oxygen (O_2) sensor circuit
22	Coolant Temperature Sensor (CTS) circuit — power loss/limited lamp is ON
23	Throttle body temperature sensor circuit
24	Throttle Position Sensor (TPS) circuit — power loss/limited lamp is ON
25	Automatic Idle Speed (AIS) control circuit
26	Peak injector current has not been replaced
27	Fuel interface circuit — internal fuel circuit problem of logic module
31	Canister purge solenoid circuit
32	Power loss lamp circuit
33	Air conditioning Wide Open Throttle (WOT) cut out relay circuit
34	Problem in spare driver circuit
35	Fan control relay circuit
36	Problem in spare driver circuit
37	Shift indicator lamp circuit — manual transmissions only
41	Charging system excess or no field circuit
42	Automatic Shut Down (ASD) relay circuit
43	Spark interface (internal) circuits
44	Battery temperature is out of range
46	Battery voltage too high — power loss/limited lamp is ON
47	Battery voltage too low
51	Closed loop fuel system problem — oxygen sensor signal stuck at the lean position
52	Oxygen sensor signal stuck at the rich position
53	Logic module problem or failure
55	End of message
88	Start of message — this code only appears on the diagnostic readout Tool C-4805 or equivalent, and means start of message

Year — 1985
Model — Dodge Omni GLH
Engine — 2.2L (135 cid) Turbo 4 cyl
Engine Code — VIN E

ECM TROUBLE CODES

Code	Explanation
88	Start of test
11	Engine not cranked since battery was disconnected
12	Memory standby power lost
13	Manifold Absolute Pressure (MAP) sensor pneumatic circuit — power loss/limited lamp is ON
14	Manifold Absolute Pressure (MAP) sensor electrical system — power loss/limited lamp is ON
15	Vehicle Speed Sensor (VSS) circuit
16	Lose of battery voltage sense — power loss/limited lamp is ON
21	Oxygen (O_2) sensor circuit
22	Coolant Temperature Sensor (CTS) circuit — power loss/limited lamp is ON
23	Throttle body temperature sensor circuit
24	Throttle Position Sensor (TPS) circuit — power loss/limited lamp is ON
25	Automatic Idle Speed (AIS) control circuit
26	Number 1 injector circuit
27	Number 2 injector circuit
31	Canister purge solenoid circuit
32	Power loss lamp circuit
33	A/C wide cut out relay circuit
34	Problem in the Exhaust Gas Recirculation (EGR) solenoid circuit
35	Fan control relay circuit
36	Wastegate solenoid circuit — power loss/limited lamp is ON
37	Barometric read solenoid circuit
41	Charging system excess or no field circuit
42	Automatic Shut Down (ASD) relay driver circuit
43	Spark interface (internal) circuits
44	Battery temperature is out of range
45	Overboost shut-off circuit — power loss/limited lamp is ON
46	Battery voltage too high — power loss/limited lamp is ON
47	Battery voltage too low
51	Closed loop fuel system problem — oxygen sensor signal stuck at the lean position
52	Oxygen sensor signal stuck at the rich position
53	Logic module problem or failure
54	Distributor sync pick-up circuit
55	End of message

Year – 1985
Model – Dodge Charger Shelby
Engine – 2.2L (135 cid) Turbo 4 cyl
Engine Code – VIN E

ECM TROUBLE CODES

Code	Explanation
88	Start of test
11	Engine not cranked since battery was disconnected
12	Memory standby power lost
13	Manifold Absolute Pressure (MAP) sensor pneumatic circuit – power loss/limited lamp is ON
14	Manifold Absolute Pressure (MAP) sensor electrical system – power loss/limited lamp is ON
15	Vehicle Speed Sensor (VSS) circuit
16	Lose of battery voltage sense – power loss/limited lamp is ON
21	Oxygen (O_2) sensor circuit
22	Coolant Temperature Sensor (CTS) circuit – power loss/limited lamp is ON
23	Throttle body temperature sensor circuit
24	Throttle Position Sensor (TPS) circuit – power loss/limited lamp is ON
25	Automatic Idle Speed (AIS) control circuit
26	Number 1 injector circuit
27	Number 2 injector circuit
31	Canister purge solenoid circuit
32	Power loss lamp circuit
33	A/C wide cut out relay circuit
34	Problem in the Exhaust Gas Recirculation (EGR) solenoid circuit
35	Fan control relay circuit
36	Wastegate solenoid circuit – power loss/limited lamp is ON
37	Barometric read solenoid circuit
41	Charging system excess or no field circuit
42	Automatic Shut Down (ASD) relay driver circuit
43	Spark interface (internal) circuits
44	Battery temperature is out of range
45	Overboost shut-off circuit – power loss/limited lamp is ON
46	Battery voltage too high – power loss/limited lamp is ON
47	Battery voltage too low
51	Closed loop fuel system problem – oxygen sensor signal stuck at the lean position
52	Oxygen sensor signal stuck at the rich position
53	Logic module problem or failure
54	Distributor sync pick-up circuit
55	End of message

Year — 1985
Model — Dodge 600 and 600SE
Engine — 2.2L (135 cid) EFI 4 cyl
Engine Code — VIN D

ECM TROUBLE CODES

Code	Explanation
88	Start of test
11	Engine not cranked since battery was disconnected
12	Memory standby power lost
13	Manifold Absolute Pressure (MAP) sensor pneumatic circuit — power loss/limited lamp is ON
14	Manifold Absolute Pressure (MAP) sensor electrical system — power loss/limited lamp is ON
15	Vehicle Speed Sensor (VSS) circuit
16	Lose of battery voltage sense — power loss/limited lamp is ON
21	Oxygen (O_2) sensor circuit
22	Coolant Temperature Sensor (CTS) circuit — power loss/limited lamp is ON
23	Throttle body temperature sensor circuit
24	Throttle Position Sensor (TPS) circuit — power loss/limited lamp is ON
25	Automatic Idle Speed (AIS) control circuit
26	Peak injector current has not been replaced
27	Fuel interface circuit — internal fuel circuit problem of logic module
31	Canister purge solenoid circuit
32	Power loss lamp circuit
33	Air conditioning Wide Open Throttle (WOT) cut out relay circuit
34	Problem in spare driver circuit
35	Fan control relay circuit
36	Problem in spare driver circuit
37	Shift indicator lamp circuit — manual transmissions only
41	Charging system excess or no field circuit
42	Automatic Shut Down (ASD) relay circuit
43	Spark interface (internal) circuits
44	Battery temperature is out of range
46	Battery voltage too high — power loss/limited lamp is ON
47	Battery voltage too low
51	Closed loop fuel system problem — oxygen sensor signal stuck at the lean position
52	Oxygen sensor signal stuck at the rich position
53	Logic module problem or failure
55	End of message
88	Start of message — this code only appears on the diagnostic readout Tool C-4805 or equivalent, and means start of message

Year — 1985
Model — Caravelle
Engine — 2.2L (135 cid) EFI 4 cyl
Engine Code — VIN D

ECM TROUBLE CODES

Code	Explanation
88	Start of test
11	Engine not cranked since battery was disconnected
12	Memory standby power lost
13	Manifold Absolute Pressure (MAP) sensor pneumatic circuit — power loss/limited lamp is ON
14	Manifold Absolute Pressure (MAP) sensor electrical system — power loss/limited lamp is ON
15	Vehicle Speed Sensor (VSS) circuit
16	Lose of battery voltage sense — power loss/limited lamp is ON
21	Oxygen (O_2) sensor circuit
22	Coolant Temperature Sensor (CTS) circuit — power loss/limited lamp is ON
23	Throttle body temperature sensor circuit
24	Throttle Position Sensor (TPS) circuit — power loss/limited lamp is ON
25	Automatic Idle Speed (AIS) control circuit
26	Peak injector current has not been replaced
27	Fuel interface circuit — internal fuel circuit problem of logic module
31	Canister purge solenoid circuit
32	Power loss lamp circuit
33	Air conditioning Wide Open Throttle (WOT) cut out relay circuit
34	Problem in spare driver circuit
35	Fan control relay circuit
36	Problem in spare driver circuit
37	Shift indicator lamp circuit — manual transmissions only
41	Charging system excess or no field circuit
42	Automatic Shut Down (ASD) relay circuit
43	Spark interface (internal) circuits
44	Battery temperature is out of range
46	Battery voltage too high — power loss/limited lamp is ON
47	Battery voltage too low
51	Closed loop fuel system problem — oxygen sensor signal stuck at the lean position
52	Oxygen sensor signal stuck at the rich position
53	Logic module problem or failure
55	End of message
88	Start of message — this code only appears on the diagnostic readout Tool C-4805 or equivalent, and means start of message

Year — 1985
Model — LeBaron
Engine — 2.2L (135 cid) EFI 4 cyl
Engine Code — VIN D

ECM TROUBLE CODES

Code	Explanation
88	Start of test
11	Engine not cranked since battery was disconnected
12	Memory standby power lost
13	Manifold Absolute Pressure (MAP) sensor pneumatic circuit — power loss/limited lamp is ON
14	Manifold Absolute Pressure (MAP) sensor electrical system — power loss/limited lamp is ON
15	Vehicle Speed Sensor (VSS) circuit
16	Lose of battery voltage sense — power loss/limited lamp is ON
21	Oxygen (O_2) sensor circuit
22	Coolant Temperature Sensor (CTS) circuit — power loss/limited lamp is ON
23	Throttle body temperature sensor circuit
24	Throttle Position Sensor (TPS) circuit — power loss/limited lamp is ON
25	Automatic Idle Speed (AIS) control circuit
26	Peak injector current has not been replaced
27	Fuel interface circuit — internal fuel circuit problem of logic module
31	Canister purge solenoid circuit
32	Power loss lamp circuit
33	Air conditioning Wide Open Throttle (WOT) cut out relay circuit
34	Problem in spare driver circuit
35	Fan control relay circuit
36	Problem in spare driver circuit
37	Shift indicator lamp circuit — manual transmissions only
41	Charging system excess or no field circuit
42	Automatic Shut Down (ASD) relay circuit
43	Spark interface (internal) circuits
44	Battery temperature is out of range
46	Battery voltage too high — power loss/limited lamp is ON
47	Battery voltage too low
51	Closed loop fuel system problem — oxygen sensor signal stuck at the lean position
52	Oxygen sensor signal stuck at the rich position
53	Logic module problem or failure
55	End of message
88	Start of message — this code only appears on the diagnostic readout Tool C-4805 or equivalent, and means start of message

Year – 1985
Model – Dodge 600 and 600SE
Engine – 2.2L (135 cid) Turbo 4 cyl
Engine Code – VIN E

ECM TROUBLE CODES

Code	Explanation
88	Start of test
11	Engine not cranked since battery was disconnected
12	Memory standby power lost
13	Manifold Absolute Pressure (MAP) sensor pneumatic circuit – power loss/limited lamp is ON
14	Manifold Absolute Pressure (MAP) sensor electrical system – power loss/limited lamp is ON
15	Vehicle Speed Sensor (VSS) circuit
16	Lose of battery voltage sense – power loss/limited lamp is ON
21	Oxygen (O_2) sensor circuit
22	Coolant Temperature Sensor (CTS) circuit – power loss/limited lamp is ON
23	Throttle body temperature sensor circuit
24	Throttle Position Sensor (TPS) circuit – power loss/limited lamp is ON
25	Automatic Idle Speed (AIS) control circuit
26	Number 1 injector circuit
27	Number 2 injector circuit
31	Canister purge solenoid circuit
32	Power loss lamp circuit
33	A/C wide cut out relay circuit
34	Problem in the Exhaust Gas Recirculation (EGR) solenoid circuit
35	Fan control relay circuit
36	Wastegate solenoid circuit – power loss/limited lamp is ON
37	Barometric read solenoid circuit
41	Charging system excess or no field circuit
42	Automatic Shut Down (ASD) relay driver circuit
43	Spark interface (internal) circuits
44	Battery temperature is out of range
45	Overboost shut-off circuit – power loss/limited lamp is ON
46	Battery voltage too high – power loss/limited lamp is ON
47	Battery voltage too low
51	Closed loop fuel system problem – oxygen sensor signal stuck at the lean position
52	Oxygen sensor signal stuck at the rich position
53	Logic module problem or failure
54	Distributor sync pick-up circuit
55	End of message

Year – 1985
Model – Caravelle
Engine – 2.2L (135 cid) Turbo 4 cyl
Engine Code – VIN E

ECM TROUBLE CODES

Code	Explanation
88	Start of test
11	Engine not cranked since battery was disconnected
12	Memory standby power lost
13	Manifold Absolute Pressure (MAP) sensor pneumatic circuit – power loss/limited lamp is ON
14	Manifold Absolute Pressure (MAP) sensor electrical system – power loss/limited lamp is ON
15	Vehicle Speed Sensor (VSS) circuit
16	Lose of battery voltage sense – power loss/limited lamp is ON
21	Oxygen (O₂) sensor circuit
22	Coolant Temperature Sensor (CTS) circuit – power loss/limited lamp is ON
23	Throttle body temperature sensor circuit
24	Throttle Position Sensor (TPS) circuit – power loss/limited lamp is ON
25	Automatic Idle Speed (AIS) control circuit
26	Number 1 injector circuit
27	Number 2 injector circuit
31	Canister purge solenoid circuit
32	Power loss lamp circuit
33	A/C wide cut out relay circuit
34	Problem in the Exhaust Gas Recirculation (EGR) solenoid circuit
35	Fan control relay circuit
36	Wastegate solenoid circuit – power loss/limited lamp is ON
37	Barometric read solenoid circuit
41	Charging system excess or no field circuit
42	Automatic Shut Down (ASD) relay driver circuit
43	Spark interface (internal) circuits
44	Battery temperature is out of range
45	Overboost shut-off circuit – power loss/limited lamp is ON
46	Battery voltage too high – power loss/limited lamp is ON
47	Battery voltage too low
51	Closed loop fuel system problem – oxygen sensor signal stuck at the lean position
52	Oxygen sensor signal stuck at the rich position
53	Logic module problem or failure
54	Distributor sync pick-up circuit
55	End of message

Year — 1985
Model — LeBaron
Engine — 2.2L (135 cid) Turbo 4 cyl
Engine Code — VIN E

ECM TROUBLE CODES

Code	Explanation
88	Start of test
11	Engine not cranked since battery was disconnected
12	Memory standby power lost
13	Manifold Absolute Pressure (MAP) sensor pneumatic circuit — power loss/limited lamp is ON
14	Manifold Absolute Pressure (MAP) sensor electrical system — power loss/limited lamp is ON
15	Vehicle Speed Sensor (VSS) circuit
16	Lose of battery voltage sense — power loss/limited lamp is ON
21	Oxygen (O_2) sensor circuit
22	Coolant Temperature Sensor (CTS) circuit — power loss/limited lamp is ON
23	Throttle body temperature sensor circuit
24	Throttle Position Sensor (TPS) circuit — power loss/limited lamp is ON
25	Automatic Idle Speed (AIS) control circuit
26	Number 1 injector circuit
27	Number 2 injector circuit
31	Canister purge solenoid circuit
32	Power loss lamp circuit
33	A/C wide cut out relay circuit
34	Problem in the Exhaust Gas Recirculation (EGR) solenoid circuit
35	Fan control relay circuit
36	Wastegate solenoid circuit — power loss/limited lamp is ON
37	Barometric read solenoid circuit
41	Charging system excess or no field circuit
42	Automatic Shut Down (ASD) relay driver circuit
43	Spark interface (internal) circuits
44	Battery temperature is out of range
45	Overboost shut-off circuit — power loss/limited lamp is ON
46	Battery voltage too high — power loss/limited lamp is ON
47	Battery voltage too low
51	Closed loop fuel system problem — oxygen sensor signal stuck at the lean position
52	Oxygen sensor signal stuck at the rich position
53	Logic module problem or failure
54	Distributor sync pick-up circuit
55	End of message

Year – 1985
Model – New Yorker
Engine – 2.2L (135 cid) Turbo 4 cyl
Engine Code – VIN E

ECM TROUBLE CODES

Code	Explanation
88	Start of test
11	Engine not cranked since battery was disconnected
12	Memory standby power lost
13	Manifold Absolute Pressure (MAP) sensor pneumatic circuit – power loss/limited lamp is ON
14	Manifold Absolute Pressure (MAP) sensor electrical system – power loss/limited lamp is ON
15	Vehicle Speed Sensor (VSS) circuit
16	Lose of battery voltage sense – power loss/limited lamp is ON
21	Oxygen (O$_2$) sensor circuit
22	Coolant Temperature Sensor (CTS) circuit – power loss/limited lamp is ON
23	Throttle body temperature sensor circuit
24	Throttle Position Sensor (TPS) circuit – power loss/limited lamp is ON
25	Automatic Idle Speed (AIS) control circuit
26	Number 1 injector circuit
27	Number 2 injector circuit
31	Canister purge solenoid circuit
32	Power loss lamp circuit
33	A/C wide cut out relay circuit
34	Problem in the Exhaust Gas Recirculation (EGR) solenoid circuit
35	Fan control relay circuit
36	Wastegate solenoid circuit – power loss/limited lamp is ON
37	Barometric read solenoid circuit
41	Charging system excess or no field circuit
42	Automatic Shut Down (ASD) relay driver circuit
43	Spark interface (internal) circuits
44	Battery temperature is out of range
45	Overboost shut-off circuit – power loss/limited lamp is ON
46	Battery voltage too high – power loss/limited lamp is ON
47	Battery voltage too low
51	Closed loop fuel system problem – oxygen sensor signal stuck at the lean position
52	Oxygen sensor signal stuck at the rich position
53	Logic module problem or failure
54	Distributor sync pick-up circuit
55	End of message

CHRYSLER CORPORATION
DIAGNOSTIC CODE DATA

Year – 1985
Model – LeBaron GTS
Engine – 2.2L (135 cid) Turbo 4 cyl
Engine Code – VIN E

ECM TROUBLE CODES

Code	Explanation
88	Start of test
11	Engine not cranked since battery was disconnected
12	Memory standby power lost
13	Manifold Absolute Pressure (MAP) sensor pneumatic circuit – power loss/limited lamp is ON
14	Manifold Absolute Pressure (MAP) sensor electrical system – power loss/limited lamp is ON
15	Vehicle Speed Sensor (VSS) circuit
16	Lose of battery voltage sense – power loss/limited lamp is ON
21	Oxygen (O_2) sensor circuit
22	Coolant Temperature Sensor (CTS) circuit – power loss/limited lamp is ON
23	Throttle body temperature sensor circuit
24	Throttle Position Sensor (TPS) circuit – power loss/limited lamp is ON
25	Automatic Idle Speed (AIS) control circuit
26	Number 1 injector circuit
27	Number 2 injector circuit
31	Canister purge solenoid circuit
32	Power loss lamp circuit
33	A/C wide cut out relay circuit
34	Problem in the Exhaust Gas Recirculation (EGR) solenoid circuit
35	Fan control relay circuit
36	Wastegate solenoid circuit – power loss/limited lamp is ON
37	Barometric read solenoid circuit
41	Charging system excess or no field circuit
42	Automatic Shut Down (ASD) relay driver circuit
43	Spark interface (internal) circuits
44	Battery temperature is out of range
45	Overboost shut-off circuit – power loss/limited lamp is ON
46	Battery voltage too high – power loss/limited lamp is ON
47	Battery voltage too low
51	Closed loop fuel system problem – oxygen sensor signal stuck at the lean position
52	Oxygen sensor signal stuck at the rich position
53	Logic module problem or failure
54	Distributor sync pick-up circuit
55	End of message

Year – 1985
Model – Lancer
Engine – 2.2L (135 cid) Turbo 4 cyl
Engine Code – VIN E

ECM TROUBLE CODES

Code	Explanation
88	Start of test
11	Engine not cranked since battery was disconnected
12	Memory standby power lost
13	Manifold Absolute Pressure (MAP) sensor pneumatic circuit – power loss/limited lamp is ON
14	Manifold Absolute Pressure (MAP) sensor electrical system – power loss/limited lamp is ON
15	Vehicle Speed Sensor (VSS) circuit
16	Lose of battery voltage sense – power loss/limited lamp is ON
21	Oxygen (O$_2$) sensor circuit
22	Coolant Temperature Sensor (CTS) circuit – power loss/limited lamp is ON
23	Throttle body temperature sensor circuit
24	Throttle Position Sensor (TPS) circuit – power loss/limited lamp is ON
25	Automatic Idle Speed (AIS) control circuit
26	Number 1 injector circuit
27	Number 2 injector circuit
31	Canister purge solenoid circuit
32	Power loss lamp circuit
33	A/C wide cut out relay circuit
34	Problem in the Exhaust Gas Recirculation (EGR) solenoid circuit
35	Fan control relay circuit
36	Wastegate solenoid circuit – power loss/limited lamp is ON
37	Barometric read solenoid circuit
41	Charging system excess or no field circuit
42	Automatic Shut Down (ASD) relay driver circuit
43	Spark interface (internal) circuits
44	Battery temperature is out of range
45	Overboost shut-off circuit – power loss/limited lamp is ON
46	Battery voltage too high – power loss/limited lamp is ON
47	Battery voltage too low
51	Closed loop fuel system problem – oxygen sensor signal stuck at the lean position
52	Oxygen sensor signal stuck at the rich position
53	Logic module problem or failure
54	Distributor sync pick-up circuit
55	End of message

Year — 1985
Model — Dodge Lancer
Engine — 2.2L (135 cid) EFI 4 cyl
Engine Code — VIN D

ECM TROUBLE CODES

Code	Explanation
88	Start of test
11	Engine not cranked since battery was disconnected
12	Memory standby power lost
13	Manifold Absolute Pressure (MAP) sensor pneumatic circuit — power loss/limited lamp is ON
14	Manifold Absolute Pressure (MAP) sensor electrical system — power loss/limited lamp is ON
15	Vehicle Speed Sensor (VSS) circuit
16	Lose of battery voltage sense — power loss/limited lamp is ON
21	Oxygen (O_2) sensor circuit
22	Coolant Temperature Sensor (CTS) circuit — power loss/limited lamp is ON
23	Throttle body temperature sensor circuit
24	Throttle Position Sensor (TPS) circuit — power loss/limited lamp is ON
25	Automatic Idle Speed (AIS) control circuit
26	Peak injector current has not been replaced
27	Fuel interface circuit — internal fuel circuit problem of logic module
31	Canister purge solenoid circuit
32	Power loss lamp circuit
33	Air conditioning Wide Open Throttle (WOT) cut out relay circuit
34	Problem in spare driver circuit
35	Fan control relay circuit
36	Problem in spare driver circuit
37	Shift indicator lamp circuit — manual transmissions only
41	Charging system excess or no field circuit
42	Automatic Shut Down (ASD) relay circuit
43	Spark interface (internal) circuits
44	Battery temperature is out of range
46	Battery voltage too high — power loss/limited lamp is ON
47	Battery voltage too low
51	Closed loop fuel system problem — oxygen sensor signal stuck at the lean position
52	Oxygen sensor signal stuck at the rich position
53	Logic module problem or failure
55	End of message
88	Start of message — this code only appears on the diagnostic readout Tool C-4805 or equivalent, and means start of message

Year – 1985
Model – LeBaron GTS
Engine – 2.2L (135 cid) EFI 4 cyl
Engine Code – VIN D

ECM TROUBLE CODES

Code	Explanation
88	Start of test
11	Engine not cranked since battery was disconnected
12	Memory standby power lost
13	Manifold Absolute Pressure (MAP) sensor pneumatic circuit – power loss/limited lamp is ON
14	Manifold Absolute Pressure (MAP) sensor electrical system – power loss/limited lamp is ON
15	Vehicle Speed Sensor (VSS) circuit
16	Lose of battery voltage sense – power loss/limited lamp is ON
21	Oxygen (O$_2$) sensor circuit
22	Coolant Temperature Sensor (CTS) circuit – power loss/limited lamp is ON
23	Throttle body temperature sensor circuit
24	Throttle Position Sensor (TPS) circuit – power loss/limited lamp is ON
25	Automatic Idle Speed (AIS) control circuit
26	Peak injector current has not been replaced
27	Fuel interface circuit – internal fuel circuit problem of logic module
31	Canister purge solenoid circuit
32	Power loss lamp circuit
33	Air conditioning Wide Open Throttle (WOT) cut out relay circuit
34	Problem in spare driver circuit
35	Fan control relay circuit
36	Problem in spare driver circuit
37	Shift indicator lamp circuit – manual transmissions only
41	Charging system excess or no field circuit
42	Automatic Shut Down (ASD) relay circuit
43	Spark interface (internal) circuits
44	Battery temperature is out of range
46	Battery voltage too high – power loss/limited lamp is ON
47	Battery voltage too low
51	Closed loop fuel system problem – oxygen sensor signal stuck at the lean position
52	Oxygen sensor signal stuck at the rich position
53	Logic module problem or failure
55	End of message
88	Start of message – this code only appears on the diagnostic readout Tool C-4805 or equivalent, and means start of message

Year – 1985
Model – Omni
Engine – 1.6L (98 cid) 4 cyl
Engine Code – VIN A

ECM TROUBLE CODES

Code	Explanation
11	Carburetor oxygen (O_2) solenoid does not respond to computer commands
12	Disregard this code
14	Battery feed for computer memory. If the battery was disconnected within the last 20–40 engine starts
16	Disregard this code
21	Distributor pickup coil. If there is no distributor signal input at the computer
22	Oxygen feedback system. If the oxygen feedback system stays rich or lean longer than 5 minutes
24	Computer. If the vacuum transducer fails
26	Engine Temperature Sensor (CTS). If the engine temperature sensor circuit does not read 100°F after 30 minutes from when the engine started. Also, if the circuit is shorted or changes too fast to be real
28	Speed sensor. If speed sensor circuit does not indicate between 2 and 150 mph
31	Battery feed for computer memory. If the engine has not been cranked since the battery was disconnected
32 & 33	Computer. If computer fails
55	End of diagnostic mode
88	Start of diagnostic mode – this code must appear first in the diagnostic mode or fault codes will be inaccurate. Indicates switch is ON in switch test mode
00	Diagnostic readout box is powered up – switch is OFF in switch test mode

Year — 1985
Model — Horizon
Engine — 1.6L (98 cid) 4 cyl
Engine Code — VIN A

ECM TROUBLE CODES

Code	Explanation
11	Carburetor oxygen (O_2) solenoid does not respond to computer commands
12	Disregard this code
14	Battery feed for computer memory. If the battery was disconnected within the last 20–40 engine starts
16	Disregard this code
21	Distributor pickup coil. If there is no distributor signal input at the computer
22	Oxygen feedback system. If the oxygen feedback system stays rich or lean longer than 5 minutes
24	Computer. If the vacuum transducer fails
26	Engine Temperature Sensor (CTS). If the engine temperature sensor circuit does not read 100°F after 30 minutes from when the engine started. Also, if the circuit is shorted or changes too fast to be real
28	Speed sensor. If speed sensor circuit does not indicate between 2 and 150 mph
31	Battery feed for computer memory. If the engine has not been cranked since the battery was disconnected
32 & 33	Computer. If computer fails
55	End of diagnostic mode
88	Start of diagnostic mode — this code must appear first in the diagnostic mode or fault codes will be inaccurate. Indicates switch is ON in switch test mode
00	Diagnostic readout box is powered up — switch is OFF in switch test mode

CHRYSLER CORPORATION
DIAGNOSTIC CODE DATA

Year — 1985
Model — Charger
Engine — 1.6L (98 cid) 4 cyl
Engine Code — VIN A

ECM TROUBLE CODES

Code	Explanation
11	Carburetor oxygen (O_2) solenoid does not respond to computer commands
12	Disregard this code
14	Battery feed for computer memory. If the battery was disconnected within the last 20–40 engine starts
16	Disregard this code
21	Distributor pickup coil. If there is no distributor signal input at the computer
22	Oxygen feedback system. If the oxygen feedback system stays rich or lean longer than 5 minutes
24	Computer. If the vacuum transducer fails
26	Engine Temperature Sensor (CTS). If the engine temperature sensor circuit does not read 100°F after 30 minutes from when the engine started. Also, if the circuit is shorted or changes too fast to be real
28	Speed sensor. If speed sensor circuit does not indicate between 2 and 150 mph
31	Battery feed for computer memory. If the engine has not been cranked since the battery was disconnected
32 & 33	Computer. If computer fails
55	End of diagnostic mode
88	Start of diagnostic mode — this code must appear first in the diagnostic mode or fault codes will be inaccurate. Indicates switch is ON in switch test mode
00	Diagnostic readout box is powered up — switch is OFF in switch test mode

Year — 1985
Model — Turismo
Engine — 1.6L (98 cid) 4 cyl
Engine Code — VIN A

ECM TROUBLE CODES

Code	Explanation
11	Carburetor oxygen (O_2) solenoid does not respond to computer commands
12	Disregard this code
14	Battery feed for computer memory. If the battery was disconnected within the last 20–40 engine starts
16	Disregard this code
21	Distributor pickup coil. If there is no distributor signal input at the computer
22	Oxygen feedback system. If the oxygen feedback system stays rich or lean longer than 5 minutes
24	Computer. If the vacuum transducer fails
26	Engine Temperature Sensor (CTS). If the engine temperature sensor circuit does not read 100°F after 30 minutes from when the engine started. Also, if the circuit is shorted or changes too fast to be real
28	Speed sensor. If speed sensor circuit does not indicate between 2 and 150 mph
31	Battery feed for computer memory. If the engine has not been cranked since the battery was disconnected
32 & 33	Computer. If computer fails
55	End of diagnostic mode
88	Start of diagnostic mode — this code must appear first in the diagnostic mode or fault codes will be inaccurate. Indicates switch is ON in switch test mode
00	Diagnostic readout box is powered up — switch is OFF in switch test mode

Year—1985
Model—Omni
Engine—2.2L (135 cid) 4 cyl
Engine Code—VIN C

ECM TROUBLE CODES

Code	Explanation
11	Carburetor oxygen (O_2) solenoid does not respond to computer commands
12	Disregard this code
13	Canister purge solenoid. If the canister purge solenoid circuit does not turn ON and OFF at the correct time
14	Battery feed for computer memory. If the battery was disconnected within the last 20–40 engine starts
16	Disregard this code
17	Electronic throttle control solenoid. If the throttle circuit control solenoid does not turn ON and OFF at the correct time
18	Vacuum Operated Secondary Control Solenoid (VOS). If the VOS control solenoid circuit does not turn ON and OFF at the correct time
21	Distributor pickup coil. If there is no distributor signal input at the computer
22	Oxygen feedback system. If the oxygen feedback system stays rich or lean longer than 5 minutes
24	Computer. If the vacuum transducer fails
25	Radiator Fan Temperature Sensor (CTS). If the engine temperature sensor circuit indicates 100°F or less and the radiator fan temperature does not agree or changes too fast to be real
26	Engine Temperature Sensor (CTS). If the engine temperature sensor circuit does not read 100°F after 30 minutes from when the engine started. Also, if the circuit is shorted or changes too fast to be real
28	Speed sensor. If speed sensor circuit does not indicate between 2 and 150 mph
31	Battery feed for computer memory. If the engine has not been cranked since the battery was disconnected
32 & 33	Computer. If computer fails
55	End of diagnostic mode
88	Start of diagnostic mode—this code must appear first in the diagnostic mode or fault codes will be inaccurate—switch is ON in switch test mode
00	Diagnostic readout box is powered up—switch is OFF in switch test mode

Year — 1985
Model — Horizon
Engine — 2.2L (135 cid) 4 cyl
Engine Code — VIN C

ECM TROUBLE CODES

Code	Explanation
11	Carburetor oxygen (O_2) solenoid does not respond to computer commands
12	Disregard this code
13	Canister purge solenoid. If the canister purge solenoid circuit does not turn ON and OFF at the correct time
14	Battery feed for computer memory. If the battery was disconnected within the last 20–40 engine starts
16	Disregard this code
17	Electronic throttle control solenoid. If the throttle circuit control solenoid does not turn ON and OFF at the correct time
18	Vacuum Operated Secondary Control Solenoid (VOS). If the VOS control solenoid circuit does not turn ON and OFF at the correct time
21	Distributor pickup coil. If there is no distributor signal input at the computer
22	Oxygen feedback system. If the oxygen feedback system stays rich or lean longer than 5 minutes
24	Computer. If the vacuum transducer fails
25	Radiator Fan Temperature Sensor (CTS). If the engine temperature sensor circuit indicates 100°F or less and the radiator fan temperature does not agree or changes too fast to be real
26	Engine Temperature Sensor (CTS). If the engine temperature sensor circuit does not read 100°F after 30 minutes from when the engine started. Also, if the circuit is shorted or changes too fast to be real
28	Speed sensor. If speed sensor circuit does not indicate between 2 and 150 mph
31	Battery feed for computer memory. If the engine has not been cranked since the battery was disconnected
32 & 33	Computer. If computer fails
55	End of diagnostic mode
88	Start of diagnostic mode — this code must appear first in the diagnostic mode or fault codes will be inaccurate — switch is ON in switch test mode
00	Diagnostic readout box is powered up — switch is OFF in switch test mode

Year – 1985
Model – Charger
Engine – 2.2L (135 cid) 4 cyl
Engine Code – VIN C

ECM TROUBLE CODES

Code	Explanation
11	Carburetor oxygen (O_2) solenoid does not respond to computer commands
12	Disregard this code
13	Canister purge solenoid. If the canister purge solenoid circuit does not turn ON and OFF at the correct time
14	Battery feed for computer memory. If the battery was disconnected within the last 20–40 engine starts
16	Disregard this code
17	Electronic throttle control solenoid. If the throttle circuit control solenoid does not turn ON and OFF at the correct time
18	Vacuum Operated Secondary Control Solenoid (VOS). If the VOS control solenoid circuit does not turn ON and OFF at the correct time
21	Distributor pickup coil. If there is no distributor signal input at the computer
22	Oxygen feedback system. If the oxygen feedback system stays rich or lean longer than 5 minutes
24	Computer. If the vacuum transducer fails
25	Radiator Fan Temperature Sensor (CTS). If the engine temperature sensor circuit indicates 100°F or less and the radiator fan temperature does not agree or changes too fast to be real
26	Engine Temperature Sensor (CTS). If the engine temperature sensor circuit does not read 100°F after 30 minutes from when the engine started. Also, if the circuit is shorted or changes too fast to be real
28	Speed sensor. If speed sensor circuit does not indicate between 2 and 150 mph
31	Battery feed for computer memory. If the engine has not been cranked since the battery was disconnected
32 & 33	Computer. If computer fails
55	End of diagnostic mode
88	Start of diagnostic mode – this code must appear first in the diagnostic mode or fault codes will be inaccurate – switch is ON in switch test mode
00	Diagnostic readout box is powered up – switch is OFF in switch test mode

Year – 1985
Model – Turismo
Engine – 2.2L (135 cid) 4 cyl
Engine Code – VIN C

ECM TROUBLE CODES

Code	Explanation
11	Carburetor oxygen (O_2) solenoid does not respond to computer commands
12	Disregard this code
13	Canister purge solenoid. If the canister purge solenoid circuit does not turn ON and OFF at the correct time
14	Battery feed for computer memory. If the battery was disconnected within the last 20–40 engine starts
16	Disregard this code
17	Electronic throttle control solenoid. If the throttle circuit control solenoid does not turn ON and OFF at the correct time
18	Vacuum Operated Secondary Control Solenoid (VOS). If the VOS control solenoid circuit does not turn ON and OFF at the correct time
21	Distributor pickup coil. If there is no distributor signal input at the computer
22	Oxygen feedback system. If the oxygen feedback system stays rich or lean longer than 5 minutes
24	Computer. If the vacuum transducer fails
25	Radiator Fan Temperature Sensor (CTS). If the engine temperature sensor circuit indicates 100°F or less and the radiator fan temperature does not agree or changes too fast to be real
26	Engine Temperature Sensor (CTS). If the engine temperature sensor circuit does not read 100°F after 30 minutes from when the engine started. Also, if the circuit is shorted or changes too fast to be real
28	Speed sensor. If speed sensor circuit does not indicate between 2 and 150 mph
31	Battery feed for computer memory. If the engine has not been cranked since the battery was disconnected
32 & 33	Computer. If computer fails
55	End of diagnostic mode
88	Start of diagnostic mode – this code must appear first in the diagnostic mode or fault codes will be inaccurate – switch is ON in switch test mode
00	Diagnostic readout box is powered up – switch is OFF in switch test mode

Year — 1985
Model — Reliant
Engine — 2.2L (135 cid) 4 cyl
Engine Code — VIN C

ECM TROUBLE CODES

Code	Explanation
11	Carburetor oxygen (O_2) solenoid does not respond to computer commands
12	Disregard this code
13	Canister purge solenoid. If the canister purge solenoid circuit does not turn ON and OFF at the correct time
14	Battery feed for computer memory. If the battery was disconnected within the last 20–40 engine starts
16	Disregard this code
17	Electronic throttle control solenoid. If the throttle circuit control solenoid does not turn ON and OFF at the correct time
18	Vacuum Operated Secondary Control Solenoid (VOS). If the VOS control solenoid circuit does not turn ON and OFF at the correct time
21	Distributor pickup coil. If there is no distributor signal input at the computer
22	Oxygen feedback system. If the oxygen feedback system stays rich or lean longer than 5 minutes
24	Computer. If the vacuum transducer fails
25	Radiator Fan Temperature Sensor (CTS). If the engine temperature sensor circuit indicates 100°F or less and the radiator fan temperature does not agree or changes too fast to be real
26	Engine Temperature Sensor (CTS). If the engine temperature sensor circuit does not read 100°F after 30 minutes from when the engine started. Also, if the circuit is shorted or changes too fast to be real
28	Speed sensor. If speed sensor circuit does not indicate between 2 and 150 mph
31	Battery feed for computer memory. If the engine has not been cranked since the battery was disconnected
32 & 33	Computer. If computer fails
55	End of diagnostic mode
88	Start of diagnostic mode — this code must appear first in the diagnostic mode or fault codes will be inaccurate — switch is ON in switch test mode
00	Diagnostic readout box is powered up — switch is OFF in switch test mode

Year — 1985
Model — Aries
Engine — 2.2L (135 cid) 4 cyl
Engine Code — VIN C

ECM TROUBLE CODES

Code	Explanation
11	Carburetor oxygen (O_2) solenoid does not respond to computer commands
12	Disregard this code
13	Canister purge solenoid. If the canister purge solenoid circuit does not turn ON and OFF at the correct time
14	Battery feed for computer memory. If the battery was disconnected within the last 20–40 engine starts
16	Disregard this code
17	Electronic throttle control solenoid. If the throttle circuit control solenoid does not turn ON and OFF at the correct time
18	Vacuum Operated Secondary Control Solenoid (VOS). If the VOS control solenoid circuit does not turn ON and OFF at the correct time
21	Distributor pickup coil. If there is no distributor signal input at the computer
22	Oxygen feedback system. If the oxygen feedback system stays rich or lean longer than 5 minutes
24	Computer. If the vacuum transducer fails
25	Radiator Fan Temperature Sensor (CTS). If the engine temperature sensor circuit indicates 100°F or less and the radiator fan temperature does not agree or changes too fast to be real
26	Engine Temperature Sensor (CTS). If the engine temperature sensor circuit does not read 100°F after 30 minutes from when the engine started. Also, if the circuit is shorted or changes too fast to be real
28	Speed sensor. If speed sensor circuit does not indicate between 2 and 150 mph
31	Battery feed for computer memory. If the engine has not been cranked since the battery was disconnected
32 & 33	Computer. If computer fails
55	End of diagnostic mode
88	Start of diagnostic mode — this code must appear first in the diagnostic mode or fault codes will be inaccurate — switch is ON in switch test mode
00	Diagnostic readout box is powered up — switch is OFF in switch test mode

Year — 1986
Model — Dodge Daytona
Engine — 2.2L (135 cid) Turbo 4 cyl
Engine Code — VIN E

ECM TROUBLE CODES

Code	Explanation
88	Start of test
11	Engine not cranked since battery was disconnected
12	Memory standby power lost
13	Manifold Absolute Pressure (MAP) sensor pneumatic circuit — power loss/limited lamp is ON
14	Manifold Absolute Pressure (MAP) sensor electrical system — power loss/limited lamp is ON
15	Vehicle Speed Sensor (VSS) circuit
16	Lose of battery voltage sense — power loss/limited lamp is ON
17	Engine is running too cool
21	Oxygen (O$_2$) sensor circuit
22	Coolant Temperature Sensor (CTS) circuit — power loss/limited lamp is ON
23	Throttle body temperature sensor circuit
24	Throttle Position Sensor (TPS) circuit — power loss/limited lamp is ON
25	Automatic Idle Speed (AIS) control circuit
26	Number 1 injector circuit
27	Number 2 injector circuit
31	Canister purge solenoid circuit
33	A/C wide cut out relay circuit
34	Problem in the Exhaust Gas Recirculation (EGR) solenoid circuit
35	Fan control relay circuit
36	Wastegate solenoid circuit — power loss/limited lamp is ON
37	Barometric read solenoid circuit
41	Charging system excess or no field circuit
42	Automatic Shut Down (ASD) relay driver circuit
43	Spark interface (internal) circuits
44	Battery temperature is out of range
45	Overboost shut-off circuit — power loss/limited lamp is ON
46	Battery voltage too high — power loss/limited lamp is ON
47	Battery voltage too low
51	Closed loop fuel system problem — oxygen sensor signal stuck at the lean position
52	Oxygen sensor signal stuck at the rich position
53	Logic module problem or failure
54	Distributor sync pick-up circuit
55	End of message

Year — 1986
Model — Plymouth Laser
Engine — 2.2L (135 cid) Turbo 4 cyl
Engine Code — VIN E

ECM TROUBLE CODES

Code	Explanation
88	Start of test
11	Engine not cranked since battery was disconnected
12	Memory standby power lost
13	Manifold Absolute Pressure (MAP) sensor pneumatic circuit — power loss/limited lamp is ON
14	Manifold Absolute Pressure (MAP) sensor electrical system — power loss/limited lamp is ON
15	Vehicle Speed Sensor (VSS) circuit
16	Lose of battery voltage sense — power loss/limited lamp is ON
17	Engine is running too cool
21	Oxygen (O_2) sensor circuit
22	Coolant Temperature Sensor (CTS) circuit — power loss/limited lamp is ON
23	Throttle body temperature sensor circuit
24	Throttle Position Sensor (TPS) circuit — power loss/limited lamp is ON
25	Automatic Idle Speed (AIS) control circuit
26	Number 1 injector circuit
27	Number 2 injector circuit
31	Canister purge solenoid circuit
33	A/C wide cut out relay circuit
34	Problem in the Exhaust Gas Recirculation (EGR) solenoid circuit
35	Fan control relay circuit
36	Wastegate solenoid circuit — power loss/limited lamp is ON
37	Barometric read solenoid circuit
41	Charging system excess or no field circuit
42	Automatic Shut Down (ASD) relay driver circuit
43	Spark interface (internal) circuits
44	Battery temperature is out of range
45	Overboost shut-off circuit — power loss/limited lamp is ON
46	Battery voltage too high — power loss/limited lamp is ON
47	Battery voltage too low
51	Closed loop fuel system problem — oxygen sensor signal stuck at the lean position
52	Oxygen sensor signal stuck at the rich position
53	Logic module problem or failure
54	Distributor sync pick-up circuit
55	End of message

Year — 1986
Model — Dodge Daytona
Engine — 2.2L (135 cid) EFI 4 cyl
Engine Code — VIN D

ECM TROUBLE CODES

Code	Explanation
88	Start of test
11	Engine not cranked since battery was disconnected
12	Memory standby power lost
13	Manifold Absolute Pressure (MAP) sensor pneumatic circuit — power loss/limited lamp is ON
14	Manifold Absolute Pressure (MAP) sensor electrical system — power loss/limited lamp is ON
15	Vehicle Speed Sensor (VSS) circuit
16	Lose of battery voltage sense — power loss/limited lamp is ON
17	Engine is running too cool
21	Oxygen (O_2) sensor circuit
22	Coolant Temperature Sensor (CTS) circuit — power loss/limited lamp is ON
23	Throttle body temperature sensor circuit
24	Throttle Position Sensor (TPS) circuit — power loss/limited lamp is ON
25	Automatic Idle Speed (AIS) control circuit
26	Peak injector current has not been replaced
27	Fuel interface circuit — internal fuel circuit problem of logic module
31	Canister purge solenoid circuit
33	Air conditioning Wide Open Throttle (WOT) cut out relay circuit
34	Problem in spare driver circuit
35	Fan control relay circuit
37	Shift indicator lamp circuit — manual transmissions only
41	Charging system excess or no field circuit
42	Automatic Shut Down (ASD) relay circuit
43	Spark interface (internal) circuits
44	Battery temperature is out of range
46	Battery voltage too high — power loss/limited lamp is ON
47	Battery voltage too low
51	Closed loop fuel system problem — oxygen sensor signal stuck at the lean position
52	Oxygen sensor signal stuck at the rich position
53	Logic module problem or failure
55	End of message
88	Start of message — this code only appears on the diagnostic readout Tool C-4805 or equivalent, and means start of message

Year — 1986
Model — Plymouth Laser
Engine — 2.2L (135 cid) EFI 4 cyl
Engine Code — VIN D

ECM TROUBLE CODES

Code	Explanation
88	Start of test
11	Engine not cranked since battery was disconnected
12	Memory standby power lost
13	Manifold Absolute Pressure (MAP) sensor pneumatic circuit — power loss/limited lamp is ON
14	Manifold Absolute Pressure (MAP) sensor electrical system — power loss/limited lamp is ON
15	Vehicle Speed Sensor (VSS) circuit
16	Lose of battery voltage sense — power loss/limited lamp is ON
17	Engine is running too cool
21	Oxygen (O_2) sensor circuit
22	Coolant Temperature Sensor (CTS) circuit — power loss/limited lamp is ON
23	Throttle body temperature sensor circuit
24	Throttle Position Sensor (TPS) circuit — power loss/limited lamp is ON
25	Automatic Idle Speed (AIS) control circuit
26	Peak injector current has not been replaced
27	Fuel interface circuit — internal fuel circuit problem of logic module
31	Canister purge solenoid circuit
33	Air conditioning Wide Open Throttle (WOT) cut out relay circuit
34	Problem in spare driver circuit
35	Fan control relay circuit
37	Shift indicator lamp circuit — manual transmissions only
41	Charging system excess or no field circuit
42	Automatic Shut Down (ASD) relay circuit
43	Spark interface (internal) circuits
44	Battery temperature is out of range
46	Battery voltage too high — power loss/limited lamp is ON
47	Battery voltage too low
51	Closed loop fuel system problem — oxygen sensor signal stuck at the lean position
52	Oxygen sensor signal stuck at the rich position
53	Logic module problem or failure
55	End of message
88	Start of message — this code only appears on the diagnostic readout Tool C-4805 or equivalent, and means start of message

Year – 1986
Model – New Yorker
Engine – 2.2L (135 cid) Turbo 4 cyl
Engine Code – VIN E

ECM TROUBLE CODES

Code	Explanation
88	Start of test
11	Engine not cranked since battery was disconnected
12	Memory standby power lost
13	Manifold Absolute Pressure (MAP) sensor pneumatic circuit – power loss/limited lamp is ON
14	Manifold Absolute Pressure (MAP) sensor electrical system – power loss/limited lamp is ON
15	Vehicle Speed Sensor (VSS) circuit
16	Lose of battery voltage sense – power loss/limited lamp is ON
17	Engine is running too cool
21	Oxygen (O$_2$) sensor circuit
22	Coolant Temperature Sensor (CTS) circuit – power loss/limited lamp is ON
23	Throttle body temperature sensor circuit
24	Throttle Position Sensor (TPS) circuit – power loss/limited lamp is ON
25	Automatic Idle Speed (AIS) control circuit
26	Number 1 injector circuit
27	Number 2 injector circuit
31	Canister purge solenoid circuit
33	A/C wide cut out relay circuit
34	Problem in the Exhaust Gas Recirculation (EGR) solenoid circuit
35	Fan control relay circuit
36	Wastegate solenoid circuit – power loss/limited lamp is ON
37	Barometric read solenoid circuit
41	Charging system excess or no field circuit
42	Automatic Shut Down (ASD) relay driver circuit
43	Spark interface (internal) circuits
44	Battery temperature is out of range
45	Overboost shut-off circuit – power loss/limited lamp is ON
46	Battery voltage too high – power loss/limited lamp is ON
47	Battery voltage too low
51	Closed loop fuel system problem – oxygen sensor signal stuck at the lean position
52	Oxygen sensor signal stuck at the rich position
53	Logic module problem or failure
54	Distributor sync pick-up circuit
55	End of message

Year – 1986
Model – LeBaron GTS
Engine – 2.2L (135 cid) Turbo 4 cyl
Engine Code – VIN E

ECM TROUBLE CODES

Code	Explanation
88	Start of test
11	Engine not cranked since battery was disconnected
12	Memory standby power lost
13	Manifold Absolute Pressure (MAP) sensor pneumatic circuit – power loss/limited lamp is ON
14	Manifold Absolute Pressure (MAP) sensor electrical system – power loss/limited lamp is ON
15	Vehicle Speed Sensor (VSS) circuit
16	Lose of battery voltage sense – power loss/limited lamp is ON
17	Engine is running too cool
21	Oxygen (O_2) sensor circuit
22	Coolant Temperature Sensor (CTS) circuit – power loss/limited lamp is ON
23	Throttle body temperature sensor circuit
24	Throttle Position Sensor (TPS) circuit – power loss/limited lamp is ON
25	Automatic Idle Speed (AIS) control circuit
26	Number 1 injector circuit
27	Number 2 injector circuit
31	Canister purge solenoid circuit
33	A/C wide cut out relay circuit
34	Problem in the Exhaust Gas Recirculation (EGR) solenoid circuit
35	Fan control relay circuit
36	Wastegate solenoid circuit – power loss/limited lamp is ON
37	Barometric read solenoid circuit
41	Charging system excess or no field circuit
42	Automatic Shut Down (ASD) relay driver circuit
43	Spark interface (internal) circuits
44	Battery temperature is out of range
45	Overboost shut-off circuit – power loss/limited lamp is ON
46	Battery voltage too high – power loss/limited lamp is ON
47	Battery voltage too low
51	Closed loop fuel system problem – oxygen sensor signal stuck at the lean position
52	Oxygen sensor signal stuck at the rich position
53	Logic module problem or failure
54	Distributor sync pick-up circuit
55	End of message

Year — 1986
Model — Lancer
Engine — 2.2L (135 cid) Turbo 4 cyl
Engine Code — VIN E

ECM TROUBLE CODES

Code	Explanation
88	Start of test
11	Engine not cranked since battery was disconnected
12	Memory standby power lost
13	Manifold Absolute Pressure (MAP) sensor pneumatic circuit — power loss/limited lamp is ON
14	Manifold Absolute Pressure (MAP) sensor electrical system — power loss/limited lamp is ON
15	Vehicle Speed Sensor (VSS) circuit
16	Lose of battery voltage sense — power loss/limited lamp is ON
17	Engine is running too cool
21	Oxygen (O_2) sensor circuit
22	Coolant Temperature Sensor (CTS) circuit — power loss/limited lamp is ON
23	Throttle body temperature sensor circuit
24	Throttle Position Sensor (TPS) circuit — power loss/limited lamp is ON
25	Automatic Idle Speed (AIS) control circuit
26	Number 1 injector circuit
27	Number 2 injector circuit
31	Canister purge solenoid circuit
33	A/C wide cut out relay circuit
34	Problem in the Exhaust Gas Recirculation (EGR) solenoid circuit
35	Fan control relay circuit
36	Wastegate solenoid circuit — power loss/limited lamp is ON
37	Barometric read solenoid circuit
41	Charging system excess or no field circuit
42	Automatic Shut Down (ASD) relay driver circuit
43	Spark interface (internal) circuits
44	Battery temperature is out of range
45	Overboost shut-off circuit — power loss/limited lamp is ON
46	Battery voltage too high — power loss/limited lamp is ON
47	Battery voltage too low
51	Closed loop fuel system problem — oxygen sensor signal stuck at the lean position
52	Oxygen sensor signal stuck at the rich position
53	Logic module problem or failure
54	Distributor sync pick-up circuit
55	End of message

Year – 1986
Model – LeBaron GTS
Engine – 2.2L (135 cid) EFI 4 cyl
Engine Code – VIN D

ECM TROUBLE CODES

Code	Explanation
88	Start of test
11	Engine not cranked since battery was disconnected
12	Memory standby power lost
13	Manifold Absolute Pressure (MAP) sensor pneumatic circuit – power loss/limited lamp is ON
14	Manifold Absolute Pressure (MAP) sensor electrical system – power loss/limited lamp is ON
15	Vehicle Speed Sensor (VSS) circuit
16	Lose of battery voltage sense – power loss/limited lamp is ON
17	Engine is running too cool
21	Oxygen (O_2) sensor circuit
22	Coolant Temperature Sensor (CTS) circuit – power loss/limited lamp is ON
23	Throttle body temperature sensor circuit
24	Throttle Position Sensor (TPS) circuit – power loss/limited lamp is ON
25	Automatic Idle Speed (AIS) control circuit
26	Peak injector current has not been replaced
27	Fuel interface circuit – internal fuel circuit problem of logic module
31	Canister purge solenoid circuit
33	Air conditioning Wide Open Throttle (WOT) cut out relay circuit
34	Problem in spare driver circuit
35	Fan control relay circuit
37	Shift indicator lamp circuit – manual transmissions only
41	Charging system excess or no field circuit
42	Automatic Shut Down (ASD) relay circuit
43	Spark interface (internal) circuits
44	Battery temperature is out of range
46	Battery voltage too high – power loss/limited lamp is ON
47	Battery voltage too low
51	Closed loop fuel system problem – oxygen sensor signal stuck at the lean position
52	Oxygen sensor signal stuck at the rich position
53	Logic module problem or failure
55	End of message
88	Start of message – this code only appears on the diagnostic readout Tool C-4805 or equivalent, and means start of message

Year – 1986
Model – Lancer
Engine – 2.2L (135 cid) EFI 4 cyl
Engine Code – VIN D

ECM TROUBLE CODES

Code	Explanation
88	Start of test
11	Engine not cranked since battery was disconnected
12	Memory standby power lost
13	Manifold Absolute Pressure (MAP) sensor pneumatic circuit – power loss/limited lamp is ON
14	Manifold Absolute Pressure (MAP) sensor electrical system – power loss/limited lamp is ON
15	Vehicle Speed Sensor (VSS) circuit
16	Lose of battery voltage sense – power loss/limited lamp is ON
17	Engine is running too cool
21	Oxygen (O_2) sensor circuit
22	Coolant Temperature Sensor (CTS) circuit – power loss/limited lamp is ON
23	Throttle body temperature sensor circuit
24	Throttle Position Sensor (TPS) circuit – power loss/limited lamp is ON
25	Automatic Idle Speed (AIS) control circuit
26	Peak injector current has not been replaced
27	Fuel interface circuit – internal fuel circuit problem of logic module
31	Canister purge solenoid circuit
33	Air conditioning Wide Open Throttle (WOT) cut out relay circuit
34	Problem in spare driver circuit
35	Fan control relay circuit
37	Shift indicator lamp circuit – manual transmissions only
41	Charging system excess or no field circuit
42	Automatic Shut Down (ASD) relay circuit
43	Spark interface (internal) circuits
44	Battery temperature is out of range
46	Battery voltage too high – power loss/limited lamp is ON
47	Battery voltage too low
51	Closed loop fuel system problem – oxygen sensor signal stuck at the lean position
52	Oxygen sensor signal stuck at the rich position
53	Logic module problem or failure
55	End of message
88	Start of message – this code only appears on the diagnostic readout Tool C-4805 or equivalent, and means start of message

Year – 1986
Model – Dodge Omni GLH
Engine – 2.2L (135 cid) Turbo 4 cyl
Engine Code – VIN E

ECM TROUBLE CODES

Code	Explanation
88	Start of test
11	Engine not cranked since battery was disconnected
12	Memory standby power lost
13	Manifold Absolute Pressure (MAP) sensor pneumatic circuit – power loss/limited lamp is ON
14	Manifold Absolute Pressure (MAP) sensor electrical system – power loss/limited lamp is ON
15	Vehicle Speed Sensor (VSS) circuit
16	Lose of battery voltage sense – power loss/limited lamp is ON
17	Engine is running too cool
21	Oxygen (O_2) sensor circuit
22	Coolant Temperature Sensor (CTS) circuit – power loss/limited lamp is ON
23	Throttle body temperature sensor circuit
24	Throttle Position Sensor (TPS) circuit – power loss/limited lamp is ON
25	Automatic Idle Speed (AIS) control circuit
26	Number 1 injector circuit
27	Number 2 injector circuit
31	Canister purge solenoid circuit
33	A/C wide cut out relay circuit
34	Problem in the Exhaust Gas Recirculation (EGR) solenoid circuit
35	Fan control relay circuit
36	Wastegate solenoid circuit – power loss/limited lamp is ON
37	Barometric read solenoid circuit
41	Charging system excess or no field circuit
42	Automatic Shut Down (ASD) relay driver circuit
43	Spark interface (internal) circuits
44	Battery temperature is out of range
45	Overboost shut-off circuit – power loss/limited lamp is ON
46	Battery voltage too high – power loss/limited lamp is ON
47	Battery voltage too low
51	Closed loop fuel system problem – oxygen sensor signal stuck at the lean position
52	Oxygen sensor signal stuck at the rich position
53	Logic module problem or failure
54	Distributor sync pick-up circuit
55	End of message

Year – 1986
Model – Dodge Charger Shelby
Engine – 2.2L (135 cid) Turbo 4 cyl
Engine Code – VIN E

ECM TROUBLE CODES

Code	Explanation
88	Start of test
11	Engine not cranked since battery was disconnected
12	Memory standby power lost
13	Manifold Absolute Pressure (MAP) sensor pneumatic circuit – power loss/limited lamp is ON
14	Manifold Absolute Pressure (MAP) sensor electrical system – power loss/limited lamp is ON
15	Vehicle Speed Sensor (VSS) circuit
16	Lose of battery voltage sense – power loss/limited lamp is ON
17	Engine is running too cool
21	Oxygen (O$_2$) sensor circuit
22	Coolant Temperature Sensor (CTS) circuit – power loss/limited lamp is ON
23	Throttle body temperature sensor circuit
24	Throttle Position Sensor (TPS) circuit – power loss/limited lamp is ON
25	Automatic Idle Speed (AIS) control circuit
26	Number 1 injector circuit
27	Number 2 injector circuit
31	Canister purge solenoid circuit
33	A/C wide cut out relay circuit
34	Problem in the Exhaust Gas Recirculation (EGR) solenoid circuit
35	Fan control relay circuit
36	Wastegate solenoid circuit – power loss/limited lamp is ON
37	Barometric read solenoid circuit
41	Charging system excess or no field circuit
42	Automatic Shut Down (ASD) relay driver circuit
43	Spark interface (internal) circuits
44	Battery temperature is out of range
45	Overboost shut-off circuit – power loss/limited lamp is ON
46	Battery voltage too high – power loss/limited lamp is ON
47	Battery voltage too low
51	Closed loop fuel system problem – oxygen sensor signal stuck at the lean position
52	Oxygen sensor signal stuck at the rich position
53	Logic module problem or failure
54	Distributor sync pick-up circuit
55	End of message

Year — 1986
Model — Dodge 600 and 600SE
Engine — 2.2L (135 cid) EFI 4 cyl
Engine Code — VIN D

ECM TROUBLE CODES

Code	Explanation
88	Start of test
11	Engine not cranked since battery was disconnected
12	Memory standby power lost
13	Manifold Absolute Pressure (MAP) sensor pneumatic circuit — power loss/limited lamp is ON
14	Manifold Absolute Pressure (MAP) sensor electrical system — power loss/limited lamp is ON
15	Vehicle Speed Sensor (VSS) circuit
16	Lose of battery voltage sense — power loss/limited lamp is ON
17	Engine is running too cool
21	Oxygen (O$_2$) sensor circuit
22	Coolant Temperature Sensor (CTS) circuit — power loss/limited lamp is ON
23	Throttle body temperature sensor circuit
24	Throttle Position Sensor (TPS) circuit — power loss/limited lamp is ON
25	Automatic Idle Speed (AIS) control circuit
26	Peak injector current has not been replaced
27	Fuel interface circuit — internal fuel circuit problem of logic module
31	Canister purge solenoid circuit
33	Air conditioning Wide Open Throttle (WOT) cut out relay circuit
34	Problem in spare driver circuit
35	Fan control relay circuit
37	Shift indicator lamp circuit — manual transmissions only
41	Charging system excess or no field circuit
42	Automatic Shut Down (ASD) relay circuit
43	Spark interface (internal) circuits
44	Battery temperature is out of range
46	Battery voltage too high — power loss/limited lamp is ON
47	Battery voltage too low
51	Closed loop fuel system problem — oxygen sensor signal stuck at the lean position
52	Oxygen sensor signal stuck at the rich position
53	Logic module problem or failure
55	End of message
88	Start of message — this code only appears on the diagnostic readout Tool C-4805 or equivalent, and means start of message

Year – 1986
Model – Plymouth Caravelle
Engine – 2.2L (135 cid) EFI 4 cyl
Engine Code – VIN D

ECM TROUBLE CODES

Code	Explanation
88	Start of test
11	Engine not cranked since battery was disconnected
12	Memory standby power lost
13	Manifold Absolute Pressure (MAP) sensor pneumatic circuit – power loss/limited lamp is ON
14	Manifold Absolute Pressure (MAP) sensor electrical system – power loss/limited lamp is ON
15	Vehicle Speed Sensor (VSS) circuit
16	Lose of battery voltage sense – power loss/limited lamp is ON
17	Engine is running too cool
21	Oxygen (O₂) sensor circuit
22	Coolant Temperature Sensor (CTS) circuit – power loss/limited lamp is ON
23	Throttle body temperature sensor circuit
24	Throttle Position Sensor (TPS) circuit – power loss/limited lamp is ON
25	Automatic Idle Speed (AIS) control circuit
26	Peak injector current has not been replaced
27	Fuel interface circuit – internal fuel circuit problem of logic module
31	Canister purge solenoid circuit
33	Air conditioning Wide Open Throttle (WOT) cut out relay circuit
34	Problem in spare driver circuit
35	Fan control relay circuit
37	Shift indicator lamp circuit – manual transmissions only
41	Charging system excess or no field circuit
42	Automatic Shut Down (ASD) relay circuit
43	Spark interface (internal) circuits
44	Battery temperature is out of range
46	Battery voltage too high – power loss/limited lamp is ON
47	Battery voltage too low
51	Closed loop fuel system problem – oxygen sensor signal stuck at the lean position
52	Oxygen sensor signal stuck at the rich position
53	Logic module problem or failure
55	End of message
88	Start of message – this code only appears on the diagnostic readout Tool C-4805 or equivalent, and means start of message

Year — 1986
Model — Dodge 600 and 600SE
Engine — 2.2L (135 cid) Turbo 4 cyl
Engine Code — VIN E

ECM TROUBLE CODES

Code	Explanation
88	Start of test
11	Engine not cranked since battery was disconnected
12	Memory standby power lost
13	Manifold Absolute Pressure (MAP) sensor pneumatic circuit — power loss/limited lamp is ON
14	Manifold Absolute Pressure (MAP) sensor electrical system — power loss/limited lamp is ON
15	Vehicle Speed Sensor (VSS) circuit
16	Lose of battery voltage sense — power loss/limited lamp is ON
17	Engine is running too cool
21	Oxygen (O_2) sensor circuit
22	Coolant Temperature Sensor (CTS) circuit — power loss/limited lamp is ON
23	Throttle body temperature sensor circuit
24	Throttle Position Sensor (TPS) circuit — power loss/limited lamp is ON
25	Automatic Idle Speed (AIS) control circuit
26	Number 1 injector circuit
27	Number 2 injector circuit
31	Canister purge solenoid circuit
33	A/C wide cut out relay circuit
34	Problem in the Exhaust Gas Recirculation (EGR) solenoid circuit
35	Fan control relay circuit
36	Wastegate solenoid circuit — power loss/limited lamp is ON
37	Barometric read solenoid circuit
41	Charging system excess or no field circuit
42	Automatic Shut Down (ASD) relay driver circuit
43	Spark interface (internal) circuits
44	Battery temperature is out of range
45	Overboost shut-off circuit — power loss/limited lamp is ON
46	Battery voltage too high — power loss/limited lamp is ON
47	Battery voltage too low
51	Closed loop fuel system problem — oxygen sensor signal stuck at the lean position
52	Oxygen sensor signal stuck at the rich position
53	Logic module problem or failure
54	Distributor sync pick-up circuit
55	End of message

Year — 1986
Model — Plymouth Caravelle
Engine — 2.2L (135 cid) Turbo 4 cyl
Engine Code — VIN E

ECM TROUBLE CODES

Code	Explanation
88	Start of test
11	Engine not cranked since battery was disconnected
12	Memory standby power lost
13	Manifold Absolute Pressure (MAP) sensor pneumatic circuit — power loss/limited lamp is ON
14	Manifold Absolute Pressure (MAP) sensor electrical system — power loss/limited lamp is ON
15	Vehicle Speed Sensor (VSS) circuit
16	Lose of battery voltage sense — power loss/limited lamp is ON
17	Engine is running too cool
21	Oxygen (O_2) sensor circuit
22	Coolant Temperature Sensor (CTS) circuit — power loss/limited lamp is ON
23	Throttle body temperature sensor circuit
24	Throttle Position Sensor (TPS) circuit — power loss/limited lamp is ON
25	Automatic Idle Speed (AIS) control circuit
26	Number 1 injector circuit
27	Number 2 injector circuit
31	Canister purge solenoid circuit
33	A/C wide cut out relay circuit
34	Problem in the Exhaust Gas Recirculation (EGR) solenoid circuit
35	Fan control relay circuit
36	Wastegate solenoid circuit — power loss/limited lamp is ON
37	Barometric read solenoid circuit
41	Charging system excess or no field circuit
42	Automatic Shut Down (ASD) relay driver circuit
43	Spark interface (internal) circuits
44	Battery temperature is out of range
45	Overboost shut-off circuit — power loss/limited lamp is ON
46	Battery voltage too high — power loss/limited lamp is ON
47	Battery voltage too low
51	Closed loop fuel system problem — oxygen sensor signal stuck at the lean position
52	Oxygen sensor signal stuck at the rich position
53	Logic module problem or failure
54	Distributor sync pick-up circuit
55	End of message

Year — 1986
Model — Dodge Aries
Engine — 2.2L (135 cid) EFI 4 cyl
Engine Code — VIN D

ECM TROUBLE CODES

Code	Explanation
88	Start of test
11	Engine not cranked since battery was disconnected
12	Memory standby power lost
13	Manifold Absolute Pressure (MAP) sensor pneumatic circuit — power loss/limited lamp is ON
14	Manifold Absolute Pressure (MAP) sensor electrical system — power loss/limited lamp is ON
15	Vehicle Speed Sensor (VSS) circuit
16	Lose of battery voltage sense — power loss/limited lamp is ON
17	Engine is running too cool
21	Oxygen (O$_2$) sensor circuit
22	Coolant Temperature Sensor (CTS) circuit — power loss/limited lamp is ON
23	Throttle body temperature sensor circuit
24	Throttle Position Sensor (TPS) circuit — power loss/limited lamp is ON
25	Automatic Idle Speed (AIS) control circuit
26	Peak injector current has not been replaced
27	Fuel interface circuit — internal fuel circuit problem of logic module
31	Canister purge solenoid circuit
33	Air conditioning Wide Open Throttle (WOT) cut out relay circuit
34	Problem in spare driver circuit
35	Fan control relay circuit
37	Shift indicator lamp circuit — manual transmissions only
41	Charging system excess or no field circuit
42	Automatic Shut Down (ASD) relay circuit
43	Spark interface (internal) circuits
44	Battery temperature is out of range
46	Battery voltage too high — power loss/limited lamp is ON
47	Battery voltage too low
51	Closed loop fuel system problem — oxygen sensor signal stuck at the lean position
52	Oxygen sensor signal stuck at the rich position
53	Logic module problem or failure
55	End of message
88	Start of message — this code only appears on the diagnostic readout Tool C-4805 or equivalent, and means start of message

Year—1986
Model—Plymouth Reliant
Engine—2.2L (135 cid) EFI 4 cyl
Engine Code—VIN D

ECM TROUBLE CODES

Code	Explanation
88	Start of test
11	Engine not cranked since battery was disconnected
12	Memory standby power lost
13	Manifold Absolute Pressure (MAP) sensor pneumatic circuit—power loss/limited lamp is ON
14	Manifold Absolute Pressure (MAP) sensor electrical system—power loss/limited lamp is ON
15	Vehicle Speed Sensor (VSS) circuit
16	Lose of battery voltage sense—power loss/limited lamp is ON
17	Engine is running too cool
21	Oxygen (O₂) sensor circuit
22	Coolant Temperature Sensor (CTS) circuit—power loss/limited lamp is ON
23	Throttle body temperature sensor circuit
24	Throttle Position Sensor (TPS) circuit—power loss/limited lamp is ON
25	Automatic Idle Speed (AIS) control circuit
26	Peak injector current has not been replaced
27	Fuel interface circuit—internal fuel circuit problem of logic module
31	Canister purge solenoid circuit
33	Air conditioning Wide Open Throttle (WOT) cut out relay circuit
34	Problem in spare driver circuit
35	Fan control relay circuit
37	Shift indicator lamp circuit—manual transmissions only
41	Charging system excess or no field circuit
42	Automatic Shut Down (ASD) relay circuit
43	Spark interface (internal) circuits
44	Battery temperature is out of range
46	Battery voltage too high—power loss/limited lamp is ON
47	Battery voltage too low
51	Closed loop fuel system problem—oxygen sensor signal stuck at the lean position
52	Oxygen sensor signal stuck at the rich position
53	Logic module problem or failure
55	End of message
88	Start of message—this code only appears on the diagnostic readout Tool C-4805 or equivalent, and means start of message

Year — 1987
Model — Dodge Charger Shelby
Engine — 2.2L (135 cid) Turbo 4 cyl
Engine Code — VIN E

ECM TROUBLE CODES

Code	Explanation
88	Start of test
11	Engine not cranked since battery was disconnected
12	Memory standby power lost
13	Manifold Absolute Pressure (MAP) sensor pneumatic circuit — power loss/limited lamp is ON
14	Manifold Absolute Pressure (MAP) sensor electrical system — power loss/limited lamp is ON
15	Vehicle Speed Sensor (VSS) circuit
16	Lose of battery voltage sense — power loss/limited lamp is ON
17	Engine is running too cool
21	Oxygen (O_2) sensor circuit
22	Coolant Temperature Sensor (CTS) circuit — power loss/limited lamp is ON
23	Throttle body temperature sensor circuit
24	Throttle Position Sensor (TPS) circuit — power loss/limited lamp is ON
25	Automatic Idle Speed (AIS) control circuit
26	Number 1 injector circuit
27	Number 2 injector circuit
31	EGR/purge solenoid circuit
33	A/C wide cut out relay circuit
34	Speed control malfunction
35	Fan control relay circuit
36	Wastegate solenoid circuit — power loss/limited lamp is ON
37	Barometric read solenoid circuit
41	Charging system excess or no field circuit
42	Automatic Shut Down (ASD) relay driver circuit
43	Spark interface (internal) circuits
44	Battery temperature is out of range
45	Overboost shut-off circuit — power loss/limited lamp is ON
46	Battery voltage too high — power loss/limited lamp is ON
47	Battery voltage too low
51	Closed loop fuel system problem — oxygen sensor signal stuck at the lean position
52	Oxygen sensor signal stuck at the rich position
53	Logic module problem or failure
54	Distributor sync pick-up circuit
55	End of message

Year — 1987
Model — LeBaron CP
Engine — 2.2L (135 cid) Turbo 4 cyl
Engine Code — VIN E

ECM TROUBLE CODES

Code	Explanation
88	Start of test
11	Engine not cranked since battery was disconnected
12	Memory standby power lost
13	Manifold Absolute Pressure (MAP) sensor pneumatic circuit — power loss/limited lamp is ON
14	Manifold Absolute Pressure (MAP) sensor electrical system — power loss/limited lamp is ON
15	Vehicle Speed Sensor (VSS) circuit
16	Lose of battery voltage sense — power loss/limited lamp is ON
17	Engine is running too cool
21	Oxygen (O_2) sensor circuit
22	Coolant Temperature Sensor (CTS) circuit — power loss/limited lamp is ON
23	Throttle body temperature sensor circuit
24	Throttle Position Sensor (TPS) circuit — power loss/limited lamp is ON
25	Automatic Idle Speed (AIS) control circuit
26	Number 1 injector circuit
27	Number 2 injector circuit
31	EGR/purge solenoid circuit
33	A/C wide cut out relay circuit
34	Speed control malfunction
35	Fan control relay circuit
36	Wastegate solenoid circuit — power loss/limited lamp is ON
37	Barometric read solenoid circuit
41	Charging system excess or no field circuit
42	Automatic Shut Down (ASD) relay driver circuit
43	Spark interface (internal) circuits
44	Battery temperature is out of range
45	Overboost shut-off circuit — power loss/limited lamp is ON
46	Battery voltage too high — power loss/limited lamp is ON
47	Battery voltage too low
51	Closed loop fuel system problem — oxygen sensor signal stuck at the lean position
52	Oxygen sensor signal stuck at the rich position
53	Logic module problem or failure
54	Distributor sync pick-up circuit
55	End of message

Year — 1987
Model — LeBaron CP
Engine — 2.5L (153 cid) EFI 4 cyl
Engine Code — VIN K

ECM TROUBLE CODES

Code	Explanation
88	Start of test
11	Engine not cranked since battery was disconnected
12	Memory standby power lost
13	Manifold Absolute Pressure (MAP) sensor pneumatic circuit — power loss/limited lamp is ON
14	Manifold Absolute Pressure (MAP) sensor electrical system — power loss/limited lamp is ON
15	Vehicle Speed Sensor (VSS) circuit
16	Lose of battery voltage sense — power loss/limited lamp is ON
17	Engine is running too cool
21	Oxygen (O_2) sensor circuit
22	Coolant Temperature Sensor (CTS) circuit — power loss/limited lamp is ON
23	Throttle body temperature sensor circuit
24	Throttle Position Sensor (TPS) circuit — power loss/limited lamp is ON
25	Automatic Idle Speed (AIS) control circuit
26	Peak injector current has not been replaced
27	Fuel interface circuit — internal fuel circuit problem of logic module
31	Canister purge solenoid circuit
33	Air conditioning Wide Open Throttle (WOT) cut out relay circuit
34	Problem in spare driver circuit
35	Fan control relay circuit
37	Shift indicator lamp circuit — manual transmissions only
41	Charging system excess or no field circuit
42	Automatic Shut Down (ASD) relay circuit
43	Spark interface (internal) circuits
44	Battery temperature is out of range
46	Battery voltage too high — power loss/limited lamp is ON
47	Battery voltage too low
51	Closed loop fuel system problem — oxygen sensor signal stuck at the lean position
52	Oxygen sensor signal stuck at the rich position
53	Logic module problem or failure
55	End of message
88	Start of message — this code only appears on the diagnostic readout Tool C-4805 or equivalent, and means start of message

Year — 1987
Model — Dodge Shadow
Engine — 2.2L (135 cid) EFI 4 cyl
Engine Code — VIN D

ECM TROUBLE CODES

Code	Explanation
88	Start of test
11	Engine not cranked since battery was disconnected
12	Memory standby power lost
13	Manifold Absolute Pressure (MAP) sensor pneumatic circuit — power loss/limited lamp is ON
14	Manifold Absolute Pressure (MAP) sensor electrical system — power loss/limited lamp is ON
15	Vehicle Speed Sensor (VSS) circuit
16	Lose of battery voltage sense — power loss/limited lamp is ON
17	Engine is running too cool
21	Oxygen (O_2) sensor circuit
22	Coolant Temperature Sensor (CTS) circuit — power loss/limited lamp is ON
23	Throttle body temperature sensor circuit
24	Throttle Position Sensor (TPS) circuit — power loss/limited lamp is ON
25	Automatic Idle Speed (AIS) control circuit
26	Peak injector current has not been replaced
27	Fuel interface circuit — internal fuel circuit problem of logic module
31	Canister purge solenoid circuit
33	Air conditioning Wide Open Throttle (WOT) cut out relay circuit
34	Problem in spare driver circuit
35	Fan control relay circuit
37	Shift indicator lamp circuit — manual transmissions only
41	Charging system excess or no field circuit
42	Automatic Shut Down (ASD) relay circuit
43	Spark interface (internal) circuits
44	Battery temperature is out of range
46	Battery voltage too high — power loss/limited lamp is ON
47	Battery voltage too low
51	Closed loop fuel system problem — oxygen sensor signal stuck at the lean position
52	Oxygen sensor signal stuck at the rich position
53	Logic module problem or failure
55	End of message
88	Start of message — this code only appears on the diagnostic readout Tool C-4805 or equivalent, and means start of message

Year – 1987
Model – Plymouth Sundance
Engine – 2.2L (135 cid) EFI 4 cyl
Engine Code – VIN D

ECM TROUBLE CODES

Code	Explanation
88	Start of test
11	Engine not cranked since battery was disconnected
12	Memory standby power lost
13	Manifold Absolute Pressure (MAP) sensor pneumatic circuit – power loss/limited lamp is ON
14	Manifold Absolute Pressure (MAP) sensor electrical system – power loss/limited lamp is ON
15	Vehicle Speed Sensor (VSS) circuit
16	Lose of battery voltage sense – power loss/limited lamp is ON
17	Engine is running too cool
21	Oxygen (O$_2$) sensor circuit
22	Coolant Temperature Sensor (CTS) circuit – power loss/limited lamp is ON
23	Throttle body temperature sensor circuit
24	Throttle Position Sensor (TPS) circuit – power loss/limited lamp is ON
25	Automatic Idle Speed (AIS) control circuit
26	Peak injector current has not been replaced
27	Fuel interface circuit – internal fuel circuit problem of logic module
31	Canister purge solenoid circuit
33	Air conditioning Wide Open Throttle (WOT) cut out relay circuit
34	Problem in spare driver circuit
35	Fan control relay circuit
37	Shift indicator lamp circuit – manual transmissions only
41	Charging system excess or no field circuit
42	Automatic Shut Down (ASD) relay circuit
43	Spark interface (internal) circuits
44	Battery temperature is out of range
46	Battery voltage too high – power loss/limited lamp is ON
47	Battery voltage too low
51	Closed loop fuel system problem – oxygen sensor signal stuck at the lean position
52	Oxygen sensor signal stuck at the rich position
53	Logic module problem or failure
55	End of message
88	Start of message – this code only appears on the diagnostic readout Tool C-4805 or equivalent, and means start of message

Year – 1987
Model – Dodge Shadow
Engine – 2.2L (135 cid) Turbo 4 cyl
Engine Code – VIN E

ECM TROUBLE CODES

Code	Explanation
88	Start of test
11	Engine not cranked since battery was disconnected
12	Memory standby power lost
13	Manifold Absolute Pressure (MAP) sensor pneumatic circuit—power loss/limited lamp is ON
14	Manifold Absolute Pressure (MAP) sensor electrical system—power loss/limited lamp is ON
15	Vehicle Speed Sensor (VSS) circuit
16	Lose of battery voltage sense—power loss/limited lamp is ON
17	Engine is running too cool
21	Oxygen (O_2) sensor circuit
22	Coolant Temperature Sensor (CTS) circuit—power loss/limited lamp is ON
23	Throttle body temperature sensor circuit
24	Throttle Position Sensor (TPS) circuit—power loss/limited lamp is ON
25	Automatic Idle Speed (AIS) control circuit
26	Number 1 injector circuit
27	Number 2 injector circuit
31	EGR/purge solenoid circuit
33	A/C wide cut out relay circuit
34	Speed control malfunction
35	Fan control relay circuit
36	Wastegate solenoid circuit—power loss/limited lamp is ON
37	Barometric read solenoid circuit
41	Charging system excess or no field circuit
42	Automatic Shut Down (ASD) relay driver circuit
43	Spark interface (internal) circuits
44	Battery temperature is out of range
45	Overboost shut-off circuit—power loss/limited lamp is ON
46	Battery voltage too high—power loss/limited lamp is ON
47	Battery voltage too low
51	Closed loop fuel system problem—oxygen sensor signal stuck at the lean position
52	Oxygen sensor signal stuck at the rich position
53	Logic module problem or failure
54	Distributor sync pick-up circuit
55	End of message

Year — 1987
Model — Plymouth Sundance
Engine — 2.2L (135 cid) Turbo 4 cyl
Engine Code — VIN E

ECM TROUBLE CODES

Code	Explanation
88	Start of test
11	Engine not cranked since battery was disconnected
12	Memory standby power lost
13	Manifold Absolute Pressure (MAP) sensor pneumatic circuit — power loss/limited lamp is ON
14	Manifold Absolute Pressure (MAP) sensor electrical system — power loss/limited lamp is ON
15	Vehicle Speed Sensor (VSS) circuit
16	Lose of battery voltage sense — power loss/limited lamp is ON
17	Engine is running too cool
21	Oxygen (O_2) sensor circuit
22	Coolant Temperature Sensor (CTS) circuit — power loss/limited lamp is ON
23	Throttle body temperature sensor circuit
24	Throttle Position Sensor (TPS) circuit — power loss/limited lamp is ON
25	Automatic Idle Speed (AIS) control circuit
26	Number 1 injector circuit
27	Number 2 injector circuit
31	EGR/purge solenoid circuit
33	A/C wide cut out relay circuit
34	Speed control malfunction
35	Fan control relay circuit
36	Wastegate solenoid circuit — power loss/limited lamp is ON
37	Barometric read solenoid circuit
41	Charging system excess or no field circuit
42	Automatic Shut Down (ASD) relay driver circuit
43	Spark interface (internal) circuits
44	Battery temperature is out of range
45	Overboost shut-off circuit — power loss/limited lamp is ON
46	Battery voltage too high — power loss/limited lamp is ON
47	Battery voltage too low
51	Closed loop fuel system problem — oxygen sensor signal stuck at the lean position
52	Oxygen sensor signal stuck at the rich position
53	Logic module problem or failure
54	Distributor sync pick-up circuit
55	End of message

Year — 1987
Model — Chrysler LeBaron GTS
Engine — 2.2L (135 cid) EFI 4 cyl
Engine Code — VIN D

ECM TROUBLE CODES

Code	Explanation
88	Start of test
11	Engine not cranked since battery was disconnected
12	Memory standby power lost
13	Manifold Absolute Pressure (MAP) sensor pneumatic circuit — power loss/limited lamp is ON
14	Manifold Absolute Pressure (MAP) sensor electrical system — power loss/limited lamp is ON
15	Vehicle Speed Sensor (VSS) circuit
16	Lose of battery voltage sense — power loss/limited lamp is ON
17	Engine is running too cool
21	Oxygen (O_2) sensor circuit
22	Coolant Temperature Sensor (CTS) circuit — power loss/limited lamp is ON
23	Throttle body temperature sensor circuit
24	Throttle Position Sensor (TPS) circuit — power loss/limited lamp is ON
25	Automatic Idle Speed (AIS) control circuit
26	Peak injector current has not been replaced
27	Fuel interface circuit — internal fuel circuit problem of logic module
31	Canister purge solenoid circuit
33	Air conditioning Wide Open Throttle (WOT) cut out relay circuit
34	Problem in spare driver circuit
35	Fan control relay circuit
37	Shift indicator lamp circuit — manual transmissions only
41	Charging system excess or no field circuit
42	Automatic Shut Down (ASD) relay circuit
43	Spark interface (internal) circuits
44	Battery temperature is out of range
46	Battery voltage too high — power loss/limited lamp is ON
47	Battery voltage too low
51	Closed loop fuel system problem — oxygen sensor signal stuck at the lean position
52	Oxygen sensor signal stuck at the rich position
53	Logic module problem or failure
55	End of message
88	Start of message — this code only appears on the diagnostic readout Tool C-4805 or equivalent, and means start of message

Year — 1987
Model — Lancer
Engine — 2.2L (135 cid) EFI 4 cyl
Engine Code — VIN D

ECM TROUBLE CODES

Code	Explanation
88	Start of test
11	Engine not cranked since battery was disconnected
12	Memory standby power lost
13	Manifold Absolute Pressure (MAP) sensor pneumatic circuit — power loss/limited lamp is ON
14	Manifold Absolute Pressure (MAP) sensor electrical system — power loss/limited lamp is ON
15	Vehicle Speed Sensor (VSS) circuit
16	Lose of battery voltage sense — power loss/limited lamp is ON
17	Engine is running too cool
21	Oxygen (O_2) sensor circuit
22	Coolant Temperature Sensor (CTS) circuit — power loss/limited lamp is ON
23	Throttle body temperature sensor circuit
24	Throttle Position Sensor (TPS) circuit — power loss/limited lamp is ON
25	Automatic Idle Speed (AIS) control circuit
26	Peak injector current has not been replaced
27	Fuel interface circuit — internal fuel circuit problem of logic module
31	Canister purge solenoid circuit
33	Air conditioning Wide Open Throttle (WOT) cut out relay circuit
34	Problem in spare driver circuit
35	Fan control relay circuit
37	Shift indicator lamp circuit — manual transmissions only
41	Charging system excess or no field circuit
42	Automatic Shut Down (ASD) relay circuit
43	Spark interface (internal) circuits
44	Battery temperature is out of range
46	Battery voltage too high — power loss/limited lamp is ON
47	Battery voltage too low
51	Closed loop fuel system problem — oxygen sensor signal stuck at the lean position
52	Oxygen sensor signal stuck at the rich position
53	Logic module problem or failure
55	End of message
88	Start of message — this code only appears on the diagnostic readout Tool C-4805 or equivalent, and means start of message

Year – 1987
Model – Chrysler LeBaron GTS
Engine – 2.2L (135 cid) Turbo 4 cyl
Engine Code – VIN E

ECM TROUBLE CODES

Code	Explanation
88	Start of test
11	Engine not cranked since battery was disconnected
12	Memory standby power lost
13	Manifold Absolute Pressure (MAP) sensor pneumatic circuit – power loss/limited lamp is ON
14	Manifold Absolute Pressure (MAP) sensor electrical system – power loss/limited lamp is ON
15	Vehicle Speed Sensor (VSS) circuit
16	Lose of battery voltage sense – power loss/limited lamp is ON
17	Engine is running too cool
21	Oxygen (O_2) sensor circuit
22	Coolant Temperature Sensor (CTS) circuit – power loss/limited lamp is ON
23	Throttle body temperature sensor circuit
24	Throttle Position Sensor (TPS) circuit – power loss/limited lamp is ON
25	Automatic Idle Speed (AIS) control circuit
26	Number 1 injector circuit
27	Number 2 injector circuit
31	EGR/purge solenoid circuit
33	A/C wide cut out relay circuit
34	Speed control malfunction
35	Fan control relay circuit
36	Wastegate solenoid circuit – power loss/limited lamp is ON
37	Barometric read solenoid circuit
41	Charging system excess or no field circuit
42	Automatic Shut Down (ASD) relay driver circuit
43	Spark interface (internal) circuits
44	Battery temperature is out of range
45	Overboost shut-off circuit – power loss/limited lamp is ON
46	Battery voltage too high – power loss/limited lamp is ON
47	Battery voltage too low
51	Closed loop fuel system problem – oxygen sensor signal stuck at the lean position
52	Oxygen sensor signal stuck at the rich position
53	Logic module problem or failure
54	Distributor sync pick-up circuit
55	End of message

Year – 1987
Model – Lancer
Engine – 2.2L (135 cid) Turbo 4 cyl
Engine Code – VIN E

ECM TROUBLE CODES

Code	Explanation
88	Start of test
11	Engine not cranked since battery was disconnected
12	Memory standby power lost
13	Manifold Absolute Pressure (MAP) sensor pneumatic circuit – power loss/limited lamp is ON
14	Manifold Absolute Pressure (MAP) sensor electrical system – power loss/limited lamp is ON
15	Vehicle Speed Sensor (VSS) circuit
16	Lose of battery voltage sense – power loss/limited lamp is ON
17	Engine is running too cool
21	Oxygen (O_2) sensor circuit
22	Coolant Temperature Sensor (CTS) circuit – power loss/limited lamp is ON
23	Throttle body temperature sensor circuit
24	Throttle Position Sensor (TPS) circuit – power loss/limited lamp is ON
25	Automatic Idle Speed (AIS) control circuit
26	Number 1 injector circuit
27	Number 2 injector circuit
31	EGR/purge solenoid circuit
33	A/C wide cut out relay circuit
34	Speed control malfunction
35	Fan control relay circuit
36	Wastegate solenoid circuit – power loss/limited lamp is ON
37	Barometric read solenoid circuit
41	Charging system excess or no field circuit
42	Automatic Shut Down (ASD) relay driver circuit
43	Spark interface (internal) circuits
44	Battery temperature is out of range
45	Overboost shut-off circuit – power loss/limited lamp is ON
46	Battery voltage too high – power loss/limited lamp is ON
47	Battery voltage too low
51	Closed loop fuel system problem – oxygen sensor signal stuck at the lean position
52	Oxygen sensor signal stuck at the rich position
53	Logic module problem or failure
54	Distributor sync pick-up circuit
55	End of message

Year – 1987
Model – Chrysler LeBaron GTS
Engine – 2.5L (153 cid) Turbo 4 cyl
Engine Code – VIN J

ECM TROUBLE CODES

Code	Explanation
88	Start of test
11	Engine not cranked since battery was disconnected
12	Memory standby power lost
13	Manifold Absolute Pressure (MAP) sensor pneumatic circuit – power loss/limited lamp is ON
14	Manifold Absolute Pressure (MAP) sensor electrical system – power loss/limited lamp is ON
15	Vehicle Speed Sensor (VSS) circuit
16	Lose of battery voltage sense – power loss/limited lamp is ON
17	Engine is running too cool
21	Oxygen (O_2) sensor circuit
22	Coolant Temperature Sensor (CTS) circuit – power loss/limited lamp is ON
23	Throttle body temperature sensor circuit
24	Throttle Position Sensor (TPS) circuit – power loss/limited lamp is ON
25	Automatic Idle Speed (AIS) control circuit
26	Number 1 injector circuit
27	Number 2 injector circuit
31	EGR/purge solenoid circuit
33	A/C wide cut out relay circuit
34	Speed control malfunction
35	Fan control relay circuit
36	Wastegate solenoid circuit – power loss/limited lamp is ON
37	Barometric read solenoid circuit
41	Charging system excess or no field circuit
42	Automatic Shut Down (ASD) relay driver circuit
43	Spark interface (internal) circuits
44	Battery temperature is out of range
45	Overboost shut-off circuit – power loss/limited lamp is ON
46	Battery voltage too high – power loss/limited lamp is ON
47	Battery voltage too low
51	Closed loop fuel system problem – oxygen sensor signal stuck at the lean position
52	Oxygen sensor signal stuck at the rich position
53	Logic module problem or failure
54	Distributor sync pick-up circuit
55	End of message

Year — 1987
Model — New Yorker
Engine — 2.2L (135 cid) Turbo 4 cyl
Engine Code — VIN E

ECM TROUBLE CODES

Code	Explanation
88	Start of test
11	Engine not cranked since battery was disconnected
12	Memory standby power lost
13	Manifold Absolute Pressure (MAP) sensor pneumatic circuit — power loss/limited lamp is ON
14	Manifold Absolute Pressure (MAP) sensor electrical system — power loss/limited lamp is ON
15	Vehicle Speed Sensor (VSS) circuit
16	Lose of battery voltage sense — power loss/limited lamp is ON
17	Engine is running too cool
21	Oxygen (O_2) sensor circuit
22	Coolant Temperature Sensor (CTS) circuit — power loss/limited lamp is ON
23	Throttle body temperature sensor circuit
24	Throttle Position Sensor (TPS) circuit — power loss/limited lamp is ON
25	Automatic Idle Speed (AIS) control circuit
26	Number 1 injector circuit
27	Number 2 injector circuit
31	EGR/purge solenoid circuit
33	A/C wide cut out relay circuit
34	Speed control malfunction
35	Fan control relay circuit
36	Wastegate solenoid circuit — power loss/limited lamp is ON
37	Barometric read solenoid circuit
41	Charging system excess or no field circuit
42	Automatic Shut Down (ASD) relay driver circuit
43	Spark interface (internal) circuits
44	Battery temperature is out of range
45	Overboost shut-off circuit — power loss/limited lamp is ON
46	Battery voltage too high — power loss/limited lamp is ON
47	Battery voltage too low
51	Closed loop fuel system problem — oxygen sensor signal stuck at the lean position
52	Oxygen sensor signal stuck at the rich position
53	Logic module problem or failure
54	Distributor sync pick-up circuit
55	End of message

Year – 1987
Model – New Yorker
Engine – 2.5L (153 cid) EFI 4 cyl
Engine Code – VIN K

ECM TROUBLE CODES

Code	Explanation
88	Start of test
11	Engine not cranked since battery was disconnected
12	Memory standby power lost
13	Manifold Absolute Pressure (MAP) sensor pneumatic circuit – power loss/limited lamp is ON
14	Manifold Absolute Pressure (MAP) sensor electrical system – power loss/limited lamp is ON
15	Vehicle Speed Sensor (VSS) circuit
16	Lose of battery voltage sense – power loss/limited lamp is ON
17	Engine is running too cool
21	Oxygen (O_2) sensor circuit
22	Coolant Temperature Sensor (CTS) circuit – power loss/limited lamp is ON
23	Throttle body temperature sensor circuit
24	Throttle Position Sensor (TPS) circuit – power loss/limited lamp is ON
25	Automatic Idle Speed (AIS) control circuit
26	Peak injector current has not been replaced
27	Fuel interface circuit – internal fuel circuit problem of logic module
31	Canister purge solenoid circuit
33	Air conditioning Wide Open Throttle (WOT) cut out relay circuit
34	Problem in spare driver circuit
35	Fan control relay circuit
37	Shift indicator lamp circuit – manual transmissions only
41	Charging system excess or no field circuit
42	Automatic Shut Down (ASD) relay circuit
43	Spark interface (internal) circuits
44	Battery temperature is out of range
46	Battery voltage too high – power loss/limited lamp is ON
47	Battery voltage too low
51	Closed loop fuel system problem – oxygen sensor signal stuck at the lean position
52	Oxygen sensor signal stuck at the rich position
53	Logic module problem or failure
55	End of message
88	Start of message – this code only appears on the diagnostic readout Tool C-4805 or equivalent, and means start of message

Year — 1987
Model — Dodge Aries
Engine — 2.2L (135 cid) EFI 4 cyl
Engine Code — VIN D

ECM TROUBLE CODES

Code	Explanation
88	Start of test
11	Engine not cranked since battery was disconnected
12	Memory standby power lost
13	Manifold Absolute Pressure (MAP) sensor pneumatic circuit — power loss/limited lamp is ON
14	Manifold Absolute Pressure (MAP) sensor electrical system — power loss/limited lamp is ON
15	Vehicle Speed Sensor (VSS) circuit
16	Lose of battery voltage sense — power loss/limited lamp is ON
17	Engine is running too cool
21	Oxygen (O$_2$) sensor circuit
22	Coolant Temperature Sensor (CTS) circuit — power loss/limited lamp is ON
23	Throttle body temperature sensor circuit
24	Throttle Position Sensor (TPS) circuit — power loss/limited lamp is ON
25	Automatic Idle Speed (AIS) control circuit
26	Peak injector current has not been replaced
27	Fuel interface circuit — internal fuel circuit problem of logic module
31	Canister purge solenoid circuit
33	Air conditioning Wide Open Throttle (WOT) cut out relay circuit
34	Problem in spare driver circuit
35	Fan control relay circuit
37	Shift indicator lamp circuit — manual transmissions only
41	Charging system excess or no field circuit
42	Automatic Shut Down (ASD) relay circuit
43	Spark interface (internal) circuits
44	Battery temperature is out of range
46	Battery voltage too high — power loss/limited lamp is ON
47	Battery voltage too low
51	Closed loop fuel system problem — oxygen sensor signal stuck at the lean position
52	Oxygen sensor signal stuck at the rich position
53	Logic module problem or failure
55	End of message
88	Start of message — this code only appears on the diagnostic readout Tool C-4805 or equivalent, and means start of message

Year – 1987
Model – Plymouth Reliant
Engine – 2.2L (135 cid) EFI 4 cyl
Engine Code – VIN D

ECM TROUBLE CODES

Code	Explanation
88	Start of test
11	Engine not cranked since battery was disconnected
12	Memory standby power lost
13	Manifold Absolute Pressure (MAP) sensor pneumatic circuit – power loss/limited lamp is ON
14	Manifold Absolute Pressure (MAP) sensor electrical system – power loss/limited lamp is ON
15	Vehicle Speed Sensor (VSS) circuit
16	Lose of battery voltage sense – power loss/limited lamp is ON
17	Engine is running too cool
21	Oxygen (O_2) sensor circuit
22	Coolant Temperature Sensor (CTS) circuit – power loss/limited lamp is ON
23	Throttle body temperature sensor circuit
24	Throttle Position Sensor (TPS) circuit – power loss/limited lamp is ON
25	Automatic Idle Speed (AIS) control circuit
26	Peak injector current has not been replaced
27	Fuel interface circuit – internal fuel circuit problem of logic module
31	Canister purge solenoid circuit
33	Air conditioning Wide Open Throttle (WOT) cut out relay circuit
34	Problem in spare driver circuit
35	Fan control relay circuit
37	Shift indicator lamp circuit – manual transmissions only
41	Charging system excess or no field circuit
42	Automatic Shut Down (ASD) relay circuit
43	Spark interface (internal) circuits
44	Battery temperature is out of range
46	Battery voltage too high – power loss/limited lamp is ON
47	Battery voltage too low
51	Closed loop fuel system problem – oxygen sensor signal stuck at the lean position
52	Oxygen sensor signal stuck at the rich position
53	Logic module problem or failure
55	End of message
88	Start of message – this code only appears on the diagnostic readout Tool C-4805 or equivalent, and means start of message

Year – 1987
Model – Dodge Aries
Engine – 2.5L (153 cid) EFI 4 cyl
Engine Code – VIN K

ECM TROUBLE CODES

Code	Explanation
88	Start of test
11	Engine not cranked since battery was disconnected
12	Memory standby power lost
13	Manifold Absolute Pressure (MAP) sensor pneumatic circuit – power loss/limited lamp is ON
14	Manifold Absolute Pressure (MAP) sensor electrical system – power loss/limited lamp is ON
15	Vehicle Speed Sensor (VSS) circuit
16	Lose of battery voltage sense – power loss/limited lamp is ON
17	Engine is running too cool
21	Oxygen (O₂) sensor circuit
22	Coolant Temperature Sensor (CTS) circuit – power loss/limited lamp is ON
23	Throttle body temperature sensor circuit
24	Throttle Position Sensor (TPS) circuit – power loss/limited lamp is ON
25	Automatic Idle Speed (AIS) control circuit
26	Peak injector current has not been replaced
27	Fuel interface circuit – internal fuel circuit problem of logic module
31	Canister purge solenoid circuit
33	Air conditioning Wide Open Throttle (WOT) cut out relay circuit
34	Problem in spare driver circuit
35	Fan control relay circuit
37	Shift indicator lamp circuit – manual transmissions only
41	Charging system excess or no field circuit
42	Automatic Shut Down (ASD) relay circuit
43	Spark interface (internal) circuits
44	Battery temperature is out of range
46	Battery voltage too high – power loss/limited lamp is ON
47	Battery voltage too low
51	Closed loop fuel system problem – oxygen sensor signal stuck at the lean position
52	Oxygen sensor signal stuck at the rich position
53	Logic module problem or failure
55	End of message
88	Start of message – this code only appears on the diagnostic readout Tool C-4805 or equivalent, and means start of message

CHRYSLER CORPORATION
DIAGNOSTIC CODE DATA

Year – 1987
Model – Plymouth Reliant
Engine – 2.5L (153 cid) EFI 4 cyl
Engine Code – VIN K

ECM TROUBLE CODES

Code	Explanation
88	Start of test
11	Engine not cranked since battery was disconnected
12	Memory standby power lost
13	Manifold Absolute Pressure (MAP) sensor pneumatic circuit—power loss/limited lamp is ON
14	Manifold Absolute Pressure (MAP) sensor electrical system—power loss/limited lamp is ON
15	Vehicle Speed Sensor (VSS) circuit
16	Lose of battery voltage sense—power loss/limited lamp is ON
17	Engine is running too cool
21	Oxygen (O_2) sensor circuit
22	Coolant Temperature Sensor (CTS) circuit—power loss/limited lamp is ON
23	Throttle body temperature sensor circuit
24	Throttle Position Sensor (TPS) circuit—power loss/limited lamp is ON
25	Automatic Idle Speed (AIS) control circuit
26	Peak injector current has not been replaced
27	Fuel interface circuit—internal fuel circuit problem of logic module
31	Canister purge solenoid circuit
33	Air conditioning Wide Open Throttle (WOT) cut out relay circuit
34	Problem in spare driver circuit
35	Fan control relay circuit
37	Shift indicator lamp circuit—manual transmissions only
41	Charging system excess or no field circuit
42	Automatic Shut Down (ASD) relay circuit
43	Spark interface (internal) circuits
44	Battery temperature is out of range
46	Battery voltage too high—power loss/limited lamp is ON
47	Battery voltage too low
51	Closed loop fuel system problem—oxygen sensor signal stuck at the lean position
52	Oxygen sensor signal stuck at the rich position
53	Logic module problem or failure
55	End of message
88	Start of message—this code only appears on the diagnostic readout Tool C-4805 or equivalent, and means start of message

Year — 1987
Model — Chrysler LeBaron GTS
Engine — 2.2L (135 cid) EFI 4 cyl
Engine Code — VIN D

ECM TROUBLE CODES

Code	Explanation
88	Start of test
11	Engine not cranked since battery was disconnected
12	Memory standby power lost
13	Manifold Absolute Pressure (MAP) sensor pneumatic circuit — power loss/limited lamp is ON
14	Manifold Absolute Pressure (MAP) sensor electrical system — power loss/limited lamp is ON
15	Vehicle Speed Sensor (VSS) circuit
16	Lose of battery voltage sense — power loss/limited lamp is ON
17	Engine is running too cool
21	Oxygen (O_2) sensor circuit
22	Coolant Temperature Sensor (CTS) circuit — power loss/limited lamp is ON
23	Throttle body temperature sensor circuit
24	Throttle Position Sensor (TPS) circuit — power loss/limited lamp is ON
25	Automatic Idle Speed (AIS) control circuit
26	Peak injector current has not been replaced
27	Fuel interface circuit — internal fuel circuit problem of logic module
31	Canister purge solenoid circuit
33	Air conditioning Wide Open Throttle (WOT) cut out relay circuit
34	Problem in spare driver circuit
35	Fan control relay circuit
37	Shift indicator lamp circuit — manual transmissions only
41	Charging system excess or no field circuit
42	Automatic Shut Down (ASD) relay circuit
43	Spark interface (internal) circuits
44	Battery temperature is out of range
46	Battery voltage too high — power loss/limited lamp is ON
47	Battery voltage too low
51	Closed loop fuel system problem — oxygen sensor signal stuck at the lean position
52	Oxygen sensor signal stuck at the rich position
53	Logic module problem or failure
55	End of message
88	Start of message — this code only appears on the diagnostic readout Tool C-4805 or equivalent, and means start of message

Year – 1987
Model – Lancer
Engine – 2.2L (135 cid) EFI 4 cyl
Engine Code – VIN D

ECM TROUBLE CODES

Code	Explanation
88	Start of test
11	Engine not cranked since battery was disconnected
12	Memory standby power lost
13	Manifold Absolute Pressure (MAP) sensor pneumatic circuit – power loss/limited lamp is ON
14	Manifold Absolute Pressure (MAP) sensor electrical system – power loss/limited lamp is ON
15	Vehicle Speed Sensor (VSS) circuit
16	Lose of battery voltage sense – power loss/limited lamp is ON
17	Engine is running too cool
21	Oxygen (O_2) sensor circuit
22	Coolant Temperature Sensor (CTS) circuit – power loss/limited lamp is ON
23	Throttle body temperature sensor circuit
24	Throttle Position Sensor (TPS) circuit – power loss/limited lamp is ON
25	Automatic Idle Speed (AIS) control circuit
26	Peak injector current has not been replaced
27	Fuel interface circuit – internal fuel circuit problem of logic module
31	Canister purge solenoid circuit
33	Air conditioning Wide Open Throttle (WOT) cut out relay circuit
34	Problem in spare driver circuit
35	Fan control relay circuit
37	Shift indicator lamp circuit – manual transmissions only
41	Charging system excess or no field circuit
42	Automatic Shut Down (ASD) relay circuit
43	Spark interface (internal) circuits
44	Battery temperature is out of range
46	Battery voltage too high – power loss/limited lamp is ON
47	Battery voltage too low
51	Closed loop fuel system problem – oxygen sensor signal stuck at the lean position
52	Oxygen sensor signal stuck at the rich position
53	Logic module problem or failure
55	End of message
88	Start of message – this code only appears on the diagnostic readout Tool C-4805 or equivalent, and means start of message

Year – 1987
Model – Dodge 600 and 600SE
Engine – 2.2L (135 cid) Turbo 4 cyl
Engine Code – VIN E

ECM TROUBLE CODES

Code	Explanation
88	Start of test
11	Engine not cranked since battery was disconnected
12	Memory standby power lost
13	Manifold Absolute Pressure (MAP) sensor pneumatic circuit – power loss/limited lamp is ON
14	Manifold Absolute Pressure (MAP) sensor electrical system – power loss/limited lamp is ON
15	Vehicle Speed Sensor (VSS) circuit
16	Lose of battery voltage sense – power loss/limited lamp is ON
17	Engine is running too cool
21	Oxygen (O_2) sensor circuit
22	Coolant Temperature Sensor (CTS) circuit – power loss/limited lamp is ON
23	Throttle body temperature sensor circuit
24	Throttle Position Sensor (TPS) circuit – power loss/limited lamp is ON
25	Automatic Idle Speed (AIS) control circuit
26	Number 1 injector circuit
27	Number 2 injector circuit
31	EGR/purge solenoid circuit
33	A/C wide cut out relay circuit
34	Speed control malfunction
35	Fan control relay circuit
36	Wastegate solenoid circuit – power loss/limited lamp is ON
37	Barometric read solenoid circuit
41	Charging system excess or no field circuit
42	Automatic Shut Down (ASD) relay driver circuit
43	Spark interface (internal) circuits
44	Battery temperature is out of range
45	Overboost shut-off circuit – power loss/limited lamp is ON
46	Battery voltage too high – power loss/limited lamp is ON
47	Battery voltage too low
51	Closed loop fuel system problem – oxygen sensor signal stuck at the lean position
52	Oxygen sensor signal stuck at the rich position
53	Logic module problem or failure
54	Distributor sync pick-up circuit
55	End of message

Year – 1987
Model – Plymouth Caravelle
Engine – 2.2L (135 cid) Turbo 4 cyl
Engine Code – VIN E

ECM TROUBLE CODES

Code	Explanation
88	Start of test
11	Engine not cranked since battery was disconnected
12	Memory standby power lost
13	Manifold Absolute Pressure (MAP) sensor pneumatic circuit – power loss/limited lamp is ON
14	Manifold Absolute Pressure (MAP) sensor electrical system – power loss/limited lamp is ON
15	Vehicle Speed Sensor (VSS) circuit
16	Lose of battery voltage sense – power loss/limited lamp is ON
17	Engine is running too cool
21	Oxygen (O$_2$) sensor circuit
22	Coolant Temperature Sensor (CTS) circuit – power loss/limited lamp is ON
23	Throttle body temperature sensor circuit
24	Throttle Position Sensor (TPS) circuit – power loss/limited lamp is ON
25	Automatic Idle Speed (AIS) control circuit
26	Number 1 injector circuit
27	Number 2 injector circuit
31	EGR/purge solenoid circuit
33	A/C wide cut out relay circuit
34	Speed control malfunction
35	Fan control relay circuit
36	Wastegate solenoid circuit – power loss/limited lamp is ON
37	Barometric read solenoid circuit
41	Charging system excess or no field circuit
42	Automatic Shut Down (ASD) relay driver circuit
43	Spark interface (internal) circuits
44	Battery temperature is out of range
45	Overboost shut-off circuit – power loss/limited lamp is ON
46	Battery voltage too high – power loss/limited lamp is ON
47	Battery voltage too low
51	Closed loop fuel system problem – oxygen sensor signal stuck at the lean position
52	Oxygen sensor signal stuck at the rich position
53	Logic module problem or failure
54	Distributor sync pick-up circuit
55	End of message

Year — 1987
Model — Dodge 600 and 600SE
Engine — 2.5L (153 cid) EFI 4 cyl
Engine Code — VIN K

ECM TROUBLE CODES

Code	Explanation
88	Start of test
11	Engine not cranked since battery was disconnected
12	Memory standby power lost
13	Manifold Absolute Pressure (MAP) sensor pneumatic circuit — power loss/limited lamp is ON
14	Manifold Absolute Pressure (MAP) sensor electrical system — power loss/limited lamp is ON
15	Vehicle Speed Sensor (VSS) circuit
16	Lose of battery voltage sense — power loss/limited lamp is ON
17	Engine is running too cool
21	Oxygen (O_2) sensor circuit
22	Coolant Temperature Sensor (CTS) circuit — power loss/limited lamp is ON
23	Throttle body temperature sensor circuit
24	Throttle Position Sensor (TPS) circuit — power loss/limited lamp is ON
25	Automatic Idle Speed (AIS) control circuit
26	Peak injector current has not been replaced
27	Fuel interface circuit — internal fuel circuit problem of logic module
31	Canister purge solenoid circuit
33	Air conditioning Wide Open Throttle (WOT) cut out relay circuit
34	Problem in spare driver circuit
35	Fan control relay circuit
37	Shift indicator lamp circuit — manual transmissions only
41	Charging system excess or no field circuit
42	Automatic Shut Down (ASD) relay circuit
43	Spark interface (internal) circuits
44	Battery temperature is out of range
46	Battery voltage too high — power loss/limited lamp is ON
47	Battery voltage too low
51	Closed loop fuel system problem — oxygen sensor signal stuck at the lean position
52	Oxygen sensor signal stuck at the rich position
53	Logic module problem or failure
55	End of message
88	Start of message — this code only appears on the diagnostic readout Tool C-4805 or equivalent, and means start of message

Year – 1987
Model – Plymouth Caravelle
Engine – 2.5L (153 cid) EFI 4 cyl
Engine Code – VIN K

ECM TROUBLE CODES

Code	Explanation
88	Start of test
11	Engine not cranked since battery was disconnected
12	Memory standby power lost
13	Manifold Absolute Pressure (MAP) sensor pneumatic circuit—power loss/limited lamp is ON
14	Manifold Absolute Pressure (MAP) sensor electrical system—power loss/limited lamp is ON
15	Vehicle Speed Sensor (VSS) circuit
16	Lose of battery voltage sense—power loss/limited lamp is ON
17	Engine is running too cool
21	Oxygen (O_2) sensor circuit
22	Coolant Temperature Sensor (CTS) circuit—power loss/limited lamp is ON
23	Throttle body temperature sensor circuit
24	Throttle Position Sensor (TPS) circuit—power loss/limited lamp is ON
25	Automatic Idle Speed (AIS) control circuit
26	Peak injector current has not been replaced
27	Fuel interface circuit—internal fuel circuit problem of logic module
31	Canister purge solenoid circuit
33	Air conditioning Wide Open Throttle (WOT) cut out relay circuit
34	Problem in spare driver circuit
35	Fan control relay circuit
37	Shift indicator lamp circuit—manual transmissions only
41	Charging system excess or no field circuit
42	Automatic Shut Down (ASD) relay circuit
43	Spark interface (internal) circuits
44	Battery temperature is out of range
46	Battery voltage too high—power loss/limited lamp is ON
47	Battery voltage too low
51	Closed loop fuel system problem—oxygen sensor signal stuck at the lean position
52	Oxygen sensor signal stuck at the rich position
53	Logic module problem or failure
55	End of message
88	Start of message—this code only appears on the diagnostic readout Tool C-4805 or equivalent, and means start of message

Year – 1988
Model – Daytona
Engine – 2.2L (135 cid) Turbo 4 cyl
Engine Code – VIN E

ECM TROUBLE CODES

Code	Explanation
88	Start of test
11	Engine not cranked since battery was disconnected
12	Memory standby power lost
13	Manifold Absolute Pressure (MAP) sensor pneumatic circuit – power loss/limited lamp is ON
14	Manifold Absolute Pressure (MAP) sensor electrical system – power loss/limited lamp is ON
15	Vehicle Speed Sensor (VSS) circuit
16	Lose of battery voltage sense – power loss/limited lamp is ON
17	Engine is running too cool
21	Oxygen (O_2) sensor circuit
22	Coolant Temperature Sensor (CTS) circuit – power loss/limited lamp is ON
23	Throttle body temperature sensor circuit
24	Throttle Position Sensor (TPS) circuit – power loss/limited lamp is ON
25	Automatic Idle Speed (AIS) control circuit
26	Number 1 injector circuit
27	Number 2 injector circuit
31	Exhaust Gas Recirculation (EGR)/purge solenoid circuit
33	A/C wide cut out relay circuit
35	Fan control relay circuit
36	Wastegate solenoid circuit – power loss/limited lamp is ON
37	Barometric read solenoid circuit
41	Charging system excess or no field circuit
42	Automatic Shut Down (ASD) relay driver circuit
43	Spark interface (internal) circuits
44	Battery temperature is out of range
45	Overboost shut-off circuit – power loss/limited lamp is ON
46	Battery voltage too high – power loss/limited lamp is ON
47	Battery voltage too low
51	Closed loop fuel system problem – oxygen sensor signal stuck at the lean position
52	Oxygen sensor signal stuck at the rich position
53	Logic module problem or failure
54	Distributor sync pick-up circuit
55	End of message

Year – 1988
Model – Daytona
Engine – 2.5L (153 cid) EFI 4 cyl
Engine Code – VIN K

ECM TROUBLE CODES

Code	Explanation
88	Start of test
11	Engine not cranked since battery was disconnected
12	Memory standby power lost
13	Manifold Absolute Pressure (MAP) sensor pneumatic circuit – power loss/limited lamp is ON
14	Manifold Absolute Pressure (MAP) sensor electrical system – power loss/limited lamp is ON
15	Vehicle Speed Sensor (VSS) circuit
16	Lose of battery voltage sense – power loss/limited lamp is ON
17	Engine is running too cool
21	Oxygen (O₂) sensor circuit
22	Coolant Temperature Sensor (CTS) circuit – power loss/limited lamp is ON
23	Throttle body temperature sensor circuit
24	Throttle Position Sensor (TPS) circuit – power loss/limited lamp is ON
25	Automatic Idle Speed (AIS) control circuit
26	Peak injector current has not been replaced
27	Fuel interface circuit – internal fuel circuit problem of logic module
31	Canister purge solenoid circuit
33	Air conditioning Wide Open Throttle (WOT) cut out relay circuit
34	Problem in spare driver circuit
35	Fan control relay circuit
37	Shift indicator lamp circuit – manual transmissions only
41	Charging system excess or no field circuit
42	Automatic Shut Down (ASD) relay circuit
43	Spark interface (internal) circuits
44	Battery temperature is out of range
46	Battery voltage too high – power loss/limited lamp is ON
47	Battery voltage too low
51	Closed loop fuel system problem – oxygen sensor signal stuck at the lean position
52	Oxygen sensor signal stuck at the rich position
53	Logic module problem or failure
55	End of message
88	Start of message – this code only appears on the diagnostic readout Tool C-4805 or equivalent, and means start of message

Year – 1988
Model – Daytona
Engine – 2.2L (135 cid) EFI 4 cyl
Engine Code – VIN D

ECM TROUBLE CODES

Code	Explanation
88	Start of test
11	Engine not cranked since battery was disconnected
12	Memory standby power lost
13	Manifold Absolute Pressure (MAP) sensor pneumatic circuit – power loss/limited lamp is ON
14	Manifold Absolute Pressure (MAP) sensor electrical system – power loss/limited lamp is ON
15	Vehicle Speed Sensor (VSS) circuit
16	Lose of battery voltage sense – power loss/limited lamp is ON
17	Engine is running too cool
21	Oxygen (O_2) sensor circuit
22	Coolant Temperature Sensor (CTS) circuit – power loss/limited lamp is ON
23	Throttle body temperature sensor circuit
24	Throttle Position Sensor (TPS) circuit – power loss/limited lamp is ON
25	Automatic Idle Speed (AIS) control circuit
26	Peak injector current has not been replaced
27	Fuel interface circuit – internal fuel circuit problem of logic module
31	Canister purge solenoid circuit
33	Air conditioning Wide Open Throttle (WOT) cut out relay circuit
34	Problem in spare driver circuit
35	Fan control relay circuit
37	Shift indicator lamp circuit – manual transmissions only
41	Charging system excess or no field circuit
42	Automatic Shut Down (ASD) relay circuit
43	Spark interface (internal) circuits
44	Battery temperature is out of range
46	Battery voltage too high – power loss/limited lamp is ON
47	Battery voltage too low
51	Closed loop fuel system problem – oxygen sensor signal stuck at the lean position
52	Oxygen sensor signal stuck at the rich position
53	Logic module problem or failure
55	End of message
88	Start of message – this code only appears on the diagnostic readout Tool C-4805 or equivalent, and means start of message

Year — 1988
Model — Dodge 600
Engine — 2.5L (153 cid) EFI 4 cyl
Engine Code — VIN K

ECM TROUBLE CODES

Code	Explanation
88	Start of test
11	Engine not cranked since battery was disconnected
12	Memory standby power lost
13	Manifold Absolute Pressure (MAP) sensor pneumatic circuit — power loss/limited lamp is ON
14	Manifold Absolute Pressure (MAP) sensor electrical system — power loss/limited lamp is ON
15	Vehicle Speed Sensor (VSS) circuit
16	Lose of battery voltage sense — power loss/limited lamp is ON
17	Engine is running too cool
21	Oxygen (O_2) sensor circuit
22	Coolant Temperature Sensor (CTS) circuit — power loss/limited lamp is ON
23	Throttle body temperature sensor circuit
24	Throttle Position Sensor (TPS) circuit — power loss/limited lamp is ON
25	Automatic Idle Speed (AIS) control circuit
26	Peak injector current has not been replaced
27	Fuel interface circuit — internal fuel circuit problem of logic module
31	Canister purge solenoid circuit
33	Air conditioning Wide Open Throttle (WOT) cut out relay circuit
34	Problem in spare driver circuit
35	Fan control relay circuit
37	Shift indicator lamp circuit — manual transmissions only
41	Charging system excess or no field circuit
42	Automatic Shut Down (ASD) relay circuit
43	Spark interface (internal) circuits
44	Battery temperature is out of range
46	Battery voltage too high — power loss/limited lamp is ON
47	Battery voltage too low
51	Closed loop fuel system problem — oxygen sensor signal stuck at the lean position
52	Oxygen sensor signal stuck at the rich position
53	Logic module problem or failure
55	End of message
88	Start of message — this code only appears on the diagnostic readout Tool C-4805 or equivalent, and means start of message

Year – 1988
Model – Caravelle
Engine – 2.5L (153 cid) EFI 4 cyl
Engine Code – VIN K

ECM TROUBLE CODES

Code	Explanation
88	Start of test
11	Engine not cranked since battery was disconnected
12	Memory standby power lost
13	Manifold Absolute Pressure (MAP) sensor pneumatic circuit – power loss/limited lamp is ON
14	Manifold Absolute Pressure (MAP) sensor electrical system – power loss/limited lamp is ON
15	Vehicle Speed Sensor (VSS) circuit
16	Lose of battery voltage sense – power loss/limited lamp is ON
17	Engine is running too cool
21	Oxygen (O₂) sensor circuit
22	Coolant Temperature Sensor (CTS) circuit – power loss/limited lamp is ON
23	Throttle body temperature sensor circuit
24	Throttle Position Sensor (TPS) circuit – power loss/limited lamp is ON
25	Automatic Idle Speed (AIS) control circuit
26	Peak injector current has not been replaced
27	Fuel interface circuit – internal fuel circuit problem of logic module
31	Canister purge solenoid circuit
33	Air conditioning Wide Open Throttle (WOT) cut out relay circuit
34	Problem in spare driver circuit
35	Fan control relay circuit
37	Shift indicator lamp circuit – manual transmissions only
41	Charging system excess or no field circuit
42	Automatic Shut Down (ASD) relay circuit
43	Spark interface (internal) circuits
44	Battery temperature is out of range
46	Battery voltage too high – power loss/limited lamp is ON
47	Battery voltage too low
51	Closed loop fuel system problem – oxygen sensor signal stuck at the lean position
52	Oxygen sensor signal stuck at the rich position
53	Logic module problem or failure
55	End of message
88	Start of message – this code only appears on the diagnostic readout Tool C-4805 or equivalent, and means start of message

Year – 1988
Model – Dodge 600
Engine – 2.2L (135 cid) Turbo 4 cyl
Engine Code – VIN E

ECM TROUBLE CODES

Code	Explanation
88	Start of test
11	Engine not cranked since battery was disconnected
12	Memory standby power lost
13	Manifold Absolute Pressure (MAP) sensor pneumatic circuit – power loss/limited lamp is ON
14	Manifold Absolute Pressure (MAP) sensor electrical system – power loss/limited lamp is ON
15	Vehicle Speed Sensor (VSS) circuit
16	Lose of battery voltage sense – power loss/limited lamp is ON
17	Engine is running too cool
21	Oxygen (O_2) sensor circuit
22	Coolant Temperature Sensor (CTS) circuit – power loss/limited lamp is ON
23	Throttle body temperature sensor circuit
24	Throttle Position Sensor (TPS) circuit – power loss/limited lamp is ON
25	Automatic Idle Speed (AIS) control circuit
26	Number 1 injector circuit
27	Number 2 injector circuit
31	Exhaust Gas Recirculation (EGR)/purge solenoid circuit
33	A/C wide cut out relay circuit
35	Fan control relay circuit
36	Wastegate solenoid circuit – power loss/limited lamp is ON
37	Barometric read solenoid circuit
41	Charging system excess or no field circuit
42	Automatic Shut Down (ASD) relay driver circuit
43	Spark interface (internal) circuits
44	Battery temperature is out of range
45	Overboost shut-off circuit – power loss/limited lamp is ON
46	Battery voltage too high – power loss/limited lamp is ON
47	Battery voltage too low
51	Closed loop fuel system problem – oxygen sensor signal stuck at the lean position
52	Oxygen sensor signal stuck at the rich position
53	Logic module problem or failure
54	Distributor sync pick-up circuit
55	End of message

Year – 1988
Model – Caravelle
Engine – 2.2L (135 cid) Turbo 4 cyl
Engine Code – VIN E

ECM TROUBLE CODES

Code	Explanation
88	Start of test
11	Engine not cranked since battery was disconnected
12	Memory standby power lost
13	Manifold Absolute Pressure (MAP) sensor pneumatic circuit – power loss/limited lamp is ON
14	Manifold Absolute Pressure (MAP) sensor electrical system – power loss/limited lamp is ON
15	Vehicle Speed Sensor (VSS) circuit
16	Lose of battery voltage sense – power loss/limited lamp is ON
17	Engine is running too cool
21	Oxygen (O₂) sensor circuit
22	Coolant Temperature Sensor (CTS) circuit – power loss/limited lamp is ON
23	Throttle body temperature sensor circuit
24	Throttle Position Sensor (TPS) circuit – power loss/limited lamp is ON
25	Automatic Idle Speed (AIS) control circuit
26	Number 1 injector circuit
27	Number 2 injector circuit
31	Exhaust Gas Recirculation (EGR)/purge solenoid circuit
33	A/C wide cut out relay circuit
35	Fan control relay circuit
36	Wastegate solenoid circuit – power loss/limited lamp is ON
37	Barometric read solenoid circuit
41	Charging system excess or no field circuit
42	Automatic Shut Down (ASD) relay driver circuit
43	Spark interface (internal) circuits
44	Battery temperature is out of range
45	Overboost shut-off circuit – power loss/limited lamp is ON
46	Battery voltage too high – power loss/limited lamp is ON
47	Battery voltage too low
51	Closed loop fuel system problem – oxygen sensor signal stuck at the lean position
52	Oxygen sensor signal stuck at the rich position
53	Logic module problem or failure
54	Distributor sync pick-up circuit
55	End of message

Year – 1988
Model – Dodge 600
Engine – 2.2L (135 cid) EFI 4 cyl
Engine Code – VIN D

ECM TROUBLE CODES

Code	Explanation
88	Start of test
11	Engine not cranked since battery was disconnected
12	Memory standby power lost
13	Manifold Absolute Pressure (MAP) sensor pneumatic circuit – power loss/limited lamp is ON
14	Manifold Absolute Pressure (MAP) sensor electrical system – power loss/limited lamp is ON
15	Vehicle Speed Sensor (VSS) circuit
16	Lose of battery voltage sense – power loss/limited lamp is ON
17	Engine is running too cool
21	Oxygen (O$_2$) sensor circuit
22	Coolant Temperature Sensor (CTS) circuit – power loss/limited lamp is ON
23	Throttle body temperature sensor circuit
24	Throttle Position Sensor (TPS) circuit – power loss/limited lamp is ON
25	Automatic Idle Speed (AIS) control circuit
26	Peak injector current has not been replaced
27	Fuel interface circuit – internal fuel circuit problem of logic module
31	Canister purge solenoid circuit
33	Air conditioning Wide Open Throttle (WOT) cut out relay circuit
34	Problem in spare driver circuit
35	Fan control relay circuit
37	Shift indicator lamp circuit – manual transmissions only
41	Charging system excess or no field circuit
42	Automatic Shut Down (ASD) relay circuit
43	Spark interface (internal) circuits
44	Battery temperature is out of range
46	Battery voltage too high – power loss/limited lamp is ON
47	Battery voltage too low
51	Closed loop fuel system problem – oxygen sensor signal stuck at the lean position
52	Oxygen sensor signal stuck at the rich position
53	Logic module problem or failure
55	End of message
88	Start of message – this code only appears on the diagnostic readout Tool C-4805 or equivalent, and means start of message

Year – 1988
Model – Caravelle
Engine – 2.2L (135 cid) EFI 4 cyl
Engine Code – VIN D

ECM TROUBLE CODES

Code	Explanation
88	Start of test
11	Engine not cranked since battery was disconnected
12	Memory standby power lost
13	Manifold Absolute Pressure (MAP) sensor pneumatic circuit – power loss/limited lamp is ON
14	Manifold Absolute Pressure (MAP) sensor electrical system – power loss/limited lamp is ON
15	Vehicle Speed Sensor (VSS) circuit
16	Lose of battery voltage sense – power loss/limited lamp is ON
17	Engine is running too cool
21	Oxygen (O$_2$) sensor circuit
22	Coolant Temperature Sensor (CTS) circuit – power loss/limited lamp is ON
23	Throttle body temperature sensor circuit
24	Throttle Position Sensor (TPS) circuit – power loss/limited lamp is ON
25	Automatic Idle Speed (AIS) control circuit
26	Peak injector current has not been replaced
27	Fuel interface circuit – internal fuel circuit problem of logic module
31	Canister purge solenoid circuit
33	Air conditioning Wide Open Throttle (WOT) cut out relay circuit
34	Problem in spare driver circuit
35	Fan control relay circuit
37	Shift indicator lamp circuit – manual transmissions only
41	Charging system excess or no field circuit
42	Automatic Shut Down (ASD) relay circuit
43	Spark interface (internal) circuits
44	Battery temperature is out of range
46	Battery voltage too high – power loss/limited lamp is ON
47	Battery voltage too low
51	Closed loop fuel system problem – oxygen sensor signal stuck at the lean position
52	Oxygen sensor signal stuck at the rich position
53	Logic module problem or failure
55	End of message
88	Start of message – this code only appears on the diagnostic readout Tool C-4805 or equivalent, and means start of message

Year — 1988
Model — Dynasty
Engine — 2.5L (153 cid) EFI 4 cyl
Engine Code — VIN K

ECM TROUBLE CODES

Code	Explanation
88	Start of test
11	Engine not cranked since battery was disconnected
12	Memory standby power lost
13	Manifold Absolute Pressure (MAP) sensor pneumatic circuit — power loss/limited lamp is ON
14	Manifold Absolute Pressure (MAP) sensor electrical system — power loss/limited lamp is ON
15	Vehicle Speed Sensor (VSS) circuit
16	Lose of battery voltage sense — power loss/limited lamp is ON
17	Engine is running too cool
21	Oxygen (O_2) sensor circuit
22	Coolant Temperature Sensor (CTS) circuit — power loss/limited lamp is ON
23	Throttle body temperature sensor circuit
24	Throttle Position Sensor (TPS) circuit — power loss/limited lamp is ON
25	Automatic Idle Speed (AIS) control circuit
26	Peak injector current has not been replaced
27	Fuel interface circuit — internal fuel circuit problem of logic module
31	Canister purge solenoid circuit
33	Air conditioning Wide Open Throttle (WOT) cut out relay circuit
34	Problem in spare driver circuit
35	Fan control relay circuit
37	Shift indicator lamp circuit — manual transmissions only
41	Charging system excess or no field circuit
42	Automatic Shut Down (ASD) relay circuit
43	Spark interface (internal) circuits
44	Battery temperature is out of range
46	Battery voltage too high — power loss/limited lamp is ON
47	Battery voltage too low
51	Closed loop fuel system problem — oxygen sensor signal stuck at the lean position
52	Oxygen sensor signal stuck at the rich position
53	Logic module problem or failure
55	End of message
88	Start of message — this code only appears on the diagnostic readout Tool C-4805 or equivalent, and means start of message

Year – 1988
Model – Dynasty
Engine – 3.0L (181 cid) EFI 4 cyl
Engine Code – VIN 3

ECM TROUBLE CODES

Code	Explanation
88	Start of test
11	Engine not cranked since battery was disconnected
12	Memory standby power lost
13	Manifold Absolute Pressure (MAP) sensor pneumatic circuit – power loss/limited lamp is ON
14	Manifold Absolute Pressure (MAP) sensor electrical system – power loss/limited lamp is ON
15	Vehicle Speed Sensor (VSS) circuit
16	Lose of battery voltage sense – power loss/limited lamp is ON
17	Engine is running too cool
21	Oxygen (O₂) sensor circuit
22	Coolant Temperature Sensor (CTS) circuit – power loss/limited lamp is ON
23	Throttle body temperature sensor circuit
24	Throttle Position Sensor (TPS) circuit – power loss/limited lamp is ON
25	Automatic Idle Speed (AIS) control circuit
26	Peak injector current has not been replaced
27	Fuel interface circuit – internal fuel circuit problem of logic module
31	Canister purge solenoid circuit
33	Air conditioning Wide Open Throttle (WOT) cut out relay circuit
34	Problem in spare driver circuit
35	Fan control relay circuit
37	Shift indicator lamp circuit – manual transmissions only
41	Charging system excess or no field circuit
42	Automatic Shut Down (ASD) relay circuit
43	Spark interface (internal) circuits
44	Battery temperature is out of range
46	Battery voltage too high – power loss/limited lamp is ON
47	Battery voltage too low
51	Closed loop fuel system problem – oxygen sensor signal stuck at the lean position
52	Oxygen sensor signal stuck at the rich position
53	Logic module problem or failure
55	End of message
88	Start of message – this code only appears on the diagnostic readout Tool C-4805 or equivalent, and means start of message

Year – 1988
Model – New Yorker
Engine – 3.0L (181 cid) EFI 4 cyl
Engine Code – VIN 3

ECM TROUBLE CODES

Code	Explanation
88	Start of test
11	Engine not cranked since battery was disconnected
12	Memory standby power lost
13	Manifold Absolute Pressure (MAP) sensor pneumatic circuit – power loss/limited lamp is ON
14	Manifold Absolute Pressure (MAP) sensor electrical system – power loss/limited lamp is ON
15	Vehicle Speed Sensor (VSS) circuit
16	Lose of battery voltage sense – power loss/limited lamp is ON
17	Engine is running too cool
21	Oxygen (O_2) sensor circuit
22	Coolant Temperature Sensor (CTS) circuit – power loss/limited lamp is ON
23	Throttle body temperature sensor circuit
24	Throttle Position Sensor (TPS) circuit – power loss/limited lamp is ON
25	Automatic Idle Speed (AIS) control circuit
26	Peak injector current has not been replaced
27	Fuel interface circuit – internal fuel circuit problem of logic module
31	Canister purge solenoid circuit
33	Air conditioning Wide Open Throttle (WOT) cut out relay circuit
34	Problem in spare driver circuit
35	Fan control relay circuit
37	Shift indicator lamp circuit – manual transmissions only
41	Charging system excess or no field circuit
42	Automatic Shut Down (ASD) relay circuit
43	Spark interface (internal) circuits
44	Battery temperature is out of range
46	Battery voltage too high – power loss/limited lamp is ON
47	Battery voltage too low
51	Closed loop fuel system problem – oxygen sensor signal stuck at the lean position
52	Oxygen sensor signal stuck at the rich position
53	Logic module problem or failure
55	End of message
88	Start of message – this code only appears on the diagnostic readout Tool C-4805 or equivalent, and means start of message

Year — 1988
Model — New Yorker
Engine — 2.2L (135 cid) Turbo 4 cyl
Engine Code — VIN E

ECM TROUBLE CODES

Code	Explanation
88	Start of test
11	Engine not cranked since battery was disconnected
12	Memory standby power lost
13	Manifold Absolute Pressure (MAP) sensor pneumatic circuit — power loss/limited lamp is ON
14	Manifold Absolute Pressure (MAP) sensor electrical system — power loss/limited lamp is ON
15	Vehicle Speed Sensor (VSS) circuit
16	Lose of battery voltage sense — power loss/limited lamp is ON
17	Engine is running too cool
21	Oxygen (O_2) sensor circuit
22	Coolant Temperature Sensor (CTS) circuit — power loss/limited lamp is ON
23	Throttle body temperature sensor circuit
24	Throttle Position Sensor (TPS) circuit — power loss/limited lamp is ON
25	Automatic Idle Speed (AIS) control circuit
26	Number 1 injector circuit
27	Number 2 injector circuit
31	Exhaust Gas Recirculation (EGR)/purge solenoid circuit
33	A/C wide cut out relay circuit
35	Fan control relay circuit
36	Wastegate solenoid circuit — power loss/limited lamp is ON
37	Barometric read solenoid circuit
41	Charging system excess or no field circuit
42	Automatic Shut Down (ASD) relay driver circuit
43	Spark interface (internal) circuits
44	Battery temperature is out of range
45	Overboost shut-off circuit — power loss/limited lamp is ON
46	Battery voltage too high — power loss/limited lamp is ON
47	Battery voltage too low
51	Closed loop fuel system problem — oxygen sensor signal stuck at the lean position
52	Oxygen sensor signal stuck at the rich position
53	Logic module problem or failure
54	Distributor sync pick-up circuit
55	End of message

Year – 1988
Model – Aries
Engine – 2.2L (135 cid) EFI 4 cyl
Engine Code – VIN D

ECM TROUBLE CODES

Code	Explanation
88	Start of test
11	Engine not cranked since battery was disconnected
12	Memory standby power lost
13	Manifold Absolute Pressure (MAP) sensor pneumatic circuit – power loss/limited lamp is ON
14	Manifold Absolute Pressure (MAP) sensor electrical system – power loss/limited lamp is ON
15	Vehicle Speed Sensor (VSS) circuit
16	Lose of battery voltage sense – power loss/limited lamp is ON
17	Engine is running too cool
21	Oxygen (O_2) sensor circuit
22	Coolant Temperature Sensor (CTS) circuit – power loss/limited lamp is ON
23	Throttle body temperature sensor circuit
24	Throttle Position Sensor (TPS) circuit – power loss/limited lamp is ON
25	Automatic Idle Speed (AIS) control circuit
26	Peak injector current has not been replaced
27	Fuel interface circuit – internal fuel circuit problem of logic module
31	Canister purge solenoid circuit
33	Air conditioning Wide Open Throttle (WOT) cut out relay circuit
34	Problem in spare driver circuit
35	Fan control relay circuit
37	Shift indicator lamp circuit – manual transmissions only
41	Charging system excess or no field circuit
42	Automatic Shut Down (ASD) relay circuit
43	Spark interface (internal) circuits
44	Battery temperature is out of range
46	Battery voltage too high – power loss/limited lamp is ON
47	Battery voltage too low
51	Closed loop fuel system problem – oxygen sensor signal stuck at the lean position
52	Oxygen sensor signal stuck at the rich position
53	Logic module problem or failure
55	End of message
88	Start of message – this code only appears on the diagnostic readout Tool C-4805 or equivalent, and means start of message

Year — 1988
Model — Reliant
Engine — 2.2L (135 cid) EFI 4 cyl
Engine Code — VIN D

ECM TROUBLE CODES

Code	Explanation
88	Start of test
11	Engine not cranked since battery was disconnected
12	Memory standby power lost
13	Manifold Absolute Pressure (MAP) sensor pneumatic circuit — power loss/limited lamp is ON
14	Manifold Absolute Pressure (MAP) sensor electrical system — power loss/limited lamp is ON
15	Vehicle Speed Sensor (VSS) circuit
16	Lose of battery voltage sense — power loss/limited lamp is ON
17	Engine is running too cool
21	Oxygen (O_2) sensor circuit
22	Coolant Temperature Sensor (CTS) circuit — power loss/limited lamp is ON
23	Throttle body temperature sensor circuit
24	Throttle Position Sensor (TPS) circuit — power loss/limited lamp is ON
25	Automatic Idle Speed (AIS) control circuit
26	Peak injector current has not been replaced
27	Fuel interface circuit — internal fuel circuit problem of logic module
31	Canister purge solenoid circuit
33	Air conditioning Wide Open Throttle (WOT) cut out relay circuit
34	Problem in spare driver circuit
35	Fan control relay circuit
37	Shift indicator lamp circuit — manual transmissions only
41	Charging system excess or no field circuit
42	Automatic Shut Down (ASD) relay circuit
43	Spark interface (internal) circuits
44	Battery temperature is out of range
46	Battery voltage too high — power loss/limited lamp is ON
47	Battery voltage too low
51	Closed loop fuel system problem — oxygen sensor signal stuck at the lean position
52	Oxygen sensor signal stuck at the rich position
53	Logic module problem or failure
55	End of message
88	Start of message — this code only appears on the diagnostic readout Tool C-4805 or equivalent, and means start of message

Year — 1988
Model — Aries
Engine — 2.5L (153 cid) EFI 4 cyl
Engine Code — VIN K

ECM TROUBLE CODES

Code	Explanation
88	Start of test
11	Engine not cranked since battery was disconnected
12	Memory standby power lost
13	Manifold Absolute Pressure (MAP) sensor pneumatic circuit — power loss/limited lamp is ON
14	Manifold Absolute Pressure (MAP) sensor electrical system — power loss/limited lamp is ON
15	Vehicle Speed Sensor (VSS) circuit
16	Lose of battery voltage sense — power loss/limited lamp is ON
17	Engine is running too cool
21	Oxygen (O$_2$) sensor circuit
22	Coolant Temperature Sensor (CTS) circuit — power loss/limited lamp is ON
23	Throttle body temperature sensor circuit
24	Throttle Position Sensor (TPS) circuit — power loss/limited lamp is ON
25	Automatic Idle Speed (AIS) control circuit
26	Peak injector current has not been replaced
27	Fuel interface circuit — internal fuel circuit problem of logic module
31	Canister purge solenoid circuit
33	Air conditioning Wide Open Throttle (WOT) cut out relay circuit
34	Problem in spare driver circuit
35	Fan control relay circuit
37	Shift indicator lamp circuit — manual transmissions only
41	Charging system excess or no field circuit
42	Automatic Shut Down (ASD) relay circuit
43	Spark interface (internal) circuits
44	Battery temperature is out of range
46	Battery voltage too high — power loss/limited lamp is ON
47	Battery voltage too low
51	Closed loop fuel system problem — oxygen sensor signal stuck at the lean position
52	Oxygen sensor signal stuck at the rich position
53	Logic module problem or failure
55	End of message
88	Start of message — this code only appears on the diagnostic readout Tool C-4805 or equivalent, and means start of message

Year — 1988
Model — Reliant
Engine — 2.5L (153 cid) EFI 4 cyl
Engine Code — VIN K

ECM TROUBLE CODES

Code	Explanation
88	Start of test
11	Engine not cranked since battery was disconnected
12	Memory standby power lost
13	Manifold Absolute Pressure (MAP) sensor pneumatic circuit — power loss/limited lamp is ON
14	Manifold Absolute Pressure (MAP) sensor electrical system — power loss/limited lamp is ON
15	Vehicle Speed Sensor (VSS) circuit
16	Lose of battery voltage sense — power loss/limited lamp is ON
17	Engine is running too cool
21	Oxygen (O$_2$) sensor circuit
22	Coolant Temperature Sensor (CTS) circuit — power loss/limited lamp is ON
23	Throttle body temperature sensor circuit
24	Throttle Position Sensor (TPS) circuit — power loss/limited lamp is ON
25	Automatic Idle Speed (AIS) control circuit
26	Peak injector current has not been replaced
27	Fuel interface circuit — internal fuel circuit problem of logic module
31	Canister purge solenoid circuit
33	Air conditioning Wide Open Throttle (WOT) cut out relay circuit
34	Problem in spare driver circuit
35	Fan control relay circuit
37	Shift indicator lamp circuit — manual transmissions only
41	Charging system excess or no field circuit
42	Automatic Shut Down (ASD) relay circuit
43	Spark interface (internal) circuits
44	Battery temperature is out of range
46	Battery voltage too high — power loss/limited lamp is ON
47	Battery voltage too low
51	Closed loop fuel system problem oxygen sensor signal stuck at the lean position
52	Oxygen sensor signal stuck at the rich position
53	Logic module problem or failure
55	End of message
88	Start of message — this code only appears on the diagnostic readout Tool C-4805 or equivalent, and means start of message

CHRYSLER CORPORATION
DIAGNOSTIC CODE DATA

Year—1988
Model—Omni
Engine—2.2L (135 cid) EFI 4 cyl
Engine Code—VIN D

ECM TROUBLE CODES

Code	Explanation
88	Start of test
11	Engine not cranked since battery was disconnected
12	Memory standby power lost
13	Manifold Absolute Pressure (MAP) sensor pneumatic circuit—power loss/limited lamp is ON
14	Manifold Absolute Pressure (MAP) sensor electrical system—power loss/limited lamp is ON
15	Vehicle Speed Sensor (VSS) circuit
16	Lose of battery voltage sense—power loss/limited lamp is ON
17	Engine is running too cool
21	Oxygen (O_2) sensor circuit
22	Coolant Temperature Sensor (CTS) circuit—power loss/limited lamp is ON
23	Throttle body temperature sensor circuit
24	Throttle Position Sensor (TPS) circuit—power loss/limited lamp is ON
25	Automatic Idle Speed (AIS) control circuit
26	Peak injector current has not been replaced
27	Fuel interface circuit—internal fuel circuit problem of logic module
31	Canister purge solenoid circuit
33	Air conditioning Wide Open Throttle (WOT) cut out relay circuit
34	Problem in spare driver circuit
35	Fan control relay circuit
37	Shift indicator lamp circuit—manual transmissions only
41	Charging system excess or no field circuit
42	Automatic Shut Down (ASD) relay circuit
43	Spark interface (internal) circuits
44	Battery temperature is out of range
46	Battery voltage too high—power loss/limited lamp is ON
47	Battery voltage too low
51	Closed loop fuel system problem—oxygen sensor signal stuck at the lean position
52	Oxygen sensor signal stuck at the rich position
53	Logic module problem or failure
55	End of message
88	Start of message—this code only appears on the diagnostic readout Tool C-4805 or equivalent, and means start of message

Year – 1988
Model – Horizon
Engine – 2.2L (135 cid) EFI 4 cyl
Engine Code – VIN D

ECM TROUBLE CODES

Code	Explanation
88	Start of test
11	Engine not cranked since battery was disconnected
12	Memory standby power lost
13	Manifold Absolute Pressure (MAP) sensor pneumatic circuit – power loss/limited lamp is ON
14	Manifold Absolute Pressure (MAP) sensor electrical system – power loss/limited lamp is ON
15	Vehicle Speed Sensor (VSS) circuit
16	Lose of battery voltage sense – power loss/limited lamp is ON
17	Engine is running too cool
21	Oxygen (O_2) sensor circuit
22	Coolant Temperature Sensor (CTS) circuit – power loss/limited lamp is ON
23	Throttle body temperature sensor circuit
24	Throttle Position Sensor (TPS) circuit – power loss/limited lamp is ON
25	Automatic Idle Speed (AIS) control circuit
26	Peak injector current has not been replaced
27	Fuel interface circuit – internal fuel circuit problem of logic module
31	Canister purge solenoid circuit
33	Air conditioning Wide Open Throttle (WOT) cut out relay circuit
34	Problem in spare driver circuit
35	Fan control relay circuit
37	Shift indicator lamp circuit – manual transmissions only
41	Charging system excess or no field circuit
42	Automatic Shut Down (ASD) relay circuit
43	Spark interface (internal) circuits
44	Battery temperature is out of range
46	Battery voltage too high – power loss/limited lamp is ON
47	Battery voltage too low
51	Closed loop fuel system problem oxygen sensor signal stuck at the lean position
52	Oxygen sensor signal stuck at the rich position
53	Logic module problem or failure
55	End of message
88	Start of message – this code only appears on the diagnostic readout Tool C-4805 or equivalent, and means start of message

Year – 1988
Model – LeBaron
Engine – 2.2L (135 cid) EFI 4 cyl
Engine Code – VIN D

ECM TROUBLE CODES

Code	Explanation
88	Start of test
11	Engine not cranked since battery was disconnected
12	Memory standby power lost
13	Manifold Absolute Pressure (MAP) sensor pneumatic circuit – power loss/limited lamp is ON
14	Manifold Absolute Pressure (MAP) sensor electrical system – power loss/limited lamp is ON
15	Vehicle Speed Sensor (VSS) circuit
16	Lose of battery voltage sense – power loss/limited lamp is ON
17	Engine is running too cool
21	Oxygen (O_2) sensor circuit
22	Coolant Temperature Sensor (CTS) circuit – power loss/limited lamp is ON
23	Throttle body temperature sensor circuit
24	Throttle Position Sensor (TPS) circuit – power loss/limited lamp is ON
25	Automatic Idle Speed (AIS) control circuit
26	Peak injector current has not been replaced
27	Fuel interface circuit – internal fuel circuit problem of logic module
31	Canister purge solenoid circuit
33	Air conditioning Wide Open Throttle (WOT) cut out relay circuit
34	Problem in spare driver circuit
35	Fan control relay circuit
37	Shift indicator lamp circuit – manual transmissions only
41	Charging system excess or no field circuit
42	Automatic Shut Down (ASD) relay circuit
43	Spark interface (internal) circuits
44	Battery temperature is out of range
46	Battery voltage too high – power loss/limited lamp is ON
47	Battery voltage too low
51	Closed loop fuel system problem – oxygen sensor signal stuck at the lean position
52	Oxygen sensor signal stuck at the rich position
53	Logic module problem or failure
55	End of message
88	Start of message – this code only appears on the diagnostic readout Tool C-4805 or equivalent, and means start of message

Year – 1988
Model – Lancer
Engine – 2.2L (135 cid) EFI 4 cyl
Engine Code – VIN D

ECM TROUBLE CODES

Code	Explanation
88	Start of test
11	Engine not cranked since battery was disconnected
12	Memory standby power lost
13	Manifold Absolute Pressure (MAP) sensor pneumatic circuit – power loss/limited lamp is ON
14	Manifold Absolute Pressure (MAP) sensor electrical system – power loss/limited lamp is ON
15	Vehicle Speed Sensor (VSS) circuit
16	Lose of battery voltage sense – power loss/limited lamp is ON
17	Engine is running too cool
21	Oxygen (O_2) sensor circuit
22	Coolant Temperature Sensor (CTS) circuit – power loss/limited lamp is ON
23	Throttle body temperature sensor circuit
24	Throttle Position Sensor (TPS) circuit – power loss/limited lamp is ON
25	Automatic Idle Speed (AIS) control circuit
26	Peak injector current has not been replaced
27	Fuel interface circuit – internal fuel circuit problem of logic module
31	Canister purge solenoid circuit
33	Air conditioning Wide Open Throttle (WOT) cut out relay circuit
34	Problem in spare driver circuit
35	Fan control relay circuit
37	Shift indicator lamp circuit – manual transmissions only
41	Charging system excess or no field circuit
42	Automatic Shut Down (ASD) relay circuit
43	Spark interface (internal) circuits
44	Battery temperature is out of range
46	Battery voltage too high – power loss/limited lamp is ON
47	Battery voltage too low
51	Closed loop fuel system problem – oxygen sensor signal stuck at the lean position
52	Oxygen sensor signal stuck at the rich position
53	Logic module problem or failure
55	End of message
88	Start of message – this code only appears on the diagnostic readout Tool C-4805 or equivalent, and means start of message

Year – 1988
Model – LeBaron
Engine – 2.2L (135 cid) Turbo 4 cyl
Engine Code – VIN E

ECM TROUBLE CODES

Code	Explanation
88	Start of test
11	Engine not cranked since battery was disconnected
12	Memory standby power lost
13	Manifold Absolute Pressure (MAP) sensor pneumatic circuit – power loss/limited lamp is ON
14	Manifold Absolute Pressure (MAP) sensor electrical system – power loss/limited lamp is ON
15	Vehicle Speed Sensor (VSS) circuit
16	Lose of battery voltage sense – power loss/limited lamp is ON
17	Engine is running too cool
21	Oxygen (O₂) sensor circuit
22	Coolant Temperature Sensor (CTS) circuit – power loss/limited lamp is ON
23	Throttle body temperature sensor circuit
24	Throttle Position Sensor (TPS) circuit – power loss/limited lamp is ON
25	Automatic Idle Speed (AIS) control circuit
26	Number 1 injector circuit
27	Number 2 injector circuit
31	Exhaust Gas Recirculation (EGR)/purge solenoid circuit
33	A/C wide cut out relay circuit
35	Fan control relay circuit
36	Wastegate solenoid circuit – power loss/limited lamp is ON
37	Barometric read solenoid circuit
41	Charging system excess or no field circuit
42	Automatic Shut Down (ASD) relay driver circuit
43	Spark interface (internal) circuits
44	Battery temperature is out of range
45	Overboost shut-off circuit – power loss/limited lamp is ON
46	Battery voltage too high – power loss/limited lamp is ON
47	Battery voltage too low
51	Closed loop fuel system problem – oxygen sensor signal stuck at the lean position
52	Oxygen sensor signal stuck at the rich position
53	Logic module problem or failure
54	Distributor sync pick-up circuit
55	End of message

Year – 1988
Model – Lancer
Engine – 2.2L (135 cid) Turbo 4 cyl
Engine Code – VIN E

ECM TROUBLE CODES

Code	Explanation
88	Start of test
11	Engine not cranked since battery was disconnected
12	Memory standby power lost
13	Manifold Absolute Pressure (MAP) sensor pneumatic circuit – power loss/limited lamp is ON
14	Manifold Absolute Pressure (MAP) sensor electrical system – power loss/limited lamp is ON
15	Vehicle Speed Sensor (VSS) circuit
16	Lose of battery voltage sense – power loss/limited lamp is ON
17	Engine is running too cool
21	Oxygen (O₂) sensor circuit
22	Coolant Temperature Sensor (CTS) circuit – power loss/limited lamp is ON
23	Throttle body temperature sensor circuit
24	Throttle Position Sensor (TPS) circuit – power loss/limited lamp is ON
25	Automatic Idle Speed (AIS) control circuit
26	Number 1 injector circuit
27	Number 2 injector circuit
31	Exhaust Gas Recirculation (EGR)/purge solenoid circuit
33	A/C wide cut out relay circuit
35	Fan control relay circuit
36	Wastegate solenoid circuit – power loss/limited lamp is ON
37	Barometric read solenoid circuit
41	Charging system excess or no field circuit
42	Automatic Shut Down (ASD) relay driver circuit
43	Spark interface (internal) circuits
44	Battery temperature is out of range
45	Overboost shut-off circuit – power loss/limited lamp is ON
46	Battery voltage too high – power loss/limited lamp is ON
47	Battery voltage too low
51	Closed loop fuel system problem – oxygen sensor signal stuck at the lean position
52	Oxygen sensor signal stuck at the rich position
53	Logic module problem or failure
54	Distributor sync pick-up circuit
55	End of message

Year — 1988
Model — LeBaron
Engine — 2.5L (153 cid) EFI 4 cyl
Engine Code — VIN K

ECM TROUBLE CODES

Code	Explanation
88	Start of test
11	Engine not cranked since battery was disconnected
12	Memory standby power lost
13	Manifold Absolute Pressure (MAP) sensor pneumatic circuit — power loss/limited lamp is ON
14	Manifold Absolute Pressure (MAP) sensor electrical system — power loss/limited lamp is ON
15	Vehicle Speed Sensor (VSS) circuit
16	Lose of battery voltage sense — power loss/limited lamp is ON
17	Engine is running too cool
21	Oxygen (O_2) sensor circuit
22	Coolant Temperature Sensor (CTS) circuit — power loss/limited lamp is ON
23	Throttle body temperature sensor circuit
24	Throttle Position Sensor (TPS) circuit — power loss/limited lamp is ON
25	Automatic Idle Speed (AIS) control circuit
26	Peak injector current has not been replaced
27	Fuel interface circuit — internal fuel circuit problem of logic module
31	Canister purge solenoid circuit
33	Air conditioning Wide Open Throttle (WOT) cut out relay circuit
34	Problem in spare driver circuit
35	Fan control relay circuit
37	Shift indicator lamp circuit — manual transmissions only
41	Charging system excess or no field circuit
42	Automatic Shut Down (ASD) relay circuit
43	Spark interface (internal) circuits
44	Battery temperature is out of range
46	Battery voltage too high — power loss/limited lamp is ON
47	Battery voltage too low
51	Closed loop fuel system problem — oxygen sensor signal stuck at the lean position
52	Oxygen sensor signal stuck at the rich position
53	Logic module problem or failure
55	End of message
88	Start of message — this code only appears on the diagnostic readout Tool C-4805 or equivalent, and means start of message

Year — 1988
Model — Lancer
Engine — 2.5L (153 cid) EFI 4 cyl
Engine Code — VIN K

ECM TROUBLE CODES

Code	Explanation
88	Start of test
11	Engine not cranked since battery was disconnected
12	Memory standby power lost
13	Manifold Absolute Pressure (MAP) sensor pneumatic circuit — power loss/limited lamp is ON
14	Manifold Absolute Pressure (MAP) sensor electrical system — power loss/limited lamp is ON
15	Vehicle Speed Sensor (VSS) circuit
16	Lose of battery voltage sense — power loss/limited lamp is ON
17	Engine is running too cool
21	Oxygen (O_2) sensor circuit
22	Coolant Temperature Sensor (CTS) circuit — power loss/limited lamp is ON
23	Throttle body temperature sensor circuit
24	Throttle Position Sensor (TPS) circuit — power loss/limited lamp is ON
25	Automatic Idle Speed (AIS) control circuit
26	Peak injector current has not been replaced
27	Fuel interface circuit — internal fuel circuit problem of logic module
31	Canister purge solenoid circuit
33	Air conditioning Wide Open Throttle (WOT) cut out relay circuit
34	Problem in spare driver circuit
35	Fan control relay circuit
37	Shift indicator lamp circuit — manual transmissions only
41	Charging system excess or no field circuit
42	Automatic Shut Down (ASD) relay circuit
43	Spark interface (internal) circuits
44	Battery temperature is out of range
46	Battery voltage too high — power loss/limited lamp is ON
47	Battery voltage too low
51	Closed loop fuel system problem — oxygen sensor signal stuck at the lean position
52	Oxygen sensor signal stuck at the rich position
53	Logic module problem or failure
55	End of message
88	Start of message — this code only appears on the diagnostic readout Tool C-4805 or equivalent, and means start of message

Year – 1988
Model – Shadow
Engine – 2.2L (135 cid) EFI 4 cyl
Engine Code – VIN D

ECM TROUBLE CODES

Code	Explanation
88	Start of test
11	Engine not cranked since battery was disconnected
12	Memory standby power lost
13	Manifold Absolute Pressure (MAP) sensor pneumatic circuit – power loss/limited lamp is ON
14	Manifold Absolute Pressure (MAP) sensor electrical system – power loss/limited lamp is ON
15	Vehicle Speed Sensor (VSS) circuit
16	Lose of battery voltage sense – power loss/limited lamp is ON
17	Engine is running too cool
21	Oxygen (O$_2$) sensor circuit
22	Coolant Temperature Sensor (CTS) circuit – power loss/limited lamp is ON
23	Throttle body temperature sensor circuit
24	Throttle Position Sensor (TPS) circuit – power loss/limited lamp is ON
25	Automatic Idle Speed (AIS) control circuit
26	Peak injector current has not been replaced
27	Fuel interface circuit – internal fuel circuit problem of logic module
31	Canister purge solenoid circuit
33	Air conditioning Wide Open Throttle (WOT) cut out relay circuit
34	Problem in spare driver circuit
35	Fan control relay circuit
37	Shift indicator lamp circuit – manual transmissions only
41	Charging system excess or no field circuit
42	Automatic Shut Down (ASD) relay circuit
43	Spark interface (internal) circuits
44	Battery temperature is out of range
46	Battery voltage too high – power loss/limited lamp is ON
47	Battery voltage too low
51	Closed loop fuel system problem – oxygen sensor signal stuck at the lean position
52	Oxygen sensor signal stuck at the rich position
53	Logic module problem or failure
55	End of message
88	Start of message – this code only appears on the diagnostic readout Tool C-4805 or equivalent, and means start of message

Year — 1988
Model — Sundance
Engine — 2.2L (135 cid) EFI 4 cyl
Engine Code — VIN D

ECM TROUBLE CODES

Code	Explanation
88	Start of test
11	Engine not cranked since battery was disconnected
12	Memory standby power lost
13	Manifold Absolute Pressure (MAP) sensor pneumatic circuit — power loss/limited lamp is ON
14	Manifold Absolute Pressure (MAP) sensor electrical system — power loss/limited lamp is ON
15	Vehicle Speed Sensor (VSS) circuit
16	Lose of battery voltage sense — power loss/limited lamp is ON
17	Engine is running too cool
21	Oxygen (O_2) sensor circuit
22	Coolant Temperature Sensor (CTS) circuit — power loss/limited lamp is ON
23	Throttle body temperature sensor circuit
24	Throttle Position Sensor (TPS) circuit — power loss/limited lamp is ON
25	Automatic Idle Speed (AIS) control circuit
26	Peak injector current has not been replaced
27	Fuel interface circuit — internal fuel circuit problem of logic module
31	Canister purge solenoid circuit
33	Air conditioning Wide Open Throttle (WOT) cut out relay circuit
34	Problem in spare driver circuit
35	Fan control relay circuit
37	Shift indicator lamp circuit — manual transmissions only
41	Charging system excess or no field circuit
42	Automatic Shut Down (ASD) relay circuit
43	Spark interface (internal) circuits
44	Battery temperature is out of range
46	Battery voltage too high — power loss/limited lamp is ON
47	Battery voltage too low
51	Closed loop fuel system problem — oxygen sensor signal stuck at the lean position
52	Oxygen sensor signal stuck at the rich position
53	Logic module problem or failure
55	End of message
88	Start of message — this code only appears on the diagnostic readout Tool C-4805 or equivalent, and means start of message

Year — 1988
Model — Shadow
Engine — 2.5L (153 cid) EFI 4 cyl
Engine Code — VIN K

ECM TROUBLE CODES

Code	Explanation
88	Start of test
11	Engine not cranked since battery was disconnected
12	Memory standby power lost
13	Manifold Absolute Pressure (MAP) sensor pneumatic circuit — power loss/limited lamp is ON
14	Manifold Absolute Pressure (MAP) sensor electrical system — power loss/limited lamp is ON
15	Vehicle Speed Sensor (VSS) circuit
16	Lose of battery voltage sense — power loss/limited lamp is ON
17	Engine is running too cool
21	Oxygen (O_2) sensor circuit
22	Coolant Temperature Sensor (CTS) circuit — power loss/limited lamp is ON
23	Throttle body temperature sensor circuit
24	Throttle Position Sensor (TPS) circuit — power loss/limited lamp is ON
25	Automatic Idle Speed (AIS) control circuit
26	Peak injector current has not been replaced
27	Fuel interface circuit — internal fuel circuit problem of logic module
31	Canister purge solenoid circuit
33	Air conditioning Wide Open Throttle (WOT) cut out relay circuit
34	Problem in spare driver circuit
35	Fan control relay circuit
37	Shift indicator lamp circuit — manual transmissions only
41	Charging system excess or no field circuit
42	Automatic Shut Down (ASD) relay circuit
43	Spark interface (internal) circuits
44	Battery temperature is out of range
46	Battery voltage too high — power loss/limited lamp is ON
47	Battery voltage too low
51	Closed loop fuel system problem — oxygen sensor signal stuck at the lean position
52	Oxygen sensor signal stuck at the rich position
53	Logic module problem or failure
55	End of message
88	Start of message — this code only appears on the diagnostic readout Tool C-4805 or equivalent, and means start of message

Year — 1988
Model — Sundance
Engine — 2.5L (153 cid) EFI 4 cyl
Engine Code — VIN K

ECM TROUBLE CODES

Code	Explanation
88	Start of test
11	Engine not cranked since battery was disconnected
12	Memory standby power lost
13	Manifold Absolute Pressure (MAP) sensor pneumatic circuit — power loss/limited lamp is ON
14	Manifold Absolute Pressure (MAP) sensor electrical system — power loss/limited lamp is ON
15	Vehicle Speed Sensor (VSS) circuit
16	Lose of battery voltage sense — power loss/limited lamp is ON
17	Engine is running too cool
21	Oxygen (O_2) sensor circuit
22	Coolant Temperature Sensor (CTS) circuit — power loss/limited lamp is ON
23	Throttle body temperature sensor circuit
24	Throttle Position Sensor (TPS) circuit — power loss/limited lamp is ON
25	Automatic Idle Speed (AIS) control circuit
26	Peak injector current has not been replaced
27	Fuel interface circuit — internal fuel circuit problem of logic module
31	Canister purge solenoid circuit
33	Air conditioning Wide Open Throttle (WOT) cut out relay circuit
34	Problem in spare driver circuit
35	Fan control relay circuit
37	Shift indicator lamp circuit — manual transmissions only
41	Charging system excess or no field circuit
42	Automatic Shut Down (ASD) relay circuit
43	Spark interface (internal) circuits
44	Battery temperature is out of range
46	Battery voltage too high — power loss/limited lamp is ON
47	Battery voltage too low
51	Closed loop fuel system problem — oxygen sensor signal stuck at the lean position
52	Oxygen sensor signal stuck at the rich position
53	Logic module problem or failure
55	End of message
88	Start of message — this code only appears on the diagnostic readout Tool C-4805 or equivalent, and means start of message

Year – 1988
Model – Shadow
Engine – 2.2L (135 cid) Turbo 4 cyl
Engine Code – VIN E

ECM TROUBLE CODES

Code	Explanation
88	Start of test
11	Engine not cranked since battery was disconnected
12	Memory standby power lost
13	Manifold Absolute Pressure (MAP) sensor pneumatic circuit – power loss/limited lamp is ON
14	Manifold Absolute Pressure (MAP) sensor electrical system – power loss/limited lamp is ON
15	Vehicle Speed Sensor (VSS) circuit
16	Lose of battery voltage sense – power loss/limited lamp is ON
17	Engine is running too cool
21	Oxygen (O_2) sensor circuit
22	Coolant Temperature Sensor (CTS) circuit – power loss/limited lamp is ON
23	Throttle body temperature sensor circuit
24	Throttle Position Sensor (TPS) circuit – power loss/limited lamp is ON
25	Automatic Idle Speed (AIS) control circuit
26	Number 1 injector circuit
27	Number 2 injector circuit
31	Exhaust Gas Recirculation (EGR)/purge solenoid circuit
33	A/C wide cut out relay circuit
35	Fan control relay circuit
36	Wastegate solenoid circuit – power loss/limited lamp is ON
37	Barometric read solenoid circuit
41	Charging system excess or no field circuit
42	Automatic Shut Down (ASD) relay driver circuit
43	Spark interface (internal) circuits
44	Battery temperature is out of range
45	Overboost shut-off circuit – power loss/limited lamp is ON
46	Battery voltage too high – power loss/limited lamp is ON
47	Battery voltage too low
51	Closed loop fuel system problem – oxygen sensor signal stuck at the lean position
52	Oxygen sensor signal stuck at the rich position
53	Logic module problem or failure
54	Distributor sync pick-up circuit
55	End of message

Year — 1988
Model — Sundance
Engine — 2.2L (135 cid) Turbo 4 cyl
Engine Code — VIN E

ECM TROUBLE CODES

Code	Explanation
88	Start of test
11	Engine not cranked since battery was disconnected
12	Memory standby power lost
13	Manifold Absolute Pressure (MAP) sensor pneumatic circuit — power loss/limited lamp is ON
14	Manifold Absolute Pressure (MAP) sensor electrical system — power loss/limited lamp is ON
15	Vehicle Speed Sensor (VSS) circuit
16	Lose of battery voltage sense — power loss/limited lamp is ON
17	Engine is running too cool
21	Oxygen (O_2) sensor circuit
22	Coolant Temperature Sensor (CTS) circuit — power loss/limited lamp is ON
23	Throttle body temperature sensor circuit
24	Throttle Position Sensor (TPS) circuit — power loss/limited lamp is ON
25	Automatic Idle Speed (AIS) control circuit
26	Number 1 injector circuit
27	Number 2 injector circuit
31	Exhaust Gas Recirculation (EGR)/purge solenoid circuit
33	A/C wide cut out relay circuit
35	Fan control relay circuit
36	Wastegate solenoid circuit — power loss/limited lamp is ON
37	Barometric read solenoid circuit
41	Charging system excess or no field circuit
42	Automatic Shut Down (ASD) relay driver circuit
43	Spark interface (internal) circuits
44	Battery temperature is out of range
45	Overboost shut-off circuit — power loss/limited lamp is ON
46	Battery voltage too high — power loss/limited lamp is ON
47	Battery voltage too low
51	Closed loop fuel system problem — oxygen sensor signal stuck at the lean position
52	Oxygen sensor signal stuck at the rich position
53	Logic module problem or failure
54	Distributor sync pick-up circuit
55	End of message

Year – 1989
Model – LeBaron
Engine – 2.2L (135 cid) Turbo II 4 cyl
Engine Code – VIN A

ECM TROUBLE CODES

Code	Explanation
11	IGN REFERENCE SIGNAL – No distributor reference signal detected during engine cranking
12	No. or key-on's since last fault or since faults were erased – Direct battery input to controller disconnected within the last 50–100 ignition key-on's
13	a) MAP PNEUMATIC SIGNAL – No variation in Manifold Absolute Pressure (MAP) sensor signal is detected – check engine lamp ON – California only b) MAP PNEUMATIC CHANGE – No difference is recognized between the engine Manifold Absolute Pressure (MAP) reading and the stored barometric pressure reading – check engine lamp ON – California only
14	a) MAP VOLTAGE TOO LOW – Manifold Absolute Pressure (MAP) sensor input below minimum acceptable voltage – check engine lamp ON – California only b) MAP VOLTAGE TOO HIGH – Manifold Absolute Pressure (MAP) sensor input above maximum acceptable voltage – check engine lamp ON – California only
15	VEHICLE SPEED SIGNAL – No distance sensor signal detected during road load conditions – check engine lamp ON – California only
16	BATTERY INPUT SENSE – Battery voltage sense input not detected during engine running – check engine lamp ON – California only
17	LOW ENGINE TEMP – Engine coolant temperature remains below normal operating temperatures during vehicle travel – thermostat
21	OXYGEN SENSOR SIGNAL – Neither rich or lean condition is detected from the oxygen sensor input – check engine lamp ON – California only
22	a) COOLANT VOLTAGE LOW – Coolant Temperature Sensor (CTS) input below the minimum acceptable voltage – check engine lamp ON – California only b) COOLANT VOLTAGE HIGH – Coolant Temperature Sensor (CTS) input above the maximum acceptable voltage – check engine lamp ON – California only
24	a) TPS VOLTAGE LOW – Throttle Position Sensor (TPS) input below the minimum acceptable voltage – check engine lamp ON – California only b) TPS VOLTAGE HIGH – Throttle Position Sensor (TPS) input above the maximum acceptable voltage – check engine lamp ON – California only
25	AIS MOTOR CIRCUITS – A shorted condition detected in 1 or more of the AIS control circuits – check engine lamp ON – California only
26	a) INJ 1 PEAK CURRENT – High resistance condition detected in the INJ 1 injector bank circuit b) INJ 2 PEAK CURRENT – High resistance condition detected in the INJ 2 injector bank circuit
27	a) INJ 1 CONTROL CKT – INJ 1 injector bank driver stage does not respond properly to the control signal b) INJ 2 CONTROL CKT – INJ 2 injector bank driver stage does not respond properly to the control signal

ECM TROUBLE CODES (cont'd)

Code	Explanation
31	PURGE SOLENOID CKT — An open or shorted condition detected in the purge solenoid circuit
32	a) EGR SOLENOID CIRCUIT — An open or shorted condition detected in the Exhaust Gas Recirculation (EGR) solenoid circuit — check engine lamp ON — California only b) EGR SYSTEM CIRCUIT — Required change in fuel/air ratio not detected during diagnostic test — check engine lamp ON — California only
33	A/C CLUTCH RELAY CKT — An open or shorted condition detected in the air conditioning clutch relay circuit
34	S/C SERVO SOLENOIDS — An open or shorted condition detected in the speed control vacuum or vent solenoid circuits
35	RADIATOR FAN RELAY — An open or shorted condition detected in the radiator fan relay circuit
36	WASTEGATE SOLENOID — An open or shorted condition detected in the turbocharger wastegate control solenoid circuit — check engine lamp ON — California only
41	CHARGING SYSTEM CKT — Output driver stage for alternator field does not respond properly to the voltage regulator control signal
42	a) ASD RELAY CIRCUIT — An open or shorted condition detected in the auto shutdown relay circuit b) Z1 VOLTAGE SENSE — No Z1 voltage sensed when the auto shutdown relay is energized
43	IGNITION CONTROL CKT — Output driver stage for ignition coil does not respond properly to the dwell control signal
44	FJ2 VOLTAGE SENSE — No FJ2 voltage present at the logic board during controller operation
45	BOOST LIMIT EXCEEDED — Manifold Absolute Pressure (MAP) reading above overboost limit detected during controller operation
46	BATTERY VOLTAGE HIGH — Battery voltage sense input above target charging voltage during engine operation — check engine lamp ON — California only
47	BATTERY VOLTAGE LOW — Battery voltage sense input below target charging voltage during engine operation
51	LEAN F/A CONDITION — Oxygen sensor signal input indcates lean fuel/air ratio condition during engine operation — check engine lamp ON — California only
52	RICK F/A CONDITION — Oxygen sensor signal input indicates righ fuel/air ratio condition during engine operation — check engine lamp ON — California only
53	INTERNAL SELF-TEST — Internal engine controller fault condition detected
54	SYNC PICK-UP SIGNAL — No fuel sync signal detected during engine rotation.
55	Completion of fault code display on the "Check Engine" lamp
61	BARO READ SOLENOID — An open or shorted condition detected in the baro read solenoid circuit — check engine lamp ON
62	EMR MILAGE ACCUM — Unsuccessful attempt to update EMR mileage in the controller EEPROM
63	EEPROM WRITE DENIED — Unsuccessful attempt to write to an EEPROM location by the controller or unrecognized fault ID received by the DRB-II
	FAULT CODE ERROR — Unrecognized fault ID received by the DRB-II

Year – 1989
Model – LeBaron
Engine – 2.2L (135 cid) EFI 4 cyl
Engine Code – VIN D

ECM TROUBLE CODES

Code	Explanation
11	IGN REFERENCE SIGNAL – No distributor reference signal detected during engine cranking
12	No. of key-on's since last fault or since faults were erased – Direct battery input to controller disconnected within the last 50–100 ignition key-on's
13	a) MAP PNEUMATIC SIGNAL – No variation in Manifold Absolute Pressure (MAP) sensor signal is detected – check engine lamp ON – California only b) MAP PNEUMATIC CHANGE – No difference is recognized between the engine Manifold Absolute Pressure (MAP) reading and the stored barometric pressure reading – check engine lamp ON – California only
14	a) MAP VOLTAGE TOO LOW – Manifold Absolute Pressure (MAP) sensor input below minimum acceptable voltage – check engine lamp ON – California only b) MAP VOLTAGE TOO HIGH – Manifold Absolute Pressure (MAP) sensor input above maximum acceptable voltage – check engine lamp ON – California only
15	VEHICLE SPEED SIGNAL – No distance sensor signal detected during road load conditions – check engine lamp ON – California only
16	BATTERY INPUT SENSE – Battery voltage sense input not detected during engine running – check engine lamp ON – California only
17	LOW ENGINE TEMP – Engine coolant temperature remains below normal operating temperatures during vehicle travel – thermostat
21	OXYGEN SENSOR SIGNAL – Neither rich or lean condition is detected from the oxygen sensor input – check engine lamp ON – California only
22	a) COOLANT VOLTAGE LOW – Coolant Temperature Sensor (CTS) input below the minimum acceptable voltage – check engine lamp ON – California only b) COOLANT VOLTAGE HIGH – Coolant Temperature Sensor (CTS) input above the maximum acceptable voltage – check engine lamp ON – California only
23	a) T/B TEMP VOLTAGE LOW – Throttle body temperature sensor input below the minimum acceptable voltage b) T/B TEMP VOLTAGE HI – Throttle body temperature sensor input above the maximum acceptable voltage
24	a) TPS VOLTAGE LOW – Throttle Position Sensor (TPS) input below the minimum acceptable voltage – check engine lamp ON – California only b) TPS VOLTAGE HIGH – Throttle Position Sensor (TPS) input above the maximum acceptable voltage – check engine lamp ON – California only
25	AIS MOTOR CIRCUITS – A shorted condition detected in 1 or more of the AIS control circuits – check engine lamp ON – California only
26	INJ 1 PEAK CURRENT – High resistance condition detected in the injector output circuit
27	INJ 1 CONTROL CKT – Injector output driver stage does not respond properly to the control signal
31	PURGE SOLENOID CKT – An open or shorted condition detected in the purge solenoid circuit – check engine lamp ON – California only
32	a) EGR SOLENOID CIRCUIT – An open or shorted condition detected in the Exhaust Gas Recirculation (EGR) solenoid circuit – check engine lamp ON – California only b) EGR SYSTEM FAILURE – Required change in fuel/air ratio not detected during diagnostic test – check engine lamp ON – California only
33	A/C CLUTCH RELAY CKT – An open or shorted condition detected in the air conditioning clutch relay circuit
34	S/C SERVO SOLENOIDS – An open or shorted condition detected in the speed control vacuum or vent solenoid circuits

ECM TROUBLE CODES (cont'd)

Code	Explanation
35	RADIATOR FAN RELAY—An open or shorted condition detected in the radiator fan relay circuit
37	PTU SOLENOID CIRCUIT—An open or shorted condition detected in the torque converter part throttle unlock solenoid circuit
41	CHARGING SYSTEM CKT—Output driver stage for alternator field does not respond properly to the voltage regulator control signal
42	ASD RELAY CIRCUIT—An open or shorted condition detected in the auto shutdown relay circuit
43	IGNITION CONTROL CKT—Output driver stage for ignition coil does not respond properly to the dwell control signal
44	FJ2 VOLTAGE SENSE—No FJ2 voltage present at the logic board during controller operation
46	BATTERY VOLTAGE HIGH—Battery voltage sense input above target charging voltage during engine operation—check engine lamp ON—California only
47	BATTERY VOLTAGE LOW—Battery voltage sense input below target charging voltage during engine operation
51	LEAN F/A CONDITION—Oxygen sensor signal input indcates lean fuel/air ratio condition during engine operation—check engine lamp ON—California only
52	a) RICH F/A CONDITION—Oxygen sensor signal input indicates righ fuel/air ratio condition during engine operation—check engine lamp ON—California only b) EXCESSIVE LEANING—Adaptive fuel value leaned excessively due to a sustained rich condition—check engine lamp ON—California only
53	INTERNAL SELF-TEST—Internal engine controller fault condition detected
55	Completion of fault code display on the "Check Engine" lamp
62	EMR MILEAGE ACCUM—Unsuccessful attempt to update EMR mileage in the controller EEPROM
63	EEPROM WRITE DENIED—Unsuccessful attempt to write to an EEPROM location by the controller
	FAULT CODE ERROR—Unrecognized fault ID received by the DRB-II

Year—1989
Model—LeBaron
Engine—2.5L (153 cid) Turbo I 4 cyl
Engine Code—VIN J

ECM TROUBLE CODES

Code	Explanation
11	IGN REFERENCE SIGNAL—No distributor reference signal detected during engine cranking
12	No. or key-on's since last fault or since faults were erased—Direct battery input to controller disconnected within the last 50–100 ignition key-on's
13	a) MAP PNEUMATIC SIGNAL—No variation in Manifold Absolute Pressure (MAP) sensor signal is detected—check engine lamp ON—California only b) MAP PNEUMATIC CHANGE—No differrence is recognized between the engine Manifold Absolute Pressure (MAP) reading and the stored barometric pressure reading—check engine lamp ON—California only
14	a) MAP VOLTAGE TOO LOW—Manifold Absolute Pressure (MAP) sensor input below minimum acceptable voltage—check engine lamp ON—California only b) MAP VOLTAGE TOO HIGH—Manifold Absolute Pressure (MAP) sensor input above maximum acceptable voltage—check engine lamp ON—California only
15	VEHICLE SPEED SIGNAL—No distance sensor signal detected during road load conditions—check engine lamp ON—California only
16	BATTERY INPUT SENSE—Battery voltage sense input not detected during engine running—check engine lamp ON—California only

ECM TROUBLE CODES (cont'd)

Code	Explanation
17	LOW ENGINE TEMP—Engine coolant temperature remains below normal operating temperatures during vehicle travel—thermostat
21	OXYGEN SENSOR SIGNAL—Neither rich or lean condition is detected from the oxygen sensor input—check engine lamp ON—California only
22	a) COOLANT VOLTAGE LOW—Coolant Temperature Sensor (CTS) input below the minimum acceptable voltage—check engine lamp ON—California only b) COOLANT VOLTAGE HIGH—Coolant Temperature Sensor (CTS) input above the maximum acceptable voltage—check engine lamp ON—California only
24	a) TPS VOLTAGE LOW—Throttle Position Sensor (TPS) input below the minimum acceptable voltage—check engine lamp ON—California only b) TPS VOLTAGE HIGH—Throttle Position Sensor (TPS) input above the maximum acceptable voltage—check engine lamp ON—California only
25	AIS MOTOR CIRCUITS—A shorted condition detected in 1 or more of the AIS control circuits—check engine lamp ON—California only
26	a) INJ 1 PEAK CURRENT—High resistance condition detected in the INJ 1 injector bank circuit b) INJ 2 PEAK CURRENT—High resistance condition detected in the INJ 2 injector bank circuit
27	a) INJ 1 CONTROL CKT—INJ 1 injector bank driver stage does not respond properly to the control signal b) INJ 2 CONTROL CKT—INJ 2 injector bank driver stage does not respond properly to the control signal
31	PURGE SOLENOID CKT—An open or shorted condition detected in the purge solenoid circuit
32	a) EGR SOLENOID CIRCUIT—An open or shorted condition detected in the Exhaust Gas Recirculation (EGR) solenoid circuit—check engine lamp ON—California only b) EGR SYSTEM CIRCUIT—Required change in fuel/air ratio not detected during diagnostic test—check engine lamp ON—California only
33	A/C CLUTCH RELAY CKT—An open or shorted condition detected in the air conditioning clutch relay circuit
34	S/C SERVO SOLENOIDS—An open or shorted condition detected in the speed control vacuum or vent solenoid circuits
35	RADIATOR FAN RELAY—An open or shorted condition detected in the radiator fan relay circuit
36	WASTEGATE SOLENOID—An open or shorted condition detected in the turbocharger wastegate control solenoid circuit—check engine lamp ON—California only
41	CHARGING SYSTEM CKT—Output driver stage for alternator field does not respond properly to the voltage regulator control signal
42	a) ASD RELAY CIRCUIT—An open or shorted condition detected in the auto shutdown relay circuit b) Z1 VOLTAGE SENSE—No Z1 voltage sensed when the auto shutdown relay is energized
43	IGNITION CONTROL CKT—Output driver stage for ignition coil does not respond properly to the dwell control signal
44	FJ2 VOLTAGE SENSE—No FJ2 voltage present at the logic board during controller operation
45	BOOST LIMIT EXCEEDED—Manifold Absolute Pressure (MAP) reading above overboost limit detected during controller operation
46	BATTERY VOLTAGE HIGH—Battery voltage sense input above target charging voltage during engine operation—check engine lamp ON—California only
47	BATTERY VOLTAGE LOW—Battery voltage sense input below target charging voltage during engine operation
51	LEAN F/A CONDITION—Oxygen sensor signal input indcates lean fuel/air ratio condition during engine operation—check engine lamp ON—California only
52	RICK F/A CONDITION—Oxygen sensor signal input indicates righ fuel/air ratio condition during engine operation—check engine lamp ON—California only
53	INTERNAL SELF-TEST—Internal engine controller fault condition detected
54	SYNC PICK-UP SIGNAL—No fuel sync signal detected during engine rotation.

ECM TROUBLE CODES (cont'd)

Code	Explanation
55	Completion of fault code display on the "Check Engine" lamp
61	BARO READ SOLENOID—An open or shorted condition detected in the baro read solenoid circuit—check engine lamp ON
62	EMR MILAGE ACCUM—Unsuccessful attempt to update EMR mileage in the controller EEPROM
63	EEPROM WRITE DENIED—Unsuccessful attempt to write to an EEPROM location by the controller or unrecognized fault ID received by the DRB-II
	FAULT CODE ERROR—Unrecognized fault ID received by the DRB-II

Year—1989
Model—LeBaron
Engine—2.5L (153 cid) EFI 4 cyl
Engine Code—VIN K

ECM TROUBLE CODES

Code	Explanation
11	IGN REFERENCE SIGNAL—No distributor reference signal detected during engine cranking
12	No. of key-on's since last fault or since faults were erased—Direct battery input to controller disconnected within the last 50–100 ignition key-on's
13	a) MAP PNEUMATIC SIGNAL—No variation in Manifold Absolute Pressure (MAP) sensor signal is detected—check engine lamp ON—California only b) MAP PNEUMATIC CHANGE—No differrence is recognized between the engine Manifold Absolute Pressure (MAP) reading and the stored barometric pressure reading—check engine lamp ON—California only
14	a) MAP VOLTAGE TOO LOW—Manifold Absolute Pressure (MAP) sensor input below minimum acceptable voltage—check engine lamp ON—California only b) MAP VOLTAGE TOO HIGH—Manifold Absolute Pressure (MAP) sensor input above maximum acceptable voltage—check engine lamp ON—California only
15	VEHICLE SPEED SIGNAL—No distance sensor signal detected during road load conditions—check engine lamp ON—California only
16	BATTERY INPUT SENSE—Battery voltage sense input not detected during engine running—check engine lamp ON—California only
17	LOW ENGINE TEMP—Engine coolant temperature remains below normal operating temperatures during vehicle travel—thermostat
21	OXYGEN SENSOR SIGNAL—Neither rich or lean condition is detected from the oxygen sensor input—check engine lamp ON—California only
22	a) COOLANT VOLTAGE LOW—Coolant Temperature Sensor (CTS) input below the minimum acceptable voltage—check engine lamp ON—California only b) COOLANT VOLTAGE HIGH—Coolant Temperature Sensor (CTS) input above the maximum acceptable voltage—check engine lamp ON—California only
23	a) T/B TEMP VOLTAGE LOW—Throttle body temperature sensor input below the minimum acceptable voltage b) T/B TEMP VOLTAGE HI—Throttle body temperature sensor input above the maximum acceptable voltage
24	a) TPS VOLTAGE LOW—Throttle Position Sensor (TPS) input below the minimum acceptable voltage—check engine lamp ON—California only b) TPS VOLTAGE HIGH—Throttle Position Sensor (TPS) input above the maximum acceptable voltage—check engine lamp ON—California only
25	AIS MOTOR CIRCUITS—A shorted condition detected in 1 or more of the AIS control circuits—check engine lamp ON—California only

ECM TROUBLE CODES (cont'd)

Code	Explanation
26	INJ 1 PEAK CURRENT — High resistance condition detected in the injector output circuit
27	INJ 1 CONTROL CKT — Injector output driver stage does not respond properly to the control signal
31	PURGE SOLENOID CKT — An open or shorted condition detected in the purge solenoid circuit — check engine lamp ON — California only
32	a) EGR SOLENOID CIRCUIT — An open or shorted condition detected in the Exhaust Gas Recirculation (EGR) solenoid circuit — check engine lamp ON — California only b) EGR SYSTEM FAILURE — Required change in fuel/air ratio not detected during diagnostic test — check engine lamp ON — California only
33	A/C CLUTCH RELAY CKT — An open or shorted condition detected in the air conditioning clutch relay circuit
34	S/C SERVO SOLENOIDS — An open or shorted condition detected in the speed control vacuum or vent solenoid circuits
35	RADIATOR FAN RELAY — An open or shorted condition detected in the radiator fan relay circuit
37	PTU SOLENOID CIRCUIT — An open or shorted condition detected in the torque converter part throttle unlock solenoid circuit
41	CHARGING SYSTEM CKT — Output driver stage for alternator field does not respond properly to the voltage regulator control signal
42	ASD RELAY CIRCUIT — An open or shorted condition detected in the auto shutdown relay circuit
43	IGNITION CONTROL CKT — Output driver stage for ignition coil does not respond properly to the dwell control signal
44	FJ2 VOLTAGE SENSE — No FJ2 voltage present at the logic board during controller operation
46	BATTERY VOLTAGE HIGH — Battery voltage sense input above target charging voltage during engine operation — check engine lamp ON — California only
47	BATTERY VOLTAGE LOW — Battery voltage sense input below target charging voltage during engine operation
51	LEAN F/A CONDITION — Oxygen sensor signal input indcates lean fuel/air ratio condition during engine operation — check engine lamp ON — California only
52	a) RICH F/A CONDITION — Oxygen sensor signal input indicates righ fuel/air ratio condition during engine operation — check engine lamp ON — California only b) EXCESSIVE LEANING — Adaptive fuel value leaned excessively due to a sustained rich condition — check engine lamp ON — California only
53	INTERNAL SELF-TEST — Internal engine controller fault condition detected
55	Completion of fault code display on the "Check Engine" lamp
62	EMR MILEAGE ACCUM — Unsuccessful attempt to update EMR mileage in the controller EEPROM
63	EEPROM WRITE DENIED — Unsuccessful attempt to write to an EEPROM location by the controller
	FAULT CODE ERROR — Unrecognized fault ID received by the DRB-II

Year — 1989
Model — New Yorker
Engine — 3.0L (181 cid) MPFI V6
Engine Code — VIN 3

ECM TROUBLE CODES

Code	Explanation
11	IGN REFERENCE SIGNAL — No distributor reference signal detected during engine cranking
12	No. or key-on's since last fault or since faults were erased — Direct battery input to controller disconnected within the last 50–100 ignition key-on's

ECM TROUBLE CODES (cont'd)

Code	Explanation
13	a) MAP PNEUMATIC SIGNAL—No variation in Manifold Absolute Pressure (MAP) sensor signal is detected—check engine lamp ON—California only b) MAP PNEUMATIC CHANGE—No differrence is recognized between the engine Manifold Absolute Pressure (MAP) reading and the stored barometric pressure reading—check engine lamp ON—California only
14	a) MAP VOLTAGE TOO LOW—Manifold Absolute Pressure (MAP) sensor input below minimum acceptable voltage—check engine lamp ON—California only b) MAP VOLTAGE TOO HIGH—Manifold Absolute Pressure (MAP) above maximum acceptable voltage—check engine lamp ON—California only
15	VEHICLE SPEED SIGNAL—No distance sensor signal detected during road load conditions—check engine lamp ON—California only
16	BATTERY INPUT SENSE—Battery voltage sense input not detected during engine running—check engine lamp ON—California only
17	LOW ENGINE TEMP—Engine coolant temperature remains below normal operating temperatures during vehicle travel—thermostat
21	OXYGEN SENSOR SIGNAL—Neither rich or lean condition is detected from the oxygen sensor input—check engine lamp ON—California only
22	a) COOLANT VOLTAGE LOW—Coolant Temperature Sensor (CTS) input below the minimum acceptable voltage—check engine lamp ON—California only b) COOLANT VOLTAGE HIGH—Coolant Temperature Sensor (CTS) input above the maximum acceptable voltage—check engine lamp ON—California only
24	a) TPS VOLTAGE LOW—Throttle Position Sensor (TPS) input below the minimum acceptable voltage b) TPS VOLTAGE HIGH—Throttle Position Sensor (TPS) input above the maximum acceptable voltage
25	AIS MOTOR CIRCUITS—A shorted condition detected in 1 or more of the AIS control circuits
26	a) INJ 1 PEAK CURRENT—High resistance condition detected in the INJ 1 injector bank circuit—check engine lamp ON—California only b) INJ 2 PEAK CURRENT—High resistance condition detected in the INJ 2 injector bank circuit—check engine lamp ON—California only c) INJ 3 PEAK CURRENT—High resistance condition detected in the INJ 3 injector bank circuit—check engine lamp ON—California only
27	a) INJ 1 CONTROL CKT—INJ 1 injector bank driver stage does not respond properly to the control signal—check engine lamp ON—California only b) INJ 2 CONTROL CKT—INJ 2 injector bank driver stage does not respond properly to the control signal—check engine lamp ON—California only c) INJ 3 CONTROL CKT—INJ 3 injector bank driver stage does not respond properly to the control signal—check engine lamp ON—California only
31	PURGE SOLENOID CKT—An open or shorted condition detected in the purge solenoid circuit—check engine lamp ON—California only
32	a) EGR SOLENOID CIRCUIT—An open or shorted condition detected in the Exhaust Gas Recirculation (EGR) solenoid circuit—check engine lamp ON—California only b) EGR SYSTEM FAILURE—Required change in fuel/air ratio not detected during diagnostic test—check engine lamp ON—California only
33	A/C CLUTCH RELAY CKT—An open or shorted condition detected in the air conditioning clutch relay circuit
34	S/C SERVO SOLENOIDS—An open or shorted condition detected in the speed control vacuum or vent solenoid circuits
35	RADIATOR FAN RELAY—An open or shorted condition detected in the radiator fan relay circuit
41	CHARGING SYSTEM CKT—Output driver stage for alternator field does not respond properly to the voltage regulator control signal
42	a) ASD RELAY CIRCUIT—An open or shorted condition detected in the auto shutdown relay circuit b) Z1 VOLTAGE SENSE—No Z1 voltage sensed when the auto shutdown relay is energized

ECM TROUBLE CODES (cont'd)

Code	Explanation
43	IGNITION CONTROL CKT — Output driver stage for ignition coil does not respond properly to the dwell control signal
46	BATTERY VOLTAGE HIGH — Battery voltage sense input above target charging voltage during engine operation — check engine lamp ON — California only
47	BATTERY VOLTAGE LOW — Battery voltage sense input below target charging voltage during engine operation
51	LEAN F/A CONDITION — Oxygen sensor signal input indcates lean fuel/air ratio condition during engine operation
52	RICH F/A CONDITION — Oxygen sensor signal input indicates righ fuel/air ratio condition during engine operation
53	INTERNAL SELF-TEST — Internal engine controller fault condition detected
54	SYNC PICK-UP SIGNAL — No high data rate signal detected during engine rotation — check engine lamp ON — California only
55	Completion of fault code display on the "Check Engine" lamp
62	EMR MILEAGE ACCUM — Unsuccessful attempt to update EMR mileage in the controller EEPROM
63	EEPROM WRITE DENIED — Unsuccessful attempt to write to an EEPROM location by the controller or unrecognized fault ID received by the DRB-II
	FAULT CODE ERROR — Unrecognized fault ID received by the DRB-II

Year — 1989
Model — New Yorker Landau
Engine — 3.0L (181 cid) MPFI V6
Engine Code — VIN 3

ECM TROUBLE CODES

Code	Explanation
11	IGN REFERENCE SIGNAL — No distributor reference signal detected during engine cranking
12	No. or key-on's since last fault or since faults were erased — Direct battery input to controller disconnected within the last 50–100 ignition key-on's
13	a) MAP PNEUMATIC SIGNAL — No variation in Manifold Absolute Pressure (MAP) sensor signal is detected — check engine lamp ON — California only b) MAP PNEUMATIC CHANGE — No differrence is recognized between the engine Manifold Absolute Pressure (MAP) reading and the stored barometric pressure reading — check engine lamp ON — California only
14	a) MAP VOLTAGE TOO LOW — Manifold Absolute Pressure (MAP) sensor input below minimum acceptable voltage — check engine lamp ON — California only b) MAP VOLTAGE TOO HIGH — Manifold Absolute Pressure (MAP) above maximum acceptable voltage — check engine lamp ON — California only
15	VEHICLE SPEED SIGNAL — No distance sensor signal detected during road load conditions — check engine lamp ON — California only
16	BATTERY INPUT SENSE — Battery voltage sense input not detected during engine running — check engine lamp ON — California only
17	LOW ENGINE TEMP — Engine coolant temperature remains below normal operating temperatures during vehicle travel — thermostat
21	OXYGEN SENSOR SIGNAL — Neither rich or lean condition is detected from the oxygen sensor input — check engine lamp ON — California only

ECM TROUBLE CODES (cont'd)

Code	Explanation
22	a) COOLANT VOLTAGE LOW—Coolant Temperature Sensor (CTS) input below the minimum acceptable voltage—check engine lamp ON—California only b) COOLANT VOLTAGE HIGH—Coolant Temperature Sensor (CTS) input above the maximum acceptable voltage—check engine lamp ON—California only
24	a) TPS VOLTAGE LOW—Throttle Position Sensor (TPS) input below the minimum acceptable voltage b) TPS VOLTAGE HIGH—Throttle Position Sensor (TPS) input above the maximum acceptable voltage
25	AIS MOTOR CIRCUITS—A shorted condition detected in 1 or more of the AIS control circuits
26	a) INJ 1 PEAK CURRENT—High resistance condition detected in the INJ 1 injector bank circuit—check engine lamp ON—California only b) INJ 2 PEAK CURRENT—High resistance condition detected in the INJ 2 injector bank circuit—check engine lamp ON—California only c) INJ 3 PEAK CURRENT—High resistance condition detected in the INJ 3 injector bank circuit—check engine lamp ON—California only
27	a) INJ 1 CONTROL CKT—INJ 1 injector bank driver stage does not respond properly to the control signal—check engine lamp ON—California only b) INJ 2 CONTROL CKT—INJ 2 injector bank driver stage does not respond properly to the control signal—check engine lamp ON—California only c) INJ 3 CONTROL CKT—INJ 3 injector bank driver stage does not respond properly to the control signal—check engine lamp ON—California only
31	PURGE SOLENOID CKT—An open or shorted condition detected in the purge solenoid circuit—check engine lamp ON—California only
32	a) EGR SOLENOID CIRCUIT—An open or shorted condition detected in the Exhaust Gas Recirculation (EGR) solenoid circuit—check engine lamp ON—California only b) EGR SYSTEM FAILURE—Required change in fuel/air ratio not detected during diagnostic test—check engine lamp ON—California only
33	A/C CLUTCH RELAY CKT—An open or shorted condition detected in the air conditioning clutch relay circuit
34	S/C SERVO SOLENOIDS—An open or shorted condition detected in the speed control vacuum or vent solenoid circuits
35	RADIATOR FAN RELAY—An open or shorted condition detected in the radiator fan relay circuit
41	CHARGING SYSTEM CKT—Output driver stage for alternator field does not respond properly to the voltage regulator control signal
42	a) ASD RELAY CIRCUIT—An open or shorted condition detected in the auto shutdown relay circuit b) Z1 VOLTAGE SENSE—No Z1 voltage sensed when the auto shutdown relay is energized
43	IGNITION CONTROL CKT—Output driver stage for ignition coil does not respond properly to the dwell control signal
46	BATTERY VOLTAGE HIGH—Battery voltage sense input above target charging voltage during engine operation—check engine lamp ON—California only
47	BATTERY VOLTAGE LOW—Battery voltage sense input below target charging voltage during engine operation
51	LEAN F/A CONDITION—Oxygen sensor signal input indcates lean fuel/air ratio condition during engine operation
52	RICH F/A CONDITION—Oxygen sensor signal input indicates rich fuel/air ratio condition during engine operation
53	INTERNAL SELF-TEST—Internal engine controller fault condition detected
54	SYNC PICK-UP SIGNAL—No high data rate signal detected during engine rotation—check engine lamp ON—California only
55	Completion of fault code display on the "Check Engine" lamp
62	EMR MILEAGE ACCUM—Unsuccessful attempt to update EMR mileage in the controller EEPROM
63	EEPROM WRITE DENIED—Unsuccessful attempt to write to an EEPROM location by the controller or unrecognized fault ID received by the DRB-II
	FAULT CODE ERROR—Unrecognized fault ID received by the DRB-II

Year — 1989
Model — Omni
Engine — 2.2L (135 cid) EFI 4 cyl
Engine Code — VIN D

ECM TROUBLE CODES

Code	Explanation
11	IGN REFERENCE SIGNAL — No distributor reference signal detected during engine cranking
12	No. of key-on's since last fault or since faults were erased — Direct battery input to controller disconnected within the last 50–100 ignition key-on's
13	a) MAP PNEUMATIC SIGNAL — No variation in Manifold Absolute Pressure (MAP) sensor signal is detected — check engine lamp ON — California only b) MAP PNEUMATIC CHANGE — No differrence is recognized between the engine Manifold Absolute Pressure (MAP) reading and the stored barometric pressure reading — check engine lamp ON — California only
14	a) MAP VOLTAGE TOO LOW — Manifold Absolute Pressure (MAP) sensor input below minimum acceptable voltage — check engine lamp ON — California only b) MAP VOLTAGE TOO HIGH — Manifold Absolute Pressure (MAP) sensor input above maximum acceptable voltage — check engine lamp ON — California only
15	VEHICLE SPEED SIGNAL — No distance sensor signal detected during road load conditions — check engine lamp ON — California only
16	BATTERY INPUT SENSE — Battery voltage sense input not detected during engine running — check engine lamp ON — California only
17	LOW ENGINE TEMP — Engine coolant temperature remains below normal operating temperatures during vehicle travel — thermostat
21	OXYGEN SENSOR SIGNAL — Neither rich or lean condition is detected from the oxygen sensor input — check engine lamp ON — California only
22	a) COOLANT VOLTAGE LOW — Coolant Temperature Sensor (CTS) input below the minimum acceptable voltage — check engine lamp ON — California only b) COOLANT VOLTAGE HIGH — Coolant Temperature Sensor (CTS) input above the maximum acceptable voltage — check engine lamp ON — California only
23	a) T/B TEMP VOLTAGE LOW — Throttle body temperature sensor input below the minimum acceptable voltage b) T/B TEMP VOLTAGE HI — Throttle body temperature sensor input above the maximum acceptable voltage
24	a) TPS VOLTAGE LOW — Throttle Position Sensor (TPS) input below the minimum acceptable voltage — check engine lamp ON — California only b) TPS VOLTAGE HIGH — Throttle Position Sensor (TPS) input above the maximum acceptable voltage — check engine lamp ON — California only
25	AIS MOTOR CIRCUITS — A shorted condition detected in 1 or more of the AIS control circuits — check engine lamp ON — California only
26	INJ 1 PEAK CURRENT — High resistance condition detected in the injector output circuit
27	INJ 1 CONTROL CKT — Injector output driver stage does not respond properly to the control signal
31	PURGE SOLENOID CKT — An open or shorted condition detected in the purge solenoid circuit — check engine lamp ON — California only
32	a) EGR SOLENOID CIRCUIT — An open or shorted condition detected in the Exhaust Gas Recirculation (EGR) solenoid circuit — check engine lamp ON — California only b) EGR SYSTEM FAILURE — Required change in fuel/air ratio not detected during diagnostic test — check engine lamp ON — California only
33	A/C CLUTCH RELAY CKT — An open or shorted condition detected in the air conditioning clutch relay circuit
34	S/C SERVO SOLENOIDS — An open or shorted condition detected in the speed control vacuum or vent solenoid circuits

ECM TROUBLE CODES (cont'd)

Code	Explanation
35	RADIATOR FAN RELAY — An open or shorted condition detected in the radiator fan relay circuit
37	PTU SOLENOID CIRCUIT — An open or shorted condition detected in the torque converter part throttle unlock solenoid circuit
41	CHARGING SYSTEM CKT — Output driver stage for alternator field does not respond properly to the voltage regulator control signal
42	ASD RELAY CIRCUIT — An open or shorted condition detected in the auto shutdown relay circuit
43	IGNITION CONTROL CKT — Output driver stage for ignition coil does not respond properly to the dwell control signal
44	FJ2 VOLTAGE SENSE — No FJ2 voltage present at the logic board during controller operation
46	BATTERY VOLTAGE HIGH — Battery voltage sense input above target charging voltage during engine operation — check engine lamp ON — California only
47	BATTERY VOLTAGE LOW — Battery voltage sense input below target charging voltage during engine operation
51	LEAN F/A CONDITION — Oxygen sensor signal input indcates lean fuel/air ratio condition during engine operation — check engine lamp ON — California only
52	a) RICH F/A CONDITION — Oxygen sensor signal input indicates righ fuel/air ratio condition during engine operation — check engine lamp ON — California only b) EXCESSIVE LEANING — Adaptive fuel value leaned excessively due to a sustained rich condition — check engine lamp ON — California only
53	INTERNAL SELF-TEST — Internal engine controller fault condition detected
55	Completion of fault code display on the "Check Engine" lamp
62	EMR MILEAGE ACCUM — Unsuccessful attempt to update EMR mileage in the controller EEPROM
63	EEPROM WRITE DENIED — Unsuccessful attempt to write to an EEPROM location by the controller
	FAULT CODE ERROR — Unrecognized fault ID received by the DRB-II

Year — 1989
Model — Aries
Engine — 2.2L (135 cid) EFI 4 cyl
Engine Code — VIN D

ECM TROUBLE CODES

Code	Explanation
11	IGN REFERENCE SIGNAL — No distributor reference signal detected during engine cranking
12	No. of key-on's since last fault or since faults were erased — Direct battery input to controller disconnected within the last 50–100 ignition key-on's
13	a) MAP PNEUMATIC SIGNAL — No variation in Manifold Absolute Pressure (MAP) sensor signal is detected — check engine lamp ON — California only b) MAP PNEUMATIC CHANGE — No differrence is recognized between the engine Manifold Absolute Pressure (MAP) reading and the stored barometric pressure reading — check engine lamp ON — California only
14	a) MAP VOLTAGE TOO LOW — Manifold Absolute Pressure (MAP) sensor input below minimum acceptable voltage — check engine lamp ON — California only b) MAP VOLTAGE TOO HIGH — Manifold Absolute Pressure (MAP) sensor input above maximum acceptable voltage — check engine lamp ON — California only
15	VEHICLE SPEED SIGNAL — No distance sensor signal detected during road load conditions — check engine lamp ON — California only
16	BATTERY INPUT SENSE — Battery voltage sense input not detected during engine running — check engine lamp ON — California only

ECM TROUBLE CODES (cont'd)

Code	Explanation
17	LOW ENGINE TEMP—Engine coolant temperature remains below normal operating temperatures during vehicle travel—thermostat
21	OXYGEN SENSOR SIGNAL—Neither rich or lean condition is detected from the oxygen sensor input—check engine lamp ON—California only
22	a) COOLANT VOLTAGE LOW—Coolant Temperature Sensor (CTS) input below the minimum acceptable voltage—check engine lamp ON—California only
	b) COOLANT VOLTAGE HIGH—Coolant Temperature Sensor (CTS) input above the maximum acceptable voltage—check engine lamp ON—California only
23	a) T/B TEMP VOLTAGE LOW—Throttle body temperature sensor input below the minimum acceptable voltage
	b) T/B TEMP VOLTAGE HI—Throttle body temperature sensor input above the maximum acceptable voltage
24	a) TPS VOLTAGE LOW—Throttle Position Sensor (TPS) input below the minimum acceptable voltage—check engine lamp ON—California only
	b) TPS VOLTAGE HIGH—Throttle Position Sensor (TPS) input above the maximum acceptable voltage—check engine lamp ON—California only
25	AIS MOTOR CIRCUITS—A shorted condition detected in 1 or more of the AIS control circuits—check engine lamp ON—California only
26	INJ 1 PEAK CURRENT—High resistance condition detected in the injector output circuit
27	INJ 1 CONTROL CKT—Injector output driver stage does not respond properly to the control signal
31	PURGE SOLENOID CKT—An open or shorted condition detected in the purge solenoid circuit—check engine lamp ON—California only
32	a) EGR SOLENOID CIRCUIT—An open or shorted condition detected in the Exhaust Gas Recirculation (EGR) solenoid circuit—check engine lamp ON—California only
	b) EGR SYSTEM FAILURE—Required change in fuel/air ratio not detected during diagnostic test—check engine lamp ON—California only
33	A/C CLUTCH RELAY CKT—An open or shorted condition detected in the air conditioning clutch relay circuit
34	S/C SERVO SOLENOIDS—An open or shorted condition detected in the speed control vacuum or vent solenoid circuits
35	RADIATOR FAN RELAY—An open or shorted condition detected in the radiator fan relay circuit
37	PTU SOLENOID CIRCUIT—An open or shorted condition detected in the torque converter part throttle unlock solenoid circuit
41	CHARGING SYSTEM CKT—Output driver stage for alternator field does not respond properly to the voltage regulator control signal
42	ASD RELAY CIRCUIT—An open or shorted condition detected in the auto shutdown relay circuit
43	IGNITION CONTROL CKT—Output driver stage for ignition coil does not respond properly to the dwell control signal
44	FJ2 VOLTAGE SENSE—No FJ2 voltage present at the logic board during controller operation
46	BATTERY VOLTAGE HIGH—Battery voltage sense input above target charging voltage during engine operation—check engine lamp ON—California only
47	BATTERY VOLTAGE LOW—Battery voltage sense input below target charging voltage during engine operation
51	LEAN F/A CONDITION—Oxygen sensor signal input indcates lean fuel/air ratio condition during engine operation—check engine lamp ON—California only
52	a) RICH F/A CONDITION—Oxygen sensor signal input indicates righ fuel/air ratio condition during engine operation—check engine lamp ON—California only
	b) EXCESSIVE LEANING—Adaptive fuel value leaned excessively due to a sustained rich condition—check engine lamp ON—California only
53	INTERNAL SELF-TEST—Internal engine controller fault condition detected
55	Completion of fault code display on the ''Check Engine'' lamp
62	EMR MILEAGE ACCUM—Unsuccessful attempt to update EMR mileage in the controller EEPROM

ECM TROUBLE CODES (cont'd)

Code	Explanation
63	EEPROM WRITE DENIED — Unsuccessful attempt to write to an EEPROM location by the controller
	FAULT CODE ERROR — Unrecognized fault ID received by the DRB-II

Year — 1989
Model — Aries
Engine — 2.2L (135 cid) EFI 4 cyl
Engine Code — VIN D

ECM TROUBLE CODES

Code	Explanation
11	IGN REFERENCE SIGNAL — No distributor reference signal detected during engine cranking
12	No. of key-on's since last fault or since faults were erased — Direct battery input to controller disconnected within the last 50–100 ignition key-on's
13	a) MAP PNEUMATIC SIGNAL — No variation in Manifold Absolute Pressure (MAP) sensor signal is detected — check engine lamp ON — California only b) MAP PNEUMATIC CHANGE — No differrence is recognized between the engine Manifold Absolute Pressure (MAP) reading and the stored barometric pressure reading — check engine lamp ON — California only
14	a) MAP VOLTAGE TOO LOW — Manifold Absolute Pressure (MAP) sensor input below minimum acceptable voltage — check engine lamp ON — California only b) MAP VOLTAGE TOO HIGH — Manifold Absolute Pressure (MAP) sensor input above maximum acceptable voltage — check engine lamp ON — California only
15	VEHICLE SPEED SIGNAL — No distance sensor signal detected during road load conditions — check engine lamp ON — California only
16	BATTERY INPUT SENSE — Battery voltage sense input not detected during engine running — check engine lamp ON — California only
17	LOW ENGINE TEMP — Engine coolant temperature remains below normal operating temperatures during vehicle travel — thermostat
21	OXYGEN SENSOR SIGNAL — Neither rich or lean condition is detected from the oxygen sensor input — check engine lamp ON — California only
22	a) COOLANT VOLTAGE LOW — Coolant Temperature Sensor (CTS) input below the minimum acceptable voltage — check engine lamp ON — California only b) COOLANT VOLTAGE HIGH — Coolant Temperature Sensor (CTS) input above the maximum acceptable voltage — check engine lamp ON — California only
23	a) T/B TEMP VOLTAGE LOW — Throttle body temperature sensor input below the minimum acceptable voltage b) T/B TEMP VOLTAGE HI — Throttle body temperature sensor input above the maximum acceptable voltage
24	a) TPS VOLTAGE LOW — Throttle Position Sensor (TPS) input below the minimum acceptable voltage — check engine lamp ON — California only b) TPS VOLTAGE HIGH — Throttle Position Sensor (TPS) input above the maximum acceptable voltage — check engine lamp ON — California only
25	AIS MOTOR CIRCUITS — A shorted condition detected in 1 or more of the AIS control circuits — check engine lamp ON — California only
26	INJ 1 PEAK CURRENT — High resistance condition detected in the injector output circuit
27	INJ 1 CONTROL CKT — Injector output driver stage does not respond properly to the control signal
31	PURGE SOLENOID CKT — An open or shorted condition detected in the purge solenoid circuit — check engine lamp ON — California only

ECM TROUBLE CODES (cont'd)

Code	Explanation
32	a) EGR SOLENOID CIRCUIT—An open or shorted condition detected in the Exhaust Gas Recirculation (EGR) solenoid circuit—check engine lamp ON—California only b) EGR SYSTEM FAILURE—Required change in fuel/air ratio not detected during diagnostic test—check engine lamp ON—California only
33	A/C CLUTCH RELAY CKT—An open or shorted condition detected in the air conditioning clutch relay circuit
34	S/C SERVO SOLENOIDS—An open or shorted condition detected in the speed control vacuum or vent solenoid circuits
35	RADIATOR FAN RELAY—An open or shorted condition detected in the radiator fan relay circuit
37	PTU SOLENOID CIRCUIT—An open or shorted condition detected in the torque converter part throttle unlock solenoid circuit
41	CHARGING SYSTEM CKT—Output driver stage for alternator field does not respond properly to the voltage regulator control signal
42	ASD RELAY CIRCUIT—An open or shorted condition detected in the auto shutdown relay circuit
43	IGNITION CONTROL CKT—Output driver stage for ignition coil does not respond properly to the dwell control signal
44	FJ2 VOLTAGE SENSE—No FJ2 voltage present at the logic board during controller operation
46	BATTERY VOLTAGE HIGH—Battery voltage sense input above target charging voltage during engine operation—check engine lamp ON—California only
47	BATTERY VOLTAGE LOW—Battery voltage sense input below target charging voltage during engine operation
51	LEAN F/A CONDITION—Oxygen sensor signal input indcates lean fuel/air ratio condition during engine operation—check engine lamp ON—California only
52	a) RICH F/A CONDITION—Oxygen sensor signal input indicates righ fuel/air ratio condition during engine operation—check engine lamp ON—California only b) EXCESSIVE LEANING—Adaptive fuel value leaned excessively due to a sustained rich condition—check engine lamp ON—California only
53	INTERNAL SELF-TEST—Internal engine controller fault condition detected
55	Completion of fault code display on the "Check Engine" lamp
62	EMR MILEAGE ACCUM—Unsuccessful attempt to update EMR mileage in the controller EEPROM
63	EEPROM WRITE DENIED—Unsuccessful attempt to write to an EEPROM location by the controller
	FAULT CODE ERROR—Unrecognized fault ID received by the DRB-II

Year—1989
Model—Aries
Engine—2.5L (153 cid) EFI 4 cyl
Engine Code—VIN K

ECM TROUBLE CODES

Code	Explanation
11	IGN REFERENCE SIGNAL—No distributor reference signal detected during engine cranking
12	No. of key-on's since last fault or since faults were erased—Direct battery input to controller disconnected within the last 50–100 ignition key-on's
13	a) MAP PNEUMATIC SIGNAL—No variation in Manifold Absolute Pressure (MAP) sensor signal is detected—check engine lamp ON—California only b) MAP PNEUMATIC CHANGE—No differrence is recognized between the engine Manifold Absolute Pressure (MAP) reading and the stored barometric pressure reading—check engine lamp ON—California only

ECM TROUBLE CODES (cont'd)

Code	Explanation
14	a) MAP VOLTAGE TOO LOW—Manifold Absolute Pressure (MAP) sensor input below minimum acceptable voltage—check engine lamp ON—California only b) MAP VOLTAGE TOO HIGH—Manifold Absolute Pressure (MAP) sensor input above maximum acceptable voltage—check engine lamp ON—California only
15	VEHICLE SPEED SIGNAL—No distance sensor signal detected during road load conditions—check engine lamp ON—California only
16	BATTERY INPUT SENSE—Battery voltage sense input not detected during engine running—check engine lamp ON—California only
17	LOW ENGINE TEMP—Engine coolant temperature remains below normal operating temperatures during vehicle travel—thermostat
21	OXYGEN SENSOR SIGNAL—Neither rich or lean condition is detected from the oxygen sensor input—check engine lamp ON—California only
22	a) COOLANT VOLTAGE LOW—Coolant Temperature Sensor (CTS) input below the minimum acceptable voltage—check engine lamp ON—California only b) COOLANT VOLTAGE HIGH—Coolant Temperature Sensor (CTS) input above the maximum acceptable voltage—check engine lamp ON—California only
23	a) T/B TEMP VOLTAGE LOW—Throttle body temperature sensor input below the minimum acceptable voltage b) T/B TEMP VOLTAGE HI—Throttle body temperature sensor input above the maximum acceptable voltage
24	a) TPS VOLTAGE LOW—Throttle Position Sensor (TPS) input below the minimum acceptable voltage—check engine lamp ON—California only b) TPS VOLTAGE HIGH—Throttle Position Sensor (TPS) input above the maximum acceptable voltage—check engine lamp ON—California only
25	AIS MOTOR CIRCUITS—A shorted condition detected in 1 or more of the AIS control circuits—check engine lamp ON—California only
26	INJ 1 PEAK CURRENT—High resistance condition detected in the injector output circuit
27	INJ 1 CONTROL CKT—Injector output driver stage does not respond properly to the control signal
31	PURGE SOLENOID CKT—An open or shorted condition detected in the purge solenoid circuit—check engine lamp ON—California only
32	a) EGR SOLENOID CIRCUIT—An open or shorted condition detected in the Exhaust Gas Recirculation (EGR) solenoid circuit—check engine lamp ON—California only b) EGR SYSTEM FAILURE—Required change in fuel/air ratio not detected during diagnostic test—check engine lamp ON—California only
33	A/C CLUTCH RELAY CKT—An open or shorted condition detected in the air conditioning clutch relay circuit
34	S/C SERVO SOLENOIDS—An open or shorted condition detected in the speed control vacuum or vent solenoid circuits
35	RADIATOR FAN RELAY—An open or shorted condition detected in the radiator fan relay circuit
37	PTU SOLENOID CIRCUIT—An open or shorted condition detected in the torque converter part throttle unlock solenoid circuit
41	CHARGING SYSTEM CKT—Output driver stage for alternator field does not respond properly to the voltage regulator control signal
42	ASD RELAY CIRCUIT—An open or shorted condition detected in the auto shutdown relay circuit
43	IGNITION CONTROL CKT—Output driver stage for ignition coil does not respond properly to the dwell control signal
44	FJ2 VOLTAGE SENSE—No FJ2 voltage present at the logic board during controller operation
46	BATTERY VOLTAGE HIGH—Battery voltage sense input above target charging voltage during engine operation—check engine lamp ON—California only
47	BATTERY VOLTAGE LOW—Battery voltage sense input below target charging voltage during engine operation

ECM TROUBLE CODES (cont'd)

Code	Explanation
51	LEAN F/A CONDITION — Oxygen sensor signal input indcates lean fuel/air ratio condition during engine operation — check engine lamp ON — California only
52	a) RICH F/A CONDITION — Oxygen sensor signal input indicates righ fuel/air ratio condition during engine operation — check engine lamp ON — California only
	b) EXCESSIVE LEANING — Adaptive fuel value leaned excessively due to a sustained rich condition — check engine lamp ON — California only
53	INTERNAL SELF-TEST — Internal engine controller fault condition detected
55	Completion of fault code display on the "Check Engine" lamp
62	EMR MILEAGE ACCUM — Unsuccessful attempt to update EMR mileage in the controller EEPROM
63	EEPROM WRITE DENIED — Unsuccessful attempt to write to an EEPROM location by the controller
	FAULT CODE ERROR — Unrecognized fault ID received by the DRB-II

Year — 1989
Model — Spirit
Engine — 2.5L (153 cid) Turbo I 4 cyl
Engine Code — VIN J

ECM TROUBLE CODES

Code	Explanation
11	IGN REFERENCE SIGNAL — No distributor reference signal detected during engine cranking
12	No. or key-on's since last fault or since faults were erased — Direct battery input to controller disconnected within the last 50–100 ignition key-on's
13	a) MAP PNEUMATIC SIGNAL — No variation in Manifold Absolute Pressure (MAP) sensor signal is detected — check engine lamp ON — California only
	b) MAP PNEUMATIC CHANGE — No differrence is recognized between the engine Manifold Absolute Pressure (MAP) reading and the stored barometric pressure reading — check engine lamp ON — California only
14	a) MAP VOLTAGE TOO LOW — Manifold Absolute Pressure (MAP) sensor input below minimum acceptable voltage — check engine lamp ON — California only
	b) MAP VOLTAGE TOO HIGH — Manifold Absolute Pressure (MAP) sensor input above maximum acceptable voltage — check engine lamp ON — California only
15	VEHICLE SPEED SIGNAL — No distance sensor signal detected during road load conditions — check engine lamp ON — California only
16	BATTERY INPUT SENSE — Battery voltage sense input not detected during engine running — check engine lamp ON — California only
17	LOW ENGINE TEMP — Engine coolant temperature remains below normal operating temperatures during vehicle travel — thermostat
21	OXYGEN SENSOR SIGNAL — Neither rich or lean condition is detected from the oxygen sensor input — check engine lamp ON — California only
22	a) COOLANT VOLTAGE LOW — Coolant Temperature Sensor (CTS) input below the minimum acceptable voltage — check engine lamp ON — California only
	b) COOLANT VOLTAGE HIGH — Coolant Temperature Sensor (CTS) input above the maximum acceptable voltage — check engine lamp ON — California only
24	a) TPS VOLTAGE LOW — Throttle Position Sensor (TPS) input below the minimum acceptable voltage — check engine lamp ON — California only
	b) TPS VOLTAGE HIGH — Throttle Position Sensor (TPS) input above the maximum acceptable voltage — check engine lamp ON — California only
25	AIS MOTOR CIRCUITS — A shorted condition detected in 1 or more of the AIS control circuits — check engine lamp ON — California only

ECM TROUBLE CODES (cont'd)

Code	Explanation
26	a) INJ 1 PEAK CURRENT—High resistance condition detected in the INJ 1 injector bank circuit
	b) INJ 2 PEAK CURRENT—High resistance condition detected in the INJ 2 injector bank circuit
27	a) INJ 1 CONTROL CKT—INJ 1 injector bank driver stage does not respond properly to the control signal
	b) INJ 2 CONTROL CKT—INJ 2 injector bank driver stage does not respond properly to the control signal
31	PURGE SOLENOID CKT—An open or shorted condition detected in the purge solenoid circuit
32	a) EGR SOLENOID CIRCUIT—An open or shorted condition detected in the Exhaust Gas Recirculation (EGR) solenoid circuit—check engine lamp ON—California only
	b) EGR SYSTEM CIRCUIT—Required change in fuel/air ratio not detected during diagnostic test—check engine lamp ON—California only
33	A/C CLUTCH RELAY CKT—An open or shorted condition detected in the air conditioning clutch relay circuit
34	S/C SERVO SOLENOIDS—An open or shorted condition detected in the speed control vacuum or vent solenoid circuits
35	RADIATOR FAN RELAY—An open or shorted condition detected in the radiator fan relay circuit
36	WASTEGATE SOLENOID—An open or shorted condition detected in the turbocharger wastegate control solenoid circuit—check engine lamp ON—California only
41	CHARGING SYSTEM CKT—Output driver stage for alternator field does not respond properly to the voltage regulator control signal
42	a) ASD RELAY CIRCUIT—An open or shorted condition detected in the auto shutdown relay circuit
	b) Z1 VOLTAGE SENSE—No Z1 voltage sensed when the auto shutdown relay is energized
43	IGNITION CONTROL CKT—Output driver stage for ignition coil does not respond properly to the dwell control signal
44	FJ2 VOLTAGE SENSE—No FJ2 voltage present at the logic board during controller operation
45	BOOST LIMIT EXCEEDED—Manifold Absolute Pressure (MAP) reading above overboost limit detected during controller operation
46	BATTERY VOLTAGE HIGH—Battery voltage sense input above target charging voltage during engine operation—check engine lamp ON—California only
47	BATTERY VOLTAGE LOW—Battery voltage sense input below target charging voltage during engine operation
51	LEAN F/A CONDITION—Oxygen sensor signal input indcates lean fuel/air ratio condition during engine operation—check engine lamp ON—California only
52	RICK F/A CONDITION—Oxygen sensor signal input indicates righ fuel/air ratio condition during engine operation—check engine lamp ON—California only
53	INTERNAL SELF-TEST—Internal engine controller fault condition detected
54	SYNC PICK-UP SIGNAL—No fuel sync signal detected during engine rotation.
55	Completion of fault code display on the "Check Engine" lamp
61	BARO READ SOLENOID—An open or shorted condition detected in the baro read solenoid circuit—check engine lamp ON
62	EMR MILAGE ACCUM—Unsuccessful attempt to update EMR mileage in the controller EEPROM
63	EEPROM WRITE DENIED—Unsuccessful attempt to write to an EEPROM location by the controller or unrecognized fault ID received by the DRB-II
	FAULT CODE ERROR—Unrecognized fault ID received by the DRB-II

Year – 1989
Model – Spirit
Engine – 2.5L (153 cid) EFI 4 cyl
Engine Code – VIN K

ECM TROUBLE CODES

Code	Explanation
11	IGN REFERENCE SIGNAL – No distributor reference signal detected during engine cranking
12	No. of key-on's since last fault or since faults were erased – Direct battery input to controller disconnected within the last 50–100 ignition key-on's
13	a) MAP PNEUMATIC SIGNAL – No variation in Manifold Absolute Pressure (MAP) sensor signal is detected – check engine lamp ON – California only
	b) MAP PNEUMATIC CHANGE – No differrence is recognized between the engine Manifold Absolute Pressure (MAP) reading and the stored barometric pressure reading – check engine lamp ON – California only
14	a) MAP VOLTAGE TOO LOW – Manifold Absolute Pressure (MAP) sensor input below minimum acceptable voltage – check engine lamp ON – California only
	b) MAP VOLTAGE TOO HIGH – Manifold Absolute Pressure (MAP) sensor input above maximum acceptable voltage – check engine lamp ON – California only
15	VEHICLE SPEED SIGNAL – No distance sensor signal detected during road load conditions – check engine lamp ON – California only
16	BATTERY INPUT SENSE – Battery voltage sense input not detected during engine running – check engine lamp ON – California only
17	LOW ENGINE TEMP – Engine coolant temperature remains below normal operating temperatures during vehicle travel – thermostat
21	OXYGEN SENSOR SIGNAL – Neither rich or lean condition is detected from the oxygen sensor input – check engine lamp ON – California only
22	a) COOLANT VOLTAGE LOW – Coolant Temperature Sensor (CTS) input below the minimum acceptable voltage – check engine lamp ON – California only
	b) COOLANT VOLTAGE HIGH – Coolant Temperature Sensor (CTS) input above the maximum acceptable voltage – check engine lamp ON – California only
23	a) T/B TEMP VOLTAGE LOW – Throttle body temperature sensor input below the minimum acceptable voltage
	b) T/B TEMP VOLTAGE HI – Throttle body temperature sensor input above the maximum acceptable voltage
24	a) TPS VOLTAGE LOW – Throttle Position Sensor (TPS) input below the minimum acceptable voltage – check engine lamp ON – California only
	b) TPS VOLTAGE HIGH – Throttle Position Sensor (TPS) input above the maximum acceptable voltage – check engine lamp ON – California only
25	AIS MOTOR CIRCUITS – A shorted condition detected in 1 or more of the AIS control circuits – check engine lamp ON – California only
26	INJ 1 PEAK CURRENT – High resistance condition detected in the injector output circuit
27	INJ 1 CONTROL CKT – Injector output driver stage does not respond properly to the control signal
31	PURGE SOLENOID CKT – An open or shorted condition detected in the purge solenoid circuit – check engine lamp ON – California only
32	a) EGR SOLENOID CIRCUIT – An open or shorted condition detected in the Exhaust Gas Recirculation (EGR) solenoid circuit – check engine lamp ON – California only
	b) EGR SYSTEM FAILURE – Required change in fuel/air ratio not detected during diagnostic test – check engine lamp ON – California only
33	A/C CLUTCH RELAY CKT – An open or shorted condition detected in the air conditioning clutch relay circuit
34	S/C SERVO SOLENOIDS – An open or shorted condition detected in the speed control vacuum or vent solenoid circuits

ECM TROUBLE CODES (cont'd)

Code	Explanation
35	RADIATOR FAN RELAY—An open or shorted condition detected in the radiator fan relay circuit
37	PTU SOLENOID CIRCUIT—An open or shorted condition detected in the torque converter part throttle unlock solenoid circuit
41	CHARGING SYSTEM CKT—Output driver stage for alternator field does not respond properly to the voltage regulator control signal
42	ASD RELAY CIRCUIT—An open or shorted condition detected in the auto shutdown relay circuit
43	IGNITION CONTROL CKT—Output driver stage for ignition coil does not respond properly to the dwell control signal
44	FJ2 VOLTAGE SENSE—No FJ2 voltage present at the logic board during controller operation
46	BATTERY VOLTAGE HIGH—Battery voltage sense input above target charging voltage during engine operation—check engine lamp ON—California only
47	BATTERY VOLTAGE LOW—Battery voltage sense input below target charging voltage during engine operation
51	LEAN F/A CONDITION—Oxygen sensor signal input indcates lean fuel/air ratio condition during engine operation—check engine lamp ON—California only
52	a) RICH F/A CONDITION—Oxygen sensor signal input indicates righ fuel/air ratio condition during engine operation—check engine lamp ON—California only b) EXCESSIVE LEANING—Adaptive fuel value leaned excessively due to a sustained rich condition—check engine lamp ON—California only
53	INTERNAL SELF-TEST—Internal engine controller fault condition detected
55	Completion of fault code display on the "Check Engine" lamp
62	EMR MILEAGE ACCUM—Unsuccessful attempt to update EMR mileage in the controller EEPROM
63	EEPROM WRITE DENIED—Unsuccessful attempt to write to an EEPROM location by the controller
	FAULT CODE ERROR—Unrecognized fault ID received by the DRB-II

Year—1989
Model—Spirit
Engine—3.0L (181 cid) MPFI V6
Engine Code—VIN 3

ECM TROUBLE CODES

Code	Explanation
11	IGN REFERENCE SIGNAL—No distributor reference signal detected during engine cranking
12	No. or key-on's since last fault or since faults were erased—Direct battery input to controller disconnected within the last 50–100 ignition key-on's
13	a) MAP PNEUMATIC SIGNAL—No variation in Manifold Absolute Pressure (MAP) sensor signal is detected—check engine lamp ON—California only b) MAP PNEUMATIC CHANGE—No differrence is recognized between the engine Manifold Absolute Pressure (MAP) reading and the stored barometric pressure reading—check engine lamp ON—California only
14	a) MAP VOLTAGE TOO LOW—Manifold Absolute Pressure (MAP) sensor input below minimum acceptable voltage—check engine lamp ON—California only b) MAP VOLTAGE TOO HIGH—Manifold Absolute Pressure (MAP) above maximum acceptable voltage—check engine lamp ON—California only
15	VEHICLE SPEED SIGNAL—No distance sensor signal detected during road load conditions—check engine lamp ON—California only
16	BATTERY INPUT SENSE—Battery voltage sense input not detected during engine running—check engine lamp ON—California only

ECM TROUBLE CODES (cont'd)

Code	Explanation
17	LOW ENGINE TEMP—Engine coolant temperature remains below normal operating temperatures during vehicle travel—thermostat
21	OXYGEN SENSOR SIGNAL—Neither rich or lean condition is detected from the oxygen sensor input—check engine lamp ON—California only
22	a) COOLANT VOLTAGE LOW—Coolant Temperature Sensor (CTS) input below the minimum acceptable voltage—check engine lamp ON—California only b) COOLANT VOLTAGE HIGH—Coolant Temperature Sensor (CTS) input above the maximum acceptable voltage—check engine lamp ON—California only
24	a) TPS VOLTAGE LOW—Throttle Position Sensor (TPS) input below the minimum acceptable voltage b) TPS VOLTAGE HIGH—Throttle Position Sensor (TPS) input above the maximum acceptable voltage
25	AIS MOTOR CIRCUITS—A shorted condition detected in 1 or more of the AIS control circuits
26	a) INJ 1 PEAK CURRENT—High resistance condition detected in the INJ 1 injector bank circuit—check engine lamp ON—California only b) INJ 2 PEAK CURRENT—High resistance condition detected in the INJ 2 injector bank circuit—check engine lamp ON—California only c) INJ 3 PEAK CURRENT—High resistance condition detected in the INJ 3 injector bank circuit—check engine lamp ON—California only
27	a) INJ 1 CONTROL CKT—INJ 1 injector bank driver stage does not respond properly to the control signal—check engine lamp ON—California only b) INJ 2 CONTROL CKT—INJ 2 injector bank driver stage does not respond properly to the control signal—check engine lamp ON—California only c) INJ 3 CONTROL CKT—INJ 3 injector bank driver stage does not respond properly to the control signal—check engine lamp ON—California only
31	PURGE SOLENOID CKT—An open or shorted condition detected in the purge solenoid circuit—check engine lamp ON—California only
32	a) EGR SOLENOID CIRCUIT—An open or shorted condition detected in the Exhaust Gas Recirculation (EGR) solenoid circuit—check engine lamp ON—California only b) EGR SYSTEM FAILURE—Required change in fuel/air ratio not detected during diagnostic test—check engine lamp ON—California only
33	A/C CLUTCH RELAY CKT—An open or shorted condition detected in the air conditioning clutch relay circuit
34	S/C SERVO SOLENOIDS—An open or shorted condition detected in the speed control vacuum or vent solenoid circuits
35	RADIATOR FAN RELAY—An open or shorted condition detected in the radiator fan relay circuit
41	CHARGING SYSTEM CKT—Output driver stage for alternator field does not respond properly to the voltage regulator control signal
42	a) ASD RELAY CIRCUIT—An open or shorted condition detected in the auto shutdown relay circuit b) Z1 VOLTAGE SENSE—No Z1 voltage sensed when the auto shutdown relay is energized
43	IGNITION CONTROL CKT—Output driver stage for ignition coil does not respond properly to the dwell control signal
46	BATTERY VOLTAGE HIGH—Battery voltage sense input above target charging voltage during engine operation—check engine lamp ON—California only
47	BATTERY VOLTAGE LOW—Battery voltage sense input below target charging voltage during engine operation
51	LEAN F/A CONDITION—Oxygen sensor signal input indcates lean fuel/air ratio condition during engine operation
52	RICH F/A CONDITION—Oxygen sensor signal input indicates righ fuel/air ratio condition during engine operation
53	INTERNAL SELF-TEST—Internal engine controller fault condition detected
54	SYNC PICK-UP SIGNAL—No high data rate signal detected during engine rotation—check engine lamp ON—California only

ECM TROUBLE CODES (cont'd)

Code	Explanation
55	Completion of fault code display on the "Check Engine" lamp
62	EMR MILEAGE ACCUM — Unsuccessful attempt to update EMR mileage in the controller EEPROM
63	EEPROM WRITE DENIED — Unsuccessful attempt to write to an EEPROM location by the controller or unrecognized fault ID received by the DRB-II
	FAULT CODE ERROR — Unrecognized fault ID received by the DRB-II

Year — 1989
Model — Lancer
Engine — 2.2L (135 cid) Turbo II 4 cyl
Engine Code — VIN A

ECM TROUBLE CODES

Code	Explanation
11	IGN REFERENCE SIGNAL — No distributor reference signal detected during engine cranking
12	No. or key-on's since last fault or since faults were erased — Direct battery input to controller disconnected within the last 50–100 ignition key-on's
13	a) MAP PNEUMATIC SIGNAL — No variation in Manifold Absolute Pressure (MAP) sensor signal is detected — check engine lamp ON — California only b) MAP PNEUMATIC CHANGE — No differrence is recognized between the engine Manifold Absolute Pressure (MAP) reading and the stored barometric pressure reading — check engine lamp ON — California only
14	a) MAP VOLTAGE TOO LOW — Manifold Absolute Pressure (MAP) sensor input below minimum acceptable voltage — check engine lamp ON — California only b) MAP VOLTAGE TOO HIGH — Manifold Absolute Pressure (MAP) sensor input above maximum acceptable voltage — check engine lamp ON — California only
15	VEHICLE SPEED SIGNAL — No distance sensor signal detected during road load conditions — check engine lamp ON — California only
16	BATTERY INPUT SENSE — Battery voltage sense input not detected during engine running — check engine lamp ON — California only
17	LOW ENGINE TEMP — Engine coolant temperature remains below normal operating temperatures during vehicle travel — thermostat
21	OXYGEN SENSOR SIGNAL — Neither rich or lean condition is detected from the oxygen sensor input — check engine lamp ON — California only
22	a) COOLANT VOLTAGE LOW — Coolant Temperature Sensor (CTS) input below the minimum acceptable voltage — check engine lamp ON — California only b) COOLANT VOLTAGE HIGH — Coolant Temperature Sensor (CTS) input above the maximum acceptable voltage — check engine lamp ON — California only
24	a) TPS VOLTAGE LOW — Throttle Position Sensor (TPS) input below the minimum acceptable voltage — check engine lamp ON — California only b) TPS VOLTAGE HIGH — Throttle Position Sensor (TPS) input above the maximum acceptable voltage — check engine lamp ON — California only
25	AIS MOTOR CIRCUITS — A shorted condition detected in 1 or more of the AIS control circuits — check engine lamp ON — California only
26	a) INJ 1 PEAK CURRENT — High resistance condition detected in the INJ 1 injector bank circuit b) INJ 2 PEAK CURRENT — High resistance condition detected in the INJ 2 injector bank circuit
27	a) INJ 1 CONTROL CKT — INJ 1 injector bank driver stage does not respond properly to the control signal b) INJ 2 CONTROL CKT — INJ 2 injector bank driver stage does not respond properly to the control signal
31	PURGE SOLENOID CKT — An open or shorted condition detected in the purge solenoid circuit

ECM TROUBLE CODES (cont'd)

Code	Explanation
32	a) EGR SOLENOID CIRCUIT—An open or shorted condition detected in the Exhaust Gas Recirculation (EGR) solenoid circuit—check engine lamp ON—California only b) EGR SYSTEM CIRCUIT—Required change in fuel/air ratio not detected during diagnostic test—check engine lamp ON—California only
33	A/C CLUTCH RELAY CKT—An open or shorted condition detected in the air conditioning clutch relay circuit
34	S/C SERVO SOLENOIDS—An open or shorted condition detected in the speed control vacuum or vent solenoid circuits
35	RADIATOR FAN RELAY—An open or shorted condition detected in the radiator fan relay circuit
36	WASTEGATE SOLENOID—An open or shorted condition detected in the turbocharger wastegate control solenoid circuit—check engine lamp ON—California only
41	CHARGING SYSTEM CKT—Output driver stage for alternator field does not respond properly to the voltage regulator control signal
42	a) ASD RELAY CIRCUIT—An open or shorted condition detected in the auto shutdown relay circuit b) Z1 VOLTAGE SENSE—No Z1 voltage sensed when the auto shutdown relay is energized
43	IGNITION CONTROL CKT—Output driver stage for ignition coil does not respond properly to the dwell control signal
44	FJ2 VOLTAGE SENSE—No FJ2 voltage present at the logic board during controller operation
45	BOOST LIMIT EXCEEDED—Manifold Absolute Pressure (MAP) reading above overboost limit detected during controller operation
46	BATTERY VOLTAGE HIGH—Battery voltage sense input above target charging voltage during engine operation—check engine lamp ON—California only
47	BATTERY VOLTAGE LOW—Battery voltage sense input below target charging voltage during engine operation
51	LEAN F/A CONDITION—Oxygen sensor signal input indcates lean fuel/air ratio condition during engine operation—check engine lamp ON—California only
52	RICK F/A CONDITION—Oxygen sensor signal input indicates righ fuel/air ratio condition during engine operation—check engine lamp ON—California only
53	INTERNAL SELF-TEST—Internal engine controller fault condition detected
54	SYNC PICK-UP SIGNAL—No fuel sync signal detected during engine rotation.
55	Completion of fault code display on the "Check Engine" lamp
61	BARO READ SOLENOID—An open or shorted condition detected in the baro read solenoid circuit—check engine lamp ON
62	EMR MILAGE ACCUM—Unsuccessful attempt to update EMR mileage in the controller EEPROM
63	EEPROM WRITE DENIED—Unsuccessful attempt to write to an EEPROM location by the controller or unrecognized fault ID received by the DRB-II
	FAULT CODE ERROR—Unrecognized fault ID received by the DRB-II

Year—1989
Model—Lancer
Engine—2.2L (135 cid) EFI 4 cyl
Engine Code—VIN D

ECM TROUBLE CODES

Code	Explanation
11	IGN REFERENCE SIGNAL—No distributor reference signal detected during engine cranking
12	No. of key-on's since last fault or since faults were erased—Direct battery input to controller disconnected within the last 50–100 ignition key-on's

ECM TROUBLE CODES (cont'd)

Code	Explanation
13	a) MAP PNEUMATIC SIGNAL — No variation in Manifold Absolute Pressure (MAP) sensor signal is detected — check engine lamp ON — California only b) MAP PNEUMATIC CHANGE — No differrence is recognized between the engine Manifold Absolute Pressure (MAP) reading and the stored barometric pressure reading — check engine lamp ON — California only
14	a) MAP VOLTAGE TOO LOW — Manifold Absolute Pressure (MAP) sensor input below minimum acceptable voltage — check engine lamp ON — California only b) MAP VOLTAGE TOO HIGH — Manifold Absolute Pressure (MAP) sensor input above maximum acceptable voltage — check engine lamp ON — California only
15	VEHICLE SPEED SIGNAL — No distance sensor signal detected during road load conditions — check engine lamp ON — California only
16	BATTERY INPUT SENSE — Battery voltage sense input not detected during engine running — check engine lamp ON — California only
17	LOW ENGINE TEMP — Engine coolant temperature remains below normal operating temperatures during vehicle travel — thermostat
21	OXYGEN SENSOR SIGNAL — Neither rich or lean condition is detected from the oxygen sensor input — check engine lamp ON — California only
22	a) COOLANT VOLTAGE LOW — Coolant Temperature Sensor (CTS) input below the minimum acceptable voltage — check engine lamp ON — California only b) COOLANT VOLTAGE HIGH — Coolant Temperature Sensor (CTS) input above the maximum acceptable voltage — check engine lamp ON — California only
23	a) T/B TEMP VOLTAGE LOW — Throttle body temperature sensor input below the minimum acceptable voltage b) T/B TEMP VOLTAGE HI — Throttle body temperature sensor input above the maximum acceptable voltage
24	a) TPS VOLTAGE LOW — Throttle Position Sensor (TPS) input below the minimum acceptable voltage — check engine lamp ON — California only b) TPS VOLTAGE HIGH — Throttle Position Sensor (TPS) input above the maximum acceptable voltage — check engine lamp ON — California only
25	AIS MOTOR CIRCUITS — A shorted condition detected in 1 or more of the AIS control circuits — check engine lamp ON — California only
26	INJ 1 PEAK CURRENT — High resistance condition detected in the injector output circuit
27	INJ 1 CONTROL CKT — Injector output driver stage does not respond properly to the control signal
31	PURGE SOLENOID CKT — An open or shorted condition detected in the purge solenoid circuit — check engine lamp ON — California only
32	a) EGR SOLENOID CIRCUIT — An open or shorted condition detected in the Exhaust Gas Recirculation (EGR) solenoid circuit — check engine lamp ON — California only b) EGR SYSTEM FAILURE — Required change in fuel/air ratio not detected during diagnostic test — check engine lamp ON — California only
33	A/C CLUTCH RELAY CKT — An open or shorted condition detected in the air conditioning clutch relay circuit
34	S/C SERVO SOLENOIDS — An open or shorted condition detected in the speed control vacuum or vent solenoid circuits
35	RADIATOR FAN RELAY — An open or shorted condition detected in the radiator fan relay circuit
37	PTU SOLENOID CIRCUIT — An open or shorted condition detected in the torque converter part throttle unlock solenoid circuit
41	CHARGING SYSTEM CKT — Output driver stage for alternator field does not respond properly to the voltage regulator control signal
42	ASD RELAY CIRCUIT — An open or shorted condition detected in the auto shutdown relay circuit
43	IGNITION CONTROL CKT — Output driver stage for ignition coil does not respond properly to the dwell control signal
44	FJ2 VOLTAGE SENSE — No FJ2 voltage present at the logic board during controller operation

ECM TROUBLE CODES (cont'd)

Code	Explanation
46	BATTERY VOLTAGE HIGH—Battery voltage sense input above target charging voltage during engine operation—check engine lamp ON—California only
47	BATTERY VOLTAGE LOW—Battery voltage sense input below target charging voltage during engine operation
51	LEAN F/A CONDITION—Oxygen sensor signal input indcates lean fuel/air ratio condition during engine operation—check engine lamp ON—California only
52	a) RICH F/A CONDITION—Oxygen sensor signal input indicates righ fuel/air ratio condition during engine operation—check engine lamp ON—California only
	b) EXCESSIVE LEANING—Adaptive fuel value leaned excessively due to a sustained rich condition—check engine lamp ON—California only
53	INTERNAL SELF-TEST—Internal engine controller fault condition detected
55	Completion of fault code display on the "Check Engine" lamp
62	EMR MILEAGE ACCUM—Unsuccessful attempt to update EMR mileage in the controller EEPROM
63	EEPROM WRITE DENIED—Unsuccessful attempt to write to an EEPROM location by the controller
	FAULT CODE ERROR—Unrecognized fault ID received by the DRB-II

Year—1989
Model—Lancer
Engine—2.5L (153 cid) Turbo I 4 cyl
Engine Code—VIN J

ECM TROUBLE CODES

Code	Explanation
11	IGN REFERENCE SIGNAL—No distributor reference signal detected during engine cranking
12	No. or key-on's since last fault or since faults were erased—Direct battery input to controller disconnected within the last 50–100 ignition key-on's
13	a) MAP PNEUMATIC SIGNAL—No variation in Manifold Absolute Pressure (MAP) sensor signal is detected—check engine lamp ON—California only
	b) MAP PNEUMATIC CHANGE—No differrence is recognized between the engine Manifold Absolute Pressure (MAP) reading and the stored barometric pressure reading—check engine lamp ON—California only
14	a) MAP VOLTAGE TOO LOW—Manifold Absolute Pressure (MAP) sensor input below minimum acceptable voltage—check engine lamp ON—California only
	b) MAP VOLTAGE TOO HIGH—Manifold Absolute Pressure (MAP) sensor input above maximum acceptable voltage—check engine lamp ON—California only
15	VEHICLE SPEED SIGNAL—No distance sensor signal detected during road load conditions—check engine lamp ON—California only
16	BATTERY INPUT SENSE—Battery voltage sense input not detected during engine running—check engine lamp ON—California only
17	LOW ENGINE TEMP—Engine coolant temperature remains below normal operating temperatures during vehicle travel—thermostat
21	OXYGEN SENSOR SIGNAL—Neither rich or lean condition is detected from the oxygen sensor input—check engine lamp ON—California only
22	a) COOLANT VOLTAGE LOW—Coolant Temperature Sensor (CTS) input below the minimum acceptable voltage—check engine lamp ON—California only
	b) COOLANT VOLTAGE HIGH—Coolant Temperature Sensor (CTS) input above the maximum acceptable voltage—check engine lamp ON—California only

ECM TROUBLE CODES (cont'd)

Code	Explanation
24	a) TPS VOLTAGE LOW—Throttle Position Sensor (TPS) input below the minimum acceptable voltage—check engine lamp ON—California only b) TPS VOLTAGE HIGH—Throttle Position Sensor (TPS) input above the maximum acceptable voltage—check engine lamp ON—California only
25	AIS MOTOR CIRCUITS—A shorted condition detected in 1 or more of the AIS control circuits—check engine lamp ON—California only
26	a) INJ 1 PEAK CURRENT—High resistance condition detected in the INJ 1 injector bank circuit b) INJ 2 PEAK CURRENT—High resistance condition detected in the INJ 2 injector bank circuit
27	a) INJ 1 CONTROL CKT—INJ 1 injector bank driver stage does not respond properly to the control signal b) INJ 2 CONTROL CKT—INJ 2 injector bank driver stage does not respond properly to the control signal
31	PURGE SOLENOID CKT—An open or shorted condition detected in the purge solenoid circuit
32	a) EGR SOLENOID CIRCUIT—An open or shorted condition detected in the Exhaust Gas Recirculation (EGR) solenoid circuit—check engine lamp ON—California only b) EGR SYSTEM CIRCUIT—Required change in fuel/air ratio not detected during diagnostic test—check engine lamp ON—California only
33	A/C CLUTCH RELAY CKT—An open or shorted condition detected in the air conditioning clutch relay circuit
34	S/C SERVO SOLENOIDS—An open or shorted condition detected in the speed control vacuum or vent solenoid circuits
35	RADIATOR FAN RELAY—An open or shorted condition detected in the radiator fan relay circuit
36	WASTEGATE SOLENOID—An open or shorted condition detected in the turbocharger wastegate control solenoid circuit—check engine lamp ON—California only
41	CHARGING SYSTEM CKT—Output driver stage for alternator field does not respond properly to the voltage regulator control signal
42	a) ASD RELAY CIRCUIT—An open or shorted condition detected in the auto shutdown relay circuit b) Z1 VOLTAGE SENSE—No Z1 voltage sensed when the auto shutdown relay is energized
43	IGNITION CONTROL CKT—Output driver stage for ignition coil does not respond properly to the dwell control signal
44	FJ2 VOLTAGE SENSE—No FJ2 voltage present at the logic board during controller operation
45	BOOST LIMIT EXCEEDED—Manifold Absolute Pressure (MAP) reading above overboost limit detected during controller operation
46	BATTERY VOLTAGE HIGH—Battery voltage sense input above target charging voltage during engine operation—check engine lamp ON—California only
47	BATTERY VOLTAGE LOW—Battery voltage sense input below target charging voltage during engine operation
51	LEAN F/A CONDITION—Oxygen sensor signal input indicates lean fuel/air ratio condition during engine operation—check engine lamp ON—California only
52	RICK F/A CONDITION—Oxygen sensor signal input indicates righ fuel/air ratio condition during engine operation—check engine lamp ON—California only
53	INTERNAL SELF-TEST—Internal engine controller fault condition detected
54	SYNC PICK-UP SIGNAL—No fuel sync signal detected during engine rotation.
55	Completion of fault code display on the ''Check Engine'' lamp
61	BARO READ SOLENOID—An open or shorted condition detected in the baro read solenoid circuit—check engine lamp ON
62	EMR MILAGE ACCUM—Unsuccessful attempt to update EMR mileage in the controller EEPROM
63	EEPROM WRITE DENIED—Unsuccessful attempt to write to an EEPROM location by the controller or unrecognized fault ID received by the DRB-II
	FAULT CODE ERROR—Unrecognized fault ID received by the DRB-II

Year — 1989
Model — Lancer
Engine — 2.5L (153 cid) EFI 4 cyl
Engine Code — VIN K

ECM TROUBLE CODES

Code	Explanation
11	IGN REFERENCE SIGNAL — No distributor reference signal detected during engine cranking
12	No. of key-on's since last fault or since faults were erased — Direct battery input to controller disconnected within the last 50–100 ignition key-on's
13	a) MAP PNEUMATIC SIGNAL — No variation in Manifold Absolute Pressure (MAP) sensor signal is detected — check engine lamp ON — California only b) MAP PNEUMATIC CHANGE — No difference is recognized between the engine Manifold Absolute Pressure (MAP) reading and the stored barometric pressure reading — check engine lamp ON — California only
14	a) MAP VOLTAGE TOO LOW — Manifold Absolute Pressure (MAP) sensor input below minimum acceptable voltage — check engine lamp ON — California only b) MAP VOLTAGE TOO HIGH — Manifold Absolute Pressure (MAP) sensor input above maximum acceptable voltage — check engine lamp ON — California only
15	VEHICLE SPEED SIGNAL — No distance sensor signal detected during road load conditions — check engine lamp ON — California only
16	BATTERY INPUT SENSE — Battery voltage sense input not detected during engine running — check engine lamp ON — California only
17	LOW ENGINE TEMP — Engine coolant temperature remains below normal operating temperatures during vehicle travel — thermostat
21	OXYGEN SENSOR SIGNAL — Neither rich or lean condition is detected from the oxygen sensor input — check engine lamp ON — California only
22	a) COOLANT VOLTAGE LOW — Coolant Temperature Sensor (CTS) input below the minimum acceptable voltage — check engine lamp ON — California only b) COOLANT VOLTAGE HIGH — Coolant Temperature Sensor (CTS) input above the maximum acceptable voltage — check engine lamp ON — California only
23	a) T/B TEMP VOLTAGE LOW — Throttle body temperature sensor input below the minimum acceptable voltage b) T/B TEMP VOLTAGE HI — Throttle body temperature sensor input above the maximum acceptable voltage
24	a) TPS VOLTAGE LOW — Throttle Position Sensor (TPS) input below the minimum acceptable voltage — check engine lamp ON — California only b) TPS VOLTAGE HIGH — Throttle Position Sensor (TPS) input above the maximum acceptable voltage — check engine lamp ON — California only
25	AIS MOTOR CIRCUITS — A shorted condition detected in 1 or more of the AIS control circuits — check engine lamp ON — California only
26	INJ 1 PEAK CURRENT — High resistance condition detected in the injector output circuit
27	INJ 1 CONTROL CKT — Injector output driver stage does not respond properly to the control signal
31	PURGE SOLENOID CKT — An open or shorted condition detected in the purge solenoid circuit — check engine lamp ON — California only
32	a) EGR SOLENOID CIRCUIT — An open or shorted condition detected in the Exhaust Gas Recirculation (EGR) solenoid circuit — check engine lamp ON — California only b) EGR SYSTEM FAILURE — Required change in fuel/air ratio not detected during diagnostic test — check engine lamp ON — California only
33	A/C CLUTCH RELAY CKT — An open or shorted condition detected in the air conditioning clutch relay circuit
34	S/C SERVO SOLENOIDS — An open or shorted condition detected in the speed control vacuum or vent solenoid circuits

ECM TROUBLE CODES (cont'd)

Code	Explanation
35	RADIATOR FAN RELAY—An open or shorted condition detected in the radiator fan relay circuit
37	PTU SOLENOID CIRCUIT—An open or shorted condition detected in the torque converter part throttle unlock solenoid circuit
41	CHARGING SYSTEM CKT—Output driver stage for alternator field does not respond properly to the voltage regulator control signal
42	ASD RELAY CIRCUIT—An open or shorted condition detected in the auto shutdown relay circuit
43	IGNITION CONTROL CKT—Output driver stage for ignition coil does not respond properly to the dwell control signal
44	FJ2 VOLTAGE SENSE—No FJ2 voltage present at the logic board during controller operation
46	BATTERY VOLTAGE HIGH—Battery voltage sense input above target charging voltage during engine operation—check engine lamp ON—California only
47	BATTERY VOLTAGE LOW—Battery voltage sense input below target charging voltage during engine operation
51	LEAN F/A CONDITION—Oxygen sensor signal input indcates lean fuel/air ratio condition during engine operation—check engine lamp ON—California only
52	a) RICH F/A CONDITION—Oxygen sensor signal input indicates righ fuel/air ratio condition during engine operation—check engine lamp ON—California only b) EXCESSIVE LEANING—Adaptive fuel value leaned excessively due to a sustained rich condition—check engine lamp ON—California only
53	INTERNAL SELF-TEST—Internal engine controller fault condition detected
55	Completion of fault code display on the "Check Engine" lamp
62	EMR MILEAGE ACCUM—Unsuccessful attempt to update EMR mileage in the controller EEPROM
63	EEPROM WRITE DENIED—Unsuccessful attempt to write to an EEPROM location by the controller
	FAULT CODE ERROR—Unrecognized fault ID received by the DRB-II

Year—1989
Model—Daytona
Engine—2.2L (135 cid) Turbo II 4 cyl
Engine Code—VIN A

ECM TROUBLE CODES

Code	Explanation
11	IGN REFERENCE SIGNAL—No distributor reference signal detected during engine cranking
12	No. or key-on's since last fault or since faults were erased—Direct battery input to controller disconnected within the last 50–100 ignition key-on's
13	a) MAP PNEUMATIC SIGNAL—No variation in Manifold Absolute Pressure (MAP) sensor signal is detected—check engine lamp ON—California only b) MAP PNEUMATIC CHANGE—No differrence is recognized between the engine Manifold Absolute Pressure (MAP) reading and the stored barometric pressure reading—check engine lamp ON—California only
14	a) MAP VOLTAGE TOO LOW—Manifold Absolute Pressure (MAP) sensor input below minimum acceptable voltage—check engine lamp ON—California only b) MAP VOLTAGE TOO HIGH—Manifold Absolute Pressure (MAP) sensor input above maximum acceptable voltage—check engine lamp ON—California only
15	VEHICLE SPEED SIGNAL—No distance sensor signal detected during road load conditions—check engine lamp ON—California only
16	BATTERY INPUT SENSE—Battery voltage sense input not detected during engine running—check engine lamp ON—California only

ECM TROUBLE CODES (cont'd)

Code	Explanation
17	LOW ENGINE TEMP—Engine coolant temperature remains below normal operating temperatures during vehicle travel—thermostat
21	OXYGEN SENSOR SIGNAL—Neither rich or lean condition is detected from the oxygen sensor input—check engine lamp ON—California only
22	a) COOLANT VOLTAGE LOW—Coolant Temperature Sensor (CTS) input below the minimum acceptable voltage—check engine lamp ON—California only b) COOLANT VOLTAGE HIGH—Coolant Temperature Sensor (CTS) input above the maximum acceptable voltage—check engine lamp ON—California only
24	a) TPS VOLTAGE LOW—Throttle Position Sensor (TPS) input below the minimum acceptable voltage—check engine lamp ON—California only b) TPS VOLTAGE HIGH—Throttle Position Sensor (TPS) input above the maximum acceptable voltage—check engine lamp ON—California only
25	AIS MOTOR CIRCUITS—A shorted condition detected in 1 or more of the AIS control circuits—check engine lamp ON—California only
26	a) INJ 1 PEAK CURRENT—High resistance condition detected in the INJ 1 injector bank circuit b) INJ 2 PEAK CURRENT—High resistance condition detected in the INJ 2 injector bank circuit
27	a) INJ 1 CONTROL CKT—INJ 1 injector bank driver stage does not respond properly to the control signal b) INJ 2 CONTROL CKT—INJ 2 injector bank driver stage does not respond properly to the control signal
31	PURGE SOLENOID CKT—An open or shorted condition detected in the purge solenoid circuit
32	a) EGR SOLENOID CIRCUIT—An open or shorted condition detected in the Exhaust Gas Recirculation (EGR) solenoid circuit—check engine lamp ON—California only b) EGR SYSTEM CIRCUIT—Required change in fuel/air ratio not detected during diagnostic test—check engine lamp ON—California only
33	A/C CLUTCH RELAY CKT—An open or shorted condition detected in the air conditioning clutch relay circuit
34	S/C SERVO SOLENOIDS—An open or shorted condition detected in the speed control vacuum or vent solenoid circuits
35	RADIATOR FAN RELAY—An open or shorted condition detected in the radiator fan relay circuit
36	WASTEGATE SOLENOID—An open or shorted condition detected in the turbocharger wastegate control solenoid circuit—check engine lamp ON—California only
41	CHARGING SYSTEM CKT—Output driver stage for alternator field does not respond properly to the voltage regulator control signal
42	a) ASD RELAY CIRCUIT—An open or shorted condition detected in the auto shutdown relay circuit b) Z1 VOLTAGE SENSE—No Z1 voltage sensed when the auto shutdown relay is energized
43	IGNITION CONTROL CKT—Output driver stage for ignition coil does not respond properly to the dwell control signal
44	FJ2 VOLTAGE SENSE—No FJ2 voltage present at the logic board during controller operation
45	BOOST LIMIT EXCEEDED—Manifold Absolute Pressure (MAP) reading above overboost limit detected during controller operation
46	BATTERY VOLTAGE HIGH—Battery voltage sense input above target charging voltage during engine operation—check engine lamp ON—California only
47	BATTERY VOLTAGE LOW—Battery voltage sense input below target charging voltage during engine operation
51	LEAN F/A CONDITION—Oxygen sensor signal input indcates lean fuel/air ratio condition during engine operation—check engine lamp ON—California only
52	RICK F/A CONDITION—Oxygen sensor signal input indicates righ fuel/air ratio condition during engine operation—check engine lamp ON—California only
53	INTERNAL SELF-TEST—Internal engine controller fault condition detected
54	SYNC PICK-UP SIGNAL—No fuel sync signal detected during engine rotation.
55	Completion of fault code display on the ''Check Engine'' lamp

ECM TROUBLE CODES (cont'd)

Code	Explanation
61	BARO READ SOLENOID — An open or shorted condition detected in the baro read solenoid circuit — check engine lamp ON
62	EMR MILAGE ACCUM — Unsuccessful attempt to update EMR mileage in the controller EEPROM
63	EEPROM WRITE DENIED — Unsuccessful attempt to write to an EEPROM location by the controller or unrecognized fault ID received by the DRB-II
	FAULT CODE ERROR — Unrecognized fault ID received by the DRB-II

Year — 1989
Model — Daytona
Engine — 2.5L (153 cid) Turbo I 4 cyl
Engine Code — VIN J

ECM TROUBLE CODES

Code	Explanation
11	IGN REFERENCE SIGNAL — No distributor reference signal detected during engine cranking
12	No. or key-on's since last fault or since faults were erased — Direct battery input to controller disconnected within the last 50–100 ignition key-on's
13	a) MAP PNEUMATIC SIGNAL — No variation in Manifold Absolute Pressure (MAP) sensor signal is detected — check engine lamp ON — California only b) MAP PNEUMATIC CHANGE — No differrence is recognized between the engine Manifold Absolute Pressure (MAP) reading and the stored barometric pressure reading — check engine lamp ON — California only
14	a) MAP VOLTAGE TOO LOW — Manifold Absolute Pressure (MAP) sensor input below minimum acceptable voltage — check engine lamp ON — California only b) MAP VOLTAGE TOO HIGH — Manifold Absolute Pressure (MAP) sensor input above maximum acceptable voltage — check engine lamp ON — California only
15	VEHICLE SPEED SIGNAL — No distance sensor signal detected during road load conditions — check engine lamp ON — California only
16	BATTERY INPUT SENSE — Battery voltage sense input not detected during engine running — check engine lamp ON — California only
17	LOW ENGINE TEMP — Engine coolant temperature remains below normal operating temperatures during vehicle travel — thermostat
21	OXYGEN SENSOR SIGNAL — Neither rich or lean condition is detected from the oxygen sensor input — check engine lamp ON — California only
22	a) COOLANT VOLTAGE LOW — Coolant Temperature Sensor (CTS) input below the minimum acceptable voltage — check engine lamp ON — California only b) COOLANT VOLTAGE HIGH — Coolant Temperature Sensor (CTS) input above the maximum acceptable voltage — check engine lamp ON — California only
24	a) TPS VOLTAGE LOW — Throttle Position Sensor (TPS) input below the minimum acceptable voltage — check engine lamp ON — California only b) TPS VOLTAGE HIGH — Throttle Position Sensor (TPS) input above the maximum acceptable voltage — check engine lamp ON — California only
25	AIS MOTOR CIRCUITS — A shorted condition detected in 1 or more of the AIS control circuits — check engine lamp ON — California only
26	a) INJ 1 PEAK CURRENT — High resistance condition detected in the INJ 1 injector bank circuit b) INJ 2 PEAK CURRENT — High resistance condition detected in the INJ 2 injector bank circuit
27	a) INJ 1 CONTROL CKT — INJ 1 injector bank driver stage does not respond properly to the control signal b) INJ 2 CONTROL CKT — INJ 2 injector bank driver stage does not respond properly to the control signal

ECM TROUBLE CODES (cont'd)

Code	Explanation
31	PURGE SOLENOID CKT—An open or shorted condition detected in the purge solenoid circuit
32	a) EGR SOLENOID CIRCUIT—An open or shorted condition detected in the Exhaust Gas Recirculation (EGR) solenoid circuit—check engine lamp ON—California only b) EGR SYSTEM CIRCUIT—Required change in fuel/air ratio not detected during diagnostic test—check engine lamp ON—California only
33	A/C CLUTCH RELAY CKT—An open or shorted condition detected in the air conditioning clutch relay circuit
34	S/C SERVO SOLENOIDS—An open or shorted condition detected in the speed control vacuum or vent solenoid circuits
35	RADIATOR FAN RELAY—An open or shorted condition detected in the radiator fan relay circuit
36	WASTEGATE SOLENOID—An open or shorted condition detected in the turbocharger wastegate control solenoid circuit—check engine lamp ON—California only
41	CHARGING SYSTEM CKT—Output driver stage for alternator field does not respond properly to the voltage regulator control signal
42	a) ASD RELAY CIRCUIT—An open or shorted condition detected in the auto shutdown relay circuit b) Z1 VOLTAGE SENSE—No Z1 voltage sensed when the auto shutdown relay is energized
43	IGNITION CONTROL CKT—Output driver stage for ignition coil does not respond properly to the dwell control signal
44	FJ2 VOLTAGE SENSE—No FJ2 voltage present at the logic board during controller operation
45	BOOST LIMIT EXCEEDED—Manifold Absolute Pressure (MAP) reading above overboost limit detected during controller operation
46	BATTERY VOLTAGE HIGH—Battery voltage sense input above target charging voltage during engine operation—check engine lamp ON—California only
47	BATTERY VOLTAGE LOW—Battery voltage sense input below target charging voltage during engine operation
51	LEAN F/A CONDITION—Oxygen sensor signal input indcates lean fuel/air ratio condition during engine operation—check engine lamp ON—California only
52	RICK F/A CONDITION—Oxygen sensor signal input indicates righ fuel/air ratio condition during engine operation—check engine lamp ON—California only
53	INTERNAL SELF-TEST—Internal engine controller fault condition detected
54	SYNC PICK-UP SIGNAL—No fuel sync signal detected during engine rotation.
55	Completion of fault code display on the "Check Engine" lamp
61	BARO READ SOLENOID—An open or shorted condition detected in the baro read solenoid circuit—check engine lamp ON
62	EMR MILAGE ACCUM—Unsuccessful attempt to update EMR mileage in the controller EEPROM
63	EEPROM WRITE DENIED—Unsuccessful attempt to write to an EEPROM location by the controller or unrecognized fault ID received by the DRB-II
	FAULT CODE ERROR—Unrecognized fault ID received by the DRB-II

Year – 1989
Model – Daytona
Engine – 2.5L (153 cid) EFI 4 cyl
Engine Code – VIN K

ECM TROUBLE CODES

Code	Explanation
11	IGN REFERENCE SIGNAL – No distributor reference signal detected during engine cranking
12	No. of key-on's since last fault or since faults were erased – Direct battery input to controller disconnected within the last 50–100 ignition key-on's
13	a) MAP PNEUMATIC SIGNAL – No variation in Manifold Absolute Pressure (MAP) sensor signal is detected – check engine lamp ON – California only b) MAP PNEUMATIC CHANGE – No difference is recognized between the engine Manifold Absolute Pressure (MAP) reading and the stored barometric pressure reading – check engine lamp ON – California only
14	a) MAP VOLTAGE TOO LOW – Manifold Absolute Pressure (MAP) sensor input below minimum acceptable voltage – check engine lamp ON – California only b) MAP VOLTAGE TOO HIGH – Manifold Absolute Pressure (MAP) sensor input above maximum acceptable voltage – check engine lamp ON – California only
15	VEHICLE SPEED SIGNAL – No distance sensor signal detected during road load conditions – check engine lamp ON – California only
16	BATTERY INPUT SENSE – Battery voltage sense input not detected during engine running – check engine lamp ON – California only
17	LOW ENGINE TEMP – Engine coolant temperature remains below normal operating temperatures during vehicle travel – thermostat
21	OXYGEN SENSOR SIGNAL – Neither rich or lean condition is detected from the oxygen sensor input – check engine lamp ON – California only
22	a) COOLANT VOLTAGE LOW – Coolant Temperature Sensor (CTS) input below the minimum acceptable voltage – check engine lamp ON – California only b) COOLANT VOLTAGE HIGH – Coolant Temperature Sensor (CTS) input above the maximum acceptable voltage – check engine lamp ON – California only
23	a) T/B TEMP VOLTAGE LOW – Throttle body temperature sensor input below the minimum acceptable voltage b) T/B TEMP VOLTAGE HI – Throttle body temperature sensor input above the maximum acceptable voltage
24	a) TPS VOLTAGE LOW – Throttle Position Sensor (TPS) input below the minimum acceptable voltage – check engine lamp ON – California only b) TPS VOLTAGE HIGH – Throttle Position Sensor (TPS) input above the maximum acceptable voltage – check engine lamp ON – California only
25	AIS MOTOR CIRCUITS – A shorted condition detected in 1 or more of the AIS control circuits – check engine lamp ON – California only
26	INJ 1 PEAK CURRENT – High resistance condition detected in the injector output circuit
27	INJ 1 CONTROL CKT – Injector output driver stage does not respond properly to the control signal
31	PURGE SOLENOID CKT – An open or shorted condition detected in the purge solenoid circuit – check engine lamp ON – California only
32	a) EGR SOLENOID CIRCUIT – An open or shorted condition detected in the Exhaust Gas Recirculation (EGR) solenoid circuit – check engine lamp ON – California only b) EGR SYSTEM FAILURE – Required change in fuel/air ratio not detected during diagnostic test – check engine lamp ON – California only
33	A/C CLUTCH RELAY CKT – An open or shorted condition detected in the air conditioning clutch relay circuit
34	S/C SERVO SOLENOIDS – An open or shorted condition detected in the speed control vacuum or vent solenoid circuits

ECM TROUBLE CODES (cont'd)

Code	Explanation
35	RADIATOR FAN RELAY—An open or shorted condition detected in the radiator fan relay circuit
37	PTU SOLENOID CIRCUIT—An open or shorted condition detected in the torque converter part throttle unlock solenoid circuit
41	CHARGING SYSTEM CKT—Output driver stage for alternator field does not respond properly to the voltage regulator control signal
42	ASD RELAY CIRCUIT—An open or shorted condition detected in the auto shutdown relay circuit
43	IGNITION CONTROL CKT—Output driver stage for ignition coil does not respond properly to the dwell control signal
44	FJ2 VOLTAGE SENSE—No FJ2 voltage present at the logic board during controller operation
46	BATTERY VOLTAGE HIGH—Battery voltage sense input above target charging voltage during engine operation—check engine lamp ON—California only
47	BATTERY VOLTAGE LOW—Battery voltage sense input below target charging voltage during engine operation
51	LEAN F/A CONDITION—Oxygen sensor signal input indcates lean fuel/air ratio condition during engine operation—check engine lamp ON—California only
52	a) RICH F/A CONDITION—Oxygen sensor signal input indicates righ fuel/air ratio condition during engine operation—check engine lamp ON—California only
	b) EXCESSIVE LEANING—Adaptive fuel value leaned excessively due to a sustained rich condition—check engine lamp ON—California only
53	INTERNAL SELF-TEST—Internal engine controller fault condition detected
55	Completion of fault code display on the "Check Engine" lamp
62	EMR MILEAGE ACCUM—Unsuccessful attempt to update EMR mileage in the controller EEPROM
63	EEPROM WRITE DENIED—Unsuccessful attempt to write to an EEPROM location by the controller
	FAULT CODE ERROR—Unrecognized fault ID received by the DRB-II

Year—1989
Model—Shadow
Engine—2.2L (135 cid) EFI 4 cyl
Engine Code—VIN D

ECM TROUBLE CODES

Code	Explanation
11	IGN REFERENCE SIGNAL—No distributor reference signal detected during engine cranking
12	No. of key-on's since last fault or since faults were erased—Direct battery input to controller disconnected within the last 50–100 ignition key-on's
13	a) MAP PNEUMATIC SIGNAL—No variation in Manifold Absolute Pressure (MAP) sensor signal is detected—check engine lamp ON—California only
	b) MAP PNEUMATIC CHANGE—No differrence is recognized between the engine Manifold Absolute Pressure (MAP) reading and the stored barometric pressure reading—check engine lamp ON—California only
14	a) MAP VOLTAGE TOO LOW—Manifold Absolute Pressure (MAP) sensor input below minimum acceptable voltage—check engine lamp ON—California only
	b) MAP VOLTAGE TOO HIGH—Manifold Absolute Pressure (MAP) sensor input above maximum acceptable voltage—check engine lamp ON—California only
15	VEHICLE SPEED SIGNAL—No distance sensor signal detected during road load conditions—check engine lamp ON—California only
16	BATTERY INPUT SENSE—Battery voltage sense input not detected during engine running—check engine lamp ON—California only

ECM TROUBLE CODES (cont'd)

Code	Explanation
17	LOW ENGINE TEMP — Engine coolant temperature remains below normal operating temperatures during vehicle travel — thermostat
21	OXYGEN SENSOR SIGNAL — Neither rich or lean condition is detected from the oxygen sensor input — check engine lamp ON — California only
22	a) COOLANT VOLTAGE LOW — Coolant Temperature Sensor (CTS) input below the minimum acceptable voltage — check engine lamp ON — California only b) COOLANT VOLTAGE HIGH — Coolant Temperature Sensor (CTS) input above the maximum acceptable voltage — check engine lamp ON — California only
23	a) T/B TEMP VOLTAGE LOW — Throttle body temperature sensor input below the minimum acceptable voltage b) T/B TEMP VOLTAGE HI — Throttle body temperature sensor input above the maximum acceptable voltage
24	a) TPS VOLTAGE LOW — Throttle Position Sensor (TPS) input below the minimum acceptable voltage — check engine lamp ON — California only b) TPS VOLTAGE HIGH — Throttle Position Sensor (TPS) input above the maximum acceptable voltage — check engine lamp ON — California only
25	AIS MOTOR CIRCUITS — A shorted condition detected in 1 or more of the AIS control circuits — check engine lamp ON — California only
26	INJ 1 PEAK CURRENT — High resistance condition detected in the injector output circuit
27	INJ 1 CONTROL CKT — Injector output driver stage does not respond properly to the control signal
31	PURGE SOLENOID CKT — An open or shorted condition detected in the purge solenoid circuit — check engine lamp ON — California only
32	a) EGR SOLENOID CIRCUIT — An open or shorted condition detected in the Exhaust Gas Recirculation (EGR) solenoid circuit — check engine lamp ON — California only b) EGR SYSTEM FAILURE — Required change in fuel/air ratio not detected during diagnostic test — check engine lamp ON — California only
33	A/C CLUTCH RELAY CKT — An open or shorted condition detected in the air conditioning clutch relay circuit
34	S/C SERVO SOLENOIDS — An open or shorted condition detected in the speed control vacuum or vent solenoid circuits
35	RADIATOR FAN RELAY — An open or shorted condition detected in the radiator fan relay circuit
37	PTU SOLENOID CIRCUIT — An open or shorted condition detected in the torque converter part throttle unlock solenoid circuit
41	CHARGING SYSTEM CKT — Output driver stage for alternator field does not respond properly to the voltage regulator control signal
42	ASD RELAY CIRCUIT — An open or shorted condition detected in the auto shutdown relay circuit
43	IGNITION CONTROL CKT — Output driver stage for ignition coil does not respond properly to the dwell control signal
44	FJ2 VOLTAGE SENSE — No FJ2 voltage present at the logic board during controller operation
46	BATTERY VOLTAGE HIGH — Battery voltage sense input above target charging voltage during engine operation — check engine lamp ON — California only
47	BATTERY VOLTAGE LOW — Battery voltage sense input below target charging voltage during engine operation
51	LEAN F/A CONDITION — Oxygen sensor signal input indcates lean fuel/air ratio condition during engine operation — check engine lamp ON — California only
52	a) RICH F/A CONDITION — Oxygen sensor signal input indicates righ fuel/air ratio condition during engine operation — check engine lamp ON — California only b) EXCESSIVE LEANING — Adaptive fuel value leaned excessively due to a sustained rich condition — check engine lamp ON — California only
53	INTERNAL SELF-TEST — Internal engine controller fault condition detected
55	Completion of fault code display on the ''Check Engine'' lamp
62	EMR MILEAGE ACCUM — Unsuccessful attempt to update EMR mileage in the controller EEPROM

ECM TROUBLE CODES (cont'd)

Code	Explanation
63	EEPROM WRITE DENIED — Unsuccessful attempt to write to an EEPROM location by the controller
	FAULT CODE ERROR — Unrecognized fault ID received by the DRB-II

Year — 1989
Model — Shadow
Engine — 2.5L (153 cid) EFI 4 cyl
Engine Code — VIN K

ECM TROUBLE CODES

Code	Explanation
11	IGN REFERENCE SIGNAL — No distributor reference signal detected during engine cranking
12	No. of key-on's since last fault or since faults were erased — Direct battery input to controller disconnected within the last 50–100 ignition key-on's
13	a) MAP PNEUMATIC SIGNAL — No variation in Manifold Absolute Pressure (MAP) sensor signal is detected — check engine lamp ON — California only b) MAP PNEUMATIC CHANGE — No differrence is recognized between the engine Manifold Absolute Pressure (MAP) reading and the stored barometric pressure reading — check engine lamp ON — California only
14	a) MAP VOLTAGE TOO LOW — Manifold Absolute Pressure (MAP) sensor input below minimum acceptable voltage — check engine lamp ON — California only b) MAP VOLTAGE TOO HIGH — Manifold Absolute Pressure (MAP) sensor input above maximum acceptable voltage — check engine lamp ON — California only
15	VEHICLE SPEED SIGNAL — No distance sensor signal detected during road load conditions — check engine lamp ON — California only
16	BATTERY INPUT SENSE — Battery voltage sense input not detected during engine running — check engine lamp ON — California only
17	LOW ENGINE TEMP — Engine coolant temperature remains below normal operating temperatures during vehicle travel — thermostat
21	OXYGEN SENSOR SIGNAL — Neither rich or lean condition is detected from the oxygen sensor input — check engine lamp ON — California only
22	a) COOLANT VOLTAGE LOW — Coolant Temperature Sensor (CTS) input below the minimum acceptable voltage — check engine lamp ON — California only b) COOLANT VOLTAGE HIGH — Coolant Temperature Sensor (CTS) input above the maximum acceptable voltage — check engine lamp ON — California only
23	a) T/B TEMP VOLTAGE LOW — Throttle body temperature sensor input below the minimum acceptable voltage b) T/B TEMP VOLTAGE HI — Throttle body temperature sensor input above the maximum acceptable voltage
24	a) TPS VOLTAGE LOW — Throttle Position Sensor (TPS) input below the minimum acceptable voltage — check engine lamp ON — California only b) TPS VOLTAGE HIGH — Throttle Position Sensor (TPS) input above the maximum acceptable voltage — check engine lamp ON — California only
25	AIS MOTOR CIRCUITS — A shorted condition detected in 1 or more of the AIS control circuits — check engine lamp ON — California only
26	INJ 1 PEAK CURRENT — High resistance condition detected in the injector output circuit
27	INJ 1 CONTROL CKT — Injector output driver stage does not respond properly to the control signal
31	PURGE SOLENOID CKT — An open or shorted condition detected in the purge solenoid circuit — check engine lamp ON — California only

ECM TROUBLE CODES (cont'd)

Code	Explanation
32	a) EGR SOLENOID CIRCUIT—An open or shorted condition detected in the Exhaust Gas Recirculation (EGR) solenoid circuit—check engine lamp ON—California only b) EGR SYSTEM FAILURE—Required change in fuel/air ratio not detected during diagnostic test—check engine lamp ON—California only
33	A/C CLUTCH RELAY CKT—An open or shorted condition detected in the air conditioning clutch relay circuit
34	S/C SERVO SOLENOIDS—An open or shorted condition detected in the speed control vacuum or vent solenoid circuits
35	RADIATOR FAN RELAY—An open or shorted condition detected in the radiator fan relay circuit
37	PTU SOLENOID CIRCUIT—An open or shorted condition detected in the torque converter part throttle unlock solenoid circuit
41	CHARGING SYSTEM CKT—Output driver stage for alternator field does not respond properly to the voltage regulator control signal
42	ASD RELAY CIRCUIT—An open or shorted condition detected in the auto shutdown relay circuit
43	IGNITION CONTROL CKT—Output driver stage for ignition coil does not respond properly to the dwell control signal
44	FJ2 VOLTAGE SENSE—No FJ2 voltage present at the logic board during controller operation
46	BATTERY VOLTAGE HIGH—Battery voltage sense input above target charging voltage during engine operation—check engine lamp ON—California only
47	BATTERY VOLTAGE LOW—Battery voltage sense input below target charging voltage during engine operation
51	LEAN F/A CONDITION—Oxygen sensor signal input indcates lean fuel/air ratio condition during engine operation—check engine lamp ON—California only
52	a) RICH F/A CONDITION—Oxygen sensor signal input indicates righ fuel/air ratio condition during engine operation—check engine lamp ON—California only b) EXCESSIVE LEANING—Adaptive fuel value leaned excessively due to a sustained rich condition—check engine lamp ON—California only
53	INTERNAL SELF-TEST—Internal engine controller fault condition detected
55	Completion of fault code display on the ''Check Engine'' lamp
62	EMR MILEAGE ACCUM—Unsuccessful attempt to update EMR mileage in the controller EEPROM
63	EEPROM WRITE DENIED—Unsuccessful attempt to write to an EEPROM location by the controller
	FAULT CODE ERROR—Unrecognized fault ID received by the DRB-II

Year—1989
Model—Shadow
Engine—2.5L (153 cid) Turbo I 4 cyl
Engine Code—VIN J

ECM TROUBLE CODES

Code	Explanation
11	IGN REFERENCE SIGNAL—No distributor reference signal detected during engine cranking
12	No. or key-on's since last fault or since faults were erased—Direct battery input to controller disconnected within the last 50–100 ignition key-on's
13	a) MAP PNEUMATIC SIGNAL—No variation in Manifold Absolute Pressure (MAP) sensor signal is detected—check engine lamp ON—California only b) MAP PNEUMATIC CHANGE—No differrence is recognized between the engine Manifold Absolute Pressure (MAP) reading and the stored barometric pressure reading—check engine lamp ON—California only

ECM TROUBLE CODES (cont'd)

Code	Explanation
14	a) MAP VOLTAGE TOO LOW—Manifold Absolute Pressure (MAP) sensor input below minimum acceptable voltage—check engine lamp ON—California only b) MAP VOLTAGE TOO HIGH—Manifold Absolute Pressure (MAP) sensor input above maximum acceptable voltage—check engine lamp ON—California only
15	VEHICLE SPEED SIGNAL—No distance sensor signal detected during road load conditions—check engine lamp ON—California only
16	BATTERY INPUT SENSE—Battery voltage sense input not detected during engine running—check engine lamp ON—California only
17	LOW ENGINE TEMP—Engine coolant temperature remains below normal operating temperatures during vehicle travel—thermostat
21	OXYGEN SENSOR SIGNAL—Neither rich or lean condition is detected from the oxygen sensor input—check engine lamp ON—California only
22	a) COOLANT VOLTAGE LOW—Coolant Temperature Sensor (CTS) input below the minimum acceptable voltage—check engine lamp ON—California only b) COOLANT VOLTAGE HIGH—Coolant Temperature Sensor (CTS) input above the maximum acceptable voltage—check engine lamp ON—California only
24	a) TPS VOLTAGE LOW—Throttle Position Sensor (TPS) input below the minimum acceptable voltage—check engine lamp ON—California only b) TPS VOLTAGE HIGH—Throttle Position Sensor (TPS) input above the maximum acceptable voltage—check engine lamp ON—California only
25	AIS MOTOR CIRCUITS—A shorted condition detected in 1 or more of the AIS control circuits—check engine lamp ON—California only
26	a) INJ 1 PEAK CURRENT—High resistance condition detected in the INJ 1 injector bank circuit b) INJ 2 PEAK CURRENT—High resistance condition detected in the INJ 2 injector bank circuit
27	a) INJ 1 CONTROL CKT—INJ 1 injector bank driver stage does not respond properly to the control signal b) INJ 2 CONTROL CKT—INJ 2 injector bank driver stage does not respond properly to the control signal
31	PURGE SOLENOID CKT—An open or shorted condition detected in the purge solenoid circuit
32	a) EGR SOLENOID CIRCUIT—An open or shorted condition detected in the Exhaust Gas Recirculation (EGR) solenoid circuit—check engine lamp ON—California only b) EGR SYSTEM CIRCUIT—Required change in fuel/air ratio not detected during diagnostic test—check engine lamp ON—California only
33	A/C CLUTCH RELAY CKT—An open or shorted condition detected in the air conditioning clutch relay circuit
34	S/C SERVO SOLENOIDS—An open or shorted condition detected in the speed control vacuum or vent solenoid circuits
35	RADIATOR FAN RELAY—An open or shorted condition detected in the radiator fan relay circuit
36	WASTEGATE SOLENOID—An open or shorted condition detected in the turbocharger wastegate control solenoid circuit—check engine lamp ON—California only
41	CHARGING SYSTEM CKT—Output driver stage for alternator field does not respond properly to the voltage regulator control signal
42	a) ASD RELAY CIRCUIT—An open or shorted condition detected in the auto shutdown relay circuit b) Z1 VOLTAGE SENSE—No Z1 voltage sensed when the auto shutdown relay is energized
43	IGNITION CONTROL CKT—Output driver stage for ignition coil does not respond properly to the dwell control signal
44	FJ2 VOLTAGE SENSE—No FJ2 voltage present at the logic board during controller operation
45	BOOST LIMIT EXCEEDED—Manifold Absolute Pressure (MAP) reading above overboost limit detected during controller operation
46	BATTERY VOLTAGE HIGH—Battery voltage sense input above target charging voltage during engine operation—check engine lamp ON—California only

ECM TROUBLE CODES (cont'd)

Code	Explanation
47	BATTERY VOLTAGE LOW — Battery voltage sense input below target charging voltage during engine operation
51	LEAN F/A CONDITION — Oxygen sensor signal input indcates lean fuel/air ratio condition during engine operation — check engine lamp ON — California only
52	RICK F/A CONDITION — Oxygen sensor signal input indicates righ fuel/air ratio condition during engine operation — check engine lamp ON — California only
53	INTERNAL SELF-TEST — Internal engine controller fault condition detected
54	SYNC PICK-UP SIGNAL — No fuel sync signal detected during engine rotation.
55	Completion of fault code display on the "Check Engine" lamp
61	BARO READ SOLENOID — An open or shorted condition detected in the baro read solenoid circuit — check engine lamp ON
62	EMR MILAGE ACCUM — Unsuccessful attempt to update EMR mileage in the controller EEPROM
63	EEPROM WRITE DENIED — Unsuccessful attempt to write to an EEPROM location by the controller or unrecognized fault ID received by the DRB-II
	FAULT CODE ERROR — Unrecognized fault ID received by the DRB-II

Year — 1989
Model — Dynasty
Engine — 2.5L (153 cid) EFI 4 cyl
Engine Code — VIN K

ECM TROUBLE CODES

Code	Explanation
11	IGN REFERENCE SIGNAL — No distributor reference signal detected during engine cranking
12	No. of key-on's since last fault or since faults were erased — Direct battery input to controller disconnected within the last 50–100 ignition key-on's
13	a) MAP PNEUMATIC SIGNAL — No variation in Manifold Absolute Pressure (MAP) sensor signal is detected — check engine lamp ON — California only b) MAP PNEUMATIC CHANGE — No differrence is recognized between the engine Manifold Absolute Pressure (MAP) reading and the stored barometric pressure reading — check engine lamp ON — California only
14	a) MAP VOLTAGE TOO LOW — Manifold Absolute Pressure (MAP) sensor input below minimum acceptable voltage — check engine lamp ON — California only b) MAP VOLTAGE TOO HIGH — Manifold Absolute Pressure (MAP) sensor input above maximum acceptable voltage — check engine lamp ON — California only
15	VEHICLE SPEED SIGNAL — No distance sensor signal detected during road load conditions — check engine lamp ON — California only
16	BATTERY INPUT SENSE — Battery voltage sense input not detected during engine running — check engine lamp ON — California only
17	LOW ENGINE TEMP — Engine coolant temperature remains below normal operating temperatures during vehicle travel — thermostat
21	OXYGEN SENSOR SIGNAL — Neither rich or lean condition is detected from the oxygen sensor input — check engine lamp ON — California only
22	a) COOLANT VOLTAGE LOW — Coolant Temperature Sensor (CTS) input below the minimum acceptable voltage — check engine lamp ON — California only b) COOLANT VOLTAGE HIGH — Coolant Temperature Sensor (CTS) input above the maximum acceptable voltage — check engine lamp ON — California only

ECM TROUBLE CODES (cont'd)

Code	Explanation
23	a) T/B TEMP VOLTAGE LOW — Throttle body temperature sensor input below the minimum acceptable voltage b) T/B TEMP VOLTAGE HI — Throttle body temperature sensor input above the maximum acceptable voltage
24	a) TPS VOLTAGE LOW — Throttle Position Sensor (TPS) input below the minimum acceptable voltage — check engine lamp ON — California only b) TPS VOLTAGE HIGH — Throttle Position Sensor (TPS) input above the maximum acceptable voltage — check engine lamp ON — California only
25	AIS MOTOR CIRCUITS — A shorted condition detected in 1 or more of the AIS control circuits — check engine lamp ON — California only
26	INJ 1 PEAK CURRENT — High resistance condition detected in the injector output circuit
27	INJ 1 CONTROL CKT — Injector output driver stage does not respond properly to the control signal
31	PURGE SOLENOID CKT — An open or shorted condition detected in the purge solenoid circuit — check engine lamp ON — California only
32	a) EGR SOLENOID CIRCUIT — An open or shorted condition detected in the Exhaust Gas Recirculation (EGR) solenoid circuit — check engine lamp ON — California only b) EGR SYSTEM FAILURE — Required change in fuel/air ratio not detected during diagnostic test — check engine lamp ON — California only
33	A/C CLUTCH RELAY CKT — An open or shorted condition detected in the air conditioning clutch relay circuit
34	S/C SERVO SOLENOIDS — An open or shorted condition detected in the speed control vacuum or vent solenoid circuits
35	RADIATOR FAN RELAY — An open or shorted condition detected in the radiator fan relay circuit
37	PTU SOLENOID CIRCUIT — An open or shorted condition detected in the torque converter part throttle unlock solenoid circuit
41	CHARGING SYSTEM CKT — Output driver stage for alternator field does not respond properly to the voltage regulator control signal
42	ASD RELAY CIRCUIT — An open or shorted condition detected in the auto shutdown relay circuit
43	IGNITION CONTROL CKT — Output driver stage for ignition coil does not respond properly to the dwell control signal
44	FJ2 VOLTAGE SENSE — No FJ2 voltage present at the logic board during controller operation
46	BATTERY VOLTAGE HIGH — Battery voltage sense input above target charging voltage during engine operation — check engine lamp ON — California only
47	BATTERY VOLTAGE LOW — Battery voltage sense input below target charging voltage during engine operation
51	LEAN F/A CONDITION — Oxygen sensor signal input indcates lean fuel/air ratio condition during engine operation — check engine lamp ON — California only
52	a) RICH F/A CONDITION — Oxygen sensor signal input indicates righ fuel/air ratio condition during engine operation — check engine lamp ON — California only b) EXCESSIVE LEANING — Adaptive fuel value leaned excessively due to a sustained rich condition — check engine lamp ON — California only
53	INTERNAL SELF-TEST — Internal engine controller fault condition detected
55	Completion of fault code display on the "Check Engine" lamp
62	EMR MILEAGE ACCUM — Unsuccessful attempt to update EMR mileage in the controller EEPROM
63	EEPROM WRITE DENIED — Unsuccessful attempt to write to an EEPROM location by the controller
	FAULT CODE ERROR — Unrecognized fault ID received by the DRB-II

Year – 1989
Model – Dynasty
Engine – 3.0L (181 cid) MPFI V6
Engine Code – VIN 3

ECM TROUBLE CODES

Code	Explanation
11	IGN REFERENCE SIGNAL — No distributor reference signal detected during engine cranking
12	No. or key-on's since last fault or since faults were erased — Direct battery input to controller disconnected within the last 50–100 ignition key-on's
13	a) MAP PNEUMATIC SIGNAL — No variation in Manifold Absolute Pressure (MAP) sensor signal is detected — check engine lamp ON — California only b) MAP PNEUMATIC CHANGE — No differrence is recognized between the engine Manifold Absolute Pressure (MAP) reading and the stored barometric pressure reading — check engine lamp ON — California only
14	a) MAP VOLTAGE TOO LOW — Manifold Absolute Pressure (MAP) sensor input below minimum acceptable voltage — check engine lamp ON — California only b) MAP VOLTAGE TOO HIGH — Manifold Absolute Pressure (MAP) above maximum acceptable voltage — check engine lamp ON — California only
15	VEHICLE SPEED SIGNAL — No distance sensor signal detected during road load conditions — check engine lamp ON — California only
16	BATTERY INPUT SENSE — Battery voltage sense input not detected during engine running — check engine lamp ON — California only
17	LOW ENGINE TEMP — Engine coolant temperature remains below normal operating temperatures during vehicle travel — thermostat
21	OXYGEN SENSOR SIGNAL — Neither rich or lean condition is detected from the oxygen sensor input — check engine lamp ON — California only
22	a) COOLANT VOLTAGE LOW — Coolant Temperature Sensor (CTS) input below the minimum acceptable voltage — check engine lamp ON — California only b) COOLANT VOLTAGE HIGH — Coolant Temperature Sensor (CTS) input above the maximum acceptable voltage — check engine lamp ON — California only
24	a) TPS VOLTAGE LOW — Throttle Position Sensor (TPS) input below the minimum acceptable voltage b) TPS VOLTAGE HIGH — Throttle Position Sensor (TPS) input above the maximum acceptable voltage
25	AIS MOTOR CIRCUITS — A shorted condition detected in 1 or more of the AIS control circuits
26	a) INJ 1 PEAK CURRENT — High resistance condition detected in the INJ 1 injector bank circuit — check engine lamp ON — California only b) INJ 2 PEAK CURRENT — High resistance condition detected in the INJ 2 injector bank circuit — check engine lamp ON — California only c) INJ 3 PEAK CURRENT — High resistance condition detected in the INJ 3 injector bank circuit — check engine lamp ON — California only
27	a) INJ 1 CONTROL CKT — INJ 1 injector bank driver stage does not respond properly to the control signal — check engine lamp ON — California only b) INJ 2 CONTROL CKT — INJ 2 injector bank driver stage does not respond properly to the control signal — check engine lamp ON — California only c) INJ 3 CONTROL CKT — INJ 3 injector bank driver stage does not respond properly to the control signal — check engine lamp ON — California only
31	PURGE SOLENOID CKT — An open or shorted condition detected in the purge solenoid circuit — check engine lamp ON — California only
32	a) EGR SOLENOID CIRCUIT — An open or shorted condition detected in the Exhaust Gas Recirculation (EGR) solenoid circuit — check engine lamp ON — California only b) EGR SYSTEM FAILURE — Required change in fuel/air ratio not detected during diagnostic test — check engine lamp ON — California only

ECM TROUBLE CODES (cont'd)

Code	Explanation
33	A/C CLUTCH RELAY CKT — An open or shorted condition detected in the air conditioning clutch relay circuit
34	S/C SERVO SOLENOIDS — An open or shorted condition detected in the speed control vacuum or vent solenoid circuits
35	RADIATOR FAN RELAY — An open or shorted condition detected in the radiator fan relay circuit
41	CHARGING SYSTEM CKT — Output driver stage for alternator field does not respond properly to the voltage regulator control signal
42	a) ASD RELAY CIRCUIT — An open or shorted condition detected in the auto shutdown relay circuit b) Z1 VOLTAGE SENSE — No Z1 voltage sensed when the auto shutdown relay is energized
43	IGNITION CONTROL CKT — Output driver stage for ignition coil does not respond properly to the dwell control signal
46	BATTERY VOLTAGE HIGH — Battery voltage sense input above target charging voltage during engine operation — check engine lamp ON — California only
47	BATTERY VOLTAGE LOW — Battery voltage sense input below target charging voltage during engine operation
51	LEAN F/A CONDITION — Oxygen sensor signal input indcates lean fuel/air ratio condition during engine operation
52	RICH F/A CONDITION — Oxygen sensor signal input indicates righ fuel/air ratio condition during engine operation
53	INTERNAL SELF-TEST — Internal engine controller fault condition detected
54	SYNC PICK-UP SIGNAL — No high data rate signal detected during engine rotation — check engine lamp ON — California only
55	Completion of fault code display on the "Check Engine" lamp
62	EMR MILEAGE ACCUM — Unsuccessful attempt to update EMR mileage in the controller EEPROM
63	EEPROM WRITE DENIED — Unsuccessful attempt to write to an EEPROM location by the controller or unrecognized fault ID received by the DRB-II
	FAULT CODE ERROR — Unrecognized fault ID received by the DRB-II

Year — 1989

Model — Horizon

Engine — 2.2L (135 cid) EFI 4 cyl

Engine Code — VIN D

ECM TROUBLE CODES

Code	Explanation
11	IGN REFERENCE SIGNAL — No distributor reference signal detected during engine cranking
12	No. of key-on's since last fault or since faults were erased — Direct battery input to controller disconnected within the last 50–100 ignition key-on's
13	a) MAP PNEUMATIC SIGNAL — No variation in Manifold Absolute Pressure (MAP) sensor signal is detected — check engine lamp ON — California only b) MAP PNEUMATIC CHANGE — No differrence is recognized between the engine Manifold Absolute Pressure (MAP) reading and the stored barometric pressure reading — check engine lamp ON — California only
14	a) MAP VOLTAGE TOO LOW — Manifold Absolute Pressure (MAP) sensor input below minimum acceptable voltage — check engine lamp ON — California only b) MAP VOLTAGE TOO HIGH — Manifold Absolute Pressure (MAP) sensor input above maximum acceptable voltage — check engine lamp ON — California only
15	VEHICLE SPEED SIGNAL — No distance sensor signal detected during road load conditions — check engine lamp ON — California only

ECM TROUBLE CODES (cont'd)

Code	Explanation
16	BATTERY INPUT SENSE—Battery voltage sense input not detected during engine running—check engine lamp ON—California only
17	LOW ENGINE TEMP—Engine coolant temperature remains below normal operating temperatures during vehicle travel—thermostat
21	OXYGEN SENSOR SIGNAL—Neither rich or lean condition is detected from the oxygen sensor input—check engine lamp ON—California only
22	a) COOLANT VOLTAGE LOW—Coolant Temperature Sensor (CTS) input below the minimum acceptable voltage—check engine lamp ON—California only b) COOLANT VOLTAGE HIGH—Coolant Temperature Sensor (CTS) input above the maximum acceptable voltage—check engine lamp ON—California only
23	a) T/B TEMP VOLTAGE LOW—Throttle body temperature sensor input below the minimum acceptable voltage b) T/B TEMP VOLTAGE HI—Throttle body temperature sensor input above the maximum acceptable voltage
24	a) TPS VOLTAGE LOW—Throttle Position Sensor (TPS) input below the minimum acceptable voltage—check engine lamp ON—California only b) TPS VOLTAGE HIGH—Throttle Position Sensor (TPS) input above the maximum acceptable voltage—check engine lamp ON—California only
25	AIS MOTOR CIRCUITS—A shorted condition detected in 1 or more of the AIS control circuits—check engine lamp ON—California only
26	INJ 1 PEAK CURRENT—High resistance condition detected in the injector output circuit
27	INJ 1 CONTROL CKT—Injector output driver stage does not respond properly to the control signal
31	PURGE SOLENOID CKT—An open or shorted condition detected in the purge solenoid circuit—check engine lamp ON—California only
32	a) EGR SOLENOID CIRCUIT—An open or shorted condition detected in the Exhaust Gas Recirculation (EGR) solenoid circuit—check engine lamp ON—California only b) EGR SYSTEM FAILURE—Required change in fuel/air ratio not detected during diagnostic test—check engine lamp ON—California only
33	A/C CLUTCH RELAY CKT—An open or shorted condition detected in the air conditioning clutch relay circuit
34	S/C SERVO SOLENOIDS—An open or shorted condition detected in the speed control vacuum or vent solenoid circuits
35	RADIATOR FAN RELAY—An open or shorted condition detected in the radiator fan relay circuit
37	PTU SOLENOID CIRCUIT—An open or shorted condition detected in the torque converter part throttle unlock solenoid circuit
41	CHARGING SYSTEM CKT—Output driver stage for alternator field does not respond properly to the voltage regulator control signal
42	ASD RELAY CIRCUIT—An open or shorted condition detected in the auto shutdown relay circuit
43	IGNITION CONTROL CKT—Output driver stage for ignition coil does not respond properly to the dwell control signal
44	FJ2 VOLTAGE SENSE—No FJ2 voltage present at the logic board during controller operation
46	BATTERY VOLTAGE HIGH—Battery voltage sense input above target charging voltage during engine operation—check engine lamp ON—California only
47	BATTERY VOLTAGE LOW—Battery voltage sense input below target charging voltage during engine operation
51	LEAN F/A CONDITION—Oxygen sensor signal input indcates lean fuel/air ratio condition during engine operation—check engine lamp ON—California only
52	a) RICH F/A CONDITION—Oxygen sensor signal input indicates righ fuel/air ratio condition during engine operation—check engine lamp ON—California only b) EXCESSIVE LEANING—Adaptive fuel value leaned excessively due to a sustained rich condition—check engine lamp ON—California only
53	INTERNAL SELF-TEST—Internal engine controller fault condition detected

ECM TROUBLE CODES (cont'd)

Code	Explanation
55	Completion of fault code display on the "Check Engine" lamp
62	EMR MILEAGE ACCUM—Unsuccessful attempt to update EMR mileage in the controller EEPROM
63	EEPROM WRITE DENIED—Unsuccessful attempt to write to an EEPROM location by the controller
	FAULT CODE ERROR—Unrecognized fault ID received by the DRB-II

Year—1989
Model—Sundance
Engine—2.2L (135 cid) EFI 4 cyl
Engine Code—VIN D

ECM TROUBLE CODES

Code	Explanation
11	IGN REFERENCE SIGNAL—No distributor reference signal detected during engine cranking
12	No. of key-on's since last fault or since faults were erased—Direct battery input to controller disconnected within the last 50–100 ignition key-on's
13	a) MAP PNEUMATIC SIGNAL—No variation in Manifold Absolute Pressure (MAP) sensor signal is detected—check engine lamp ON—California only b) MAP PNEUMATIC CHANGE—No differrence is recognized between the engine Manifold Absolute Pressure (MAP) reading and the stored barometric pressure reading—check engine lamp ON—California only
14	a) MAP VOLTAGE TOO LOW—Manifold Absolute Pressure (MAP) sensor input below minimum acceptable voltage—check engine lamp ON—California only b) MAP VOLTAGE TOO HIGH—Manifold Absolute Pressure (MAP) sensor input above maximum acceptable voltage—check engine lamp ON—California only
15	VEHICLE SPEED SIGNAL—No distance sensor signal detected during road load conditions—check engine lamp ON—California only
16	BATTERY INPUT SENSE—Battery voltage sense input not detected during engine running—check engine lamp ON—California only
17	LOW ENGINE TEMP—Engine coolant temperature remains below normal operating temperatures during vehicle travel—thermostat
21	OXYGEN SENSOR SIGNAL—Neither rich or lean condition is detected from the oxygen sensor input—check engine lamp ON—California only
22	a) COOLANT VOLTAGE LOW—Coolant Temperature Sensor (CTS) input below the minimum acceptable voltage—check engine lamp ON—California only b) COOLANT VOLTAGE HIGH—Coolant Temperature Sensor (CTS) input above the maximum acceptable voltage—check engine lamp ON—California only
23	a) T/B TEMP VOLTAGE LOW—Throttle body temperature sensor input below the minimum acceptable voltage b) T/B TEMP VOLTAGE HI—Throttle body temperature sensor input above the maximum acceptable voltage
24	a) TPS VOLTAGE LOW—Throttle Position Sensor (TPS) input below the minimum acceptable voltage—check engine lamp ON—California only b) TPS VOLTAGE HIGH—Throttle Position Sensor (TPS) input above the maximum acceptable voltage—check engine lamp ON—California only
25	AIS MOTOR CIRCUITS—A shorted condition detected in 1 or more of the AIS control circuits—check engine lamp ON—California only
26	INJ 1 PEAK CURRENT—High resistance condition detected in the injector output circuit
27	INJ 1 CONTROL CKT—Injector output driver stage does not respond properly to the control signal
31	PURGE SOLENOID CKT—An open or shorted condition detected in the purge solenoid circuit—check engine lamp ON—California only

ECM TROUBLE CODES (cont'd)

Code	Explanation
32	a) EGR SOLENOID CIRCUIT—An open or shorted condition detected in the Exhaust Gas Recirculation (EGR) solenoid circuit—check engine lamp ON—California only b) EGR SYSTEM FAILURE—Required change in fuel/air ratio not detected during diagnostic test—check engine lamp ON—California only
33	A/C CLUTCH RELAY CKT—An open or shorted condition detected in the air conditioning clutch relay circuit
34	S/C SERVO SOLENOIDS—An open or shorted condition detected in the speed control vacuum or vent solenoid circuits
35	RADIATOR FAN RELAY—An open or shorted condition detected in the radiator fan relay circuit
37	PTU SOLENOID CIRCUIT—An open or shorted condition detected in the torque converter part throttle unlock solenoid circuit
41	CHARGING SYSTEM CKT—Output driver stage for alternator field does not respond properly to the voltage regulator control signal
42	ASD RELAY CIRCUIT—An open or shorted condition detected in the auto shutdown relay circuit
43	IGNITION CONTROL CKT—Output driver stage for ignition coil does not respond properly to the dwell control signal
44	FJ2 VOLTAGE SENSE—No FJ2 voltage present at the logic board during controller operation
46	BATTERY VOLTAGE HIGH—Battery voltage sense input above target charging voltage during engine operation—check engine lamp ON—California only
47	BATTERY VOLTAGE LOW—Battery voltage sense input below target charging voltage during engine operation
51	LEAN F/A CONDITION—Oxygen sensor signal input indcates lean fuel/air ratio condition during engine operation—check engine lamp ON—California only
52	a) RICH F/A CONDITION—Oxygen sensor signal input indicates righ fuel/air ratio condition during engine operation—check engine lamp ON—California only b) EXCESSIVE LEANING—Adaptive fuel value leaned excessively due to a sustained rich condition—check engine lamp ON—California only
53	INTERNAL SELF-TEST—Internal engine controller fault condition detected
55	Completion of fault code display on the "Check Engine" lamp
62	EMR MILEAGE ACCUM—Unsuccessful attempt to update EMR mileage in the controller EEPROM
63	EEPROM WRITE DENIED—Unsuccessful attempt to write to an EEPROM location by the controller
	FAULT CODE ERROR—Unrecognized fault ID received by the DRB-II

Year—1989
Model—Sundance
Engine—2.5L (153 cid) Turbo I 4 cyl
Engine Code—VIN J

ECM TROUBLE CODES

Code	Explanation
11	IGN REFERENCE SIGNAL—No distributor reference signal detected during engine cranking
12	No. or key-on's since last fault or since faults were erased—Direct battery input to controller disconnected within the last 50–100 ignition key-on's
13	a) MAP PNEUMATIC SIGNAL—No variation in Manifold Absolute Pressure (MAP) sensor signal is detected—check engine lamp ON—California only b) MAP PNEUMATIC CHANGE—No differrence is recognized between the engine Manifold Absolute Pressure (MAP) reading and the stored barometric pressure reading—check engine lamp ON—California only

ECM TROUBLE CODES (cont'd)

Code	Explanation
14	a) MAP VOLTAGE TOO LOW—Manifold Absolute Pressure (MAP) sensor input below minimum acceptable voltage—check engine lamp ON—California only b) MAP VOLTAGE TOO HIGH—Manifold Absolute Pressure (MAP) sensor input above maximum acceptable voltage—check engine lamp ON—California only
15	VEHICLE SPEED SIGNAL—No distance sensor signal detected during road load conditions—check engine lamp ON—California only
16	BATTERY INPUT SENSE—Battery voltage sense input not detected during engine running—check engine lamp ON—California only
17	LOW ENGINE TEMP—Engine coolant temperature remains below normal operating temperatures during vehicle travel—thermostat
21	OXYGEN SENSOR SIGNAL—Neither rich or lean condition is detected from the oxygen sensor input—check engine lamp ON—California only
22	a) COOLANT VOLTAGE LOW—Coolant Temperature Sensor (CTS) input below the minimum acceptable voltage—check engine lamp ON—California only b) COOLANT VOLTAGE HIGH—Coolant Temperature Sensor (CTS) input above the maximum acceptable voltage—check engine lamp ON—California only
24	a) TPS VOLTAGE LOW—Throttle Position Sensor (TPS) input below the minimum acceptable voltage—check engine lamp ON—California only b) TPS VOLTAGE HIGH—Throttle Position Sensor (TPS) input above the maximum acceptable voltage—check engine lamp ON—California only
25	AIS MOTOR CIRCUITS—A shorted condition detected in 1 or more of the AIS control circuits—check engine lamp ON—California only
26	a) INJ 1 PEAK CURRENT—High resistance condition detected in the INJ 1 injector bank circuit b) INJ 2 PEAK CURRENT—High resistance condition detected in the INJ 2 injector bank circuit
27	a) INJ 1 CONTROL CKT—INJ 1 injector bank driver stage does not respond properly to the control signal b) INJ 2 CONTROL CKT—INJ 2 injector bank driver stage does not respond properly to the control signal
31	PURGE SOLENOID CKT—An open or shorted condition detected in the purge solenoid circuit
32	a) EGR SOLENOID CIRCUIT—An open or shorted condition detected in the Exhaust Gas Recirculation (EGR) solenoid circuit—check engine lamp ON—California only b) EGR SYSTEM CIRCUIT—Required change in fuel/air ratio not detected during diagnostic test—check engine lamp ON—California only
33	A/C CLUTCH RELAY CKT—An open or shorted condition detected in the air conditioning clutch relay circuit
34	S/C SERVO SOLENOIDS—An open or shorted condition detected in the speed control vacuum or vent solenoid circuits
35	RADIATOR FAN RELAY—An open or shorted condition detected in the radiator fan relay circuit
36	WASTEGATE SOLENOID—An open or shorted condition detected in the turbocharger wastegate control solenoid circuit—check engine lamp ON—California only
41	CHARGING SYSTEM CKT—Output driver stage for alternator field does not respond properly to the voltage regulator control signal
42	a) ASD RELAY CIRCUIT—An open or shorted condition detected in the auto shutdown relay circuit b) Z1 VOLTAGE SENSE—No Z1 voltage sensed when the auto shutdown relay is energized
43	IGNITION CONTROL CKT—Output driver stage for ignition coil does not respond properly to the dwell control signal
44	FJ2 VOLTAGE SENSE—No FJ2 voltage present at the logic board during controller operation
45	BOOST LIMIT EXCEEDED—Manifold Absolute Pressure (MAP) reading above overboost limit detected during controller operation
46	BATTERY VOLTAGE HIGH—Battery voltage sense input above target charging voltage during engine operation—check engine lamp ON—California only

ECM TROUBLE CODES (cont'd)

Code	Explanation
47	BATTERY VOLTAGE LOW — Battery voltage sense input below target charging voltage during engine operation
51	LEAN F/A CONDITION — Oxygen sensor signal input indcates lean fuel/air ratio condition during engine operation — check engine lamp ON — California only
52	RICK F/A CONDITION — Oxygen sensor signal input indicates righ fuel/air ratio condition during engine operation — check engine lamp ON — California only
53	INTERNAL SELF-TEST — Internal engine controller fault condition detected
54	SYNC PICK-UP SIGNAL — No fuel sync signal detected during engine rotation.
55	Completion of fault code display on the "Check Engine" lamp
61	BARO READ SOLENOID — An open or shorted condition detected in the baro read solenoid circuit — check engine lamp ON
62	EMR MILAGE ACCUM — Unsuccessful attempt to update EMR mileage in the controller EEPROM
63	EEPROM WRITE DENIED — Unsuccessful attempt to write to an EEPROM location by the controller or unrecognized fault ID received by the DRB-II
	FAULT CODE ERROR — Unrecognized fault ID received by the DRB-II

Year — 1989
Model — Sundance
Engine — 2.5L (153 cid) EFI 4 cyl
Engine Code — VIN K

ECM TROUBLE CODES

Code	Explanation
11	IGN REFERENCE SIGNAL — No distributor reference signal detected during engine cranking
12	No. of key-on's since last fault or since faults were erased — Direct battery input to controller disconnected within the last 50–100 ignition key-on's
13	a) MAP PNEUMATIC SIGNAL — No variation in Manifold Absolute Pressure (MAP) sensor signal is detected — check engine lamp ON — California only b) MAP PNEUMATIC CHANGE — No differrence is recognized between the engine Manifold Absolute Pressure (MAP) reading and the stored barometric pressure reading — check engine lamp ON — California only
14	a) MAP VOLTAGE TOO LOW — Manifold Absolute Pressure (MAP) sensor input below minimum acceptable voltage — check engine lamp ON — California only b) MAP VOLTAGE TOO HIGH — Manifold Absolute Pressure (MAP) sensor input above maximum acceptable voltage — check engine lamp ON — California only
15	VEHICLE SPEED SIGNAL — No distance sensor signal detected during road load conditions — check engine lamp ON — California only
16	BATTERY INPUT SENSE — Battery voltage sense input not detected during engine running — check engine lamp ON — California only
17	LOW ENGINE TEMP — Engine coolant temperature remains below normal operating temperatures during vehicle travel — thermostat
21	OXYGEN SENSOR SIGNAL — Neither rich or lean condition is detected from the oxygen sensor input — check engine lamp ON — California only
22	a) COOLANT VOLTAGE LOW — Coolant Temperature Sensor (CTS) input below the minimum acceptable voltage — check engine lamp ON — California only b) COOLANT VOLTAGE HIGH — Coolant Temperature Sensor (CTS) input above the maximum acceptable voltage — check engine lamp ON — California only

ECM TROUBLE CODES (cont'd)

Code	Explanation
23	a) T/B TEMP VOLTAGE LOW — Throttle body temperature sensor input below the minimum acceptable voltage b) T/B TEMP VOLTAGE HI — Throttle body temperature sensor input above the maximum acceptable voltage
24	a) TPS VOLTAGE LOW — Throttle Position Sensor (TPS) input below the minimum acceptable voltage — check engine lamp ON — California only b) TPS VOLTAGE HIGH — Throttle Position Sensor (TPS) input above the maximum acceptable voltage — check engine lamp ON — California only
25	AIS MOTOR CIRCUITS — A shorted condition detected in 1 or more of the AIS control circuits — check engine lamp ON — California only
26	INJ 1 PEAK CURRENT — High resistance condition detected in the injector output circuit
27	INJ 1 CONTROL CKT — Injector output driver stage does not respond properly to the control signal
31	PURGE SOLENOID CKT — An open or shorted condition detected in the purge solenoid circuit — check engine lamp ON — California only
32	a) EGR SOLENOID CIRCUIT — An open or shorted condition detected in the Exhaust Gas Recirculation (EGR) solenoid circuit — check engine lamp ON — California only b) EGR SYSTEM FAILURE — Required change in fuel/air ratio not detected during diagnostic test — check engine lamp ON — California only
33	A/C CLUTCH RELAY CKT — An open or shorted condition detected in the air conditioning clutch relay circuit
34	S/C SERVO SOLENOIDS — An open or shorted condition detected in the speed control vacuum or vent solenoid circuits
35	RADIATOR FAN RELAY — An open or shorted condition detected in the radiator fan relay circuit
37	PTU SOLENOID CIRCUIT — An open or shorted condition detected in the torque converter part throttle unlock solenoid circuit
41	CHARGING SYSTEM CKT — Output driver stage for alternator field does not respond properly to the voltage regulator control signal
42	ASD RELAY CIRCUIT — An open or shorted condition detected in the auto shutdown relay circuit
43	IGNITION CONTROL CKT — Output driver stage for ignition coil does not respond properly to the dwell control signal
44	FJ2 VOLTAGE SENSE — No FJ2 voltage present at the logic board during controller operation
46	BATTERY VOLTAGE HIGH — Battery voltage sense input above target charging voltage during engine operation — check engine lamp ON — California only
47	BATTERY VOLTAGE LOW — Battery voltage sense input below target charging voltage during engine operation
51	LEAN F/A CONDITION — Oxygen sensor signal input indcates lean fuel/air ratio condition during engine operation — check engine lamp ON — California only
52	a) RICH F/A CONDITION — Oxygen sensor signal input indicates righ fuel/air ratio condition during engine operation — check engine lamp ON — California only b) EXCESSIVE LEANING — Adaptive fuel value leaned excessively due to a sustained rich condition — check engine lamp ON — California only
53	INTERNAL SELF-TEST — Internal engine controller fault condition detected
55	Completion of fault code display on the "Check Engine" lamp
62	EMR MILEAGE ACCUM — Unsuccessful attempt to update EMR mileage in the controller EEPROM
63	EEPROM WRITE DENIED — Unsuccessful attempt to write to an EEPROM location by the controller
	FAULT CODE ERROR — Unrecognized fault ID received by the DRB-II

Year — 1989
Model — Acclaim
Engine — 2.5L (153 cid) EFI 4 cyl
Engine Code — VIN K

ECM TROUBLE CODES

Code	Explanation
11	IGN REFERENCE SIGNAL — No distributor reference signal detected during engine cranking
12	No. of key-on's since last fault or since faults were erased — Direct battery input to controller disconnected within the last 50–100 ignition key-on's
13	a) MAP PNEUMATIC SIGNAL — No variation in Manifold Absolute Pressure (MAP) sensor signal is detected — check engine lamp ON — California only b) MAP PNEUMATIC CHANGE — No differrence is recognized between the engine Manifold Absolute Pressure (MAP) reading and the stored barometric pressure reading — check engine lamp ON — California only
14	a) MAP VOLTAGE TOO LOW — Manifold Absolute Pressure (MAP) sensor input below minimum acceptable voltage — check engine lamp ON — California only b) MAP VOLTAGE TOO HIGH — Manifold Absolute Pressure (MAP) sensor input above maximum acceptable voltage — check engine lamp ON — California only
15	VEHICLE SPEED SIGNAL — No distance sensor signal detected during road load conditions — check engine lamp ON — California only
16	BATTERY INPUT SENSE — Battery voltage sense input not detected during engine running — check engine lamp ON — California only
17	LOW ENGINE TEMP — Engine coolant temperature remains below normal operating temperatures during vehicle travel — thermostat
21	OXYGEN SENSOR SIGNAL — Neither rich or lean condition is detected from the oxygen sensor input — check engine lamp ON — California only
22	a) COOLANT VOLTAGE LOW — Coolant Temperature Sensor (CTS) input below the minimum acceptable voltage — check engine lamp ON — California only b) COOLANT VOLTAGE HIGH — Coolant Temperature Sensor (CTS) input above the maximum acceptable voltage — check engine lamp ON — California only
23	a) T/B TEMP VOLTAGE LOW — Throttle body temperature sensor input below the minimum acceptable voltage b) T/B TEMP VOLTAGE HI — Throttle body temperature sensor input above the maximum acceptable voltage
24	a) TPS VOLTAGE LOW — Throttle Position Sensor (TPS) input below the minimum acceptable voltage — check engine lamp ON — California only b) TPS VOLTAGE HIGH — Throttle Position Sensor (TPS) input above the maximum acceptable voltage — check engine lamp ON — California only
25	AIS MOTOR CIRCUITS — A shorted condition detected in 1 or more of the AIS control circuits — check engine lamp ON — California only
26	INJ 1 PEAK CURRENT — High resistance condition detected in the injector output circuit
27	INJ 1 CONTROL CKT — Injector output driver stage does not respond properly to the control signal
31	PURGE SOLENOID CKT — An open or shorted condition detected in the purge solenoid circuit — check engine lamp ON — California only
32	a) EGR SOLENOID CIRCUIT — An open or shorted condition detected in the Exhaust Gas Recirculation (EGR) solenoid circuit — check engine lamp ON — California only b) EGR SYSTEM FAILURE — Required change in fuel/air ratio not detected during diagnostic test — check engine lamp ON — California only
33	A/C CLUTCH RELAY CKT — An open or shorted condition detected in the air conditioning clutch relay circuit
34	S/C SERVO SOLENOIDS — An open or shorted condition detected in the speed control vacuum or vent solenoid circuits

ECM TROUBLE CODES (cont'd)

Code	Explanation
35	RADIATOR FAN RELAY—An open or shorted condition detected in the radiator fan relay circuit
37	PTU SOLENOID CIRCUIT—An open or shorted condition detected in the torque converter part throttle unlock solenoid circuit
41	CHARGING SYSTEM CKT—Output driver stage for alternator field does not respond properly to the voltage regulator control signal
42	ASD RELAY CIRCUIT—An open or shorted condition detected in the auto shutdown relay circuit
43	IGNITION CONTROL CKT—Output driver stage for ignition coil does not respond properly to the dwell control signal
44	FJ2 VOLTAGE SENSE—No FJ2 voltage present at the logic board during controller operation
46	BATTERY VOLTAGE HIGH—Battery voltage sense input above target charging voltage during engine operation—check engine lamp ON—California only
47	BATTERY VOLTAGE LOW—Battery voltage sense input below target charging voltage during engine operation
51	LEAN F/A CONDITION—Oxygen sensor signal input indcates lean fuel/air ratio condition during engine operation—check engine lamp ON—California only
52	a) RICH F/A CONDITION—Oxygen sensor signal input indicates righ fuel/air ratio condition during engine operation—check engine lamp ON—California only b) EXCESSIVE LEANING—Adaptive fuel value leaned excessively due to a sustained rich condition—check engine lamp ON—California only
53	INTERNAL SELF-TEST—Internal engine controller fault condition detected
55	Completion of fault code display on the "Check Engine" lamp
62	EMR MILEAGE ACCUM—Unsuccessful attempt to update EMR mileage in the controller EEPROM
63	EEPROM WRITE DENIED—Unsuccessful attempt to write to an EEPROM location by the controller
	FAULT CODE ERROR—Unrecognized fault ID received by the DRB-II

Year—1989
Model—Acclaim
Engine—2.5L (153 cid) Turbo I 4 cyl
Engine Code—VIN J

ECM TROUBLE CODES

Code	Explanation
11	IGN REFERENCE SIGNAL—No distributor reference signal detected during engine cranking
12	No. or key-on's since last fault or since faults were erased—Direct battery input to controller disconnected within the last 50–100 ignition key-on's
13	a) MAP PNEUMATIC SIGNAL—No variation in Manifold Absolute Pressure (MAP) sensor signal is detected—check engine lamp ON—California only b) MAP PNEUMATIC CHANGE—No differrence is recognized between the engine Manifold Absolute Pressure (MAP) reading and the stored barometric pressure reading—check engine lamp ON—California only
14	a) MAP VOLTAGE TOO LOW—Manifold Absolute Pressure (MAP) sensor input below minimum acceptable voltage—check engine lamp ON—California only b) MAP VOLTAGE TOO HIGH—Manifold Absolute Pressure (MAP) sensor input above maximum acceptable voltage—check engine lamp ON—California only
15	VEHICLE SPEED SIGNAL—No distance sensor signal detected during road load conditions—check engine lamp ON—California only
16	BATTERY INPUT SENSE—Battery voltage sense input not detected during engine running—check engine lamp ON—California only

ECM TROUBLE CODES (cont'd)

Code	Explanation
17	LOW ENGINE TEMP — Engine coolant temperature remains below normal operating temperatures during vehicle travel — thermostat
21	OXYGEN SENSOR SIGNAL — Neither rich or lean condition is detected from the oxygen sensor input — check engine lamp ON — California only
22	a) COOLANT VOLTAGE LOW — Coolant Temperature Sensor (CTS) input below the minimum acceptable voltage — check engine lamp ON — California only b) COOLANT VOLTAGE HIGH — Coolant Temperature Sensor (CTS) input above the maximum acceptable voltage — check engine lamp ON — California only
24	a) TPS VOLTAGE LOW — Throttle Position Sensor (TPS) input below the minimum acceptable voltage — check engine lamp ON — California only b) TPS VOLTAGE HIGH — Throttle Position Sensor (TPS) input above the maximum acceptable voltage — check engine lamp ON — California only
25	AIS MOTOR CIRCUITS — A shorted condition detected in 1 or more of the AIS control circuits — check engine lamp ON — California only
26	a) INJ 1 PEAK CURRENT — High resistance condition detected in the INJ 1 injector bank circuit b) INJ 2 PEAK CURRENT — High resistance condition detected in the INJ 2 injector bank circuit
27	a) INJ 1 CONTROL CKT — INJ 1 injector bank driver stage does not respond properly to the control signal b) INJ 2 CONTROL CKT — INJ 2 injector bank driver stage does not respond properly to the control signal
31	PURGE SOLENOID CKT — An open or shorted condition detected in the purge solenoid circuit
32	a) EGR SOLENOID CIRCUIT — An open or shorted condition detected in the Exhaust Gas Recirculation (EGR) solenoid circuit — check engine lamp ON — California only b) EGR SYSTEM CIRCUIT — Required change in fuel/air ratio not detected during diagnostic test — check engine lamp ON — California only
33	A/C CLUTCH RELAY CKT — An open or shorted condition detected in the air conditioning clutch relay circuit
34	S/C SERVO SOLENOIDS — An open or shorted condition detected in the speed control vacuum or vent solenoid circuits
35	RADIATOR FAN RELAY — An open or shorted condition detected in the radiator fan relay circuit
36	WASTEGATE SOLENOID — An open or shorted condition detected in the turbocharger wastegate control solenoid circuit — check engine lamp ON — California only
41	CHARGING SYSTEM CKT — Output driver stage for alternator field does not respond properly to the voltage regulator control signal
42	a) ASD RELAY CIRCUIT — An open or shorted condition detected in the auto shutdown relay circuit b) Z1 VOLTAGE SENSE — No Z1 voltage sensed when the auto shutdown relay is energized
43	IGNITION CONTROL CKT — Output driver stage for ignition coil does not respond properly to the dwell control signal
44	FJ2 VOLTAGE SENSE — No FJ2 voltage present at the logic board during controller operation
45	BOOST LIMIT EXCEEDED — Manifold Absolute Pressure (MAP) reading above overboost limit detected during controller operation
46	BATTERY VOLTAGE HIGH — Battery voltage sense input above target charging voltage during engine operation — check engine lamp ON — California only
47	BATTERY VOLTAGE LOW — Battery voltage sense input below target charging voltage during engine operation
51	LEAN F/A CONDITION — Oxygen sensor signal input indcates lean fuel/air ratio condition during engine operation — check engine lamp ON — California only
52	RICK F/A CONDITION — Oxygen sensor signal input indicates righ fuel/air ratio condition during engine operation — check engine lamp ON — California only
53	INTERNAL SELF-TEST — Internal engine controller fault condition detected
54	SYNC PICK-UP SIGNAL — No fuel sync signal detected during engine rotation.
55	Completion of fault code display on the "Check Engine" lamp

ECM TROUBLE CODES (cont'd)

Code	Explanation
61	BARO READ SOLENOID — An open or shorted condition detected in the baro read solenoid circuit — check engine lamp ON
62	EMR MILAGE ACCUM — Unsuccessful attempt to update EMR mileage in the controller EEPROM
63	EEPROM WRITE DENIED — Unsuccessful attempt to write to an EEPROM location by the controller or unrecognized fault ID received by the DRB-II
	FAULT CODE ERROR — Unrecognized fault ID received by the DRB-II

Year — 1989
Model — Acclaim
Engine — 3.0L (181 cid) MPFI V6
Engine Code — VIN 3

ECM TROUBLE CODES

Code	Explanation
11	IGN REFERENCE SIGNAL — No distributor reference signal detected during engine cranking
12	No. or key-on's since last fault or since faults were erased — Direct battery input to controller disconnected within the last 50–100 ignition key-on's
13	a) MAP PNEUMATIC SIGNAL — No variation in Manifold Absolute Pressure (MAP) sensor signal is detected — check engine lamp ON — California only b) MAP PNEUMATIC CHANGE — No differrence is recognized between the engine Manifold Absolute Pressure (MAP) reading and the stored barometric pressure reading — check engine lamp ON — California only
14	a) MAP VOLTAGE TOO LOW — Manifold Absolute Pressure (MAP) sensor input below minimum acceptable voltage — check engine lamp ON — California only b) MAP VOLTAGE TOO HIGH — Manifold Absolute Pressure (MAP) above maximum acceptable voltage — check engine lamp ON — California only
15	VEHICLE SPEED SIGNAL — No distance sensor signal detected during road load conditions — check engine lamp ON — California only
16	BATTERY INPUT SENSE — Battery voltage sense input not detected during engine running — check engine lamp ON — California only
17	LOW ENGINE TEMP — Engine coolant temperature remains below normal operating temperatures during vehicle travel — thermostat
21	OXYGEN SENSOR SIGNAL — Neither rich or lean condition is detected from the oxygen sensor input — check engine lamp ON — California only
22	a) COOLANT VOLTAGE LOW — Coolant Temperature Sensor (CTS) input below the minimum acceptable voltage — check engine lamp ON — California only b) COOLANT VOLTAGE HIGH — Coolant Temperature Sensor (CTS) input above the maximum acceptable voltage — check engine lamp ON — California only
24	a) TPS VOLTAGE LOW — Throttle Position Sensor (TPS) input below the minimum acceptable voltage b) TPS VOLTAGE HIGH — Throttle Position Sensor (TPS) input above the maximum acceptable voltage
25	AIS MOTOR CIRCUITS — A shorted condition detected in 1 or more of the AIS control circuits
26	a) INJ 1 PEAK CURRENT — High resistance condition detected in the INJ 1 injector bank circuit — check engine lamp ON — California only b) INJ 2 PEAK CURRENT — High resistance condition detected in the INJ 2 injector bank circuit — check engine lamp ON — California only c) INJ 3 PEAK CURRENT — High resistance condition detected in the INJ 3 injector bank circuit — check engine lamp ON — California only

ECM TROUBLE CODES (cont'd)

Code	Explanation
27	a) INJ 1 CONTROL CKT—INJ 1 injector bank driver stage does not respond properly to the control signal—check engine lamp ON—California only b) INJ 2 CONTROL CKT—INJ 2 injector bank driver stage does not respond properly to the control signal—check engine lamp ON—California only c) INJ 3 CONTROL CKT—INJ 3 injector bank driver stage does not respond properly to the control signal—check engine lamp ON—California only
31	PURGE SOLENOID CKT—An open or shorted condition detected in the purge solenoid circuit—check engine lamp ON—California only
32	a) EGR SOLENOID CIRCUIT—An open or shorted condition detected in the Exhaust Gas Recirculation (EGR) solenoid circuit—check engine lamp ON—California only b) EGR SYSTEM FAILURE—Required change in fuel/air ratio not detected during diagnostic test—check engine lamp ON—California only
33	A/C CLUTCH RELAY CKT—An open or shorted condition detected in the air conditioning clutch relay circuit
34	S/C SERVO SOLENOIDS—An open or shorted condition detected in the speed control vacuum or vent solenoid circuits
35	RADIATOR FAN RELAY—An open or shorted condition detected in the radiator fan relay circuit
41	CHARGING SYSTEM CKT—Output driver stage for alternator field does not respond properly to the voltage regulator control signal
42	a) ASD RELAY CIRCUIT—An open or shorted condition detected in the auto shutdown relay circuit b) Z1 VOLTAGE SENSE—No Z1 voltage sensed when the auto shutdown relay is energized
43	IGNITION CONTROL CKT—Output driver stage for ignition coil does not respond properly to the dwell control signal
46	BATTERY VOLTAGE HIGH—Battery voltage sense input above target charging voltage during engine operation—check engine lamp ON—California only
47	BATTERY VOLTAGE LOW—Battery voltage sense input below target charging voltage during engine operation
51	LEAN F/A CONDITION—Oxygen sensor signal input indcates lean fuel/air ratio condition during engine operation
52	RICH F/A CONDITION—Oxygen sensor signal input indicates righ fuel/air ratio condition during engine operation
53	INTERNAL SELF-TEST—Internal engine controller fault condition detected
54	SYNC PICK-UP SIGNAL—No high data rate signal detected during engine rotation—check engine lamp ON—California only
55	Completion of fault code display on the "Check Engine" lamp
62	EMR MILEAGE ACCUM—Unsuccessful attempt to update EMR mileage in the controller EEPROM
63	EEPROM WRITE DENIED—Unsuccessful attempt to write to an EEPROM location by the controller or unrecognized fault ID received by the DRB-II
	FAULT CODE ERROR—Unrecognized fault ID received by the DRB-II

Year — 1989
Model — Reliant
Engine — 2.2L (135 cid) EFI 4 cyl
Engine Code — VIN D

ECM TROUBLE CODES

Code	Explanation
11	IGN REFERENCE SIGNAL — No distributor reference signal detected during engine cranking
12	No. of key-on's since last fault or since faults were erased — Direct battery input to controller disconnected within the last 50–100 ignition key-on's
13	a) MAP PNEUMATIC SIGNAL — No variation in Manifold Absolute Pressure (MAP) sensor signal is detected — check engine lamp ON — California only b) MAP PNEUMATIC CHANGE — No difference is recognized between the engine Manifold Absolute Pressure (MAP) reading and the stored barometric pressure reading — check engine lamp ON — California only
14	a) MAP VOLTAGE TOO LOW — Manifold Absolute Pressure (MAP) sensor input below minimum acceptable voltage — check engine lamp ON — California only b) MAP VOLTAGE TOO HIGH — Manifold Absolute Pressure (MAP) sensor input above maximum acceptable voltage — check engine lamp ON — California only
15	VEHICLE SPEED SIGNAL — No distance sensor signal detected during road load conditions — check engine lamp ON — California only
16	BATTERY INPUT SENSE — Battery voltage sense input not detected during engine running — check engine lamp ON — California only
17	LOW ENGINE TEMP — Engine coolant temperature remains below normal operating temperatures during vehicle travel — thermostat
21	OXYGEN SENSOR SIGNAL — Neither rich or lean condition is detected from the oxygen sensor input — check engine lamp ON — California only
22	a) COOLANT VOLTAGE LOW — Coolant Temperature Sensor (CTS) input below the minimum acceptable voltage — check engine lamp ON — California only b) COOLANT VOLTAGE HIGH — Coolant Temperature Sensor (CTS) input above the maximum acceptable voltage — check engine lamp ON — California only
23	a) T/B TEMP VOLTAGE LOW — Throttle body temperature sensor input below the minimum acceptable voltage b) T/B TEMP VOLTAGE HI — Throttle body temperature sensor input above the maximum acceptable voltage
24	a) TPS VOLTAGE LOW — Throttle Position Sensor (TPS) input below the minimum acceptable voltage — check engine lamp ON — California only b) TPS VOLTAGE HIGH — Throttle Position Sensor (TPS) input above the maximum acceptable voltage — check engine lamp ON — California only
25	AIS MOTOR CIRCUITS — A shorted condition detected in 1 or more of the AIS control circuits — check engine lamp ON — California only
26	INJ 1 PEAK CURRENT — High resistance condition detected in the injector output circuit
27	INJ 1 CONTROL CKT — Injector output driver stage does not respond properly to the control signal
31	PURGE SOLENOID CKT — An open or shorted condition detected in the purge solenoid circuit — check engine lamp ON — California only
32	a) EGR SOLENOID CIRCUIT — An open or shorted condition detected in the Exhaust Gas Recirculation (EGR) solenoid circuit — check engine lamp ON — California only b) EGR SYSTEM FAILURE — Required change in fuel/air ratio not detected during diagnostic test — check engine lamp ON — California only
33	A/C CLUTCH RELAY CKT — An open or shorted condition detected in the air conditioning clutch relay circuit
34	S/C SERVO SOLENOIDS — An open or shorted condition detected in the speed control vacuum or vent solenoid circuits
35	RADIATOR FAN RELAY — An open or shorted condition detected in the radiator fan relay circuit

ECM TROUBLE CODES (cont'd)

Code	Explanation
37	PTU SOLENOID CIRCUIT—An open or shorted condition detected in the torque converter part throttle unlock solenoid circuit
41	CHARGING SYSTEM CKT—Output driver stage for alternator field does not respond properly to the voltage regulator control signal
42	ASD RELAY CIRCUIT—An open or shorted condition detected in the auto shutdown relay circuit
43	IGNITION CONTROL CKT—Output driver stage for ignition coil does not respond properly to the dwell control signal
44	FJ2 VOLTAGE SENSE—No FJ2 voltage present at the logic board during controller operation
46	BATTERY VOLTAGE HIGH—Battery voltage sense input above target charging voltage during engine operation—check engine lamp ON—California only
47	BATTERY VOLTAGE LOW—Battery voltage sense input below target charging voltage during engine operation
51	LEAN F/A CONDITION—Oxygen sensor signal input indcates lean fuel/air ratio condition during engine operation—check engine lamp ON—California only
52	a) RICH F/A CONDITION—Oxygen sensor signal input indicates righ fuel/air ratio condition during engine operation—check engine lamp ON—California only b) EXCESSIVE LEANING—Adaptive fuel value leaned excessively due to a sustained rich condition—check engine lamp ON—California only
53	INTERNAL SELF-TEST—Internal engine controller fault condition detected
55	Completion of fault code display on the "Check Engine" lamp
62	EMR MILEAGE ACCUM—Unsuccessful attempt to update EMR mileage in the controller EEPROM
63	EEPROM WRITE DENIED—Unsuccessful attempt to write to an EEPROM location by the controller
	FAULT CODE ERROR—Unrecognized fault ID received by the DRB-II

Year—1989
Model—Reliant
Engine—2.5L (153 cid) EFI 4 cyl
Engine Code—VIN K

ECM TROUBLE CODES

Code	Explanation
11	IGN REFERENCE SIGNAL—No distributor reference signal detected during engine cranking
12	No. of key-on's since last fault or since faults were erased—Direct battery input to controller disconnected within the last 50–100 ignition key-on's
13	a) MAP PNEUMATIC SIGNAL—No variation in Manifold Absolute Pressure (MAP) sensor signal is detected—check engine lamp ON—California only b) MAP PNEUMATIC CHANGE—No differrence is recognized between the engine Manifold Absolute Pressure (MAP) reading and the stored barometric pressure reading—check engine lamp ON—California only
14	a) MAP VOLTAGE TOO LOW—Manifold Absolute Pressure (MAP) sensor input below minimum acceptable voltage—check engine lamp ON—California only b) MAP VOLTAGE TOO HIGH—Manifold Absolute Pressure (MAP) sensor input above maximum acceptable voltage—check engine lamp ON—California only
15	VEHICLE SPEED SIGNAL—No distance sensor signal detected during road load conditions—check engine lamp ON—California only
16	BATTERY INPUT SENSE—Battery voltage sense input not detected during engine running—check engine lamp ON—California only
17	LOW ENGINE TEMP—Engine coolant temperature remains below normal operating temperatures during vehicle travel—thermostat
21	OXYGEN SENSOR SIGNAL—Neither rich or lean condition is detected from the oxygen sensor input—check engine lamp ON—California only

ECM TROUBLE CODES (cont'd)

Code	Explanation
22	a) COOLANT VOLTAGE LOW—Coolant Temperature Sensor (CTS) input below the minimum acceptable voltage—check engine lamp ON—California only b) COOLANT VOLTAGE HIGH—Coolant Temperature Sensor (CTS) input above the maximum acceptable voltage—check engine lamp ON—California only
23	a) T/B TEMP VOLTAGE LOW—Throttle body temperature sensor input below the minimum acceptable voltage b) T/B TEMP VOLTAGE HI—Throttle body temperature sensor input above the maximum acceptable voltage
24	a) TPS VOLTAGE LOW—Throttle Position Sensor (TPS) input below the minimum acceptable voltage—check engine lamp ON—California only b) TPS VOLTAGE HIGH—Throttle Position Sensor (TPS) input above the maximum acceptable voltage—check engine lamp ON—California only
25	AIS MOTOR CIRCUITS—A shorted condition detected in 1 or more of the AIS control circuits—check engine lamp ON—California only
26	INJ 1 PEAK CURRENT—High resistance condition detected in the injector output circuit
27	INJ 1 CONTROL CKT—Injector output driver stage does not respond properly to the control signal
31	PURGE SOLENOID CKT—An open or shorted condition detected in the purge solenoid circuit—check engine lamp ON—California only
32	a) EGR SOLENOID CIRCUIT—An open or shorted condition detected in the Exhaust Gas Recirculation (EGR) solenoid circuit—check engine lamp ON—California only b) EGR SYSTEM FAILURE—Required change in fuel/air ratio not detected during diagnostic test—check engine lamp ON—California only
33	A/C CLUTCH RELAY CKT—An open or shorted condition detected in the air conditioning clutch relay circuit
34	S/C SERVO SOLENOIDS—An open or shorted condition detected in the speed control vacuum or vent solenoid circuits
35	RADIATOR FAN RELAY—An open or shorted condition detected in the radiator fan relay circuit
37	PTU SOLENOID CIRCUIT—An open or shorted condition detected in the torque converter part throttle unlock solenoid circuit
41	CHARGING SYSTEM CKT—Output driver stage for alternator field does not respond properly to the voltage regulator control signal
42	ASD RELAY CIRCUIT—An open or shorted condition detected in the auto shutdown relay circuit
43	IGNITION CONTROL CKT—Output driver stage for ignition coil does not respond properly to the dwell control signal
44	FJ2 VOLTAGE SENSE—No FJ2 voltage present at the logic board during controller operation
46	BATTERY VOLTAGE HIGH—Battery voltage sense input above target charging voltage during engine operation—check engine lamp ON—California only
47	BATTERY VOLTAGE LOW—Battery voltage sense input below target charging voltage during engine operation
51	LEAN F/A CONDITION—Oxygen sensor signal input indcates lean fuel/air ratio condition during engine operation—check engine lamp ON—California only
52	a) RICH F/A CONDITION—Oxygen sensor signal input indicates righ fuel/air ratio condition during engine operation—check engine lamp ON—California only b) EXCESSIVE LEANING—Adaptive fuel value leaned excessively due to a sustained rich condition—check engine lamp ON—California only
53	INTERNAL SELF-TEST—Internal engine controller fault condition detected
55	Completion of fault code display on the "Check Engine" lamp
62	EMR MILEAGE ACCUM—Unsuccessful attempt to update EMR mileage in the controller EEPROM
63	EEPROM WRITE DENIED—Unsuccessful attempt to write to an EEPROM location by the controller
	FAULT CODE ERROR—Unrecognized fault ID received by the DRB-II

CHRYSLER CORPORATION TRUCK

Year – 1985
Model – Dodge Mini Ram Van (FWD)
Engine – 2.2L (135 cid) 4 cyl
Engine Code – VIN C

ECM TROUBLE CODES

Code	Explanation
00	Diagnostic readout tool is receiving power.
11	Problem in the O_2 solenoid control circuit.
13	Problem in the canister purge solenoid circuit.
14	Battery has been disconnected.
17	Problem in the electronic throttle control vacuum solenoid system.
18	Problem in the vacuum operated secondary control solenoid system.
21	Problem in the distributor pick-up system.
22	O_2 system is stuck in either the full rich or full lean position.
24	Problem in the computer.
25	Problem in the radiator fan coolant sensor portion of the engine temperature dual sensor system.
26	Problem in the engine temperature portion of the engine temperature dual sensor system.
28	Problem in the distance sensor system with manual transmission.
31	Engine has not been cranked since battery was disconnected.
32	Problem in the computer.
33	Problem in the computer.
55	End of message.
88	Start of message.

Year—1985
Model—Dodge Caravan
Engine—2.2L (135 cid) 4 cyl
Engine Code—VIN C

ECM TROUBLE CODES

Code	Explanation
00	Diagnostic readout tool is receiving power.
11	Problem in the O_2 solenoid control circuit.
13	Problem in the canister purge solenoid circuit.
14	Battery has been disconnected.
17	Problem in the electronic throttle control vacuum solenoid system.
18	Problem in the vacuum operated secondary control solenoid system.
21	Problem in the distributor pick-up system.
22	O_2 system is stuck in either the full rich or full lean position.
24	Problem in the computer.
25	Problem in the radiator fan coolant sensor portion of the engine temperature dual sensor system.
26	Problem in the engine temperature portion of the engine temperature dual sensor system.
28	Problem in the distance sensor system with manual transmission.
31	Engine has not been cranked since battery was disconnected.
32	Problem in the computer.
33	Problem in the computer.
55	End of message.
88	Start of message.

Year – 1985
Model – Plymouth Voyager
Engine – 2.2L (135 cid) 4 cyl
Engine Code – VIN C

ECM TROUBLE CODES

Code	Explanation
00	Diagnostic readout tool is receiving power.
11	Problem in the O_2 solenoid control circuit.
13	Problem in the canister purge solenoid circuit.
14	Battery has been disconnected.
17	Problem in the electronic throttle control vacuum solenoid system.
18	Problem in the vacuum operated secondary control solenoid system.
21	Problem in the distributor pick-up system.
22	O_2 system is stuck in either the full rich or full lean position.
24	Problem in the computer.
25	Problem in the radiator fan coolant sensor portion of the engine temperature dual sensor system.
26	Problem in the engine temperature portion of the engine temperature dual sensor system.
28	Problem in the distance sensor system with manual transmission.
31	Engine has not been cranked since battery was disconnected.
32	Problem in the computer.
33	Problem in the computer.
55	End of message.
88	Start of message.

CHRYSLER CORPORATION
DIAGNOSTIC CODE DATA

Year – 1985
Model – Dodge D & W 100–350 (RWD)
Engine – 3.7L (225 cid) 6 cyl
Engine Code – VIN H

ECM TROUBLE CODES

Code	Explanation
00	Diagnostic readout tool is receiving power.
11	Problem in the O_2 solenoid control circuit.
13	Problem in the canister purge solenoid circuit.
14	Battery has been disconnected.
17	Problem in the electronic throttle control vacuum solenoid system.
18	Problem in the vacuum operated secondary control solenoid system.
21	Problem in the distributor pick-up system.
22	O_2 system is stuck in either the full rich or full lean position.
24	Problem in the computer.
25	Problem in the radiator fan coolant sensor portion of the engine temperature dual sensor system.
26	Problem in the engine temperature portion of the engine temperature dual sensor system.
28	Problem in the distance sensor system with manual transmission.
31	Engine has not been cranked since battery was disconnected.
32	Problem in the computer.
33	Problem in the computer.
55	End of message.
88	Start of message.

Year — 1985
Model — Vans
Engine — 3.7L (225 cid) 6 cyl
Engine Code — VIN H

ECM TROUBLE CODES

Code	Explanation
00	Diagnostic readout tool is receiving power.
11	Problem in the O_2 solenoid control circuit.
13	Problem in the canister purge solenoid circuit.
14	Battery has been disconnected.
17	Problem in the electronic throttle control vacuum solenoid system.
18	Problem in the vacuum operated secondary control solenoid system.
21	Problem in the distributor pick-up system.
22	O_2 system is stuck in either the full rich or full lean position.
24	Problem in the computer.
25	Problem in the radiator fan coolant sensor portion of the engine temperature dual sensor system.
26	Problem in the engine temperature portion of the engine temperature dual sensor system.
28	Problem in the distance sensor system with manual transmission.
31	Engine has not been cranked since battery was disconnected.
32	Problem in the computer.
33	Problem in the computer.
55	End of message.
88	Start of message.

Year — 1985
Model — Dodge D & W 100–350 (RWD)
Engine — 5.2L (318 cid) V8
Engine Code — VIN T

ECM TROUBLE CODES

Code	Explanation
00	Diagnostic readout tool is receiving power.
11	Problem in the O_2 solenoid control circuit.
13	Problem in the air Switching control solenoid circuit.
14	Battery has been disconnected within the last 20–40 key-on's.
17	Problem in the electronic throttle control solenoid system.
18	Problem in the exhaust gas recirculation solenoid.
21	Problem in the distributor pick-up system.
22	O_2 system is stuck in either the full rich or full lean position.
24	Problem in the computer.
26	Problem in the engine charge temperature sensor circuit.
31	Engine has not been cranked since battery was disconnected.
32	Problem in the computer.
33	Problem in the computer.
55	End of message.
88	Start of message.

Year – 1985
Model – Ramcharger
Engine – 5.2L (318 cid) V8
Engine Code – VIN T

ECM TROUBLE CODES

Code	Explanation
00	Diagnostic readout tool is receiving power.
11	Problem in the O_2 solenoid control circuit.
13	Problem in the air Switching control solenoid circuit.
14	Battery has been disconnected within the last 20–40 key-on's.
17	Problem in the electronic throttle control solenoid system.
18	Problem in the exhaust gas recirculation solenoid.
21	Problem in the distributor pick-up system.
22	O_2 system is stuck in either the full rich or full lean position.
24	Problem in the computer.
26	Problem in the engine charge temperature sensor circuit.
31	Engine has not been cranked since battery was disconnected.
32	Problem in the computer.
33	Problem in the computer.
55	End of message.
88	Start of message.

Year – 1985
Model – Vans
Engine – 5.2L (318 cid) V8
Engine Code – VIN T

ECM TROUBLE CODES

Code	Explanation
00	Diagnostic readout tool is receiving power.
11	Problem in the O_2 solenoid control circuit.
13	Problem in the air Switching control solenoid circuit.
14	Battery has been disconnected within the last 20–40 key-on's.
17	Problem in the electronic throttle control solenoid system.
18	Problem in the exhaust gas recirculation solenoid.
21	Problem in the distributor pick-up system.
22	O_2 system is stuck in either the full rich or full lean position.
24	Problem in the computer.
26	Problem in the engine charge temperature sensor circuit.
31	Engine has not been cranked since battery was disconnected.
32	Problem in the computer.
33	Problem in the computer.
55	End of message.
88	Start of message.

Year – 1986
Model – Plymouth Voyager (FWD)
Engine – 2.2L (135 cid) 4 cyl
Engine Code – VIN C

ECM TROUBLE CODES

Code	Explanation
00	Diagnostic readout tool is receiving power.
11	Problem in the O_2 solenoid control circuit.
13	Problem in the vacuum operated secondary control solenoid circuit.
14	Battery has been disconnected.
17	Problem in the electronic throttle control vacuum solenoid system.
18	Problem in the canister purge solenoid system.
21	Problem in the distributor pick-up system.
22	O_2 system is stuck in the full lean position.
23	O_2 system is stuck in the full rich position.
24	Problem in the computer.
25	Problem in the radiator fan coolant sensor portion of the engine temperature dual sensor system.
26	Problem in the engine temperature portion of the engine temperature dual sensor system.
28	Problem in the distance sensor system.
31	Engine has not been cranked since battery was disconnected.
32	Problem in the computer.
33	Problem in the computer.
55	End of message.
88	Start of message.

Year – 1986
Model – Dodge Mini Ram Van
Engine – 2.2L (135 cid) 4 cyl
Engine Code – VIN C

ECM TROUBLE CODES

Code	Explanation
00	Diagnostic readout tool is receiving power.
11	Problem in the O_2 solenoid control circuit.
13	Problem in the vacuum operated secondary control solenoid circuit.
14	Battery has been disconnected.
17	Problem in the electronic throttle control vacuum solenoid system.
18	Problem in the canister purge solenoid system.
21	Problem in the distributor pick-up system.
22	O_2 system is stuck in the full lean position.
23	O_2 system is stuck in the full rich position.
24	Problem in the computer.
25	Problem in the radiator fan coolant sensor portion of the engine temperature dual sensor system.
26	Problem in the engine temperature portion of the engine temperature dual sensor system.
28	Problem in the distance sensor system.
31	Engine has not been cranked since battery was disconnected.
32	Problem in the computer.
33	Problem in the computer.
55	End of message.
88	Start of message.

Year — 1986
Model — Dodge Caravan
Engine — 2.2L (135 cid) 4 cyl
Engine Code — VIN C

ECM TROUBLE CODES

Code	Explanation
00	Diagnostic readout tool is receiving power.
11	Problem in the O_2 solenoid control circuit.
13	Problem in the vacuum operated secondary control solenoid circuit.
14	Battery has been disconnected.
17	Problem in the electronic throttle control vacuum solenoid system.
18	Problem in the canister purge solenoid system.
21	Problem in the distributor pick-up system.
22	O_2 system is stuck in the full lean position.
23	O_2 system is stuck in the full rich position.
24	Problem in the computer.
25	Problem in the radiator fan coolant sensor portion of the engine temperature dual sensor system.
26	Problem in the engine temperature portion of the engine temperature dual sensor system.
28	Problem in the distance sensor system.
31	Engine has not been cranked since battery was disconnected.
32	Problem in the computer.
33	Problem in the computer.
55	End of message.
88	Start of message.

Year — 1986
Model — Dodge D & W 100–350 (RWD)
Engine — 3.7L (225 cid) 6 cyl
Engine Code — VIN H

ECM TROUBLE CODES

Code	Explanation
00	Diagnostic readout tool is receiving power.
11	Problem in the O_2 solenoid control circuit.
12	Problem in the transmission unlock relay. Ignore fault code 12 on manual transmission T–115.
13	Problem in the air switching control solenoid circuit.
14	Battery has been disconnected within the last 20–40 key-on's.
17	Problem in the electronic throttle control solenoid system.
18	Problem in the exhaust gas recirculation solenoid.
21	Problem in the distributor pick-up system.
22	O_2 system is stuck in the full lean or full rich position.
24	Problem in the computer.
25	Problem in the charge temperature switch circuit.
26	Problem in the engine temperature sensor circuit.
28	Problem in the distance sensor system.
31	Engine has not been cranked since battery was disconnected.
32	Problem in the computer.
33	Problem in the computer.
55	End of message.
88	Start of message.

Year – 1986
Model – Vans
Engine – 3.7L (225 cid) 6 cyl
Engine Code – VIN H

ECM TROUBLE CODES

Code	Explanation
00	Diagnostic readout tool is receiving power.
11	Problem in the O_2 solenoid control circuit.
12	Problem in the transmission unlock relay. Ignore fault code 12 on manual transmission T–115.
13	Problem in the air switching control solenoid circuit.
14	Battery has been disconnected within the last 20–40 key-on's.
17	Problem in the electronic throttle control solenoid system.
18	Problem in the exhaust gas recirculation solenoid.
21	Problem in the distributor pick-up system.
22	O_2 system is stuck in the full lean or full rich position.
24	Problem in the computer.
25	Problem in the charge temperature switch circuit.
26	Problem in the engine temperature sensor circuit.
28	Problem in the distance sensor system.
31	Engine has not been cranked since battery was disconnected.
32	Problem in the computer.
33	Problem in the computer.
55	End of message.
88	Start of message.

Year – 1986
Model – Ramcharger
Engine – 5.2L (318 cid) V8
Engine Code – VIN T

ECM TROUBLE CODES

Code	Explanation
00	Diagnostic readout tool is receiving power.
11	Problem in the O_2 solenoid control circuit.
12	Problem in the transmission unlock relay. Ignore fault code 12 on manual transmission T–115.
13	Problem in the air switching control solenoid circuit.
14	Battery has been disconnected within the last 20–40 key-on's.
17	Problem in the electronic throttle control solenoid system.
18	Problem in the exhaust gas recirculation solenoid.
21	Problem in the distributor pick-up system.
22	O_2 system is stuck in the full lean or full rich position.
24	Problem in the computer.
26	Problem in the charge temperature sensor circuit.
31	Engine has not been cranked since battery was disconnected.
32	Problem in the computer.
33	Problem in the computer.
55	End of message.
88	Start of message.

Year — 1986
Model — Dodge D & W 100–350 (RWD)
Engine — 5.2L (318 cid) V8
Engine Code — VIN T

ECM TROUBLE CODES

Code	Explanation
00	Diagnostic readout tool is receiving power.
11	Problem in the O_2 solenoid control circuit.
12	Problem in the transmission unlock relay. Ignore fault code 12 on manual transmission T–115.
13	Problem in the air switching control solenoid circuit.
14	Battery has been disconnected within the last 20–40 key-on's.
17	Problem in the electronic throttle control solenoid system.
18	Problem in the exhaust gas recirculation solenoid.
21	Problem in the distributor pick-up system.
22	O_2 system is stuck in the full lean or full rich position.
24	Problem in the computer.
26	Problem in the charge temperature sensor circuit.
31	Engine has not been cranked since battery was disconnected.
32	Problem in the computer.
33	Problem in the computer.
55	End of message.
88	Start of message.

Year – 1986
Model – Vans
Engine – 5.2L (318 cid) V8
Engine Code – VIN T

ECM TROUBLE CODES

Code	Explanation
00	Diagnostic readout tool is receiving power.
11	Problem in the O_2 solenoid control circuit.
12	Problem in the transmission unlock relay. Ignore fault code 12 on manual transmission T–115.
13	Problem in the air switching control solenoid circuit.
14	Battery has been disconnected within the last 20–40 key-on's.
17	Problem in the electronic throttle control solenoid system.
18	Problem in the exhaust gas recirculation solenoid.
21	Problem in the distributor pick-up system.
22	O_2 system is stuck in the full lean or full rich position.
24	Problem in the computer.
26	Problem in the charge temperature sensor circuit.
31	Engine has not been cranked since battery was disconnected.
32	Problem in the computer.
33	Problem in the computer.
55	End of message.
88	Start of message.

Year – 1987
Model – Dodge Mini Ram Van
Engine – 3.0L (181 cid) EFI V6
Engine Code – VIN 3

ECM TROUBLE CODES

Code	Explanation
11	No distributor reference pickup signal is present since the engine control module memory was cleared.
12	Memory of the engine control module has been cleared within the last 20–40 engine starts.
13	No variance in the MAP signal is detected between ignition pulses.
14	MAP sensor signal is below 0.02 or above 4.9 volts.
15	No speed sensor signal is detected over an 11 second period.
16	Battery sensing voltage drops below 4 volts for more than 4 seconds.
17	Engine coolant temperature does not reach 160°F within 8 minutes of vehicle speeds greater than 28 mph.
21	No lean or rich condition is indicated for a 2 minute time period.
22	Coolant sensor voltage is above 4.96 volts when the engine is cold or below 0.51 volts when the engine is warm.
23	Charge temperature sensor voltage is below 0.04 or above 4.96 when engine coolant temperature is above 77°F.
24	Throttle position sensor signal is below 0.16 or above 4.7 volts.
25	Proper voltage in the AIS system is not present; open circuit will not activate code.
26	Current through any of the fuel injector pairs does not reach its proper peak level.
27	Fuel control interface fails to switch properly.
31	Solenoid does not turn ON and OFF when it should.
33	Relay does not turn ON and OFF when it should.
34	Servo does not turn ON and OFF when it should.
35	Relay does not turn ON and OFF when it should.
37	Lockup solenoid does not turn ON and OFF when it should.
41	Field control fails to switch properly.
42	Relay does not turn ON and OFF when it should.
43	Spark control interface fails to switch properly.
44	Fused J2 is not present in the logic board of the engine control module.
46	Battery sense voltage is more than 1 volt above the desired control voltage for more than 20 seconds.
47	Battery sense voltage is less than 1 volt below the desired control voltage for more than 20 seconds.
51	O_2 sensor indicates a lean condition for more than 2 minutes.
52	O_2 sensor indicates a rich condition for more than 2 minutes.
53	Logic board fails.
54	No distributor synchronizer pick-up signal.
55	End of diagnostic mode.
88	Start of diagnostic mode. NOTE: This code must appear first in the diagnostic mode or fault codes will be inaccurate.
0	Oxygen feedback system is lean with the engine running.
1	Oxygen feedback system is rich with engine running.

Year – 1987
Model – Dodge Caravan
Engine – 3.0L (181 cid) EFI V6
Engine Code – VIN 3

ECM TROUBLE CODES

Code	Explanation
11	No distributor reference pickup signal is present since the engine control module memory was cleared.
12	Memory of the engine control module has been cleared within the last 20–40 engine starts.
13	No variance in the MAP signal is detected between ignition pulses.
14	MAP sensor signal is below 0.02 or above 4.9 volts.
15	No speed sensor signal is detected over an 11 second period.
16	Battery sensing voltage drops below 4 volts for more than 4 seconds.
17	Engine coolant temperature does not reach 160°F within 8 minutes of vehicle speeds greater than 28 mph.
21	No lean or rich condition is indicated for a 2 minute time period.
22	Coolant sensor voltage is above 4.96 volts when the engine is cold or below 0.51 volts when the engine is warm.
23	Charge temperature sensor voltage is below 0.04 or above 4.96 when engine coolant temperature is above 77°F.
24	Throttle position sensor signal is below 0.16 or above 4.7 volts.
25	Proper voltage in the AIS system is not present; open circuit will not activate code.
26	Current through any of the fuel injector pairs does not reach its proper peak level.
27	Fuel control interface fails to switch properly.
31	Solenoid does not turn ON and OFF when it should.
33	Relay does not turn ON and OFF when it should.
34	Servo does not turn ON and OFF when it should.
35	Relay does not turn ON and OFF when it should.
37	Lockup solenoid does not turn ON and OFF when it should.
41	Field control fails to switch properly.
42	Relay does not turn ON and OFF when it should.
43	Spark control interface fails to switch properly.
44	Fused J2 is not present in the logic board of the engine control module.
46	Battery sense voltage is more than 1 volt above the desired control voltage for more than 20 seconds.
47	Battery sense voltage is less than 1 volt below the desired control voltage for more than 20 seconds.
51	O$_2$ sensor indicates a lean condition for more than 2 minutes.
52	O$_2$ sensor indicates a rich condition for more than 2 minutes.
53	Logic board fails.
54	No distributor synchronizer pick-up signal.
55	End of diagnostic mode.
88	Start of diagnostic mode. NOTE: This code must appear first in the diagnostic mode or fault codes will be inaccurate.
0	Oxygen feedback system is lean with the engine running.
1	Oxygen feedback system is rich with engine running.

Year — 1987
Model — Plymouth Voyager
Engine — 3.0L (181 cid) EFI V6
Engine Code — VIN 3

ECM TROUBLE CODES

Code	Explanation
11	No distributor reference pickup signal is present since the engine control module memory was cleared.
12	Memory of the engine control module has been cleared within the last 20–40 engine starts.
13	No variance in the MAP signal is detected between ignition pulses.
14	MAP sensor signal is below 0.02 or above 4.9 volts.
15	No speed sensor signal is detected over an 11 second period.
16	Battery sensing voltage drops below 4 volts for more than 4 seconds.
17	Engine coolant temperature does not reach 160°F within 8 minutes of vehicle speeds greater than 28 mph.
21	No lean or rich condition is indicated for a 2 minute time period.
22	Coolant sensor voltage is above 4.96 volts when the engine is cold or below 0.51 volts when the engine is warm.
23	Charge temperature sensor voltage is below 0.04 or above 4.96 when engine coolant temperature is above 77°F.
24	Throttle position sensor signal is below 0.16 or above 4.7 volts.
25	Proper voltage in the AIS system is not present; open circuit will not activate code.
26	Current through any of the fuel injector pairs does not reach its proper peak level.
27	Fuel control interface fails to switch properly.
31	Solenoid does not turn ON and OFF when it should.
33	Relay does not turn ON and OFF when it should.
34	Servo does not turn ON and OFF when it should.
35	Relay does not turn ON and OFF when it should.
37	Lockup solenoid does not turn ON and OFF when it should.
41	Field control fails to switch properly.
42	Relay does not turn ON and OFF when it should.
43	Spark control interface fails to switch properly.
44	Fused J2 is not present in the logic board of the engine control module.
46	Battery sense voltage is more than 1 volt above the desired control voltage for more than 20 seconds.
47	Battery sense voltage is less than 1 volt below the desired control voltage for more than 20 seconds.
51	O_2 sensor indicates a lean condition for more than 2 minutes.
52	O_2 sensor indicates a rich condition for more than 2 minutes.
53	Logic board fails.
54	No distributor synchronizer pick-up signal.
55	End of diagnostic mode.
88	Start of diagnostic mode. NOTE: This code must appear first in the diagnostic mode or fault codes will be inaccurate.
0	Oxygen feedback system is lean with the engine running.
1	Oxygen feedback system is rich with engine running.

Year – 1987
Model – Dodge Mini Ram Van
Engine – 2.5L (153 cid) EFI 4 cyl
Engine Code – VIN K

ECM TROUBLE CODES

Code	Explanation
11	No distributor reference pickup signal is present since the engine control module memory was cleared.
12	Memory of the engine control module has been cleared within the last 20–40 engine starts.
13	No variance in the MAP signal is detected between ignition pulses.
14	MAP sensor signal is below 0.02 or above 4.9 volts.
15	No speed sensor signal is detected over an 11 second period.
16	Battery sensing voltage drops below 4 volts for more than 4 seconds.
17	Engine coolant temperature does not reach 160°F within 8 minutes of vehicle speeds greater than 28 mph.
21	No lean or rich condition is indicated for a 2 minute time period.
22	Coolant sensor voltage is above 4.96 volts when the engine is cold or below 0.51 volts when the engine is warm.
23	Charge temperature sensor voltage is below 0.04 or above 4.96 when engine coolant temperature is above 77°F.
24	Throttle position sensor signal is below 0.16 or above 4.7 volts.
25	Proper voltage in the AIS system is not present; open circuit will not activate code.
26	Current through any of the fuel injector pairs does not reach its proper peak level.
27	Fuel control interface fails to switch properly.
31	Solenoid does not turn ON and OFF when it should.
33	Relay does not turn ON and OFF when it should.
34	Servo does not turn ON and OFF when it should.
35	Relay does not turn ON and OFF when it should.
37	Lockup solenoid does not turn ON and OFF when it should.
41	Field control fails to switch properly.
42	Relay does not turn ON and OFF when it should.
43	Spark control interface fails to switch properly.
44	Fused J2 is not present in the logic board of the engine control module.
46	Battery sense voltage is more than 1 volt above the desired control voltage for more than 20 seconds.
47	Battery sense voltage is less than 1 volt below the desired control voltage for more than 20 seconds.
51	O$_2$ sensor indicates a lean condition for more than 2 minutes.
52	O$_2$ sensor indicates a rich condition for more than 2 minutes.
53	Logic board fails.
54	No distributor synchronizer pick-up signal.
55	End of diagnostic mode.
88	Start of diagnostic mode. NOTE: This code must appear first in the diagnostic mode or fault codes will be inaccurate.
0	Oxygen feedback system is lean with the engine running.
1	Oxygen feedback system is rich with engine running.

Year — 1987
Model — Dodge Caravan
Engine — 2.5L (153 cid) EFI 4 cyl
Engine Code — VIN K

ECM TROUBLE CODES

Code	Explanation
11	No distributor reference pickup signal is present since the engine control module memory was cleared.
12	Memory of the engine control module has been cleared within the last 20–40 engine starts.
13	No variance in the MAP signal is detected between ignition pulses.
14	MAP sensor signal is below 0.02 or above 4.9 volts.
15	No speed sensor signal is detected over an 11 second period.
16	Battery sensing voltage drops below 4 volts for more than 4 seconds.
17	Engine coolant temperature does not reach 160°F within 8 minutes of vehicle speeds greater than 28 mph.
21	No lean or rich condition is indicated for a 2 minute time period.
22	Coolant sensor voltage is above 4.96 volts when the engine is cold or below 0.51 volts when the engine is warm.
23	Charge temperature sensor voltage is below 0.04 or above 4.96 when engine coolant temperature is above 77°F.
24	Throttle position sensor signal is below 0.16 or above 4.7 volts.
25	Proper voltage in the AIS system is not present; open circuit will not activate code.
26	Current through any of the fuel injector pairs does not reach its proper peak level.
27	Fuel control interface fails to switch properly.
31	Solenoid does not turn ON and OFF when it should.
33	Relay does not turn ON and OFF when it should.
34	Servo does not turn ON and OFF when it should.
35	Relay does not turn ON and OFF when it should.
37	Lockup solenoid does not turn ON and OFF when it should.
41	Field control fails to switch properly.
42	Relay does not turn ON and OFF when it should.
43	Spark control interface fails to switch properly.
44	Fused J2 is not present in the logic board of the engine control module.
46	Battery sense voltage is more than 1 volt above the desired control voltage for more than 20 seconds.
47	Battery sense voltage is less than 1 volt below the desired control voltage for more than 20 seconds.
51	O$_2$ sensor indicates a lean condition for more than 2 minutes.
52	O$_2$ sensor indicates a rich condition for more than 2 minutes.
53	Logic board fails.
54	No distributor synchronizer pick-up signal.
55	End of diagnostic mode.
88	Start of diagnostic mode. NOTE: This code must appear first in the diagnostic mode or fault codes will be inaccurate.
0	Oxygen feedback system is lean with the engine running.
1	Oxygen feedback system is rich with engine running.

Year—1987
Model—Plymouth Voyager
Engine—2.5L (153 cid) EFI 4 cyl
Engine Code—VIN K

ECM TROUBLE CODES

Code	Explanation
11	No distributor reference pickup signal is present since the engine control module memory was cleared.
12	Memory of the engine control module has been cleared within the last 20–40 engine starts.
13	No variance in the MAP signal is detected between ignition pulses.
14	MAP sensor signal is below 0.02 or above 4.9 volts.
15	No speed sensor signal is detected over an 11 second period.
16	Battery sensing voltage drops below 4 volts for more than 4 seconds.
17	Engine coolant temperature does not reach 160°F within 8 minutes of vehicle speeds greater than 28 mph.
21	No lean or rich condition is indicated for a 2 minute time period.
22	Coolant sensor voltage is above 4.96 volts when the engine is cold or below 0.51 volts when the engine is warm.
23	Charge temperature sensor voltage is below 0.04 or above 4.96 when engine coolant temperature is above 77°F.
24	Throttle position sensor signal is below 0.16 or above 4.7 volts.
25	Proper voltage in the AIS system is not present; open circuit will not activate code.
26	Current through any of the fuel injector pairs does not reach its proper peak level.
27	Fuel control interface fails to switch properly.
31	Solenoid does not turn ON and OFF when it should.
33	Relay does not turn ON and OFF when it should.
34	Servo does not turn ON and OFF when it should.
35	Relay does not turn ON and OFF when it should.
37	Lockup solenoid does not turn ON and OFF when it should.
41	Field control fails to switch properly.
42	Relay does not turn ON and OFF when it should.
43	Spark control interface fails to switch properly.
44	Fused J2 is not present in the logic board of the engine control module.
46	Battery sense voltage is more than 1 volt above the desired control voltage for more than 20 seconds.
47	Battery sense voltage is less than 1 volt below the desired control voltage for more than 20 seconds.
51	O_2 sensor indicates a lean condition for more than 2 minutes.
52	O_2 sensor indicates a rich condition for more than 2 minutes.
53	Logic board fails.
54	No distributor synchronizer pick-up signal.
55	End of diagnostic mode.
88	Start of diagnostic mode. NOTE: This code must appear first in the diagnostic mode or fault codes will be inaccurate.
0	Oxygen feedback system is lean with the engine running.
1	Oxygen feedback system is rich with engine running.

Year — 1987
Model — Dodge Dakota
Engine — 2.2L (135 cid) 4 cyl
Engine Code — VIN C

ECM TROUBLE CODES

Code	Explanation
00	Diagnostic readout tool is receiving power.
11	Problem in the O_2 solenoid control circuit.
13	Problem in the Vacuum Operated Secondary (VOS).
14	Battery has been disconnected within the last 20–40 key-ons.
17	Problem in the electronic throttle control vacuum solenoid system.
18	Problem in the canister purge solenoid system.
21	Problem in the distributor pick-up system.
22	O_2 system is stuck in the full lean position.
23	O_2 system is stuck in the full rich position.
24	Problem in the computer.
25	Problem in the radiator fan coolant sensor portion of the engine temperature dual sensor system.
26	Problem in the engine temperature portion of the engine temperature dual sensor system.
28	Problem in the distance sensor system.
31	Engine has not been cranked since battery was disconnected.
32	Problem in the computer.
33	Problem in the computer.
55	End of message.
88	Start of message.

Year — 1987
Model — Dodge Dakota
Engine — 3.9L (239 cid) V6
Engine Code — VIN M

ECM TROUBLE CODES

Code	Explanation
00	Diagnostic readout tool is receiving power.
11	Problem in the O_2 solenoid control circuit.
12	Problem in transmission unlock relay.
13	Disregard this code.
14	Battery has been disconnected within the last 20–40 key-ons.
17	Problem in the electronic throttle control solenoid system.
18	Problem in the canister purge solenoid system.
21	Problem in the distributor pick-up system.
22	O_2 system is stuck in the full lean or full rich position.
24	Problem in the computer.
25	Problem in the change temperature switch circuit.
26	Problem in the engine temperature portion of the engine temperature dual sensor system or the engine coolant temperature sensor.
28	Problem in the distance sensor system.
31	Engine has not been cranked since battery was disconnected.
32	Problem in the computer.
33	Problem in the computer.
55	End of message.
88	Start of message.

Year — 1987
Model — D & W 100–250
Engine — 3.7L (225 cid) 6 cyl
Engine Code — VIN H

ECM TROUBLE CODES

Code	Explanation
00	Diagnostic readout tool is receiving power.
11	Problem in the O_2 solenoid control circuit.
12	Problem in the transmission unlock relay. Ignore fault code 12 on manual transmission T–115.
13	Problem in the air switching control solenoid circuit.
14	Battery has been disconnected within the last 20–40 key-on's.
17	Problem in the electronic throttle control solenoid system.
18	Problem in the exhaust gas recirculation solenoid.
21	Problem in the distributor pick-up system.
22	O_2 system is stuck in the full lean or full rich position.
24	Problem in the computer.
25	Problem in the charge temperature switch circuit.
26	Problem in the engine temperature sensor circuit.
28	Problem in the distance sensor system.
31	Engine has not been cranked since battery was disconnected.
32	Problem in the computer.
33	Problem in the computer.
55	End of message.
88	Start of message.

Year – 1987
Model – Vans
Engine – 3.7L (225 cid) 6 cyl
Engine Code – VIN H

ECM TROUBLE CODES

Code	Explanation
00	Diagnostic readout tool is receiving power.
11	Problem in the O_2 solenoid control circuit.
12	Problem in the transmission unlock relay. Ignore fault code 12 on manual transmission T–115.
13	Problem in the air switching control solenoid circuit.
14	Battery has been disconnected within the last 20–40 key-on's.
17	Problem in the electronic throttle control solenoid system.
18	Problem in the exhaust gas recirculation solenoid.
21	Problem in the distributor pick-up system.
22	O_2 system is stuck in the full lean or full rich position.
24	Problem in the computer.
25	Problem in the charge temperature switch circuit.
26	Problem in the engine temperature sensor circuit.
28	Problem in the distance sensor system.
31	Engine has not been cranked since battery was disconnected.
32	Problem in the computer.
33	Problem in the computer.
55	End of message.
88	Start of message.

Year — 1987
Model — Ramcharger
Engine — 5.2L (318 cid) V8
Engine Code — VIN T

ECM TROUBLE CODES

Code	Explanation
00	Diagnostic readout tool is receiving power.
11	Problem in the O_2 solenoid control circuit.
12	Problem in the transmission unlock relay. Ignore fault code 12 on manual transmission T–115.
13	Problem in the air switching control solenoid circuit.
14	Battery has been disconnected within the last 20–40 key-on's.
17	Problem in the electronic throttle control solenoid system.
18	Problem in the exhaust gas recirculation solenoid.
21	Problem in the distributor pick-up system.
22	O_2 system is stuck in the full lean or full rich position.
24	Problem in the computer.
26	Problem in the charge temperature sensor circuit.
31	Engine has not been cranked since battery was disconnected.
32	Problem in the computer.
33	Problem in the computer.
55	End of message.
88	Start of message.

CHRYSLER CORPORATION
DIAGNOSTIC CODE DATA

Year – 1987
Model – D & W 100–350
Engine – 5.2L (318 cid) V8
Engine Code – VIN T

ECM TROUBLE CODES

Code	Explanation
00	Diagnostic readout tool is receiving power.
11	Problem in the O_2 solenoid control circuit.
12	Problem in the transmission unlock relay. Ignore fault code 12 on manual transmission T–115.
13	Problem in the air switching control solenoid circuit.
14	Battery has been disconnected within the last 20–40 key-on's.
17	Problem in the electronic throttle control solenoid system.
18	Problem in the exhaust gas recirculation solenoid.
21	Problem in the distributor pick-up system.
22	O_2 system is stuck in the full lean or full rich position.
24	Problem in the computer.
26	Problem in the charge temperature sensor circuit.
31	Engine has not been cranked since battery was disconnected.
32	Problem in the computer.
33	Problem in the computer.
55	End of message.
88	Start of message.

Year — 1987
Model — Vans
Engine — 5.2L (318 cid) V8
Engine Code — VIN T

ECM TROUBLE CODES

Code	Explanation
00	Diagnostic readout tool is receiving power.
11	Problem in the O_2 solenoid control circuit.
12	Problem in the transmission unlock relay. Ignore fault code 12 on manual transmission T–115.
13	Problem in the air switching control solenoid circuit.
14	Battery has been disconnected within the last 20–40 key-on's.
17	Problem in the electronic throttle control solenoid system.
18	Problem in the exhaust gas recirculation solenoid.
21	Problem in the distributor pick-up system.
22	O_2 system is stuck in the full lean or full rich position.
24	Problem in the computer.
26	Problem in the charge temperature sensor circuit.
31	Engine has not been cranked since battery was disconnected.
32	Problem in the computer.
33	Problem in the computer.
55	End of message.
88	Start of message.

Year – 1988
Model – Dodge Mini Ram Van
Engine – 3.0L (181 cid) EFI V6
Engine Code – VIN 3

ECM TROUBLE CODES

Code	Explanation
88	Start of test.
11	Engine not cranked since battery was disconnected.
12	Memory stand-by power lost.
13	MAP sensor pneumatic circuit; check engine lamp ON.
14	MAP sensor electrical circuit; check engine lamp ON.
15	Vehicle distance sensor; check engine lamp ON, California only.
16	Loss of battery voltage sense; check engine lamp ON.
17	Engine running too cool.
21	Oxygen sensor circuit; check engine lamp ON, California only.
22	Coolant temperature sensor circuit; check engine lamp ON.
23	Charge temperature sensor.
24	Throttle position sensor; check engine lamp ON.
25	AIS motor driver circuit; check engine lamp ON, California only.
26	Fuel injector drivers.
27	Fuel injector control problem.
31	Canister purge solenoid circuit; check engine lamp ON, California only.
32	EGR diagnostics; check engine lamp ON, California only.
33	A/C cutout relay circuit.
34	Speed control solenoid driver circuit.
35	Radiator fan control relay circuit.
37	Transmission lockup solenoid.
41	Charging system excess or no field circuit.
42	Auto shutdown relay driver.
43	Spark interface circuit.
44	Loss of FJ2 to logic board.
46	Battery voltage too high; check engine lamp ON.
47	Battery voltage too low.
51	Lean condition indicated; check engine lamp ON, California only.
52	Rich condition indicated; check engine lamp ON, California only.
53	Internal logic module problem.
55	End of message.

Year — 1988
Model — Dodge Caravan
Engine — 3.0L (181 cid) EFI V6
Engine Code — VIN 3

ECM TROUBLE CODES

Code	Explanation
88	Start of test.
11	Engine not cranked since battery was disconnected.
12	Memory stand-by power lost.
13	MAP sensor pneumatic circuit; check engine lamp ON.
14	MAP sensor electrical circuit; check engine lamp ON.
15	Vehicle distance sensor; check engine lamp ON, California only.
16	Loss of battery voltage sense; check engine lamp ON.
17	Engine running too cool.
21	Oxygen sensor circuit; check engine lamp ON, California only.
22	Coolant temperature sensor circuit; check engine lamp ON.
23	Charge temperature sensor.
24	Throttle position sensor; check engine lamp ON.
25	AIS motor driver circuit; check engine lamp ON, California only.
26	Fuel injector drivers.
27	Fuel injector control problem.
31	Canister purge solenoid circuit; check engine lamp ON, California only.
32	EGR diagnostics; check engine lamp ON, California only.
33	A/C cutout relay circuit.
34	Speed control solenoid driver circuit.
35	Radiator fan control relay circuit.
37	Transmission lockup solenoid.
41	Charging system excess or no field circuit.
42	Auto shutdown relay driver.
43	Spark interface circuit.
44	Loss of FJ2 to logic board.
46	Battery voltage too high; check engine lamp ON.
47	Battery voltage too low.
51	Lean condition indicated; check engine lamp ON, California only.
52	Rich condition indicated; check engine lamp ON, California only.
53	Internal logic module problem.
55	End of message.

Year — 1988
Model — Plymouth Voyager
Engine — 3.0L (181 cid) EFI V6
Engine Code — VIN 3

ECM TROUBLE CODES

Code	Explanation
88	Start of test.
11	Engine not cranked since battery was disconnected.
12	Memory stand-by power lost.
13	MAP sensor pneumatic circuit; check engine lamp ON.
14	MAP sensor electrical circuit; check engine lamp ON.
15	Vehicle distance sensor; check engine lamp ON, California only.
16	Loss of battery voltage sense; check engine lamp ON.
17	Engine running too cool.
21	Oxygen sensor circuit; check engine lamp ON, California only.
22	Coolant temperature sensor circuit; check engine lamp ON.
23	Charge temperature sensor.
24	Throttle position sensor; check engine lamp ON.
25	AIS motor driver circuit; check engine lamp ON, California only.
26	Fuel injector drivers.
27	Fuel injector control problem.
31	Canister purge solenoid circuit; check engine lamp ON, California only.
32	EGR diagnostics; check engine lamp ON, California only.
33	A/C cutout relay circuit.
34	Speed control solenoid driver circuit.
35	Radiator fan control relay circuit.
37	Transmission lockup solenoid.
41	Charging system excess or no field circuit.
42	Auto shutdown relay driver.
43	Spark interface circuit.
44	Loss of FJ2 to logic board.
46	Battery voltage too high; check engine lamp ON.
47	Battery voltage too low.
51	Lean condition indicated; check engine lamp ON, California only.
52	Rich condition indicated; check engine lamp ON, California only.
53	Internal logic module problem.
55	End of message.

Year – 1988
Model – Dodge Mini Ram Van
Engine – 2.5L (153 cid) EFI 4 cyl
Engine Code – VIN K

ECM TROUBLE CODES

Code	Explanation
88	Start of test.
11	Engine not cranked since battery was disconnected.
12	Memory stand-by power lost.
13	MAP sensor pneumatic circuit; check engine lamp ON.
14	MAP sensor electrical circuit; check engine lamp ON.
15	Vehicle distance sensor; check engine lamp ON, California only.
16	Loss of battery voltage sense; check engine lamp ON.
17	Engine running too cool.
21	Oxygen sensor circuit; check engine lamp ON, California only.
22	Coolant temperature sensor circuit; check engine lamp ON.
23	Throttle body temperature sensor circuit.
24	Throttle position sensor; check engine lamp ON.
25	AIS motor driver circuit; check engine lamp ON, California only.
26	Fuel injector drivers.
27	Fuel injector control problem.
31	Canister purge solenoid circuit; check engine lamp ON, California only.
32	EGR diagnostics; check engine lamp ON, California only.
33	A/C cutout relay circuit.
34	Speed control solenoid driver circuit.
35	Radiator fan control relay circuit.
37	Transmission lockup solenoid.
41	Charging system excess or no field circuit.
42	Auto shutdown relay driver.
43	Spark interface circuit.
44	Loss of FJ2 to logic board.
46	Battery voltage too high; check engine lamp ON
47	Battery voltage too low.
51	Lean condition indicated; check engine lamp ON, California only.
52	Rich condition indicated; check engine lamp ON, California only.
53	Internal logic module problem.
55	End of message.

Year — 1988
Model — Dodge Caravan
Engine — 2.5L (153 cid) EFI 4 cyl
Engine Code — VIN K

ECM TROUBLE CODES

Code	Explanation
88	Start of test.
11	Engine not cranked since battery was disconnected.
12	Memory stand-by power lost.
13	MAP sensor pneumatic circuit; check engine lamp ON.
14	MAP sensor electrical circuit; check engine lamp ON.
15	Vehicle distance sensor; check engine lamp ON, California only.
16	Loss of battery voltage sense; check engine lamp ON.
17	Engine running too cool.
21	Oxygen sensor circuit; check engine lamp ON, California only.
22	Coolant temperature sensor circuit; check engine lamp ON.
23	Throttle body temperature sensor circuit.
24	Throttle position sensor; check engine lamp ON.
25	AIS motor driver circuit; check engine lamp ON, California only.
26	Fuel injector drivers.
27	Fuel injector control problem.
31	Canister purge solenoid circuit; check engine lamp ON, California only.
32	EGR diagnostics; check engine lamp ON, California only.
33	A/C cutout relay circuit.
34	Speed control solenoid driver circuit.
35	Radiator fan control relay circuit.
37	Transmission lockup solenoid.
41	Charging system excess or no field circuit.
42	Auto shutdown relay driver.
43	Spark interface circuit.
44	Loss of FJ2 to logic board.
46	Battery voltage too high; check engine lamp ON.
47	Battery voltage too low.
51	Lean condition indicated; check engine lamp ON, California only.
52	Rich condition indicated; check engine lamp ON, California only.
53	Internal logic module problem.
55	End of message.

Year — 1988
Model — Plymouth Voyager
Engine — 2.5L (153 cid) EFI 4 cyl
Engine Code — VIN K

ECM TROUBLE CODES

Code	Explanation
88	Start of test.
11	Engine not cranked since battery was disconnected.
12	Memory stand-by power lost.
13	MAP sensor pneumatic circuit; check engine lamp ON.
14	MAP sensor electrical circuit; check engine lamp ON.
15	Vehicle distance sensor; check engine lamp ON, California only.
16	Loss of battery voltage sense; check engine lamp ON.
17	Engine running too cool.
21	Oxygen sensor circuit; check engine lamp ON, California only.
22	Coolant temperature sensor circuit; check engine lamp ON.
23	Throttle body temperature sensor circuit.
24	Throttle position sensor; check engine lamp ON.
25	AIS motor driver circuit; check engine lamp ON, California only.
26	Fuel injector drivers.
27	Fuel injector control problem.
31	Canister purge solenoid circuit; check engine lamp ON, California only.
32	EGR diagnostics; check engine lamp ON, California only.
33	A/C cutout relay circuit.
34	Speed control solenoid driver circuit.
35	Radiator fan control relay circuit.
37	Transmission lockup solenoid.
41	Charging system excess or no field circuit.
42	Auto shutdown relay driver.
43	Spark interface circuit.
44	Loss of FJ2 to logic board.
46	Battery voltage too high; check engine lamp ON.
47	Battery voltage too low.
51	Lean condition indicated; check engine lamp ON, California only.
52	Rich condition indicated; check engine lamp ON, California only.
53	Internal logic module problem.
55	End of message.

Year – 1988
Model – Dodge Dakota
Engine – 3.9L (239 cid) EFI V6
Engine Code – VIN M

ECM TROUBLE CODES

Code	Explanation
88	Start of test.
11	Engine not cranked since battery was disconnected.
12	Memory stand-by power lost.
13	MAP sensor pneumatic circuit; check engine lamp ON.
14	MAP sensor electrical circuit; check engine lamp ON.
15	Vehicle distance sensor; check engine lamp ON, California only.
16	Loss of battery voltage sense; check engine lamp ON.
17	Engine running too cool.
21	Oxygen sensor circuit; check engine lamp ON, California only.
22	Coolant temperature sensor circuit; check engine lamp ON.
24	Throttle position sensor; check engine lamp ON.
25	AIS motor
26	Peak injector current has not been reached; check engine lamp ON.
27	Fuel injector control problem.
31	Canister purge solenoid circuit; check engine lamp ON, California only.
32	EGR diagnostics; check engine lamp ON, California only.
33	A/C cutout relay circuit.
35	Idle switch circuit.
36	Air switching solenoid circuit; check engine lamp ON, California only.
37	Part throttle unlock solenoid driver circuit, automatic only.
41	Charging system excess or no field circuit.
42	Auto shutdown relay driver circuit.
43	Ignition coil control circuit.
44	Loss of FJ2 to logic board.
46	Battery voltage too high; check engine lamp ON.
47	Battery voltage too low.
51	Lean condition indicated; check engine lamp ON, California only.
52	Rich condition indicated; check engine lamp ON, California only.
53	Internal logic module problem.
55	End of message.

Year — 1988
Model — Dodge Dakota
Engine — 2.2L (135 cid) 4 cyl
Engine Code — VIN C

ECM TROUBLE CODES

Code	Explanation
00	Diagnostic readout tool is receiving power.
11	Problem in the O_2 solenoid control circuit.
12	Problem in transmission unlock relay.
13	Problem in the Vacuum Operated Secondary (VOS).
14	Battery has been disconnected within the last 20–40 key-ons.
17	Problem in the electronic throttle control vacuum solenoid system.
18	Problem in the canister purge solenoid system.
21	Problem in the distributor pick-up system.
22	O_2 system is stuck in the full lean position.
23	O_2 system is stuck in the full rich position.
24	Problem in the vacuum transducer circuit.
25	Problem in the radiator fan coolant sensor portion of the engine temperature dual sensor system.
26	Problem in the engine temperature portion of the engine temperature dual sensor system.
28	Problem in the distance sensor system.
31	Engine has not been cranked since battery was disconnected.
32	Problem in the computer.
33	Problem in the computer.
55	End of message.
88	Start of message.

Year—1988
Model—D & W 100–350
Engine—5.2L (318 cid) EFI V8
Engine Code—VIN Y

ECM TROUBLE CODES

Code	Explanation
88	Start of test.
11	Engine not cranked since battery was disconnected.
12	Memory stand-by power lost.
13	MAP sensor pneumatic circuit; check engine lamp ON.
14	MAP sensor electrical circuit; check engine lamp ON.
15	Vehicle distance sensor; check engine lamp ON, California only.
16	Loss of battery voltage sense; check engine lamp ON.
17	Engine running too cool.
21	Oxygen sensor circuit; check engine lamp ON, California only.
22	Coolant temperature sensor circuit; check engine lamp ON.
23	Charge temperature sensor.
24	Throttle position sensor; check engine lamp ON.
25	ISC motor driver circuit.
26	Peak injector current has not been reached; check engine lamp ON.
27	Fuel injector control problem.
31	Canister purge solenoid circuit; check engine lamp ON, California only.
32	EGR diagnostics; check engine lamp ON, California only.
33	A/C cutout relay circuit.
35	Idle switch circuit.
36	Air switching solenoid circuit; check engine lamp ON, California only.
37	Part throttle unlock solenoid driver circuit, automatic only.
41	Charging system excess or no field circuit.
42	Auto shutdown relay driver circuit.
43	Ignition coil control circuit.
44	Loss of FJ2 to logic board.
46	Battery voltage too high; check engine lamp ON.
47	Battery voltage too low.
51	Lean condition indicated; check engine lamp ON, California only.
52	Rich condition indicated; check engine lamp ON, California only.
53	Internal logic module problem.
55	End of message.

Year – 1988
Model – Ramcharger
Engine – 5.2L (318 cid) EFI V8
Engine Code – VIN Y

ECM TROUBLE CODES

Code	Explanation
88	Start of test.
11	Engine not cranked since battery was disconnected.
12	Memory stand-by power lost.
13	MAP sensor pneumatic circuit; check engine lamp ON.
14	MAP sensor electrical circuit; check engine lamp ON.
15	Vehicle distance sensor; check engine lamp ON, California only.
16	Loss of battery voltage sense; check engine lamp ON.
17	Engine running too cool.
21	Oxygen sensor circuit; check engine lamp ON, California only.
22	Coolant temperature sensor circuit; check engine lamp ON.
23	Charge temperature sensor.
24	Throttle position sensor; check engine lamp ON.
25	ISC motor driver circuit.
26	Peak injector current has not been reached; check engine lamp ON.
27	Fuel injector control problem.
31	Canister purge solenoid circuit; check engine lamp ON, California only.
32	EGR diagnostics; check engine lamp ON, California only.
33	A/C cutout relay circuit.
35	Idle switch circuit.
36	Air switching solenoid circuit; check engine lamp ON, California only.
37	Part throttle unlock solenoid driver circuit, automatic only.
41	Charging system excess or no field circuit.
42	Auto shutdown relay driver circuit.
43	Ignition coil control circuit.
44	Loss of FJ2 to logic board.
46	Battery voltage too high; check engine lamp ON.
47	Battery voltage too low.
51	Lean condition indicated; check engine lamp ON, California only.
52	Rich condition indicated; check engine lamp ON, California only.
53	Internal logic module problem.
55	End of message.

Year — 1988
Model — Vans
Engine — 5.2L (318 cid) EFI V8
Engine Code — VIN Y

ECM TROUBLE CODES

Code	Explanation
88	Start of test.
11	Engine not cranked since battery was disconnected.
12	Memory stand-by power lost.
13	MAP sensor pneumatic circuit; check engine lamp ON.
14	MAP sensor electrical circuit; check engine lamp ON.
15	Vehicle distance sensor; check engine lamp ON, California only.
16	Loss of battery voltage sense; check engine lamp ON.
17	Engine running too cool.
21	Oxygen sensor circuit; check engine lamp ON, California only.
22	Coolant temperature sensor circuit; check engine lamp ON.
23	Charge temperature sensor.
24	Throttle position sensor; check engine lamp ON.
25	ISC motor driver circuit.
26	Peak injector current has not been reached; check engine lamp ON.
27	Fuel injector control problem.
31	Canister purge solenoid circuit; check engine lamp ON, California only.
32	EGR diagnostics; check engine lamp ON, California only.
33	A/C cutout relay circuit.
35	Idle switch circuit.
36	Air switching solenoid circuit; check engine lamp ON, California only.
37	Part throttle unlock solenoid driver circuit, automatic only.
41	Charging system excess or no field circuit.
42	Auto shutdown relay driver circuit.
43	Ignition coil control circuit.
44	Loss of FJ2 to logic board.
46	Battery voltage too high; check engine lamp ON.
47	Battery voltage too low.
51	Lean condition indicated; check engine lamp ON, California only.
52	Rich condition indicated; check engine lamp ON, California only.
53	Internal logic module problem.
55	End of message.

Year – 1988
Model – D & W 100–250
Engine – 3.9L (239 cid) EFI V6
Engine Code – VIN X

ECM TROUBLE CODES

Code	Explanation
88	Start of test.
11	Engine not cranked since battery was disconnected.
12	Memory stand-by power lost.
13	MAP sensor pneumatic circuit; check engine lamp ON.
14	MAP sensor electrical circuit; check engine lamp ON.
15	Vehicle distance sensor; check engine lamp ON, California only.
16	Loss of battery voltage sense; check engine lamp ON.
17	Engine running too cool.
21	Oxygen sensor circuit; check engine lamp ON, California only.
22	Coolant temperature sensor circuit; check engine lamp ON.
23	Throttle body temperature sensor circuit.
24	Throttle position sensor; check engine lamp ON.
25	AIS motor
26	Peak injector current has not been reached; check engine lamp ON.
27	Fuel injector control problem; check engine lamp ON.
31	Canister purge solenoid circuit; check engine lamp ON, California only.
32	EGR diagnostics; check engine lamp ON, California only.
33	A/C cutout relay circuit.
35	Idle switch circuit.
36	Air switching solenoid circuit; check engine lamp ON, California only.
37	Part throttle unlock solenoid driver circuit, automatic only.
41	Charging system excess or no field circuit.
42	Auto shutdown relay driver circuit.
43	Ignition coil control circuit.
44	Loss of FJ2 to logic board.
46	Battery voltage too high; check engine lamp ON.
47	Battery voltage too low.
51	Lean condition indicated; check engine lamp ON, California only.
52	Rich condition indicated; check engine lamp ON, California only.
53	Internal logic module problem.
55	End of message.

Year — 1988
Model — Vans
Engine — 3.9L (239 cid) EFI V6
Engine Code — VIN X

ECM TROUBLE CODES

Code	Explanation
88	Start of test.
11	Engine not cranked since battery was disconnected.
12	Memory stand-by power lost.
13	MAP sensor pneumatic circuit; check engine lamp ON.
14	MAP sensor electrical circuit; check engine lamp ON.
15	Vehicle distance sensor; check engine lamp ON, California only.
16	Loss of battery voltage sense; check engine lamp ON.
17	Engine running too cool.
21	Oxygen sensor circuit; check engine lamp ON, California only.
22	Coolant temperature sensor circuit; check engine lamp ON.
23	Throttle body temperature sensor circuit.
24	Throttle position sensor; check engine lamp ON.
25	AIS motor
26	Peak injector current has not been reached; check engine lamp ON.
27	Fuel injector control problem; check engine lamp ON.
31	Canister purge solenoid circuit; check engine lamp ON, California only.
32	EGR diagnostics; check engine lamp ON, California only.
33	A/C cutout relay circuit.
35	Idle switch circuit.
36	Air switching solenoid circuit; check engine lamp ON, California only.
37	Part throttle unlock solenoid driver circuit, automatic only.
41	Charging system excess or no field circuit.
42	Auto shutdown relay driver circuit.
43	Ignition coil control circuit.
44	Loss of FJ2 to logic board.
46	Battery voltage too high; check engine lamp ON.
47	Battery voltage too low.
51	Lean condition indicated; check engine lamp ON, California only.
52	Rich condition indicated; check engine lamp ON, California only.
53	Internal logic module problem.
55	End of message.

Year — 1989
Model — Dodge Caravan
Engine — 2.5L (153 cid) Turbo 4 cyl
Engine Code — VIN J

ECM TROUBLE CODES

Code	Explanation
11	No distributor reference signal detected during engine cranking.
12	Direct battery input to controller disconnected within the last 50–100 ignition key-on's.
13	No variation in MAP sensor signal is detected or no difference is recognized between the engine MAP reading and the stored barometric pressure reading; check engine lamp ON, California only.
14	MAP sensor input below or above the minimum acceptable voltage; check engine lamp ON, California only.
15	No distance sensor signal detected during road load conditions. Check engine lamp ON, California only.
16	Battery voltage sense input not detected during engine running; check engine lamp ON, California only.
17	Engine coolant temperature remains below normal operating temperatures during vehicle travel (thermostat).
21	Neither rich or lean condition is detected from the oxygen sensor input; check engine lamp ON, California only.
22	Coolant temperature sensor input below or above the maximum acceptable voltage; check engine lamp ON, California only.
24	Throttle position sensor input below or above the maximum acceptable voltage; check engine lamp ON, California only.
25	A shorted condition detected in one or more of the AIS control circuits; check engine lamp ON, California only.
26	High resistance condition detected in the INJ 1 or INJ 2 injector bank circuit.
27	INJ 1 or INJ 2 injector bank output driver stage does not respond properly to the control signal.
31	An open or shorted condition detected in the purge solenoid circuit; check engine lamp ON, California only.
33	An open or shorted condition detected in the A/C clutch relay circuit.
34	An open or shorted condition detected in the speed control vacuum or vent solenoid circuits.
35	An open or shorted condition detected in the radiator fan relay circuit.
36	An open or shorted condition detected in the turbocharger wastegate control solenoid circuit; check engine lamp ON, California only.
41	Output driver stage for alternator field does not respond properly to the voltage regulator control signal.
42	An open or shorted condition detected in the auto shutdown relay circuit or no Z1 voltage sensed when the auto shutdown relay is energized.
43	Output driver stage for ignition coil does not respond properly to the dwell control signal.
44	No FJ2 voltage present at the logic board during controller operation.
45	MAP reading above overboost limit detected during engine operation.
46	Battery voltage sense input above target charging voltage during engine operation; check engine lamp ON, California only.
47	Battery voltage sense input below target charging voltage during engine operation.
51	Oxygen sensor signal input indicates lean fuel/air ratio condition during engine operation; check engine lamp ON, California only.
52	Oxygen sensor signal input indicates rich fuel/air ratio condition during engine operation; check engine lamp ON, California only.

ECM TROUBLE CODES (cont'd)

Code	Explanation
53	Internal engine controller fault condition detected.
54	No fuel sync signal detected during engine rotation. Completion of fault code display on the CHECK ENGINE lamp.
55	Completion of fault code display on the check engine lamp.
61	An open or shorted condition detected in the baro read solenoid circuit; check engine lamp ON.
62	Unsuccessful attempt to update EMR mileage in the controller EEPROM.
63	Unsuccessful attempt to write to an EEPROM location by the controller or an unrecognized fault ID received by DRBII.

Year – 1989
Model – Plymouth Voyager
Engine – 2.5L (153 cid) Turbo 4 cyl
Engine Code – VIN J

ECM TROUBLE CODES

Code	Explanation
11	No distributor reference signal detected during engine cranking.
12	Direct battery input to controller disconnected within the last 50–100 ignition key-on's.
13	No variation in MAP sensor signal is detected or no difference is recognized between the engine MAP reading and the stored barometric pressure reading; check engine lamp ON, California only.
14	MAP sensor input below or above the minimum acceptable voltage; check engine lamp ON, California only.
15	No distance sensor signal detected during road load conditions. Check engine lamp ON, California only.
16	Battery voltage sense input not detected during engine running; check engine lamp ON, California only.
17	Engine coolant temperature remains below normal operating temperatures during vehicle travel (thermostat).
21	Neither rich or lean condition is detected from the oxygen sensor input; check engine lamp ON, California only.
22	Coolant temperature sensor input below or above the minimum acceptable voltage; check engine lamp ON, California only.
24	Throttle position sensor input below or above the maximum acceptable voltage.
25	A shorted condition detected in one or more of the AIS control circuits.
26	High resistance condition detected in the INJ 1, INJ 2 or INJ 3 injector bank circuit; check engine lamp ON, California only.
27	INJ 1, INJ 2 or INJ 3 injector bank output driver stage does not respond properly to the control signal; check engine lamp ON, California only.
31	An open or shorted condition detected in the purge solenoid circuit; check engine lamp ON, California only.
33	An open or shorted condition detected in the A/C clutch relay circuit.
34	An open or shorted condition detected in the speed control vacuum or vent solenoid circuits.
35	An open or shorted condition detected in the radiator fan relay circuit.
41	Output driver stage for alternator field does not respond properly to the voltage regulator control signal.

ECM TROUBLE CODES (cont'd)

Code	Explanation
42	An open or shorted condition detected in the auto shutdown relay circuit or no Z1 voltage sensed when the auto shutdown relay is energized.
43	Output driver stage for ignition coil does not respond properly to the dwell control signal.
44	No FJ2 voltage present at the logic board during controller operation.
46	Battery voltage sense input above target charging voltage during engine operation; check engine lamp ON, California only.
47	Battery voltage sense input below target charging voltage during engine operation.
51	Oxygen sensor signal input indicates lean fuel/air ratio condition during engine operation.
52	Oxygen sensor signal input indicates rich fuel/air ratio condition during engine operation; check engine lamp ON, California only.
53	Internal engine controller fault condition detected.
54	No high data rate signal detected during engine rotation.
55	Completion of fault code display on the check engine lamp.
61	An open or shorted condition detected in the baro read solenoid circuit; check engine lamp ON.
62	Unsuccessful attempt to update EMR mileage in the controller EEPROM.
63	Unsuccessful attempt to write to an EEPROM location by the controller or an unrecognized fault ID received by DRBII.

Year — 1989
Model — Dodge Mini Ram Van
Engine — 3.0L (181 cid) EFI V6
Engine Code — VIN 3

ECM TROUBLE CODES

Code	Explanation
11	No distributor reference signal detected during engine cranking.
12	Direct battery input to controller disconnected within the last 50–100 ignition key-on's.
13	No variation in MAP sensor signal is detected or no difference is recognized between the engine MAP reading and the stored barometric pressure reading; check engine lamp ON, California only.
14	MAP sensor input below or above minimum acceptable voltage; check engine lamp ON, California only.
15	No distance sensor signal detected during road load conditions. Check engine lamp ON, California only.
16	Battery voltage sense input not detected during engine running; check engine lamp ON, California only.
17	Engine coolant temperature remains below normal operating temperatures during vehicle travel (thermostat).
21	Neither rich or lean condition is detected from the oxygen sensor input; check engine lamp ON, California only.
22	Coolant temperature sensor input below or above the maximum acceptable voltage; check engine lamp ON, California only.
24	Throttle position sensor input below or above the maximum acceptable voltage; check engine lamp ON, California only.
25	A shorted condition detected in one or more of the AIS control circuits; check engine lamp ON, California only.
26	High resistance condition detected in the INJ 1 or INJ 2 injector bank circuit.

ECM TROUBLE CODES (cont'd)

Code	Explanation
27	INJ 1 or INJ 2 injector bank output driver stage does not respond properly to the control signal.
31	An open or shorted condition detected in the purge solenoid circuit; check engine lamp ON, California only.
33	An open or shorted condition detected in the A/C clutch relay circuit.
34	An open or shorted condition detected in the speed control vacuum or vent solenoid circuits.
35	An open or shorted condition detected in the radiator fan relay circuit.
36	An open or shorted condition detected in the turbocharger wastegate control solenoid circuit; check engine lamp ON, California only.
41	Output driver stage for alternator field does not respond properly to the voltage regulator control signal.
42	An open or shorted condition detected in the auto shutdown relay circuit or no Z1 voltage sensed when the auto shutdown relay is energized.
43	Output driver stage for ignition coil does not respond properly to the dwell control signal.
44	No FJ2 voltage present at the logic board during controller operation.
45	MAP reading above overboost limit detected during engine operation.
46	Battery voltage sense input above target charging voltage during engine operation; check engine lamp ON, California only.
47	Battery voltage sense input below target charging voltage during engine operation.
51	Oxygen sensor signal input indicates lean fuel/air ratio condition during engine operation; check engine lamp ON, California only.
52	Oxygen sensor signal input indicates rich fuel/air ratio condition during engine operation; check engine lamp ON, California only.
53	Internal engine controller fault condition detected.
54	No fuel sync signal detected during engine rotation; check engine lamp ON, California only.
55	Completion of fault code display on the check engine lamp.
62	Unsuccessful attempt to update EMR mileage in the controller EEPROM.
63	Unsuccessful attempt to write to an EEPROM location by the controller or an unrecognized fault ID received by DRBII.

Year – 1989
Model – Dodge Caravan
Engine – 3.0L (181 cid) EFI V6
Engine Code – VIN 3

ECM TROUBLE CODES

Code	Explanation
11	No distributor reference signal detected during engine cranking.
12	Direct battery input to controller disconnected within the last 50–100 ignition key-on's.
13	No variation in MAP sensor signal is detected or no difference is recognized between the engine MAP reading and the stored barometric pressure reading; check engine lamp ON, California only.
14	MAP sensor input below or above minimum acceptable voltage; check engine lamp ON, California only.
15	No distance sensor signal detected during road load conditions. Check engine lamp ON, California only.

ECM TROUBLE CODES (cont'd)

Code	Explanation
16	Battery voltage sense input not detected during engine running; check engine lamp ON, California only.
17	Engine coolant temperature remains below normal operating temperatures during vehicle travel (thermostat).
21	Neither rich or lean condition is detected from the oxygen sensor input; check engine lamp ON, California only.
22	Coolant temperature sensor input below or above the maximum acceptable voltage; check engine lamp ON, California only.
24	Throttle position sensor input below or above the maximum acceptable voltage; check engine lamp ON, California only.
25	A shorted condition detected in one or more of the AIS control circuits; check engine lamp ON, California only.
26	High resistance condition detected in the INJ 1 or INJ 2 injector bank circuit.
27	INJ 1 or INJ 2 injector bank output driver stage does not respond properly to the control signal.
31	An open or shorted condition detected in the purge solenoid circuit; check engine lamp ON, California only.
33	An open or shorted condition detected in the A/C clutch relay circuit.
34	An open or shorted condition detected in the speed control vacuum or vent solenoid circuits.
35	An open or shorted condition detected in the radiator fan relay circuit.
36	An open or shorted condition detected in the turbocharger wastegate control solenoid circuit; check engine lamp ON, California only.
41	Output driver stage for alternator field does not respond properly to the voltage regulator control signal.
42	An open or shorted condition detected in the auto shutdown relay circuit or no Z1 voltage sensed when the auto shutdown relay is energized.
43	Output driver stage for ignition coil does not respond properly to the dwell control signal.
44	No FJ2 voltage present at the logic board during controller operation.
45	MAP reading above overboost limit detected during engine operation.
46	Battery voltage sense input above target charging voltage during engine operation; check engine lamp ON, California only.
47	Battery voltage sense input below target charging voltage during engine operation.
51	Oxygen sensor signal input indicates lean fuel/air ratio condition during engine operation; check engine lamp ON, California only.
52	Oxygen sensor signal input indicates rich fuel/air ratio condition during engine operation; check engine lamp ON, California only.
53	Internal engine controller fault condition detected.
54	No fuel sync signal detected during engine rotation; check engine lamp ON, California only.
55	Completion of fault code display on the check engine lamp.
62	Unsuccessful attempt to update EMR mileage in the controller EEPROM.
63	Unsuccessful attempt to write to an EEPROM location by the controller or an unrecognized fault ID received by DRBII.

Year — 1989
Model — Plymouth Voyager
Engine — 3.0L (181 cid) EFI V6
Engine Code — VIN 3

ECM TROUBLE CODES

Code	Explanation
11	No distributor reference signal detected during engine cranking.
12	Direct battery input to controller disconnected within the last 50–100 ignition key-on's.
13	No variation in MAP sensor signal is detected or no difference is recognized between the engine MAP reading and the stored barometric pressure reading; check engine lamp ON, California only.
14	MAP sensor input below or above minimum acceptable voltage; check engine lamp ON, California only.
15	No distance sensor signal detected during road load conditions. Check engine lamp ON, California only.
16	Battery voltage sense input not detected during engine running; check engine lamp ON, California only.
17	Engine coolant temperature remains below normal operating temperatures during vehicle travel (thermostat).
21	Neither rich or lean condition is detected from the oxygen sensor input; check engine lamp ON, California only.
22	Coolant temperature sensor input below or above the maximum acceptable voltage; check engine lamp ON, California only.
24	Throttle position sensor input below or above the maximum acceptable voltage; check engine lamp ON, California only.
25	A shorted condition detected in one or more of the AIS control circuits; check engine lamp ON, California only.
26	High resistance condition detected in the INJ 1 or INJ 2 injector bank circuit.
27	INJ 1 or INJ 2 injector bank output driver stage does not respond properly to the control signal.
31	An open or shorted condition detected in the purge solenoid circuit; check engine lamp ON, California only.
33	An open or shorted condition detected in the A/C clutch relay circuit.
34	An open or shorted condition detected in the speed control vacuum or vent solenoid circuits.
35	An open or shorted condition detected in the radiator fan relay circuit.
36	An open or shorted condition detected in the turbocharger wastegate control solenoid circuit; check engine lamp ON, California only.
41	Output driver stage for alternator field does not respond properly to the voltage regulator control signal.
42	An open or shorted condition detected in the auto shutdown relay circuit or no Z1 voltage sensed when the auto shutdown relay is energized.
43	Output driver stage for ignition coil does not respond properly to the dwell control signal.
44	No FJ2 voltage present at the logic board during controller operation.
45	MAP reading above overboost limit detected during engine operation.
46	Battery voltage sense input above target charging voltage during engine operation; check engine lamp ON, California only.
47	Battery voltage sense input below target charging voltage during engine operation.
51	Oxygen sensor signal input indicates lean fuel/air ratio condition during engine operation; check engine lamp ON, California only.
52	Oxygen sensor signal input indicates rich fuel/air ratio condition during engine operation; check engine lamp ON, California only.

ECM TROUBLE CODES (cont'd)

Code	Explanation
53	Internal engine controller fault condition detected.
54	No fuel sync signal detected during engine rotation; check engine lamp ON, California only.
55	Completion of fault code display on the check engine lamp.
62	Unsuccessful attempt to update EMR mileage in the controller EEPROM.
63	Unsuccessful attempt to write to an EEPROM location by the controller or an unrecognized fault ID received by DRBII.

Year — 1989
Model — Dodge Mini Ram Van
Engine — 2.5L (153 cid) EFI 4 cyl
Engine Code — VIN K

ECM TROUBLE CODES

Code	Explanation
11	No distributor reference signal detected during engine cranking.
12	Direct battery input to controller disconnected within the last 50–100 ignition key-on's.
13	No variation in MAP sensor signal is detected or no difference is recognized between the engine MAP reading and the stored barometric pressure reading; check engine lamp ON, California only.
14	MAP sensor input below or above the minimum acceptable voltage; check engine lamp ON, California only.
15	No distance sensor signal detected during road load conditions. Check engine lamp ON, California only.
16	Battery voltage sense input not detected during engine running; check engine lamp ON, California only.
17	Engine coolant temperature remains below normal operating temperatures during vehicle travel (thermostat).
21	Neither rich or lean condition is detected from the oxygen sensor input; check engine lamp ON, California only.
22	Coolant temperature sensor input below or above the maximum acceptable voltage; check engine lamp ON, California only.
23	Throttle body temperature sensor input below or above the minimum acceptable voltage.
24	Throttle position sensor input below or above the minimum acceptable voltage; check engine lamp ON, California only.
25	A shorted condition detected in one or more of the AIS control circuits; check engine lamp ON, California only.
26	High resistance condition detected in the INJ 1 injector bank circuit. Injector output driver stage does not respond properly to the control signal.
31	An open or shorted condition detected in the purge solenoid circuit; check engine lamp ON, California only.
32	An open or shorted condition detected in the EGR solenoid circuit or required change in fuel/air ratio not detected during diagnostic test; check engine lamp ON, California only.
33	An open or shorted condition detected in the A/C clutch relay circuit.
34	An open or shorted condition detected in the speed control vacuum or vent solenoid circuits.
35	An open or shorted condition detected in the radiator fan relay circuit.
41	Output driver stage for alternator field does not respond properly to the voltage regulator control signal.

ECM TROUBLE CODES (cont'd)

Code	Explanation
42	An open or shorted condition detected in the auto shutdown relay circuit.
43	Output driver stage for ignition coil does not respond properly to the dwell control signal.
44	No FJ2 voltage present at the logic board during controller operation.
46	Battery voltage sense input above target charging voltage during engine operation; check engine lamp ON, California only.
47	Battery voltage sense input below target charging voltage during engine operation.
51	Oxygen sensor signal input indicates lean fuel/air ratio condition during engine operation; check engine lamp ON, California only.
52	Oxygen sensor signal input indicates rich fuel/air ratio condition during engine operation or adaptive fuel value leaned excessively due to a sustained rich condition; check engine lamp ON, California only.
53	Internal engine controller fault condition detected.
55	Completion of fault code display on the check engine lamp.
62	Unsuccessful attempt to update EMR mileage in the controller EEPROM.
63	Unsuccessful attempt to write to an EEPROM location by the controller or an unrecognized fault ID received by DRBII.

Year – 1989
Model – Dodge Caravan
Engine – 2.5L (153 cid) EFI 4 cyl
Engine Code – VIN K

ECM TROUBLE CODES

Code	Explanation
11	No distributor reference signal detected during engine cranking.
12	Direct battery input to controller disconnected within the last 50–100 ignition key-on's.
13	No variation in MAP sensor signal is detected or no difference is recognized between the engine MAP reading and the stored barometric pressure reading; check engine lamp ON, California only.
14	MAP sensor input below or above the minimum acceptable voltage; check engine lamp ON, California only.
15	No distance sensor signal detected during road load conditions. Check engine lamp ON, California only.
16	Battery voltage sense input not detected during engine running; check engine lamp ON, California only.
17	Engine coolant temperature remains below normal operating temperatures during vehicle travel (thermostat).
21	Neither rich or lean condition is detected from the oxygen sensor input; check engine lamp ON, California only.
22	Coolant temperature sensor input below or above the maximum acceptable voltage; check engine lamp ON, California only.
23	Throttle body temperature sensor input below or above the minimum acceptable voltage.
24	Throttle position sensor input below or above the minimum acceptable voltage; check engine lamp ON, California only.
25	A shorted condition detected in one or more of the AIS control circuits; check engine lamp ON, California only.

ECM TROUBLE CODES (cont'd)

Code	Explanation
26	High resistance condition detected in the INJ 1 injector bank circuit. Injector output driver stage does not respond properly to the control signal.
31	An open or shorted condition detected in the purge solenoid circuit; check engine lamp ON, California only.
32	An open or shorted condition detected in the EGR solenoid circuit or required change in fuel/air ratio not detected during diagnostic test; check engine lamp ON, California only.
33	An open or shorted condition detected in the A/C clutch relay circuit.
34	An open or shorted condition detected in the speed control vacuum or vent solenoid circuits.
35	An open or shorted condition detected in the radiator fan relay circuit.
41	Output driver stage for alternator field does not respond properly to the voltage regulator control signal.
42	An open or shorted condition detected in the auto shutdown relay circuit.
43	Output driver stage for ignition coil does not respond properly to the dwell control signal.
44	No FJ2 voltage present at the logic board during controller operation.
46	Battery voltage sense input above target charging voltage during engine operation; check engine lamp ON, California only.
47	Battery voltage sense input below target charging voltage during engine operation.
51	Oxygen sensor signal input indicates lean fuel/air ratio condition during engine operation; check engine lamp ON, California only.
52	Oxygen sensor signal input indicates rich fuel/air ratio condition during engine operation or adaptive fuel value leaned excessively due to a sustained rich condition; check engine lamp ON, California only.
53	Internal engine controller fault condition detected.
55	Completion of fault code display on the check engine lamp.
62	Unsuccessful attempt to update EMR mileage in the controller EEPROM.
63	Unsuccessful attempt to write to an EEPROM location by the controller or an unrecognized fault ID received by DRBII.

Year — 1989
Model — Plymouth Voyager
Engine — 2.5L (153 cid) EFI 4 cyl
Engine Code — VIN K

ECM TROUBLE CODES

Code	Explanation
11	No distributor reference signal detected during engine cranking.
12	Direct battery input to controller disconnected within the last 50–100 ignition key-on's.
13	No variation in MAP sensor signal is detected or no difference is recognized between the engine MAP reading and the stored barometric pressure reading; check engine lamp ON, California only.
14	MAP sensor input below or above the minimum acceptable voltage; check engine lamp ON, California only.
15	No distance sensor signal detected during road load conditions. Check engine lamp ON, California only.
16	Battery voltage sense input not detected during engine running; check engine lamp ON, California only.

ECM TROUBLE CODES (cont'd)

Code	Explanation
17	Engine coolant temperature remains below normal operating temperatures during vehicle travel (thermostat).
21	Neither rich or lean condition is detected from the oxygen sensor input; check engine lamp ON, California only.
22	Coolant temperature sensor input below or above the maximum acceptable voltage; check engine lamp ON, California only.
23	Throttle body temperature sensor input below or above the minimum acceptable voltage.
24	Throttle position sensor input below or above the minimum acceptable voltage; check engine lamp ON, California only.
25	A shorted condition detected in one or more of the AIS control circuits; check engine lamp ON, California only.
26	High resistance condition detected in the INJ 1 injector bank circuit. Injector output driver stage does not respond properly to the control signal.
31	An open or shorted condition detected in the purge solenoid circuit; check engine lamp ON, California only.
32	An open or shorted condition detected in the EGR solenoid circuit or required change in fuel/air ratio not detected during diagnostic test; check engine lamp ON, California only.
33	An open or shorted condition detected in the A/C clutch relay circuit.
34	An open or shorted condition detected in the speed control vacuum or vent solenoid circuits.
35	An open or shorted condition detected in the radiator fan relay circuit.
41	Output driver stage for alternator field does not respond properly to the voltage regulator control signal.
42	An open or shorted condition detected in the auto shutdown relay circuit.
43	Output driver stage for ignition coil does not respond properly to the dwell control signal.
44	No FJ2 voltage present at the logic board during controller operation.
46	Battery voltage sense input above target charging voltage during engine operation; check engine lamp ON, California only.
47	Battery voltage sense input below target charging voltage during engine operation.
51	Oxygen sensor signal input indicates lean fuel/air ratio condition during engine operation; check engine lamp ON, California only.
52	Oxygen sensor signal input indicates rich fuel/air ratio condition during engine operation or adaptive fuel value leaned excessively due to a sustained rich condition; check engine lamp ON, California only.
53	Internal engine controller fault condition detected.
55	Completion of fault code display on the check engine lamp.
62	Unsuccessful attempt to update EMR mileage in the controller EEPROM.
63	Unsuccessful attempt to write to an EEPROM location by the controller or an unrecognized fault ID received by DRBII.

Year — 1989
Model — Dodge Dakota
Engine — 2.5L (153 cid) TBI 4 cyl
Engine Code — VIN K

ECM TROUBLE CODES

Code	Explanation
11	No distributor reference signal detected during engine cranking.
12	Direct battery input to controller disconnected within the last 50–100 ignition key-on's.
13	No variation in MAP sensor signal is detected or no difference is recognized between the engine MAP reading and the stored barometric pressure reading; check engine lamp ON, California only.
14	MAP sensor input below or above the minimum acceptable voltage; check engine lamp ON, California only.
15	No distance sensor signal detected during road load conditions. Check engine lamp ON, California only.
16	Battery voltage sense input not detected during engine running; check engine lamp ON, California only.
17	Engine coolant temperature remains below normal operating temperatures during vehicle travel (thermostat).
21	Neither rich or lean condition is detected from the oxygen sensor input; check engine lamp ON, California only.
22	Coolant temperature sensor input below or above the maximum acceptable voltage; check engine lamp ON, California only.
23	Throttle body temperature sensor input below or above the minimum acceptable voltage.
24	Throttle position sensor input below or above the minimum acceptable voltage; check engine lamp ON, California only.
25	A shorted condition detected in one or more of the AIS control circuits; check engine lamp ON, California only.
26	High resistance condition detected in the INJ 1 injector bank circuit.
31	An open or shorted condition detected in the purge solenoid circuit; check engine lamp ON, California only.
32	An open or shorted condition detected in the EGR solenoid circuit or required change in fuel/air ratio not detected during diagnostic test; check engine lamp ON, California only.
33	An open or shorted condition detected in the A/C clutch relay circuit.
34	An open or shorted condition detected in the speed control vacuum or vent solenoid circuits.
35	An open or shorted condition detected in the radiator fan relay circuit.
37	An open or shorted condition detected in the converter part throttle unlock solenoid circuit.
41	Output driver stage for alternator field does not respond properly to the voltage regulator control signal.
42	An open or shorted condition detected in the auto shutdown relay circuit.
43	Output driver stage for ignition coil does not respond properly to the dwell control signal.
44	No FJ2 voltage present at the logic board during controller operation.
46	Battery voltage sense input above target charging voltage during engine operation; check engine lamp ON, California only.
47	Battery voltage sense input below target charging voltage during engine operation.
51	Oxygen sensor signal input indicates lean fuel/air ratio condition during engine operation; check engine lamp ON, California only.
52	Oxygen sensor signal input indicates rich fuel/air ratio condition during engine operation or adaptive fuel value leaned excessively due to a sustained rich condition; check engine lamp ON, California only.

CHRYSLER CORPORATION
DIAGNOSTIC CODE DATA

ECM TROUBLE CODES (cont'd)

Code	Explanation
53	Internal engine controller fault condition detected.
55	Completion of fault code display on the check engine lamp.
62	Unsuccessful attempt to update EMR mileage in the controller EEPROM.
63	Unsuccessful attempt to write to an EEPROM location by the controller or an unrecognized fault ID received by DRBII.

Year – 1989
Model – Dodge Dakota
Engine – 3.0L (181 cid) EFI V6
Engine Code – VIN X

ECM TROUBLE CODES

Code	Explanation
11	No distributor reference signal detected during engine cranking.
12	Direct battery input to controller disconnected within the last 50–100 ignition key-on's.
13	No variation in MAP sensor signal is detected or no difference is recognized between the engine MAP reading and the stored barometric pressure reading; check engine lamp ON, California only.
14	MAP sensor input below or above minimum acceptable voltage; check engine lamp ON, California only.
15	No distance sensor signal detected during road load conditions. Check engine lamp ON, California only.
16	Battery voltage sense input not detected during engine running; check engine lamp ON, California only.
17	Engine coolant temperature remains below normal operating temperatures during vehicle travel (thermostat).
21	Neither rich or lean condition is detected from the oxygen sensor input; check engine lamp ON, California only.
22	Coolant temperature sensor input below or above the maximum acceptable voltage; check engine lamp ON, California only.
23	Throttle body temperature sensor input below or above the minimum acceptable voltage.
24	Throttle position sensor input below or above the maximum acceptable voltage; check engine lamp ON, California only.
25	A shorted condition detected in one or more of the AIS control circuits; check engine lamp ON, California only.
26	High resistance condition detected in the INJ 1 or INJ 2 injector bank circuit.
27	INJ 1 or INJ 2 injector bank output driver stage does not respond properly to the control signal.
31	An open or shorted condition detected in the purge solenoid circuit; check engine lamp ON, California only.
32	An open or shorted condition detected in the EGR solenoid circuit or required change in fuel/air ratio not detected during diagnostic test; check engine lamp ON, California only.
33	An open or shorted condition detected in the A/C clutch relay circuit.
34	An open or shorted condition detected in the speed control vacuum or vent solenoid circuits.
35	Idle contact switch input circuit shorted to ground or circuit open.
36	An open or shorted condition detected in the air switching solenoid circuit.
37	An open or shorted condition detected in the converter part throttle unlock solenoid circuit, automatic transmission only.

ECM TROUBLE CODES (cont'd)

Code	Explanation
41	Output driver stage for alternator field does not respond properly to the voltage regulator control signal.
42	An open or shorted condition detected in the auto shutdown relay circuit or no Z1 voltage sensed when the auto shutdown relay is energized.
43	Output driver stage for ignition coil does not respond properly to the dwell control signal.
44	No FJ2 voltage present at the logic board during controller operation.
45	An open or shorted condition detected in the overdrive solenoid circuit, automatic transmission only.
46	Battery voltage sense input above target charging voltage during engine operation; check engine lamp ON, California only.
47	Battery voltage sense input below target charging voltage during engine operation.
51	Oxygen sensor signal input indicates lean fuel/air ratio condition during engine operation; check engine lamp ON, California only.
52	Oxygen sensor signal input indicates rich fuel/air ratio condition during engine operation or adaptive fuel value leaned excessively due to a sustained rich condition; check engine lamp ON, California only.
53	Internal engine controller fault condition detected.
55	Completion of fault code display on the check engine lamp.
62	Unsuccessful attempt to update EMR mileage in the controller EEPROM.
63	Unsuccessful attempt to write to an EEPROM location by the controller or an unrecognized fault ID received by DRBII.

Year – 1989
Model – D & W 100–250
Engine – 3.9L (239 cid) EFI V6
Engine Code – VIN X

ECM TROUBLE CODES

Code	Explanation
11	No distributor reference signal detected during engine cranking.
12	Direct battery input to controller disconnected within the last 50–100 ignition key-on's.
13	No variation in MAP sensor signal is detected or no difference is recognized between the engine MAP reading and the stored barometric pressure reading; check engine lamp ON, California only.
14	MAP sensor input below or above minimum acceptable voltage; check engine lamp ON, California only.
15	No distance sensor signal detected during road load conditions. Check engine lamp ON, California only.
16	Battery voltage sense input not detected during engine running; check engine lamp ON, California only.
17	Engine coolant temperature remains below normal operating temperatures during vehicle travel (thermostat).
21	Neither rich or lean condition is detected from the oxygen sensor input; check engine lamp ON, California only.
22	Coolant temperature sensor input below or above the maximum acceptable voltage; check engine lamp ON, California only.
23	Throttle body temperature sensor input below or above the minimum acceptable voltage.

ECM TROUBLE CODES (cont'd)

Code	Explanation
24	Throttle position sensor input below or above the maximum acceptable voltage; check engine lamp ON, California only.
25	A shorted condition detected in one or more of the ISC control circuits; check engine lamp ON, California only.
26	High resistance condition detected in the INJ 1 or INJ 2 injector bank circuit.
27	INJ 1 or INJ 2 injector bank output driver stage does not respond properly to the control signal.
31	An open or shorted condition detected in the purge solenoid circuit; check engine lamp ON, California only.
32	An open or shorted condition detected in the EGR solenoid circuit or required change in fuel/air ratio not detected during diagnostic test; check engine lamp ON, California only.
33	An open or shorted condition detected in the A/C clutch relay circuit.
34	An open or shorted condition detected in the speed control vacuum or vent solenoid circuits.
35	Idle contact switch input circuit shorted to ground or circuit open.
36	An open or shorted condition detected in the air switching solenoid circuit.
37	An open or shorted condition detected in the torque converter part throttle unlock solenoid circuit, automatic transmission only.
41	Output driver stage for alternator field does not respond properly to the voltage regulator control signal.
42	An open or shorted condition detected in the auto shutdown relay circuit or no Z1 voltage sensed when the auto shutdown relay is energized.
43	Output driver stage for ignition coil does not respond properly to the dwell control signal.
44	No FJ2 voltage present at the logic board during controller operation.
45	An open or shorted condition detected in the overdrive solenoid circuit, automatic transmission only.
46	Battery voltage sense input above target charging voltage during engine operation; check engine lamp ON, California only.
47	Battery voltage sense input below target charging voltage during engine operation.
51	Oxygen sensor signal input indicates lean fuel/air ratio condition during engine operation; check engine lamp ON, California only.
52	Oxygen sensor signal input indicates rich fuel/air ratio condition during engine operation or adaptive fuel value leaned excessively due to a sustained rich condition; check engine lamp ON, California only.
53	Internal engine controller fault condition detected.
55	Completion of fault code display on the check engine lamp.
62	Unsuccessful attempt to update EMR mileage in the controller EEPROM.
63	Unsuccessful attempt to write to an EEPROM location by the controller or an unrecognized fault ID received by DRBII.

Year – 1989

Model – Vans

Engine – 3.9L (239 cid) EFI V6

Engine Code – VIN X

ECM TROUBLE CODES

Code	Explanation
11	No distributor reference signal detected during engine cranking.
12	Direct battery input to controller disconnected within the last 50–100 ignition key-on's.
13	No variation in MAP sensor signal is detected or no difference is recognized between the engine MAP reading and the stored barometric pressure reading; check engine lamp ON, California only.

ECM TROUBLE CODES (cont'd)

Code	Explanation
14	MAP sensor input below or above minimum acceptable voltage; check engine lamp ON, California only.
15	No distance sensor signal detected during road load conditions. Check engine lamp ON, California only.
16	Battery voltage sense input not detected during engine running; check engine lamp ON, California only.
17	Engine coolant temperature remains below normal operating temperatures during vehicle travel (thermostat).
21	Neither rich or lean condition is detected from the oxygen sensor input; check engine lamp ON, California only.
22	Coolant temperature sensor input below or above the maximum acceptable voltage; check engine lamp ON, California only.
23	Throttle body temperature sensor input below or above the minimum acceptable voltage.
24	Throttle position sensor input below or above the maximum acceptable voltage; check engine lamp ON, California only.
25	A shorted condition detected in one or more of the ISC control circuits; check engine lamp ON, California only.
26	High resistance condition detected in the INJ 1 or INJ 2 injector bank circuit.
27	INJ 1 or INJ 2 injector bank output driver stage does not respond properly to the control signal.
31	An open or shorted condition detected in the purge solenoid circuit; check engine lamp ON, California only.
32	An open or shorted condition detected in the EGR solenoid circuit or required change in fuel/air ratio not detected during diagnostic test; check engine lamp ON, California only.
33	An open or shorted condition detected in the A/C clutch relay circuit.
34	An open or shorted condition detected in the speed control vacuum or vent solenoid circuits.
35	Idle contact switch input circuit shorted to ground or circuit open.
36	An open or shorted condition detected in the air switching solenoid circuit.
37	An open or shorted condition detected in the torque converter part throttle unlock solenoid circuit, automatic transmission only.
41	Output driver stage for alternator field does not respond properly to the voltage regulator control signal.
42	An open or shorted condition detected in the auto shutdown relay circuit or no Z1 voltage sensed when the auto shutdown relay is energized.
43	Output driver stage for ignition coil does not respond properly to the dwell control signal.
44	No FJ2 voltage present at the logic board during controller operation.
45	An open or shorted condition detected in the overdrive solenoid circuit, automatic transmission only.
46	Battery voltage sense input above target charging voltage during engine operation; check engine lamp ON, California only.
47	Battery voltage sense input below target charging voltage during engine operation.
51	Oxygen sensor signal input indicates lean fuel/air ratio condition during engine operation; check engine lamp ON, California only.
52	Oxygen sensor signal input indicates rich fuel/air ratio condition during engine operation or adaptive fuel value leaned excessively due to a sustained rich condition; check engine lamp ON, California only.
53	Internal engine controller fault condition detected.
55	Completion of fault code display on the check engine lamp.
62	Unsuccessful attempt to update EMR mileage in the controller EEPROM.
63	Unsuccessful attempt to write to an EEPROM location by the controller or an unrecognized fault ID received by DRBII.

Year – 1989
Model – D & W 100–350
Engine – 5.2L (318 cid) EFI V8
Engine Code – VIN Y

ECM TROUBLE CODES

Code	Explanation
11	No distributor reference signal detected during engine cranking.
12	Direct battery input to controller disconnected within the last 50–100 ignition key-on's.
13	No variation in MAP sensor signal is detected or no difference is recognized between the engine MAP reading and the stored barometric pressure reading; check engine lamp ON, California only.
14	MAP sensor input below or above minimum acceptable voltage; check engine lamp ON, California only.
15	No distance sensor signal detected during road load conditions. Check engine lamp ON, California only.
16	Battery voltage sense input not detected during engine running; check engine lamp ON, California only.
17	Engine coolant temperature remains below normal operating temperatures during vehicle travel (thermostat).
21	Neither rich or lean condition is detected from the oxygen sensor input; check engine lamp ON, California only.
22	Coolant temperature sensor input below or above the maximum acceptable voltage; check engine lamp ON, California only.
23	Throttle body temperature sensor input below or above the minimum acceptable voltage.
24	Throttle position sensor input below or above the maximum acceptable voltage; check engine lamp ON, California only.
25	A shorted condition detected in one or more of the ISC control circuits; check engine lamp ON, California only.
26	High resistance condition detected in the INJ 1 or INJ 2 injector bank circuit.
27	INJ 1 or INJ 2 injector bank output driver stage does not respond properly to the control signal.
31	An open or shorted condition detected in the purge solenoid circuit; check engine lamp ON, California only.
32	An open or shorted condition detected in the EGR solenoid circuit or required change in fuel/air ratio not detected during diagnostic test; check engine lamp ON, California only.
33	An open or shorted condition detected in the A/C clutch relay circuit.
34	An open or shorted condition detected in the speed control vacuum or vent solenoid circuits.
35	Idle contact switch input circuit shorted to ground or circuit open.
36	An open or shorted condition detected in the air switching solenoid circuit.
37	An open or shorted condition detected in the torque converter part throttle unlock solenoid circuit, automatic transmission only.
41	Output driver stage for alternator field does not respond properly to the voltage regulator control signal.
42	An open or shorted condition detected in the auto shutdown relay circuit or no Z1 voltage sensed when the auto shutdown relay is energized.
43	Output driver stage for ignition coil does not respond properly to the dwell control signal.
44	No FJ2 voltage present at the logic board during controller operation.
45	An open or shorted condition detected in the overdrive solenoid circuit, automatic transmission only.
46	Battery voltage sense input above target charging voltage during engine operation; check engine lamp ON, California only.

ECM TROUBLE CODES (cont'd)

Code	Explanation
47	Battery voltage sense input below target charging voltage during engine operation.
51	Oxygen sensor signal input indicates lean fuel/air ratio condition during engine operation; check engine lamp ON, California only.
52	Oxygen sensor signal input indicates rich fuel/air ratio condition during engine operation or adaptive fuel value leaned excessively due to a sustained rich condition; check engine lamp ON, California only.
53	Internal engine controller fault condition detected.
55	Completion of fault code display on the check engine lamp.
62	Unsuccessful attempt to update EMR mileage in the controller EEPROM.
63	Unsuccessful attempt to write to an EEPROM location by the controller or an unrecognized fault ID received by DRBII.

Year — 1989
Model — Dodge Ramcharger
Engine — 5.2L (318 cid) EFI V8
Engine Code — VIN Y

ECM TROUBLE CODES

Code	Explanation
11	No distributor reference signal detected during engine cranking.
12	Direct battery input to controller disconnected within the last 50–100 ignition key-on's.
13	No variation in MAP sensor signal is detected or no difference is recognized between the engine MAP reading and the stored barometric pressure reading; check engine lamp ON, California only.
14	MAP sensor input below or above minimum acceptable voltage; check engine lamp ON, California only.
15	No distance sensor signal detected during road load conditions. Check engine lamp ON, California only.
16	Battery voltage sense input not detected during engine running; check engine lamp ON, California only.
17	Engine coolant temperature remains below normal operating temperatures during vehicle travel (thermostat).
21	Neither rich or lean condition is detected from the oxygen sensor input; check engine lamp ON, California only.
22	Coolant temperature sensor input below or above the maximum acceptable voltage; check engine lamp ON, California only.
23	Throttle body temperature sensor input below or above the minimum acceptable voltage.
24	Throttle position sensor input below or above the maximum acceptable voltage; check engine lamp ON, California only.
25	A shorted condition detected in one or more of the ISC control circuits; check engine lamp ON, California only.
26	High resistance condition detected in the INJ 1 or INJ 2 injector bank circuit.
27	INJ 1 or INJ 2 injector bank output driver stage does not respond properly to the control signal.
31	An open or shorted condition detected in the purge solenoid circuit; check engine lamp ON, California only.
32	An open or shorted condition detected in the EGR solenoid circuit or required change in fuel/air ratio not detected during diagnostic test; check engine lamp ON, California only.
33	An open or shorted condition detected in the A/C clutch relay circuit.

ECM TROUBLE CODES (cont'd)

Code	Explanation
34	An open or shorted condition detected in the speed control vacuum or vent solenoid circuits.
35	Idle contact switch input circuit shorted to ground or circuit open.
36	An open or shorted condition detected in the air switching solenoid circuit.
37	An open or shorted condition detected in the torque converter part throttle unlock solenoid circuit, automatic transmission only.
41	Output driver stage for alternator field does not respond properly to the voltage regulator control signal.
42	An open or shorted condition detected in the auto shutdown relay circuit or no Z1 voltage sensed when the auto shutdown relay is energized.
43	Output driver stage for ignition coil does not respond properly to the dwell control signal.
44	No FJ2 voltage present at the logic board during controller operation.
45	An open or shorted condition detected in the overdrive solenoid circuit, automatic transmission only.
46	Battery voltage sense input above target charging voltage during engine operation; check engine lamp ON, California only.
47	Battery voltage sense input below target charging voltage during engine operation.
51	Oxygen sensor signal input indicates lean fuel/air ratio condition during engine operation; check engine lamp ON, California only.
52	Oxygen sensor signal input indicates rich fuel/air ratio condition during engine operation or adaptive fuel value leaned excessively due to a sustained rich condition; check engine lamp ON, California only.
53	Internal engine controller fault condition detected.
55	Completion of fault code display on the check engine lamp.
62	Unsuccessful attempt to update EMR mileage in the controller EEPROM.
63	Unsuccessful attempt to write to an EEPROM location by the controller or an unrecognized fault ID received by DRBII.

Year – 1989

Model – Vans

Engine – 5.2L (318 cid) EFI V8

Engine Code – VIN Y

ECM TROUBLE CODES

Code	Explanation
11	No distributor reference signal detected during engine cranking.
12	Direct battery input to controller disconnected within the last 50–100 ignition key-on's.
13	No variation in MAP sensor signal is detected or no difference is recognized between the engine MAP reading and the stored barometric pressure reading; check engine lamp ON, California only.
14	MAP sensor input below or above minimum acceptable voltage; check engine lamp ON, California only.
15	No distance sensor signal detected during road load conditions. Check engine lamp ON, California only.
16	Battery voltage sense input not detected during engine running; check engine lamp ON, California only.
17	Engine coolant temperature remains below normal operating temperatures during vehicle travel (thermostat).

ECM TROUBLE CODES (cont'd)

Code	Explanation
21	Neither rich or lean condition is detected from the oxygen sensor input; check engine lamp ON, California only.
22	Coolant temperature sensor input below or above the maximum acceptable voltage; check engine lamp ON, California only.
23	Throttle body temperature sensor input below or above the minimum acceptable voltage.
24	Throttle position sensor input below or above the maximum acceptable voltage; check engine lamp ON, California only.
25	A shorted condition detected in one or more of the ISC control circuits; check engine lamp ON, California only.
26	High resistance condition detected in the INJ 1 or INJ 2 injector bank circuit.
27	INJ 1 or INJ 2 injector bank output driver stage does not respond properly to the control signal.
31	An open or shorted condition detected in the purge solenoid circuit; check engine lamp ON, California only.
32	An open or shorted condition detected in the EGR solenoid circuit or required change in fuel/air ratio not detected during diagnostic test; check engine lamp ON, California only.
33	An open or shorted condition detected in the A/C clutch relay circuit.
34	An open or shorted condition detected in the speed control vacuum or vent solenoid circuits.
35	Idle contact switch input circuit shorted to ground or circuit open.
36	An open or shorted condition detected in the air switching solenoid circuit.
37	An open or shorted condition detected in the torque converter part throttle unlock solenoid circuit, automatic transmission only.
41	Output driver stage for alternator field does not respond properly to the voltage regulator control signal.
42	An open or shorted condition detected in the auto shutdown relay circuit or no Z1 voltage sensed when the auto shutdown relay is energized.
43	Output driver stage for ignition coil does not respond properly to the dwell control signal.
44	No FJ2 voltage present at the logic board during controller operation.
45	An open or shorted condition detected in the overdrive solenoid circuit, automatic transmission only.
46	Battery voltage sense input above target charging voltage during engine operation; check engine lamp ON, California only.
47	Battery voltage sense input below target charging voltage during engine operation.
51	Oxygen sensor signal input indicates lean fuel/air ratio condition during engine operation; check engine lamp ON, California only.
52	Oxygen sensor signal input indicates rich fuel/air ratio condition during engine operation or adaptive fuel value learned excessively due to a sustained rich condition; check engine lamp ON, California only.
53	Internal engine controller fault condition detected.
55	Completion of fault code display on the check engine lamp.
62	Unsuccessful attempt to update EMR mileage in the controller EEPROM.
63	Unsuccessful attempt to write to an EEPROM location by the controller or an unrecognized fault ID received by DRBII.

Year — 1989
Model — D & W 250–350
Engine — 5.9L (360 cid) EFI V8
Engine Code — VIN W

ECM TROUBLE CODES

Code	Explanation
11	No distributor reference signal detected during engine cranking.
12	Direct battery input to controller disconnected within the last 50–100 ignition key-on's.
13	No variation in MAP sensor signal is detected or no difference is recognized between the engine MAP reading and the stored barometric pressure reading; check engine lamp ON, California only.
14	MAP sensor input below or above minimum acceptable voltage; check engine lamp ON, California only.
15	No distance sensor signal detected during road load conditions. Check engine lamp ON, California only.
16	Battery voltage sense input not detected during engine running; check engine lamp ON, California only.
17	Engine coolant temperature remains below normal operating temperatures during vehicle travel (thermostat).
21	Neither rich or lean condition is detected from the oxygen sensor input; check engine lamp ON, California only.
22	Coolant temperature sensor input below or above the maximum acceptable voltage; check engine lamp ON, California only.
23	Throttle body temperature sensor input below or above the minimum acceptable voltage.
24	Throttle position sensor input below or above the maximum acceptable voltage; check engine lamp ON, California only.
25	A shorted condition detected in one or more of the ISC control circuits; check engine lamp ON, California only.
26	High resistance condition detected in the INJ 1 or INJ 2 injector bank circuit.
27	INJ 1 or INJ 2 injector bank output driver stage does not respond properly to the control signal.
31	An open or shorted condition detected in the purge solenoid circuit; check engine lamp ON, California only.
32	An open or shorted condition detected in the EGR solenoid circuit or required change in fuel/air ratio not detected during diagnostic test; check engine lamp ON, California only.
33	An open or shorted condition detected in the A/C clutch relay circuit.
34	An open or shorted condition detected in the speed control vacuum or vent solenoid circuits.
35	Idle contact switch input circuit shorted to ground or circuit open.
36	An open or shorted condition detected in the air switching solenoid circuit.
37	An open or shorted condition detected in the torque converter part throttle unlock solenoid circuit, automatic transmission only.
41	Output driver stage for alternator field does not respond properly to the voltage regulator control signal.
42	An open or shorted condition detected in the auto shutdown relay circuit or no Z1 voltage sensed when the auto shutdown relay is energized.
43	Output driver stage for ignition coil does not respond properly to the dwell control signal.
44	No FJ2 voltage present at the logic board during controller operation.
45	An open or shorted condition detected in the overdrive solenoid circuit, automatic transmission only.
46	Battery voltage sense input above target charging voltage during engine operation; check engine lamp ON, California only.

ECM TROUBLE CODES (cont'd)

Code	Explanation
47	Battery voltage sense input below target charging voltage during engine operation.
51	Oxygen sensor signal input indicates lean fuel/air ratio condition during engine operation; check engine lamp ON, California only.
52	Oxygen sensor signal input indicates rich fuel/air ratio condition during engine operation or adaptive fuel value leaned excessively due to a sustained rich condition; check engine lamp ON, California only.
53	Internal engine controller fault condition detected.
55	Completion of fault code display on the check engine lamp.
62	Unsuccessful attempt to update EMR mileage in the controller EEPROM.
63	Unsuccessful attempt to write to an EEPROM location by the controller or an unrecognized fault ID received by DRBII.

Year — 1989
Model — Dodge Ramcharger
Engine — 5.9L (360 cid) EFI V8
Engine Code — VIN W

ECM TROUBLE CODES

Code	Explanation
11	No distributor reference signal detected during engine cranking.
12	Direct battery input to controller disconnected within the last 50–100 ignition key-on's.
13	No variation in MAP sensor signal is detected or no difference is recognized between the engine MAP reading and the stored barometric pressure reading; check engine lamp ON, California only.
14	MAP sensor input below or above minimum acceptable voltage; check engine lamp ON, California only.
15	No distance sensor signal detected during road load conditions. Check engine lamp ON, California only.
16	Battery voltage sense input not detected during engine running; check engine lamp ON, California only.
17	Engine coolant temperature remains below normal operating temperatures during vehicle travel (thermostat).
21	Neither rich or lean condition is detected from the oxygen sensor input; check engine lamp ON, California only.
22	Coolant temperature sensor input below or above the maximum acceptable voltage; check engine lamp ON, California only.
23	Throttle body temperature sensor input below or above the minimum acceptable voltage.
24	Throttle position sensor input below or above the maximum acceptable voltage; check engine lamp ON, California only.
25	A shorted condition detected in one or more of the ISC control circuits; check engine lamp ON, California only.
26	High resistance condition detected in the INJ 1 or INJ 2 injector bank circuit.
27	INJ 1 or INJ 2 injector bank output driver stage does not respond properly to the control signal.
31	An open or shorted condition detected in the purge solenoid circuit; check engine lamp ON, California only.
32	An open or shorted condition detected in the EGR solenoid circuit or required change in fuel/air ratio not detected during diagnostic test; check engine lamp ON, California only.
33	An open or shorted condition detected in the A/C clutch relay circuit.

ECM TROUBLE CODES (cont'd)

Code	Explanation
34	An open or shorted condition detected in the speed control vacuum or vent solenoid circuits.
35	Idle contact switch input circuit shorted to ground or circuit open.
36	An open or shorted condition detected in the air switching solenoid circuit.
37	An open or shorted condition detected in the torque converter part throttle unlock solenoid circuit, automatic transmission only.
41	Output driver stage for alternator field does not respond properly to the voltage regulator control signal.
42	An open or shorted condition detected in the auto shutdown relay circuit or no Z1 voltage sensed when the auto shutdown relay is energized.
43	Output driver stage for ignition coil does not respond properly to the dwell control signal.
44	No FJ2 voltage present at the logic board during controller operation.
45	An open or shorted condition detected in the overdrive solenoid circuit, automatic transmission only.
46	Battery voltage sense input above target charging voltage during engine operation; check engine lamp ON, California only.
47	Battery voltage sense input below target charging voltage during engine operation.
51	Oxygen sensor signal input indicates lean fuel/air ratio condition during engine operation; check engine lamp ON, California only.
52	Oxygen sensor signal input indicates rich fuel/air ratio condition during engine operation or adaptive fuel value leaned excessively due to a sustained rich condition; check engine lamp ON, California only.
53	Internal engine controller fault condition detected.
55	Completion of fault code display on the check engine lamp.
62	Unsuccessful attempt to update EMR mileage in the controller EEPROM.
63	Unsuccessful attempt to write to an EEPROM location by the controller or an unrecognized fault ID received by DRBII.

Year – 1989
Model – D & W 250–350/ Dodge Ramcharger/Vans
Engine – 5.9L (360 cid) EFI V8
Engine Code – VIN W

ECM TROUBLE CODES

Code	Explanation
11	No distributor reference signal detected during engine cranking.
12	Direct battery input to controller disconnected within the last 50–100 ignition key-on's.
13	No variation in MAP sensor signal is detected or no difference is recognized between the engine MAP reading and the stored barometric pressure reading; check engine lamp ON, California only.
14	MAP sensor input below or above minimum acceptable voltage; check engine lamp ON, California only.
15	No distance sensor signal detected during road load conditions. Check engine lamp ON, California only.
16	Battery voltage sense input not detected during engine running; check engine lamp ON, California only.

ECM TROUBLE CODES (cont'd)

Code	Explanation
17	Engine coolant temperature remains below normal operating temperatures during vehicle travel (thermostat).
21	Neither rich or lean condition is detected from the oxygen sensor input; check engine lamp ON, California only.
22	Coolant temperature sensor input below or above the maximum acceptable voltage; check engine lamp ON, California only.
23	Throttle body temperature sensor input below or above the minimum acceptable voltage.
24	Throttle position sensor input below or above the maximum acceptable voltage; check engine lamp ON, California only.
25	A shorted condition detected in one or more of the ISC control circuits; check engine lamp ON, California only.
26	High resistance condition detected in the INJ 1 or INJ 2 injector bank circuit.
27	INJ 1 or INJ 2 injector bank output driver stage does not respond properly to the control signal.
31	An open or shorted condition detected in the purge solenoid circuit; check engine lamp ON, California only.
32	An open or shorted condition detected in the EGR solenoid circuit or required change in fuel/air ratio not detected during diagnostic test; check engine lamp ON, California only.
33	An open or shorted condition detected in the A/C clutch relay circuit.
34	An open or shorted condition detected in the speed control vacuum or vent solenoid circuits.
35	Idle contact switch input circuit shorted to ground or circuit open.
36	An open or shorted condition detected in the air switching solenoid circuit.
37	An open or shorted condition detected in the torque converter part throttle unlock solenoid circuit, automatic transmission only.
41	Output driver stage for alternator field does not respond properly to the voltage regulator control signal.
42	An open or shorted condition detected in the auto shutdown relay circuit or no Z1 voltage sensed when the auto shutdown relay is energized.
43	Output driver stage for ignition coil does not respond properly to the dwell control signal.
44	No FJ2 voltage present at the logic board during controller operation.
45	An open or shorted condition detected in the overdrive solenoid circuit, automatic transmission only.
46	Battery voltage sense input above target charging voltage during engine operation; check engine lamp ON, California only.
47	Battery voltage sense input below target charging voltage during engine operation.
51	Oxygen sensor signal input indicates lean fuel/air ratio condition during engine operation; check engine lamp ON, California only.
52	Oxygen sensor signal input indicates rich fuel/air ratio condition during engine operation or adaptive fuel value leaned excessively due to a sustained rich condition; check engine lamp ON, California only.
53	Internal engine controller fault condition detected.
55	Completion of fault code display on the check engine lamp.
62	Unsuccessful attempt to update EMR mileage in the controller EEPROM.
63	Unsuccessful attempt to write to an EEPROM location by the controller or an unrecognized fault ID received by DRBII.

Year – 1989
Model – Vans
Engine – 5.9L (360 cid) EFI V8
Engine Code – VIN W

ECM TROUBLE CODES

Code	Explanation
11	No distributor reference signal detected during engine cranking.
12	Direct battery input to controller disconnected within the last 50–100 ignition key-on's.
13	No variation in MAP sensor signal is detected or no difference is recognized between the engine MAP reading and the stored barometric pressure reading; check engine lamp ON, California only.
14	MAP sensor input below or above minimum acceptable voltage; check engine lamp ON, California only.
15	No distance sensor signal detected during road load conditions. Check engine lamp ON, California only.
16	Battery voltage sense input not detected during engine running; check engine lamp ON, California only.
17	Engine coolant temperature remains below normal operating temperatures during vehicle travel (thermostat).
21	Neither rich or lean condition is detected from the oxygen sensor input; check engine lamp ON, California only.
22	Coolant temperature sensor input below or above the maximum acceptable voltage; check engine lamp ON, California only.
23	Throttle body temperature sensor input below or above the minimum acceptable voltage.
24	Throttle position sensor input below or above the maximum acceptable voltage; check engine lamp ON, California only.
25	A shorted condition detected in one or more of the ISC control circuits; check engine lamp ON, California only.
26	High resistance condition detected in the INJ 1 or INJ 2 injector bank circuit.
27	INJ 1 or INJ 2 injector bank output driver stage does not respond properly to the control signal.
31	An open or shorted condition detected in the purge solenoid circuit; check engine lamp ON, California only.
32	An open or shorted condition detected in the EGR solenoid circuit or required change in fuel/air ratio not detected during diagnostic test; check engine lamp ON, California only.
33	An open or shorted condition detected in the A/C clutch relay circuit.
34	An open or shorted condition detected in the speed control vacuum or vent solenoid circuits.
35	Idle contact switch input circuit shorted to ground or circuit open.
36	An open or shorted condition detected in the air switching solenoid circuit.
37	An open or shorted condition detected in the torque converter part throttle unlock solenoid circuit, automatic transmission only.
41	Output driver stage for alternator field does not respond properly to the voltage regulator control signal.
42	An open or shorted condition detected in the auto shutdown relay circuit or no Z1 voltage sensed when the auto shutdown relay is energized.
43	Output driver stage for ignition coil does not respond properly to the dwell control signal.
44	No FJ2 voltage present at the logic board during controller operation.
45	An open or shorted condition detected in the overdrive solenoid circuit, automatic transmission only.
46	Battery voltage sense input above target charging voltage during engine operation; check engine lamp ON, California only.

ECM TROUBLE CODES (cont'd)

Code	Explanation
47	Battery voltage sense input below target charging voltage during engine operation.
51	Oxygen sensor signal input indicates lean fuel/air ratio condition during engine operation; check engine lamp ON, California only.
52	Oxygen sensor signal input indicates rich fuel/air ratio condition during engine operation or adaptive fuel value leaned excessively due to a sustained rich condition; check engine lamp ON, California only.
53	Internal engine controller fault condition detected.
55	Completion of fault code display on the check engine lamp.
62	Unsuccessful attempt to update EMR mileage in the controller EEPROM.
63	Unsuccessful attempt to write to an EEPROM location by the controller or an unrecognized fault ID received by DRB-II.

Year – 1989
Model – Cherokee
Engine – 2.5L (150 cid) 4 cyl
Engine Code – VIN E

ECM TROUBLE CODES

Code	Explanation
1000	Ignition line low
1001	Ignition line high
1004	Battery voltage low
1005	Sensor ground line out of limits
1006	Exhaust Gas Recirculation (EGR)/EVAP solenoid line low
1007	Exhaust Gas Recirculation (EGR)/EVAP solenoid line high
1008	Power steering line low
1009	Power steering line high
1012	Manifold Absolute Pressure (MAP) line low
1013	Manifold Absolute Pressure (MAP) line high
1014	Fuel pump line low
1015	Fuel pump line high
1016	Charge Air Temperature (CAT) sensor line low
1017	Charge Air Temperature (CAT) sensor line high
1018	No serial data (automatic or manual transmission)
1019	Power latch not set
1021	Engine failed to start due to mechanical, fuel or ignition problem
1022	Start line low
1027	Electronic Control Unit (ECU) sees Wide Open Throttle (WOT)
1028	Electronic Control Unit (ECU) does not see Wide Open Throttle (WOT)
1029	Closed throttle line low
1030	Closed throttle line high
1031	Electronic Control Unit (ECU) sees closed throttle
1032	Electronic Control Unit (ECU) does not see closed throttle
1033	Idle speed increase line low

ECM TROUBLE CODES (cont'd)

Code	Explanation
1034	Idle speed increase line high
1035	Idle speed decrease line low
1036	Idle speed decrease line high
1037	Throttle Position Sensor (TPS) reads low
1038	Park/Neutral line high—automatic or manual transmission
1039	Park/Neutral line low with manual transmission
1040	Latched B+ line low
1041	Latched B+ line high
1042	No latched B+, ½ volt drop
1043	Shift light circuit grounded
1044	Fault in shift light circuit—automatic or manual transmission
1045	Shift light circuit open
1047	Wrong Electronic Control Unit (ECU)
1048	Manual vehicle equipped with automatic Electronic Control Unit (ECU)
1049	Automatic vehicle equipped with manual Electronic Control Unit (ECU)
1050	Idle rpm's less than 500
1051	Idle rpm's greater than 2000
1052	Manifold Absolute Pressure (MAP) sensor out of limits
1053	Change in Manifold Absolute Pressure (MAP) reading out of limits
1054	Coolant Temperature Sensor (CTS) line low
1055	Coolant Temperature Sensor (CTS) line high
1056	Inactive Coolant Temperature Sensor (CTS)
1059	Air conditioning request line low
1060	Air conditioning request line high
1061	Air conditioning select line low
1062	Air conditioning select line high
1063	Air conditioning clutch line low
1064	Air conditioning clutch line high
1065	Oxygen sensor reads rich
1066	Oxygen sensor reads lean
1067	Latch relay line low
1068	Latch relay line high
1069	No tach
1074	Electronic Control Unit (ECU) does not see speed sensor signal

Year – 1989
Model – Cherokee
Engine – 4.0L (242 cid) V6
Engine Code – VIN M

ECM TROUBLE CODES

Code	Explanation
1000	Ignition line low
1001	Ignition line high
1002	Oxygen heater line high
1004	Battery voltage low
1005	Sensor ground line out of limits
1013	Manifold Absolute Pressure (MAP) line high
1014	Fuel pump line low
1015	Fuel pump line high
1016	Charge Air Temperature (CAT) sensor line low
1017	Charge Air Temperature (CAT) sensor line high
1018	No serial data
1020	No SYNC pulse seen
1021	Engine failed to start due to mechanical, fuel or ignition problem
1022	Start line low
1027	Electronic Control Unit (ECU) sees Wide Open Throttle (WOT)
1028	Electronic Control Unit (ECU) does not see Wide Open Throttle (WOT)
1031	Electronic Control Unit (ECU) sees closed throttle
1032	Electronic Control Unit (ECU) does not see closed throttle
1037	Throttle Position Sensor (TPS) reads low
1038	Park/Neutral line high (automatic transmission)
1040	Latched B + line low
1041	Latched B + line high
1042	No latched B +, ½ volt drop
1044	Fault in shift light circuit (manual transmission)
1047	Wrong Electronic Control Unit (ECU)
1048	Manual vehicle equipped with automatic Electronic Control Unit (ECU)
1049	Automatic vehicle equipped with manual Electronic Control Unit (ECU)
1050	Idle rpm's less than 500
1051	Idle rpm's greater than 2000
1052	Manifold Absolute Pressure (MAP) sensor out of limits
1053	Change in Manifold Absolute Pressure (MAP) reading out of limits
1054	Coolant Temperature Sensor (CTS) line low
1055	Coolant Temperature Sensor (CTS) line high
1056	Inactive Coolant Temperature Sensor (CTS)
1057	Knock circuit shorted
1058	Knock value out of limits
1059	Air conditioning request line low
1060	Air conditioning request line high
1061	Air conditioning select line low

ECM TROUBLE CODES (cont'd)

Code	Explanation
1062	Air conditioning select line high
1063	Air conditioning clutch line low
1064	Air conditioning clutch line high
1065	Oxygen sensor reads rich
1066	Oxygen sensor reads lean
1067	Latch relay line low
1068	Latch relay line high
1069	No tach
1072	IAS motor cannot control idle
1073	Electronic Control Unit (ECU) does not see speed sensor signal
1200	Electronic Control Unit (ECU) defective
1201	Injector short to B+
1202	All injectors shorted to ground
1203–1208	Injector N shorted to ground
1209	All injectors open
1210–1215	Injector N circuit open
1216	No voltage at Electronic Control Unit (ECU) from air conditioning relay
1217	No voltage at Electronic Control Unit (ECU) from oxygen heater relay
1218	No voltage at Electronic Control Unit (ECU) from shift light
1220	No voltage at Electronic Control Unit (ECU) from Exhaust Gas Recirculation (EGR) solenoid
1222	Manifold Absolute Pressure (MAP) not grounded
1223	No Electronic Control Unit (ECU) test run

Ford Motor Company

INDEX

FORD MOTOR COMPANY

Microprocessor Control Unit (MCU) System

SELF-DIAGNOSTIC SYSTEM

Description

The MCU has the capability to diagnose a malfunction within its own system. However, it is not designed to diagnose malfunctions outside the MCU system.

Through the use of trouble code indicators, the system will indicate where to look for MCU problems through the use of a self-test computer program, built into the MCU module. Standard test equipment, such as an analog voltmeter, can be used to check the system or a special tester can be used to simplify the testing procedure on the MCU self-test connector.

When the analog voltmeter or the special tester is connected to the test connector and the system is triggered, the self-test simulates a variety of engine operating conditions and evaluates all the responses received from the various MCU components, so that any abnormal operating condition can be detected.

A routine visual inspection should be the first step in diagnosis of the MCU system. Broken or frayed wires, loose connections, obvious shorts, disconnected or damaged vacuum hoses are among the areas that should be inspected and corrected before any tests are done.

Entering Diagnostic Mode

The MCU system incorporates a self-test connector, located near the MCU module in the engine compartment on one of the fender aprons, for isolating problems in the system.

A received response to the initiated self-test is reported, through the self-test connector to 1 of 2 testing devices, an analog voltmeter or a Self-Test Automatic Readout (STAR) tester, which in turn indicates codes as a series of pulses, displayed on the testers' meter.

The codes are displayed by a series of electrical pulses which indicate a 2-digit number. This 2-digit service code indicates the source of MCU system's malfunction.

ANALOG VOLTMETER

1. With the ignition key in the **OFF** position, connect a jumper wire between circuit 60 and 201 on the self-test connector.
2. Connect an analog voltmeter from the battery positive post to the self-test output on the self-test connector.
3. Set the voltmeter on the DC volt range to read from 0–15V.

NOTE: One quick initialization pulse may occur on the voltmeter immediately after turning the ignition key ON. The output service code will occur approximately 5 seconds.

STAR TESTER

1. With the ignition key in the **OFF** position, connect the black negative lead to the battery's negative post.
2. Connect the red lead to the self-test output terminal on the self-test connector.
3. Connect the white lead to the self-test trigger on the self-test connector.

NOTE: Operating instructions for the STAR tester are located on the back panel of the tester.

Operation

With the analog voltmeter connected and the ignition switch

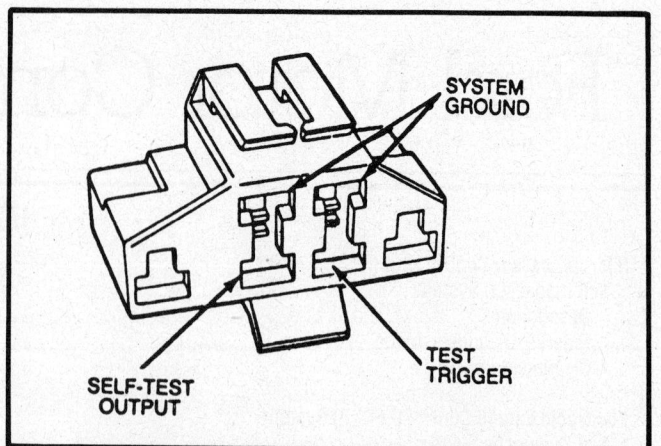

MCU self-test connector

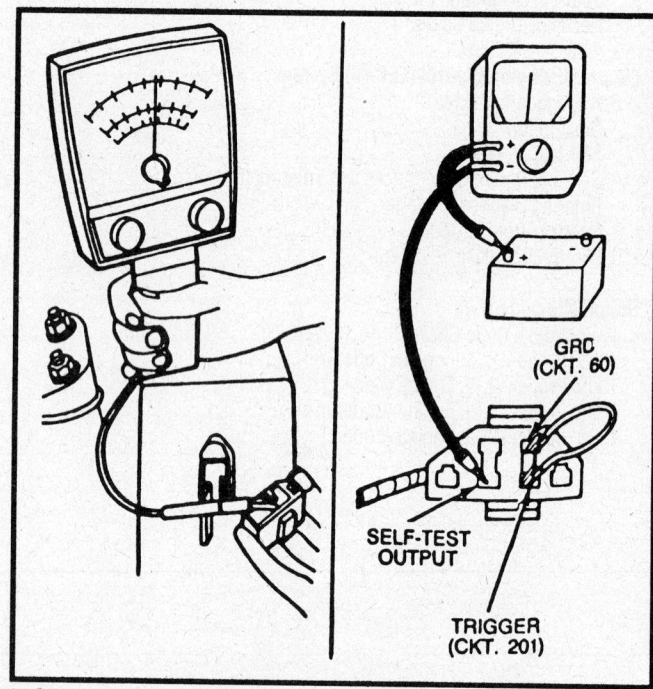

MCU self-test with analog voltmeter

turned **ON**, without the engine operating, the MCU system is placed in its reporting service code display mode.

When a service code is reported on the analog meter, it will represent itself as a pulsing or sweeping movement of the voltmeter scale's needle across the dial face of the meter. Therefore, a single digit number of 3 will be indicated by 3 pulses (sweeps) of the needle across the dial. Since the codes are indicated by a 2-digit number, such as 32, the self-test's service code 32 will be displayed as 3 pulses (sweeps) of the meter's needle with a ½ second pause between pulses (sweeps) and a 2 second pause between digits. When more than 1 service code is indicated, a 5 second pause between codes will occur.

SELF-TEST AUTOMATIC READOUT (STAR) TESTER

After connecting the tester and turning **ON** its power switch, the tester will run a display check with a code 88 beginning to flash in the display window. A steady 00 will then appear to signify that the tester is ready to start the self-test and receive the stored codes.

In order to receive the codes, press the button on the front of the tester. The button will latch down and a colon will appear in the display window on front of the Code 00 (:00). The colon must be displayed before the trouble codes can be received.

Follow the instructions accompanying the tester to complete the self-test procedure.

OTHER CIRCUIT AND SELF-TEST UNITS

Numerous other self-test units have been developed to assist the technician in obtaining the stored trouble codes. Should these units be used in determining malfunctions or to retrieve stored trouble codes from the system, the manufacturer's operating procedures must be followed to prevent damage to the MCU system and/or the test unit.

Clearing Diagnostic Memory

To exit the MCU system, turn the ignition key to the **OFF** position and disconnect the read-out meter from the self-test connector.

Electronic Engine Control (EEC-III) System

SELF-DIAGNOSTIC SYSTEM

Description

The EEC-III system is equipped with a self-test feature to aid in diagnosis. The self-test is a set of instructions programmed in the computer memory of the calibration assembly. When the program is activated, the computer performs a system test. This verifies the proper connection and operation of the various sensors and actuators. The self-test program controls vehicle operation during the test sequence. Basically, the self-test program does the following:

1. Sends commands to the solenoids and checks for proper response.
2. Checks for reasonable readings from the sensors.
3. Produces numbered codes that inform the technician of a trouble area or of "all okay" operation.

To further test and service the EEC-III system, perform what is called a "Quick Test" first and if the vehicle passes these tests, the EEC-III system is functioning properly and the vehicle's problem exists somewhere other than in the EEC-III system. Should the "Quick Test" fail in 1 or more catagories, tests known as "Pin Tests" should be initiated to located the malfunction.

A Self Test is used in conjunction with the Quick Test, to perform proper diagnostics. The EEC-III system includes self test capabilities in the computer memory of the processor and when a Self Test is activated during a Quick Test, the ECA performs the EEC system test to verify that various sensors and actuators are connected and operating properly.

Before attempting any repairs or extensive diagnosis, visually examine the vehicle for obvious faults.

1. Remove air cleaner assembly. Check for dirt, foreign matter or other contamination in and around filter element.
2. Examine vacuum hose for proper routing and connection. Also check for broken, cracked or pinched hoses or fittings.
3. Examine each portion of the EEC-III wiring harness. Check for the following at each location.
   a. Proper connection to sensors and solenoids.
   b. Loose or disconnected connectors.
   c. Broken or disconnected wires.
   d. Partially seated connectors.
   e. Broken or frayed wires.
   f. Shorting between wires.

g. Corrosion.
4. Inspect sensor for obvious physical damage.
5. Operate engine and inspect exhaust manifold and exhaust gas oxygen sensor for leaks.
6. Repair faults as necessary. Reinstall air cleaner. If the problem has not been corrected, proceed to self-test.

Entering Diagnostic Mode

SELF-TEST OPERATION

The EEC diagnostic tester includes provisions for the self-test feature. In this case, the technician monitors the test panel for flashes of the thermactor solenoids operation. The series of light flashes represent a service code. The test can also be accomplished using a vacuum pump and gauges. In this case, the technician must actually monitor the solenoids for pulses or observe corresponding vacuum signals caused by the pulses. In all cases, the starting method for the self-test is the same.

The technician should activate the self-test only after proper engine preparation. The engine should be run until the radiator hose is hot and pressurized.

DISPLAYING CODES WITH TEST METER

Codes are displayed by a series of pulses on both the thermactor air lights (TAB and TAD) on the Test meter. The pulses form 2-digit numbers. Each pulse is ON for ½ second then off for ½ second for each count. A full second pause separates the digits, a 5 second pause separates service code numbers. A digital Volt/Ohmmeter can also be used and connected to the EEC-III tester.

NOTE: Complete connection and operational instructions accompany the tester and are located on the inside of the tester cover. Refer to the instructions before initiating test.

The begin the test, the test meter cables must be connected in the following manner:

1. Turn the ignition switch **OFF** and disconnect the EEC-III harness from the ECA.
2. Connect the EFI adapter harness and tester harness as per the tester's instructions.
3. If the tester lamps are illuminated with the ignition OFF, check for a short circuit between the vehicle battery and

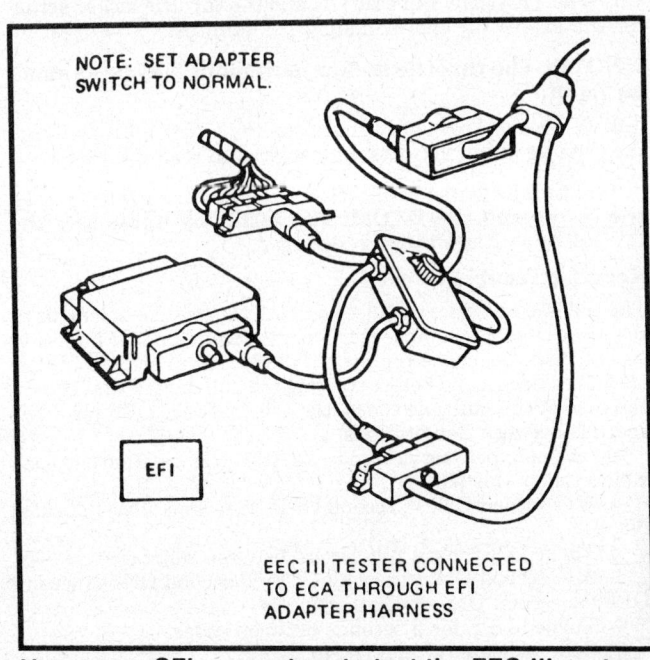

NOTE: SET ADAPTER SWITCH TO NORMAL.

EFI

EEC III TESTER CONNECTED TO ECA THROUGH EFI ADAPTER HARNESS

Necessary CFI connectors to test the EEC-III system

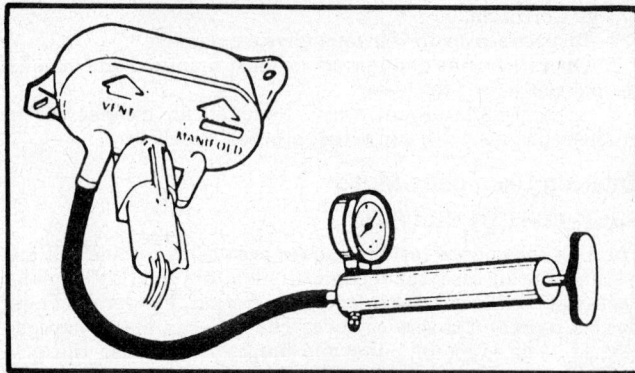

Triggering the EEC-III self-test sequence

the ECA power circuit or an open circuit in the ECC-III ground circuits.

4. Turn the ignition switch **ON**. Press and hold the "Test Light" button. All lights on the control panel of the tester should turn ON.

5. If the lights do not display, a problem exists within the tester.

TRIGGERING SELF-TEST

1. Start the engine.

2. Operate the engine at 1800 rpm for 1–2 minutes until the upper radiator hose is pressurized and hot or have the engine near normal operating temperature.

3. Set the tester switch to A-8 position.

4. Attach a vacuum pump to the B/MAP sensor vent port and apply vacuum (approximately 20 in. Hg) until the DVOM reading is 2.85V and hold for for approximately 8 seconds.

NOTE: It maybe necessary to hold the vacuum for a longer time interval in order to trigger the system.

5. Release the vacuum on the vent port of the B/MAP sensor and observe the lights on the tester console.

6. The throttle kicker light (TKS) will blink the ON light, then, OFF. An interval of 2 seconds will elapse and the TKS ON light will blink.

7. The TKS light will stay ON and the throttle kicker actuator will extend for approximately 1½ minutes.

NOTE: The throttle kicker movement may be as small as 1/16 in.

8. When the TKS light turns from the ON to OFF light and the throttle kicker retracts, be prepared to read the codes.

NOTE: The pulse indications can be observed on both the tester and the DVOM. The tester by lights and the DVOM by voltage pulse readings.

Reading Trouble Codes

The codes are a series of pulses on both thermactor solenoids at the same time. Each pulse is ON for ½ second and OFF for a ½ second. This sequence represents the No. 1. The solenoids are OFF for a full second before starting the 2nd digit of the code. In the case of the multiple codes, the solenoids are OFF for 5 full seconds between 2-digit codes.

As an example, service code 23 (throttle position sensor), would follow this pattern.

1. A ½ second ON, ½ second OFF, ½ second ON—indicates No. 2.

2. Turned OFF for a full second between numbers.

3. A ½ second ON, ½ second OFF, ½ second ON; ½ second OFF, ½ second ON—indicates No. 3.

4. Turned OFF for 5 seconds between codes.

5. Code indicated would be No. 23.

The vehicle remains in self-test for 15 seconds after completing the last code, with the tester's Ccanister Purge (CANP) light turned ON for 15 seconds; the system then returns to normal operation. When beginning diagnosis and repairs, consider the final code first. In the above case of 23, then 41, begin with diagnosis of code 41 (fuel control lean), and then continue with code 23 (throttle position sensor).

NOTE: On some engine calibrations, both the CANP lights (ON and OFF) could be illuminated during the test.

DISPLAYING CODES WITHOUT TEST METER

1. Tee a vacuum gauge into the hose that connects the air injection pump diverter valve and the Thermactor Air Diverter Solenoid valve.

2. Have the engine at normal operating temperature.

3. Attach the vacuum pump hose to the VENT port on the B/MAP sensor.

4. Apply 20 in. Hg of vacuum and hold for approximately 60 seconds.

5. The Throttle Kicker actuator (TKS) will extend and then retract when the vacuum is released.

6. The vacuum gauge needle will pulse twice on the EFI system to indicate the system is ready to check its self out.

7. If the needle doesn't move, either the diagnostic circuit inside the ECA is faulty or the Thermactor pump is faulty.

8. The system will activate the Throttle Kicker Actuator again. As the system starts through its self examination, the vacuum gauge reading will rise and jump a few times and then the Throttle Kicker Actuator will pull in.

9. This operation means the diagnosis is completed and the system is ready to communicate the findings to the technician.

10. To translate the findings, count the pulses noted on the vacuum gauge.

11. As an example, 2 pulses, pause, 3 pulses represent code 23.

12. If there are more than malfunction, the system sends out trouble codes, 1 at a time, with a long pause between then.

Trouble Codes

CODE 11 — System is OK.
CODE 12 — No rpm signal to the ECA.
CODE 21 — ECT sensor wiring faulty.
CODE 22 — B/MAP faulty.
CODE 23 — TP sensor faulty.
CODE 31 — EVP sensor not moving to open position.
CODE 32 — EVP sensor not moving to closed position.
CODE 41 — Air/fuel mixture too lean.
CODE 42 — Air/fuel mixture too rich.
CODE 43 — Coolant temperature below 120°F.
CODE 44 — Thermactor system faulty.

Electronic Engine Control (EEC-IV) System

NOTE: This EEC-IV system is for 1984–89 vehicles.

SELF-DIAGNOSTIC SYSTEM

Description

The EEC-IV system has a Keep Alive Memory, which the other systems did not have. The ECA retains any intermittent trouble codes stored within the last 20 engine restarts. With this system, the memory is not erased when the key is turned **OFF**. Trouble codes retained in the ECA are used by the technicians to evaluate and diagnose the EEC-IV system.

NOTE: In the EEC-IV system, the reference voltage is 5V, instead of the 9V sed with the other EEC systems and

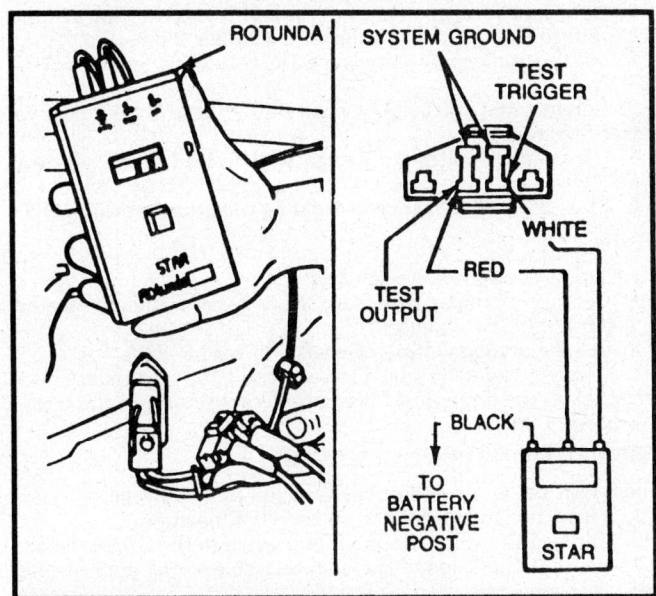

MCU self-tester with STAR tester

a power relay is used to provide all necessary power required for the EEC-IV system.

A short learning period will occur on new vehicles, when the battery has been disconnected during normal service and when an EEC-IV component is disconnected or replaced.

If an EEC-IV component is replaced, due to damage or age, the memory may need to be cleared to eliminate the adjustments that were made to correct for the replaced component. It is possible for the engine operation to actually deteriorate because the new component will be controlled as if it were still the replaced component.

During the adjustment or learning period, usually under 5 but sometimes as much as 10 miles of driving, some vehicles could exhibit abnormal drive symptoms, such as surge, hesitation, high idle speed, etc., which should clear up after the learning period.

Improvements have been made on the EEC-IV system to provide better driveability when 1 or more sensors fail. The basic improvement within the ECA is that each sensor now has an input operating range. The ECA monitors whether the sensor is operating within it operating limits. When an out of limit condition occurs, the ECA will store a diagnostic code in its memory and will substitute an in-limit signal.

By substituting an in-limit signal, an alternate system strategy comes into operation, which allows the vehicle to continue running. Prior to this change, the engine may have stalled or may not have run at all. With the addition of the Failure Mode Effects Management (FMEM), the vehicle can now be started and operated. When in this Limp In mode, the vehicle may not run well, but it will allow the operator to drive the vehicle to a service center. When the FMEM system is in effect, the computer will display Code 98 and the "Check Engine" light will turn ON during the duration of FMEM.

The EEC-IV system has the capability of checking the electronic components in the system. This self-test, often referred to as a QUICK TEST, is an internal function performed by the Electronic Control Assembly (ECA), in which the ECA checks the operational status of every circuit and component in the EEC-IV system.

Self-test only checks the system components, such as sensors, relays, switches and solenoids. It cannot provide information on

driveability/engine performance problems, unless related to 1 of the system's components.

During the self-test, the ECA reads and evaluates signals received from the system input components. The input components are checked by the ECA during a Key On/Engine Off and during the Engine Running portion of the test.

This self-test also allows the technician to determine if the ECA is capable of controlling the ignition timing of the engine, since different engine operating modes require the timing be advanced or retarded. The ECA must do this automatically or the engine will not perform properly.

NOTE: EEC-IV system engines have an in-line base timing connector that must be disconnected to check the base ignition timing. The connector is part of the SPOUT circuit and when disconnected, interrupts the electronic timing signal and locks the system into a fixed timing base. The SPOUT connector is located within 6 in. of the distributor on all EEC-IV applications.

The self-test can be performed by an analog voltmeter, Self-Test Automatic Readout (STAR or Super STAR II) tester or equivalent, Malfunction Indicator Light (MIL) or Message Center (Continental only). Other types of automatic testers are marketed and are available to the technicians. With each of the automatic testers, it is important that the technician follow the manufacturer's instructions on hook-up and display procedures.

Self-Test Modes
KEY ON/ENGINE OFF (KOEO)

In this segment of the test, the system inputs and outputs are checked for existing faults. These type of faults are referred to as hard faults in this test procedure because they represent a failure that is always present. Also, the system is checked for intermediate faults, which indicate that a problem did exist recently somewhere in the system. The fault is not now present but it did occur some time recently. This usually indicates a loose wire, a bad connection, a broken wire that opens periodically or some failure similar to these. Some times, recent work that may have been done to the vehicle is a good place to start when trying to determine the root of an intermediate problem.

Key On/Engine Off Sequence
FAST CODES
At the very beginning of the Key On/Engine Off self-test sequence, the ECA generates standard codes at a rate of approximately 100 times faster than a voltmeter can respond. These fast codes are read by special computer type machines in the assembly plants and maybe observed on the voltmeter by a slight deflection of the needle. They have no practical application in the service field.
ON-DEMAND CODES
The on-demand codes indicate there is something wrong somewhere in the EEC-IV system at the time of the self-test. This type of malfunction is considered to be a hard fault.
SEPARATOR CODES
The separator codes or pulses, cause the voltmeter needle to sweep once, indicating that on-demand codes have ceased and memory codes are about to begin.
MEMORY CODES
Memory codes indicate there was a recent problem, somewhere in the EEC-IV system, such as an open or short circuit, though it is not present at the time of the self-test. These codes are often referred to as intermediate faults.
CONTINUOUS MEMORY CODES
Continuous memory codes are issued as a result of the information displayed during the continuous self-test, while the vehicle was in normal operation. These codes are displayed only during the Key On/Engine Off. These codes are displayed only during

Key On/Engine Off testing and after the separator code. These codes should be used for diagnosis only when Key On/Engine Off and Engine Running self-tests result in Code 11 and the whole quick tests have been completed.

KEY ON ENGINE RUNNING (KOER)

In this portion of the test, the system is checked under all operating conditions. The output devices are all activated to check for proper operation. Only Hard Faults are noted during this test.

Engine Running Segment
ENGINE IDENTIFICATION CODES

The engine identification codes have no practical application in the service field but are part of the assembly process. When the self-test is initiated at the beginning of the engine running segment, the voltmeter needle will sweep 2, 3 or 4 times to denote a 4, 6 or 8 cylinder engine. The I.D. code multiplied by 2 equals the number of engine cylinders.

DYNAMIC RESPONSE CODE

The dynamic response code is indicated by the needle sweeping once, signals the operator to perform a brief wide open throttle. This allows the ECA to check for proper movement of the throttle position sensor and operation of the manifold absolute pressure sensor, The operator has 15 seconds to "goose" the engine after the dynamic response code appears. Otherwise a Code 77 (operator did not do goose test) will appear.

ON-DEMAND CODES

The on-demand codes indicate there is something wrong in the EEC-IV system at this time. These faults or malfunctions are referred to as hard faults.

Self-Test Preliminary checks and Equipment Hook-Up
PRELIMINARY CHECKS

A routine inspection should be the first procedure the technician should use to begin the diagnosis of the system. Before proceeding with the test, perform the following:

Check the air cleaner and air cleaner ducting.

Check all engine vacuum hoses for damage, proper routing, cracks, deformation, blockage, etc.

Check the engine control system wiring for proper connections, bent or broken pins, proper routing, corrosion, loose wires, etc.

Check the processor, sensors and actuators for physical damage.

Check the engine coolant for proper level.

The technician performing the self-test must know what to expect when the self-test is activated and what to do when the codes are displayed.

CONNECTION OF ANALOG VOLTMETER
Except 1983 1.6L EEC-VI/EFI and Probe

1. Set the analog voltmeter on a DC voltage range to read from 0–15V. Insert 1 end of a jumper wire into the No. 4 pin on the self-test output connector. Clamp the negative lead from the analog voltmeter to the other end of the jumper wire.
2. Clamp the positive lead from the voltmeter to the positive terminal of the battery.
3. Insert the end of a second jumper wire into the number 2 terminal of the self-test output connector. Insert the other end of the jumper wire into the self-test input wire connector.

NOTE: The final connection to the self-test input wire connector also activates the self-test sequence inside the ECA when the ignition switch is turned ON.

1983 1.6L EEC-IV/EFI

The system has only 1 self-test connector. Connect the analog voltmeter in the following manner:

1. Connect a jumper wire from the self-test connector's number 5 pin to the self-test connector's number 2 pin.
2. Set the analog voltmeter on a DC voltage range to read 5–15V.
3. Connect the voltmeter's positive (+) lead to the postive battery terminal.
4. Connect the voltmeter's negative (−) lead to the self-test connector's No. 4 pin.
5. Start the test sequence by turning the ignition switch **ON**.

Probe

1. Turn the ignition switch **ON**.
2. Connect a jumper wire from the Self-Test input connector to ground.
3. Set the analog voltmeter on DC to read 0–20V.
4. Connect the voltmeter between the light green/black (+) terminal on the 6-pin Self-Test output connector and the negative battery terminal.

CONNECTION OF STAR TESTER

The STAR tester is used on all vehicles, except Probe.
1. Turn the ignition switch to the **OFF** position.
2. Connect the color coded adapter cable to the STAR tester.
3. Connect the leads of the adapter cable to the appropriate self-test connectors.
4. Connect a timing light.

CONNECTION OF SUPER STAR II TESTER

NOTE: The Super STAR II tester is used on the Probe only.

1. Turn the ignition switch to the **OFF** position.
2. Connect the color coded adapter cable to the Super STAR II tester.
3. Connect the leads of the adapter cable to the appropriate self-test connectors.
4. Ground the adapter cable.
5. Move the tester switch to the **MECS** position.
6. Move the FAST/SLOW switch to **SLOW**.
7. Turn the switch **ON**. The tester will initiate a display routine and the No. **888** will flash in the display window. Then a steady **00** will appear when the center button is unlatched, to announce that the tester is ready to receive service codes. To receive the service codes, press the button at the front of the tester, turn the ignition switch **ON**, unlatch and relatch the center button.

Entering Diagnostic Mode

The self-test is divided into the following specialized tests: Key On/Engine Off self-test, Engine Running self-test and Continuous self-test.

The self-test is not a conclusive test by itself but is used as part of the functional QUICK TEST diagnostic procedure. The processor stores the self-test program in its permanent memory. When activated, the processor checks the electronic engine control system by testing the memory integrity and processing capability and makes sure the various engine sensors and actuating devices are operating properly.

Also, intermittent trouble codes are not erased if the fault is not removed after 40 vehicle starts. Consequently, any intermittent code will be stored in the computer's permanent memory until it is erased. The codes for output devices are not stored in the computer's memory and can only be accessed during the Key On testing. Input device codes are stored in the permanent memory and must be erased after service.

SYSTEM DISPLAYS
Analog Voltmeter

After the EEC-IV system completes its self-test, it communicates with the operator by way of the analog voltmeter needle and scale.

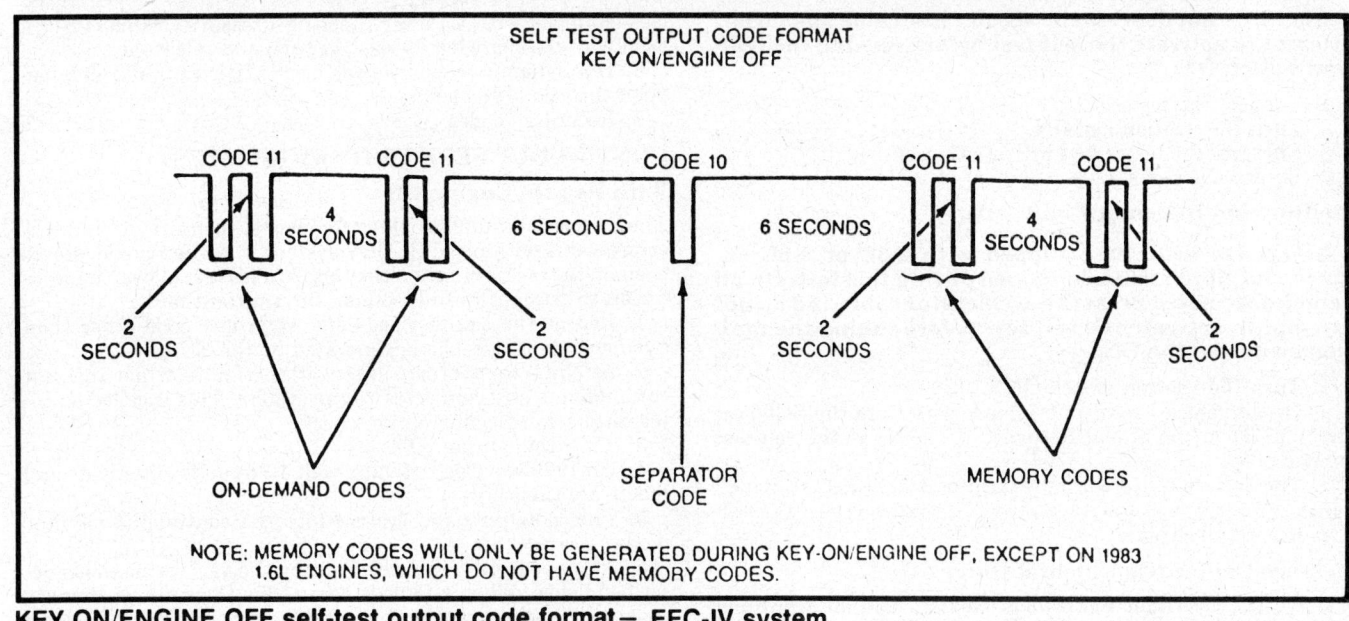

SELF TEST OUTPUT CODE FORMAT
KEY ON/ENGINE OFF

NOTE: MEMORY CODES WILL ONLY BE GENERATED DURING KEY-ON/ENGINE OFF, EXCEPT ON 1983 1.6L ENGINES, WHICH DO NOT HAVE MEMORY CODES.

KEY ON/ENGINE OFF self-test output code format— EEC-IV system

When a service code is reported on the analog meter, it will represent itself as a pulsing or sweeping movement of the voltmeter scale's needle across the dial face of the meter. Therefore, a single digit number of 3 will be indicated by 3 pulses (sweeps) of the needle across the dial. Since the codes are indicated by a 2-digit number, such as 32, the self-test's service Code 32 will be displayed as 3 pulses (sweeps) of the meter's needle with a ½ second pause between pulses (sweeps) and a 2 second pause between digits. When more than 1 service code is indicated, a 4 second pause between codes will occur.

Separator and dynamic response codes (numeral 10 in both cases), are represented by a single pulse or sweep of the needle. There are no pulses or sweeps generated for the digit 0; there will be a 6 second pause before each one of these.

Continuous memory codes are separated from Key On/Engine Off codes by a 6 second delay, a single ½ second sweep followed by another 6 second delay. The continuous memory codes are produced in the same manner as the Key On/Engine Off codes.

The key to sorting out the codes on the voltmeter is to keep the pulses and the pauses straight.

1. Each digit is separated by a 2 second pause.
2. Each code is separated by a 4 second pause.
3. Separator and dynamic response codes are separated from previous and subsequent codes by 6 second (or longer) pauses.
4. Continuous memory codes are separated from Key On/Engine Off codes by a 6 second delay, a single ½ second sweep, followed by another 6 second delay.

The self-test consists of 2 segments: Key On/Engine Off and the Engine Running. Each segment displays its own set of codes.

Malfunction Indicator Light (MIL)

During the self-test, a service code is displayed by the "Check Engine" light. The code is represented as a flash of the "Check Engine" light on the display panel on the dash. For example a Code 3 will be represented as 3 flashes of the light.

If the service code is a 2-digit number, such as a 23, the code will appear on the light as 2 flashes, then a 2 second pause, followed by 3 flashes of the light.

Continuous memory codes are separated from Key On/Engine Off codes by a 6 second delay, a single ½ second sweep followed by another 6 second delay.

Message Center (Continental Only)

The EEC-IV sends the "Check Engine" message to the message display center through the Data Communications Link (DCL). Self-Test codes may be read from the message display on the electronic instrument cluster.

Reading Trouble Codes

KEY ON/ENGINE OFF TEST

Analog Voltmeter

NOTE: On vehicles equipped with the 2.5L and 4.9L engines, the clutch must be depressed during this test. Do not depress the accelerator cable and do not attempt to activate the self-test before turning the ignition switch ON.

1. Set the voltmeter to a range that covers 0–15V DC and connect it as previously explained.
2. On all vehicles, except Probe, connect a jumper wire from the No. 2 pin on the self-test connector to the self-test input connector. On Probe, connect the jumper wire from the self-test input connector to ground.
3. Turn the ignition switch ON.
4. Assuming the system inputs check out OK for hard and intermediate faults, codes should be registering as follows:
   a. The needle will fluctuate between 0–3V for fast codes.
   b. Next the needle will sweep twice, with a 2 second pause in between, representing a Code 11 (system pass). The Code 11 will be repeated once (in case it was missed the first time). There is a 4 second pause in between the codes.
   c. A 6 second pause is next, followed by a single sweep of the needle (representing the separator code). Another 6 second pause follows the separator pulse.
   d. Finally, the Code 11 is repeated twice, again with a 4 second pause in between.
5. Record all codes. After the codes are recorded, erase them and retest. Address only those that appear during the retest.

STAR and Super STAR II Testers

NOTE: On vehicles equipped with 2.5L or 4.9L engines, the clutch must depressed during this test. On all vehicles, do not depress the accelerator cable and do not attempt to activate the self-test before turning the ignition switch ON.

1. Connect the tester.
2. Turn the ignition key **ON**.
3. Energize the tester and activate the self-test.
4. Record the codes.

Malfunction Indicator Light (MIL)

NOTE: On vehicles equipped with 2.5L or 4.9L engines, the clutch must depressed during this test. On all vehicles, do not depress the accelerator cable and do not attempt to activate the self-test before tuning the ignition switch to the ON.

1. Turn the ignition switch **ON**.
2. On all vehicles connect a jumper wire from the Self-Test Input (STI) to the Signal Return (SIG RTN) at the self-test connectors.
3. The serivce codes will now flash on the "Check Engine" light.
4. Record all codes.

Message Center (Continental Only)

1. On the electronic instrument cluster, hold all 3 buttons (SELECT, RESET and SYSTEM CHECK) in at the same time.
2. While holding the buttons in, turn the ignition switch **ON** and release the buttons.
3. Press the **SELECT** button 3 times.
4. To activate the self-test, connect a jumper wire from the Self-Test Input (STI) to the Signal Return (SIG RTN) at the self-test connectors or uses a STAR tester and latch the center button in the down position.
5. Look at the message display. A base readout of the numerals 2554 (1988 vehicles) or 4255 (1989 vehicles) indicates that the system has been entered properly.
6. Output of the codes will appear on the right 3 digits of the message display.
7. To exit the test, turn the ignition switch **OFF** and remove the jumper wire or the tester.

ENGINE RUNNING TEST

1. Before proceeding with this test, take note of the following:
   a. If equipped with a Brake ON/OFF (BOO) switch, depress the brake pedal and release it after an ID code is displayed.
   b. If equipped with a Power Steering Pressure Switch (PSPS), within 1–2 seconds after the ID code is displayed, turn the steering wheel at least ½ turn and release it.
   c. On 1989 vehicles equipped with E40D transmissions, the Overdrive Cancel Switch (OCS) must be cycled after the ID code.
   d. On 1989 vehicles, the Dynamic Response code will appear as a single pulse (if using a voltmeter) or as a Code 10 (if using the STAR tester) approximately 6–20 seconds after the engine ID code. When this code appears, perform a brief wide-open throttle.

NOTE: Do not depress the throttle unless a dynamic response code is displayed.

2. If not already done, deactivate the Key On/Engine Off self-test.
3. Start the engine and run at approximately 2000 rpm for 2 minutes to warm the EGO sensor.
4. Turn the engine **OFF** and wait 10 seconds.
5. Start the engine.
6. Activate the self-test as described above in Key/On Engine Off self test.
7. After the ID code is displayed, depress and release the brake pedal, if equipped with a Brake ON/OFF switch. On vehi-

cles equipped with a Power Steering Pressure Switch (PSPS), turn the steering whel at least ½ turn and release it.

8. If a dynamic response code occurs, perform a brief wide-open throttle (1989 vehicles).
9. Record all codes.

CONTINUOUT SELF-TEST (WIGGLE TEST)

With Key On/Engine Off

The ECA is continually looking for shorts, open circuits and other problems within the EEC-IV system and when noted, stores them in the memory, when they occur. This test allows the technician to attempt to re-create an intermittent fault.

1. Repeat the self-test segment when any code other than System Pass (Code 11), is generated by the ECA.
2. Attempt to re-create intermittent faults while the test equipment is still connected to the system. This is called an intermittent fault confirmation check.
3. Turn the ignition **ON**.
4. On 1989 vehicles, activate, wait 10 seconds, deactivate and reactivate the self-test.
5. This now puts the system into the continuous monitor mode.
6. Attempt to re-create the fault by the various methods described below. When a fault is detected, a Continuous Memory code will be stored in the computer's memory. On the tester a fault will be indicated by a red LED light or a steady tone; the "Check Engine" lamp will illuminate or the voltmeter needle will sweep depending what type of display equipment is being used.

NOTE: Remember that the cause of the some of the continuous memory codes may have been cleared during the either the Key On/Engine Off or Engine Running self-tests. Address only those continuous memory codes for those faults that have not been serviced. If the fault has already be corrected, clear the continuous memory.

With Engine Running

The ECA is continually looking for shorts, open circuits and other problems within the EEC-IV system and when noted, stores them in the memory, when they occur. This test allows the technician to attempt to re-create an intermittent fault.

1. Connnect the STAR tester or voltmeter to the engine.
2. Turn the ignition **OFF** and wait 10 seconds.
3. Start the engine.
4. Activate the self-test, wait 10 seconds, deactivate and activate the self-test; do not turn the engine **OFF**.
5. The engine is now in the running continuous monitor mode.
6. Attempt to re-create the fault by the various methods described below. When a fault is detected, a Continuous Memory code will be stored in the computer's memory. On the tester a fault will be indicated by a red LED light or a steady tone; the "Check Engine" lamp will illuminate or the voltmeter needle will sweep depending what type of display equipment is being used.

NOTE: Remember that the cause of the some of the continuous memory codes may have been cleared during the Engine Running self-test. Address only those continuous memory codes for those faults that have not been serviced. If the fault has already be corrected, clear the continuous memory.

RE-CREATING INTERMITTENT FAULTS

Intermittent faults can generally be recreated by the following methods:

1. Wiggling connectors and harnesses.
2. Manipulating moveable sensors and actuators.
3. Heating thermistor-type sensors with a heat gun.

Suspected components, such as the sensors, actuators and

harnesses, are identified by matching codes obtained during the Key On/Engine Off segment of the self-test.

When an intermittent fault is re-created, the voltmeter needle will sweep back and forth across the scale or sweep to the right and stay there or the tester will display a code.

Malfunctioning components identified with this procedure can be repaired or replaced without further diagnostic testing. Further testing must be done for hard faults and for intermittent faults that can not be re-created by the above method.

OUTPUT CYCLING TEST

This test is performed during the Key On/Engine Off test segment, after the memory codes have been generated. Without deactivating the self-test sequence, momentarily depress the throttle to the floor, then release it. Most of the EEC-IV actuators will be energized and the solenoid armatures should move (open or close) accordingly. Another throttle depression will de-energize the actuators. This cycle can be repeated as many times as necessary.

Malfunctiuoning actuators identified in this fashion, should be repaired or replaced. Further diagnostics are required for faults that cannot be isolated by the above method.

Clearing Diagnostic Memory
CONTINUOUS MEMORY CODES

NOTE: DO NOT disconnect the negative battery cable

to clear continuous memory codes. Doing this will erase the "Keep Alive Memory" (KAM) information which may lead to a driveability problem.

1. Perform the Key On/Engine Off self-test.
2. With a STAR tester, unlatch center button to the up position. With voltmeter, Malfunction Indicator Light (MIL) and Message Center (Continental), remove the jumper wire between the Self-Test Input (STI) connector and the Signal Return Pin of self-test connector.
3. The continuous memory codes will be erased from the computer's memory.

KEEP ALIVE MEMORY (KAM)

The processor stores information on vehicle operating conditions and uses this inforamation to compensate for operating parameters. When the EGR, HEGO, injectors, MAP/BP, TPS or VAF are replaced, the Keep Alive Memory must be cleared to erase the information from the original component.

To clear the memory, disconnect the negative battery cable for a minimum of 5 minutes.

After the memory is cleared, the vehicle may exhibit certain drivability problems. If this occurs, drive the vehicle 10 miles or more to allow the processor to relearn the values for optimum driveability and engine performance.

Check the engine coolant for proper level.

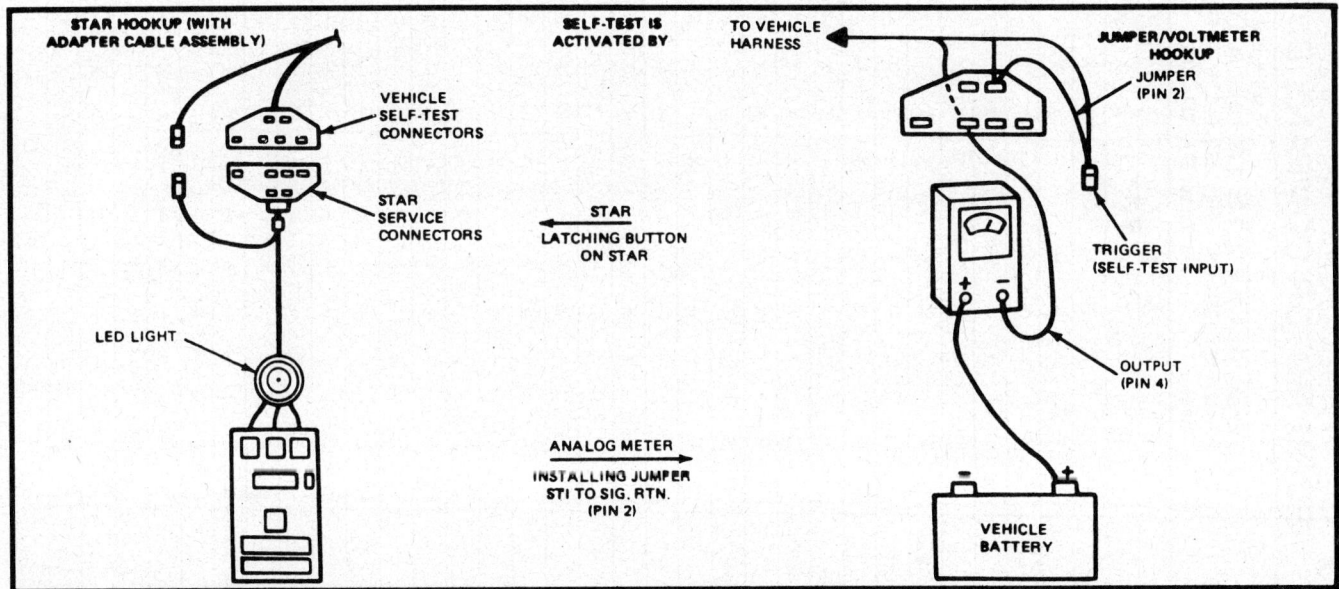

Making the self test equipment hookups

FORD MOTOR COMPANY DIAGNOSTIC TROUBLE CODES

Trouble Codes	Quick Test Mode	1.9L EFI	1.9L CFI	2.3L OHC EFI	2.3L EFI Turbo	2.3L HSC CFI	2.5L CLC CFI	MTX CFI	3.0L EFI	3.0L SEFI SHO	3.8L SEFI AXOD	3.8L SEFI RWD	3.8L SEFI SC	5.0L SEFI MA	5.0L SEFI SEFI	2.3L TPH EFI	2.9L EFI	3.0L EFI	4.9L EFI	5.0L EFI	5.8L EFI	5.8L E40D EFI	7.5L EFI	7.5L E40D EFI
		Car Engines														Truck Engines								
11—System pass	O/R/C	X	X	X	X	X	X	X	X	X	X	X	X	X	X	X	X	X	X	X	X	X	X	X
12—Rpm unable to reach upper test limit	R	X	X	X	X	X	X	X	X	X	X	X	X	X	X	X	X	X	X	X	X	X	X	X
13—Rpm unable to reach lower test limit	R	X	X	–	–	X	X	X	X	X	X	X	X	X	X	X	X	X	X	X	X	–	X	X
13—DC motor did not move	O	–	–	–	–	X	–	X	–	–	–	–	–	–	–	–	–	–	–	–	–	–	–	–
13—DC motor did follow dashpot	O	–	X	–	–	X	–	X	–	–	–	–	–	–	–	–	–	–	–	–	–	–	–	–
14—PIP circuit failure	C	X	X	X	X	X	X	X	X	X	X	X	X	X	X	X	X	X	X	X	X	X	X	X
15—ROM test failure	O	X	X	X	X	X	X	X	X	X	X	X	X	X	X	X	X	X	X	X	X	X	X	X
15—Power interrupted to keep alive memory	C	X	X	X	X	X	X	X	X	X	X	X	X	X	X	X	X	X	X	X	X	X	X	X
16—Rpm above self-test limit, set too high	R	①	–	X	–	–	–	–	⑦	⑦	–	–	–	⑦	–	–	–	–	–	–	–	–	–	X
16—Rpm too low to perform test	R	–	–	X	–	X	X	–	X	X	X	X	X	X	X	–	–	–	X	–	–	–	X	X
17—Rpm below self-test limit, set too low	R	①	X	–	–	X	X	X	X	X	X	X	X	X	X	–	–	–	–	–	–	–	–	–
18—Loss of tach input to ECU, spout grounded	C	X	X	X	X	X	X	X	X	X	X	X	X	X	X	⑭	X	X	X	X	X	X	X	X
18—Spout circuit open	R	X	X	–	–	X	X	X	X	X	X	X	X	X	X	X	X	X	X	X	X	X	X	X
19—Erratic rpm during test or rpm too low	R	①	⑦	X	–	–	–	–	X	X	X	X	X	X	X	X	X	X	X	X	X	X	X	X
19—Failure of EEC power supply	O	–	–	X	X	–	–	–	X	–	X	X	–	X	X	–	–	–	–	–	–	X	–	X
19—CID sensor input failed	C	–	–	–	–	–	–	–	X	X	X	X	X	X	X	–	–	–	–	–	–	–	–	–
21—ECT sensor input out of test range	O/R	X	X	X	X	X	X	X	X	X	X	X	X	X	X	X	X	X	X	X	X	X	X	X
22—BP sensor input out of test range	O/R/C	X	–	X	X	–	–	⑦	⑦	–	–	–	⑦	⑦	–	–	–	–	–	–	–	–	X	X
22—MAP sensor input out of test range	O/R/C	–	X	X	–	X	X	X	–	X	X	X	X	X	X	X	X	X	X	X	X	X	X	X
23—TP sensor input out of test range	O/R	X	③	X	X	③	③	③	X	X	X	X	X	X	X	X	X	X	X	X	X	X	X	X
24—ACT sensor input out of test range	O/R	–	X	X	–	X	X	X	X	X	X	X	X	X	X	X	X	X	X	X	X	X	X	X
24—VAT sensor input out of test range	O/R	X	–	–	–	–	–	–	X	–	X	X	–	X	X	–	–	–	–	–	–	–	–	–
25—KS sensor not detected during test	R	–	–	X	X	–	–	–	–	X	X	X	X	X	X	X	–	X	X	–	–	–	–	–
26—VAF sensor input out of test range	O/R	X	–	X	X	–	–	–	–	X	X	X	X	X	X	–	–	–	–	–	–	–	–	–
26—MAF sensor input out of test range	O/R	–	–	–	–	–	–	X	X	–	X	X	X	X	X	–	–	–	–	X	X	X	X	X
26—TOT sensor input out of test range	O/R	–	–	–	–	–	–	–	X	X	X	X	X	X	X	–	–	–	–	–	–	X	–	X
28—VAT sensor input out of test range	O/R	X	–	X	–	–	–	–	X	–	X	X	–	X	X	–	–	–	–	–	X	X	–	–
28—Loss of primary tach, right side	C	–	–	–	–	–	–	–	X	X	X	X	X	X	X	X	–	–	–	–	–	–	–	–
29—Insufficient input from vehicle speed sensor	C	–	X	X	X	X	X	X	X	X	X	X	X	X	X	X	X	X	X	X	X	X	X	X
31—PFE circuit below minimum voltage	O/R/C	X	–	–	–	–	–	–	–	–	X	X	–	X	X	X	–	–	–	X	X	X	X	X
31—EVP circuit below minimum voltage	O/R/C	–	X	X	X	X	X	X	X	X	X	X	X	X	X	X	X	X	X	X	X	X	X	X
32—EGR valve not seated	R/C	–	X	⑥	–	X	X	–	–	–	X	X	–	X	X	X	–	–	–	–	X	X	X	X
32—EVP voltage below closed limit	O/R/C	X	–	–	–	–	–	X	X	X	X	X	X	X	X	X	–	X	X	X	X	X	X	X
33—EGR valve not opening	R/C	X	–	X	X	X	X	X	X	X	X	X	X	X	X	X	–	X	X	X	X	X	X	X

Trouble Codes	Quick Test Mode	1.9L CFI EFI	1.9L EFI	2.3L OHC EFI	2.3L EFI Turbo	2.3L HSC EFI	2.5L CLC CFI	2.5L CFI	3.0L EFI	3.0L SHO SEFI	3.8L AXOD SEFI	3.8L RWD SEFI	5.0L SC SEFI	5.0L SEFI MA	5.0L SEFI	2.3L TPH EFI	2.9L EFI	3.0L EFI	4.9L EFI	5.0L EFI	5.8L EFI	5.8L E40D EFI	7.5L EFI	7.5L E40D EFI
		Car Engines														Truck Engines								
33—EVP not closing in limits	R	—	X	—	X	—	—	—	—	—	—	—	—	—	—	—	—	—	—	—	—	—	—	—
34—Insufficient EGR flow	R	—	—	X	X	—	—	—	—	—	—	—	—	—	—	—	—	—	—	—	—	—	—	—
34—Defective PFE sensor	O	—	X	—	—	X	—	—	X	X	X	X	—	—	—	—	—	—	—	—	—	—	—	—
34—Excess exhaust back pressure	R/C	—	X	—	—	X	—	—	X	X	X	X	—	—	—	—	—	—	—	—	—	—	—	—
34—EVP voltage above closed limit	O/R/C	—	—	—	—	—	X	X	—	—	—	—	—	—	—	X	X	X	X	X	X	X	X	X
35—EVP circuit above maximum voltage	O/R/C	—	—	—	—	—	X	X	—	—	X	X	X	X	—	X	X	X	X	X	X	X	X	X
35—PFE circuit above maximum voltage	O/R/C	—	X	—	—	X	—	—	X	X	X	X	—	—	—	—	—	—	—	—	—	—	—	—
35—Rpm too low for EGR test	R	—	X	—	—	—	—	—	—	—	—	—	—	—	—	—	—	—	—	—	—	—	—	—
38—Idle track switch circuit open	C	X	—	—	—	—	X	X	—	—	X	X	—	—	—	—	—	—	—	—	—	—	—	—
39—AXOD by-pass clutch not applying properly	C	—	—	—	—	—	—	—	—	—	X	—	—	—	—	—	—	—	—	—	—	—	—	—
41—EGO/HEGO circuit shows system lean	R	X	X	X	X	X	X	X	X	⑩	⑩	⑩	⑩	⑩	⑩	X	X	X	X	X	X	X	X	X
41—No EGO/HEGO switching detected, system lean	C	X	X	X	X	X	X	X	X	⑩	⑩	⑩	⑩	⑩	⑩	X	X	X	X	X	X	X	X	X
42—EGO/HEGO shows system rich	R	X	X	X	X	X	X	X	X	⑩	⑩	⑩	⑩	⑩	⑩	X	X	X	X	X	X	X	X	X
42—No EGO/HEGO switching detected, system rich	C	X	—	X	—	—	X	X	—	—	—	—	—	—	—	—	—	—	—	—	—	—	—	—
43—EGO/HEGO lean at wide open throttle	C	X	—	—	—	—	X	—	—	—	—	—	—	—	—	—	—	—	—	—	—	—	—	—
44—Thermactor air system inoperative (cyl. 1–4)	R	—	—	X	—	—	X	X	—	—	—	X	—	X	X	—	X	X	X	X	X	X	X	X
45—DIS coil Pack 3 circuit failure	C	—	—	—	—	—	—	—	X	—	—	—	X	—	—	—	—	—	—	—	—	—	—	—
45—Thermactor air upstream during self test	R	X	X	—	—	—	—	—	—	—	—	—	—	X	X	—	X	X	X	X	X	X	X	X
46—DIS coil Pack 1 circuit failure	C	—	—	—	—	—	—	—	X	—	—	—	X	—	—	—	—	—	—	—	—	—	—	—
46—Thermactor air not bypassed during self-test	R	—	—	X	—	X	X	X	—	—	—	—	—	—	—	—	X	X	X	X	X	X	X	X
47—Airflow at base idle	R	X	X	—	—	—	—	—	—	—	—	—	—	—	—	—	—	—	—	—	—	—	—	—
47—4x4 switch is closed	O	—	—	—	—	—	—	—	—	—	—	—	—	—	—	—	—	—	—	—	—	—	—	X
48—Airflow high at base idle	R	X	X	—	—	—	—	—	—	—	—	—	—	—	—	—	—	—	—	—	—	—	—	—
48—DIS coil pack 2 circuit failure	C	—	—	X	—	—	—	—	X	—	—	—	X	—	—	—	—	X	—	—	X	—	—	—
48—Loss of secondary tach, left side	C	—	—	—	—	—	X	X	—	X	—	—	—	—	—	X	—	—	—	—	—	—	—	—
49—1-2 shift error	C	—	—	—	—	—	X	X	—	—	—	—	—	—	—	—	—	—	—	—	—	—	—	—
49—Spout signal defaulted to 10 degrees BTDC	C	X	X	—	—	—	X	X	X	X	X	X	X	X	X	X	X	X	X	X	X	X	X	X
51—ECT sensor input exceeds test max.	O/C	X	X	X	X	X	X	X	X	X	X	X	X	X	X	X	X	X	X	X	X	X	X	X
52—PSPS circuit open	O	—	—	X	—	—	X	X	—	—	—	X	—	—	—	X	—	—	X	—	—	—	—	—
52—PSPS always open or always closed	R	X	X	—	—	—	X	X	X	—	—	X	—	X	X	X	X	X	X	X	X	X	X	X
53—TP sensor input exceeds test maximum	O/C	X	X	X	X	X	X	X	X	X	X	X	X	X	X	X	X	X	X	X	X	X	X	X
54—ACT sensor input exceeds test maximum	O/C	—	—	X	X	X	X	X	X	X	X	X	X	X	X	X	X	X	X	X	X	X	X	X
54—VAT sensor input exceed test maximum	O/C	—	—	X	—	—	X	X	—	—	—	—	—	—	—	—	—	—	—	—	—	—	—	—
55—Key power input to processor is open	R	—	X	—	—	—	X	X	—	—	—	—	—	—	—	—	—	—	—	—	—	—	—	—

FORD MOTOR COMPANY DIAGNOSTIC TROUBLE CODES

Trouble Codes	Quick Test Mode	Car Engines 1.9L EFI	1.9L CFI	2.3L OHC EFI	2.3L EFI Turbo	2.3L HSC CFI	2.5L CLC CFI	3.0L MTX EFI	3.0L SEFI	3.8L SEFI AXOD	3.8L SEFI RWD	3.8L SEFI SC	5.0L SEFI MA	5.0L SEFI	Truck Engines 2.3L TPH EFI	2.9L EFI	3.0L EFI	4.9L EFI	5.0L EFI	5.8L EFI	5.8L E40D EFI	7.5L EFI	7.5L E40D EFI
56—VAF sensor input exceeds test maximum	O/C	X	—	—	—	—	—	—	—	—	—	—	—	—	—	—	—	—	—	—	—	—	—
56—MAF sensor input exceeds test maximum	O/C	—	—	—	—	—	—	—	X	—	—	X	X	X	—	—	—	—	X	X	—	X	—
56—TOT sensor input exceeds test maximum	O/C	—	—	—	—	—	—	—	—	X	—	—	—	—	—	—	—	—	—	—	X	—	X
57—AXOD neutral pressure switch failed open	C	—	—	—	X	—	—	X	X	X	X	X	X	X	—	X	X	X	X	X	—	X	—
58—VAT sensor input exceeds test maximum	O/C	X	—	—	—	—	—	—	—	—	—	—	—	—	—	—	—	—	—	—	—	—	—
58—Idle tracking switch circuit closed	R	—	X	—	—	X	X	—	—	—	—	—	—	—	—	—	—	—	—	—	—	—	—
58—Idle tracking switch circuit open	O	—	X	—	—	X	X	—	—	—	—	—	—	—	—	—	—	—	—	—	—	—	—
59—AXOD 4/3 pressure switch failed open	C	—	—	—	X	—	—	X	X	X	X	X	X	X	—	X	X	X	X	X	—	X	—
59—Low speed fuel pump circuit failure	O/C	—	—	—	—	—	—	X	X	X	—	—	—	—	—	—	—	—	—	—	—	—	—
59—AXOD 4/3 pressure switch failed closed	O	—	—	—	X	—	—	X	X	X	X	X	X	X	—	—	—	—	—	—	—	—	X
59—2-3 shift error	C	—	—	—	—	—	—	—	—	—	—	—	—	—	—	—	—	—	—	—	X	—	X
61—ECT test sensor input below test minimum	O/C	X	X	X	X	X	X	X	X	X	X	X	X	X	X	X	X	X	X	X	X	X	X
62—AXOD 4/3 or 3/2 pressure switch failed closed	O	—	—	—	—	—	—	X	X	X	X	X	X	X	—	—	—	—	—	—	—	—	—
63—Converter clutch failure	C	—	—	—	—	—	—	—	—	—	—	—	—	—	—	—	—	—	—	—	X	—	X
63—TP sensor below test minimum	O/C	X	X	X	X	X	X	X	X	X	X	X	X	X	X	X	X	X	X	X	X	X	X
64—ACT sensor input below test minimum	O/C	—	X	X	X	X	X	X	X	X	X	X	X	X	X	X	X	X	X	X	X	X	X
64—VAT sensor input below test minimum	O/C	—	—	X	—	—	—	—	—	—	—	—	—	—	—	—	—	—	—	—	—	—	—
65—Failed to enter closed loop mode	C	X	X	X	—	X	X	X	X	X	X	X	X	X	X	X	X	X	X	X	X	X	X
65—Overdrive cancel switch not changing state	R	—	—	—	—	—	—	—	—	—	—	—	—	—	—	—	—	—	—	—	X	—	X
66—VAF sensor input below test minimum	O/C	X	—	X	—	—	—	—	—	—	—	—	—	—	—	—	—	—	—	—	—	—	—
66—MAF sensor input below test minimum	C	—	—	—	—	—	—	—	X	—	—	X	X	X	—	—	—	—	X	X	—	X	—
66—TOT sensor input below test minimum	O/C	—	—	—	—	—	—	—	—	X	—	—	—	X	—	—	—	—	—	—	X	—	X
67—Neutral drive switch open, A/C input high	O	X	(4)	X	X	X	X	X	(8)	X	(9)	X	(12)	X	X	X	X	X	X	X	X	X	X
67—Clutch switch circuit failure	C	X	X	—	X	X	X	X	X	X	X	X	X	X	—	X	—	—	—	—	—	—	—
67—AXOD neutral pressure switch failed closed	O	—	—	—	—	—	—	—	—	X	—	—	—	—	—	—	—	—	—	—	—	—	—
67—MLP sensor out of range, A/C input high	O/C	—	—	—	—	—	—	—	—	—	—	—	X	X	—	—	—	—	—	—	X	—	X
68—VAT sensor input below test minimum	O/C	X	—	X	—	—	—	—	—	—	—	—	—	—	—	—	—	—	—	—	—	—	—
68—Idle tracking switch circuit open	R	—	X	—	—	X	X	—	—	—	—	—	—	—	—	—	—	—	—	—	—	—	—
68—Idle tracking switch closed	O	—	X	—	—	X	X	—	—	—	—	—	—	—	—	—	—	—	—	—	—	—	—
68—AXOD temperature switch failed open	O/R/C	—	—	—	—	—	—	X	X	X	—	—	—	—	—	—	—	—	—	—	—	—	—
69—AXOD 3/4 pressure switch failed open	C	—	—	—	—	—	—	X	X	X	X	X	X	X	—	—	—	—	—	—	—	—	—
69—AXOD 3/2 pressure switch failed closed	O	—	—	—	—	—	—	X	X	X	—	—	—	—	—	—	—	—	—	—	—	—	—
69—3-4 shift error	C	—	—	—	—	—	—	—	—	—	—	—	—	—	—	—	—	—	—	—	X	—	X

Trouble Codes	Quick Test Mode	1.9L CFI EFI	1.9L CFI	2.3L OHC EFI	2.3L EFI Turbo	2.3L HSC EFI	2.5L CLC CFI	2.5L MTX CFI	3.0L EFI	3.0L SHO SEFI	3.8L AXOD SEFI	3.8L RWD SEFI	3.8L SC SEFI	5.0L SEFI	5.0L MA SEFI	5.0L SEFI	2.3L TPH EFI	2.9L EFI	3.0L EFI	4.9L EFI	5.0L EFI	5.8L EFI	5.8L E40D EFI	7.5L E40D EFI	7.5L E400 EFI
70—EEC-IV data transmission link failed	C	—	—	—	—	—	—	—	—	—	X	—	—	—	—	—	—	—	—	—	—	—	—	—	—
71—Software re-initialization detected	C	②	—	—	—	—	—	—	—	—	—	—	—	—	—	—	—	—	—	—	—	—	—	—	—
71—Idle tracking switch closed on pre-position	C	—	—	X	—	X	—	—	—	—	—	—	—	—	—	—	—	—	—	—	—	—	—	—	—
71—Cluster control assembly circuit failed	C	—	—	—	—	—	—	—	—	X	—	—	—	—	—	—	—	—	—	—	—	—	—	—	—
72—Power interrupt detected	C	X	—	X	—	X	—	X	—	—	—	—	—	—	—	—	X	—	—	—	—	—	—	—	—
72—Insufficient BP change during test	R	—	—	—	—	—	—	—	—	X	—	—	X	—	—	—	—	—	—	—	—	—	—	—	—
72—Insufficient MAP output change during test	R	—	—	—	—	X	—	—	X	X	X	X	X	—	—	—	X	X	—	X	X	X	X	—	X
72—Message center control circuit failed	C	—	—	—	—	—	—	—	—	—	—	—	X	—	—	—	—	—	—	—	—	—	—	—	—
73—Insufficient TP output change during test	R	X	—	X	—	X	—	—	X	X	X	X	X	—	—	—	X	X	X	X	X	X	X	—	X
73—Insufficient TP change	O	—	—	—	X	—	X	X	—	—	—	—	—	—	—	—	—	—	—	—	—	—	—	—	—
74—Brake on/off circuit open, not on during test	R	X	—	X	—	X	—	—	X	X	X	X	X	X	X	X	X	X	X	X	X	X	X	X	X
75—Brake on/off circuit closed, always high	R	—	—	X	—	—	—	—	—	X	—	—	X	—	—	—	—	—	—	—	—	—	—	—	—
76—Insufficient VAF output change during test	R	X	—	X	—	X	—	—	—	—	—	—	—	—	—	—	—	—	—	—	—	—	—	—	—
77—Wide open throttle not sensed during test	R	X	—	X	—	X	—	—	X	X	X	X	X	—	X	X	X	X	X	X	X	X	X	—	X
79—A/C on during self test	O	—	—	—	—	—	—	—	X	X	X	X	X	X	X	X	—	—	—	—	—	—	—	—	—
81—Insufficient IAS output during test	O	—	—	—	—	—	—	—	—	X	—	—	X	—	—	—	—	—	—	—	—	—	—	—	—
81—Air management 2 circuit failure	O	—	—	—	—	—	—	—	—	—	—	—	—	X	X	X	—	—	—	X	X	X	X	X	X
82—Supercharger bypass circuit failure	O	—	—	—	—	—	—	—	—	—	—	—	X	—	—	—	—	—	—	—	—	—	—	—	—
82—Air management 1 circuit failure	O	—	—	—	—	—	—	—	—	—	—	—	—	X	X	X	—	—	—	X	X	X	X	X	X
83—EGRC solenoid circuit failure	O	—	—	X	—	X	—	—	—	—	—	—	—	—	—	—	—	—	—	—	—	—	—	—	—
83—High speed electro drive fan circuit failure	O	—	—	—	—	—	—	—	—	X	X	X	X	—	—	—	—	—	—	—	—	—	—	—	—
83—Low speed fuel pump relay circuit open	O/C	X	—	X	—	X	X	X	X	X	X	X	X	X	X	X	X	X	X	X	X	X	X	X	X
84—EGR VAC regulator circuit failure	O	④	—	X	—	—	—	—	—	—	—	—	—	—	—	—	—	④	—	—	—	—	—	—	—
84—EGRV solenoid circuit failure	O	—	—	X	—	—	—	—	—	—	—	—	—	—	—	—	—	—	—	—	—	—	—	—	—
85—Adaptive lean limit reached	C	X	—	—	—	X	—	—	—	—	—	—	—	—	—	—	X	—	—	—	—	—	—	—	—
85—Canister purge circuit failure	O	④	—	—	—	—	—	—	—	X	X	X	X	X	X	X	—	—	X	X	X	X	X	—	X
86—Adaptive rich limit reached	C	X	—	—	—	X	—	—	—	—	—	—	—	—	—	—	X	—	—	—	—	—	—	—	—
86—3-4 shift solenoid circuit failure	O	—	—	—	—	—	—	—	—	—	—	—	X	—	—	—	—	—	—	—	—	—	—	—	—
87—Fuel pump primary circuit failure	O/C	④	—	⑤	—	X	X	X	X	X	X	X	X	X	X	X	X	X	X	X	X	X	X	X	X
88—Electro drive fan circuit failure	O	—	—	—	—	—	—	—	—	X	—	—	—	—	—	—	—	—	—	—	—	—	—	—	—
88—Loss of dual plug input control	C	—	—	X	—	X	—	—	—	—	—	—	—	—	—	—	X	—	—	—	—	—	—	—	—
89—Clutch converter overdrive circuit failure	O	—	—	—	—	—	—	—	—	—	—	—	—	—	—	—	—	—	—	—	—	—	X	X	X
89—AXOD lock-up solenoid circuit failure	O	—	—	—	—	—	—	—	—	—	⑩	⑩	⑩	⑩	⑩	⑩	—	—	—	—	—	—	—	—	—
91—HEGO sensor circuit shows system lean	R	—	—	—	—	—	—	—	—	⑪	⑪	⑪	⑪	⑪	⑪	⑪	—	—	—	—	—	—	—	—	—

FORD MOTOR COMPANY DIAGNOSTIC TROUBLE CODES

Trouble Codes	Quick Test Mode	Car Engines													Truck Engines								
		1.9L EFI	1.9L CFI	2.3L OHC EFI Turbo	2.3L EFI	2.3L HSC CFI	2.5L CLC CFI	3.0L MTX CFI	3.0L SEFI	3.8L SEFI AXOD	3.8L SEFI RWD	3.8L SEFI SC	5.0L SEFI MA	5.0L SEFI SEFI	2.3L TPH EFI	2.9L EFI	3.0L EFI	4.9L EFI	5.0L EFI	5.8L EFI	5.8L E4OD EFI	7.5L EFI	7.5L E4OD EFI
91—Shift solenoid 1 circuit failure	O	–	–	–	–	–	–	–	–	–	–	–	–	–	–	–	–	–	–	–	X	–	X
91—No HEGO switching sensed	C	–	–	–	–	–	–	–	[11]	[11]	[11]	[11]	[11]	[11]	–	–	–	–	–	–	–	–	–
92—HEGO sensor circuit shows system rich	R	–	–	–	–	–	–	–	[11]	[11]	[11]	[11]	[11]	[11]	–	–	–	–	–	–	–	–	–
92—Shift solenoid 2 circuit failure	O	–	–	–	–	–	–	–	–	–	–	–	–	–	–	–	–	–	–	–	X	–	X
93—TP sensor input low at max DC motor extension	O	–	X	–	–	–	X	X	–	–	–	–	–	–	–	–	–	–	–	–	–	–	–
94—Thermactor air system inoperative (cyl. 5–8)	R	–	–	–	–	–	–	–	–	–	–	–	X	X	–	–	–	–	–	–	–	–	–
94—Converter clutch solenoid circuit failure	O	–	–	–	–	–	–	–	–	X	–	–	–	–	–	X	X	X	X	X	X	X	X
95—Fuel pump secondary circuit failure	O/C	–	–	X	X	–	–	–	X	X	X	X	X	X	X	X	X	X	X	X	X	X	X
96—Fuel pump secondary circuit failure	O/C	–	–	X	X	–	–	–	X	X	X	X	X	X	X	X	X	X	X	X	X	X	X
96—High speed fuel pump relay circuit open	O/C	–	–	X	–	–	–	–	–	–	–	X	–	–	–	–	–	–	–	–	–	–	–
97—Overdrive cancel indicator circuit failure	O	–	–	–	–	–	–	–	X	–	–	–	–	–	–	–	–	–	–	–	–	–	–
98—Hard fault is present	R	X	X	X	X	X	X	X	X	X	X	X	X	X	X	X	X	X	X	X	X	X	X
98—Electronic pressure control driver failure	O	–	–	–	–	–	–	–	–	–	–	–	–	–	–	–	–	–	–	–	X	–	X
99—EEC system has not learned to control idle	R	–	X	–	–	–	X	–	–	–	–	–	–	–	–	–	–	–	–	–	–	–	–
99—Electronic pressure control circuit failure	O/C	–	–	–	–	–	–	–	–	–	–	–	–	–	–	–	–	–	–	–	X	–	X
No code—unable to run self-test or output codes	[13]	X	X	X	X	X	X	X	X	X	X	X	X	X	X	X	X	X	X	X	X	X	X
Code not listed—does not apply to vehicle tested	[13]	X	X	X	X	X	X	X	X	X	X	X	X	X	X	X	X	X	X	X	X	X	X

O— Key on, engine off
R— Engine running
C— Continuous memory

① ISC off
② 1989 only
③ Occurs also in continuous memory (C)
④ Occurs also with the engine running (R)
⑤ Occurs only in key on, engine off (O)
⑥ Occurs only with the engine running (R)
⑦ Occurs only in key on, engine off (O) or continuous memory (C)
⑧ A/C input high only
⑨ Neutral pressure switch open
⑩ Right side HEGO
⑪ Left side HEGO
⑫ N–D switch only (no A/C signal)
⑬ Refer to system diagnostics
⑭ Erratic input to processor

FORD MOTOR COMPANY

Year — 1989
Model — Probe
Engine — 2.2L (133 cid) 4 cyl
Engine Code — VIN C

ECM TROUBLE CODES

Code	Explanation
1	Ignition module
8	Vane airflow meter
9	Engine coolant temperature sensor
10	Vane air temperature sensor
12	Throttle position sensor
14	Barometric pressure sensor
15	Exhaust Gas Oxygen (EGO) sensor
16	EGR valve position sensor — California only
17	Exhaust Gas Oxygen (EGO) sensor
25	Pressure regulator control
26	Canister purge solenoid valve
28	Exhaust Gas Recirculation (EGR) control solenoid valve
34	Idle speed control solenoid valve

Year – 1989
Model – Probe
Engine – 2.2L (133 cid) Turbo 4 cyl
Engine Code – VIN L

ECM TROUBLE CODES

Code	Explanation
1	Ignition module
2	Crankshaft position sensor
3	Cylinder identification sensor A
4	Cylinder identification sensor B
5	Knock sensor or knock control unit
8	Vane airflow meter
9	Engine coolant temperature sensor
10	Vane air temperature sensor
12	Throttle position sensor
14	Barometric pressure sensor
15	Exhaust Gas Oxygen (EGO) sensor
16	Exhaust Gas Recirculation (EGR) valve position sensor
17	Exhaust Gas Oxygen (EGO) sensor
25	Pressure regulator control
26	Canister purge solenoid valve
28	Exhaust Gas Recirculation (EGR) control solenoid valve
29	Exhaust Gas Recirculation (EGR) vent solenoid valve
34	Idle speed control solenoid valve
42	Turbocharger boost control solenoid valve

Year — 1990
Model — Probe
Engine — 2.2L (133 cid) 4 cyl
Engine Code — VIN C

ECM TROUBLE CODES

Code	Explanation
1	Ignition module
8	Vane airflow meter
9	Engine coolant temperature sensor
10	Vane air temperature sensor
12	Throttle position sensor
14	Barometric pressure sensor
15	Exhaust Gas Oxygen (EGO) sensor
16	Exhaust Gas Recirculation (EGR) valve position sensor — California only
17	Exhaust Gas Oxygen (EGO) sensor
25	Pressure regulator control
26	Canister purge solenoid valve
28	Exhaust Gas Recirculation (EGR) control solenoid valve
34	Idle speed control solenoid valve

Year – 1990
Model – Probe
Engine – 2.2L (133 cid) Turbo 4 cyl
Engine Code – VIN L

ECM TROUBLE CODES

Code	Explanation
1	Ignition module
2	Crankshaft position sensor
3	Cylinder identification sensor A
4	Cylinder identification sensor B
5	Knock sensor or knock control unit
8	Vane airflow meter
9	Engine coolant temperature sensor
10	Vane air temperature sensor
12	Throttle position sensor
14	Barometric pressure sensor
15	Exhaust Gas Oxygen (EGO) sensor
16	Exhaust Gas Recirculation (EGR) valve position sensor
17	Exhaust Gas Oxygen (EGO) sensor
25	Pressure regulator control
26	Canister purge solenoid valve
28	Exhaust Gas Recirculation (EGR) control solenoid valve
29	Exhaust Gas Recirculation (EGR) vent solenoid valve
34	Idle speed control solenoid valve
42	Turbocharger boost control solenoid valve

General Motors Corporation

INDEX

GENERAL MOTORS CORPORATION

Digital Electronic Fuel Injection (DEFI) System

1984–85 RWD DEVILLE AND FLEETWOOD

Description

The ECM is designed to withstand normal current draws associated with the vehicle operation. However, care must be exercised to avoid overloading any of these circuits. In testing for opens or shorts, do not ground or apply voltage to any of the ECM circuits, unless instructed to do so by a diagnostic procedure. These circuits should only be tested using a high impedance multimeter, should they remain connected to the ECM.

Power should never be applied to the ECM with the ignition **ON**. Before removing or connecting battery cables, ECM fuses or ECM connectors, always turn the ignition **OFF**.

The ECM has a learning ability that allows the fuel control calibration to be tailored to account for minor differences in the fuel control system and the engine mechanical system. This allows the ECM to better adapt the vehicle to changing environmental conditions. If the battery is disconnected or if an ECM is replaced, the ECM in the vehicle will have to begin the learning process all over again. A change in vehicle driveability may be noted after a battery disconnect or ECM replacement. To teach the ECM, operate the vehicle at normal operating temperature, at part throttle and at idle until driveability and performance returns

Trouble Codes

The dash mounted "Service Now" and "Service Soon" indicator lamps are used to detected system malfunctions or system abnormalities. These malfunctions may be related to the various operating sensors or to the ECM itself. The light that turns ON automatically, goes out if the fault clears, such as an intermediate malfunction. However, the ECM stores the trouble code associated with the detected failure until the diagnostic system is cleared or until 50 OFF/ON ignition switch cycles have occurred without any fault reappearing.

Proper operation of "Service Now" or the "Service Soon" indicator lamps are as follows:

1. Both lamps are normally OFF.
2. A bulb check is performed with both bulbs ON, when the ignition switch is in the CRANK position only. When the engine starts, both lamps go out.
3. Depending upon the trouble code set, either the "Service Soon" or the "Service Now" lamps will turn ON and stay ON when a constant malfunction is detected.
4. If the malfunction is intermittent, the lamp that turned ON previously, will go out when the malfunction is no longer detected. The lamp will turn ON each time the malfunction is again detected and will either be bright or flickering.
5. When a "Service Soon" malfunction is detected at the same time a "Service Now" malfunction is detected, only the "Service Now" lamp will be ON.
6. Both lamps will stay ON when the system is displaying the diagnostic routines.

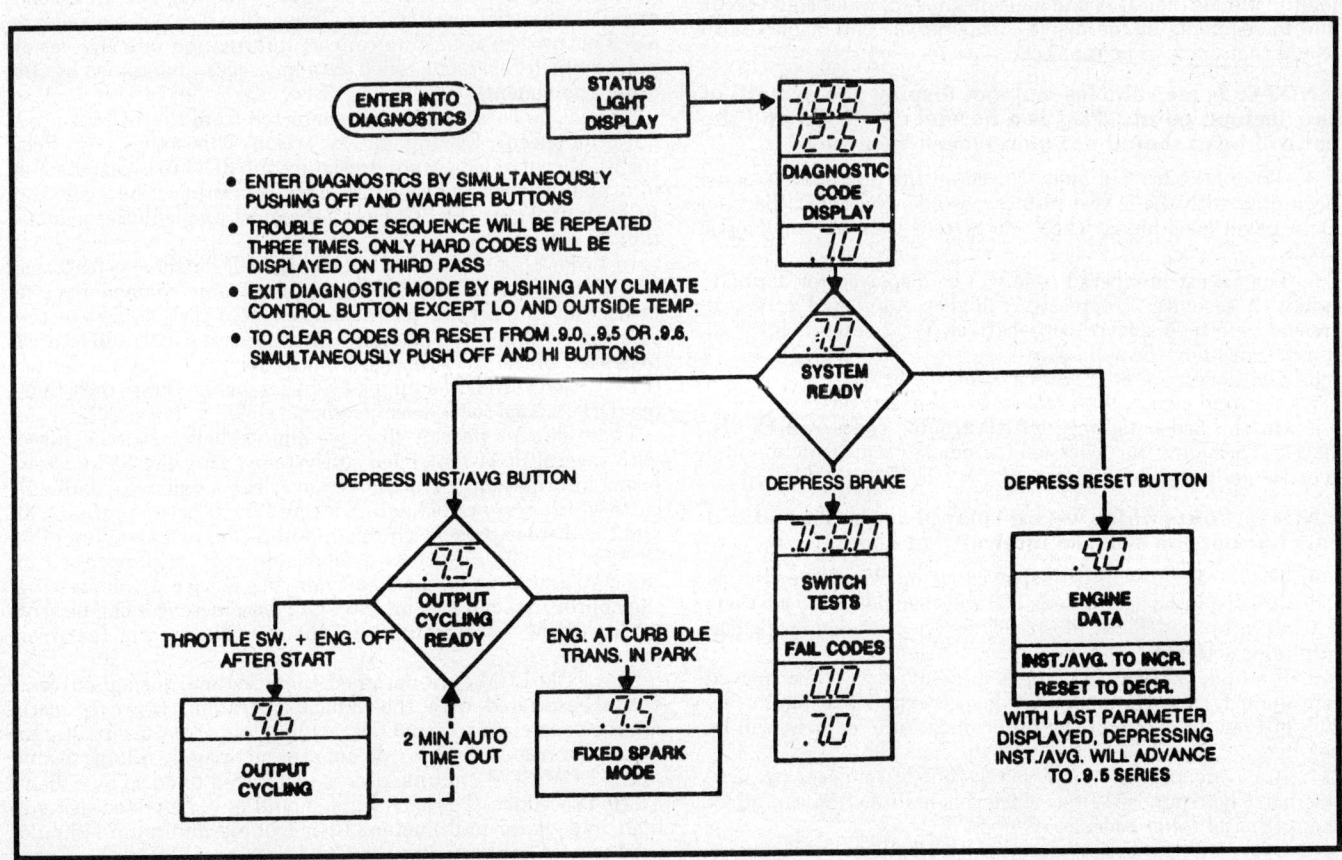

DFI diagnostics – 1984–85 RWD models

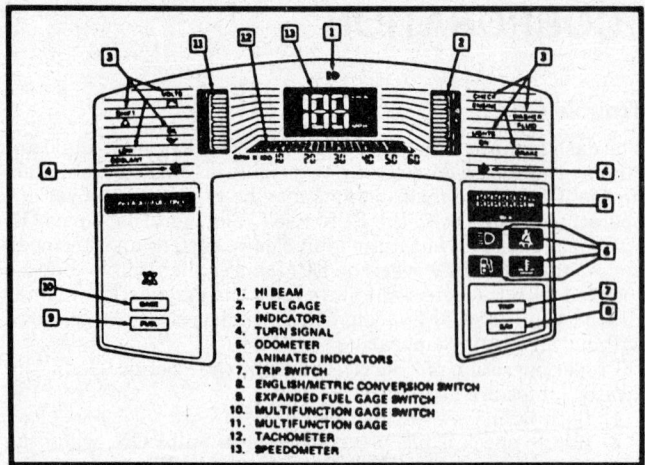

1. HI BEAM
2. FUEL GAGE
3. INDICATORS
4. TURN SIGNAL
5. ODOMETER
6. ANIMATED INDICATORS
7. TRIP SWITCH
8. ENGLISH/METRIC CONVERSION SWITCH
9. EXPANDED FUEL GAGE SWITCH
10. MULTIFUNCTION GAGE SWITCH
11. MULTIFUNCTION GAGE
12. TACHOMETER
13. SPEEDOMETER

Electronic Instrument Cluster assembly

NOTE: The dash mounted digital display panel, normally used for the ECC system, can be temporarily directed to display trouble codes stored in the ECM.

Entering Diagnostic Mode

To enter diagnostics, proceed as follows.
  1. Turn the ignition ON.
  2. Depress the OFF and WARMER buttons on the ECC panel simultaneously and hold until ".." appears. "–1.8.8" will then be displayed, which indicates the beginning of the diagnostic readout.
  3. If "–1.8.8" does not display or is partically displayed, a malfunction is indicated and a misdiagnose of codes could occur due to segments of the display inoperative. The display head would then have to be replaced.

NOTE: Some vehicles may not display one or both of the decimal points. This is a normal condition and the control head should not be replaced because of it.

  4. Trouble codes will be displayed on the digital ECC panel beginning with the lowest numbered code. Note that the Fuel Data panel goes blank when the system is in the diagnostic mode.
  5. The lowest numbered code will be displayed for approximately 2 seconds. Progressively higher numbered codes, if present, will be displayed consecutively for 2 seconds until all stored codes have been displayed.
  6. The Code "–1.8.8" will be displayed again.
  7. A second pass will be repeated of the first pass.
  8. On the 3rd pass, only HARD trouble codes will be displayed. These are the codes which indicate a malfunction and keep the indicator lamp ON.

NOTE: Codes which were displayed on the 1st and 2nd pass but not the 3rd, are intermittent codes.

  9. The "–1.8.8" will be displayed again. When the trouble codes are displayed again, Code .7.0 will then be displayed. Code .7.0 indicates that the ECM is ready for the next diagnostic feature to be selected.
  10. If a Code 51 (PROM error) is present, it will be displayed continuously until the diagnostic mode is exited. During the display of Code 51, none of the other diagnostic features will be possible.
  11. If a Code 16 (alternator voltage out of range) is present, this must be diagnosed first, since this malfunction can affect the setting of other codes.
  12. If no trouble codes are present, "–1.8.8" will be displayed for 2 seconds and then the ECM will display the Code .7.0, which

indicates the ECM is ready for the next diagnostic feature to be selected.

Clearing Diagnostic Memory

Trouble codes stored in the ECM's memory may be cleared (erased) by entering the diagnostic mode and then depressing the OFF and HI buttons on the CCP simultaneously. Hold the buttons in until "E.0.0" appears on the display. Trouble codes stored in the BCM's memory may be cleared by depressing the OFF and LO buttons simultaneously until "F.0.0" appears. After "E.0.0" or "F.0.0" is displayed, ".7.0." will appear. With the ".7.0" displayed, turn the ignition OFF for at least ten seconds before re-entering the diagnostic mode.

Exiting Diagnostic Mode

To get out of the diagnostic mode, depress the AUTO button or turn the ignition switch OFF for 10 seconds. Trouble codes are not erased when this is done. The temperature setting will reappear in the display panel.

1985–89 FWD DEVILLE AND FLEETWOOD

Description

At the center of the self-diagnostic system is the Body Computer Module (BCM), located behind the glove compartment opening. An internal microprocessor is used to control various vehicle function, based on monitored sensor and switch inputs. The ECM is located on the right side of the instrument panel and is the major factor in providing self-diagnostic capabilities for those subsection which it controls.

When both the BCM and ECM are used, a communication process has been incorporated which allows the 2 modules to share information and thereby provide for additional control capability. In a method similar to a telegraph key operator, each module's internal circuitry rapidly switches a circuit between 0–5V. This process is used to convert information into a series of pulses which represent coded data messages understood by the other components.

One of the data messages transferred from the BCM is a request for specific ECM diagnostic action. This action may affect the ECM controlled output or require the ECM to transfer some information back to the BCM. This communication gives the BCM control over the ECM's self-diagnostic capabilities in addition to its own.

In order to access and control the self-diagnostic features, available to the BCM, 2 additional electronic components are utilized by the service technician. Located to the right of the steering column is the Climate Control Panel (CCP) and located to the left of the steering column is either the Fuel Data Center (FDC), used with DFI equipped vehicles, or the Diesel Data Center (DDC), used with diesel engines.

These devices provide displays and keyboard switches used with several BCM controlled subsystems. This display and keyboard information is transferred over the single wire data circuits which carry coded data back and forth between the BCM and the display panels. This communication process allows the BCM to transfer any of its available diagnostic information to the instrument panel for display during service. By depressing the appropriate buttons on the CCP, data messages can be sent to the BCM, requesting the specific diagnostic features required.

The ECM/BCMs are designed to withstand normal current draws associated with the vehicle operation. However, care must be exercised to avoid overloading any of these circuits. In testing for opens or shorts, do not ground or apply voltage to any of the ECM/BCM circuits, unless instructed to do so by a diagnostic procedure. These circuits should only be tested using a high impedance multimeter (10 megohms minimum), should they remain connected to the ECM/BCM.

Power should never be applied to the ECM with the ignition

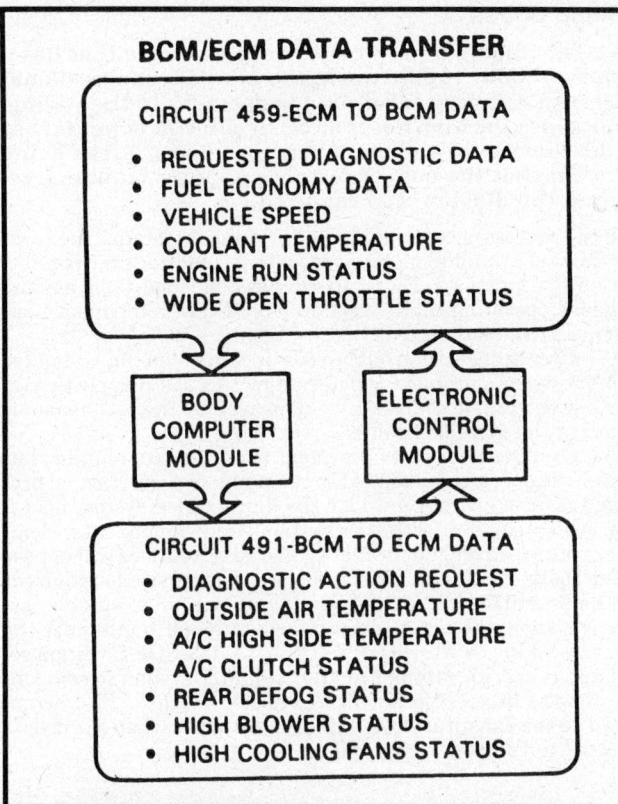

BCM/ECM DATA TRANSFER

CIRCUIT 459-ECM TO BCM DATA

- REQUESTED DIAGNOSTIC DATA
- FUEL ECONOMY DATA
- VEHICLE SPEED
- COOLANT TEMPERATURE
- ENGINE RUN STATUS
- WIDE OPEN THROTTLE STATUS

BODY COMPUTER MODULE   ELECTRONIC CONTROL MODULE

CIRCUIT 491-BCM TO ECM DATA

- DIAGNOSTIC ACTION REQUEST
- OUTSIDE AIR TEMPERATURE
- A/C HIGH SIDE TEMPERATURE
- A/C CLUTCH STATUS
- REAR DEFOG STATUS
- HIGH BLOWER STATUS
- HIGH COOLING FANS STATUS

BCM/ECM data transfer method—1985–89 FWD Deville and Fleetwood

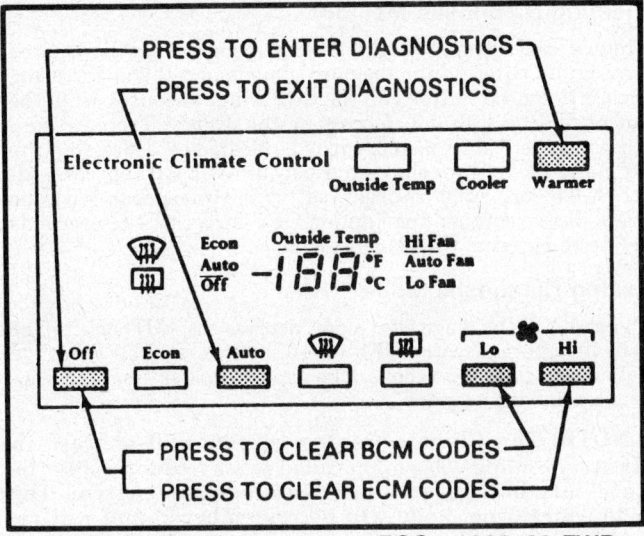

Entering diagnostic system on ECC—1985–89 FWD Deville and Fleetwood

ON. Before removing or connecting battery cables, ECM/BCM fuses or ECM/BCM connectors, always turn the ignition **OFF**.

Trouble Codes

In the process of controlling its various subsystems, the ECM and BCM continually monitor the operating conditions for possible system malfunctions. By comparing system conditions against standard operating limits, certain circuit and component malfunctions can be detected. A 2-digit numerical trouble code is stored in the computer's memory when a problem is detected by this self-diagnostic system. These trouble codes can later be displayed by the service technician as an aid in system repair.

If a particular malfunction would result in unacceptable system operation, the self-diagnostics will attempt to minimize the effect by taking FAIL-SAFE action. FAIL-SAFE action refers to any specific attempt by the computer system to compensate for the detected problem. A typical FAIL-SAFE action would be the substitution of a fixed input value when a sensor/circuit is detected to be open or shorted.

Entering Diagnostic Mode

To enter the diagnostic mode, proceed as follows:
1. Turn the ignition switch **ON**.
2. Depress the **OFF** and the **WARMER** buttons on the CCP, simultaneously and hold them in until all display segments illuminate, which indicated the beginning of the diagnostic readout.

NOTE: If any of the segments are inoperative, the diagnosis should not be attempted, as this could lead to misdiagnosis. The display in question would have to be replaced before the diagnosis procedure is initiated.

Trouble Code Display

After the display segment check is completed, any trouble codes stored in the computer memory will be displayed on the Data Center panel as follows:
1. Display of the trouble codes will begin with an "8.8.8" on the data center panel for approximately 1 second. "..E" will then be displayed which indicates the beginning of the ECM stored trouble codes.
2. This first pass of ECM codes includes all detected malfunctions whether they are currently present or not. If no ECM trouble codes are stored, the "..E" display will be bypassed.
3. Following the display of "..E", the lowest numbered ECM trouble code will be displayed for approximately 2 seconds. All ECM trouble codes will be prefixed with the letter "E". (i.e. E12, E13, etc.).
4. Progressively higher numbered trouble codes will be displayed, until the highest code present has been displayed.
5. ".E.E" will then be displayed, which indicates the beginning of the second pass of the ECM trouble codes.
6. On the 2nd pass, only "HARD" trouble codes will be displayed. These are the codes which indicate a currently present malfunction.
7. Codes which are displayed during the 1st pass but not on the 2nd, are classified as "intermittent" trouble codes. If all the ECM codes are considered "intermittent", the ".E.E" display will be bypassed.
8. When all the ECM trouble codes have been displayed, the BCM codes will then displayed in a similar fashion. The only exceptions during the BCM code display are as follows:
    a. "..F" precedes the first display pass.
    b. The BCM codes are prefixed by an "F".
    c. ".F.F" precedes the second display pass.
9. After all the ECM and BCM trouble codes have been displayed or if no codes are present, Code ".7.0" will be displayed. This code indicates that the system is ready for the next diagnostic feature to be selected.

NOTE: If a Code E51 is detected, it will be displayed continuously until the diagnostic mode is exited. During this display of Code E51, none of the other diagnostic features will be possible.

Clearing Diagnostic Memory

Trouble codes stored in the ECM's memory may be cleared (erased) by entering the diagnostic mode and then depressing the **OFF** and **HI** buttons on the CCP simultaneously. Hold the buttons in until "E.0.0"appears on the display. Trouble codes stored in the BCM's memory may be cleared by depressing the **OFF** and **LO** buttons simultaneously until "F.0.0" appears. After "E.0.0" or "F.0.0" is displayed, ".7.0." will appear. With the ".7.0"displayed, turn the ignition **OFF** for at least ten seconds before re-entering the diagnostic mode.

Exiting Diagnostic Mode

To get out of the diagnostic mode, depress the AUTO button or turn the ignition switch **OFF** for 10 seconds. Trouble codes are not erased when this is done. The temperature setting will reappear in the display panel.

NOTE: The Climate Control system will operate in whatever mode was commanded prior to depressing the necessary buttons to enter the diagnostic system. The prior operating mode will be remembered and will resume after the diagnostic mode is entered.

1986–89 FWD ELDORADO AND SEVILLE

Description

The Electronic Control Module (ECM) is located under the instrument panel and is the control center of the engine control and fuel injection systems. It constantly examines the information from the various sensors and controls the systems that affect the vehicle performance. The ECM performs the diagnostic function of the system by recognizing operational problems, alert the operator through an "Engine Control System" lamp and will store a code or codes which identify the problem areas to aid the technician in determining what repairs are to be made.

The ECM consists of 3 parts; a controller, (the ECM without the PROM), A separate calibrator (PROM – Programmable Read Only Memory) and a resistor network (CALPAK) which provides the calibrated backup fuel calibrations and ECM/BCM communication instructions.

In addition to the ECM, the vehicle contains a Body Computer Module (BCM), which is used to control various vehicle functions, based on data sensors and switch inputs.

Both the ECM and BCM have the capability to diagnose faults with the various inputs and systems they control. When the ECM recognizes a problem, an "Engine Control System" indicator lamp is illuminated on the instrument panel to alert the operator that a malfunction has occurred.

The ECM supplies either 5 or 12 volts to power the various sensors or switched. This is done through resistances in the ECM which are so high in value that a conventional test lamp will not illuminate when connected to a circuit. In some cases, a conventional shop voltmeter will not give accurate readings because its resistance is to low. Therefore, a 10 megohm input impedance digital voltmeter is required to assure accurate voltage readings.

The ECM has a learning ability that allows the fuel control calibration to be tailored to account for minor differences in fuel control systems and engine mechanical systems and to better adapt the vehicle to changing environmental conditions.

If the battery is disconnected or if an ECM is replaced, the ECM in the vehicle will have to begin the learning process all over again. A change in vehicle driveability may be noted after a battery disconnect or ECM replacement. To teach the ECM, operate the vehicle at normal operating temperature, at part throttle and at idle, until the driveability and performance returns.

Trouble Codes

NOTE: Should a problem exist in a vehicle that has a history of body repair work, the area of repairs should be scrutinzed very carefully for damages to the wiring, connectors, vacuum hoses or other sub-components that could contribute to component problems. After being satisfied that the concerned area appears trouble free, expand the diagnosis as required.

In the process of controlling the various subsystems, the ECM and BCM continually monitor operating conditions for possible system malfunctions. By comparing system conditions against standard operating limits, certain circuit and component malfunctions can be detected.

A 3-digit numerical trouble code is stored in the computer memory when a problem is detected by this self diagnostic system. These trouble codes can be displayed by the technician as an aid in the system repairs.

The occurrence of certain system malfunctions require that the vehicle operator be alerted to the problem so as to avoid prolonged vehicle operation under the downgraded system operation, which could affect other systems and components. Computer controlled diagnostic messages and/or telltales will appear under these conditions which indicate that service is required.

If a particular malfunction would result in unacceptable system operation, the self diagnostics will attempt to minimize the effect by taking "FAIL-SOFT" action. "FAIL-SOFT" action refers to any specific attempt by the computer system to compensate for the detected problem. A typical "FAIL-SAFE" action would be the substitution of a fixed input value when a sensor is detected to be open or shorted.

Entering Diagnostic Mode

To enter the diagnostic mode, proceed as follows:
1. Turn the ignition switch **ON**.
2. Touch the **OFF** and the **WARM** buttons on the Climate Control panel simultaneously and hold until a segment check is displayed on the Instrument Panel Cluster (IPC) and Climate Control Driver Information Center, usually around 3 seconds.

NOTE: Operating the vehicle in the "Service Mode" for extended time periods (exceeding ½ hour) without the engine operating or without a "Trickle" type charger connected to the battery, can cause the the battery to discharge, resulting in possible relaying of false diagnostic information or causing a no-start condition.

Trouble Code Display

After the Service Mode is entered, any trouble codes stored in the computer memory will be displayed. ECM codes will be displayed first. If no ECM trouble codes are stored, a "NO ECM CODES" message will be displayed. All ECM codes will be prefixed with a "E". Examples are E013, E014 and etc.

The lowest numbered ECM code will be displayed first, followed by progressively higher numbered codes present in the system. Following the highest ECM code present or the "NO ECM CODES" message, the BCM codes will be displayed. All BCM codes will be prefixed with a letter "B". Examples are B110, B111 and etc.

Progressively higher numbered BCM codes, if present, will be displayed consecutively for 2 second intervals until the highest code present has been displayed. If no BCM trouble codes are stored, "NO BCM CODES" message will be displayed.

Any BCM and ECM codes displayed will also be accompanied by "CURRENT" or "HISTORY". "HISTORY" indicates the failure was not present the last time the code was tested and "CURRENT" indicates the fault still exists.

At any time during the display of ECM or BCM codes, if the

"LO" fan button on the ECC is depressed, the display of codes will be bypassed.

At any time during the display of trouble codes, if the "RESET/RECALL" button on the DIC is depressed, the system will exit the Service Mode and go back to normal vehicle operation.

NOTE: Upon entering the Service Mode, the climate control will operate in whatever mode was being commanded just prior to depressing the OFF and WARM buttons. Even though the displays may change just as the buttons are touched, the prior operating mode is remembered and will resume after the Service Mode is entered. Extended Compressor at Idle (ECI) is not allowed while in the diagnostic mode. This allows observation of system parameters during normal compressor cycles.

Selecting "CLEAR CODES?"

Selection of the "CLEAR CODES?" test type will result in the message "CODES CLEAR" being displayed along with the selected system name. This message will appear for 3 seconds to indicate that all stored trouble codes have been erased from that system's memory. After 3 seconds, the display will automatically return to the next available test type for the selected system

Selecting "SNAPSHOT?"

Selection of "SNAPSHOT?" test type will result in the message "SNAPSHOT TAKEN" being displayed with the selected system name proceeding it. This message will appear for 3 seconds to indicate that all system data and inputs have been stored in memory. After 3 seconds, the display will automatically proceed to the first available snapshot test type, for example "SNAP DATA". While selecting a snapshot test type, any of the following actions can be taken to control the display;

1. Pressing the **OFF** button on the CCP will stop the test type selection process and return the display to the next available system selection.
2. Pressing the **LO** button on the CCP will display the next available snapshot test type.
3. This allows the display to be stepped through all available choices. This list of snapshot test types can be repeated following the display of the last choice.
4. Pressing the **HI** button with "SNAP DATA?" or "SNAP INPUT?" displayed, will select that test type. At this point, the display is controlled as it would be for non-snapshot data and inputs displays. However, all values and status information represents memorized vehicle conditions.
5. Pressing the **HI** button on the CCP with "SNAPSHOT?" displayed will again display the "SNAPSHOT TAKEN" message to indicate that new information has been stored in the memory. Access to this information is obtained the same as previously outlined.

Clearing Diagnostic Mode

To exit the Service Mode, press the RESET/RECALL button on the DIC or turn the ignition switch **OFF**. Trouble codes are not erased when this is done.

Electronic Engine Control System

1986–87 RIVIERA

Description

The Electronic Control Module (ECM) is the controlling unit of the electronic engine control system. Though it communicates with the other vehicle computers, it alone has the primary responsibility of maintaining proper emissions while delivering optimum driveability characteristics.

The ECM monitors inputs from the engine as well as other vehicle sensors. It then correlates this information with data

stored in the PROM. After all the information is evaluated, the ECM calulates the necessary changes to compensate for all driving conditions.

The ECM is able to detect malfunctions in most of the systems it monitors. It will turn on the "Service Engine Soon" indicator lamp, set a trouble code, or both if it detects a fault.

NOTE: Always repair all code malfunctions before any driveability or emission problem repairs are attempted. If more than 1 code is set, always repair the lowest numbered code first.

The ECM trouble codes are displayed on the Cathode Ray Tube (CRT) when in the diagnostic mode. Other service related information that can be displayed are as follows:

1. ECM data.
2. ECM Discrete inputs.
3. ECM output cycling.
4. ECM trouble codes

All displays except for the output mode cycling can be viewed under the following conditions:

1. The ignition switch **ON**.
2. The engine NOT operating.
3. The engine at idle.
4. The vehicle being driven.

The output mode cycling function is only operational with the ignition switch **ON** and the engine not operating.

Accessing BCM Self Diagnostics

In order to access and control the BCM self-diagnostic features, 2 additional electronic components are necessary, the CRTC and the CRT picture tube. As part of the CRT's Service Mode page, a 22 character display area is used to display diagnostic information. When a malfunction is sensed by the computer system, 1 of the driver warning messages is displayed on the CRT under the "DIAGNOSTIC" category. When the Service Mode is entered, the various BCM, ECM, or IPC parameters, fault codes, inputs, outputs as well as override commands and clearing code capability are displayed when commanded through the CRT.

The CRT becomes the device to enter the diagnostics and access the Service Diagnostic routines. The CRTC is the device which controls the display on the CRT and interprets the switches touched on the CRT and passes this information along to the BCM. This communication process allows the BCM to transfer any of its available diagnostic information to the CRT for display during Service Mode.

By touching the appropriate pads on the CRT, data messages can be sent to the BCM from the CRTC over the data line, requesting the specific diagnostic feature required.

ALDL CONNECTOR

The Assembly Line Diagnostic Link (ALDL) is a diagnostic connector located in the passenger compartment. Along with the assembly plant usage for proper engine operation before leaving the plant, it may also be used to access the SERIAL DATA circuit, using a service diagnostic tool, specifically designed and calibrated for that purpose.

The ALDL cover contains a jumper, which is part of the redundant SERIAL DATA CKT "800" and if removed for any reason, must be replaced before returning the vehicle to service. The missing ALDL cover could create a loss of SERIAL DATA communication if CKT "800" was already open elsewhere. This would result in the message "ELECTRICAL PROBLEM", accompanied by a "SERIAL DATA" loss code and potential driveability complaints.

Trouble Codes

In the process of controlling the various subsystems, the ECM and the BCM continually monitor operating conditions for possible malfunctions. By comparing systems conditions against standard operating limits, certain circuit and component malfunctions can be detected. A 3-digit numerical trouble code is stored in the computer memory when a problem is detected by this self-diagnostic system. These trouble codes can later be displayed by the service technician as an aid in system repair.

The occurrence of certain system malfunctions require the vehicle operator be alerted to the problem so as to avoid prolonged operation of the vehicle under degrading system operations. The computer controlled diagnostic messages and/or telltales will appear under these conditions which indicate service or repairs are required.

If a particular malfunction would result in unacceptable system operation, the self-diagnostics will attempt to minimize the effect by taking a "FAIL–SOFT" action. "FAIL–SOFT" action refers to any specific attempt by the computer system to compensate for the detected problem. A typical "FAIL–SOFT" action would be the substitution of a fixed input value when a sensor is detected to have an open or shorted circuit.

Entering Diagnostic Mode

1. Turn the ignition switch **ON**.
2. Touch the **OFF** and the **WARM** pads on the CRT's climate control page, simultaneously and hold until a double "BEEP" is heard or a page entitled "Service Mode" appears on the CRT.

NOTE: Operating the vehicle in the Service Mode for an extended time period without the engine operating or without a trickle battery charger attached to the battery, can cause the battery to become discharged and possibly relate false diagnostic information or cause an engine no-start. Avoid lengthy (over ½ hour) Service Mode operation.

Trouble Code Display

After the Service Mode is entered, any trouble codes stored in the computer memory will be displayed. ECM codes will be displayed first. If no ECM codes are stored, the CRT will display a "NO ECM CODES" message for approximately 2 seconds. All ECM codes will be prefixed with an "E" (Example: EO13, EO23, etc.).

The lowest numbered ECM code will be displayed first, followed by progressively higher numbered codes present. Codes will be displayed consecutively for 2 second intervals until the highest code present has been displayed. When all ECM codes have been displayed, BCM codes will be displayed. Following the highest ECM code present or the "NO ECM CODES" message, the lowest numbered BCM code will be displayed for approximately 2 seconds. BCM codes displayed will also be accompanied by "CURRENT" or "HISTORY". "HISTORY" indicates the failure was not present the last time the code was tested and "CURRENT" indicates the fault still exists. Since the ECM is not capable of making this determination, these messages do not appear when the ECM codes are being displayed.

All BCM codes will be prefixed with the letter "B" (Example: B110 and etc.). Progressively higher numbered BCM codes, if present, will be displayed for approximately 2 second intervals until the highest code present has been displayed. If no BCM trouble codes are stored, "NO BCM CODES" message will be displayed. At any time during the display of the ECM or BCM codes, if the "NO" pad is touched, the display will bypass the codes. At any time during the display of trouble codes, if the "EXIT" pad is touched, the CRT will exit the "Service Mode" and go back to normal vehicle operation.

Selecting "CODE RESET?"

Selection of "CODE RESET?" test type will result in the message "CODES CLEAR" being displayed with the selected system name above it after the "YES" pad has been touched. This

message will appear for 3 seconds to indicate all stored trouble codes have been erased from that system's memory. After 3 seconds, the display will automatically return to the next available test type for the selected system.

Clearing Service Mode

To exit the Service Mode, repeatedly touch the "EXIT" pad until the Service Mode page disappears or turn the ignition switch **OFF**. Trouble codes are not erased when this is done.

1988–89 RIVIERA AND REATTA

Description

Numerous electronic components are located on the vehicle as a part of an electrical network, designed to control various engine and body subsystems.

At the heart of the computer system is the Body Computer Module (BCM). The BCM is located on the front driver's side of the floor console and has an internal microprocessor, which is the center for communication with all other components in the system. All sensors and switches are monitored by the BCM or other major components that complete the computer system. The components are as follows:

1. Electronic Control Module (ECM)
2. Instrument Panel Cluster (IPC)
3. Cathode Ray Tube Controller (CRTC)
4. Programmer/Heating/Ventilation/Air Conditioning

A combination of inputs from these major components and the other sensors and switches communicate together to the BCM, either as individual inputs, or on the common communication link called the serial data line. The various inputs to the BCM combine with program instructions within the system memory to provide accurate control over the many subsystems involved. When a subsystem circuit exceeds pre-programmed limits, a system malfunction is indicated and may provide certain back-up functions. Providing control over the many subsystems from the BCM is done by controlling system outputs. This can be either direct or transmitted along the serial data line to 1 of the other major components. The process of receiving, storing, testing and controlling information is continuous. The data communication gives the BCM control over the ECM's self-diagnostic capacities in addition to its own.

Between the BCM and the other 4 major components of the computer system, a communication process has been incorporated which allows the devices to share information and thereby provide for additional control capabilities. In a method similar to that used by a telegraph system, the BCM's internal circuitry rapidly switches to a circuit 0–5V like a telegraph key. This process is used to convert information into a series of pulses which represents coded data messages understood by other components. Also, much like a telegraph system, each major component has its own recognition code. When a message is sent out on the serial data line, only the component or station that matches the assigned recognition code will pay attention and the rest of the components or stations will ignore it. This data transfer of information is most important in understanding how the system operates and how to diagnosis possible malfunctions within the system.

In order to access and control the BCM self-diagnostic features, additional electronic components are necessary, which are the Cathode Ray Tube Controller (CRTC) and the Graphic Control Center (GCC) picture tube. As part of the GCC's Service Mode page, a 22 character display area is used to display diagnostic information. When a malfunction is sensed by the computer system, a driver warning messages is displayed on the GCC under the Diagnostic category. When the Service Mode is entered, the various BCM, ECM, or IPC parameters, fault codes, inputs, outputs as well as override commands and clearing code capability are displayed when commanded through the GCC.

The GCC becomes the device to enter the diagnostics and access the Service Diagnostic routines. The CRTC is the device which controls the display on the GCC and interprets the switches touched on the GCC and passes this information along to the BCM. This communication process allows the BCM to transfer any of its available diagnostic information to the GCC for display during Service Mode.

By touching the appropriate pads on the GCC, data messages can be sent to the BCM from the CRTC over the data line, requesting the specific diagnostic feature required.

Trouble Codes

In the process of controlling the various subsystems, the ECM and the BCM continually monitor operating conditions for possible malfunctions. By comparing systems conditions against standard operating limits, certain circuit and component malfunctions can be detected. A 3-digit numerical trouble code is stored in the computer memory when a problem is detected by this self-diagnostic system. These trouble codes can later be displayed by the service technician as an aid in system repair.

The occurrence of certain system malfunctions require that the vehicle operator be alerted to the problem so as to avoid prolonged operation of the vehicle under degrading system operations. The computer controlled diagnostic messages and/or telltales will appear under these conditions which indicate that service or repairs are required.

If a particular malfunction would result in unacceptable system operation, the self-diagnostics will attempt to minimize the effect by taking a FAIL-SOFT action. FAIL-SOFT action refers to any specific attempt by the computer system to compensate for the detected problem. A typical FAIL-SOFT action would be the substitution of a fixed input value when a sensor is detected to have an open or shorted circuit.

Entering Diagnostic Mode

1. Turn the ignition switch **ON**.
2. Touch the **OFF** and the **WARM** pads on the CRT's climate control page, simultaneously and hold until a double BEEP is heard or a page entitled Service Mode appears on the CRT.

NOTE: Operating the vehicle in the Service Mode for an extended time period without the engine operating or without a trickle battery charger attached to the battery, can cause the battery to become discharged and possibly relate false diagnostic information or cause an engine no-start. Avoid lengthy (over ½ hour) Service Mode operation.

Clearing Diagnostic Memory

To exit the Service Mode, repeatedly touch the EXIT pad until the Service Mode page disappears or turn the ignition switch OFF. Trouble codes are not erased when this is done.

1986–89 TORONADO

Decsription

The Electronic Control Module (ECM) is the controlling unit of the Electronic Engine Control System. Though it communicates with the other vehicle computers, it alone has the primary responsibility of maintaining proper emissions while delivering optimum driveability characteristics.

The ECM monitors inputs from the engine as well as other vehicle sensors. It then correlates this information with data stored in the PROM. After all the information is evaluated, the ECM calculates the necessary changes to compensate for all driving conditions. The ECM is able to detect malfunctions in most of the systems it monitors. It will turn ON the "Service

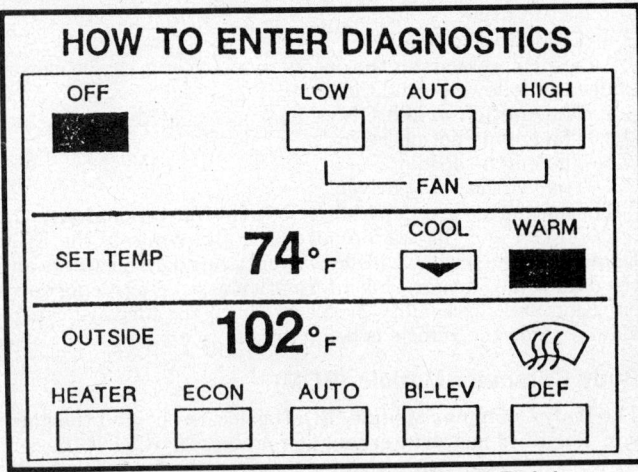

How to enter diagnostic mode – 1988–89 Buick Riviera and Reatta

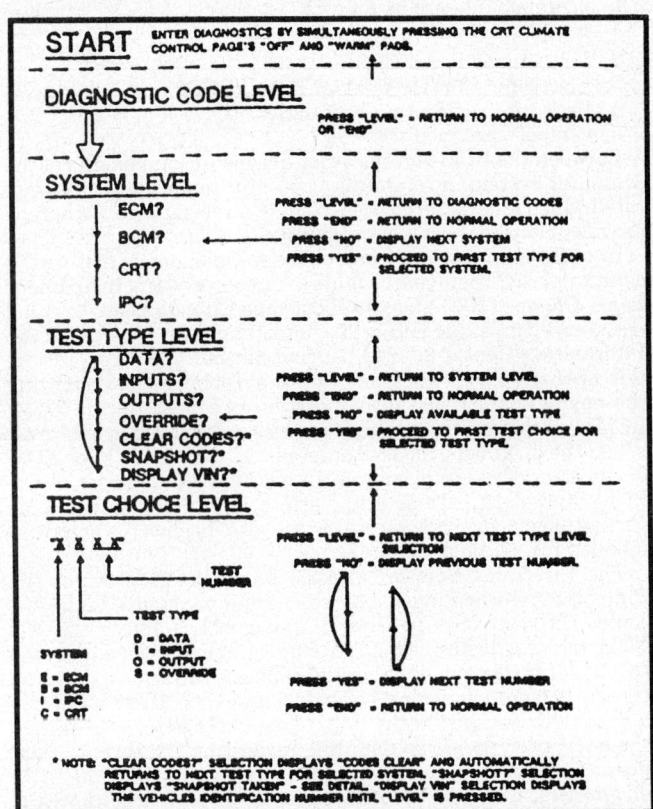

Self-diagnostic system flow chart – 1988–89 Buick Riviera and Reatta

Engine Soon" lamp, set a trouble code, or both if it detects a fault.

NOTE: Always repair all code malfunctions before any driveability or emission problem repairs are attempted. If more than 1 code is set, always repair the lowest numbered code first.

The ECM trouble codes are displayed on the Instrument Panel Cluster (IPC) when in the diagnostic mode. Other service related information that can be displayed are as follows:
1. ECM data.
2. ECM Discrete inputs.

3. ECM output cycling.
4. ECM trouble codes

All displays, except for the output mode cycling, can be viewed under the following conditions:
1. The ignition switch **ON**.
2. The engine not operating.
3. The engine at idle.
4. The vehicle being driven.

The output mode cycling function is only operational with the ignition **ON** and the engine not operating. While in the ECM Data mode, the display will show twenty-one data messages and the data value of each. This information assists in tracing down emission and driveability problems, since the displays can be viewed while the vehicle is being driven.

Body Computer Module (BCM)

The Body Computer Module (BCM) is located behind the glove box. The BCM has an internal microprocessor, which is the center for communication with all other components in the system. All sensors and switches are monitored by the BCM or 1 of the 5 other major components that complete the computer system. The 5 components are as follows:

1. Electronic Control Module (ECM)
2. Instrument Panel Cluster (IPC)
3. Electronic Climate Control Panel (ECC)
4. Programmer/Heating/Ventilation/AC
5. Chime/Voice module

Between the BCM and the other five major components of the computer system, a communication process has been incorporated which allows the devices to share information and thereby provide additional control capabilities.

In order to access and control the self diagnostic features, 2 additional electronic components are necessary, the Instrument Panel Cluster (IPC) and the Electronic Climate Control panel (ECC). As part of the IPC, a 20 character display area called the Information Center is used. During normal engine operation, this area displays "Toronado" or is a Tachometer, displaying the engine rpm. When a malfunction is sensed by the ECM/BCM, 1 of the driver warning messages is displayed in this area. When the diagnostic mode is entered, the various BCM or ECM diagnostic codes are displayed. In addition to the codes of the ECM/BCM data parameters, discrete inputs and outputs, as well as output override messages are also displayed when commanded for, through the ECC.

The Electronic Comfort Control Panel (ECC) provides the controls for the heating and air conditioning systems. It also becomes the controller to enter the diagnostics and access the BCM self-diagnostics. This communication process allows the BCM to transfer any of its available diagnostic information top the instrument panel for display during service. By pressing the appropriate buttons on the ECC, data messages can be sent to the BCM over the serial data line requesting the specific diagnostic features desired. When in the Override mode of the BCM diagnostics, the amount of Override is displayed at the ECC where the outside and set temperatures are normally displayed.

Trouble Codes

In the process of controlling the various subsystems, the ECM and BCM continually monitor operating conditions for possible system malfunctions. By comparing system conditions against standard operating limits, certain circuit and component malfunctions can be detected. A 3-digit numerical trouble code is stored in the computer memory when a problem is detected by this self diagnostic system. These trouble codes can be displayed by the technician as an aid in the system repairs.

The occurrence of certain system malfunctions require the vehicle operator be alerted to the problem so as to avoid prolonged vehicle operation under the downgraded system operation, which could affect other systems and components. Com-

puter Controlled diagnostic messages and/or telltales will appear under these conditions which indicate service is required.

If a particular malfunction would result in unacceptable system operation, the self diagnostics will attempt to minimize the effect by taking "FAIL-SOFT" action. "FAIL-SOFT" action refers to any specific attempt by the computer system to compensate for the detected problem. A typical "FAIL-SAFE" action would be the substitution of a fixed input value when a sensor is detected to be open or shorted.

Entering Diagnostic Mode

To enter the diagnostic mode, proceed as follows:
1. Turn the ignition switch **ON**.
2. Touch the **OFF** and the **WARM** buttons on the Electronic Climate Control (ECC) panel simultaneously and hold until a segment check is displayed on the Instrument Panel Cluster (IPC) and Electronic Climate Control (ECC), usually around 3 seconds.

NOTE: Operating the vehicle in the Service Mode for extended time periods (exceeding ½ hour) without the engine operating or without a trickle-type charger connected to the battery, can cause the the battery to discharge, resulting in possible relaying of false diagnostic information or causing a no-start condition.

Trouble Code Display

After the Service Mode is entered, any trouble codes stored in the computer memory will be displayed. ECM codes will be displayed first. If no ECM trouble codes are stored, the IPC will display a "NO ECM CODES" message for approximately 2 seconds. All ECM codes will be prefixed with a "E". Examples are E013, E014 and etc. The lowest numbered ECM code will be displayed 1st, followed by progressively higher numbered codes present in the system.

The codes will be displayed consecutively for 2 second intervals until the highest code present has been displayed. When all ECM codes have been displayed, the BCM codes will be displayed. The lowest numbered BCM code will be displayed for appropriately 2 seconds. BCM codes accompanied by "CURRENT" indicates the fault still exits. Since the ECM is not capable of making this determination, this message does not appear when the ECM codes are being displayed. All BCM codes will be prefixed with a letter "B". Examples are B110, B111 and etc.

Progressively higher numbered BCM codes, if present, will be displayed consecutively for 2 second intervals until the highest code present has been displayed. If no BCM trouble codes are stored, "NO BCM CODES" message will be displayed. At any time during the display of ECM or BCM codes, if the "LO" fan button on the ECC is depressed, the display of codes will be bypassed. At any time during the display of trouble codes, if the "BI-LEV" button is depressed, the BCM will exit the Service Mode and go back to normal vehicle operation.

NOTE: Upon entering the Service Mode, the climate control will operate in whatever mode was being commanded just prior to depressing the OFF and WARM buttons. Even though the displays may change just as the buttons are touched, the prior operating mode is remembered and will resume after the Service Mode is entered.

Clearing Diagnostic Mode

To exit the Service Mode, press the BI-LEV button. Trouble codes are not erased when this is done. Any mode button will exit diagnostics, however, BI-LEV was chosen for procedural consistency.

EXCEPT E, K AND CADILLAC C-BODY

Description

The ECM is equipped with a self-diagnostic capability which can detect system failures and aids the technician by identifying the fault via a trouble code system and a dash mounted indicator light, marked either "Service Engine Soon" or "Check Engine". The light is mounted on the instrument panel and has 2 functions:

1. It is used to inform the operator that a problem has occurred and the vehicle should be taken in for service as soon as reasonably possible.

2. It is used by the technician to read out stored trouble codes in order to localize malfunction areas during the diagnosis and repair phases.

As a bulb and system check, the light will turn ON with the ignition key turned **ON** and the engine not operating. When the engine is started, the light will turn OFF. If the light does not turn OFF, the self diagnostic system has detected a problem in the system. If the problem goes away, the light will go out, in most cases after 10 second, but a trouble code will be set in the ECM's memory.

Assembly Line Communication Link (ALCL)

In order to access the ECM to provide the trouble codes stored in its memory, the Assembly Line Communication Link (also known as the Assembly Line Diagnostic Link or ALDL) is used.

NOTE: This connector is utilized at the assembly plant to insure the engine is operating properly before the vehicle is shipped.

Terminal **B** of the diagnostic connnector is the diagnostic terminal and it can be connected to terminal **A**, or ground, to enter the diagnostic mode, or the field Service Mode on fuel injection models.

Entering Diagnostic Mode

If the diagnostic terminal is grounded with the ignition turned **ON** and the engine stopped, the system will enter the diagnostic mode. In this mode, the ECM will accomplish the following:

1. The ECM will display a Code 12 by flashing the "Service Engine Soon" or "Check Engine" light, which indicates the system is working. A Code 12 consists of 1 flash, followed by a short pause, then 2 flashes in quick succession.

a. This code will be flashed 3 times. If no other codes are stored, Code 12 will continue to flash until the diagnostic terminal is disconnected from the ground circuit.

b. On a carbureted engine, the engine should not be started with the diagnostic terminal grounded, because it may continue to flash a Code 12 with the engine running. Also, if the test terminal is grounded after the engine is running any stored codes will flash but Code 12 will flash only if there is a problem with the distributor reference signal.

c. On fuel injected engines, codes can only be obtained with the engine stopped. Grounding the diagnostic terminal with the engine running activates the Field Service Mode.

2. The ECM will display any stored codes by flashing the "Service Engine Soon" or "Check Engine" light. Each code will be flashed 3 times, then Code 12 will be flashed again.

a. On carbureted engines, if a trouble code is displayed, the memory is cleared, then the engine is operated to see if the code is a hard or intermittent failure.

b. If the code represents a hard failure, a diagnostic code chart is used to locate the area of the failure.

c. If an intermittent failure is determined, the problem circuits can be examined physically for reasons of failure.

d. On fuel injected engines, if a trouble code is displayed, a diagnostic code chart is used to locate the area of failure.

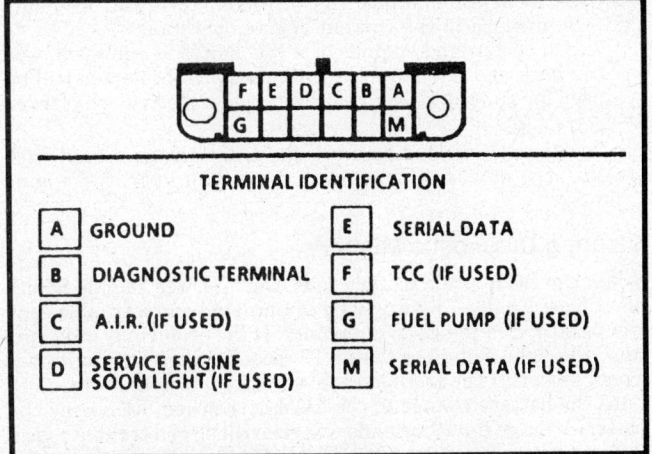

TERMINAL IDENTIFICATION

A	GROUND	**E**	SERIAL DATA
B	DIAGNOSTIC TERMINAL	**F**	TCC (IF USED)
C	A.I.R. (IF USED)	**G**	FUEL PUMP (IF USED)
D	SERVICE ENGINE SOON LIGHT (IF USED)	**M**	SERIAL DATA (IF USED)

Assembly Line Communication Link (ALCL) or Assembly Line Data Link (ALDL) — Typical

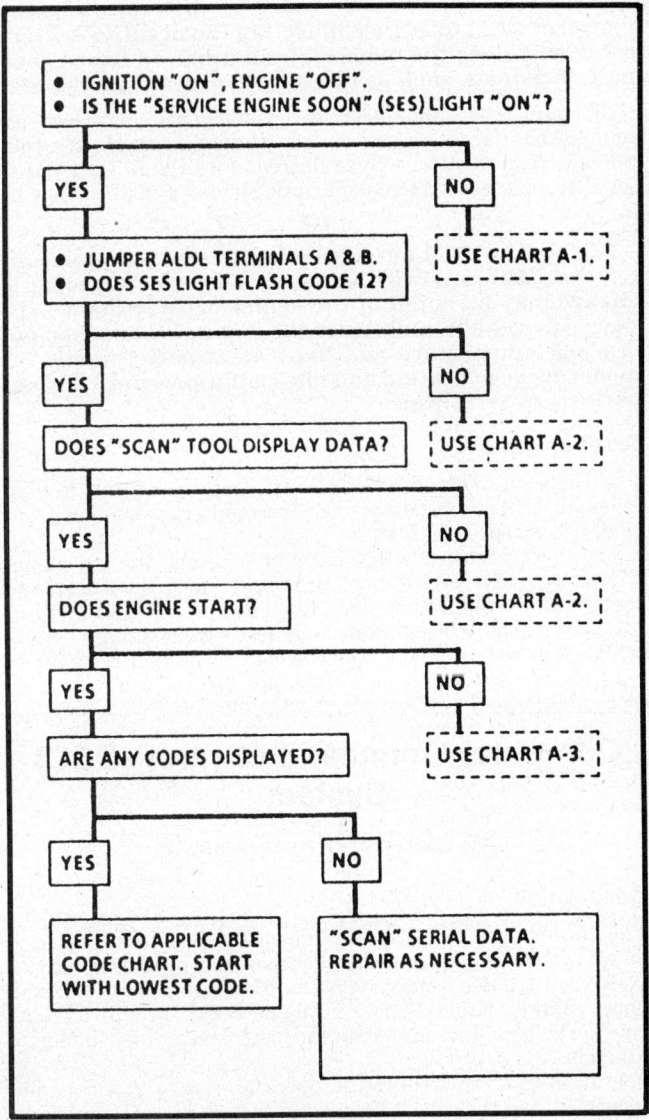

Diagnostic flow chart — Typical

3. The ECM will energize all controlled relays and solenoids that are involved in the current engine operation.

   a. On carbureted engines, the ISC motor, if equipped, will move back and forth and the mixture control solenoid will be pulsed for 25 seconds or until the engine is started, which ever occurs 1st.

   b. On fuel injected engines, the IAC valve is moved back and forth or is fully extended, depending upon the engine family.

Clearing Diagnostic Memory

When the ECM sets a trouble code, the "Service Engine Soon" or "Check Engine" light will be illuminated and a trouble code will be stored in the ECM's memory. If the problem is intermittent, the light will go out after 10 seconds when the fault goes away, however, the trouble code will stay in the ECM memory until the battery voltage to the ECM is removed. Removing the battery voltage for 10 seconds will clear all stored trouble codes.

To prevent damage to the ECM, the ignition key must be turned **OFF** when disconnecting or reconnecting the power to the ECM through the battery cable, ECM pigtail, ECM fuse, jumper cables, etc.

NOTE: If posiable clear codes by disconnecting the pigtail or ECM fuse. Disconnecting the negative battery cable will clear the memory from other on-board computers systems, such as pre-set radio, seat control, etc.

All trouble codes should be cleared after repairs have been accomplished. In some cases, such as through a diagnoistic routine, the codes may have to be cleared first to allow the ECM to set a trouble code during the test, should a malfunction be present.

NOTE: The ECM has a learning ability to perform after the battery power has been disconnected to it. A change may be noted in the vehicle's performance. To teach the vehicle, make sure the engine is at normal operating temperature and drive it at part throttle, at moderate acceleration and idle conditions, until normal performance returns.

Trouble Codes

The Diagnostic Trouble Code chart contains all the trouble codes for all General Motors car and light truck engines from 1988–89, except E-body series.

The chart is labeled with the engine (in liters) and the engine VIN designation at the top of the chart. Along the side of the chart are the trouble codes and the abbreviated function. Within the chart are all the applicable body series letter designation. If a particular code applies the all the body series that is equipped with the listed engine, then the word "ALL" will appear in block.

Computer Command Control (CCC) System

CARBURETED MODELS

Description

The ECM is equipped with a self-diagnostic capability which can detect system failures and aids the technician by identifying the fault via a trouble code system and a dash mounted indicator lamp, marked either "Service Engine Soon" or "Check Engine". The lamp is mounted on the instrument panel and has 2 functions:

1. It is used to inform the operator that a problem has occurrred, and the vehicle should be taken in for service as soon as possible.

2. It is used by the technician to read out trouble codes in order to localize malfunction areas during the diagnosis and repair phases.

As a bulb and system check, the light will turn ON with the ignition key **ON** and the engine not operating. When the engine is started, the light will turn OFF. If the light does not turn OFF, the self diagnostic system has detected a problem in the system. If the problem goes away, the light will go out, in most cases after ten second, but a trouble code will be set in the ECM's memory.

Assembly Line Communication Link (ALCL)

In order to access the ECM to provide the trouble codes stored in its memory, the Assembly Line Communication Link (also known as the Assembly Line Diagnostic Link or ALDL) is used.

NOTE: This connector is utilized at the assembly plant to insure the engine is operating properly before the vehicle is shipped.

Terminal **B** of the diagnostic connnector is the diagnostic terminal and it can be connected to terminal **A**, or ground, to enter the diagnostic mode, or the field Service Mode on fuel injection models.

Entering Diagnostic Mode

If the diagnostic terminal is grounded with the ignition **ON** and the engine stopped, the system will enter the diagnostic mode. In this mode, the ECM will accomplish the following:

1. The ECM will display a Code 12 by flashing the "Service Engine Soon" or "Check Engine" light, which indicates the system is working. A Code 12 consists of 1 flash, followed by a short pause, then 2 flashes in quick succession.

   a. This code will be flashed 3 times. If no other codes are stored, Code 12 will continue to flash until the diagnostic terminal is disconnected from the ground circuit.

   b. On a carbureted engine, the engine should not be started with the diagnostic terminal grounded, because it may continue to flash a Code 12 with the engine running. Also, if the test terminal is grounded after the engine is running any stored codes will flash, but Code 12 will flash only if there is a problem with the distributor reference signal.

   c. On fuel injected engines, codes can only be obtained with the engine stopped. Grounding the diagnostic terminal with the engine running activates the "Field Service Mode".

2. The ECM will display any stored codes by flashing the "Service Engine Soon" or "Check Engine" light. Each code will be flashed 3 times, then Code 12 will be flashed again.

   a. On carbureted engines, if a trouble code is displayed, the memory is cleared, then the engine is operated to see if the code is a hard or intermittent failure.

   b. If the code represents a hard failure, a diagnostic code chart is used to locate the area of the failure.

   c. If an intermittent failure is determined, the problem circuits can be examined physically for reasons of failure.

   d. On fuel injected engines, if a trouble code is displayed, a diagnostic code chart is used to locate the area of failure.

3. The ECM will energize all controlled relays and solenoids that are involved in the current engine operation.

   a. On carbureted engines, the ISC motor, if equipped, will move back and forth and the mixture control solenoid will be pulsed for 25 seconds or until the engine is started, which ever occurs 1st.

   b. On fuel injected engines, the IAC valve is moved back and forth or is fully extended, depending upon the engine family.

Clearing Diagnostic Memory

When the Electronic Control Module (ECM) sets a trouble code, the "Service Engine Soon" or "Check Engine" lamp will be illuminated and a trouble code will be stored in the ECM's memory. If the problem is intermittent, the light will go out after 10 seconds when the fault goes away, however, the trouble code will stay in the ECM memory until the battery voltage to the ECM is removed. Removing the battery voltage for ten seconds will clear all stored trouble codes.

To prevent damage to the ECM, the ignition key must be turned **OFF** when disconnecting or reconnecting the power to the ECM through the battery cable, ECM pigtail, ECM fuse, jumper cables, etc.

All trouble codes should be cleared after repairs have been accomplished. In some cases, such as through a diagnostic routine, the codes may have to be cleared first to allow the ECM to set a trouble code during the test, should a malfunction be present.

NOTE: The ECM has a learning ability to perform after the battery power has been disconnected to it. A change may be noted in the vehicle's performance. To teach the vehicle, make sure the engine is at normal operating temperature and drive it at part throttle, at moderate acceleration and idle conditions, until normal performance returns.

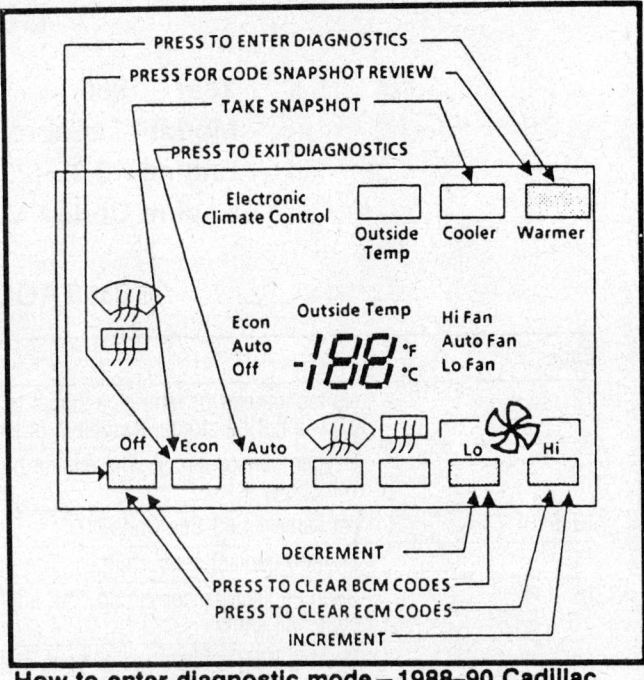

How to enter diagnostic mode – 1988–90 Cadillac Eldorado and Seville

ECM DIAGNOSTIC CODES

CODE	DESCRIPTION	COMMENTS	CODE	DESCRIPTION	COMMENTS
E012	No Distributor Signal		E038	Open MAT Sensor Circuit [AIR]	
E013	Oxygen Sensor Not Ready [AIR & CL]		E039	VCC Engagement Problem	
E014	Shorted Coolant Sensor Circuit [AIR]		E040	Open Power Steering Pressure Switch Circuit	
E015	Open Coolant Sensor Circuit [AIR]		E044	Lean Exhaust Signal [AIR & CL]	
E016	Generator Voltage Out Of Range [All Solenoids]		E045	Rich Exhaust Signal [AIR & CL]	
E018	Open Crank Signal Circuit		E047	BCM—ECM Data Problem [A/C Clutch]	
E019	Shorted Fuel Pump Circuit		E048	EGR System Fault [EGR]	
E020	Open Fuel Pump Circuit		E052	ECM Memory Reset Indicator	
E021	Shorted Throttle Position Sensor Circuit		E053	Distributor Signal Interrupt	
E022	Open Throttle Position Sensor Circuit		E055	TPS Misadjusted	
			E058	Pass Key Fuel Enable	
E023	EST/Bypass Circuit Problem [AIR & EGR]		E059	VCC Temperature Sensor Circuit Problem	
E024	Speed Sensor Circuit Problem [VCC & Cruise]		E060	Cruise—Transmission Not In Drive [Cruise]	
E026	Shorted Throttle Switch Circuit		E063	Cruise—Car Speed And Set Speed	
E027	Open Throttle Switch Circuit			Difference Too High [Cruise]	
E028	Open Third Or Fourth Gear Circuit		E064	Cruise—Car Acceleration Too High [Cruise]	
E030	RPM Error Too Great		E065	Cruise—Coolant Temperature Too High [Cruise]	
E031	Shorted MAP Sensor Circuit [AIR]		E066	Cruise—Engine RPM Too High [Cruise]	
E032	Open MAP Sensor Circuit [AIR]		E067	Cruise—Cruise Switch Shorted During	
E034	MAP Sensor Signal Too High [AIR]			Enable [Cruise]	
E037	Shorted MAT Sensor Circuit [AIR]				

BCM DIAGNOSTIC CODES

CODE	DESCRIPTION	COMMENTS	CODE	DESCRIPTION	COMMENTS
B110	Outside Air Temperature Circuit Problem		B410	Charging System Problem	
B111	A/C High Side Temperature Circuit Problem		B411	Battery Volts Too Low	
B112	A/C Low Side Temperature Circuit Problem [A/C Clutch]		B412	Battery Volts Too High	
B113	In-Car Temperature Circuit Problem		B420	Relay Circuit Problem	
B115	Sunload Temperature Circuit Problem		B440	Air Mix Door Problem	
B119	Twilight Sentinel Photosensor Circuit Problem		B441	Cooling Fans Problem	
B120	Twilight Sentinel Delay Pot Circuit Problem		B446	Low A/C Refrigerant Condition Warning	
B121	Twilight Sentinel Enable Circuit Problem		B447	Very Low A/C Refrigerant Condition Warning [A/C Clutch]	
B122	Panel Lamp Dimming Pot Circuit Problem		B448	Very Low A/C Refrigerant Pressure Condition [A/C Clutch]	
B123	Panel Lamp Enable Circuit Problem		B449	A/C High Side Temperature Too High [A/C Clutch]	
B124	Speed Sensor Circuit Problem		B450	Coolant Temperature Too High [A/C Clutch]	
B127	PRND321 Sensor Circuit Problem		B552	BCM Memory Reset Indicator	
B334	Loss Of ECM Data [A/C Clutch]		B554	BCM EEPROM Error	
B335	Loss Of CCDIC Data				
B336	Loss Of IPC Data				
B337	Loss Of Programmer Data				

DIAGNOSTIC CODE COMMENTS

	Turns On "SERVICE ENGINE SOON" Light.		Displays Square Box Around Each PRND321 Position On IPC.
	Displays "SERVICE CAR SOON" On DIC.		Displays "Error" In Season Odometer.
	Displays Status Message On DIC.		Switches ECC Mode To ECON.
	Does Not Turn On Any Telltale Light Or Display Any Message.		Forces Cooling Fans On Full Speed.
	Causes System To Operate On Bypass Spark.		Enables Canister Purge.
	Disengages VCC For Entire Ignition Cycle.		Disables Cruise Control For Ignition Cycle.
		[ ]	Functions Within Bracket Are Disengaged While Specified Malfunction Remains Current.

Diagnostic trouble codes – 1988–90 Cadillac Eldorado and Seville

BUICK

Year – 1980
Model – LeSabre
Engine – 3.8L (231 cid) V6
Engine Code – VIN A

ECM TROUBLE CODES

Code	Explanation
12	No tachometer or reference signal to ECM, this code will only be present while a fault exisits. Code 12 will not be stored if problem is intermittent
13	Oxygen sensor circuit. The engine has to operate for about 18 minutes at part throttle before code will show.
13 & 14	(At same time.) See Code 43
14	Shorted coolant sensor circuit. The engine has to run 2 minutes before this code will show
15	Open coolant sensor circuit. The engine has to operate for about 5 minutes at part throttle before this code will show
21	Shorted WOT switch and/or open closed throttle switch circuit (when used)
21	(After 10 seconds and below 800 rpm) throttle position sensor circuit
23	Open or grounded carburetor solenoid circuit
32	Barometric Pressure Sensor (BARO) output low
32 & 55	(At same time) grounded + 8V, V (REF) or faulty ECM
34	(After 10 seconds and below 800 rpm) Manifold Absolute Pressure (MAP) sensor output high
43	Throttle position sensor adjustment
44	Lean oxygen sensor. Engine must be run for approximately 5 minutes in closed loop mode and part throttle at roadload (drive car) before this code will show
45	Rich oxygen sensor. Engine must run for approximately 5 minutes in closed loop mode and part throttle before this code will show
44 & 45	(At same time) faulty oxygen sensor
51	Faulty Calibration Unit (PROM) or improper PROM installation
52 & 53	Check engine light OFF – intermittent ECM problem Check engine light ON – faulty ECM (replace)
54	Faulty carburetor solenoid and/or ECM
55	Faulty oxygen sensor, open MAP sensor or ECM

Year — 1980
Model — LeSabre
Engine — 3.8L (231 cid) V6
Engine Code — VIN 3

ECM TROUBLE CODES

Code	Explanation
12	No tachometer or reference signal to ECM, this code will only be present while a fault exisits. Code 12 will not be stored if problem is intermittent
13	Oxygen sensor circuit. The engine has to operate for about 18 minutes at part throttle before code will show.
13 & 14	(At same time.) See Code 43
14	Shorted coolant sensor circuit. The engine has to run 2 minutes before this code will show
15	Open coolant sensor circuit. The engine has to operate for about 5 minutes at part throttle before this code will show
21	Shorted WOT switch and/or open closed throttle switch circuit (when used)
21	(After 10 seconds and below 800 rpm) throttle position sensor circuit
23	Open or grounded carburetor solenoid circuit
32	Barometric Pressure Sensor (BARO) output low
32 & 55	(At same time) grounded +8V, V (REF) or faulty ECM
34	(After 10 seconds and below 800 rpm) Manifold Absolute Pressure (MAP) sensor output high
43	Throttle position sensor adjustment
44	Lean oxygen sensor. Engine must be run for approximately 5 minutes in closed loop mode and part throttle at roadload (drive car) before this code will show
45	Rich oxygen sensor. Engine must run for approximately 5 minutes in closed loop mode and part throttle before this code will show
44 & 45	(At same time) faulty oxygen sensor
51	Faulty Calibration Unit (PROM) or improper PROM installation
52 & 53	Check engine light OFF — intermittent ECM problem Check engine light ON — faulty ECM (replace)
54	Faulty carburetor solenoid and/or ECM
55	Faulty oxygen sensor, open MAP sensor or ECM

Year — 1980
Model — LeSabre
Engine — 4.1L (252 cid) V6
Engine Code — VIN 4

ECM TROUBLE CODES

Code	Explanation
12	No tachometer or reference signal to ECM, this code will only be present while a fault exisits. Code 12 will not be stored if problem is intermittent
13	Oxygen sensor circuit. The engine has to operate for about 18 minutes at part throttle before code will show.
13 & 14	(At same time.) See Code 43
14	Shorted coolant sensor circuit. The engine has to run 2 minutes before this code will show
15	Open coolant sensor circuit. The engine has to operate for about 5 minutes at part throttle before this code will show
21	Shorted WOT switch and/or open closed throttle switch circuit (when used)
21	(After 10 seconds and below 800 rpm) throttle position sensor circuit
23	Open or grounded carburetor solenoid circuit
32	Barometric Pressure Sensor (BARO) output low
32 & 55	(At same time) grounded +8V, V (REF) or faulty ECM
34	(After 10 seconds and below 800 rpm) Manifold Absolute Pressure (MAP) sensor output high
43	Throttle position sensor adjustment
44	Lean oxygen sensor. Engine must be run for approximately 5 minutes in closed loop mode and part throttle at roadload (drive car) before this code will show
45	Rich oxygen sensor. Engine must run for approximately 5 minutes in closed loop mode and part throttle before this code will show
44 & 45	(At same time) faulty oxygen sensor
51	Faulty Calibration Unit (PROM) or improper PROM installation
52 & 53	Check engine light OFF—intermittent ECM problem Check engine light ON—faulty ECM (replace)
54	Faulty carburetor solenoid and/or ECM
55	Faulty throttle position sensor or ECM

Year — 1980
Model — LeSabre Sport Coupe
Engine — 4.9L (301 cid) V8
Engine Code — VIN W

ECM TROUBLE CODES

Code	Explanation
12	No tachometer or reference signal to ECM, this code will only be present while a fault exisits. Code 12 will not be stored if problem is intermittent
13	Oxygen sensor circuit. The engine has to operate for about 18 minutes at part throttle before code will show.
13 & 14	(At same time.) See Code 43
14	Shorted coolant sensor circuit. The engine has to run 2 minutes before this code will show
15	Open coolant sensor circuit. The engine has to operate for about 5 minutes at part throttle before this code will show
21	Shorted WOT switch and/or open closed throttle switch circuit (when used)
21	(After 10 seconds and below 800 rpm) throttle position sensor circuit
23	Open or grounded carburetor solenoid circuit
32	Barometric Pressure Sensor (BARO) output low
32 & 55	(At same time) grounded +8V, V (REF) or faulty ECM
34	(After 10 seconds and below 800 rpm) Manifold Absolute Pressure (MAP) sensor output high
43	Throttle position sensor adjustment
44	Lean oxygen sensor. Engine must be run for approximately 5 minutes in closed loop mode and part throttle at roadload (drive car) before this code will show
45	Rich oxygen sensor. Engine must run for approximately 5 minutes in closed loop mode and part throttle before this code will show
44 & 45	(At same time) faulty oxygen sensor
51	Faulty Calibration Unit (PROM) or improper PROM installation
52 & 53	Check engine light OFF — intermittent ECM problem Check engine light ON — faulty ECM (replace)
54	Faulty carburetor solenoid and/or ECM
55	Faulty throttle position sensor or ECM

Year — 1980
Model — LeSabre
Engine — 5.7L (350 cid) V8
Engine Code — VIN R

ECM TROUBLE CODES

Code	Explanation
12	No tachometer or reference signal to ECM, this code will only be present while a fault exisits. Code 12 will not be stored if problem is intermittent
13	Oxygen sensor circuit. The engine has to operate for about 18 minutes at part throttle before code will show.
13 & 14	(At same time.) See Code 43
14	Shorted coolant sensor circuit. The engine has to run 2 minutes before this code will show
15	Open coolant sensor circuit. The engine has to operate for about 5 minutes at part throttle before this code will show
21	Shorted WOT switch and/or open closed throttle switch circuit (when used)
21	(After 10 seconds and below 800 rpm) throttle position sensor circuit
23	Open or grounded carburetor solenoid circuit
32	Barometric Pressure Sensor (BARO) output low
32 & 55	(At same time) grounded +8V, V (REF) or faulty ECM
34	(After 10 seconds and below 800 rpm) Manifold Absolute Pressure (MAP) sensor output high
43	Throttle position sensor adjustment
44	Lean oxygen sensor. Engine must be run for approximately 5 minutes in closed loop mode and part throttle at roadload (drive car) before this code will show
45	Rich oxygen sensor. Engine must run for approximately 5 minutes in closed loop mode and part throttle before this code will show
44 & 45	(At same time) faulty oxygen sensor
51	Faulty Calibration Unit (PROM) or improper PROM installation
52 & 53	Check engine light OFF — intermittent ECM problem Check engine light ON — faulty ECM (replace)
54	Faulty carburetor solenoid and/or ECM
55	Faulty throttle position sensor or ECM

Year — 1980
Model — LaSabre
Engine — 5.7L (350 cid) V8
Engine Code — VIN X

ECM TROUBLE CODES

Code	Explanation
12	No tachometer or reference signal to ECM, this code will only be present while a fault exisits. Code 12 will not be stored if problem is intermittent
13	Oxygen sensor circuit. The engine has to operate for about 18 minutes at part throttle before code will show.
13 & 14	(At same time.) See Code 43
14	Shorted coolant sensor circuit. The engine has to run 2 minutes before this code will show
15	Open coolant sensor circuit. The engine has to operate for about 5 minutes at part throttle before this code will show
21	Shorted WOT switch and/or open closed throttle switch circuit (when used)
21	(After 10 seconds and below 800 rpm) throttle position sensor circuit
23	Open or grounded carburetor solenoid circuit
32	Barometric Pressure Sensor (BARO) output low
32 & 55	(At same time) grounded +8V, V (REF) or faulty ECM
34	(After 10 seconds and below 800 rpm) Manifold Absolute Pressure (MAP) sensor output high
43	Throttle position sensor adjustment
44	Lean oxygen sensor. Engine must be run for approximately 5 minutes in closed loop mode and part throttle at roadload (drive car) before this code will show
45	Rich oxygen sensor. Engine must run for approximately 5 minutes in closed loop mode and part throttle before this code will show
44 & 45	(At same time) faulty oxygen sensor
51	Faulty Calibration Unit (PROM) or improper PROM installation
52 & 53	Check engine light OFF — intermittent ECM problem Check engine light ON — faulty ECM (replace)
54	Faulty carburetor solenoid and/or ECM
55	Faulty throttle position sensor or ECM

Year — 1980
Model — LeSabre Estate Wagon
Engine — 5.7L (350 cid) V8
Engine Code — VIN X

ECM TROUBLE CODES

Code	Explanation
12	No tachometer or reference signal to ECM, this code will only be present while a fault exisits. Code 12 will not be stored if problem is intermittent
13	Oxygen sensor circuit. The engine has to operate for about 18 minutes at part throttle before code will show.
13 & 14	(At same time.) See Code 43
14	Shorted coolant sensor circuit. The engine has to run 2 minutes before this code will show
15	Open coolant sensor circuit. The engine has to operate for about 5 minutes at part throttle before this code will show
21	Shorted WOT switch and/or open closed throttle switch circuit (when used)
21	(After 10 seconds and below 800 rpm) throttle position sensor circuit
23	Open or grounded carburetor solenoid circuit
32	Barometric Pressure Sensor (BARO) output low
32 & 55	(At same time) grounded +8V, V (REF) or faulty ECM
34	(After 10 seconds and below 800 rpm) Manifold Absolute Pressure (MAP) sensor output high
43	Throttle position sensor adjustment
44	Lean oxygen sensor. Engine must be run for approximately 5 minutes in closed loop mode and part throttle at roadload (drive car) before this code will show
45	Rich oxygen sensor. Engine must run for approximately 5 minutes in closed loop mode and part throttle before this code will show
44 & 45	(At same time) faulty oxygen sensor
51	Faulty Calibration Unit (PROM) or improper PROM installation
52 & 53	Check engine light OFF — intermittent ECM problem Check engine light ON — faulty ECM (replace)
54	Faulty carburetor solenoid and/or ECM
55	Faulty throttle position sensor or ECM

Year – 1980
Model – Electra
Engine – 5.7L (350 cid) V8
Engine Code – VIN R

ECM TROUBLE CODES

Code	Explanation
12	No tachometer or reference signal to ECM, this code will only be present while a fault exisits. Code 12 will not be stored if problem is intermittent
13	Oxygen sensor circuit. The engine has to operate for about 18 minutes at part throttle before code will show.
13 & 14	(At same time.) See Code 43
14	Shorted coolant sensor circuit. The engine has to run 2 minutes before this code will show
15	Open coolant sensor circuit. The engine has to operate for about 5 minutes at part throttle before this code will show
21	Shorted WOT switch and/or open closed throttle switch circuit (when used)
21	(After 10 seconds and below 800 rpm) throttle position sensor circuit
23	Open or grounded carburetor solenoid circuit
32	Barometric Pressure Sensor (BARO) output low
32 & 55	(At same time) grounded +8V, V (REF) or faulty ECM
34	(After 10 seconds and below 800 rpm) Manifold Absolute Pressure (MAP) sensor output high
43	Throttle position sensor adjustment
44	Lean oxygen sensor. Engine must be run for approximately 5 minutes in closed loop mode and part throttle at roadload (drive car) before this code will show
45	Rich oxygen sensor. Engine must run for approximately 5 minutes in closed loop mode and part throttle before this code will show
44 & 45	(At same time) faulty oxygen sensor
51	Faulty Calibration Unit (PROM) or improper PROM installation
52 & 53	Check engine light OFF – intermittent ECM problem Check engine light ON – faulty ECM (replace)
54	Faulty carburetor solenoid and/or ECM
55	Faulty throttle position sensor or ECM

Year – 1980
Model – Electra
Engine – 4.1L (252 cid) V6
Engine Code – VIN 4

ECM TROUBLE CODES

Code	Explanation
12	No tachometer or reference signal to ECM, this code will only be present while a fault exisits. Code 12 will not be stored if problem is intermittent
13	Oxygen sensor circuit. The engine has to operate for about 18 minutes at part throttle before code will show.
13 & 14	(At same time.) See Code 43
14	Shorted coolant sensor circuit. The engine has to run 2 minutes before this code will show
15	Open coolant sensor circuit. The engine has to operate for about 5 minutes at part throttle before this code will show
21	Shorted WOT switch and/or open closed throttle switch circuit (when used)
21	(After 10 seconds and below 800 rpm) throttle position sensor circuit
23	Open or grounded carburetor solenoid circuit
32	Barometric Pressure Sensor (BARO) output low
32 & 55	(At same time) grounded +8V, V (REF) or faulty ECM
34	(After 10 seconds and below 800 rpm) Manifold Absolute Pressure (MAP) sensor output high
43	Throttle position sensor adjustment
44	Lean oxygen sensor. Engine must be run for approximately 5 minutes in closed loop mode and part throttle at roadload (drive car) before this code will show
45	Rich oxygen sensor. Engine must run for approximately 5 minutes in closed loop mode and part throttle before this code will show
44 & 45	(At same time) faulty oxygen sensor
51	Faulty Calibration Unit (PROM) or improper PROM installation
52 & 53	Check engine light OFF – intermittent ECM problem Check engine light ON – faulty ECM (replace)
54	Faulty carburetor solenoid and/or ECM
55	Faulty throttle position sensor or ECM

Year — 1980
Model — Electra Park Avenue
Engine — 5.7L (350 cid) V8
Engine Code — VIN X

ECM TROUBLE CODES

Code	Explanation
12	No tachometer or reference signal to ECM, this code will only be present while a fault exisits. Code 12 will not be stored if problem is intermittent
13	Oxygen sensor circuit. The engine has to operate for about 18 minutes at part throttle before code will show.
13 & 14	(At same time.) See Code 43
14	Shorted coolant sensor circuit. The engine has to run 2 minutes before this code will show
15	Open coolant sensor circuit. The engine has to operate for about 5 minutes at part throttle before this code will show
21	Shorted WOT switch and/or open closed throttle switch circuit (when used)
21	(After 10 seconds and below 800 rpm) throttle position sensor circuit
23	Open or grounded carburetor solenoid circuit
32	Barometric Pressure Sensor (BARO) output low
32 & 55	(At same time) grounded +8V, V (REF) or faulty ECM
34	(After 10 seconds and below 800 rpm) Manifold Absolute Pressure (MAP) sensor output high
43	Throttle position sensor adjustment
44	Lean oxygen sensor. Engine must be run for approximately 5 minutes in closed loop mode and part throttle at roadload (drive car) before this code will show
45	Rich oxygen sensor. Engine must run for approximately 5 minutes in closed loop mode and part throttle before this code will show
44 & 45	(At same time) faulty oxygen sensor
51	Faulty Calibration Unit (PROM) or improper PROM installation
52 & 53	Check engine light OFF — intermittent ECM problem Check engine light ON — faulty ECM (replace)
54	Faulty carburetor solenoid and/or ECM
55	Faulty throttle position sensor or ECM

Year — 1980
Model — Electra Estate Wagon
Engine — 5.7L (350 cid) V8
Engine Code — VIN X

ECM TROUBLE CODES

Code	Explanation
12	No tachometer or reference signal to ECM, this code will only be present while a fault exisits. Code 12 will not be stored if problem is intermittent
13	Oxygen sensor circuit. The engine has to operate for about 18 minutes at part throttle before code will show.
13 & 14	(At same time.) See Code 43
14	Shorted coolant sensor circuit. The engine has to run 2 minutes before this code will show
15	Open coolant sensor circuit. The engine has to operate for about 5 minutes at part throttle before this code will show
21	Shorted WOT switch and/or open closed throttle switch circuit (when used)
21	(After 10 seconds and below 800 rpm) throttle position sensor circuit
23	Open or grounded carburetor solenoid circuit
32	Barometric Pressure Sensor (BARO) output low
32 & 55	(At same time) grounded +8V, V (REF) or faulty ECM
34	(After 10 seconds and below 800 rpm) Manifold Absolute Pressure (MAP) sensor output high
43	Throttle position sensor adjustment
44	Lean oxygen sensor. Engine must be run for approximately 5 minutes in closed loop mode and part throttle at roadload (drive car) before this code will show
45	Rich oxygen sensor. Engine must run for approximately 5 minutes in closed loop mode and part throttle before this code will show
44 & 45	(At same time) faulty oxygen sensor
51	Faulty Calibration Unit (PROM) or improper PROM installation
52 & 53	Check engine light OFF — intermittent ECM problem Check engine light ON — faulty ECM (replace)
54	Faulty carburetor solenoid and/or ECM
55	Faulty throttle position sensor or ECM

Year — 1980
Model — Century
Engine — 3.8L (231 cid) V6
Engine Code — VIN A

ECM TROUBLE CODES

Code	Explanation
12	No tachometer or reference signal to ECM, this code will only be present while a fault exisits. Code 12 will not be stored if problem is intermittent
13	Oxygen sensor circuit. The engine has to operate for about 18 minutes at part throttle before code will show.
13 & 14	(At same time.) See Code 43
14	Shorted coolant sensor circuit. The engine has to run 2 minutes before this code will show
15	Open coolant sensor circuit. The engine has to operate for about 5 minutes at part throttle before this code will show
21	Shorted WOT switch and/or open closed throttle switch circuit (when used)
21	(After 10 seconds and below 800 rpm) throttle position sensor circuit
23	Open or grounded carburetor solenoid circuit
32	Barometric Pressure Sensor (BARO) output low
32 & 55	(At same time) grounded +8V, V (REF) or faulty ECM
34	(After 10 seconds and below 800 rpm) Manifold Absolute Pressure (MAP) sensor output high
43	Throttle position sensor adjustment
44	Lean oxygen sensor. Engine must be run for approximately 5 minutes in closed loop mode and part throttle at roadload (drive car) before this code will show
45	Rich oxygen sensor. Engine must run for approximately 5 minutes in closed loop mode and part throttle before this code will show
44 & 45	(At same time) faulty oxygen sensor
51	Faulty Calibration Unit (PROM) or improper PROM installation
52 & 53	Check engine light OFF—intermittent ECM problem Check engine light ON—faulty ECM (replace)
54	Faulty carburetor solenoid and/or ECM
55	Faulty oxygen sensor, open MAP sensor or ECM

Year — 1980
Model — Century
Engine — 3.8L (231 cid) Turbo V6
Engine Code — VIN 3

ECM TROUBLE CODES

Code	Explanation
12	No tachometer or reference signal to ECM, this code will only be present while a fault exisits. Code 12 will not be stored if problem is intermittent
13	Oxygen sensor circuit. The engine has to operate for about 18 minutes at part throttle before code will show.
13 & 14	(At same time.) See Code 43
14	Shorted coolant sensor circuit. The engine has to run 2 minutes before this code will show
15	Open coolant sensor circuit. The engine has to operate for about 5 minutes at part throttle before this code will show
21	Shorted WOT switch and/or open closed throttle switch circuit (when used)
21	(After 10 seconds and below 800 rpm) throttle position sensor circuit
23	Open or grounded carburetor solenoid circuit
32	Barometric Pressure Sensor (BARO) output low
32 & 55	(At same time) grounded +8V, V (REF) or faulty ECM
34	(After 10 seconds and below 800 rpm) Manifold Absolute Pressure (MAP) sensor output high
43	Throttle position sensor adjustment
44	Lean oxygen sensor. Engine must be run for approximately 5 minutes in closed loop mode and part throttle at roadload (drive car) before this code will show
45	Rich oxygen sensor. Engine must run for approximately 5 minutes in closed loop mode and part throttle before this code will show
44 & 45	(At same time) faulty oxygen sensor
51	Faulty Calibration Unit (PROM) or improper PROM installation
52 & 53	Check engine light OFF — intermittent ECM problem Check engine light ON — faulty ECM (replace)
54	Faulty carburetor solenoid and/or ECM
55	Faulty oxygen sensor, open MAP sensor or ECM

Year — 1980
Model — Century Sport Coupe
Engine — 4.3L (265 cid) V8
Engine Code — VIN S

ECM TROUBLE CODES

Code	Explanation
12	No tachometer or reference signal to ECM, this code will only be present while a fault exisits. Code 12 will not be stored if problem is intermittent
13	Oxygen sensor circuit. The engine has to operate for about 18 minutes at part throttle before code will show.
13 & 14	(At same time.) See Code 43
14	Shorted coolant sensor circuit. The engine has to run 2 minutes before this code will show
15	Open coolant sensor circuit. The engine has to operate for about 5 minutes at part throttle before this code will show
21	Shorted WOT switch and/or open closed throttle switch circuit (when used)
21	(After 10 seconds and below 800 rpm) throttle position sensor circuit
23	Open or grounded carburetor solenoid circuit
32	Barometric Pressure Sensor (BARO) output low
32 & 55	(At same time) grounded +8V, V (REF) or faulty ECM
34	(After 10 seconds and below 800 rpm) Manifold Absolute Pressure (MAP) sensor output high
43	Throttle position sensor adjustment
44	Lean oxygen sensor. Engine must be run for approximately 5 minutes in closed loop mode and part throttle at roadload (drive car) before this code will show
45	Rich oxygen sensor. Engine must run for approximately 5 minutes in closed loop mode and part throttle before this code will show
44 & 45	(At same time) faulty oxygen sensor
51	Faulty Calibration Unit (PROM) or improper PROM installation
52 & 53	Check engine light OFF—intermittent ECM problem Check engine light ON—faulty ECM (replace)
54	Faulty carburetor solenoid and/or ECM
55	Faulty throttle position sensor or ECM

Year – 1980
Model – Century
Engine – 4.9L (301 cid) V8
Engine Code – VIN W

ECM TROUBLE CODES

Code	Explanation
12	No tachometer or reference signal to ECM, this code will only be present while a fault exisits. Code 12 will not be stored if problem is intermittent
13	Oxygen sensor circuit. The engine has to operate for about 18 minutes at part throttle before code will show.
13 & 14	(At same time.) See Code 43
14	Shorted coolant sensor circuit. The engine has to run 2 minutes before this code will show
15	Open coolant sensor circuit. The engine has to operate for about 5 minutes at part throttle before this code will show
21	Shorted WOT switch and/or open closed throttle switch circuit (when used)
21	(After 10 seconds and below 800 rpm) throttle position sensor circuit
23	Open or grounded carburetor solenoid circuit
32	Barometric Pressure Sensor (BARO) output low
32 & 55	(At same time) grounded +8V, V (REF) or faulty ECM
34	(After 10 seconds and below 800 rpm) Manifold Absolute Pressure (MAP) sensor output high
43	Throttle position sensor adjustment
44	Lean oxygen sensor. Engine must be run for approximately 5 minutes in closed loop mode and part throttle at roadload (drive car) before this code will show
45	Rich oxygen sensor. Engine must run for approximately 5 minutes in closed loop mode and part throttle before this code will show
44 & 45	(At same time) faulty oxygen sensor
51	Faulty Calibration Unit (PROM) or improper PROM installation
52 & 53	Check engine light OFF – intermittent ECM problem Check engine light ON – faulty ECM (replace)
54	Faulty carburetor solenoid and/or ECM
55	Faulty throttle position sensor or ECM

Year — 1980
Model — Regal
Engine — 3.8L (231 cid) V6
Engine Code — VIN A

ECM TROUBLE CODES

Code	Explanation
12	No tachometer or reference signal to ECM, this code will only be present while a fault exisits. Code 12 will not be stored if problem is intermittent
13	Oxygen sensor circuit. The engine has to operate for about 18 minutes at part throttle before code will show.
13 & 14	(At same time.) See Code 43
14	Shorted coolant sensor circuit. The engine has to run 2 minutes before this code will show
15	Open coolant sensor circuit. The engine has to operate for about 5 minutes at part throttle before this code will show
21	Shorted WOT switch and/or open closed throttle switch circuit (when used)
21	(After 10 seconds and below 800 rpm) throttle position sensor circuit
23	Open or grounded carburetor solenoid circuit
32	Barometric Pressure Sensor (BARO) output low
32 & 55	(At same time) grounded + 8V, V (REF) or faulty ECM
34	(After 10 seconds and below 800 rpm) Manifold Absolute Pressure (MAP) sensor output high
43	Throttle position sensor adjustment
44	Lean oxygen sensor. Engine must be run for approximately 5 minutes in closed loop mode and part throttle at roadload (drive car) before this code will show
45	Rich oxygen sensor. Engine must run for approximately 5 minutes in closed loop mode and part throttle before this code will show
44 & 45	(At same time) faulty oxygen sensor
51	Faulty Calibration Unit (PROM) or improper PROM installation
52 & 53	Check engine light OFF — intermittent ECM problem Check engine light ON — faulty ECM (replace)
54	Faulty carburetor solenoid and/or ECM
55	Faulty oxygen sensor, open MAP sensor or ECM

Year—1980
Model—Regal
Engine—3.8L (231 cid) Turbo V6
Engine Code—VIN 3

ECM TROUBLE CODES

Code	Explanation
12	No tachometer or reference signal to ECM, this code will only be present while a fault exisits. Code 12 will not be stored if problem is intermittent
13	Oxygen sensor circuit. The engine has to operate for about 18 minutes at part throttle before code will show.
13 & 14	(At same time.) See Code 43
14	Shorted coolant sensor circuit. The engine has to run 2 minutes before this code will show
15	Open coolant sensor circuit. The engine has to operate for about 5 minutes at part throttle before this code will show
21	Shorted WOT switch and/or open closed throttle switch circuit (when used)
21	(After 10 seconds and below 800 rpm) throttle position sensor circuit
23	Open or grounded carburetor solenoid circuit
32	Barometric Pressure Sensor (BARO) output low
32 & 55	(At same time) grounded +8V, V (REF) or faulty ECM
34	(After 10 seconds and below 800 rpm) Manifold Absolute Pressure (MAP) sensor output high
43	Throttle position sensor adjustment
44	Lean oxygen sensor. Engine must be run for approximately 5 minutes in closed loop mode and part throttle at roadload (drive car) before this code will show
45	Rich oxygen sensor. Engine must run for approximately 5 minutes in closed loop mode and part throttle before this code will show
44 & 45	(At same time) faulty oxygen sensor
51	Faulty Calibration Unit (PROM) or improper PROM installation
52 & 53	Check engine light OFF—intermittent ECM problem Check engine light ON—faulty ECM (replace)
54	Faulty carburetor solenoid and/or ECM
55	Faulty oxygen sensor, open MAP sensor or ECM

Year – 1980
Model – Regal
Engine – 5.0L (305 cid) V8
Engine Code – VIN H

ECM TROUBLE CODES

Code	Explanation
12	No tachometer or reference signal to ECM, this code will only be present while a fault exisits. Code 12 will not be stored if problem is intermittent
13	Oxygen sensor circuit. The engine has to operate for about 18 minutes at part throttle before code will show.
13 & 14	(At same time.) See Code 43
14	Shorted coolant sensor circuit. The engine has to run 2 minutes before this code will show
15	Open coolant sensor circuit. The engine has to operate for about 5 minutes at part throttle before this code will show
21	Shorted WOT switch and/or open closed throttle switch circuit (when used)
21	(After 10 seconds and below 800 rpm) throttle position sensor circuit
23	Open or grounded carburetor solenoid circuit
32	Barometric Pressure Sensor (BARO) output low
32 & 55	(At same time) grounded +8V, V (REF) or faulty ECM
34	(After 10 seconds and below 800 rpm) Manifold Absolute Pressure (MAP) sensor output high
43	Throttle position sensor adjustment
44	Lean oxygen sensor. Engine must be run for approximately 5 minutes in closed loop mode and part throttle at roadload (drive car) before this code will show
45	Rich oxygen sensor. Engine must run for approximately 5 minutes in closed loop mode and part throttle before this code will show
44 & 45	(At same time) faulty oxygen sensor
51	Faulty Calibration Unit (PROM) or improper PROM installation
52 & 53	Check engine light OFF – intermittent ECM problem Check engine light ON – faulty ECM (replace)
54	Faulty carburetor solenoid and/or ECM
55	Faulty oxygen sensor, open MAP sensor or ECM

Year – 1980
Model – Skylark
Engine – 2.5L (151 cid) 4 cyl
Engine Code – VIN 5

ECM TROUBLE CODES

Code	Explanation
12	No tachometer or reference signal to ECM, this code will only be present while a fault exisits. Code 12 will not be stored if problem is intermittent
13	Oxygen sensor circuit. The engine has to operate for about 5 minutes at part throttle before code will show.
14	Shorted coolant sensor circuit. The engine has to run 2 minutes before this code will show
15	Open coolant sensor circuit. The engine has to operate for about 5 minutes at part throttle before this code will show
21 & 22	(At the same time) grounded WOT switch circuit
22	Grounded closed throttle or WOT switch circuit
23	Open or grounded carburetor solenoid circuit
44	Lean oxygen sensor. Engine must be run for approximately 5 minutes in closed loop mode and part throttle at roadload (drive car) before this code will show
45	Rich oxygen sensor. Engine must run for approximately 5 minutes in closed loop mode and part throttle before this code will show
51	On service unit, check calibration unit (PROM) installation. On factory installed unit, replace ECM
52 & 53	Replace the ECM
54	Faulty carburetor solenoid and/or ECM
55	Replace the ECM

Year — 1980
Model — Skylark
Engine — 2.8L (171 cid) V6
Engine Code — VIN 7

ECM TROUBLE CODES

Code	Explanation
12	No tachometer or reference signal to ECM, this code will only be present while a fault exisits. Code 12 will not be stored if problem is intermittent
13	Oxygen sensor circuit. The engine has to operate for about 5 minutes at part throttle before code will show.
13 & 43	(At the same time) Throttle position sensor adjustment
14	Shorted coolant sensor circuit. The engine has to run 2 minutes before this code will show
15	Open coolant sensor circuit. The engine has to operate for about 5 minutes at part throttle before this code will show
21	Throttle position sensor circuit
23	Open or grounded carburetor solenoid circuit
44	Lean oxygen sensor. Engine must be run for approximately 5 minutes in closed loop mode and part throttle at roadload (drive car) before this code will show
45	Rich oxygen sensor. Engine must run for approximately 5 minutes in closed loop mode and part throttle before this code will show
51	On service unit, check calibration unit (PROM) installation. On factory installed unit, replace ECM
52 & 53	Replace the ECM
54	Faulty carburetor solenoid and/or ECM
55	Faulty throttle position sensor or ECM

Year — 1980
Model — Skyhawk
Engine — 3.8L (231 cid) V6
Engine Code — VIN A

ECM TROUBLE CODES

Code	Explanation
12	No tachometer or reference signal to ECM, this code will only be present while a fault exisits. Code 12 will not be stored if problem is intermittent
13	Oxygen sensor circuit. The engine has to operate for about 18 minutes at part throttle before code will show.
13 & 14	(At same time.) See Code 43
14	Shorted coolant sensor circuit. The engine has to run 2 minutes before this code will show
15	Open coolant sensor circuit. The engine has to operate for about 5 minutes at part throttle before this code will show
21	Shorted WOT switch and/or open closed throttle switch circuit (when used)
21	(After 10 seconds and below 800 rpm) throttle position sensor circuit
23	Open or grounded carburetor solenoid circuit
32	Barometric Pressure Sensor (BARO) output low
32 & 55	(At same time) grounded +8V, V (REF) or faulty ECM
34	(After 10 seconds and below 800 rpm) Manifold Absolute Pressure (MAP) sensor output high
43	Throttle position sensor adjustment
44	Lean oxygen sensor. Engine must be run for approximately 5 minutes in closed loop mode and part throttle at roadload (drive car) before this code will show
45	Rich oxygen sensor. Engine must run for approximately 5 minutes in closed loop mode and part throttle before this code will show
44 & 45	(At same time) faulty oxygen sensor
51	Faulty Calibration Unit (PROM) or improper PROM installation
52 & 53	Check engine light OFF — intermittent ECM problem Check engine light ON — faulty ECM (replace)
54	Faulty carburetor solenoid and/or ECM
55	Faulty oxygen sensor, open MAP sensor or ECM

Year — 1980
Model — Riviera
Engine — 3.8L (231 cid) Turbo V6
Engine Code — VIN 3

ECM TROUBLE CODES

Code	Explanation
12	No tachometer or reference signal to ECM, this code will only be present while a fault exisits. Code 12 will not be stored if problem is intermittent
13	Oxygen sensor circuit. The engine has to operate for about 18 minutes at part throttle before code will show.
13 & 14	(At same time.) See Code 43
14	Shorted coolant sensor circuit. The engine has to run 2 minutes before this code will show
15	Open coolant sensor circuit. The engine has to operate for about 5 minutes at part throttle before this code will show
21	Shorted WOT switch and/or open closed throttle switch circuit (when used)
21	(After 10 seconds and below 800 rpm) throttle position sensor circuit
23	Open or grounded carburetor solenoid circuit
32	Barometric Pressure Sensor (BARO) output low
32 & 55	(At same time) grounded +8V, V (REF) or faulty ECM
34	(After 10 seconds and below 800 rpm) Manifold Absolute Pressure (MAP) sensor output high
43	Throttle position sensor adjustment
44	Lean oxygen sensor. Engine must be run for approximately 5 minutes in closed loop mode and part throttle at roadload (drive car) before this code will show
45	Rich oxygen sensor. Engine must run for approximately 5 minutes in closed loop mode and part throttle before this code will show
44 & 45	(At same time) faulty oxygen sensor
51	Faulty Calibration Unit (PROM) or improper PROM installation
52 & 53	Check engine light OFF—intermittent ECM problem Check engine light ON—faulty ECM (replace)
54	Faulty carburetor solenoid and/or ECM
55	Faulty oxygen sensor, open MAP sensor or ECM

GENERAL MOTORS CORPORATION
DIAGNOSTIC CODE DATA

Year — 1980
Model — Riviera
Engine — 5.0L (307 cid) V8
Engine Code — VIN Y

ECM TROUBLE CODES

Code	Explanation
12	No reference pulses to the ECM. This code is not stored in memory and will only flash while the fault is present
13	Oxygen sensor circuit — the engine must run up to 5 minutes at part throttle, under road load, before this code will set
14	Shorted coolant sensor circuit — the engine must run up to 2 minutes before this code will set
15	Open coolant sensor circuit — the engine must run up to 5 minutes before this code will set
21	Throttle position sensor circuit — the engine must run up to 25 seconds, below 800 rpm, before this code will set
23	Open or grounded M/C solenoid circuit
24	Vehicle Speed Sensor (VSS) circuit — the car must operate up to 5 minutes at road speed before this code will set
32	Barometric Pressure Sensor (BARO) circuit low
34	Manifold Absolute Pressure (MAP) or Vacuum Sensor circuit. The engine must run up to 5 minutes, below 800 rpm, before this code will set
35	Idle Speed Control (ISC) Switch circuit shorted. (Over ½ throttle for over 2 seconds)
42	Electronic Spark Timing (EST) Bypass circuit grounded
44	Lean oxygen sensor indication — the engine must run up to 5 minutes, in closed loop, at part throttle and road load before this code will set
44 & 45	(At same time) — Faulty oxygen sensor circuit
45	Rich system indication — the engine must run up to 5 minutes, in closed loop, at part throttle and road load before this code will set
51	Faulty calibration unit (PROM) or installation. It takes up to 30 seconds before this code will set
52	Faulty ECM
53	Faulty ECM
54	Shorted M/C solenoid circuit and/or faulty ECM
55	Grounded +8 volts, V ref, faulty oxygen sensor or ECM

Year – 1980
Model – Riviera
Engine – 5.7L (350 cid) V8
Engine Code – VIN R

ECM TROUBLE CODES

Code	Explanation
12	No tachometer or reference signal to ECM, this code will only be present while a fault exisits. Code 12 will not be stored if problem is intermittent
13	Oxygen sensor circuit. The engine has to operate for about 18 minutes at part throttle before code will show.
13 & 14	(At same time.) See Code 43
14	Shorted coolant sensor circuit. The engine has to run 2 minutes before this code will show
15	Open coolant sensor circuit. The engine has to operate for about 5 minutes at part throttle before this code will show
21	Shorted WOT switch and/or open closed throttle switch circuit (when used)
21	(After 10 seconds and below 800 rpm) throttle position sensor circuit
23	Open or grounded carburetor solenoid circuit
32	Barometric Pressure Sensor (BARO) output low
32 & 55	(At same time) grounded +8V, V (REF) or faulty ECM
34	(After 10 seconds and below 800 rpm) Manifold Absolute Pressure (MAP) sensor output high
43	Throttle position sensor adjustment
44	Lean oxygen sensor. Engine must be run for approximately 5 minutes in closed loop mode and part throttle at roadload (drive car) before this code will show
45	Rich oxygen sensor. Engine must run for approximately 5 minutes in closed loop mode and part throttle before this code will show
44 & 45	(At same time) faulty oxygen sensor
51	Faulty Calibration Unit (PROM) or improper PROM installation
52 & 53	Check engine light OFF – intermittent ECM problem Check engine light ON – faulty ECM (replace)
54	Faulty carburetor solenoid and/or ECM
55	Faulty throttle position sensor or ECM

Year — 1981
Model — LeSabre
Engine — 3.8L (231 cid) V6
Engine Code — VIN A

ECM TROUBLE CODES

Code	Explanation
12	No reference pulses to the ECM. This code is not stored in memory and will only flash while the fault is present
13	Oxygen sensor circuit — the engine must run up to 5 minutes at part throttle, under road load, before this code will set
14	Shorted coolant sensor circuit — the engine must run up to 2 minutes before this code will set
15	Open coolant sensor circuit — the engine must run up to 5 minutes before this code will set
21	Throttle position sensor circuit — the engine must run up to 25 seconds, below 800 rpm, before this code will set
23	Open or grounded M/C solenoid circuit
24	Vehicle Speed Sensor (VSS) circuit — the car must operate up to 5 minutes at road speed before this code will set
32	Barometric Pressure Sensor (BARO) circuit low
34	Manifold Absolute Pressure (MAP) or Vacuum Sensor circuit. The engine must run up to 5 minutes, below 800 rpm, before this code will set
35	Idle Speed Control (ISC) Switch circuit shorted. (Over ½ throttle for over 2 seconds)
42	Electronic Spark Timing (EST) Bypass circuit grounded
44	Lean oxygen sensor indication — the engine must run up to 5 minutes, in closed loop, at part throttle and road load before this code will set
44 & 45	(At same time) — Faulty oxygen sensor circuit
45	Rich system indication — the engine must run up to 5 minutes, in closed loop, at part throttle and road load before this code will set
51	Faulty calibration unit (PROM) or installation. It takes up to 30 seconds before this code will set
52	Faulty ECM
53	Faulty ECM
54	Shorted M/C solenoid circuit and/or faulty ECM
55	Grounded +8 volts, V ref, faulty oxygen sensor or ECM

Year — 1981
Model — LeSabre
Engine — 4.1L (252 cid) V6
Engine Code — VIN 4

ECM TROUBLE CODES

Code	Explanation
12	No reference pulses to the ECM. This code is not stored in memory and will only flash while the fault is present
13	Oxygen sensor circuit — the engine must run up to 5 minutes at part throttle, under road load, before this code will set
14	Shorted coolant sensor circuit — the engine must run up to 2 minutes before this code will set
15	Open coolant sensor circuit — the engine must run up to 5 minutes before this code will set
21	Throttle position sensor circuit — the engine must run up to 25 seconds, below 800 rpm, before this code will set
23	Open or grounded M/C solenoid circuit
24	Vehicle Speed Sensor (VSS) circuit — the car must operate up to 5 minutes at road speed before this code will set
32	Barometric Pressure Sensor (BARO) circuit low
34	Manifold Absolute Pressure (MAP) or Vacuum Sensor circuit. The engine must run up to 5 minutes, below 800 rpm, before this code will set
35	Idle Speed Control (ISC) Switch circuit shorted. (Over ½ throttle for over 2 seconds)
42	Electronic Spark Timing (EST) Bypass circuit grounded
44	Lean oxygen sensor indication — the engine must run up to 5 minutes, in closed loop, at part throttle and road load before this code will set
44 & 45	(At same time) — Faulty oxygen sensor circuit
45	Rich system indication — the engine must run up to 5 minutes, in closed loop, at part throttle and road load before this code will set
51	Faulty calibration unit (PROM) or installation. It takes up to 30 seconds before this code will set
52	Faulty ECM
53	Faulty ECM
54	Shorted M/C solenoid circuit and/or faulty ECM
55	Grounded +8 volts, V ref, faulty oxygen sensor or ECM

Year—1981
Model—LeSabre
Engine—5.0L (307 cid) V8
Engine Code—VIN Y

ECM TROUBLE CODES

Code	Explanation
12	No reference pulses to the ECM. This code is not stored in memory and will only flash while the fault is present
13	Oxygen sensor circuit—the engine must run up to 5 minutes at part throttle, under road load, before this code will set
14	Shorted coolant sensor circuit—the engine must run up to 2 minutes before this code will set
15	Open coolant sensor circuit—the engine must run up to 5 minutes before this code will set
21	Throttle position sensor circuit—the engine must run up to 25 seconds, below 800 rpm, before this code will set
23	Open or grounded M/C solenoid circuit
24	Vehicle Speed Sensor (VSS) circuit—the car must operate up to 5 minutes at road speed before this code will set
32	Barometric Pressure Sensor (BARO) circuit low
34	Manifold Absolute Pressure (MAP) or Vacuum Sensor circuit. The engine must run up to 5 minutes, below 800 rpm, before this code will set
35	Idle Speed Control (ISC) Switch circuit shorted. (Over ½ throttle for over 2 seconds)
42	Electronic Spark Timing (EST) Bypass circuit grounded
44	Lean oxygen sensor indication—the engine must run up to 5 minutes, in closed loop, at part throttle and road load before this code will set
44 & 45	(At same time)—Faulty oxygen sensor circuit
45	Rich system indication—the engine must run up to 5 minutes, in closed loop, at part throttle and road load before this code will set
51	Faulty calibration unit (PROM) or installation. It takes up to 30 seconds before this code will set
52	Faulty ECM
53	Faulty ECM
54	Shorted M/C solenoid circuit and/or faulty ECM
55	Grounded +8 volts, V ref, faulty oxygen sensor or ECM

Year — 1981
Model — Electra
Engine — 4.1L (252 cid) V6
Engine Code — VIN 4

ECM TROUBLE CODES

Code	Explanation
12	No reference pulses to the ECM. This code is not stored in memory and will only flash while the fault is present
13	Oxygen sensor circuit — the engine must run up to 5 minutes at part throttle, under road load, before this code will set
14	Shorted coolant sensor circuit — the engine must run up to 2 minutes before this code will set
15	Open coolant sensor circuit — the engine must run up to 5 minutes before this code will set
21	Throttle position sensor circuit — the engine must run up to 25 seconds, below 800 rpm, before this code will set
23	Open or grounded M/C solenoid circuit
24	Vehicle Speed Sensor (VSS) circuit — the car must operate up to 5 minutes at road speed before this code will set
32	Barometric Pressure Sensor (BARO) circuit low
34	Manifold Absolute Pressure (MAP) or Vacuum Sensor circuit. The engine must run up to 5 minutes, below 800 rpm, before this code will set
35	Idle Speed Control (ISC) Switch circuit shorted. (Over ½ throttle for over 2 seconds)
42	Electronic Spark Timing (EST) Bypass circuit grounded
44	Lean oxygen sensor indication — the engine must run up to 5 minutes, in closed loop, at part throttle and road load before this code will set
44 & 45	(At same time) — Faulty oxygen sensor circuit
45	Rich system indication — the engine must run up to 5 minutes, in closed loop, at part throttle and road load before this code will set
51	Faulty calibration unit (PROM) or installation. It takes up to 30 seconds before this code will set
52	Faulty ECM
53	Faulty ECM
54	Shorted M/C solenoid circuit and/or faulty ECM
55	Grounded + 8 volts, V ref, faulty oxygen sensor or ECM

Year — 1981
Model — Electra
Engine — 5.0L (307 cid) V8
Engine Code — VIN Y

ECM TROUBLE CODES

Code	Explanation
12	No reference pulses to the ECM. This code is not stored in memory and will only flash while the fault is present
13	Oxygen sensor circuit — the engine must run up to 5 minutes at part throttle, under road load, before this code will set
14	Shorted coolant sensor circuit — the engine must run up to 2 minutes before this code will set
15	Open coolant sensor circuit — the engine must run up to 5 minutes before this code will set
21	Throttle position sensor circuit — the engine must run up to 25 seconds, below 800 rpm, before this code will set
23	Open or grounded M/C solenoid circuit
24	Vehicle Speed Sensor (VSS) circuit — the car must operate up to 5 minutes at road speed before this code will set
32	Barometric Pressure Sensor (BARO) circuit low
34	Manifold Absolute Pressure (MAP) or Vacuum Sensor circuit. The engine must run up to 5 minutes, below 800 rpm, before this code will set
35	Idle Speed Control (ISC) Switch circuit shorted. (Over ½ throttle for over 2 seconds)
42	Electronic Spark Timing (EST) Bypass circuit grounded
44	Lean oxygen sensor indication — the engine must run up to 5 minutes, in closed loop, at part throttle and road load before this code will set
44 & 45	(At same time) — Faulty oxygen sensor circuit
45	Rich system indication — the engine must run up to 5 minutes, in closed loop, at part throttle and road load before this code will set
51	Faulty calibration unit (PROM) or installation. It takes up to 30 seconds before this code will set
52	Faulty ECM
53	Faulty ECM
54	Shorted M/C solenoid circuit and/or faulty ECM
55	Grounded +8 volts, V ref, faulty oxygen sensor or ECM

Year — 1981
Model — Century
Engine — 3.8L (231 cid) V6
Engine Code — VIN A

ECM TROUBLE CODES

Code	Explanation
12	No reference pulses to the ECM. This code is not stored in memory and will only flash while the fault is present
13	Oxygen sensor circuit—the engine must run up to 5 minutes at part throttle, under road load, before this code will set
14	Shorted coolant sensor circuit—the engine must run up to 2 minutes before this code will set
15	Open coolant sensor circuit—the engine must run up to 5 minutes before this code will set
21	Throttle position sensor circuit—the engine must run up to 25 seconds, below 800 rpm, before this code will set
23	Open or grounded M/C solenoid circuit
24	Vehicle Speed Sensor (VSS) circuit—the car must operate up to 5 minutes at road speed before this code will set
32	Barometric Pressure Sensor (BARO) circuit low
34	Manifold Absolute Pressure (MAP) or Vacuum Sensor circuit. The engine must run up to 5 minutes, below 800 rpm, before this code will set
35	Idle Speed Control (ISC) Switch circuit shorted. (Over ½ throttle for over 2 seconds)
42	Electronic Spark Timing (EST) Bypass circuit grounded
44	Lean oxygen sensor indication—the engine must run up to 5 minutes, in closed loop, at part throttle and road load before this code will set
44 & 45	(At same time)—Faulty oxygen sensor circuit
45	Rich system indication—the engine must run up to 5 minutes, in closed loop, at part throttle and road load before this code will set
51	Faulty calibration unit (PROM) or installation. It takes up to 30 seconds before this code will set
52	Faulty ECM
53	Faulty ECM
54	Shorted M/C solenoid circuit and/or faulty ECM
55	Grounded +8 volts, V ref, faulty oxygen sensor or ECM

Year — 1981
Model — Century
Engine — 3.8L (231 cid) Turbo V6
Engine Code — VIN 3

ECM TROUBLE CODES

Code	Explanation
12	No reference pulses to the ECM. This code is not stored in memory and will only flash while the fault is present
13	Oxygen sensor circuit — the engine must run up to 5 minutes at part throttle, under road load, before this code will set
14	Shorted coolant sensor circuit — the engine must run up to 2 minutes before this code will set
15	Open coolant sensor circuit — the engine must run up to 5 minutes before this code will set
21	Throttle position sensor circuit — the engine must run up to 25 seconds, below 800 rpm, before this code will set
23	Open or grounded M/C solenoid circuit
24	Vehicle Speed Sensor (VSS) circuit — the car must operate up to 5 minutes at road speed before this code will set
32	Barometric Pressure Sensor (BARO) circuit low
34	Manifold Absolute Pressure (MAP) or Vacuum Sensor circuit. The engine must run up to 5 minutes, below 800 rpm, before this code will set
35	Idle Speed Control (ISC) Switch circuit shorted. (Over ½ throttle for over 2 seconds)
42	Electronic Spark Timing (EST) Bypass circuit grounded
44	Lean oxygen sensor indication — the engine must run up to 5 minutes, in closed loop, at part throttle and road load before this code will set
44 & 45	(At same time) — Faulty oxygen sensor circuit
45	Rich system indication — the engine must run up to 5 minutes, in closed loop, at part throttle and road load before this code will set
51	Faulty calibration unit (PROM) or installation. It takes up to 30 seconds before this code will set
52	Faulty ECM
53	Faulty ECM
54	Shorted M/C solenoid circuit and/or faulty ECM
55	Grounded +8 volts, V ref, faulty oxygen sensor or ECM

Year — 1981
Model — Century Limited
Engine — 4.3L (265 cid) V8
Engine Code — VIN S

ECM TROUBLE CODES

Code	Explanation
12	No reference pulses to the ECM. This code is not stored in memory and will only flash while the fault is present
13	Oxygen sensor circuit — the engine must run up to 5 minutes at part throttle, under road load, before this code will set
14	Shorted coolant sensor circuit — the engine must run up to 2 minutes before this code will set
15	Open coolant sensor circuit — the engine must run up to 5 minutes before this code will set
21	Throttle position sensor circuit — the engine must run up to 25 seconds, below 800 rpm, before this code will set
23	Open or grounded M/C solenoid circuit
24	Vehicle Speed Sensor (VSS) circuit — the car must operate up to 5 minutes at road speed before this code will set
32	Barometric Pressure Sensor (BARO) circuit low
34	Manifold Absolute Pressure (MAP) or Vacuum Sensor circuit. The engine must run up to 5 minutes, below 800 rpm, before this code will set
35	Idle Speed Control (ISC) Switch circuit shorted. (Over ½ throttle for over 2 seconds)
42	Electronic Spark Timing (EST) Bypass circuit grounded
44	Lean oxygen sensor indication — the engine must run up to 5 minutes, in closed loop, at part throttle and road load before this code will set
44 & 45	(At same time) — Faulty oxygen sensor circuit
45	Rich system indication — the engine must run up to 5 minutes, in closed loop, at part throttle and road load before this code will set
51	Faulty calibration unit (PROM) or installation. It takes up to 30 seconds before this code will set
52	Faulty ECM
53	Faulty ECM
54	Shorted M/C solenoid circuit and/or faulty ECM
55	Grounded + 8 volts, V ref, faulty oxygen sensor or ECM

Year—1981
Model—Regal
Engine—3.8L (231 cid) V6
Engine Code—VIN A

ECM TROUBLE CODES

Code	Explanation
12	No tachometer or reference signal to ECM, this code will only be present while a fault exisits. Code 12 will not be stored if problem is intermittent
13	Oxygen sensor circuit. The engine has to operate for about 18 minutes at part throttle before code will show.
13 & 14	(At same time.) See Code 43
14	Shorted coolant sensor circuit. The engine has to run 2 minutes before this code will show
15	Open coolant sensor circuit. The engine has to operate for about 5 minutes at part throttle before this code will show
21	Shorted WOT switch and/or open closed throttle switch circuit (when used)
21	(After 10 seconds and below 800 rpm) throttle position sensor circuit
23	Open or grounded carburetor solenoid circuit
32	Barometric Pressure Sensor (BARO) output low
32 & 55	(At same time) grounded +8V, V (REF) or faulty ECM
34	(After 10 seconds and below 800 rpm) Manifold Absolute Pressure (MAP) sensor output high
43	Throttle position sensor adjustment
44	Lean oxygen sensor. Engine must be run for approximately 5 minutes in closed loop mode and part throttle at roadload (drive car) before this code will show
45	Rich oxygen sensor. Engine must run for approximately 5 minutes in closed loop mode and part throttle before this code will show
44 & 45	(At same time) faulty oxygen sensor
51	Faulty Calibration Unit (PROM) or improper PROM installation
52 & 53	Check engine light OFF—intermittent ECM problem Check engine light ON—faulty ECM (replace)
54	Faulty carburetor solenoid and/or ECM
55	Faulty oxygen sensor, open MAP sensor or ECM

Year – 1981
Model – Regal
Engine – 3.8L (231 cid) Turbo V6
Engine Code – VIN 3

ECM TROUBLE CODES

Code	Explanation
12	No tachometer or reference signal to ECM, this code will only be present while a fault exisits. Code 12 will not be stored if problem is intermittent
13	Oxygen sensor circuit. The engine has to operate for about 18 minutes at part throttle before code will show.
13 & 14	(At same time.) See Code 43
14	Shorted coolant sensor circuit. The engine has to run 2 minutes before this code will show
15	Open coolant sensor circuit. The engine has to operate for about 5 minutes at part throttle before this code will show
21	Shorted WOT switch and/or open closed throttle switch circuit (when used)
21	(After 10 seconds and below 800 rpm) throttle position sensor circuit
23	Open or grounded carburetor solenoid circuit
32	Barometric Pressure Sensor (BARO) output low
32 & 55	(At same time) grounded + 8V, V (REF) or faulty ECM
34	(After 10 seconds and below 800 rpm) Manifold Absolute Pressure (MAP) sensor output high
43	Throttle position sensor adjustment
44	Lean oxygen sensor. Engine must be run for approximately 5 minutes in closed loop mode and part throttle at roadload (drive car) before this code will show
45	Rich oxygen sensor. Engine must run for approximately 5 minutes in closed loop mode and part throttle before this code will show
44 & 45	(At same time) faulty oxygen sensor
51	Faulty Calibration Unit (PROM) or improper PROM installation
52 & 53	Check engine light OFF – intermittent ECM problem Check engine light ON – faulty ECM (replace)
54	Faulty carburetor solenoid and/or ECM
55	Faulty oxygen sensor, open MAP sensor or ECM

Year – 1981
Model – Regal
Engine – 4.1L (252 cid) V6
Engine Code – VIN 4

ECM TROUBLE CODES

Code	Explanation
12	No reference pulses to the ECM. This code is not stored in memory and will only flash while the fault is present
13	Oxygen sensor circuit — the engine must run up to 5 minutes at part throttle, under road load, before this code will set
14	Shorted coolant sensor circuit — the engine must run up to 2 minutes before this code will set
15	Open coolant sensor circuit — the engine must run up to 5 minutes before this code will set
21	Throttle position sensor circuit — the engine must run up to 25 seconds, below 800 rpm, before this code will set
23	Open or grounded M/C solenoid circuit
24	Vehicle Speed Sensor (VSS) circuit — the car must operate up to 5 minutes at road speed before this code will set
32	Barometric Pressure Sensor (BARO) circuit low
34	Manifold Absolute Pressure (MAP) or Vacuum Sensor circuit. The engine must run up to 5 minutes, below 800 rpm, before this code will set
35	Idle Speed Control (ISC) Switch circuit shorted. (Over ½ throttle for over 2 seconds)
42	Electronic Spark Timing (EST) Bypass circuit grounded
44	Lean oxygen sensor indication — the engine must run up to 5 minutes, in closed loop, at part throttle and road load before this code will set
44 & 45	(At same time) — Faulty oxygen sensor circuit
45	Rich system indication — the engine must run up to 5 minutes, in closed loop, at part throttle and road load before this code will set
51	Faulty calibration unit (PROM) or installation. It takes up to 30 seconds before this code will set
52	Faulty ECM
53	Faulty ECM
54	Shorted M/C solenoid circuit and/or faulty ECM
55	Grounded +8 volts, V ref, faulty oxygen sensor or ECM

Year — 1981
Model — Regal
Engine — 5.0L (305 cid) V8
Engine Code — VIN H

ECM TROUBLE CODES

Code	Explanation
12	No tachometer or reference signal to ECM, this code will only be present while a fault exisits. Code 12 will not be stored if problem is intermittent
13	Oxygen sensor circuit. The engine has to operate for about 18 minutes at part throttle before code will show.
13 & 14	(At same time.) See Code 43
14	Shorted coolant sensor circuit. The engine has to run 2 minutes before this code will show
15	Open coolant sensor circuit. The engine has to operate for about 5 minutes at part throttle before this code will show
21	Shorted WOT switch and/or open closed throttle switch circuit (when used)
21	(After 10 seconds and below 800 rpm) throttle position sensor circuit
23	Open or grounded carburetor solenoid circuit
32	Barometric Pressure Sensor (BARO) output low
32 & 55	(At same time) grounded +8V, V (REF) or faulty ECM
34	(After 10 seconds and below 800 rpm) Manifold Absolute Pressure (MAP) sensor output high
43	Throttle position sensor adjustment
44	Lean oxygen sensor. Engine must be run for approximately 5 minutes in closed loop mode and part throttle at roadload (drive car) before this code will show
45	Rich oxygen sensor. Engine must run for approximately 5 minutes in closed loop mode and part throttle before this code will show
44 & 45	(At same time) faulty oxygen sensor
51	Faulty Calibration Unit (PROM) or improper PROM installation
52 & 53	Check engine light OFF — intermittent ECM problem Check engine light ON — faulty ECM (replace)
54	Faulty carburetor solenoid and/or ECM
55	Faulty oxygen sensor, open MAP sensor or ECM

Year – 1981
Model – Skylark
Engine – 2.5L (151 cid) 4 cyl
Engine Code – VIN 5

ECM TROUBLE CODES

Code	Explanation
12	No reference pulses to the ECM. This code is not stored in memory and will only flash while the fault is present
13	Oxygen sensor circuit—the engine must run up to 5 minutes at part throttle, under road load, before this code will set
14	Shorted coolant sensor circuit—the engine must run up to 2 minutes before this code will set
15	Open coolant sensor circuit—the engine must run up to 5 minutes before this code will set
21	Throttle position sensor circuit—the engine must run up to 25 seconds, below 800 rpm, before this code will set
23	Open or grounded M/C solenoid circuit
34	Vacuum Sensor circuit. The engine must run up to 5 minutes, below 800 rpm, before this code will set
35	Idle Speed Control (ISC) Switch circuit shorted. (Over ½ throttle for over 2 seconds)
42	Electronic Spark Timing (EST) Bypass circuit grounded
44	Lean oxygen sensor indication—the engine must run up to 5 minutes, in closed loop, at part throttle and road load before this code will set
44 & 45	(At same time)—Faulty oxygen sensor circuit
45	Rich system indication—the engine must run up to 5 minutes, in closed loop, at part throttle and road load before this code will set
51	Faulty calibration unit (PROM) or installation. It takes up to 30 seconds before this code will set
52	Faulty ECM
53	Faulty ECM
54	Shorted M/C solenoid circuit and/or faulty ECM
55	Grounded +8 volts, V ref, faulty oxygen sensor or ECM

Year — 1981
Model — Skylark
Engine — 2.8L (171 cid) V6
Engine Code — VIN X

ECM TROUBLE CODES

Code	Explanation
12	No reference pulses to the ECM. This code is not stored in memory and will only flash while the fault is present
13	Oxygen sensor circuit — the engine must run up to 5 minutes at part throttle, under road load, before this code will set
14	Shorted coolant sensor circuit — the engine must run up to 2 minutes before this code will set
15	Open coolant sensor circuit — the engine must run up to 5 minutes before this code will set
21	Throttle position sensor circuit — the engine must run up to 25 seconds, below 800 rpm, before this code will set
23	Open or grounded M/C solenoid circuit
34	Vacuum Sensor circuit. The engine must run up to 5 minutes, below 800 rpm, before this code will set
35	Idle Speed Control (ISC) Switch circuit shorted. (Over ½ throttle for over 2 seconds)
42	Electronic Spark Timing (EST) Bypass circuit grounded
44	Lean oxygen sensor indication — the engine must run up to 5 minutes, in closed loop, at part throttle and road load before this code will set
44 & 45	(At same time) — Faulty oxygen sensor circuit
45	Rich system indication — the engine must run up to 5 minutes, in closed loop, at part throttle and road load before this code will set
51	Faulty calibration unit (PROM) or installation. It takes up to 30 seconds before this code will set
52	Faulty ECM
53	Faulty ECM
54	Shorted M/C solenoid circuit and/or faulty ECM
55	Grounded + 8 volts, V ref, faulty oxygen sensor or ECM

Year – 1981
Model – Riviera
Engine – 3.8L (231 cid) Turbo V6
Engine Code – VIN 3

ECM TROUBLE CODES

Code	Explanation
12	No reference pulses to the ECM. This code is not stored in memory and will only flash while the fault is present
13	Oxygen sensor circuit – the engine must run up to 5 minutes at part throttle, under road load, before this code will set
14	Shorted coolant sensor circuit – the engine must run up to 2 minutes before this code will set
15	Open coolant sensor circuit – the engine must run up to 5 minutes before this code will set
21	Throttle position sensor circuit – the engine must run up to 25 seconds, below 800 rpm, before this code will set
23	Open or grounded M/C solenoid circuit
24	Vehicle Speed Sensor (VSS) circuit – the car must operate up to 5 minutes at road speed before this code will set
32	Barometric Pressure Sensor (BARO) circuit low
34	Manifold Absolute Pressure (MAP) or Vacuum Sensor circuit. The engine must run up to 5 minutes, below 800 rpm, before this code will set
35	Idle Speed Control (ISC) Switch circuit shorted. (Over ½ throttle for over 2 seconds)
42	Electronic Spark Timing (EST) Bypass circuit grounded
44	Lean oxygen sensor indication – the engine must run up to 5 minutes, in closed loop, at part throttle and road load before this code will set
44 & 45	(At same time) – Faulty oxygen sensor circuit
45	Rich system indication – the engine must run up to 5 minutes, in closed loop, at part throttle and road load before this code will set
51	Faulty calibration unit (PROM) or installation. It takes up to 30 seconds before this code will set
52	Faulty ECM
53	Faulty ECM
54	Shorted M/C solenoid circuit and/or faulty ECM
55	Grounded +8 volts, V ref, faulty oxygen sensor or ECM

Year — 1981
Model — Riviera
Engine — 4.1L (252 cid) V6
Engine Code — VIN 4

ECM TROUBLE CODES

Code	Explanation
12	No reference pulses to the ECM. This code is not stored in memory and will only flash while the fault is present
13	Oxygen sensor circuit — the engine must run up to 5 minutes at part throttle, under road load, before this code will set
14	Shorted coolant sensor circuit — the engine must run up to 2 minutes before this code will set
15	Open coolant sensor circuit — the engine must run up to 5 minutes before this code will set
21	Throttle position sensor circuit — the engine must run up to 25 seconds, below 800 rpm, before this code will set
23	Open or grounded M/C solenoid circuit
24	Vehicle Speed Sensor (VSS) circuit — the car must operate up to 5 minutes at road speed before this code will set
32	Barometric Pressure Sensor (BARO) circuit low
34	Manifold Absolute Pressure (MAP) or Vacuum Sensor circuit. The engine must run up to 5 minutes, below 800 rpm, before this code will set
35	Idle Speed Control (ISC) Switch circuit shorted. (Over ½ throttle for over 2 seconds)
42	Electronic Spark Timing (EST) Bypass circuit grounded
44	Lean oxygen sensor indication — the engine must run up to 5 minutes, in closed loop, at part throttle and road load before this code will set
44 & 45	(At same time) — Faulty oxygen sensor circuit
45	Rich system indication — the engine must run up to 5 minutes, in closed loop, at part throttle and road load before this code will set
51	Faulty calibration unit (PROM) or installation. It takes up to 30 seconds before this code will set
52	Faulty ECM
53	Faulty ECM
54	Shorted M/C solenoid circuit and/or faulty ECM
55	Grounded + 8 volts, V ref, faulty oxygen sensor or ECM

Year—1981
Model—Riviera
Engine—5.0L (307 cid) V8
Engine Code—VIN Y

ECM TROUBLE CODES

Code	Explanation
12	No reference pulses to the ECM. This code is not stored in memory and will only flash while the fault is present
13	Oxygen sensor circuit—the engine must run up to 5 minutes at part throttle, under road load, before this code will set
14	Shorted coolant sensor circuit—the engine must run up to 2 minutes before this code will set
15	Open coolant sensor circuit—the engine must run up to 5 minutes before this code will set
21	Throttle position sensor circuit—the engine must run up to 25 seconds, below 800 rpm, before this code will set
23	Open or grounded M/C solenoid circuit
24	Vehicle Speed Sensor (VSS) circuit—the car must operate up to 5 minutes at road speed before this code will set
32	Barometric Pressure Sensor (BARO) circuit low
34	Manifold Absolute Pressure (MAP) or Vacuum Sensor circuit. The engine must run up to 5 minutes, below 800 rpm, before this code will set
35	Idle Speed Control (ISC) Switch circuit shorted. (Over ½ throttle for over 2 seconds)
42	Electronic Spark Timing (EST) Bypass circuit grounded
44	Lean oxygen sensor indication—the engine must run up to 5 minutes, in closed loop, at part throttle and road load before this code will set
44 & 45	(At same time)—Faulty oxygen sensor circuit
45	Rich system indication—the engine must run up to 5 minutes, in closed loop, at part throttle and road load before this code will set
51	Faulty calibration unit (PROM) or installation. It takes up to 30 seconds before this code will set
52	Faulty ECM
53	Faulty ECM
54	Shorted M/C solenoid circuit and/or faulty ECM
55	Grounded +8 volts, V ref, faulty oxygen sensor or ECM

Year – 1982
Model – LeSabre
Engine – 3.8L (231 cid) V6
Engine Code – VIN A

ECM TROUBLE CODES

Code	Explanation
12	No reference pulses to the ECM. This code is not stored in memory and will only flash while the fault is present. Normal code with ignition ON engine not running
13	Oxygen sensor circuit – the engine must run up to 5 minutes at part throttle, under road load, before this code will set
14	Shorted coolant sensor circuit – the engine must run up to 2 minutes before this code will set
15	Open coolant sensor circuit – the engine must run up to 5 minutes before this code will set
21	Throttle position sensor circuit – the engine must run up to 25 seconds, at specified curb idle speed, before this code will set
23	Open or grounded M/C solenoid circuit
24	Vehicle Speed Sensor (VSS) circuit – the car must operate up to 5 minutes at road speed before this code will set
32	Barometric Pressure Sensor (BARO) circuit low
34	Manifold Absolute Pressure (MAP) or vacuum sensor circuit. The engine must run up to 5 minutes, at specified curb idle speed, before this code will set
35	Idle Speed Control (ISC) switch circuit shorted. (Over ½ throttle for over two seconds)
41	No distributor reference pulses at specified engine vacuum. This code will store
42	Electronic Spark Timing (EST) bypass circuit grounded or open
43	ESC retard signal for too long; causes a retard in EST signal
44	Lean oxygen sensor indication – the engine must run up to 5 minutes, in closed loop, at part throttle before this code will set
44 & 45	(At same time) – Faulty oxygen sensor circuit
45	Rich system indication – the engine must run up to 5 minutes, in closed loop, at part throttle before this code will set
51	Faulty calibration unit (PROM) or installation. It takes up to 30 seconds before this code will set
54	Shorted M/C solenoid circuit and/or faulty ECM
55	Grounded V ref (term. 21), faulty oxygen sensor or ECM

Year — 1982
Model — LeSabre
Engine — 4.1L (252 cid) V6
Engine Code — VIN 4

ECM TROUBLE CODES

Code	Explanation
12	No reference pulses to the ECM. This code is not stored in memory and will only flash while the fault is present. Normal code with ignition ON engine not running
13	Oxygen sensor circuit — the engine must run up to 5 minutes at part throttle, under road load, before this code will set
14	Shorted coolant sensor circuit — the engine must run up to 2 minutes before this code will set
15	Open coolant sensor circuit — the engine must run up to 5 minutes before this code will set
21	Throttle position sensor circuit — the engine must run up to 25 seconds, at specified curb idle speed, before this code will set
23	Open or grounded M/C solenoid circuit
24	Vehicle Speed Sensor (VSS) circuit — the car must operate up to 5 minutes at road speed before this code will set
32	Barometric Pressure Sensor (BARO) circuit low
34	Manifold Absolute Pressure (MAP) or vacuum sensor circuit. The engine must run up to 5 minutes, at specified curb idle speed, before this code will set
35	Idle Speed Control (ISC) switch circuit shorted. (Over ½ throttle for over two seconds)
41	No distributor reference pulses at specified engine vacuum. This code will store
42	Electronic Spark Timing (EST) bypass circuit grounded or open
43	ESC retard signal for too long; causes a retard in EST signal
44	Lean oxygen sensor indication — the engine must run up to 5 minutes, in closed loop, at part throttle before this code will set
44 & 45	(At same time) — Faulty oxygen sensor circuit
45	Rich system indication — the engine must run up to 5 minutes, in closed loop, at part throttle before this code will set
51	Faulty calibration unit (PROM) or installation. It takes up to 30 seconds before this code will set
54	Shorted M/C solenoid circuit and/or faulty ECM
55	Grounded V ref (term. 21), faulty oxygen sensor or ECM

Year – 1982
Model – LeSabre
Engine – 5.0L (307 cid) V8
Engine Code – VIN Y

ECM TROUBLE CODES

Code	Explanation
12	No reference pulses to the ECM. This code is not stored in memory and will only flash while the fault is present. Normal code with ignition ON engine not running
13	Oxygen sensor circuit – the engine must run up to 5 minutes at part throttle, under road load, before this code will set
14	Shorted coolant sensor circuit – the engine must run up to 2 minutes before this code will set
15	Open coolant sensor circuit – the engine must run up to 5 minutes before this code will set
21	Throttle position sensor circuit – the engine must run up to 25 seconds, at specified curb idle speed, before this code will set
23	Open or grounded M/C solenoid circuit
24	Vehicle Speed Sensor (VSS) circuit – the car must operate up to 5 minutes at road speed before this code will set
32	Barometric Pressure Sensor (BARO) circuit low
34	Manifold Absolute Pressure (MAP) or vacuum sensor circuit. The engine must run up to 5 minutes, at specified curb idle speed, before this code will set
35	Idle Speed Control (ISC) switch circuit shorted. (Over ½ throttle for over two seconds)
41	No distributor reference pulses at specified engine vacuum. This code will store
42	Electronic Spark Timing (EST) bypass circuit grounded or open
43	ESC retard signal for too long; causes a retard in EST signal
44	Lean oxygen sensor indication – the engine must run up to 5 minutes, in closed loop, at part throttle before this code will set
44 & 45	(At same time) – Faulty oxygen sensor circuit
45	Rich system indication – the engine must run up to 5 minutes, in closed loop, at part throttle before this code will set
51	Faulty calibration unit (PROM) or installation. It takes up to 30 seconds before this code will set
54	Shorted M/C solenoid circuit and/or faulty ECM
55	Grounded V ref (term. 21), faulty oxygen sensor or ECM

Year – 1982
Model – LeSabre Estate Wagon
Engine – 5.0L (307 cid) V8
Engine Code – VIN Y

ECM TROUBLE CODES

Code	Explanation
12	No reference pulses to the ECM. This code is not stored in memory and will only flash while the fault is present. Normal code with ignition ON engine not running
13	Oxygen sensor circuit – the engine must run up to 5 minutes at part throttle, under road load, before this code will set
14	Shorted coolant sensor circuit – the engine must run up to 2 minutes before this code will set
15	Open coolant sensor circuit – the engine must run up to 5 minutes before this code will set
21	Throttle position sensor circuit – the engine must run up to 25 seconds, at specified curb idle speed, before this code will set
23	Open or grounded M/C solenoid circuit
24	Vehicle Speed Sensor (VSS) circuit – the car must operate up to 5 minutes at road speed before this code will set
32	Barometric Pressure Sensor (BARO) circuit low
34	Manifold Absolute Pressure (MAP) or vacuum sensor circuit. The engine must run up to 5 minutes, at specified curb idle speed, before this code will set
35	Idle Speed Control (ISC) switch circuit shorted. (Over ½ throttle for over two seconds)
41	No distributor reference pulses at specified engine vacuum. This code will store
42	Electronic Spark Timing (EST) bypass circuit grounded or open
43	ESC retard signal for too long; causes a retard in EST signal
44	Lean oxygen sensor indication – the engine must run up to 5 minutes, in closed loop, at part throttle before this code will set
44 & 45	(At same time) – Faulty oxygen sensor circuit
45	Rich system indication – the engine must run up to 5 minutes, in closed loop, at part throttle before this code will set
51	Faulty calibration unit (PROM) or installation. It takes up to 30 seconds before this code will set
54	Shorted M/C solenoid circuit and/or faulty ECM
55	Grounded V ref (term. 21), faulty oxygen sensor or ECM

Year — 1982
Model — Electra Limited
Engine — 4.1L (252 cid) V6
Engine Code — VIN 4

ECM TROUBLE CODES

Code	Explanation
12	No reference pulses to the ECM. This code is not stored in memory and will only flash while the fault is present. Normal code with ignition ON engine not running
13	Oxygen sensor circuit — the engine must run up to 5 minutes at part throttle, under road load, before this code will set
14	Shorted coolant sensor circuit — the engine must run up to 2 minutes before this code will set
15	Open coolant sensor circuit — the engine must run up to 5 minutes before this code will set
21	Throttle position sensor circuit — the engine must run up to 25 seconds, at specified curb idle speed, before this code will set
23	Open or grounded M/C solenoid circuit
24	Vehicle Speed Sensor (VSS) circuit — the car must operate up to 5 minutes at road speed before this code will set
32	Barometric Pressure Sensor (BARO) circuit low
34	Manifold Absolute Pressure (MAP) or vacuum sensor circuit. The engine must run up to 5 minutes, at specified curb idle speed, before this code will set
35	Idle Speed Control (ISC) switch circuit shorted. (Over ½ throttle for over two seconds)
41	No distributor reference pulses at specified engine vacuum. This code will store
42	Electronic Spark Timing (EST) bypass circuit grounded or open
43	ESC retard signal for too long; causes a retard in EST signal
44	Lean oxygen sensor indication — the engine must run up to 5 minutes, in closed loop, at part throttle before this code will set
44 & 45	(At same time) — Faulty oxygen sensor circuit
45	Rich system indication — the engine must run up to 5 minutes, in closed loop, at part throttle before this code will set
51	Faulty calibration unit (PROM) or installation. It takes up to 30 seconds before this code will set
54	Shorted M/C solenoid circuit and/or faulty ECM
55	Grounded V ref (term. 21), faulty oxygen sensor or ECM

Year — 1982
Model — Electra Limited
Engine — 5.0L (307 cid) V8
Engine Code — VIN Y

ECM TROUBLE CODES

Code	Explanation
12	No reference pulses to the ECM. This code is not stored in memory and will only flash while the fault is present. Normal code with ignition ON engine not running
13	Oxygen sensor circuit — the engine must run up to 5 minutes at part throttle, under road load, before this code will set
14	Shorted coolant sensor circuit — the engine must run up to 2 minutes before this code will set
15	Open coolant sensor circuit — the engine must run up to 5 minutes before this code will set
21	Throttle position sensor circuit — the engine must run up to 25 seconds, at specified curb idle speed, before this code will set
23	Open or grounded M/C solenoid circuit
24	Vehicle Speed Sensor (VSS) circuit — the car must operate up to 5 minutes at road speed before this code will set
32	Barometric Pressure Sensor (BARO) circuit low
34	Manifold Absolute Pressure (MAP) or vacuum sensor circuit. The engine must run up to 5 minutes, at specified curb idle speed, before this code will set
35	Idle Speed Control (ISC) switch circuit shorted. (Over ½ throttle for over two seconds)
41	No distributor reference pulses at specified engine vacuum. This code will store
42	Electronic Spark Timing (EST) bypass circuit grounded or open
43	ESC retard signal for too long; causes a retard in EST signal
44	Lean oxygen sensor indication — the engine must run up to 5 minutes, in closed loop, at part throttle before this code will set
44 & 45	(At same time) — Faulty oxygen sensor circuit
45	Rich system indication — the engine must run up to 5 minutes, in closed loop, at part throttle before this code will set
51	Faulty calibration unit (PROM) or installation. It takes up to 30 seconds before this code will set
54	Shorted M/C solenoid circuit and/or faulty ECM
55	Grounded V ref (term. 21), faulty oxygen sensor or ECM

Year — 1982
Model — Electra Estate Wagon
Engine — 5.0L (307 cid) V8
Engine Code — VIN Y

ECM TROUBLE CODES

Code	Explanation
12	No reference pulses to the ECM. This code is not stored in memory and will only flash while the fault is present. Normal code with ignition ON engine not running
13	Oxygen sensor circuit — the engine must run up to 5 minutes at part throttle, under road load, before this code will set
14	Shorted coolant sensor circuit — the engine must run up to 2 minutes before this code will set
15	Open coolant sensor circuit — the engine must run up to 5 minutes before this code will set
21	Throttle position sensor circuit — the engine must run up to 25 seconds, at specified curb idle speed, before this code will set
23	Open or grounded M/C solenoid circuit
24	Vehicle Speed Sensor (VSS) circuit — the car must operate up to 5 minutes at road speed before this code will set
32	Barometric Pressure Sensor (BARO) circuit low
34	Manifold Absolute Pressure (MAP) or vacuum sensor circuit. The engine must run up to 5 minutes, at specified curb idle speed, before this code will set
35	Idle Speed Control (ISC) switch circuit shorted. (Over ½ throttle for over two seconds)
41	No distributor reference pulses at specified engine vacuum. This code will store
42	Electronic Spark Timing (EST) bypass circuit grounded or open
43	ESC retard signal for too long; causes a retard in EST signal
44	Lean oxygen sensor indication — the engine must run up to 5 minutes, in closed loop, at part throttle before this code will set
44 & 45	(At same time) — Faulty oxygen sensor circuit
45	Rich system indication — the engine must run up to 5 minutes, in closed loop, at part throttle before this code will set
51	Faulty calibration unit (PROM) or installation. It takes up to 30 seconds before this code will set
54	Shorted M/C solenoid circuit and/or faulty ECM
55	Grounded V ref (term. 21), faulty oxygen sensor or ECM

GENERAL MOTORS CORPORATION
DIAGNOSTIC CODE DATA

Year – 1982
Model – Century
Engine – 2.5L (151 cid) 4 cyl EFI
Engine Code – VIN R

ECM TROUBLE CODES

Code	Explanation
12	No reference pulses to the ECM. This code is not stored in memory and will only flash while the fault is present. Normal code with ignition ON engine not running
13	Oxygen sensor circuit—the engine must run up to 5 minutes at part throttle, under road load, before this code will set
14	Shorted coolant sensor circuit—the engine must run up to 2 minutes before this code will set
15	Open coolant sensor circuit—the engine must run up to 5 minutes before this code will set
21	Throttle position sensor circuit—the engine must run up to 25 seconds, at specified curb idle speed, before this code will set
23	Open or grounded M/C solenoid circuit
24	Vehicle Speed Sensor (VSS) circuit—the car must operate up to 5 minutes at road speed before this code will set
32	Barometric Pressure Sensor (BARO) circuit low
34	Manifold Absolute Pressure (MAP) or vacuum sensor circuit. The engine must run up to 5 minutes, at specified curb idle speed, before this code will set
35	Idle Speed Control (ISC) switch circuit shorted. (Over ½ throttle for over two seconds)
41	No distributor reference pulses at specified engine vacuum. This code will store
42	Electronic Spark Timing (EST) bypass circuit grounded or open
44	Lean oxygen sensor indication—the engine must run up to 5 minutes, in closed loop, at part throttle before this code will set
44 & 45	(At same time)—Faulty oxygen sensor circuit
45	Rich system indication—the engine must run up to 5 minutes, in closed loop, at part throttle before this code will set

Year — 1982
Model — Century
Engine — 2.5L (151 cid) 4 cyl EFI
Engine Code — VIN 5

ECM TROUBLE CODES

Code	Explanation
12	No reference pulses to the ECM. This code is not stored in memory and will only flash while the fault is present. Normal code with ignition ON engine not running
13	Oxygen sensor circuit — the engine must run up to 5 minutes at part throttle, under road load, before this code will set
14	Shorted coolant sensor circuit — the engine must run up to 2 minutes before this code will set
15	Open coolant sensor circuit — the engine must run up to 5 minutes before this code will set
21	Throttle position sensor circuit — the engine must run up to 25 seconds, at specified curb idle speed, before this code will set
23	Open or grounded M/C solenoid circuit
24	Vehicle Speed Sensor (VSS) circuit — the car must operate up to 5 minutes at road speed before this code will set
32	Barometric Pressure Sensor (BARO) circuit low
34	Manifold Absolute Pressure (MAP) or vacuum sensor circuit. The engine must run up to 5 minutes, at specified curb idle speed, before this code will set
35	Idle Speed Control (ISC) switch circuit shorted. (Over ½ throttle for over two seconds)
41	No distributor reference pulses at specified engine vacuum. This code will store
42	Electronic Spark Timing (EST) bypass circuit grounded or open
44	Lean oxygen sensor indication — the engine must run up to 5 minutes, in closed loop, at part throttle before this code will set
44 & 45	(At same time) — Faulty oxygen sensor circuit
45	Rich system indication — the engine must run up to 5 minutes, in closed loop, at part throttle before this code will set

Year – 1982
Model – Century
Engine – 2.8L (181 cid) V6 EFI
Engine Code – VIN Z

ECM TROUBLE CODES

Code	Explanation
12	No reference pulses to the ECM. This code is not stored in memory and will only flash while the fault is present. Normal code with ignition ON engine not running
13	Oxygen sensor circuit – the engine must run up to 5 minutes at part throttle, under road load, before this code will set
14	Shorted coolant sensor circuit – the engine must run up to 2 minutes before this code will set
15	Open coolant sensor circuit – the engine must run up to 5 minutes before this code will set
21	Throttle position sensor circuit – the engine must run up to 25 seconds, at specified curb idle speed, before this code will set
23	Open or grounded M/C solenoid circuit
24	Vehicle Speed Sensor (VSS) circuit – the car must operate up to 5 minutes at road speed before this code will set
32	Barometric Pressure Sensor (BARO) circuit low
34	Manifold Absolute Pressure (MAP) or vacuum sensor circuit. The engine must run up to 5 minutes, at specified curb idle speed, before this code will set
35	Idle Speed Control (ISC) switch circuit shorted. (Over ½ throttle for over two seconds)
41	No distributor reference pulses at specified engine vacuum. This code will store
42	Electronic Spark Timing (EST) bypass circuit grounded or open
44	Lean oxygen sensor indication – the engine must run up to 5 minutes, in closed loop, at part throttle before this code will set
44 & 45	(At same time) – Faulty oxygen sensor circuit
45	Rich system indication – the engine must run up to 5 minutes, in closed loop, at part throttle before this code will set

Year — 1982
Model — Century
Engine — 2.8L (181 cid) V6 EFI
Engine Code — VIN X

ECM TROUBLE CODES

Code	Explanation
12	No reference pulses to the ECM. This code is not stored in memory and will only flash while the fault is present. Normal code with ignition ON engine not running
13	Oxygen sensor circuit — the engine must run up to 5 minutes at part throttle, under road load, before this code will set
14	Shorted coolant sensor circuit — the engine must run up to 2 minutes before this code will set
15	Open coolant sensor circuit — the engine must run up to 5 minutes before this code will set
21	Throttle position sensor circuit — the engine must run up to 25 seconds, at specified curb idle speed, before this code will set
23	Open or grounded M/C solenoid circuit
24	Vehicle Speed Sensor (VSS) circuit — the car must operate up to 5 minutes at road speed before this code will set
32	Barometric Pressure Sensor (BARO) circuit low
34	Manifold Absolute Pressure (MAP) or vacuum sensor circuit. The engine must run up to 5 minutes, at specified curb idle speed, before this code will set
35	Idle Speed Control (ISC) switch circuit shorted. (Over ½ throttle for over two seconds)
41	No distributor reference pulses at specified engine vacuum. This code will store
42	Electronic Spark Timing (EST) bypass circuit grounded or open
43	ESC retard signal for too long; causes a retard in EST signal
44	Lean oxygen sensor indication — the engine must run up to 5 minutes, in closed loop, at part throttle before this code will set
44 & 45	(At same time) — Faulty oxygen sensor circuit
45	Rich system indication — the engine must run up to 5 minutes, in closed loop, at part throttle before this code will set
51	Faulty calibration unit (PROM) or installation. It takes up to 30 seconds before this code will set
54	Shorted M/C solenoid circuit and/or faulty ECM
55	Grounded V ref (term. 21), faulty oxygen sensor or ECM

Year – 1982
Model – Century
Engine – 3.0L (181 cid) V6 EFI
Engine Code – VIN E

ECM TROUBLE CODES

Code	Explanation
12	No reference pulses to the ECM. This code is not stored in memory and will only flash while the fault is present. Normal code with ignition ON engine not running
13	Oxygen sensor circuit – the engine must run up to 5 minutes at part throttle, under road load, before this code will set
14	Shorted coolant sensor circuit – the engine must run up to 2 minutes before this code will set
15	Open coolant sensor circuit – the engine must run up to 5 minutes before this code will set
21	Throttle position sensor circuit – the engine must run up to 25 seconds, at specified curb idle speed, before this code will set
23	Open or grounded M/C solenoid circuit
24	Vehicle Speed Sensor (VSS) circuit – the car must operate up to 5 minutes at road speed before this code will set
32	Barometric Pressure Sensor (BARO) circuit low
34	Manifold Absolute Pressure (MAP) or vacuum sensor circuit. The engine must run up to 5 minutes, at specified curb idle speed, before this code will set
35	Idle Speed Control (ISC) switch circuit shorted. (Over ½ throttle for over two seconds)
41	No distributor reference pulses at specified engine vacuum. This code will store
42	Electronic Spark Timing (EST) bypass circuit grounded or open
44	Lean oxygen sensor indication – the engine must run up to 5 minutes, in closed loop, at part throttle before this code will set
44 & 45	(At same time) – Faulty oxygen sensor circuit
45	Rich system indication – the engine must run up to 5 minutes, in closed loop, at part throttle before this code will set

Year — 1982
Model — Regal
Engine — 3.8L (231 cid) V6
Engine Code — VIN A

ECM TROUBLE CODES

Code	Explanation
12	No reference pulses to the ECM. This code is not stored in memory and will only flash while the fault is present. Normal code with ignition ON engine not running
13	Oxygen sensor circuit — the engine must run up to 5 minutes at part throttle, under road load, before this code will set
14	Shorted coolant sensor circuit — the engine must run up to 2 minutes before this code will set
15	Open coolant sensor circuit — the engine must run up to 5 minutes before this code will set
21	Throttle position sensor circuit — the engine must run up to 25 seconds, at specified curb idle speed, before this code will set
23	Open or grounded M/C solenoid circuit
24	Vehicle Speed Sensor (VSS) circuit — the car must operate up to 5 minutes at road speed before this code will set
32	Barometric Pressure Sensor (BARO) circuit low
34	Manifold Absolute Pressure (MAP) or vacuum sensor circuit. The engine must run up to 5 minutes, at specified curb idle speed, before this code will set
35	Idle Speed Control (ISC) switch circuit shorted. (Over ½ throttle for over two seconds)
41	No distributor reference pulses at specified engine vacuum. This code will store
42	Electronic Spark Timing (EST) bypass circuit grounded or open
43	ESC retard signal for too long; causes a retard in EST signal
44	Lean oxygen sensor indication — the engine must run up to 5 minutes, in closed loop, at part throttle before this code will set
44 & 45	(At same time) — Faulty oxygen sensor circuit
45	Rich system indication — the engine must run up to 5 minutes, in closed loop, at part throttle before this code will set
51	Faulty calibration unit (PROM) or installation. It takes up to 30 seconds before this code will set
54	Shorted M/C solenoid circuit and/or faulty ECM
55	Grounded V ref (term. 21), faulty oxygen sensor or ECM

Year – 1982
Model – Regal
Engine – 3.8L (231 cid) Turbo V6
Engine Code – VIN 3

ECM TROUBLE CODES

Code	Explanation
12	No reference pulses to the ECM. This code is not stored in memory and will only flash while the fault is present. Normal code with ignition ON engine not running
13	Oxygen sensor circuit – the engine must run up to 5 minutes at part throttle, under road load, before this code will set
14	Shorted coolant sensor circuit – the engine must run up to 2 minutes before this code will set
15	Open coolant sensor circuit – the engine must run up to 5 minutes before this code will set
21	Throttle position sensor circuit – the engine must run up to 25 seconds, at specified curb idle speed, before this code will set
23	Open or grounded M/C solenoid circuit
24	Vehicle Speed Sensor (VSS) circuit – the car must operate up to 5 minutes at road speed before this code will set
32	Barometric Pressure Sensor (BARO) circuit low
34	Manifold Absolute Pressure (MAP) or vacuum sensor circuit. The engine must run up to 5 minutes, at specified curb idle speed, before this code will set
35	Idle Speed Control (ISC) switch circuit shorted. (Over ½ throttle for over two seconds)
41	No distributor reference pulses at specified engine vacuum. This code will store
42	Electronic Spark Timing (EST) bypass circuit grounded or open
43	ESC retard signal for too long; causes a retard in EST signal
44	Lean oxygen sensor indication – the engine must run up to 5 minutes, in closed loop, at part throttle before this code will set
44 & 45	(At same time) – Faulty oxygen sensor circuit
45	Rich system indication – the engine must run up to 5 minutes, in closed loop, at part throttle before this code will set
51	Faulty calibration unit (PROM) or installation. It takes up to 30 seconds before this code will set
54	Shorted M/C solenoid circuit and/or faulty ECM
55	Grounded V ref (term. 21), faulty oxygen sensor or ECM

Year — 1982
Model — Regal
Engine — 4.1L (252 cid) V6
Engine Code — VIN 4

ECM TROUBLE CODES

Code	Explanation
12	No reference pulses to the ECM. This code is not stored in memory and will only flash while the fault is present. Normal code with ignition ON engine not running
13	Oxygen sensor circuit — the engine must run up to 5 minutes at part throttle, under road load, before this code will set
14	Shorted coolant sensor circuit — the engine must run up to 2 minutes before this code will set
15	Open coolant sensor circuit — the engine must run up to 5 minutes before this code will set
21	Throttle position sensor circuit — the engine must run up to 25 seconds, at specified curb idle speed, before this code will set
23	Open or grounded M/C solenoid circuit
24	Vehicle Speed Sensor (VSS) circuit — the car must operate up to 5 minutes at road speed before this code will set
32	Barometric Pressure Sensor (BARO) circuit low
34	Manifold Absolute Pressure (MAP) or vacuum sensor circuit. The engine must run up to 5 minutes, at specified curb idle speed, before this code will set
35	Idle Speed Control (ISC) switch circuit shorted. (Over ½ throttle for over two seconds)
41	No distributor reference pulses at specified engine vacuum. This code will store
42	Electronic Spark Timing (EST) bypass circuit grounded or open
43	ESC retard signal for too long; causes a retard in EST signal
44	Lean oxygen sensor indication — the engine must run up to 5 minutes, in closed loop, at part throttle before this code will set
44 & 45	(At same time) — Faulty oxygen sensor circuit
45	Rich system indication — the engine must run up to 5 minutes, in closed loop, at part throttle before this code will set
51	Faulty calibration unit (PROM) or installation. It takes up to 30 seconds before this code will set
54	Shorted M/C solenoid circuit and/or faulty ECM
55	Grounded V ref (term. 21), faulty oxygen sensor or ECM

Year — 1982
Model — Regal Limited
Engine — 3.8L (231 cid) V6
Engine Code — VIN A

ECM TROUBLE CODES

Code	Explanation
12	No reference pulses to the ECM. This code is not stored in memory and will only flash while the fault is present. Normal code with ignition ON engine not running
13	Oxygen sensor circuit — the engine must run up to 5 minutes at part throttle, under road load, before this code will set
14	Shorted coolant sensor circuit — the engine must run up to 2 minutes before this code will set
15	Open coolant sensor circuit — the engine must run up to 5 minutes before this code will set
21	Throttle position sensor circuit — the engine must run up to 25 seconds, at specified curb idle speed, before this code will set
23	Open or grounded M/C solenoid circuit
24	Vehicle Speed Sensor (VSS) circuit — the car must operate up to 5 minutes at road speed before this code will set
32	Barometric Pressure Sensor (BARO) circuit low
34	Manifold Absolute Pressure (MAP) or vacuum sensor circuit. The engine must run up to 5 minutes, at specified curb idle speed, before this code will set
35	Idle Speed Control (ISC) switch circuit shorted. (Over ½ throttle for over two seconds)
41	No distributor reference pulses at specified engine vacuum. This code will store
42	Electronic Spark Timing (EST) bypass circuit grounded or open
43	ESC retard signal for too long; causes a retard in EST signal
44	Lean oxygen sensor indication — the engine must run up to 5 minutes, in closed loop, at part throttle before this code will set
44 & 45	(At same time) — Faulty oxygen sensor circuit
45	Rich system indication — the engine must run up to 5 minutes, in closed loop, at part throttle before this code will set
51	Faulty calibration unit (PROM) or installation. It takes up to 30 seconds before this code will set
54	Shorted M/C solenoid circuit and/or faulty ECM
55	Grounded V ref (term. 21), faulty oxygen sensor or ECM

Year — 1982
Model — Regal Limited
Engine — 3.8L (231 cid) Turbo V6
Engine Code — VIN 3

ECM TROUBLE CODES

Code	Explanation
12	No reference pulses to the ECM. This code is not stored in memory and will only flash while the fault is present. Normal code with ignition ON engine not running
13	Oxygen sensor circuit — the engine must run up to 5 minutes at part throttle, under road load, before this code will set
14	Shorted coolant sensor circuit — the engine must run up to 2 minutes before this code will set
15	Open coolant sensor circuit — the engine must run up to 5 minutes before this code will set
21	Throttle position sensor circuit — the engine must run up to 25 seconds, at specified curb idle speed, before this code will set
23	Open or grounded M/C solenoid circuit
24	Vehicle Speed Sensor (VSS) circuit — the car must operate up to 5 minutes at road speed before this code will set
32	Barometric Pressure Sensor (BARO) circuit low
34	Manifold Absolute Pressure (MAP) or vacuum sensor circuit. The engine must run up to 5 minutes, at specified curb idle speed, before this code will set
35	Idle Speed Control (ISC) switch circuit shorted. (Over ½ throttle for over two seconds)
41	No distributor reference pulses at specified engine vacuum. This code will store
42	Electronic Spark Timing (EST) bypass circuit grounded or open
43	ESC retard signal for too long; causes a retard in EST signal
44	Lean oxygen sensor indication — the engine must run up to 5 minutes, in closed loop, at part throttle before this code will set
44 & 45	(At same time) — Faulty oxygen sensor circuit
45	Rich system indication — the engine must run up to 5 minutes, in closed loop, at part throttle before this code will set
51	Faulty calibration unit (PROM) or installation. It takes up to 30 seconds before this code will set
54	Shorted M/C solenoid circuit and/or faulty ECM
55	Grounded V ref (term. 21), faulty oxygen sensor or ECM

Year – 1982
Model – Regal Limited
Engine – 4.1L (252 cid) V6
Engine Code – VIN 4

ECM TROUBLE CODES

Code	Explanation
12	No reference pulses to the ECM. This code is not stored in memory and will only flash while the fault is present. Normal code with ignition ON engine not running
13	Oxygen sensor circuit—the engine must run up to 5 minutes at part throttle, under road load, before this code will set
14	Shorted coolant sensor circuit—the engine must run up to 2 minutes before this code will set
15	Open coolant sensor circuit—the engine must run up to 5 minutes before this code will set
21	Throttle position sensor circuit—the engine must run up to 25 seconds, at specified curb idle speed, before this code will set
23	Open or grounded M/C solenoid circuit
24	Vehicle Speed Sensor (VSS) circuit—the car must operate up to 5 minutes at road speed before this code will set
32	Barometric Pressure Sensor (BARO) circuit low
34	Manifold Absolute Pressure (MAP) or vacuum sensor circuit. The engine must run up to 5 minutes, at specified curb idle speed, before this code will set
35	Idle Speed Control (ISC) switch circuit shorted. (Over ½ throttle for over two seconds)
41	No distributor reference pulses at specified engine vacuum. This code will store
42	Electronic Spark Timing (EST) bypass circuit grounded or open
43	ESC retard signal for too long; causes a retard in EST signal
44	Lean oxygen sensor indication—the engine must run up to 5 minutes, in closed loop, at part throttle before this code will set
44 & 45	(At same time)—Faulty oxygen sensor circuit
45	Rich system indication—the engine must run up to 5 minutes, in closed loop, at part throttle before this code will set
51	Faulty calibration unit (PROM) or installation. It takes up to 30 seconds before this code will set
54	Shorted M/C solenoid circuit and/or faulty ECM
55	Grounded V ref (term. 21), faulty oxygen sensor or ECM

Year – 1982
Model – Skylark
Engine – 2.5L (151 cid) 4 cyl EFI
Engine Code – VIN R

ECM TROUBLE CODES

Code	Explanation
12	No reference pulses to the ECM. This code is not stored in memory and will only flash while the fault is present. Normal code with ignition ON engine not running
13	Oxygen sensor circuit—the engine must run up to 5 minutes at part throttle, under road load, before this code will set
14	Shorted coolant sensor circuit—the engine must run up to 2 minutes before this code will set
15	Open coolant sensor circuit—the engine must run up to 5 minutes before this code will set
21	Throttle position sensor circuit—the engine must run up to 25 seconds, at specified curb idle speed, before this code will set
23	Open or grounded M/C solenoid circuit
24	Vehicle Speed Sensor (VSS) circuit—the car must operate up to 5 minutes at road speed before this code will set
32	Barometric Pressure Sensor (BARO) circuit low
34	Manifold Absolute Pressure (MAP) or vacuum sensor circuit. The engine must run up to 5 minutes, at specified curb idle speed, before this code will set
35	Idle Speed Control (ISC) switch circuit shorted. (Over ½ throttle for over two seconds)
41	No distributor reference pulses at specified engine vacuum. This code will store
42	Electronic Spark Timing (EST) bypass circuit grounded or open
44	Lean oxygen sensor indication—the engine must run up to 5 minutes, in closed loop, at part throttle before this code will set
44 & 45	(At same time)—Faulty oxygen sensor circuit
45	Rich system indication—the engine must run up to 5 minutes, in closed loop, at part throttle before this code will set

GENERAL MOTORS CORPORATION
DIAGNOSTIC CODE DATA

Year — 1982
Model — Skylark
Engine — 2.5L (151 cid) 4 cyl EFI
Engine Code — VIN 5

ECM TROUBLE CODES

Code	Explanation
12	No reference pulses to the ECM. This code is not stored in memory and will only flash while the fault is present. Normal code with ignition ON engine not running
13	Oxygen sensor circuit — the engine must run up to 5 minutes at part throttle, under road load, before this code will set
14	Shorted coolant sensor circuit — the engine must run up to 2 minutes before this code will set
15	Open coolant sensor circuit — the engine must run up to 5 minutes before this code will set
21	Throttle position sensor circuit — the engine must run up to 25 seconds, at specified curb idle speed, before this code will set
23	Open or grounded M/C solenoid circuit
24	Vehicle Speed Sensor (VSS) circuit — the car must operate up to 5 minutes at road speed before this code will set
32	Barometric Pressure Sensor (BARO) circuit low
34	Manifold Absolute Pressure (MAP) or vacuum sensor circuit. The engine must run up to 5 minutes, at specified curb idle speed, before this code will set
35	Idle Speed Control (ISC) switch circuit shorted. (Over ½ throttle for over two seconds)
41	No distributor reference pulses at specified engine vacuum. This code will store
42	Electronic Spark Timing (EST) bypass circuit grounded or open
44	Lean oxygen sensor indication — the engine must run up to 5 minutes, in closed loop, at part throttle before this code will set
44 & 45	(At same time) — Faulty oxygen sensor circuit
45	Rich system indication — the engine must run up to 5 minutes, in closed loop, at part throttle before this code will set

Year – 1982
Model – Skylark
Engine – 2.8L (181 cid) V6 EFI
Engine Code – VIN Z

ECM TROUBLE CODES

Code	Explanation
12	No reference pulses to the ECM. This code is not stored in memory and will only flash while the fault is present. Normal code with ignition ON engine not running
13	Oxygen sensor circuit – the engine must run up to 5 minutes at part throttle, under road load, before this code will set
14	Shorted coolant sensor circuit – the engine must run up to 2 minutes before this code will set
15	Open coolant sensor circuit – the engine must run up to 5 minutes before this code will set
21	Throttle position sensor circuit – the engine must run up to 25 seconds, at specified curb idle speed, before this code will set
23	Open or grounded M/C solenoid circuit
24	Vehicle Speed Sensor (VSS) circuit – the car must operate up to 5 minutes at road speed before this code will set
32	Barometric Pressure Sensor (BARO) circuit low
34	Manifold Absolute Pressure (MAP) or vacuum sensor circuit. The engine must run up to 5 minutes, at specified curb idle speed, before this code will set
35	Idle Speed Control (ISC) switch circuit shorted. (Over ½ throttle for over two seconds)
41	No distributor reference pulses at specified engine vacuum. This code will store
42	Electronic Spark Timing (EST) bypass circuit grounded or open
44	Lean oxygen sensor indication – the engine must run up to 5 minutes, in closed loop, at part throttle before this code will set
44 & 45	(At same time) – Faulty oxygen sensor circuit
45	Rich system indication – the engine must run up to 5 minutes, in closed loop, at part throttle before this code will set

Year—1982
Model—Skylark
Engine—2.8L (181 cid) V6 EFI
Engine Code—VIN X

ECM TROUBLE CODES

Code	Explanation
12	No reference pulses to the ECM. This code is not stored in memory and will only flash while the fault is present. Normal code with ignition ON engine not running
13	Oxygen sensor circuit—the engine must run up to 5 minutes at part throttle, under road load, before this code will set
14	Shorted coolant sensor circuit—the engine must run up to 2 minutes before this code will set
15	Open coolant sensor circuit—the engine must run up to 5 minutes before this code will set
21	Throttle position sensor circuit—the engine must run up to 25 seconds, at specified curb idle speed, before this code will set
23	Open or grounded M/C solenoid circuit
24	Vehicle Speed Sensor (VSS) circuit—the car must operate up to 5 minutes at road speed before this code will set
32	Barometric Pressure Sensor (BARO) circuit low
34	Manifold Absolute Pressure (MAP) or vacuum sensor circuit. The engine must run up to 5 minutes, at specified curb idle speed, before this code will set
35	Idle Speed Control (ISC) switch circuit shorted. (Over ½ throttle for over two seconds)
41	No distributor reference pulses at specified engine vacuum. This code will store
42	Electronic Spark Timing (EST) bypass circuit grounded or open
44	Lean oxygen sensor indication—the engine must run up to 5 minutes, in closed loop, at part throttle before this code will set
44 & 45	(At same time)—Faulty oxygen sensor circuit
45	Rich system indication—the engine must run up to 5 minutes, in closed loop, at part throttle before this code will set

Year – 1982
Model – Skylark
Engine – 3.0L (181 cid) V6 EFI
Engine Code – VIN E

ECM TROUBLE CODES

Code	Explanation
12	No reference pulses to the ECM. This code is not stored in memory and will only flash while the fault is present. Normal code with ignition ON engine not running
13	Oxygen sensor circuit – the engine must run up to 5 minutes at part throttle, under road load, before this code will set
14	Shorted coolant sensor circuit – the engine must run up to 2 minutes before this code will set
15	Open coolant sensor circuit – the engine must run up to 5 minutes before this code will set
21	Throttle position sensor circuit – the engine must run up to 25 seconds, at specified curb idle speed, before this code will set
23	Open or grounded M/C solenoid circuit
24	Vehicle Speed Sensor (VSS) circuit – the car must operate up to 5 minutes at road speed before this code will set
32	Barometric Pressure Sensor (BARO) circuit low
34	Manifold Absolute Pressure (MAP) or vacuum sensor circuit. The engine must run up to 5 minutes, at specified curb idle speed, before this code will set
35	Idle Speed Control (ISC) switch circuit shorted. (Over ½ throttle for over two seconds)
41	No distributor reference pulses at specified engine vacuum. This code will store
42	Electronic Spark Timing (EST) bypass circuit grounded or open
44	Lean oxygen sensor indication – the engine must run up to 5 minutes, in closed loop, at part throttle before this code will set
44 & 45	(At same time) – Faulty oxygen sensor circuit
45	Rich system indication – the engine must run up to 5 minutes, in closed loop, at part throttle before this code will set

Year – 1982
Model – Skyhawk
Engine – 1.8L (111 cid) 4 cyl
Engine Code – VIN G

ECM TROUBLE CODES

Code	Explanation
12	No reference pulses to the ECM. This code is not stored in memory and will only flash while the fault is present. Normal code with ignition ON engine not running
13	Oxygen sensor circuit – the engine must run up to 5 minutes at part throttle, under road load, before this code will set
14	Shorted coolant sensor circuit – the engine must run up to 2 minutes before this code will set
15	Open coolant sensor circuit – the engine must run up to 5 minutes before this code will set
21	Throttle position sensor circuit – the engine must run up to 25 seconds, at specified curb idle speed, before this code will set
23	Open or grounded M/C solenoid circuit
24	Vehicle Speed Sensor (VSS) circuit – the car must operate up to 5 minutes at road speed before this code will set
32	Barometric Pressure Sensor (BARO) circuit low
34	Manifold Absolute Pressure (MAP) or vacuum sensor circuit. The engine must run up to 5 minutes, at specified curb idle speed, before this code will set
35	Idle Speed Control (ISC) switch circuit shorted. (Over ½ throttle for over two seconds)
41	No distributor reference pulses at specified engine vacuum. This code will store
42	Electronic Spark Timing (EST) bypass circuit grounded or open
43	ESC retard signal for too long; causes a retard in EST signal
44	Lean oxygen sensor indication – the engine must run up to 5 minutes, in closed loop, at part throttle before this code will set
44 & 45	(At same time) – Faulty oxygen sensor circuit
45	Rich system indication – the engine must run up to 5 minutes, in closed loop, at part throttle before this code will set
51	Faulty calibration unit (PROM) or installation. It takes up to 30 seconds before this code will set
54	Shorted M/C solenoid circuit and/or faulty ECM
55	Grounded V ref (term. 21), faulty oxygen sensor or ECM

Year – 1982
Model – Skyhawk
Engine – 1.8L (111 cid) TBI 4 cyl
Engine Code – VIN O

ECM TROUBLE CODES

Code	Explanation
12	No reference pulses to the ECM. This code is not stored in memory and will only flash while the fault is present. Normal code with ignition ON engine not running
13	Oxygen sensor circuit – the engine must run up to 5 minutes at part throttle, under road load, before this code will set
14	Shorted coolant sensor circuit – the engine must run up to 2 minutes before this code will set
15	Open coolant sensor circuit – the engine must run up to 5 minutes before this code will set
21	Throttle position sensor circuit – the engine must run up to 25 seconds, at specified curb idle speed, before this code will set
23	Open or grounded M/C solenoid circuit
24	Vehicle Speed Sensor (VSS) circuit – the car must operate up to 5 minutes at road speed before this code will set
32	Barometric Pressure Sensor (BARO) circuit low
34	Manifold Absolute Pressure (MAP) or vacuum sensor circuit. The engine must run up to 5 minutes, at specified curb idle speed, before this code will set
35	Idle Speed Control (ISC) switch circuit shorted. (Over ½ throttle for over two seconds)
41	No distributor reference pulses at specified engine vacuum. This code will store
42	Electronic Spark Timing (EST) bypass circuit grounded or open
43	ESC retard signal for too long; causes a retard in EST signal
44	Lean oxygen sensor indication – the engine must run up to 5 minutes, in closed loop, at part throttle before this code will set
44 & 45	(At same time) – Faulty oxygen sensor circuit
45	Rich system indication – the engine must run up to 5 minutes, in closed loop, at part throttle before this code will set
51	Faulty calibration unit (PROM) or installation. It takes up to 30 seconds before this code will set
54	Shorted M/C solenoid circuit and/or faulty ECM
55	Grounded V ref (term. 21), faulty oxygen sensor or ECM

Year — 1982
Model — Skyhawk
Engine — 2.0L (121 cid) 4 cyl
Engine Code — VIN B

ECM TROUBLE CODES

Code	Explanation
12	No reference pulses to the ECM. This code is not stored in memory and will only flash while the fault is present. Normal code with ignition ON engine not running
13	Oxygen sensor circuit — the engine must run up to 5 minutes at part throttle, under road load, before this code will set
14	Shorted coolant sensor circuit — the engine must run up to 2 minutes before this code will set
15	Open coolant sensor circuit — the engine must run up to 5 minutes before this code will set
21	Throttle position sensor circuit — the engine must run up to 25 seconds, at specified curb idle speed, before this code will set
23	Open or grounded M/C solenoid circuit
24	Vehicle Speed Sensor (VSS) circuit — the car must operate up to 5 minutes at road speed before this code will set
32	Barometric Pressure Sensor (BARO) circuit low
34	Manifold Absolute Pressure (MAP) or vacuum sensor circuit. The engine must run up to 5 minutes, at specified curb idle speed, before this code will set
35	Idle Speed Control (ISC) switch circuit shorted. (Over ½ throttle for over two seconds)
41	No distributor reference pulses at specified engine vacuum. This code will store
42	Electronic Spark Timing (EST) bypass circuit grounded or open
43	ESC retard signal for too long; causes a retard in EST signal
44	Lean oxygen sensor indication — the engine must run up to 5 minutes, in closed loop, at part throttle before this code will set
44 & 45	(At same time) — Faulty oxygen sensor circuit
45	Rich system indication — the engine must run up to 5 minutes, in closed loop, at part throttle before this code will set
51	Faulty calibration unit (PROM) or installation. It takes up to 30 seconds before this code will set
54	Shorted M/C solenoid circuit and/or faulty ECM
55	Grounded V ref (term. 21), faulty oxygen sensor or ECM

Year — 1982
Model — Riviera T-Type
Engine — 3.9L (231 cid) Turbo V6
Engine Code — VIN 3

ECM TROUBLE CODES

Code	Explanation
12	No reference pulses to the ECM. This code is not stored in memory and will only flash while the fault is present. Normal code with ignition ON engine not running
13	Oxygen sensor circuit — the engine must run up to 5 minutes at part throttle, under road load, before this code will set
14	Shorted coolant sensor circuit — the engine must run up to 2 minutes before this code will set
15	Open coolant sensor circuit — the engine must run up to 5 minutes before this code will set
21	Throttle position sensor circuit — the engine must run up to 25 seconds, at specified curb idle speed, before this code will set
23	Open or grounded M/C solenoid circuit
24	Vehicle Speed Sensor (VSS) circuit — the car must operate up to 5 minutes at road speed before this code will set
32	Barometric Pressure Sensor (BARO) circuit low
34	Manifold Absolute Pressure (MAP) or vacuum sensor circuit. The engine must run up to 5 minutes, at specified curb idle speed, before this code will set
35	Idle Speed Control (ISC) switch circuit shorted. (Over ½ throttle for over two seconds)
41	No distributor reference pulses at specified engine vacuum. This code will store
42	Electronic Spark Timing (EST) bypass circuit grounded or open
43	ESC retard signal for too long; causes a retard in EST signal
44	Lean oxygen sensor indication — the engine must run up to 5 minutes, in closed loop, at part throttle before this code will set
44 & 45	(At same time) — Faulty oxygen sensor circuit
45	Rich system indication — the engine must run up to 5 minutes, in closed loop, at part throttle before this code will set
51	Faulty calibration unit (PROM) or installation. It takes up to 30 seconds before this code will set
54	Shorted M/C solenoid circuit and/or faulty ECM
55	Grounded V ref (term. 21), faulty oxygen sensor or ECM

Year – 1982
Model – Riviera
Engine – 4.1L (252 cid) V6
Engine Code – VIN 4

ECM TROUBLE CODES

Code	Explanation
12	No reference pulses to the ECM. This code is not stored in memory and will only flash while the fault is present. Normal code with ignition ON engine not running
13	Oxygen sensor circuit—the engine must run up to 5 minutes at part throttle, under road load, before this code will set
14	Shorted coolant sensor circuit—the engine must run up to 2 minutes before this code will set
15	Open coolant sensor circuit—the engine must run up to 5 minutes before this code will set
21	Throttle position sensor circuit—the engine must run up to 25 seconds, at specified curb idle speed, before this code will set
23	Open or grounded M/C solenoid circuit
24	Vehicle Speed Sensor (VSS) circuit—the car must operate up to 5 minutes at road speed before this code will set
32	Barometric Pressure Sensor (BARO) circuit low
34	Manifold Absolute Pressure (MAP) or vacuum sensor circuit. The engine must run up to 5 minutes, at specified curb idle speed, before this code will set
35	Idle Speed Control (ISC) switch circuit shorted. (Over ½ throttle for over two seconds)
41	No distributor reference pulses at specified engine vacuum. This code will store
42	Electronic Spark Timing (EST) bypass circuit grounded or open
43	ESC retard signal for too long; causes a retard in EST signal
44	Lean oxygen sensor indication—the engine must run up to 5 minutes, in closed loop, at part throttle before this code will set
44 & 45	(At same time)—Faulty oxygen sensor circuit
45	Rich system indication—the engine must run up to 5 minutes, in closed loop, at part throttle before this code will set
51	Faulty calibration unit (PROM) or installation. It takes up to 30 seconds before this code will set
54	Shorted M/C solenoid circuit and/or faulty ECM
55	Grounded V ref (term. 21), faulty oxygen sensor or ECM

Year — 1982
Model — Riviera
Engine — 5.0L (307 cid) V8
Engine Code — VIN Y

ECM TROUBLE CODES

Code	Explanation
12	No reference pulses to the ECM. This code is not stored in memory and will only flash while the fault is present. Normal code with ignition ON engine not running
13	Oxygen sensor circuit — the engine must run up to 5 minutes at part throttle, under road load, before this code will set
14	Shorted coolant sensor circuit — the engine must run up to 2 minutes before this code will set
15	Open coolant sensor circuit — the engine must run up to 5 minutes before this code will set
21	Throttle position sensor circuit — the engine must run up to 25 seconds, at specified curb idle speed, before this code will set
23	Open or grounded M/C solenoid circuit
24	Vehicle Speed Sensor (VSS) circuit — the car must operate up to 5 minutes at road speed before this code will set
32	Barometric Pressure Sensor (BARO) circuit low
34	Manifold Absolute Pressure (MAP) or vacuum sensor circuit. The engine must run up to 5 minutes, at specified curb idle speed, before this code will set
35	Idle Speed Control (ISC) switch circuit shorted. (Over ½ throttle for over two seconds)
41	No distributor reference pulses at specified engine vacuum. This code will store
42	Electronic Spark Timing (EST) bypass circuit grounded or open
43	ESC retard signal for too long; causes a retard in EST signal
44	Lean oxygen sensor indication — the engine must run up to 5 minutes, in closed loop, at part throttle before this code will set
44 & 45	(At same time) — Faulty oxygen sensor circuit
45	Rich system indication — the engine must run up to 5 minutes, in closed loop, at part throttle before this code will set
51	Faulty calibration unit (PROM) or installation. It takes up to 30 seconds before this code will set
54	Shorted M/C solenoid circuit and/or faulty ECM
55	Grounded V ref (term. 21), faulty oxygen sensor or ECM

Year – 1983
Model – LeSabre
Engine – 3.8L (231 cid) V6
Engine Code – VIN A

ECM TROUBLE CODES

Code	Explanation
12	No distributor reference pulses to the ECM. This code is not stored in memory and will only flash while the fault is present. Normal code with ignition ON, engine not running
13	Oxygen sensor circuit—the engine must run up to 5 minutes at part throttle, under road load, before this code will set
14	Shorted coolant sensor circuit—the engine must run up to 5 minutes before this code will set
15	Open coolant sensor circuit—the engine must run up to 5 minutes before this code will set
21	Throttle position sensor circuit—the engine must run up to 25 seconds, at specified curb idle speed, before this code will set
23	M/C solenoid circuit open or grounded
24	Vehicle Speed Sensor (VSS) circuit—the vehicle must operate up to 5 minutes at road speed, before this code will set
32	Barometric Pressure Sensor (BARO) circuit low
34	Vacuum sensor or Manifold Absolute Pressure (MAP) circuit—the engine must run up to 5 minutes, at specified curb idle, before this code will set
35	Idle Speed Control (ISC) switch circuit shorted. (Over 50% throttle for over 2 seconds)
41	No distributor reference pulses to the ECM at specified engine vacuum. This code will store in memory
42	Electronic Spark Timing (EST) bypass circuit or EST circuit grounded or open
43	Electronic Spark Control (ESC) retard signal for too long a time; causes retard in EST signal
44	Lean exhaust indication—the engine must run up to 5 minutes, in closed loop and at part throttle, before this code will set.
45	Rich exhaust indication—the engine must run up to 5 minutes, in closed loop and at part throttle, before this code will set
51	Faulty or improperly installed calibration unit (PROM). It takes up to 30 seconds before this code will set
54	Shorted M/C solenoid circuit and/or faulty ECM
55	Grounded V ref (terminal 21), high voltage on oxygen sensor circuit or ECM

Year — 1983
Model — LeSabre
Engine — 4.1L (252 cid) V6
Engine Code — VIN 4

ECM TROUBLE CODES

Code	Explanation
12	No distributor reference pulses to the ECM. This code is not stored in memory and will only flash while the fault is present. Normal code with ignition ON, engine not running
13	Oxygen sensor circuit — the engine must run up to 5 minutes at part throttle, under road load, before this code will set
14	Shorted coolant sensor circuit — the engine must run up to 5 minutes before this code will set
15	Open coolant sensor circuit — the engine must run up to 5 minutes before this code will set
21	Throttle position sensor circuit — the engine must run up to 25 seconds, at specified curb idle speed, before this code will set
23	M/C solenoid circuit open or grounded
24	Vehicle Speed Sensor (VSS) circuit — the vehicle must operate up to 5 minutes at road speed, before this code will set
32	Barometric Pressure Sensor (BARO) circuit low
34	Vacuum sensor or Manifold Absolute Pressure (MAP) circuit — the engine must run up to 5 minutes, at specified curb idle, before this code will set
35	Idle Speed Control (ISC) switch circuit shorted. (Over 50% throttle for over 2 seconds)
41	No distributor reference pulses to the ECM at specified engine vacuum. This code will store in memory
42	Electronic Spark Timing (EST) bypass circuit or EST circuit grounded or open
43	Electronic Spark Control (ESC) retard signal for too long a time; causes retard in EST signal
44	Lean exhaust indication — the engine must run up to 5 minutes, in closed loop and at part throttle, before this code will set.
45	Rich exhaust indication — the engine must run up to 5 minutes, in closed loop and at part throttle, before this code will set
51	Faulty or improperly installed calibration unit (PROM). It takes up to 30 seconds before this code will set
54	Shorted M/C solenoid circuit and/or faulty ECM
55	Grounded V ref (terminal 21), high voltage on oxygen sensor circuit or ECM

Year – 1983
Model – LeSabre
Engine – 5.0L (307 cid) V8
Engine Code – VIN Y

ECM TROUBLE CODES

Code	Explanation
12	No distributor reference pulses to the ECM. This code is not stored in memory and will only flash while the fault is present. Normal code with ignition ON, engine not running
13	Oxygen sensor circuit—the engine must run up to 5 minutes at part throttle, under road load, before this code will set
14	Shorted coolant sensor circuit—the engine must run up to 5 minutes before this code will set
15	Open coolant sensor circuit—the engine must run up to 5 minutes before this code will set
21	Throttle position sensor circuit—the engine must run up to 25 seconds, at specified curb idle speed, before this code will set
23	M/C solenoid circuit open or grounded
24	Vehicle Speed Sensor (VSS) circuit—the vehicle must operate up to 5 minutes at road speed, before this code will set
32	Barometric Pressure Sensor (BARO) circuit low
34	Vacuum sensor or Manifold Absolute Pressure (MAP) circuit—the engine must run up to 5 minutes, at specified curb idle, before this code will set
35	Idle Speed Control (ISC) switch circuit shorted. (Over 50% throttle for over 2 seconds)
41	No distributor reference pulses to the ECM at specified engine vacuum. This code will store in memory
42	Electronic Spark Timing (EST) bypass circuit or EST circuit grounded or open
43	Electronic Spark Control (ESC) retard signal for too long a time; causes retard in EST signal
44	Lean exhaust indication—the engine must run up to 5 minutes, in closed loop and at part throttle, before this code will set.
45	Rich exhaust indication—the engine must run up to 5 minutes, in closed loop and at part throttle, before this code will set
51	Faulty or improperly installed calibration unit (PROM). It takes up to 30 seconds before this code will set
54	Shorted M/C solenoid circuit and/or faulty ECM
55	Grounded V ref (terminal 21), high voltage on oxygen sensor circuit or ECM

Year – 1983
Model – LeSabre Estate Wagon
Engine – 5.0L (307 cid) V8
Engine Code – VIN Y

ECM TROUBLE CODES

Code	Explanation
12	No distributor reference pulses to the ECM. This code is not stored in memory and will only flash while the fault is present. Normal code with ignition ON, engine not running
13	Oxygen sensor circuit – the engine must run up to 5 minutes at part throttle, under road load, before this code will set
14	Shorted coolant sensor circuit – the engine must run up to 5 minutes before this code will set
15	Open coolant sensor circuit – the engine must run up to 5 minutes before this code will set
21	Throttle position sensor circuit – the engine must run up to 25 seconds, at specified curb idle speed, before this code will set
23	M/C solenoid circuit open or grounded
24	Vehicle Speed Sensor (VSS) circuit – the vehicle must operate up to 5 minutes at road speed, before this code will set
32	Barometric Pressure Sensor (BARO) circuit low
34	Vacuum sensor or Manifold Absolute Pressure (MAP) circuit – the engine must run up to 5 minutes, at specified curb idle, before this code will set
35	Idle Speed Control (ISC) switch circuit shorted. (Over 50% throttle for over 2 seconds)
41	No distributor reference pulses to the ECM at specified engine vacuum. This code will store in memory
42	Electronic Spark Timing (EST) bypass circuit or EST circuit grounded or open
43	Electronic Spark Control (ESC) retard signal for too long a time; causes retard in EST signal
44	Lean exhaust indication – the engine must run up to 5 minutes, in closed loop and at part throttle, before this code will set.
45	Rich exhaust indication – the engine must run up to 5 minutes, in closed loop and at part throttle, before this code will set
51	Faulty or improperly installed calibration unit (PROM). It takes up to 30 seconds before this code will set
54	Shorted M/C solenoid circuit and/or faulty ECM
55	Grounded V ref (terminal 21), high voltage on oxygen sensor circuit or ECM

Year – 1983
Model – Electra Limited
Engine – 4.1L (252 cid) V6
Engine Code – VIN 4

ECM TROUBLE CODES

Code	Explanation
12	No distributor reference pulses to the ECM. This code is not stored in memory and will only flash while the fault is present. Normal code with ignition ON, engine not running
13	Oxygen sensor circuit – the engine must run up to 5 minutes at part throttle, under road load, before this code will set
14	Shorted coolant sensor circuit – the engine must run up to 5 minutes before this code will set
15	Open coolant sensor circuit – the engine must run up to 5 minutes before this code will set
21	Throttle position sensor circuit – the engine must run up to 25 seconds, at specified curb idle speed, before this code will set
23	M/C solenoid circuit open or grounded
24	Vehicle Speed Sensor (VSS) circuit – the vehicle must operate up to 5 minutes at road speed, before this code will set
32	Barometric Pressure Sensor (BARO) circuit low
34	Vacuum sensor or Manifold Absolute Pressure (MAP) circuit – the engine must run up to 5 minutes, at specified curb idle, before this code will set
35	Idle Speed Control (ISC) switch circuit shorted. (Over 50% throttle for over 2 seconds)
41	No distributor reference pulses to the ECM at specified engine vacuum. This code will store in memory
42	Electronic Spark Timing (EST) bypass circuit or EST circuit grounded or open
43	Electronic Spark Control (ESC) retard signal for too long a time; causes retard in EST signal
44	Lean exhaust indication – the engine must run up to 5 minutes, in closed loop and at part throttle, before this code will set.
45	Rich exhaust indication – the engine must run up to 5 minutes, in closed loop and at part throttle, before this code will set
51	Faulty or improperly installed calibration unit (PROM). It takes up to 30 seconds before this code will set
54	Shorted M/C solenoid circuit and/or faulty ECM
55	Grounded V ref (terminal 21), high voltage on oxygen sensor circuit or ECM

Year – 1983
Model – Electra Limited
Engine – 5.0L (307 cid) V8
Engine Code – VIN Y

ECM TROUBLE CODES

Code	Explanation
12	No distributor reference pulses to the ECM. This code is not stored in memory and will only flash while the fault is present. Normal code with ignition ON, engine not running
13	Oxygen sensor circuit – the engine must run up to 5 minutes at part throttle, under road load, before this code will set
14	Shorted coolant sensor circuit – the engine must run up to 5 minutes before this code will set
15	Open coolant sensor circuit – the engine must run up to 5 minutes before this code will set
21	Throttle position sensor circuit – the engine must run up to 25 seconds, at specified curb idle speed, before this code will set
23	M/C solenoid circuit open or grounded
24	Vehicle Speed Sensor (VSS) circuit – the vehicle must operate up to 5 minutes at road speed, before this code will set
32	Barometric Pressure Sensor (BARO) circuit low
34	Vacuum sensor or Manifold Absolute Pressure (MAP) circuit – the engine must run up to 5 minutes, at specified curb idle, before this code will set
35	Idle Speed Control (ISC) switch circuit shorted. (Over 50% throttle for over 2 seconds)
41	No distributor reference pulses to the ECM at specified engine vacuum. This code will store in memory
42	Electronic Spark Timing (EST) bypass circuit or EST circuit grounded or open
43	Electronic Spark Control (ESC) retard signal for too long a time; causes retard in EST signal
44	Lean exhaust indication – the engine must run up to 5 minutes, in closed loop and at part throttle, before this code will set.
45	Rich exhaust indication – the engine must run up to 5 minutes, in closed loop and at part throttle, before this code will set
51	Faulty or improperly installed calibration unit (PROM). It takes up to 30 seconds before this code will set
54	Shorted M/C solenoid circuit and/or faulty ECM
55	Grounded V ref (terminal 21), high voltage on oxygen sensor circuit or ECM

Year – 1983
Model – Electra Park Avenue
Engine – 4.1L (252 cid) V6
Engine Code – VIN 4

ECM TROUBLE CODES

Code	Explanation
12	No distributor reference pulses to the ECM. This code is not stored in memory and will only flash while the fault is present. Normal code with ignition ON, engine not running
13	Oxygen sensor circuit – the engine must run up to 5 minutes at part throttle, under road load, before this code will set
14	Shorted coolant sensor circuit – the engine must run up to 5 minutes before this code will set
15	Open coolant sensor circuit – the engine must run up to 5 minutes before this code will set
21	Throttle position sensor circuit – the engine must run up to 25 seconds, at specified curb idle speed, before this code will set
23	M/C solenoid circuit open or grounded
24	Vehicle Speed Sensor (VSS) circuit – the vehicle must operate up to 5 minutes at road speed, before this code will set
32	Barometric Pressure Sensor (BARO) circuit low
34	Vacuum sensor or Manifold Absolute Pressure (MAP) circuit – the engine must run up to 5 minutes, at specified curb idle, before this code will set
35	Idle Speed Control (ISC) switch circuit shorted. (Over 50% throttle for over 2 seconds)
41	No distributor reference pulses to the ECM at specified engine vacuum. This code will store in memory
42	Electronic Spark Timing (EST) bypass circuit or EST circuit grounded or open
43	Electronic Spark Control (ESC) retard signal for too long a time; causes retard in EST signal
44	Lean exhaust indication – the engine must run up to 5 minutes, in closed loop and at part throttle, before this code will set.
45	Rich exhaust indication – the engine must run up to 5 minutes, in closed loop and at part throttle, before this code will set
51	Faulty or improperly installed calibration unit (PROM). It takes up to 30 seconds before this code will set
54	Shorted M/C solenoid circuit and/or faulty ECM
55	Grounded V ref (terminal 21), high voltage on oxygen sensor circuit or ECM

Year — 1983
Model — Electra Estate Wagon
Engine — 5.0L (307 cid) V8
Engine Code — VIN Y

ECM TROUBLE CODES

Code	Explanation
12	No distributor reference pulses to the ECM. This code is not stored in memory and will only flash while the fault is present. Normal code with ignition ON, engine not running
13	Oxygen sensor circuit — the engine must run up to 5 minutes at part throttle, under road load, before this code will set
14	Shorted coolant sensor circuit — the engine must run up to 5 minutes before this code will set
15	Open coolant sensor circuit — the engine must run up to 5 minutes before this code will set
21	Throttle position sensor circuit — the engine must run up to 25 seconds, at specified curb idle speed, before this code will set
23	M/C solenoid circuit open or grounded
24	Vehicle Speed Sensor (VSS) circuit — the vehicle must operate up to 5 minutes at road speed, before this code will set
32	Barometric Pressure Sensor (BARO) circuit low
34	Vacuum sensor or Manifold Absolute Pressure (MAP) circuit — the engine must run up to 5 minutes, at specified curb idle, before this code will set
35	Idle Speed Control (ISC) switch circuit shorted. (Over 50% throttle for over 2 seconds)
41	No distributor reference pulses to the ECM at specified engine vacuum. This code will store in memory
42	Electronic Spark Timing (EST) bypass circuit or EST circuit grounded or open
43	Electronic Spark Control (ESC) retard signal for too long a time; causes retard in EST signal
44	Lean exhaust indication — the engine must run up to 5 minutes, in closed loop and at part throttle, before this code will set.
45	Rich exhaust indication — the engine must run up to 5 minutes, in closed loop and at part throttle, before this code will set
51	Faulty or improperly installed calibration unit (PROM). It takes up to 30 seconds before this code will set
54	Shorted M/C solenoid circuit and/or faulty ECM
55	Grounded V ref (terminal 21), high voltage on oxygen sensor circuit or ECM

Year — 1983
Model — Electra Park Avenue
Engine — 5.0L (307 cid) V8
Engine Code — VIN Y

ECM TROUBLE CODES

Code	Explanation
12	No distributor reference pulses to the ECM. This code is not stored in memory and will only flash while the fault is present. Normal code with ignition ON, engine not running
13	Oxygen sensor circuit — the engine must run up to 5 minutes at part throttle, under road load, before this code will set
14	Shorted coolant sensor circuit — the engine must run up to 5 minutes before this code will set
15	Open coolant sensor circuit — the engine must run up to 5 minutes before this code will set
21	Throttle position sensor circuit — the engine must run up to 25 seconds, at specified curb idle speed, before this code will set
23	M/C solenoid circuit open or grounded
24	Vehicle Speed Sensor (VSS) circuit — the vehicle must operate up to 5 minutes at road speed, before this code will set
32	Barometric Pressure Sensor (BARO) circuit low
34	Vacuum sensor or Manifold Absolute Pressure (MAP) circuit — the engine must run up to 5 minutes, at specified curb idle, before this code will set
35	Idle Speed Control (ISC) switch circuit shorted. (Over 50% throttle for over 2 seconds)
41	No distributor reference pulses to the ECM at specified engine vacuum. This code will store in memory
42	Electronic Spark Timing (EST) bypass circuit or EST circuit grounded or open
43	Electronic Spark Control (ESC) retard signal for too long a time; causes retard in EST signal
44	Lean exhaust indication — the engine must run up to 5 minutes, in closed loop and at part throttle, before this code will set.
45	Rich exhaust indication — the engine must run up to 5 minutes, in closed loop and at part throttle, before this code will set
51	Faulty or improperly installed calibration unit (PROM). It takes up to 30 seconds before this code will set
54	Shorted M/C solenoid circuit and/or faulty ECM
55	Grounded V ref (terminal 21), high voltage on oxygen sensor circuit or ECM

Year – 1983
Model – Century
Engine – 2.5L (151 cid) TBI 4 cyl
Engine Code – VIN R

ECM TROUBLE CODES

Code	Explanation
12	No distributor reference pulses to the ECM. This code is not stored in memory and will only flash while the fault is present. Normal code with ignition ON, engine not running
13	Oxygen sensor circuit – the engine must run up to 5 minutes at part throttle, under road load, before this code will set
14	Shorted coolant sensor circuit – the engine must run up to 5 minutes before this code will set
15	Open coolant sensor circuit – the engine must run up to 5 minutes before this code will set
21	Throttle position sensor circuit – the engine must run up to 25 seconds, at specified curb idle speed, before this code will set
23	M/C solenoid circuit open or grounded
24	Vehicle Speed Sensor (VSS) circuit – the vehicle must operate up to 5 minutes at road speed, before this code will set
32	Barometric Pressure Sensor (BARO) circuit low
34	Vacuum sensor or Manifold Absolute Pressure (MAP) circuit – the engine must run up to 5 minutes, at specified curb idle, before this code will set
35	Idle Speed Control (ISC) switch circuit shorted. (Over 50% throttle for over 2 seconds)
41	No distributor reference pulses to the ECM at specified engine vacuum. This code will store in memory
42	Electronic Spark Timing (EST) bypass circuit or EST circuit grounded or open
43	Electronic Spark Control (ESC) retard signal for too long a time; causes retard in EST signal
44	Lean exhaust indication – the engine must run up to 5 minutes, in closed loop and at part throttle, before this code will set.
45	Rich exhaust indication – the engine must run up to 5 minutes, in closed loop and at part throttle, before this code will set
51	Faulty or improperly installed calibration unit (PROM). It takes up to 30 seconds before this code will set
54	Shorted M/C solenoid circuit and/or faulty ECM
55	Grounded V ref (terminal 21), high voltage on oxygen sensor circuit or ECM

Year – 1983
Model – Century
Engine – 3.0L (181 cid) V6
Engine Code – VIN E

ECM TROUBLE CODES

Code	Explanation
12	No distributor reference pulses to the ECM. This code is not stored in memory and will only flash while the fault is present. Normal code with ignition ON, engine not running
13	Oxygen sensor circuit – the engine must run up to 5 minutes at part throttle, under road load, before this code will set
14	Shorted coolant sensor circuit – the engine must run up to 5 minutes before this code will set
15	Open coolant sensor circuit – the engine must run up to 5 minutes before this code will set
21	Throttle position sensor circuit – the engine must run up to 25 seconds, at specified curb idle speed, before this code will set
23	M/C solenoid circuit open or grounded
24	Vehicle Speed Sensor (VSS) circuit – the vehicle must operate up to 5 minutes at road speed, before this code will set
32	Barometric Pressure Sensor (BARO) circuit low
34	Vacuum sensor or Manifold Absolute Pressure (MAP) circuit – the engine must run up to 5 minutes, at specified curb idle, before this code will set
35	Idle Speed Control (ISC) switch circuit shorted. (Over 50% throttle for over 2 seconds)
41	No distributor reference pulses to the ECM at specified engine vacuum. This code will store in memory
42	Electronic Spark Timing (EST) bypass circuit or EST circuit grounded or open
43	Electronic Spark Control (ESC) retard signal for too long a time; causes retard in EST signal
44	Lean exhaust indication – the engine must run up to 5 minutes, in closed loop and at part throttle, before this code will set.
45	Rich exhaust indication – the engine must run up to 5 minutes, in closed loop and at part throttle, before this code will set
51	Faulty or improperly installed calibration unit (PROM). It takes up to 30 seconds before this code will set
54	Shorted M/C solenoid circuit and/or faulty ECM
55	Grounded V ref (terminal 21), high voltage on oxygen sensor circuit or ECM

Year – 1983
Model – Regal
Engine – 3.8L (231 cid) V6
Engine Code – VIN A

ECM TROUBLE CODES

Code	Explanation
12	No distributor reference pulses to the ECM. This code is not stored in memory and will only flash while the fault is present. Normal code with ignition ON, engine not running
13	Oxygen sensor circuit – the engine must run up to 5 minutes at part throttle, under road load, before this code will set
14	Shorted coolant sensor circuit – the engine must run up to 5 minutes before this code will set
15	Open coolant sensor circuit – the engine must run up to 5 minutes before this code will set
21	Throttle position sensor circuit – the engine must run up to 25 seconds, at specified curb idle speed, before this code will set
23	M/C solenoid circuit open or grounded
24	Vehicle Speed Sensor (VSS) circuit – the vehicle must operate up to 5 minutes at road speed, before this code will set
32	Barometric Pressure Sensor (BARO) circuit low
34	Vacuum sensor or Manifold Absolute Pressure (MAP) circuit – the engine must run up to 5 minutes, at specified curb idle, before this code will set
35	Idle Speed Control (ISC) switch circuit shorted. (Over 50% throttle for over 2 seconds)
41	No distributor reference pulses to the ECM at specified engine vacuum. This code will store in memory
42	Electronic Spark Timing (EST) bypass circuit or EST circuit grounded or open
43	Electronic Spark Control (ESC) retard signal for too long a time; causes retard in EST signal
44	Lean exhaust indication – the engine must run up to 5 minutes, in closed loop and at part throttle, before this code will set.
45	Rich exhaust indication – the engine must run up to 5 minutes, in closed loop and at part throttle, before this code will set
51	Faulty or improperly installed calibration unit (PROM). It takes up to 30 seconds before this code will set
54	Shorted M/C solenoid circuit and/or faulty ECM
55	Grounded V ref (terminal 21), high voltage on oxygen sensor circuit or ECM

Year – 1983
Model – Regal
Engine – 3.8L (231 cid) Turbo V6
Engine Code – VIN 8

ECM TROUBLE CODES

Code	Explanation
12	No distributor reference pulses to the ECM. This code is not stored in memory and will only flash while the fault is present. Normal code with ignition ON, engine not running
13	Oxygen sensor circuit – the engine must run up to 5 minutes at part throttle, under road load, before this code will set
14	Shorted coolant sensor circuit – the engine must run up to 5 minutes before this code will set
15	Open coolant sensor circuit – the engine must run up to 5 minutes before this code will set
21	Throttle position sensor circuit – the engine must run up to 25 seconds, at specified curb idle speed, before this code will set
23	M/C solenoid circuit open or grounded
24	Vehicle Speed Sensor (VSS) circuit – the vehicle must operate up to 5 minutes at road speed, before this code will set
32	Barometric Pressure Sensor (BARO) circuit low
34	Vacuum sensor or Manifold Absolute Pressure (MAP) circuit – the engine must run up to 5 minutes, at specified curb idle, before this code will set
35	Idle Speed Control (ISC) switch circuit shorted. (Over 50% throttle for over 2 seconds)
41	No distributor reference pulses to the ECM at specified engine vacuum. This code will store in memory
42	Electronic Spark Timing (EST) bypass circuit or EST circuit grounded or open
43	Electronic Spark Control (ESC) retard signal for too long a time; causes retard in EST signal
44	Lean exhaust indication – the engine must run up to 5 minutes, in closed loop and at part throttle, before this code will set.
45	Rich exhaust indication – the engine must run up to 5 minutes, in closed loop and at part throttle, before this code will set
51	Faulty or improperly installed calibration unit (PROM). It takes up to 30 seconds before this code will set
54	Shorted M/C solenoid circuit and/or faulty ECM
55	Grounded V ref (terminal 21), high voltage on oxygen sensor circuit or ECM

Year — 1983
Model — Regal
Engine — 4.1L (252 cid) V6
Engine Code — VIN 4

ECM TROUBLE CODES

Code	Explanation
12	No distributor reference pulses to the ECM. This code is not stored in memory and will only flash while the fault is present. Normal code with ignition ON, engine not running
13	Oxygen sensor circuit — the engine must run up to 5 minutes at part throttle, under road load, before this code will set
14	Shorted coolant sensor circuit — the engine must run up to 5 minutes before this code will set
15	Open coolant sensor circuit — the engine must run up to 5 minutes before this code will set
21	Throttle position sensor circuit — the engine must run up to 25 seconds, at specified curb idle speed, before this code will set
23	M/C solenoid circuit open or grounded
24	Vehicle Speed Sensor (VSS) circuit — the vehicle must operate up to 5 minutes at road speed, before this code will set
32	Barometric Pressure Sensor (BARO) circuit low
34	Vacuum sensor or Manifold Absolute Pressure (MAP) circuit — the engine must run up to 5 minutes, at specified curb idle, before this code will set
35	Idle Speed Control (ISC) switch circuit shorted. (Over 50% throttle for over 2 seconds)
41	No distributor reference pulses to the ECM at specified engine vacuum. This code will store in memory
42	Electronic Spark Timing (EST) bypass circuit or EST circuit grounded or open
43	Electronic Spark Control (ESC) retard signal for too long a time; causes retard in EST signal
44	Lean exhaust indication — the engine must run up to 5 minutes, in closed loop and at part throttle, before this code will set.
45	Rich exhaust indication — the engine must run up to 5 minutes, in closed loop and at part throttle, before this code will set
51	Faulty or improperly installed calibration unit (PROM). It takes up to 30 seconds before this code will set
54	Shorted M/C solenoid circuit and/or faulty ECM
55	Grounded V ref (terminal 21), high voltage on oxygen sensor circuit or ECM

Year – 1983
Model – Skylark
Engine – 2.5L (151 cid) TBI 4 cyl
Engine Code – VIN R

ECM TROUBLE CODES

Code	Explanation
12	No distributor reference pulses to the ECM. This code is not stored in memory and will only flash while the fault is present. Normal code with ignition ON, engine not running
13	Oxygen sensor circuit – the engine must run up to 5 minutes at part throttle, under road load, before this code will set
14	Shorted coolant sensor circuit – the engine must run up to 5 minutes before this code will set
15	Open coolant sensor circuit – the engine must run up to 5 minutes before this code will set
21	Throttle position sensor circuit – the engine must run up to 25 seconds, at specified curb idle speed, before this code will set
23	M/C solenoid circuit open or grounded
24	Vehicle Speed Sensor (VSS) circuit – the vehicle must operate up to 5 minutes at road speed, before this code will set
32	Barometric Pressure Sensor (BARO) circuit low
34	Vacuum sensor or Manifold Absolute Pressure (MAP) circuit – the engine must run up to 5 minutes, at specified curb idle, before this code will set
35	Idle Speed Control (ISC) switch circuit shorted. (Over 50% throttle for over 2 seconds)
41	No distributor reference pulses to the ECM at specified engine vacuum. This code will store in memory
42	Electronic Spark Timing (EST) bypass circuit or EST circuit grounded or open
43	Electronic Spark Control (ESC) retard signal for too long a time; causes retard in EST signal
44	Lean exhaust indication – the engine must run up to 5 minutes, in closed loop and at part throttle, before this code will set.
45	Rich exhaust indication – the engine must run up to 5 minutes, in closed loop and at part throttle, before this code will set
51	Faulty or improperly installed calibration unit (PROM). It takes up to 30 seconds before this code will set
54	Shorted M/C solenoid circuit and/or faulty ECM
55	Grounded V ref (terminal 21), high voltage on oxygen sensor circuit or ECM

Year – 1983
Model – Skylark
Engine – 2.8L (171 cid) V6
Engine Code – VIN X

ECM TROUBLE CODES

Code	Explanation
12	No distributor reference pulses to the ECM. This code is not stored in memory and will only flash while the fault is present. Normal code with ignition ON, engine not running
13	Oxygen sensor circuit – the engine must run up to 5 minutes at part throttle, under road load, before this code will set
14	Shorted coolant sensor circuit – the engine must run up to 5 minutes before this code will set
15	Open coolant sensor circuit – the engine must run up to 5 minutes before this code will set
21	Throttle position sensor circuit – the engine must run up to 25 seconds, at specified curb idle speed, before this code will set
23	M/C solenoid circuit open or grounded
24	Vehicle Speed Sensor (VSS) circuit – the vehicle must operate up to 5 minutes at road speed, before this code will set
32	Barometric Pressure Sensor (BARO) circuit low
34	Vacuum sensor or Manifold Absolute Pressure (MAP) circuit – the engine must run up to 5 minutes, at specified curb idle, before this code will set
35	Idle Speed Control (ISC) switch circuit shorted. (Over 50% throttle for over 2 seconds)
41	No distributor reference pulses to the ECM at specified engine vacuum. This code will store in memory
42	Electronic Spark Timing (EST) bypass circuit or EST circuit grounded or open
43	Electronic Spark Control (ESC) retard signal for too long a time; causes retard in EST signal
44	Lean exhaust indication – the engine must run up to 5 minutes, in closed loop and at part throttle, before this code will set.
45	Rich exhaust indication – the engine must run up to 5 minutes, in closed loop and at part throttle, before this code will set
51	Faulty or improperly installed calibration unit (PROM). It takes up to 30 seconds before this code will set
54	Shorted M/C solenoid circuit and/or faulty ECM
55	Grounded V ref (terminal 21), high voltage on oxygen sensor circuit or ECM

Year – 1983
Model – Skylark
Engine – 2.8L (171 cid) V6
Engine Code – VIN Z

ECM TROUBLE CODES

Code	Explanation
12	No distributor reference pulses to the ECM. This code is not stored in memory and will only flash while the fault is present. Normal code with ignition ON, engine not running
13	Oxygen sensor circuit – the engine must run up to 5 minutes at part throttle, under road load, before this code will set
14	Shorted coolant sensor circuit – the engine must run up to 5 minutes before this code will set
15	Open coolant sensor circuit – the engine must run up to 5 minutes before this code will set
21	Throttle position sensor circuit – the engine must run up to 25 seconds, at specified curb idle speed, before this code will set
23	M/C solenoid circuit open or grounded
24	Vehicle Speed Sensor (VSS) circuit – the vehicle must operate up to 5 minutes at road speed, before this code will set
32	Barometric Pressure Sensor (BARO) circuit low
34	Vacuum sensor or Manifold Absolute Pressure (MAP) circuit – the engine must run up to 5 minutes, at specified curb idle, before this code will set
35	Idle Speed Control (ISC) switch circuit shorted. (Over 50% throttle for over 2 seconds)
41	No distributor reference pulses to the ECM at specified engine vacuum. This code will store in memory
42	Electronic Spark Timing (EST) bypass circuit or EST circuit grounded or open
43	Electronic Spark Control (ESC) retard signal for too long a time; causes retard in EST signal
44	Lean exhaust indication – the engine must run up to 5 minutes, in closed loop and at part throttle, before this code will set.
45	Rich exhaust indication – the engine must run up to 5 minutes, in closed loop and at part throttle, before this code will set
51	Faulty or improperly installed calibration unit (PROM). It takes up to 30 seconds before this code will set
54	Shorted M/C solenoid circuit and/or faulty ECM
55	Grounded V ref (terminal 21), high voltage on oxygen sensor circuit or ECM

Year – 1983
Model – Skyhawk
Engine – 1.8L (111 cid) TBI 4 cyl
Engine Code – VIN O

ECM TROUBLE CODES

Code	Explanation
12	No distributor reference pulses to the ECM. This code is not stored in memory and will only flash while the fault is present. Normal code with ignition ON, engine not running
13	Oxygen sensor circuit – the engine must run up to 5 minutes at part throttle, under road load, before this code will set
14	Shorted coolant sensor circuit – the engine must run up to 5 minutes before this code will set
15	Open coolant sensor circuit – the engine must run up to 5 minutes before this code will set
21	Throttle position sensor circuit – the engine must run up to 25 seconds, at specified curb idle speed, before this code will set
23	M/C solenoid circuit open or grounded
24	Vehicle Speed Sensor (VSS) circuit – the vehicle must operate up to 5 minutes at road speed, before this code will set
32	Barometric Pressure Sensor (BARO) circuit low
34	Vacuum sensor or Manifold Absolute Pressure (MAP) circuit – the engine must run up to 5 minutes, at specified curb idle, before this code will set
35	Idle Speed Control (ISC) switch circuit shorted. (Over 50% throttle for over 2 seconds)
41	No distributor reference pulses to the ECM at specified engine vacuum. This code will store in memory
42	Electronic Spark Timing (EST) bypass circuit or EST circuit grounded or open
43	Electronic Spark Control (ESC) retard signal for too long a time; causes retard in EST signal
44	Lean exhaust indication – the engine must run up to 5 minutes, in closed loop and at part throttle, before this code will set.
45	Rich exhaust indication – the engine must run up to 5 minutes, in closed loop and at part throttle, before this code will set
51	Faulty or improperly installed calibration unit (PROM). It takes up to 30 seconds before this code will set
54	Shorted M/C solenoid circuit and/or faulty ECM
55	Grounded V ref (terminal 21), high voltage on oxygen sensor circuit or ECM

Year – 1983
Model – Skyhawk
Engine – 2.0L (121 cid) TBI 4 cyl
Engine Code – VIN P

ECM TROUBLE CODES

Code	Explanation
12	No distributor reference pulses to the ECM. This code is not stored in memory and will only flash while the fault is present. Normal code with ignition ON, engine not running
13	Oxygen sensor circuit—the engine must run up to 5 minutes at part throttle, under road load, before this code will set
14	Shorted coolant sensor circuit—the engine must run up to 5 minutes before this code will set
15	Open coolant sensor circuit—the engine must run up to 5 minutes before this code will set
21	Throttle position sensor circuit—the engine must run up to 25 seconds, at specified curb idle speed, before this code will set
23	M/C solenoid circuit open or grounded
24	Vehicle Speed Sensor (VSS) circuit—the vehicle must operate up to 5 minutes at road speed, before this code will set
32	Barometric Pressure Sensor (BARO) circuit low
34	Vacuum sensor or Manifold Absolute Pressure (MAP) circuit—the engine must run up to 5 minutes, at specified curb idle, before this code will set
35	Idle Speed Control (ISC) switch circuit shorted. (Over 50% throttle for over 2 seconds)
41	No distributor reference pulses to the ECM at specified engine vacuum. This code will store in memory
42	Electronic Spark Timing (EST) bypass circuit or EST circuit grounded or open
43	Electronic Spark Control (ESC) retard signal for too long a time; causes retard in EST signal
44	Lean exhaust indication—the engine must run up to 5 minutes, in closed loop and at part throttle, before this code will set.
45	Rich exhaust indication—the engine must run up to 5 minutes, in closed loop and at part throttle, before this code will set
51	Faulty or improperly installed calibration unit (PROM). It takes up to 30 seconds before this code will set
54	Shorted M/C solenoid circuit and/or faulty ECM
55	Grounded V ref (terminal 21), high voltage on oxygen sensor circuit or ECM

Year – 1983
Model – Riviera T-Type
Engine – 3.8L (231 cid) Turbo V6
Engine Code – VIN 8

ECM TROUBLE CODES

Code	Explanation
12	No distributor reference pulses to the ECM. This code is not stored in memory and will only flash while the fault is present. Normal code with ignition ON, engine not running
13	Oxygen sensor circuit – the engine must run up to 5 minutes at part throttle, under road load, before this code will set
14	Shorted coolant sensor circuit – the engine must run up to 5 minutes before this code will set
15	Open coolant sensor circuit – the engine must run up to 5 minutes before this code will set
21	Throttle position sensor circuit – the engine must run up to 25 seconds, at specified curb idle speed, before this code will set
23	M/C solenoid circuit open or grounded
24	Vehicle Speed Sensor (VSS) circuit – the vehicle must operate up to 5 minutes at road speed, before this code will set
32	Barometric Pressure Sensor (BARO) circuit low
34	Vacuum sensor or Manifold Absolute Pressure (MAP) circuit – the engine must run up to 5 minutes, at specified curb idle, before this code will set
35	Idle Speed Control (ISC) switch circuit shorted. (Over 50% throttle for over 2 seconds)
41	No distributor reference pulses to the ECM at specified engine vacuum. This code will store in memory
42	Electronic Spark Timing (EST) bypass circuit or EST circuit grounded or open
43	Electronic Spark Control (ESC) retard signal for too long a time; causes retard in EST signal
44	Lean exhaust indication – the engine must run up to 5 minutes, in closed loop and at part throttle, before this code will set.
45	Rich exhaust indication – the engine must run up to 5 minutes, in closed loop and at part throttle, before this code will set
51	Faulty or improperly installed calibration unit (PROM). It takes up to 30 seconds before this code will set
54	Shorted M/C solenoid circuit and/or faulty ECM
55	Grounded V ref (terminal 21), high voltage on oxygen sensor circuit or ECM

Year — 1983
Model — Riviera
Engine — 4.1L (252 cid) V6
Engine Code — VIN 4

ECM TROUBLE CODES

Code	Explanation
12	No distributor reference pulses to the ECM. This code is not stored in memory and will only flash while the fault is present. Normal code with ignition ON, engine not running
13	Oxygen sensor circuit — the engine must run up to 5 minutes at part throttle, under road load, before this code will set
14	Shorted coolant sensor circuit — the engine must run up to 5 minutes before this code will set
15	Open coolant sensor circuit — the engine must run up to 5 minutes before this code will set
21	Throttle position sensor circuit — the engine must run up to 25 seconds, at specified curb idle speed, before this code will set
23	M/C solenoid circuit open or grounded
24	Vehicle Speed Sensor (VSS) circuit — the vehicle must operate up to 5 minutes at road speed, before this code will set
32	Barometric Pressure Sensor (BARO) circuit low
34	Vacuum sensor or Manifold Absolute Pressure (MAP) circuit — the engine must run up to 5 minutes, at specified curb idle, before this code will set
35	Idle Speed Control (ISC) switch circuit shorted. (Over 50% throttle for over 2 seconds)
41	No distributor reference pulses to the ECM at specified engine vacuum. This code will store in memory
42	Electronic Spark Timing (EST) bypass circuit or EST circuit grounded or open
43	Electronic Spark Control (ESC) retard signal for too long a time; causes retard in EST signal
44	Lean exhaust indication — the engine must run up to 5 minutes, in closed loop and at part throttle, before this code will set.
45	Rich exhaust indication — the engine must run up to 5 minutes, in closed loop and at part throttle, before this code will set
51	Faulty or improperly installed calibration unit (PROM). It takes up to 30 seconds before this code will set
54	Shorted M/C solenoid circuit and/or faulty ECM
55	Grounded V ref (terminal 21), high voltage on oxygen sensor circuit or ECM

Year — 1983
Model — Riviera
Engine — 5.0L (307 cid) V8
Engine Code — VIN Y

ECM TROUBLE CODES

Code	Explanation
12	No distributor reference pulses to the ECM. This code is not stored in memory and will only flash while the fault is present. Normal code with ignition ON, engine not running
13	Oxygen sensor circuit — the engine must run up to 5 minutes at part throttle, under road load, before this code will set
14	Shorted coolant sensor circuit — the engine must run up to 5 minutes before this code will set
15	Open coolant sensor circuit — the engine must run up to 5 minutes before this code will set
21	Throttle position sensor circuit — the engine must run up to 25 seconds, at specified curb idle speed, before this code will set
23	M/C solenoid circuit open or grounded
24	Vehicle Speed Sensor (VSS) circuit — the vehicle must operate up to 5 minutes at road speed, before this code will set
32	Barometric Pressure Sensor (BARO) circuit low
34	Vacuum sensor or Manifold Absolute Pressure (MAP) circuit — the engine must run up to 5 minutes, at specified curb idle, before this code will set
35	Idle Speed Control (ISC) switch circuit shorted. (Over 50% throttle for over 2 seconds)
41	No distributor reference pulses to the ECM at specified engine vacuum. This code will store in memory
42	Electronic Spark Timing (EST) bypass circuit or EST circuit grounded or open
43	Electronic Spark Control (ESC) retard signal for too long a time; causes retard in EST signal
44	Lean exhaust indication — the engine must run up to 5 minutes, in closed loop and at part throttle, before this code will set.
45	Rich exhaust indication — the engine must run up to 5 minutes, in closed loop and at part throttle, before this code will set
51	Faulty or improperly installed calibration unit (PROM). It takes up to 30 seconds before this code will set
54	Shorted M/C solenoid circuit and/or faulty ECM
55	Grounded V ref (terminal 21), high voltage on oxygen sensor circuit or ECM

Year—1984
Model—LeSabre
Engine—3.8L (231 cid) V6
Engine Code—VIN A

ECM TROUBLE CODES

Code	Explanation
12	No distributor reference pulses to the ECM. This code is not stored in memory and will only flash while the fault is present. Normal code with ignition ON, engine not running
13	Oxygen sensor circuit—the engine must run up to 4 minutes at part throttle, under road load, before this code will set
14	Shorted coolant sensor circuit—the engine must run 2 minutes before this code will set
15	Open coolant sensor circuit—the engine must run 5 minutes before this code will set
21	Throttle Position Sensor (TPS) circuit voltage high (open circuit or misadjusted TPS). The engine must run 10 seconds, at specified curb idle speed, before this code will set
22	Throttle Position Sensor (TPS) circuit voltage low (grounded circuit or misadjusted TPS). Engine must run 20 seconds, at specified curb idle speed, to set code
23	M/C solenoid circuit open or grounded
24	Vehicle Speed Sensor (VSS) circuit—the vehicle must operate up to 2 minutes, at road speed, before this code will set
32	Barometric Pressure Sensor (BARO) circuit low
34	Vacuum sensor or Manifold Absolute Pressure (MAP) circuit—the engine must run up to 2 minutes, at specified curb idle, before this code will set
35	Idle Speed Control (ISC) switch circuit shorted. (Up to 70% TPS for over 5 seconds)
41	No distributor reference pulses to the ECM at specified engine vacuum. This code will store in memory
42	Electronic Spark Timing (EST) bypass circuit or EST circuit grounded or open
43	Electronic Spark Control (ESC) retard signal for too long a time; causes retard in EST signal
44	Lean exhaust indication—the engine must run 2 minutes, in closed loop and at part throttle, before this code will set
45	Rich exhaust indication—the engine must run 2 minutes, in closed loop and at part throttle, before this code will set
51	Faulty or improperly installed calibration unit (PROM). It takes up to 30 seconds before this code will set
53	Exhaust Gas Recirculation (EGR) valve vacuum sensor has seen improper EGR vacuum
54	Shorted M/C solenoid circuit and/or faulty ECM
55	Grounded V ref (terminal 21), high voltage on oxygen sensor circuit or ECM

Year – 1984
Model – LeSabre
Engine – 4.1L (252 cid) V6
Engine Code – VIN 4

ECM TROUBLE CODES

Code	Explanation
12	No distributor reference pulses to the ECM. This code is not stored in memory and will only flash while the fault is present. Normal code with ignition ON, engine not running
13	Oxygen sensor circuit – the engine must run up to 4 minutes at part throttle, under road load, before this code will set
14	Shorted coolant sensor circuit – the engine must run 2 minutes before this code will set
15	Open coolant sensor circuit – the engine must run 5 minutes before this code will set
21	Throttle Position Sensor (TPS) circuit voltage high (open circuit or misadjusted TPS). The engine must run 10 seconds, at specified curb idle speed, before this code will set
22	Throttle Position Sensor (TPS) circuit voltage low (grounded circuit or misadjusted TPS). Engine must run 20 seconds, at specified curb idle speed, to set code
23	M/C solenoid circuit open or grounded
24	Vehicle Speed Sensor (VSS) circuit – the vehicle must operate up to 2 minutes, at road speed, before this code will set
32	Barometric Pressure Sensor (BARO) circuit low
34	Vacuum sensor or Manifold Absolute Pressure (MAP) circuit – the engine must run up to 2 minutes, at specified curb idle, before this code will set
35	Idle Speed Control (ISC) switch circuit shorted. (Up to 70% TPS for over 5 seconds)
41	No distributor reference pulses to the ECM at specified engine vacuum. This code will store in memory
42	Electronic Spark Timing (EST) bypass circuit or EST circuit grounded or open
43	Electronic Spark Control (ESC) retard signal for too long a time; causes retard in EST signal
44	Lean exhaust indication – the engine must run 2 minutes, in closed loop and at part throttle, before this code will set
45	Rich exhaust indication – the engine must run 2 minutes, in closed loop and at part throttle, before this code will set
51	Faulty or improperly installed calibration unit (PROM). It takes up to 30 seconds before this code will set
53	Exhaust Gas Recirculation (EGR) valve vacuum sensor has seen improper EGR vacuum
54	Shorted M/C solenoid circuit and/or faulty ECM
55	Grounded V ref (terminal 21), high voltage on oxygen sensor circuit or ECM

Year – 1984
Model – LeSabre
Engine – 5.0L (307 cid) V8
Engine Code – VIN Y

ECM TROUBLE CODES

Code	Explanation
12	No distributor reference pulses to the ECM. This code is not stored in memory and will only flash while the fault is present. Normal code with ignition ON, engine not running
13	Oxygen sensor circuit—the engine must run up to 4 minutes at part throttle, under road load, before this code will set
14	Shorted coolant sensor circuit—the engine must run 2 minutes before this code will set
15	Open coolant sensor circuit—the engine must run 5 minutes before this code will set
21	Throttle Position Sensor (TPS) circuit voltage high (open circuit or misadjusted TPS). The engine must run 10 seconds, at specified curb idle speed, before this code will set
22	Throttle Position Sensor (TPS) circuit voltage low (grounded circuit or misadjusted TPS). Engine must run 20 seconds, at specified curb idle speed, to set code
23	M/C solenoid circuit open or grounded
24	Vehicle Speed Sensor (VSS) circuit—the vehicle must operate up to two minutes, at road speed, before this code will set
32	Barometric Pressure Sensor (BARO) circuit low
34	Vacuum sensor or Manifold Absolute Pressure (MAP) circuit—the engine must run up to 2 minutes, at specified curb idle, before this code will set
35	Idle Speed Control (ISC) switch circuit shorted. (Up to 70% TPS for over 5 seconds)
41	No distributor reference pulses to the ECM at specified engine vacuum. This code will store in memory
42	Electronic Spark Timing (EST) bypass circuit or EST circuit grounded or open
43	Electronic Spark Control (ESC) retard signal for too long a time; causes retard in EST signal
44	Lean exhaust indication—the engine must run 2 minutes, in closed loop and at part throttle, before this code will set
45	Rich exhaust indication—the engine must run 2 minutes, in closed loop and at part throttle, before this code will set
51	Faulty or improperly installed calibration unit (PROM). It takes up to 30 seconds before this code will set
53	Exhaust Gas Recirculation (EGR) valve vacuum sensor has seen improper EGR vacuum
54	Shorted M/C solenoid circuit and/or faulty ECM
55	Grounded V ref (terminal 21), high voltage on oxygen sensor circuit or ECM

Year – 1984
Model – Electra
Engine – 4.1L (252 cid) V6
Engine Code – VIN 4

ECM TROUBLE CODES

Code	Explanation
12	No distributor reference pulses to the ECM. This code is not stored in memory and will only flash while the fault is present. Normal code with ignition ON, engine not running
13	Oxygen sensor circuit – the engine must run up to 4 minutes at part throttle, under road load, before this code will set
14	Shorted coolant sensor circuit – the engine must run 2 minutes before this code will set
15	Open coolant sensor circuit – the engine must run five minutes before this code will set
21	Throttle Position Sensor (TPS) circuit voltage high (open circuit or misadjusted TPS). The engine must run 10 seconds, at specified curb idle speed, before this code will set
22	Throttle Position Sensor (TPS) circuit voltage low (grounded circuit or misadjusted TPS). Engine must run 20 seconds, at specified curb idle speed, to set code
23	M/C solenoid circuit open or grounded
24	Vehicle Speed Sensor (VSS) circuit – the vehicle must operate up to 2 minutes, at road speed, before this code will set
32	Barometric Pressure Sensor (BARO) circuit low
34	Vacuum sensor or Manifold Absolute Pressure (MAP) circuit – the engine must run up to 2 minutes, at specified curb idle, before this code will set
35	Idle Speed Control (ISC) switch circuit shorted. (Up to 70% TPS for over 5 seconds)
41	No distributor reference pulses to the ECM at specified engine vacuum. This code will store in memory
42	Electronic Spark Timing (EST) bypass circuit or EST circuit grounded or open
43	Electronic Spark Control (ESC) retard signal for too long a time; causes retard in EST signal
44	Lean exhaust indication – the engine must run 2 minutes, in closed loop and at part throttle, before this code will set
45	Rich exhaust indication – the engine must run 2 minutes, in closed loop and at part throttle, before this code will set
51	Faulty or improperly installed calibration unit (PROM). It takes up to 30 seconds before this code will set
53	Exhaust Gas Recirculation (EGR) valve vacuum sensor has seen improper EGR vacuum
54	Shorted M/C solenoid circuit and/or faulty ECM
55	Grounded V ref (terminal 21), high voltage on oxygen sensor circuit or ECM

Year – 1984
Model – Electra
Engine – 5.0L (307 cid) V8
Engine Code – VIN Y

ECM TROUBLE CODES

Code	Explanation
12	No distributor reference pulses to the ECM. This code is not stored in memory and will only flash while the fault is present. Normal code with ignition ON, engine not running
13	Oxygen sensor circuit—the engine must run up to 4 minutes at part throttle, under road load, before this code will set
14	Shorted coolant sensor circuit—the engine must run 2 minutes before this code will set
15	Open coolant sensor circuit—the engine must run 5 minutes before this code will set
21	Throttle Position Sensor (TPS) circuit voltage high (open circuit or misadjusted TPS). The engine must run 10 seconds, at specified curb idle speed, before this code will set
22	Throttle Position Sensor (TPS) circuit voltage low (grounded circuit or misadjusted TPS). Engine must run 20 seconds, at specified curb idle speed, to set code
23	M/C solenoid circuit open or grounded
24	Vehicle Speed Sensor (VSS) circuit—the vehicle must operate up to 2 minutes, at road speed, before this code will set
32	Barometric Pressure Sensor (BARO) circuit low
34	Vacuum sensor or Manifold Absolute Pressure (MAP) circuit—the engine must run up to 2 minutes, at specified curb idle, before this code will set
35	Idle Speed Control (ISC) switch circuit shorted. (Up to 70% TPS for over 5 seconds)
41	No distributor reference pulses to the ECM at specified engine vacuum. This code will store in memory
42	Electronic Spark Timing (EST) bypass circuit or EST circuit grounded or open
43	Electronic Spark Control (ESC) retard signal for too long a time; causes retard in EST signal
44	Lean exhaust indication—the engine must run 2 minutes, in closed loop and at part throttle, before this code will set
45	Rich exhaust indication—the engine must run 2 minutes, in closed loop and at part throttle, before this code will set
51	Faulty or improperly installed calibration unit (PROM). It takes up to 30 seconds before this code will set
53	Exhaust Gas Recirculation (EGR) valve vacuum sensor has seen improper EGR vacuum
54	Shorted M/C solenoid circuit and/or faulty ECM
55	Grounded V ref (terminal 21), high voltage on oxygen sensor circuit or ECM

Year — 1984
Model — Century
Engine — 2.5L (151 cid) TBI 4 cyl
Engine Code — VIN R

ECM TROUBLE CODES

Code	Explanation
12	No distributor reference pulses to the ECM. This code is not stored in memory and will only flash while the fault is present. Normal code with ignition ON, engine not running
13	Oxygen sensor circuit—the engine must run up to 4 minutes at part throttle, under road load, before this code will set
14	Shorted coolant sensor circuit—the engine must run 2 minutes before this code will set
15	Open coolant sensor circuit—the engine must run 5 minutes before this code will set
21	Throttle Position Sensor (TPS) circuit voltage high (open circuit or misadjusted TPS). The engine must run 10 seconds, at specified curb idle speed, before this code will set
22	Throttle Position Sensor (TPS) circuit voltage low (grounded circuit or misadjusted TPS). Engine must run 20 seconds, at specified curb idle speed, to set code
23	M/C solenoid circuit open or grounded
24	Vehicle Speed Sensor (VSS) circuit—the vehicle must operate up to 2 minutes, at road speed, before this code will set
32	Barometric Pressure Sensor (BARO) circuit low
34	Vacuum sensor or Manifold Absolute Pressure (MAP) circuit—the engine must run up to 2 minutes, at specified curb idle, before this code will set
35	Idle Speed Control (ISC) switch circuit shorted. (Up to 70% TPS for over 5 seconds)
41	No distributor reference pulses to the ECM at specified engine vacuum. This code will store in memory
42	Electronic Spark Timing (EST) bypass circuit or EST circuit grounded or open
43	Electronic Spark Control (ESC) retard signal for too long a time; causes retard in EST signal
44	Lean exhaust indication—the engine must run 2 minutes, in closed loop and at part throttle, before this code will set
45	Rich exhaust indication—the engine must run 2 minutes, in closed loop and at part throttle, before this code will set
51	Faulty or improperly installed calibration unit (PROM). It takes up to 30 seconds before this code will set
53	Exhaust Gas Recirculation (EGR) valve vacuum sensor has seen improper EGR vacuum
54	Shorted M/C solenoid circuit and/or faulty ECM
55	Grounded V ref (terminal 21), high voltage on oxygen sensor circuit or ECM

Year – 1984
Model – Century
Engine – 3.0L (181 cid) V6
Engine Code – VIN E

ECM TROUBLE CODES

Code	Explanation
12	No distributor reference pulses to the ECM. This code is not stored in memory and will only flash while the fault is present. Normal code with ignition ON, engine not running
13	Oxygen sensor circuit – the engine must run up to 4 minutes at part throttle, under road load, before this code will set
14	Shorted coolant sensor circuit – the engine must run 2 minutes before this code will set
15	Open coolant sensor circuit – the engine must run 5 minutes before this code will set
21	Throttle Position Sensor (TPS) circuit voltage high (open circuit or misadjusted TPS). The engine must run 10 seconds, at specified curb idle speed, before this code will set
22	Throttle Position Sensor (TPS) circuit voltage low (grounded circuit or misadjusted TPS). Engine must run 20 seconds, at specified curb idle speed, to set code
23	M/C solenoid circuit open or grounded
24	Vehicle Speed Sensor (VSS) circuit – the vehicle must operate up to 2 minutes, at road speed, before this code will set
32	Barometric Pressure Sensor (BARO) circuit low
34	Vacuum sensor or Manifold Absolute Pressure (MAP) circuit – the engine must run up to 2 minutes, at specified curb idle, before this code will set
35	Idle Speed Control (ISC) switch circuit shorted. (Up to 70% TPS for over 5 seconds)
41	No distributor reference pulses to the ECM at specified engine vacuum. This code will store in memory
42	Electronic Spark Timing (EST) bypass circuit or EST circuit grounded or open
43	Electronic Spark Control (ESC) retard signal for too long a time; causes retard in EST signal
44	Lean exhaust indication – the engine must run 2 minutes, in closed loop and at part throttle, before this code will set
45	Rich exhaust indication – the engine must run 2 minutes, in closed loop and at part throttle, before this code will set
51	Faulty or improperly installed calibration unit (PROM). It takes up to 30 seconds before this code will set
53	Exhaust Gas Recirculation (EGR) valve vacuum sensor has seen improper EGR vacuum
54	Shorted M/C solenoid circuit and/or faulty ECM
55	Grounded V ref (terminal 21), high voltage on oxygen sensor circuit or ECM

Year — 1984
Model — Century
Engine — 3.8L (231 cid) MFI V6
Engine Code — VIN 3

ECM TROUBLE CODES

Code	Explanation
12	No distributor reference pulses to the ECM. This code is not stored in memory and will only flash while the fault is present. Normal code with ignition ON, engine not running
13	Oxygen sensor circuit—the engine must run up to 4 minutes at part throttle, under road load, before this code will set
14	Shorted coolant sensor circuit—the engine must run 2 minutes before this code will set
15	Open coolant sensor circuit—the engine must run 5 minutes before this code will set
21	Throttle Position Sensor (TPS) circuit voltage high (open circuit or misadjusted TPS). The engine must run 10 seconds, at specified curb idle speed, before this code will set
22	Throttle Position Sensor (TPS) circuit voltage low (grounded circuit or misadjusted TPS). Engine must run 20 seconds, at specified curb idle speed, to set code
23	M/C solenoid circuit open or grounded
24	Vehicle Speed Sensor (VSS) circuit—the vehicle must operate up to 2 minutes, at road speed, before this code will set
32	Barometric Pressure Sensor (BARO) circuit low
34	Vacuum sensor or Manifold Absolute Pressure (MAP) circuit—the engine must run up to 2 minutes, at specified curb idle, before this code will set
35	Idle Speed Control (ISC) switch circuit shorted. (Up to 70% TPS for over 5 seconds)
41	No distributor reference pulses to the ECM at specified engine vacuum. This code will store in memory
42	Electronic Spark Timing (EST) bypass circuit or EST circuit grounded or open
43	Electronic Spark Control (ESC) retard signal for too long a time; causes retard in EST signal
44	Lean exhaust indication—the engine must run 2 minutes, in closed loop and at part throttle, before this code will set
45	Rich exhaust indication—the engine must run 2 minutes, in closed loop and at part throttle, before this code will set
51	Faulty or improperly installed calibration unit (PROM). It takes up to 30 seconds before this code will set
53	Exhaust Gas Recirculation (EGR) valve vacuum sensor has seen improper EGR vacuum
54	Shorted M/C solenoid circuit and/or faulty ECM
55	Grounded V ref (terminal 21), high voltage on oxygen sensor circuit or ECM

Year — 1984
Model — Century
Engine — 3.8L (231 cid) V6
Engine Code — VIN A

ECM TROUBLE CODES

Code	Explanation
12	No distributor reference pulses to the ECM. This code is not stored in memory and will only flash while the fault is present. Normal code with ignition ON, engine not running
13	Oxygen sensor circuit — the engine must run up to 4 minutes at part throttle, under road load, before this code will set
14	Shorted coolant sensor circuit — the engine must run 2 minutes before this code will set
15	Open coolant sensor circuit — the engine must run 5 minutes before this code will set
21	Throttle Position Sensor (TPS) circuit voltage high (open circuit or misadjusted TPS). The engine must run 10 seconds, at specified curb idle speed, before this code will set
22	Throttle Position Sensor (TPS) circuit voltage low (grounded circuit or misadjusted TPS). Engine must run 20 seconds, at specified curb idle speed, to set code
23	M/C solenoid circuit open or grounded
24	Vehicle Speed Sensor (VSS) circuit — the vehicle must operate up to 2 minutes, at road speed, before this code will set
32	Barometric Pressure Sensor (BARO) circuit low
34	Vacuum sensor or Manifold Absolute Pressure (MAP) circuit — the engine must run up to 2 minutes, at specified curb idle, before this code will set
35	Idle Speed Control (ISC) switch circuit shorted. (Up to 70% TPS for over 5 seconds)
41	No distributor reference pulses to the ECM at specified engine vacuum. This code will store in memory
42	Electronic Spark Timing (EST) bypass circuit or EST circuit grounded or open
43	Electronic Spark Control (ESC) retard signal for too long a time; causes retard in EST signal
44	Lean exhaust indication — the engine must run 2 minutes, in closed loop and at part throttle, before this code will set
45	Rich exhaust indication — the engine must run 2 minutes, in closed loop and at part throttle, before this code will set
51	Faulty or improperly installed calibration unit (PROM). It takes up to 30 seconds before this code will set
53	Exhaust Gas Recirculation (EGR) valve vacuum sensor has seen improper EGR vacuum
54	Shorted M/C solenoid circuit and/or faulty ECM
55	Grounded V ref (terminal 21), high voltage on oxygen sensor circuit or ECM

Year – 1984
Model – Regal
Engine – 3.8L (231 cid) V6
Engine Code – VIN A

ECM TROUBLE CODES

Code	Explanation
12	No distributor reference pulses to the ECM. This code is not stored in memory and will only flash while the fault is present. Normal code with ignition ON, engine not running
13	Oxygen sensor circuit – the engine must run up to 4 minutes at part throttle, under road load, before this code will set
14	Shorted coolant sensor circuit – the engine must run 2 minutes before this code will set
15	Open coolant sensor circuit – the engine must run 5 minutes before this code will set
21	Throttle Position Sensor (TPS) circuit voltage high (open circuit or misadjusted TPS). The engine must run 10 seconds, at specified curb idle speed, before this code will set
22	Throttle Position Sensor (TPS) circuit voltage low (grounded circuit or misadjusted TPS). Engine must run 20 seconds, at specified curb idle speed, to set code
23	M/C solenoid circuit open or grounded
24	Vehicle Speed Sensor (VSS) circuit – the vehicle must operate up to 2 minutes, at road speed, before this code will set
32	Barometric Pressure Sensor (BARO) circuit low
34	Vacuum sensor or Manifold Absolute Pressure (MAP) circuit – the engine must run up to 2 minutes, at specified curb idle, before this code will set
35	Idle Speed Control (ISC) switch circuit shorted. (Up to 70% TPS for over 5 seconds)
41	No distributor reference pulses to the ECM at specified engine vacuum. This code will store in memory
42	Electronic Spark Timing (EST) bypass circuit or EST circuit grounded or open
43	Electronic Spark Control (ESC) retard signal for too long a time; causes retard in EST signal
44	Lean exhaust indication – the engine must run 2 minutes, in closed loop and at part throttle, before this code will set
45	Rich exhaust indication – the engine must run 2 minutes, in closed loop and at part throttle, before this code will set
51	Faulty or improperly installed calibration unit (PROM). It takes up to 30 seconds before this code will set
53	Exhaust Gas Recirculation (EGR) valve vacuum sensor has seen improper EGR vacuum
54	Shorted M/C solenoid circuit and/or faulty ECM
55	Grounded V ref (terminal 21), high voltage on oxygen sensor circuit or ECM

Year – 1984
Model – Regal
Engine – 3.8L (231 cid) SFI V6 Turbo
Engine Code – VIN 9

ECM TROUBLE CODES

Code	Explanation
12	No distributor reference pulses to the ECM. This code is not stored in memory and will only flash while the fault is present. Normal code with ignition ON, engine not running
13	Oxygen sensor circuit – the engine must run up to 4 minutes at part throttle, under road load, before this code will set
14	Shorted coolant sensor circuit – the engine must run 2 minutes before this code will set
15	Open coolant sensor circuit – the engine must run 5 minutes before this code will set
21	Throttle Position Sensor (TPS) circuit voltage high (open circuit or misadjusted TPS). The engine must run 10 seconds, at specified curb idle speed, before this code will set
22	Throttle Position Sensor (TPS) circuit voltage low (grounded circuit or misadjusted TPS). Engine must run 20 seconds, at specified curb idle speed, to set code
23	M/C solenoid circuit open or grounded
24	Vehicle Speed Sensor (VSS) circuit – the vehicle must operate up to 2 minutes, at road speed, before this code will set
32	Barometric Pressure Sensor (BARO) circuit low
34	Vacuum sensor or Manifold Absolute Pressure (MAP) circuit – the engine must run up to 2 minutes, at specified curb idle, before this code will set
35	Idle Speed Control (ISC) switch circuit shorted. (Up to 70% TPS for over 5 seconds)
41	No distributor reference pulses to the ECM at specified engine vacuum. This code will store in memory
42	Electronic Spark Timing (EST) bypass circuit or EST circuit grounded or open
43	Electronic Spark Control (ESC) retard signal for too long a time; causes retard in EST signal
44	Lean exhaust indication – the engine must run 2 minutes, in closed loop and at part throttle, before this code will set
45	Rich exhaust indication – the engine must run 2 minutes, in closed loop and at part throttle, before this code will set
51	Faulty or improperly installed calibration unit (PROM). It takes up to 30 seconds before this code will set
53	Exhaust Gas Recirculation (EGR) valve vacuum sensor has seen improper EGR vacuum
54	Shorted M/C solenoid circuit and/or faulty ECM
55	Grounded V ref (terminal 21), high voltage on oxygen sensor circuit or ECM

Year – 1984
Model – Regal
Engine – 4.1L (252 cid) V6
Engine Code – VIN 4

ECM TROUBLE CODES

Code	Explanation
12	No distributor reference pulses to the ECM. This code is not stored in memory and will only flash while the fault is present. Normal code with ignition ON, engine not running
13	Oxygen sensor circuit – the engine must run up to 4 minutes at part throttle, under road load, before this code will set
14	Shorted coolant sensor circuit – the engine must run 2 minutes before this code will set
15	Open coolant sensor circuit – the engine must run 5 minutes before this code will set
21	Throttle Position Sensor (TPS) circuit voltage high (open circuit or misadjusted TPS). The engine must run 10 seconds, at specified curb idle speed, before this code will set
22	Throttle Position Sensor (TPS) circuit voltage low (grounded circuit or misadjusted TPS). Engine must run 20 seconds, at specified curb idle speed, to set code
23	M/C solenoid circuit open or grounded
24	Vehicle Speed Sensor (VSS) circuit – the vehicle must operate up to 2 minutes, at road speed, before this code will set
32	Barometric Pressure Sensor (BARO) circuit low
34	Vacuum sensor or Manifold Absolute Pressure (MAP) circuit – the engine must run up to 2 minutes, at specified curb idle, before this code will set
35	Idle Speed Control (ISC) switch circuit shorted. (Up to 70% TPS for over 5 seconds)
41	No distributor reference pulses to the ECM at specified engine vacuum. This code will store in memory
42	Electronic Spark Timing (EST) bypass circuit or EST circuit grounded or open
43	Electronic Spark Control (ESC) retard signal for too long a time; causes retard in EST signal
44	Lean exhaust indication – the engine must run 2 minutes, in closed loop and at part throttle, before this code will set
45	Rich exhaust indication – the engine must run 2 minutes, in closed loop and at part throttle, before this code will set
51	Faulty or improperly installed calibration unit (PROM). It takes up to 30 seconds before this code will set
53	Exhaust Gas Recirculation (EGR) valve vacuum sensor has seen improper EGR vacuum
54	Shorted M/C solenoid circuit and/or faulty ECM
55	Grounded V ref (terminal 21), high voltage on oxygen sensor circuit or ECM

Year – 1984
Model – Skylark
Engine – 2.5L (151 cid) TBI 4 cyl
Engine Code – VIN R

ECM TROUBLE CODES

Code	Explanation
12	No distributor reference pulses to the ECM. This code is not stored in memory and will only flash while the fault is present. Normal code with ignition ON, engine not running
13	Oxygen sensor circuit – the engine must run up to 4 minutes at part throttle, under road load, before this code will set
14	Shorted coolant sensor circuit – the engine must run 2 minutes before this code will set
15	Open coolant sensor circuit – the engine must run 5 minutes before this code will set
21	Throttle Position Sensor (TPS) circuit voltage high (open circuit or misadjusted TPS). The engine must run 10 seconds, at specified curb idle speed, before this code will set
22	Throttle Position Sensor (TPS) circuit voltage low (grounded circuit or misadjusted TPS). Engine must run 20 seconds, at specified curb idle speed, to set code
23	M/C solenoid circuit open or grounded
24	Vehicle Speed Sensor (VSS) circuit – the vehicle must operate up to 2 minutes, at road speed, before this code will set
32	Barometric Pressure Sensor (BARO) circuit low
34	Vacuum sensor or Manifold Absolute Pressure (MAP) circuit – the engine must run up to 2 minutes, at specified curb idle, before this code will set
35	Idle Speed Control (ISC) switch circuit shorted. (Up to 70% TPS for over 5 seconds)
41	No distributor reference pulses to the ECM at specified engine vacuum. This code will store in memory
42	Electronic Spark Timing (EST) bypass circuit or EST circuit grounded or open
43	Electronic Spark Control (ESC) retard signal for too long a time; causes retard in EST signal
44	Lean exhaust indication – the engine must run 2 minutes, in closed loop and at part throttle, before this code will set
45	Rich exhaust indication – the engine must run 2 minutes, in closed loop and at part throttle, before this code will set
51	Faulty or improperly installed calibration unit (PROM). It takes up to 30 seconds before this code will set
53	Exhaust Gas Recirculation (EGR) valve vacuum sensor has seen improper EGR vacuum
54	Shorted M/C solenoid circuit and/or faulty ECM
55	Grounded V ref (terminal 21), high voltage on oxygen sensor circuit or ECM

Year—1984
Model—Skylark
Engine—2.8L (171 cid) V6
Engine Code—VIN Z

ECM TROUBLE CODES

Code	Explanation
12	No distributor reference pulses to the ECM. This code is not stored in memory and will only flash while the fault is present. Normal code with ignition ON, engine not running
13	Oxygen sensor circuit—the engine must run up to 4 minutes at part throttle, under road load, before this code will set
14	Shorted coolant sensor circuit—the engine must run 2 minutes before this code will set
15	Open coolant sensor circuit—the engine must run 5 minutes before this code will set
21	Throttle Position Sensor (TPS) circuit voltage high (open circuit or misadjusted TPS). The engine must run 10 seconds, at specified curb idle speed, before this code will set
22	Throttle Position Sensor (TPS) circuit voltage low (grounded circuit or misadjusted TPS). Engine must run 20 seconds, at specified curb idle speed, to set code
23	M/C solenoid circuit open or grounded
24	Vehicle Speed Sensor (VSS) circuit—the vehicle must operate up to 2 minutes, at road speed, before this code will set
32	Barometric Pressure Sensor (BARO) circuit low
34	Vacuum sensor or Manifold Absolute Pressure (MAP) circuit—the engine must run up to 2 minutes, at specified curb idle, before this code will set
35	Idle Speed Control (ISC) switch circuit shorted. (Up to 70% TPS for over 5 seconds)
41	No distributor reference pulses to the ECM at specified engine vacuum. This code will store in memory
42	Electronic Spark Timing (EST) bypass circuit or EST circuit grounded or open
43	Electronic Spark Control (ESC) retard signal for too long a time; causes retard in EST signal
44	Lean exhaust indication—the engine must run 2 minutes, in closed loop and at part throttle, before this code will set
45	Rich exhaust indication—the engine must run 2 minutes, in closed loop and at part throttle, before this code will set
51	Faulty or improperly installed calibration unit (PROM). It takes up to 30 seconds before this code will set
53	Exhaust Gas Recirculation (EGR) valve vacuum sensor has seen improper EGR vacuum
54	Shorted M/C solenoid circuit and/or faulty ECM
55	Grounded V ref (terminal 21), high voltage on oxygen sensor circuit or ECM

Year — 1984
Model — Skylark
Engine — 2.8L (171 cid) V6
Engine Code — VIN X

ECM TROUBLE CODES

Code	Explanation
12	No distributor reference pulses to the ECM. This code is not stored in memory and will only flash while the fault is present. Normal code with ignition ON, engine not running
13	Oxygen sensor circuit—the engine must run up to 4 minutes at part throttle, under road load, before this code will set
14	Shorted coolant sensor circuit—the engine must run 2 minutes before this code will set
15	Open coolant sensor circuit—the engine must run 5 minutes before this code will set
21	Throttle Position Sensor (TPS) circuit voltage high (open circuit or misadjusted TPS). The engine must run 10 seconds, at specified curb idle speed, before this code will set
22	Throttle Position Sensor (TPS) circuit voltage low (grounded circuit or misadjusted TPS). Engine must run 20 seconds, at specified curb idle speed, to set code
23	M/C solenoid circuit open or grounded
24	Vehicle Speed Sensor (VSS) circuit—the vehicle must operate up to 2 minutes, at road speed, before this code will set
32	Barometric Pressure Sensor (BARO) circuit low
34	Vacuum sensor or Manifold Absolute Pressure (MAP) circuit—the engine must run up to 2 minutes, at specified curb idle, before this code will set
35	Idle Speed Control (ISC) switch circuit shorted. (Up to 70% TPS for over 5 seconds)
41	No distributor reference pulses to the ECM at specified engine vacuum. This code will store in memory
42	Electronic Spark Timing (EST) bypass circuit or EST circuit grounded or open
43	Electronic Spark Control (ESC) retard signal for too long a time; causes retard in EST signal
44	Lean exhaust indication—the engine must run 2 minutes, in closed loop and at part throttle, before this code will set
45	Rich exhaust indication—the engine must run 2 minutes, in closed loop and at part throttle, before this code will set
51	Faulty or improperly installed calibration unit (PROM). It takes up to 30 seconds before this code will set
53	Exhaust Gas Recirculation (EGR) valve vacuum sensor has seen improper EGR vacuum
54	Shorted M/C solenoid circuit and/or faulty ECM
55	Grounded V ref (terminal 21), high voltage on oxygen sensor circuit or ECM

Year – 1984
Model – Skylark
Engine – 3.0L (181 cid) V6
Engine Code – VIN E

ECM TROUBLE CODES

Code	Explanation
12	No distributor reference pulses to the ECM. This code is not stored in memory and will only flash while the fault is present. Normal code with ignition ON, engine not running
13	Oxygen sensor circuit – the engine must run up to 4 minutes at part throttle, under road load, before this code will set
14	Shorted coolant sensor circuit – the engine must run 2 minutes before this code will set
15	Open coolant sensor circuit – the engine must run 5 minutes before this code will set
21	Throttle Position Sensor (TPS) circuit voltage high (open circuit or misadjusted TPS). The engine must run 10 seconds, at specified curb idle speed, before this code will set
22	Throttle Position Sensor (TPS) circuit voltage low (grounded circuit or misadjusted TPS). Engine must run 20 seconds, at specified curb idle speed, to set code
23	M/C solenoid circuit open or grounded
24	Vehicle Speed Sensor (VSS) circuit – the vehicle must operate up to 2 minutes, at road speed, before this code will set
32	Barometric Pressure Sensor (BARO) circuit low
34	Vacuum sensor or Manifold Absolute Pressure (MAP) circuit – the engine must run up to 2 minutes, at specified curb idle, before this code will set
35	Idle Speed Control (ISC) switch circuit shorted. (Up to 70% TPS for over 5 seconds)
41	No distributor reference pulses to the ECM at specified engine vacuum. This code will store in memory
42	Electronic Spark Timing (EST) bypass circuit or EST circuit grounded or open
43	Electronic Spark Control (ESC) retard signal for too long a time; causes retard in EST signal
44	Lean exhaust indication – the engine must run 2 minutes, in closed loop and at part throttle, before this code will set
45	Rich exhaust indication – the engine must run 2 minutes, in closed loop and at part throttle, before this code will set
51	Faulty or improperly installed calibration unit (PROM). It takes up to 30 seconds before this code will set
53	Exhaust Gas Recirculation (EGR) valve vacuum sensor has seen improper EGR vacuum
54	Shorted M/C solenoid circuit and/or faulty ECM
55	Grounded V ref (terminal 21), high voltage on oxygen sensor circuit or ECM

Year — 1984
Model — Skyhawk
Engine — 1.8L (111 cid) TBI 4 cyl
Engine Code — VIN O

ECM TROUBLE CODES

Code	Explanation
12	No distributor reference pulses to the ECM. This code is not stored in memory and will only flash while the fault is present. Normal code with ignition ON, engine not running
13	Oxygen sensor circuit — the engine must run up to 4 minutes at part throttle, under road load, before this code will set
14	Shorted coolant sensor circuit — the engine must run 2 minutes before this code will set
15	Open coolant sensor circuit — the engine must run 5 minutes before this code will set
21	Throttle Position Sensor (TPS) circuit voltage high (open circuit or misadjusted TPS). The engine must run 10 seconds, at specified curb idle speed, before this code will set
22	Throttle Position Sensor (TPS) circuit voltage low (grounded circuit or misadjusted TPS). Engine must run 20 seconds, at specified curb idle speed, to set code
23	M/C solenoid circuit open or grounded
24	Vehicle Speed Sensor (VSS) circuit — the vehicle must operate up to 2 minutes, at road speed, before this code will set
32	Barometric Pressure Sensor (BARO) circuit low
34	Vacuum sensor or Manifold Absolute Pressure (MAP) circuit — the engine must run up to 2 minutes, at specified curb idle, before this code will set
35	Idle Speed Control (ISC) switch circuit shorted. (Up to 70% TPS for over 5 seconds)
41	No distributor reference pulses to the ECM at specified engine vacuum. This code will store in memory
42	Electronic Spark Timing (EST) bypass circuit or EST circuit grounded or open
43	Electronic Spark Control (ESC) retard signal for too long a time; causes retard in EST signal
44	Lean exhaust indication — the engine must run 2 minutes, in closed loop and at part throttle, before this code will set
45	Rich exhaust indication — the engine must run 2 minutes, in closed loop and at part throttle, before this code will set
51	Faulty or improperly installed calibration unit (PROM). It takes up to 30 seconds before this code will set
53	Exhaust Gas Recirculation (EGR) valve vacuum sensor has seen improper EGR vacuum
54	Shorted M/C solenoid circuit and/or faulty ECM
55	Grounded V ref (terminal 21), high voltage on oxygen sensor circuit or ECM

Year – 1984
Model – Skyhawk
Engine – 1.8L (111 cid) MFI Turbo
Engine Code – VIN J

ECM TROUBLE CODES

Code	Explanation
12	No distributor reference pulses to the ECM. This code is not stored in memory and will only flash while the fault is present. Normal code with ignition ON, engine not running
13	Oxygen sensor circuit – the engine must run up to 4 minutes at part throttle, under road load, before this code will set
14	Shorted coolant sensor circuit – the engine must run 2 minutes before this code will set
15	Open coolant sensor circuit – the engine must run 5 minutes before this code will set
21	Throttle Position Sensor (TPS) circuit voltage high (open circuit or misadjusted TPS). The engine must run 10 seconds, at specified curb idle speed, before this code will set
22	Throttle Position Sensor (TPS) circuit voltage low (grounded circuit or misadjusted TPS). Engine must run 20 seconds, at specified curb idle speed, to set code
23	M/C solenoid circuit open or grounded
24	Vehicle Speed Sensor (VSS) circuit – the vehicle must operate up to 2 minutes, at road speed, before this code will set
32	Barometric Pressure Sensor (BARO) circuit low
34	Vacuum sensor or Manifold Absolute Pressure (MAP) circuit – the engine must run up to 2 minutes, at specified curb idle, before this code will set
35	Idle Speed Control (ISC) switch circuit shorted. (Up to 70% TPS for over 5 seconds)
41	No distributor reference pulses to the ECM at specified engine vacuum. This code will store in memory
42	Electronic Spark Timing (EST) bypass circuit or EST circuit grounded or open
43	Electronic Spark Control (ESC) retard signal for too long a time; causes retard in EST signal
44	Lean exhaust indication – the engine must run 2 minutes, in closed loop and at part throttle, before this code will set
45	Rich exhaust indication – the engine must run 2 minutes, in closed loop and at part throttle, before this code will set
51	Faulty or improperly installed calibration unit (PROM). It takes up to 30 seconds before this code will set
53	Exhaust Gas Recirculation (EGR) valve vacuum sensor has seen improper EGR vacuum
54	Shorted M/C solenoid circuit and/or faulty ECM
55	Grounded V ref (terminal 21), high voltage on oxygen sensor circuit or ECM

Year — 1984
Model — Skyhawk
Engine — 2.0L (121 cid) TBI 4 cyl
Engine Code — VIN P

ECM TROUBLE CODES

Code	Explanation
12	No distributor reference pulses to the ECM. This code is not stored in memory and will only flash while the fault is present. Normal code with ignition ON, engine not running
13	Oxygen sensor circuit — the engine must run up to 4 minutes at part throttle, under road load, before this code will set
14	Shorted coolant sensor circuit — the engine must run 2 minutes before this code will set
15	Open coolant sensor circuit — the engine must run 5 minutes before this code will set
21	Throttle Position Sensor (TPS) circuit voltage high (open circuit or misadjusted TPS). The engine must run 10 seconds, at specified curb idle speed, before this code will set
22	Throttle Position Sensor (TPS) circuit voltage low (grounded circuit or misadjusted TPS). Engine must run 20 seconds, at specified curb idle speed, to set code
23	M/C solenoid circuit open or grounded
24	Vehicle Speed Sensor (VSS) circuit — the vehicle must operate up to 2 minutes, at road speed, before this code will set
32	Barometric Pressure Sensor (BARO) circuit low
34	Vacuum sensor or Manifold Absolute Pressure (MAP) circuit — the engine must run up to 2 minutes, at specified curb idle, before this code will set
35	Idle Speed Control (ISC) switch circuit shorted. (Up to 70% TPS for over 5 seconds)
41	No distributor reference pulses to the ECM at specified engine vacuum. This code will store in memory
42	Electronic Spark Timing (EST) bypass circuit or EST circuit grounded or open
43	Electronic Spark Control (ESC) retard signal for too long a time; causes retard in EST signal
44	Lean exhaust indication — the engine must run 2 minutes, in closed loop and at part throttle, before this code will set
45	Rich exhaust indication — the engine must run 2 minutes, in closed loop and at part throttle, before this code will set
51	Faulty or improperly installed calibration unit (PROM). It takes up to 30 seconds before this code will set
53	Exhaust Gas Recirculation (EGR) valve vacuum sensor has seen improper EGR vacuum
54	Shorted M/C solenoid circuit and/or faulty ECM
55	Grounded V ref (terminal 21), high voltage on oxygen sensor circuit or ECM

Year – 1984
Model – Riviera
Engine – 3.8L (231 cid) SFI V6 Turbo
Engine Code – VIN 9

ECM TROUBLE CODES

Code	Explanation
12	No distributor reference pulses to the ECM. This code is not stored in memory and will only flash while the fault is present. Normal code with ignition ON, engine not running
13	Oxygen sensor circuit – the engine must run up to 4 minutes at part throttle, under road load, before this code will set
14	Shorted coolant sensor circuit – the engine must run 2 minutes before this code will set
15	Open coolant sensor circuit – the engine must run 5 minutes before this code will set
21	Throttle Position Sensor (TPS) circuit voltage high (open circuit or misadjusted TPS). The engine must run 10 seconds, at specified curb idle speed, before this code will set
22	Throttle Position Sensor (TPS) circuit voltage low (grounded circuit or misadjusted TPS). Engine must run 20 seconds, at specified curb idle speed, to set code
23	M/C solenoid circuit open or grounded
24	Vehicle Speed Sensor (VSS) circuit – the vehicle must operate up to 2 minutes, at road speed, before this code will set
32	Barometric Pressure Sensor (BARO) circuit low
34	Vacuum sensor or Manifold Absolute Pressure (MAP) circuit – the engine must run up to 2 minutes, at specified curb idle, before this code will set
35	Idle Speed Control (ISC) switch circuit shorted. (Up to 70% TPS for over 5 seconds)
41	No distributor reference pulses to the ECM at specified engine vacuum. This code will store in memory
42	Electronic Spark Timing (EST) bypass circuit or EST circuit grounded or open
43	Electronic Spark Control (ESC) retard signal for too long a time; causes retard in EST signal
44	Lean exhaust indication – the engine must run 2 minutes, in closed loop and at part throttle, before this code will set
45	Rich exhaust indication – the engine must run 2 minutes, in closed loop and at part throttle, before this code will set
51	Faulty or improperly installed calibration unit (PROM). It takes up to 30 seconds before this code will set
53	Exhaust Gas Recirculation (EGR) valve vacuum sensor has seen improper EGR vacuum
54	Shorted M/C solenoid circuit and/or faulty ECM
55	Grounded V ref (terminal 21), high voltage on oxygen sensor circuit or ECM

Year — 1984
Model — Riviera
Engine — 4.1L (252 cid) V6
Engine Code — VIN 4

ECM TROUBLE CODES

Code	Explanation
12	No distributor reference pulses to the ECM. This code is not stored in memory and will only flash while the fault is present. Normal code with ignition ON, engine not running
13	Oxygen sensor circuit — the engine must run up to 4 minutes at part throttle, under road load, before this code will set
14	Shorted coolant sensor circuit — the engine must run 2 minutes before this code will set
15	Open coolant sensor circuit — the engine must run 5 minutes before this code will set
21	Throttle Position Sensor (TPS) circuit voltage high (open circuit or misadjusted TPS). The engine must run 10 seconds, at specified curb idle speed, before this code will set
22	Throttle Position Sensor (TPS) circuit voltage low (grounded circuit or misadjusted TPS). Engine must run 20 seconds, at specified curb idle speed, to set code
23	M/C solenoid circuit open or grounded
24	Vehicle Speed Sensor (VSS) circuit — the vehicle must operate up to 2 minutes, at road speed, before this code will set
32	Barometric Pressure Sensor (BARO) circuit low
34	Vacuum sensor or Manifold Absolute Pressure (MAP) circuit — the engine must run up to 2 minutes, at specified curb idle, before this code will set
35	Idle Speed Control (ISC) switch circuit shorted. (Up to 70% TPS for over 5 seconds)
41	No distributor reference pulses to the ECM at specified engine vacuum. This code will store in memory
42	Electronic Spark Timing (EST) bypass circuit or EST circuit grounded or open
43	Electronic Spark Control (ESC) retard signal for too long a time; causes retard in EST signal
44	Lean exhaust indication — the engine must run 2 minutes, in closed loop and at part throttle, before this code will set
45	Rich exhaust indication — the engine must run 2 minutes, in closed loop and at part throttle, before this code will set
51	Faulty or improperly installed calibration unit (PROM). It takes up to 30 seconds before this code will set
53	Exhaust Gas Recirculation (EGR) valve vacuum sensor has seen improper EGR vacuum
54	Shorted M/C solenoid circuit and/or faulty ECM
55	Grounded V ref (terminal 21), high voltage on oxygen sensor circuit or ECM

Year – 1984
Model – Riviera
Engine – 5.0L (307 cid) V8
Engine Code – VIN Y

ECM TROUBLE CODES

Code	Explanation
12	No distributor reference pulses to the ECM. This code is not stored in memory and will only flash while the fault is present. Normal code with ignition ON, engine not running
13	Oxygen sensor circuit – the engine must run up to 4 minutes at part throttle, under road load, before this code will set
14	Shorted coolant sensor circuit – the engine must run 2 minutes before this code will set
15	Open coolant sensor circuit – the engine must run 5 minutes before this code will set
21	Throttle Position Sensor (TPS) circuit voltage high (open circuit or misadjusted TPS). The engine must run 10 seconds, at specified curb idle speed, before this code will set
22	Throttle Position Sensor (TPS) circuit voltage low (grounded circuit or misadjusted TPS). Engine must run 20 seconds, at specified curb idle speed, to set code
23	M/C solenoid circuit open or grounded
24	Vehicle Speed Sensor (VSS) circuit – the vehicle must operate up to 2 minutes, at road speed, before this code will set
32	Barometric Pressure Sensor (BARO) circuit low
34	Vacuum sensor or Manifold Absolute Pressure (MAP) circuit – the engine must run up to 2 minutes, at specified curb idle, before this code will set
35	Idle Speed Control (ISC) switch circuit shorted. (Up to 70% TPS for over 5 seconds)
41	No distributor reference pulses to the ECM at specified engine vacuum. This code will store in memory
42	Electronic Spark Timing (EST) bypass circuit or EST circuit grounded or open
43	Electronic Spark Control (ESC) retard signal for too long a time; causes retard in EST signal
44	Lean exhaust indication – the engine must run 2 minutes, in closed loop and at part throttle, before this code will set
45	Rich exhaust indication – the engine must run 2 minutes, in closed loop and at part throttle, before this code will set
51	Faulty or improperly installed calibration unit (PROM). It takes up to 30 seconds before this code will set
53	Exhaust Gas Recirculation (EGR) valve vacuum sensor has seen improper EGR vacuum
54	Shorted M/C solenoid circuit and/or faulty ECM
55	Grounded V rcf (terminal 21), high voltage on oxygen sensor circuit or ECM

Year — 1985
Model — LeSabre
Engine — 3.8L (231 cid) V6
Engine Code — VIN A

ECM TROUBLE CODES

Code	Explanation
12	No distributor reference pulses to the ECM. This code is not stored in memory and will only flash while the fault is present. Normal code with ignition ON, engine not running
13	Oxygen sensor circuit–the engine must run up to 4 minutes at part throttle, under road load, before this code will set
14	Shorted coolant sensor circuit—the engine must run 2 minutes before this code will set
15	Open coolant sensor circuit—the engine must run 5 minutes before this code will set
21	Throttle Position Sensor (TPS) circuit voltage high (open circuit or misadjusted TPS). The engine must run 10 seconds, at specified curb idle speed, before this code will set
22	Throttle Position Sensor (TPS) circuit voltage low (grounded circuit or misadjusted TPS). Engine must run 20 seconds, at specified curb idle speed, to set code
23	M/C solenoid circuit open or grounded
24	Vehicle Speed Sensor (VSS) circuit—the vehicle must operate up to 2 minutes, at road speed, before this code will set
32	Barometric Pressure Sensor (BARO) circuit low
34	Vacuum sensor or Manifold Absolute Pressure (MAP) circuit—the engine must run up to 2 minutes, at specified curb idle, before this code will set
35	Idle Speed Control (ISC) switch circuit shorted. (Up to 70% TPS for over 5 seconds)
41	No distributor reference pulses to the ECM at specified engine vacuum. This code will store in memory
42	Electronic Spark Timing (EST) bypass circuit or EST circuit grounded or open
43	Electronic Spark Control (ESC) retard signal for too long a time; causes retard in EST signal
44	Lean exhaust indication—the engine must run 2 minutes, in closed loop and at part throttle, before this code will set
45	Rich exhaust indication—the engine must run 2 minutes, in closed loop and at part throttle, before this code will set
51	Faulty or improperly installed calibration unit (PROM). It takes up to 30 seconds before this code will set
53	Exhaust Gas Recirculation (EGR) valve vacuum sensor has seen improper EGR vacuum
54	Shorted M/C solenoid circuit and/or faulty ECM
55	Grounded V ref (terminal 21), high voltage on oxygen sensor circuit or ECM

Year — 1985
Model — LeSabre
Engine — 4.1L (252 cid) V6
Engine Code — VIN 4

ECM TROUBLE CODES

Code	Explanation
12	No distributor reference pulses to the ECM. This code is not stored in memory and will only flash while the fault is present. Normal code with ignition ON, engine not running
13	Oxygen sensor circuit — the engine must run up to 4 minutes at part throttle, under road load, before this code will set
14	Shorted coolant sensor circuit — the engine must run 2 minutes before this code will set
15	Open coolant sensor circuit — the engine must run 5 minutes before this code will set
21	Throttle Position Sensor (TPS) circuit voltage high (open circuit or misadjusted TPS). The engine must run 10 seconds, at specified curb idle speed, before this code will set
22	Throttle Position Sensor (TPS) circuit voltage low (grounded circuit or misadjusted TPS). Engine must run 20 seconds, at specified curb idle speed, to set code
23	M/C solenoid circuit open or grounded
24	Vehicle Speed Sensor (VSS) circuit — the vehicle must operate up to 2 minutes, at road speed, before this code will set
32	Barometric Pressure Sensor (BARO) circuit low
34	Vacuum sensor or Manifold Absolute Pressure (MAP) circuit — the engine must run up to 2 minutes, at specified curb idle, before this code will set
35	Idle Speed Control (ISC) switch circuit shorted. (Up to 70% TPS for over 5 seconds)
41	No distributor reference pulses to the ECM at specified engine vacuum. This code will store in memory
42	Electronic Spark Timing (EST) bypass circuit or EST circuit grounded or open
43	Electronic Spark Control (ESC) retard signal for too long a time; causes retard in EST signal
44	Lean exhaust indication — the engine must run 2 minutes, in closed loop and at part throttle, before this code will set
45	Rich exhaust indication — the engine must run 2 minutes, in closed loop and at part throttle, before this code will set
51	Faulty or improperly installed calibration unit (PROM). It takes up to 30 seconds before this code will set
53	Exhaust Gas Recirculation (EGR) valve vacuum sensor has seen improper EGR vacuum
54	Shorted M/C solenoid circuit and/or faulty ECM
55	Grounded V ref (terminal 21), high voltage on oxygen sensor circuit or ECM

Year — 1985
Model — LeSabre
Engine — 5.0L (307 cid) V8
Engine Code — VIN Y

ECM TROUBLE CODES

Code	Explanation
12	No distributor reference pulses to the ECM. This code is not stored in memory and will only flash while the fault is present. Normal code with ignition ON, engine not running
13	Oxygen sensor circuit — the engine must run up to 4 minutes at part throttle, under road load, before this code will set
14	Shorted coolant sensor circuit — the engine must run 2 minutes before this code will set
15	Open coolant sensor circuit — the engine must run 5 minutes before this code will set
21	Throttle Position Sensor (TPS) circuit voltage high (open circuit or misadjusted TPS). The engine must run 10 seconds, at specified curb idle speed, before this code will set
22	Throttle Position Sensor (TPS) circuit voltage low (grounded circuit or misadjusted TPS). Engine must run 20 seconds, at specified curb idle speed, to set code
23	M/C solenoid circuit open or grounded
24	Vehicle Speed Sensor (VSS) circuit — the vehicle must operate up to two minutes, at road speed, before this code will set
32	Barometric Pressure Sensor (BARO) circuit low
34	Vacuum sensor or Manifold Absolute Pressure (MAP) circuit — the engine must run up to 2 minutes, at specified curb idle, before this code will set
35	Idle Speed Control (ISC) switch circuit shorted. (Up to 70% TPS for over 5 seconds)
41	No distributor reference pulses to the ECM at specified engine vacuum. This code will store in memory
42	Electronic Spark Timing (EST) bypass circuit or EST circuit grounded or open
43	Electronic Spark Control (ESC) retard signal for too long a time; causes retard in EST signal
44	Lean exhaust indication — the engine must run 2 minutes, in closed loop and at part throttle, before this code will set
45	Rich exhaust indication — the engine must run 2 minutes, in closed loop and at part throttle, before this code will set
51	Faulty or improperly installed calibration unit (PROM). It takes up to 30 seconds before this code will set
53	Exhaust Gas Recirculation (EGR) valve vacuum sensor has seen improper EGR vacuum
54	Shorted M/C solenoid circuit and/or faulty ECM
55	Grounded V ref (terminal 21), high voltage on oxygen sensor circuit or ECM

Year – 1985
Model – LeSabre Estate Wagon
Engine – 5.0L (307 cid) V8
Engine Code – VIN Y

ECM TROUBLE CODES

Code	Explanation
12	No distributor reference signal to the ECM. This code is not stored in memory and will only flash while the fault is present. Normal code with ignition ON, engine not running
13	Oxygen sensor circuit – the engine must run up to 4 minutes at part throttle, under road load, before this code will set
14	Shorted coolant sensor circuit – the engine must run 2 minutes before this code will set
15	Open coolant sensor circuit – the engine must run 5 minutes before this code will set
21	Throttle Position Sensor (TPS) circuit voltage high (open circuit or misadjusted TPS). The engine must run 10 seconds, at specified curb idle speed, before this code will set
22	Throttle Position Sensor (TPS) circuit voltage low (grounded circuit or misadjusted TPS). Engine must run 20 seconds, at specified curb idle speed, to set code
23	M/C solenoid circuit open or grounded
24	Vehicle Speed Sensor (VSS) circuit – the vehicle must operate up to 2 minutes, at road speed, before this code will set
32	Barometric Pressure Sensor (BARO) circuit low
34	Vacuum sensor or Manifold Absolute Pressure (MAP) circuit – the engine must run up to 2 minutes, at specified curb idle, before this code will set
35	Idle Speed Control (ISC) switch circuit shorted (Up to 70% TPS for over 5 seconds)
41	No distributor reference signal to the ECM at specified engine vacuum. This code will store in memory
42	Electronic Spark Timing (EST) bypass circuit or EST circuit grounded or open
43	Electronic Spark Control (ESC) retard signal for too long a time; causes retard in EST signal
44	Lean exhaust indication – the engine must run 2 minutes, in closed loop and at part throttle, before this code will set
45	Rich exhaust indication – the engine must run 2 minutes, in closed loop and at part throttle, before this code will set
51	Faulty or improperly installed calibration unit (PROM). It takes up to 30 seconds before this code will set
53	Exhaust Gas Recirculation (EGR) valve vacuum sensor has seen improper EGR control vacuum
54	M/C solenoid voltage high at ECM as a result of a shorted M/C solenoid circuit and/or faulty ECM

GENERAL MOTORS CORPORATION
DIAGNOSTIC CODE DATA

Year – 1985
Model – Electra
Engine – 3.8L (231 cid) SFI V6
Engine Code – VIN B

ECM TROUBLE CODES

Code	Explanation
12	No distributor reference signal to the ECM. This code is not stored in memory and will only flash while the fault is present. Normal code with ignition ON, engine not running
13	Oxygen sensor circuit—the engine must run up to 4 minutes at part throttle, under road load, before this code will set
14	Shorted coolant sensor circuit—the engine must run 2 minutes before this code will set
15	Open coolant sensor circuit—the engine must run 5 minutes before this code will set
21	Throttle Position Sensor (TPS) circuit voltage high (open circuit or misadjusted TPS). The engine must run 10 seconds, at specified curb idle speed, before this code will set
22	Throttle Position Sensor (TPS) circuit voltage low (grounded circuit or misadjusted TPS). Engine must run 20 seconds, at specified curb idle speed, to set code
23	M/C solenoid circuit open or grounded
24	Vehicle Speed Sensor (VSS) circuit—the vehicle must operate up to 2 minutes, at road speed, before this code will set
32	Barometric Pressure Sensor (BARO) circuit low
34	Vacuum sensor or Manifold Absolute Pressure (MAP) circuit—the engine must run up to 2 minutes, at specified curb idle, before this code will set
35	Idle Speed Control (ISC) switch circuit shorted (Up to 70% TPS for over 5 seconds)
41	No distributor reference signal to the ECM at specified engine vacuum. This code will store in memory
42	Electronic Spark Timing (EST) bypass circuit or EST circuit grounded or open
43	Electronic Spark Control (ESC) retard signal for too long a time; causes retard in EST signal
44	Lean exhaust indication—the engine must run 2 minutes, in closed loop and at part throttle, before this code will set
45	Rich exhaust indication—the engine must run 2 minutes, in closed loop and at part throttle, before this code will set
51	Faulty or improperly installed calibration unit (PROM). It takes up to 30 seconds before this code will set
53	Exhaust Gas Recirculation (EGR) valve vacuum sensor has seen improper EGR control vacuum
54	M/C solenoid voltage high at ECM as a result of a shorted M/C solenoid circuit and/or faulty ECM

Year – 1985
Model – Electra Estate Wagon
Engine – 5.0L (307 cid) V8
Engine Code – VIN Y

ECM TROUBLE CODES

Code	Explanation
12	No distributor reference signal to the ECM. This code is not stored in memory and will only flash while the fault is present. Normal code with ignition ON, engine not running
13	Oxygen sensor circuit – the engine must run up to 4 minutes at part throttle, under road load, before this code will set
14	Shorted coolant sensor circuit – the engine must run 2 minutes before this code will set
15	Open coolant sensor circuit – the engine must run 5 minutes before this code will set
21	Throttle Position Sensor (TPS) circuit voltage high (open circuit or misadjusted TPS). The engine must run 10 seconds, at specified curb idle speed, before this code will set
22	Throttle Position Sensor (TPS) circuit voltage low (grounded circuit or misadjusted TPS). Engine must run 20 seconds, at specified curb idle speed, to set code
23	M/C solenoid circuit open or grounded
24	Vehicle Speed Sensor (VSS) circuit – the vehicle must operate up to 2 minutes, at road speed, before this code will set
32	Barometric Pressure Sensor (BARO) circuit low
34	Vacuum sensor or Manifold Absolute Pressure (MAP) circuit – the engine must run up to 2 minutes, at specified curb idle, before this code will set
35	Idle Speed Control (ISC) switch circuit shorted (Up to 70% TPS for over 5 seconds)
41	No distributor reference signal to the ECM at specified engine vacuum This code will store in memory
42	Electronic Spark Timing (EST) bypass circuit or EST circuit grounded or open
43	Electronic Spark Control (ESC) retard signal for too long a time; causes retard in EST signal
44	Lean exhaust indication – the engine must run 2 minutes, in closed loop and at part throttle, before this code will set
45	Rich exhaust indication – the engine must run 2 minutes, in closed loop and at part throttle, before this code will set
51	Faulty or improperly installed calibration unit (PROM). It takes up to 30 seconds before this code will set
53	Exhaust Gas Recirculation (EGR) valve vacuum sensor has seen improper EGR control vacuum
54	M/C solenoid voltage high at ECM as a result of a shorted M/C solenoid circuit and/or faulty ECM

Year — 1985
Model — Century
Engine — 2.5L (151 cid) 4 cyl
Engine Code — VIN R

ECM TROUBLE CODES

Code	Explanation
12	No distributor reference signal to the ECM. This code is not stored in memory and will only flash while the fault is present. Normal code with ignition ON, engine not running
13	Oxygen sensor circuit — the engine must run up to 4 minutes at part throttle, under road load, before this code will set
14	Shorted coolant sensor circuit — the engine must run 2 minutes before this code will set
15	Open coolant sensor circuit — the engine must run 5 minutes before this code will set
21	Throttle Position Sensor (TPS) circuit voltage high (open circuit or misadjusted TPS). The engine must run 10 seconds, at specified curb idle speed, before this code will set
22	Throttle Position Sensor (TPS) circuit voltage low (grounded circuit or misadjusted TPS). Engine must run 20 seconds, at specified curb idle speed, to set code
23	M/C solenoid circuit open or grounded
24	Vehicle Speed Sensor (VSS) circuit — the vehicle must operate up to 2 minutes, at road speed, before this code will set
32	Barometric Pressure Sensor (BARO) circuit low
34	Vacuum sensor or Manifold Absolute Pressure (MAP) circuit — the engine must run up to 2 minutes, at specified curb idle, before this code will set
35	Idle Speed Control (ISC) switch circuit shorted (Up to 70% TPS for over 5 seconds)
41	No distributor reference signal to the ECM at specified engine vacuum. This code will store in memory
42	Electronic Spark Timing (EST) bypass circuit or EST circuit grounded or open
43	Electronic Spark Control (ESC) retard signal for too long a time; causes retard in EST signal
44	Lean exhaust indication — the engine must run 2 minutes, in closed loop and at part throttle, before this code will set
45	Rich exhaust indication — the engine must run 2 minutes, in closed loop and at part throttle, before this code will set
51	Faulty or improperly installed calibration unit (PROM). It takes up to 30 seconds before this code will set
53	Exhaust Gas Recirculation (EGR) valve vacuum sensor has seen improper EGR control vacuum
54	M/C solenoid voltage high at ECM as a result of a shorted M/C solenoid circuit and/or faulty ECM

Year — 1985
Model — Century
Engine — 2.8L (171 cid) V6
Engine Code — VIN X

ECM TROUBLE CODES

Code	Explanation
12	No distributor reference signal to the ECM. This code is not stored in memory and will only flash while the fault is present. Normal code with ignition ON, engine not running
13	Oxygen sensor circuit — the engine must run up to 4 minutes at part throttle, under road load, before this code will set
14	Shorted coolant sensor circuit — the engine must run 2 minutes before this code will set
15	Open coolant sensor circuit — the engine must run 5 minutes before this code will set
21	Throttle Position Sensor (TPS) circuit voltage high (open circuit or misadjusted TPS). The engine must run 10 seconds, at specified curb idle speed, before this code will set
22	Throttle Position Sensor (TPS) circuit voltage low (grounded circuit or misadjusted TPS). Engine must run 20 seconds, at specified curb idle speed, to set code
23	M/C solenoid circuit open or grounded
24	Vehicle Speed Sensor (VSS) circuit — the vehicle must operate up to 2 minutes, at road speed, before this code will set
32	Barometric Pressure Sensor (BARO) circuit low
34	Vacuum sensor or Manifold Absolute Pressure (MAP) circuit — the engine must run up to 2 minutes, at specified curb idle, before this code will set
35	Idle Speed Control (ISC) switch circuit shorted (Up to 70% TPS for over 5 seconds)
41	No distributor reference signal to the ECM at specified engine vacuum. This code will store in memory
42	Electronic Spark Timing (EST) bypass circuit or EST circuit grounded or open
43	Electronic Spark Control (ESC) retard signal for too long a time; causes retard in EST signal
44	Lean exhaust indication — the engine must run 2 minutes, in closed loop and at part throttle, before this code will set
45	Rich exhaust indication — the engine must run 2 minutes, in closed loop and at part throttle, before this code will set
51	Faulty or improperly installed calibration unit (PROM) It takes up to 30 seconds before this code will set.
53	Exhaust Gas Recirculation (EGR) valve vacuum sensor has seen improper EGR control vacuum
54	M/C solenoid voltage high at ECM as a result of a shorted M/C solenoid circuit and/or faulty ECM

Year – 1985
Model – Century
Engine – 3.8L (231cid) SFI V6
Engine Code – VIN B

ECM TROUBLE CODES

Code	Explanation
12	No distributor reference signal to the ECM. This code is not stored in memory and will only flash while the fault is present. Normal code with ignition ON, engine not running
13	Oxygen sensor circuit – the engine must run up to 4 minutes at part throttle, under road load, before this code will set
14	Shorted coolant sensor circuit – the engine must run 2 minutes before this code will set
15	Open coolant sensor circuit – the engine must run 5 minutes before this code will set
21	Throttle Position Sensor (TPS) circuit voltage high (open circuit or misadjusted TPS). The engine must run 10 seconds, at specified curb idle speed, before this code will set
22	Throttle Position Sensor (TPS) circuit voltage low (grounded circuit or misadjusted TPS). Engine must run 20 seconds, at specified curb idle speed, to set code
23	M/C solenoid circuit open or grounded
24	Vehicle Speed Sensor (VSS) circuit – the vehicle must operate up to 2 minutes, at road speed, before this code will set
32	Barometric Pressure Sensor (BARO) circuit low
34	Vacuum sensor or Manifold Absolute Pressure (MAP) circuit – the engine must run up to 2 minutes, at specified curb idle, before this code will set
35	Idle Speed Control (ISC) switch circuit shorted (Up to 70% TPS for over 5 seconds)
41	No distributor reference signal to the ECM at specified engine vacuum This code will store in memory.
42	Electronic Spark Timing (EST) bypass circuit or EST circuit grounded or open
43	Electronic Spark Control (ESC) retard signal for too long a time; causes retard in EST signal
44	Lean exhaust indication – the engine must run 2 minutes, in closed loop and at part throttle, before this code will set
45	Rich exhaust indication – the engine must run 2 minutes, in closed loop and at part throttle, before this code will set
51	Faulty or improperly installed calibration unit (PROM). It takes up to 30 seconds before this code will set
53	Exhaust Gas Recirculation (EGR) valve vacuum sensor has seen improper EGR control vacuum
54	M/C solenoid voltage high at ECM as a result of a shorted M/C solenoid circuit and/or faulty ECM

Year – 1985
Model – Century
Engine – 3.8L (231 cid) SFI V6
Engine Code – VIN 3

ECM TROUBLE CODES

Code	Explanation
12	No distributor reference signal to the ECM. This code is not stored in memory and will only flash while the fault is present. Normal code with ignition ON, engine not running
13	Oxygen sensor circuit – the engine must run up to 4 minutes at part throttle, under road load, before this code will set
14	Shorted coolant sensor circuit – the engine must run 2 minutes before this code will set
15	Open coolant sensor circuit – the engine must run 5 minutes before this code will set
21	Throttle Position Sensor (TPS) circuit voltage high (open circuit or misadjusted TPS). The engine must run 10 seconds, at specified curb idle speed, before this code will set
22	Throttle Position Sensor (TPS) circuit voltage low (grounded circuit or misadjusted TPS). Engine must run 20 seconds, at specified curb idle speed, to set code
23	M/C solenoid circuit open or grounded
24	Vehicle Speed Sensor (VSS) circuit – the vehicle must operate up to 2 minutes, at road speed, before this code will set
32	Barometric Pressure Sensor (BARO) circuit low
34	Vacuum sensor or Manifold Absolute Pressure (MAP) circuit – the engine must run up to 2 minutes, at specified curb idle, before this code will set
35	Idle Speed Control (ISC) switch circuit shorted (Up to 70% TPS for over 5 seconds)
41	No distributor reference signal to the ECM at specified engine vacuum. This code will store in memory
42	Electronic Spark Timing (EST) bypass circuit or EST circuit grounded or open
43	Electronic Spark Control (ESC) retard signal for too long a time; causes retard in EST signal
44	Lean exhaust indication – the engine must run 2 minutes, in closed loop and at part throttle, before this code will set
45	Rich exhaust indication – the engine must run 2 minutes, in closed loop and at part throttle, before this code will set
51	Faulty or improperly installed calibration unit (PROM). It takes up to 30 seconds before this code will set
53	Exhaust Gas Recirculation (EGR) valve vacuum sensor has seen improper EGR control vacuum
54	M/C solenoid voltage high at ECM as a result of a shorted M/C solenoid circuit and/or faulty ECM

Year — 1985
Model — Regal
Engine — 3.8L (231 cid) V6
Engine Code — VIN A

ECM TROUBLE CODES

Code	Explanation
12	No distributor reference signal to the ECM. This code is not stored in memory and will only flash while the fault is present. Normal code with ignition ON, engine not running
13	Oxygen sensor circuit — the engine must run up to 4 minutes at part throttle, under road load, before this code will set
14	Shorted coolant sensor circuit — the engine must run 2 minutes before this code will set
15	Open coolant sensor circuit — the engine must run 5 minutes before this code will set
21	Throttle Position Sensor (TPS) circuit voltage high (open circuit or misadjusted TPS). The engine must run 10 seconds, at specified curb idle speed, before this code will set
22	Throttle Position Sensor (TPS) circuit voltage low (grounded circuit or misadjusted TPS). Engine must run 20 seconds, at specified curb idle speed, to set code
23	M/C solenoid circuit open or grounded
24	Vehicle Speed Sensor (VSS) circuit — the vehicle must operate up to 2 minutes, at road speed, before this code will set
32	Barometric Pressure Sensor (BARO) circuit low
34	Vacuum sensor or Manifold Absolute Pressure (MAP) circuit — the engine must run up to 2 minutes, at specified curb idle, before this code will set
35	Idle Speed Control (ISC) switch circuit shorted (Up to 70% TPS for over 5 seconds)
41	No distributor reference signal to the ECM at specified engine vacuum. This code will store in memory
42	Electronic Spark Timing (EST) bypass circuit or EST circuit grounded or open
43	Electronic Spark Control (ESC) retard signal for too long a time; causes retard in EST signal
44	Lean exhaust indication — the engine must run 2 minutes, in closed loop and at part throttle, before this code will set
45	Rich exhaust indication — the engine must run 2 minutes, in closed loop and at part throttle, before this code will set
51	Faulty or improperly installed calibration unit (PROM). It takes up to 30 seconds before this code will set
53	Exhaust Gas Recirculation (EGR) valve vacuum sensor has seen improper EGR control vacuum
54	M/C solenoid voltage high at ECM as a result of a shorted M/C solenoid circuit and/or faulty ECM

Year – 1985
Model – Regal
Engine – 3.8L (231 cid) SFI V6
Engine Code – VIN 7

ECM TROUBLE CODES

Code	Explanation
12	No distributor reference signal to the ECM. This code is not stored in memory and will only flash while the fault is present. Normal code with ignition ON, engine not running
13	Oxygen sensor circuit — the engine must run up to 4 minutes at part throttle, under road load, before this code will set
14	Shorted coolant sensor circuit — the engine must run 2 minutes before this code will set
15	Open coolant sensor circuit — the engine must run 5 minutes before this code will set
21	Throttle Position Sensor (TPS) circuit voltage high (open circuit or misadjusted TPS). The engine must run 10 seconds, at specified curb idle speed, before this code will set
22	Throttle Position Sensor (TPS) circuit voltage low (grounded circuit or misadjusted TPS). Engine must run 20 seconds, at specified curb idle speed, to set code
23	M/C solenoid circuit open or grounded
24	Vehicle Speed Sensor (VSS) circuit — the vehicle must operate up to 2 minutes, at road speed, before this code will set
32	Barometric Pressure Sensor (BARO) circuit low
34	Vacuum sensor or Manifold Absolute Pressure (MAP) circuit — the engine must run up to 2 minutes, at specified curb idle, before this code will set
35	Idle Speed Control (ISC) switch circuit shorted (Up to 70% TPS for over 5 seconds)
41	No distributor reference signal to the ECM at specified engine vacuum. This code will store in memory
42	Electronic Spark Timing (EST) bypass circuit or EST circuit grounded or open
43	Electronic Spark Control (ESC) retard signal for too long a time; causes retard in EST signal
44	Lean exhaust indication — the engine must run 2 minutes, in closed loop and at part throttle, before this code will set
45	Rich exhaust indication — the engine must run 2 minutes, in closed loop and at part throttle, before this code will set
51	Faulty or improperly installed calibration unit (PROM). It takes up to 30 seconds before this code will set
53	Exhaust Gas Recirculation (EGR) valve vacuum sensor has seen improper EGR control vacuum
54	M/C solenoid voltage high at ECM as a result of a shorted M/C solenoid circuit and/or faulty ECM

Year – 1985
Model – Regal
Engine – 5.0L (305 cid) V8
Engine Code – VIN H

ECM TROUBLE CODES

Code	Explanation
12	No distributor reference signal to the ECM. This code is not stored in memory and will only flash while the fault is present. Normal code with ignition ON, engine not running
13	Oxygen sensor circuit – the engine must run up to 4 minutes at part throttle, under road load, before this code will set
14	Shorted coolant sensor circuit – the engine must run 2 minutes before this code will set
15	Open coolant sensor circuit – the engine must run 5 minutes before this code will set
21	Throttle Position Sensor (TPS) circuit voltage high (open circuit or misadjusted TPS). The engine must run 10 seconds, at specified curb idle speed, before this code will set
22	Throttle Position Sensor (TPS) circuit voltage low (grounded circuit or misadjusted TPS). Engine must run 20 seconds, at specified curb idle speed, to set code
23	M/C solenoid circuit open or grounded
24	Vehicle Speed Sensor (VSS) circuit – the vehicle must operate up to 2 minutes, at road speed, before this code will set
32	Barometric Pressure Sensor (BARO) circuit low
34	Vacuum sensor or Manifold Absolute Pressure (MAP) circuit – the engine must run up to 2 minutes, at specified curb idle, before this code will set
35	Idle Speed Control (ISC) switch circuit shorted (Up to 70% TPS for over 5 seconds)
41	No distributor reference signal to the ECM at specified engine vacuum. This code will store in memory
42	Electronic Spark Timing (EST) bypass circuit or EST circuit grounded or open
43	Electronic Spark Control (ESC) retard signal for too long a time; causes retard in EST signal
44	Lean exhaust indication – the engine must run 2 minutes, in closed loop and at part throttle, before this code will set
45	Rich exhaust indication – the engine must run 2 minutes, in closed loop and at part throttle, before this code will set
51	Faulty or improperly installed calibration unit (PROM). It takes up to 30 seconds before this code will set
53	Exhaust Gas Recirculation (EGR) valve vacuum sensor has seen improper EGR control vacuum
54	M/C solenoid voltage high at ECM as a result of a shorted M/C solenoid circuit and/or faulty ECM

Year – 1985
Model – Skylark
Engine – 2.5L (151 cid) TBI 4 cyl
Engine Code – VIN U

ECM TROUBLE CODES

Code	Explanation
12	No distributor reference signal to the ECM. This code is not stored in memory and will only flash while the fault is present. Normal code with ignition ON, engine not running
13	Oxygen sensor circuit – the engine must run up to 4 minutes at part throttle, under road load, before this code will set
14	Shorted coolant sensor circuit – the engine must run 2 minutes before this code will set
15	Open coolant sensor circuit – the engine must run 5 minutes before this code will set
21	Throttle Position Sensor (TPS) circuit voltage high (open circuit or misadjusted TPS). The engine must run 10 seconds, at specified curb idle speed, before this code will set
22	Throttle Position Sensor (TPS) circuit voltage low (grounded circuit or misadjusted TPS). Engine must run 20 seconds, at specified curb idle speed, to set code
23	M/C solenoid circuit open or grounded
24	Vehicle Speed Sensor (VSS) circuit – the vehicle must operate up to 2 minutes, at road speed, before this code will set
32	Barometric Pressure Sensor (BARO) circuit low
34	Vacuum sensor or Manifold Absolute Pressure (MAP) circuit – the engine must run up to 2 minutes, at specified curb idle, before this code will set
35	Idle Speed Control (ISC) switch circuit shorted (Up to 70% TPS for over 5 seconds)
41	No distributor reference signal to the ECM at specified engine vacuum. This code will store in memory
42	Electronic Spark Timing (EST) bypass circuit or EST circuit grounded or open
43	Electronic Spark Control (ESC) retard signal for too long a time; causes retard in EST signal
44	Lean exhaust indication – the engine must run 2 minutes, in closed loop and at part throttle, before this code will set
45	Rich exhaust indication – the engine must run 2 minutes, in closed loop and at part throttle, before this code will set
51	Faulty or improperly installed calibration unit (PROM). It takes up to 30 seconds before this code will set
53	Exhaust Gas Recirculation (EGR) valve vacuum sensor has seen improper EGR control vacuum
54	M/C solenoid voltage high at ECM as a result of a shorted M/C solenoid circuit and/or faulty ECM

Year – 1985
Model – Skylark
Engine – 3.0L (181 cid) MFI V6
Engine Code – VIN L

ECM TROUBLE CODES

Code	Explanation
12	No distributor reference signal to the ECM. This code is not stored in memory and will only flash while the fault is present. Normal code with ignition ON, engine not running.
13	Oxygen sensor circuit – the engine must run up to 4 minutes at part throttle, under road load, before this code will set
14	Shorted coolant sensor circuit – the engine must run 2 minutes before this code will set
15	Open coolant sensor circuit – the engine must run 5 minutes before this code will set
21	Throttle Position Sensor (TPS) circuit voltage high (open circuit or misadjusted TPS). The engine must run 10 seconds, at specified curb idle speed, before this code will set
22	Throttle Position Sensor (TPS) circuit voltage low (grounded circuit or misadjusted TPS). Engine must run 20 seconds, at specified curb idle speed, to set code
23	M/C solenoid circuit open or grounded
24	Vehicle Speed Sensor (VSS) circuit – the vehicle must operate up to 2 minutes, at road speed, before this code will set
32	Barometric Pressure Sensor (BARO) circuit low
34	Vacuum sensor or Manifold Absolute Pressure (MAP) circuit – the engine must run up to 2 minutes, at specified curb idle, before this code will set
35	Idle Speed Control (ISC) switch circuit shorted (Up to 70% TPS for over 5 seconds)
41	No distributor reference signal to the ECM at specified engine vacuum This code will store in memory
42	Electronic Spark Timing (EST) bypass circuit or EST circuit grounded or open
43	Electronic Spark Control (ESC) retard signal for too long a time; causes retard in EST signal
44	Lean exhaust indication – the engine must run 2 minutes, in closed loop and at part throttle, before this code will set
45	Rich exhaust indication – the engine must run 2 minutes, in closed loop and at part throttle, before this code will set
51	Faulty or improperly installed calibration unit (PROM). It takes up to 30 seconds before this code will set
53	Exhaust Gas Recirculation (EGR) valve vacuum sensor has seen improper EGR control vacuum
54	M/C solenoid voltage high at ECM as a result of a shorted M/C solenoid circuit and/or faulty ECM

Year — 1985
Model — Somerset
Engine — 2.5L (151 cid) TBI 4 cyl
Engine Code — VIN U

ECM TROUBLE CODES

Code	Explanation
12	No distributor reference signal to the ECM. This code is not stored in memory and will only flash while the fault is present. Normal code with ignition ON, engine not running
13	Oxygen sensor circuit — the engine must run up to 4 minutes at part throttle, under road load, before this code will set
14	Shorted coolant sensor circuit — the engine must run 2 minutes before this code will set
15	Open coolant sensor circuit — the engine must run 5 minutes before this code will set
21	Throttle Position Sensor (TPS) circuit voltage high (open circuit or misadjusted TPS). The engine must run 10 seconds, at specified curb idle speed, before this code will set
22	Throttle Position Sensor (TPS) circuit voltage low (grounded circuit or misadjusted TPS). Engine must run 20 seconds, at specified curb idle speed, to set code
23	M/C solenoid circuit open or grounded
24	Vehicle Speed Sensor (VSS) circuit — the vehicle must operate up to 2 minutes, at road speed, before this code will set
32	Barometric Pressure Sensor (BARO) circuit low
34	Vacuum sensor or Manifold Absolute Pressure (MAP) circuit — the engine must run up to 2 minutes, at specified curb idle, before this code will set
35	Idle Speed Control (ISC) switch circuit shorted (Up to 70% TPS for over 5 seconds)
41	No distributor reference signal to the ECM at specified engine vacuum. This code will store in memory
42	Electronic Spark Timing (EST) bypass circuit or EST circuit grounded or open
43	Electronic Spark Control (ESC) retard signal for too long a time; causes retard in EST signal
44	Lean exhaust indication — the engine must run 2 minutes, in closed loop and at part throttle, before this code will set
45	Rich exhaust indication — the engine must run 2 minutes, in closed loop and at part throttle, before this code will set
51	Faulty or improperly installed calibration unit (PROM). It takes up to 30 seconds before this code will set
53	Exhaust Gas Recirculation (EGR) valve vacuum sensor has seen improper EGR control vacuum
54	M/C solenoid voltage high at ECM as a result of a shorted M/C solenoid circuit and/or faulty ECM

Year – 1985
Model – Somerset
Engine – 3.0L (181 cid) MFI V6
Engine Code – VIN L

ECM TROUBLE CODES

Code	Explanation
12	No distributor reference signal to the ECM. This code is not stored in memory and will only flash while the fault is present. Normal code with ignition ON, engine not running.
13	Oxygen sensor circuit—the engine must run up to 4 minutes at part throttle, under road load, before this code will set
14	Shorted coolant sensor circuit—the engine must run 2 minutes before this code will set
15	Open coolant sensor circuit—the engine must run 5 minutes before this code will set
21	Throttle Position Sensor (TPS) circuit voltage high (open circuit or misadjusted TPS). The engine must run 10 seconds, at specified curb idle speed, before this code will set
22	Throttle Position Sensor (TPS) circuit voltage low (grounded circuit or misadjusted TPS). Engine must run 20 seconds, at specified curb idle speed, to set code
23	M/C solenoid circuit open or grounded
24	Vehicle Speed Sensor (VSS) circuit—the vehicle must operate up to 2 minutes, at road speed, before this code will set
32	Barometric Pressure Sensor (BARO) circuit low
34	Vacuum sensor or Manifold Absolute Pressure (MAP) circuit—the engine must run up to 2 minutes, at specified curb idle, before this code will set
35	Idle Speed Control (ISC) switch circuit shorted (Up to 70% TPS for over 5 seconds)
41	No distributor reference signal to the ECM at specified engine vacuum This code will store in memory
42	Electronic Spark Timing (EST) bypass circuit or EST circuit grounded or open
43	Electronic Spark Control (ESC) retard signal for too long a time; causes retard in EST signal
44	Lean exhaust indication—the engine must run 2 minutes, in closed loop and at part throttle, before this code will set
45	Rich exhaust indication—the engine must run 2 minutes, in closed loop and at part throttle, before this code will set
51	Faulty or improperly installed calibration unit (PROM). It takes up to 30 seconds before this code will set
53	Exhaust Gas Recirculation (EGR) valve vacuum sensor has seen improper EGR control vacuum
54	M/C solenoid voltage high at ECM as a result of a shorted M/C solenoid circuit and/or faulty ECM

Year – 1985
Model – Skyhawk
Engine – 1.8L (111 cid) MFI Turbo 4 cyl
Engine Code – VIN J

ECM TROUBLE CODES

Code	Explanation
12	No distributor reference signal to the ECM. This code is not stored in memory and will only flash while the fault is present. Normal code with ignition ON, engine not running.
13	Oxygen sensor circuit – the engine must run up to 4 minutes at part throttle, under road load, before this code will set
14	Shorted coolant sensor circuit – the engine must run 2 minutes before this code will set
15	Open coolant sensor circuit – the engine must run 5 minutes before this code will set
21	Throttle Position Sensor (TPS) circuit voltage high (open circuit or misadjusted TPS). The engine must run 10 seconds, at specified curb idle speed, before this code will set
22	Throttle Position Sensor (TPS) circuit voltage low (grounded circuit or misadjusted TPS). Engine must run 20 seconds, at specified curb idle speed, to set code
23	M/C solenoid circuit open or grounded
24	Vehicle Speed Sensor (VSS) circuit – the vehicle must operate up to 2 minutes, at road speed, before this code will set
32	Barometric Pressure Sensor (BARO) circuit low
34	Vacuum sensor or Manifold Absolute Pressure (MAP) circuit – the engine must run up to 2 minutes, at specified curb idle, before this code will set
35	Idle Speed Control (ISC) switch circuit shorted (Up to 70% TPS for over 5 seconds)
41	No distributor reference signal to the ECM at specified engine vacuum. This code will store in memory
42	Electronic Spark Timing (EST) bypass circuit or EST circuit grounded or open
43	Electronic Spark Control (ESC) retard signal for too long a time; causes retard in EST signal
44	Lean exhaust indication – the engine must run 2 minutes, in closed loop and at part throttle, before this code will set
45	Rich exhaust indication – the engine must run 2 minutes, in closed loop and at part throttle, before this code will set
51	Faulty or improperly installed calibration unit (PROM). It takes up to 30 seconds before this code will set
53	Exhaust Gas Recirculation (EGR) valve vacuum sensor has seen improper EGR control vacuum
54	M/C solenoid voltage high at ECM as a result of a shorted M/C solenoid circuit and/or faulty ECM

Year — 1985
Model — Skyhawk
Engine — 1.8L (111 cid) TBI Turbo 4 cyl
Engine Code — VIN 0

ECM TROUBLE CODES

Code	Explanation
12	No distributor reference signal to the ECM. This code is not stored in memory and will only flash while the fault is present. Normal code with ignition ON, engine not running.
13	Oxygen sensor circuit — the engine must run up to 4 minutes at part throttle, under road load, before this code will set
14	Shorted coolant sensor circuit — the engine must run 2 minutes before this code will set
15	Open coolant sensor circuit — the engine must run 5 minutes before this code will set
21	Throttle Position Sensor (TPS) circuit voltage high (open circuit or misadjusted TPS). The engine must run 10 seconds, at specified curb idle speed, before this code will set
22	Throttle Position Sensor (TPS) circuit voltage low (grounded circuit or misadjusted TPS). Engine must run 20 seconds, at specified curb idle speed, to set code
23	M/C solenoid circuit open or grounded
24	Vehicle Speed Sensor (VSS) circuit — the vehicle must operate up to 2 minutes, at road speed, before this code will set
32	Barometric Pressure Sensor (BARO) circuit low
34	Vacuum sensor or Manifold Absolute Pressure (MAP) circuit — the engine must run up to 2 minutes, at specified curb idle, before this code will set
35	Idle Speed Control (ISC) switch circuit shorted (Up to 70% TPS for over 5 seconds)
41	No distributor reference signal to the ECM at specified engine vacuum. This code will store in memory
42	Electronic Spark Timing (EST) bypass circuit or EST circuit grounded or open
43	Electronic Spark Control (ESC) retard signal for too long a time; causes retard in EST signal
44	Lean exhaust indication — the engine must run 2 minutes, in closed loop and at part throttle, before this code will set
45	Rich exhaust indication — the engine must run 2 minutes, in closed loop and at part throttle, before this code will set
51	Faulty or improperly installed calibration unit (PROM). It takes up to 30 seconds before this code will set
53	Exhaust Gas Recirculation (EGR) valve vacuum sensor has seen improper EGR control vacuum
54	M/C solenoid voltage high at ECM as a result of a shorted M/C solenoid circuit and/or faulty ECM

Year – 1985
Model – Skyhawk
Engine – 2.0L (121 cid) TBI 4 cyl
Engine Code – VIN P

ECM TROUBLE CODES

Code	Explanation
12	No distributor reference signal to the ECM. This code is not stored in memory and will only flash while the fault is present. Normal code with ignition ON, engine not running.
13	Oxygen sensor circuit – the engine must run up to 4 minutes at part throttle, under road load, before this code will set
14	Shorted coolant sensor circuit – the engine must run 2 minutes before this code will set
15	Open coolant sensor circuit – the engine must run 5 minutes before this code will set
21	Throttle Position Sensor (TPS) circuit voltage high (open circuit or misadjusted TPS). The engine must run 10 seconds, at specified curb idle speed, before this code will set
22	Throttle Position Sensor (TPS) circuit voltage low (grounded circuit or misadjusted TPS). Engine must run 20 seconds, at specified curb idle speed, to set code
23	M/C solenoid circuit open or grounded
24	Vehicle Speed Sensor (VSS) circuit – the vehicle must operate up to 2 minutes, at road speed, before this code will set
32	Barometric Pressure Sensor (BARO) circuit low
34	Vacuum sensor or Manifold Absolute Pressure (MAP) circuit – the engine must run up to 2 minutes, at specified curb idle, before this code will set
35	Idle Speed Control (ISC) switch circuit shorted (Up to 70% TPS for over 5 seconds)
41	No distributor reference signal to the ECM at specified engine vacuum. This code will store in memory
42	Electronic Spark Timing (EST) bypass circuit or EST circuit grounded or open
43	Electronic Spark Control (ESC) retard signal for too long a time; causes retard in EST signal
44	Lean exhaust indication – the engine must run 2 minutes, in closed loop and at part throttle, before this code will set
45	Rich exhaust indication – the engine must run 2 minutes, in closed loop and at part throttle, before this code will set
51	Faulty or improperly installed calibration unit (PROM). It takes up to 30 seconds before this code will set
53	Exhaust Gas Recirculation (EGR) valve vacuum sensor has seen improper EGR control vacuum
54	M/C solenoid voltage high at ECM as a result of a shorted M/C solenoid circuit and/or faulty ECM

Year — 1985
Model — Riviera
Engine — 3.8L (231 cid) SFI V6 Turbo
Engine Code — VIN 9

ECM TROUBLE CODES

Code	Explanation
12	No distributor reference pulses to the ECM. This code is not stored in memory and will only flash while the fault is present. Normal code with ignition ON, engine not running
13	Oxygen sensor circuit — the engine must run up to 4 minutes at part throttle, under road load, before this code will set
14	Shorted coolant sensor circuit — the engine must run 2 minutes before this code will set
15	Open coolant sensor circuit — the engine must run 5 minutes before this code will set
21	Throttle Position Sensor (TPS) circuit voltage high (open circuit or misadjusted TPS). The engine must run 10 seconds, at specified curb idle speed, before this code will set
22	Throttle Position Sensor (TPS) circuit voltage low (grounded circuit or misadjusted TPS). Engine must run 20 seconds, at specified curb idle speed, to set code
23	M/C solenoid circuit open or grounded
24	Vehicle Speed Sensor (VSS) circuit — the vehicle must operate up to 2 minutes, at road speed, before this code will set
32	Barometric Pressure Sensor (BARO) circuit low
34	Vacuum sensor or Manifold Absolute Pressure (MAP) circuit — the engine must run up to 2 minutes, at specified curb idle, before this code will set
35	Idle Speed Control (ISC) switch circuit shorted. (Up to 70% TPS for over 5 seconds)
41	No distributor reference pulses to the ECM at specified engine vacuum. This code will store in memory
42	Electronic Spark Timing (EST) bypass circuit or EST circuit grounded or open
43	Electronic Spark Control (ESC) retard signal for too long a time; causes retard in EST signal
44	Lean exhaust indication — the engine must run 2 minutes, in closed loop and at part throttle, before this code will set
45	Rich exhaust indication — the engine must run 2 minutes, in closed loop and at part throttle, before this code will set
51	Faulty or improperly installed calibration unit (PROM). It takes up to 30 seconds before this code will set
53	Exhaust Gas Recirculation (EGR) valve vacuum sensor has seen improper EGR vacuum
54	Shorted M/C solenoid circuit and/or faulty ECM
55	Grounded V ref (terminal 21), high voltage on oxygen sensor circuit or ECM

Year — 1985
Model — Riviera
Engine — 4.1L (252 cid) V6
Engine Code — VIN 4

ECM TROUBLE CODES

Code	Explanation
12	No distributor reference pulses to the ECM. This code is not stored in memory and will only flash while the fault is present. Normal code with ignition ON, engine not running
13	Oxygen sensor circuit — the engine must run up to 4 minutes at part throttle, under road load, before this code will set
14	Shorted coolant sensor circuit — the engine must run 2 minutes before this code will set
15	Open coolant sensor circuit — the engine must run 5 minutes before this code will set
21	Throttle Position Sensor (TPS) circuit voltage high (open circuit or misadjusted TPS). The engine must run 10 seconds, at specified curb idle speed, before this code will set
22	Throttle Position Sensor (TPS) circuit voltage low (grounded circuit or misadjusted TPS). Engine must run 20 seconds, at specified curb idle speed, to set code
23	M/C solenoid circuit open or grounded
24	Vehicle Speed Sensor (VSS) circuit — the vehicle must operate up to 2 minutes, at road speed, before this code will set
32	Barometric Pressure Sensor (BARO) circuit low
34	Vacuum sensor or Manifold Absolute Pressure (MAP) circuit — the engine must run up to 2 minutes, at specified curb idle, before this code will set
35	Idle Speed Control (ISC) switch circuit shorted. (Up to 70% TPS for over 5 seconds)
41	No distributor reference pulses to the ECM at specified engine vacuum. This code will store in memory
42	Electronic Spark Timing (EST) bypass circuit or EST circuit grounded or open
43	Electronic Spark Control (ESC) retard signal for too long a time; causes retard in EST signal
44	Lean exhaust indication — the engine must run 2 minutes, in closed loop and at part throttle, before this code will set
45	Rich exhaust indication — the engine must run 2 minutes, in closed loop and at part throttle, before this code will set
51	Faulty or improperly installed calibration unit (PROM). It takes up to 30 seconds before this code will set
53	Exhaust Gas Recirculation (EGR) valve vacuum sensor has seen improper EGR vacuum
54	Shorted M/C solenoid circuit and/or faulty ECM
55	Grounded V ref (terminal 21), high voltage on oxygen sensor circuit or ECM

Year – 1985
Model – Riviera
Engine – 5.0L (307 cid) V8
Engine Code – VIN Y

ECM TROUBLE CODES

Code	Explanation
12	No distributor reference pulses to the ECM. This code is not stored in memory and will only flash while the fault is present. Normal code with ignition ON, engine not running
13	Oxygen sensor circuit – the engine must run up to 4 minutes at part throttle, under road load, before this code will set
14	Shorted coolant sensor circuit – the engine must run 2 minutes before this code will set
15	Open coolant sensor circuit – the engine must run 5 minutes before this code will set
21	Throttle Position Sensor (TPS) circuit voltage high (open circuit or misadjusted TPS). The engine must run 10 seconds, at specified curb idle speed, before this code will set
22	Throttle Position Sensor (TPS) circuit voltage low (grounded circuit or misadjusted TPS). Engine must run 20 seconds, at specified curb idle speed, to set code
23	M/C solenoid circuit open or grounded
24	Vehicle Speed Sensor (VSS) circuit – the vehicle must operate up to 2 minutes, at road speed, before this code will set
32	Barometric Pressure Sensor (BARO) circuit low
34	Vacuum sensor or Manifold Absolute Pressure (MAP) circuit – the engine must run up to 2 minutes, at specified curb idle, before this code will set
35	Idle Speed Control (ISC) switch circuit shorted. (Up to 70% TPS for over 5 seconds)
41	No distributor reference pulses to the ECM at specified engine vacuum. This code will store in memory
42	Electronic Spark Timing (EST) bypass circuit or EST circuit grounded or open
43	Electronic Spark Control (ESC) retard signal for too long a time; causes retard in EST signal
44	Lean exhaust indication – the engine must run 2 minutes, in closed loop and at part throttle, before this code will set
45	Rich exhaust indication – the engine must run 2 minutes, in closed loop and at part throttle, before this code will set
51	Faulty or improperly installed calibration unit (PROM). It takes up to 30 seconds before this code will set
53	Exhaust Gas Recirculation (EGR) valve vacuum sensor has seen improper EGR vacuum
54	Shorted M/C solenoid circuit and/or faulty ECM
55	Grounded V ref (terminal 21), high voltage on oxygen sensor circuit or ECM

Year – 1986
Model – LeSabre
Engine – 3.0L (181 cid) MFI V6
Engine Code – VIN L

ECM TROUBLE CODES

Code	Explanation
12	No distributor reference signal to the ECM. This code is not stored in memory and will only flash while the fault is present. Normal code with ignition ON, engine not running
13	Oxygen sensor circuit – the engine must run up to 4 minutes at part throttle, under road load, before this code will set
14	Shorted coolant sensor circuit – the engine must run 2 minutes before this code will set
15	Open coolant sensor circuit – the engine must run 5 minutes before this code will set
21	Throttle Position Sensor (TPS) circuit voltage high (open circuit or misadjusted TPS). The engine must run 10 seconds, at specified curb idle speed, before this code will set
22	Throttle Position Sensor (TPS) circuit voltage low (grounded circuit or misadjusted TPS). Engine must run 20 seconds, at specified curb idle speed, to set code
23	M/C solenoid circuit open or grounded
24	Vehicle Speed Sensor (VSS) circuit – the vehicle must operate up to 2 minutes, at road speed, before this code will set
32	Barometric Pressure Sensor (BARO) circuit low
34	Vacuum sensor or Manifold Absolute Pressure (MAP) circuit – the engine must run up to 2 minutes, at specified curb idle, before this code will set
35	Idle Speed Control (ISC) switch circuit shorted. (Up to 70% TPS for over 5 seconds)
41	No distributor reference signal to the ECM at specified engine vacuum. This code will store in memory
42	Electronic Spark Timing (EST) bypass circuit or EST circuit grounded or open
43	Electronic Spark Control (ESC) retard signal for too long a time; causes retard in EST signal
44	Lean exhaust indication – the engine must run 2 minutes, in closed loop and at part throttle, before this code will set
45	Rich exhaust indication – the engine must run 2 minutes, in closed loop and at part throttle, before this code will set
51	Faulty or improperly installed calibration unit (PROM). It takes up to 30 seconds before this code will set
53	Exhaust Gas Recirculation (EGR) valve vacuum sensor has seen improper EGR control vacuum
54	M/C solenoid voltage high at ECM as a result of a shorted M/C solenoid circuit and/or faulty ECM

Year — 1986
Model — LeSabre
Engine — 3.8L (231 cid) SFI V6
Engine Code — VIN 3

ECM TROUBLE CODES

Code	Explanation
12	No distributor reference signal to the ECM. This code is not stored in memory and will only flash while the fault is present. Normal code with ignition ON, engine not running
13	Oxygen sensor circuit — the engine must run up to 4 minutes at part throttle, under road load, before this code will set
14	Shorted coolant sensor circuit — the engine must run 2 minutes before this code will set
15	Open coolant sensor circuit — the engine must run 5 minutes before this code will set
21	Throttle Position Sensor (TPS) circuit voltage high (open circuit or misadjusted TPS). The engine must run 10 seconds, at specified curb idle speed, before this code will set
22	Throttle Position Sensor (TPS) circuit voltage low (grounded circuit or misadjusted TPS). Engine must run 20 seconds, at specified curb idle speed, to set code
23	M/C solenoid circuit open or grounded
24	Vehicle Speed Sensor (VSS) circuit — the vehicle must operate up to 2 minutes, at road speed, before this code will set
32	Barometric Pressure Sensor (BARO) circuit low
34	Vacuum sensor or Manifold Absolute Pressure (MAP) circuit — the engine must run up to 2 minutes, at specified curb idle, before this code will set
35	Idle Speed Control (ISC) switch circuit shorted. (Up to 70% TPS for over 5 seconds)
41	No distributor reference signal to the ECM at specified engine vacuum. This code will store in memory
42	Electronic Spark Timing (EST) bypass circuit or EST circuit grounded or open
43	Electronic Spark Control (ESC) retard signal for too long a time; causes retard in EST signal
44	Lean exhaust indication — the engine must run 2 minutes, in closed loop and at part throttle, before this code will set
45	Rich exhaust indication — the engine must run 2 minutes, in closed loop and at part throttle, before this code will set
51	Faulty or improperly installed calibration unit (PROM). It takes up to 30 seconds before this code will set
53	Exhaust Gas Recirculation (EGR) valve vacuum sensor has seen improper EGR control vacuum
54	M/C solenoid voltage high at ECM as a result of a shorted M/C solenoid circuit and/or faulty ECM

Year — 1986
Model — LeSabre
Engine — 3.8L (231 cid) SFI V6
Engine Code — VIN B

ECM TROUBLE CODES

Code	Explanation
12	No distributor reference signal to the ECM. This code is not stored in memory and will only flash while the fault is present. Normal code with ignition ON, engine not running
13	Oxygen sensor circuit — the engine must run up to 4 minutes at part throttle, under road load, before this code will set
14	Shorted coolant sensor circuit — the engine must run 2 minutes before this code will set
15	Open coolant sensor circuit — the engine must run 5 minutes before this code will set
21	Throttle Position Sensor (TPS) circuit voltage high (open circuit or misadjusted TPS). The engine must run 10 seconds, at specified curb idle speed, before this code will set
22	Throttle Position Sensor (TPS) circuit voltage low (grounded circuit or misadjusted TPS). Engine must run 20 seconds, at specified curb idle speed, to set code
23	M/C solenoid circuit open or grounded
24	Vehicle Speed Sensor (VSS) circuit — the vehicle must operate up to 2 minutes, at road speed, before this code will set
32	Barometric Pressure Sensor (BARO) circuit low
34	Vacuum sensor or Manifold Absolute Pressure (MAP) circuit — the engine must run up to 2 minutes, at specified curb idle, before this code will set
35	Idle Speed Control (ISC) switch circuit shorted. (Up to 70% TPS for over 5 seconds)
41	No distributor reference signal to the ECM at specified engine vacuum. This code will store in memory
42	Electronic Spark Timing (EST) bypass circuit or EST circuit grounded or open
43	Electronic Spark Control (ESC) retard signal for too long a time; causes retard in EST signal
44	Lean exhaust indication — the engine must run 2 minutes, in closed loop and at part throttle, before this code will set
45	Rich exhaust indication — the engine must run 2 minutes, in closed loop and at part throttle, before this code will set
51	Faulty or improperly installed calibration unit (PROM). It takes up to 30 seconds before this code will set
53	Exhaust Gas Recirculation (EGR) valve vacuum sensor has seen improper EGR control vacuum
54	M/C solenoid voltage high at ECM as a result of a shorted M/C solenoid circuit and/or faulty ECM

Year — 1986
Model — LeSabre Estate Wagon
Engine — 5.0L (307 cid) V8
Engine Code — VIN Y

ECM TROUBLE CODES

Code	Explanation
12	No distributor reference signal to the ECM. This code is not stored in memory and will only flash while the fault is present. Normal code with ignition ON, engine not running
13	Oxygen sensor circuit — the engine must run up to 4 minutes at part throttle, under road load, before this code will set
14	Shorted coolant sensor circuit — the engine must run 2 minutes before this code will set
15	Open coolant sensor circuit — the engine must run 5 minutes before this code will set
21	Throttle Position Sensor (TPS) circuit voltage high (open circuit or misadjusted TPS). The engine must run 10 seconds, at specified curb idle speed, before this code will set
22	Throttle Position Sensor (TPS) circuit voltage low (grounded circuit or misadjusted TPS). Engine must run 20 seconds, at specified curb idle speed, to set code
23	M/C solenoid circuit open or grounded
24	Vehicle Speed Sensor (VSS) circuit — the vehicle must operate up to 2 minutes, at road speed, before this code will set
32	Barometric Pressure Sensor (BARO) circuit low
34	Vacuum sensor or Manifold Absolute Pressure (MAP) circuit — the engine must run up to 2 minutes, at specified curb idle, before this code will set
35	Idle Speed Control (ISC) switch circuit shorted. (Up to 70% TPS for over 5 seconds)
41	No distributor reference signal to the ECM at specified engine vacuum. This code will store in memory
42	Electronic Spark Timing (EST) bypass circuit or EST circuit grounded or open
43	Electronic Spark Control (ESC) retard signal for too long a time; causes retard in EST signal
44	Lean exhaust indication — the engine must run 2 minutes, in closed loop and at part throttle, before this code will set
45	Rich exhaust indication — the engine must run 2 minutes, in closed loop and at part throttle, before this code will set
51	Faulty or improperly installed calibration unit (PROM). It takes up to 30 seconds before this code will set
53	Exhaust Gas Recirculation (EGR) valve vacuum sensor has seen improper EGR control vacuum
54	M/C solenoid voltage high at ECM as a result of a shorted M/C solenoid circuit and/or faulty ECM

Year – 1986
Model – Electra
Engine – 3.8L (231 cid) SFI V6
Engine Code – VIN B

ECM TROUBLE CODES

Code	Explanation
12	No distributor reference signal to the ECM. This code is not stored in memory and will only flash while the fault is present. Normal code with ignition ON, engine not running
13	Oxygen sensor circuit – the engine must run up to 4 minutes at part throttle, under road load, before this code will set
14	Shorted coolant sensor circuit – the engine must run 2 minutes before this code will set
15	Open coolant sensor circuit – the engine must run 5 minutes before this code will set
21	Throttle Position Sensor (TPS) circuit voltage high (open circuit or misadjusted TPS). The engine must run 10 seconds, at specified curb idle speed, before this code will set
22	Throttle Position Sensor (TPS) circuit voltage low (grounded circuit or misadjusted TPS). Engine must run 20 seconds, at specified curb idle speed, to set code
23	M/C solenoid circuit open or grounded
24	Vehicle Speed Sensor (VSS) circuit – the vehicle must operate up to 2 minutes, at road speed, before this code will set
32	Barometric Pressure Sensor (BARO) circuit low
34	Vacuum sensor or Manifold Absolute Pressure (MAP) circuit – the engine must run up to 2 minutes, at specified curb idle, before this code will set
35	Idle Speed Control (ISC) switch circuit shorted. (Up to 70% TPS for over 5 seconds)
41	No distributor reference signal to the ECM at specified engine vacuum. This code will store in memory
42	Electronic Spark Timing (EST) bypass circuit or EST circuit grounded or open
43	Electronic Spark Control (ESC) retard signal for too long a time; causes retard in EST signal
44	Lean exhaust indication – the engine must run 2 minutes, in closed loop and at part throttle, before this code will set
45	Rich exhaust indication – the engine must run 2 minutes, in closed loop and at part throttle, before this code will set
51	Faulty or improperly installed calibration unit (PROM). It takes up to 30 seconds before this code will set
53	Exhaust Gas Recirculation (EGR) valve vacuum sensor has seen improper EGR control vacuum
54	M/C solenoid voltage high at ECM as a result of a shorted M/C solenoid circuit and/or faulty ECM

Year – 1986
Model – Electra Estate Wagon
Engine – 5.0L (307 cid) V8
Engine Code – VIN Y

ECM TROUBLE CODES

Code	Explanation
12	No distributor reference signal to the ECM. This code is not stored in memory and will only flash while the fault is present. Normal code with ignition ON, engine not running
13	Oxygen sensor circuit—the engine must run up to 4 minutes at part throttle, under road load, before this code will set
14	Shorted coolant sensor circuit—the engine must run 2 minutes before this code will set
15	Open coolant sensor circuit—the engine must run 5 minutes before this code will set
21	Throttle Position Sensor (TPS) circuit voltage high (open circuit or misadjusted TPS). The engine must run 10 seconds, at specified curb idle speed, before this code will set
22	Throttle Position Sensor (TPS) circuit voltage low (grounded circuit or misadjusted TPS). Engine must run 20 seconds, at specified curb idle speed, to set code
23	M/C solenoid circuit open or grounded
24	Vehicle Speed Sensor (VSS) circuit—the vehicle must operate up to 2 minutes, at road speed, before this code will set
32	Barometric Pressure Sensor (BARO) circuit low
34	Vacuum sensor or Manifold Absolute Pressure (MAP) circuit—the engine must run up to 2 minutes, at specified curb idle, before this code will set
35	Idle Speed Control (ISC) switch circuit shorted. (Up to 70% TPS for over 5 seconds)
41	No distributor reference signal to the ECM at specified engine vacuum. This code will store in memory
42	Electronic Spark Timing (EST) bypass circuit or EST circuit grounded or open
43	Electronic Spark Control (ESC) retard signal for too long a time; causes retard in EST signal
44	Lean exhaust indication—the engine must run 2 minutes, in closed loop and at part throttle, before this code will set
45	Rich exhaust indication—the engine must run 2 minutes, in closed loop and at part throttle, before this code will set
51	Faulty or improperly installed calibration unit (PROM). It takes up to 30 seconds before this code will set
53	Exhaust Gas Recirculation (EGR) valve vacuum sensor has seen improper EGR control vacuum
54	M/C solenoid voltage high at ECM as a result of a shorted M/C solenoid circuit and/or faulty ECM

Year – 1986
Model – Regal
Engine – 3.8L (231 cid) V6
Engine Code – VIN A

ECM TROUBLE CODES

Code	Explanation
12	No distributor reference signal to the ECM. This code is not stored in memory and will only flash while the fault is present. Normal code with ignition ON, engine not running
13	Oxygen sensor circuit—the engine must run up to 4 minutes at part throttle, under road load, before this code will set
14	Shorted coolant sensor circuit—the engine must run 2 minutes before this code will set
15	Open coolant sensor circuit—the engine must run 5 minutes before this code will set
21	Throttle Position Sensor (TPS) circuit voltage high (open circuit or misadjusted TPS). The engine must run 10 seconds, at specified curb idle speed, before this code will set
22	Throttle Position Sensor (TPS) circuit voltage low (grounded circuit or misadjusted TPS). Engine must run 20 seconds, at specified curb idle speed, to set code
23	M/C solenoid circuit open or grounded
24	Vehicle Speed Sensor (VSS) circuit—the vehicle must operate up to 2 minutes, at road speed, before this code will set
32	Barometric Pressure Sensor (BARO) circuit low
34	Vacuum sensor or Manifold Absolute Pressure (MAP) circuit—the engine must run up to 2 minutes, at specified curb idle, before this code will set
35	Idle Speed Control (ISC) switch circuit shorted. (Up to 70% TPS for over 5 seconds)
41	No distributor reference signal to the ECM at specified engine vacuum. This code will store in memory
42	Electronic Spark Timing (EST) bypass circuit or EST circuit grounded or open
43	Electronic Spark Control (ESC) retard signal for too long a time; causes retard in EST signal
44	Lean exhaust indication—the engine must run 2 minutes, in closed loop and at part throttle, before this code will set
45	Rich exhaust indication—the engine must run 2 minutes, in closed loop and at part throttle, before this code will set
51	Faulty or improperly installed calibration unit (PROM). It takes up to 30 seconds before this code will set
53	Exhaust Gas Recirculation (EGR) valve vacuum sensor has seen improper EGR control vacuum
54	M/C solenoid voltage high at ECM as a result of a shorted M/C solenoid circuit and/or faulty ECM

Year – 1986
Model – Regal
Engine – 3.8L (231 cid) SFI V6
Engine Code – VIN 7

ECM TROUBLE CODES

Code	Explanation
12	No distributor reference signal to the ECM. This code is not stored in memory and will only flash while the fault is present. Normal code with ignition ON, engine not running
13	Oxygen sensor circuit – the engine must run up to 4 minutes at part throttle, under road load, before this code will set
14	Shorted coolant sensor circuit – the engine must run 2 minutes before this code will set
15	Open coolant sensor circuit – the engine must run 5 minutes before this code will set
21	Throttle Position Sensor (TPS) circuit voltage high (open circuit or misadjusted TPS). The engine must run 10 seconds, at specified curb idle speed, before this code will set
22	Throttle Position Sensor (TPS) circuit voltage low (grounded circuit or misadjusted TPS). Engine must run 20 seconds, at specified curb idle speed, to set code
23	M/C solenoid circuit open or grounded
24	Vehicle Speed Sensor (VSS) circuit – the vehicle must operate up to 2 minutes, at road speed, before this code will set
32	Barometric Pressure Sensor (BARO) circuit low
34	Vacuum sensor or Manifold Absolute Pressure (MAP) circuit – the engine must run up to 2 minutes, at specified curb idle, before this code will set
35	Idle Speed Control (ISC) switch circuit shorted. (Up to 70% TPS for over 5 seconds)
41	No distributor reference signal to the ECM at specified engine vacuum. This code will store in memory
42	Electronic Spark Timing (EST) bypass circuit or EST circuit grounded or open
43	Electronic Spark Control (ESC) retard signal for too long a time; causes retard in EST signal
44	Lean exhaust indication – the engine must run 2 minutes, in closed loop and at part throttle, before this code will set
45	Rich exhaust indication – the engine must run 2 minutes, in closed loop and at part throttle, before this code will set
51	Faulty or improperly installed calibration unit (PROM). It takes up to 30 seconds before this code will set
53	Exhaust Gas Recirculation (EGR) valve vacuum sensor has seen improper EGR control vacuum
54	M/C solenoid voltage high at ECM as a result of a shorted M/C solenoid circuit and/or faulty ECM

Year – 1986
Model – Regal
Engine – 5.0L (305 cid) V8
Engine Code – VIN H

ECM TROUBLE CODES

Code	Explanation
12	No distributor reference signal to the ECM. This code is not stored in memory and will only flash while the fault is present. Normal code with ignition ON, engine not running
13	Oxygen sensor circuit – the engine must run up to 4 minutes at part throttle, under road load, before this code will set
14	Shorted coolant sensor circuit – the engine must run 2 minutes before this code will set
15	Open coolant sensor circuit – the engine must run 5 minutes before this code will set
21	Throttle Position Sensor (TPS) circuit voltage high (open circuit or misadjusted TPS). The engine must run 10 seconds, at specified curb idle speed, before this code will set
22	Throttle Position Sensor (TPS) circuit voltage low (grounded circuit or misadjusted TPS). Engine must run 20 seconds, at specified curb idle speed, to set code
23	M/C solenoid circuit open or grounded
24	Vehicle Speed Sensor (VSS) circuit – the vehicle must operate up to 2 minutes, at road speed, before this code will set
32	Barometric Pressure Sensor (BARO) circuit low
34	Vacuum sensor or Manifold Absolute Pressure (MAP) circuit – the engine must run up to 2 minutes, at specified curb idle, before this code will set
35	Idle Speed Control (ISC) switch circuit shorted. (Up to 70% TPS for over 5 seconds)
41	No distributor reference signal to the ECM at specified engine vacuum. This code will store in memory
42	Electronic Spark Timing (EST) bypass circuit or EST circuit grounded or open
43	Electronic Spark Control (ESC) retard signal for too long a time; causes retard in EST signal
44	Lean exhaust indication – the engine must run 2 minutes, in closed loop and at part throttle, before this code will set
45	Rich exhaust indication – the engine must run 2 minutes, in closed loop and at part throttle, before this code will set
51	Faulty or improperly installed calibration unit (PROM). It takes up to 30 seconds before this code will set
53	Exhaust Gas Recirculation (EGR) valve vacuum sensor has seen improper EGR control vacuum
54	M/C solenoid voltage high at ECM as a result of a shorted M/C solenoid circuit and/or faulty ECM

Year – 1986
Model – Century
Engine – 2.5L (151 cid) EFI 4 cyl
Engine Code – VIN R

ECM TROUBLE CODES

Code	Explanation
12	No distributor reference signal to the ECM. This code is not stored in memory and will only flash while the fault is present. Normal code with ignition ON, engine not running
13	Oxygen sensor circuit – the engine must run up to 4 minutes at part throttle, under road load, before this code will set
14	Shorted coolant sensor circuit – the engine must run 2 minutes before this code will set
15	Open coolant sensor circuit – the engine must run 5 minutes before this code will set
21	Throttle Position Sensor (TPS) circuit voltage high (open circuit or misadjusted TPS). The engine must run 10 seconds, at specified curb idle speed, before this code will set
22	Throttle Position Sensor (TPS) circuit voltage low (grounded circuit or misadjusted TPS). Engine must run 20 seconds, at specified curb idle speed, to set code
23	M/C solenoid circuit open or grounded
24	Vehicle Speed Sensor (VSS) circuit – the vehicle must operate up to 2 minutes, at road speed, before this code will set
32	Barometric Pressure Sensor (BARO) circuit low
34	Vacuum sensor or Manifold Absolute Pressure (MAP) circuit – the engine must run up to 2 minutes, at specified curb idle, before this code will set
35	Idle Speed Control (ISC) switch circuit shorted. (Up to 70% TPS for over 5 seconds)
41	No distributor reference signal to the ECM at specified engine vacuum. This code will store in memory
42	Electronic Spark Timing (EST) bypass circuit or EST circuit grounded or open
43	Electronic Spark Control (ESC) retard signal for too long a time; causes retard in EST signal
44	Lean exhaust indication – the engine must run 2 minutes, in closed loop and at part throttle, before this code will set
45	Rich exhaust indication – the engine must run 2 minutes, in closed loop and at part throttle, before this code will set
51	Faulty or improperly installed calibration unit (PROM). It takes up to 30 seconds before this code will set
53	Exhaust Gas Recirculation (EGR) valve vacuum sensor has seen improper EGR control vacuum
54	M/C solenoid voltage high at ECM as a result of a shorted M/C solenoid circuit and/or faulty ECM

Year — 1986
Model — Century
Engine — 2.8L (171 cid) V6
Engine Code — VIN X

ECM TROUBLE CODES

Code	Explanation
12	No distributor reference signal to the ECM. This code is not stored in memory and will only flash while the fault is present. Normal code with ignition ON, engine not running
13	Oxygen sensor circuit — the engine must run up to 4 minutes at part throttle, under road load, before this code will set
14	Shorted coolant sensor circuit — the engine must run 2 minutes before this code will set
15	Open coolant sensor circuit — the engine must run 5 minutes before this code will set
21	Throttle Position Sensor (TPS) circuit voltage high (open circuit or misadjusted TPS). The engine must run 10 seconds, at specified curb idle speed, before this code will set
22	Throttle Position Sensor (TPS) circuit voltage low (grounded circuit or misadjusted TPS). Engine must run 20 seconds, at specified curb idle speed, to set code
23	M/C solenoid circuit open or grounded
24	Vehicle Speed Sensor (VSS) circuit — the vehicle must operate up to 2 minutes, at road speed, before this code will set
32	Barometric Pressure Sensor (BARO) circuit low
34	Vacuum sensor or Manifold Absolute Pressure (MAP) circuit — the engine must run up to 2 minutes, at specified curb idle, before this code will set
35	Idle Speed Control (ISC) switch circuit shorted. (Up to 70% TPS for over 5 seconds)
41	No distributor reference signal to the ECM at specified engine vacuum. This code will store in memory
42	Electronic Spark Timing (EST) bypass circuit or EST circuit grounded or open
43	Electronic Spark Control (ESC) retard signal for too long a time; causes retard in EST signal
44	Lean exhaust indication — the engine must run 2 minutes, in closed loop and at part throttle, before this code will set
45	Rich exhaust indication — the engine must run 2 minutes, in closed loop and at part throttle, before this code will set
51	Faulty or improperly installed calibration unit (PROM). It takes up to 30 seconds before this code will set
53	Exhaust Gas Recirculation (EGR) valve vacuum sensor has seen improper EGR control vacuum
54	M/C solenoid voltage high at ECM as a result of a shorted M/C solenoid circuit and/or faulty ECM

Year – 1986
Model – Century
Engine – 3.8L (231 cid) SFI V6
Engine Code – VIN B

ECM TROUBLE CODES

Code	Explanation
12	No distributor reference signal to the ECM. This code is not stored in memory and will only flash while the fault is present. Normal code with ignition ON, engine not running
13	Oxygen sensor circuit—the engine must run up to 4 minutes at part throttle, under road load, before this code will set
14	Shorted coolant sensor circuit—the engine must run 2 minutes before this code will set
15	Open coolant sensor circuit—the engine must run 5 minutes before this code will set
21	Throttle Position Sensor (TPS) circuit voltage high (open circuit or misadjusted TPS). The engine must run 10 seconds, at specified curb idle speed, before this code will set
22	Throttle Position Sensor (TPS) circuit voltage low (grounded circuit or misadjusted TPS). Engine must run 20 seconds, at specified curb idle speed, to set code
23	M/C solenoid circuit open or grounded
24	Vehicle Speed Sensor (VSS) circuit—the vehicle must operate up to 2 minutes, at road speed, before this code will set
32	Barometric Pressure Sensor (BARO) circuit low
34	Vacuum sensor or Manifold Absolute Pressure (MAP) circuit—the engine must run up to 2 minutes, at specified curb idle, before this code will set
35	Idle Speed Control (ISC) switch circuit shorted. (Up to 70% TPS for over 5 seconds)
41	No distributor reference signal to the ECM at specified engine vacuum. This code will store in memory
42	Electronic Spark Timing (EST) bypass circuit or EST circuit grounded or open
43	Electronic Spark Control (ESC) retard signal for too long a time; causes retard in EST signal
44	Lean exhaust indication—the engine must run 2 minutes, in closed loop and at part throttle, before this code will set
45	Rich exhaust indication—the engine must run 2 minutes, in closed loop and at part throttle, before this code will set
51	Faulty or improperly installed calibration unit (PROM). It takes up to 30 seconds before this code will set
53	Exhaust Gas Recirculation (EGR) valve vacuum sensor has seen improper EGR control vacuum
54	M/C solenoid voltage high at ECM as a result of a shorted M/C solenoid circuit and/or faulty ECM

Year – 1986
Model – Century
Engine – 3.8L (231 cid) SFI V6
Engine Code – VIN 3

ECM TROUBLE CODES

Code	Explanation
12	No distributor reference signal to the ECM. This code is not stored in memory and will only flash while the fault is present. Normal code with ignition ON, engine not running
13	Oxygen sensor circuit—the engine must run up to 4 minutes at part throttle, under road load, before this code will set
14	Shorted coolant sensor circuit—the engine must run 2 minutes before this code will set
15	Open coolant sensor circuit—the engine must run 5 minutes before this code will set
21	Throttle Position Sensor (TPS) circuit voltage high (open circuit or misadjusted TPS). The engine must run 10 seconds, at specified curb idle speed, before this code will set
22	Throttle Position Sensor (TPS) circuit voltage low (grounded circuit or misadjusted TPS). Engine must run 20 seconds, at specified curb idle speed, to set code
23	M/C solenoid circuit open or grounded
24	Vehicle Speed Sensor (VSS) circuit—the vehicle must operate up to 2 minutes, at road speed, before this code will set
32	Barometric Pressure Sensor (BARO) circuit low
34	Vacuum sensor or Manifold Absolute Pressure (MAP) circuit—the engine must run up to 2 minutes, at specified curb idle, before this code will set
35	Idle Speed Control (ISC) switch circuit shorted. (Up to 70% TPS for over 5 seconds)
41	No distributor reference signal to the ECM at specified engine vacuum. This code will store in memory
42	Electronic Spark Timing (EST) bypass circuit or EST circuit grounded or open
43	Electronic Spark Control (ESC) retard signal for too long a time; causes retard in EST signal
44	Lean exhaust indication—the engine must run 2 minutes, in closed loop and at part throttle, before this code will set
45	Rich exhaust indication—the engine must run 2 minutes, in closed loop and at part throttle, before this code will set
51	Faulty or improperly installed calibration unit (PROM). It takes up to 30 seconds before this code will set
53	Exhaust Gas Recirculation (EGR) valve vacuum sensor has seen improper EGR control vacuum
54	M/C solenoid voltage high at ECM as a result of a shorted M/C solenoid circuit and/or faulty ECM

GENERAL MOTORS CORPORATION
DIAGNOSTIC CODE DATA

Year—1986
Model—Skylark
Engine—2.5L (151 cid) TBI 4 cyl
Engine Code—VIN U

ECM TROUBLE CODES

Code	Explanation
12	No distributor reference signal to the ECM. This code is not stored in memory and will only flash while the fault is present. Normal code with ignition ON, engine not running
13	Oxygen sensor circuit—the engine must run up to 4 minutes at part throttle, under road load, before this code will set
14	Shorted coolant sensor circuit—the engine must run 2 minutes before this code will set
15	Open coolant sensor circuit—the engine must run 5 minutes before this code will set
21	Throttle Position Sensor (TPS) circuit voltage high (open circuit or misadjusted TPS). The engine must run 10 seconds, at specified curb idle speed, before this code will set
22	Throttle Position Sensor (TPS) circuit voltage low (grounded circuit or misadjusted TPS). Engine must run 20 seconds, at specified curb idle speed, to set code
23	M/C solenoid circuit open or grounded
24	Vehicle Speed Sensor (VSS) circuit—the vehicle must operate up to 2 minutes, at road speed, before this code will set
32	Barometric Pressure Sensor (BARO) circuit low
34	Vacuum sensor or Manifold Absolute Pressure (MAP) circuit—the engine must run up to 2 minutes, at specified curb idle, before this code will set
35	Idle Speed Control (ISC) switch circuit shorted. (Up to 70% TPS for over 5 seconds)
41	No distributor reference signal to the ECM at specified engine vacuum. This code will store in memory
42	Electronic Spark Timing (EST) bypass circuit or EST circuit grounded or open
43	Electronic Spark Control (ESC) retard signal for too long a time; causes retard in EST signal
44	Lean exhaust indication—the engine must run 2 minutes, in closed loop and at part throttle, before this code will set
45	Rich exhaust indication—the engine must run 2 minutes, in closed loop and at part throttle, before this code will set
51	Faulty or improperly installed calibration unit (PROM). It takes up to 30 seconds before this code will set
53	Exhaust Gas Recirculation (EGR) valve vacuum sensor has seen improper EGR control vacuum
54	M/C solenoid voltage high at ECM as a result of a shorted M/C solenoid circuit and/or faulty ECM

Year — 1986

Model — Skylark

Engine — 3.0L (181 cid) MFI V6

Engine Code — VIN L

ECM TROUBLE CODES

Code	Explanation
12	No distributor reference signal to the ECM. This code is not stored in memory and will only flash while the fault is present. Normal code with ignition ON, engine not running
13	Oxygen sensor circuit — the engine must run up to 4 minutes at part throttle, under road load, before this code will set
14	Shorted coolant sensor circuit — the engine must run 2 minutes before this code will set
15	Open coolant sensor circuit — the engine must run 5 minutes before this code will set
21	Throttle Position Sensor (TPS) circuit voltage high (open circuit or misadjusted TPS). The engine must run 10 seconds, at specified curb idle speed, before this code will set
22	Throttle Position Sensor (TPS) circuit voltage low (grounded circuit or misadjusted TPS). Engine must run 20 seconds, at specified curb idle speed, to set code
23	M/C solenoid circuit open or grounded
24	Vehicle Speed Sensor (VSS) circuit — the vehicle must operate up to 2 minutes, at road speed, before this code will set
32	Barometric Pressure Sensor (BARO) circuit low
34	Vacuum sensor or Manifold Absolute Pressure (MAP) circuit — the engine must run up to 2 minutes, at specified curb idle, before this code will set
35	Idle Speed Control (ISC) switch circuit shorted. (Up to 70% TPS for over 5 seconds)
41	No distributor reference signal to the ECM at specified engine vacuum. This code will store in memory
42	Electronic Spark Timing (EST) bypass circuit or EST circuit grounded or open
43	Electronic Spark Control (ESC) retard signal for too long a time; causes retard in EST signal
44	Lean exhaust indication — the engine must run 2 minutes, in closed loop and at part throttle, before this code will set
45	Rich exhaust indication — the engine must run 2 minutes, in closed loop and at part throttle, before this code will set
51	Faulty or improperly installed calibration unit (PROM). It takes up to 30 seconds before this code will set
53	Exhaust Gas Recirculation (EGR) valve vacuum sensor has seen improper EGR control vacuum
54	M/C solenoid voltage high at ECM as a result of a shorted M/C solenoid circuit and/or faulty ECM

Year — 1986
Model — Somerset
Engine — 2.5L (151 cid) TBI 4 cyl
Engine Code — VIN U

ECM TROUBLE CODES

Code	Explanation
12	No distributor reference signal to the ECM. This code is not stored in memory and will only flash while the fault is present. Normal code with ignition ON, engine not running
13	Oxygen sensor circuit—the engine must run up to 4 minutes at part throttle, under road load, before this code will set
14	Shorted coolant sensor circuit—the engine must run 2 minutes before this code will set
15	Open coolant sensor circuit—the engine must run 5 minutes before this code will set
21	Throttle Position Sensor (TPS) circuit voltage high (open circuit or misadjusted TPS). The engine must run 10 seconds, at specified curb idle speed, before this code will set
22	Throttle Position Sensor (TPS) circuit voltage low (grounded circuit or misadjusted TPS). Engine must run 20 seconds, at specified curb idle speed, to set code
23	M/C solenoid circuit open or grounded
24	Vehicle Speed Sensor (VSS) circuit—the vehicle must operate up to 2 minutes, at road speed, before this code will set
32	Barometric Pressure Sensor (BARO) circuit low
34	Vacuum sensor or Manifold Absolute Pressure (MAP) circuit—the engine must run up to 2 minutes, at specified curb idle, before this code will set
35	Idle Speed Control (ISC) switch circuit shorted (Up to 70% TPS for over 5 seconds)
41	No distributor reference signal to the ECM at specified engine vacuum. This code will store in memory
42	Electronic Spark Timing (EST) bypass circuit or EST circuit grounded or open
43	Electronic Spark Control (ESC) retard signal for too long a time; causes retard in EST signal
44	Lean exhaust indication—the engine must run 2 minutes, in closed loop and at part throttle, before this code will set
45	Rich exhaust indication—the engine must run 2 minutes, in closed loop and at part throttle, before this code will set
51	Faulty or improperly installed calibration unit (PROM). It takes up to 30 seconds before this code will set
53	Exhaust Gas Recirculation (EGR) valve vacuum sensor has seen improper EGR control vacuum
54	M/C solenoid voltage high at ECM as a result of a shorted M/C solenoid circuit and/or faulty ECM

Year — 1986
Model — Somerset
Engine — 3.0L (181 cid) MFI V6
Engine Code — VIN L

ECM TROUBLE CODES

Code	Explanation
12	No distributor reference signal to the ECM. This code is not stored in memory and will only flash while the fault is present. Normal code with ignition ON, engine not running.
13	Oxygen sensor circuit — the engine must run up to 4 minutes at part throttle, under road load, before this code will set
14	Shorted coolant sensor circuit — the engine must run 2 minutes before this code will set
15	Open coolant sensor circuit — the engine must run 5 minutes before this code will set
21	Throttle Position Sensor (TPS) circuit voltage high (open circuit or misadjusted TPS). The engine must run 10 seconds, at specified curb idle speed, before this code will set
22	Throttle Position Sensor (TPS) circuit voltage low (grounded circuit or misadjusted TPS). Engine must run 20 seconds, at specified curb idle speed, to set code
23	M/C solenoid circuit open or grounded
24	Vehicle Speed Sensor (VSS) circuit — the vehicle must operate up to 2 minutes, at road speed, before this code will set
32	Barometric Pressure Sensor (BARO) circuit low
34	Vacuum sensor or Manifold Absolute Pressure (MAP) circuit — the engine must run up to 2 minutes, at specified curb idle, before this code will set
35	Idle Speed Control (ISC) switch circuit shorted (Up to 70% TPS for over 5 seconds)
41	No distributor reference signal to the ECM at specified engine vacuum This code will store in memory
42	Electronic Spark Timing (EST) bypass circuit or EST circuit grounded or open
43	Electronic Spark Control (ESC) retard signal for too long a time; causes retard in EST signal
44	Lean exhaust indication — the engine must run 2 minutes, in closed loop and at part throttle, before this code will set
45	Rich exhaust indication — the engine must run 2 minutes, in closed loop and at part throttle, before this code will set
51	Faulty or improperly installed calibration unit (PROM). It takes up to 30 seconds before this code will set
53	Exhaust Gas Recirculation (EGR) valve vacuum sensor has seen improper EGR control vacuum
54	M/C solenoid voltage high at ECM as a result of a shorted M/C solenoid circuit and/or faulty ECM

GENERAL MOTORS CORPORATION
DIAGNOSTIC CODE DATA

Year – 1986
Model – Skyhawk
Engine – 1.8L (111 cid) TBI 4 cyl
Engine Code – VIN O

ECM TROUBLE CODES

Code	Explanation
12	No distributor reference signal to the ECM. This code is not stored in memory and will only flash while the fault is present. Normal code with ignition ON, engine not running
13	Oxygen sensor circuit – the engine must run up to 4 minutes at part throttle, under road load, before this code will set
14	Shorted coolant sensor circuit – the engine must run 2 minutes before this code will set
15	Open coolant sensor circuit – the engine must run 5 minutes before this code will set
21	Throttle Position Sensor (TPS) circuit voltage high (open circuit or misadjusted TPS). The engine must run 10 seconds, at specified curb idle speed, before this code will set
22	Throttle Position Sensor (TPS) circuit voltage low (grounded circuit or misadjusted TPS). Engine must run 20 seconds, at specified curb idle speed, to set code
23	M/C solenoid circuit open or grounded
24	Vehicle Speed Sensor (VSS) circuit – the vehicle must operate up to 2 minutes, at road speed, before this code will set
32	Barometric Pressure Sensor (BARO) circuit low
34	Vacuum sensor or Manifold Absolute Pressure (MAP) circuit – the engine must run up to 2 minutes, at specified curb idle, before this code will set
35	Idle Speed Control (ISC) switch circuit shorted. (Up to 70% TPS for over 5 seconds)
41	No distributor reference signal to the ECM at specified engine vacuum. This code will store in memory
42	Electronic Spark Timing (EST) bypass circuit or EST circuit grounded or open
43	Electronic Spark Control (ESC) retard signal for too long a time; causes retard in EST signal
44	Lean exhaust indication – the engine must run 2 minutes, in closed loop and at part throttle, before this code will set
45	Rich exhaust indication – the engine must run 2 minutes, in closed loop and at part throttle, before this code will set
51	Faulty or improperly installed calibration unit (PROM). It takes up to 30 seconds before this code will set
53	Exhaust Gas Recirculation (EGR) valve vacuum sensor has seen improper EGR control vacuum
54	M/C solenoid voltage high at ECM as a result of a shorted M/C solenoid circuit and/or faulty ECM

Year — 1986
Model — Skyhawk
Engine — 1.8L (111 cid) MFI Turbo 4 cyl
Engine Code — VIN J

ECM TROUBLE CODES

Code	Explanation
12	No distributor reference signal to the ECM. This code is not stored in memory and will only flash while the fault is present. Normal code with ignition ON, engine not running
13	Oxygen sensor circuit — the engine must run up to 4 minutes at part throttle, under road load, before this code will set
14	Shorted coolant sensor circuit — the engine must run 2 minutes before this code will set
15	Open coolant sensor circuit — the engine must run 5 minutes before this code will set
21	Throttle Position Sensor (TPS) circuit voltage high (open circuit or misadjusted TPS). The engine must run 10 seconds, at specified curb idle speed, before this code will set
22	Throttle Position Sensor (TPS) circuit voltage low (grounded circuit or misadjusted TPS). Engine must run 20 seconds, at specified curb idle speed, to set code
23	M/C solenoid circuit open or grounded
24	Vehicle Speed Sensor (VSS) circuit — the vehicle must operate up to 2 minutes, at road speed, before this code will set
32	Barometric Pressure Sensor (BARO) circuit low
34	Vacuum sensor or Manifold Absolute Pressure (MAP) circuit — the engine must run up to 2 minutes, at specified curb idle, before this code will set
35	Idle Speed Control (ISC) switch circuit shorted. (Up to 70% TPS for over 5 seconds)
41	No distributor reference signal to the ECM at specified engine vacuum. This code will store in memory
42	Electronic Spark Timing (EST) bypass circuit or EST circuit grounded or open
43	Electronic Spark Control (ESC) retard signal for too long a time; causes retard in EST signal
44	Lean exhaust indication — the engine must run 2 minutes, in closed loop and at part throttle, before this code will set
45	Rich exhaust indication — the engine must run 2 minutes, in closed loop and at part throttle, before this code will set
51	Faulty or improperly installed calibration unit (PROM). It takes up to 30 seconds before this code will set
53	Exhaust Gas Recirculation (EGR) valve vacuum sensor has seen improper EGR control vacuum
54	M/C solenoid voltage high at ECM as a result of a shorted M/C solenoid circuit and/or faulty ECM

Year – 1986
Model – Skyhawk
Engine – 2.0L (121 cid) TBI 4 cyl
Engine Code – VIN P

ECM TROUBLE CODES

Code	Explanation
12	No distributor reference signal to the ECM. This code is not stored in memory and will only flash while the fault is present. Normal code with ignition ON, engine not running
13	Oxygen sensor circuit – the engine must run up to 4 minutes at part throttle, under road load, before this code will set
14	Shorted coolant sensor circuit – the engine must run 2 minutes before this code will set
15	Open coolant sensor circuit – the engine must run 5 minutes before this code will set
21	Throttle Position Sensor (TPS) circuit voltage high (open circuit or misadjusted TPS). The engine must run 10 seconds, at specified curb idle speed, before this code will set
22	Throttle Position Sensor (TPS) circuit voltage low (grounded circuit or misadjusted TPS). Engine must run 20 seconds, at specified curb idle speed, to set code
23	M/C solenoid circuit open or grounded
24	Vehicle Speed Sensor (VSS) circuit – the vehicle must operate up to 2 minutes, at road speed, before this code will set
32	Barometric Pressure Sensor (BARO) circuit low
34	Vacuum sensor or Manifold Absolute Pressure (MAP) circuit – the engine must run up to 2 minutes, at specified curb idle, before this code will set
35	Idle Speed Control (ISC) switch circuit shorted. (Up to 70% TPS for over 5 seconds)
41	No distributor reference signal to the ECM at specified engine vacuum. This code will store in memory
42	Electronic Spark Timing (EST) bypass circuit or EST circuit grounded or open
43	Electronic Spark Control (ESC) retard signal for too long a time; causes retard in EST signal
44	Lean exhaust indication – the engine must run 2 minutes, in closed loop and at part throttle, before this code will set
45	Rich exhaust indication – the engine must run 2 minutes, in closed loop and at part throttle, before this code will set
51	Faulty or improperly installed calibration unit (PROM). It takes up to 30 seconds before this code will set
53	Exhaust Gas Recirculation (EGR) valve vacuum sensor has seen improper EGR control vacuum
54	M/C solenoid voltage high at ECM as a result of a shorted M/C solenoid circuit and/or faulty ECM

Year — 1986
Model — Riviera
Engine — 3.8L (231 cid) SFI V6
Engine Code — VIN B

ECM TROUBLE CODES

Code	Explanation
12	No distributor reference signal to the ECM. This code is not stored in memory and will only flash while the fault is present. Normal code with ignition ON, engine not running
13	Oxygen sensor circuit — the engine must run up to 4 minutes at part throttle, under road load, before this code will set
14	Shorted coolant sensor circuit — the engine must run 2 minutes before this code will set
15	Open coolant sensor circuit — the engine must run 5 minutes before this code will set
21	Throttle Position Sensor (TPS) circuit voltage high (open circuit or misadjusted TPS). The engine must run 10 seconds, at specified curb idle speed, before this code will set
22	Throttle Position Sensor (TPS) circuit voltage low (grounded circuit or misadjusted TPS). Engine must run 20 seconds, at specified curb idle speed, to set code
23	M/C solenoid circuit open or grounded
24	Vehicle Speed Sensor (VSS) circuit — the vehicle must operate up to 2 minutes, at road speed, before this code will set
32	Barometric Pressure Sensor (BARO) circuit low
34	Vacuum sensor or Manifold Absolute Pressure (MAP) circuit — the engine must run up to 2 minutes, at specified curb idle, before this code will set
35	Idle Speed Control (ISC) switch circuit shorted. (Up to 70% TPS for over 5 seconds)
41	No distributor reference signal to the ECM at specified engine vacuum. This code will store in memory
42	Electronic Spark Timing (EST) bypass circuit or EST circuit grounded or open
43	Electronic Spark Control (ESC) retard signal for too long a time; causes retard in EST signal
44	Lean exhaust indication — the engine must run 2 minutes, in closed loop and at part throttle, before this code will set
45	Rich exhaust indication — the engine must run 2 minutes, in closed loop and at part throttle, before this code will set
51	Faulty or improperly installed calibration unit (PROM). It takes up to 30 seconds before this code will set
53	Exhaust Gas Recirculation (EGR) valve vacuum sensor has seen improper EGR control vacuum
54	M/C solenoid voltage high at ECM as a result of a shorted M/C solenoid circuit and/or faulty ECM

Year – 1986
Model – Riviera
Engine – 3.8L (231 cid) SFI V6
Engine Code – VIN B

ECM TROUBLE CODES

Code	Explanation
12	No distributor reference signal to the ECM. This code is not stored in memory and will only flash while the fault is present. Normal code with ignition ON, engine not running
13	Oxygen sensor circuit—the engine must run up to 4 minutes at part throttle, under road load, before this code will set
14	Shorted coolant sensor circuit—the engine must run 2 minutes before this code will set
15	Open coolant sensor circuit—the engine must run 5 minutes before this code will set
21	Throttle Position Sensor (TPS) circuit voltage high (open circuit or misadjusted TPS). The engine must run 10 seconds, at specified curb idle speed, before this code will set
22	Throttle Position Sensor (TPS) circuit voltage low (grounded circuit or misadjusted TPS). Engine must run 20 seconds, at specified curb idle speed, to set code
23	M/C solenoid circuit open or grounded
24	Vehicle Speed Sensor (VSS) circuit—the vehicle must operate up to 2 minutes, at road speed, before this code will set
32	Barometric Pressure Sensor (BARO) circuit low
34	Vacuum sensor or Manifold Absolute Pressure (MAP) circuit—the engine must run up to 2 minutes, at specified curb idle, before this code will set
35	Idle Speed Control (ISC) switch circuit shorted. (Up to 70% TPS for over 5 seconds)
41	No distributor reference signal to the ECM at specified engine vacuum. This code will store in memory
42	Electronic Spark Timing (EST) bypass circuit or EST circuit grounded or open
43	Electronic Spark Control (ESC) retard signal for too long a time; causes retard in EST signal
44	Lean exhaust indication—the engine must run 2 minutes, in closed loop and at part throttle, before this code will set
45	Rich exhaust indication—the engine must run 2 minutes, in closed loop and at part throttle, before this code will set
51	Faulty or improperly installed calibration unit (PROM). It takes up to 30 seconds before this code will set
53	Exhaust Gas Recirculation (EGR) valve vacuum sensor has seen improper EGR control vacuum
54	M/C solenoid voltage high at ECM as a result of a shorted M/C solenoid circuit and/or faulty ECM

Year — 1987
Model — LeSabre
Engine — 3.8L (231 cid) SFI V6
Engine Code — VIN 3

ECM TROUBLE CODES

Code	Explanation
12	No distributor reference signal to the ECM. This code is not stored in memory and will only flash while the fault is present. Normal code with ignition ON, engine not running
13	Oxygen sensor circuit — the engine must run up to 4 minutes at part throttle, under road load, before this code will set
14	Shorted coolant sensor circuit — the engine must run 2 minutes before this code will set
15	Open coolant sensor circuit — the engine must run 5 minutes before this code will set
21	Throttle Position Sensor (TPS) circuit voltage high (open circuit or misadjusted TPS). The engine must run 10 seconds, at specified curb idle speed, before this code will set
22	Throttle Position Sensor (TPS) circuit voltage low (grounded circuit or misadjusted TPS). Engine must run 20 seconds, at specified curb idle speed, to set code
23	M/C solenoid circuit open or grounded
24	Vehicle Speed Sensor (VSS) circuit — the vehicle must operate up to 2 minutes, at road speed, before this code will set
32	Barometric Pressure Sensor (BARO) circuit low
34	Vacuum sensor or Manifold Absolute Pressure (MAP) circuit — the engine must run up to 2 minutes, at specified curb idle, before this code will set
35	Idle Speed Control (ISC) switch circuit shorted. (Up to 70% TPS for over 5 seconds)
41	No distributor reference signal to the ECM at specified engine vacuum. This code will store in memory
42	Electronic Spark Timing (EST) bypass circuit or EST circuit grounded or open
43	Electronic Spark Control (ESC) retard signal for too long a time; causes retard in EST signal
44	Lean exhaust indication — the engine must run 2 minutes, in closed loop and at part throttle, before this code will set
45	Rich exhaust indication — the engine must run 2 minutes, in closed loop and at part throttle, before this code will set
51	Faulty or improperly installed calibration unit (PROM). It takes up to 30 seconds before this code will set
53	Exhaust Gas Recirculation (EGR) valve vacuum sensor has seen improper EGR control vacuum
54	M/C solenoid voltage high at ECM as a result of a shorted M/C solenoid circuit and/or faulty ECM

Year – 1987
Model – LeSabre Estate Wagon
Engine – 5.0L (307 cid) V8
Engine Code – VIN Y

ECM TROUBLE CODES

Code	Explanation
12	No distributor reference signal to the ECM. This code is not stored in memory and will only flash while the fault is present. Normal code with ignition ON, engine not running
13	Oxygen sensor circuit—the engine must run up to 4 minutes at part throttle, under road load, before this code will set
14	Shorted coolant sensor circuit—the engine must run 2 minutes before this code will set
15	Open coolant sensor circuit—the engine must run 5 minutes before this code will set
21	Throttle Position Sensor (TPS) circuit voltage high (open circuit or misadjusted TPS). The engine must run 10 seconds, at specified curb idle speed, before this code will set
22	Throttle Position Sensor (TPS) circuit voltage low (grounded circuit or misadjusted TPS). Engine must run 20 seconds, at specified curb idle speed, to set code
23	M/C solenoid circuit open or grounded
24	Vehicle Speed Sensor (VSS) circuit—the vehicle must operate up to 2 minutes, at road speed, before this code will set
32	Barometric Pressure Sensor (BARO) circuit low
34	Vacuum sensor or Manifold Absolute Pressure (MAP) circuit — the engine must run up to 2 minutes, at specified curb idle, before this code will set
35	Idle Speed Control (ISC) switch circuit shorted. (Up to 70% TPS for over 5 seconds)
41	No distributor reference signal to the ECM at specified engine vacuum. This code will store in memory
42	Electronic Spark Timing (EST) bypass circuit or EST circuit grounded or open
43	Electronic Spark Control (ESC) retard signal for too long a time; causes retard in EST signal
44	Lean exhaust indication—the engine must run 2 minutes, in closed loop and at part throttle, before this code will set
45	Rich exhaust indication—the engine must run 2 minutes, in closed loop and at part throttle, before this code will set
51	Faulty or improperly installed calibration unit (PROM). It takes up to 30 seconds before this code will set
53	Exhaust Gas Recirculation (EGR) valve vacuum sensor has seen improper EGR control vacuum
54	M/C solenoid voltage high at ECM as a result of a shorted M/C solenoid circuit and/or faulty ECM

Year – 1987
Model – Electra
Engine – 3.8L (231 cid) SFI V6
Engine Code – VIN 3

ECM TROUBLE CODES

Code	Explanation
12	No distributor reference signal to the ECM. This code is not stored in memory and will only flash while the fault is present. Normal code with ignition ON, engine not running
13	Oxygen sensor circuit – the engine must run up to 4 minutes at part throttle, under road load, before this code will set
14	Shorted coolant sensor circuit – the engine must run 2 minutes before this code will set
15	Open coolant sensor circuit – the engine must run 5 minutes before this code will set
21	Throttle Position Sensor (TPS) circuit voltage high (open circuit or misadjusted TPS). The engine must run 10 seconds, at specified curb idle speed, before this code will set
22	Throttle Position Sensor (TPS) circuit voltage low (grounded circuit or misadjusted TPS). Engine must run 20 seconds, at specified curb idle speed, to set code
23	M/C solenoid circuit open or grounded
24	Vehicle Speed Sensor (VSS) circuit – the vehicle must operate up to 2 minutes, at road speed, before this code will set
32	Barometric Pressure Sensor (BARO) circuit low
34	Vacuum sensor or Manifold Absolute Pressure (MAP) circuit – the engine must run up to 2 minutes, at specified curb idle, before this code will set
35	Idle Speed Control (ISC) switch circuit shorted. (Up to 70% TPS for over 5 seconds)
41	No distributor reference signal to the ECM at specified engine vacuum. This code will store in memory
42	Electronic Spark Timing (EST) bypass circuit or EST circuit grounded or open
43	Electronic Spark Control (ESC) retard signal for too long a time; causes retard in EST signal
44	Lean exhaust indication – the engine must run 2 minutes, in closed loop and at part throttle, before this code will set
45	Rich exhaust indication – the engine must run 2 minutes, in closed loop and at part throttle, before this code will set
51	Faulty or improperly installed calibration unit (PROM). It takes up to 30 seconds before this code will set
53	Exhaust Gas Recirculation (EGR) valve vacuum sensor has seen improper EGR control vacuum
54	M/C solenoid voltage high at ECM as a result of a shorted M/C solenoid circuit and/or faulty ECM

Year — 1987
Model — Electra Estate Wagon
Engine — 5.0L (307 cid) V8
Engine Code — VIN Y

ECM TROUBLE CODES

Code	Explanation
12	No distributor reference signal to the ECM. This code is not stored in memory and will only flash while the fault is present. Normal code with ignition ON, engine not running
13	Oxygen sensor circuit — the engine must run up to 4 minutes at part throttle, under road load, before this code will set
14	Shorted coolant sensor circuit — the engine must run 2 minutes before this code will set
15	Open coolant sensor circuit — the engine must run 5 minutes before this code will set
21	Throttle Position Sensor (TPS) circuit voltage high (open circuit or misadjusted TPS). The engine must run 10 seconds, at specified curb idle speed, before this code will set
22	Throttle Position Sensor (TPS) circuit voltage low (grounded circuit or misadjusted TPS). Engine must run 20 seconds, at specified curb idle speed, to set code
23	M/C solenoid circuit open or grounded
24	Vehicle Speed Sensor (VSS) circuit — the vehicle must operate up to 2 minutes, at road speed, before this code will set
32	Barometric Pressure Sensor (BARO) circuit low
34	Vacuum sensor or Manifold Absolute Pressure (MAP) circuit — the engine must run up to 2 minutes, at specified curb idle, before this code will set
35	Idle Speed Control (ISC) switch circuit shorted. (Up to 70% TPS for over 5 seconds)
41	No distributor reference signal to the ECM at specified engine vacuum. This code will store in memory
42	Electronic Spark Timing (EST) bypass circuit or EST circuit grounded or open
43	Electronic Spark Control (ESC) retard signal for too long a time; causes retard in EST signal
44	Lean exhaust indication — the engine must run 2 minutes, in closed loop and at part throttle, before this code will set
45	Rich exhaust indication — the engine must run 2 minutes, in closed loop and at part throttle, before this code will set
51	Faulty or improperly installed calibration unit (PROM). It takes up to 30 seconds before this code will set
53	Exhaust Gas Recirculation (EGR) valve vacuum sensor has seen improper EGR control vacuum
54	M/C solenoid voltage high at ECM as a result of a shorted M/C solenoid circuit and/or faulty ECM

Year — 1987
Model — Century
Engine — 2.5L (151 cid) EFI 4 cyl
Engine Code — VIN R

ECM TROUBLE CODES

Code	Explanation
12	No distributor reference signal to the ECM. This code is not stored in memory and will only flash while the fault is present. Normal code with ignition ON, engine not running
13	Oxygen sensor circuit — the engine must run up to 4 minutes at part throttle, under road load, before this code will set
14	Shorted coolant sensor circuit — the engine must run 2 minutes before this code will set
15	Open coolant sensor circuit — the engine must run 5 minutes before this code will set
21	Throttle Position Sensor (TPS) circuit voltage high (open circuit or misadjusted TPS). The engine must run 10 seconds, at specified curb idle speed, before this code will set
22	Throttle Position Sensor (TPS) circuit voltage low (grounded circuit or misadjusted TPS). Engine must run 20 seconds, at specified curb idle speed, to set code
23	M/C solenoid circuit open or grounded
24	Vehicle Speed Sensor (VSS) circuit — the vehicle must operate up to 2 minutes, at road speed, before this code will set
32	Barometric Pressure Sensor (BARO) circuit low
34	Vacuum sensor or Manifold Absolute Pressure (MAP) circuit — the engine must run up to 2 minutes, at specified curb idle, before this code will set
35	Idle Speed Control (ISC) switch circuit shorted. (Up to 70% TPS for over 5 seconds)
41	No distributor reference signal to the ECM at specified engine vacuum. This code will store in memory
42	Electronic Spark Timing (EST) bypass circuit or EST circuit grounded or open
43	Electronic Spark Control (ESC) retard signal for too long a time; causes retard in EST signal
44	Lean exhaust indication — the engine must run 2 minutes, in closed loop and at part throttle, before this code will set
45	Rich exhaust indication — the engine must run 2 minutes, in closed loop and at part throttle, before this code will set
51	Faulty or improperly installed calibration unit (PROM). It takes up to 30 seconds before this code will set
53	Exhaust Gas Recirculation (EGR) valve vacuum sensor has seen improper EGR control vacuum
54	M/C solenoid voltage high at ECM as a result of a shorted M/C solenoid circuit and/or faulty ECM

Year – 1987
Model – Century
Engine – 2.8L (171 cid) V6
Engine Code – VIN W

ECM TROUBLE CODES

Code	Explanation
12	No distributor reference signal to the ECM. This code is not stored in memory and will only flash while the fault is present. Normal code with ignition ON, engine not running
13	Oxygen sensor circuit – the engine must run up to 4 minutes at part throttle, under road load, before this code will set
14	Shorted coolant sensor circuit – the engine must run 2 minutes before this code will set
15	Open coolant sensor circuit – the engine must run 5 minutes before this code will set
21	Throttle Position Sensor (TPS) circuit voltage high (open circuit or misadjusted TPS). The engine must run 10 seconds, at specified curb idle speed, before this code will set
22	Throttle Position Sensor (TPS) circuit voltage low (grounded circuit or misadjusted TPS). Engine must run 20 seconds, at specified curb idle speed, to set code
23	M/C solenoid circuit open or grounded
24	Vehicle Speed Sensor (VSS) circuit – the vehicle must operate up to 2 minutes, at road speed, before this code will set
32	Barometric Pressure Sensor (BARO) circuit low
34	Vacuum sensor or Manifold Absolute Pressure (MAP) circuit – the engine must run up to 2 minutes, at specified curb idle, before this code will set
35	Idle Speed Control (ISC) switch circuit shorted. (Up to 70% TPS for over 5 seconds)
41	No distributor reference signal to the ECM at specified engine vacuum. This code will store in memory
42	Electronic Spark Timing (EST) bypass circuit or EST circuit grounded or open
43	Electronic Spark Control (ESC) retard signal for too long a time; causes retard in EST signal
44	Lean exhaust indication – the engine must run 2 minutes, in closed loop and at part throttle, before this code will set
45	Rich exhaust indication – the engine must run 2 minutes, in closed loop and at part throttle, before this code will set
51	Faulty or improperly installed calibration unit (PROM). It takes up to 30 seconds before this code will set
53	Exhaust Gas Recirculation (EGR) valve vacuum sensor has seen improper EGR control vacuum
54	M/C solenoid voltage high at ECM as a result of a shorted M/C solenoid circuit and/or faulty ECM

Year — 1987
Model — Century
Engine — 3.8L (231 cid) SFI V6
Engine Code — VIN 3

ECM TROUBLE CODES

Code	Explanation
12	No distributor reference signal to the ECM. This code is not stored in memory and will only flash while the fault is present. Normal code with ignition ON, engine not running
13	Oxygen sensor circuit — the engine must run up to 4 minutes at part throttle, under road load, before this code will set
14	Shorted coolant sensor circuit — the engine must run 2 minutes before this code will set
15	Open coolant sensor circuit — the engine must run 5 minutes before this code will set
21	Throttle Position Sensor (TPS) circuit voltage high (open circuit or misadjusted TPS). The engine must run 10 seconds, at specified curb idle speed, before this code will set
22	Throttle Position Sensor (TPS) circuit voltage low (grounded circuit or misadjusted TPS). Engine must run 20 seconds, at specified curb idle speed, to set code
23	M/C solenoid circuit open or grounded
24	Vehicle Speed Sensor (VSS) circuit — the vehicle must operate up to 2 minutes, at road speed, before this code will set
32	Barometric Pressure Sensor (BARO) circuit low
34	Vacuum sensor or Manifold Absolute Pressure (MAP) circuit — the engine must run up to 2 minutes, at specified curb idle, before this code will set
35	Idle Speed Control (ISC) switch circuit shorted. (Up to 70% TPS for over 5 seconds)
41	No distributor reference signal to the ECM at specified engine vacuum. This code will store in memory
42	Electronic Spark Timing (EST) bypass circuit or EST circuit grounded or open
43	Electronic Spark Control (ESC) retard signal for too long a time; causes retard in EST signal
44	Lean exhaust indication — the engine must run 2 minutes, in closed loop and at part throttle, before this code will set
45	Rich exhaust indication — the engine must run 2 minutes, in closed loop and at part throttle, before this code will set
51	Faulty or improperly installed calibration unit (PROM). It takes up to 30 seconds before this code will set
53	Exhaust Gas Recirculation (EGR) valve vacuum sensor has seen improper EGR control vacuum
54	M/C solenoid voltage high at ECM as a result of a shorted M/C solenoid circuit and/or faulty ECM

Year — 1987
Model — Regal
Engine — 3.8L (231 cid) V6
Engine Code — VIN A

ECM TROUBLE CODES

Code	Explanation
12	No distributor reference signal to the ECM. This code is not stored in memory and will only flash while the fault is present. Normal code with ignition ON, engine not running
13	Oxygen sensor circuit — the engine must run up to 4 minutes at part throttle, under road load, before this code will set
14	Shorted coolant sensor circuit — the engine must run 2 minutes before this code will set
15	Open coolant sensor circuit — the engine must run 5 minutes before this code will set
21	Throttle Position Sensor (TPS) circuit voltage high (open circuit or misadjusted TPS). The engine must run 10 seconds, at specified curb idle speed, before this code will set
22	Throttle Position Sensor (TPS) circuit voltage low (grounded circuit or misadjusted TPS). Engine must run 20 seconds, at specified curb idle speed, to set code
23	M/C solenoid circuit open or grounded
24	Vehicle Speed Sensor (VSS) circuit — the vehicle must operate up to 2 minutes, at road speed, before this code will set
32	Barometric Pressure Sensor (BARO) circuit low
34	Vacuum sensor or Manifold Absolute Pressure (MAP) circuit — the engine must run up to 2 minutes, at specified curb idle, before this code will set
35	Idle Speed Control (ISC) switch circuit shorted. (Up to 70% TPS for over 5 seconds)
41	No distributor reference signal to the ECM at specified engine vacuum. This code will store in memory
42	Electronic Spark Timing (EST) bypass circuit or EST circuit grounded or open
43	Electronic Spark Control (ESC) retard signal for too long a time; causes retard in EST signal
44	Lean exhaust indication — the engine must run 2 minutes, in closed loop and at part throttle, before this code will set
45	Rich exhaust indication — the engine must run 2 minutes, in closed loop and at part throttle, before this code will set
51	Faulty or improperly installed calibration unit (PROM). It takes up to 30 seconds before this code will set
53	Exhaust Gas Recirculation (EGR) valve vacuum sensor has seen improper EGR control vacuum
54	M/C solenoid voltage high at ECM as a result of a shorted M/C solenoid circuit and/or faulty ECM

Year — 1987
Model — Regal
Engine — 3.8L (231 cid) SFI V6
Engine Code — VIN 7

ECM TROUBLE CODES

Code	Explanation
12	No distributor reference signal to the ECM. This code is not stored in memory and will only flash while the fault is present. Normal code with ignition ON, engine not running
13	Oxygen sensor circuit — the engine must run up to 4 minutes at part throttle, under road load, before this code will set
14	Shorted coolant sensor circuit — the engine must run 2 minutes before this code will set
15	Open coolant sensor circuit — the engine must run 5 minutes before this code will set
21	Throttle Position Sensor (TPS) circuit voltage high (open circuit or misadjusted TPS). The engine must run 10 seconds, at specified curb idle speed, before this code will set
22	Throttle Position Sensor (TPS) circuit voltage low (grounded circuit or misadjusted TPS). Engine must run 20 seconds, at specified curb idle speed, to set code
23	M/C solenoid circuit open or grounded
24	Vehicle Speed Sensor (VSS) circuit — the vehicle must operate up to 2 minutes, at road speed, before this code will set
32	Barometric Pressure Sensor (BARO) circuit low
34	Vacuum sensor or Manifold Absolute Pressure (MAP) circuit — the engine must run up to 2 minutes, at specified curb idle, before this code will set
35	Idle Speed Control (ISC) switch circuit shorted. (Up to 70% TPS for over 5 seconds)
41	No distributor reference signal to the ECM at specified engine vacuum. This code will store in memory
42	Electronic Spark Timing (EST) bypass circuit or EST circuit grounded or open
43	Electronic Spark Control (ESC) retard signal for too long a time; causes retard in EST signal
44	Lean exhaust indication — the engine must run 2 minutes, in closed loop and at part throttle, before this code will set
45	Rich exhaust indication — the engine must run 2 minutes, in closed loop and at part throttle, before this code will set
51	Faulty or improperly installed calibration unit (PROM). It takes up to 30 seconds before this code will set
53	Exhaust Gas Recirculation (EGR) valve vacuum sensor has seen improper EGR control vacuum
54	M/C solenoid voltage high at ECM as a result of a shorted M/C solenoid circuit and/or faulty ECM

Year — 1987
Model — Regal
Engine — 5.0L (305 cid) V8
Engine Code — VIN H

ECM TROUBLE CODES

Code	Explanation
12	No distributor reference signal to the ECM. This code is not stored in memory and will only flash while the fault is present. Normal code with ignition ON, engine not running
13	Oxygen sensor circuit — the engine must run up to 4 minutes at part throttle, under road load, before this code will set
14	Shorted coolant sensor circuit — the engine must run 2 minutes before this code will set
15	Open coolant sensor circuit — the engine must run 5 minutes before this code will set
21	Throttle Position Sensor (TPS) circuit voltage high (open circuit or misadjusted TPS). The engine must run 10 seconds, at specified curb idle speed, before this code will set
22	Throttle Position Sensor (TPS) circuit voltage low (grounded circuit or misadjusted TPS). Engine must run 20 seconds, at specified curb idle speed, to set code
23	M/C solenoid circuit open or grounded
24	Vehicle Speed Sensor (VSS) circuit — the vehicle must operate up to 2 minutes, at road speed, before this code will set
32	Barometric Pressure Sensor (BARO) circuit low
34	Vacuum sensor or Manifold Absolute Pressure (MAP) circuit — the engine must run up to 2 minutes, at specified curb idle, before this code will set
35	Idle Speed Control (ISC) switch circuit shorted. (Up to 70% TPS for over 5 seconds)
41	No distributor reference signal to the ECM at specified engine vacuum. This code will store in memory
42	Electronic Spark Timing (EST) bypass circuit or EST circuit grounded or open
43	Electronic Spark Control (ESC) retard signal for too long a time; causes retard in EST signal
44	Lean exhaust indication — the engine must run 2 minutes, in closed loop and at part throttle, before this code will set
45	Rich exhaust indication — the engine must run 2 minutes, in closed loop and at part throttle, before this code will set
51	Faulty or improperly installed calibration unit (PROM). It takes up to 30 seconds before this code will set
53	Exhaust Gas Recirculation (EGR) valve vacuum sensor has seen improper EGR control vacuum
54	M/C solenoid voltage high at ECM as a result of a shorted M/C solenoid circuit and/or faulty ECM

Year – 1987
Model – Skylark
Engine – 2.5L (151 cid) TBI 4 cyl
Engine Code – VIN U

ECM TROUBLE CODES

Code	Explanation
12	No distributor reference signal to the ECM. This code is not stored in memory and will only flash while the fault is present. Normal code with ignition ON, engine not running
13	Oxygen sensor circuit – the engine must run up to 4 minutes at part throttle, under road load, before this code will set
14	Shorted coolant sensor circuit – the engine must run 2 minutes before this code will set
15	Open coolant sensor circuit – the engine must run 5 minutes before this code will set
21	Throttle Position Sensor (TPS) circuit voltage high (open circuit or misadjusted TPS). The engine must run 10 seconds, at specified curb idle speed, before this code will set
22	Throttle Position Sensor (TPS) circuit voltage low (grounded circuit or misadjusted TPS). Engine must run 20 seconds, at specified curb idle speed, to set code
23	M/C solenoid circuit open or grounded
24	Vehicle Speed Sensor (VSS) circuit – the vehicle must operate up to 2 minutes, at road speed, before this code will set
32	Barometric Pressure Sensor (BARO) circuit low
34	Vacuum sensor or Manifold Absolute Pressure (MAP) circuit — the engine must run up to 2 minutes, at specified curb idle, before this code will set
35	Idle Speed Control (ISC) switch circuit shorted. (Up to 70% TPS for over 5 seconds)
41	No distributor reference signal to the ECM at specified engine vacuum. This code will store in memory
42	Electronic Spark Timing (EST) bypass circuit or EST circuit grounded or open
43	Electronic Spark Control (ESC) retard signal for too long a time; causes retard in EST signal
44	Lean exhaust indication – the engine must run 2 minutes, in closed loop and at part throttle, before this code will set
45	Rich exhaust indication – the engine must run 2 minutes, in closed loop and at part throttle, before this code will set
51	Faulty or improperly installed calibration unit (PROM). It takes up to 30 seconds before this code will set
53	Exhaust Gas Recirculation (EGR) valve vacuum sensor has seen improper EGR control vacuum
54	M/C solenoid voltage high at ECM as a result of a shorted M/C solenoid circuit and/or faulty ECM

Year — 1987
Model — Skylark
Engine — 3.0L (181 cid) MFI V6
Engine Code — VIN L

ECM TROUBLE CODES

Code	Explanation
12	No distributor reference signal to the ECM. This code is not stored in memory and will only flash while the fault is present. Normal code with ignition ON, engine not running
13	Oxygen sensor circuit—the engine must run up to 4 minutes at part throttle, under road load, before this code will set
14	Shorted coolant sensor circuit—the engine must run 2 minutes before this code will set
15	Open coolant sensor circuit—the engine must run 5 minutes before this code will set
21	Throttle Position Sensor (TPS) circuit voltage high (open circuit or misadjusted TPS). The engine must run 10 seconds, at specified curb idle speed, before this code will set
22	Throttle Position Sensor (TPS) circuit voltage low (grounded circuit or misadjusted TPS). Engine must run 20 seconds, at specified curb idle speed, to set code
23	M/C solenoid circuit open or grounded
24	Vehicle Speed Sensor (VSS) circuit—the vehicle must operate up to 2 minutes, at road speed, before this code will set
32	Barometric Pressure Sensor (BARO) circuit low
34	Vacuum sensor or Manifold Absolute Pressure (MAP) circuit — the engine must run up to 2 minutes, at specified curb idle, before this code will set
35	Idle Speed Control (ISC) switch circuit shorted. (Up to 70% TPS for over 5 seconds)
41	No distributor reference signal to the ECM at specified engine vacuum. This code will store in memory
42	Electronic Spark Timing (EST) bypass circuit or EST circuit grounded or open
43	Electronic Spark Control (ESC) retard signal for too long a time; causes retard in EST signal
44	Lean exhaust indication—the engine must run 2 minutes, in closed loop and at part throttle, before this code will set
45	Rich exhaust indication—the engine must run 2 minutes, in closed loop and at part throttle, before this code will set
51	Faulty or improperly installed calibration unit (PROM). It takes up to 30 seconds before this code will set
53	Exhaust Gas Recirculation (EGR) valve vacuum sensor has seen improper EGR control vacuum
54	M/C solenoid voltage high at ECM as a result of a shorted M/C solenoid circuit and/or faulty ECM

Year – 1987
Model – Skyhawk
Engine – 2.0L (121 cid) TBI 4 cyl
Engine Code – VIN K

ECM TROUBLE CODES

Code	Explanation
12	No distributor reference signal to the ECM. This code is not stored in memory and will only flash while the fault is present. Normal code with ignition ON, engine not running
13	Oxygen sensor circuit – the engine must run up to 4 minutes at part throttle, under road load, before this code will set
14	Shorted coolant sensor circuit – the engine must run 2 minutes before this code will set
15	Open coolant sensor circuit – the engine must run 5 minutes before this code will set
21	Throttle Position Sensor (TPS) circuit voltage high (open circuit or misadjusted TPS). The engine must run 10 seconds, at specified curb idle speed, before this code will set
22	Throttle Position Sensor (TPS) circuit voltage low (grounded circuit or misadjusted TPS). Engine must run 20 seconds, at specified curb idle speed, to set code
23	M/C solenoid circuit open or grounded
24	Vehicle Speed Sensor (VSS) circuit – the vehicle must operate up to 2 minutes, at road speed, before this code will set
32	Barometric Pressure Sensor (BARO) circuit low
34	Vacuum sensor or Manifold Absolute Pressure (MAP) circuit — the engine must run up to 2 minutes, at specified curb idle, before this code will set
35	Idle Speed Control (ISC) switch circuit shorted. (Up to 70% TPS for over 5 seconds)
41	No distributor reference signal to the ECM at specified engine vacuum. This code will store in memory
42	Electronic Spark Timing (EST) bypass circuit or EST circuit grounded or open
43	Electronic Spark Control (ESC) retard signal for too long a time; causes retard in EST signal
44	Lean exhaust indication – the engine must run 2 minutes, in closed loop and at part throttle, before this code will set
45	Rich exhaust indication – the engine must run 2 minutes, in closed loop and at part throttle, before this code will set
51	Faulty or improperly installed calibration unit (PROM). It takes up to 30 seconds before this code will set
53	Exhaust Gas Recirculation (EGR) valve vacuum sensor has seen improper EGR control vacuum
54	M/C solenoid voltage high at ECM as a result of a shorted M/C solenoid circuit and/or faulty ECM

Year — 1987
Model — Skyhawk
Engine — 2.0L (121 cid) TBI 4 cyl
Engine Code — VIN I

ECM TROUBLE CODES

Code	Explanation
12	No distributor reference signal to the ECM. This code is not stored in memory and will only flash while the fault is present. Normal code with ignition ON, engine not running
13	Oxygen sensor circuit — the engine must run up to 4 minutes at part throttle, under road load, before this code will set
14	Shorted coolant sensor circuit — the engine must run 2 minutes before this code will set
15	Open coolant sensor circuit — the engine must run 5 minutes before this code will set
21	Throttle Position Sensor (TPS) circuit voltage high (open circuit or misadjusted TPS). The engine must run 10 seconds, at specified curb idle speed, before this code will set
22	Throttle Position Sensor (TPS) circuit voltage low (grounded circuit or misadjusted TPS). Engine must run 20 seconds, at specified curb idle speed, to set code
23	M/C solenoid circuit open or grounded
24	Vehicle Speed Sensor (VSS) circuit — the vehicle must operate up to 2 minutes, at road speed, before this code will set
32	Barometric Pressure Sensor (BARO) circuit low
34	Vacuum sensor or Manifold Absolute Pressure (MAP) circuit — the engine must run up to 2 minutes, at specified curb idle, before this code will set
35	Idle Speed Control (ISC) switch circuit shorted. (Up to 70% TPS for over 5 seconds)
41	No distributor reference signal to the ECM at specified engine vacuum. This code will store in memory
42	Electronic Spark Timing (EST) bypass circuit or EST circuit grounded or open
43	Electronic Spark Control (ESC) retard signal for too long a time; causes retard in EST signal
44	Lean exhaust indication — the engine must run 2 minutes, in closed loop and at part throttle, before this code will set
45	Rich exhaust indication — the engine must run 2 minutes, in closed loop and at part throttle, before this code will set
51	Faulty or improperly installed calibration unit (PROM). It takes up to 30 seconds before this code will set
53	Exhaust Gas Recirculation (EGR) valve vacuum sensor has seen improper EGR control vacuum
54	M/C solenoid voltage high at ECM as a result of a shorted M/C solenoid circuit and/or faulty ECM

Year — 1987
Model — Skyhawk
Engine — 2.0L (121 cid) MFI Turbo
Engine Code — VIN M

ECM TROUBLE CODES

Code	Explanation
12	No distributor reference signal to the ECM. This code is not stored in memory and will only flash while the fault is present. Normal code with ignition ON, engine not running
13	Oxygen sensor circuit — the engine must run up to 4 minutes at part throttle, under road load, before this code will set
14	Shorted coolant sensor circuit — the engine must run 2 minutes before this code will set
15	Open coolant sensor circuit — the engine must run 5 minutes before this code will set
21	Throttle Position Sensor (TPS) circuit voltage high (open circuit or misadjusted TPS). The engine must run 10 seconds, at specified curb idle speed, before this code will set
22	Throttle Position Sensor (TPS) circuit voltage low (grounded circuit or misadjusted TPS). Engine must run 20 seconds, at specified curb idle speed, to set code
23	M/C solenoid circuit open or grounded
24	Vehicle Speed Sensor (VSS) circuit — the vehicle must operate up to 2 minutes, at road speed, before this code will set
32	Barometric Pressure Sensor (BARO) circuit low
34	Vacuum sensor or Manifold Absolute Pressure (MAP) circuit — the engine must run up to 2 minutes, at specified curb idle, before this code will set
35	Idle Speed Control (ISC) switch circuit shorted. (Up to 70% TPS for over 5 seconds)
41	No distributor reference signal to the ECM at specified engine vacuum. This code will store in memory
42	Electronic Spark Timing (EST) bypass circuit or EST circuit grounded or open
43	Electronic Spark Control (ESC) retard signal for too long a time; causes retard in EST signal
44	Lean exhaust indication — the engine must run 2 minutes, in closed loop and at part throttle, before this code will set
45	Rich exhaust indication — the engine must run 2 minutes, in closed loop and at part throttle, before this code will set
51	Faulty or improperly installed calibration unit (PROM). It takes up to 30 seconds before this code will set
53	Exhaust Gas Recirculation (EGR) valve vacuum sensor has seen improper EGR control vacuum
54	M/C solenoid voltage high at ECM as a result of a shorted M/C solenoid circuit and/or faulty ECM

Year — 1987
Model — Riviera
Engine — 3.8L (231 cid) SFI V6
Engine Code — VIN 3

ECM TROUBLE CODES

Code	Explanation
E012	Reference pulse; indicates ECM's diagnostic system is operating
E013	Open oxygen sensor circuit — "Service Engine Soon" message displayed
E014	Coolant temperature sensor circuit — high temperature — "Service Engine Soon" message displayed and forces cooling fans ON
E015	Coolant temperature sensor circuit — low temperature — "Service Engine Soon" message displayed
E016	System voltage out of range — all solenoids — "Service Engine Soon" message displayed
E021	Throttle Position Sensor (TPS) circuit (signal voltage high) — "Service Engine Soon" message displayed
E022	Throttle Position Sensor (TPS) circuit (signal voltage low) — "Service Engine Soon" message displayed
E024	Vehicle Speed Sensor (VSS) circuit failure — TCC functions are disengaged while specified malfunctions remains current — "Service Engine Soon" message displayed
E029	4th gear switch circuit — "Service Engine Soon" message displayed
E032	EGR vacuum control system fault — "Service Engine Soon" message displayed
E033	Mass Aif Flow (MAF) sensor signal frequency high — "Service Engine Soon" message displayed
E034	Mass Air Flow (MAF) sensor frequency low — "Service Engine Soon" message displayed
E037	MAT sensor high temperature indicated — "Service Engine Soon" message displayed
E038	MAT sensor low temperature inciated — "Service Engine Soon" message displayed
E040	Power steering pressure switch circuit open — A/C clutch and cruise functions are disengaged while specified malfunctions remains current — "Service Engine Soon" message displayed
E041	Cam sensor circuit failure — C^{3}I module to ECM — "Service Engine Soon" message displayed
E042	C^{3}I-EST or bypass circuit failure — "Service Engine Soon" message displayed and causes system to operate in bypass spark mode
E043	Electronic Spark Control (ESC) system failure — "Service Engine Soon" message displayed
E044	Lean exhaust indication — "Service Engine Soon" message displayed and forces open loop operation
E045	Rich exhaust indication — "Service Engine Soon" message displayed and forces open loop operation
E047	ECM-BCM data — A/C clutch and cruise functions are disengaged while specified malfunctions remains current — "Service Engine Soon" message displayed
E051	ECM PROM error — "Service Engine Soon" message displayed, causes system to operate in bypass spark mode and/or back-up fuel mode
E052	Calpak error — "Service Engine Soon" message displayed
E055	ECM error — "Service Engine Soon" message displayed

Year – 1988
Model – LeSabre
Engine – 3.8L (231 cid) SFI V6
Engine Code – VIN C

ECM TROUBLE CODES

Code	Explanation
12	Reference pulse; indicates ECM's diagnostic system is operating
13	Oxygen sensor circuit (open circuit)
14	Coolant temperature sensor circuit (high temperature indicated)
15	Coolant temperature sensor circuit (low temperature indicated)
16	System voltage high
21	Throttle Position Sensor (TPS) circuit (signal voltage high)
22	Throttle Position Sensor (TPS) circuit (signal voltage low)
23	Manifold Air Temperature (MAT) sensor circuit (low temperature indicated)
24	Vehicle Speed Sensor (VSS) circuit
25	Manifold Air Temperature (MAT) sensor circuit (high temperature indicated)
26	Quad Driver (QDM) error
27, 28, 29	Gear switch diagnosis
31	Park/Neutral Switch circuit
34	Mass Air Flow (MAF) sensor circuit (GM/SEC low)
38	Brake switch circuit
39	Torque converter clutch circuit diagnosis
41	Cam sensor circuit
42	Electronic Spark Timing (EST) circuit
43	Electronic Spark Control (ESC) circuit
44	Oxygen sensor circuit (lean exhaust indicated)
45	Oxygen sensor circuit (rich exhaust indicated)
46	Power steering press switch
48	Misfire
51	Mem–Cal error
63, 64, 65	Exhaust Gas Recirculation (EGR) circuit

Year – 1988
Model – LeSabre
Engine – 3.8L (231 cid) SFI V6
Engine Code – VIN 3

ECM TROUBLE CODES

Code	Explanation
12	Reference pulse; indicates ECM's diagnostic system is operating
13	Oxygen sensor circuit (open circuit)
14	Coolant temperature sensor circuit (high temperature indicated)
15	Coolant temperature sensor circuit (low temperature indicated)
21	Throttle Position Sensor (TPS) circuit (signal voltage high)
22	Throttle Position Sensor (TPS) circuit (signal voltage low)
23	Manifold Air Temperature (MAT) sensor circuit (low temperature indicated)
24	Vehicle Speed Sensor (VSS) circuit
25	Manifold Air Temperature (MAT) sensor circuit (high temperature indicated)
32	Exhaust Gas Recirculation (EGR) circuit
33	Mass Air Flow (MAF) sensor circuit (GM/SEC high)
34	Mass Air Flow (MAF) sensor circuit (GM/SEC low)
41	Cam sensor circuit
42	Electronic Spark Timing (EST) circuit
43	Electronic Spark Control (ESC) circuit
44	Oxygen sensor circuit (lean exhaust indicated)
45	Oxygen sensor circuit (rich exhaust indicated)
51	PROM error (faulty or incorrect PROM)
52	Calpak error (faulty or incorrect calpak)
55	ECM error

Year – 1988
Model – LeSabre Estate Wagon
Engine – 5.0L (307cid) V8
Engine Code – VIN Y

ECM TROUBLE CODES

Code	Explanation
12	No distributor reference signal to ECM. This code is not stored in memory and will only flash while the fault is present. This is a normal code with ignition ON, engine not running
13	Oxygen sensor circuit – the engine must run up to 4 minutes at part throttle under road load before this code will set
14	Shorted coolant temperature sensor circuit – the engine must run 2 minutes before this code will set
15	Open coolant temperature sensor circuit – the engine must run 5 minutes before this code will set
21	Throttle Position Sensor (TPS) circuit voltage high (open circuit or misadjusted TPS). The engine must run 10 seconds at specified curb idle speed before this code will set
22	Throttle Position Sensor (TPS) circuit signal voltage low (grounded circuit or misadjusted TPS). Engine must run 20 seconds at specified curb idle speed to set code
23	M/C solenoid circuit open or grounded
24	Vehicle Speed Sensor (VSS) circuit – the vehicle must operate up to 2 minutes at road speed before this code will set
31	Canister purge solenoid voltage high to ECM above idle rpm will set this code
34	Manifold Absolute Pressure (MAP) sensor circuit – too high or too low voltage signal at a specified amount time and rpm will cause this code to set
41	No distributor reference signal to the ECM at specified engine vacuum. This code will store in memory
42	Electronic Spark Timing (EST) bypass circuit or EST circuit grounded or open
43	Electronic Spark Control (ESC) retard signal for too long a time, causes retard in EST signal
44	Lean exhaust indication – the engione must run 2 minutes, in closed loop and at part throttle before this code will set
45	Rich exhaust indication – the engine must run 2 minutes in closed loop and at part throttle before this code will set
51	Faulty or improperly installed calibration unit (PROM). It takes up to 30 seconds before this code will set
53	Exhaust Gas Recirculation (EGR) valve vacuum sensor has seen improper EGR control vacuum – California only
55	M/C solenoid voltage high, at ECM, as a result of a shorted M/C solenoid circuit and/or faulty ECM

GENERAL MOTORS CORPORATION
DIAGNOSTIC CODE DATA

Year–1988
Model–Electra
Engine–3.8L (231 cid) SFI V6
Engine Code–VIN 3

ECM TROUBLE CODES

Code	Explanation
12	Reference pulse; indicates ECM's diagnostic system is operating
13	Oxygen sensor circuit (open circuit)
14	Coolant temperature sensor circuit (high temperature indicated)
15	Coolant temperature sensor circuit (low temperature indicated)
21	Throttle Position Sensor (TPS) circuit (signal voltage high)
22	Throttle Position Sensor (TPS) circuit (signal voltage low)
23	Manifold Air Temperature (MAT) sensor circuit (low temperature indicated)
24	Vehicle Speed Sensor (VSS) circuit
25	Manifold Air Temperature (MAT) sensor circuit (high temperature indicated)
32	Exhaust Gas Recirculation (EGR) circuit
33	Mass Air Flow (MAF) sensor circuit (GM/SEC high)
34	Mass Air Flow (MAF) sensor circuit (GM/SEC low)
41	Cam sensor circuit
42	Electronic Spark Timing (EST) circuit
43	Electronic Spark Control (ESC) circuit
44	Oxygen sensor circuit (lean exhaust indicated)
45	Oxygen sensor circuit (rich exhaust indicated)
51	PROM error (faulty or incorrect PROM)
53	Calpak error (faulty or incorrect calpak)
55	ECM error

Year — 1988
Model — Electra
Engine — 3.8L (231 cid) SFI V6
Engine Code — VIN C

ECM TROUBLE CODES

Code	Explanation
12	Reference pulse; indicates ECM's diagnostic system is operating
13	Oxygen sensor circuit (open circuit)
14	Coolant temperature sensor circuit (high temperature indicated)
15	Coolant temperature sensor circuit (low temperature indicated)
16	System voltage high
21	Throttle Position Sensor (TPS) circuit (signal voltage high)
22	Throttle Position Sensor (TPS) circuit (signal voltage low)
23	Manifold Air Temperature (MAT) sensor circuit (low temperature indicated)
24	Vehicle Speed Sensor (VSS) circuit
25	Manifold Air Temperature (MAT) sensor circuit (high temperature indicated)
26	Quad Driver (QDM) error
27, 28, 29	Gear switch diagnosis
31	Park/Neutral Switch circuit
34	Mass Air Flow (MAF) sensor circuit (GM/SEC low)
38	Brake switch circuit
39	Torque converter clutch circuit diagnosis
41	Cam sensor circuit
42	Electronic Spark Timing (EST) circuit
43	Electronic Spark Control (ESC) circuit
44	Oxygen sensor circuit (lean exhaust indicated)
45	Oxygen sensor circuit (rich exhaust indicated)
46	Power steering press switch
48	Misfire
51	Mem–Cal error
63, 64, 65	Exhaust Gas Recirculation (EGR) circuit

GENERAL MOTORS CORPORATION
DIAGNOSTIC CODE DATA

Year – 1988
Model – Electra Estate Wagon
Engine – 5.0L (307 cid) V8
Engine Code – VIN Y

ECM TROUBLE CODES

Code	Explanation
12	No distributor reference signal to ECM. This code is not stored in memory and will only flash while the fault is present. This is a normal code with ignition ON, engine not running
13	Oxygen sensor circuit—the engine must run up to 4 minutes at part throttle under road load before this code will set
14	Shorted coolant temperature sensor circuit—the engine must run 2 minutes before this code will set
15	Open coolant temperature sensor circuit—the engine must run 5 minutes before this code will set
21	Throttle Position Sensor (TPS) circuit voltage high (open circuit or misadjusted TPS). The engine must run 10 seconds at specified curb idle speed before this code will set
22	Throttle Position Sensor (TPS) circuit signal voltage low (grounded circuit or misadjusted TPS). Engine must run 20 seconds at specified curb idle speed to set code
23	M/C solenoid circuit open or grounded
24	Vehicle Speed Sensor (VSS) circuit—the vehicle must operate up to 2 minutes at road speed before this code will set
31	Canister purge solenoid voltage high to ECM above idle rpm will set this code
34	Manifold Absolute Pressure (MAP) sensor circuit—too high or too low voltage signal at a specified amount time and rpm will cause this code to set
41	No distributor reference signal to the ECM at specified engine vacuum. This code will store in memory
42	Electronic Spark Timing (EST) bypass circuit or EST circuit grounded or open
43	Electronic Spark Control (ESC) retard signal for too long a time, causes retard in EST signal
44	Lean exhaust indication—the engione must run 2 minutes, in closed loop and at part throttle before this code will set
45	Rich exhaust indication—the engine must run 2 minutes in closed loop and at part throttle before this code will set
51	Faulty or improperly installed calibration unit (PROM). It takes up to 30 seconds before this code will set
53	Exhaust Gas Recirculation (EGR) valve vacuum sensor has seen improper EGR control vacuum— California only
55	M/C solenoid voltage high, at ECM, as a result of a shorted M/C solenoid circuit and/or faulty ECM

Year – 1988
Model – Century
Engine – 2.5L (151 cid) EFI 4 cyl
Engine Code – VIN R

ECM TROUBLE CODES

Code	Explanation
12	Reference pulse; indicates ECM's diagnostic system is operating
13	Oxygen sensor circuit (open circuit)
14	Coolant temperature sensor circuit (high temperature indicated)
15	Coolant temperature sensor circuit (low temperature indicated)
21	Throttle Position Sensor (TPS) circuit (signal voltage high)
22	Throttle Position Sensor (TPS) circuit (signal voltage low)
23	Manifold Air Temperature (MAT) sensor circuit (low temperature indicated)
24	Vehicle Speed Sensor (VSS) circuit
25	Manifold Air Temperature (MAT) sensor circuit (high temperature indicated)
33	Manifold Absolute Pressure (MAP) sensor circuit (signal voltage high – low vacuum)
34	Manifold Absolute Pressure (MAP) sensor circuit (signal voltage low – high vacuum)
35	Idle speed error
42	Electronic Spark Timing (EST) circuit
44	Oxygen sensor circuit (lean exhaust indicated)
45	Oxygen sensor circuit (rich exhaust indicated)
51	Prom error (faulty or incorrect PROM)
53	System over voltage

Year – 1988
Model – Century
Engine – 2.8L (171 cid) MPFI V6
Engine Code – VIN W

ECM TROUBLE CODES

Code	Explanation
12	Reference pulse; indicates ECM's diagnostic system is operating
13	Oxygen sensor circuit (open circuit)
14	Coolant temperature sensor circuit (high temperature indicated)
15	Coolant temperature sensor circuit (low temperature indicated)
21	Throttle Position Sensor (TPS) circuit (signal voltage high)
22	Throttle Position Sensor (TPS) circuit (signal voltage low)
23	Manifold Air Temperature (MAT) sensor circuit (low temperature indicated)
24	Vehicle Speed Sensor (VSS) circuit
25	Manifold Air Temperature (MAT) sensor circuit (high temperature indicated)
33	Mass Air Flow (MAF) sensor circuit (GM/SEC high)
34	Mass Air Flow (MAF) sensor circuit (GM/SEC low)
35	Idle speed circuit
41	Cylinder select error (faulty or incorrect Mem-Cal)
42	Electronic Spark Timing (EST) circuit
43	Electronic Spark Control (ESC) circuit
44	Oxygen sensor circuit (lean exhaust indicated)
45	Oxygen sensor circuit (rich exhaust indicated)
51	Mem–Cal error (faulty or incorrect Mem-Cal)
52	Calpak error (faulty or incorrect calpak)
53	System over voltage
54	Fuel pump circuit (low voltage)
61	Degraded oxygen sensor
63	Manifold Absolute Pressure (MAP) sensor circuit (signal voltage high)
64	Manifold Absolute Pressure (MAP) sensor circuit (signal voltage low)

Year — 1988
Model — Century
Engine — 3.8L (231 cid) SFI V6
Engine Code — VIN 3

ECM TROUBLE CODES

Code	Explanation
12	Reference pulse; indicates ECM's diagnostic system is operating
13	Oxygen sensor circuit (open circuit)
14	Coolant temperature sensor circuit (high temperature indicated)
15	Coolant temperature sensor circuit (low temperature indicated)
21	Throttle Position Sensor (TPS) circuit (signal voltage high)
22	Throttle Position Sensor (TPS) circuit (signal voltage low)
23	Manifold Air Temperature (MAT) sensor circuit (low temperature indicated)
24	Vehicle Speed Sensor (VSS) circuit
25	Manifold Air Temperature (MAT) sensor circuit (high temperature indicated)
32	Exhaust Gas Recirculation (EGR) circuit
33	Mass Air Flow (MAF) sensor circuit (GM/SEC high)
34	Mass Air Flow (MAF) sensor circuit (GM/SEC low)
41	Cam sensor circuit
42	Electronic Spark Timing (EST) circuit
43	Electronic Spark Control (ESC) circuit
44	Oxygen sensor circuit (lean exhaust indicated)
45	Oxygen sensor circuit (rich exhaust indicated)
51	PROM error (faulty or incorrect PROM)
52	Calpak error (faulty or incorrect calpak)
55	ECM error

Year – 1988
Model – Regal
Engine – 2.8L (171 cid) MFI V6
Engine Code – VIN W

ECM TROUBLE CODES

Code	Explanation
12	Reference pulse; indicates ECM's diagnostic system is operating
13	Oxygen sensor circuit (open circuit)
14	Coolant temperature sensor circuit (high temperature indicated)
15	Coolant temperature sensor circuit (low temperature indicated)
21	Throttle Position Sensor (TPS) circuit (signal voltage high)
22	Throttle Position Sensor (TPS) circuit (signal voltage low)
23	Manifold Air Temperature (MAT) sensor circuit (low temperature indicated)
24	Vehicle Speed Sensor (VSS) circuit
25	Manifold Air Temperature (MAT) sensor circuit (high temperature indicated)
33	Mass Air Flow (MAF) sensor circuit (GM/SEC high)
34	Mass Air Flow (MAF) sensor circuit (GM/SEC low)
35	Idle speed circuit
41	Cylinder select error (faulty or incorrect Mem-Cal)
42	Electronic Spark Timing (EST) circuit
43	Electronic Spark Control (ESC) circuit
44	Oxygen sensor circuit (lean exhaust indicated)
45	Oxygen sensor circuit (rich exhaust indicated)
51	Mem–Cal error (faulty or incorrect Mem-Cal)
52	Calpak error (faulty or incorrect calpak)
53	System over voltage
54	Fuel pump circuit (low voltage)
61	Degraded oxygen sensor

Year – 1988
Model – Skylark
Engine – 2.3L (140 cid) 4 cyl
Engine Code – VIN D

ECM TROUBLE CODES

Code	Explanation
12	Reference pulse; indicates ECM's diagnostic system is operating
13	Oxygen sensor circuit (open circuit)
14	Coolant temperature sensor circuit (high temperature indicated)
15	Coolant temperature sensor circuit (low temperature indicated)
21	Throttle Position Sensor (TPS) circuit (signal voltage high)
22	Throttle Position Sensor (TPS) circuit (signal voltage low)
23	Manifold Air Temperature (MAT) sensor circuit (low temperature indicated)
24	Vehicle Speed Sensor (VSS) circuit
25	Manifold Air Temperature (MAT) sensor circuit (high temperature indicated)
26	Quad Drive (QDM) error
33	Manifold Absolute Pressure (MAP) sensor (signal voltage high)
34	Manifold Absolute Pressure (MAP) sensor (signal voltage low)
36	Closed throttle air flow too high
42	Electronic Spark Timing (EST) circuit
43	Electronic Spark Control (ESC) circuit
44	Oxygen sensor circuit (lean exhaust indicated)
45	Oxygen sensor circuit (rich exhaust indicated)
51	Mem–Cal error (faulty or incorrect Mem-Cal)
53	Battery voltage too high
62	Transmission gear switches circuit
65	Fuel injector circuit (low circuit)
66	A/C pressure sensor circuit

Year — 1988
Model — Skylark
Engine — 2.5L (151 cid) TBI 4 cyl
Engine Code — VIN U

ECM TROUBLE CODES

Code	Explanation
12	Reference pulse; indicates ECM's diagnostic system is operating
13	Oxygen sensor circuit (open circuit)
14	Coolant temperature sensor circuit (high temperature indicated)
15	Coolant temperature sensor circuit (low temperature indicated)
21	Throttle Position Sensor (TPS) circuit (signal voltage high)
22	Throttle Position Sensor (TPS) circuit (signal voltage low)
23	Manifold Air Temperature (MAT) sensor circuit (low temperature indicated)
24	Vehicle Speed Sensor (VSS) circuit
25	Manifold Air Temperature (MAT) sensor circuit (high temperature indicated)
33	Manifold Absolute Pressure (MAP) sensor circuit (signal voltage high — low vacuum)
34	Manifold Absolute Pressure (MAP) sensor circuit (signal voltage low — high vacuum)
35	Idle speed error
42	Electronic Spark Timing (EST) circuit
44	Oxygen sensor circuit (lean exhaust indicated)
45	Oxygen sensor circuit (rich exhaust indicated)
51	Prom error (faulty or incorrect PROM)
53	System over voltage

Year – 1988
Model – Skylark
Engine – 3.0L (181 cid) MFI V6
Engine Code – VIN L

ECM TROUBLE CODES

Code	Explanation
12	Reference pulse; indicates ECM's diagnostic system is operating
13	Oxygen sensor circuit (open circuit)
14	Coolant temperature sensor circuit (high temperature indicated)
15	Coolant temperature sensor circuit (low temperature indicated)
21	Throttle Position Sensor (TPS) circuit (signal voltage high)
22	Throttle Position Sensor (TPS) circuit (signal voltage low)
23	Manifold Air Temperature (MAT) sensor circuit (low temperature indicated)
24	Vehicle Speed Sensor (VSS) circuit
25	Manifold Air Temperature (MAT) sensor circuit (high temperature indicated)
33	Mass Air Flow (MAF) sensor circuit (GM/SEC high)
34	Mass Air Flow (MAF) sensor circuit (GM/SEC low)
42	Electronic Spark Timing (EST) circuit
43	Electronic Spark Control (ESC) circuit
44	Oxygen sensor circuit (lean exhaust indicated)
45	Oxygen sensor circuit (rich exhaust indicated)
51	PROM error (faulty or incorrect PROM)
52	Calpak error (faulty or incorrect calpak)
55	ECM error

Year — 1988
Model — Skyhawk
Engine — 2.0L OHC (121 cid) 4 cyl
Engine Code — VIN K

ECM TROUBLE CODES

Code	Explanation
12	Reference pulse; indicates ECM's diagnostic system is operating
13	Oxygen sensor circuit (open circuit)
14	Coolant temperature sensor circuit (high temperature indicated)
15	Coolant temperature sensor circuit (low temperature indicated)
21	Throttle Position Sensor (TPS) circuit (signal voltage high)
22	Throttle Position Sensor (TPS) circuit (signal voltage low)
23	Manifold Air Temperature (MAT) sensor circuit (low temperature indicated)
24	Vehicle Speed Sensor (VSS) circuit
25	Manifold Air Temperature (MAT) sensor circuit (high temperature indicated)
32	Exhaust Gas Recirculation (EGR) system failure
33	Manifold Absolute Pressure (MAP) sensor circuit (signal voltage high — low vacuum)
34	Manifold Absolute Pressure (MAP) sensor circuit (signal voltage low — high vacuum)
35	Idle speed error
42	Electronic Spark Timing (EST) circuit
44	Oxygen sensor circuit (lean exhaust indicated)
45	Oxygen sensor circuit (rich exhaust indicated)
51	Prom error (faulty or incorrect PROM)
53	System over voltage

Year — 1988
Model — Riviera
Engine — 3.8L (231 cid) V6
Engine Code — VIN C

ECM TROUBLE CODES

Code	Explanation
EO12	Reference pulse; indicates ECM's diagnostic system is operating
EO13	Open oxygen sensor circuit — "Service Engine Soon" message displayed
EO14	Coolant temperature sensor circuit — high temperature — "Service Engine Soon" message displayed and forces cooling fans ON
EO15	Coolant temperature sensor circuit — low temperature — "Service Engine Soon" message displayed
EO16	System voltage out of range — all solenoids — "Service Engine Soon" message displayed
EO21	Throttle Position Sensor (TPS) circuit (signal voltage high) — "Service Engine Soon" message displayed
EO22	Throttle Position Sensor (TPS) circuit (signal voltage low) — "Service Engine Soon" message displayed
EO23	Manifold Air Temperature (MAT) sensor circuit (low temperature indicated) — "Service Engine Soon" message displayed
EO24	Vehicle Speed Sensor (VSS) circuit — "Service Engine Soon" message displayed
EO25	Manifold Air Temperature (MAT) sensor circuit (high temperature indicated) — "Service Engine Soon" message displayed
EO26	Quad Driver (QDM) error — "Service Engine Soon" message displayed
EO27	2nd gear switch circuit — "Service Engine Soon" message displayed
EO28	3rd gear switch circuit — "Service Engine Soon" message displayed
EO29	4th gear switch circuit — "Service Engine Soon" message displayed
EO31	Park/Neutral Switch circuit — "Service Engine Soon" message displayed
EO34	Mass Air Flow (MAF) sensor frequency low — "Service Engine Soon" message displayed
EO38	Brake switch circuit — "Service Engine Soon" message displayed
EO39	Torque Converter Clutch (TCC) circuit — "Service Engine Soon" message displayed
EO41	Cam sensor circuit — C^3I module to ECM — "Service Engine Soon" message displayed
EO42	Electronic Spark Timing (EST) or bypass circuit failure — "Service Engine Soon" message displayed and causes system to operate in bypass spark mode
EO43	Electronic Spark Control (ESC) system failure — "Service Engine Soon" message displayed
EO44	Lean exhaust indication — "Service Engine Soon" message displayed and forces open loop operation
EO45	Rich exhaust indication — "Service Engine Soon" message displayed and forces open loop operation
EO46	Power steering pressure switch circuit open — A/C clutch and cruise — "Service Engine Soon" message displayed
EO47	ECM-BCM data — A/C clutch and cruise — "Service Engine Soon" message displayed
EO48	Misfire — "Service Engine Soon" message displayed, causes system to operate in bypass spark mode and/or back-up fuel mode
EO63	Small Exhaust Gas Recirculation (EGR) flow problem — "Service Engine Soon" message displayed
EO64	Medium Exhaust Gas Recirculation (EGR) circuit flow problem — "Service Engine Soon" message displayed
EO65	Large Exhaust Gas Recirculation (EGR) circuit flow problem — "Service Engine Soon" message displayed

Year – 1988
Model – Reatta
Engine – 3.8L (231 cid) V6
Engine Code – VIN C

ECM TROUBLE CODES

Code	Explanation
E012	Reference pulse; indicates ECM's diagnostic system is operating
E013	Open oxygen sensor circuit – "Service Engine Soon" message displayed
E014	Coolant temperature sensor circuit – high temperature – "Service Engine Soon" message displayed and forces cooling fans ON
E015	Coolant temperature sensor circuit – low temperature – "Service Engine Soon" message displayed
E016	System voltage out of range – all solenoids – "Service Engine Soon" message displayed
E021	Throttle Position Sensor (TPS) circuit (signal voltage high) – "Service Engine Soon" message displayed
E022	Throttle Position Sensor (TPS) circuit (signal voltage low) – "Service Engine Soon" message displayed
E023	Manifold Air Temperature (MAT) sensor circuit (low temperature indicated) – "Service Engine Soon" message displayed
E024	Vehicle Speed Sensor (VSS) circuit – "Service Engine Soon" message displayed
E025	Manifold Air Temperature (MAT) sensor circuit (high temperature indicated) – "Service Engine Soon" message displayed
E026	Quad Driver (QDM) error – "Service Engine Soon" message displayed
E027	2nd gear switch circuit – "Service Engine Soon" message displayed
E028	3rd gear switch circuit – "Service Engine Soon" message displayed
E029	4th gear switch circuit – "Service Engine Soon" message displayed
E031	Park/Neutral Switch circuit – "Service Engine Soon" message displayed
E034	Mass Air Flow (MAF) sensor frequency low – "Service Engine Soon" message displayed
E038	Brake switch circuit – "Service Engine Soon" message displayed
E039	Torque Converter Clutch (TCC) circuit – "Service Engine Soon" message displayed
E041	Cam sensor circuit – C^{3}I module to ECM – "Service Engine Soon" message displayed
E042	Electronic Spark Timing (EST) or bypass circuit failure – "Service Engine Soon" message displayed and causes system to operate in bypass spark mode
E043	Electronic Spark Control (ESC) system failure – "Service Engine Soon" message displayed
E044	Lean exhaust indication – "Service Engine Soon" message displayed and forces open loop operation
E045	Rich exhaust indication – "Service Engine Soon" message displayed and forces open loop operation
E046	Power steering pressure switch circuit open – A/C clutch and cruise – "Service Engine Soon" message displayed
E047	ECM-BCM data – A/C clutch and cruise – "Service Engine Soon" message displayed
E048	Misfire – "Service Engine Soon" message displayed, causes system to operate in bypass spark mode and/or back-up fuel mode
E063	Small Exhaust Gas Recirculation (EGR) flow problem – "Service Engine Soon" message displayed
E064	Medium Exhaust Gas Recirculation (EGR) circuit flow problem – "Service Engine Soon" message displayed
E065	Large Exhaust Gas Recirculation (EGR) circuit flow problem – "Service Engine Soon" message displayed

Year – 1989
Model – LeSabre
Engine – 3.8L (231 cid) V6
Engine Code – VIN C

ECM TROUBLE CODES

Code	Explanation
12	Reference pulse; indicates ECM's diagnostic system is operating
13	Oxygen sensor circuit (open circuit)
14	Coolant temperature sensor circuit (high temperature indicated)
15	Coolant temperature sensor circuit (low temperature indicated)
16	System voltage high
21	Throttle Position Sensor (TPS) circuit (signal voltage high)
22	Throttle Position Sensor (TPS) circuit (signal voltage low)
23	Manifold Air Temperature (MAT) sensor circuit (low temperature indicated)
24	Vehicle Speed Sensor (VSS) circuit
25	Manifold Air Temperature (MAT) sensor circuit (high temperature indicated)
26	Quad-Driver Module (QDM) circuit
27, 28, 29	Gear switch diagnosis
31	Park/Neutral switch circuit
34	Mass Air Flow (MAF) sensor circuit (GM/SEC low)
38	Brake input circuit
39	Torque Converter Clutch (TCC) circuit
41	Cam sensor circuit
42	Electronic Spark Timing (EST) circuit
43	Electronic Spark Control (ESC) circuit
44	Oxygen sensor circuit (lean exhaust indicated)
45	Oxygen sensor circuit (rich exhaust indicated)
46	Power steering pressure switch circuit
48	Misfire diagnosis
51	Mem-Cal Error (faulty or incorrect Mem-Cal)
63, 64, 65	Exhaust Gas Recirculation (EGR) flow check

Year – 1989
Model – Electra
Engine – 3.8L (231 cid) V6
Engine Code – VIN C

ECM TROUBLE CODES

Code	Explanation
12	Reference pulse; indicates ECM's diagnostic system is operating
13	Oxygen sensor circuit (open circuit)
14	Coolant temperature sensor circuit (high temperature indicated)
15	Coolant temperature sensor circuit (low temperature indicated)
16	System voltage high
21	Throttle Position Sensor (TPS) circuit (signal voltage high)
22	Throttle Position Sensor (TPS) circuit (signal voltage low)
23	Manifold Air Temperature (MAT) sensor circuit (low temperature indicated)
24	Vehicle Speed Sensor (VSS) circuit
25	Manifold Air Temperature (MAT) sensor circuit (high temperature indicated)
26	Quad-Driver Module (QDM) circuit
27, 28, 29	Gear switch diagnosis
31	Park/Neutral switch circuit
34	Mass Air Flow (MAF) sensor circuit (GM/SEC low)
38	Brake input circuit
39	Torque Converter Clutch (TCC) circuit
41	Cam sensor circuit
42	Electronic Spark Timing (EST) circuit
43	Electronic Spark Control (ESC) circuit
44	Oxygen sensor circuit (lean exhaust indicated)
45	Oxygen sensor circuit (rich exhaust indicated)
46	Power steering pressure switch circuit
48	Misfire diagnosis
51	Mem-Cal Error (faulty or incorrect Mem-Cal)
63, 64, 65	Exhaust Gas Recirculation (EGR) flow check

Year – 1989
Model – LeSabre Estate Wagon
Engine – 5.0L (307 cid) V8
Engine Code – VIN Y

ECM TROUBLE CODES

Code	Explanation
12	No distributor reference signal to ECM. This code is not stored in memory and will only flash while the fault is present. This is a normal code with ignition ON, engine not running
13	Oxygen sensor circuit — the engine must run up to 4 minutes at part throttle under road load before this code will set
14	Shorted coolant temperature sensor circuit — the engine must run 2 minutes before this code will set
15	Open coolant temperature sensor circuit — the engine must run 5 minutes before this code will set
21	Throttle Position Sensor (TPS) circuit voltage high (open circuit or misadjusted TPS). The engine must run 10 seconds at specified curb idle speed before this code will set
22	Throttle Position Sensor (TPS) circuit signal voltage low (grounded circuit or misadjusted TPS). Engine must run 20 seconds at specified curb idle speed to set code
23	M/C solenoid circuit open or grounded
24	Vehicle Speed Sensor (VSS) circuit — the vehicle must operate up to 2 minutes at road speed before this code will set
31	Canister purge solenoid voltage high to ECM above idle rpm will set this code
34	Manifold Absolute Pressure (MAP) sensor circuit — too high or too low voltage signal at a specified amount time and rpm will cause this code to set
41	No distributor reference signal to the ECM at specified engine vacuum. This code will store in memory
42	Electronic Spark Timing (EST) bypass circuit or EST circuit grounded or open
43	Electronic Spark Control (ESC) retard signal for too long a time, causes retard in EST signal
44	Lean exhaust indication — the engione must run 2 minutes, in closed loop and at part throttle before this code will set
45	Rich exhaust indication — the engine must run 2 minutes in closed loop and at part throttle before this code will set
51	Faulty or improperly installed calibration unit (PROM). It takes up to 30 seconds before this code will set
53	Exhaust Gas Recirculation (EGR) valve vacuum sensor has seen improper EGR control vacuum — California only
55	M/C solenoid voltage high, at ECM, as a result of a shorted M/C solenoid circuit and/or faulty ECM

Year – 1989
Model – Electra Estate Wagon
Engine – 5.0L (307 cid) V8
Engine Code – VIN Y

ECM TROUBLE CODES

Code	Explanation
12	No distributor reference signal to ECM. This code is not stored in memory and will only flash while the fault is present. This is a normal code with ignition ON, engine not running
13	Oxygen sensor circuit – the engine must run up to 4 minutes at part throttle under road load before this code will set
14	Shorted coolant temperature sensor circuit – the engine must run 2 minutes before this code will set
15	Open coolant temperature sensor circuit – the engine must run 5 minutes before this code will set
21	Throttle Position Sensor (TPS) circuit voltage high (open circuit or misadjusted TPS). The engine must run 10 seconds at specified curb idle speed before this code will set
22	Throttle Position Sensor (TPS) circuit signal voltage low (grounded circuit or misadjusted TPS). Engine must run 20 seconds at specified curb idle speed to set code
23	M/C solenoid circuit open or grounded
24	Vehicle Speed Sensor (VSS) circuit – the vehicle must operate up to 2 minutes at road speed before this code will set
31	Canister purge solenoid voltage high to ECM above idle rpm will set this code
34	Manifold Absolute Pressure (MAP) sensor circuit – too high or too low voltage signal at a specified amount time and rpm will cause this code to set
41	No distributor reference signal to the ECM at specified engine vacuum. This code will store in memory
42	Electronic Spark Timing (EST) bypass circuit or EST circuit grounded or open
43	Electronic Spark Control (ESC) retard signal for too long a time, causes retard in EST signal
44	Lean exhaust indication – the engiene must run 2 minutes, in closed loop and at part throttle before this code will set
45	Rich exhaust indication – the engine must run 2 minutes in closed loop and at part throttle before this code will set
51	Faulty or improperly installed calibration unit (PROM). It takes up to 30 seconds before this code will set
53	Exhaust Gas Recirculation (EGR) valve vacuum sensor has seen improper EGR control vacuum – California only
55	M/C solenoid voltage high, at ECM, as a result of a shorted M/C solenoid circuit and/or faulty ECM

Year — 1989
Model — Century
Engine — 2.5L (151 cid) 4 cyl
Engine Code — VIN R

ECM TROUBLE CODES

Code	Explanation
12	Reference pulse; indicates ECM's diagnostic system is operating
13	Oxygen sensor circuit (open circuit)
14	Coolant temperature sensor circuit (high temperature indicated)
15	Coolant temperature sensor circuit (low temperature indicated)
21	Throttle Position Sensor (TPS) circuit (signal voltage high)
22	Throttle Position Sensor (TPS) circuit (signal voltage low)
23	Manifold Air Temperature (MAT) sensor circuit (low temperature indicated)
24	Vehicle Speed Sensor (VSS) circuit
25	Manifold Air Temperature (MAT) sensor circuit (high temperature indicated)
32	Exhaust Gas Recirculation (EGR) system failure
33	Manifold Absolute Pressure (MAP) sensor circuit (signal voltage high-low vacuum)
34	Manifold Absolute Pressure (MAP) sensor circuit (Signal voltage low-high vacuum)
35	Idle speed error
42	Electronic Spark Timing (EST) circuit
44	Oxygen sensor circuit (lean exhaust indicated)
45	Oxygen sensor circuit (rich exhaust indicated)
51	Mem-Cal Error (faulty or incorrect Mem-Cal)
53	System over voltage

Year — 1989
Model — Century
Engine — 2.8L (173 cid) MPI V6
Engine Code — VIN W

ECM TROUBLE CODES

Code	Explanation
12	Reference pulse; indicates ECM's diagnostic system is operating
13	Oxygen sensor circuit (open circuit)
14	Coolant temperature sensor circuit (high temperature indicated)
15	Coolant temperature sensor circuit (low temperature indicated)
21	Throttle Position Sensor (TPS) circuit (signal voltage high)
22	Throttle Position Sensor (TPS) circuit (signal voltage low)
23	Manifold Air Temperature (MAT) sensor circuit (low temperature indicated)
24	Vehicle Speed Sensor (VSS) circuit
25	Manifold Air Temperature (MAT) sensor circuit (high temperature indicated)
32	Exhaust Gas Recirculation (EGR) circuit
33	Manifold Absolute Pressure (MAP) sensor circuit (signal voltage high)
34	Manifold Absolute Pressure (MAP) sensor circuit (signal voltage low)
35	Idle speed error
41	Cylinder select error (faulty or incorret Mem-Cal)
42	Electronic Spark Timing (EST) circuit
43	Electronic Spark Control (ESC) circuit
44	Oxygen sensor circuit (lean exhaust indicated)
45	Oxygen sensor circuit (rich exhaust indicated)
51	Mem-Cal error (faulty or incorrect Mem-Cal)
52	Calpak error
53	System over voltage
54	Fuel pump circuit (low voltage)
61	Degraded oxygen sensor

Year – 1989
Model – Century
Engine – 3.3L (231 cid) SFI V6
Engine Code – VIN N

ECM TROUBLE CODES

Code	Explanation
12	Reference pulse; indicates ECM's diagnostic system is operating
13	Oxygen sensor circuit (open circuit)
14	Coolant temperature sensor circuit (high temperature indicated)
15	Coolant temperature sensor circuit (low temperature indicated)
16	System voltage high
21	Throttle Position Sensor (TPS) circuit (signal voltage high)
22	Throttle Position Sensor (TPS) circuit (signal voltage low)
24	Vehicle Speed Sensor (VSS) circuit
26	Quad-Driver Module (QDM) circuit
27, 28	Gear switch diagnosis
31	Park/Neutral switch circuit
34	Mass Air Flow (MAF) sensor circuit (GM/SEC low)
38	Brake switch circuit
39	Torque Converter Clutch (TCC) circuit
42	Electronic Spark Timing (EST) circuit
43	Electronic Spark Control (ESC) circuit
44	Oxygen sensor circuit (lean exhaust indicated)
45	Oxygen sensor circuit (rich exhaust indicated)
46	Power steering pressure switch circuit
48	Misfire diagnosis
51	Mem-Cal Error (faulty or incorrect Mem-Cal)
66	A/C pressure sensor circuit

GENERAL MOTORS CORPORATION
DIAGNOSTIC CODE DATA

Year – 1989
Model – Regal
Engine – 2.8L (173 cid) V6
Engine Code – VIN W

ECM TROUBLE CODES

Code	Explanation
12	Reference pulse; indicates ECM's diagnostic system is operating
13	Oxygen sensor circuit (open circuit)
14	Coolant temperature sensor circuit (high temperature indicated)
15	Coolant temperature sensor circuit (low temperature indicated)
21	Throttle Position Sensor (TPS) circuit (signal voltage high)
22	Throttle Position Sensor (TPS) circuit (signal voltage low)
23	Manifold Air Temperature (MAT) sensor circuit (low temperature indicated)
24	Vehicle Speed Sensor (VSS) circuit
25	Manifold Air Temperature (MAT) sensor circuit (high temperature indicated)
26	Quad-Driver Module (QDM) circuit
32	Exhaust Gas Recirculation (EGR) circuit
33	Manifold Absolute Pressure (MAP) sensor circuit (signal voltage high-low vacuum)
34	Manifold Absolute Pressure (MAP) sensor circuit (signal voltage low-high vacuum)
35	Idle Speed Control (ISC) circuit
41	Cylinder select error (faulty or incorrect Mem-Cal)
42	Electronic Spark Timing (EST) circuit
43	Electronic Spark Control (ESC) circuit
44	Oxygen sensor circuit (lean exhaust indicated)
45	Oxygen sensor circuit (rich exhaust indicated)
51	Mem-Cal Error (faulty or incorrect Mem-Cal)
52	Cal Pak error
53	System over voltage
54	Fuel pump circuit (low voltage)
55	ECM error
61	Degraded oxygen sensor

Year — 1989
Model — Regal
Engine — 3.1L (192 cid) V6
Engine Code — VIN T

ECM TROUBLE CODES

Code	Explanation
12	Reference pulse; indicates ECM's diagnostic system is operating
13	Oxygen sensor circuit (open circuit)
14	Coolant temperature sensor circuit (high temperature indicated)
15	Coolant temperature sensor circuit (low temperature indicated)
21	Throttle Position Sensor (TPS) circuit (signal voltage high)
22	Throttle Position Sensor (TPS) circuit (signal voltage low)
23	Manifold Air Temperature (MAT) sensor circuit (low temperature indicated)
24	Vehicle Speed Sensor (VSS) circuit
25	Manifold Air Temperature (MAT) sensor circuit (high temperature indicated)
26	Quad-Driver Module (QDM) circuit
32	Exhaust Gas Recirculation (EGR) circuit
33	Manifold Absolute Pressure (MAP) sensor circuit (signal voltage high-low vacuum)
34	Manifold Absolute Presssure (MAP) sensor circuit (signal voltage low-high vacuum)
35	Idle Speed Control (ISC) circuit
41	Cylinder select error (faulty or incorrect Mem-Cal)
42	Electronic Spark Timing (EST) circuit
43	Electronic Spark Control (ESC) circuit
44	Oxygen sensor circuit (lean exhaust indicated)
45	Oxygen sensor circuit (rich exhaust indicated)
51	Mem-Cal error (faulty or incorrect Mem-Cal)
53	System over voltage
54	Fuel pump circuit (low voltage)
55	ECM error
61	Degraded oxygen sensor

Year – 1989
Model – Skylark
Engine – 2.3L (138 cid) 4 cyl
Engine Code – VIN D

ECM TROUBLE CODES

Code	Explanation
12	Reference pulse; indicates ECM's diagnostic system is operating
13	Oxygen sensor circuit (open circuit)
14	Coolant temperature sensor circuit (high temperature indicated)
15	Coolant temperature sensor circuit (low temperature indicated)
21	Throttle Position Sensor (TPS) circuit (signal voltage high)
22	Throttle Position Sensor (TPS) circuit (signal voltage low)
23	Manifold Air Temperature (MAT) sensor circuit (low temperature indicated)
24	Vehicle Speed Sensor (VSS) circuit
25	Manifold Air Temperature (MAT) sensor circuit (high temperature indicated)
26	Quad-Driver Module (QDM) circuit
33	Manifold Absolute Pressure (MAP) sensor circuit (signal voltage high-low vacuum)
34	Manifold Absolute Pressure (MAP) sensor circuit (signal voltage low-high vacuum)
35	Idle speed error
41	Ignition reference circuit
42	Electronic Spark Timing (EST) circuit
43	Electronic Spark Control (ESC) circuit
44	Oxygen sensor circuit (lean exhaust indicated)
45	Oxygen sensor circuit (rich exhaust indicated)
51	Mem-Cal Error (faulty or incorrect Mem-Cal)
53	Battery voltage too high
62	Transmission gear switches circuit
65	Fuel injector circuit (low current)
66	A/C pressure sensor circuit

Year – 1989
Model – Skylark
Engine – 2.5L (151 cid) 4 cyl
Engine Code – VIN U

ECM TROUBLE CODES

Code	Explanation
12	Reference pulse; indicates ECM's diagnostic system is operating
13	Oxygen sensor circuit (open circuit)
14	Coolant temperature sensor circuit (high temperature indicated)
15	Coolant temperature sensor circuit (low temperature indicated)
21	Throttle Position Sensor (TPS) circuit (signal voltage high)
22	Throttle Position Sensor (TPS) circuit (signal voltage low)
23	Manifold Air Temperature (MAT) sensor circuit (low temperature indicated)
24	Vehicle Speed Sensor (VSS) circuit
25	Manifold Air Temperature (MAT) sensor circuit (high temperature indicated)
33	Manifold Air Pressure (MAP) sensor circuit (signal voltage high-low vacuum)
34	Manifold Air Pressure (MAP) sensor circuit (signal voltage low-high vacuum)
35	Idle speed error
42	Electronic Spark Timing (EST) circuit
44	Oxygen sensor circuit (lean exhaust indicated)
45	Oxygen sensor circuit (rich exhaust indicated)
51	PROM error (faulty or incorrect PROM)
53	System over voltage

Year – 1989
Model – Skylark
Engine – 3.3L (231 cid) SFI V6
Engine Code – VIN N

ECM TROUBLE CODES

Code	Explanation
12	Reference pulse; indicates ECM's diagnostic system is operating
13	Oxygen sensor circuit (open circuit)
14	Coolant temperature sensor circuit (high temperature indicated)
15	Coolant temperature sensor circuit (low temperature indicated)
16	System voltage high
21	Throttle Position Sensor (TPS) circuit (signal voltage high)
22	Throttle Position Sensor (TPS) circuit (signal voltage low)
23	Manifold Air Temperature (MAT) sensor circuit (low temperature indicated)
24	Vehicle Speed Sensor (VSS) circuit
27, 28	Gear switch diagnosis
31	Park/Neutral switch circuit
34	Mass Air Flow (MAF) sensor circuit (GM/SEC low)
38	Brake input circuit
39	Torque Converter Clutch (TCC) circuit
42	Electronic Spark Timing (EST) circuit
43	Electronic Spark Control (ESC) circuit
44	Oxygen sensor circuit (lean exhaust indicated)
45	Oxygen sensor circuit (rich exhaust indicated)
46	Power steering pressure switch circuit
48	Misfire diagnosis
51	Mem-Cal Error (faulty or incorrect Mem-Cal)
66	A/C Pressure Sensor Circuit

Year — 1989
Model — Skyhawk
Engine — 2.0L (120 cid) TBI 4 cyl
Engine Code — VIN 1

ECM TROUBLE CODES

Code	Explanation
12	Reference pulse; indicates ECM's diagnostic system is operating
13	Oxygen sensor circuit (open circuit)
14	Coolant temperature sensor circuit (high temperature indicated)
15	Coolant temperature sensor circuit (low temperature indicated)
21	Throttle Position Sensor (TPS) circuit (signal voltage high)
22	Throttle Position Sensor (TPS) circuit (signal voltage low)
23	Manifold Air Temperature (MAT) sensor circuit (low temperature indicated)
24	Vehicle Speed Sensor (VSS) circuit
25	Manifold Air Temperature (MAT) sensor circuit (high temperature indicated)
32	Exhaust Gas Recirculation (EGR) system failure
33	Manifold Absolute Pressure (MAP) sensor circuit (signal voltage high-low vacuum)
34	Manifold Absolute Pressure (MAP) sensor circuit (signal voltage low-high vacuum)
42	Electronic Spark Timing (EST) circuit
44	Oxygen sensor circuit (lean exhaust indicated)
45	Oxygen sensor circuit (rich exhaust indicated)
51	PROM error (faulty of incorrect PROM)

Year — 1989
Model — Riviera
Engine — 3.8L (231 cid) V6
Engine Code — VIN C

ECM TROUBLE CODES

Code	Explanation
E012	Reference pulse; indicates ECM's diagnostic system is operating
E013	Open oxygen sensor circuit — "Service Engine Soon" message displayed
E014	Coolant temperature sensor circuit — high temperature — "Service Engine Soon" message displayed and forces cooling fans ON
E015	Coolant temperature sensor circuit — low temperature — "Service Engine Soon" message displayed
E016	System voltage out of range — all solenoids — "Service Engine Soon" message displayed
E021	Throttle Position Sensor (TPS) circuit (signal voltage high) — "Service Engine Soon" message displayed
E022	Throttle Position Sensor (TPS) circuit (signal voltage low) — "Service Engine Soon" message displayed
E023	Manifold Air Temperature (MAT) sensor circuit (low temperature indicated) — "Service Engine Soon" message displayed
E024	Vehicle Speed Sensor (VSS) circuit — "Service Engine Soon" message displayed
E025	Manifold Air Temperature (MAT) sensor circuit (high temperature indicated) — "Service Engine Soon" message displayed
E026	Quad Driver Module (QDM) error — "Service Engine Soon" message displayed
E027	2nd gear switch circuit — "Service Engine Soon" message displayed
E028	3rd gear switch circuit — "Service Engine Soon" message displayed
E029	4th gear switch circuit — "Service Engine Soon" message displayed
E031	Park/Neutral Switch circuit — "Service Engine Soon" message displayed
E034	Mass Air Flow (MAF) sensor frequency low — "Service Engine Soon" message displayed
E038	Brake switch circuit — "Service Engine Soon" message displayed
E039	Torque Converter Clutch (TCC) circuit — "Service Engine Soon" message displayed
E041	Cam sensor circuit — C^3I module to ECM — "Service Engine Soon" message displayed
E042	Electronic Spark Timing (EST) or bypass circuit failure — "Service Engine Soon" message displayed and causes system to operate in bypass spark mode
E043	Electronic Spark Control (ESC) system failure — "Service Engine Soon" message displayed
E044	Lean exhaust indication — "Service Engine Soon" message displayed and forces open loop operation
E045	Rich exhaust indication — "Service Engine Soon" message displayed and forces open loop operation
E046	Power steering pressure switch circuit open — A/C clutch and cruise — "Service Engine Soon" message displayed
E047	ECM-BCM data — A/C clutch and cruise — "Service Engine Soon" message displayed
E048	Misfire — "Service Engine Soon" message displayed, causes system to operate in bypass spark mode and/or back-up fuel mode
E063	Small Exhaust Gas Recirculation (EGR) flow problem — "Service Engine Soon" message displayed
E064	Medium Exhaust Gas Recirculation (EGR) circuit flow problem — "Service Engine Soon" message displayed
E065	Large Exhaust Gas Recirculation (EGR) circuit flow problem — "Service Engine Soon" message displayed

Year – 1989
Model – Reatta
Engine – 3.8L (231 cid) V6
Engine Code – VIN C

ECM TROUBLE CODES

Code	Explanation
E012	Reference pulse; indicates ECM's diagnostic system is operating
E013	Open oxygen sensor circuit – "Service Engine Soon" message displayed
E014	Coolant temperature sensor circuit – high temperature – "Service Engine Soon" message displayed and forces cooling fans ON
E015	Coolant temperature sensor circuit – low temperature – "Service Engine Soon" message displayed
E016	System voltage out of range – all solenoids – "Service Engine Soon" message displayed
E021	Throttle Position Sensor (TPS) circuit (signal voltage high) – "Service Engine Soon" message displayed
E022	Throttle Position Sensor (TPS) circuit (signal voltage low) – "Service Engine Soon" message displayed
E023	Manifold Air Temperature (MAT) sensor circuit (low temperature indicated) – "Service Engine Soon" message displayed
E024	Vehicle Speed Sensor (VSS) circuit – "Service Engine Soon" message displayed
E025	Manifold Air Temperature (MAT) sensor circuit (high temperature indicated) – "Service Engine Soon" message displayed
E026	Quad Driver Module (QDM) error – "Service Engine Soon" message displayed
E027	2nd gear switch circuit – "Service Engine Soon" message displayed
E028	3rd gear switch circuit – "Service Engine Soon" message displayed
E029	4th gear switch circuit – "Service Engine Soon" message displayed
E031	Park/Neutral Switch circuit – "Service Engine Soon" message displayed
E034	Mass Air Flow (MAF) sensor frequency low – "Service Engine Soon" message displayed
E038	Brake switch circuit – "Service Engine Soon" message displayed
E039	Torque Converter Clutch (TCC) circuit – "Service Engine Soon" message displayed
E041	Cam sensor circuit – C³I module to ECM – "Service Engine Soon" message displayed
E042	Electronic Spark Timing (EST) or bypass circuit failure – "Service Engine Soon" message displayed and causes system to operate in bypass spark mode
E043	Electronic Spark Control (ESC) system failure – "Service Engine Soon" message displayed
E044	Lean exhaust indication – "Service Engine Soon" message displayed and forces open loop operation
E045	Rich exhaust indication – "Service Engine Soon" message displayed and forces open loop operation
E046	Power steering pressure switch circuit open – A/C clutch and cruise – "Service Engine Soon" message displayed
E047	ECM-BCM data – A/C clutch and cruise – "Service Engine Soon" message displayed
E048	Misfire – "Service Engine Soon" message displayed, causes system to operate in bypass spark mode and/or back-up fuel mode
E063	Small Exhaust Gas Recirculation (EGR) flow problem – "Service Engine Soon" message displayed
E064	Medium Exhaust Gas Recirculation (EGR) circuit flow problem – "Service Engine Soon" message displayed
E065	Large Exhaust Gas Recirculation (EGR) circuit flow problem – "Service Engine Soon" message displayed

CADILLAC

Year — 1980
Model — DeVille
Engine — 6.0L (368 cid) V8
Engine Code — VIN 6

ECM TROUBLE CODES

Code	Explanation
12	No tach signal to the Electronic Control Module (ECM). This code will only be present while a fault is present. It will not be stored with an intermittent problem
13	Oxygen sensor circuit. The engine has to run for about 5 minutes at part throttle before this code will show
13 & 43	Same time — Throttle Position Sensor (TPS) adjustment — part throttle — after 10 seconds
14	Shorted coolant sensor circuit. The engine has to run 2 minutes before this code will show
15	Open coolant sensor circuit. The engine has to operate for about 5 minutes before this code will show
21	Throttle Position Sensor (TPS) — Wide Open Throttle (WOT) error — after 10 seconds and below 800 RPM
23	Open or grounded carburetor M/C solenoid
43	Throttle Position Sensor (TPS) adjustment — part throttle — after 10 seconds
44	Lean oxygen sensor. The engine has to run for about 3 minutes in closed loop and part throttle at road load before this code will show
44 & 45	(At same time) — faulty oxygen sensor
45	Rich oxygen sensor indication. The engine has to run for about 3 minutes in closed loop and part throttle at road load before this code will show
51	Faulty calibration unit (PROM) or installation
52 & 53	Light OFF — intermittent Electronic Control Module (ECM) problem. Light ON — faulty ECM.
54	Faulty M/C solenoid or Electronic Control Module (ECM)
55	Faulty Throttle Position Sensor (TPS) or Electronic Control Module (ECM)

Year – 1980
Model – Fleetwood
Engine – 6.0L (368 cid) V8
Engine Code – VIN 6

ECM TROUBLE CODES

Code	Explanation
12	No tach signal to the Electronic Control Module (ECM). This code will only be present while a fault is present. It will not be stored with an intermittent problem
13	Oxygen sensor circuit. The engine has to run for about 5 minutes at part throttle before this code will show
13 & 43	Same time – Throttle Position Sensor (TPS) adjustment – part throttle – after 10 seconds
14	Shorted coolant sensor circuit. The engine has to run 2 minutes before this code will show
15	Open coolant sensor circuit. The engine has to operate for about 5 minutes before this code will show
21	Throttle Position Sensor (TPS) – Wide Open Throttle (WOT) error – after 10 seconds and below 800 RPM
23	Open or grounded carburetor M/C solenoid
43	Throttle Position Sensor (TPS) adjustment – part throttle – after 10 seconds
44	Lean oxygen sensor. The engine has to run for about 3 minutes in closed loop and part throttle at road load before this code will show
44 & 55	(At same time) – faulty oxygen sensor
45	Rich oxygen sensor indication. The engine has to run for about 3 minutes in closed loop and part throttle at road load before this code will show
51	Faulty calibration unit (PROM) or installation
52 & 53	Light OFF – intermittent Electronic Control Module (ECM) problem. Light ON – faulty ECM.
54	Faulty M/C solenoid or Electronic Control Module (ECM)
55	Faulty Throttle Position Sensor (TPS) or Electronic Control Module (ECM)

Year — 1980
Model — Seville
Engine — 5.7L (350 cid) EFI V8
Engine Code — VIN 8

ECM TROUBLE CODES

Code	Explanation
12	No tach signal to the Electronic Control Module (ECM). This code will be present while a fault is present. It will not be stored with an intermittent problem
13	Oxygen sensor circuit. The engine has to run for about 5 minutes at part throttle before this code will show
13 & 43	Same time — Throttle Position Sensor (TPS) adjustment — part throttle — after 10 seconds
14	Shorted coolant sensor circuit. The engine has to run 2 minutes before this code will show
15	Open coolant sensor circuit. The engine has to operate for about 5 minutes before this code will show
21	Throttle Position Sensor (TPS) — Wide Open Throttle (WOT) error — after 10 seconds and below 800 RPM
23	Open or grounded carburetor M/C solenoid
43	Throttle Position Sensor (TPS) adjustment — part throttle — after 10 seconds
44	Lean oxygen sensor. The engine has to run for about 3 minutes in closed loop and part throttle at road load before this code will show
44 & 55	(At same time) — faulty oxygen sensor
45	Rich oxygen sensor indication. The engine has to run for about 3 minutes in closed loop and part throttle at road load before this code will show
51	Faulty calibration unit (PROM) or installation
52 & 53	Light OFF — intermittent Electronic Control Module (ECM) problem. Light ON — faulty ECM.
54	Faulty M/C solenoid or Electronic Control Module (ECM)
55	Faulty Throttle Position Sensor (TPS) or Electronic Control Module (ECM)

Year — 1980
Model — Seville
Engine — 6.0L (368 cid) DEFI V8
Engine Code — VIN 9

ECM TROUBLE CODES

Code	Explanation
12	No tach signal to the Electronic Control Module (ECM). This code will only be present while a fault is present. It will not be stored with an intermittent problem
13	Oxygen sensor circuit. The engine has to run for about 5 minutes at part throttle before this code will show
13 & 43	Same time — Throttle Position Sensor (TPS) adjustment — part throttle — after 10 seconds
14	Shorted coolant sensor circuit. The engine has to run 2 minutes before this code will show
15	Open coolant sensor circuit. The engine has to operate for about 5 minutes before this code will show
21	Throttle Position Sensor (TPS) — Wide Open Throttle (WOT) error — after 10 seconds and below 800 RPM
23	Open or grounded carburetor M/C solenoid
43	Throttle Position Sensor (TPS) adjustment — part throttle — after 10 seconds
44	Lean oxygen sensor. The engine has to run for about 3 minutes in closed loop and part throttle at road load before this code will show
44 & 55	(At same time) — faulty oxygen sensor
45	Rich oxygen sensor indication. The engine has to run for about 3 minutes in closed loop and part throttle at road load before this code will show
51	Faulty calibration unit (PROM) or installation
52 & 53	Light OFF — intermittent Electronic Control Module (ECM) problem. Light ON — faulty ECM.
54	Faulty M/C solenoid or Electronic Control Module (ECM)
55	Faulty Throttle Position Sensor (TPS) or Electronic Control Module (ECM)

Year — 1980
Model — Eldorado
Engine — 5.7L (350 cid) EFI V8
Engine Code — VIN 8

ECM TROUBLE CODES

Code	Explanation
12	No tach signal to the Electronic Control Module (ECM). This code will only be present while a fault is present. It will not be stored with an intermittent problem
13	Oxygen sensor circuit. The engine has to run for about 5 minutes at part throttle before this code will show
13 & 43	Same time — Throttle Position Sensor (TPS) adjustment — part throttle — after 10 seconds
14	Shorted coolant sensor circuit. The engine has to run 2 minutes before this code will show
15	Open coolant sensor circuit. The engine has to operate for about 5 minutes before this code will show
21	Throttle Position Sensor (TPS) — Wide Open Throttle (WOT) error — after 10 seconds and below 800 RPM
23	Open or grounded carburetor M/C solenoid
43	Throttle Position Sensor (TPS) adjustment — part throttle — after 10 seconds
44	Lean oxygen sensor. The engine has to run for about 3 minutes in closed loop and part throttle at road load before this code will show
44 & 55	(At same time), faulty oxygen sensor
45	Rich oxygen sensor indication. The engine has to run for about 3 minutes in closed loop and part throttle at road load before this code will show
51	Faulty calibration unit (PROM) or installation
52 & 53	Light OFF — intermittent Electronic Control Module (ECM) problem. Light ON — faulty ECM.
54	Faulty M/C solenoid or Electronic Control Module (ECM)
55	Faulty Throttle Position Sensor (TPS) or Electronic Control Module (ECM)

Year — 1980
Model — Eldorado
Engine — 6.0L (368 cid) DEFI V8
Engine Code — VIN 9

ECM TROUBLE CODES

Code	Explanation
12	No tach signal to the Electronic Control Module (ECM). This code will only be present while a fault is present. It will not be stored with an intermittent problem
13	Oxygen sensor circuit. The engine has to run for about 5 minutes at part throttle before this code will show
13 & 43	Same time — Throttle Position Sensor (TPS) adjustment — part throttle — after 10 seconds
14	Shorted coolant sensor circuit. The engine has to run 2 minutes before this code will show
15	Open coolant sensor circuit. The engine has to operate for about 5 minutes before this code will show
21	Throttle Position Sensor (TPS) — Wide Open Throttle (WOT) error — after 10 seconds and below 800 RPM
23	Open or grounded carburetor M/C solenoid
43	Throttle Position Sensor (TPS) adjustment — part throttle — after 10 seconds
44	Lean oxygen sensor. The engine has to run for about 3 minutes in closed loop and part throttle at road load before this code will show
44 & 55	(At same time), faulty oxygen sensor
45	Rich oxygen sensor indication. The engine has to run for about 3 minutes in closed loop and part throttle at road load before this code will show
51	Faulty calibration unit (PROM) or installation
52 & 53	Light OFF — intermittent Electronic Control Module (ECM) problem. Light ON — faulty ECM.
54	Faulty M/C solenoid or Electronic Control Module (ECM)
55	Faulty Throttle Position Sensor (TPS) or Electronic Control Module (ECM)

GENERAL MOTORS CORPORATION
DIAGNOSTIC CODE DATA

Year – 1981
Model – DeVille
Engine – 4.1L (252 cid) V6
Engine Code – VIN 4

ECM TROUBLE CODES

Code	Explanation
12	No reference pulses to the Electronic Control Module (ECM). This code is not stored in memory and will only flash while the fault is present
13	Oxygen sensor circuit — the engine must run up to 5 minutes at part throttle, under road load, before this code will set
14	Shorted Coolant Temperature Sensor (CTS) circuit — the engine must run up to 2 minutes before this code will set
15	Open Coolant Temperature Sensor (CTS) circuit — the engine must run up to 5 minutes before this code will set
21	Throttle Position Sensor (TPS) circuit — the engine must run up to 25 seconds, below 800 RPM, before this code will set
23	Open or grounded M/C solenoid circuit
24	Vehicle Speed Sensor (VSS) circuit — the car must operate up to 5 minutes at road speed before this code will set
32	Barometric Pressure Sensor (BARO) circuit low
34	Manifold Absolute Pressure (MAP) or vacuum sensor circuit. The engine must run up to 5 minutes, below 800 RPM, before this code will set
35	Idle Speed Control (ISC) switch circuit shorted — over ½ throttle for over 2 seconds
42	Electronic Spark Timing (EST) bypass circuit grounded
44	Lean oxygen sensor indication — the engine must run up to 5 minutes, in closed loop, at part throttle and road load before this code will set
44 & 45	(At same time) — faulty oxygen sensor circuit
45	Rich system indication — the engine must run up to 5 minutes, in closed loop, at part throttle and road load before this code will set
51	Faulty calibration unit (PROM) or installation. It takes up to 30 seconds before this code will set
52	Faulty Electronic Control Module (ECM)
53	Faulty Electronic Control Module (ECM)
54	Shorted M/C solenoid circuit
55	Grounded +8 volts, V/ref, faulty oxygen sensor or Electronic Control Module (ECM)

Year — 1981
Model — DeVille
Engine — 6.0L (368 cid) DFI V8
Engine Code — VIN 9

ECM TROUBLE CODES

Code	Explanation
12	No tach signal
13	Oxygen sensor not ready
14	Shorted Coolant Temperature Sensor (CTS)
15	Open Coolant Temperature Sensor (CTS) circuit
16	Generator voltage out of range
17	Crank signal circuit high
18	Open crank signal circuit
19	Fuel pump circuit high
20	Open fuel pump circuit
21	Shorted Throttle Position Sensor (TPS) circuit
22	Open Throttle Position Sensor (TPS) circuit
23	Electronic Spark Timing (EST)/bypass circuit shorted or open
24	Speed sensor failure
25	Modulated displacement failure
26	Shorted throttle switch circuit
27	Open throttle switch circuit
30	Idle Speed Control (ISC) circuit
31	Short Manifold Absolute Pressure (MAP) sensor circuit
32	Open Manifold Absolute Pressure (MAP) sensor circuit
33	Manifold Absolute Pressure (MAP)/Barometric Pressure (BARO) sensor correlation
34	Manifold Absolute Pressure (MAP) hose
35	Shorted Barometric Pressure (BARO) sensor circuit
36	Open Barometric Pressure (BARO) sensor circuit
37	Shorted Manifold Air Temperature (MAT) sensor circuit
38	Open Manifold Air Temperature (MAT) sensor circuit
44	Oxygen sensor lean
45	Oxygen sensor rich
51	PROM insertion faulty
60	Drive (ADL) switch circuit
61	Set and resume switch circuit
62	Car speed exceeds maximum limit
63	Car and set speed tolerance exceeded
64	Car acceleration exceeds maximum limit
65	Coolant temperature exceeds maximum limit
66	Engine RPM exceeds maximum limit
68	Set and resume switch circuit
70	System ready — switch tests
71	Brake light switch
72	Idle Speed Control (ISC) throttle switch

ECM TROUBLE CODES (cont'd)

Code	Explanation
73	Drive (ADL) switch
74	Back-up lamp switch
75	Cruise on/off circuit
76	Set/coast circuit
77	Resume/acceleration circuit
78	Instant/average MPG button
79	Reset MPG button
80	Air conditioning clutch circuit
88	Display check
90	System ready to display engine data
95	System ready for actuator cycling
96	Actuator cycling
97	Modulated Displacement (MD) cylinder solenoid cycling
00	All diagnostic complete

Year – 1981
Model – Fleetwood
Engine – 4.1L (252 cid) V6
Engine Code – VIN 4

ECM TROUBLE CODES

Code	Explanation
12	No reference pulses to the Electronic Control Module (ECM). This code is not stored in memory and will only flash while the fault is present
13	Oxygen sensor circuit—the engine must run up to 5 minutes at part throttle, under road load, before this code will set
14	Shorted Coolant Temperature Sensor (CTS) circuit—the engine must run up to 2 minutes before this code will set
15	Open Coolant Temperature Sensor (CTS) circuit—the engine must run up to 5 minutes before this code will set
21	Throttle Position Sensor (TPS) circuit—the engine must run up to 25 seconds, below 800 RPM, before this code will set
23	Open or grounded M/C solenoid circuit
24	Vehicle Speed Sensor (VSS) circuit—the car must operate up to 5 minutes at road speed before this code will set
32	Barometric Pressure Sensor (BARO) circuit low
34	Manifold Absolute Pressure (MAP) or vacuum sensor circuit. The engine must run up to 5 minutes, below 800 RPM, before this code will set
35	Idle Speed Control (ISC) switch circuit shorted—over ½ throttle for over 2 seconds
42	Electronic Spark Timing (EST) bypass circuit grounded
44	Lean oxygen sensor indication—the engine must run up to 5 minutes, in closed loop, at part throttle and road load before this code will set
44 & 45	(At same time)—faulty oxygen sensor circuit
45	Rich system indication—the engine must run up to 5 minutes, in closed loop, at part throttle and road load before this code will set

ECM TROUBLE CODES (cont'd)

Code	Explanation
51	Faulty calibration unit (PROM) or installation. It takes up to 30 seconds before this code will set
52	Faulty Electronic Control Module (ECM)
53	Faulty Electronic Control Module (ECM)
54	Shorted M/C solenoid circuit
55	Grounded +8 volts, V/ref, faulty oxygen sensor or Electronic Control Module (ECM)

Year – 1981
Model – Fleetwood
Engine – 6.0L (368 cid) DFI V8
Engine Code – VIN 9

ECM TROUBLE CODES

Code	Explanation
12	No tach signal
13	Oxygen sensor not ready
14	Shorted Coolant Temperature Sensor (CTS)
15	Open Coolant Temperature Sensor (CTS) circuit
16	Generator voltage out of range
17	Crank signal circuit high
18	Open crank signal circuit
19	Fuel pump circuit high
20	Open fuel pump circuit
21	Shorted Throttle Position Sensor (TPS) circuit
22	Open Throttle Position Sensor (TPS) circuit
23	Electronic Spark Timing (EST)/bypass circuit shorted or open
24	Speed sensor failure
25	Modulated displacement failure
26	Shorted throttle switch circuit
27	Open throttle switch circuit
30	Idle Speed Control (ISC) circuit
31	Short Manifold Absolute Pressure (MAP) sensor circuit
32	Open Manifold Absolute Pressure (MAP) sensor circuit
33	Manifold Absolute Pressure (MAP)/Barometric Pressure (BARO) sensor correlation
34	Manifold Absolute Pressure (MAP) hose
35	Shorted Barometric Pressure (BARO) sensor circuit
36	Open Barometric Pressure (BARO) sensor circuit
37	Shorted Manifold Air Temperature (MAT) sensor circuit
38	Open Manifold Air Temperature (MAT) sensor circuit
44	Oxygen sensor lean
45	Oxygen sensor rich
51	PROM insertion faulty
60	Drive (ADL) switch circuit
61	Set and resume switch circuit

ECM TROUBLE CODES (cont'd)

Code	Explanation
62	Car speed exceeds maximum limit
63	Car and set speed tolerance exceeded
64	Car acceleration exceeds maximum limit
65	Coolant temperature exceeds maximum limit
66	Engine RPM exceeds maximum limit
68	Set and resume switch circuit
70	System ready — switch tests
71	Brake light switch
72	Idle Speed Control (ISC) throttle switch
73	Drive (ADL) switch
74	Back-up lamp switch
75	Cruise on/off circuit
76	Set/coast circuit
77	Resume/acceleration circuit
78	Instant/average MPG button
79	Reset MPG button
80	Air conditioning clutch circuit
88	Display check
90	System ready to display engine data
95	System ready for actuator cycling
96	Actuator cycling
97	Modulated Displacement (MD) cylinder solenoid cycling
00	All diagnostic complete

Year — 1981
Model — Seville
Engine — 4.1L (252 cid) V6
Engine Code — VIN 4

ECM TROUBLE CODES

Code	Explanation
12	No reference pulses to the Electronic Control Module (ECM). This code is not stored in memory and will only flash while the fault is present
13	Oxygen sensor circuit — the engine must run up to 5 minutes at part throttle, under road load, before this code will set
14	Shorted Coolant Temperature Sensor (CTS) circuit — the engine must run up to 2 minutes before this code will set
15	Open Coolant Temperature Sensor (CTS) circuit — the engine must run up to 5 minutes before this code will set
21	Throttle Position Sensor (TPS) circuit — the engine must run up to 25 seconds, below 800 RPM, before this code will set
23	Open or grounded M/C solenoid circuit
24	Vehicle Speed Sensor (VSS) circuit — the car must operate up to 5 minutes at road speed before this code will set
32	Barometric Pressure Sensor (BARO) circuit low

ECM TROUBLE CODES (cont'd)

Code	Explanation
34	Manifold Absolute Pressure (MAP) or vacuum sensor circuit. The engine must run up to 5 minutes, below 800 RPM, before this code will set
35	Idle Speed Control (ISC) switch circuit shorted—over ½ throttle for over 2 seconds
42	Electronic Spark Timing (EST) bypass circuit grounded
44	Lean oxygen sensor indication—the engine must run up to 5 minutes, in closed loop, at part throttle and road load before this code will set
44 & 45	(At same time)—faulty oxygen sensor circuit
45	Rich system indication—the engine must run up to 5 minutes, in closed loop, at part throttle and road load before this code will set
51	Faulty calibration unit (PROM) or installation. It takes up to 30 seconds before this code will set
52	Faulty Electronic Control Module (ECM)
53	Faulty Electronic Control Module (ECM)
54	Shorted M/C solenoid circuit
55	Grounded +8 volts, V/ref, faulty oxygen sensor or Electronic Control Module (ECM)

Year — 1981
Model — Seville
Engine — 6.0L (368 cid) DFI V8
Engine Code — VIN 9

ECM TROUBLE CODES

Code	Explanation
12	No tach signal
13	Oxygen sensor not ready
14	Shorted Coolant Temperature Sensor (CTS)
15	Open Coolant Temperature Sensor (CTS) circuit
16	Generator voltage out of range
17	Crank signal circuit high
18	Open crank signal circuit
19	Fuel pump circuit high
20	Open fuel pump circuit
21	Shorted Throttle Position Sensor (TPS) circuit
22	Open Throttle Position Sensor (TPS) circuit
23	Electronic Spark Timing (EST)/bypass circuit shorted or open
24	Speed sensor failure
25	Modulated displacement failure
26	Shorted throttle switch circuit
27	Open throttle switch circuit
30	Idle Speed Control (ISC) circuit
31	Short Manifold Absolute Pressure (MAP) sensor circuit
32	Open Manifold Absolute Pressure (MAP) sensor circuit
33	Manifold Absolute Pressure (MAP)/Barometric Pressure (BARO) sensor correlation
34	Manifold Absolute Pressure (MAP) hose
35	Shorted Barometric Pressure (BARO) sensor circuit

ECM TROUBLE CODES (cont'd)

Code	Explanation
36	Open Barometric Pressure (BARO) sensor circuit
37	Shorted Manifold Air Temperature (MAT) sensor circuit
38	Open Manifold Air Temperature (MAT) sensor circuit
44	Oxygen sensor lean
45	Oxygen sensor rich
51	PROM insertion faulty
60	Drive (ADL) switch circuit
61	Set and resume switch circuit
62	Car speed exceeds maximum limit
63	Car and set speed tolerance exceeded
64	Car acceleration exceeds maximum limit
65	Coolant temperature exceeds maximum limit
66	Engine RPM exceeds maximum limit
68	Set and resume switch circuit
70	System ready — switch tests
71	Brake light switch
72	Idle Speed Control (ISC) throttle switch
73	Drive (ADL) switch
74	Back-up lamp switch
75	Cruise on/off circuit
76	Set/coast circuit
77	Resume/acceleration circuit
78	Instant/average MPG button
79	Reset MPG button
80	Air conditioning clutch circuit
88	Display check
90	System ready to display engine data
95	System ready for actuator cycling
96	Actuator cycling
97	Modulated Displacement (MD) cylinder solenoid cycling
00	All diagnostic complete

Year — 1981
Model — Eldorado
Engine — 4.1L (252 cid) V6
Engine Code — VIN 4

ECM TROUBLE CODES

Code	Explanation
12	No reference pulses to the Electronic Control Module (ECM). This code is not stored in memory and will only flash while the fault is present
13	Oxygen sensor circuit — the engine must run up to 5 minutes at part throttle, under road load, before this code will set

ECM TROUBLE CODES (cont'd)

Code	Explanation
14	Shorted Coolant Temperature Sensor (CTS) circuit—the engine must run up to 2 minutes before this code will set
15	Open Coolant Temperature Sensor (CTS) circuit—the engine must run up to 5 minutes before this code will set
21	Throttle Position Sensor (TPS) circuit—the engine must run up to 25 seconds, below 800 RPM, before this code will set
23	Open or grounded M/C solenoid circuit
24	Vehicle Speed Sensor (VSS) circuit—the car must operate up to 5 minutes at road speed before this code will set
32	Barometric Pressure Sensor (BARO) circuit low
34	Manifold Absolute Pressure (MAP) or vacuum sensor circuit. The engine must run up to 5 minutes, below 800 RPM, before this code will set
35	Idle Speed Control (ISC) switch circuit shorted—over ½ throttle for over 2 seconds
42	Electronic Spark Timing (EST) bypass circuit grounded
44	Lean oxygen sensor indication—the engine must run up to 5 minutes, in closed loop, at part throttle and road load before this code will set
44 & 45	(At same time)—faulty oxygen sensor circuit
45	Rich system indication—the engine must run up to 5 minutes, in closed loop, at part throttle and road load before this code will set
51	Faulty calibration unit (PROM) or installation. It takes up to 30 seconds before this code will set
52	Faulty Electronic Control Module (ECM)
53	Faulty Electronic Control Module (ECM)
54	Shorted M/C solenoid circuit
55	Grounded +8 volts, V/ref, faulty oxygen sensor or Electronic Control Module (ECM)

Year—1981
Model—Eldorado
Engine—6.0L (368 cid) DFI V8
Engine Code—VIN 9

ECM TROUBLE CODES

Code	Explanation
12	No tach signal
13	Oxygen sensor not ready
14	Shorted Coolant Temperature Sensor (CTS)
15	Open Coolant Temperature Sensor (CTS) circuit
16	Generator voltage out of range
17	Crank signal circuit high
18	Open crank signal circuit
19	Fuel pump circuit high
20	Open fuel pump circuit
21	Shorted Throttle Position Sensor (TPS) circuit
22	Open Throttle Position Sensor (TPS) circuit
23	Electronic Spark Timing (EST)/bypass circuit shorted or open
24	Speed sensor failure

ECM TROUBLE CODES (cont'd)

Code	Explanation
25	Modulated displacement failure
26	Shorted throttle switch circuit
27	Open throttle switch circuit
30	Idle Speed Control (ISC) circuit
31	Short Manifold Absolute Pressure (MAP) sensor circuit
32	Open Manifold Absolute Pressure (MAP) sensor circuit
33	Manifold Absolute Pressure (MAP)/Barometric Pressure (BARO) sensor correlation
34	Manifold Absolute Pressure (MAP) hose
35	Shorted Barometric Pressure (BARO) sensor circuit
36	Open Barometric Pressure (BARO) sensor circuit
37	Shorted Manifold Air Temperature (MAT) sensor circuit
38	Open Manifold Air Temperature (MAT) sensor circuit
44	Oxygen sensor lean
45	Oxygen sensor rich
51	PROM insertion faulty
60	Drive (ADL) switch circuit
61	Set and resume switch circuit
62	Car speed exceeds maximum limit
63	Car and set speed tolerance exceeded
64	Car acceleration exceeds maximum limit
65	Coolant temperature exceeds maximum limit
66	Engine RPM exceeds maximum limit
68	Set and resume switch circuit
70	System ready—switch tests
71	Brake light switch
72	Idle Speed Control (ISC) throttle switch
73	Drive (ADL) switch
74	Back-up lamp switch
75	Cruise on/off circuit
76	Set/coast circuit
77	Resume/acceleration circuit
78	Instant/average MPG button
79	Reset MPG button
80	Air conditioning clutch circuit
88	Display check
90	System ready to display engine data
95	System ready for actuator cycling
96	Actuator cycling
97	Modulated Displacement (MD) cylinder solenoid cycling
00	All diagnostic complete

Year — 1982
Model — Deville
Engine — 4.1L (252 cid) V6
Engine Code — VIN 4

ECM TROUBLE CODES

Code	Explanation
12	No reference pulses to the ECM. This code is not stored in memory and will only flash while the fault is present. Normal code with ignition ON, engine not running
13	Oxygen sensor circuit — the engine must run up to 5 minutes at part throttle, under road load, before this code will set
14	Shorted Coolant Temperature Sensor (CTS) circuit — the engine must run up to 2 minutes before this code will set
15	Open Coolant Temperature Sensor (CTS) circuit — the engine must run up to 5 minutes before this code will set
21	Throttle Position Sensor (TPS) circuit — the engine must run up to 25 seconds, at specified curb idle speed, before this code will set
23	Open or grounded M/C solenoid circuit
24	Vehicle Speed Sensor (VSS) circuit — the car must operate up to 5 minutes at road speed before this code will set
32	Barometric Pressure Sensor (BARO) circuit low
34	Manifold Absolute Pressure (MAP) or vacuum sensor circuit. The engine must run up to 5 minutes, at specified curb idle speed, before this code will set
35	Idle Speed Control (ISC) switch circuit shorted — over ½ throttle for over 2 seconds
41	No distributor reference pulses at specified engine vacuum. This code will store
42	Electronic Spark Timing (EST) bypass circuit grounded or open
43	Electronic Spark Control (ESC) retard signal for too long; causes a retard in Electronic Spark Timing (EST) signal
44	Lean oxygen sensor indication — the engine must run up to 5 minutes, in closed loop, at part throttle before this code will set
44 & 55	(At same time) — faulty oxygen sensor circuit
45	Rich system indication — the engine must run up to 5 minutes, in closed loop, at part throttle before this code will set
51	Faulty calibration unit (PROM) or installation. It takes up to 30 seconds before this code will set
54	Shorted M/C solenoid circuit and/or faulty ECM
55	Grounded V/ref (terminal 21), faulty oxygen sensor or ECM

Year — 1982
Model — DeVille
Engine — 4.1L (250 cid) DFI V8
Engine Code — VIN 8

ECM TROUBLE CODES

Code	Explanation
12	No distributor (tach) signal
13	Oxygen sensor not ready
14	Shorted Coolant Temperature Sensor (CTS) circuit
15	Open Coolant Temperature Sensor (CTS) circuit
16	Generator voltage out of range
18	Open crank signal circuit
19	Shorted fuel pump circuit
20	Open fuel pump circuit
21	Shorted Throttle Position Sensor (TPS) circuit
22	Open Throttle Position Sensor (TPS) circuit
23	Electronic Spark Timing (EST) circuit problem in run mode
24	Speed sensor circuit problem
25	Electronic Spark Timing (EST) circuit problem in bypass mode
26	Shorted throttle switch circuit
27	Open throttle switch circuit
28	Open fourth gear circuit
29	Shorted fourth gear circuit
30	Idle Speed Control (ISC) circuit problem
31	Short Manifold Absolute Pressure (MAP) sensor circuit
32	Open Manifold Absolute Pressure (MAP) sensor circuit
33	Manifold Absolute Pressure (MAP)/BARO sensor correlation
34	Manifold Absolute Pressure (MAP) signal too high
35	Shorted Barometric Pressure (BARO) sensor circuit
36	Open Barometric Pressure (BARO) sensor circuit
37	Shorted Manifold Air Temperature (MAT) sensor circuit
38	Open Manifold Air Temperature (MAT) sensor circuit
39	Torque Converter Clutch (TCC) engagement problem
44	Lean exhaust signal
45	Rich exhaust signal
51	PROM error indicator
52	ECM memory reset indicator
60	Transmission not in Drive
63	Car and set speed tolerance exceeded
64	Car acceleration exceeds maximum limit
65	Coolant temperature exceeds maximum limit
66	Engine RPM exceeds maximum limit
67	Shorted set or resume circuit
.7.0	System ready for further tests
.7.1	Cruise control brake circuit test

ECM TROUBLE CODES (cont'd)

Code	Explanation
.7.2	Throttle switch circuit test
.7.3	Drive (ADL) circuit test
.7.4	Reverse circuit test
.7.5	Cruise on/off circuit test
.7.6	"Set/coast" circuit test
.7.7	"Resume/acceleration" circuit test
.7.8	"Instant/average" circuit test
.7.9	"Reset" circuit test
.8.0	Air conditioning clutch circuit test
− 1.8.8	Display check
.9.0	System ready to display engine data
.9.5	System ready for output cycling or in fixed spark mode
.9.6	Output cycling
.0.0	All diagnostics complete

Year — 1982
Model — Fleetwood
Engine — 4.1L (252 cid) V6
Engine Code — VIN 4

ECM TROUBLE CODES

Code	Explanation
12	No reference pulses to the ECM. This code is not stored in memory and will only flash while the fault is present. Normal code with ignition ON, engine not running
13	Oxygen sensor circuit — the engine must run up to 5 minutes at part throttle, under road load, before this code will set
14	Shorted Coolant Temperature Sensor (CTS) circuit — the engine must run up to 2 minutes before this code will set
15	Open Coolant Temperature Sensor (CTS) circuit — the engine must run up to 5 minutes before this code will set
21	Throttle Position Sensor (TPS) circuit — the engine must run up to 25 seconds, at specified curb idle speed, before this code will set
23	Open or grounded M/C solenoid circuit
24	Vehicle Speed Sensor (VSS) circuit — the car must operate up to 5 minutes at road speed before this code will set
32	Barometric Pressure Sensor (BARO) circuit low
34	Manifold Absolute Pressure (MAP) or vacuum sensor circuit. The engine must run up to 5 minutes, at specified curb idle speed, before this code will set
35	Idle Speed Control (ISC) switch circuit shorted — over ½ throttle for over 2 seconds
41	No distributor reference pulses at specified engine vacuum. This code will store
42	Electronic Spark Timing (EST) bypass circuit grounded or open
43	Electronic Spark Control (ESC) retard signal for too long; causes a retard in Electronic Spark Timing (EST) signal
44	Lean oxygen sensor indication — the engine must run up to 5 minutes, in closed loop, at part throttle before this code will set
44 & 55	(At same time) — Faulty oxygen sensor circuit

ECM TROUBLE CODES (cont'd)

Code	Explanation
45	Rich system indication—the engine must run up to 5 minutes, in closed loop, at part throttle before this code will set
51	Faulty calibration unit (PROM) or installation. It takes up to 30 seconds before this code will set
54	Shorted M/C solenoid circuit and/or faulty ECM
55	Grounded V/ref (terminal 21), faulty oxygen sensor or ECM

Year – 1982
Model – Fleetwood
Engine – 4.1L (250 cid) DFI V8
Engine Code – VIN 8

ECM TROUBLE CODES

Code	Explanation
12	No distributor (tach) signal
13	Oxygen sensor not ready
14	Shorted Coolant Temperature Sensor (CTS) circuit
15	Open Coolant Temperature Sensor (CTS) circuit
16	Generator voltage out of range
18	Open crank signal circuit
19	Shorted fuel pump circuit
20	Open fuel pump circuit
21	Shorted Throttle Position Sensor (TPS) circuit
22	Open Throttle Position Sensor (TPS) circuit
23	Electronic Spark Timing (EST) circuit problem in run mode
24	Speed sensor circuit problem
25	Electronic Spark Timing (EST) circuit problem in bypass mode
26	Shorted throttle switch circuit
27	Open throttle switch circuit
28	Open fourth gear circuit
29	Shorted fourth gear circuit
30	Idle Speed Control (ISC) circuit problem
31	Short Manifold Absolute Pressure (MAP) sensor circuit
32	Open Manifold Absolute Pressure (MAP) sensor circuit
33	Manifold Absolute Pressure (MAP)/Barometric Pressure (BARO) sensor correlation
34	Manifold Absolute Pressure (MAP) signal too high
35	Shorted Barometric Pressure (BARO) sensor circuit
36	Open Barometric Pressure (BARO) sensor circuit
37	Shorted Manifold Air Temperature (MAT) sensor circuit
38	Open Manifold Air Temperature (MAT) sensor circuit
39	Torque Converter Clutch (TCC) engagement problem
44	Lean exhaust signal
45	Rich exhaust signal
51	PROM error indicator

ECM TROUBLE CODES (cont'd)

Code	Explanation
52	ECM memory reset indicator
60	Transmission not in Drive
63	Car and set speed tolerance exceeded
64	Car acceleration exceeds maximum limit
65	Coolant temperature exceeds maximum limit
66	Engine RPM exceeds maximum limit
67	Shorted set or resume circuit
.7.0	System ready for further tests
.7.1	Cruise control brake circuit test
.7.2	Throttle switch circuit test
.7.3	Drive (ADL) circuit test
.7.4	Reverse circuit test
.7.5	Cruise on/off circuit test
.7.6	"Set/coast" circuit test
.7.7	"Resume/acceleration" circuit test
.7.8	"Instant/average" circuit test
.7.9	"Reset" circuit test
.8.0	Air conditioning clutch circuit test
— 1.8.8	Display check
.9.0	System ready to display engine data
.9.5	System ready for output cycling or in fixed spark mode
.9.6	Output cycling
.0.0	All diagnostics complete

Year — 1982
Model — Fleetwood Limousine
Engine — 6.0L (368 cid) DEFI V8
Engine Code — VIN 9

ECM TROUBLE CODES

Code	Explanation
12	No tach signal to the ECM. This code will only be present while a fault is present. It will not be stored with an intermittent problem
13	Oxygen sensor circuit — the engine has to run for about 5 minutes at part throttle, before this code will show
13 & 43	Throttle Position Sensor (TPS) adjustment — part throttle — after 10 seconds
14	Shorted Coolant Temperature Sensor (CTS) circuit — the engine has to run 2 minutes before this code will show
15	Open Coolant Temperature Sensor (CTS) circuit — the engine has to operate for about 5 minutes before this code will show
21	Throttle Position Sensor (TPS) — Wide Open Throttle (WOT) error — After 10 seconds and below 800 RPM
23	Open or grounded carburetor M/C solenoid
43	Throttle Position Sensor (TPS) adjustment — part throttle — after 10 seconds

ECM TROUBLE CODES (cont'd)

Code	Explanation
44	Lean oxygen sensor. The engine has to run for about 3 minutes in closed loop and part throttle at road load before this code will show
44 & 55	(At same time) — faulty oxygen sensor circuit
45	Rich oxygen sensor indication. The engine has to run for about 3 minutes in closed loop and part throttle at road load before this code will show
51	Faulty calibration unit (PROM) or installation
52 & 53	Light OFF — Intermittent ECM problem. Light ON — faulty ECM
54	Faulty M/C solenoid or ECM
55	Faulty Throttle Position Sensor (TPS) or ECM

Year — 1982
Model — Seville
Engine — 4.1L (252 cid) V6
Engine Code — VIN 4

ECM TROUBLE CODES

Code	Explanation
12	No reference pulses to the ECM. This code is not stored in memory and will only flash while the fault is present. Normal code with ignition ON, engine not running
13	Oxygen sensor circuit — the engine must run up to 5 minutes at part throttle, under road load, before this code will set
14	Shorted Coolant Temperature Sensor (CTS) circuit — the engine must run up to 2 minutes before this code will set
15	Open Coolant Temperature Sensor (CTS) circuit — the engine must run up to 5 minutes before this code will set
21	Throttle Position Sensor (TPS) circuit — the engine must run up to 25 seconds, at specified curb idle speed, before this code will set
23	Open or grounded M/C solenoid circuit
24	Vehicle Speed Sensor (VSS) circuit — the car must operate up to 5 minutes at road speed before this code will set
32	Barometric Pressure Sensor (BARO) circuit low
34	Manifold Absolute Pressure (MAP) or vacuum sensor circuit. The engine must run up to 5 minutes, at specified curb idle speed, before this code will set
35	Idle Speed Control (ISC) switch circuit shorted — over ½ throttle for over 2 seconds
41	No distributor reference pulses at specified engine vacuum. This code will store
42	Electronic Spark Timing (EST) bypass circuit grounded or open
43	Electronic Spark Control (ESC) retard signal for too long; causes a retard in Electronic Spark Timing (EST) signal
44	Lean oxygen sensor indication — the engine must run up to 5 minutes, in closed loop, at part throttle before this code will set
44 & 55	(At same time) — faulty oxygen sensor circuit
45	Rich system indication — the engine must run up to 5 minutes, in closed loop, at part throttle before this code will set
51	Faulty calibration unit (PROM) or installation. It takes up to 30 seconds before this code will set
54	Shorted M/C solenoid circuit and/or faulty ECM
55	Grounded V/ref (terminal 21), faulty oxygen sensor or ECM

Year—1982
Model—Seville
Engine—4.1L (250 cid) DFI V8
Engine Code—VIN 8

ECM TROUBLE CODES

Code	Explanation
12	No distributor (tach) signal
13	Oxygen sensor not ready
14	Shorted Coolant Temperature Sensor (CTS) circuit
15	Open Coolant Temperature Sensor (CTS) circuit
16	Generator voltage out of range
18	Open crank signal circuit
19	Shorted fuel pump circuit
20	Open fuel pump circuit
21	Shorted Throttle Position Sensor (TPS) circuit
22	Open Throttle Position Sensor (TPS) circuit
23	Electronic Spark Timing (EST) circuit problem in run mode
24	Speed sensor circuit problem
25	Electronic Spark Timing (EST) circuit problem in bypass mode
26	Shorted throttle switch circuit
27	Open throttle switch circuit
28	Open fourth gear circuit
29	Shorted fourth gear circuit
30	Idle Speed Control (ISC) circuit problem
31	Short Manifold Absolute Pressure (MAP) sensor circuit
32	Open Manifold Absolute Pressure (MAP) sensor circuit
33	Manifold Absolute Pressure (MAP)/Barometric Pressure (BARO) sensor correlation
34	Manifold Absolute Pressure (MAP) signal too high
35	Shorted Barometric Pressure (BARO) sensor circuit
36	Open Barometric Pressure (BARO) sensor circuit
37	Shorted Manifold Air Temperature (MAT) sensor circuit
38	Open Manifold Air Temperature (MAT) sensor circuit
39	Torque Converter Clutch (TCC) engagement problem
44	Lean exhaust signal
45	Rich exhaust signal
51	PROM error indicator
52	ECM memory reset indicator
60	Transmission not in Drive
63	Car and set speed tolerance exceeded
64	Car acceleration exceeds maximum limit
65	Coolant temperature exceeds maximum limit
66	Engine RPM exceeds maximum limit
67	Shorted set or resume circuit
.7.0	System ready for further tests
.7.1	Cruise control brake circuit test

ECM TROUBLE CODES (cont'd)

Code	Explanation
.7.2	Throttle switch circuit test
.7.3	Drive (ADL) circuit test
.7.4	Reverse circuit test
.7.5	Cruise on/off circuit test
.7.6	"Set/coast" circuit test
.7.7	"Resume/acceleration" circuit test
.7.8	"Instant/average" circuit test
.7.9	"Reset" circuit test
.8.0	Air conditioning clutch circuit test
−1.8.8	Display check
.9.0	System ready to display engine data
.9.5	System ready for output cycling or in fixed spark mode
.9.6	Output cycling
.0.0	All diagnostics complete

Year – 1982
Model – Eldorado
Engine – 4.1L (250 cid) DFI V8
Engine Code – VIN 8

ECM TROUBLE CODES

Code	Explanation
12	No distributor (tach) signal
13	Oxygen sensor not ready
14	Shorted Coolant Temperature Sensor (CTS) circuit
15	Open Coolant Temperature Sensor (CTS) circuit
16	Generator voltage out of range
18	Open crank signal circuit
19	Shorted fuel pump circuit
20	Open fuel pump circuit
21	Shorted Throttle Position Sensor (TPS) circuit
22	Open Throttle Position Sensor (TPS) circuit
23	Electronic Spark Timing (EST) circuit problem in run mode
24	Speed sensor circuit problem
25	Electronic Spark Timing (EST) circuit problem in bypass mode
26	Shorted throttle switch circuit
27	Open throttle switch circuit
28	Open fourth gear circuit
29	Shorted fourth gear circuit
30	Idle Speed Control (ISC) circuit problem
31	Short Manifold Absolute Pressure (MAP) sensor circuit
32	Open Manifold Absolute Pressure (MAP) sensor circuit
33	Manifold Absolute Pressure (MAP)/Barometric Pressure (BARO) sensor correlation

ECM TROUBLE CODES (cont'd)

Code	Explanation
34	Manifold Absolute Pressure (MAP) signal too high
35	Shorted Barometric Pressure (BARO) sensor circuit
36	Open Barometric Pressure (BARO) sensor circuit
37	Shorted Manifold Air Temperature (MAT) sensor circuit
38	Open Manifold Air Temperature (MAT) sensor circuit
39	Torque Converter Clutch (TCC) engagement problem
44	Lean exhaust signal
45	Rich exhaust signal
51	PROM error indicator
52	ECM memory reset indicator
60	Transmission not in Drive
63	Car and set speed tolerance exceeded
64	Car acceleration exceeds maximum limit
65	Coolant temperature exceeds maximum limit
66	Engine RPM exceeds maximum limit
67	Shorted set or resume circuit
.7.0	System ready for further tests
.7.1	Cruise control brake circuit test
.7.2	Throttle switch circuit test
.7.3	Drive (ADL) circuit test
.7.4	Reverse circuit test
.7.5	Cruise on/off circuit test
.7.6	"Set/coast" circuit test
.7.7	"Resume/acceleration" circuit test
.7.8	"Instant/average" circuit test
.7.9	"Reset" circuit test
.8.0	Air conditioning clutch circuit test
−1.8.8	Display check
.9.0	System ready to display engine data
.9.5	System ready for output cycling or in fixed spark mode
.9.6	Output cycling
.0.0	All diagnostics complete

Year — 1982
Model — Eldorado
Engine — 4.1L (252 cid) V6
Engine Code — VIN 4

ECM TROUBLE CODES

Code	Explanation
12	No reference pulses to the ECM. This code is not stored in memory and will only flash while the fault is present. Normal code with ignition ON, engine not running
13	Oxygen sensor circuit — the engine must run up to 5 minutes at part throttle, under road load, before this code will set
14	Shorted Coolant Temperature Sensor (CTS) circuit — the engine must run up to 2 minutes before this code will set
15	Open Coolant Temperature Sensor (CTS) circuit — the engine must run up to 5 minutes before this code will set
21	Throttle Position Sensor (TPS) circuit — the engine must run up to 25 seconds, at specified curb idle speed, before this code will set
23	Open or grounded M/C solenoid circuit
24	Vehicle Speed Sensor (VSS) circuit — the car must operate up to 5 minutes at road speed before this code will set
32	Barometric Pressure Sensor (BARO) circuit low
34	Manifold Absolute Pressure (MAP) or vacuum sensor circuit. The engine must run up to 5 minutes, at specified curb idle speed, before this code will set
35	Idle Speed Control (ISC) switch circuit shorted — over ½ throttle for over 2 seconds
41	No distributor reference pulses at specified engine vacuum. This code will store
42	Electronic Spark Timing (EST) bypass circuit grounded or open
43	Electronic Spark Control (ESC) retard signal for too long; causes a retard in Electronic Spark Timing (EST) signal
44	Lean oxygen sensor indication — the engine must run up to 5 minutes, in closed loop, at part throttle before this code will set
44 & 55	(At same time) — faulty oxygen sensor circuit
45	Rich system indication — the engine must run up to 5 minutes, in closed loop, at part throttle before this code will set
51	Faulty calibration unit (PROM) or installation. It takes up to 30 seconds before this code will set
54	Shorted M/C solenoid circuit and/or faulty ECM
55	Grounded V/ref (terminal 21), faulty oxygen sensor or ECM

Year — 1982
Model — Cimarron
Engine — 1.8L (112 cid) 4 cyl
Engine Code — VIN G

ECM TROUBLE CODES

Code	Explanation
12	No distributor reference pulses to the ECM. This code is not stored in memory and will only flash while the fault is present
13	Oxygen sensor circuit — the engine must run up to 5 minutes at part throttle, under road load, before this code will set
14	Shorted Coolant Temperature Sensor (CTS) circuit — the engine must run up to 2 minutes before this code will set
15	Open Coolant Temperature Sensor (CTS) circuit — the engine must run up to 5 minutes before this code will set
21	Throttle Position Sensor (TPS) circuit — the engine must run up to 25 seconds, below 800 RPM, before this code will set
23	Open or grounded M/C solenoid circuit
24	Vehicle Speed Sensor (VSS) circuit — the car must operate up to 5 minutes at road speed before this code will set
32	Altitude compensator circuit
34	Vacuum sensor circuit. The engine must run up to 5 minutes at specified curb idle before this code will set
35	Idle Speed Control (ISC) switch circuit shorted — over ½ throttle for over 2 seconds
41	No distributor reference pulses to ECM at specified engine vacuum. This code will store in memory
42	Electronic Spark Timing (EST) bypass circuit grounded
44	Lean oxygen sensor indication — the engine must run up to 5 minutes, in closed loop, at part throttle and road load before this code will set
44 & 55	(At same time) — faulty oxygen sensor circuit
45	Rich system indication — the engine must run up to 5 minutes, in closed loop, at part throttle and road load before this code will set
51	Faulty calibration unit (PROM) or installation. It takes up to 30 seconds before this code will set
54	Shorted M/C solenoid circuit and/or faulty ECM
55	Grounded V/ref (terminal 21), faulty oxygen sensor or ECM

GENERAL MOTORS CORPORATION
DIAGNOSTIC CODE DATA

Year — 1983
Model — DeVille
Engine — 4.1L (250 cid) DFI V8
Engine Code — VIN 8

ECM TROUBLE CODES

Code	Explanation
12	No distributor (tach) signal — turns ON "Sevice Now" light
13	Oxygen sensor not ready — turns ON "Sevice Soon" light
14	Shorted Coolant Temperature Sensor (CTS) circuit — turns ON "Sevice Soon" light
15	Open Coolant Temperature Sensor (CTS) circuit — turns ON "Sevice Soon" light
16	Generator voltage out of range — turns ON "Sevice Now" light
18	Open crank signal circuit — turns ON "Sevice Soon" light
19	Shorted fuel pump circuit — turns ON "Sevice Soon" light
20	Open fuel pump circuit — turns ON "Sevice Now" light
21	Shorted Throttle Position Sensor (TPS) circuit — turns ON "Sevice Soon" light
22	Open Throttle Position Sensor (TPS) circuit — turns ON "Sevice Soon" light
23	Electronic Spark Timing (EST) circuit problem in run mode — turns ON "Sevice Soon" light
24	Speed sensor circuit problem — turns ON "Sevice Soon" light
26	Shorted throttle switch circuit — turns ON "Sevice Soon" light
27	Open throttle switch circuit — turns ON "Sevice Soon" light
28	Open fourth gear circuit — turns ON "Sevice Soon" light
29	Shorted fourth gear circuit — turns ON "Sevice Soon" light
30	Idle Speed Control (ISC) circuit problem — turns ON "Sevice Soon" light
31	Short Manifold Absolute Pressure (MAP) sensor circuit — turns ON "Sevice Now" light
32	Open Manifold Absolute Pressure (MAP) sensor circuit — turns ON "Sevice Now" light
33	Manifold Absolute Pressure (MAP)/Barometric Pressure (BARO) sensor correlation — turns ON "Sevice Now" light
34	Manifold Absolute Pressure (MAP) signal too high — turns ON "Sevice Soon" light
35	Shorted Barometric Pressure (BARO) sensor circuit — turns ON "Sevice Soon" light
36	Open Barometric Pressure (BARO) sensor circuit — turns ON "Sevice Soon" light
37	Shorted Manifold Air Temperature (MAT) sensor circuit — turns ON "Sevice Soon" light
38	Open Manifold Air Temperature (MAT) sensor circuit — turns ON "Sevice Soon" light
39	Torque Converter Clutch (TCC) engagement problem — turns ON "Sevice Soon" light
44	Lean exhaust signal — turns ON "Sevice Now" light
45	Rich exhaust signal — turns ON "Sevice Now" light
51	PROM error indicator — turns ON "Sevice Now" light
52	Electronic Control Module (ECM) memory reset indicator — does not turn ON any telltale light
53	Distributor signal interrupt — does not turn ON any telltale light
60	Transmission not in Drive — does not turn ON any telltale light
63	Car and set speed tolerance exceeded — does not turn ON any telltale light
64	Car acceleration exceeds maximum limit — does not turn ON any telltale light
65	Coolant temperature exceeds maximum limit — does not turn ON any telltale light
66	Engine RPM exceeds maximum limit — does not turn ON any telltale light
67	Shorted set or resume circuit — does not turn ON any telltale light
.7.0	System ready for further tests

ECM TROUBLE CODES (cont'd)

Code	Explanation
.7.1	Cruise control brake circuit test
.7.2	Throttle switch circuit test
.7.3	Drive (ADL) circuit test
.7.4	Reverse circuit test
.7.5	Cruise on/off circuit test
.7.6	"Set/coast" circuit test
.7.7	"Resume/acceleration" circuit test
.7.8	"Instant/average" circuit test
.7.9	"Reset" circuit test
.8.0	Air conditioning clutch circuit test
−1.8.8	Display check
.9.0	System ready to display engine data
.9.5	System ready for output cycling or in fixed spark mode
.9.6	Output cycling
.0.0	All diagnostics complete

Year—1983
Model—Fleetwood Brougham
Engine—4.1L (250 cid) DFI V8
Engine Code—VIN 8

ECM TROUBLE CODES

Code	Explanation
12	No distributor (tach) signal—turns ON "Sevice Now" light
13	Oxygen sensor not ready—turns ON "Sevice Soon" light
14	Shorted Coolant Temperature Sensor (CTS) circuit—turns ON "Sevice Soon" light
15	Open Coolant Temperature Sensor (CTS) circuit—turns ON "Sevice Soon" light
16	Generator voltage out of range—turns ON "Sevice Now" light
18	Open crank signal circuit—turns ON "Sevice Soon" light
19	Shorted fuel pump circuit—turns ON "Sevice Soon" light
20	Open fuel pump circuit—turns ON "Sevice Now" light
21	Shorted Throttle Position Sensor (TPS) circuit—turns ON "Sevice Soon" light
22	Open Throttle Position Sensor (TPS) circuit—turns ON "Sevice Soon" light
23	Electronic Spark Timing (EST) circuit problem in run mode—turns ON "Sevice Soon" light
24	Speed sensor circuit problem—turns ON "Sevice Soon" light
26	Shorted throttle switch circuit—turns ON "Sevice Soon" light
27	Open throttle switch circuit—turns ON "Sevice Soon" light
28	Open fourth gear circuit—turns ON "Sevice Soon" light
29	Shorted fourth gear circuit—turns ON "Sevice Soon" light
30	Idle Speed Control (ISC) circuit problem—turns ON "Sevice Soon" light
31	Short Manifold Absolute Pressure (MAP) sensor circuit—turns ON "Sevice Now" light
32	Open Manifold Absolute Pressure (MAP) sensor circuit—turns ON "Sevice Now" light

ECM TROUBLE CODES (cont'd)

Code	Explanation
33	Manifold Absolute Pressure (MAP)/Barometric Pressure (BARO) sensor correlation—turns ON "Sevice Now" light
34	Manifold Absolute Pressure (MAP) signal too high—turns ON "Sevice Soon" light
35	Shorted Barometric Pressure (BARO) sensor circuit—turns ON "Sevice Soon" light
36	Open Barometric Pressure (BARO) sensor circuit—turns ON "Sevice Soon" light
37	Shorted Manifold Air Temperature (MAT) sensor circuit—turns ON "Sevice Soon" light
38	Open Manifold Air Temperature (MAT) sensor circuit—turns ON "Sevice Soon" light
39	Torque Converter Clutch (TCC) engagement problem—turns ON "Sevice Soon" light
44	Lean exhaust signal—turns ON "Sevice Now" light
45	Rich exhaust signal—turns ON "Sevice Now" light
51	PROM error indicator—turns ON "Sevice Now" light
52	Electronic Control Module (ECM) memory reset indicator—does not turn ON any telltale light
53	Distributor signal interrupt—does not turn ON any telltale light
60	Transmission not in Drive—does not turn ON any telltale light
63	Car and set speed tolerance exceeded—does not turn ON any telltale light
64	Car acceleration exceeds maximum limit—does not turn ON any telltale light
65	Coolant temperature exceeds maximum limit—does not turn ON any telltale light
66	Engine RPM exceeds maximum limit—does not turn ON any telltale light
67	Shorted set or resume circuit—does not turn ON any telltale light
.7.0	System ready for further tests
.7.1	Cruise control brake circuit test
.7.2	Throttle switch circuit test
.7.3	Drive (ADL) circuit test
.7.4	Reverse circuit test
.7.5	Cruise on/off circuit test
.7.6	"Set/coast" circuit test
.7.7	"Resume/acceleration" circuit test
.7.8	"Instant/average" circuit test
.7.9	"Reset" circuit test
.8.0	Air conditioning clutch circuit test
−1.8.8	Display check
.9.0	System ready to display engine data
.9.5	System ready for output cycling or in fixed spark mode
.9.6	Output cycling
.0.0	All diagnostics complete

Year – 1983
Model – Fleetwood Limousine
Engine – 6.0L (368 cid) DEFI V8
Engine Code – VIN 9

ECM TROUBLE CODES

Code	Explanation
12	No tach signal to the Electronic Control Module (ECM). This code will only be present while a fault is present. It will not be stored with an intermittent problem
13	Oxygen sensor circuit—the engine has to run for about 5 minutes at part throttle, before this code will show
13 & 43	Throttle Position Sensor (TPS) adjustment—part throttle—after 10 seconds
14	Shorted Coolant Temperature Sensor (CTS) circuit—the engine has to run 2 minutes before this code will show
15	Open Coolant Temperature Sensor (CTS) circuit—the engine has to operate for about 5 minutes before this code will show
21	Throttle Position Sensor (TPS)—Wide Open Throttle (WOT) error—After 10 seconds and below 800 RPM
23	Open or grounded carburetor M/C solenoid
43	Throttle Position Sensor (TPS) adjustment—part throttle—after 10 seconds
44	Lean oxygen sensor. The engine has to run for about 3 minutes in closed loop and part throttle at road load before this code will show
44 & 55	(At same time)—faulty oxygen sensor circuit
45	Rich oxygen sensor indication. The engine has to run for about 3 minutes in closed loop and part throttle at road load before this code will show
51	Faulty calibration unit (PROM) or installation
52 & 53	Light OFF—Intermittent Electronic Control Module (ECM) problem. Light ON—faulty ECM
54	Faulty M/C solenoid or Electronic Control Module (ECM)
55	Faulty Throttle Position Sensor (TPS) or Electronic Control Module (ECM)

GENERAL MOTORS CORPORATION
DIAGNOSTIC CODE DATA

Year – 1983
Model – Seville
Engine – 4.1L (250 cid) DFI V8
Engine Code – VIN 8

ECM TROUBLE CODES

Code	Explanation
12	No distributor (tach) signal – turns ON "Sevice Now" light
13	Oxygen sensor not ready – turns ON "Sevice Soon" light
14	Shorted Coolant Temperature Sensor (CTS) circuit – turns ON "Sevice Soon" light
15	Open Coolant Temperature Sensor (CTS) circuit – turns ON "Sevice Soon" light
16	Generator voltage out of range – turns ON "Sevice Now" light
18	Open crank signal circuit – turns ON "Sevice Soon" light
19	Shorted fuel pump circuit – turns ON "Sevice Soon" light
20	Open fuel pump circuit – turns ON "Sevice Now" light
21	Shorted Throttle Position Sensor (TPS) circuit – turns ON "Sevice Soon" light
22	Open Throttle Position Sensor (TPS) circuit – turns ON "Sevice Soon" light
23	Electronic Spark Timing (EST) circuit problem in run mode – turns ON "Sevice Soon" light
24	Speed sensor circuit problem – turns ON "Sevice Soon" light
26	Shorted throttle switch circuit – turns ON "Sevice Soon" light
27	Open throttle switch circuit – turns ON "Sevice Soon" light
28	Open fourth gear circuit – turns ON "Sevice Soon" light
29	Shorted fourth gear circuit – turns ON "Sevice Soon" light
30	Idle Speed Control (ISC) circuit problem – turns ON "Sevice Soon" light
31	Short Manifold Absolute Pressure (MAP) sensor circuit – turns ON "Sevice Now" light
32	Open Manifold Absolute Pressure (MAP) sensor circuit – turns ON "Sevice Now" light
33	Manifold Absolute Pressure (MAP)/Barometric Pressure (BARO) sensor correlation – turns ON "Sevice Now" light
34	Manifold Absolute Pressure (MAP) signal too high – turns ON "Sevice Soon" light
35	Shorted Barometric Pressure (BARO) sensor circuit – turns ON "Sevice Soon" light
36	Open Barometric Pressure (BARO) sensor circuit – turns ON "Sevice Soon" light
37	Shorted Manifold Air Temperature (MAT) sensor circuit – turns ON "Sevice Soon" light
38	Open Manifold Air Temperature (MAT) sensor circuit – turns ON "Sevice Soon" light
39	Torque Converter Clutch (TCC) engagement problem – turns ON "Sevice Soon" light
44	Lean exhaust signal – turns ON "Sevice Now" light
45	Rich exhaust signal – turns ON "Sevice Now" light
51	PROM error indicator – turns ON "Sevice Now" light
52	Electronic Control Module (ECM) memory reset indicator – does not turn ON any telltale light
53	Distributor signal interrupt – does not turn ON any telltale light
60	Transmission not in Drive – does not turn ON any telltale light
63	Car and set speed tolerance exceeded – does not turn ON any telltale light
64	Car acceleration exceeds maximum limit – does not turn ON any telltale light
65	Coolant temperature exceeds maximum limit – does not turn ON any telltale light
66	Engine RPM exceeds maximum limit – does not turn ON any telltale light
67	Shorted set or resume circuit – does not turn ON any telltale light
.7.0	System ready for further tests
.7.1	Cruise control brake circuit test

ECM TROUBLE CODES (cont'd)

Code	Explanation
.7.2	Throttle switch circuit test
.7.3	Drive (ADL) circuit test
.7.4	Reverse circuit test
.7.5	Cruise on/off circuit test
.7.6	"Set/coast" circuit test
.7.7	"Resume/acceleration" circuit test
.7.8	"Instant/average" circuit test
.7.9	"Reset" circuit test
.8.0	Air conditioning clutch circuit test
−1.8.8	Display check
.9.0	System ready to display engine data
.9.5	System ready for output cycling or in fixed spark mode
.9.6	Output cycling
.0.0	All diagnostics complete

Year – 1983
Model – Eldorado
Engine – 4.1L (250 cid) DFI V8
Engine Code – VIN 8

ECM TROUBLE CODES

Code	Explanation
12	No distributor (tach) signal – turns ON "Sevice Now" light
13	Oxygen sensor not ready – turns ON "Sevice Soon" light
14	Shorted Coolant Temperature Sensor (CTS) circuit – turns ON "Sevice Soon" light
15	Open Coolant Temperature Sensor (CTS) circuit – turns ON "Sevice Soon" light
16	Generator voltage out of range – turns ON "Sevice Now" light
18	Open crank signal circuit – turns ON "Sevice Soon" light
19	Shorted fuel pump circuit – turns ON "Sevice Soon" light
20	Open fuel pump circuit – turns ON "Sevice Now" light
21	Shorted Throttle Position Sensor (TPS) circuit – turns ON "Sevice Soon" light
22	Open Throttle Position Sensor (TPS) circuit – turns ON "Sevice Soon" light
23	Electronic Spark Timing (EST) circuit problem in run mode – turns ON "Sevice Soon" light
24	Speed sensor circuit problem – turns ON "Sevice Soon" light
26	Shorted throttle switch circuit – turns ON "Sevice Soon" light
27	Open throttle switch circuit – turns ON "Sevice Soon" light
28	Open fourth gear circuit – turns ON "Sevice Soon" light
29	Shorted fourth gear circuit – turns ON "Sevice Soon" light
30	Idle Speed Control (ISC) circuit problem – turns ON "Sevice Soon" light
31	Short Manifold Absolute Pressure (MAP) sensor circuit – turns ON "Sevice Now" light
32	Open Manifold Absolute Pressure (MAP) sensor circuit – turns ON "Sevice Now" light
33	Manifold Absolute Pressure (MAP)/Barometric Pressure (BARO) sensor correlation – turns ON "Sevice Now" light

GENERAL MOTORS CORPORATION
DIAGNOSTIC CODE DATA

ECM TROUBLE CODES (cont'd)

Code	Explanation
34	Manifold Absolute Pressure (MAP) signal too high—turns ON "Sevice Soon" light
35	Shorted Barometric Pressure (BARO) sensor circuit—turns ON "Sevice Soon" light
36	Open Barometric Pressure (BARO) sensor circuit—turns ON "Sevice Soon" light
37	Shorted Manifold Air Temperature (MAT) sensor circuit—turns ON "Sevice Soon" light
38	Open Manifold Air Temperature (MAT) sensor circuit—turns ON "Sevice Soon" light
39	Torque Converter Clutch (TCC) engagement problem—turns ON "Sevice Soon" light
44	Lean exhaust signal—turns ON "Sevice Now" light
45	Rich exhaust signal—turns ON "Sevice Now" light
51	PROM error indicator—turns ON "Sevice Now" light
52	Electronic Control Module (ECM) memory reset indicator—does not turn ON any telltale light
53	Distributor signal interrupt—does not turn ON any telltale light
60	Transmission not in Drive—does not turn ON any telltale light
63	Car and set speed tolerance exceeded—does not turn ON any telltale light
64	Car acceleration exceeds maximum limit—does not turn ON any telltale light
65	Coolant temperature exceeds maximum limit—does not turn ON any telltale light
66	Engine RPM exceeds maximum limit—does not turn ON any telltale light
67	Shorted set or resume circuit—does not turn ON any telltale light
.7.0	System ready for further tests
.7.1	Cruise control brake circuit test
.7.2	Throttle switch circuit test
.7.3	Drive (ADL) circuit test
.7.4	Reverse circuit test
.7.5	Cruise on/off circuit test
.7.6	"Set/coast" circuit test
.7.7	"Resume/acceleration" circuit test
.7.8	"Instant/average" circuit test
.7.9	"Reset" circuit test
.8.0	Air conditioning clutch circuit test
− 1.8.8	Display check
.9.0	System ready to display engine data
.9.5	System ready for output cycling or in fixed spark mode
.9.6	Output cycling
.0.0	All diagnostics complete

Year — 1983
Model — Cimarron
Engine — 2.0L (121 cid) TBI 4 cyl
Engine Code — VIN P

ECM TROUBLE CODES

Code	Explanation
15	Engine running 10 seconds with no coolant sensor signal voltage. Coolant sensor circuit signal voltagehigh. Engine running with coolant sensor signal too high for 60 seconds. If fault occurs with ignition "OFF," engine will crank, but may not start
21	Throttle Position Sensor (TPS) signal too high. Engine running below 1600 RPM, and TPS is above 50% (2.5 volts) for 2 seconds
22	Throttle Position Sensor (TPS) signal too low. Engine running with TPS signal voltage too low
24	Vehicle Speed Sensor (VSS). Vehicle speed about 40—45 MPH while decelerating with no VSS signal for one minute
33	Manifold Absolute Pressure (MAP) signal too high (low vacuum). Engine idling and MAP signal is high for 5 seconds
34	Manifold Absolute Pressure (MAP) signal too low. Engine running code will set within 2 seconds with MAP signal voltage too low
42	Electronic Spark Timing (EST). Open or grounded EST line, open or grounded bypass line, and engine speed above 500 RPM
44	Lean exhaust system. Engine running in closed loop at normal operating temperature with oxygen sensor signal less than 200mv. for 1 minute. Forces open loop operation. May require drive position to set on some engines
45	Rich exhaust system. Engine idling in closed loop at normal operating temperature with oxygen sensor signal above 750mv. for 20 seconds. Forces open loop operation. May require drive position to set on some engines
51	Faulty Calibration Unit (PROM) or installation.
55	Electronic Control Module (ECM) error. Analog to digital conversion error in ECM

GENERAL MOTORS CORPORATION
DIAGNOSTIC CODE DATA

Year — 1984
Model — DeVille
Engine — 4.1L (252 cid) DFI V8
Engine Code — VIN 8

ECM TROUBLE CODES

Code	Explanation
12	No distributor (tach) signal — turns ON "Sevice Now" light
13	Oxygen sensor not ready — turns ON "Sevice Soon" light
14	Shorted Coolant Temperature Sensor (CTS) circuit — turns ON "Sevice Soon" light
15	Open Coolant Temperature Sensor (CTS) circuit — turns ON "Sevice Soon" light
16	Generator voltage out of range — turns ON "Sevice Now" light
18	Open crank signal circuit — turns ON "Sevice Soon" light
19	Shorted fuel pump circuit — turns ON "Sevice Soon" light
20	Open fuel pump circuit — turns ON "Sevice Now" light
21	Shorted Throttle Position Sensor (TPS) circuit — turns ON "Sevice Soon" light
22	Open Throttle Position Sensor (TPS) circuit — turns ON "Sevice Soon" light
23	Electronic Spark Timing (EST) circuit problem in run mode — turns ON "Sevice Soon" light
24	Speed sensor circuit problem — turns ON "Sevice Soon" light
26	Shorted throttle switch circuit — turns ON "Sevice Soon" light
27	Open throttle switch circuit — turns ON "Sevice Soon" light
28	Open fourth gear circuit — turns ON "Sevice Soon" light
29	Shorted fourth gear circuit — turns ON "Sevice Soon" light
30	Idle Speed Control (ISC) circuit problem — turns ON "Sevice Soon" light
31	Short Manifold Absolute Pressure (MAP) sensor circuit — turns ON "Sevice Now" light
32	Open Manifold Absolute Pressure (MAP) sensor circuit — turns ON "Sevice Now" light
33	Manifold Absolute Pressure (MAP)/Barometric Pressure (BARO) sensor correlation — turns ON "Sevice Now" light
34	Manifold Absolute Pressure (MAP) signal too high — turns ON "Sevice Now" light
35	Shorted Barometric Pressure (BARO) sensor circuit — turns ON "Sevice Soon" light
36	Open Barometric Pressure (BARO) sensor circuit — turns ON "Sevice Soon" light
37	Shorted Manifold Air Temperature (MAT) sensor circuit — turns ON "Sevice Soon" light
38	Open Manifold Air Temperature (MAT) sensor circuit — turns ON "Sevice Soon" light
39	Torque Converter Clutch (TCC) engagement problem — turns ON "Sevice Soon" light
44	Lean exhaust signal — turns ON "Sevice Now" light
45	Rich exhaust signal — turns ON "Sevice Now" light
51	PROM error indicator — turns ON "Sevice Now" light
52	Electronic Control Module (ECM) memory reset indicator — does not turn ON any telltale light
53	Distributor signal interrupt — does not turn ON any telltale light
60	Transmission not in Drive — does not turn ON any telltale light
63	Car and set speed tolerance exceeded — does not turn ON any telltale light
64	Car acceleration exceeds maximum limit — does not turn ON any telltale light
65	Coolant temperature exceeds maximum limit — does not turn ON any telltale light
66	Engine RPM exceeds maximum limit — does not turn ON any telltale light
67	Shorted set or resume circuit — does not turn ON any telltale light
.7.0	System ready for further tests

ECM TROUBLE CODES (cont'd)

Code	Explanation
.7.1	Cruise control brake circuit test
.7.2	Throttle switch circuit test
.7.3	Drive (ADL) circuit test
.7.4	Reverse circuit test
.7.5	Cruise on/off circuit test
.7.6	"Set/coast" circuit test
.7.7	"Resume/acceleration" circuit test
.7.8	"Instant/average" circuit test
.7.9	"Reset" circuit test
.8.0	Air conditioning clutch circuit test
−1.8.8	Display check
.9.0	System ready to display engine data
.9.5	System ready for output cycling or in fixed spark mode
.9.6	Output cycling
.0.0	All diagnostics complete

Year – 1984
Model – Fleetwood Brougham
Engine – 4.1L (252 cid) DFI V8
Engine Code – VIN 8

ECM TROUBLE CODES

Code	Explanation
12	No distributor (tach) signal – turns ON "Sevice Now" light
13	Oxygen sensor not ready – turns ON "Sevice Soon" light
14	Shorted Coolant Temperature Sensor (CTS) circuit – turns ON "Sevice Soon" light
15	Open Coolant Temperature Sensor (CTS) circuit – turns ON "Sevice Soon" light
16	Generator voltage out of range – turns ON "Sevice Now" light
18	Open crank signal circuit – turns ON "Sevice Soon" light
19	Shorted fuel pump circuit – turns ON "Sevice Soon" light
20	Open fuel pump circuit – turns ON "Sevice Now" light
21	Shorted Throttle Position Sensor (TPS) circuit – turns ON "Sevice Soon" light
22	Open Throttle Position Sensor (TPS) circuit – turns ON "Sevice Soon" light
23	Electronic Spark Timing (EST) circuit problem in run mode – turns ON "Sevice Soon" light
24	Speed sensor circuit problem – turns ON "Sevice Soon" light
26	Shorted throttle switch circuit – turns ON "Sevice Soon" light
27	Open throttle switch circuit – turns ON "Sevice Soon" light
28	Open fourth gear circuit – turns ON "Sevice Soon" light
29	Shorted fourth gear circuit – turns ON "Sevice Soon" light
30	Idle Speed Control (ISC) circuit problem – turns ON "Sevice Soon" light
31	Short Manifold Absolute Pressure (MAP) sensor circuit – turns ON "Sevice Now" light
32	Open Manifold Absolute Pressure (MAP) sensor circuit – turns ON "Sevice Now" light

ECM TROUBLE CODES (cont'd)

Code	Explanation
33	Manifold Absolute Pressure (MAP)/Barometric Pressure (BARO) sensor correlation—turns ON "Sevice Now" light
34	Manifold Absolute Pressure (MAP) signal too high—turns ON "Sevice Now" light
35	Shorted Barometric Pressure (BARO) sensor circuit—turns ON "Sevice Soon" light
36	Open Barometric Pressure (BARO) sensor circuit—turns ON "Sevice Soon" light
37	Shorted Manifold Air Temperature (MAT) sensor circuit—turns ON "Sevice Soon" light
38	Open Manifold Air Temperature (MAT) sensor circuit—turns ON "Sevice Soon" light
39	Torque Converter Clutch (TCC) engagement problem—turns ON "Sevice Soon" light
44	Lean exhaust signal—turns ON "Sevice Now" light
45	Rich exhaust signal—turns ON "Sevice Now" light
51	PROM error indicator—turns ON "Sevice Now" light
52	Electronic Control Module (ECM) memory reset indicator—does not turn ON any telltale light
53	Distributor signal interrupt—does not turn ON any telltale light
60	Transmission not in Drive—does not turn ON any telltale light
63	Car and set speed tolerance exceeded—does not turn ON any telltale light
64	Car acceleration exceeds maximum limit—does not turn ON any telltale light
65	Coolant temperature exceeds maximum limit—does not turn ON any telltale light
66	Engine RPM exceeds maximum limit—does not turn ON any telltale light
67	Shorted set or resume circuit—does not turn ON any telltale light
.7.0	System ready for further tests
.7.1	Cruise control brake circuit test
.7.2	Throttle switch circuit test
.7.3	Drive (ADL) circuit test
.7.4	Reverse circuit test
.7.5	Cruise on/off circuit test
.7.6	"Set/coast" circuit test
.7.7	"Resume/acceleration" circuit test
.7.8	"Instant/average" circuit test
.7.9	"Reset" circuit test
.8.0	Air conditioning clutch circuit test
−1.8.8	Display check
.9.0	System ready to display engine data
.9.5	System ready for output cycling or in fixed spark mode
.9.6	Output cycling
.0.0	All diagnostics complete

Year — 1984
Model — Fleetwood Limousine
Engine — 6.0L (368 cid) DEFI V8
Engine Code — VIN 9

ECM TROUBLE CODES

Code	Explanation
12	No tach signal to the Electronic Control Module (ECM). This code will only be present while a fault is present. It will not be stored with an intermittent problem
13	Oxygen sensor circuit — the engine has to run for about 5 minutes at part throttle, before this code will show
13 & 43	Throttle Position Sensor (TPS) adjustment — part throttle — after 10 seconds
14	Shorted Coolant Temperature Sensor (CTS) circuit — the engine has to run 2 minutes before this code will show
15	Open Coolant Temperature Sensor (CTS) circuit — the engine has to operate for about 5 minutes before this code will show
21	Throttle Position Sensor (TPS) — Wide Open Throttle (WOT) error — After 10 seconds and below 800 RPM
23	Open or grounded carburetor M/C solenoid
43	Throttle Position Sensor (TPS) adjustment — part throttle — after 10 seconds
44	Lean oxygen sensor. The engine has to run for about 3 minutes in closed loop and part throttle at road load before this code will show
44 & 55	(At same time) — faulty oxygen sensor circuit
45	Rich oxygen sensor indication. The engine has to run for about 3 minutes in closed loop and part throttle at road load before this code will show
51	Faulty calibration unit (PROM) or installation
52 & 53	Light OFF — Intermittent Electronic Control Module (ECM) problem. Light ON — faulty ECM
54	Faulty M/C solenoid or Electronic Control Module (ECM)
55	Faulty Throttle Position Sensor (TPS) or Electronic Control Module (ECM)

GENERAL MOTORS CORPORATION
DIAGNOSTIC CODE DATA

Year — 1984
Model — Seville
Engine — 4.1L (252 cid) DFI V8
Engine Code — VIN 8

ECM TROUBLE CODES

Code	Explanation
12	No distributor (tach) signal—turns ON "Sevice Now" light
13	Oxygen sensor not ready—turns ON "Sevice Soon" light
14	Shorted Coolant Temperature Sensor (CTS) circuit—turns ON "Sevice Soon" light
15	Open Coolant Temperature Sensor (CTS) circuit—turns ON "Sevice Soon" light
16	Generator voltage out of range—turns ON "Sevice Now" light
18	Open crank signal circuit—turns ON "Sevice Soon" light
19	Shorted fuel pump circuit—turns ON "Sevice Soon" light
20	Open fuel pump circuit—turns ON "Sevice Now" light
21	Shorted Throttle Position Sensor (TPS) circuit—turns ON "Sevice Soon" light
22	Open Throttle Position Sensor (TPS) circuit—turns ON "Sevice Soon" light
23	Electronic Spark Timing (EST) circuit problem in run mode—turns ON "Sevice Soon" light
24	Speed sensor circuit problem—turns ON "Sevice Soon" light
26	Shorted throttle switch circuit—turns ON "Sevice Soon" light
27	Open throttle switch circuit—turns ON "Sevice Soon" light
28	Open fourth gear circuit—turns ON "Sevice Soon" light
29	Shorted fourth gear circuit—turns ON "Sevice Soon" light
30	Idle Speed Control (ISC) circuit problem—turns ON "Sevice Soon" light
31	Short Manifold Absolute Pressure (MAP) sensor circuit—turns ON "Sevice Now" light
32	Open Manifold Absolute Pressure (MAP) sensor circuit—turns ON "Sevice Now" light
33	Manifold Absolute Pressure (MAP)/Barometric Pressure (BARO) sensor correlation—turns ON "Sevice Now" light
34	Manifold Absolute Pressure (MAP) signal too high—turns ON "Sevice Now" light
35	Shorted Barometric Pressure (BARO) sensor circuit—turns ON "Sevice Soon" light
36	Open Barometric Pressure (BARO) sensor circuit—turns ON "Sevice Soon" light
37	Shorted Manifold Air Temperature (MAT) sensor circuit—turns ON "Sevice Soon" light
38	Open Manifold Air Temperature (MAT) sensor circuit—turns ON "Sevice Soon" light
39	Torque Converter Clutch (TCC) engagement problem—turns ON "Sevice Soon" light
44	Lean exhaust signal—turns ON "Sevice Now" light
45	Rich exhaust signal—turns ON "Sevice Now" light
51	PROM error indicator—turns ON "Sevice Now" light
52	Electronic Control Module (ECM) memory reset indicator—does not turn ON any telltale light
53	Distributor signal interrupt—does not turn ON any telltale light
60	Transmission not in Drive—does not turn ON any telltale light
63	Car and set speed tolerance exceeded—does not turn ON any telltale light
64	Car acceleration exceeds maximum limit—does not turn ON any telltale light
65	Coolant temperature exceeds maximum limit—does not turn ON any telltale light
66	Engine RPM exceeds maximum limit—does not turn ON any telltale light
67	Shorted set or resume circuit—does not turn ON any telltale light
.7.0	System ready for further tests

ECM TROUBLE CODES (cont'd)

Code	Explanation
.7.1	Cruise control brake circuit test
.7.2	Throttle switch circuit test
.7.3	Drive (ADL) circuit test
.7.4	Reverse circuit test
.7.5	Cruise on/off circuit test
.7.6	"Set/coast" circuit test
.7.7	"Resume/acceleration" circuit test
.7.8	"Instant/average" circuit test
.7.9	"Reset" circuit test
.8.0	Air conditioning clutch circuit test
—1.8.8	Display check
.9.0	System ready to display engine data
.9.5	System ready for output cycling or in fixed spark mode
.9.6	Output cycling
.0.0	All diagnostics complete

Year — 1984
Model — Eldorado
Engine — 4.1L (252 cid) DFI V8
Engine Code — VIN 8

ECM TROUBLE CODES

Code	Explanation
12	No distributor (tach) signal — turns ON "Sevice Now" light
13	Oxygen sensor not ready — turns ON "Sevice Soon" light
14	Shorted Coolant Temperature Sensor (CTS) circuit — turns ON "Sevice Soon" light
15	Open Coolant Temperature Sensor (CTS) circuit — turns ON "Sevice Soon" light
16	Generator voltage out of range — turns ON "Sevice Now" light
18	Open crank signal circuit — turns ON "Sevice Soon" light
19	Shorted fuel pump circuit — turns ON "Sevice Soon" light
20	Open fuel pump circuit — turns ON "Sevice Now" light
21	Shorted Throttle Position Sensor (TPS) circuit — turns ON "Sevice Soon" light
22	Open Throttle Position Sensor (TPS) circuit — turns ON "Sevice Soon" light
23	Electronic Spark Timing (EST) circuit problem in run mode — turns ON "Sevice Soon" light
24	Speed sensor circuit problem — turns ON "Sevice Soon" light
26	Shorted throttle switch circuit — turns ON "Sevice Soon" light
27	Open throttle switch circuit — turns ON "Sevice Soon" light
28	Open fourth gear circuit — turns ON "Sevice Soon" light
29	Shorted fourth gear circuit — turns ON "Sevice Soon" light
30	Idle Speed Control (ISC) circuit problem — turns ON "Sevice Soon" light
31	Short Manifold Absolute Pressure (MAP) sensor circuit — turns ON "Sevice Now" light
32	Open Manifold Absolute Pressure (MAP) sensor circuit — turns ON "Sevice Now" light

ECM TROUBLE CODES (cont'd)

Code	Explanation
33	Manifold Absolute Pressure (MAP)/Barometric Pressure (BARO) sensor correlation—turns ON "Sevice Now" light
34	Manifold Absolute Pressure (MAP) signal too high—turns ON "Sevice Now" light
35	Shorted Barometric Pressure (BARO) sensor circuit—turns ON "Sevice Soon" light
36	Open Barometric Pressure (BARO) sensor circuit—turns ON "Sevice Soon" light
37	Shorted Manifold Air Temperature (MAT) sensor circuit—turns ON "Sevice Soon" light
38	Open Manifold Air Temperature (MAT) sensor circuit—turns ON "Sevice Soon" light
39	Torque Converter Clutch (TCC) engagement problem—turns ON "Sevice Soon" light
44	Lean exhaust signal—turns ON "Sevice Now" light
45	Rich exhaust signal—turns ON "Sevice Now" light
51	PROM error indicator—turns ON "Sevice Now" light
52	Electronic Control Module (ECM) memory reset indicator—does not turn ON any telltale light
53	Distributor signal interrupt—does not turn ON any telltale light
60	Transmission not in Drive—does not turn ON any telltale light
63	Car and set speed tolerance exceeded—does not turn ON any telltale light
64	Car acceleration exceeds maximum limit—does not turn ON any telltale light
65	Coolant temperature exceeds maximum limit—does not turn ON any telltale light
66	Engine RPM exceeds maximum limit—does not turn ON any telltale light
67	Shorted set or resume circuit—does not turn ON any telltale light
.7.0	System ready for further tests
.7.1	Cruise control brake circuit test
.7.2	Throttle switch circuit test
.7.3	Drive (ADL) circuit test
.7.4	Reverse circuit test
.7.5	Cruise on/off circuit test
.7.6	"Set/coast" circuit test
.7.7	"Resume/acceleration" circuit test
.7.8	"Instant/average" circuit test
.7.9	"Reset" circuit test
.8.0	Air conditioning clutch circuit test
−1.8.8	Display check
.9.0	System ready to display engine data
.9.5	System ready for output cycling or in fixed spark mode
.9.6	Output cycling
.0.0	All diagnostics complete

Year – 1984
Model – Cimarron
Engine – 2.0L (121 cid) TBI 4 cyl
Engine Code – VIN P

ECM TROUBLE CODES

Code	Explanation
13	Oxygen sensor circuit
14	Coolant Temperature Sensor (CTS) voltage low
15	Coolant Temperature Sensor (CTS) voltage high
21	Throttle Position Sensor (TPS) voltage high
22	Throttle Position Sensor (TPS) voltage low
24	Vehicle Speed Sensor (VSS)
33	Manifold Absolute Pressure (MAP) sensor voltage low
34	Manifold Absolute Pressure (MAP) sensor voltage high
42	Electronic Spark Timing (EST)
44	Lean exhaust indication
45	Rich exhaust indication
51	PROM
55	Electronic Control Module (ECM)

GENERAL MOTORS CORPORATION
DIAGNOSTIC CODE DATA

Year — 1985
Model — DeVille
Engine — 4.1L (250 cid) DFI V8
Engine Code — VIN 8

ECM TROUBLE CODES

Code	Explanation
E12	No distributor signal — turns ON "Sevice Now" light
E13	Oxygen sensor not ready — canister purge disengaged — turns ON "Sevice Soon" light
E14	Shorted coolant sensor circuit — turns ON "Sevice Soon" light
E15	Open Coolant Temperature Sensor (CTS) circuit — turns ON "Sevice Soon" light
E16	Generator voltage out of range — all solenoids are disengaged — turns ON "Sevice Now" light
E18	Open crank signal circuit — turns ON "Sevice Soon" light
E19	Shorted fuel pump circuit — turns ON "Sevice Soon" light
E20	Open fuel pump circuit — turns ON "Sevice Now" light
E21	Shorted Throttle Position Sensor (TPS) circuit — turns ON "Sevice Soon" light
E22	Open Throttle Position Sensor (TPS) circuit — turns ON "Sevice Soon" light
E23	Electronic Spark Timing (EST)/Bypass circuit problem — Air Injector Reaction (AIR) system disengaged — turns ON "Sevice Soon" light
E24	Speed sensor circuit problem — Viscous Converter Clutch (VCC) disengaged — turns ON "Sevice Soon" light
E26	Shorted throttle switch circuit — turns ON "Sevice Soon" light
E27	Open throttle switch circuit — turns ON "Sevice Soon" light
E28	Open third or fourth gear circuit — turns ON "Sevice Soon" light
E30	Idle Speed Control (ISC) circuit problem — turns ON "Sevice Soon" light
E31	Shorted Manifold Absolute Pressure (MAP) sensor circuit — Air Injection Reaction (AIR) system disengaged — turns ON "Sevice Now" light
E32	Open Manifold Absolute Pressure (MAP) sensor circuit — Air Injection Reaction (AIR) system disengaged — turns ON "Sevice Now" light
E34	Manifold Absolute Pressure (MAP) sensor signal too high — Air Injection Reaction (AIR) system disengaged — turns ON "Sevice Now" light
E37	Shorted Manifold Air Temperature (MAT) sensor circuit — turns ON "Sevice Soon" light
E38	Open Manifold Air Temperature (MAT) sensor circuit — turns ON "Sevice Soon" light
E39	Viscous Converter Clutch (VCC) engagement problem — turns ON "Sevice Soon" light
E40	Open power steering pressure circuit — turns ON "Sevice Soon" light
E44	Lean exhaust signal — Air Injector Reaction (AIR), CL and canister purge disengaged — turns ON "Sevice Now" light
E45	Rich exhaust signal — Air Injector Reaction (AIR), CL and canister purge disengaged — turns ON "Sevice Now" light
E47	Body Control Module (BCM) — Electronic Control Module (ECM) data problem — turns ON "Sevice Soon" light
E51	Electronic Control Module (ECM) PROM error — turns ON "Sevice Now" light
E52	Electronic Control Module (ECM) memory reset indicator — does not turn ON any telltale light
E53	Distributor signal interrupt — does not turn ON any telltale light
E59	Viscous Converter Clutch (VCC) temperature sensor circuit — does not turn ON any telltale light
E60	Transmission not in Drive — does not turn ON any telltale light
E63	Car speed and set speed difference too high — does not turn ON any telltale light
E64	Car acceleration too high — does not turn ON any telltale light

ECM TROUBLE CODES (cont'd)

Code	Explanation
E65	Coolant temperature too high — does not turn ON any telltale light
E66	Engine RPM too high — does not turn ON any telltale light
E67	Cruise switch shorted during enable — does not turn ON any telltale light

Year — 1985
Model — Fleetwood Brougham
Engine — 4.1L (250 cid) DFI V8
Engine Code — VIN 8

ECM TROUBLE CODES

Code	Explanation
E12	No distributor signal
E13	Oxygen sensor not ready — canister purge disengaged
E14	Shorted Coolant Temperature Sensor (CTS) circuit
E15	Open Coolant Temperature Sensor (CTS) circuit
E16	Generator voltage out of range — all solenoids disengaged
E18	Open crank signal circuit
E19	Shorted fuel pump circuit
E20	Open fuel pump circuit
E21	Shorted Throttle Position Sensor (TPS) circuit
E22	Open Throttle Position Sensor (TPS) circuit
E23	Electronic Spark Timing (EST)/Bypass circuit problem — Air Injection Reaction (AIR) system disengaged
E24	Speed sensor circuit problem — Viscous Converter Clutch (VCC) disengaged
E26	Shorted throttle switch circuit
E27	Open throttle switch circuit
E28	Open third or fourth gear circuit
E30	Idle Speed Control (ISC) circuit problem
E31	Shorted Manifold Absolute Pressure (MAP) sensor circuit — Air Injection Reaction (AIR) system disengaged
E32	Open Manifold Absolute Pressure (MAP) sensor circuit — Air Injection Reaction (AIR) system disengaged
E34	Manifold Absolute Pressure (MAP) sensor signal too high — Air Injection Reaction (AIR) system disengaged
E37	Shorted Manifold Air Temperature (MAT) sensor circuit
E38	Open Manifold Air Temperature (MAT) sensor circuit
E39	Viscous Converter Clutch (VCC) engagement problem
E40	Open power steering pressure circuit
E44	Lean exhaust signal — Air Injector Reaction (AIR), CL and canister purge disengaged
E45	Rich exhaust signal — Air Injector Reaction (AIR), CL and canister purge disengaged
E47	Body Control Module (BCM) — Electronic Control Module (ECM) data problem
E51	Electronic Control Module (ECM) PROM error
E52	Electronic Control Module (ECM) memory reset indicator
E53	Distributor signal interrupt

ECM TROUBLE CODES (cont'd)

Code	Explanation
E59	Viscous Converter Clutch (VCC) temperature sensor circuit
E60	Transmission not in Drive
E63	Car speed and set speed difference too high
E64	Car acceleration too high
E65	Coolant temperature too high
E66	Engine RPM too high
E67	Cruise switch shorted during enable

Year — 1985
Model — Fleetwood Limousine
Engine — 6.0L (368 cid) DEFI V8
Engine Code — VIN 9

ECM TROUBLE CODES

Code	Explanation
12	No tach signal to the Electronic Control Module (ECM). This code will only be present while a fault is present. It will not be stored with an intermittent problem
13	Oxygen sensor circuit — the engine has to run for about 5 minutes at part throttle, before this code will show
13 & 43	Throttle Position Sensor (TPS) adjustment — part throttle — after 10 seconds
14	Shorted Coolant Temperature Sensor (CTS) circuit — the engine has to run 2 minutes before this code will show
15	Open Coolant Temperature Sensor (CTS) circuit — the engine has to operate for about 5 minutes before this code will show
21	Throttle Position Sensor (TPS) — Wide Open Throttle (WOT) error — After 10 seconds and below 800 RPM
23	Open or grounded carburetor M/C solenoid
43	Throttle Position Sensor (TPS) adjustment — part throttle — after 10 seconds
44	Lean oxygen sensor. The engine has to run for about 3 minutes in closed loop and part throttle at road load before this code will show
44 & 55	(At same time) — faulty oxygen sensor circuit
45	Rich oxygen sensor indication. The engine has to run for about 3 minutes in closed loop and part throttle at road load before this code will show
51	Faulty calibration unit (PROM) or installation
52 & 53	Light OFF — intermittent Electronic Control Module (ECM) problem. Light ON — faulty ECM
54	Faulty M/C solenoid or Electronic Control Module (ECM)
55	Faulty Throttle Position Sensor (TPS) or Electronic Control Module (ECM)

Year — 1985
Model — Seville
Engine — 4.1L (250 cid) DFI V8
Engine Code — VIN 8

ECM TROUBLE CODES

Code	Explanation
E12	No distributor signal
E13	Oxygen sensor not ready — canister purge disengaged
E14	Shorted Coolant Temperature Sensor (CTS) circuit
E15	Open Coolant Temperature Sensor (CTS) circuit
E16	Generator voltage out of range — all solenoids disengaged
E18	Open crank signal circuit
E19	Shorted fuel pump circuit
E20	Open fuel pump circuit
E21	Shorted Throttle Position Sensor (TPS) circuit
E22	Open Throttle Position Sensor (TPS) circuit
E23	Electronic Spark Timing (EST)/Bypass circuit problem — Air Injection Reaction (AIR) system disengaged
E24	Speed sensor circuit problem — Viscous Converter Clutch (VCC) disengaged
E26	Shorted throttle switch circuit
E27	Open throttle switch circuit
E28	Open third or fourth gear circuit
E30	Idle Speed Control (ISC) circuit problem
E31	Shorted Manifold Absolute Pressure (MAP) sensor circuit — Air Injection Reaction (AIR) system disengaged
E32	Open Manifold Absolute Pressure (MAP) sensor circuit — Air Injection Reaction (AIR) system disengaged
E34	Manifold Absolute Pressure (MAP) sensor signal too high — Air Injection Reaction (AIR) system disengaged
E37	Shorted Manifold Air Temperature (MAT) sensor circuit
E38	Open Manifold Air Temperature (MAT) sensor circuit
E39	Viscous Converter Clutch (VCC) engagement problem
E40	Open power steering pressure circuit
E44	Lean exhaust signal — Air Injector Reaction (AIR), CL and canister purge disengaged
E45	Rich exhaust signal — Air Injector Reaction (AIR), CL and canister purge disengaged
E47	Body Control Module (BCM) — Electronic Control Module (ECM) data problem
E51	Electronic Control Module (ECM) PROM error
E52	Electronic Control Module (ECM) memory reset indicator
E53	Distributor signal interrupt
E59	Viscous Converter Clutch (VCC) temperature sensor circuit
E60	Transmission not in Drive
E63	Car speed and set speed difference too high
E64	Car acceleration too high
E65	Coolant temperature too high
E66	Engine RPM too high
E67	Cruise switch shorted during enable

GENERAL MOTORS CORPORATION
DIAGNOSTIC CODE DATA

Year – 1985
Model – Eldorado
Engine – 4.1L (250 cid) DFI V8
Engine Code – VIN 8

ECM TROUBLE CODES

Code	Explanation
E12	No distributor signal
E13	Oxygen sensor not ready – canister purge disengaged
E14	Shorted Coolant Temperature Sensor (CTS) circuit
E15	Open Coolant Temperature Sensor (CTS) circuit
E16	Generator voltage out of range – all solenoids disengaged
E18	Open crank signal circuit
E19	Shorted fuel pump circuit
E20	Open fuel pump circuit
E21	Shorted Throttle Position Sensor (TPS) circuit
E22	Open Throttle Position Sensor (TPS) circuit
E23	Electronic Spark Timing (EST)/Bypass circuit problem – Air Injection Reaction (AIR) system disengaged
E24	Speed sensor circuit problem – Viscous Converter Clutch (VCC) disengaged
E26	Shorted throttle switch circuit
E27	Open throttle switch circuit
E28	Open third or fourth gear circuit
E30	Idle Speed Control (ISC) circuit problem
E31	Shorted Manifold Absolute Pressure (MAP) sensor circuit – Air Injection Reaction (AIR) system disengaged
E32	Open Manifold Absolute Pressure (MAP) sensor circuit – Air Injection Reaction (AIR) system disengaged
E34	Manifold Absolute Pressure (MAP) sensor signal too high – Air Injection Reaction (AIR) system disengaged
E37	Shorted Manifold Air Temperature (MAT) sensor circuit
E38	Open Manifold Air Temperature (MAT) sensor circuit
E39	Viscous Converter Clutch (VCC) engagement problem
E40	Open power steering pressure circuit
E44	Lean exhaust signal – Air Injector Reaction (AIR), CL and canister purge disengaged
E45	Rich exhaust signal – Air Injector Reaction (AIR), CL and canister purge disengaged
E47	Body Control Module (BCM) – Electronic Control Module (ECM) data problem
E51	Electronic Control Module (ECM) PROM error
E52	Electronic Control Module (ECM) memory reset indicator
E53	Distributor signal interrupt
E59	Viscous Converter Clutch (VCC) temperature sensor circuit
E60	Transmission not in Drive
E63	Car speed and set speed difference too high
E64	Car acceleration too high
E65	Coolant temperature too high
E66	Engine RPM too high
E67	Cruise switch shorted during enable

Year – 1985
Model – Cimarron
Engine – 2.0L (121 cid) EFI 4 cyl
Engine Code – VIN P

ECM TROUBLE CODES

Code	Explanation
13	Oxygen sensor circuit
14	Coolant Temperature Sensor (CTS) low
15	Coolant Temperature Sensor (CTS) high
21	Throttle Postion Sensor (TPS) high
22	Throttle Postion Sensor (TPS) low
24	Vehicle Speed Sensor (VSS)
33	Manifold Absolute Pressure (MAP) sensor high
34	Manifold Absolute Pressure (MAP) sensor low
42	Electronic Spark Timing (EST)
44	Lean exhaust
45	Rich exhaust
54	Fuel pump circuit low
51	PROM
52	Calpac
55	Electronic Control Module (ECM)

Year – 1985
Model – Cimarron
Engine – 2.8L (173 cid) MPFI V6
Engine Code – VIN W

ECM TROUBLE CODES

Code	Explanation
13	Oxygen sensor circuit
14	Coolant Temperature Sensor (CTS)
15	Coolant Temperature Sensor (CTS)
21	Throttle Postion Sensor (TPS)
22	Throttle Postion Sensor (TPS)
23	Manifold Air Temperature (MAT) sensor
24	Vehicle Speed Sensor (VSS)
25	Manifold Air Temperature (MAT) sensor
32	Exhaust Gas Recirculation (EGR)
34	Mass Air Flow (MAF) sensor
41	Cylinder select error
42	Electronic Spark Timing (EST)
44	Lean exhaust indication
45	Rich exhaust indication
51	PROM
52	Calpak
53	System over voltage
54	Fuel pump voltage low
55	Electronic Control Module (ECM)

Year – 1986
Model – DeVille
Engine – 4.1L (250 cid) DFI V8
Engine Code – VIN 8

ECM TROUBLE CODES

Code	Explanation
E12	No distributor signal – turns ON "Service Now" light
E13	Oxygen sensor not ready – Air Injector Reaction (AIR), CL and canister purge disengaged – turns ON "Service Soon" light
E14	Shorted Coolant Temperature Sensor (CTS) circuit – Air Injector Reaction (AIR) disengaged – turns ON "Service Soon" light – forces cooling fans on full speed
E15	Open Coolant Temperature Sensor (CTS) circuit – Air Injector Reaction (AIR) disengaged – turns ON "Service Soon" light – forces cooling fans on full speed
E16	Generator voltage out of range – all solenoids disengaged – turns ON "Service Now" light – disengages VCC for entire ignition cycle
E18	Open crank signal circuit – turns ON "Service Soon" light
E19	Shorted fuel pump circuit – turns ON "Service Soon" light
E20	Open fuel pump circuit – turns ON "Service Now" light
E21	Shorted Throttle Posiion Sensor (TPS) circuit – turns ON "Service Soon" light
E22	Open Throttle Posiion Sensor (TPS) circuit – turns ON "Service Soon" light
E23	Electronic Spark Timing (EST)/bypass circuit problem – Air Injector Reaction (AIR) disengaged – turns ON "Service Soon" light – causes system to operate on bypass spark
E24	Speed sensor circuit problem – Viscous Converter Clutch (VCC) and cruise disengaged – turns ON "Service Soon" light – disables cruise for entire ignition cycle – disengages VCC for entire ignition cycle
E26	Shorted throttle switch circuit – turns on "Service Soon" light
E27	Open throttle switch circuit – turns ON "Service Soon" light
E28	Open third or fourth gear circuit – turns ON "Service Soon" light
E30	Idle Speed Control (ISC) circuit problem – turns ON "Service Soon" light
E31	Shorted Manifold Absolute Pressure (MAP) sensor circuit – Air Injector Reaction (AIR) disengaged – turns ON "Service Now" light
E32	Open Manifold Absolute Pressure (MAP) sensor circuit – Air Injector Reaction (AIR) disengaged – turns ON "Service Now" light
E34	Manifold Absolute Pressure (MAP) sensor signal too high – Air Injector Reaction (AIR) disengaged – turns ON "Service Now" light
E37	Shorted Manifold Air Temperature (MAT) sensor circuit – Air Injector Reaction (AIR) disengaged – turns ON "Service Soon" light
E38	Open Manifold Air Temperature (MAT) sensor circuit – Air Injector Reaction (AIR) disengaged – turns ON "Service Soon" light
E39	Viscous Converter Clutch (VCC) engagement problem – turns ON "Service Soon" light
E40	Open Power Steering Pressure Switch (PSPS) circuit – turns ON "Service Soon" light
E44	Lean exhaust signal – Air Injector Reaction (AIR), CL and canister purge disengaged – turns ON "Service Now" light
E45	Rich exhaust signal – Air Injector Reaction (AIR), CL and canister purge disengaged – turns ON "Service Now" light
E47	Body Control Module (BCM) – Electronic Control Module (ECM) data problem – turns ON "Service Soon" light
E48	Exhaust Gas Recirculation (EGR) system fault – turns ON "Service Soon" light
E51	Electronic Control Module (ECM) PROM error – turns ON "Service Now" light

ECM TROUBLE CODES (cont'd)

Code	Explanation
E52	Electronic Control Module (ECM) memory reset indicator—does not turn on any telltale light
E53	Distributor signal interrupt—does not turn on any telltale light
E55	Throttle Position Sensor (TPS) misadjusted—does not turn on any telltale light
E59	Viscous Converter Clutch (VCC) temperature sensor circuit problem—does not turn on any telltale light
E60	Cruise—transmission not in Drive—cruise disengaged—does not turn on any telltale light
E63	Cruise—car speed and set speed difference too high—cruise disengaged—does not turn on any telltale light
E64	Cruise—car acceleration too high—cruise disengaged—does not turn on any telltale light
E65	Cruise—coolant temperature too high—cruise disengaged—does not turn on any telltale light
E66	Cruise—engine RPM too high—cruise disengaged—does not turn on any telltale light
E67	Cruise—cruise switch shorted during enable—cruise disengaged—does not turn on any telltale light—disables cruise for entire ignition cycle

Year—1986
Model—Fleetwood Brougham
Engine—5.0L (307 cid) V8
Engine Code—VIN Y

ECM TROUBLE CODES

Code	Explanation
12	No distributor reference signal to the Electronic Control Module (ECM). This code is not stored in memory and will only flash wh e the fault is present. Normal code with ignition ON, engine not running
13	Oxygen sensor circuit—the engine must run up to 4 minutes at part throttle, under road load, before this code will set
14	Shorted Coolant Temperature Sensor (CTS) circuit—the engine must run 2 minutes before this code will set
15	Open Coolant Temperature Sensor (CTS) circuit—the engine must run 5 minutes before this code will set
21	Throttle Position Sensor (TPS) circuit voltage high—open circuit or misadjusted TPS). The engine must run 10 seconds, at specified curb idle speed, before this code will set
22	Throttle Position Sensor (TPS) circuit voltage low—grounded circuit or misadjusted TPS). Engine must run 20 seconds at specified curb idle speed, to set code
23	M/C solenoid circuit open or grounded
24	Vehicle Speed Sensor (VSS) circuit—the vehicle must operate up to 2 minutes, at road speed, before this code will set
32	Barometric Pressure Sensor (BARO) circuit low
34	Vacuum sensor or Manifold Absolute Pressure (MAP) circuit—the engine must run up to 2 minutes, at specified curb idle, before this code will set
35	Idle Speed Control (ISC) switch circuit shorted—up to 70% Throttle Position Sensor (TPS) for over 5 seconds
41	No distributor reference signal to the Electronic Control Module (ECM) at specified engine vacuum. This code will store in memory
42	Electronic Spark Timing (EST) bypass circuit or EST circuit grounded or open
43	Electronic Spark Control (ESC) retard signal for too long a time; causes retard in EST signal

ECM TROUBLE CODES (cont'd)

Code	Explanation
44	Lean exhaust indication — the engine must run 2 minutes, in closed loop and at part throttle, before this code will set
45	Rich exhaust indication — the engine must run 2 minutes, in closed loop and at part throttle, before this code will set
51	Faulty or improperly installed calibration unit (PROM). It takes up to 30 seconds before this code will set
53	Exhaust Gas Recirculation (EGR) valve vacuum sensor has seen improper EGR control vacuum
54	M/C solenoid voltage high at Electronic Control Module (ECM) as a result of a shorted M/C solenoid circuit and/or faulty Electronic Control Module (ECM)

Year — 1986
Model — Fleetwood Limousine
Engine — 4.1L (250 cid) DFI V8
Engine Code — VIN 8

ECM TROUBLE CODES

Code	Explanation
E12	No distributor signal — turns ON "Service Now" light
E13	Oxygen sensor not ready — Air Injector Reaction (AIR), CL and canister purge disengaged — turns ON "Service Soon" light
E14	Shorted Coolant Temperature Sensor (CTS) circuit — Air Injector Reaction (AIR) disengaged — turns ON "Service Soon" light — forces cooling fans on full speed
E15	Open Coolant Temperature Sensor (CTS) circuit — Air Injector Reaction (AIR) disengaged — turns ON "Service Soon" light — forces cooling fans on full speed
E16	Generator voltage out of range — all solenoids disengaged — turns ON "Service Now" light — disengages Viscous Converter Clutch (VCC) for entire ignition cycle
E18	Open crank signal circuit — turns ON "Service Soon" light
E19	Shorted fuel pump circuit — turns ON "Service Soon" light
E20	Open fuel pump circuit — turns ON "Service Now" light
E21	Shorted Throttle Posiion Sensor (TPS) circuit — turns ON "Service Soon" light
E22	Open Throttle Posiion Sensor (TPS) circuit — turns ON "Service Soon" light
E23	Electronic Spark Timing (EST)/bypass circuit problem — Air Injector Reaction (AIR) disengaged — turns ON "Service Soon" light — causes system to operate on bypass spark
E24	Speed sensor circuit problem — Viscous Converter Clutch (VCC) and cruise disengaged — turns ON "Service Soon" light — disables cruise for entire ignition cycle — disengages Viscous Converter Clutch (VCC) for entire ignition cycle
E26	Shorted throttle switch circuit — turns ON "Service Soon" light
E27	Open throttle switch circuit — turns ON "Service Soon" light
E28	Open third or fourth gear circuit — turns ON "Service Soon" light
E30	Idle Speed Control (ISC) circuit problem — turns ON "Service Soon" light
E31	Shorted Manifold Absolute Pressure (MAP) sensor circuit — Air Injector Reaction (AIR) disengaged — turns ON "Service Now" light
E32	Open Manifold Absolute Pressure (MAP) sensor circuit — Air Injector Reaction (AIR) disengaged — turns ON "Service Now" light
E34	Manifold Absolute Pressure (MAP) sensor signal too high — Air Injector Reaction (AIR) disengaged — turns ON "Service Now" light

ECM TROUBLE CODES (cont'd)

Code	Explanation
E37	Shorted Manifold Air Temperature (MAT) sensor circuit—Air Injector Reaction (AIR) disengaged—turns ON "Service Soon" light
E38	Open Manifold Air Temperature (MAT) sensor circuit—Air Injector Reaction (AIR) disengaged—turns ON "Service Soon" light
E39	Viscous Converter Clutch (VCC) engagement problem—turns ON "Service Soon" light
E40	Open Power Steering Pressure Switch (PSPS) circuit—turns ON "Service Soon" light
E44	Lean exhaust signal—Air Injector Reaction (AIR), CL and canister purge disengaged—turns ON "Service Now" light
E45	Rich exhaust signal—Air Injector Reaction (AIR), CL and canister purge disengaged—turns ON "Service Now" light
E47	Body Control Module (BCM)—Electronic Control Module (ECM) data problem—turns ON "Service Soon" light
E48	Exhaust Gas Recirculation (EGR) system fault—turns ON "Service Soon" light
E51	Electronic Control Module (ECM) PROM error—turns ON "Service Now" light
E52	Electronic Control Module (ECM) memory reset indicator—does not turn on any telltale light
E53	Distributor signal interrupt—does not turn on any telltale light
E55	Throttle Position Sensor (TPS) misadjusted—does not turn on any telltale light
E59	Viscous Converter Clutch (VCC) temperature sensor circuit problem—does not turn on any telltale light
E60	Cruise—transmission not in Drive—cruise disengaged—does not turn on any telltale light
E63	Cruise—car speed and set speed difference too high—cruise disengaged—does not turn on any telltale light
E64	Cruise—car acceleration too high—cruise disengaged—does not turn on any telltale light
E65	Cruise—coolant temperature too high—cruise disengaged—does not turn on any telltale light
E66	Cruise—engine RPM too high—cruise disengaged—does not turn on any telltale light
E67	Cruise—cruise switch shorted during enable—cruise disengaged—does not turn on any telltale light—disables cruise for entire ignition cycle

Year—1986

Model—Seville

Engine—4.1L (250 cid) DFI V8

Engine Code—VIN 8

ECM TROUBLE CODES

Code	Explanation
E012	No distributor signal—displays "Service Now" message and turns ON "Engine Control System" light
E013	Oxygen sensor not ready—Air Injector Reaction (AIR), CL and canister purge disengaged—displays "Service Soon" message and turns ON "Engine Control System"
E014	Shorted Coolant Temperature Sensor (CTS) circuit—Air Injector Reaction (AIR) disengaged—displays "Service Soon" message and turns ON "Engine Control System" light—forces cooling fans on full speed
E015	Open Coolant Temperature Sensor (CTS) circuit—Air Injector Reaction (AIR) disengaged—displays "Service Soon" message and turns ON "Engine Control System" light—forces cooling fans on full speed
E016	Generator voltage out of range—all solenoids disengaged—displays "Service Now" message and turns ON "Engine Control System" light—disengages Viscous Converter Clutch (VCC) for entire ignition cycle
E018	Open crank signal circuit—displays "Service Soon" message and turns ON "Engine Control System" light

ECM TROUBLE CODES (cont'd)

Code	Explanation
E019	Shorted fuel pump circuit – displays "Service Soon" message and turns ON "Engine Control System" light
E020	Open fuel pump circuit – displays "Service Now" message and turns ON "Engine Control System" light
E021	Shorted Throttle Posiion Sensor (TPS) circuit – displays "Service Soon" message and turns ON "Engine Control System" light
E022	Open Throttle Posiion Sensor (TPS) circuit – displays "Service Soon" message and turns ON "Engine Control System" light
E023	Electronic Spark Timing (EST)/bypass circuit problem – Air Injector Reaction (AIR) disengaged – displays "Service Soon" message and turns ON "Engine Control System" light – causes system to operate on bypass spark
E024	Speed sensor circuit problem – Viscous Converter Clutch (VCC) disengaged – displays "Service Soon" message and turns ON "Engine Control System" light – disables Viscous Converter Clutch (VCC) for entire ignition cycle
E026	Shorted throttle switch circuit – displays "Service Soon" message and turns ON "Engine Control System" light
E027	Open throttle switch circuit – displays "Service Soon" message and turns ON "Engine Control System" light
E028	Open third or fourth gear circuit – displays "Service Soon" message and turns ON "Engine Control System" light
E030	Idle Speed Control (ISC) circuit problem – displays "Service Soon" message and turns ON "Engine Control System" light
E031	Shorted Manifold Absolute Pressure (MAP) sensor circuit – Air Injector Reaction (AIR) disengaged – displays "Service Now" message and turns ON "Engine Control System" light
E032	Open Manifold Absolute Pressure (MAP) sensor circuit – Air Injector Reaction (AIR) disengaged – displays "Service Now" message and turns ON "Engine Control System" light
E034	Manifold Absolute Pressure (MAP) sensor signal too high – Air Injector Reaction (AIR) disengaged – displays "Service Now" message and turns ON "Engine Control System" light
E037	Shorted Manifold Air Temperature (MAT) sensor circuit – Air Injector Reaction (AIR) disengaged – displays "Service Soon" message and turns ON "Engine Control System" light
E038	Open Manifold Air Temperature (MAT) sensor circuit – Air Injector Reaction (AIR) disengaged – displays "Service Soon" message and turns ON "Engine Control System" light
E039	Viscous Converter Clutch (VCC) engagement problem – displays "Service Soon" message and turns ON "Engine Control System" light
E040	Open Power Steering Pressure Switch (PSPS) circuit – displays "Service Soon" message and turns ON "Engine Control System" light
E044	Lean exhaust signal – Air Injector Reaction (AIR), CL and canister purge disengaged – displays "Service Now" message and turns ON "Engine Control System" light
E045	Rich exhaust signal – Air Injector Reaction (AIR), CL and canister purge disengaged – displays "Service Now" message and turns ON "Engine Control System" light
E047	Body Control Module (BCM) – Electronic Control Module (ECM) data problem – displays "Service Soon" message and turns ON "Engine Control System" light
E048	Exhaust Gas Recirculation (EGR) system fault – displays "Service Soon" message and turns ON "Engine Control System" light
E051	Electronic Control Module (ECM) PROM error – displays "Service Now" message and turns ON "Engine Control System" light
E052	Electronic Control Module (ECM) memory reset indicator – does not turn on any telltale light or display any message
E053	Distributor signal interrupt – does not turn on any telltale light or display any message
E055	Throttle Position Sensor (TPS) misadjusted – does not turn on any telltale light or display any message
E059	Viscous Converter Clutch (VCC) temperature sensor circuit problem – does not turn on any telltale light or display any message

Year – 1986
Model – Eldorado
Engine – 4.1L (250 cid) DFI V8
Engine Code – VIN 8

ECM TROUBLE CODES

Code	Explanation
E012	No distributor signal – displays "Service Now" message and turns ON "Engine Control System" light
E013	Oxygen sensor not ready – Air Injector Reaction (AIR), CL and canister purge disengaged – displays "Service Soon" message and turns ON "Engine Control System"
E014	Shorted Coolant Temperature Sensor (CTS) circuit – Air Injector Reaction (AIR) disengaged – displays "Service Soon" message and turns ON "Engine Control System" light – forces cooling fans on full speed
E015	Open Coolant Temperature Sensor (CTS) circuit – Air Injector Reaction (AIR) disengaged – displays "Service Soon" message and turns ON "Engine Control System" light – forces cooling fans on full speed
E016	Generator voltage out of range – all solenoids disengaged – displays "Service Now" message and turns ON "Engine Control System" light – disengages Viscous Converter Clutch (VCC) for entire ignition cycle
E018	Open crank signal circuit – displays "Service Soon" message and turns ON "Engine Control System" light
E019	Shorted fuel pump circuit – displays "Service Soon" message and turns ON "Engine Control System" light
E020	Open fuel pump circuit – displays "Service Now" message and turns ON "Engine Control System" light
E021	Shorted Throttle Posiion Sensor (TPS) circuit – displays "Service Soon" message and turns ON "Engine Control System" light
E022	Open Throttle Posiion Sensor (TPS) circuit – displays "Service Soon" message and turns ON "Engine Control System" light
E023	Electronic Spark Timing (EST)/bypass circuit problem – Air Injector Reaction (AIR) disengaged – displays "Service Soon" message and turns ON "Engine Control System" light – causes system to operate on bypass spark
E024	Speed sensor circuit problem – Viscous Converter Clutch (VCC) disengaged – displays "Service Soon" message and turns ON "Engine Control System" light – disables Viscous Converter Clutch (VCC) for entire ignition cycle
E026	Shorted throttle switch circuit – displays "Service Soon" message and turns ON "Engine Control System" light
E027	Open throttle switch circuit – displays "Service Soon" message and turns ON "Engine Control System" light
E028	Open third or fourth gear circuit – displays "Service Soon" message and turns ON "Engine Control System" light
E030	Idle Speed Control (ISC) circuit problem – displays "Service Soon" message and turns ON "Engine Control System" light
E031	Shorted Manifold Absolute Pressure (MAP) sensor circuit – Air Injector Reaction (AIR) disengaged – displays "Service Now" message and turns ON "Engine Control System" light
E032	Open Manifold Absolute Pressure (MAP) sensor circuit – Air Injector Reaction (AIR) disengaged – displays "Service Now" message and turns ON "Engine Control System" light
E034	Manifold Absolute Pressure (MAP) sensor signal too high – Air Injector Reaction (AIR) disengaged – displays "Service Now" message and turns ON "Engine Control System" light
E037	Shorted Manifold Air Temperature (MAT) sensor circuit – Air Injector Reaction (AIR) disengaged – displays "Service Soon" message and turns ON "Engine Control System" light

ECM TROUBLE CODES (cont'd)

Code	Explanation
E038	Open Manifold Air Temperature (MAT) sensor circuit—Air Injector Reaction (AIR) disengaged—displays "Service Soon" message and turns ON "Engine Control System" light
E039	Viscous Converter Clutch (VCC) engagement problem—displays "Service Soon" message and turns ON "Engine Control System" light
E040	Open Power Steering Pressure Switch (PSPS) circuit—displays "Service Soon" message and turns ON "Engine Control System" light
E044	Lean exhaust signal—Air Injector Reaction (AIR), CL and canister purge disengaged—displays "Service Now" message and turns ON "Engine Control System" light
E045	Rich exhaust signal—Air Injector Reaction (AIR), CL and canister purge disengaged—displays "Service Now" message and turns ON "Engine Control System" light
E047	Body Control Module (BCM)—Electronic Control Module (ECM) data problem—displays "Service Soon" message and turns ON "Engine Control System" light
E048	Exhaust Gas Recirculation (EGR) system fault—displays "Service Soon" message and turns ON "Engine Control System" light
E051	Electronic Control Module (ECM) PROM error—displays "Service Now" message and turns ON "Engine Control System" light
E052	Electronic Control Module (ECM) memory reset indicator—does not turn on any telltale light or display any message
E053	Distributor signal interrupt—does not turn on any telltale light or display any message
E055	Throttle Position Sensor (TPS) misadjusted—does not turn on any telltale light or display any message
E059	Viscous Converter Clutch (VCC) temperature sensor circuit problem—does not turn on any telltale light or display any message

Year—1986
Model—Cimarron
Engine—2.8L (173 cid) MPFI V6
Engine Code—VIN W

ECM TROUBLE CODES

Code	Explanation
13	Oxygen sensor circuit open
14	Coolant Temperature Sensor (CTS) circuit high
15	Coolant Temperature Sensor (CTS) circuit low
21	Throttle Position Sensor (TPS) circuit—signal voltage high
22	Throttle Position Sensor (TPS) circuit—signal voltage low
23	Manifold Air Temperature (MAT) sensor circuit—low temperature indicated
24	Vehicle Speed Sensor (VSS) circuit
25	Manifold Air Temperature (MAT) sensor circuit—high temperature indicated
33	Manifold Absolute Pressure (MAP) sensor circuit—signal voltage high—low vacuum
34	Manifold Absolute Pressure (MAP) sensor circuit—signal voltage low—high vacuum
35	Idle speed error
41	Cylinder select error—faulty or incorrect Mem-Cal
42	Electronic Spark Timing (EST) circuit
43	Electronic Spark Control (ESC) circuit
44	Oxygen sensor circuit—lean exhaust indicated

ECM TROUBLE CODES (cont'd)

Code	Explanation
45	Oxygen sensor circuit—rich exhaust indicated
54	Fuel pump circuit—low voltage
51	Mem-Cal error—faulty or incorrect Mem-Cal
52	Calpak error—faulty or incorrect calpak
53	System over voltage
61	Degraded oxygen sensor

Year—1987
Model—DeVille
Engine—4.1L (250 cid) DFI V8
Engine Code—VIN 8

ECM TROUBLE CODES

Code	Explanation
E12	No distributor signal—turns ON "Service Now" light
E13	Oxygen sensor not ready—Air Injector Reaction (AIR), CL and canister purge disengaged—turns ON "Service Soon" light
E14	Shorted Coolant Temperature Sensor (CTS) circuit—Air Injector Reaction (AIR) disengaged—turns ON "Service Soon" light—forces cooling fans on full speed
E15	Open Coolant Temperature Sensor (CTS) circuit—Air Injector Reaction (AIR) disengaged—turns ON "Service Soon" light—forces cooling fans on full speed
E16	Generator voltage out of range—all solenoids disengaged—turns ON "Service Now" light—disengages Viscous Converter Clutch (VCC) for entire ignition cycle
E18	Open crank signal circuit—turns ON "Service Soon" light
E19	Shorted fuel pump circuit—turns ON "Service Soon" light
E20	Open fuel pump circuit—turns ON "Service Now" light
E21	Shorted Throttle Position Sensor (TPS) circuit—turns ON "Service Soon" light
E22	Open Throttle Position Sensor (TPS) circuit—turns ON "Service Soon" light
E23	Electronic Spark Timing (EST)/bypass circuit problem—Air Injector Reaction (AIR) disengaged—turns ON "Service Soon" light—causes system to operate on bypass spark
E24	Speed sensor circuit problem—Viscous Converter Clutch (VCC) and cruise disengaged—turns ON "Service Soon" light—disables cruise for entire ignition cycle—disengages Viscous Converter Clutch (VCC) for entire ignition cycle
E26	Shorted throttle switch circuit—turns ON "Service Soon" light
E27	Open throttle switch circuit—turns ON "Service Soon" light
E28	Open third or fourth gear circuit—turns ON "Service Soon" light
E30	Idle Speed Control (ISC) circuit problem—turns ON "Service Soon" light
E31	Shorted Manifold Absolute Pressure (MAP) sensor circuit—Air Injector Reaction (AIR) disengaged—turns ON "Service Now" light
E32	Open Manifold Absolute Pressure (MAP) sensor circuit—Air Injector Reaction (AIR) disengaged—turns ON "Service Now" light
E34	Manifold Absolute Pressure (MAP) sensor signal too high—Air Injector Reaction (AIR) disengaged—turns ON "Service Now" light
E37	Shorted Manifold Air Temperature (MAT) sensor circuit—Air Injector Reaction (AIR) disengaged—turns ON "Service Soon" light

ECM TROUBLE CODES (cont'd)

Code	Explanation
E38	Open Manifold Air Temperature (MAT) sensor circuit — Air Injector Reaction (AIR) disengaged — turns ON "Service Soon" light
E39	Viscous Converter Clutch (VCC) engagement problem — turns ON "Service Soon" light
E40	Open Power Steering Pressure Switch (PSPS) circuit — turns ON "Service Soon" light
E44	Lean exhaust signal — Air Injector Reaction (AIR), CL and canister purge disengaged — turns ON "Service Now" light
E45	Rich exhaust signal — Air Injector Reaction (AIR), CL and canister purge disengaged — turns ON "Service Now" light
E47	Body Control Module (BCM) — Electronic Control Module (ECM) data problem — turns ON "Service Soon" light
E48	Exhaust Gas Recirculation (EGR) system fault — turns ON "Service Soon" light
E51	Electronic Control Module (ECM) PROM error — turns ON "Service Now" light
E52	Electronic Control Module (ECM) memory reset indicator — does not turn on any telltale light
E53	Distributor signal interrupt — does not turn on any telltale light
E55	Throttle Position Sensor (TPS) misadjusted — does not turn on any telltale light
E59	Viscous Converter Clutch (VCC) temperature sensor circuit problem — does not turn on any telltale light
E60	Cruise — transmission not in Drive — cruise disengaged — does not turn on any telltale light
E63	Cruise — car speed and set speed difference too high — cruise disengaged — does not turn on any telltale light
E64	Cruise — car acceleration too high — cruise disengaged — does not turn on any telltale light
E65	Cruise — coolant temperature too high — cruise disengaged — does not turn on any telltale light
E66	Cruise — engine RPM too high — cruise disengaged — does not turn on any telltale light
E67	Cruise — cruise switch shorted during enable — cruise disengaged — does not turn on any telltale light — disables cruise for entire ignition cycle

BCM TROUBLE CODES

Code	Explanation
F10	Outside temperature sensor CKT — does not turn on any light
F11	Air conditioning high side temperature sensor CKT — does not turn on any light — turns ON cooling fans when air conditioning clutch is engaged
F12	Air conditioning low side temperature sensor CKT — does not turn on any light — disengages air conditioning clutch
F13	In-car temperature sensor CKT — does not turn on any light
F30	Climate Control Panel (CCP) to Body Control Module (BCM) data CKT — does not turn on any light — turns ON ft. defog at 75°F
F31	Fuel Data Center (FDC) to Body Control Module (BCM) data CKT — does not turn on any light
F32	Electronic Control Module (ECM) — Body Control Module (BCM) data CKT's — does not turn on any light — turns ON cooling fans
F40	Air mix door problem — does not turn on any light
F41	Cooling fans problem — does not turn on any light — turns ON "Coolant Temp/Fans" light when fans should be on
F46	Low refrigerant warning — turns ON "Service Air Cond" light
F47	Low refrigerant condition — turns ON "Service Air Cond" light — switches from "Auto" to "Econ"
F48	Low refrigerant pressure — turns ON "Service Air Cond" light — switches from "Auto" to "Econ"
F49	High temperature clutch disengage — does not turn on any light
F51	Body Control Module (BCM) PROM error — does not turn on any light

GENERAL MOTORS CORPORATION
DIAGNOSTIC CODE DATA

Year — 1987
Model — Brougham
Engine — 5.0L (307 cid) V8
Engine Code — VIN Y

ECM TROUBLE CODES

Code	Explanation
12	No distributor reference signal to the Electronic Control Module (ECM). This code is not stored in memory and will only flash while the fault is present. This is a normal code with ignition ON, engine not running
13	Oxygen sensor circuit—the engine must run up to 4 minutes at part throttle, under road load, before this code will set
14	Shorted Coolant Temperature Sensor (CTS) circuit—the engine must run 2 minutes before this code will set
15	Open Coolant Temperature Sensor (CTS) circuit—the engine must run 5 minutes before this code will set
21	Throttle Position Sensor (TPS) circuit voltage high—open circuit or misadjusted TPS. The engine must run 10 seconds, at specified curb idle speed, before this code will set
22	Throttle Position Sensor (TPS) circuit voltage low—grounded circuit of misadjusted TPS. Engine must run 20 seconds at specified curb idle speed, to set code
23	M/C solenoid circuit open or grounded
24	Vehicle Speed Sensor (VSS) circuit—the vehicle must operate up to 2 minutes at road speed, before this code will set
32	Barometric Pressure Sensor (BARO) circuit low
34	Manifold Absolute Pressure (MAP) or vacuum sensor circuit. The engine must run up to 2 minutes at specified curb idle speed, before this code will set
35	Idle Speed Control (ISC) switch circuit shorted—up to 70% Throttle Position Sensor (TPS) for over 5 seconds
41	No distributor reference signal to the Electronic Control Module (ECM) at specified engine vacuum. This code will store in memory
42	Electronic Spark Timing (EST) bypass circuit or EST circuit grounded or open
43	Electronic Spark Control (ESC) retard signal for too long; causes a retard in Electronic Spark Timing (EST) signal
44	Lean exhaust indication—the engine must run 2 minutes, in closed loop and at part throttle, before this code will set
45	Rich exhaust indication—the engine must run 2 minutes, in closed loop and at part throttle, before this code will set
51	Faulty or improperly installed calibration unit (PROM). It takes up to 30 seconds before this code will set
53	Exhaust Gas Recirculation (EGR) valve vacuum sensor has seen improper EGR control vacuum
54	M/C solenoid voltage high, at Electronic Control Module (ECM), as a result of a shorted M/C solenoid circuit and/or faulty ECM

Year — 1987
Model — Fleetwood
Engine — 4.1L (250 cid) DFI V8
Engine Code — VIN 8

ECM TROUBLE CODES

Code	Explanation
E12	No distributor signal — turns ON "Service Now" light
E13	Oxygen sensor not ready — Air Injector Reaction (AIR), CL and canister purge disengaged — turns ON "Service Soon" light
E14	Shorted Coolant Temperature Sensor (CTS) circuit — Air Injector Reaction (AIR) disengaged — turns ON "Service Soon" light — forces cooling fans on full speed
E15	Open Coolant Temperature Sensor (CTS) circuit — Air Injector Reaction (AIR) disengaged — turns ON "Service Soon" light — forces cooling fans on full speed
E16	Generator voltage out of range — all solenoids disengaged — turns ON "Service Now" light — disengages Viscous Converter Clutch (VCC) for entire ignition cycle
E18	Open crank signal circuit — turns ON "Service Soon" light
E19	Shorted fuel pump circuit — turns ON "Service Soon" light
E20	Open fuel pump circuit — turns ON "Service Now" light
E21	Shorted Throttle Position Sensor (TPS) circuit — turns ON "Service Soon" light
E22	Open Throttle Position Sensor (TPS) circuit — turns ON "Service Soon" light
E23	Electronic Spark Timing (EST)/bypass circuit problem — Air Injector Reaction (AIR) disengaged — turns ON "Service Soon" light — causes system to operate on bypass spark
E24	Speed sensor circuit problem — Viscous Converter Clutch (VCC) and cruise disengaged — turns ON "Service Soon" light — disables cruise for entire ignition cycle — disengages Viscous Converter Clutch (VCC) for entire ignition cycle
E26	Shorted throttle switch circuit — turns ON "Service Soon" light
E27	Open throttle switch circuit — turns ON "Service Soon" light
E28	Open third or fourth gear circuit — turns ON "Service Soon" light
E30	Idle Speed Control (ISC) circuit problem — turns ON "Service Soon" light
E31	Shorted Manifold Absolute Pressure (MAP) sensor circuit — Air Injector Reaction (AIR) disengaged — turns ON "Service Now" light
E32	Open Manifold Absolute Pressure (MAP) sensor circuit — Air Injector Reaction (AIR) disengaged — turns ON "Service Now" light
E34	Manifold Absolute Pressure (MAP) sensor signal too high — Air Injector Reaction (AIR) disengaged — turns ON "Service Now" light
E37	Shorted Manifold Air Temperature (MAT) sensor circuit — Air Injector Reaction (AIR) disengaged — turns ON "Service Soon" light
E38	Open Manifold Air Temperature (MAT) sensor circuit — Air Injector Reaction (AIR) disengaged — turns ON "Service Soon" light
E39	Viscous Converter Clutch (VCC) engagement problem — turns ON "Service Soon" light
E40	Open Power Steering Pressure Switch (PSPS) circuit — turns ON "Service Soon" light
E44	Lean exhaust signal — Air Injector Reaction (AIR), CL and canister purge disengaged — turns ON "Service Now" light
E45	Rich exhaust signal — Air Injector Reaction (AIR), CL and canister purge disengaged — turns ON "Service Now" light
E47	Body Control Module (BCM) — Electronic Control Module (ECM) data problem — turns ON "Service Soon" light
E48	Exhaust Gas Recirculation (EGR) system fault — turns ON "Service Soon" light
E51	Electronic Control Module (ECM) PROM error — turns ON "Service Now" light

ECM TROUBLE CODES (cont'd)

Code	Explanation
E52	Electronic Control Module (ECM) memory reset indicator—does not turn on any telltale light
E53	Distributor signal interrupt—does not turn on any telltale light
E55	Throttle Position Sensor (TPS) misadjusted—does not turn on any telltale light
E59	Viscous Converter Clutch (VCC) temperature Sensor (CTS) circuit problem—does not turn on any telltale light
E60	Cruise—transmission not in Drive—cruise disengaged—does not turn on any telltale light
E63	Cruise—car speed and set speed difference too high—cruise disengaged—does not turn on any telltale light
E64	Cruise—car acceleration too high—cruise disengaged—does not turn on any telltale light
E65	Cruise—coolant temperature too high—cruise disengaged—does not turn on any telltale light
E66	Cruise—engine RPM too high—cruise disengaged—does not turn on any telltale light
E67	Cruise—cruise switch shorted during enable—cruise disengaged—does not turn on any telltale light—disables cruise for entire ignition cycle

BCM TROUBLE CODES

Code	Explanation
F10	Outside temperature sensor CKT—does not turn on any light
F11	Air conditioning high side temperature sensor CKT—does not turn on any light—turns ON cooling fans when air conditioning clutch is engaged
F12	Air conditioning low side temperature sensor CKT—does not turn on any light—disengages air conditioning clutch
F13	In-car temperature sensor CKT—does not turn on any light
F30	Climate Control Panel (CCP) to Body Control Module (BCM) data CKT—does not turn on any light—turns ON ft. defog at 75°F
F31	Fuel Data Center (FDC) to Body Control Module (BCM) data CKT—does not turn on any light
F32	Electronic Control Module (ECM)—Body Control Module (BCM) data CKT's—does not turn on any light—turns ON cooling fans
F40	Air mix door problem—does not turn on any light
F41	Cooling fans problem—does not turn on any light—turns ON "Coolant Temp/Fans" light when fans should be on
F46	Low refrigerant warning—turns ON "Service Air Cond" light
F47	Low refrigerant condition—turns ON "Service Air Cond" light—switches from "Auto" to "Econ"
F48	Low refrigerant pressure—turns ON "Service Air Cond" light—switches from "Auto" to "Econ"
F49	High temperature clutch disengage—does not turn on any light
F51	Body Control Module (BCM) PROM error—does not turn on any light

Year — 1987
Model — Seville
Engine — 4.1L (250 cid) DFI V8
Engine Code — VIN 8

ECM TROUBLE CODES

Code	Explanation
E012	No distributor signal — displays "Service Now" message and turns ON "Engine Control System" light
E013	Oxygen sensor not ready — Air Injector Reaction (AIR), CL and canister purge disengaged — displays "Service Soon" message and turns ON "Engine Control System"
E014	Shorted Coolant Temperature Sensor (CTS) circuit — Air Injector Reaction (AIR) disengaged — displays "Service Soon" message and turns ON "Engine Control System" light — forces cooling fans on full speed
E015	Open Coolant Temperature Sensor (CTS) circuit — Air Injector Reaction (AIR) disengaged — displays "Service Soon" message and turns ON "Engine Control System" light — forces cooling fans on full speed
E016	Generator voltage out of range — all solenoids disengaged — displays "Service Now" message and turns ON "Engine Control System" light — disengages Viscous Converter Clutch (VCC) for entire ignition cycle
E018	Open crank signal circuit — displays "Service Soon" message and turns ON "Engine Control System" light
E019	Shorted fuel pump circuit — displays "Service Soon" message and turns ON "Engine Control System" light
E020	Open fuel pump circuit — displays "Service Now" message and turns ON "Engine Control System" light
E021	Shorted Throttle Position Sensor (TPS) circuit — displays "Service Soon" message and turns ON "Engine Control System" light
E022	Open Throttle Position Sensor (TPS) circuit — displays "Service Soon" message and turns ON "Engine Control System" light
E023	Electronic Spark Timing (EST)/bypass circuit problem — Air Injector Reaction (AIR) disengaged — displays "Service Soon" message and turns ON "Engine Control System" light — causes system to operate on bypass spark
E024	Speed sensor circuit problem — Viscous Converter Clutch (VCC) disengaged — displays "Service Soon" message and turns ON "Engine Control System" light — disables Viscous Converter Clutch (VCC) for entire ignition cycle
E026	Shorted throttle switch circuit — displays "Service Soon" message and turns ON "Engine Control System" light
E027	Open throttle switch circuit — displays "Service Soon" message and turns ON "Engine Control System" light
E028	Open third or fourth gear circuit — displays "Service Soon" message and turns ON "Engine Control System" light
E030	Idle Speed Control (ISC) circuit problem — displays "Service Soon" message and turns ON "Engine Control System" light
E031	Shorted Manifold Absolute Pressure (MAP) sensor circuit — Air Injector Reaction (AIR) disengaged — displays "Service Now" message and turns ON "Engine Control System" light
E032	Open Manifold Absolute Pressure (MAP) sensor circuit — Air Injector Reaction (AIR) disengaged — displays "Service Now" message and turns ON "Engine Control System" light
E034	Manifold Absolute Pressure (MAP) sensor signal too high — Air Injector Reaction (AIR) disengaged — displays "Service Now" message and turns ON "Engine Control System" light
E037	Shorted Manifold Air Temperature (MAT) sensor circuit — Air Injector Reaction (AIR) disengaged — displays "Service Soon" message and turns ON "Engine Control System" light
E038	Open Manifold Air Temperature (MAT) sensor circuit — Air Injector Reaction (AIR) disengaged — displays "Service Soon" message and turns ON "Engine Control System" light

ECM TROUBLE CODES (cont'd)

Code	Explanation
E039	Viscous Converter Clutch (VCC) engagement problem—displays "Service Soon" message and turns ON "Engine Control System" light
E040	Open Power Steering Pressure Switch (PSPS) circuit—displays "Service Soon" message and turns ON "Engine Control System" light
E044	Lean exhaust signal—Air Injector Reaction (AIR), CL and canister purge disengaged—displays "Service Now" message and turns ON "Engine Control System" light
E045	Rich exhaust signal—Air Injector Reaction (AIR), CL and canister purge disengaged—displays "Service Now" message and turns ON "Engine Control System" light
E047	Body Control Module (BCM)—Electronic Control Module (ECM) data problem—displays "Service Soon" message and turns ON "Engine Control System" light
E048	Exhaust Gas Recirculation (EGR) system fault—displays "Service Soon" message and turns ON "Engine Control System" light
E051	Electronic Control Module (ECM) PROM error—displays "Service Now" message and turns ON "Engine Control System" light
E052	Electronic Control Module (ECM) memory reset indicator—does not turn on any telltale light or display any message
E053	Distributor signal interrupt—does not turn on any telltale light or display any message
E055	Throttle Position Sensor (TPS) misadjusted—does not turn on any telltale light or display any message
E059	Viscous Converter Clutch (VCC) temperature sensor circuit problem—does not turn on any telltale light or display any message

BCM TROUBLE CODES

Code	Explanation
B110	Outside temperature sensor
B111	Air conditioning Hi side temperature sensor
B112	Air conditioning Lo side temperature sensor
B113	In-car temperature sensor
B115	Sunload temperature sensor
B118	Door jamb/AJAR
B119	Twilight photocell
B120	Twilight delay pot
B121	Twilight enable switch
B122	Panel lamp dimming pot
B123	Courtesy light switch
B124	Vehicle Speed Sensor (VSS)
B127	PRND321 sensor
B128	Bulb reference circuit
B334	Electronic Control Module (ECM) data
B335	CCDIC data
B336	Instrument Panel Control (IPC) data
B37	Programmer data
B410	Regulator
B411	Battery low
B412	Battery high
B420	Relays

BCM TROUBLE CODES (cont'd)

Code	Explanation
B440	Air mix door
B441	Cooling fans
B446	Low Refrigerant warning
B447	Very low refrigerant problem
B448	Low refrigerant pressure
B449	Air conditioning Hi temperature
B450	Coolant high temp — air conditioning
B552	Body Control Module (BCM) memory reset
B556	Odometer EE PROM error
B660	Cruise — not in drive
B663	Cruise — speed difference
B664	Cruise — acceleration
B665	Cruise — coolant temperature too high
B666	Cruise — RPM too high
B667	Cruise — switch shorted
B671	Cruise — position sensor
B672	Cruise — vent solenoid
B673	Cruise — vacuum solenoid

Year — 1987
Model — Eldorado
Engine — 4.1L (250 cid) DFI V8
Engine Code — VIN 8

ECM TROUBLE CODES

Code	Explanation
E012	No distributor signal — displays "Service Now" message and turns ON "Engine Control System" light
E013	Oxygen sensor not ready — Air Injector Reaction (AIR), CL and canister purge disengaged — displays "Service Soon" message and turns ON "Engine Control System"
E014	Shorted Coolant Temperature Sensor (CTS) circuit — Air Injector Reaction (AIR) disengaged — displays "Service Soon" message and turns ON "Engine Control System" light — forces cooling fans on full speed
E015	Open Coolant Temperature Sensor (CTS) circuit — Air Injector Reaction (AIR) disengaged — displays "Service Soon" message and turns ON "Engine Control System" light — forces cooling fans on full speed
E016	Generator voltage out of range — all solenoids disengaged — displays "Service Now" message and turns ON "Engine Control System" light — disengages Viscous Converter Clutch (VCC) for entire ignition cycle
E018	Open crank signal circuit — displays "Service Soon" message and turns ON "Engine Control System" light
E019	Shorted fuel pump circuit — displays "Service Soon" message and turns ON "Engine Control System" light
E020	Open fuel pump circuit — displays "Service Now" message and turns ON "Engine Control System" light
E021	Shorted Throttle Position Sensor (TPS) circuit — displays "Service Soon" message and turns ON "Engine Control System" light

ECM TROUBLE CODES (cont'd)

Code	Explanation
E022	Open Throttle Position Sensor (TPS) circuit—displays "Service Soon" message and turns ON "Engine Control System" light
E023	Electronic Spark Timing (EST)/bypass circuit problem—Air Injector Reaction (AIR) disengaged—displays "Service Soon" message and turns ON "Engine Control System" light—causes system to operate on bypass spark
E024	Speed sensor circuit problem—Viscous Converter Clutch (VCC) disengaged—displays "Service Soon" message and turns ON "Engine Control System" light—disables Viscous Converter Clutch (VCC) for entire ignition cycle
E026	Shorted throttle switch circuit—displays "Service Soon" message and turns ON "Engine Control System" light
E027	Open throttle switch circuit—displays "Service Soon" message and turns ON "Engine Control System" light
E028	Open third or fourth gear circuit—displays "Service Soon" message and turns ON "Engine Control System" light
E030	Idle Speed Control (ISC) circuit problem—displays "Service Soon" message and turns ON "Engine Control System" light
E031	Shorted Manifold Absolute Pressure (MAP) sensor circuit—Air Injector Reaction (AIR) disengaged—displays "Service Now" message and turns ON "Engine Control System" light
E032	Open Manifold Absolute Pressure (MAP) sensor circuit—Air Injector Reaction (AIR) disengaged—displays "Service Now" message and turns ON "Engine Control System" light
E034	Manifold Absolute Pressure (MAP) sensor signal too high—Air Injector Reaction (AIR) disengaged—displays "Service Now" message and turns ON "Engine Control System" light
E037	Shorted Manifold Air Temperature (MAT) sensor circuit—Air Injector Reaction (AIR) disengaged—displays "Service Soon" message and turns ON "Engine Control System" light
E038	Open Manifold Air Temperature (MAT) sensor circuit—Air Injector Reaction (AIR) disengaged—displays "Service Soon" message and turns ON "Engine Control System" light
E039	Viscous Converter Clutch (VCC) engagement problem—displays "Service Soon" message and turns ON "Engine Control System" light
E040	Open Power Steering Pressure Switch (PSPS) circuit—displays "Service Soon" message and turns ON "Engine Control System" light
E044	Lean exhaust signal—Air Injector Reaction (AIR), CL and canister purge disengaged—displays "Service Now" message and turns ON "Engine Control System" light
E045	Rich exhaust signal—Air Injector Reaction (AIR), CL and canister purge disengaged—displays "Service Now" message and turns ON "Engine Control System" light
E047	Body Control Module (BCM)—Electronic Control Module (ECM) data problem—displays "Service Soon" message and turns ON "Engine Control System" light
E048	Exhaust Gas Recirculation (EGR) system fault—displays "Service Soon" message and turns ON "Engine Control System" light
E051	Electronic Control Module (ECM) PROM error—displays "Service Now" message and turns ON "Engine Control System" light
E052	Electronic Control Module (ECM) memory reset indicator—does not turn on any telltale light or display any message
E053	Distributor signal interrupt—does not turn on any telltale light or display any message
E055	Throttle Position Sensor (TPS) misadjusted—does not turn on any telltale light or display any message
E059	Viscous Converter Clutch (VCC) temperature sensor circuit problem—does not turn on any telltale light or display any message

BCM TROUBLE CODES

Code	Explanation
B110	Outside temperature sensor
B111	Air conditioning Hi side temperature sensor
B112	Air conditioning Lo side temperature sensor
B113	In-car temperature sensor
B115	Sunload temperature sensor
B118	Door jamb/AJAR
B119	Twilight photocell
B120	Twilight delay pot
B121	Twilight enable switch
B122	Panel lamp dimming pot
B123	Courtesy light switch
B124	Vehicle Speed Sensor (VSS)
B127	PRND321 sensor
B128	Bulb reference circuit
B334	Electronic Control Module (ECM) data
B335	CCDIC data
B336	Instrument Panel Control (IPC) data
B37	Programmer data
B410	Regulator
B411	Battery low
B412	Battery high
B420	Relays
B440	Air mix door
B441	Cooling fans
B446	Low Refrigerant warning
B447	Very low refrigerant problem
B448	Low refrigerant pressure
B449	Air conditioning Hi temperature
B450	Coolant high temperature — air conditioning
B552	Body Control Module (BCM) memory reset
B556	Odometer EE PROM error
B660	Cruise — not in drive
B663	Cruise — speed difference
B664	Cruise — acceleration
B665	Cruise — coolant temperature too high
B666	Cruise — RPM too high
B667	Cruise — switch shorted
B671	Cruise — position sensor
B672	Cruise — vent solenoid
B673	Cruise — vacuum solenoid

Year – 1987
Model – Allante
Engine – 4.1L (250 cid) MPFI V8
Engine Code – VIN 7

ECM TROUBLE CODES

Code	Explanation
E012	No distributor signal – displays "Service Now" message and turns ON "Engine Control System" light
E013	Right oxygen sensor not ready – Air Injector Reaction (AIR), CL and canister purge disengaged – displays "Service Soon" message and turns ON "Engine Control System" – enables canister purge, diverts air, and disables closed loop only if a problem is detected with both the left and the right sensors
E014	Shorted Coolant Temperature Sensor (CTS) circuit – Air Injector Reaction (AIR) disengaged – displays "Service Soon" message and turns ON "Engine Control System" light – forces cooling fans on full speed
E015	Open Coolant Temperature Sensor (CTS) circuit – Air Injector Reaction (AIR) disengaged – displays "Service Soon" message and turns ON "Engine Control System" light – forces cooling fans on full speed
E016	Generator voltage out of range – all solenoids, except shift solenoids disengaged – displays "Service Now" message and turns ON "Engine Control System" light
E017	Left oxygen sensor not ready – Air Injector Reaction (AIR), CL and canister purge disengaged – displays "Service Soon" message and turns o Engine Control System" – enables canister purge, diverts air, and disables closed loop only if a problem is detected with both the left and the right sensors
E019	Shorted fuel pump circuit – displays "Service Soon" message and turns ON "Engine Control System" light
E020	Open fuel pump circuit – displays "Service Now" message and turns ON "Engine Control System" light
E021	Shorted Throttle Position Sensor (TPS) circuit – Viscous Converter Clutch (VCC) disengaged – displays "Service Soon" message and turns ON "Engine Control System" light
E022	Open Throttle Position Sensor (TPS) circuit – Viscous Converter Clutch (VCC) disengaged – displays "Service Soon" message and turns ON "Engine Control System" light
E023	Electronic Spark Timing (EST)/bypass circuit problem – Air Injector Reaction (AIR) disengaged – displays "Service Soon" message and turns ON "Engine Control System" light – causes system to operate on bypass spark
E024	Speed sensor circuit problem – Viscous Converter Clutch (VCC) and cruise disengaged – displays "Service Soon" message and turns ON "Engine Control System" light
E026	Shorted throttle switch circuit – Exhaust Gas Recirculation (EGR) – displays "Service Soon" message and turns ON "Engine Control System" light
E027	Open throttle switch circuit – Exhaust Gas Recirculation (EGR) – displays "Service Soon" message and turns ON "Engine Control System" light
E028	Open third gear switch circuit or shorted 2–3 shift solenoid – Viscous Converter Clutch (VCC) and cruise disengaged – displays "Service Soon" message and turns ON "Engine Control System" light
E029	Shorted third gear switch circuit or open 2–3 shift solenoid – Viscous Converter Clutch (VCC) and cruise disengaged – displays "Service Soon" message and turns ON "Engine Control System" light
E030	Idle Speed Control (ISC) circuit problem – displays "Service Soon" message and turns ON "Engine Control System" light
E031	Shorted Manifold Absolute Pressure (MAP) sensor circuit – Air Injector Reaction (AIR) disengaged – displays "Service Now" message and turns ON "Engine Control System" light
E032	Open Manifold Absolute Pressure (MAP) sensor circuit – Air Injector Reaction (AIR) disengaged – displays "Service Now" message and turns ON "Engine Control System" light
E034	Manifold Absolute Pressure (MAP) sensor signal too high – Air Injector Reaction (AIR) disengaged – displays "Service Now" message and turns ON "Engine Control System" light

ECM TROUBLE CODES (cont'd)

Code	Explanation
E037	Shorted Manifold Air Temperature (MAT) sensor circuit — Air Injector Reaction (AIR) disengaged — displays "Service Soon" message and turns ON "Engine Control System" light
E038	Open Manifold Air Temperature (MAT) sensor circuit — Air Injector Reaction (AIR) disengaged — displays "Service Soon" message and turns ON "Engine Control System" light
E039	Viscous Converter Clutch (VCC) engagement problem — Viscous Converter Clutch (VCC) disengaged — displays "Service Soon" message and turns ON "Engine Control System" light — disengages Viscous Converter Clutch (VCC) for entire ignition cycle
E040	Power Steering Pressure sensor circuit — displays "Service Soon" message and turns ON "Engine Control System" light
E041	Cam sensor circuit problem — displays "Service Soon" message and turns ON "Engine Control System" light
E042	Left oxygen sensor signal lean — Air Injector Reaction (AIR), CL and canister purge disengaged — displays "Service Now" message and turns ON "Engine Control System" light — enables canister purge, diverts air, and disables closed loop only if a problem is detected with both the left and the right sensor
E043	Left oxygen sensor signal rich — Air Injector Reaction (AIR), CL and canister purge disengaged — displays "Service Now" message and turns ON "Engine Control System" light — enables canister purge, diverts air, and disables closed loop only if a problem is detected with both the left and the right sensors
E044	Right oxygen sensor signal lean — Air Injector Reaction (AIR), CL and canister purge disengaged — displays "Service Now" message and turns ON "Engine Control System" light — enables canister purge, diverts air, and disables closed loop only if a problem is detected with both the left and the right sensors
E045	Right oxygen sensor signal rich — Air Injector Reaction (AIR), CL and canister purge disengaged — displays "Service Now" message and turns ON "Engine Control System" light — enables canister purge, diverts air, and disables closed loop only if a problem is detected with both the left and the right se
E046	Right to left bank fueling imbalance — displays "Service Now" message and turns ON "Engine Control System" light
E047	Body Control Module (BCM) — Electronic Control Module (ECM) data problem — displays "Service Soon" message and turns ON "Engine Control System" light
E048	Exhaust Gas Recirculation (EGR) system fault — displays "Service Soon" message and turns ON "Engine Control System" light
E049	Air management system fault — Air Injector Reaction (AIR) disengaged — does not turn on any telltale light or display and message
E052	Electronic Control Module (ECM) memory reset indicator — does not turn on any telltale light or display any message
E053	Distributor signal interrupt — does not turn on any telltale light or display any message
E055	Throttle Position Sensor (TPS) misadjusted — does not turn on any telltale light or display any message
E056	Open fourth gear switch or shorted 3 — 4 shift solenoid (VCC) — displays "Service Soon" message and turns on "Engine Control System" light
E057	Shorted fourth gear switch circuit or open 3 — 4 shift solenoid (VCC) — displays "Service Soon" message and turns on "Engine Control System" light t
E059	Transmission temperature sensor circuit problem — Viscous Converter Clutch (VCC) disengaged — displays "Engine Soon" message and turns on "Engine Control System" light
E060	Cruise — transmission not in Drive — cruise disengaged — does not turn on any telltale light or display any message
E061	Cruise — vent solenoid circuit problem — cruise disengaged — does not turn on any telltale light or display any message
E062	Cruise — vacuum solenoid circuit problem — cruise disengaged — does not turn on any telltale light or display any message
E063	Cruise — car speed and set speed difference too high — cruise disengaged — does not turn on any telltale light or display any message

ECM TROUBLE CODES (cont'd)

Code	Explanation
E064	Cruise—car acceleration too high—cruise disengaged—does not turn on any telltale light or display any message
E065	Cruise—cruise servo position sensor failure—cruise disengaged—does not turn on any telltale light or display any message
E066	Cruise—engine RPM too high—cruise disengaged—does not turn on any telltale light or display any message
E067	Cruise—switch shorted during enable—cruise disengaged—does not turn on any telltale light or display any message

BCM TROUBLE CODES

Code	Explanation
B110	Outside temp sensor
B111	Air conditioning HI side temperature sensor
B112	Air conditioning LO side temperature sensor
B113	In-car temperatire sensor
B115	Sunload temperature sensor
B119	Twilight photocell
B120	Twilight delay pot
B122	Panel lamp dimming pot
B124	Vehicle Speed Sensor (VSS)
B127	PRND321 sensor
B132	Oil pressure sensor
B334	Electronic Control Module (ECM) data
B335	CCDIC data
B336	Instrument Panel Control (IPC) data
B337	Programmer data
B409	Charging system fault
B410	Regulator fault
B411	Battery low
B412	Battery high
B420	Body Control Module (BCM) output driver No. 1
B421	Body Control Module (BCM) output driver No. 2
B440	Air mix door
B441	Cooling fans
B446	Low refrigerant warning
B447	Very low refrigerant problem
B448	Low refrigerant pressure
B449	Air conditioning HI temperature
B450	Coolant high temperature—air conditioning
B480	Anti—lock data problem
B481	Anti—lock fault
B552	Body Control Module (BCM) memory reset
B556	Odometer EE PROM error

Year – 1987
Model – Cimmarron
Engine – 2.8L (173 cid) MPFI V6
Engine Code – VIN W

ECM TROUBLE CODES

Code	Explanation
13	Open oxygen sensor circuit
14	Coolant Temperature Sensor (CTS) circuit
15	Coolant Temperature Sensor (CTS) circuit
21	Throttle Position Sensor (TPS)
22	Throttle Position Sensor (TPS)
23	Manifold Air Temperature (MAT) sensor
24	Vehicle Speed Sensor (VSS)
25	Manifold Air Temperature (MAT) sensor
33	Mass Air Flow (MAF) sensor
34	Mass Air Flow (MAF) sensor
35	Idle speed error
41	Cylinder select error – faulty or incorrect Mem-Cal
42	Electronic Spark Timing (EST)
43	Electronic Spark Control (ESC)
44	Lean exhaust indication
45	Rich exhaust indication
54	Fuel pump circuit – low voltage
51	Faulty Mem-Cal
53	System over voltage
55	Electronic Control Module (ECM)
61	Degraded oxygen sensor
63	Manifold Absolute Pressure (MAP) sensor
64	Manifold Absolute Pressure (MAP) sensor

GENERAL MOTORS CORPORATION
DIAGNOSTIC CODE DATA

Year – 1988
Model – DeVille
Engine – 4.5L (273 cid) DFI V8
Engine Code – VIN 5

ECM TROUBLE CODES

Code	Explanation
E012	No distributor signal – turns ON "Service Now" message and "Engine Control System" light
E013	Oxygen sensor not ready – Air Injector Reaction (AIR) and closed loop disengaged – turns ON "Service Soon" message and "Engine Control System" light – engages canister purge
E014	Shorted coolant sensor circuit – Air Injector Reaction (AIR) disengaged – turns ON "Service Soon" message and "Engine Control System" light – forces cooling fans on full speed
E015	Open coolant sensor circuit – Air Injector Reaction (AIR) disengaged – turns ON "Service Soon" message and "Engine Control System" light – forces cooling fans on full speed
E016	Generator voltage out of range – all solenoids disengaged – turns ON "Service Now" message and "Engine Control System" light – disengages Viscous Converter Clutch (VCC) for entire ignition cycle
E018	Open crank signal circuit – turns ON "Service Soon" message and "Engine Control System" light
E019	Shorted fuel pump circuit – turns ON "Service Soon" message and "Engine Control System" light
E020	Open fuel pump circuit – turns ON "Service Now" message and "Engine Control System" light
E021	Shorted Throttle Position Sensor (TPS) circuit – turns ON "Service Soon" message and "Engine Control System" light – disables cruise control for entire ignition cycle
E022	Open Throttle Position Sensor (TPS) circuit – turns ON "Service Soon" message and "Engine Control System" light – disables cruise control for entire ignition cycle
E023	Electronic Spark Timing (EST)/bypass circuit problem – Air Injector Reaction (AIR) disengaged – turns ON "Service Soon" message and "Engine Control System" light – causes system to operate on bypass spark
E024	Speed sensor circuit problem – Viscous Converter Clutch (VCC) and cruise disengaged – turns ON "Service Soon" message and "Engine Control System" light – disengages Viscous Converter Clutch (VCC) for entire ignition cycle
E026	Shorted throttle switch circuit – turns ON "Service Soon" message and "Engine Control System" light
E027	Open throttle switch circuit – turns ON "Service Soon" message and "Engine Control System" light
E028	Open third or fourth gear circuit – turns ON "Service Soon" message and "Engine Control System" light
E030	Idle Speed Control (ISC) circuit problem – turns ON "Service Soon" message and "Engine Control System" light
E031	Shorted Manifold Absolute Pressure (MAP) sensor circuit – Air Injector Reaction (AIR) disengaged – turns ON "Service Now" message and "Engine Control System" light – disenges Viscous Converter Clutch (VCC) for entire ignition cycle
E032	Open Manifold Absolute Pressure (MAP) sensor circuit – Air Injector Reaction (AIR) disengaged – turns ON "Service Now" message and "Engine Control System" light – disengages Viscous Converter Clucth (VCC) for entire ignition cycle
E034	Manifold Absolute Pressure (MAP) sensor signal too high – Air Injector Reaction (AIR) disengaged – turns ON "Service Now" message and "Engine Control System" light – disengages Viscous Converter Clutch (VCC) for entire ignition cycle
E037	Shorted Manifold Air Temperature (MAT) sensor circuit – Air Injector Reaction (AIR) disengaged – turns ON "Service Soon" message and "Engine Control System" light
E038	Open Manifold Air Temperature (MAT) sensor circuit – Air Injector Reaction (AIR) disengaged – turns ON "Service Soon" message and "Engine Control System" light
E039	Viscous Converter Clutch (VCC) engagement problem – turns ON "Service Soon" message and "Engine Control System" light – disengages Viscous Converter Clutch (VCC) for entire ignition cycle
E040	Open Power Steering Pressure Switch (PSPS) circuit – Exhaust Gas Recirculation (EGR) disengaged – turns ON "Service Soon" message and "Engine Control System" light

ECM TROUBLE CODES (cont'd)

Code	Explanation
E044	Lean exhaust signal—Air Injector Reaction (AIR) and closed loop disengaged—turns ON "Service Now" message and "Engine Control System" light—engages canister purge
E045	Rich exhaust signal—Air Injector Reaction (AIR) and closed loop disengaged—turns ON "Service Now" message and "Engine Control System" light—engages canister purge
E047	Body Control Module (BCM)—Electronic Control Module (ECM) data problem—turns ON "Service Soon" message and "Engine Control System" light
E048	Exhaust Gas Recirculation (EGR) system fault—EGR disengaged—turns ON "Service Soon" message and "Engine Control System" light
E052	Electronic Control Module (ECM) memory reset indicator—does not turn on any telltale light or display any message
E053	Distributor signal interrupt—does not turn on any telltale light or display any message
E055	Throttle Position Sensor (TPS) misadjusted—does not turn on any telltale light or display any message
E059	Viscous Converter Clutch (VCC) temperature sensor circuit problem—does not turn on any telltale light or display any message—disengages Viscous Converter Clutch (VCC) for entire ignition problem
E060	Cruise—transmission not in Drive—cruise disengaged—does not turn on any telltale light or display any message
E063	Cruise—car speed and set speed difference too high—cruise disengaged—does not turn on any telltale light or display any message
E064	Cruise—car acceleration too high—cruise disengaged—does not turn on any telltale light or display any message
E065	Cruise—servo position sensor failure—does not turn on any telltale light or display any message
E066	Cruise—engine RPM too high—cruise disengaged—does not turn on any telltale light or display any message
E067	Cruise—cruise switch shorted during enable—does not turn on any telltale light or display any message

BCM TROUBLE CODES

Code	Explanation
B110	Outside temperature sensor
B111	Air conditioning HI side temperature sensor
B112	Air conditioning LO side temperature sensor
B113	In-car temperature sensor
B115	Sunload temperature sensor
B119	Twilight photocell
B120	Twilight delay pot
B121	Twilight enable switch
B122	Panel lamp dimming pot
B123	Courtesy light switch
B124	Vehicle Speed Sensor (VSS)
B127	PRND321
B334	Electronic Control Module (ECM) data
B335	Electronic Climate Control (ECC) data
B336	Instrument Panel Control (IPC) data
B337	Programmer data
B410	Regulator
B411	Battery low

BCM TROUBLE CODES (cont'd)

Code	Explanation
B412	Battery high
B420	Relays
B440	Air mix door—valve
B441	Cooling fans
B446	Low refrigerant warning
B447	Very low refrigerant problem
B448	Low refrigerant pressure
B449	Air conditioning HI temperature
B450	Coolant HI temperature—air conditioning
B552	Body Control Module (BCM) memory reset
B556	EE PROM

Year—1988
Model—Fleetwood
Engine—4.5L (273 cid) DFI V8
Engine Code—VIN 5

ECM TROUBLE CODES

Code	Explanation
E012	No distributor signal—turns ON "Service Now" message and "Engine Control System" light
E013	Oxygen sensor not ready—Air Injector Reaction (AIR) and closed loop disengaged—turns ON "Service Soon" message and "Engine Control System" light—engages canister purge
E014	Shorted coolant sensor circuit—Air Injector Reaction (AIR) disengaged—turns ON "Service Soon" message and "Engine Control System" light—forces cooling fans on full speed
E015	Open coolant sensor circuit—Air Injector Reaction (AIR) disengaged—turns ON "Service Soon" message and "Engine Control System" light—forces cooling fans on full speed
E016	Generator voltage out of range—all solenoids disengaged—turns ON "Service Now" message and "Engine Control System" light—disengages Viscous Converter Clutch (VCC) for entire ignition cycle
E018	Open crank signal circuit—turns ON "Service Soon" message and "Engine Control System" light
E019	Shorted fuel pump circuit—turns ON "Service Soon" message and "Engine Control System" light
E020	Open fuel pump circuit—turns ON "Service Now" message and "Engine Control System" light
E021	Shorted Throttle Position Sensor (TPS) circuit—turns ON "Service Soon" message and "Engine Control System" light—disables cruise control for entire ignition cycle
E022	Open Throttle Position Sensor (TPS) circuit—turns ON "Service Soon" message and "Engine Control System" light—disables cruise control for entire ignition cycle
E023	Electronic Spark Timing (EST)/bypass circuit problem—Air Injector Reaction (AIR) disengaged—turns ON "Service Soon" message and "Engine Control System" light—causes system to operate on bypass spark
E024	Speed sensor circuit problem—Viscous Converter Clutch (VCC) and cruise disengaged—turns ON "Service Soon" message and "Engine Control System" light—disengages Viscous Converter Clutch (VCC) for entire ignition cycle
E026	Shorted throttle switch circuit—turns ON "Service Soon" message and "Engine Control System" light
E027	Open throttle switch circuit—turns ON "Service Soon" message and "Engine Control System" light
E028	Open third or fourth gear circuit—turns ON "Service Soon" message and "Engine Control System" light

ECM TROUBLE CODES (cont'd)

Code	Explanation
E030	Idle Speed Control (ISC) circuit problem—turns ON "Service Soon" message and "Engine Control System" light
E031	Shorted Manifold Absolute Pressure (MAP) sensor circuit—Air Injector Reaction (AIR) disengaged—turns ON "Service Now" message and "Engine Control System" light—disenges Viscous Converter Clutch (VCC) for entire ignition cycle
E032	Open Manifold Absolute Pressure (MAP) sensor circuit—Air Injector Reaction (AIR) disengaged—turns ON "Service Now" message and "Engine Control System" light—disengages Viscous Converter Clucth (VCC) for entire ignition cycle
E034	Manifold Absolute Pressure (MAP) sensor signal too high—Air Injector Reaction (AIR) disengaged—turns ON "Service Now" message and "Engine Control System" light—disengages Viscous Converter Clutch (VCC) for entire ignition cycle
E037	Shorted Manifold Air Temperature (MAT) sensor circuit—Air Injector Reaction (AIR) disengaged—turns ON "Service Soon" message and "Engine Control System" light
E038	Open Manifold Air Temperature (MAT) sensor circuit—Air Injector Reaction (AIR) disengaged—turns ON "Service Soon" message and "Engine Control System" light
E039	Viscous Converter Clutch (VCC) engagement problem—turns ON "Service Soon" message and "Engine Control System" light—disengages Viscous Converter Clutch (VCC) for entire ignition cycle
E040	Open Power Steering Pressure Switch (PSPS) circuit—Exhaust Gas Recirculation (EGR) disengaged—turns ON "Service Soon" message and "Engine Control System" light
E044	Lean exhaust signal—Air Injector Reaction (AIR) and closed loop disengaged—turns ON "Service Now" message and "Engine Control System" light—engages canister purge
E045	Rich exhaust signal—Air Injector Reaction (AIR) and closed loop disengaged—turns ON "Service Now" message and "Engine Control System" light—engages canister purge
E047	Body Control Module (BCM)—Electronic Control Module (ECM) data problem—turns ON "Service Soon" message and "Engine Control System" light
E048	Exhaust Gas Recirculation (EGR) system fault—EGR disengaged—turns ON "Service Soon" message and "Engine Control System" light
E052	Electronic Control Module (ECM) memory reset indicator—does not turn on any telltale light or display any message
E053	Distributor signal interrupt—does not turn on any telltale light or display any message
E055	Throttle Position Sensor (TPS) misadjusted—does not turn on any telltale light or display any message
E059	Viscous Converter Clutch (VCC) temperature sensor circuit problem—does not turn on any telltale light or display any message—disengages Viscous Converter Clutch (VCC) for entire ignition problem
E060	Cruise—transmission not in Drive—cruise disengaged—does not turn on any telltale light or display any message
E063	Cruise—car speed and set speed difference too high—cruise disengaged—does not turn on any telltale light or display any message
E064	Cruise—car acceleration too high—cruise disengaged—does not turn on any telltale light or display any message
E065	Cruise—servo position sensor failure—does not turn on any telltale light or display any message
E066	Cruise—engine RPM too high—cruise disengaged—does not turn on any telltale light or display any message
E067	Cruise—cruise switch shorted during enable—does not turn on any telltale light or display any message

GENERAL MOTORS CORPORATION
DIAGNOSTIC CODE DATA

BCM TROUBLE CODES

Code	Explanation
B110	Outside temperature sensor
B111	Air conditioning HI side temperature sensor
B112	Air conditioning LO side temperature sensor
B113	In-car temperature sensor
B115	Sunload temperature sensor
B119	Twilight photocell
B120	Twilight delay pot
B121	Twilight enable switch
B122	Panel lamp dimming pot
B123	Courtesy light switch
B124	Vehicle Speed Sensor (VSS)
B127	PRND321
B334	Electronic Control Module (ECM) data
B335	Electronic Climate Control (ECC) data
B336	Instrument Panel Control (IPC) data
B337	Programmer data
B410	Regulator
B411	Battery low
B412	Battery high
B420	Relays
B440	Air mix door — valve
B441	Cooling fans
B446	Low refrigerant warning
B447	Very low refrigerant problem
B448	Low refrigerant pressure
B449	Air conditioning HI temperature
B450	Coolant HI temperature — air conditioning
B552	Body Control Module (BCM) memory reset
B556	EE PROM

Year — 1988
Model — Brougham
Engine — 5.0L (307 cid) V8
Engine Code — VIN Y

ECM TROUBLE CODES

Code	Explanation
12	No engine speed reference pulse
13	Open oxygen sensor circuit
14	Coolant Temperature Sensor (CTS) circuit — high temperature indicated
15	Coolant Temperature Sensor (CTS) circuit — low temperature indicated
21	Throttle Position Sensor (TPS) circuit — signal voltage high
22	Throttle Position Sensor (TPS) circuit — signal voltage low
23	Mixture Control (M/C) solenoid circuit — signal voltage low
24	Vehicle Speed Sensor (VSS) circuit
31	Canister purge solenoid diagnosis
34	Pressure sensor circuit — signal voltage out of range
41	No distributor reference pulse
42	Electronic Spark Timing (EST) circuit
43	Electronic Spark Control (ESC) circuit
44	Oxygen sensor circuit — lean exhaust indicated
45	Oxygen sensor circuit — rich exhaust indicated
51	PROM error — faulty or incorrect PROM
54	Mixture Control (M/C) solenoid circuit — signal voltage high

GENERAL MOTORS CORPORATION
DIAGNOSTIC CODE DATA

Year – 1988
Model – Seville
Engine – 4.5L (273 cid) DFI V8
Engine Code – VIN 5

ECM TROUBLE CODES

Code	Explanation
E012	No distributor signal – turns ON "Service Now" message and "Engine Control System" light
E013	Oxygen sensor not ready – Air Injector Reaction (AIR) and closed loop disengaged – turns ON "Service Soon" message and "Engine Control System" light – engages canister purge
E014	Shorted coolant sensor circuit – Air Injector Reaction (AIR) disengaged – turns ON "Service Soon" message and "Engine Control System" light – forces cooling fans on full speed
E015	Open coolant sensor circuit – Air Injector Reaction (AIR) disengaged – turns ON "Service Soon" message and "Engine Control System" light – forces cooling fans on full speed
E016	Generator voltage out of range – all solenoids disengaged – turns ON "Service Now" message and "Engine Control System" light – disengages Viscous Converter Clutch (VCC) for entire ignition cycle
E018	Open crank signal circuit – turns ON "Service Soon" message and "Engine Control System" light
E019	Shorted fuel pump circuit – turns ON "Service Soon" message and "Engine Control System" light
E020	Open fuel pump circuit – turns ON "Service Now" message and "Engine Control System" light
E021	Shorted Throttle Position Sensor (TPS) circuit – turns ON "Service Soon" message and "Engine Control System" light – disables cruise control for entire ignition cycle
E022	Open Throttle Position Sensor (TPS) circuit – turns ON "Service Soon" message and "Engine Control System" light – disables cruise control for entire ignition cycle
E023	Electronic Spark Timing (EST)/bypass circuit problem – Air Injector Reaction (AIR) disengaged – turns ON "Service Soon" message and "Engine Control System" light – causes system to operate on bypass spark
E024	Speed sensor circuit problem – Viscous Converter Clutch (VCC) and cruise disengaged – turns ON "Service Soon" message and "Engine Control System" light – disengages Viscous Converter Clutch (VCC) for entire ignition cycle
E026	Shorted throttle switch circuit – turns ON "Service Soon" message and "Engine Control System" light
E027	Open throttle switch circuit – turns ON "Service Soon" message and "Engine Control System" light
E028	Open third or fourth gear circuit – turns ON "Service Soon" message and "Engine Control System" light
E030	Idle Speed Control (ISC) circuit problem – turns ON "Service Soon" message and "Engine Control System" light
E031	Shorted Manifold Absolute Pressure (MAP) sensor circuit – Air Injector Reaction (AIR) disengaged – turns ON "Service Now" message and "Engine Control System" light – disenges Viscous Converter Clutch (VCC) for entire ignition cycle
E032	Open Manifold Absolute Pressure (MAP) sensor circuit – Air Injector Reaction (AIR) disengaged – turns ON "Service Now" message and "Engine Control System" light – disengages Viscous Converter Clucth (VCC) for entire ignition cycle
E034	Manifold Absolute Pressure (MAP) sensor signal too high – Air Injector Reaction (AIR) disengaged – turns ON "Service Now" message and "Engine Control System" light – disengages Viscous Converter Clutch (VCC) for entire ignition cycle
E037	Shorted Manifold Air Temperature (MAT) sensor circuit – Air Injector Reaction (AIR) disengaged – turns ON "Service Soon" message and "Engine Control System" light
E038	Open Manifold Air Temperature (MAT) sensor circuit – Air Injector Reaction (AIR) disengaged – turns ON "Service Soon" message and "Engine Control System" light
E039	Viscous Converter Clutch (VCC) engagement problem – turns ON "Service Soon" message and "Engine Control System" light – disengages Viscous Converter Clutch (VCC) for entire ignition cycle
E040	Open Power Steering Pressure Switch (PSPS) circuit – Exhaust Gas Recirculation (EGR) disengaged – turns ON "Service Soon" message and "Engine Control System" light

ECM TROUBLE CODES (cont'd)

Code	Explanation
E044	Lean exhaust signal—Air Injector Reaction (AIR) and closed loop disengaged—turns ON "Service Now" message and "Engine Control System" light—engages canister purge
E045	Rich exhaust signal—Air Injector Reaction (AIR) and closed loop disengaged—turns ON "Service Now" message and "Engine Control System" light—engages canister purge
E047	Body Control Module (BCM)—Electronic Control Module (ECM) data problem—turns ON "Service Soon" message and "Engine Control System" light
E048	Exhaust Gas Recirculation (EGR) system fault—EGR disengaged—turns ON "Service Soon" message and "Engine Control System" light
E052	Electronic Control Module (ECM) memory reset indicator—does not turn on any telltale light or display any message
E053	Distributor signal interrupt—does not turn on any telltale light or display any message
E055	Throttle Position Sensor (TPS) misadjusted—does not turn on any telltale light or display any message
E059	Viscous Converter Clutch (VCC) temperature sensor circuit problem—does not turn on any telltale light or display any message—disengages Viscous Converter Clutch (VCC) for entire ignition problem
E060	Cruise—transmission not in Drive—cruise disengaged—does not turn on any telltale light or display any message
E063	Cruise—car speed and set speed difference too high—cruise disengaged—does not turn on any telltale light or display any message
E064	Cruise—car acceleration too high—cruise disengaged—does not turn on any telltale light or display any message
E065	Cruise—servo position sensor failure—does not turn on any telltale light or display any message
E066	Cruise—engine RPM too high—cruise disengaged—does not turn on any telltale light or display any message
E067	Cruise—cruise switch shorted during enable—does not turn on any telltale light or display any message

BCM TROUBLE CODES

Code	Explanation
B110	Outside temperature sensor
B111	Air conditioning HI side temperature sensor
B112	Air conditioning LO side temperature sensor
B113	In-car temperature sensor
B115	Sunload temperature sensor
B119	Twilight photocell
B120	Twilight delay pot
B121	Twilight enable switch
B122	Panel lamp dimming pot
B123	Courtesy light switch
B124	Vehicle Speed Sensor (VSS)
B127	PRND321
B334	Electronic Control Module (ECM) data
B335	Electronic Climate Control (ECC) data
B336	Instrument Panel Control (IPC) data
B337	Programmer data
B410	Regulator
B411	Battery low

BCM TROUBLE CODES (cont'd)

Code	Explanation
B412	Battery high
B420	Relays
B440	Air mix door—valve
B441	Cooling fans
B446	Low refrigerant warning
B447	Very low refrigerant problem
B448	Low refrigerant pressure
B449	Air conditioning HI temperature
B450	Coolant HI temperature—air conditioning
B552	Body Control Module (BCM) memory reset
B556	EE PROM

Year—1988
Model—Eldorado
Engine—4.5L (273 cid) DFI V8
Engine Code—VIN 5

ECM TROUBLE CODES

Code	Explanation
E012	No distributor signal—turns ON "Service Now" message and "Engine Control System" light
E013	Oxygen sensor not ready—Air Injector Reaction (AIR) and closed loop disengaged—turns ON "Service Soon" message and "Engine Control System" light—engages canister purge
E014	Shorted coolant sensor circuit—Air Injector Reaction (AIR) disengaged—turns ON "Service Soon" message and "Engine Control System" light—forces cooling fans on full speed
E015	Open coolant sensor circuit—Air Injector Reaction (AIR) disengaged—turns ON "Service Soon" message and "Engine Control System" light—forces cooling fans on full speed
E016	Generator voltage out of range—all solenoids disengaged—turns ON "Service Now" message and "Engine Control System" light—disengages Viscous Converter Clutch (VCC) for entire ignition cycle
E018	Open crank signal circuit—turns ON "Service Soon" message and "Engine Control System" light
E019	Shorted fuel pump circuit—turns ON "Service Soon" message and "Engine Control System" light
E020	Open fuel pump circuit—turns ON "Service Now" message and "Engine Control System" light
E021	Shorted Throttle Position Sensor (TPS) circuit—turns ON "Service Soon" message and "Engine Control System" light—disables cruise control for entire ignition cycle
E022	Open Throttle Position Sensor (TPS) circuit—turns ON "Service Soon" message and "Engine Control System" light—disables cruise control for entire ignition cycle
E023	Electronic Spark Timing (EST)/bypass circuit problem—Air Injector Reaction (AIR) disengaged—turns ON "Service Soon" message and "Engine Control System" light—causes system to operate on bypass spark
E024	Speed sensor circuit problem—Viscous Converter Clutch (VCC) and cruise disengaged—turns ON "Service Soon" message and "Engine Control System" light—disengages Viscous Converter Clutch (VCC) for entire ignition cycle
E026	Shorted throttle switch circuit—turns ON "Service Soon" message and "Engine Control System" light
E027	Open throttle switch circuit—turns ON "Service Soon" message and "Engine Control System" light
E028	Open third or fourth gear circuit—turns ON "Service Soon" message and "Engine Control System" light

ECM TROUBLE CODES (cont'd)

Code	Explanation
E030	Idle Speed Control (ISC) circuit problem — turns ON "Service Soon" message and "Engine Control System" light
E031	Shorted Manifold Absolute Pressure (MAP) sensor circuit — Air Injector Reaction (AIR) disengaged — turns ON "Service Now" message and "Engine Control System" light — disenges Viscous Converter Clutch (VCC) for entire ignition cycle
E032	Open Manifold Absolute Pressure (MAP) sensor circuit — Air Injector Reaction (AIR) disengaged — turns ON "Service Now" message and "Engine Control System" light — disengages Viscous Converter Clucth (VCC) for entire ignition cycle
E034	Manifold Absolute Pressure (MAP) sensor signal too high — Air Injector Reaction (AIR) disengaged — turns ON "Service Now" message and "Engine Control System" light — disengages Viscous Converter Clutch (VCC) for entire ignition cycle
E037	Shorted Manifold Air Temperature (MAT) sensor circuit — Air Injector Reaction (AIR) disengaged — turns ON "Service Soon" message and "Engine Control System" light
E038	Open Manifold Air Temperature (MAT) sensor circuit — Air Injector Reaction (AIR) disengaged — turns ON "Service Soon" message and "Engine Control System" light
E039	Viscous Converter Clutch (VCC) engagement problem — turns ON "Service Soon" message and "Engine Control System" light — disengages Viscous Converter Clutch (VCC) for entire ignition cycle
E040	Open Power Steering Pressure Switch (PSPS) circuit — Exhaust Gas Recirculation (EGR) disengaged — turns ON "Service Soon" message and "Engine Control System" light
E044	Lean exhaust signal — Air Injector Reaction (AIR) and closed loop disengaged — turns ON "Service Now" message and "Engine Control System" light — engages canister purge
E045	Rich exhaust signal — Air Injector Reaction (AIR) and closed loop disengaged — turns ON "Service Now" message and "Engine Control System" light — engages canister purge
E047	Body Control Module (BCM) — Electronic Control Module (ECM) data problem — turns ON "Service Soon" message and "Engine Control System" light
E048	Exhaust Gas Recirculation (EGR) system fault — EGR disengaged — turns ON "Service Soon" message and "Engine Control System" light
E052	Electronic Control Module (ECM) memory reset indicator — does not turn on any telltale light or display any message
E053	Distributor signal interrupt — does not turn on any telltale light or display any message
E055	Throttle Position Sensor (TPS) misadjusted — does not turn on any telltale light or display any message
E059	Viscous Converter Clutch (VCC) temperature sensor circuit problem — does not turn on any telltale light or display any message — disengages Viscous Converter Clutch (VCC) for entire ignition problem
E060	Cruise — transmission not in Drive — cruise disengaged — does not turn on any telltale light or display any message
E063	Cruise — car speed and set speed difference too high — cruise disengaged — does not turn on any telltale light or display any message
E064	Cruise — car acceleration too high — cruise disengaged — does not turn on any telltale light or display any message
E065	Cruise — servo position sensor failure — does not turn on any telltale light or display any message
E066	Cruise — engine RPM too high — cruise disengaged — does not turn on any telltale light or display any message
E067	Cruise — cruise switch shorted during enable — does not turn on any telltale light or display any message

BCM TROUBLE CODES

Code	Explanation
B110	Outside temperature sensor
B111	Air conditioning HI side temperature sensor

BCM TROUBLE CODES (cont'd)

Code	Explanation
B112	Air conditioning LO side temperature sensor
B113	In-car temperature sensor
B115	Sunload temperature sensor
B119	Twilight photocell
B120	Twilight delay pot
B121	Twilight enable switch
B122	Panel lamp dimming pot
B123	Courtesy light switch
B124	Vehicle Speed Sensor (VSS)
B127	PRND321
B334	Electronic Control Module (ECM) data
B335	Electronic Climate Control (ECC) data
B336	Instrument Panel Control (IPC) data
B337	Programmer data
B410	Regulator
B411	Battery low
B412	Battery high
B420	Relays
B440	Air mix door—valve
B441	Cooling fans
B446	Low refrigerant warning
B447	Very low refrigerant problem
B448	Low refrigerant pressure
B449	Air conditioning HI temperature
B450	Coolant HI temperature—air conditioning
B552	Body Control Module (BCM) memory reset
B556	EE PROM

Year—1988
Model—Allante
Engine—4.1L (250 cid) MPFI V8
Engine Code—VIN 7

ECM TROUBLE CODES

Code	Explanation
E012	No distributor signal
E013	Right oxygen sensor not ready
E014	Shorted coolant sensor circuit
E015	Open coolant sensor circuit
E016	Generator voltage out of range
E017	Left oxygen sensor not ready
E019	Shorted fuel pump circuit
E020	Open fuel pump circuit

ECM TROUBLE CODES (cont'd)

Code	Explanation
E021	Shorted Throttle Position Sensor (TPS) circuit
E022	Open Throttle Position Sensor (TPS) circuit
E023	Electronic Spark Timing (EST)/bypass circuit problem
E024	Speed sensor circuit problem
E026	Shorted throttle switch circuit
E027	Open throttle switch circuit
E028	Open 3rd gear switch or shorted 2–3 shift solenoid
E029	Shorted 3rd gear switch or open 2–3 shift solenoid
E030	Idle Speed Control (ISC) circuit problem
E031	Shorted Manifold Absolute Pressure (MAP) sensor circuit
E032	Open Manifold Absolute Pressure (MAP) sensor circuit
E034	Manifold Absolute Pressure (MAP) sensor signal too high
E037	Shorted Manifold Air Temperature (MAT) sensor circuit
E038	Open Manifold Air Temperature (MAT) sensor circuit
E039	Viscous Converter Clutch (VCC) engagement problem
E040	Open power steering pressure switch circuit
E041	CAM sensor problem

BCM TROUBLE CODES

Code	Explanation
B110	Outside air temperature circuit problem
B111	Air conditioning high side temperature circuit problem
B112	Air conditioning low side temperature circuit problem
B113	In-car temperature circuit problem
B115	Sunload temperature circuit problem
B119	Twilight sentinel photosensor circuit problem
B120	Twilight sentinel delay pot circuit problem
B122	Panel lamp dimming pot circuit problem
B124	Speed sensor circuit problem
B127	PRND321 sensor circuit problem
B132	Oil pressure sensor failure
B334	Loss of Electronic Control Module (ECM) data
B335	Loss of CCDIC data
B336	Loss of Instrument Panel Control (IPC) data
B337	Loss of programmer data
B409	Charging system failure
B410	Charging system problem
B411	Battery volts too low
B412	Battery volts too high
B420	Body Control Module (BCM) output driver 1 failure
B421	Body Control Module (BCM) output driver 2 failure
B440	Air mix door problem
B441	Cooling fans problem

BCM TROUBLE CODES (cont'd)

Code	Explanation
B446	Low air conditioning refrigerant condition warning
B447	Very low air conditioning refrigerant condition warning
B448	Very low air conditioning refrigerant pressure condition
B449	Air conditioning high side temperature too high
B450	Coolant temperature too high
B480	Loss of anti-lock data
B481	Anti-lock fault
B552	Body Control Module (BCM) memory reset indicator
B556	Body Control Module (BCM) EEPROM error

Year – 1988
Model – Cimarron
Engine – 2.8L (173 cid) MPFI V6
Engine Code – VIN W

ECM TROUBLE CODES

Code	Explanation
13	Oxygen sensor circuit – open circuit
14	Coolant Temperature Sensor (CTS) circuit – high temperature indicated
15	Coolant Temperature Sensor (CTS) circuit – low temperature indicated
21	Throttle Position Sensor (TPS) circuit – signal voltage high
22	Throttle Position Sensor (TPS) circuit – signal voltage low
23	Manifold Air Temperature (MAT) sensor circuit – low temperature indicated
24	Vehicle Speed Sensor (VSS) circuit
25	Manifold Air Temperature (MAT) sensor circuit – high temperature indicated
33	Manifold Absolute Pressure (MAP) sensor circuit – signal voltage high – low vacuum
34	Manifold Absolute Pressure (MAP) sensor circuit – signal voltage low – high vacuum
35	Idle speed error
41	Cylinder select error – faulty or incorrect Mem-Cal
42	Electronic Spark Timing (EST) circuit
43	Electronic Spark Control (ESC) circuit
44	Oxygen sensor circuit – lean exhaust indicated
45	Oxygen sensor circuit – rich exhaust indicated
54	Fuel pump circuit – low voltage
51	Mem-Cal error – faulty or incorrect Mem-Cal
52	Calpak error – faulty or incorrect calpak
53	System over voltage
61	Degraded oxygen sensor

Year – 1989
Model – DeVille
Engine – 4.5L (273 cid) DFI V8
Engine Code – VIN 5

ECM TROUBLE CODES

Code	Explanation
E12	No distributor signal – turns ON "Service Engine Soon" light
E13	Oxygen sensor not ready – Air Injector Reaction (AIR) and closed loop disengaged – turns ON "Service Engine Soon" light – enable canister purge
E14	Shorted coolant sensor circuit – Air Injector Reaction (AIR) disengaged – turns ON "Service Engine Soon" light – forces cooling fans on full speed
E15	Open coolant sensor circuit – Air Injector Reaction (AIR) disengaged – turns ON "Service Engine Soon" light – forces cooling fans on full speed
E16	Generator voltage out of range – all solenoids disengaged – turns ON "Service Vehicle Soon" light – disengages Viscous Converter Clutch (VCC) for entire ignition cycle
E18	Open crank signal circuit – turns ON "Service Vehicle Soon" light
E19	Shorted fuel pump circuit – turns ON "Service Vehicle Soon" light
E20	Open fuel pump circuit – turns ON "Service Vehicle Soon" light
E21	Shorted Throttle Position Sensor (TPS) circuit – turns ON "Service Engine Soon" light – disables cruise for entire ignition cycle
E22	Open Throttle Position Sensor (TPS) circuit – turns ON "Service Engine Soon" light – disables cruise for entire ignition cycle
E23	Electronic Spark Timing (EST)/bypass circuit problem – Air Injector Reaction (AIR) disengaged – Exhaust Gas Recirculation (EGR) disengaged – turns ON "Service Engine Soon" light – causes system to operate on bypass spark
E24	Speed sensor circuit problem – Viscous Converter Clutch (VCC) and cruise disengaged – turns ON "Service Engine Soon" light – disables cruise for entire ignition cycle – disengages Viscous Converter Clutch (VCC) for entire ignition cycle
E26	Shorted throttle switch circuit – turns ON "Service Engine Soon" light
E27	Open throttle switch circuit – turns ON "Service Engine Soon" light
E28	Open 3rd or 4th gear circuit – turns ON "Service Engine Soon" light
E30	RPM error too great – turns ON "Service Engine Soon" light
E31	Shorted Manifold Absolute Pressure (MAP) sensor circuit – Air Injector Reaction (AIR) disengaged – turns ON "Service Engine Soon" light – disengages Viscous Converter Clutch (VCC) for entire ignition cycle
E32	Open Manifold Absolute Pressure (MAP) sensor circuit – Air Injector Reaction (AIR) disengaged – turns ON "Service Engine Soon" light – disengages Viscous Converter Clutch (VCC) for entire ignition cycle
E34	Manifold Absolute Pressure (MAP) sensor signal too high – Air Injector Reaction (AIR) disengaged – turns ON "Service Engine Soon" light – disengages Viscous Converter Clutch (VCC) for entire ignition cycle
E37	Shorted Manifold Air Temperature (MAT) sensor circuit – Air Injector Reaction (AIR) disengaged – turns ON "Service Engine Soon" light
E38	Open Manifold Air Temperature (MAT) sensor circuit – Air Injector Reaction (AIR) disengaged – turns ON "Service Engine Soon" light
E39	Viscous Converter Clutch (VCC) engagement problem – turns ON "Service Engine Soon" light – disengages Viscous Converter Clutch (VCC) for entire ignition cycle
E40	Open Power Steering Pressure Switch (PSPS) circuit – turns ON "Service Engine Soon" light
E44	Lean exhaust signal – Air Injector Reaction (AIR) and closed loop disengaged – turns ON "Service Engine Soon" light – enable canister purge

ECM TROUBLE CODES (cont'd)

Code	Explanation
E45	Rich exhaust signal—Air Injector Reaction (AIR) and closed loop disengaged—turns ON "Service Engine Soon" light—enable canister purge
E47	Body Control Module (BCM)—Electronic Control Module (ECM) data problem—air conditioning clutch disengaged—turns ON "Service Engine Soon" light
E48	Exhaust Gas Recirculation (EGR) system fault—EGR disengaged—turns ON "Service Engine Soon" light
E52	Electronic Control Module (ECM) memory reset indicator—does not turn on any telltale light
E53	Distributor signal interrupt—does not turn on any telltale light
E55	Throttle Position Sensor (TPS) misadjusted—does not turn on any telltale light
E59	Viscous Converter Clutch (VCC) temperature sensor circuit problem—turns ON "Service Engine Soon" light—disengages Viscous Converter Clutch (VCC) for entire ignition problem
E60	Cruise—transmission not in Drive—cruise disengaged—does not turn on any telltale light
E63	Cruise—car speed and set speed difference too high—cruise disengaged—does not turn on any telltale light
E64	Cruise—car acceleration too high—cruise disengaged—does not turn on any telltale light
E65	Cruise—coolant temperature too high—cruise disengaged—does not turn on any telltale light
E66	Cruise—engine RPM too high—cruise disengaged—does not turn on any telltale light
E67	Cruise—cruise switch shorted during enable—cruise disengaged—does not turn on any telltale light

BCM TROUBLE CODES

Code	Explanation
F10	Outside air temperature circuit problem—does not turn on any telltale light
F11	Air conditioning high side temperature circuit problem—does not turn on any telltale light—turns ON cooling fans whenever air conditioning clutch is engaged
F12	Air conditioning low side temperature circuit problem—air conditioning clutch disengaged—does not turn on any telltale light
F13	In-car temperature circuit problem—does not turn on any telltale light
F30	Climate Control Panel (CCP) to Body Control Module (BCM) data problem—does not turn on any telltale light—displays "c" for clock problem or "d" for data problem—turns ON front defog at 75°F
F31	FDC to Body Control Module (BCM) data problem—does not turn on any telltale light—displays "c" for clock problem or "d" for data problem
F32	Electronic Control Module (ECM)—Body Control Module (BCM) data problem—does not turn on any telltale light—forces cooling fans on full speed
F40	Air mix door problem—does not turn on any telltale light
F43	Heated windshield failure—does not turn on any telltale light
F46	Low air conditioning refrigerant condition warning—turns ON "Service Air Cond" light for a period of time
F47	Very low air conditioning refrigerant condition warning—air conditioning clutch disengaged—turns ON "Service Air Cond" light for a period of time, & switches ECC mode to Econ
F48	Very low air conditioning refrigerant pressure condition—air conditioning clutch disengaged—turns ON "Service Air Cond" light for a period of time, & switches ECC mode to Econ
F49	High temperature clutch disengage—air conditioning clutch disengaged—does not turn on any telltale light
F51	Body Control Module (BCM) PROM error—does not turn on any telltale light—displays "—151" on Climate Control Panel (CCP) and turns ON front defog

Year — 1989
Model — Fleetwood
Engine — 4.5L (273 cid) DFI V8
Engine Code — VIN 5

ECM TROUBLE CODES

Code	Explanation
E012	No distributor signal — turns ON "Service Now" message and "Engine Control System" light
E013	Oxygen sensor not ready — Air Injector Reaction (AIR) and closed loop disengaged — turns ON "Service Soon" message and "Engine Control System" light — engages canister purge
E014	Shorted coolant sensor circuit — Air Injector Reaction (AIR) disengaged — turns ON "Service Soon" message and "Engine Control System" light — forces cooling fans on full speed
E015	Open coolant sensor circuit — Air Injector Reaction (AIR) disengaged — turns ON "Service Soon" message and "Engine Control System" light — forces cooling fans on full speed
E016	Generator voltage out of range — all solenoids disengaged — turns ON "Service Now" message and "Engine Control System" light — disengages Viscous Converter Clutch (VCC) for entire ignition cycle
E018	Open crank signal circuit — turns ON "Service Soon" message and "Engine Control System" light
E019	Shorted fuel pump circuit — turns ON "Service Soon" message and "Engine Control System" light
E020	Open fuel pump circuit — turns ON "Service Now" message and "Engine Control System" light
E021	Shorted Throttle Position Sensor (TPS) circuit — turns ON "Service Soon" message and "Engine Control System" light — disables cruise control for entire ignition cycle
E022	Open Throttle Position Sensor (TPS) circuit — turns ON "Service Soon" message and "Engine Control System" light — disables cruise control for entire ignition cycle
E023	Electronic Spark Timing (EST)/bypass circuit problem — Air Injector Reaction (AIR) disengaged — turns ON "Service Soon" message and "Engine Control System" light — causes system to operate on bypass spark
E024	Speed sensor circuit problem — Viscous Converter Clutch (VCC) disengaged — turns ON "Service Soon" message and "Engine Control System" light — disengages Viscous Converter Clutch (VCC) for entire ignition cycle
E026	Shorted throttle switch circuit — turns ON "Service Soon" message and "Engine Control System" light
E027	Open throttle switch circuit — turns ON "Service Soon" message and "Engine Control System" light
E028	Open 3rd or 4th gear circuit — turns ON "Service Soon" message and "Engine Control System" light
E030	Idle Speed Control (ISC) circuit problem — turns ON "Service Soon" message and "Engine Control System" light
E031	Shorted Manifold Absolute Pressure (MAP) sensor circuit — Air Injector Reaction (AIR) disengaged — turns ON "Service Now" message and "Engine Control System" light — disenges Viscous Converter Clutch (VCC) for entire ignition cycle
E032	Open Manifold Absolute Pressure (MAP) sensor circuit — Air Injector Reaction (AIR) disengaged — turns ON "Service Now" message and "Engine Control System" light — disengages Viscous Converter Clucth (VCC) for entire ignition cycle
E034	Manifold Absolute Pressure (MAP) sensor signal too high — Air Injector Reaction (AIR) disengaged — turns ON "Service Now" message and "Engine Control System" light — disengages Viscous Converter Clutch (VCC) for entire ignition cycle
E037	Shorted Manifold Air Temperature (MAT) sensor circuit — Air Injector Reaction (AIR) disengaged — turns ON "Service Soon" message and "Engine Control System" light
E038	Open Manifold Air Temperature (MAT) sensor circuit — Air Injector Reaction (AIR) disengaged — turns ON "Service Soon" message and "Engine Control System" light
E039	Viscous Converter Clutch (VCC) engagement problem — turns ON "Service Soon" message and "Engine Control System" light — disengages Viscous Converter Clutch (VCC) for entire ignition cycle
E040	Open Power Steering Pressure Switch (PSPS) circuit — Exhaust Gas Recirculation (EGR) disengaged — turns ON "Service Soon" message and "Engine Control System" light

ECM TROUBLE CODES (cont'd)

Code	Explanation
E044	Lean exhaust signal—Air Injector Reaction (AIR) and closed loop disengaged—turns ON "Service Now" message and "Engine Control System" light—engages canister purge
E045	Rich exhaust signal—Air Injector Reaction (AIR) and closed loop disengaged—turns ON "Service Now" message and "Engine Control System" light—engages canister purge
E047	Body Control Module (BCM)—Electronic Control Module (ECM) data problem—turns ON "Service Soon" message and "Engine Control System" light
E048	Exhaust Gas Recirculation (EGR) system fault—EGR disengaged—turns ON "Service Soon" message and "Engine Control System" light
E052	Electronic Control Module (ECM) memory reset indicator—does not turn on any telltale light or display any message
E053	Distributor signal interrupt—does not turn on any telltale light or display any message
E055	Throttle Position Sensor (TPS) misadjusted—does not turn on any telltale light or display any message
E059	Viscous Converter Clutch (VCC) temperature sensor circuit problem—does not turn on any telltale light or display any message—disengages Viscous Converter Clutch (VCC) for entire ignition problem
E060	Cruise—transmission not in Drive—cruise disengaged—does not turn on any telltale light or display any message
E063	Cruise—car speed and set speed difference too high—cruise disengaged—does not turn on any telltale light or display any message
E064	Cruise—car acceleration too high—cruise disengaged—does not turn on any telltale light or display any message
E065	Cruise—servo position sensor failure—does not turn on any telltale light or display any message
E066	Cruise—engine RPM too high—cruise disengaged—does not turn on any telltale light or display any message
E067	Cruise—cruise switch shorted during enable—does not turn on any telltale light or display any message

BCM TROUBLE CODES

Code	Explanation
B110	Outside temperature sensor
B111	Air conditioning HI side temperature sensor
B112	Air conditioning LO side temperature sensor
B113	In-car temperature sensor
B115	Sunload temperature sensor
B119	Twilight photocell
B120	Twilight delay pot
B121	Twilight enable switch
B122	Panel lamp dimming pot
B123	Courtesy light switch
B124	Vehicle Speed Sensor (VSS)
B127	PRND321
B334	Electronic Control Module (ECM) data
B335	Electronic Climate Control (ECC) data
B336	Instrument Panel Control (IPC) data
B337	Programmer data
B410	Regulator
B411	Battery low

BCM TROUBLE CODES (cont'd)

Code	Explanation
B412	Battery high
B420	Relays
B440	Air mix door—valve
B441	Cooling fans
B446	Low refrigerant warning
B447	Very low refrigerant problem
B448	Low refrigerant pressure
B449	Air conditioning HI temperature
B450	Coolant HI temperature—air conditioning
B552	Body Control Module (BCM) memory reset
B556	EE PROM

Year — 1989
Model — Brougham
Engine — 5.0L (307 cid) V8
Engine Code — VIN Y

ECM TROUBLE CODES

Code	Explanation
12	No engine speed reference pulse
13	Open oxygen sensor circuit
14	Coolant Temperature Sensor (CTS) circuit—high temperature indicated
15	Coolant Temperature Sensor (CTS) circuit—low temperature indicated
21	Throttle Position Sensor (TPS) circuit—signal voltage high
22	Throttle Position Sensor (TPS) circuit—signal voltage low
23	Mixture Control (M/C) solenoid circuit—signal voltage low
24	Vehicle Speed Sensor (VSS) circuit
31	Canister purge solenoid diagnosis
34	Pressure sensor circuit—signal voltage out of range
41	No distributor reference pulse
42	Electronic Spark Timing (EST) circuit
43	Electronic Spark Control (ESC) circuit
44	Oxygen sensor circuit—lean exhaust indicated
45	Oxygen sensor circuit—rich exhaust indicated
51	PROM error—faulty or incorrect PROM
54	Mixture Control (M/C) solenoid circuit—signal voltage high

GENERAL MOTORS CORPORATION
DIAGNOSTIC CODE DATA

Year — 1989
Model — Seville
Engine — 4.5L (273 cid) DFI V8
Engine Code — VIN 5

ECM TROUBLE CODES

Code	Explanation
E012	No distributor signal — turns ON "Service Engine Soon" light
E013	Oxygen sensor not ready — Air Injector Reaction (AIR) and closed loop disengaged — turns ON "Service Engine Soon" light — enables canister purge
E014	Shorted coolant sensor circuit — Air Injector Reaction (AIR) disengaged — turns ON "Service Engine Soon" light — forces cooling fans on full speed
E015	Open coolant sensor circuit — Air Injector Reaction (AIR) disengaged — turns ON "Service Engine Soon" light — forces cooling fans on full speed
E016	Generator voltage out of range — all solenoids disengaged — displays "Service Car Soon" on Driver Information Center (DIC) — disengages Viscous Converter Clutch (VCC) for entire ignition cycle
E018	Open crank signal circuit — displays "Service Car Soon" on Driver Information Center (DIC)
E019	Shorted fuel pump circuit — displays "Service Car Soon" on Driver Information Center (DIC)
E020	Open fuel pump circuit — displays "Service Car Soon" on Driver Information Center (DIC)
E021	Shorted Throttle Position Sensor (TPS) circuit — turns ON "Service Engine Soon" light — disables cruise control for ignition cycle
E022	Open Throttle Position Sensor (TPS) circuit — turns ON "Service Engine Soon" light — disables cruise control for ignition cycle
E023	Electronic Spark Timing (EST)/bypass circuit problem — Air Injector Reaction (AIR) disengaged — Exhaust Gas Recirculation (EGR) disengaged — turns ON "Service Engine Soon" light — causes system to operate on bypass spark
E024	Speed sensor circuit problem — Viscous Converter Clutch (VCC) and cruise disengaged — turns ON "Service Engine Soon" light — disengages Viscous Converter Clutch (VCC) for entire ignition cycle
E026	Shorted throttle switch circuit — turns ON "Service Engine Soon" light
E027	Open throttle switch circuit — turns ON "Service Engine Soon" light
E028	Open 3rd or 4th gear circuit — turns ON "Service Engine Soon" light
E030	RPM error too great — turns ON "Service Engine Soon" light
E031	Shorted Manifold Absolute Pressure (MAP) sensor circuit — Air Injector Reaction (AIR) disengaged — turns ON "Service Engine Soon" light — disengages Viscous Converter Clutch (VCC) for entire ignition cycle
E032	Open Manifold Absolute Pressure (MAP) sensor circuit — Air Injector Reaction (AIR) disengaged — turns ON "Service Engine Soon" light — disengages Viscous Converter Clucth (VCC) for entire ignition cycle
E034	Manifold Absolute Pressure (MAP) sensor signal too high — Air Injector Reaction (AIR) disengaged — turns ON "Service Engine Soon" light — disengages Viscous Converter Clutch (VCC) for entire ignition cycle
E037	Shorted Manifold Air Temperature (MAT) sensor circuit — Air Injector Reaction (AIR) disengaged — turns ON "Service Engine Soon" light
E038	Open Manifold Air Temperature (MAT) sensor circuit — Air Injector Reaction (AIR) disengaged — turns ON "Service Engine Soon" light
E039	Viscous Converter Clutch (VCC) engagement problem — turns ON "Service Engine Soon" light — disengages Viscous Converter Clutch (VCC) for entire ignition cycle
E040	Open Power Steering Pressure Switch (PSPS) circuit — turns ON "Service Engine Soon" light
E044	Lean exhaust signal — Air Injector Reaction (AIR) and closed loop disengaged — turns ON "Service Engine Soon" light — enables canister purge
E045	Rich exhaust signal — Air Injector Reaction (AIR) and closed loop disengaged — turns ON "Service Engine Soon" light — enables canister purge

ECM TROUBLE CODES (cont'd)

Code	Explanation
E047	Body Control Module (BCM)—Electronic Control Module (ECM) data problem—turns ON "Service Engine Soon" light
E048	Exhaust Gas Recirculation (EGR) system fault—EGR disengaged—turns ON "Service Engine Soon" light
E052	Electronic Control Module (ECM) memory reset indicator—does not turn on any telltale light or display any message
E053	Distributor signal interrupt—does not turn on any telltale light or display any message
E055	Throttle Position Sensor (TPS) misadjusted—does not turn on any telltale light or display any message
E058	Pass key fuel enable—displays status message on Driver Information Center (DIC)
E059	Viscous Converter Clutch (VCC) temperature sensor circuit problem—turns ON "Service Engine Soon" light—disengages Viscous Converter Clutch (VCC) for entire ignition problem
E060	Cruise—transmission not in Drive—cruise disengaged—does not turn on any telltale light or display any message
E063	Cruise—car speed and set speed difference too high—cruise disengaged—does not turn on any telltale light or display any message
E064	Cruise—car acceleration too high—cruise disengaged—does not turn on any telltale light or display any message
E065	Cruise—coolant temperature too high—cruise disengaged—does not turn on any telltale light or display any message
E066	Cruise—engine RPM too high—cruise disengaged—does not turn on any telltale light or display any message
E067	Cruise—cruise switch shorted during enable—cruise disengaged—does not turn on any telltale light or display any message

BCM TROUBLE CODES

Code	Explanation
B110	Outside air temperature circuit problem—displays status message on Driver Information Center (DIC)
B111	Air conditioning HI side temperature circuit problem—forces cooling fans on full speed
B112	Air conditioning LO side temperature circuit problem—air conditioning clutch disengaged—displays status message on Driver Information Center (DIC)
B113	In-car temperature circuit problem—displays status message on Driver Information Center (DIC)
B115	Sunload temperature circuit problem—displays status message on Driver Information Center (DIC)
B119	Twilight sentinel photosensor circuit problem—does not turn on any telltale light or display any message
B120	Twilight sentinel delay pot circuit problem—does not turn on any telltale light or display any message
B121	Twilight sentinel enable circuit problem—does not turn on any telltale light or display any message
B122	Panel lamp dimming pot circuit problem—does not turn on any telltale light or display any message
B123	Panel lamp enable circuit problem—does not turn on any telltale light or display any message
B124	Speed sensor circuit problem—does not turn on any telltale light or display any message
B127	PRND321 sensor circuit problem—displays square box around each PRND321 position on Instrument Panel Cluster (IPC)—displays status message on Driver Information Center (DIC)
B334	Loss of Electronic Control Module (ECM) data—air conditioning clutch—displays status message on Driver Information Center (DIC)—forces cooling fans on full speed
B335	Loss of Climate Control/Driver Information Center (CCDIC) data—displays status message on Driver Information Center (DIC)
B336	Loss of Instrument Panel Control (IPC) data—displays status message on Driver Information Center (DIC)

BCM TROUBLE CODES (cont'd)

Code	Explanation
B337	Loss of programmer data—displays status message on Driver Information Center (DIC)
B410	Charging system problem—displays status message on Driver Information Center (DIC)
B411	Battery volts too low—displays status message on Driver Information Center (DIC)
B412	Battery volts too high—displays status message on Driver Information Center (DIC)
B420	Relay circuit problem—does not turn on any telltale light or display any message
B440	Air mix door problem—does not turn on any telltale light or display any message
B441	Cooling fans problem—displays status message on Driver Information Center (DIC)—forces cooling fans on full speed
B446	Low air conditioning refrigerant condition warning—displays status message on Driver Information Center (DIC)
B447	Very low air conditioning refrigerant condition warning—air conditioning clutch—displays status message on Driver Information Center (DIC)—switches ECC mode to ECON
B448	Very low air conditioning refrigerant pressure condition—displays status message on Driver Information Center (DIC)—switches ECC mode to ECON
B449	Air conditioning HI side temperature too high—air conditioning clutch—displays status message on Driver Information Center (DIC)
B450	Coolant temperature too HI—air conditioning clutch—displays status message on Driver Information Center (DIC)
B552	Body Control Module (BCM) memory reset indicator—does not turn on any telltale light or display any message
B556	Body Control Module (BCM) EE PROM error—displays "Error" in season odometer

Year—1989
Model—Eldorado
Engine—4.5L (273 cid) DFI V8
Engine Code—VIN 5

ECM TROUBLE CODES

Code	Explanation
E012	No distributor signal—turns ON "Service Engine Soon" light
E013	Oxygen sensor not ready—Air Injector Reaction (AIR) and closed loop disengaged—turns ON "Service Engine Soon" light—enables canister purge
E014	Shorted coolant sensor circuit—Air Injector Reaction (AIR) disengaged—turns ON "Service Engine Soon" light—forces cooling fans on full speed
E015	Open coolant sensor circuit—Air Injector Reaction (AIR) disengaged—turns ON "Service Engine Soon" light—forces cooling fans on full speed
E016	Generator voltage out of range—all solenoids disengaged—displays "Service Car Soon" on Driver Information Center (DIC)—disengages Viscous Converter Clutch (VCC) for entire ignition cycle
E018	Open crank signal circuit—displays "Service Car Soon" on Driver Information Center (DIC)
E019	Shorted fuel pump circuit—displays "Service Car Soon" on Driver Information Center (DIC)
E020	Open fuel pump circuit—displays "Service Car Soon" on Driver Information Center (DIC)
E021	Shorted Throttle Position Sensor (TPS) circuit—turns ON "Service Engine Soon" light—disables cruise control for ignition cycle
E022	Open Throttle Position Sensor (TPS) circuit—turns ON "Service Engine Soon" light—disables cruise control for ignition cycle

ECM TROUBLE CODES (cont'd)

Code	Explanation
E023	Electronic Spark Timing (EST)/bypass circuit problem—Air Injector Reaction (AIR) disengaged—Exhaust Gas Recirculation (EGR) disengaged—turns ON "Service Engine Soon" light—causes system to operate on bypass spark
E024	Speed sensor circuit problem—Viscous Converter Clutch (VCC) and cruise disengaged—turns ON "Service Engine Soon" light—disengages Viscous Converter Clutch (VCC) for entire ignition cycle
E026	Shorted throttle switch circuit—turns ON "Service Engine Soon" light
E027	Open throttle switch circuit—turns ON "Service Engine Soon" light
E028	Open 3rd or 4th gear circuit—turns ON "Service Engine Soon" light
E030	RPM error too great—turns ON "Service Engine Soon" light
E031	Shorted Manifold Absolute Pressure (MAP) sensor circuit—Air Injector Reaction (AIR) disengaged—turns ON "Service Engine Soon" light—disengages Viscous Converter Clutch (VCC) for entire ignition cycle
E032	Open Manifold Absolute Pressure (MAP) sensor circuit—Air Injector Reaction (AIR) disengaged—turns ON "Service Engine Soon" light—disengages Viscous Converter Clucth (VCC) for entire ignition cycle
E034	Manifold Absolute Pressure (MAP) sensor signal too high—Air Injector Reaction (AIR) disengaged—turns ON "Service Engine Soon" light—disengages Viscous Converter Clutch (VCC) for entire ignition cycle
E037	Shorted Manifold Air Temperature (MAT) sensor circuit—Air Injector Reaction (AIR) disengaged—turns ON "Service Engine Soon" light
E038	Open Manifold Air Temperature (MAT) sensor circuit—Air Injector Reaction (AIR) disengaged—turns ON "Service Engine Soon" light
E039	Viscous Converter Clutch (VCC) engagement problem—turns ON "Service Engine Soon" light—disengages Viscous Converter Clutch (VCC) for entire ignition cycle
E040	Open Power Steering Pressure Switch (PSPS) circuit—turns ON "Service Engine Soon" light
E044	Lean exhaust signal—Air Injector Reaction (AIR) and closed loop disengaged—turns ON "Service Engine Soon" light—enables canister purge
E045	Rich exhaust signal—Air Injector Reaction (AIR) and closed loop disengaged—turns ON "Service Engine Soon" light—enables canister purge
E047	Body Control Module (BCM)—Electronic Control Module (ECM) data problem—turns ON "Service Engine Soon" light
E048	Exhaust Gas Recirculation (EGR) system fault—EGR disengaged—turns ON "Service Engine Soon" light
E052	Electronic Control Module (ECM) memory reset indicator—does not turn on any telltale light or display any message
E053	Distributor signal interrupt—does not turn on any telltale light or display any message
E055	Throttle Position Sensor (TPS) misadjusted—does not turn on any telltale light or display any message
E058	Pass key fuel enable—displays status message on Driver Information Center (DIC)
E059	Viscous Converter Clutch (VCC) temperature sensor circuit problem—turns ON "Service Engine Soon" light—disengages Viscous Converter Clutch (VCC) for entire ignition problem
E060	Cruise—transmission not in Drive—cruise disengaged—does not turn on any telltale light or display any message
E063	Cruise—car speed and set speed difference too high—cruise disengaged—does not turn on any telltale light or display any message
E064	Cruise—car acceleration too high—cruise disengaged—does not turn on any telltale light or display any message
E065	Cruise—coolant temperature too high—cruise disengaged—does not turn on any telltale light or display any message

ECM TROUBLE CODES (cont'd)

Code	Explanation
E066	Cruise—engine RPM too high—cruise disengaged—does not turn on any telltale light or display any message
E067	Cruise—cruise switch shorted during enable—cruise disengaged—does not turn on any telltale light or display any message

BCM TROUBLE CODES

Code	Explanation
B110	Outside air temperature circuit problem—displays status message on Driver Information Center (DIC)
B111	Air conditioning HI side temperature circuit problem—forces cooling fans on full speed
B112	Air conditioning LO side temperature circuit problem—(air conditioning clutch)—displays status message on Driver Information Center (DIC)
B113	In-car temperature circuit problem—displays status message on Driver Information Center (DIC)
B115	Sunload temperature circuit problem—displays status message on Driver Information Center (DIC)
B119	Twilight sentinel photosensor circuit problem—does not turn on any telltale light or display any message
B120	Twilight sentinel delay pot circuit problem—does not turn on any telltale light or display any message
B121	Twilight sentinel enable circuit problem—does not turn on any telltale light or display any message
B122	Panel lamp dimming pot circuit problem—does not turn on any telltale light or display any message
B123	Panel lamp enable circuit problem—does not turn on any telltale light or display any message
B124	Speed sensor circuit problem—does not turn on any telltale light or display any message
B127	PRND321 sensor circuit problem—displays square box around each PRND321 position on Instrument Panel Cluster (IPC)—displays status message on Driver Information Center (DIC)
B334	Loss of Electronic Control Module (ECM) data—air conditioning clutch—displays status message on Driver Information Center (DIC)—forces cooling fans on full speed
B335	Loss of Climate Control/Driver Information Center (CCDIC) data—displays status message on Driver Information Center (DIC)
B336	Loss of Instrument Panel Control (IPC) data—displays status message on Driver Information Center (DIC)
B337	Loss of programmer data—displays status message on Driver Information Center (DIC)
B410	Charging system problem—displays status message on Driver Information Center (DIC)
B411	Battery volts too low—displays status message on Driver Information Center (DIC)
B412	Battery volts too high—displays status message on Driver Information Center (DIC)
B420	Relay circuit problem—does not turn on any telltale light or display any message
B440	Air mix door problem—does not turn on any telltale light or display any message
B441	Cooling fans problem—displays status message on Driver Information Center (DIC)—forces cooling fans on full speed
B446	Low air conditioning refrigerant condition warning—displays status message on Driver Information Center (DIC)
B447	Very low air conditioning refrigerant condition warning—air conditioning clutch—displays status message on Driver Information Center (DIC)—switches ECC mode to ECON
B448	Very low air conditioning refrigerant pressure condition—displays status message on Driver Information Center (DIC)—switches ECC mode to ECON
B449	Air conditioning HI side temperature too high—air conditioning clutch—displays status message on Driver Information Center (DIC)
B450	Coolant temperature too HI—air conditioning clutch—displays status message on Driver Information Center (DIC)
B552	Body Control Module (BCM) memory reset indicator—does not turn on any telltale light or display any message
B556	Body Control Module (BCM) EE PROM error—displays "Error" in season odometer

Year — 1989
Model — Cimarron
Engine — 2.8L (173 cid) MPFI V6
Engine Code — VIN W

ECM TROUBLE CODES

Code	Explanation
13	Open oxygen sensor circuit
14	Coolant Temperature Sensor (CTS) circuit — high temperature indicated
15	Coolant Temperature Sensor (CTS) circuit — low temperature indicated
21	Throttle Position Sensor (TPS) circuit — signal voltage high
22	Throttle Position Sensor (TPS) circuit — signal voltage low
23	Manifold Air Temperature (MAT) sensor circuit — low temperature indicated
24	Vehicle Speed Sensor (VSS) circuit
25	Manifold Air Temperature (MAT) sensor circuit — high temperature indicated
33	Manifold Absolute Pressure (MAP) sensor circuit — signal voltage high — low vacuum
34	Manifold Absolute Pressure (MAP) sensor circuit — signal voltage low — high vacuum
35	Idle speed error
41	Cylinder select error — faulty or incorrect Mem-Cal
42	Electronic Spark Timing (EST) circuit
43	Electronic Spark Control (ESC) circuit
44	Oxygen sensor circuit — lean exhaust indicated
45	Oxygen sensor circuit — rich exhaust indicated
54	Fuel pump circuit — low voltage
51	Mem-Cal error — faulty or incorrect Mem-Cal
52	Calpak error — faulty or incorrect calpak
53	System over voltage
61	Degraded oxygen sensor

Year — 1989
Model — Allante
Engine — 4.1L (250 cid) MPFI V8
Engine Code — VIN 7

ECM TROUBLE CODES

Code	Explanation
E012	No distributor signal—turns ON "Engine Control System Fault" light
E013	Right oxygen sensor not ready—closed loop and canister purge disengaged—turns ON "Engine Control System Fault" light—enables canister purge, and disables closed loop only if a problem is detected with both the left and the right sensors
E014	Shorted Coolant Temperature Sensor (CTS) circuit—turns ON "Engine Control System Fault" light—forces cooling fans on full speed
E015	Open Coolant Temperature Sensor (CTS) circuit—turns ON "Engine Control System Fault" light—forces cooling fans on full speed
E016	Generator voltage out of range—all solenoids, except shift solenoids disengaged—displays "Service Soon" message on Driver Information Center (DIC)
E017	Left oxygen sensor not ready—closed loop and canister purge disengaged—turns ON "Engine Control System Fault" light—enables canister purge, and disables closed loop only if a problem is detected with both the left and the right sensors
E019	Shorted fuel pump circuit—displays "Service Soon" message on Climate Control/Driver Information Center (CCDIC)
E020	Open fuel pump circuit—displays "Service Now" message on Climate Control/Driver Information Center (CCDIC)
E021	Shorted Throttle Position Sensor (TPS) circuit—Viscous Converter Clutch (VCC) disengaged—turns ON "Engine Control System Fault" light
E022	Open Throttle Position Sensor (TPS) circuit—Viscous Converter Clutch (VCC) disengaged—turns ON "Engine Control System Fault" light
E023	Electronic Spark Timing (EST)/bypass circuit problem—turns ON "Engine Control System Fault" light—causes system to operate on bypass spark
E024	Speed sensor circuit problem—Viscous Converter Clutch (VCC) and cruise disengaged—turns ON "Engine Control System Fault" light
E026	Shorted throttle switch circuit—turns ON "Engine Control System Fault" light
E027	Open throttle switch circuit—turns ON "Engine Control System Fault" light
E030	RPM error too great—turns ON "Engine Control System Fault" light
E031	Shorted Manifold Absolute Pressure (MAP) sensor circuit—turns ON "Engine Control System Fault" light
E032	Open Manifold Absolute Pressure (MAP) sensor circuit—turns ON "Engine Control System Fault" light
E034	Manifold Absolute Pressure (MAP) sensor signal too high—turns ON "Engine Control System Fault" light
E037	Shorted Manifold Air Temperature (MAT) sensor circuit—turns ON "Engine Control System Fault" light
E038	Open Manifold Air Temperature (MAT) sensor circuit—turns ON "Engine Control System Fault" light
E039	Viscous Converter Clutch (VCC) engagement problem—Viscous Converter Clutch (VCC) disengaged—turns ON "Engine Control System Fault" light—disengages Viscous Converter Clutch (VCC) for entire ignition cycle
E040	Power Steering Pressure sensor circuit—turns ON "Engine Control System Fault" light
E041	Cam sensor circuit problem—turns ON "Engine Control System Fault" light
E042	Left oxygen sensor signal lean—closed loop and canister purge disengaged—turns ON "Engine Control System Fault" light—enables canister purge, and disables closed loop only if a problem is detected with both the left and the right sensor

ECM TROUBLE CODES (cont'd)

Code	Explanation
E043	Left oxygen sensor signal rich—closed loop and canister purge disengaged—turns ON "Engine Control System Fault" light—enables canister purge, and disables closed loop only if a problem is detected with both the left and the right sensors
E044	Right oxygen sensor signal lean—closed loop and canister purge disengaged—urns ON "Engine Control System Fault" light—enables canister purge, and disables closed loop only if a problem is detected with both the left and the right sensors
E045	Right oxygen sensor signal rich—closed loop and canister purge disengaged—turns ON "Engine Control System Fault" light—enables canister purge, and disables closed loop only if a problem is detected with both the left and the right sensors
E046	Right to left bank fueling imbalance—turns ON "Engine Control System Fault" light
E047	Body Control Module (BCM)—Electronic Control Module (ECM) data problem—turns ON "Engine Control System Fault" light
E050	Second gear pressure circuit—does not turn on any telltale light or display any message
E052	Electronic Control Module (ECM) memory reset indicator—does not turn on any telltale light or display any message
E053	Distributor signal interrupt—does not turn on any telltale light or display any message
E055	Throttle Position Sensor (TPS) misadjusted—does not turn on any telltale light or display any message
E058	"PASS Key" anti-theft system—displays status message on Driver Information Center (DIC)
E060	Cruise—transmission not in Drive—cruise disengaged—does not turn on any telltale light or display any message
E061	Cruise—vent solenoid circuit problem—cruise disengaged—does not turn on any telltale light or display any message
E062	Cruise—vacuum solenoid circuit problem—cruise disengaged—does not turn on any telltale light or display any message
E063	Cruise—car speed and set speed difference too high—cruise disengaged—does not turn on any telltale light or display any message
E064	Cruise—car acceleration too high—cruise disengaged—does not turn on any telltale light or display any message
E065	Cruise—cruise servo position sensor failure—cruise disengaged—does not turn on any telltale light or display any message
E066	Cruise—engine RPM too high—cruise disengaged—does not turn on any telltale light or display any message
E067	Cruise—switch shorted during enable—cruise disengaged—does not turn on any telltale light or display any message

BCM TROUBLE CODES

Code	Explanation
B110	Outside air temperature circuit problem—displays status message on Driver Information Center (DIC)
B111	Air conditioning HI side temperature circuit problem—forces cooling fans on full speed
B112	Air conditioning LO side temperature circuit problem—(air conditioning clutch)—displays status message on Driver Information Center (DIC)
B113	In-car temperature circuit problem—displays status message on Driver Information Center (DIC)
B115	Sunload temperature circuit problem—displays status message on Driver Information Center (DIC)
B119	Twilight sentinel photosensor circuit problem—does not turn on any telltale light or display any message
B120	Twilight sentinel delay pot circuit problem—does not turn on any telltale light or display any message
B121	Twilight sentinel enable circuit problem—does not turn on any telltale light or display any message

BCM TROUBLE CODES (cont'd)

Code	Explanation
B122	Panel lamp dimming pot circuit problem—does not turn on any telltale light or display any message
B123	Panel lamp enable circuit problem—does not turn on any telltale light or display any message
B124	Speed sensor circuit problem—does not turn on any telltale light or display any message
B127	PRND321 sensor circuit problem—displays square box around each PRND321 position on Instrument Panel Cluster (IPC)—displays status message on Driver Information Center (DIC)
B334	Loss of Electronic Control Module (ECM) data—air conditioning clutch—displays status message on Driver Information Center (DIC)—forces cooling fans on full speed
B335	Loss of Climate Control/Driver Information Center (CCDIC) data—displays status message on Driver Information Center (DIC)
B336	Loss of Instrument Panel Control (IPC) data—displays status message on Driver Information Center (DIC)
B337	Loss of programmer data—displays status message on Driver Information Center (DIC)
B410	Charging system problem—displays status message on Driver Information Center (DIC)
B411	Battery volts too low—displays status message on Driver Information Center (DIC)
B412	Battery volts too high—displays status message on Driver Information Center (DIC)
B420	Relay circuit problem—does not turn on any telltale light or display any message
B440	Air mix door problem—does not turn on any telltale light or display any message
B441	Cooling fans problem—displays status message on Driver Information Center (DIC)—forces cooling fans on full speed
B446	Low air conditioning refrigerant condition warning—displays status message on Driver Information Center (DIC)
B447	Very low air conditioning refrigerant condition warning—air conditioning clutch—displays status message on Driver Information Center (DIC)—switches ECC mode to ECON
B448	Very low air conditioning refrigerant pressure condition—displays status message on Driver Information Center (DIC)—switches ECC mode to ECON
B449	Air conditioning HI side temperature too high—air conditioning clutch—displays status message on Driver Information Center (DIC)
B450	Coolant temperature too HI—air conditioning clutch—displays status message on Driver Information Center (DIC)
B552	Body Control Module (BCM) memory reset indicator—does not turn on any telltale light or display any message
B556	Body Control Module (BCM) EE PROM error—displays "Error" in season odometer

ANTI-LOCK TROUBLE CODES

Code	Explanation
1	Left front valve problem
2	Right front valve problem
3	Right rear valve problem
4	Left rear valve problem
5	Left front Wheel Speed Sensor (WSS) low output
6	Right front Wheel Speed Sensor (WSS) low output
7	Right rear Wheel Speed Sensor (WSS) low output
8	Left rear Wheel Speed Sensor (WSS) low output
9	Left front/right rear Wheel Speed Sensor (WSS) signal error
10	Right front/left rear Wheel Speed Sensor (WSS) signal error
11	Replenishing valve circuit problem

ANTI-LOCK TROUBLE CODES

Code	Explanation
12	Valve ready circuit problem
13	Improper booster switch sequence — pressure
14	Improper booster switch sequence — piston travel
15	Improper booster switch sequence — brake light switch
16	Electronic Brake Control Module (EBCM) error

LIGHTING TROUBLE CODES

Code	Explanation
L010	Redundant tail lamp relay failure — displays status message on Driver Information Center (DIC)
L011	Redundant headlamp relay failure — displays status message on Driver Information Center (DIC)
L110	Left Switch Pod (LSP) communication failure — displays status message on Driver Information Center (DIC)
L202	Output Switching Module (OSM) No. 2 communication failure — displays status message on Driver Information Center (DIC)
L203	Output Switching Module (OSM) No. 3 communication failure — displays status message on Driver Information Center (DIC)
L204	Output Switching Module (OSM) No. 4 communication failure — displays status message on Driver Information Center (DIC)
L205	Output Switching Module (OSM) No. 5 communication failure — displays status message on Driver Information Center (DIC)
L206	Output Switching Module (OSM) No. 6 communication failure — displays status message on Driver Information Center (DIC)
L207	Output Switching Module (OSM) No. 7 communication failure — displays status message on Driver Information Center (DIC)
L208	Output Switching Module (OSM) No. 8 communication failure — displays status message on Driver Information Center (DIC) — lamp substitution possible
L209	Output Switching Module (OSM) No. 9 communication failure — displays status message on Driver Information Center (DIC) — lamp substitution possible
L210	Output Switching Module (OSM) No. 10 communication failure — displays status message on Driver Information Center (DIC) — lamp substitution possible
L302	Output Switching Module (OSM) No. 2 output failure — displays status message on Driver Information Center (DIC)
L303	Output Switching Module (OSM) No. 3 output failure — displays status message on Driver Information Center (DIC)
L304	Output Switching Module (OSM) No. 4 output failure — displays status message on Driver Information Center (DIC)
L305	Output Switching Module (OSM) No. 5 output failure — displays status message on Driver Information Center (DIC)
L306	Output Switching Module (OSM) No. 6 output failure — displays status message on Driver Information Center (DIC)
L307	Output Switching Module (OSM) No. 7 output failure — displays status message on Driver Information Center (DIC)
L308	Output Switching Module (OSM) No. 8 output failure — displays status message on Driver Information Center (DIC) — lamp substitution possible
L309	Output Switching Module (OSM) No. 9 output failure — displays status message on Driver Information Center (DIC) — lamp substitution possible
L310	Output Switching Module (OSM) No. 10 output failure — displays status message on Driver Information Center (DIC) — lamp substitution possible
L411	Lighting system low voltage warning — displays status message on Driver Information Center (DIC)

CHEVROLET

Year – 1980
Model – Citation
Engine – 2.5L (151 cid) 4 cyl
Engine Code – VIN 5

ECM TROUBLE CODES

Code	Explanation
12	No tachometer signal to the Electronic Control Module (ECM)
13	Oxygen sensor circuit. The engine has to operate for about 5 minutes at part throttle before this code will show
14	Shorted coolant sensor circuit. The engine has to run 2 minutes before this code will show
15	Open coolant sensor circuit. The engine has to operate for about 5 minutes at part throttle before this code will show
21 & 22	(At same time) – grounded Wide Open Throttle (WOT) switch circuit
22	Grounded closed throttle or Wide Open Throttle (WOT) switch circuit
23	Carburetor solenoid circuit
44	Lean oxygen sensor
45	Rich oxygen sensor
51	On service unit, check calibration unit (PROM) installation. On factory installed unit, replace Electronic Control Module (ECM)
52, 53	Replace Electronic Control Module (ECM)
55	Replace Electronic Control Module (ECM)

Year — 1980
Model — Citation
Engine — 2.8L (171 cid) V6
Engine Code — VIN 7

ECM TROUBLE CODES

Code	Explanation
12	No tachometer signal to the Electronic Control Module (ECM)
13	Oxygen sensor circuit. The engine has to operate for about 5 minutes at part throttle before this code will show
13 & 43	Same time — Electronic Spark Control (ESC) signal for too long
14	Shorted coolant sensor circuit. The engine has to run 2 minutes before this code will show
15	Open coolant sensor circuit. The engine has to operate for about 5 minutes at part throttle before this code will show
21	Throttle position sensor circuit
23	Carburetor solenoid circuit
44	Lean oxygen sensor
45	Rich oxygen sensor
51	On service unit, check calibration unit (PROM) installation. On factory installed unit, replace Electronic Control Module (ECM)
54	Faulty carburetor solenoid and/or Electronic Control Module (ECM)
52, 53	Replace Electronic Control Module (ECM)
55	Replace Electronic Control Module (ECM)

Year — 1981
Model — Caprice Classic
Engine — 3.8L (231 cid) V6
Engine Code — VIN A

ECM TROUBLE CODES

Code	Explanation
12	No reference pulses to the Electronic Control Module (ECM). This code is not stored in memory and will only flash while the fault is present
13	Oxygen sensor circuit — the engine must run up to 5 minutes at part throttle, under road load, before this code will set
14	Shorted Coolant Temperature Sensor (CTS) circuit — the engine must run up to 2 minutes before this code will set
15	Open Coolant Temperature Sensor (CTS) circuit — the engine must run up to 5 minutes before this code will set
21	Throttle Position Sensor (TPS) circuit — the engine must run up to 25 seconds, below 800 RPM, before this code will set
23	Open or grounded Mixture Control (M/C) solenoid circuit
24	Vehicle Speed Sensor (VSS) circuit — the car must operate up to 5 minutes at road speed before this code will set
32	Barometric Pressure Sensor (BARO) circuit low
34	Manifold Absolute Pressure (MAP) or vacuum sensor circuit. The engine must run up to 5 minutes, below 800 RPM, before this code will set
35	Idle Speed Control (ISC) switch circuit shorted — over ½ throttle for over 2 seconds
42	Electronic Spark Timing (EST) bypass circuit grounded
44	Lean oxygen sensor indication — the engine must run up to 5 minutes, in closed loop, at part throttle and road load before this code will set
44 & 45	At same time — faulty oxygen sensor circuit
45	Rich system indication — the engine must run up to 5 minutes, in closed loop, at part throttle and road load before this code will set
51	Faulty calibration unit (PROM) or installation. It takes up to 30 seconds before this code will set
52	Faulty Electronic Control Module (ECM)
53	Faulty Electronic Control Module (ECM)
54	Shorted Mixture Control (M/C) solenoid circuit
55	Grounded +8 volts, V/ref, faulty oxygen sensor or Electronic Control Module (ECM)

Year – 1981
Model – Caprice Classic
Engine – 3.8L (231 cid) V6
Engine Code – VIN K

ECM TROUBLE CODES

Code	Explanation
12	No reference pulses to the Electronic Control Module (ECM). This code is not stored in memory and will only flash while the fault is present
13	Oxygen sensor circuit – the engine must run up to 5 minutes at part throttle, under road load, before this code will set
14	Shorted Coolant Temperature Sensor (CTS) circuit – the engine must run up to 2 minutes before this code will set
15	Open Coolant Temperature Sensor (CTS) circuit – the engine must run up to 5 minutes before this code will set
21	Throttle Position Sensor (TPS) circuit – the engine must run up to 25 seconds, below 800 RPM, before this code will set
23	Open or grounded Mixture Control (M/C) solenoid circuit
24	Vehicle Speed Sensor (VSS) circuit – the car must operate up to 5 minutes at road speed before this code will set
32	Barometric Pressure Sensor (BARO) circuit low
34	Manifold Absolute Pressure (MAP) or vacuum sensor circuit. The engine must run up to 5 minutes, below 800 RPM, before this code will set
35	Idle Speed Control (ISC) switch circuit shorted – over ½ throttle for over 2 seconds
42	Electronic Spark Timing (EST) bypass circuit grounded
44	Lean oxygen sensor indication – the engine must run up to 5 minutes, in closed loop, at part throttle and road load before this code will set
44 & 45	At same time – faulty oxygen sensor circuit
45	Rich system indication – the engine must run up to 5 minutes, in closed loop, at part throttle and road load before this code will set
51	Faulty calibration unit (PROM) or installation. It takes up to 30 seconds before this code will set
52	Faulty Electronic Control Module (ECM)
53	Faulty Electronic Control Module (ECM)
54	Shorted Mixture Control (M/C) solenoid circuit
55	Grounded +8 volts, V/ref, faulty oxygen sensor or Electronic Control Module (ECM)

Year—1981
Model—Caprice Classic
Engine—4.4L (267 cid) V8
Engine Code—VIN J

ECM TROUBLE CODES

Code	Explanation
12	No reference pulses to the Electronic Control Module (ECM). This code is not stored in memory and will only flash while the fault is present
13	Oxygen sensor circuit—the engine must run up to 5 minutes at part throttle, under road load, before this code will set
14	Shorted Coolant Temperature Sensor (CTS) circuit—the engine must run up to 2 minutes before this code will set
15	Open Coolant Temperature Sensor (CTS) circuit—the engine must run up to 5 minutes before this code will set
21	Throttle Position Sensor (TPS) circuit—the engine must run up to 25 seconds, below 800 RPM, before this code will set
23	Open or grounded Mixture Control (M/C) solenoid circuit
24	Vehicle Speed Sensor (VSS) circuit—the car must operate up to 5 minutes at road speed before this code will set
32	Barometric Pressure Sensor (BARO) circuit low
34	Manifold Absolute Pressure (MAP) or vacuum sensor circuit. The engine must run up to 5 minutes, below 800 RPM, before this code will set
35	Idle Speed Control (ISC) switch circuit shorted—over ½ throttle for over 2 seconds
42	Electronic Spark Timing (EST) bypass circuit grounded
44	Lean oxygen sensor indication—the engine must run up to 5 minutes, in closed loop, at part throttle and road load before this code will set
44 & 45	At same time—faulty oxygen sensor circuit
45	Rich system indication—the engine must run up to 5 minutes, in closed loop, at part throttle and road load before this code will set
51	Faulty calibration unit (PROM) or installation. It takes up to 30 seconds before this code will set
52	Faulty Electronic Control Module (ECM)
53	Faulty Electronic Control Module (ECM)
54	Shorted Mixture Control (M/C) solenoid circuit
55	Grounded +8 volts, V/ref, faulty oxygen sensor or Electronic Control Module (ECM)

Year — 1981
Model — Caprice Classic
Engine — 5.0L (305 cid) V8
Engine Code — VIN H

ECM TROUBLE CODES

Code	Explanation
12	No reference pulses to the Electronic Control Module (ECM). This code is not stored in memory and will only flash while the fault is present
13	Oxygen sensor circuit — the engine must run up to 5 minutes at part throttle, under road load, before this code will set
14	Shorted Coolant Temperature Sensor (CTS) circuit — the engine must run up to 2 minutes before this code will set
15	Open Coolant Temperature Sensor (CTS) circuit — the engine must run up to 5 minutes before this code will set
21	Throttle Position Sensor (TPS) circuit — the engine must run up to 25 seconds, below 800 RPM, before this code will set
23	Open or grounded Mixture Control (M/C) solenoid circuit
24	Vehicle Speed Sensor (VSS) circuit — the car must operate up to 5 minutes at road speed before this code will set
32	Barometric Pressure Sensor (BARO) circuit low
34	Manifold Absolute Pressure (MAP) or vacuum sensor circuit. The engine must run up to 5 minutes, below 800 RPM, before this code will set
35	Idle Speed Control (ISC) switch circuit shorted — over ½ throttle for over 2 seconds
42	Electronic Spark Timing (EST) bypass circuit grounded
44	Lean oxygen sensor indication — the engine must run up to 5 minutes, in closed loop, at part throttle and road load before this code will set
44 & 45	At same time — faulty oxygen sensor circuit
45	Rich system indication — the engine must run up to 5 minutes, in closed loop, at part throttle and road load before this code will set
51	Faulty calibration unit (PROM) or installation. It takes up to 30 seconds before this code will set
52	Faulty Electronic Control Module (ECM)
53	Faulty Electronic Control Module (ECM)
54	Shorted Mixture Control (M/C) solenoid circuit
55	Grounded +8 volts, V/ref, faulty oxygen sensor or Electronic Control Module (ECM)

Year — 1981
Model — Caprice Classic
Engine — 5.7L (350 cid) V8
Engine Code — VIN L

ECM TROUBLE CODES

Code	Explanation
12	No reference pulses to the Electronic Control Module (ECM). This code is not stored in memory and will only flash while the fault is present
13	Oxygen sensor circuit — the engine must run up to 5 minutes at part throttle, under road load, before this code will set
14	Shorted Coolant Temperature Sensor (CTS) circuit — the engine must run up to 2 minutes before this code will set
15	Open Coolant Temperature Sensor (CTS) circuit — the engine must run up to 5 minutes before this code will set
21	Throttle Position Sensor (TPS) circuit — the engine must run up to 25 seconds, below 800 RPM, before this code will set
23	Open or grounded Mixture Control (M/C) solenoid circuit
24	Vehicle Speed Sensor (VSS) circuit — the car must operate up to 5 minutes at road speed before this code will set
32	Barometric Pressure Sensor (BARO) circuit low
34	Manifold Absolute Pressure (MAP) or vacuum sensor circuit. The engine must run up to 5 minutes, below 800 RPM, before this code will set
35	Idle Speed Control (ISC) switch circuit shorted — over ½ throttle for over 2 seconds
42	Electronic Spark Timing (EST) bypass circuit grounded
44	Lean oxygen sensor indication — the engine must run up to 5 minutes, in closed loop, at part throttle and road load before this code will set
44 & 45	At same time — faulty oxygen sensor circuit
45	Rich system indication — the engine must run up to 5 minutes, in closed loop, at part throttle and road load before this code will set
51	Faulty calibration unit (PROM) or installation. It takes up to 30 seconds before this code will set
52	Faulty Electronic Control Module (ECM)
53	Faulty Electronic Control Module (ECM)
54	Shorted Mixture Control (M/C) solenoid circuit
55	Grounded +8 volts, V/ref, faulty oxygen sensor or Electronic Control Module (ECM)

Year — 1981
Model — Impala
Engine — 3.8L (231 cid) V6
Engine Code — VIN A

ECM TROUBLE CODES

Code	Explanation
12	No reference pulses to the Electronic Control Module (ECM). This code is not stored in memory and will only flash while the fault is present
13	Oxygen sensor circuit — the engine must run up to 5 minutes at part throttle, under road load, before this code will set
14	Shorted Coolant Temperature Sensor (CTS) circuit — the engine must run up to 2 minutes before this code will set
15	Open Coolant Temperature Sensor (CTS) circuit — the engine must run up to 5 minutes before this code will set
21	Throttle Position Sensor (TPS) circuit — the engine must run up to 25 seconds, below 800 RPM, before this code will set
23	Open or grounded Mixture Control (M/C) solenoid circuit
24	Vehicle Speed Sensor (VSS) circuit — the car must operate up to 5 minutes at road speed before this code will set
32	Barometric Pressure Sensor (BARO) circuit low
34	Manifold Absolute Pressure (MAP) or vacuum sensor circuit. The engine must run up to 5 minutes, below 800 RPM, before this code will set
35	Idle Speed Control (ISC) switch circuit shorted — over ½ throttle for over 2 seconds
42	Electronic Spark Timing (EST) bypass circuit grounded
44	Lean oxygen sensor indication — the engine must run up to 5 minutes, in closed loop, at part throttle and road load before this code will set
44 & 45	At same time — faulty oxygen sensor circuit
45	Rich system indication — the engine must run up to 5 minutes, in closed loop, at part throttle and road load before this code will set
51	Faulty calibration unit (PROM) or installation. It takes up to 30 seconds before this code will set
52	Faulty Electronic Control Module (ECM)
53	Faulty Electronic Control Module (ECM)
54	Shorted Mixture Control (M/C) solenoid circuit
55	Grounded +8 volts, V/ref, faulty oxygen sensor or Electronic Control Module (ECM)

GENERAL MOTORS CORPORATION
DIAGNOSTIC CODE DATA

Year – 1981
Model – Impala
Engine – 3.8L (229 cid) V6
Engine Code – VIN K

ECM TROUBLE CODES

Code	Explanation
12	No reference pulses to the Electronic Control Module (ECM). This code is not stored in memory and will only flash while the fault is present
13	Oxygen sensor circuit – the engine must run up to 5 minutes at part throttle, under road load, before this code will set
14	Shorted Coolant Temperature Sensor (CTS) circuit – the engine must run up to 2 minutes before this code will set
15	Open Coolant Temperature Sensor (CTS) circuit – the engine must run up to 5 minutes before this code will set
21	Throttle Position Sensor (TPS) circuit – the engine must run up to 25 seconds, below 800 RPM, before this code will set
23	Open or grounded Mixture Control (M/C) solenoid circuit
24	Vehicle Speed Sensor (VSS) circuit – the car must operate up to 5 minutes at road speed before this code will set
32	Barometric Pressure Sensor (BARO) circuit low
34	Manifold Absolute Pressure (MAP) or vacuum sensor circuit. The engine must run up to 5 minutes, below 800 RPM, before this code will set
35	Idle Speed Control (ISC) switch circuit shorted – over ½ throttle for over 2 seconds
42	Electronic Spark Timing (EST) bypass circuit grounded
44	Lean oxygen sensor indication – the engine must run up to 5 minutes, in closed loop, at part throttle and road load before this code will set
44 & 45	At same time – faulty oxygen sensor circuit
45	Rich system indication – the engine must run up to 5 minutes, in closed loop, at part throttle and road load before this code will set
51	Faulty calibration unit (PROM) or installation. It takes up to 30 seconds before this code will set
52	Faulty Electronic Control Module (ECM)
53	Faulty Electronic Control Module (ECM)
54	Shorted Mixture Control (M/C) solenoid circuit
55	Grounded + 8 volts, V/ref, faulty oxygen sensor or Electronic Control Module (ECM)

Year — 1981
Model — Impala
Engine — 4.4L (267 cid) V8
Engine Code — VIN J

ECM TROUBLE CODES

Code	Explanation
12	No reference pulses to the Electronic Control Module (ECM). This code is not stored in memory and will only flash while the fault is present
13	Oxygen sensor circuit — the engine must run up to 5 minutes at part throttle, under road load, before this code will set
14	Shorted Coolant Temperature Sensor (CTS) circuit — the engine must run up to 2 minutes before this code will set
15	Open Coolant Temperature Sensor (CTS) circuit — the engine must run up to 5 minutes before this code will set
21	Throttle Position Sensor (TPS) circuit — the engine must run up to 25 seconds, below 800 RPM, before this code will set
23	Open or grounded Mixture Control (M/C) solenoid circuit
24	Vehicle Speed Sensor (VSS) circuit — the car must operate up to 5 minutes at road speed before this code will set
32	Barometric Pressure Sensor (BARO) circuit low
34	Manifold Absolute Pressure (MAP) or vacuum sensor circuit. The engine must run up to 5 minutes, below 800 RPM, before this code will set
35	Idle Speed Control (ISC) switch circuit shorted — over ½ throttle for over 2 seconds
42	Electronic Spark Timing (EST) bypass circuit grounded
44	Lean oxygen sensor indication — the engine must run up to 5 minutes, in closed loop, at part throttle and road load before this code will set
44 & 45	At same time — faulty oxygen sensor circuit
45	Rich system indication — the engine must run up to 5 minutes, in closed loop, at part throttle and road load before this code will set
51	Faulty calibration unit (PROM) or installation. It takes up to 30 seconds before this code will set
52	Faulty Electronic Control Module (ECM)
53	Faulty Electronic Control Module (ECM)
54	Shorted Mixture Control (M/C) solenoid circuit
55	Grounded +8 volts, V/ref, faulty oxygen sensor or Electronic Control Module (ECM)

Year — 1981
Model — Impala
Engine — 5.0L (305 cid) V8
Engine Code — VIN H

ECM TROUBLE CODES

Code	Explanation
12	No reference pulses to the Electronic Control Module (ECM). This code is not stored in memory and will only flash while the fault is present
13	Oxygen sensor circuit — the engine must run up to 5 minutes at part throttle, under road load, before this code will set
14	Shorted Coolant Temperature Sensor (CTS) circuit — the engine must run up to 2 minutes before this code will set
15	Open Coolant Temperature Sensor (CTS) circuit — the engine must run up to 5 minutes before this code will set
21	Throttle Position Sensor (TPS) circuit — the engine must run up to 25 seconds, below 800 RPM, before this code will set
23	Open or grounded Mixture Control (M/C) solenoid circuit
24	Vehicle Speed Sensor (VSS) circuit — the car must operate up to 5 minutes at road speed before this code will set
32	Barometric Pressure Sensor (BARO) circuit low
34	Manifold Absolute Pressure (MAP) or vacuum sensor circuit. The engine must run up to 5 minutes, below 800 RPM, before this code will set
35	Idle Speed Control (ISC) switch circuit shorted — over ½ throttle for over 2 seconds
42	Electronic Spark Timing (EST) bypass circuit grounded
44	Lean oxygen sensor indication — the engine must run up to 5 minutes, in closed loop, at part throttle and road load before this code will set
44 & 45	At same time — faulty oxygen sensor circuit
45	Rich system indication — the engine must run up to 5 minutes, in closed loop, at part throttle and road load before this code will set
51	Faulty calibration unit (PROM) or installation. It takes up to 30 seconds before this code will set
52	Faulty Electronic Control Module (ECM)
53	Faulty Electronic Control Module (ECM)
54	Shorted Mixture Control (M/C) solenoid circuit
55	Grounded +8 volts, V/ref, faulty oxygen sensor or Electronic Control Module (ECM)

Year—1981
Model—Impala
Engine—5.7L (350 cid) V8
Engine Code—VIN L

ECM TROUBLE CODES

Code	Explanation
12	No reference pulses to the Electronic Control Module (ECM). This code is not stored in memory and will only flash while the fault is present
13	Oxygen sensor circuit—the engine must run up to 5 minutes at part throttle, under road load, before this code will set
14	Shorted Coolant Temperature Sensor (CTS) circuit—the engine must run up to 2 minutes before this code will set
15	Open Coolant Temperature Sensor (CTS) circuit—the engine must run up to 5 minutes before this code will set
21	Throttle Position Sensor (TPS) circuit—the engine must run up to 25 seconds, below 800 RPM, before this code will set
23	Open or grounded Mixture Control (M/C) solenoid circuit
24	Vehicle Speed Sensor (VSS) circuit—the car must operate up to 5 minutes at road speed before this code will set
32	Barometric Pressure Sensor (BARO) circuit low
34	Manifold Absolute Pressure (MAP) or vacuum sensor circuit. The engine must run up to 5 minutes, below 800 RPM, before this code will set
35	Idle Speed Control (ISC) switch circuit shorted—over ½ throttle for over 2 seconds
42	Electronic Spark Timing (EST) bypass circuit grounded
44	Lean oxygen sensor indication—the engine must run up to 5 minutes, in closed loop, at part throttle and road load before this code will set
44 & 45	At same time—faulty oxygen sensor circuit
45	Rich system indication—the engine must run up to 5 minutes, in closed loop, at part throttle and road load before this code will set
51	Faulty calibration unit (PROM) or installation. It takes up to 30 seconds before this code will set
52	Faulty Electronic Control Module (ECM)
53	Faulty Electronic Control Module (ECM)
54	Shorted Mixture Control (M/C) solenoid circuit
55	Grounded +8 volts, V/ref, faulty oxygen sensor or Electronic Control Module (ECM)

GENERAL MOTORS CORPORATION
DIAGNOSTIC CODE DATA

Year — 1981
Model — Monte Carlo
Engine — 3.8L (229 cid) V6
Engine Code — VIN K

ECM TROUBLE CODES

Code	Explanation
12	No reference pulses to the Electronic Control Module (ECM). This code is not stored in memory and will only flash while the fault is present
13	Oxygen sensor circuit — the engine must run up to 5 minutes at part throttle, under road load, before this code will set
14	Shorted Coolant Temperature Sensor (CTS) circuit — the engine must run up to 2 minutes before this code will set
15	Open Coolant Temperature Sensor (CTS) circuit — the engine must run up to 5 minutes before this code will set
21	Throttle Position Sensor (TPS) circuit — the engine must run up to 25 seconds, below 800 RPM, before this code will set
23	Open or grounded Mixture Control (M/C) solenoid circuit
24	Vehicle Speed Sensor (VSS) circuit — the car must operate up to 5 minutes at road speed before this code will set
32	Barometric Pressure Sensor (BARO) circuit low
34	Manifold Absolute Pressure (MAP) or vacuum sensor circuit. The engine must run up to 5 minutes, below 800 RPM, before this code will set
35	Idle Speed Control (ISC) switch circuit shorted — over ½ throttle for over 2 seconds
42	Electronic Spark Timing (EST) bypass circuit grounded
44	Lean oxygen sensor indication — the engine must run up to 5 minutes, in closed loop, at part throttle and road load before this code will set
44 & 45	At same time — faulty oxygen sensor circuit
45	Rich system indication — the engine must run up to 5 minutes, in closed loop, at part throttle and road load before this code will set
51	Faulty calibration unit (PROM) or installation. It takes up to 30 seconds before this code will set
52	Faulty Electronic Control Module (ECM)
53	Faulty Electronic Control Module (ECM)
54	Shorted Mixture Control (M/C) solenoid circuit
55	Grounded +8 volts, V/ref, faulty oxygen sensor or Electronic Control Module (ECM)

Year – 1981
Model – Monte Carlo
Engine – 3.8L (231 cid) V8
Engine Code – VIN A

ECM TROUBLE CODES

Code	Explanation
12	No reference pulses to the Electronic Control Module (ECM). This code is not stored in memory and will only flash while the fault is present
13	Oxygen sensor circuit – the engine must run up to 5 minutes at part throttle, under road load, before this code will set
14	Shorted Coolant Temperature Sensor (CTS) circuit – the engine must run up to 2 minutes before this code will set
15	Open Coolant Temperature Sensor (CTS) circuit – the engine must run up to 5 minutes before this code will set
21	Throttle Position Sensor (TPS) circuit – the engine must run up to 25 seconds, below 800 RPM, before this code will set
23	Open or grounded Mixture Control (M/C) solenoid circuit
24	Vehicle Speed Sensor (VSS) circuit – the car must operate up to 5 minutes at road speed before this code will set
32	Barometric Pressure Sensor (BARO) circuit low
34	Manifold Absolute Pressure (MAP) or vacuum sensor circuit. The engine must run up to 5 minutes, below 800 RPM, before this code will set
35	Idle Speed Control (ISC) switch circuit shorted – over ½ throttle for over 2 seconds
42	Electronic Spark Timing (EST) bypass circuit grounded
44	Lean oxygen sensor indication – the engine must run up to 5 minutes, in closed loop, at part throttle and road load before this code will set
44 & 45	At same time – faulty oxygen sensor circuit
45	Rich system indication – the engine must run up to 5 minutes, in closed loop, at part throttle and road load before this code will set
51	Faulty calibration unit (PROM) or installation. It takes up to 30 seconds before this code will set
52	Faulty Electronic Control Module (ECM)
53	Faulty Electronic Control Module (ECM)
54	Shorted Mixture Control (M/C) solenoid circuit
55	Grounded +8 volts, V/ref, faulty oxygen sensor or Electronic Control Module (ECM)

Year — 1981
Model — Monte Carlo
Engine — 4.4L (267 cid) V6
Engine Code — VIN J

ECM TROUBLE CODES

Code	Explanation
12	No reference pulses to the Electronic Control Module (ECM). This code is not stored in memory and will only flash while the fault is present
13	Oxygen sensor circuit — the engine must run up to 5 minutes at part throttle, under road load, before this code will set
14	Shorted Coolant Temperature Sensor (CTS) circuit — the engine must run up to 2 minutes before this code will set
15	Open Coolant Temperature Sensor (CTS) circuit — the engine must run up to 5 minutes before this code will set
21	Throttle Position Sensor (TPS) circuit — the engine must run up to 25 seconds, below 800 RPM, before this code will set
23	Open or grounded Mixture Control (M/C) solenoid circuit
24	Vehicle Speed Sensor (VSS) circuit — the car must operate up to 5 minutes at road speed before this code will set
32	Barometric Pressure Sensor (BARO) circuit low
34	Manifold Absolute Pressure (MAP) or vacuum sensor circuit. The engine must run up to 5 minutes, below 800 RPM, before this code will set
35	Idle Speed Control (ISC) switch circuit shorted — over ½ throttle for over 2 seconds
42	Electronic Spark Timing (EST) bypass circuit grounded
44	Lean oxygen sensor indication — the engine must run up to 5 minutes, in closed loop, at part throttle and road load before this code will set
44 & 45	At same time — faulty oxygen sensor circuit
45	Rich system indication — the engine must run up to 5 minutes, in closed loop, at part throttle and road load before this code will set
51	Faulty calibration unit (PROM) or installation. It takes up to 30 seconds before this code will set
52	Faulty Electronic Control Module (ECM)
53	Faulty Electronic Control Module (ECM)
54	Shorted Mixture Control (M/C) solenoid circuit
55	Grounded + 8 volts, V/ref, faulty oxygen sensor or Electronic Control Module (ECM)

Year — 1981
Model — Monte Carlo
Engine — 3.8L (229 cid) V6
Engine Code — VIN 3

ECM TROUBLE CODES

Code	Explanation
12	No reference pulses to the Electronic Control Module (ECM). This code is not stored in memory and will only flash while the fault is present
13	Oxygen sensor circuit — the engine must run up to 5 minutes at part throttle, under road load, before this code will set
14	Shorted Coolant Temperature Sensor (CTS) circuit — the engine must run up to 2 minutes before this code will set
15	Open Coolant Temperature Sensor (CTS) circuit — the engine must run up to 5 minutes before this code will set
21	Throttle Position Sensor (TPS) circuit — the engine must run up to 25 seconds, below 800 RPM, before this code will set
23	Open or grounded Mixture Control (M/C) solenoid circuit
24	Vehicle Speed Sensor (VSS) circuit — the car must operate up to 5 minutes at road speed before this code will set
32	Barometric Pressure Sensor (BARO) circuit low
34	Manifold Absolute Pressure (MAP) or vacuum sensor circuit. The engine must run up to 5 minutes, below 800 RPM, before this code will set
35	Idle Speed Control (ISC) switch circuit shorted — over ½ throttle for over 2 seconds
42	Electronic Spark Timing (EST) bypass circuit grounded
44	Lean oxygen sensor indication — the engine must run up to 5 minutes, in closed loop, at part throttle and road load before this code will set
44 & 45	At same time — faulty oxygen sensor circuit
45	Rich system indication — the engine must run up to 5 minutes, in closed loop, at part throttle and road load before this code will set
51	Faulty calibration unit (PROM) or installation. It takes up to 30 seconds before this code will set
52	Faulty Electronic Control Module (ECM)
53	Faulty Electronic Control Module (ECM)
54	Shorted Mixture Control (M/C) solenoid circuit
55	Grounded +8 volts, V/ref, faulty oxygen sensor or Electronic Control Module (ECM)

Year — 1981
Model — Monte Carlo
Engine — 5.0L (305 cid) V8
Engine Code — VIN H

ECM TROUBLE CODES

Code	Explanation
12	No reference pulses to the Electronic Control Module (ECM). This code is not stored in memory and will only flash while the fault is present
13	Oxygen sensor circuit — the engine must run up to 5 minutes at part throttle, under road load, before this code will set
14	Shorted Coolant Temperature Sensor (CTS) circuit — the engine must run up to 2 minutes before this code will set
15	Open Coolant Temperature Sensor (CTS) circuit — the engine must run up to 5 minutes before this code will set
21	Throttle Position Sensor (TPS) circuit — the engine must run up to 25 seconds, below 800 RPM, before this code will set
23	Open or grounded Mixture Control (M/C) solenoid circuit
24	Vehicle Speed Sensor (VSS) circuit — the car must operate up to 5 minutes at road speed before this code will set
32	Barometric Pressure Sensor (BARO) circuit low
34	Manifold Absolute Pressure (MAP) or vacuum sensor circuit. The engine must run up to 5 minutes, below 800 RPM, before this code will set
35	Idle Speed Control (ISC) switch circuit shorted — over ½ throttle for over 2 seconds
42	Electronic Spark Timing (EST) bypass circuit grounded
44	Lean oxygen sensor indication — the engine must run up to 5 minutes, in closed loop, at part throttle and road load before this code will set
44 & 45	At same time — faulty oxygen sensor circuit
45	Rich system indication — the engine must run up to 5 minutes, in closed loop, at part throttle and road load before this code will set
51	Faulty calibration unit (PROM) or installation. It takes up to 30 seconds before this code will set
52	Faulty Electronic Control Module (ECM)
53	Faulty Electronic Control Module (ECM)
54	Shorted Mixture Control (M/C) solenoid circuit
55	Grounded +8 volts, V/ref, faulty oxygen sensor or Electronic Control Module (ECM)

Year – 1981
Model – Camaro
Engine – 3.8L (231 cid) V6
Engine Code – VIN A

ECM TROUBLE CODES

Code	Explanation
12	No reference pulses to the Electronic Control Module (ECM). This code is not stored in memory and will only flash while the fault is present
13	Oxygen sensor circuit – the engine must run up to 5 minutes at part throttle, under road load, before this code will set
14	Shorted Coolant Temperature Sensor (CTS) circuit – the engine must run up to 2 minutes before this code will set
15	Open Coolant Temperature Sensor (CTS) circuit – the engine must run up to 5 minutes before this code will set
21	Throttle Position Sensor (TPS) circuit – the engine must run up to 25 seconds, below 800 RPM, before this code will set
23	Open or grounded Mixture Control (M/C) solenoid circuit
24	Vehicle Speed Sensor (VSS) circuit – the car must operate up to 5 minutes at road speed before this code will set
32	Barometric Pressure Sensor (BARO) circuit low
34	Manifold Absolute Pressure (MAP) or vacuum sensor circuit. The engine must run up to 5 minutes, below 800 RPM, before this code will set
35	Idle Speed Control (ISC) switch circuit shorted – over ½ throttle for over 2 seconds
42	Electronic Spark Timing (EST) bypass circuit grounded
44	Lean oxygen sensor indication – the engine must run up to 5 minutes, in closed loop, at part throttle and road load before this code will set
44 & 45	At same time – faulty oxygen sensor circuit
45	Rich system indication – the engine must run up to 5 minutes, in closed loop, at part throttle and road load before this code will set
51	Faulty calibration unit (PROM) or installation. It takes up to 30 seconds before this code will set
52	Faulty Electronic Control Module (ECM)
53	Faulty Electronic Control Module (ECM)
54	Shorted Mixture Control (M/C) solenoid circuit
55	Grounded + 8 volts, V/ref, faulty oxygen sensor or Electronic Control Module (ECM)

Year – 1981
Model – Camaro
Engine – 3.8L (229 cid) V6
Engine Code – VIN K

ECM TROUBLE CODES

Code	Explanation
12	No reference pulses to the Electronic Control Module (ECM). This code is not stored in memory and will only flash while the fault is present
13	Oxygen sensor circuit—the engine must run up to 5 minutes at part throttle, under road load, before this code will set
14	Shorted Coolant Temperature Sensor (CTS) circuit—the engine must run up to 2 minutes before this code will set
15	Open Coolant Temperature Sensor (CTS) circuit—the engine must run up to 5 minutes before this code will set
21	Throttle Position Sensor (TPS) circuit—the engine must run up to 25 seconds, below 800 RPM, before this code will set
23	Open or grounded Mixture Control (M/C) solenoid circuit
24	Vehicle Speed Sensor (VSS) circuit—the car must operate up to 5 minutes at road speed before this code will set
32	Barometric Pressure Sensor (BARO) circuit low
34	Manifold Absolute Pressure (MAP) or vacuum sensor circuit. The engine must run up to 5 minutes, below 800 RPM, before this code will set
35	Idle Speed Control (ISC) switch circuit shorted—over ½ throttle for over 2 seconds
42	Electronic Spark Timing (EST) bypass circuit grounded
44	Lean oxygen sensor indication—the engine must run up to 5 minutes, in closed loop, at part throttle and road load before this code will set
44 & 45	At same time—faulty oxygen sensor circuit
45	Rich system indication—the engine must run up to 5 minutes, in closed loop, at part throttle and road load before this code will set
51	Faulty calibration unit (PROM) or installation. It takes up to 30 seconds before this code will set
52	Faulty Electronic Control Module (ECM)
53	Faulty Electronic Control Module (ECM)
54	Shorted Mixture Control (M/C) solenoid circuit
55	Grounded +8 volts, V/ref, faulty oxygen sensor or Electronic Control Module (ECM)

Year – 1981
Model – Camaro
Engine – 4.4L (267 cid) V8
Engine Code – VIN J

ECM TROUBLE CODES

Code	Explanation
12	No reference pulses to the Electronic Control Module (ECM). This code is not stored in memory and will only flash while the fault is present
13	Oxygen sensor circuit – the engine must run up to 5 minutes at part throttle, under road load, before this code will set
14	Shorted Coolant Temperature Sensor (CTS) circuit – the engine must run up to 2 minutes before this code will set
15	Open Coolant Temperature Sensor (CTS) circuit – the engine must run up to 5 minutes before this code will set
21	Throttle Position Sensor (TPS) circuit – the engine must run up to 25 seconds, below 800 RPM, before this code will set
23	Open or grounded Mixture Control (M/C) solenoid circuit
24	Vehicle Speed Sensor (VSS) circuit – the car must operate up to 5 minutes at road speed before this code will set
32	Barometric Pressure Sensor (BARO) circuit low
34	Manifold Absolute Pressure (MAP) or vacuum sensor circuit. The engine must run up to 5 minutes, below 800 RPM, before this code will set
35	Idle Speed Control (ISC) switch circuit shorted – over ½ throttle for over 2 seconds
42	Electronic Spark Timing (EST) bypass circuit grounded
44	Lean oxygen sensor indication – the engine must run up to 5 minutes, in closed loop, at part throttle and road load before this code will set
44 & 45	At same time – faulty oxygen sensor circuit
45	Rich system indication – the engine must run up to 5 minutes, in closed loop, at part throttle and road load before this code will set
51	Faulty calibration unit (PROM) or installation. It takes up to 30 seconds before this code will set
52	Faulty Electronic Control Module (ECM)
53	Faulty Electronic Control Module (ECM)
54	Shorted Mixture Control (M/C) solenoid circuit
55	Grounded +8 volts, V/ref, faulty oxygen sensor or Electronic Control Module (ECM)

Year — 1981
Model — Camaro
Engine — 5.0L (305 cid) V8
Engine Code — VIN H

ECM TROUBLE CODES

Code	Explanation
12	No reference pulses to the Electronic Control Module (ECM). This code is not stored in memory and will only flash while the fault is present
13	Oxygen sensor circuit — the engine must run up to 5 minutes at part throttle, under road load, before this code will set
14	Shorted Coolant Temperature Sensor (CTS) circuit — the engine must run up to 2 minutes before this code will set
15	Open Coolant Temperature Sensor (CTS) circuit — the engine must run up to 5 minutes before this code will set
21	Throttle Position Sensor (TPS) circuit — the engine must run up to 25 seconds, below 800 RPM, before this code will set
23	Open or grounded Mixture Control (M/C) solenoid circuit
24	Vehicle Speed Sensor (VSS) circuit — the car must operate up to 5 minutes at road speed before this code will set
32	Barometric Pressure Sensor (BARO) circuit low
34	Manifold Absolute Pressure (MAP) or vacuum sensor circuit. The engine must run up to 5 minutes, below 800 RPM, before this code will set
35	Idle Speed Control (ISC) switch circuit shorted — over ½ throttle for over 2 seconds
42	Electronic Spark Timing (EST) bypass circuit grounded
44	Lean oxygen sensor indication — the engine must run up to 5 minutes, in closed loop, at part throttle and road load before this code will set
44 & 45	At same time — faulty oxygen sensor circuit
45	Rich system indication — the engine must run up to 5 minutes, in closed loop, at part throttle and road load before this code will set
51	Faulty calibration unit (PROM) or installation. It takes up to 30 seconds before this code will set
52	Faulty Electronic Control Module (ECM)
53	Faulty Electronic Control Module (ECM)
54	Shorted Mixture Control (M/C) solenoid circuit
55	Grounded +8 volts, V/ref, faulty oxygen sensor or Electronic Control Module (ECM)

Year – 1981
Model – Camaro
Engine – 5.7L (350 cid) V8
Engine Code – VIN L

ECM TROUBLE CODES

Code	Explanation
12	No reference pulses to the Electronic Control Module (ECM). This code is not stored in memory and will only flash while the fault is present
13	Oxygen sensor circuit—the engine must run up to 5 minutes at part throttle, under road load, before this code will set
14	Shorted Coolant Temperature Sensor (CTS) circuit—the engine must run up to 2 minutes before this code will set
15	Open Coolant Temperature Sensor (CTS) circuit—the engine must run up to 5 minutes before this code will set
21	Throttle Position Sensor (TPS) circuit—the engine must run up to 25 seconds, below 800 RPM, before this code will set
23	Open or grounded Mixture Control (M/C) solenoid circuit
24	Vehicle Speed Sensor (VSS) circuit—the car must operate up to 5 minutes at road speed before this code will set
32	Barometric Pressure Sensor (BARO) circuit low
34	Manifold Absolute Pressure (MAP) or vacuum sensor circuit. The engine must run up to 5 minutes, below 800 RPM, before this code will set
35	Idle Speed Control (ISC) switch circuit shorted—over ½ throttle for over 2 seconds
42	Electronic Spark Timing (EST) bypass circuit grounded
44	Lean oxygen sensor indication—the engine must run up to 5 minutes, in closed loop, at part throttle and road load before this code will set
44 & 45	At same time—faulty oxygen sensor circuit
45	Rich system indication—the engine must run up to 5 minutes, in closed loop, at part throttle and road load before this code will set
51	Faulty calibration unit (PROM) or installation. It takes up to 30 seconds before this code will set
52	Faulty Electronic Control Module (ECM)
53	Faulty Electronic Control Module (ECM)
54	Shorted Mixture Control (M/C) solenoid circuit
55	Grounded + 8 volts, V/ref, faulty oxygen sensor or Electronic Control Module (ECM)

Year – 1981
Model – Corvette
Engine – 5.7L (350 cid) V8
Engine Code – VIN 6

ECM TROUBLE CODES

Code	Explanation
12	No reference pulses to the Electronic Control Module (ECM). This code is not stored in memory and will only flash while the fault is present
13	Oxygen sensor circuit – the engine must run up to 5 minutes at part throttle, under road load, before this code will set
14	Shorted Coolant Temperature Sensor (CTS) circuit – the engine must run up to 2 minutes before this code will set
15	Open Coolant Temperature Sensor (CTS) circuit – the engine must run up to 5 minutes before this code will set
21	Throttle Position Sensor (TPS) circuit – the engine must run up to 25 seconds, below 800 RPM, before this code will set
23	Open or grounded Mixture Control (M/C) solenoid circuit
24	Vehicle Speed Sensor (VSS) circuit – the car must operate up to 5 minutes at road speed before this code will set
34	Vacuum sensor circuit. The engine must run up to 5 minutes, below 800 RPM, before this code will set
42	Electronic Spark Timing (EST) bypass circuit grounded
44	Lean oxygen sensor indication – the engine must run up to 5 minutes, in closed loop, at part throttle and road load before this code will set
44 & 45	At same time – faulty oxygen sensor circuit
45	Rich system indication – the engine must run up to 5 minutes, in closed loop, at part throttle and road load before this code will set
51	Faulty calibration unit (PROM) or installation. It takes up to 30 seconds before this code will set
52	Faulty Electronic Control Module (ECM)
53	Faulty Electronic Control Module (ECM)
54	Shorted Mixture Control (M/C) solenoid circuit
55	Grounded +8 volts, V/ref, faulty oxygen sensor or Electronic Control Module (ECM)

Year – 1981
Model – Chevette
Engine – 1.6L (98 cid) 4 cyl
Engine Code – VIN 9

ECM TROUBLE CODES

Code	Explanation
12	No reference pulses to the Electronic Control Module (ECM). This code is not stored in memory and will only flash while the fault is present
13	Oxygen sensor circuit – the engine must run up to 5 minutes at part throttle, under road load, before this code will set
14	Shorted Coolant Temperature Sensor (CTS) circuit – the engine must run up to 2 minutes before this code will set
15	Open Coolant Temperature Sensor (CTS) circuit – the engine must run up to 5 minutes before this code will set
21	Throttle Position Sensor (TPS) circuit – the engine must run up to 25 seconds, below 800 RPM, before this code will set
23	Open or grounded Mixture Control (M/C) solenoid circuit
24	Vehicle Speed Sensor (VSS) circuit – the car must operate up to 5 minutes at road speed before this code will set
34	Vacuum sensor circuit. The engine must run up to 5 minutes, below 800 RPM, before this code will set
42	Electronic Spark Timing (EST) bypass circuit grounded
44	Lean oxygen sensor indication – the engine must run up to 5 minutes, in closed loop, at part throttle and road load before this code will set
44 & 45	At same time – faulty oxygen sensor circuit
45	Rich system indication – the engine must run up to 5 minutes, in closed loop, at part throttle and road load before this code will set
51	Faulty calibration unit (PROM) or installation. It takes up to 30 seconds before this code will set
52	Faulty Electronic Control Module (ECM)
53	Faulty Electronic Control Module (ECM)
54	Shorted Mixture Control (M/C) solenoid circuit
55	Grounded + 8 volts, V/ref, faulty oxygen sensor or Electronic Control Module (ECM)

GENERAL MOTORS CORPORATION
DIAGNOSTIC CODE DATA

Year – 1981
Model – Malibu
Engine – 3.8L (231 cid) V6
Engine Code – VIN A

ECM TROUBLE CODES

Code	Explanation
12	No reference pulses to the Electronic Control Module (ECM). This code is not stored in memory and will only flash while the fault is present
13	Oxygen sensor circuit—the engine must run up to 5 minutes at part throttle, under road load, before this code will set
14	Shorted Coolant Temperature Sensor (CTS) circuit—the engine must run up to 2 minutes before this code will set
15	Open Coolant Temperature Sensor (CTS) circuit—the engine must run up to 5 minutes before this code will set
21	Throttle Position Sensor (TPS) circuit—the engine must run up to 25 seconds, below 800 RPM, before this code will set
23	Open or grounded Mixture Control (M/C) solenoid circuit
24	Vehicle Speed Sensor (VSS) circuit—the car must operate up to 5 minutes at road speed before this code will set
32	Barometric Pressure Sensor (BARO) circuit low
34	Manifold Absolute Pressure (MAP) or vacuum sensor circuit. The engine must run up to 5 minutes, below 800 RPM, before this code will set
35	Idle Speed Control (ISC) switch circuit shorted—over ½ throttle for over 2 seconds
42	Electronic Spark Timing (EST) bypass circuit grounded
44	Lean oxygen sensor indication—the engine must run up to 5 minutes, in closed loop, at part throttle and road load before this code will set
44 & 45	At same time—faulty oxygen sensor circuit
45	Rich system indication—the engine must run up to 5 minutes, in closed loop, at part throttle and road load before this code will set
51	Faulty calibration unit (PROM) or installation. It takes up to 30 seconds before this code will set
52	Faulty Electronic Control Module (ECM)
53	Faulty Electronic Control Module (ECM)
54	Shorted Mixture Control (M/C) solenoid circuit
55	Grounded + 8 volts, V/ref, faulty oxygen sensor or Electronic Control Module (ECM)

Year — 1981
Model — Malibu
Engine — 3.8L (229 cid) V6
Engine Code — VIN K

ECM TROUBLE CODES

Code	Explanation
12	No reference pulses to the Electronic Control Module (ECM). This code is not stored in memory and will only flash while the fault is present
13	Oxygen sensor circuit — the engine must run up to 5 minutes at part throttle, under road load, before this code will set
14	Shorted Coolant Temperature Sensor (CTS) circuit — the engine must run up to 2 minutes before this code will set
15	Open Coolant Temperature Sensor (CTS) circuit — the engine must run up to 5 minutes before this code will set
21	Throttle Position Sensor (TPS) circuit — the engine must run up to 25 seconds, below 800 RPM, before this code will set
23	Open or grounded Mixture Control (M/C) solenoid circuit
24	Vehicle Speed Sensor (VSS) circuit — the car must operate up to 5 minutes at road speed before this code will set
32	Barometric Pressure Sensor (BARO) circuit low
34	Manifold Absolute Pressure (MAP) or vacuum sensor circuit. The engine must run up to 5 minutes, below 800 RPM, before this code will set
35	Idle Speed Control (ISC) switch circuit shorted — over ½ throttle for over 2 seconds
42	Electronic Spark Timing (EST) bypass circuit grounded
44	Lean oxygen sensor indication — the engine must run up to 5 minutes, in closed loop, at part throttle and road load before this code will set
44 & 45	At same time — faulty oxygen sensor circuit
45	Rich system indication — the engine must run up to 5 minutes, in closed loop, at part throttle and road load before this code will set
51	Faulty calibration unit (PROM) or installation. It takes up to 30 seconds before this code will set
52	Faulty Electronic Control Module (ECM)
53	Faulty Electronic Control Module (ECM)
54	Shorted Mixture Control (M/C) solenoid circuit
55	Grounded +8 volts, V/ref, faulty oxygen sensor or Electronic Control Module (ECM)

Year — 1981
Model — Malibu
Engine — 4.4L (267 cid) V8
Engine Code — VIN J

ECM TROUBLE CODES

Code	Explanation
12	No reference pulses to the Electronic Control Module (ECM). This code is not stored in memory and will only flash while the fault is present
13	Oxygen sensor circuit — the engine must run up to 5 minutes at part throttle, under road load, before this code will set
14	Shorted Coolant Temperature Sensor (CTS) circuit — the engine must run up to 2 minutes before this code will set
15	Open Coolant Temperature Sensor (CTS) circuit — the engine must run up to 5 minutes before this code will set
21	Throttle Position Sensor (TPS) circuit — the engine must run up to 25 seconds, below 800 RPM, before this code will set
23	Open or grounded Mixture Control (M/C) solenoid circuit
24	Vehicle Speed Sensor (VSS) circuit — the car must operate up to 5 minutes at road speed before this code will set
32	Barometric Pressure Sensor (BARO) circuit low
34	Manifold Absolute Pressure (MAP) or vacuum sensor circuit. The engine must run up to 5 minutes, below 800 RPM, before this code will set
35	Idle Speed Control (ISC) switch circuit shorted — over ½ throttle for over 2 seconds
42	Electronic Spark Timing (EST) bypass circuit grounded
44	Lean oxygen sensor indication — the engine must run up to 5 minutes, in closed loop, at part throttle and road load before this code will set
44 & 45	At same time — faulty oxygen sensor circuit
45	Rich system indication — the engine must run up to 5 minutes, in closed loop, at part throttle and road load before this code will set
51	Faulty calibration unit (PROM) or installation. It takes up to 30 seconds before this code will set
52	Faulty Electronic Control Module (ECM)
53	Faulty Electronic Control Module (ECM)
54	Shorted Mixture Control (M/C) solenoid circuit
55	Grounded +8 volts, V/ref, faulty oxygen sensor or Electronic Control Module (ECM)

Year — 1981
Model — Malibu
Engine — 5.0L (305 cid) V8
Engine Code — VIN H

ECM TROUBLE CODES

Code	Explanation
12	No reference pulses to the Electronic Control Module (ECM). This code is not stored in memory and will only flash while the fault is present
13	Oxygen sensor circuit — the engine must run up to 5 minutes at part throttle, under road load, before this code will set
14	Shorted Coolant Temperature Sensor (CTS) circuit — the engine must run up to 2 minutes before this code will set
15	Open Coolant Temperature Sensor (CTS) circuit — the engine must run up to 5 minutes before this code will set
21	Throttle Position Sensor (TPS) circuit — the engine must run up to 25 seconds, below 800 RPM, before this code will set
23	Open or grounded Mixture Control (M/C) solenoid circuit
24	Vehicle Speed Sensor (VSS) circuit — the car must operate up to 5 minutes at road speed before this code will set
32	Barometric Pressure Sensor (BARO) circuit low
34	Manifold Absolute Pressure (MAP) or vacuum sensor circuit. The engine must run up to 5 minutes, below 800 RPM, before this code will set
35	Idle Speed Control (ISC) switch circuit shorted — over ½ throttle for over 2 seconds
42	Electronic Spark Timing (EST) bypass circuit grounded
44	Lean oxygen sensor indication — the engine must run up to 5 minutes, in closed loop, at part throttle and road load before this code will set
44 & 45	At same time — faulty oxygen sensor circuit
45	Rich system indication — the engine must run up to 5 minutes, in closed loop, at part throttle and road load before this code will set
51	Faulty calibration unit (PROM) or installation. It takes up to 30 seconds before this code will set
52	Faulty Electronic Control Module (ECM)
53	Faulty Electronic Control Module (ECM)
54	Shorted Mixture Control (M/C) solenoid circuit
55	Grounded + 8 volts, V/ref, faulty oxygen sensor or Electronic Control Module (ECM)

Year – 1981
Model – Citation
Engine – 2.5L (151 cid) 4 cyl
Engine Code – VIN 5

ECM TROUBLE CODES

Code	Explanation
12	No reference pulses to the Electronic Control Module (ECM). This code is not stored in memory and will only flash while the fault is present
13	Oxygen sensor circuit – the engine must run up to 5 minutes at part throttle, under road load, before this code will set
14	Shorted Coolant Temperature Sensor (CTS) circuit – the engine must run up to 2 minutes before this code will set
15	Open Coolant Temperature Sensor (CTS) circuit – the engine must run up to 5 minutes before this code will set
21	Throttle Position Sensor (TPS) circuit – the engine must run up to 25 seconds, below 800 RPM, before this code will set
23	Open or grounded Mixture Control (M/C) solenoid circuit
34	Vacuum sensor circuit. The engine must run up to 5 minutes, below 800 RPM, before this code will set
35	Idle Speed Control (ISC) switch circuit shorted – over ½ throttle for over 2 seconds
42	Electronic Spark Timing (EST) bypass circuit grounded
44	Lean oxygen sensor indication – the engine must run up to 5 minutes, in closed loop, at part throttle and road load before this code will set
44 & 45	At same time – faulty oxygen sensor circuit
45	Rich system indication – the engine must run up to 5 minutes, in closed loop, at part throttle and road load before this code will set
51	Faulty calibration unit (PROM) or installation. It takes up to 30 seconds before this code will set
52	Faulty Electronic Control Module (ECM)
53	Faulty Electronic Control Module (ECM)
54	Shorted Mixture Control (M/C) solenoid circuit
55	Grounded + 8 volts, V/ref, faulty oxygen sensor or Electronic Control Module (ECM)

Year – 1981
Model – Citation
Engine – 2.8L (173 cid) V6
Engine Code – VIN X

ECM TROUBLE CODES

Code	Explanation
12	No reference pulses to the Electronic Control Module (ECM). This code is not stored in memory and will only flash while the fault is present
13	Oxygen sensor circuit – the engine must run up to 5 minutes at part throttle, under road load, before this code will set
14	Shorted Coolant Temperature Sensor (CTS) circuit – the engine must run up to 2 minutes before this code will set
15	Open Coolant Temperature Sensor (CTS) circuit – the engine must run up to 5 minutes before this code will set
21	Throttle Position Sensor (TPS) circuit – the engine must run up to 25 seconds, below 800 RPM, before this code will set
23	Open or grounded Mixture Control (M/C) solenoid circuit
34	Vacuum sensor circuit. The engine must run up to 5 minutes, below 800 RPM, before this code will set
35	Idle Speed Control (ISC) switch circuit shorted – over ½ throttle for over 2 seconds
42	Electronic Spark Timing (EST) bypass circuit grounded
44	Lean oxygen sensor indication – the engine must run up to 5 minutes, in closed loop, at part throttle and road load before this code will set
44 & 45	At same time – faulty oxygen sensor circuit
45	Rich system indication – the engine must run up to 5 minutes, in closed loop, at part throttle and road load before this code will set
51	Faulty calibration unit (PROM) or installation. It takes up to 30 seconds before this code will set
52	Faulty Electronic Control Module (ECM)
53	Faulty Electronic Control Module (ECM)
54	Shorted Mixture Control (M/C) solenoid circuit
55	Grounded +8 volts, V/ref, faulty oxygen sensor or Electronic Control Module (ECM)

Year—1981
Model—Citation
Engine—2.8L (173 cid) V6
Engine Code—VIN Z

ECM TROUBLE CODES

Code	Explanation
12	No reference pulses to the Electronic Control Module (ECM). This code is not stored in memory and will only flash while the fault is present
13	Oxygen sensor circuit—the engine must run up to 5 minutes at part throttle, under road load, before this code will set
14	Shorted Coolant Temperature Sensor (CTS) circuit—the engine must run up to 2 minutes before this code will set
15	Open Coolant Temperature Sensor (CTS) circuit—the engine must run up to 5 minutes before this code will set
21	Throttle Position Sensor (TPS) circuit—the engine must run up to 25 seconds, below 800 RPM, before this code will set
23	Open or grounded Mixture Control (M/C) solenoid circuit
34	Vacuum sensor circuit. The engine must run up to 5 minutes, below 800 RPM, before this code will set
35	Idle Speed Control (ISC) switch circuit shorted—over ½ throttle for over 2 seconds
42	Electronic Spark Timing (EST) bypass circuit grounded
44	Lean oxygen sensor indication—the engine must run up to 5 minutes, in closed loop, at part throttle and road load before this code will set
44 & 45	At same time—faulty oxygen sensor circuit
45	Rich system indication—the engine must run up to 5 minutes, in closed loop, at part throttle and road load before this code will set
51	Faulty calibration unit (PROM) or installation. It takes up to 30 seconds before this code will set
52	Faulty Electronic Control Module (ECM)
53	Faulty Electronic Control Module (ECM)
54	Shorted Mixture Control (M/C) solenoid circuit
55	Grounded +8 volts, V/ref, faulty oxygen sensor or Electronic Control Module (ECM)

Year — 1982
Model — Caprice Classic
Engine — 3.8L (229 cid) V6
Engine Code — VIN K

ECM TROUBLE CODES

Code	Explanation
12	No distributor reference pulses to the ECM. This code is not stored in memory and will only flash while the fault is present. Normal code with ignition ON, engine not running
13	Oxygen sensor circuit—the engine must run up to 5 minutes at part throttle, under road load, before this code will set
14	Shorted Coolant Temperature Sensor (CTS) circuit—the engine must run up to 5 minutes before this code will set
15	Open Coolant Temperature Sensor (CTS) circuit—the engine must run up to 5 minutes before this code will set
21	Throttle Position Sensor (TPS) circuit—the engine must run up to 25 seconds, at specified curb idle speed, before this code will set
23	Open or grounded Mixture Control (M/C) solenoid circuit
24	Vehicle Speed Sensor (VSS) circuit—the car must operate up to 5 minutes at road speed before this code will set
32	Barometric Pressure Sensor (BARO) circuit low
34	Manifold Absolute Pressure (MAP) or vacuum sensor circuit. The engine must run up to 5 minutes, at specified curb idle, before this code will set
35	Idle Speed Control (ISC) switch circuit shorted—over ½ throttle for over 2 seconds
41	No distributor reference pules to the Electronic Control Module (ECM) at specified engine vacuum. This code will store in memory
42	Electronic Spark Timing (EST) bypass circuit or EST circuit grounded or open
44	Lean exhaust sensor indication—the engine must run up to 5 minutes, in closed loop and at part throttle before this code will set
44 & 45	At same time—faulty oxygen sensor circuit
45	Rich exhaust indication—the engine must run up to 5 minutes, in closed loop and at part throttle before this code will set
51	Faulty calibration unit (PROM) or installation. It takes up to 30 seconds before this code will set
54	Shorted Mixture Control (M/C) solenoid circuit and/or faulty Electronic Control Module (ECM)
55	Grounded V/ref (terminal 21), faulty oxygen sensor or Electronic Control Module (ECM)

Year – 1982
Model – Caprice Classic
Engine – 4.4L (262 cid) V8
Engine Code – VIN J

ECM TROUBLE CODES

Code	Explanation
12	No distributor reference pulses to the Electronic Control Module (ECM). This code is not stored in memory and will only flash while the fault is present. Normal code with ignition ON, engine not running
13	Oxygen sensor circuit – the engine must run up to 5 minutes at part throttle, under road load, before this code will set
14	Shorted Coolant Temperature Sensor (CTS) circuit – the engine must run up to 5 minutes before this code will set
15	Open Coolant Temperature Sensor (CTS) circuit – the engine must run up to 5 minutes before this code will set
21	Throttle Position Sensor (TPS) circuit – the engine must run up to 25 seconds, at specified curb idle speed, before this code will set
23	Open or grounded Mixture Control (M/C) solenoid circuit
24	Vehicle Speed Sensor (VSS) circuit – the car must operate up to 5 minutes at road speed before this code will set
32	Barometric Pressure Sensor (BARO) circuit low
34	Manifold Absolute Pressure (MAP) or vacuum sensor circuit. The engine must run up to 5 minutes, at specified curb idle, before this code will set
35	Idle Speed Control (ISC) switch circuit shorted – over ½ throttle for over 2 seconds
41	No distributor reference pules to the Electronic Control Module (ECM) at specified engine vacuum. This code will store in memory
42	Electronic Spark Timing (EST) bypass circuit or EST circuit grounded or open
44	Lean exhaust sensor indication – the engine must run up to 5 minutes, in closed loop and at part throttle before this code will set
44 & 45	At same time – faulty oxygen sensor circuit
45	Rich exhaust indication – the engine must run up to 5 minutes, in closed loop and at part throttle before this code will set
51	Faulty calibration unit (PROM) or installation. It takes up to 30 seconds before this code will set
54	Shorted Mixture Control (M/C) solenoid circuit and/or faulty Electronic Control Module (ECM)
55	Grounded V/ref (terminal 21), faulty oxygen sensor or Electronic Control Module (ECM)

Year – 1982
Model – Caprice Classic
Engine – 3.8L (231 cid) V6
Engine Code – VIN A

ECM TROUBLE CODES

Code	Explanation
12	No distributor reference pulses to the Electronic Control Module (ECM). This code is not stored in memory and will only flash while the fault is present. Normal code with ignition ON, engine not running
13	Oxygen sensor circuit—the engine must run up to 5 minutes at part throttle, under road load, before this code will set
14	Shorted Coolant Temperature Sensor (CTS) circuit—the engine must run up to 5 minutes before this code will set
15	Open Coolant Temperature Sensor (CTS) circuit—the engine must run up to 5 minutes before this code will set
21	Throttle Position Sensor (TPS) circuit—the engine must run up to 25 seconds, at specified curb idle speed, before this code will set
23	Open or grounded Mixture Control (M/C) solenoid circuit
24	Vehicle Speed Sensor (VSS) circuit—the car must operate up to 5 minutes at road speed before this code will set
32	Barometric Pressure Sensor (BARO) circuit low
34	Manifold Absolute Pressure (MAP) or vacuum sensor circuit. The engine must run up to 5 minutes, at specified curb idle, before this code will set
35	Idle Speed Control (ISC) switch circuit shorted—over ½ throttle for over 2 seconds
41	No distributor reference pules to the Electronic Control Module (ECM) at specified engine vacuum. This code will store in memory
42	Electronic Spark Timing (EST) bypass circuit or EST circuit grounded or open
44	Lean exhaust sensor indication—the engine must run up to 5 minutes, in closed loop and at part throttle before this code will set
44 & 45	At same time—faulty oxygen sensor circuit
45	Rich exhaust indication—the engine must run up to 5 minutes, in closed loop and at part throttle before this code will set
51	Faulty calibration unit (PROM) or installation. It takes up to 30 seconds before this code will set
54	Shorted Mixture Control (M/C) solenoid circuit and/or faulty Electronic Control Module (ECM)
55	Grounded V/ref (terminal 21), faulty oxygen sensor or Electronic Control Module (ECM)

GENERAL MOTORS CORPORATION
DIAGNOSTIC CODE DATA

Year – 1982
Model – Caprice Classic
Engine – 5.0L (305 cid) V8
Engine Code – VIN H

ECM TROUBLE CODES

Code	Explanation
12	No distributor reference pulses to the Electronic Control Module (ECM). This code is not stored in memory and will only flash while the fault is present. Normal code with ignition ON, engine not running
13	Oxygen sensor circuit – the engine must run up to 5 minutes at part throttle, under road load, before this code will set
14	Shorted Coolant Temperature Sensor (CTS) circuit – the engine must run up to 5 minutes before this code will set
15	Open Coolant Temperature Sensor (CTS) circuit – the engine must run up to 5 minutes before this code will set
21	Throttle Position Sensor (TPS) circuit – the engine must run up to 25 seconds, at specified curb idle speed, before this code will set
23	Open or grounded Mixture Control (M/C) solenoid circuit
24	Vehicle Speed Sensor (VSS) circuit – the car must operate up to 5 minutes at road speed before this code will set
32	Barometric Pressure Sensor (BARO) circuit low
34	Manifold Absolute Pressure (MAP) or vacuum sensor circuit. The engine must run up to 5 minutes, at specified curb idle, before this code will set
35	Idle Speed Control (ISC) switch circuit shorted – over ½ throttle for over 2 seconds
41	No distributor reference pules to the Electronic Control Module (ECM) at specified engine vacuum. This code will store in memory
42	Electronic Spark Timing (EST) bypass circuit or EST circuit grounded or open
44	Lean exhaust sensor indication – the engine must run up to 5 minutes, in closed loop and at part throttle before this code will set
44 & 45	At same time – faulty oxygen sensor circuit
45	Rich exhaust indication – the engine must run up to 5 minutes, in closed loop and at part throttle before this code will set
51	Faulty calibration unit (PROM) or installation. It takes up to 30 seconds before this code will set
54	Shorted Mixture Control (M/C) solenoid circuit and/or faulty Electronic Control Module (ECM)
55	Grounded V/ref (terminal 21), faulty oxygen sensor or Electronic Control Module (ECM)

Year – 1982
Model – Caprice Classic
Engine – 5.7L (350 cid) V8
Engine Code – VIN L

ECM TROUBLE CODES

Code	Explanation
12	No distributor reference pulses to the Electronic Control Module (ECM). This code is not stored in memory and will only flash while the fault is present. Normal code with ignition ON, engine not running
13	Oxygen sensor circuit – the engine must run up to 5 minutes at part throttle, under road load, before this code will set
14	Shorted Coolant Temperature Sensor (CTS) circuit – the engine must run up to 5 minutes before this code will set
15	Open Coolant Temperature Sensor (CTS) circuit – the engine must run up to 5 minutes before this code will set
21	Throttle Position Sensor (TPS) circuit – the engine must run up to 25 seconds, at specified curb idle speed, before this code will set
23	Open or grounded Mixture Control (M/C) solenoid circuit
24	Vehicle Speed Sensor (VSS) circuit – the car must operate up to 5 minutes at road speed before this code will set
32	Barometric Pressure Sensor (BARO) circuit low
34	Manifold Absolute Pressure (MAP) or vacuum sensor circuit. The engine must run up to 5 minutes, at specified curb idle, before this code will set
35	Idle Speed Control (ISC) switch circuit shorted – over ½ throttle for over 2 seconds
41	No distributor reference pules to the Electronic Control Module (ECM) at specified engine vacuum. This code will store in memory
42	Electronic Spark Timing (EST) bypass circuit or EST circuit grounded or open
44	Lean exhaust sensor indication – the engine must run up to 5 minutes, in closed loop and at part throttle before this code will set
44 & 45	At same time – faulty oxygen sensor circuit
45	Rich exhaust indication – the engine must run up to 5 minutes, in closed loop and at part throttle before this code will set
51	Faulty calibration unit (PROM) or installation. It takes up to 30 seconds before this code will set
54	Shorted Mixture Control (M/C) solenoid circuit and/or faulty Electronic Control Module (ECM)
55	Grounded V/ref (terminal 21), faulty oxygen sensor or Electronic Control Module (ECM)

Year — 1982
Model — Impala
Engine — 3.8L (231 cid) V6
Engine Code — VIN A

ECM TROUBLE CODES

Code	Explanation
12	No distributor reference pulses to the Electronic Control Module (ECM). This code is not stored in memory and will only flash while the fault is present. Normal code with ignition ON, engine not running
13	Oxygen sensor circuit—the engine must run up to 5 minutes at part throttle, under road load, before this code will set
14	Shorted Coolant Temperature Sensor (CTS) circuit—the engine must run up to 5 minutes before this code will set
15	Open Coolant Temperature Sensor (CTS) circuit—the engine must run up to 5 minutes before this code will set
21	Throttle Position Sensor (TPS) circuit—the engine must run up to 25 seconds, at specified curb idle speed, before this code will set
23	Open or grounded Mixture Control (M/C) solenoid circuit
24	Vehicle Speed Sensor (VSS) circuit—the car must operate up to 5 minutes at road speed before this code will set
32	Barometric Pressure Sensor (BARO) circuit low
34	Manifold Absolute Pressure (MAP) or vacuum sensor circuit. The engine must run up to 5 minutes, at specified curb idle, before this code will set
35	Idle Speed Control (ISC) switch circuit shorted—over ½ throttle for over 2 seconds
41	No distributor reference pules to the Electronic Control Module (ECM) at specified engine vacuum. This code will store in memory
42	Electronic Spark Timing (EST) bypass circuit or EST circuit grounded or open
44	Lean exhaust sensor indication—the engine must run up to 5 minutes, in closed loop and at part throttle before this code will set
44 & 45	At same time—faulty oxygen sensor circuit
45	Rich exhaust indication—the engine must run up to 5 minutes, in closed loop and at part throttle before this code will set
51	Faulty calibration unit (PROM) or installation. It takes up to 30 seconds before this code will set
54	Shorted Mixture Control (M/C) solenoid circuit and/or faulty Electronic Control Module (ECM)
55	Grounded V/ref (terminal 21), faulty oxygen sensor or Electronic Control Module (ECM)

Year – 1982
Model – Impala
Engine – 3.8L (229 cid) V6
Engine Code – VIN K

ECM TROUBLE CODES

Code	Explanation
12	No distributor reference pulses to the Electronic Control Module (ECM). This code is not stored in memory and will only flash while the fault is present. Normal code with ignition ON, engine not running
13	Oxygen sensor circuit – the engine must run up to 5 minutes at part throttle, under road load, before this code will set
14	Shorted Coolant Temperature Sensor (CTS) circuit – the engine must run up to 5 minutes before this code will set
15	Open Coolant Temperature Sensor (CTS) circuit – the engine must run up to 5 minutes before this code will set
21	Throttle Position Sensor (TPS) circuit – the engine must run up to 25 seconds, at specified curb idle speed, before this code will set
23	Open or grounded Mixture Control (M/C) solenoid circuit
24	Vehicle Speed Sensor (VSS) circuit – the car must operate up to 5 minutes at road speed before this code will set
32	Barometric Pressure Sensor (BARO) circuit low
34	Manifold Absolute Pressure (MAP) or vacuum sensor circuit. The engine must run up to 5 minutes, at specified curb idle, before this code will set
35	Idle Speed Control (ISC) switch circuit shorted – over ½ throttle for over 2 seconds
41	No distributor reference pules to the Electronic Control Module (ECM) at specified engine vacuum. This code will store in memory
42	Electronic Spark Timing (EST) bypass circuit or EST circuit grounded or open
44	Lean exhaust sensor indication – the engine must run up to 5 minutes, in closed loop and at part throttle before this code will set
44 & 45	At same time – faulty oxygen sensor circuit
45	Rich exhaust indication – the engine must run up to 5 minutes, in closed loop and at part throttle before this code will set
51	Faulty calibration unit (PROM) or installation. It takes up to 30 seconds before this code will set
54	Shorted Mixture Control (M/C) solenoid circuit and/or faulty Electronic Control Module (ECM)
55	Grounded V/ref (terminal 21), faulty oxygen sensor or Electronic Control Module (ECM)

Year — 1982
Model — Impala
Engine — 4.4L (262 cid) V8
Engine Code — VIN J

ECM TROUBLE CODES

Code	Explanation
12	No distributor reference pulses to the Electronic Control Module (ECM). This code is not stored in memory and will only flash while the fault is present. Normal code with ignition ON, engine not running
13	Oxygen sensor circuit — the engine must run up to 5 minutes at part throttle, under road load, before this code will set
14	Shorted Coolant Temperature Sensor (CTS) circuit — the engine must run up to 5 minutes before this code will set
15	Open Coolant Temperature Sensor (CTS) circuit — the engine must run up to 5 minutes before this code will set
21	Throttle Position Sensor (TPS) circuit — the engine must run up to 25 seconds, at specified curb idle speed, before this code will set
23	Open or grounded Mixture Control (M/C) solenoid circuit
24	Vehicle Speed Sensor (VSS) circuit — the car must operate up to 5 minutes at road speed before this code will set
32	Barometric Pressure Sensor (BARO) circuit low
34	Manifold Absolute Pressure (MAP) or vacuum sensor circuit. The engine must run up to 5 minutes, at specified curb idle, before this code will set
35	Idle Speed Control (ISC) switch circuit shorted — over ½ throttle for over 2 seconds
41	No distributor reference pules to the Electronic Control Module (ECM) at specified engine vacuum. This code will store in memory
42	Electronic Spark Timing (EST) bypass circuit or EST circuit grounded or open
44	Lean exhaust sensor indication — the engine must run up to 5 minutes, in closed loop and at part throttle before this code will set
44 & 45	At same time — faulty oxygen sensor circuit
45	Rich exhaust indication — the engine must run up to 5 minutes, in closed loop and at part throttle before this code will set
51	Faulty calibration unit (PROM) or installation. It takes up to 30 seconds before this code will set
54	Shorted Mixture Control (M/C) solenoid circuit and/or faulty Electronic Control Module (ECM)
55	Grounded V/ref (terminal 21), faulty oxygen sensor or Electronic Control Module (ECM)

Year – 1982
Model – Impala
Engine – 5.0L (305 cid) V8
Engine Code – VIN H

ECM TROUBLE CODES

Code	Explanation
12	No distributor reference pulses to the Electronic Control Module (ECM). This code is not stored in memory and will only flash while the fault is present. Normal code with ignition ON, engine not running
13	Oxygen sensor circuit—the engine must run up to 5 minutes at part throttle, under road load, before this code will set
14	Shorted Coolant Temperature Sensor (CTS) circuit—the engine must run up to 5 minutes before this code will set
15	Open Coolant Temperature Sensor (CTS) circuit—the engine must run up to 5 minutes before this code will set
21	Throttle Position Sensor (TPS) circuit—the engine must run up to 25 seconds, at specified curb idle speed, before this code will set
23	Open or grounded Mixture Control (M/C) solenoid circuit
24	Vehicle Speed Sensor (VSS) circuit—the car must operate up to 5 minutes at road speed before this code will set
32	Barometric Pressure Sensor (BARO) circuit low
34	Manifold Absolute Pressure (MAP) or vacuum sensor circuit. The engine must run up to 5 minutes, at specified curb idle, before this code will set
35	Idle Speed Control (ISC) switch circuit shorted—over ½ throttle for over 2 seconds
41	No distributor reference pules to the Electronic Control Module (ECM) at specified engine vacuum. This code will store in memory
42	Electronic Spark Timing (EST) bypass circuit or EST circuit grounded or open
44	Lean exhaust sensor indication—the engine must run up to 5 minutes, in closed loop and at part throttle before this code will set
44 & 45	At same time—faulty oxygen sensor circuit
45	Rich exhaust indication—the engine must run up to 5 minutes, in closed loop and at part throttle before this code will set
51	Faulty calibration unit (PROM) or installation. It takes up to 30 seconds before this code will set
54	Shorted Mixture Control (M/C) solenoid circuit and/or faulty Electronic Control Module (ECM)
55	Grounded V/ref (terminal 21), faulty oxygen sensor or Electronic Control Module (ECM)

Year — 1982
Model — Impala
Engine — 5.7L (350 cid) V8
Engine Code — VIN L

ECM TROUBLE CODES

Code	Explanation
12	No distributor reference pulses to the Electronic Control Module (ECM). This code is not stored in memory and will only flash while the fault is present. Normal code with ignition ON, engine not running
13	Oxygen sensor circuit — the engine must run up to 5 minutes at part throttle, under road load, before this code will set
14	Shorted Coolant Temperature Sensor (CTS) circuit — the engine must run up to 5 minutes before this code will set
15	Open Coolant Temperature Sensor (CTS) circuit — the engine must run up to 5 minutes before this code will set
21	Throttle Position Sensor (TPS) circuit — the engine must run up to 25 seconds, at specified curb idle speed, before this code will set
23	Open or grounded Mixture Control (M/C) solenoid circuit
24	Vehicle Speed Sensor (VSS) circuit — the car must operate up to 5 minutes at road speed before this code will set
32	Barometric Pressure Sensor (BARO) circuit low
34	Manifold Absolute Pressure (MAP) or vacuum sensor circuit. The engine must run up to 5 minutes, at specified curb idle, before this code will set
35	Idle Speed Control (ISC) switch circuit shorted — over ½ throttle for over 2 seconds
41	No distributor reference pules to the Electronic Control Module (ECM) at specified engine vacuum. This code will store in memory
42	Electronic Spark Timing (EST) bypass circuit or EST circuit grounded or open
44	Lean exhaust sensor indication — the engine must run up to 5 minutes, in closed loop and at part throttle before this code will set
44 & 45	At same time — faulty oxygen sensor circuit
45	Rich exhaust indication — the engine must run up to 5 minutes, in closed loop and at part throttle before this code will set
51	Faulty calibration unit (PROM) or installation. It takes up to 30 seconds before this code will set
54	Shorted Mixture Control (M/C) solenoid circuit and/or faulty Electronic Control Module (ECM)
55	Grounded V/ref (terminal 21), faulty oxygen sensor or Electronic Control Module (ECM)

Year — 1982
Model — Monte Carlo
Engine — 3.8L (231 cid) V6
Engine Code — VIN A

ECM TROUBLE CODES

Code	Explanation
12	No distributor reference pulses to the Electronic Control Module (ECM). This code is not stored in memory and will only flash while the fault is present. Normal code with ignition ON, engine not running
13	Oxygen sensor circuit — the engine must run up to 5 minutes at part throttle, under road load, before this code will set
14	Shorted Coolant Temperature Sensor (CTS) circuit — the engine must run up to 5 minutes before this code will set
15	Open Coolant Temperature Sensor (CTS) circuit — the engine must run up to 5 minutes before this code will set
21	Throttle Position Sensor (TPS) circuit — the engine must run up to 25 seconds, at specified curb idle speed, before this code will set
23	Open or grounded Mixture Control (M/C) solenoid circuit
24	Vehicle Speed Sensor (VSS) circuit — the car must operate up to 5 minutes at road speed before this code will set
32	Barometric Pressure Sensor (BARO) circuit low
34	Manifold Absolute Pressure (MAP) or vacuum sensor circuit. The engine must run up to 5 minutes, at specified curb idle, before this code will set
35	Idle Speed Control (ISC) switch circuit shorted — over ½ throttle for over 2 seconds
41	No distributor reference pules to the Electronic Control Module (ECM) at specified engine vacuum. This code will store in memory
42	Electronic Spark Timing (EST) bypass circuit or EST circuit grounded or open
44	Lean exhaust sensor indication — the engine must run up to 5 minutes, in closed loop and at part throttle before this code will set
44 & 45	At same time — faulty oxygen sensor circuit
45	Rich exhaust indication — the engine must run up to 5 minutes, in closed loop and at part throttle before this code will set
51	Faulty calibration unit (PROM) or installation. It takes up to 30 seconds before this code will set
54	Shorted Mixture Control (M/C) solenoid circuit and/or faulty Electronic Control Module (ECM)
55	Grounded V/ref (terminal 21), faulty oxygen sensor or Electronic Control Module (ECM)

Year — 1982
Model — Monte Carlo
Engine — 3.8L (229 cid) V6
Engine Code — VIN K

ECM TROUBLE CODES

Code	Explanation
12	No distributor reference pulses to the Electronic Control Module (ECM). This code is not stored in memory and will only flash while the fault is present. Normal code with ignition ON, engine not running
13	Oxygen sensor circuit—the engine must run up to 5 minutes at part throttle, under road load, before this code will set
14	Shorted Coolant Temperature Sensor (CTS) circuit—the engine must run up to 5 minutes before this code will set
15	Open Coolant Temperature Sensor (CTS) circuit—the engine must run up to 5 minutes before this code will set
21	Throttle Position Sensor (TPS) circuit—the engine must run up to 25 seconds, at specified curb idle speed, before this code will set
23	Open or grounded Mixture Control (M/C) solenoid circuit
24	Vehicle Speed Sensor (VSS) circuit—the car must operate up to 5 minutes at road speed before this code will set
32	Barometric Pressure Sensor (BARO) circuit low
34	Manifold Absolute Pressure (MAP) or vacuum sensor circuit. The engine must run up to 5 minutes, at specified curb idle, before this code will set
35	Idle Speed Control (ISC) switch circuit shorted—over ½ throttle for over 2 seconds
41	No distributor reference pules to the Electronic Control Module (ECM) at specified engine vacuum. This code will store in memory
42	Electronic Spark Timing (EST) bypass circuit or EST circuit grounded or open
44	Lean exhaust sensor indication—the engine must run up to 5 minutes, in closed loop and at part throttle before this code will set
44 & 45	At same time—faulty oxygen sensor circuit
45	Rich exhaust indication—the engine must run up to 5 minutes, in closed loop and at part throttle before this code will set
51	Faulty calibration unit (PROM) or installation. It takes up to 30 seconds before this code will set
54	Shorted Mixture Control (M/C) solenoid circuit and/or faulty Electronic Control Module (ECM)
55	Grounded V/ref (terminal 21), faulty oxygen sensor or Electronic Control Module (ECM)

Year — 1982
Model — Monte Carlo
Engine — 4.4L (267 cid) V8
Engine Code — VIN J

ECM TROUBLE CODES

Code	Explanation
12	No distributor reference pulses to the Electronic Control Module (ECM). This code is not stored in memory and will only flash while the fault is present. Normal code with ignition ON, engine not running
13	Oxygen sensor circuit — the engine must run up to 5 minutes at part throttle, under road load, before this code will set
14	Shorted Coolant Temperature Sensor (CTS) circuit — the engine must run up to 5 minutes before this code will set
15	Open Coolant Temperature Sensor (CTS) circuit — the engine must run up to 5 minutes before this code will set
21	Throttle Position Sensor (TPS) circuit — the engine must run up to 25 seconds, at specified curb idle speed, before this code will set
23	Open or grounded Mixture Control (M/C) solenoid circuit
24	Vehicle Speed Sensor (VSS) circuit — the car must operate up to 5 minutes at road speed before this code will set
32	Barometric Pressure Sensor (BARO) circuit low
34	Manifold Absolute Pressure (MAP) or vacuum sensor circuit. The engine must run up to 5 minutes, at specified curb idle, before this code will set
35	Idle Speed Control (ISC) switch circuit shorted — over ½ throttle for over 2 seconds
41	No distributor reference pules to the Electronic Control Module (ECM) at specified engine vacuum. This code will store in memory
42	Electronic Spark Timing (EST) bypass circuit or EST circuit grounded or open
44	Lean exhaust sensor indication — the engine must run up to 5 minutes, in closed loop and at part throttle before this code will set
44 & 45	At same time — faulty oxygen sensor circuit
45	Rich exhaust indication — the engine must run up to 5 minutes, in closed loop and at part throttle before this code will set
51	Faulty calibration unit (PROM) or installation. It takes up to 30 seconds before this code will set
54	Shorted Mixture Control (M/C) solenoid circuit and/or faulty Electronic Control Module (ECM)
55	Grounded V/ref (terminal 21), faulty oxygen sensor or Electronic Control Module (ECM)

Year — 1982
Model — Monte Carlo
Engine — 5.0L (305 cid) V8
Engine Code — VIN H

ECM TROUBLE CODES

Code	Explanation
12	No distributor reference pulses to the Electronic Control Module (ECM). This code is not stored in memory and will only flash while the fault is present. Normal code with ignition ON, engine not running
13	Oxygen sensor circuit — the engine must run up to 5 minutes at part throttle, under road load, before this code will set
14	Shorted Coolant Temperature Sensor (CTS) circuit — the engine must run up to 5 minutes before this code will set
15	Open Coolant Temperature Sensor (CTS) circuit — the engine must run up to 5 minutes before this code will set
21	Throttle Position Sensor (TPS) circuit — the engine must run up to 25 seconds, at specified curb idle speed, before this code will set
23	Open or grounded Mixture Control (M/C) solenoid circuit
24	Vehicle Speed Sensor (VSS) circuit — the car must operate up to 5 minutes at road speed before this code will set
32	Barometric Pressure Sensor (BARO) circuit low
34	Manifold Absolute Pressure (MAP) or vacuum sensor circuit. The engine must run up to 5 minutes, at specified curb idle, before this code will set
35	Idle Speed Control (ISC) switch circuit shorted — over ½ throttle for over 2 seconds
41	No distributor reference pules to the Electronic Control Module (ECM) at specified engine vacuum. This code will store in memory
42	Electronic Spark Timing (EST) bypass circuit or EST circuit grounded or open
44	Lean exhaust sensor indication — the engine must run up to 5 minutes, in closed loop and at part throttle before this code will set
44 & 45	At same time — faulty oxygen sensor circuit
45	Rich exhaust indication — the engine must run up to 5 minutes, in closed loop and at part throttle before this code will set
51	Faulty calibration unit (PROM) or installation. It takes up to 30 seconds before this code will set
54	Shorted Mixture Control (M/C) solenoid circuit and/or faulty Electronic Control Module (ECM)
55	Grounded V/ref (terminal 21), faulty oxygen sensor or Electronic Control Module (ECM)

Year – 1982
Model – Camaro
Engine – 2.5L (151 cid) 4 cyl
Engine Code – VIN 9

ECM TROUBLE CODES

Code	Explanation
12	No reference pulses to the Electronic Control Module (ECM). This code is not stored in memory and will only flash while the fault is present. Normal code with ignition ON, engine not running
13	Oxygen sensor circuit—the engine must run up to 5 minutes at part throttle, under road load, before this code will set
14	Shorted Coolant Temperature Sensor (CTS) circuit—the engine must run up to 2 minutes before this code will set
15	Open Coolant Temperature Sensor (CTS) circuit—the engine must run up to 5 minutes before this code will set
21	Throttle Position Sensor (TPS) circuit—the engine must run up to 25 seconds, at specified curb idle speed, before this code will set
23	Open or grounded Mixture Control (M/C) solenoid circuit
24	Vehicle Speed Sensor (VSS) circuit—the car must operate up to 5 minutes at road speed before this code will set
34	Vacuum sensor circuit. The engine must run up to 5 minutes, at specfied curb idle speed, before this code will set
41	No distributor reference pulses at specified engine vacuum. This code will store
42	Electronic Spark Timing (EST) bypass circuit grounded or open
44	Lean oxygen sensor indication—the engine must run up to 5 minutes, in closed loop, at part throttle before this code will set
44 & 45	At same time—faulty oxygen sensor circuit
45	Rich system indication—the engine must run up to 5 minutes, in closed loop, at part throttle before this code will set
51	Faulty calibration unit (PROM) or installation. It takes up to 30 seconds before this code will set
54	Shorted Mixture Control (M/C) solenoid circuit and/or faulty Electronic Control Module (ECM)
55	Grounded V/ref (terminal 21), faulty oxygen sensor or Electronic Control Module (ECM)

GENERAL MOTORS CORPORATION
DIAGNOSTIC CODE DATA

Year — 1982
Model — Camaro
Engine — 2.5L (151 cid) TBI 4 cyl
Engine Code — VIN 2

ECM TROUBLE CODES

Code	Explanation
13	Open oxygen sensor circuit — the engine must run up to 2 minutes at part throttle under road load before this code will set
14	Shorted coolant sensor — the engine must run up to 2 minutes before this code will set
15	Open coolant sensor circuit — the engine must run up to 2 minutes before this code will set
21	Throttle Position Sensor (TPS) circuit — high output
22	Throttle Position Sensor (TPS) circuit — low output
24	Vehicle Speed Sensor (VSS) circuit
33	Manifold Absolute Pressure (MAP) sensor circuit — high output
34	Manifolf Absolute Pressure (MAP) sensor circuit — low output
42	Electronic Spark Timing (EST) monitor — bypass circuit open or grounded
43	Electronic Spark Control (ESC) signal for too long.
44	Lean exhaust system indication
45	Rich exhaust system indication
51	Faulty calibration unit (PROM) or installation
55	Replace Electronic Control Module (ECM) — faulty

Year — 1982
Model — Camaro
Engine — 2.8L (173 cid) V6
Engine Code — VIN 1

ECM TROUBLE CODES

Code	Explanation
12	No reference pulses to the Electronic Control Module (ECM). This code is not stored in memory and will only flash while the fault is present. Normal code with ignition ON, engine not running
13	Oxygen sensor circuit — the engine must run up to 5 minutes at part throttle, under road load, before this code will set
14	Shorted Coolant Temperature Sensor (CTS) circuit — the engine must run up to 2 minutes before this code will set
15	Open Coolant Temperature Sensor (CTS) circuit — the engine must run up to 5 minutes before this code will set
21	Throttle Position Sensor (TPS) circuit — the engine must run up to 25 seconds, at specified curb idle speed, before this code will set
23	Open or grounded Mixture Control (M/C) solenoid circuit
24	Vehicle Speed Sensor (VSS) circuit — the car must operate up to 5 minutes at road speed before this code will set
34	Vacuum sensor circuit. The engine must run up to 5 minutes, at specfied curb idle speed, before this code will set
41	No distributor reference pulses at specified engine vacuum. This code will store
42	Electronic Spark Timing (EST) bypass circuit grounded or open
44	Lean oxygen sensor indication — the engine must run up to 5 minutes, in closed loop, at part throttle before this code will set
44 & 45	At same time — faulty oxygen sensor circuit
45	Rich system indication — the engine must run up to 5 minutes, in closed loop, at part throttle before this code will set
51	Faulty calibration unit (PROM) or installation. It takes up to 30 seconds before this code will set
54	Shorted Mixture Control (M/C) solenoid circuit and/or faulty Electronic Control Module (ECM)
55	Grounded V/ref (terminal 21), faulty oxygen sensor or Electronic Control Module (ECM)

Year — 1982
Model — Camaro
Engine — 5.0L (305 cid) V8
Engine Code — VIN H

ECM TROUBLE CODES

Code	Explanation
12	No reference pulses to the Electronic Control Module (ECM). This code is not stored in memory and will only flash while the fault is present. Normal code with ignition ON, engine not running
13	Oxygen sensor circuit — the engine must run up to 5 minutes at part throttle, under road load, before this code will set
14	Shorted Coolant Temperature Sensor (CTS) circuit — the engine must run up to 2 minutes before this code will set
15	Open Coolant Temperature Sensor (CTS) circuit — the engine must run up to 5 minutes before this code will set
21	Throttle Position Sensor (TPS) circuit — the engine must run up to 25 seconds, at specified curb idle speed, before this code will set
23	Open or grounded Mixture Control (M/C) solenoid circuit
24	Vehicle Speed Sensor (VSS) circuit — the car must operate up to 5 minutes at road speed before this code will set
34	Vacuum sensor circuit. The engine must run up to 5 minutes, at specfied curb idle speed, before this code will set
41	No distributor reference pulses at specified engine vacuum. This code will store
42	Electronic Spark Timing (EST) bypass circuit grounded or open
44	Lean oxygen sensor indication — the engine must run up to 5 minutes, in closed loop, at part throttle before this code will set
44 & 45	At same time — faulty oxygen sensor circuit
45	Rich system indication — the engine must run up to 5 minutes, in closed loop, at part throttle before this code will set
51	Faulty calibration unit (PROM) or installation. It takes up to 30 seconds before this code will set
54	Shorted Mixture Control (M/C) solenoid circuit and/or faulty Electronic Control Module (ECM)
55	Grounded V/ref (terminal 21), faulty oxygen sensor or Electronic Control Module (ECM)

Year — 1982
Model — Camaro
Engine — 5.0L (305 cid) TBI V8
Engine Code — VIN 7

ECM TROUBLE CODES

Code	Explanation
13	Open oxygen sensor circuit — the engine must run up to 2 minutes at part throttle under road load before this code will set
14	Shorted coolant sensor — the engine must run up to 2 minutes before this code will set
15	Open coolant sensor circuit — the engine must run up to 2 minutes before this code will set
21	Throttle Position Sensor (TPS) circuit — high output
22	Throttle Position Sensor (TPS) circuit — low output
24	Vehicle Speed Sensor (VSS) circuit
33	Manifold Absolute Pressure (MAP) sensor circuit — high output
34	Manifolf Absolute Pressure (MAP) sensor circuit — low output
42	Electronic Spark Timing (EST) monitor — bypass circuit open or grounded
43	Electronic Spark Control (ESC) signal for too long.
44	Lean exhaust system indication
45	Rich exhaust system indication
51	Faulty calibration unit (PROM) or installation
55	Replace Electronic Control Module (ECM) — faulty

Year — 1982
Model — Corvette
Engine — 5.7L (350 cid) V8
Engine Code — VIN 6

ECM TROUBLE CODES

Code	Explanation
12	Indicates that the distributor spark — tuning reference pulses, which are generated by the pickup coil, are not being received by the Electronic Control Module (ECM)
13	Indicates that the oxygen sensor will not swing above or below its cold voltage of approximately 0.5V and that the system will not go to closed loop circuitry
14	Indicates that the coolant sensor signal voltage is too low because of shorted circuitry
15	Indicates that the coolant sensor signal voltage is too high because of an open circuit
21	Indicates that the voltage signal from the Throttle Position Sensor (TPS) is too high
22	Indicates that the voltage signal from the Throttle Position Sensor (TPS) is too low
24	Indicates that the speed signal is not being received by the Electronic Control Module (ECM)
33	Manifold Absolute Pressure (MAP) sensor circuit
34	Manifold Absolute Pressure (MAP) sensor circuit
42	Indicates that the Electronic Control Module (ECM) is not receiving the proper bypass signal voltage through the High Energy Ignition (HEI) bypass feedback circuit
43	Electronic Spark Control (ESC) signal — ESC signal circuit in retard mode all the time
44	Indicates that the oxygen sensor voltage reading is below 0.30V and will not swing above. If the voltage remains in this low range, the Electronic Control Module (ECM) will set Code 44 and return the system to open loop operation
45	Indicates that the oxygen sensor voltage reading is above 0.60V and will not swing below. If the voltage remains in this low range, the Electronic Control Module (ECM) will set Code 45 and return the system to open loop operation
51	Indicates that the calibration PROMS are not being read properly by the Electronic Control Module (ECM). PROMS installed backwards or PROMS installed with their pins bent or missing may cause this code to set
55	Indicates a faulty Electronic Control Module (ECM)

Year — 1982
Model — Chevette
Engine — 1.6L (98 cid) 4 cyl
Engine Code — VIN C

ECM TROUBLE CODES

Code	Explanation
12	No distributor reference pulses to the Electronic Control Module (ECM). This code is not stored in memory and will only flash while the fault is present
15	Open coolant sensor circuit — the engine must run up to 10 minutes before this code will set
21	Throttle position sensor circuit at WOT — the engine must run up to 10 seconds below 1000 RPM, before this code will set
23	Mixture Control (M/C) solenoid circuit — must be in closed loop before this code will set
44	Lean exhaust indication — the engine must run up to 1 minute in closed loop and at part throttle above 2000 RPM before this code will set
45	Rich exhaust indication — the engine must run up to 1 minute, in closed loop and at part throttle above 2000 RPM before this code will set
51	Faulty calibration unit (PROM) or installation — turns OFF Electronic Control Module (ECM)

GENERAL MOTORS CORPORATION
DIAGNOSTIC CODE DATA

Year – 1982
Model – Celebrity
Engine – 2.5L (151 cid) TBI 4 cyl
Engine Code – VIN R

ECM TROUBLE CODES

Code	Explanation
13	Open oxygen sensor circuit—the engine must run up to 2 minutes at part throttle under road load before this code will set
14	Shorted coolant sensor—the engine must run up to 2 minutes before this code will set
15	Open coolant sensor circuit—the engine must run up to 2 minutes before this code will set
22	Throttle Position Sensor (TPS) circuit—low output
24	Vehicle Speed Sensor (VSS) circuit
33	Manifold Absolute Pressure (MAP) sensor circuit—high output
34	Manifolf Absolute Pressure (MAP) sensor circuit—low output
42	Electronic Spark Timing (EST) monitor—bypass circuit open or grounded
44	Lean exhaust system indication
45	Rich exhaust system indication
51	Faulty calibration unit (PROM) or installation
55	Replace Electronic Control Module (ECM)—faulty

Year — 1982
Model — Celebrity
Engine — 2.8L (173 cid) V6
Engine Code — VIN X

ECM TROUBLE CODES

Code	Explanation
12	No reference pulses to the Electronic Control Module (ECM). This code is not stored in memory and will only flash while the fault is present. Normal code with ignition ON, engine not running
13	Oxygen sensor circuit — the engine must run up to 5 minutes at part throttle, under road load, before this code will set
14	Shorted Coolant Temperature Sensor (CTS) circuit — the engine must run up to 5 minutes before this code will set
15	Open Coolant Temperature Sensor (CTS) circuit — the engine must run up to 5 minutes before this code will set
21	Throttle Position Sensor (TPS) circuit — the engine must run up to 25 seconds, at specified curb idle speed, before this code will set
23	Open or grounded Mixture Control (M/C) solenoid circuit
24	Vehicle Speed Sensor (VSS) circuit — the car must operate up to 5 minutes at road speed before this code will set
32	Barometric Pressure Sensor (BARO) circuit low
34	Manifold Absolute Pressure (MAP) or vacuum sensor circuit — the engine must run up to 5 minutes, at specfied curb idle speed, before this code will set
35	Idle Speed Control (ISC) switch circuitr — over 50% throttle for over 2 seconds
42	Electronic Spark Timing (EST) bypass circuit or EST circuit grounded or open
44	Lean exhaust indication — the engine must run up to 5 minutes, in closed loop, at part throttle before this code will set
44 & 45	At same time — faulty oxygen sensor circuit
45	Rich exhaust indication — the engine must run up to 5 minutes, in closed loop, at part throttle before this code will set
51	Faulty calibration unit (PROM) or installation. It takes up to 30 seconds before this code will set
54	Shorted Mixture Control (M/C) solenoid
55	Grounded V/ref (terminal 21), faulty oxygen sensor or Electronic Control Module (ECM)

Year — 1982
Model — Citation
Engine — 2.5L (151 cid) 4 cyl
Engine Code — VIN 5

ECM TROUBLE CODES

Code	Explanation
12	No reference pulses to the Electronic Control Module (ECM). This code is not stored in memory and will only flash while the fault is present. Normal code with ignition ON, engine not running
13	Oxygen sensor circuit — the engine must run up to 5 minutes at part throttle, under road load, before this code will set
14	Shorted Coolant Temperature Sensor (CTS) circuit — the engine must run up to 5 minutes before this code will set
15	Open Coolant Temperature Sensor (CTS) circuit — the engine must run up to 5 minutes before this code will set
21	Throttle Position Sensor (TPS) circuit — the engine must run up to 25 seconds, at specified curb idle speed, before this code will set
23	Open or grounded Mixture Control (M/C) solenoid circuit
24	Vehicle Speed Sensor (VSS) circuit — the car must operate up to 5 minutes at road speed before this code will set
32	Barometric Pressure Sensor (BARO) circuit low
34	Manifold Absolute Pressure (MAP) or vacuum sensor circuit — the engine must run up to 5 minutes, at specfied curb idle speed, before this code will set
35	Idle Speed Control (ISC) switch circuitr — over 50% throttle for over 2 seconds
42	Electronic Spark Timing (EST) bypass circuit or EST circuit grounded or open
44	Lean exhaust indication — the engine must run up to 5 minutes, in closed loop, at part throttle before this code will set
44 & 45	At same time — faulty oxygen sensor circuit
45	Rich exhaust indication — the engine must run up to 5 minutes, in closed loop, at part throttle before this code will set
51	Faulty calibration unit (PROM) or installation. It takes up to 30 seconds before this code will set
54	Shorted Mixture Control (M/C) solenoid
55	Grounded V/ref (terminal 21), faulty oxygen sensor or Electronic Control Module (ECM)

Year — 1982
Model — Citation
Engine — 2.5L (151 cid) TBI 4 cyl
Engine Code — VIN R

ECM TROUBLE CODES

Code	Explanation
13	Open oxygen sensor circuit — the engine must run up to 2 minutes at part throttle under road load before this code will set
14	Shorted coolant sensor — the engine must run up to 2 minutes before this code will set
15	Open coolant sensor circuit — the engine must run up to 2 minutes before this code will set
22	Throttle Position Sensor (TPS) circuit — low output
24	Vehicle Speed Sensor (VSS) circuit
33	Manifold Absolute Pressure (MAP) sensor circuit — high output
34	Manifolf Absolute Pressure (MAP) sensor circuit — low output
42	Electronic Spark Timing (EST) monitor — bypass circuit open or grounded
44	Lean exhaust system indication
45	Rich exhaust system indication
51	Faulty calibration unit (PROM) or installation
55	Replace Electronic Control Module (ECM) — faulty

Year – 1982
Model – Citation
Engine – 2.8L (171 cid) V6
Engine Code – VIN X

ECM TROUBLE CODES

Code	Explanation
12	No reference pulses to the Electronic Control Module (ECM). This code is not stored in memory and will only flash while the fault is present. Normal code with ignition ON, engine not running
13	Oxygen sensor circuit – the engine must run up to 5 minutes at part throttle, under road load, before this code will set
14	Shorted Coolant Temperature Sensor (CTS) circuit – the engine must run up to 5 minutes before this code will set
15	Open Coolant Temperature Sensor (CTS) circuit – the engine must run up to 5 minutes before this code will set
21	Throttle Position Sensor (TPS) circuit – the engine must run up to 25 seconds, at specified curb idle speed, before this code will set
23	Open or grounded Mixture Control (M/C) solenoid circuit
24	Vehicle Speed Sensor (VSS) circuit – the car must operate up to 5 minutes at road speed before this code will set
32	Barometric Pressure Sensor (BARO) circuit low
34	Manifold Absolute Pressure (MAP) or vacuum sensor circuit – the engine must run up to 5 minutes, at specfied curb idle speed, before this code will set
35	Idle Speed Control (ISC) switch circuitr – over 50% throttle for over 2 seconds
42	Electronic Spark Timing (EST) bypass circuit or EST circuit grounded or open
44	Lean exhaust indication – the engine must run up to 5 minutes, in closed loop, at part throttle before this code will set
44 & 45	At same time – faulty oxygen sensor circuit
45	Rich exhaust indication – the engine must run up to 5 minutes, in closed loop, at part throttle before this code will set
51	Faulty calibration unit (PROM) or installation. It takes up to 30 seconds before this code will set
54	Shorted Mixture Control (M/C) solenoid
55	Grounded V/ref (terminal 21), faulty oxygen sensor or Electronic Control Module (ECM)

Year — 1982
Model — Citation
Engine — 2.8L (171 cid) V6
Engine Code — VIN Z

ECM TROUBLE CODES

Code	Explanation
12	No reference pulses to the Electronic Control Module (ECM). This code is not stored in memory and will only flash while the fault is present. Normal code with ignition ON, engine not running
13	Oxygen sensor circuit — the engine must run up to 5 minutes at part throttle, under road load, before this code will set
14	Shorted Coolant Temperature Sensor (CTS) circuit — the engine must run up to 5 minutes before this code will set
15	Open Coolant Temperature Sensor (CTS) circuit — the engine must run up to 5 minutes before this code will set
21	Throttle Position Sensor (TPS) circuit — the engine must run up to 25 seconds, at specified curb idle speed, before this code will set
23	Open or grounded Mixture Control (M/C) solenoid circuit
24	Vehicle Speed Sensor (VSS) circuit — the car must operate up to 5 minutes at road speed before this code will set
32	Barometric Pressure Sensor (BARO) circuit low
34	Manifold Absolute Pressure (MAP) or vacuum sensor circuit — the engine must run up to 5 minutes, at specfied curb idle speed, before this code will set
35	Idle Speed Control (ISC) switch circuitr — over 50% throttle for over 2 seconds
42	Electronic Spark Timing (EST) bypass circuit or EST circuit grounded or open
44	Lean exhaust indication — the engine must run up to 5 minutes, in closed loop, at part throttle before this code will set
44 & 45	At same time — faulty oxygen sensor circuit
45	Rich exhaust indication — the engine must run up to 5 minutes, in closed loop, at part throttle before this code will set
51	Faulty calibration unit (PROM) or installation. It takes up to 30 seconds before this code will set
54	Shorted Mixture Control (M/C) solenoid
55	Grounded V/ref (terminal 21), faulty oxygen sensor or Electronic Control Module (ECM)

Year – 1982
Model – Cavalier
Engine – 1.8L (112 cid) 4 cyl
Engine Code – VIN G

ECM TROUBLE CODES

Code	Explanation
12	No reference pulses to the Electronic Control Module (ECM). This code is not stored in memory and will only flash while the fault is present. Normal code with ignition ON, engine not running
13	Oxygen sensor circuit – the engine must run up to 5 minutes at part throttle, under road load, before this code will set
14	Shorted Coolant Temperature Sensor (CTS) circuit – the engine must run up to 5 minutes before this code will set
15	Open Coolant Temperature Sensor (CTS) circuit – the engine must run up to 5 minutes before this code will set
21	Throttle Position Sensor (TPS) circuit – the engine must run up to 25 seconds, at specified curb idle speed, before this code will set
23	Open or grounded Mixture Control (M/C) solenoid circuit
24	Vehicle Speed Sensor (VSS) circuit – the car must operate up to 5 minutes at road speed before this code will set
32	Barometric Pressure Sensor (BARO) circuit low
34	Manifold Absolute Pressure (MAP) or vacuum sensor circuit – the engine must run up to 5 minutes, at specfied curb idle speed, before this code will set
35	Idle Speed Control (ISC) switch circuitr – over 50% throttle for over 2 seconds
42	Electronic Spark Timing (EST) bypass circuit or EST circuit grounded or open
44	Lean exhaust indication – the engine must run up to 5 minutes, in closed loop, at part throttle before this code will set
44 & 45	At same time – faulty oxygen sensor circuit
45	Rich exhaust indication – the engine must run up to 5 minutes, in closed loop, at part throttle before this code will set
51	Faulty calibration unit (PROM) or installation. It takes up to 30 seconds before this code will set
54	Shorted Mixture Control (M/C) solenoid
55	Grounded V/ref (terminal 21), faulty oxygen sensor or Electronic Control Module (ECM)

Year — 1983
Model — Caprice Classic
Engine — 3.8L (231 cid) V6
Engine Code — VIN A

ECM TROUBLE CODES

Code	Explanation
12	No distributor reference pulses to the Electronic Control Module (ECM). This code is not stored in memory and will only flash while the fault is present. Normal code with ignition ON, engine not running
13	Oxygen sensor circuit — the engine must run up to 5 minutes at part throttle, under road load, before this code will set
14	Shorted Coolant Temperature Sensor (CTS) circuit — the engine must run up to 5 minutes before this code will set
15	Open Coolant Temperature Sensor (CTS) circuit — the engine must run up to 5 minutes before this code will set
21	Throttle Position Sensor (TPS) circuit — the engine must run up to 25 seconds, at specified curb idle speed, before this code will set
23	Open or grounded Mixture Control (M/C) solenoid circuit
24	Vehicle Speed Sensor (VSS) circuit — the car must operate up to 5 minutes at road speed before this code will set
32	Barometric Pressure Sensor (BARO) circuit low
34	Manifold Absolute Pressure (MAP) or vacuum sensor circuit. The engine must run up to 5 minutes at specified curb idle speed, before this code will set
35	Idle Speed Control (ISC) switch circuit shorted — over ½ throttle for over 2 seconds
41	No distributor reference pulses at specified engine vacuum. This code will store
42	Electronic Spark Timing (EST) bypass circuit grounded or open
44	Lean exhaust indication — the engine must run up to 5 minutes, in closed loop, at part throttle before this code will set
45	Rich exhaust indication — the engine must run up to 5 minutes, in closed loop, at part throttle before this code will set
51	Faulty or improperly installed calibration unit (PROM). It takes up to 30 seconds before this code will set
54	Shorted Mixture Control (M/C) solenoid circuit and/or faulty Electronic Control Module (ECM)
55	Grounded V/ref, (terminal 21) hush voltage on oxygen sensor circuit

Year – 1983
Model – Caprice Classic
Engine – 3.8L (229 cid) V6
Engine Code – VIN K

ECM TROUBLE CODES

Code	Explanation
12	No distributor reference pulses to the Electronic Control Module (ECM). This code is not stored in memory and will only flash while the fault is present. Normal code with ignition ON, engine not running
13	Oxygen sensor circuit—the engine must run up to 5 minutes at part throttle, under road load, before this code will set
14	Shorted Coolant Temperature Sensor (CTS) circuit—the engine must run up to 5 minutes before this code will set
15	Open Coolant Temperature Sensor (CTS) circuit—the engine must run up to 5 minutes before this code will set
21	Throttle Position Sensor (TPS) circuit—the engine must run up to 25 seconds, at specified curb idle speed, before this code will set
23	Open or grounded Mixture Control (M/C) solenoid circuit
24	Vehicle Speed Sensor (VSS) circuit—the car must operate up to 5 minutes at road speed before this code will set
32	Barometric Pressure Sensor (BARO) circuit low
34	Manifold Absolute Pressure (MAP) or vacuum sensor circuit. The engine must run up to 5 minutes at specified curb idle speed, before this code will set
35	Idle Speed Control (ISC) switch circuit shorted—over ½ throttle for over 2 seconds
41	No distributor reference pulses at specified engine vacuum. This code will store
42	Electronic Spark Timing (EST) bypass circuit grounded or open
44	Lean exhaust indication—the engine must run up to 5 minutes, in closed loop, at part throttle before this code will set
45	Rich exhaust indication—the engine must run up to 5 minutes, in closed loop, at part throttle before this code will set
51	Faulty or improperly installed calibration unit (PROM). It takes up to 30 seconds before this code will set
54	Shorted Mixture Control (M/C) solenoid circuit and/or faulty Electronic Control Module (ECM)
55	Grounded V/ref, (terminal 21) hush voltage on oxygen sensor circuit

Year — 1983
Model — Caprice Classic
Engine — 5.0L (305 cid) V8
Engine Code — VIN H

ECM TROUBLE CODES

Code	Explanation
12	No distributor reference pulses to the Electronic Control Module (ECM). This code is not stored in memory and will only flash while the fault is present. Normal code with ignition ON, engine not running
13	Oxygen sensor circuit — the engine must run up to 5 minutes at part throttle, under road load, before this code will set
14	Shorted Coolant Temperature Sensor (CTS) circuit — the engine must run up to 5 minutes before this code will set
15	Open Coolant Temperature Sensor (CTS) circuit — the engine must run up to 5 minutes before this code will set
21	Throttle Position Sensor (TPS) circuit — the engine must run up to 25 seconds, at specified curb idle speed, before this code will set
23	Open or grounded Mixture Control (M/C) solenoid circuit
24	Vehicle Speed Sensor (VSS) circuit — the car must operate up to 5 minutes at road speed before this code will set
32	Barometric Pressure Sensor (BARO) circuit low
34	Manifold Absolute Pressure (MAP) or vacuum sensor circuit. The engine must run up to 5 minutes at specified curb idle speed, before this code will set
35	Idle Speed Control (ISC) switch circuit shorted — over ½ throttle for over 2 seconds
41	No distributor reference pulses at specified engine vacuum. This code will store
42	Electronic Spark Timing (EST) bypass circuit grounded or open
44	Lean exhaust indication — the engine must run up to 5 minutes, in closed loop, at part throttle before this code will set
45	Rich exhaust indication — the engine must run up to 5 minutes, in closed loop, at part throttle before this code will set
51	Faulty or improperly installed calibration unit (PROM). It takes up to 30 seconds before this code will set
54	Shorted Mixture Control (M/C) solenoid circuit and/or faulty Electronic Control Module (ECM)
55	Grounded V/ref, (terminal 21) hush voltage on oxygen sensor circuit

Year — 1983
Model — Impala
Engine — 3.8L (231 cid) V6
Engine Code — VIN A

ECM TROUBLE CODES

Code	Explanation
12	No distributor reference pulses to the Electronic Control Module (ECM). This code is not stored in memory and will only flash while the fault is present. Normal code with ignition ON, engine not running
13	Oxygen sensor circuit — the engine must run up to 5 minutes at part throttle, under road load, before this code will set
14	Shorted Coolant Temperature Sensor (CTS) circuit — the engine must run up to 5 minutes before this code will set
15	Open Coolant Temperature Sensor (CTS) circuit — the engine must run up to 5 minutes before this code will set
21	Throttle Position Sensor (TPS) circuit — the engine must run up to 25 seconds, at specified curb idle speed, before this code will set
23	Open or grounded Mixture Control (M/C) solenoid circuit
24	Vehicle Speed Sensor (VSS) circuit — the car must operate up to 5 minutes at road speed before this code will set
32	Barometric Pressure Sensor (BARO) circuit low
34	Manifold Absolute Pressure (MAP) or vacuum sensor circuit. The engine must run up to 5 minutes at specified curb idle speed, before this code will set
35	Idle Speed Control (ISC) switch circuit shorted — over ½ throttle for over 2 seconds
41	No distributor reference pulses at specified engine vacuum. This code will store
42	Electronic Spark Timing (EST) bypass circuit grounded or open
44	Lean exhaust indication — the engine must run up to 5 minutes, in closed loop, at part throttle before this code will set
45	Rich exhaust indication — the engine must run up to 5 minutes, in closed loop, at part throttle before this code will set
51	Faulty or improperly installed calibration unit (PROM). It takes up to 30 seconds before this code will set
54	Shorted Mixture Control (M/C) solenoid circuit and/or faulty Electronic Control Module (ECM)
55	Grounded V/ref, (terminal 21) hush voltage on oxygen sensor circuit

Year — 1983
Model — Impala
Engine — 3.8L (229 cid) V6
Engine Code — VIN K

ECM TROUBLE CODES

Code	Explanation
12	No distributor reference pulses to the Electronic Control Module (ECM). This code is not stored in memory and will only flash while the fault is present. Normal code with ignition ON, engine not running
13	Oxygen sensor circuit — the engine must run up to 5 minutes at part throttle, under road load, before this code will set
14	Shorted Coolant Temperature Sensor (CTS) circuit — the engine must run up to 5 minutes before this code will set
15	Open Coolant Temperature Sensor (CTS) circuit — the engine must run up to 5 minutes before this code will set
21	Throttle Position Sensor (TPS) circuit — the engine must run up to 25 seconds, at specified curb idle speed, before this code will set
23	Open or grounded Mixture Control (M/C) solenoid circuit
24	Vehicle Speed Sensor (VSS) circuit — the car must operate up to 5 minutes at road speed before this code will set
32	Barometric Pressure Sensor (BARO) circuit low
34	Manifold Absolute Pressure (MAP) or vacuum sensor circuit. The engine must run up to 5 minutes at specified curb idle speed, before this code will set
35	Idle Speed Control (ISC) switch circuit shorted — over ½ throttle for over 2 seconds
41	No distributor reference pulses at specified engine vacuum. This code will store
42	Electronic Spark Timing (EST) bypass circuit grounded or open
44	Lean exhaust indication — the engine must run up to 5 minutes, in closed loop, at part throttle before this code will set
45	Rich exhaust indication — the engine must run up to 5 minutes, in closed loop, at part throttle before this code will set
51	Faulty or improperly installed calibration unit (PROM). It takes up to 30 seconds before this code will set
54	Shorted Mixture Control (M/C) solenoid circuit and/or faulty Electronic Control Module (ECM)
55	Grounded V/rcf, (terminal 21) hush voltage on oxygen sensor circuit

GENERAL MOTORS CORPORATION
DIAGNOSTIC CODE DATA

Year – 1983
Model – Impala
Engine – 5.0L (305 cid) V8
Engine Code – VIN H

ECM TROUBLE CODES

Code	Explanation
12	No distributor reference pulses to the Electronic Control Module (ECM). This code is not stored in memory and will only flash while the fault is present. Normal code with ignition ON, engine not running
13	Oxygen sensor circuit – the engine must run up to 5 minutes at part throttle, under road load, before this code will set
14	Shorted Coolant Temperature Sensor (CTS) circuit – the engine must run up to 5 minutes before this code will set
15	Open Coolant Temperature Sensor (CTS) circuit – the engine must run up to 5 minutes before this code will set
21	Throttle Position Sensor (TPS) circuit – the engine must run up to 25 seconds, at specified curb idle speed, before this code will set
23	Open or grounded Mixture Control (M/C) solenoid circuit
24	Vehicle Speed Sensor (VSS) circuit – the car must operate up to 5 minutes at road speed before this code will set
32	Barometric Pressure Sensor (BARO) circuit low
34	Manifold Absolute Pressure (MAP) or vacuum sensor circuit. The engine must run up to 5 minutes at specified curb idle speed, before this code will set
35	Idle Speed Control (ISC) switch circuit shorted – over ½ throttle for over 2 seconds
41	No distributor reference pulses at specified engine vacuum. This code will store
42	Electronic Spark Timing (EST) bypass circuit grounded or open
44	Lean exhaust indication – the engine must run up to 5 minutes, in closed loop, at part throttle before this code will set
45	Rich exhaust indication – the engine must run up to 5 minutes, in closed loop, at part throttle before this code will set
51	Faulty or improperly installed calibration unit (PROM). It takes up to 30 seconds before this code will set
54	Shorted Mixture Control (M/C) solenoid circuit and/or faulty Electronic Control Module (ECM)
55	Grounded V/ref, (terminal 21) hush voltage on oxygen sensor circuit

Year – 1983
Model – Camaro
Engine – 2.5L (151 cid) 4 cyl
Engine Code – VIN F

ECM TROUBLE CODES

Code	Explanation
12	No reference pulses to the Electronic Control Module (ECM). This code is not stored in memory and will only flash while the fault is present. Normal code with ignition ON, engine not running
13	Oxygen sensor circuit—the engine must run up to 5 minutes at part throttle, under road load, before this code will set
14	Shorted Coolant Temperature Sensor (CTS) circuit—the engine must run up to 2 minutes before this code will set
15	Open Coolant Temperature Sensor (CTS) circuit—the engine must run up to 5 minutes before this code will set
21	Throttle Position Sensor (TPS) circuit—the engine must run up to 25 seconds, at specified curb idle speed, before this code will set
23	Open or grounded Mixture Control (M/C) solenoid circuit
24	Vehicle Speed Sensor (VSS) circuit—the car must operate up to 5 minutes at road speed before this code will set
34	Vacuum sensor circuit—the engine must run up to 5 minutes at specified curb idle speed, before this code will set
41	No distributor reference pulses at specified engine vacuum. This code will store
42	Electronic Spark Timing (EST) bypass circuit grounded or open
44	Lean oxygen sensor indication—the engine must run up to 5 minutes, in closed loop, at part throttle before this code will set
44 & 45	At same time—faulty oxygen sensor circuit
45	Rich system indication—the engine must run up to 5 minutes, in closed loop, at part throttle before this code will set
51	Faulty calibration unit (PROM) or installation. It takes up to 30 seconds before this code will set
54	Shorted Mixture Control (M/C) solenoid circuit and/or faulty Electronic Control Module (ECM)
55	Grounded V/ref (terminal 21), faulty oxygen sensor or Electronic Control Module (ECM)

GENERAL MOTORS CORPORATION
DIAGNOSTIC CODE DATA

Year – 1983
Model – Camaro
Engine – 2.5L (151 cid) 4 cyl
Engine Code – VIN 2

ECM TROUBLE CODES

Code	Explanation
13	Oxygen sensor circuit—warm engine running at normal operating temperature for at least 3 minutes at part throttle with oxygen sensor signal missing (open) for 60 seconds
14	Coolant Temperature Sensor (CTS) circuit signal voltage low—engine running 10 seconds with no coolant sensor signal voltage
15	Coolant Temperature Sensor (CTS) circuit signal voltage high—engine running with coolant sensor signal too high for 60 seconds. If fault occurs with ignition OFF, engine will crank but may not start
21	Throttle Position Sensor (TPS) signal too high—engine running below 1600 RPM, and TPS is above 50% (2.5V) for 2 seconds
22	Throttle Position Sensor (TPS) signal too low—engine running with TPS signal voltage too low
24	Vehicle Speed Sensor (VSS)—vehicle speed decelerating with no VSS for 1 minute
33	Manifold Absolute Pressure (MAP) signal too high, low vacuum—engine idling and MAP signal is high for 5 seconds
34	Manifold Absolute Pressure (MAP) signal too low—engine running 0.2 second (200m seconds) with MAP signal voltage too low
42	Electronic Spark Timing (EST)—open or grounded EST line, open or grounded bypass line, and engine speed above 500 RPM
43	Electronic Spark Control (ESC)—full retard—engine running and ESC signal at Electronic Control Module (ECM) is low for 4 seconds.
44	Lean exhaust system—engine running in closed loop at normal operating temperature with oxygen sensor signal less than 200mv for 1 minute. Forces open loop operation. May require drive position to set on some engines
45	Rich exhaust system—engine idling in closed loop at normal operating temperature with oxygen sensor signal above 750mv for 20 seconds. Forces open loop operation. May require drive position to set on some engines
51	Faulty calibration unit (PROM) or installation
55	Replace faulty Electronic Control Module (ECM)

Year — 1983
Model — Camaro
Engine — 2.8L (173 cid) V6
Engine Code — VIN 1

ECM TROUBLE CODES

Code	Explanation
12	No reference pulses to the Electronic Control Module (ECM). This code is not stored in memory and will only flash while the fault is present. Normal code with ignition ON, engine not running
13	Oxygen sensor circuit — the engine must run up to 5 minutes at part throttle, under road load, before this code will set
14	Shorted Coolant Temperature Sensor (CTS) circuit — the engine must run up to 2 minutes before this code will set
15	Open Coolant Temperature Sensor (CTS) circuit — the engine must run up to 5 minutes before this code will set
21	Throttle Position Sensor (TPS) circuit — the engine must run up to 25 seconds, at specified curb idle speed, before this code will set
23	Open or grounded Mixture Control (M/C) solenoid circuit
24	Vehicle Speed Sensor (VSS) circuit — the car must operate up to 5 minutes at road speed before this code will set
34	Vacuum sensor circuit — the engine must run up to 5 minutes at specified curb idle speed, before this code will set
41	No distributor reference pulses at specified engine vacuum. This code will store
42	Electronic Spark Timing (EST) bypass circuit grounded or open
44	Lean oxygen sensor indication — the engine must run up to 5 minutes, in closed loop, at part throttle before this code will set
44 & 45	At same time — faulty oxygen sensor circuit
45	Rich system indication — the engine must run up to 5 minutes, in closed loop, at part throttle before this code will set
51	Faulty calibration unit (PROM) or installation. It takes up to 30 seconds before this code will set
54	Shorted Mixture Control (M/C) solenoid circuit and/or faulty Electronic Control Module (ECM)
55	Grounded V/ref (terminal 21), faulty oxygen sensor or Electronic Control Module (ECM)

Year – 1983
Model – Camaro
Engine – 2.8L (173 cid) V6
Engine Code – VIN L

ECM TROUBLE CODES

Code	Explanation
12	No reference pulses to the Electronic Control Module (ECM). This code is not stored in memory and will only flash while the fault is present. Normal code with ignition ON, engine not running
13	Oxygen sensor circuit – the engine must run up to 5 minutes at part throttle, under road load, before this code will set
14	Shorted Coolant Temperature Sensor (CTS) circuit – the engine must run up to 2 minutes before this code will set
15	Open Coolant Temperature Sensor (CTS) circuit – the engine must run up to 5 minutes before this code will set
21	Throttle Position Sensor (TPS) circuit – the engine must run up to 25 seconds, at specified curb idle speed, before this code will set
23	Open or grounded Mixture Control (M/C) solenoid circuit
24	Vehicle Speed Sensor (VSS) circuit – the car must operate up to 5 minutes at road speed before this code will set
34	Vacuum sensor circuit – the engine must run up to 5 minutes at specified curb idle speed, before this code will set
41	No distributor reference pulses at specified engine vacuum. This code will store
42	Electronic Spark Timing (EST) bypass circuit grounded or open
44	Lean oxygen sensor indication – the engine must run up to 5 minutes, in closed loop, at part throttle before this code will set
44 & 45	At same time – faulty oxygen sensor circuit
45	Rich system indication – the engine must run up to 5 minutes, in closed loop, at part throttle before this code will set
51	Faulty calibration unit (PROM) or installation. It takes up to 30 seconds before this code will set
54	Shorted Mixture Control (M/C) solenoid circuit and/or faulty Electronic Control Module (ECM)
55	Grounded V/ref (terminal 21), faulty oxygen sensor or Electronic Control Module (ECM)

Year — 1983
Model — Camaro
Engine — 5.0L (305 cid) V8
Engine Code — VIN H

ECM TROUBLE CODES

Code	Explanation
12	No reference pulses to the Electronic Control Module (ECM). This code is not stored in memory and will only flash while the fault is present. Normal code with ignition ON, engine not running
13	Oxygen sensor circuit — the engine must run up to 5 minutes at part throttle, under road load, before this code will set
14	Shorted Coolant Temperature Sensor (CTS) circuit — the engine must run up to 2 minutes before this code will set
15	Open Coolant Temperature Sensor (CTS) circuit — the engine must run up to 5 minutes before this code will set
21	Throttle Position Sensor (TPS) circuit — the engine must run up to 25 seconds, at specified curb idle speed, before this code will set
23	Open or grounded Mixture Control (M/C) solenoid circuit
24	Vehicle Speed Sensor (VSS) circuit — the car must operate up to 5 minutes at road speed before this code will set
34	Vacuum sensor circuit — the engine must run up to 5 minutes at specified curb idle speed, before this code will set
41	No distributor reference pulses at specified engine vacuum. This code will store
42	Electronic Spark Timing (EST) bypass circuit grounded or open
44	Lean oxygen sensor indication — the engine must run up to 5 minutes, in closed loop, at part throttle before this code will set
44 & 45	At same time — faulty oxygen sensor circuit
45	Rich system indication — the engine must run up to 5 minutes, in closed loop, at part throttle before this code will set
51	Faulty calibration unit (PROM) or installation. It takes up to 30 seconds before this code will set
54	Shorted Mixture Control (M/C) solenoid circuit and/or faulty Electronic Control Module (ECM)
55	Grounded V/ref (terminal 21), faulty oxygen sensor or Electronic Control Module (ECM)

Year – 1983
Model – Camaro
Engine – 5.0L (305 cid) EFE V8
Engine Code – VIN S

ECM TROUBLE CODES

Code	Explanation
13	Oxygen sensor circuit – warm engine running at normal operating temperature for at least 3 minutes at part throttle with oxygen sensor signal missing (open) for 60 seconds
14	Coolant Temperature Sensor (CTS) circuit signal voltage low – engine running 10 seconds with no coolant sensor signal voltage
15	Coolant Temperature Sensor (CTS) circuit signal voltage high – engine running with coolant sensor signal too high for 60 seconds. If fault occurs with ignition OFF, engine will crank but may not start
21	Throttle Position Sensor (TPS) signal too high – engine running below 1600 RPM, and TPS is above 50% (2.5V) for 2 seconds
22	Throttle Position Sensor (TPS) signal too low – engine running with TPS signal voltage too low
24	Vehicle Speed Sensor (VSS) – vehicle speed about 40–45 mph, steady throttle signal with no VSS for 1 minute
33	Manifold Absolute Pressure (MAP) signal too high, low vacuum – engine idling and MAP signal is high for 5 seconds
34	Manifold Absolute Pressure (MAP) signal too low – engine running 0.2 second (200m seconds) with MAP signal voltage too low
42	Electronic Spark Timing (EST) – open or grounded EST line, open or grounded bypass line, and engine speed above 500 RPM
43	Electronic Spark Control (ESC) – full retard – engine running and ESC signal at Electronic Control Module (ECM) is low for 4 seconds.
44	Lean exhaust system – engine running in closed loop at normal operating temperature with oxygen sensor signal less than 200mv for 1 minute. Forces open loop operation. May require drive position to set on some engines
45	Rich exhaust system – engine idling in closed loop at normal operating temperature with oxygen sensor signal above 750mv for 20 seconds. Forces open loop operation. May require drive position to set on some engines
51	Faulty calibration unit (PROM) or installation
55	Replace faulty Electronic Control Module (ECM)

Year – 1983
Model – Malibu Classic
Engine – 3.8L (231 cid) V6
Engine Code – VIN A

ECM TROUBLE CODES

Code	Explanation
12	No distributor reference pulses to the Electronic Control Module (ECM). This code is not stored in memory and will only flash while the fault is present. Normal code with ignition ON, engine not running
13	Oxygen sensor circuit – the engine must run up to 5 minutes at part throttle, under road load, before this code will set
14	Shorted Coolant Temperature Sensor (CTS) circuit – the engine must run up to 5 minutes before this code will set
15	Open Coolant Temperature Sensor (CTS) circuit – the engine must run up to 5 minutes before this code will set
21	Throttle Position Sensor (TPS) circuit – the engine must run up to 25 seconds, at specified curb idle speed, before this code will set
23	Open or grounded Mixture Control (M/C) solenoid circuit
24	Vehicle Speed Sensor (VSS) circuit – the car must operate up to 5 minutes at road speed before this code will set
32	Barometric Pressure Sensor (BARO) circuit low
34	Manifold Absolute Pressure (MAP) or vacuum sensor circuit. The engine must run up to 5 minutes at specified curb idle speed, before this code will set
35	Idle Speed Control (ISC) switch circuit shorted – over ½ throttle for over 2 seconds
41	No distributor reference pulses at specified engine vacuum. This code will store
42	Electronic Spark Timing (EST) bypass circuit grounded or open
44	Lean exhaust indication – the engine must run up to 5 minutes, in closed loop, at part throttle before this code will set
45	Rich exhaust indication – the engine must run up to 5 minutes, in closed loop, at part throttle before this code will set
51	Faulty or improperly installed calibration unit (PROM). It takes up to 30 seconds before this code will set
54	Shorted Mixture Control (M/C) solenoid circuit and/or faulty Electronic Control Module (ECM)
55	Grounded V/ref, (terminal 21) hush voltage on oxygen sensor circuit

GENERAL MOTORS CORPORATION
DIAGNOSTIC CODE DATA

Year – 1983
Model – Malibu Classic
Engine – 3.8L (229 cid) V6
Engine Code – VIN 9

ECM TROUBLE CODES

Code	Explanation
12	No distributor reference pulses to the Electronic Control Module (ECM). This code is not stored in memory and will only flash while the fault is present. Normal code with ignition ON, engine not running
13	Oxygen sensor circuit—the engine must run up to 5 minutes at part throttle, under road load, before this code will set
14	Shorted Coolant Temperature Sensor (CTS) circuit—the engine must run up to 5 minutes before this code will set
15	Open Coolant Temperature Sensor (CTS) circuit—the engine must run up to 5 minutes before this code will set
21	Throttle Position Sensor (TPS) circuit—the engine must run up to 25 seconds, at specified curb idle speed, before this code will set
23	Open or grounded Mixture Control (M/C) solenoid circuit
24	Vehicle Speed Sensor (VSS) circuit—the car must operate up to 5 minutes at road speed before this code will set
32	Barometric Pressure Sensor (BARO) circuit low
34	Manifold Absolute Pressure (MAP) or vacuum sensor circuit. The engine must run up to 5 minutes at specified curb idle speed, before this code will set
35	Idle Speed Control (ISC) switch circuit shorted—over ½ throttle for over 2 seconds
41	No distributor reference pulses at specified engine vacuum. This code will store
42	Electronic Spark Timing (EST) bypass circuit grounded or open
44	Lean exhaust indication—the engine must run up to 5 minutes, in closed loop, at part throttle before this code will set
45	Rich exhaust indication—the engine must run up to 5 minutes, in closed loop, at part throttle before this code will set
51	Faulty or improperly installed calibration unit (PROM). It takes up to 30 seconds before this code will set
54	Shorted Mixture Control (M/C) solenoid circuit and/or faulty Electronic Control Module (ECM)
55	Grounded V/ref, (terminal 21) hush voltage on oxygen sensor circuit

Year — 1983
Model — Malibu Classic
Engine — 5.0L (305 cid) V8
Engine Code — VIN H

ECM TROUBLE CODES

Code	Explanation
12	No distributor reference pulses to the Electronic Control Module (ECM). This code is not stored in memory and will only flash while the fault is present. Normal code with ignition ON, engine not running
13	Oxygen sensor circuit — the engine must run up to 5 minutes at part throttle, under road load, before this code will set
14	Shorted Coolant Temperature Sensor (CTS) circuit — the engine must run up to 5 minutes before this code will set
15	Open Coolant Temperature Sensor (CTS) circuit — the engine must run up to 5 minutes before this code will set
21	Throttle Position Sensor (TPS) circuit — the engine must run up to 25 seconds, at specified curb idle speed, before this code will set
23	Open or grounded Mixture Control (M/C) solenoid circuit
24	Vehicle Speed Sensor (VSS) circuit — the car must operate up to 5 minutes at road speed before this code will set
32	Barometric Pressure Sensor (BARO) circuit low
34	Manifold Absolute Pressure (MAP) or vacuum sensor circuit. The engine must run up to 5 minutes at specified curb idle speed, before this code will set
35	Idle Speed Control (ISC) switch circuit shorted — over ½ throttle for over 2 seconds
41	No distributor reference pulses at specified engine vacuum. This code will store
42	Electronic Spark Timing (EST) bypass circuit grounded or open
44	Lean exhaust indication — the engine must run up to 5 minutes, in closed loop, at part throttle before this code will set
45	Rich exhaust indication — the engine must run up to 5 minutes, in closed loop, at part throttle before this code will set
51	Faulty or improperly installed calibration unit (PROM). It takes up to 30 seconds before this code will set
54	Shorted Mixture Control (M/C) solenoid circuit and/or faulty Electronic Control Module (ECM)
55	Grounded V/ref, (terminal 21) hush voltage on oxygen sensor circuit

GENERAL MOTORS CORPORATION
DIAGNOSTIC CODE DATA

Year – 1983
Model – Monte Carlo
Engine – 3.8L (231 cid) V6
Engine Code – VIN A

ECM TROUBLE CODES

Code	Explanation
12	No distributor reference pulses to the Electronic Control Module (ECM). This code is not stored in memory and will only flash while the fault is present. Normal code with ignition ON, engine not running
13	Oxygen sensor circuit – the engine must run up to 5 minutes at part throttle, under road load, before this code will set
14	Shorted Coolant Temperature Sensor (CTS) circuit – the engine must run up to 5 minutes before this code will set
15	Open Coolant Temperature Sensor (CTS) circuit – the engine must run up to 5 minutes before this code will set
21	Throttle Position Sensor (TPS) circuit – the engine must run up to 25 seconds, at specified curb idle speed, before this code will set
23	Open or grounded Mixture Control (M/C) solenoid circuit
24	Vehicle Speed Sensor (VSS) circuit – the car must operate up to 5 minutes at road speed before this code will set
32	Barometric Pressure Sensor (BARO) circuit low
34	Manifold Absolute Pressure (MAP) or vacuum sensor circuit. The engine must run up to 5 minutes at specified curb idle speed, before this code will set
35	Idle Speed Control (ISC) switch circuit shorted – over ½ throttle for over 2 seconds
41	No distributor reference pulses at specified engine vacuum. This code will store
42	Electronic Spark Timing (EST) bypass circuit grounded or open
44	Lean exhaust indication – the engine must run up to 5 minutes, in closed loop, at part throttle before this code will set
45	Rich exhaust indication – the engine must run up to 5 minutes, in closed loop, at part throttle before this code will set
51	Faulty or improperly installed calibration unit (PROM). It takes up to 30 seconds before this code will set
54	Shorted Mixture Control (M/C) solenoid circuit and/or faulty Electronic Control Module (ECM)
55	Grounded V/ref, (terminal 21) hush voltage on oxygen sensor circuit

Year — 1983
Model — Monte Carlo
Engine — 3.8L (229 cid) V6
Engine Code — VIN 9

ECM TROUBLE CODES

Code	Explanation
12	No distributor reference pulses to the Electronic Control Module (ECM). This code is not stored in memory and will only flash while the fault is present. Normal code with ignition ON, engine not running
13	Oxygen sensor circuit — the engine must run up to 5 minutes at part throttle, under road load, before this code will set
14	Shorted Coolant Temperature Sensor (CTS) circuit — the engine must run up to 5 minutes before this code will set
15	Open Coolant Temperature Sensor (CTS) circuit — the engine must run up to 5 minutes before this code will set
21	Throttle Position Sensor (TPS) circuit — the engine must run up to 25 seconds, at specified curb idle speed, before this code will set
23	Open or grounded Mixture Control (M/C) solenoid circuit
24	Vehicle Speed Sensor (VSS) circuit — the car must operate up to 5 minutes at road speed before this code will set
32	Barometric Pressure Sensor (BARO) circuit low
34	Manifold Absolute Pressure (MAP) or vacuum sensor circuit. The engine must run up to 5 minutes at specified curb idle speed, before this code will set
35	Idle Speed Control (ISC) switch circuit shorted — over ½ throttle for over 2 seconds
41	No distributor reference pulses at specified engine vacuum. This code will store
42	Electronic Spark Timing (EST) bypass circuit grounded or open
44	Lean exhaust indication — the engine must run up to 5 minutes, in closed loop, at part throttle before this code will set
45	Rich exhaust indication — the engine must run up to 5 minutes, in closed loop, at part throttle before this code will set
51	Faulty or improperly installed calibration unit (PROM). It takes up to 30 seconds before this code will set
54	Shorted Mixture Control (M/C) solenoid circuit and/or faulty Electronic Control Module (ECM)
55	Grounded V/ref, (terminal 21) hush voltage on oxygen sensor circuit

Year – 1983
Model – Monte Carlo
Engine – 5.0L (305 cid) V8
Engine Code – VIN H

ECM TROUBLE CODES

Code	Explanation
12	No distributor reference pulses to the Electronic Control Module (ECM). This code is not stored in memory and will only flash while the fault is present. Normal code with ignition ON, engine not running
13	Oxygen sensor circuit – the engine must run up to 5 minutes at part throttle, under road load, before this code will set
14	Shorted Coolant Temperature Sensor (CTS) circuit – the engine must run up to 5 minutes before this code will set
15	Open Coolant Temperature Sensor (CTS) circuit – the engine must run up to 5 minutes before this code will set
21	Throttle Position Sensor (TPS) circuit – the engine must run up to 25 seconds, at specified curb idle speed, before this code will set
23	Open or grounded Mixture Control (M/C) solenoid circuit
24	Vehicle Speed Sensor (VSS) circuit – the car must operate up to 5 minutes at road speed before this code will set
32	Barometric Pressure Sensor (BARO) circuit low
34	Manifold Absolute Pressure (MAP) or vacuum sensor circuit. The engine must run up to 5 minutes at specified curb idle speed, before this code will set
35	Idle Speed Control (ISC) switch circuit shorted – over ½ throttle for over 2 seconds
41	No distributor reference pulses at specified engine vacuum. This code will store
42	Electronic Spark Timing (EST) bypass circuit grounded or open
44	Lean exhaust indication – the engine must run up to 5 minutes, in closed loop, at part throttle before this code will set
45	Rich exhaust indication – the engine must run up to 5 minutes, in closed loop, at part throttle before this code will set
51	Faulty or improperly installed calibration unit (PROM). It takes up to 30 seconds before this code will set
54	Shorted Mixture Control (M/C) solenoid circuit and/or faulty Electronic Control Module (ECM)
55	Grounded V/ref, (terminal 21) hush voltage on oxygen sensor circuit

Year – 1983
Model – Monte Carlo
Engine – 5.0L (305 cid) V8
Engine Code – VIN 7

ECM TROUBLE CODES

Code	Explanation
12	No distributor reference pulses to the Electronic Control Module (ECM). This code is not stored in memory and will only flash while the fault is present. Normal code with ignition ON, engine not running
13	Oxygen sensor circuit — the engine must run up to 5 minutes at part throttle, under road load, before this code will set
14	Shorted Coolant Temperature Sensor (CTS) circuit — the engine must run up to 5 minutes before this code will set
15	Open Coolant Temperature Sensor (CTS) circuit — the engine must run up to 5 minutes before this code will set
21	Throttle Position Sensor (TPS) circuit — the engine must run up to 25 seconds, at specified curb idle speed, before this code will set
23	Open or grounded Mixture Control (M/C) solenoid circuit
24	Vehicle Speed Sensor (VSS) circuit — the car must operate up to 5 minutes at road speed before this code will set
32	Barometric Pressure Sensor (BARO) circuit low
34	Manifold Absolute Pressure (MAP) or vacuum sensor circuit. The engine must run up to 5 minutes at specified curb idle speed, before this code will set
35	Idle Speed Control (ISC) switch circuit shorted — over ½ throttle for over 2 seconds
41	No distributor reference pulses at specified engine vacuum. This code will store
42	Electronic Spark Timing (EST) bypass circuit grounded or open
44	Lean exhaust indication — the engine must run up to 5 minutes, in closed loop, at part throttle before this code will set
45	Rich exhaust indication — the engine must run up to 5 minutes, in closed loop, at part throttle before this code will set
51	Faulty or improperly installed calibration unit (PROM). It takes up to 30 seconds before this code will set
54	Shorted Mixture Control (M/C) solenoid circuit and/or faulty Electronic Control Module (ECM)
55	Grounded V/ref, (terminal 21) hush voltage on oxygen sensor circuit

Year – 1983
Model – Cavalier
Engine – 2.0L (121 cid) EFI 4 cyl
Engine Code – VIN B

ECM TROUBLE CODES

Code	Explanation
13	Oxygen sensor circuit – warm engine running at normal operating temperature for at least 3 minutes at part throttle with oxygen sensor signal missing (open) for 60 seconds
14	Coolant Temperature Sensor (CTS) circuit signal voltage low – engine running 10 seconds with no coolant sensor signal voltage
15	Coolant Temperature Sensor (CTS) circuit signal voltage high – engine running with coolant sensor signal too high for 60 seconds. If fault occurs with ignition OFF, engine will crank but may not start
21	Throttle Position Sensor (TPS) signal too high – engine running below 1600 RPM, and TPS is above 50% (2.5V) for 2 seconds
22	Throttle Position Sensor (TPS) signal too low – engine running with TPS signal voltage too low
24	Vehicle Speed Sensor (VSS) – vehicle speed decelerating with no VSS for 1 minute
33	Manifold Absolute Pressure (MAP) signal too high, low vacuum – engine idling and MAP signal is high for 5 seconds
34	Manifold Absolute Pressure (MAP) signal too low – engine running 0.2 second (200m seconds) with MAP signal voltage too low
42	Electronic Spark Timing (EST) – open or grounded EST line, open or grounded bypass line, and engine speed above 500 RPM
43	Electronic Spark Control (ESC) – full retard – engine running and ESC signal at Electronic Control Module (ECM) is low for 4 seconds.
44	Lean exhaust system – engine running in closed loop at normal operating temperature with oxygen sensor signal less than 200mv for 1 minute. Forces open loop operation. May require drive position to set on some engines
45	Rich exhaust system – engine idling in closed loop at normal operating temperature with oxygen sensor signal above 750mv for 20 seconds. Forces open loop operation. May require drive position to set on some engines
51	Faulty calibration unit (PROM) or installation
55	Replace faulty Electronic Control Module (ECM)

Year — 1983
Model — Cavalier
Engine — 2.0L (121 cid) EFI 4 cyl
Engine Code — VIN P

ECM TROUBLE CODES

Code	Explanation
13	Oxygen sensor circuit — warm engine running at normal operating temperature for at least 3 minutes at part throttle with oxygen sensor signal missing (open) for 60 seconds
14	Coolant Temperature Sensor (CTS) circuit signal voltage low — engine running 10 seconds with no coolant sensor signal voltage
15	Coolant Temperature Sensor (CTS) circuit signal voltage high — engine running with coolant sensor signal too high for 60 seconds. If fault occurs with ignition OFF, engine will crank but may not start
21	Throttle Position Sensor (TPS) signal too high — engine running below 1600 RPM, and TPS is above 50% (2.5V) for 2 seconds
22	Throttle Position Sensor (TPS) signal too low — engine running with TPS signal voltage too low
24	Vehicle Speed Sensor (VSS) — vehicle speed decelerating with no VSS for 1 minute
33	Manifold Absolute Pressure (MAP) signal too high, low vacuum — engine idling and MAP signal is high for 5 seconds
34	Manifold Absolute Pressure (MAP) signal too low — engine running 0.2 second (200m seconds) with MAP signal voltage too low
42	Electronic Spark Timing (EST) — open or grounded EST line, open or grounded bypass line, and engine speed above 500 RPM
43	Electronic Spark Control (ESC) — full retard — engine running and ESC signal at Electronic Control Module (ECM) is low for 4 seconds.
44	Lean exhaust system — engine running in closed loop at normal operating temperature with oxygen sensor signal less than 200mv for 1 minute. Forces open loop operation. May require drive position to set on some engines
45	Rich exhaust system — engine idling in closed loop at normal operating temperature with oxygen sensor signal above 750mv for 20 seconds. Forces open loop operation. May require drive position to set on some engines
51	Faulty calibration unit (PROM) or installation
55	Replace faulty Electronic Control Module (ECM)

Year — 1983
Model — Citation
Engine — 2.5L (151 cid) 4 cyl
Engine Code — VIN 5

ECM TROUBLE CODES

Code	Explanation
12	No reference pulses to the controller. This code does not stored in memory. It will only flash while the fault is present. The code is normal when the ignition is ON and the engine is not running
13	Open in the oxygen sensor circuit to Electronic Control Module (ECM) assembly terminal 9 — the engine must run for up to 5 minutes at part throttle, under road load, before this code will be stored
14	Shorted Coolant Temperature Sensor (CTS) circuit — the engine must run for up to 2 minutes before this code will be stored
15	Open Coolant Temperature Sensor (CTS) circuit — the engine must run for up to 5 minutes before this code will be stored
21	Throttle Position Sensor (TPS) circuit — the engine must run for up to 25 seconds, at the specified curb idle speed, before this code will be stored
23	Open or grounded Mixture Control (M/C) solenoid circuit
24	Vehicle Speed Sensor (VSS) circuit — the car must operate for up to 5 minutes at road speed before this code will be stored
32	Barometric Pressure Sensor (BARO) circuit low
34	Manifold Absolute Pressure (MAP) or vacuum sensor circuit. The engine must run for up to 5 minutes at the specified curb idle speed, before this code will be stored
41	No distributor reference pulses at the specified engine vacuum
42	Electronic Spark Timing (EST) bypass circuit grounded or open
43	Electronic Spark Control (ESC) retard signal for too long, causes a retard in EST signal
44	Lean oxygen sensor indication — the engine must run, in closed loop, for up to 2 minutes at part throttle before this code will be stored
44 & 45	At same time — faulty oxygen sensor circuit
45	Rich system indication — the engine must run, in closed loop, for up to 2 minutes at part throttle before this code will be stored
51	Faulty calibrator (PROM) or faulty calibrator installation. It takes up to 30 seconds before this code will be stored
54	Shorted Mixture Control (M/C) solenoid circuit and/or faulty controller
55	Grounded V/ref, (terminal 22), faulty oxygen sensor or controller

Year – 1983
Model – Citation
Engine – 2.5L (151 cid) EFI 4 cyl
Engine Code – VIN R

ECM TROUBLE CODES

Code	Explanation
13	Oxygen sensor circuit – warm engine running at normal operating temperature for at least 3 minutes at part throttle with oxygen sensor signal missing (open) for 60 seconds
14	Coolant Temperature Sensor (CTS) circuit signal voltage low – engine running 10 seconds with no coolant sensor signal voltage
15	Coolant Temperature Sensor (CTS) circuit signal voltage high – engine running with coolant sensor signal too high for 60 seconds. If fault occurs with ignition OFF, engine will crank but may not start
21	Throttle Position Sensor (TPS) signal too high – engine running below 1600 RPM, and TPS is above 50% (2.5V) for 2 seconds
22	Throttle Position Sensor (TPS) signal too low – engine running with TPS signal voltage too low
24	Vehicle Speed Sensor (VSS) – vehicle speed decelerating with no VSS for 1 minute
33	Manifold Absolute Pressure (MAP) signal too high, low vacuum – engine idling and MAP signal is high for 5 seconds
34	Manifold Absolute Pressure (MAP) signal too low – engine running code will set within 0.2 second with MAP signal voltage too low
42	Electronic Spark Timing (EST) – open or grounded EST line, open or grounded bypass line, and engine speed above 500 RPM
44	Lean exhaust system – engine running in closed loop at normal operating temperature with oxygen sensor signal less than 200mv for 1 minute. Forces open loop operation. May require drive position to set on some engines
45	Rich exhaust system – engine idling in closed loop at normal operating temperature with oxygen sensor signal above 750mv for 20 seconds. Forces open loop operation. May require drive position to set on some engines
51	Faulty calibration unit (PROM) or installation
55	Replace faulty Electronic Control Module (ECM)

Year – 1983
Model – Citation
Engine – 2.8L (173 cid) V6
Engine Code – VIN X

ECM TROUBLE CODES

Code	Explanation
12	No reference pulses to the controller. This code does not stored in memory. It will only flash while the fault is present. The code is normal when the ignition is ON and the engine is not running
13	Open in the oxygen sensor circuit to Electronic Control Module (ECM) assembly terminal 9 – the engine must run for up to 5 minutes at part throttle, under road load, before this code will be stored
14	Shorted Coolant Temperature Sensor (CTS) circuit – the engine must run for up to 2 minutes before this code will be stored
15	Open Coolant Temperature Sensor (CTS) circuit – the engine must run for up to 5 minutes before this code will be stored
21	Throttle Position Sensor (TPS) circuit – the engine must run for up to 25 seconds, at the specified curb idle speed, before this code will be stored
23	Open or grounded Mixture Control (M/C) solenoid circuit
24	Vehicle Speed Sensor (VSS) circuit – the car must operate for up to 5 minutes at road speed before this code will be stored
32	Barometric Pressure Sensor (BARO) circuit low
34	Manifold Absolute Pressure (MAP) or vacuum sensor circuit. The engine must run for up to 5 minutes at the specified curb idle speed, before this code will be stored
41	No distributor reference pulses at the specified engine vacuum
42	Electronic Spark Timing (EST) bypass circuit grounded or open
43	Electronic Spark Control (ESC) retard signal for too long, causes a retard in EST signal
44	Lean oxygen sensor indication – the engine must run, in closed loop, for up to 2 minutes at part throttle before this code will be stored
44 & 45	At same time – faulty oxygen sensor circuit
45	Rich system indication – the engine must run, in closed loop, for up to 2 minutes at part throttle before this code will be stored
51	Faulty calibrator (PROM) or faulty calibrator installation. It takes up to 30 seconds before this code will be stored
54	Shorted Mixture Control (M/C) solenoid circuit and/or faulty controller
55	Grounded V/ref, (terminal 22), faulty oxygen sensor or controller

Year – 1983
Model – Citation
Engine – 2.8L (173 cid) V6
Engine Code – VIN Z

ECM TROUBLE CODES

Code	Explanation
12	No reference pulses to the controller. This code does not stored in memory. It will only flash while the fault is present. The code is normal when the ignition is ON and the engine is not running
13	Open in the oxygen sensor circuit to Electronic Control Module (ECM) assembly terminal 9 – the engine must run for up to 5 minutes at part throttle, under road load, before this code will be stored
14	Shorted Coolant Temperature Sensor (CTS) circuit – the engine must run for up to 2 minutes before this code will be stored
15	Open Coolant Temperature Sensor (CTS) circuit – the engine must run for up to 5 minutes before this code will be stored
21	Throttle Position Sensor (TPS) circuit – the engine must run for up to 25 seconds, at the specified curb idle speed, before this code will be stored
23	Open or grounded Mixture Control (M/C) solenoid circuit
24	Vehicle Speed Sensor (VSS) circuit – the car must operate for up to 5 minutes at road speed before this code will be stored
32	Barometric Pressure Sensor (BARO) circuit low
34	Manifold Absolute Pressure (MAP) or vacuum sensor circuit. The engine must run for up to 5 minutes at the specified curb idle speed, before this code will be stored
41	No distributor reference pulses at the specified engine vacuum
42	Electronic Spark Timing (EST) bypass circuit grounded or open
43	Electronic Spark Control (ESC) retard signal for too long, causes a retard in EST signal
44	Lean oxygen sensor indication – the engine must run, in closed loop, for up to 2 minutes at part throttle before this code will be stored
44 & 45	At same time – faulty oxygen sensor circuit
45	Rich system indication – the engine must run, in closed loop, for up to 2 minutes at part throttle before this code will be stored
51	Faulty calibrator (PROM) or faulty calibrator installation. It takes up to 30 seconds before this code will be stored
54	Shorted Mixture Control (M/C) solenoid circuit and/or faulty controller
55	Grounded V/ref, (terminal 22), faulty oxygen sensor or controller

GENERAL MOTORS CORPORATION
DIAGNOSTIC CODE DATA

Year – 1983
Model – Celebrity
Engine – 2.5L (151 cid) 4 cyl
Engine Code – VIN 5

ECM TROUBLE CODES

Code	Explanation
12	No reference pulses to the controller. This code does not stored in memory. It will only flash while the fault is present. The code is normal when the ignition is ON and the engine is not running
13	Open in the oxygen sensor circuit to Electronic Control Module (ECM) assembly terminal 9 – the engine must run for up to 5 minutes at part throttle, under road load, before this code will be stored
14	Shorted Coolant Temperature Sensor (CTS) circuit – the engine must run for up to 2 minutes before this code will be stored
15	Open Coolant Temperature Sensor (CTS) circuit – the engine must run for up to 5 minutes before this code will be stored
21	Throttle Position Sensor (TPS) circuit – the engine must run for up to 25 seconds, at the specified curb idle speed, before this code will be stored
23	Open or grounded Mixture Control (M/C) solenoid circuit
24	Vehicle Speed Sensor (VSS) circuit – the car must operate for up to 5 minutes at road speed before this code will be stored
32	Barometric Pressure Sensor (BARO) circuit low
34	Manifold Absolute Pressure (MAP) or vacuum sensor circuit. The engine must run for up to 5 minutes at the specified curb idle speed, before this code will be stored
41	No distributor reference pulses at the specified engine vacuum
42	Electronic Spark Timing (EST) bypass circuit grounded or open
43	Electronic Spark Control (ESC) retard signal for too long, causes a retard in EST signal
44	Lean oxygen sensor indication – the engine must run, in closed loop, for up to 2 minutes at part throttle before this code will be stored
44 & 45	At same time – faulty oxygen sensor circuit
45	Rich system indication – the engine must run, in closed loop, for up to 2 minutes at part throttle before this code will be stored
51	Faulty calibrator (PROM) or faulty calibrator installation. It takes up to 30 seconds before this code will be stored
54	Shorted Mixture Control (M/C) solenoid circuit and/or faulty controller
55	Grounded V/ref, (terminal 22), faulty oxygen sensor or controller

Year — 1983
Model — Celebrity
Engine — 2.5L (151 cid) EFI 4 cyl
Engine Code — VIN R

ECM TROUBLE CODES

Code	Explanation
13	Oxygen sensor circuit—warm engine running at normal operating temperature for at least 3 minutes at part throttle with oxygen sensor signal missing (open) for 60 seconds
14	Coolant Temperature Sensor (CTS) circuit signal voltage low—engine running 10 seconds with no coolant sensor signal voltage
15	Coolant Temperature Sensor (CTS) circuit signal voltage high—engine running with coolant sensor signal too high for 60 seconds. If fault occurs with ignition OFF, engine will crank but may not start
21	Throttle Position Sensor (TPS) signal too high—engine running below 1600 RPM, and TPS is above 50% (2.5V) for 2 seconds
22	Throttle Position Sensor (TPS) signal too low—engine running with TPS signal voltage too low
24	Vehicle Speed Sensor (VSS)—vehicle speed decelerating with no VSS for 1 minute
33	Manifold Absolute Pressure (MAP) signal too high, low vacuum—engine idling and MAP signal is high for 5 seconds
34	Manifold Absolute Pressure (MAP) signal too low—engine running code will set within .2 second with MAP signal voltage too low
42	Electronic Spark Timing (EST)—open or grounded EST line, open or grounded bypass line, and engine speed above 500 RPM
44	Lean exhaust system—engine running in closed loop at normal operating temperature with oxygen sensor signal less than 200mv for 1 minute. Forces open loop operation. May require drive position to set on some engines
45	Rich exhaust system—engine idling in closed loop at normal operating temperature with oxygen sensor signal above 750mv for 20 seconds. Forces open loop operation. May require drive position to set on some engines
51	Faulty calibration unit (PROM) or installation
55	Replace faulty Electronic Control Module (ECM)

Year — 1983
Model — Celebrity
Engine — 2.8L (151 cid) V6
Engine Code — VIN X

ECM TROUBLE CODES

Code	Explanation
12	No reference pulses to the controller. This code does not stored in memory. It will only flash while the fault is present. The code is normal when the ignition is ON and the engine is not running
13	Open in the oxygen sensor circuit to Electronic Control Module (ECM) assembly terminal 9 — the engine must run for up to 5 minutes at part throttle, under road load, before this code will be stored
14	Shorted Coolant Temperature Sensor (CTS) circuit — the engine must run for up to 2 minutes before this code will be stored
15	Open Coolant Temperature Sensor (CTS) circuit — the engine must run for up to 5 minutes before this code will be stored
21	Throttle Position Sensor (TPS) circuit — the engine must run for up to 25 seconds, at the specified curb idle speed, before this code will be stored
23	Open or grounded Mixture Control (M/C) solenoid circuit
24	Vehicle Speed Sensor (VSS) circuit — the car must operate for up to 5 minutes at road speed before this code will be stored
32	Barometric Pressure Sensor (BARO) circuit low
34	Manifold Absolute Pressure (MAP) or vacuum sensor circuit. The engine must run for up to 5 minutes at the specified curb idle speed, before this code will be stored
41	No distributor reference pulses at the specified engine vacuum
42	Electronic Spark Timing (EST) bypass circuit grounded or open
43	Electronic Spark Control (ESC) retard signal for too long, causes a retard in EST signal
44	Lean oxygen sensor indication — the engine must run, in closed loop, for up to 2 minutes at part throttle before this code will be stored
44 & 45	At same time — faulty oxygen sensor circuit
45	Rich system indication — the engine must run, in closed loop, for up to 2 minutes at part throttle before this code will be stored
51	Faulty calibrator (PROM) or faulty calibrator installation. It takes up to 30 seconds before this code will be stored
54	Shorted Mixture Control (M/C) solenoid circuit and/or faulty controller
55	Grounded V/ref, (terminal 22), faulty oxygen sensor or controller

Year — 1983
Model — Chevette
Engine — 1.6L (98 cid) 4 cyl
Engine Code — VIN C

ECM TROUBLE CODES

Code	Explanation
12	No distributor reference pulses to the Electronic Control Module (ECM)
15	Open coolant sensor circuit — the engine must run up to 10 minutes before this code will set
21	Throttle position sensor circuit at Wide Open Throttle (WOT). The engine must run up to 10 seconds below 1000 RPM, before this code will set
23	Mixture Control (M/C) solenoid circuit
44	Lean exhaust indication — the engine must run up to 1 minute in closed loop and at part throttle above 2000 RPM before this code will set
45	Rich exhaust indication — the engine must run up to 1 minute, in closed loop and at part throttle above 2000 RPM before this code will set
51	Faulty calibration unit (PROM) or installation. Turns OFF Electronic Control Module (ECM)

Year – 1984
Model – Caprice Classic
Engine – 3.8L (231 cid) V6
Engine Code – VIN A

ECM TROUBLE CODES

Code	Explanation
12	No distributor reference pulses to the Electronic Control Module (ECM). This code is not stored in memory and will only flash while the fault is present. Normal code with ignition ON, engine not running
13	Oxygen sensor circuit – the engine must run up to 4 minutes at part throttle, under road load, before this code will set
14	Shorted Coolant Temperature Sensor (CTS) circuit – the engine must run 2 minutes before this code will set
15	Open Coolant Temperature Sensor (CTS) circuit – the engine must run 5 minutes before this code will set
21	Throttle Position Sensor (TPS) circuit voltage high – open circuit or misadjusted TPS – the engine must run 10 seconds, at specified curb idle speed, before this code will set
22	Throttle Position Sensor (TPS) voltage low – grounded circuit or misadjusted TPS – engine must run 20 seconds at specified curb idle speed, to set code
23	Mixture Control (M/C) solenoid circuit open or grounded
24	Vehicle Speed Sensor (VSS) circuit – the vehicle must operate up to 2 minutes at road speed, before this code will set
32	Barometric Pressure Sensor (BARO) circuit low
34	Manifold Absolute Pressure (MAP) or vacuum sensor circuit. The engine must run up to 2 minutes at specified curb idle speed, before this code will set
35	Idle Speed Control (ISC) switch circuit shorted – up to 70% TPS for over 5 seconds
41	No distributor reference pulses to the Electronic Control Module (ECM) at specified engine vacuum. This code will store in memory
42	Electronic Spark Timing (EST) bypass circuit or EST circuit grounded or open
43	Electronic Spark Control (ESC) retard signal for too long a time; causes retard in Electronic Spark Timing (EST) signal
44	Lean exhaust indication – the engine must run 2 minutes, in closed loop and at part throttle, before this code will set
45	Rich exhaust indication – the engine must run 2 minutes, in closed loop and at part throttle, before this code will set
51	Faulty or improperly installed calibration unit (PROM). It takes up to 30 seconds before this code will set
53	Exhaust Gas Recirculation (EGR) valve vacuum sensor has seen improper EGR vacuum
54	Shorted Mixture Control (M/C) solenoid circuit and/or faulty Electronic Control Module (ECM)

Year – 1984
Model – Caprice Classic
Engine – 3.8L (229 cid) V6
Engine Code – VIN 9

ECM TROUBLE CODES

Code	Explanation
12	No distributor reference pulses to the Electronic Control Module (ECM). This code is not stored in memory and will only flash while the fault is present. Normal code with ignition ON, engine not running
13	Oxygen sensor circuit – the engine must run up to 4 minutes at part throttle, under road load, before this code will set
14	Shorted Coolant Temperature Sensor (CTS) circuit – the engine must run 2 minutes before this code will set
15	Open Coolant Temperature Sensor (CTS) circuit – the engine must run 5 minutes before this code will set
21	Throttle Position Sensor (TPS) circuit voltage high – open circuit or misadjusted TPS – the engine must run 10 seconds, at specified curb idle speed, before this code will set
22	Throttle Position Sensor (TPS) voltage low – grounded circuit or misadjusted TPS – engine must run 20 seconds at specified curb idle speed, to set code
23	Mixture Control (M/C) solenoid circuit open or grounded
24	Vehicle Speed Sensor (VSS) circuit – the vehicle must operate up to 2 minutes at road speed, before this code will set
32	Barometric Pressure Sensor (BARO) circuit low
34	Manifold Absolute Pressure (MAP) or vacuum sensor circuit. The engine must run up to 2 minutes at specified curb idle speed, before this code will set
35	Idle Speed Control (ISC) switch circuit shorted – up to 70% Throttle Position Sensor (TPS) for over 5 seconds
41	No distributor reference pulses to the Electronic Control Module (ECM) at specified engine vacuum. This code will store in memory
42	Electronic Spark Timing (EST) bypass circuit or EST circuit grounded or open
43	Electronic Spark Control (ESC) retard signal for too long a time; causes retard in Electronic Spark Timing (EST) signal
44	Lean exhaust indication – the engine must run 2 minutes, in closed loop and at part throttle, before this code will set
45	Rich exhaust indication – the engine must run 2 minutes, in closed loop and at part throttle, before this code will set
51	Faulty or improperly installed calibration unit (PROM). It takes up to 30 seconds before this code will set
53	Exhaust Gas Recirculation (EGR) valve vacuum sensor has seen improper EGR vacuum
54	Shorted Mixture Control (M/C) solenoid circuit and/or faulty Electronic Control Module (ECM)

Year – 1984
Model – Caprice Classic
Engine – 5.0L (305 cid) V8
Engine Code – VIN H

ECM TROUBLE CODES

Code	Explanation
12	No distributor reference pulses to the Electronic Control Module (ECM). This code is not stored in memory and will only flash while the fault is present. Normal code with ignition ON, engine not running
13	Oxygen sensor circuit – the engine must run up to 4 minutes at part throttle, under road load, before this code will set
14	Shorted Coolant Temperature Sensor (CTS) circuit – the engine must run 2 minutes before this code will set
15	Open Coolant Temperature Sensor (CTS) circuit – the engine must run 5 minutes before this code will set
21	Throttle Position Sensor (TPS) circuit voltage high – open circuit or misadjusted TPS – the engine must run 10 seconds, at specified curb idle speed, before this code will set
22	Throttle Position Sensor (TPS) voltage low – grounded circuit or misadjusted TPS – engine must run 20 seconds at specified curb idle speed, to set code
23	Mixture Control (M/C) solenoid circuit open or grounded
24	Vehicle Speed Sensor (VSS) circuit – the vehicle must operate up to 2 minutes at road speed, before this code will set
32	Barometric Pressure Sensor (BARO) circuit low
34	Manifold Absolute Pressure (MAP) or vacuum sensor circuit. The engine must run up to 2 minutes at specified curb idle speed, before this code will set
35	Idle Speed Control (ISC) switch circuit shorted – up to 70% Throttle Position Sensor (TPS) for over 5 seconds
41	No distributor reference pulses to the Electronic Control Module (ECM) at specified engine vacuum. This code will store in memory
42	Electronic Spark Timing (EST) bypass circuit or EST circuit grounded or open
43	Electronic Spark Control (ESC) retard signal for too long a time; causes retard in Electronic Spark Timing (EST) signal
44	Lean exhaust indication – the engine must run 2 minutes, in closed loop and at part throttle, before this code will set
45	Rich exhaust indication – the engine must run 2 minutes, in closed loop and at part throttle, before this code will set
51	Faulty or improperly installed calibration unit (PROM). It takes up to 30 seconds before this code will set
53	Exhaust Gas Recirculation (EGR) valve vacuum sensor has seen improper EGR vacuum
54	Shorted Mixture Control (M/C) solenoid circuit and/or faulty Electronic Control Module (ECM)

Year — 1984
Model — Impala
Engine — 3.8L (231 cid) V6
Engine Code — VIN A

ECM TROUBLE CODES

Code	Explanation
12	No distributor reference pulses to the Electronic Control Module (ECM). This code is not stored in memory and will only flash while the fault is present. Normal code with ignition ON, engine not running
13	Oxygen sensor circuit — the engine must run up to 4 minutes at part throttle, under road load, before this code will set
14	Shorted Coolant Temperature Sensor (CTS) circuit — the engine must run 2 minutes before this code will set
15	Open Coolant Temperature Sensor (CTS) circuit — the engine must run 5 minutes before this code will set
21	Throttle Position Sensor (TPS) circuit voltage high — open circuit or misadjusted TPS — the engine must run 10 seconds, at specified curb idle speed, before this code will set
22	Throttle Position Sensor (TPS) voltage low — grounded circuit or misadjusted TPS — engine must run 20 seconds at specified curb idle speed, to set code
23	Mixture Control (M/C) solenoid circuit open or grounded
24	Vehicle Speed Sensor (VSS) circuit — the vehicle must operate up to 2 minutes at road speed, before this code will set
32	Barometric Pressure Sensor (BARO) circuit low
34	Manifold Absolute Pressure (MAP) or vacuum sensor circuit. The engine must run up to 2 minutes at specified curb idle speed, before this code will set
35	Idle Speed Control (ISC) switch circuit shorted — up to 70% Throttle Position Sensor (TPS) for over 5 seconds
41	No distributor reference pulses to the Electronic Control Module (ECM) at specified engine vacuum. This code will store in memory
42	Electronic Spark Timing (EST) bypass circuit or EST circuit grounded or open
43	Electronic Spark Control (ESC) retard signal for too long a time; causes retard in Electronic Spark Timing (EST) signal
44	Lean exhaust indication — the engine must run 2 minutes, in closed loop and at part throttle, before this code will set
45	Rich exhaust indication — the engine must run 2 minutes, in closed loop and at part throttle, before this code will set
51	Faulty or improperly installed calibration unit (PROM). It takes up to 30 seconds before this code will set
53	Exhaust Gas Recirculation (EGR) valve vacuum sensor has seen improper EGR vacuum
54	Shorted Mixture Control (M/C) solenoid circuit and/or faulty Electronic Control Module (ECM)

Year – 1984
Model – Impala
Engine – 3.8L (229 cid) V6
Engine Code – VIN 9

ECM TROUBLE CODES

Code	Explanation
12	No distributor reference pulses to the Electronic Control Module (ECM). This code is not stored in memory and will only flash while the fault is present. Normal code with ignition ON, engine not running
13	Oxygen sensor circuit—the engine must run up to 4 minutes at part throttle, under road load, before this code will set
14	Shorted Coolant Temperature Sensor (CTS) circuit—the engine must run 2 minutes before this code will set
15	Open Coolant Temperature Sensor (CTS) circuit—the engine must run 5 minutes before this code will set
21	Throttle Position Sensor (TPS) circuit voltage high—open circuit or misadjusted TPS—the engine must run 10 seconds, at specified curb idle speed, before this code will set
22	Throttle Position Sensor (TPS) voltage low—grounded circuit or misadjusted TPS—engine must run 20 seconds at specified curb idle speed, to set code
23	Mixture Control (M/C) solenoid circuit open or grounded
24	Vehicle Speed Sensor (VSS) circuit—the vehicle must operate up to 2 minutes at road speed, before this code will set
32	Barometric Pressure Sensor (BARO) circuit low
34	Manifold Absolute Pressure (MAP) or vacuum sensor circuit. The engine must run up to 2 minutes at specified curb idle speed, before this code will set
35	Idle Speed Control (ISC) switch circuit shorted—up to 70% Throttle Position Sensor (TPS) for over 5 seconds
41	No distributor reference pulses to the Electronic Control Module (ECM) at specified engine vacuum. This code will store in memory
42	Electronic Spark Timing (EST) bypass circuit or EST circuit grounded or open
43	Electronic Spark Control (ESC) retard signal for too long a time; causes retard in Electronic Spark Timing (EST) signal
44	Lean exhaust indication—the engine must run 2 minutes, in closed loop and at part throttle, before this code will set
45	Rich exhaust indication—the engine must run 2 minutes, in closed loop and at part throttle, before this code will set
51	Faulty or improperly installed calibration unit (PROM). It takes up to 30 seconds before this code will set
53	Exhaust Gas Recirculation (EGR) valve vacuum sensor has seen improper EGR vacuum
54	Shorted Mixture Control (M/C) solenoid circuit and/or faulty Electronic Control Module (ECM)

Year – 1984
Model – Impala
Engine – 5.0L (305 cid) V8
Engine Code – VIN H

ECM TROUBLE CODES

Code	Explanation
12	No distributor reference pulses to the Electronic Control Module (ECM). This code is not stored in memory and will only flash while the fault is present. Normal code with ignition ON, engine not running
13	Oxygen sensor circuit—the engine must run up to 4 minutes at part throttle, under road load, before this code will set
14	Shorted Coolant Temperature Sensor (CTS) circuit—the engine must run 2 minutes before this code will set
15	Open Coolant Temperature Sensor (CTS) circuit—the engine must run 5 minutes before this code will set
21	Throttle Position Sensor (TPS) circuit voltage high—open circuit or misadjusted TPS—the engine must run 10 seconds, at specified curb idle speed, before this code will set
22	Throttle Position Sensor (TPS) voltage low—grounded circuit or misadjusted TPS—engine must run 20 seconds at specified curb idle speed, to set code
23	Mixture Control (M/C) solenoid circuit open or grounded
24	Vehicle Speed Sensor (VSS) circuit—the vehicle must operate up to 2 minutes at road speed, before this code will set
32	Barometric Pressure Sensor (BARO) circuit low
34	Manifold Absolute Pressure (MAP) or vacuum sensor circuit. The engine must run up to 2 minutes at specified curb idle speed, before this code will set
35	Idle Speed Control (ISC) switch circuit shorted—up to 70% Throttle Position Sensor (TPS) for over 5 seconds
41	No distributor reference pulses to the Electronic Control Module (ECM) at specified engine vacuum. This code will store in memory
42	Electronic Spark Timing (EST) bypass circuit or EST circuit grounded or open
43	Electronic Spark Control (ESC) retard signal for too long a time; causes retard in Electronic Spark Timing (EST) signal
44	Lean exhaust indication—the engine must run 2 minutes, in closed loop and at part throttle, before this code will set
45	Rich exhaust indication—the engine must run 2 minutes, in closed loop and at part throttle, before this code will set
51	Faulty or improperly installed calibration unit (PROM). It takes up to 30 seconds before this code will set
53	Exhaust Gas Recirculation (EGR) valve vacuum sensor has seen improper EGR vacuum
54	Shorted Mixture Control (M/C) solenoid circuit and/or faulty Electronic Control Module (ECM)

Year – 1984
Model – Monte Carlo
Engine – 3.8L (229 cid) V6
Engine Code – VIN 9

ECM TROUBLE CODES

Code	Explanation
12	No distributor reference pulses to the Electronic Control Module (ECM). This code is not stored in memory and will only flash while the fault is present. Normal code with ignition ON, engine not running
13	Oxygen sensor circuit – the engine must run up to 4 minutes at part throttle, under road load, before this code will set
14	Shorted Coolant Temperature Sensor (CTS) circuit – the engine must run 2 minutes before this code will set
15	Open Coolant Temperature Sensor (CTS) circuit – the engine must run 5 minutes before this code will set
21	Throttle Position Sensor (TPS) circuit voltage high – open circuit or misadjusted TPS – the engine must run 10 seconds, at specified curb idle speed, before this code will set
22	Throttle Position Sensor (TPS) voltage low – grounded circuit or misadjusted TPS – engine must run 20 seconds at specified curb idle speed, to set code
23	Mixture Control (M/C) solenoid circuit open or grounded
24	Vehicle Speed Sensor (VSS) circuit – the vehicle must operate up to 2 minutes at road speed, before this code will set
32	Barometric Pressure Sensor (BARO) circuit low
34	Manifold Absolute Pressure (MAP) or vacuum sensor circuit. The engine must run up to 2 minutes at specified curb idle speed, before this code will set
35	Idle Speed Control (ISC) switch circuit shorted – up to 70% Throttle Position Sensor (TPS) for over 5 seconds
41	No distributor reference pulses to the Electronic Control Module (ECM) at specified engine vacuum. This code will store in memory
42	Electronic Spark Timing (EST) bypass circuit or EST circuit grounded or open
43	Electronic Spark Control (ESC) retard signal for too long a time; causes retard in Electronic Spark Timing (EST) signal
44	Lean exhaust indication – the engine must run 2 minutes, in closed loop and at part throttle, before this code will set
45	Rich exhaust indication – the engine must run 2 minutes, in closed loop and at part throttle, before this code will set
51	Faulty or improperly installed calibration unit (PROM). It takes up to 30 seconds before this code will set
53	Exhaust Gas Recirculation (EGR) valve vacuum sensor has seen improper EGR vacuum
54	Shorted Mixture Control (M/C) solenoid circuit and/or faulty Electronic Control Module (ECM)

Year — 1984
Model — Monte Carlo
Engine — 3.8L (231 cid) V6
Engine Code — VIN A

ECM TROUBLE CODES

Code	Explanation
12	No distributor reference pulses to the Electronic Control Module (ECM). This code is not stored in memory and will only flash while the fault is present. Normal code with ignition ON, engine not running
13	Oxygen sensor circuit — the engine must run up to 4 minutes at part throttle, under road load, before this code will set
14	Shorted Coolant Temperature Sensor (CTS) circuit — the engine must run 2 minutes before this code will set
15	Open Coolant Temperature Sensor (CTS) circuit — the engine must run 5 minutes before this code will set
21	Throttle Position Sensor (TPS) circuit voltage high — open circuit or misadjusted TPS — the engine must run 10 seconds, at specified curb idle speed, before this code will set
22	Throttle Position Sensor (TPS) voltage low — grounded circuit or misadjusted TPS — engine must run 20 seconds at specified curb idle speed, to set code
23	Mixture Control (M/C) solenoid circuit open or grounded
24	Vehicle Speed Sensor (VSS) circuit — the vehicle must operate up to 2 minutes at road speed, before this code will set
32	Barometric Pressure Sensor (BARO) circuit low
34	Manifold Absolute Pressure (MAP) or vacuum sensor circuit. The engine must run up to 2 minutes at specified curb idle speed, before this code will set
35	Idle Speed Control (ISC) switch circuit shorted — up to 70% Throttle Position Sensor (TPS) for over 5 seconds
41	No distributor reference pulses to the Electronic Control Module (ECM) at specified engine vacuum. This code will store in memory
42	Electronic Spark Timing (EST) bypass circuit or EST circuit grounded or open
43	Electronic Spark Control (ESC) retard signal for too long a time; causes retard in Electronic Spark Timing (EST) signal
44	Lean exhaust indication — the engine must run 2 minutes, in closed loop and at part throttle, before this code will set
45	Rich exhaust indication — the engine must run 2 minutes, in closed loop and at part throttle, before this code will set
51	Faulty or improperly installed calibration unit (PROM). It takes up to 30 seconds before this code will set
53	Exhaust Gas Recirculation (EGR) valve vacuum sensor has seen improper EGR vacuum
54	Shorted Mixture Control (M/C) solenoid circuit and/or faulty Electronic Control Module (ECM)

Year — 1984
Model — Monte Carlo
Engine — 5.0L (305 cid) V8
Engine Code — VIN H

ECM TROUBLE CODES

Code	Explanation
12	No distributor reference pulses to the Electronic Control Module (ECM). This code is not stored in memory and will only flash while the fault is present. Normal code with ignition ON, engine not running
13	Oxygen sensor circuit — the engine must run up to 4 minutes at part throttle, under road load, before this code will set
14	Shorted Coolant Temperature Sensor (CTS) circuit — the engine must run 2 minutes before this code will set
15	Open Coolant Temperature Sensor (CTS) circuit — the engine must run 5 minutes before this code will set
21	Throttle Position Sensor (TPS) circuit voltage high — open circuit or misadjusted TPS — the engine must run 10 seconds, at specified curb idle speed, before this code will set
22	Throttle Position Sensor (TPS) voltage low — grounded circuit or misadjusted TPS — engine must run 20 seconds at specified curb idle speed, to set code
23	Mixture Control (M/C) solenoid circuit open or grounded
24	Vehicle Speed Sensor (VSS) circuit — the vehicle must operate up to 2 minutes at road speed, before this code will set
32	Barometric Pressure Sensor (BARO) circuit low
34	Manifold Absolute Pressure (MAP) or vacuum sensor circuit. The engine must run up to 2 minutes at specified curb idle speed, before this code will set
35	Idle Speed Control (ISC) switch circuit shorted — up to 70% Throttle Position Sensor (TPS) for over 5 seconds
41	No distributor reference pulses to the Electronic Control Module (ECM) at specified engine vacuum. This code will store in memory
42	Electronic Spark Timing (EST) bypass circuit or EST circuit grounded or open
43	Electronic Spark Control (ESC) retard signal for too long a time; causes retard in Electronic Spark Timing (EST) signal
44	Lean exhaust indication — the engine must run 2 minutes, in closed loop and at part throttle, before this code will set
45	Rich exhaust indication — the engine must run 2 minutes, in closed loop and at part throttle, before this code will set
51	Faulty or improperly installed calibration unit (PROM). It takes up to 30 seconds before this code will set
53	Exhaust Gas Recirculation (EGR) valve vacuum sensor has seen improper EGR vacuum
54	Shorted Mixture Control (M/C) solenoid circuit and/or faulty Electronic Control Module (ECM)

Year — 1984
Model — Camaro
Engine — 2.5L (151 cid) TBI 4 cyl
Engine Code — VIN 2

ECM TROUBLE CODES

Code	Explanation
13	Oxygen sensor circuit
14	Coolant Temperature Sensor (CTS) — voltage low
15	Coolant Temperature Sensor (CTS) — voltage high
21	Throttle Position Sensor (TPS) — voltage high
22	Throttle Position Sensor (TPS) — voltage low
24	Vehicle Speed Sensor (VSS)
33	Manifold Absolute Pressure (MAP) — voltage low
34	Manifold Absolute Pressure (MAP) — voltage high
42	Electronic Spark Timing (EST)
44	Lean exhaust indication
45	Rich exhaust indication
51	PROM
55	Electronic Control Module (ECM)

Year – 1984
Model – Camaro
Engine – 2.8L (173 cid) V6
Engine Code – VIN 1

ECM TROUBLE CODES

Code	Explanation
12	No distributor reference pulses to the Electronic Control Module (ECM). This code is not stored in memory and will only flash while the fault is present. Normal code with ignition ON, engine not running
13	Oxygen sensor circuit – the engine must run up to 4 minutes at part throttle, under road load, before this code will set
14	Shorted Coolant Temperature Sensor (CTS) circuit – the engine must run 2 minutes before this code will set
15	Open Coolant Temperature Sensor (CTS) circuit – the engine must run 5 minutes before this code will set
21	Throttle Position Sensor (TPS) circuit voltage high – open circuit or misadjusted TPS – the engine must run 10 seconds, at specified curb idle speed, before this code will set
22	Throttle Position Sensor (TPS) voltage low – grounded circuit or misadjusted TPS – engine must run 20 seconds at specified curb idle speed, to set code
23	Mixture Control (M/C) solenoid circuit open or grounded
24	Vehicle Speed Sensor (VSS) circuit – the vehicle must operate up to 2 minutes at road speed, before this code will set
32	Barometric Pressure Sensor (BARO) circuit low
34	Manifold Absolute Pressure (MAP) or vacuum sensor circuit. The engine must run up to 2 minutes at specified curb idle speed, before this code will set
35	Idle Speed Control (ISC) switch circuit shorted – up to 70% Throttle Position Sensor (TPS) for over 5 seconds
41	No distributor reference pulses to the Electronic Control Module (ECM) at specified engine vacuum. This code will store in memory
42	Electronic Spark Timing (EST) bypass circuit or EST circuit grounded or open
43	Electronic Spark Control (ESC) retard signal for too long a time; causes retard in Electronic Spark Timing (EST) signal
44	Lean exhaust indication – the engine must run 2 minutes, in closed loop and at part throttle, before this code will set
45	Rich exhaust indication – the engine must run 2 minutes, in closed loop and at part throttle, before this code will set
51	Faulty or improperly installed calibration unit (PROM). It takes up to 30 seconds before this code will set
53	Exhaust Gas Recirculation (EGR) valve vacuum sensor has seen improper EGR vacuum
54	Shorted Mixture Control (M/C) solenoid circuit and/or faulty Electronic Control Module (ECM)

Year — 1984
Model — Camaro
Engine — 2.8L (173 cid) V6
Engine Code — VIN L

ECM TROUBLE CODES

Code	Explanation
12	No distributor reference pulses to the Electronic Control Module (ECM). This code is not stored in memory and will only flash while the fault is present. Normal code with ignition ON, engine not running
13	Oxygen sensor circuit — the engine must run up to 4 minutes at part throttle, under road load, before this code will set
14	Shorted Coolant Temperature Sensor (CTS) circuit — the engine must run 2 minutes before this code will set
15	Open Coolant Temperature Sensor (CTS) circuit — the engine must run 5 minutes before this code will set
21	Throttle Position Sensor (TPS) circuit voltage high — open circuit or misadjusted TPS — the engine must run 10 seconds, at specified curb idle speed, before this code will set
22	Throttle Position Sensor (TPS) voltage low — grounded circuit or misadjusted TPS — engine must run 20 seconds at specified curb idle speed, to set code
23	Mixture Control (M/C) solenoid circuit open or grounded
24	Vehicle Speed Sensor (VSS) circuit — the vehicle must operate up to 2 minutes at road speed, before this code will set
32	Barometric Pressure Sensor (BARO) circuit low
34	Manifold Absolute Pressure (MAP) or vacuum sensor circuit. The engine must run up to 2 minutes at specified curb idle speed, before this code will set
35	Idle Speed Control (ISC) switch circuit shorted — up to 70% Throttle Position Sensor (TPS) for over 5 seconds
41	No distributor reference pulses to the Electronic Control Module (ECM) at specified engine vacuum. This code will store in memory
42	Electronic Spark Timing (EST) bypass circuit or EST circuit grounded or open
43	Electronic Spark Control (ESC) retard signal for too long a time; causes retard in Electronic Spark Timing (EST) signal
44	Lean exhaust indication — the engine must run 2 minutes, in closed loop and at part throttle, before this code will set
45	Rich exhaust indication — the engine must run 2 minutes, in closed loop and at part throttle, before this code will set
51	Faulty or improperly installed calibration unit (PROM). It takes up to 30 seconds before this code will set
53	Exhaust Gas Recirculation (EGR) valve vacuum sensor has seen improper EGR vacuum
54	Shorted Mixture Control (M/C) solenoid circuit and/or faulty Electronic Control Module (ECM)

Year – 1984
Model – Camaro
Engine – 5.0L (305 cid) V8
Engine Code – VIN G

ECM TROUBLE CODES

Code	Explanation
12	No distributor reference pulses to the Electronic Control Module (ECM). This code is not stored in memory and will only flash while the fault is present. Normal code with ignition ON, engine not running
13	Oxygen sensor circuit – the engine must run up to 4 minutes at part throttle, under road load, before this code will set
14	Shorted Coolant Temperature Sensor (CTS) circuit – the engine must run 2 minutes before this code will set
15	Open Coolant Temperature Sensor (CTS) circuit – the engine must run 5 minutes before this code will set
21	Throttle Position Sensor (TPS) circuit voltage high – open circuit or misadjusted TPS – the engine must run 10 seconds, at specified curb idle speed, before this code will set
22	Throttle Position Sensor (TPS) voltage low – grounded circuit or misadjusted TPS – engine must run 20 seconds at specified curb idle speed, to set code
23	Mixture Control (M/C) solenoid circuit open or grounded
24	Vehicle Speed Sensor (VSS) circuit – the vehicle must operate up to 2 minutes at road speed, before this code will set
32	Barometric Pressure Sensor (BARO) circuit low
34	Manifold Absolute Pressure (MAP) or vacuum sensor circuit. The engine must run up to 2 minutes at specified curb idle speed, before this code will set
35	Idle Speed Control (ISC) switch circuit shorted – up to 70% Throttle Position Sensor (TPS) for over 5 seconds
41	No distributor reference pulses to the Electronic Control Module (ECM) at specified engine vacuum. This code will store in memory
42	Electronic Spark Timing (EST) bypass circuit or EST circuit grounded or open
43	Electronic Spark Control (ESC) retard signal for too long a time; causes retard in Electronic Spark Timing (EST) signal
44	Lean exhaust indication – the engine must run 2 minutes, in closed loop and at part throttle, before this code will set
45	Rich exhaust indication – the engine must run 2 minutes, in closed loop and at part throttle, before this code will set
51	Faulty or improperly installed calibration unit (PROM). It takes up to 30 seconds before this code will set
53	Exhaust Gas Recirculation (EGR) valve vacuum sensor has seen improper EGR vacuum
54	Shorted Mixture Control (M/C) solenoid circuit and/or faulty Electronic Control Module (ECM)

Year – 1984
Model – Camaro
Engine – 5.0L (305 cid) V8
Engine Code – VIN H

ECM TROUBLE CODES

Code	Explanation
12	No distributor reference pulses to the Electronic Control Module (ECM). This code is not stored in memory and will only flash while the fault is present. Normal code with ignition ON, engine not running
13	Oxygen sensor circuit – the engine must run up to 4 minutes at part throttle, under road load, before this code will set
14	Shorted Coolant Temperature Sensor (CTS) circuit – the engine must run 2 minutes before this code will set
15	Open Coolant Temperature Sensor (CTS) circuit – the engine must run 5 minutes before this code will set
21	Throttle Position Sensor (TPS) circuit voltage high – open circuit or misadjusted TPS – the engine must run 10 seconds, at specified curb idle speed, before this code will set
22	Throttle Position Sensor (TPS) voltage low – grounded circuit or misadjusted TPS – engine must run 20 seconds at specified curb idle speed, to set code
23	Mixture Control (M/C) solenoid circuit open or grounded
24	Vehicle Speed Sensor (VSS) circuit – the vehicle must operate up to 2 minutes at road speed, before this code will set
32	Barometric Pressure Sensor (BARO) circuit low
34	Manifold Absolute Pressure (MAP) or vacuum sensor circuit. The engine must run up to 2 minutes at specified curb idle speed, before this code will set
35	Idle Speed Control (ISC) switch circuit shorted – up to 70% Throttle Position Sensor (TPS) for over 5 seconds
41	No distributor reference pulses to the Electronic Control Module (ECM) at specified engine vacuum. This code will store in memory
42	Electronic Spark Timing (EST) bypass circuit or EST circuit grounded or open
43	Electronic Spark Control (ESC) retard signal for too long a time; causes retard in Electronic Spark Timing (EST) signal
44	Lean exhaust indication – the engine must run 2 minutes, in closed loop and at part throttle, before this code will set
45	Rich exhaust indication – the engine must run 2 minutes, in closed loop and at part throttle, before this code will set
51	Faulty or improperly installed calibration unit (PROM). It takes up to 30 seconds before this code will set
53	Exhaust Gas Recirculation (EGR) valve vacuum sensor has seen improper EGR vacuum
54	Shorted Mixture Control (M/C) solenoid circuit and/or faulty Electronic Control Module (ECM)

GENERAL MOTORS CORPORATION
DIAGNOSTIC CODE DATA

Year — 1984
Model — Corvette
Engine — 5.7L (350 cid) EFI V8
Engine Code — VIN 8

ECM TROUBLE CODES

Code	Explanation
13	Oxygen sensor circuit
14	Coolant Temperature Sensor (CTS) — voltage low
15	Coolant Temperature Sensor (CTS) — voltage high
21	Throttle Position Sensor (TPS) — voltage high
22	Throttle Position Sensor (TPS) — voltage low
24	Vehicle Speed Sensor (VSS)
33	Manifold Absolute Pressure (MAP) — voltage low
34	Manifold Absolute Pressure (MAP) — voltage high
42	Electronic Spark Timing (EST)
43	Electronic Spark Control (ESC)
44	Lean exhaust indication
45	Rich exhaust indication
51	PROM
55	Electronic Control Module (ECM)

Year — 1984
Model — Chevette
Engine — 1.6L (97.6 cid) 4 cyl
Engine Code — VIN C

ECM TROUBLE CODES

Code	Explanation
12	No distributor performance pulse
15	Coolant Temperature Sensor (CTS) open
21	Throttle Position Sensor (TPS)
23	Mixture Control (M/C) solenoid circuit low
44	Lean exhaust indication
45	Rich exhaust indication
51	PROM

Year – 1984
Model – Celebrity
Engine – 2.5L (151 cid) EFI 4 cyl
Engine Code – VIN R

ECM TROUBLE CODES

Code	Explanation
13	Oxygen sensor circuit
14	Coolant Temperature Sensor (CTS) – voltage low
15	Coolant Temperature Sensor (CTS) – voltage high
21	Throttle Position Sensor (TPS) – voltage high
22	Throttle Position Sensor (TPS) – voltage low
24	Vehicle Speed Sensor (VSS)
33	Manifold Absolute Pressure (MAP) – voltage low
34	Manifold Absolute Pressure (MAP) – voltage high
42	Electronic Spark Timing (EST)
44	Lean exhaust indication
45	Rich exhaust indication
51	PROM
55	Electronic Control Module (ECM)

Year – 1984
Model – Celebrity
Engine – 2.8L (173 cid) V6
Engine Code – VIN X

ECM TROUBLE CODES

Code	Explanation
12	No distributor reference pulses to the Electronic Control Module (ECM). This code is not stored in memory and will only flash while the fault is present. Normal code with ignition ON, engine not running
13	Oxygen sensor circuit – the engine must run up to 4 minutes at part throttle, under road load, before this code will set
14	Shorted Coolant Temperature Sensor (CTS) circuit – the engine must run 2 minutes before this code will set
15	Open Coolant Temperature Sensor (CTS) circuit – the engine must run 5 minutes before this code will set
21	Throttle Position Sensor (TPS) circuit voltage high – open circuit or misadjusted TPS – the engine must run 10 seconds, at specified curb idle speed, before this code will set
22	Throttle Position Sensor (TPS) voltage low – grounded circuit or misadjusted TPS – engine must run 20 seconds at specified curb idle speed, to set code
23	Mixture Control (M/C) solenoid circuit open or grounded
24	Vehicle Speed Sensor (VSS) circuit – the vehicle must operate up to 2 minutes at road speed, before this code will set
32	Barometric Pressure Sensor (BARO) circuit low
34	Manifold Absolute Pressure (MAP) or vacuum sensor circuit. The engine must run up to 2 minutes at specified curb idle speed, before this code will set
35	Idle Speed Control (ISC) switch circuit shorted – up to 70% Throttle Position Sensor (TPS) for over 5 seconds
41	No distributor reference pulses to the Electronic Control Module (ECM) at specified engine vacuum. This code will store in memory
42	Electronic Spark Timing (EST) bypass circuit or EST circuit grounded or open
43	Electronic Spark Control (ESC) retard signal for too long a time; causes retard in Electronic Spark Timing (EST) signal
44	Lean exhaust indication – the engine must run 2 minutes, in closed loop and at part throttle, before this code will set
45	Rich exhaust indication – the engine must run 2 minutes, in closed loop and at part throttle, before this code will set
51	Faulty or improperly installed calibration unit (PROM). It takes up to 30 seconds before this code will set
53	Exhaust Gas Recirculation (EGR) valve vacuum sensor has seen improper EGR vacuum
54	Shorted Mixture Control (M/C) solenoid circuit and/or faulty Electronic Control Module (ECM)

Year — 1984
Model — Cavalier
Engine — 2.0L (121 cid) TBI 4 cyl
Engine Code — VIN P

ECM TROUBLE CODES

Code	Explanation
13	Oxygen sensor circuit
14	Coolant Temperature Sensor (CTS) — voltage low
15	Coolant Temperature Sensor (CTS) — voltage high
21	Throttle Position Sensor (TPS) — voltage high
22	Throttle Position Sensor (TPS) — voltage low
24	Vehicle Speed Sensor (VSS)
33	Manifold Absolute Pressure (MAP) — voltage low
34	Manifold Absolute Pressure (MAP) — voltage high
42	Electronic Spark Timing (EST)
44	Lean exhaust indication
45	Rich exhaust indication
51	PROM
52	Calpak
55	Electronic Control Module (ECM)

Year – 1984
Model – Citation II
Engine – 2.5L (151 cid) EFI 4 cyl
Engine Code – VIN R

ECM TROUBLE CODES

Code	Explanation
13	Oxygen sensor circuit
14	Coolant Temperature Sensor (CTS) – voltage low
15	Coolant Temperature Sensor (CTS) – voltage high
21	Throttle Position Sensor (TPS) – voltage high
22	Throttle Position Sensor (TPS) – voltage low
24	Vehicle Speed Sensor (VSS)
33	Manifold Absolute Pressure (MAP) – voltage low
34	Manifold Absolute Pressure (MAP) – voltage high
42	Electronic Spark Timing (EST)
44	Lean exhaust indication
45	Rich exhaust indication
51	PROM
55	Electronic Control Module (ECM)

GENERAL MOTORS CORPORATION
DIAGNOSTIC CODE DATA

Year – 1984
Model – Citation II
Engine – 2.8L (173 cid) V6
Engine Code – VIN X

ECM TROUBLE CODES

Code	Explanation
12	No distributor reference pulses to the Electronic Control Module (ECM). This code is not stored in memory and will only flash while the fault is present. Normal code with ignition ON, engine not running
13	Oxygen sensor circuit – the engine must run up to 4 minutes at part throttle, under road load, before this code will set
14	Shorted Coolant Temperature Sensor (CTS) circuit – the engine must run 2 minutes before this code will set
15	Open Coolant Temperature Sensor (CTS) circuit – the engine must run 5 minutes before this code will set
21	Throttle Position Sensor (TPS) circuit voltage high – open circuit or misadjusted TPS – the engine must run 10 seconds, at specified curb idle speed, before this code will set
22	Throttle Position Sensor (TPS) voltage low – grounded circuit or misadjusted TPS – engine must run 20 seconds at specified curb idle speed, to set code
23	Mixture Control (M/C) solenoid circuit open or grounded
24	Vehicle Speed Sensor (VSS) circuit – the vehicle must operate up to 2 minutes at road speed, before this code will set
32	Barometric Pressure Sensor (BARO) circuit low
34	Manifold Absolute Pressure (MAP) or vacuum sensor circuit. The engine must run up to 2 minutes at specified curb idle speed, before this code will set
35	Idle Speed Control (ISC) switch circuit shorted – up to 70% Throttle Position Sensor (TPS) for over 5 seconds
41	No distributor reference pulses to the Electronic Control Module (ECM) at specified engine vacuum. This code will store in memory
42	Electronic Spark Timing (EST) bypass circuit or EST circuit grounded or open
43	Electronic Spark Control (ESC) retard signal for too long a time; causes retard in Electronic Spark Timing (EST) signal
44	Lean exhaust indication – the engine must run 2 minutes, in closed loop and at part throttle, before this code will set
45	Rich exhaust indication – the engine must run 2 minutes, in closed loop and at part throttle, before this code will set
51	Faulty or improperly installed calibration unit (PROM). It takes up to 30 seconds before this code will set
53	Exhaust Gas Recirculation (EGR) valve vacuum sensor has seen improper EGR vacuum
54	Shorted Mixture Control (M/C) solenoid circuit and/or faulty Electronic Control Module (ECM)

Year — 1984
Model — Citation II
Engine — 2.8L (173 cid) V6
Engine Code — VIN Z

ECM TROUBLE CODES

Code	Explanation
12	No distributor reference pulses to the Electronic Control Module (ECM). This code is not stored in memory and will only flash while the fault is present. Normal code with ignition ON, engine not running
13	Oxygen sensor circuit — the engine must run up to 4 minutes at part throttle, under road load, before this code will set
14	Shorted Coolant Temperature Sensor (CTS) circuit — the engine must run 2 minutes before this code will set
15	Open Coolant Temperature Sensor (CTS) circuit — the engine must run 5 minutes before this code will set
21	Throttle Position Sensor (TPS) circuit voltage high — open circuit or misadjusted TPS — the engine must run 10 seconds, at specified curb idle speed, before this code will set
22	Throttle Position Sensor (TPS) voltage low — grounded circuit or misadjusted TPS — engine must run 20 seconds at specified curb idle speed, to set code
23	Mixture Control (M/C) solenoid circuit open or grounded
24	Vehicle Speed Sensor (VSS) circuit — the vehicle must operate up to 2 minutes at road speed, before this code will set
32	Barometric Pressure Sensor (BARO) circuit low
34	Manifold Absolute Pressure (MAP) or vacuum sensor circuit. The engine must run up to 2 minutes at specified curb idle speed, before this code will set
35	Idle Speed Control (ISC) switch circuit shorted — up to 70% Throttle Position Sensor (TPS) for over 5 seconds
41	No distributor reference pulses to the Electronic Control Module (ECM) at specified engine vacuum. This code will store in memory
42	Electronic Spark Timing (EST) bypass circuit or EST circuit grounded or open
43	Electronic Spark Control (ESC) retard signal for too long a time; causes retard in Electronic Spark Timing (EST) signal
44	Lean exhaust indication — the engine must run 2 minutes, in closed loop and at part throttle, before this code will set
45	Rich exhaust indication — the engine must run 2 minutes, in closed loop and at part throttle, before this code will set
51	Faulty or improperly installed calibration unit (PROM). It takes up to 30 seconds before this code will set
53	Exhaust Gas Recirculation (EGR) valve vacuum sensor has seen improper EGR vacuum
54	Shorted Mixture Control (M/C) solenoid circuit and/or faulty Electronic Control Module (ECM)

Year — 1985
Model — Caprice Classic
Engine — 4.3L (262 cid) EFI V6
Engine Code — VIN Z

ECM TROUBLE CODES

Code	Explanation
13	Oxygen sensor circuit
14	Coolant Temperature Sensor (CTS) — low
15	Coolant Temperature Sensor (CTS) — high
21	Throttle Position Sensor (TPS) — high
22	Throttle Position Sensor (TPS) — low
24	Vehicle Speed Sensor (VSS)
32	Exhaust Gas Recirculation (EGR) system failure
33	Manifold Absolute Pressure (MAP) sensor — high
34	Manifold Absolute Pressure (MAP) sensor — low
42	Electronic Spark Timing (EST)
43	Electronic Spark Control (ESC)
44	Lean exhaust
45	Rich exhaust
51	PROM
52	Calpak missing
55	Electronic Control Module (ECM)

Year – 1985
Model – Caprice Classic
Engine – 5.0L (305 cid) V8
Engine Code – VIN H

ECM TROUBLE CODES

Code	Explanation
12	No distributor reference pulses to the Electronic Control Module (ECM). This code is not stored in memory and will only flash while the fault is present. Normal code with ignition ON, engine not running
13	Oxygen sensor circuit – the engine must run up to 4 minutes at part throttle, under road load, before this code will set
14	Shorted Coolant Temperature Sensor (CTS) circuit – the engine must run 2 minutes before this code will set
15	Open Coolant Temperature Sensor (CTS) circuit – the engine must run 5 minutes before this code will set
21	Throttle Position Sensor (TPS) circuit voltage high – open circuit or misadjusted TPS – the engine must run 10 seconds, at specified curb idle speed, before this code will set
22	Throttle Position Sensor (TPS) circuit voltage low – grounded circuit or misadjusted TPS – engine must run 20 seconds at specified curb idle speed, to set code
23	Mixture Control (M/C) solenoid circuit open or grounded
24	Vehicle Speed Sensor (VSS) circuit – the vehicle must operate up to 2 minutes at road speed, before this code will set
32	Barometric Pressure Sensor (BARO) circuit low
34	Manifold Absolute Pressure (MAP) or vacuum sensor circuit. The engine must run up to 2 minutes at specified curb idle speed, before this code will set
35	Idle Speed Control (ISC) switch circuit shorted – up to 70% Throttle Position Sensor (TPS) for over 5 seconds
41	No distributor reference pulses to the Electronic Control Module (ECM) at specified engine vacuum. This code will store in memory
42	Electronic Spark Timing (EST) bypass circuit or EST circuit grounded or open
43	Electronic Spark Control (ESC) retard signal for too long a time – causes retard in Electronic Spark Timing (EST) signal
44	Lean exhaust indication – the engine must run 2 minutes, in closed loop and at part throttle, before this code will set
45	Rich exhaust indication – the engine must run 2 minutes, in closed loop and at part throttle, before this code will set
51	Faulty or improperly installed calibration unit (PROM). It takes up to 30 seconds before this code will set
53	Exhaust Gas Recirculation (EGR) valve vacuum sensor has seen improper EGR vacuum
54	Shorted Mixture Control (M/C) solenoid circuit and/or faulty Electronic Control Module (ECM)

GENERAL MOTORS CORPORATION
DIAGNOSTIC CODE DATA

Year — 1985
Model — Caprice Classic
Engine — 5.7L (350 cid) V8
Engine Code — VIN 6

ECM TROUBLE CODES

Code	Explanation
12	No distributor reference pulses to the Electronic Control Module (ECM). This code is not stored in memory and will only flash while the fault is present. Normal code with ignition ON, engine not running
13	Oxygen sensor circuit — the engine must run up to 4 minutes at part throttle, under road load, before this code will set
14	Shorted Coolant Temperature Sensor (CTS) circuit — the engine must run 2 minutes before this code will set
15	Open Coolant Temperature Sensor (CTS) circuit — the engine must run 5 minutes before this code will set
21	Throttle Position Sensor (TPS) circuit voltage high — open circuit or misadjusted TPS — the engine must run 10 seconds, at specified curb idle speed, before this code will set
22	Throttle Position Sensor (TPS) circuit voltage low — grounded circuit or misadjusted TPS — engine must run 20 seconds at specified curb idle speed, to set code
23	Mixture Control (M/C) solenoid circuit open or grounded
24	Vehicle Speed Sensor (VSS) circuit — the vehicle must operate up to 2 minutes at road speed, before this code will set
32	Barometric Pressure Sensor (BARO) circuit low
34	Manifold Absolute Pressure (MAP) or vacuum sensor circuit. The engine must run up to 2 minutes at specified curb idle speed, before this code will set
35	Idle Speed Control (ISC) switch circuit shorted — up to 70% Throttle Position Sensor (TPS) for over 5 seconds
41	No distributor reference pulses to the Electronic Control Module (ECM) at specified engine vacuum. This code will store in memory
42	Electronic Spark Timing (EST) bypass circuit or EST circuit grounded or open
43	Electronic Spark Control (ESC) retard signal for too long a time — causes retard in Electronic Spark Timing (EST) signal
44	Lean exhaust indication — the engine must run 2 minutes, in closed loop and at part throttle, before this code will set
45	Rich exhaust indication — the engine must run 2 minutes, in closed loop and at part throttle, before this code will set
51	Faulty or improperly installed calibration unit (PROM). It takes up to 30 seconds before this code will set
53	Exhaust Gas Recirculation (EGR) valve vacuum sensor has seen improper EGR vacuum
54	Shorted Mixture Control (M/C) solenoid circuit and/or faulty Electronic Control Module (ECM)

Year – 1985
Model – Impala
Engine – 4.3L (262 cid) EFI V6
Engine Code – VIN Z

ECM TROUBLE CODES

Code	Explanation
13	Oxygen sensor circuit
14	Coolant Temperature Sensor (CTS) – low
15	Coolant Temperature Sensor (CTS) – high
21	Throttle Position Sensor (TPS) – high
22	Throttle Position Sensor (TPS) – low
24	Vehicle Speed Sensor (VSS)
32	Exhaust Gas Recirculation (EGR) system failure
33	Manifold Absolute Pressure (MAP) sensor – high
34	Manifold Absolute Pressure (MAP) sensor – low
42	Electronic Spark Timing (EST)
43	Electronic Spark Control (ESC)
44	Lean exhaust
45	Rich exhaust
51	PROM
52	Calpak missing
55	Electronic Control Module (ECM)

Year — 1985
Model — Impala
Engine — 5.0L (305 cid) V8
Engine Code — VIN H

ECM TROUBLE CODES

Code	Explanation
12	No distributor reference pulses to the Electronic Control Module (ECM). This code is not stored in memory and will only flash while the fault is present. Normal code with ignition ON, engine not running
13	Oxygen sensor circuit — the engine must run up to 4 minutes at part throttle, under road load, before this code will set
14	Shorted Coolant Temperature Sensor (CTS) circuit — the engine must run 2 minutes before this code will set
15	Open Coolant Temperature Sensor (CTS) circuit — the engine must run 5 minutes before this code will set
21	Throttle Position Sensor (TPS) circuit voltage high — open circuit or misadjusted TPS — the engine must run 10 seconds, at specified curb idle speed, before this code will set
22	Throttle Position Sensor (TPS) circuit voltage low — grounded circuit or misadjusted TPS — engine must run 20 seconds at specified curb idle speed, to set code
23	Mixture Control (M/C) solenoid circuit open or grounded
24	Vehicle Speed Sensor (VSS) circuit — the vehicle must operate up to 2 minutes at road speed, before this code will set
32	Barometric Pressure Sensor (BARO) circuit low
34	Manifold Absolute Pressure (MAP) or vacuum sensor circuit. The engine must run up to 2 minutes at specified curb idle speed, before this code will set
35	Idle Speed Control (ISC) switch circuit shorted — up to 70% Throttle Position Sensor (TPS) for over 5 seconds
41	No distributor reference pulses to the Electronic Control Module (ECM) at specified engine vacuum. This code will store in memory
42	Electronic Spark Timing (EST) bypass circuit or EST circuit grounded or open
43	Electronic Spark Control (ESC) retard signal for too long a time — causes retard in Electronic Spark Timing (EST) signal
44	Lean exhaust indication — the engine must run 2 minutes, in closed loop and at part throttle, before this code will set
45	Rich exhaust indication — the engine must run 2 minutes, in closed loop and at part throttle, before this code will set
51	Faulty or improperly installed calibration unit (PROM). It takes up to 30 seconds before this code will set
53	Exhaust Gas Recirculation (EGR) valve vacuum sensor has seen improper EGR vacuum
54	Shorted Mixture Control (M/C) solenoid circuit and/or faulty Electronic Control Module (ECM)

Year — 1985

Model — Impala

Engine — 5.7L (350 cid) V8

Engine Code — VIN 6

ECM TROUBLE CODES

Code	Explanation
12	No distributor reference pulses to the Electronic Control Module (ECM). This code is not stored in memory and will only flash while the fault is present. Normal code with ignition ON, engine not running
13	Oxygen sensor circuit—the engine must run up to 4 minutes at part throttle, under road load, before this code will set
14	Shorted Coolant Temperature Sensor (CTS) circuit—the engine must run 2 minutes before this code will set
15	Open Coolant Temperature Sensor (CTS) circuit—the engine must run 5 minutes before this code will set
21	Throttle Position Sensor (TPS) circuit voltage high—open circuit or misadjusted TPS—the engine must run 10 seconds, at specified curb idle speed, before this code will set
22	Throttle Position Sensor (TPS) circuit voltage low—grounded circuit or misadjusted TPS—engine must run 20 seconds at specified curb idle speed, to set code
23	Mixture Control (M/C) solenoid circuit open or grounded
24	Vehicle Speed Sensor (VSS) circuit—the vehicle must operate up to 2 minutes at road speed, before this code will set
32	Barometric Pressure Sensor (BARO) circuit low
34	Manifold Absolute Pressure (MAP) or vacuum sensor circuit. The engine must run up to 2 minutes at specified curb idle speed, before this code will set
35	Idle Speed Control (ISC) switch circuit shorted—up to 70% Throttle Position Sensor (TPS) for over 5 seconds
41	No distributor reference pulses to the Electronic Control Module (ECM) at specified engine vacuum. This code will store in memory
42	Electronic Spark Timing (EST) bypass circuit or EST circuit grounded or open
43	Electronic Spark Control (ESC) retard signal for too long a time—causes retard in Electronic Spark Timing (EST) signal
44	Lean exhaust indication—the engine must run 2 minutes, in closed loop and at part throttle, before this code will set
45	Rich exhaust indication—the engine must run 2 minutes, in closed loop and at part throttle, before this code will set
51	Faulty or improperly installed calibration unit (PROM). It takes up to 30 seconds before this code will set
53	Exhaust Gas Recirculation (EGR) valve vacuum sensor has seen improper EGR vacuum
54	Shorted Mixture Control (M/C) solenoid circuit and/or faulty Electronic Control Module (ECM)

Year – 1985
Model – Monte Carlo
Engine – 4.3L (262 cid) EFI V6
Engine Code – VIN Z

ECM TROUBLE CODES

Code	Explanation
13	Oxygen sensor circuit
14	Coolant Temperature Sensor (CTS) – low
15	Coolant Temperature Sensor (CTS) – high
21	Throttle Position Sensor (TPS) – high
22	Throttle Position Sensor (TPS) – low
24	Vehicle Speed Sensor (VSS)
32	Exhaust Gas Recirculation (EGR) system failure
33	Manifold Absolute Pressure (MAP) sensor – high
34	Manifold Absolute Pressure (MAP) sensor – low
42	Electronic Spark Timing (EST)
43	Electronic Spark Control (ESC)
44	Lean exhaust
45	Rich exhaust
51	PROM
52	Calpak missing
55	Electronic Control Module (ECM)

Year—1985
Model—Monte Carlo
Engine—5.0L (305 cid) V8
Engine Code—VIN G

ECM TROUBLE CODES

Code	Explanation
12	No distributor reference pulses to the Electronic Control Module (ECM). This code is not stored in memory and will only flash while the fault is present. Normal code with ignition ON, engine not running
13	Oxygen sensor circuit—the engine must run up to 4 minutes at part throttle, under road load, before this code will set
14	Shorted Coolant Temperature Sensor (CTS) circuit—the engine must run 2 minutes before this code will set
15	Open Coolant Temperature Sensor (CTS) circuit—the engine must run 5 minutes before this code will set
21	Throttle Position Sensor (TPS) circuit voltage high—open circuit or misadjusted TPS—the engine must run 10 seconds, at specified curb idle speed, before this code will set
22	Throttle Position Sensor (TPS) circuit voltage low—grounded circuit or misadjusted TPS—engine must run 20 seconds at specified curb idle speed, to set code
23	Mixture Control (M/C) solenoid circuit open or grounded
24	Vehicle Speed Sensor (VSS) circuit—the vehicle must operate up to 2 minutes at road speed, before this code will set
32	Barometric Pressure Sensor (BARO) circuit low
34	Manifold Absolute Pressure (MAP) or vacuum sensor circuit. The engine must run up to 2 minutes at specified curb idle speed, before this code will set
35	Idle Speed Control (ISC) switch circuit shorted—up to 70% Throttle Position Sensor (TPS) for over 5 seconds
41	No distributor reference pulses to the Electronic Control Module (ECM) at specified engine vacuum. This code will store in memory
42	Electronic Spark Timing (EST) bypass circuit or EST circuit grounded or open
43	Electronic Spark Control (ESC) retard signal for too long a time—causes retard in Electronic Spark Timing (EST) signal
44	Lean exhaust indication—the engine must run 2 minutes, in closed loop and at part throttle, before this code will set
45	Rich exhaust indication—the engine must run 2 minutes, in closed loop and at part throttle, before this code will set
51	Faulty or improperly installed calibration unit (PROM). It takes up to 30 seconds before this code will set
53	Exhaust Gas Recirculation (EGR) valve vacuum sensor has seen improper EGR vacuum
54	Shorted Mixture Control (M/C) solenoid circuit and/or faulty Electronic Control Module (ECM)

Year — 1985
Model — Monte Carlo
Engine — 5.0L (305 cid) V8
Engine Code — VIN H

ECM TROUBLE CODES

Code	Explanation
12	No distributor reference pulses to the Electronic Control Module (ECM). This code is not stored in memory and will only flash while the fault is present. Normal code with ignition ON, engine not running
13	Oxygen sensor circuit — the engine must run up to 4 minutes at part throttle, under road load, before this code will set
14	Shorted Coolant Temperature Sensor (CTS) circuit — the engine must run 2 minutes before this code will set
15	Open Coolant Temperature Sensor (CTS) circuit — the engine must run 5 minutes before this code will set
21	Throttle Position Sensor (TPS) circuit voltage high — open circuit or misadjusted TPS — the engine must run 10 seconds, at specified curb idle speed, before this code will set
22	Throttle Position Sensor (TPS) circuit voltage low — grounded circuit or misadjusted TPS — engine must run 20 seconds at specified curb idle speed, to set code
23	Mixture Control (M/C) solenoid circuit open or grounded
24	Vehicle Speed Sensor (VSS) circuit — the vehicle must operate up to 2 minutes at road speed, before this code will set
32	Barometric Pressure Sensor (BARO) circuit low
34	Manifold Absolute Pressure (MAP) or vacuum sensor circuit. The engine must run up to 2 minutes at specified curb idle speed, before this code will set
35	Idle Speed Control (ISC) switch circuit shorted — up to 70% Throttle Position Sensor (TPS) for over 5 seconds
41	No distributor reference pulses to the Electronic Control Module (ECM) at specified engine vacuum. This code will store in memory
42	Electronic Spark Timing (EST) bypass circuit or EST circuit grounded or open
43	Electronic Spark Control (ESC) retard signal for too long a time — causes retard in Electronic Spark Timing (EST) signal
44	Lean exhaust indication — the engine must run 2 minutes, in closed loop and at part throttle, before this code will set
45	Rich exhaust indication — the engine must run 2 minutes, in closed loop and at part throttle, before this code will set
51	Faulty or improperly installed calibration unit (PROM). It takes up to 30 seconds before this code will set
53	Exhaust Gas Recirculation (EGR) valve vacuum sensor has seen improper EGR vacuum
54	Shorted Mixture Control (M/C) solenoid circuit and/or faulty Electronic Control Module (ECM)

Year — 1985
Model — Camaro
Engine — 2.5L (151 cid) EFI 4 cyl
Engine Code — VIN 2

ECM TROUBLE CODES

Code	Explanation
13	Oxygen sensor circuit
14	Coolant Temperature Sensor (CTS) — low
15	Coolant Temperature Sensor (CTS) — high
21	Throttle Position Sensor (TPS) — high
22	Throttle Position Sensor (TPS) — low
24	Vehicle Speed Sensor (VSS)
33	Manifold Absolute Pressure (MAP) sensor — high
34	Manifold Absolute Pressure (MAP) sensor — low
35	Idle Air Control (IAC)
42	Electronic Spark Timing (EST)
44	Lean exhaust
45	Rich exhaust
51	PROM
55	Electronic Control Module (ECM)

Year – 1985
Model – Camaro
Engine – 2.8L (173 cid) MPI V6
Engine Code – VIN 1

ECM TROUBLE CODES

Code	Explanation
13	Oxygen sensor circuit
14	Coolant Temperature Sensor (CTS)
15	Coolant Temperature Sensor (CTS)
21	Throttle Position Sensor (TPS)
22	Throttle Position Sensor (TPS)
23	Manifold Air Temperature (MAT) sensor
24	Vehicle Speed Sensor (VSS)
25	Manifold Air Temperature (MAT) sensor
32	Exhaust Gas Recirculation (EGR) control
34	MAF sensor
41	Cylinder select
42	Electronic Spark Timing (EST)
44	Lean exhaust
45	Rich exhaust
51	PROM
52	Calpak
53	System over voltage
54	Fuel pump voltage low
55	Electronic Control Module (ECM)

Year – 1985
Model – Camaro
Engine – 5.0L (305 cid) V8
Engine Code – VIN H

ECM TROUBLE CODES

Code	Explanation
12	No distributor reference pulses to the Electronic Control Module (ECM). This code is not stored in memory and will only flash while the fault is present. Normal code with ignition ON, engine not running
13	Oxygen sensor circuit—the engine must run up to 4 minutes at part throttle, under road load, before this code will set
14	Shorted Coolant Temperature Sensor (CTS) circuit—the engine must run 2 minutes before this code will set
15	Open Coolant Temperature Sensor (CTS) circuit—the engine must run 5 minutes before this code will set
21	Throttle Position Sensor (TPS) circuit voltage high—open circuit or misadjusted TPS—the engine must run 10 seconds, at specified curb idle speed, before this code will set
22	Throttle Position Sensor (TPS) circuit voltage low—grounded circuit or misadjusted TPS—engine must run 20 seconds at specified curb idle speed, to set code
23	Mixture Control (M/C) solenoid circuit open or grounded
24	Vehicle Speed Sensor (VSS) circuit—the vehicle must operate up to 2 minutes at road speed, before this code will set
32	Barometric Pressure Sensor (BARO) circuit low
34	Manifold Absolute Pressure (MAP) or vacuum sensor circuit. The engine must run up to 2 minutes at specified curb idle speed, before this code will set
35	Idle Speed Control (ISC) switch circuit shorted—up to 70% Throttle Position Sensor (TPS) for over 5 seconds
41	No distributor reference pulses to the Electronic Control Module (ECM) at specified engine vacuum. This code will store in memory
42	Electronic Spark Timing (EST) bypass circuit or EST circuit grounded or open
43	Electronic Spark Control (ESC) retard signal for too long a time—causes retard in Electronic Spark Timing (EST) signal
44	Lean exhaust indication—the engine must run 2 minutes, in closed loop and at part throttle, before this code will set
45	Rich exhaust indication—the engine must run 2 minutes, in closed loop and at part throttle, before this code will set
51	Faulty or improperly installed calibration unit (PROM). It takes up to 30 seconds before this code will set
53	Exhaust Gas Recirculation (EGR) valve vacuum sensor has seen improper EGR vacuum
54	Shorted Mixture Control (M/C) solenoid circuit and/or faulty Electronic Control Module (ECM)

Year – 1985
Model – Camaro
Engine – 5.0L (305 cid) V8
Engine Code – VIN G

ECM TROUBLE CODES

Code	Explanation
12	No distributor reference pulses to the Electronic Control Module (ECM). This code is not stored in memory and will only flash while the fault is present. Normal code with ignition ON, engine not running
13	Oxygen sensor circuit – the engine must run up to 4 minutes at part throttle, under road load, before this code will set
14	Shorted Coolant Temperature Sensor (CTS) circuit – the engine must run 2 minutes before this code will set
15	Open Coolant Temperature Sensor (CTS) circuit – the engine must run 5 minutes before this code will set
21	Throttle Position Sensor (TPS) circuit voltage high – open circuit or misadjusted TPS – the engine must run 10 seconds, at specified curb idle speed, before this code will set
22	Throttle Position Sensor (TPS) circuit voltage low – grounded circuit or misadjusted TPS – engine must run 20 seconds at specified curb idle speed, to set code
23	Mixture Control (M/C) solenoid circuit open or grounded
24	Vehicle Speed Sensor (VSS) circuit – the vehicle must operate up to 2 minutes at road speed, before this code will set
32	Barometric Pressure Sensor (BARO) circuit low
34	Manifold Absolute Pressure (MAP) or vacuum sensor circuit. The engine must run up to 2 minutes at specified curb idle speed, before this code will set
35	Idle Speed Control (ISC) switch circuit shorted – up to 70% Throttle Position Sensor (TPS) for over 5 seconds
41	No distributor reference pulses to the Electronic Control Module (ECM) at specified engine vacuum. This code will store in memory
42	Electronic Spark Timing (EST) bypass circuit or EST circuit grounded or open
43	Electronic Spark Control (ESC) retard signal for too long a time – causes retard in Electronic Spark Timing (EST) signal
44	Lean exhaust indication – the engine must run 2 minutes, in closed loop and at part throttle, before this code will set
45	Rich exhaust indication – the engine must run 2 minutes, in closed loop and at part throttle, before this code will set
51	Faulty or improperly installed calibration unit (PROM). It takes up to 30 seconds before this code will set
53	Exhaust Gas Recirculation (EGR) valve vacuum sensor has seen improper EGR vacuum
54	Shorted Mixture Control (M/C) solenoid circuit and/or faulty Electronic Control Module (ECM)

Year – 1985
Model – Camaro
Engine – 5.0L (305 cid) MPI V8
Engine Code – VIN F

ECM TROUBLE CODES

Code	Explanation
13	Oxygen sensor circuit
14	Coolant Temperature Sensor (CTS)
15	Coolant Temperature Sensor (CTS)
21	Throttle Position Sensor (TPS)
22	Throttle Position Sensor (TPS)
23	Manifold Air Temperature (MAT) sensor
24	Vehicle Speed Sensor (VSS)
25	Manifold Air Temperature (MAT) sensor
32	Exhaust Gas Recirculation (EGR) control
34	Mass Air Flow (MAF) sensor
41	Cylinder select
42	Electronic Spark Timing (EST)
44	Lean exhaust
45	Rich exhaust
51	PROM
52	Calpak
53	System over voltage
54	Fuel pump voltage low
55	Electronic Control Module (ECM)

Year — 1985
Model — Corvette
Engine — 5.7L (350 cid) V8
Engine Code — VIN 8

ECM TROUBLE CODES

Code	Explanation
13	Oxygen sensor circuit
14	Coolant Temperature Sensor (CTS) — voltage low
15	Coolant Temperature Sensor (CTS) — voltage high
21	Throttle Position Sensor (TPS) — voltage high
22	Throttle Position Sensor (TPS) — voltage low
23	Manifold Air Temperature (MAT) sensor — voltage high
24	Vehicle Speed Sensor (VSS)
25	Manifold Air Temperature (MAT) sensor — voltage low
34	Mass Air Flow (MAF) sensor — voltage high
41	Cylinder select
42	Electronic Spark Timing (EST)
43	Electronic Spark Control (ESC)
44	Lean exhaust indication
45	Rich exhaust indication
51	PROM
52	Calpak — missing
53	System over voltage
54	Fuel pump voltage low
55	Electronic Control Module (ECM)

Year — 1985
Model — Chevette
Engine — 1.6L (98 cid) 4 cyl
Engine Code — VIN C

ECM TROUBLE CODES

Code	Explanation
12	No distributor reference pulses to the Electronic Control Module (ECM)
15	Open Coolant Temperature Sensor (CTS) circuit — the engine must run up to 10 minutes before this code will set
21	Throttle Position Sensor (TPS) circuit at WOT — the engine must run up to 10 seconds below 1000 RPM, before this code will set
23	Mixture Control (M/C) solenoid circuit
44	Lean exhaust indication — the engine must run up to 1 minute in closed loop and at part throttle above 2000 rpm before this code will set
45	Rich exhaust indication — the engine must run up to 1 minute in closed loop and at part throttle above 2000 rpm before this code will set
51	Faulty calibration unit (PROM) or installation — turns Electronic Control Module (ECM) off

Year — 1985
Model — Celebrity
Engine — 2.5L (151 cid) TBI 4 cyl
Engine Code — VIN R

ECM TROUBLE CODES

Code	Explanation
13	Oxygen sensor circuit
14	Coolant Temperature Sensor (CTS) — voltage low
15	Coolant Temperature Sensor (CTS) — voltage high
21	Throttle Position Sensor (TPS) — voltage high
22	Throttle Position Sensor (TPS) — voltage low
24	Vehicle Speed Sensor (VSS)
33	Manifold Absolute Pressure (MAP) sensor — voltage low
34	Manifold Absolute Pressure (MAP) sensor — voltage high
35	Idle Air Control (IAC)
42	Electronic Spark Timing (EST)
44	Lean exhaust indication
45	Rich exhaust indication
51	PROM
55	Electronic Control Module (ECM)

Year — 1985
Model — Celebrity
Engine — 2.8L (173 cid) V6
Engine Code — VIN X

ECM TROUBLE CODES

Code	Explanation
12	No distributor reference pulses to the Electronic Control Module (ECM). This code is not stored in memory and will only flash while the fault is present. Normal code with ignition ON, engine not running
13	Oxygen sensor circuit — the engine must run up to 4 minutes at part throttle, under road load, before this code will set
14	Shorted Coolant Temperature Sensor (CTS) circuit — the engine must run 2 minutes before this code will set
15	Open Coolant Temperature Sensor (CTS) circuit — the engine must run 5 minutes before this code will set
21	Throttle Position Sensor (TPS) circuit voltage high — open circuit or misadjusted TPS — the engine must run 10 seconds, at specified curb idle speed, before this code will set
22	Throttle Position Sensor (TPS) circuit voltage low — grounded circuit or misadjusted TPS — engine must run 20 seconds at specified curb idle speed, to set code
23	Mixture Control (M/C) solenoid circuit open or grounded
24	Vehicle Speed Sensor (VSS) circuit — the vehicle must operate up to 2 minutes at road speed, before this code will set
32	Barometric Pressure Sensor (BARO) circuit low
34	Manifold Absolute Pressure (MAP) or vacuum sensor circuit. The engine must run up to 2 minutes at specified curb idle speed, before this code will set
35	Idle Speed Control (ISC) switch circuit shorted — up to 70% Throttle Position Sensor (TPS) for over 5 seconds
41	No distributor reference pulses to the Electronic Control Module (ECM) at specified engine vacuum. This code will store in memory
42	Electronic Spark Timing (EST) bypass circuit or EST circuit grounded or open
43	Electronic Spark Control (ESC) retard signal for too long a time — causes retard in Electronic Spark Timing (EST) signal
44	Lean exhaust indication — the engine must run 2 minutes, in closed loop and at part throttle, before this code will set
45	Rich exhaust indication — the engine must run 2 minutes, in closed loop and at part throttle, before this code will set
51	Faulty or improperly installed calibration unit (PROM). It takes up to 30 seconds before this code will set
53	Exhaust Gas Recirculation (EGR) valve vacuum sensor has seen improper EGR vacuum
54	Shorted Mixture Control (M/C) solenoid circuit and/or faulty Electronic Control Module (ECM)

Year — 1985
Model — Celebrity
Engine — 2.8L (173 cid) MFI V6
Engine Code — VIN W

ECM TROUBLE CODES

Code	Explanation
13	Oxygen sensor circuit
14	Coolant Temperature Sensor (CTS) — signal low
15	Coolant Temperature Sensor (CTS) — signal high
21	Throttle Position Sensor (TPS) — voltage high
22	Throttle Position Sensor (TPS) — voltage low
23	Manifold Air Temperature (MAT) sensor — voltage high
24	Vehicle Speed Sensor (VSS)
25	Manifold Air Temperature (MAT) sensor — voltage low
32	Exhaust Gas Recirculation (EGR)
34	Mass Air Flow (MAF) sensor — signal low
41	Cylinder select
42	Electronic Spark Timing (EST)
44	Lean exhaust indication
45	Rich exhaust indication
51	PROM
52	Calpak
53	System over voltage
54	Fuel pump voltage low
55	Electronic Control Module (ECM)

Year — 1985
Model — Cavalier
Engine — 2.0L (121 cid) TBI 4 cyl
Engine Code — VIN P

ECM TROUBLE CODES

Code	Explanation
13	Oxygen sensor circuit
14	Coolant Temperature Sensor (CTS) — low
15	Coolant Temperature Sensor (CTS) — high
21	Throttle Position Sensor (TPS) — high
22	Throttle Position Sensor (TPS) — low
24	Vehicle Speed Sensor (VSS)
33	Manifold Absolute Pressure (MAP) sensor — high
34	Manifold Absolute Pressure (MAP) sensor — low
42	Electronic Spark Timing (EST)
44	Lean exhaust
45	Rich exhaust
51	PROM
52	Calpak
54	Fuel pump circuit — low
55	Electronic Control Module (ECM)

Year – 1985
Model – Cavalier

Engine – 2.8L (173 cid) MFI V6
Engine Code – VIN W

ECM TROUBLE CODES

Code	Explanation
13	Oxygen sensor circuit
14	Coolant Temperature Sensor (CTS)
15	Coolant Temperature Sensor (CTS)
21	Throttle Position Sensor (TPS)
22	Throttle Position Sensor (TPS)
23	Manifold Air Temperature (MAT) sensor
24	Vehicle Speed Sensor (VSS)
25	Manifold Air Temperature (MAT) sensor
32	Exhaust Gas Recirculation (EGR)
34	Mass Air Flow (MAF) sensor
41	Cylinder select error
42	Electronic Spark Timing (EST)
44	Lean exhaust indication
45	Rich exhaust indication
51	PROM
52	Calpak
53	System over voltage
54	Fuel pump voltage low
55	Electronic Control Module (ECM)

Year — 1985
Model — Citation
Engine — 2.5L (151 cid) TBI 4 cyl
Engine Code — VIN R

ECM TROUBLE CODES

Code	Explanation
13	Oxygen sensor circuit
14	Coolant Temperature Sensor (CTS) — voltage low
15	Coolant Temperature Sensor (CTS) — voltage high
21	Throttle Position Sensor (TPS) — voltage high
22	Throttle Position Sensor (TPS) — voltage low
24	Vehicle Speed Sensor (VSS)
33	Manifold Absolute Pressure (MAP) sensor — voltage low
34	Manifold Absolute Pressure (MAP) sensor — voltage high
35	Idle Air Control (IAC)
42	Electronic Spark Timing (EST)
44	Lean exhaust indication
45	Rich exhaust indication
51	PROM
55	Electronic Control Module (ECM)

Year — 1985
Model — Citation
Engine — 2.8L (173 cid) V6
Engine Code — VIN X

ECM TROUBLE CODES

Code	Explanation
12	No distributor reference pulses to the Electronic Control Module (ECM). This code is not stored in memory and will only flash while the fault is present. Normal code with ignition ON, engine not running
13	Oxygen sensor circuit—the engine must run up to 4 minutes at part throttle, under road load, before this code will set
14	Shorted Coolant Temperature Sensor (CTS) circuit—the engine must run 2 minutes before this code will set
15	Open Coolant Temperature Sensor (CTS) circuit—the engine must run 5 minutes before this code will set
21	Throttle Position Sensor (TPS) circuit voltage high—open circuit or misadjusted TPS—the engine must run 10 seconds, at specified curb idle speed, before this code will set
22	Throttle Position Sensor (TPS) circuit voltage low—grounded circuit or misadjusted TPS—engine must run 20 seconds at specified curb idle speed, to set code
23	Mixture Control (M/C) solenoid circuit open or grounded
24	Vehicle Speed Sensor (VSS) circuit—the vehicle must operate up to 2 minutes at road speed, before this code will set
32	Barometric Pressure Sensor (BARO) circuit low
34	Manifold Absolute Pressure (MAP) or vacuum sensor circuit. The engine must run up to 2 minutes at specified curb idle speed, before this code will set
35	Idle Speed Control (ISC) switch circuit shorted—up to 70% Throttle Position Sensor (TPS) for over 5 seconds
41	No distributor reference pulses to the Electronic Control Module (ECM) at specified engine vacuum. This code will store in memory
42	Electronic Spark Timing (EST) bypass circuit or EST circuit grounded or open
43	Electronic Spark Control (ESC) retard signal for too long a time—causes retard in Electronic Spark Timing (EST) signal
44	Lean exhaust indication—the engine must run 2 minutes, in closed loop and at part throttle, before this code will set
45	Rich exhaust indication—the engine must run 2 minutes, in closed loop and at part throttle, before this code will set
51	Faulty or improperly installed calibration unit (PROM). It takes up to 30 seconds before this code will set
53	Exhaust Gas Recirculation (EGR) valve vacuum sensor has seen improper EGR vacuum
54	Shorted Mixture Control (M/C) solenoid circuit and/or faulty Electronic Control Module (ECM)

Year — 1985
Model — Citation
Engine — 2.8L (173 cid) MFI V6
Engine Code — VIN W

ECM TROUBLE CODES

Code	Explanation
13	Oxygen sensor circuit
14	Coolant Temperature Sensor (CTS) — signal low
15	Coolant Temperature Sensor (CTS) — signal high
21	Throttle Position Sensor (TPS) — voltage high
22	Throttle Position Sensor (TPS) — voltage low
23	Manifold Air Temperature (MAT) sensor — signal high
24	Vehicle Speed Sensor (VSS)
25	Manifold Air Temperature (MAT) sensor — signal low
32	Exhaust Gas Recirculation (EGR)
34	Mass Air Flow (MAF) sensor — signal low
41	Cylinder select
42	Electronic Spark Timing (EST)
44	Lean exhaust indication
45	Rich exhaust indication
51	PROM
52	Calpak
53	System over voltage
54	Fuel pump voltage low
55	Electronic Control Module (ECM)

Year – 1986
Model – Caprice
Engine – 4.3L (262 cid) TBI V6
Engine Code – VIN Z

ECM TROUBLE CODES

Code	Explanation
13	Oxygen sensor circuit
14	Coolant Temperature Sensor (CTS) – low
15	Coolant Temperature Sensor (CTS) – high
21	Throttle Position Sensor (TPS) – high
22	Throttle Position Sensor (TPS) – low
24	Vehicle Speed Sensor (VSS)
32	Exhaust Gas Recirculation (EGR) system failure
33	Manifold Absolute Pressure (MAP) sensor – high
34	Manifold Absolute Pressure (MAP) sensor – low
42	Electronic Spark Timing (EST)
43	Electronic Spark Control (ESC)
44	Lean exhaust indication
45	Rich exhaust indication
51	PROM – Mem-Cal
52	Calpak – missing
54	Fuel pump voltage low
55	Electronic Control Module (ECM)

Year — 1986
Model — Caprice
Engine — 5.0L (307 cid) V8
Engine Code — VIN Y

ECM TROUBLE CODES

Code	Explanation
12	No distributor reference pulses to the Electronic Control Module (ECM). This code is not stored in memory and will only flash while the fault is present. Normal code with ignition ON, engine not running
13	Oxygen sensor circuit—the engine must run up to 4 minutes at part throttle, under road load, before this code will set
14	Shorted Coolant Temperature Sensor (CTS) circuit—the engine must run 2 minutes before this code will set
15	Open Coolant Temperature Sensor (CTS) circuit—the engine must run 5 minutes before this code will set
21	Throttle Position Sensor (TPS) circuit voltage high—open circuit or misadjusted TPS—the engine must run 10 seconds, at specified curb idle speed, before this code will set
22	Throttle Position Sensor (TPS) circuitt voltage low—grounded circuit or misadjusted TPS—engine must run 20 seconds at specified curb idle speed, to set code
23	Mixture Control (M/C) solenoid circuit open or grounded
24	Vehicle Speed Sensor (VSS) circuit—the vehicle must operate up to 2 minutes at road speed, before this code will set
32	Barometric Pressure Sensor (BARO) circuit low
34	Manifold Absolute Pressure (MAP) or vacuum sensor circuit. The engine must run up to 2 minutes at specified curb idle speed, before this code will set
35	Idle Speed Control (ISC) switch circuit shorted—up to 70% Throttle Position Sensor (TPS) for over 5 seconds
41	No distributor reference pulses to the Electronic Control Module (ECM) at specified engine vacuum. This code will store in memory
42	Electronic Spark Timing (EST) bypass circuit or EST circuit grounded or open
43	Electronic Spark Control (ESC) retard signal for too long a time—causes retard in Electronic Spark Timing (EST) signal
44	Lean exhaust indication—the engine must run 2 minutes, in closed loop and at part throttle, before this code will set
45	Rich exhaust Indication—the engine must run 2 minutes, in closed loop and at part throttle, before this code will set
51	Faulty or improperly installed calibration unit (PROM). It takes up to 30 seconds before this code will set
53	Exhaust Gas Recirculation (EGR) valve vacuum sensor has seen improper EGR vacuum
54	Shorted Mixture Control (M/C) solenoid circuit and/or faulty Electronic Control Module (ECM)

Year – 1986
Model – Caprice
Engine – 5.0L (305 cid) V8
Engine Code – VIN H

ECM TROUBLE CODES

Code	Explanation
12	No distributor reference pulses to the Electronic Control Module (ECM). This code is not stored in memory and will only flash while the fault is present. Normal code with ignition ON, engine not running
13	Oxygen sensor circuit – the engine must run up to 4 minutes at part throttle, under road load, before this code will set
14	Shorted Coolant Temperature Sensor (CTS) circuit – the engine must run 2 minutes before this code will set
15	Open Coolant Temperature Sensor (CTS) circuit – the engine must run 5 minutes before this code will set
21	Throttle Position Sensor (TPS) circuit voltage high – open circuit or misadjusted TPS – the engine must run 10 seconds, at specified curb idle speed, before this code will set
22	Throttle Position Sensor (TPS) circuitt voltage low – grounded circuit or misadjusted TPS – engine must run 20 seconds at specified curb idle speed, to set code
23	Mixture Control (M/C) solenoid circuit open or grounded
24	Vehicle Speed Sensor (VSS) circuit – the vehicle must operate up to 2 minutes at road speed, before this code will set
32	Barometric Pressure Sensor (BARO) circuit low
34	Manifold Absolute Pressure (MAP) or vacuum sensor circuit. The engine must run up to 2 minutes at specified curb idle speed, before this code will set
35	Idle Speed Control (ISC) switch circuit shorted – up to 70% Throttle Position Sensor (TPS) for over 5 seconds
41	No distributor reference pulses to the Electronic Control Module (ECM) at specified engine vacuum. This code will store in memory
42	Electronic Spark Timing (EST) bypass circuit or EST circuit grounded or open
43	Electronic Spark Control (ESC) retard signal for too long a time – causes retard in Electronic Spark Timing (EST) signal
44	Lean exhaust indication – the engine must run 2 minutes, in closed loop and at part throttle, before this code will set
45	Rich exhaust indication – the engine must run 2 minutes, in closed loop and at part throttle, before this code will set
51	Faulty or improperly installed calibration unit (PROM). It takes up to 30 seconds before this code will set
53	Exhaust Gas Recirculation (EGR) valve vacuum sensor has seen improper EGR vacuum
54	Shorted Mixture Control (M/C) solenoid circuit and/or faulty Electronic Control Module (ECM)

Year — 1986
Model — Caprice
Engine — 5.7L (350 cid) V8
Engine Code — VIN 6

ECM TROUBLE CODES

Code	Explanation
12	No distributor reference pulses to the Electronic Control Module (ECM). This code is not stored in memory and will only flash while the fault is present. Normal code with ignition ON, engine not running
13	Oxygen sensor circuit—the engine must run up to 4 minutes at part throttle, under road load, before this code will set
14	Shorted Coolant Temperature Sensor (CTS) circuit—the engine must run 2 minutes before this code will set
15	Open Coolant Temperature Sensor (CTS) circuit—the engine must run 5 minutes before this code will set
21	Throttle Position Sensor (TPS) circuit voltage high—open circuit or misadjusted TPS—the engine must run 10 seconds, at specified curb idle speed, before this code will set
22	Throttle Position Sensor (TPS) circuitt voltage low—grounded circuit or misadjusted TPS—engine must run 20 seconds at specified curb idle speed, to set code
23	Mixture Control (M/C) solenoid circuit open or grounded
24	Vehicle Speed Sensor (VSS) circuit—the vehicle must operate up to 2 minutes at road speed, before this code will set
32	Barometric Pressure Sensor (BARO) circuit low
34	Manifold Absolute Pressure (MAP) or vacuum sensor circuit. The engine must run up to 2 minutes at specified curb idle speed, before this code will set
35	Idle Speed Control (ISC) switch circuit shorted—up to 70% Throttle Position Sensor (TPS) for over 5 seconds
41	No distributor reference pulses to the Electronic Control Module (ECM) at specified engine vacuum. This code will store in memory
42	Electronic Spark Timing (EST) bypass circuit or EST circuit grounded or open
43	Electronic Spark Control (ESC) retard signal for too long a time—causes retard in Electronic Spark Timing (EST) signal
44	Lean exhaust indication—the engine must run 2 minutes, in closed loop and at part throttle, before this code will set
45	Rich exhaust indication—the engine must run 2 minutes, in closed loop and at part throttle, before this code will set
51	Faulty or improperly installed calibration unit (PROM). It takes up to 30 seconds before this code will set
53	Exhaust Gas Recirculation (EGR) valve vacuum sensor has seen improper EGR vacuum
54	Shorted Mixture Control (M/C) solenoid circuit and/or faulty Electronic Control Module (ECM)

Year – 1986
Model – Monte Carlo
Engine – 4.3L (262 cid) TBI V6
Engine Code – VIN Z

ECM TROUBLE CODES

Code	Explanation
13	Oxygen sensor circuit
14	Coolant Temperature Sensor (CTS) – low
15	Coolant Temperature Sensor (CTS) – high
21	Throttle Position Sensor (TPS) – high
22	Throttle Position Sensor (TPS) – low
24	Vehicle Speed Sensor (VSS)
32	Exhaust Gas Recirculation (EGR) system failure
33	Manifold Absolute Pressure (MAP) sensor – high
34	Manifold Absolute Pressure (MAP) sensor – low
42	Electronic Spark Timing (EST)
43	Electronic Spark Control (ESC)
44	Lean exhaust indication
45	Rich exhaust indication
51	PROM – Mem-Cal
52	Calpak – missing
54	Fuel pump voltage low
55	Electronic Control Module (ECM)

Year—1986
Model—Monte Carlo
Engine—5.0L (305 cid) V8
Engine Code—VIN H

ECM TROUBLE CODES

Code	Explanation
12	No distributor reference pulses to the Electronic Control Module (ECM). This code is not stored in memory and will only flash while the fault is present. Normal code with ignition ON, engine not running
13	Oxygen sensor circuit—the engine must run up to 4 minutes at part throttle, under road load, before this code will set
14	Shorted Coolant Temperature Sensor (CTS) circuit—the engine must run 2 minutes before this code will set
15	Open Coolant Temperature Sensor (CTS) circuit—the engine must run 5 minutes before this code will set
21	Throttle Position Sensor (TPS) circuit voltage high—open circuit or misadjusted TPS—the engine must run 10 seconds, at specified curb idle speed, before this code will set
22	Throttle Position Sensor (TPS) circuitt voltage low—grounded circuit or misadjusted TPS—engine must run 20 seconds at specified curb idle speed, to set code
23	Mixture Control (M/C) solenoid circuit open or grounded
24	Vehicle Speed Sensor (VSS) circuit—the vehicle must operate up to 2 minutes at road speed, before this code will set
32	Barometric Pressure Sensor (BARO) circuit low
34	Manifold Absolute Pressure (MAP) or vacuum sensor circuit. The engine must run up to 2 minutes at specified curb idle speed, before this code will set
35	Idle Speed Control (ISC) switch circuit shorted—up to 70% Throttle Position Sensor (TPS) for over 5 seconds
41	No distributor reference pulses to the Electronic Control Module (ECM) at specified engine vacuum. This code will store in memory
42	Electronic Spark Timing (EST) bypass circuit or EST circuit grounded or open
43	Electronic Spark Control (ESC) retard signal for too long a time—causes retard in Electronic Spark Timing (EST) signal
44	Lean exhaust indication—the engine must run 2 minutes, in closed loop and at part throttle, before this code will set
45	Rich exhaust indication—the engine must run 2 minutes, in closed loop and at part throttle, before this code will set
51	Faulty or improperly installed calibration unit (PROM). It takes up to 30 seconds before this code will set
53	Exhaust Gas Recirculation (EGR) valve vacuum sensor has seen improper EGR vacuum
54	Shorted Mixture Control (M/C) solenoid circuit and/or faulty Electronic Control Module (ECM)

Year – 1986
Model – El Camino
Engine – 4.3L (262 cid) TBI V6
Engine Code – VIN Z

ECM TROUBLE CODES

Code	Explanation
13	Oxygen sensor circuit
14	Coolant Temperature Sensor (CTS) – low
15	Coolant Temperature Sensor (CTS) – high
21	Throttle Position Sensor (TPS) – high
22	Throttle Position Sensor (TPS) – low
24	Vehicle Speed Sensor (VSS)
32	Exhaust Gas Recirculation (EGR) system failure
33	Manifold Absolute Pressure (MAP) sensor – high
34	Manifold Absolute Pressure (MAP) sensor – low
42	Electronic Spark Timing (EST)
43	Electronic Spark Control (ESC)
44	Lean exhaust indication
45	Rich exhaust indication
51	PROM – Mem-Cal
52	Calpak – missing
54	Fuel pump voltage low
55	Electronic Control Module (ECM)

Year – 1986
Model – El Camino
Engine – 5.0L (305 cid) V8
Engine Code – VIN H

ECM TROUBLE CODES

Code	Explanation
12	No distributor reference pulses to the Electronic Control Module (ECM). This code is not stored in memory and will only flash while the fault is present. Normal code with ignition ON, engine not running
13	Oxygen sensor circuit – the engine must run up to 4 minutes at part throttle, under road load, before this code will set
14	Shorted Coolant Temperature Sensor (CTS) circuit – the engine must run 2 minutes before this code will set
15	Open Coolant Temperature Sensor (CTS) circuit – the engine must run 5 minutes before this code will set
21	Throttle Position Sensor (TPS) circuit voltage high – open circuit or misadjusted TPS – the engine must run 10 seconds, at specified curb idle speed, before this code will set
22	Throttle Position Sensor (TPS) circuitt voltage low – grounded circuit or misadjusted TPS – engine must run 20 seconds at specified curb idle speed, to set code
23	Mixture Control (M/C) solenoid circuit open or grounded
24	Vehicle Speed Sensor (VSS) circuit – the vehicle must operate up to 2 minutes at road speed, before this code will set
32	Barometric Pressure Sensor (BARO) circuit low
34	Manifold Absolute Pressure (MAP) or vacuum sensor circuit. The engine must run up to 2 minutes at specified curb idle speed, before this code will set
35	Idle Speed Control (ISC) switch circuit shorted – up to 70% Throttle Position Sensor (TPS) for over 5 seconds
41	No distributor reference pulses to the Electronic Control Module (ECM) at specified engine vacuum. This code will store in memory
42	Electronic Spark Timing (EST) bypass circuit or EST circuit grounded or open
43	Electronic Spark Control (ESC) retard signal for too long a time – causes retard in Electronic Spark Timing (EST) signal
44	Lean exhaust indication – the engine must run 2 minutes, in closed loop and at part throttle, before this code will set
45	Rich exhaust indication – the engine must run 2 minutes, in closed loop and at part throttle, before this code will set
51	Faulty or improperly installed calibration unit (PROM). It takes up to 30 seconds before this code will set
53	Exhaust Gas Recirculation (EGR) valve vacuum sensor has seen improper EGR vacuum
54	Shorted Mixture Control (M/C) solenoid circuit and/or faulty Electronic Control Module (ECM)

Year – 1986
Model – Camaro
Engine – 2.5L (151 cid) EFI 4 cyl
Engine Code – VIN 2

ECM TROUBLE CODES

Code	Explanation
13	Oxygen sensor circuit
14	Coolant Temperature Sensor (CTS)
15	Coolant Temperature Sensor (CTS)
21	Throttle Position Sensor (TPS)
22	Throttle Position Sensor (TPS)
24	Vehicle Speed Sensor (VSS)
33	Manifold Absolute Pressure (MAP) sensor
34	Manifold Absolute Pressure (MAP) sensor
35	Idle Air Control (IAC)
42	Electronic Spark Timing (EST)
44	Lean exhaust
45	Rich exhaust
51	PROM
55	Electronic Control Module (ECM)

Year — 1986
Model — Camaro
Engine — 2.8L (173 cid) MPI V6
Engine Code — VIN S

ECM TROUBLE CODES

Code	Explanation
13	Oxygen sensor circuit
14	Coolant Temperature Sensor (CTS)
15	Coolant Temperature Sensor (CTS)
21	Throttle Position Sensor (TPS)
22	Throttle Position Sensor (TPS)
23	Manifold Air Temperature (MAT) sensor
24	Vehicle Speed Sensor (VSS)
25	Manifold Air Temperature (MAT) sensor
32	Exhaust Gas Recirculation (EGR) control
33	Mass Air Flow (MAF) sensor
34	Mass Air Flow (MAF) sensor
41	Cylinder select
42	Electronic Spark Timing (EST)
44	Lean exhaust indication
45	Rich exhaust indication
51	PROM
52	Calpak — missing
53	System over voltage
54	Fuel pump voltage low
55	Electronic Control Module (ECM)

Year — 1986
Model — Camaro
Engine — 5.0L (305 cid) V8
Engine Code — VIN F

ECM TROUBLE CODES

Code	Explanation
13	Oxygen sensor circuit
14	Coolant Temperature Sensor (CTS)
15	Coolant Temperature Sensor (CTS)
21	Throttle Position Sensor (TPS)
22	Throttle Position Sensor (TPS)
23	Manifold Air Temperature (MAT) sensor
24	Vehicle Speed Sensor (VSS)
25	Manifold Air Temperature (MAT) sensor
32	Exhaust Gas Recirculation (EGR)
33	Mass Air Flow (MAF) sensor
34	Mass Air Flow (MAF) sensor
36	Burn-off function fault
41	Cylinder select
42	Electronic Spark Timing (EST)
43	Electronic Spark Control (ESC)
44	Lean exhaust indication
45	Rich exhaust indication
51	Mem-Cal
53	System over voltage
54	Fuel pump voltage low
55	Electronic Control Module (ECM)

Year – 1986
Model – Camaro
Engine – 5.0L (305 cid) V8
Engine Code – VIN G

ECM TROUBLE CODES

Code	Explanation
12	No distributor reference pulses to the Electronic Control Module (ECM). This code is not stored in memory and will only flash while the fault is present. Normal code with ignition ON, engine not running
13	Oxygen sensor circuit – the engine must run up to 4 minutes at part throttle, under road load, before this code will set
14	Shorted Coolant Temperature Sensor (CTS) circuit – the engine must run 2 minutes before this code will set
15	Open Coolant Temperature Sensor (CTS) circuit – the engine must run 5 minutes before this code will set
21	Throttle Position Sensor (TPS) circuit voltage high – open circuit or misadjusted TPS – the engine must run 10 seconds, at specified curb idle speed, before this code will set
22	Throttle Position Sensor (TPS) circuitt voltage low – grounded circuit or misadjusted TPS – engine must run 20 seconds at specified curb idle speed, to set code
23	Mixture Control (M/C) solenoid circuit open or grounded
24	Vehicle Speed Sensor (VSS) circuit – the vehicle must operate up to 2 minutes at road speed, before this code will set
32	Barometric Pressure Sensor (BARO) circuit low
34	Manifold Absolute Pressure (MAP) or vacuum sensor circuit. The engine must run up to 2 minutes at specified curb idle speed, before this code will set
35	Idle Speed Control (ISC) switch circuit shorted – up to 70% Throttle Position Sensor (TPS) for over 5 seconds
41	No distributor reference pulses to the Electronic Control Module (ECM) at specified engine vacuum. This code will store in memory
42	Electronic Spark Timing (EST) bypass circuit or EST circuit grounded or open
43	Electronic Spark Control (ESC) retard signal for too long a time – causes retard in Electronic Spark Timing (EST) signal
44	Lean exhaust indication – the engine must run 2 minutes, in closed loop and at part throttle, before this code will set
45	Rich exhaust indication – the engine must run 2 minutes, in closed loop and at part throttle, before this code will set
51	Faulty or improperly installed calibration unit (PROM). It takes up to 30 seconds before this code will set
53	Exhaust Gas Recirculation (EGR) valve vacuum sensor has seen improper EGR vacuum
54	Shorted Mixture Control (M/C) solenoid circuit and/or faulty Electronic Control Module (ECM)

Year – 1986
Model – Camaro
Engine – 5.0L (305 cid) V8
Engine Code – VIN H

ECM TROUBLE CODES

Code	Explanation
12	No distributor reference pulses to the Electronic Control Module (ECM). This code is not stored in memory and will only flash while the fault is present. Normal code with ignition ON, engine not running
13	Oxygen sensor circuit – the engine must run up to 4 minutes at part throttle, under road load, before this code will set
14	Shorted Coolant Temperature Sensor (CTS) circuit – the engine must run 2 minutes before this code will set
15	Open Coolant Temperature Sensor (CTS) circuit – the engine must run 5 minutes before this code will set
21	Throttle Position Sensor (TPS) circuit voltage high – open circuit or misadjusted TPS – the engine must run 10 seconds, at specified curb idle speed, before this code will set
22	Throttle Position Sensor (TPS) circuitt voltage low – grounded circuit or misadjusted TPS – engine must run 20 seconds at specified curb idle speed, to set code
23	Mixture Control (M/C) solenoid circuit open or grounded
24	Vehicle Speed Sensor (VSS) circuit – the vehicle must operate up to 2 minutes at road speed, before this code will set
32	Barometric Pressure Sensor (BARO) circuit low
34	Manifold Absolute Pressure (MAP) or vacuum sensor circuit. The engine must run up to 2 minutes at specified curb idle speed, before this code will set
35	Idle Speed Control (ISC) switch circuit shorted – up to 70% Throttle Position Sensor (TPS) for over 5 seconds
41	No distributor reference pulses to the Electronic Control Module (ECM) at specified engine vacuum. This code will store in memory
42	Electronic Spark Timing (EST) bypass circuit or EST circuit grounded or open
43	Electronic Spark Control (ESC) retard signal for too long a time – causes retard in Electronic Spark Timing (EST) signal
44	Lean exhaust indication – the engine must run 2 minutes, in closed loop and at part throttle, before this code will set
45	Rich exhaust indication – the engine must run 2 minutes, in closed loop and at part throttle, before this code will set
51	Faulty or improperly installed calibration unit (PROM). It takes up to 30 seconds before this code will set
53	Exhaust Gas Recirculation (EGR) valve vacuum sensor has seen improper EGR vacuum
54	Shorted Mixture Control (M/C) solenoid circuit and/or faulty Electronic Control Module (ECM)

Year — 1986
Model — Corvette
Engine — 5.7L (350 cid) TPI V8
Engine Code — VIN 8

ECM TROUBLE CODES

Code	Explanation
13	Oxygen sensor circuit
14	Coolant Temperature Sensor (CTS)
15	Coolant Temperature Sensor (CTS)
21	Throttle Position Sensor (TPS)
22	Throttle Position Sensor (TPS)
23	Manifold Air Temperature (MAT) sensor
24	Vehicle Speed Sensor (VSS)
25	Manifold Air Temperature (MAT) sensor
32	Exhaust Gas Recirculation (EGR)
33	Mass Air Flow (MAF) sensor
34	Mass Air Flow (MAF) sensor
36	Burn-off function fault
41	Cylinder select
42	Electronic Spark Timing (EST)
43	Electronic Spark Control (ESC)
44	Lean exhaust indication
45	Rich exhaust indication
46	Vehicle Anti-Theft fault
51	Mem-Cal
53	System over voltage
54	Fuel pump voltage low
55	Electronic Control Module (ECM)

Year—1986
Model—Chevette
Engine—1.6L (98 cid) 4 cyl
Engine Code—VIN C

ECM TROUBLE CODES

Code	Explanation
12	No distributor reference pulses to the Electronic Control Module (ECM)
15	Open coolant Temperature Sensor (CTS) circuit—the engine must run up to 10 minutes before this code will set
21	Throttle Position Sensor (TPS) circuit at WOT—the engine must run up to 10 seconds below 1000 RPM, before this code will set
23	Mixture Control (M/C) solenoid circuit
44	Lean exhaust indication—the engine must run up to 1 minute in closed loop and at part throttle above 2000 rpm before this code will set
45	Rich exhaust indication—the engine must run up to 1 minute in closed loop and at part throttle above 2000 rpm before this code will set
51	Faulty calibration unit (PROM) or installation—turns Electronic Control Module (ECM) OFF

Year – 1986
Model – Celebrity
Engine – 2.5L (151 cid) TBI 4 cyl
Engine Code – VIN R

ECM TROUBLE CODES

Code	Explanation
13	Oxygen sensor circuit
14	Coolant Temperature Sensor (CTS)
15	Coolant Temperature Sensor (CTS)
21	Throttle Position Sensor (TPS)
22	Throttle Position Sensor (TPS)
24	Vehicle Speed Sensor (VSS)
33	Mass Air Flow (MAF) sensor
34	Mass Air Flow (MAF) sensor
35	Idle Air Control (IAC)
42	Electronic Spark Timing (EST)
44	Lean exhaust indication
45	Rich exhaust indication
51	PROM
55	Electronic Control Module (ECM)

Year – 1986
Model – Celebrity
Engine – 2.8L (173 cid) V6
Engine Code – VIN X

ECM TROUBLE CODES

Code	Explanation
12	No distributor reference signal to the Electronic Control Module (ECM). This code is not stored in memory and will only flash while the fault is present. Normal code with ignition ON, engine not running
13	Oxygen sensor circuit – the engine must run up to 4 minutes at part throttle, under road load, before this code will set
14	Shorted Coolant Temperature Sensor (CTS) circuit – the engine must run 2 minutes before this code will set
15	Open Coolant Temperature Sensor (CTS) circuit – the engine must run 5 minutes before this code will set
21	Throttle Position Sensor (TPS) circuit voltage high – open circuit or misadjusted TPS – the engine must run 10 seconds, at specified curb idle speed, before this code will set
23	Mixture Control (M/C) solenoid circuit open or grounded
24	Vehicle Speed Sensor (VSS) circuit – the vehicle must operate up to 2 minutes at road speed, before this code will set
32	Barometric Pressure Sensor (BARO) circuit low
34	Manifold Absolute Pressure (MAP) or vacuum sensor circuit. The engine must run up to 2 minutes at specified curb idle speed, before this code will set
41	No distributor reference signal to the Electronic Control Module (ECM) at specified engine vacuum. This code will store in memory
42	Electronic Spark Timing (EST) bypass circuit or EST circuit grounded or open
44	Lean exhaust indication – the engine must run 2 minutes, in closed loop and at part throttle, before this code will set
45	Rich exhaust indication – the engine must run 2 minutes, in closed loop and at part throttle, before this code will set
51	Faulty or improperly installed calibration unit (PROM). It takes up to 30 seconds before this code will set
54	Mixture Control (M/C) solenoid voltage high at Electronic Control Module (ECM) as a result of a shorted M/C solenoid circuit and/or faulty ECM

Year — 1986
Model — Celebrity
Engine — 2.8L (173 cid) MFI V6
Engine Code — VIN W

ECM TROUBLE CODES

Code	Explanation
13	Oxygen sensor circuit
14	Coolant Temperature Sensor (CTS)
15	Coolant Temperature Sensor (CTS)
21	Throttle Position Sensor (TPS)
22	Throttle Position Sensor (TPS)
23	Manifold Air Temperature (MAT) sensor
24	Vehicle Speed Sensor (VSS)
25	Manifold Air Temperature (MAT) sensor
32	Exhaust Gas Recirculation (EGR) system failure
33	Mass Air Flow (MAF) sensor
34	Mass Air Flow (MAF) sensor
41	Cylinder select
42	Electronic Spark Timing (EST)
44	Lean exhaust indication
45	Rich exhaust indication
51	PROM
52	Calpak — missing
53	System over voltage
54	Fuel pump voltage low
55	Electronic Control Module (ECM)

GENERAL MOTORS CORPORATION
DIAGNOSTIC CODE DATA

Year – 1986
Model – Cavalier
Engine – 2.0L (121 cid)
Engine Code – VIN P

ECM TROUBLE CODES

Code	Explanation
13	Oxygen sensor circuit
14	Coolant Temperature Sensor (CTS)
15	Coolant Temperature Sensor (CTS)
21	Throttle Position Sensor (TPS)
22	Throttle Position Sensor (TPS)
24	Vehicle Speed Sensor (VSS)
33	Manifold Absolute Pressure (MAP) sensor
34	Manifold Absolure Pressure (MAP) sensor
42	Electronic Spark Timing (EST)
44	Lean exhaust indication
45	Rich exhaust indication
51	PROM – Mem-Cal
52	Calpak – missing
54	Fuel pump voltage low
55	Electronic Control Module (ECM)

Year — 1986
Model — Cavalier
Engine — 2.8L (173 cid) V6
Engine Code — VIN W

ECM TROUBLE CODES

Code	Explanation
13	Oxygen sensor circuit
14	Coolant Temperature Sensor (CTS)
15	Coolant Temperature Sensor (CTS)
21	Throttle Position Sensor (TPS)
22	Throttle Position Sensor (TPS)
23	Manifold Air Temperature (MAT) sensor
24	Vehicle Speed Sensor (VSS)
25	Manifold Air Temperature (MAT) sensor
32	Exhaust Gas Recirculation (EGR) system failure
33	Mass Air Flow (MAF) sensor
34	Mass Air Flow (MAF) sensor
41	Cylinder select
42	Electronic Spark Timing (EST)
44	Lean exhaust indication
45	Rich exhaust indication
51	PROM
52	Calpak — missing
53	System over voltage
54	Fuel pump voltage low
55	Electronic Control Module (ECM)

GENERAL MOTORS CORPORATION
DIAGNOSTIC CODE DATA

Year – 1987
Model – Caprice Classic
Engine – 4.3L (262 cid) TBI V6
Engine Code – VIN Z

ECM TROUBLE CODES

Code	Explanation
13	Open oxygen sensor circuit
14	Coolant Temperature Sensor (CTS) circuit
15	Coolant Temperature Sensor (CTS) circuit
21	Throttle Position Sensor (TPS)
22	Throttle Position Sensor (TPS)
24	Vehicle Speed Sensor (VSS)
32	Exhaust Gas Recirculation (EGR) system failure
33	Manifold Absolute Pressure (MAP) sensor circuit
34	Manifold Absolute Pressure (MAP) sensor circuit
42	Electronic Spark Timing (EST)
43	Electronic Spark Control (ESC)
44	Lean exhaust indicated
45	Rich exhaust indicated
54	Fuel pump circuit
51	PROM problem
52	Fuel calpak missing
55	Electronic Control Module (ECM)

Year — 1987
Model — Caprice Classic
Engine — 5.0L (305 cid) V8
Engine Code — VIN H

ECM TROUBLE CODES

Code	Explanation
12	No distributor reference signal to the Electronic Control Module (ECM). This code is not stored in memory and will only flash while the fault is present. Normal code with ignition ON, engine not running
13	Oxygen sensor circuit — the engine must run up to 4 minutes at part throttle, under road load, before this code will set
14	Shorted Coolant Temperature Sensor (CTS) circuit — the engine must run 2 minutes before this code will set
15	Open Coolant Temperature Sensor (CTS) circuit — the engine must run 5 minutes before this code will set
21	Throttle Position Sensor (TPS) circuit voltage high — open circuit or misadjusted TPS — the engine must run 10 seconds, at specified curb idle speed, before this code will set
22	Throttle Position Sensor (TPS) circuit voltage low — grounded circuit or misadjusted TPS — engine must run 20 seconds at specified curb idle speed, to set code
23	Mixture Control (M/C) solenoid circuit open or grounded
24	Vehicle Speed Sensor (VSS) circuit — the vehicle must operate up to 2 minutes at road speed, before this code will set
32	Barometric Pressure Sensor (BARO) circuit low
34	Manifold Absolute Pressure (MAP) or vacuum sensor circuit. The engine must run up to 2 minutes at specified curb idle speed, before this code will set
35	Idle Speed Control (ISC) switch circuit shorted — up to 70% Throttle Position Sensor (TPS) for over 5 seconds
41	No distributor reference signal to the Electronic Control Module (ECM) at specified engine vacuum. This code will store in memory
42	Electronic Spark Timing (EST) bypass circuit or EST circuit grounded or open
43	Electronic Spark Control (ESC) retard signal for too long a time — causes retard in Electronic Spark Timing (EST) signal
44	Lean exhaust indication — the engine must run 2 minutes, in closed loop and at part throttle, before this code will set
45	Rich exhaust indication — the engine must run 2 minutes, in closed loop and at part throttle, before this code will set
51	Faulty or improperly installed calibration unit (PROM). It takes up to 30 seconds before this code will set
53	Exhaust Gas Recirculation (EGR) valve vacuum sensor has seen improper EGR vacuum
54	Mixture Control (M/C) solenoid voltage high, at Electronic Control Module (ECM), as a result of a shorted M/C solenoid circuit and/or faulty ECM

Year – 1987
Model – Caprice Classic
Engine – 5.0L (307 cid) V8
Engine Code – VIN Y

ECM TROUBLE CODES

Code	Explanation
12	No distributor reference signal to the Electronic Control Module (ECM). This code is not stored in memory and will only flash while the fault is present. Normal code with ignition ON, engine not running
13	Oxygen sensor circuit – the engine must run up to 4 minutes at part throttle, under road load, before this code will set
14	Shorted Coolant Temperature Sensor (CTS) circuit – the engine must run 2 minutes before this code will set
15	Open Coolant Temperature Sensor (CTS) circuit – the engine must run 5 minutes before this code will set
21	Throttle Position Sensor (TPS) circuit voltage high – open circuit or misadjusted TPS – the engine must run 10 seconds, at specified curb idle speed, before this code will set
22	Throttle Position Sensor (TPS) circuit voltage low – grounded circuit or misadjusted TPS – engine must run 20 seconds at specified curb idle speed, to set code
23	Mixture Control (M/C) solenoid circuit open or grounded
24	Vehicle Speed Sensor (VSS) circuit – the vehicle must operate up to 2 minutes at road speed, before this code will set
32	Barometric Pressure Sensor (BARO) circuit low
34	Manifold Absolute Pressure (MAP) or vacuum sensor circuit. The engine must run up to 2 minutes at specified curb idle speed, before this code will set
35	Idle Speed Control (ISC) switch circuit shorted – up to 70% Throttle Position Sensor (TPS) for over 5 seconds
41	No distributor reference signal to the Electronic Control Module (ECM) at specified engine vacuum. This code will store in memory
42	Electronic Spark Timing (EST) bypass circuit or EST circuit grounded or open
43	Electronic Spark Control (ESC) retard signal for too long a time – causes retard in Electronic Spark Timing (EST) signal
44	Lean exhaust indication – the engine must run 2 minutes, in closed loop and at part throttle, before this code will set
45	Rich exhaust indication – the engine must run 2 minutes, in closed loop and at part throttle, before this code will set
51	Faulty or improperly installed calibration unit (PROM). It takes up to 30 seconds before this code will set
53	Exhaust Gas Recirculation (EGR) valve vacuum sensor has seen improper EGR vacuum
54	Mixture Control (M/C) solenoid voltage high, at Electronic Control Module (ECM), as a result of a shorted M/C solenoid circuit and/or faulty ECM

Year — 1987
Model — Caprice Classic
Engine — 5.7L (350 cid) V8
Engine Code — VIN 6

ECM TROUBLE CODES

Code	Explanation
12	No distributor reference signal to the Electronic Control Module (ECM). This code is not stored in memory and will only flash while the fault is present. Normal code with ignition ON, engine not running
13	Oxygen sensor circuit — the engine must run up to 4 minutes at part throttle, under road load, before this code will set
14	Shorted Coolant Temperature Sensor (CTS) circuit — the engine must run 2 minutes before this code will set
15	Open Coolant Temperature Sensor (CTS) circuit — the engine must run 5 minutes before this code will set
21	Throttle Position Sensor (TPS) circuit voltage high — open circuit or misadjusted TPS — the engine must run 10 seconds, at specified curb idle speed, before this code will set
22	Throttle Position Sensor (TPS) circuit voltage low — grounded circuit or misadjusted TPS — engine must run 20 seconds at specified curb idle speed, to set code
23	Mixture Control (M/C) solenoid circuit open or grounded
24	Vehicle Speed Sensor (VSS) circuit — the vehicle must operate up to 2 minutes at road speed, before this code will set
32	Barometric Pressure Sensor (BARO) circuit low
34	Manifold Absolute Pressure (MAP) or vacuum sensor circuit. The engine must run up to 2 minutes at specified curb idle speed, before this code will set
35	Idle Speed Control (ISC) switch circuit shorted — up to 70% Throttle Position Sensor (TPS) for over 5 seconds
41	No distributor reference signal to the Electronic Control Module (ECM) at specified engine vacuum. This code will store in memory
42	Electronic Spark Timing (EST) bypass circuit or EST circuit grounded or open
43	Electronic Spark Control (ESC) retard signal for too long a time — causes retard in Electronic Spark Timing (EST) signal
44	Lean exhaust indication — the engine must run 2 minutes, in closed loop and at part throttle, before this code will set
45	Rich exhaust indication — the engine must run 2 minutes, in closed loop and at part throttle, before this code will set
51	Faulty or improperly installed calibration unit (PROM). It takes up to 30 seconds before this code will set
53	Exhaust Gas Recirculation (EGR) valve vacuum sensor has seen improper EGR vacuum
54	Mixture Control (M/C) solenoid voltage high, at Electronic Control Module (ECM), as a result of a shorted M/C solenoid circuit and/or faulty ECM

Year — 1987
Model — Monte Carlo
Engine — 4.3L (262 cid) EFI V6
Engine Code — VIN Z

ECM TROUBLE CODES

Code	Explanation
13	Open oxygen sensor circuit
14	Coolant Temperature Sensor (CTS) circuit
15	Coolant Temperature Sensor (CTS) circuit
21	Throttle Position Sensor (TPS)
22	Throttle Position Sensor (TPS)
24	Vehicle Speed Sensor (VSS)
32	Exhaust Gas Recirculation (EGR) system failure
33	Manifold Absolute Pressure (MAP) sensor circuit
34	Manifold Absolute Pressure (MAP) sensor circuit
42	Electronic Spark Timing (EST)
43	Electronic Spark Control (ESC)
44	Lean exhaust indicated
45	Rich exhaust indicated
54	Fuel pump circuit
51	PROM problem
52	Fuel calpak missing
55	Electronic Control Module (ECM)

Year – 1987
Model – Monte Carlo
Engine – 5.0L (305 cid) V8
Engine Code – VIN G

ECM TROUBLE CODES

Code	Explanation
12	No distributor reference signal to the Electronic Control Module (ECM). This code is not stored in memory and will only flash while the fault is present. Normal code with ignition ON, engine not running
13	Oxygen sensor circuit – the engine must run up to 4 minutes at part throttle, under road load, before this code will set
14	Shorted Coolant Temperature Sensor (CTS) circuit – the engine must run 2 minutes before this code will set
15	Open Coolant Temperature Sensor (CTS) circuit – the engine must run 5 minutes before this code will set
21	Throttle Position Sensor (TPS) circuit voltage high – open circuit or misadjusted TPS – the engine must run 10 seconds, at specified curb idle speed, before this code will set
22	Throttle Position Sensor (TPS) circuit voltage low – grounded circuit or misadjusted TPS – engine must run 20 seconds at specified curb idle speed, to set code
23	Mixture Control (M/C) solenoid circuit open or grounded
24	Vehicle Speed Sensor (VSS) circuit – the vehicle must operate up to 2 minutes at road speed, before this code will set
32	Barometric Pressure Sensor (BARO) circuit low
34	Manifold Absolute Pressure (MAP) or vacuum sensor circuit. The engine must run up to 2 minutes at specified curb idle speed, before this code will set
35	Idle Speed Control (ISC) switch circuit shorted – up to 70% Throttle Position Sensor (TPS) for over 5 seconds
41	No distributor reference signal to the Electronic Control Module (ECM) at specified engine vacuum. This code will store in memory
42	Electronic Spark Timing (EST) bypass circuit or EST circuit grounded or open
43	Electronic Spark Control (ESC) retard signal for too long a time – causes retard in Electronic Spark Timing (EST) signal
44	Lean exhaust indication – the engine must run 2 minutes, in closed loop and at part throttle, before this code will set
45	Rich exhaust indication – the engine must run 2 minutes, in closed loop and at part throttle, before this code will set
51	Faulty or improperly installed calibration unit (PROM). It takes up to 30 seconds before this code will set
53	Exhaust Gas Recirculation (EGR) valve vacuum sensor has seen improper EGR vacuum
54	Mixture Control (M/C) solenoid voltage high, at Electronic Control Module (ECM), as a result of a shorted M/C solenoid circuit and/or faulty ECM

Year — 1987
Model — Monte Carlo
Engine — 5.0L (305 cid) V8
Engine Code — VIN H

ECM TROUBLE CODES

Code	Explanation
12	No distributor reference signal to the Electronic Control Module (ECM). This code is not stored in memory and will only flash while the fault is present. Normal code with ignition ON, engine not running
13	Oxygen sensor circuit — the engine must run up to 4 minutes at part throttle, under road load, before this code will set
14	Shorted Coolant Temperature Sensor (CTS) circuit — the engine must run 2 minutes before this code will set
15	Open Coolant Temperature Sensor (CTS) circuit — the engine must run 5 minutes before this code will set
21	Throttle Position Sensor (TPS) circuit voltage high — open circuit or misadjusted TPS — the engine must run 10 seconds, at specified curb idle speed, before this code will set
22	Throttle Position Sensor (TPS) circuit voltage low — grounded circuit or misadjusted TPS — engine must run 20 seconds at specified curb idle speed, to set code
23	Mixture Control (M/C) solenoid circuit open or grounded
24	Vehicle Speed Sensor (VSS) circuit — the vehicle must operate up to 2 minutes at road speed, before this code will set
32	Barometric Pressure Sensor (BARO) circuit low
34	Manifold Absolute Pressure (MAP) or vacuum sensor circuit. The engine must run up to 2 minutes at specified curb idle speed, before this code will set
35	Idle Speed Control (ISC) switch circuit shorted — up to 70% Throttle Position Sensor (TPS) for over 5 seconds
41	No distributor reference signal to the Electronic Control Module (ECM) at specified engine vacuum. This code will store in memory
42	Electronic Spark Timing (EST) bypass circuit or EST circuit grounded or open
43	Electronic Spark Control (ESC) retard signal for too long a time — causes retard in Electronic Spark Timing (EST) signal
44	Lean exhaust indication — the engine must run 2 minutes, in closed loop and at part throttle, before this code will set
45	Rich exhaust indication — the engine must run 2 minutes, in closed loop and at part throttle, before this code will set
51	Faulty or improperly installed calibration unit (PROM). It takes up to 30 seconds before this code will set
53	Exhaust Gas Recirculation (EGR) valve vacuum sensor has seen improper EGR vacuum
54	Mixture Control (M/C) solenoid voltage high, at Electronic Control Module (ECM), as a result of a shorted M/C solenoid circuit and/or faulty ECM

Year — 1987
Model — Camaro
Engine — 2.8L (173 cid) MPI V6
Engine Code — VIN S

ECM TROUBLE CODES

Code	Explanation
13	Oxygen sensor circuit
14	Coolant Temperature Sensor (CTS)
15	Coolant Temperature Sensor (CTS)
21	Throttle Position Sensor (TPS)
22	Throttle Position Sensor (TPS)
23	Manifold Air Temperature (MAT) sensor
24	Vehicle Speed Sensor (VSS)
25	Manifold Air Temperature (MAT) sensor
32	Exhaust Gas Recirculation (EGR)
33	Mass Air Flow (MAF) sensor
34	Mass Air Flow (MAF) sensor
41	Cylinder select error
42	Electronic Spark Timing (EST) fault
44	Lean exhaust indication
45	Rich exhaust indication
51	PROM
52	Calpak — missing
53	System over voltage
54	Fuel pump voltage low
55	Electronic Control Module (ECM)

Year – 1987
Model – Camaro
Engine – 5.0L (305 cid) V8
Engine Code – VIN H

ECM TROUBLE CODES

Code	Explanation
13	Oxygen sensor circuit
14	Coolant Temperature Sensor (CTS)
15	Coolant Temperature Sensor (CTS)
21	Throttle Position Sensor (TPS)
22	Throttle Position Sensor (TPS)
23	Manifold Air Temperature (MAT) sensor
24	Vehicle Speed Sensor (VSS)
25	Manifold Air Temperature (MAT) sensor
32	Exhaust Gas Recirculation (EGR)
33	Mass Air Flow (MAF) sensor
34	Mass Air Flow (MAF) sensor
36	Mass Air Flow (MAF) sensor burn-off function fault
41	Cylinder select error
42	Electronic Spark Timing (EST) fault
43	Electronic Spark Control (ESC)
44	Lean exhaust indication
45	Rich exhaust indication
51	Mem/Cal
53	System over voltage
54	Fuel pump voltage low
55	Electronic Control Module (ECM)

Year — 1987
Model — Camaro
Engine — 5.0L (350 cid) TPI V8
Engine Code — VIN 8

ECM TROUBLE CODES

Code	Explanation
13	Oxygen sensor circuit
14	Coolant Temperature Sensor (CTS)
15	Coolant Temperature Sensor (CTS)
21	Throttle Position Sensor (TPS)
22	Throttle Position Sensor (TPS)
23	Manifold Air Temperature (MAT) sensor
24	Vehicle Speed Sensor (VSS)
25	Manifold Air Temperature (MAT) sensor
32	Exhaust Gas Recirculation (EGR)
33	Mass Air Flow (MAF) sensor
34	Mass Air Flow (MAF) sensor
36	Mass Air Flow (MAF) sensor burn-off function fault
41	Cylinder select error
42	Electronic Spark Timing (EST) fault
43	Electronic Spark Control (ESC)
44	Lean exhaust indication
45	Rich exhaust indication
51	Mem/Cal
53	System over voltage
54	Fuel pump voltage low
55	Electronic Control Module (ECM)

GENERAL MOTORS CORPORATION
DIAGNOSTIC CODE DATA

Year — 1987
Model — Camaro
Engine — 5.0L (305 cid) TPI V8
Engine Code — VIN F

ECM TROUBLE CODES

Code	Explanation
13	Oxygen sensor circuit — open circuit
14	Coolant Temperature Sensor (CTS) circuit — high temperature indicated
15	Coolant Temperature Sensor (CTS) circuit — low temperature indicated
21	Throttle Position Sensor (TPS) circuit — signal voltage high
22	Throttle Position Sensor (TPS) circuit — signal voltage low
23	Manifold Air Temperature (MAT) sensor circuit — low temperature indicated
24	Vehicle Speed Sensor (VSS) circuit
25	Manifold Air Temperature (MAT) sensor circuit — high temperature indicated
32	Exhaust Gas Recirculation (EGR) circuit
33	Mass Air Flow (MAF) sensor circuit — GM/SEC high
34	Mass Air Flow (MAF) sensor circuit — GM/SEC low
36	Mass Air Flow (MAF) sensor burn-off circuit
41	Cylinder select error — faulty or incorrect Mem-Cal
42	Electronic Spark Timing (EST) circuit
43	Electronic Spark Control (ESC) circuit
44	Oxygen sensor circuit — lean exhaust indication
45	Oxygen sensor circuit — rich exhaust indication
46	Vehicle Anti-Theft system (VATS) circuit
51	Mem-Cal error — faulty or incorrect Mem-Cal
52	Calpak error — faulty or incorrect calpak
53	System over voltage
54	Fuel pump circuit — low voltage

Year — 1987
Model — Corvette
Engine — 5.7L (350 cid) TPI V8
Engine Code — VIN 8

ECM TROUBLE CODES

Code	Explanation
13	Oxygen sensor circuit — open circuit
14	Coolant Temperature Sensor (CTS) circuit — high temperature indicated
15	Coolant Temperature Sensor (CTS) circuit — low temperature indicated
21	Throttle Position Sensor (TPS) circuit — signal voltage high
22	Throttle Position Sensor (TPS) circuit — signal voltage low
23	Manifold Air Temperature (MAT) sensor circuit — low temperature indicated
24	Vehicle Speed Sensor (VSS) circuit
25	Manifold Air Temperature (MAT) sensor circuit — high temperature indicated
32	Exhaust Gas Recirculation (EGR) circuit
33	Mass Air Flow (MAF) sensor circuit — GM/SEC high
34	Mass Air Flow (MAF) sensor circuit — GM/SEC low
36	Mass Air Flow (MAF) sensor burn-off circuit
41	Cylinder select error — faulty or incorrect Mem-Cal
42	Electronic Spark Timing (EST) circuit
43	Electronic Spark Control (ESC) circuit
44	Oxygen sensor circuit — lean exhaust indication
45	Oxygen sensor circuit — rich exhaust indication
46	Vehicle Anti-Theft system (VATS) circuit
51	Mem-Cal error — faulty or incorrect Mem-Cal
52	Calpak error — faulty or incorrect calpak
53	System over voltage
54	Fuel pump circuit — low voltage

Year — 1987
Model — Chevette
Engine — 1.6L (98 cid) 4 cyl
Engine Code — VIN C

ECM TROUBLE CODES

Code	Explanation
12	No distributor reference pulses to the Electronic Control Module (ECM)
15	Open Coolant Temperature Sensor (CTS) circuit — the engine must run up to 10 minutes before this code will set
21	Throttle Position Sensor (TPS) circuit at Wide Open Throttle (WOT) — the engine must run up to 10 seconds below 1000 rpm, before this code will set
23	Mixture Control (M/C) solenoid circuit
44	Lean exhaust indication — the engine must run up to 1 minute in closed loop and at part throttle above 2000 rpm before this code will set
45	Rich exhaust indication — the engine must run up to 1 minute in closed loop and at part throttle above 2000 rpm before this code will set
51	Faulty calibration unit (PROM) or installation — turns Electronic Control Module (ECM) OFF

Year — 1987
Model — Corsica
Engine — 2.0L (121 cid) TPI 4 cyl
Engine Code — VIN 1

ECM TROUBLE CODES

Code	Explanation
13	Oxygen sensor circuit — open circuit
14	Coolant Temperature Sensor (CTS) circuit — high temperature indicated
15	Coolant Temperature Sensor (CTS) circuit — low temperature indicated
21	Throttle Position Sensor (TPS) circuit — signal voltage high
22	Throttle Position Sensor (TPS) circuit — signal voltage low
23	Manifold Air Temperature (MAT) sensor circuit — low temperature indicated
24	Vehicle Speed Sensor (VSS) circuit
25	Manifold Air Temperature (MAT) sensor circuit — high temperature indicated
33	Manifold Absolute Pressure (MAP) sensor circuit — signal voltage high
34	Manifold Absolute Pressure (MAP) sensor circuit — signal voltage low
42	Electronic Spark Timing (EST) circuit
44	Oxygen sensor circuit — lean exhaust indication
45	Oxygen sensor circuit — rich exhaust indication
51	Mem-Cal error — faulty or incorrect Mem-Cal

GENERAL MOTORS CORPORATION
DIAGNOSTIC CODE DATA

Year — 1987
Model — Corsica
Engine — 2.8L (173 cid) MFI V6
Engine Code — VIN W

ECM TROUBLE CODES

Code	Explanation
13	Oxygen sensor circuit — open circuit
14	Coolant Temperature Sensor (CTS) circuit — high temperature indicated
15	Coolant Temperature Sensor (CTS) circuit — low temperature indicated
21	Throttle Position Sensor (TPS) circuit — signal voltage high
22	Throttle Position Sensor (TPS) circuit — signal voltage low
23	Manifold Air Temperature (MAT) sensor circuit — low temperature indicated
24	Vehicle Speed Sensor (VSS) circuit
25	Manifold Air Temperature (MAT) sensor circuit — high temperature indicated
33	Mass Air Flow (MAF) sensor circuit — GM/SEC high
34	Mass Air Flow (MAF) sensor circuit — GM/SEC low
35	Idle speed error
41	Cylinder select error — faulty or incorrect Mem-Cal
42	Electronic Spark Timing (EST) circuit
43	Electronic Spark Control (ESC) circuit
44	Oxygen sensor circuit — lean exhaust indication
45	Oxygen sensor circuit — rich exhaust indication
54	Fuel pump circuit — low voltage
51	Mem-Cal error — faulty or incorrect Mem-Cal
52	Calpak error — faulty or incorrect calpak
53	System over voltage
61	Degraded oxygen sensor
63	Manifold Absolute Pressure (MAP) sensor circuit — signal voltage high
64	Manifold Absolute Pressure (MAP) sensor circuit — signal voltage low

Year – 1987
Model – Beretta
Engine – 2.0L (121 cid) TPI 4 cyl
Engine Code – VIN 1

ECM TROUBLE CODES

Code	Explanation
13	Oxygen sensor circuit – open circuit
14	Coolant Temperature Sensor (CTS) circuit – high temperature indicated
15	Coolant Temperature Sensor (CTS) circuit – low temperature indicated
21	Throttle Position Sensor (TPS) circuit – signal voltage high
22	Throttle Position Sensor (TPS) circuit – signal voltage low
23	Manifold Air Temperature (MAT) sensor circuit – low temperature indicated
24	Vehicle Speed Sensor (VSS) circuit
25	Manifold Air Temperature (MAT) sensor circuit – high temperature indicated
33	Manifold Absolute Pressure (MAP) sensor circuit – signal voltage high
34	Manifold Absolute Pressure (MAP) sensor circuit – signal voltage low
42	Electronic Spark Timing (EST) circuit
44	Oxygen sensor circuit – lean exhaust indication
45	Oxygen sensor circuit – rich exhaust indication
51	Mem-Cal error – faulty or incorrect Mem-Cal

Year – 1987
Model – Beretta
Engine – 2.8L (173 cid) MFI V6
Engine Code – VIN W

ECM TROUBLE CODES

Code	Explanation
13	Oxygen sensor circuit—open circuit
14	Coolant Temperature Sensor (CTS) circuit—high temperature indicated
15	Coolant Temperature Sensor (CTS) circuit—low temperature indicated
21	Throttle Position Sensor (TPS) circuit—signal voltage high
22	Throttle Position Sensor (TPS) circuit—signal voltage low
23	Manifold Air Temperature (MAT) sensor circuit—low temperature indicated
24	Vehicle Speed Sensor (VSS) circuit
25	Manifold Air Temperature (MAT) sensor circuit—high temperature indicated
33	Mass Air Flow (MAF) sensor circuit—GM/SEC high
34	Mass Air Flow (MAF) sensor circuit—GM/SEC low
35	Idle speed error
41	Cylinder select error—faulty or incorrect Mem-Cal
42	Electronic Spark Timing (EST) circuit
43	Electronic Spark Control (ESC) circuit
44	Oxygen sensor circuit—lean exhaust indication
45	Oxygen sensor circuit—rich exhaust indication
54	Fuel pump circuit—low voltage
51	Mem-Cal error—faulty or incorrect Mem-Cal
52	Calpak error—faulty or incorrect calpak
53	System over voltage
61	Degraded oxygen sensor
63	Manifold Absolute Pressure (MAP) sensor circuit—signal voltage high
64	Manifold Absolute Pressure (MAP) sensor circuit—signal voltage low

Year — 1987
Model — Celebrity
Engine — 2.5L (151 cid) TPI 4 cyl
Engine Code — VIN R

ECM TROUBLE CODES

Code	Explanation
13	Oxygen sensor circuit — open circuit
14	Coolant Temperature Sensor (CTS) circuit — high temperature indicated
15	Coolant Temperature Sensor (CTS) circuit — low temperature indicated
21	Throttle Position Sensor (TPS) circuit — signal voltage high
22	Throttle Position Sensor (TPS) circuit — signal voltage low
23	Manifold Air Temperature (MAT) sensor circuit — low temperature indicated
24	Vehicle Speed Sensor (VSS) circuit
25	Manifold Air Temperature (MAT) sensor circuit — high temperature indicated
33	Manifold Absolute Pressure (MAP) sensor circuit — signal voltage high — low vacuum
34	Manifold Absolute Pressure (MAP) sensor circuit — signal voltage low — high vacuum
35	Idle Speed Control (ISC) circuit
42	Electronic Spark Timing (EST) circuit
44	Oxygen sensor circuit — lean exhaust indicated
45	Oxygen sensor circuit — rich exhaust indicated
51	Faulty PROM
53	System over voltage

Year – 1987
Model – Celebrity
Engine – 2.8L (173 cid) MFI V6
Engine Code – VIN W

ECM TROUBLE CODES

Code	Explanation
13	Oxygen sensor circuit—open circuit
14	Coolant Temperature Sensor (CTS) circuit—high temperature indicated
15	Coolant Temperature Sensor (CTS) circuit—low temperature indicated
21	Throttle Position Sensor (TPS) circuit—signal voltage high
22	Throttle Position Sensor (TPS) circuit—signal voltage low
23	Manifold Air Temperature (MAT) sensor circuit—low temperature indicated
24	Vehicle Speed Sensor (VSS) circuit
25	Manifold Air Temperature (MAT) sensor circuit—high temperature indicated
33	Mass Air Flow (MAF) sensor circuit—high GM/SEC indicated
34	Mass Air Flow (MAF) sensor circuit—low GM/SEC indicated
35	Idle speed circuit
41	Cylinder select error—faulty or incorrect Mem-Cal
42	Electronic Spark Timing (EST)
43	Electronic Spark Control (ESC)
44	Lean exhaust indicated
45	Rich exhaust indicated
54	Fuel pump circuit—low voltage
51	Faulty Mem-Cal
53	System over voltage
55	Electronic Control Module (ECM)
61	Degraded oxygen sensor
63	Manifold Absolute Pressure (MAP) sensor circuit—signal voltage high
64	Manifold Absolute Pressure (MAP) sensor circuit—signal voltage low

Year — 1987
Model — Cavalier
Engine — 2.0L (121 cid) 4 cyl
Engine Code — VIN P

ECM TROUBLE CODES

Code	Explanation
13	Oxygen sensor circuit
14	Coolant Temperature Sensor (CTS)
15	Coolant Temperature Sensor (CTS)
21	Throttle Position Sensor (TPS)
22	Throttle Position Sensor (TPS)
24	Vehicle Speed Sensor (VSS)
33	Manifold Absolute Pressure (MAP) sensor
34	Manifold Absolure Pressure (MAP) sensor
42	Electronic Spark Timing (EST)
44	Lean exhaust indication
45	Rich exhaust indication
51	PROM — Mem-Cal
52	Calpak — missing
54	Fuel pump voltage low
55	Electronic Control Module (ECM)

Year – 1987
Model – Cavalier
Engine – 2.8L (173 cid) V6
Engine Code – VIN W

ECM TROUBLE CODES

Code	Explanation
13	Oxygen sensor circuit
14	Coolant Temperature Sensor (CTS)
15	Coolant Temperature Sensor (CTS)
21	Throttle Position Sensor (TPS)
22	Throttle Position Sensor (TPS)
23	Manifold Air Temperature (MAT) sensor
24	Vehicle Speed Sensor (VSS)
25	Manifold Air Temperature (MAT) sensor
32	Exhaust Gas Recirculation (EGR) system failure
33	Mass Air Flow (MAF) sensor
34	Mass Air Flow (MAF) sensor
41	Cylinder select
42	Electronic Spark Timing (EST)
44	Lean exhaust indication
45	Rich exhaust indication
51	PROM
52	Calpak – missing
53	System over voltage
54	Fuel pump voltage low
55	Electronic Control Module (ECM)

Year — 1988
Model — Caprice
Engine — 4.3L (262 cid) EFI V6
Engine Code — VIN Z

ECM TROUBLE CODES

Code	Explanation
12	Speed reference pulse
13	Open oxygen sensor circuit
14	Coolant Temperature Sensor (CTS) circuit — temperature too high
15	Coolant Temperature Sensor (CTS) circuit — temperature too low
21	Throttle Position Sensor (TPS) — signal voltage high
22	Throttle Position Sensor (TPS) — signal voltage low
23	Manifold Air Temperature (MAT) sensor circuit — low temperature indicated
24	Vehicle Speed Sensor (VSS) circuit
32	Exhaust Gas Recirculation (EGR) system failure
33	Manifold Absolute Pressure (MAP) sensor circuit signal voltage high — Low vacuum
34	Manifold Absolute Pressure (MAP) sensor circuit signal voltage low — high vacuum
42	Electronic Spark Timing (EST)
43	Electronic Spark Control (ESC)
44	Lean exhaust indicated
45	Rich exhaust indicated
51	PROM or Mem-Cal error
52	Fuel Calpak missing
54	Fuel pump circuit
55	Electronic Control Module (ECM)

Year – 1988
Model – Caprice
Engine – 5.0L (305 cid) V8
Engine Code – VIN H

ECM TROUBLE CODES

Code	Explanation
12	No distributor reference signal to the Electronic Control Module (ECM). This code is not stored in memory and will only flash while the fault is present. Normal code with ignition ON, engine not running
13	Oxygen sensor circuit – the engine must run up to 4 minutes at part throttle, under road load, before this code will set
14	Shorted Coolant Temperature Sensor (CTS) circuit – the engine must run 2 minutes before this code will set
15	Open Coolant Temperature Sensor (CTS) circuit – the engine must run 5 minutes before this code will set
21	Throttle Position Sensor (TPS) circuit voltage high – open circuit or misadjusted TPS – the engine must run 10 seconds, at specified curb idle speed, before this code will set
22	Throttle Position Sensor (TPS) circuit voltage low – grounded circuit or misadjusted TPS – engine must run 20 seconds at specified curb idle speed, to set code
23	Mixture Control (M/C) solenoid circuit open or grounded
24	Vehicle Speed Sensor (VSS) circuit – the vehicle must operate up to 2 minutes at road speed, before this code will set
31	Canister Purge Solenoid (CPS) voltage high to Electronic Control Module (ECM) above idle RPM will set this code
34	Vacuum sensor circuit – the engine must run up to 2 minutes at specified curb idle speed, before this code will set
41	No distributor reference signal to the Electronic Control Module (ECM) at specified engine vacuum. This code will store in memory
42	Electronic Spark Timing (EST) bypass circuit or EST circuit grounded or open
43	Electronic Spark Control (ESC) retard signal for too long a time; causes retard in Electronic Spark Timing (EST) signal
44	Lean exhaust indication – the engine must run 2 minutes, in closed loop and at part throttle, before this code will set
45	Rich exhaust indication – the engine must run 2 minutes, in closed loop and at part throttle, before this code will set
51	Faulty or improperly installed calibration unit (PROM). It takes up to 30 seconds before this code will set
53	Exhaust Gas Recirculation (EGR) valve vacuum sensor has seen improper EGR control vacuum
54	Mixture Control (M/C) solenoid voltage high, at Electronic Control Module (ECM), as a result of a shorted M/C solenoid circuit and/or faulty ECM

Year — 1988
Model — Monte Carlo
Engine — 4.3L (262 cid) EFI V6
Engine Code — VIN Z

ECM TROUBLE CODES

Code	Explanation
12	Speed reference pulse
13	Open oxygen sensor circuit
14	Coolant Temperature Sensor (CTS) circuit — temperature too high
15	Coolant Temperature Sensor (CTS) circuit — temperature too low
21	Throttle Position Sensor (TPS) — signal voltage high
22	Throttle Position Sensor (TPS) — signal voltage low
23	Manifold Air Temperature (MAT) sensor circuit — low temperature indicated
24	Vehicle Speed Sensor (VSS) circuit
25	Manifold Air Temperature (MAT) — temperature high
32	Exhaust Gas Recirculation (EGR) system failure
33	Manifold Absolute Pressure (MAP) sensor circuit signal voltage high — Low vacuum
34	Manifold Absolute Pressure (MAP) sensor circuit signal voltage low — high vacuum
42	Electronic Spark Timing (EST)
43	Electronic Spark Control (ESC)
44	Lean exhaust indicated
45	Rich exhaust indicated
51	PROM or Mem-Cal error
52	Fuel Calpak missing
54	Fuel pump circuit
55	Electronic Control Module (ECM)

GENERAL MOTORS CORPORATION
DIAGNOSTIC CODE DATA

Year — 1988
Model — Monte Carlo
Engine — 5.0L (305 cid) V8
Engine Code — VIN G

ECM TROUBLE CODES

Code	Explanation
12	No distributor reference signal to the Electronic Control Module (ECM). This code is not stored in memory and will only flash while the fault is present. Normal code with ignition ON, engine not running
13	Oxygen sensor circuit — the engine must run up to 4 minutes at part throttle, under road load, before this code will set
14	Shorted Coolant Temperature Sensor (CTS) circuit — the engine must run 2 minutes before this code will set
15	Open Coolant Temperature Sensor (CTS) circuit — the engine must run 5 minutes before this code will set
21	Throttle Position Sensor (TPS) circuit voltage high — open circuit or misadjusted TPS — the engine must run 10 seconds, at specified curb idle speed, before this code will set
22	Throttle Position Sensor (TPS) circuit voltage low — grounded circuit or misadjusted TPS — engine must run 20 seconds at specified curb idle speed, to set code
23	Mixture Control (M/C) solenoid circuit open or grounded
24	Vehicle Speed Sensor (VSS) circuit — the vehicle must operate up to 2 minutes at road speed, before this code will set
31	Canister Purge Solenoid (CPS) voltage high to Electronic Control Module (ECM) above idle RPM will set this code
32	Barometric Pressure Sensor (BARO) low
34	Vacuum sensor circuit — the engine must run up to 2 minutes at specified curb idle speed, before this code will set
41	No distributor reference signal to the Electronic Control Module (ECM) at specified engine vacuum. This code will store in memory
42	Electronic Spark Timing (EST) bypass circuit or EST circuit grounded or open
43	Electronic Spark Control (ESC) retard signal for too long a time; causes retard in Electronic Spark Timing (EST) signal
44	Lean exhaust indication — the engine must run 2 minutes, in closed loop and at part throttle, before this code will set
45	Rich exhaust indication — the engine must run 2 minutes, in closed loop and at part throttle, before this code will set
51	Faulty or improperly installed calibration unit (PROM). It takes up to 30 seconds before this code will set
53	Exhaust Gas Recirculation (EGR) valve vacuum sensor has seen improper EGR control vacuum
54	Mixture Control (M/C) solenoid voltage high, at Electronic Control Module (ECM), as a result of a shorted M/C solenoid circuit and/or faulty ECM

Year – 1988
Model – Monte Carlo
Engine – 5.0L (305 cid) V8
Engine Code – VIN H

ECM TROUBLE CODES

Code	Explanation
12	No distributor reference signal to the Electronic Control Module (ECM). This code is not stored in memory and will only flash while the fault is present. Normal code with ignition ON, engine not running
13	Oxygen sensor circuit – the engine must run up to 4 minutes at part throttle, under road load, before this code will set
14	Shorted Coolant Temperature Sensor (CTS) circuit – the engine must run 2 minutes before this code will set
15	Open Coolant Temperature Sensor (CTS) circuit – the engine must run 5 minutes before this code will set
21	Throttle Position Sensor (TPS) circuit voltage high – open circuit or misadjusted TPS – the engine must run 10 seconds, at specified curb idle speed, before this code will set
22	Throttle Position Sensor (TPS) circuit voltage low – grounded circuit or misadjusted TPS – engine must run 20 seconds at specified curb idle speed, to set code
23	Mixture Control (M/C) solenoid circuit open or grounded
24	Vehicle Speed Sensor (VSS) circuit – the vehicle must operate up to 2 minutes at road speed, before this code will set
31	Canister Purge Solenoid (CPS) voltage high to Electronic Control Module (ECM) above idle RPM will set this code
32	Barometric Pressure Sensor (BARO) low
34	Vacuum sensor circuit – the engine must run up to 2 minutes at specified curb idle speed, before this code will set
41	No distributor reference signal to the Electronic Control Module (ECM) at specified engine vacuum. This code will store in memory
42	Electronic Spark Timing (EST) bypass circuit or EST circuit grounded or open
43	Electronic Spark Control (ESC) retard signal for too long a time; causes retard in Electronic Spark Timing (EST) signal
44	Lean exhaust indication – the engine must run 2 minutes, in closed loop and at part throttle, before this code will set
45	Rich exhaust indication – the engine must run 2 minutes, in closed loop and at part throttle, before this code will set
51	Faulty or improperly installed calibration unit (PROM). It takes up to 30 seconds before this code will set
53	Exhaust Gas Recirculation (EGR) valve vacuum sensor has seen improper EGR control vacuum
54	Mixture Control (M/C) solenoid voltage high, at Electronic Control Module (ECM), as a result of a shorted M/C solenoid circuit and/or faulty ECM

Year – 1988
Model – Camaro
Engine – 2.8L (173 cid) MFI V6
Engine Code – VIN S

ECM TROUBLE CODES

Code	Explanation
12	Speed reference pulse
13	Oxygen sensor circui – open circuit
14	Coolant Temperature Sensor (CTS) circuit – high temperature indicated
15	Coolant Temperature Sensor (CTS) circuit – low temperature indicated
21	Throttle Position Sensor (TPS) circuit – signal voltage high
22	Throttle Position Sensor (TPS) circuit – signal voltage low
23	Manifold Air Temperature (MAT) sensor circuit – iow temperature indicated
24	Vehicle Speed Sensor (VSS) circuit
25	Manifold Air Temperature (MAT) sensor circuit – high temperature indicated
32	Exhaust Gas Recirculation (EGR) failure
33	Mass Air Flow (MAF) sensor circuit – GM/SEC high
34	Mass Air Flow (MAF) sensor circuit – GM/SEC low
41	Cylinder select error
42	Electronic Spark Timing (EST) fault
44	Oxygen sensor circuit – lean exhaust indicated
45	Oxygen sensor circuit – rich exhaust indicated
51	PROM error – faulty or incorrect PROM
52	Calpak error – faulty or incorrect Calpak
53	System over voltage
54	Fuel pump circuit – low voltage

Year — 1988
Model — Camaro
Engine — 5.0L (305 cid) EFI V8
Engine Code — VIN E

ECM TROUBLE CODES

Code	Explanation
12	Speed reference pulse
13	Oxygen sensor circuit
14	Coolant Temperature Sensor (CTS) circuit — high
15	Coolant Temperature Sensor (CTS) circuit — low
21	Throttle Position Sensor (TPS) circuit — high
22	Throttle Position Sensor (TPS) circuit — low
23	Manifold Air Temperature (MAT) sensor circuit — low
24	Vehicle Speed Sensor (VSS) circuit
25	Manifold Air Temperature (MAT) sensor circuit — high
32	Exhaust Gas Recirculation (EGR) circuit
33	Mass Air Flow (MAF) sensor circuit — GM/SEC high
34	Mass Air Flow (MAF) sensor circuit — GM/SEC low
42	Electronic Spark Timing (EST) circuit
43	Electronic Spark Control (ESC) circuit
44	Oxygen sensor circuit — lean
45	Oxygen sensor circuit — rich
51	Mem-Cal
52	Calpak error
53	System over voltage
54	Fuel pump circuit

Year – 1988
Model – Camaro
Engine – 5.7L (350 cid) TPI V8
Engine Code – VIN 8

ECM TROUBLE CODES

Code	Explanation
12	Speed reference pulse
13	Oxygen sensor circuit
14	Coolant Temperature Sensor (CTS) circuit – high
15	Coolant Temperature Sensor (CTS) circuit – low
21	Throttle Position Sensor (TPS) circuit – high
22	Throttle Position Sensor (TPS) circuit – low
23	Manifold Air Temperature (MAT) sensor circuit – low
24	Vehicle Speed Sensor (VSS) circuit
25	Manifold Air Temperature (MAT) sensor circuit – high
32	Exhaust Gas Recirculation (EGR) circuit
33	Mass Air Flow (MAF) sensor circuit – high
34	Mass Air Flow (MAF) sensor circuit – low
36	Mass Air Flow (MAF) sensor burn-off circuit
41	Cylinder select error
42	Electronic Spark Timing (EST) circuit
43	Electronic Spark Control (ESC) circuit
44	Oxygen sensor circuit – lean
45	Oxygen sensor circuit – rich
51	Mem-Cal
52	Calpak error
53	System over voltage
54	Fuel pump circuit
55	Electronic Control Module (ECM) error

Year – 1988
Model – Corvette
Engine – 5.7L (350 cid) TPI V8
Engine Code – VIN 8

ECM TROUBLE CODES

Code	Explanation
12	Speed reference pulse
13	Oxygen sensor circuit – open circuit
14	Coolant temperature Sensor (CTS) circuit – high temperature indicated
15	Coolant Temperature Sensor (CTS) circuit – low temperature indicated
21	Throttle Position Sensor (TPS) circuit – signal voltage high
22	Throttle Position Sensor (TPS) circuit – signal voltage low
23	Manifold Air Temperature (MAT) sensor circuit – low temperature indicated
24	Vehicle Speed Sensor (VSS) circuit
25	Manifold Air Temperature (MAT) sensor circuit – high temperature indicated
32	Exhaust Gas Recirculation (EGR) circuit
33	Mass Air Flow (MAF) sensor circuit – GM/SEC high
34	Mass Air Flow (MAF) sensor circuit – GM/SEC low
36	Mass Air Flow (MAF) sensor burn-off circuit
41	Cylinder select error – faulty or incorrect Mem-Cal
42	Electronic Spark Timing (EST) circuit
43	Electronic Spark Control (ESC) circuit
44	Oxygen sensor circuit – lean exhaust indication
45	Oxygen sensor circuit – rich exhaust indication
46	Vehicle Anti-Theft system (VATS) circuit
51	Mem-Cal error – faulty or inorrect Mem-Cal
52	Calpak error – faulty or incorrect Calpak
53	System over voltage
54	Fuel pump circuit – low voltage
55	Electronic Control Module (ECM) error

Year — 1988
Model — Corsica
Engine — 2.0L (122 cid) TBI 4 cyl
Engine Code — VIN 1

ECM TROUBLE CODES

Code	Explanation
12	Speed reference pulse
13	Oxygen sensor circui — open circuit
14	Coolant Temperature Sensor (CTS) circuit — high temperature indicated
15	Coolant Temperature Sensor (CTS) circuit — low temperature indicated
21	Throttle Position Sensor (TPS) circuit — signal voltage high
22	Throttle Position Sensor (TPS) circuit — signal voltage low
23	Manifold Air Temperature (MAT) sensor circuit — low temperature indicated
24	Vehicle Speed Sensor (VSS) circuit
25	Manifold Air Temperature (MAT) sensor circuit — high temperature indicated
33	Manifold Absolute Pressure (MAP) sensor circuit — signal voltage high
34	Manifold Absolute Pressure (MAP) sensor circuit — signal voltage low
42	Electronic Spark Timing (EST) circuit
44	Oxygen sensor circuit — lean exhaust indicated
45	Oxygen sensor circuit — rich exhaust indicated
51	Mem-Cal error — faulty or incorrect Mem-Cal

Year — 1988
Model — Corsica
Engine — 2.8L (173 cid) MFI V6
Engine Code — VIN W

ECM TROUBLE CODES

Code	Explanation
12	Speed reference pulse
13	Oxygen sensor circui — open circuit
14	Coolant Temperature Sensor (CTS) circuit — high temperature indicated
15	Coolant Temperature Sensor (CTS) circuit — low temperature indicated
21	Throttle Position Sensor (TPS) circuit — signal voltage high
22	Throttle Position Sensor (TPS) circuit — signal voltage low
23	Manifold Air Temperature (MAT) sensor circuit — low temperature indicated
24	Vehicle Speed Sensor (VSS) circuit
25	Manifold Air Temperature (MAT) sensor circuit — high temperature indicated
33	Mass Air Flow (MAF) sensor circuit — GM/SEC high
34	Mass Air Flow (MAF) sensor circuit — GM/SEC low
35	Idle speed error
41	Cylinder select error — faulty or incorrect Mem-Cal
42	Electronic Spark Timing (EST) circuit
43	Electronic Spark Control (ESC) circuit
44	Oxygen sensor circuit — lean exhaust indicated
45	Oxygen sensor circuit — rich exhaust indicated
51	Mem-Cal error — faulty or incorrect Mem-Cal
52	Calpak error — faulty or incorrect Calpak
53	System over voltage
54	Fuel pump circuit — low voltage
61	Degraded oxygen sensor
63	Manifold Absolute Pressure (MAP) sensor circuit — signal voltage high
64	Manifold Absolute Pressure (MAP) sensor circuit — signal voltage low

Year — 1988
Model — Beretta
Engine — 2.0L (122 cid) TBI 4 cyl
Engine Code — VIN 1

ECM TROUBLE CODES

Code	Explanation
12	Speed reference pulse
13	Oxygen sensor circuit — open circuit
14	Coolant Temperature Sensor (CTS) circuit — high temperature indicated
15	Coolant Temperature Sensor (CTS) circuit — low temperature indicated
21	Throttle Position Sensor (TPS) circuit — signal voltage high
22	Throttle Position Sensor (TPS) circuit — signal voltage low
23	Manifold Air Temperature (MAT) sensor circuit — low temperature indicated
24	Vehicle Speed Sensor (VSS) circuit
25	Manifold Air Temperature (MAT) sensor circuit — high temperature indicated
33	Manifold Absolute Pressure (MAP) sensor circuit — signal voltage high
34	Manifold Absolute Pressure (MAP) sensor circuit — signal voltage low
42	Electronic Spark Timing (EST) circuit
44	Oxygen sensor circuit — lean exhaust indicated
45	Oxygen sensor circuit — rich exhaust indicated
51	Mem-Cal error — faulty or incorrect Mem-Cal

Year – 1988
Model – Beretta
Engine – 2.8L (173 cid) MFI V6
Engine Code – VIN W

ECM TROUBLE CODES

Code	Explanation
12	Speed reference pulse
13	Oxygen sensor circui – open circuit
14	Coolant Temperature Sensor (CTS) circuit – high temperature indicated
15	Coolant Temperature Sensor (CTS) circuit – low temperature indicated
21	Throttle Position Sensor (TPS) circuit – signal voltage high
22	Throttle Position Sensor (TPS) circuit – signal voltage low
23	Manifold Air Temperature (MAT) sensor circuit – low temperature indicated
24	Vehicle Speed Sensor (VSS) circuit
25	Manifold Air Temperature (MAT) sensor circuit – high temperature indicated
33	Mass Air Flow (MAF) sensor circuit – GM/SEC high
34	Mass Air Flow (MAF) sensor circuit – GM/SEC low
35	Idle speed error
41	Cylinder select error – faulty or incorrect Mem-Cal
42	Electronic Spark Timing (EST) circuit
43	Electronic Spark Control (ESC) circuit
44	Oxygen sensor circuit – lean exhaust indicated
45	Oxygen sensor circuit – rich exhaust indicated
51	Mem-Cal error – faulty or incorrect Mem-Cal
52	Calpak error – faulty or incorrect Calpak
53	System over voltage
54	Fuel pump circuit – low voltage
61	Degraded oxygen sensor
63	Manifold Absolute Pressure (MAP) sensor circuit – signal voltage high
64	Manifold Absolute Pressure (MAP) sensor circuit – signal voltage low

Year — 1988
Model — Celebrity
Engine — 2.5L (151 cid) 4 cyl
Engine Code — VIN R

ECM TROUBLE CODES

Code	Explanation
12	Speed reference pulse
13	Oxygen sensor circuit — open circuit
14	Coolant Temperature Sensor (CTS) circuit — high temperature indicated
15	Coolant Temperature Sensor (CTS) circuit — low temperature indicated
21	Throttle Position Sensor (TPS) circuit — signal voltage high
22	Throttle Position Sensor (TPS) circuit — signal voltage low
23	Manifold Air Temperature (MAT) sensor circuit — low temperature indicated
24	Vehicle Speed Sensor (VSS) circuit
25	Manifold Air Temperature (MAT) sensor circuit — high temperature indicated
33	Manifold Absolute Pressure (MAP) sensor circuit — signal voltage high — low vacuum
34	Manifold Absolute Pressure (MAP) sensor circuit — signal voltage low — high vacuum
35	Idle speed error
42	Electronic Spark Timing (EST) circuit
44	Oxygen sensor circuit — lean exhaust indicated
45	Oxygen sensor circuit — rich exhaust indicated
51	PROM error — faulty or incorrect PROM
53	System over voltage

Year — 1988
Model — Celebrity
Engine — 2.8L (173 cid) V6
Engine Code — VIN W

ECM TROUBLE CODES

Code	Explanation
12	Speed reference pulse
13	Oxygen sensor circui — open circuit
14	Coolant Temperature Sensor (CTS) circuit — high temperature indicated
15	Coolant Temperature Sensor (CTS) circuit — low temperature indicated
21	Throttle Position Sensor (TPS) circuit — signal voltage high
22	Throttle Position Sensor (TPS) circuit — signal voltage low
23	Manifold Air Temperature (MAT) sensor circuit — low temperature indicated
24	Vehicle Speed Sensor (VSS) circuit
25	Manifold Air Temperature (MAT) sensor circuit — high temperature indicated
33	Mass Air Flow (MAF) sensor circuit — high GM/SEC indicated
34	Mass Air Flow (MAF) sensor circuit — low GM/SEC indicated
35	Idle speed error
41	Cylinder select error — faulty or incorrect Mem-Cal
42	Electronic Spark Timing (EST) circuit
43	Electronic Spark Control (ESC) circuit
44	Oxygen sensor circuit — lean exhaust indicated
45	Oxygen sensor circuit — rich exhaust indicated
51	Mem-Cal error — faulty or incorrect Mem-Cal
52	Calpak error — faulty or incorrect Calpak
53	System over voltage
54	Fuel pump circuit — low voltage
61	Degraded oxygen sensor
63	Manifold Absolute Pressure (MAP) sensor circuit — signal voltage high
64	Manifold Absolute Pressure (MAP) sensor circuit — signal voltage low

GENERAL MOTORS CORPORATION
DIAGNOSTIC CODE DATA

Year — 1988
Model — Cavalier
Engine — 2.0L (122 cid) TBI 4 cyl
Engine Code — VIN 1

ECM TROUBLE CODES

Code	Explanation
12	Speed reference pulse
13	Oxygen sensor circuit — open circuit
14	Coolant Temperature Sensor (CTS) circuit — high temperature indicated
15	Coolant Temperature Sensor (CTS) circuit — low temperature indicated
21	Throttle Position Sensor (TPS) circuit — signal voltage high
22	Throttle Position Sensor (TPS) circuit — signal voltage low
23	Manifold Air Temperature (MAT) sensor circuit — low temperature indicated
24	Vehicle Speed Sensor (VSS) circuit
25	Manifold Air Temperature (MAT) sensor circuit — high temperature indicated
32	Exhaust Gas Recirculation (EGR) system error
33	Manifold Absolute Pressure (MAP) sensor circuit — signal voltage high — low vacuum
34	Manifold Absolute Pressure (MAP) sensor circuit — signal voltage low — high vacuum
42	Electronic Spark Timing (EST) circuit
44	Oxygen sensor circuit — lean exhaust indicated
45	Oxygen sensor circuit — rich exhaust indicated
51	PROM error — faulty or incorrect PROM
53	System over voltage

Year — 1988
Model — Cavalier
Engine — 2.8L (173 cid) MPFI V6
Engine Code — VIN W

ECM TROUBLE CODES

Code	Explanation
12	Speed reference pulse
13	Oxygen sensor circui — open circuit
14	Coolant Temperature Sensor (CTS) circuit — high temperature indicated
15	Coolant Temperature Sensor (CTS) circuit — low temperature indicated
21	Throttle Position Sensor (TPS) circuit — signal voltage high
22	Throttle Position Sensor (TPS) circuit — signal voltage low
23	Manifold Air Temperature (MAT) sensor circuit — low temperature indicated
24	Vehicle Speed Sensor (VSS) circuit
25	Manifold Air Temperature (MAT) sensor circuit — high temperature indicated
33	Manifold Absolute Pressure (MAP) sensor circuit — signal voltage high — low vacuum
34	Manifold Absolure Pressure (MAP) sensor circuit — signal voltage low — high vacuum
35	Idle speed error
41	Cylinder select error — faulty or incorrect Mem-Cal
42	Electronic Spark Timing (EST) circuit
43	Electronic Spark Control (ESC) circuit
44	Oxygen sensor circuit — lean exhaust indicated
45	Oxygen sensor circuit — rich exhaust indicated
51	Mem-Cal error — faulty or incorrect Mem-Cal
52	Calpak error — faulty or incorrect Calpak
53	System over voltage
54	Fuel pump circuit — low voltage
61	Degraded oxygen sensor

Year — 1988
Model — Spectrum
Engine — 1.5L (90 cid) 4 cyl
Engine Code — VIN 7

ECM TROUBLE CODES

Code	Explanation
12	No distributor reference pulses to the Electronic Control Module (ECM). This code is not stored and will only flash while the fault is present
13	Oxygen sensor circuit — the engine must run up to 2 minutes at part throttle, under road load, before this code will set
14	Shorted Coolant Temperature Sensor (CTS) circuit — the engine must run up to 2 minutes before this code will set
15	Open Coolant Temperature Sensor (CTS) circuit — the engine must run up to 5 minutes before this code will set
21	Idle switch misadjusted and/or circuit open. This code will set if engine speed falls below 600 rpm for longer than 32 seconds, or if Throttle Position Sensor (TPS) and idle switch are faulty or misadjusted. This code will set if the Electronic Control Module (ECM) detects both idle and Wide Open Throttle (WOT) condition at the same time
22	Fuel cut-off relay and/or circuit open
23	Open or grounded Mixture Control (M/C) circuit
42	Lean oxygen sensor condition — the engine must run up to 2 minutes, in closed loop, at part throttle, under road load, before this code will set. This code will not set when the coolant temperature is below 70°C and/or the air temperature in air cleaner is below 0°C, in a "low altitude" condition. This code will not set in a "high altitude" condition
45	Rich exhaust indication — the engine must run up to 2 minutes, in closed loop, at part throttle, under road load, before this code will set. This code will not set when the engine is not 1500–2500 rpm and/or the coolant temperature is below 70°C and/or at "high altitude condition"
51	Faulty calibration unit (PROM) or installation. It takes up to 30 seconds before this code will set
54	Shorted Mixture Control (M/C) solenoid circuit and/or faulty Electronic Control Module (ECM)
55	Faulty Electronic Control Module (ECM) — problem in A/D converter in ECM

Year – 1989
Model – Caprice, Caprice Classic
Engine – 4.3L (262 cid) FI V6
Engine Code – VIN Z

ECM TROUBLE CODES

Code	Explanation
13	Oxygen sensor circuit – open circuit
14	Coolant Temperature Sensor (CTS) circuit – high temperature indicated
15	Coolant Temperature Sensor (CTS) circuit – low temperature indicated
21	Throttle Position Sensor (TPS) circuit – signal voltage high
22	Throttle Position Sensor (TPS) circuit – signal voltage low
23	Manifold Air Temperature (MAT) sensor circuit – low temperature indicated
24	Vehicle Speed Sensor (VSS) circuit
25	Manifold Air Temperature (MAT) sensor circuit – high temperature indicated
32	Exhaust Gas Recirculation (EGR) circuit
33	Manifold Absolute Pressure (MAP) sensor circuit – signal voltage high – low vacuum
34	Manifold Absolute Pressure (MAP) sensor circuit – signal voltage low – high vacuum
42	Electronic Spark Timing (EST) circuit
43	Electronic Spark Control (ESC) circuit
44	Oxygen sensor circuit – lean exhaust indicated
45	Oxygen sensor circuit – rich exhaust indicated
51	PROM error – faulty or incorrect PROM
52	Calpak error – faulty or incorrect Calpak
54	Fuel pump circuit – low voltage
55	Electronic Control Module (ECM) error

GENERAL MOTORS CORPORATION
DIAGNOSTIC CODE DATA

Year – 1989
Model – Caprice, Caprice Classic
Engine – 5.0L (305 cid) 4-bbl V8
Engine Code – VIN H

ECM TROUBLE CODES

Code	Explanation
12	No engine speed reference pulse
13	Oxygen sensor circuit – open circuit
14	Coolant Temperature Sensor (CTS) circuit – high temperature indicated
15	Coolant Temperature Sensor (CTS) circuit – low temperature indicated
21	Throttle Position Sensor (TPS) circuit – signal voltage high
22	Throttle Position Sensor (TPS) circuit – signal voltage low
23	Mixture Control (M/C) solenoid circuit – signal voltage low
24	Vehicle Speed Sensor (VSS) circuit
24B	Park/Neutral (P/N) circuit
31	Canister Purge Solenoid (CPS) circuit
34	Pressure sensor circuit – signal voltage out or range
41	No distributor reference pulse
42	Electronic Spark Timing (EST) circuit
43	Electronic Spark Control (ESC) circuit
44	Oxygen sensor circuit – lean exhaust indicated
45	Oxygen sensor circuit – rich exhaust indicated
51	PROM error – faulty or incorrect PROM
53	Exhaust Gas Recirculation (EGR) system malfunction – California only
54	Mixture Control (M/C) solenoid circuit – signal voltage high

Year—1989
Model—Caprice Wagon
Engine—5.0L (307 cid) V8
Engine Code—VIN Y

ECM TROUBLE CODES

Code	Explanation
12	Speed reference pulse
13	Oxygen sensor circuit—open circuit
14	Coolant Temperature Sensor (CTS) circuit—high temperature indicated
15	Coolant Temperature Sensor (CTS) circuit—low temperature indicated
21	Throttle Position Sensor (TPS) circuit—signal voltage high
22	Throttle Position Sensor (TPS) circuit—signal voltage low
23	Manifold Air Temperature (MAT) sensor circuit—low temperature indicated
24	Vehicle Speed Sensor (VSS) circuit
25	Manifold Air Temperature (MAT) sensor circuit—high temperature indicated
32	Exhaust Gas Recirculation (EGR) circuit
33	Manifold Absolute Pressure (MAP) sensor circuit—signal voltage high—low vacuum
34	Manifold Absolute Pressure (MAP) sensor circuit—signal voltage low—high vacuum
42	Electronic Spark Timing (EST) circuit
43	Electronic Spark Control (ESC) circuit
44	Oxygen sensor circuit—lean exhaust indicated
45	Oxygen sensor circuit—rich exhaust indicated
51	PROM error—faulty or incorrect PROM
52	Calpak error—faulty or incorrect Calpak
54	Fuel pump circuit—low voltage
55	Electronic Control Module (ECM) error

Year — 1989
Model — Camaro
Engine — 2.8L (173 cid) MPFI V6
Engine Code — VIN S

ECM TROUBLE CODES

Code	Explanation
12	Speed reference pulse
13	Oxygen sensor circuit — open circuit
14	Coolant Temperature Sensor (CTS) circuit — high temperature indicated
15	Coolant Temperature Sensor (CTS) circuit — low temperature indicated
21	Throttle Position Sensor (TPS) circuit — signal voltage high
22	Throttle Position Sensor (TPS) circuit — signal voltage low
23	Manifold Air Temperature (MAT) sensor circuit — low temperature indicated
24	Vehicle Speed Sensor (VSS) circuit
25	Manifold Air Temperature (MAT) sensor circuit — high temperature indicated
32	Exhaust Gas Recirculation (EGR) circuit
33	Mass Air Flow (MAF) sensor circuit — GM/SEC high
34	Mass Air Flow (MAF) sensor circuit — GM/SEC low
41	Cylinder select error — faulty or incorrect Mem-Cal
42	Electronic Spark Timing (EST) circuit
44	Oxygen sensor circuit — lean exhaust indicated
45	Oxygen sensor circuit — rich exhaust indicated
51	PROM error — faulty or incorrect PROM
52	Calpak error — faulty or incorrect Calpak
53	System over voltage
54	Fuel pump circuit — low voltage

Year — 1989
Model — Camaro
Engine — 5.0L (305 cid) TBI V8
Engine Code — VIN E

ECM TROUBLE CODES

Code	Explanation
12	Speed reference signal
13	Oxygen sensor circuit — open circuit
14	Coolant Temperature Sensor (CTS) circuit — high temperature indicated
15	Coolant Temperature Sensor (CTS) circuit — low temperature indicated
21	Throttle Position Sensor (TPS) circuit — signal voltage high
22	Throttle Position Sensor (TPS) circuit — signal voltage low
23	Manifold Air Temperature (MAT) sensor circuit — low temperature indicated
24	Vehicle Speed Sensor (VSS) circuit
25	Manifold Air Temperature (MAT) sensor circuit — high temperature indicated
32	Exhaust Gas Recirculation (EGR) circuit
33	Manifold Absolute Pressure (MAP) sensor circuit — signal voltage high — low vacuum
34	Manifold Absolute Pressure (MAP) sensor circuit — signal voltage low — high vacuum
42	Electronic Spark Timing (EST) circuit
43	Electronic Spark Control (ESC) circuit
44	Oxygen sensor circuit — lean exhaust indicated
45	Oxygen sensor circuit — rich exhaust indicated
51	PROM error — faulty or incorrect PROM
52	Calpak error — faulty or incorrect Calpak
53	Vehicle Anti-Theft System (VATS) circuit
54	Fuel pump circuit — low voltage

Year – 1989
Model – Camaro
Engine – 5.0L (305 cid) TPI V8
Engine Code – VIN F

ECM TROUBLE CODES

Code	Explanation
12	Speed reference signal
13	Oxygen sensor circuit — open circuit
14	Coolant Temperature Sensor (CTS) circuit — high temperature indicated
15	Coolant Temperature Sensor (CTS) circuit — low temperature indicated
21	Throttle Position Sensor (TPS) circuit — signal voltage high
22	Throttle Position Sensor (TPS) circuit — signal voltage low
23	Manifold Air Temperature (MAT) sensor circuit — low temperature indicated
24	Vehicle Speed Sensor (VSS) circuit
25	Manifold Air Temperature (MAT) sensor circuit — high temperature indicated
32	Exhaust Gas Recirculation (EGR) circuit
33	Mass Air Flow (MAF) sensor circuit — GM/SEC high
34	Mass Air Flow (MAF) sensor circuit — GM/SEC low
36	Mass Air Flow (MAF) sensor burn-off circuit
41	Cylinder select error — faulty or incorrect Mem-Cal
42	Electronic Spark Timing (EST) circuit
43	Electronic Spark Control (ESC) circuit
44	Oxygen sensor circuit — lean exhaust indicated
45	Oxygen sensor circuit — rich exhaust indicated
46	Vehicle Anti-Theft System (VATS) circuit
51	Mem-Cal — faulty or incorrect Mem-Cal
52	Calpak error — faulty or incorrect Calpak
53	System over voltage
54	Fuel pump circuit — low voltage

Year — 1989
Model — Camaro
Engine — 5.7L (350 cid) TPI V8
Engine Code — VIN 8

ECM TROUBLE CODES

Code	Explanation
12	Speed reference pulse
13	Oxygen sensor circuit — open circuit
14	Coolant Temperature Sensor (CTS) circuit — high temperature indicated
15	Coolant Temperature Sensor (CTS) circuit — low temperature indicated
21	Throttle Position Sensor (TPS) circuit — signal voltage high
22	Throttle Position Sensor (TPS) circuit — signal voltage low
23	Manifold Air Temperature (MAT) sensor circuit — low temperature indicated
24	Vehicle Speed Sensor (VSS) circuit
25	Manifold Air Temperature (MAT) sensor circuit — high temperature indicated
32	Exhaust Gas Recirculation (EGR) circuit
33	Mass Air Flow (MAF) sensor circuit — GM/SEC high
34	Mass Air Flow (MAF) sensor circuit — GM/SEC low
36	Mass Air Flow (MAF) sensor burn-off circuit
41	Cylinder select error — faulty or incorrect Mem-Cal
42	Electronic Spark Timing (EST) circuit
43	Electronic Spark Control (ESC) circuit
44	Oxygen sensor circuit — lean exhaust indicated
45	Oxygen sensor circuit — rich exhaust indicated
46	Vehicle Anti-Theft System (VATS) circuit
51	Mem-Cal — faulty or incorrect Mem-Cal
52	Calpak error — faulty or incorrect Calpak
53	System over voltage
54	Fuel pump circuit — low voltage
55	Electronic Control Module (ECM) error

GENERAL MOTORS CORPORATION
DIAGNOSTIC CODE DATA

Year — 1989
Model — Corvette
Engine — 5.7L (350 cid) TPI V8
Engine Code — VIN 8

ECM TROUBLE CODES

Code	Explanation
12	Speed reference pulse
13	Oxygen sensor circuit — open circuit
14	Coolant Temperature Sensor (CTS) circuit — high temperature indicated
15	Coolant Temperature Sensor (CTS) circuit — low temperature indicated
21	Throttle Position Sensor (TPS) circuit — signal voltage high
22	Throttle Position Sensor (TPS) circuit — signal voltage low
23	Manifold Air Temperature (MAT) sensor circuit — low temperature indicated
24	Vehicle Speed Sensor (VSS) circuit
25	Manifold Air Temperature (MAT) sensor circuit — high temperature indicated
32	Exhaust Gas Recirculation (EGR) circuit
33	Mass Air Flow (MAF) sensor circuit — GM/SEC high
34	Mass Air Flow (MAF) sensor circuit — GM/SEC low
36	Mass Air Flow (MAF) sensor burn-off circuit
41	Cylinder select error — faulty or incorrect Mem-Cal
42	Electronic Spark Timing (EST) circuit
43	Electronic Spark Control (ESC) circuit
44	Oxygen sensor circuit — lean exhaust indicated
45	Oxygen sensor circuit — rich exhaust indicated
46	Vehicle Anti-Theft System (VATS) circuit
51	Mem-Cal error — faulty or incorrect Mem-Cal
52	Calpak error — faulty or incorrect Calpak
53	System over voltage
54	Fuel pump circuit — low voltage
55	Electronic Control Module (ECM) error

Year — 1989
Model — Beretta
Engine — 2.0L (121 cid) TBI 4 cyl
Engine Code — VIN 1

ECM TROUBLE CODES

Code	Explanation
12	Speed reference pulse
13	Oxygen sensor circuit — open circuit
14	Coolant Temperature Sensor (CTS) circuit — high temperature indicated
15	Coolant Temperature Sensor (CTS) circuit — low temperature indicated
21	Throttle Position Sensor (TPS) circuit — signal voltage high
22	Throttle Position Sensor (TPS) circuit — signal voltage low
23	Manifold Air Temperature (MAT) sensor circuit — low temperature indicated
24	Vehicle Speed Sensor (VSS) circuit
25	Manifold Air Temperature (MAT) sensor circuit — high temperature indicated
33	Manifold Absolute Pressure (MAP) sensor circuit — signal voltage high — low vacuum
34	Manifold Absolute Pressure (MAP) sensor circuit — signal voltage low — high vacuum
42	Electronic Spark Timing (EST) circuit
44	Oxygen sensor circuit — lean exhaust indicated
45	Oxygen sensor circuit — rich exhaust indicated
51	PROM error — faulty or incorrect PROM

Year – 1989
Model – Corsica
Engine – 2.0L (121 cid) TBI 4 cyl
Engine Code – VIN 1

ECM TROUBLE CODES

Code	Explanation
12	Speed reference pulse
13	Oxygen sensor circuit – open circuit
14	Coolant Temperature Sensor (CTS) circuit – high temperature indicated
15	Coolant Temperature Sensor (CTS) circuit – low temperature indicated
21	Throttle Position Sensor (TPS) circuit – signal voltage high
22	Throttle Position Sensor (TPS) circuit – signal voltage low
23	Manifold Air Temperature (MAT) sensor circuit – low temperature indicated
24	Vehicle Speed Sensor (VSS) circuit
25	Manifold Air Temperature (MAT) sensor circuit – high temperature indicated
33	Manifold Absolute Pressure (MAP) sensor circuit – signal voltage high – low vacuum
34	Manifold Absolute Pressure (MAP) sensor circuit – signal voltage low – high vacuum
42	Electronic Spark Timing (EST) circuit
44	Oxygen sensor circuit – lean exhaust indicated
45	Oxygen sensor circuit – rich exhaust indicated
51	PROM error – faulty or incorrect PROM

Year—1989
Model—Beretta
Engine—2.8L (173 cid) MFI V6
Engine Code—VIN W

ECM TROUBLE CODES

Code	Explanation
12	Speed reference pulse
13	Oxygen sensor circuit—open circuit
14	Coolant Temperature Sensor (CTS) circuit—high temperature indicated
15	Coolant Temperature Sensor (CTS) circuit—low temperature indicated
21	Throttle Position Sensor (TPS) circuit—signal voltage high
22	Throttle Position Sensor (TPS) circuit—signal voltage low
23	Manifold Air Temperature (MAT) sensor circuit—low temperature indicated
24	Vehicle Speed Sensor (VSS) circuit
25	Manifold Air Temperature (MAT) sensor circuit—high temperature indicated
32	Exhaust Gas Recirculation (EGR) circuit
33	Manifold Absolute Pressure (MAP) sensor circuit—signal voltage high
34	Manifold Absolute Pressure (MAP) sensor circuit—signal voltage low
35	Idle speed error
41	Cylinder select error—faulty or incorrect Mem-Cal
42	Electronic Spark Timing (EST) circuit
43	Electronic Spark Control (ESC) circuit
44	Oxygen sensor circuit—lean exhaust indicated
45	Oxygen sensor circuit—rich exhaust indicated
51	Mem-Cal error—faulty or incorrect Mem-Cal
52	Calpak error—faulty or incorrect Calpak
53	System over voltage
54	Fuel pump circuit—low voltage
61	Degraded oxygen sensor

GENERAL MOTORS CORPORATION
DIAGNOSTIC CODE DATA

Year — 1989
Model — Corsica
Engine — 2.8L (173 cid) MFI V6
Engine Code — VIN W

ECM TROUBLE CODES

Code	Explanation
12	Speed reference pulse
13	Oxygen sensor circuit — open circuit
14	Coolant Temperature Sensor (CTS) circuit — high temperature indicated
15	Coolant Temperature Sensor (CTS) circuit — low temperature indicated
21	Throttle Position Sensor (TPS) circuit — signal voltage high
22	Throttle Position Sensor (TPS) circuit — signal voltage low
23	Manifold Air Temperature (MAT) sensor circuit — low temperature indicated
24	Vehicle Speed Sensor (VSS) circuit
25	Manifold Air Temperature (MAT) sensor circuit — high temperature indicated
32	Exhaust Gas Recirculation (EGR) circuit
33	Manifold Absolute Pressure (MAP) sensor circuit — signal voltage high
34	Manifold Absolute Pressure (MAP) sensor circuit — signal voltage low
35	Idle speed error
41	Cylinder select error — faulty or incorrect Mem-Cal
42	Electronic Spark Timing (EST) circuit
43	Electronic Spark Control (ESC) circuit
44	Oxygen sensor circuit — lean exhaust indicated
45	Oxygen sensor circuit — rich exhaust indicated
51	Mem-Cal error — faulty or incorrect Mem-Cal
52	Calpak error — faulty or incorrect Calpak
53	System over voltage
54	Fuel pump circuit — low voltage
61	Degraded oxygen sensor

Year – 1989
Model – Celebrity
Engine – 2.5L (151 cid) TBI 4 cyl
Engine Code – VIN R

ECM TROUBLE CODES

Code	Explanation
12	Speed reference signal
13	Oxygen sensor circuit – open circuit
14	Coolant Temperature Sensor (CTS) circuit – high temperature indicated
15	Coolant Temperature Sensor (CTS) circuit – low temperature indicated
21	Throttle Position Sensor (TPS) circuit – signal voltage high
22	Throttle Position Sensor (TPS) circuit – signal voltage low
23	Manifold Air Temperature (MAT) sensor circuit – low temperature indicated
24	Vehicle Speed Sensor (VSS) circuit
25	Manifold Air Temperature (MAT) sensor circuit – high temperature indicated
32	Exhaust Gas Recirculation (EGR) circuit
33	Manifold Absolute Pressure (MAP) sensor circuit – signal voltage high
34	Manifold Absolute Pressure (MAP) sensor circuit – signal voltage low
35	Idle speed error
42	Electronic Spark Timing (EST) circuit
44	Oxygen sensor circuit – lean exhaust indicated
45	Oxygen sensor circuit – rich exhaust indicated
51	PROM error – faulty or incorrect PROM
53	System over voltage

Year – 1989
Model – Celebrity
Engine – 2.8L (173 cid) MFI V6
Engine Code – VIN W

ECM TROUBLE CODES

Code	Explanation
12	Speed reference pulse
13	Oxygen sensor circuit – open circuit
14	Coolant Temperature Sensor (CTS) circuit – high temperature indicated
15	Coolant Temperature Sensor (CTS) circuit – low temperature indicated
21	Throttle Position Sensor (TPS) circuit – signal voltage high
22	Throttle Position Sensor (TPS) circuit – signal voltage low
23	Manifold Air Temperature (MAT) sensor circuit – low temperature indicated
24	Vehicle Speed Sensor (VSS) circuit
25	Manifold Air Temperature (MAT) sensor circuit – high temperature indicated
32	Exhaust Gas Recirculation (EGR) circuit
33	Manifold Absolute Pressure (MAP) sensor circuit – signal voltage high
34	Manifold Absolute Pressure (MAP) sensor circuit – signal voltage low
35	Idle speed error
41	Cylinder select error – faulty or incorrect Mem-Cal
42	Electronic Spark Timing (EST) circuit
43	Electronic Spark Control (ESC) circuit
44	Oxygen sensor circuit – lean exhaust indicated
45	Oxygen sensor circuit – rich exhaust indicated
51	Mem-Cal error – faulty or incorrect Mem-Cal
52	Calpak error – faulty or incorrect Calpak
53	System over voltage
54	Fuel pump circuit – low voltage
61	Degraded oxygen sensor

Year – 1989
Model – Cavalier
Engine – 2.0L (122 cid) TBI 4 cyl
Engine Code – VIN 1

ECM TROUBLE CODES

Code	Explanation
12	Speed reference pulse
13	Oxygen sensor circuit – open circuit
14	Coolant Temperature Sensor (CTS) circuit – high temperature indicated
15	Coolant Temperature Sensor (CTS) circuit – low temperature indicated
21	Throttle Position Sensor (TPS) circuit – signal voltage high
22	Throttle Position Sensor (TPS) circuit – signal voltage low
23	Manifold Air Temperature (MAT) sensor circuit – low temperature indicated
24	Vehicle Speed Sensor (VSS) circuit
25	Manifold Air Temperature (MAT) sensor circuit – high temperature indicated
32	Exhaust Gas Recirculation (EGR) system failure
33	Manifold Absolute Pressure (MAP) sensor circuit – signal voltage high – low vacuum
34	Manifold Absolute Pressure (MAP) sensor circuit – signal voltage low – high vacuum
42	Electronic Spark Timing (EST) circuit
44	Oxygen sensor circuit – lean exhaust indicated
45	Oxygen sensor circuit – rich exhaust indicated
51	PROM error – faulty or incorrect PROM

Year – 1989
Model – Cavalier
Engine – 2.8L (173 cid) MFI V6
Engine Code – VIN W

ECM TROUBLE CODES

Code	Explanation
12	Speed reference pulse
13	Oxygen sensor circuit — open circuit
14	Coolant Temperature Sensor (CTS) circuit — high temperature indicated
15	Coolant Temperature Sensor (CTS) circuit — low temperature indicated
21	Throttle Position Sensor (TPS) circuit — signal voltage high
22	Throttle Position Sensor (TPS) circuit — signal voltage low
23	Manifold Air Temperature (MAT) sensor circuit — low temperature indicated
24	Vehicle Speed Sensor (VSS) circuit
25	Manifold Air Temperature (MAT) sensor circuit — high temperature indicated
32	Exhaust Gas Recirculation (EGR) circuit
33	Manifold Absolute Pressure (MAP) sensor circuit — signal voltage high
34	Manifold Absolute Pressure (MAP) sensor circuit — signal voltage low
35	Idle speed error
41	Cylinder select error — faulty or incorrect Mem-Cal
42	Electronic Spark Timing (EST) circuit
43	Electronic Spark Control (ESC) circuit
44	Oxygen sensor circuit — lean exhaust indicated
45	Oxygen sensor circuit — rich exhaust indicated
51	Mem-Cal error — faulty or incorrect Mem-Cal
52	Calpak error — faulty or incorrect Calpak
53	System over voltage
54	Fuel pump circuit — low voltage
61	Degraded oxygen sensor

OLDSMOBILE

Year — 1980
Model — Delta 88
Engine — 3.8L (231 cid) V6
Engine Code — VIN A

ECM TROUBLE CODES

Code	Explanation
12	No tachometer or reference signal to ECM, this code will only be present while a fault exists. Code 12 will not be stored if problem is intermittent
13	Oxygen sensor circuit. The engine has to operate for about 18 minutes at part throttle before this code will show
13 & 14	(At same time) Throttle Position Sensor (TPS) adjustment
14	Shorted coolant sensor circuit. The engine has to run 2 minutes before this code will show
15	Open coolant sensor circuit. The engine has to operate for about 5 minutes at part throttle before this code will show
21	Shorted Wide Open Throttle (WOT) switch and/or open "Closed Throttle" switch circuit (when used)
21	Throttle Position Sensor (TPS) circuit (After 10 seconds and below 800 rpm)
23	Open or grounded carburetor solenoid circuit
32	Barometric Pressure Sensor (BARO) output low
32 & 55	(At same time) grounded +8V, V/ref or faulty ECM
34	Manifold Absolute Pressure (MAP) sensor output high. (After 10 seconds and below 800 rpm)
43	Throttle Position Sensor (TPS) adjustment
44	Lean oxygen sensor. Engine must run for approximately 5 minutes in closed loop mode and part throttle at road load (drive car) before this code will show
45	Rich oxygen sensor. Engine must be run for approximately 5 minutes in closed loop mode and part throttle before this code will show
44 & 45	(At same time) faulty oxygen sensor or open sensor
51	Faulty Calibration Unit (PROM) or improper PROM installation
52 & 53	"Check Engine" light OFF — Intermittent ECM problem "Check Engine" light ON — Faulty ECM (replace)
54	Faulty carburetor solenoid and/or ECM
55	Faulty oxygen sensor, open MAP sensor or ECM

GENERAL MOTORS CORPORATION
DIAGNOSTIC CODE DATA

Year—1980
Model—Delta 88
Engine—5.0L (307 cid) V8
Engine Code—VIN Y

ECM TROUBLE CODES

Code	Explanation
12	No tachometer or reference signal to ECM, this code will only be present while a fault exists. Code 12 will not be stored if problem is intermittent
13	Oxygen sensor circuit. The engine has to operate for about 18 minutes at part throttle before this code will show
13 & 14	(At same time) Throttle Position Sensor (TPS) adjustment
14	Shorted coolant sensor circuit. The engine has to run 2 minutes before this code will show
15	Open coolant sensor circuit. The engine has to operate for about 5 minutes at part throttle before this code will show
21	Shorted Wide Open Throttle (WOT) switch and/or open "Closed Throttle" switch circuit (when used)
21	Throttle Position Sensor (TPS) circuit (After 10 seconds and below 800 rpm)
23	Open or grounded carburetor solenoid circuit
32	Barometric Pressure Sensor (BARO) output low
32 & 55	(At same time) grounded +8V, V/ref or faulty ECM
34	Manifold Absolute Pressure (MAP) sensor output high. (After 10 seconds and below 800 rpm)
43	Throttle Position Sensor (TPS) adjustment
44	Lean oxygen sensor. Engine must run for approximately 5 minutes in closed loop mode and part throttle at road load (drive car) before this code will show
45	Rich oxygen sensor. Engine must be run for approximately 5 minutes in closed loop mode and part throttle before this code will show
44 & 45	(At same time) faulty oxygen sensor or open sensor
51	Faulty Calibration Unit (PROM) or improper PROM installation
52 & 53	"Check Engine" light OFF—Intermittent ECM problem "Check Engine" light ON—Faulty ECM (replace)
54	Faulty carburetor solenoid and/or ECM
55	Faulty oxygen sensor, open MAP sensor or ECM

Year – 1980
Model – Delta 88
Engine – 5.7L (350 cid) V8
Engine Code – VIN R

ECM TROUBLE CODES

Code	Explanation
12	No tachometer or reference signal to ECM, this code will only be present while a fault exists. Code 12 will not be stored if problem is intermittent
13	Oxygen sensor circuit. The engine has to operate for about 18 minutes at part throttle before this code will show
13 & 14	(At same time) Throttle Position Sensor (TPS) adjustment
14	Shorted coolant sensor circuit. The engine has to run 2 minutes before this code will show
15	Open coolant sensor circuit. The engine has to operate for about 5 minutes at part throttle before this code will show
21	Shorted Wide Open Throttle (WOT) switch and/or open "Closed Throttle" switch circuit (when used)
21	Throttle Position Sensor (TPS) circuit (After 10 seconds and below 800 rpm)
23	Open or grounded carburetor solenoid circuit
32	Barometric Pressure Sensor (BARO) output low
32 & 55	(At same time) grounded +8V, V/ref or faulty ECM
34	Manifold Absolute Pressure (MAP) sensor output high. (After 10 seconds and below 800 rpm)
43	Throttle Position Sensor (TPS) adjustment
44	Lean oxygen sensor. Engine must run for approximately 5 minutes in closed loop mode and part throttle at road load (drive car) before this code will show
45	Rich oxygen sensor. Engine must be run for approximately 5 minutes in closed loop mode and part throttle before this code will show
44 & 45	(At same time) faulty oxygen sensor or open sensor
51	Faulty Calibration Unit (PROM) or improper PROM installation
52 & 53	"Check Engine" light OFF – Intermittent ECM problem "Check Engine" light ON – Faulty ECM (replace)
54	Faulty carburetor solenoid and/or ECM
55	Faulty oxygen sensor, open MAP sensor or ECM

GENERAL MOTORS CORPORATION
DIAGNOSTIC CODE DATA

Year — 1980
Model — Ninety-Eight
Engine — 5.0L (307 cid) V8
Engine Code — VIN Y

ECM TROUBLE CODES

Code	Explanation
12	No tachometer or reference signal to ECM, this code will only be present while a fault exists. Code 12 will not be stored if problem is intermittent
13	Oxygen sensor circuit. The engine has to operate for about 18 minutes at part throttle before this code will show
13 & 14	(At same time) Throttle Position Sensor (TPS) adjustment
14	Shorted coolant sensor circuit. The engine has to run 2 minutes before this code will show
15	Open coolant sensor circuit. The engine has to operate for about 5 minutes at part throttle before this code will show
21	Shorted Wide Open Throttle (WOT) switch and/or open "Closed Throttle" switch circuit (when used)
21	Throttle Position Sensor (TPS) circuit (After 10 seconds and below 800 rpm)
23	Open or grounded carburetor solenoid circuit
32	Barometric Pressure Sensor (BARO) output low
32 & 55	(At same time) grounded +8V, V/ref or faulty ECM
34	Manifold Absolute Pressure (MAP) sensor output high. (After 10 seconds and below 800 rpm)
43	Throttle Position Sensor (TPS) adjustment
44	Lean oxygen sensor. Engine must run for approximately 5 minutes in closed loop mode and part throttle at road load (drive car) before this code will show
45	Rich oxygen sensor. Engine must be run for approximately 5 minutes in closed loop mode and part throttle before this code will show
44 & 45	(At same time) faulty oxygen sensor or open sensor
51	Faulty Calibration Unit (PROM) or improper PROM installation
52 & 53	"Check Engine" light OFF — Intermittent ECM problem "Check Engine" light ON — Faulty ECM (replace)
54	Faulty carburetor solenoid and/or ECM
55	Faulty oxygen sensor, open MAP sensor or ECM

Year — 1980
Model — Ninety-Eight
Engine — 5.7L (350 cid) V8
Engine Code — VIN R

ECM TROUBLE CODES

Code	Explanation
12	No tachometer or reference signal to ECM, this code will only be present while a fault exists. Code 12 will not be stored if problem is intermittent
13	Oxygen sensor circuit. The engine has to operate for about 18 minutes at part throttle before this code will show
13 & 14	(At same time) Throttle Position Sensor (TPS) adjustment
14	Shorted coolant sensor circuit. The engine has to run 2 minutes before this code will show
15	Open coolant sensor circuit. The engine has to operate for about 5 minutes at part throttle before this code will show
21	Shorted Wide Open Throttle (WOT) switch and/or open "Closed Throttle" switch circuit (when used)
21	Throttle Position Sensor (TPS) circuit (After 10 seconds and below 800 rpm)
23	Open or grounded carburetor solenoid circuit
32	Barometric Pressure Sensor (BARO) output low
32 & 55	(At same time) grounded +8V, V/ref or faulty ECM
34	Manifold Absolute Pressure (MAP) sensor output high. (After 10 seconds and below 800 rpm)
43	Throttle Position Sensor (TPS) adjustment
44	Lean oxygen sensor. Engine must run for approximately 5 minutes in closed loop mode and part throttle at road load (drive car) before this code will show
45	Rich oxygen sensor. Engine must be run for approximately 5 minutes in closed loop mode and part throttle before this code will show
44 & 45	(At same time) faulty oxygen sensor or open sensor
51	Faulty Calibration Unit (PROM) or improper PROM installation
52 & 53	"Check Engine" light OFF—Intermittent ECM problem "Check Engine" light ON—Faulty ECM (replace)
54	Faulty carburetor solenoid and/or ECM
55	Faulty oxygen sensor, open MAP sensor or ECM

GENERAL MOTORS CORPORATION
DIAGNOSTIC CODE DATA

Year — 1980
Model — Cutlass
Engine — 3.8L (231 cid) V6
Engine Code — VIN A

ECM TROUBLE CODES

Code	Explanation
12	No tachometer or reference signal to ECM, this code will only be present while a fault exists. Code 12 will not be stored if problem is intermittent
13	Oxygen sensor circuit. The engine has to operate for about 18 minutes at part throttle before this code will show
13 & 14	(At same time) Throttle Position Sensor (TPS) adjustment
14	Shorted coolant sensor circuit. The engine has to run 2 minutes before this code will show
15	Open coolant sensor circuit. The engine has to operate for about 5 minutes at part throttle before this code will show
21	Shorted Wide Open Throttle (WOT) switch and/or open "Closed Throttle" switch circuit (when used)
21	Throttle Position Sensor (TPS) circuit (After 10 seconds and below 800 rpm)
23	Open or grounded carburetor solenoid circuit
32	Barometric Pressure Sensor (BARO) output low
32 & 55	(At same time) grounded +8V, V/ref or faulty ECM
34	Manifold Absolute Pressure (MAP) sensor output high. (After 10 seconds and below 800 rpm)
43	Throttle Position Sensor (TPS) adjustment
44	Lean oxygen sensor. Engine must run for approximately 5 minutes in closed loop mode and part throttle at road load (drive car) before this code will show
45	Rich oxygen sensor. Engine must be run for approximately 5 minutes in closed loop mode and part throttle before this code will show
44 & 45	(At same time) faulty oxygen sensor or open sensor
51	Faulty Calibration Unit (PROM) or improper PROM installation
52 & 53	"Check Engine" light OFF — Intermittent ECM problem "Check Engine" light ON — Faulty ECM (replace)
54	Faulty carburetor solenoid and/or ECM
55	Faulty oxygen sensor, open MAP sensor or ECM

Year – 1980
Model – Cutlass
Engine – 4.3L (260 cid) V8
Engine Code – VIN F

ECM TROUBLE CODES

Code	Explanation
12	No tachometer or reference signal to ECM, this code will only be present while a fault exists. Code 12 will not be stored if problem is intermittent
13	Oxygen sensor circuit. The engine has to operate for about 18 minutes at part throttle before this code will show
13 & 14	(At same time) Throttle Position Sensor (TPS) adjustment
14	Shorted coolant sensor circuit. The engine has to run 2 minutes before this code will show
15	Open coolant sensor circuit. The engine has to operate for about 5 minutes at part throttle before this code will show
21	Shorted Wide Open Throttle (WOT) switch and/or open "Closed Throttle" switch circuit (when used)
21	Throttle Position Sensor (TPS) circuit (After 10 seconds and below 800 rpm)
23	Open or grounded carburetor solenoid circuit
32	Barometric Pressure Sensor (BARO) output low
32 & 55	(At same time) grounded +8V, V/ref or faulty ECM
34	Manifold Absolute Pressure (MAP) sensor output high. (After 10 seconds and below 800 rpm)
43	Throttle Position Sensor (TPS) adjustment
44	Lean oxygen sensor. Engine must run for approximately 5 minutes in closed loop mode and part throttle at road load (drive car) before this code will show
45	Rich oxygen sensor. Engine must be run for approximately 5 minutes in closed loop mode and part throttle before this code will show
44 & 45	(At same time) faulty oxygen sensor or open sensor
51	Faulty Calibration Unit (PROM) or improper PROM installation
52 & 53	"Check Engine" light OFF – Intermittent ECM problem "Check Engine" light ON – Faulty ECM (replace)
54	Faulty carburetor solenoid and/or ECM
55	Faulty oxygen sensor, open MAP sensor or ECM

Year — 1980
Model — Cutlass
Engine — 5.0L (305 cid) V8
Engine Code — VIN H

ECM TROUBLE CODES

Code	Explanation
12	No tachometer or reference signal to ECM, this code will only be present while a fault exists. Code 12 will not be stored if problem is intermittent
13	Oxygen sensor circuit. The engine has to operate for about 18 minutes at part throttle before this code will show
13 & 14	(At same time) Throttle Position Sensor (TPS) adjustment
14	Shorted coolant sensor circuit. The engine has to run 2 minutes before this code will show
15	Open coolant sensor circuit. The engine has to operate for about 5 minutes at part throttle before this code will show
21	Shorted Wide Open Throttle (WOT) switch and/or open "Closed Throttle" switch circuit (when used)
21	Throttle Position Sensor (TPS) circuit (After 10 seconds and below 800 rpm)
23	Open or grounded carburetor solenoid circuit
32	Barometric Pressure Sensor (BARO) output low
32 & 55	(At same time) grounded +8V, V/ref or faulty ECM
34	Manifold Absolute Pressure (MAP) sensor output high. (After 10 seconds and below 800 rpm)
43	Throttle Position Sensor (TPS) adjustment
44	Lean oxygen sensor. Engine must run for approximately 5 minutes in closed loop mode and part throttle at road load (drive car) before this code will show
45	Rich oxygen sensor. Engine must be run for approximately 5 minutes in closed loop mode and part throttle before this code will show
44 & 45	(At same time) faulty oxygen sensor or open sensor
51	Faulty Calibration Unit (PROM) or improper PROM installation
52 & 53	"Check Engine" light OFF—Intermittent ECM problem "Check Engine" light ON—Faulty ECM (replace)
54	Faulty carburetor solenoid and/or ECM
55	Faulty oxygen sensor, open MAP sensor or ECM

Year — 1980
Model — Custom Cruiser
Engine — 5.0L (307 cid) V8
Engine Code — VIN Y

ECM TROUBLE CODES

Code	Explanation
12	No tachometer or reference signal to ECM, this code will only be present while a fault exists. Code 12 will not be stored if problem is intermittent
13	Oxygen sensor circuit. The engine has to operate for about 18 minutes at part throttle before this code will show
13 & 14	(At same time) Throttle Position Sensor (TPS) adjustment
14	Shorted coolant sensor circuit. The engine has to run 2 minutes before this code will show
15	Open coolant sensor circuit. The engine has to operate for about 5 minutes at part throttle before this code will show
21	Shorted Wide Open Throttle (WOT) switch and/or open "Closed Throttle" switch circuit (when used)
21	Throttle Position Sensor (TPS) circuit (After 10 seconds and below 800 rpm)
23	Open or grounded carburetor solenoid circuit
32	Barometric Pressure Sensor (BARO) output low
32 & 55	(At same time) grounded +8V, V/ref or faulty ECM
34	Manifold Absolute Pressure (MAP) sensor output high. (After 10 seconds and below 800 rpm)
43	Throttle Position Sensor (TPS) adjustment
44	Lean oxygen sensor. Engine must run for approximately 5 minutes in closed loop mode and part throttle at road load (drive car) before this code will show
45	Rich oxygen sensor. Engine must be run for approximately 5 minutes in closed loop mode and part throttle before this code will show
44 & 45	(At same time) faulty oxygen sensor or open sensor
51	Faulty Calibration Unit (PROM) or improper PROM installation
52 & 53	"Check Engine" light OFF — Intermittent ECM problem "Check Engine" light ON — Faulty ECM (replace)
54	Faulty carburetor solenoid and/or ECM
55	Faulty oxygen sensor, open MAP sensor or ECM

GENERAL MOTORS CORPORATION
DIAGNOSTIC CODE DATA

Year — 1980
Model — Custom Cruiser
Engine — 5.7L (350 cid) V8
Engine Code — VIN R

ECM TROUBLE CODES

Code	Explanation
12	No tachometer or reference signal to ECM, this code will only be present while a fault exists. Code 12 will not be stored if problem is intermittent
13	Oxygen sensor circuit. The engine has to operate for about 18 minutes at part throttle before this code will show
13 & 14	(At same time) Throttle Position Sensor (TPS) adjustment
14	Shorted coolant sensor circuit. The engine has to run 2 minutes before this code will show
15	Open coolant sensor circuit. The engine has to operate for about 5 minutes at part throttle before this code will show
21	Shorted Wide Open Throttle (WOT) switch and/or open "Closed Throttle" switch circuit (when used)
21	Throttle Position Sensor (TPS) circuit (After 10 seconds and below 800 rpm)
23	Open or grounded carburetor solenoid circuit
32	Barometric Pressure Sensor (BARO) output low
32 & 55	(At same time) grounded +8V, V/ref or faulty ECM
34	Manifold Absolute Pressure (MAP) sensor output high. (After 10 seconds and below 800 rpm)
43	Throttle Position Sensor (TPS) adjustment
44	Lean oxygen sensor. Engine must run for approximately 5 minutes in closed loop mode and part throttle at road load (drive car) before this code will show
45	Rich oxygen sensor. Engine must be run for approximately 5 minutes in closed loop mode and part throttle before this code will show
44 & 45	(At same time) faulty oxygen sensor or open sensor
51	Faulty Calibration Unit (PROM) or improper PROM installation
52 & 53	"Check Engine" light OFF — Intermittent ECM problem "Check Engine" light ON — Faulty ECM (replace)
54	Faulty carburetor solenoid and/or ECM
55	Faulty oxygen sensor, open MAP sensor or ECM

Year – 1980
Model – Starfire
Engine – 2.5L (151 cid) 4 cyl
Engine Code – VIN V

ECM TROUBLE CODES

Code	Explanation
12	No tachometer or reference signal to ECM, this code will only be present while a fault exists. Code 12 will not be stored if problem is intermittent
13	Oxygen sensor circuit. The engine has to operate for about 18 minutes at part throttle before this code will show
13 & 14	(At same time) Throttle Position Sensor (TPS) adjustment
14	Shorted coolant sensor circuit. The engine has to run 2 minutes before this code will show
15	Open coolant sensor circuit. The engine has to operate for about 5 minutes at part throttle before this code will show
21	Shorted Wide Open Throttle (WOT) switch and/or open "Closed Throttle" switch circuit (when used)
21	Throttle Position Sensor (TPS) circuit (After 10 seconds and below 800 rpm)
22	Grounded "Closed Throttle" or Wide Open Throttle (WOT) switch circuit
21 & 22	(At the same time) grounded Wide Open Throttle (WOT) switch circuit
23	Open or grounded carburetor solenoid circuit
32	Barometric Pressure Sensor (BARO) output low
32 & 55	(At same time) grounded +8V, V/ref or faulty ECM
34	Manifold Absolute Pressure (MAP) sensor output high. (After 10 seconds and below 800 rpm)
43	Throttle Position Sensor (TPS) adjustment
44	Lean oxygen sensor. Engine must run for approximately 5 minutes in closed loop mode and part throttle at road load (drive car) before this code will show
45	Rich oxygen sensor. Engine must be run for approximately 5 minutes in closed loop mode and part throttle before this code will show
44 & 45	(At same time) faulty oxygen sensor or open sensor
51	Faulty Calibration Unit (PROM) or improper PROM installation
52 & 53	"Check Engine" light OFF – Intermittent ECM problem "Check Engine" light ON – Faulty ECM (replace)
54	Faulty carburetor solenoid and/or ECM
55	Faulty oxygen sensor, open MAP sensor or ECM
55	Faulty ECM

Year — 1980
Model — Starfire
Engine — 3.8L (231 cid) V6
Engine Code — VIN A

ECM TROUBLE CODES

Code	Explanation
12	No tachometer or reference signal to ECM, this code will only be present while a fault exists. Code 12 will not be stored if problem is intermittent
13	Oxygen sensor circuit. The engine has to operate for about 18 minutes at part throttle before this code will show
13 & 14	(At same time) Throttle Position Sensor (TPS) adjustment
14	Shorted coolant sensor circuit. The engine has to run 2 minutes before this code will show
15	Open coolant sensor circuit. The engine has to operate for about 5 minutes at part throttle before this code will show
21	Shorted Wide Open Throttle (WOT) switch and/or open "Closed Throttle" switch circuit (when used)
21	Throttle Position Sensor (TPS) circuit (After 10 seconds and below 800 rpm)
23	Open or grounded carburetor solenoid circuit
32	Barometric Pressure Sensor (BARO) output low
32 & 55	(At same time) grounded +8V, V/ref or faulty ECM
34	Manifold Absolute Pressure (MAP) sensor output high. (After 10 seconds and below 800 rpm)
43	Throttle Position Sensor (TPS) adjustment
44	Lean oxygen sensor. Engine must run for approximately 5 minutes in closed loop mode and part throttle at road load (drive car) before this code will show
45	Rich oxygen sensor. Engine must be run for approximately 5 minutes in closed loop mode and part throttle before this code will show
44 & 45	(At same time) faulty oxygen sensor or open sensor
51	Faulty Calibration Unit (PROM) or improper PROM installation
52 & 53	"Check Engine" light OFF — Intermittent ECM problem "Check Engine" light ON — Faulty ECM (replace)
54	Faulty carburetor solenoid and/or ECM
55	Faulty oxygen sensor, open MAP sensor or ECM

Year — 1980
Model — Toronado
Engine — 5.0L (307 cid) V8
Engine Code — VIN Y

ECM TROUBLE CODES

Code	Explanation
12	No tachometer or reference signal to ECM, this code will only be present while a fault exists. Code 12 will not be stored if problem is intermittent
13	Oxygen sensor circuit. The engine has to operate for about 18 minutes at part throttle before this code will show
13 & 14	(At same time) Throttle Position Sensor (TPS) adjustment
14	Shorted coolant sensor circuit. The engine has to run 2 minutes before this code will show
15	Open coolant sensor circuit. The engine has to operate for about 5 minutes at part throttle before this code will show
21	Shorted Wide Open Throttle (WOT) switch and/or open "Closed Throttle" switch circuit (when used)
21	Throttle Position Sensor (TPS) circuit (After 10 seconds and below 800 rpm)
23	Open or grounded carburetor solenoid circuit
32	Barometric Pressure Sensor (BARO) output low
32 & 55	(At same time) grounded +8V, V/ref or faulty ECM
34	Manifold Absolute Pressure (MAP) sensor output high. (After 10 seconds and below 800 rpm)
43	Throttle Position Sensor (TPS) adjustment
44	Lean oxygen sensor. Engine must run for approximately 5 minutes in closed loop mode and part throttle at road load (drive car) before this code will show
45	Rich oxygen sensor. Engine must be run for approximately 5 minutes in closed loop mode and part throttle before this code will show
44 & 45	(At same time) faulty oxygen sensor or open sensor
51	Faulty Calibration Unit (PROM) or improper PROM installation
52 & 53	"Check Engine" light OFF — Intermittent ECM problem "Check Engine" light ON — Faulty ECM (replace)
54	Faulty carburetor solenoid and/or ECM
55	Faulty oxygen sensor, open MAP sensor or ECM

Year – 1980
Model – Toronado
Engine – 5.7L (350 cid) V8
Engine Code – VIN R

ECM TROUBLE CODES

Code	Explanation
12	No tachometer or reference signal to ECM, this code will only be present while a fault exists. Code 12 will not be stored if problem is intermittent
13	Oxygen sensor circuit. The engine has to operate for about 18 minutes at part throttle before this code will show
13 & 14	(At same time) Throttle Position Sensor (TPS) adjustment
14	Shorted coolant sensor circuit. The engine has to run 2 minutes before this code will show
15	Open coolant sensor circuit. The engine has to operate for about 5 minutes at part throttle before this code will show
21	Shorted Wide Open Throttle (WOT) switch and/or open "Closed Throttle" switch circuit (when used)
21	Throttle Position Sensor (TPS) circuit (After 10 seconds and below 800 rpm)
23	Open or grounded carburetor solenoid circuit
32	Barometric Pressure Sensor (BARO) output low
32 & 55	(At same time) grounded +8V, V/ref or faulty ECM
34	Manifold Absolute Pressure (MAP) sensor output high. (After 10 seconds and below 800 rpm)
43	Throttle Position Sensor (TPS) adjustment
44	Lean oxygen sensor. Engine must run for approximately 5 minutes in closed loop mode and part throttle at road load (drive car) before this code will show
45	Rich oxygen sensor. Engine must be run for approximately 5 minutes in closed loop mode and part throttle before this code will show
44 & 45	(At same time) faulty oxygen sensor or open sensor
51	Faulty Calibration Unit (PROM) or improper PROM installation
52 & 53	"Check Engine" light OFF – Intermittent ECM problem "Check Engine" light ON – Faulty ECM (replace)
54	Faulty carburetor solenoid and/or ECM
55	Faulty oxygen sensor, open MAP sensor or ECM

Year – 1981
Model – Delta 88
Engine – 3.8L (231 cid) V6
Engine Code – VIN A

ECM TROUBLE CODES

Code	Explanation
12	No reference pulses to the ECM. This code is not stored in memory and will only flash while the fault is present
13	Oxygen sensor circuit—the engine must run up to 5 minutes at part throttle, under road load, before this code will set
14	Shorted coolant sensor circuit—the engine must run up to 2 minutes before this code will set
15	Open coolant sensor circuit—the engine must run up to 5 minutes before this code will set
21	Throttle position sensor circuit—the engine must run up to 25 seconds, at specified curb idle speed, before this code will set
23	Open or grounded M/C solenoid circuit
24	Vehicle Speed Sensor (VSS) circuit—the car must operate up to 5 minutes at road speed before this code will set
32	Barometric Pressure Sensor (BARO) circuit low
34	Manifold Absolute Pressure (MAP) or vacuum sensor cirucit. The engine must run up to 5 minutes at specified curb idle speed, before this code will set
35	Idle Speed Control (ISC) switch circuit shorted. (Over ½ throttle for over 2 seconds)
41	No distributor reference pulses at specified engine vacuum. This code will store
42	Electronic Spark Timing (EST) Bypass circuit grounded
43	Electronic Spark Control (ESC) retard signal for too long; causes a retard in Electronic Spark Timing (EST) signal
44	Lean oxygen sensor indication—the engine must run up to 5 minutes, in closed loop, at part throttle before this code will set
44 & 45	(At same time)—faulty oxygen sensor circuit
45	Rich system indication—the engine must run up to 5 minutes, in closed loop, at part throttle and road load before this code will set
51	Faulty calibration unit (PROM) or installation. It takes up to 30 seconds before this code will set
54	Shorted M/C solenoid circuit and/or faulty ECM
55	Grounded V ref, (terminal 21) faulty oxygen sensor or ECM

Year – 1981
Model – Delta 88
Engine – 4.3L (260 cid) V8
Engine Code – VIN 8

ECM TROUBLE CODES

Code	Explanation
12	No reference pulses to the ECM. This code is not stored in memory and will only flash while the fault is present
13	Oxygen sensor circuit – the engine must run up to 5 minutes at part throttle, under road load, before this code will set
14	Shorted coolant sensor circuit – the engine must run up to 2 minutes before this code will set
15	Open coolant sensor circuit – the engine must run up to 5 minutes before this code will set
21	Throttle position sensor circuit – the engine must run up to 25 seconds, at specified curb idle speed, before this code will set
23	Open or grounded M/C solenoid circuit
24	Vehicle Speed Sensor (VSS) circuit – the car must operate up to 5 minutes at road speed before this code will set
32	Barometric Pressure Sensor (BARO) circuit low
34	Manifold Absolute Pressure (MAP) or vacuum sensor cirucit. The engine must run up to 5 minutes at specified curb idle speed, before this code will set
35	Idle Speed Control (ISC) switch circuit shorted. (Over ½ throttle for over 2 seconds)
41	No distributor reference pulses at specified engine vacuum. This code will store
42	Electronic Spark Timing (EST) Bypass circuit grounded
43	Electronic Spark Control (ESC) retard signal for too long; causes a retard in Electronic Spark Timing (EST) signal
44	Lean oxygen sensor indication – the engine must run up to 5 minutes, in closed loop, at part throttle before this code will set
44 & 45	(At same time) – faulty oxygen sensor circuit
45	Rich system indication – the engine must run up to 5 minutes, in closed loop, at part throttle and road load before this code will set
51	Faulty calibration unit (PROM) or installation. It takes up to 30 seconds before this code will set
54	Shorted M/C solenoid circuit and/or faulty ECM
55	Grounded V ref, (terminal 21) faulty oxygen sensor or ECM

Year — 1981
Model — Ninety–Eight
Engine — 4.1L (252 cid) V6
Engine Code — VIN 4

ECM TROUBLE CODES

Code	Explanation
12	No reference pulses to the ECM. This code is not stored in memory and will only flash while the fault is present
13	Oxygen sensor circuit — the engine must run up to 5 minutes at part throttle, under road load, before this code will set
14	Shorted coolant sensor circuit — the engine must run up to 2 minutes before this code will set
15	Open coolant sensor circuit — the engine must run up to 5 minutes before this code will set
21	Throttle position sensor circuit — the engine must run up to 25 seconds, at specified curb idle speed, before this code will set
23	Open or grounded M/C solenoid circuit
24	Vehicle Speed Sensor (VSS) circuit — the car must operate up to 5 minutes at road speed before this code will set
32	Barometric Pressure Sensor (BARO) circuit low
34	Manifold Absolute Pressure (MAP) or vacuum sensor cirucit. The engine must run up to 5 minutes at specified curb idle speed, before this code will set
35	Idle Speed Control (ISC) switch circuit shorted. (Over ½ throttle for over 2 seconds)
41	No distributor reference pulses at specified engine vacuum. This code will store
42	Electronic Spark Timing (EST) Bypass circuit grounded
43	Electronic Spark Control (ESC) retard signal for too long; causes a retard in Electronic Spark Timing (EST) signal
44	Lean oxygen sensor indication — the engine must run up to 5 minutes, in closed loop, at part throttle before this code will set
44 & 45	(At same time) — faulty oxygen sensor circuit
45	Rich system indication — the engine must run up to 5 minutes, in closed loop, at part throttle and road load before this code will set
51	Faulty calibration unit (PROM) or installation. It takes up to 30 seconds before this code will set
54	Shorted M/C solenoid circuit and/or faulty ECM
55	Grounded V ref, (terminal 21) faulty oxygen sensor or ECM

Year — 1981
Model — Ninety-Eight
Engine — 5.0L (307 cid) V8
Engine Code — VIN Y

ECM TROUBLE CODES

Code	Explanation
12	No reference pulses to the ECM. This code is not stored in memory and will only flash while the fault is present
13	Oxygen sensor circuit — the engine must run up to 5 minutes at part throttle, under road load, before this code will set
14	Shorted coolant sensor circuit — the engine must run up to 2 minutes before this code will set
15	Open coolant sensor circuit — the engine must run up to 5 minutes before this code will set
21	Throttle position sensor circuit — the engine must run up to 25 seconds, at specified curb idle speed, before this code will set
23	Open or grounded M/C solenoid circuit
24	Vehicle Speed Sensor (VSS) circuit — the car must operate up to 5 minutes at road speed before this code will set
32	Barometric Pressure Sensor (BARO) circuit low
34	Manifold Absolute Pressure (MAP) or vacuum sensor cirucit. The engine must run up to 5 minutes at specified curb idle speed, before this code will set
35	Idle Speed Control (ISC) switch circuit shorted. (Over ½ throttle for over 2 seconds)
41	No distributor reference pulses at specified engine vacuum. This code will store
42	Electronic Spark Timing (EST) Bypass circuit grounded
43	Electronic Spark Control (ESC) retard signal for too long; causes a retard in Electronic Spark Timing (EST) signal
44	Lean oxygen sensor indication — the engine must run up to 5 minutes, in closed loop, at part throttle before this code will set
44 & 45	(At same time) — faulty oxygen sensor circuit
45	Rich system indication — the engine must run up to 5 minutes, in closed loop, at part throttle and road load before this code will set
51	Faulty calibration unit (PROM) or installation. It takes up to 30 seconds before this code will set
54	Shorted M/C solenoid circuit and/or faulty ECM
55	Grounded V ref, (terminal 21) faulty oxygen sensor or ECM

Year — 1981
Model — Cutlass
Engine — 3.8L (231 cid) V6
Engine Code — VIN A

ECM TROUBLE CODES

Code	Explanation
12	No reference pulses to the ECM. This code is not stored in memory and will only flash while the fault is present
13	Oxygen sensor circuit — the engine must run up to 5 minutes at part throttle, under road load, before this code will set
14	Shorted coolant sensor circuit — the engine must run up to 2 minutes before this code will set
15	Open coolant sensor circuit — the engine must run up to 5 minutes before this code will set
21	Throttle position sensor circuit — the engine must run up to 25 seconds, at specified curb idle speed, before this code will set
23	Open or grounded M/C solenoid circuit
24	Vehicle Speed Sensor (VSS) circuit — the car must operate up to 5 minutes at road speed before this code will set
32	Barometric Pressure Sensor (BARO) circuit low
34	Manifold Absolute Pressure (MAP) or vacuum sensor cirucit. The engine must run up to 5 minutes at specified curb idle speed, before this code will set
35	Idle Speed Control (ISC) switch circuit shorted. (Over ½ throttle for over 2 seconds)
41	No distributor reference pulses at specified engine vacuum. This code will store
42	Electronic Spark Timing (EST) Bypass circuit grounded
43	Electronic Spark Control (ESC) retard signal for too long; causes a retard in Electronic Spark Timing (EST) signal
44	Lean oxygen sensor indication — the engine must run up to 5 minutes, in closed loop, at part throttle before this code will set
44 & 45	(At same time) — faulty oxygen sensor circuit
45	Rich system indication — the engine must run up to 5 minutes, in closed loop, at part throttle and road load before this code will set
51	Faulty calibration unit (PROM) or installation. It takes up to 30 seconds before this code will set
54	Shorted M/C solenoid circuit and/or faulty ECM
55	Grounded V ref, (terminal 21) faulty oxygen sensor or ECM

Year — 1981
Model — Cutlass
Engine — 4.3L (260 cid) V8
Engine Code — VIN 8

ECM TROUBLE CODES

Code	Explanation
12	No reference pulses to the ECM. This code is not stored in memory and will only flash while the fault is present
13	Oxygen sensor circuit — the engine must run up to 5 minutes at part throttle, under road load, before this code will set
14	Shorted coolant sensor circuit — the engine must run up to 2 minutes before this code will set
15	Open coolant sensor circuit — the engine must run up to 5 minutes before this code will set
21	Throttle position sensor circuit — the engine must run up to 25 seconds, at specified curb idle speed, before this code will set
23	Open or grounded M/C solenoid circuit
24	Vehicle Speed Sensor (VSS) circuit — the car must operate up to 5 minutes at road speed before this code will set
32	Barometric Pressure Sensor (BARO) circuit low
34	Manifold Absolute Pressure (MAP) or vacuum sensor cirucit. The engine must run up to 5 minutes at specified curb idle speed, before this code will set
35	Idle Speed Control (ISC) switch circuit shorted. (Over ½ throttle for over 2 seconds)
41	No distributor reference pulses at specified engine vacuum. This code will store
42	Electronic Spark Timing (EST) Bypass circuit grounded
43	Electronic Spark Control (ESC) retard signal for too long; causes a retard in Electronic Spark Timing (EST) signal
44	Lean oxygen sensor indication — the engine must run up to 5 minutes, in closed loop, at part throttle before this code will set
44 & 45	(At same time) — faulty oxygen sensor circuit
45	Rich system indication — the engine must run up to 5 minutes, in closed loop, at part throttle and road load before this code will set
51	Faulty calibration unit (PROM) or installation. It takes up to 30 seconds before this code will set
54	Shorted M/C solenoid circuit and/or faulty ECM
55	Grounded V ref, (terminal 21) faulty oxygen sensor or ECM

Year — 1981
Model — Cutlass Cruiser
Engine — 5.0L (307 cid) V8
Engine Code — VIN Y

ECM TROUBLE CODES

Code	Explanation
12	No reference pulses to the ECM. This code is not stored in memory and will only flash while the fault is present
13	Oxygen sensor circuit — the engine must run up to 5 minutes at part throttle, under road load, before this code will set
14	Shorted coolant sensor circuit — the engine must run up to 2 minutes before this code will set
15	Open coolant sensor circuit — the engine must run up to 5 minutes before this code will set
21	Throttle position sensor circuit — the engine must run up to 25 seconds, at specified curb idle speed, before this code will set
23	Open or grounded M/C solenoid circuit
24	Vehicle Speed Sensor (VSS) circuit — the car must operate up to 5 minutes at road speed before this code will set
32	Barometric Pressure Sensor (BARO) circuit low
34	Manifold Absolute Pressure (MAP) or vacuum sensor cirucit. The engine must run up to 5 minutes at specified curb idle speed, before this code will set
35	Idle Speed Control (ISC) switch circuit shorted. (Over ½ throttle for over 2 seconds)
41	No distributor reference pulses at specified engine vacuum. This code will store
42	Electronic Spark Timing (EST) Bypass circuit grounded
43	Electronic Spark Control (ESC) retard signal for too long; causes a retard in Electronic Spark Timing (EST) signal
44	Lean oxygen sensor indication — the engine must run up to 5 minutes, in closed loop, at part throttle before this code will set
44 & 45	(At same time) — faulty oxygen sensor circuit
45	Rich system indication — the engine must run up to 5 minutes, in closed loop, at part throttle and road load before this code will set
51	Faulty calibration unit (PROM) or installation. It takes up to 30 seconds before this code will set
54	Shorted M/C solenoid circuit and/or faulty ECM
55	Grounded V ref, (terminal 21) faulty oxygen sensor or ECM

Year — 1981
Model — Firenza
Engine — 1.8L (111 cid) 4 cyl
Engine Code — VIN G

ECM TROUBLE CODES

Code	Explanation
12	No distributor reference signal to the ECM. This code is not stored in memory and will only flash while the fault is present. Normal code with ignition ON, engine not running
13	Oxygen sensor circuit — the engine must run up to 5 minutes at part throttle, under road load, before this code will set
14	Shorted coolant sensor circuit — the engine must run up to 5 minutes before this code will set
15	Open coolant sensor circuit — the engine must run 5 minutes before this code will set
21	Throttle Position Sensor (TPS) circuit. The engine must run up to 25 seconds, below the specified curb idle speed, before this code will set
23	M/C solenoid circuit open or grounded
24	Vehicle Speed Sensor (VSS) circuit — the vehicle must operate up to 5 minutes, at road speed, before this code will set
32	Altitude compensator circuit low
34	Vacuum sensor circuit — the engine must run up to 5 minutes, at specified curb idle, before this code will set
35	Idle Speed Control (ISC) switch circuit shorted. (Over ½ throttle for over 2 seconds)
41	No distributor reference signal to the ECM at specified engine vacuum. This code will store in memory
42	Electronic Spark Timing (EST) bypass circuit or EST circuit grounded or open
44	Lean exhaust indication — the engine must run up to 5 minutes, in closed loop, at part throttle and road load, before this code will set
44 & 55	(At the same time) — Faulty oxygen sensor circuit
45	Rich exhaust indication — the engine must run up to 5 minutes, in closed loop, at part throttle and road load, before this code will set
51	Faulty or improperly installed calibration unit (PROM). It takes up to 30 seconds before this code will set
54	Shorted M/C solenoid circuit and/or faulty ECM
55	Grounded V/ref (terminal 21), faulty oxygen sensor or ECM

Year — 1981
Model — Firenza
Engine — 2.0L (121 cid) 4 cyl
Engine Code — VIN R

ECM TROUBLE CODES

Code	Explanation
12	No distributor reference signal to the ECM. This code is not stored in memory and will only flash while the fault is present. Normal code with ignition ON, engine not running
13	Oxygen sensor circuit — the engine must run up to 5 minutes at part throttle, under road load, before this code will set
14	Shorted coolant sensor circuit — the engine must run up to 5 minutes before this code will set
15	Open coolant sensor circuit — the engine must run 5 minutes before this code will set
21	Throttle Position Sensor (TPS) circuit. The engine must run up to 25 seconds, below the specified curb idle speed, before this code will set
23	M/C solenoid circuit open or grounded
24	Vehicle Speed Sensor (VSS) circuit — the vehicle must operate up to 5 minutes, at road speed, before this code will set
32	Altitude compensator circuit low
34	Vacuum sensor circuit — the engine must run up to 5 minutes, at specified curb idle, before this code will set
35	Idle Speed Control (ISC) switch circuit shorted. (Over ½ throttle for over 2 seconds)
41	No distributor reference signal to the ECM at specified engine vacuum. This code will store in memory
42	Electronic Spark Timing (EST) bypass circuit or EST circuit grounded or open
44	Lean exhaust indication — the engine must run up to 5 minutes, in closed loop, at part throttle and road load, before this code will set
44 & 55	(At the same time) — Faulty oxygen sensor circuit
45	Rich exhaust indication — the engine must run up to 5 minutes, in closed loop, at part throttle and road load, before this code will set
51	Faulty or improperly installed calibration unit (PROM). It takes up to 30 seconds before this code will set
54	Shorted M/C solenoid circuit and/or faulty ECM
55	Grounded V/ref (terminal 21), faulty oxygen sensor or ECM

GENERAL MOTORS CORPORATION
DIAGNOSTIC CODE DATA

Year – 1981
Model – Toronado
Engine – 4.1L (252 cid) V6
Engine Code – VIN 8

ECM TROUBLE CODES

Code	Explanation
12	No reference pulses to the ECM. This code is not stored in memory and will only flash while the fault is present
13	Oxygen sensor circuit – the engine must run up to 5 minutes at part throttle, under road load, before this code will set
14	Shorted coolant sensor circuit – the engine must run up to 2 minutes before this code will set
15	Open coolant sensor circuit – the engine must run up to 5 minutes before this code will set
21	Throttle position sensor circuit – the engine must run up to 25 seconds, at specified curb idle speed, before this code will set
23	Open or grounded M/C solenoid circuit
24	Vehicle Speed Sensor (VSS) circuit – the car must operate up to 5 minutes at road speed before this code will set
32	Barometric Pressure Sensor (BARO) circuit low
34	Manifold Absolute Pressure (MAP) or vacuum sensor cirucit. The engine must run up to 5 minutes at specified curb idle speed, before this code will set
35	Idle Speed Control (ISC) switch circuit shorted. (Over ½ throttle for over 2 seconds)
41	No distributor reference pulses at specified engine vacuum. This code will store
42	Electronic Spark Timing (EST) Bypass circuit grounded
43	Electronic Spark Control (ESC) retard signal for too long; causes a retard in Electronic Spark Timing (EST) signal
44	Lean oxygen sensor indication – the engine must run up to 5 minutes, in closed loop, at part throttle before this code will set
44 & 45	(At same time) – faulty oxygen sensor circuit
45	Rich system indication – the engine must run up to 5 minutes, in closed loop, at part throttle and road load before this code will set
51	Faulty calibration unit (PROM) or installation. It takes up to 30 seconds before this code will set
54	Shorted M/C solenoid circuit and/or faulty ECM
55	Grounded V ref, (terminal 21) faulty oxygen sensor or ECM

Year – 1981
Model – Toronado
Engine – 5.0L (307 cid) V8
Engine Code – VIN Y

ECM TROUBLE CODES

Code	Explanation
12	No reference pulses to the ECM. This code is not stored in memory and will only flash while the fault is present
13	Oxygen sensor circuit—the engine must run up to 5 minutes at part throttle, under road load, before this code will set
14	Shorted coolant sensor circuit—the engine must run up to 2 minutes before this code will set
15	Open coolant sensor circuit—the engine must run up to 5 minutes before this code will set
21	Throttle position sensor circuit—the engine must run up to 25 seconds, at specified curb idle speed, before this code will set
23	Open or grounded M/C solenoid circuit
24	Vehicle Speed Sensor (VSS) circuit—the car must operate up to 5 minutes at road speed before this code will set
32	Barometric Pressure Sensor (BARO) circuit low
34	Manifold Absolute Pressure (MAP) or vacuum sensor cirucit. The engine must run up to 5 minutes at specified curb idle speed, before this code will set
35	Idle Speed Control (ISC) switch circuit shorted. (Over ½ throttle for over 2 seconds)
41	No distributor reference pulses at specified engine vacuum. This code will store
42	Electronic Spark Timing (EST) Bypass circuit grounded
43	Electronic Spark Control (ESC) retard signal for too long; causes a retard in Electronic Spark Timing (EST) signal
44	Lean oxygen sensor indication—the engine must run up to 5 minutes, in closed loop, at part throttle before this code will set
44 & 45	(At same time)—faulty oxygen sensor circuit
45	Rich system indication—the engine must run up to 5 minutes, in closed loop, at part throttle and road load before this code will set
51	Faulty calibration unit (PROM) or installation. It takes up to 30 seconds before this code will set
54	Shorted M/C solenoid circuit and/or faulty ECM
55	Grounded V ref, (terminal 21) faulty oxygen sensor or ECM

Year – 1982
Model – Delta 88
Engine – 3.8L (231 cid) V6
Engine Code – VIN A

ECM TROUBLE CODES

Code	Explanation
12	No reference pulses to the ECM. This code is not stored in memory and will only flash while the fault is present
13	Oxygen sensor circuit—the engine must run up to 5 minutes at part throttle, under road load, before this code will set
14	Shorted coolant sensor circuit—the engine must run up to 2 minutes before this code will set
15	Open coolant sensor circuit—the engine must run up to 5 minutes before this code will set
21	Throttle Position Sensor (TPS) circuit—the engine must run up to 25 seconds, at specified curb idle speed, before this code will set
23	Open or grounded M/C solenoid circuit
24	Vehicle Speed Sensor (VSS) circuit—the car must operate up to 5 minutes at road speed before this code will set
32	Barometric Pressure Sensor (BARO) circuit low
34	Manifold Absolute Pressure (MAP) or vacuum sensor circuit. The engine must run up to 5 minutes at specified curb idle speed, before this code will set
35	Idle Speed Control (ISC) switch circuit shorted. (Over ½ throttle for over 2 seconds)
41	No distributor reference pulses at specified engine vacuum. This code will store
42	Electronic Spark Timing (EST) bypass circuit grounded
43	Electronic Spark Control (ESC) retard signal for too long; causes a retard in EST signal
44	Lean oxygen sensor indication—the engine must run up to 5 minutes, in closed loop, at part throttle before this code will set
44 & 45	(At same time)—Faulty oxygen sensor circuit
45	Rich system indication—the engine must run up to 5 minutes, in closed loop, at part throttle and road load before this code will set
51	Faulty calibration unit (PROM) or installation. It takes up to 30 seconds before this code will set
54	Shorted M/C solenoid circuit and/or faulty ECM
55	Grounded V/ref, (terminal 21) faulty oxygen sensor or ECM

Year – 1982
Model – Delta 88
Engine – 4.3L (260 cid) V8
Engine Code – VIN 8

ECM TROUBLE CODES

Code	Explanation
12	No reference pulses to the ECM. This code is not stored in memory and will only flash while the fault is present
13	Oxygen sensor circuit – the engine must run up to 5 minutes at part throttle, under road load, before this code will set
14	Shorted coolant sensor circuit – the engine must run up to 2 minutes before this code will set
15	Open coolant sensor circuit – the engine must run up to 5 minutes before this code will set
21	Throttle Position Sensor (TPS) circuit – the engine must run up to 25 seconds, at specified curb idle speed, before this code will set
23	Open or grounded M/C solenoid circuit
24	Vehicle Speed Sensor (VSS) circuit – the car must operate up to 5 minutes at road speed before this code will set
32	Barometric Pressure Sensor (BARO) circuit low
34	Manifold Absolute Pressure (MAP) or vacuum sensor circuit. The engine must run up to 5 minutes at specified curb idle speed, before this code will set
35	Idle Speed Control (ISC) switch circuit shorted. (Over ½ throttle for over 2 seconds)
41	No distributor reference pulses at specified engine vacuum. This code will store
42	Electronic Spark Timing (EST) bypass circuit grounded
43	Electronic Spark Control (ESC) retard signal for too long; causes a retard in EST signal
44	Lean oxygen sensor indication – the engine must run up to 5 minutes, in closed loop, at part throttle before this code will set
44 & 45	(At same time) – Faulty oxygen sensor circuit
45	Rich system indication – the engine must run up to 5 minutes, in closed loop, at part throttle and road load before this code will set
51	Faulty calibration unit (PROM) or installation. It takes up to 30 seconds before this code will set
54	Shorted M/C solenoid circuit and/or faulty ECM
55	Grounded V/ref, (terminal 21) faulty oxygen sensor or ECM

Year – 1982
Model – Ninety–Eight
Engine – 4.1L (252 cid) V6
Engine Code – VIN 4

ECM TROUBLE CODES

Code	Explanation
12	No reference pulses to the ECM. This code is not stored in memory and will only flash while the fault is present
13	Oxygen sensor circuit – the engine must run up to 5 minutes at part throttle, under road load, before this code will set
14	Shorted coolant sensor circuit – the engine must run up to 2 minutes before this code will set
15	Open coolant sensor circuit – the engine must run up to 5 minutes before this code will set
21	Throttle Position Sensor (TPS) circuit – the engine must run up to 25 seconds, at specified curb idle speed, before this code will set
23	Open or grounded M/C solenoid circuit
24	Vehicle Speed Sensor (VSS) circuit – the car must operate up to 5 minutes at road speed before this code will set
32	Barometric Pressure Sensor (BARO) circuit low
34	Manifold Absolute Pressure (MAP) or vacuum sensor circuit. The engine must run up to 5 minutes at specified curb idle speed, before this code will set
35	Idle Speed Control (ISC) switch circuit shorted. (Over ½ throttle for over 2 seconds)
41	No distributor reference pulses at specified engine vacuum. This code will store
42	Electronic Spark Timing (EST) bypass circuit grounded
43	Electronic Spark Control (ESC) retard signal for too long; causes a retard in EST signal
44	Lean oxygen sensor indication – the engine must run up to 5 minutes, in closed loop, at part throttle before this code will set
44 & 45	(At same time) – Faulty oxygen sensor circuit
45	Rich system indication – the engine must run up to 5 minutes, in closed loop, at part throttle and road load before this code will set
51	Faulty calibration unit (PROM) or installation. It takes up to 30 seconds before this code will set
54	Shorted M/C solenoid circuit and/or faulty ECM
55	Grounded V/ref, (terminal 21) faulty oxygen sensor or ECM

Year — 1982
Model — Ninety–Eight
Engine — 5.0L (307 cid) V8
Engine Code — VIN Y

ECM TROUBLE CODES

Code	Explanation
12	No reference pulses to the ECM. This code is not stored in memory and will only flash while the fault is present
13	Oxygen sensor circuit — the engine must run up to 5 minutes at part throttle, under road load, before this code will set
14	Shorted coolant sensor circuit — the engine must run up to 2 minutes before this code will set
15	Open coolant sensor circuit — the engine must run up to 5 minutes before this code will set
21	Throttle Position Sensor (TPS) circuit — the engine must run up to 25 seconds, at specified curb idle speed, before this code will set
23	Open or grounded M/C solenoid circuit
24	Vehicle Speed Sensor (VSS) circuit — the car must operate up to 5 minutes at road speed before this code will set
32	Barometric Pressure Sensor (BARO) circuit low
34	Manifold Absolute Pressure (MAP) or vacuum sensor circuit. The engine must run up to 5 minutes at specified curb idle speed, before this code will set
35	Idle Speed Control (ISC) switch circuit shorted. (Over ½ throttle for over 2 seconds)
41	No distributor reference pulses at specified engine vacuum. This code will store
42	Electronic Spark Timing (EST) bypass circuit grounded
43	Electronic Spark Control (ESC) retard signal for too long; causes a retard in EST signal
44	Lean oxygen sensor indication — the engine must run up to 5 minutes, in closed loop, at part throttle before this code will set
44 & 45	(At same time) — Faulty oxygen sensor circuit
45	Rich system indication — the engine must run up to 5 minutes, in closed loop, at part throttle and road load before this code will set
51	Faulty calibration unit (PROM) or installation. It takes up to 30 seconds before this code will set
54	Shorted M/C solenoid circuit and/or faulty ECM
55	Grounded V/ref, (terminal 21) faulty oxygen sensor or ECM

Year – 1982
Model – Cutlass
Engine – 3.8L (231 cid) V6
Engine Code – VIN A

ECM TROUBLE CODES

Code	Explanation
12	No reference pulses to the ECM. This code is not stored in memory and will only flash while the fault is present
13	Oxygen sensor circuit – the engine must run up to 5 minutes at part throttle, under road load, before this code will set
14	Shorted coolant sensor circuit – the engine must run up to 2 minutes before this code will set
15	Open coolant sensor circuit – the engine must run up to 5 minutes before this code will set
21	Throttle Position Sensor (TPS) circuit – the engine must run up to 25 seconds, at specified curb idle speed, before this code will set
23	Open or grounded M/C solenoid circuit
24	Vehicle Speed Sensor (VSS) circuit – the car must operate up to 5 minutes at road speed before this code will set
32	Barometric Pressure Sensor (BARO) circuit low
34	Manifold Absolute Pressure (MAP) or vacuum sensor circuit. The engine must run up to 5 minutes at specified curb idle speed, before this code will set
35	Idle Speed Control (ISC) switch circuit shorted. (Over ½ throttle for over 2 seconds)
41	No distributor reference pulses at specified engine vacuum. This code will store
42	Electronic Spark Timing (EST) bypass circuit grounded
43	Electronic Spark Control (ESC) retard signal for too long; causes a retard in EST signal
44	Lean oxygen sensor indication – the engine must run up to 5 minutes, in closed loop, at part throttle before this code will set
44 & 45	(At same time) – Faulty oxygen sensor circuit
45	Rich system indication – the engine must run up to 5 minutes, in closed loop, at part throttle and road load before this code will set
51	Faulty calibration unit (PROM) or installation. It takes up to 30 seconds before this code will set
54	Shorted M/C solenoid circuit and/or faulty ECM
55	Grounded V/ref, (terminal 21) faulty oxygen sensor or ECM

Year – 1982
Model – Cutlass
Engine – 4.3L (260 cid) V8
Engine Code – VIN 8

ECM TROUBLE CODES

Code	Explanation
12	No reference pulses to the ECM. This code is not stored in memory and will only flash while the fault is present
13	Oxygen sensor circuit – the engine must run up to 5 minutes at part throttle, under road load, before this code will set
14	Shorted coolant sensor circuit – the engine must run up to 2 minutes before this code will set
15	Open coolant sensor circuit – the engine must run up to 5 minutes before this code will set
21	Throttle Position Sensor (TPS) circuit – the engine must run up to 25 seconds, at specified curb idle speed, before this code will set
23	Open or grounded M/C solenoid circuit
24	Vehicle Speed Sensor (VSS) circuit – the car must operate up to 5 minutes at road speed before this code will set
32	Barometric Pressure Sensor (BARO) circuit low
34	Manifold Absolute Pressure (MAP) or vacuum sensor circuit. The engine must run up to 5 minutes at specified curb idle speed, before this code will set
35	Idle Speed Control (ISC) switch circuit shorted. (Over ½ throttle for over 2 seconds)
41	No distributor reference pulses at specified engine vacuum. This code will store
42	Electronic Spark Timing (EST) bypass circuit grounded
43	Electronic Spark Control (ESC) retard signal for too long; causes a retard in EST signal
44	Lean oxygen sensor indication – the engine must run up to 5 minutes, in closed loop, at part throttle before this code will set
44 & 45	(At same time) – Faulty oxygen sensor circuit
45	Rich system indication – the engine must run up to 5 minutes, in closed loop, at part throttle and road load before this code will set
51	Faulty calibration unit (PROM) or installation. It takes up to 30 seconds before this code will set
54	Shorted M/C solenoid circuit and/or faulty ECM
55	Grounded V/ref, (terminal 21) faulty oxygen sensor or ECM

Year — 1982
Model — Cutlass Cruiser
Engine — 5.0L (307 cid) V8
Engine Code — VIN Y

ECM TROUBLE CODES

Code	Explanation
12	No reference pulses to the ECM. This code is not stored in memory and will only flash while the fault is present
13	Oxygen sensor circuit — the engine must run up to 5 minutes at part throttle, under road load, before this code will set
14	Shorted coolant sensor circuit — the engine must run up to 2 minutes before this code will set
15	Open coolant sensor circuit — the engine must run up to 5 minutes before this code will set
21	Throttle Position Sensor (TPS) circuit — the engine must run up to 25 seconds, at specified curb idle speed, before this code will set
23	Open or grounded M/C solenoid circuit
24	Vehicle Speed Sensor (VSS) circuit — the car must operate up to 5 minutes at road speed before this code will set
32	Barometric Pressure Sensor (BARO) circuit low
34	Manifold Absolute Pressure (MAP) or vacuum sensor circuit. The engine must run up to 5 minutes at specified curb idle speed, before this code will set
35	Idle Speed Control (ISC) switch circuit shorted. (Over ½ throttle for over 2 seconds)
41	No distributor reference pulses at specified engine vacuum. This code will store
42	Electronic Spark Timing (EST) bypass circuit grounded
43	Electronic Spark Control (ESC) retard signal for too long; causes a retard in EST signal
44	Lean oxygen sensor indication — the engine must run up to 5 minutes, in closed loop, at part throttle before this code will set
44 & 45	(At same time) — Faulty oxygen sensor circuit
45	Rich system indication — the engine must run up to 5 minutes, in closed loop, at part throttle and road load before this code will set
51	Faulty calibration unit (PROM) or installation. It takes up to 30 seconds before this code will set
54	Shorted M/C solenoid circuit and/or faulty ECM
55	Grounded V/ref, (terminal 21) faulty oxygen sensor or ECM

Year — 1982
Model — Firenza
Engine — 1.8L (111 cid) 4 cyl
Engine Code — VIN G

ECM TROUBLE CODES

Code	Explanation
12	No distributor reference pulses to the ECM. This code is not stored in memory and will only flash while the fault is present. Normal code with ignition ON ,engine not running
13	Oxygen sensor circuit — the engine must run up to 5 minutes at part throttle, under road load, before this code will set
14	Shorted coolant sensor circuit — the engine must run up to 5 minutes before this code will set
15	Open coolant sensor circuit — the engine must run up to 5 minutes before this code will set
21	Throttle Position Sensor (TPS) circuit — the engine must run up to 25 seconds, below specified curb idle speed, before this code will set
23	Open or grounded M/C solenoid circuit
24	Vehicle Speed Sensor (VSS) circuit — the car must operate up to 5 minutes at road speed before this code will set
32	Altitude compensator circuit low
34	vacuum sensor circuit — the engine must run up to 5 minutes at specified curb idle speed, before this code will set
35	Idle Speed Control (ISC) switch circuit shorted. (Over ½ throttle for over 2 seconds)
41	No distributor reference pulses to the ECM at specified engine vacuum. This code will store in memory
42	Electronic Spark Timing (EST) bypass circuit or EST circuit grounded or open
44	Lean exhaust indication — the engine must run up to 5 minutes, in closed loop, at part throttle and road load before this code will set
44 & 45	(At same time) — Faulty oxygen sensor circuit
45	Rich system indication — the engine must run up to 5 minutes, in closed loop, at part throttle and road load before this code will set
51	Faulty calibration unit (PROM) or installation. It takes up to 30 seconds before this code will set
54	Shorted M/C solenoid circuit and/or faulty ECM
55	Grounded V/ref, (terminal 21) faulty oxygen sensor or ECM

Year – 1982
Model – Firenza
Engine – 2.0L (121 cid) 4 cyl
Engine Code – VIN B

ECM TROUBLE CODES

Code	Explanation
12	No distributor reference pulses to the ECM. This code is not stored in memory and will only flash while the fault is present. Normal code with ignition ON , engine not running
13	Oxygen sensor circuit – the engine must run up to 5 minutes at part throttle, under road load, before this code will set
14	Shorted coolant sensor circuit – the engine must run up to 5 minutes before this code will set
15	Open coolant sensor circuit – the engine must run up to 5 minutes before this code will set
21	Throttle Position Sensor (TPS) circuit – the engine must run up to 25 seconds, below specified curb idle speed, before this code will set
23	Open or grounded M/C solenoid circuit
24	Vehicle Speed Sensor (VSS) circuit – the car must operate up to 5 minutes at road speed before this code will set
32	Altitude compensator circuit low
34	Vacuum sensor circuit – the engine must run up to 5 minutes at specified curb idle speed before this code will set
35	Idle Speed Control (ISC) switch circuit shorted. (Over ½ throttle for over 2 seconds)
41	No distributor reference pulses to the ECM at specified engine vacuum. This code will store in memory
42	Electronic Spark Timing (EST) bypass circuit or EST circuit grounded or open
44	Lean exhaust indication – the engine must run up to 5 minutes, in closed loop, at part throttle and road load before this code will set
44 & 45	(At same time) – Faulty oxygen sensor circuit
45	Rich system indication – the engine must run up to 5 minutes, in closed loop, at part throttle and road load before this code will set
51	Faulty calibration unit (PROM) or installation. It takes up to 30 seconds before this code will set
54	Shorted M/C solenoid circuit and/or faulty ECM
55	Grounded V/ref, (terminal 21) faulty oxygen sensor or ECM

Year – 1982
Model – Toronado
Engine – 4.1L (252 cid) V6
Engine Code – VIN 8

ECM TROUBLE CODES

Code	Explanation
12	No reference pulses to the ECM. This code is not stored in memory and will only flash while the fault is present
13	Oxygen sensor circuit – the engine must run up to 5 minutes at part throttle, under road load, before this code will set
14	Shorted coolant sensor circuit – the engine must run up to 2 minutes before this code will set
15	Open coolant sensor circuit – the engine must run up to 5 minutes before this code will set
21	Throttle Position Sensor (TPS) circuit – the engine must run up to 25 seconds, at specified curb idle speed, before this code will set
23	Open or grounded M/C solenoid circuit
24	Vehicle Speed Sensor (VSS) circuit – the car must operate up to 5 minutes at road speed before this code will set
32	Barometric Pressure Sensor (BARO) circuit low
34	Manifold Absolute Pressure (MAP) or vacuum sensor circuit. The engine must run up to 5 minutes at specified curb idle speed, before this code will set
35	Idle Speed Control (ISC) switch circuit shorted. (Over ½ throttle for over 2 seconds)
41	No distributor reference pulses at specified engine vacuum. This code will store
42	Electronic Spark Timing (EST) bypass circuit grounded
43	Electronic Spark Control (ESC) retard signal for too long; causes a retard in EST signal
44	Lean oxygen sensor indication – the engine must run up to 5 minutes, in closed loop, at part throttle before this code will set
44 & 45	(At same time) – Faulty oxygen sensor circuit
45	Rich system indication – the engine must run up to 5 minutes, in closed loop, at part throttle and road load before this code will set
51	Faulty calibration unit (PROM) or installation. It takes up to 30 seconds before this code will set
54	Shorted M/C solenoid circuit and/or faulty ECM
55	Grounded V/ref, (terminal 21) faulty oxygen sensor or ECM

Year – 1982
Model – Toronado
Engine – 5.0L (307 cid) V8
Engine Code – VIN Y

ECM TROUBLE CODES

Code	Explanation
12	No reference pulses to the ECM. This code is not stored in memory and will only flash while the fault is present
13	Oxygen sensor circuit – the engine must run up to 5 minutes at part throttle, under road load, before this code will set
14	Shorted coolant sensor circuit – the engine must run up to 2 minutes before this code will set
15	Open coolant sensor circuit – the engine must run up to 5 minutes before this code will set
21	Throttle Position Sensor (TPS) circuit – the engine must run up to 25 seconds, at specified curb idle speed, before this code will set
23	Open or grounded M/C solenoid circuit
24	Vehicle Speed Sensor (VSS) circuit – the car must operate up to 5 minutes at road speed before this code will set
32	Barometric Pressure Sensor (BARO) circuit low
34	Manifold Absolute Pressure (MAP) or vacuum sensor circuit. The engine must run up to 5 minutes at specified curb idle speed, before this code will set
35	Idle Speed Control (ISC) switch circuit shorted. (Over ½ throttle for over 2 seconds)
41	No distributor reference pulses at specified engine vacuum. This code will store
42	Electronic Spark Timing (EST) bypass circuit grounded
43	Electronic Spark Control (ESC) retard signal for too long; causes a retard in EST signal
44	Lean oxygen sensor indication – the engine must run up to 5 minutes, in closed loop, at part throttle before this code will set
44 & 45	(At same time) – Faulty oxygen sensor circuit
45	Rich system indication – the engine must run up to 5 minutes, in closed loop, at part throttle and road load before this code will set
51	Faulty calibration unit (PROM) or installation. It takes up to 30 seconds before this code will set
54	Shorted M/C solenoid circuit and/or faulty ECM
55	Grounded V/ref, (terminal 21) faulty oxygen sensor or ECM

Year – 1983
Model – Delta 88
Engine – 3.8L (231 cid) V6
Engine Code – VIN A

ECM TROUBLE CODES

Code	Explanation
12	No distributor reference pulses to the ECM. This code is not stored in memory and will only flash while the fault is present. Normal code with ignition ON ,engine not running
13	Oxygen sensor circuit – the engine must run up to 5 minutes at part throttle, under road load, before this code will set
14	Shorted coolant sensor circuit – the engine must run up to 5 minutes before this code will set
15	Open coolant sensor circuit – the engine must run up to 5 minutes before this code will set
21	Throttle Position Sensor (TPS) circuit – the engine must run up to 25 seconds, at specified curb idle speed, before this code will set
23	M/C solenoid circuit open or grounded
24	Vehicle Speed Sensor (VSS) circuit – the vehicle must operate up to 5 minutes at road speed before this code will set
32	Barometric Pressure Sensor (BARO) circuit low
34	Manifold Absolute Pressure (MAP) or vacuum sensor circuit. The engine must run up to 5 minutes at specified curb idle speed before this code will set
35	Idle Speed Control (ISC) switch circuit shorted. (Over ½ throttle for over 2 seconds)
41	No distributor reference pulses to the ECM at specified engine vacuum. This code will store in memory
42	Electronic Spark Timing (EST) bypass circuit or EST circuit grounded or open
43	Electronic Spark Control (ESC) retard signal for too long; causes a retard in EST signal
44	Lean exhaust indication – the engine must run up to 5 minutes, in closed loop, at part throttle before this code will set
45	Rich exhaust indication – the engine must run up to 5 minutes, in closed loop and at part throttle, before this code will set
51	Faulty or improperly installed calibration unit (PROM). It takes up to 30 seconds before this code will set
54	Shorted M/C solenoid circuit and/or faulty ECM
55	Grounded V/ref, (terminal 21) high voltage on oxygen sensor circuit or ECM

Year — 1983
Model — Delta 88
Engine — 5.0L (307 cid) V8
Engine Code — VIN Y

ECM TROUBLE CODES

Code	Explanation
12	No distributor reference pulses to the ECM. This code is not stored in memory and will only flash while the fault is present. Normal code with ignition ON engine not running
13	Oxygen sensor circuit — the engine must run up to 5 minutes at part throttle, under road load, before this code will set
14	Shorted coolant sensor circuit — the engine must run up to 5 minutes before this code will set
15	Open coolant sensor circuit — the engine must run up to 5 minutes before this code will set
21	Throttle Position Sensor (TPS) circuit — the engine must run up to 25 seconds, at specified curb idle speed, before this code will set
23	M/C solenoid circuit open or grounded
24	Vehicle Speed Sensor (VSS) circuit — the vehicle must operate up to 5 minutes at road speed before this code will set
32	Barometric Pressure Sensor (BARO) circuit low
34	Manifold Absolute Pressure (MAP) or vacuum sensor circuit. The engine must run up to 5 minutes at specified curb idle speed before this code will set
35	Idle Speed Control (ISC) switch circuit shorted. (Over ½ throttle for over 2 seconds)
41	No distributor reference pulses to the ECM at specified engine vacuum. This code will store in memory
42	Electronic Spark Timing (EST) bypass circuit or EST circuit grounded or open
43	Electronic Spark Control (ESC) retard signal for too long; causes a retard in EST signal
44	Lean exhaust indication — the engine must run up to 5 minutes, in closed loop, at part throttle before this code will set
45	Rich exhaust indication — the engine must run up to 5 minutes, in closed loop and at part throttle, before this code will set
51	Faulty or improperly installed calibration unit (PROM). It takes up to 30 seconds before this code will set
54	Shorted M/C solenoid circuit and/or faulty ECM
55	Grounded V/ref, (terminal 21) high voltage on oxygen sensor circuit or ECM

Year — 1983
Model — Ninety–Eight
Engine — 4.1L (252 cid) V6
Engine Code — VIN 4

ECM TROUBLE CODES

Code	Explanation
12	No distributor reference pulses to the ECM. This code is not stored in memory and will only flash while the fault is present. Normal code with ignition ON engine not running
13	Oxygen sensor circuit — the engine must run up to 5 minutes at part throttle, under road load, before this code will set
14	Shorted coolant sensor circuit — the engine must run up to 5 minutes before this code will set
15	Open coolant sensor circuit — the engine must run up to 5 minutes before this code will set
21	Throttle Position Sensor (TPS) circuit — the engine must run up to 25 seconds, at specified curb idle speed, before this code will set
23	M/C solenoid circuit open or grounded
24	Vehicle Speed Sensor (VSS) circuit — the vehicle must operate up to 5 minutes at road speed before this code will set
32	Barometric Pressure Sensor (BARO) circuit low
34	Manifold Absolute Pressure (MAP) or vacuum sensor circuit. The engine must run up to 5 minutes at specified curb idle speed before this code will set
35	Idle Speed Control (ISC) switch circuit shorted. (Over ½ throttle for over 2 seconds)
41	No distributor reference pulses to the ECM at specified engine vacuum. This code will store in memory
42	Electronic Spark Timing (EST) bypass circuit or EST circuit grounded or open
43	Electronic Spark Control (ESC) retard signal for too long; causes a retard in EST signal
44	Lean exhaust indication — the engine must run up to 5 minutes, in closed loop, at part throttle before this code will set
45	Rich exhaust indication — the engine must run up to 5 minutes, in closed loop and at part throttle, before this code will set
51	Faulty or improperly installed calibration unit (PROM). It takes up to 30 seconds before this code will set
54	Shorted M/C solenoid circuit and/or faulty ECM
55	Grounded V/ref, (terminal 21) high voltage on oxygen sensor circuit or ECM

Year – 1983
Model – Ninety-Eight
Engine – 5.0L (307 cid) V8
Engine Code – VIN Y

ECM TROUBLE CODES

Code	Explanation
12	No distributor reference pulses to the ECM. This code is not stored in memory and will only flash while the fault is present. Normal code with ignition ON engine not running
13	Oxygen sensor circuit – the engine must run up to 5 minutes at part throttle, under road load, before this code will set
14	Shorted coolant sensor circuit – the engine must run up to 5 minutes before this code will set
15	Open coolant sensor circuit – the engine must run up to 5 minutes before this code will set
21	Throttle Position Sensor (TPS) circuit – the engine must run up to 25 seconds, at specified curb idle speed, before this code will set
23	M/C solenoid circuit open or grounded
24	Vehicle Speed Sensor (VSS) circuit – the vehicle must operate up to 5 minutes at road speed before this code will set
32	Barometric Pressure Sensor (BARO) circuit low
34	Manifold Absolute Pressure (MAP) or vacuum sensor circuit. The engine must run up to 5 minutes at specified curb idle speed before this code will set
35	Idle Speed Control (ISC) switch circuit shorted. (Over ½ throttle for over 2 seconds)
41	No distributor reference pulses to the ECM at specified engine vacuum. This code will store in memory
42	Electronic Spark Timing (EST) bypass circuit or EST circuit grounded or open
43	Electronic Spark Control (ESC) retard signal for too long; causes a retard in EST signal
44	Lean exhaust indication – the engine must run up to 5 minutes, in closed loop, at part throttle before this code will set
45	Rich exhaust indication – the engine must run up to 5 minutes, in closed loop and at part throttle, before this code will set
51	Faulty or improperly installed calibration unit (PROM). It takes up to 30 seconds before this code will set
54	Shorted M/C solenoid circuit and/or faulty ECM
55	Grounded V/ref, (terminal 21) high voltage on oxygen sensor circuit or ECM

Year — 1983
Model — Cutlass Ciera
Engine — 2.5L (151 cid) EFI 4 cyl
Engine Code — VIN R

ECM TROUBLE CODES

Code	Explanation
12	No distributor reference pulses to the ECM. This code is not stored in memory and will only flash while the fault is present. Normal code with ignition ON engine not running
13	Oxygen sensor circuit — the engine must run up to 5 minutes at part throttle, under road load, before this code will set
14	Shorted coolant sensor circuit — the engine must run up to 5 minutes before this code will set
15	Open coolant sensor circuit — the engine must run up to 5 minutes before this code will set
21	Throttle Position Sensor (TPS) circuit — the engine must run up to 25 seconds, at specified curb idle speed, before this code will set
23	M/C solenoid circuit open or grounded
24	Vehicle Speed Sensor (VSS) circuit — the vehicle must operate up to 5 minutes at road speed before this code will set
32	Barometric Pressure Sensor (BARO) circuit low
34	Manifold Absolute Pressure (MAP) or vacuum sensor circuit. The engine must run up to 5 minutes at specified curb idle speed before this code will set
35	Idle Speed Control (ISC) switch circuit shorted. (Over ½ throttle for over 2 seconds)
41	No distributor reference pulses to the ECM at specified engine vacuum. This code will store in memory
42	Electronic Spark Timing (EST) bypass circuit or EST circuit grounded or open
43	Electronic Spark Control (ESC) retard signal for too long; causes a retard in EST signal
44	Lean exhaust indication — the engine must run up to 5 minutes, in closed loop, at part throttle before this code will set
45	Rich exhaust indication — the engine must run up to 5 minutes, in closed loop and at part throttle, before this code will set
51	Faulty or improperly installed calibration unit (PROM). It takes up to 30 seconds before this code will set
54	Shorted M/C solenoid circuit and/or faulty ECM
55	Grounded V/ref, (terminal 21) high voltage on oxygen sensor circuit or ECM

GENERAL MOTORS CORPORATION
DIAGNOSTIC CODE DATA

Year – 1983
Model – Cutlass Ciera
Engine – 3.0L (183 cid) V6
Engine Code – VIN E

ECM TROUBLE CODES

Code	Explanation
12	No distributor reference pulses to the ECM. This code is not stored in memory and will only flash while the fault is present. Normal code with ignition ON engine not running
13	Oxygen sensor circuit – the engine must run up to 5 minutes at part throttle, under road load, before this code will set
14	Shorted coolant sensor circuit – the engine must run up to 5 minutes before this code will set
15	Open coolant sensor circuit – the engine must run up to 5 minutes before this code will set
21	Throttle Position Sensor (TPS) circuit – the engine must run up to 25 seconds, at specified curb idle speed, before this code will set
23	M/C solenoid circuit open or grounded
24	Vehicle Speed Sensor (VSS) circuit – the vehicle must operate up to 5 minutes at road speed before this code will set
32	Barometric Pressure Sensor (BARO) circuit low
34	Manifold Absolute Pressure (MAP) or vacuum sensor circuit. The engine must run up to 5 minutes at specified curb idle speed before this code will set
35	Idle Speed Control (ISC) switch circuit shorted. (Over ½ throttle for over 2 seconds)
41	No distributor reference pulses to the ECM at specified engine vacuum. This code will store in memory
42	Electronic Spark Timing (EST) bypass circuit or EST circuit grounded or open
43	Electronic Spark Control (ESC) retard signal for too long; causes a retard in EST signal
44	Lean exhaust indication – the engine must run up to 5 minutes, in closed loop, at part throttle before this code will set
45	Rich exhaust indication – the engine must run up to 5 minutes, in closed loop and at part throttle, before this code will set
51	Faulty or improperly installed calibration unit (PROM). It takes up to 30 seconds before this code will set
54	Shorted M/C solenoid circuit and/or faulty ECM
55	Grounded V/ref, (terminal 21) high voltage on oxygen sensor circuit or ECM

Year — 1983
Model — Cutlass
Engine — 3.8L (231 cid) V6
Engine Code — VIN A

ECM TROUBLE CODES

Code	Explanation
12	No distributor reference pulses to the ECM. This code is not stored in memory and will only flash while the fault is present. Normal code with ignition ON engine not running
13	Oxygen sensor circuit — the engine must run up to 5 minutes at part throttle, under road load, before this code will set
14	Shorted coolant sensor circuit — the engine must run up to 5 minutes before this code will set
15	Open coolant sensor circuit — the engine must run up to 5 minutes before this code will set
21	Throttle Position Sensor (TPS) circuit — the engine must run up to 25 seconds, at specified curb idle speed, before this code will set
23	M/C solenoid circuit open or grounded
24	Vehicle Speed Sensor (VSS) circuit — the vehicle must operate up to 5 minutes at road speed before this code will set
32	Barometric Pressure Sensor (BARO) circuit low
34	Manifold Absolute Pressure (MAP) or vacuum sensor circuit. The engine must run up to 5 minutes at specified curb idle speed before this code will set
35	Idle Speed Control (ISC) switch circuit shorted. (Over ½ throttle for over 2 seconds)
41	No distributor reference pulses to the ECM at specified engine vacuum. This code will store in memory
42	Electronic Spark Timing (EST) bypass circuit or EST circuit grounded or open
43	Electronic Spark Control (ESC) retard signal for too long; causes a retard in EST signal
44	Lean exhaust indication — the engine must run up to 5 minutes, in closed loop, at part throttle before this code will set
45	Rich exhaust indication — the engine must run up to 5 minutes, in closed loop and at part throttle, before this code will set
51	Faulty or improperly installed calibration unit (PROM). It takes up to 30 seconds before this code will set
54	Shorted M/C solenoid circuit and/or faulty ECM
55	Grounded V/ref, (terminal 21) high voltage on oxygen sensor circuit or ECM

GENERAL MOTORS CORPORATION
DIAGNOSTIC CODE DATA

Year – 1983
Model – Cutlass
Engine – 5.0L (307 cid) V8

Engine Code – VIN Y

ECM TROUBLE CODES

Code	Explanation
12	No distributor reference pulses to the ECM. This code is not stored in memory and will only flash while the fault is present. Normal code with ignition ON engine not running
13	Oxygen sensor circuit – the engine must run up to 5 minutes at part throttle, under road load, before this code will set
14	Shorted coolant sensor circuit – the engine must run up to 5 minutes before this code will set
15	Open coolant sensor circuit – the engine must run up to 5 minutes before this code will set
21	Throttle Position Sensor (TPS) circuit – the engine must run up to 25 seconds, at specified curb idle speed, before this code will set
23	M/C solenoid circuit open or grounded
24	Vehicle Speed Sensor (VSS) circuit – the vehicle must operate up to 5 minutes at road speed before this code will set
32	Barometric Pressure Sensor (BARO) circuit low
34	Manifold Absolute Pressure (MAP) or vacuum sensor circuit. The engine must run up to 5 minutes at specified curb idle speed before this code will set
35	Idle Speed Control (ISC) switch circuit shorted. (Over ½ throttle for over 2 seconds)
41	No distributor reference pulses to the ECM at specified engine vacuum. This code will store in memory
42	Electronic Spark Timing (EST) bypass circuit or EST circuit grounded or open
43	Electronic Spark Control (ESC) retard signal for too long; causes a retard in EST signal
44	Lean exhaust indication – the engine must run up to 5 minutes, in closed loop, at part throttle before this code will set
45	Rich exhaust indication – the engine must run up to 5 minutes, in closed loop and at part throttle, before this code will set
51	Faulty or improperly installed calibration unit (PROM). It takes up to 30 seconds before this code will set
54	Shorted M/C solenoid circuit and/or faulty ECM
55	Grounded V/ref, (terminal 21) high voltage on oxygen sensor circuit or ECM

Year — 1983
Model — Omega
Engine — 2.5L (151 cid) EFI 4 cyl
Engine Code — VIN R

ECM TROUBLE CODES

Code	Explanation
12	No distributor reference pulses to the ECM. This code is not stored in memory and will only flash while the fault is present. Normal code with ignition ON engine not running
13	Oxygen sensor circuit — the engine must run up to 5 minutes at part throttle, under road load, before this code will set
14	Shorted coolant sensor circuit — the engine must run up to 5 minutes before this code will set
15	Open coolant sensor circuit — the engine must run up to 5 minutes before this code will set
21	Throttle Position Sensor (TPS) circuit — the engine must run up to 25 seconds, at specified curb idle speed, before this code will set
23	M/C solenoid circuit open or grounded
24	Vehicle Speed Sensor (VSS) circuit — the vehicle must operate up to 5 minutes at road speed before this code will set
32	Barometric Pressure Sensor (BARO) circuit low
34	Manifold Absolute Pressure (MAP) or vacuum sensor circuit. The engine must run up to 5 minutes at specified curb idle speed before this code will set
35	Idle Speed Control (ISC) switch circuit shorted. (Over ½ throttle for over 2 seconds)
41	No distributor reference pulses to the ECM at specified engine vacuum. This code will store in memory
42	Electronic Spark Timing (EST) bypass circuit or EST circuit grounded or open
43	Electronic Spark Control (ESC) retard signal for too long; causes a retard in EST signal
44	Lean exhaust indication — the engine must run up to 5 minutes, in closed loop, at part throttle before this code will set
45	Rich exhaust indication — the engine must run up to 5 minutes, in closed loop and at part throttle, before this code will set
51	Faulty or improperly installed calibration unit (PROM). It takes up to 30 seconds before this code will set
54	Shorted M/C solenoid circuit and/or faulty ECM
55	Grounded V/ref, (terminal 21) high voltage on oxygen sensor circuit or ECM

Year — 1983

Model — Omega

Engine — 2.8L (173 cid) V6

Engine Code — VIN Z

ECM TROUBLE CODES

Code	Explanation
12	No distributor reference pulses to the ECM. This code is not stored in memory and will only flash while the fault is present. Normal code with ignition ON engine not running
13	Oxygen sensor circuit — the engine must run up to 5 minutes at part throttle, under road load, before this code will set
14	Shorted coolant sensor circuit — the engine must run up to 5 minutes before this code will set
15	Open coolant sensor circuit — the engine must run up to 5 minutes before this code will set
21	Throttle Position Sensor (TPS) circuit — the engine must run up to 25 seconds, at specified curb idle speed, before this code will set
23	M/C solenoid circuit open or grounded
24	Vehicle Speed Sensor (VSS) circuit — the vehicle must operate up to 5 minutes at road speed before this code will set
32	Barometric Pressure Sensor (BARO) circuit low
34	Manifold Absolute Pressure (MAP) or vacuum sensor circuit. The engine must run up to 5 minutes at specified curb idle speed before this code will set
35	Idle Speed Control (ISC) switch circuit shorted. (Over ½ throttle for over 2 seconds)
41	No distributor reference pulses to the ECM at specified engine vacuum. This code will store in memory
42	Electronic Spark Timing (EST) bypass circuit or EST circuit grounded or open
43	Electronic Spark Control (ESC) retard signal for too long; causes a retard in EST signal
44	Lean exhaust indication — the engine must run up to 5 minutes, in closed loop, at part throttle before this code will set
45	Rich exhaust indication — the engine must run up to 5 minutes, in closed loop and at part throttle, before this code will set
51	Faulty or improperly installed calibration unit (PROM). It takes up to 30 seconds before this code will set
54	Shorted M/C solenoid circuit and/or faulty ECM
55	Grounded V/ref, (terminal 21) high voltage on oxygen sensor circuit or ECM

Year — 1983
Model — Omega
Engine — 2.8L (173 cid) V6
Engine Code — VIN X

ECM TROUBLE CODES

Code	Explanation
12	No distributor reference pulses to the ECM. This code is not stored in memory and will only flash while the fault is present. Normal code with ignition ON engine not running
13	Oxygen sensor circuit — the engine must run up to 5 minutes at part throttle, under road load, before this code will set
14	Shorted coolant sensor circuit — the engine must run up to 5 minutes before this code will set
15	Open coolant sensor circuit — the engine must run up to 5 minutes before this code will set
21	Throttle Position Sensor (TPS) circuit — the engine must run up to 25 seconds, at specified curb idle speed, before this code will set
23	M/C solenoid circuit open or grounded
24	Vehicle Speed Sensor (VSS) circuit — the vehicle must operate up to 5 minutes at road speed before this code will set
32	Barometric Pressure Sensor (BARO) circuit low
34	Manifold Absolute Pressure (MAP) or vacuum sensor circuit. The engine must run up to 5 minutes at specified curb idle speed before this code will set
35	Idle Speed Control (ISC) switch circuit shorted. (Over ½ throttle for over 2 seconds)
41	No distributor reference pulses to the ECM at specified engine vacuum. This code will store in memory
42	Electronic Spark Timing (EST) bypass circuit or EST circuit grounded or open
43	Electronic Spark Control (ESC) retard signal for too long; causes a retard in EST signal
44	Lean exhaust indication — the engine must run up to 5 minutes, in closed loop, at part throttle before this code will set
45	Rich exhaust indication — the engine must run up to 5 minutes, in closed loop and at part throttle, before this code will set
51	Faulty or improperly installed calibration unit (PROM). It takes up to 30 seconds before this code will set
54	Shorted M/C solenoid circuit and/or faulty ECM
55	Grounded V/ref, (terminal 21) high voltage on oxygen sensor circuit or ECM

Year – 1983
Model – Firenza
Engine – 2.0L (121 cid) EFI 4 cyl
Engine Code – VIN P

ECM TROUBLE CODES

Code	Explanation
12	No distributor reference pulses to the ECM. This code is not stored in memory and will only flash while the fault is present. Normal code with ignition ON engine not running
13	Oxygen sensor circuit – the engine must run up to 5 minutes at part throttle, under road load, before this code will set
14	Shorted coolant sensor circuit – the engine must run up to 5 minutes before this code will set
15	Open coolant sensor circuit – the engine must run up to 5 minutes before this code will set
21	Throttle Position Sensor (TPS) circuit – the engine must run up to 25 seconds, at specified curb idle speed, before this code will set
23	M/C solenoid circuit open or grounded
24	Vehicle Speed Sensor (VSS) circuit – the vehicle must operate up to 5 minutes at road speed before this code will set
32	Barometric Pressure Sensor (BARO) circuit low
34	Manifold Absolute Pressure (MAP) or vacuum sensor circuit. The engine must run up to 5 minutes at specified curb idle speed before this code will set
35	Idle Speed Control (ISC) switch circuit shorted. (Over ½ throttle for over 2 seconds)
41	No distributor reference pulses to the ECM at specified engine vacuum. This code will store in memory
42	Electronic Spark Timing (EST) bypass circuit or EST circuit grounded or open
43	Electronic Spark Control (ESC) retard signal for too long; causes a retard in EST signal
44	Lean exhaust indication – the engine must run up to 5 minutes, in closed loop, at part throttle before this code will set
45	Rich exhaust indication – the engine must run up to 5 minutes, in closed loop and at part throttle, before this code will set
51	Faulty or improperly installed calibration unit (PROM). It takes up to 30 seconds before this code will set
54	Shorted M/C solenoid circuit and/or faulty ECM
55	Grounded V/ref, (terminal 21) high voltage on oxygen sensor circuit or ECM

Year – 1983
Model – Toronado
Engine – 4.1L (252 cid) V6
Engine Code – VIN 4

ECM TROUBLE CODES

Code	Explanation
12	No distributor reference pulses to the ECM. This code is not stored in memory and will only flash while the fault is present. Normal code with ignition ON engine not running
13	Oxygen sensor circuit—the engine must run up to 5 minutes at part throttle, under road load, before this code will set
14	Shorted coolant sensor circuit—the engine must run up to 5 minutes before this code will set
15	Open coolant sensor circuit—the engine must run up to 5 minutes before this code will set
21	Throttle Position Sensor (TPS) circuit—the engine must run up to 25 seconds, at specified curb idle speed, before this code will set
23	M/C solenoid circuit open or grounded
24	Vehicle Speed Sensor (VSS) circuit—the vehicle must operate up to 5 minutes at road speed before this code will set
32	Barometric Pressure Sensor (BARO) circuit low
34	Manifold Absolute Pressure (MAP) or vacuum sensor circuit. The engine must run up to 5 minutes at specified curb idle speed before this code will set
35	Idle Speed Control (ISC) switch circuit shorted. (Over ½ throttle for over 2 seconds)
41	No distributor reference pulses to the ECM at specified engine vacuum. This code will store in memory
42	Electronic Spark Timing (EST) bypass circuit or EST circuit grounded or open
43	Electronic Spark Control (ESC) retard signal for too long; causes a retard in EST signal
44	Lean exhaust indication—the engine must run up to 5 minutes, in closed loop, at part throttle before this code will set
45	Rich exhaust indication—the engine must run up to 5 minutes, in closed loop and at part throttle, before this code will set
51	Faulty or improperly installed calibration unit (PROM). It takes up to 30 seconds before this code will set
54	Shorted M/C solenoid circuit and/or faulty ECM
55	Grounded V/ref, (terminal 21) high voltage on oxygen sensor circuit or ECM

Year – 1983
Model – Toronado
Engine – 5.0L (307 cid) V8
Engine Code – VIN Y

ECM TROUBLE CODES

Code	Explanation
12	No distributor reference pulses to the ECM. This code is not stored in memory and will only flash while the fault is present. Normal code with ignition ON engine not running
13	Oxygen sensor circuit – the engine must run up to 5 minutes at part throttle, under road load, before this code will set
14	Shorted coolant sensor circuit – the engine must run up to 5 minutes before this code will set
15	Open coolant sensor circuit – the engine must run up to 5 minutes before this code will set
21	Throttle Position Sensor (TPS) circuit – the engine must run up to 25 seconds, at specified curb idle speed, before this code will set
23	M/C solenoid circuit open or grounded
24	Vehicle Speed Sensor (VSS) circuit – the vehicle must operate up to 5 minutes at road speed before this code will set
32	Barometric Pressure Sensor (BARO) circuit low
34	Manifold Absolute Pressure (MAP) or vacuum sensor circuit. The engine must run up to 5 minutes at specified curb idle speed before this code will set
35	Idle Speed Control (ISC) switch circuit shorted. (Over ½ throttle for over 2 seconds)
41	No distributor reference pulses to the ECM at specified engine vacuum. This code will store in memory
42	Electronic Spark Timing (EST) bypass circuit or EST circuit grounded or open
43	Electronic Spark Control (ESC) retard signal for too long; causes a retard in EST signal
44	Lean exhaust indication – the engine must run up to 5 minutes, in closed loop, at part throttle before this code will set
45	Rich exhaust indication – the engine must run up to 5 minutes, in closed loop and at part throttle, before this code will set
51	Faulty or improperly installed calibration unit (PROM). It takes up to 30 seconds before this code will set
54	Shorted M/C solenoid circuit and/or faulty ECM
55	Grounded V/ref, (terminal 21) high voltage on oxygen sensor circuit or ECM

Year — 1984
Model — Delta 88
Engine — 3.8L (231 cid) V6
Engine Code — VIN A

ECM TROUBLE CODES

Code	Explanation
12	No distributor reference pulses to the ECM. This code is not stored in memory and will only flash while the fault is present. Normal code with ignition ON, engine not running
13	Oxygen sensor circuit
14	Coolant sensor — voltage low
15	Coolant sensor — voltage high
21	Throttle Position Sensor (TPS) — voltage high
22	Throttle Position Sensor (TPS) — voltage low
24	Vehicle Speed Sensor (VSS) — A series standard cluster or digital cluster
32	Exhaust Gas Recirculation (EGR) vacuum control
33	Mass Air Flow (MAF) sensor
34	Mass Air Flow (MAF) sensor
42	Electronic Spark Timing (EST)
43	Electronic Spark Control (ESC)
44	Lean exhaust indication
45	Rich exhaust indication
51	PROM
52	Calpak
55	ECM

Year — 1984

Model — Delta 88

Engine — 5.0L (307 cid) V8

Engine Code — VIN Y

ECM TROUBLE CODES

Code	Explanation
12	No distributor reference pulses to the ECM. This code is not stored in memory and will only flash while the fault is present. Normal code with ignition ON, engine not running
13	Oxygen sensor circuit — the engine must run up to 4 minutes at part throttle, under road load, before this code will set
14	Shorted coolant sensor circuit — the engine must run up to 2 minutes before this code will set
15	Open coolant sensor circuit — the engine must run 5 minutes before this code will set
21	Throttle Position Sensor (TPS) circuit voltage high (open circuit or misadjusted TPS). The engine must run 10 seconds, at specified curb idle speed, before this code will set
22	Throttle Position Sensor (TPS) circuit voltage low (grounded circuit or misadjusted TPS). Engine must run 20 seconds at specified curb idle speed, to set code
23	M/C solenoid circuit open or grounded
24	Vehicle Speed Sensor (VSS) circuit — the vehicle must operate up to 2 minutes at road speed before this code will set
32	Barometric Pressure Sensor (BARO) circuit low
34	Manifold Absolute Pressure (MAP) sensor or vacuum sensor circuit. The engine must run up to 2 minutes, at specified curb idle speed, before this code will set
35	Idle Speed Control (ISC) switch circuit shorted. (Up to 70% TPS value for over 5 seconds)
41	No distributor reference pulses to the ECM at specified engine vacuum. This code will store in memory
42	Electronic Spark Timing (EST) bypass circuit or EST circuit grounded or open
43	Electronic Spark Control (ESC) retard signal for too long; causes a retard in EST signal
44	Lean exhaust indication — the engine must run 2 minutes, in closed loop and at part throttle, before this code will set
45	Rich exhaust indication — the engine must run 2 minutes, in closed loop and at part throttle, before this code will set
51	Faulty or improperly installed calibration unit (PROM). It takes up to 30 seconds before this code will set
53	Exhaust Gas Recirculation (EGR) valve vacuum sensor has seen improper EGR vacuum
54	Shorted M/C solenoid circuit and/or faulty ECM

Year — 1984
Model — Ninety–Eight
Engine — 4.1L (252 cid) V6
Engine Code — VIN 4

ECM TROUBLE CODES

Code	Explanation
12	No distributor reference pulses to the ECM. This code is not stored in memory and will only flash while the fault is present. Normal code with ignition ON engine not running
13	Oxygen sensor circuit — the engine must run up to 5 minutes at part throttle, under road load, before this code will set
14	Shorted coolant sensor circuit — the engine must run up to 5 minutes before this code will set
15	Open coolant sensor circuit — the engine must run up to 5 minutes before this code will set
21	Throttle Position Sensor (TPS) circuit — the engine must run up to 25 seconds, at specified curb idle speed, before this code will set
23	M/C solenoid circuit open or grounded
24	Vehicle Speed Sensor (VSS) circuit — the vehicle must operate up to 5 minutes at road speed before this code will set
32	Barometric Pressure Sensor (BARO) circuit low
34	Manifold Absolute Pressure (MAP) or vacuum sensor circuit. The engine must run up to 5 minutes at specified curb idle speed before this code will set
35	Idle Speed Control (ISC) switch circuit shorted. (Over ½ throttle for over 2 seconds)
41	No distributor reference pulses to the ECM at specified engine vacuum. This code will store in memory
42	Electronic Spark Timing (EST) bypass circuit or EST circuit grounded or open
43	Electronic Spark Control (ESC) retard signal for too long; causes a retard in EST signal
44	Lean exhaust indication — the engine must run up to 5 minutes, in closed loop, at part throttle before this code will set
45	Rich exhaust indication — the engine must run up to 5 minutes, in closed loop and at part throttle, before this code will set
51	Faulty or improperly installed calibration unit (PROM). It takes up to 30 seconds before this code will set
54	Shorted M/C solenoid circuit and/or faulty ECM
55	Grounded V/ref, (terminal 21) high voltage on oxygen sensor circuit or ECM

Year – 1984
Model – Ninety–Eight
Engine – 5.0L (307 cid) V8
Engine Code – VIN Y

ECM TROUBLE CODES

Code	Explanation
12	No distributor reference pulses to the ECM. This code is not stored in memory and will only flash while the fault is present. Normal code with ignition ON engine not running
13	Oxygen sensor circuit—the engine must run up to 5 minutes at part throttle, under road load, before this code will set
14	Shorted coolant sensor circuit—the engine must run up to 5 minutes before this code will set
15	Open coolant sensor circuit—the engine must run up to 5 minutes before this code will set
21	Throttle Position Sensor (TPS) circuit—the engine must run up to 25 seconds, at specified curb idle speed, before this code will set
23	M/C solenoid circuit open or grounded
24	Vehicle Speed Sensor (VSS) circuit—the vehicle must operate up to 5 minutes at road speed before this code will set
32	Barometric Pressure Sensor (BARO) circuit low
34	Manifold Absolute Pressure (MAP) or vacuum sensor circuit. The engine must run up to 5 minutes at specified curb idle speed before this code will set
35	Idle Speed Control (ISC) switch circuit shorted. (Over ½ throttle for over 2 seconds)
41	No distributor reference pulses to the ECM at specified engine vacuum. This code will store in memory
42	Electronic Spark Timing (EST) bypass circuit or EST circuit grounded or open
43	Electronic Spark Control (ESC) retard signal for too long; causes a retard in EST signal
44	Lean exhaust indication—the engine must run up to 5 minutes, in closed loop, at part throttle before this code will set
45	Rich exhaust indication—the engine must run up to 5 minutes, in closed loop and at part throttle, before this code will set
51	Faulty or improperly installed calibration unit (PROM). It takes up to 30 seconds before this code will set
54	Shorted M/C solenoid circuit and/or faulty ECM
55	Grounded V/ref, (terminal 21) high voltage on oxygen sensor circuit or ECM

Year — 1984
Model — Cutlass Ciera
Engine — 2.5L (151 cid) EFI 4 cyl
Engine Code — VIN R

ECM TROUBLE CODES

Code	Explanation
12	No distributor reference pulses to the ECM. This code is not stored in memory and will only flash while the fault is present. Normal code with ignition ON, engine not running
13	Oxygen sensor circuit
14	Coolant sensor — voltage low
15	Coolant sensor — voltage high
21	Throttle Position Sensor (TPS) — voltage high
22	Throttle Position Sensor (TPS) — voltage low
24	Vehicle Speed Sensor (VSS) — Integral buffer, digital cluster or remote buffer
33	Mass Air Flow (MAF) sensor — voltage high
34	Mass Air Flow (MAF) sensor — voltage low
42	Electronic Spark Timing (EST)
44	Lean exhaust indication
45	Rich exhaust indication
51	PROM
55	ECM

Year – 1984
Model – Cutlass Ciera
Engine – 3.0L (183 cid) V6
Engine Code – VIN E

ECM TROUBLE CODES

Code	Explanation
12	No distributor reference pulses to the ECM. This code is not stored in memory and will only flash while the fault is present. Normal code with ignition ON, engine not running
13	Oxygen sensor circuit – the engine must run up to 4 minutes at part throttle, under road load, before this code will set
14	Shorted coolant sensor circuit – the engine must run up to 2 minutes before this code will set
15	Open coolant sensor circuit – the engine must run 5 minutes before this code will set
21	Throttle Position Sensor (TPS) circuit voltage high (open circuit or misadjusted TPS). The engine must run 10 seconds, at specified curb idle speed, before this code will set
22	Throttle Position Sensor (TPS) circuit voltage low (grounded circuit or misadjusted TPS). Engine must run 20 seconds at specified curb idle speed, to set code
23	M/C solenoid circuit open or grounded
24	Vehicle Speed Sensor (VSS) circuit – the vehicle must operate up to 2 minutes at road speed before this code will set
32	Barometric Pressure Sensor (BARO) circuit low
34	Manifold Absolute Pressure (MAP) sensor or vacuum sensor circuit. The engine must run up to 2 minutes, at specified curb idle speed, before this code will set
35	Idle Speed Control (ISC) switch circuit shorted. (Up to 70% TPS value for over 5 seconds)
41	No distributor reference pulses to the ECM at specified engine vacuum. This code will store in memory
42	Electronic Spark Timing (EST) bypass circuit or EST circuit grounded or open
43	Electronic Spark Control (ESC) retard signal for too long; causes a retard in EST signal
44	Lean exhaust indication – the engine must run 2 minutes, in closed loop and at part throttle, before this code will set
45	Rich exhaust indication – the engine must run 2 minutes, in closed loop and at part throttle, before this code will set
51	Faulty or improperly installed calibration unit (PROM). It takes up to 30 seconds before this code will set
53	Exhaust Gas Recirculation (EGR) valve vacuum sensor has seen improper EGR vacuum
54	Shorted M/C solenoid circuit and/or faulty ECM

Year — 1984
Model — Cutlass Ciera
Engine — 3.8L (231 cid) MPFI V6
Engine Code — VIN 3

ECM TROUBLE CODES

Code	Explanation
12	No distributor reference pulses to the ECM. This code is not stored in memory and will only flash while the fault is present. Normal code with ignition ON, engine not running
13	Oxygen sensor circuit
14	Coolant sensor — voltage low
15	Coolant sensor — voltage high
21	Throttle Position Sensor (TPS) — voltage high
22	Throttle Position Sensor (TPS) — voltage low
24	Vehicle Speed Sensor (VSS) — A series standard cluster or digital cluster
32	Exhaust Gas Recirculation (EGR) vacuum control
33	Mass Air Flow (MAF) sensor
34	Mass Air Flow (MAF) sensor
42	Electronic Spark Timing (EST)
43	Electronic Spark Control (ESC)
44	Lean exhaust indication
45	Rich exhaust indication
51	PROM
52	Calpak
55	ECM

GENERAL MOTORS CORPORATION
DIAGNOSTIC CODE DATA

Year—1984
Model—Cutlass
Engine—3.8L (231 cid) V6
Engine Code—VIN A

ECM TROUBLE CODES

Code	Explanation
12	No distributor reference pulses to the ECM. This code is not stored in memory and will only flash while the fault is present. Normal code with ignition ON, engine not running
13	Oxygen sensor circuit
14	Coolant sensor—voltage low
15	Coolant sensor—voltage high
21	Throttle Position Sensor (TPS)—voltage high
22	Throttle Position Sensor (TPS)—voltage low
24	Vehicle Speed Sensor (VSS)—A series standard cluster or digital cluster
32	Exhaust Gas Recirculation (EGR) vacuum control
33	Mass Air Flow (MAF) sensor
34	Mass Air Flow (MAF) sensor
42	Electronic Spark Timing (EST)
43	Electronic Spark Control (ESC)
44	Lean exhaust indication
45	Rich exhaust indication
51	PROM
52	Calpak
55	ECM

Year – 1984
Model – Cutlass
Engine – 5.0L (307 cid) V8
Engine Code – VIN Y

ECM TROUBLE CODES

Code	Explanation
12	No distributor reference pulses to the ECM. This code is not stored in memory and will only flash while the fault is present. Normal code with ignition ON, engine not running
13	Oxygen sensor circuit—the engine must run up to 4 minutes at part throttle, under road load, before this code will set
14	Shorted coolant sensor circuit—the engine must run 2 minutes before this code will set
15	Open coolant sensor circuit—the engine must run 5 minutes before this code will set
21	Throttle Position Sensor (TPS) circuit voltage high (open circuit or misadjusted TPS). The engine must run 10 seconds, at specified curb idle speed, before this code will set
22	Throttle Position Sensor (TPS) circuit voltage low (grounded circuit or misadjusted TPS). Engine must run 20 seconds at specified curb idle speed, to set code
23	M/C solenoid circuit open or grounded
24	Vehicle Speed Sensor (VSS) circuit—the vehicle must operate up to 2 minutes at road speed before this code will set
32	Barometric Pressure Sensor (BARO) circuit low
34	Manifold Absolute Pressure (MAP) sensor or vacuum sensor circuit. The engine must run up to 2 minutes, at specified curb idle speed, before this code will set
35	Idle Speed Control (ISC) switch circuit shorted. (Up to 70% TPS value for over 5 seconds)
41	No distributor reference pulses to the ECM at specified engine vacuum. This code will store in memory
42	Electronic Spark Timing (EST) bypass circuit or EST circuit grounded or open
43	Electronic Spark Control (ESC) retard signal for too long; causes a retard in EST signal
44	Lean exhaust indication—the engine must run 2 minutes, in closed loop and at part throttle, before this code will set
45	Rich exhaust indication—the engine must run 2 minutes, in closed loop and at part throttle, before this code will set
51	Faulty or improperly installed calibration unit (PROM). It takes up to 30 seconds before this code will set
53	Exhaust Gas Recirculation (EGR) valve vacuum sensor has seen improper EGR vacuum
54	Shorted M/C solenoid circuit and/or faulty ECM

Year – 1984
Model – Cutlass
Engine – 5.0L (307 cid) V8
Engine Code – VIN 9

ECM TROUBLE CODES

Code	Explanation
12	No distributor reference pulses to the ECM. This code is not stored in memory and will only flash while the fault is present. Normal code with ignition ON, engine not running
13	Oxygen sensor circuit – the engine must run up to 4 minutes at part throttle, under road load, before this code will set
14	Shorted coolant sensor circuit – the engine must run up to 2 minutes before this code will set
15	Open coolant sensor circuit – the engine must run 5 minutes before this code will set
21	Throttle Position Sensor (TPS) circuit voltage high (open circuit or misadjusted TPS). The engine must run 10 seconds, at specified curb idle speed, before this code will set
22	Throttle Position Sensor (TPS) circuit voltage low (grounded circuit or misadjusted TPS). Engine must run 20 seconds at specified curb idle speed, to set code
23	M/C solenoid circuit open or grounded
24	Vehicle Speed Sensor (VSS) circuit – the vehicle must operate up to 2 minutes at road speed before this code will set
32	Barometric Pressure Sensor (BARO) circuit low
34	Manifold Absolute Pressure (MAP) sensor or vacuum sensor circuit. The engine must run up to 2 minutes, at specified curb idle speed, before this code will set
35	Idle Speed Control (ISC) switch circuit shorted. (Up to 70% TPS value for over 5 seconds)
41	No distributor reference pulses to the ECM at specified engine vacuum. This code will store in memory
42	Electronic Spark Timing (EST) bypass circuit or EST circuit grounded or open
43	Electronic Spark Control (ESC) retard signal for too long; causes a retard in EST signal
44	Lean exhaust indication – the engine must run 2 minutes, in closed loop and at part throttle, before this code will set
45	Rich exhaust indication – the engine must run 2 minutes, in closed loop and at part throttle, before this code will set
51	Faulty or improperly installed calibration unit (PROM). It takes up to 30 seconds before this code will set
53	Exhaust Gas Recirculation (EGR) valve vacuum sensor has seen improper EGR vacuum
54	Shorted M/C solenoid circuit and/or faulty ECM

Year – 1984
Model – Custom Cruiser
Engine – 5.0L (307 cid) V8
Engine Code – VIN Y

ECM TROUBLE CODES

Code	Explanation
12	No distributor reference pulses to the ECM. This code is not stored in memory and will only flash while the fault is present. Normal code with ignition ON, engine not running
13	Oxygen sensor circuit – the engine must run up to 4 minutes at part throttle, under road load, before this code will set
14	Shorted coolant sensor circuit – the engine must run up to 2 minutes before this code will set
15	Open coolant sensor circuit – the engine must run 5 minutes before this code will set
21	Throttle Position Sensor (TPS) circuit voltage high (open circuit or misadjusted TPS). The engine must run 10 seconds, at specified curb idle speed, before this code will set
22	Throttle Position Sensor (TPS) circuit voltage low (grounded circuit or misadjusted TPS). Engine must run 20 seconds at specified curb idle speed, to set code
23	M/C solenoid circuit open or grounded
24	Vehicle Speed Sensor (VSS) circuit – the vehicle must operate up to 2 minutes at road speed before this code will set
32	Barometric Pressure Sensor (BARO) circuit low
34	Manifold Absolute Pressure (MAP) sensor or vacuum sensor circuit. The engine must run up to 2 minutes, at specified curb idle speed, before this code will set
35	Idle Speed Control (ISC) switch circuit shorted. (Up to 70% TPS value for over 5 seconds)
41	No distributor reference pulses to the ECM at specified engine vacuum. This code will store in memory
42	Electronic Spark Timing (EST) bypass circuit or EST circuit grounded or open
43	Electronic Spark Control (ESC) retard signal for too long; causes a retard in EST signal
44	Lean exhaust indication – the engine must run 2 minutes, in closed loop and at part throttle, before this code will set
45	Rich exhaust indication – the engine must run 2 minutes, in closed loop and at part throttle, before this code will set
51	Faulty or improperly installed calibration unit (PROM). It takes up to 30 seconds before this code will set
53	Exhaust Gas Recirculation (EGR) valve vacuum sensor has seen improper EGR vacuum
54	Shorted M/C solenoid circuit and/or faulty ECM

Year — 1984
Model — Omega
Engine — 2.5L (151 cid) EFI 4 cyl
Engine Code — VIN R

ECM TROUBLE CODES

Code	Explanation
12	No distributor reference pulses to the ECM. This code is not stored in memory and will only flash while the fault is present. Normal code with ignition ON, engine not running
13	Oxygen sensor circuit
14	Coolant sensor — voltage low
15	Coolant sensor — voltage high
21	Throttle Position Sensor (TPS) — voltage high
22	Throttle Position Sensor (TPS) — voltage low
24	Vehicle Speed Sensor (VSS)
33	Manifold Absolute Pressure (MAP) — voltage high
34	Manifold Absolute Pressure (MAP) — voltage low
42	Electronic Spark Timing (EST)
44	Lean exhaust indication
45	Rich exhaust indication
51	PROM
52	Calpak
54	Fuel pump circuit — voltage low
55	ECM

Year – 1984
Model – Omega
Engine – 2.8L (173 cid) V6
Engine Code – VIN X

ECM TROUBLE CODES

Code	Explanation
12	No distributor reference pulses to the ECM. This code is not stored in memory and will only flash while the fault is present. Normal code with ignition ON, engine not running
13	Oxygen sensor circuit – the engine must run up to 4 minutes at part throttle, under road load, before this code will set
14	Shorted coolant sensor circuit – the engine must run up to 2 minutes before this code will set
15	Open coolant sensor circuit – the engine must run 5 minutes before this code will set
21	Throttle Position Sensor (TPS) circuit voltage high (open circuit or misadjusted TPS). The engine must run 10 seconds, at specified curb idle speed, before this code will set
22	Throttle Position Sensor (TPS) circuit voltage low (grounded circuit or misadjusted TPS). Engine must run 20 seconds at specified curb idle speed, to set code
23	M/C solenoid circuit open or grounded
24	Vehicle Speed Sensor (VSS) circuit – the vehicle must operate up to 2 minutes at road speed before this code will set
32	Barometric Pressure Sensor (BARO) circuit low
34	Manifold Absolute Pressure (MAP) sensor or vacuum sensor circuit. The engine must run up to 2 minutes, at specified curb idle speed, before this code will set
35	Idle Speed Control (ISC) switch circuit shorted. (Up to 70% TPS value for over 5 seconds)
41	No distributor reference pulses to the ECM at specified engine vacuum. This code will store in memory
42	Electronic Spark Timing (EST) bypass circuit or EST circuit grounded or open
43	Electronic Spark Control (ESC) retard signal for too long; causes a retard in EST signal
44	Lean exhaust indication – the engine must run 2 minutes, in closed loop and at part throttle, before this code will set
45	Rich exhaust indication – the engine must run 2 minutes, in closed loop and at part throttle, before this code will set
51	Faulty or improperly installed calibration unit (PROM). It takes up to 30 seconds before this code will set
53	Exhaust Gas Recirculation (EGR) valve vacuum sensor has seen improper EGR vacuum
54	Shorted M/C solenoid circuit and/or faulty ECM

GENERAL MOTORS CORPORATION
DIAGNOSTIC CODE DATA

Year – 1984
Model – Omega
Engine – 2.8L (173 cid) V6
Engine Code – VIN Z

ECM TROUBLE CODES

Code	Explanation
12	No distributor reference pulses to the ECM. This code is not stored in memory and will only flash while the fault is present. Normal code with ignition ON, engine not running
13	Oxygen sensor circuit—the engine must run up to 4 minutes at part throttle, under road load, before this code will set
14	Shorted coolant sensor circuit—the engine must run up to 2 minutes before this code will set
15	Open coolant sensor circuit—the engine must run 5 minutes before this code will set
21	Throttle Position Sensor (TPS) circuit voltage high (open circuit or misadjusted TPS). The engine must run 10 seconds, at specified curb idle speed, before this code will set
22	Throttle Position Sensor (TPS) circuit voltage low (grounded circuit or misadjusted TPS). Engine must run 20 seconds at specified curb idle speed, to set code
23	M/C solenoid circuit open or grounded
24	Vehicle Speed Sensor (VSS) circuit—the vehicle must operate up to 2 minutes at road speed before this code will set
32	Barometric Pressure Sensor (BARO) circuit low
34	Manifold Absolute Pressure (MAP) sensor or vacuum sensor circuit. The engine must run up to 2 minutes, at specified curb idle speed, before this code will set
35	Idle Speed Control (ISC) switch circuit shorted. (Up to 70% TPS value for over 5 seconds)
41	No distributor reference pulses to the ECM at specified engine vacuum. This code will store in memory
42	Electronic Spark Timing (EST) bypass circuit or EST circuit grounded or open
43	Electronic Spark Control (ESC) retard signal for too long; causes a retard in EST signal
44	Lean exhaust indication—the engine must run 2 minutes, in closed loop and at part throttle, before this code will set
45	Rich exhaust indication—the engine must run 2 minutes, in closed loop and at part throttle, before this code will set
51	Faulty or improperly installed calibration unit (PROM). It takes up to 30 seconds before this code will set
53	Exhaust Gas Recirculation (EGR) valve vacuum sensor has seen improper EGR vacuum
54	Shorted M/C solenoid circuit and/or faulty ECM

Year — 1984
Model — Firenza
Engine — 1.8L (111 cid) EFI 4 cyl
Engine Code — VIN O

ECM TROUBLE CODES

Code	Explanation
12	No distributor reference pulses to the ECM. This code is not stored in memory and will only flash while the fault is present. Normal code with ignition ON, engine not running
13	Oxygen sensor circuit
14	Coolant sensor — voltage low
15	Coolant sensor — voltage high
21	Throttle Position Sensor (TPS) — voltage high
22	Throttle Position Sensor (TPS) — voltage low
24	Vehicle Speed Sensor (VSS) — Integral buffer, digital cluster or remote buffer
33	Manifold Absolute Pressure (MAP) — voltage high
34	Manifold Absolure Pressure (MAP) — voltage high
42	Electronic Spark Timing (EST)
44	Lean exhaust indication
45	Rich exhaust indication
51	PROM
55	ECM

Year – 1984
Model – Firenza
Engine – 2.0L (121 cid) EFI 4 cyl
Engine Code – VIN P

ECM TROUBLE CODES

Code	Explanation
12	No distributor reference pulses to the ECM. This code is not stored in memory and will only flash while the fault is present. Normal code with ignition ON, engine not running
13	Oxygen sensor circuit
14	Coolant sensor – voltage low
15	Coolant sensor – voltage high
21	Throttle Position Sensor (TPS) – voltage high
22	Throttle Position Sensor (TPS) – voltage low
24	Vehicle Speed Sensor (VSS) – Integral buffer, digital cluster or remote buffer
33	Manifold Absolute Pressure (MAP) – voltage high
34	Manifold Absolute Pressure (MAP) – voltage low
42	Electronic Spark Timing (EST)
44	Lean exhaust indication
45	Rich exhaust indication
51	PROM
52	Calpak
55	ECM

Year – 1984
Model – Toronado
Engine – 4.1L (252 cid) V6
Engine Code – VIN 4

ECM TROUBLE CODES

Code	Explanation
12	No distributor reference pulses to the ECM. This code is not stored in memory and will only flash while the fault is present. Normal code with ignition ON engine not running
13	Oxygen sensor circuit – the engine must run up to 5 minutes at part throttle, under road load, before this code will set
14	Shorted coolant sensor circuit – the engine must run up to 5 minutes before this code will set
15	Open coolant sensor circuit – the engine must run up to 5 minutes before this code will set
21	Throttle Position Sensor (TPS) circuit – the engine must run up to 25 seconds, at specified curb idle speed, before this code will set
23	M/C solenoid circuit open or grounded
24	Vehicle Speed Sensor (VSS) circuit – the vehicle must operate up to 5 minutes at road speed before this code will set
32	Barometric Pressure Sensor (BARO) circuit low
34	Manifold Absolute Pressure (MAP) or vacuum sensor circuit. The engine must run up to 5 minutes at specified curb idle speed before this code will set
35	Idle Speed Control (ISC) switch circuit shorted. (Over ½ throttle for over 2 seconds)
41	No distributor reference pulses to the ECM at specified engine vacuum. This code will store in memory
42	Electronic Spark Timing (EST) bypass circuit or EST circuit grounded or open
43	Electronic Spark Control (ESC) retard signal for too long; causes a retard in EST signal
44	Lean exhaust indication – the engine must run up to 5 minutes, in closed loop, at part throttle before this code will set
45	Rich exhaust indication – the engine must run up to 5 minutes, in closed loop and at part throttle, before this code will set
51	Faulty or improperly installed calibration unit (PROM). It takes up to 30 seconds before this code will set
54	Shorted M/C solenoid circuit and/or faulty ECM
55	Grounded V/ref, (terminal 21) high voltage on oxygen sensor circuit or ECM

Year — 1984
Model — Toronado
Engine — 5.0L (307 cid) V8
Engine Code — VIN Y

ECM TROUBLE CODES

Code	Explanation
12	No distributor reference pulses to the ECM. This code is not stored in memory and will only flash while the fault is present. Normal code with ignition ON, engine not running
13	Oxygen sensor circuit — the engine must run up to 4 minutes at part throttle, under road load, before this code will set
14	Shorted coolant sensor circuit — the engine must run up to 2 minutes before this code will set
15	Open coolant sensor circuit — the engine must run 5 minutes before this code will set
21	Throttle Position Sensor (TPS) circuit voltage high (open circuit or misadjusted TPS). The engine must run 10 seconds, at specified curb idle speed, before this code will set
22	Throttle Position Sensor (TPS) circuit voltage low (grounded circuit or misadjusted TPS). Engine must run 20 seconds at specified curb idle speed, to set code
23	M/C solenoid circuit open or grounded
24	Vehicle Speed Sensor (VSS) circuit — the vehicle must operate up to 2 minutes at road speed before this code will set
32	Barometric Pressure Sensor (BARO) circuit low
34	Manifold Absolute Pressure (MAP) sensor or vacuum sensor circuit. The engine must run up to 2 minutes, at specified curb idle speed, before this code will set
35	Idle Speed Control (ISC) switch circuit shorted. (Up to 70% TPS value for over 5 seconds)
41	No distributor reference pulses to the ECM at specified engine vacuum. This code will store in memory
42	Electronic Spark Timing (EST) bypass circuit or EST circuit grounded or open
43	Electronic Spark Control (ESC) retard signal for too long; causes a retard in EST signal
44	Lean exhaust indication — the engine must run 2 minutes, in closed loop and at part throttle, before this code will set
45	Rich exhaust indication — the engine must run 2 minutes, in closed loop and at part throttle, before this code will set
51	Faulty or improperly installed calibration unit (PROM). It takes up to 30 seconds before this code will set
53	Exhaust Gas Recirculation (EGR) valve vacuum sensor has seen improper EGR vacuum
54	Shorted M/C solenoid circuit and/or faulty ECM

Year — 1985
Model — Delta 88
Engine — 3.8L (231 cid) V6
Engine Code — VIN A

ECM TROUBLE CODES

Code	Explanation
12	No distributor reference pulses to the ECM. This code is not stored in memory and will only flash while the fault is present. Normal code with ignition ON, engine not running
13	Oxygen sensor circuit — the engine must run up to 4 minutes at part throttle, under road load, before this code will set
14	Shorted coolant sensor circuit — the engine must run 2 minutes before this code will set
15	Open coolant sensor circuit — the engine must run up to 5 minutes before this code will set
21	Throttle Position Sensor (TPS) circuit voltage high (open circuit or misadjusted TPS). The engine must run 10 seconds, at specified curb idle speed, before this code will set
22	Throttle Position Sensor (TPS) circuit voltage low (grounded circuit or misadjusted TPS). Engine must run 20 seconds at specified curb idle speed, to set code
23	M/C solenoid circuit open or grounded
24	Vehicle Speed Sensor (VSS) circuit — the vehicle must operate up to 2 minutes at road speed before this code will set
32	Barometric Pressure Sensor (BARO) circuit low
34	Manifold Absolute Pressure (MAP) sensor or vacuum sensor circuit. The engine must run up to 2 minutes, at specified curb idle speed, before this code will set
35	Idle Speed Control (ISC) switch circuit shorted. (Up to 70% TPS value for over 5 seconds)
41	No distributor reference pulses to the ECM at specified engine vacuum. This code will store in memory
42	Electronic Spark Timing (EST) bypass circuit or EST circuit grounded or open
43	Electronic Spark Control (ESC) retard signal for too long; causes a retard in EST signal
44	Lean exhaust indication — the engine must run 2 minutes, in closed loop and at part throttle, before this code will set
45	Rich exhaust indication — the engine must run 2 minutes, in closed loop and at part throttle, before this code will set
51	Faulty or improperly installed calibration unit (PROM). It takes up to 30 seconds before this code will set
53	Exhaust Gas Recirculation (EGR) valve vacuum sensor has seen improper EGR vacuum
54	Shorted M/C solenoid circuit and/or faulty ECM

Year – 1985
Model – Delta 88
Engine – 5.0L (307 cid) V8
Engine Code – VIN Y

ECM TROUBLE CODES

Code	Explanation
12	No distributor reference pulses to the ECM. This code is not stored in memory and will only flash while the fault is present. Normal code with ignition ON, engine not running
13	Oxygen sensor circuit – the engine must run up to 4 minutes at part throttle, under road load, before this code will set
14	Shorted coolant sensor circuit – the engine must run 2 minutes before this code will set
15	Open coolant sensor circuit – the engine must run up to 5 minutes before this code will set
21	Throttle Position Sensor (TPS) circuit voltage high (open circuit or misadjusted TPS). The engine must run 10 seconds, at specified curb idle speed, before this code will set
22	Throttle Position Sensor (TPS) circuit voltage low (grounded circuit or misadjusted TPS). Engine must run 20 seconds at specified curb idle speed, to set code
23	M/C solenoid circuit open or grounded
24	Vehicle Speed Sensor (VSS) circuit – the vehicle must operate up to 2 minutes at road speed before this code will set
32	Barometric Pressure Sensor (BARO) circuit low
34	Manifold Absolute Pressure (MAP) sensor or vacuum sensor circuit. The engine must run up to 2 minutes, at specified curb idle speed, before this code will set
35	Idle Speed Control (ISC) switch circuit shorted. (Up to 70% TPS value for over 5 seconds)
41	No distributor reference pulses to the ECM at specified engine vacuum. This code will store in memory
42	Electronic Spark Timing (EST) bypass circuit or EST circuit grounded or open
43	Electronic Spark Control (ESC) retard signal for too long; causes a retard in EST signal
44	Lean exhaust indication – the engine must run 2 minutes, in closed loop and at part throttle, before this code will set
45	Rich exhaust indication – the engine must run 2 minutes, in closed loop and at part throttle, before this code will set
51	Faulty or improperly installed calibration unit (PROM). It takes up to 30 seconds before this code will set
53	Exhaust Gas Recirculation (EGR) valve vacuum sensor has seen improper EGR vacuum
54	Shorted M/C solenoid circuit and/or faulty ECM

Year — 1985
Model — Ninety-Eight
Engine — 3.0L (183 cid) V6
Engine Code — VIN E

ECM TROUBLE CODES

Code	Explanation
12	No distributor reference pulses to the ECM. This code is not stored in memory and will only flash while the fault is present. Normal code with ignition ON, engine not running
13	Oxygen sensor circuit — the engine must run up to 4 minutes at part throttle, under road load, before this code will set
14	Shorted coolant sensor circuit — the engine must run 2 minutes before this code will set
15	Open coolant sensor circuit — the engine must run up to 5 minutes before this code will set
21	Throttle Position Sensor (TPS) circuit voltage high (open circuit or misadjusted TPS). The engine must run 10 seconds, at specified curb idle speed, before this code will set
22	Throttle Position Sensor (TPS) circuit voltage low (grounded circuit or misadjusted TPS). Engine must run 20 seconds at specified curb idle speed, to set code
23	M/C solenoid circuit open or grounded
24	Vehicle Speed Sensor (VSS) circuit — the vehicle must operate up to 2 minutes at road speed before this code will set
32	Barometric Pressure Sensor (BARO) circuit low
34	Manifold Absolute Pressure (MAP) sensor or vacuum sensor circuit. The engine must run up to 2 minutes, at specified curb idle speed, before this code will set
35	Idle Speed Control (ISC) switch circuit shorted. (Up to 70% TPS value for over 5 seconds)
41	No distributor reference pulses to the ECM at specified engine vacuum. This code will store in memory
42	Electronic Spark Timing (EST) bypass circuit or EST circuit grounded or open
43	Electronic Spark Control (ESC) retard signal for too long; causes a retard in EST signal
44	Lean exhaust indication — the engine must run 2 minutes, in closed loop and at part throttle, before this code will set
45	Rich exhaust indication — the engine must run 2 minutes, in closed loop and at part throttle, before this code will set
51	Faulty or improperly installed calibration unit (PROM). It takes up to 30 seconds before this code will set
53	Exhaust Gas Recirculation (EGR) valve vacuum sensor has seen improper EGR vacuum
54	Shorted M/C solenoid circuit and/or faulty ECM

Year – 1985
Model – Ninety–Eight
Engine – 3.8L (231 cid) MPFI V6
Engine Code – VIN 3

ECM TROUBLE CODES

Code	Explanation
12	No distributor reference pulses to the ECM. This code is not stored in memory and will only flash while the fault is present. Normal code with ignition ON, engine not running
13	Oxygen sensor circuit – the engine must run up to 4 minutes at part throttle, under road load, before this code will set
14	Shorted coolant sensor circuit – the engine must run 2 minutes before this code will set
15	Open coolant sensor circuit – the engine must run up to 5 minutes before this code will set
21	Throttle Position Sensor (TPS) circuit voltage high (open circuit or misadjusted TPS). The engine must run 10 seconds, at specified curb idle speed, before this code will set
22	Throttle Position Sensor (TPS) circuit voltage low (grounded circuit or misadjusted TPS). Engine must run 20 seconds at specified curb idle speed, to set code
23	M/C solenoid circuit open or grounded
24	Vehicle Speed Sensor (VSS) circuit – the vehicle must operate up to 2 minutes at road speed before this code will set
32	Barometric Pressure Sensor (BARO) circuit low
34	Manifold Absolute Pressure (MAP) sensor or vacuum sensor circuit. The engine must run up to 2 minutes, at specified curb idle speed, before this code will set
35	Idle Speed Control (ISC) switch circuit shorted. (Up to 70% TPS value for over 5 seconds)
41	No distributor reference pulses to the ECM at specified engine vacuum. This code will store in memory
42	Electronic Spark Timing (EST) bypass circuit or EST circuit grounded or open
43	Electronic Spark Control (ESC) retard signal for too long; causes a retard in EST signal
44	Lean exhaust indication – the engine must run 2 minutes, in closed loop and at part throttle, before this code will set
45	Rich exhaust indication – the engine must run 2 minutes, in closed loop and at part throttle, before this code will set
51	Faulty or improperly installed calibration unit (PROM). It takes up to 30 seconds before this code will set
53	Exhaust Gas Recirculation (EGR) valve vacuum sensor has seen improper EGR vacuum
54	Shorted M/C solenoid circuit and/or faulty ECM

Year – 1985
Model – Cutlass Ciera
Engine – 2.5L (151 cid) EFI 4 cyl
Engine Code – VIN R

ECM TROUBLE CODES

Code	Explanation
12	No distributor reference pulses to the ECM. This code is not stored in memory and will only flash while the fault is present. Normal code with ignition ON, engine not running
13	Oxygen sensor circuit
14	Coolant sensor – voltage low
15	Coolant sensor – voltage high
21	Throttle Position Sensor (TPS) – voltage high
22	Throttle Position Sensor (TPS) – voltage low
24	Vehicle Speed Sensor (VSS)
33	Manifold Absolute Pressure (MAP) – voltage high
34	Manifold Absolute Pressure (MAP) – voltage low
35	Idle Air Control (IAC)
42	Electronic Spark Timing (EST)
44	Lean exhaust indication
45	Rich exhaust indication
51	PROM
55	ECM

Year — 1985
Model — Cutlass Ciera
Engine — 3.0L (183 cid) V6
Engine Code — VIN E

ECM TROUBLE CODES

Code	Explanation
12	No distributor reference pulses to the ECM. This code is not stored in memory and will only flash while the fault is present. Normal code with ignition ON, engine not running
13	Oxygen sensor circuit—the engine must run up to 4 minutes at part throttle, under road load, before this code will set
14	Shorted coolant sensor circuit—the engine must run 2 minutes before this code will set
15	Open coolant sensor circuit—the engine must run up to 5 minutes before this code will set
21	Throttle Position Sensor (TPS) circuit voltage high (open circuit or misadjusted TPS). The engine must run 10 seconds, at specified curb idle speed, before this code will set
22	Throttle Position Sensor (TPS) circuit voltage low (grounded circuit or misadjusted TPS). Engine must run 20 seconds at specified curb idle speed, to set code
23	M/C solenoid circuit open or grounded
24	Vehicle Speed Sensor (VSS) circuit—the vehicle must operate up to 2 minutes at road speed before this code will set
32	Barometric Pressure Sensor (BARO) circuit low
34	Manifold Absolute Pressure (MAP) or vacuum sensor circuit. The engine must run up to 2 minutes at specified curb idle speed, before this code will set
35	Idle Speed Control (ISC) switch circuit shorted. (Up to 70% TPS for over 5 seconds)
41	No distributor reference pulses to the ECM at specified engine vacuum. This code will store in memory
42	Electronic Spark Timing (EST) bypass circuit or EST circuit grounded or open
43	Electronic Spark Control (ESC) retard signal for too long; causes a retard in EST signal
44	Lean exhaust indication—the engine must run 2 minutes, in closed loop and at part throttle, before this code will set
45	Rich exhaust indication—the engine must run 2 minutes, in closed loop and at part throttle, before this code will set
51	Faulty or improperly installed calibration unit (PROM). It takes up to 30 seconds before this code will set
53	Exhaust Gas Recirculation (EGR) valve vacuum sensor has seen improper EGR vacuum
54	Shorted M/C solenoid circuit and/or faulty ECM

Year—1985
Model—Cutlass Ciera
Engine—3.8L (231 cid) MPFI V6
Engine Code—VIN 3

ECM TROUBLE CODES

Code	Explanation
12	No distributor reference pulses to the ECM. This code is not stored in memory and will only flash while the fault is present. Normal code with ignition ON, engine not running
13	Oxygen sensor circuit
14	Coolant sensor—voltage low
15	Coolant sensor—voltage high
21	Throttle Position Sensor (TPS)—voltage high
22	Throttle Position Sensor (TPS)—voltage low
24	Vehicle Speed Sensor (VSS)—A series standard cluster or digital cluster,C series digital cluster
32	Exhaust Gas Recirculation (EGR) vacuum control
33	Mass Air Flow (MAF) sensor—high output
34	Mass Air Flow (MAF) sensor—low output
42	Electronic Spark Timing (EST)
43	Electronic Spark Control (ESC)
44	Lean exhaust indication
45	Rich exhaust indication
51	PROM
52	Calpak
55	ECM

Year — 1985
Model — Calais
Engine — 3.0L (183 cid) MPFI V6
Engine Code — VIN L

ECM TROUBLE CODES

Code	Explanation
12	No distributor reference pulses to the ECM. This code is not stored in memory and will only flash while the fault is present. Normal code with ignition ON, engine not running
13	Oxygen sensor circuit
14	Coolant sensor — voltage low
15	Coolant sensor — voltage high
21	Throttle Position Sensor (TPS) — voltage high
22	Throttle Position Sensor (TPS) — voltage low
23	Air Temperature Sensor (ATS) — signal high
24	Vehicle Speed Sensor (VSS)
25	Air Temperature Sensor (ATS) — signal low
32	Exhaust Gas Recirculation (EGR) vacuum control
33	Mass Air Flow (MAF) sensor — high output
34	Mass Air Flow (MAF) sensor — low output
42	C^3I Ignition
43	Electronic Spark Control (ESC)
44	Lean exhaust indication
45	Rich exhaust indication
51	PROM
52	Calpak
55	ECM
52	Calpak

Year – 1985
Model – Calais
Engine – 2.5L (151 cid) EFI 4 cyl
Engine Code – VIN U

ECM TROUBLE CODES

Code	Explanation
12	No distributor reference pulses to the ECM. This code is not stored in memory and will only flash while the fault is present. Normal code with ignition ON, engine not running
13	Oxygen sensor circuit
14	Coolant sensor – voltage low
15	Coolant sensor – voltage high
21	Throttle Position Sensor (TPS) – voltage high
22	Throttle Position Sensor (TPS) – voltage low
24	Vehicle Speed Sensor (VSS)
33	Manifold Absolute Pressure (MAP) – voltage high
34	Manifold Absolute Pressure (MAP) – voltage low
35	Idle Air Control (IAC)
42	Electronic Spark Timing (EST)
43	Electronic Spark Control (ESC)
44	Lean exhaust indication
45	Rich exhaust indication
51	PROM
52	Calpak
55	ECM

Year – 1985
Model – Cutlass
Engine – 3.8L (231 cid) V6
Engine Code – VIN A

ECM TROUBLE CODES

Code	Explanation
12	No distributor reference pulses to the ECM. This code is not stored in memory and will only flash while the fault is present. Normal code with ignition ON, engine not running
13	Oxygen sensor circuit – the engine must run up to 4 minutes at part throttle, under road load, before this code will set
14	Shorted coolant sensor circuit – the engine must run 2 minutes before this code will set
15	Open coolant sensor circuit – the engine must run up to 5 minutes before this code will set
21	Throttle Position Sensor (TPS) circuit voltage high (open circuit or misadjusted TPS). The engine must run 10 seconds, at specified curb idle speed, before this code will set
22	Throttle Position Sensor (TPS) circuit voltage low (grounded circuit or misadjusted TPS). Engine must run 20 seconds at specified curb idle speed, to set code
23	M/C solenoid circuit open or grounded
24	Vehicle Speed Sensor (VSS) circuit – the vehicle must operate up to 2 minutes at road speed before this code will set
32	Barometric Pressure Sensor (BARO) circuit low
34	Manifold Absolute Pressure (MAP) sensor or vacuum sensor circuit. The engine must run up to 2 minutes, at specified curb idle speed, before this code will set
35	Idle Speed Control (ISC) switch circuit shorted. (Up to 70% TPS value for over 5 seconds)
41	No distributor reference pulses to the ECM at specified engine vacuum. This code will store in memory
42	Electronic Spark Timing (EST) bypass circuit or EST circuit grounded or open
43	Electronic Spark Control (ESC) retard signal for too long; causes a retard in EST signal
44	Lean exhaust indication – the engine must run 2 minutes, in closed loop and at part throttle, before this code will set
45	Rich exhaust indication – the engine must run 2 minutes, in closed loop and at part throttle, before this code will set
51	Faulty or improperly installed calibration unit (PROM). It takes up to 30 seconds before this code will set
53	Exhaust Gas Recirculation (EGR) valve vacuum sensor has seen improper EGR vacuum
54	Shorted M/C solenoid circuit and/or faulty ECM

Year – 1985
Model – Cutlass Salon
Engine – 5.0L (307 cid) V8
Engine Code – VIN 9

ECM TROUBLE CODES

Code	Explanation
12	No distributor reference pulses to the ECM. This code is not stored in memory and will only flash while the fault is present. Normal code with ignition ON, engine not running
13	Oxygen sensor circuit – the engine must run up to 4 minutes at part throttle, under road load, before this code will set
14	Shorted coolant sensor circuit – the engine must run 2 minutes before this code will set
15	Open coolant sensor circuit – the engine must run up to 5 minutes before this code will set
21	Throttle Position Sensor (TPS) circuit voltage high (open circuit or misadjusted TPS). The engine must run 10 seconds, at specified curb idle speed, before this code will set
22	Throttle Position Sensor (TPS) circuit voltage low (grounded circuit or misadjusted TPS). Engine must run 20 seconds at specified curb idle speed, to set code
23	M/C solenoid circuit open or grounded
24	Vehicle Speed Sensor (VSS) circuit – the vehicle must operate up to 2 minutes at road speed before this code will set
32	Barometric Pressure Sensor (BARO) circuit low
34	Manifold Absolute Pressure (MAP) sensor or vacuum sensor circuit. The engine must run up to 2 minutes, at specified curb idle speed, before this code will set
35	Idle Speed Control (ISC) switch circuit shorted. (Up to 70% TPS value for over 5 seconds)
41	No distributor reference pulses to the ECM at specified engine vacuum. This code will store in memory
42	Electronic Spark Timing (EST) bypass circuit or EST circuit grounded or open
43	Electronic Spark Control (ESC) retard signal for too long; causes a retard in EST signal
44	Lean exhaust indication – the engine must run 2 minutes, in closed loop and at part throttle, before this code will set
45	Rich exhaust indication – the engine must run 2 minutes, in closed loop and at part throttle, before this code will set
51	Faulty or improperly installed calibration unit (PROM). It takes up to 30 seconds before this code will set
53	Exhaust Gas Recirculation (EGR) valve vacuum sensor has seen improper EGR vacuum
54	Shorted M/C solenoid circuit and/or faulty ECM

GENERAL MOTORS CORPORATION
DIAGNOSTIC CODE DATA

Year – 1985
Model – Cutlass
Engine – 5.0L (307 cid) V8
Engine Code – VIN Y

ECM TROUBLE CODES

Code	Explanation
12	No distributor reference pulses to the ECM. This code is not stored in memory and will only flash while the fault is present. Normal code with ignition ON, engine not running
13	Oxygen sensor circuit – the engine must run up to 4 minutes at part throttle, under road load, before this code will set
14	Shorted coolant sensor circuit – the engine must run 2 minutes before this code will set
15	Open coolant sensor circuit – the engine must run up to 5 minutes before this code will set
21	Throttle Position Sensor (TPS) circuit voltage high (open circuit or misadjusted TPS). The engine must run 10 seconds, at specified curb idle speed, before this code will set
22	Throttle Position Sensor (TPS) circuit voltage low (grounded circuit or misadjusted TPS). Engine must run 20 seconds at specified curb idle speed, to set code
23	M/C solenoid circuit open or grounded
24	Vehicle Speed Sensor (VSS) circuit – the vehicle must operate up to 2 minutes at road speed before this code will set
32	Barometric Pressure Sensor (BARO) circuit low
34	Manifold Absolute Pressure (MAP) sensor or vacuum sensor circuit. The engine must run up to 2 minutes, at specified curb idle speed, before this code will set
35	Idle Speed Control (ISC) switch circuit shorted. (Up to 70% TPS value for over 5 seconds)
41	No distributor reference pulses to the ECM at specified engine vacuum. This code will store in memory
42	Electronic Spark Timing (EST) bypass circuit or EST circuit grounded or open
43	Electronic Spark Control (ESC) retard signal for too long; causes a retard in EST signal
44	Lean exhaust indication – the engine must run 2 minutes, in closed loop and at part throttle, before this code will set
45	Rich exhaust indication – the engine must run 2 minutes, in closed loop and at part throttle, before this code will set
51	Faulty or improperly installed calibration unit (PROM). It takes up to 30 seconds before this code will set
53	Exhaust Gas Recirculation (EGR) valve vacuum sensor has seen improper EGR vacuum
54	Shorted M/C solenoid circuit and/or faulty ECM

Year — 1985
Model — Custom Cruiser
Engine — 5.0L (307 cid) V8
Engine Code — VIN Y

ECM TROUBLE CODES

Code	Explanation
12	No distributor reference pulses to the ECM. This code is not stored in memory and will only flash while the fault is present. Normal code with ignition ON, engine not running
13	Oxygen sensor circuit — the engine must run up to 4 minutes at part throttle, under road load, before this code will set
14	Shorted coolant sensor circuit — the engine must run 2 minutes before this code will set
15	Open coolant sensor circuit — the engine must run up to 5 minutes before this code will set
21	Throttle Position Sensor (TPS) circuit voltage high (open circuit or misadjusted TPS). The engine must run 10 seconds, at specified curb idle speed, before this code will set
22	Throttle Position Sensor (TPS) circuit voltage low (grounded circuit or misadjusted TPS). Engine must run 20 seconds at specified curb idle speed, to set code
23	M/C solenoid circuit open or grounded
24	Vehicle Speed Sensor (VSS) circuit — the vehicle must operate up to 2 minutes at road speed before this code will set
32	Barometric Pressure Sensor (BARO) circuit low
34	Manifold Absolute Pressure (MAP) sensor or vacuum sensor circuit. The engine must run up to 2 minutes, at specified curb idle speed, before this code will set
35	Idle Speed Control (ISC) switch circuit shorted. (Up to 70% TPS value for over 5 seconds)
41	No distributor reference pulses to the ECM at specified engine vacuum. This code will store in memory
42	Electronic Spark Timing (EST) bypass circuit or EST circuit grounded or open
43	Electronic Spark Control (ESC) retard signal for too long; causes a retard in EST signal
44	Lean exhaust indication — the engine must run 2 minutes, in closed loop and at part throttle, before this code will set
45	Rich exhaust indication — the engine must run 2 minutes, in closed loop and at part throttle, before this code will set
51	Faulty or improperly installed calibration unit (PROM). It takes up to 30 seconds before this code will set
53	Exhaust Gas Recirculation (EGR) valve vacuum sensor has seen improper EGR vacuum
54	Shorted M/C solenoid circuit and/or faulty ECM

Year — 1985
Model — Firenza
Engine — 1.8L (111 cid) EFI 4 cyl
Engine Code — VIN O

ECM TROUBLE CODES

Code	Explanation
12	No distributor reference pulses to the ECM. This code is not stored in memory and will only flash while the fault is present. Normal code with ignition ON, engine not running
13	Oxygen sensor circuit
14	Coolant sensor — voltage low
15	Coolant sensor — voltage high
21	Throttle Position Sensor (TPS) — voltage high
22	Throttle Position Sensor (TPS) — voltage low
24	Vehicle Speed Sensor (VSS)
33	Manifold Absolute Pressure (MAP) — voltage high
34	Manifold Absolute Pressure (MAP) — voltage low
35	Idle Air Control (IAC)
42	Electronic Spark Timing (EST)
44	Lean exhaust indication
45	Rich exhaust indication
51	PROM
55	ECM

Year — 1985
Model — Firenza
Engine — 2.0L (121 cid) EFI 4 cyl
Engine Code — VIN P

ECM TROUBLE CODES

Code	Explanation
12	No distributor reference pulses to the ECM. This code is not stored in memory and will only flash while the fault is present. Normal code with ignition ON, engine not running
13	Oxygen sensor circuit
14	Coolant sensor — voltage low
15	Coolant sensor — voltage high
21	Throttle Position Sensor (TPS) — voltage high
22	Throttle Position Sensor (TPS) — voltage low
24	Vehicle Speed Sensor (VSS)
33	Manifold Absolute Pressure (MAP) — voltage high
34	Manifold Absolute Pressure (MAP) — voltage low
42	Electronic Spark Timing (EST)
44	Lean exhaust indication
45	Rich exhaust indication
51	PROM
52	Calpak
54	Fuel pump circuit — voltage low
55	ECM

Year — 1985
Model — Firenza
Engine — 2.8L (173 cid) MPFI V6
Engine Code — VIN W

ECM TROUBLE CODES

Code	Explanation
12	No distributor reference pulses to the ECM. This code is not stored in memory and will only flash while the fault is present. Normal code with ignition ON, engine not running
13	Oxygen sensor circuit
14	Coolant sensor — voltage low
15	Coolant sensor — voltage high
21	Throttle Position Sensor (TPS) — voltage high
22	Throttle Position Sensor (TPS) — voltage low
23	Manifold Air Temperature (MAT) sensor
24	Vehicle Speed Sensor (VSS)
25	Manifold Air Temperature (MAT) sensor
32	Exhaust Gas Recirculation (EGR) vacuum control
34	Mass Air Flow (MAF) sensor
41	Cylinder select error
42	Electronic Spark Timing (EST)
44	Lean exhaust indication
45	Rich exhaust indication
51	PROM
52	Calpak
53	System over voltage
54	Fuel pump voltage low
55	ECM

Year — 1985
Model — Toronado
Engine — 5.0L (307 cid) V8
Engine Code — VIN Y

ECM TROUBLE CODES

Code	Explanation
12	No distributor reference pulses to the ECM. This code is not stored in memory and will only flash while the fault is present. Normal code with ignition ON, engine not running
13	Oxygen sensor circuit — the engine must run up to 4 minutes at part throttle, under road load, before this code will set
14	Shorted coolant sensor circuit — the engine must run 2 minutes before this code will set
15	Open coolant sensor circuit — the engine must run up to 5 minutes before this code will set
21	Throttle Position Sensor (TPS) circuit voltage high (open circuit or misadjusted TPS). The engine must run 10 seconds, at specified curb idle speed, before this code will set
22	Throttle Position Sensor (TPS) circuit voltage low (grounded circuit or misadjusted TPS). Engine must run 20 seconds at specified curb idle speed, to set code
23	M/C solenoid circuit open or grounded
24	Vehicle Speed Sensor (VSS) circuit — the vehicle must operate up to 2 minutes at road speed before this code will set
32	Barometric Pressure Sensor (BARO) circuit low
34	Manifold Absolute Pressure (MAP) sensor or vacuum sensor circuit. The engine must run up to 2 minutes, at specified curb idle speed, before this code will set
35	Idle Speed Control (ISC) switch circuit shorted. (Up to 70% TPS value for over 5 seconds)
41	No distributor reference pulses to the ECM at specified engine vacuum. This code will store in memory
42	Electronic Spark Timing (EST) bypass circuit or EST circuit grounded or open
43	Electronic Spark Control (ESC) retard signal for too long; causes a retard in EST signal
44	Lean exhaust indication — the engine must run 2 minutes, in closed loop and at part throttle, before this code will set
45	Rich exhaust indication — the engine must run 2 minutes, in closed loop and at part throttle, before this code will set
51	Faulty or improperly installed calibration unit (PROM). It takes up to 30 seconds before this code will set
53	Exhaust Gas Recirculation (EGR) valve vacuum sensor has seen improper EGR vacuum
54	Shorted M/C solenoid circuit and/or faulty ECM

Year – 1986
Model – Delta 88
Engine – 3.0L (183 cid) MPFI V6
Engine Code – VIN L

ECM TROUBLE CODES

Code	Explanation
12	No distributor reference pulses to the ECM. This code is not stored in memory and will only flash while the fault is present. Normal code with ignition ON, engine not running
13	Oxygen sensor circuit
14	Coolant sensor – voltage low
15	Coolant sensor – voltage high
21	Throttle Position Sensor (TPS) – voltage high
22	Throttle Position Sensor (TPS) – voltage low
23	Manifold Air Temperature (MAT) sensor
24	Vehicle Speed Sensor (VSS)
25	Manifold Air Temperature (MAT) sensor
32	Exhaust Gas Recirculation (EGR) system failure
33	Mass Air Flow (MAF) sensor – voltage high
34	Mass Air Flow (MAF) sensor – voltage low
42	Electronic Spark Timing (EST)
43	Electronic Spark Control (ESC)
44	Lean exhaust indication
45	Rich exhaust indication
51	PROM, Mem–Cal
52	Calpak (missing)
55	ECM

Year — 1986
Model — Delta 88
Engine — 3.8L (231 cid) SFI V6
Engine Code — VIN B

ECM TROUBLE CODES

Code	Explanation
12	No distributor reference pulses to the ECM. This code is not stored in memory and will only flash while the fault is present. Normal code with ignition ON, engine not running
13	Oxygen sensor circuit
14	Coolant sensor — voltage low
15	Coolant sensor — voltage high
21	Throttle Position Sensor (TPS) — voltage high
22	Throttle Position Sensor (TPS) — voltage low
23	Manifold Air Temperature (MAT) sensor
24	Vehicle Speed Sensor (VSS)
25	Manifold Air Temperature (MAT) sensor
32	Exhaust Gas Recirculation (EGR) vacuum control
33	Mass Air Flow (MAF) sensor — voltage high
34	Mass Air Flow (MAF) sensor — voltage low
41	C^3I Ignition Cam sensor signal
42	C^3I Ignition
43	Electronic Spark Control (ESC)
44	Lean exhaust indication
45	Rich exhaust indication
51	PROM
52	Calpak (missing)
55	ECM

Year — 1986
Model — Delta 88
Engine — 3.8L (231 cid) SFI V6
Engine Code — VIN 3

ECM TROUBLE CODES

Code	Explanation
12	No distributor reference pulses to the ECM. This code is not stored in memory and will only flash while the fault is present. Normal code with ignition ON, engine not running
13	Oxygen sensor circuit
14	Coolant sensor — voltage low
15	Coolant sensor — voltage high
21	Throttle Position Sensor (TPS) — voltage high
22	Throttle Position Sensor (TPS) — voltage low
23	Manifold Air Temperature (MAT) sensor
24	Vehicle Speed Sensor (VSS)
25	Manifold Air Temperature (MAT) sensor
32	Exhaust Gas Recirculation (EGR) vacuum control
33	Mass Air Flow (MAF) sensor — voltage high
34	Mass Air Flow (MAF) sensor — voltage low
41	C^3I Ignition Cam sensor signal
42	C^3I Ignition
43	Electronic Spark Control (ESC)
44	Lean exhaust indication
45	Rich exhaust indication
51	PROM
52	Calpak
55	ECM

Year — 1986
Model — Ninety — Eight
Engine — 3.8L (231 cid) SFI V6
Engine Code — VIN 3

ECM TROUBLE CODES

Code	Explanation
12	No distributor reference pulses to the ECM. This code is not stored in memory and will only flash while the fault is present. Normal code with ignition ON, engine not running
13	Oxygen sensor circuit
14	Coolant sensor — voltage low
15	Coolant sensor — voltage high
21	Throttle Position Sensor (TPS) — voltage high
22	Throttle Position Sensor (TPS) — voltage low
23	Manifold Air Temperature (MAT) sensor
24	Vehicle Speed Sensor (VSS)
25	Manifold Air Temperature (MAT) sensor
32	Exhaust Gas Recirculation (EGR) vacuum control
33	Mass Air Flow (MAF) sensor — voltage high
34	Mass Air Flow (MAF) sensor — voltage low
41	C^{3}I Ignition Cam sensor signal
42	C^{3}I Ignition
43	Electronic Spark Control (ESC)
44	Lean exhaust indication
45	Rich exhaust indication
51	PROM
52	Calpak (missing)
55	ECM

Year – 1986
Model – Cutlass Ciera
Engine – 2.8L (173 cid) V6
Engine Code – VIN X

ECM TROUBLE CODES

Code	Explanation
12	No distributor reference signal to the ECM. This code is not stored in memory and will only flash while the fault is present. This is a normal code with ignition ON, engine not running
13	Oxygen sensor circuit – the engine must run up to 2 minutes at part throttle, under road load, before this code will set
14	Shorted coolant sensor circuit – the engine must run 2 minutes before this code will set
15	Open coolant sensor circuit – the engine must run 5 minutes before this code will set
21	Throttle Position Sensor (TPS) circuit voltage high (open circuit or misadjusted TPS). The engine must run 10 seconds, at specified curb idle speed, before this code will set
23	M/C solenoid circuit open or grounded
24	Vehicle Speed Sensor (VSS) circuit – the vehicle must operate up to 2 minutes, at road speed, before this code will set
32	Barometric Pressure Sensor (BARO) circuit low
34	Manifold Absolute Pressure (MAP) sensor or vacuum sensor circuit. The engine must run up to 2 minutes, at specified curb idle speed, before this code will set
41	No distributor reference signal to the ECM at specified engine vacuum. This code will store in memory
42	Electronic Spark Timing (EST) bypass circuit or EST circuit grounded or open
44	Lean exhaust indication – the engine must run 2 minutes, in closed loop and at part throttle, before this code will set
45	Rich exhaust indication – the engine must run 2 minutes, in closed loop and at part throttle, before this code will set
51	Faulty or improperly installed calibration unit (PROM). It takes up to 30 seconds before this code will set
54	M/C solenoid voltage high at ECM as a result of a shorted M/C solenoid circuit and/or faulty ECM

Year — 1986
Model — Cutlass Ciera
Engine — 2.5L (151 cid) EFI 4 cyl
Engine Code — VIN R

ECM TROUBLE CODES

Code	Explanation
12	No distributor reference pulses to the ECM. This code is not stored in memory and will only flash while the fault is present. Normal code with ignition ON, engine not running
13	Oxygen sensor circuit
14	Coolant sensor — voltage low
15	Coolant sensor — voltage high
21	Throttle Position Sensor (TPS) — voltage high
22	Throttle Position Sensor (TPS) — voltage low
24	Vehicle Speed Sensor (VSS)
33	Manifold Absolute Pressure (MAP) — voltage high
34	Manifold Absolute Pressure (MAP) — voltage low
35	Idle Air Control (IAC)
42	Electronic Spark Timing (EST)
44	Lean exhaust indication
45	Rich exhaust indication
51	PROM
55	ECM

Year – 1986
Model – Cutlass Ciera
Engine – 2.8L (173 cid) MPFI V6
Engine Code – VIN W

ECM TROUBLE CODES

Code	Explanation
12	No distributor reference pulses to the ECM. This code is not stored in memory and will only flash while the fault is present. Normal code with ignition ON, engine not running
13	Oxygen Sensor Circuit
14	Coolant Sensor
15	Coolant Sensor
21	Throttle Position Sensor (TPS) – voltage high
22	Throttle Position Sensor (TPS) – voltage low
23	Manifold Air Temperature (MAT) sensor – voltage high
24	Vehicle Speed Sensor (VSS)
25	Manifold Air Temperature (MAT) sensor – voltage low
32	Exhaust Gas Recirculation (EGR) – vacuum control
33	Manifold Absolute Pressure (MAP) – voltage high
34	Manifold Absolute Pressure (MAP) – voltage low
41	Cylinder select error
42	Electronic Spark Timing (EST)
44	Lean Exhaust Indication
45	Rich Exhaust Indication
51	PROM
52	Calpak (missing)
53	System over voltage
54	Fuel pump voltage low
55	ECM

Year — 1986
Model — Cutlass Ciera
Engine — 3.8L (231 cid) SFI V6
Engine Code — VIN B

ECM TROUBLE CODES

Code	Explanation
12	No distributor reference pulses to the ECM. This code is not stored in memory and will only flash while the fault is present. Normal code with ignition ON, engine not running
13	Oxygen sensor circuit
14	Coolant sensor — voltage low
15	Coolant sensor — voltage high
21	Throttle Position Sensor (TPS) — voltage high
22	Throttle Position Sensor (TPS) — voltage low
23	Manifold Air Temperature (MAT) sensor
24	Vehicle Speed Sensor (VSS)
25	Manifold Air Temperature (MAT) sensor
32	Exhaust Gas Recirculation (EGR) vacuum control
33	Mass Air Flow (MAF) sensor — voltage high
34	Mass Air Flow (MAF) sensor — voltage low
41	C^3I Ignition Cam sensor signal
42	C^3I Ignition
43	Electronic Spark Control (ESC)
44	Lean exhaust indication
45	Rich exhaust indication
51	PROM
52	Calpak (missing)
55	ECM

Year — 1986
Model — Cutlass Ciera
Engine — 3.8L (231 cid) SFI V6
Engine Code — VIN 3

ECM TROUBLE CODES

Code	Explanation
12	No distributor reference pulses to the ECM. This code is not stored in memory and will only flash while the fault is present. Normal code with ignition ON, engine not running
13	Oxygen sensor circuit
14	Coolant sensor — voltage low
15	Coolant sensor — voltage high
21	Throttle Position Sensor (TPS) — voltage high
22	Throttle Position Sensor (TPS) — voltage low
23	Manifold Air Temperature (MAT) sensor
24	Vehicle Speed Sensor (VSS)
25	Manifold Air Temperature (MAT) sensor
32	Exhaust Gas Recirculation (EGR) vacuum control
33	Mass Air Flow (MAF) sensor — voltage high
34	Mass Air Flow (MAF) sensor — voltage low
41	C^3I Ignition Cam sensor signal
42	C^3I Ignition
43	Electronic Spark Control (ESC)
44	Lean exhaust indication
45	Rich exhaust indication
51	PROM
52	Calpak
55	ECM

Year — 1986
Model — Calais
Engine — 3.0L (183 cid) MPFI V6
Engine Code — VIN L

ECM TROUBLE CODES

Code	Explanation
12	No distributor reference pulses to the ECM. This code is not stored in memory and will only flash while the fault is present. Normal code with ignition ON, engine not running
13	Oxygen sensor circuit
14	Coolant sensor — voltage low
15	Coolant sensor — voltage high
21	Throttle Position Sensor (TPS) — voltage high
22	Throttle Position Sensor (TPS) — voltage low
23	Manifold Air Temperature (MAT) sensor
24	Vehicle Speed Sensor (VSS)
25	Manifold Air Temperature (MAT) sensor
32	Exhaust Gas Recirculation (EGR) vacuum control
33	Mass Air Flow (MAF) sensor — voltage high
34	Mass Air Flow (MAF) sensor — voltage low
41	C^3I Ignition — Cam sensor signal
42	C^3I Ignition
43	Electronic Spark Control (ESC)
44	Lean exhaust indication
45	Rich exhaust indication
51	PROM
52	Calpak
55	ECM

Year — 1986
Model — Cutlass
Engine — 3.8L (231 cid) V6
Engine Code — VIN A

ECM TROUBLE CODES

Code	Explanation
12	No distributor reference signal to the ECM. This code is not stored in memory and will only flash while the fault is present. This is a normal code with ignition ON, engine not running
13	Oxygen sensor circuit — the engine must run up to 4 minutes at part throttle, under road load, before this code will set
14	Shorted coolant sensor circuit — the engine must run 2 minutes before this code will set
15	Open coolant sensor circuit — the engine must run 5 minutes before this code will set
21	Throttle Position Sensor (TPS) circuit voltage high (open circuit or misadjusted TPS). The engine must run 10 seconds, at specified curb idle speed, before this code will set
22	Throttle Position Sensor (TPS) circuit voltage low (grounded circuit or misadjusted TPS). Engine must run 20 seconds at specified curb idle speed, to set code
23	M/C solenoid circuit open or grounded
24	Vehicle Speed Sensor (VSS) circuit — the vehicle must operate up to 2 minutes, at road speed, before this code will set
32	Barometric Pressure Sensor (BARO) circuit low
34	Manifold Absolute Pressure (MAP) or vacuum sensor circuit. The engine must run up to 2 minutes at specified curb idle speed, before this code will set
35	Idle Speed Control (ISC) switch circuit shorted. (Up to 70% TPS for over 5 seconds)
41	No distributor reference signal to the ECM at specified engine vacuum. This code will store in memory
42	Electronic Spark Timing (EST) bypass circuit or EST circuit grounded or open
43	Electronic Spark Control (ESC) retard signal for too long a time; causes retard in (EST) signal
44	Lean exhaust indication — the engine must run 2 minutes, in closed loop and at part throttle, before this code will set
45	Rich exhaust indication — the engine must run 2 minutes, in closed loop and at part throttle, before this code will set
51	Faulty or improperly installed calibration unit (PROM). It takes up to 30 seconds before this code will set
53	Exhaust Gas Recirculation (EGR) valve vacuum sensor has seen improper EGR control vacuum
54	M/C solenoid voltage high at ECM as a result of a shorted M/C solenoid circuit and/or faulty ECM

Year — 1986
Model — Cutlass
Engine — 5.0L (307 cid) V8
Engine Code — VIN Y

ECM TROUBLE CODES

Code	Explanation
12	No distributor reference signal to the ECM. This code is not stored in memory and will only flash while the fault is present. This is a normal code with ignition ON, engine not running
13	Oxygen sensor circuit — the engine must run up to 4 minutes at part throttle, under road load, before this code will set
14	Shorted coolant sensor circuit — the engine must run 2 minutes before this code will set
15	Open coolant sensor circuit — the engine must run 5 minutes before this code will set
21	Throttle Position Sensor (TPS) circuit voltage high (open circuit or misadjusted TPS). The engine must run 10 seconds, at specified curb idle speed, before this code will set
22	Throttle Position Sensor (TPS) circuit voltage low (grounded circuit or misadjusted TPS). Engine must run 20 seconds at specified curb idle speed, to set code
23	M/C solenoid circuit open or grounded
24	Vehicle Speed Sensor (VSS) circuit — the vehicle must operate up to 2 minutes, at road speed, before this code will set
32	Barometric Pressure Sensor (BARO) circuit low
34	Manifold Absolute Pressure (MAP) sensor or vacuum sensor circuit. The engine must run up to 2 minutes, at specified curb idle speed, before this code will set
35	Idle Speed Control (ISC) switch circuit shorted. (Up to 70% TPS value for over 5 seconds)
41	No distributor reference signal to the ECM at specified engine vacuum. This code will store in memory
42	Electronic Spark Timing (EST) bypass circuit or EST circuit grounded or open
43	Electronic Spark Control (ESC) retard signal for too long a time; causes retard in (EST) signal
44	Lean exhaust indication — the engine must run 2 minutes, in closed loop and at part throttle, before this code will set
45	Rich exhaust indication — the engine must run 2 minutes, in closed loop and at part throttle, before this code will set
51	Faulty or improperly installed calibration unit (PROM). It takes up to 30 seconds before this code will set
53	Exhaust Gas Recirculation (EGR) valve vacuum sensor has seen improper EGR control vacuum
54	M/C solenoid voltage high at ECM as a result of a shorted M/C solenoid circuit and/or faulty ECM

Year—1986
Model—Cutlass
Engine—5.0L (307 cid) V8
Engine Code—VIN 9

ECM TROUBLE CODES

Code	Explanation
12	No distributor reference signal to the ECM. This code is not stored in memory and will only flash while the fault is present. This is a normal code with ignition ON, engine not running
13	Oxygen sensor circuit—the engine must run up to 4 minutes at part throttle, under road load, before this code will set
14	Shorted coolant sensor circuit—the engine must run 2 minutes before this code will set
15	Open coolant sensor circuit—the engine must run 5 minutes before this code will set
21	Throttle Position Sensor (TPS) circuit voltage high (open circuit or misadjusted TPS). The engine must run 10 seconds, at specified curb idle speed, before this code will set
22	Throttle Position Sensor (TPS) circuit voltage low (grounded circuit or misadjusted TPS). Engine must run 20 seconds at specified curb idle speed, to set code
23	M/C solenoid circuit open or grounded
24	Vehicle Speed Sensor (VSS) circuit—the vehicle must operate up to 2 minutes, at road speed, before this code will set
32	Barometric Pressure Sensor (BARO) circuit low
34	Manifold Absolute Pressure (MAP) sensor or vacuum sensor circuit. The engine must run up to 2 minutes, at specified curb idle speed, before this code will set
35	Idle Speed Control (ISC) switch circuit shorted. (Up to 70% TPS value for over 5 seconds)
41	No distributor reference signal to the ECM at specified engine vacuum. This code will store in memory
42	Electronic Spark Timing (EST) bypass circuit or EST circuit grounded or open
43	Electronic Spark Control (ESC) retard signal for too long a time; causes retard in (EST) signal
44	Lean exhaust indication—the engine must run 2 minutes, in closed loop and at part throttle, before this code will set
45	Rich exhaust indication—the engine must run 2 minutes, in closed loop and at part throttle, before this code will set
51	Faulty or improperly installed calibration unit (PROM). It takes up to 30 seconds before this code will set
53	Exhaust Gas Recirculation (EGR) valve vacuum sensor has seen improper EGR control vacuum
54	M/C solenoid voltage high at ECM as a result of a shorted M/C solenoid circuit and/or faulty ECM

Year — 1986
Model — Custom Cruiser
Engine — 5.0L (307 cid) V8
Engine Code — VIN Y

ECM TROUBLE CODES

Code	Explanation
12	No distributor reference signal to the ECM. This code is not stored in memory and will only flash while the fault is present. This is a normal code with ignition ON, engine not running
13	Oxygen sensor circuit — the engine must run up to 4 minutes at part throttle, under road load, before this code will set
14	Shorted coolant sensor circuit — the engine must run 2 minutes before this code will set
15	Open coolant sensor circuit — the engine must run 5 minutes before this code will set
21	Throttle Position Sensor (TPS) circuit voltage high (open circuit or misadjusted TPS). The engine must run 10 seconds, at specified curb idle speed, before this code will set
22	Throttle Position Sensor (TPS) circuit voltage low (grounded circuit or misadjusted TPS). Engine must run 20 seconds at specified curb idle speed, to set code
23	M/C solenoid circuit open or grounded
24	Vehicle Speed Sensor (VSS) circuit — the vehicle must operate up to 2 minutes, at road speed, before this code will set
32	Barometric Pressure Sensor (BARO) circuit low
34	Manifold Absolute Pressure (MAP) sensor or vacuum sensor circuit. The engine must run up to 2 minutes, at specified curb idle speed, before this code will set
35	Idle Speed Control (ISC) switch circuit shorted. (Up to 70% TPS value for over 5 seconds)
41	No distributor reference signal to the ECM at specified engine vacuum. This code will store in memory
42	Electronic Spark Timing (EST) bypass circuit or EST circuit grounded or open
43	Electronic Spark Control (ESC) retard signal for too long a time; causes retard in (EST) signal
44	Lean exhaust indication — the engine must run 2 minutes, in closed loop and at part throttle, before this code will set
45	Rich exhaust indication — the engine must run 2 minutes, in closed loop and at part throttle, before this code will set
51	Faulty or improperly installed calibration unit (PROM). It takes up to 30 seconds before this code will set
53	Exhaust Gas Recirculation (EGR) valve vacuum sensor has seen improper EGR control vacuum
54	M/C solenoid voltage high at ECM as a result of a shorted M/C solenoid circuit and/or faulty ECM

Year – 1986
Model – Firenza
Engine – 1.8L (111 cid) EFI 4 cyl
Engine Code – VIN O

ECM TROUBLE CODES

Code	Explanation
12	No distributor reference pulses to the ECM. This code is not stored in memory and will only flash while the fault is present. Normal code with ignition ON, engine not running
13	Oxygen sensor circuit
14	Coolant sensor – voltage low
15	Coolant sensor – voltage high
21	Throttle Position Sensor (TPS) – voltage high
22	Throttle Position Sensor (TPS) – voltage low
24	Vehicle Speed Sensor (VSS)
33	Manifold Absolute Pressure (MAP) – voltage high
34	Manifold Absolute Pressure (MAP) – voltage low
35	Idle Air Control (IAC)
42	Electronic Spark Timing (EST)
44	Lean exhaust indication
45	Rich exhaust indication
51	PROM
55	ECM

Year — 1986
Model — Firenza
Engine — 2.0L (121 cid) EFI 4 cyl
Engine Code — VIN P

ECM TROUBLE CODES

Code	Explanation
12	No distributor reference pulses to the ECM. This code is not stored in memory and will only flash while the fault is present. Normal code with ignition ON, engine not running
13	Oxygen sensor circuit
14	Coolant sensor — voltage low
15	Coolant sensor — voltage high
21	Throttle Position Sensor (TPS) — voltage high
22	Throttle Position Sensor (TPS) — voltage low
24	Vehicle Speed Sensor (VSS)
33	Manifold Absolute Pressure (MAP) — voltage high
34	Manifold Absolute Pressure (MAP) — voltage low
35	Idle Air Control (IAC)
42	Electronic Spark Timing (EST)
44	Lean exhaust indication
45	Rich exhaust indication
51	PROM
55	ECM

Year — 1986
Model — Firenza
Engine — 2.8L (173 cid) MPFI V6
Engine Code — VIN W

ECM TROUBLE CODES

Code	Explanation
12	No distributor reference pulses to the ECM. This code is not stored in memory and will only flash while the fault is present. Normal code with ignition ON, engine not running
13	Oxygen sensor circuit
14	Coolant sensor — voltage low
15	Coolant sensor — voltage high
21	Throttle Position Sensor (TPS) — voltage high
22	Throttle Position Sensor (TPS) — voltage low
23	Manifold Air Temperature (MAT) sensor
24	Vehicle Speed Sensor (VSS)
25	Manifold Air Temperature (MAT) sensor
32	Exhaust Gas Recirculation (EGR) vacuum control
33	Manifold Absolute Pressure (MAP) — voltage high
34	Manifold Absolute Pressure (MAP) — voltage low
41	Cylinder select error
42	Electronic Spark Timing (EST)
44	Lean exhaust indication
45	Rich exhaust indication
51	PROM
52	Calpak (missing)
53	System over voltage
54	Fuel pump circuit — voltage low
55	ECM

Year — 1986
Model — Calais
Engine — 2.5L (151 cid) EFI 4 cyl
Engine Code — VIN U

ECM TROUBLE CODES

Code	Explanation
12	No distributor reference pulses to the ECM. This code is not stored in memory and will only flash while the fault is present. Normal code with ignition ON, engine not running
13	Oxygen sensor circuit
14	Coolant sensor — voltage low
15	Coolant sensor — voltage high
21	Throttle Position Sensor (TPS) — voltage high
22	Throttle Position Sensor (TPS) — voltage low
24	Vehicle Speed Sensor (VSS)
33	Manifold Absolute Pressure (MAP) — voltage high
34	Manifold Absolute Pressure (MAP) — voltage low
35	Idle Air Control (IAC)
42	Electronic Spark Timing (EST)
44	Lean exhaust indication
45	Rich exhaust indication
51	PROM
55	ECM

Year – 1986
Model – Toronado
Engine – 3.8L (231 cid) SFI V6
Engine Code – VIN B

ECM TROUBLE CODES

Code	Explanation
E012	No distributor reference pulses to the ECM. This code is not stored in memory and will only flash while the fault is present. Normal code with ignition ON, engine not running
E013	Oxygen sensor circuit – "Service Engine Soon" indicator light – canister purge function disengaged while malfunction exists
E014	Coolant sensor – signal voltage low – "Service Engine Soon" indicator light – forces cooling fans ON
E015	Coolant sensor – signal voltage high – "Service Engine Soon" indicator light – forces cooling fans ON
E016	System voltage out of range – "Service Engine Soon" indicator light – all solenoids disengaged while malfunction exists
E021	Throttle Position Sensor (TPS) – signal voltage high – "Service Engine Soon" indicator light – Transaxle Converter Clutch (TCC) disengaged while malfunction exists
E022	Throttle Position Sensor (TPS) – signal voltage low – "Service Engine Soon" indicator light – Transaxle Converter Clutch (TCC) disengaged while malfunction exists
E024	Vehicle Speed Sensor (VSS) circuit – "Service Engine Soon" indicator light – Transaxle Converter Clutch (TCC) disengaged while malfunction exists
E029	Fourth gear circuit open – "Service Engine Soon" indicator light
E032	EGR vacuum control system fault – "Service Engine Soon" indicator light
E033	Mass Air Flow (MAF) sensor – signal frequency high – "Service Engine Soon" indicator light
E034	Mass Air Flow (MAF) sensor – Signal frequency low – "Service Engine Soon" indicator light
E037	Manifold Air Temperature (MAT) sensor – temperature too high – "Service Engine Soon" indicator light
E038	Manifold Air Temperature (MAT) sensor – temperature too low – "Service Engine Soon" indicator light
E040	Power steering pressure switch circuit open – "Service Engine Soon" indicator light – A/C Clutch and Cruise Control disengaged while malfunction exists
E041	C^3I Ignition – Cam sensor circuit – "Service Engine Soon" indicator light
E042	C^3I Ignition – Electronic Spark Timing (EST) circuit – "Service Engine Soon" indicator light – causes system to operate in bypass spark mode
E043	Electronic Spark Control (ESC) – "Service Engine Soon" indicator light
E044	Lean exhaust indication – "Service Engine Soon" indicator light – forces open loop operation
E045	Rich exhaust indication – "Service Engine Soon" indicator light – forces open loop operation
E047	BCM to ECM data link – "Service Engine Soon" indication light – A/C Clutch and Cruise Control disengaged while malfunction exists
E051	ECM PROM Error – "Service Engine Soon" indication light – causes system to operate in bypass spark mode – causes system to operate in back–up fuel mode
E052	Calpack error – "Service Engine Soon" indicator light
E055	ECM Error – "Service Engine Soon" indicator light

BCM TROUBLE CODES

Code	Explanation
B110	Outside temperature sensor
B111	Air conditioning high side temperature sensor

BCM TROUBLE CODES

Code	Explanation
B112	Air conditioning low side temperature sensor
B113	In-car temperature sensor
B115	Sunload temperature sensor
B118	Door ajar/jamb switch
B119	Twilight photocell
B120	Twilight delay pot
B122	Panel lamp dimming pot
B123	Courtesy light switch
B124	Vehicle Speed Sensor (VSS)
B127	PRNDL sensor
B131	Oil pressure sensor
B132	Oil pressure sensor
B334	Electronic Control Module (ECM) data
B335	Electronic Comfort Control (ECC) data
B336	Instrument Panel Cluster (IPC) data
B337	Programmer data
B338	Chime/Voice data
B409	Generator
B411	Battery low
B412	Battery high
B440	Air mix door
B445	Air conditioning clutch
B446	Low refrigerant warning
B447	Very low refrigerant problem
B448	Low refrigerant pressure
B449	A/C high temperature
B450	Coolant high temperature–air conditioning
B552	Body Control Module (BCM) memory reset
B556	E^2 PROM
B660	Cruise – not in drive
B663	Cruise – speed difference
B664	Cruise – acceleration
B667	Cruise – switch shorted
B671	Cruise – position sensor
B672	Cruise – vent solenoid
B673	Cruise – vacuum solenoid

Year – 1987
Model – Delta 88
Engine – 3.8L (231 cid) SFI V6
Engine Code – VIN 3

ECM TROUBLE CODES

Code	Explanation
13	Oxygen sensor circuit – open circuit
14	Coolant Temperature Sensor (CTS) circuit – high temperature indicated
15	Coolant Temperature Sensor (CTS) circuit – low temperature indicated
21	Throttle Position Sensor (TPS) circuit – signal voltage high
22	Throttle Position Sensor (TPS) circuit – signal voltage Low
23	Manifold Air Temperature (MAT) sensor – low temperature indicated
24	Vehicle Speed Sensor (VSS) circuit
25	Manifold Air Temperature (MAT) sensor – high temperature indicated
32	Exhaust Gas Recirculation (EGR) system fault
33	Mass Air Flow (MAF) sensor circuit – GM/SEC high
34	Mass Air Flow (MAF) sensor – GM/SEC low
41	Cam sensor circuit
42	Electronic Spark Control (ESC) circuit – C^{3}I EST or bypass circuit
43	Electronic Spark Control (ESC) circuit
44	Oxygen sensor circuit – lean exhaust indicated
45	Oxygen sensor circuit – rich exhaust indicated
51	PROM error
52	Calpak error
55	ECM error

Year — 1987
Model — Ninety — Eight
Engine — 3.8L (231 cid) SFI V6
Engine Code — VIN 3

ECM TROUBLE CODES

Code	Explanation
13	Oxygen sensor circuit — open circuit
14	Coolant Temperature Sensor (CTS) circuit — high temperature indicated
15	Coolant Temperature Sensor (CTS) circuit — low temperature indicated
21	Throttle Position Sensor (TPS) circuit — signal voltage high
22	Throttle Position Sensor (TPS) circuit — signal voltage low
23	Manifold Air Temperature (MAT) sensor — low temperature indicated
24	Vehicle Speed Sensor (VSS) circuit
25	Manifold Air Temperature (MAT) sensor — high temperature indicated
32	Exhaust Gas Recirculation (EGR) system fault
33	Mass Air Flow (MAF) sensor circuit — GM/SEC high
34	Mass Air Flow (MAF) sensor — GM/SEC low
41	Cam sensor circuit
42	Electronic Spark Control (ESC) circuit — C^{3}I EST or bypass circuit
43	Electronic Spark Control (ESC) circuit
44	Oxygen sensor circuit — lean exhaust indicated
45	Oxygen sensor circuit — rich exhaust indicated
51	PROM error
52	Calpak error
55	ECM error

Year — 1987
Model — Cutlass Ciera
Engine — 2.5L (151 cid) EFI 4 cyl
Engine Code — VIN R

ECM TROUBLE CODES

Code	Explanation
13	Oxygen sensor circuit — open circuit
14	Coolant Temperature Sensor (CTS) circuit — high temperature indicated
15	Coolant Temperature Sensor (CTS) circuit — low temperature indicated
21	Throttle Position Sensor (TPS) circuit — signal voltage high
22	Throttle Position Sensor (TPS) circuit — signal voltage low
23	Manifold Air Temperature (MAT) sensor circuit — low temperature indicated
24	Vehicle Speed Sensor (VSS) circuit
25	Manifold Air Temperature (MAT) sensor — high temperature indicated
33	Manifold Absolute Pressure (MAP) sensor circuit — signal voltage high
34	Manifold Absolute Pressure (MAP) sensor circuit — signal voltage low
35	Idle speed error
42	Electronic Spark Timing (EST) circuit
44	Oxygen sensor circuit — lean exhaust indicated
45	Oxygen sensor circuit — rich exhaust indicated
51	PROM error
53	System over voltage

Year — 1987
Model — Cutlass Ciera
Engine — 2.8L (173 cid) MPFI V6
Engine Code — VIN W

ECM TROUBLE CODES

Code	Explanation
13	Oxygen sensor circuit — open
14	Coolant sensor circuit — high temperature indicated
15	Coolant sensor circuit — low temperature indicated
21	Throttle Position Sensor (TPS) signal voltage high
22	Throttle Position Sensor (TPS) signal voltage low
23	Manifold Air Temperature (MAT) sensor circuit — low temperature indicated
24	Vehicle Speed Sensor (VSS) circuit
25	Manifold Air Temperature (MAT) sensor circuit — high temperature indicated
33	Mass Air Flow (MAF) high GM/SEC indicated
34	Mass Air Flow (MAF) low GM/SEC indicated
35	Idle speed error
41	Cylinder select error — faulty or incorrect Mem-Cal
42	Electronic Spark Timing (EST) circuit
43	Electronic Spark Control (ESC) circuit
44	Oxygen sensor circuit — lean exhaust indicated
45	Oxygen sensor circuit — rich exhaust indicated
54	Fuel Pump circuit — low voltage
51	Mem-Cal error — faulty or incorrect Mem-Cal
52	Calpak error — faulty or incorrect Calpak
53	System over voltage
61	Degraded oxygen sensor
63	Manifold Absolute Pressure (MAP) sensor circuit — signal voltage high — low vacuum
64	Manifold Absolute Pressure (MAP) sensor circuit — signal voltage low — high vacuum

Year – 1987
Model – Cutlass Ciera
Engine – 3.8L (231 cid) SFI V6
Engine Code – VIN 3

ECM TROUBLE CODES

Code	Explanation
13	Oxygen sensor circuit—open circuit
14	Coolant Temperature Sensor (CTS) circuit—high temperature indicated
15	Coolant Temperature Sensor (CTS) circuit—low temperature indicated
21	Throttle Position Sensor (TPS) circuit—signal voltage high
22	Throttle Position Sensor (TPS) circuit—signal voltage low
23	Manifold Air Temperature (MAT) sensor—low temperature indicated
24	Vehicle Speed Sensor (VSS) circuit
25	Manifold Air Temperature (MAT) sensor—high temperature indicated
32	Exhaust Gas Recirculation (EGR) system fault
33	Mass Air Flow (MAF) sensor circuit—GM/SEC high
34	Mass Air Flow (MAF) sensor—GM/SEC low
41	Cam sensor circuit
42	Electronic Spark Control (ESC) circuit—C^{3}I EST or bypass circuit
43	Electronic Spark Control (ESC) circuit
44	Oxygen sensor circuit—lean exhaust indicated
45	Oxygen sensor circuit—rich exhaust indicated
51	PROM error
52	Calpak error
55	ECM error

Year — 1987
Model — Calais
Engine — 2.5L (151 cid) EFI 4 cyl
Engine Code — VIN U

ECM TROUBLE CODES

Code	Explanation
13	Oxygen sensor circuit—open circuit
14	Coolant Temperature Sensor (CTS) circuit—high temperature indicated
15	Coolant Temperature Sensor (CTS) circuit—low temperature indicated
21	Throttle Position Sensor (TPS) circuit—signal voltage high
22	Throttle Position Sensor (TPS) circuit—signal voltage low
23	Manifold Air Temperature (MAT) sensor circuit—low temperature indicated
24	Vehicle Speed Sensor (VSS) circuit
25	Manifold Air Temperature (MAT) sensor—high temperature indicated
33	Manifold Absolute Pressure (MAP) sensor circuit—signal voltage high
34	Manifold Absolute Pressure (MAP) sensor circuit—signal voltage low
35	Idle speed error
42	Electronic Spark Timing (EST) circuit
44	Oxygen sensor circuit—lean exhaust indicated
45	Oxygen sensor circuit—rich exhaust indicated
51	PROM error
53	System over voltage

Year — 1987
Model — Calais
Engine — 3.0L (183 cid) MPFI V6
Engine Code — VIN L

ECM TROUBLE CODES

Code	Explanation
13	Oxygen sensor circuit — open circuit
14	Coolant Temperature Sensor (CTS) circuit — high temperature indicated
15	Coolant Temperature Sensor (CTS) circuit — low temperature indicated
21	Throttle Position Sensor (TPS) circuit — signal voltage high
22	Throttle Position Sensor (TPS) circuit — signal voltage low
23	Manifold Air Temperature (MAT) sensor — low temperature indicated
24	Vehicle Speed Sensor (VSS) circuit
25	Manifold Air Temperature (MAT) sensor — high temperature indicated
32	Exhaust Gas Recirculation (EGR) system fault
33	Mass Air Flow (MAF) sensor circuit — GM/SEC high
34	Mass Air Flow (MAF) sensor — GM/SEC low
41	Cam sensor circuit
42	Electronic Spark Control (ESC) circuit — C^3I EST or bypass circuit
43	Electronic Spark Control (ESC) circuit
44	Oxygen sensor circuit — lean exhaust indicated
45	Oxygen sensor circuit — rich exhaust indicated
51	PROM error
52	Calpak error
55	ECM error

Year – 1987
Model – Cutlass Supreme
Engine – 3.8L (231 cid) V6
Engine Code – VIN A

ECM TROUBLE CODES

Code	Explanation
12	No distributor reference signal to the ECM. This code is not stored in memory and will only flash while the fault is present. This is a normal code with ignition ON, engine not running
13	Oxygen sensor circuit – the engine must run up to 4 minutes at part throttle, under road load, before this code will set
14	Shorted Coolant Temperature Sensor (CTS) circuit – the engine must run 2 minutes before this code will set
15	Open coolant sensor circuit – the engine must run 5 minutes before this code will set
21	Throttle Position Sensor (TPS) circuit voltage high – open circuit or misadjusted TPS. The engine must run 10 seconds, at specified curb idle speed, before this code will set
22	Throttle Position Sensor (TPS) circuit voltage low – grounded circuit or misadjusted TPS. Engine must run 20 seconds at specified curb idle speed, to set code
23	M/C solenoid circuit open or grounded
24	Vehicle Speed Sensor (VSS) circuit – the vehicle must operate up to 2 minutes, at road speed, before this code will set
32	Barometric Pressure Sensor (BARO) circuit low
34	Vacuum sensor or Manifold Absolute Pressure (MAP) circuit – the engine must run up to 2 minutes, at specified curb idle, before this code will set
35	Idle Speed Control (ISC) switch circuit shorted – Up to 70% TPS for over 5 seconds
41	No distributor reference signal to the ECM at specified engine vacuum. This code will store in memory
42	Electronic Spark Timing (EST) bypass circuit or EST circuit grounded or open
43	Electronic Spark Control (ESC) retard signal for too long; causes retard in EST signal
44	Lean exhaust indication – the engine must run 2 minutes, in closed loop and at part throttle, before this code will set
45	Rich exhaust indication – the engine must run 2 minutes, in closed loop and at part throttle, before this code will set
51	Faulty or improperly installed calibration unit (PROM). It takes up to 30 seconds before this code will set
53	Exhaust Gas Recirculation (EGR) valve vacuum sensor has seen improper EGR control vacuum
54	M/C solenoid voltage high, at ECM, as a result of a shorted M/C solenoid circuit and/or faulty ECM

Year – 1987
Model – Cutlass Supreme
Engine – 5.0L (307 cid) V8
Engine Code – VIN Y

ECM TROUBLE CODES

Code	Explanation
12	No distributor reference signal to the ECM. This code is not stored in memory and will only flash while the fault is present. This is a normal code with ignition ON, engine not running
13	Oxygen sensor circuit – the engine must run up to 4 minutes at part throttle, under road load, before this code will set
14	Shorted Coolant Temperature Sensor (CTS) circuit – the engine must run 2 minutes before this code will set
15	Open coolant sensor circuit – the engine must run 5 minutes before this code will set
21	Throttle Position Sensor (TPS) circuit voltage high – open circuit or misadjusted TPS. The engine must run 10 seconds, at specified curb idle speed, before this code will set
22	Throttle Position Sensor (TPS) circuit voltage low – grounded circuit or misadjusted TPS. Engine must run 20 seconds at specified curb idle speed, to set code
23	M/C solenoid circuit open or grounded
24	Vehicle Speed Sensor (VSS) circuit – the vehicle must operate up to 2 minutes, at road speed, before this code will set
32	Barometric Pressure Sensor (BARO) circuit low
34	Vacuum sensor or Manifold Absolute Pressure (MAP) circuit – the engine must run up to 2 minutes, at specified curb idle, before this code will set
35	Idle Speed Control (ISC) switch circuit shorted – up to 70% TPS for over 5 seconds
41	No distributor reference signal to the ECM at specified engine vacuum. This code will store in memory
42	Electronic Spark Timing (EST) bypass circuit or EST circuit grounded or open
43	Electronic Spark Control (ESC) retard signal for too long; causes retard in EST signal
44	Lean exhaust indication – the engine must run 2 minutes, in closed loop and at part throttle, before this code will set
45	Rich exhaust indication – the engine must run 2 minutes, in closed loop and at part throttle, before this code will set
51	Faulty or improperly installed calibration unit (PROM). It takes up to 30 seconds before this code will set
53	Exhaust Gas Recirculation (EGR) valve vacuum sensor has seen improper EGR control vacuum
54	M/C solenoid voltage high, at ECM, as a result of a shorted M/C solenoid circuit and/or faulty ECM

Year — 1987
Model — Cutlass Supreme
Engine — 5.0L (307 cid) V8
Engine Code — VIN 9

ECM TROUBLE CODES

Code	Explanation
12	No distributor reference signal to the ECM. This code is not stored in memory and will only flash while the fault is present. This is a normal code with ignition ON, engine not running
13	Oxygen sensor circuit — the engine must run up to 4 minutes at part throttle, under road load, before this code will set
14	Shorted Coolant Temperature Sensor (CTS) circuit — the engine must run 2 minutes before this code will set
15	Open coolant sensor circuit — the engine must run 5 minutes before this code will set
21	Throttle Position Sensor (TPS) circuit voltage high — open circuit or misadjusted TPS. The engine must run 10 seconds, at specified curb idle speed, before this code will set
22	Throttle Position Sensor (TPS) circuit voltage low — grounded circuit or misadjusted TPS. Engine must run 20 seconds at specified curb idle speed, to set code
23	M/C solenoid circuit open or grounded
24	Vehicle Speed Sensor (VSS) circuit — the vehicle must operate up to 2 minutes, at road speed, before this code will set
32	Barometric Pressure Sensor (BARO) circuit low
34	Vacuum sensor or Manifold Absolute Pressure (MAP) circuit — the engine must run up to 2 minutes, at specified curb idle, before this code will set
35	Idle Speed Control (ISC) switch circuit shorted — Up to 70% TPS for over 5 seconds
41	No distributor reference signal to the ECM at specified engine vacuum. This code will store in memory
42	Electronic Spark Timing (EST) bypass circuit or EST circuit grounded or open
43	Electronic Spark Control (ESC) retard signal for too long; causes retard in EST signal
44	Lean exhaust indication — the engine must run 2 minutes, in closed loop and at part throttle, before this code will set
45	Rich exhaust indication — the engine must run 2 minutes, in closed loop and at part throttle, before this code will set
51	Faulty or improperly installed calibration unit (PROM). It takes up to 30 seconds before this code will set
53	Exhaust Gas Recirculation (EGR) valve vacuum sensor has seen improper EGR control vacuum
54	M/C solenoid voltage high, at ECM, as a result of a shorted M/C solenoid circuit and/or faulty ECM

Year—1987
Model—Cutlass Supreme Brougham
Engine—3.8L (231 cid) V6
Engine Code—VIN A

ECM TROUBLE CODES

Code	Explanation
12	No distributor reference signal to the ECM. This code is not stored in memory and will only flash while the fault is present. This is a normal code with ignition ON, engine not running
13	Oxygen sensor circuit—the engine must run up to 4 minutes at part throttle, under road load, before this code will set
14	Shorted Coolant Temperature Sensor (CTS) circuit—the engine must run 2 minutes before this code will set
15	Open coolant sensor circuit—the engine must run 5 minutes before this code will set
21	Throttle Position Sensor (TPS) circuit voltage high—open circuit or misadjusted TPS. The engine must run 10 seconds, at specified curb idle speed, before this code will set
22	Throttle Position Sensor (TPS) circuit voltage low—grounded circuit or misadjusted TPS. Engine must run 20 seconds at specified curb idle speed, to set code
23	M/C solenoid circuit open or grounded
24	Vehicle Speed Sensor (VSS) circuit—the vehicle must operate up to 2 minutes, at road speed, before this code will set
32	Barometric Pressure Sensor (BARO) circuit low
34	Vacuum sensor or Manifold Absolute Pressure (MAP) circuit—the engine must run up to 2 minutes, at specified curb idle, before this code will set
35	Idle Speed Control (ISC) switch circuit shorted—Up to 70% TPS for over 5 seconds
41	No distributor reference signal to the ECM at specified engine vacuum. This code will store in memory
42	Electronic Spark Timing (EST) bypass circuit or EST circuit grounded or open
43	Electronic Spark Control (ESC) retard signal for too long; causes retard in EST signal
44	Lean exhaust indication—the engine must run 2 minutes, in closed loop and at part throttle, before this code will set
45	Rich exhaust indication—the engine must run 2 minutes, in closed loop and at part throttle, before this code will set
51	Faulty or improperly installed calibration unit (PROM). It takes up to 30 seconds before this code will set
53	Exhaust Gas Recirculation (EGR) valve vacuum sensor has seen improper EGR control vacuum
54	M/C solenoid voltage high, at ECM, as a result of a shorted M/C solenoid circuit and/or faulty ECM

Year – 1987
Model – Cutlass Supreme Brougham
Engine – 5.0L (307 cid) V8
Engine Code – VIN Y

ECM TROUBLE CODES

Code	Explanation
12	No distributor reference signal to the ECM. This code is not stored in memory and will only flash while the fault is present. This is a normal code with ignition ON, engine not running
13	Oxygen sensor circuit—the engine must run up to 4 minutes at part throttle, under road load, before this code will set
14	Shorted Coolant Temperature Sensor (CTS) circuit—the engine must run 2 minutes before this code will set
15	Open coolant sensor circuit—the engine must run 5 minutes before this code will set
21	Throttle Position Sensor (TPS) circuit voltage high—open circuit or misadjusted TPS. The engine must run 10 seconds, at specified curb idle speed, before this code will set
22	Throttle Position Sensor (TPS) circuit voltage low—grounded circuit or misadjusted TPS. Engine must run 20 seconds at specified curb idle speed, to set code
23	M/C solenoid circuit open or grounded
24	Vehicle Speed Sensor (VSS) circuit—the vehicle must operate up to 2 minutes, at road speed, before this code will set
32	Barometric Pressure Sensor (BARO) circuit low
34	Vacuum sensor or Manifold Absolute Pressure (MAP) circuit—the engine must run up to 2 minutes, at specified curb idle, before this code will set
35	Idle Speed Control (ISC) switch circuit shorted—Up to 70% TPS for over 5 seconds
41	No distributor reference signal to the ECM at specified engine vacuum. This code will store in memory
42	Electronic Spark Timing (EST) bypass circuit or EST circuit grounded or open
43	Electronic Spark Control (ESC) retard signal for too long, causes retard in EST signal
44	Lean exhaust indication—the engine must run 2 minutes, in closed loop and at part throttle, before this code will set
45	Rich exhaust indication—the engine must run 2 minutes, in closed loop and at part throttle, before this code will set
51	Faulty or improperly installed calibration unit (PROM). It takes up to 30 seconds before this code will set
53	Exhaust Gas Recirculation (EGR) valve vacuum sensor has seen improper EGR control vacuum
54	M/C solenoid voltage high, at ECM, as a result of a shorted M/C solenoid circuit and/or faulty ECM

Year — 1987
Model — Cutlass Supreme Brougham
Engine — 5.0L (307 cid) V8
Engine Code — VIN 9

ECM TROUBLE CODES

Code	Explanation
12	No distributor reference signal to the ECM. This code is not stored in memory and will only flash while the fault is present. This is a normal code with ignition ON, engine not running
13	Oxygen sensor circuit — the engine must run up to 4 minutes at part throttle, under road load, before this code will set
14	Shorted Coolant Temperature Sensor (CTS) circuit — the engine must run 2 minutes before this code will set
15	Open coolant sensor circuit — the engine must run 5 minutes before this code will set
21	Throttle Position Sensor (TPS) circuit voltage high — open circuit or misadjusted TPS. The engine must run 10 seconds, at specified curb idle speed, before this code will set
22	Throttle Position Sensor (TPS) circuit voltage low — grounded circuit or misadjusted TPS. Engine must run 20 seconds at specified curb idle speed, to set code
23	M/C solenoid circuit open or grounded
24	Vehicle Speed Sensor (VSS) circuit — the vehicle must operate up to 2 minutes, at road speed, before this code will set
32	Barometric Pressure Sensor (BARO) circuit low
34	Vacuum sensor or Manifold Absolute Pressure (MAP) circuit — the engine must run up to 2 minutes, at specified curb idle, before this code will set
35	Idle Speed Control (ISC) switch circuit shorted — up to 70% TPS for over 5 seconds
41	No distributor reference signal to the ECM at specified engine vacuum. This code will store in memory
42	Electronic Spark Timing (EST) bypass circuit or EST circuit grounded or open
43	Electronic Spark Control (ESC) retard signal for too long, causes retard in EST signal
44	Lean exhaust indication — the engine must run 2 minutes, in closed loop and at part throttle, before this code will set
45	Rich exhaust indication — the engine must run 2 minutes, in closed loop and at part throttle, before this code will set
51	Faulty or improperly installed calibration unit (PROM). It takes up to 30 seconds before this code will set
53	Exhaust Gas Recirculation (EGR) valve vacuum sensor has seen improper EGR control vacuum
54	M/C solenoid voltage high, at ECM, as a result of a shorted M/C solenoid circuit and/or faulty ECM

Year – 1987
Model – Cutlass Salon
Engine – 3.8L (231 cid) V6
Engine Code – VIN A

ECM TROUBLE CODES

Code	Explanation
12	No distributor reference signal to the ECM. This code is not stored in memory and will only flash while the fault is present. This is a normal code with ignition ON, engine not running
13	Oxygen sensor circuit – the engine must run up to 4 minutes at part throttle, under road load, before this code will set
14	Shorted Coolant Temperature Sensor (CTS) circuit – the engine must run 2 minutes before this code will set
15	Open coolant sensor circuit – the engine must run 5 minutes before this code will set
21	Throttle Position Sensor (TPS) circuit voltage high – open circuit or misadjusted TPS. The engine must run 10 seconds, at specified curb idle speed, before this code will set
22	Throttle Position Sensor (TPS) circuit voltage low – grounded circuit or misadjusted TPS. Engine must run 20 seconds at specified curb idle speed, to set code
23	M/C solenoid circuit open or grounded
24	Vehicle Speed Sensor (VSS) circuit – the vehicle must operate up to 2 minutes, at road speed, before this code will set
32	Barometric Pressure Sensor (BARO) circuit low
34	Vacuum sensor or Manifold Absolute Pressure (MAP) circuit – the engine must run up to 2 minutes, at specified curb idle, before this code will set
35	Idle Speed Control (ISC) switch circuit shorted – up to 70% TPS for over 5 seconds
41	No distributor reference signal to the ECM at specified engine vacuum. This code will store in memory
42	Electronic Spark Timing (EST) bypass circuit or EST circuit grounded or open
43	Electronic Spark Control (ESC) retard signal for too long; causes retard in EST signal
44	Lean exhaust indication – the engine must run 2 minutes, in closed loop and at part throttle, before this code will set
45	Rich exhaust indication – the engine must run 2 minutes, in closed loop and at part throttle, before this code will set
51	Faulty or improperly installed calibration unit (PROM). It takes up to 30 seconds before this code will set
53	Exhaust Gas Recirculation (EGR) valve vacuum sensor has seen improper EGR control vacuum
54	M/C solenoid voltage high, at ECM, as a result of a shorted M/C solenoid circuit and/or faulty ECM

Year – 1987
Model – Cutlass Salon
Engine – 5.0L (307 cid) V8
Engine Code – VIN Y

ECM TROUBLE CODES

Code	Explanation
12	No distributor reference signal to the ECM. This code is not stored in memory and will only flash while the fault is present. This is a normal code with ignition ON, engine not running
13	Oxygen sensor circuit – the engine must run up to 4 minutes at part throttle, under road load, before this code will set
14	Shorted Coolant Temperature Sensor (CTS) circuit – the engine must run 2 minutes before this code will set
15	Open coolant sensor circuit – the engine must run 5 minutes before this code will set
21	Throttle Position Sensor (TPS) circuit voltage high – open circuit or misadjusted TPS. The engine must run 10 seconds, at specified curb idle speed, before this code will set
22	Throttle Position Sensor (TPS) circuit voltage low – grounded circuit or misadjusted TPS. Engine must run 20 seconds at specified curb idle speed, to set code
23	M/C solenoid circuit open or grounded
24	Vehicle Speed Sensor (VSS) circuit – the vehicle must operate up to 2 minutes, at road speed, before this code will set
32	Barometric Pressure Sensor (BARO) circuit low
34	Vacuum sensor or Manifold Absolute Pressure (MAP) circuit – the engine must run up to 2 minutes, at specified curb idle, before this code will set
35	Idle Speed Control (ISC) switch circuit shorted – up to 70% TPS for over 5 seconds
41	No distributor reference signal to the ECM at specified engine vacuum. This code will store in memory
42	Electronic Spark Timing (EST) bypass circuit or EST circuit grounded or open
43	Electronic Spark Control (ESC) retard signal for too long; causes retard in EST signal
44	Lean exhaust indication – the engine must run 2 minutes, in closed loop and at part throttle, before this code will set
45	Rich exhaust indication – the engine must run 2 minutes, in closed loop and at part throttle, before this code will set
51	Faulty or improperly installed calibration unit (PROM). It takes up to 30 seconds before this code will set
53	Exhaust Gas Recirculation (EGR) valve vacuum sensor has seen improper EGR control vacuum
54	M/C solenoid voltage high, at ECM, as a result of a shorted M/C solenoid circuit and/or faulty ECM

Year – 1987
Model – Cutlass Salon
Engine – 5.0L (307 cid) V8
Engine Code – VIN 9

ECM TROUBLE CODES

Code	Explanation
12	No distributor reference signal to the ECM. This code is not stored in memory and will only flash while the fault is present. This is a normal code with ignition ON, engine not running
13	Oxygen sensor circuit – the engine must run up to 4 minutes at part throttle, under road load, before this code will set
14	Shorted Coolant Temperature Sensor (CTS) circuit – the engine must run 2 minutes before this code will set
15	Open coolant sensor circuit – the engine must run 5 minutes before this code will set
21	Throttle Position Sensor (TPS) circuit voltage high – open circuit or misadjusted TPS. The engine must run 10 seconds, at specified curb idle speed, before this code will set
22	Throttle Position Sensor (TPS) circuit voltage low – grounded circuit or misadjusted TPS. Engine must run 20 seconds at specified curb idle speed, to set code
23	M/C solenoid circuit open or grounded
24	Vehicle Speed Sensor (VSS) circuit – the vehicle must operate up to 2 minutes, at road speed, before this code will set
32	Barometric Pressure Sensor (BARO) circuit low
34	Vacuum sensor or Manifold Absolute Pressure (MAP) circuit – the engine must run up to 2 minutes, at specified curb idle, before this code will set
35	Idle Speed Control (ISC) switch circuit shorted – up to 70% TPS for over 5 seconds
41	No distributor reference signal to the ECM at specified engine vacuum. This code will store in memory
42	Electronic Spark Timing (EST) bypass circuit or EST circuit grounded or open
43	Electronic Spark Control (ESC) retard signal for too long; causes retard in EST signal
44	Lean exhaust indication – the engine must run 2 minutes, in closed loop and at part throttle, before this code will set
45	Rich exhaust indication – the engine must run 2 minutes, in closed loop and at part throttle, before this code will set
51	Faulty or improperly installed calibration unit (PROM). It takes up to 30 seconds before this code will set
53	Exhaust Gas Recirculation (EGR) valve vacuum sensor has seen improper EGR control vacuum
54	M/C solenoid voltage high, at ECM, as a result of a shorted M/C solenoid circuit and/or faulty ECM

Year — 1987
Model — Custom Cruiser
Engine — 5.0L (307 cid) V8
Engine Code — VIN Y

ECM TROUBLE CODES

Code	Explanation
12	No distributor reference signal to the ECM. This code is not stored in memory and will only flash while the fault is present. This is a normal code with ignition ON, engine not running
13	Oxygen sensor circuit — the engine must run up to 4 minutes at part throttle, under road load, before this code will set
14	Shorted Coolant Temperature Sensor (CTS) circuit — the engine must run 2 minutes before this code will set
15	Open coolant sensor circuit — the engine must run 5 minutes before this code will set
21	Throttle Position Sensor (TPS) circuit voltage high — open circuit or misadjusted TPS. The engine must run 10 seconds, at specified curb idle speed, before this code will set
22	Throttle Position Sensor (TPS) circuit voltage low — grounded circuit or misadjusted TPS. Engine must run 20 seconds at specified curb idle speed, to set code
23	M/C solenoid circuit open or grounded
24	Vehicle Speed Sensor (VSS) circuit — the vehicle must operate up to 2 minutes, at road speed, before this code will set
32	Barometric Pressure Sensor (BARO) circuit low
34	Vacuum sensor or Manifold Absolute Pressure (MAP) circuit — the engine must run up to 2 minutes, at specified curb idle, before this code will set
35	Idle Speed Control (ISC) switch circuit shorted — up to 70% TPS for over 5 seconds
41	No distributor reference signal to the ECM at specified engine vacuum. This code will store in memory
42	Electronic Spark Timing (EST) bypass circuit or EST circuit grounded or open
43	Electronic Spark Control (ESC) retard signal for too long; causes retard in EST signal
44	Lean exhaust indication — the engine must run 2 minutes, in closed loop and at part throttle, before this code will set
45	Rich exhaust indication — the engine must run 2 minutes, in closed loop and at part throttle, before this code will set
51	Faulty or improperly installed calibration unit (PROM). It takes up to 30 seconds before this code will set
53	Exhaust Gas Recirculation (EGR) valve vacuum sensor has seen improper EGR control vacuum
54	M/C solenoid voltage high, at ECM, as a result of a shorted M/C solenoid circuit and/or faulty ECM

Year — 1987
Model — Firenza
Engine — 2.0L (121 cid) EFI 4 cyl
Engine Code — VIN I

ECM TROUBLE CODES

Code	Explanation
13	Oxygen sensor circuit — open circuit
14	Coolant Temperature Sensor (CTS) circuit — high temperature indicated
15	Coolant Temperature Sensor (CTS) circuit — low temperature indicated
21	Throttle Position Sensor (TPS) circuit — signal voltage high
22	Throttle Position Sensor (TPS) circuit — signal voltage low
23	Manifold Air Temperature (MAT) sensor circuit — low temperature indicated
24	Vehicle Speed Sensor (VSS) circuit
25	Manifold Air Temperature (MAT) sensor circuit — high temperature indicated
33	Manifold Air Pressure (MAP) sensor circuit — signal voltage high — low vacuum
34	Manifold Air Pressure (MAP) sensor circuit — signal voltage low — high vacuum
42	Electronic Spark Timing (EST) circuit
44	Oxygen sensor circuit — lean exhaust indication
45	Oxygen sensor circuit — rich exhaust indication
51	Faulty Mem-Cal

Year — 1987
Model — Firenza
Engine — 2.0L (121 cid) OHC EFI 4 cyl
Engine Code — VIN K

ECM TROUBLE CODES

Code	Explanation
13	Oxygen sensor circuit — open circuit
14	Coolant Temperature Sensor (CTS) circuit — high temperature indicated
15	Coolant Temperature Sensor (CTS) circuit — low temperature indicated
21	Throttle Position Sensor (TPS) circuit — signal voltage high
22	Throttle Position Sensor (TPS) circuit — signal voltage low
23	Manifold Air Temperature (MAT) sensor circuit — low temperature indicated
24	Vehicle Speed Sensor (VSS) circuit
25	Manifold Air Temperature (MAT) sensor circuit — high temperature indicated
33	Manifold Absolute Pressure (MAP) sensor circuit — signal voltage high
34	Manifold Absolute Pressure (MAP) sensor circuit — signal voltage low
35	Idle speed error
42	Electronic Spark Timing (EST) circuit
44	Oxygen sensor circuit — lean exhaust indicated
45	Oxygen sensor circuit — rich exhaust indicated
51	PROM error
53	System over voltage

Year – 1987
Model – Firenza
Engine – 2.8L (173 cid) MPFI V6
Engine Code – VIN W

ECM TROUBLE CODES

Code	Explanation
13	Oxygen sensor circuit – open
14	Coolant sensor circuit – high temperature indicated
15	Coolant sensor circuit – low temperature indicated
21	Throttle Position Sensor (TPS) signal voltage high
22	Throttle Position Sensor (TPS) signal voltage low
23	Manifold Air Temperature (MAT) sensor circuit – low temperature indicated
24	Vehicle Speed Sensor (VSS) circuit
25	Manifold Air Temperature (MAT) sensor circuit – high temperature indicated
33	Mass Air Flow (MAF) high GM/SEC indicated
34	Mass Air Flow (MAF) low GM/SEC indicated
35	Idle speed error
41	Cylinder select error – faulty or incorrect Mem-Cal
42	Electronic Spark Timing (EST) circuit
43	Electronic Spark Control (ESC) circuit
44	Oxygen sensor circuit – lean exhaust indicated
45	Oxygen sensor circuit – rich exhaust indicated
51	Mem-Cal error – faulty or incorrect Mem-Cal
52	Calpak error – faulty or incorrect Calpak
53	System over voltage
54	Fuel Pump circuit – low voltage
61	Degraded oxygen sensor
63	Manifold Absolute Pressure (MAP) sensor circuit – signal voltage high – low vacuum
64	Manifold Absolute Pressure (MAP) sensor circuit – signal voltage low – high vacuum

Year — 1987
Model — Toronado
Engine — 3.8L (231 cid) SFI V6
Engine Code — VIN 3

ECM TROUBLE CODES

Code	Explanation
E013	Open oxygen sensor circuit — canister purge functions are desengaged while specified malfunctions remain current — "Service Engine Soon" message displayed
E014	Coolant sensor circuit — high temperature — "Service Engine Soon" message displayed — forces cooling fans ON
E015	Coolant sensor circuit — low temperature — "Service Engine Soon" message displayed — forces cooling fans ON
E016	System voltage out of range — all solenoid functions are desengaged while specified malfunctions remain current — "Service Engine Soon" message displayed
E021	Throttle Position Sensor (TPS) circuit failure — signal voltage high — Torque Converter Clutch (TCC) functions are desengaged while specified malfunctions remain current — "Service Engine Soon" message displayed
E022	Throttle Position Sensor (TPS) circuit failure — signal voltage low — Torque Converter Clutch (TCC) functions are desengaged while specified malfunctions remain current — "Service Engine Soon" message displayed
E024	Vehicle Speed Sensor (VSS) circuit failure — Torque Converter Clutch (TCC) functions are desengaged while specified malfunctions remain current — "Service Engine Soon" message displayed
E029	Fourth gear switch circuit open — "Service Engine Soon" message displayed
E032	Exhaust Gas Recirculation (EGR) vacuum control system fault — "Service Engine Soon" message displayed
E033	Mass Air Flow (MAF) sensor frequency high — "Service Engine Soon" message displayed
E034	Mass Air Flow (MAF) sensor frequency low — "Service Engine Soon" message displayed
E037	Manifold Absolute Temperature (MAT) sensor circuit — high temperature — "Service Engine Soon" message displayed
E038	Manifold Absolute Temperature (MAT) sensor circuit — low temperature — "Service Engine Soon" message displayed
E040	Power steering pressure switch circuit open — air conditioning clutch and cruise functions are desengaged while specified malfunctions remain current — "Service Engine Soon" message displayed
E041	CAM sensor circuit — C^3I module to ECM — "Service Engine Soon" message displayed
E042	C^3I Electronic Spark Timing (EST) or bypass circuit failure — "Service Engine Soon" message displayed — causes system to operate in bypass spark mode
E043	Electronic Spark Control (ESC) system failure — "Service Engine Soon" message displayed
E044	Lean exhaust indication — "Service Engine Soon" message displayed — forces "Open Loop" operation
E045	Rich exhaust indication — "Service Engine Soon" message displayed — forces "Open Loop" operation
E047	ECM — BCM data — air conditioning clutch and cruise functions are desengaged while specified malfunctions remain current — "Service Engine Soon" message displayed
E051	ECM PROM error — "Service Engine Soon" message displayed — causes system to operate in bypass spark mode — causes system to operate in back-up fuel mode
E052	Calpak error — "Service Engine Soon" message displayed
E055	ECM error — "Service Engine Soon" message displayed

BCM TROUBLE CODES

Code	Explanation
B110	Outside temperature sensor circuit
B111	Air conditioning Hi side temperature sensor
B112	Air conditioning Lo side temperature sensor
B113	In-car temperature sensor
B115	Sunload temperature sensor
B118	Door ajar/jamb switch
B119	Twilight photocell circuit
B120	Twilight delay switch pot and panel dimming
B122	Panel dimming switch
B123	Courtesy light switch
B124	Vehicle Speed Sensor (VSS) circuit
B127	PRNDL sensor
B131	Engine oil pressure sensor
B132	Engine oil pressure sensor circuit
B334	ECM data
B335	Electronic Climate Control (ECC) data
B336	Instrument Panel Control (IPC) data
B337	Programmer data
B338	Chime/voice data
B409	Charging system problem
B411	Battery voltage too low
B412	Battery voltage too high
B440	Air mix door circuit – valve
B445	Air conditioning clutch engaged
B446	Low refrigerant warning
B447	Very low refrigerant problem
B448	Low refrigerant pressure
B449	Air conditioning Hi temperature
B450	Coolant Hi temperature – air conditioning
B552	BCM memory reset
B556	Odometer (E^2) PROM error
B660	Cruise control not in drive
B663	Cruise vehicle speed too high – above set speed
B664	Cruise acceleration too high
B667	Cruise set/coast or resume/acceleration switch shorted
B671	Cruise – servo position sensor circuit
B672	Cruise – vent solenoid circuit
B673	Cruise – vacuum solenoid circuit

Year – 1988
Model – Delta 88
Engine – 3.8L (231 cid) SFI V6
Engine Code – VIN C

ECM TROUBLE CODES

Code	Explanation
13	Oxygen sensor circuit – open
14	Coolant Temperature Sensor (CTS)
15	Coolant Temperature Sensor (CTS)
16	System voltage high
21	Throttle Position Sensor (TPS)
22	Throttle Position Sensor (TPS)
23	Manifold Air Temperature (MAT)
24	Vehicle Speed Sensor (VSS)
25	Manifold Air Temperature (MAT)
26	Quad Driver Module (QDM) error
27, 28, 29	Gear switch diagnosis
31	Park/Neutral switch circuit
34	Mass Air Flow (MAF)
38	Brake switch circuit
39	Torque Converter Clutch (TCC)
41	Cam sensor circuit
42	Electronic Spark Timing (EST)
43	Electronic Spark Control (ESC)
44	Oxygen sensor circuit – lean
45	Oxygen sensor circuit – rich
48	Misfire
51	Mem-Cal error
63, 64, 65	Exhaust Gas Recirculation (EGR)

Year – 1988
Model – Delta 88
Engine – 3.8L (231 cid) SFI V6
Engine Code – VIN 3

ECM TROUBLE CODES

Code	Explanation
13	Oxygen sensor circuit – open
14	Coolant Temperature Sensor (CTS)
15	Coolant Temperature Sensor (CTS)
16	System voltage high
21	Throttle Position Sensor (TPS)
22	Throttle Position Sensor (TPS)
23	Manifold Air Temperature (MAT)
24	Vehicle Speed Sensor (VSS)
25	Manifold Air Temperature (MAT)
26	Quad Driver Module (QDM) error
27, 28, 29	Gear switch diagnosis
31	Park/Neutral switch circuit
34	Mass Air Flow (MAF)
38	Brake switch circuit
39	Torque Converter Clutch (TCC)
41	Cam sensor circuit
42	Electronic Spark Timing (EST)
43	Electronic Spark Control (ESC)
44	Oxygen sensor circuit – lean
45	Oxygen sensor circuit – rich
48	Misfire
51	Mem-Cal error
63, 64, 65	Exhaust Gas Recirculation (EGR)

GENERAL MOTORS CORPORATION
DIAGNOSTIC CODE DATA

Year — 1988
Model — Ninety — Eight
Engine — 3.8L (231 cid) SFI V6
Engine Code — VIN C

ECM TROUBLE CODES

Code	Explanation
13	Oxygen sensor circuit — open
14	Coolant Temperature Sensor (CTS)
15	Coolant Temperature Sensor (CTS)
16	System voltage high
21	Throttle Position Sensor (TPS)
22	Throttle Position Sensor (TPS)
23	Manifold Air Temperature (MAT)
24	Vehicle Speed Sensor (VSS)
25	Manifold Air Temperature (MAT)
26	Quad Driver Module (QDM) error
27, 28, 29	Gear switch diagnosis
31	Park/Neutral switch circuit
34	Mass Air Flow (MAF)
38	Brake switch circuit
39	Torque Converter Clutch (TCC)
41	Cam sensor circuit
42	Electronic Spark Timing (EST)
43	Electronic Spark Control (ESC)
44	Oxygen sensor circuit — lean
45	Oxygen sensor circuit — rich
48	Misfire
51	Mem-Cal error
63, 64, 65	Exhaust Gas Recirculation (EGR)

Year—1988
Model—Cutlass Ciera
Engine—2.5L (151 cid) EFI 4 cyl
Engine Code—VIN R

ECM TROUBLE CODES

Code	Explanation
13	Oxygen sensor circuit—open circuit
14	Coolant Temperature Sensor (CTS) circuit—high temperature indicated
15	Coolant Temperature Sensor (CTS) circuit—low temperature indicated
21	Throttle Position Sensor (TPS) circuit—signal voltage high
22	Throttle Position Sensor (TPS) circuit—signal voltage low
23	Manifold Air Temperature (MAT) sensor circuit—low temperature indicated
24	Vehicle Speed Sensor (VSS) circuit
25	Manifold Air Temperature (MAT) sensor circuit—high temperature indicated
33	Manifold Absolute Pressure (MAP) sensor circuit—signal voltage high—low vacuum
34	Manifold Absolute Pressure (MAP) sensor circuit—signal voltage low—high vacuum
35	Idle speed error
42	Electronic Spark Timing (EST) circuit
44	Oxygen sensor circuit—lean exhaust indicated
45	Oxygen sensor circuit—rich exhaust indicated
51	PROM error—faulty or incorrect PROM
53	System over voltage

Year — 1988
Model — Cutlass Ciera
Engine — 2.8L (173 cid) MPFI V6
Engine Code — VIN W

ECM TROUBLE CODES

Code	Explanation
13	Oxygen sensor circuit — open circuit
14	Coolant Temperature Sensor (CTS) circuit — high temperature indicated
15	Coolant Temperature Sensor (CTS) circuit — low temperature indicated
21	Throttle Position Sensor (TPS) circuit — signal voltage high
22	Throttle Position Sensor (TPS) circuit — signal voltage low
23	Manifold Air Temperature (MAT) sensor circuit — low temperature indicated
24	Vehicle Speed Sensor (VSS) circuit
25	Manifold Air Temperature (MAT) sensor circuit — high temperature indicated
33	Mass Air Flow (MAF) sensor circuit — GM/SEC high
34	Mass Air Flow (MAF) sensor circuit — GM/SEC low
35	Idle speed error
41	Cylinder select error — faulty or incorrect Mem-Cal
42	Electronic Spark Timing (EST) circuit
43	Electronic Spark Control (ESC) circuit
44	Oxygen sensor circuit — lean exhaust indicated
45	Oxygen sensor circuit — rich exhaust indicated
51	Mem-Cal error — faulty or incorrect Mem-Cal
52	Calpak error — faulty or incorrect Calpak
53	System over voltage
54	Fuel pump circuit — low voltage
61	Degraded oxygen sensor
63	Manifold Absolute Pressure (MAP) sensor circuit — signal voltage high
64	Manifold Absolute Pressure (MAP) sensor circuit — signal voltage low

Year — 1988
Model — Cutlass Ciera
Engine — 3.8L (231 cid) SFI V6
Engine Code — VIN 3

ECM TROUBLE CODES

Code	Explanation
13	Oxygen sensor circuit — open circuit
14	Coolant Temperature Sensor (CTS) circuit — high temperature indicated
15	Coolant Temperature Sensor (CTS) circuit — low temperature indicated
21	Throttle Position Sensor (TPS) circuit — signal voltage high
22	Throttle Position Sensor (TPS) circuit — signal voltage low
23	Manifold Air Temperature (MAT) sensor circuit — low temperature indicated
24	Vehicle Speed Sensor (VSS) circuit
25	Manifold Air Temperature (MAT) sensor circuit — high temperature indicated
32	Exhaust Gas Recirculation (EGR) circuit
33	Mass Air Flow (MAF) sensor circuit — GM/SEC high
34	Mass Air Flow (MAF) sensor circuit — GM/SEC low
41	Cam sensor circuit
42	Electronic Spark Timing (EST) circuit
43	Electronic Spark Control (ESC) circuit
44	Oxygen sensor circuit — lean exhaust indicated
45	Oxygen sensor circuit — rich exhaust indicated
51	PROM error — faulty or incorrect PROM
52	Calpak error — faulty or incorrect Calpak
55	ECM error

Year — 1988
Model — Cutlass Supreme
Engine — 2.8L (173 cid) MPFI V6
Engine Code — VIN W

ECM TROUBLE CODES

Code	Explanation
13	Oxygen sensor circuit — open circuit
14	Coolant Temperature Sensor (CTS) circuit — high temperature indicated
15	Coolant Temperature Sensor (CTS) circuit — low temperature indicated
21	Throttle Position Sensor (TPS) circuit — signal voltage high
22	Throttle Position Sensor (TPS) circuit — signal voltage low
23	Manifold Air Temperature (MAT) sensor circuit — low temperature indicated
24	Vehicle Speed Sensor (VSS) circuit
25	Manifold Air Temperature (MAT) sensor circuit — high temperature indicated
26	Quad Driver Module (QDM) error
32	Exhaust Gas Recirculation (EGR) circuit
33	Mass Air Flow (MAF) sensor circuit — GM/SEC high
34	Mass Air Flow (MAF) sensor circuit — GM/SEC low
35	Idle Speed Control (ISC) circuit
41	Cylinder select error — faulty or incorrect Mem-Cal
42	Electronic Spark Timing (EST) circuit
43	Electronic Spark Control (ESC) circuit
44	Oxygen sensor circuit — lean exhaust indicated
45	Oxygen sensor circuit — rich exhaust indicated
51	Mem-Cal error — faulty or incorrect Mem-Cal
53	System over voltage
54	Fuel Pump circuit — low voltage
55	ECM error
61	Degraded oxygen sensor

Year — 1988
Model — Cutlass Supreme Classic
Engine — 5.0L (307 cid) V8
Engine Code — VIN Y

ECM TROUBLE CODES

Code	Explanation
12	No engine speed reference pulse
13	Oxygen sensor circuit — open circuit
14	Coolant Temperature Sensor (CTS) circuit — high temperature indicated
15	Coolant Temperature Sensor (CTS) circuit — low temperature indicated
21	Throttle Position Sensor (TPS) circuit — signal voltage high
22	Throttle Position Sensor (TPS) circuit — signal voltage low
23	Mixture Control (M/C) Solenoid circuit — signal voltage low
24	Vehicle Speed Sensor (VSS) circuit
24B	Park/Neutral (P/N) circuit
32	Barometric Pressure (BARO) sensor circuit — signal voltage low
34	Differential Pressure (VAC) sensor circuit
41	No distributor reference pulse
42	Electronic Spark Timing (EST) circuit
44	Oxygen sensor circuit — lean exhaust indicated
45	Oxygen sensor circuit — rich exhaust indicated
51	PROM error — faulty or incorrect PROM
54	Mixture Control (M/C) solenoid circuit — signal voltage high

Year — 1988
Model — Cutlass Cruiser
Engine — 5.0L (307 cid) V8
Engine Code — VIN Y

ECM TROUBLE CODES

Code	Explanation
13	Oxygen sensor circuit — open circuit
14	Coolant Temperature Sensor (CTS) circuit — high temperature indicated
15	Coolant Temperature Sensor (CTS) circuit — low temperature indicated
21	Throttle Position Sensor (TPS) circuit — signal voltage high
22	Throttle Position Sensor (TPS) circuit — signal voltage low
23	Mixture Control (M/C) solenoid circuit — signal voltage low
24	Vehicle Speed Sensor (VSS) circuit
24B	Park/Neutral (P/N) circuit
31	Canister purge solenoid diagnosis
34	Pressure sensor circuit — signal voltage out of range
41	No distributor reference pulse
42	Electronic Spark Timing (EST) circuit
43	Electronic Spark Control (ESC) circuit
44	Oxygen sensor circuit — lean exhaust indicated
45	Oxygen sensor circuit — rich exhaust indicated
51	PROM error — faulty or incorrect PROM
54	Mixture Control (M/C) Solenoid circuit — signal voltage high

Year – 1988
Model – Cutlass Calais
Engine – 2.3L (140 cid) MPFI 4 cyl
Engine Code – VIN D

ECM TROUBLE CODES

Code	Explanation
13	Oxygen sensor circuit – open circuit
14	Coolant Temperature Sensor (CTS) circuit – high temperature indicated
15	Coolant Temperature Sensor (CTS) circuit – low temperature indicated
21	Throttle Position Sensor (TPS) circuit – signal voltage high
22	Throttle Position Sensor (TPS) circuit – signal voltage low
23	Manifold Air Temperature (MAT) sensor circuit – low temperature indicated
24	Vehicle Speed Sensor (VSS) circuit
25	Manifold Air Temperature (MAT) sensor circuit – high temperature indicated
26	Quad Driver Module (QDM) circuit
33	Manifold Absolute Pressure (MAP) sensor circuit – signal voltage high – low vacuum
34	Manifold Absolute Pressure (MAP) sensor circuit – signal voltage low – high vacuum
36	Closed throttle air flow too high
42	Electronic Spark Timing (EST) circuit
43	Electronic Spark Control (ESC) circuit
44	Oxygen sensor circuit – lean exhaust indicated
45	Oxygen sensor circuit – rich exhaust indicated
51	Mem-Cal error – faulty or incorrect Mem-Cal
53	Battery voltage too high
62	Transmission gear switches circuit
65	Fuel injector circuit – low current
66	Air conditioning pressure sensor circuit

Year — 1988
Model — Cutlass Calais
Engine — 3.0L (183 cid) MPFI V6
Engine Code — VIN L

ECM TROUBLE CODES

Code	Explanation
13	Oxygen sensor circuit — open circuit
14	Coolant Temperature Sensor (CTS) circuit — high temperature indicated
15	Coolant Temperature Sensor (CTS) circuit — low temperature indicated
21	Throttle Position Sensor (TPS) circuit — signal voltage high
22	Throttle Position Sensor (TPS) circuit — signal voltage low
23	Manifold Air Temperature (MAT) sensor circuit — low temperature indicated
24	Vehicle Speed Sensor (VSS) circuit
25	Manifold Air Temperature (MAT) sensor circuit — high temperature indicated
32	Exhaust Gas Recirculation (EGR) circuit
33	Mass Air Flow (MAF) sensor circuit — GM/SEC high
34	Mass Air Flow (MAF) sensor circuit — GM/SEC low
42	Electronic Spark Timing (EST) circuit
43	Electronic Spark Control (ESC) circuit
44	Oxygen sensor circuit — lean exhaust indicated
45	Oxygen sensor circuit — rich exhaust indicated
51	PROM error — faulty or incorrect PROM
52	Calpak error — faulty or incorrect Calpak
55	ECM error

Year — 1988
Model — Cutlass Calais
Engine — 2.5L (151 cid) EFI 4 cyl
Engine Code — VIN U

ECM TROUBLE CODES

Code	Explanation
13	Oxygen sensor circuit — open circuit
14	Coolant Temperature Sensor (CTS) circuit — high temperature indicated
15	Coolant Temperature Sensor (CTS) circuit — low temperature indicated
21	Throttle Position Sensor (TPS) circuit — signal voltage high
22	Throttle Position Sensor (TPS) circuit — signal voltage low
23	Manifold Air Temperature (MAT) sensor circuit — low temperature indicated
24	Vehicle Speed Sensor (VSS) circuit
25	Manifold Air Temperature (MAT) sensor circuit — high temperature indicated
33	Manifold Absolute Pressure (MAP) sensor circuit — signal voltage high — low vacuum
34	Manifold Absolute Pressure (MAP) sensor circuit — signal voltage low — high vacuum
35	Idle speed error
42	Electronic Spark Timing (EST) circuit
44	Oxygen sensor circuit — lean exhaust indicated
45	Oxygen sensor circuit — rich exhaust indicated
51	PROM error — faulty or incorrect PROM
53	System over voltage

Year — 1988
Model — Firenza
Engine — 2.0L (121 cid) TBI 4 cyl
Engine Code — VIN 1

ECM TROUBLE CODES

Code	Explanation
13	Oxygen sensor circuit — open circuit
14	Coolant Temperature Sensor (CTS) circuit — high temperature indicated
15	Coolant Temperature Sensor (CTS) circuit — low temperature indicated
21	Throttle Position Sensor (TPS) circuit — signal voltage high
22	Throttle Position Sensor (TPS) circuit — signal voltage low
23	Manifold Air Temperature (MAT) sensor circuit — low temperature indicated
24	Vehicle Speed Sensor (VSS) circuit
25	Manifold Air Temperature (MAT) sensor circuit — high temperature indicated
32	Exhaust Gas Recirculation (EGR) — system failure
33	Manifold Air Pressure (MAP) sensor circuit — signal voltage high — low vacuum
34	Manifold Air Pressure (MAP) sensor circuit — signal voltage low — high vacuum
42	Electronic Spark Timing (EST) circuit
44	Oxygen sensor circuit — lean exhaust indicated
45	Oxygen sensor circuit — rich exhaust indicated
51	PROM error — faulty or incorrect PROM

Year – 1988
Model – Firenza
Engine – 2.0L (121 cid) OHC 4 cyl
Engine Code – VIN K

ECM TROUBLE CODES

Code	Explanation
13	Oxygen sensor circuit – open circuit
14	Coolant Temperature Sensor (CTS) circuit – high temperature indicated
15	Coolant Temperature Sensor (CTS) circuit – low temperature indicated
21	Throttle Position Sensor (TPS) circuit – signal voltage high
22	Throttle Position Sensor (TPS) circuit – signal voltage low
23	Manifold Air Temperature (MAT) sensor circuit – low temperature indicated
24	Vehicle Speed Sensor (VSS) circuit
25	Manifold Air Temperature (MAT) sensor circuit – high temperature indicated
32	Exhaust Gas Recirculation (EGR) – system failure
33	Manifold Absolute Pressure (MAP) sensor circuit – signal voltage high – low vacuum
34	Manifold Absolute Pressure (MAP) sensor circuit – signal voltage low – high vacuum
35	Idle speed error
42	Electronic Spark Timing (EST) circuit
44	Oxygen sensor circuit – lean exhaust indicated
45	Oxygen sensor circuit – rich exhaust indicated
51	PROM error – faulty or incorrect PROM
53	System over voltage

Year – 1988
Model – Toronado
Engine – 3.8L (231 cid) SFI V6
Engine Code – VIN C

ECM TROUBLE CODES

Code	Explanation
E013	Open oxygen sensor circuit – canister purge functions are desengaged while specified malfunctions remain current – "Service Engine Soon" message displayed
E014	Coolant sensor circuit – high temperature – "Service Engine Soon" message displayed – forces cooling fans ON
E015	Coolant sensor circuit – low temperature – "Service Engine Soon" message displayed – forces cooling fans ON
E016	System voltage out of range – all solenoid functions are desengaged while specified malfunctions remain current – "Service Engine Soon" message displayed
E021	Throttle Position Sensor (TPS) circuit failure – signal voltage high – Torque Converter Clutch (TCC) functions are desengaged while specified malfunctions remain current – "Service Engine Soon" message displayed
E022	Throttle Position Sensor (TPS) circuit failure – signal voltage low – Torque Converter Clutch (TCC) functions are desengaged while specified malfunctions remain current – "Service Engine Soon" message displayed
E023	Manifold Air Temperature (MAT) – low temperature indicated – "Service Engine Soon" message displayed
E024	Vehicle Speed Sensor (VSS) circuit Failure – Torque Converter Clutch (TCC) functions are desengaged while specified malfunctions remain current – "Service Engine Soon" message displayed
E025	Manifold Air Temperature (MAT) – high temperature indicated – "Service Engine Soon" message displayed
E026	Quad Driver Module (QDM) error – "Service Engine Soon" message displayed
E027	Second gear switch circuit – "Service Engine Soon" message displayed
E028	Third gear switch circuit – "Service Engine Soon" message displayed
E029	Fourth gear switch circuit open – "Service Engine Soon" message displayed
E031	Park/Neutral switch circuit – "Service Engine Soon" message displayed
E034	Mass Air Flow (MAF) sensor frequency low – "Service Engine Soon" message displayed
E038	Brake switch circuit – "Service Engine Soon" message displayed
E039	Torque Converter Clutch (TCC) circuit – "Service Engine Soon" message displayed
E041	CAM sensor circuit – C^{3}I module to ECM – "Service Engine Soon" message displayed
E042	Electronic Spark Timing (EST) or bypass circuit failure – "Service Engine Soon" message displayed – causes system to operate in bypass spark mode
E043	Electronic Spark Control (ESC) – system failure – "Service Engine Soon" message displayed
E044	Lean exhaust indication – "Service Engine Soon" message displayed – forces "Open Loop" operation
E045	Rich exhaust indication – "Service Engine Soon" message displayed – forces "Open Loop" operation
E046	Power steering pressure switch circuit open – air conditioning clutch and cruise functions are desengaged while specified malfunctions remain current – "Service Engine Soon" message displayed
E047	ECM – BCM data – air conditioning clutch and cruise functions are desengaged while specified malfunctions remain current – "Service Engine Soon" message displayed
E048	Misfire – "Service Engine Soon" message displayed
E063	Exhaust Gas Recirculation (EGR) – flow problem small – "Service Engine Soon" message displayed – causes system to operate in bypass spark mode – causes system to operate in back-up fuel mode
E064	Exhaust Gas Recirculation (EGR) – flow problem medium – "Service Engine Soon" message displayed
E065	Exhaust Gas Recirculation (EGR) – flow problem large – "Service Engine Soon" message displayed

BCM TROUBLE CODES

Code	Explanation
B110	Outside temperature sensor circuit
B111	Air conditioning Hi side temperature sensor
B112	Air conditioning Lo side temperature sensor
B113	In-car temperature sensor
B115	Sunload temperature sensor
B119	Twilight photocell circuit
B120	Twilight delay switch pot and panel dimming
B122	Panel dimming switch
B123	Courtesy light switch
B124	Vehicle Speed Sensor (VSS) circuit
B127	PRNDL sensor
B132	Engine oil pressure sensor
B334	ECM data
B335	Electronic Climate Control (ECC) data
B336	Instrument Panel Control (IPC) data
B337	Programmer data
B410	Charging system problem
B411	Battery voltage too low
B412	Battery voltage too high
B420	Relay circuit problem
B440	Air mix door circuit—valve
B446	low refrigerant warning
B447	Very low refrigerant problem
B448	low refrigerant pressure
B449	Air conditioning Hi temperature
B450	Coolant Hi temperature—air conditioning
B482	Anti-lock pressure
B552	BCM memory reset
B556	Odometer (E^2) PROM error
B660	Cruise control not in drive
B663	Cruise vehicle speed too high—above set speed
B664	Cruise acceleration too high
B667	Cruise set/coast or resume/acceleration switch shorted
B671	Cruise—servo position sensor circuit
B672	Cruise—vent solenoid circuit
B673	Cruise vacuum solenoid circuit

GENERAL MOTORS CORPORATION
DIAGNOSTIC CODE DATA

Year — 1988
Model — Trofeo
Engine — 3.8L (231 cid) SFI V6
Engine Code — VIN C

ECM TROUBLE CODES

Code	Explanation
E013	Open oxygen sensor circuit — canister purge functions are desengaged while specified malfunctions remain current — "Service Engine Soon" message displayed
E014	Coolant sensor circuit — high temperature — "Service Engine Soon" message displayed — forces cooling fans ON
E015	Coolant sensor circuit — low temperature — "Service Engine Soon" message displayed — forces cooling fans ON
E016	System voltage out of range — all solenoid functions are desengaged while specified malfunctions remain current — "Service Engine Soon" message displayed
E021	Throttle Position Sensor (TPS) circuit failure — signal voltage high — Torque Converter Clutch (TCC) functions are desengaged while specified malfunctions remain current — "Service Engine Soon" message displayed
E022	Throttle Position Sensor (TPS) circuit failure — signal voltage low — Torque Converter Clutch (TCC) functions are desengaged while specified malfunctions remain current — "Service Engine Soon" message displayed
E023	Manifold Air Temperature (MAT) — low temperature indicated — "Service Engine Soon" message displayed
E024	Vehicle Speed Sensor (VSS) circuit failure — Torque Converter Clutch (TCC) functions are desengaged while specified malfunctions remain current — "Service Engine Soon" message displayed
E025	Manifold Air Temperature (MAT) — high temperature indicated — "Service Engine Soon" message displayed
E026	Quad Driver Module (QDM) error — "Service Engine Soon" message displayed
E027	Second gear switch circuit — "Service Engine Soon" message displayed
E028	Third gear switch circuit — "Service Engine Soon" message displayed
E029	Fourth gear switch circuit open — "Service Engine Soon" message displayed
E031	Park/Neutral switch circuit — "Service Engine Soon" message displayed
E034	Mass Air Flow (MAF) sensor frequency low — "Service Engine Soon" message displayed
E038	Brake switch circuit — "Service Engine Soon" message displayed
E039	Torque Converter Clutch (TCC) circuit — "Service Engine Soon" message displayed
E041	CAM sensor circuit — C^3I module to ECM — "Service Engine Soon" message displayed
E042	Electronic Spark Timing (EST) or bypass circuit failure — "Service Engine Soon" message displayed — causes system to operate in bypass spark mode
E043	Electronic Spark Control (ESC) — system failure — "Service Engine Soon" message displayed
E044	Lean exhaust indication — "Service Engine Soon" message displayed — forces "Open Loop" operation
E045	Rich exhaust indication — "Service Engine Soon" message displayed — forces "Open Loop" operation
E046	Power steering pressure switch circuit Open — air conditioning clutch and cruise functions are desengaged while specified malfunctions remain current — "Service Engine Soon" message displayed
E047	ECM — BCM data — air conditioning clutch and cruise functions are desengaged while specified malfunctions remain current — "Service Engine Soon" message displayed
E048	Misfire — "Service Engine Soon" message displayed
E063	Exhaust Gas Recirculation (EGR) — flow problem small — "Service Engine Soon" message displayed — causes system to operate in bypass spark mode — causes system to operate in back-up fuel mode
E064	Exhaust Gas Recirculation (EGR) — flow problem medium — "Service Engine Soon" message displayed
E065	Exhaust Gas Recirculation (EGR) — flow problem large — "Service Engine Soon" message displayed

BCM TROUBLE CODES

Code	Explanation
B110	Outside temperature sensor
B111	Air conditioning Hi side temperature sensor
B112	Air conditioning Lo side temperature sensor
B113	In-car temperature sensor
B115	Sunload temperature sensor
B119	Twilight photocell circuit
B120	Twilight delay switch pot and panel dimming
B122	Panel dimming switch
B123	Courtesy light switch
B124	Vehicle Speed Sensor (VSS) circuit
B127	PRNDL sensor
B132	Engine oil pressure sensor
B334	ECM data
B335	Electronic Climate Control (ECC) data
B336	Instrument Panel Control (IPC) data
B337	Programmer data
B410	Charging system problem
B411	Battery voltage too low
B412	Battery voltage too high
B420	Relay circuit problem
B440	Air mix door circuit—valve
B446	low refrigerant warning
B447	Very low refrigerant problem
B448	low refrigerant pressure
B449	Air conditioning Hi temperature
B450	Coolant Hi temperature—air conditioning
B482	Anti-lock pressure
B552	BCM memory reset
B556	Odometer (E^2) PROM
B660	Cruise control not in drive
B663	Cruise vehicle speed too high—above set speed
B664	Cruise acceleration too high
B667	Cruise set/coast or resume/acceleration switch shorted
B671	Cruise—servo position sensor circuit
B672	Cruise—vent solenoid circuit
B673	Cruise—vacuum solenoid circuit

Year – 1989
Model – Eighty Eight Royale
Engine – 3.8L (231 cid) V6 PFI
Engine Code – VIN C

ECM TROUBLE CODES

Code	Explanation
13	Oxygen sensor circuit – open circuit
14	Coolant Temperature Sensor (CTS) circuit – high temperature indicated
15	Coolant Temperature Sensor (CTS) circuit – low temperature indicated
16	System voltage high
21	Throttle Position Sensor (TPS) circuit – signal voltage high
22	Throttle Position Sensor (TPS) circuit – signal voltage low
23	Manifold Air Temperature (MAT) sensor circuit – low temperature indicated
24	Vehicle Speed Sensor (VSS) circuit
25	Manifold Air Temperature (MAT) sensor circuit – high temperature indicated
26	Quad Driver Module (QDM) circuit
27, 28, 29	Gear switch diagnosis
31	Park/Neutral switch circuit
34	Mass Air Flow (MAF) sensor circuit – GM/SEC low
38	Brake switch circuit
39	Torque Converter Clutch (TCC) circuit
41	Cam sensor circuit
42	Electronic Spark Timing (EST) circuit
43	Electronic Spark Control (ESC) circuit
44	Oxygen sensor circuit – lean exhaust indicated
45	Oxygen sensor circuit – rich exhaust indicated
46	Power Steering Pressure Switch (PSPS) circuit
48	Misfire diagnosis
51	Mem-Cal error – faulty or incorrect Mem-Cal
63, 64, 65	Exhaust Gas Recirculation (EGR) flow check

Year — 1989
Model — Ninety — Eight Regency
Engine — 3.8L (231 cid) V6 PFI
Engine Code — VIN C

ECM TROUBLE CODES

Code	Explanation
13	Oxygen sensor circuit — open circuit
14	Coolant Temperature Sensor (CTS) circuit — high temperature indicated
15	Coolant Temperature Sensor (CTS) circuit — low temperature indicated
16	System voltage high
21	Throttle Position Sensor (TPS) circuit — signal voltage high
22	Throttle Position Sensor (TPS) circuit — signal voltage low
23	Manifold Air Temperature (MAT) sensor circuit — low temperature indicated
24	Vehicle Speed Sensor (VSS) circuit
25	Manifold Air Temperature (MAT) sensor circuit — high temperature indicated
26	Quad Driver Module (QDM) circuit
27, 28, 29	Gear switch diagnosis
31	Park/Neutral switch circuit
34	Mass Air Flow (MAF) sensor circuit — GM/SEC low
38	Brake switch circuit
39	Torque Converter Clutch (TCC) circuit
41	Cam sensor circuit
42	Electronic Spark Timing (EST) circuit
43	Electronic Spark Control (ESC) circuit
44	Oxygen sensor circuit — lean exhaust indicated
45	Oxygen sensor circuit — rich exhaust indicated
46	Power Steering Pressure Switch (PSPS) circuit
48	Misfire diagnosis
51	Mem-Cal error — faulty or incorrect Mem-Cal
63, 64, 65	Exhaust Gas Recirculation (EGR) flow check

Year — 1989
Model — Cutlass Ciera
Engine — 2.5L (151 cid) EFI 4 cyl
Engine Code — VIN R

ECM TROUBLE CODES

Code	Explanation
13	Oxygen sensor circuit — open circuit
14	Coolant Temperature Sensor (CTS) circuit — high temperature indicated
15	Coolant Temperature Sensor (CTS) circuit — low temperature indicated
21	Throttle Position Sensor (TPS) circuit — signal voltage high
22	Throttle Position Sensor (TPS) circuit — signal voltage low
23	Manifold Air Temperature (MAT) sensor circuit — low temperature indicated
24	Vehicle Speed Sensor (VSS) circuit
25	Manifold Air Temperature (MAT) sensor circuit — high temperature indicated
32	Exhaust Gas Recirculation (EGR) system failure
33	Manifold Absolute Pressure (MAP) sensor circuit — signal voltage high — low vacuum
34	Manifold Absolute Pressure (MAP) sensor circuit — signal voltage low — high vacuum
35	Idle speed error
42	Electronic Spark Timing (EST) circuit
44	Oxygen sensor circuit — lean exhaust indicated
45	Oxygen sensor circuit — rich exhaust indicated
51	PROM error — faulty or incorrect PROM
53	System over voltage

Year – 1989
Model – Cutlass Ciera
Engine – 2.8L (173 cid) MPFI V6
Engine Code – VIN W

ECM TROUBLE CODES

Code	Explanation
13	Oxygen sensor circuit – open circuit
14	Coolant Temperature Sensor (CTS) circuit – high temperature indicated
15	Coolant Temperature Sensor (CTS) circuit – low temperature indicated
21	Throttle Position Sensor (TPS) circuit – signal voltage high
22	Throttle Position Sensor (TPS) circuit – signal voltage low
23	Manifold Air Temperature (MAT) sensor circuit – low temperature indicated
24	Vehicle Speed Sensor (VSS) circuit
25	Manifold Air Temperature (MAT) sensor circuit – high temperature indicated
32	Exhaust Gas Recirculation (EGR) circuit
33	Manifold Absolute Pressure (MAP) sensor circuit – signal voltage high
34	Manifold Absolute Pressure (MAP) sensor circuit – signal voltage low
35	Idle speed error
41	Cylinder select error – faulty or incorrect Mem-Cal
42	Electronic Spark Timing (EST) circuit
43	Electronic Spark Control (ESC) circuit
44	Oxygen sensor circuit – lean exhaust indicated
45	Oxygen sensor circuit – rich exhaust indicated
54	Fuel pump circuit – low voltage
51	Mem-Cal error
52	Calpak error
53	System over voltage
61	Degraded oxygen sensor

Year—1989
Model—Cutlass Cruiser
Engine—3.3L (231 cid) V6 SFI
Engine Code—VIN N

ECM TROUBLE CODES

Code	Explanation
13	Oxygen sensor circuit—open circuit
14	Coolant Temperature Sensor (CTS) circuit—high temperature indicated
15	Coolant Temperature Sensor (CTS) circuit—low temperature indicated
16	System voltage high
21	Throttle Position Sensor (TPS) circuit—signal voltage high
22	Throttle Position Sensor (TPS) circuit—signal voltage low
24	Vehicle Speed Sensor (VSS) circuit
26	Quad Driver Module (QDM) circuit (125-C only)
26	Quad Driver Module (QDM) circuit (440-T4 only)
27, 28	Gear switch diagnosis (125-C only)
28, 29	Gear switch diagnosis (440-T4 only)
31	Park/Neutral switch circuit
34	Mass Air Flow (MAF) sensor circuit—GM/SEC low
38	Brake switch circuit
39	Torque Converter Clutch (TCC) circuit (125-C only)
39	Torque Converter Clutch (TCC) circuit (440-T4 only)
42	Electronic Spark Timing (EST) circuit
43	Electronic Spark Control (ESC) circuit
44	Oxygen sensor circuit—lean exhaust indicated
45	Oxygen sensor circuit—rich exhaust indicated
46	Power Steering Pressure Switch (PSPS) circuit
48	Misfire diagnosis
51	Mem-Cal error—faulty or incorrect Mem-Cal

Year — 1989
Model — Cutlass Supreme
Engine — 2.8L (173 cid) V6
Engine Code — VIN W

ECM TROUBLE CODES

Code	Explanation
13	Oxygen sensor circuit — open circuit
14	Coolant Temperature Sensor (CTS) circuit — high temperature indicated
15	Coolant Temperature Sensor (CTS) circuit — low temperature indicated
21	Throttle Position Sensor (TPS) circuit — signal voltage high
22	Throttle Position Sensor (TPS) circuit — signal voltage low
23	Manifold Air Temperature (MAT) sensor circuit — low temperature indicated
24	Vehicle Speed Sensor (VSS) circuit
25	Manifold Air Temperature (MAT) sensor circuit — high temperature indicated
26	Quad — Driver (QDM) error (1 of 3)
32	Exhaust Gas Recirculation (EGR) circuit
33	Manifold Absolute Pressure (MAP) sensor circuit — signal voltage high — low vacuum
34	Manifold Absolute Pressure (MAP) sensor circuit — signal voltage low — high vacuum
35	Idle Speed Control (ISC) circuit
41	Cylinder Select Error — faulty or incorrect Mem-Cal
42	Electronic Spark Timing (EST) circuit
43	Electronic Spark Control (ESC) circuit
44	Oxygen sensor circuit — lean exhaust indicated
45	Oxygen sensor circuit — rich exhaust indicated
53	System over voltage
54	Fuel pump circuit — low voltage
51	Mem-Cal error — faulty or incorrect Mem-Cal
55	ECM error
61	Degraded oxygen sensor

Year — 1989
Model — Cutlass Supreme
Engine — 3.1L (188 cid) V6
Engine Code — VIN T

ECM TROUBLE CODES

Code	Explanation
13	Oxygen sensor circuit — open circuit
14	Coolant Temperature Sensor (CTS) circuit — high temperature indicated
15	Coolant Temperature Sensor (CTS) circuit — low temperature indicated
21	Throttle Position Sensor (TPS) circuit — signal voltage high
22	Throttle Position Sensor (TPS) circuit — signal voltage low
23	Manifold Air Temperature (MAT) sensor circuit — low temperature indicated
24	Vehicle Speed Sensor (VSS) circuit
25	Manifold Air Temperature (MAT) sensor circuit — high temperature indicated
26	Quad Driver Module (QDM) error (1 of 3)
32	Exhaust Gas Recirculation (EGR) circuit
33	Manifold Absolute Pressure (MAP) sensor circuit — signal voltage high — low vacuum
34	Manifold Absolute Pressure (MAP) sensor circuit — signal voltage low — high vacuum
35	Idle Speed Control (ISC) circuit
41	Cylinder Select error — faulty or incorrect Mem-Cal
42	Electronic Spark Timing (EST) circuit
43	Electronic Spark Control (ESC) circuit
44	Oxygen sensor circuit — lean exhaust indicated
45	Oxygen sensor circuit — rich exhaust indicated
53	System over voltage
54	Fuel pump circuit — low voltage
51	Mem-Cal error — faulty or incorrect Mem-Cal
55	ECM error
61	Degraded oxygen sensor

Year – 1989
Model – Cutlass Calais
Engine – 2.3L (138 cid) 4 cyl
Engine Code – VIN A

ECM TROUBLE CODES

Code	Explanation
13	Oxygen sensor circuit – open circuit
14	Coolant Temperature Sensor (CTS) circuit – high temperature indicated
15	Coolant Temperature Sensor (CTS) circuit – low temperature indicated
21	Throttle Position Sensor (TPS) circuit – signal voltage high
22	Throttle Position Sensor (TPS) circuit – signal voltage low
23	Manifold Air Temperature (MAT) sensor circuit – low temperature indicated
24	Vehicle Speed Sensor (VSS) circuit
25	Manifold Air Temperature (MAT) sensor circuit – high temperature indicated
26	Quad – Driver (QDM) error (1 of 3)
33	Manifold Absolute Pressure (MAP) sensor circuit – signal voltage high – low vacuum
34	Manifold Absolute Pressure (MAP) sensor circuit – signal voltage low – high vacuum
35	Idle Speed error
41	1X Reference circuit
42	Electronic Spark Timing (EST) circuit
43	Electronic Spark Control (ESC) circuit
44	Oxygen sensor circuit – lean exhaust indicated
45	Oxygen sensor circuit – rich exhaust indicated
51	Mem-Cal error – faulty or incorrect Mem-Cal
53	Battery voltage too high
62	Transmission gear switches circuit
65	Fuel injector circuit – low current (1 of 2)
66	Air conditioning pressure sensor circuit

GENERAL MOTORS CORPORATION
DIAGNOSTIC CODE DATA

Year — 1989
Model — Cutlass Calais
Engine — 2.3L (138 cid) 4 cyl PFI
Engine Code — VIN D

ECM TROUBLE CODES

Code	Explanation
13	Oxygen sensor circuit — open circuit
14	Coolant Temperature Sensor (CTS) circuit — high temperature indicated
15	Coolant Temperature Sensor (CTS) circuit — low temperature indicated
21	Throttle Position Sensor (TPS) circuit — signal voltage high
22	Throttle Position Sensor (TPS) circuit — signal voltage low
23	Manifold Air Temperature (MAT) sensor circuit — low temperature indicated
24	Vehicle Speed Sensor (VSS) circuit
25	Manifold Air Temperature (MAT) sensor circuit — high temperature indicated
26	Quad Driver Module (QDM) error (1 of 3)
33	Manifold Absolute Pressure (MAP) sensor circuit — signal voltage high — low vacuum
34	Manifold Absolute Pressure (MAP) sensor circuit — signal voltage low — high vacuum
35	Idle speed error
41	1X reference circuit
42	Electronic Spark Timing (EST) circuit
43	Electronic Spark Control (ESC) circuit
44	Oxygen sensor circuit — lean exhaust indicated
45	Oxygen sensor circuit — rich exhaust indicated
51	Mem-Cal error — faulty or incorrect Mem-Cal
53	Battery voltage too high
62	Transmission gear switches circuit
65	Fuel injector circuit — low current (1 of 2)
66	Air conditioning pressure sensor circuit

Year – 1989
Model – Cutlass Calais
Engine – 2.5L (151 cid) 4 cyl TBI
Engine Code – VIN U

ECM TROUBLE CODES

Code	Explanation
13	Oxygen sensor circuit – open circuit
14	Coolant Temperature Sensor (CTS) circuit – high temperature indicated
15	Coolant Temperature Sensor (CTS) circuit – low temperature indicated
21	Throttle Position Sensor (TPS) circuit – signal voltage high
22	Throttle Position Sensor (TPS) circuit – signal voltage low
23	Manifold Air Temperature (MAT) sensor circuit – low temperature indicated
24	Vehicle Speed Sensor (VSS) circuit
25	Manifold Air Temperature (MAT) sensor circuit – high temperature indicated
33	Manifold Absolute Pressure (MAP) sensor circuit – signal voltage high – low vacuum
34	Manifold Absolute Pressure (MAP) sensor circuit – signal voltage low – high vacuum
35	Idle speed error
42	Electronic Spark Timing (EST) circuit
44	Oxygen sensor circuit – lean exhaust indicated
45	Oxygen sensor circuit – rich exhaust indicated
51	PROM error – faulty or incorrect PROM
53	System over voltage

Year — 1989
Model — Cutlass Calais
Engine — 3.3L (231 cid) V6 SFI
Engine Code — VIN N

ECM TROUBLE CODES

Code	Explanation
13	Oxygen sensor circuit — open circuit
14	Coolant Temperature Sensor (CTS) circuit — high temperature indicated
15	Coolant Temperature Sensor (CTS) circuit — low temperature indicated
16	System voltage high
21	Throttle Position Sensor (TPS) circuit — signal voltage high
22	Throttle Position Sensor (TPS) circuit — signal voltage low
24	Vehicle Speed Sensor (VSS) circuit
26	Quad Driver Module (QDM) circuit
27, 28	Gear switch circuits
31	Park/Neutral switch circuit
34	Mass Air Flow (MAF) sensor circuit — GM/SEC low
38	Brake switch circuit
39	Torque Converter Clutch (TCC) circuit
42	Electronic Spark Timing (EST) circuit
43	Electronic Spark Control (ESC) circuit
44	Oxygen sensor circuit — lean exhaust indicated
45	Oxygen sensor circuit — rich exhaust indicated
46	Power Steering Pressure Switch (PSPS) circuit
48	Misfire diagnosis
51	Mem-Cal error — faulty or incorrect Mem-Cal
66	Air conditioning pressure sensor circuit

Year — 1989
Model — Cutlass Cruiser
Engine — 5.0L (307 cid) V8 FI
Engine Code — VIN E

ECM TROUBLE CODES

Code	Explanation
13	Oxygen sensor circuit — open circuit
14	Coolant Temperature Sensor (CTS) circuit — high temperature indicated
15	Coolant Temperature Sensor (CTS) circuit — low temperature indicated
21	Throttle Position Sensor (TPS) circuit — signal voltage high
22	Throttle Position Sensor (TPS) circuit — signal voltage low
23	Manifold Air Temperature (MAT) sensor circuit — low temperature indicated
24	Vehicle Speed Sensor (VSS) circuit
25	Manifold Air Temperature (MAT) sensor circuit — high temperature indicated
32	Exhaust Gas Recirculation (EGR) circuit
33	Manifold Absolute Pressure (MAP) sensor circuit — signal voltage high — low vacuum
34	Manifold Absolute Pressure (MAP) sensor circuit — signal voltage low — high vacuum
42	Electronic Spark Timing (EST) circuit
43	Electronic Spark Control (ESC) circuit
44	Oxygen sensor circuit — lean exhaust indicated
45	Oxygen sensor circuit — rich exhaust indicated
54	Fuel pump circuit — low voltage
51	PROM error — faulty or incorrect PROM
52	Calpak error — faulty or incorrect Calpak
55	ECM error

Year – 1989
Model – Toronado
Engine – 3.8L (231 cid) SFI V6
Engine Code – VIN C

ECM TROUBLE CODES

Code	Explanation
E013	Open oxygen sensor circuit—canister purge functions are desengaged while specified malfunctions remain current—"Service Engine Soon" message displayed
E014	Coolant sensor circuit—high temperature—"Service Engine Soon" message displayed—forces cooling fans ON
E015	Coolant sensor circuit—low temperature—"Service Engine Soon" message displayed—forces cooling fans ON
E016	System voltage out of range—all solenoid functions are desengaged while specified malfunctions remain current—"Service Engine Soon" message displayed
E021	Throttle Position Sensor (TPS) circuit failure—signal voltage high—Torque Converter Clutch (TCC) functions are desengaged while specified malfunctions remain current—"Service Engine Soon" message displayed
E022	Throttle Position Sensor (TPS) circuit failure—signal voltage low—Torque Converter Clutch (TCC) functions are desengaged while specified malfunctions remain current—"Service Engine Soon" message displayed
E023	Manifold Air Temperature (MAT)—low temperature indicated—"Service Engine Soon" message displayed
E024	Vehicle Speed Sensor (VSS) circuit Failure—Torque Converter Clutch (TCC) functions are desengaged while specified malfunctions remain current—"Service Engine Soon" message displayed
E025	Manifold Air Temperature (MAT)—high temperature indicated—"Service Engine Soon" message displayed
E026	Quad Driver Module (QDM) error—"Service Engine Soon" message displayed
E027	Second gear switch circuit—"Service Engine Soon" message displayed
E028	Third gear switch circuit—"Service Engine Soon" message displayed
E029	Fourth gear switch circuit open—"Service Engine Soon" message displayed
E031	Park/Neutral switch circuit—"Service Engine Soon" message displayed
E034	Mass Air Flow (MAF) sensor frequency low—"Service Engine Soon" message displayed
E038	Brake switch circuit—"Service Engine Soon" message displayed
E039	Torque Converter Clutch (TCC) circuit—"Service Engine Soon" message displayed
E041	CAM sensor circuit—C^3I module to ECM—"Service Engine Soon" message displayed
E042	Electronic Spark Timing (EST) or bypass circuit failure—"Service Engine Soon" message displayed—causes system to operate in bypass spark mode
E043	Electronic Spark Control (ESC)—system failure—"Service Engine Soon" message displayed
E044	Lean exhaust indication—"Service Engine Soon" message displayed—forces "Open Loop" operation
E045	Rich exhaust indication—"Service Engine Soon" message displayed—forces "Open Loop" operation
E046	Power steering pressure switch circuit open—air conditioning clutch and cruise functions are desengaged while specified malfunctions remain current—"Service Engine Soon" message displayed
E047	ECM—BCM data—air conditioning clutch and cruise functions are desengaged while specified malfunctions remain current—"Service Engine Soon" message displayed
E048	Misfire—"Service Engine Soon" message displayed
E063	Exhaust Gas Recirculation (EGR)—flow problem small—"Service Engine Soon" message displayed—causes system to operate in bypass spark mode—causes system to operate in back-up fuel mode
E064	Exhaust Gas Recirculation (EGR)—flow problem medium—"Service Engine Soon" message displayed
E065	Exhaust Gas Recirculation (EGR)—flow problem large—"Service Engine Soon" message displayed

BCM TROUBLE CODES

Code	Explanation
B110	Outside temperature sensor circuit—displays diagnostic message on Instrument Panel Control (IPC)
B111	Air conditioning Hi side temperature sensor—displays diagnostic message on Instrument Panel Control (IPC)—forces cooling fans ON
B112	Air conditioning Lo side temperature sensor—displays diagnostic message on Instrument Panel Control (IPC)
B113	In-car temperature sensor—displays diagnostic message on Instrument Panel Control (IPC)
B115	Sunload temperature sensor—displays diagnostic message on Instrument Panel Control (IPC)
B119	Twilight photocell circuit—displays diagnostic message on Instrument Panel Control (IPC)
B120	Twilight delay switch pot and panel dimming—displays diagnostic message on Instrument Panel Control (IPC)
B122	Panel dimming switch—no telltale light or message
B123	Courtesy light switch—no telltale light or message
B124	Vehicle Speed Sensor (VSS) circuit—"Service Engine Soon" telltale in Instrument Panel Control (IPC) turned ON
B127	PRNDL sensor—displays diagnostic message on Instrument Panel Control (IPC)
B132	Engine oil pressure sensor—displays diagnostic message on Instrument Panel Control (IPC)
B140	Phone system problem
B332	Loss of compass data
B334	ECM data—"Service Engine Soon" telltale in Instrument Panel Control (IPC) turned ON—displays diagnostic message on Instrument Panel Control (IPC)
B335	Electronic Climate Control (ECC) data
B336	Instrument Panel Control (IPC) data
B337	Programmer data—displays diagnostic message on Instrument Panel Control (IPC)
B410	Charging system problem—displays diagnostic message on Instrument Panel Control (IPC)
B411	Battery voltage too low—displays diagnostic message on Instrument Panel Control (IPC)
B412	Battery voltage too high—displays diagnostic message on Instrument Panel Control (IPC)
B420	Relay circuit problem—no telltale light or message
B440	Air mix door circuit—valve—no telltale light or message
B446	low refrigerant warning—displays diagnostic message on Instrument Panel Control (IPC)
B447	Very low refrigerant problem—displays diagnostic message on Instrument Panel Control (IPC)
B448	low refrigerant pressure—displays diagnostic message on Instrument Panel Control (IPC)
B449	Air conditioning Hi temperature—displays diagnostic message on Instrument Panel Control (IPC)—forces cooling fans ON
B450	Coolant Hi temperature—air conditioning—displays diagnostic message on Instrument Panel Control (IPC)—forces cooling fans ON
B482	Anti-lock brake pressure circuit problem—displays diagnostic message on Instrument Panel Control (IPC)
B552	BCM memory reset—no telltale light or message
B556	Odometer (E^2) PROM error—displays "Error" in reason odometer
B660	Cruise control not in drive—no telltale light or message
B663	Cruise vehicle speed too high—above set speed—no telltale light or message
B664	Cruise acceleration too high—no telltale light or message
B667	Cruise set/coast or resume/acceleration switch shorted—displays diagnostic message on Instrument Panel Control (IPC)
B671	Cruise—servo position sensor circuit—displays diagnostic message on Instrument Panel Control (IPC)
B672	Cruise—vent solenoid circuit—displays diagnostic message on Instrument Panel Control (IPC)
B673	Cruise vacuum solenoid circuit—displays diagnostic message on Instrument Panel Control (IPC)

GENERAL MOTORS CORPORATION
DIAGNOSTIC CODE DATA

CRT TROUBLE CODES

Code	Explanation
C553	CRT keep alive memory reset—no telltale light or message
C710	CRT–CRTC communications problem—no telltale light or message

Year—1989
Model—Trofeo
Engine—3.8L (231 cid) SFI V6
Engine Code—VIN C

ECM TROUBLE CODES

Code	Explanation
E013	Open oxygen sensor circuit—canister purge functions are desengaged while specified malfunctions remain current—"Service Engine Soon" message displayed
E014	Coolant sensor circuit—high temperature—"Service Engine Soon" message displayed—forces cooling fans ON
E015	Coolant sensor circuit—low temperature—"Service Engine Soon" message displayed—forces cooling fans ON
E016	System voltage out of range—all solenoid functions are desengaged while specified malfunctions remain current—"Service Engine Soon" message displayed
E021	Throttle Position Sensor (TPS) circuit failure—signal voltage high—Torque Converter Clutch (TCC) functions are desengaged while specified malfunctions remain current—"Service Engine Soon" message displayed
E022	Throttle Position Sensor (TPS) circuit failure—signal voltage low—Torque Converter Clutch (TCC) functions are desengaged while specified malfunctions remain current—"Service Engine Soon" message displayed
E023	Manifold Air Temperature (MAT)—low temperature indicated—"Service Engine Soon" message displayed
E024	Vehicle Speed Sensor (VSS) circuit failure—Torque Converter Clutch (TCC) functions are desengaged while specified malfunctions remain current—"Service Engine Soon" message displayed
E025	Manifold Air Temperature (MAT)—high temperature indicated—"Service Engine Soon" message displayed
E026	Quad Driver Module (QDM) error—"Service Engine Soon" message displayed
E027	Second gear switch circuit—"Service Engine Soon" message displayed
E028	Third gear switch circuit—"Service Engine Soon" message displayed
E029	Fourth gear switch circuit open—"Service Engine Soon" message displayed
E031	Park/Neutral switch circuit—"Service Engine Soon" message displayed
E034	Mass Air Flow (MAF) sensor frequency low—"Service Engine Soon" message displayed
E038	Brake switch circuit—"Service Engine Soon" message displayed
E039	Torque Converter Clutch (TCC) circuit—"Service Engine Soon" message displayed
E041	CAM sensor circuit—C^{3}I module to ECM—"Service Engine Soon" message displayed
E042	Electronic Spark Timing (EST) or bypass circuit failure—"Service Engine Soon" message displayed—causes system to operate in bypass spark mode
E043	Electronic Spark Control (ESC)—system failure—"Service Engine Soon" message displayed
E044	Lean exhaust indication—"Service Engine Soon" message displayed—forces "Open Loop" operation
E045	Rich exhaust indication—"Service Engine Soon" message displayed—forces "Open Loop" operation
E046	Power steering pressure switch circuit Open—air conditioning clutch and cruise functions are desengaged while specified malfunctions remain current—"Service Engine Soon" message displayed
E047	ECM—BCM data—air conditioning clutch and cruise functions are desengaged while specified malfunctions remain current—"Service Engine Soon" message displayed

ECM TROUBLE CODES

Code	Explanation
E048	Misfire—"Service Engine Soon" message displayed
E063	Exhaust Gas Recirculation (EGR)—flow problem small—"Service Engine Soon" message displayed—causes system to operate in bypass spark mode—causes system to operate in back-up fuel mode
E064	Exhaust Gas Recirculation (EGR)—flow problem medium—"Service Engine Soon" message displayed
E065	Exhaust Gas Recirculation (EGR)—flow problem large—"Service Engine Soon" message displayed

BCM TROUBLE CODES

Code	Explanation
B110	Outside temperature sensor
B111	Air conditioning Hi side temperature sensor
B112	Air conditioning Lo side temperature sensor
B113	In-car temperature sensor
B115	Sunload temperature sensor
B119	Twilight photocell circuit
B120	Twilight delay switch pot and panel dimming
B122	Panel dimming switch
B123	Courtesy light switch
B124	Vehicle Speed Sensor (VSS) circuit
B127	PRNDL sensor
B132	Engine oil pressure sensor
B334	ECM data
B335	Electronic Climate Control (ECC) data
B336	Instrument Panel Control (IPC) data
B337	Programmer data
B410	Charging system problem
B411	Battery voltage too low
B412	Battery voltage too high
B420	Relay circuit problem
B440	Air mix door circuit—valve
B446	low refrigerant warning
B447	Very low refrigerant problem
B448	low refrigerant pressure
B449	Air conditioning Hi temperature
B450	Coolant Hi temperature—air conditioning
B482	Anti-lock pressure
B552	BCM memory reset
B556	Odometer (E^2) PROM
B660	Cruise control not in drive
B663	Cruise vehicle speed too high—above set speed
B664	Cruise acceleration too high
B667	Cruise set/coast or resume/acceleration switch shorted
B671	Cruise—servo position sensor circuit
B672	Cruise—vent solenoid circuit
B673	Cruise—vacuum solenoid circuit

PONTIAC

Year – 1980
Model – Bonneville
Engine – 3.8L (231 cid) V6
Engine Code – VIN A

ECM TROUBLE CODES

Code	Explanation
12	No tachometer or reference signal to ECM. This code will only be present while a fault exists. Code 12 will not be stored if problem is intermittent
13	Oxygen sensor circuit. The engine has to operate for about 5 minutes at part throttle before this code will show
13 & 43	(At same time) throttle position sensor adjustment
14	Shorted coolant sensor circuit. The engine has to run 2 minutes before this code will show
15	Open coolant sensor circuit. The engine has to operate for about 5 minutes at part throttle before this code will show
21	Shorted Wide Open Throttle (WOT) switch circuit and/or open "Closed Throttle" switch circuit, when used. After 10 seconds and below 800 rpm, check throttle position sensor circuit, when used
22	Grounded closed throttle or Wide Open Throttle (WOT) switch circuit
21 & 22	(At same time) grounded Wide Open Throttle (WOT) switch circuit
23	Open or grounded carburetor mixture control solenoid circuit
32	Barometric Pressure Sensor (BARO) output low
32 & 35	(At same time) grounded +8V, V/ref or faulty ECM
34	(After 10 seconds and below 800 RPM) Manifold Absolute Pressure (MAP) Sensor output high
43	Throttle position sensor adjustment
44	Lean oxygen sensor. Engine must run for approximately 5 minutes in close loop mode and part throttle at road load (drive car) before this code will show
45	Rich oxygen sensor indication. Engine must be run for approximately 5 minutes in closed loop mode and part throttle at road load (drive car) before this code will show
44 & 45	(At same time) faulty oxygen sensor or open oxygen sensor lead
51	Faulty calibration unit (PROM) or improper PROM installation
52 & 53	(At same time) "Check Engine" light OFF, intermittent ECM problem; "Check Engine" light ON, faulty ECM (replace)
54	Faulty carburetor solenoid and/or ECM.
55	Faulty oxygen sensor, open MAP sensor, faulty throttle position sensor (when used) or ECM

Year — 1980
Model — Bonneville
Engine — 4.3L (265 cid) V8
Engine Code — VIN S

ECM TROUBLE CODES

Code	Explanation
12	No tachometer or reference signal to ECM. This code will only be present while a fault exists. Code 12 will not be stored if problem is intermittent
13	Oxygen sensor circuit. The engine has to operate for about 5 minutes at part throttle before this code will show
13 & 43	(At same time) throttle position sensor adjustment
14	Shorted coolant sensor circuit. The engine has to run 2 minutes before this code will show
15	Open coolant sensor circuit. The engine has to operate for about 5 minutes at part throttle before this code will show
21	Shorted Wide Open Throttle (WOT) switch circuit and/or open "Closed Throttle" switch circuit, when used. After 10 seconds and below 800 rpm, check throttle position sensor circuit, when used
22	Grounded closed throttle or Wide Open Throttle (WOT) switch circuit
21 & 22	(At same time) grounded Wide Open Throttle (WOT) switch circuit
23	Open or grounded carburetor mixture control solenoid circuit
32	Barometric Pressure Sensor (BARO) output low
32 & 35	(At same time) grounded +8V, V/ref or faulty ECM
34	(After 10 seconds and below 800 RPM) Manifold Absolute Pressure (MAP) Sensor output high
43	Throttle position sensor adjustment
44	Lean oxygen sensor. Engine must run for approximately 5 minutes in close loop mode and part throttle at road load (drive car) before this code will show
45	Rich oxygen sensor indication. Engine must be run for approximately 5 minutes in closed loop mode and part throttle at road load (drive car) before this code will show
44 & 45	(At same time) faulty oxygen sensor or open oxygen sensor lead
51	Faulty calibration unit (PROM) or improper PROM installation
52 & 53	(At same time) "Check Engine" light OFF, intermittent ECM problem; "Check Engine" light ON; faulty ECM (replace)
54	Faulty carburetor solenoid and/or ECM.
55	Faulty throttle position sensor (when used) or ECM

Year — 1980
Model — Bonneville
Engine — 4.9L (301 cid) V8
Engine Code — VIN W

ECM TROUBLE CODES

Code	Explanation
12	No tachometer or reference signal to ECM. This code will only be present while a fault exists. Code 12 will not be stored if problem is intermittent
13	Oxygen sensor circuit. The engine has to operate for about 5 minutes at part throttle before this code will show
13 & 43	(At same time) throttle position sensor adjustment
14	Shorted coolant sensor circuit. The engine has to run 2 minutes before this code will show
15	Open coolant sensor circuit. The engine has to operate for about 5 minutes at part throttle before this code will show
21	Shorted Wide Open Throttle (WOT) switch circuit and/or open "Closed Throttle" switch circuit, when used. After 10 seconds and below 800 rpm) throttle position sensor circuit, when used
22	Grounded closed throttle or Wide Open Throttle (WOT) switch circuit
21 & 22	(At same time) grounded Wide Open Throttle (WOT) switch circuit
23	Open or grounded carburetor mixture control solenoid circuit
32	Barometric Pressure Sensor (BARO) output low
32 & 35	(At same time) grounded +8V, V/ref or faulty ECM
34	(After 10 seconds and below 800 RPM) Manifold Absolute Pressure (MAP) Sensor output high
43	Throttle position sensor adjustment
44	Lean oxygen sensor. Engine must run for approximately 5 minutes in close loop mode and part throttle at road load (drive car) before this code will show
45	Rich oxygen sensor indication. Engine must be run for approximately 5 minutes in closed loop mode and part throttle at road load (drive car) before this code will show
44 & 45	(At same time) faulty oxygen sensor or open oxygen sensor lead
51	Faulty calibration unit (PROM) or improper PROM installation
52 & 53	(At same time) "Check Engine" light OFF, intermittent ECM problem; "Check Engine" light ON, faulty ECM (replace)
54	Faulty carburetor solenoid and/or ECM.
55	Faulty throttle position sensor (when used) or ECM

Year – 1980
Model – Bonneville
Engine – 5.7L (350 cid) V8
Engine Code – VIN R

ECM TROUBLE CODES

Code	Explanation
12	No tachometer or reference signal to ECM, this code will only be present while a fault exisits. Code 12 will not be stored if problem is intermittent
13	Oxygen sensor circuit. The engine has to operate for about 18 minutes at part throttle before code will show.
13 & 14	(At same time.) See Code 43
14	Shorted coolant sensor circuit. The engine has to run 2 minutes before this code will show
15	Open coolant sensor circuit. The engine has to operate for about 5 minutes at part throttle before this code will show
21	Shorted WOT switch and/or open closed throttle switch circuit (when used)
21	(After 10 seconds and below 800 rpm) throttle position sensor circuit
23	Open or grounded carburetor solenoid circuit
32	Barometric Pressure Sensor (BARO) output low
32 & 55	(At same time) grounded +8V, V (REF) or faulty ECM
34	(After 10 seconds and below 800 rpm) Manifold Absolute Pressure (MAP) sensor output high
43	Throttle position sensor adjustment
44	Lean oxygen sensor. Engine must be run for approximately 5 minutes in closed loop mode and part throttle at roadload (drive car) before this code will show
45	Rich oxygen sensor. Engine must run for approximately 5 minutes in closed loop mode and part throttle before this code will show
44 & 45	(At same time) faulty oxygen sensor
51	Faulty Calibration Unit (PROM) or improper PROM installation
52 & 53	Check engine light OFF – intermittent ECM problem
	Check engine light ON – faulty ECM (replace)
54	Faulty carburetor solenoid and/or ECM
55	Faulty throttle position sensor or ECM

Year — 1980
Model — Bonneville
Engine — 5.7L (350 cid) V8
Engine Code — Vin X

ECM TROUBLE CODES

Code	Explanation
12	No tachometer or reference signal to ECM, this code will only be present while a fault exisits. Code 12 will not be stored if problem is intermittent
13	Oxygen sensor circuit. The engine has to operate for about 18 minutes at part throttle before code will show.
13 & 14	(At same time.) See Code 43
14	Shorted coolant sensor circuit. The engine has to run 2 minutes before this code will show
15	Open coolant sensor circuit. The engine has to operate for about 5 minutes at part throttle before this code will show
21	Shorted WOT switch and/or open closed throttle switch circuit (when used)
21	(After 10 seconds and below 800 rpm) throttle position sensor circuit
23	Open or grounded carburetor solenoid circuit
32	Barometric Pressure Sensor (BARO) output low
32 & 55	(At same time) grounded +8V, V (REF) or faulty ECM
34	(After 10 seconds and below 800 rpm) Manifold Absolute Pressure (MAP) sensor output high
43	Throttle position sensor adjustment
44	Lean oxygen sensor. Engine must be run for approximately 5 minutes in closed loop mode and part throttle at roadload (drive car) before this code will show
45	Rich oxygen sensor. Engine must run for approximately 5 minutes in closed loop mode and part throttle before this code will show
44 & 45	(At same time) faulty oxygen sensor
51	Faulty Calibration Unit (PROM) or improper PROM installation
52 & 53	Check engine light OFF — intermittent ECM problem
	Check engine light ON — faulty ECM (replace)
54	Faulty carburetor solenoid and/or ECM
55	Faulty throttle position sensor or ECM

Year – 1980
Model – Grand Prix
Engine – 3.8L (231 cid) V6
Engine Code – VIN A

ECM TROUBLE CODES

Code	Explanation
12	No tachometer or reference signal to ECM. This code will only be present while a fault exists. Code 12 will not be stored if problem is intermittent
13	Oxygen sensor circuit. The engine has to operate for about 5 minutes at part throttle before this code will show
13 & 43	(At same time) throttle position sensor adjustment
14	Shorted coolant sensor circuit. The engine has to run 2 minutes before this code will show
15	Open coolant sensor circuit. The engine has to operate for about 5 minutes at part throttle before this code will show
21	Shorted Wide Open Throttle (WOT) switch circuit and/or open "Closed Throttle" switch circuit, when used. After 10 seconds and below 800 rpm, check throttle position sensor circuit, when used
22	Grounded closed throttle or Wide Open Throttle (WOT) switch circuit
21 & 22	(At same time) grounded Wide Open Throttle (WOT) switch circuit
23	Open or grounded carburetor mixture control solenoid circuit
32	Barometric Pressure Sensor (BARO) output low
32 & 35	(At same time) grounded +8V, V/ref or faulty ECM
34	(After 10 seconds and below 800 RPM) Manifold Absolute Pressure (MAP) Sensor output high
43	Throttle position sensor adjustment
44	Lean oxygen sensor. Engine must run for approximately 5 minutes in close loop mode and part throttle at road load (drive car) before this code will show
45	Rich oxygen sensor indication. Engine must be run for approximately 5 minutes in closed loop mode and part throttle at road load (drive car) before this code will show
44 & 45	(At same time) faulty oxygen sensor or open oxygen sensor lead
51	Faulty calibration unit (PROM) or improper PROM installation
52 & 53	(At same time) "Check Engine" light OFF, intermittent ECM problem; "Check Engine" light ON, faulty ECM (replace)
54	Faulty carburetor solenoid and/or ECM.
55	Faulty oxygen sensor, open MAP sensor or ECM

Year – 1980
Model – Grand Prix
Engine – 4.3L (265 cid) V8
Engine Code – VIN S

ECM TROUBLE CODES

Code	Explanation
12	No tachometer or reference signal to ECM. This code will only be present while a fault exists. Code 12 will not be stored if problem is intermittent
13	Oxygen sensor circuit. The engine has to operate for about 5 minutes at part throttle before this code will show
13 & 43	(At same time) throttle position sensor adjustment
14	Shorted coolant sensor circuit. The engine has to run 2 minutes before this code will show
15	Open coolant sensor circuit. The engine has to operate for about 5 minutes at part throttle before this code will show
21	Shorted Wide Open Throttle (WOT) switch circuit and/or open "Closed Throttle" switch circuit, when used. After 10 seconds and below 800 rpm, check throttle position sensor circuit, when used
22	Grounded closed throttle or Wide Open Throttle (WOT) switch circuit
21 & 22	(At same time) grounded Wide Open Throttle (WOT) switch circuit
23	Open or grounded carburetor mixture control solenoid circuit
32	Barometric Pressure Sensor (BARO) output low
32 & 35	(At same time) grounded +8V, V/ref or faulty ECM
34	(After 10 seconds and below 800 RPM) Manifold Absolute Pressure (MAP) Sensor output high
43	Throttle position sensor adjustment
44	Lean oxygen sensor. Engine must run for approximately 5 minutes in close loop mode and part throttle at road load (drive car) before this code will show
45	Rich oxygen sensor indication. Engine must be run for approximately 5 minutes in closed loop mode and part throttle at road load (drive car) before this code will show
44 & 45	(At same time) faulty oxygen sensor or open oxygen sensor lead
51	Faulty calibration unit (PROM) or improper PROM installation
52 & 53	(At same time) "Check Engine" light OFF, intermittent ECM problem; "Check Engine" light ON; faulty ECM (replace)
54	Faulty carburetor solenoid and/or ECM.
55	Faulty throttle position sensor (when used) or ECM

Year – 1980
Model – Grand Prix
Engine – 4.9L (301 cid) V8
Engine Code – VIN W

ECM TROUBLE CODES

Code	Explanation
12	No tachometer or reference signal to ECM. This code will only be present while a fault exists. Code 12 will not be stored if problem is intermittent
13	Oxygen sensor circuit. The engine has to operate for about 5 minutes at part throttle before this code will show
13 & 43	(At same time) throttle position sensor adjustment
14	Shorted coolant sensor circuit. The engine has to run 2 minutes before this code will show
15	Open coolant sensor circuit. The engine has to operate for about 5 minutes at part throttle before this code will show
21	Shorted Wide Open Throttle (WOT) switch circuit and/or open "Closed Throttle" switch circuit, when used. After 10 seconds and below 800 rpm) throttle position sensor circuit, when used
22	Grounded closed throttle or Wide Open Throttle (WOT) switch circuit
21 & 22	(At same time) grounded Wide Open Throttle (WOT) switch circuit
23	Open or grounded carburetor mixture control solenoid circuit
32	Barometric Pressure Sensor (BARO) output low
32 & 35	(At same time) grounded +8V, V/ref or faulty ECM
34	(After 10 seconds and below 800 RPM) Manifold Absolute Pressure (MAP) Sensor output high
43	Throttle position sensor adjustment
44	Lean oxygen sensor. Engine must run for approximately 5 minutes in close loop mode and part throttle at road load (drive car) before this code will show
45	Rich oxygen sensor indication. Engine must be run for approximately 5 minutes in closed loop mode and part throttle at road load (drive car) before this code will show
44 & 45	(At same time) faulty oxygen sensor or open oxygen sensor lead
51	Faulty calibration unit (PROM) or improper PROM installation
52 & 53	(At same time) "Check Engine" light OFF, intermittent ECM problem; "Check Engine" light ON, faulty ECM (replace)
54	Faulty carburetor solenoid and/or ECM.
55	Faulty throttle position sensor (when used) or ECM

Year — 1980
Model — Grand Prix
Engine — 5.0L (305 cid) V8
Engine Code — VIN H

ECM TROUBLE CODES

Code	Explanation
12	No tachometer or reference signal to ECM. This code will only be present while a fault exists. Code 12 will not be stored if problem is intermittent
13	Oxygen sensor circuit. The engine has to operate for about 5 minutes at part throttle before this code will show
13 & 43	(At same time) throttle position sensor adjustment
14	Shorted coolant sensor circuit. The engine has to run 2 minutes before this code will show
15	Open coolant sensor circuit. The engine has to operate for about 5 minutes at part throttle before this code will show
21	Shorted Wide Open Throttle (WOT) switch circuit and/or open "Closed Throttle" switch circuit, when used. After 10 seconds and below 800 rpm, check throttle position sensor circuit, when used
22	Grounded closed throttle or Wide Open Throttle (WOT) switch circuit
21 & 22	(At same time) grounded Wide Open Throttle (WOT) switch circuit
23	Open or grounded carburetor mixture control solenoid circuit
32	Barometric Pressure Sensor (BARO) output low
32 & 35	(At same time) grounded +8V, V/ref or faulty ECM
34	(After 10 seconds and below 800 RPM) Manifold Absolute Pressure (MAP) Sensor output high
43	Throttle position sensor adjustment
44	Lean oxygen sensor. Engine must run for approximately 5 minutes in close loop mode and part throttle at road load (drive car) before this code will show
45	Rich oxygen sensor indication. Engine must be run for approximately 5 minutes in closed loop mode and part throttle at road load (drive car) before this code will show
44 & 45	(At same time) faulty oxygen sensor or open oxygen sensor lead
51	Faulty calibration unit (PROM) or improper PROM installation
52 & 53	(At same time) "Check Engine" light OFF, intermittent ECM problem; "Check Engine" light ON, faulty ECM (replace)
54	Faulty carburetor solenoid and/or ECM.
55	Faulty throttle position sensor (when used) or ECM

Year — 1980
Model — Catalina
Engine — 3.8L (231 cid) V6
Engine Code — VIN A

ECM TROUBLE CODES

Code	Explanation
12	No tachometer or reference signal to ECM. This code will only be present while a fault exists. Code 12 will not be stored if problem is intermittent
13	Oxygen sensor circuit. The engine has to operate for about 5 minutes at part throttle before this code will show
13 & 43	(At same time) throttle position sensor adjustment
14	Shorted coolant sensor circuit. The engine has to run 2 minutes before this code will show
15	Open coolant sensor circuit. The engine has to operate for about 5 minutes at part throttle before this code will show
21	Shorted Wide Open Throttle (WOT) switch circuit and/or open "Closed Throttle" switch circuit, when used. After 10 seconds and below 800 rpm, check throttle position sensor circuit, when used
22	Grounded closed throttle or Wide Open Throttle (WOT) switch circuit
21 & 22	(At same time) grounded Wide Open Throttle (WOT) switch circuit
23	Open or grounded carburetor mixture control solenoid circuit
32	Barometric Pressure Sensor (BARO) output low
32 & 35	(At same time) grounded +8V, V/ref or faulty ECM
34	(After 10 seconds and below 800 RPM) Manifold Absolute Pressure (MAP) Sensor output high
43	Throttle position sensor adjustment
44	Lean oxygen sensor. Engine must run for approximately 5 minutes in close loop mode and part throttle at road load (drive car) before this code will show
45	Rich oxygen sensor indication. Engine must be run for approximately 5 minutes in closed loop mode and part throttle at road load (drive car) before this code will show
44 & 45	(At same time) faulty oxygen sensor or open oxygen sensor lead
51	Faulty calibration unit (PROM) or improper PROM installation
52 & 53	(At same time) "Check Engine" light OFF, intermittent ECM problem; "Check Engine" light ON, faulty ECM (replace)
54	Faulty carburetor solenoid and/or ECM.
55	Faulty oxygen sensor, open MAP sensor or ECM

Year – 1980
Model – Catalina
Engine – 4.3L (265 cid) V8
Engine Code – VIN S

ECM TROUBLE CODES

Code	Explanation
12	No tachometer or reference signal to ECM. This code will only be present while a fault exists. Code 12 will not be stored if problem is intermittent
13	Oxygen sensor circuit. The engine has to operate for about 5 minutes at part throttle before this code will show
13 & 43	(At same time) throttle position sensor adjustment
14	Shorted coolant sensor circuit. The engine has to run 2 minutes before this code will show
15	Open coolant sensor circuit. The engine has to operate for about 5 minutes at part throttle before this code will show
21	Shorted Wide Open Throttle (WOT) switch circuit and/or open "Closed Throttle" switch circuit, when used. After 10 seconds and below 800 rpm, check throttle position sensor circuit when used
22	Grounded closed throttle or Wide Open Throttle (WOT) switch circuit
21 & 22	(At same time) grounded Wide Open Throttle (WOT) switch circuit
23	Open or grounded carburetor mixture control solenoid circuit
32	Barometric Pressure Sensor (BARO) output low
32 & 35	(At same time) grounded +8V, V/ref or faulty ECM
34	(After 10 seconds and below 800 RPM) Manifold Absolute Pressure (MAP) Sensor output high
43	Throttle position sensor adjustment
44	Lean oxygen sensor. Engine must run for approximately 5 minutes in close loop mode and part throttle at road load (drive car) before this code will show
45	Rich oxygen sensor indication. Engine must be run for approximately 5 minutes in closed loop mode and part throttle at road load (drive car) before this code will show
44 & 45	(At same time) faulty oxygen sensor or open oxygen sensor lead
51	Faulty calibration unit (PROM) or improper PROM installation
52 & 53	(At same time) "Check Engine" light OFF, intermittent ECM problem; "Check Engine" light ON, faulty ECM (replace)
54	Faulty carburetor solenoid and/or ECM.
55	Faulty throttle position sensor (when used) or ECM

Year – 1980
Model – Catalina
Engine – 4.9L (301 cid) V8
Engine Code – VIN W

ECM TROUBLE CODES

Code	Explanation
12	No tachometer or reference signal to ECM. This code will only be present while a fault exists. Code 12 will not be stored if problem is intermittent
13	Oxygen sensor circuit. The engine has to operate for about 5 minutes at part throttle before this code will show
13 & 43	(At same time) throttle position sensor adjustment
14	Shorted coolant sensor circuit. The engine has to run 2 minutes before this code will show
15	Open coolant sensor circuit. The engine has to operate for about 5 minutes at part throttle before this code will show
21	Shorted Wide Open Throttle (WOT) switch circuit and/or open "Closed Throttle" switch circuit, when used. After 10 seconds and below 800 rpm) throttle position sensor circuit, when used
22	Grounded closed throttle or Wide Open Throttle (WOT) switch circuit
21 & 22	(At same time) grounded Wide Open Throttle (WOT) switch circuit
23	Open or grounded carburetor mixture control solenoid circuit
32	Barometric Pressure Sensor (BARO) output low
32 & 35	(At same time) grounded +8V, V/ref or faulty ECM
34	(After 10 seconds and below 800 RPM) Manifold Absolute Pressure (MAP) Sensor output high
43	Throttle position sensor adjustment
44	Lean oxygen sensor. Engine must run for approximately 5 minutes in close loop mode and part throttle at road load (drive car) before this code will show
45	Rich oxygen sensor indication. Engine must be run for approximately 5 minutes in closed loop mode and part throttle at road load (drive car) before this code will show
44 & 45	(At same time) faulty oxygen sensor or open oxygen sensor lead
51	Faulty calibration unit (PROM) or improper PROM installation
52 & 53	(At same time) "Check Engine" light OFF, intermittent ECM problem; "Check Engine" light ON, faulty ECM (replace)
54	Faulty carburetor solenoid and/or ECM.
55	Faulty throttle position sensor (when used) or ECM

Year – 1980
Model – Catalina
Engine – 5.7L (350 cid) V8
Engine Code – VIN R

ECM TROUBLE CODES

Code	Explanation
12	No tachometer or reference signal to ECM, this code will only be present while a fault exisits. Code 12 will not be stored if problem is intermittent
13	Oxygen sensor circuit. The engine has to operate for about 18 minutes at part throttle before code will show.
13 & 14	(At same time.) See Code 43
14	Shorted coolant sensor circuit. The engine has to run 2 minutes before this code will show
15	Open coolant sensor circuit. The engine has to operate for about 5 minutes at part throttle before this code will show
21	Shorted WOT switch and/or open closed throttle switch circuit (when used)
21	(After 10 seconds and below 800 rpm) throttle position sensor circuit
23	Open or grounded carburetor solenoid circuit
32	Barometric Pressure Sensor (BARO) output low
32 & 55	(At same time) grounded +8V, V (REF) or faulty ECM
34	(After 10 seconds and below 800 rpm) Manifold Absolute Pressure (MAP) sensor output high
43	Throttle position sensor adjustment
44	Lean oxygen sensor. Engine must be run for approximately 5 minutes in closed loop mode and part throttle at roadload (drive car) before this code will show
45	Rich oxygen sensor. Engine must run for approximately 5 minutes in closed loop mode and part throttle before this code will show
44 & 45	(At same time) faulty oxygen sensor
51	Faulty Calibration Unit (PROM) or improper PROM installation
52 & 53	Check engine light OFF – intermittent ECM problem
	Check engine light ON – faulty ECM (replace)
54	Faulty carburetor solenoid and/or ECM
55	Faulty throttle position sensor or ECM

Year – 1980
Model – Catalina
Engine – 5.7L (350 cid) V8
Engine Code – Vin X

ECM TROUBLE CODES

Code	Explanation
12	No tachometer or reference signal to ECM, this code will only be present while a fault exisits. Code 12 will not be stored if problem is intermittent
13	Oxygen sensor circuit. The engine has to operate for about 18 minutes at part throttle before code will show.
13 & 14	(At same time.) See Code 43
14	Shorted coolant sensor circuit. The engine has to run 2 minutes before this code will show
15	Open coolant sensor circuit. The engine has to operate for about 5 minutes at part throttle before this code will show
21	Shorted WOT switch and/or open closed throttle switch circuit (when used)
21	(After 10 seconds and below 800 rpm) throttle position sensor circuit
23	Open or grounded carburetor solenoid circuit
32	Barometric Pressure Sensor (BARO) output low
32 & 55	(At same time) grounded +8V, V (REF) or faulty ECM
34	(After 10 seconds and below 800 rpm) Manifold Absolute Pressure (MAP) sensor output high
43	Throttle position sensor adjustment
44	Lean oxygen sensor. Engine must be run for approximately 5 minutes in closed loop mode and part throttle at roadload (drive car) before this code will show
45	Rich oxygen sensor. Engine must run for approximately 5 minutes in closed loop mode and part throttle before this code will show
44 & 45	(At same time) faulty oxygen sensor
51	Faulty Calibration Unit (PROM) or improper PROM installation
52 & 53	Check engine light OFF – intermittent ECM problem
	Check engine light ON – faulty ECM (replace)
54	Faulty carburetor solenoid and/or ECM
55	Faulty throttle position sensor or ECM

GENERAL MOTORS CORPORATION
DIAGNOSTIC CODE DATA

Year – 1980
Model – Firebird
Engine – 3.8L (231 cid) V6
Engine Code – VIN A

ECM TROUBLE CODES

Code	Explanation
12	No tachometer or reference signal to ECM. This code will only be present while a fault exists. Code 12 will not be stored if problem is intermittent
13	Oxygen sensor circuit. The engine has to operate for about 5 minutes at part throttle before this code will show
13 & 43	(At same time) throttle position sensor adjustment
14	Shorted coolant sensor circuit. The engine has to run 2 minutes before this code will show
15	Open coolant sensor circuit. The engine has to operate for about 5 minutes at part throttle before this code will show
21	Shorted Wide Open Throttle (WOT) switch circuit and/or open "Closed Throttle" switch circuit, when used. After 10 seconds and below 800 rpm, check throttle position sensor circuit, when used
22	Grounded closed throttle or Wide Open Throttle (WOT) switch circuit
21 & 22	(At same time) grounded Wide Open Throttle (WOT) switch circuit
23	Open or grounded carburetor mixture control solenoid circuit
32	Barometric Pressure Sensor (BARO) output low
32 & 35	(At same time) grounded +8V, V/ref or faulty ECM
34	(After 10 seconds and below 800 RPM) Manifold Absolute Pressure (MAP) Sensor output high
43	Throttle position sensor adjustment
44	Lean oxygen sensor. Engine must run for approximately 5 minutes in close loop mode and part throttle at road load (drive car) before this code will show
45	Rich oxygen sensor indication. Engine must be run for approximately 5 minutes in closed loop mode and part throttle at road load (drive car) before this code will show
44 & 45	(At same time) faulty oxygen sensor or open oxygen sensor lead
51	Faulty calibration unit (PROM) or improper PROM installation
52 & 53	(At same time) "Check Engine" light OFF, intermittent ECM problem; "Check Engine" light ON, faulty ECM (replace)
54	Faulty carburetor solenoid and/or ECM.
55	Faulty oxygen sensor, open MAP sensor or ECM

Year – 1980
Model – Firebird
Engine – 4.3L (265 cid) V8
Engine Code – VIN S

ECM TROUBLE CODES

Code	Explanation
12	No tachometer or reference signal to ECM. This code will only be present while a fault exists. Code 12 will not be stored if problem is intermittent
13	Oxygen sensor circuit. The engine has to operate for about 5 minutes at part throttle before this code will show
13 & 43	(At same time) throttle position sensor adjustment
14	Shorted coolant sensor circuit. The engine has to run 2 minutes before this code will show
15	Open coolant sensor circuit. The engine has to operate for about 5 minutes at part throttle before this code will show
21	Shorted Wide Open Throttle (WOT) switch circuit and/or open "Closed Throttle" switch circuit, when used. After 10 seconds and below 800 rpm, check throttle position sensor circuit, when used
22	Grounded closed throttle or Wide Open Throttle (WOT) switch circuit
21 & 22	(At same time) grounded Wide Open Throttle (WOT) switch circuit
23	Open or grounded carburetor mixture control solenoid circuit
32	Barometric Pressure Sensor (BARO) output low
32 & 35	(At same time) grounded +8V, V/ref or faulty ECM
34	(After 10 seconds and below 800 RPM) Manifold Absolute Pressure (MAP) Sensor output high
43	Throttle position sensor adjustment
44	Lean oxygen sensor. Engine must run for approximately 5 minutes in close loop mode and part throttle at road load (drive car) before this code will show
45	Rich oxygen sensor indication. Engine must be run for approximately 5 minutes in closed loop mode and part throttle at road load (drive car) before this code will show
44 & 45	(At same time) faulty oxygen sensor or open oxygen sensor lead
51	Faulty calibration unit (PROM) or improper PROM installation
52 & 53	(At same time) "Check Engine" light OFF, intermittent ECM problem; "Check Engine" light ON, faulty ECM (replace)
54	Faulty carburetor solenoid and/or ECM.
55	Faulty throttle position sensor (when used) or ECM

Year – 1980
Model – Firebird
Engine – 4.9L (301 cid) V8
Engine Code – VIN W

ECM TROUBLE CODES

Code	Explanation
12	No tachometer or reference signal to ECM. This code will only be present while a fault exists. Code 12 will not be stored if problem is intermittent
13	Oxygen sensor circuit. The engine has to operate for about 5 minutes at part throttle before this code will show
13 & 43	(At same time) throttle position sensor adjustment
14	Shorted coolant sensor circuit. The engine has to run 2 minutes before this code will show
15	Open coolant sensor circuit. The engine has to operate for about 5 minutes at part throttle before this code will show
21	Shorted Wide Open Throttle (WOT) switch circuit and/or open ''Closed Throttle'' switch circuit, when used. After 10 seconds and below 800 rpm, check throttle position sensor circuit, when used
22	Grounded closed throttle or Wide Open Throttle (WOT) switch circuit
21 & 22	(At same time) grounded Wide Open Throttle (WOT) switch circuit
23	Open or grounded carburetor mixture control solenoid circuit
32	Barometric Pressure Sensor (BARO) output low
32 & 35	(At same time) grounded +8V, V/ref or faulty ECM
34	(After 10 seconds and below 800 RPM) Manifold Absolute Pressure (MAP) Sensor output high
43	Throttle position sensor adjustment
44	Lean oxygen sensor. Engine must run for approximately 5 minutes in close loop mode and part throttle at road load (drive car) before this code will show
45	Rich oxygen sensor indication. Engine must be run for approximately 5 minutes in closed loop mode and part throttle at road load (drive car) before this code will show
44 & 45	(At same time) faulty oxygen sensor or open oxygen sensor lead
51	Faulty calibration unit (PROM) or improper PROM installation
52 & 53	(At same time) ''Check Engine'' light OFF, intermittent ECM problem; ''Check Engine'' light ON, faulty ECM (replace)
54	Faulty carburetor solenoid and/or ECM.
55	Faulty throttle position sensor (when used) or ECM

Year – 1980
Model – Firebird
Engine – 5.0L (305 cid) V8
Engine Code – VIN H

ECM TROUBLE CODES

Code	Explanation
12	No tachometer or reference signal to ECM. This code will only be present while a fault exists. Code 12 will not be stored if problem is intermittent
13	Oxygen sensor circuit. The engine has to operate for about 5 minutes at part throttle before this code will show
13 & 43	(At same time) throttle position sensor adjustment
14	Shorted coolant sensor circuit. The engine has to run 2 minutes before this code will show
15	Open coolant sensor circuit. The engine has to operate for about 5 minutes at part throttle before this code will show
21	Shorted Wide Open Throttle (WOT) switch circuit and/or open "Closed Throttle" switch circuit, when used. After 10 seconds and below 800 rpm, check throttle position sensor circuit, when used
22	Grounded closed throttle or Wide Open Throttle (WOT) switch circuit
21 & 22	(At same time) grounded Wide Open Throttle (WOT) switch circuit
23	Open or grounded carburetor mixture control solenoid circuit
32	Barometric Pressure Sensor (BARO) output low
32 & 35	(At same time) grounded +8V, V/ref or faulty ECM
34	(After 10 seconds and below 800 RPM) Manifold Absolute Pressure (MAP) Sensor output high
43	Throttle position sensor adjustment
44	Lean oxygen sensor. Engine must run for approximately 5 minutes in close loop mode and part throttle at road load (drive car) before this code will show
45	Rich oxygen sensor indication. Engine must be run for approximately 5 minutes in closed loop mode and part throttle at road load (drive car) before this code will show
44 & 45	(At same time) faulty oxygen sensor or open oxygen sensor lead
51	Faulty calibration unit (PROM) or improper PROM installation
52 & 53	(At same time) "Check Engine" light OFF, intermittent ECM problem; "Check Engine" light ON, faulty ECM (replace)
54	Faulty carburetor solenoid and/or ECM.
55	Faulty throttle position sensor (when used) or ECM

Year – 1980
Model – Trans Am
Engine – 4.9L (301 cid) V8 Turbo
Engine Code – VIN T

ECM TROUBLE CODES

Code	Explanation
12	No tachometer or reference signal to ECM. This code will only be present while a fault exists. Code 12 will not be stored if problem is intermittent
13	Oxygen sensor circuit. The engine has to operate for about 5 minutes at part throttle before this code will show
13 & 43	(At same time) throttle position sensor adjustment
14	Shorted coolant sensor circuit. The engine has to run 2 minutes before this code will show
15	Open coolant sensor circuit. The engine has to operate for about 5 minutes at part throttle before this code will show
21	Shorted Wide Open Throttle (WOT) switch circuit and/or open "Closed Throttle" switch circuit, when used. After 10 seconds and below 800 rpm, check throttle position sensor circuit, when used
22	Grounded closed throttle or Wide Open Throttle (WOT) switch circuit
21 & 22	(At same time) grounded Wide Open Throttle (WOT) switch circuit
23	Open or grounded carburetor mixture control solenoid circuit
32	Barometric Pressure Sensor (BARO) output low
32 & 35	(At same time) grounded + 8V, V/ref or faulty ECM
34	(After 10 seconds and below 800 RPM) Manifold Absolute Pressure (MAP) Sensor output high
43	Throttle position sensor adjustment
44	Lean oxygen sensor. Engine must run for approximately 5 minutes in close loop mode and part throttle at road load (drive car) before this code will show
45	Rich oxygen sensor indication. Engine must be run for approximately 5 minutes in closed loop mode and part throttle at road load (drive car) before this code will show
44 & 45	(At same time) faulty oxygen sensor or open oxygen sensor lead
51	Faulty calibration unit (PROM) or improper PROM installation
52 & 53	(At same time) "Check Engine" light OFF, intermittent ECM problem; "Check Engine" light ON, faulty ECM (replace)
54	Faulty carburetor solenoid and/or ECM.
55	Faulty oxygen sensor, open MAP sensor or ECM

Year — 1980
Model — LeMans
Engine — 3.8L (231 cid) V6
Engine Code — VIN C

ECM TROUBLE CODES

Code	Explanation
12	No tachometer or reference signal to ECM. This code will only be present while a fault exists. Code 12 will not be stored if problem is intermittent
13	Oxygen sensor circuit. The engine has to operate for about 5 minutes at part throttle before this code will show
13 & 43	(At same time) throttle position sensor adjustment
14	Shorted coolant sensor circuit. The engine has to run 2 minutes before this code will show
15	Open coolant sensor circuit. The engine has to operate for about 5 minutes at part throttle before this code will show
21	Shorted Wide Open Throttle (WOT) switch circuit and/or open "Closed Throttle" switch circuit, when used. After 10 seconds and below 800 rpm, check throttle position sensor circuit, when used
22	Grounded closed throttle or Wide Open Throttle (WOT) switch circuit
21 & 22	(At same time) grounded Wide Open Throttle (WOT) switch circuit
23	Open or grounded carburetor mixture control solenoid circuit
32	Barometric Pressure Sensor (BARO) output low
32 & 35	(At same time) grounded +8V, V/ref or faulty ECM
34	(After 10 seconds and below 800 RPM) Manifold Absolute Pressure (MAP) Sensor output high
43	Throttle position sensor adjustment
44	Lean oxygen sensor. Engine must run for approximately 5 minutes in close loop mode and part throttle at road load (drive car) before this code will show
45	Rich oxygen sensor indication. Engine must be run for approximately 5 minutes in closed loop mode and part throttle at road load (drive car) before this code will show
44 & 45	(At same time) faulty oxygen sensor or open oxygen sensor lead
51	Faulty calibration unit (PROM) or improper PROM installation
52 & 53	(At same time) "Check Engine" light OFF, intermittent ECM problem; "Check Engine" light ON, faulty ECM (replace)
54	Faulty carburetor solenoid and/or ECM.
55	Faulty oxygen sensor, open MAP sensor or ECM

Year – 1980
Model – LeMans
Engine – 3.7L (229 cid) V6
Engine Code – VIN K

ECM TROUBLE CODES

Code	Explanation
12	No tachometer or reference signal to ECM. This code will only be present while a fault exists. Code 12 will not be stored if problem is intermittent
13	Oxygen sensor circuit. The engine has to operate for about 5 minutes at part throttle before this code will show
13 & 43	(At same time) throttle position sensor adjustment
14	Shorted coolant sensor circuit. The engine has to run 2 minutes before this code will show
15	Open coolant sensor circuit. The engine has to operate for about 5 minutes at part throttle before this code will show
21	Shorted Wide Open Throttle (WOT) switch circuit and/or open "Closed Throttle" switch circuit, when used. After 10 seconds and below 800 rpm, check throttle position sensor circuit, when used
22	Grounded closed throttle or Wide Open Throttle (WOT) switch circuit
21 & 22	(At same time) grounded Wide Open Throttle (WOT) switch circuit
23	Open or grounded carburetor mixture control solenoid circuit
32	Barometric Pressure Sensor (BARO) output low
32 & 35	(At same time) grounded +8V, V/ref or faulty ECM
34	(After 10 seconds and below 800 RPM) Manifold Absolute Pressure (MAP) Sensor output high
43	Throttle position sensor adjustment
44	Lean oxygen sensor. Engine must run for approximately 5 minutes in close loop mode and part throttle at road load (drive car) before this code will show
45	Rich oxygen sensor indication. Engine must be run for approximately 5 minutes in closed loop mode and part throttle at road load (drive car) before this code will show
44 & 45	(At same time) faulty oxygen sensor or open oxygen sensor lead
51	Faulty calibration unit (PROM) or improper PROM installation
52 & 53	(At same time) "Check Engine" light OFF, intermittent ECM problem; "Check Engine" light ON, faulty ECM (replace)
54	Faulty carburetor solenoid and/or ECM.
55	Faulty throttle position sensor (when used) or ECM

Year — 1980
Model — LeMans
Engine — 4.3L (265 cid) V8
Engine Code — VIN S

ECM TROUBLE CODES

Code	Explanation
12	No tachometer or reference signal to ECM. This code will only be present while a fault exists. Code 12 will not be stored if problem is intermittent
13	Oxygen sensor circuit. The engine has to operate for about 5 minutes at part throttle before this code will show
13 & 43	(At same time) throttle position sensor adjustment
14	Shorted coolant sensor circuit. The engine has to run 2 minutes before this code will show
15	Open coolant sensor circuit. The engine has to operate for about 5 minutes at part throttle before this code will show
21	Shorted Wide Open Throttle (WOT) switch circuit and/or open "Closed Throttle" switch circuit, when used. After 10 seconds and below 800 rpm, check throttle position sensor circuit, when used
22	Grounded closed throttle or Wide Open Throttle (WOT) switch circuit
21 & 22	(At same time) grounded Wide Open Throttle (WOT) switch circuit
23	Open or grounded carburetor mixture control solenoid circuit
32	Barometric Pressure Sensor (BARO) output low
32 & 35	(At same time) grounded +8V, V/ref or faulty ECM
34	(After 10 seconds and below 800 RPM) Manifold Absolute Pressure (MAP) Sensor output high
43	Throttle position sensor adjustment
44	Lean oxygen sensor. Engine must run for approximately 5 minutes in close loop mode and part throttle at road load (drive car) before this code will show
45	Rich oxygen sensor indication. Engine must be run for approximately 5 minutes in closed loop mode and part throttle at road load (drive car) before this code will show
44 & 45	(At same time) faulty oxygen sensor or open oxygen sensor lead
51	Faulty calibration unit (PROM) or improper PROM installation
52 & 53	(At same time) "Check Engine" light OFF, intermittent ECM problem; "Check Engine" light ON, faulty ECM (replace)
54	Faulty carburetor solenoid and/or ECM.
55	Faulty throttle position sensor (when used) or ECM

Year – 1980
Model – LeMans
Engine – 4.9L (301 cid) V8
Engine Code – VIN W

ECM TROUBLE CODES

Code	Explanation
12	No tachometer or reference signal to ECM. This code will only be present while a fault exists. Code 12 will not be stored if problem is intermittent
13	Oxygen sensor circuit. The engine has to operate for about 5 minutes at part throttle before this code will show
13 & 43	(At same time) throttle position sensor adjustment
14	Shorted coolant sensor circuit. The engine has to run 2 minutes before this code will show
15	Open coolant sensor circuit. The engine has to operate for about 5 minutes at part throttle before this code will show
21	Shorted Wide Open Throttle (WOT) switch circuit and/or open "Closed Throttle" switch circuit, when used. After 10 seconds and below 800 rpm, check throttle position sensor circuit, when used
22	Grounded closed throttle or Wide Open Throttle (WOT) switch circuit
21 & 22	(At same time) grounded Wide Open Throttle (WOT) switch circuit
23	Open or grounded carburetor mixture control solenoid circuit
32	Barometric Pressure Sensor (BARO) output low
32 & 35	(At same time) grounded +8V, V/ref or faulty ECM
34	(After 10 seconds and below 800 RPM) Manifold Absolute Pressure (MAP) Sensor output high
43	Throttle position sensor adjustment
44	Lean oxygen sensor. Engine must run for approximately 5 minutes in close loop mode and part throttle at road load (drive car) before this code will show
45	Rich oxygen sensor indication. Engine must be run for approximately 5 minutes in closed loop mode and part throttle at road load (drive car) before this code will show
44 & 45	(At same time) faulty oxygen sensor or open oxygen sensor lead
51	Faulty calibration unit (PROM) or improper PROM installation
52 & 53	(At same time) "Check Engine" light OFF, intermittent ECM problem; "Check Engine" light ON, faulty ECM (replace)
54	Faulty carburetor solenoid and/or ECM.
55	Faulty throttle position sensor (when used) or ECM

Year — 1980
Model — LeMans
Engine — 5.0L (305 cid) V8
Engine Code — VIN H

ECM TROUBLE CODES

Code	Explanation
12	No tachometer or reference signal to ECM. This code will only be present while a fault exists. Code 12 will not be stored if problem is intermittent
13	Oxygen sensor circuit. The engine has to operate for about 5 minutes at part throttle before this code will show
13 & 43	(At same time) throttle position sensor adjustment
14	Shorted coolant sensor circuit. The engine has to run 2 minutes before this code will show
15	Open coolant sensor circuit. The engine has to operate for about 5 minutes at part throttle before this code will show
21	Shorted Wide Open Throttle (WOT) switch circuit and/or open "Closed Throttle" switch circuit, when used. After 10 seconds and below 800 rpm, check throttle position sensor circuit, when used
22	Grounded closed throttle or Wide Open Throttle (WOT) switch circuit
21 & 22	(At same time) grounded Wide Open Throttle (WOT) switch circuit
23	Open or grounded carburetor mixture control solenoid circuit
32	Barometric Pressure Sensor (BARO) output low
32 & 35	(At same time) grounded +8V, V/ref or faulty ECM
34	(After 10 seconds and below 800 RPM) Manifold Absolute Pressure (MAP) Sensor output high
43	Throttle position sensor adjustment
44	Lean oxygen sensor. Engine must run for approximately 5 minutes in close loop mode and part throttle at road load (drive car) before this code will show
45	Rich oxygen sensor indication. Engine must be run for approximately 5 minutes in closed loop mode and part throttle at road load (drive car) before this code will show
44 & 45	(At same time) faulty oxygen sensor or open oxygen sensor lead
51	Faulty calibration unit (PROM) or improper PROM installation
52 & 53	(At same time) "Check Engine" light OFF, intermittent ECM problem; "Check Engine" light ON, faulty ECM (replace)
54	Faulty carburetor solenoid and/or ECM.
55	Faulty throttle position sensor (when used) or ECM

Year — 1980
Model — Phoenix
Engine — 2.5L (151 cid) 4 cyl
Engine Code — VIN 5

ECM TROUBLE CODES

Code	Explanation
12	No tachometer or reference signal to ECM
13	Oxygen sensor circuit. The engine has to operate for about 5 minutes at part throttle before this code will show
14	Shorted coolant sensor circuit. The engine has to run 2 minutes before this code will show
15	Open coolant sensor circuit. The engine has to operate for about 5 minutes at part throttle before this code will show
21 & 22	(At same time) grounded Wide Open Throttle (WOT) switch circuit
22	Grounded closed throttle or Wide Open Throttle (WOT) switch circuit
23	Carburetor solenoid circuit

Year — 1980
Model — Phoenix
Engine — 2.8L (171 cid) V6
Engine Code — VIN 7

ECM TROUBLE CODES

Code	Explanation
12	No tachometer or reference signal to ECM
13	Oxygen sensor circuit. The engine has to operate for about 5 minutes at part throttle before this code will show
14	Shorted coolant sensor circuit. The engine has to run 2 minutes before this code will show
15	Open coolant sensor circuit. The engine has to operate for about 5 minutes at part throttle before this code will show
21	Throttle position sensor circuit
22	Grounded closed throttle or Wide Open Throttle (WOT) switch circuit
23	Carburetor solenoid circuit
44	Lean oxygen sensor
45	Rich oxygen sensor
51	On service unit, check calibration unit (PROM) installation. On factory installed unit, replace ECM

Year — 1980
Model — Sunbird
Engine — 2.5L (151 cid) 4 cyl
Engine Code — VIN V

ECM TROUBLE CODES

Code	Explanation
12	No tachometer or reference signal to ECM. This code will only be present while a fault exists. Code 12 will not be stored if problem is intermittent
13	Oxygen sensor circuit. The engine has to operate for about 5 minutes at part throttle before this code will show
13 & 43	(At same time) throttle position sensor adjustment
14	Shorted coolant sensor circuit. The engine has to run 2 minutes before this code will show
15	Open coolant sensor circuit. The engine has to operate for about 5 minutes at part throttle before this code will show
21	Shorted Wide Open Throttle (WOT) switch circuit and/or open "Closed Throttle" switch circuit, when used. After 10 seconds and below 800 rpm, check throttle position sensor circuit, when used
22	Grounded closed throttle or Wide Open Throttle (WOT) switch circuit
21 & 22	(At same time) grounded Wide Open Throttle (WOT) switch circuit
23	Open or grounded carburetor mixture control solenoid circuit
32	Barometric Pressure Sensor (BARO) output low
32 & 35	(At same time) grounded +8V, V/ref or faulty ECM
34	(After 10 seconds and below 800 RPM) Manifold Absolute Pressure (MAP) Sensor output high
43	Throttle position sensor adjustment
44	Lean oxygen sensor. Engine must run for approximately 5 minutes in close loop mode and part throttle at road load (drive car) before this code will show
45	Rich oxygen sensor indication. Engine must be run for approximately 5 minutes in closed loop mode and part throttle at road load (drive car) before this code will show
44 & 45	(At same time) faulty oxygen sensor or open oxygen sensor lead
51	Faulty calibration unit (PROM) or improper PROM installation
52 & 53	(At same time) "Check Engine" light OFF, intermittent ECM problem; "Check Engine" light ON, faulty ECM (replace)
54	Faulty carburetor solenoid and/or ECM.
55	Faulty throttle position sensor (when used) or ECM

Year – 1980
Model – Sunbird
Engine – 3.8L (231 cid) V6
Engine Code – VIN A

ECM TROUBLE CODES

Code	Explanation
12	No tachometer or reference signal to ECM. This code will only be present while a fault exists. Code 12 will not be stored if problem is intermittent
13	Oxygen sensor circuit. The engine has to operate for about 5 minutes at part throttle before this code will show
13 & 43	(At same time) throttle position sensor adjustment
14	Shorted coolant sensor circuit. The engine has to run 2 minutes before this code will show
15	Open coolant sensor circuit. The engine has to operate for about 5 minutes at part throttle before this code will show
21	Shorted Wide Open Throttle (WOT) switch circuit and/or open "Closed Throttle" switch circuit, when used. After 10 seconds and below 800 rpm, check throttle position sensor circuit, when used
22	Grounded closed throttle or Wide Open Throttle (WOT) switch circuit
21 & 22	(At same time) grounded Wide Open Throttle (WOT) switch circuit
23	Open or grounded carburetor mixture control solenoid circuit
32	Barometric Pressure Sensor (BARO) output low
32 & 35	(At same time) grounded +8V, V/ref or faulty ECM
34	(After 10 seconds and below 800 RPM) Manifold Absolute Pressure (MAP) Sensor output high
43	Throttle position sensor adjustment
44	Lean oxygen sensor. Engine must run for approximately 5 minutes in close loop mode and part throttle at road load (drive car) before this code will show
45	Rich oxygen sensor indication. Engine must be run for approximately 5 minutes in closed loop mode and part throttle at road load (drive car) before this code will show
44 & 45	(At same time) faulty oxygen sensor or open oxygen sensor lead
51	Faulty calibration unit (PROM) or improper PROM installation
52 & 53	(At same time) "Check Engine" light OFF, intermittent ECM problem; "Check Engine" light ON, faulty ECM (replace)
54	Faulty carburetor solenoid and/or ECM.
55	Faulty oxygen sensor, open MAP sensor or ECM

GENERAL MOTORS CORPORATION
DIAGNOSTIC CODE DATA

Year — 1981
Model — Bonneville
Engine — 3.8L (231 cid) V6
Engine Code — VIN A

ECM TROUBLE CODES

Code	Explanation
12	No reference pulses to the ECM. This code is not stored in memory and will only flash while the fault is present
13	Oxygen sensor circuit — the engine must run up to 5 minutes at part throttle, under road load, before this code will set
14	Shorted coolant sensor circuit — the engine must run up to 2 minutes before this code will set
15	Open coolant sensor circuit — the engine must run up to 5 minutes before this code will set
21	Throttle position sensor circuit — the engine must run up to 25 seconds, below 800 rpm, before this code will set
23	Open or grounded M/C solenoid circuit
24	Vehicle Speed Sensor (VSS) circuit — the car must operate up to 5 minutes at road speed before this code will set
32	Barometric Pressure Sensor (BARO) circuit low
34	Manifold Absolute Pressure (MAP) or vacuum sensor circuit. The engine must run up to 5 minutes, below 800 rpm, before this code will set
35	Idle Speed Control (ISC) switch circuit shorted. (Over ½ throttle for over 2 seconds)
36	Electronic Spark Timing (EST) bypass circuit grounded
44	Lean oxygen sensor indication — the engine must run up to 5 minutes, in closed loop, at part throttle and road load before this code will set
44 & 45	(At same time) — faulty oxygen sensor circuit
45	Rich system indication — the engine must run up to 5 minutes, in closed loop, at part throttle and road load before this code will set
51	Faulty calibration unit (PROM) or installation. It takes up to 30 seconds before this code will set
52	Faulty ECM
53	Faulty ECM
54	Shorted M/C solenoid circuit and/or faulty ECM
55	Grounded +8 volts, V ref, faulty oxygen sensor or ECM

Year – 1981
Model – Bonneville
Engine – 4.3L (265 cid) V8
Engine Code – VIN S

ECM TROUBLE CODES

Code	Explanation
12	No reference pulses to the ECM. This code is not stored in memory and will only flash while the fault is present
13	Oxygen sensor circuit – the engine must run up to 5 minutes at part throttle, under road load, before this code will set
14	Shorted coolant sensor circuit – the engine must run up to 2 minutes before this code will set
15	Open coolant sensor circuit – the engine must run up to 5 minutes before this code will set
21	Throttle position sensor circuit – the engine must run up to 25 seconds, below 800 rpm, before this code will set
23	Open or grounded M/C solenoid circuit
24	Vehicle Speed Sensor (VSS) circuit – the car must operate up to 5 minutes at road speed before this code will set
32	Barometric Pressure Sensor (BARO) circuit low
34	Manifold Absolute Pressure (MAP) or vacuum sensor circuit. The engine must run up to 5 minutes, below 800 rpm, before this code will set
35	Idle Speed Control (ISC) switch circuit shorted. (Over ½ throttle for over 2 seconds)
36	Electronic Spark Timing (EST) bypass circuit grounded
44	Lean oxygen sensor indication – the engine must run up to 5 minutes, in closed loop, at part throttle and road load before this code will set
44 & 45	(At same time) – faulty oxygen sensor circuit
45	Rich system indication – the engine must run up to 5 minutes, in closed loop, at part throttle and road load before this code will set
51	Faulty calibration unit (PROM) or installation. It takes up to 30 seconds before this code will set
52	Faulty ECM
53	Faulty ECM
54	Shorted M/C solenoid circuit and/or faulty ECM
55	Grounded +8 volts, V ref, faulty oxygen sensor or ECM

Year — 1981
Model — Bonneville
Engine — 5.0L (307 cid) V8
Engine Code — VIN Y

ECM TROUBLE CODES

Code	Explanation
12	No reference pulses to the ECM. This code is not stored in memory and will only flash while the fault is present
13	Oxygen sensor circuit — the engine must run up to 5 minutes at part throttle, under road load, before this code will set
14	Shorted coolant sensor circuit — the engine must run up to 2 minutes before this code will set
15	Open coolant sensor circuit — the engine must run up to 5 minutes before this code will set
21	Throttle position sensor circuit — the engine must run up to 25 seconds, below 800 rpm, before this code will set
23	Open or grounded M/C solenoid circuit
24	Vehicle Speed Sensor (VSS) circuit — the car must operate up to 5 minutes at road speed before this code will set
32	Barometric Pressure Sensor (BARO) circuit low
34	Manifold Absolute Pressure (MAP) or vacuum sensor circuit. The engine must run up to 5 minutes, below 800 rpm, before this code will set
35	Idle Speed Control (ISC) switch circuit shorted. (Over ½ throttle for over 2 seconds)
36	Electronic Spark Timing (EST) bypass circuit grounded
44	Lean oxygen sensor indication — the engine must run up to 5 minutes, in closed loop, at part throttle and road load before this code will set
44 & 45	(At same time) — faulty oxygen sensor circuit
45	Rich system indication — the engine must run up to 5 minutes, in closed loop, at part throttle and road load before this code will set
51	Faulty calibration unit (PROM) or installation. It takes up to 30 seconds before this code will set
52	Faulty ECM
53	Faulty ECM
54	Shorted M/C solenoid circuit and/or faulty ECM
55	Grounded +8 volts, V ref, faulty oxygen sensor or ECM

Year — 1981
Model — Grand Prix
Engine — 3.8L (231 cid) V6
Engine Code — VIN A

ECM TROUBLE CODES

Code	Explanation
12	No reference pulses to the ECM. This code is not stored in memory and will only flash while the fault is present
13	Oxygen sensor circuit — the engine must run up to 5 minutes at part throttle, under road load, before this code will set
14	Shorted coolant sensor circuit — the engine must run up to 2 minutes before this code will set
15	Open coolant sensor circuit — the engine must run up to 5 minutes before this code will set
21	Throttle position sensor circuit — the engine must run up to 25 seconds, below 800 rpm, before this code will set
23	Open or grounded M/C solenoid circuit
24	Vehicle Speed Sensor (VSS) circuit — the car must operate up to 5 minutes at road speed before this code will set
32	Barometric Pressure Sensor (BARO) circuit low
34	Manifold Absolute Pressure (MAP) or vacuum sensor circuit. The engine must run up to 5 minutes, below 800 rpm, before this code will set
35	Idle Speed Control (ISC) switch circuit shorted. (Over ½ throttle for over 2 seconds)
36	Electronic Spark Timing (EST) bypass circuit grounded
44	Lean oxygen sensor indication — the engine must run up to 5 minutes, in closed loop, at part throttle and road load before this code will set
44 & 45	(At same time) — faulty oxygen sensor circuit
45	Rich system indication — the engine must run up to 5 minutes, in closed loop, at part throttle and road load before this code will set
51	Faulty calibration unit (PROM) or installation. It takes up to 30 seconds before this code will set
52	Faulty ECM
53	Faulty ECM
54	Shorted M/C solenoid circuit and/or faulty ECM
55	Grounded +8 volts, V ref, faulty oxygen sensor or ECM

Year – 1981
Model – Grand Prix
Engine – 4.3L (265 cid) V8
Engine Code – VIN S

ECM TROUBLE CODES

Code	Explanation
12	No reference pulses to the ECM. This code is not stored in memory and will only flash while the fault is present
13	Oxygen sensor circuit—the engine must run up to 5 minutes at part throttle, under road load, before this code will set
14	Shorted coolant sensor circuit—the engine must run up to 2 minutes before this code will set
15	Open coolant sensor circuit—the engine must run up to 5 minutes before this code will set
21	Throttle position sensor circuit—the engine must run up to 25 seconds, below 800 rpm, before this code will set
23	Open or grounded M/C solenoid circuit
24	Vehicle Speed Sensor (VSS) circuit—the car must operate up to 5 minutes at road speed before this code will set
32	Barometric Pressure Sensor (BARO) circuit low
34	Manifold Absolute Pressure (MAP) or vacuum sensor circuit. The engine must run up to 5 minutes, below 800 rpm, before this code will set
35	Idle Speed Control (ISC) switch circuit shorted. (Over ½ throttle for over 2 seconds)
36	Electronic Spark Timing (EST) bypass circuit grounded
44	Lean oxygen sensor indication—the engine must run up to 5 minutes, in closed loop, at part throttle and road load before this code will set
44 & 45	(At same time)—faulty oxygen sensor circuit
45	Rich system indication—the engine must run up to 5 minutes, in closed loop, at part throttle and road load before this code will set
51	Faulty calibration unit (PROM) or installation. It takes up to 30 seconds before this code will set
52	Faulty ECM
53	Faulty ECM
54	Shorted M/C solenoid circuit and/or faulty ECM
55	Grounded +8 volts, V ref, faulty oxygen sensor or ECM

Year – 1981
Model – Catalina
Engine – 3.8L (231 cid) V6
Engine Code – VIN A

ECM TROUBLE CODES

Code	Explanation
12	No reference pulses to the ECM. This code is not stored in memory and will only flash while the fault is present
13	Oxygen sensor circuit – the engine must run up to 5 minutes at part throttle, under road load, before this code will set
14	Shorted coolant sensor circuit – the engine must run up to 2 minutes before this code will set
15	Open coolant sensor circuit – the engine must run up to 5 minutes before this code will set
21	Throttle position sensor circuit – the engine must run up to 25 seconds, below 800 rpm, before this code will set
23	Open or grounded M/C solenoid circuit
24	Vehicle Speed Sensor (VSS) circuit – the car must operate up to 5 minutes at road speed before this code will set
32	Barometric Pressure Sensor (BARO) circuit low
34	Manifold Absolute Pressure (MAP) or vacuum sensor circuit. The engine must run up to 5 minutes, below 800 rpm, before this code will set
35	Idle Speed Control (ISC) switch circuit shorted. (Over ½ throttle for over 2 seconds)
36	Electronic Spark Timing (EST) bypass circuit grounded
44	Lean oxygen sensor indication – the engine must run up to 5 minutes, in closed loop, at part throttle and road load before this code will set
44 & 45	(At same time) – faulty oxygen sensor circuit
45	Rich system indication – the engine must run up to 5 minutes, in closed loop, at part throttle and road load before this code will set
51	Faulty calibration unit (PROM) or installation. It takes up to 30 seconds before this code will set
52	Faulty ECM
53	Faulty ECM
54	Shorted M/C solenoid circuit and/or faulty ECM
55	Grounded +8 volts, V ref, faulty oxygen sensor or ECM

Year — 1981
Model — Catalina
Engine — 4.3L (265 cid) V8
Engine Code — VIN S

ECM TROUBLE CODES

Code	Explanation
12	No reference pulses to the ECM. This code is not stored in memory and will only flash while the fault is present
13	Oxygen sensor circuit — the engine must run up to 5 minutes at part throttle, under road load, before this code will set
14	Shorted coolant sensor circuit — the engine must run up to 2 minutes before this code will set
15	Open coolant sensor circuit — the engine must run up to 5 minutes before this code will set
21	Throttle position sensor circuit — the engine must run up to 25 seconds, below 800 rpm, before this code will set
23	Open or grounded M/C solenoid circuit
24	Vehicle Speed Sensor (VSS) circuit — the car must operate up to 5 minutes at road speed before this code will set
32	Barometric Pressure Sensor (BARO) circuit low
34	Manifold Absolute Pressure (MAP) or vacuum sensor circuit. The engine must run up to 5 minutes, below 800 rpm, before this code will set
35	Idle Speed Control (ISC) switch circuit shorted. (Over ½ throttle for over 2 seconds)
36	Electronic Spark Timing (EST) bypass circuit grounded
44	Lean oxygen sensor indication — the engine must run up to 5 minutes, in closed loop, at part throttle and road load before this code will set
44 & 45	(At same time) — faulty oxygen sensor circuit
45	Rich system indication — the engine must run up to 5 minutes, in closed loop, at part throttle and road load before this code will set
51	Faulty calibration unit (PROM) or installation. It takes up to 30 seconds before this code will set
52	Faulty ECM
53	Faulty ECM
54	Shorted M/C solenoid circuit and/or faulty ECM
55	Grounded +8 volts, V ref, faulty oxygen sensor or ECM

Year – 1981
Model – Catalina
Engine – 5.0L (307 cid) V8
Engine Code – VIN Y

ECM TROUBLE CODES

Code	Explanation
12	No reference pulses to the ECM. This code is not stored in memory and will only flash while the fault is present
13	Oxygen sensor circuit – the engine must run up to 5 minutes at part throttle, under road load, before this code will set
14	Shorted coolant sensor circuit – the engine must run up to 2 minutes before this code will set
15	Open coolant sensor circuit – the engine must run up to 5 minutes before this code will set
21	Throttle position sensor circuit – the engine must run up to 25 seconds, below 800 rpm, before this code will set
23	Open or grounded M/C solenoid circuit
24	Vehicle Speed Sensor (VSS) circuit – the car must operate up to 5 minutes at road speed before this code will set
32	Barometric Pressure Sensor (BARO) circuit low
34	Manifold Absolute Pressure (MAP) or vacuum sensor circuit. The engine must run up to 5 minutes, below 800 rpm, before this code will set
35	Idle Speed Control (ISC) switch circuit shorted. (Over ½ throttle for over 2 seconds)
36	Electronic Spark Timing (EST) bypass circuit grounded
44	Lean oxygen sensor indication – the engine must run up to 5 minutes, in closed loop, at part throttle and road load before this code will set
44 & 45	(At same time) – faulty oxygen sensor circuit
45	Rich system indication – the engine must run up to 5 minutes, in closed loop, at part throttle and road load before this code will set
51	Faulty calibration unit (PROM) or installation. It takes up to 30 seconds before this code will set
52	Faulty ECM
53	Faulty ECM
54	Shorted M/C solenoid circuit and/or faulty ECM
55	Grounded + 8 volts, V ref, faulty oxygen sensor or ECM

Year—1981
Model—Phoenix
Engine—2.5L (151 cid) 4 cyl
Engine Code—VIN 5

ECM TROUBLE CODES

Code	Explanation
12	No reference pulses to the ECM. This code is not stored in memory and will only flash while the fault is present
13	Oxygen sensor circuit—the engine must run up to 5 minutes at part throttle, under road load, before this code will set
14	Shorted coolant sensor circuit—the engine must run up to 2 minutes before this code will set
15	Open coolant sensor circuit—the engine must run up to 5 minutes before this code will set
21	Throttle position sensor circuit—the engine must run up to 25 seconds, below 800 rpm, before this code will set
23	Open or grounded M/C solenoid circuit
34	Vacuum sensor circuit. The engine must run up to 5 minutes, below 800 rpm, before this code will set
35	Idle Speed Control (ISC) switch circuit shorted. (Over ½ throttle for over 2 seconds)
42	Electronic Spark Timing (EST) bypass circuit grounded
44	Lean oxygen sensor indication—the engine must run up to 5 minutes, in closed loop, at part throttle and road load before this code will set
44 & 45	(At same time)—faulty oxygen sensor circuit
45	Rich system indication—the engine must run up to 5 minutes, in closed loop, at part throttle and road load before this code will set
51	Faulty calibration unit (PROM) or installation. It takes up to 30 seconds before this code will set
52	Faulty ECM
53	Faulty ECM
54	Shorted M/C solenoid circuit and/or faulty ECM
55	Grounded +8 volts, V ref, faulty oxygen sensor or ECM

Year — 1981
Model — Phoenix
Engine — 2.8L (171 cid) V6
Engine Code — VIN X

ECM TROUBLE CODES

Code	Explanation
12	No reference pulses to the ECM. This code is not stored in memory and will only flash while the fault is present
13	Oxygen sensor circuit — the engine must run up to 5 minutes at part throttle, under road load, before this code will set
14	Shorted coolant sensor circuit — the engine must run up to 2 minutes before this code will set
15	Open coolant sensor circuit — the engine must run up to 5 minutes before this code will set
21	Throttle position sensor circuit — the engine must run up to 25 seconds, below 800 rpm, before this code will set
23	Open or grounded M/C solenoid circuit
34	Vacuum sensor circuit. The engine must run up to 5 minutes, below 800 rpm, before this code will set
35	Idle Speed Control (ISC) switch circuit shorted. (Over ½ throttle for over 2 seconds)
42	Electronic Spark Timing (EST) bypass circuit grounded
44	Lean oxygen sensor indication — the engine must run up to 5 minutes; in closed loop, at part throttle and road load before this code will set
44 & 45	(At same time) — faulty oxygen sensor circuit
45	Rich system indication — the engine must run up to 5 minutes, in closed loop, at part throttle and road load before this code will set
51	Faulty calibration unit (PROM) or installation. It takes up to 30 seconds before this code will set
52	Faulty ECM
53	Faulty ECM
54	Shorted M/C solenoid circuit and/or faulty ECM
55	Grounded +8 volts, V ref, faulty oxygen sensor or ECM

Year — 1981
Model — Firebird
Engine — 3.8L (231 cid) V6
Engine Code — VIN A

ECM TROUBLE CODES

Code	Explanation
12	No reference pulses to the ECM. This code is not stored in memory and will only flash while the fault is present
13	Oxygen sensor circuit—the engine must run up to 5 minutes at part throttle, under road load, before this code will set
14	Shorted coolant sensor circuit—the engine must run up to 2 minutes before this code will set
15	Open coolant sensor circuit—the engine must run up to 5 minutes before this code will set
21	Throttle position sensor circuit—the engine must run up to 25 seconds, below 800 rpm, before this code will set
23	Open or grounded M/C solenoid circuit
24	Vehicle Speed Sensor (VSS) circuit—the car must operate up to 5 minutes at road speed before this code will set
32	Barometric Pressure Sensor (BARO) circuit low
34	Manifold Absolute Pressure (MAP) or vacuum sensor circuit. The engine must run up to 5 minutes, below 800 rpm, before this code will set
35	Idle Speed Control (ISC) switch circuit shorted. (Over ½ throttle for over 2 seconds)
36	Electronic Spark Timing (EST) bypass circuit grounded
44	Lean oxygen sensor indication—the engine must run up to 5 minutes, in closed loop, at part throttle and road load before this code will set
44 & 45	(At same time)—faulty oxygen sensor circuit
45	Rich system indication—the engine must run up to 5 minutes, in closed loop, at part throttle and road load before this code will set
51	Faulty calibration unit (PROM) or installation. It takes up to 30 seconds before this code will set
52	Faulty ECM
53	Faulty ECM
54	Shorted M/C solenoid circuit and/or faulty ECM
55	Grounded +8 volts, V ref, faulty oxygen sensor or ECM

Year — 1981
Model — Firebird
Engine — 4.3L (265 cid) V8
Engine Code — VIN S

ECM TROUBLE CODES

Code	Explanation
12	No reference pulses to the ECM. This code is not stored in memory and will only flash while the fault is present
13	Oxygen sensor circuit — the engine must run up to 5 minutes at part throttle, under road load, before this code will set
14	Shorted coolant sensor circuit — the engine must run up to 2 minutes before this code will set
15	Open coolant sensor circuit — the engine must run up to 5 minutes before this code will set
21	Throttle position sensor circuit — the engine must run up to 25 seconds, below 800 rpm, before this code will set
23	Open or grounded M/C solenoid circuit
24	Vehicle Speed Sensor (VSS) circuit — the car must operate up to 5 minutes at road speed before this code will set
32	Barometric Pressure Sensor (BARO) circuit low
34	Manifold Absolute Pressure (MAP) or vacuum sensor circuit. The engine must run up to 5 minutes, below 800 rpm, before this code will set
35	Idle Speed Control (ISC) switch circuit shorted. (Over ½ throttle for over 2 seconds)
36	Electronic Spark Timing (EST) bypass circuit grounded
44	Lean oxygen sensor indication — the engine must run up to 5 minutes, in closed loop, at part throttle and road load before this code will set
44 & 45	(At same time) — faulty oxygen sensor circuit
45	Rich system indication — the engine must run up to 5 minutes, in closed loop, at part throttle and road load before this code will set
51	Faulty calibration unit (PROM) or installation. It takes up to 30 seconds before this code will set
52	Faulty ECM
53	Faulty ECM
54	Shorted M/C solenoid circuit and/or faulty ECM
55	Grounded +8 volts, V ref, faulty oxygen sensor or ECM

Year – 1981
Model – Firebird
Engine – 4.9L (301 cid) V8
Engine Code – VIN W

ECM TROUBLE CODES

Code	Explanation
12	No reference pulses to the ECM. This code is not stored in memory and will only flash while the fault is present
13	Oxygen sensor circuit – the engine must run up to 5 minutes at part throttle, under road load, before this code will set
14	Shorted coolant sensor circuit – the engine must run up to 2 minutes before this code will set
15	Open coolant sensor circuit – the engine must run up to 5 minutes before this code will set
21	Throttle position sensor circuit – the engine must run up to 25 seconds, below 800 rpm, before this code will set
23	Open or grounded M/C solenoid circuit
24	Vehicle Speed Sensor (VSS) circuit – the car must operate up to 5 minutes at road speed before this code will set
32	Barometric Pressure Sensor (BARO) circuit low
34	Manifold Absolute Pressure (MAP) or vacuum sensor circuit. The engine must run up to 5 minutes, below 800 rpm, before this code will set
35	Idle Speed Control (ISC) switch circuit shorted. (Over ½ throttle for over 2 seconds)
36	Electronic Spark Timing (EST) bypass circuit grounded
44	Lean oxygen sensor indication – the engine must run up to 5 minutes, in closed loop, at part throttle and road load before this code will set
44 & 45	(At same time) – faulty oxygen sensor circuit
45	Rich system indication – the engine must run up to 5 minutes, in closed loop, at part throttle and road load before this code will set
51	Faulty calibration unit (PROM) or installation. It takes up to 30 seconds before this code will set
52	Faulty ECM
53	Faulty ECM
54	Shorted M/C solenoid circuit and/or faulty ECM
55	Grounded +8 volts, V ref, faulty oxygen sensor or ECM

Year — 1981
Model — Firebird
Engine — 5.0L (305 cid) V8
Engine Code — VIN H

ECM TROUBLE CODES

Code	Explanation
12	No reference pulses to the ECM. This code is not stored in memory and will only flash while the fault is present
13	Oxygen sensor circuit—the engine must run up to 5 minutes at part throttle, under road load, before this code will set
14	Shorted coolant sensor circuit—the engine must run up to 2 minutes before this code will set
15	Open coolant sensor circuit—the engine must run up to 5 minutes before this code will set
21	Throttle position sensor circuit—the engine must run up to 25 seconds, below 800 rpm, before this code will set
23	Open or grounded M/C solenoid circuit
24	Vehicle Speed Sensor (VSS) circuit—the car must operate up to 5 minutes at road speed before this code will set
32	Barometric Pressure Sensor (BARO) circuit low
34	Manifold Absolute Pressure (MAP) or vacuum sensor circuit. The engine must run up to 5 minutes, below 800 rpm, before this code will set
35	Idle Speed Control (ISC) switch circuit shorted. (Over ½ throttle for over 2 seconds)
36	Electronic Spark Timing (EST) bypass circuit grounded
44	Lean oxygen sensor indication—the engine must run up to 5 minutes, in closed loop, at part throttle and road load before this code will set
44 & 45	(At same time)—faulty oxygen sensor circuit
45	Rich system indication—the engine must run up to 5 minutes, in closed loop, at part throttle and road load before this code will set
51	Faulty calibration unit (PROM) or installation. It takes up to 30 seconds before this code will set
52	Faulty ECM
53	Faulty ECM
54	Shorted M/C solenoid circuit and/or faulty ECM
55	Grounded + 8 volts, V ref, faulty oxygen sensor or ECM

Year — 1981
Model — T1000
Engine — 1.6L (98 cid) 4 cyl
Engine Code — VIN 9

ECM TROUBLE CODES

Code	Explanation
12	No reference pulses to the ECM. This code is not stored in memory and will only flash while the fault is present
13	Oxygen sensor circuit — the engine must run up to 5 minutes at part throttle, under road load, before this code will set
14	Shorted coolant sensor circuit — the engine must run up to 2 minutes before this code will set
15	Open coolant sensor circuit — the engine must run up to 5 minutes before this code will set
21	Throttle position sensor circuit — the engine must run up to 25 seconds, below 800 rpm, before this code will set
23	Open or grounded M/C solenoid circuit
34	Vacuum sensor circuit. The engine must run up to 5 minutes, below 800 rpm, before this code will set
35	Idle Speed Control (ISC) switch circuit shorted. (Over ½ throttle for over 2 seconds)
36	Electronic Spark Timing (EST) bypass circuit grounded
44	Lean oxygen sensor indication — the engine must run up to 5 minutes, in closed loop, at part throttle and road load before this code will set
44 & 45	(At same time) — faulty oxygen sensor circuit
45	Rich system indication — the engine must run up to 5 minutes, in closed loop, at part throttle and road load before this code will set
51	Faulty calibration unit (PROM) or installation. It takes up to 30 seconds before this code will set
52	Faulty ECM
53	Faulty ECM
54	Shorted M/C solenoid circuit and/or faulty ECM
55	Grounded +8 volts, V ref, faulty oxygen sensor or ECM

Year — 1981
Model — LeMans
Engine — 3.8L (231 cid) V6
Engine Code — VIN A

ECM TROUBLE CODES

Code	Explanation
12	No reference pulses to the ECM. This code is not stored in memory and will only flash while the fault is present
13	Oxygen sensor circuit — the engine must run up to 5 minutes at part throttle, under road load, before this code will set
14	Shorted coolant sensor circuit — the engine must run up to 2 minutes before this code will set
15	Open coolant sensor circuit — the engine must run up to 5 minutes before this code will set
21	Throttle position sensor circuit — the engine must run up to 25 seconds, below 800 rpm, before this code will set
23	Open or grounded M/C solenoid circuit
24	Vehicle Speed Sensor (VSS) circuit — the car must operate up to 5 minutes at road speed before this code will set
32	Barometric Pressure Sensor (BARO) circuit low
34	Manifold Absolute Pressure (MAP) or vacuum sensor circuit. The engine must run up to 5 minutes, below 800 rpm, before this code will set
35	Idle Speed Control (ISC) switch circuit shorted. (Over ½ throttle for over 2 seconds)
36	Electronic Spark Timing (EST) bypass circuit grounded
44	Lean oxygen sensor indication — the engine must run up to 5 minutes, in closed loop, at part throttle and road load before this code will set
44 & 45	(At same time) — faulty oxygen sensor circuit
45	Rich system indication — the engine must run up to 5 minutes, in closed loop, at part throttle and road load before this code will set
51	Faulty calibration unit (PROM) or installation. It takes up to 30 seconds before this code will set
52	Faulty ECM
53	Faulty ECM
54	Shorted M/C solenoid circuit and/or faulty ECM
55	Grounded +8 volts, V ref, faulty oxygen sensor or ECM

Year — 1981
Model — LeMans
Engine — 4.3L (265 cid) V8
Engine Code — VIN S

ECM TROUBLE CODES

Code	Explanation
12	No reference pulses to the ECM. This code is not stored in memory and will only flash while the fault is present
13	Oxygen sensor circuit — the engine must run up to 5 minutes at part throttle, under road load, before this code will set
14	Shorted coolant sensor circuit — the engine must run up to 2 minutes before this code will set
15	Open coolant sensor circuit — the engine must run up to 5 minutes before this code will set
21	Throttle position sensor circuit — the engine must run up to 25 seconds, below 800 rpm, before this code will set
23	Open or grounded M/C solenoid circuit
24	Vehicle Speed Sensor (VSS) circuit — the car must operate up to 5 minutes at road speed before this code will set
32	Barometric Pressure Sensor (BARO) circuit low
34	Manifold Absolute Pressure (MAP) or vacuum sensor circuit. The engine must run up to 5 minutes, below 800 rpm, before this code will set
35	Idle Speed Control (ISC) switch circuit shorted. (Over ½ throttle for over 2 seconds)
36	Electronic Spark Timing (EST) bypass circuit grounded
44	Lean oxygen sensor indication — the engine must run up to 5 minutes, in closed loop, at part throttle and road load before this code will set
44 & 45	(At same time) — faulty oxygen sensor circuit
45	Rich system indication — the engine must run up to 5 minutes, in closed loop, at part throttle and road load before this code will set
51	Faulty calibration unit (PROM) or installation. It takes up to 30 seconds before this code will set
52	Faulty ECM
53	Faulty ECM
54	Shorted M/C solenoid circuit and/or faulty ECM
55	Grounded +8 volts, V ref, faulty oxygen sensor or ECM

Year — 1981
Model — LeMans Safari
Engine — 4.9L (301 cid) V8
Engine Code — VIN W

ECM TROUBLE CODES

Code	Explanation
12	No reference pulses to the ECM. This code is not stored in memory and will only flash while the fault is present
13	Oxygen sensor circuit — the engine must run up to 5 minutes at part throttle, under road load, before this code will set
14	Shorted coolant sensor circuit — the engine must run up to 2 minutes before this code will set
15	Open coolant sensor circuit — the engine must run up to 5 minutes before this code will set
21	Throttle position sensor circuit — the engine must run up to 25 seconds, below 800 rpm, before this code will set
23	Open or grounded M/C solenoid circuit
24	Vehicle Speed Sensor (VSS) circuit — the car must operate up to 5 minutes at road speed before this code will set
32	Barometric Pressure Sensor (BARO) circuit low
34	Manifold Absolute Pressure (MAP) or vacuum sensor circuit. The engine must run up to 5 minutes, below 800 rpm, before this code will set
35	Idle Speed Control (ISC) switch circuit shorted. (Over ½ throttle for over 2 seconds)
36	Electronic Spark Timing (EST) bypass circuit grounded
44	Lean oxygen sensor indication — the engine must run up to 5 minutes, in closed loop, at part throttle and road load before this code will set
44 & 45	(At same time) — faulty oxygen sensor circuit
45	Rich system indication — the engine must run up to 5 minutes, in closed loop, at part throttle and road load before this code will set
51	Faulty calibration unit (PROM) or installation. It takes up to 30 seconds before this code will set
52	Faulty ECM
53	Faulty ECM
54	Shorted M/C solenoid circuit and/or faulty ECM
55	Grounded +8 volts, V ref, faulty oxygen sensor or ECM

Year – 1982
Model – Bonneville
Engine – 3.8L (231 cid) 2bbl V6
Engine Code – VIN A

ECM TROUBLE CODES

Code	Explanation
12	No reference pulses to the ECM. This code is not stored in memory and will only flash while the fault is present. Normal code with ignition ON, engine not running
13	Oxygen sensor circuit – the engine must run up to 5 minutes at part throttle, under road load, before this code will set
14	Shorted coolant sensor circuit – the engine must run up to 2 minutes before this code will set
15	Open coolant sensor circuit – the engine must run up to 5 minutes before this code will set
21	Throttle position sensor circuit – the engine must run up to 25 seconds, at specified curb idle speed, before this code will set
23	Open or grounded M/C solenoid circuit
24	Vehicle Speed Sensor (VSS) circuit – the car must operate up to 5 minutes at road speed before this code will set
32	Barometric Pressure Sensor (BARO) circuit low
34	Manifold Absolute Pressure (MAP) or Vacuum sensor circuit. The engine must run up to 5 minutes, at specified curb idle speed, before this code will set
35	Idle Speed Control (ISC) switch circuit shorted. (Over ½ throttle for over 2 seconds)
41	No distributor reference pulses at specified engine vacuum. This code will store
42	Electronic Spark Timing (EST) bypass circuit grounded or open
43	ESC retard signal for too long; causes a retard in EST signal
44	Lean oxygen sensor indication – the engine must run up to 5 minutes, in closed loop, at part throttle before this code will set
44 & 45	(At same time) – Faulty oxygen sensor circuit.
45	Rich system indication – the engine must run up to 5 minutes, in closed loop, at part throttle before this code will set
51	Faulty calibration unit (PROM) or installation. It takes up to 30 seconds before this code will set
54	Shorted M/C solenoid circuit and/or faulty ECM
55	Grounded V ref (terminal 21), faulty oxygen sensor or ECM

Year – 1982
Model – Bonneville
Engine – 4.1L (252 cid) 4bbl V6
Engine Code – VIN 4

ECM TROUBLE CODES

Code	Explanation
12	No reference pulses to the ECM. This code is not stored in memory and will only flash while the fault is present. Normal code with ignition ON, engine not running
13	Oxygen sensor circuit – the engine must run up to 5 minutes at part throttle, under road load, before this code will set
14	Shorted coolant sensor circuit – the engine must run up to 2 minutes before this code will set
15	Open coolant sensor circuit – the engine must run up to 5 minutes before this code will set
21	Throttle position sensor circuit – the engine must run up to 25 seconds, at specified curb idle speed, before this code will set
23	Open or grounded M/C solenoid circuit
24	Vehicle Speed Sensor (VSS) circuit – the car must operate up to 5 minutes at road speed before this code will set
32	Barometric Pressure Sensor (BARO) circuit low
34	Manifold Absolute Pressure (MAP) or Vacuum sensor circuit. The engine must run up to 5 minutes, at specified curb idle speed, before this code will set
35	Idle Speed Control (ISC) switch circuit shorted. (Over ½ throttle for over 2 seconds)
41	No distributor reference pulses at specified engine vacuum. This code will store
42	Electronic Spark Timing (EST) bypass circuit grounded or open
43	ESC retard signal for too long; causes a retard in EST signal
44	Lean oxygen sensor indication – the engine must run up to 5 minutes, in closed loop, at part throttle before this code will set
44 & 45	(At same time) – Faulty oxygen sensor circuit.
45	Rich system indication – the engine must run up to 5 minutes, in closed loop, at part throttle before this code will set
51	Faulty calibration unit (PROM) or installation. It takes up to 30 seconds before this code will set
54	Shorted M/C solenoid circuit and/or faulty ECM
55	Grounded V ref (terminal 21), faulty oxygen sensor or ECM

Year – 1982
Model – Grand Prix
Engine – 3.8L (231 cid) 2bbl V6
Engine Code – VIN A

ECM TROUBLE CODES

Code	Explanation
12	No reference pulses to the ECM. This code is not stored in memory and will only flash while the fault is present. Normal code with ignition ON, engine not running
13	Oxygen sensor circuit – the engine must run up to 5 minutes at part throttle, under road load, before this code will set
14	Shorted coolant sensor circuit – the engine must run up to 2 minutes before this code will set
15	Open coolant sensor circuit – the engine must run up to 5 minutes before this code will set
21	Throttle position sensor circuit – the engine must run up to 25 seconds, at specified curb idle speed, before this code will set
23	Open or grounded M/C solenoid circuit
24	Vehicle Speed Sensor (VSS) circuit – the car must operate up to 5 minutes at road speed before this code will set
32	Barometric Pressure Sensor (BARO) circuit low
34	Manifold Absolute Pressure (MAP) or Vacuum sensor circuit. The engine must run up to 5 minutes, at specified curb idle speed, before this code will set
35	Idle Speed Control (ISC) switch circuit shorted. (Over ½ throttle for over 2 seconds)
41	No distributor reference pulses at specified engine vacuum. This code will store
42	Electronic Spark Timing (EST) bypass circuit grounded or open
43	ESC retard signal for too long; causes a retard in EST signal
44	Lean oxygen sensor indication – the engine must run up to 5 minutes, in closed loop, at part throttle before this code will set
44 & 45	(At same time) – Faulty oxygen sensor circuit.
45	Rich system indication – the engine must run up to 5 minutes, in closed loop, at part throttle before this code will set
51	Faulty calibration unit (PROM) or installation. It takes up to 30 seconds before this code will set
54	Shorted M/C solenoid circuit and/or faulty ECM
55	Grounded V ref (terminal 21), faulty oxygen sensor or ECM

Year – 1982
Model – Grand Prix
Engine – 4.1L (252 cid) 4bbl V6
Engine Code – VIN 4

ECM TROUBLE CODES

Code	Explanation
12	No reference pulses to the ECM. This code is not stored in memory and will only flash while the fault is present. Normal code with ignition ON, engine not running
13	Oxygen sensor circuit – the engine must run up to 5 minutes at part throttle, under road load, before this code will set
14	Shorted coolant sensor circuit – the engine must run up to 2 minutes before this code will set
15	Open coolant sensor circuit – the engine must run up to 5 minutes before this code will set
21	Throttle position sensor circuit – the engine must run up to 25 seconds, at specified curb idle speed, before this code will set
23	Open or grounded M/C solenoid circuit
24	Vehicle Speed Sensor (VSS) circuit – the car must operate up to 5 minutes at road speed before this code will set
32	Barometric Pressure Sensor (BARO) circuit low
34	Manifold Absolute Pressure (MAP) or Vacuum sensor circuit. The engine must run up to 5 minutes, at specified curb idle speed, before this code will set
35	Idle Speed Control (ISC) switch circuit shorted. (Over ½ throttle for over 2 seconds)
41	No distributor reference pulses at specified engine vacuum. This code will store
42	Electronic Spark Timing (EST) bypass circuit grounded or open
43	ESC retard signal for too long; causes a retard in EST signal
44	Lean oxygen sensor indication – the engine must run up to 5 minutes, in closed loop, at part throttle before this code will set
44 & 45	(At same time) – Faulty oxygen sensor circuit.
45	Rich system indication – the engine must run up to 5 minutes, in closed loop, at part throttle before this code will set
51	Faulty calibration unit (PROM) or installation. It takes up to 30 seconds before this code will set
54	Shorted M/C solenoid circuit and/or faulty ECM
55	Grounded V ref (terminal 21), faulty oxygen sensor or ECM

GENERAL MOTORS CORPORATION
DIAGNOSTIC CODE DATA

Year – 1982
Model – Firebird
Engine – 2.5L (151 cid) EFI 4 cyl
Engine Code – VIN Z

ECM TROUBLE CODES

Code	Explanation
12	No reference pulses to the ECM. This code is not stored in memory and will only flash while the fault is present. Normal code with ignition ON, engine not running
13	Open oxygen sensor circuit – the engine must run up to 2 minutes before this code will set
14	Shorted coolant sensor circuit – the engine must run up to 2 minutes before this code will set
15	Open coolant sensor circuit – the engine must run up to 2 minutes before this code will set
21	Throttle position sensor circuit – high output
22	Throttle position sensor circuit – low output
24	Vehicle Speed Sensor (VSS) circuit
33	Manifold Absolute Pressure (MAP) sensor circuit – high output
34	Manifold Absolute Pressure (MAP) sensor circuit – low output
42	Electronic Spark Timing (EST) monitor – bypass circuit grounded or open
43	Electronic Spark Control (ESC) signal for too long
44	Lean exhaust system indication
45	Rich exhaust system indication
51	Faulty calibration unit (PROM) or installation
55	Replace ECM (faulty)

Year — 1982
Model — Firebird
Engine — 2.8L (173 cid) V6
Engine Code — VIN 1

ECM TROUBLE CODES

Code	Explanation
12	No reference pulses to the ECM. This code is not stored in memory and will only flash while the fault is present. Normal code with ignition ON, engine not running
13	Oxygen sensor circuit — the engine must run up to 5 minutes at part throttle, under road load, before this code will set
14	Shorted coolant sensor circuit — the engine must run up to 2 minutes before this code will set
15	Open coolant sensor circuit — the engine must run up to 5 minutes before this code will set
21	Throttle position sensor circuit — the engine must run up to 25 seconds, at specified curb idle speed, before this code will set
23	Open or grounded M/C solenoid circuit
24	Vehicle Speed Sensor (VSS) circuit — the car must operate up to 5 minutes at road speed before this code will set
34	Manifold Absolute Pressure (MAP) or Vacuum sensor circuit. The engine must run up to 5 minutes, at specified curb idle speed, before this code will set
41	No distributor reference pulses at specified engine vacuum. This code will store
42	Electronic Spark Timing (EST) bypass circuit grounded or open
44	Lean oxygen sensor indication — the engine must run up to 5 minutes, in closed loop, at part throttle before this code will set
44 & 45	(At same time) — Faulty oxygen sensor circuit.
45	Rich system indication — the engine must run up to 5 minutes, in closed loop, at part throttle before this code will set
51	Faulty calibration unit (PROM) or installation. It takes up to 30 seconds before this code will set
54	Shorted M/C solenoid circuit and/or faulty ECM
55	Grounded V ref (terminal 21), faulty oxygen sensor or ECM

Year — 1982
Model — Firebird
Engine — 5.0L (305 cid) V8
Engine Code — VIN H

ECM TROUBLE CODES

Code	Explanation
12	No reference pulses to the ECM. This code is not stored in memory and will only flash while the fault is present. Normal code with ignition ON, engine not running
13	Oxygen sensor circuit — the engine must run up to 5 minutes at part throttle, under road load, before this code will set
14	Shorted coolant sensor circuit — the engine must run up to 2 minutes before this code will set
15	Open coolant sensor circuit — the engine must run up to 5 minutes before this code will set
21	Throttle position sensor circuit — the engine must run up to 25 seconds, at specified curb idle speed, before this code will set
23	Open or grounded M/C solenoid circuit
24	Vehicle Speed Sensor (VSS) circuit — the car must operate up to 5 minutes at road speed before this code will set
34	Manifold Absolute Pressure (MAP) or Vacuum sensor circuit. The engine must run up to 5 minutes, at specified curb idle speed, before this code will set
41	No distributor reference pulses at specified engine vacuum. This code will store
42	Electronic Spark Timing (EST) bypass circuit grounded or open
44	Lean oxygen sensor indication — the engine must run up to 5 minutes, in closed loop, at part throttle before this code will set
44 & 45	(At same time) — Faulty oxygen sensor circuit.
45	Rich system indication — the engine must run up to 5 minutes, in closed loop, at part throttle before this code will set
51	Faulty calibration unit (PROM) or installation. It takes up to 30 seconds before this code will set
54	Shorted M/C solenoid circuit and/or faulty ECM
55	Grounded V ref (terminal 21), faulty oxygen sensor or ECM

Year — 1982
Model — Firebird
Engine — 5.0L (305 cid) V8
Engine Code — VIN 7

ECM TROUBLE CODES

Code	Explanation
12	No reference pulses to the ECM. This code is not stored in memory and will only flash while the fault is present. Normal code with ignition ON, engine not running
13	Open oxygen sensor circuit — the engine must run up to 2 minutes before this code will set
14	Shorted coolant sensor circuit — the engine must run up to 2 minutes before this code will set
15	Open coolant sensor circuit — the engine must run up to 2 minutes before this code will set
21	Throttle position sensor circuit — high output
22	Throttle position sensor circuit — low output
24	Vehicle Speed Sensor (VSS) circuit
33	Manifold Absolute Pressure (MAP) sensor circuit — high output
34	Manifold Absolute Pressure (MAP) sensor circuit — low output
42	Electronic Spark Timing (EST) monitor — bypass circuit grounded or open
43	Electronic Spark Control (ESC) signal for too long
44	Lean exhaust system indication
45	Rich exhaust system indication
51	Faulty calibration unit (PROM) or installation
55	Replace ECM (faulty)

Year – 1982
Model – Pontiac 6000
Engine – 2.5L (151 cid) EFI 4 cyl
Engine Code – VIN R

ECM TROUBLE CODES

Code	Explanation
12	No reference pulses to the ECM. This code is not stored in memory and will only flash while the fault is present. Normal code with ignition ON, engine not running
13	Open oxygen sensor circuit – the engine must run up to 2 minutes before this code will set
14	Shorted coolant sensor circuit – the engine must run up to 2 minutes before this code will set
15	Open coolant sensor circuit – the engine must run up to 2 minutes before this code will set
21	Throttle position sensor circuit – high output
22	Throttle position sensor circuit – low output
24	Vehicle Speed Sensor (VSS) circuit
33	Manifold Absolute Pressure (MAP) sensor circuit – high output
34	Manifold Absolute Pressure (MAP) sensor circuit – low output
42	Electronic Spark Timing (EST) monitor – bypass circuit grounded or open
43	Electronic Spark Control (ESC) signal for too long
44	Lean exhaust system indication
45	Rich exhaust system indication
51	Faulty calibration unit (PROM) or installation
55	Replace ECM (faulty)

Year — 1982
Model — Pontiac 6000
Engine — 2.8L (173 cid) 2bbl V6
Engine Code — VIN X

ECM TROUBLE CODES

Code	Explanation
12	No reference pulses to the ECM. This code is not stored in memory and will only flash while the fault is present. Normal code with ignition ON, engine not running
13	Oxygen sensor circuit — the engine must run up to 5 minutes at part throttle, under road load, before this code will set
14	Shorted coolant sensor circuit — the engine must run up to 2 minutes before this code will set
15	Open coolant sensor circuit — the engine must run up to 5 minutes before this code will set
21	Throttle position sensor circuit — the engine must run up to 25 seconds, at specified curb idle speed, before this code will set
23	Open or grounded M/C solenoid circuit
24	Vehicle Speed Sensor (VSS) circuit — the car must operate up to 5 minutes at road speed before this code will set
32	Barometric Pressure Sensor (BARO) circuit low
34	Manifold Absolute Pressure (MAP) or Vacuum sensor circuit. The engine must run up to 5 minutes, at specified curb idle speed, before this code will set
35	Idle Speed Control (ISC) switch circuit shorted. (Over ½ throttle for over 2 seconds)
42	Electronic Spark Timing (EST) bypass circuit grounded or open
44	Lean oxygen sensor indication — the engine must run up to 5 minutes, in closed loop, at part throttle before this code will set
44 & 45	(At same time) — Faulty oxygen sensor circuit.
45	Rich system indication — the engine must run up to 5 minutes, in closed loop, at part throttle before this code will set
51	Faulty calibration unit (PROM) or installation. It takes up to 30 seconds before this code will set
54	Shorted M/C solenoid circuit and/or faulty ECM
55	Grounded V ref (terminal 21), faulty oxygen sensor or ECM

Year – 1982
Model – Pontiac 6000
Engine – 2.8L (173 cid) 2bbl V6
Engine Code – VIN Z

ECM TROUBLE CODES

Code	Explanation
12	No reference pulses to the ECM. This code is not stored in memory and will only flash while the fault is present. Normal code with ignition ON, engine not running
13	Oxygen sensor circuit—the engine must run up to 5 minutes at part throttle, under road load, before this code will set
14	Shorted coolant sensor circuit—the engine must run up to 2 minutes before this code will set
15	Open coolant sensor circuit—the engine must run up to 5 minutes before this code will set
21	Throttle position sensor circuit—the engine must run up to 25 seconds, at specified curb idle speed, before this code will set
23	Open or grounded M/C solenoid circuit
24	Vehicle Speed Sensor (VSS) circuit—the car must operate up to 5 minutes at road speed before this code will set
32	Barometric Pressure Sensor (BARO) circuit low
34	Manifold Absolute Pressure (MAP) or Vacuum sensor circuit. The engine must run up to 5 minutes, at specified curb idle speed, before this code will set
35	Idle Speed Control (ISC) switch circuit shorted. (Over ½ throttle for over 2 seconds)
42	Electronic Spark Timing (EST) bypass circuit grounded or open
44	Lean oxygen sensor indication—the engine must run up to 5 minutes, in closed loop, at part throttle before this code will set
44 & 45	(At same time)—Faulty oxygen sensor circuit.
45	Rich system indication—the engine must run up to 5 minutes, in closed loop, at part throttle before this code will set
51	Faulty calibration unit (PROM) or installation. It takes up to 30 seconds before this code will set
54	Shorted M/C solenoid circuit and/or faulty ECM
55	Grounded V ref (terminal 21), faulty oxygen sensor or ECM

Year – 1982
Model – Phoenix
Engine – 2.5L (151 cid) EFI 4 cyl
Engine Code – VIN R

ECM TROUBLE CODES

Code	Explanation
12	No reference pulses to the ECM. This code is not stored in memory and will only flash while the fault is present. Normal code with ignition ON, engine not running
13	Open oxygen sensor circuit – the engine must run up to 2 minutes before this code will set
14	Shorted coolant sensor circuit – the engine must run up to 2 minutes before this code will set
15	Open coolant sensor circuit – the engine must run up to 2 minutes before this code will set
21	Throttle position sensor circuit – high output
22	Throttle position sensor circuit – low output
24	Vehicle Speed Sensor (VSS) circuit
33	Manifold Absolute Pressure (MAP) sensor circuit – high output
34	Manifold Absolute Pressure (MAP) sensor circuit – low output
42	Electronic Spark Timing (EST) monitor – bypass circuit grounded or open
43	Electronic Spark Control (ESC) signal for too long
44	Lean exhaust system indication
45	Rich exhaust system indication
51	Faulty calibration unit (PROM) or installation
55	Replace ECM (faulty)

Year — 1982
Model — Phoenix
Engine — 2.8L (173 cid) 2bbl V6
Engine Code — VIN X

ECM TROUBLE CODES

Code	Explanation
12	No reference pulses to the ECM. This code is not stored in memory and will only flash while the fault is present. Normal code with ignition ON, engine not running
13	Oxygen sensor circuit—the engine must run up to 5 minutes at part throttle, under road load, before this code will set
14	Shorted coolant sensor circuit—the engine must run up to 2 minutes before this code will set
15	Open coolant sensor circuit—the engine must run up to 5 minutes before this code will set
21	Throttle position sensor circuit—the engine must run up to 25 seconds, at specified curb idle speed, before this code will set
23	Open or grounded M/C solenoid circuit
24	Vehicle Speed Sensor (VSS) circuit—the car must operate up to 5 minutes at road speed before this code will set
32	Barometric Pressure Sensor (BARO) circuit low
34	Manifold Absolute Pressure (MAP) or Vacuum sensor circuit. The engine must run up to 5 minutes, at specified curb idle speed, before this code will set
35	Idle Speed Control (ISC) switch circuit shorted. (Over ½ throttle for over 2 seconds)
42	Electronic Spark Timing (EST) bypass circuit grounded or open
44	Lean oxygen sensor indication—the engine must run up to 5 minutes, in closed loop, at part throttle before this code will set
44 & 45	(At same time)—Faulty oxygen sensor circuit.
45	Rich system indication—the engine must run up to 5 minutes, in closed loop, at part throttle before this code will set
51	Faulty calibration unit (PROM) or installation. It takes up to 30 seconds before this code will set
54	Shorted M/C solenoid circuit and/or faulty ECM
55	Grounded V ref (terminal 21), faulty oxygen sensor or ECM

Year — 1982
Model — Phoenix
Engine — 2.8L (173 cid) 2bbl V6
Engine Code — VIN Z

ECM TROUBLE CODES

Code	Explanation
12	No reference pulses to the ECM. This code is not stored in memory and will only flash while the fault is present. Normal code with ignition ON, engine not running
13	Oxygen sensor circuit — the engine must run up to 5 minutes at part throttle, under road load, before this code will set
14	Shorted coolant sensor circuit — the engine must run up to 2 minutes before this code will set
15	Open coolant sensor circuit — the engine must run up to 5 minutes before this code will set
21	Throttle position sensor circuit — the engine must run up to 25 seconds, at specified curb idle speed, before this code will set
23	Open or grounded M/C solenoid circuit
24	Vehicle Speed Sensor (VSS) circuit — the car must operate up to 5 minutes at road speed before this code will set
32	Barometric Pressure Sensor (BARO) circuit low
34	Manifold Absolute Pressure (MAP) or Vacuum sensor circuit. The engine must run up to 5 minutes, at specified curb idle speed, before this code will set
35	Idle Speed Control (ISC) switch circuit shorted. (Over ½ throttle for over 2 seconds)
42	Electronic Spark Timing (EST) bypass circuit grounded or open
44	Lean oxygen sensor indication — the engine must run up to 5 minutes, in closed loop, at part throttle before this code will set
44 & 45	(At same time) — Faulty oxygen sensor circuit.
45	Rich system indication — the engine must run up to 5 minutes, in closed loop, at part throttle before this code will set
51	Faulty calibration unit (PROM) or installation. It takes up to 30 seconds before this code will set
54	Shorted M/C solenoid circuit and/or faulty ECM
55	Grounded V ref (terminal 21), faulty oxygen sensor or ECM

Year — 1982
Model — Pontiac T1000
Engine — 1.6L (98 cid) 2bbl 4 cyl
Engine Code — VIN 9

ECM TROUBLE CODES

Code	Explanation
12	No reference pulses to the ECM. This code is not stored in memory and will only flash while the fault is present
15	Open coolant sensor circuit — the engine must run up to 10 minutes before this code will set
21	Throttle position sensor circuit at WOT — the engine must run up to 10 seconds below 1000 rpm, before this code will set
23	M/C solenoid circuit. Must be in closed loop before this code will set
44	Lean exhaust indication — the engine must run up to 1 minute, in closed loop and at part throttle, before this code will set
45	Rich exhaust indication — the engine must run up to 1 minute, in closed loop and at part throttle, above 2000 rpm, before this code will set
51	Faulty calibration unit (PROM) or installation. Turns the ECM OFF

Year — 1982
Model — Pontiac J2000
Engine — 1.8L (111 cid) 4 cyl
Engine Code — VIN G

ECM TROUBLE CODES

Code	Explanation
12	No reference pulses to the ECM. This code is not stored in memory and will only flash while the fault is present. Normal code with ignition ON, engine not running
13	Oxygen sensor circuit — the engine must run up to 5 minutes at part throttle, under road load, before this code will set
14	Shorted coolant sensor circuit — the engine must run up to 2 minutes before this code will set
15	Open coolant sensor circuit — the engine must run up to 5 minutes before this code will set
21	Throttle position sensor circuit — the engine must run up to 25 seconds, at specified curb idle speed, before this code will set
23	Open or grounded M/C solenoid circuit
24	Vehicle Speed Sensor (VSS) circuit — the car must operate up to 5 minutes at road speed before this code will set
32	Barometric Pressure Sensor (BARO) circuit low
34	Vacuum sensor circuit. The engine must run up to 5 minutes, at specified curb idle speed, before this code will set
35	Idle Speed Control (ISC) switch circuit shorted. (Over ½ throttle for over 2 seconds)
41	No distributor reference pulses at specified engine vacuum. This code will store
42	Electronic Spark Timing (EST) bypass circuit grounded or open
43	ESC retard signal for too long; causes a retard in EST signal
44	Lean oxygen sensor indication — the engine must run up to 5 minutes, in closed loop, at part throttle before this code will set
44 & 45	(At same time) — Faulty oxygen sensor circuit.
45	Rich system indication — the engine must run up to 5 minutes, in closed loop, at part throttle before this code will set
51	Faulty calibration unit (PROM) or installation. It takes up to 30 seconds before this code will set
54	Shorted M/C solenoid circuit and/or faulty ECM
55	Grounded V ref (terminal 21), faulty oxygen sensor or ECM

Year – 1983
Model – Bonneville
Engine – 3.8L (231 cid) 2bbl V6
Engine Code – VIN A

ECM TROUBLE CODES

Code	Explanation
13	Oxygen sensor circuit — warm engine running at normal operating temperature for at least 3 minutes at part throttle with oxygen sensor signal missing (open) for 60 seconds
14	Coolant sensor circuit signal voltage low — engine running 10 seconds with no coolant sensor signal voltage
15	Coolant sensor circuit signal voltage high — engine running with coolant sensor signal too high for 60 seconds. If fault occurs with ignition OFF, engine will crank, but may not start
21	Throttle position sensor signal too high — engine running below 1600 RPM, and TPS is above 50% (2.5 volts) for 2 seconds
22	Throttle position sensor signal too low — engine running with TPS signal voltage too low
24	Vehicle Speed Sensor (VSS) — vehicle speed about 40–45 MPH steady throttle signal with no VSS for 1 minute
33	Manifold Absolute Pressure (MAP) signal too high (LOW VACUUM) — engine idling and MAP signal is high for 5 seconds
34	Manifold Absolute Pressure (MAP) signal too low — engine running 0.2 second (200m seconds) with MAP signal voltage too low
42	Electronic Spark Timing (EST) — open or grounded EST line, open or grounded bypass line, and engine speed above 500 RPM
43	Electronic spark control — full retard — engine running and ESC signal at ECM is low for 4 seconds
44	Lean exhaust system — Engine running in closed loop at normal operating temperature with oxygen sensor signal less than 200mv. for 1 minute. Forces open loop operation. May require drive position to set on some engines
45	Rich exhaust system — Engine idling in closed loop at normal operating temperature with oxygen sensor signal above 750mv. for 20 seconds. Forces open loop operation. May require drive position to set on some engines
51	Faulty Calibration Unit (PROM) or installation
55	Replace ECM (faulty)

Year — 1983
Model — Bonneville
Engine — 5.0L (305 cid) 4bbl V8
Engine Code — VIN H

ECM TROUBLE CODES

Code	Explanation
13	Oxygen sensor circuit — warm engine running at normal operating temperature for at least 3 minutes at part throttle with oxygen sensor signal missing (open) for 60 seconds
14	Coolant sensor circuit signal voltage low — engine running 10 seconds with no coolant sensor signal voltage
15	Coolant sensor circuit signal voltage high — engine running with coolant sensor signal too high for 60 seconds. If fault occurs with ignition OFF, engine will crank, but may not start
21	Throttle position sensor signal too high — engine running below 1600 RPM, and TPS is above 50% (2.5 volts) for 2 seconds
22	Throttle position sensor signal too low — engine running with TPS signal voltage too low
24	Vehicle Speed Sensor (VSS) — vehicle speed about 40–45 MPH steady throttle signal with no VSS for 1 minute
33	Manifold Absolute Pressure (MAP) signal too high (LOW VACUUM) — engine idling and MAP signal is high for 5 seconds
34	Manifold Absolute Pressure (MAP) signal too low — engine running 0.2 second (200m seconds) with MAP signal voltage too low
42	Electronic Spark Timing (EST) — open or grounded EST line, open or grounded bypass line, and engine speed above 500 RPM
43	Electronic spark control — full retard — engine running and ESC signal at ECM is low for 4 seconds
44	Lean exhaust system — Engine running in closed loop at normal operating temperature with oxygen sensor signal less than 200mv. for 1 minute. Forces open loop operation. May require drive position to set on some engines
45	Rich exhaust system — Engine idling in closed loop at normal operating temperature with oxygen sensor signal above 750mv. for 20 seconds. Forces open loop operation. May require drive position to set on some engines
51	Faulty Calibration Unit (PROM) or installation
55	Replace ECM (faulty)

Year – 1983
Model – Grand Prix
Engine – 2.8L (171 cid) 2bbl V6
Engine Code – VIN L

ECM TROUBLE CODES

Code	Explanation
13	Oxygen sensor circuit—warm engine running at normal operating temperature for at least 3 minutes at part throttle with oxygen sensor signal missing (open) for 60 seconds
14	Coolant sensor circuit signal voltage low—engine running 10 seconds with no coolant sensor signal voltage
15	Coolant sensor circuit signal voltage high—engine running with coolant sensor signal too high for 60 seconds. If fault occurs with ignition OFF, engine will crank, but may not start
21	Throttle position sensor signal too high—engine running below 1600 RPM, and TPS is above 50% (2.5 volts) for 2 seconds
22	Throttle position sensor signal too low—engine running with TPS signal voltage too low
24	Vehicle Speed Sensor (VSS)—vehicle speed about 40–45 MPH steady throttle signal with no VSS for 1 minute
33	Manifold Absolute Pressure (MAP) signal too high (LOW VACUUM)—engine idling and MAP signal is high for 5 seconds
34	Manifold Absolute Pressure (MAP) signal too low—engine running 0.2 second (200m seconds) with MAP signal voltage too low
42	Electronic Spark Timing (EST)—open or grounded EST line, open or grounded bypass line, and engine speed above 500 RPM
43	Electronic spark control—full retard—engine running and ESC signal at ECM is low for 4 seconds
44	Lean exhaust system—Engine running in closed loop at normal operating temperature with oxygen sensor signal less than 200mv. for 1 minute. Forces open loop operation. May require drive position to set on some engines
45	Rich exhaust system—Engine idling in closed loop at normal operating temperature with oxygen sensor signal above 750mv. for 20 seconds. Forces open loop operation. May require drive position to set on some engines
51	Faulty Calibration Unit (PROM) or installation
55	Replace ECM (faulty)

Year — 1983
Model — Grand Prix
Engine — 3.8L (231 cid) 2bbl V6
Engine Code — VIN A

ECM TROUBLE CODES

Code	Explanation
13	Oxygen sensor circuit — warm engine running at normal operating temperature for at least 3 minutes at part throttle with oxygen sensor signal missing (open) for 60 seconds
14	Coolant sensor circuit signal voltage low — engine running 10 seconds with no coolant sensor signal voltage
15	Coolant sensor circuit signal voltage high — engine running with coolant sensor signal too high for 60 seconds. If fault occurs with ignition OFF, engine will crank, but may not start
21	Throttle position sensor signal too high — engine running below 1600 RPM, and TPS is above 50% (2.5 volts) for 2 seconds
22	Throttle position sensor signal too low — engine running with TPS signal voltage too low
24	Vehicle Speed Sensor (VSS) — vehicle speed about 40–45 MPH steady throttle signal with no VSS for 1 minute
33	Manifold Absolute Pressure (MAP) signal too high (LOW VACUUM) — engine idling and MAP signal is high for 5 seconds
34	Manifold Absolute Pressure (MAP) signal too low — engine running 0.2 second (200m seconds) with MAP signal voltage too low
42	Electronic Spark Timing (EST) — open or grounded EST line, open or grounded bypass line, and engine speed above 500 RPM
43	Electronic spark control — full retard — engine running and ESC signal at ECM is low for 4 seconds
44	Lean exhaust system — Engine running in closed loop at normal operating temperature with oxygen sensor signal less than 200mv. for 1 minute. Forces open loop operation. May require drive position to set on some engines
45	Rich exhaust system — Engine idling in closed loop at normal operating temperature with oxygen sensor signal above 750mv. for 20 seconds. Forces open loop operation. May require drive position to set on some engines
51	Faulty Calibration Unit (PROM) or installation
55	Replace ECM (faulty)

GENERAL MOTORS CORPORATION
DIAGNOSTIC CODE DATA

Year — 1983
Model — Grand Prix
Engine — 5.0L (305 cid) 4bbl V8
Engine Code — VIN H

ECM TROUBLE CODES

Code	Explanation
13	Oxygen sensor circuit — warm engine running at normal operating temperature for at least 3 minutes at part throttle with oxygen sensor signal missing (open) for 60 seconds
14	Coolant sensor circuit signal voltage low — engine running 10 seconds with no coolant sensor signal voltage
15	Coolant sensor circuit signal voltage high — engine running with coolant sensor signal too high for 60 seconds. If fault occurs with ignition OFF, engine will crank, but may not start
21	Throttle position sensor signal too high — engine running below 1600 RPM, and TPS is above 50% (2.5 volts) for 2 seconds
22	Throttle position sensor signal too low — engine running with TPS signal voltage too low
24	Vehicle Speed Sensor (VSS) — vehicle speed about 40–45 MPH steady throttle signal with no VSS for 1 minute
33	Manifold Absolute Pressure (MAP) signal too high (LOW VACUUM) — engine idling and MAP signal is high for 5 seconds
34	Manifold Absolute Pressure (MAP) signal too low — engine running 0.2 second (200m seconds) with MAP signal voltage too low
42	Electronic Spark Timing (EST) — open or grounded EST line, open or grounded bypass line, and engine speed above 500 RPM
43	Electronic spark control — full retard — engine running and ESC signal at ECM is low for 4 seconds
44	Lean exhaust system — Engine running in closed loop at normal operating temperature with oxygen sensor signal less than 200mv. for 1 minute. Forces open loop operation. May require drive position to set on some engines
45	Rich exhaust system — Engine idling in closed loop at normal operating temperature with oxygen sensor signal above 750mv. for 20 seconds. Forces open loop operation. May require drive position to set on some engines
51	Faulty Calibration Unit (PROM) or installation
55	Replace ECM (faulty)

Year – 1983
Model – Firebird
Engine – 2.5L (151 cid) EFI 4 cyl
Engine Code – VIN R

ECM TROUBLE CODES

Code	Explanation
13	Oxygen sensor circuit – warm engine running at normal operating temperature for at least 3 minutes at part throttle with oxygen sensor signal missing (open) for 60 seconds
14	Coolant sensor circuit signal voltage low – engine running 10 seconds with no coolant sensor signal voltage
15	Coolant sensor circuit signal voltage high – engine running with coolant sensor signal too high for 60 seconds. If fault occurs with ignition OFF, engine will crank, but may not start
21	Throttle position sensor signal too high – engine running below 1600 RPM, and TPS is above 50% (2.5 volts) for 2 seconds
22	Throttle position sensor signal too low – engine running with TPS signal voltage too low
24	Vehicle Speed Sensor (VSS) – vehicle speed about 40–45 MPH steady throttle signal, decelerating, with no VSS for 1 minute
33	Manifold Absolute Pressure (MAP) signal too high (LOW VACUUM) – engine idling and MAP signal is high for 5 seconds
34	Manifold Absolute Pressure (MAP) signal too low – engine running 0.2 second (200m seconds) with MAP signal voltage too low
42	Electronic Spark Timing (EST) – open or grounded EST line, open or grounded bypass line, and engine speed above 500 RPM
43	Electronic spark control – full retard – engine running and ESC signal at ECM is low for 4 seconds
44	Lean exhaust system – Engine running in closed loop at normal operating temperature with oxygen sensor signal less than 200mv. for 1 minute. Forces open loop operation. May require drive position to set on some engines
45	Rich exhaust system – Engine idling in closed loop at normal operating temperature with oxygen sensor signal above 750mv. for 20 seconds. Forces open loop operation. May require drive position to set on some engines
51	Faulty Calibration Unit (PROM) or installation
55	Replace ECM (faulty)

Year – 1983
Model – Firebird
Engine – 2.8L (173 cid) 2bbl V6
Engine Code – VIN L

ECM TROUBLE CODES

Code	Explanation
13	Oxygen sensor circuit – warm engine running at normal operating temperature for at least 3 minutes at part throttle with oxygen sensor signal missing (open) for 60 seconds
14	Coolant sensor circuit signal voltage low – engine running 10 seconds with no coolant sensor signal voltage
15	Coolant sensor circuit signal voltage high – engine running with coolant sensor signal too high for 60 seconds. If fault occurs with ignition OFF, engine will crank, but may not start
21	Throttle position sensor signal too high – engine running below 1600 RPM, and TPS is above 50% (2.5 volts) for 2 seconds
22	Throttle position sensor signal too low – engine running with TPS signal voltage too low
24	Vehicle Speed Sensor (VSS) – vehicle speed about 40–45 MPH steady throttle signal with no VSS for 1 minute
33	Manifold Absolute Pressure (MAP) signal too high (LOW VACUUM) – engine idling and MAP signal is high for 5 seconds
34	Manifold Absolute Pressure (MAP) signal too low – engine running 0.2 second (200m seconds) with MAP signal voltage too low
42	Electronic Spark Timing (EST) – open or grounded EST line, open or grounded bypass line, and engine speed above 500 RPM
43	Electronic spark control – full retard – engine running and ESC signal at ECM is low for 4 seconds
44	Lean exhaust system – Engine running in closed loop at normal operating temperature with oxygen sensor signal less than 200mv. for 1 minute. Forces open loop operation. May require drive position to set on some engines
45	Rich exhaust system – Engine idling in closed loop at normal operating temperature with oxygen sensor signal above 750mv. for 20 seconds. Forces open loop operation. May require drive position to set on some engines
51	Faulty Calibration Unit (PROM) or installation
55	Replace ECM (faulty)

Year – 1983
Model – Firebird
Engine – 5.0L (305 cid) 4bbl V8
Engine Code – VIN H

ECM TROUBLE CODES

Code	Explanation
13	Oxygen sensor circuit — warm engine running at normal operating temperature for at least 3 minutes at part throttle with oxygen sensor signal missing (open) for 60 seconds
14	Coolant sensor circuit signal voltage low — engine running 10 seconds with no coolant sensor signal voltage
15	Coolant sensor circuit signal voltage high — engine running with coolant sensor signal too high for 60 seconds. If fault occurs with ignition OFF, engine will crank, but may not start
21	Throttle position sensor signal too high — engine running below 1600 RPM, and TPS is above 50% (2.5 volts) for 2 seconds
22	Throttle position sensor signal too low — engine running with TPS signal voltage too low.
24	Vehicle Speed Sensor (VSS) — vehicle speed about 40–45 MPH steady throttle signal with no VSS for 1 minute
33	Manifold Absolute Pressure (MAP) signal too high (LOW VACUUM) — engine idling and MAP signal is high for 5 seconds
34	Manifold Absolute Pressure (MAP) signal too low — engine running 0.2 second (200m seconds) with MAP signal voltage too low
42	Electronic Spark Timing (EST) — open or grounded EST line, open or grounded bypass line, and engine speed above 500 RPM
43	Electronic spark control — full retard — engine running and ESC signal at ECM is low for 4 seconds
44	Lean exhaust system — Engine running in closed loop at normal operating temperature with oxygen sensor signal less than 200mv. for 1 minute. Forces open loop operation. May require drive position to set on some engines
45	Rich exhaust system — Engine idling in closed loop at normal operating temperature with oxygen sensor signal above 750mv. for 20 seconds. Forces open loop operation. May require drive position to set on some engines
51	Faulty Calibration Unit (PROM) or installation
55	Replace ECM (faulty)

Year – 1983
Model – Firebird
Engine – 5.0L (305 cid) EFI V8
Engine Code – VIN X

ECM TROUBLE CODES

Code	Explanation
13	Oxygen sensor circuit—warm engine running at normal operating temperature for at least 3 minutes at part throttle with oxygen sensor signal missing (open) for 60 seconds
14	Coolant sensor circuit signal voltage low—engine running 10 seconds with no coolant sensor signal voltage
15	Coolant sensor circuit signal voltage high—engine running with coolant sensor signal too high for 60 seconds. If fault occurs with ignition OFF, engine will crank, but may not start
21	Throttle position sensor signal too high—engine running below 1600 RPM, and TPS is above 50% (2.5 volts) for 2 seconds
22	Throttle position sensor signal too low—engine running with TPS signal voltage too low
24	Vehicle Speed Sensor (VSS)—vehicle speed about 40–45 MPH steady throttle signal with no VSS for 1 minute
33	Manifold Absolute Pressure (MAP) signal too high (LOW VACUUM)—engine idling and MAP signal is high for 5 seconds
34	Manifold Absolute Pressure (MAP) signal too low—engine running 0.2 second (200m seconds) with MAP signal voltage too low
42	Electronic Spark Timing (EST)—open or grounded EST line, open or grounded bypass line, and engine speed above 500 RPM
43	Electronic spark control—full retard—engine running and ESC signal at ECM is low for 4 seconds
44	Lean exhaust system—Engine running in closed loop at normal operating temperature with oxygen sensor signal less than 200mv. for 1 minute. Forces open loop operation. May require drive position to set on some engines
45	Rich exhaust system—Engine idling in closed loop at normal operating temperature with oxygen sensor signal above 750mv. for 20 seconds. Forces open loop operation. May require drive position to set on some engines
51	Faulty Calibration Unit (PROM) or installation
55	Replace ECM (faulty)

Year — 1983
Model — Parisienne
Engine — 3.8L (231 cid) 2bbl V6
Engine Code — VIN A

ECM TROUBLE CODES

Code	Explanation
13	Oxygen sensor circuit — warm engine running at normal operating temperature for at least 3 minutes at part throttle with oxygen sensor signal missing (open) for 60 seconds
14	Coolant sensor circuit signal voltage low — engine running 10 seconds with no coolant sensor signal voltage
15	Coolant sensor circuit signal voltage high — engine running with coolant sensor signal too high for 60 seconds. If fault occurs with ignition OFF, engine will crank, but may not start
21	Throttle position sensor signal too high — engine running below 1600 RPM, and TPS is above 50% (2.5 volts) for 2 seconds
22	Throttle position sensor signal too low — engine running with TPS signal voltage too low
24	Vehicle Speed Sensor (VSS) — vehicle speed about 40–45 MPH steady throttle signal with no VSS for 1 minute
33	Manifold Absolute Pressure (MAP) signal too high (LOW VACUUM) — engine idling and MAP signal is high for 5 seconds
34	Manifold Absolute Pressure (MAP) signal too low — engine running 0.2 second (200m seconds) with MAP signal voltage too low
42	Electronic Spark Timing (EST) — open or grounded EST line, open or grounded bypass line, and engine speed above 500 RPM
43	Electronic spark control — full retard — engine running and ESC signal at ECM is low for 4 seconds
44	Lean exhaust system — Engine running in closed loop at normal operating temperature with oxygen sensor signal less than 200mv. for 1 minute. Forces open loop operation. May require drive position to set on some engines
45	Rich exhaust system — Engine idling in closed loop at normal operating temperature with oxygen sensor signal above 750mv. for 20 seconds. Forces open loop operation. May require drive position to set on some engines
51	Faulty Calibration Unit (PROM) or installation
55	Replace ECM (faulty)

Year—1983
Model—Parisienne
Engine—5.0L (305 cid) 4bbl V8
Engine Code—VIN H

ECM TROUBLE CODES

Code	Explanation
13	Oxygen sensor circuit—warm engine running at normal operating temperature for at least 3 minutes at part throttle with oxygen sensor signal missing (open) for 60 seconds
14	Coolant sensor circuit signal voltage low—engine running 10 seconds with no coolant sensor signal voltage
15	Coolant sensor circuit signal voltage high—engine running with coolant sensor signal too high for 60 seconds. If fault occurs with ignition OFF, engine will crank, but may not start
21	Throttle position sensor signal too high—engine running below 1600 RPM, and TPS is above 50% (2.5 volts) for 2 seconds
22	Throttle position sensor signal too low—engine running with TPS signal voltage too low
24	Vehicle Speed Sensor (VSS)—vehicle speed about 40–45 MPH steady throttle signal with no VSS for 1 minute
33	Manifold Absolute Pressure (MAP) signal too high (LOW VACUUM)—engine idling and MAP signal is high for 5 seconds
34	Manifold Absolute Pressure (MAP) signal too low—engine running 0.2 second (200m seconds) with MAP signal voltage too low
42	Electronic Spark Timing (EST)—open or grounded EST line, open or grounded bypass line, and engine speed above 500 RPM
43	Electronic spark control—full retard—engine running and ESC signal at ECM is low for 4 seconds
44	Lean exhaust system—Engine running in closed loop at normal operating temperature with oxygen sensor signal less than 200mv. for 1 minute. Forces open loop operation. May require drive position to set on some engines
45	Rich exhaust system—Engine idling in closed loop at normal operating temperature with oxygen sensor signal above 750mv. for 20 seconds. Forces open loop operation. May require drive position to set on some engines
51	Faulty Calibration Unit (PROM) or installation
55	Replace ECM (faulty)

Year — 1983
Model — Pontiac 1000
Engine — 1.6L (98 cid) 2bbl 4 cyl
Engine Code — VIN C

ECM TROUBLE CODES

Code	Explanation
12	No distributor reference pulses to the ECM
15	Open coolant sensor circuit — The engine must run up to 10 minutes before this code will set
21	Throttle position sensor circuit at WOT. The engine must run up to 10 seconds below 1000 rpm, before this code will set
23	M/C solenoid circuit
44	Lean exhaust indication — The engine must run up to 1 minute, in closed loop and at part throttle above 2000 rpm before this code will set
45	Rich exhaust indication — The engine must run up to 1 minute, in closed loop and at part throttle above 2000 rpm before this code will set
51	Faulty Calibration Unit (PROM) or installation. Turns ECM OFF
55	Replace ECM (faulty)

Year — 1983
Model — Pontiac 2000
Engine — 1.8L (111 cid) EFI 4 cyl
Engine Code — VIN O

ECM TROUBLE CODES

Code	Explanation
13	Oxygen sensor circuit — warm engine running at normal operating temperature for at least 3 minutes at part throttle with oxygen sensor signal missing (open) for 60 seconds
14	Coolant sensor circuit signal voltage low — engine running 10 seconds with no coolant sensor signal voltage
15	Coolant sensor circuit signal voltage high — engine running with coolant sensor signal too high for 60 seconds. If fault occurs with ignition OFF, engine will crank, but may not start
21	Throttle position sensor signal too high — engine running below 1600 RPM, and TPS is above 50% (2.5 volts) for 2 seconds
22	Throttle position sensor signal too low — engine running with TPS signal voltage too low
24	Vehicle Speed Sensor (VSS) — vehicle speed about 40–45 MPH steady throttle signal with no VSS for 1 minute
33	Manifold Absolute Pressure (MAP) signal too high (LOW VACUUM) — engine idling and MAP signal is high for 5 seconds
34	Manifold Absolute Pressure (MAP) signal too low — engine running 0.2 second (200m seconds) with MAP signal voltage too low
42	Electronic Spark Timing (EST) — open or grounded EST line, open or grounded bypass line, and engine speed above 500 RPM
43	Electronic spark control — full retard — engine running and ESC signal at ECM is low for 4 seconds
44	Lean exhaust system — Engine running in closed loop at normal operating temperature with oxygen sensor signal less than 200mv. for 1 minute. Forces open loop operation. May require drive position to set on some engines
45	Rich exhaust system — Engine idling in closed loop at normal operating temperature with oxygen sensor signal above 750mv. for 20 seconds. Forces open loop operation. May require drive position to set on some engines
51	Faulty Calibration Unit (PROM) or installation
55	Replace ECM (faulty)

Year – 1983
Model – Pontiac 2000
Engine – 2.0L (121 cid) EFI 4 cyl
Engine Code – VIN P

ECM TROUBLE CODES

Code	Explanation
13	Oxygen sensor circuit — warm engine running at normal operating temperature for at least 3 minutes at part throttle with oxygen sensor signal missing (open) for 60 seconds
14	Coolant sensor circuit signal voltage low — engine running 10 seconds with no coolant sensor signal voltage
15	Coolant sensor circuit signal voltage high — engine running with coolant sensor signal too high for 60 seconds. If fault occurs with ignition OFF, engine will crank, but may not start
21	Throttle position sensor signal too high — engine running below 1600 RPM, and TPS is above 50% (2.5 volts) for 2 seconds
22	Throttle position sensor signal too low — engine running with TPS signal voltage too low
24	Vehicle Speed Sensor (VSS) — vehicle speed about 40–45 MPH steady throttle signal, decelerating, with no VSS for 1 minute
33	Manifold Absolute Pressure (MAP) signal too high (LOW VACUUM) — engine idling and MAP signal is high for 5 seconds
34	Manifold Absolute Pressure (MAP) signal too low — engine running 0.2 second (200m seconds) with MAP signal voltage too low
42	Electronic Spark Timing (EST) — open or grounded EST line, open or grounded bypass line, and engine speed above 500 RPM
43	Electronic spark control — full retard — engine running and ESC signal at ECM is low for 4 seconds
44	Lean exhaust system — Engine running in closed loop at normal operating temperature with oxygen sensor signal less than 200mv. for 1 minute. Forces open loop operation. May require drive position to set on some engines
45	Rich exhaust system — Engine idling in closed loop at normal operating temperature with oxygen sensor signal above 750mv. for 20 seconds. Forces open loop operation. May require drive position to set on some engines
51	Faulty Calibration Unit (PROM) or installation
55	Replace ECM (faulty)

Year — 1983
Model — Pontiac 6000
Engine — 2.5L (151 cid) EFI 4 cyl
Engine Code — VIN R

ECM TROUBLE CODES

Code	Explanation
13	Oxygen sensor circuit — warm engine running at normal operating temperature for at least 3 minutes at part throttle with oxygen sensor signal missing (open) for 60 seconds
14	Coolant sensor circuit signal voltage low — engine running 10 seconds with no coolant sensor signal voltage
15	Coolant sensor circuit signal voltage high — engine running with coolant sensor signal too high for 60 seconds. If fault occurs with ignition OFF, engine will crank, but may not start
21	Throttle position sensor signal too high — engine running below 1600 RPM, and TPS is above 50% (2.5 volts) for 2 seconds
22	Throttle position sensor signal too low — engine running with TPS signal voltage too low
24	Vehicle Speed Sensor (VSS) — vehicle speed about 40–45 MPH steady throttle signal, decelerating, with no VSS for 1 minute
33	Manifold Absolute Pressure (MAP) signal too high (LOW VACUUM) — engine idling and MAP signal is high for 5 seconds
34	Manifold Absolute Pressure (MAP) signal too low — engine running 0.2 second (200m seconds) with MAP signal voltage too low
42	Electronic Spark Timing (EST) — open or grounded EST line, open or grounded bypass line, and engine speed above 500 RPM
43	Electronic spark control — full retard — engine running and ESC signal at ECM is low for 4 seconds
44	Lean exhaust system — Engine running in closed loop at normal operating temperature with oxygen sensor signal less than 200mv. for 1 minute. Forces open loop operation. May require drive position to set on some engines
45	Rich exhaust system — Engine idling in closed loop at normal operating temperature with oxygen sensor signal above 750mv. for 20 seconds. Forces open loop operation. May require drive position to set on some engines
51	Faulty Calibration Unit (PROM) or installation
55	Replace ECM (faulty)

Year — 1983
Model — Pontiac 6000
Engine — 2.8L (173 cid) 2bbl V6
Engine Code — VIN L

ECM TROUBLE CODES

Code	Explanation
13	Oxygen sensor circuit — warm engine running at normal operating temperature for at least 3 minutes at part throttle with oxygen sensor signal missing (open) for 60 seconds
14	Coolant sensor circuit signal voltage low — engine running 10 seconds with no coolant sensor signal voltage
15	Coolant sensor circuit signal voltage high — engine running with coolant sensor signal too high for 60 seconds. If fault occurs with ignition OFF, engine will crank, but may not start
21	Throttle position sensor signal too high — engine running below 1600 RPM, and TPS is above 50% (2.5 volts) for 2 seconds
22	Throttle position sensor signal too low — engine running with TPS signal voltage too low
24	Vehicle Speed Sensor (VSS) — vehicle speed about 40–45 MPH steady throttle signal with no VSS for 1 minute
33	Manifold Absolute Pressure (MAP) signal too high (LOW VACUUM) — engine idling and MAP signal is high for 5 seconds
34	Manifold Absolute Pressure (MAP) signal too low — engine running 0.2 second (200m seconds) with MAP signal voltage too low
42	Electronic Spark Timing (EST) — open or grounded EST line, open or grounded bypass line, and engine speed above 500 RPM
43	Electronic spark control — full retard — engine running and ESC signal at ECM is low for 4 seconds
44	Lean exhaust system — Engine running in closed loop at normal operating temperature with oxygen sensor signal less than 200mv. for 1 minute. Forces open loop operation. May require drive position to set on some engines
45	Rich exhaust system — Engine idling in closed loop at normal operating temperature with oxygen sensor signal above 750mv. for 20 seconds. Forces open loop operation. May require drive position to set on some engines
51	Faulty Calibration Unit (PROM) or installation
55	Replace ECM (faulty)

Year – 1983
Model – Phoenix
Engine – 2.5L (151 cid) EFI 4 cyl
Engine Code – VIN R

ECM TROUBLE CODES

Code	Explanation
13	Oxygen sensor circuit – warm engine running at normal operating temperature for at least 3 minutes at part throttle with oxygen sensor signal missing (open) for 60 seconds
14	Coolant sensor circuit signal voltage low – engine running 10 seconds with no coolant sensor signal voltage
15	Coolant sensor circuit signal voltage high – engine running with coolant sensor signal too high for 60 seconds. If fault occurs with ignition OFF, engine will crank, but may not start
21	Throttle position sensor signal too high – engine running below 1600 RPM, and TPS is above 50% (2.5 volts) for 2 seconds
22	Throttle position sensor signal too low – engine running with TPS signal voltage too low
24	Vehicle Speed Sensor (VSS) – vehicle speed about 40–45 MPH steady throttle signal, decelerating, with no VSS for 1 minute
33	Manifold Absolute Pressure (MAP) signal too high (LOW VACUUM) – engine idling and MAP signal is high for 5 seconds
34	Manifold Absolute Pressure (MAP) signal too low – engine running 0.2 second (200m seconds) with MAP signal voltage too low
42	Electronic Spark Timing (EST) – open or grounded EST line, open or grounded bypass line, and engine speed above 500 RPM
43	Electronic spark control – full retard – engine running and ESC signal at ECM is low for 4 seconds
44	Lean exhaust system – Engine running in closed loop at normal operating temperature with oxygen sensor signal less than 200mv. for 1 minute. Forces open loop operation. May require drive position to set on some engines
45	Rich exhaust system – Engine idling in closed loop at normal operating temperature with oxygen sensor signal above 750mv. for 20 seconds. Forces open loop operation. May require drive position to set on some engines
51	Faulty Calibration Unit (PROM) or installation
55	Replace ECM (faulty)

Year — 1983
Model — Phoenix
Engine — 2.8L (173 cid) 2bbl V6
Engine Code — VIN L

ECM TROUBLE CODES

Code	Explanation
13	Oxygen sensor circuit — warm engine running at normal operating temperature for at least 3 minutes at part throttle with oxygen sensor signal missing (open) for 60 seconds
14	Coolant sensor circuit signal voltage low — engine running 10 seconds with no coolant sensor signal voltage
15	Coolant sensor circuit signal voltage high — engine running with coolant sensor signal too high for 60 seconds. If fault occurs with ignition OFF, engine will crank, but may not start
21	Throttle position sensor signal too high — engine running below 1600 RPM, and TPS is above 50% (2.5 volts) for 2 seconds
22	Throttle position sensor signal too low — engine running with TPS signal voltage too low
24	Vehicle Speed Sensor (VSS) — vehicle speed about 40–45 MPH steady throttle signal with no VSS for 1 minute
33	Manifold Absolute Pressure (MAP) signal too high (LOW VACUUM) — engine idling and MAP signal is high for 5 seconds
34	Manifold Absolute Pressure (MAP) signal too low — engine running 0.2 second (200m seconds) with MAP signal voltage too low
42	Electronic Spark Timing (EST) — open or grounded EST line, open or grounded bypass line, and engine speed above 500 RPM
43	Electronic spark control — full retard — engine running and ESC signal at ECM is low for 4 seconds
44	Lean exhaust system — Engine running in closed loop at normal operating temperature with oxygen sensor signal less than 200mv. for 1 minute. Forces open loop operation. May require drive position to set on some engines
45	Rich exhaust system — Engine idling in closed loop at normal operating temperature with oxygen sensor signal above 750mv. for 20 seconds. Forces open loop operation. May require drive position to set on some engines
51	Faulty Calibration Unit (PROM) or installation
55	Replace ECM (faulty)

Year — 1984
Model — Bonneville
Engine — 3.8L (231 cid) V6
Engine Code — VIN A

ECM TROUBLE CODES

Code	Explanation
12	No distributor reference pulses to the ECM. This code is not stored in memory and will only flash while the fault is present. Normal code with ignition ON, engine not running
13	Oxygen sensor circuit — the engine must run up to 4 minutes at part throttle, under road load, before this code will set
14	Shorted coolant sensor circuit — the engine must run 2 minutes before this code will set
15	Open coolant sensor circuit — the engine must run 5 minutes before this code will set
21	Throttle Position Sensor (TPS) circuit voltage high (open circuit or misadjusted TPS). The engine must run 10 seconds, at specified curb idle speed, before this code will set
22	Throttle Position Sensor (TPS) circuit voltage low (grounded circuit or misadjusted TPS). Engine must run 20 seconds, at specified curb idle speed, to set code
23	M/C solenoid circuit open or grounded
24	Vehicle Speed Sensor (VSS) circuit — the vehicle must operate up to 2 minutes at road speed, before this code will set
32	Barometric Pressure Sensor (BARO) circuit low
34	Vacuum sensor or Manifold Absolute Pressure (MAP) circuit — the engine must run up to 2 minutes, at specified curb idle, before this code will set
35	Idle Speed Control (ISC) switch circuit shorted. (Up to 70% TPS for over 5 seconds)
41	No distributor reference pulses to the ECM at specified engine vacuum. This code will store in memory
42	Electronic Spark Timing (EST) bypass circuit or EST circuit grounded or open
43	Electronic Spark Control (ESC) retard signal for too long a time; causes retard in EST signal
44	Lean exhaust indication — the engine must run 2 minutes, in closed loop and at part throttle, before this code will set
45	Rich exhaust indication — the engine must run 2 minutes, in closed loop and at part throttle, before this code will set
51	Faulty or improperly installed calibration unit (PROM). It takes up to 30 seconds before this code will set
53	Exhaust Gas Recirculation (EGR) valve vacuum sensor has seen improper EGR vacuum
54	Shorted M/C solenoid circuit and/or faulty ECM

Year – 1984
Model – Bonneville
Engine – 5.0L (305 cid) V8
Engine Code – VIN H

ECM TROUBLE CODES

Code	Explanation
12	No distributor reference pulses to the ECM. This code is not stored in memory and will only flash while the fault is present. Normal code with ignition ON, engine not running
13	Oxygen sensor circuit – the engine must run up to 4 minutes at part throttle, under road load, before this code will set
14	Shorted coolant sensor circuit – the engine must run 2 minutes before this code will set
15	Open coolant sensor circuit – the engine must run 5 minutes before this code will set
21	Throttle Position Sensor (TPS) circuit voltage high (open circuit or misadjusted TPS). The engine must run 10 seconds, at specified curb idle speed, before this code will set
22	Throttle Position Sensor (TPS) circuit voltage low (grounded circuit or misadjusted TPS). Engine must run 20 seconds, at specified curb idle speed, to set code
23	M/C solenoid circuit open or grounded
24	Vehicle Speed Sensor (VSS) circuit – the vehicle must operate up to 2 minutes at road speed, before this code will set
32	Barometric Pressure Sensor (BARO) circuit low
34	Vacuum sensor or Manifold Absolute Pressure (MAP) circuit – the engine must run up to 2 minutes, at specified curb idle, before this code will set
35	Idle Speed Control (ISC) switch circuit shorted. (Up to 70% TPS for over 5 seconds)
41	No distributor reference pulses to the ECM at specified engine vacuum. This code will store in memory
42	Electronic Spark Timing (EST) bypass circuit or EST circuit grounded or open
43	Electronic Spark Control (ESC) retard signal for too long a time; causes retard in EST signal
44	Lean exhaust indication – the engine must run 2 minutes, in closed loop and at part throttle, before this code will set
45	Rich exhaust indication – the engine must run 2 minutes, in closed loop and at part throttle, before this code will set
51	Faulty or improperly installed calibration unit (PROM). It takes up to 30 seconds before this code will set
53	Exhaust Gas Recirculation (EGR) valve vacuum sensor has seen improper EGR vacuum
54	Shorted M/C solenoid circuit and/or faulty ECM

Year – 1984

Model – Grand Prix

Engine – 3.8L (231 cid) V6

Engine Code – VIN A

ECM TROUBLE CODES

Code	Explanation
12	No distributor reference pulses to the ECM. This code is not stored in memory and will only flash while the fault is present. Normal code with ignition ON, engine not running
13	Oxygen sensor circuit – the engine must run up to 4 minutes at part throttle, under road load, before this code will set
14	Shorted coolant sensor circuit – the engine must run 2 minutes before this code will set
15	Open coolant sensor circuit – the engine must run 5 minutes before this code will set
21	Throttle Position Sensor (TPS) circuit voltage high (open circuit or misadjusted TPS). The engine must run 10 seconds, at specified curb idle speed, before this code will set
22	Throttle Position Sensor (TPS) circuit voltage low (grounded circuit or misadjusted TPS). Engine must run 20 seconds, at specified curb idle speed, to set code
23	M/C solenoid circuit open or grounded
24	Vehicle Speed Sensor (VSS) circuit – the vehicle must operate up to 2 minutes at road speed, before this code will set
32	Barometric Pressure Sensor (BARO) circuit low
34	Vacuum sensor or Manifold Absolute Pressure (MAP) circuit – the engine must run up to 2 minutes, at specified curb idle, before this code will set
35	Idle Speed Control (ISC) switch circuit shorted. (Up to 70% TPS for over 5 seconds)
41	No distributor reference pulses to the ECM at specified engine vacuum. This code will store in memory
42	Electronic Spark Timing (EST) bypass circuit or EST circuit grounded or open
43	Electronic Spark Control (ESC) retard signal for too long a time; causes retard in EST signal
44	Lean exhaust indication – the engine must run 2 minutes, in closed loop and at part throttle, before this code will set
45	Rich exhaust indication – the engine must run 2 minutes, in closed loop and at part throttle, before this code will set
51	Faulty or improperly installed calibration unit (PROM). It takes up to 30 seconds before this code will set
53	Exhaust Gas Recirculation (EGR) valve vacuum sensor has seen improper EGR vacuum
54	Shorted M/C solenoid circuit and/or faulty ECM

Year — 1984
Model — Grand Prix
Engine — 5.0L (305 cid) V8
Engine Code — VIN H

ECM TROUBLE CODES

Code	Explanation
12	No distributor reference pulses to the ECM. This code is not stored in memory and will only flash while the fault is present. Normal code with ignition ON, engine not running
13	Oxygen sensor circuit — the engine must run up to 4 minutes at part throttle, under road load, before this code will set
14	Shorted coolant sensor circuit — the engine must run 2 minutes before this code will set
15	Open coolant sensor circuit — the engine must run 5 minutes before this code will set
21	Throttle Position Sensor (TPS) circuit voltage high (open circuit or misadjusted TPS). The engine must run 10 seconds, at specified curb idle speed, before this code will set
22	Throttle Position Sensor (TPS) circuit voltage low (grounded circuit or misadjusted TPS). Engine must run 20 seconds, at specified curb idle speed, to set code
23	M/C solenoid circuit open or grounded
24	Vehicle Speed Sensor (VSS) circuit — the vehicle must operate up to 2 minutes at road speed, before this code will set
32	Barometric Pressure Sensor (BARO) circuit low
34	Vacuum sensor or Manifold Absolute Pressure (MAP) circuit — the engine must run up to 2 minutes, at specified curb idle, before this code will set
35	Idle Speed Control (ISC) switch circuit shorted. (Up to 70% TPS for over 5 seconds)
41	No distributor reference pulses to the ECM at specified engine vacuum. This code will store in memory
42	Electronic Spark Timing (EST) bypass circuit or EST circuit grounded or open
43	Electronic Spark Control (ESC) retard signal for too long a time; causes retard in EST signal
44	Lean exhaust indication — the engine must run 2 minutes, in closed loop and at part throttle, before this code will set
45	Rich exhaust indication — the engine must run 2 minutes, in closed loop and at part throttle, before this code will set
51	Faulty or improperly installed calibration unit (PROM). It takes up to 30 seconds before this code will set
53	Exhaust Gas Recirculation (EGR) valve vacuum sensor has seen improper EGR vacuum
54	Shorted M/C solenoid circuit and/or faulty ECM

Year – 1984
Model – Firebird
Engine – 2.5L (151 cid) TBI 4 cyl
Engine Code – VIN 2

ECM TROUBLE CODES

Code	Explanation
12	No distributor reference pulses to the ECM. This code is not stored in memory and will only flash while the fault is present. Normal code with ignition ON, engine not running
13	Oxygen sensor circuit – the engine must run up to 4 minutes at part throttle, under road load, before this code will set
14	Shorted coolant sensor circuit – the engine must run 2 minutes before this code will set
15	Open coolant sensor circuit – the engine must run 5 minutes before this code will set
21	Throttle Position Sensor (TPS) circuit voltage high (open circuit or misadjusted TPS). The engine must run 10 seconds, at specified curb idle speed, before this code will set
22	Throttle Position Sensor (TPS) circuit voltage low (grounded circuit or misadjusted TPS). Engine must run 20 seconds, at specified curb idle speed, to set code
24	Vehicle Speed Sensor (VSS) circuit – the vehicle must operate up to 2 minutes at road speed, before this code will set
33	Manifold Absolute Pressure (MAP) sensor (voltage low)
34	Manifold Absolute Pressure (MAP) sensor (voltage high)
42	Electronic Spark Timing (EST) bypass circuit or EST circuit grounded or open
44	Lean exhaust indication – the engine must run 2 minutes, in closed loop and at part throttle, before this code will set
45	Rich exhaust indication – the engine must run 2 minutes, in closed loop and at part throttle, before this code will set
51	Faulty or improperly installed calibration unit (PROM). It takes up to 30 seconds before this code will set
55	ECM error

Year — 1984
Model — Firebird
Engine — 2.8L (173 cid) V6
Engine Code — VIN 1

ECM TROUBLE CODES

Code	Explanation
12	No distributor reference pulses to the ECM. This code is not stored in memory and will only flash while the fault is present. Normal code with ignition ON, engine not running
13	Oxygen sensor circuit — the engine must run up to 4 minutes at part throttle, under road load, before this code will set
14	Shorted coolant sensor circuit — the engine must run 2 minutes before this code will set
15	Open coolant sensor circuit — the engine must run 5 minutes before this code will set
21	Throttle Position Sensor (TPS) circuit voltage high (open circuit or misadjusted TPS). The engine must run 10 seconds, at specified curb idle speed, before this code will set
22	Throttle Position Sensor (TPS) circuit voltage low (grounded circuit or misadjusted TPS): Engine must run 20 seconds, at specified curb idle speed, to set code
23	M/C solenoid circuit open or grounded
24	Vehicle Speed Sensor (VSS) circuit — the vehicle must operate up to 2 minutes at road speed, before this code will set
32	Barometric Pressure Sensor (BARO) circuit low
34	Vacuum sensor or Manifold Absolute Pressure (MAP) circuit — the engine must run up to 2 minutes, at specified curb idle, before this code will set
35	Idle Speed Control (ISC) switch circuit shorted. (Up to 70% TPS for over 5 seconds)
41	No distributor reference pulses to the ECM at specified engine vacuum. This code will store in memory
42	Electronic Spark Timing (EST) bypass circuit or EST circuit grounded or open
43	Electronic Spark Control (ESC) retard signal for too long a time; causes retard in EST signal
44	Lean exhaust indication — the engine must run 2 minutes, in closed loop and at part throttle, before this code will set
45	Rich exhaust indication — the engine must run 2 minutes, in closed loop and at part throttle, before this code will set
51	Faulty or improperly installed calibration unit (PROM). It takes up to 30 seconds before this code will set
53	Exhaust Gas Recirculation (EGR) valve vacuum sensor has seen improper EGR vacuum
54	Shorted M/C solenoid circuit and/or faulty ECM

Year — 1984
Model — Firebird
Engine — 2.8L (173 cid) V6
Engine Code — VIN L

ECM TROUBLE CODES

Code	Explanation
12	No distributor reference pulses to the ECM. This code is not stored in memory and will only flash while the fault is present. Normal code with ignition ON, engine not running
13	Oxygen sensor circuit — the engine must run up to 4 minutes at part throttle, under road load, before this code will set
14	Shorted coolant sensor circuit — the engine must run 2 minutes before this code will set
15	Open coolant sensor circuit — the engine must run 5 minutes before this code will set
21	Throttle Position Sensor (TPS) circuit voltage high (open circuit or misadjusted TPS). The engine must run 10 seconds, at specified curb idle speed, before this code will set
22	Throttle Position Sensor (TPS) circuit voltage low (grounded circuit or misadjusted TPS). Engine must run 20 seconds, at specified curb idle speed, to set code
23	M/C solenoid circuit open or grounded
24	Vehicle Speed Sensor (VSS) circuit — the vehicle must operate up to 2 minutes at road speed, before this code will set
32	Barometric Pressure Sensor (BARO) circuit low
34	Vacuum sensor or Manifold Absolute Pressure (MAP) circuit — the engine must run up to 2 minutes, at specified curb idle, before this code will set
35	Idle Speed Control (ISC) switch circuit shorted. (Up to 70% TPS for over 5 seconds)
41	No distributor reference pulses to the ECM at specified engine vacuum. This code will store in memory
42	Electronic Spark Timing (EST) bypass circuit or EST circuit grounded or open
43	Electronic Spark Control (ESC) retard signal for too long a time; causes retard in EST signal
44	Lean exhaust indication — the engine must run 2 minutes, in closed loop and at part throttle, before this code will set
45	Rich exhaust indication — the engine must run 2 minutes, in closed loop and at part throttle, before this code will set
51	Faulty or improperly installed calibration unit (PROM). It takes up to 30 seconds before this code will set
53	Exhaust Gas Recirculation (EGR) valve vacuum sensor has seen improper EGR vacuum
54	Shorted M/C solenoid circuit and/or faulty ECM

Year – 1984
Model – Firebird
Engine – 5.0L (305 cid) V8
Engine Code – VIN G

ECM TROUBLE CODES

Code	Explanation
12	No distributor reference pulses to the ECM. This code is not stored in memory and will only flash while the fault is present. Normal code with ignition ON, engine not running
13	Oxygen sensor circuit—the engine must run up to 4 minutes at part throttle, under road load, before this code will set
14	Shorted coolant sensor circuit—the engine must run 2 minutes before this code will set
15	Open coolant sensor circuit—the engine must run 5 minutes before this code will set
21	Throttle Position Sensor (TPS) circuit voltage high (open circuit or misadjusted TPS). The engine must run 10 seconds, at specified curb idle speed, before this code will set
22	Throttle Position Sensor (TPS) circuit voltage low (grounded circuit or misadjusted TPS). Engine must run 20 seconds, at specified curb idle speed, to set code
23	M/C solenoid circuit open or grounded
24	Vehicle Speed Sensor (VSS) circuit—the vehicle must operate up to 2 minutes at road speed, before this code will set
32	Barometric Pressure Sensor (BARO) circuit low
34	Vacuum sensor or Manifold Absolute Pressure (MAP) circuit—the engine must run up to 2 minutes, at specified curb idle, before this code will set
35	Idle Speed Control (ISC) switch circuit shorted. (Up to 70% TPS for over 5 seconds)
41	No distributor reference pulses to the ECM at specified engine vacuum. This code will store in memory
42	Electronic Spark Timing (EST) bypass circuit or EST circuit grounded or open
43	Electronic Spark Control (ESC) retard signal for too long a time; causes retard in EST signal
44	Lean exhaust indication—the engine must run 2 minutes, in closed loop and at part throttle, before this code will set
45	Rich exhaust indication—the engine must run 2 minutes, in closed loop and at part throttle, before this code will set
51	Faulty or improperly installed calibration unit (PROM). It takes up to 30 seconds before this code will set
53	Exhaust Gas Recirculation (EGR) valve vacuum sensor has seen improper EGR vacuum
54	Shorted M/C solenoid circuit and/or faulty ECM

Year – 1984
Model – Firebird
Engine – 5.0L (305 cid) V8
Engine Code – VIN H

ECM TROUBLE CODES

Code	Explanation
12	No distributor reference pulses to the ECM. This code is not stored in memory and will only flash while the fault is present. Normal code with ignition ON, engine not running
13	Oxygen sensor circuit – the engine must run up to 4 minutes at part throttle, under road load, before this code will set
14	Shorted coolant sensor circuit – the engine must run 2 minutes before this code will set
15	Open coolant sensor circuit – the engine must run 5 minutes before this code will set
21	Throttle Position Sensor (TPS) circuit voltage high (open circuit or misadjusted TPS). The engine must run 10 seconds, at specified curb idle speed, before this code will set
22	Throttle Position Sensor (TPS) circuit voltage low (grounded circuit or misadjusted TPS). Engine must run 20 seconds, at specified curb idle speed, to set code
23	M/C solenoid circuit open or grounded
24	Vehicle Speed Sensor (VSS) circuit – the vehicle must operate up to 2 minutes at road speed, before this code will set
32	Barometric Pressure Sensor (BARO) circuit low
34	Vacuum sensor or Manifold Absolute Pressure (MAP) circuit – the engine must run up to 2 minutes, at specified curb idle, before this code will set
35	Idle Speed Control (ISC) switch circuit shorted. (Up to 70% TPS for over 5 seconds)
41	No distributor reference pulses to the ECM at specified engine vacuum. This code will store in memory
42	Electronic Spark Timing (EST) bypass circuit or EST circuit grounded or open
43	Electronic Spark Control (ESC) retard signal for too long a time; causes retard in EST signal
44	Lean exhaust indication – the engine must run 2 minutes, in closed loop and at part throttle, before this code will set
45	Rich exhaust indication – the engine must run 2 minutes, in closed loop and at part throttle, before this code will set
51	Faulty or improperly installed calibration unit (PROM). It takes up to 30 seconds before this code will set
53	Exhaust Gas Recirculation (EGR) valve vacuum sensor has seen improper EGR vacuum
54	Shorted M/C solenoid circuit and/or faulty ECM

Year — 1984
Model — Parisienne
Engine — 3.8L (231 cid) V6
Engine Code — VIN A

ECM TROUBLE CODES

Code	Explanation
12	No distributor reference pulses to the ECM. This code is not stored in memory and will only flash while the fault is present. Normal code with ignition ON, engine not running
13	Oxygen sensor circuit — the engine must run up to 4 minutes at part throttle, under road load, before this code will set
14	Shorted coolant sensor circuit — the engine must run 2 minutes before this code will set
15	Open coolant sensor circuit — the engine must run 5 minutes before this code will set
21	Throttle Position Sensor (TPS) circuit voltage high (open circuit or misadjusted TPS). The engine must run 10 seconds, at specified curb idle speed, before this code will set
22	Throttle Position Sensor (TPS) circuit voltage low (grounded circuit or misadjusted TPS). Engine must run 20 seconds, at specified curb idle speed, to set code
23	M/C solenoid circuit open or grounded
24	Vehicle Speed Sensor (VSS) circuit — the vehicle must operate up to 2 minutes at road speed, before this code will set
32	Barometric Pressure Sensor (BARO) circuit low
34	Vacuum sensor or Manifold Absolute Pressure (MAP) circuit — the engine must run up to 2 minutes, at specified curb idle, before this code will set
35	Idle Speed Control (ISC) switch circuit shorted. (Up to 70% TPS for over 5 seconds)
41	No distributor reference pulses to the ECM at specified engine vacuum. This code will store in memory
42	Electronic Spark Timing (EST) bypass circuit or EST circuit grounded or open
43	Electronic Spark Control (ESC) retard signal for too long a time; causes retard in EST signal
44	Lean exhaust indication — the engine must run 2 minutes, in closed loop and at part throttle, before this code will set
45	Rich exhaust indication — the engine must run 2 minutes, in closed loop and at part throttle, before this code will set
51	Faulty or improperly installed calibration unit (PROM). It takes up to 30 seconds before this code will set
53	Exhaust Gas Recirculation (EGR) valve vacuum sensor has seen improper EGR vacuum
54	Shorted M/C solenoid circuit and/or faulty ECM

Year — 1984
Model — Parisienne
Engine — 5.0L (305 cid) V8
Engine Code — VIN H

ECM TROUBLE CODES

Code	Explanation
12	No distributor reference pulses to the ECM. This code is not stored in memory and will only flash while the fault is present. Normal code with ignition ON, engine not running
13	Oxygen sensor circuit — the engine must run up to 4 minutes at part throttle, under road load, before this code will set
14	Shorted coolant sensor circuit — the engine must run 2 minutes before this code will set
15	Open coolant sensor circuit — the engine must run 5 minutes before this code will set
21	Throttle Position Sensor (TPS) circuit voltage high (open circuit or misadjusted TPS). The engine must run 10 seconds, at specified curb idle speed, before this code will set
22	Throttle Position Sensor (TPS) circuit voltage low (grounded circuit or misadjusted TPS). Engine must run 20 seconds, at specified curb idle speed, to set code
23	M/C solenoid circuit open or grounded
24	Vehicle Speed Sensor (VSS) circuit — the vehicle must operate up to 2 minutes at road speed, before this code will set
32	Barometric Pressure Sensor (BARO) circuit low
34	Vacuum sensor or Manifold Absolute Pressure (MAP) circuit — the engine must run up to 2 minutes, at specified curb idle, before this code will set
35	Idle Speed Control (ISC) switch circuit shorted. (Up to 70% TPS for over 5 seconds)
41	No distributor reference pulses to the ECM at specified engine vacuum. This code will store in memory
42	Electronic Spark Timing (EST) bypass circuit or EST circuit grounded or open
43	Electronic Spark Control (ESC) retard signal for too long a time; causes retard in EST signal
44	Lean exhaust indication — the engine must run 2 minutes, in closed loop and at part throttle, before this code will set
45	Rich exhaust indication — the engine must run 2 minutes, in closed loop and at part throttle, before this code will set
51	Faulty or improperly installed calibration unit (PROM). It takes up to 30 seconds before this code will set
53	Exhaust Gas Recirculation (EGR) valve vacuum sensor has seen improper EGR vacuum
54	Shorted M/C solenoid circuit and/or faulty ECM

Year – 1984
Model – Pontiac 1000
Engine – 1.6L (98 cid) 4 cyl
Engine Code – VIN C

ECM TROUBLE CODES

Code	Explanation
12	No distributor reference pulses to the ECM. This code is not stored in memory and will only flash while the fault is present. Normal code with ignition ON, engine not running
15	Open coolant sensor circuit – the engine must run up to 10 minutes before this code will set
21	Throttle Position Sensor (TPS) circuit at WOT (Wide Open Throttle). The engine must run up to 10 seconds below 1000 rpm before this code will set
23	M/C solenoid circuit open or grounded
44	Lean exhaust indication – the engine must run up to one minute in closed loop and at part throttle above 2000 rpm before this code will set
45	Rich exhaust indication – the engine must run up to one minute in cosed loop and at part throttle above 2000 rpm before this code will set
51	Faulty or improperly installed calibration unit (PROM). Turns ECM off

Year – 1984
Model – 2000 Sunbird
Engine – 1.8L (111 cid) TBI 4 cyl
Engine Code – VIN O

ECM TROUBLE CODES

Code	Explanation
12	No distributor reference pulses to the ECM. This code is not stored in memory and will only flash while the fault is present. Normal code with ignition ON, engine not running
13	Oxygen sensor circuit
14	Coolant sensor (voltage low)
15	Coolant sensor (voltage high)
21	Throttle Position Sensor (TPS) circuit voltage high (open circuit or misadjusted TPS).
22	Throttle Position Sensor (TPS) circuit voltage low (grounded circuit or misadjusted TPS).
24	Vehicle Speed Sensor (VSS)
33	Manifold Absolute Pressure (MAP) sensor (voltage low)
34	Manifold Absloute Pressure (MAP) sensor (voltage high)
42	Electronic Spark Timing (EST) bypass circuit or EST circuit grounded or open
44	Lean exhaust indication
45	Rich exhaust indication
51	Faulty or improperly installed calibration unit (PROM)
52	Calpac
53	ECM error

Year — 1984
Model — 2000 Sunbird
Engine — 1.8L (111 cid) EFI Turbo 4 cyl
Engine Code — VIN J

ECM TROUBLE CODES

Code	Explanation
12	No distributor reference pulses to the ECM. This code is not stored in memory and will only flash while the fault is present. Normal code with ignition ON, engine not running
13	Oxygen sensor circuit
14	Coolant sensor circuit (voltage low)
15	Coolant sensor circuit (voltage high)
21	Throttle Position Sensor (TPS) circuit (voltage high)
22	Throttle Position Sensor (TPS) circuit (voltage low)
23	Manifold Air Temperature (MAT) sensor (voltage low)
24	Vehicle Speed Sensor (VSS) circuit
25	Manifold Air Temperature (MAT) sensor (voltage high)
31	Wastgate solenoid
33	Manifold Absolute Pressure (MAP) sensor (voltage low)
34	Manifold Absolute Pressure (MAP) sensor (voltage high)
42	Electronic Spark Timing (EST) bypass circuit or EST circuit grounded or open
43	Electronic Spark Control (ESC) retard signal for too long a time; causes retard in EST signal
44	Lean exhaust indication
45	Rich exhaust indication
51	Faulty or improperly installed calibration unit (PROM)
52	Calpak error
55	ECM error

GENERAL MOTORS CORPORATION
DIAGNOSTIC CODE DATA

Year – 1984
Model – 2000 Sunbird
Engine – 2.0L (121 cid) TBI 4 cyl
Engine Code – VIN P

ECM TROUBLE CODES

Code	Explanation
12	No distributor reference pulses to the ECM. This code is not stored in memory and will only flash while the fault is present. Normal code with ignition ON, engine not running
13	Oxygen sensor circuit
14	Coolant sensor circuit (voltage low)
15	Coolant sensor circuit (voltage high)
21	Throttle Position Sensor (TPS) circuit (voltage high)
22	Throttle Position Sensor (TPS) circuit (voltage low)
24	Vehicle Speed Sensor (VSS) circuit
33	Manifold Absolute Pressure (MAP) sensor (voltage low)
34	Manifold Absolute Pressure (MAP) sensor (voltage high)
42	Electronic Spark Timing (EST) bypass circuit or EST circuit grounded or open
44	Lean exhaust indication
45	Rich exhaust indication
51	Faulty or improperly installed calibration unit (PROM)
52	Calpac error
55	ECM error

Year – 1984
Model – Pontiac 6000, LE, STE
Engine – 2.5L (151 cid) TBI 4 cyl
Engine Code – VIN R

ECM TROUBLE CODES

Code	Explanation
12	No distributor reference pulses to the ECM. This code is not stored in memory and will only flash while the fault is present. Normal code with ignition ON, engine not running
13	Oxygen sensor circuit
14	Coolant sensor circuit (voltage low)
15	Coolant sensor circuit (voltage high)
21	Throttle Position Sensor (TPS) circuit (voltage high)
22	Throttle Position Sensor (TPS) circuit (voltage low)
24	Vehicle Speed Sensor (VSS) circuit
33	Manifold Absolute Pressure (MAP) sensor (voltage low)
34	Manifold Absolute Pressure (MAP) sensor (voltage high)
42	Electronic Spark Timing (EST) bypass circuit or EST circuit grounded or open
44	Lean exhaust indication
45	Rich exhaust indication
51	Faulty or improperly installed calibration unit (PROM)
55	ECM error

Year — 1984
Model — Pontiac 6000, LE, STE
Engine — 2.8L (173 cid) V6
Engine Code — VIN X

ECM TROUBLE CODES

Code	Explanation
12	No distributor reference pulses to the ECM. This code is not stored in memory and will only flash while the fault is present. Normal code with ignition ON, engine not running
13	Oxygen sensor circuit — the engine must run up to 4 minutes at part throttle, under road load, before this code will set
14	Shorted coolant sensor circuit — the engine must run 2 minutes before this code will set
15	Open coolant sensor circuit — the engine must run 5 minutes before this code will set
21	Throttle Position Sensor (TPS) circuit voltage high (open circuit or misadjusted TPS). The engine must run 10 seconds, at specified curb idle speed, before this code will set
22	Throttle Position Sensor (TPS) circuit voltage low (grounded circuit or misadjusted TPS). Engine must run 20 seconds, at specified curb idle speed, to set code
23	M/C solenoid circuit open or grounded
24	Vehicle Speed Sensor (VSS) circuit — the vehicle must operate up to 2 minutes at road speed, before this code will set
32	Barometric Pressure Sensor (BARO) circuit low
34	Vacuum sensor or Manifold Absolute Pressure (MAP) circuit — the engine must run up to 2 minutes, at specified curb idle, before this code will set
35	Idle Speed Control (ISC) switch circuit shorted. (Up to 70% TPS for over 5 seconds)
41	No distributor reference pulses to the ECM at specified engine vacuum. This code will store in memory
42	Electronic Spark Timing (EST) bypass circuit or EST circuit grounded or open
43	Electronic Spark Control (ESC) retard signal for too long a time; causes retard in EST signal
44	Lean exhaust indication — the engine must run 2 minutes, in closed loop and at part throttle, before this code will set
45	Rich exhaust indication — the engine must run 2 minutes, in closed loop and at part throttle, before this code will set
51	Faulty or improperly installed calibration unit (PROM). It takes up to 30 seconds before this code will set
53	Exhaust Gas Recirculation (EGR) valve vacuum sensor has seen improper EGR vacuum
54	Shorted M/C solenoid circuit and/or faulty ECM

Year — 1984
Model — Phoenix, LE, SE
Engine — 2.5L (151 cid) TBI 4 cyl
Engine Code — VIN R

ECM TROUBLE CODES

Code	Explanation
12	No distributor reference pulses to the ECM. This code is not stored in memory and will only flash while the fault is present. Normal code with ignition ON, engine not running
13	Oxygen sensor circuit
14	Coolant sensor circuit (voltage low)
15	Coolant sensor circuit (voltage high)
21	Throttle Position Sensor (TPS) circuit (voltage high)
22	Throttle Position Sensor (TPS) circuit (voltage low)
24	Vehicle Speed Sensor (VSS) circuit
33	Manifold Absolute Pressure (MAP) sensor (voltage low)
34	Manifold Absolute Pressure (MAP) sensor (voltage high)
42	Electronic Spark Timing (EST) bypass circuit or EST circuit grounded or open
44	Lean exhaust indication
45	Rich exhaust indication
51	Faulty or improperly installed calibration unit (PROM)
55	ECM error

Year — 1984
Model — Phoenix, LE, SE
Engine — 2.8L (173 cid) V6
Engine Code — VIN Z

ECM TROUBLE CODES

Code	Explanation
12	No distributor reference pulses to the ECM. This code is not stored in memory and will only flash while the fault is present. Normal code with ignition ON, engine not running
13	Oxygen sensor circuit — the engine must run up to 4 minutes at part throttle, under road load, before this code will set
14	Shorted coolant sensor circuit — the engine must run 2 minutes before this code will set
15	Open coolant sensor circuit — the engine must run 5 minutes before this code will set
21	Throttle Position Sensor (TPS) circuit voltage high (open circuit or misadjusted TPS). The engine must run 10 seconds, at specified curb idle speed, before this code will set
22	Throttle Position Sensor (TPS) circuit voltage low (grounded circuit or misadjusted TPS). Engine must run 20 seconds, at specified curb idle speed, to set code
23	M/C solenoid circuit open or grounded
24	Vehicle Speed Sensor (VSS) circuit — the vehicle must operate up to 2 minutes at road speed, before this code will set
32	Barometric Pressure Sensor (BARO) circuit low
34	Vacuum sensor or Manifold Absolute Pressure (MAP) circuit — the engine must run up to 2 minutes, at specified curb idle, before this code will set
35	Idle Speed Control (ISC) switch circuit shorted. (Up to 70% TPS for over 5 seconds)
41	No distributor reference pulses to the ECM at specified engine vacuum. This code will store in memory
42	Electronic Spark Timing (EST) bypass circuit or EST circuit grounded or open
43	Electronic Spark Control (ESC) retard signal for too long a time; causes retard in EST signal
44	Lean exhaust indication — the engine must run 2 minutes, in closed loop and at part throttle, before this code will set
45	Rich exhaust indication — the engine must run 2 minutes, in closed loop and at part throttle, before this code will set
51	Faulty or improperly installed calibration unit (PROM). It takes up to 30 seconds before this code will set
53	Exhaust Gas Recirculation (EGR) valve vacuum sensor has seen improper EGR vacuum
54	Shorted M/C solenoid circuit and/or faulty ECM

Year — 1984
Model — Fiero
Engine — 2.5L (151 cid) TBI 4 cyl
Engine Code — VIN R

ECM TROUBLE CODES

Code	Explanation
12	No distributor reference pulses to the ECM. This code is not stored in memory and will only flash while the fault is present. Normal code with ignition ON, engine not running
13	Oxygen sensor circuit
14	Coolant sensor circuit (voltage low)
15	Coolant sensor circuit (voltage high)
21	Throttle Position Sensor (TPS) circuit (voltage high)
22	Throttle Position Sensor (TPS) circuit (voltage low)
24	Vehicle Speed Sensor (VSS) circuit
33	Manifold Absolute Pressure (MAP) sensor (voltage low)
34	Manifold Absolute Pressure (MAP) sensor (voltage high)
42	Electronic Spark Timing (EST) bypass circuit or EST circuit grounded or open
44	Lean exhaust indication
45	Rich exhaust indication
51	Faulty or improperly installed calibration unit (PROM)
55	ECM error

GENERAL MOTORS CORPORATION
DIAGNOSTIC CODE DATA

Year — 1985
Model — Bonneville
Engine — 3.8L (231 cid) V6
Engine Code — VIN A

ECM TROUBLE CODES

Code	Explanation
12	No distributor reference signal to the ECM. This code is not stored in memory and will only flash while the fault is present. Normal code with ignition ON, engine not running
13	Oxygen sensor circuit — the engine must run up to 4 minutes at part throttle, under road load, before this code will set
14	Shorted coolant sensor circuit — the engine must run 2 minutes before this code will set
15	Open coolant sensor circuit — the engine must run 5 minutes before this code will set
21	Throttle Position Sensor (TPS) circuit voltage high (open circuit or misadjusted TPS). The engine must run 10 seconds, at specified curb idle speed, before this code will set
22	Throttle Position Sensor (TPS) circuit voltage low (grounded circuit or misadjusted TPS). Engine must run 20 seconds, at specified curb idle speed, to set code
23	M/C solenoid circuit open or grounded
24	Vehicle Speed Sensor (VSS) circuit — the vehicle must operate up to 2 minutes at road speed, before this code will set
32	Barometric Pressure Sensor (BARO) circuit low
34	Vacuum sensor or Manifold Absolute Pressure (MAP) circuit — the engine must run up to 2 minutes, at specified curb idle, before this code will set
35	Idle Speed Control (ISC) switch circuit shorted. (Up to 70% TPS for over 5 seconds)
41	No distributor reference signal to the ECM at specified engine vacuum. This code will store in memory
42	Electronic Spark Timing (EST) bypass circuit or EST circuit grounded or open
43	Electronic Spark Control (ESC) retard signal for too long a time; causes retard in EST signal
44	Lean exhaust indication — the engine must run 2 minutes, in closed loop and at part throttle, before this code will set
45	Rich exhaust indication — the engine must run 2 minutes, in closed loop and at part throttle, before this code will set
51	Faulty or improperly installed calibration unit (PROM). It takes up to 30 seconds before this code will set
53	Exhaust Gas Recirculation (EGR) valve vacuum sensor has seen improper EGR vacuum
54	M/C solenoid voltage high at ECM as a result of a shorted M/C solenoid circuit and/or faulty ECM

Year – 1985
Model – Bonneville
Engine – 4.3L (262 cid) TBI V6
Engine Code – VIN Z

ECM TROUBLE CODES

Code	Explanation
12	No distributor reference pulses to the ECM. This code is not stored in memory and will only flash while the fault is present. Normal code with ignition ON, engine not running
13	Oxygen sensor circuit – the engine must run up to 4 minutes at part throttle, under road load, before this code will set
14	Shorted coolant sensor circuit – the engine must run 2 minutes before this code will set
15	Open coolant sensor circuit – the engine must run 5 minutes before this code will set
21	Throttle Position Sensor (TPS) circuit voltage high (open circuit or misadjusted TPS). The engine must run 10 seconds, at specified curb idle speed, before this code will set
22	Throttle Position Sensor (TPS) circuit voltage low (grounded circuit or misadjusted TPS). Engine must run 20 seconds, at specified curb idle speed, to set code
24	Vehicle Speed Sensor (VSS) circuit – the vehicle must operate up to 2 minutes at road speed, before this code will set
32	Exhaust Gas Recirculation (EGR) system failure
33	Manifold Absolute Pressure (MAP) sensor (voltage high)
34	Manifold Absolute Pressure (MAP) sensor (voltage low)
42	Electronic Spark Timing (EST) bypass circuit or EST circuit grounded or open
43	Electronic Spark Control (ESC)
44	Lean exhaust indication – the engine must run 2 minutes, in closed loop and at part throttle, before this code will set
45	Rich exhaust indication – the engine must run 2 minutes, in closed loop and at part throttle, before this code will set
51	Faulty or improperly installed calibration unit (PROM). It takes up to 30 seconds before this code will set
52	Calpak error
55	ECM error

Year – 1985
Model – Bonneville
Engine – 5.0L (305 cid) 4 bbl V8
Engine Code – VIN H

ECM TROUBLE CODES

Code	Explanation
12	No distributor reference signal to the ECM. This code is not stored in memory and will only flash while the fault is present. Normal code with ignition ON, engine not running
13	Oxygen sensor circuit—the engine must run up to 4 minutes at part throttle, under road load, before this code will set
14	Shorted coolant sensor circuit—the engine must run 2 minutes before this code will set
15	Open coolant sensor circuit—the engine must run 5 minutes before this code will set
21	Throttle Position Sensor (TPS) circuit voltage high (open circuit or misadjusted TPS). The engine must run 10 seconds, at specified curb idle speed, before this code will set
22	Throttle Position Sensor (TPS) circuit voltage low (grounded circuit or misadjusted TPS). Engine must run 20 seconds, at specified curb idle speed, to set code
23	M/C solenoid circuit open or grounded
24	Vehicle Speed Sensor (VSS) circuit—the vehicle must operate up to 2 minutes at road speed, before this code will set
32	Barometric Pressure Sensor (BARO) circuit low
34	Vacuum sensor or Manifold Absolute Pressure (MAP) circuit—the engine must run up to 2 minutes, at specified curb idle, before this code will set
35	Idle Speed Control (ISC) switch circuit shorted. (Up to 70% TPS for over 5 seconds)
41	No distributor reference signal to the ECM at specified engine vacuum. This code will store in memory
42	Electronic Spark Timing (EST) bypass circuit or EST circuit grounded or open
43	Electronic Spark Control (ESC) retard signal for too long a time; causes retard in EST signal
44	Lean exhaust indication—the engine must run 2 minutes, in closed loop and at part throttle, before this code will set
45	Rich exhaust indication—the engine must run 2 minutes, in closed loop and at part throttle, before this code will set
51	Faulty or improperly installed calibration unit (PROM). It takes up to 30 seconds before this code will set
53	Exhaust Gas Recirculation (EGR) valve vacuum sensor has seen improper EGR vacuum
54	M/C solenoid voltage high at ECM as a result of a shorted M/C solenoid circuit and/or faulty ECM

Year — 1985
Model — Grand Prix
Engine — 3.8L (231 cid) V6
Engine Code — VIN A

ECM TROUBLE CODES

Code	Explanation
12	No distributor reference signal to the ECM. This code is not stored in memory and will only flash while the fault is present. Normal code with ignition ON, engine not running
13	Oxygen sensor circuit — the engine must run up to 4 minutes at part throttle, under road load, before this code will set
14	Shorted coolant sensor circuit — the engine must run 2 minutes before this code will set
15	Open coolant sensor circuit — the engine must run 5 minutes before this code will set
21	Throttle Position Sensor (TPS) circuit voltage high (open circuit or misadjusted TPS). The engine must run 10 seconds, at specified curb idle speed, before this code will set
22	Throttle Position Sensor (TPS) circuit voltage low (grounded circuit or misadjusted TPS). Engine must run 20 seconds, at specified curb idle speed, to set code
23	M/C solenoid circuit open or grounded
24	Vehicle Speed Sensor (VSS) circuit — the vehicle must operate up to 2 minutes at road speed, before this code will set
32	Barometric Pressure Sensor (BARO) circuit low
34	Vacuum sensor or Manifold Absolute Pressure (MAP) circuit — the engine must run up to 2 minutes, at specified curb idle, before this code will set
35	Idle Speed Control (ISC) switch circuit shorted. (Up to 70% TPS for over 5 seconds)
41	No distributor reference signal to the ECM at specified engine vacuum. This code will store in memory
42	Electronic Spark Timing (EST) bypass circuit or EST circuit grounded or open
43	Electronic Spark Control (ESC) retard signal for too long a time; causes retard in EST signal
44	Lean exhaust indication — the engine must run 2 minutes, in closed loop and at part throttle, before this code will set
45	Rich exhaust indication — the engine must run 2 minutes, in closed loop and at part throttle, before this code will set
51	Faulty or improperly installed calibration unit (PROM). It takes up to 30 seconds before this code will set
53	Exhaust Gas Recirculation (EGR) valve vacuum sensor has seen improper EGR vacuum
54	M/C solenoid voltage high at ECM as a result of a shorted M/C solenoid circuit and/or faulty ECM

Year – 1985
Model – Grand Prix
Engine – 4.3L (262 cid) TBI V6
Engine Code – VIN Z

ECM TROUBLE CODES

Code	Explanation
12	No distributor reference pulses to the ECM. This code is not stored in memory and will only flash while the fault is present. Normal code with ignition ON, engine not running
13	Oxygen sensor circuit – the engine must run up to 4 minutes at part throttle, under road load, before this code will set
14	Shorted coolant sensor circuit – the engine must run 2 minutes before this code will set
15	Open coolant sensor circuit – the engine must run 5 minutes before this code will set
21	Throttle Position Sensor (TPS) circuit voltage high (open circuit or misadjusted TPS). The engine must run 10 seconds, at specified curb idle speed, before this code will set
22	Throttle Position Sensor (TPS) circuit voltage low (grounded circuit or misadjusted TPS). Engine must run 20 seconds, at specified curb idle speed, to set code
24	Vehicle Speed Sensor (VSS) circuit – the vehicle must operate up to 2 minutes at road speed, before this code will set
32	Exhaust Gas Recirculation (EGR) system failure
33	Manifold Absolute Pressure (MAP) sensor (voltage high)
34	Manifold Absolute Pressure (MAP) sensor (voltage low)
42	Electronic Spark Timing (EST) bypass circuit or EST circuit grounded or open
43	Electronic Spark Control (ESC)
44	Lean exhaust indication – the engine must run 2 minutes, in closed loop and at part throttle, before this code will set
45	Rich exhaust indication – the engine must run 2 minutes, in closed loop and at part throttle, before this code will set
51	Faulty or improperly installed calibration unit (PROM). It takes up to 30 seconds before this code will set
52	Calpak error
55	ECM error

Year — 1985
Model — Grand Prix
Engine — 5.0L (305 cid) 4 bbl V8
Engine Code — VIN H

ECM TROUBLE CODES

Code	Explanation
12	No distributor reference signal to the ECM. This code is not stored in memory and will only flash while the fault is present. Normal code with ignition ON, engine not running
13	Oxygen sensor circuit — the engine must run up to 4 minutes at part throttle, under road load, before this code will set
14	Shorted coolant sensor circuit — the engine must run 2 minutes before this code will set
15	Open coolant sensor circuit — the engine must run 5 minutes before this code will set
21	Throttle Position Sensor (TPS) circuit voltage high (open circuit or misadjusted TPS). The engine must run 10 seconds, at specified curb idle speed, before this code will set
22	Throttle Position Sensor (TPS) circuit voltage low (grounded circuit or misadjusted TPS). Engine must run 20 seconds, at specified curb idle speed, to set code
23	M/C solenoid circuit open or grounded
24	Vehicle Speed Sensor (VSS) circuit — the vehicle must operate up to 2 minutes at road speed, before this code will set
32	Barometric Pressure Sensor (BARO) circuit low
34	Vacuum sensor or Manifold Absolute Pressure (MAP) circuit — the engine must run up to 2 minutes, at specified curb idle, before this code will set
35	Idle Speed Control (ISC) switch circuit shorted. (Up to 70% TPS for over 5 seconds)
41	No distributor reference signal to the ECM at specified engine vacuum. This code will store in memory
42	Electronic Spark Timing (EST) bypass circuit or EST circuit grounded or open
43	Electronic Spark Control (ESC) retard signal for too long a time; causes retard in EST signal
44	Lean exhaust indication — the engine must run 2 minutes, in closed loop and at part throttle, before this code will set
45	Rich exhaust indication — the engine must run 2 minutes, in closed loop and at part throttle, before this code will set
51	Faulty or improperly installed calibration unit (PROM). It takes up to 30 seconds before this code will set
53	Exhaust Gas Recirculation (EGR) valve vacuum sensor has seen improper EGR vacuum
54	M/C solenoid voltage high at ECM as a result of a shorted M/C solenoid circuit and/or faulty ECM

GENERAL MOTORS CORPORATION
DIAGNOSTIC CODE DATA

Year — 1985
Model — Firebird
Engine — 2.5L (151 cid) TBI 4 cyl
Engine Code — VIN 2

ECM TROUBLE CODES

Code	Explanation
12	No distributor reference pulses to the ECM. This code is not stored in memory and will only flash while the fault is present. Normal code with ignition ON, engine not running
13	Oxygen sensor circuit — the engine must run up to 4 minutes at part throttle, under road load, before this code will set
14	Shorted coolant sensor circuit — low temperature indicated — the engine must run 2 minutes before this code will set
15	Open coolant sensor circuit — high temperature indicated — the engine must run 5 minutes before this code will set
21	Throttle Position Sensor (TPS) circuit voltage high (open circuit or misadjusted TPS). The engine must run 10 seconds, at specified curb idle speed, before this code will set
22	Throttle Position Sensor (TPS) circuit voltage low (grounded circuit or misadjusted TPS). Engine must run 20 seconds, at specified curb idle speed, to set code
24	Vehicle Speed Sensor (VSS) circuit — the vehicle must operate up to 2 minutes at road speed, before this code will set
33	Manifold Absolute Pressure (MAP) sensor (voltage high)
34	Manifold Absolute Pressure (MAP) sensor (voltage low)
35	Idle Air Control (IAC) sensor
42	Electronic Spark Timing (EST) bypass circuit or EST circuit grounded or open
44	Lean exhaust indication — the engine must run 2 minutes, in closed loop and at part throttle, before this code will set
45	Rich exhaust indication — the engine must run 2 minutes, in closed loop and at part throttle, before this code will set
51	Faulty or improperly installed calibration unit (PROM). It takes up to 30 seconds before this code will set
55	ECM error

Year — 1985
Model — Firebird
Engine — 2.8L (173 cid) EFI V6
Engine Code — VIN S

ECM TROUBLE CODES

Code	Explanation
12	No distributor reference pulses to the ECM. This code is not stored in memory and will only flash while the fault is present. Normal code with ignition ON, engine not running
13	Oxygen sensor circuit — the engine must run up to 4 minutes at part throttle, under road load, before this code will set
14	Shorted coolant sensor circuit — the engine must run 2 minutes before this code will set
15	Open coolant sensor circuit — the engine must run 5 minutes before this code will set
21	Throttle Position Sensor (TPS) circuit voltage high (open circuit or misadjusted TPS). The engine must run 10 seconds, at specified curb idle speed, before this code will set
22	Throttle Position Sensor (TPS) circuit voltage low (grounded circuit or misadjusted TPS). Engine must run 20 seconds, at specified curb idle speed, to set code
24	Vehicle Speed Sensor (VSS) circuit — the vehicle must operate up to 2 minutes at road speed, before this code will set
25	Manifold Absolute Temperature (MAT) sensor
32	Exhaust Gas Recirculation (EGR) system failure
34	Mass Air Flow (MAF) sensor (voltage low)
41	Cylinder select error
42	Electronic Spark Timing (EST) bypass circuit or EST circuit grounded or open
44	Lean exhaust indication — the engine must run 2 minutes, in closed loop and at part throttle, before this code will set
45	Rich exhaust indication — the engine must run 2 minutes, in closed loop and at part throttle, before this code will set
51	Faulty or improperly installed calibration unit (PROM). It takes up to 30 seconds before this code will set
52	Calpak error
53	System over voltage
54	Fuel pump voltage low
55	ECM error

Year — 1985
Model — Firebird
Engine — 5.0L (305 cid) EFI V8
Engine Code — VIN F

ECM TROUBLE CODES

Code	Explanation
12	No distributor reference pulses to the ECM. This code is not stored in memory and will only flash while the fault is present. Normal code with ignition ON, engine not running
13	Oxygen sensor circuit—the engine must run up to 4 minutes at part throttle, under road load, before this code will set
14	Shorted coolant sensor circuit—the engine must run 2 minutes before this code will set
15	Open coolant sensor circuit—the engine must run 5 minutes before this code will set
21	Throttle Position Sensor (TPS) circuit voltage high (open circuit or misadjusted TPS). The engine must run 10 seconds, at specified curb idle speed, before this code will set
22	Throttle Position Sensor (TPS) circuit voltage low (grounded circuit or misadjusted TPS). Engine must run 20 seconds, at specified curb idle speed, to set code
24	Vehicle Speed Sensor (VSS) circuit—the vehicle must operate up to 2 minutes at road speed, before this code will set
25	Manifold Absolute Temperature (MAT) sensor
32	Exhaust Gas Recirculation (EGR) system failure
34	Mass Air Flow (MAF) sensor (voltage low)
41	Cylinder select error
42	Electronic Spark Timing (EST) bypass circuit or EST circuit grounded or open
44	Lean exhaust indication—the engine must run 2 minutes, in closed loop and at part throttle, before this code will set
45	Rich exhaust indication—the engine must run 2 minutes, in closed loop and at part throttle, before this code will set
51	Faulty or improperly installed calibration unit (PROM). It takes up to 30 seconds before this code will set
52	Calpak error
53	System over voltage
54	Fuel pump voltage low
55	ECM error

Year – 1985
Model – Firebird
Engine – 5.0L (305 cid) V8
Engine Code – VIN G

ECM TROUBLE CODES

Code	Explanation
12	No distributor reference signal to the ECM. This code is not stored in memory and will only flash while the fault is present. Normal code with ignition ON, engine not running
13	Oxygen sensor circuit—the engine must run up to 4 minutes at part throttle, under road load, before this code will set
14	Shorted coolant sensor circuit—the engine must run 2 minutes before this code will set
15	Open coolant sensor circuit—the engine must run 5 minutes before this code will set
21	Throttle Position Sensor (TPS) circuit voltage high (open circuit or misadjusted TPS). The engine must run 10 seconds, at specified curb idle speed, before this code will set
23	M/C solenoid circuit open or grounded
24	Vehicle Speed Sensor (VSS) circuit—the vehicle must operate up to 2 minutes at road speed, before this code will set
32	Barometric Pressure Sensor (BARO) circuit low
34	Vacuum sensor or Manifold Absolute Pressure (MAP) circuit—the engine must run up to 2 minutes, at specified curb idle, before this code will set
41	No distributor reference signal to the ECM at specified engine vacuum. This code will store in memory
42	Electronic Spark Timing (EST) bypass circuit or EST circuit grounded or open
43	Electronic Spark Control (ESC) retard signal for too long a time; causes retard in EST signal
44	Lean exhaust indication—the engine must run 2 minutes, in closed loop and at part throttle, before this code will set
45	Rich exhaust indication—the engine must run 2 minutes, in closed loop and at part throttle, before this code will set
51	Faulty or improperly installed calibration unit (PROM). It takes up to 30 seconds before this code will set
53	Exhaust Gas Recirculation (EGR) valve vacuum sensor has seen improper EGR vacuum
54	M/C solenoid voltage high at ECM as a result of a shorted M/C solenoid circuit and/or faulty ECM

Year – 1985
Model – Firebird
Engine – 5.0L (305 cid) 4 bbl V8
Engine Code – VIN H

ECM TROUBLE CODES

Code	Explanation
12	No distributor reference signal to the ECM. This code is not stored in memory and will only flash while the fault is present. Normal code with ignition ON, engine not running
13	Oxygen sensor circuit – the engine must run up to 4 minutes at part throttle, under road load, before this code will set
14	Shorted coolant sensor circuit – the engine must run 2 minutes before this code will set
15	Open coolant sensor circuit – the engine must run 5 minutes before this code will set
21	Throttle Position Sensor (TPS) circuit voltage high (open circuit or misadjusted TPS). The engine must run 10 seconds, at specified curb idle speed, before this code will set
23	M/C solenoid circuit open or grounded
24	Vehicle Speed Sensor (VSS) circuit – the vehicle must operate up to 2 minutes at road speed, before this code will set
32	Barometric Pressure Sensor (BARO) circuit low
34	Vacuum sensor or Manifold Absolute Pressure (MAP) circuit – the engine must run up to 2 minutes, at specified curb idle, before this code will set
41	No distributor reference signal to the ECM at specified engine vacuum. This code will store in memory
42	Electronic Spark Timing (EST) bypass circuit or EST circuit grounded or open
43	Electronic Spark Control (ESC) retard signal for too long a time; causes retard in EST signal
44	Lean exhaust indication – the engine must run 2 minutes, in closed loop and at part throttle, before this code will set
45	Rich exhaust indication – the engine must run 2 minutes, in closed loop and at part throttle, before this code will set
51	Faulty or improperly installed calibration unit (PROM). It takes up to 30 seconds before this code will set
53	Exhaust Gas Recirculation (EGR) valve vacuum sensor has seen improper EGR vacuum
54	M/C solenoid voltage high at ECM as a result of a shorted M/C solenoid circuit and/or faulty ECM

Year – 1985
Model – Grand Am
Engine – 2.5L (151 cid) TBI 4 cyl
Engine Code – VIN U

ECM TROUBLE CODES

Code	Explanation
12	No distributor reference pulses to the ECM. This code is not stored in memory and will only flash while the fault is present. Normal code with ignition ON, engine not running
13	Oxygen sensor circuit – the engine must run up to 4 minutes at part throttle, under road load, before this code will set
14	Shorted coolant sensor circuit – low temperature indicated – the engine must run 2 minutes before this code will set
15	Open coolant sensor circuit – high temperature indicated – the engine must run 5 minutes before this code will set
21	Throttle Position Sensor (TPS) circuit voltage high (open circuit or misadjusted TPS). The engine must run 10 seconds, at specified curb idle speed, before this code will set
22	Throttle Position Sensor (TPS) circuit voltage low (grounded circuit or misadjusted TPS). Engine must run 20 seconds, at specified curb idle speed, to set code
24	Vehicle Speed Sensor (VSS) circuit – the vehicle must operate up to 2 minutes at road speed, before this code will set
33	Manifold Absolute Pressure (MAP) sensor (voltage low)
34	Manifold Absolute Pressure (MAP) sensor (voltage high)
35	Idle Air Control (IAC) sensor
42	Electronic Spark Timing (EST) bypass circuit or EST circuit grounded or open
44	Lean exhaust indication – the engine must run 2 minutes, in closed loop and at part throttle, before this code will set
45	Rich exhaust indication – the engine must run 2 minutes, in closed loop and at part throttle, before this code will set
51	Faulty or improperly installed calibration unit (PROM). It takes up to 30 seconds before this code will set
55	ECM error

GENERAL MOTORS CORPORATION
DIAGNOSTIC CODE DATA

Year—1985
Model—Grand Am
Engine—3.0L (181 cid) EFI V6
Engine Code—VIN L

ECM TROUBLE CODES

Code	Explanation
12	No distributor reference pulses to the ECM. This code is not stored in memory and will only flash while the fault is present. Normal code with ignition ON, engine not running
13	Oxygen sensor circuit—the engine must run up to 4 minutes at part throttle, under road load, before this code will set
14	Shorted coolant sensor circuit—low temperature indicated—the engine must run 2 minutes before this code will set
15	Open coolant sensor circuit—high temperature indicated—the engine must run 5 minutes before this code will set
21	Throttle Position Sensor (TPS) circuit voltage high (open circuit or misadjusted TPS). The engine must run 10 seconds, at specified curb idle speed, before this code will set
22	Throttle Position Sensor (TPS) circuit voltage low (grounded circuit or misadjusted TPS). Engine must run 20 seconds, at specified curb idle speed, to set code
23	Air Temperature Sensor (ATS) voltage high
24	Vehicle Speed Sensor (VSS) circuit—the vehicle must operate up to 2 minutes at road speed, before this code will set
25	Air Temperature Sensor (ATS) voltage low
32	Exhaust Gas Recirculation (EGR) system failure
33	Mass Air Flow (MAF) sensor
34	Mass Air Flow (MAF) sensor
42	Electronic Spark Timing (EST) bypass circuit or EST circuit grounded or open
43	Electronic Spark Control (ESC)
44	Lean exhaust indication—the engine must run 2 minutes, in closed loop and at part throttle, before this code will set
45	Rich exhaust indication—the engine must run 2 minutes, in closed loop and at part throttle, before this code will set
51	Faulty or improperly installed calibration unit (PROM). It takes up to 30 seconds before this code will set
52	Calpak error
55	ECM error

Year — 1985
Model — Parisienne
Engine — 4.3L (262 cid) TBI V6
Engine Code — VIN Z

ECM TROUBLE CODES

Code	Explanation
12	No distributor reference pulses to the ECM. This code is not stored in memory and will only flash while the fault is present. Normal code with ignition ON, engine not running
13	Oxygen sensor circuit — the engine must run up to 4 minutes at part throttle, under road load, before this code will set
14	Shorted coolant sensor circuit — low temperature indicated — the engine must run 2 minutes before this code will set
15	Open coolant sensor circuit — high temperature indicated — the engine must run 5 minutes before this code will set
21	Throttle Position Sensor (TPS) circuit voltage high (open circuit or misadjusted TPS). The engine must run 10 seconds, at specified curb idle speed, before this code will set
22	Throttle Position Sensor (TPS) circuit voltage low (grounded circuit or misadjusted TPS). Engine must run 20 seconds, at specified curb idle speed, to set code
24	Vehicle Speed Sensor (VSS) circuit — the vehicle must operate up to 2 minutes at road speed, before this code will set
32	Exhaust Gas Recirculation (EGR) system failure
33	Manifold Absolute Pressure (MAP) sensor (voltage high)
34	Manifold Absolute Pressure (MAP) sensor (voltage low)
42	Electronic Spark Timing (EST) bypass circuit or EST circuit grounded or open
43	Electronic Spark Control (ESC)
44	Lean exhaust indication — the engine must run 2 minutes, in closed loop and at part throttle, before this code will set
45	Rich exhaust indication — the engine must run 2 minutes, in closed loop and at part throttle, before this code will set
51	Faulty or improperly installed calibration unit (PROM). It takes up to 30 seconds before this code will set
52	Calpak error
55	ECM error

Year – 1985
Model – Parisienne
Engine – 5.0L (305 cid) 4 bbl V8
Engine Code – VIN H

ECM TROUBLE CODES

Code	Explanation
12	No distributor reference signal to the ECM. This code is not stored in memory and will only flash while the fault is present. Normal code with ignition ON, engine not running
13	Oxygen sensor circuit—the engine must run up to 4 minutes at part throttle, under road load, before this code will set
14	Shorted coolant sensor circuit—the engine must run 2 minutes before this code will set
15	Open coolant sensor circuit—the engine must run 5 minutes before this code will set
21	Throttle Position Sensor (TPS) circuit voltage high (open circuit or misadjusted TPS). The engine must run 10 seconds, at specified curb idle speed, before this code will set
22	Throttle Position Sensor (TPS) circuit voltage low (grounded circuit or misadjusted TPS). Engine must run 20 seconds, at specified curb idle speed, to set code
23	M/C solenoid circuit open or grounded
24	Vehicle Speed Sensor (VSS) circuit—the vehicle must operate up to 2 minutes at road speed, before this code will set
32	Barometric Pressure Sensor (BARO) circuit low
34	Vacuum sensor or Manifold Absolute Pressure (MAP) circuit—the engine must run up to 2 minutes, at specified curb idle, before this code will set
35	Idle Speed Control (ISC) switch circuit shorted. (Up to 70% TPS for over 5 seconds)
41	No distributor reference signal to the ECM at specified engine vacuum. This code will store in memory
42	Electronic Spark Timing (EST) bypass circuit or EST circuit grounded or open
43	Electronic Spark Control (ESC) retard signal for too long a time; causes retard in EST signal
44	Lean exhaust indication—the engine must run 2 minutes, in closed loop and at part throttle, before this code will set
45	Rich exhaust indication—the engine must run 2 minutes, in closed loop and at part throttle, before this code will set
51	Faulty or improperly installed calibration unit (PROM). It takes up to 30 seconds before this code will set
53	Exhaust Gas Recirculation (EGR) valve vacuum sensor has seen improper EGR vacuum
54	M/C solenoid voltage high at ECM as a result of a shorted M/C solenoid circuit and/or faulty ECM

Year — 1985
Model — Pontiac 1000
Engine — 1.6L (98 cid) 4 cyl
Engine Code — VIN C

ECM TROUBLE CODES

Code	Explanation
12	No distributor reference signal to the ECM. This code is not stored in memory and will only flash while the fault is present. Normal code with ignition ON, engine not running
15	Open coolant sensor circuit — the engine must run 10 minutes before this code will set
21	Throttle Position Sensor (TPS) circuit at WOT. The engine must run up to 10 seconds, below 1000 rpm, before this code will set
23	M/C solenoid circuit open or grounded
44	Lean exhaust indication — the engine must run up to 1 minute, in closed loop and at part throttle above 2000 rpm, before this code will set
45	Rich exhaust indication — the engine must run up to 1 minute, in closed loop and at part throttle above 2000 rpm, before this code will set
51	Faulty or improperly installed calibration unit (PROM). Turns the ECM OFF

Year — 1985
Model — Sunbird
Engine — 1.8L (111 cid) TBI 4 cyl
Engine Code — VIN O

ECM TROUBLE CODES

Code	Explanation
12	No distributor reference pulses to the ECM. This code is not stored in memory and will only flash while the fault is present. Normal code with ignition ON, engine not running
13	Oxygen sensor circuit — the engine must run up to 4 minutes at part throttle, under road load, before this code will set
14	Shorted coolant sensor circuit — low temperature indicated — the engine must run 2 minutes before this code will set
15	Open coolant sensor circuit — high temperature indicated — the engine must run 5 minutes before this code will set
21	Throttle Position Sensor (TPS) circuit voltage high (open circuit or misadjusted TPS). The engine must run 10 seconds, at specified curb idle speed, before this code will set
22	Throttle Position Sensor (TPS) circuit voltage low (grounded circuit or misadjusted TPS). Engine must run 20 seconds, at specified curb idle speed, to set code
24	Vehicle Speed Sensor (VSS) circuit — the vehicle must operate up to 2 minutes at road speed, before this code will set
33	Manifold Absolute Pressure (MAP) sensor (voltage high)
34	Manifold Absolute Pressure (MAP) sensor (voltage low)
35	Idle Air Control (IAC)
42	Electronic Spark Timing (EST) bypass circuit or EST circuit grounded or open
44	Lean exhaust indication — the engine must run 2 minutes, in closed loop and at part throttle, before this code will set
45	Rich exhaust indication — the engine must run 2 minutes, in closed loop and at part throttle, before this code will set
51	Faulty or improperly installed calibration unit (PROM). It takes up to 30 seconds before this code will set
55	ECM error

Year — 1985
Model — Sunbird
Engine — 1.8L (111 cid) EFI Turbo 4 cyl
Engine Code — VIN J

ECM TROUBLE CODES

Code	Explanation
12	No distributor reference pulses to the ECM. This code is not stored in memory and will only flash while the fault is present. Normal code with ignition ON, engine not running
13	Oxygen sensor circuit — the engine must run up to 4 minutes at part throttle, under road load, before this code will set
14	Shorted coolant sensor circuit — low temperature indicated — the engine must run 2 minutes before this code will set
15	Open coolant sensor circuit — high temperature indicated — the engine must run 5 minutes before this code will set
21	Throttle Position Sensor (TPS) circuit voltage high (open circuit or misadjusted TPS). The engine must run 10 seconds, at specified curb idle speed, before this code will set
22	Throttle Position Sensor (TPS) circuit voltage low (grounded circuit or misadjusted TPS). Engine must run 20 seconds, at specified curb idle speed, to set code
24	Vehicle Speed Sensor (VSS) circuit — the vehicle must operate up to 2 minutes at road speed, before this code will set
25	Manifold Absolute Temperature (MAT) sensor
31	Wastegate solenoid
33	Manifold Absolute Pressure (MAP) sensor
34	Manifold Absolute Pressure (MAP) sensor
42	Electronic Spark Timing (EST) bypass circuit or EST circuit grounded or open
43	Electronic Spark Control (ESC)
44	Lean exhaust indication — the engine must run 2 minutes, in closed loop and at part throttle, before this code will set
45	Rich exhaust indication — the engine must run 2 minutes, in closed loop and at part throttle, before this code will set
51	Faulty or improperly installed calibration unit (PROM). It takes up to 30 seconds before this code will set
52	Calpak error
55	ECM error

Year – 1985
Model – Pontiac 6000, LE, STE
Engine – 2.5L (151 cid) TBI 4 cyl
Engine Code – VIN R

ECM TROUBLE CODES

Code	Explanation
12	No distributor reference pulses to the ECM. This code is not stored in memory and will only flash while the fault is present. Normal code with ignition ON, engine not running
13	Oxygen sensor circuit – the engine must run up to 4 minutes at part throttle, under road load, before this code will set
14	Shorted coolant sensor circuit – low temperature indicated – the engine must run 2 minutes before this code will set
15	Open coolant sensor circuit – high temperature indicated – the engine must run 5 minutes before this code will set
21	Throttle Position Sensor (TPS) circuit voltage high (open circuit or misadjusted TPS). The engine must run 10 seconds, at specified curb idle speed, before this code will set
22	Throttle Position Sensor (TPS) circuit voltage low (grounded circuit or misadjusted TPS). Engine must run 20 seconds, at specified curb idle speed, to set code
24	Vehicle Speed Sensor (VSS) circuit – the vehicle must operate up to 2 minutes at road speed, before this code will set
33	Manifold Absolute Pressure (MAP) sensor (voltage high)
34	Manifold Absolute Pressure (MAP) sensor (voltage low)
35	Idle Air Control (IAC)
42	Electronic Spark Timing (EST) bypass circuit or EST circuit grounded or open
44	Lean exhaust indication – the engine must run 2 minutes, in closed loop and at part throttle, before this code will set
45	Rich exhaust indication – the engine must run 2 minutes, in closed loop and at part throttle, before this code will set
51	Faulty or improperly installed calibration unit (PROM). It takes up to 30 seconds before this code will set
55	ECM error

Year — 1985
Model — Pontiac 6000, LE, STE
Engine — 2.8L (173 cid) V6
Engine Code — VIN X

ECM TROUBLE CODES

Code	Explanation
12	No distributor reference signal to the ECM. This code is not stored in memory and will only flash while the fault is present. Normal code with ignition ON, engine not running
13	Oxygen sensor circuit — the engine must run up to 4 minutes at part throttle, under road load, before this code will set
14	Shorted coolant sensor circuit — the engine must run 2 minutes before this code will set
15	Open coolant sensor circuit — the engine must run 5 minutes before this code will set
21	Throttle Position Sensor (TPS) circuit voltage high (open circuit or misadjusted TPS). The engine must run 10 seconds, at specified curb idle speed, before this code will set
23	M/C solenoid circuit open or grounded
24	Vehicle Speed Sensor (VSS) circuit — the vehicle must operate up to 2 minutes at road speed, before this code will set
32	Barometric Pressure Sensor (BARO) circuit low
34	Vacuum sensor or Manifold Absolute Pressure (MAP) circuit — the engine must run up to 2 minutes, at specified curb idle, before this code will set
41	No distributor reference signal to the ECM at specified engine vacuum. This code will store in memory
42	Electronic Spark Timing (EST) bypass circuit or EST circuit grounded or open
43	Electronic Spark Control (ESC) retard signal for too long a time; causes retard in EST signal
44	Lean exhaust indication — the engine must run 2 minutes, in closed loop and at part throttle, before this code will set
45	Rich exhaust indication — the engine must run 2 minutes, in closed loop and at part throttle, before this code will set
51	Faulty or improperly installed calibration unit (PROM). It takes up to 30 seconds before this code will set
54	M/C solenoid voltage high at ECM as a result of a shorted M/C solenoid circuit and/or faulty ECM

Year – 1985
Model – Pontiac 6000, LE, STE
Engine – 2.8L (173 cid) EFI V6
Engine Code – VIN W

ECM TROUBLE CODES

Code	Explanation
12	No distributor reference pulses to the ECM. This code is not stored in memory and will only flash while the fault is present. Normal code with ignition ON, engine not running
13	Oxygen sensor circuit – the engine must run up to 4 minutes at part throttle, under road load, before this code will set
14	Shorted coolant sensor circuit – the engine must run 2 minutes before this code will set
15	Open coolant sensor circuit – the engine must run 5 minutes before this code will set
21	Throttle Position Sensor (TPS) circuit voltage high (open circuit or misadjusted TPS). The engine must run 10 seconds, at specified curb idle speed, before this code will set
22	Throttle Position Sensor (TPS) circuit voltage low (grounded circuit or misadjusted TPS). Engine must run 20 seconds, at specified curb idle speed, to set code
23	Manifold Air Temperature (MAT) sensor
24	Vehicle Speed Sensor (VSS) circuit – the vehicle must operate up to 2 minutes at road speed, before this code will set
25	Manifold Air Temperature (MAT) sensor
32	Exhaust Gas Recirculation (EGR) system failure
34	Manifold Air Flow (MAF) sensor
41	Cylinder select error
42	Electronic Spark Timing (EST) bypass circuit or EST circuit grounded or open
44	Lean exhaust indication – the engine must run 2 minutes, in closed loop and at part throttle, before this code will set
45	Rich exhaust indication – the engine must run 2 minutes, in closed loop and at part throttle, before this code will set
51	Faulty or improperly installed calibration unit (PROM). It takes up to 30 seconds before this code will set
52	Calpak error
53	System over voltage
54	Fuel pump voltage low
55	ECM error

Year — 1985
Model — Fiero
Engine — 2.5L (151 cid) TBI 4 cyl
Engine Code — VIN R

ECM TROUBLE CODES

Code	Explanation
12	No distributor reference pulses to the ECM. This code is not stored in memory and will only flash while the fault is present. Normal code with ignition ON, engine not running
13	Oxygen sensor circuit — the engine must run up to 4 minutes at part throttle, under road load, before this code will set
14	Shorted coolant sensor circuit — low temperature indicated — the engine must run 2 minutes before this code will set
15	Open coolant sensor circuit — high temperature indicated — the engine must run 5 minutes before this code will set
21	Throttle Position Sensor (TPS) circuit voltage high (open circuit or misadjusted TPS). The engine must run 10 seconds, at specified curb idle speed, before this code will set
22	Throttle Position Sensor (TPS) circuit voltage low (grounded circuit or misadjusted TPS). Engine must run 20 seconds, at specified curb idle speed, to set code
24	Vehicle Speed Sensor (VSS) circuit — the vehicle must operate up to 2 minutes at road speed, before this code will set
33	Manifold Absolute Pressure (MAP) sensor (voltage high)
34	Manifold Air Flow (MAF) sensor (voltage low)
35	Idle Air Control (IAC)
42	Electronic Spark Timing (EST) bypass circuit or EST circuit grounded or open
44	Lean exhaust indication — the engine must run 2 minutes, in closed loop and at part throttle, before this code will set
45	Rich exhaust indication — the engine must run 2 minutes, in closed loop and at part throttle, before this code will set
51	Faulty or improperly installed calibration unit (PROM). It takes up to 30 seconds before this code will set
55	ECM error

Year — 1985
Model — Fiero
Engine — 2.8L (173 cid) EFI V6
Engine Code — VIN 9

ECM TROUBLE CODES

Code	Explanation
12	No distributor reference pulses to the ECM. This code is not stored in memory and will only flash while the fault is present. Normal code with ignition ON, engine not running
13	Oxygen sensor circuit — the engine must run up to 4 minutes at part throttle, under road load, before this code will set
14	Shorted coolant sensor circuit — low temperature indicated — the engine must run 2 minutes before this code will set
15	Open coolant sensor circuit — high temperature indicated — the engine must run 5 minutes before this code will set
21	Throttle Position Sensor (TPS) circuit voltage high (open circuit or misadjusted TPS). The engine must run 10 seconds, at specified curb idle speed, before this code will set
22	Throttle Position Sensor (TPS) circuit voltage low (grounded circuit or misadjusted TPS). Engine must run 20 seconds, at specified curb idle speed, to set code
23	Manifold Air Temperature (MAT) sensor
24	Vehicle Speed Sensor (VSS) circuit — the vehicle must operate up to 2 minutes at road speed, before this code will set
25	Manifold Air Temperature (MAT) sensor
32	Exhaust Gas Recirculation (EGR) vacuum control
33	Manifold Absolute Pressure (MAP) sensor
34	Manifold Absolute Pressure (MAP) sensor
35	Idle Air Control (IAC)
42	Electronic Spark Timing (EST) bypass circuit or EST circuit grounded or open
44	Lean exhaust indication — the engine must run 2 minutes, in closed loop and at part throttle, before this code will set
45	Rich exhaust indication — the engine must run 2 minutes, in closed loop and at part throttle, before this code will set
51	Faulty or improperly installed calibration unit (PROM). It takes up to 30 seconds before this code will set
52	Calpak error
55	ECM error

Year — 1986
Model — Bonneville
Engine — 3.8L (231 cid) 2bbl V6
Engine Code — VIN A

ECM TROUBLE CODES

Code	Explanation
12	No distributor reference signal to the ECM. This code is not stored in memory and will only flash while the fault is present. This is a normal code with ignition ON, engine not running
13	Oxygen sensor circuit — the engine must run up to 4 minutes at part throttle, under road load, before this code will set
14	Shorted coolant sensor circuit — the engine must run 2 minutes before this code will set
15	Open coolant sensor circuit — the engine must run 5 minutes before this code will set
21	Throttle Position Sensor (TPS) circuit voltage high (open circuit or misadjusted TPS). The engine must run 10 seconds, at specified curb idle speed, before this code will set
22	Throttle Position Sensor (TPS) circuit voltage low (grounded circuit or misadjusted TPS). Engine must run 20 seconds, at specified curb idle speed, to set code
23	M/C solenoid circuit open or grounded
24	Vehicle Speed Sensor (VSS) circuit — the vehicle must operate up to 2 minutes at road speed, before this code will set
32	Barometric Pressure Sensor (BARO) circuit low
34	Vacuum sensor or Manifold Absolute Pressure (MAP) circuit — the engine must run up to 2 minutes, at specified curb idle, before this code will set
35	Idle Speed Control (ISC) switch circuit shorted. (Up to 70% TPS for over 5 seconds)
41	No distributor reference signal to the ECM at specified engine vacuum. This code will store in memory
42	Electronic Spark Timing (EST) bypass circuit or EST circuit grounded or open
43	Electronic Spark Control (ESC) retard signal for too long a time; causes retard in EST signal
44	Lean exhaust indication — the engine must run 2 minutes, in closed loop and at part throttle, before this code will set
45	Rich exhaust indication — the engine must run 2 minutes, in closed loop and at part throttle, before this code will set
51	Faulty or improperly installed calibration unit (PROM). It takes up to 30 seconds before this code will set
53	Exhaust Gas Recirculation (EGR) valve vacuum sensor has seen improper EGR control vacuum
54	M/C solenoid voltage high at ECM as a result of a shorted M/C solenoid circuit and/or faulty ECM

Year — 1986
Model — Bonneville
Engine — 4.3L (262 cid) TBI V6
Engine Code — VIN Z

ECM TROUBLE CODES

Code	Explanation
12	No distributor reference signal to the ECM. This code is not stored in memory and will only flash while the fault is present. This is a normal code with ignition ON, engine not running
13	Oxygen sensor circuit
14	Coolant sensor circuit (voltage low)
15	Coolant sensor circuit (voltage high)
21	Throttle Position Sensor (TPS) circuit (voltage high)
22	Throttle Position Sensor (TPS) circuit (voltage low)
24	Vehicle Speed Sensor (VSS) circuit
32	Exhaust Gas Recirculation (EGR) system failure
33	Manifold Absolute Pressure (MAP) sensor (voltage high)
34	Manifold Absolute Pressure (MAP) sensor (voltage low)
42	Electronic Spark Timing (EST) bypass circuit or EST circuit grounded or open
43	Electronic Spark Control (ESC) retard signal for too long a time; causes retard in EST signal
44	Lean exhaust indication
45	Rich exhaust indication
51	Faulty or improperly installed calibration unit (PROM)
52	Calpak (missing)
54	Fuel pump voltage low
55	ECM error

Year – 1986
Model – Bonneville
Engine – 5.0L (305 cid) V8
Engine Code – VIN H

ECM TROUBLE CODES

Code	Explanation
12	No distributor reference signal to the ECM. This code is not stored in memory and will only flash while the fault is present. This is a normal code with ignition ON, engine not running
13	Oxygen sensor circuit – the engine must run up to 4 minutes at part throttle, under road load, before this code will set
14	Shorted coolant sensor circuit – the engine must run 2 minutes before this code will set
15	Open coolant sensor circuit – the engine must run 5 minutes before this code will set
21	Throttle Position Sensor (TPS) circuit voltage high (open circuit or misadjusted TPS). The engine must run 10 seconds, at specified curb idle speed, before this code will set
22	Throttle Position Sensor (TPS) circuit voltage low (grounded circuit or misadjusted TPS). Engine must run 20 seconds, at specified curb idle speed, to set code
23	M/C solenoid circuit open or grounded
24	Vehicle Speed Sensor (VSS) circuit – the vehicle must operate up to 2 minutes at road speed, before this code will set
32	Barometric Pressure Sensor (BARO) circuit low
34	Vacuum sensor or Manifold Absolute Pressure (MAP) circuit – the engine must run up to 2 minutes, at specified curb idle, before this code will set
35	Idle Speed Control (ISC) switch circuit shorted. (Up to 70% TPS for over 5 seconds)
41	No distributor reference signal to the ECM at specified engine vacuum. This code will store in memory
42	Electronic Spark Timing (EST) bypass circuit or EST circuit grounded or open
43	Electronic Spark Control (ESC) retard signal for too long a time; causes retard in EST signal
44	Lean exhaust indication – the engine must run 2 minutes, in closed loop and at part throttle, before this code will set
45	Rich exhaust indication – the engine must run 2 minutes, in closed loop and at part throttle, before this code will set
51	Faulty or improperly installed calibration unit (PROM). It takes up to 30 seconds before this code will set
53	Exhaust Gas Recirculation (EGR) valve vacuum sensor has seen improper EGR control vacuum
54	M/C solenoid voltage high at ECM as a result of a shorted M/C solenoid circuit and/or faulty ECM

Year — 1986
Model — Bonneville
Engine — 5.0L (305 cid) 4bbl V8
Engine Code — VIN Y

ECM TROUBLE CODES

Code	Explanation
12	No distributor reference signal to the ECM. This code is not stored in memory and will only flash while the fault is present. This is a normal code with ignition ON, engine not running
13	Oxygen sensor circuit—the engine must run up to 4 minutes at part throttle, under road load, before this code will set
14	Shorted coolant sensor circuit—the engine must run 2 minutes before this code will set
15	Open coolant sensor circuit—the engine must run 5 minutes before this code will set
21	Throttle Position Sensor (TPS) circuit voltage high (open circuit or misadjusted TPS). The engine must run 10 seconds, at specified curb idle speed, before this code will set
22	Throttle Position Sensor (TPS) circuit voltage low (grounded circuit or misadjusted TPS). Engine must run 20 seconds, at specified curb idle speed, to set code
23	M/C solenoid circuit open or grounded
24	Vehicle Speed Sensor (VSS) circuit—the vehicle must operate up to 2 minutes at road speed, before this code will set
32	Barometric Pressure Sensor (BARO) circuit low
34	Vacuum sensor or Manifold Absolute Pressure (MAP) circuit—the engine must run up to 2 minutes, at specified curb idle, before this code will set
35	Idle Speed Control (ISC) switch circuit shorted. (Up to 70% TPS for over 5 seconds)
41	No distributor reference signal to the ECM at specified engine vacuum. This code will store in memory
42	Electronic Spark Timing (EST) bypass circuit or EST circuit grounded or open
43	Electronic Spark Control (ESC) retard signal for too long a time; causes retard in EST signal
44	Lean exhaust indication—the engine must run 2 minutes, in closed loop and at part throttle, before this code will set
45	Rich exhaust indication—the engine must run 2 minutes, in closed loop and at part throttle, before this code will set
51	Faulty or improperly installed calibration unit (PROM). It takes up to 30 seconds before this code will set
53	Exhaust Gas Recirculation (EGR) valve vacuum sensor has seen improper EGR control vacuum
54	M/C solenoid voltage high at ECM as a result of a shorted M/C solenoid circuit and/or faulty ECM

Year — 1986
Model — Grand Prix
Engine — 3.8L (231 cid) 2bbl V6
Engine Code — VIN A

ECM TROUBLE CODES

Code	Explanation
12	No distributor reference signal to the ECM. This code is not stored in memory and will only flash while the fault is present. This is a normal code with ignition ON, engine not running
13	Oxygen sensor circuit — the engine must run up to 4 minutes at part throttle, under road load, before this code will set
14	Shorted coolant sensor circuit — the engine must run 2 minutes before this code will set
15	Open coolant sensor circuit — the engine must run 5 minutes before this code will set
21	Throttle Position Sensor (TPS) circuit voltage high (open circuit or misadjusted TPS). The engine must run 10 seconds, at specified curb idle speed, before this code will set
22	Throttle Position Sensor (TPS) circuit voltage low (grounded circuit or misadjusted TPS). Engine must run 20 seconds, at specified curb idle speed, to set code
23	M/C solenoid circuit open or grounded
24	Vehicle Speed Sensor (VSS) circuit — the vehicle must operate up to 2 minutes at road speed, before this code will set
32	Barometric Pressure Sensor (BARO) circuit low
34	Vacuum sensor or Manifold Absolute Pressure (MAP) circuit — the engine must run up to 2 minutes, at specified curb idle, before this code will set
35	Idle Speed Control (ISC) switch circuit shorted. (Up to 70% TPS for over 5 seconds)
41	No distributor reference signal to the ECM at specified engine vacuum. This code will store in memory
42	Electronic Spark Timing (EST) bypass circuit or EST circuit grounded or open
43	Electronic Spark Control (ESC) retard signal for too long a time; causes retard in EST signal
44	Lean exhaust indication — the engine must run 2 minutes, in closed loop and at part throttle, before this code will set
45	Rich exhaust indication — the engine must run 2 minutes, in closed loop and at part throttle, before this code will set
51	Faulty or improperly installed calibration unit (PROM). It takes up to 30 seconds before this code will set
53	Exhaust Gas Recirculation (EGR) valve vacuum sensor has seen improper EGR control vacuum
54	M/C solenoid voltage high at ECM as a result of a shorted M/C solenoid circuit and/or faulty ECM

Year — 1986
Model — Grand Prix
Engine — 4.3L (262 cid) TBI V6
Engine Code — VIN Z

ECM TROUBLE CODES

Code	Explanation
12	No distributor reference signal to the ECM. This code is not stored in memory and will only flash while the fault is present. This is a normal code with ignition ON, engine not running
13	Oxygen sensor circuit
14	Coolant sensor circuit (voltage low)
15	Coolant sensor circuit (voltage high)
21	Throttle Position Sensor (TPS) circuit (voltage high)
22	Throttle Position Sensor (TPS) circuit (voltage low)
24	Vehicle Speed Sensor (VSS) circuit
32	Exhaust Gas Recirculation (EGR) system failure
33	Manifold Absolute Pressure (MAP) sensor (voltage high)
34	Manifold Absolute Pressure (MAP) sensor (voltage low)
42	Electronic Spark Timing (EST) bypass circuit or EST circuit grounded or open
43	Electronic Spark Control (ESC) retard signal for too long a time; causes retard in EST signal
44	Lean exhaust indication
45	Rich exhaust indication
51	Faulty or improperly installed calibration unit (PROM)
52	Calpak (missing)
54	Fuel pump voltage low
55	ECM error

Year – 1986
Model – Grand Prix
Engine – 5.0L (305 cid) 4bbl V8
Engine Code – VIN H

ECM TROUBLE CODES

Code	Explanation
12	No distributor reference signal to the ECM. This code is not stored in memory and will only flash while the fault is present. This is a normal code with ignition ON, engine not running
13	Oxygen sensor circuit – the engine must run up to 4 minutes at part throttle, under road load, before this code will set
14	Shorted coolant sensor circuit – the engine must run 2 minutes before this code will set
15	Open coolant sensor circuit – the engine must run 5 minutes before this code will set
21	Throttle Position Sensor (TPS) circuit voltage high (open circuit or misadjusted TPS). The engine must run 10 seconds, at specified curb idle speed, before this code will set
22	Throttle Position Sensor (TPS) circuit voltage low (grounded circuit or misadjusted TPS). Engine must run 20 seconds, at specified curb idle speed, to set code
23	M/C solenoid circuit open or grounded
24	Vehicle Speed Sensor (VSS) circuit – the vehicle must operate up to 2 minutes at road speed, before this code will set
32	Barometric Pressure Sensor (BARO) circuit low
34	Vacuum sensor or Manifold Absolute Pressure (MAP) circuit – the engine must run up to 2 minutes, at specified curb idle, before this code will set
35	Idle Speed Control (ISC) switch circuit shorted. (Up to 70% TPS for over 5 seconds)
41	No distributor reference signal to the ECM at specified engine vacuum. This code will store in memory
42	Electronic Spark Timing (EST) bypass circuit or EST circuit grounded or open
43	Electronic Spark Control (ESC) retard signal for too long a time; causes retard in EST signal
44	Lean exhaust indication – the engine must run 2 minutes, in closed loop and at part throttle, before this code will set
45	Rich exhaust indication – the engine must run 2 minutes, in closed loop and at part throttle, before this code will set
51	Faulty or improperly installed calibration unit (PROM). It takes up to 30 seconds before this code will set
53	Exhaust Gas Recirculation (EGR) valve vacuum sensor has seen improper EGR control vacuum
54	M/C solenoid voltage high at ECM as a result of a shorted M/C solenoid circuit and/or faulty ECM

Year — 1986
Model — Grand Prix
Engine — 5.0L (305 cid) 4bbl V8
Engine Code — VIN Y

ECM TROUBLE CODES

Code	Explanation
12	No distributor reference signal to the ECM. This code is not stored in memory and will only flash while the fault is present. This is a normal code with ignition ON, engine not running
13	Oxygen sensor circuit — the engine must run up to 4 minutes at part throttle, under road load, before this code will set
14	Shorted coolant sensor circuit — the engine must run 2 minutes before this code will set
15	Open coolant sensor circuit — the engine must run 5 minutes before this code will set
21	Throttle Position Sensor (TPS) circuit voltage high (open circuit or misadjusted TPS). The engine must run 10 seconds, at specified curb idle speed, before this code will set
22	Throttle Position Sensor (TPS) circuit voltage low (grounded circuit or misadjusted TPS). Engine must run 20 seconds, at specified curb idle speed, to set code
23	M/C solenoid circuit open or grounded
24	Vehicle Speed Sensor (VSS) circuit — the vehicle must operate up to 2 minutes at road speed, before this code will set
32	Barometric Pressure Sensor (BARO) circuit low
34	Vacuum sensor or Manifold Absolute Pressure (MAP) circuit — the engine must run up to 2 minutes, at specified curb idle, before this code will set
35	Idle Speed Control (ISC) switch circuit shorted. (Up to 70% TPS for over 5 seconds)
41	No distributor reference signal to the ECM at specified engine vacuum. This code will store in memory
42	Electronic Spark Timing (EST) bypass circuit or EST circuit grounded or open
43	Electronic Spark Control (ESC) retard signal for too long a time; causes retard in EST signal
44	Lean exhaust indication — the engine must run 2 minutes, in closed loop and at part throttle, before this code will set
45	Rich exhaust indication — the engine must run 2 minutes, in closed loop and at part throttle, before this code will set
51	Faulty or improperly installed calibration unit (PROM). It takes up to 30 seconds before this code will set
53	Exhaust Gas Recirculation (EGR) valve vacuum sensor has seen improper EGR control vacuum
54	M/C solenoid voltage high at ECM as a result of a shorted M/C solenoid circuit and/or faulty ECM

Year – 1986
Model – Firebird
Engine – 2.5L (151 cid) TBI 4 cyl
Engine Code – VIN 2

ECM TROUBLE CODES

Code	Explanation
12	No distributor reference signal to the ECM. This code is not stored in memory and will only flash while the fault is present. This is a normal code with ignition ON, engine not running
13	Oxygen sensor circuit
14	Coolant sensor circuit
15	Coolant sensor circuit
21	Throttle Position Sensor (TPS) circuit
22	Throttle Position Sensor (TPS) circuit
24	Vehicle Speed Sensor (VSS) circuit
33	Manifold Absolute Pressure (MAP) sensor
34	Manifold Absolute Pressure (MAP) sensor
35	Idle air control
42	Electronic Spark Timing (EST) bypass circuit or EST circuit grounded or open
44	Lean exhaust indication
45	Rich exhaust indication
51	Faulty or improperly installed calibration unit (PROM)
55	ECM error

Year – 1986
Model – Firebird
Engine – 2.8L (173 cid) TBI V6
Engine Code – VIN Z

ECM TROUBLE CODES

Code	Explanation
12	No distributor reference signal to the ECM. This code is not stored in memory and will only flash while the fault is present. This is a normal code with ignition ON, engine not running
13	Oxygen sensor circuit
14	Coolant sensor circuit
15	Coolant sensor circuit
21	Throttle Position Sensor (TPS) circuit
22	Throttle Position Sensor (TPS) circuit
23	Manifold Air Temperature (MAT) sensor
24	Vehicle Speed Sensor (VSS) circuit
25	Manifold Air Temperature (MAT) sensor
32	Exhaust Gas Recirculation (EGR)
33	Mass Air Flow (MAF) sensor
34	Mass Air Flow (MAF) sensor
41	Cylinder select
42	Electronic Spark Timing (EST) bypass circuit or EST circuit grounded or open
44	Lean exhaust indication
45	Rich exhaust indication
51	Faulty or improperly installed calibration unit (PROM)
52	Calpak (missing)
53	System over voltage
54	Fuel pump voltage low
55	ECM error

Year – 1986
Model – Firebird
Engine – 5.0L (305 cid) 4bbl V8
Engine Code – VIN G

ECM TROUBLE CODES

Code	Explanation
12	No distributor reference signal to the ECM. This code is not stored in memory and will only flash while the fault is present. This is a normal code with ignition ON, engine not running
13	Oxygen sensor circuit – the engine must run up to 4 minutes at part throttle, under road load, before this code will set
14	Shorted coolant sensor circuit – the engine must run 2 minutes before this code will set
15	Open coolant sensor circuit – the engine must run 5 minutes before this code will set
21	Throttle Position Sensor (TPS) circuit voltage high (open circuit or misadjusted TPS). The engine must run 10 seconds, at specified curb idle speed, before this code will set
22	Throttle Position Sensor (TPS) circuit voltage low (grounded circuit or misadjusted TPS). Engine must run 20 seconds, at specified curb idle speed, to set code
23	M/C solenoid circuit open or grounded
24	Vehicle Speed Sensor (VSS) circuit – the vehicle must operate up to 2 minutes at road speed, before this code will set
32	Barometric Pressure Sensor (BARO) circuit low
34	Vacuum sensor or Manifold Absolute Pressure (MAP) circuit – the engine must run up to 2 minutes, at specified curb idle, before this code will set
35	Idle Speed Control (ISC) switch circuit shorted. (Up to 70% TPS for over 5 seconds)
41	No distributor reference signal to the ECM at specified engine vacuum. This code will store in memory
42	Electronic Spark Timing (EST) bypass circuit or EST circuit grounded or open
43	Electronic Spark Control (ESC) retard signal for too long a time; causes retard in EST signal
44	Lean exhaust indication – the engine must run 2 minutes, in closed loop and at part throttle, before this code will set
45	Rich exhaust indication – the engine must run 2 minutes, in closed loop and at part throttle, before this code will set
51	Faulty or improperly installed calibration unit (PROM). It takes up to 30 seconds before this code will set
53	Exhaust Gas Recirculation (EGR) valve vacuum sensor has seen improper EGR control vacuum
54	M/C solenoid voltage high at ECM as a result of a shorted M/C solenoid circuit and/or faulty ECM

Year – 1986
Model – Firebird
Engine – 5.0L (305 cid) 4bbl V8
Engine Code – VIN H

ECM TROUBLE CODES

Code	Explanation
12	No distributor reference signal to the ECM. This code is not stored in memory and will only flash while the fault is present. This is a normal code with ignition ON, engine not running
13	Oxygen sensor circuit – the engine must run up to 4 minutes at part throttle, under road load, before this code will set
14	Shorted coolant sensor circuit – the engine must run 2 minutes before this code will set
15	Open coolant sensor circuit – the engine must run 5 minutes before this code will set
21	Throttle Position Sensor (TPS) circuit voltage high (open circuit or misadjusted TPS). The engine must run 10 seconds, at specified curb idle speed, before this code will set
22	Throttle Position Sensor (TPS) circuit voltage low (grounded circuit or misadjusted TPS). Engine must run 20 seconds, at specified curb idle speed, to set code
23	M/C solenoid circuit open or grounded
24	Vehicle Speed Sensor (VSS) circuit – the vehicle must operate up to 2 minutes at road speed, before this code will set
32	Barometric Pressure Sensor (BARO) circuit low
34	Vacuum sensor or Manifold Absolute Pressure (MAP) circuit – the engine must run up to 2 minutes, at specified curb idle, before this code will set
35	Idle Speed Control (ISC) switch circuit shorted. (Up to 70% TPS for over 5 seconds)
41	No distributor reference signal to the ECM at specified engine vacuum. This code will store in memory
42	Electronic Spark Timing (EST) bypass circuit or EST circuit grounded or open
43	Electronic Spark Control (ESC) retard signal for too long a time; causes retard in EST signal
44	Lean exhaust indication – the engine must run 2 minutes, in closed loop and at part throttle, before this code will set
45	Rich exhaust indication – the engine must run 2 minutes, in closed loop and at part throttle, before this code will set
51	Faulty or improperly installed calibration unit (PROM). It takes up to 30 seconds before this code will set
53	Exhaust Gas Recirculation (EGR) valve vacuum sensor has seen improper EGR control vacuum
54	M/C solenoid voltage high at ECM as a result of a shorted M/C solenoid circuit and/or faulty ECM

Year — 1986
Model — Firebird
Engine — 5.0L (305 cid) MPFI V8
Engine Code — VIN F

ECM TROUBLE CODES

Code	Explanation
12	No distributor reference signal to the ECM. This code is not stored in memory and will only flash while the fault is present. This is a normal code with ignition ON, engine not running
13	Oxygen sensor circuit
14	Coolant sensor circuit
15	Coolant sensor circuit
21	Throttle Position Sensor (TPS) circuit
22	Throttle Position Sensor (TPS) circuit
23	Manifold Air Temperature (MAT) sensor
24	Vehicle Speed Sensor (VSS) circuit
25	Manifold Air Temperature (MAT) sensor
32	Exhaust Gas Recirculation (EGR)
33	Mass Air Flow (MAF) sensor
34	Mass Air Flow (MAF) sensor
36	Burn-off function fault
41	Cylinder select
42	Electronic Spark Timing (EST) bypass circuit or EST circuit grounded or open
43	Electronic Spark Control (ESC) retard signal for too long a time; causes retard in EST signal
44	Lean exhaust indication
45	Rich exhaust indication
51	Faulty or improperly installed calibration unit (PROM)
53	System over voltage
54	Fuel pump voltage low
55	ECM error

Year – 1986
Model – Firebird
Engine – 5.7L (350 cid) MPFI V8
Engine Code – VIN 8

ECM TROUBLE CODES

Code	Explanation
12	No distributor reference signal to the ECM. This code is not stored in memory and will only flash while the fault is present. This is a normal code with ignition ON, engine not running
13	Oxygen sensor circuit
14	Coolant sensor circuit
15	Coolant sensor circuit
21	Throttle Position Sensor (TPS) circuit
22	Throttle Position Sensor (TPS) circuit
23	Manifold Air Temperature (MAT) sensor
24	Vehicle Speed Sensor (VSS) circuit
25	Manifold Air Temperature (MAT) sensor
32	Exhaust Gas Recirculation (EGR)
33	Mass Air Flow (MAF) sensor
34	Mass Air Flow (MAF) sensor
36	Burn-off function fault
41	Cylinder select
42	Electronic Spark Timing (EST) bypass circuit or EST circuit grounded or open
43	Electronic Spark Control (ESC) retard signal for too long a time; causes retard in EST signal
44	Lean exhaust indication
45	Rich exhaust indication
51	Faulty or improperly installed calibration unit (PROM)
53	System over voltage
54	Fuel pump voltage low
55	ECM error

Year — 1986
Model — Parisienne
Engine — 3.8L (231 cid) 2bbl V6
Engine Code — VIN A

ECM TROUBLE CODES

Code	Explanation
12	No distributor reference signal to the ECM. This code is not stored in memory and will only flash while the fault is present. This is a normal code with ignition ON, engine not running
13	Oxygen sensor circuit — the engine must run up to 4 minutes at part throttle, under road load, before this code will set
14	Shorted coolant sensor circuit — the engine must run 2 minutes before this code will set
15	Open coolant sensor circuit — the engine must run 5 minutes before this code will set
21	Throttle Position Sensor (TPS) circuit voltage high (open circuit or misadjusted TPS). The engine must run 10 seconds, at specified curb idle speed, before this code will set
22	Throttle Position Sensor (TPS) circuit voltage low (grounded circuit or misadjusted TPS). Engine must run 20 seconds, at specified curb idle speed, to set code
23	M/C solenoid circuit open or grounded
24	Vehicle Speed Sensor (VSS) circuit — the vehicle must operate up to 2 minutes at road speed, before this code will set
32	Barometric Pressure Sensor (BARO) circuit low
34	Vacuum sensor or Manifold Absolute Pressure (MAP) circuit — the engine must run up to 2 minutes, at specified curb idle, before this code will set
35	Idle Speed Control (ISC) switch circuit shorted. (Up to 70% TPS for over 5 seconds)
41	No distributor reference signal to the ECM at specified engine vacuum. This code will store in memory
42	Electronic Spark Timing (EST) bypass circuit or EST circuit grounded or open
43	Electronic Spark Control (ESC) retard signal for too long a time; causes retard in EST signal
44	Lean exhaust indication — the engine must run 2 minutes, in closed loop and at part throttle, before this code will set
45	Rich exhaust indication — the engine must run 2 minutes, in closed loop and at part throttle, before this code will set
51	Faulty or improperly installed calibration unit (PROM). It takes up to 30 seconds before this code will set
53	Exhaust Gas Recirculation (EGR) valve vacuum sensor has seen improper EGR control vacuum
54	M/C solenoid voltage high at ECM as a result of a shorted M/C solenoid circuit and/or faulty ECM

Year – 1986
Model – Parisienne
Engine – 4.3L (262 cid) TBI V6
Engine Code – VIN Z

ECM TROUBLE CODES

Code	Explanation
12	No distributor reference signal to the ECM. This code is not stored in memory and will only flash while the fault is present. This is a normal code with ignition ON, engine not running
13	Oxygen sensor circuit
14	Coolant sensor circuit (voltage low)
15	Coolant sensor circuit (voltage high)
21	Throttle Position Sensor (TPS) circuit (voltage high)
22	Throttle Position Sensor (TPS) circuit (voltage low)
24	Vehicle Speed Sensor (VSS) circuit
32	Exhaust Gas Recirculation (EGR) system failure
33	Manifold Absolute Pressure (MAP) sensor (voltage high)
34	Manifold Absolute Pressure (MAP) sensor (voltage low)
42	Electronic Spark Timing (EST) bypass circuit or EST circuit grounded or open
43	Electronic Spark Control (ESC) retard signal for too long a time; causes retard in EST signal
44	Lean exhaust indication
45	Rich exhaust indication
51	Faulty or improperly installed calibration unit (PROM)
52	Calpak (missing)
54	Fuel pump voltage low
55	ECM error

Year — 1986
Model — Parisienne
Engine — 5.0L (305 cid) 4bbl V8
Engine Code — VIN H

ECM TROUBLE CODES

Code	Explanation
12	No distributor reference signal to the ECM. This code is not stored in memory and will only flash while the fault is present. This is a normal code with ignition ON, engine not running
13	Oxygen sensor circuit — the engine must run up to 4 minutes at part throttle, under road load, before this code will set
14	Shorted coolant sensor circuit — the engine must run 2 minutes before this code will set
15	Open coolant sensor circuit — the engine must run 5 minutes before this code will set
21	Throttle Position Sensor (TPS) circuit voltage high (open circuit or misadjusted TPS). The engine must run 10 seconds, at specified curb idle speed, before this code will set
22	Throttle Position Sensor (TPS) circuit voltage low (grounded circuit or misadjusted TPS). Engine must run 20 seconds, at specified curb idle speed, to set code
23	M/C solenoid circuit open or grounded
24	Vehicle Speed Sensor (VSS) circuit — the vehicle must operate up to 2 minutes at road speed, before this code will set
32	Barometric Pressure Sensor (BARO) circuit low
34	Vacuum sensor or Manifold Absolute Pressure (MAP) circuit — the engine must run up to 2 minutes, at specified curb idle, before this code will set
35	Idle Speed Control (ISC) switch circuit shorted. (Up to 70% TPS for over 5 seconds)
41	No distributor reference signal to the ECM at specified engine vacuum. This code will store in memory
42	Electronic Spark Timing (EST) bypass circuit or EST circuit grounded or open
43	Electronic Spark Control (ESC) retard signal for too long a time; causes retard in EST signal
44	Lean exhaust indication — the engine must run 2 minutes, in closed loop and at part throttle, before this code will set
45	Rich exhaust indication — the engine must run 2 minutes, in closed loop and at part throttle, before this code will set
51	Faulty or improperly installed calibration unit (PROM). It takes up to 30 seconds before this code will set
53	Exhaust Gas Recirculation (EGR) valve vacuum sensor has seen improper EGR control vacuum
54	M/C solenoid voltage high at ECM as a result of a shorted M/C solenoid circuit and/or faulty ECM

GENERAL MOTORS CORPORATION
DIAGNOSTIC CODE DATA

Year – 1986
Model – Parisienne
Engine – 5.0L (305 cid) 4bbl V8
Engine Code – VIN Y

ECM TROUBLE CODES

Code	Explanation
12	No distributor reference signal to the ECM. This code is not stored in memory and will only flash while the fault is present. This is a normal code with ignition ON, engine not running
13	Oxygen sensor circuit – the engine must run up to 4 minutes at part throttle, under road load, before this code will set
14	Shorted coolant sensor circuit – the engine must run 2 minutes before this code will set
15	Open coolant sensor circuit – the engine must run 5 minutes before this code will set
21	Throttle Position Sensor (TPS) circuit voltage high (open circuit or misadjusted TPS). The engine must run 10 seconds, at specified curb idle speed, before this code will set
22	Throttle Position Sensor (TPS) circuit voltage low (grounded circuit or misadjusted TPS). Engine must run 20 seconds, at specified curb idle speed, to set code
23	M/C solenoid circuit open or grounded
24	Vehicle Speed Sensor (VSS) circuit – the vehicle must operate up to 2 minutes at road speed, before this code will set
32	Barometric Pressure Sensor (BARO) circuit low
34	Vacuum sensor or Manifold Absolute Pressure (MAP) circuit – the engine must run up to 2 minutes, at specified curb idle, before this code will set
35	Idle Speed Control (ISC) switch circuit shorted. (Up to 70% TPS for over 5 seconds)
41	No distributor reference signal to the ECM at specified engine vacuum. This code will store in memory
42	Electronic Spark Timing (EST) bypass circuit or EST circuit grounded or open
43	Electronic Spark Control (ESC) retard signal for too long a time; causes retard in EST signal
44	Lean exhaust indication – the engine must run 2 minutes, in closed loop and at part throttle, before this code will set
45	Rich exhaust indication – the engine must run 2 minutes, in closed loop and at part throttle, before this code will set
51	Faulty or improperly installed calibration unit (PROM). It takes up to 30 seconds before this code will set
53	Exhaust Gas Recirculation (EGR) valve vacuum sensor has seen improper EGR control vacuum
54	M/C solenoid voltage high at ECM as a result of a shorted M/C solenoid circuit and/or faulty ECM

Year — 1986
Model — Grand Am
Engine — 2.5L (151 cid) TBI 4 cyl
Engine Code — VIN U

ECM TROUBLE CODES

Code	Explanation
12	No distributor reference signal to the ECM. This code is not stored in memory and will only flash while the fault is present. This is a normal code with ignition ON, engine not running
13	Oxygen sensor circuit
14	Coolant sensor circuit
15	Coolant sensor circuit
21	Throttle Position Sensor (TPS) circuit
22	Throttle Position Sensor (TPS) circuit
24	Vehicle Speed Sensor (VSS) circuit
33	Manifold Absolute Pressure (MAP) sensor
34	Manifold Absolute Pressure (MAP) sensor
35	Idle Air Control
42	Electronic Spark Timing (EST) bypass circuit or EST circuit grounded or open
44	Lean exhaust indication
45	Rich exhaust indication
51	Faulty or improperly installed calibration unit (PROM)
55	ECM error

Year – 1986
Model – Grand Am
Engine – 3.0L (181 cid) MPFI V6
Engine Code – VIN L

ECM TROUBLE CODES

Code	Explanation
12	No distributor reference signal to the ECM. This code is not stored in memory and will only flash while the fault is present. This is a normal code with ignition ON, engine not running
13	Oxygen sensor circuit
14	Coolant sensor circuit (voltage low)
15	Coolant sensor circuit (voltage high)
21	Throttle Position Sensor (TPS) circuit (voltage high)
22	Throttle Position Sensor (TPS) circuit (voltage low)
23	Manifold Air Temperature (MAT) sensor (voltage high)
24	Vehicle Speed Sensor (VSS) circuit
25	Manifold Air Temperature (MAT) sensor (voltage low)
32	Exhaust Gas Recirculation (EGR) system failure
33	Manifold Absolute Pressure (MAP) sensor (voltage high)
34	Manifold Absolute Pressure (MAP) sensor (voltage low)
42	Electronic Spark Timing (EST) bypass circuit or EST circuit grounded or open
43	Electronic Spark Control (ESC) retard signal for too long a time; causes retard in EST signal
44	Lean exhaust indication
45	Rich exhaust indication
51	Faulty or improperly installed calibration unit (PROM)
52	Calpak (missing)
55	ECM error

Year — 1986
Model — Pontiac 1000
Engine — 1.6L (98 cid) 2bbl 4 cyl
Engine Code — VIN C

ECM TROUBLE CODES

Code	Explanation
12	No distributor reference signal to the ECM. This code is not stored in memory and will only flash while the fault is present. This is a normal code with ignition ON, engine not running
15	Open coolant sensor circuit — the engine must run up to 10 minutes before this code will set
21	Throttle Position Sensor (TPS) circuit at WOT. The engine must run up to 10 seconds below 1000 rpm, before this code will set
23	M/C solenoid circuit
44	Lean exhaust indication — the engine must run up to 1 minute in closed loop and at part throttle above 2000 rpm before this code will set
45	Rich exhaust indication — the engine must run up to 1 minute in closed loop and at part throttle above 2000 rpm before this code will set
51	Faulty or improperly installed calibration unit (PROM). Turns ECM off

Year – 1986
Model – Sunbird
Engine – 1.8L (111 cid) TBI 4 cyl
Engine Code – VIN O

ECM TROUBLE CODES

Code	Explanation
12	No distributor reference signal to the ECM. This code is not stored in memory and will only flash while the fault is present. This is a normal code with ignition ON, engine not running
13	Oxygen sensor circuit
14	Coolant sensor circuit (voltage low)
15	Coolant sensor circuit (voltage high)
21	Throttle Position Sensor (TPS) circuit (voltage high)
22	Throttle Position Sensor (TPS) circuit (voltage low)
24	Vehicle Speed Sensor (VSS) circuit
33	Manifold Absolute Pressure (MAP) sensor (voltage high)
34	Manifold Absolute Pressure (MAP) sensor (voltage low)
35	Idle Air Control
42	Electronic Spark Timing
44	Lean exhaust indication
45	Rich exhaust indication
51	Faulty or improperly installed calibration unit (PROM)
55	ECM error

Year — 1986
Model — Sunbird
Engine — 1.8L (111 cid) MPFI Turbo 4 cyl
Engine Code — VIN J

ECM TROUBLE CODES

Code	Explanation
12	No distributor reference signal to the ECM. This code is not stored in memory and will only flash while the fault is present. This is a normal code with ignition ON, engine not running
13	Oxygen sensor circuit
14	Coolant sensor circuit
15	Coolant sensor circuit
21	Throttle Position Sensor (TPS) circuit
22	Throttle Position Sensor (TPS) circuit
23	Manifold Air Temperature (MAT) sensor
24	Vehicle Speed Sensor (VSS) circuit
25	Manifold Air Temperature (MAT) sensor
31	Wastegate solenoid
33	Manifold Absolute Pressure (MAP) sensor
34	Manifold Absolute Pressure (MAP) sensor
35	Idle air control
42	Electronic Spark Timing (EST) bypass circuit or EST circuit grounded or open
43	Electronic Spark Control (ESC) retard signal for too long a time; causes retard in EST signal
44	Lean exhaust indication
45	Rich exhaust indication
51	Faulty or improperly installed calibration unit (PROM)
52	Calpak (missing)
55	ECM error

Year — 1986
Model — Pontiac 6000, LE, SE, STE
Engine — 2.5L (151 cid) TBI 4 cyl
Engine Code — VIN R

ECM TROUBLE CODES

Code	Explanation
12	No distributor reference signal to the ECM. This code is not stored in memory and will only flash while the fault is present. This is a normal code with ignition ON, engine not running
13	Oxygen sensor circuit
14	Coolant sensor circuit
15	Coolant sensor circuit
21	Throttle Position Sensor (TPS) circuit
22	Throttle Position Sensor (TPS) circuit
24	Vehicle Speed Sensor (VSS) circuit
33	Mass Air Flow (MAF) sensor
34	Mass Air Flow (MAF) sensor
35	Idle air control
42	Electronic Spark Timing (EST) bypass circuit or EST circuit grounded or open
44	Lean exhaust indication
45	Rich exhaust indication
51	Faulty or improperly installed calibration unit (PROM)
55	ECM error

Year – 1986
Model – Pontiac 6000, LE, SE, STE
Engine – 2.8L (173 cid) 2bbl V6
Engine Code – VIN X

ECM TROUBLE CODES

Code	Explanation
12	No distributor reference signal to the ECM. This code is not stored in memory and will only flash while the fault is present. This is a normal code with ignition ON, engine not running
13	Oxygen sensor circuit – the engine must run up to 4 minutes at part throttle, under road load, before this code will set
14	Shorted coolant sensor circuit – the engine must run 2 minutes before this code will set
15	Open coolant sensor circuit – the engine must run 5 minutes before this code will set
21	Throttle Position Sensor (TPS) circuit voltage high (open circuit or misadjusted TPS). The engine must run 10 seconds, at specified curb idle speed, before this code will set
22	Throttle Position Sensor (TPS) circuit voltage low (grounded circuit or misadjusted TPS). Engine must run 20 seconds, at specified curb idle speed, to set code
23	M/C solenoid circuit open or grounded
24	Vehicle Speed Sensor (VSS) circuit – the vehicle must operate up to 2 minutes at road speed, before this code will set
32	Barometric Pressure Sensor (BARO) circuit low
34	Vacuum sensor or Manifold Absolute Pressure (MAP) circuit – the engine must run up to 2 minutes, at specified curb idle, before this code will set
35	Idle Speed Control (ISC) switch circuit shorted. (Up to 70% TPS for over 5 seconds)
41	No distributor reference signal to the ECM at specified engine vacuum. This code will store in memory
42	Electronic Spark Timing (EST) bypass circuit or EST circuit grounded or open
43	Electronic Spark Control (ESC) retard signal for too long a time; causes retard in EST signal
44	Lean exhaust indication – the engine must run 2 minutes, in closed loop and at part throttle, before this code will set
45	Rich exhaust indication – the engine must run 2 minutes, in closed loop and at part throttle, before this code will set
51	Faulty or improperly installed calibration unit (PROM). It takes up to 30 seconds before this code will set
54	M/C solenoid voltage high at ECM as a result of a shorted M/C solenoid circuit and/or faulty ECM

Year — 1986
Model — Pontiac 6000, LE, SE, STE
Engine — 2.8L (173 cid) MPFI V6
Engine Code — VIN W

ECM TROUBLE CODES

Code	Explanation
12	No distributor reference signal to the ECM. This code is not stored in memory and will only flash while the fault is present. This is a normal code with ignition ON, engine not running
13	Oxygen sensor circuit
14	Coolant sensor circuit
15	Coolant sensor circuit
21	Throttle Position Sensor (TPS) circuit
22	Throttle Position Sensor (TPS) circuit
23	Manifold Air Temperature (MAT) sensor
24	Vehicle Speed Sensor (VSS) circuit
25	Manifold Air Temperature (MAT) sensor
32	Exhaust Gas Recirculation (EGR)
33	Mass Air Flow (MAF) sensor
34	Mass Air Flow (MAF) sensor
41	Cylinder select
42	Electronic Spark Timing (EST) bypass circuit or EST circuit grounded or open
44	Lean exhaust indication
45	Rich exhaust indication
51	Faulty or improperly installed calibration unit (PROM)
52	Calpak (missing)
53	System over voltage
54	Fuel pump voltage low
55	ECM error

Year — 1986
Model — Fiero
Engine — 2.5L (151 cid) TBI 4 cyl
Engine Code — VIN R

ECM TROUBLE CODES

Code	Explanation
12	No distributor reference signal to the ECM. This code is not stored in memory and will only flash while the fault is present. This is a normal code with ignition ON, engine not running
13	Oxygen sensor circuit
14	Coolant sensor circuit (voltage low)
15	Coolant sensor circuit (voltage high)
21	Throttle Position Sensor (TPS) circuit (voltage high)
22	Throttle Position Sensor (TPS) circuit (voltage low)
24	Vehicle Speed Sensor (VSS) circuit
33	Manifold Absolute Pressure (MAP) sensor
34	Manifold Absolute Pressure (MAP) sensor
35	Idle air control
42	Electronic Spark Timing (EST) bypass circuit or EST circuit grounded or open
44	Lean exhaust indication
45	Rich exhaust indication
51	Faulty or improperly installed calibration unit (PROM)
55	ECM error

GENERAL MOTORS CORPORATION
DIAGNOSTIC CODE DATA

Year – 1986
Model – Fiero
Engine – 2.8L (173 cid) MPFI V6
Engine Code – VIN 9

ECM TROUBLE CODES

Code	Explanation
12	No distributor reference signal to the ECM. This code is not stored in memory and will only flash while the fault is present. This is a normal code with ignition ON, engine not running
13	Oxygen sensor circuit
14	Coolant sensor circuit (voltage low)
15	Coolant sensor circuit (voltage high)
21	Throttle Position Sensor (TPS) circuit (voltage high)
22	Throttle Position Sensor (TPS) circuit (voltage low)
23	Manifold Air Temperature (MAT) sensor (voltage high)
24	Vehicle Speed Sensor (VSS) circuit
25	Manifold Air Temperature (MAT) sensor (voltage low)
32	Exhaust Gas Recirculation (EGR) system failure
33	Manifold Absolute Pressure (MAP) sensor (voltage high)
34	Manifold Absolute Pressure (MAP) sensor (voltage low)
35	Idle air control
42	Electronic Spark Timing (EST) bypass circuit or EST circuit grounded or open
44	Lean exhaust indication
45	Rich exhaust indication
51	Faulty or improperly installed calibration unit (PROM)
52	Calpak (missing)
53	System over voltage
55	ECM error

Year – 1987
Model – Bonneville
Engine – 3.8L (231 cid) SFI V6
Engine Code – VIN 3

ECM TROUBLE CODES

Code	Explanation
12	No distributor reference signal to the ECM
13	Oxygen sensor circuit – open circuit
14	Coolant sensor circuit – high temperature indicated
15	Coolant sensor circuit – low temperature indicated
21	Throttle Position Sensor (TPS) – signal voltage high
22	Throttle Position Sensor (TPS) – signal voltage low
23	Manifold Air Temperature (MAT) sensor – low temperature indicated
24	Vehicle Speed Sensor (VSS) circuit fault
25	Manifold Air Temperature (MAT) sensor – high temperature indicated
32	Exhaust Gas Recirculation (EGR) system fault
33	Mass Air Flow (MAF) sensor – high GM/SEC indicated
34	Mass Air Flow (MAF) sensor – low GM/SEC indicated
41	Cam sensor circuit failure
42	C^3I EST or bypass circuit failure
43	Electronic Spark Control (ESC) circuit
44	Oxygen sensor circuit – lean exhaust indicated
45	Oxygen sensor circuit – rich exhaust indicated
51	PROM error
52	Calpak error
55	ECM error

Year – 1987
Model – Grand Prix
Engine – 3.8L (231 cid) V6
Engine Code – VIN A

ECM TROUBLE CODES

Code	Explanation
12	No distributor reference signal to the ECM. This code is not stored in memory and will only flash while the fault is present. Normal code with ignition ON, engine not running
13	Oxygen sensor circuit—the engine must run up to 4 minutes at part throttle, under road load, before this code will set
14	Shorted coolant sensor circuit—the engine must run 2 minutes before this code will set
15	Open coolant sensor circuit—the engine must run 5 minutes before this code will set
21	Throttle Position Sensor (TPS) circuit voltage high (open circuit or misadjusted TPS). The engine must run 10 seconds, at specified curb idle speed, before this code will set
22	Throttle Position Sensor (TPS) circuit voltage low (grounded circuit or misadjusted TPS). Engine must run 20 seconds, at specified curb idle speed, to set code
23	M/C solenoid circuit open or grounded
24	Vehicle Speed Sensor (VSS) circuit—the vehicle must operate up to 2 minutes at road speed, before this code will set
32	Barometric Pressure Sensor (BARO) circuit low
34	Vacuum sensor or Manifold Absolute Pressure (MAP) circuit—the engine must run up to 2 minutes, at specified curb idle, before this code will set
35	Idle Speed Control (ISC) switch circuit shorted. (Up to 70% TPS for over 5 seconds)
41	No distributor reference signal to the ECM at specified engine vacuum. This code will store in memory
42	Electronic Spark Timing (EST) bypass circuit or EST circuit grounded or open
43	Electronic Spark Control (ESC) retard signal for too long a time; causes retard in EST signal
44	Lean exhaust indication—the engine must run 2 minutes, in closed loop and at part throttle, before this code will set
45	Rich exhaust indication—the engine must run 2 minutes, in closed loop and at part throttle, before this code will set
51	Faulty or improperly installed calibration unit (PROM). It takes up to 30 seconds before this code will set
53	Exhaust Gas Recirculation (EGR) valve vacuum sensor has seen improper EGR vacuum
54	M/C solenoid voltage high at ECM as a result of a shorted M/C solenoid circuit and/or faulty ECM

Year — 1987
Model — Grand Prix
Engine — 4.3L (262 cid) TBI V6
Engine Code — VIN Z

ECM TROUBLE CODES

Code	Explanation
12	No distributor reference signal to the ECM
13	Oxygen sensor circuit — open circuit
14	Coolant sensor circuit — high temperature indicated
15	Coolant sensor circuit — low temperature indicated
21	Throttle Position Sensor (TPS) — signal voltage high
22	Throttle Position Sensor (TPS) — signal voltage low
24	Vehicle Speed Sensor (VSS) circuit fault
32	Exhaust Gas Recirculation (EGR) system fault
33	Manifold Absolute Pressure (MAP) signal voltage high — low vacuum
34	Manifold Absolute Pressure (MAP) signal voltage low — high vacuum
42	Electronic Spark Timing (EST)
43	Electronic Spark Control (ESC) circuit
44	Oxygen sensor circuit — lean exhaust indicated
45	Oxygen sensor circuit — rich exhaust indicated
52	Fuel Calpak missing
54	Fuel pump circuit
55	ECM error

GENERAL MOTORS CORPORATION
DIAGNOSTIC CODE DATA

Year – 1987
Model – Grand Prix
Engine – 5.0L (305 cid) V8
Engine Code – VIN G

ECM TROUBLE CODES

Code	Explanation
12	No distributor reference signal to the ECM. This code is not stored in memory and will only flash while the fault is present. Normal code with ignition ON, engine not running
13	Oxygen sensor circuit – the engine must run up to 4 minutes at part throttle, under road load, before this code will set
14	Shorted coolant sensor circuit – the engine must run 2 minutes before this code will set
15	Open coolant sensor circuit – the engine must run 5 minutes before this code will set
21	Throttle Position Sensor (TPS) circuit voltage high (open circuit or misadjusted TPS). The engine must run 10 seconds, at specified curb idle speed, before this code will set
22	Throttle Position Sensor (TPS) circuit voltage low (grounded circuit or misadjusted TPS). Engine must run 20 seconds, at specified curb idle speed, to set code
23	M/C solenoid circuit open or grounded
24	Vehicle Speed Sensor (VSS) circuit – the vehicle must operate up to 2 minutes at road speed, before this code will set
32	Barometric Pressure Sensor (BARO) circuit low
34	Vacuum sensor or Manifold Absolute Pressure (MAP) circuit – the engine must run up to 2 minutes, at specified curb idle, before this code will set
35	Idle Speed Control (ISC) switch circuit shorted. (Up to 70% TPS for over 5 seconds)
41	No distributor reference signal to the ECM at specified engine vacuum. This code will store in memory
42	Electronic Spark Timing (EST) bypass circuit or EST circuit grounded or open
43	Electronic Spark Control (ESC) retard signal for too long a time; causes retard in EST signal
44	Lean exhaust indication – the engine must run 2 minutes, in closed loop and at part throttle, before this code will set
45	Rich exhaust indication – the engine must run 2 minutes, in closed loop and at part throttle, before this code will set
51	Faulty or improperly installed calibration unit (PROM). It takes up to 30 seconds before this code will set
53	Exhaust Gas Recirculation (EGR) valve vacuum sensor has seen improper EGR vacuum
54	M/C solenoid voltage high at ECM as a result of a shorted M/C solenoid circuit and/or faulty ECM

Year – 1987
Model – Firebird
Engine – 2.8L (173 cid) V6
Engine Code – VIN S

ECM TROUBLE CODES

Code	Explanation
12	No distributor reference signal to the ECM
13	Oxygen sensor circuit – open circuit
14	Coolant sensor circuit – high temperature indicated
15	Coolant sensor circuit – low temperature indicated
21	Throttle Position Sensor (TPS) – signal voltage high
22	Throttle Position Sensor (TPS) – signal voltage low
23	Manifold Air Temperature (MAT) sensor – low temperature indicated
24	Vehicle Speed Sensor (VSS) circuit fault
25	Manifold Air Temperature (MAT) sensor – high temperature indicated
32	Exhaust Gas Recirculation (EGR) system fault
33	Mass Air Flow (MAF) sensor – high GM/SEC indicated
34	Mass Air Flow (MAF) sensor – low GM/SEC indicated
41	Cylinder select error
42	Electonic Spark Timing (EST) fault
44	Oxygen sensor circuit – lean exhaust indicated
45	Oxygen sensor circuit – rich exhaust indicated
51	PROM error
52	Calpak missing
53	System over voltage
54	Fuel pump voltage low
55	ECM error

Year – 1987
Model – Firebird
Engine – 5.0L (305 cid) V8
Engine Code – VIN H

ECM TROUBLE CODES

Code	Explanation
12	No distributor reference signal to the ECM. This code is not stored in memory and will only flash while the fault is present. Normal code with ignition ON, engine not running
13	Oxygen sensor circuit – the engine must run up to 4 minutes at part throttle, under road load, before this code will set
14	Shorted coolant sensor circuit – the engine must run 2 minutes before this code will set
15	Open coolant sensor circuit – the engine must run 5 minutes before this code will set
21	Throttle Position Sensor (TPS) circuit voltage high (open circuit or misadjusted TPS). The engine must run 10 seconds, at specified curb idle speed, before this code will set
22	Throttle Position Sensor (TPS) circuit voltage low (grounded circuit or misadjusted TPS). Engine must run 20 seconds, at specified curb idle speed, to set code
23	M/C solenoid circuit open or grounded
24	Vehicle Speed Sensor (VSS) circuit – the vehicle must operate up to 2 minutes at road speed, before this code will set
32	Barometric Pressure Sensor (BARO) circuit low
34	Vacuum sensor or Manifold Absolute Pressure (MAP) circuit – the engine must run up to 2 minutes, at specified curb idle, before this code will set
35	Idle Speed Control (ISC) switch circuit shorted. (Up to 70% TPS for over 5 seconds)
41	No distributor reference signal to the ECM at specified engine vacuum. This code will store in memory
42	Electronic Spark Timing (EST) bypass circuit or EST circuit grounded or open
43	Electronic Spark Control (ESC) retard signal for too long a time; causes retard in EST signal
44	Lean exhaust indication – the engine must run 2 minutes, in closed loop and at part throttle, before this code will set
45	Rich exhaust indication – the engine must run 2 minutes, in closed loop and at part throttle, before this code will set
51	Faulty or improperly installed calibration unit (PROM). It takes up to 30 seconds before this code will set
53	Exhaust Gas Recirculation (EGR) valve vacuum sensor has seen improper EGR vacuum
54	M/C solenoid voltage high at ECM as a result of a shorted M/C solenoid circuit and/or faulty ECM

Year — 1987
Model — Firebird
Engine — 5.0L (305 cid) MPFI V8
Engine Code — VIN F

ECM TROUBLE CODES

Code	Explanation
12	No distributor reference signal to the ECM
13	Oxygen sensor circuit — open circuit
14	Coolant sensor circuit — high temperature indicated
15	Coolant sensor circuit — low temperature indicated
21	Throttle Position Sensor (TPS) — signal voltage high
22	Throttle Position Sensor (TPS) — signal voltage low
23	Manifold Air Temperature (MAT) sensor — low temperature indicated
24	Vehicle Speed Sensor (VSS) circuit fault
25	Manifold Air Temperature (MAT) sensor — high temperature indicated
32	Exhaust Gas Recirculation (EGR) system fault
33	Mass Air Flow (MAF) sensor — high GM/SEC indicated
34	Mass Air Flow (MAF) sensor — low GM/SEC indicated
36	Mass Air Flow (MAF) sensor burn-off function fault
41	Cylinder select error
42	Electronic Spark Timing (EST) failure
43	Electronic Spark Control (ESC) circuit
44	Oxygen sensor circuit — lean exhaust indicated
45	Oxygen sensor circuit — rich exhaust indicated
51	PROM error
53	System over voltage
54	Fuel pump voltage low
55	ECM error

Year – 1987
Model – Firebird
Engine – 5.7L (350 cid) TBI V8
Engine Code – VIN 8

ECM TROUBLE CODES

Code	Explanation
12	No distributor reference signal to the ECM
13	Oxygen sensor circuit – open circuit
14	Coolant sensor circuit – high temperature indicated
15	Coolant sensor circuit – low temperature indicated
21	Throttle Position Sensor (TPS) – signal voltage high
22	Throttle Position Sensor (TPS) – signal voltage low
23	Manifold Air Temperature (MAT) sensor – low temperature indicated
24	Vehicle Speed Sensor (VSS) circuit fault
25	Manifold Air Temperature (MAT) sensor – high temperature indicated
32	Exhaust Gas Recirculation (EGR) system fault
33	Mass Air Flow (MAF) sensor – high GM/SEC indicated
34	Mass Air Flow (MAF) sensor – low GM/SEC indicated
36	Mass Air Flow (MAF) sensor burn-off function fault
41	Cylinder select error
42	Electronic Spark Timing (EST) failure
43	Electronic Spark Control (ESC) circuit
44	Oxygen sensor circuit – lean exhaust indicated
45	Oxygen sensor circuit – rich exhaust indicated
51	PROM error
53	System over voltage
54	Fuel pump voltage low
55	ECM error

Year – 1987
Model – Grand Am
Engine – 2.0L (121 cid) MPFI Turbo 4 cyl
Engine Code – VIN M

ECM TROUBLE CODES

Code	Explanation
12	No distributor reference signal to the ECM
13	Oxygen sensor circuit – open circuit
14	Coolant sensor circuit – high temperature indicated
15	Coolant sensor circuit – low temperature indicated
21	Throttle Position Sensor (TPS) – signal voltage high
22	Throttle Position Sensor (TPS) – signal voltage low
23	Manifold Air Temperature (MAT) sensor – low temperature indicated
24	Vehicle Speed Sensor (VSS) circuit fault
25	Manifold Air Temperature (MAT) sensor – high temperature indicated
31	Wastegate overboost
32	Exhaust Gas Recirculation (EGR) system fault
33	Manifold Absolute Pressure (MAP) sensor – high GM/SEC indicated
34	Manifold Absolute Pressure (MAP) sensor – low GM/SEC indicated
35	Idle speed error
42	Electonic Spark Timing (EST)
43	Electronic Spark Control (ESC) circuit
44	Oxygen sensor circuit – lean exhaust indicated
45	Oxygen sensor circuit – rich exhaust indicated
51	PROM error

Year — 1987
Model — Grand Am
Engine — 2.5L (151 cid) TBI 4 cyl
Engine Code — VIN U

ECM TROUBLE CODES

Code	Explanation
12	No distributor reference signal to the ECM
13	Oxygen sensor circuit — open circuit
14	Coolant sensor circuit — high temperature indicated
15	Coolant sensor circuit — low temperature indicated
21	Throttle Position Sensor (TPS) — signal voltage high
22	Throttle Position Sensor (TPS) — signal voltage low
23	Manifold Air Temperature (MAT) sensor — low temperature indicated
24	Vehicle Speed Sensor (VSS) circuit fault
25	Manifold Air Temperature (MAT) sensor — high temperature indicated
33	Manifold Absolute Pressure (MAP) sensor — signal voltage high — vacuum low
34	Manifold Absolute Pressure (MAP) sensor — signal voltage low — vacuum high
42	Electronic Spark Timing (EST)
44	Oxygen sensor circuit — lean exhaust indicated
45	Oxygen sensor circuit — rich exhaust indicated
51	PROM error
53	System over voltage

Year – 1987
Model – Grand Am
Engine – 3.0L (181 cid) MPFI V6
Engine Code – VIN L

ECM TROUBLE CODES

Code	Explanation
12	No distributor reference signal to the ECM
13	Oxygen sensor circuit – open circuit
14	Coolant sensor circuit – high temperature indicated
15	Coolant sensor circuit – low temperature indicated
21	Throttle Position Sensor (TPS) – signal voltage high
22	Throttle Position Sensor (TPS) – signal voltage low
23	Manifold Air Temperature (MAT) sensor – low temperature indicated
24	Vehicle Speed Sensor (VSS) circuit fault
25	Manifold Air Temperature (MAT) sensor – high temperature indicated
32	Exhaust Gas Recirculation (EGR) system fault
33	Mass Air Flow (MAF) sensor – high GM/SEC indicated
34	Mass Air Flow (MAF) sensor – low GM/SEC indicated
42	Electronic Spark Timing (EST)
43	Electronic Spark Control (ESC) circuit
44	Oxygen sensor circuit – lean exhaust indicated
45	Oxygen sensor circuit – rich exhaust indicated
51	PROM error
52	Calpak error
55	ECM error

Year—1987
Model—Pontiac 1000
Engine—1.6L (98 cid) 4 cyl
Engine Code—VIN C

ECM TROUBLE CODES

Code	Explanation
12	No distributor reference pulses to the ECM
15	Open coolant sensor circuit—the engine must run up to 10 minutes before this code will set
21	Throttle Position Sensor (TPS) circuit at WOT. The engine must run 10 seconds below 1000 rpm, before this code will set
23	M/C solenoid circuit
44	Lean exhaust indicated—the engine must run up to 1 minute in closed loop and at part throttle above 2000 rpm, before this code will set
45	Rich exhaust indicated—the engine must run up to 1 minute in closed loop and at part throttle above 2000 rpm, before this code will set
51	Faulty calibration unit (PROM) or installation. Turns OFF them ECM

Year — 1987
Model — Sunbird
Engine — 2.0L (121 cid) TBI OHC 4 cyl
Engine Code — VIN K

ECM TROUBLE CODES

Code	Explanation
12	No distributor reference signal to the ECM
13	Oxygen sensor circuit — open circuit
14	Coolant sensor circuit — high temperature indicated
15	Coolant sensor circuit — low temperature indicated
21	Throttle Position Sensor (TPS) — signal voltage high
22	Throttle Position Sensor (TPS) — signal voltage low
23	Manifold Air Temperature (MAT) sensor — low temperature indicated
24	Vehicle Speed Sensor (VSS) circuit fault
25	Manifold Air Temperature (MAT) sensor — high temperature indicated
33	Manifold Absolute Pressure (MAP) sensor — signal voltage high — low vacuum
34	Manifold Absolute Pressure (MAP) sensor — signal voltage low — high vacuum
35	Idle speed error
42	Electronic Spark Timing (EST) circuit
44	Oxygen sensor circuit — lean exhaust indicated
45	Oxygen sensor circuit — rich exhaust indicated
51	PROM error
53	System over voltage

Year – 1987
Model – Sunbird
Engine – 2.0L (121 cid) Turbo 4 cyl
Engine Code – VIN M

ECM TROUBLE CODES

Code	Explanation
12	No distributor reference signal to the ECM
13	Oxygen sensor circuit – open circuit
14	Coolant sensor circuit – high temperature indicated
15	Coolant sensor circuit – low temperature indicated
21	Throttle Position Sensor (TPS) – signal voltage high
22	Throttle Position Sensor (TPS) – signal voltage low
23	Manifold Air Temperature (MAT) sensor – low temperature indicated
24	Vehicle Speed Sensor (VSS) circuit fault
25	Manifold Air Temperature (MAT) sensor – high temperature indicated
31	Turbo wastegate overboost
32	Exhaust Gas Recirculation (EGR) circuit
33	Manifold Absolute Pressure (MAP) sensor – signal voltage high
34	Manifold Absolute Pressure (MAP) sensor – signal voltage low
35	Idle speed error
42	Electronic Spark Timing (EST) circuit
43	Electronic Spark Control (ESC) circuit
44	Oxygen sensor circuit – lean exhaust indicated
45	Oxygen sensor circuit – rich exhaust indicated
51	PROM error

Year — 1987
Model — Pontiac 6000, LE, SE, STE
Engine — 2.5L (151 cid) TBI 4 cyl
Engine Code — VIN R

ECM TROUBLE CODES

Code	Explanation
12	No distributor reference signal to the ECM
13	Oxygen sensor circuit — open circuit
14	Coolant sensor circuit — high temperature indicated
15	Coolant sensor circuit — low temperature indicated
21	Throttle Position Sensor (TPS) — signal voltage high
22	Throttle Position Sensor (TPS) — signal voltage low
23	Manifold Air Temperature (MAT) sensor — low temperature indicated
24	Vehicle Speed Sensor (VSS) circuit fault
25	Manifold Air Temperature (MAT) sensor — high temperature indicated
33	Manifold Absolute Pressure (MAP) sensor — signal voltage high — low vacuum
34	Manifold Absolute Pressure (MAP) sensor — signal voltage low — high vacuum
35	Idle speed error
42	Electronic Spark Timing (EST) circuit
44	Oxygen sensor circuit — lean exhaust indicated
45	Oxygen sensor circuit — rich exhaust indicated
51	PROM error
53	System over voltage

GENERAL MOTORS CORPORATION
DIAGNOSTIC CODE DATA

Year—1987
Model—Pontiac 6000, LE, SE, STE
Engine—2.8L (173 cid) MPFI V6
Engine Code—VIN W

ECM TROUBLE CODES

Code	Explanation
12	No distributor reference signal to the ECM
13	Oxygen sensor circuit—open circuit
14	Coolant sensor circuit—high temperature indicated
15	Coolant sensor circuit—low temperature indicated
21	Throttle Position Sensor (TPS)—signal voltage high
22	Throttle Position Sensor (TPS)—signal voltage low
23	Manifold Air Temperature (MAT) sensor—low temperature indicated
24	Vehicle Speed Sensor (VSS) circuit fault
25	Manifold Air Temperature (MAT) sensor—high temperature indicated
33	Mass Air Flow (MAF) sensor—high GM/SEC indicated
34	Mass Air Flow (MAF) sensor—low GM/SEC indicated
35	Idle speed error
41	Cylinder select error
42	Electronic Spark Timing (EST)
43	Electronic Spark Control (ESC) circuit
44	Oxygen sensor circuit—lean exhaust indicated
45	Oxygen sensor circuit—rich exhaust indicated
51	PROM error
53	System over voltage
54	Fuel pump circuit
55	ECM error
61	Degraded oxygen sensor
63	Manifold Absolute Pressure (MAP) sensor circuit
64	Manifold Absolute Pressure (MAP) sensor circuit

Year — 1987
Model — Fiero
Engine — 2.5L (151 cid) TBI 4 cyl
Engine Code — VIN R

ECM TROUBLE CODES

Code	Explanation
12	No distributor reference signal to the ECM
13	Oxygen sensor circuit — open circuit
14	Coolant sensor circuit — high temperature indicated
15	Coolant sensor circuit — low temperature indicated
21	Throttle Position Sensor (TPS) — signal voltage high
22	Throttle Position Sensor (TPS) — signal voltage low
23	Manifold Air Temperature (MAT) sensor — low temperature indicated
24	Vehicle Speed Sensor (VSS) circuit fault
25	Manifold Air Temperature (MAT) sensor — high temperature indicated
33	Manifold Absolute Pressure (MAP) sensor — signal voltage high — low vacuum
34	Manifold Absolute Pressure (MAP) sensor — signal voltage low — high vacuum
35	Idle speed error
42	Electronic Spark Timing (EST) circuit
44	Oxygen sensor circuit — lean exhaust indicated
45	Oxygen sensor circuit — rich exhaust indicated
51	PROM error
53	System over voltage

GENERAL MOTORS CORPORATION
DIAGNOSTIC CODE DATA

Year – 1987
Model – Safari
Engine – 5.0L (305 cid) V8
Engine Code – VIN H

ECM TROUBLE CODES

Code	Explanation
12	No distributor reference signal to the ECM. This code is not stored in memory and will only flash while the fault is present. Normal code with ignition ON, engine not running
13	Oxygen sensor circuit – the engine must run up to 4 minutes at part throttle, under road load, before this code will set
14	Shorted coolant sensor circuit – the engine must run 2 minutes before this code will set
15	Open coolant sensor circuit – the engine must run 5 minutes before this code will set
21	Throttle Position Sensor (TPS) circuit voltage high (open circuit or misadjusted TPS). The engine must run 10 seconds, at specified curb idle speed, before this code will set
22	Throttle Position Sensor (TPS) circuit voltage low (grounded circuit or misadjusted TPS). Engine must run 20 seconds, at specified curb idle speed, to set code
23	M/C solenoid circuit open or grounded
24	Vehicle Speed Sensor (VSS) circuit – the vehicle must operate up to 2 minutes at road speed, before this code will set
32	Barometric Pressure Sensor (BARO) circuit low
34	Vacuum sensor or Manifold Absolute Pressure (MAP) circuit – the engine must run up to 2 minutes, at specified curb idle, before this code will set
35	Idle Speed Control (ISC) switch circuit shorted. (Up to 70% TPS for over 5 seconds)
41	No distributor reference signal to the ECM at specified engine vacuum. This code will store in memory
42	Electronic Spark Timing (EST) bypass circuit or EST circuit grounded or open
43	Electronic Spark Control (ESC) retard signal for too long a time; causes retard in EST signal
44	Lean exhaust indication – the engine must run 2 minutes, in closed loop and at part throttle, before this code will set
45	Rich exhaust indication – the engine must run 2 minutes, in closed loop and at part throttle, before this code will set
51	Faulty or improperly installed calibration unit (PROM). It takes up to 30 seconds before this code will set
53	Exhaust Gas Recirculation (EGR) valve vacuum sensor has seen improper EGR vacuum
54	M/C solenoid voltage high at ECM as a result of a shorted M/C solenoid circuit and/or faulty ECM

Year – 1987
Model – Safari
Engine – 5.0L (305 cid) V8
Engine Code – VIN Y

ECM TROUBLE CODES

Code	Explanation
12	No distributor reference signal to the ECM. This code is not stored in memory and will only flash while the fault is present. Normal code with ignition ON, engine not running
13	Oxygen sensor circuit – the engine must run up to 4 minutes at part throttle, under road load, before this code will set
14	Shorted coolant sensor circuit – the engine must run 2 minutes before this code will set
15	Open coolant sensor circuit – the engine must run 5 minutes before this code will set
21	Throttle Position Sensor (TPS) circuit voltage high (open circuit or misadjusted TPS). The engine must run 10 seconds, at specified curb idle speed, before this code will set
22	Throttle Position Sensor (TPS) circuit voltage low (grounded circuit or misadjusted TPS). Engine must run 20 seconds, at specified curb idle speed, to set code
23	M/C solenoid circuit open or grounded
24	Vehicle Speed Sensor (VSS) circuit – the vehicle must operate up to 2 minutes at road speed, before this code will set
32	Barometric Pressure Sensor (BARO) circuit low
34	Vacuum sensor or Manifold Absolute Pressure (MAP) circuit – the engine must run up to 2 minutes, at specified curb idle, before this code will set
35	Idle Speed Control (ISC) switch circuit shorted. (Up to 70% TPS for over 5 seconds)
41	No distributor reference signal to the ECM at specified engine vacuum. This code will store in memory
42	Electronic Spark Timing (EST) bypass circuit or EST circuit grounded or open
43	Electronic Spark Control (ESC) retard signal for too long a time; causes retard in EST signal
44	Lean exhaust indication – the engine must run 2 minutes, in closed loop and at part throttle, before this code will set
45	Rich exhaust indication – the engine must run 2 minutes, in closed loop and at part throttle, before this code will set
51	Faulty or improperly installed calibration unit (PROM). It takes up to 30 seconds before this code will set
53	Exhaust Gas Recirculation (EGR) valve vacuum sensor has seen improper EGR vacuum
54	M/C solenoid voltage high at ECM as a result of a shorted M/C solenoid circuit and/or faulty ECM

Year – 1987
Model – Safari
Engine – 5.7L (350 cid) V8
Engine Code – VIN 6

ECM TROUBLE CODES

Code	Explanation
12	No distributor reference signal to the ECM. This code is not stored in memory and will only flash while the fault is present. Normal code with ignition ON, engine not running
13	Oxygen sensor circuit – the engine must run up to 4 minutes at part throttle, under road load, before this code will set
14	Shorted coolant sensor circuit – the engine must run 2 minutes before this code will set
15	Open coolant sensor circuit – the engine must run 5 minutes before this code will set
21	Throttle Position Sensor (TPS) circuit voltage high (open circuit or misadjusted TPS). The engine must run 10 seconds, at specified curb idle speed, before this code will set
22	Throttle Position Sensor (TPS) circuit voltage low (grounded circuit or misadjusted TPS). Engine must run 20 seconds, at specified curb idle speed, to set code
23	M/C solenoid circuit open or grounded
24	Vehicle Speed Sensor (VSS) circuit – the vehicle must operate up to 2 minutes at road speed, before this code will set
32	Barometric Pressure Sensor (BARO) circuit low
34	Vacuum sensor or Manifold Absolute Pressure (MAP) circuit – the engine must run up to 2 minutes, at specified curb idle, before this code will set
35	Idle Speed Control (ISC) switch circuit shorted. (Up to 70% TPS for over 5 seconds)
41	No distributor reference signal to the ECM at specified engine vacuum. This code will store in memory
42	Electronic Spark Timing (EST) bypass circuit or EST circuit grounded or open
43	Electronic Spark Control (ESC) retard signal for too long a time; causes retard in EST signal
44	Lean exhaust indication – the engine must run 2 minutes, in closed loop and at part throttle, before this code will set
45	Rich exhaust indication – the engine must run 2 minutes, in closed loop and at part throttle, before this code will set
51	Faulty or improperly installed calibration unit (PROM). It takes up to 30 seconds before this code will set
53	Exhaust Gas Recirculation (EGR) valve vacuum sensor has seen improper EGR vacuum
54	M/C solenoid voltage high at ECM as a result of a shorted M/C solenoid circuit and/or faulty ECM

Year — 1988
Model — Bonneville
Engine — 3.8L (231 cid) SFI V6
Engine Code — VIN 3

ECM TROUBLE CODES

Code	Explanation
12	Speed reference pulse
13	Oxygen sensor circuit — open circuit
14	Coolant temperature sensor circuit — high temperature indicated
15	Coolant temperature sensor circuit — low temperature indicated
21	Throttle Position Sensor (TPS) circuit — signal voltage high
22	Throttle Position Sensor (TPS) circuit — signal voltage low
23	Manifold Air Temperature (MAT) sensor circuit — low temperature indicated
24	Vehicle Speed Sensor (VSS) circuit
25	Manifold Air Temperature (MAT) sensor circuit — high temperature indicated
32	Exhaust Gas Recirculation (EGR) circuit
33	Mass Air Flow (MAF) sensor circuit — GM/SEC high
34	Mass Air Flow (MAF) sensor circuit — GM/SEC low
41	CAM sensor circuit
42	Electric Spark Timing (EST)
43	Electronic Spark Control (ESC) Circuit
44	Oxygen sensor circuit — lean exhaust indicated
45	Oxygen sensor circuit — rich exhaust indicated
51	PROM error — faulty or incorrect PROM
52	Calpak error — faulty or incorrect Calpak
55	ECM error

Year — 1988
Model — Bonneville
Engine — 3.8L (229 cid) SFI V6
Engine Code — VIN C

ECM TROUBLE CODES

Code	Explanation
12	Speed reference pulse
13	Oxygen sensor circuit — open circuit
14	Coolant temperature sensor circuit — high temperature indicated
15	Coolant temperature sensor circuit — low temperature indicated
16	System voltage high
21	Throttle Position Sensor (TPS) circuit — signal voltage high
22	Throttle Position Sensor (TPS) circuit — signal voltage low
23	Manifold Air Temperature (MAT) sensor circuit — low temperature indicated
24	Vehicle Speed Sensor (VSS) circuit
25	Manifold Air Temperature (MAT) sensor circuit — high temperature indicated
26	Quad Driver Module (QDM) error
28 & 29	Gear switch diagnosis
31	Park/neutral switch circuit
34	Mass Air Flow (MAF) sensor circuit — GM/SEC low
38	Brake switch circuit
39	Torque Converter Clutch (TCC) circuit diagnosis
41	CAM sensor circuit
42	Electric Spark Timing (EST)
43	Electronic Spark Control (ESC) Circuit
44	Oxygen sensor circuit — lean exhaust indicated
45	Oxygen sensor circuit — rich exhaust indicated
46	Power steering pressure switch
48	Misfire
51	PROM error — faulty or incorrect PROM
63, 64, 65	Exhaust Gas Recirculation (EGR) circuit

Year — 1988
Model — Grand Prix
Engine — 2.8L (173 cid) MFI V6
Engine Code — VIN W

ECM TROUBLE CODES

Code	Explanation
12	Speed reference pulse
13	Oxygen sensor circuit — open circuit
14	Coolant temperature sensor circuit — high temperature indicated
15	Coolant temperature sensor circuit — low temperature indicated
21	Throttle Position Sensor (TPS) circuit — signal voltage high
22	Throttle Position Sensor (TPS) circuit — signal voltage low
23	Manifold Air Temperature (MAT) sensor circuit — low temperature indicated
24	Vehicle Speed Sensor (VSS) circuit
25	Manifold Air Temperature (MAT) sensor circuit — high temperature indicated
26	Quad drive (QDM) error
32	Exhaust Gas Recirculation (EGR) circuit
33	Mass Air Flow (MAF) sensor circuit — GM/SEC high
34	Mass Air Flow (MAF) sensor circuit — GM/SEC low
35	Idle Speed Control (ISC) circuit
41	Cylinder select error — faulty or incorrect Mem-Cal
42	Electric Spark Timing (EST)
43	Electronic Spark Control (ESC) Circuit
44	Oxygen sensor circuit — lean exhaust indicated
45	Oxygen sensor circuit — rich exhaust indicated
51	PROM error — faulty or incorrect PROM
53	System over voltage
54	Fuel pump circuit — low voltage
61	Degraded oxygen sensor

Year – 1988
Model – Firebird
Engine – 2.8L (173 cid) MPFI V6
Engine Code – VIN S

ECM TROUBLE CODES

Code	Explanation
12	Speed reference pulse
13	Oxygen sensor circuit – open circuit
14	Coolant temperature sensor circuit – high temperature indicated
15	Coolant temperature sensor circuit – low temperature indicated
21	Throttle Position Sensor (TPS) circuit – signal voltage high
22	Throttle Position Sensor (TPS) circuit – signal voltage low
23	Manifold Air Temperature (MAT) sensor circuit – low temperature indicated
24	Vehicle Speed Sensor (VSS) circuit
25	Manifold Air Temperature (MAT) sensor circuit – high temperature indicated
32	Exhaust Gas Recirculation (EGR) circuit
33	Mass Air Flow (MAF) sensor circuit – GM/SEC high
34	Mass Air Flow (MAF) sensor circuit – GM/SEC low
41	Cylinder select error
42	Electric Spark Timing (EST) fault
44	Oxygen sensor circuit – lean exhaust indicated
45	Oxygen sensor circuit – rich exhaust indicated
51	PROM error – faulty or incorrect PROM
52	Calpak error – faulty or incorrect Calpak
53	System over voltage
55	ECM error

Year — 1988
Model — Firebird
Engine — 5.0L (305 cid) TBI V8
Engine Code — VIN E

ECM TROUBLE CODES

Code	Explanation
12	Speed reference pulse
13	Oxygen sensor circuit — open circuit
14	Coolant temperature sensor circuit — high temperature indicated
15	Coolant temperature sensor circuit — low temperature indicated
21	Throttle Position Sensor (TPS) circuit — signal voltage high
22	Throttle Position Sensor (TPS) circuit — signal voltage low
23	Manifold Air Temperature (MAT) sensor circuit — low temperature indicated
24	Vehicle Speed Sensor (VSS) circuit
25	Manifold Air Temperature (MAT) sensor circuit — high temperature indicated
32	Exhaust Gas Recirculation (EGR) circuit
33	Manifold Absolute Pressure (MAP) sensor circuit — signal voltage high — low vacuum
34	Manifold Absolute Pressure (MAP) sensor circuit — signal voltage low — high vacuum
42	Electric Spark Timing (EST)
43	Electronic Spark Control (ESC) Circuit
44	Oxygen sensor circuit — lean exhaust indicated
45	Oxygen sensor circuit — rich exhaust indicated
51	PROM error — faulty or incorrect PROM
52	Calpak error — faulty or incorrect Calpak
54	Fuel pump circuit — low voltage
55	ECM error

GENERAL MOTORS CORPORATION
DIAGNOSTIC CODE DATA

Year – 1988
Model – Firebird
Engine – 5.0L (305 cid) MPFI V8
Engine Code – VIN F

ECM TROUBLE CODES

Code	Explanation
12	Speed reference pulse
13	Oxygen sensor circuit – open circuit
14	Coolant temperature sensor circuit – high temperature indicated
15	Coolant temperature sensor circuit – low temperature indicated
21	Throttle Position Sensor (TPS) circuit – signal voltage high
22	Throttle Position Sensor (TPS) circuit – signal voltage low
23	Manifold Air Temperature (MAT) sensor circuit – low temperature indicated
24	Vehicle Speed Sensor (VSS) circuit
25	Manifold Air Temperature (MAT) sensor circuit – high temperature indicated
32	Exhaust Gas Recirculation (EGR) circuit
33	Mass Air Flow (MAF) sensor circuit – GM/SEC high
34	Mass Air Flow (MAF) sensor circuit – GM/SEC low
36	Mass Air Flow (MAF) sensor burn-off circuit
41	Cylinder select error
42	Electric Spark Timing (EST)
43	Electronic Spark Control (ESC) Circuit
44	Oxygen sensor circuit – lean exhaust indicated
45	Oxygen sensor circuit – rich exhaust indicated
46	Vehicle Anti-Theft System (VATS)
51	PROM error – faulty or incorrect PROM
52	Calpak error – faulty or incorrect Calpak
53	System over voltage
54	Fuel pump circuit – low voltage

Year — 1988
Model — Firebird
Engine — 5.7L (350 cid) V8
Engine Code — VIN 8

ECM TROUBLE CODES

Code	Explanation
12	Speed reference pulse
13	Oxygen sensor circuit — open circuit
14	Coolant temperature sensor circuit — high temperature indicated
15	Coolant temperature sensor circuit — low temperature indicated
21	Throttle Position Sensor (TPS) circuit — signal voltage high
22	Throttle Position Sensor (TPS) circuit — signal voltage low
23	Manifold Air Temperature (MAT) sensor circuit — low temperature indicated
24	Vehicle Speed Sensor (VSS) circuit
25	Manifold Air Temperature (MAT) sensor circuit — high temperature indicated
32	Exhaust Gas Recirculation (EGR) circuit
33	Mass Air Flow (MAF) sensor circuit — GM/SEC high
34	Mass Air Flow (MAF) sensor circuit — GM/SEC low
36	Mass Air Flow (MAF) sensor burn-off circuit
41	Cylinder select error
42	Electric Spark Timing (EST)
43	Electronic Spark Control (ESC) Circuit
44	Oxygen sensor circuit — lean exhaust indicated
45	Oxygen sensor circuit — rich exhaust indicated
46	Vehicle Anti-Theft System (VATS)
51	PROM error — faulty or incorrect PROM
52	Calpak error — faulty or incorrect Calpak
53	System over voltage
54	Fuel pump circuit — low voltage

Year – 1988
Model – Grand Am
Engine – 2.0L (121 cid) TBI Turbo 4 cyl
Engine Code – VIN M

ECM TROUBLE CODES

Code	Explanation
12	Speed reference pulse
13	Oxygen sensor circuit – open circuit
14	Coolant temperature sensor circuit – high temperature indicated
15	Coolant temperature sensor circuit – low temperature indicated
21	Throttle Position Sensor (TPS) circuit – signal voltage high
22	Throttle Position Sensor (TPS) circuit – signal voltage low
23	Manifold Air Temperature (MAT) sensor circuit – low temperature indicated
24	Vehicle Speed Sensor (VSS) circuit
25	Manifold Air Temperature (MAT) sensor circuit – high temperature indicated
31	Turbo wastegate overboost
32	Exhaust Gas Recirculation (EGR) circuit
33	Mass Air Flow (MAF) sensor circuit – GM/SEC high
34	Mass Air Flow (MAF) sensor circuit – GM/SEC low
35	Idle speed error
42	Electric Spark Timing (EST)
43	Electronic Spark Control (ESC) Circuit
44	Oxygen sensor circuit – lean exhaust indicated
45	Oxygen sensor circuit – rich exhaust indicated
51	PROM error – faulty or incorrect PROM

Year — 1988
Model — Grand Am
Engine — 2.3L (140 cid) TBI 4 cyl
Engine Code — VIN D

ECM TROUBLE CODES

Code	Explanation
12	Speed reference pulse
13	Oxygen sensor circuit — open circuit
14	Coolant temperature sensor circuit — high temperature indicated
15	Coolant temperature sensor circuit — low temperature indicated
21	Throttle Position Sensor (TPS) circuit — signal voltage high
22	Throttle Position Sensor (TPS) circuit — signal voltage low
23	Manifold Air Temperature (MAT) sensor circuit — low temperature indicated
24	Vehicle Speed Sensor (VSS) circuit
25	Manifold Air Temperature (MAT) sensor circuit — high temperature indicated
26	Quad Driver Module (QDM) fault
33	Manifold Absolute Pressure (MAP) sensor circuit — signal voltage high
34	Manifold Absolute Pressure (MAP) sensor circuit — signal voltage low
36	Closed throttle air flow too high
42	Electric Spark Timing (EST)
43	Electronic Spark Control (ESC) Circuit
44	Oxygen sensor circuit — lean exhaust indicated
45	Oxygen sensor circuit — rich exhaust indicated
51	PROM error — faulty or incorrect PROM
53	Battery voltage too high
62	Transmission gear switches circuit
65	Fuel injector circuit — low current
66	A/C pressure sensor circuit

Year – 1988
Model – Grand Am
Engine – 2.5L (151 cid) TBI 4 cyl
Engine Code – VIN U

ECM TROUBLE CODES

Code	Explanation
12	Speed reference pulse
13	Oxygen sensor circuit – open circuit
14	Coolant temperature sensor circuit – high temperature indicated
15	Coolant temperature sensor circuit – low temperature indicated
21	Throttle Position Sensor (TPS) circuit – signal voltage high
22	Throttle Position Sensor (TPS) circuit – signal voltage low
23	Manifold Air Temperature (MAT) sensor circuit – low temperature indicated
24	Vehicle Speed Sensor (VSS) circuit
25	Manifold Air Temperature (MAT) sensor circuit – high temperature indicated
33	Manifold Absolute Pressure (MAP) sensor circuit – signal voltage high – low vacuum
34	Manifold Absolute Pressure (MAP) sensor circuit – signal voltage low – high vacuum
35	Idle speed error
42	Electric Spark Timing (EST)
44	Oxygen sensor circuit – lean exhaust indicated
45	Oxygen sensor circuit – rich exhaust indicated
51	PROM error – faulty or incorrect PROM
53	System over voltage

Year — 1988
Model — Sunbird
Engine — 2.0L (121 cid) OHC TBI 4 cyl
Engine Code — VIN K

ECM TROUBLE CODES

Code	Explanation
12	Speed reference pulse
13	Oxygen sensor circuit — open circuit
14	Coolant temperature sensor circuit — high temperature indicated
15	Coolant temperature sensor circuit — low temperature indicated
21	Throttle Position Sensor (TPS) circuit — signal voltage high
22	Throttle Position Sensor (TPS) circuit — signal voltage low
23	Manifold Air Temperature (MAT) sensor circuit — low temperature indicated
24	Vehicle Speed Sensor (VSS) circuit
25	Manifold Air Temperature (MAT) sensor circuit — high temperature indicated
32	Exhaust Gas Recirculation (EGR) system error
33	Manifold Absolute Pressure (MAP) sensor circuit — signal voltage high — low vacuum
34	Manifold Absolute Pressure (MAP) sensor circuit — signal voltage low — high vacuum
35	Idle speed error
42	Electric Spark Timing (EST)
44	Oxygen sensor circuit — lean exhaust indicated
45	Oxygen sensor circuit — rich exhaust indicated
51	PROM error — faulty or incorrect PROM
53	System over voltage

GENERAL MOTORS CORPORATION
DIAGNOSTIC CODE DATA

Year — 1988
Model — Sunbird
Engine — 2.0L (121 cid) TBI 4 cyl
Engine Code — VIN M

ECM TROUBLE CODES

Code	Explanation
12	Speed reference pulse
13	Oxygen sensor circuit — open circuit
14	Coolant temperature sensor circuit — high temperature indicated
15	Coolant temperature sensor circuit — low temperature indicated
21	Throttle Position Sensor (TPS) circuit — signal voltage high
22	Throttle Position Sensor (TPS) circuit — signal voltage low
23	Manifold Air Temperature (MAT) sensor circuit — low temperature indicated
24	Vehicle Speed Sensor (VSS) circuit
25	Manifold Air Temperature (MAT) sensor circuit — high temperature indicated
31	Turbo wastegate overboost
32	Exhaust Gas Recirculation (EGR) circuit
33	Mass Air Flow (MAF) sensor circuit — GM/SEC high
34	Mass Air Flow (MAF) sensor circuit — GM/SEC low
35	Idle speed error
42	Electric Spark Timing (EST)
43	Electronic Spark Control (ESC) Circuit
44	Oxygen sensor circuit — lean exhaust indicated
45	Oxygen sensor circuit — rich exhaust indicated
51	PROM error — faulty or incorrect PROM

Year – 1988
Model – Pontiac 6000, LE, SE, STE
Engine – 2.5L (151 cid) TBI 4 cyl
Engine Code – VIN R

ECM TROUBLE CODES

Code	Explanation
12	Speed reference pulse
13	Oxygen sensor circuit – open circuit
14	Coolant temperature sensor circuit – high temperature indicated
15	Coolant temperature sensor circuit – low temperature indicated
21	Throttle Position Sensor (TPS) circuit – signal voltage high
22	Throttle Position Sensor (TPS) circuit – signal voltage low
23	Manifold Air Temperature (MAT) sensor circuit – low temperature indicated
24	Vehicle Speed Sensor (VSS) circuit
25	Manifold Air Temperature (MAT) sensor circuit – high temperature indicated
33	Manifold Absolute Pressure (MAP) sensor circuit – signal voltage high – low vacuum
34	Manifold Absolute Pressure (MAP) sensor circuit – signal voltage low – high vacuum
35	Idle speed error
42	Electric Spark Timing (EST)
44	Oxygen sensor circuit – lean exhaust indicated
45	Oxygen sensor circuit – rich exhaust indicated
51	PROM error – faulty or incorrect PROM
53	System over voltage

Year – 1988
Model – Pontiac 6000, LE, SE, STE
Engine – 2.8L (173 cid) MPFI V6
Engine Code – VIN W

ECM TROUBLE CODES

Code	Explanation
12	Speed reference pulse
13	Oxygen sensor circuit – open circuit
14	Coolant temperature sensor circuit – high temperature indicated
15	Coolant temperature sensor circuit – low temperature indicated
21	Throttle Position Sensor (TPS) circuit – signal voltage high
22	Throttle Position Sensor (TPS) circuit – signal voltage low
23	Manifold Air Temperature (MAT) sensor circuit – low temperature indicated
24	Vehicle Speed Sensor (VSS) circuit
25	Manifold Air Temperature (MAT) sensor circuit – high temperature indicated
33	Mass Air Flow (MAF) sensor circuit – GM/SEC high
34	Mass Air Flow (MAF) sensor circuit – GM/SEC low
41	Cylinder select error – faulty or incorrect Mem-Cal
42	Electric Spark Timing (EST)
43	Electronic Spark Control (ESC) Circuit
44	Oxygen sensor circuit – lean exhaust indicated
45	Oxygen sensor circuit – rich exhaust indicated
51	PROM error – faulty or incorrect PROM
52	Calpak error – faulty or incorrect Calpak
53	System over voltage
54	Fuel pump circuit – low voltage
61	Degraded oxygen sensor
63	Manifold Absolute Pressure (MAP) sensor circuit – signal voltage high
64	Manifold Absolute Pressure (MAP) sensor circuit – signal voltage low

Year – 1988
Model – LeMans
Engine – 1.6L (98 cid) TBI 4 cyl
Engine Code – VIN 6

ECM TROUBLE CODES

Code	Explanation
12	Speed reference pulse
13	Oxygen sensor circuit – open circuit
14	Coolant temperature sensor circuit – high temperature indicated
15	Coolant temperature sensor circuit – low temperature indicated
21	Throttle Position Sensor (TPS) circuit – signal voltage high
22	Throttle Position Sensor (TPS) circuit – signal voltage low
24	Vehicle Speed Sensor (VSS) circuit
33	Manifold Absolute Pressure (MAP) sensor circuit – signal voltage high – low vacuum
34	Manifold Absolute Pressure (MAP) sensor circuit – signal voltage low – high vacuum
35	Idle speed error
42	Electric Spark Timing (EST)
44	Oxygen sensor circuit – lean exhaust indicated
45	Oxygen sensor circuit – rich exhaust indicated
51	PROM error – faulty or incorrect PROM
53	System over voltage

GENERAL MOTORS CORPORATION
DIAGNOSTIC CODE DATA

Year — 1988
Model — Fiero
Engine — 2.5L (151 cid) TBI 4 cyl
Engine Code — VIN R

ECM TROUBLE CODES

Code	Explanation
12	Speed reference pulse
13	Oxygen sensor circuit — open circuit
14	Coolant temperature sensor circuit — high temperature indicated
15	Coolant temperature sensor circuit — low temperature indicated
21	Throttle Position Sensor (TPS) circuit — signal voltage high
22	Throttle Position Sensor (TPS) circuit — signal voltage low
24	Vehicle Speed Sensor (VSS) circuit
25	Manifold Air Temperature (MAT) sensor circuit — high temperature indicated
33	Manifold Absolute Pressure (MAP) sensor circuit — signal voltage high — low vacuum
34	Manifold Absolute Pressure (MAP) sensor circuit — signal voltage low — high vacuum
35	Idle speed error
42	Electric Spark Timing (EST)
44	Oxygen sensor circuit — lean exhaust indicated
45	Oxygen sensor circuit — rich exhaust indicated
51	PROM error — faulty or incorrect PROM
53	System over voltage

Year—1988
Model—Fiero
Engine—2.5L (151 cid) TBI 4 cyl
Engine Code—VIN U

ECM TROUBLE CODES

Code	Explanation
12	Speed reference pulse
13	Oxygen sensor circuit—open circuit
14	Coolant temperature sensor circuit—high temperature indicated
15	Coolant temperature sensor circuit—low temperature indicated
21	Throttle Position Sensor (TPS) circuit—signal voltage high
22	Throttle Position Sensor (TPS) circuit—signal voltage low
24	Vehicle Speed Sensor (VSS) circuit
25	Manifold Air Temperature (MAT) sensor circuit—high temperature indicated
33	Manifold Absolute Pressure (MAP) sensor circuit—signal voltage high—low vacuum
34	Manifold Absolute Pressure (MAP) sensor circuit—signal voltage low—high vacuum
35	Idle speed error
42	Electric Spark Timing (EST)
44	Oxygen sensor circuit—lean exhaust indicated
45	Oxygen sensor circuit—rich exhaust indicated
51	PROM error—faulty or incorrect PROM
53	System over voltage

GENERAL MOTORS CORPORATION
DIAGNOSTIC CODE DATA

Year – 1988
Model – Fiero
Engine – 2.8L (173 cid) MPFI V6
Engine Code – VIN 9

ECM TROUBLE CODES

Code	Explanation
12	Speed reference pulse
13	Oxygen sensor circuit – open circuit
14	Coolant temperature sensor circuit – high temperature indicated
15	Coolant temperature sensor circuit – low temperature indicated
21	Throttle Position Sensor (TPS) circuit – signal voltage high
22	Throttle Position Sensor (TPS) circuit – signal voltage low
23	Manifold Air Temperature (MAT) sensor circuit – low temperature indicated
24	Vehicle Speed Sensor (VSS) circuit
25	Manifold Air Temperature (MAT) sensor circuit – high temperature indicated
32	Exhaust Gas Recirculation (EGR) circuit
33	Manifold Absolute Pressure (MAP) sensor circuit – signal voltage high – low vacuum
34	Manifold Absolute Pressure (MAP) sensor circuit – signal voltage low – high vacuum
35	Idle speed error
42	Electric Spark Timing (EST)
44	Oxygen sensor circuit – lean exhaust indicated
45	Oxygen sensor circuit – rich exhaust indicated
51	PROM error – faulty or incorrect PROM
52	Calpak error – faulty or incorrect Calpak
53	System over voltage
55	ECM error

Year — 1988
Model — Safari Wagon
Engine — 5.0L (307 cid) V8
Engine Code — VIN Y

ECM TROUBLE CODES

Code	Explanation
12	No distributor reference signal to the ECM. This code is not stored in memory and will only flash while the fault is present. Normal code with ignition ON, engine not running
13	Oxygen sensor circuit — the engine must run up to 4 minutes at part throttle, under road load, before this code will set
14	Shorted coolant sensor circuit — the engine must run 2 minutes before this code will set
15	Open coolant sensor circuit — the engine must run 5 minutes before this code will set
21	Throttle Position Sensor (TPS) circuit voltage high (open circuit or misadjusted TPS). The engine must run 10 seconds, at specified curb idle speed, before this code will set
22	Throttle Position Sensor (TPS) circuit voltage low (grounded circuit or misadjusted TPS). Engine must run 20 seconds, at specified curb idle speed, to set code
23	M/C solenoid circuit open or grounded
24	Vehicle Speed Sensor (VSS) circuit — the vehicle must operate up to 2 minutes at road speed, before this code will set
31	Canister purge solenoid voltage high to ECM, above idle rpm, will set this code
34	Manifold Absolute Pressure (MAP) sensor circuit — too high or too low voltage signal, at a specified amount of time and rpm, will cause this code to set
41	No distributor reference signal to the ECM at specified engine vacuum. This code will store in memory
42	Electronic Spark Timing (EST) bypass circuit or EST circuit grounded or open
43	Electronic Spark Control (ESC) retard signal for too long a time; causes retard in EST signal
44	Lean exhaust indication — the engine must run 2 minutes, in closed loop and at part throttle, before this code will set
45	Rich exhaust indication — the engine must run 2 minutes, in closed loop and at part throttle, before this code will set
51	Faulty or improperly installed calibration unit (PROM). It takes up to 30 seconds before this code will set
53	Exhaust Gas Recirculation (EGR) valve vacuum sensor has seen improper EGR vacuum
54	M/C solenoid voltage high at ECM as a result of a shorted M/C solenoid circuit and/or faulty ECM — California models

GENERAL MOTORS CORPORATION
DIAGNOSTIC CODE DATA

Year – 1989
Model – Bonneville
Engine – 3.8L (231 cid) SFI V6
Engine Code – VIN C

ECM TROUBLE CODES

Code	Explanation
12	Reference pulse; indicates ECM's diagnostic system is operating
13	Oxygen sensor circuit – open circuit
14	Coolant Temperature Sensor (CTS) circuit – high temperature indicated
15	Coolant Temperature Sensor (CTS) circuit – low temperature indicated
16	System voltage high
21	Throttle Position Sensor (TPS) circuit – signal voltage high
22	Throttle Position Sensor (TPS) circuit – signal voltage low
23	Manifold Air Temperature (MAT) sensor circuit – low temperature indicated
24	Vehicle Speed Sensor (VSS) circuit
25	Manifold Air Temperature (MAT) sensor circuit – high temperature indicated
26	Quad–Driver Module (QDM) circuit
28, 29	Gear switch diagnosis
31	Park/Neutral switch circuit
34	Mass Air Flow (MAF) sensor circuit – GM/SEC low
38	Brake input circuit
39	Torque Converter Clutch (TCC) circuit
41	Cam sensor circuit
42	Electronic Spark Timing (EST) circuit
43	Electronic Spark Control (ESC) circuit
44	Oxygen sensor circuit – lean exhaust indicated
45	Oxygen sensor circuit – rich exhaust indicated
46	Power steering pressure switch circuit
48	Misfire diagnosis
51	Mem–Cal error – faulty or incorrect Mem–Cal
63, 64, 65	Exhaust Gas Recirculation (EGR) flow check

Year – 1989
Model – Grand Prix
Engine – 2.8L (173 cid) MFI V6
Engine Code – VIN W

ECM TROUBLE CODES

Code	Explanation
12	Reference pulse; indicates ECM's diagnostic system is operating
13	Oxygen sensor circuit – open circuit
14	Coolant Temperature Sensor (CTS) circuit – high temperature indicated
15	Coolant Temperature Sensor (CTS) circuit – low temperature indicated
21	Throttle Position Sensor (TPS) circuit – signal voltage high
22	Throttle Position Sensor (TPS) circuit – signal voltage low
23	Manifold Air Temperature (MAT) sensor circuit – low temperature indicated
24	Vehicle Speed Sensor (VSS) circuit
25	Manifold Air Temperature (MAT) sensor circuit – high temperature indicated
26	Quad–Driver Module (QDM) circuit error
32	Exhaust Gas Recirculation (EGR) circuit
33	Manifold Absolute Pressure (MAP) sensor circuit – signal voltage high–low vacuum
34	Manifold Absolute Pressure (MAP) sensor circuit – signal voltage low–high vacuum
35	Idle Speed Control (ISC) circuit
41	Cylinder select error – faulty or incorrect Mem-Cal
42	Electronic Spark Timing (EST) circuit
43	Electronic Spark Control (ESC) circuit
44	Oxygen sensor circuit – lean exhaust indicated
45	Oxygen sensor circuit – rich exhaust indicated
51	Mem–Cal error – faulty or incorrect Mem–Cal
53	System over voltage
54	Fuel pump circuit – low voltage
55	ECM error
61	Degraded oxygen sensor

GENERAL MOTORS CORPORATION
DIAGNOSTIC CODE DATA

Year — 1989
Model — Grand Prix
Engine — 3.1L (192 cid) PFI V6
Engine Code — VIN T

ECM TROUBLE CODES

Code	Explanation
12	Reference pulse; indicates ECM's diagnostic system is operating
13	Oxygen sensor circuit — open circuit
14	Coolant Temperature Sensor (CTS) circuit — high temperature indicated
15	Coolant Temperature Sensor (CTS) circuit — low temperature indicated
21	Throttle Position Sensor (TPS) circuit — signal voltage high
22	Throttle Position Sensor (TPS) circuit — signal voltage low
23	Manifold Air Temperature (MAT) sensor circuit — low temperature indicated
24	Vehicle Speed Sensor (VSS) circuit
25	Manifold Air Temperature (MAT) sensor circuit — high temperature indicated
26	Quad–Driver Module (QDM) circuit error
32	Exhaust Gas Recirculation (EGR) circuit
33	Manifold Absolute Pressure (MAP) sensor circuit — signal voltage high–low vacuum
34	Manifold Absolute Pressure (MAP) sensor circuit — signal voltage low–high vacuum
35	Idle Speed Control (ISC) circuit
41	Cylinder select error — faulty or incorrect Mem-Cal
42	Electronic Spark Timing (EST) circuit
43	Electronic Spark Control (ESC) circuit
44	Oxygen sensor circuit — lean exhaust indicated
45	Oxygen sensor circuit — rich exhaust indicated
51	Mem–Cal error — faulty or incorrect Mem–Cal
53	System over voltage
54	Fuel pump circuit — low voltage
55	ECM error
61	Degraded oxygen sensor

Year – 1989
Model – Firebird
Engine – 2.8L (173 cid) PFI V6
Engine Code – VIN S

ECM TROUBLE CODES

Code	Explanation
12	Reference pulse; indicates ECM's diagnostic system is operating
13	Oxygen sensor circuit – open circuit
14	Coolant Temperature Sensor (CTS) circuit – high temperature indicated
15	Coolant Temperature Sensor (CTS) circuit – low temperature indicated
21	Throttle Position Sensor (TPS) circuit – signal voltage high
22	Throttle Position Sensor (TPS) circuit – signal voltage low
23	Manifold Air Temperature (MAT) sensor circuit – low temperature indicated
24	Vehicle Speed Sensor (VSS) circuit
25	Manifold Air Temperature (MAT) sensor circuit – high temperature indicated
32	Exhaust Gas Recirculation (EGR) circuit
33	Mass Air Flow (MAF) sensor circuit – GM/SEC high
34	Mass Air Flow (MAF) sensor circuit – GM/SEC low
41	Cylinder select error – faulty or incorrect Mem–Cal
42	Electronic Spark Timing (EST) circuit
44	Oxygen sensor circuit – lean exhaust indicated
45	Oxygen sensor circuit – rich exhaust indicated
51	PROM error – faulty or incorrect PROM
52	Calpak error – faulty or incorrect Calpak
53	System over voltage
54	Fuel pump circuit – low voltage
55	ECM error

Year – 1989
Model – Firebird
Engine – 5.0L (305 cid) TBI V8
Engine Code – VIN E

ECM TROUBLE CODES

Code	Explanation
12	Reference pulse; indicates ECM's diagnostic system is operating
13	Oxygen sensor circuit – open circuit
14	Coolant Temperature Sensor (CTS) circuit – high temperature indicated
15	Coolant Temperature Sensor (CTS) circuit – low temperature indicated
21	Throttle Position Sensor (TPS) circuit – signal voltage high
22	Throttle Position Sensor (TPS) circuit – signal voltage low
23	Manifold Air Temperature (MAT) sensor circuit – low temperature indicated
24	Vehicle Speed Sensor (VSS) circuit
25	Manifold Air Temperature (MAT) sensor circuit – high temperature indicated
32	Exhaust Gas Recirculation (EGR) circuit
33	Manifold Absolute Pressure (MAP) sensor circuit – signal voltage high – low vacuum
34	Manifold Absolute Pressure (MAP) sensor circuit – signal voltage low – high vacuum
42	Electronic Spark Timing (EST) circuit
43	Electronic Spark Control (ESC) circuit
44	Oxygen sensor circuit – lean exhaust indicated
45	Oxygen sensor circuit – rich exhaust indicated
51	PROM error – faulty or incorrect PROM
52	Calpak error – faulty or incorrect Calpak
53	Vehicle Anti–Theft System (VATS) circuit
54	Fuel pump circuit – low voltage
55	ECM error

Year – 1989
Model – Firebird
Engine – 5.0L (305 cid) TBI V8
Engine Code – VIN F

ECM TROUBLE CODES

Code	Explanation
12	Reference pulse; indicates ECM's diagnostic system is operating
13	Oxygen sensor circuit – open circuit
14	Coolant Temperature Sensor (CTS) circuit – high temperature indicated
15	Coolant Temperature Sensor (CTS) circuit – low temperature indicated
21	Throttle Position Sensor (TPS) circuit – signal voltage high
22	Throttle Position Sensor (TPS) circuit – signal voltage low
23	Manifold Air Temperature (MAT) sensor circuit – low temperature indicated
24	Vehicle Speed Sensor (VSS) circuit
25	Manifold Air Temperature (MAT) sensor circuit – high temperature indicated
32	Exhaust Gas Recirculation (EGR) circuit
33	Mass Air Flow (MAF) sensor circuit – GM/SEC high
34	Mass Air Flow (MAF) sensor circuit – GM/SEC low
36	Mass Air Flow (MAF) sensor burn–off circuit
41	Cylinder select error – faulty or incorrect Mem–Cal
42	Electronic Spark Timing (EST) circuit
43	Electronic Spark Control (ESC) circuit
44	Oxygen sensor circuit – lean exhaust indicated
45	Oxygen sensor circuit – rich exhaust indicated
46	Vehicle Anti–Theft System (VATS) circuit
51	Mem–Cal error – faulty or incorrect Mem–Cal
52	Calpak error – faulty or incorrect Calpak
53	System over voltage
54	Fuel pump circuit – low voltage

Year – 1989
Model – Firebird
Engine – 5.7L (350 cid) PFI V8
Engine Code – VIN 8

ECM TROUBLE CODES

Code	Explanation
12	Reference pulse; indicates ECM's diagnostic system is operating
13	Oxygen sensor circuit – open circuit
14	Coolant Temperature Sensor (CTS) circuit – high temperature indicated
15	Coolant Temperature Sensor (CTS) circuit – low temperature indicated
21	Throttle Position Sensor (TPS) circuit – signal voltage high
22	Throttle Position Sensor (TPS) circuit – signal voltage low
23	Manifold Air Temperature (MAT) sensor circuit – low temperature indicated
24	Vehicle Speed Sensor (VSS) circuit
25	Manifold Air Temperature (MAT) sensor circuit – high temperature indicated
32	Exhaust Gas Recirculation (EGR) circuit
33	Mass Air Flow (MAF) sensor circuit – GM/SEC high
34	Mass Air Flow (MAF) sensor circuit – GM/SEC low
36	Mass Air Flow (MAF) sensor burn–off circuit
41	Cylinder select error – faulty or incorrect Mem–Cal
42	Electronic Spark Timing (EST) circuit
43	Electronic Spark Control (ESC) circuit
44	Oxygen sensor circuit – lean exhaust indicated
45	Oxygen sensor circuit – rich exhaust indicated
46	Vehicle Anti–Theft System (VATS) circuit
51	Mem–Cal error – faulty or incorrect Mem–Cal
52	Calpak error – faulty or incorrect Calpak
53	System over voltage
54	Fuel pump circuit – low voltage

Year — 1989
Model — Grand Am
Engine — 2.0L (121 cid) Turbo 4 cyl
Engine Code — VIN M

ECM TROUBLE CODES

Code	Explanation
12	Reference pulse; indicates ECM's diagnostic system is operating
13	Oxygen sensor circuit — open circuit
14	Coolant Temperature Sensor (CTS) (CTS) circuit — high temperature indicated
15	Coolant Temperature Sensor (CTS) (CTS) circuit — low temperature indicated
21	Throttle Position Sensor (TPS) circuit — signal voltage high
22	Throttle Position Sensor (TPS) circuit — signal voltage low
23	Manifold Air Temperature (MAT) sensor circuit — low temperature indicated
24	Vehicle Speed Sensor (VSS) circuit
25	Manifold Air Temperature (MAT) sensor circuit — high temperature indicated
31	Turbo wastegate overboost
32	Exhaust Gas Recirculation (EGR) circuit
33	Manifold Absolute Pressure (MAP) sensor circuit — signal voltage high
34	Manifold Absolute Pressure (MAP) sensor circuit — signal voltage low
35	Idle speed error
42	Electronic Spark Timing (EST) circuit
43	Electronic Spark Control (ESC) circuit
44	Oxygen sensor circuit — lean exhaust indicated
45	Oxygen sensor circuit — rich exhaust indicated
51	PROM error — faulty or incorrect PROM

Year — 1989
Model — Grand Am
Engine — 2.3L (138 cid) 4 cyl
Engine Code — VIN A

ECM TROUBLE CODES

Code	Explanation
12	Reference pulse; indicates ECM's diagnostic system is operating
13	Oxygen sensor circuit — open circuit
14	Coolant Temperature Sensor (CTS) circuit — high temperature indicated
15	Coolant Temperature Sensor (CTS) circuit — low temperature indicated
21	Throttle Position Sensor (TPS) circuit — signal voltage high
22	Throttle Position Sensor (TPS) circuit — signal voltage low
23	Manifold Air Temperature (MAT) sensor circuit — low temperature indicated
24	Vehicle Speed Sensor (VSS) circuit
25	Manifold Air Temperature (MAT) sensor circuit — high temperature indicated
26	Quad–Driver Module (QDM) circuit
33	Manifold Absolute Pressure (MAP) sensor circuit — signal voltage high–low vacuum
34	Manifold Absolute Pressure (MAP) sensor circuit — signal voltage low–high vacuum
35	Idle speed error
41	Reference circuit
42	Electronic Spark Timing (EST) circuit
43	Electronic Spark Control (ESC) circuit
44	Oxygen sensor circuit — lean exhaust indicated
45	Oxygen sensor circuit — rich exhaust indicated
51	Mem–Cal error — faulty or incorrect Mem–Cal
53	Battery voltage too high
62	Transmission gear switches circuit
65	Fuel injector circuit — low current
66	A/C pressure sensor circuit

Year – 1989
Model – Grand Am
Engine – 2.3L (138 cid) 4 cyl
Engine Code – VIN D

ECM TROUBLE CODES

Code	Explanation
12	Reference pulse; indicates ECM's diagnostic system is operating
13	Oxygen sensor circuit – open circuit
14	Coolant Temperature Sensor (CTS) circuit – high temperature indicated
15	Coolant Temperature Sensor (CTS) circuit – low temperature indicated
21	Throttle Position Sensor (TPS) circuit – signal voltage high
22	Throttle Position Sensor (TPS) circuit – signal voltage low
23	Manifold Air Temperature (MAT) sensor circuit – low temperature indicated
24	Vehicle Speed Sensor (VSS) circuit
25	Manifold Air Temperature (MAT) sensor circuit – high temperature indicated
26	Quad–Driver Module (QDM) circuit
33	Manifold Absolute Pressure (MAP) sensor circuit – signal voltage high–low vacuum
34	Manifold Absolute Pressure (MAP) sensor circuit signal voltage low–high vacuum
35	Idle speed error
41	Reference circuit
42	Electronic Spark Timing (EST) circuit
43	Electronic Spark Control (ESC) circuit
44	Oxygen sensor circuit – lean exhaust indicated
45	Oxygen sensor circuit – rich exhaust indicated
51	Mem–Cal error – faulty or incorrect Mem–Cal
53	Battery voltage too high
62	Transmission gear switches circuit
65	Fuel injector circuit – low current
66	A/C pressure sensor circuit

Year — 1989
Model — Grand Am
Engine — 2.5L (151 cid) 4 cyl
Engine Code — VIN U

ECM TROUBLE CODES

Code	Explanation
12	Reference pulse; indicates ECM's diagnostic system is operating
13	Oxygen sensor circuit—open circuit
14	Coolant Temperature Sensor (CTS) circuit—high temperature indicated
15	Coolant Temperature Sensor (CTS) circuit—low temperature indicated
21	Throttle Position Sensor (TPS) circuit—signal voltage high
22	Throttle Position Sensor (TPS) circuit—signal voltage low
23	Manifold Air Temperature (MAT) sensor circuit—low temperature indicated
24	Vehicle Speed Sensor (VSS) circuit
25	Manifold Air Temperature (MAT) sensor circuit—high temperature indicated
33	Manifold Absolute Pressure (MAP) sensor circuit—signal voltage high–low vacuum
34	Manifold Absolute Pressure (MAP) sensor circuit—signal voltage low–high vacuum
35	Idle speed error
42	Electronic Spark Timing (EST) circuit
44	Oxygen sensor circuit—lean exhaust indicated
45	Oxygen sensor circuit—rich exhaust indicated
51	PROM error—faulty or incorrect PROM
52	System over voltage

Year – 1989
Model – Sunbird
Engine – 2.0L (122 cid) TBI 4 cyl
Engine Code – VIN K

ECM TROUBLE CODES

Code	Explanation
12	Reference pulse; indicates ECM's diagnostic system is operating
13	Oxygen sensor circuit – open circuit
14	Coolant Temperature Sensor (CTS) circuit – high temperature indicated
15	Coolant Temperature Sensor (CTS) circuit – low temperature indicated
21	Throttle Position Sensor (TPS) circuit – signal voltage high
22	Throttle Position Sensor (TPS) circuit – signal voltage low
23	Manifold Air Temperature (MAT) sensor circuit – low temperature indicated
24	Vehicle Speed Sensor (VSS) circuit
25	Manifold Air Temperature (MAT) sensor circuit – high temperature indicated
32	Exhaust Gas Recirculation (EGR) system failure
33	Manifold Absolute Pressure (MAP) sensor circuit – signal voltage high–low vacuum
34	Manifold Absolute Pressure (MAP) sensor circuit – signal voltage low–high vacuum
35	Idle speed error
42	Electronic Spark Timing (EST) circuit
44	Oxygen sensor circuit – lean exhaust indicated
45	Oxygen sensor circuit – rich exhaust indicated
51	PROM error – faulty or incorrect PROM
53	System over voltage

Year – 1989
Model – Sunbird
Engine – 2.0L (122 cid) MFI 4 cyl Turbo
Engine Code – VIN M

ECM TROUBLE CODES

Code	Explanation
12	Reference pulse; indicates ECM's diagnostic system is operating
13	Oxygen sensor circuit – open circuit
14	Coolant Temperature Sensor (CTS) circuit – high temperature indicated
15	Coolant Temperature Sensor (CTS) circuit – low temperature indicated
21	Throttle Position Sensor (TPS) circuit – signal voltage high
22	Throttle Position Sensor (TPS) circuit – signal voltage low
23	Manifold Air Temperature (MAT) sensor circuit – low temperature indicated
24	Vehicle Speed Sensor (VSS) circuit
25	Manifold Air Temperature (MAT) sensor circuit – high temperature indicated
31	Turbo wastegate overboost
32	Exhaust Gas Recirculation (EGR) circuit
33	Manifold Absolute Pressure (MAP) sensor circuit – signal voltage high–low vacuum
34	Manifold Absolute Pressure (MAP) sensor circuit – signal voltage low–high vacuum
35	Idle speed error
42	Electronic Spark Timing (EST) circuit
43	Electronic Spark Control (ESC) circuit
44	Oxygen sensor circuit – lean exhaust indicated
45	Oxygen sensor circuit – rich exhaust indicated
51	PROM error – faulty or incorrect PROM

Year — 1989
Model — LeMans
Engine — 1.6L (98 cid) TBI 4 cyl
Engine Code — VIN 6

ECM TROUBLE CODES

Code	Explanation
12	Reference pulse; indicates ECM's diagnostic system is operating
13	Oxygen sensor circuit — open circuit
14	Coolant Temperature Sensor (CTS) circuit — high temperature indicated
15	Coolant Temperature Sensor (CTS) circuit — low temperature indicated
21	Throttle Position Sensor (TPS) circuit — signal voltage high
22	Throttle Position Sensor (TPS) circuit — signal voltage low
23	Manifold Air Temperature (MAT) sensor circuit — low temperature indicated
24	Vehicle Speed Sensor (VSS) circuit
25	Manifold Air Temperature (MAT) sensor circuit — high temperature indicated
32	Exhaust Gas Recirculation (EGR) system error
33	Manifold Absolute Pressure (MAP) sensor circuit — signal voltage high–low vacuum
34	Manifold Absolute Pressure (MAP) sensor circuit — signal voltage low–high vacuum
35	Idle speed error
42	Electronic Spark Timing (EST) circuit
44	Oxygen sensor circuit — lean exhaust indicated
45	Oxygen sensor circuit — rich exhaust indicated
51	Mem-Cal error — faulty or incorrect Mem-Cal
53	System over voltage

Year – 1989
Model – LeMans
Engine – 2.0L (122 cid) TBI 4 cyl
Engine Code – VIN K

ECM TROUBLE CODES

Code	Explanation
12	Reference pulse; indicates ECM's diagnostic system is operating
13	Oxygen sensor circuit – open circuit
14	Coolant Temperature Sensor (CTS) circuit – high temperature indicated
15	Coolant Temperature Sensor (CTS) circuit – low temperature indicated
21	Throttle Position Sensor (TPS) circuit – signal voltage high
22	Throttle Position Sensor (TPS) circuit – signal voltage low
23	Manifold Air Temperature (MAT) sensor circuit – low temperature indicated
24	Vehicle Speed Sensor (VSS) circuit
25	Manifold Air Temperature (MAT) sensor circuit – high temperature indicated
32	Exhaust Gas Recirculation (EGR) system error
33	Manifold Absolute Pressure (MAP) sensor circuit – signal voltage high–low vacuum
34	Manifold Absolute Pressure (MAP) sensor circuit – signal voltage low–high vacuum
35	Idle speed error
42	Electronic Spark Timing (EST) circuit
44	Oxygen sensor circuit – lean exhaust indicated
45	Oxygen sensor circuit – rich exhaust indicated
51	Mem–Cal error – faulty or incorrect Mem–Cal
53	System over voltage

Year – 1989
Model – Pontiac 6000
Engine – 2.5L (151 cid) TPI 4 cyl
Engine Code – VIN R

ECM TROUBLE CODES

Code	Explanation
12	Reference pulse; indicates ECM's diagnostic system is operating
13	Oxygen sensor circuit – open circuit
14	Coolant Temperature Sensor (CTS) circuit – high temperature indicated
15	Coolant Temperature Sensor (CTS) circuit – low temperature indicated
21	Throttle Position Sensor (TPS) circuit – signal voltage high
22	Throttle Position Sensor (TPS) circuit – signal voltage low
23	Manifold Air Temperature (MAT) sensor circuit – low temperature indicated
24	Vehicle Speed Sensor (VSS) circuit
25	Manifold Air Temperature (MAT) sensor circuit – high temperature indicated
32	Exhaust Gas Recirculation (EGR) system failure
33	Manifold Absolute Pressure (MAP) sensor circuit – signal voltage high–low vacuum
34	Manifold Absolute Pressure (MAP) sensor circuit – signal voltage low–high vacuum
35	Idle speed error
42	Electronic Spark Timing (EST) circuit
44	Oxygen sensor circuit – lean exhaust indicated
45	Oxygen sensor circuit – rich exhaust indicated
51	PROM error – faulty or incorrect PROM
53	System over voltage

Year – 1989
Model – Pontiac 6000
Engine – 2.8L (173 cid) PFI V6
Engine Code – VIN W

ECM TROUBLE CODES

Code	Explanation
12	Reference pulse; indicates ECM's diagnostic system is operating
13	Oxygen sensor circuit – open circuit
14	Coolant Temperature Sensor (CTS) circuit – high temperature indicated
15	Coolant Temperature Sensor (CTS) circuit – low temperature indicated
21	Throttle Position Sensor (TPS) circuit – signal voltage high
22	Throttle Position Sensor (TPS) circuit – signal voltage low
23	Manifold Air Temperature (MAT) sensor circuit – low temperature indicated
24	Vehicle Speed Sensor (VSS) circuit
25	Manifold Air Temperature (MAT) sensor circuit – high temperature indicated
32	Exhaust Gas Recirculation (EGR) circuit
33	Manifold Absolute Pressure (MAP) sensor circuit – signal voltage high
34	Manifold Absolute Pressure (MAP) sensor circuit – signal voltage low
35	Idle speed error
41	Cylinder select error – faulty or incorrect Mem–Cal
42	Electronic Spark Timing (EST) circuit
43	Electronic Spark Control (ESC) circuit
44	Oxygen sensor circuit – lean exhaust indicated
45	Oxygen sensor circuit – rich exhaust indicated
51	Mem–Cal error – faulty or incorrect Mem–Cal
52	Calpak error
53	System over voltage
54	Fuel pump circuit – low voltage
61	Degraded oxygen sensor

Year – 1989
Model – Pontiac 6000
Engine – 3.1L (192 cid) PFI V6
Engine Code – VIN T

ECM TROUBLE CODES

Code	Explanation
12	Reference pulse; indicates ECM's diagnostic system is operating
13	Oxygen sensor circuit – open circuit
14	Coolant Temperature Sensor (CTS) circuit – high temperature indicated
15	Coolant Temperature Sensor (CTS) circuit – low temperature indicated
21	Throttle Position Sensor (TPS) circuit – signal voltage high
22	Throttle Position Sensor (TPS) circuit – signal voltage low
23	Manifold Air Temperature (MAT) sensor circuit – low temperature indicated
24	Vehicle Speed Sensor (VSS) circuit
25	Manifold Air Temperature (MAT) sensor circuit – high temperature indicated
32	Exhaust Gas Recirculation (EGR) circuit
33	Manifold Absolute Pressure (MAP) sensor circuit – signal voltage high–low vacuum
34	Manifold Absolute Pressure (MAP) sensor circuit – signal voltage low–high vacuum
35	Idle Speed Control (ISC) circuit
41	Cylinder select error – faulty or incorrect Mem-Cal
42	Electronic Spark Timing (EST) circuit
43	Electronic Spark Control (ESC) circuit
44	Oxygen sensor circuit – lean exhaust indicated
45	Oxygen sensor circuit – rich exhaust indicated
51	Mem–Cal error – faulty or incorrect Mem–Cal
52	Calpak error – faulty or incorrect Calpak
53	System over voltage
54	Fuel pump circuit – low voltage
61	Degraded oxygen sensor

Year — 1989
Model — Fiero
Engine — 2.5L (151 cid) TBI 4 cyl
Engine Code — VIN U

ECM TROUBLE CODES

Code	Explanation
12	Reference pulse; indicates ECM's diagnostic system is operating
13	Oxygen sensor circuit — open circuit
14	Coolant Temperature Sensor (CTS) circuit — high temperature indicated
15	Coolant Temperature Sensor (CTS) circuit — low temperature indicated
21	Throttle Position Sensor (TPS) circuit — signal voltage high
22	Throttle Position Sensor (TPS) circuit — signal voltage low
23	Manifold Air Temperature (MAT) sensor circuit — low temperature indicated
24	Vehicle Speed Sensor (VSS) circuit
25	Manifold Air Temperature (MAT) sensor circuit — high temperature indicated
33	Manifold Absolute Pressure (MAP) sensor circuit — signal voltage high – low vacuum
34	Manifold Absolute Pressure (MAP) sensor circuit — signal voltage low – high vacuum
35	Idle speed error
42	Electronic Spark Timing (EST) circuit
44	Oxygen sensor circuit — lean exhaust indicated
45	Oxygen sensor circuit — rich exhaust indicated
51	PROM error — faulty or incorrect PROM
53	System over voltage

Year – 1989
Model – Fiero
Engine – 2.8L (173 cid) MPFI V6
Engine Code – VIN 9

ECM TROUBLE CODES

Code	Explanation
12	Reference pulse; indicates ECM's diagnostic system is operating
13	Oxygen sensor circuit – open circuit
14	Coolant Temperature Sensor (CTS) circuit – high temperature indicated
15	Coolant Temperature Sensor (CTS) circuit – low temperature indicated
21	Throttle Position Sensor (TPS) circuit – signal voltage high
22	Throttle Position Sensor (TPS) circuit – signal voltage low
23	Manifold Air Temperature (MAT) sensor circuit – low temperature indicated
24	Vehicle Speed Sensor (VSS) circuit
25	Manifold Air Temperature (MAT) sensor circuit – high temperature indicated
32	Exhaust Gas Recirculation (EGR) circuit
33	Manifold Absolute Pressure (MAP) sensor circuit – signal voltage high–low vacuum
34	Manifold Absolute Pressure (MAP) sensor circuit – signal voltage low–high vacuum
35	Idle Speed Control (ISC) circuit
42	Electronic Spark Timing (EST) circuit
44	Oxygen sensor circuit – lean exhaust indicated
45	Oxygen sensor circuit – rich exhaust indicated
51	PROM error – faulty or incorrect PROM
52	Calpak error – faulty or incorrect Calpak
53	System over voltage
55	ECM error

Year – 1989
Model – Safari Wagon
Engine – 5.0L (307 cid) V8
Engine Code – VIN Y

ECM TROUBLE CODES

Code	Explanation
12	Reference pulse; indicates ECM's diagnostic system is operating
13	Oxygen sensor circuit – open circuit
14	Coolant Temperature Sensor (CTS) circuit – high temperature indicated
15	Coolant Temperature Sensor (CTS) circuit – low temperature indicated
21	Throttle Position Sensor (TPS) circuit – signal voltage high
22	Throttle Position Sensor (TPS) circuit – signal voltage low
23	Manifold Air Temperature (MAT) sensor circuit – low temperature indicated
24	Vehicle Speed Sensor (VSS) circuit
25	Manifold Air Temperature (MAT) sensor circuit – high temperature indicated
32	Exhaust Gas Recirculation (EGR) circuit
33	Manifold Absolute Pressure (MAP) sensor circuit – signal voltage high–low vacuum
34	Manifold Absolute Pressure (MAP) sensor circuit – signal voltage low–high vacuum
42	Electronic Spark Timing (EST) circuit
43	Electronic Spark Control (ESC) circuit
44	Oxygen sensor circuit – lean exhaust indicated
45	Oxygen sensor circuit – rich exhaust indicated
51	PROM error – faulty or incorrect PROM
52	Calpak error – faulty or incorrect Calpak
54	Fuel pump circuit – low voltage
55	ECM error

CHEVROLET/GMC TRUCKS

Year – 1982
Model – S-Series
Engine – 1.9L (119 cid) 4 cyl
Engine Code – VIN A

ECM TROUBLE CODES

Code	Explanation
12	Idle Position Switch (IPS) high output – this code indicates that the idle position switch output terminal was in a high voltage state when it should have been in a low voltage state
13	Idle Position Switch (IPS) low output – this code indicates that the idle position switch ouput terminal was in a low voltage state when it should have been in a high voltage state
14	Wide Open Throttle (WOT) switch high output – this code indicates that the WOT position switch output terminal was in a high voltage state when it should have been in a low voltage state
15	Wide Open Throttle (WOT) switch low output – this code indicates that the WOT position switch outtput terminal was in a low voltage state when it should have been in a high voltage state
21	Vacuum Control Solenoid (VCS) high output – this code indicates that the vacuum solenoid signal output terminal was in a high voltage state when it should have been in a low voltage state
22	Vacuum Control Solenoid (VCS) low output – this code indicates that the vacuum solenoid signal output terminal was in a low voltage state when it should have been in a high voltage state.
23	Oxygen sensor – this code indicates that the oxygen sensor output terminal was in a low voltage state when it should have been in a high voltage state
24	Coolant Temperature Switch (CTS) – this code indicates that the coolant temperature switch output terminal was in a low voltage state when it should have been in a high voltage state
25	Random Access Memory (RAM) Error

GENERAL MOTORS CORPORATION
DIAGNOSTIC CODE DATA

Year — 1982
Model — S-Series
Engine — 2.8L (173 cid) V6
Engine Code — VIN B

ECM TROUBLE CODES

Code	Explanation
12	No distributor reference pulses to the Electronic Control Module (ECM). This code is not stored in memory and will only flash while the fault is present. Normal code with ignition ON, engine not running
13	Oxygen sensor circuit — the engine must run up to 5 minutes at part throttle, under road load, before this code will set
14	Shorted Coolant Temperature Sensor (CTS) circuit — the engine must run up to 5 minutes before this code will set
15	Open Coolant Temperature Sensor (CTS) circuit — the engine must run up to 5 minutes before this code will set
21	Throttle Position Sensor (TPS) circuit — the engine must run up to 25 seconds at specified curb idle speed before this code will set
23	Open or grounded Mixture Control (M/C) solenoid circuit
34	Vacuum sensor — the engine must run up to 5 minutes at specified curb idle before this code will set
41	No distribuitor reference pulses to the Electronic Control Module (ECM) at specified engine vacuum. This code will store in memory
42	Electronic Spark Timing (EST) bypass circuit or EST circuit grounded or open
44	Lean exhaust indication — the engine must run up to 5 minutes, in closed loop and at part throttle before this code will set
44	Lean exhaust indication — the engine must run up to 5 minutes, in closed loop and at part throttle before this code will set
44 & 45	At same time — faulty oxygen sensor circuit
45	Rich exhaust indication — the engine must run up to 5 minutes, in closed loop and at part throttle before this code will set
51	Faulty calibration unit (PROM) or installation. It takes up to 30 seconds before this code will set
54	Shorted Mixture Control (M/C) solenoid circuit and/or faulty Electronic Control Module (ECM)
55	Grounded V/ref (terminal 21), faulty oxygen sensor or Electronic Control Module (ECM)

Year — 1982
Model — Caballero/El Camino
Engine — 3.8L (231 cid) V6
Engine Code — VIN A

ECM TROUBLE CODES

Code	Explanation
12	No distributor reference pulses to the Electronic Control Module (ECM). This code is not stored in memory and will only flash while the fault is present. Normal code with ignition ON, engine not running
13	Oxygen sensor circuit — the engine must run up to 5 minutes at part throttle, under road load, before this code will set
14	Shorted Coolant Temperature Sensor (CTS) circuit — the engine must run up to 5 minutes before this code will set
15	Open Coolant Temperature Sensor (CTS) circuit — the engine must run up to 5 minutes before this code will set
21	Throttle Position Sensor (TPS) circuit — the engine must run up to 25 seconds, at specified curb idle speed, before this code will set
23	Mixture Control (M/C) solenoid circuit open or grounded
24	Vehicle Speed Sensor (VSS) circuit — the vehicle must operate up to 5 minutes ar road speed before this code will set.
32	Barometric Pressure Sensor (BARO) Circuit low
34	Vacuum sensor circuit — the engine must run up to 5 minutes, at specified curb idle speed, before this code will set
35	Idle Speed Control (ISC) switch circuit shorted — over 50% throttle for over 2 sec.
41	No distributor reference pulses at specified engine vacuum. This code will store in memory
42	Electronic Spark Timing (EST) bypass circuit or EST circuit grounded or open
44	Lean exhaust indication — the engine must run up to 5 minutes, in closed loop and at part throttle, before this code will set
45	Rich exhaust indication — the engine must run up to 5 minutes, in closed loop and at part throttle, before this code will set
51	Faulty or improperly installed calibration unit (PROM). It takes up to 30 seconds before this code will set
54	Shorted Mixture Control (M/C) solenoid circuit and or faulty Electronic Control Module (ECM)
55	Grounded V/ref (terminal 21), high voltage on oxygen sensor circuit or Electronic Control Module (ECM)

Year — 1982
Model — Caballero/El Camino
Engine — 3.8L (229 cid) V6
Engine Code — VIN 9

ECM TROUBLE CODES

Code	Explanation
12	No distributor reference pulses to the Electronic Control Module (ECM). This code is not stored in memory and will only flash while the fault is present. Normal code with ignition ON, engine not running
13	Oxygen sensor circuit — the engine must run up to 5 minutes at part throttle, under road load, before this code will set
14	Shorted Coolant Temperature Sensor (CTS) circuit — the engine must run up to 5 minutes before this code will set
15	Open Coolant Temperature Sensor (CTS) circuit — the engine must run up to 5 minutes before this code will set
21	Throttle Position Sensor (TPS) circuit — the engine must run up to 25 seconds, at specified curb idle speed, before this code will set
23	Mixture Control (M/C) solenoid circuit open or grounded
24	Vehicle Speed Sensor (VSS) circuit — the vehicle must operate up to 5 minutes at road speed before this code will set
32	Barometric Pressure Sensor (BARO) Circuit low.
34	Manifold Absolute Pressure (MAP) or Vacuum sensor circuit. The engine must run up to 5 minutes at specified curb idle speed, before this code will set
35	Idle Speed Control (ISC) switch circuit shorted — over 50% throttle for over 2 seconds
41	No distributor reference pulses at specified engine vacuum. This code will store in memory
42	Electronic Spark Timing (EST) bypass circuit or EST circuit grounded or open
44	Lean exhaust indication — the engine must run up to 5 minutes, in closed loop and at part throttle, before this code will set
45	Rich exhaust indication — the engine must run up to 5 minutes, in closed loop and at part throttle, before this code will set
51	Faulty or improperly installed calibration unit (PROM). It takes up to 30 seconds before this code will set
54	Shorted Mixture Control (M/C) solenoid circuit and or faulty Electronic Control Module (ECM)
55	Grounded V/ref (terminal 21), high voltage on oxygen sensor circuit or Electronic Control Module (ECM)

Year – 1982
Model – Caballero/El Camino
Engine – 5.0L (305 cid) V8
Engine Code – VIN H

ECM TROUBLE CODES

Code	Explanation
12	No distributor reference pulses to the Electronic Control Module (ECM). This code is not stored in memory and will only flash while the fault is present. Normal code with ignition ON, engine not running
13	Oxygen sensor circuit – the engine must run up to 5 minutes at part throttle, under road load, before this code will set
14	Shorted Coolant Temperature Sensor (CTS) circuit – the engine must run up to 5 minutes before this code will set
15	Open Coolant Temperature Sensor (CTS) circuit – the engine must run up to 5 minutes before this code will set
21	Throttle Position Sensor (TPS) circuit – the engine must run up to 25 seconds, at specified curb idle speed, before this code will set
23	Mixture Control (M/C) solenoid circuit open or grounded
24	Vehicle Speed Sensor (VSS) circuit – the vehicle must operate up to 5 minutes at road speed before this code will set
32	Barometric Pressure Sensor (BARO) Circuit low
34	Manifold Absolute Pressure (MAP) or Vacuum sensor circuit. The engine must run up to 5 minutes at specified curb idle speed, before this code will set
35	Idle Speed Control (ISC) switch circuit shorted – over 50% throttle for over 2 sec.)
41	No distributor reference pulses at specified engine vacuum. This code will store in memory
42	Electronic Spark Timing (EST) bypass circuit or EST circuit grounded or open
44	Lean exhaust indication – the engine must run up to 5 minutes, in closed loop and at part throttle, before this code will set
45	Rich exhaust indication – the engine must run up to 5 minutes, in closed loop and at part throttle, before this code will set
51	Faulty or improperly installed calibration unit (PROM). It takes up to 30 seconds before this code will set
54	Shorted Mixture Control (M/C) solenoid circuit and or faulty Electronic Control Module (ECM)
55	Grounded V/ref (terminal 21), high voltage on oxygen sensor circuit or Electronic Control Module (ECM)

Year – 1983
Model – S-Series
Engine – 1.9L (119 cid) 4 cyl
Engine Code – VIN A

ECM TROUBLE CODES

Code	Explanation
12	No ignition reference. Pulses to the Electronic Control Module (ECM). This code is not stored in memory and will only flash while the fault is present
13	Oxygen sensor circuit – the engine must run up 1 minute at part throttle, under road load, before this code will set. This code does not set when the coolant temperature is below 70°C and/or the time since engine start has not exceeded 2 minutes
14	Shorted Coolant Temperature Sensor circuit – the engine must run up to 2 minutes before this code will set
15	Open Coolant Temperature Sensor circuit – the engine must run up to 5 minutes before this code will set
21	Idle switch circuit open or Wide Open Throttle (WOT) switch circuit shorted – the engine must run up to 10 seconds at following 2 conditions concurrently before this code will set. Idle switch output is in a low voltage state. WOT switch output is in a high voltage state
22	Fuel Cut Solenoid (FCS) circuit open or grounded – the engine must run under the decelerating condition over 2000 engine rpm before this code will set
23	Vacuum Control Solenoid (VCS) circuit open or grounded
25	Air Switching Solenoid (ASS) circuit open or grounded
31	No ignition reference pulses to the Electronic Control Module (ECM) for 10 seconds at part throttle, under road load. This code will store in memory
44	Lean oxygen sensor indication – the engine must run up to 2 minutes at part throttle, under road load, before this code will set. This code does not set when the coolant temperature is below 70°C and/or the air temperature in air cleaner is below 0°C
45	Rich system indication – the engine must run up to 2 minutes at part throttle, under road load, before this code will set. This code does not set when the engine exceeds 2500 rpm and/or the coolant temperature is below 70°C and/or the barometric pressure is below 23 in. Hg above 1800 ft. (2500m) altitude
51	Shorted Fuel Cut Solenoid (FCS) circuit and/or faulty Electronic Control Module (ECM)
52	Faulty Electronic Control Module (ECM) – problem of Random Access Memory (RAM) in ECM
53	Shorted Air Switching Solenoid (ASS) and/or faulty Electronic Control Module (ECM)
54	Shorted Vacuum Control Solenoid (VCS) and/or faulty Electronic Control Module (ECM)
55	Faulty Electronic Control Module (ECM) – fault of A/D converter in Electronic Control Module (ECM)

Year – 1983
Model – S-Series
Engine – 2.0L (121 cid) 4 cyl
Engine Code – VIN Y

ECM TROUBLE CODES

Code	Explanation
12	No distributor reference pulses to the Electronic Control Module (ECM). This code is not stored in memory and will only flash while the fault is present. Normal code with ignition ON, engine not running
13	Oxygen sensor circuit – the engine must run up to 5 minutes at part throttle, under road load, before this code will set
14	Shorted Coolant Temperature Sensor (CTS) circuit – the engine must run up to 5 minutes before this code will set
15	Open Coolant Temperature Sensor (CTS) circuit – the engine must run up to 5 minutes before this code will set
21	Throttle Position Sensor (TPS) circuit – the engine must run up to 25 seconds, at specified curb idle speed, before this code will set
23	Mixture Control (M/C) solenoid circuit open or grounded
24	Vehicle Speed Sensor (VSS) circuit – the vehicle must operate up to 5 minutes, at road speed, before this code will set
32	Barometric pressure sensor (BARO) circuit low
34	Vacuum sensor or Manifold Absolute Pressure (MAP) circuit – the engine must run up to 5 minutes, at specified curb idle, before this code will set
35	Idle Speed Control (ISC) switch circuit shorted – over 50% throttle for over 2 seconds
41	No distributor reference pulses to the Electronic Control Module (ECM) at specified engine vacuum. This code will store in memory
42	Electronic Spark Timing (EST) bypass circuit or EST circuit grounded or open
43	Electronic Spark Control (ESC) retard signal for too long a time – causes retard in Electronic Spark Timing (EST) signal
44	Lean exhaust indication – the engine must run up to 5 minutes, in closed loop and at part throttle, before this code will set
45	Rich exhaust indication – the engine must run up to 5 minutes, in closed loop and at part throttle, before this code will set
51	Faulty or improperly installed calibration unit (PROM). It takes up to 30 seconds before this code will set
54	Shorted Mixture Control (M/C) solenoid circuit and or faulty Electronic Control Module (ECM)
55	Grounded V/ref (terminal 21), high voltage on oxygen sensor circuit or Electronic Control Module (ECM)

Year — 1983
Model — S-Series
Engine — 2.8L (173 cid) V6
Engine Code — VIN B

ECM TROUBLE CODES

Code	Explanation
12	No distributor reference pulses to the Electronic Control Module (ECM). This code is not stored in memory and will only flash while the fault is present. Normal code with ignition ON, engine not running
13	Oxygen sensor circuit — the engine must run up to 5 minutes at part throttle, under road load, before this code will set
14	Shorted Coolant Temperature Sensor (CTS) circuit — the engine must run up to 5 minutes before this code will set
15	Open Coolant Temperature Sensor (CTS) circuit — the engine must run up to 5 minutes before this code will set
21	Throttle Position Sensor (TPS) circuit — the engine must run up to 25 seconds, at specified curb idle speed, before this code will set
23	Mixture Control (M/C) solenoid circuit open or grounded
24	Vehicle Speed Sensor (VSS) circuit — the vehicle must operate up to 5 minutes, at road speed, before this code will set
32	Barometric pressure sensor (BARO) circuit low
34	Vacuum sensor or Manifold Absolute Pressure (MAP) circuit — the engine must run up to 5 minutes, at specified curb idle, before this code will set
35	Idle Speed Control (ISC) switch circuit shorted — over 50% throttle for over 2 seconds
41	No distributor reference pulses to the Electronic Control Module (ECM) at specified engine vacuum. This code will store in memory
42	Electronic Spark Timing (EST) bypass circuit or EST circuit grounded or open
43	Electronic Spark Control (ESC) retard signal for too long a time — causes retard in Electronic Spark Timing (EST) signal
44	Lean exhaust indication — the engine must run up to 5 minutes, in closed loop and at part throttle, before this code will set
45	Rich exhaust indication — the engine must run up to 5 minutes, in closed loop and at part throttle, before this code will set
51	Faulty or improperly installed calibration unit (PROM). It takes up to 30 seconds before this code will set
54	Shorted Mixture Control (M/C) solenoid circuit and or faulty Electronic Control Module (ECM)
55	Grounded V/ref (terminal 21), high voltage on oxygen sensor circuit or Electronic Control Module (ECM)

Year – 1983
Model – G-Series Vans
Engine – 4.1L (252 cid) 6 cyl
Engine Code – VIN D

ECM TROUBLE CODES

Code	Explanation
12	No distributor reference pulses to the Electronic Control Module (ECM). This code is not stored in memory and will only flash while the fault is present. Normal code with ignition ON, engine not running
13	Oxygen sensor circuit – the engine must run up to 5 minutes at part throttle, under road load, before this code will set
14	Shorted Coolant Temperature Sensor (CTS) circuit – the engine must run up to 5 minutes before this code will set
15	Open Coolant Temperature Sensor (CTS) circuit – the engine must run up to 5 minutes before this code will set
21	Throttle Position Sensor (TPS) circuit – the engine must run up to 25 seconds, at specified curb idle speed, before this code will set
23	Mixture Control (M/C) solenoid circuit open or grounded
34	Vacuum sensor or Manifold Absolute Pressure (MAP) circuit – the engine must run up to 5 minutes, at specified curb idle, before this code will set
41	No distributor reference pulses to the Electronic Control Module (ECM) at specified engine vacuum. This code will store in memory
42	Electronic Spark Timing (EST) bypass circuit or EST circuit grounded or open
44	Lean exhaust indication – the engine must run up to 5 minutes, in closed loop and at part throttle, before this code will set
45	Rich exhaust indication – the engine must run up to 5 minutes, in closed loop and at part throttle, before this code will set
51	Faulty or improperly installed calibration unit (PROM). It takes up to 30 seconds before this code will set
54	Shorted Mixture Control (M/C) solenoid circuit and or faulty Electronic Control Module (ECM)
55	Grounded V/ref (terminal 21), high voltage on oxygen sensor circuit or Electronic Control Module (ECM)

GENERAL MOTORS CORPORATION
DIAGNOSTIC CODE DATA

Year — 1983
Model — G-Series Vans
Engine — 5.0L (305 cid) V8
Engine Code — VIN F

ECM TROUBLE CODES

Code	Explanation
12	No distributor reference pulses to the Electronic Control Module (ECM). This code is not stored in memory and will only flash while the fault is present. Normal code with ignition ON, engine not running
13	Oxygen sensor circuit — the engine must run up to 5 minutes at part throttle, under road load, before this code will set
14	Shorted Coolant Temperature Sensor (CTS) circuit — the engine must run up to 5 minutes before this code will set
15	Open Coolant Temperature Sensor (CTS) circuit — the engine must run up to 5 minutes before this code will set
21	Throttle Position Sensor (TPS) circuit — the engine must run up to 25 seconds, at specified curb idle speed, before this code will set
23	Mixture Control (M/C) solenoid circuit open or grounded
34	Vacuum sensor circuit — the engine must run up to 5 minutes, at specified curb idle speed, before this code will set
41	No distributor reference pulses at specified engine vacuum. This code will store in memory
42	Electronic Spark Timing (EST) bypass circuit or EST circuit grounded or open
44	Lean exhaust indication — the engine must run up to 5 minutes, in closed loop and at part throttle, before this code will set
45	Rich exhaust indication — the engine must run up to 5 minutes, in closed loop and at part throttle, before this code will set
51	Faulty or improperly installed calibration unit (PROM). It takes up to 30 seconds before this code will set
54	Shorted Mixture Control (M/C) solenoid circuit and or faulty Electronic Control Module (ECM)
55	Grounded V/ref (terminal 21), high voltage on oxygen sensor circuit or Electronic Control Module (ECM)

Year – 1983
Model – G-Series Vans
Engine – 5.0L (305 cid) V8
Engine Code – VIN H

ECM TROUBLE CODES

Code	Explanation
12	No distributor reference pulses to the Electronic Control Module (ECM). This code is not stored in memory and will only flash while the fault is present. Normal code with ignition ON, engine not running
13	Oxygen sensor circuit – the engine must run up to 5 minutes at part throttle, under road load, before this code will set
14	Shorted Coolant Temperature Sensor (CTS) circuit – the engine must run up to 5 minutes before this code will set
15	Open Coolant Temperature Sensor (CTS) circuit – the engine must run up to 5 minutes before this code will set
21	Throttle Position Sensor (TPS) circuit – the engine must run up to 25 seconds, at specified curb idle speed, before this code will set
23	Mixture Control (M/C) solenoid circuit open or grounded
34	Vacuum sensor circuit – the engine must run up to 5 minutes, at specified curb idle speed, before this code will set
41	No distributor reference pulses at specified engine vacuum. This code will store in memory
42	Electronic Spark Timing (EST) bypass circuit or EST circuit grounded or open
44	Lean exhaust indication – the engine must run up to 5 minutes, in closed loop and at part throttle, before this code will set
45	Rich exhaust indication – the engine must run up to 5 minutes, in closed loop and at part throttle, before this code will set
51	Faulty or improperly installed calibration unit (PROM). It takes up to 30 seconds before this code will set
54	Shorted Mixture Control (M/C) solenoid circuit and or faulty Electronic Control Module (ECM)
55	Grounded V/ref (terminal 21), high voltage on oxygen sensor circuit or Electronic Control Module (ECM)

Year – 1983
Model – G-Series Vans
Engine – 5.7L (350 cid) V8
Engine Code – VIN L

ECM TROUBLE CODES

Code	Explanation
12	No distributor reference pulses to the Electronic Control Module (ECM). This code is not stored in memory and will only flash while the fault is present. Normal code with ignition ON, engine not running
13	Oxygen sensor circuit—the engine must run up to 5 minutes at part throttle, under road load, before this code will set
14	Shorted Coolant Temperature Sensor (CTS) circuit—the engine must run up to 5 minutes before this code will set
15	Open Coolant Temperature Sensor (CTS) circuit—the engine must run up to 5 minutes before this code will set
21	Throttle Position Sensor (TPS) circuit—the engine must run up to 25 seconds, at specified curb idle speed, before this code will set
23	Mixture Control (M/C) solenoid circuit open or grounded
34	Vacuum sensor circuit—the engine must run up to 5 minutes, at specified curb idle speed, before this code will set
41	No distributor reference pulses at specified engine vacuum. This code will store in memory
42	Electronic Spark Timing (EST) bypass circuit or EST circuit grounded or open
44	Lean exhaust indication—the engine must run up to 5 minutes, in closed loop and at part throttle, before this code will set
45	Rich exhaust indication—the engine must run up to 5 minutes, in closed loop and at part throttle, before this code will set
51	Faulty or improperly installed calibration unit (PROM). It takes up to 30 seconds before this code will set
54	Shorted Mixture Control (M/C) solenoid circuit and or faulty Electronic Control Module (ECM)
55	Grounded V/ref (terminal 21), high voltage on oxygen sensor circuit or Electronic Control Module (ECM)

Year – 1983
Model – G-Series Vans
Engine – 5.7L (350 cid) V8
Engine Code – VIN M

ECM TROUBLE CODES

Code	Explanation
12	No distributor reference pulses to the Electronic Control Module (ECM). This code is not stored in memory and will only flash while the fault is present. Normal code with ignition ON, engine not running
13	Oxygen sensor circuit – the engine must run up to 5 minutes at part throttle, under road load, before this code will set
14	Shorted Coolant Temperature Sensor (CTS) circuit – the engine must run up to 5 minutes before this code will set
15	Open Coolant Temperature Sensor (CTS) circuit – the engine must run up to 5 minutes before this code will set
21	Throttle Position Sensor (TPS) circuit – the engine must run up to 25 seconds, at specified curb idle speed, before this code will set
23	Mixture Control (M/C) solenoid circuit open or grounded
34	Vacuum sensor circuit – the engine must run up to 5 minutes, at specified curb idle speed, before this code will set
41	No distributor reference pulses at specified engine vacuum. This code will store in memory
42	Electronic Spark Timing (EST) bypass circuit or EST circuit grounded or open
44	Lean exhaust indication – the engine must run up to 5 minutes, in closed loop and at part throttle, before this code will set
45	Rich exhaust indication – the engine must run up to 5 minutes, in closed loop and at part throttle, before this code will set
51	Faulty or improperly installed calibration unit (PROM). It takes up to 30 seconds before this code will set
54	Shorted Mixture Control (M/C) solenoid circuit and or faulty Electronic Control Module (ECM)
55	Grounded V/ref (terminal 21), high voltage on oxygen sensor circuit or Electronic Control Module (ECM)

Year — 1983
Model — C, K & P Models
Engine — 4.8L (292 cid) 6 cyl
Engine Code — VIN T

ECM TROUBLE CODES

Code	Explanation
12	No distributor reference pulses to the Electronic Control Module (ECM). This code is not stored in memory and will only flash while the fault is present. Normal code with ignition ON, engine not running
13	Oxygen sensor circuit — the engine must run up to 5 minutes at part throttle, under road load, before this code will set
14	Shorted Coolant Temperature Sensor (CTS) circuit — the engine must run up to 5 minutes before this code will set
15	Open Coolant Temperature Sensor (CTS) circuit — the engine must run up to 5 minutes before this code will set
21	Throttle Position Sensor (TPS) circuit — the engine must run up to 25 seconds, at specified curb idle speed, before this code will set
23	Mixture Control (M/C) solenoid circuit open or grounded
34	Vacuum sensor circuit — the engine must run up to 5 minutes, at specified curb idle speed, before this code will set
41	No distributor reference pulses at specified engine vacuum. This code will store in memory
42	Electronic Spark Timing (EST) bypass circuit or EST circuit grounded or open
44	Lean exhaust indication — the engine must run up to 5 minutes, in closed loop and at part throttle, before this code will set
45	Rich exhaust indication — the engine must run up to 5 minutes, in closed loop and at part throttle, before this code will set
51	Faulty or improperly installed calibration unit (PROM). It takes up to 30 seconds before this code will set
54	Shorted Mixture Control (M/C) solenoid circuit and or faulty Electronic Control Module (ECM)
55	Grounded V/ref (terminal 21), high voltage on oxygen sensor circuit or Electronic Control Module (ECM)

Year — 1983
Model — C & K Models
Engine — 5.0L (305 cid) V8
Engine Code — VIN F

ECM TROUBLE CODES

Code	Explanation
12	No distributor reference pulses to the Electronic Control Module (ECM). This code is not stored in memory and will only flash while the fault is present. Normal code with ignition ON, engine not running
13	Oxygen sensor circuit — the engine must run up to 5 minutes at part throttle, under road load, before this code will set
14	Shorted Coolant Temperature Sensor (CTS) circuit — the engine must run up to 5 minutes before this code will set
15	Open Coolant Temperature Sensor (CTS) circuit — the engine must run up to 5 minutes before this code will set
21	Throttle Position Sensor (TPS) circuit — the engine must run up to 25 seconds, at specified curb idle speed, before this code will set
23	Mixture Control (M/C) solenoid circuit open or grounded
34	Vacuum sensor circuit — the engine must run up to 5 minutes, at specified curb idle speed, before this code will set
41	No distributor reference pulses at specified engine vacuum. This code will store in memory
42	Electronic Spark Timing (EST) bypass circuit or EST circuit grounded or open
44	Lean exhaust indication — the engine must run up to 5 minutes, in closed loop and at part throttle, before this code will set
45	Rich exhaust indication — the engine must run up to 5 minutes, in closed loop and at part throttle, before this code will set
51	Faulty or improperly installed calibration unit (PROM). It takes up to 30 seconds before this code will set
54	Shorted Mixture Control (M/C) solenoid circuit and or faulty Electronic Control Module (ECM)
55	Grounded V/ref (terminal 21), high voltage on oxygen sensor circuit or Electronic Control Module (ECM)

Year — 1983
Model — C & K Models
Engine — 5.0L (305 cid) V8
Engine Code — VIN H

ECM TROUBLE CODES

Code	Explanation
12	No distributor reference pulses to the Electronic Control Module (ECM). This code is not stored in memory and will only flash while the fault is present. Normal code with ignition ON, engine not running
13	Oxygen sensor circuit — the engine must run up to 5 minutes at part throttle, under road load, before this code will set
14	Shorted Coolant Temperature Sensor (CTS) circuit — the engine must run up to 5 minutes before this code will set
15	Open Coolant Temperature Sensor (CTS) circuit — the engine must run up to 5 minutes before this code will set
21	Throttle Position Sensor (TPS) circuit — the engine must run up to 25 seconds, at specified curb idle speed, before this code will set
23	Mixture Control (M/C) solenoid circuit open or grounded
34	Vacuum sensor circuit — the engine must run up to 5 minutes, at specified curb idle speed, before this code will set
41	No distributor reference pulses at specified engine vacuum. This code will store in memory
42	Electronic Spark Timing (EST) bypass circuit or EST circuit grounded or open
44	Lean exhaust indication — the engine must run up to 5 minutes, in closed loop and at part throttle, before this code will set
45	Rich exhaust indication — the engine must run up to 5 minutes, in closed loop and at part throttle, before this code will set
51	Faulty or improperly installed calibration unit (PROM). It takes up to 30 seconds before this code will set
54	Shorted Mixture Control (M/C) solenoid circuit and or faulty Electronic Control Module (ECM)
55	Grounded V/ref (terminal 21), high voltage on oxygen sensor circuit or Electronic Control Module (ECM)

Year — 1983
Model — C & K Models
Engine — 5.7L (350 cid) V8
Engine Code — VIN L

ECM TROUBLE CODES

Code	Explanation
12	No distributor reference pulses to the Electronic Control Module (ECM). This code is not stored in memory and will only flash while the fault is present. Normal code with ignition ON, engine not running
13	Oxygen sensor circuit — the engine must run up to 5 minutes at part throttle, under road load, before this code will set
14	Shorted Coolant Temperature Sensor (CTS) circuit — the engine must run up to 5 minutes before this code will set
15	Open Coolant Temperature Sensor (CTS) circuit — the engine must run up to 5 minutes before this code will set
21	Throttle Position Sensor (TPS) circuit — the engine must run up to 25 seconds, at specified curb idle speed, before this code will set
23	Mixture Control (M/C) solenoid circuit open or grounded
34	Vacuum sensor circuit — the engine must run up to 5 minutes, at specified curb idle speed, before this code will set
41	No distributor reference pulses at specified engine vacuum. This code will store in memory
42	Electronic Spark Timing (EST) bypass circuit or EST circuit grounded or open
44	Lean exhaust indication — the engine must run up to 5 minutes, in closed loop and at part throttle, before this code will set
45	Rich exhaust indication — the engine must run up to 5 minutes, in closed loop and at part throttle, before this code will set
51	Faulty or improperly installed calibration unit (PROM). It takes up to 30 seconds before this code will set
54	Shorted Mixture Control (M/C) solenoid circuit and or faulty Electronic Control Module (ECM)
55	Grounded V/ref (terminal 21), high voltage on oxygen sensor circuit or Electronic Control Module (ECM)

Year – 1983
Model – C, K & P Models
Engine – 5.7L (350 cid) V8
Engine Code – VIN M

ECM TROUBLE CODES

Code	Explanation
12	No distributor reference pulses to the Electronic Control Module (ECM). This code is not stored in memory and will only flash while the fault is present. Normal code with ignition ON, engine not running
13	Oxygen sensor circuit – the engine must run up to 5 minutes at part throttle, under road load, before this code will set
14	Shorted Coolant Temperature Sensor (CTS) circuit – the engine must run up to 5 minutes before this code will set
15	Open Coolant Temperature Sensor (CTS) circuit – the engine must run up to 5 minutes before this code will set
21	Throttle Position Sensor (TPS) circuit – the engine must run up to 25 seconds, at specified curb idle speed, before this code will set
23	Mixture Control (M/C) solenoid circuit open or grounded
34	Vacuum sensor circuit – the engine must run up to 5 minutes, at specified curb idle speed, before this code will set
41	No distributor reference pulses at specified engine vacuum. This code will store in memory
42	Electronic Spark Timing (EST) bypass circuit or EST circuit grounded or open
44	Lean exhaust indication – the engine must run up to 5 minutes, in closed loop and at part throttle, before this code will set
45	Rich exhaust indication – the engine must run up to 5 minutes, in closed loop and at part throttle, before this code will set
51	Faulty or improperly installed calibration unit (PROM). It takes up to 30 seconds before this code will set
54	Shorted Mixture Control (M/C) solenoid circuit and or faulty Electronic Control Module (ECM)
55	Grounded V/ref (terminal 21), high voltage on oxygen sensor circuit or Electronic Control Module (ECM)

Year — 1983
Model — C & K Models
Engine — 5.7L (350 cid) V8
Engine Code — VIN P

ECM TROUBLE CODES

Code	Explanation
12	No distributor reference pulses to the Electronic Control Module (ECM). This code is not stored in memory and will only flash while the fault is present. Normal code with ignition ON, engine not running.
13	Oxygen sensor circuit — the engine must run up to 5 minutes at part throttle, under road load, before this code will set
14	Shorted Coolant Temperature Sensor (CTS) circuit — the engine must run up to 5 minutes before this code will set
15	Open Coolant Temperature Sensor (CTS) circuit — the engine must run up to 5 minutes before this code will set
21	Throttle Position Sensor (TPS) circuit — the engine must run up to 25 seconds, at specified curb idle speed, before this code will set
23	Mixture Control (M/C) solenoid circuit open or grounded
34	Vacuum sensor circuit — the engine must run up to 5 minutes, at specified curb idle speed, before this code will set
41	No distributor reference pulses at specified engine vacuum. This code will store in memory
42	Electronic Spark Timing (EST) bypass circuit or EST circuit grounded or open
44	Lean exhaust indication — the engine must run up to 5 minutes, in closed loop and at part throttle, before this code will set
45	Rich exhaust indication — the engine must run up to 5 minutes, in closed loop and at part throttle, before this code will set
51	Faulty or improperly installed calibration unit (PROM). It takes up to 30 seconds before this code will set
54	Shorted Mixture Control (M/C) solenoid circuit and or faulty Electronic Control Module (ECM)
55	Grounded V/ref (terminal 21), high voltage on oxygen sensor circuit or Electronic Control Module (ECM)

Year – 1983
Model – Caballero/El Camino
Engine – 3.8L (231 cid) V6
Engine Code – VIN A

ECM TROUBLE CODES

Code	Explanation
12	No distributor reference pulses to the Electronic Control Module (ECM). This code is not stored in memory and will only flash while the fault is present. Normal code with ignition ON, engine not running
13	Oxygen sensor circuit – the engine must run up to 5 minutes at part throttle, under road load, before this code will set
14	Shorted Coolant Temperature Sensor (CTS) circuit – the engine must run up to 5 minutes before this code will set
15	Open Coolant Temperature Sensor (CTS) circuit – the engine must run up to 5 minutes before this code will set
21	Throttle Position Sensor (TPS) circuit – the engine must run up to 25 seconds, at specified curb idle speed, before this code will set
23	Mixture Control (M/C) solenoid circuit open or grounded
24	Vehicle Speed Sensor (VSS) circuit – the vehicle must operate up to 5 minutes ar road speed before this code will set.
32	Barometric Pressure Sensor (BARO) Circuit low
34	Vacuum sensor circuit – the engine must run up to 5 minutes, at specified curb idle speed, before this code will set
35	Idle Speed Control (ISC) switch circuit shorted – over 50% throttle for over 2 sec.
41	No distributor reference pulses at specified engine vacuum. This code will store in memory
42	Electronic Spark Timing (EST) bypass circuit or EST circuit grounded or open
44	Lean exhaust indication – the engine must run up to 5 minutes, in closed loop and at part throttle, before this code will set
45	Rich exhaust indication – the engine must run up to 5 minutes, in closed loop and at part throttle, before this code will set
51	Faulty or improperly installed calibration unit (PROM). It takes up to 30 seconds before this code will set
54	Shorted Mixture Control (M/C) solenoid circuit and or faulty Electronic Control Module (ECM)
55	Grounded V/ref (terminal 21), high voltage on oxygen sensor circuit or Electronic Control Module (ECM)

Year — 1983
Model — Caballero/El Camino
Engine — 3.8L (229 cid) V6
Engine Code — VIN 9

ECM TROUBLE CODES

Code	Explanation
12	No distributor reference pulses to the Electronic Control Module (ECM). This code is not stored in memory and will only flash while the fault is present. Normal code with ignition ON, engine not running
13	Oxygen sensor circuit — the engine must run up to 5 minutes at part throttle, under road load, before this code will set
14	Shorted Coolant Temperature Sensor (CTS) circuit — the engine must run up to 5 minutes before this code will set
15	Open Coolant Temperature Sensor (CTS) circuit — the engine must run up to 5 minutes before this code will set
21	Throttle Position Sensor (TPS) circuit — the engine must run up to 25 seconds, at specified curb idle speed, before this code will set
23	Mixture Control (M/C) solenoid circuit open or grounded
24	Vehicle Speed Sensor (VSS) circuit — the vehicle must operate up to 5 minutes at road speed before this code will set
32	Barometric Pressure Sensor (BARO) Circuit low.
34	Manifold Absolute Pressure (MAP) or Vacuum sensor circuit. The engine must run up to 5 minutes at specified curb idle speed, before this code will set
35	Idle Speed Control (ISC) switch circuit shorted — over 50% throttle for over 2 seconds
41	No distributor reference pulses at specified engine vacuum. This code will store in memory
42	Electronic Spark Timing (EST) bypass circuit or EST circuit grounded or open
44	Lean exhaust indication — the engine must run up to 5 minutes, in closed loop and at part throttle, before this code will set
45	Rich exhaust indication — the engine must run up to 5 minutes, in closed loop and at part throttle, before this code will set
51	Faulty or improperly installed calibration unit (PROM). It takes up to 30 seconds before this code will set
54	Shorted Mixture Control (M/C) solenoid circuit and or faulty Electronic Control Module (ECM)
55	Grounded V/ref (terminal 21), high voltage on oxygen sensor circuit or Electronic Control Module (ECM)

Year – 1983
Model – Caballero/El Camino
Engine – 5.0L (305 cid) V8
Engine Code – VIN H

ECM TROUBLE CODES

Code	Explanation
12	No distributor reference pulses to the Electronic Control Module (ECM). This code is not stored in memory and will only flash while the fault is present. Normal code with ignition ON, engine not running
13	Oxygen sensor circuit – the engine must run up to 5 minutes at part throttle, under road load, before this code will set
14	Shorted Coolant Temperature Sensor (CTS) circuit – the engine must run up to 5 minutes before this code will set
15	Open Coolant Temperature Sensor (CTS) circuit – the engine must run up to 5 minutes before this code will set
21	Throttle Position Sensor (TPS) circuit – the engine must run up to 25 seconds, at specified curb idle speed, before this code will set
23	Mixture Control (M/C) solenoid circuit open or grounded
24	Vehicle Speed Sensor (VSS) circuit – the vehicle must operate up to 5 minutes at road speed before this code will set
32	Barometric Pressure Sensor (BARO) Circuit low
34	Manifold Absolute Pressure (MAP) or Vacuum sensor circuit. The engine must run up to 5 minutes at specified curb idle speed, before this code will set
35	Idle Speed Control (ISC) switch circuit shorted – over 50% throttle for over 2 sec.)
41	No distributor reference pulses at specified engine vacuum. This code will store in memory
42	Electronic Spark Timing (EST) bypass circuit or EST circuit grounded or open
44	Lean exhaust indication – the engine must run up to 5 minutes, in closed loop and at part throttle, before this code will set
45	Rich exhaust indication – the engine must run up to 5 minutes, in closed loop and at part throttle, before this code will set
51	Faulty or improperly installed calibration unit (PROM). It takes up to 30 seconds before this code will set
54	Shorted Mixture Control (M/C) solenoid circuit and or faulty Electronic Control Module (ECM)
55	Grounded V/ref (terminal 21), high voltage on oxygen sensor circuit or Electronic Control Module (ECM)

Year – 1984
Model – S-Series
Engine – 1.9L (119 cid) 4 cyl
Engine Code – VIN A

ECM TROUBLE CODES

Code	Explanation
12	No ignition reference. Pulses to the Electronic Control Module (ECM). This code is not stored in memory and will only flash while the fault is present
13	Oxygen sensor circuit—the engine must run up 1 minute at part throttle, under road load, before this code will set. This code does not set when the coolant temperature is below 70°C and/or the time since engine start has not exceeded 2 minutes
14	Shorted Coolant Temperature Sensor (CTS) circuit—the engine must run up to 2 minutes before this code will set
15	Open Coolant Temperature Sensor (CTS) circuit—the engine must run up to 5 minutes before this code will set
21	Idle switch circuit open or Wide Open Throttle (WOT) switch circuit shorted—the engine must run up to 10 seconds at following 2 conditions concurrently before this code will set. Idle switch output is in a low voltage state. WOT switch output is in a high voltage state
22	Fuel cut solenoid circuit open or grounded—the engine must run under the decelerating condition over 2000 engine rpm before this code will set
23	Vacuum control solenoid circuit open or grounded
25	Air switching solenoid circuit open or grounded
31	No ignition reference pulses to the Electronic Control Module (ECM) for 10 seconds at part throttle, under road load. This code will store in memory
44	Lean oxygen sensor indication—the engine must run up to 2 minutes at part throttle, under road load, before this code will set. This code does not set when the coolant temperature is below 70°C and/or the air temperature in air cleaner is below 0°C
45	Rich System indication—the engine must run up to 2 minutes at part throttle, under road load, before this code will set. This code does not set when the engine exceeds 2500 rpm and/or the coolant temperature is below 70°C and/or the barometric pressure is below 23 in. Hg above 1800 ft. (2500m) altitude
51	Shorted fuel cut solenoid circuit and/or faulty Electronic Control Module (ECM)
52	Faulty Electronic Control Module (ECM)—problem of Random Access Memory (RAM) in ECM
53	Shorted air switching solenoid and/or faulty Electronic Control Module (ECM)
54	Shorted vacuum control solenoid and/or faulty Electronic Control Module (ECM)
55	Faulty Electronic Control Module (ECM)—fault of A/D converter in ECM

Year – 1984
Model – S-Series
Engine – 2.0L (121 cid) 4 cyl
Engine Code – VIN Y

ECM TROUBLE CODES

Code	Explanation
12	No distributor reference pulses to the Electronic Control Module (ECM). This code is not stored in memory and will only flash while the fault is present. Normal code with ignition ON, engine not running
13	Oxygen Sensor Circuit – the engine must run up to 5 minutes at part throttle, under road load, before this code will set
14	Shorted Coolant Temperature Sensor (CTS) circuit – the engine must run up to 5 minutes before this code will set
15	Open Coolant Temperature Sensor (CTS) circuit – the engine must run up to 5 minutes before this code will set
21	Throttle position sensor circuit – the engine must run up to 25 seconds, at specified curb idle speed, before this code will set
23	Mixture Control (M/C) solenoid circuit open or grounded
24	Vehicle Speed Sensor (VSS) circuit – the vehicle must operate up to 5 minutes, at road speed, before this code will set
32	Barometric Pressure Sensor (BARO) circuit low
34	Vacuum sensor or Manifold Absolute Pressure (MAP) circuit – the engine must run up to 5 minutes, at specified curb idle, before this code will set
35	Idle Speed Control (ISC) switch circuit shorted – over 50% throttle for over 2 seconds
41	No distributor reference pulses to the Electronic Control Module (ECM) at specified engine vacuum. This code wiil store in memory
42	Electronic Spark Timing (EST) bypass circuit or EST circuit grounded or open
43	Electronic Spark Control (ESC) retard signal for too long a time; causes retard in EST signal
44	Lean exhaust indication – the engine must run up to 5 minutes, in closed loop and at part throttle, before this code will set
45	Rich exhaust indication – the engine must run up to 5 minutes, in closed loop and at part throttle, before this code will set
51	Faulty or improperly installed calibration unit (PROM). It takes up to 30 seconds before this code will set
54	Shorted Mixture Control (M/C) solenoid circuit and or faulty Electronic Control Module (ECM)
55	Grounded V/ref (terminal 21), high voltage on oxygen sensor circuit or Electronic Control Module (ECM)

Year — 1984
Model — S-Series
Engine — 2.8L (173 cid) V6
Engine Code — VIN B

ECM TROUBLE CODES

Code	Explanation
12	No distributor reference pulses to the Electronic Control Module (ECM). This code is not stored in memory and will only flash while the fault is present. Normal code with ignition ON, engine not running
13	Oxygen sensor circuit — the engine must run up to 5 minutes at part throttle, under road load, before this code will set
14	Shorted Coolant Temperature Sensor (CTS) circuit — the engine must run up to 5 minutes before this code will set
15	Open Coolant Temperature Sensor (CTS) circuit — the engine must run up to 5 minutes before this code will set
21	Throttle Position Sensor (TPS) circuit — the engine must run up to 25 seconds, at specified curb idle speed, before this code will set
23	Mixture Control (M/C) solenoid circuit open or grounded
24	Vehicle Speed Sensor (VSS) circuit — the vehicle must operate up to 5 minutes, at road speed, before this code will set
32	Barometric Pressure Sensor (BARO) circuit low
34	Vacuum sensor or Manifold Absolute Pressure (MAP) circuit — the engine must run up to 5 minutes, at specified curb idle, before this code will set
35	Idle Speed Control (ISC) switch circuit shorted — over 50% throttle for over 2 seconds
41	No distributor reference pulses to the Electronic Control Module (ECM) at specified engine vacuum. This code will store in memory
42	Electronic Spark Timing (EST) bypass circuit or EST circuit grounded or open
43	Electronic Spark Control (ESC) retard signal for too long a time; causes retard in EST signal
44	Lean exhaust indication — the engine must run up to 5 minutes, in closed loop and at part throttle, before this code will set
45	Rich exhaust indication — the engine must run up to 5 minutes, in closed loop and at part throttle, before this code will set
51	Faulty or improperly installed calibration unit (PROM). It takes up to 30 seconds before this code will set
54	Shorted Mixture Control (M/C) solenoid circuit and or faulty Electronic Control Module (ECM)
55	Grounded V/ref (terminal 21), high voltage on oxygen sensor circuit or Electronic Control Module (ECM)

Year – 1984
Model – G-Series Vans
Engine – 4.1L (252 cid) 6 cyl
Engine Code – VIN D

ECM TROUBLE CODES

Code	Explanation
12	No distributor reference pulses to the Electronic Control Module (ECM). This code is not stored in memory and will only flash while the fault is present. Normal code with ignition ON, engine not running
13	Oxygen sensor circuit – the engine must run up to 5 minutes at part throttle, under road load, before this code will set
14	Shorted Coolant Temperature Sensor (CTS) circuit – the engine must run up to 5 minutes before this code will set
15	Open Coolant Temperature Sensor (CTS) circuit – the engine must run up to 5 minutes before this code will set
21	Throttle Position Sensor (TPS) circuit voltage high (open circuit or misadjusted TPS). The engine must run up to 10 seconds, at specified curb idle speed, before this code will set
23	Mixture Control (M/C) solenoid circuit open or grounded
34	Differential pressure (vacuum) sensor circuit – the engine must run up to 2 minutes, at specified curb idle, before this code will set
41	No distributor reference pulses to the Electronic Control Module (ECM) at specified engine vacuum. This code will store in memory
42	Electronic Spark Timing (EST) bypass circuit or EST circuit grounded or open
44	Lean exhaust indication – the engine must run up to 2 minutes, in closed loop and at part throttle, before this code will set
45	Rich exhaust indication – the engine must run up to 2 minutes, in closed loop and at part throttle, before this code will set
51	Faulty or improperly installed calibration unit (PROM). It takes up to 30 seconds before this code will set
54	Shorted Mixture Control (M/C) solenoid circuit and or faulty Electronic Control Module (ECM)
55	Grounded V/ref (terminal 21), high voltage on oxygen sensor circuit or Electronic Control Module (ECM)

Year – 1984
Model – G-Series Vans
Engine – 5.0L (305 cid) V8
Engine Code – VIN F

ECM TROUBLE CODES

Code	Explanation
12	No distributor reference pulses to the Electronic Control Module (ECM). This code is not stored in memory and will only flash while the fault is present. Normal code with ignition ON, engine not running
13	Oxygen sensor circuit – the engine must run up to 4 minutes at part throttle, under road load, before this code will set
14	Shorted Coolant Temperature Sensor (CTS) circuit – the engine must run up to 2 minutes before this code will set
15	Open Coolant Temperature Sensor (CTS) circuit – the engine must run up to 5 minutes before this code will set
21	Throttle Position Sensor (TPS) circuit voltage high – open circuit or misadjusted TPS. The engine must run up to 10 seconds, at specified curb idle speed, before this code will set
23	Mixture Control (M/C) solenoid circuit open or grounded
34	Differential pressure (vacuum) sensor circuit – the engine must run up to 2 minutes, at specified curb idle speed, before this code will set
41	No distributor reference pulses at specified engine vacuum. This code will store in memory
42	Electronic Spark Timing (EST) bypass circuit or EST circuit grounded or open
44	Lean exhaust indication – the engine must run up to 2 minutes, in closed loop and at part throttle, before this code will set
45	Rich exhaust indication – the engine must run up to 2 minutes, in closed loop and at part throttle, before this code will set
51	Faulty or improperly installed calibration unit (PROM). It takes up to 30 seconds before this code will set
54	Shorted Mixture Control (M/C) solenoid circuit and or faulty Electronic Control Module (ECM)
55	Grounded V/ref (terminal 21), high voltage on oxygen sensor circuit or Electronic Control Module (ECM)

Year — 1984
Model — G-Series Vans
Engine — 5.0L (305 cid) V8
Engine Code — VIN H

ECM TROUBLE CODES

Code	Explanation
12	No distributor reference pulses to the Electronic Control Module (ECM). This code is not stored in memory and will only flash while the fault is present. Normal code with ignition ON, engine not running
13	Oxygen sensor circuit — the engine must run up to 4 minutes at part throttle, under road load, before this code will set
14	Shorted Coolant Temperature Sensor (CTS) circuit — the engine must run up to 2 minutes before this code will set
15	Open Coolant Temperature Sensor (CTS) circuit — the engine must run up to 5 minutes before this code will set
21	Throttle Position Sensor (TPS) circuit voltage high — open circuit or misadjusted TPS. Tthe engine must run up to 10 seconds, at specified curb idle speed, before this code will set
23	Mixture Control (M/C) solenoid circuit open or grounded
34	Differential pressure (vacuum) sensor circuit — the engine must run up to 2 minutes, at specified curb idle speed, before this code will set
41	No distributor reference pulses to the Electronic Control Module (ECM) at specified engine vacuum. This code will store in memory
42	Electronic Spark Timing (EST) bypass circuit or EST circuit grounded or open
44	Lean exhaust indication — the engine must run up to 2 minutes, in closed loop and at part throttle, before this code will set
45	Rich exhaust indication — the engine must run up to 2 minutes, in closed loop and at part throttle, before this code will set
51	Faulty or improperly installed calibration unit (PROM). It takes up to 30 seconds before this code will set
54	Shorted Mixture Control (M/C) solenoid circuit and or faulty Electronic Control Module (ECM)
55	Grounded V/ref (terminal 21), high voltage on oxygen sensor circuit or Electronic Control Module (ECM)

Year – 1984
Model – G-Series Vans
Engine – 5.7L (350 cid) V8
Engine Code – VIN L

ECM TROUBLE CODES

Code	Explanation
12	No distributor reference pulses to the Electronic Control Module (ECM). This code is not stored in memory and will only flash while the fault is present. Normal code with ignition ON, engine not running
13	Oxygen sensor circuit—the engine must run up to 4 minutes at part throttle, under road load, before this code will set
14	Shorted Coolant Temperature Sensor (CTS) circuit—the engine must run up to 2 minutes before this code will set
15	Open Coolant Temperature Sensor (CTS) circuit—the engine must run up to 5 minutes before this code will set
21	Throttle Position Sensor (TPS) circuit voltage high—open circuit or misadjusted TPS. The engine must run up to 10 seconds, at specified curb idle speed, before this code will set
23	Mixture Control (M/C) solenoid circuit open or grounded
34	Differential pressure (vacuum) sensor circuit—the engine must run up to 2 minutes, at specified curb idle speed, before this code will set
41	No distributor reference pulses to the Electronic Control Module (ECM) at specified engine vacuum. This code will store in memory
42	Electronic Spark Timing (EST) bypass circuit or EST circuit grounded or open
44	Lean exhaust indication—the engine must run up to 2 minutes, in closed loop and at part throttle, before this code will set
45	Rich exhaust indication—the engine must run up to 2 minutes, in closed loop and at part throttle, before this code will set
51	Faulty or improperly installed calibration unit (PROM). It takes up to 30 seconds before this code will set
54	Shorted Mixture Control (M/C) solenoid circuit and or faulty Electronic Control Module (ECM)
55	Grounded V/ref (terminal 21), high voltage on oxygen sensor circuit or Electronic Control Module (ECM)

Year — 1984
Model — G-Series Vans
Engine — 5.7L (305 cid) V8
Engine Code — VIN M

ECM TROUBLE CODES

Code	Explanation
12	No distributor reference pulses to the Electronic Control Module (ECM). This code is not stored in memory and will only flash while the fault is present. Normal code with ignition ON, engine not running
13	Oxygen sensor circuit — the engine must run up to 4 minutes at part throttle, under road load, before this code will set
14	Shorted Coolant Temperature Sensor (CTS) circuit — the engine must run up to 2 minutes before this code will set
15	Open Coolant Temperature Sensor (CTS) circuit — the engine must run up to 5 minutes before this code will set
21	Throttle Position Sensor (TPS) circuit voltage high — open circuit or misadjusted TPS. The engine must run up to 10 seconds, at specified curb idle speed, before this code will set
23	Mixture Control (M/C) solenoid circuit open or grounded
34	Differential pressure (vacuum) sensor circuit — the engine must run up to 2 minutes, at specified curb idle speed, before this code will set
41	No distributor reference pulses to the Electronic Control Module (ECM) at specified engine vacuum. This code will store in memory
42	Electronic Spark Timing (EST) bypass circuit or EST circuit grounded or open
44	Lean exhaust indication — the engine must run up to 2 minutes, in closed loop and at part throttle, before this code will set
45	Rich exhaust indication — the engine must run up to 2 minutes, in closed loop and at part throttle, before this code will set
51	Faulty or improperly installed calibration unit (PROM). It takes up to 30 seconds before this code will set
54	Shorted Mixture Control (M/C) solenoid circuit and or faulty Electronic Control Module (ECM)
55	Grounded V/ref (terminal 21), high voltage on oxygen sensor circuit or Electronic Control Module (ECM)

Year — 1984
Model — C, K & P Models
Engine — 4.8L (292 cid) 6 cyl
Engine Code — VIN T

ECM TROUBLE CODES

Code	Explanation
12	No distributor reference pulses to the Electronic Control Module (ECM). This code is not stored in memory and will only flash while the fault is present. Normal code with ignition ON, engine not running
13	Oxygen sensor circuit — the engine must run up to 4 minutes at part throttle, under road load, before this code will set
14	Shorted Coolant Temperature Sensor (CTS) circuit — the engine must run up to 2 minutes before this code will set
15	Open Coolant Temperature Sensor (CTS) circuit — the engine must run up to 5 minutes before this code will set
21	Throttle Position Sensor (TPS) circuit voltage high — open circuit or misadjusted TPS. The engine must run up to 10 seconds, at specified curb idle speed, before this code will set
23	Mixture Control (M/C) solenoid circuit open or grounded
34	Differential pressure (vacuum) sensor circuit — the engine must run up to 2 minutes, at specified curb idle speed, before this code will set
41	No distributor reference pulses to the Electronic Control Module (ECM) at specified engine vacuum. This code will store in memory
42	Electronic Spark Timing (EST) bypass circuit or EST circuit grounded or open
44	Lean exhaust indication — the engine must run up to 2 minutes, in closed loop and at part throttle, before this code will set
45	Rich exhaust indication — the engine must run up to 2 minutes, in closed loop and at part throttle, before this code will set
51	Faulty or improperly installed calibration unit (PROM). It takes up to 30 seconds before this code will set
54	Shorted Mixture Control (M/C) solenoid circuit and or faulty Electronic Control Module (ECM)
55	Grounded V/ref (terminal 21), high voltage on oxygen sensor circuit or Electronic Control Module (ECM)

Year — 1984
Model — C & K Models
Engine — 5.0L (305 cid) V8
Engine Code — VIN F

ECM TROUBLE CODES

Code	Explanation
12	No distributor reference pulses to the Electronic Control Module (ECM). This code is not stored in memory and will only flash while the fault is present. Normal code with ignition ON, engine not running
13	Oxygen sensor circuit — the engine must run up to 4 minutes at part throttle, under road load, before this code will set
14	Shorted Coolant Temperature Sensor (CTS) circuit — the engine must run up to 2 minutes before this code will set
15	Open Coolant Temperature Sensor (CTS) circuit — the engine must run up to 5 minutes before this code will set
21	Throttle Position Sensor (TPS) circuit voltage high — open circuit or misadjusted TPS. The engine must run up to 10 seconds, at specified curb idle speed, before this code will set
23	Mixture Control (M/C) solenoid circuit open or grounded
34	Differential pressure (vacuum) sensor circuit — the engine must run up to 2 minutes, at specified curb idle speed, before this code will set
41	No distributor reference pulses to the Electronic Control Module (ECM) at specified engine vacuum. This code will store in memory
42	Electronic Spark Timing (EST) bypass circuit or EST circuit grounded or open
44	Lean exhaust indication — the engine must run up to 2 minutes, in closed loop and at part throttle, before this code will set
45	Rich exhaust indication — the engine must run up to 2 minutes, in closed loop and at part throttle, before this code will set
51	Faulty or improperly installed calibration unit (PROM). It takes up to 30 seconds before this code will set
54	Shorted Mixture Control (M/C) solenoid circuit and or faulty Electronic Control Module (ECM)
55	Grounded V/ref (terminal 21), high voltage on oxygen sensor circuit or Electronic Control Module (ECM)

Year — 1984
Model — C & K Models
Engine — 5.0L (305 cid) V8
Engine Code — VIN H

ECM TROUBLE CODES

Code	Explanation
12	No distributor reference pulses to the Electronic Control Module (ECM). This code is not stored in memory and will only flash while the fault is present. Normal code with ignition ON, engine not running
13	Oxygen sensor circuit — the engine must run up to 4 minutes at part throttle, under road load, before this code will set
14	Shorted Coolant Temperature Sensor (CTS) circuit — the engine must run up to 2 minutes before this code will set
15	Open Coolant Temperature Sensor (CTS) circuit — the engine must run up to 5 minutes before this code will set
21	Throttle Position Sensor (TPS) circuit voltage high — open circuit or misadjusted TPS. The engine must run up to 10 seconds, at specified curb idle speed, before this code will set
23	Mixture Control (M/C) solenoid circuit open or grounded
34	Differential pressure (vacuum) sensor circuit — the engine must run up to 2 minutes, at specified curb idle speed, before this code will set
41	No distributor reference pulses to the Electronic Control Module (ECM) at specified engine vacuum. This code will store in memory
42	Electronic Spark Timing (EST) bypass circuit or EST circuit grounded or open
44	Lean exhaust indication — the engine must run up to 2 minutes, in closed loop and at part throttle, before this code will set
45	Rich exhaust indication — the engine must run up to 2 minutes, in closed loop and at part throttle, before this code will set
51	Faulty or improperly installed calibration unit (PROM). It takes up to 30 seconds before this code will set
54	Shorted Mixture Control (M/C) solenoid circuit and or faulty Electronic Control Module (ECM)
55	Grounded V/ref (terminal 21), high voltage on oxygen sensor circuit or Electronic Control Module (ECM)

Year – 1984
Model – C & K Models
Engine – 5.7L (350 cid) V8
Engine Code – VIN L

ECM TROUBLE CODES

Code	Explanation
12	No distributor reference pulses to the Electronic Control Module (ECM). This code is not stored in memory and will only flash while the fault is present. Normal code with ignition ON, engine not running
13	Oxygen sensor circuit – the engine must run up to 4 minutes at part throttle, under road load, before this code will set
14	Shorted Coolant Temperature Sensor (CTS) circuit – the engine must run up to 2 minutes before this code will set
15	Open Coolant Temperature Sensor (CTS) circuit – the engine must run up to 5 minutes before this code will set
21	Throttle Position Sensor (TPS) circuit voltage high – open circuit or misadjusted TPS. The engine must run up to 25 seconds, at specified curb idle speed, before this code will set
23	Mixture Control (M/C) solenoid circuit open or grounded
34	Differential pressure (vacuum) sensor circuit – the engine must run up to 2 minutes, at specified curb idle speed, before this code will set
41	No distributor reference pulses to the Electronic Control Module (ECM) at specified engine vacuum. This code will store in memory
42	Electronic Spark Timing (EST) bypass circuit or EST circuit grounded or open
44	Lean exhaust indication – the engine must run up to 2 minutes, in closed loop and at part throttle, before this code will set
45	Rich exhaust indication – the engine must run up to 2 minutes, in closed loop and at part throttle, before this code will set
51	Faulty or improperly installed calibration unit (PROM). It takes up to 30 seconds before this code will set
54	Shorted Mixture Control (M/C) solenoid circuit and or faulty Electronic Control Module (ECM)
55	Grounded V/ref (terminal 21), high voltage on oxygen sensor circuit or Electronic Control Module (ECM)

Year — 1984
Model — C, K & P Models
Engine — 5.7L (350 cid) V8
Engine Code — VIN M

ECM TROUBLE CODES

Code	Explanation
12	No distributor reference pulses to the Electronic Control Module (ECM). This code is not stored in memory and will only flash while the fault is present. Normal code with ignition ON, engine not running
13	Oxygen sensor circuit — the engine must run up to 4 minutes at part throttle, under road load, before this code will set
14	Shorted Coolant Temperature Sensor (CTS) circuit — the engine must run up to 2 minutes before this code will set
15	Open Coolant Temperature Sensor (CTS) circuit — the engine must run up to 5 minutes before this code will set
21	Throttle Position Sensor (TPS) circuit voltage high — open circuit of misadjusted TPS. The engine must run up to 10 seconds, at specified curb idle speed, before this code will set
23	Mixture Control (M/C) solenoid circuit open or grounded
34	Differential pressure (vacuum) sensor circuit — the engine must run up to 2 minutes, at specified curb idle speed, before this code will set
41	No distributor reference pulses to the Electronic Control Module (ECM) at specified engine vacuum. This code will store in memory
42	Electronic Spark Timing (EST) bypass circuit or EST circuit grounded or open
44	Lean exhaust indication — the engine must run up to 2 minutes, in closed loop and at part throttle, before this code will set
45	Rich exhaust indication — the engine must run up to 2 minutes, in closed loop and at part throttle, before this code will set
51	Faulty or improperly installed calibration unit (PROM). It takes up to 30 seconds before this code will set
54	Shorted Mixture Control (M/C) solenoid circuit and or faulty Electronic Control Module (ECM)
55	Grounded V/ref (terminal 21), high voltage on oxygen sensor circuit or Electronic Control Module (ECM)

Year – 1984
Model – C & K Models
Engine – 5.7L (350 cid) V8
Engine Code – VIN P

ECM TROUBLE CODES

Code	Explanation
12	No distributor reference pulses to the Electronic Control Module (ECM). This code is not stored in memory and will only flash while the fault is present. Normal code with ignition ON, engine not running
13	Oxygen sensor circuit – the engine must run up to 4 minutes at part throttle, under road load, before this code will set
14	Shorted Coolant Temperature Sensor (CTS) circuit – the engine must run up to 2 minutes before this code will set
15	Open Coolant Temperature Sensor (CTS) circuit – the engine must run up to 5 minutes before this code will set
21	Throttle position sensor (TPS) circuit voltage high – open ciruc uit or misadjusted TPS. The engine must run up to 10 seconds, at specified curb idle speed, before this code will set
23	Mixture Control (M/C) solenoid circuit open or grounded
34	Differential pressure (vacuum) sensor circuit – the engine must run up to 2 minutes, at specified curb idle speed, before this code will set
41	No distributor reference pulses to the Electronic Control Module (ECM) at specified engine vacuum. This code will store in memory
42	Electronic Spark Timing (EST) bypass circuit or EST circuit grounded or open
44	Lean exhaust indication – the engine must run up to 2 minutes, in closed loop and at part throttle, before this code will set
45	Rich exhaust indication – the engine must run up to 2 minutes, in closed loop and at part throttle, before this code will set
51	Faulty or improperly installed calibration unit (PROM). It takes up to 30 seconds before this code will set
54	Shorted Mixture Control (M/C) solenoid circuit and or faulty Electronic Control Module (ECM)
55	Grounded V/ref (terminal 21), high voltage on oxygen sensor circuit or Electronic Control Module (ECM)

Year — 1984
Model — C, K & P Models
Engine — 7.4L (454 cid) V8
Engine Code — VIN W

ECM TROUBLE CODES

Code	Explanation
12	No distributor reference pulses to the Electronic Control Module (ECM). This code is not stored in memory and will only flash while the fault is present. Normal code with ignition ON, engine not running
13	Oxygen sensor circuit — the engine must run up to 4 minutes at part throttle, under road load, before this code will set
14	Shorted Coolant Temperature Sensor (CTS) circuit — the engine must run up to 2 minutes before this code will set
15	Open Coolant Temperature Sensor (CTS) circuit — the engine must run up to 5 minutes before this code will set
21	Throttle Position Sensor (TPS) circuit voltage high — open circuit or misadjusted TPS. The engine must run up to 10 seconds, at specified curb idle speed, before this code will set
23	Mixture Control (M/C) solenoid circuit open or grounded
34	Differential pressure (vacuum) sensor circuit — the engine must run up to 2 minutes, at specified curb idle speed, before this code will set
41	No distributor reference pulses to the Electronic Control Module (ECM) at specified engine vacuum. This code will store in memory
42	Electronic Spark Timing (EST) bypass circuit or EST circuit grounded or open
44	Lean exhaust indication — the engine must run up to 2 minutes, in closed loop and at part throttle, before this code will set
45	Rich exhaust indication — the engine must run up to 2 minutes, in closed loop and at part throttle, before this code will set
51	Faulty or improperly installed calibration unit (PROM). It takes up to 30 seconds before this code will set
54	Shorted Mixture Control (M/C) solenoid circuit and or faulty Electronic Control Module (ECM)
55	Grounded V/ref (terminal 21), high voltage on oxygen sensor circuit or Electronic Control Module (ECM)

Year — 1985
Model — S-10 Models
Engine — 2.5L (151 cid) TBI 4 cyl
Engine Code — VIN E

ECM TROUBLE CODES

Code	Explanation
13	Oxygen sensor circuit
14	Coolant Temperature Sensor (CTS) — voltage low
15	Coolant Temperature Sensor (CTS) — voltage high
21	Throttle Position Sensor (TPS) — voltage high
22	Throttle Position Sensor (TPS) — voltage low
24	Vehicle Speed Sensor (VSS)
33	Manifold Absolute Pressure (MAP) sensor — voltage low
34	Manifold Absolute Pressure (MAP) sensor — voltage high
35	Idle Air Control (IAC)
42	Electronic Spark Timing (EST)
44	Lean exhaust indication
45	Rich exhaust indication
51	PROM
55	Electronic Control Module (ECM)

Year — 1985
Model — S-10 Models
Engine — 2.8L (173 cid) V6
Engine Code — VIN B

ECM TROUBLE CODES

Code	Explanation
12	No distributor reference pulses to the Electronic Control Module (ECM). This code is not stored in memory and will only flash while the fault is present. Normal code with ignition ON, engine not running
13	Oxygen sensor circuit — the engine must run up to 4 minutes at part throttle, under road load, before this code will set
14	Shorted Coolant Temperature Sensor (CTS) circuit — the engine must run 2 minutes before this code will set
15	Open Coolant Temperature Sensor (CTS) circuit — the engine must run 5 minutes before this code will set
21	Throttle Position Sensor (TPS) circuit voltage high — open circuit or misadjusted TPS — the engine must run 10 seconds, at specified curb idle speed, before this code will set
22	Throttle Position Sensor (TPS) circuit voltage low — grounded circuit or misadjusted TPS — the engine must run 20 seconds, at specified curb idle speed, before this code will set
23	Mixture Control (M/C) solenoid circuit open or grounded
24	Vehicle Speed Sensor (VSS) circuit — the vehicle must operate up to 2 minutes at road speed before this code will set
32	Barometric Pressure Sensor (BARO) circuit low
34	Manifold Absolute Pressure (MAP) or vacuum sensor circuit. The engine must run up to 2 minutes at specified curb idle speed, before this code will set
35	Idle Speed Control (ISC) switch circuit shorted — up to 70% Throttle Position Sensor (TPS) for over 5 seconds
41	No distributor reference pulses to the Electronic Control Module (ECM) at specified engine vacuum. This code will store in memory
42	Electronic Spark Timing (EST) bypass circuit or EST circuit grounded or open
43	Electronic Spark Control (ESC) retard signal for too long — causes retard in Electronic Spark Timing (EST) signal
44	Lean exhaust indication — the engine must run 2 minutes, in closed loop and at part throttle, before this code will set
45	Rich exhaust indication — the engine must run 2 minutes, in closed loop and at part throttle, before this code will set
51	Faulty or improperly installed calibration unit (PROM). It takes up to 30 seconds before this code will set
53	Exhaust Gas Recirculation (EGR) valve vacuum sensor has seen improper EGR vacuum
54	Shorted Mixture Control (M/C) solenoid circuit and/or faulty Electronic Control Module (ECM)

Year — 1985
Model — G-Series Vans
Engine — 4.3L (262 cid) V6
Engine Code — VIN N

ECM TROUBLE CODES

Code	Explanation
12	No distributor reference pulses to the Electronic Control Module (ECM). This code is not stored in memory and will only flash while the fault is present. Normal code with ignition ON, engine not running
13	Oxygen sensor circuit — the engine must run up to 4 minutes at part throttle, under road load, before this code will set
14	Shorted Coolant Temperature Sensor (CTS) circuit — the engine must run 2 minutes before this code will set
15	Open Coolant Temperature Sensor (CTS) circuit — the engine must run 5 minutes before this code will set
21	Throttle Position Sensor (TPS) circuit voltage high — open circuit or misadjusted TPS — the engine must run 10 seconds, at specified curb idle speed, before this code will set
22	Throttle Position Sensor (TPS) circuit voltage low — grounded circuit or misadjusted TPS — the engine must run 20 seconds, at specified curb idle speed, before this code will set
23	Mixture Control (M/C) solenoid circuit open or grounded
24	Vehicle Speed Sensor (VSS) circuit — the vehicle must operate up to 2 minutes at road speed before this code will set
32	Barometric Pressure Sensor (BARO) circuit low
34	Manifold Absolute Pressure (MAP) or vacuum sensor circuit. The engine must run up to 2 minutes at specified curb idle speed, before this code will set
35	Idle Speed Control (ISC) switch circuit shorted — up to 70% Throttle Position Sensor (TPS) for over 5 seconds
41	No distributor reference pulses to the Electronic Control Module (ECM) at specified engine vacuum. This code will store in memory
42	Electronic Spark Timing (EST) bypass circuit or EST circuit grounded or open
43	Electronic Spark Control (ESC) retard signal for too long — causes retard in Electronic Spark Timing (EST) signal
44	Lean exhaust indication — the engine must run 2 minutes, in closed loop and at part throttle, before this code will set
45	Rich exhaust indication — the engine must run 2 minutes, in closed loop and at part throttle, before this code will set
51	Faulty or improperly installed calibration unit (PROM). It takes up to 30 seconds before this code will set
53	Exhaust Gas Recirculation (EGR) valve vacuum sensor has seen improper EGR vacuum
54	Shorted Mixture Control (M/C) solenoid circuit and/or faulty Electronic Control Module (ECM)

Year — 1985
Model — G-Series Vans
Engine — 5.0L (305 cid) V8
Engine Code — VIN F

ECM TROUBLE CODES

Code	Explanation
12	No distributor reference pulses to the Electronic Control Module (ECM). This code is not stored in memory and will only flash while the fault is present. Normal code with ignition ON, engine not running
13	Oxygen sensor circuit — the engine must run up to 4 minutes at part throttle, under road load, before this code will set
14	Shorted Coolant Temperature Sensor (CTS) circuit — the engine must run 2 minutes before this code will set
15	Open Coolant Temperature Sensor (CTS) circuit — the engine must run 5 minutes before this code will set
21	Throttle Position Sensor (TPS) circuit voltage high — open circuit or misadjusted TPS — the engine must run 10 seconds, at specified curb idle speed, before this code will set
22	Throttle Position Sensor (TPS) circuit voltage low — grounded circuit or misadjusted TPS — the engine must run 20 seconds, at specified curb idle speed, before this code will set
23	Mixture Control (M/C) solenoid circuit open or grounded
24	Vehicle Speed Sensor (VSS) circuit — the vehicle must operate up to 2 minutes at road speed before this code will set
32	Barometric Pressure Sensor (BARO) circuit low
34	Manifold Absolute Pressure (MAP) or vacuum sensor circuit. The engine must run up to 2 minutes at specified curb idle speed, before this code will set
35	Idle Speed Control (ISC) switch circuit shorted — up to 70% Throttle Position Sensor (TPS) for over 5 seconds
41	No distributor reference pulses to the Electronic Control Module (ECM) at specified engine vacuum. This code will store in memory
42	Electronic Spark Timing (EST) bypass circuit or EST circuit grounded or open
43	Electronic Spark Control (ESC) retard signal for too long — causes retard in Electronic Spark Timing (EST) signal
44	Lean exhaust indication — the engine must run 2 minutes, in closed loop and at part throttle, before this code will set
45	Rich exhaust indication — the engine must run 2 minutes, in closed loop and at part throttle, before this code will set
51	Faulty or improperly installed calibration unit (PROM). It takes up to 30 seconds before this code will set
53	Exhaust Gas Recirculation (EGR) valve vacuum sensor has seen improper EGR vacuum
54	Shorted Mixture Control (M/C) solenoid circuit and/or faulty Electronic Control Module (ECM)

Year – 1985
Model – G-Series Vans
Engine – 5.0L (305 cid) V8
Engine Code – VIN H

ECM TROUBLE CODES

Code	Explanation
12	No distributor reference pulses to the Electronic Control Module (ECM). This code is not stored in memory and will only flash while the fault is present. Normal code with ignition ON, engine not running
13	Oxygen sensor circuit – the engine must run up to 4 minutes at part throttle, under road load, before this code will set
14	Shorted Coolant Temperature Sensor (CTS) circuit – the engine must run 2 minutes before this code will set
15	Open Coolant Temperature Sensor (CTS) circuit – the engine must run 5 minutes before this code will set
21	Throttle Position Sensor (TPS) circuit voltage high – open circuit or misadjusted TPS – the engine must run 10 seconds, at specified curb idle speed, before this code will set
22	Throttle Position Sensor (TPS) circuit voltage low – grounded circuit or misadjusted TPS – the engine must run 20 seconds, at specified curb idle speed, before this code will set
23	Mixture Control (M/C) solenoid circuit open or grounded
24	Vehicle Speed Sensor (VSS) circuit – the vehicle must operate up to 2 minutes at road speed before this code will set
32	Barometric Pressure Sensor (BARO) circuit low
34	Manifold Absolute Pressure (MAP) or vacuum sensor circuit. The engine must run up to 2 minutes at specified curb idle speed, before this code will set
35	Idle Speed Control (ISC) switch circuit shorted – up to 70% Throttle Position Sensor (TPS) for over 5 seconds
41	No distributor reference pulses to the Electronic Control Module (ECM) at specified engine vacuum. This code will store in memory
42	Electronic Spark Timing (EST) bypass circuit or EST circuit grounded or open
43	Electronic Spark Control (ESC) retard signal for too long – causes retard in Electronic Spark Timing (EST) signal
44	Lean exhaust indication – the engine must run 2 minutes, in closed loop and at part throttle, before this code will set
45	Rich exhaust indication – the engine must run 2 minutes, in closed loop and at part throttle, before this code will set
51	Faulty or improperly installed calibration unit (PROM). It takes up to 30 seconds before this code will set
53	Exhaust Gas Recirculation (EGR) valve vacuum sensor has seen improper EGR vacuum
54	Shorted Mixture Control (M/C) solenoid circuit and/or faulty Electronic Control Module (ECM)

Year – 1985
Model – G-Series Vans
Engine – 5.7L (350 cid) V8
Engine Code – VIN L

ECM TROUBLE CODES

Code	Explanation
12	No distributor reference pulses to the Electronic Control Module (ECM). This code is not stored in memory and will only flash while the fault is present. Normal code with ignition ON, engine not running
13	Oxygen sensor circuit – the engine must run up to 4 minutes at part throttle, under road load, before this code will set
14	Shorted Coolant Temperature Sensor (CTS) circuit – the engine must run 2 minutes before this code will set
15	Open Coolant Temperature Sensor (CTS) circuit – the engine must run 5 minutes before this code will set
21	Throttle Position Sensor (TPS) circuit voltage high – open circuit or misadjusted TPS – the engine must run 10 seconds, at specified curb idle speed, before this code will set
22	Throttle Position Sensor (TPS) circuit voltage low – grounded circuit or misadjusted TPS – the engine must run 20 seconds, at specified curb idle speed, before this code will set
23	Mixture Control (M/C) solenoid circuit open or grounded
24	Vehicle Speed Sensor (VSS) circuit – the vehicle must operate up to 2 minutes at road speed before this code will set
32	Barometric Pressure Sensor (BARO) circuit low
34	Manifold Absolute Pressure (MAP) or vacuum sensor circuit. The engine must run up to 2 minutes at specified curb idle speed, before this code will set
35	Idle Speed Control (ISC) switch circuit shorted – up to 70% Throttle Position Sensor (TPS) for over 5 seconds
41	No distributor reference pulses to the Electronic Control Module (ECM) at specified engine vacuum. This code will store in memory
42	Electronic Spark Timing (EST) bypass circuit or EST circuit grounded or open
43	Electronic Spark Control (ESC) retard signal for too long – causes retard in Electronic Spark Timing (EST) signal
44	Lean exhaust indication – the engine must run 2 minutes, in closed loop and at part throttle, before this code will set
45	Rich exhaust indication – the engine must run 2 minutes, in closed loop and at part throttle, before this code will set
51	Faulty or improperly installed calibration unit (PROM). It takes up to 30 seconds before this code will set
53	Exhaust Gas Recirculation (EGR) valve vacuum sensor has seen improper EGR vacuum
54	Shorted Mixture Control (M/C) solenoid circuit and/or faulty Electronic Control Module (ECM)

Year – 1985
Model – G-Series Vans
Engine – 5.7L (350 cid) V8
Engine Code – VIN M

ECM TROUBLE CODES

Code	Explanation
12	No distributor reference pulses to the Electronic Control Module (ECM). This code is not stored in memory and will only flash while the fault is present. Normal code with ignition ON, engine not running
13	Oxygen sensor circuit – the engine must run up to 4 minutes at part throttle, under road load, before this code will set
14	Shorted Coolant Temperature Sensor (CTS) circuit – the engine must run 2 minutes before this code will set
15	Open Coolant Temperature Sensor (CTS) circuit – the engine must run 5 minutes before this code will set
21	Throttle Position Sensor (TPS) circuit voltage high – open circuit or misadjusted TPS – the engine must run 10 seconds, at specified curb idle speed, before this code will set
22	Throttle Position Sensor (TPS) circuit voltage low – grounded circuit or misadjusted TPS – the engine must run 20 seconds, at specified curb idle speed, before this code will set
23	Mixture Control (M/C) solenoid circuit open or grounded
24	Vehicle Speed Sensor (VSS) circuit – the vehicle must operate up to 2 minutes at road speed before this code will set
32	Barometric Pressure Sensor (BARO) circuit low
34	Manifold Absolute Pressure (MAP) or vacuum sensor circuit. The engine must run up to 2 minutes at specified curb idle speed, before this code will set
35	Idle Speed Control (ISC) switch circuit shorted – up to 70% Throttle Position Sensor (TPS) for over 5 seconds
41	No distributor reference pulses to the Electronic Control Module (ECM) at specified engine vacuum. This code will store in memory
42	Electronic Spark Timing (EST) bypass circuit or EST circuit grounded or open
43	Electronic Spark Control (ESC) retard signal for too long – causes retard in Electronic Spark Timing (EST) signal
44	Lean exhaust indication – the engine must run 2 minutes, in closed loop and at part throttle, before this code will set
45	Rich exhaust indication – the engine must run 2 minutes, in closed loop and at part throttle, before this code will set
51	Faulty or improperly installed calibration unit (PROM). It takes up to 30 seconds before this code will set
53	Exhaust Gas Recirculation (EGR) valve vacuum sensor has seen improper EGR vacuum
54	Shorted Mixture Control (M/C) solenoid circuit and/or faulty Electronic Control Module (ECM)

Year – 1985
Model – C & K Models
Engine – 4.3L (262 cid) V6
Engine Code – VIN N

ECM TROUBLE CODES

Code	Explanation
12	No distributor reference pulses to the Electronic Control Module (ECM). This code is not stored in memory and will only flash while the fault is present. Normal code with ignition ON, engine not running
13	Oxygen sensor circuit – the engine must run up to 4 minutes at part throttle, under road load, before this code will set
14	Shorted Coolant Temperature Sensor (CTS) circuit – the engine must run 2 minutes before this code will set
15	Open Coolant Temperature Sensor (CTS) circuit – the engine must run 5 minutes before this code will set
21	Throttle Position Sensor (TPS) circuit voltage high – open circuit or misadjusted TPS – the engine must run 10 seconds, at specified curb idle speed, before this code will set
22	Throttle Position Sensor (TPS) circuit voltage low – grounded circuit or misadjusted TPS – the engine must run 20 seconds, at specified curb idle speed, before this code will set
23	Mixture Control (M/C) solenoid circuit open or grounded
24	Vehicle Speed Sensor (VSS) circuit – the vehicle must operate up to 2 minutes at road speed before this code will set
32	Barometric Pressure Sensor (BARO) circuit low
34	Manifold Absolute Pressure (MAP) or vacuum sensor circuit. The engine must run up to 2 minutes at specified curb idle speed, before this code will set
35	Idle Speed Control (ISC) switch circuit shorted – up to 70% Throttle Position Sensor (TPS) for over 5 seconds
41	No distributor reference pulses to the Electronic Control Module (ECM) at specified engine vacuum. This code will store in memory
42	Electronic Spark Timing (EST) bypass circuit or EST circuit grounded or open
43	Electronic Spark Control (ESC) retard signal for too long – causes retard in Electronic Spark Timing (EST) signal
44	Lean exhaust indication – the engine must run 2 minutes, in closed loop and at part throttle, before this code will set
45	Rich exhaust indication – the engine must run 2 minutes, in closed loop and at part throttle, before this code will set
51	Faulty or improperly installed calibration unit (PROM). It takes up to 30 seconds before this code will set
53	Exhaust Gas Recirculation (EGR) valve vacuum sensor has seen improper EGR vacuum
54	Shorted Mixture Control (M/C) solenoid circuit and/or faulty Electronic Control Module (ECM)

Year—1985
Model—C, K & P Models
Engine—4.8L (292 cid) V6
Engine Code—VIN T

ECM TROUBLE CODES

Code	Explanation
12	No distributor reference pulses to the Electronic Control Module (ECM). This code is not stored in memory and will only flash while the fault is present. Normal code with ignition ON, engine not running
13	Oxygen sensor circuit—the engine must run up to 4 minutes at part throttle, under road load, before this code will set
14	Shorted Coolant Temperature Sensor (CTS) circuit—the engine must run 2 minutes before this code will set
15	Open Coolant Temperature Sensor (CTS) circuit—the engine must run 5 minutes before this code will set
21	Throttle Position Sensor (TPS) circuit voltage high—open circuit or misadjusted TPS—the engine must run 10 seconds, at specified curb idle speed, before this code will set
22	Throttle Position Sensor (TPS) circuit voltage low—grounded circuit or misadjusted TPS—the engine must run 20 seconds, at specified curb idle speed, before this code will set
23	Mixture Control (M/C) solenoid circuit open or grounded
24	Vehicle Speed Sensor (VSS) circuit—the vehicle must operate up to 2 minutes at road speed before this code will set
32	Barometric Pressure Sensor (BARO) circuit low
34	Manifold Absolute Pressure (MAP) or vacuum sensor circuit. The engine must run up to 2 minutes at specified curb idle speed, before this code will set
35	Idle Speed Control (ISC) switch circuit shorted—up to 70% Throttle Position Sensor (TPS) for over 5 seconds
41	No distributor reference pulses to the Electronic Control Module (ECM) at specified engine vacuum. This code will store in memory
42	Electronic Spark Timing (EST) bypass circuit or EST circuit grounded or open
43	Electronic Spark Control (ESC) retard signal for too long—causes retard in Electronic Spark Timing (EST) signal
44	Lean exhaust indication—the engine must run 2 minutes, in closed loop and at part throttle, before this code will set
45	Rich exhaust indication—the engine must run 2 minutes, in closed loop and at part throttle, before this code will set
51	Faulty or improperly installed calibration unit (PROM). It takes up to 30 seconds before this code will set
53	Exhaust Gas Recirculation (EGR) valve vacuum sensor has seen improper EGR vacuum
54	Shorted Mixture Control (M/C) solenoid circuit and/or faulty Electronic Control Module (ECM)

Year – 1985
Model – C & K Models
Engine – 5.0L (305 cid) V8
Engine Code – VIN H

ECM TROUBLE CODES

Code	Explanation
12	No distributor reference pulses to the Electronic Control Module (ECM). This code is not stored in memory and will only flash while the fault is present. Normal code with ignition ON, engine not running
13	Oxygen sensor circuit – the engine must run up to 4 minutes at part throttle, under road load, before this code will set
14	Shorted Coolant Temperature Sensor (CTS) circuit – the engine must run 2 minutes before this code will set
15	Open Coolant Temperature Sensor (CTS) circuit – the engine must run 5 minutes before this code will set
21	Throttle Position Sensor (TPS) circuit voltage high – open circuit or misadjusted TPS – the engine must run 10 seconds, at specified curb idle speed, before this code will set
22	Throttle Position Sensor (TPS) circuit voltage low – grounded circuit or misadjusted TPS – the engine must run 20 seconds, at specified curb idle speed, before this code will set
23	Mixture Control (M/C) solenoid circuit open or grounded
24	Vehicle Speed Sensor (VSS) circuit – the vehicle must operate up to 2 minutes at road speed before this code will set
32	Barometric Pressure Sensor (BARO) circuit low
34	Manifold Absolute Pressure (MAP) or vacuum sensor circuit. The engine must run up to 2 minutes at specified curb idle speed, before this code will set
35	Idle Speed Control (ISC) switch circuit shorted – up to 70% Throttle Position Sensor (TPS) for over 5 seconds
41	No distributor reference pulses to the Electronic Control Module (ECM) at specified engine vacuum. This code will store in memory
42	Electronic Spark Timing (EST) bypass circuit or EST circuit grounded or open
43	Electronic Spark Control (ESC) retard signal for too long – causes retard in Electronic Spark Timing (EST) signal
44	Lean exhaust indication – the engine must run 2 minutes, in closed loop and at part throttle, before this code will set
45	Rich exhaust indication – the engine must run 2 minutes, in closed loop and at part throttle, before this code will set
51	Faulty or improperly installed calibration unit (PROM). It takes up to 30 seconds before this code will set
53	Exhaust Gas Recirculation (EGR) valve vacuum sensor has seen improper EGR vacuum
54	Shorted Mixture Control (M/C) solenoid circuit and/or faulty Electronic Control Module (ECM)

GENERAL MOTORS CORPORATION
DIAGNOSTIC CODE DATA

Year — 1985
Model — C & K Models
Engine — 5.0L (305 cid) V8
Engine Code — VIN F

ECM TROUBLE CODES

Code	Explanation
12	No distributor reference pulses to the Electronic Control Module (ECM). This code is not stored in memory and will only flash while the fault is present. Normal code with ignition ON, engine not running
13	Oxygen sensor circuit — the engine must run up to 4 minutes at part throttle, under road load, before this code will set
14	Shorted Coolant Temperature Sensor (CTS) circuit — the engine must run 2 minutes before this code will set
15	Open Coolant Temperature Sensor (CTS) circuit — the engine must run 5 minutes before this code will set
21	Throttle Position Sensor (TPS) circuit voltage high — open circuit or misadjusted TPS — the engine must run 10 seconds, at specified curb idle speed, before this code will set
22	Throttle Position Sensor (TPS) circuit voltage low — grounded circuit or misadjusted TPS — the engine must run 20 seconds, at specified curb idle speed, before this code will set
23	Mixture Control (M/C) solenoid circuit open or grounded
24	Vehicle Speed Sensor (VSS) circuit — the vehicle must operate up to 2 minutes at road speed before this code will set
32	Barometric Pressure Sensor (BARO) circuit low
34	Manifold Absolute Pressure (MAP) or vacuum sensor circuit. The engine must run up to 2 minutes at specified curb idle speed, before this code will set
35	Idle Speed Control (ISC) switch circuit shorted — up to 70% Throttle Position Sensor (TPS) for over 5 seconds
41	No distributor reference pulses to the Electronic Control Module (ECM) at specified engine vacuum. This code will store in memory
42	Electronic Spark Timing (EST) bypass circuit or EST circuit grounded or open
43	Electronic Spark Control (ESC) retard signal for too long — causes retard in Electronic Spark Timing (EST) signal
44	Lean exhaust indication — the engine must run 2 minutes, in closed loop and at part throttle, before this code will set
45	Rich exhaust indication — the engine must run 2 minutes, in closed loop and at part throttle, before this code will set
51	Faulty or improperly installed calibration unit (PROM). It takes up to 30 seconds before this code will set
53	Exhaust Gas Recirculation (EGR) valve vacuum sensor has seen improper EGR vacuum
54	Shorted Mixture Control (M/C) solenoid circuit and/or faulty Electronic Control Module (ECM)

Year — 1985
Model — C & K Models
Engine — 5.7L (350 cid) V8
Engine Code — VIN L

ECM TROUBLE CODES

Code	Explanation
12	No distributor reference pulses to the Electronic Control Module (ECM). This code is not stored in memory and will only flash while the fault is present. Normal code with ignition ON, engine not running
13	Oxygen sensor circuit — the engine must run up to 4 minutes at part throttle, under road load, before this code will set
14	Shorted Coolant Temperature Sensor (CTS) circuit — the engine must run 2 minutes before this code will set
15	Open Coolant Temperature Sensor (CTS) circuit — the engine must run 5 minutes before this code will set
21	Throttle Position Sensor (TPS) circuit voltage high — open circuit or misadjusted TPS — the engine must run 10 seconds, at specified curb idle speed, before this code will set
22	Throttle Position Sensor (TPS) circuit voltage low — grounded circuit or misadjusted TPS — the engine must run 20 seconds, at specified curb idle speed, before this code will set
23	Mixture Control (M/C) solenoid circuit open or grounded
24	Vehicle Speed Sensor (VSS) circuit — the vehicle must operate up to 2 minutes at road speed before this code will set
32	Barometric Pressure Sensor (BARO) circuit low
34	Manifold Absolute Pressure (MAP) or vacuum sensor circuit. The engine must run up to 2 minutes at specified curb idle speed, before this code will set
35	Idle Speed Control (ISC) switch circuit shorted — up to 70% Throttle Position Sensor (TPS) for over 5 seconds
41	No distributor reference pulses to the Electronic Control Module (ECM) at specified engine vacuum. This code will store in memory
42	Electronic Spark Timing (EST) bypass circuit or EST circuit grounded or open
43	Electronic Spark Control (ESC) retard signal for too long — causes retard in Electronic Spark Timing (EST) signal
44	Lean exhaust indication — the engine must run 2 minutes, in closed loop and at part throttle, before this code will set
45	Rich exhaust indication — the engine must run 2 minutes, in closed loop and at part throttle, before this code will set
51	Faulty or improperly installed calibration unit (PROM). It takes up to 30 seconds before this code will set
53	Exhaust Gas Recirculation (EGR) valve vacuum sensor has seen improper EGR vacuum
54	Shorted Mixture Control (M/C) solenoid circuit and/or faulty Electronic Control Module (ECM)

Year—1985
Model—C, K & P Models
Engine—5.7L (350 cid) V8
Engine Code—VIN M

ECM TROUBLE CODES

Code	Explanation
12	No distributor reference pulses to the Electronic Control Module (ECM). This code is not stored in memory and will only flash while the fault is present. Normal code with ignition ON, engine not running
13	Oxygen sensor circuit—the engine must run up to 4 minutes at part throttle, under road load, before this code will set
14	Shorted Coolant Temperature Sensor (CTS) circuit—the engine must run 2 minutes before this code will set
15	Open Coolant Temperature Sensor (CTS) circuit—the engine must run 5 minutes before this code will set
21	Throttle Position Sensor (TPS) circuit voltage high—open circuit or misadjusted TPS—the engine must run 10 seconds, at specified curb idle speed, before this code will set
22	Throttle Position Sensor (TPS) circuit voltage low—grounded circuit or misadjusted TPS—the engine must run 20 seconds, at specified curb idle speed, before this code will set
23	Mixture Control (M/C) solenoid circuit open or grounded
24	Vehicle Speed Sensor (VSS) circuit—the vehicle must operate up to 2 minutes at road speed before this code will set
32	Barometric Pressure Sensor (BARO) circuit low
34	Manifold Absolute Pressure (MAP) or vacuum sensor circuit. The engine must run up to 2 minutes at specified curb idle speed, before this code will set
35	Idle Speed Control (ISC) switch circuit shorted—up to 70% Throttle Position Sensor (TPS) for over 5 seconds
41	No distributor reference pulses to the Electronic Control Module (ECM) at specified engine vacuum. This code will store in memory
42	Electronic Spark Timing (EST) bypass circuit or EST circuit grounded or open
43	Electronic Spark Control (ESC) retard signal for too long—causes retard in Electronic Spark Timing (EST) signal
44	Lean exhaust indication—the engine must run 2 minutes, in closed loop and at part throttle, before this code will set
45	Rich exhaust indication—the engine must run 2 minutes, in closed loop and at part throttle, before this code will set
51	Faulty or improperly installed calibration unit (PROM). It takes up to 30 seconds before this code will set
53	Exhaust Gas Recirculation (EGR) valve vacuum sensor has seen improper EGR vacuum
54	Shorted Mixture Control (M/C) solenoid circuit and/or faulty Electronic Control Module (ECM)

Year—1985
Model—C, K & P Models
Engine—7.4L (454 cid) V8
Engine Code—VIN W

ECM TROUBLE CODES

Code	Explanation
12	No distributor reference pulses to the Electronic Control Module (ECM). This code is not stored in memory and will only flash while the fault is present. Normal code with ignition ON, engine not running
13	Oxygen sensor circuit—the engine must run up to 4 minutes at part throttle, under road load, before this code will set
14	Shorted Coolant Temperature Sensor (CTS) circuit—the engine must run 2 minutes before this code will set
15	Open Coolant Temperature Sensor (CTS) circuit—the engine must run 5 minutes before this code will set
21	Throttle Position Sensor (TPS) circuit voltage high—open circuit or misadjusted TPS—the engine must run 10 seconds, at specified curb idle speed, before this code will set
22	Throttle Position Sensor (TPS) circuit voltage low—grounded circuit or misadjusted TPS—the engine must run 20 seconds, at specified curb idle speed, before this code will set
23	Mixture Control (M/C) solenoid circuit open or grounded
24	Vehicle Speed Sensor (VSS) circuit—the vehicle must operate up to 2 minutes at road speed before this code will set
32	Barometric Pressure Sensor (BARO) circuit low
34	Manifold Absolute Pressure (MAP) or vacuum sensor circuit. The engine must run up to 2 minutes at specified curb idle speed, before this code will set
35	Idle Speed Control (ISC) switch circuit shorted—up to 70% Throttle Position Sensor (TPS) for over 5 seconds
41	No distributor reference pulses to the Electronic Control Module (ECM) at specified engine vacuum. This code will store in memory
42	Electronic Spark Timing (EST) bypass circuit or EST circuit grounded or open
43	Electronic Spark Control (ESC) retard signal for too long—causes retard in Electronic Spark Timing (EST) signal
44	Lean exhaust indication—the engine must run 2 minutes, in closed loop and at part throttle, before this code will set
45	Rich exhaust indication—the engine must run 2 minutes, in closed loop and at part throttle, before this code will set
51	Faulty or improperly installed calibration unit (PROM). It takes up to 30 seconds before this code will set
53	Exhaust Gas Recirculation (EGR) valve vacuum sensor has seen improper EGR vacuum
54	Shorted Mixture Control (M/C) solenoid circuit and/or faulty Electronic Control Module (ECM)

Year — 1985
Model — M-Series Vans (Astro)
Engine — 2.5L (151 cid) TBI 4 cyl
Engine Code — VIN E

ECM TROUBLE CODES

Code	Explanation
13	Oxygen sensor circuit
14	Coolant Temperature Sensor (CTS) — voltage low
15	Coolant Temperature Sensor (CTS) — voltage high
21	Throttle Position Sensor (TPS) — voltage high
22	Throttle Position Sensor (TPS) — voltage low
24	Vehicle Speed Sensor (VSS)
33	Manifold Absolute Pressure (MAP) sensor — voltage low
34	Manifold Absolute Pressure (MAP) sensor — voltage high
35	Idle Air Control (IAC)
42	Electronic Spark Timing (EST)
44	Lean exhaust indication
45	Rich exhaust indication
51	PROM
55	Electronic Control Module (ECM)

Year — 1985
Model — M-Series Vans (Astro)
Engine — 4.3L (262 cid) V6
Engine Code — VIN N

ECM TROUBLE CODES

Code	Explanation
12	No distributor reference pulses to the Electronic Control Module (ECM). This code is not stored in memory and will only flash while the fault is present. Normal code with ignition ON, engine not running
13	Oxygen sensor circuit — the engine must run up to 4 minutes at part throttle, under road load, before this code will set
14	Shorted Coolant Temperature Sensor (CTS) circuit — the engine must run 2 minutes before this code will set
15	Open Coolant Temperature Sensor (CTS) circuit — the engine must run 5 minutes before this code will set
21	Throttle Position Sensor (TPS) circuit voltage high — open circuit or misadjusted TPS — the engine must run 10 seconds, at specified curb idle speed, before this code will set
22	Throttle Position Sensor (TPS) circuit voltage low — grounded circuit or misadjusted TPS — the engine must run 20 seconds, at specified curb idle speed, before this code will set
23	Mixture Control (M/C) solenoid circuit open or grounded
24	Vehicle Speed Sensor (VSS) circuit — the vehicle must operate up to 2 minutes at road speed before this code will set
32	Barometric Pressure Sensor (BARO) circuit low
34	Manifold Absolute Pressure (MAP) or vacuum sensor circuit. The engine must run up to 2 minutes at specified curb idle speed, before this code will set
35	Idle Speed Control (ISC) switch circuit shorted — up to 70% Throttle Position Sensor (TPS) for over 5 seconds
41	No distributor reference pulses to the Electronic Control Module (ECM) at specified engine vacuum. This code will store in memory
42	Electronic Spark Timing (EST) bypass circuit or EST circuit grounded or open
43	Electronic Spark Control (ESC) retard signal for too long — causes retard in Electronic Spark Timing (EST) signal
44	Lean exhaust indication — the engine must run 2 minutes, in closed loop and at part throttle, before this code will set
45	Rich exhaust indication — the engine must run 2 minutes, in closed loop and at part throttle, before this code will set
51	Faulty or improperly installed calibration unit (PROM). It takes up to 30 seconds before this code will set
53	Exhaust Gas Recirculation (EGR) valve vacuum sensor has seen improper EGR vacuum
54	Shorted Mixture Control (M/C) solenoid circuit and/or faulty Electronic Control Module (ECM)

Year — 1985
Model — M-Series Vans (Astro)
Engine — 4.3L (262 cid) V6
Engine Code — VIN N

ECM TROUBLE CODES

Code	Explanation
12	No distributor reference pulses to the Electronic Control Module (ECM). This code is not stored in memory and will only flash while the fault is present. Normal code with ignition ON, engine not running
13	Oxygen sensor circuit — the engine must run up to 4 minutes at part throttle, under road load, before this code will set
14	Shorted Coolant Temperature Sensor (CTS) circuit — the engine must run 2 minutes before this code will set
15	Open Coolant Temperature Sensor (CTS) circuit — the engine must run 5 minutes before this code will set
21	Throttle Position Sensor (TPS) circuit voltage high — open circuit or misadjusted TPS — the engine must run 10 seconds, at specified curb idle speed, before this code will set
22	Throttle Position Sensor (TPS) circuit voltage low — grounded circuit or misadjusted TPS — the engine must run 20 seconds, at specified curb idle speed, before this code will set
23	Mixture Control (M/C) solenoid circuit open or grounded
24	Vehicle Speed Sensor (VSS) circuit — the vehicle must operate up to 2 minutes at road speed before this code will set
32	Barometric Pressure Sensor (BARO) circuit low
34	Manifold Absolute Pressure (MAP) or vacuum sensor circuit. The engine must run up to 2 minutes at specified curb idle speed, before this code will set
35	Idle Speed Control (ISC) switch circuit shorted — up to 70% Throttle Position Sensor (TPS) for over 5 seconds
41	No distributor reference pulses to the Electronic Control Module (ECM) at specified engine vacuum. This code will store in memory
42	Electronic Spark Timing (EST) bypass circuit or EST circuit grounded or open
43	Electronic Spark Control (ESC) retard signal for too long — causes retard in Electronic Spark Timing (EST) signal
44	Lean exhaust indication — the engine must run 2 minutes, in closed loop and at part throttle, before this code will set
45	Rich exhaust indication — the engine must run 2 minutes, in closed loop and at part throttle, before this code will set
51	Faulty or improperly installed calibration unit (PROM). It takes up to 30 seconds before this code will set
53	Exhaust Gas Recirculation (EGR) valve vacuum sensor has seen improper EGR vacuum
54	Shorted Mixture Control (M/C) solenoid circuit and/or faulty Electronic Control Module (ECM)

Year – 1985
Model – El Camino
Engine – 4.3L (262 cid) EFI V6
Engine Code – VIN Z

ECM TROUBLE CODES

Code	Explanation
13	Oxygen sensor circuit
14	Coolant Temperature Sensor (CTS) – low
15	Coolant Temperature Sensor (CTS) – high
21	Throttle Position Sensor (TPS) – high
22	Throttle Position Sensor (TPS) – low
24	Vehicle Speed Sensor (VSS)
32	Exhaust Gas Recirculation (EGR) system failure
33	Manifold Absolute Pressure (MAP) sensor – high
34	Manifold Absolute Pressure (MAP) sensor – low
42	Electronic Spark Timing (EST)
43	Electronic Spark Control (ESC)
44	Lean exhaust
45	Rich exhaust
51	PROM
52	Calpak missing
55	Electronic Control Module (ECM)

Year—1985
Model—El Camino
Engine—5.0L (305 cid) V8
Engine Code—VIN H

ECM TROUBLE CODES

Code	Explanation
12	No distributor reference pulses to the Electronic Control Module (ECM). This code is not stored in memory and will only flash while the fault is present. Normal code with ignition ON, engine not running
13	Oxygen sensor circuit—the engine must run up to 4 minutes at part throttle, under road load, before this code will set
14	Shorted Coolant Temperature Sensor (CTS) circuit—the engine must run 2 minutes before this code will set
15	Open Coolant Temperature Sensor (CTS) circuit—the engine must run 5 minutes before this code will set
21	Throttle Position Sensor (TPS) circuit voltage high—open circuit or misadjusted TPS—the engine must run 10 seconds, at specified curb idle speed, before this code will set
22	Throttle Position Sensor (TPS) circuit voltage low—grounded circuit or misadjusted TPS—engine must run 20 seconds at specified curb idle speed, to set code
23	Mixture Control (M/C) solenoid circuit open or grounded
24	Vehicle Speed Sensor (VSS) circuit—the vehicle must operate up to 2 minutes at road speed, before this code will set
32	Barometric Pressure Sensor (BARO) circuit low
34	Manifold Absolute Pressure (MAP) or vacuum sensor circuit. The engine must run up to 2 minutes at specified curb idle speed, before this code will set
35	Idle Speed Control (ISC) switch circuit shorted—up to 70% Throttle Position Sensor (TPS) for over 5 seconds
41	No distributor reference pulses to the Electronic Control Module (ECM) at specified engine vacuum. This code will store in memory
42	Electronic Spark Timing (EST) bypass circuit or EST circuit grounded or open
43	Electronic Spark Control (ESC) retard signal for too long a time—causes retard in Electronic Spark Timing (EST) signal
44	Lean exhaust indication—the engine must run 2 minutes, in closed loop and at part throttle, before this code will set
45	Rich exhaust indication—the engine must run 2 minutes, in closed loop and at part throttle, before this code will set
51	Faulty or improperly installed calibration unit (PROM). It takes up to 30 seconds before this code will set
53	Exhaust Gas Recirculation (EGR) valve vacuum sensor has seen improper EGR vacuum
54	Shorted Mixture Control (M/C) solenoid circuit and/or faulty Electronic Control Module (ECM)

Year — 1986
Model — S-10 Series
Engine — 2.5L (151 cid) TBI 4 cyl
Engine Code — VIN E

ECM TROUBLE CODES

Code	Explanation
13	Oxygen sensor circuit — open oxygen sensor — indicates that the oxygen sensor circuit or sensor was open for one minute while off idle
14	Coolant Temperature Sensor (CTS) — low signal voltage — sets if the sensor or signal line becomes grounded for 3 seconds
15	Coolant Temperature Sensor (CTS) — high signal voltage — sets if the sensor, connections or wires open for 3 seconds
21	Throttle Position Sensor (TPS) — high signal voltage — TPS voltage greater than 2.5V for 3 seconds with less than 1200 rpm
22	Throttle Position Sensor (TPS) — low signal voltage — short to ground or open signal circuit will set in 3 seconds
24	Vehicle Speed Sensor (VSS) circuit — no VSS — no vehicle speed present during a road load deceleration
32	Exhaust Gas Recirculation (EGR) — diagnostic switch shorted to ground on start up or switch not closed after the Electronic Control Module (ECM) has commanded EGR for a specified period of time
33	Manifold Absolute Pressure (MAP) sensor — high signal — MAP sensor output too high for 5 seconds or an open signal circuit
34	Manifold Absolute Pressure (MAP) sensor — low or no signal — low or no output from sensor with engine running
35	Idle Air Control (IAC) — IAC error
42	Electronic Spark Timing (EST) — Electronic Control Module (ECM) has seen an open or grounded EST or bypass circuit
43	Electronic Spark Control (ESC) — signal to the Electronic Control Module (ECM) has remained low for too long or the system has failed a functional check
44	Lean exhaust indication — sets if oxygen sensor voltage remains below 0.2V for about 20 seconds
45	Rich exhaust indication — sets if oxygen sensor voltage remains above .7 volts for about 1 minute
51	Faulty PROM or Electronic Control Module (ECM)
53	Fuel Calpak missing or faulty
54	Low fuel pump voltage — sets when the fuel pump voltage is less than 2V when reference pulses are being received
55	Faulty Electronic Control Module (ECM)

Year – 1986
Model – S-10 Series
Engine – 2.8L (173 cid) TBI V6
Engine Code – VIN R

ECM TROUBLE CODES

Code	Explanation
13	Oxygen sensor circuit – open oxygen sensor – indicates that the oxygen sensor circuit or sensor was open for one minute while off idle
14	Coolant Temperature Sensor (CTS) – low signal voltage – sets if the sensor or signal line becomes grounded for 3 seconds
15	Coolant Temperature Sensor (CTS) – high signal voltage – sets if the sensor, connections or wires open for 3 seconds
21	Throttle Position Sensor (TPS) – high signal voltage – TPS voltage greater than 2.5V for 3 seconds with less than 1200 rpm
22	Throttle Position Sensor (TPS) – low signal voltage – shorted to ground or open signal circuit will set in 3 seconds
24	Vehicle Speed Sensor (VSS) circuit – no VSS – no vehicle speed present during a road load deceleration
32	Exhaust Gas Recirculation (EGR) – diagnostic switch shorted to ground on start up or switch not closed after the Electronic Control Module (ECM) has commanded EGR for a specified period of time
33	Manifold Absolute Pressure (MAP) sensor – high signal – MAP sensor output too high for 5 seconds or an open signal circuit
34	Manifold Absolute Pressure (MAP) sensor – low or no signal – low or no output from sensor with engine running
35	Idle Air Control (IAC) – IAC error
42	Electronic Spark Timing (EST) – Electronic Control Module (ECM) has seen an open or grounded EST or bypass circuit
43	Electronic Spark Control (ESC) – signal to the Electronic Control Module (ECM) has remained low for too long or the system has failed a functional check
44	Lean exhaust indication – sets if oxygen sensor voltage remains below 0.2V for about 20 seconds
45	Rich exhaust indication – sets if oxygen sensor voltage remains above 0.7V for about 1 minute
51	Faulty PROM or Electronic Control Module (ECM)
53	Fuel Calpak missing or faulty
54	Low fuel pump voltage – sets when the fuel pump voltage is less than 2V when reference pulses are being received
55	Faulty Electronic Control Module (ECM)

Year — 1986
Model — G-Series Vans
Engine — 4.3L (262 cid) V6
Engine Code — VIN N

ECM TROUBLE CODES

Code	Explanation
12	No distributor reference signal to the Electronic Control Module (ECM). This code is not stored in memory and will only flash while the fault is present. Normal code with ignition ON, engine not running
13	Oxygen sensor circuit — the engine must run up to 4 minutes at part throttle, under road load, before this code will set
14	Shorted Coolant Temperature Sensor (CTS) circuit — the engine must run 2 minutes before this code will set
15	Open Coolant Temperature Sensor (CTS) circuit — the engine must run 5 minutes before this code will set
21	Throttle Position Sensor (TPS) circuit voltage high — open circuit or misadjusted TPS — the engine must run 10 seconds, at specified curb idle speed, before this code will set
23	Mixture Control (M/C) solenoid circuit open or grounded
34	Differential pressure (vacuum) sensor circuit — the engine must run up to 2 minutes, at specified curb idle, before this code will set
41	No distributor reference signal to the Electronic Control Module (ECM) at specified engine vacuum. This code will store in memory
42	Electronic Spark Timing (EST) bypass circuit or EST circuit grounded or open
43	Electronic Spark Control (ESC) retard signal for too long — causes retard in Electronic Spark Timing (EST) signal
44	Lean exhaust indication — the engine must run 2 minutes, in closed loop and at part throttle, before this code will set
45	Rich exhaust indication — the engine must run 2 minutes, in closed loop and at part throttle, before this code will set
51	Faulty or improperly installed calibration unit (PROM). It takes up to 30 seconds before this code will set
54	Mixture Control (M/C) solenoid voltage high at Electronic Control Module (ECM) as a result of a shorted M/C solenoid circuit and/or faulty Electronic Control Module (ECM)

Year — 1986
Model — G-Series Vans
Engine — 4.8L (292 cid) 6 cyl
Engine Code — VIN T

ECM TROUBLE CODES

Code	Explanation
12	No distributor reference signal to the Electronic Control Module (ECM). This code is not stored in memory and will only flash while the fault is present. Normal code with ignition ON, engine not running
13	Oxygen sensor circuit — the engine must run up to 4 minutes at part throttle, under road load, before this code will set
14	Shorted Coolant Temperature Sensor (CTS) circuit — the engine must run 2 minutes before this code will set
15	Open Coolant Temperature Sensor (CTS) circuit — the engine must run 5 minutes before this code will set
21	Throttle Position Sensor (TPS) circuit voltage high — open circuit or misadjusted TPS — the engine must run 10 seconds, at specified curb idle speed, before this code will set
23	Mixture Control (M/C) solenoid circuit open or grounded
34	Differential pressure (vacuum) sensor circuit — the engine must run up to 2 minutes, at specified curb idle, before this code will set
41	No distributor reference signal to the Electronic Control Module (ECM) at specified engine vacuum. This code will store in memory
42	Electronic Spark Timing (EST) bypass circuit or EST circuit grounded or open
43	Electronic Spark Control (ESC) retard signal for too long — causes retard in Electronic Spark Timing (EST) signal
44	Lean exhaust indication — the engine must run 2 minutes, in closed loop and at part throttle, before this code will set
45	Rich exhaust indication — the engine must run 2 minutes, in closed loop and at part throttle, before this code will set
51	Faulty or improperly installed calibration unit (PROM). It takes up to 30 seconds before this code will set
54	Mixture Control (M/C) solenoid voltage high at Electronic Control Module (ECM) as a result of a shorted M/C solenoid circuit and/or faulty ECM

Year – 1986
Model – G-Series Vans
Engine – 5.0L (305 cid) V8
Engine Code – VIN H

ECM TROUBLE CODES

Code	Explanation
12	No distributor reference signal to the Electronic Control Module (ECM). This code is not stored in memory and will only flash while the fault is present. Normal code with ignition ON, engine not running
13	Oxygen sensor circuit – the engine must run up to 4 minutes at part throttle, under road load, before this code will set
14	Shorted Coolant Temperature Sensor (CTS) circuit – the engine must run 2 minutes before this code will set
15	Open Coolant Temperature Sensor (CTS) circuit – the engine must run 5 minutes before this code will set
21	Throttle Position Sensor (TPS) circuit voltage high – open circuit or misadjusted TPS – the engine must run 10 seconds, at specified curb idle speed, before this code will set
23	Mixture Control (M/C) solenoid circuit open or grounded
34	Differential pressure (vacuum) sensor circuit – the engine must run up to 2 minutes, at specified curb idle, before this code will set
41	No distributor reference signal to the Electronic Control Module (ECM) at specified engine vacuum. This code will store in memory
42	Electronic Spark Timing (EST) bypass circuit or EST circuit grounded or open
43	Electronic Spark Control (ESC) retard signal for too long – causes retard in Electronic Spark Timing (EST) signal
44	Lean exhaust indication – the engine must run 2 minutes, in closed loop and at part throttle, before this code will set
45	Rich exhaust indication – the engine must run 2 minutes, in closed loop and at part throttle, before this code will set
51	Faulty or improperly installed calibration unit (PROM). It takes up to 30 seconds before this code will set
54	Mixture Control (M/C) solenoid voltage high at Electronic Control Module (ECM) as a result of a shorted M/C solenoid circuit and/or faulty ECM

GENERAL MOTORS CORPORATION
DIAGNOSTIC CODE DATA

Year – 1986
Model – G-Series Vans
Engine – 5.0L (305 cid) V8
Engine Code – VIN F

ECM TROUBLE CODES

Code	Explanation
12	No distributor reference signal to the Electronic Control Module (ECM). This code is not stored in memory and will only flash while the fault is present. Normal code with ignition ON, engine not running
13	Oxygen sensor circuit – the engine must run up to 4 minutes at part throttle, under road load, before this code will set
14	Shorted Coolant Temperature Sensor (CTS) circuit – the engine must run 2 minutes before this code will set
15	Open Coolant Temperature Sensor (CTS) circuit – the engine must run 5 minutes before this code will set
21	Throttle Position Sensor (TPS) circuit voltage high – open circuit or misadjusted TPS – the engine must run 10 seconds, at specified curb idle speed, before this code will set
23	Mixture Control (M/C) solenoid circuit open or grounded
34	Differential pressure (vacuum) sensor circuit – the engine must run up to 2 minutes, at specified curb idle, before this code will set
41	No distributor reference signal to the Electronic Control Module (ECM) at specified engine vacuum. This code will store in memory
42	Electronic Spark Timing (EST) bypass circuit or EST circuit grounded or open
43	Electronic Spark Control (ESC) retard signal for too long – causes retard in Electronic Spark Timing (EST) signal
44	Lean exhaust indication – the engine must run 2 minutes, in closed loop and at part throttle, before this code will set
45	Rich exhaust indication – the engine must run 2 minutes, in closed loop and at part throttle, before this code will set
51	Faulty or improperly installed calibration unit (PROM). It takes up to 30 seconds before this code will set
54	Mixture Control (M/C) solenoid voltage high at Electronic Control Module (ECM) as a result of a shorted M/C solenoid circuit and/or faulty ECM

Year — 1986
Model — G-Series Vans
Engine — 5.7L (350 cid) V8
Engine Code — VIN L

ECM TROUBLE CODES

Code	Explanation
12	No distributor reference signal to the Electronic Control Module (ECM). This code is not stored in memory and will only flash while the fault is present. Normal code with ignition ON, engine not running
13	Oxygen sensor circuit — the engine must run up to 4 minutes at part throttle, under road load, before this code will set
14	Shorted Coolant Temperature Sensor (CTS) circuit — the engine must run 2 minutes before this code will set
15	Open Coolant Temperature Sensor (CTS) circuit — the engine must run 5 minutes before this code will set
21	Throttle Position Sensor (TPS) circuit voltage high — open circuit or misadjusted TPS — the engine must run 10 seconds, at specified curb idle speed, before this code will set
23	Mixture Control (M/C) solenoid circuit open or grounded
34	Differential pressure (vacuum) sensor circuit — the engine must run up to 2 minutes, at specified curb idle, before this code will set
41	No distributor reference signal to the Electronic Control Module (ECM) at specified engine vacuum. This code will store in memory
42	Electronic Spark Timing (EST) bypass circuit or EST circuit grounded or open
43	Electronic Spark Control (ESC) retard signal for too long — causes retard in Electronic Spark Timing (EST) signal
44	Lean exhaust indication — the engine must run 2 minutes, in closed loop and at part throttle, before this code will set
45	Rich exhaust indication — the engine must run 2 minutes, in closed loop and at part throttle, before this code will set
51	Faulty or improperly installed calibration unit (PROM). It takes up to 30 seconds before this code will set
54	Mixture Control (M/C) solenoid voltage high at Electronic Control Module (ECM) as a result of a shorted M/C solenoid circuit and/or faulty ECM

Year – 1986
Model – G-Series Vans
Engine – 5.7L (350 cid) V8
Engine Code – VIN M

ECM TROUBLE CODES

Code	Explanation
12	No distributor reference signal to the Electronic Control Module (ECM). This code is not stored in memory and will only flash while the fault is present. Normal code with ignition ON, engine not running
13	Oxygen sensor circuit – the engine must run up to 4 minutes at part throttle, under road load, before this code will set
14	Shorted Coolant Temperature Sensor (CTS) circuit – the engine must run 2 minutes before this code will set
15	Open Coolant Temperature Sensor (CTS) circuit – the engine must run 5 minutes before this code will set
21	Throttle Position Sensor (TPS) circuit voltage high – open circuit or misadjusted TPS – the engine must run 10 seconds, at specified curb idle speed, before this code will set
23	Mixture Control (M/C) solenoid circuit open or grounded
34	Differential pressure (vacuum) sensor circuit – the engine must run up to 2 minutes, at specified curb idle, before this code will set
41	No distributor reference signal to the Electronic Control Module (ECM) at specified engine vacuum. This code will store in memory
42	Electronic Spark Timing (EST) bypass circuit or EST circuit grounded or open
43	Electronic Spark Control (ESC) retard signal for too long – causes retard in Electronic Spark Timing (EST) signal
44	Lean exhaust indication – the engine must run 2 minutes, in closed loop and at part throttle, before this code will set
45	Rich exhaust indication – the engine must run 2 minutes, in closed loop and at part throttle, before this code will set
51	Faulty or improperly installed calibration unit (PROM). It takes up to 30 seconds before this code will set
54	Mixture Control (M/C) solenoid voltage high at Electronic Control Module (ECM) as a result of a shorted M/C solenoid circuit and/or faulty ECM

Year – 1986
Model – G-Series Vans
Engine – 7.4L (454 cid) V8
Engine Code – VIN W

ECM TROUBLE CODES

Code	Explanation
12	No distributor reference signal to the Electronic Control Module (ECM). This code is not stored in memory and will only flash while the fault is present. Normal code with ignition ON, engine not running
13	Oxygen sensor circuit – the engine must run up to 4 minutes at part throttle, under road load, before this code will set
14	Shorted Coolant Temperature Sensor (CTS) circuit – the engine must run 2 minutes before this code will set
15	Open Coolant Temperature Sensor (CTS) circuit – the engine must run 5 minutes before this code will set
21	Throttle Position Sensor (TPS) circuit voltage high – open circuit or misadjusted TPS – the engine must run 10 seconds, at specified curb idle speed, before this code will set
23	Mixture Control (M/C) solenoid circuit open or grounded
34	Differential pressure (vacuum) sensor circuit – the engine must run up to 2 minutes, at specified curb idle, before this code will set
41	No distributor reference signal to the Electronic Control Module (ECM) at specified engine vacuum. This code will store in memory
42	Electronic Spark Timing (EST) bypass circuit or EST circuit grounded or open
43	Electronic Spark Control (ESC) retard signal for too long – causes retard in Electronic Spark Timing (EST) signal
44	Lean exhaust indication – the engine must run 2 minutes, in closed loop and at part throttle, before this code will set
45	Rich exhaust indication – the engine must run 2 minutes, in closed loop and at part throttle, before this code will set
51	Faulty or improperly installed calibration unit (PROM). It takes up to 30 seconds before this code will set
54	Mixture Control (M/C) solenoid voltage high at Electronic Control Module (ECM) as a result of a shorted M/C solenoid circuit and/or faulty ECM

GENERAL MOTORS CORPORATION
DIAGNOSTIC CODE DATA

Year – 1986
Model – C, K & P Models
Engine – 4.3L (262 cid) V6
Engine Code – VIN N

ECM TROUBLE CODES

Code	Explanation
12	No distributor reference signal to the Electronic Control Module (ECM). This code is not stored in memory and will only flash while the fault is present. Normal code with ignition ON, engine not running
13	Oxygen sensor circuit – the engine must run up to 4 minutes at part throttle, under road load, before this code will set
14	Shorted Coolant Temperature Sensor (CTS) circuit – the engine must run 2 minutes before this code will set
15	Open Coolant Temperature Sensor (CTS) circuit – the engine must run 5 minutes before this code will set
21	Throttle Position Sensor (TPS) circuit voltage high – open circuit or misadjusted TPS – the engine must run 10 seconds, at specified curb idle speed, before this code will set
23	Mixture Control (M/C) solenoid circuit open or grounded
34	Differential pressure (vacuum) sensor circuit – the engine must run up to 2 minutes, at specified curb idle, before this code will set
41	No distributor reference signal to the Electronic Control Module (ECM) at specified engine vacuum. This code will store in memory
42	Electronic Spark Timing (EST) bypass circuit or EST circuit grounded or open
43	Electronic Spark Control (ESC) retard signal for too long – causes retard in Electronic Spark Timing (EST) signal
44	Lean exhaust indication – the engine must run 2 minutes, in closed loop and at part throttle, before this code will set
45	Rich exhaust indication – the engine must run 2 minutes, in closed loop and at part throttle, before this code will set
51	Faulty or improperly installed calibration unit (PROM). It takes up to 30 seconds before this code will set
54	Mixture Control (M/C) solenoid voltage high at Electronic Control Module (ECM) as a result of a shorted M/C solenoid circuit and/or faulty ECM

Year – 1986
Model – C, K & P Models
Engine – 4.8L (292 cid) 6 cyl
Engine Code – VIN T

ECM TROUBLE CODES

Code	Explanation
12	No distributor reference signal to the Electronic Control Module (ECM). This code is not stored in memory and will only flash while the fault is present. Normal code with ignition ON, engine not running
13	Oxygen sensor circuit – the engine must run up to 4 minutes at part throttle, under road load, before this code will set
14	Shorted Coolant Temperature Sensor (CTS) circuit – the engine must run 2 minutes before this code will set
15	Open Coolant Temperature Sensor (CTS) circuit – the engine must run 5 minutes before this code will set
21	Throttle Position Sensor (TPS) circuit voltage high – open circuit or misadjusted TPS – the engine must run 10 seconds, at specified curb idle speed, before this code will set
23	Mixture Control (M/C) solenoid circuit open or grounded
34	Differential pressure (vacuum) sensor circuit – the engine must run up to 2 minutes, at specified curb idle, before this code will set
41	No distributor reference signal to the Electronic Control Module (ECM) at specified engine vacuum. This code will store in memory
42	Electronic Spark Timing (EST) bypass circuit or EST circuit grounded or open
43	Electronic Spark Control (ESC) retard signal for too long – causes retard in Electronic Spark Timing (EST) signal
44	Lean exhaust indication – the engine must run 2 minutes, in closed loop and at part throttle, before this code will set
45	Rich exhaust indication – the engine must run 2 minutes, in closed loop and at part throttle, before this code will set
51	Faulty or improperly installed calibration unit (PROM). It takes up to 30 seconds before this code will set
54	Mixture Control (M/C) solenoid voltage high at Electronic Control Module (ECM) as a result of a shorted M/C solenoid circuit and/or faulty ECM

Year – 1986
Model – C, K & P Models
Engine – 5.0L (305 cid) V8
Engine Code – VIN H

ECM TROUBLE CODES

Code	Explanation
12	No distributor reference signal to the Electronic Control Module (ECM). This code is not stored in memory and will only flash while the fault is present. Normal code with ignition ON, engine not running
13	Oxygen sensor circuit – the engine must run up to 4 minutes at part throttle, under road load, before this code will set
14	Shorted Coolant Temperature Sensor (CTS) circuit – the engine must run 2 minutes before this code will set
15	Open Coolant Temperature Sensor (CTS) circuit – the engine must run 5 minutes before this code will set
21	Throttle Position Sensor (TPS) circuit voltage high – open circuit or misadjusted TPS – the engine must run 10 seconds, at specified curb idle speed, before this code will set
23	Mixture Control (M/C) solenoid circuit open or grounded
34	Differential pressure (vacuum) sensor circuit – the engine must run up to 2 minutes, at specified curb idle, before this code will set
41	No distributor reference signal to the Electronic Control Module (ECM) at specified engine vacuum. This code will store in memory
42	Electronic Spark Timing (EST) bypass circuit or EST circuit grounded or open
43	Electronic Spark Control (ESC) retard signal for too long – causes retard in Electronic Spark Timing (EST) signal
44	Lean exhaust indication – the engine must run 2 minutes, in closed loop and at part throttle, before this code will set
45	Rich exhaust indication – the engine must run 2 minutes, in closed loop and at part throttle, before this code will set
51	Faulty or improperly installed calibration unit (PROM). It takes up to 30 seconds before this code will set
54	Mixture Control (M/C) solenoid voltage high at Electronic Control Module (ECM) as a result of a shorted M/C solenoid circuit and/or faulty ECM

Year — 1986
Model — C, K & P Models
Engine — 5.0L (305 cid) V8
Engine Code — VIN F

ECM TROUBLE CODES

Code	Explanation
12	No distributor reference signal to the Electronic Control Module (ECM). This code is not stored in memory and will only flash while the fault is present. Normal code with ignition ON, engine not running
13	Oxygen sensor circuit — the engine must run up to 4 minutes at part throttle, under road load, before this code will set
14	Shorted Coolant Temperature Sensor (CTS) circuit — the engine must run 2 minutes before this code will set
15	Open Coolant Temperature Sensor (CTS) circuit — the engine must run 5 minutes before this code will set
21	Throttle Position Sensor (TPS) circuit voltage high — open circuit or misadjusted TPS — the engine must run 10 seconds, at specified curb idle speed, before this code will set
23	Mixture Control (M/C) solenoid circuit open or grounded
34	Differential pressure (vacuum) sensor circuit — the engine must run up to 2 minutes, at specified curb idle, before this code will set
41	No distributor reference signal to the Electronic Control Module (ECM) at specified engine vacuum. This code will store in memory
42	Electronic Spark Timing (EST) bypass circuit or EST circuit grounded or open
43	Electronic Spark Control (ESC) retard signal for too long — causes retard in Electronic Spark Timing (EST) signal
44	Lean exhaust indication — the engine must run 2 minutes, in closed loop and at part throttle, before this code will set
45	Rich exhaust indication — the engine must run 2 minutes, in closed loop and at part throttle, before this code will set
51	Faulty or improperly installed calibration unit (PROM). It takes up to 30 seconds before this code will set
54	Mixture Control (M/C) solenoid voltage high at Electronic Control Module (ECM) as a result of a shorted M/C solenoid circuit and/or faulty ECM

Year — 1986
Model — C, K & P Models
Engine — 5.7L (350 cid) V8
Engine Code — VIN L

ECM TROUBLE CODES

Code	Explanation
12	No distributor reference signal to the Electronic Control Module (ECM). This code is not stored in memory and will only flash while the fault is present. Normal code with ignition ON, engine not running
13	Oxygen sensor circuit — the engine must run up to 4 minutes at part throttle, under road load, before this code will set
14	Shorted Coolant Temperature Sensor (CTS) circuit — the engine must run 2 minutes before this code will set
15	Open Coolant Temperature Sensor (CTS) circuit — the engine must run 5 minutes before this code will set
21	Throttle Position Sensor (TPS) circuit voltage high — open circuit or misadjusted TPS — the engine must run 10 seconds, at specified curb idle speed, before this code will set
23	Mixture Control (M/C) solenoid circuit open or grounded
34	Differential pressure (vacuum) sensor circuit — the engine must run up to 2 minutes, at specified curb idle, before this code will set
41	No distributor reference signal to the Electronic Control Module (ECM) at specified engine vacuum. This code will store in memory
42	Electronic Spark Timing (EST) bypass circuit or EST circuit grounded or open
43	Electronic Spark Control (ESC) retard signal for too long — causes retard in Electronic Spark Timing (EST) signal
44	Lean exhaust indication — the engine must run 2 minutes, in closed loop and at part throttle, before this code will set
45	Rich exhaust indication — the engine must run 2 minutes, in closed loop and at part throttle, before this code will set
51	Faulty or improperly installed calibration unit (PROM). It takes up to 30 seconds before this code will set
54	Mixture Control (M/C) solenoid voltage high at Electronic Control Module (ECM) as a result of a shorted M/C solenoid circuit and/or faulty ECM

Year – 1986
Model – C, K & P Models
Engine – 5.7L (350 cid) V8
Engine Code – VIN M

ECM TROUBLE CODES

Code	Explanation
12	No distributor reference signal to the Electronic Control Module (ECM). This code is not stored in memory and will only flash while the fault is present. Normal code with ignition ON, engine not running
13	Oxygen sensor circuit – the engine must run up to 4 minutes at part throttle, under road load, before this code will set
14	Shorted Coolant Temperature Sensor (CTS) circuit – the engine must run 2 minutes before this code will set
15	Open Coolant Temperature Sensor (CTS) circuit – the engine must run 5 minutes before this code will set
21	Throttle Position Sensor (TPS) circuit voltage high – open circuit or misadjusted TPS – the engine must run 10 seconds, at specified curb idle speed, before this code will set
23	Mixture Control (M/C) solenoid circuit open or grounded
34	Differential pressure (vacuum) sensor circuit – the engine must run up to 2 minutes, at specified curb idle, before this code will set
41	No distributor reference signal to the Electronic Control Module (ECM) at specified engine vacuum. This code will store in memory
42	Electronic Spark Timing (EST) bypass circuit or EST circuit grounded or open
43	Electronic Spark Control (ESC) retard signal for too long – causes retard in Electronic Spark Timing (EST) signal
44	Lean exhaust indication – the engine must run 2 minutes, in closed loop and at part throttle, before this code will set
45	Rich exhaust indication – the engine must run 2 minutes, in closed loop and at part throttle, before this code will set
51	Faulty or improperly installed calibration unit (PROM). It takes up to 30 seconds before this code will set
54	Mixture Control (M/C) solenoid voltage high at Electronic Control Module (ECM) as a result of a shorted M/C solenoid circuit and/or faulty ECM

Year – 1986
Model – C, K & P Models
Engine – 7.4L (454 cid) V8
Engine Code – VIN W

ECM TROUBLE CODES

Code	Explanation
12	No distributor reference signal to the Electronic Control Module (ECM). This code is not stored in memory and will only flash while the fault is present. Normal code with ignition ON, engine not running
13	Oxygen sensor circuit – the engine must run up to 4 minutes at part throttle, under road load, before this code will set
14	Shorted Coolant Temperature Sensor (CTS) circuit – the engine must run 2 minutes before this code will set
15	Open Coolant Temperature Sensor (CTS) circuit – the engine must run 5 minutes before this code will set
21	Throttle Position Sensor (TPS) circuit voltage high – open circuit or misadjusted TPS – the engine must run 10 seconds, at specified curb idle speed, before this code will set
23	Mixture Control (M/C) solenoid circuit open or grounded
34	Differential pressure (vacuum) sensor circuit – the engine must run up to 2 minutes, at specified curb idle, before this code will set
41	No distributor reference signal to the Electronic Control Module (ECM) at specified engine vacuum. This code will store in memory
42	Electronic Spark Timing (EST) bypass circuit or EST circuit grounded or open
43	Electronic Spark Control (ESC) retard signal for too long – causes retard in Electronic Spark Timing (EST) signal
44	Lean exhaust indication – the engine must run 2 minutes, in closed loop and at part throttle, before this code will set
45	Rich exhaust indication – the engine must run 2 minutes, in closed loop and at part throttle, before this code will set
51	Faulty or improperly installed calibration unit (PROM). It takes up to 30 seconds before this code will set
54	Mixture Control (M/C) solenoid voltage high at Electronic Control Module (ECM) as a result of a shorted M/C solenoid circuit and/or faulty ECM

Year — 1986
Model — M Vans (Astro/Safari)
Engine — 2.5L (151 cid) TBI 4 cyl
Engine Code — VIN E

ECM TROUBLE CODES

Code	Explanation
13	Oxygen sensor circuit
14	Coolant Temperature Sensor (CTS) — low
15	Coolant Temperature Sensor (CTS) — high
21	Throttle Position Sensor (TPS) — high
22	Throttle Position Sensor (TPS) — low
24	Vehicle Speed Sensor (VSS)
33	Manifold Absolute Pressure (MAP) sensor — high
34	Manifold Absolute Pressure (MAP) sensor — low
35	Idle Air Control (IAC)
42	Electronic Spark Timing (EST)
44	Lean exhaust indication
45	Rich exhaust indication
51	PROM
55	Electronic Control Module (ECM)

Year — 1986
Model — M Vans (Astro/Safari)
Engine — 4.3L (262 cid) TBI V6
Engine Code — VIN Z

ECM TROUBLE CODES

Code	Explanation
13	Oxygen sensor circuit
14	Coolant Temperature Sensor (CTS) — low
15	Coolant Temperature Sensor (CTS) — high
21	Throttle Position Sensor (TPS) — high
22	Throttle Position Sensor (TPS) — low
24	Vehicle Speed Sensor (VSS)
32	Exhaust Gas Recirculation (EGR) system failure
33	Manifold Absolute Pressure (MAP) sensor — high
34	Manifold Absolute Pressure (MAP) sensor — low
42	Electronic Spark Timing (EST)
43	Electronic Spark Control (ESC)
44	Lean exhaust indication
45	Rich exhaust indication
51	PROM
52	Calpak
54	Fuel pump relay circuit
55	Electronic Control Module (ECM)

Year — 1986
Model — El Camino
Engine — 4.3L (262 cid) EFI V6
Engine Code — VIN Z

ECM TROUBLE CODES

Code	Explanation
13	Open oxygen sensor circuit
14	Coolant Temperature Sensor (CTS) circuit
15	Coolant Temperature Sensor (CTS) circuit
21	Throttle Position Sensor (TPS)
22	Throttle Position Sensor (TPS)
24	Vehicle Speed Sensor (VSS)
32	Exhaust Gas Recirculation (EGR) system failure
33	Manifold Absolute Pressure (MAP) sensor circuit
34	Manifold Absolute Pressure (MAP) sensor circuit
42	Electronic Spark Timing (EST)
43	Electronic Spark Control (ESC)
44	Lean exhaust indicated
45	Rich exhaust indicated
54	Fuel pump circuit
51	PROM problem
52	Fuel calpak missing
55	Electronic Control Module (ECM)

Year – 1986
Model – El Camino
Engine – 5.0L (305 cid) V8
Engine Code – VIN H

ECM TROUBLE CODES

Code	Explanation
12	No distributor reference signal to the Electronic Control Module (ECM). This code is not stored in memory and will only flash while the fault is present. Normal code with ignition ON, engine not running
13	Oxygen sensor circuit – the engine must run up to 4 minutes at part throttle, under road load, before this code will set
14	Shorted Coolant Temperature Sensor (CTS) circuit – the engine must run 2 minutes before this code will set
15	Open Coolant Temperature Sensor (CTS) circuit – the engine must run 5 minutes before this code will set
21	Throttle Position Sensor (TPS) circuit voltage high – open circuit or misadjusted TPS – the engine must run 10 seconds, at specified curb idle speed, before this code will set
22	Throttle Position Sensor (TPS) circuit voltage low – grounded circuit or misadjusted TPS – engine must run 20 seconds at specified curb idle speed, to set code
23	Mixture Control (M/C) solenoid circuit open or grounded
24	Vehicle Speed Sensor (VSS) circuit – the vehicle must operate up to 2 minutes at road speed, before this code will set
32	Barometric Pressure Sensor (BARO) circuit low
34	Manifold Absolute Pressure (MAP) or vacuum sensor circuit. The engine must run up to 2 minutes at specified curb idle speed, before this code will set
35	Idle Speed Control (ISC) switch circuit shorted – up to 70% Throttle Position Sensor (TPS) for over 5 seconds
41	No distributor reference signal to the Electronic Control Module (ECM) at specified engine vacuum. This code will store in memory
42	Electronic Spark Timing (EST) bypass circuit or EST circuit grounded or open
43	Electronic Spark Control (ESC) retard signal for too long a time – causes retard in Electronic Spark Timing (EST) signal
44	Lean exhaust indication – the engine must run 2 minutes, in closed loop and at part throttle, before this code will set
45	Rich exhaust indication – the engine must run 2 minutes, in closed loop and at part throttle, before this code will set
51	Faulty or improperly installed calibration unit (PROM). It takes up to 30 seconds before this code will set
53	Exhaust Gas Recirculation (EGR) valve vacuum sensor has seen improper EGR vacuum
54	Mixture Control (M/C) solenoid voltage high, at Electronic Control Module (ECM), as a result of a shorted M/C solenoid circuit and/or faulty ECM

Year – 1987
Model – S-10/15 Series
Engine – 2.5L (151 cid) TBI 4 cyl
Engine Code – VIN E

ECM TROUBLE CODES

Code	Explanation
13	Oxygen sensor circuit – open oxygen sensor – indicates that the oxygen sensor circuit or sensor was open for 1 minute while off idle
14	Coolant Temperature Sensor (CTS) – high temperature indication – sets if the sensor or signal line becomes grounded for 3 seconds
15	Coolant Temperature Sensor (CTS) – low temperature indication – sets if the sensor, connections, or wires open for 3 seconds
21	Throttle Position Sensor (TPS) – signal voltage high – TPS voltage greater than 2.5V for 3 seconds with less than 1200 rpm
22	Throttle Position Sensor (TPS) – signal voltage low – short to ground or open signal circuit will set in 3 seconds
23	Manifold Air Temperature (MAT) – low temperature indication – sets if the sensor, connections or wires open for 3 seconds
24	Vehicle Speed Sensor (VSS) circuit – no vehicle speed indication – no vehicle speed present during a road load deceleration
25	Manifold Air Temperature (MAT) – high temperature indication – sets if the sensor or signal line becomes grounded for 3 seconds
32	Exhaust Gas Recirculation (EGR) – vacuum switch shorted to ground on start up or switch not closed after the Electronic Control Module (ECM) has commanded EGR for a specified period of time or EGR solenoid circuit open for a specified period of time
33	Manifold Absolute Pressure (MAP) sensor – low vacuum – MAP sensor output too high for 5 seconds or an open signal circuit
34	Manifold Absolute Pressure (MAP) sensor – high vacuum – low or no output from sensor with engine running
35	Idle Air Control (IAC) – IAC error
42	Electronic Spark Timing (EST) – Electronic Control Module (ECM) has seen an open or grounded EST or bypass circuit
43	Electronic Spark Control (ESC) – signal to the Electronic Control Module (ECM) has remained low for too long or the system has failed a functional check
44	Lean exhaust indication – sets if oxygen sensor voltage remains below 0.2V for about 20 seconds
45	Rich exhaust indication – sets if oxygen sensor voltage remains above 0.7V for about 1 minute
51	Faulty Mem-Cal, PROM or Electronic Control Module (ECM)
52	Fuel Calpak missing or faulty
54	Fuel pump – low voltage – sets when the fuel pump voltage is less than 2V when reference pulses are being received
55	Faulty Electronic Control Module (ECM)

GENERAL MOTORS CORPORATION
DIAGNOSTIC CODE DATA

Year – 1987
Model – S-10/15 Series
Engine – 2.8L (173 cid) TBI V6
Engine Code – VIN R

ECM TROUBLE CODES

Code	Explanation
13	Oxygen sensor circuit – open oxygen sensor – indicates that the oxygen sensor circuit or sensor was open for 1 minute while off idle
14	Coolant Temperature Sensor (CTS) – high temperature indication – sets if the sensor or signal line becomes grounded for 3 seconds
15	Coolant Temperature Sensor (CTS) – low temperature indication – sets if the sensor, connections or wires open for 3 seconds
21	Throttle Position Sensor (TPS) – signal voltage high – TPS voltage greater than 2.5V for 3 seconds with less than 1200 rpm
22	Throttle Position Sensor (TPS) – signal voltage low – short to ground or open signal circuit will set in 3 seconds
23	Manifold Air Temperature (MAT) – low temperature indication – sets if the sensor, connections or wires open for 3 seconds
24	Vehicle Speed Sensor (VSS) circuit – no vehicle speed indication – no vehicle speed present during a road load deceleration
25	Manifold Air Temperature (MAT) – high temperature indication – sets if the sensor or signal line becomes grounded for 3 seconds
32	Exhaust Gas Recirculation (EGR) – vacuum switch shorted to ground on start up or switch not closed after the Electronic Control Module (ECM) has commanded EGR for a specified period of time or EGR solenoid circuit open for a specified period of time
33	Manifold Absolute Pressure (MAP) sensor – low vacuum – MAP sensor output too high for 5 seconds or an open signal circuit
34	Manifold Absolute Pressure (MAP) sensor – high vacuum – low or no output from sensor with engine running
35	Idle Air Control (IAC) – IAC error
42	Electronic Spark Timing (EST) – Electronic Control Module (ECM) has seen an open or grounded EST or bypass circuit
43	Electronic Spark Control (ESC) – signal to the Electronic Control Module (ECM) has remained low for too long or the system has failed a functional check
44	Lean exhaust indication – sets if oxygen sensor voltage remains below 0.2V for about 20 seconds
45	Rich exhaust indication – sets if oxygen sensor voltage remains above 0.7V for about 1 minute
51	Faulty Mem-Cal, PROM or Electronic Control Module (ECM)
52	Fuel Calpak missing or faulty
54	Fuel pump – low voltage – sets when the fuel pump voltage is less than 2V when reference pulses are being received
55	Faulty Electronic Control Module (ECM)

Year – 1987
Model – Astro Van/GMC Safari
Engine – 2.5L (151 cid) TBI 4 cyl
Engine Code – VIN E

ECM TROUBLE CODES

Code	Explanation
13	Oxygen sensor circuit – open oxygen sensor – indicates that the oxygen sensor circuit or sensor was open for 1 minute while off idle
14	Coolant Temperature Sensor (CTS) – high temperature indication – sets if the sensor or signal line becomes grounded for 3 seconds
15	Coolant Temperature Sensor (CTS) – low temperature indication – sets if the sensor, connections or wires open for 3 seconds
21	Throttle Position Sensor (TPS) – signal voltage high – TPS voltage greater than 2.5V for 3 seconds with less than 1200 rpm
22	Throttle Position Sensor (TPS) – signal voltage low – short to ground or open signal circuit will set in 3 seconds
23	Manifold Air Temperature (MAT) – low temperature indication – sets if the sensor, connections or wires open for 3 seconds
24	Vehicle Speed Sensor (VSS) circuit – no vehicle speed indication – no vehicle speed present during a road load deceleration
25	Manifold Air Temperature (MAT) – high temperature indication – sets if the sensor or signal line becomes grounded for 3 seconds
32	Exhaust Gas Recirculation (EGR) – vacuum switch shorted to ground on start up or switch not closed after the Electronic Control Module (ECM) has commanded EGR for a specified period of time or EGR solenoid circuit open for a specified period of time
33	Manifold Absolute Pressure (MAP) sensor – low vacuum – MAP sensor output too high for 5 seconds or an open signal circuit
34	Manifold Absolute Pressure (MAP) sensor – high vacuum – low or no output from sensor with engine running
35	Idle Air Control (IAC) – IAC error
42	Electronic Spark Timing (EST) – Electronic Control Module (ECM) has seen an open or grounded EST or bypass circuit
43	Electronic Spark Control (ESC) – signal to the Electronic Control Module (ECM) has remained low for too long or the system has failed a functional check
44	Lean exhaust indication – sets if oxygen sensor voltage remains below 0.2V for about 20 seconds
45	Rich exhaust indication – sets if oxygen sensor voltage remains above 0.7V for about 1 minute
51	Faulty Mem-Cal, PROM or Electronic Control Module (ECM)
52	Fuel Calpak missing or faulty
54	Fuel pump – low voltage – sets when the fuel pump voltage is less than 2V when reference pulses are being received
55	Faulty Electronic Control Module (ECM)

Year – 1987
Model – Astro Van/GMC Safari
Engine – 4.3L (262 cid) TBI V6
Engine Code – VIN Z

ECM TROUBLE CODES

Code	Explanation
13	Oxygen sensor circuit – open oxygen sensor – indicates that the oxygen sensor circuit or sensor was open for 1 minute while off idle
14	Coolant Temperature Sensor (CTS) – high temperature indication – sets if the sensor or signal line becomes grounded for 3 seconds
15	Coolant Temperature Sensor (CTS) – low temperature indication – sets if the sensor, connections or wires open for 3 seconds
21	Throttle Position Sensor (TPS) – signal voltage high – TPS voltage greater than 2.5V for 3 seconds with less than 1200 rpm
22	Throttle Position Sensor (TPS) – signal voltage low – short to ground or open signal circuit will set in 3 seconds
23	Manifold Air Temperature (MAT) – low temperature indication – sets if the sensor, connections or wires open for 3 seconds
24	Vehicle Speed Sensor (VSS) circuit – no vehicle speed indication – no vehicle speed present during a road load deceleration
25	Manifold Air Temperature (MAT) – high temperature indication – sets if the sensor or signal line becomes grounded for 3 seconds
32	Exhaust Gas Recirculation (EGR) – vacuum switch shorted to ground on start up or switch not closed after the Electronic Control Module (ECM) has commanded EGR for a specified period of time or EGR solenoid circuit open for a specified period of time
33	Manifold Absolute Pressure (MAP) sensor – low vacuum – MAP sensor output too high for 5 seconds or an open signal circuit
34	Manifold Absolute Pressure (MAP) sensor – high vacuum – low or no output from sensor with engine running
35	Idle Air Control (IAC) – IAC error
42	Electronic Spark Timing (EST) – Electronic Control Module (ECM) has seen an open or grounded EST or bypass circuit
43	Electronic Spark Control (ESC) – signal to the Electronic Control Module (ECM) has remained low for too long or the system has failed a functional check
44	Lean exhaust indication – sets if oxygen sensor voltage remains below 0.2V for about 20 seconds
45	Rich exhaust indication – sets if oxygen sensor voltage remains above 0.7V for about 1 minute
51	Faulty Mem-Cal, PROM or Electronic Control Module (ECM)
52	Fuel Calpak missing or faulty
54	Fuel pump – low voltage – sets when the fuel pump voltage is less than 2V when reference pulses are being received
55	Faulty Electronic Control Module (ECM)

Year – 1987
Model – R & V Pick-Ups
Engine – 4.3L (262 cid) TBI V6
Engine Code – VIN Z

ECM TROUBLE CODES

Code	Explanation
13	Oxygen sensor circuit – open oxygen sensor – indicates that the oxygen sensor circuit or sensor was open for 1 minute while off idle
14	Coolant Temperature Sensor (CTS) – high temperature indication – sets if the sensor or signal line becomes grounded for 3 seconds
15	Coolant Temperature Sensor (CTS) – low temperature indication – sets if the sensor, connections or wires open for 3 seconds
21	Throttle Position Sensor (TPS) – signal voltage high – TPS voltage greater than 2.5V for 3 seconds with less than 1200 rpm
22	Throttle Position Sensor (TPS) – signal voltage low – short to ground or open signal circuit will set in 3 seconds
23	Manifold Air Temperature (MAT) – low temperature indication – sets if the sensor, connections or wires open for 3 seconds
24	Vehicle Speed Sensor (VSS) circuit – no vehicle speed indication – no vehicle speed present during a road load deceleration
25	Manifold Air Temperature (MAT) – high temperature indication – sets if the sensor or signal line becomes grounded for 3 seconds
32	Exhaust Gas Recirculation (EGR) – vacuum switch shorted to ground on start up or switch not closed after the Electronic Control Module (ECM) has commanded EGR for a specified period of time or EGR solenoid circuit open for a specified period of time
33	Manifold Absolute Pressure (MAP) sensor – low vacuum – MAP sensor output too high for 5 seconds or an open signal circuit
34	Manifold Absolute Pressure (MAP) sensor – high vacuum – low or no output from sensor with engine running
35	Idle Air Control (IAC) – IAC error
42	Electronic Spark Timing (EST) – Electronic Control Module (ECM) has seen an open or grounded EST or bypass circuit
43	Electronic Spark Control (ESC) – signal to the Electronic Control Module (ECM) has remained low for too long or the system has failed a functional check
44	Lean exhaust indication – sets if oxygen sensor voltage remains below 0.2V for about 20 seconds
45	Rich exhaust indication – sets if oxygen sensor voltage remains above 0.7V for about 1 minute
51	Faulty Mem-Cal, PROM or Electronic Control Module (ECM)
52	Fuel Calpak missing or faulty
54	Fuel pump – low voltage – sets when the fuel pump voltage is less than 2V when reference pulses are being received
55	Faulty Electronic Control Module (ECM)

Year – 1987
Model – R & V Pick-Ups
Engine – 5.0L (305 cid) TBI V8
Engine Code – VIN H

ECM TROUBLE CODES

Code	Explanation
13	Oxygen sensor circuit – open oxygen sensor – indicates that the oxygen sensor circuit or sensor was open for 1 minute while off idle
14	Coolant Temperature Sensor (CTS) – high temperature indication – sets if the sensor or signal line becomes grounded for 3 seconds
15	Coolant Temperature Sensor (CTS) – low temperature indication – sets if the sensor, connections or wires open for 3 seconds
21	Throttle Position Sensor (TPS) – signal voltage high – TPS voltage greater than 2.5V for 3 seconds with less than 1200 rpm
22	Throttle Position Sensor (TPS) – signal voltage low – short to ground or open signal circuit will set in 3 seconds
23	Manifold Air Temperature (MAT) – low temperature indication – sets if the sensor, connections or wires open for 3 seconds
24	Vehicle Speed Sensor (VSS) circuit – no vehicle speed indication – no vehicle speed present during a road load deceleration
25	Manifold Air Temperature (MAT) – high temperature indication – sets if the sensor or signal line becomes grounded for 3 seconds
32	Exhaust Gas Recirculation (EGR) – vacuum switch shorted to ground on start up or switch not closed after the Electronic Control Module (ECM) has commanded EGR for a specified period of time or EGR solenoid circuit open for a specified period of time
33	Manifold Absolute Pressure (MAP) sensor – low vacuum – MAP sensor output too high for 5 seconds or an open signal circuit
34	Manifold Absolute Pressure (MAP) sensor – high vacuum – low or no output from sensor with engine running
35	Idle Air Control (IAC) – IAC error
42	Electronic Spark Timing (EST) – Electronic Control Module (ECM) has seen an open or grounded EST or bypass circuit
43	Electronic Spark Control (ESC) – signal to the Electronic Control Module (ECM) has remained low for too long or the system has failed a functional check
44	Lean exhaust indication – sets if oxygen sensor voltage remains below 0.2V for about 20 seconds
45	Rich exhaust indication – sets if oxygen sensor voltage remains above 0.7V for about 1 minute
51	Faulty Mem-Cal, PROM or Electronic Control Module (ECM)
52	Fuel Calpak missing or faulty
54	Fuel pump – low voltage – sets when the fuel pump voltage is less than 2V when reference pulses are being received
55	Faulty Electronic Control Module (ECM)

Year — 1987
Model — R & V Pick-Ups
Engine — 5.7L (350 cid) TBI V8
Engine Code — VIN K

ECM TROUBLE CODES

Code	Explanation
13	Oxygen sensor circuit — open oxygen sensor — indicates that the oxygen sensor circuit or sensor was open for 1 minute while off idle
14	Coolant Temperature Sensor (CTS) — high temperature indication — sets if the sensor or signal line becomes grounded for 3 seconds
15	Coolant Temperature Sensor (CTS) — low temperature indication — sets if the sensor, connections or wires open for 3 seconds
21	Throttle Position Sensor (TPS) — signal voltage high — TPS voltage greater than 2.5V for 3 seconds with less than 1200 rpm
22	Throttle Position Sensor (TPS) — signal voltage low — short to ground or open signal circuit will set in 3 seconds
23	Manifold Air Temperature (MAT) — low temperature indication — sets if the sensor, connections or wires open for 3 seconds
24	Vehicle Speed Sensor (VSS) circuit — no vehicle speed indication — no vehicle speed present during a road load deceleration
25	Manifold Air Temperature (MAT) — high temperature indication — sets if the sensor or signal line becomes grounded for 3 seconds
32	Exhaust Gas Recirculation (EGR) — vacuum switch shorted to ground on start up or switch not closed after the Electronic Control Module (ECM) has commanded EGR for a specified period of time or EGR solenoid circuit open for a specified period of time
33	Manifold Absolute Pressure (MAP) sensor — low vacuum — MAP sensor output too high for 5 seconds or an open signal circuit
34	Manifold Absolute Pressure (MAP) sensor — high vacuum — low or no output from sensor with engine running
35	Idle Air Control (IAC) — IAC error
42	Electronic Spark Timing (EST) — Electronic Control Module (ECM) has seen an open or grounded EST or bypass circuit
43	Electronic Spark Control (ESC) — signal to the Electronic Control Module (ECM) has remained low for too long or the system has failed a functional check
44	Lean exhaust indication — sets if oxygen sensor voltage remains below 0.2V for about 20 seconds
45	Rich exhaust indication — sets if oxygen sensor voltage remains above 0.7V for about 1 minute
51	Faulty Mem-Cal, PROM or Electronic Control Module (ECM)
52	Fuel Calpak missing or faulty
54	Fuel pump — low voltage — sets when the fuel pump voltage is less than 2V when reference pulses are being received
55	Faulty Electronic Control Module (ECM)

Year – 1987
Model – R & V Pick-Ups
Engine – 7.4L (454 cid) TBI V8
Engine Code – VIN N

ECM TROUBLE CODES

Code	Explanation
13	Oxygen sensor circuit – open oxygen sensor – indicates that the oxygen sensor circuit or sensor was open for 1 minute while off idle
14	Coolant Temperature Sensor (CTS) – high temperature indication – sets if the sensor or signal line becomes grounded for 3 seconds
15	Coolant Temperature Sensor (CTS) – low temperature indication – sets if the sensor, connections or wires open for 3 seconds
21	Throttle Position Sensor (TPS) – signal voltage high – TPS voltage greater than 2.5V for 3 seconds with less than 1200 rpm
22	Throttle Position Sensor (TPS) – signal voltage low – short to ground or open signal circuit will set in 3 seconds
23	Manifold Air Temperature (MAT) – low temperature indication – sets if the sensor, connections or wires open for 3 seconds
24	Vehicle Speed Sensor (VSS) circuit – no vehicle speed indication – no vehicle speed present during a road load deceleration
25	Manifold Air Temperature (MAT) – high temperature indication – sets if the sensor or signal line becomes grounded for 3 seconds
32	Exhaust Gas Recirculation (EGR) – vacuum switch shorted to ground on start up or switch not closed after the Electronic Control Module (ECM) has commanded EGR for a specified period of time or EGR solenoid circuit open for a specified period of time
33	Manifold Absolute Pressure (MAP) sensor – low vacuum – MAP sensor output too high for 5 seconds or an open signal circuit
34	Manifold Absolute Pressure (MAP) sensor – high vacuum – low or no output from sensor with engine running
35	Idle Air Control (IAC) – IAC error
42	Electronic Spark Timing (EST) – Electronic Control Module (ECM) has seen an open or grounded EST or bypass circuit
43	Electronic Spark Control (ESC) – signal to the Electronic Control Module (ECM) has remained low for too long or the system has failed a functional check
44	Lean exhaust indication – sets if oxygen sensor voltage remains below 0.2V for about 20 seconds
45	Rich exhaust indication – sets if oxygen sensor voltage remains above 0.7V for about 1 minute
51	Faulty Mem-Cal, PROM or Electronic Control Module (ECM)
52	Fuel Calpak missing or faulty
54	Fuel pump – low voltage – sets when the fuel pump voltage is less than 2V when reference pulses are being received
55	Faulty Electronic Control Module (ECM)

Year — 1987
Model — G-Series Vans
Engine — 4.3L (260 cid) TBI V6
Engine Code — VIN Z

ECM TROUBLE CODES

Code	Explanation
13	Oxygen sensor circuit — open oxygen sensor — indicates that the oxygen sensor circuit or sensor was open for 1 minute while off idle
14	Coolant Temperature Sensor (CTS) — high temperature indication — sets if the sensor or signal line becomes grounded for 3 seconds
15	Coolant Temperature Sensor (CTS) — low temperature indication — sets if the sensor, connections or wires open for 3 seconds
21	Throttle Position Sensor (TPS) — signal voltage high — TPS voltage greater than 2.5V for 3 seconds with less than 1200 rpm
22	Throttle Position Sensor (TPS) — signal voltage low — short to ground or open signal circuit will set in 3 seconds
23	Manifold Air Temperature (MAT) — low temperature indication — sets if the sensor, connections or wires open for 3 seconds
24	Vehicle Speed Sensor (VSS) circuit — no vehicle speed indication — no vehicle speed present during a road load deceleration
25	Manifold Air Temperature (MAT) — high temperature indication — sets if the sensor or signal line becomes grounded for 3 seconds
32	Exhaust Gas Recirculation (EGR) — vacuum switch shorted to ground on start up or switch not closed after the Electronic Control Module (ECM) has commanded EGR for a specified period of time or EGR solenoid circuit open for a specified period of time
33	Manifold Absolute Pressure (MAP) sensor — low vacuum — MAP sensor output too high for 5 seconds or an open signal circuit
34	Manifold Absolute Pressure (MAP) sensor — high vacuum — low or no output from sensor with engine running
35	Idle Air Control (IAC) — IAC error
42	Electronic Spark Timing (EST) — Electronic Control Module (ECM) has seen an open or grounded EST or bypass circuit
43	Electronic Spark Control (ESC) — signal to the Electronic Control Module (ECM) has remained low for too long or the system has failed a functional check
44	Lean exhaust indication — sets if oxygen sensor voltage remains below 0.2V for about 20 seconds
45	Rich exhaust indication — sets if oxygen sensor voltage remains above 0.7V for about 1 minute
51	Faulty Mem-Cal, PROM or Electronic Control Module (ECM)
52	Fuel Calpak missing or faulty
54	Fuel pump — low voltage — sets when the fuel pump voltage is less than 2V when reference pulses are being received
55	Faulty Electronic Control Module (ECM)

GENERAL MOTORS CORPORATION
DIAGNOSTIC CODE DATA

Year — 1987
Model — G-Series Vans
Engine — 5.0L (305 cid) TBI V8
Engine Code — VIN H

ECM TROUBLE CODES

Code	Explanation
13	Oxygen sensor circuit — open oxygen sensor — indicates that the oxygen sensor circuit or sensor was open for 1 minute while off idle
14	Coolant Temperature Sensor (CTS) — high temperature indication — sets if the sensor or signal line becomes grounded for 3 seconds
15	Coolant Temperature Sensor (CTS) — low temperature indication — sets if the sensor, connections or wires open for 3 seconds
21	Throttle Position Sensor (TPS) — signal voltage high — TPS voltage greater than 2.5V for 3 seconds with less than 1200 rpm
22	Throttle Position Sensor (TPS) — signal voltage low — short to ground or open signal circuit will set in 3 seconds
23	Manifold Air Temperature (MAT) — low temperature indication — sets if the sensor, connections or wires open for 3 seconds
24	Vehicle Speed Sensor (VSS) circuit — no vehicle speed indication — no vehicle speed present during a road load deceleration
25	Manifold Air Temperature (MAT) — high temperature indication — sets if the sensor or signal line becomes grounded for 3 seconds
32	Exhaust Gas Recirculation (EGR) — vacuum switch shorted to ground on start up or switch not closed after the Electronic Control Module (ECM) has commanded EGR for a specified period of time or EGR solenoid circuit open for a specified period of time
33	Manifold Absolute Pressure (MAP) sensor — low vacuum — MAP sensor output too high for 5 seconds or an open signal circuit
34	Manifold Absolute Pressure (MAP) sensor — high vacuum — low or no output from sensor with engine running
35	Idle Air Control (IAC) — IAC error
42	Electronic Spark Timing (EST) — Electronic Control Module (ECM) has seen an open or grounded EST or bypass circuit
43	Electronic Spark Control (ESC) — signal to the Electronic Control Module (ECM) has remained low for too long or the system has failed a functional check
44	Lean exhaust indication — sets if oxygen sensor voltage remains below 0.2V for about 20 seconds
45	Rich exhaust indication — sets if oxygen sensor voltage remains above 0.7V for about 1 minute
51	Faulty Mem-Cal, PROM or Electronic Control Module (ECM)
52	Fuel Calpak missing or faulty
54	Fuel pump — low voltage — sets when the fuel pump voltage is less than 2V when reference pulses are being received
55	Faulty Electronic Control Module (ECM)

Year — 1987
Model — G-Series Vans
Engine — 5.7L (350 cid) TBI V8
Engine Code — VIN K

ECM TROUBLE CODES

Code	Explanation
13	Oxygen sensor circuit — open oxygen sensor — indicates that the oxygen sensor circuit or sensor was open for 1 minute while off idle
14	Coolant Temperature Sensor (CTS) — high temperature indication — sets if the sensor or signal line becomes grounded for 3 seconds
15	Coolant Temperature Sensor (CTS) — low temperature indication — sets if the sensor, connections or wires open for 3 seconds
21	Throttle Position Sensor (TPS) — signal voltage high — TPS voltage greater than 2.5V for 3 seconds with less than 1200 rpm
22	Throttle Position Sensor (TPS) — signal voltage low — short to ground or open signal circuit will set in 3 seconds
23	Manifold Air Temperature (MAT) — low temperature indication — sets if the sensor, connections or wires open for 3 seconds
24	Vehicle Speed Sensor (VSS) circuit — no vehicle speed indication — no vehicle speed present during a road load deceleration
25	Manifold Air Temperature (MAT) — high temperature indication — sets if the sensor or signal line becomes grounded for 3 seconds
32	Exhaust Gas Recirculation (EGR) — vacuum switch shorted to ground on start up or switch not closed after the Electronic Control Module (ECM) has commanded EGR for a specified period of time or EGR solenoid circuit open for a specified period of time
33	Manifold Absolute Pressure (MAP) sensor — low vacuum — MAP sensor output too high for 5 seconds or an open signal circuit
34	Manifold Absolute Pressure (MAP) sensor — high vacuum — low or no output from sensor with engine running
35	Idle Air Control (IAC) — IAC error
42	Electronic Spark Timing (EST) — Electronic Control Module (ECM) has seen an open or grounded EST or bypass circuit
43	Electronic Spark Control (ESC) — signal to the Electronic Control Module (ECM) has remained low for too long or the system has failed a functional check
44	Lean exhaust indication — sets if oxygen sensor voltage remains below 0.2V for about 20 seconds
45	Rich exhaust indication — sets if oxygen sensor voltage remains above 0.7V for about 1 minute
51	Faulty Mem-Cal, PROM or Electronic Control Module (ECM)
52	Fuel Calpak missing or faulty
54	Fuel pump — low voltage — sets when the fuel pump voltage is less than 2V when reference pulses are being received
55	Faulty Electronic Control Module (ECM)

GENERAL MOTORS CORPORATION
DIAGNOSTIC CODE DATA

Year – 1987
Model – P-Series Models
Engine – 5.7L (350 cid) TBI V8
Engine Code – VIN K

ECM TROUBLE CODES

Code	Explanation
13	Oxygen sensor circuit—open oxygen sensor—indicates that the oxygen sensor circuit or sensor was open for 1 minute while off idle
14	Coolant Temperature Sensor (CTS)—high temperature indication—sets if the sensor or signal line becomes grounded for 3 seconds
15	Coolant Temperature Sensor (CTS)—low temperature indication—sets if the sensor, connections or wires open for 3 seconds
21	Throttle Position Sensor (TPS)—signal voltage high—TPS voltage greater than 2.5V for 3 seconds with less than 1200 rpm
22	Throttle Position Sensor (TPS)—signal voltage low—short to ground or open signal circuit will set in 3 seconds
23	Manifold Air Temperature (MAT)—low temperature indication—sets if the sensor, connections or wires open for 3 seconds
24	Vehicle Speed Sensor (VSS) circuit—no vehicle speed indication—no vehicle speed present during a road load deceleration
25	Manifold Air Temperature (MAT)—high temperature indication—sets if the sensor or signal line becomes grounded for 3 seconds
32	Exhaust Gas Recirculation (EGR)—vacuum switch shorted to ground on start up or switch not closed after the Electronic Control Module (ECM) has commanded EGR for a specified period of time or EGR solenoid circuit open for a specified period of time
33	Manifold Absolute Pressure (MAP) sensor—low vacuum—MAP sensor output too high for 5 seconds or an open signal circuit
34	Manifold Absolute Pressure (MAP) sensor—high vacuum—low or no output from sensor with engine running
35	Idle Air Control (IAC)—IAC error
42	Electronic Spark Timing (EST)—Electronic Control Module (ECM) has seen an open or grounded EST or bypass circuit
43	Electronic Spark Control (ESC)—signal to the Electronic Control Module (ECM) has remained low for too long or the system has failed a functional check
44	Lean exhaust indication—sets if oxygen sensor voltage remains below 0.2V for about 20 seconds
45	Rich exhaust indication—sets if oxygen sensor voltage remains above 0.7V for about 1 minute
51	Faulty Mem-Cal, PROM or Electronic Control Module (ECM)
52	Fuel Calpak missing or faulty
54	Fuel pump—low voltage—sets when the fuel pump voltage is less than 2V when reference pulses are being received
55	Faulty Electronic Control Module (ECM)

Year — 1987
Model — P-Series Models
Engine — 7.4L (455 cid) TBI V8
Engine Code — VIN N

ECM TROUBLE CODES

Code	Explanation
13	Oxygen sensor circuit — open oxygen sensor — indicates that the oxygen sensor circuit or sensor was open for 1 minute while off idle
14	Coolant Temperature Sensor (CTS) — high temperature indication — sets if the sensor or signal line becomes grounded for 3 seconds
15	Coolant Temperature Sensor (CTS) — low temperature indication — sets if the sensor, connections or wires open for 3 seconds
21	Throttle Position Sensor (TPS) — signal voltage high — TPS voltage greater than 2.5V for 3 seconds with less than 1200 rpm
22	Throttle Position Sensor (TPS) — signal voltage low — short to ground or open signal circuit will set in 3 seconds
23	Manifold Air Temperature (MAT) — low temperature indication — sets if the sensor, connections or wires open for 3 seconds
24	Vehicle Speed Sensor (VSS) circuit — no vehicle speed indication — no vehicle speed present during a road load deceleration
25	Manifold Air Temperature (MAT) — high temperature indication — sets if the sensor or signal line becomes grounded for 3 seconds
32	Exhaust Gas Recirculation (EGR) — vacuum switch shorted to ground on start up or switch not closed after the Electronic Control Module (ECM) has commanded EGR for a specified period of time or EGR solenoid circuit open for a specified period of time
33	Manifold Absolute Pressure (MAP) sensor — low vacuum — MAP sensor output too high for 5 seconds or an open signal circuit
34	Manifold Absolute Pressure (MAP) sensor — high vacuum — low or no output from sensor with engine running
35	Idle Air Control (IAC) — IAC error
42	Electronic Spark Timing (EST) — Electronic Control Module (ECM) has seen an open or grounded EST or bypass circuit
43	Electronic Spark Control (ESC) — signal to the Electronic Control Module (ECM) has remained low for too long or the system has failed a functional check
44	Lean exhaust indication — sets if oxygen sensor voltage remains below 0.2V for about 20 seconds
45	Rich exhaust indication — sets if oxygen sensor voltage remains above 0.7V for about 1 minute
51	Faulty Mem-Cal, PROM or Electronic Control Module (ECM)
52	Fuel Calpak missing or faulty
54	Fuel pump — low voltage — sets when the fuel pump voltage is less than 2V when reference pulses are being received
55	Faulty Electronic Control Module (ECM)

Year – 1987
Model – El Camino
Engine – 4.3L (262 cid) EFI V6
Engine Code – VIN Z

ECM TROUBLE CODES

Code	Explanation
13	Open oxygen sensor circuit
14	Coolant Temperature Sensor (CTS) circuit
15	Coolant Temperature Sensor (CTS) circuit
21	Throttle Position Sensor (TPS)
22	Throttle Position Sensor (TPS)
24	Vehicle Speed Sensor (VSS)
32	Exhaust Gas Recirculation (EGR) system failure
33	Manifold Absolute Pressure (MAP) sensor circuit
34	Manifold Absolute Pressure (MAP) sensor circuit
42	Electronic Spark Timing (EST)
43	Electronic Spark Control (ESC)
44	Lean exhaust indicated
45	Rich exhaust indicated
54	Fuel pump circuit
51	PROM problem
52	Fuel calpak missing
55	Electronic Control Module (ECM)

Year – 1987
Model – El Camino
Engine – 5.0L (305 cid) V8
Engine Code – VIN H

ECM TROUBLE CODES

Code	Explanation
12	No distributor reference signal to the Electronic Control Module (ECM). This code is not stored in memory and will only flash while the fault is present. Normal code with ignition ON, engine not running
13	Oxygen sensor circuit – the engine must run up to 4 minutes at part throttle, under road load, before this code will set
14	Shorted Coolant Temperature Sensor (CTS) circuit – the engine must run 2 minutes before this code will set
15	Open Coolant Temperature Sensor (CTS) circuit – the engine must run 5 minutes before this code will set
21	Throttle Position Sensor (TPS) circuit voltage high – open circuit or misadjusted TPS – the engine must run 10 seconds, at specified curb idle speed, before this code will set
22	Throttle Position Sensor (TPS) circuit voltage low – grounded circuit or misadjusted TPS – engine must run 20 seconds at specified curb idle speed, to set code
23	Mixture Control (M/C) solenoid circuit open or grounded
24	Vehicle Speed Sensor (VSS) circuit – the vehicle must operate up to 2 minutes at road speed, before this code will set
32	Barometric Pressure Sensor (BARO) circuit low
34	Manifold Absolute Pressure (MAP) or vacuum sensor circuit. The engine must run up to 2 minutes at specified curb idle speed, before this code will set
35	Idle Speed Control (ISC) switch circuit shorted – up to 70% Throttle Position Sensor (TPS) for over 5 seconds
41	No distributor reference signal to the Electronic Control Module (ECM) at specified engine vacuum. This code will store in memory
42	Electronic Spark Timing (EST) bypass circuit or EST circuit grounded or open
43	Electronic Spark Control (ESC) retard signal for too long a time – causes retard in Electronic Spark Timing (EST) signal
44	Lean exhaust indication – the engine must run 2 minutes, in closed loop and at part throttle, before this code will set
45	Rich exhaust indication – the engine must run 2 minutes, in closed loop and at part throttle, before this code will set
51	Faulty or improperly installed calibration unit (PROM). It takes up to 30 seconds before this code will set
53	Exhaust Gas Recirculation (EGR) valve vacuum sensor has seen improper EGR vacuum
54	Mixture Control (M/C) solenoid voltage high, at Electronic Control Module (ECM), as a result of a shorted M/C solenoid circuit and/or faulty ECM

Year – 1988
Model – S & T Series
Engine – 2.5L (151 cid) TBI 4 cyl
Engine Code – VIN E

ECM TROUBLE CODES

Code	Explanation
13	Oxygen sensor circuit – open oxygen sensor – indicates that the oxygen sensor circuit or sensor was open for 1 minute while off idle
14	Coolant Temperature Sensor (CTS) – high temperature indication – sets if the sensor or signal line becomes grounded for 3 seconds
15	Coolant Temperature Sensor (CTS) – low temperature indication – sets if the sensor, connections or wires open for 3 seconds
21	Throttle Position Sensor (TPS) – signal voltage high – TPS voltage greater than 2.5V for 3 seconds with less than 1200 rpm
22	Throttle Position Sensor (TPS) – signal voltage low – short to ground or open signal circuit will set in 3 seconds
23	Manifold Air Temperature (MAT) – low temperature indication – sets if the sensor, connections or wires open for 3 seconds
24	Vehicle Speed Sensor (VSS) circuit – no vehicle speed indication – no vehicle speed present during a road load deceleration
25	Manifold Air Temperature (MAT) – high temperature indication – sets if the sensor or signal line becomes grounded for 3 seconds
32	Exhaust Gas Recirculation (EGR) – vacuum switch shorted to ground on start up or switch not closed after the Electronic Control Module (ECM) has commanded EGR for a specified period of time or EGR solenoid circuit open for a specified period of time
33	Manifold Absolute Pressure (MAP) sensor – low vacuum – MAP sensor output too high for 5 seconds or an open signal circuit
34	Manifold Absolute Pressure (MAP) sensor – high vacuum – low or no output from sensor with engine running
35	Idle Air Control (IAC) – IAC error
42	Electronic Spark Timing (EST) – Electronic Control Module (ECM) has seen an open or grounded EST or bypass circuit
43	Electronic Spark Control (ESC) – signal to the Electronic Control Module (ECM) has remained low for too long or the system has failed a functional check
44	Lean exhaust indication – sets if oxygen sensor voltage remains below 0.2V for about 20 seconds
45	Rich exhaust indication – sets if oxygen sensor voltage remains above 0.7V for about 1 minute
51	Faulty Mem-Cal, PROM or Electronic Control Module (ECM)
52	Fuel Calpak missing or faulty
53	System overvoltage – indicates a basic generator problem
54	Fuel pump – low voltage – sets when the fuel pump voltage is less than 2V when reference pulses are being received
55	Faulty Electronic Control Module (ECM)

Year – 1988
Model – S & T Series
Engine – 2.8L (173 cid) TBI V6
Engine Code – VIN R

ECM TROUBLE CODES

Code	Explanation
13	Oxygen sensor circuit – open oxygen sensor – indicates that the oxygen sensor circuit or sensor was open for 1 minute while off idle
14	Coolant Temperature Sensor (CTS) – high temperature indication – sets if the sensor or signal line becomes grounded for 3 seconds
15	Coolant Temperature Sensor (CTS) – low temperature indication – sets if the sensor, connections or wires open for 3 seconds
21	Throttle Position Sensor (TPS) – signal voltage high – TPS voltage greater than 2.5V for 3 seconds with less than 1200 rpm
22	Throttle Position Sensor (TPS) – signal voltage low – short to ground or open signal circuit will set in 3 seconds
23	Manifold Air Temperature (MAT) – low temperature indication – sets if the sensor, connections or wires open for 3 seconds
24	Vehicle Speed Sensor (VSS) circuit – no vehicle speed indication – no vehicle speed present during a road load deceleration
25	Manifold Air Temperature (MAT) – high temperature indication – sets if the sensor or signal line becomes grounded for 3 seconds
32	Exhaust Gas Recirculation (EGR) – vacuum switch shorted to ground on start up or switch not closed after the Electronic Control Module (ECM) has commanded EGR for a specified period of time or EGR solenoid circuit open for a specified period of time
33	Manifold Absolute Pressure (MAP) sensor – low vacuum – MAP sensor output too high for 5 seconds or an open signal circuit
34	Manifold Absolute Pressure (MAP) sensor – high vacuum – low or no output from sensor with engine running
35	Idle Air Control (IAC) – IAC error
42	Electronic Spark Timing (EST) – Electronic Control Module (ECM) has seen an open or grounded EST or bypass circuit
43	Electronic Spark Control (ESC) – signal to the Electronic Control Module (ECM) has remained low for too long or the system has failed a functional check
44	Lean exhaust indication – sets if oxygen sensor voltage remains below 0.2V for about 20 seconds
45	Rich exhaust indication – sets if oxygen sensor voltage remains above 0.7V for about 1 minute
51	Faulty Mem-Cal, PROM or Electronic Control Module (ECM)
52	Fuel Calpak missing or faulty
53	System overvoltage – indicates a basic generator problem
54	Fuel pump – low voltage – sets when the fuel pump voltage is less than 2V when reference pulses are being received
55	Faulty Electronic Control Module (ECM)

Year — 1988
Model — S & T Series
Engine — 4.3L (262 cid) TBI V6
Engine Code — VIN Z

ECM TROUBLE CODES

Code	Explanation
13	Oxygen sensor circuit — open oxygen sensor — indicates that the oxygen sensor circuit or sensor was open for 1 minute while off idle
14	Coolant Temperature Sensor (CTS) — high temperature indication — sets if the sensor or signal line becomes grounded for 3 seconds
15	Coolant Temperature Sensor (CTS) — low temperature indication — sets if the sensor, connections or wires open for 3 seconds
21	Throttle Position Sensor (TPS) — signal voltage high — TPS voltage greater than 2.5V for 3 seconds with less than 1200 rpm
22	Throttle Position Sensor (TPS) — signal voltage low — short to ground or open signal circuit will set in 3 seconds
23	Manifold Air Temperature (MAT) — low temperature indication — sets if the sensor, connections or wires open for 3 seconds
24	Vehicle Speed Sensor (VSS) circuit — no vehicle speed indication — no vehicle speed present during a road load deceleration
25	Manifold Air Temperature (MAT) — high temperature indication — sets if the sensor or signal line becomes grounded for 3 seconds
32	Exhaust Gas Recirculation (EGR) — vacuum switch shorted to ground on start up or switch not closed after the Electronic Control Module (ECM) has commanded EGR for a specified period of time or EGR solenoid circuit open for a specified period of time
33	Manifold Absolute Pressure (MAP) sensor — low vacuum — MAP sensor output too high for 5 seconds or an open signal circuit
34	Manifold Absolute Pressure (MAP) sensor — high vacuum — low or no output from sensor with engine running
35	Idle Air Control (IAC) — IAC error
42	Electronic Spark Timing (EST) — Electronic Control Module (ECM) has seen an open or grounded EST or bypass circuit
43	Electronic Spark Control (ESC) — signal to the Electronic Control Module (ECM) has remained low for too long or the system has failed a functional check
44	Lean exhaust indication — sets if oxygen sensor voltage remains below 0.2V for about 20 seconds
45	Rich exhaust indication — sets if oxygen sensor voltage remains above 0.7V for about 1 minute
51	Faulty Mem-Cal, PROM or Electronic Control Module (ECM)
52	Fuel Calpak missing or faulty
53	System overvoltage — indicates a basic generator problem
54	Fuel pump — low voltage — sets when the fuel pump voltage is less than 2V when reference pulses are being received
55	Faulty Electronic Control Module (ECM)

Year — 1988
Model — M Vans (Astro Van)
Engine — 2.5L (151 cid) TBI 4 cyl
Engine Code — VIN E

ECM TROUBLE CODES

Code	Explanation
13	Oxygen sensor circuit — open oxygen sensor — indicates that the oxygen sensor circuit or sensor was open for 1 minute while off idle
14	Coolant Temperature Sensor (CTS) — high temperature indication — sets if the sensor or signal line becomes grounded for 3 seconds
15	Coolant Temperature Sensor (CTS) — low temperature indication — sets if the sensor, connections or wires open for 3 seconds
21	Throttle Position Sensor (TPS) — signal voltage high — TPS voltage greater than 2.5V for 3 seconds with less than 1200 rpm
22	Throttle Position Sensor (TPS) — signal voltage low — short to ground or open signal circuit will set in 3 seconds
23	Manifold Air Temperature (MAT) — low temperature indication — sets if the sensor, connections or wires open for 3 seconds
24	Vehicle Speed Sensor (VSS) circuit — no vehicle speed indication — no vehicle speed present during a road load deceleration
25	Manifold Air Temperature (MAT) — high temperature indication — sets if the sensor or signal line becomes grounded for 3 seconds
32	Exhaust Gas Recirculation (EGR) — vacuum switch shorted to ground on start up or switch not closed after the Electronic Control Module (ECM) has commanded EGR for a specified period of time or EGR solenoid circuit open for a specified period of time
33	Manifold Absolute Pressure (MAP) sensor — low vacuum — MAP sensor output too high for 5 seconds or an open signal circuit
34	Manifold Absolute Pressure (MAP) sensor — high vacuum — low or no output from sensor with engine running
35	Idle Air Control (IAC) — IAC error
42	Electronic Spark Timing (EST) — Electronic Control Module (ECM) has seen an open or grounded EST or bypass circuit
43	Electronic Spark Control (ESC) — signal to the Electronic Control Module (ECM) has remained low for too long or the system has failed a functional check
44	Lean exhaust indication — sets if oxygen sensor voltage remains below 0.2V for about 20 seconds
45	Rich exhaust indication — sets if oxygen sensor voltage remains above 0.7V for about 1 minute
51	Faulty Mem-Cal, PROM or Electronic Control Module (ECM)
52	Fuel Calpak missing or faulty
53	System overvoltage — indicates a basic generator problem
54	Fuel pump — low voltage — sets when the fuel pump voltage is less than 2V when reference pulses are being received
55	Faulty Electronic Control Module (ECM)

Year – 1988
Model – M Vans (Astro Van)
Engine – 4.3L (262 cid) TBI V6
Engine Code – VIN Z

ECM TROUBLE CODES

Code	Explanation
13	Oxygen sensor circuit – open oxygen sensor – indicates that the oxygen sensor circuit or sensor was open for 1 minute while off idle
14	Coolant Temperature Sensor (CTS) – high temperature indication – sets if the sensor or signal line becomes grounded for 3 seconds
15	Coolant Temperature Sensor (CTS) – low temperature indication – sets if the sensor, connections or wires open for 3 seconds
21	Throttle Position Sensor (TPS) – signal voltage high – TPS voltage greater than 2.5V for 3 seconds with less than 1200 rpm
22	Throttle Position Sensor (TPS) – signal voltage low – short to ground or open signal circuit will set in 3 seconds
23	Manifold Air Temperature (MAT) – low temperature indication – sets if the sensor, connections or wires open for 3 seconds
24	Vehicle Speed Sensor (VSS) circuit – no vehicle speed indication – no vehicle speed present during a road load deceleration
25	Manifold Air Temperature (MAT) – high temperature indication – sets if the sensor or signal line becomes grounded for 3 seconds
32	Exhaust Gas Recirculation (EGR) – vacuum switch shorted to ground on start up or switch not closed after the Electronic Control Module (ECM) has commanded EGR for a specified period of time or EGR solenoid circuit open for a specified period of time
33	Manifold Absolute Pressure (MAP) sensor – low vacuum – MAP sensor output too high for 5 seconds or an open signal circuit
34	Manifold Absolute Pressure (MAP) sensor – high vacuum – low or no output from sensor with engine running
35	Idle Air Control (IAC) – IAC error
42	Electronic Spark Timing (EST) – Electronic Control Module (ECM) has seen an open or grounded EST or bypass circuit
43	Electronic Spark Control (ESC) – signal to the Electronic Control Module (ECM) has remained low for too long or the system has failed a functional check
44	Lean exhaust indication – sets if oxygen sensor voltage remains below 0.2V for about 20 seconds
45	Rich exhaust indication – sets if oxygen sensor voltage remains above 0.7V for about 1 minute
51	Faulty Mem-Cal, PROM or Electronic Control Module (ECM)
52	Fuel Calpak missing or faulty
53	System overvoltage – indicates a basic generator problem
54	Fuel pump – low voltage – sets when the fuel pump voltage is less than 2V when reference pulses are being received
55	Faulty Electronic Control Module (ECM)

Year – 1988
Model – G-Series Vans
Engine – 4.3L (262 cid) TBI V6
Engine Code – VIN Z

ECM TROUBLE CODES

Code	Explanation
13	Oxygen sensor circuit – open oxygen sensor – indicates that the oxygen sensor circuit or sensor was open for 1 minute while off idle
14	Coolant Temperature Sensor (CTS) – high temperature indication – sets if the sensor or signal line becomes grounded for 3 seconds
15	Coolant Temperature Sensor (CTS) – low temperature indication – sets if the sensor, connections or wires open for 3 seconds
21	Throttle Position Sensor (TPS) – signal voltage high – TPS voltage greater than 2.5V for 3 seconds with less than 1200 rpm
22	Throttle Position Sensor (TPS) – signal voltage low – short to ground or open signal circuit will set in 3 seconds
23	Manifold Air Temperature (MAT) – low temperature indication – sets if the sensor, connections or wires open for 3 seconds
24	Vehicle Speed Sensor (VSS) circuit – no vehicle speed indication – no vehicle speed present during a road load deceleration
25	Manifold Air Temperature (MAT) – high temperature indication – sets if the sensor or signal line becomes grounded for 3 seconds
32	Exhaust Gas Recirculation (EGR) – vacuum switch shorted to ground on start up or switch not closed after the Electronic Control Module (ECM) has commanded EGR for a specified period of time or EGR solenoid circuit open for a specified period of time
33	Manifold Absolute Pressure (MAP) sensor – low vacuum – MAP sensor output too high for 5 seconds or an open signal circuit
34	Manifold Absolute Pressure (MAP) sensor – high vacuum – low or no output from sensor with engine running
35	Idle Air Control (IAC) – IAC error
42	Electronic Spark Timing (EST) – Electronic Control Module (ECM) has seen an open or grounded EST or bypass circuit
43	Electronic Spark Control (ESC) – signal to the Electronic Control Module (ECM) has remained low for too long or the system has failed a functional check
44	Lean exhaust indication – sets if oxygen sensor voltage remains below 0.2V for about 20 seconds
45	Rich exhaust indication – sets if oxygen sensor voltage remains above 0.7V for about 1 minute
51	Faulty Mem-Cal, PROM or Electronic Control Module (ECM)
52	Fuel Calpak missing or faulty
53	System overvoltage – indicates a basic generator problem
54	Fuel pump – low voltage – sets when the fuel pump voltage is less than 2V when reference pulses are being received
55	Faulty Electronic Control Module (ECM)

Year – 1988
Model – G-Series Vans
Engine – 5.0L (305 cid) TBI V8
Engine Code – VIN H

ECM TROUBLE CODES

Code	Explanation
13	Oxygen sensor circuit—open oxygen sensor—indicates that the oxygen sensor circuit or sensor was open for 1 minute while off idle
14	Coolant Temperature Sensor (CTS)—high temperature indication—sets if the sensor or signal line becomes grounded for 3 seconds
15	Coolant Temperature Sensor (CTS)—low temperature indication—sets if the sensor, connections or wires open for 3 seconds
21	Throttle Position Sensor (TPS)—signal voltage high—TPS voltage greater than 2.5V for 3 seconds with less than 1200 rpm
22	Throttle Position Sensor (TPS)—signal voltage low—short to ground or open signal circuit will set in 3 seconds
23	Manifold Air Temperature (MAT)—low temperature indication—sets if the sensor, connections or wires open for 3 seconds
24	Vehicle Speed Sensor (VSS) circuit—no vehicle speed indication—no vehicle speed present during a road load deceleration
25	Manifold Air Temperature (MAT)—high temperature indication—sets if the sensor or signal line becomes grounded for 3 seconds
32	Exhaust Gas Recirculation (EGR)—vacuum switch shorted to ground on start up or switch not closed after the Electronic Control Module (ECM) has commanded EGR for a specified period of time or EGR solenoid circuit open for a specified period of time
33	Manifold Absolute Pressure (MAP) sensor—low vacuum—MAP sensor output too high for 5 seconds or an open signal circuit
34	Manifold Absolute Pressure (MAP) sensor—high vacuum—low or no output from sensor with engine running
35	Idle Air Control (IAC)—IAC error
42	Electronic Spark Timing (EST)—Electronic Control Module (ECM) has seen an open or grounded EST or bypass circuit
43	Electronic Spark Control (ESC)—signal to the Electronic Control Module (ECM) has remained low for too long or the system has failed a functional check
44	Lean exhaust indication—sets if oxygen sensor voltage remains below 0.2V for about 20 seconds
45	Rich exhaust indication—sets if oxygen sensor voltage remains above 0.7V for about 1 minute
51	Faulty Mem-Cal, PROM or Electronic Control Module (ECM)
52	Fuel Calpak missing or faulty
53	System overvoltage—indicates a basic generator problem
54	Fuel pump—low voltage—sets when the fuel pump voltage is less than 2V when reference pulses are being received
55	Faulty Electronic Control Module (ECM)

Year — 1988
Model — G-Series Vans
Engine — 5.7L (350 cid) TBI V8
Engine Code — VIN K

ECM TROUBLE CODES

Code	Explanation
13	Oxygen sensor circuit — open oxygen sensor — indicates that the oxygen sensor circuit or sensor was open for 1 minute while off idle
14	Coolant Temperature Sensor (CTS) — high temperature indication — sets if the sensor or signal line becomes grounded for 3 seconds
15	Coolant Temperature Sensor (CTS) — low temperature indication — sets if the sensor, connections or wires open for 3 seconds
21	Throttle Position Sensor (TPS) — signal voltage high — TPS voltage greater than 2.5V for 3 seconds with less than 1200 rpm
22	Throttle Position Sensor (TPS) — signal voltage low — short to ground or open signal circuit will set in 3 seconds
23	Manifold Air Temperature (MAT) — low temperature indication — sets if the sensor, connections or wires open for 3 seconds
24	Vehicle Speed Sensor (VSS) circuit — no vehicle speed indication — no vehicle speed present during a road load deceleration
25	Manifold Air Temperature (MAT) — high temperature indication — sets if the sensor or signal line becomes grounded for 3 seconds
32	Exhaust Gas Recirculation (EGR) — vacuum switch shorted to ground on start up or switch not closed after the Electronic Control Module (ECM) has commanded EGR for a specified period of time or EGR solenoid circuit open for a specified period of time
33	Manifold Absolute Pressure (MAP) sensor — low vacuum — MAP sensor output too high for 5 seconds or an open signal circuit
34	Manifold Absolute Pressure (MAP) sensor — high vacuum — low or no output from sensor with engine running
35	Idle Air Control (IAC) — IAC error
42	Electronic Spark Timing (EST) — Electronic Control Module (ECM) has seen an open or grounded EST or bypass circuit
43	Electronic Spark Control (ESC) — signal to the Electronic Control Module (ECM) has remained low for too long or the system has failed a functional check
44	Lean exhaust indication — sets if oxygen sensor voltage remains below 0.2V for about 20 seconds
45	Rich exhaust indication — sets if oxygen sensor voltage remains above 0.7V for about 1 minute
51	Faulty Mem-Cal, PROM or Electronic Control Module (ECM)
52	Fuel Calpak missing or faulty
53	System overvoltage — indicates a basic generator problem
54	Fuel pump — low voltage — sets when the fuel pump voltage is less than 2V when reference pulses are being received
55	Faulty Electronic Control Module (ECM)

GENERAL MOTORS CORPORATION
DIAGNOSTIC CODE DATA

Year – 1988
Model – G-Series Vans
Engine – 7.4L (454 cid) TBI V8
Engine Code – VIN N

ECM TROUBLE CODES

Code	Explanation
13	Oxygen sensor circuit – open oxygen sensor – indicates that the oxygen sensor circuit or sensor was open for 1 minute while off idle
14	Coolant Temperature Sensor (CTS) – high temperature indication – sets if the sensor or signal line becomes grounded for 3 seconds
15	Coolant Temperature Sensor (CTS) – low temperature indication – sets if the sensor, connections or wires open for 3 seconds
21	Throttle Position Sensor (TPS) – signal voltage high – TPS voltage greater than 2.5V for 3 seconds with less than 1200 rpm
22	Throttle Position Sensor (TPS) – signal voltage low – short to ground or open signal circuit will set in 3 seconds
23	Manifold Air Temperature (MAT) – low temperature indication – sets if the sensor, connections or wires open for 3 seconds
24	Vehicle Speed Sensor (VSS) circuit – no vehicle speed indication – no vehicle speed present during a road load deceleration
25	Manifold Air Temperature (MAT) – high temperature indication – sets if the sensor or signal line becomes grounded for 3 seconds
32	Exhaust Gas Recirculation (EGR) – vacuum switch shorted to ground on start up or switch not closed after the Electronic Control Module (ECM) has commanded EGR for a specified period of time or EGR solenoid circuit open for a specified period of time
33	Manifold Absolute Pressure (MAP) sensor – low vacuum – MAP sensor output too high for 5 seconds or an open signal circuit
34	Manifold Absolute Pressure (MAP) sensor – high vacuum – low or no output from sensor with engine running
35	Idle Air Control (IAC) – IAC error
42	Electronic Spark Timing (EST) – Electronic Control Module (ECM) has seen an open or grounded EST or bypass circuit
43	Electronic Spark Control (ESC) – signal to the Electronic Control Module (ECM) has remained low for too long or the system has failed a functional check
44	Lean exhaust indication – sets if oxygen sensor voltage remains below 0.2V for about 20 seconds
45	Rich exhaust indication – sets if oxygen sensor voltage remains above 0.7V for about 1 minute
51	Faulty Mem-Cal, PROM or Electronic Control Module (ECM)
52	Fuel Calpak missing or faulty
53	System overvoltage – indicates a basic generator problem
54	Fuel pump – low voltage – sets when the fuel pump voltage is less than 2V when reference pulses are being received
55	Faulty Electronic Control Module (ECM)

Year — 1988
Model — R & V Series
Engine — 4.3L (262 cid) TBI V6
Engine Code — VIN Z

ECM TROUBLE CODES

Code	Explanation
13	Oxygen sensor circuit — open oxygen sensor — indicates that the oxygen sensor circuit or sensor was open for 1 minute while off idle
14	Coolant Temperature Sensor (CTS) — high temperature indication — sets if the sensor or signal line becomes grounded for 3 seconds
15	Coolant Temperature Sensor (CTS) — low temperature indication — sets if the sensor, connections or wires open for 3 seconds
21	Throttle Position Sensor (TPS) — signal voltage high — TPS voltage greater than 2.5V for 3 seconds with less than 1200 rpm
22	Throttle Position Sensor (TPS) — signal voltage low — short to ground or open signal circuit will set in 3 seconds
23	Manifold Air Temperature (MAT) — low temperature indication — sets if the sensor, connections or wires open for 3 seconds
24	Vehicle Speed Sensor (VSS) circuit — no vehicle speed indication — no vehicle speed present during a road load deceleration
25	Manifold Air Temperature (MAT) — high temperature indication — sets if the sensor or signal line becomes grounded for 3 seconds
32	Exhaust Gas Recirculation (EGR) — vacuum switch shorted to ground on start up or switch not closed after the Electronic Control Module (ECM) has commanded EGR for a specified period of time or EGR solenoid circuit open for a specified period of time
33	Manifold Absolute Pressure (MAP) sensor — low vacuum — MAP sensor output too high for 5 seconds or an open signal circuit
34	Manifold Absolute Pressure (MAP) sensor — high vacuum — low or no output from sensor with engine running
35	Idle Air Control (IAC) — IAC error
42	Electronic Spark Timing (EST) — Electronic Control Module (ECM) has seen an open or grounded EST or bypass circuit
43	Electronic Spark Control (ESC) — signal to the Electronic Control Module (ECM) has remained low for too long or the system has failed a functional check
44	Lean exhaust indication — sets if oxygen sensor voltage remains below 0.2V for about 20 seconds
45	Rich exhaust indication — sets if oxygen sensor voltage remains above 0.7V for about 1 minute
51	Faulty Mem-Cal, PROM or Electronic Control Module (ECM)
52	Fuel Calpak missing or faulty
53	System overvoltage — indicates a basic generator problem
54	Fuel pump — low voltage — sets when the fuel pump voltage is less than 2V when reference pulses are being received
55	Faulty Electronic Control Module (ECM)

Year – 1988
Model – R & V Series
Engine – 5.0L (305 cid) TBI V8
Engine Code – VIN H

ECM TROUBLE CODES

Code	Explanation
13	Oxygen sensor circuit – open oxygen sensor – indicates that the oxygen sensor circuit or sensor was open for 1 minute while off idle
14	Coolant Temperature Sensor (CTS) – high temperature indication – sets if the sensor or signal line becomes grounded for 3 seconds
15	Coolant Temperature Sensor (CTS) – low temperature indication – sets if the sensor, connections or wires open for 3 seconds
21	Throttle Position Sensor (TPS) – signal voltage high – TPS voltage greater than 2.5V for 3 seconds with less than 1200 rpm
22	Throttle Position Sensor (TPS) – signal voltage low – short to ground or open signal circuit will set in 3 seconds
23	Manifold Air Temperature (MAT) – low temperature indication – sets if the sensor, connections or wires open for 3 seconds
24	Vehicle Speed Sensor (VSS) circuit – no vehicle speed indication – no vehicle speed present during a road load deceleration
25	Manifold Air Temperature (MAT) – high temperature indication – sets if the sensor or signal line becomes grounded for 3 seconds
32	Exhaust Gas Recirculation (EGR) – vacuum switch shorted to ground on start up or switch not closed after the Electronic Control Module (ECM) has commanded EGR for a specified period of time or EGR solenoid circuit open for a specified period of time
33	Manifold Absolute Pressure (MAP) sensor – low vacuum – MAP sensor output too high for 5 seconds or an open signal circuit
34	Manifold Absolute Pressure (MAP) sensor – high vacuum – low or no output from sensor with engine running
35	Idle Air Control (IAC) – IAC error
42	Electronic Spark Timing (EST) – Electronic Control Module (ECM) has seen an open or grounded EST or bypass circuit
43	Electronic Spark Control (ESC) – signal to the Electronic Control Module (ECM) has remained low for too long or the system has failed a functional check
44	Lean exhaust indication – sets if oxygen sensor voltage remains below 0.2V for about 20 seconds
45	Rich exhaust indication – sets if oxygen sensor voltage remains above 0.7V for about 1 minute
51	Faulty Mem-Cal, PROM or Electronic Control Module (ECM)
52	Fuel Calpak missing or faulty
53	System overvoltage – indicates a basic generator problem
54	Fuel pump – low voltage – sets when the fuel pump voltage is less than 2V when reference pulses are being received
55	Faulty Electronic Control Module (ECM)

Year – 1988
Model – R & V Series
Engine – 5.7L (350 cid) TBI V8
Engine Code – VIN K

ECM TROUBLE CODES

Code	Explanation
13	Oxygen sensor circuit—open oxygen sensor—indicates that the oxygen sensor circuit or sensor was open for 1 minute while off idle
14	Coolant Temperature Sensor (CTS)—high temperature indication—sets if the sensor or signal line becomes grounded for 3 seconds
15	Coolant Temperature Sensor (CTS)—low temperature indication—sets if the sensor, connections or wires open for 3 seconds
21	Throttle Position Sensor (TPS)—signal voltage high—TPS voltage greater than 2.5V for 3 seconds with less than 1200 rpm
22	Throttle Position Sensor (TPS)—signal voltage low—short to ground or open signal circuit will set in 3 seconds
23	Manifold Air Temperature (MAT)—low temperature indication—sets if the sensor, connections or wires open for 3 seconds
24	Vehicle Speed Sensor (VSS) circuit—no vehicle speed indication—no vehicle speed present during a road load deceleration
25	Manifold Air Temperature (MAT)—high temperature indication—sets if the sensor or signal line becomes grounded for 3 seconds
32	Exhaust Gas Recirculation (EGR)—vacuum switch shorted to ground on start up or switch not closed after the Electronic Control Module (ECM) has commanded EGR for a specified period of time or EGR solenoid circuit open for a specified period of time
33	Manifold Absolute Pressure (MAP) sensor—low vacuum—MAP sensor output too high for 5 seconds or an open signal circuit
34	Manifold Absolute Pressure (MAP) sensor—high vacuum—low or no output from sensor with engine running
35	Idle Air Control (IAC)—IAC error
42	Electronic Spark Timing (EST)—Electronic Control Module (ECM) has seen an open or grounded EST or bypass circuit
43	Electronic Spark Control (ESC)—signal to the Electronic Control Module (ECM) has remained low for too long or the system has failed a functional check
44	Lean exhaust indication—sets if oxygen sensor voltage remains below 0.2V for about 20 seconds
45	Rich exhaust indication—sets if oxygen sensor voltage remains above 0.7V for about 1 minute
51	Faulty Mem-Cal, PROM or Electronic Control Module (ECM)
52	Fuel Calpak missing or faulty
53	System overvoltage—indicates a basic generator problem
54	Fuel pump—low voltage—sets when the fuel pump voltage is less than 2V when reference pulses are being received
55	Faulty Electronic Control Module (ECM)

GENERAL MOTORS CORPORATION
DIAGNOSTIC CODE DATA

Year — 1988
Model — R & V Series
Engine — 7.4L (454 cid) TBI V8
Engine Code — VIN N

ECM TROUBLE CODES

Code	Explanation
13	Oxygen sensor circuit — open oxygen sensor — indicates that the oxygen sensor circuit or sensor was open for 1 minute while off idle
14	Coolant Temperature Sensor (CTS) — high temperature indication — sets if the sensor or signal line becomes grounded for 3 seconds
15	Coolant Temperature Sensor (CTS) — low temperature indication — sets if the sensor, connections or wires open for 3 seconds
21	Throttle Position Sensor (TPS) — signal voltage high — TPS voltage greater than 2.5V for 3 seconds with less than 1200 rpm
22	Throttle Position Sensor (TPS) — signal voltage low — short to ground or open signal circuit will set in 3 seconds
23	Manifold Air Temperature (MAT) — low temperature indication — sets if the sensor, connections or wires open for 3 seconds
24	Vehicle Speed Sensor (VSS) circuit — no vehicle speed indication — no vehicle speed present during a road load deceleration
25	Manifold Air Temperature (MAT) — high temperature indication — sets if the sensor or signal line becomes grounded for 3 seconds
32	Exhaust Gas Recirculation (EGR) — vacuum switch shorted to ground on start up or switch not closed after the Electronic Control Module (ECM) has commanded EGR for a specified period of time or EGR solenoid circuit open for a specified period of time
33	Manifold Absolute Pressure (MAP) sensor — low vacuum — MAP sensor output too high for 5 seconds or an open signal circuit
34	Manifold Absolute Pressure (MAP) sensor — high vacuum — low or no output from sensor with engine running
35	Idle Air Control (IAC) — IAC error
42	Electronic Spark Timing (EST) — Electronic Control Module (ECM) has seen an open or grounded EST or bypass circuit
43	Electronic Spark Control (ESC) — signal to the Electronic Control Module (ECM) has remained low for too long or the system has failed a functional check
44	Lean exhaust indication — sets if oxygen sensor voltage remains below 0.2V for about 20 seconds
45	Rich exhaust indication — sets if oxygen sensor voltage remains above 0.7V for about 1 minute
51	Faulty Mem-Cal, PROM or Electronic Control Module (ECM)
52	Fuel Calpak missing or faulty
53	System overvoltage — indicates a basic generator problem
54	Fuel pump — low voltage — sets when the fuel pump voltage is less than 2V when reference pulses are being received
55	Faulty Electronic Control Module (ECM)

Year – 1988
Model – C & K Series
Engine – 4.3L (262 cid) TBI V6
Engine Code – VIN Z

ECM TROUBLE CODES

Code	Explanation
13	Oxygen sensor circuit – open oxygen sensor – indicates that the oxygen sensor circuit or sensor was open for 1 minute while off idle
14	Coolant Temperature Sensor (CTS) – high temperature indication – sets if the sensor or signal line becomes grounded for 3 seconds
15	Coolant Temperature Sensor (CTS) – low temperature indication – sets if the sensor, connections or wires open for 3 seconds
21	Throttle Position Sensor (TPS) – signal voltage high – TPS voltage greater than 2.5V for 3 seconds with less than 1200 rpm
22	Throttle Position Sensor (TPS) – signal voltage low – short to ground or open signal circuit will set in 3 seconds
23	Manifold Air Temperature (MAT) – low temperature indication – sets if the sensor, connections or wires open for 3 seconds
24	Vehicle Speed Sensor (VSS) circuit – no vehicle speed indication – no vehicle speed present during a road load deceleration
25	Manifold Air Temperature (MAT) – high temperature indication – sets if the sensor or signal line becomes grounded for 3 seconds
32	Exhaust Gas Recirculation (EGR) – vacuum switch shorted to ground on start up or switch not closed after the Electronic Control Module (ECM) has commanded EGR for a specified period of time or EGR solenoid circuit open for a specified period of time
33	Manifold Absolute Pressure (MAP) sensor – low vacuum – MAP sensor output too high for 5 seconds or an open signal circuit
34	Manifold Absolute Pressure (MAP) sensor – high vacuum – low or no output from sensor with engine running
35	Idle Air Control (IAC) – IAC error
42	Electronic Spark Timing (EST) – Electronic Control Module (ECM) has seen an open or grounded EST or bypass circuit
43	Electronic Spark Control (ESC) – signal to the Electronic Control Module (ECM) has remained low for too long or the system has failed a functional check
44	Lean exhaust indication – sets if oxygen sensor voltage remains below 0.2V for about 20 seconds
45	Rich exhaust indication – sets if oxygen sensor voltage remains above 0.7V for about 1 minute
51	Faulty Mem-Cal, PROM or Electronic Control Module (ECM)
52	Fuel Calpak missing or faulty
53	System overvoltage – indicates a basic generator problem
54	Fuel pump – low voltage – sets when the fuel pump voltage is less than 2V when reference pulses are being received
55	Faulty Electronic Control Module (ECM)

Year—1988
Model—C & K Series
Engine—5.0L (305 cid) TBI V8
Engine Code—VIN H

ECM TROUBLE CODES

Code	Explanation
13	Oxygen sensor circuit—open oxygen sensor—indicates that the oxygen sensor circuit or sensor was open for 1 minute while off idle
14	Coolant Temperature Sensor (CTS)—high temperature indication—sets if the sensor or signal line becomes grounded for 3 seconds
15	Coolant Temperature Sensor (CTS)—low temperature indication—sets if the sensor, connections or wires open for 3 seconds
21	Throttle Position Sensor (TPS)—signal voltage high—TPS voltage greater than 2.5V for 3 seconds with less than 1200 rpm
22	Throttle Position Sensor (TPS)—signal voltage low—short to ground or open signal circuit will set in 3 seconds
23	Manifold Air Temperature (MAT)—low temperature indication—sets if the sensor, connections or wires open for 3 seconds
24	Vehicle Speed Sensor (VSS) circuit—no vehicle speed indication—no vehicle speed present during a road load deceleration
25	Manifold Air Temperature (MAT)—high temperature indication—sets if the sensor or signal line becomes grounded for 3 seconds
32	Exhaust Gas Recirculation (EGR)—vacuum switch shorted to ground on start up or switch not closed after the Electronic Control Module (ECM) has commanded EGR for a specified period of time or EGR solenoid circuit open for a specified period of time
33	Manifold Absolute Pressure (MAP) sensor—low vacuum—MAP sensor output too high for 5 seconds or an open signal circuit
34	Manifold Absolute Pressure (MAP) sensor—high vacuum—low or no output from sensor with engine running
35	Idle Air Control (IAC)—IAC error
42	Electronic Spark Timing (EST)—Electronic Control Module (ECM) has seen an open or grounded EST or bypass circuit
43	Electronic Spark Control (ESC)—signal to the Electronic Control Module (ECM) has remained low for too long or the system has failed a functional check
44	Lean exhaust indication—sets if oxygen sensor voltage remains below 0.2V for about 20 seconds
45	Rich exhaust indication—sets if oxygen sensor voltage remains above 0.7V for about 1 minute
51	Faulty Mem-Cal, PROM or Electronic Control Module (ECM)
52	Fuel Calpak missing or faulty
53	System overvoltage—indicates a basic generator problem
54	Fuel pump—low voltage—sets when the fuel pump voltage is less than 2V when reference pulses are being received
55	Faulty Electronic Control Module (ECM)

Year — 1988
Model — C & K Series
Engine — 5.7L (350 cid) TBI V8
Engine Code — VIN K

ECM TROUBLE CODES

Code	Explanation
13	Oxygen sensor circuit — open oxygen sensor — indicates that the oxygen sensor circuit or sensor was open for 1 minute while off idle
14	Coolant Temperature Sensor (CTS) — high temperature indication — sets if the sensor or signal line becomes grounded for 3 seconds
15	Coolant Temperature Sensor (CTS) — low temperature indication — sets if the sensor, connections or wires open for 3 seconds
21	Throttle Position Sensor (TPS) — signal voltage high — TPS voltage greater than 2.5V for 3 seconds with less than 1200 rpm
22	Throttle Position Sensor (TPS) — signal voltage low — short to ground or open signal circuit will set in 3 seconds
23	Manifold Air Temperature (MAT) — low temperature indication — sets if the sensor, connections or wires open for 3 seconds
24	Vehicle Speed Sensor (VSS) circuit — no vehicle speed indication — no vehicle speed present during a road load deceleration
25	Manifold Air Temperature (MAT) — high temperature indication — sets if the sensor or signal line becomes grounded for 3 seconds
32	Exhaust Gas Recirculation (EGR) — vacuum switch shorted to ground on start up or switch not closed after the Electronic Control Module (ECM) has commanded EGR for a specified period of time or EGR solenoid circuit open for a specified period of time
33	Manifold Absolute Pressure (MAP) sensor — low vacuum — MAP sensor output too high for 5 seconds or an open signal circuit
34	Manifold Absolute Pressure (MAP) sensor — high vacuum — low or no output from sensor with engine running
35	Idle Air Control (IAC) — IAC error
42	Electronic Spark Timing (EST) — Electronic Control Module (ECM) has seen an open or grounded EST or bypass circuit
43	Electronic Spark Control (ESC) — signal to the Electronic Control Module (ECM) has remained low for too long or the system has failed a functional check
44	Lean exhaust indication — sets if oxygen sensor voltage remains below 0.2V for about 20 seconds
45	Rich exhaust indication — sets if oxygen sensor voltage remains above 0.7V for about 1 minute
51	Faulty Mem-Cal, PROM or Electronic Control Module (ECM)
52	Fuel Calpak missing or faulty
53	System overvoltage — indicates a basic generator problem
54	Fuel pump — low voltage — sets when the fuel pump voltage is less than 2V when reference pulses are being received
55	Faulty Electronic Control Module (ECM)

Year – 1988
Model – C & K Series
Engine – 7.4L (454 cid) TBI V8
Engine Code – VIN N

ECM TROUBLE CODES

Code	Explanation
13	Oxygen sensor circuit—open oxygen sensor—indicates that the oxygen sensor circuit or sensor was open for 1 minute while off idle
14	Coolant Temperature Sensor (CTS)—high temperature indication—sets if the sensor or signal line becomes grounded for 3 seconds
15	Coolant Temperature Sensor (CTS)—low temperature indication—sets if the sensor, connections or wires open for 3 seconds
21	Throttle Position Sensor (TPS)—signal voltage high—TPS voltage greater than 2.5V for 3 seconds with less than 1200 rpm
22	Throttle Position Sensor (TPS)—signal voltage low—short to ground or open signal circuit will set in 3 seconds
23	Manifold Air Temperature (MAT)—low temperature indication—sets if the sensor, connections or wires open for 3 seconds
24	Vehicle Speed Sensor (VSS) circuit—no vehicle speed indication—no vehicle speed present during a road load deceleration
25	Manifold Air Temperature (MAT)—high temperature indication—sets if the sensor or signal line becomes grounded for 3 seconds
32	Exhaust Gas Recirculation (EGR)—vacuum switch shorted to ground on start up or switch not closed after the Electronic Control Module (ECM) has commanded EGR for a specified period of time or EGR solenoid circuit open for a specified period of time
33	Manifold Absolute Pressure (MAP) sensor—low vacuum—MAP sensor output too high for 5 seconds or an open signal circuit
34	Manifold Absolute Pressure (MAP) sensor—high vacuum—low or no output from sensor with engine running
35	Idle Air Control (IAC)—IAC error
42	Electronic Spark Timing (EST)—Electronic Control Module (ECM) has seen an open or grounded EST or bypass circuit
43	Electronic Spark Control (ESC)—signal to the Electronic Control Module (ECM) has remained low for too long or the system has failed a functional check
44	Lean exhaust indication—sets if oxygen sensor voltage remains below 0.2V for about 20 seconds
45	Rich exhaust indication—sets if oxygen sensor voltage remains above 0.7V for about 1 minute
51	Faulty Mem-Cal, PROM or Electronic Control Module (ECM)
52	Fuel Calpak missing or faulty
53	System overvoltage—indicates a basic generator problem
54	Fuel pump—low voltage—sets when the fuel pump voltage is less than 2V when reference pulses are being received
55	Faulty Electronic Control Module (ECM)

Year – 1988
Model – P-Series
Engine – 5.7L (350 cid) TBI V8
Engine Code – VIN K

ECM TROUBLE CODES

Code	Explanation
13	Oxygen sensor circuit – open oxygen sensor – indicates that the oxygen sensor circuit or sensor was open for 1 minute while off idle
14	Coolant Temperature Sensor (CTS) – high temperature indication – sets if the sensor or signal line becomes grounded for 3 seconds
15	Coolant Temperature Sensor (CTS) – low temperature indication – sets if the sensor, connections or wires open for 3 seconds
21	Throttle Position Sensor (TPS) – signal voltage high – TPS voltage greater than 2.5V for 3 seconds with less than 1200 rpm
22	Throttle Position Sensor (TPS) – signal voltage low – short to ground or open signal circuit will set in 3 seconds
23	Manifold Air Temperature (MAT) – low temperature indication – sets if the sensor, connections or wires open for 3 seconds
24	Vehicle Speed Sensor (VSS) circuit – no vehicle speed indication – no vehicle speed present during a road load deceleration
25	Manifold Air Temperature (MAT) – high temperature indication – sets if the sensor or signal line becomes grounded for 3 seconds
32	Exhaust Gas Recirculation (EGR) – vacuum switch shorted to ground on start up or switch not closed after the Electronic Control Module (ECM) has commanded EGR for a specified period of time or EGR solenoid circuit open for a specified period of time
33	Manifold Absolute Pressure (MAP) sensor – low vacuum – MAP sensor output too high for 5 seconds or an open signal circuit
34	Manifold Absolute Pressure (MAP) sensor – high vacuum – low or no output from sensor with engine running
35	Idle Air Control (IAC) – IAC error
42	Electronic Spark Timing (EST) – Electronic Control Module (ECM) has seen an open or grounded EST or bypass circuit
43	Electronic Spark Control (ESC) – signal to the Electronic Control Module (ECM) has remained low for too long or the system has failed a functional check
44	Lean exhaust indication – sets if oxygen sensor voltage remains below 0.2V for about 20 seconds
45	Rich exhaust indication – sets if oxygen sensor voltage remains above 0.7V for about 1 minute
51	Faulty Mem-Cal, PROM or Electronic Control Module (ECM)
52	Fuel Calpak missing or faulty
53	System overvoltage – indicates a basic generator problem
54	Fuel pump – low voltage – sets when the fuel pump voltage is less than 2V when reference pulses are being received
55	Faulty Electronic Control Module (ECM)

Year – 1989
Model – S-Series
Engine – 2.5L (151 cid) TBI 4 cyl
Engine Code – VIN E

ECM TROUBLE CODES

Code	Explanation
13	Oxygen sensor circuit – open oxygen sensor – indicates that the oxygen sensor circuit or sensor was open for 1 minute while off idle
14	Coolant Temperature Sensor (CTS) – high temperature indication – sets if the sensor or signal line becomes grounded for 3 seconds
15	Coolant Temperature Sensor (CTS) – low temperature indication – sets if the sensor, connections or wires open for 3 seconds
21	Throttle Position Sensor (TPS) – signal voltage high – TPS voltage greater than 2.5V for 3 seconds with less than 1200 rpm
22	Throttle Position Sensor (TPS) – signal voltage low – short to ground or open signal circuit will set in 3 seconds
23	Manifold Air Temperature (MAT) – low temperature indication – sets if the sensor, connections or wires open for 3 seconds
24	Vehicle Speed Sensor (VSS) circuit – no vehicle speed indication – no vehicle speed present during a road load deceleration
25	Manifold Air Temperature (MAT) – high temperature indication – sets if the sensor or signal line becomes grounded for 3 seconds
32	Exhaust Gas Recirculation (EGR) – vacuum switch shorted to ground on start up or switch not closed after the Electronic Control Module (ECM) has commanded EGR for a specified period of time or EGR solenoid circuit open for a specified period of time
33	Manifold Absolute Pressure (MAP) sensor – low vacuum – MAP sensor output too high for 5 seconds or an open signal circuit
34	Manifold Absolute Pressure (MAP) sensor – high vacuum – low or no output from sensor with engine running
35	Idle Air Control (IAC) – IAC error
42	Electronic Spark Timing (EST) – Electronic Control Module (ECM) has seen an open or grounded EST or bypass circuit
43	Electronic Spark Control (ESC) – signal to the Electronic Control Module (ECM) has remained low for too long or the system has failed a functional check
44	Lean exhaust indication – sets if oxygen sensor voltage remains below 0.2V for about 20 seconds
45	Rich exhaust indication – sets if oxygen sensor voltage remains above 0.7V for about 1 minute
51	Faulty Mem-Cal, PROM or Electronic Control Module (ECM)
52	Fuel Calpak missing or faulty
53	System overvoltage – indicates a basic generator problem
54	Fuel pump – low voltage – sets when the fuel pump voltage is less than 2V when reference pulses are being received
55	Faulty Electronic Control Module (ECM)

Year – 1989
Model – S & T Series
Engine – 2.8L (173 cid) TBI V6
Engine Code – VIN R

ECM TROUBLE CODES

Code	Explanation
13	Oxygen sensor circuit – open oxygen sensor – indicates that the oxygen sensor circuit or sensor was open for 1 minute while off idle
14	Coolant Temperature Sensor (CTS) – high temperature indication – sets if the sensor or signal line becomes grounded for 3 seconds
15	Coolant Temperature Sensor (CTS) – low temperature indication – sets if the sensor, connections or wires open for 3 seconds
21	Throttle Position Sensor (TPS) – signal voltage high – TPS voltage greater than 2.5V for 3 seconds with less than 1200 rpm
22	Throttle Position Sensor (TPS) – signal voltage low – short to ground or open signal circuit will set in 3 seconds
23	Manifold Air Temperature (MAT) – low temperature indication – sets if the sensor, connections or wires open for 3 seconds
24	Vehicle Speed Sensor (VSS) circuit – no vehicle speed indication – no vehicle speed present during a road load deceleration
25	Manifold Air Temperature (MAT) – high temperature indication – sets if the sensor or signal line becomes grounded for 3 seconds
32	Exhaust Gas Recirculation (EGR) – vacuum switch shorted to ground on start up or switch not closed after the Electronic Control Module (ECM) has commanded EGR for a specified period of time or EGR solenoid circuit open for a specified period of time
33	Manifold Absolute Pressure (MAP) sensor – low vacuum – MAP sensor output too high for 5 seconds or an open signal circuit
34	Manifold Absolute Pressure (MAP) sensor – high vacuum – low or no output from sensor with engine running
35	Idle Air Control (IAC) – IAC error
42	Electronic Spark Timing (EST) – Electronic Control Module (ECM) has seen an open or grounded EST or bypass circuit
43	Electronic Spark Control (ESC) – signal to the Electronic Control Module (ECM) has remained low for too long or the system has failed a functional check
44	Lean exhaust indication – sets if oxygen sensor voltage remains below 0.2V for about 20 seconds
45	Rich exhaust indication – sets if oxygen sensor voltage remains above 0.7V for about 1 minute
51	Faulty Mem-Cal, PROM or Electronic Control Module (ECM)
52	Fuel Calpak missing or faulty
53	System overvoltage – indicates a basic generator problem
54	Fuel pump – low voltage – sets when the fuel pump voltage is less than 2V when reference pulses are being received
55	Faulty Electronic Control Module (ECM)

Year — 1989
Model — S & T Series
Engine — 4.3L (262 cid) TBI V6
Engine Code — VIN Z

ECM TROUBLE CODES

Code	Explanation
13	Oxygen sensor circuit — open oxygen sensor — indicates that the oxygen sensor circuit or sensor was open for 1 minute while off idle
14	Coolant Temperature Sensor (CTS) — high temperature indication — sets if the sensor or signal line becomes grounded for 3 seconds
15	Coolant Temperature Sensor (CTS) — low temperature indication — sets if the sensor, connections or wires open for 3 seconds
21	Throttle Position Sensor (TPS) — signal voltage high — TPS voltage greater than 2.5V for 3 seconds with less than 1200 rpm
22	Throttle Position Sensor (TPS) — signal voltage low — short to ground or open signal circuit will set in 3 seconds
23	Manifold Air Temperature (MAT) — low temperature indication — sets if the sensor, connections or wires open for 3 seconds
24	Vehicle Speed Sensor (VSS) circuit — no vehicle speed indication — no vehicle speed present during a road load deceleration
25	Manifold Air Temperature (MAT) — high temperature indication — sets if the sensor or signal line becomes grounded for 3 seconds
32	Exhaust Gas Recirculation (EGR) — vacuum switch shorted to ground on start up or switch not closed after the Electronic Control Module (ECM) has commanded EGR for a specified period of time or EGR solenoid circuit open for a specified period of time
33	Manifold Absolute Pressure (MAP) sensor — low vacuum — MAP sensor output too high for 5 seconds or an open signal circuit
34	Manifold Absolute Pressure (MAP) sensor — high vacuum — low or no output from sensor with engine running
35	Idle Air Control (IAC) — IAC error
42	Electronic Spark Timing (EST) — Electronic Control Module (ECM) has seen an open or grounded EST or bypass circuit
43	Electronic Spark Control (ESC) — signal to the Electronic Control Module (ECM) has remained low for too long or the system has failed a functional check
44	Lean exhaust indication — sets if oxygen sensor voltage remains below 0.2V for about 20 seconds
45	Rich exhaust indication — sets if oxygen sensor voltage remains above 0.7V for about 1 minute
51	Faulty Mem-Cal, PROM or Electronic Control Module (ECM)
52	Fuel Calpak missing or faulty
53	System overvoltage — indicates a basic generator problem
54	Fuel pump — low voltage — sets when the fuel pump voltage is less than 2V when reference pulses are being received
55	Faulty Electronic Control Module (ECM)

Year – 1989
Model – M Van (Astro Van)
Engine – 2.5L (151 cid) TBI 4 cyl
Engine Code – VIN E

ECM TROUBLE CODES

Code	Explanation
13	Oxygen sensor circuit – open oxygen sensor – indicates that the oxygen sensor circuit or sensor was open for 1 minute while off idle
14	Coolant Temperature Sensor (CTS) – high temperature indication – sets if the sensor or signal line becomes grounded for 3 seconds
15	Coolant Temperature Sensor (CTS) – low temperature indication – sets if the sensor, connections or wires open for 3 seconds
21	Throttle Position Sensor (TPS) – signal voltage high – TPS voltage greater than 2.5V for 3 seconds with less than 1200 rpm
22	Throttle Position Sensor (TPS) – signal voltage low – short to ground or open signal circuit will set in 3 seconds
23	Manifold Air Temperature (MAT) – low temperature indication – sets if the sensor, connections or wires open for 3 seconds
24	Vehicle Speed Sensor (VSS) circuit – no vehicle speed indication – no vehicle speed present during a road load deceleration
25	Manifold Air Temperature (MAT) – high temperature indication – sets if the sensor or signal line becomes grounded for 3 seconds
32	Exhaust Gas Recirculation (EGR) – vacuum switch shorted to ground on start up or switch not closed after the Electronic Control Module (ECM) has commanded EGR for a specified period of time or EGR solenoid circuit open for a specified period of time
33	Manifold Absolute Pressure (MAP) sensor – low vacuum – MAP sensor output too high for 5 seconds or an open signal circuit
34	Manifold Absolute Pressure (MAP) sensor – high vacuum – low or no output from sensor with engine running
35	Idle Air Control (IAC) – IAC error
42	Electronic Spark Timing (EST) – Electronic Control Module (ECM) has seen an open or grounded EST or bypass circuit
43	Electronic Spark Control (ESC) – signal to the Electronic Control Module (ECM) has remained low for too long or the system has failed a functional check
44	Lean exhaust indication – sets if oxygen sensor voltage remains below 0.2V for about 20 seconds
45	Rich exhaust indication – sets if oxygen sensor voltage remains above 0.7V for about 1 minute
51	Faulty Mem-Cal, PROM or Electronic Control Module (ECM)
52	Fuel Calpak missing or faulty
53	System overvoltage – indicates a basic generator problem
54	Fuel pump – low voltage – sets when the fuel pump voltage is less than 2V when reference pulses are being received
55	Faulty Electronic Control Module (ECM)

GENERAL MOTORS CORPORATION
DIAGNOSTIC CODE DATA

Year – 1989
Model – M Van (Astro Van)
Engine – 4.3L (262 cid) TBI V6
Engine Code – VIN Z

ECM TROUBLE CODES

Code	Explanation
13	Oxygen sensor circuit – open oxygen sensor – indicates that the oxygen sensor circuit or sensor was open for 1 minute while off idle
14	Coolant Temperature Sensor (CTS) – high temperature indication – sets if the sensor or signal line becomes grounded for 3 seconds
15	Coolant Temperature Sensor (CTS) – low temperature indication – sets if the sensor, connections or wires open for 3 seconds
21	Throttle Position Sensor (TPS) – signal voltage high – TPS voltage greater than 2.5V for 3 seconds with less than 1200 rpm
22	Throttle Position Sensor (TPS) – signal voltage low – short to ground or open signal circuit will set in 3 seconds
23	Manifold Air Temperature (MAT) – low temperature indication – sets if the sensor, connections or wires open for 3 seconds
24	Vehicle Speed Sensor (VSS) circuit – no vehicle speed indication – no vehicle speed present during a road load deceleration
25	Manifold Air Temperature (MAT) – high temperature indication – sets if the sensor or signal line becomes grounded for 3 seconds
32	Exhaust Gas Recirculation (EGR) – vacuum switch shorted to ground on start up or switch not closed after the Electronic Control Module (ECM) has commanded EGR for a specified period of time or EGR solenoid circuit open for a specified period of time
33	Manifold Absolute Pressure (MAP) sensor – low vacuum – MAP sensor output too high for 5 seconds or an open signal circuit
34	Manifold Absolute Pressure (MAP) sensor – high vacuum – low or no output from sensor with engine running
35	Idle Air Control (IAC) – IAC error
42	Electronic Spark Timing (EST) – Electronic Control Module (ECM) has seen an open or grounded EST or bypass circuit
43	Electronic Spark Control (ESC) – signal to the Electronic Control Module (ECM) has remained low for too long or the system has failed a functional check
44	Lean exhaust indication – sets if oxygen sensor voltage remains below 0.2V for about 20 seconds
45	Rich exhaust indication – sets if oxygen sensor voltage remains above 0.7V for about 1 minute
51	Faulty Mem-Cal, PROM or Electronic Control Module (ECM)
52	Fuel Calpak missing or faulty
53	System overvoltage – indicates a basic generator problem
54	Fuel pump – low voltage – sets when the fuel pump voltage is less than 2V when reference pulses are being received
55	Faulty Electronic Control Module (ECM)

Year – 1989
Model – G-Series Vans
Engine – 4.3L (262 cid) TBI V6
Engine Code – VIN Z

ECM TROUBLE CODES

Code	Explanation
13	Oxygen sensor circuit – open oxygen sensor – indicates that the oxygen sensor circuit or sensor was open for 1 minute while off idle
14	Coolant Temperature Sensor (CTS) – high temperature indication – sets if the sensor or signal line becomes grounded for 3 seconds
15	Coolant Temperature Sensor (CTS) – low temperature indication – sets if the sensor, connections or wires open for 3 seconds
21	Throttle Position Sensor (TPS) – signal voltage high – TPS voltage greater than 2.5V for 3 seconds with less than 1200 rpm
22	Throttle Position Sensor (TPS) – signal voltage low – short to ground or open signal circuit will set in 3 seconds
23	Manifold Air Temperature (MAT) – low temperature indication – sets if the sensor, connections or wires open for 3 seconds
24	Vehicle Speed Sensor (VSS) circuit – no vehicle speed indication – no vehicle speed present during a road load deceleration
25	Manifold Air Temperature (MAT) – high temperature indication – sets if the sensor or signal line becomes grounded for 3 seconds
32	Exhaust Gas Recirculation (EGR) – vacuum switch shorted to ground on start up or switch not closed after the Electronic Control Module (ECM) has commanded EGR for a specified period of time or EGR solenoid circuit open for a specified period of time
33	Manifold Absolute Pressure (MAP) sensor – low vacuum – MAP sensor output too high for 5 seconds or an open signal circuit
34	Manifold Absolute Pressure (MAP) sensor – high vacuum – low or no output from sensor with engine running
35	Idle Air Control (IAC) – IAC error
42	Electronic Spark Timing (EST) – Electronic Control Module (ECM) has seen an open or grounded EST or bypass circuit
43	Electronic Spark Control (ESC) – signal to the Electronic Control Module (ECM) has remained low for too long or the system has failed a functional check
44	Lean exhaust indication – sets if oxygen sensor voltage remains below 0.2V for about 20 seconds
45	Rich exhaust indication – sets if oxygen sensor voltage remains above 0.7V for about 1 minute
51	Faulty Mem-Cal, PROM or Electronic Control Module (ECM)
52	Fuel Calpak missing or faulty
53	System overvoltage – indicates a basic generator problem
54	Fuel pump – low voltage – sets when the fuel pump voltage is less than 2V when reference pulses are being received
55	Faulty Electronic Control Module (ECM)

Year – 1989
Model – G-Series Vans
Engine – 5.0L (305 cid) TBI V8
Engine Code – VIN H

ECM TROUBLE CODES

Code	Explanation
13	Oxygen sensor circuit – open oxygen sensor – indicates that the oxygen sensor circuit or sensor was open for 1 minute while off idle
14	Coolant Temperature Sensor (CTS) – high temperature indication – sets if the sensor or signal line becomes grounded for 3 seconds
15	Coolant Temperature Sensor (CTS) – low temperature indication – sets if the sensor, connections or wires open for 3 seconds
21	Throttle Position Sensor (TPS) – signal voltage high – TPS voltage greater than 2.5V for 3 seconds with less than 1200 rpm
22	Throttle Position Sensor (TPS) – signal voltage low – short to ground or open signal circuit will set in 3 seconds
23	Manifold Air Temperature (MAT) – low temperature indication – sets if the sensor, connections or wires open for 3 seconds
24	Vehicle Speed Sensor (VSS) circuit – no vehicle speed indication – no vehicle speed present during a road load deceleration
25	Manifold Air Temperature (MAT) – high temperature indication – sets if the sensor or signal line becomes grounded for 3 seconds
32	Exhaust Gas Recirculation (EGR) – vacuum switch shorted to ground on start up or switch not closed after the Electronic Control Module (ECM) has commanded EGR for a specified period of time or EGR solenoid circuit open for a specified period of time
33	Manifold Absolute Pressure (MAP) sensor – low vacuum – MAP sensor output too high for 5 seconds or an open signal circuit
34	Manifold Absolute Pressure (MAP) sensor – high vacuum – low or no output from sensor with engine running
35	Idle Air Control (IAC) – IAC error
42	Electronic Spark Timing (EST) – Electronic Control Module (ECM) has seen an open or grounded EST or bypass circuit
43	Electronic Spark Control (ESC) – signal to the Electronic Control Module (ECM) has remained low for too long or the system has failed a functional check
44	Lean exhaust indication – sets if oxygen sensor voltage remains below 0.2V for about 20 seconds
45	Rich exhaust indication – sets if oxygen sensor voltage remains above 0.7V for about 1 minute
51	Faulty Mem-Cal, PROM or Electronic Control Module (ECM)
52	Fuel Calpak missing or faulty
53	System overvoltage – indicates a basic generator problem
54	Fuel pump – low voltage – sets when the fuel pump voltage is less than 2V when reference pulses are being received
55	Faulty Electronic Control Module (ECM)

Year – 1989
Model – G-Series Vans
Engine – 5.7L (350 cid) TBI V8
Engine Code – VIN K

ECM TROUBLE CODES

Code	Explanation
13	Oxygen sensor circuit—open oxygen sensor—indicates that the oxygen sensor circuit or sensor was open for 1 minute while off idle
14	Coolant Temperature Sensor (CTS)—high temperature indication—sets if the sensor or signal line becomes grounded for 3 seconds
15	Coolant Temperature Sensor (CTS)—low temperature indication—sets if the sensor, connections or wires open for 3 seconds
21	Throttle Position Sensor (TPS)—signal voltage high—TPS voltage greater than 2.5V for 3 seconds with less than 1200 rpm
22	Throttle Position Sensor (TPS)—signal voltage low—short to ground or open signal circuit will set in 3 seconds
23	Manifold Air Temperature (MAT)—low temperature indication—sets if the sensor, connections or wires open for 3 seconds
24	Vehicle Speed Sensor (VSS) circuit—no vehicle speed indication—no vehicle speed present during a road load deceleration
25	Manifold Air Temperature (MAT)—high temperature indication—sets if the sensor or signal line becomes grounded for 3 seconds
32	Exhaust Gas Recirculation (EGR)—vacuum switch shorted to ground on start up or switch not closed after the Electronic Control Module (ECM) has commanded EGR for a specified period of time or EGR solenoid circuit open for a specified period of time
33	Manifold Absolute Pressure (MAP) sensor—low vacuum—MAP sensor output too high for 5 seconds or an open signal circuit
34	Manifold Absolute Pressure (MAP) sensor—high vacuum—low or no output from sensor with engine running
35	Idle Air Control (IAC)—IAC error
42	Electronic Spark Timing (EST)—Electronic Control Module (ECM) has seen an open or grounded EST or bypass circuit
43	Electronic Spark Control (ESC)—signal to the Electronic Control Module (ECM) has remained low for too long or the system has failed a functional check
44	Lean exhaust indication—sets if oxygen sensor voltage remains below 0.2V for about 20 seconds
45	Rich exhaust indication—sets if oxygen sensor voltage remains above 0.7V for about 1 minute
51	Faulty Mem-Cal, PROM or Electronic Control Module (ECM)
52	Fuel Calpak missing or faulty
53	System overvoltage—indicates a basic generator problem
54	Fuel pump—low voltage—sets when the fuel pump voltage is less than 2V when reference pulses are being received
55	Faulty Electronic Control Module (ECM)

Year — 1989
Model — G-Series Vans
Engine — 7.4L (454 cid) TBI V8
Engine Code — VIN N

ECM TROUBLE CODES

Code	Explanation
13	Oxygen sensor circuit — open oxygen sensor — indicates that the oxygen sensor circuit or sensor was open for 1 minute while off idle
14	Coolant Temperature Sensor (CTS) — high temperature indication — sets if the sensor or signal line becomes grounded for 3 seconds
15	Coolant Temperature Sensor (CTS) — low temperature indication — sets if the sensor, connections or wires open for 3 seconds
21	Throttle Position Sensor (TPS) — signal voltage high — TPS voltage greater than 2.5V for 3 seconds with less than 1200 rpm
22	Throttle Position Sensor (TPS) — signal voltage low — short to ground or open signal circuit will set in 3 seconds
23	Manifold Air Temperature (MAT) — low temperature indication — sets if the sensor, connections or wires open for 3 seconds
24	Vehicle Speed Sensor (VSS) circuit — no vehicle speed indication — no vehicle speed present during a road load deceleration
25	Manifold Air Temperature (MAT) — high temperature indication — sets if the sensor or signal line becomes grounded for 3 seconds
32	Exhaust Gas Recirculation (EGR) — vacuum switch shorted to ground on start up or switch not closed after the Electronic Control Module (ECM) has commanded EGR for a specified period of time or EGR solenoid circuit open for a specified period of time
33	Manifold Absolute Pressure (MAP) sensor — low vacuum — MAP sensor output too high for 5 seconds or an open signal circuit
34	Manifold Absolute Pressure (MAP) sensor — high vacuum — low or no output from sensor with engine running
35	Idle Air Control (IAC) — IAC error
42	Electronic Spark Timing (EST) — Electronic Control Module (ECM) has seen an open or grounded EST or bypass circuit
43	Electronic Spark Control (ESC) — signal to the Electronic Control Module (ECM) has remained low for too long or the system has failed a functional check
44	Lean exhaust indication — sets if oxygen sensor voltage remains below 0.2V for about 20 seconds
45	Rich exhaust indication — sets if oxygen sensor voltage remains above 0.7V for about 1 minute
51	Faulty Mem-Cal, PROM or Electronic Control Module (ECM)
52	Fuel Calpak missing or faulty
53	System overvoltage — indicates a basic generator problem
54	Fuel pump — low voltage — sets when the fuel pump voltage is less than 2V when reference pulses are being received
55	Faulty Electronic Control Module (ECM)

Year — 1989
Model — R & V Series
Engine — 5.7L (350 cid) TBI V8
Engine Code — VIN K

ECM TROUBLE CODES

Code	Explanation
13	Oxygen sensor circuit—open oxygen sensor—indicates that the oxygen sensor circuit or sensor was open for 1 minute while off idle
14	Coolant Temperature Sensor (CTS)—high temperature indication—sets if the sensor or signal line becomes grounded for 3 seconds
15	Coolant Temperature Sensor (CTS)—low temperature indication—sets if the sensor, connections or wires open for 3 seconds
21	Throttle Position Sensor (TPS)—signal voltage high—TPS voltage greater than 2.5V for 3 seconds with less than 1200 rpm
22	Throttle Position Sensor (TPS)—signal voltage low—short to ground or open signal circuit will set in 3 seconds
23	Manifold Air Temperature (MAT)—low temperature indication—sets if the sensor, connections or wires open for 3 seconds
24	Vehicle Speed Sensor (VSS) circuit—no vehicle speed indication—no vehicle speed present during a road load deceleration
25	Manifold Air Temperature (MAT)—high temperature indication—sets if the sensor or signal line becomes grounded for 3 seconds
32	Exhaust Gas Recirculation (EGR)—vacuum switch shorted to ground on start up or switch not closed after the Electronic Control Module (ECM) has commanded EGR for a specified period of time or EGR solenoid circuit open for a specified period of time
33	Manifold Absolute Pressure (MAP) sensor—low vacuum—MAP sensor output too high for 5 seconds or an open signal circuit
34	Manifold Absolute Pressure (MAP) sensor—high vacuum—low or no output from sensor with engine running
35	Idle Air Control (IAC)—IAC error
42	Electronic Spark Timing (EST)—Electronic Control Module (ECM) has seen an open or grounded EST or bypass circuit
43	Electronic Spark Control (ESC)—signal to the Electronic Control Module (ECM) has remained low for too long or the system has failed a functional check
44	Lean exhaust indication—sets if oxygen sensor voltage remains below 0.2V for about 20 seconds
45	Rich exhaust indication—sets if oxygen sensor voltage remains above 0.7V for about 1 minute
51	Faulty Mem-Cal, PROM or Electronic Control Module (ECM)
52	Fuel Calpak missing or faulty
53	System overvoltage—indicates a basic generator problem
54	Fuel pump—low voltage—sets when the fuel pump voltage is less than 2V when reference pulses are being received
55	Faulty Electronic Control Module (ECM)

Year – 1989
Model – R & V Series
Engine – 7.4L (454 cid) TBI V8
Engine Code – VIN N

ECM TROUBLE CODES

Code	Explanation
13	Oxygen sensor circuit—open oxygen sensor—indicates that the oxygen sensor circuit or sensor was open for 1 minute while off idle
14	Coolant Temperature Sensor (CTS)—high temperature indication—sets if the sensor or signal line becomes grounded for 3 seconds
15	Coolant Temperature Sensor (CTS)—low temperature indication—sets if the sensor, connections or wires open for 3 seconds
21	Throttle Position Sensor (TPS)—signal voltage high—TPS voltage greater than 2.5V for 3 seconds with less than 1200 rpm
22	Throttle Position Sensor (TPS)—signal voltage low—short to ground or open signal circuit will set in 3 seconds
23	Manifold Air Temperature (MAT)—low temperature indication—sets if the sensor, connections or wires open for 3 seconds
24	Vehicle Speed Sensor (VSS) circuit—no vehicle speed indication—no vehicle speed present during a road load deceleration
25	Manifold Air Temperature (MAT)—high temperature indication—sets if the sensor or signal line becomes grounded for 3 seconds
32	Exhaust Gas Recirculation (EGR)—vacuum switch shorted to ground on start up or switch not closed after the Electronic Control Module (ECM) has commanded EGR for a specified period of time or EGR solenoid circuit open for a specified period of time
33	Manifold Absolute Pressure (MAP) sensor—low vacuum—MAP sensor output too high for 5 seconds or an open signal circuit
34	Manifold Absolute Pressure (MAP) sensor—high vacuum—low or no output from sensor with engine running
35	Idle Air Control (IAC)—IAC error
42	Electronic Spark Timing (EST)—Electronic Control Module (ECM) has seen an open or grounded EST or bypass circuit
43	Electronic Spark Control (ESC)—signal to the Electronic Control Module (ECM) has remained low for too long or the system has failed a functional check
44	Lean exhaust indication—sets if oxygen sensor voltage remains below 0.2V for about 20 seconds
45	Rich exhaust indication—sets if oxygen sensor voltage remains above 0.7V for about 1 minute
51	Faulty Mem-Cal, PROM or Electronic Control Module (ECM)
52	Fuel Calpak missing or faulty
53	System overvoltage—indicates a basic generator problem
54	Fuel pump—low voltage—sets when the fuel pump voltage is less than 2V when reference pulses are being received
55	Faulty Electronic Control Module (ECM)

Year – 1989
Model – 10–30 Series
Engine – 6.2L (388 cid) V8 Diesel
Engine Code – VIN C

ECM TROUBLE CODES

Code	Explanation
12	No engine speed reference pulse – no engine speed sensor reference pulses to the Electronic Control Module (ECM). This code is not stored in memory and will only flash while the fault is present. Normal code with ignition ON, engine not running
14	Coolant Temperature Sensor (CTS) – high temperature indication – sets if the sensor or signal line becomes grounded for 5 minutes
15	Coolant Temperature Sensor (CTS) – low temperature indication – sets if the sensor, connections or wires open for 5 minutes
21	Throttle Position Sensor (TPS) – signal voltage high – Throttle Position Sensor (TPS) circuit voltage high – open circuit or misadjusted TPS – engine must run 30 seconds, at curb idle speed, before this code will set
22	Throttle Position Sensor (TPS) – signal voltage low – Throttle Position Sensor (TPS) circuit voltage low – grounded circuit – engine must run 2 minutes at 1250 rpm or above before this code will set
23	Throttle Position Sensor (TPS) – not calibrated – Throttle Position Sensor (TPS) circuit – voltage not between 0.25 – 1.3V at curb idle speed – engine must run for 30 seconds, at curb idle, before this code will set
24	Vehicle Speed Sensor (VSS) circuit – no vehicle speed indication – Vehicle Speed Sensor (VSS) circuit – open or grounded circuit – vehicle must operate at road speed for 10 seconds before this code will set
31	Manifold Absolute Pressure (MAP) sensor too low – Manifold Absolute Pressure (MAP) circuit signal voltage too low – engine must run at curb idle for 10 seconds before this code will set
32	Exhaust Gas Recirculation (EGR) – loop error – Exhaust Gas Recirculation (EGR) vacuum has seen improper EGR vacuum – vehicle must be running at road speed approximately 30 mph (48 Km/h) for 10 seconds before this code will set
33	Manifold Absolute Pressure (MAP) sensor too high – Manifold Absolute Pressure (MAP) circuit signal voltage too high – engine must run at curb idle for 10 seconds before this code will set
51	PROM – Faulty or improperly installed PROM. It takes approximately 10 seconds before this code will set
52	Electronic Control Module (ECM) – fault in ECM circuit. It takes 10 seconds before this code will set
53	Five volt reference overloaod – 5V reference (V/ref) circuit overloaded – grounded circuit – it takes 10 seconds before this code will set

Year – 1989
Model – C & K Series
Engine – 4.3L (262 cid) TBI V6
Engine Code – VIN Z

ECM TROUBLE CODES

Code	Explanation
13	Oxygen sensor circuit – open oxygen sensor – indicates that the oxygen sensor circuit or sensor was open for 1 minute while off idle
14	Coolant Temperature Sensor (CTS) – high temperature indication – sets if the sensor or signal line becomes grounded for 3 seconds
15	Coolant Temperature Sensor (CTS) – low temperature indication – sets if the sensor, connections or wires open for 3 seconds
21	Throttle Position Sensor (TPS) – signal voltage high – TPS voltage greater than 2.5V for 3 seconds with less than 1200 rpm
22	Throttle Position Sensor (TPS) – signal voltage low – short to ground or open signal circuit will set in 3 seconds
23	Manifold Air Temperature (MAT) – low temperature indication – sets if the sensor, connections or wires open for 3 seconds
24	Vehicle Speed Sensor (VSS) circuit – no vehicle speed indication – no vehicle speed present during a road load deceleration
25	Manifold Air Temperature (MAT) – high temperature indication – sets if the sensor or signal line becomes grounded for 3 seconds
32	Exhaust Gas Recirculation (EGR) – vacuum switch shorted to ground on start up or switch not closed after the Electronic Control Module (ECM) has commanded EGR for a specified period of time or EGR solenoid circuit open for a specified period of time
33	Manifold Absolute Pressure (MAP) sensor – low vacuum – MAP sensor output too high for 5 seconds or an open signal circuit
34	Manifold Absolute Pressure (MAP) sensor – high vacuum – low or no output from sensor with engine running
35	Idle Air Control (IAC) – IAC error
42	Electronic Spark Timing (EST) – Electronic Control Module (ECM) has seen an open or grounded EST or bypass circuit
43	Electronic Spark Control (ESC) – signal to the Electronic Control Module (ECM) has remained low for too long or the system has failed a functional check
44	Lean exhaust indication – sets if oxygen sensor voltage remains below 0.2V for about 20 seconds
45	Rich exhaust indication – sets if oxygen sensor voltage remains above 0.7V for about 1 minute
51	Faulty Mem-Cal, PROM or Electronic Control Module (ECM)
52	Fuel Calpak missing or faulty
53	System overvoltage – indicates a basic generator problem
54	Fuel pump – low voltage – sets when the fuel pump voltage is less than 2V when reference pulses are being received
55	Faulty Electronic Control Module (ECM)

Year — 1989
Model — C & K Series
Engine — 5.0L (305 cid) TBI V8
Engine Code — VIN H

ECM TROUBLE CODES

Code	Explanation
13	Oxygen sensor circuit — open oxygen sensor — indicates that the oxygen sensor circuit or sensor was open for 1 minute while off idle
14	Coolant Temperature Sensor (CTS) — high temperature indication — sets if the sensor or signal line becomes grounded for 3 seconds
15	Coolant Temperature Sensor (CTS) — low temperature indication — sets if the sensor, connections or wires open for 3 seconds
21	Throttle Position Sensor (TPS) — signal voltage high — TPS voltage greater than 2.5V for 3 seconds with less than 1200 rpm
22	Throttle Position Sensor (TPS) — signal voltage low — short to ground or open signal circuit will set in 3 seconds
23	Manifold Air Temperature (MAT) — low temperature indication — sets if the sensor, connections or wires open for 3 seconds
24	Vehicle Speed Sensor (VSS) circuit — no vehicle speed indication — no vehicle speed present during a road load deceleration
25	Manifold Air Temperature (MAT) — high temperature indication — sets if the sensor or signal line becomes grounded for 3 seconds
32	Exhaust Gas Recirculation (EGR) — vacuum switch shorted to ground on start up or switch not closed after the Electronic Control Module (ECM) has commanded EGR for a specified period of time or EGR solenoid circuit open for a specified period of time
33	Manifold Absolute Pressure (MAP) sensor — low vacuum — MAP sensor output too high for 5 seconds or an open signal circuit
34	Manifold Absolute Pressure (MAP) sensor — high vacuum — low or no output from sensor with engine running
35	Idle Air Control (IAC) — IAC error
42	Electronic Spark Timing (EST) — Electronic Control Module (ECM) has seen an open or grounded EST or bypass circuit
43	Electronic Spark Control (ESC) — signal to the Electronic Control Module (ECM) has remained low for too long or the system has failed a functional check
44	Lean exhaust indication — sets if oxygen sensor voltage remains below 0.2V for about 20 seconds
45	Rich exhaust indication — sets if oxygen sensor voltage remains above 0.7V for about 1 minute
51	Faulty Mem-Cal, PROM or Electronic Control Module (ECM)
52	Fuel Calpak missing or faulty
53	System overvoltage — indicates a basic generator problem
54	Fuel pump — low voltage — sets when the fuel pump voltage is less than 2V when reference pulses are being received
55	Faulty Electronic Control Module (ECM)

Year – 1989
Model – C & K Series
Engine – 5.7L (350 cid) TBI V8
Engine Code – VIN K

ECM TROUBLE CODES

Code	Explanation
13	Oxygen sensor circuit – open oxygen sensor – indicates that the oxygen sensor circuit or sensor was open for 1 minute while off idle
14	Coolant Temperature Sensor (CTS) – high temperature indication – sets if the sensor or signal line becomes grounded for 3 seconds
15	Coolant Temperature Sensor (CTS) – low temperature indication – sets if the sensor, connections or wires open for 3 seconds
21	Throttle Position Sensor (TPS) – signal voltage high – TPS voltage greater than 2.5V for 3 seconds with less than 1200 rpm
22	Throttle Position Sensor (TPS) – signal voltage low – short to ground or open signal circuit will set in 3 seconds
23	Manifold Air Temperature (MAT) – low temperature indication – sets if the sensor, connections or wires open for 3 seconds
24	Vehicle Speed Sensor (VSS) circuit – no vehicle speed indication – no vehicle speed present during a road load deceleration
25	Manifold Air Temperature (MAT) – high temperature indication – sets if the sensor or signal line becomes grounded for 3 seconds
32	Exhaust Gas Recirculation (EGR) – vacuum switch shorted to ground on start up or switch not closed after the Electronic Control Module (ECM) has commanded EGR for a specified period of time or EGR solenoid circuit open for a specified period of time
33	Manifold Absolute Pressure (MAP) sensor – low vacuum – MAP sensor output too high for 5 seconds or an open signal circuit
34	Manifold Absolute Pressure (MAP) sensor – high vacuum – low or no output from sensor with engine running
35	Idle Air Control (IAC) – IAC error
42	Electronic Spark Timing (EST) – Electronic Control Module (ECM) has seen an open or grounded EST or bypass circuit
43	Electronic Spark Control (ESC) – signal to the Electronic Control Module (ECM) has remained low for too long or the system has failed a functional check
44	Lean exhaust indication – sets if oxygen sensor voltage remains below 0.2V for about 20 seconds
45	Rich exhaust indication – sets if oxygen sensor voltage remains above 0.7V for about 1 minute
51	Faulty Mem-Cal, PROM or Electronic Control Module (ECM)
52	Fuel Calpak missing or faulty
53	System overvoltage – indicates a basic generator problem
54	Fuel pump – low voltage – sets when the fuel pump voltage is less than 2V when reference pulses are being received
55	Faulty Electronic Control Module (ECM)

Year — 1989
Model — C & K Pick-Ups
Engine — 6.2L (388 cid) V8 Diesel
Engine Code — VIN C

ECM TROUBLE CODES

Code	Explanation
12	No engine speed reference pulse — no engine speed sensor reference pulses to the Electronic Control Module (ECM). This code is not stored in memory and will only flash while the fault is present. Normal code with ignition ON, engine not running
14	Coolant Temperature Sensor (CTS) — high temperature indication — sets if the sensor or signal line becomes grounded for 5 minutes
15	Coolant Temperature Sensor (CTS) — low temperature indication — sets if the sensor, connections or wires open for 5 minutes
21	Throttle Position Sensor (TPS) — signal voltage high — Throttle Position Sensor (TPS) circuit voltage high — open circuit or misadjusted TPS — engine must run 30 seconds, at curb idle speed, before this code will set
22	Throttle Position Sensor (TPS) — signal voltage low — Throttle Position Sensor (TPS) circuit voltage low — grounded circuit — engine must run 2 minutes at 1250 rpm or above before this code will set
23	Throttle Position Sensor (TPS) — not calibrated — Throttle Position Sensor (TPS) circuit — voltage not between 0.25 – 1.3V at curb idle speed — engine must run for 30 seconds, at curb idle, before this code will set
24	Vehicle Speed Sensor (VSS) circuit — no vehicle speed indication — Vehicle Speed Sensor (VSS) circuit — open or grounded circuit — vehicle must operate at road speed for 10 seconds before this code will set
31	Manifold Absolute Pressure (MAP) sensor too low — Manifold Absolute Pressure (MAP) circuit signal voltage too low — engine must run at curb idle for 10 seconds before this code will set
32	Exhaust Gas Recirculation (EGR) — loop error — Exhaust Gas Recirculation (EGR) vacuum has seen improper EGR vacuum — vehicle must be running at road speed approximately 30 mph (48 Km/h) for 10 seconds before this code will set
33	Manifold Absolute Pressure (MAP) sensor too high — Manifold Absolute Pressure (MAP) circuit signal voltage too high — engine must run at curb idle for 10 seconds before this code will set
51	PROM — Faulty or improperly installed PROM. It takes approximately 10 seconds before this code will set
52	Electronic Control Module (ECM) — fault in ECM circuit. It takes 10 seconds before this code will set
53	Five volt reference overlaod — 5 volt reference (Vref) circuit overloaded — grounded circuit — it takes 10 seconds before this code will set

GENERAL MOTORS CORPORATION
DIAGNOSTIC CODE DATA

Year – 1989
Model – C & K Series
Engine – 7.4L (454 cid) TBI V8
Engine Code – VIN N

ECM TROUBLE CODES

Code	Explanation
13	Oxygen sensor circuit—open oxygen sensor—indicates that the oxygen sensor circuit or sensor was open for 1 minute while off idle
14	Coolant Temperature Sensor (CTS)—high temperature indication—sets if the sensor or signal line becomes grounded for 3 seconds
15	Coolant Temperature Sensor (CTS)—low temperature indication—sets if the sensor, connections or wires open for 3 seconds
21	Throttle Position Sensor (TPS)—signal voltage high—TPS voltage greater than 2.5V for 3 seconds with less than 1200 rpm
22	Throttle Position Sensor (TPS)—signal voltage low—short to ground or open signal circuit will set in 3 seconds
23	Manifold Air Temperature (MAT)—low temperature indication—sets if the sensor, connections or wires open for 3 seconds
24	Vehicle Speed Sensor (VSS) circuit—no vehicle speed indication—no vehicle speed present during a road load deceleration
25	Manifold Air Temperature (MAT)—high temperature indication—sets if the sensor or signal line becomes grounded for 3 seconds
32	Exhaust Gas Recirculation (EGR)—vacuum switch shorted to ground on start up or switch not closed after the Electronic Control Module (ECM) has commanded EGR for a specified period of time or EGR solenoid circuit open for a specified period of time
33	Manifold Absolute Pressure (MAP) sensor—low vacuum—MAP sensor output too high for 5 seconds or an open signal circuit
34	Manifold Absolute Pressure (MAP) sensor—high vacuum—low or no output from sensor with engine running
35	Idle Air Control (IAC)—IAC error
42	Electronic Spark Timing (EST)—Electronic Control Module (ECM) has seen an open or grounded EST or bypass circuit
43	Electronic Spark Control (ESC)—signal to the Electronic Control Module (ECM) has remained low for too long or the system has failed a functional check
44	Lean exhaust indication—sets if oxygen sensor voltage remains below 0.2V for about 20 seconds
45	Rich exhaust indication—sets if oxygen sensor voltage remains above 0.7V for about 1 minute
51	Faulty Mem-Cal, PROM or Electronic Control Module (ECM)
52	Fuel Calpak missing or faulty
53	System overvoltage—indicates a basic generator problem
54	Fuel pump—low voltage—sets when the fuel pump voltage is less than 2V when reference pulses are being received
55	Faulty Electronic Control Module (ECM)

Year — 1989
Model — P-Series Pick-Ups
Engine — 5.7L (350 cid) TBI V8
Engine Code — VIN K

ECM TROUBLE CODES

Code	Explanation
13	Oxygen sensor circuit — open oxygen sensor — indicates that the oxygen sensor circuit or sensor was open for 1 minute while off idle
14	Coolant Temperature Sensor (CTS) — high temperature indication — sets if the sensor or signal line becomes grounded for 3 seconds
15	Coolant Temperature Sensor (CTS) — low temperature indication — sets if the sensor, connections or wires open for 3 seconds
21	Throttle Position Sensor (TPS) — signal voltage high — TPS voltage greater than 2.5V for 3 seconds with less than 1200 rpm
22	Throttle Position Sensor (TPS) — signal voltage low — short to ground or open signal circuit will set in 3 seconds
23	Manifold Air Temperature (MAT) — low temperature indication — sets if the sensor, connections or wires open for 3 seconds
24	Vehicle Speed Sensor (VSS) circuit — no vehicle speed indication — no vehicle speed present during a road load deceleration
25	Manifold Air Temperature (MAT) — high temperature indication — sets if the sensor or signal line becomes grounded for 3 seconds
32	Exhaust Gas Recirculation (EGR) — vacuum switch shorted to ground on start up or switch not closed after the Electronic Control Module (ECM) has commanded EGR for a specified period of time or EGR solenoid circuit open for a specified period of time
33	Manifold Absolute Pressure (MAP) sensor — low vacuum — MAP sensor output too high for 5 seconds or an open signal circuit
34	Manifold Absolute Pressure (MAP) sensor — high vacuum — low or no output from sensor with engine running
35	Idle Air Control (IAC) — IAC error
42	Electronic Spark Timing (EST) — Electronic Control Module (ECM) has seen an open or grounded EST or bypass circuit
43	Electronic Spark Control (ESC) — signal to the Electronic Control Module (ECM) has remained low for too long or the system has failed a functional check
44	Lean exhaust indication — sets if oxygen sensor voltage remains below 0.2V for about 20 seconds
45	Rich exhaust indication — sets if oxygen sensor voltage remains above 0.7V for about 1 minute
51	Faulty Mem-Cal, PROM or Electronic Control Module (ECM)
52	Fuel Calpak missing or faulty
53	System overvoltage — indicates a basic generator problem
54	Fuel pump — low voltage — sets when the fuel pump voltage is less than 2V when reference pulses are being received
55	Faulty Electronic Control Module (ECM)

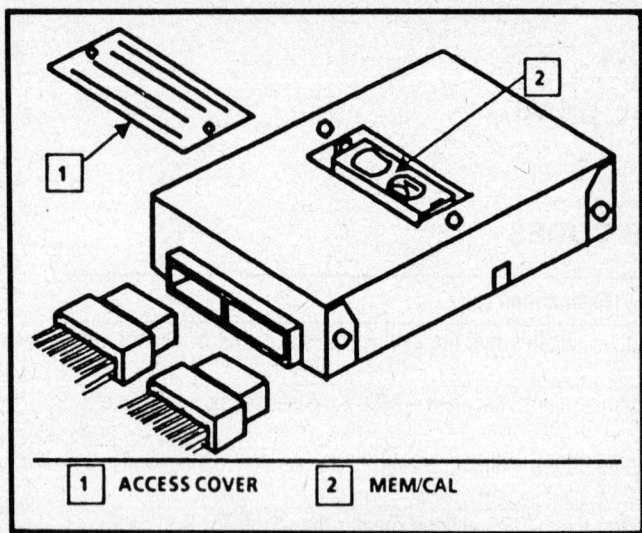

1	ACCESS COVER	2	MEM/CAL

Electronic control module—4 cylinder

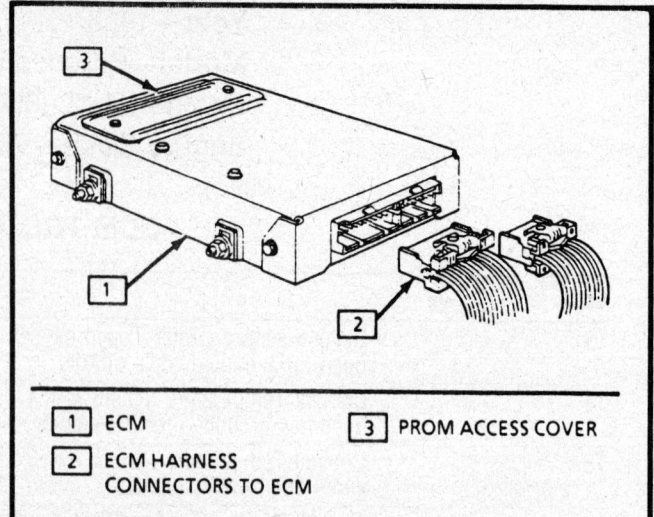

1	ECM	3	PROM ACCESS COVER
2	ECM HARNESS CONNECTORS TO ECM		

Electronic control module—except 4 cylinder

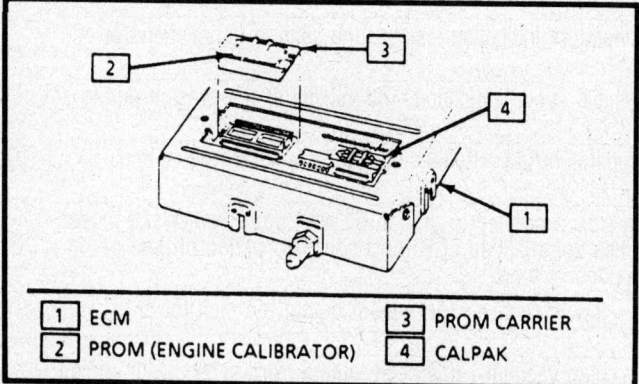

1	ECM	3	PROM CARRIER
2	PROM (ENGINE CALIBRATOR)	4	CALPAK

PROM and CalPak—V6 and V8 engines

Acura/ Sterling 6 SECTION

INDEX

ACURA/STERLING

Programmed Fuel Injection (PGM-FI)

SELF-DIAGNOSTIC SYSTEM

Diagnosis and Testing

The vehicles are equipped with a self-diagnosis function. When an abnormality in the emission control system is detected, the ECU energizes the "PGM-FI" warning light on the dashboard and the LED display. The LED display is part of the ECU which is located inside the vehicle. On 1986-89 Integra and Legend models, the ECU is located under the passenger's seat. On 1987-89 Legend Coupe models, the ECU is located behind the floor kick panel in front of the passenger's seat.

There are 2 types of LED displays: on Integra models for 1986-89, there is only 1 LED; on Legend models for 1986-89 and Legend Coupe models for 1987-89, a dual LED display is employed. The display contains a red and a yellow LED. The yellow LED is for idle speed adjustment and is not related to the self-diagnosis function of the system. On both types of displays, the location of the malfunction is determined by observing the red LED and counting the number of flashes. The flashes correspond to a code which identifies the malfunctioning component or system; refer to related chart. The ECU flashes the code once, followed by a 2 second pause, the code repeats, followed by another 2 second pause, then moves on to the next code. This sequence continues in ascending order through all codes stored in the ECU.

Sometimes the dash warning light and/or ECU LED will turn ON, indicating a system problem, when, in fact there is only a bad or intermittent electrical connection. To troubleshoot a bad connection, note the LED pattern that is lit, refer to the diagnosis chart and check the connectors associated with the items mentioned for the LED pattern. If necessary, disconnect, clean or repair and reconnect the connections, then, reset the ECU memory. Start and drive vehicle for a few minutes, then, recheck the LED(s). If the same pattern is observed, begin system troubleshooting; if not, the problem was a bad connection.

Clearing Diagnostic Memory

The memory for the "PGM-FI" warning light on the dashboard will be erased when the ignition switch is turned **OFF**; however, the memory for the LED display will not be canceled. Thus, the warning light will not turn ON when the ignition switch is turned **ON**, unless the trouble is detected once more. Troubleshooting should be done according to the LED display even if the warning light is OFF.

After making repairs, disconnect the negative battery cable from the negative battery terminal for at least 10 seconds in order to reset the ECU memory. After reconnecting the cable, make sure the LED display is turned OFF.

Other ECU Information

Turn the ignition switch **ON**. The "PGM-FI" warning light should turn ON for about 2 seconds. If the warning light does not turn ON, check for a blown warning light bulb, a blown fuse — causing faulty back-up light, seat belt alarm, clock and/or memory function of the car radio and/or an open circuit in the yellow wire between fuse and gauge assembly.

After the "PGM-FI" warning light and self-diagnosis indicators have been turned ON, turn the ignition switch **OFF**. If the LED display fails to turn ON, when the ignition switch is turned **ON**, check for a blown fuse and/or an open circuit in wire between ECU's A-17 terminal and fuse.

Replace the ECU only after making sure all couplers and connectors are connected securely.

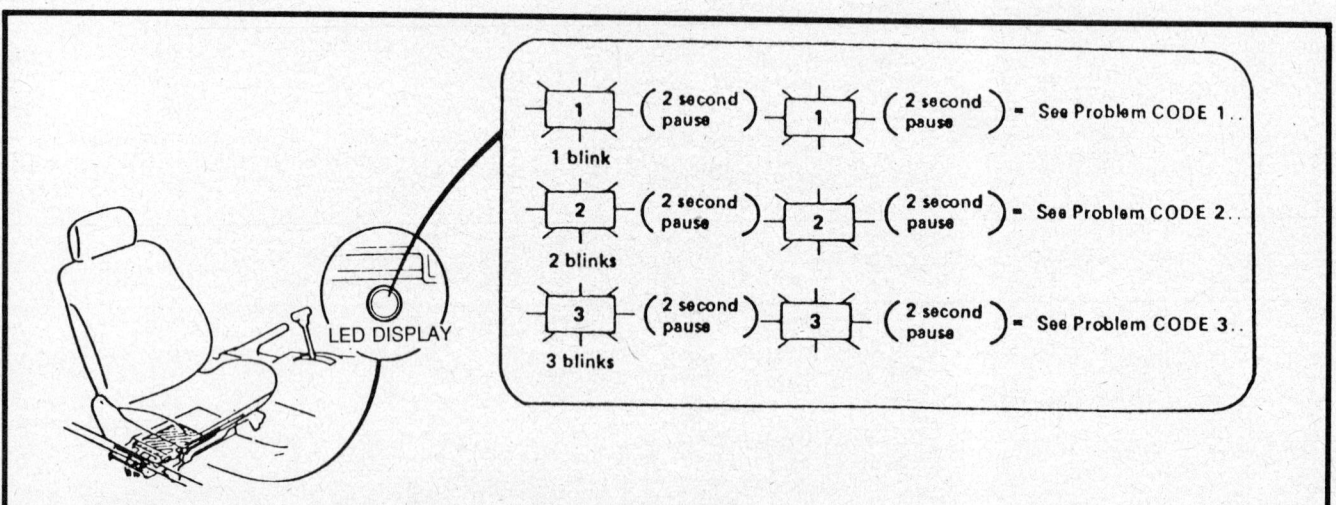

ECU location and self-diagnostic LED display—1986- 89 Acura Integra

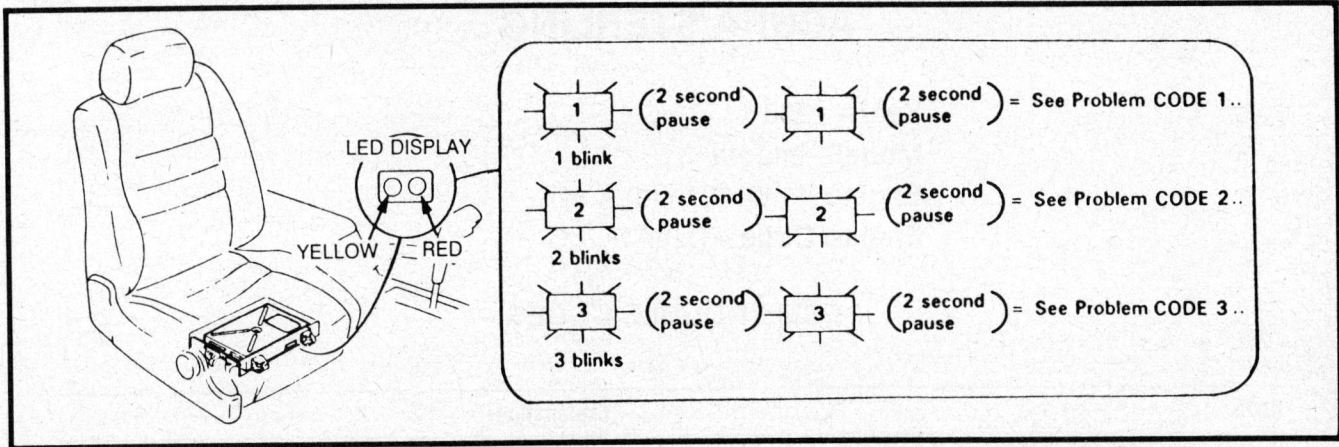

ECU location and self-diagnostic LED display—1986–89 Acura Legend Sedan and 1987–89 Sterling

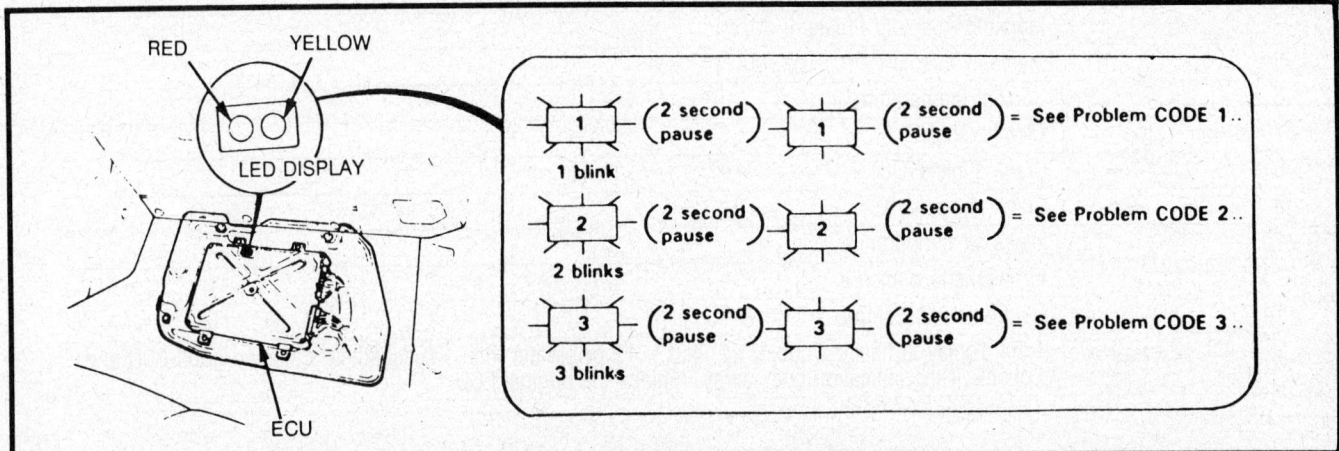

ECU location and self-diagnostic LED display—1987–89 Acura Legend Coupe

ACURA/STERLING

Year — 1986
Model — Integra
Engine — 1.6L (97 cid) 4 cyl
Engine Code — D16A1

ECM TROUBLE CODES

Code	Explanation
0	Electronic Control Unit (ECU)
1	Oxygen content
3	Manifold Absolute Pressure (MAP)
5	Manifold Absolute Pressure (MAP)
6	Coolant temperature
7	Throttle angle
8	Crank angle (TDC)
9	Crank angle (cyl)
10	Intake air temperature
13	Atmospheric pressure
14	Electronic idle control
2, 4, 11, 12 or 14+	If the display is flashing code(s) 2, 4, 11, 12 or greater than 14, substitute a known-good ECU and recheck. If the indication goes away, replace the original ECU.

Year — 1986
Model — Legend
Engine — 2.5L (152 cid) V6
Engine Code — C25A1

ECM TROUBLE CODES

Code	Explanation
0	Electronic Control Unit (ECU)
1	Front oxygen content
2	Rear oxygen content
3	Manifold Absolute Pressure (MAP)
5	Manifold Absolute Pressure (MAP)
6	Coolant temperature
7	Throttle angle
8	Crank angle — Top Dead Center (TDC)
9	Crank angle — cylinder
10	Intake air temperature
11	Idle Mixture Adjustment (IMA)
12	Exhaust Gas Recirculation (EGR) system
13	Atmospheric pressure
14	Electronic idle control
4 or 14 +	If the display is flashing code(s) 4 or greater than 14, substitute a known-good ECU and recheck. If the indication goes away, replace the original ECU.

Year – 1987
Model – Integra
Engine – 1.6L (97 cid) 4 cyl
Engine Code – D16A1

ECM TROUBLE CODES

Code	Explanation
0	Electronic Control Unit (ECU)
1	Oxygen content
3	Manifold Absolute Pressure (MAP)
5	Manifold Absolute Pressure (MAP)
6	Coolant temperature
7	Throttle angle
8	Crank angle (TDC)
9	Crank angle (cyl)
10	Intake air temperature
13	Atmospheric pressure
14	Electronic idle control
2, 4, 11, 12 or 14 +	If the display is flashing code(s) 2, 4, 11, 12 or greater than 14, substitute a known-good ECU and recheck. If the indication goes away, replace the original ECU.

Year — 1987
Model — Legend
Engine — 2.5L (152 cid) V6
Engine Code — C25A1

ECM TROUBLE CODES

Code	Explanation
0	Electronic Control Unit (ECU)
1	Front oxygen content
2	Rear oxygen content
3	Manifold Absolute Pressure (MAP)
5	Manifold Absolute Pressure (MAP)
6	Coolant temperature
7	Throttle angle
8	Crank angle — Top Dead Center (TDC)
9	Crank angle — cylinder
10	Intake air temperature
11	Idle Mixture Adjustment (IMA)
12	Exhaust Gas Recirculation (EGR) system
13	Atmospheric pressure
14	Electronic idle control
4 or 14 +	If the display is flashing code(s) 4 or greater than 14, substitute a known-good ECU and recheck. If the indication goes away, replace the original ECU.

Year — 1987
Model — Legend Coupe
Engine — 2.7L (163 cid) V6
Engine Code — C27A1

ECM TROUBLE CODES

Code	Explanation
0	Electronic Control Unit (ECU)
1	Front oxygen content
2	Rear oxygen content
3	Manifold Absolute Pressure (MAP)
5	Manifold Absolute Pressure (MAP)
4	Crank angle
6	Coolant temperature
7	Throttle angle
8	Top Dead Center (TDC) position
9	Number 1 cylinder position
10	Intake air temperature
12	Exhaust Gas Recirculation (EGR) system
13	Atmospheric pressure
14	Electronic idle control
15	Ignition output signal
17	Vehicle speed pulser
18	Ignition timing adjustment
18+	If the display is flashing code(s) greater than 18, substitute a known-good ECU and recheck. If the indication goes away, replace the original ECU.

Year – 1987
Model – 825S and 825SL
Engine – 2.5L (152 cid) V6
Engine Code – C25A1 P

ECM TROUBLE CODES

Code	Explanation
0	Electronic Control Unit (ECU)
1	Front oxygen content
2	Rear oxygen content
3	Manifold Absolute Pressure (MAP)
5	Manifold Absolute Pressure (MAP)
4	Crank angle
6	Coolant temperature
7	Throttle angle
8	Top Dead Center (TDC) position
9	Number 1 cylinder position
10	Intake air temperature
12	Exhaust Gas Recirculation (EGR) system
13	Atmospheric pressure
14	Electronic idle control
15	Ignition output signal
17	Vehicle speed pulser
18	Ignition timing adjustment
4, 11, 16 or 18 +	If the display is flashing code(s) 4, 11, 16 or greater than 18, substitute a known-good ECU and recheck. If the indication goes away, replace the original ECU.

Year — 1988
Model — Integra
Engine — 1.6L (97 cid) 4 cyl
Engine Code — D16A1

ECM TROUBLE CODES

Code	Explanation
0	Electronic Control Unit (ECU)
1	Oxygen content
3	Manifold Absolute Pressure (MAP)
5	Manifold Absolute Pressure (MAP)
6	Coolant temperature
7	Throttle angle
8	Crank angle — Top Dead Center (TDC)
9	Crank angle — cylinder
10	Intake air temperature
13	Atmospheric pressure
14	Electronic idle control
2, 4, 11, 12 or 14+	If the display is flashing code(s) 2, 4, 11, 12 or greater than 14, substitute a known-good ECU and recheck. If the indication goes away, replace the original ECU.

Year – 1988
Model – Legend
Engine – 2.7L (163 cid) V6
Engine Code – C27A1

ECM TROUBLE CODES

Code	Explanation
0	Electronic Control Unit (ECU)
1	Front oxygen content
2	Rear oxygen content
3	Manifold Absolute Pressure (MAP)
5	Manifold Absolute Pressure (MAP)
4	Crank angle
6	Coolant temperature
7	Throttle angle
8	Top Dead Center (TDC) position
9	Number 1 cylinder position
10	Intake air temperature
12	Exhaust Gas Recirculation (EGR) system
13	Atmospheric pressure
14	Electronic idle control
15	Ignition output signal
17	Vehicle speed pulser
18	Ignition timing adjustment
18 +	If the display is flashing code(s) greater than 18, substitute a known-good ECU and recheck. If the indication goes away, replace the original ECU.

Year – 1988
Model – Legend Coupe
Engine – 2.7L (163 cid) V6
Engine Code – C27A1

ECM TROUBLE CODES

Code	Explanation
0	Electronic Control Unit (ECU)
1	Front oxygen content
2	Rear oxygen content
3	Manifold Absolute Pressure (MAP)
5	Manifold Absolute Pressure (MAP)
4	Crank angle
6	Coolant temperature
7	Throttle angle
8	Top Dead Center (TDC) position
9	Number 1 cylinder position
10	Intake air temperature
12	Exhaust Gas Recirculation (EGR) system
13	Atmospheric pressure
14	Electronic idle control
15	Ignition output signal
17	Vehicle speed pulser
18	Ignition timing adjustment
18+	If the display is flashing code(s) greater than 18, substitute a known-good ECU and recheck. If the indication goes away, replace the original ECU.

Year—1988
Model—825S and 825SL
Engine—2.5L (152 cid) V6
Engine Code— C25A1

ECM TROUBLE CODES

Code	Explanation
0	Electronic Control Unit (ECU)
1	Front oxygen content
2	Rear oxygen content
3	Manifold Absolute Pressure (MAP)
5	Manifold Absolute Pressure (MAP)
4	Crank angle
6	Coolant temperature
7	Throttle angle
8	Top Dead Center (TDC) position
9	Number 1 cylinder position
10	Intake air temperature
12	Exhaust Gas Recirculation (EGR) system
13	Atmospheric pressure
14	Electronic idle control
15	Ignition output signal
17	Vehicle speed pulser
18	Ignition timing adjustment
4, 11, 16 or 18 +	If the display is flashing code(s) 4, 11, 16 or greater than 18, substitute a known-good ECU and recheck. If the indication goes away, replace the original ECU.

Year—1989
Model—Integra
Engine—1.6L (97 cid) 4 cyl
Engine Code—D16A1

ECM TROUBLE CODES

Code	Explanation
0	Electronic Control Unit (ECU)
1	Oxygen content
3	Manifold Absolute Pressure (MAP)
5	Manifold Absolute Pressure (MAP)
4	Crank angle
6	Coolant temperature
7	Throttle angle
8	Top Dead Center (TDC) position
9	Number 1 cylinder position
10	Intake air temperature
13	Atmospheric pressure
14	Electronic idle control
15	Ignition output signal
16	Fuel injector
17	Vehicle Speed Sensor (VSS)
19	Lock-up control solenoid valve
20	Electric load
20+	If the display is flashing code(s) greater than 20, substitute a known-good ECU and recheck. If the indication goes away, replace the original ECU.

Year – 1989
Model – Legend
Engine – 2.7L (163 cid) V6
Engine Code – C27A1

ECM TROUBLE CODES

Code	Explanation
0	Electronic Control Unit (ECU)
1	Front oxygen content
2	Rear oxygen content
3	Manifold Absolute Pressure (MAP)
5	Manifold Absolute Pressure (MAP)
4	Crank angle
6	Coolant temperature
7	Throttle angle
8	Top Dead Center (TDC) position
9	Number 1 cylinder position
10	Intake air temperature
12	Exhaust Gas Recirculation (EGR) system
13	Atmospheric pressure
14	Electronic idle control
15	Ignition output signal
17	Vehicle speed pulser
18	Ignition timing adjustment
18 +	If the display is flashing code(s) greater than 18, substitute a known-good ECU and recheck. If the indication goes away, replace the original ECU.

Year — 1989
Model — Legend Coupe
Engine — 2.7L (163 cid) V6
Engine Code — C27A1

ECM TROUBLE CODES

Code	Explanation
0	Electronic Control Unit (ECU)
1	Front oxygen content
2	Rear oxygen content
3	Manifold Absolute Pressure (MAP)
5	Manifold Absolute Pressure (MAP)
4	Crank angle
6	Coolant temperature
7	Throttle angle
8	Top Dead Center (TDC) position
9	Number 1 cylinder position
10	Intake air temperature
12	Exhaust Gas Recirculation (EGR) system
13	Atmospheric pressure
14	Electronic idle control
15	Ignition output signal
17	Vehicle speed pulser
18	Ignition timing adjustment
18 +	If the display is flashing code(s) greater than 18, substitute a known-good ECU and re-check. If the indication goes away, replace the original ECU.

Year – 1989
Model – 825S and 825SL
Engine – 2.5L (152 cid) V6
Engine Code – C25A1

ECM TROUBLE CODES

Code	Explanation
0	Electronic Control Unit (ECU)
1	Front oxygen content
2	Rear oxygen content
3	Manifold Absolute Pressure (MAP)
5	Manifold Absolute Pressure (MAP)
4	Crank angle
6	Coolant temperature
7	Throttle angle
8	Top Dead Center (TDC) position
9	Number 1 cylinder position
10	Intake air temperature
12	Exhaust Gas Recirculation (EGR) system
13	Atmospheric pressure
14	Electronic idle control
15	Ignition output signal
17	Vehicle speed pulser
18	Ignition timing adjustment
4, 11, 16 or 18 +	If the display is flashing code(s) 4, 11, 16 or greater than 18, substitute a known-good ECU and recheck. If the indication goes away, replace the original ECU.

Year — 1989
Model — 827S, SL, Si and SLi
Engine — 2.7L (163 cid) V6
Engine Code — C27A1

ECM TROUBLE CODES

Code	Explanation
0	Electronic Control Unit (ECU)
1	Front oxygen content
2	Rear oxygen content
3	Manifold Absolute Pressure (MAP)
5	Manifold Absolute Pressure (MAP)
4	Crank angle
6	Coolant temperature
7.	Throttle angle
8	Top Dead Center (TDC) position
9	Number 1 cylinder position
10	Intake air temperature
12	Exhaust Gas Recirculation (EGR) system
13	Atmospheric pressure
14	Electronic idle control
15	Ignition output signal
17	Vehicle speed pulser
18	Ignition timing adjustment
18+	If the display is flashing code(s) greater than 18, substitute a known-good ECU and recheck. If the indication goes away, replace the original ECU.

Audi

AUDI

CIS-E III FUEL INJECTION SYSTEMS

SELF-DIAGNOSTIC SYSTEM

Description

The self-diagnostic function on all Audi models is used to detect component malfunctions which may occur during vehicle operation. The ECU will store these malfunctions for self-diagnosis. The ECU consists of permanent fault code memory (Federal and Calif.), as well as a temporary fault code memory (Calif. only). When the ECU detects a temporary fault, the Fault Indicator Light (FIL) on the instrument panel will flash. The FIL will continue to flash until the ignition switch is turned OFF. The ECU may clear the fault on the next engine start, and the FIL will not flash unless the fault is detected again. The vehicle must be driven for at least 5 minutes to reset the fault. When the ECU detects a permanent fault, the FIL will flash, but the fault will remain in the ECU memory until erased.

Entering Diagnostic Mode

1985–87 Vehicles

NOTE: To test inputs the vehicle must be driven for a minimum of 5 minutes in order to set codes. If the engine has a no-start condition, crank engine for at least 5 seconds. In either instance, do not turn the ignition switch OFF before reading the codes as this will erase the trouble code memory.

1. Insert fuse into the opening on top of the fuel pump relay for 4 seconds.
2. Remove fuse from fuel pump relay.
3. Fault code will be displayed by observing the indicator light in the instrument cluster and counting the flashes.
4. To display the next code repeat steps 1 and 2.
5. Each code will repeat until the fuse is inserted into the fuel pump relay.
6. Diagnosis procedure will be cancelled if the engine speed in raised above 2000 rpm or the ignition switch is turned OFF.

1988 Vehicles

On all 1988 models, retrieving fault codes can be accomplished as follows:

1. Connect LED Tester US 1115 or equivalent, to test connector No. 1 and to the battery positive (+) terminal. The LED tester light must turn ON.
2. Turn the ignition switch ON but do not operate starter.
3. Install spare fuse into the fuse pump relay for at least 4 seconds, then remove fuse. The steady lighting on the LED tester should turn into flashes. Count and note flashes.
4. To switch to the next fault code, repeat Step 3. Continue testing until fault code flashes 0000.
5. After faults have been corrected, erase the fault memory as outlined.

1989 Vehicles

On 1989 models, it will no longer be possible to activate the fault memory by means of the fuel pump relay. New diagnostic test connectors have been installed in the driver's side footwell. Retrieving fault codes can be accomplished as follows:

1. Connect the positive terminal of the US 1115 LED Tester or equivalent, to the positive terminal in connector (A).
2. Connect the negative terminal of LED tester to the terminal in connector (B).
3. Connect a jumper wire to the negative terminal in connector (A) and touch the other end to the terminal in connector (B)

for approximately 4 seconds. Fault codes should now display on the LED tester.
4. To retrieve the next fault code, touch the end of the jumper wire to the terminal in connector (B) again for a minimum of 4 seconds.
5. After faults have been corrected, erase the fault memory as outlined.

Clearing Diagnostic Memory

1. Ensure that LED tester is connected and ignition switch turned OFF.
2. Install a spare fuse in the top of the fuel pump relay.
3. Turn ignition switch ON; the LED tester lioght must turn ON.
4. Remove the fuse after approximately 4 seconds. LED tester must go OFF, then begin flahing fault code 0000.
5. Install fuse again for approximately 10 seconds, then remove. LED tester should light and stay ON. Fault memory has been erased.

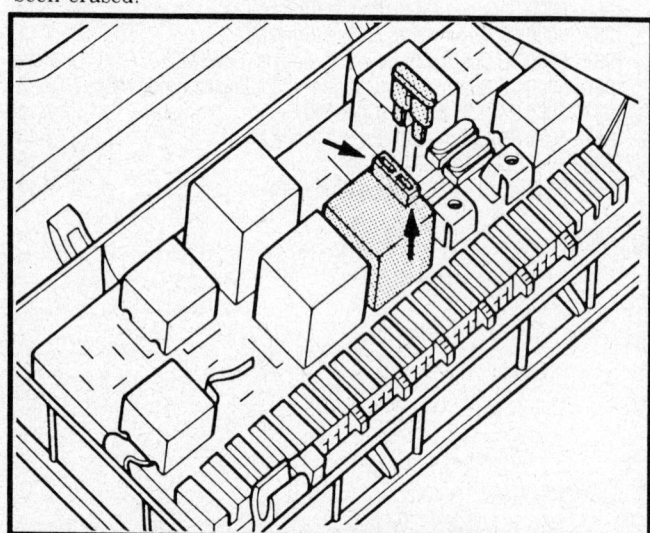

Location of fuel pump relay in fuse panel

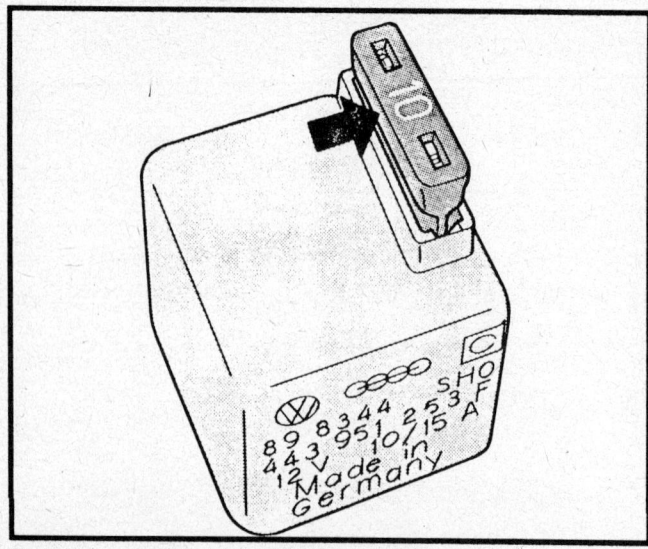

Fuse inserted into fuel pump relay

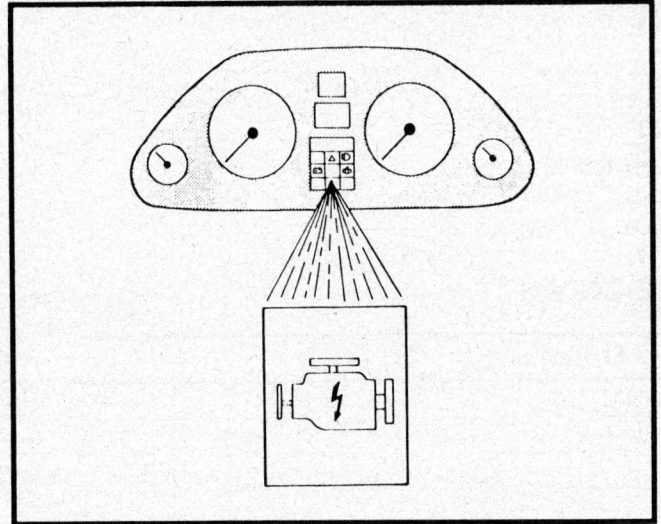

Location of fault indicator light in instrument panel

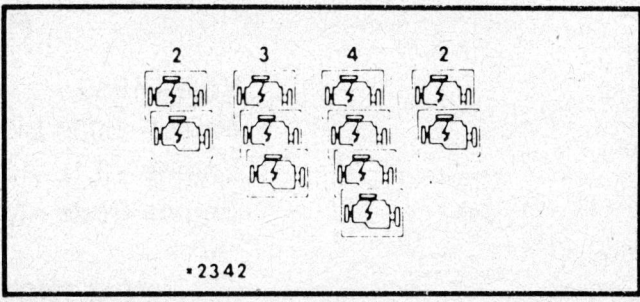

Example of indicator light flashing sequence for code 2342

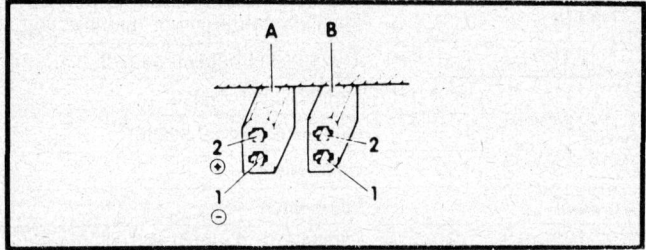

Diagnostic connector – 1989

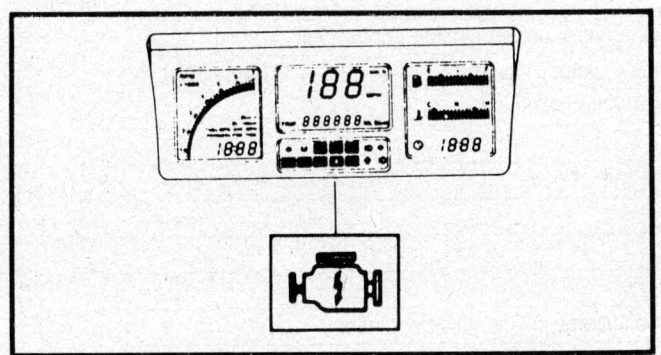

Location of fault indicator light in instrument panel

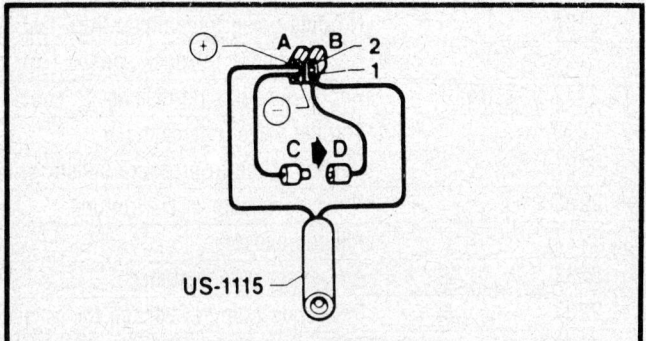

Proper connection to activate fault memory

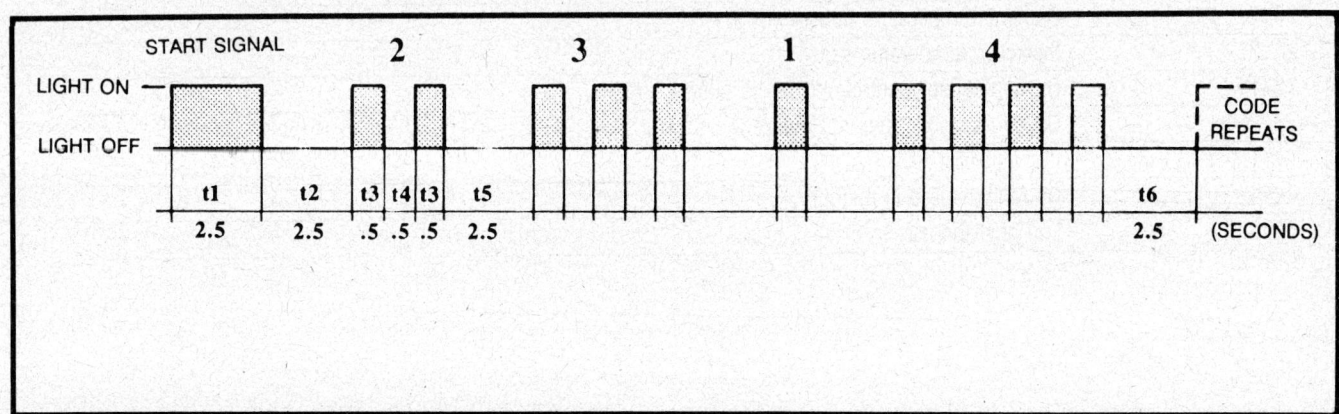

Example of display pattern for diagnosis code 2314

AUDI

Year – 1985
Model – 5000 S Turbo
Engine – 2.1L (131 cid) CIS-E 5 cyl
Engine Code – MC

ECM TROUBLE CODES

Code	Explanation
1111	Ignition control unit or fuel injection control unit
1231	Transmission speed sensor
2111	Engine speed sensor
2112	Ignition reference sensor
2113	Hall sensor
2121	Idle switch
2122	Engine speed signal or Hall sender
2123	Full throttle switch
2132	No data being transmitted from fuel injection control unit to ignition control unit
2141 or 2143	Knock control 1, knock sensor 1 for cylinder 2; knock control 2, knock sensor 2 for cylinder 4
2142 or 2144	Knock sensor 1 on cylinder 2; knock sensor 2 on cylinder 4
2212	Throttle valve potentiometer
2221	Vacuum hose to pressure sensor in control unit
2222	Pressure sensor in control unit
2223	Altitude sensor
2232	Air sensor potentiometer
2233	Reference (supply) voltage for air sensor potentiometer and altitude sensor
2234	MPI control unit supply voltage
2242	CO potentiometer
2312	Coolant Temperature Sensor (CTS)
2322	Intake air temperatue sensor
2341	Oxygen sensor control unit (at its control limit)
2342	Oxygen sensor (does not control)
4431	Idle stabilizer valve
4444	No faults stored in memory
0000	End of diagnosis

Year—1986
Model—5000 Turbo
Engine—2.2L (136 cid) CIS-E 5 cyl
Engine Code—MC

ECM TROUBLE CODES

Code	Explanation
1111	Ignition control unit or fuel injection control unit
1231	Transmission speed sensor
2111	Engine speed sensor
2112	Ignition reference sensor
2113	Hall sensor
2121	Idle switch
2122	Engine speed signal or Hall sender
2123	Full throttle switch
2132	No data being transmitted from fuel injection control unit to ignition control unit
2141 or 2143	Knock control 1, knock sensor 1 for cylinder 2; knock control 2, knock sensor 2 for cylinder 4
2142 or 2144	Knock sensor 1 on cylinder 2; knock sensor 2 on cylinder 4
2212	Throttle valve potentiometer
2221	Vacuum hose to pressure sensor in control unit
2222	Pressure sensor in control unit
2223	Altitude sensor
2232	Air sensor potentiometer
2233	Reference (supply) voltage for air sensor potentiometer and altitude sensor
2234	MPI control unit supply voltage
2242	CO potentiometer
2312	Coolant Temperature Sensor (CTS)
2322	Intake air temperatue sensor
2341	Oxygen sensor control unit (at its control limit)
2342	Oxygen sensor (does not control)
4431	Idle stabilizer valve
4444	No faults stored in memory
0000	End of diagnosis

Year – 1986
Model – 5000 CS Turbo
Engine – 2.2L (136 cid) CIS-E 5 cyl
Engine Code – MC

ECM TROUBLE CODES

Code	Explanation
1111	Ignition control unit or fuel injection control unit
1231	Transmission speed sensor
2111	Engine speed sensor
2112	Ignition reference sensor
2113	Hall sensor
2121	Idle switch
2122	Engine speed signal or Hall sender
2123	Full throttle switch
2132	No data being transmitted from fuel injection control unit to ignition control unit
2141 or 2143	Knock control 1, knock sensor 1 for cylinder 2; knock control 2, knock sensor 2 for cylinder 4
2142 or 2144	Knock sensor 1 on cylinder 2; knock sensor 2 on cylinder 4
2212	Throttle valve potentiometer
2221	Vacuum hose to pressure sensor in control unit
2222	Pressure sensor in control unit
2223	Altitude sensor
2232	Air sensor potentiometer
2233	Reference (supply) voltage for air sensor potentiometer and altitude sensor
2234	MPI control unit supply voltage
2242	CO potentiometer
2312	Coolant Temperature Sensor (CTS)
2322	Intake air temperatue sensor
2341	Oxygen sensor control unit (at its control limit)
2342	Oxygen sensor (does not control)
4431	Idle stabilizer valve
4444	No faults stored in memory
0000	End of diagnosis

Year — 1986
Model — 5000 CS Quattro Turbo
Engine — 2.2L (136 cid) CIS-E 5 cyl
Engine Code — MC

ECM TROUBLE CODES

Code	Explanation
1111	Ignition control unit or fuel injection control unit
1231	Transmission speed sensor
2111	Engine speed sensor
2112	Ignition reference sensor
2113	Hall sensor
2121	Idle switch
2122	Engine speed signal or Hall sender
2123	Full throttle switch
2132	No data being transmitted from fuel injection control unit to ignition control unit
2141 or 2143	Knock control 1, knock sensor 1 for cylinder 2; knock control 2, knock sensor 2 for cylinder 4
2142 or 2144	Knock sensor 1 on cylinder 2; knock sensor 2 on cylinder 4
2212	Throttle valve potentiometer
2221	Vacuum hose to pressure sensor in control unit
2222	Pressure sensor in control unit
2223	Altitude sensor
2232	Air sensor potentiometer
2233	Reference (supply) voltage for air sensor potentiometer and altitude sensor
2234	MPI control unit supply voltage
2242	CO potentiometer
2312	Coolant Temperature Sensor (CTS)
2322	Intake air temperatue sensor
2341	Oxygen sensor control unit (at its control limit)
2342	Oxygen sensor (does not control)
4431	Idle stabilizer valve
4444	No faults stored in memory
0000	End of diagnosis

Year — 1986
Model — 5000 CS Quattro Turbo Wagon
Engine — 2.2L (136 cid) CIS-E 5 cyl
Engine Code — MC

ECM TROUBLE CODES

Code	Explanation
1111	Ignition control unit or fuel injection control unit
1231	Transmission speed sensor
2111	Engine speed sensor
2112	Ignition reference sensor
2113	Hall sensor
2121	Idle switch
2122	Engine speed signal or Hall sender
2123	Full throttle switch
2132	No data being transmitted from fuel injection control unit to ignition control unit
2141 or 2143	Knock control 1, knock sensor 1 for cylinder 2; knock control 2, knock sensor 2 for cylinder 4
2142 or 2144	Knock sensor 1 on cylinder 2; knock sensor 2 on cylinder 4
2212	Throttle valve potentiometer
2221	Vacuum hose to pressure sensor in control unit
2222	Pressure sensor in control unit
2223	Altitude sensor
2232	Air sensor potentiometer
2233	Reference (supply) voltage for air sensor potentiometer and altitude sensor
2234	MPI control unit supply voltage
2242	CO potentiometer
2312	Coolant Temperature Sensor (CTS)
2322	Intake air temperatue sensor
2341	Oxygen sensor control unit (at its control limit)
2342	Oxygen sensor (does not control)
4431	Idle stabilizer valve
4444	No faults stored in memory
0000	End of diagnosis

Year – 1986
Model – 5000 S
Engine – 2.2L (136 cid) CIS-E 5 cyl
Engine Code – MC

ECM TROUBLE CODES

Code	Explanation
1111	Ignition control unit or fuel injection control unit
1231	Transmission speed sensor
2111	Engine speed sensor
2112	Ignition reference sensor
2113	Hall sensor
2121	Idle switch
2122	Engine speed signal or Hall sender
2123	Full throttle switch
2132	No data being transmitted from fuel injection control unit to ignition control unit
2141 or 2143	Knock control 1, knock sensor 1 for cylinder 2; knock control 2, knock sensor 2 for cylinder 4
2142 or 2144	Knock sensor 1 on cylinder 2; knock sensor 2 on cylinder 4
2212	Throttle valve potentiometer
2221	Vacuum hose to pressure sensor in control unit
2222	Pressure sensor in control unit
2223	Altitude sensor
2232	Air sensor potentiometer
2233	Reference (supply) voltage for air sensor potentiometer and altitude sensor
2234	MPI control unit supply voltage
2242	CO potentiometer
2312	Coolant Temperature Sensor (CTS)
2322	Intake air temperatue sensor
2341	Oxygen sensor control unit (at its control limit)
2342	Oxygen sensor (does not control)
4431	Idle stabilizer valve
4444	No faults stored in memory
0000	End of diagnosis

Year — 1986
Model — 5000 S Wagon
Engine — 2.2L (136 cid) CIS-E 5 cyl
Engine Code — MC

ECM TROUBLE CODES

Code	Explanation
1111	Ignition control unit or fuel injection control unit
1231	Transmission speed sensor
2111	Engine speed sensor
2112	Ignition reference sensor
2113	Hall sensor
2121	Idle switch
2122	Engine speed signal or Hall sender
2123	Full throttle switch
2132	No data being transmitted from fuel injection control unit to ignition control unit
2141 or 2143	Knock control 1, knock sensor 1 for cylinder 2; knock control 2, knock sensor 2 for cylinder 4
2142 or 2144	Knock sensor 1 on cylinder 2; knock sensor 2 on cylinder 4
2212	Throttle valve potentiometer
2221	Vacuum hose to pressure sensor in control unit
2222	Pressure sensor in control unit
2223	Altitude sensor
2232	Air sensor potentiometer
2233	Reference (supply) voltage for air sensor potentiometer and altitude sensor
2234	MPI control unit supply voltage
2242	CO potentiometer
2312	Coolant Temperature Sensor (CTS)
2322	Intake air temperatue sensor
2341	Oxygen sensor control unit (at its control limit)
2342	Oxygen sensor (does not control)
4431	Idle stabilizer valve
4444	No faults stored in memory
0000	End of diagnosis

Year – 1987
Model – 5000 CS Turbo
Engine – 2.2L (136 cid) CIS-E 5 cyl
Engine Code – MC

ECM TROUBLE CODES

Code	Explanation
1111	Ignition control unit or fuel injection control unit
1231	Transmission speed sensor
2111	Engine speed sensor
2112	Ignition reference sensor
2113	Hall sensor
2121	Idle switch
2122	Engine speed signal or Hall sender
2123	Full throttle switch
2132	No data being transmitted from fuel injection control unit to ignition control unit
2141 or 2143	Knock control 1, knock sensor 1 for cylinder 2; knock control 2, knock sensor 2 for cylinder 4
2142 or 2144	Knock sensor 1 on cylinder 2; knock sensor 2 on cylinder 4
2212	Throttle valve potentiometer
2221	Vacuum hose to pressure sensor in control unit
2222	Pressure sensor in control unit
2223	Altitude sensor
2232	Air sensor potentiometer
2233	Reference (supply) voltage for air sensor potentiometer and altitude sensor
2234	MPI control unit supply voltage
2242	CO potentiometer
2312	Coolant Temperature Sensor (CTS)
2322	Intake air temperatue sensor
2341	Oxygen sensor control unit (at its control limit)
2342	Oxygen sensor (does not control)
4431	Idle stabilizer valve
4444	No faults stored in memory
0000	End of diagnosis

Year — 1987
Model — 5000 CS Quattro Turbo
Engine — 2.2L (136 cid) CIS-E 5 cyl
Engine Code — MC

ECM TROUBLE CODES

Code	Explanation
1111	Ignition control unit or fuel injection control unit
1231	Transmission speed sensor
2111	Engine speed sensor
2112	Ignition reference sensor
2113	Hall sensor
2121	Idle switch
2122	Engine speed signal or Hall sender
2123	Full throttle switch
2132	No data being transmitted from fuel injection control unit to ignition control unit
2141 or 2143	Knock control 1, knock sensor 1 for cylinder 2; knock control 2, knock sensor 2 for cylinder 4
2142 or 2144	Knock sensor 1 on cylinder 2; knock sensor 2 on cylinder 4
2212	Throttle valve potentiometer
2221	Vacuum hose to pressure sensor in control unit
2222	Pressure sensor in control unit
2223	Altitude sensor
2232	Air sensor potentiometer
2233	Reference (supply) voltage for air sensor potentiometer and altitude sensor
2234	MPI control unit supply voltage
2242	CO potentiometer
2312	Coolant Temperature Sensor (CTS)
2322	Intake air temperatue sensor
2341	Oxygen sensor control unit (at its control limit)
2342	Oxygen sensor (does not control)
4431	Idle stabilizer valve
4444	No faults stored in memory
0000	End of diagnosis

Year – 1987
Model – 5000 CS Quattro Turbo Wagon
Engine – 2.2L (136 cid) CIS-E 5 cyl
Engine Code – MC

ECM TROUBLE CODES

Code	Explanation
1111	Ignition control unit or fuel injection control unit
1231	Transmission speed sensor
2111	Engine speed sensor
2112	Ignition reference sensor
2113	Hall sensor
2121	Idle switch
2122	Engine speed signal or Hall sender
2123	Full throttle switch
2132	No data being transmitted from fuel injection control unit to ignition control unit
2141 or 2143	Knock control 1, knock sensor 1 for cylinder 2; knock control 2, knock sensor 2 for cylinder 4
2142 or 2144	Knock sensor 1 on cylinder 2; knock sensor 2 on cylinder 4
2212	Throttle valve potentiometer
2221	Vacuum hose to pressure sensor in control unit
2222	Pressure sensor in control unit
2223	Altitude sensor
2232	Air sensor potentiometer
2233	Reference (supply) voltage for air sensor potentiometer and altitude sensor
2234	MPI control unit supply voltage
2242	CO potentiometer
2312	Coolant Temperature Sensor (CTS)
2322	Intake air temperatue sensor
2341	Oxygen sensor control unit (at its control limit)
2342	Oxygen sensor (does not control)
4431	Idle stabilizer valve
4444	No faults stored in memory
0000	End of diagnosis

Year — 1987
Model — 5000 S
Engine — 2.2L (136 cid) CIS-E 5 cyl
Engine Code — MC

ECM TROUBLE CODES

Code	Explanation
1111	Ignition control unit or fuel injection control unit
1231	Transmission speed sensor
2111	Engine speed sensor
2112	Ignition reference sensor
2113	Hall sensor
2121	Idle switch
2122	Engine speed signal or Hall sender
2123	Full throttle switch
2132	No data being transmitted from fuel injection control unit to ignition control unit
2141 or 2143	Knock control 1, knock sensor 1 for cylinder 2; knock control 2, knock sensor 2 for cylinder 4
2142 or 2144	Knock sensor 1 on cylinder 2; knock sensor 2 on cylinder 4
2212	Throttle valve potentiometer
2221	Vacuum hose to pressure sensor in control unit
2222	Pressure sensor in control unit
2223	Altitude sensor
2232	Air sensor potentiometer
2233	Reference (supply) voltage for air sensor potentiometer and altitude sensor
2234	MPI control unit supply voltage
2242	CO potentiometer
2312	Coolant Temperature Sensor (CTS)
2322	Intake air temperatue sensor
2341	Oxygen sensor control unit (at its control limit)
2342	Oxygen sensor (does not control)
4431	Idle stabilizer valve
4444	No faults stored in memory
0000	End of diagnosis

Year — 1987
Model — 5000 S Wagon
Engine — 2.2L (136 cid) CIS-E 5 cyl
Engine Code — MC

ECM TROUBLE CODES

Code	Explanation
1111	Ignition control unit or fuel injection control unit
1231	Transmission speed sensor
2111	Engine speed sensor
2112	Ignition reference sensor
2113	Hall sensor
2121	Idle switch
2122	Engine speed signal or Hall sender
2123	Full throttle switch
2132	No data being transmitted from fuel injection control unit to ignition control unit
2141 or 2143	Knock control 1, knock sensor 1 for cylinder 2; knock control 2, knock sensor 2 for cylinder 4
2142 or 2144	Knock sensor 1 on cylinder 2; knock sensor 2 on cylinder 4
2212	Throttle valve potentiometer
2221	Vacuum hose to pressure sensor in control unit
2222	Pressure sensor in control unit
2223	Altitude sensor
2232	Air sensor potentiometer
2233	Reference (supply) voltage for air sensor potentiometer and altitude sensor
2234	MPI control unit supply voltage
2242	CO potentiometer
2312	Coolant Temperature Sensor (CTS)
2322	Intake air temperatue sensor
2341	Oxygen sensor control unit (at its control limit)
2342	Oxygen sensor (does not control)
4431	Idle stabilizer valve
4444	No faults stored in memory
0000	End of diagnosis

Year — 1988
Model — 80
Engine — 2.0L (121 cid) CIS-M 4 cyl
Engine Code — 3A

ECM TROUBLE CODES

Code	Explanation
1111	Ignition control unit or fuel injection control unit
1231	Transmission speed sensor
2111	Engine speed sensor
2112	Ignition reference sensor
2113	Hall sensor
2121	Idle switch
2122	Engine speed signal or Hall sender
2123	Full throttle switch
2132	No data being transmitted from fuel injection control unit to ignition control unit
2141 or 2143	Knock control 1, knock sensor 1 for cylinder 2; knock control 2, knock sensor 2 for cylinder 4
2142 or 2144	Knock sensor 1 on cylinder 2; knock sensor 2 on cylinder 4
2212	Throttle valve potentiometer
2221	Vacuum hose to pressure sensor in control unit
2222	Pressure sensor in control unit
2223	Altitude sensor
2232	Air sensor potentiometer
2233	Reference (supply) voltage for air sensor potentiometer and altitude sensor
2234	MPI control unit supply voltage
2242	CO potentiometer
2312	Coolant Temperature Sensor (CTS)
2322	Intake air temperatue sensor
2341	Oxygen sensor control unit (at its control limit)
2342	Oxygen sensor (does not control)
4431	Idle stabilizer valve
4444	No faults stored in memory
0000	End of diagnosis

Year — 1988
Model — 80 Quattro
Engine — 2.3L (141 cid) CIS-E 5 cyl
Engine Code — NG

ECM TROUBLE CODES

Code	Explanation
1111	Ignition control unit or fuel injection control unit
1231	Transmission speed sensor
2111	Engine speed sensor
2112	Ignition reference sensor
2113	Hall sensor
2121	Idle switch
2122	Engine speed signal or Hall sender
2123	Full throttle switch
2132	No data being transmitted from fuel injection control unit to ignition control unit
2141 or 2143	Knock control 1, knock sensor 1 for cylinder 2; knock control 2, knock sensor 2 for cylinder 4
2142 or 2144	Knock sensor 1 on cylinder 2; knock sensor 2 on cylinder 4
2212	Throttle valve potentiometer
2221	Vacuum hose to pressure sensor in control unit
2222	Pressure sensor in control unit
2223	Altitude sensor
2232	Air sensor potentiometer
2233	Reference (supply) voltage for air sensor potentiometer and altitude sensor
2234	MPI control unit supply voltage
2242	CO potentiometer
2312	Coolant Temperature Sensor (CTS)
2322	Intake air temperatue sensor
2341	Oxygen sensor control unit (at its control limit)
2342	Oxygen sensor (does not control)
4431	Idle stabilizer valve
4444	No faults stored in memory
0000	End of diagnosis

Year – 1988
Model – 90 With Automatic Transmission
Engine – 2.0L (121 cid) CIS-M 4 cyl
Engine Code – 3A

ECM TROUBLE CODES

Code	Explanation
1111	Ignition control unit or fuel injection control unit
1231	Transmission speed sensor
2111	Engine speed sensor
2112	Ignition reference sensor
2113	Hall sensor
2121	Idle switch
2122	Engine speed signal or Hall sender
2123	Full throttle switch
2132	No data being transmitted from fuel injection control unit to ignition control unit
2141 or 2143	Knock control 1, knock sensor 1 for cylinder 2; knock control 2, knock sensor 2 for cylinder 4
2142 or 2144	Knock sensor 1 on cylinder 2; knock sensor 2 on cylinder 4
2212	Throttle valve potentiometer
2221	Vacuum hose to pressure sensor in control unit
2222	Pressure sensor in control unit
2223	Altitude sensor
2232	Air sensor potentiometer
2233	Reference (supply) voltage for air sensor potentiometer and altitude sensor
2234	MPI control unit supply voltage
2242	CO potentiometer
2312	Coolant Temperature Sensor (CTS)
2322	Intake air temperatue sensor
2341	Oxygen sensor control unit (at its control limit)
2342	Oxygen sensor (does not control)
4431	Idle stabilizer valve
4444	No faults stored in memory
0000	End of diagnosis

Year — 1988
Model — 90
Engine — 2.3L (141 cid) CIS-E 5 cyl
Engine Code — NG

ECM TROUBLE CODES

Code	Explanation
1111	Ignition control unit or fuel injection control unit
1231	Transmission speed sensor
2111	Engine speed sensor
2112	Ignition reference sensor
2113	Hall sensor
2121	Idle switch
2122	Engine speed signal or Hall sender
2123	Full throttle switch
2132	No data being transmitted from fuel injection control unit to ignition control unit
2141 or 2143	Knock control 1, knock sensor 1 for cylinder 2; knock control 2, knock sensor 2 for cylinder 4
2142 or 2144	Knock sensor 1 on cylinder 2; knock sensor 2 on cylinder 4
2212	Throttle valve potentiometer
2221	Vacuum hose to pressure sensor in control unit
2222	Pressure sensor in control unit
2223	Altitude sensor
2232	Air sensor potentiometer
2233	Reference (supply) voltage for air sensor potentiometer and altitude sensor
2234	MPI control unit supply voltage
2242	CO potentiometer
2312	Coolant Temperature Sensor (CTS)
2322	Intake air temperatue sensor
2341	Oxygen sensor control unit (at its control limit)
2342	Oxygen sensor (does not control)
4431	Idle stabilizer valve
4444	No faults stored in memory
0000	End of diagnosis

Year — 1988
Model — 90 Quattro
Engine — 2.3L (141 cid) CIS-E 5 cyl
Engine Code — NG

ECM TROUBLE CODES

Code	Explanation
1111	Ignition control unit or fuel injection control unit
1231	Transmission speed sensor
2111	Engine speed sensor
2112	Ignition reference sensor
2113	Hall sensor
2121	Idle switch
2122	Engine speed signal or Hall sender
2123	Full throttle switch
2132	No data being transmitted from fuel injection control unit to ignition control unit
2141 or 2143	Knock control 1, knock sensor 1 for cylinder 2; knock control 2, knock sensor 2 for cylinder 4
2142 or 2144	Knock sensor 1 on cylinder 2; knock sensor 2 on cylinder 4
2212	Throttle valve potentiometer
2221	Vacuum hose to pressure sensor in control unit
2222	Pressure sensor in control unit
2223	Altitude sensor
2232	Air sensor potentiometer
2233	Reference (supply) voltage for air sensor potentiometer and altitude sensor
2234	MPI control unit supply voltage
2242	CO potentiometer
2312	Coolant Temperature Sensor (CTS)
2322	Intake air temperatue sensor
2341	Oxygen sensor control unit (at its control limit)
2342	Oxygen sensor (does not control)
4431	Idle stabilizer valve
4444	No faults stored in memory
0000	End of diagnosis

Year – 1988
Model – 5000 CS Turbo
Engine – 2.2L (136 cid) CIS-E 5 cyl
Engine Code – MC

ECM TROUBLE CODES

Code	Explanation
1111	Ignition control unit or fuel injection control unit
1231	Transmission speed sensor
2111	Engine speed sensor
2112	Ignition reference sensor
2113	Hall sensor
2121	Idle switch
2122	Engine speed signal or Hall sender
2123	Full throttle switch
2132	No data being transmitted from fuel injection control unit to ignition control unit
2141 or 2143	Knock control 1, knock sensor 1 for cylinder 2; knock control 2, knock sensor 2 for cylinder 4
2142 or 2144	Knock sensor 1 on cylinder 2; knock sensor 2 on cylinder 4
2212	Throttle valve potentiometer
2221	Vacuum hose to pressure sensor in control unit
2222	Pressure sensor in control unit
2223	Altitude sensor
2232	Air sensor potentiometer
2233	Reference (supply) voltage for air sensor potentiometer and altitude sensor
2234	MPI control unit supply voltage
2242	CO potentiometer
2312	Coolant Temperature Sensor (CTS)
2322	Intake air temperatue sensor
2341	Oxygen sensor control unit (at its control limit)
2342	Oxygen sensor (does not control)
4431	Idle stabilizer valve
4444	No faults stored in memory
0000	End of diagnosis

Year – 1988
Model – 5000 CS Quattro Turbo
Engine – 2.2L (136 cid) CIS-E 5 cyl
Engine Code – MC

ECM TROUBLE CODES

Code	Explanation
1111	Ignition control unit or fuel injection control unit
1231	Transmission speed sensor
2111	Engine speed sensor
2112	Ignition reference sensor
2113	Hall sensor
2121	Idle switch
2122	Engine speed signal or Hall sender
2123	Full throttle switch
2132	No data being transmitted from fuel injection control unit to ignition control unit
2141 or 2143	Knock control 1, knock sensor 1 for cylinder 2; knock control 2, knock sensor 2 for cylinder 4
2142 or 2144	Knock sensor 1 on cylinder 2; knock sensor 2 on cylinder 4
2212	Throttle valve potentiometer
2221	Vacuum hose to pressure sensor in control unit
2222	Pressure sensor in control unit
2223	Altitude sensor
2232	Air sensor potentiometer
2233	Reference (supply) voltage for air sensor potentiometer and altitude sensor
2234	MPI control unit supply voltage
2242	CO potentiometer
2312	Coolant Temperature Sensor (CTS)
2322	Intake air temperatue sensor
2341	Oxygen sensor control unit (at its control limit)
2342	Oxygen sensor (does not control)
4431	Idle stabilizer valve
4444	No faults stored in memory
0000	End of diagnosis

Year – 1988
Model – 5000 CS Quattro Wagon
Engine – 2.2L (136 cid) CIS-E 5 cyl
Engine Code – MC

ECM TROUBLE CODES

Code	Explanation
1111	Ignition control unit or fuel injection control unit
1231	Transmission speed sensor
2111	Engine speed sensor
2112	Ignition reference sensor
2113	Hall sensor
2121	Idle switch
2122	Engine speed signal or Hall sender
2123	Full throttle switch
2132	No data being transmitted from fuel injection control unit to ignition control unit
2141 or 2143	Knock control 1, knock sensor 1 for cylinder 2; knock control 2, knock sensor 2 for cylinder 4
2142 or 2144	Knock sensor 1 on cylinder 2; knock sensor 2 on cylinder 4
2212	Throttle valve potentiometer
2221	Vacuum hose to pressure sensor in control unit
2222	Pressure sensor in control unit
2223	Altitude sensor
2232	Air sensor potentiometer
2233	Reference (supply) voltage for air sensor potentiometer and altitude sensor
2234	MPI control unit supply voltage
2242	CO potentiometer
2312	Coolant Temperature Sensor (CTS)
2322	Intake air temperatue sensor
2341	Oxygen sensor control unit (at its control limit)
2342	Oxygen sensor (does not control)
4431	Idle stabilizer valve
4444	No faults stored in memory
0000	End of diagnosis

Year – 1988
Model – 5000 S
Engine – 2.3L (141 cid) CIS-E III 5 cyl
Engine Code – NF

ECM TROUBLE CODES

Code	Explanation
1111	Ignition control unit or fuel injection control unit
1231	Transmission speed sensor
2111	Engine speed sensor
2112	Ignition reference sensor
2113	Hall sensor
2121	Idle switch
2122	Engine speed signal or Hall sender
2123	Full throttle switch
2132	No data being transmitted from fuel injection control unit to ignition control unit
2141 or 2143	Knock control 1, knock sensor 1 for cylinder 2; knock control 2, knock sensor 2 for cylinder 4
2142 or 2144	Knock sensor 1 on cylinder 2; knock sensor 2 on cylinder 4
2212	Throttle valve potentiometer
2221	Vacuum hose to pressure sensor in control unit
2222	Pressure sensor in control unit
2223	Altitude sensor
2232	Air sensor potentiometer
2233	Reference (supply) voltage for air sensor potentiometer and altitude sensor
2234	MPI control unit supply voltage
2242	CO potentiometer
2312	Coolant Temperature Sensor (CTS)
2322	Intake air temperatue sensor
2341	Oxygen sensor control unit (at its control limit)
2342	Oxygen sensor (does not control)
4431	Idle stabilizer valve
4444	No faults stored in memory
0000	End of diagnosis

Year — 1988
Model — 5000 S Wagon
Engine — 2.3L (141 cid) CIS-E III 5 cyl
Engine Code — NF

ECM TROUBLE CODES

Code	Explanation
1111	Ignition control unit or fuel injection control unit
1231	Transmission speed sensor
2111	Engine speed sensor
2112	Ignition reference sensor
2113	Hall sensor
2121	Idle switch
2122	Engine speed signal or Hall sender
2123	Full throttle switch
2132	No data being transmitted from fuel injection control unit to ignition control unit
2141 or 2143	Knock control 1, knock sensor 1 for cylinder 2; knock control 2, knock sensor 2 for cylinder 4
2142 or 2144	Knock sensor 1 on cylinder 2; knock sensor 2 on cylinder 4
2212	Throttle valve potentiometer
2221	Vacuum hose to pressure sensor in control unit
2222	Pressure sensor in control unit
2223	Altitude sensor
2232	Air sensor potentiometer
2233	Reference (supply) voltage for air sensor potentiometer and altitude sensor
2234	MPI control unit supply voltage
2242	CO potentiometer
2312	Coolant Temperature Sensor (CTS)
2322	Intake air temperatue sensor
2341	Oxygen sensor control unit (at its control limit)
2342	Oxygen sensor (does not control)
4431	Idle stabilizer valve
4444	No faults stored in memory
0000	End of diagnosis

Year – 1988
Model – 5000 S Quattro
Engine – 2.3L (141 cid) CIS-E III 5 cyl
Engine Code – NF

ECM TROUBLE CODES

Code	Explanation
1111	Ignition control unit or fuel injection control unit
1231	Transmission speed sensor
2111	Engine speed sensor
2112	Ignition reference sensor
2113	Hall sensor
2121	Idle switch
2122	Engine speed signal or Hall sender
2123	Full throttle switch
2132	No data being transmitted from fuel injection control unit to ignition control unit
2141 or 2143	Knock control 1, knock sensor 1 for cylinder 2; knock control 2, knock sensor 2 for cylinder 4
2142 or 2144	Knock sensor 1 on cylinder 2; knock sensor 2 on cylinder 4
2212	Throttle valve potentiometer
2221	Vacuum hose to pressure sensor in control unit
2222	Pressure sensor in control unit
2223	Altitude sensor
2232	Air sensor potentiometer
2233	Reference (supply) voltage for air sensor potentiometer and altitude sensor
2234	MPI control unit supply voltage
2242	CO potentiometer
2312	Coolant Temperature Sensor (CTS)
2322	Intake air temperatue sensor
2341	Oxygen sensor control unit (at its control limit)
2342	Oxygen sensor (does not control)
4431	Idle stabilizer valve
4444	No faults stored in memory
0000	End of diagnosis

Year – 1989
Model – 80
Engine – 2.0L (121 cid) CIS 4 cyl
Engine Code – 3A

ECM TROUBLE CODES

Code	Explanation
1111	Ignition control unit or fuel injection control unit
1231	Transmission speed sensor
2111	Engine speed sensor
2112	Ignition reference sensor
2113	Hall sensor
2121	Idle switch
2122	Engine speed signal or Hall sender
2123	Full throttle switch
2132	No data being transmitted from fuel injection control unit to ignition control unit
2141 or 2143	Knock control 1, knock sensor 1 for cylinder 2; knock control 2, knock sensor 2 for cylinder 4
2142 or 2144	Knock sensor 1 on cylinder 2; knock sensor 2 on cylinder 4
2212	Throttle valve potentiometer
2221	Vacuum hose to pressure sensor in control unit
2222	Pressure sensor in control unit
2223	Altitude sensor
2232	Air sensor potentiometer
2233	Reference (supply) voltage for air sensor potentiometer and altitude sensor
2234	MPI control unit supply voltage
2242	CO potentiometer
2312	Coolant Temperature Sensor (CTS)
2322	Intake air temperatue sensor
2341	Oxygen sensor control unit (at its control limit)
2342	Oxygen sensor (does not control)
4431	Idle stabilizer valve
4444	No faults stored in memory
0000	End of diagnosis

Year – 1989
Model – 80 Quattro
Engine – 2.3L (141 cid) CIS-E III 5 cyl
Engine Code – NG

ECM TROUBLE CODES

Code	Explanation
1111	Ignition control unit or fuel injection control unit
1231	Transmission speed sensor
2111	Engine speed sensor
2112	Ignition reference sensor
2113	Hall sensor
2121	Idle switch
2122	Engine speed signal or Hall sender
2123	Full throttle switch
2132	No data being transmitted from fuel injection control unit to ignition control unit
2141 or 2143	Knock control 1, knock sensor 1 for cylinder 2; knock control 2, knock sensor 2 for cylinder 4
2142 or 2144	Knock sensor 1 on cylinder 2; knock sensor 2 on cylinder 4
2212	Throttle valve potentiometer
2221	Vacuum hose to pressure sensor in control unit
2222	Pressure sensor in control unit
2223	Altitude sensor
2232	Air sensor potentiometer
2233	Reference (supply) voltage for air sensor potentiometer and altitude sensor
2234	MPI control unit supply voltage
2242	CO potentiometer
2312	Coolant Temperature Sensor (CTS)
2322	Intake air temperatue sensor
2341	Oxygen sensor control unit (at its control limit)
2342	Oxygen sensor (does not control)
4431	Idle stabilizer valve
4444	No faults stored in memory
0000	End of diagnosis

Year—1989
Model—90 With Automatic Transmission
Engine—2.0L (121 cid) CIS 4 cyl
Engine Code—3A

ECM TROUBLE CODES

Code	Explanation
1111	Ignition control unit or fuel injection control unit
1231	Transmission speed sensor
2111	Engine speed sensor
2112	Ignition reference sensor
2113	Hall sensor
2121	Idle switch
2122	Engine speed signal or Hall sender
2123	Full throttle switch
2132	No data being transmitted from fuel injection control unit to ignition control unit
2141 or 2143	Knock control 1, knock sensor 1 for cylinder 2; knock control 2, knock sensor 2 for cylinder 4
2142 or 2144	Knock sensor 1 on cylinder 2; knock sensor 2 on cylinder 4
2212	Throttle valve potentiometer
2221	Vacuum hose to pressure sensor in control unit
2222	Pressure sensor in control unit
2223	Altitude sensor
2232	Air sensor potentiometer
2233	Reference (supply) voltage for air sensor potentiometer and altitude sensor
2234	MPI control unit supply voltage
2242	CO potentiometer
2312	Coolant Temperature Sensor (CTS)
2322	Intake air temperatue sensor
2341	Oxygen sensor control unit (at its control limit)
2342	Oxygen sensor (does not control)
4431	Idle stabilizer valve
4444	No faults stored in memory
0000	End of diagnosis

Year—1989
Model—90
Engine—2.3L (141 cid) CIS-E III 5 cyl
Engine Code—NG

ECM TROUBLE CODES

Code	Explanation
1111	Ignition control unit or fuel injection control unit
1231	Transmission speed sensor
2111	Engine speed sensor
2112	Ignition reference sensor
2113	Hall sensor
2121	Idle switch
2122	Engine speed signal or Hall sender
2123	Full throttle switch
2132	No data being transmitted from fuel injection control unit to ignition control unit
2141 or 2143	Knock control 1, knock sensor 1 for cylinder 2; knock control 2, knock sensor 2 for cylinder 4
2142 or 2144	Knock sensor 1 on cylinder 2; knock sensor 2 on cylinder 4
2212	Throttle valve potentiometer
2221	Vacuum hose to pressure sensor in control unit
2222	Pressure sensor in control unit
2223	Altitude sensor
2232	Air sensor potentiometer
2233	Reference (supply) voltage for air sensor potentiometer and altitude sensor
2234	MPI control unit supply voltage
2242	CO potentiometer
2312	Coolant Temperature Sensor (CTS)
2322	Intake air temperatue sensor
2341	Oxygen sensor control unit (at its control limit)
2342	Oxygen sensor (does not control)
4431	Idle stabilizer valve
4444	No faults stored in memory
0000	End of diagnosis

Year – 1989
Model – 90 Quattro
Engine – 2.3L (141 cid) CIS-E III 5 cyl
Engine Code – NG

ECM TROUBLE CODES

Code	Explanation
1111	Ignition control unit or fuel injection control unit
1231	Transmission speed sensor
2111	Engine speed sensor
2112	Ignition reference sensor
2113	Hall sensor
2121	Idle switch
2122	Engine speed signal or Hall sender
2123	Full throttle switch
2132	No data being transmitted from fuel injection control unit to ignition control unit
2141 or 2143	Knock control 1, knock sensor 1 for cylinder 2; knock control 2, knock sensor 2 for cylinder 4
2142 or 2144	Knock sensor 1 on cylinder 2; knock sensor 2 on cylinder 4
2212	Throttle valve potentiometer
2221	Vacuum hose to pressure sensor in control unit
2222	Pressure sensor in control unit
2223	Altitude sensor
2232	Air sensor potentiometer
2233	Reference (supply) voltage for air sensor potentiometer and altitude sensor
2234	MPI control unit supply voltage
2242	CO potentiometer
2312	Coolant Temperature Sensor (CTS)
2322	Intake air temperatue sensor
2341	Oxygen sensor control unit (at its control limit)
2342	Oxygen sensor (does not control)
4431	Idle stabilizer valve
4444	No faults stored in memory
0000	End of diagnosis

Year—1989
Model—100
Engine—2.3L (141 cid) CIS-E III 5 cyl
Engine Code—NF

ECM TROUBLE CODES

Code	Explanation
1111	Ignition control unit or fuel injection control unit
1231	Transmission speed sensor
2111	Engine speed sensor
2112	Ignition reference sensor
2113	Hall sensor
2121	Idle switch
2122	Engine speed signal or Hall sender
2123	Full throttle switch
2132	No data being transmitted from fuel injection control unit to ignition control unit
2141 or 2143	Knock control 1, knock sensor 1 for cylinder 2; knock control 2, knock sensor 2 for cylinder 4
2142 or 2144	Knock sensor 1 on cylinder 2; knock sensor 2 on cylinder 4
2212	Throttle valve potentiometer
2221	Vacuum hose to pressure sensor in control unit
2222	Pressure sensor in control unit
2223	Altitude sensor
2232	Air sensor potentiometer
2233	Reference (supply) voltage for air sensor potentiometer and altitude sensor
2234	MPI control unit supply voltage
2242	CO potentiometer
2312	Coolant Temperature Sensor (CTS)
2322	Intake air temperatue sensor
2341	Oxygen sensor control unit (at its control limit)
2342	Oxygen sensor (does not control)
4431	Idle stabilizer valve
4444	No faults stored in memory
0000	End of diagnosis

Year — 1989
Model — 100 Quattro
Engine — 2.3L (141 cid) CIS-E III 5 cyl
Engine Code — NF

ECM TROUBLE CODES

Code	Explanation
1111	Ignition control unit or fuel injection control unit
1231	Transmission speed sensor
2111	Engine speed sensor
2112	Ignition reference sensor
2113	Hall sensor
2121	Idle switch
2122	Engine speed signal or Hall sender
2123	Full throttle switch
2132	No data being transmitted from fuel injection control unit to ignition control unit
2141 or 2143	Knock control 1, knock sensor 1 for cylinder 2; knock control 2, knock sensor 2 for cylinder 4
2142 or 2144	Knock sensor 1 on cylinder 2; knock sensor 2 on cylinder 4
2212	Throttle valve potentiometer
2221	Vacuum hose to pressure sensor in control unit
2222	Pressure sensor in control unit
2223	Altitude sensor
2232	Air sensor potentiometer
2233	Reference (supply) voltage for air sensor potentiometer and altitude sensor
2234	MPI control unit supply voltage
2242	CO potentiometer
2312	Coolant Temperature Sensor (CTS)
2322	Intake air temperatue sensor
2341	Oxygen sensor control unit (at its control limit)
2342	Oxygen sensor (does not control)
4431	Idle stabilizer valve
4444	No faults stored in memory
0000	End of diagnosis

Year — 1989
Model — 200 and 200 Quattro
Engine — 2.2L (136 cid) CIS-E 5 cyl
Engine Code — MC

ECM TROUBLE CODES

Code	Explanation
1111	Ignition control unit or fuel injection control unit
1231	Transmission speed sensor
2111	Engine speed sensor
2112	Ignition reference sensor
2113	Hall sensor
2121	Idle switch
2122	Engine speed signal or Hall sender
2123	Full throttle switch
2132	No data being transmitted from fuel injection control unit to ignition control unit
2141 or 2143	Knock control 1, knock sensor 1 for cylinder 2; knock control 2, knock sensor 2 for cylinder 4
2142 or 2144	Knock sensor 1 on cylinder 2; knock sensor 2 on cylinder 4
2212	Throttle valve potentiometer
2221	Vacuum hose to pressure sensor in control unit
2222	Pressure sensor in control unit
2223	Altitude sensor
2232	Air sensor potentiometer
2233	Reference (supply) voltage for air sensor potentiometer and altitude sensor
2234	MPI control unit supply voltage
2242	CO potentiometer
2312	Coolant Temperature Sensor (CTS)
2322	Intake air temperatue sensor
2341	Oxygen sensor control unit (at its control limit)
2342	Oxygen sensor (does not control)
4431	Idle stabilizer valve
4444	No faults stored in memory
0000	End of diagnosis

BMW

INDEX

BMW

Digital Motor Electronics (DME) System

SELF-DIAGNOSTIC SYSTEM

Description

The DME is a system that combines the L-Jetronic or LH-Jetronic type fuel injection with the fully electronic coil ignition. The same electronic controller is used for both system.

The DME control unit is capable of self-diagnosis. Faults can be called from the memory with a specially developed diagnosis tester, which can be connected on a diagnostic terminal connection, usually near the fuse or relay box. In addition to reading fault codes, the tester can activate certain functions and therefore check the function to these components.

The specific test functions of the tester are available with the BMW tester itself. Some vehicles are capable of flashing basic fault codes through the Check Engine lamp. These codes will only flash when the engine is not running and the ignition switch is **ON**.

The 750iL, which uses the M70 12 cylinder engine, is capable of storing 17 trouble codes for each side of the engine including x000 and x444. The first digit of the code will designate the side of the engine. The M70 uses 2 separate engine control systems. The code for each side are the same except for the first digit. If the 4 digit code starts with a 1, the code is for the right side com-

ponents, if the code starts with a 2, the control unit detected a problem with a component on the left side of the engine. A fault code of 4444, 1444 or 2444, states the fault memory is empty.

All engines except the 12 cylinder M70 can store 4 engine diagnostic codes. The codes include faulty air flow sensor, oxygen sensor, engine temperature sensor and idle speed switch or the associated circuit.

Entering Diagnostic Mode

The Check or Check Engine lamp will remain ON continuously while the engine is running, if there is a fault. The DME 1.1 system used on some 3 series vehicles is capable of 4 diagnostic codes. The DME 1.2 system used on the 750iL is capable of storing over 17 codes. Thee DME 1.3 system used on the other series vehicles is cabable of the same 4 codes as the DME 1.1 used on 3 series vehicles.

To activate the fault output on all vehicles except 3 series, turn the ignition **ON**, do not start engine. Operate the full load contact 5 times within 5 seconds. The fault output should begin. DME 1.1 on 3 series vehicles, equipped with self-diagnosis, code display should start after turning the ignition switch **ON**, while not starting the engine.

All engines except the 12 cylinder M70 can store the following 4 engine diagnostic codes:

Code 1 — faulty air flow sensor or circuit
Code 2 — faulty oxygen sensor or circuit
Code 3 — faulty engine temperature sensor or circuit
Code 4 — faulty idle speed switch

Clearing Diagnostic Memory

EXCEPT 750iL

The fault is cleared after problem has been repair and the engine has been started 5–10 times.

750iL – M70 ENGINE

Codes can cleared using the BMW tester cancel code command, if the BMW tester is available. The best way to clear codes with out the tester is to reactivate code sequence with the igni-

tion switch **ON**. While flashing code x000 is being displayed, close the full load switch for 10 seconds. Disconnecting the DME control wiring harness will also clear codes.

NOTE: Disconnecting the battery to clear codes should be avoid, some codes may not clear completely or temporary driveablitly problems can occur. The memory of the radio, seat adjustment or radio anti-theft system will be erased if the battery is disconnected.

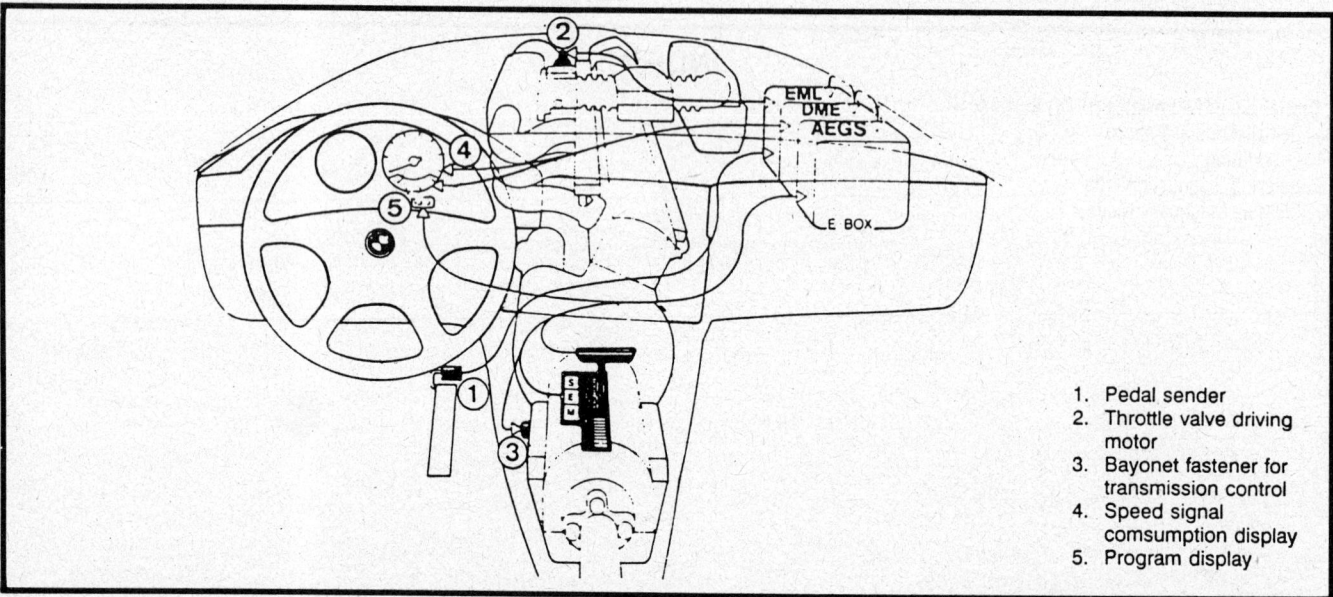

1. Pedal sender
2. Throttle valve driving motor
3. Bayonet fastener for transmission control
4. Speed signal comsumption display
5. Program display

Digital Motor Electronics (DME) component diagram

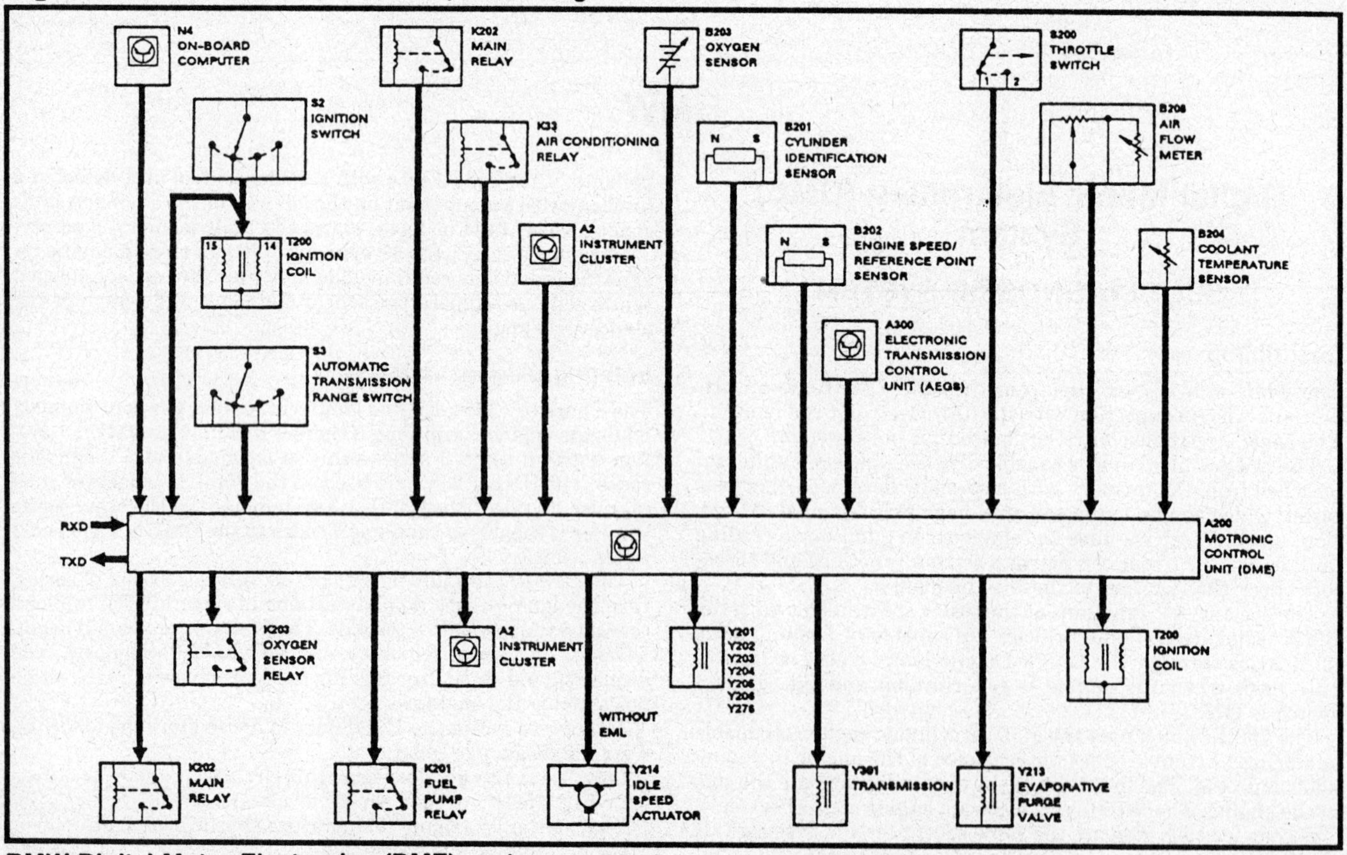

BMW Digital Motor Electronics (DME) system – typical

Chrysler Imports

9

INDEX

CHRYSLER IMPORT

Electronic Control Injection (ECI) and Multi-Port Fuel Injection (MPI) Systems

SELF-DIAGNOSTIC SYSTEM

Description

Many fuel injected engines (ECI or MPI) contain a self-diagnosis system. The Electronic Control Unit (ECU) monitors voltage signals from various engine sensors. When the ECU detects an abnormal condition, it records the condition as a trouble code, which corresponds to a particular sensor. An abnormal condition could be a voltage signal out of normal operating parameters, no voltage signal (indicating an open circuit) or an excessive voltage signal (indicating a shorted or grounded circuit). The trouble codes can be read either by using an analog voltmeter connected to the diagnostic connector. The location of the diagnostic connector varies depending upon model and year.

Diagnostic Connector Location

Conquest 1984–86—Connector located in engine compartment on right side fender well, near headlight.

Conquest 1987–89—Connector located behind glove box Colt 1984–86—Connector located in engine compartment on firewall, branched from main harness just to the left of center, near engine ground connector.

Colt 1987–88—Connector located in engine compartment on firewall, branched from main harness to the left of center.

Colt/Summit 1989—Connector located under dash on right side of heater core housing.

Colt Vista 1987—Connector located under dash on driver's side behind hood release bracket.

Colt Vista 1988–89—Connector located under glove box door on right side

Entering Diagnostic Mode

1. Turn the ignition switch **OFF**.
2. Connect analog voltmeter to correct diagnostic connector terminals.

NOTE: When connecting the analog voltmeter, be sure to observe proper polarity; otherwise, damage may occur to the Electronic Control Unit (ECU).

3. Turn ignition switch **ON**. Codes stored in ECU memory will be displayed in ascending order. The order in which the codes are displayed does not indicate the order in which the malfunction(s) occurred.

Types of Code Displays

NUMERICAL CODE DISPLAY

This type of display is used on systems with both 1 and 2-digit code numbers. Counting the number of sweeps of the pointer determines the trouble code. The sweep duration is 1.5 seconds for each multiple of 10 digit; 0.5 seconds for each unit digit. The multiple of 10 digits are displayed first, separated by 0.5 second pauses, there will be a 2 second pause and then the unit digits will be displayed also separated by 0.5 second pauses.

BINARY CODE DISPLAY

NOTE: The binary code display is used on the 1987–88 Colt Vista.

With this type of display, each code consists of 5 segments. The

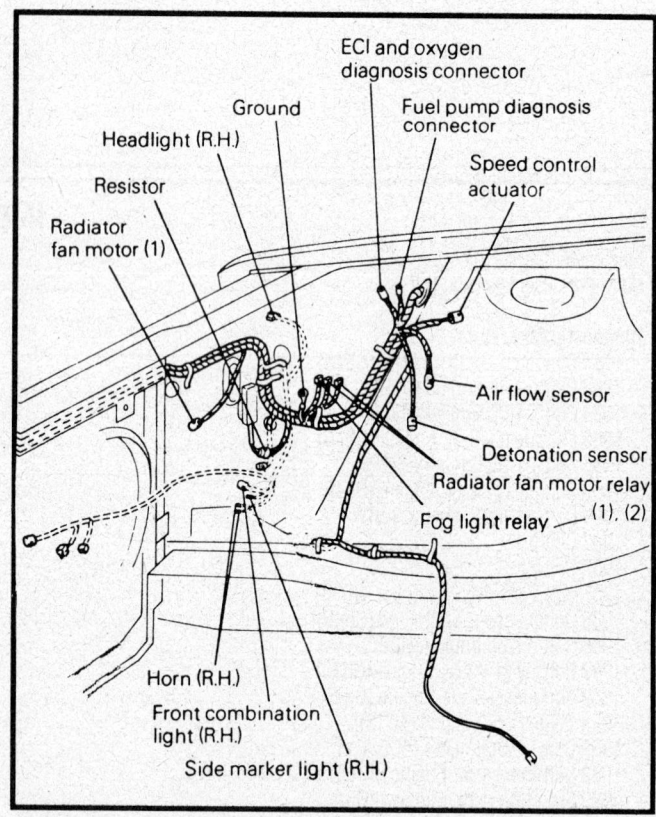

Location of self-diagnosis connector – 1984–86 Conquest

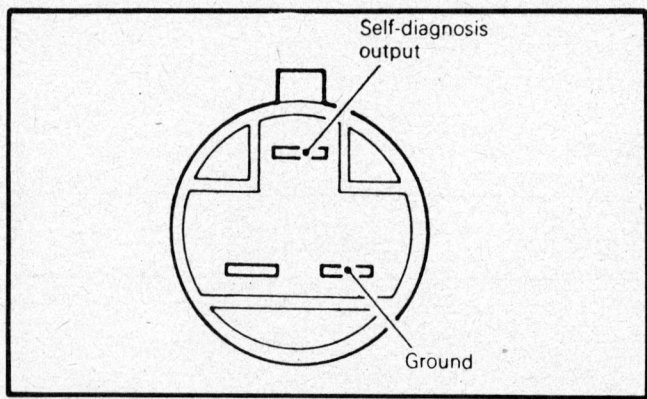

Pin locations on ECI and Oxygen sensor diagnosis connector

duration of each segment is 2.0 seconds. The value of each segment is either "0" or "1". The value is determined by measuring the duration of the pointer sweep within each 2.0 second segment. A segment with a sweep duration of 0.5 seconds is given a value of "0". A segment with a sweep duration of 1.5 seconds is given a value of "1". The series totaling five "0's" and "1's" corresponds to the trouble code. For example: the series 0 0 1 0 0 corresponds to trouble Code 4 (refer to Binary Trouble Code Chart). The trouble code display sequence begins with a steady 3.0 second sweep, followed by the five 2.0 second segments indicating the trouble code and another steady 3.0 second sweep before the next code.

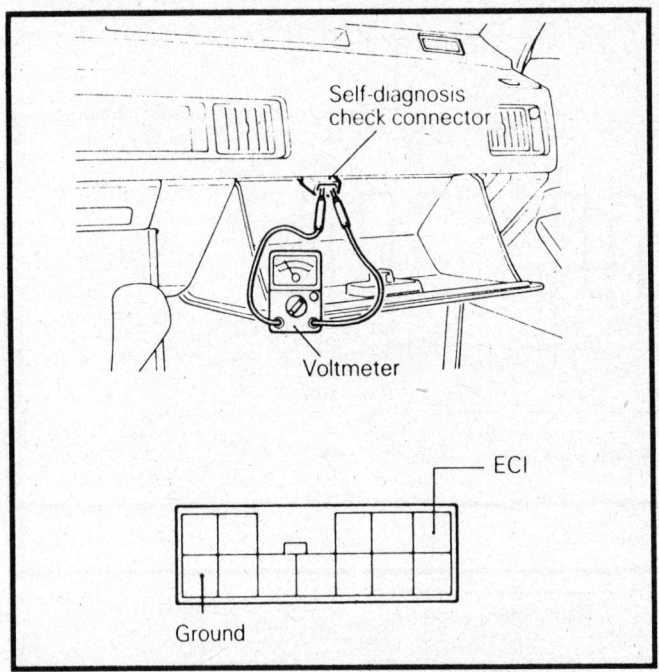

Location of self-diagnosis connector – 1987–89 Conquest

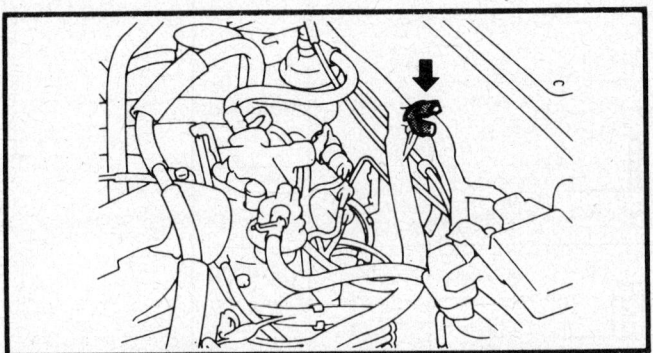

Location of self-diagnosis connector – 1987–88 Colt

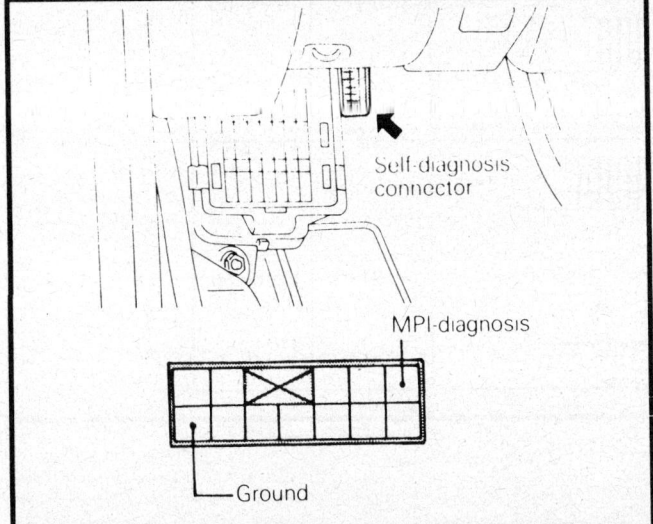

Location of self-diagnosis connector – 1989 Colt and Summit

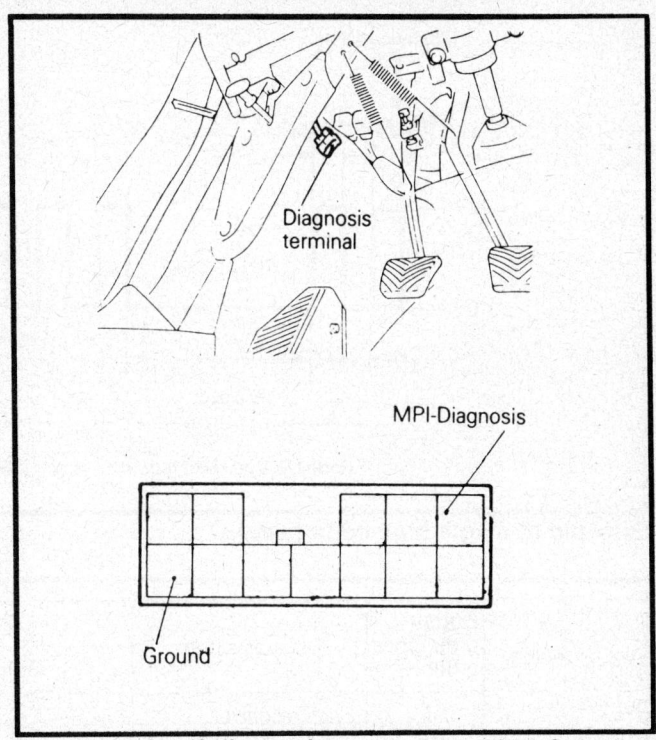

Location of self-diagnosis connector – 1987 Colt Vista

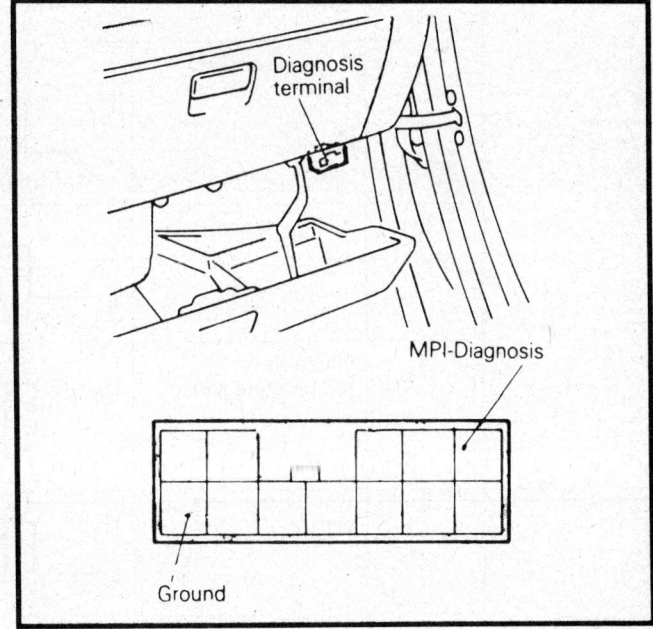

Location of self-diagnosis connector – 1988–89 Colt Vista

Clearing Diagnostic Memory

Because the ECU draws its power directly from the battery, the trouble codes stored in the ECU memory will not be erased by turning the ignition switch **OFF**. The memory may be cleared by removing the negative battery cable or by disconnecting the ECU connector for not less than 15 seconds. Insure that the ignition switch is **OFF** before disconnecting either the negative battery cable or the ECU connector.

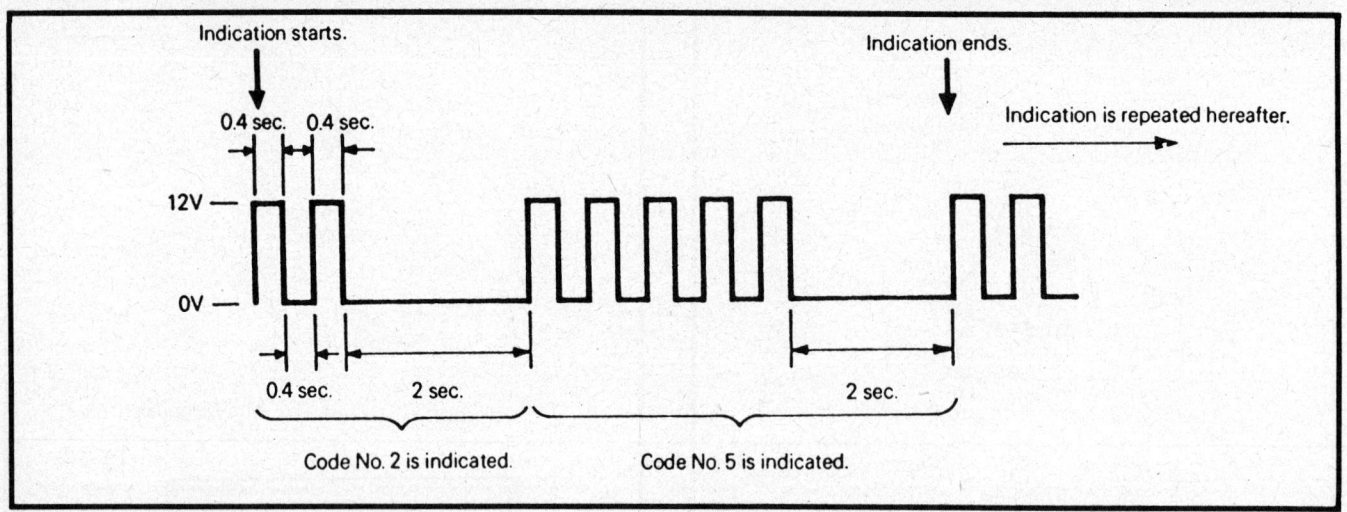

Example of single-digit code pattern

Output preference order	Diagnosis item	Malfunction code		
		Output signal pattern	No.	Memory
1	Engine control unit		–	–
2	Oxygen sensor		11	Retained
3	Air flow sensor		12	Retained
4	Intake air temperature sensor		13	Retained
5	Throttle position sensor		14	Retained
6	Engine coolant temperature sensor		21	Retained

Example of 2-digit code pattern

CHRYSLER IMPORT

Year – 1984
Model – Conquest
Engine – 2.6L (156 cid) Turbo 4 cyl
Engine Code – G54B

ECM TROUBLE CODES

Code	Explanation
1	Oxygen sensor and computer
2	Ignition pulse
3	Air Flow Sensor (AFS)
4	Pressure sensor
5	Throttle Position Sensor (TPS)
6	Idle Speed Control (ISC) motor position switch
7	Coolant Temperature Sensor (CTS)
8	Vehicle Speed Sensor (VSS)

Year – 1984
Model – Colt
Engine – 1.4L (86 cid) 4 cyl
Engine Code – G12B

ECM TROUBLE CODES

Code	Explanation
1	Oxygen sensor
2	Ignition signal
3	Air Flow Sensor (AFS)
4	Pressure sensor
5	Throttle Position Sensor (TPS)
6	Idle Speed Control (ISC) position sensor
7	Water temperature sensor
8	Car speed signal

Year — 1984
Model — Colt
Engine — 1.6L (98 cid) 4 cyl
Engine Code — G32B

ECM TROUBLE CODES

Code	Explanation
1	Oxygen sensor
2	Ignition signal
3	Air Flow Sensor (AFS)
4	Pressure sensor
5	Throttle Position Sensor (TPS)
6	Idle Speed Control (ISC) position sensor
7	Water temperature sensor
8	Car speed signal

Year – 1985
Model – Conquest
Engine – 2.6L (156 cid) Turbo 4 cyl
Engine Code – G54B

ECM TROUBLE CODES

Code	Explanation
1	Oxygen sensor
2	Ignition signal
3	Air Flow Sensor (AFS)
4	Pressure sensor
5	Throttle Position Sensor (TPS)
6	Idle Speed Control (ISC) motor position switch
7	Coolant Temperature Sensor (CTS)

Year – 1985
Model – Colt
Engine – 1.6L (97 cid) 4 cyl
Engine Code – G32B

ECM TROUBLE CODES

Code	Explanation
1	Oxygen sensor
2	Ignition signal
3	Air Flow Sensor (AFS)
4	Pressure sensor
5	Throttle Position Sensor (TPS)
6	Idle Speed Control (ISC) position sensor
7	Coolant temperature sensor
8	Vehicle speed signal

Year – 1986
Model – Conquest
Engine – 2.6L (156 cid) Turbo 4 cyl
Engine Code – G54B

ECM TROUBLE CODES

Code	Explanation
1	Oxygen sensor
2	Ignition signal
3	Air Flow Sensor (AFS)
4	Pressure sensor
5	Throttle Position Sensor (TPS)
6	Idle Speed Control (ISC) motor position switch
7	Coolant Temperature Sensor (CTS)

Year – 1986
Model – Colt
Engine – 1.6L (97 cid) 4 cyl
Engine Code – G32B

ECM TROUBLE CODES

Code	Explanation
1	Oxygen sensor and computer
2	Ignition pulse
3	Air Flow Sensor (AFS)
4	Pressure sensor
5	Throttle Position Sensor (TPS)
6	Idle Speed Control (ISC) position sensor
7	Coolant temperature sensor
8	Vehicle speed signal

Year — 1987
Model — Conquest
Engine — 2.6L (156 cid) Turbo 4 cyl
Engine Code — G54B

ECM TROUBLE CODES

Code	Explanation
1	Oxygen sensor
2	Ignition pulse (Engine speed sensor)
3	Air Flow Sensor (AFS)
5	Throttle Position Sensor (TPS)
6	Idle Speed Control (ISC) motor position switch
7	Coolant Temperature Sensor (CTS)

Year — 1987
Model — Colt
Engine — 1.6L (97 cid) 4 cyl
Engine Code — G32B

ECM TROUBLE CODES

Code	Explanation
1	Oxygen sensor
2	Ignition pulse
3	Air Flow Sensor (AFS)
5	Throttle Position Sensor (TPS)
6	Idle Speed Control (ISC) position sensor
7	Coolant temperature sensor

Year – 1987
Model – Colt Vista
Engine – 2.0L (122 cid) 4 cyl
Engine Code – G63B

ECM TROUBLE CODES

Code	Explanation
0 0 0 0 0	Normal
1 0 0 0 0	Oxygen sensor
0 1 0 0 0	Top Dead Center (TDC) sensor
1 1 0 0 0	Air Flow Sensor (AFS)
0 0 1 0 0	Atmospheric pressure sensor
1 0 1 0 0	Throttle Position Sensor (TPS)
0 1 1 0 0	Motor Position Sensor (MPS)
1 1 1 0 0	Coolant temperature sensor
0 0 0 1 0	Number 1 cylinder Top Dead Center (TDC) sensor

Year – 1988
Model – Conquest
Engine – 2.6L (156 cid) Turbo 4 cyl
Engine Code – G54B

ECM TROUBLE CODES

Code	Explanation
1	Oxygen sensor
2	Ignition pulse
3	Air Flow Sensor (AFS)
5	Throttle Position Sensor (TPS)
6	Idle Speed Control (ISC) motor position switch
7	Coolant Temperature Sensor (CTS)

Year – 1988
Model – Colt
Engine – 1.6L (97 cid) 4 cyl
Engine Code – G32B

ECM TROUBLE CODES

Code	Explanation
1	Oxygen sensor
2	Ignition pulse
3	Air Flow Sensor (AFS)
5	Throttle Position Sensor (TPS)
6	Idle Speed Control (ISC) position sensor
7	Coolant temperature sensor

Year – 1988
Model – Colt Vista
Engine – 2.0L (122 cid) 4 cyl
Engine Code – G63B

ECM TROUBLE CODES

Code	Explanation
0 0 0 0 0	Normal
1 0 0 0 0	Oxygen sensor
0 1 0 0 0	Crank angle sensor
1 1 0 0 0	Air Flow Sensor (AFS)
0 0 1 0 0	Barometric pressure sensor
1 0 1 0 0	Throttle Position Sensor (TPS)
0 1 1 0 0	Motor Position Sensor (MPS)
1 1 1 0 0	Coolant temperature sensor
0 0 0 1 0	Number 1 cylinder Top Dead Center (TDC) sensor

Year — 1989
Model — Conquest
Engine — 2.6L (156 cid) Turbo 4 cyl
Engine Code — G54B

ECM TROUBLE CODES

Code	Explanation
1	Oxygen sensor
2	Ignition pulse
3	Air Flow Sensor (AFS)
5	Throttle Position Sensor (TPS)
6	Idle Speed Control (ISC) motor position switch
7	Coolant Temperature Sensor (CTS)

Year — 1989
Model — Colt
Engine — 1.5L (96 cid) 4 cyl
Engine Code — 4G15

ECM TROUBLE CODES

Code	Explanation
11	Oxygen sensor
12	Air Flow Sensor (AFS)
13	Intake Air Temperature Sensor (ATS)
14	Throttle Position Sensor (TPS)
15	Motor Position Sensor (MPS)
21	Coolant Temperature Sensor (CTS)
22	Crank Angle Sensor (CAS)
23	Number 1 cylinder TDC sensor
24	Vehicle Speed Sensor (VSS) — reed switch
25	Barometric pressure sensor
41	Injector
42	Fuel pump
43	Exhaust Gas Recirculation (EGR) — California

Year – 1989
Model – Colt
Engine – 1.6L (98 cid) 4 cyl
Engine Code – 4G61

ECM TROUBLE CODES

Code	Explanation
11	Oxygen sensor
12	Air Flow Sensor (AFS)
13	Intake Air Temperature Sensor (ATS)
14	Throttle Position Sensor (TPS)
21	Coolant Temperature Sensor (CTS)
22	Crank Angle Sensor (CAS)
23	Number 1 cylinder TDC sensor
24	Vehicle Speed Sensor (VSS) – reed switch
25	Barometric pressure sensor
31	Detonation sensor
41	Injector
42	Fuel pump
43	Exhaust Gas Recirculation (EGR)–California
44	Ignition coil

Year – 1989
Model – Summit
Engine – 1.5L (96 cid) 4 cyl
Engine Code – 4G15

ECM TROUBLE CODES

Code	Explanation
11	Oxygen sensor
12	Air Flow Sensor (AFS)
13	Intake Air Temperature Sensor (ATS)
14	Throttle Position Sensor (TPS)
15	Motor Position Sensor (MPS)
21	Coolant Temperature Sensor (CTS)
22	Crank Angle Sensor (CAS)
23	Number 1 cylinder TDC sensor
24	Vehicle Speed Sensor (VSS) – reed switch
25	Barometric pressure sensor
41	Injector
42	Fuel pump
43	Exhaust Gas Recirculation (EGR)–California

CHRYSLER CORPORATION (IMPORTS)

Year — 1989
Model — Summit
Engine — 1.6L (98 cid) 4 cyl
Engine Code — 4G61

ECM TROUBLE CODES

Code	Explanation
11	Oxygen sensor
12	Air Flow Sensor (AFS)
13	Intake Air Temperature Sensor (ATS)
14	Throttle Position Sensor (TPS)
21	Coolant Temperature Sensor (CTS)
22	Crank Angle Sensor (CAS)
23	Number 1 cylinder TDC sensor
24	Vehicle Speed Sensor (VSS) — reed switch
25	Barometric pressure sensor
31	Detonation sensor
41	Injector
42	Fuel pump
43	Exhaust Gas Recirculation (EGR) – California
44	Ignition coil

Year – 1989
Model – Colt Vista
Engine – 2.0L (122 cid) 4 cyl
Engine Code – G63B

ECM TROUBLE CODES

Code	Explanation
11	Oxygen sensor
12	Air Flow Sensor (AFS)
13	Intake Air Temperature Sensor (ATS)
14	Throttle Position Sensor (TPS)
15	Motor Position Sensor (MPS)
21	Coolant Temperature Sensor (CTS)
22	Crank Angle Sensor (CAS)
23	Number 1 cylinder TDC sensor
24	Vehicle Speed Sensor (VSS) – reed switch
25	Barometric pressure sensor
41	Injector
42	Fuel pump
43	Exhaust Gas Recirculation (EGR)–California

INDEX

DAIHATSU

Electronic Fuel Injection (EFI)

SELF-DIAGNOSTIC SYSTEM

Description

The electronic fuel injection system consists of 3 sub-systems: air intake, electronic control and fuel supply. It controls the amount of fuel and mixture based on engine conditions and running conditions, as determined by signals input by various sensors. The ECU also controls electronic ignition timing, fuel pump operation, idle-up control, a self-diagnosis function and the fail safe and back-up functions.

If any malfunction should occur in an input signal circuit, the ECU memorizes the fault. This malfunction is indicated during the trouble diagnosis, by codes through the checking lamps. If a major malfunction is encountered, the ECU turns ON the "Check Engine" lamp to warn the driver.

FAIL-SAFE FUNCTION

When a malfunction is detected, the ECU determines, based on programmed standard values, whether the engine may be allowed to continue operation or should be stopped immediately.

BACK-UP FUNCTION

In the event the ECU detects a malfunction, the back-up function makes it possible to provide fuel injection amount and ignition timing that have been predetermined by the back-up data. This is to ensure safe driving if a single or many sensors are faulty, or if the ECU malfunctions.

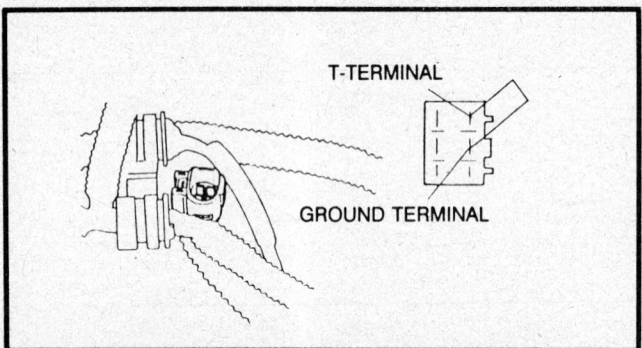

Connect the jumper wire to the test connector

Entering Diagnostic Mode

1. Make certain battery voltage is above 11V.

NOTE: The ECU may not store codes if the battery is low.

2. Make certain the throttle is closed.
3. Turn all accessories **OFF**.
4. Short the Brown **T** terminal and the Black ground terminal of the test connector.

NOTE: The check connector is located at the upper section of the transmission. The use of a special test harness SST No. 09991–87702–000 or equivalent, connected to the Check Connector may be necessary.

5. Turn the ignition switch to **ON**. Do not start the engine.
6. Read the diagnosis codes by counting the "Check Engine" lamp flashes.

Clearing Diagnostic Memory

To clear the diagnosis code from the ECU, disconnect the negative terminal from the battery or disconnect the BACK-UP fuse of the relay block assembly in the engine compartment with the ignition switch **OFF** for at least 30 seconds.

NOTE: Some vehicle computers have a learning ability. If a change is noted in vehicle performance after clearing codes, it may be due to the computers learning ability. To restore performance, warm vehicle to normal operating temperature and drive at part throttle with moderate acceleration, before performing any additional diagnosis.

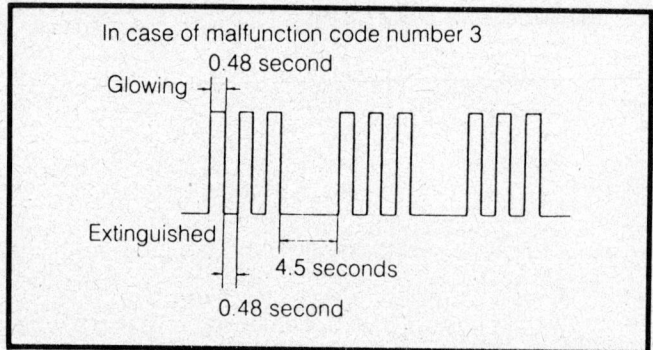

View of a Code 3 pulse

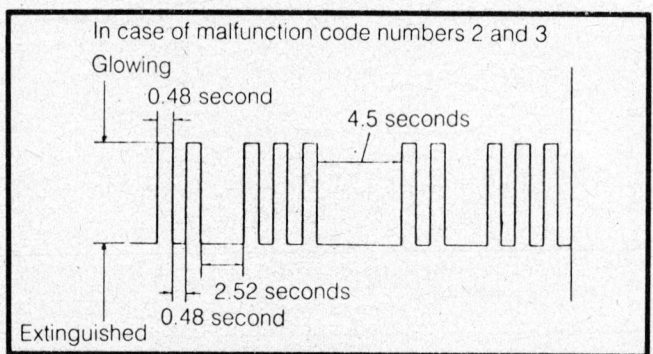

View of a Code 23 pulse

View of the check engine lamp

DAIHATSU

Year – 1988
Model – Charade
Engine – 1.0L (61 cid) EFI 3 cyl
Engine Code – CB-90

ECM TROUBLE CODES

Code	Explanation
1	Normal
2	Pressure sensor – When the signal from pressure sensor becomes open or shorted – defective pressure sensor circuit, pressure sensor or Electronic Control Unit (ECU)
3	Ignition signal – No ignition confirmation signal (IGf) is inputted – defective ignition circuit, ignitor or Electronic Control Unit (ECU)
4	Water Temperature Sensor (WTS) – When the signal from the water temperature sensor circuit becomes open or shorted – defective water temperature sensor circuit, water temperature sensor or Electronic Control Unit (ECU)
5	Oxygen sensor signal – When the oxygen sensor signal circuit becomes open or shorted – defective oxygen sensor circuit, oxygen sensor or Electronic Control Unit (ECU)
6	Revolution signal – When the Ne and/or G signal is not inputted within a few seconds after starting engine cranking or when the Ne signal of a few decade milliseconds is not inputted when the engine speed is 1000 rpm or more. Defective distributor circuit, distributor or Electronic Control Unit (ECU)
7	Throttle Position Sensor (TPS) – When the throttle position sensor signal circuit becomes open or shorted – defective throttle position sensor circuit, throttle position sensor or Electronic Control Unit (ECU)
8	Intake Air Temperature (IAT) sensor signal – When the intake air temperature signal circuit becomes open or shorted – defective air temperature sensor circuit, air temperature sensor or Electronic Control Unit (ECU)
9	Vehicle Speed Sensor (VSS) signal – When the vehicle speed sensor signal circuit becomes open or shorted – defective vehicle speed sensor circuit, vehicle speed sensor or Electronic Control Unit (ECU)
10	Starter signal – When the starter signal becomes open or shorted. However, it should be noted that this code may be memorized when the vehicle is started by being pushed – defective starter signal circuit or Electronic Control Unit (ECU)
11	Switch signal – When the air conditioner is turned ON or the idle switch is turned OFF with the terminal T̄ shorted. However, no memorizing will take place – defective air conditioner switch circuit, idle switch circuit, air conditioner switch, throttle position sensor or Electronic Control Unit (ECU)
12	Exhaust Gas Recirculation (EGR) control system – When the EGR system is not operating normally – defective EGR valve, modulator, EVSV, water temperature sensor or Electronic Control Unit (ECU)

Year – 1989
Model – Charade
Engine – 1.0L (61 cid) EFI 3 cyl
Engine Code – CB-90

ECM TROUBLE CODES

Code	Explanation
1	Normal
2	Pressure sensor – When the signal from pressure sensor becomes open or shorted – defective pressure sensor circuit, pressure sensor or Electronic Control Unit (ECU)
3	Ignition signal – No ignition confirmation signal (IGf) is inputted – defective ignition circuit, ignitor or Electronic Control Unit (ECU)
4	Water Temperature Sensor (WTS) – When the signal from the water temperature sensor circuit becomes open or shorted – defective water temperature sensor circuit, water temperature sensor or Electronic Control Unit (ECU)
5	Oxygen sensor signal – When the oxygen sensor signal circuit becomes open or shorted – defective oxygen sensor circuit, oxygen sensor or Electronic Control Unit (ECU)
6	Revolution signal – When the Ne and/or G signal is not inputted within a few seconds after starting engine cranking or when the Ne signal of a few decade milliseconds is not inputted when the engine speed is 1000 rpm or more. Defective distributor circuit, distributor or Electronic Control Unit (ECU)
7	Throttle Position Sensor (TPS) – When the throttle position sensor signal circuit becomes open or shorted – defective throttle position sensor circuit, throttle position sensor or Electronic Control Unit (ECU)
8	Intake Air Temperature (IAT) sensor signal – When the intake air temperature signal circuit becomes open or shorted – defective air temperature sensor circuit, air temperature sensor or Electronic Control Unit (ECU)
9	Vehicle Speed Sensor (VSS) signal – When the vehicle speed sensor signal circuit becomes open or shorted – defective vehicle speed sensor circuit, vehicle speed sensor or Electronic Control Unit (ECU)
10	Starter signal – When the starter signal becomes open or shorted. However, it should be noted that this code may be memorized when the vehicle is started by being pushed – defective starter signal circuit or Electronic Control Unit (ECU)
11	Switch signal – When the air conditioner is turned ON or the idle switch is turned OFF with the terminal T shorted. However, no memorizing will take place – defective air conditioner switch circuit, idle switch circuit, air conditioner switch, throttle position sensor or Electronic Control Unit (ECU)
12	Exhaust Gas Recirculation (EGR) control system – When the EGR system is not operating normally – defective EGR valve, modulator, EVSV, water temperature sensor or Electronic Control Unit (ECU)

Ford Motor Company Imports

11 SECTION

INDEX

FORD IMPORTS

Merkur
Electronic Fuel Injection (EFI)

SELF-DIAGNOSTIC SYSTEM

Description

The Merkur self diagnostic system is divided into specialized tests areas; (Key ON Engine OFF), (Engine Running) and (Continuous Memory). The self test is not a conclusive test by it self, but is used as a part of the functional quick test diagnostic procedure. When the self test mode is activated, it checks the EEC-IV system by testing its memory integrity and processing capability. It also verifies that various sensors and actuators are connected and operating properly.

The Key ON Engine OFF and Engine Running tests are functional tests which only detect faults present at the time of the self test. Continuous testing is an on going test that stores fault information for retrieval at a later time, during the self test.

Entering Diagnostic Mode
KEY ON ENGINE OFF TEST
Testing with Voltmeter

NOTE: Voltmeter testing is applicable the XR4Ti only. To obtain codes for the Scorpio use the Star tester or an equivalent testing device.

1. Turn the ignition switch OFF.
2. Connect a jumper wire from the Self Test Input (STI) to pin No. 2, Signal Return at Self Test connector.
3. Set the analog voltmeter on a DC voltage range to read 0–15 volts.
4. Connect the positive lead of the voltmeter to pin No. 4, Self Test Output (STO) of the Self test connector.
5. Connect a timing light accordingly.
6. Activate Self Test by turning the ignition switch ON.

NOTE: Do not depress the throttle during Self Test.

Codes are represented by a pulsing or sweeping movement of the voltmeter's needle across the dial face of the voltmeter. A service code is represented by a 2 digit number. For example: (Code 23). The service Code 23 will be represented as 2 pulse (sweeps) of the voltmeter's needle, followed by a 2 second pause in between and 3 pulse (sweeps) indicating 23.
7. Observe and record codes indicated by the voltmeter.
8. After diagnosis and corrections have been made, clear codes and retest.

Testing with Star tester

NOTE: Both XR4Ti and Scorpio trouble codes can be obtained, using the Star tester or an equivalent tester.

1. Turn the ignition switch OFF.
2. Connect the color coded adapter cable leads to the Star tester.
3. Connect the adapter cables service connectors to the vehicles appropriate Self test connectors.
4. Connect a timing light accordingly.
5. Using an adapter cable, connect tester to the vehicles self test connecters.
6. Turn the testers power switch ON. The tester will run a display check. The numerals 88 will begin to flash in the display window. A steady 00 will then appear to signify that the tester is prepared to begin the self test and receive the tests service codes.
7. Press the push button at the front of the tester, the button will latch down and a colon will appear in the display window in front of the 00 numerals.

NOTE: The colon must be displayed in order to receive the service codes.

8. Observe and record codes indicated.
9. After diagnosis and corrections have been made, clear codes and retest.

ENGINE RUNNING TEST
Procedure

1. Deactivate Self-Test and clear memory of codes.

NOTE: Vehicles equipped with manual transmission only. If the Star tester is connected and the Self Test is deactivated while the engine is running, after approximately 4–5 minutes from engine start up, the LED may flash ON/OFF. Do not be alarmed, this will occur if the ACT, ECT, MAP, TP OR EDT are shorted to ground or there is an open circuit.

2. Run engine at 2000 rpm for 15 minutes, to warm up the oxygen sensor.
3. Turn engine OFF and wait 10 seconds.
4. Activate the Self test.

NOTE: Do not depress the throttle during the Self Test unless a dynamic response code occurs.

5. Start the engine. The Engine Running Self Test will progress in the following sequence:
   a. Engine code will flash.
   b. Run engine at idle.
   c. When the dynamic response code occurs, perform a brief WOT.
   d. Engine Running Service codes will flash.

NOTE: The Engine ID code is equal to ½ the numbers of cylinders. (A Code 2 equals a 4 cylinder engine). The Star tester adds a 0 to all single digit readings, so a Code 20 indicates a 4 cylinder engine.

The Star tester will also indicate a 10 in the place of 1 for single digit separator code, therefore, the dynamic response code is expressed in the results column as 1(0). Some vehicles do not require a brief WOT and therefore will not display a 1(0).

6. Observe and record codes indicated.

CONTINUOUS TEST
Intermittent Fault Confirmation Check (Wiggle Test)

The ECA is continually looking for shorts, open circuits and other problems within the EEC-IV system and when noted, stores them in the memory, when they occur. Memory codes obtained during the Key ON Engine OFF segment of the self test, recalls intermittent faults from the ECA memory.

Procedure

1. Repeat the self-test segment when any code other than "System Pass", is generated by the ECA.
2. Attempt to re-create intermittent faults while the test equipment is still connected to the system. This is called an intermittent fault confirmation check.
3. During the Key ON Engine OFF segment, perform this check with self-test sequence deactivated (ECA not in the self-test mode). A fault is indicated when the VOM deflection is 10.5V or greater, or the Star LED turns OFF.
4. Activate the Self Test and perform the Engine Running Quick Test.

After the service code output has been completed, do not turn the engine **OFF** or deactivate the Self Test. Approximately 2 minutes after Code 11 has been outputted, the system will enter and remain in the continuous monitor mode until the Self Test is deactivated or the engine is turned **OFF**. A fault will be indicated in the same way as it is with the Key ON Engine OFF mode.

RECREATING INTERMITTENT FAULTS

Intermittent faults can generally be recreated by the following methods:
1. Wiggling connectors and harnesses
2. Manipulating moveable sensors and actuators
3. Heating thermistor type sensors with a heat gun

Suspected components, such as the sensors, actuators and harnesses, are identified by matching service codes obtained during the Key ON Engine OFF segment of the self-test.

If using a voltmeter; an intermittent fault is re-created, the voltmeter needle will sweep back and forth across the scale or sweep to the right and stay there.

If using the Star tester, an intermittent fault is indicated when the LED light turns **OFF**.

Malfunctioning components identified with this procedure can be repaired or replaced without further diagnostic testing. Further testing must be done for hard faults and for intermittent faults that can not be re-created by the above method.

Clearing Diagnostic Memory

1. Perform the Key ON Engine OFF test.
2. As soon as the first codes are received, disconnect the STI to the Signal Return or unlatch the Star tester connection from the vehicles test connector.

NOTE: Do not disconnect the battery cables to clear code memory.

3. Disconnect the negative battery cable.
4. To clear Continuous Memory codes, exit quick test during code output.
5. Perform the Key ON Engine OFF test to confirm the codes have cleared.

NOTE: Some vehicle computers have a learning ability. If a change is noted in vehicle performance after clearing codes, it may be due to the computers learning ability. To restore performance, warm vehicle to normal operating temperature and drive at part throttle with moderate acceleration, before performing any additional diagnosis.

Festiva and Tracer
Electronic Fuel Injection (EFI)

SELF-DIAGNOSTIC SYSTEM

Description

The Tracer fuel injection system uses an electronic engine control system similar to previous Ford EEC-IV engine control systems. The heart of the system is a microcomputer called an Electronic Control Assembly (ECA). The ECA receives data (system inputs) from sensors, switches, relays and other electronic components and issues command signals (system outputs) to various devices in order to control engine operation under a variety of loads and ambient conditions. The ECA is calibrated according to the powertrain, axle ratio and vehicle weight and options to optimize fuel economy and driveability while minimizing harmful emissions.

The Festiva fuel injection system uses an electronic engine control system identical to Tracer engine control system. Both electronic fuel injection systems are classified as a multi-port, pulse time, mass airflow, fuel injection systems. The basic fuel requirement of the engine is determined from data supplied to the ECA by the vane airflow, air temperature, atmospheric pressure, coolant temperature, engine speed, exhaust oxygen, throttle position sensors, in addition to the common sensors used on closed loop feedback engines.

MALFUNCTION INDICATOR LIGHT (MIL)

The MIL (Check Engine light) will illuminate to warn the driver of an emission related problem, when a malfunction occurs in any input sensor. The MIL can also be used to read extracted fault codes from the ECA.

READING SERVICE CODES

After the ECA system completes its self-test, it communicates with the service technician by way of the analog voltmeter needle and scale or MIL on the dash.

When a service code is obtained by the use of the MIL on the dash the codes are read as a pattern of light flashes. The MIL displays the same pattern as the voltmeter display on Ford EEC-IV systems.

When a service code is reported on the analog meter, it will represent itself as a pulsing or sweeping movement of the voltmeter scale's needle across the dial face of the meter. Therefore, a single digit number of 3 will be indicated by 3 pulses (sweeps) of the needle across the dial. Since the service codes are indicated by a 2-digit number, such as 32, the self-test's service Code of 32 will be displayed as 3 pulses (sweeps) of the meter's needle with a 1½ second pause between pulses (sweeps) and a 2 second pause between digits. When more than a single service code is indicated, a 4 second pause between service codes will occur.

Separator and dynamic response codes (numeral 10 in both cases), are represented by a single pulse or sweep of the needle. There are no pulses or sweeps generated for the digit "0". There will be a 6 second pause before each of these.

The key to sorting out the service codes on the voltmeter is to keep the pulses and the pauses straight.
1. Each digit is separated by a 2 second pause.
2. Each code is separated by a 4 second pause.
3. Separator and dynamic response codes are separated from previous and subsequent codes by 6 second (or longer) pauses.

Entering Diagnostic Mode
KEY ON ENGINE OFF TEST

MIL Equipped

On vehicle equipped with MIL on the dash, when in the Self-Test the "Check Engine" lamp will also flash the service codes.
1. Turn the ignition switch **OFF**.
2. Connect a jumper wire from the Self-Test Input (STI) connector to ground.
3. Turn the ignition switch **ON**.
4. To activate codes, disconnect and reconnect the STI ground jumper wire.
5. Record codes.
6. Clear codes and retest.

Using a Voltmeter

On vehicles not equipped with MIL, the codes can be obtained by the use of an analog voltmeter, by the same method used on other Fords with EEC-IV.
1. Set the analog voltmeter on a DC voltage range to read from 0–20V, except on non-MIL equipped Festiva, set on the 0–54V range.
2. On the Festiva, insert a voltmeter probe wire into the BL/W—EFI or GN/R—FBC terminal on the 6-pin Self-Test Output (STO) connector and the other probe to negative battery terminal. On the Tracer connect the voltmeter between the green and Black terminals of the under-dash 6-pin STO connector.
3. Jumper the Self-Test Input (STI) terminal to ground.
4. Turn the ignition switch **ON**.

5. To activate codes, disconnect and reconnect the STI ground jumper wire.

6. Record codes.

7. Clear codes and retest.

ENGINE RUNNING TEST

MIL Equipped

1. Deactivate Self-Test and clear memory of codes.

2. Run engine at 2000 rpm for 15 minutes, to warm up the oxygen sensor.

3. Ground the STI connector.

4. Turn engine **OFF**, turn ignition switch **ON** and wait 10 seconds.

5. Run engine at idle.

6. To activate codes, disconnect and reconnect the STI ground jumper wire.

7. Record codes.

Non-MIL Equipped

1. Deactivate Self-Test and clear memory of codes.

2. Run engine at 2000 rpm for 15 minutes, to warm up the oxygen sensor.

3. Ground the STI connector.

4. Turn engine **OFF**, turn ignition switch **ON** and wait 10 seconds.

5. Run engine at idle.

6. To activate codes, disconnect and reconnect the STI ground jumper wire.

7. Disconnect the STI ground wire.

8. Turn engine **OFF**, turn ignition **ON** and wait 10 seconds.

9. Run engine at idle.

10. Connect the STI ground wire.

11. Record codes.

CONTINUOUS TEST

Intermittent Fault Confirmation Check (Wiggle Test)

The ECA is continually looking for shorts, open circuits and other problems within the EEC–IV system and when noted, stores them in the memory, when they occur. Memory codes obtained during the Key ON Engine OFF segment of the self test, recalls intermittent faults from the ECA memory.

1. Repeat the self-test segment when any code other than "System Pass", is generated by the ECA.

2. Attempt to re-create intermittent faults while the test equipment is still connected to the system. This is called an intermittent fault confirmation check.

3. During the Key ON Engine OFF segment, perform this check with self-test sequence de-activated (ECA not in the self-test mode). A fault is indicated when the VOM deflection is 10.5V or greater, or the MIL flashes a code.

4. During the Key ON Engine Running mode, perform this check with self-test sequence activated (ECA in self-test mode). A fault will be indicated in the same way as it is with the Key ON Engine OFF mode.

Recreating Intermittent Faults

Intermittent faults can generally be recreated by the following methods:

1. Wiggling connectors and harnesses

2. Manipulating moveable sensors and actuators

3. Heating thermistor type sensors with a heat gun

Suspected components, such as the sensors, actuators and harnesses, are identified by matching service codes obtained during the Key ON Engine OFF segment of the self-test.

When an intermittent fault is re-created, the voltmeter needle will sweep back and forth across the scale or sweep to the right and stay there.

Malfunctioning components identified with this procedure can be repaired or replaced without further diagnostic testing. Further testing must be done for hard faults and for intermittent faults that can not be re-created by the above method.

Clearing Diagnostic Memory

1. Perform the Key ON Engine OFF test.

2. As soon as the first codes are received, disconnect the STI ground.

3. Disconnect the negative battery cable.

4. Depress the brake pedal from 10 seconds.

5. Reconnect the negative battery cable.

6. Perform the Key ON Engine OFF test to confirm the codes have cleared.

NOTE: Some vehicle computers have a learning ability. If a change is noted in vehicle performance after clearing codes, it may be due to the computers learning ability. To restore performance, warm vehicle to normal operating temperature and drive at part throttle with moderate acceleration, before performing any additional diagnosis.

FORD IMPORTS

Year — 1986
Model — XR4Ti
Engine — 2.3L (140 cid) 4 cyl
Engine Code — VIN W

ECM TROUBLE CODES

Code	Explanation
12	ENGINE RUNNING — rpm out of specification
13	ENGINE RUNNING — rpm out of specification
14	CONTINUOUS MEMORY — pip was erratic
15	KEY ON ENGINE OFF — Electronic Control Assembly (ECA) test failure CONTINUOUS MEMORY — Electronic Control Assembly (ECA) test failure
16	ENGINE RUNNING — rpm too low
18	CONTINUOUS MEMORY — no tachometer signal
19	KEY ON ENGINE OFF — power to processor
21	KEY ON ENGINE OFF — Electronic Controlled Timing (ECT) out of range ENGINE RUNNING — Electronic Controlled Timing (ECT) out of range
22	KEY ON ENGINE OFF — Manifold Absolute Pressure (MAP) out of range ENGINE RUNNING — Manifold Absolute Pressure (MAP) out of range CONTINUOUS MEMORY — Manifold Absolute Pressure (MAP) out of range
23	KEY ON ENGINE OFF — Throttle Position Sensor (TPS) out of range ENGINE RUNNING — Throttle Position Sensor (TPS) out of range
24	KEY ON ENGINE OFF — ACT out of range ENGINE RUNNING — ACT out of range
31	KEY ON ENGINE OFF — EVR/PRE out of range ENGINE RUNNING — EVR/PRE out of range CONTINUOUS MEMORY — EVR/PRE out of range
32	ENGINE RUNNING — Exhaust Gas Recirculation (EGR) not controlling CONTINUOUS MEMORY — Exhaust Gas Recirculation (EGR) not controlling
33	ENGINE RUNNING — EVR/PFE out of limits
34	KEY ON ENGINE OFF — no Exhaust Gas Recirculation (EGR) flow in test ENGINE RUNNING — no Exhaust Gas Recirculation (EGR) flow in test CONTINUOUS MEMORY — no Exhaust Gas Recirculation (EGR) flow in test
35	KEY ON ENGINE OFF — rpm too low for Exhaust Gas Recirculation (EGR) test ENGINE RUNNING — rpm too low for Exhaust Gas Recirculation (EGR) test CONTINUOUS MEMORY — rpm too low for Exhaust Gas Recirculation (EGR) test
41	ENGINE RUNNING — system always lean
42	ENGINE RUNNING — system always rich
51	KEY ON ENGINE OFF — Electronic Controlled Timing (ECT) too high CONTINUOUS MEMORY — Electronic Controlled Timing (ECT) too high
53	KEY ON ENGINE OFF — Throttle Position Sensor (TPS) input too high CONTINUOUS MEMORY — Throttle Position Sensor (TPS) input too high
54	KEY ON ENGINE OFF — ACT input too high CONTINUOUS MEMORY — ACT input too high
61	KEY ON ENGINE OFF — Electronic Controlled Timing (ECT) input too low CONTINUOUS MEMORY — Electronic Controlled Timing (ECT) input too low

ECM TROUBLE CODES (cont'd)

Code	Explanation
63	KEY ON ENGINE OFF—Throttle Position Sensor (TPS) input too low CONTINUOUS MEMORY—Throttle Position Sensor (TPS) input too low
64	KEY ON ENGINE OFF—ACT input too low CONTINUOUS MEMORY—ACT input too low
67	KEY ON ENGINE OFF—neutral drive switch
72	ENGINE RUNNING—no Manifold Absolute Pressure (MAP) change in (GOOSE) test
73	ENGINE RUNNING—no Throttle Position Sensor (TPS) change in (GOOSE) test
77	ENGINE RUNNING—operator did not do (GOOSE) test
84	KEY ON ENGINE OFF—Exhaust Gas Recirculation (EGR) circuit fault
85	KEY ON ENGINE OFF—canister purge circuit fault
87	KEY ON ENGINE OFF—fuel pump circuit fault
99	Idle Speed Control (ISC) has not learned yet

Year—1987
Model—Tracer
Engine—1.6L (98 cid) 4 cyl
Engine Code—VIN 5

ECM TROUBLE CODES

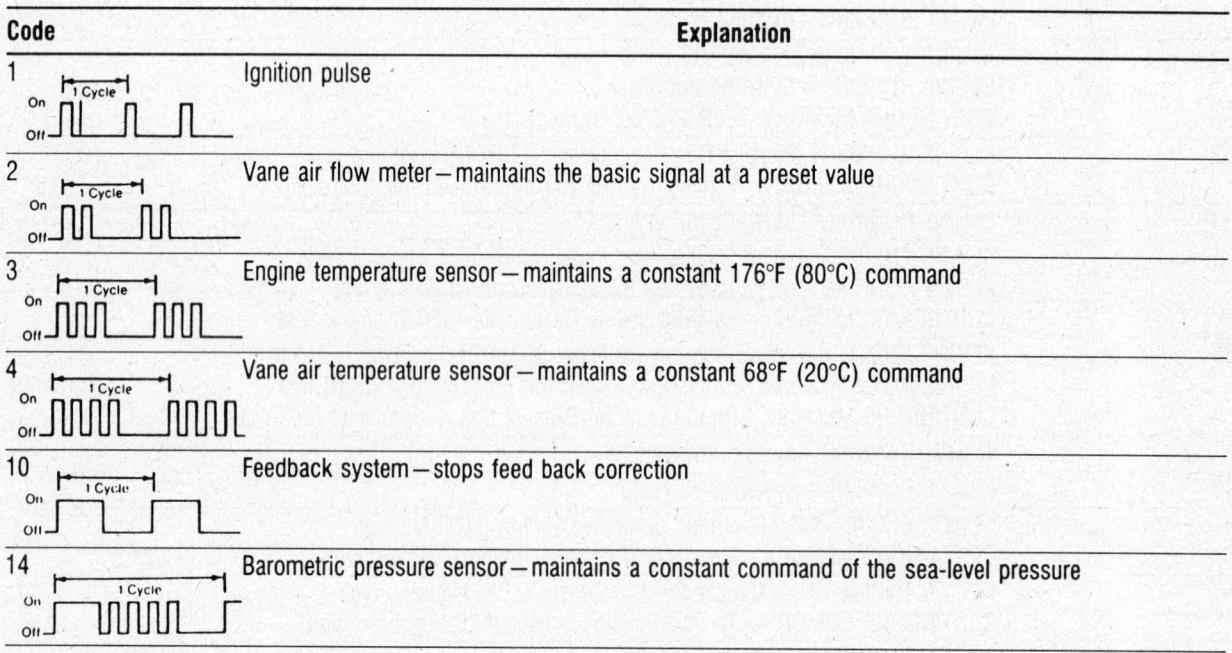

Code	Explanation
1	Ignition pulse
2	Vane air flow meter—maintains the basic signal at a preset value
3	Engine temperature sensor—maintains a constant 176°F (80°C) command
4	Vane air temperature sensor—maintains a constant 68°F (20°C) command
10	Feedback system—stops feed back correction
14	Barometric pressure sensor—maintains a constant command of the sea-level pressure

Year — 1987
Model — Tracer
Engine — 1.6L (98 cid) 4 cyl
Engine Code — VIN B

ECM TROUBLE CODES

Code	Explanation
01	Ignition pulse — broken wire, short circuit
08	Vane air flow meter — broken wire, short circuit — basic fuel injection amount fixed as for 2 driving mdes 1) idle switch: ON, 2) idle switch: OFF
09	Engine coolant temp. — broken wire, short circuit — coolant temp. input fixed at 176°F (80°C)
10	Vane air temp. sensor — broken wire, short circuit — intake air temp. input fixed at 68°F (20°C)
14	Barometric pressure sensor — broken wire, short circuit — atmospheric pressure input fixed at 29.9 in. HG (760mm Hg)
15	EGO sensor — sensor output continues less than 0.55V 120 sec after engine starts (1500 rpm) — feedback system operation cancelled
17	Feedback system — oxygen sensor output not changed 20 sec. after engine exceeds 1500 rpm — feedback system operation cancelled
25	Pressure regulator control solenoid valve
26	Canister purge regulator solenoid valve
27	Canister purge solenoid valve
34	Idle speed control solenoid valve

Year — 1987
Model — XR4Ti
Engine — 2.3L (140 cid) 4 cyl
Engine Code — VIN W

ECM TROUBLE CODES

Code	Explanation
12	ENGINE RUNNING — rpm out of specification
13	ENGINE RUNNING — rpm out of specification
14	CONTINUOUS MEMORY — pip was erratic
15	KEY ON ENGINE OFF — Electronic Control Assembly (ECA) test failure CONTINUOUS MEMORY — Electronic Control Assembly (ECA) test failure
16	ENGINE RUNNING — rpm too low
18	CONTINUOUS MEMORY — no tachometer signal
19	KEY ON ENGINE OFF — power to processor
21	KEY ON ENGINE OFF — Electronic Controlled Timing (ECT) out of range ENGINE RUNNING — Electronic Controlled Timing (ECT) out of range
22	KEY ON ENGINE OFF — Manifold Absolute Pressure (MAP) out of range ENGINE RUNNING — Manifold Absolute Pressure (MAP) out of range CONTINUOUS MEMORY — Manifold Absolute Pressure (MAP) out of range
23	KEY ON ENGINE OFF — Throttle Position Sensor (TPS) out of range ENGINE RUNNING — Throttle Position Sensor (TPS) out of range
24	KEY ON ENGINE OFF — ACT out of range ENGINE RUNNING — ACT out of range
31	KEY ON ENGINE OFF — EVR/PRE out of range ENGINE RUNNING — EVR/PRE out of range CONTINUOUS MEMORY — EVR/PRE out of range
32	ENGINE RUNNING — Exhaust Gas Recirculation (EGR) not controlling CONTINUOUS MEMORY — Exhaust Gas Recirculation (EGR) not controlling
33	ENGINE RUNNING — EVR/PFE out of limits
34	KEY ON ENGINE OFF — no Exhaust Gas Recirculation (EGR) flow in test ENGINE RUNNING — no Exhaust Gas Recirculation (EGR) flow in test CONTINUOUS MEMORY — no Exhaust Gas Recirculation (EGR) flow in test
35	KEY ON ENGINE OFF — rpm too low for Exhaust Gas Recirculation (EGR) test ENGINE RUNNING — rpm too low for Exhaust Gas Recirculation (EGR) test CONTINUOUS MEMORY — rpm too low for Exhaust Gas Recirculation (EGR) test
41	ENGINE RUNNING — system always lean
42	ENGINE RUNNING — system always rich
51	KEY ON ENGINE OFF — Electronic Controlled Timing (ECT) too high CONTINUOUS MEMORY — Electronic Controlled Timing (ECT) too high
53	KEY ON ENGINE OFF — Throttle Position Sensor (TPS) input too high CONTINUOUS MEMORY — Throttle Position Sensor (TPS) input too high
54	KEY ON ENGINE OFF — ACT input too high CONTINUOUS MEMORY — ACT input too high
61	KEY ON ENGINE OFF — Electronic Controlled Timing (ECT) input too low CONTINUOUS MEMORY — Electronic Controlled Timing (ECT) input too low
63	KEY ON ENGINE OFF — Throttle Position Sensor (TPS) input too low CONTINUOUS MEMORY — Throttle Position Sensor (TPS) input too low

ECM TROUBLE CODES (cont'd)

Code	Explanation
64	KEY ON ENGINE OFF—ACT input too low CONTINUOUS MEMORY—ACT input too low
67	KEY ON ENGINE OFF—neutral drive switch
72	ENGINE RUNNING—no Manifold Absolute Pressure (MAP) change in (GOOSE) test
73	ENGINE RUNNING—no Throttle Position Sensor (TPS) change in (GOOSE) test
77	ENGINE RUNNING—operator did not do (GOOSE) test
84	KEY ON ENGINE OFF—Exhaust Gas Recirculation (EGR) circuit fault
85	KEY ON ENGINE OFF—canister purge circuit fault
87	KEY ON ENGINE OFF—fuel pump circuit fault
99	Idle Speed Control (ISC) has not learned yet

Year—1988
Model—Tracer
Engine—1.6L (98 cid) 4 cyl
Engine Code—VIN 5

ECM TROUBLE CODES

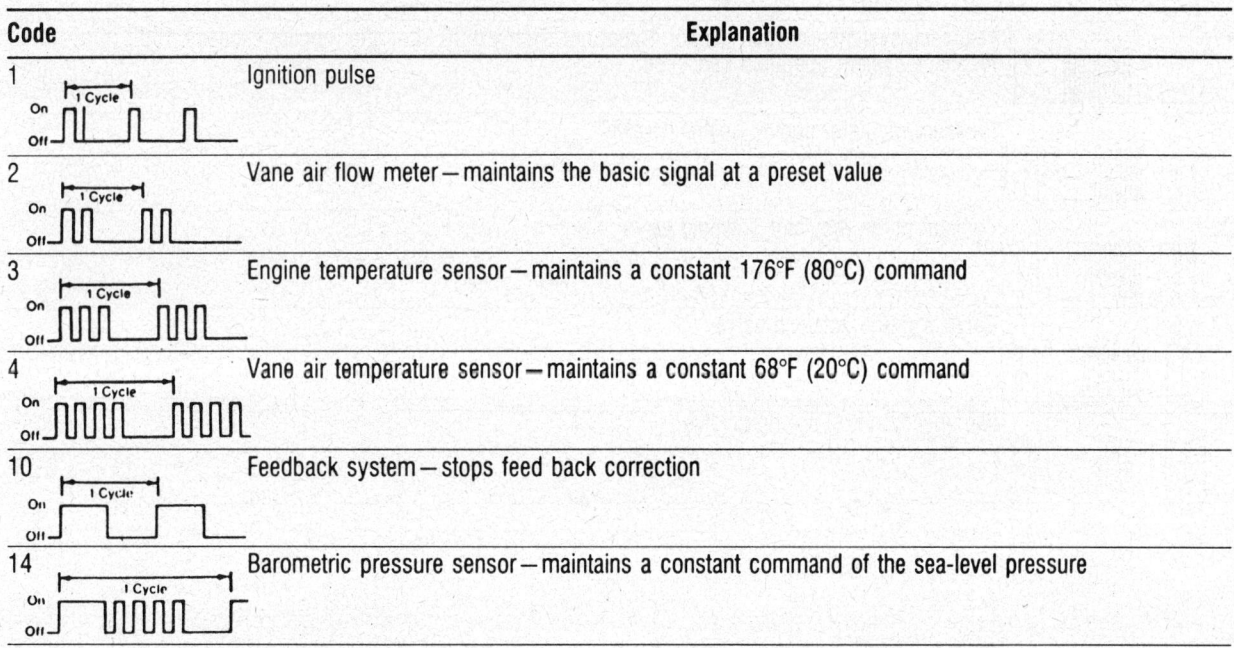

Code	Explanation
1	Ignition pulse
2	Vane air flow meter—maintains the basic signal at a preset value
3	Engine temperature sensor—maintains a constant 176°F (80°C) command
4	Vane air temperature sensor—maintains a constant 68°F (20°C) command
10	Feedback system—stops feed back correction
14	Barometric pressure sensor—maintains a constant command of the sea-level pressure

Year — 1988
Model — Tracer
Engine — 1.6L (98 cid) 4 cyl
Engine Code — VIN B

ECM TROUBLE CODES

Code	Explanation
01	Ignition pulse — broken wire, short circuit
08	Vane air flow meter — broken wire, short circuit — basic fuel injection amount fixed as for 2 driving mdes 1) idle switch: ON, 2) idle switch: OFF
09	Engine coolant temp. — broken wire, short circuit — coolant temp. input fixed at 176°F (80°C)
10	Vane air temp. sensor — broken wire, short circuit — intake air temp. input fixed at 68°F (20°C)
14	Barometric pressure sensor — broken wire, short circuit — atmospheric pressure input fixed at 29.9 in. Hg (760mm Hg)
15	EGO sensor — sensor output continues less than 0.55V 120 sec after engine starts (1500 rpm) — feedback system operation cancelled
17	Feedback system — oxygen sensor output not changed 20 sec. after engine exceeds 1500 rpm — feedback system operation cancelled
25	Pressure regulator control solenoid valve
26	Canister purge regulator solenoid valve
27	Canister purge solenoid valve
34	Idle speed control solenoid valve

Year – 1988
Model – Tracer
Engine – 1.6L (98 cid) 4 cyl
Engine Code – VIN 5

ECM TROUBLE CODES

Code	Explanation
01	Ignition pulse
08	Vane air flow meter – maintain a basic signal at a preset value
09	Engine coolant temperature sensor – maintain a constant 176°F (80°C) command
10	Vane air temperature sensor – maintains a constant 68°F (20°C) command
14	Barometric pressure sensor – maintains a constant command of the sea – level pressure
15	Exhaust gas oxygen sensor – stops feedback correction
17	Feedback system – stops feedback correction
71	Throttle position sensor

Year – 1988
Model – Festiva
Engine – 1.3L (81 cid) 4 cyl
Engine Code – VIN K

ECM TROUBLE CODES

Code	Explanation
01	Ignition coil
09	Engine coolant temperature sensor
13	Manifold Absolute Pressure (MAP) sensor
15	Exhaust Gas Oxygen (EGO) sensor
16	Exhaust Gas Recirculation (EGR) valve position sensor
17	Feedback system
18	ABC valve No. 1
19	ABC valve No. 2
20	ABC valve No. 3
21	ABC valve No. 4
22	Slow fuel cut solenoid
28	No. 1 Exhasut Gas Recirculation (EGR) solenoid vacuum valve
29	No. 2 Exhaust Gas Recirculation (EGR) solenoid vacuum valve
31	ACV solenoid valve

ECM TROUBLE CODES (cont'd)

Code	Explanation
34	E/L solenoid valve
35	Air conditioning solenoid valve
38	PTC heater relay
70	Vacuum switch

Year – 1988
Model – XR4Ti
Engine – 2.3L (140 cid) 4 cyl
Engine Code – VIN W

ECM TROUBLE CODES

Code	Explanation
12	ENGINE RUNNING – rpm out of specification
13	ENGINE RUNNING – rpm out of specification
14	CONTINUOUS MEMORY – pip was erratic
15	KEY ON ENGINE OFF – Electronic Control Assembly (ECA) test failure CONTINUOUS MEMORY – Electronic Control Assembly (ECA) test failure
16	ENGINE RUNNING – rpm too low
18	CONTINUOUS MEMORY – no tachometer signal
19	KEY ON ENGINE OFF – power to processor
21	KEY ON ENGINE OFF – Electronic Controlled Timing (ECT) out of range ENGINE RUNNING – Electronic Controlled Timing (ECT) out of range
22	KEY ON ENGINE OFF – Manifold Absolute Pressure (MAP) out of range ENGINE RUNNING – Manifold Absolute Pressure (MAP) out of range CONTINUOUS MEMORY – Manifold Absolute Pressure (MAP) out of range
23	KEY ON ENGINE OFF – Throttle Position Sensor (TPS) out of range ENGINE RUNNING – Throttle Position Sensor (TPS) out of range
24	KEY ON ENGINE OFF – ACT out of range ENGINE RUNNING – ACT out of range
31	KEY ON ENGINE OFF – EVR/PRE out of range ENGINE RUNNING – EVR/PRE out of range CONTINUOUS MEMORY – EVR/PRE out of range
32	ENGINE RUNNING – Exhaust Gas Recirculation (EGR) not controlling CONTINUOUS MEMORY – Exhaust Gas Recirculation (EGR) not controlling
33	ENGINE RUNNING – EVR/PFE out of limits

ECM TROUBLE CODES (cont'd)

Code	Explanation
34	KEY ON ENGINE OFF—no Exhaust Gas Recirculation (EGR) flow in test ENGINE RUNNING—no Exhaust Gas Recirculation (EGR) flow in test CONTINUOUS MEMORY—no Exhaust Gas Recirculation (EGR) flow in test
35	KEY ON ENGINE OFF—rpm too low for Exhaust Gas Recirculation (EGR) test ENGINE RUNNING—rpm too low for Exhaust Gas Recirculation (EGR) test CONTINUOUS MEMORY—rpm too low for Exhaust Gas Recirculation (EGR) test
41	ENGINE RUNNING—system always lean
42	ENGINE RUNNING—system always rich
51	KEY ON ENGINE OFF—Electronic Controlled Timing (ECT) too high CONTINUOUS MEMORY—Electronic Controlled Timing (ECT) too high
53	KEY ON ENGINE OFF—Throttle Position Sensor (TPS) input too high CONTINUOUS MEMORY—Throttle Position Sensor (TPS) input too high
54	KEY ON ENGINE OFF—ACT input too high CONTINUOUS MEMORY—ACT input too high
61	KEY ON ENGINE OFF—Electronic Controlled Timing (ECT) input too low CONTINUOUS MEMORY—Electronic Controlled Timing (ECT) input too low
63	KEY ON ENGINE OFF—Throttle Position Sensor (TPS) input too low CONTINUOUS MEMORY—Throttle Position Sensor (TPS) input too low
64	KEY ON ENGINE OFF—ACT input too low CONTINUOUS MEMORY—ACT input too low
67	KEY ON ENGINE OFF—neutral drive switch
72	ENGINE RUNNING—no Manifold Absolute Pressure (MAP) change in (GOOSE) test
73	ENGINE RUNNING—no Throttle Position Sensor (TPS) change in (GOOSE) test
77	ENGINE RUNNING—operator did not do (GOOSE) test
84	KEY ON ENGINE OFF—Exhaust Gas Recirculation (EGR) circuit fault
85	KEY ON ENGINE OFF—canister purge circuit fault
87	KEY ON ENGINE OFF—fuel pump circuit fault
99	Idle Speed Control (ISC) has not learned yet

Year—1988
Model—Scorpio
Engine—2.9L (177 cid) 6 cyl
Engine Code—VIN V

ECM TROUBLE CODES

Code	Explanation
12	ENGINE RUNNING—rpm out of specification
13	ENGINE RUNNING—rpm out of specification
14	CONTINUOUS MEMORY—pip was erratic
15	KEY ON ENGINE OFF—Electronic Control Assembly (ECA) test failure CONTINUOUS MEMORY—Electronic Control Assembly (ECA) test failure
16	ENGINE RUNNING—rpm too low

ECM TROUBLE CODES (cont'd)

Code	Explanation
18	CONTINUOUS MEMORY—no tachometer signal
19	KEY ON ENGINE OFF—power to processor
21	KEY ON ENGINE OFF—Electronic Controlled Timing (ECT) out of range ENGINE RUNNING—Electronic Controlled Timing (ECT) out of range
22	KEY ON ENGINE OFF—Manifold Absolute Pressure (MAP) out of range ENGINE RUNNING—Manifold Absolute Pressure (MAP) out of range CONTINUOUS MEMORY—Manifold Absolute Pressure (MAP) out of range
23	KEY ON ENGINE OFF—Throttle Position Sensor (TPS) out of range ENGINE RUNNING—Throttle Position Sensor (TPS) out of range
24	KEY ON ENGINE OFF—ACT out of range ENGINE RUNNING—ACT out of range
31	KEY ON ENGINE OFF—EVR/PRE out of range ENGINE RUNNING—EVR/PRE out of range CONTINUOUS MEMORY—EVR/PRE out of range
32	ENGINE RUNNING—Exhaust Gas Recirculation (EGR) not controlling CONTINUOUS MEMORY—Exhaust Gas Recirculation (EGR) not controlling
33	ENGINE RUNNING—EVR/PFE out of limits
34	KEY ON ENGINE OFF—no Exhaust Gas Recirculation (EGR) flow in test ENGINE RUNNING—no Exhaust Gas Recirculation (EGR) flow in test CONTINUOUS MEMORY—no Exhaust Gas Recirculation (EGR) flow in test
35	KEY ON ENGINE OFF—rpm too low for Exhaust Gas Recirculation (EGR) test ENGINE RUNNING—rpm too low for Exhaust Gas Recirculation (EGR) test CONTINUOUS MEMORY—rpm too low for Exhaust Gas Recirculation (EGR) test
41	ENGINE RUNNING—system always lean
42	ENGINE RUNNING—system always rich
51	KEY ON ENGINE OFF—Electronic Controlled Timing (ECT) too high CONTINUOUS MEMORY—Electronic Controlled Timing (ECT) too high
53	KEY ON ENGINE OFF—Throttle Position Sensor (TPS) input too high CONTINUOUS MEMORY—Throttle Position Sensor (TPS) input too high
54	KEY ON ENGINE OFF—ACT input too high CONTINUOUS MEMORY—ACT input too high
61	KEY ON ENGINE OFF—Electronic Controlled Timing (ECT) input too low CONTINUOUS MEMORY—Electronic Controlled Timing (ECT) input too low
63	KEY ON ENGINE OFF—Throttle Position Sensor (TPS) input too low CONTINUOUS MEMORY—Throttle Position Sensor (TPS) input too low
64	KEY ON ENGINE OFF—ACT input too low CONTINUOUS MEMORY—ACT input too low
67	KEY ON ENGINE OFF—neutral drive switch
72	ENGINE RUNNING—no Manifold Absolute Pressure (MAP) change in (GOOSE) test
73	ENGINE RUNNING—no Throttle Position Sensor (TPS) change in (GOOSE) test
77	ENGINE RUNNING—operator did not do (GOOSE) test
84	KEY ON ENGINE OFF—Exhaust Gas Recirculation (EGR) circuit fault
85	KEY ON ENGINE OFF—canister purge circuit fault
87	KEY ON ENGINE OFF—fuel pump circuit fault
99	Idle Speed Control (ISC) has not learned yet

Year – 1989
Model – Tracer
Engine – 1.6L (98 cid) 4 cyl
Engine Code – VIN 5

ECM TROUBLE CODES

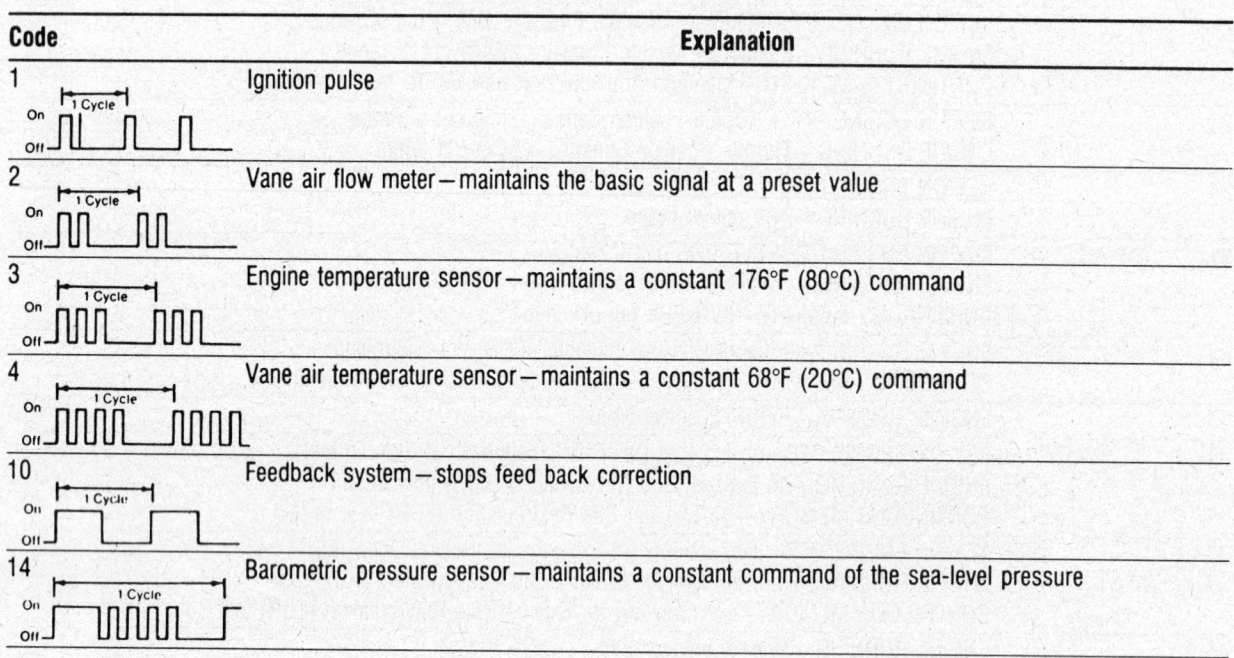

Code	Explanation
1	Ignition pulse
2	Vane air flow meter – maintains the basic signal at a preset value
3	Engine temperature sensor – maintains a constant 176°F (80°C) command
4	Vane air temperature sensor – maintains a constant 68°F (20°C) command
10	Feedback system – stops feed back correction
14	Barometric pressure sensor – maintains a constant command of the sea-level pressure

Year — 1989
Model — Tracer
Engine — 1.6L (98 cid) 4 cyl
Engine Code — VIN B

ECM TROUBLE CODES

Code	Explanation
01	Ignition pulse — broken wire, short circuit
08	Vane air flow meter — broken wire, short circuit — basic fuel injection amount fixed as for 2 driving mdes 1) idle switch: ON, 2) idle switch: OFF
09	Engine coolant temp. — broken wire, short circuit — coolant temp. input fixed at 176°F (80°C)
10	Vane air temp. sensor — broken wire, short circuit — intake air temp. input fixed at 68°F (20°C)
14	Barometric pressure sensor — broken wire, short circuit — atmospheric pressure input fixed at 29.9 in Hg (760mm Hg)
15	EGO sensor — sensor output continues less than 0.55V 120 sec after engine starts (1500 rpm) — feedback system operation cancelled
17	Feedback system — oxygen sensor output not changed 20 sec. after engine exceeds 1500 rpm — feedback system operation cancelled
25	Pressure regulator control solenoid valve
26	Canister purge regulator solenoid valve
27	Canister purge solenoid valve
34	Idle speed control solenoid valve

Year — 1989
Model — Festiva
Engine — 1.3L (81 cid) 4 cyl
Engine Code — VIN K

ECM TROUBLE CODES

Code	Explanation
01	Ignition diagnostic monitor
08	Vane airflor meter — maintains basic signal of preset value of midrange vane position
09	Engine control temperature sensor — EFI: maintains constant command — 85°F (35°C) fuel. 122°F (50°C) for ISC control use FBC: maintains constant 176°F (80°C)
10	Vane air temperature sensor — maintains constant 68°F (20°C) command
13	Manifold Absolute Pressure sensor — maintains constant command of 27.6–29.9 in. Hg manifold vacuum
14	Barometric pressure sensor — maintains constant command of sea level pressure
15	Exhaust Gas Oxygen (EGO) sensor — cancels feedback operation
16	Exhaust Gas Recirculation (EGR) valve position sensor — California only — cuts — off EGR
17	Exhaust Gas Oxygen (EGO) feedback — cancels feedback operation
70	Wide open throttle vacuum switch — maintains constant command of 27.6–29.9 in. Hg manifold vacuum

Year – 1989
Model – Festiva
Engine – 1.3L (81 cid) 4 cyl
Engine Code – VIN H

ECM TROUBLE CODES

Code	Explanation
01	Ignition diagnostic monitor
08	Vane airflor meter – maintains basic signal of preset value of midrange vane position
09	Engine control temperature sensor – EFI: maintains constant command – 85°F (35°C) fuel. 122°F (50°C) for ISC control use FBC: maintains constant 176°F (80°C)
10	Vane air temperature sensor – maintains constant 68°F (20°C) command
13	Manifold Absolute Pressure sensor – maintains constant command of 27.6–29.9 in. Hg manifold vacuum
14	Barometric pressure sensor – maintains constant command of sea level pressure
15	Exhaust Gas Oxygen (EGO) sensor – cancels feedback operation
16	Exhaust Gas Recirculation (EGR) valve position sensor – California only – cuts – off EGR
17	Exhaust Gas Oxygen (EGO) feedback – cancels feedback operation
70	Wide open throttle vacuum switch – maintains constant command of 27.6–29.9 in. Hg manifold vacuum

Year — 1989
Model — Tracer
Engine — 1.6L (98 cid) 4 cyl
Engine Code — VIN 5

ECM TROUBLE CODES

Code	Explanation
01	Ignition pulse
08	Vane air flow meter — maintain a basic signal at a preset value
09	Engine coolant temperature sensor — maintain a constant 176°F (80°C) command
10	Vane air temperature sensor — maintains a constant 68°F (20°C) command
14	Barometric pressure sensor — maintains a constant command of the sea-level pressure
15	Exhaust Gas Oxygen (EGO) sensor — stops feedback correction
17	Feedback system — stops feedback correction
71	Throttle Position Sensor (TPS)

Year – 1989
Model – XR4Ti
Engine – 2.3L (140 cid) 4 cyl
Engine Code – VIN W

ECM TROUBLE CODES

Code	Explanation
12	ENGINE RUNNING – rpm out of specification
13	ENGINE RUNNING – rpm out of specification
14	CONTINUOUS MEMORY – pip was erratic
15	KEY ON ENGINE OFF – Electronic Control Assembly (ECA) test failure
	CONTINUOUS MEMORY – Electronic Control Assembly (ECA) test failure
16	ENGINE RUNNING – rpm too low
18	CONTINUOUS MEMORY – no tachometer signal
19	KEY ON ENGINE OFF – power to processor
21	KEY ON ENGINE OFF – Electronic Controlled Timing (ECT) out of range
	ENGINE RUNNING – Electronic Controlled Timing (ECT) out of range
22	KEY ON ENGINE OFF – Manifold Absolute Pressure (MAP) out of range
	ENGINE RUNNING – Manifold Absolute Pressure (MAP) out of range
	CONTINUOUS MEMORY – Manifold Absolute Pressure (MAP) out of range
23	KEY ON ENGINE OFF – Throttle Position Sensor (TPS) out of range
	ENGINE RUNNING – Throttle Position Sensor (TPS) out of range
24	KEY ON ENGINE OFF – ACT out of range
	ENGINE RUNNING – ACT out of range
31	KEY ON ENGINE OFF – EVR/PRE out of range
	ENGINE RUNNING – EVR/PRE out of range
	CONTINUOUS MEMORY – EVR/PRE out of range
32	ENGINE RUNNING – Exhaust Gas Recirculation (EGR) not controlling
	CONTINUOUS MEMORY – Exhaust Gas Recirculation (EGR) not controlling
33	ENGINE RUNNING – EVR/PFE out of limits
34	KEY ON ENGINE OFF – no Exhaust Gas Recirculation (EGR) flow in test
	ENGINE RUNNING – no Exhaust Gas Recirculation (EGR) flow in test
	CONTINUOUS MEMORY – no Exhaust Gas Recirculation (EGR) flow in test
35	KEY ON ENGINE OFF – rpm too low for Exhaust Gas Recirculation (EGR) test
	ENGINE RUNNING – rpm too low for Exhaust Gas Recirculation (EGR) test
	CONTINUOUS MEMORY – rpm too low for Exhaust Gas Recirculation (EGR) test
41	ENGINE RUNNING – system always lean
42	ENGINE RUNNING – system always rich
51	KEY ON ENGINE OFF – Electronic Controlled Timing (ECT) too high
	CONTINUOUS MEMORY – Electronic Controlled Timing (ECT) too high
53	KEY ON ENGINE OFF – Throttle Position Sensor (TPS) input too high
	CONTINUOUS MEMORY – Throttle Position Sensor (TPS) input too high
54	KEY ON ENGINE OFF – ACT input too high
	CONTINUOUS MEMORY – ACT input too high
61	KEY ON ENGINE OFF – Electronic Controlled Timing (ECT) input too low
	CONTINUOUS MEMORY – Electronic Controlled Timing (ECT) input too low
63	KEY ON ENGINE OFF – Throttle Position Sensor (TPS) input too low
	CONTINUOUS MEMORY – Throttle Position Sensor (TPS) input too low

ECM TROUBLE CODES (cont'd)

Code	Explanation
64	KEY ON ENGINE OFF — ACT input too low CONTINUOUS MEMORY — ACT input too low
67	KEY ON ENGINE OFF — neutral drive switch
72	ENGINE RUNNING — no Manifold Absolute Pressure (MAP) change in (GOOSE) test
73	ENGINE RUNNING — no Throttle Position Sensor (TPS) change in (GOOSE) test
77	ENGINE RUNNING — operator did not do (GOOSE) test
84	KEY ON ENGINE OFF — Exhaust Gas Recirculation (EGR) circuit fault
85	KEY ON ENGINE OFF — canister purge circuit fault
87	KEY ON ENGINE OFF — fuel pump circuit fault
99	Idle Speed Control (ISC) has not learned yet

Year — 1989
Model — Scorpio
Engine — 2.9L (177 cid) 6 cyl
Engine Code — VIN V

ECM TROUBLE CODES

Code	Explanation
12	ENGINE RUNNING — rpm out of specification
13	ENGINE RUNNING — rpm out of specification
14	CONTINUOUS MEMORY — pip was erratic
15	KEY ON ENGINE OFF — Electronic Control Assembly (ECA) test failure CONTINUOUS MEMORY — Electronic Control Assembly (ECA) test failure
16	ENGINE RUNNING — rpm too low
18	CONTINUOUS MEMORY — no tachometer signal
19	KEY ON ENGINE OFF — power to processor
21	KEY ON ENGINE OFF — Electronic Controlled Timing (ECT) out of range ENGINE RUNNING — Electronic Controlled Timing (ECT) out of range
22	KEY ON ENGINE OFF — Manifold Absolute Pressure (MAP) out of range ENGINE RUNNING — Manifold Absolute Pressure (MAP) out of range CONTINUOUS MEMORY — Manifold Absolute Pressure (MAP) out of range
23	KEY ON ENGINE OFF — Throttle Position Sensor (TPS) out of range ENGINE RUNNING — Throttle Position Sensor (TPS) out of range
24	KEY ON ENGINE OFF — ACT out of range ENGINE RUNNING — ACT out of range
31	KEY ON ENGINE OFF — EVR/PRE out of range ENGINE RUNNING — EVR/PRE out of range CONTINUOUS MEMORY — EVR/PRE out of range
32	ENGINE RUNNING — Exhaust Gas Recirculation (EGR) not controlling CONTINUOUS MEMORY — Exhaust Gas Recirculation (EGR) not controlling
33	ENGINE RUNNING — EVR/PFE out of limits

ECM TROUBLE CODES (cont'd)

Code	Explanation
34	KEY ON ENGINE OFF — no Exhaust Gas Recirculation (EGR) flow in test ENGINE RUNNING — no Exhaust Gas Recirculation (EGR) flow in test CONTINUOUS MEMORY — no Exhaust Gas Recirculation (EGR) flow in test
35	KEY ON ENGINE OFF — rpm too low for Exhaust Gas Recirculation (EGR) test ENGINE RUNNING — rpm too low for Exhaust Gas Recirculation (EGR) test CONTINUOUS MEMORY — rpm too low for Exhaust Gas Recirculation (EGR) test
41	ENGINE RUNNING — system always lean
42	ENGINE RUNNING — system always rich
51	KEY ON ENGINE OFF — Electronic Controlled Timing (ECT) too high CONTINUOUS MEMORY — Electronic Controlled Timing (ECT) too high
53	KEY ON ENGINE OFF — Throttle Position Sensor (TPS) input too high CONTINUOUS MEMORY — Throttle Position Sensor (TPS) input too high
54	KEY ON ENGINE OFF — ACT input too high CONTINUOUS MEMORY — ACT input too high
61	KEY ON ENGINE OFF — Electronic Controlled Timing (ECT) input too low CONTINUOUS MEMORY — Electronic Controlled Timing (ECT) input too low
63	KEY ON ENGINE OFF — Throttle Position Sensor (TPS) input too low CONTINUOUS MEMORY — Throttle Position Sensor (TPS) input too low
64	KEY ON ENGINE OFF — ACT input too low CONTINUOUS MEMORY — ACT input too low
67	KEY ON ENGINE OFF — neutral drive switch
72	ENGINE RUNNING — no Manifold Absolute Pressure (MAP) change in (GOOSE) test
73	ENGINE RUNNING — no Throttle Position Sensor (TPS) change in (GOOSE) test
77	ENGINE RUNNING — operator did not do (GOOSE) test
84	KEY ON ENGINE OFF — Exhaust Gas Recirculation (EGR) circuit fault
85	KEY ON ENGINE OFF — canister purge circuit fault
87	KEY ON ENGINE OFF — fuel pump circuit fault
99	Idle Speed Control (ISC) has not learned yet

DISPLAY WINDOW

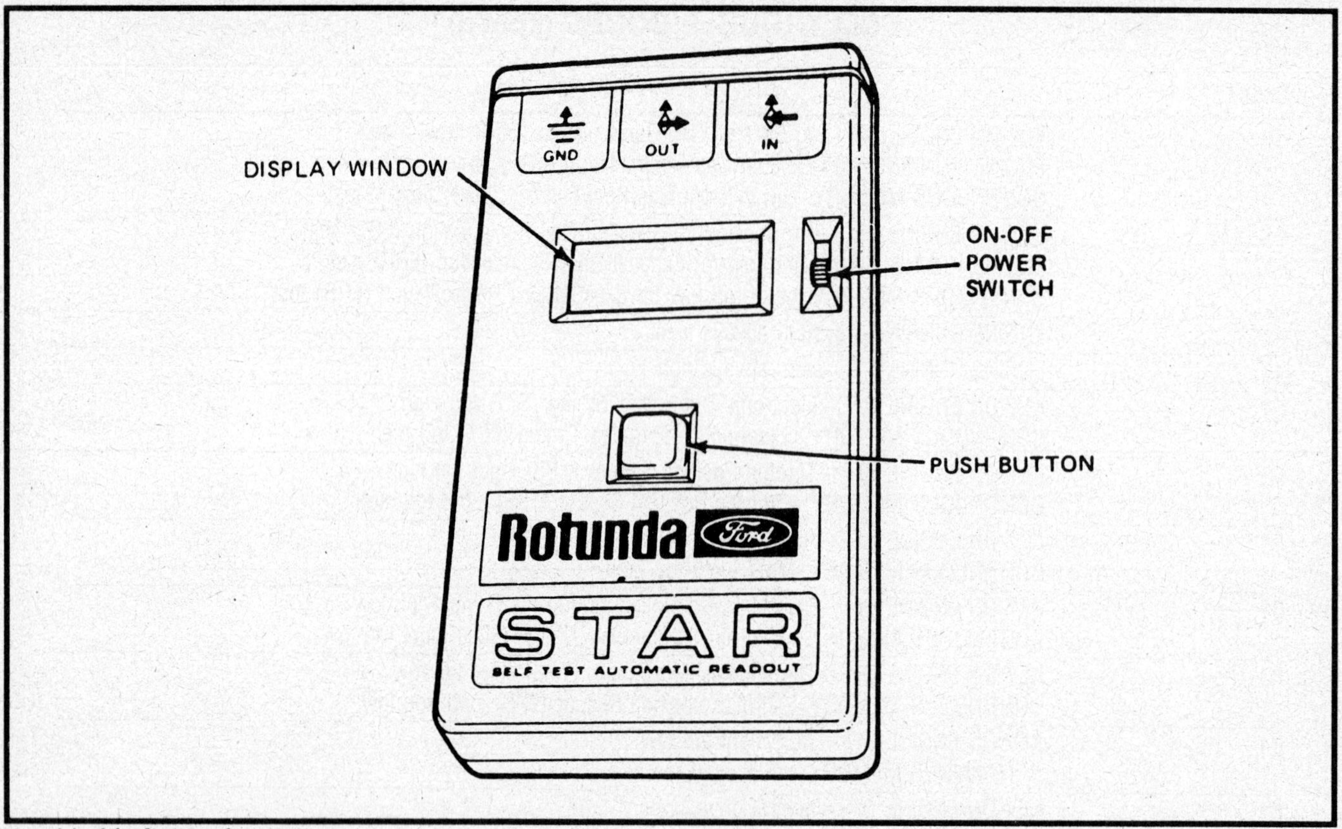

GND   OUT   IN

ON-OFF
POWER
SWITCH

PUSH BUTTON

Rotunda *Ford*

STAR
SELF TEST AUTOMATIC READOUT

Hand-held aftermarket tester

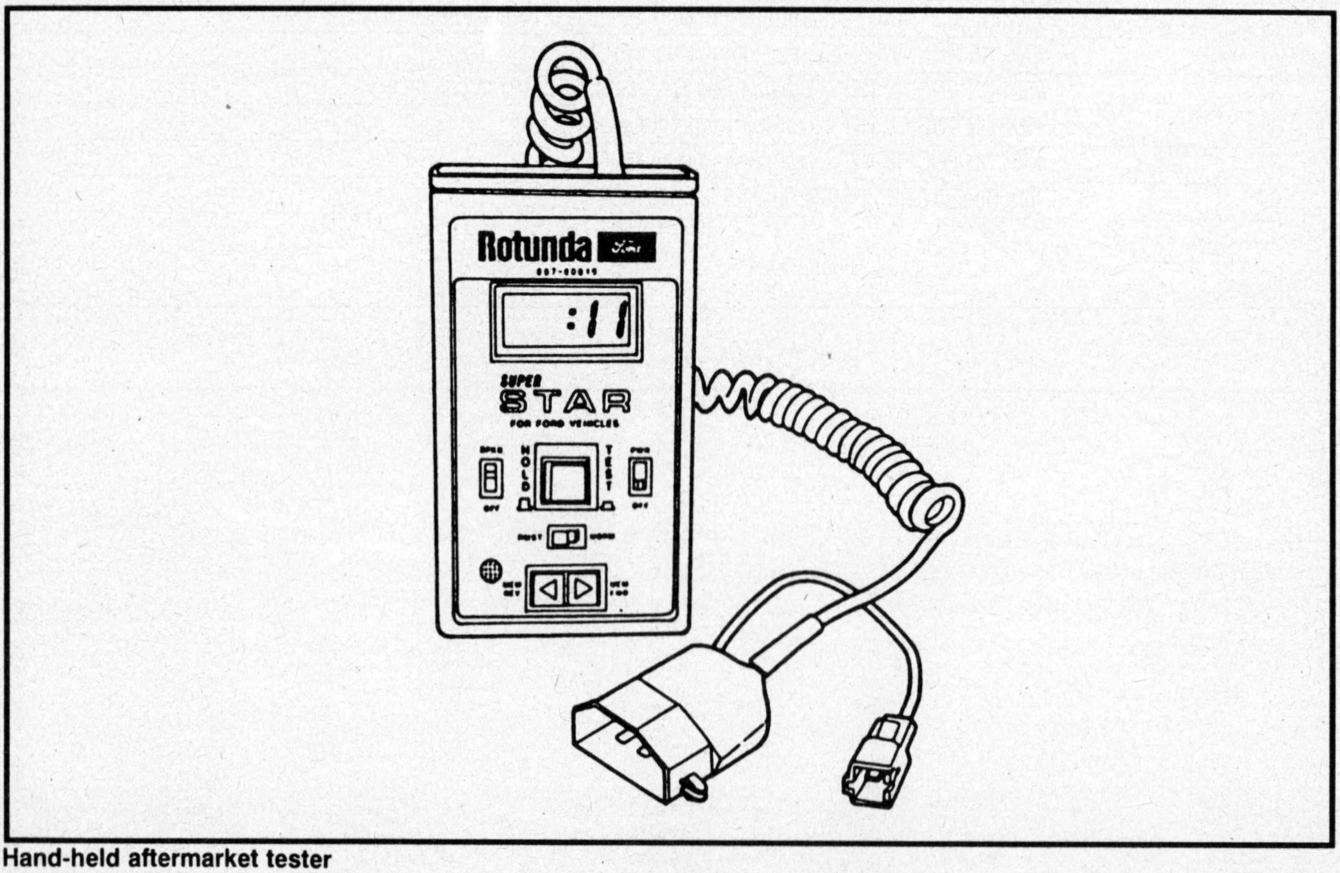

Rotunda *Ford*

:11

SUPER
STAR
FOR FORD VEHICLES

Hand-held aftermarket tester

General Motors Imports

12 SECTION

INDEX

GENERAL MOTORS IMPORTS

Sprint EFI System

SELF-DIAGNOSTIC SYSTEM

If a malfunction exists in the input signal to the ECM as a result of some trouble in the EFI components, the "Check Engine" light on the instrument panel will turn ON or flash to inform a presence of trouble.

Entering Diagnostic Mode

1. With the ignition switch **ON** with the engine not running, the light turns ON to indicate the circuit is in good condition. The light will turn OFF when the engine is started.
2. If the light stays ON after the engine is started, a malfunction exists in the signal to the ECM. The ECM will store a malfunction even if it an intermittent one. A poor contact may cause the light to come ON and then turn OFF when the circuit is completed, but the code will be stored even with the light OFF.
3. To diagnose a problem, turn **ON** the diagnostic switch located under the instrument panel. With the engine not running and the ignition switch **ON**, the "Check Engine" light will flash to indicate the diagnostic code in the ECM memory.
4. The codes consist of flashes and pauses to indicate trouble codes. Each component has a code designation. The code represents a 2-digit number.
5. If 2 or more areas are involved and that many codes are to be indicated, the "Check Engine" light indicates each code corresponding to the area of trouble 3 times in the increasing order of the code numbers and then repeats them.

NOTE: Always write down the codes as they are flashing. This memory will be lost when the power to the ECM is disconnected.

Clearing Diagnostic Memory

The code will be stored until the power from the battery to the ECM is cut off. Clear trouble codes by disconnecting the negative battery terminal for at least 30 seconds.

NOTE: Some vehicle computers have a learning ability. If a change is noted in vehicle performance after clearing codes, it may be due to the computers learning ability. To restore performance, warm vehicle to normal operating temperature and drive at part throttle with moderate acceleration, before performing any additional diagnosis.

GEO Prizm and Nova
EFI and Carbureted Systems

SELF-DIAGNOSTIC SYSTEM

If a malfunction exists in the input signal to the ECM as a result of some trouble in the EFI components, the "Check Engine" light on the instrument panel will turn ON or flash to inform a presence of trouble.

Entering Diagnostic Mode

1. With the ignition switch **ON** and the engine not running, the light turns ON to indicate the circuit is in good condition. The light will turn OFF when the engine is started.
2. If the light stays ON after the engine is started, a malfunction exists in the signal to the ECM. The ECM will store a malfunction even if it an intermittent one. A poor contact may cause

the light to come ON and then turn OFF when the circuit is completed, but the code will be stored even with the light OFF.
3. To diagnose a problem, ground the diagnostic terminal in the engine compartment with a jumper wire. With the engine not running and the ignition switch **ON**, the "Check Engine" light will flash to indicate the diagnostic code in the ECM memory.
4. The codes consist of flashes and pauses to indicate trouble codes. Each component has a code designation. The code represents a 2-digit number.
5. If 2 or more areas are involved and that many codes are to be indicated, the "Check Engine" light indicates each code corresponding to the area of trouble 3 times in the increasing order of the code numbers and then repeats them.

NOTE: Always write down the codes as they are flashing. This memory will be lost when the power to the ECM is disconnected.

Clearing Diagnostic Mode

The code will be stored until the power from the battery to the ECM is cut off. After correcting the problem, erase the memory by pulling the 15A STOP fuse located behind the drivers kick panel for 10 seconds or disconnect the battery negative cable for more than 30 seconds. Disconnecting the battery cable will cancel other memory functions such as the clock and radio.

NOTE: Some vehicle computers have a learning ability. If a change is noted in vehicle performance after clearing codes, it may be due to the computers learning ability. To restore performance, warm vehicle to normal operating temperature and drive at part throttle with moderate acceleration, before performing any additional diagnosis.

Pontiac Lemans
EFI System

SELF-DIAGNOSTIC SYSTEM

If a malfunction exists in the input signal to the ECM as a result of some trouble in the EFI components, the "Service Engine Soon" light on the instrument panel will turn ON or flash to inform a presence of trouble.

Entering Diagnostic Mode

1. With the ignition switch **ON** and the engine not running, the light turns ON to indicate the circuit is in good condition. The light will turn OFF when the engine is started.
2. If the light stays ON after the engine is started, a malfunction exists in the signal to the ECM. The ECM will store a malfunction even if it an intermittent one. A poor contact may cause the light to come ON and then turn OFF when the circuit is completed, but the code will be stored even with the light OFF.
3. To diagnose a problem, ground the Assembly Line Diagnostic Link (ALDL) terminal A and B together with a jumper wire or connect a diagnostic tool to the ALDL. The ALDL is located on the passenger side near the kick panel. With the engine not running and the ignition switch **ON**, the "Service Engine Soon" light will flash to indicate the diagnostic code in the ECM memory.
4. The codes consist of flashes and pauses to indicate trouble codes. Each component has a code designation. The code represents a 2-digit number code.
5. If 2 or more areas are involved and that many codes are to be indicated, the "Service Engine Soon" light indicates each

code corresponding to the area of trouble 3 times in the increasing order of the code numbers and then repeats them.

NOTE: Always write down the codes as they are flashing. This memory will be lost when the power to the ECM is disconnected.

Clearing Diagnostic Memory

The code will be stored until the power from the battery to the ECM is cut off. After correcting the problem, erase the memory by pulling the 20A ECM fuse (F-10) located in the fuse panel for 30 seconds or disconnect the negative battery cable for more than 30 seconds. Disconnecting the battery cable will cancel other memory functions such as the clock and radio.

NOTE: Some vehicle computers have a learning ability. If a change is noted in vehicle performance after clearing codes, it may be due to the computers learning ability. To restore performance, warm vehicle to normal operating temperature and drive at part throttle with moderate acceleration, before performing any additional diagnosis.

GEO Metro EFI System

SELF-DIAGNOSTIC SYSTEM

If a malfunction exists in the input signal to the ECM as a result of some trouble in the EFI components, the "Check Engine" light on the instrument panel will turn ON or flash to inform a presence of trouble.

Entering Diagnostic Mode

1. With the ignition switch **ON** and engine not running, the light turns ON to indicate the circuit is in good condition. The light will turn OFF when the engine is started.

2. If the light stays ON after the engine is started, a malfunction exists in the signal to the ECM. The ECM will store a malfunction even if it an intermittent one. A poor contact may cause the light to come ON and then turn OFF when the circuit is completed but the code will be stored even with the light OFF.

3. To diagnose a problem, ground the monitor connector located in the engine compartment, driver's side, near the ECM. The trouble codes can be displayed by grounding the diagnostic terminal in the fuse block or grounding the B and C terminal in the monitor connector with a jumper wire. Use a spare fuse to ground the terminal in the fuse block. Connect a Scan tool to the monitor connector for diagnosis purposes. With the engine not running and the ignition switch **ON**, the "Check Engine" light will flash to indicate the diagnostic code in the ECM memory.

4. The codes consist of flashes and pauses to indicate trouble codes. Each component has a code designation. The code represents a 2-digit number.

5. If 2 or more areas are involved and that many codes are to be indicated, the "Check Engine" light indicates each code corresponding to the area of trouble 3 times in the increasing order of the code numbers and then repeats them.

NOTE: Always write down the codes as they are flashing. This memory will be lost when the power to the ECM is disconnected.

Clearing Diagnostic Memory

The code will be stored until the power from the battery to the ECM is cut off. After correcting the problem, erase the memory by removing the 15A TAIL LAMP fuse located in the fuse panel for 30 seconds or disconnect the negative battery cable for more than 30 seconds. Disconnecting the battery cable will cancel other memory functions such as the clock and radio.

NOTE: Some vehicle computers have a learning ability. If a change is noted in vehicle performance after clearing codes, it may be due to the computers learning ability. To restore performance, warm vehicle to normal operating temperature and drive at part throttle with moderate acceleration, before performing any additional diagnosis.

GEO Tracker EFI System

SELF-DIAGNOSTIC SYSTEM

Description

If a malfunction exists in the input signal to the ECM as a result of some trouble in the EFI components, the "Check Engine" light on the instrument panel will turn ON or flash to inform a presence of trouble.

When the mileage reaches 50,000, 80,000 and 100,000 miles respectively the mileage sensor turns ON the "Check Engine" light even while the engine is running with no problems. This is to warn the driver that it is time for periodic inspection. Turn the light OFF with its cancel switch located behind the access panel below the steering column. To reset, slide the switch right or left until the light goes OFF.

Entering Diagnostic Mode

1. With the ignition switch **ON** and the engine not running, the light turns ON to indicate the circuit is in good condition. The light will turn OFF when the engine is started.

2. If the light stays ON after the engine is started, a malfunction exists in the signal to the ECM or the mileage interval has been reached. The ECM will store a malfunction even if it an intermittent code. A poor contact may cause the light to come ON and then turn OFF when the circuit is completed, but the code will be stored even with the light OFF.

3. To diagnose a problem, ground the diagnostic terminal in the fuse block. Use a spare fuse to ground the terminal in the fuse block. Connect a Scan tool to the monitor connector for diagnosis purposes. With the engine not running and the ignition switch **ON**, the "Check Engine" light will flash to indicate the diagnostic code in the ECM memory.

4. The codes consist of flashes and pauses to indicate trouble codes. Each component has a code designation. The code represents a 2-digit number.

5. If 2 or more areas are involved and that many codes are to be indicated, the "Check Engine" light indicates each code corresponding to the area of trouble 3 times in the increasing order of the code numbers and then repeats them.

NOTE: Always write down the codes as they are flashing. This memory will be lost when the power to the ECM is disconnected.

Clearing Diagnostic Memory

The code will be stored until the power from the battery to the ECM is cut off. After correcting the problem, erase the memory by removing the 15A TAIL LAMP fuse located in the fuse panel for 30 seconds or disconnect the negative battery cable for more than 30 seconds. Disconnecting the battery cable will cancel other memory functions such as the clock and radio.

NOTE: Some vehicle computers have a learning ability. If a change is noted in vehicle performance after clearing codes, it may be due to the computers learning ability. To restore performance, warm vehicle to normal operating temperature and drive at part throttle with moderate acceleration, before performing any additional diagnosis.

Spectrum Feedback Carbureted System

SELF-DIAGNOSTIC SYSTEM

Description

The ECM in the Closed Loop Emission Control system features a self-diagnosis function. The self-diagnosis function identifies troubles in the area related to the sensors, including wiring harnesses and ECM.

If a malfunction exists in the input signal to the ECM as a result of some trouble in the emission related components, the "Check Engine" light on the instrument panel will turn ON or flash to inform a presence of trouble. The system diagnosis should be performed in the following sequence:

1. Diagnostic circuit check
2. Driver complaint
3. System performance check

Entering Diagnostic Mode

1. With the ignition switch **ON** and engine not running, the light turns ON to indicate the circuit is in good condition. The light will turn OFF when the engine is started.

2. If the light stays ON after the engine is started, a malfunction exists in the signal to the ECM. The ECM will store a malfunction even if it an intermittent one. A poor contact may cause the light to come ON and then turn OFF when the circuit is completed, but the code will be stored even with the light OFF.

3. To diagnose a problem, turn **ON** the diagnostic switch located under the instrument panel. With the engine not running and the ignition switch **ON**, the "Check Engine" light will flash to indicate the diagnostic code in the ECM memory.

4. The codes consist of flashes and pauses to indicate trouble codes. Each component has a code designation. The code represents a 2-digit number.

NOTE: Code 12 is 1 flash, a short pause and 2 flashes. This code means the ECM is in the self-diagnosis mode and it is working. This code is not a problem code.

5. If 2 or more areas are involved and that many codes are to be indicated, the "Check Engine" light indicates each code corresponding to the area of trouble 3 times in the increasing order of the code numbers and then repeats them.

NOTE: Always write down the codes as they are flashing. This memory will be lost when the power to the ECM is disconnected.

Clearing Diagnostic Mode

The code will be stored until the power from the battery to the ECM is cut off. After correcting the problem, erase the memory by removing the ECM fuse in the fuse block or disconnect the negative battery cable for more than 20 seconds. Disconnecting the battery cable will cancel clock, radio and any other memory functions.

NOTE: Some vehicle computers have a learning ability. If a change is noted in vehicle performance after clearing codes, it may be due to the computers learning ability. To restore performance, warm vehicle to normal operating temperature and drive at part throttle with moderate acceleration, before performing any additional diagnosis.

GM IMPORTS

Year — 1987
Model — Sprint
Engine — 1.0L (61 cid) 4 cyl
Engine Code — VIN 5

ECM TROUBLE CODES

Code	Explanation
12	Ignition
13	Oxygen Sensor
14	Coolant Temperature Sensor (CTS)
21	Throttle Position Sensor (TPS)
23	Intake air temperature sensor
32	Ambient pressure sensor
51	Electronic Control Module (ECM)
52	Fuel cut solenoid
53	Second air solenoid
54	Mixture Control (M/C) solenoid
55	Bowl vent solenoid

Year — 1987
Model — Spectrum
Engine — 1.5L (90 cid) 4 cyl
Engine Code — VIN 7

ECM TROUBLE CODES

Code	Explanation
12	Electronic Control Module (ECM) circuit
13	Oxygen sensor circuit — The engine must run up to 2 minutes at part throttle, under road load, before this code will reset
14	Shorted coolant sensor circuit — The engine must run up to 2 minutes before this code will reset
15	Open coolant sensor circuit — The engine must run up to 5 minutes before this code will reset
21	Idle switch improperly adjusted and/or circuit open. This code will set if engine speed falls below 600 rpm for longer than 32 seconds. If Throttle Position Sensor (TPS) and idle switch are faulty or misadjusted. This code will reset
22	Fuel cut off relay and/or circuit open
23	Open or grounded Mixture Control (M/C) solenoid circuit
25	Vacuum Switching Valve (VSV) circuit open or grounded
42	Fuel cut off relay and/or cicuit open
44	Lean oxygen sensor indication — The engine must run for at least 2 minutes at part throttle and road load before this code will set. This code will not set when the coolant temperature is below 70°C. The code will not set when the air cleaner temperature is below 0°C. The code will not set in the "high altitude" condition
45	Rich system indication — The engine must run for at least 2 minutes at part throttle and road load before this code will set. This code will not set when the engine is not between 1500–2500 rpm and/or the coolant temperature is below 70°C and/or at the "high altitude" condition
51	Faulty calibration unit (PROM) or installation. It takes up to 30 seconds before this code will set
53	Shorted switching valve and/or faulty Electronic Control Module (ECM)
54	Shorted Mixture Control (M/C) soenoid circuit and/or faulty Electronic Control Module (ECM)
55	Faulty Electronic Control Module (ECM) — problem with ECM A/D converter in ECM

Year — 1988
Model — Spectrum
Engine — 1.5L (90 cid) 4 cyl
Engine Code — VIN 7

ECM TROUBLE CODES

Code	Explanation
12	No distributor reference pulses to the Electronic Control Module (ECM). This code is not stored and will only flash while the fault is present
13	Oxygen sensor circuit — The engine must run up to 2 minutes at part throttle, under road load, before this code will set
14	Shorted coolant sensor circuit — The engine must run up to 2 minutes before this code will set
15	Open coolant sensor circuit — The engine must run up to 5 minutes before this code will set
21	Idle switch misadjusted and/or cicuit open. This code will set if the speed falls below 600 rpm for longer than 32 seconds or if the TPS and idle switch are faulty or misadjusted. This code will set if the Electronic Control Module (ECM) detects both idle and WOT condition at the same time
22	Fuel cut-off relay and/or circuit open
23	Open or grounded Mixture Control (M/C) solenoid circuit
42	Fuel cut-off relay and/or circuit shorted
44	Lean oxygen sensor condition — The engine must run up to 2 minutes, in closed loop, at part throttle, under road load, before this code will set. This code will not set when the coolant temperature is below 70°C and/or the air temperature is below 0°C, in a "low altitude condition. This code will not set in a "high altitude" condition
45	Rich system indication. The engine must run up to 2 minutes, in closed loop, at part throttle, under road load, before this code will set. This code will not set when the engine is not between 1500–2500 rpm and/or the coolant temperature is below 70°C and/or at "high altitude condition"
51	Faulty calibration unit (PROM) or installation. It takes up to 30 seconds before this code will set
54	Shorted Mixture Control (M/C) solenoid circuit and/or faulty Electronic Control Module (ECM)
55	Faulty Electronic Control Module (ECM) — problem in A/D converter in ECM

Year – 1988
Model – Sprint
Engine – 1.0L (61 cid) 4 cyl
Engine Code – VIN 5

ECM TROUBLE CODES

Code	Explanation
12	Ignition
13	Oxygen Sensor
14	Coolant Temperature Sensor (CTS)
21	Throttle Position Sensor (TPS)
23	Intake air temperature sensor
32	Ambient pressure sensor
51	Electronic Control Module (ECM)
52	Fuel cut solenoid
53	Second air solenoid
54	Mixture Control (M/C) solenoid
55	Bowl vent solenoid

Year — 1988
Model — LeMans
Engine — 1.6L (98 cid) 4 cyl
Engine Code — VIN 6

ECM TROUBLE CODES

Code	Explanation
13	Oxygen sensor circuit
14	Coolant Temperature Sensor (CTS) circuit — high temperature
15	Coolant Temperature Sensor (CTS) circuit — low temperature
21	Throttle Position Sensor (TPS) circuit — high voltage
22	Throttle Position Sensor (TPS) circuit — low voltage
24	Vehicle Speed Sensor (VSS) circuit
33	Manifold absolute pressure sensor circuit — voltage high, vacuum low
34	Manifold absolute pressure sensor circuit — voltage low, vacuum high
35	Idle speed error
42	Electronic Spark Timing (EST) circuit
44	Oxygen sensor circuit — lean exhaust
45	Oxygen sensor circuit — rich exhaust
51	Faulty Mem-Cal
53	System overcharge

Year – 1989
Model – GEO Spectrum
Engine – 1.5L (90 cid) 4 cyl
Engine Code – VIN 7

ECM TROUBLE CODES

Code	Explanation
12	No distributor reference pulses to the Electronic Control Module (ECM). This code is not stored and will only flash while the fault is present
13	Oxygen sensor circuit – The engine must run up to 2 minutes at part throttle, under road load, before this code will set
14	Shorted coolant sensor circuit – The engine must run up to 2 minutes before this code will set
15	Open coolant sensor circuit – The engine must run up to 5 minutes before this code will set
21	Idle switch misadjusted and/or cicuit open. This code will set if the speed falls below 600 rpm for longer than 32 seconds or if the Throttle Position Sensor (TPS) and idle switch are faulty or misadjusted. This code will set if the Electronic Control Module (ECM) detects both idle and WOT condition at the same time
22	Fuel cut-off relay and/or circuit open
23	Open or grounded Mixture Control (M/C) solenoid circuit
42	Fuel cut-off relay and/or circuit shorted
44	Lean oxygen sensor condition – The engine must run up to 2 minutes, in closed loop, at part throttle, under road load, before this code will set. This code will not set when the coolant temperature is below 70°C and/or the air temperature is below 0°C, in a "low altitude condition. This code will not set in a "high altitude" condition
45	Rich system indication. The engine must run up to 2 minutes, in closed loop, at part throttle, under road load, before this code will set. This code will not set when the engine is not between 1500–2500 rpm and/or the coolant temperature is below 70°C and/or at "high altitude condition"
51	Faulty calibration unit (PROM) or installation. It takes up to 30 seconds before this code will set
54	Shorted Mixture Control (M/C) solenoid circuit and/or faulty Electronic Control Module (ECM)
55	Faulty Electronic Control Module (ECM) – problem in A/D converter in ECM

Year – 1989
Model – LeMans
Engine – 1.6L (98 cid) 4 cyl
Engine Code – VIN 6

ECM TROUBLE CODES

Code	Explanation
13	Oxygen sensor circuit
14	Coolant Temperature Sensor (CTS) circuit – high temperature
15	Coolant Temperature Sensor (CTS) circuit – low temperature
21	Throttle Position Sensor (TPS) circuit – high voltage
22	Throttle Position Sensor (TPS) circuit – low voltage
24	Vehicle Speed Sensor (VSS) circuit
33	Manifold absolute pressure sensor circuit – voltage high, vacuum low
34	Manifold absolute pressure sensor circuit – voltage low, vacuum high
35	Idle speed error
42	Electronic Spark Timing (TPS) circuit
44	Oxygen sensor circuit – lean exhaust
45	Oxygen sensor circuit – rich exhaust
51	Faulty Mem-Cal
53	System overcharge

Year – 1989
Model – LeMans
Engine – 2.0L (122 cid) 4 cyl
Engine Code – VIN K

ECM TROUBLE CODES

Code	Explanation
13	Oxygen sensor circuit
14	Coolant Temperature Sensor (CTS) circuit – high temperature
15	Coolant Temperature Sensor (CTS) circuit – low temperature
21	Throttle Position Sensor (TPS) circuit – high voltage
22	Throttle Position Sensor (TPS) circuit – low voltage
23	Manifold Air Temperature (MAT) sensor circuit
24	Vehicle Speed Sensor (VSS) circuit
25	Manifold Air Temperature (MAT) sensor circuit – temperature too high
32	Exhaust Gas Recirculation (EGR) system error
33	Manifold absolute pressure sensor circuit – voltage high, vacuum low
34	Manifold absolute pressure sensor circuit – voltage low, vacuum high
42	Electronic Spark Timing (EST) circuit
44	Oxygen sensor circuit – lean exhaust
45	Oxygen sensor circuit – rich exhaust
51	Faulty Mem-Cal
53	System overcharge

Year — 1989
Model — GEO Metro
Engine — 1.0L (61 cid) 4 cyl
Engine Code — VIN 6

ECM TROUBLE CODES

Code	Explanation
13	Oxygen sensor circuit — open circuit
14	Coolant Temperature Sensor (CTS) circuit — high temperature indicated
15	Coolant Temperature Sensor (CTS) circuit — low temperature indicated
21	Throttle switch circuit — manual transmission only
21	Throttle switch circuit — automatic transmission only — high voltage
22	Throttle Position Sensor (TPS) — automatic transmission only — low voltage
23	Manifold Air Temperature (MAT) sensor circuit — low temperature
24	Vehicle Speed Sensor (VSS) circuit
25	Manifold Air Temperature (MAT) sensor circuit — high temperature
31	Manifold absolute pressure sensor circuit — voltage low, vacuum high
32	Manifold absolute pressure sensor circuit — voltage high, vacuum low
41	Ignition signal circuit
42	Crank angle sensor circuit
51	Exhaust gas recirculation circuit — California

Year – 1989
Model – GEO Prism
Engine – 1.6L (97 cid) 4 cyl
Engine Code – VIN 6

ECM TROUBLE CODES

Code	Explanation
12	RPM signal
13	RPM signal
14	Ignition signal
21	Oxygen Sensor
22	Coolant Temperature Sensor (CTS)
24	Manifold Air Temperature (MAT) sensor
25	Lean air/fuel ratio
26	Rich air/fuel ratio
31	Manifold Absolute Pressure Sensor
41	Throttle Position Sensor (TPS)
43	Starter Signal
51	Switch Signal
71	Exhaust Gas Recircualion (EGR) malfunction

Year – 1989
Model – GEO Tracker
Engine – 1.6L (97 cid) 4 cyl
Engine Code – VIN U

ECM TROUBLE CODES

Code	Explanation
13	Oxygen sensor circuit
14	Water temperature circuit – low temperature
15	Water temperature circuit – high temperature
21	Throttle Position Sensor (TPS) circuit – voltage high
22	Throttle Position Sensor (TPS) circuit – voltage low
23	Air temperature sensor circuit – high temperature
25	Air temperature sensor circuit – low temperature
31	Pressure sensor circuit – high voltage, low vacuum
32	Pressure sensor circuit – low voltage, high vacuum
41	Ignition signal circuit – no signal
42	5th switch circuit grounded – manual transmission only
42	Torque converter clutch lock-up signal – automatic transmission only
44	Idle switch circuit
45	Idle switch circuit
51	Exhaust Gas Recirculation (EGR) system and recirculated exhaust gas temperature – temperature too high or too low
53	Grounded circuit – California only

INDEX

HONDA

Programmed Fuel Injection (PGM-FI) and Feedback Carburetor

SELF-DIAGNOSTIC SYSTEM

Description

Many Honda's are equipped with a self-diagnosis function. When an abnormality in the emission control system is detected, the Electronic Control Unit (ECU) energizes the LED display. The location of the malfunction is determined by observing the LED display. Honda uses 2 types of LED displays: a single LED and a 4 LED display.

Systems with a single LED, indicate the malfunction with a series of flashes. The number of flashes indicates a code which identifies the location of the component or system malfunction. The code will flash, followed by a 2 second pause, repeat, followed by another 2 second pause, then move to the next code.

On systems with 4 LED's a display pattern identifies the malfunction. The LED's are numbered 1, 2, 4 and 8 as counted from right-to-left. The code is determined by observing which LED's are lit on the display. Each code is displayed once, followed by a 2 second pause, then, the next code is displayed.

The LED(s) are part of the Electronic Control Unit (ECU), which is located inside the vehicle. The ECU location varies from model-to-model. On the Accord, the ECU is located under the driver's seat. The ECU for Prelude, 1986–87, is located behind the left side panel beside the rear seat and behind the right front kick panel for 1988–89 models. Civic models, for the years 1986–87, locate the ECU under the passenger's seat; 1988–89 models, under the carpet in front of the passenger's seat.

Entering Diagnostic Mode

Sometimes the dash warning light and/or ECU LED(s) will turn ON, indicating a system problem, when, in fact, there is only a bad or intermittent electrical connection. To troubleshoot a bad connnection, note the ECU LED code that is lit, refer to the diagnosis chart and check the connectors associated with the

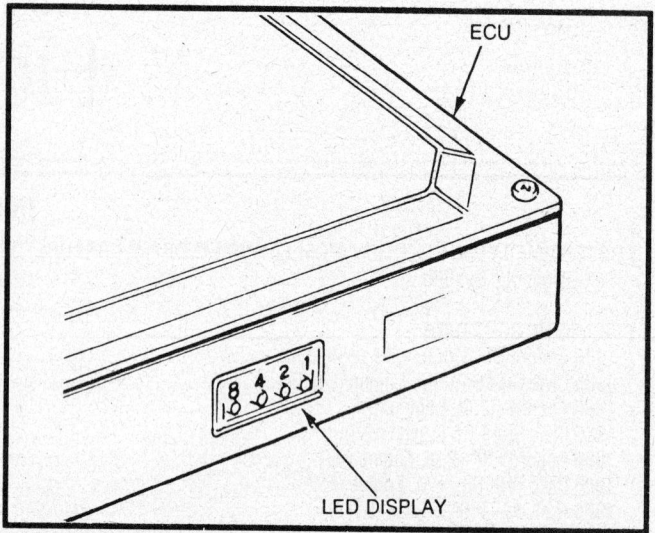

PGM-FI LED display—1985–87 Civic; CRX and 1985 Accord

items mentioned in the chart for that LED pattern; disconnect, clean or repair, if necessary, reconnect the connections and reset the ECU memory. Start the car and drive it for a few minutes and recheck the LED(s). If the same code(s) light, begin system troubleshooting; if it does not light up, the problem was only a bad connection.

Clearing Diagnostic Memory

To clear the ECU memory after making repairs, disconnect the negative battery cable from the battery negative terminal for at least 10 seconds. After reconnecting the cable, check that the LED display is turned OFF. Turn the ignition switch **ON** and all LED displays should turn ON for about 2 seconds and turn OFF.

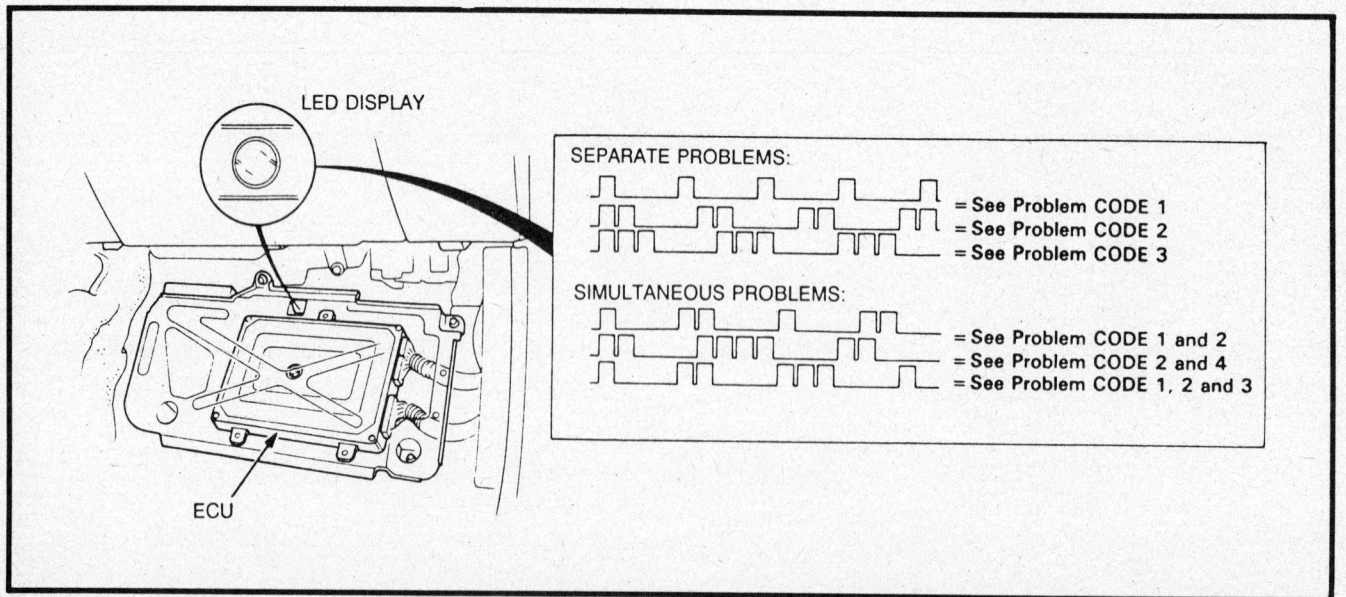

Electronic Control Unit (ECU) location—1988 Prelude carburetted and fuel injected

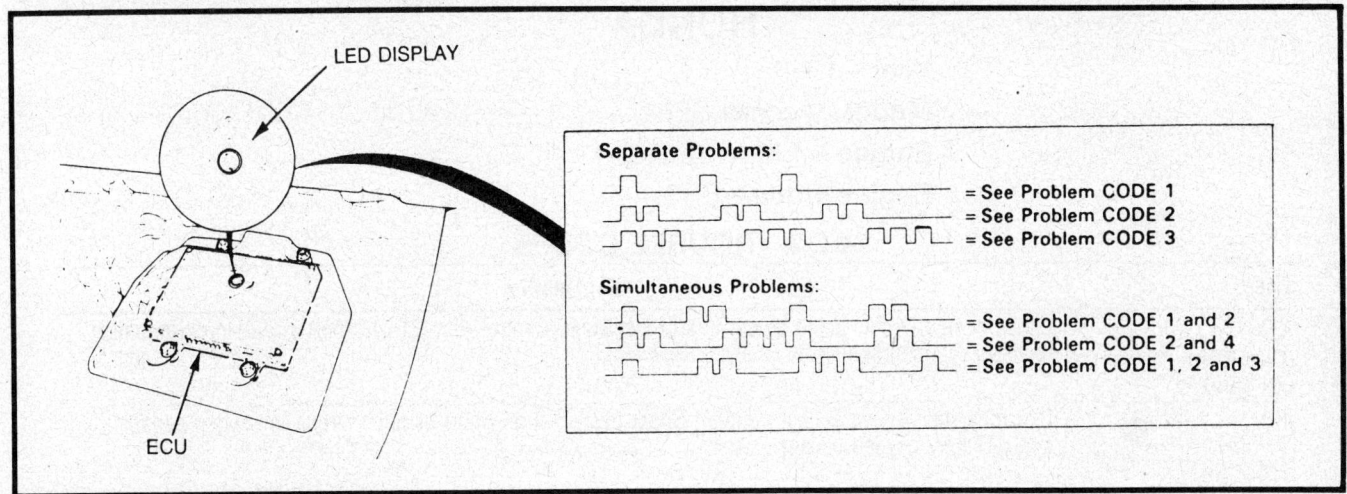

Reading codes from LED dislplay

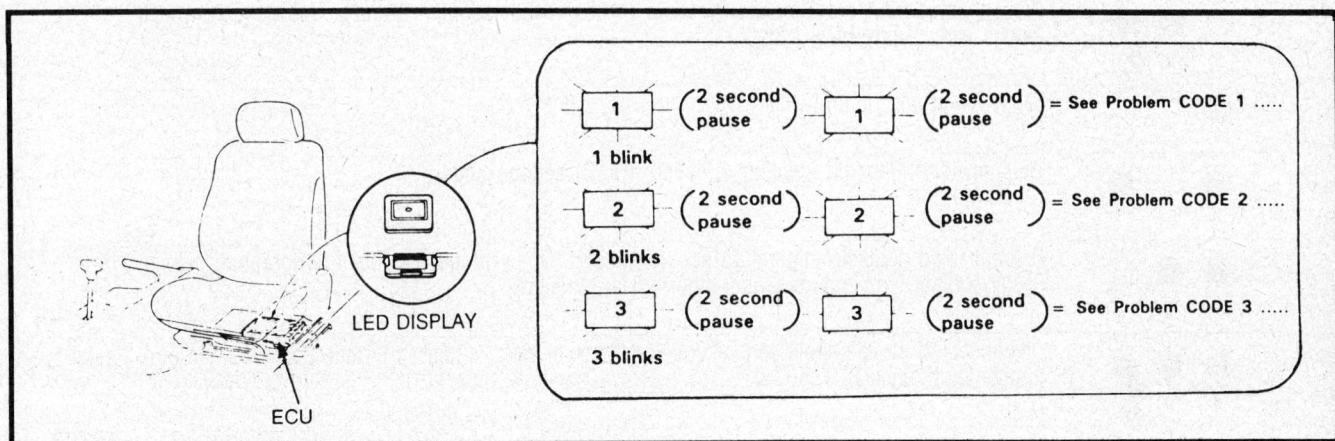

Electronic Control Unit (ECU) location—1986–88 Accord

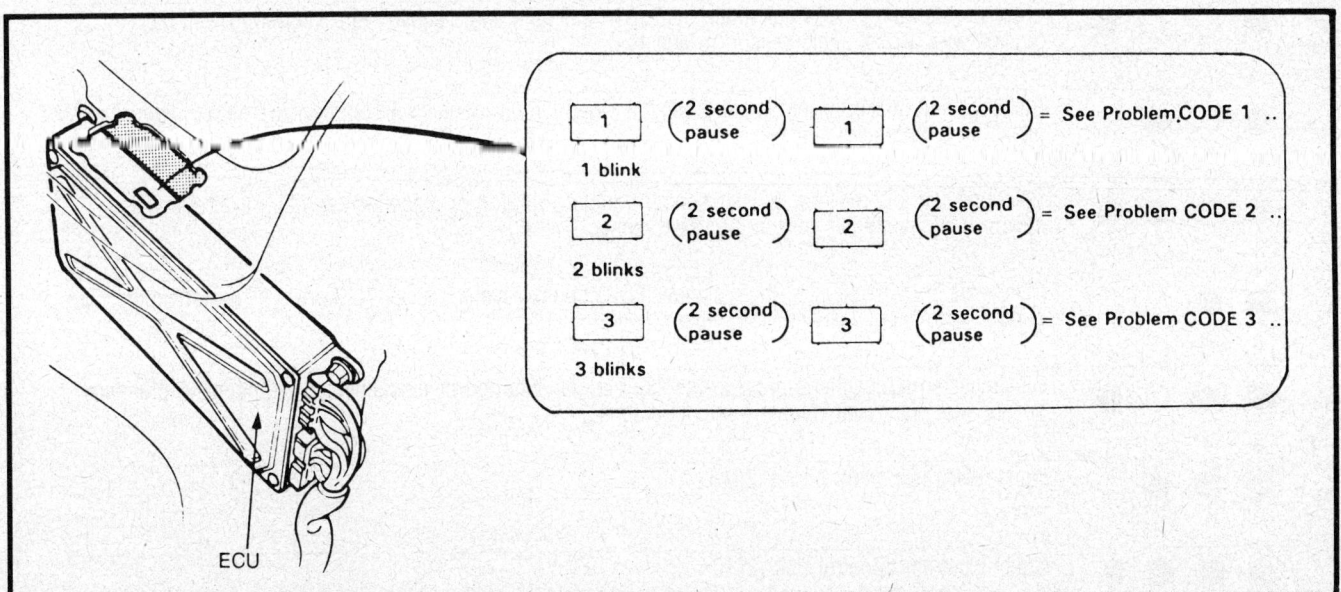

PGM-FI LED display—1986-87 Prelude shown, 1988 Prelude beneath right front carpet

HONDA

Year – 1985
Model – Accord SEi
Engine – 1.8L (112 cid) 4 cyl
Engine Code – ES3

ECM TROUBLE CODES

Code	Explanation
○ ○ ○ ○ (Dash Warning Light ON only)	Loose or poorly connected power line to Electronic Control Unit (ECU). Short circuit in combination meter or warning light wire. Faulty ECU
○ ○ ○ ● (1)	Disconnected oxygen sensor coupler. Spark plug misfire. Short or open circuit in oxygen sensor circuit. Faulty oxygen sensor
○ ○ ● ○ (2)	Faulty Electronic Control Unit (ECU)
○ ○ ● ● (2 1)	Disconnected Manifold Absolute Pressure (MAP) sensor coupler. Short or open circuit in MAP sensor wire. Faulty MAP sensor
○ ● ○ ○ (4)	Faulty Electronic Control Unit (ECU)
○ ● ○ ● (4 1)	Disconnected Manifold Absolute Pressure (MAP) sensor piping
○ ● ● ○ (4 2)	Disconnected coolant temperature sensor coupler. Open circuit in coolant temperature sensor wire. Faulty coolant temperature sensor (thermostat housing)
○ ● ● ● (4 2 1)	Disconnected throttle angle sensor coupler. Open or short circuit in throttle angle sensor wire. Faulty throttle angle sensor
● ○ ○ ○ (8)	Short or open circuit in crank angle sensor wire. Crank angle sensor wire interfering with high tension wire. Crank angle sensor at fault
● ○ ○ ● (8 1)	Short or open circuit in crank angle sensor wire. Crank angle sensor wire interfering with high tension wire. Crank angle sensor at fault
● ○ ● ○ (8 2)	Disconnected intake air temperature sensor. Open circuit in intake air temperature sensor wire. Faulty intake air temperature sensor
● ○ ● ● (8 2 1)	Disconnected idle mixture adjuster sensor coupler. Shorted or disconnected idle mixture adjuster sensor wire. Faulty idle mixture adjuster sensor
● ● ○ ○ (8 4)	Disconnected Exhaust Gas Recirculation (EGR) control system coupler. Shorted or disconnected EGR control wire. Faulty EGR control system
● ● ○ ● (8 4 1)	Disconnected atmospheric pressure sensor coupler. Shorted or disconnected atmospheric pressure sensor wire. Faulty atmospheric pressure sensor
● ● ● ○ (8 4 2)	Faulty Electronic Control Unit (ECU)
● ● ● ● (8 4 2 1)	Faulty Electronic Control Unit (ECU)

Year – 1985
Model – Civic CRX Si
Engine – 1.5L (91 cid) 4 cyl
Engine Code – EW3

ECM TROUBLE CODES

Code	Explanation
○ ○ ○ ○ (Dash Warning Light ON only)	Dash warning light ON—loose or poorly connected power line to ECU. Short circuit in combination meter or warning light wire. Faulty ECU
○ ○ ○ ● (1)	Disconnected oxygen sensor coupler. Spark plug misfire. Short or open circuit in oxygen sensor circuit. Faulty oxygen sensor
○ ○ ● ○ (2)	Faulty Electronic Control Unit (ECU)
○ ○ ● ● (2 1)	Disconnected Manifold Air Pressure (MAP) sensor coupler. Short or open circuit in MAP sensor wire. Faulty MAP sensor
○ ● ○ ○ (4)	Faulty Electronic Control Unit (ECU)
○ ● ○ ● (4 1)	Disconnected Manifold Absolute Pressure (MAP) sensor piping
○ ● ● ○ (4 2)	Disconnected Coolant Temperature Sensor (CTS) coupler. Open circuit in coolant temperature sensor wire. Faulty coolant temperature sensor (thermostat housing)
○ ● ● ● (4 2 1)	Disconnected throttle angle sensor coupler. Open or short circuit in throttle angle sensor wire. Faulty throttle angle sensor
● ○ ○ ○ (8)	Short or open circuit in crank angle sensor wire. Crank angle sensor wire interfering with high tension wire. Crank angle sensor at fault
● ○ ○ ● (8 1)	Short or open circuit in crank angle sensor wire. Crank angle sensor wire interfering with high tension wire. Crank angle sensor at fault
● ○ ● ○ (8 2)	Disconnected intake air temperature sensor. Open circuit in intake air temperature sensor wire. Faulty intake air temperature sensor
● ○ ● ● (8 2 1)	Disconnected idle mixture adjuster sensor coupler. Shorted or disconnected idle mixture adjuster sensor wire. Faulty idle mixture adjuster sensor
● ● ○ ○ (8 4)	Faulty Electronic Control Unit (ECU)
● ● ○ ● (8 4 1)	Disconnected atmospheric pressure sensor coupler. Shorted or disconnected atmospheric pressure sensor wire. Faulty atmospheric pressure sensor
● ● ● ○ (8 4 2)	Faulty Electronic Control Unit (ECU)
● ● ● ● (8 4 2 1)	Faulty Electronic Control Unit (ECU)

Year – 1986
Model – Accord
Engine – 2.0L (119 cid) 4 cyl
Engine Code – BS

ECM TROUBLE CODES

Code	Explanation
0	Dash warning light OFF – disconnected control unit ground wire. Faulty Electronic Control Unit (ECU). Dash warning light ON – loose or poorly connected power line to ECU. Disconnected control unit ground wire. Short circuit in combination meter or warning light wire. Faulty ECU
1	Disconnected oxygen sensor connector. Spark plug misfire. Short or open circuit in oxygen sensor circuit. Faulty oxygen sensor. Faulty fuel system
2	Faulty Electronic Control Unit (ECU)
3	Disconnected Manifold Absolute Pressure (MAP) sensor connector. Short or open circuit in MAP sensor wire. Faulty MAP sensor
4	Faulty Electronic Control Unit (ECU)
5	Disconnected Manifold Absolute Pressure (MAP) sensor piping
6	Disconnected Coolant Temperature Sensor (CTS) coupler. Open or short circuit in coolant temperature sensor wire. Faulty coolant temperature sensor (thermostat housing)
7	Disconnected throttle angle sensor coupler. Open or short circuit in throttle angle sensor wire. Faulty throttle angle sensor
8	Short or open circuit in crank angle sensor wire. Crank angle sensor wire interfering with spark plug wires. Crank angle sensor fault
9	Short or open circuit in crank angle sensor wire. Crank angle sensor wire interfering with spark plug wires. Crank angle sensor fault
10	Disconnected intake air temperature sensor. Open or short circuit in intake air temperature sensor wire. Faulty intake air temperature sensor
11	Faulty Electronic Control Unit (ECU)
12	Disconnected Exhaust Gas Recirculation (EGR) control system coupler. Shorted or disconnected EGR control wire. Faulty EGR control system
13	Disconnected atmosheric pressure sensor coupler. Shorted or disconnected atmospheric pressure sensor
13 +	If the number of blinks between 2 second pauses exceeds 13 or if the LED indicator stays ON, the ECU is faulty.

Year — 1986
Model — Civic Si
Engine — 1.3L (82 cid) 4 cyl
Engine Code — EVI

ECM TROUBLE CODES

Code	Explanation
○ ○ ○ ○ (Dash Warning Light ON only)	Dash warning light OFF—loose or poorly connected power line to Electronic Control Unit (ECU). Disconnected control unit ground wire. Faulty ECU
○ ○ ○ ○ (Dash warning light on)	Dash warning light ON—disconnected control unit ground wire. Faulty ECU. Short circuit in combination meter or warning light wire
○ ○ ○ ● (1)	Disconnected oxygen sensor coupler. Spark plug misfire. Short or open circuit in oxygen sensor circuit. Faulty oxygen sensor
○ ○ ● ○ (2)	Faulty Electronic Control Unit (ECU)
○ ○ ● ● (2 1)	Disconnected Manifold Absolute Pressure (MAP) sensor coupler. Short or open circuit in MAP sensor wire. Faulty MAP sensor
○ ● ○ ○ (4)	Faulty Electronic Control Unit (ECU)
○ ● ○ ● (4 1)	Disconnected Manifold Absolute Pressure (MAP) sensor piping
○ ● ● ○ (4 2)	Disconnected Coolant Temperature Sensor (CTS) coupler. Open circuit in coolant temperature sensor wire. Faulty coolant temperature sensor (thermostat housing)
○ ● ● ● (4 2 1)	Disconnected throttle angle sensor coupler. Open or short circuit in throttle angle sensor wire. Faulty throttle angle sensor
● ○ ○ ○ (8)	Short or open circuit in crank angle sensor wire. Crank angle sensor wire interfering with high tension wire. Crank angle sensor at fault
● ○ ○ ● (8)	Short or open circuit in crank angle sensor wire. Crank angle sensor wire interfering with high tension wire. Crank angle sensor at fault
● ○ ● ○ (8 2)	Disconnected intake air temperature sensor. Open circuit in intake air temperature sensor wire. Faulty intake air temperature sensor
● ○ ● ● (8 2 1)	Disconnected idle mixture adjuster sensor coupler. Shorted or disconnected idle mixture adjuster sensor wire. Faulty idle mixture adjuster sensor
● ● ○ ○ (8 4)	Faulty Electronic Control Unit (ECU)
● ● ○ ● (8 4 1)	Disconnected atmospheric pressure sensor coupler. Shorted or disconnected atmospheric pressure sensor wire. Faulty atmospheric pressure sensor
● ● ● ○ (8 4 2)	Faulty Electronic Control Unit (ECU)
● ● ● ● (8 4 2 1)	Faulty Electronic Control Unit (ECU)

Year – 1986
Model – Accord LXi
Engine – 2.0L (119 cid) 4 cyl
Engine Code – BT

ECM TROUBLE CODES

Code	Explanation
0	Electronic Control Unit (ECU)
1	Oxygen content
3	Manifold Absolute Pressure (MAP)
5	Manifold Absolute Pressure (MAP)
6	Coolant temperature
7	Throttle angle
8	Crank angle (TDC)
9	Crank angle (cyl)
10	Intake air temperature
12	Exhaust Gas Recirculation (EGR) system
13	Atmospheric pressure
2, 4, 11, or +13	Code 2, 4, 11, or exceeds 13, count the number or flashes again. If the indicator is, in fact, flashing these codes, substitute a known-good ECU and re-check. If the indication goes away, replace the original ECU.

Year – 1986
Model – Civic CRX Si
Engine – 1.5L (91 cid) 4 cyl
Engine Code – EW3

ECM TROUBLE CODES

Code	Explanation
○ ○ ○ ○ (Dash Warning Light ON only)	Dash warning light OFF—loose or poorly connected power line to Electronic Control Unit (ECU). Disconnected control unit ground wire. Faulty ECU
○ ○ ○ ○ (Dash warning light on)	Dash warning light ON—disconnected control unit ground wire. Faulty Electronic Control Unit (ECU). Short circuit in combination meter or warning light wire
○ ○ ○ ● 1	Disconnected oxygen sensor coupler. Spark plug misfire. Short or open circuit in oxygen sensor circuit. Faulty oxygen sensor
○ ○ ● ○ 2	Faulty Electronic Control Unit (ECU)
○ ○ ● ● 2 1	Disconnected Manifold Absolute Pressure (MAP) sensor coupler. Short or open circuit in MAP sensor wire. Faulty MAP sensor
○ ● ○ ○ 4	Faulty Electronic Control Unit (ECU)
○ ● ○ ● 4 1	Disconnected Manifold Absolute Pressure (MAP) sensor piping
○ ● ● ○ 4 2	Disconnected Coolant Temperature Sensor (CTS) coupler. Open circuit in coolant temperature sensor wire. Faulty coolant temperature sensor (thermostat housing)
○ ● ● ● 4 2 1	Disconnected throttle angle sensor coupler. Open or short circuit in throttle angle sensor wire. Faulty throttle angle sensor
● ○ ○ ○ 8	Short or open circuit in crank angle sensor wire. Crank angle sensor wire interfering with high tension wire. Faulty crank angle sensor
● ○ ○ ● 8	Short or open circuit in crank angle sensor wire. Crank angle sensor wire interfering with high tension wire. Faulty crank angle sensor
● ○ ● ○ 8 2	Disconnected intake air temperature sensor. Open circuit in intake air temperature sensor wire. Faulty intake air temperature sensor
● ○ ● ● 8 2 1	Disconnected idle mixture adjuster sensor coupler. Shorted or disconnected idle mixture adjuster sensor wire. Faulty idle mixture adjuster sensor
● ● ○ ○ 8 4	Faulty Electronic Control Unit (ECU)
● ● ○ ● 8 4 1	Disconnected atmospheric pressure sensor coupler. Open or short circuit in idle mixture adjuster sensor wire. Faulty atmospheric pressure sensor
● ● ● ○ 8 4 2	Faulty Electronic Control Unit (ECU)
● ● ● ● 8 4 2 1	Faulty Electronic Control Unit (ECU)

Year – 1986
Model – Prelude
Engine – 2.0L (119 cid) 4 cyl
Engine Code – BT

ECM TROUBLE CODES

Code	Explanation
0	Dash warning light OFF—disconnected control unit ground wire. Faulty Electronic Control Unit (ECU). Dash warning light ON—Loose or poorly connected power line to ECU. Disconnected control unit ground wire. Short circuit in combination meter or warning light wire. Faulty ECU
1	Disconnected oxygen sensor coupler. Spark plug misfire. Short or open circuit in oxygen sensor circuit. Faulty oxygen sensor. Faulty fuel system
2	Faulty Electronic Control Unit (ECU)
3	Disconnected Manifold Absolute Pressure (MAP) sensor coupler. Short or open circuit in MAP sensor wire. Faulty MAP sensor
4	Faulty Electronic Control Unit (ECU)
5	Disconnected Manifold Absolute Pressure (MAP) sensor piping
6	Disconnected Coolant Temperature Sensor (CTS) coupler. Open or short circuit in coolant temperature sensor wire. Faulty coolant temperature sensor (thermostat housing)
7	Disconnected throttle angle sensor coupler. Open or short circuit in throttle angle sensor wire. Faulty throttle angle sensor
8	Short or open circuit in crank angle sensor wire. Crank angle sensor wire interfering with spark plug wires. Crank angle sensor fault
9	Short or open circuit in crank angle sensor wire. Crank angle sensor wire interfering with high tension wire. Faulty crank angle sensor
10	Disconnected intake air temperature sensor. Open or short circuit in intake air temperature sensor wire. Faulty intake air temperature sensor
11	Faulty Electronic Control Unit (ECU)
12	Disconnected Exhaust Gas Recirculation (EGR) control system coupler. Shorted or disconnected EGR control wire. Faulty EGR control system
13	Disconnected atmoshperic pressure sensor coupler. Shorted or disconnected atmospheric pressure sensor
13 +	If the number of blinks between 2 second pauses exceeds 13 or if the LED indicator stays ON, the Electronic Control Unit (ECU) is faulty

Year — 1987
Model — Accord LXi
Engine — 2.0L (119 cid) 4 cyl
Engine Code — A20A3

ECM TROUBLE CODES

Code	Explanation
0	Electronic Control Unit (ECU)
1	Oxygen content
3	Manifold Absolute Pressure (MAP)
5	Manifold Absolute Pressure (MAP)
6	Coolant temperature
7	Throttle angle
8	Crank angle (TDC)
9	Crank angle (cyl)
10	Intake air temperature
12	Exhaust Gas Recirculation (EGR) system
13	Atmospheric pressure
2, 4, 11, or +13	Code 2, 4, 11, or exceeds 13, count the number or flashes again. If the indicator is, in fact, flashing these codes, substitute a known-good ECU and re-check. If the indication goes away, replace the original ECU.

Year — 1987
Model — Civic
Engine — 1.5L (91 cid) 4 cyl
Engine Code — D15A3

ECM TROUBLE CODES

Code	Explanation
○ ○ ○ ○ (Dash Warning Light ON only)	Dash warning light OFF — loose or poorly connected power line to Electronic Control Unit (ECU). Disconnected control unit ground wire. Faulty ECU
○ ○ ○ ○ (Dash wasming light on)	Dash warning light ON — disconnected control unit ground wire. Faulty ECU. Short circuit in combination meter or warning light wire
○ ○ ○ ● (1)	Disconnected oxygen sensor coupler. Spark plug misfire. Short or open circuit in oxygen sensor circuit. Faulty oxygen sensor
○ ○ ● ○ (2)	Faulty Electronic Control Unit (ECU)
○ ○ ● ● (2 1)	Disconnected Manifold Absolute Pressure (MAP) sensor connector. Short or open circuit in MAP sensor wire. Faulty MAP sensor
○ ● ○ ○ (4)	Faulty Electronic Control Unit (ECU)
○ ● ○ ● (4 1)	Disconnected Manifold Absolute Pressure (MAP) sensor piping
○ ● ● ○ (4 2)	Disconnected the Temperature Water (TW) sensor connector. Open circuit in TW sensor wire. Faulty TW sensor (thermostat housing)
○ ● ● ● (4 2 1)	Disconnected throttle angle sensor coupler. Open or short circuit in throttle angle sensor wire. Faulty throttle angle sensor
● ○ ○ ○ (8)	Short or open circuit in crank angle sensor wire. Crank angle sensor wire interfering with high tension wire. Faulty crank angle sensor
● ○ ○ ● (8)	Short or open circuit in crank angle sensor wire. Crank angle sensor wire interfering with high tension wire. Faulty crank angle sensor
● ○ ● ○ (8 2)	Disconnected Temperature Air (TA) sensor connector. Open circuit in TA sensor wire. Faulty TA sensor
● ○ ● ● (8 2 1)	Disconnected Idle Mixture Adjuster (IMA) sensor connector. Shorted or disconnected IMA sensor wire. Faulty IMA sensor
● ● ○ ○ (8 4)	Faulty Electronic Control Unit (ECU)
● ● ○ ● (8 4 1)	Disconnected Pressure Atmospheric (PA) sensor connector. Open or short circuit in PA sensor wire. Faulty PA sensor
● ● ● ○ (8 4 2)	Faulty Electronic Control Unit (ECU)
● ● ● ● (8 4 2 1)	Faulty Electronic Control Unit (ECU)

Year — 1987
Model — Civic CRX Si
Engine — 1.5L (91 cid)
Engine Code — D15A3

ECM TROUBLE CODES

Code	Explanation
8 4 2 1 ○ ○ ○ ●	Short circuit in frequency solenoid valve B (brown/black) wire
8 4 2 1 ○ ○ ● ○	Short circuit in frequency solenoid valve A (green/white) wire
8 4 2 1 ○ ○ ● ●	Disconnected Manifold Absolute Pressure (MAP) sensor connector. Short or open circuit in MAP sensor (black/white, green/white, yellow/white) wires. Faulty MAP sensor
8 4 2 1 ○ ● ○ ○	Short circuit in ignition timing control unit (red/white, blue/white) wires. Faulty ignition timing control unit
8 4 2 1 ○ ● ● ○	Disconnected Coolant Temperature Sensor (CTS) A connector. Short or open circuit in coolant temperature sensor A (light blue) wire. Faulty coolant temperature sensor A
8 4 2 1 ● ○ ○ ○	Short or open circuit in ignition coil (blue) wire
8 4 2 1 ● ● ○ ○	Disconnected Exhaust Gas Recirculation (EGR) lift sensor connector. Short or open circuit in EGR lift sensor (yellow, green/white, yellow/white) wires. Faulty EGR lift sensor
8 4 2 1 ● ● ○ ●	Disconnected atmospheric pressure sensor connector. Short or open circuit in atmospheric pressure sensor (green/black, green/white, yellow/white) wires. Faulty atmospheric pressure sensor
15 +	If the LED display pattern differs from those listed above, the Electronic Control Unit (ECU) is faulty

Year – 1987
Model – Prelude
Engine – 2.0L (119 cid) 4 cyl
Engine Code – A20A3

ECM TROUBLE CODES

Code	Explanation
0	Dash warning light OFF – disconnected control unit ground wire. Faulty Electronic Control Unit (ECU). Dash warning light ON – Loose or poorly connected power line to ECU. Disconnected control unit ground wire. Short circuit in combination meter or warning light wire. Faulty ECU
1	Disconnected oxygen sensor connector. Spark plug misfire. Short or open circuit in Manifold Absolute Pressure (MAP) sensor wire. Faulty oxygen sensor. Faulty fuel system
2	Faulty Electronic Control Unit (ECU)
3	Disconnected Manifold Absolute Pressure (MAP) sensor coupler. Short or open circuit in MAP sensor wire. Faulty MAP sensor
4	Faulty Electronic Control Unit (ECU)
5	Disconnected Manifold Absolute Pressure (MAP) sensor piping
6	Disconnected the Temperature Water (TW) sensor connector. Open or short circuit in TW sensor wire. Faulty TW sensor (thermostat housing)
7	Disconnected throttle angle sensor coupler. Open or short circuit in throttle angle sensor wire. Faulty throttle angle sensor
8	Short or open circuit in crank angle sensor wire. Crank angle sensor wire interfering with spark plug wires. Crank angle sensor fault
9	Short or open circuit in crank angle sensor wire. Crank angle sensor wire interfering with high tension wire. Faulty crank angle sensor
10	Disconnected Temperature Air (TA) sensor connector. Open or short circuit in TA sensor wire. Faulty TA sensor
11	Faulty Electronic Control Unit (ECU)
12	Disconnected Exhaust Gas Recirculation (EGR) control system connector. Shorted or disconnected EGR control wire. Faulty EGR control system
13	Disconnected Pressure, Atmospheric (PA) sensor connector. Shorted or disconnected PA sensor wire. Faulty PA sensor
13+	If the number of blinks between 2 second pauses exceeds 13 or if the LED indicator stays ON, the Electronic Control Unit (ECU) is faulty

Year — 1988
Model — Accord
Engine — 2.0L (119 cid) 4 cyl
Engine Code — A20A3

ECM TROUBLE CODES

Code	Explanation
0	Electronic Control Unit (ECU)
1	Oxygen content A
2	Oxygen content B
3	Manifold Absolute Pressure (MAP)
5	Manifold Absolute Pressure (MAP)
6	Coolant temperature
7	Throttle angle
8	Crank angle (TDC)
9	Crank angle (cyl)
10	Intake air temperature
12	Exhaust Gas Recirculation (EGR) system
13	Atmospheric pressure
14	Electronic idle control
2, 4, 11, or +14	Code 2, 4, 11, or exceeds 14, count the number or flashes again. If the indicator is, in fact, flashing these codes, substitute a known-good ECU and re-check. If the indication goes away, replace the original ECU.

Year — 1988
Model — Civic CRX Si
Engine — 1.6L (97 cid) 4 cyl
Engine Code — D16A6

ECM TROUBLE CODES

Code	Explanation
0	Electronic Control Unit (ECU)
1	Oxygen content
3	Manifold Absolute Pressure (MAP)
5	Manifold Absolute Pressure (MAP)
4	Crank angle
6	Coolant temperature
7	Throttle angle
8	Top Dead Center (TDC) position
9	Number 1 cylinder position
10	Intake air temperature
13	Atmospheric pressure
14	Electronic air control
15	Ignition output signal
16	Fuel injector
17	Vehicle Speed Sensor (VSS)
19	Lock-up control solenoid valve
20	Electric load
20 +	If codes other than those listed above are indicated, count the number of blinks again. If the indicator is in fact blinking these codes, substitute a known-good ECU and recheck. If the indication goes away, replace the original ECU

Year — 1988
Model — Prelude
Engine — 2.0L (119 cid) 4 cyl
Engine Code — A20A3

ECM TROUBLE CODES

Code	Explanation
0	Electronic Control Unit (ECU)
1	Oxygen content — A
2	Oxygen content — B
3	Manifold Absolute Pressure (MAP)
5	Manifold Absolute Pressure (MAP)
4	Crank angle
6	Coolant temperature
7	Throttle angle
8	Top Dead Center (TDC) position
9	Number 1 cylinder position
10	Intake air temperature
12	Exhaust Gas Recirculation (EGR) system
13	Atmospheric pressure
14	Electronic idle control
15	Ignition output signal
16	Fuel injector
17	Vehicle Speed Sensor (VSS)
11 or 17 +	If Code 11 or more than 17 appears, count the number of blinks again. If the indicaor is in fact blinking these codes, substitute a known-good ECU and recheck. If the indication goes away, replace the original ECU

Year — 1988
Model — Civic
Engine — 1.5L (91 cid) 4 cyl
Engine Code — D15B2

ECM TROUBLE CODES

Code	Explanation
0	Electronic Control Unit (ECU)
1	Oxygen content
3	Manifold Absolute Pressure (MAP)
5	Manifold Absolute Pressure (MAP)
4	Crank angle
6	Coolant temperature
7	Throttle angle
8	Top Dead Center (TDC) position
10	Intake air temperature
13	Atmospheric pressure
14	Electronic air control
15	Ignition output signal
16	Fuel injector
17	Vehicle Speed Sensor (VSS)
19	Lock-up control solenoid valve
20	Electric load
20 +	If codes other than those listed above are indicated, count the number of blinks again. If the indicator is in fact blinking these codes, substitute a known-good ECU and recheck. If the indication goes away, replace the original ECU

Year — 1989
Model — Accord
Engine — 2.0L (119 cid) 4 cyl
Engine Code — A20A3

ECM TROUBLE CODES

Code	Explanation
0	Electronic Control Unit (ECU)
1	Oxygen content A
2	Oxygen content B
3	Manifold Absolute Pressure (MAP)
5	Manifold Absolute Pressure (MAP)
6	Coolant temperature
7	Throttle angle
8	Crank angle (TDC)
9	Crank angle (cyl)
10	Intake air temperature
12	Exhaust Gas Recirculation (EGR) system
13	Atmospheric pressure
14	Electronic idle control
17	Vehicle Speed Sensor (VSS)
4, 11, 15, 16 or +17	Code 4, 11, 15, 16 or exceeds 17, count the number or flashes again. If the indicator is, in fact, flashing these codes, substitute a known-good ECU and re-check. If the indication goes away, replace the original ECU.

Year — 1989
Model — Prelude
Engine — 2.0L (119 cid) 4 cyl
Engine Code — B20A5

ECM TROUBLE CODES

Code	Explanation
0	Electronic Control Unit (ECU)
1	Oxygen content — A
2	Oxygen content — B
3	Manifold Absolute Pressure (MAP)
5	Manifold Absolute Pressure (MAP)
4	Crank angle
6	Coolant temperature
7	Throttle angle
8	Top Dead Center (TDC) position
9	Number 1 cylinder position
10	Intake air temperature
12	Exhaust Gas Recirculation (EGR) system
13	Atmospheric pressure
14	Electronic idle control
15	Ignition output signal
16	Fuel injector
17	Vehicle Speed Sensor (VSS)
11 or 17 +	If code 11 or more than 17 appears, count the number of blinks. If the indicator is in fact blinking these codes, substitute a jnown-good ECU and recheck. If the indication goes away, replect the original Electronic Control Unit (ECU)

Year—1989
Model—Civic CRX Si
Engine—1.6L (97 cid) 4 cyl
Engine Code—D16A6

ECM TROUBLE CODES

Code	Explanation
0	Electronic Control Unit (ECU)
1	Oxygen content
3	Manifold Absolute Pressure (MAP)
5	Manifold Absolute Pressure (MAP)
4	Crank angle
6	Coolant temperature
7	Throttle angle
8	Top Dead Center (TDC) position
9	Number 1 cylinder position
10	Intake air temperature
12	Exhaust Gas Recirculation (EGR) system
13	Atmospheric pressure
14	Electronic air control
15	Ignition output signal
16	Fuel injector
17	Vehicle Speed Sensor (VSS)
19	Lock-up control solenoid valve
20	Electric load
20 +	If codes other than those listed above are indicated, count the number of blinks again. If the indicator is in fact blinking these codes, substitute a known-good ECU and recheck. If the indication goes away, replace the original ECU

Year – 1989
Model – Civic and Civic Wagon
Engine – 1.6L (97 cid) 4 cyl
Engine Code – D16A6

ECM TROUBLE CODES

Code	Explanation
0	Electronic Control Unit (ECU)
1	Oxygen content
3	Manifold Absolute Pressure (MAP)
5	Manifold Absolute Pressure (MAP)
4	Crank angle
6	Coolant temperature
7	Throttle angle
8	Top Dead Center (TDC) position
9	Number 1 cylinder position
10	Intake air temperature
12	Exhaust Gas Recirculation (EGR) system
13	Atmospheric pressure
14	Electronic air control
15	Ignition output signal
16	Fuel injector
17	Vehicle Speed Sensor (VSS)
19	Lock-up control solenoid valve
20	Electric load
20+	If codes other than those listed above are indicated, count the number of blinks again. If the indicator is in fact blinking these codes, substitute a known-good ECU and recheck. If the indication goes away, replace the original ECU

Year — 1989
Model — Civic, Civic Wagon and Civic CRX
Engine — 1.5L (91 cid) 4 cyl
Engine Code — D15B2

ECM TROUBLE CODES

Code	Explanation
0	Electronic Control Unit (ECU)
1	Oxygen content
3	Manifold Absolute Pressure (MAP)
5	Manifold Absolute Pressure (MAP)
4	Crank angle
6	Coolant temperature
7	Throttle angle
8	Top Dead Center (TDC) position
9	Number 1 cylinder position
10	Intake air temperature
12	Exhaust Gas Recirculation (EGR) system
13	Atmospheric pressure
14	Electronic air control
15	Ignition output signal
16	Fuel injector
17	Vehicle Speed Sensor (VSS)
19	Lock-up control solenoid valve
20	Electric load
20 +	If codes other than those listed above are indicated, count the number of blinks again. If the indicator is in fact blinking these codes, substitute a known-good ECU and recheck. If the indication goes away, replace the original ECU

Year—1989
Model—Civic
Engine—1.5L (91 cid) 4 cyl
Engine Code—D15B1

ECM TROUBLE CODES

Code	Explanation
0	Electronic Control Unit (ECU)
1	Oxygen content
3	Manifold Absolute Pressure (MAP)
5	Manifold Absolute Pressure (MAP)
4	Crank angle
6	Coolant temperature
7	Throttle angle
8	Top Dead Center (TDC) position
9	Number 1 cylinder position
10	Intake air temperature
12	Exhaust Gas Recirculation (EGR) system
13	Atmospheric pressure
14	Electronic air control
15	Ignition output signal
16	Fuel injector
17	Vehicle Speed Sensor (VSS)
19	Lock-up control solenoid valve
20	Electric load
20+	If codes other than those listed above are indicated, count the number of blinks again. If the indicator is in fact blinking these codes, substitute a known-good ECU and recheck. If the indication goes away, replace the original ECU

Year — 1989
Model — Civic CRX HF
Engine — 1.5L (91 cid) 4 cyl
Engine Code — D15B6

ECM TROUBLE CODES

Code	Explanation
0	Electronic Control Unit (ECU)
1	Oxygen content
3	Manifold Absolute Pressure (MAP)
5	Manifold Absolute Pressure (MAP)
4	Crank angle
6	Coolant temperature
7	Throttle angle
8	Top Dead Center (TDC) position
9	Number 1 cylinder position
10	Intake air temperature
12	Exhaust Gas Recirculation (EGR) system
13	Atmospheric pressure
14	Electronic air control
15	Ignition output signal
16	Fuel injector
17	Vehicle Speed Sensor (VSS)
19	Lock-up control solenoid valve
20	Electric load
20 +	If codes other than those listed above are indicated, count the number of blinks again. If the indicator is in fact blinking these codes, substitute a known-good ECU and recheck. If the indication goes away, replace the original ECU.

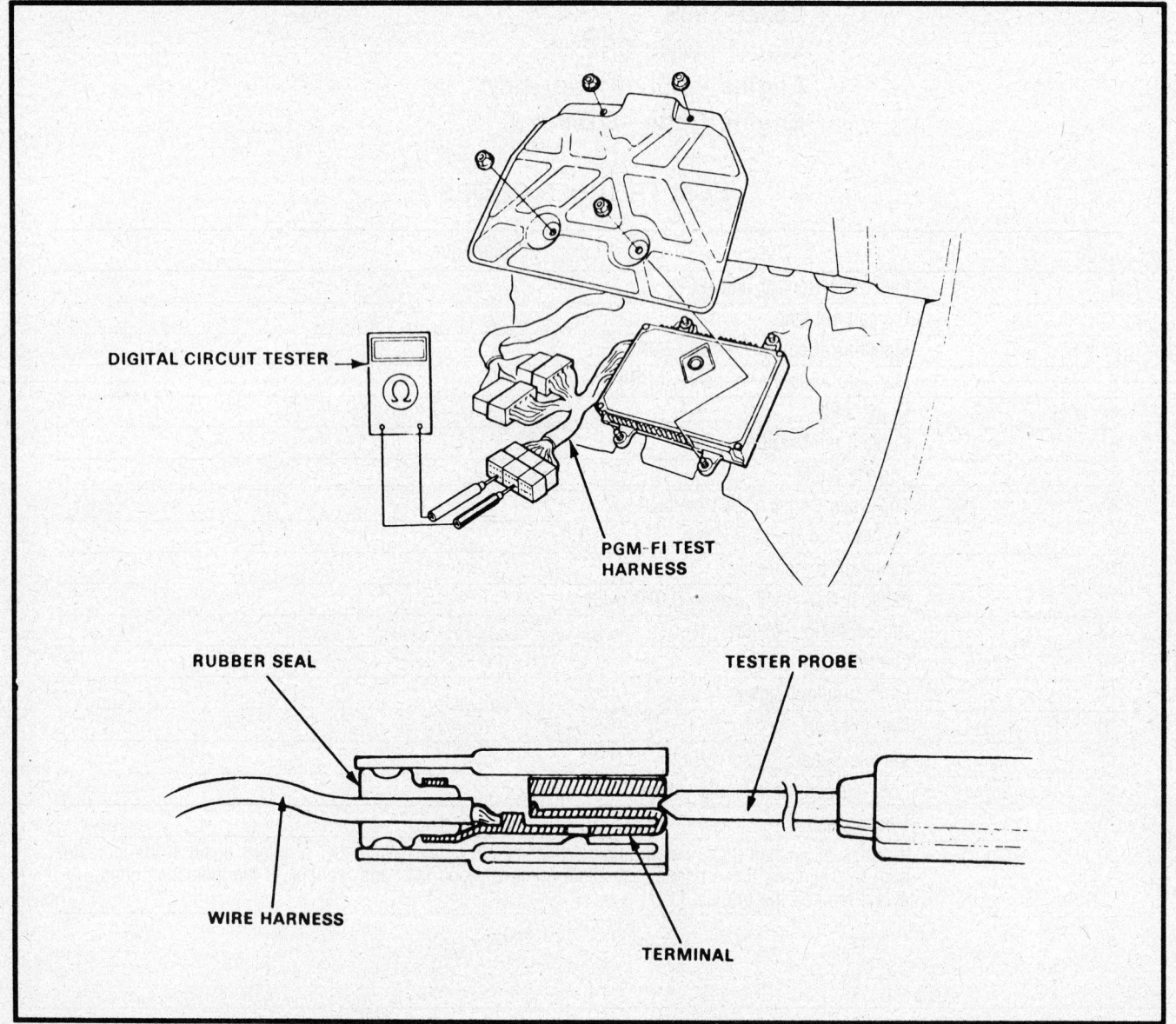

DIGITAL CIRCUIT TESTER

PGM-FI TEST
HARNESS

RUBBER SEAL

TESTER PROBE

WIRE HARNESS

TERMINAL

Diagnostic tester connection location

INDEX

ISUZU

Electronic Control System

SELF-DIAGNOSTIC SYSTEM

Description

Many Isuzu models have a self-diagnostic function as part of the Fuel Injection and Emission Control systems. The system consists of sensors and actuators connected to the Electronic Control Module (ECM). The sensors send voltage signals to the ECM, where the values are measured in order to maximize engine power and minimize exhaust emissions. When the ECM detects a malfunction, the "Check Engine" lamp, in the instrument cluster, is energized and a trouble code will be stored in the ECM trouble code memory. The lamp will remain ON with the engine running as long as there is a problem. If the malfunction is intermittent, the "Check Engine" lamp will turn OFF but the trouble code will remain stored in the ECM trouble code memory. With the ignition switch ON, engine not running, the "Check Engine" lamp should turn ON; this functions as a bulb check.

Entering Diagnostic Mode

The trouble code system is actuated by connecting a diagnostic lead to ground. The location of the diagnostic lead differs from model-to-model and, in some cases, from year-to-year within the same model.

I-Mark RWD models for 1982–85 — the trouble code test leads are usually taped to the wiring harness under the instrument panel, at the right side of the steering column and just above the accelerator pedal.

I-Mark FWD models for 1985–89 — a 3 terminal connector, also known as the Assembly Line Diagnostic Link (ALDL) or Assembly Line Communications Link (ALCL) is located near the ECM connector. Connect a jumper wire between terminals A and C.

Impulse for 1983–89 — connect diagnostic lead terminals together (one male, one female). Terminals are located under dash near the top of the driver's side kick panel.

Trooper II for 1985 — connect the diagnostic lead terminals together (one male, one female). The terminals are located under dash, on the passenger's side, behind the radio. The terminal leads for 1986–87 models are located near the ALDL connector, under dash on driver's side behind cigarette lighter. The terminal leads for 1988–89 models are located near the ECM, on center console, under the storage compartment.

Pick-Up for 1982–89 and Amigo for 1989 — connect the diagnostic lead terminals together (one male, one female). The terminals are branched from harness near the ECM, under dash on driver's side, behind hood release.

Reading Diagnostic Codes

The trouble code is determined by counting the flashes of the "Check Engine" lamp. Trouble Code 12 will flash first, indicating that the self-diagnostic system is working. Code 12 consists of 1 flash, a short pause, then 2 flashes. There will be a longer pause and Code 12 will repeat 2 more times. Each code flashes 3 times. The cycle will then repeat itself until the engine is started or the ignition is turned OFF. In most cases, the codes will be checked with the engine running since no codes other than 12 or 51 will be present on initial key ON.

Clearing Diagnostic Memory

The trouble code memory is fed a continuous 12V even with the key turned OFF. After a fault has been corrected, it will be necessary to remove this voltage for 10 seconds to clear any stored codes. Voltage can be removed by disconnecting the 14 pin ECM connector or by removing the fuse marked "ECM" or fuse No. 4 on some models. Since all memory will be lost when removing the fuse, it will be necessary to reset the clock and other electrical equipment.

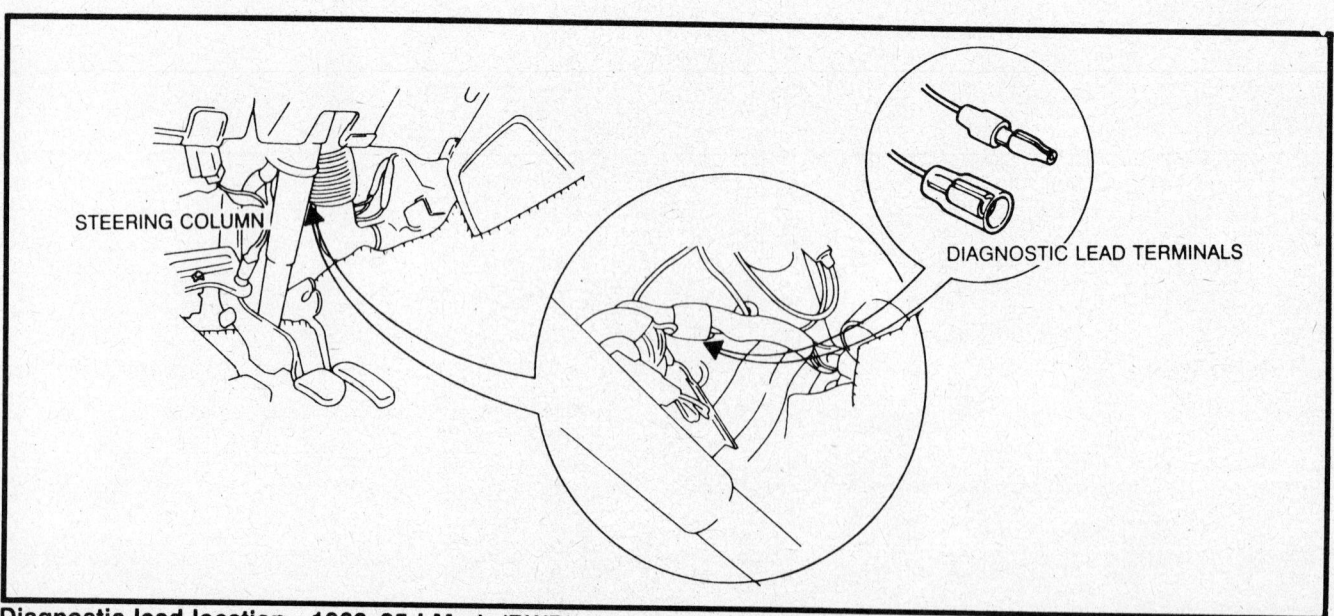

STEERING COLUMN

DIAGNOSTIC LEAD TERMINALS

Diagnostic lead location – 1982–85 I-Mark (RWD)

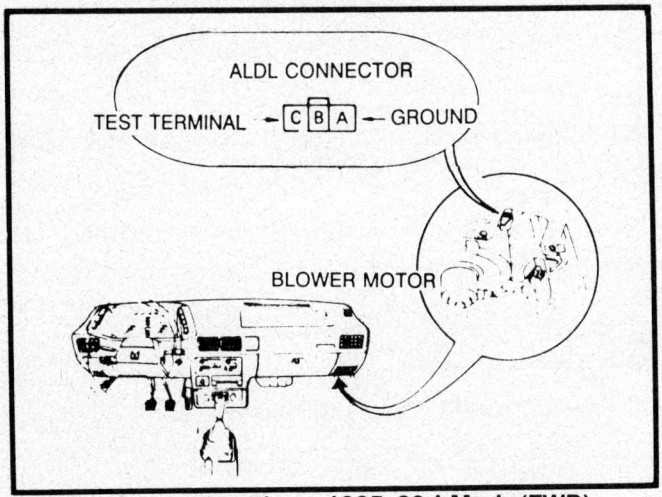

Diagnostic lead location—1985–89 I-Mark (FWD)

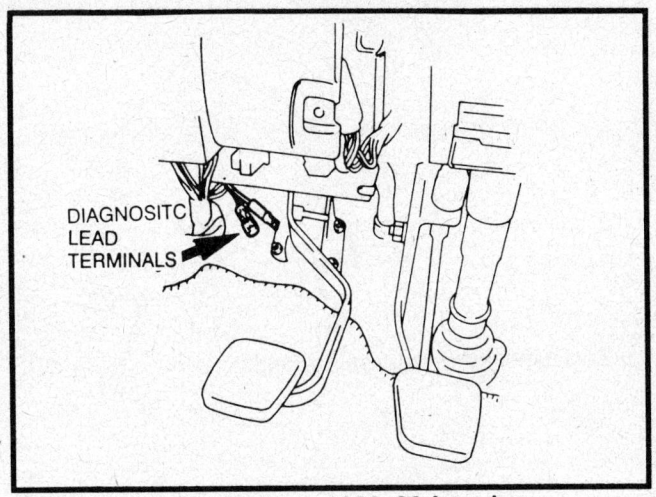

Diagnostic lead location—1983–89 Impulse

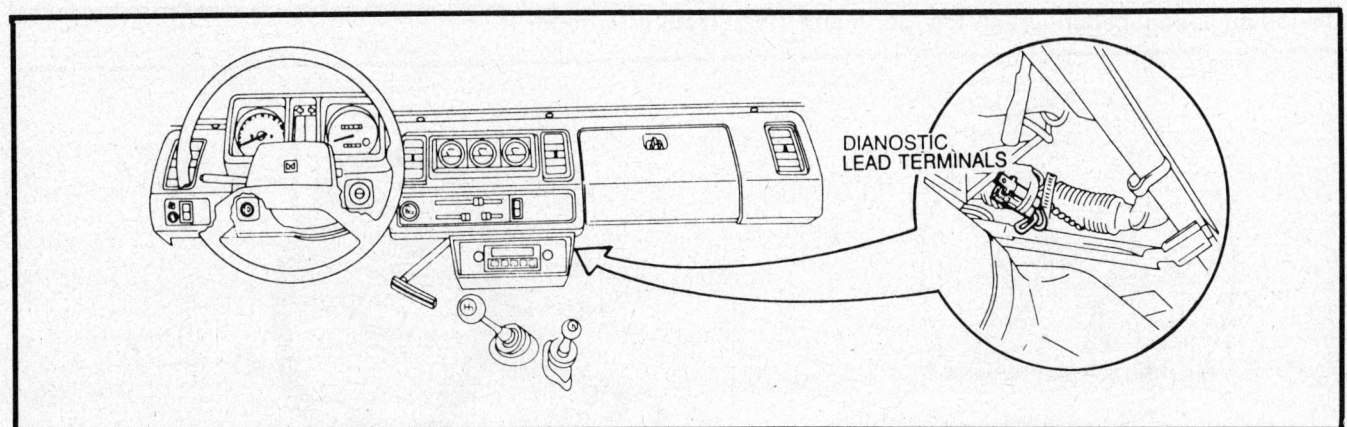

Diagnostic lead location—1985 Trooper II

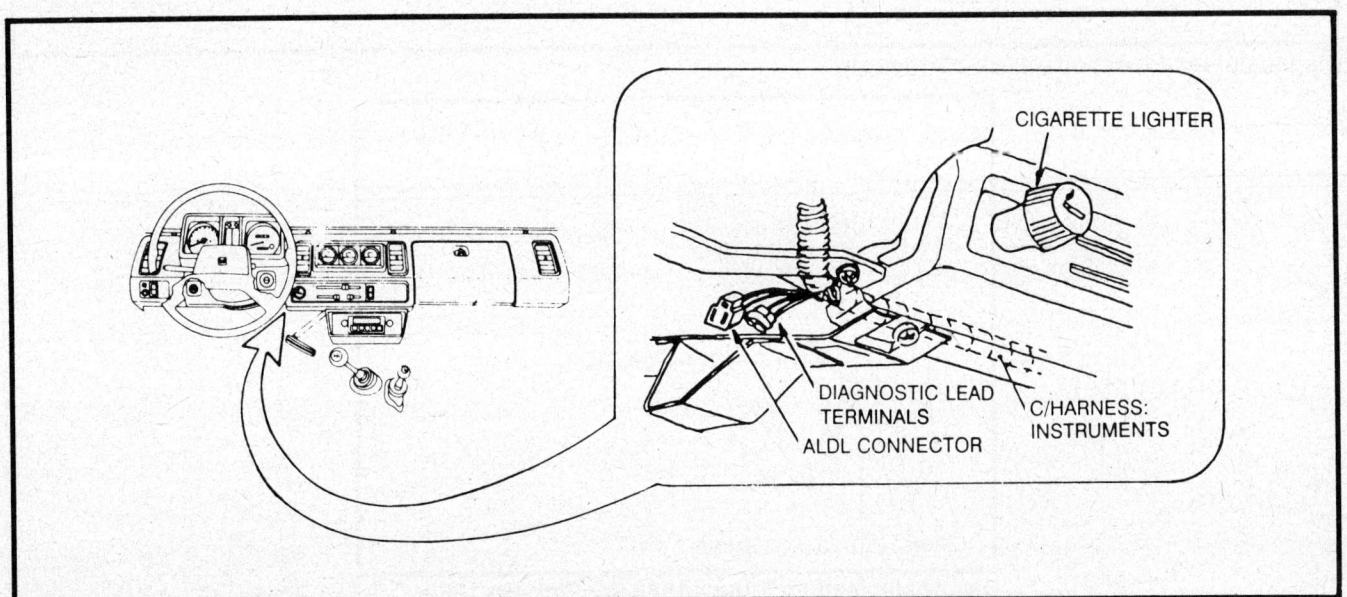

Diagnostic lead location—1986–87 Trooper II

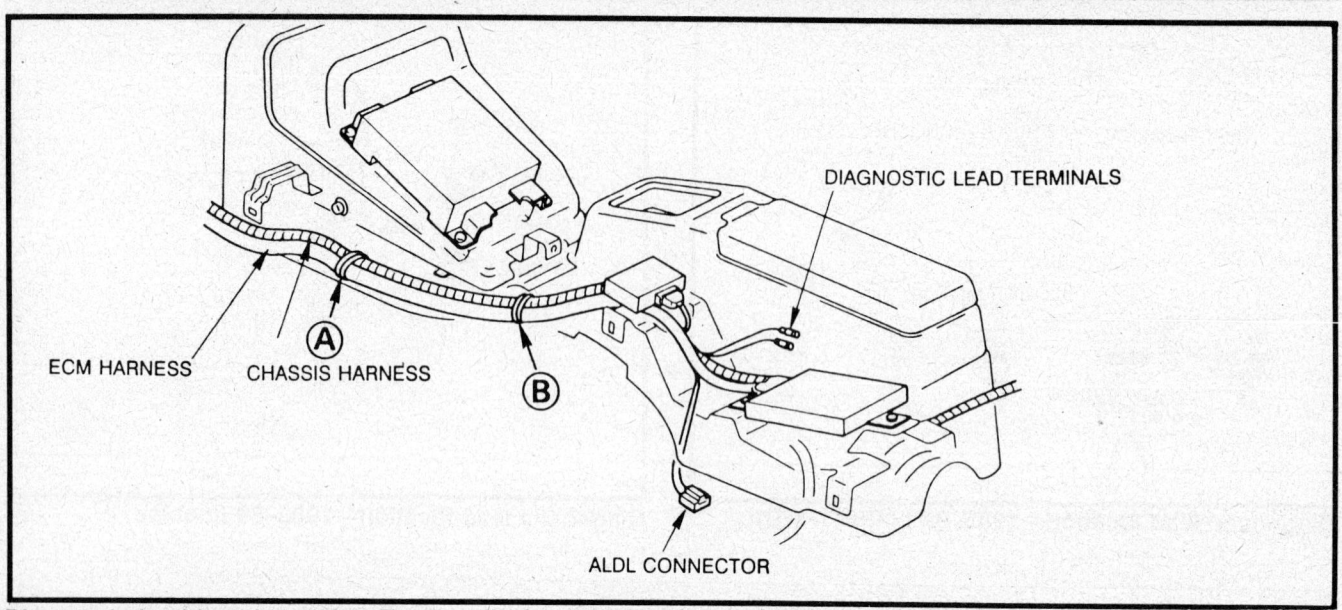

Diagnostic lead location—1988 Trooper II and 1989 Trooper/Trooper II

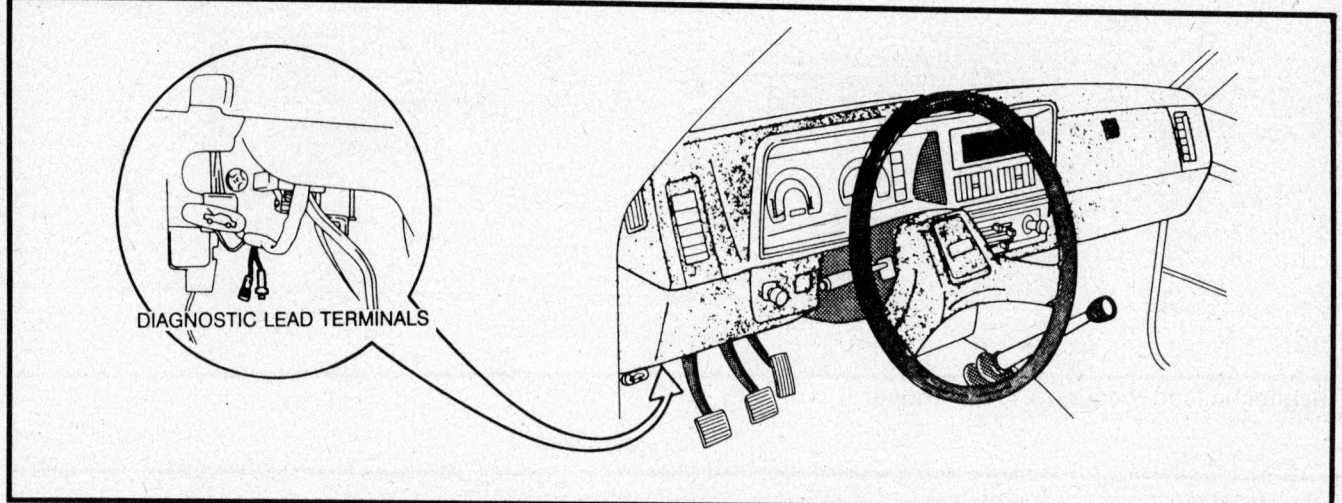

Diagnositc lead location—1982–87 Pick-Up

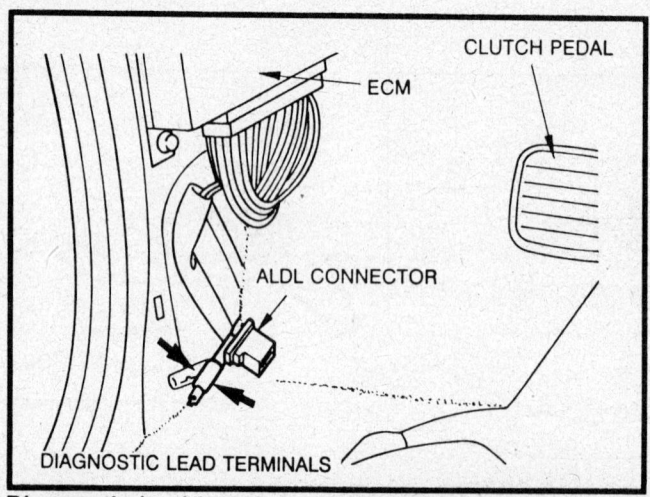

Diagnostic lead location—1988–89 Pick-Up/1989 Amigo

ISUZU

Year – 1982
Model – I-Mark
Engine – 1.8L (111 cid) 4 cyl
Engine Code – G180Z

ECM TROUBLE CODES

Code	Explanation
12	Idle switch is not turned ON
13	Idle switch is not turned OFF
14	Wide Open Throttle (WOT) switch is not turned ON
15	Wide Open Throttle (WOT) switch is not turned OFF
21	Output transistor is not turned ON
22	Output transistor is not turned OFF
23	Abnormal oxygen sensor
24	Abnormal Water Temperature Sensor (WTS) switch
25	Abnormal Random Access Memory (RAM)
12,13,14 & 15	"Check Engine" lamp not ON
21,22,23,24 & 25	"Check Engine" lamp ON

Year — 1983
Model — I-Mark
Engine — 1.8L (111 cid) 4 cyl
Engine Code — G180Z

ECM TROUBLE CODES

Code	Explanation
12	Idle switch is not turned ON
13	Idle switch is not turned OFF
14	Wide Open Throttle (WOT) switch is not turned ON
15	Wide Open Throttle (WOT) switch is not turned OFF
21	Output transistor is not turned ON
22	Output transistor is not turned OFF
23	Abnormal oxygen sensor
24	Abnormal Water Temperature Sensor (WTS) switch
25	Abnormal Random Access Memory (RAM)
12,13,14 & 15	''Check Engine'' lamp not ON
21,22,23,24 & 25	''Check Engine'' lamp ON

Year — 1983
Model — Impulse
Engine — 2.0L (119 cid) 4 cyl
Engine Code — G200Z

ECM TROUBLE CODES

Code	Explanation
12	No distributor pulses to the Electronic Control Module (ECM) and will only flash while fault is present — no fault indicated
13	Oxygen sensor system — harness open, sensor deterioration
14	Water Temperature Sensor (WTS) system grounded
15	Water Temperature Sensor (WTS) system — incorrect signal
16	Water Temperature Sensor (WTS) system — harness open
21	Throttle Valve Switch (TVS) system — idle contact and full contact make simultaneously
22	Starter signal system — no signal input
23	Ignition power transistor system — output terminal grounded
25	Vacuum Switching Valve (VSV) system — output terminal grounded or open
33	Fuel injector system — output terminal grounded or open
35	Ignition power transistor system — harness open
41	Crank Angle Sensor (CAS) system — no signal or faulty signal input
43	Throttle Valve Switch (TVS) system — idle contact closed continuously
44	Oxygen sensor system — lean signal — low voltage
45	Oxygen sensor system — rich signal — high voltage
51	Faulty Electronic Control Module (ECM)
52	Faulty Electronic Control Module (ECM)
53	Vacuum Switching Valve (VSV) system — grounded or defective power transistor
54	Ignition power transistor system — grounded or defective power transistor
55	Faulty Electronic Control Module (ECM)
61	Air Flow Sensor (AFS) system — grounded, shorted, open or broken "Hot" wire
62	Air Flow Sensor (AFS) system — broken "Cold" wire
63	Vehicle Speed Sensor (VSS) — no signal input
64	Fuel injector system — grounded or defective transistor
65	Throttle Valve Switch (TVS) system — full contact closed continuously
66	Knock sensor system — harness grounded or open

Year — 1984
Model — I-Mark
Engine — 1.8L (111 cid) 4 cyl
Engine Code — G180Z

ECM TROUBLE CODES

Code	Explanation
12	Idle switch is not turned ON
13	Idle switch is not turned OFF
14	Wide Open Throttle (WOT) switch is not turned ON
15	Wide Open Throttle (WOT) switch is not turned OFF
21	Output transistor is not turned ON
22	Output transistor is not turned OFF
23	Abnormal oxygen sensor
24	Abnormal Water Temperature Sensor (WTS) switch
25	Abnormal Random Access Memory (RAM)
12, 13, 14 and 15	"Check Engine" lamp not ON
21, 22, 23, 24 and 25	"Check Engine" lamp ON

Year — 1984
Model — Impulse
Engine — 1.9L (119 cid) 4 cyl
Engine Code — G200Z

ECM TROUBLE CODES

Code	Explanation
12	No distributor pulses to the Electronic Control Module (ECM) and will only flash while fault is present — no fault indicated
13	Oxygen sensor system — harness open, sensor deterioration
14	Water Temperature Sensor (WTS) system grounded
15	Water Temperature Sensor (WTS) system — incorrect signal
16	Water Temperature Sensor (WTS) system — harness open
21	Throttle Valve Switch (TVS) system — idle contact and full contact make simultaneously
22	Starter signal system — no signal input
23	Ignition power transistor system — output terminal grounded
25	Vacuum Switching Valve (VSV) system — output terminal grounded or open
33	Fuel injector system — output terminal grounded or open
35	Ignition power transistor system — harness open
41	Crank Angle Sensor (CAS) system — no signal or faulty signal input
43	Throttle Valve Switch (TVS) system — idle contact closed continuously
44	Oxygen sensor system — lean signal — low voltage
45	Oxygen sensor system — rich signal — high voltage
51	Faulty Electronic Control Module (ECM)
52	Faulty Electronic Control Module (ECM)
53	Vacuum Switching Valve (VSV) system — grounded or defective power transistor
54	Ignition power transistor system — grounded or defective power transistor
55	Faulty Electronic Control Module (ECM)
61	Air Flow Sensor (AFS) system — grounded, shorted, open or broken "Hot" wire
62	Air Flow Sensor (AFS) system — broken "Cold" wire
63	Vehicle Speed Sensor (VSS) — no signal input
64	Fuel injector system — grounded or defective transistor
65	Throttle Valve Switch (TVS) system — full contact closed continuously
66	Knock sensor system — harness grounded or open

Year – 1985
Model – I-Mark
Engine – 1.5L (90 cid) 4 cyl
Engine Code – 4XC1-U

ECM TROUBLE CODES

Code	Explanation
12	No distributor reference pulses to the Electronic Control Module (ECM) and will only flash while the fault is present
13	Oxygen sensor circuit — the engine must run up to 2 minutes at part throttle, under load, before this code will set
14	Shorted Coolant Temperature Sensor (CTS) circuit — the engine must run up to 2 minutes before this code will set
15	Open Coolant Temperature Sensor (CTS) circuit — the engine must run up to 5 minutes before this code will set
21	Idle switch improperly adjusted and/or circuit open. This code will set if the engine speed falls below 600 rpm for longer than 32 seconds. This code will set if TPS and idle switch are faulty or misadjusted
22	Fuel cut-off relay and/or circuit open
23	Open or grounded Mixture Control (M/C) solenoid circuit
42	Fuel cut-off relay and/or circuit shorted
44	Lean oxygen sensor indication — the engine must run for at least 2 minutes at part throttle, under load, before this code will set. Code will not set when coolant temperature is below 70°C. Code will not set when air cleaner air temperature is below 0°C — "low altitude" condition. Code will not set in "high altitude" condition.
45	Rich system indication — the engine must run for at least 2 minutes at part throttle, under load, before this code will set. Code will not set when the engine is not between 1500–2500 rpm and/or the coolant temperature is below 70°C and/or in "high altitude" condition
51	Faulty calibration unit (PROM) or installation. It takes up to 30 seconds before this code will set
54	Shorted Mixture Control (M/C) solenoid circuit and/or faulty Electronic Control Module (ECM)
55	Faulty Electronic Control Module (ECM) — problem with ECM A/D converter in ECM

Year — 1985
Model — Impulse
Engine — 1.9L (119 cid) 4 cyl
Engine Code — G200Z

ECM TROUBLE CODES

Code	Explanation
12	No distributor pulses to the Electronic Control Module (ECM) and will only flash while fault is present — no fault indicated
13	Oxygen sensor system — harness open, sensor deterioration
14	Water Temperature Sensor (WTS) system grounded
15	Water Temperature Sensor (WTS) system — incorrect signal
16	Water Temperature Sensor (WTS) system — harness open
21	Throttle Valve Switch (TVS) system — idle contact and full contact make simultaneously
22	Starter signal system — no signal input
23	Ignition power transistor system — output terminal grounded
25	Vacuum Switching Valve (VSV) system — output terminal grounded or open
33	Fuel injector system — output terminal grounded or open
35	Ignition power transistor system — harness open
41	Crank Angle Sensor (CAS) system — no signal or faulty signal input
43	Throttle Valve Switch (TVS) system — idle contact closed continuously
44	Oxygen sensor system — lean signal — low voltage
45	Oxygen sensor system — rich signal — high voltage
51	Faulty Electronic Control Module (ECM)
52	Faulty Electronic Control Module (ECM)
53	Vacuum Switching Valve (VSV) system — grounded or defective power transistor
54	Ignition power transistor system — grounded or defective power transistor
55	Faulty Electronic Control Module (ECM)
61	Air Flow Sensor (AFS) system — grounded, shorted, open or broken "Hot" wire
62	Air Flow Sensor (AFS) system — broken "Cold" wire
63	Vehicle Speed Sensor (VSS) — no signal input
64	Fuel injector system — grounded or defective transistor
65	Throttle Valve Switch (TVS) system — full contact closed continuously
66	Knock sensor system — harness grounded or open

Year – 1985
Model – Impulse
Engine – 2.0L (122 cid) Turbo 4 cyl
Engine Code – 4ZC1-T

ECM TROUBLE CODES

Code	Explanation
12	No distributor pulses to the Electronic Control Module (ECM) and will only flash while fault is present – no fault indicated
13	Oxygen sensor system – harness open, sensor deterioration
14	Water Temperature Sensor (WTS) system grounded
15	Water Temperature Sensor (WTS) system – incorrect signal
16	Water Temperature Sensor (WTS) system – harness open
21	Throttle Valve Switch (TVS) system – idle contact and full contact make simultaneously
22	Starter signal system – no signal input
23	Ignition power transistor system – output terminal grounded
25	Vacuum Switching Valve (VSV) system – output terminal grounded or open
33	Fuel injector system – output terminal grounded or open
35	Ignition power transistor system – harness open
41	Crank Angle Sensor (CAS) system – no signal or faulty signal input
43	Throttle Valve Switch (TVS) system – idle contact closed continuously
44	Oxygen sensor system – lean signal – low voltage
45	Oxygen sensor system – rich signal – high voltage
51	Faulty Electronic Control Module (ECM)
52	Faulty Electronic Control Module (ECM)
53	Vacuum Switching Valve (VSV) system – grounded or defective power transistor
54	Ignition power transistor system – grounded or defective power transistor
55	Faulty Electronic Control Module (ECM)
61	Air Flow Sensor (AFS) system – grounded, shorted, open or broken "Hot" wire
62	Air Flow Sensor (AFS) system – broken "Cold" wire
63	Vehicle Speed Sensor (VSS) – no signal input
64	Fuel injector system – grounded or defective transistor
65	Throttle Valve Switch (TVS) system – full contact closed continuously
66	Knock sensor system – harness grounded or open
71	Throttle Position Sensor (TPS) – turbo control system – abnormal signal
72	Exhaust Gas Recirculation (EGR) – Vacuum Switching Valve (VSV) – output terminal grounded or open
73	Exhaust Gas Recirculation (EGR) – Vacuum Switching Valve (VSV) – defective transistor or grounding system

Year – 1986
Model – I-Mark
Engine – 1.5L (90 cid) 4 cyl
Engine Code – 4XC1-U

ECM TROUBLE CODES

Code	Explanation
12	No distributor reference pulses to the Electronic Control Module (ECM) and will only flash while the fault is present
13	Oxygen sensor circuit—the engine must run up to 2 minutes at part throttle, under load, before this code will set
14	Shorted Coolant Temperature Sensor (CTS) circuit—the engine must run up to 2 minutes before this code will set
15	Open Coolant Temperature Sensor (CTS) circuit—the engine must run up to 5 minutes before this code will set
21	Idle switch improperly adjusted and/or circuit open. This code will set if the engine speed falls below 600 rpm for longer than 32 seconds. This code will set if Throttle Position Sensor (TPS) and idle switch are faulty or misadjusted
22	Fuel cut-off relay and/or circuit open
23	Open or grounded Mixture Control (M/C) solenoid circuit
42	Fuel cut-off relay and/or circuit shorted
44	Lean oxygen sensor indication—the engine must run for at least 2 minutes at part throttle, under load, before this code will set. Code will not set when coolant temperature is below 70°C. Code will not set when air cleaner air temperature is below 0°C—"low altitude" condition. Code will not set in "high altitude" condition
45	Rich system indication—the engine must run for at least 2 minutes at part throttle, under load, before this code will set. Code will not set when the engine is not between 1500–2500 rpm and/or the coolant temperature is below 70°C and/or in "high altitude" condition
51	Faulty calibration unit (PROM) or installation. It takes up to 30 seconds before this code will set
54	Shorted Mixture Control (M/C) solenoid circuit and/or faulty Electronic Control Module (ECM)
55	Faulty Electronic Control Module (ECM)—problem with ECM A/D converter in ECM

Year — 1986
Model — Impulse
Engine — 1.9L (119 cid) 4 cyl
Engine Code — G200Z

ECM TROUBLE CODES

Code	Explanation
12	No distributor pulses to the Electronic Control Module (ECM) and will only flash while fault is present — no fault indicated
13	Oxygen sensor system — harness open, sensor deterioration
14	Water Temperature Sensor (WTS) system grounded
15	Water Temperature Sensor (WTS) system — incorrect signal
16	Water Temperature Sensor (WTS) system — harness open
21	Throttle Valve Switch (TVS) system — idle contact and full contact make simultaneously
22	Starter signal system — no signal input
23	Ignition power transistor system — output terminal grounded
25	Vacuum Switching Valve (VSV) system — output terminal grounded or open
33	Fuel injector system — output terminal grounded or open
35	Ignition power transistor system — harness open
41	Crank Angle Sensor (CAS) system — no signal or faulty signal input
43	Throttle Valve Switch (TVS) system — idle contact closed continuously
44	Oxygen sensor system — lean signal — low voltage
45	Oxygen sensor system — rich signal — high voltage
51	Faulty Electronic Control Module (ECM)
52	Faulty Electronic Control Module (ECM)
53	Vacuum Switching Valve (VSV) system — grounded or defective power transistor
54	Ignition power transistor system — grounded or defective power transistor
55	Faulty Electronic Control Module (ECM)
61	Air Flow Sensor (AFS) system — grounded, shorted, open or broken "Hot" wire
62	Air Flow Sensor (AFS) system — broken "Cold" wire
63	Vehicle Speed Sensor (VSS) — no signal input
64	Fuel injector system — grounded or defective transistor
65	Throttle Valve Switch (TVS) system — full contact closed continuously
66	Knock sensor system — harness grounded or open

Year — 1986
Model — Impulse
Engine — 2.0L (122 cid) Turbo 4 cyl
Engine Code — 4ZC1-T

ECM TROUBLE CODES

Code	Explanation
12	No distributor pulses to the Electronic Control Module (ECM) and will only flash while fault is present — no fault indicated
13	Oxygen sensor system — harness open, sensor deterioration
14	Water Temperature Sensor (WTS) system grounded
15	Water Temperature Sensor (WTS) system — incorrect signal
16	Water Temperature Sensor (WTS) system — harness open
21	Throttle Valve Switch (TVS) system — idle contact and full contact make simultaneously
22	Starter signal system — no signal input
23	Ignition power transistor system — output terminal grounded
25	Vacuum Switching Valve (VSV) system — output terminal grounded or open
33	Fuel injector system — output terminal grounded or open
35	Ignition power transistor system — harness open
41	Crank Angle Sensor (CAS) system — no signal or faulty signal input
43	Throttle Valve Switch (TVS) system — idle contact closed continuously
44	Oxygen sensor system — lean signal — low voltage
45	Oxygen sensor system — rich signal — high voltage
51	Faulty Electronic Control Module (ECM)
52	Faulty Electronic Control Module (ECM)
53	Vacuum Switching Valve (VSV) system — grounded or defective power transistor
54	Ignition power transistor system — grounded or defective power transistor
55	Faulty Electronic Control Module (ECM)
61	Air Flow Sensor (AFS) system — grounded, shorted, open or broken "Hot" wire
62	Air Flow Sensor (AFS) system — broken "Cold" wire
63	Vehicle Speed Sensor (VSS) — no signal input
64	Fuel injector system — grounded or defective transistor
65	Throttle Valve Switch (TVS) system — full contact closed continuously
66	Knock sensor system — harness grounded or open
71	Throttle Position Sensor (TPS) — turbo control system — abnormal signal
72	Exhaust Gas Recirculation (EGR) — Vacuum Switching Valve (VSV) — output terminal grounded or open
73	Exhaust Gas Recirculation (EGR) — Vacuum Switching Valve (VSV) — defective transistor or grounding system

Year – 1987
Model – I-Mark
Engine – 1.5L (90 cid) 4 cyl
Engine Code – 4XC1-U

ECM TROUBLE CODES

Code	Explanation
12	No distributor reference pulses to the Electronic Control Module (ECM) and will only flash while the fault is present
13	Oxygen sensor circuit—the engine must run up to 2 minutes at part throttle, under load, before this code will set
14	Shorted Coolant Temperature Sensor (CTS) circuit—the engine must run up to 2 minutes before this code will set
15	Open Coolant Temperature Sensor (CTS) circuit—the engine must run up to 5 minutes before this code will set
21	Idle switch improperly adjusted and/or circuit open. This code will set if the engine speed falls below 600 rpm for longer than 32 seconds. This code will set if Throttle Position Sensor (TPS) and idle switch are faulty or misadjusted
22	Fuel cut-off relay and/or circuit open
23	Open or grounded Mixture Control (M/C) solenoid circuit
25	Vacuum Switching Valve (VSV) circuit open or grounded
42	Fuel cut-off relay and/or circuit shorted
44	Lean oxygen sensor indication—the engine must run for at least 2 minutes at part throttle, under load, before this code will set. Code will not set when coolant temperature is below 70°C. Code will not set when air cleaner air temperature is below 0°C—"low altitude" condition. Code will not set in "high altitude" condition
45	Rich system indication—the engine must run for at least 2 minutes at part throttle, under load, before this code will set. Code will not set when the engine is not between 1500–2500 rpm and/or the coolant temperature is below 70°C and/or in "high altitude" condition
51	Faulty calibration unit (PROM) or installation. It takes up to 30 seconds before this code will set
53	Shorted Switching Valve (VSV) and/or faulty Electronic Control Module (ECM)
54	Shorted Mixture Control (M/C) solenoid circuit and/or faulty Electronic Control Module (ECM)
55	Faulty Electronic Control Module (ECM)—problem with ECM A/D converter in ECM

Year — 1987
Model — Impulse
Engine — 1.9L (119 cid) 4 cyl
Engine Code — G200Z

ECM TROUBLE CODES

Code	Explanation
12	No distributor pulses to the Electronic Control Module (ECM) and will only flash while fault is present — no fault indicated
13	Oxygen sensor system — harness open, sensor deterioration
14	Water Temperature Sensor (WTS) system grounded
15	Water Temperature Sensor (WTS) system — incorrect signal
16	Water Temperature Sensor (WTS) system — harness open
21	Throttle Valve Switch (TVS) system — idle contact and full contact make simultaneously
22	Starter signal system — no signal input
23	Ignition power transistor system — output terminal grounded
25	Vacuum Switching Valve (VSV) system — output terminal grounded or open
33	Fuel injector system — output terminal grounded or open
35	Ignition power transistor system — harness open
41	Crank Angle Sensor (CAS) system — no signal or faulty signal input
43	Throttle Valve Switch (TVS) system — idle contact closed continuously
44	Oxygen sensor system — lean signal — low voltage
45	Oxygen sensor system — rich signal — high voltage
51	Faulty Electronic Control Module (ECM)
52	Faulty Electronic Control Module (ECM)
53	Vacuum Switching Valve (VSV) system — grounded or defective power transistor
54	Ignition power transistor system — grounded or defective power transistor
55	Faulty Electronic Control Module (ECM)
61	Air Flow Sensor (AFS) system — grounded, shorted, open or broken "Hot" wire
62	Air Flow Sensor (AFS) system — broken "Cold" wire
63	Vehicle Speed Sensor (VSS) — no signal input
64	Fuel injector system — grounded or defective transistor
65	Throttle Valve Switch (TVS) system — full contact closed continuously
66	Knock sensor system — harness grounded or open
71	Throttle Position Sensor (TPS) — turbo control system — abnormal signal
72	Exhaust Gas Recirculation (EGR) — Vacuum Switching Valve (VSV) — output terminal grounded or open
73	Exhaust Gas Recirculation (EGR) — Vacuum Switching Valve (VSV) — defective transistor or grounding system

Year — 1987
Model — Impulse
Engine — 2.0L (122 cid) Turbo 4 cyl
Engine Code — 4ZC1-T

ECM TROUBLE CODES

Code	Explanation
12	No distributor pulses to the Electronic Control Module (ECM) and will only flash while fault is present — no fault indicated
13	Oxygen sensor system — harness open, sensor deterioration
14	Water Temperature Sensor (WTS) system grounded
15	Water Temperature Sensor (WTS) system — incorrect signal
16	Water Temperature Sensor (WTS) system — harness open
21	Throttle Valve Switch (TVS) system — idle contact and full contact make simultaneously
22	Starter signal system — no signal input
23	Ignition power transistor system — output terminal grounded
25	Vacuum Switching Valve (VSV) system — output terminal grounded or open
33	Fuel injector system — output terminal grounded or open
35	Ignition power transistor system — harness open
41	Crank Angle Sensor (CAS) system — no signal or faulty signal input
43	Throttle Valve Switch (TVS) system — idle contact closed continuously
44	Oxygen sensor system — lean signal — low voltage
45	Oxygen sensor system — rich signal — high voltage
51	Faulty Electronic Control Module (ECM)
52	Faulty Electronic Control Module (ECM)
53	Vacuum Switching Valve (VSV) system — grounded or defective power transistor
54	Ignition power transistor system — grounded or defective power transistor
55	Faulty Electronic Control Module (ECM)
61	Air Flow Sensor (AFS) system — grounded, shorted, open or broken "Hot" wire
62	Air Flow Sensor (AFS) system — broken "Cold" wire
63	Vehicle Speed Sensor (VSS) — no signal input
64	Fuel injector system — grounded or defective transistor
65	Throttle Valve Switch (TVS) system — full contact closed continuously
66	Knock sensor system — harness grounded or open
71	Throttle Position Sensor (TPS) — turbo control system — abnormal signal
72	Exhaust Gas Recirculation (EGR) — Vacuum Switching Valve (VSV) — output terminal grounded or open
73	Exhaust Gas Recirculation (EGR) — Vacuum Switching Valve (VSV) — defective transistor or grounding system

Year — 1988
Model — I-Mark
Engine — 1.5L (90 cid) 4 cyl
Engine Code — 4XC1-U

ECM TROUBLE CODES

Code	Explanation
12	No distributor reference pulses to the Electronic Control Module (ECM) and will only flash while the fault is present
13	Oxygen sensor circuit—the engine must run up to 2 minutes at part throttle, under load, before this code will set
14	Shorted Coolant Temperature Sensor (CTS) circuit—the engine must run up to 2 minutes before this code will set
15	Open Coolant Temperature Sensor (CTS) circuit—the engine must run up to 5 minutes before this code will set
21	Idle switch improperly adjusted and/or circuit open. This code will set if the engine speed falls below 600 rpm for longer than 32 seconds. This code will set if Throttle Position Sensor (TPS) and idle switch are faulty or misadjusted
22	Fuel cut-off relay and/or circuit open
23	Open or grounded Mixture Control (M/C) solenoid circuit
25	Vacuum Switching Valve (VSV) circuit open or grounded
42	Fuel cut-off relay and/or circuit shorted
44	Lean oxygen sensor indication—the engine must run for at least 2 minutes at part throttle, under load, before this code will set. Code will not set when coolant temperature is below 70°C. Code will not set when air cleaner air temperature is below 0°C—"low altitude" condition. Code will not set in "high altitude" condition
45	Rich system indication—the engine must run for at least 2 minutes at part throttle, under load, before this code will set. Code will not set when the engine is not between 1500–2500 rpm and/or the coolant temperature is below 70°C and/or in "high altitude" condition
51	Faulty calibration unit (PROM) or installation. It takes up to 30 seconds before this code will set
53	Shorted switching valve and/or faulty Electronic Control Module (ECM)
54	Shorted Mixture Control (M/C) solenoid circuit and/or faulty Electronic Control Module (ECM)
55	Faulty Electronic Control Module (ECM)—problem with ECM A/D converter in ECM

Year – 1988
Model – I-Mark
Engine – 1.5L (90 cid) Turbo 4 cyl
Engine Code – 4XC1-T

ECM TROUBLE CODES

Code	Explanation
12	No distributor reference pulses to the Electronic Control Module (ECM) and will only flash while the fault is presesnt
13	Oxygen sensor circuit – the engine must run up to 2 minutes at part throttle, under load, before this code will set
14	Coolant Temperature Sensor (CTS) circuit – high temperature indicated
15	Coolant Temperature Sensor (CTS) circuit – low temperature indicated
21	Throttle position sensor circuit – signal voltage high
22	Throttle Position Sensor (TPS) circuit – signal voltage low
23	Manifold Air Temperature (MAT) sensor – low temperature indicated
24	Vehicle Speed Sensor (VSS) circuit
25	Manifold Air Temperature (MAT) sensor circuit – high temperature indicated
31	Turbocharger wastegate control
32	Exhaust Gas Recirculation (EGR) system fault
33	Manifold Absolute Pressure (MAP) – signal voltage high
34	Manifold Absolute Pressure (MAP) – signal voltage low
42	Electronic Spark Timing (EST) circuit
43	Electronic Spark Control (ESC) – knock control failure
44	Oxygen sensor circuit – lean exhaust indication
45	Oxygen sensor circuit – rich exhaust indication
51	Mem-Cal error – faulty or incorrect Mem-Cal

Year — 1988
Model — Impulse
Engine — 2.3L (138 cid) 4 cyl
Engine Code — 4ZD1

ECM TROUBLE CODES

Code	Explanation
12	No distributor pulses to the Electronic Control Module (ECM) and will only flash while fault is present — no fault indicated
13	Oxygen sensor system — harness open, sensor deterioration
14	Water Temperature Sensor (WTS) system grounded
15	Water Temperature Sensor (WTS) system — incorrect signal
21	Throttle Valve Switch (TVS) system — idle contact and full contact make simultaneously
22	Starter signal system — no signal input
23	Ignition power transistor system — output terminal grounded
25	Vacuum Switching Valve (VSV) system — output terminal grounded or open
26	Vacuum Switching Valve (VSV) system for canister purge — output terminal grounded or harness open
27	Vacuum Switching Valve (VSV) system for canister purge — defective transistor or grounding system
32	Exhaust Gas Recirculation (EGR) temperature sensor system — malfunction
33	Fuel injector system — output terminal grounded or open
34	Exhaust Gas Recirculation (EGR) temperature sensor system — sensor or harness defective
35	Ignition power transistor system — harness open
41	Crank Angle Sensor (CAS) system — no signal or faulty signal input
43	Throttle Valve Switch (TVS) system — idle contact closed continuously
44	Oxygen sensor system — lean signal — low voltage
45	Oxygen sensor system — rich signal — high voltage
51	Faulty Electronic Control Module (ECM)
52	Faulty Electronic Control Module (ECM)
53	Vacuum Switching Valve (VSV) system — grounded or defective power transistor
54	Ignition power transistor system — grounded or defective power transistor
61	Air Flow Sensor (AFS) system — grounded, shorted, open or broken "Hot" wire
62	Air Flow Sensor (AFS) system — broken "Cold" wire
63	Vehicle Speed Sensor (VSS) — no signal input
64	Fuel injector system — grounded or defective transistor
65	Throttle Valve Switch (TVS) system — full contact closed continuously
66	Knock sensor system — harness grounded or open
71	Throttle Position Sensor (TPS) — turbo control system — abnormal signal
72	Exhaust Gas Recirculation (EGR) — Vacuum Switching Valve (VSV) — output terminal grounded or open
73	Exhaust Gas Recirculation (EGR) — Vacuum Switching Valve (VSV) — defective transistor or grounding system

Year — 1988
Model — Impulse
Engine — 2.0L (122 cid) Turbo 4 cyl
Engine Code — 4ZC1-T

ECM TROUBLE CODES

Code	Explanation
12	No distributor pulses to the Electronic Control Module (ECM) and will only flash while fault is present — no fault indicated
13	Oxygen sensor system — harness open, sensor deterioration
14	Water Temperature Sensor (WTS) system grounded
15	Water Temperature Sensor (WTS) system — incorrect signal
21	Throttle Valve Switch (TVS) system — idle contact and full contact make simultaneously
22	Starter signal system — no signal input
23	Ignition power transistor system — output terminal grounded
25	Vacuum Switching Valve (VSV) system — output terminal grounded or open
26	Vacuum Switching Valve (VSV) system for canister purge — output terminal grounded or harness open
27	Vacuum Switching Valve (VSV) system for canister purge — defective transistor or grounding system
32	Exhaust Gas Recirculation (EGR) temperature sensor system — malfunction
33	Fuel injector system — output terminal grounded or open
34	Exhaust Gas Recirculation (EGR) temperature sensor system — sensor or harness defective
35	Ignition power transistor system — harness open
41	Crank Angle Sensor (CAS) system — no signal or faulty signal input
43	Throttle Valve Switch (TVS) system — idle contact closed continuously
44	Oxygen sensor system — lean signal — low voltage
45	Oxygen sensor system — rich signal — high voltage
51	Faulty Electronic Control Module (ECM)
52	Faulty Electronic Control Module (ECM)
53	Vacuum Switching Valve (VSV) system — grounded or defective power transistor
54	Ignition power transistor system — grounded or defective power transistor
61	Air Flow Sensor (AFS) system — grounded, shorted, open or broken "Hot" wire
62	Air Flow Sensor (AFS) system — broken "Cold" wire
63	Vehicle Speed Sensor (VSS) — no signal input
64	Fuel injector system — grounded or defective transistor
65	Throttle Valve Switch (TVS) system — full contact closed continuously
66	Knock sensor system — harness grounded or open
71	Throttle Position Sensor (TPS) — turbo control system — abnormal signal
72	Exhaust Gas Recirculation (EGR) — Vacuum Switching Valve (VSV) — output terminal grounded or open
73	Exhaust Gas Recirculation (EGR) — Vacuum Switching Valve (VSV) — defective transistor or grounding system

Year — 1989
Model — I-Mark
Engine — 1.6L (92 cid) 4 cyl
Engine Code — 4XE1

ECM TROUBLE CODES

Code	Explanation
12	No distributor reference pulses to the Electronic Control Module (ECM) and will only flash while the fault is present
13	Oxygen sensor circuit — the engine must run up to 2 minutes at part throttle, under load, before this code will set
14	Shorted Coolant Temperature Sensor (CTS) circuit — the engine must run up to 2 minutes before this code will set
15	Open Coolant Temperature Sensor (CTS) circuit — the engine must run up to 5 minutes before this code will set
21	Idle switch improperly adjusted and/or circuit open. This code will set if the engine speed falls below 600 rpm for longer than 32 seconds. This code will set if Throttle Position Sensor (TPS) and idle switch are faulty or misadjusted
22	Fuel cut-off relay and/or circuit open
23	Open or grounded Mixture Control (M/C) solenoid circuit
25	Vacuum Switching Valve (VSV) circuit open or grounded
42	Fuel cut-off relay and/or circuit shorted
44	Lean oxygen sensor indication — the engine must run for at least 2 minutes at part throttle, under load, before this code will set. Code will not set when coolant temperature is below 70°C. Code will not set when air cleaner air temperature is below 0°C — "low altitude" condition. Code will not set in "high altitude" condition
45	Rich system indication — the engine must run for at least 2 minutes at part throttle, under load, before this code will set. Code will not set when the engine is not between 1500–2500 rpm and/or the coolant temperature is below 70°C and/or in "high altitude" condition
51	Faulty calibration unit (PROM) or installation. It takes up to 30 seconds before this code will set
53	Shorted Switching Valve (VSV) and/or faulty Electronic Control Module (ECM)
54	Shorted Mixture Control (M/C) solenoid circuit and/or faulty Electronic Control Module (ECM)
55	Faulty Electronic Control Module (ECM) — problem with ECM A/D converter in ECM

Year — 1989
Model — I-Mark
Engine — 1.5L (90 cid) Turbo 4 cyl
Engine Code — 4XC1-T

ECM TROUBLE CODES

Code	Explanation
12	No distributor reference pulses to the Electronic Control Module (ECM) and will only flash while the fault is presesnt
13	Oxygen sensor circuit—the engine must run up to 2 minutes at part throttle, under load, before this code will set
14	Coolant Temperature Sensor (CTS) circuit—high temperature indicated
15	Coolant Temperature Sensor (CTS) circuit—low temperature indicated
21	Throttle Position Sensor (TPS) circuit—signal voltage high
22	Throttle Position Sensor (TPS) circuit—signal voltage low
23	Manifold Air Temperature (MAT) sensor—low temperature indicated
24	Vehicle Speed Sensor (VSS) circuit
25	Manifold Air Temperature (MAT) sensor circuit—high temperature indicated
31	Turbocharger wastegate control
32	Exhaust Gas Recirculation (EGR) system fault
33	Manifold Absolute Pressure (MAP)—signal voltage high
34	Manifold Absolute Pressure (MAP)—signal voltage low
42	Electronic Spark Timing (EST) circuit
43	Electronic Spark Control (ESC)—knock control failure
44	Oxygen sensor circuit—lean exhaust indication
45	Oxygen sensor circuit—rich exhaust indication
51	Mem-Cal error—faulty or incorrect Mem-Cal

Year — 1989
Model — I-Mark
Engine — 1.5L (90 cid) 4 cyl
Engine Code — 4XC1-U

ECM TROUBLE CODES

Code	Explanation
12	No distributor reference pulses to the Electronic Control Module (ECM) and will only flash while the fault is present
13	Oxygen sensor circuit — the engine must run up to 2 minutes at part throttle, under load, before this code will set
14	Shorted Coolant Temperature Sensor (CTS) circuit — the engine must run up to 2 minutes before this code will set
15	Open Coolant Temperature Sensor (CTS) circuit — the engine must run up to 5 minutes before this code will set
21	Idle switch improperly adjusted and/or circuit open. This code will set if the engine speed falls below 600 rpm for longer than 32 seconds. This code will set if Throttle Position Sensor (TPS) and idle switch are faulty or misadjusted
22	Fuel cut-off relay and/or circuit open
23	Open or grounded Mixture Control (M/C) solenoid circuit
25	Vacuum Switching Valve (VSV) circuit open or grounded
42	Fuel cut-off relay and/or circuit shorted
44	Lean oxygen sensor indication — the engine must run for at least 2 minutes at part throttle, under load, before this code will set. Code will not set when coolant temperature is below 70°C. Code will not set when air cleaner air temperature is below 0°C — "low altitude" condition. Code will not set in "high altitude" condition
45	Rich system indication — the engine must run for at least 2 minutes at part throttle, under load, before this code will set. Code will not set when the engine is not between 1500–2500 rpm and/or the coolant temperature is below 70°C and/or in "high altitude" condition
51	Faulty calibration unit (PROM) or installation. It takes up to 30 seconds before this code will set
53	Shorted Switching Valve (VSV) and/or faulty Electronic Control Module (ECM)
54	Shorted Mixture Control (M/C) solenoid circuit and/or faulty Electronic Control Module (ECM)
55	Faulty Electronic Control Module (ECM) — problem with ECM A/D converter in ECM

Year — 1989
Model — Impulse
Engine — 2.3L (138 cid) 4 cyl
Engine Code — 4ZD1

ECM TROUBLE CODES

Code	Explanation
12	No distributor pulses to the Electronic Control Module (ECM) and will only flash while fault is present — no fault indicated
13	Oxygen sensor system — harness open, sensor deterioration
14	Water Temperature Sensor (WTS) system grounded
15	Water Temperature Sensor (WTS) system — incorrect signal
21	Throttle Valve Switch (TVS) system — idle contact and full contact make simultaneously
22	Starter signal system — no signal input
23	Ignition power transistor system — output terminal grounded
25	Vacuum Switching Valve (VSV) system — output terminal grounded or open
26	Vacuum Switching Valve (VSV) system for canister purge — output terminal grounded or harness open
27	Vacuum Switching Valve (VSV) system for canister purge — defective transistor or grounding system
32	Exhaust Gas Recirculation (EGR) temperature sensor system — malfunction
33	Fuel injector system — output terminal grounded or open
34	Exhaust Gas Recirculation (EGR) temperature sensor system — sensor or harness defective
35	Ignition power transistor system — harness open
41	Crank Angle Sensor (CAS) system — no signal or faulty signal input
43	Throttle Valve Switch (TVS) system — idle contact closed continuously
44	Oxygen sensor system — lean signal — low voltage
45	Oxygen sensor system — rich signal — high voltage
51	Faulty Electronic Control Module (ECM)
52	Faulty Electronic Control Module (ECM)
53	Vacuum Switching Valve (VSV) system — grounded or defective power transistor
54	Ignition power transistor system — grounded or defective power transistor
61	Air Flow Sensor (AFS) system — grounded, shorted, open or broken "Hot" wire
62	Air Flow Sensor (AFS) system — broken "Cold" wire
63	Vehicle Speed Sensor (VSS) — no signal input
64	Fuel injector system — grounded or defective transistor
65	Throttle Valve Switch (TVS) system — full contact closed continuously
66	Knock sensor system — harness grounded or open
71	Throttle Position Sensor (TPS) — turbo control system — abnormal signal
72	Exhaust Gas Recirculation (EGR) — Vacuum Switching Valve (VSV) — output terminal grounded or open
73	Exhaust Gas Recirculation (EGR) — Vacuum Switching Valve (VSV) — defective transistor or grounding system

Year — 1989
Model — Impulse
Engine — 2.0L (122 cid) Turbo 4 cyl
Engine Code — 4ZC1-T

ECM TROUBLE CODES

Code	Explanation
12	No distributor pulses to the Electronic Control Module (ECM) and will only flash while fault is present — no fault indicated
13	Oxygen sensor system — harness open, sensor deterioration
14	Water Temperature Sensor (WTS) system grounded
15	Water Temperature Sensor (WTS) system — incorrect signal
21	Throttle Valve Switch (TVS) system — idle contact and full contact make simultaneously
22	Starter signal system — no signal input
23	Ignition power transistor system — output terminal grounded
25	Vacuum Switching Valve (VSV) system — output terminal grounded or open
26	Vacuum Switching Valve (VSV) system for canister purge — output terminal grounded or harness open
27	Vacuum Switching Valve (VSV) system for canister purge — defective transistor or grounding system
32	Exhaust Gas Recirculation (EGR) temperature sensor system — malfunction
33	Fuel injector system — output terminal grounded or open
34	Exhaust Gas Recirculation (EGR) temperature sensor system — sensor or harness defective
35	Ignition power transistor system — harness open
41	Crank Angle Sensor (CAS) system — no signal or faulty signal input
43	Throttle Valve Switch (TVS) system — idle contact closed continuously
44	Oxygen sensor system — lean signal — low voltage
45	Oxygen sensor system — rich signal — high voltage
51	Faulty Electronic Control Module (ECM)
52	Faulty Electronic Control Module (ECM)
53	Vacuum Switching Valve (VSV) system — grounded or defective power transistor
54	Ignition power transistor system — grounded or defective power transistor
61	Air Flow Sensor (AFS) system — grounded, shorted, open or broken "Hot" wire
62	Air Flow Sensor (AFS) system — broken "Cold" wire
63	Vehicle Speed Sensor (VSS) — no signal input
64	Fuel injector system — grounded or defective transistor
65	Throttle Valve Switch (TVS) system — full contact closed continuously
66	Knock sensor system — harness grounded or open
71	Throttle Position Sensor (TPS) — turbo control system — abnormal signal
72 & 34	Exhaust Gas Recirculation (EGR) — Vacuum Switching Valve (VSV) — output terminal grounded or open
73	Exhaust Gas Recirculation (EGR) — Vacuum Switching Valve (VSV) — defective transistor or grounding system

ISUZU TRUCKS

Year — 1982
Model — Pick-Up
Engine — 1.8L (111 cid) 4 cyl
Engine Code — G180Z

ECM TROUBLE CODES

Code	Explanation
12	Idle switch not ON
13	Idle switch not OFF
14	Wide Open Throttle (WOT) switch not ON
15	Wide Open Throttle (WOT) switch not OFF
21	Output transistor not ON
22	Output transistor not OFF
23	Abnormal oxygen sensor
24	Abnormal Water Temperature Sensor (WTS) switch
25	Abnormal Random Access Memory (RAM)
12, 13, 14 & 15	"Check Engine" lamp not ON
21, 22, 23, 24 & 25	"Check Engine" lamp ON

Year – 1983
Model – Pick-Up
Engine – 1.8L (111 cid) 4 cyl
Engine Code – G180Z

ECM TROUBLE CODES

Code	Explanation
12	No ignition reference pulses to the Electronic Control Module (ECM). This code is not stored in memory and will only flash while the fault is present
13	Oxygen sensor circuit—the engine must run up to 1 minute at part throttle, under load, before this code will set. This code does not set when the coolant temperature is below 70°C and/or the time since engine start has exceeded 2 minutes
14	Shorted Coolant Temperature Sensor (CTS) circuit—the engine must run up to 2 minutes before this code will set
15	Open Coolant Temperature Sensor (CTS) circuit—the engine must run up to 5 minutes before this code will set
21	Idle switch circuit open or Wide Open Throttle (WOT) switch circuit shorted—the engine must run up to 10 seconds at the following 2 conditions concurrently before this code will set. Idle switch output is in a low voltage state, WOT switch output is in a high voltage state
22	Fuel Cut Solenoid (FCS) circuit open or grounded—the engine must run under the decelerating condition, over 2000 rpm, before this code will set
23	Vacuum Control Solenoid (VCS) circuit open or grounded
25	Air Switching Solenoid (ASS) circuit open or grounded
31	No ignition reference pulses to the Electronic Control Module (ECM) for 10 seconds at part throttle, under load. This code will store in memory
44	Lean oxygen sensor indication—the engine must run up to 2 minutes at part throttle, under load, before this code will set
45	Rich system indication—the engine must run up to 2 minutes at part throttle, under load, before this code will set. This code does not set when the engine exceeds 2500 rpm and/or the coolant temperature is below 70°C and/or the barometric pressure is below 575mm Hg (above 2500m altitude)
51	Shorted Fuel Cut Solenoid (FCS) circuit and/or faulty Electronic Control Module (ECM)
52	Faulty Electronic Control Module (ECM)—problem of Random Access Memory (RAM) in ECM
53	Shorted Air Switching Solenoid (ASS) and/or faulty Electronic Control Module (ECM)
54	Shorted Vacuum Control Solenoid (VCS) and/or faulty Electronic Control Module (ECM)
55	Faulty Electronic Control Module (ECM)—problem of A/D converter in ECM

Year — 1984
Model — Pick-Up
Engine — 2.0L (119 cid) 4 cyl
Engine Code — G200Z

ECM TROUBLE CODES

Code	Explanation
12	No ignition reference pulses to the Electronic Control Module (ECM). This code is not stored in memory and will only flash while the fault is present
13	Oxygen sensor circuit — the engine must run up to 1 minute at part throttle, under load, before this code will set. This code does not set when the coolant temperature is below 70°C and/or the time since engine start has exceeded 2 minutes
14	Shorted Coolant Temperature Sensor (CTS) circuit — the engine must run up to 2 minutes before this code will set
15	Open Coolant Temperature Sensor (CTS) circuit — the engine must run up to 5 minutes before this code will set
21	Idle switch circuit open or Wide Open Throttle (WOT) switch circuit shorted — the engine must run up to 10 seconds at the following 2 conditions concurrently before this code will set: Idle switch output is in a low voltage state, WOT switch output is in a high voltage state
22	Fuel Cut Solenoid (FCS) circuit open or grounded — the engine must run under the decelerating condition, over 2000 rpm, before this code will set
23	Vacuum Control Solenoid (VCS) circuit open or grounded
25	Air Switching Solenoid (ASS) circuit open or grounded
31	No ignition reference pulses to the Electronic Control Module (ECM) for 10 seconds at part throttle, under load. This code will store in memory
44	Lean oxygen sensor indication — the engine must run up to 2 minutes at part throttle, under load, before this code will set
45	Rich system indication — the engine must run up to 2 minutes at part throttle, under load, before this code will set. This code does not set when the engine exceeds 2500 rpm and/or the coolant temperature is below 70°C and/or the barometric pressure is below 575mm Hg (above 2500m altitude)
51	Shorted Fuel Cut Solenoid (FCS) circuit and/or faulty Electronic Control Module (ECM)
52	Faulty Electronic Control Module (ECM) — problem of Random Access Memory (RAM) in ECM
53	Shorted Air Switching Solenoid (ASS) and/or faulty Electronic Control Module (ECM)
54	Shorted Vacuum Control Solenoid (VCS) and/or faulty Electronic Control Module (ECM)
55	Faulty Electronic Control Module (ECM) — problem of A/D converter in ECM

Year — 1985
Model — Pick-Up
Engine — 2.0L (119 cid) 4 cyl
Engine Code — G200Z

ECM TROUBLE CODES

Code	Explanation
12	No ignition reference pulses to the Electronic Control Module (ECM). This code is not stored in memory and will only flash while the fault is present
13	Oxygen sensor circuit — the engine must run up to 1 minute at part throttle, under load, before this code will set. This code does not set when the coolant temperature is below 70°C and/or the time since engine start has exceeded 2 minutes
14	Shorted Coolant Temperature Sensor (CTS) circuit — the engine must run up to 2 minutes before this code will set
15	Open Coolant Temperature Sensor (CTS) circuit — the engine must run up to 5 minutes before this code will set
21	Idle switch circuit open or Wide Open Throttle (WOT) switch circuit shorted — the engine must run up to 10 seconds at the following 2 conditions concurrently before this code will set: Idle switch output is in a low voltage state, WOT switch output is in a high voltage state
22	Fuel Cut Solenoid (FCS) circuit open or grounded — the engine must run under the decelerating condition, over 2000 rpm, before this code will set
23	Vacuum Control Solenoid (VCS) circuit open or grounded
25	Air Switching Solenoid (ASS) circuit open or grounded
31	No ignition reference pulses to the Electronic Control Module (ECM) for 10 seconds at part throttle, under load. This code will store in memory
44	Lean oxygen sensor indication — the engine must run up to 2 minutes at part throttle, under load, before this code will set
45	Rich system indication — the engine must run up to 2 minutes at part throttle, under load, before this code will set. This code does not set when the engine exceeds 2500 rpm and/or the coolant temperature is below 70°C and/or the barometric pressure is below 575mm Hg (above 2500m altitude)
51	Shorted Fuel Cut Solenoid (FCS) circuit and/or faulty Electronic Control Module (ECM)
52	Faulty Electronic Control Module (ECM) — problem of Random Access Memory (RAM) in ECM
53	Shorted Air Switching Solenoid (ASS) and/or faulty Electronic Control Module (ECM)
54	Shorted Vacuum Control Solenoid (VCS) and/or faulty Electronic Control Module (ECM)
55	Faulty Electronic Control Module (ECM) — problem of A/D converter in ECM

Year – 1985
Model – Trooper II
Engine – 2.0L (119 cid) 4 cyl
Engine Code – G200Z

ECM TROUBLE CODES

Code	Explanation
12	No ignition reference pulses to the Electronic Control Module (ECM). This code is not stored in memory and will only flash while the fault is present
13	Oxygen sensor circuit – the engine must run 1 minute at part throttle, under load, before this code will set. This code does not set when the coolant temperature is below 70°C and/or the time since engine start has exceeded 2 minutes
14	Shorted Coolant Temperature Sensor (CTS) circuit – the engine must run 2 minutes before this code will set
15	Open Coolant Temperature Sensor (CTS) circuit – the engine must run 5 minutes before this code will set
21	Idle switch circuit open or Wide Open Throttle (WOT) switch circuit shorted – the engine must run 10 seconds at following 2 conditions, concurrently, before this code will set. Idle switch output is in a low voltage state, WOT switch output is in a high voltage state
22	Fuel Cut Solenoid (FCS) circuit open or grounded – the engine must run under the decelerating condition, over 2000 rpm, before this code will set
23	Mixture Control (M/C) solenoid circuit open or grounded
25	Air Switching Solenoid (ASS) circuit open or grounded
31	No ignition reference pulses to the Electronic Control Module (ECM) for 10 seconds at part throttle, under load. This code will store in memory
44	Lean oxygen sensor indication – the engine must run up to 2 minutes at part throttle, under load, before this code will set. This code does not set when the coolant temperature is below 70°C and/or the air temperature in the air cleaner is below 0°C
45	Rich system indication – the engine must run up to 2 minutes at part throttle, under load, before this code will set. This code does not set when the engine exceeds 2500 rpm and/or the coolant temperature is below 70°C and/or the barometric pressure is below 575mm Hg (above 2500m altitude)
51	Shorted Fuel Cut Solenoid (FCS) circuit and/or faulty Electronic Control Module (ECM)
52	Faulty Electronic Control Module (ECM) – problem of Random Access Memory (RAM) in ECM
53	Shorted Air Switching Solenoid (ASS) and/or faulty Electronic Control Module (ECM)
54	Shorted Vacuum Control Solenoid (VCS) and/or faulty Electronic Control Module (ECM)
55	Faulty Electronic Control Module (ECM) – problem of A/D converter in ECM

Year — 1986
Model — Pick-Up
Engine — 2.0L (119 cid) 4 cyl
Engine Code — G200Z

ECM TROUBLE CODES

Code	Explanation
12	No ignition reference pulses to the Electronic Control Module (ECM). This code is not stored in memory and will only flash while the fault is present
13	Oxygen sensor circuit — the engine must run up to 1 minute at part throttle, under load, before this code will set. This code does not set when the coolant temperature is below 70°C and/or the time since engine start has exceeded 2 minutes
14	Shorted Coolant Temperature Sensor (CTS) circuit — the engine must run up to 2 minutes before this code will set
15	Open Coolant Temperature Sensor (CTS) circuit — the engine must run up to 5 minutes before this code will set
21	Idle switch circuit open or Wide Open Throttle (WOT) switch circuit shorted — the engine must run up to 10 seconds at the following 2 conditions concurrently before this code will set: Idle switch output is in a low voltage state, WOT switch output is in a high voltage state
22	Fuel Cut Solenoid (FCS) circuit open or grounded — the engine must run under the decelerating condition, over 2000 rpm, before this code will set
23	Vacuum Control Solenoid (VCS) circuit open or grounded
25	Air Switching Solenoid (ASS) circuit open or grounded
31	No ignition reference pulses to the Electronic Control Module (ECM) for 10 seconds at part throttle, under load. This code will store in memory
44	Lean oxygen sensor indication — the engine must run up to 2 minutes at part throttle, under load, before this code will set
45	Rich system indication — the engine must run up to 2 minutes at part throttle, under load, before this code will set. This code does not set when the engine exceeds 2500 rpm and/or the coolant temperature is below 70°C and/or the barometric pressure is below 575mm Hg (above 2500m altitude)
51	Shorted Fuel Cut Solenoid (FCS) circuit and/or faulty Electronic Control Module (ECM)
52	Faulty Electronic Control Module (ECM) — problem of Random Access Memory (RAM) in ECM
53	Shorted Air Switching Solenoid (ASS) and/or faulty Electronic Control Module (ECM)
54	Shorted Vacuum Control Solenoid (VCS) and/or faulty Electronic Control Module (ECM)
55	Faulty Electronic Control Module (ECM) — problem of A/D converter in ECM

Year—1986
Model—Pick-Up
Engine—2.3L (138 cid) 4 cyl
Engine Code—4ZD1

ECM TROUBLE CODES

Code	Explanation
12	No distributor pulses to the Electronic Control Module (ECM) and will only flash while fault is present—no fault indicated
13	Oxygen sensor circuit—the engine must run 1 minute at part throttle, under load, before this code will set. This code does not set when the coolant temperature is below 158°F (70°) and/or the time since engine start has exceeded 2 minutes
14	Shorted Coolant Temperature Sensor (CTS) circuit—the engine must run 2 minutes before this code will set
15	Open Coolant Temperature Sensor (CTS) circuit—the engine must run 5 minutes before this code will set
21	Idle switch circuit open or Wide Open Throttle (WOT) switch circuit shorted—the engine must run 10 seconds at following 2 conditions before this code will set: idle switch output is in a low voltage state, WOT switch output is in a high voltage state
22	Fuel Cut Solenoid (FCS) circuit open or grounded—the engine must run under the decelerating condition, over 2000 engine rpm, before this code will set
23	Mixture Control (M/C) solenoid circuit open or grounded
25	Air Switching Solenoid (ASS) circuit open or groundedn
31	No ignition reference pulses to the Electronic Control Module (ECM) for 10 seconds at part throttle, under load. This code will store in memory
44	Lean oxygen sensor indicaiton—the engine must run up to 2 minutes at part throttle, under load, before this code will set. This code does not set when the coolant temperature is below 158°F (70°C) and/or the air temperature in the air cleaner is below 0°C
45	Rich system indicaiont—the engine must run up to 2 minutes at part throttle, under load, before this code will set. This code does not set when the engine exceeds 2500 rpm and/or the coolant temperature is below 158°F (70°C) and/or the barometric pressure is below 23 in. Hg (575mm Hg), above 8000 ft (2500m) altitude
51	Shorted Fuel Cut Solenoid (FCS) circuit and/or faulty Electronic Control Module (ECM)
52	Faulty Electronic Control Module (ECM)—Random Access Memory (RAM) problem in ECM
53	Shorted Air Switching Solenoid (ASS) and/or faulty Electronic Control Module (ECM)
54	Shorted Vacuum Control Solenoid (VCS) and/or faulty Electronic Control Module (ECM)
55	Faulty Electronic Control Module (ECM)—problem of A/D converter in ECM

Year — 1986
Model — Trooper II
Engine — 2.3L (138 cid) 4 cyl
Engine Code — 4ZD1

ECM TROUBLE CODES

Code	Explanation
12	No ignition reference pulses to the Electronic Control Module (ECM). This code is not stored in memory and will only flash while the fault is present
13	Oxygen sensor circuit — the engine must run 1 minute at part throttle, under load, before this code will set. This code does not set when the coolant temperature is below 70°C and/or the time since engine start has exceeded 2 minutes
14	Shorted Coolant Temperature Sensor (CTS) circuit — the engine must run 2 minutes before this code will set
15	Open Coolant Temperature Sensor (CTS) circuit — the engine must run 5 minutes before this code will set
21	Idle switch circuit open or Wide Open Throttle (WOT) switch circuit shorted — the engine must run 10 seconds at following 2 conditions, concurrently, before this code will set: idle switch output is in a low voltage state, WOT switch output is in a high voltage state
22	Fuel Cut Solenoid (FCS) circuit open or grounded — the engine must run under the decelerating condition, over 2000 rpm, before this code will set
23	Mixture Control (M/C) solenoid circuit open or grounded
25	Air Switching Solenoid (ASS) circuit open or grounded
31	No ignition reference pulses to the Electronic Control Module (ECM) for 10 seconds at part throttle, under load. This code will store in memory
44	Lean oxygen sensor indication — the engine must run up to 2 minutes at part throttle, under load, before this code will set. This code does not set when the coolant temperature is below 70°C and/or the air temperature in the air cleaner is below 0°C
45	Rich system indication — the engine must run up to 2 minutes at part throttle, under load, before this code will set. This code does not set when the engine exceeds 2500 rpm and/or the coolant temperature is below 70°C and/or the barometric pressure is below 575mm Hg (above 2500m altitude)
51	Shorted Fuel Cut Solenoid (FCS) circuit and/or faulty Electronic Control Module (ECM)
52	Faulty Electronic Control Module (ECM) — problem of Random Access Memory (RAM) in ECM
53	Shorted Air Switching Solenoid (ASS) and/or faulty Electronic Control Module (ECM)
54	Shorted Vacuum Control Solenoid (VCS) and/or faulty Electronic Control Module (ECM)
55	Faulty Electronic Control Module (ECM) — problem of A/D converter in ECM

Year — 1987
Model — Pick-Up
Engine — 2.0L (119 cid) 4 cyl
Engine Code — G200Z

ECM TROUBLE CODES

Code	Explanation
12	No ignition reference pulses to the Electronic Control Module (ECM). This code is not stored in memory and will only flash while the fault is present
13	Oxygen sensor circuit — the engine must run up to 1 minute at part throttle, under load, before this code will set. This code does not set when the coolant temperature is below 70°C and/or the time since engine start has exceeded 2 minutes
14	Shorted Coolant Temperature Sensor (CTS) circuit — the engine must run up to 2 minutes before this code will set
15	Open Coolant Temperature Sensor (CTS) circuit — the engine must run up to 5 minutes before this code will set
21	Idle switch circuit open or Wide Open Throttle (WOT) switch circuit shorted — the engine must run up to 10 seconds at the following 2 conditions concurrently before this code will set: Idle switch output is in a low voltage state, WOT switch output is in a high voltage state
22	Fuel Cut Solenoid (FCS) circuit open or grounded — the engine must run under the decelerating condition, over 2000 rpm, before this code will set
23	Vacuum Control Solenoid (VCS) circuit open or grounded
25	Air Switching Solenoid (ASS) circuit open or grounded
31	No ignition reference pulses to the Electronic Control Module (ECM) for 10 seconds at part throttle, under load. This code will store in memory
44	Lean oxygen sensor indication — the engine must run up to 2 minutes at part throttle, under load, before this code will set
45	Rich system indication — the engine must run up to 2 minutes at part throttle, under load, before this code will set. This code does not set when the engine exceeds 2500 rpm and/or the coolant temperature is below 70°C and/or the barometric pressure is below 575mm Hg (above 2500m altitude)
51	Shorted Fuel Cut Solenoid (FCS) circuit and/or faulty Electronic Control Module (ECM)
52	Faulty Electronic Control Module (ECM) — problem of Random Access Memory (RAM) in ECM
53	Shorted Air Switching Solenoid (ASS) and/or faulty Electronic Control Module (ECM)
54	Shorted Vacuum Control Solenoid (VCS) and/or faulty Electronic Control Module (ECM)
55	Faulty Electronic Control Module (ECM) — problem of A/D converter in ECM

Year — 1987
Model — Pick-Up
Engine — 2.3 (138cid) 4 cyl
Engine Code — 4ZD1

ECM TROUBLE CODES

Code	Explanation
12	No ignition reference pulses to the Electronic Control Module (ECM). This code is not stored in memory and will only flash while the fault is present
13	Oxygen sensor circuit—the engine must run up to 1 minute at part throttle, under load, before this code will set. This code does not set when the coolant temperature is below 158°F (70°C) and/or the time since engine start has exceeded 2 minutes
14	Shorted Coolant Temperature Sensor (CTS) circuit—the engine must run up to 2 minutes before this code will set
15	Open Coolant Temperature Sensor (CTS) circuit—the engine must run up to 5 minutes before this code will set
21	Idle switch circuit open or Wide Open Throttle (WOT) switch circuit shorted—the engine must run up to 10 seconds at the following 2 conditions concurrently before this code will set: Idle switch output is in a low voltage state, WOT switch output is in a high voltage state
22	Fuel Cut Solenoid (FCS) circuit open or grounded—the engine must run under the decelerating condition, over 2000 rpm, before this code will set
23	Vacuum Control Solenoid (VCS) circuit open or grounded
25	Air Switching Solenoid (ASS) circuit open or grounded
31	No ignition reference pulses to the Electronic Control Module (ECM) for 10 seconds at part throttle, under load. This code will store in memory
44	Fuel metering lean—the engine must run up to 2 minutes at part throttle, under load, before this code will set. This code does not set when the coolant temperature is below 158°F (70°C) and/or the air temperature in the air cleaner is below 32°F (0°C)
45	Rich system indication—the engine must run up to 2 minutes at part throttle, under load, before this code will set. This code does not set when the engine exceeds 2500 rpm and/or the coolant temperature is below 158°F (70°C) and/or the barometric pressure is below 23 in. Hg (575mm Hg) above 8000 ft (2500m altitude)
51	Shorted Fuel Cut Solenoid (FCS) circuit and/or faulty Electronic Control Module (ECM)
52	Faulty Electronic Control Module (ECM)—problem of Random Access Memory (RAM) in ECM
53	Shorted Air Switching Solenoid (ASS) and/or faulty Electronic Control Module (ECM)
54	Shorted Vacuum Control Solenoid (VCS) and/or faulty Electronic Control Module (ECM)
55	Faulty Electronic Control Module (ECM)—problem of A/D converter in ECM

Year — 1987
Model — Trooper II
Engine — 2.3L (138 cid) 4 cyl
Engine Code — 4ZD1

ECM TROUBLE CODES

Code	Explanation
12	No ignition reference pulses to the Electronic Control Module (ECM). This code is not stored in memory and will only flash while the fault is present
13	Oxygen sensor circuit—the engine must run 1 minute at part throttle, under load, before this code will set. This code does not set when the coolant temperature is below 70°C and/or the time since engine start has exceeded 2 minutes
14	Shorted Coolant Temperature Sensor (CTS) circuit—the engine must run 2 minutes before this code will set
15	Open Coolant Temperature Sensor (CTS) circuit—the engine must run 5 minutes before this code will set
21	Idle switch circuit open or Wide Open Throttle (WOT) switch circuit shorted—the engine must run 10 seconds at following 2 conditions, concurrently, before this code will set: idle switch output is in a low voltage state, WOT switch output is in a high voltage state
22	Fuel Cut Solenoid (FCS) circuit open or grounded—the engine must run under the decelerating condition, over 2000 rpm, before this code will set
23	Mixture Control (M/C) solenoid circuit open or grounded
25	Air Switching Solenoid (ASS) circuit open or grounded
31	No ignition reference pulses to the Electronic Control Module (ECM) for 10 seconds at part throttle, under load. This code will store in memory
44	Lean oxygen sensor indication—the engine must run up to 2 minutes at part throttle, under load, before this code will set. This code does not set when the coolant temperature is below 70°C and/or the air temperature in the air cleaner is below 0°C
45	Rich system indication—the engine must run up to 2 minutes at part throttle, under load, before this code will set. This code does not set when the engine exceeds 2500 rpm and/or the coolant temperature is below 70°C and/or the barometric pressure is below 575mm Hg (above 2500m altitude)
51	Shorted Fuel Cut Solenoid (FCS) circuit and/or faulty Electronic Control Module (ECM)
52	Faulty Electronic Control Module (ECM)—problem of Random Access Memory (RAM) in ECM
53	Shorted Air Switching Solenoid (ASS) and/or faulty Electronic Control Module (ECM)
54	Shorted Vacuum Control Solenoid (VCS) and/or faulty Electronic Control Module (ECM)
55	Faulty Electronic Control Module (ECM)—problem of A/D converter in ECM

Year — 1988
Model — Pick-Up
Engine — 2.3 (138cid) 4 cyl
Engine Code — 4ZD1

ECM TROUBLE CODES

Code	Explanation
12	No ignition reference pulses to the Electronic Control Module (ECM). This code is not stored in memory and will only flash while the fault is present
13	Oxygen sensor circuit — the engine must run up to 1 minute at part throttle, under load, before this code will set. This code does not set when the coolant temperature is below 158°F (70°C) and/or the time since engine start has exceeded 2 minutes
14	Shorted Coolant Temperature Sensor (CTS) circuit — the engine must run up to 2 minutes before this code will set
15	Open Coolant Temperature Sensor (CTS) circuit — the engine must run up to 5 minutes before this code will set
21	Idle switch circuit open or Wide Open Throttle (WOT) switch circuit shorted — the engine must run up to 10 seconds at the following 2 conditions concurrently before this code will set. Idle switch output is in a low voltage state, WOT switch output is in a high voltage state
22	Fuel Cut Solenoid (FCS) circuit open or grounded — the engine must run under the decelerating condition, over 2000 rpm, before this code will set
23	Duty solenoid circuit open or grounded
25	Air Injection Reactor (AIR) Vacuum Switching Valve (VSV) circuit open or grounded
26	Canister Vacuum Switching Valve (VSV) circuit open or grounded
27	Constant high voltage from Vacuum Switching Valve (VSV) to Electronic Control Module (ECM)
31	No ignition reference pulses to the Electronic Control Module (ECM) for 10 seconds at part throttle, under load. This code will store in memory
32	Exhaust Gas Recirculation (EGR) system failure and sensor circuit failure
34	Exhaust Gas Recirculation (EGR) sensor circuit failure
44	Fuel metering lean faulty — the engine must run up to 2 minutes at part throttle, under load, before this code will set. This code does not set when the coolant temperature is below 158°F (70°C) and/or the air temperature in the air cleaner is below 32°F (0°C)
45	Fuel metering rich faulty — the engine must run up to 2 minutes at part throttle, under load, before this code will set. This code does not set when the engine exceeds 2500 rpm and/or the coolant temperature is below 158°F (70°C) and/or the barometric pressure is below 23 in. Hg (575mm Hg), above 8000 t (2500m altitude)
51	Shorted Fuel Cut Solenoid (FCS) circuit and/or faulty Electronic Control Module (ECM)
52	Faulty Electronic Control Module (ECM) — problem is Random Access Memory (RAM) in ECM
53	Shorted Air Injector Reactor (AIR), Vacuum Switching Valve (VSV) and/or faulty Electronic Control Module (ECM)
54	Shorted Vacuum Control Solenoid (VCS) and/or faulty Electronic Control Module (ECM)
55	Faulty Electronic Control Module (ECM) — problem is A/D converter in ECM

Year — 1988
Model — Pick-Up
Engine — 2.6L (156 cid) 4 cyl
Engine Code — 4ZE1

ECM TROUBLE CODES

Code	Explanation
12	No distributor pulses to the Electronic Control Module (ECM) and will only flash while fault is present — no fault indicated
13	Oxygen sensor system — harness open, sensor deterioration
14	Water Temperature Sensor (WTS) system grounded
15	Water Temperature Sensor (WTS) system — harness open
21	Throttle Valve Switch (TVS) system — idle contact and full contact make simultaneously
22	Starter signal system — no signal input
23	Ignition power transistor system — output terminal grounded
25	Vacuum Switching Valve (VSV) system for pressure regulator — grounded or open circuit VSV harness connector or inside of Electronic Control Module (ECM)
26	Vacuum Switching Valve (VSV) system for canister purge — grounded or open circuit VSV harness connector or inside Electronic Control Module (ECM)
27	Driver transistor in Electronic Control Module (ECM) open
32	Exhaust Gas Recirculation (EGR) temperature sensor system — malfunction
33	Fuel injector system — output terminal grounded or open
34	Exhaust Gas Recirculation (EGR) temperature sensor system — sensor or harness defective
35	Ignition power transistor system — harness open
41	Crank Angle Sensor (CAS) system — harnesss open or faulty signal
43	Throttle Valve Switch (TVS) system — idle contact closed continuously
44	Fuel metering system — lean signal — low voltage
45	Fuel metering system — rich signal — high voltage
51	Faulty Electronic Control Module (ECM)
52	Faulty Electronic Control Module (ECM)
53	Vacuum Switching Valve (VSV) for pressure regulator — driver transistor in Electronic Control Module (ECM) open
54	Ignition power transistor system — grounded or defective power transistor
61	Air Flow Sensor (AFS) system — grounded, shorted, open or broken "Hot" wire
62	Air Flow Sensor (AFS) system — broken "Cold" wire
63	Vehicle Speed Sensor (VSS) — harness grounded or open, vehicle speed sensor broken
64	Fuel injector system — driver transistor in Electronic Control Module (ECM) broken
65	Throttle Valve Switch (TVS) system — full contact closed continuously

Year — 1988
Model — Trooper II
Engine — 2.6L (156 cid) 4 cyl
Engine Code — 4ZE1

ECM TROUBLE CODES

Code	Explanation
12	No distributor pulses to the Electronic Control Module (ECM) and will only flash while fault is present — no fault indicated
13	Oxygen sensor system — harness open, sensor deterioration
14	Water Temperature Sensor (WTS) system grounded
15	Water Temperature Sensor (WTS) system — harness open
21	Throttle Valve Switch (TVS) system — idle contact and full contact make simultaneously
22	Starter signal system — no signal input
23	Ignition power transistor system — output terminal grounded
25	Vacuum Switching Valve (VSV) system — output terminal grounded or open
26	Vacuum Switching Valve (VSV) system for canister purge — output terminal grounded or harness open
27	Vacuum Switching Valve (VSV) system for canister purge — defective transistor or grounding system
32	Exhaust Gas Recirculation (EGR) temperature sensor system — malfunction
33	Fuel injector system — output terminal grounded or open
34	Exhaust Gas Recirculation (EGR) temperature sensor system — sensor or harness defective
35	Ignition power transistor system — harness open
41	Crank Angle Sensor (CAS) system — no signal or faulty signal input
43	Throttle Valve Switch (TVS) system — idle contact closed continuously
44	Oxygen sensor system — lean signal — low voltage
45	Oxygen sensor system — rich signal — high voltage
51	Faulty Electronic Control Module (ECM)
52	Faulty Electronic Control Module (ECM)
53	Vacuum Switching Valve (VSV) system — grounded or defective power transistor
54	Ignition power transistor system — grounded or defective power transistor
61	Air Flow Sensor (AFS) system — grounded, shorted, open or broken "Hot" wire
62	Air Flow Sensor (AFS) system — broken "Cold" wire
63	Vehicle Speed Sensor (VSS) — no signal input
64	Fuel injector system — grounded or defective transistor
65	Throttle Valve Switch (TVS) system — full contact closed continuously
72 & 34	Exhaust Gas Recirculation (EGR) — Vacuum Switching Valve (VSV) — output terminal grounded or open
73	Exhaust Gas Recirculation (EGR) — Vacuum Switching Valve (VSV) — defective transistor or grounding system

Year—1989
Model—Pick-Up
Engine—2.3L (138 cid) 4 cyl
Engine Code—4ZD1

ECM TROUBLE CODES

Code	Explanation
12	No ignition reference pulses to the Electronic Control Module (ECM). This code is not stored in memory and will only flash while the fault is present
13	Oxygen sensor circuit—the engine must run up to 1 minute at part throttle, under load, before this code will set. This code does not set when the coolant temperature is below 158°F (70°C) and/or the time since engine start has exceeded 2 minutes
14	Shorted Coolant Temperature Sensor (CTS) circuit—the engine must run up to 2 minutes before this code will set
15	Open Coolant Temperature Sensor (CTS) circuit—the engine must run up to 5 minutes before this code will set
21	Idle switch and Manifold Absolute Pressure (MAP) sensor failure: 1) Vehicle speed is 0 mph and engine speed is between 200 and 1000 rpm, MAP sensor output voltage is more than 19.7 in. Hg (500mm Hg) as input signal, for 5 seconds. 2) Idle switch is OFF. MAP sensor output voltage is less than 3.9 in. Hg (100mm Hg) as input signal, for 5 seconds. 3) MAP sensor output voltage is 15.8–17.7 in. Hg (400–450mm Hg) as input signal and engine speed is more than 1500 rpm. Idle switch is ON for more than 5 seconds. If any condition: 1, 2 or 3 exists, this code will set.
22	Fuel Cut Solenoid (FCS) circuit open or grounded—the engine must run under the decelerating condition, over 2000 rpm, before this code will set
23	Duty solenoid circuit open or grounded
25	Air Switching Solenoid (ASS) circuit open or grounded
26	Canister Vacuum Switching Valve (VSV) circuit open or grounded
27	Constant high voltage from Vacuum Switching Valve (VSV) to Electronic Control Module (ECM)
31	No ignition reference pulses to the Electronic Control Module (ECM) for 10 seconds at part throttle, under load. This code will store in memory
32	Exhaust Gas Recirculation (EGR) system failure and sensor circuit failure
34	Exhaust Gas Recirculation (EGR) sensor circuit failure—Electronic Idle Control (EIC)
44	Fuel metering lean: 1) Coolant temperature is greater than 158°F (70°C). 2) Engine throttle is partially open. 3) Engine speed is less than 2500 rpm. 4) More than 5 seconds have elapsed after fuel-cut recovery. The timer of this code will start to count when all conditions (1 to 4) exist. The Electronic Control Module (ECM) judges to use the timer information to set Code 44 except when either of the following conditions exist: Condition A—barometric MAP is less than 23.5 in. Hg (596mm Hg) ABS (high altitude condition) Condition B—Code 13 or 21 is stored in memory, or the coolant temperature is more than 302°F (150°C).
45	Fuel metering rich: 1) Coolant temperature is greater than 158°F (70°C). 2) Engine throttle is partially open. 3) Engine speed is less than 2500 rpm. 4) Vehicle speed is between 12 and 50 mph (20 and 80 km/h) or 0 mph. 5) More than 30 seconds have elapsed after starting canister purge. The timer of this code will start to count when all conditions (1 to 5) exist. This code does not set when the high altitude condition, above 8000 ft. (2500m), is judged by Electronic Control Module (ECM). ECM judges to use the timer information to set Code 45 except when either of the following conditions exist: Condition A—barometric MAP is less than 23.5 in. Hg (596mm Hg) ABS (high altitude condition) Condition B—Code 13 or 21 is stored in memory or the coolant temperature is more than 302°F (150°C).
51	Shorted Fuel Cut Solenoid (FCS) circuit and/or faulty Electronic Control Module (ECM)

ECM TROUBLE CODES

Code	Explanation
52	Faulty Electronic Control Module (ECM) — problem of Random Access Memory (RAM) in ECM
53	Shorted Air Injection Reactor (AIR), Vacuum Switching Valve (VSV) and/or faulty Electronic Control Module (ECM)
54	Shorted Vacuum Control Solenoid (VCS) and/or faulty Electronic Control Module (ECM)
55	Faulty Electronic Control Module (ECM) — problem of A/D converter in ECM

Year — 1989
Model — Pick-Up
Engine — 2.6L (156 cid) 4 cyl
Engine Code — 4ZE1

ECM TROUBLE CODES

Code	Explanation
12	No distributor pulses to the Electronic Control Module (ECM) and will only flash while fault is present — no fault indicated
13	Oxygen sensor system — harness open, sensor deterioration
14	Water Temperature Sensor (WTS) system grounded
15	Water Temperature Sensor (WTS) system — harness open
21	Throttle Valve Switch (TVS) system — idle contact and full contact make simultaneously
22	Starter signal system — harness grounded or open
23	Ignition power transistor system — output terminal grounded
25	Vacuum Switching Valve (VSV) system for pressure regulator — grounded or open circuit VSV harness connector or inside of Electronic Control Module (ECM)
26	Vacuum Switching Valve (VSV) system for canister purge — grounded or open circuit VSV harness connector or inside Electronic Control Module (ECM)
27	Driver transistor in Electronic Control Module (ECM) open
32	Exhaust Gas Recirculation (EGR) temperature sensor system — malfunction
33	Fuel injector system — grounded or open injector harness connector, dropping resistor or inside Electronic Control Module (ECM)
34	Exhaust Gas Recirculation (EGR) temperature sensor system — sensor or harness defective
35	Ignition power transistor system — harness open
41	Crank Angle Sensor (CAS) system — harnesss open or faulty signal
43	Throttle Valve Switch (TVS) system — idle contact closed continuously
44	Fuel metering system — lean signal — low voltage
45	Fuel metering system — rich signal — high voltage
51	Faulty Electronic Control Module (ECM)
52	Faulty Electronic Control Module (ECM)
53	Vacuum Switching Valve (VSV) for pressure regulator — driver transistor in Electronic Control Module (ECM) open
54	Ignition power transistor system — grounded or defective power transistor
61	Air Flow Sensor (AFS) system — grounded, shorted, open or broken "Hot" wire
62	Air Flow Sensor (AFS) system — broken "Cold" wire
63	Vehicle Speed Sensor (VSS) — harness grounded or open, vehicle speed sensor broken
64	Fuel injector system — driver transistor in Electronic Control Module (ECM) open
65	Throttle Valve Switch (TVS) system — full contact closed continuously

Year — 1989
Model — Amigo
Engine — 2.3L (138 cid) 4 cyl
Engine Code — 4ZD1

ECM TROUBLE CODES

Code	Explanation
12	No ignition reference pulses to the Electronic Control Module (ECM). This code is not stored in memory and will only flash while the fault is present
13	Oxygen sensor circuit — the engine must run up to 1 minute at part throttle, under load, before this code will set. This code does not set when the coolant temperature is below 158°F (70°C) and/or the time since engine start has exceeded 2 minutes
14	Shorted Coolant Temperature Sensor (CTS) circuit — the engine must run up to 2 minutes before this code will set
15	Open Coolant Temperature Sensor (CTS) circuit — the engine must run up to 5 minutes before this code will set
21	Idle switch and Manifold Absolute Pressure (MAP) sensor failure: 1) Vehicle speed is 0 mph and engine speed is 200–1000 rpm, MAP sensor output voltage is more than 19.7 in. Hg (500mm Hg) as input signal, for 5 seconds. 2) Idle switch is OFF — MAP sensor output voltage is less than 4 in. Hg (100mm Hg) as input signal, for 5 seconds. 3) MAP sensor output voltage is 16–18 in. Hg (400–450mm Hg) as input signal, and engine speed is more than 1500 rpm. Idle switch is ON for more than 5 seconds. If any condition: 1, 2 or 3 exists, this code will set.
22	Fuel Cut Solenoid (FCS) circuit open or grounded — the engine must run under the decelerating condition, over 2000 rpm, before this code will set
23	Duty solenoid circuit open or grounded
25	Air Switching Solenoid (ASS) circuit open or grounded
26	Canister Vacuum Switching Valve (VSV) circuit open or grounded
27	Constant high voltage from Vacuum Switching Valve (VSV) to Electronic Control Module (ECM)
31	No ignition reference pulses to the Electronic Control Module (ECM) for 10 seconds at part throttle, under load. This code will store in memory
32	Exhaust Gas Recirculation (EGR) system failure and sensor circuit failure
34	Exhaust Gas Recirculation (EGR) sensor circuit failure — Electronic Idle Control (EIC)
44	Fuel metering lean: 1) Coolant temperature is greater than 158°F (70°C). 2) Engine throttle is partially open. 3) Engine speed is less than 2500 rpm. 4) More than 5 seconds have elapsed after fuel-cut recovery. The timer of this code will start to count when all conditions (1–4) exist. The Electronic Control Module (ECM) judges to use the timer information to set Code 44 except when either of the following conditions exist: Condition A — barometric MAP is less than 24 in. Hg (596mm Hg) ABS (high altitude condition) Condition B — Code 13 or 21 is stored in memory or the coolant temperature is more than 302°F (150°C).
45	Fuel metering rich: 1) Coolant temperature is greater than 158°F (70°C). 2) Engine throttle is partially open. 3) Engine speed is less than 2500 rpm. 4) Vehicle speed is 12–50 mph (20–80 km/h) or 0 mph. 5) More than 30 seconds have elapsed after starting canister purge. The timer of this code will start to count when all conditions (1–5) exist. This code does not set when the high altitude condition, above 8000 ft. (2500m), is judged by Electronic Control Module (ECM). ECM judges to use the timer information to set Code 45 except when either of the following conditions exist: Condition A — barometric MAP is less than 24 in. Hg (596mm Hg) ABS (high altitude condition) Condition B — Code 13 or 21 is stored in memory or the coolant temperature is more than 302°F (150°C).

ECM TROUBLE CODES

Code	Explanation
51	Shorted Fuel Cut Solenoid (FCS) circuit and/or faulty Electronic Control Module (ECM)
52	Faulty Electronic Control Module (ECM)—problem of Random Access Memory (RAM) in ECM
53	Shorted Air Injection Reactor (AIR), Vacuum Switching Valve (VSV) and/or faulty Electronic Control Module (ECM)
54	Shorted Vacuum Control Solenoid (VCS) and/or faulty Electronic Control Module (ECM)
55	Faulty Electronic Control Module (ECM)—problem of A/D converter in ECM

Year—1989
Model—Amigo
Engine—2.3L (138 cid) 4 cyl
Engine Code—4ZD1

ECM TROUBLE CODES

Code	Explanation
12	No distributor pulses to the Electronic Control Module (ECM) and will only flash while fault is present—no fault indicated
13	Oxygen sensor system—harness open, sensor deterioration
14	Water Temperature Sensor (WTS) system grounded
15	Water Temperature Sensor (WTS) system—harness open
21	Throttle Valve Switch (TVS) system—idle contact and full contact make simultaneously
22	Starter signal system—harness grounded or open
23	Ignition power transistor system—output terminal grounded
25	Vacuum Switching Valve (VSV) system for pressure regulator—grounded or open circuit VSV harness connector or inside of Electronic Control Module (ECM)
26	Vacuum Switching Valve (VSV) system for canister purge—grounded or open circuit VSV harness connector or inside Electronic Control Module (ECM)
27	Driver transistor in Electronic Control Module (ECM) open
32	Exhaust Gas Recirculation (EGR) temperature sensor system—malfunction
33	Fuel injector system—grounded or open injector harness connector, dropping resistor or inside Electronic Control Module (ECM)
34	Exhaust Gas Recirculation (EGR) temperature sensor system—sensor or harness defective
35	Ignition power transistor system—harness open
41	Crank Angle Sensor (CAS) system—harness open or faulty signal
43	Throttle Valve Switch (TVS) system—idle contact closed continuously
44	Fuel metering system—lean signal—low voltage
45	Fuel metering system—rich signal—high voltage
51	Faulty Electronic Control Module (ECM)
52	Faulty Electronic Control Module (ECM)
53	Vacuum Switching Valve (VSV) for pressure regulator—driver transistor in Electronic Control Module (ECM) open
54	Ignition power transistor system—grounded or defective power transistor
61	Air Flow Sensor (AFS) system—grounded, shorted, open or broken "Hot" wire
62	Air Flow Sensor (AFS) system—broken "Cold" wire
63	Vehicle Speed Sensor (VSS)—harness grounded or open, vehicle speed sensor broken
64	Fuel injector system—driver transistor in Electronic Control Module (ECM) open
65	Throttle Valve Switch (TVS) system—full contact closed continuously

Year — 1989
Model — Trooper/Trooper II
Engine — 2.6L (156 cid) 4 cyl
Engine Code — 4ZE1

ECM TROUBLE CODES

Code	Explanation
12	No distributor pulses to the Electronic Control Module (ECM) and will only flash while fault is present — no fault indicated
13	Oxygen sensor system — harness open, sensor deterioration
14	Water Temperature Sensor (WTS) system grounded
15	Water Temperature Sensor (WTS) system — harness open
21	Throttle Valve Switch (TVS) system — idle contact and full contact make simultaneously
22	Starter signal system — no signal input
23	Ignition power transistor system — output terminal grounded
25	Vacuum Switching Valve (VSV) system — output terminal grounded or open
26	Vacuum Switching Valve (VSV) system for canister purge — output terminal grounded or harness open
27	Vacuum Switching Valve (VSV) system for canister purge — defective transistor or grounding system
32	Exhaust Gas Recirculation (EGR) temperature sensor system — malfunction
33	Fuel injector system — output terminal grounded or open
34	Exhaust Gas Recirculation (EGR) temperature sensor system — sensor or harness defective
35	Ignition power transistor system — harness open
41	Crank Angle Sensor (CAS) system — no signal or faulty signal input
43	Throttle Valve Switch (TVS) system — idle contact closed continuously
44	Oxygen sensor system — lean signal — low voltage
45	Oxygen sensor system — rich signal — high voltage
51	Faulty Electronic Control Module (ECM)
52	Faulty Electronic Control Module (ECM)
53	Vacuum Switching Valve (VSV) system — grounded or defective power transistor
54	Ignition power transistor system — grounded or defective power transistor
61	Air Flow Sensor (AFS) system — grounded, shorted, open or broken "Hot" wire
62	Air Flow Sensor (AFS) system — broken "Cold" wire
63	Vehicle Speed Sensor (VSS) — no signal input
64	Fuel injector system — grounded or defective transistor
65	Throttle Valve Switch (TVS) system — full contact closed continuously
72 & 34	Exhaust Gas Recirculation (EGR) — Vacuum Switching Valve (VSV) — output terminal grounded or open
73	Exhaust Gas Recirculation (EGR) — Vacuum Switching Valve (VSV) — defective transistor or grounding system

INDEX

JAGUAR

Microfuelling System

SELF-DIAGNOSTIC SYSTEM

Description

The XJ-S Micro Fueling System and ignition timing are controlled by a single electronic control unit (ECU), which incorporates electronic programmed memory techniques.

The ECU is mounted in the passenger's compartment under the fascia.

Ignition timing and fuel metering parameters are controlled by the ignition ECU from engine load and speed information supplied by a crankshaft sensor and an integral pressure sensor connected, via a solenoid valve (if fitted) and capillary tube, to the inlet manifold.

The ECU incorporates a Limp Home facility. If at any time a failure is experienced, the words Fuel and Fail will be displayed alternately. By using the Jaguar Diagnostic System (JDS) tester or equivalent, all fault diagnosis procedures can be checked and adjusted.

Entering Diagnostic Mode

1. Connect the JDS battery reference leads.
2. Open the passenger's door and remove the front carpet.
3. Remove the sound deadening pad.
4. Remove the ECU cover retaining nuts and the cover.
5. Connect the engine management pod to the JDS.
6. Disconnect the ECU multi-plug connectors and connect the JDS pod to the ECU multi-plugs.
7. Connect the cable harness multi-plug to the JDS multi-plugs. Connect the JDS 50-way cable.
8. To obtain any failure codes, switch the ignition **OFF**, then **ON**. After approximately 10 seconds, the failure will be noted on the display.

Clearing Diagnostic Memory

1. Turn the ignition switch **OFF**.
2. Disconnect the testing equipment; the system is exited.

JAGUAR

Year – 1988
Model – XJ6
Engine – 3.6L (220 cid) 6 cyl
Engine Code – VIN H

ECM TROUBLE CODES

Code	Explanation
FF1	Cranking signal failure, no crankshaft sensor signal detected after cranking for 6 seconds or cranking signal from the starter solenoid is present above 1550 rev/min.
FF2	Airflow meter failure – either open circuit or shorted to ground
FF3	Coolant temperature sensor failure
FF4	Feedback failure (where applicable)
FF5	Airflow meter or throttle potentiometer failure – low throttle potentiometer voltage with high airflow meter voltage
FF6	Airflow meter or throttle potentiometer failure – low throttle potentiometer voltage with low airflow meter voltage
FF7	Idle fuel adjustment potentiometer failure
FF8	Hot start sensor failure (where applicable)

Year – 1989
Model – XJ6
Engine – 3.6L (220 cid) 6 cyl
Engine Code – VIN H

ECM TROUBLE CODES

Code	Explanation
FF1	Cranking signal failure, no crankshaft sensor signal detected after cranking for 6 seconds or cranking signal from the starter solenoid is present above 1550 rev/min.
FF2	Airflow meter failure – either open circuit or shorted to ground
FF3	Coolant temperature sensor failure
FF4	Feedback failure (where applicable)
FF5	Airflow meter or throttle potentiometer failure – low throttle potentiometer voltage with high airflow meter voltage
FF6	Airflow meter or throttle potentiometer failure – low throttle potentiometer voltage with low airflow meter voltage
FF7	Idle fuel adjustment potentiometer failure
FF8	Hot start sensor failure (where applicable)

INDEX

MAZDA

Electronic Gasoline Injection (EGI) System

DIAGNOSTIC SYSTEM

Description

SYSTEM CHECKER

On models 626 and RX-7 for 1984–85, model 323 for 1986 and B-2000 Pick-Up for 1986, the System Checker No. 83 (tool No. 49-G030-920) is used to detect and indicate any problems of each sensor, damaged wiring, poor contact or a short circuit between each of the sensor control units. Trouble is indicated by a red lamp and a buzzer.

If there are more than 2 problems at the same time, the indicator lamp turns **ON** in the numerical order of the code number. Even, if the problem is corrected during indication, 1 cycle will be indicated. If after a malfunction has occured and the ignition key is switched **OFF**, the malfuction indicator for the feedback system will not be displayed on the checker.

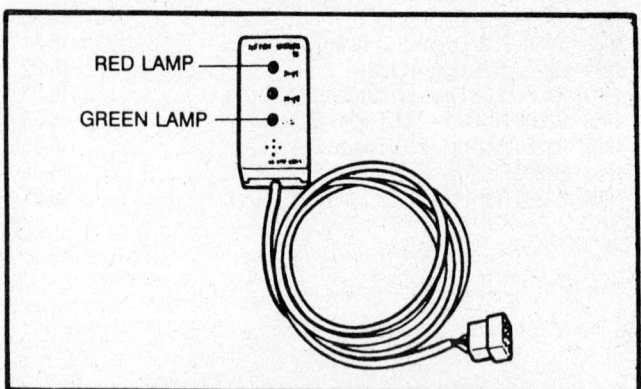

View of the System Checker 83 — Mazda

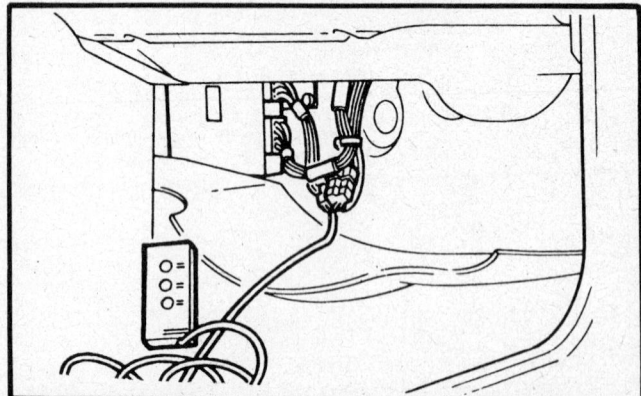

View of the System Checker 83 connected to the vehicle — Mazda

DIGITAL CODE CHECKER AND SELF-DIAGNOSIS CHECKER

The Digital Code Checker tool No. 49-G018-9A0 for 1986–87 or the Self Diagnosis Checker tool No. 49-H018-9A1 are used to retrieve code numbers of malfunctions which have happened and were memorized or are continuing. The malfunction is indicated by the code number and a buzzer.

If there is more than 1 malfunction, the code numbers will

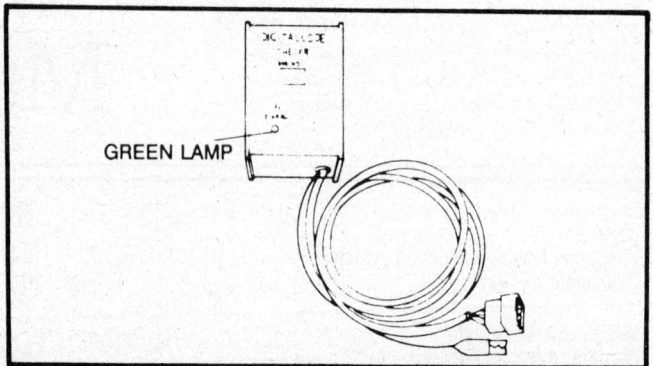

View of the Digital Code Checker — Mazda

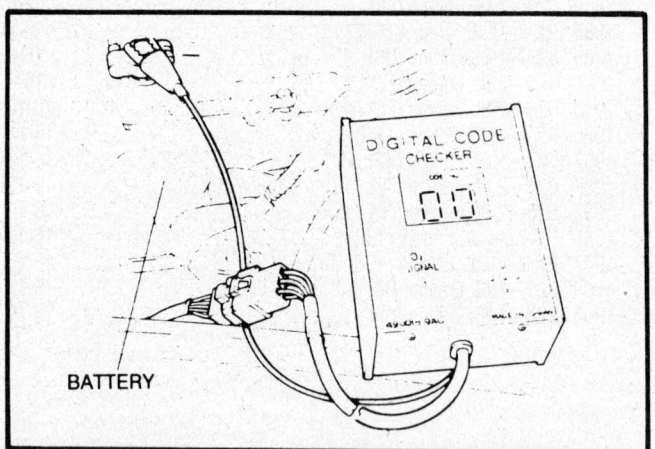

View of the Digital Code Checker connected to the vehicle — Mazda

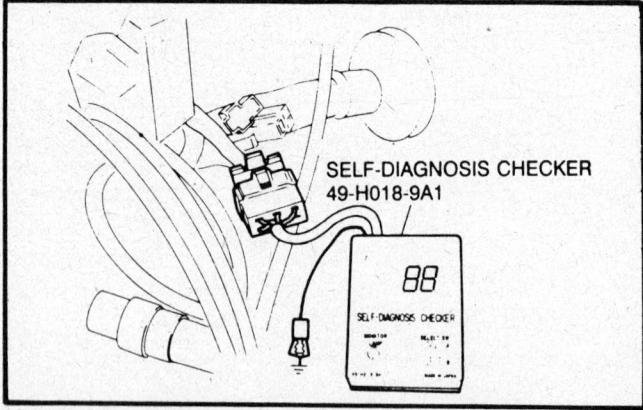

View of the Self-Diagnosis Checker — Mazda

display on the self diagnosis checker 1 by 1 in numerical order. In the case of malfunctions, 09, 13 and 01, the code numbers are displayed in a order of 01, 09 and then 13.

The memory of malfunctions is canceled by disconnecting the negative battery cable and depressing the brake pedal for at least 5 seconds.

The ECU has a built in fail-safe mechanism for the main input sensors. If a malfunction occurs, the emission control unit will substitute values; this will slightly effect the driving performance but the vehicle may still be driven.

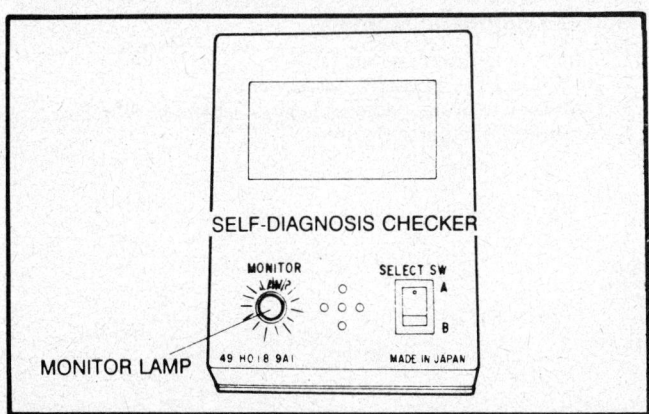

View of the Self-Diagnosis Checker connected to the vehicle—Mazda

The ECU continuously checks for malfunctions of the input devices. But, the ECU checks checks for malfunctions of the output devices within 3 seconds after turning the ignition switch to the **ON** position and the test connector is grounded.

The malfunction indicator light indicates a pattern the same as the buzzer of the self-diagnosis checker when the self-diagnosis check connector is grounded. When the self-diagnosis check connector is not grounded, the lamp illuminates steady while malfunction of the main input sensor occurs and turns **OFF** if the malfunction recovers. However, the malfunction code is memorized in the emission control unit.

Entering Diagnostic Mode

EXCEPT RX-7

1984–85

1. Operate the engine until normal temperatures are reached and run it at idle.
2. Connect the System Checker tool No. 83 (49-G030-920) to the check connector, located near the ECU.
3. Check whether the trouble indication light turns **ON**.

NOTE: Trouble is indicated by a red light and a buzzer.

4. If the light turns **ON**, check for cause problems.

1986–87

1. Warm the engine to normal operating temperatures, by keeping the engine speed below 4000 rpm.
2. Connect the Digital Code Checker No. 49-G018-9A0 to the check connector and ground the other lead.
3. Wait for 3 minutes for the code(s) to register.
4. If the code number flashes, a buzzer will automatically sound, indicating the code number.
5. Note the code numbers and check the causes, repair as necessary. Be sure to recheck the code numbers by performing the "After Repair Procedure," after repairing.

1988–89

1. Connect the Self-Diagnosis Checker No. 49-H018-9A1 to the check connector (green, 6-pin). The check connector is usually located above the right side wheel housing.
2. On the 929 models, set the select switch, on the Self-Diagnosis Checker, to the "A" position.
3. Using a jumper wire, connect it between the test connector (green, 1-pin) and a ground.
4. Turn the ignition switch to the **ON** position. Check that the number "88" flashes on the digital display and the buzzer sounds for 3 seconds after turning the ignition switch **ON**.

5. If the number "88" does not flash, check the main relay, power supply circuit and the check the check connector wiring.
6. If the number "88" flashes and the buzzer sounds continuously for more than 20 seconds, replace the ECU and perform Steps 3 and 4 again.
7. Note the code numbers and check the causes, repair as necessary. Be sure to recheck the code numbers by performing the "After Repair Procedure," after repairing.

RX-7

1985

1. Operate the engine until normal temperatures are reached and run it at idle.
2. Connect the System Checker tool No. 83 (49-G030-920) to the check connector, located near the ECU.
3. Check whether the trouble indication light turns **ON**.

NOTE: Trouble is indicated by a red light and a buzzer.

4. If the light turns **ON**, check for cause problems.

1986–87

1. Start and allow the engine to reach normal operating temperature.
2. Connect the Digital Code Checker No. 49-G018-9A0 to the check connector and the battery ground cable.
3. Check the Digital Code Checker for trouble codes.

NOTE: After turning the ignition switch to the ON position, the buzzer will sound for 3 seconds.

4. Note the code numbers and check the causes, repair as necessary. Be sure to recheck the code numbers by performing the "After Repair Procedure," after repairing.

1988–89

1. Start and allow the engine to reach normal operating temperature. Stop the engine.
2. Connect the Self-Diagnosis Checker No. 49-H018-9A1 to the check connector and the battery ground cable.
3. Set the select switch, on the Self Diagnosis Checker, to the "B" position for 1988 models or the "A" position for 1989 models.
4. On 1988 models, check the Self-Diagnosis checker for trouble codes and proceed to appropriate trouble code diagnostic chart.
5. On 1989 models, connect a jumper wire between the test connector and ground.
6. Turn the ignition switch to the **ON** position. Check that the number "88" flashes on the digital display and the buzzer sounds for 3 seconds after turning the ignition switch **ON**.
7. If the number "88" does not flash, check the main relay, the power supply circuit or the connector wiring.
9. If the number "88" flashes and the buzzer sounds continuously for more than 20 seconds, replace the ECU and perform Steps 5 and 6 again.
10. Note the code numbers and check the causes, repair as necessary. Be sure to recheck the code numbers by performing the "After Repair Procedure," after repairing.

After Repair Procedure

NOTE: This procedure is used on all vehicles 1986 and later.

1. Reset the ECU by performing the following procedures:
   a. Turn the ignition switch **OFF**.
   b. Disconnect the negative battery cable.
   c. Depress the brake pedal at least 5 seconds.
   d. Reconnect the battery cable.
2. Connect the Digital Code Checker or the Self-Diagnosis Checker to the test connector.

3. If necessary to use a jumper wire, connect it between the test connector (green: pin 1) and a ground.

4. Turn the ignition switch **ON** but do not start the engine for 6 seconds.

5. Operate the engine until normal operating temperatures are reached, then, run it at 2000 rpm for 2 minutes.

6. Verify that no code numbers are displayed.

Clearing Diagnostic Memory
1. Turn the ignition switch **OFF**.
2. Disconnect the negative battery cable.
3. Depress the brake pedal at least 5 seconds.
4. Reconnect the battery cable.

MAZDA

Year – 1984
Model – 626
Engine – 2.0L (122 cid) 4 cyl
Engine Code – FE

ECM TROUBLE CODES

Code no.	Location of problem	Indication
1	Engine speed	
2	Water thermo-sensor	
3	Oxygen (O$_2$) sensor	
4	Vacuum sensor	
5	EGR position sensor	

Year – 1984
Model – RX-7
Engine – 1.3L (80 cid) Rotary
Engine Code – 13B

ECM TROUBLE CODES

Code No.	Location of problem	Indication	Checking procedure
1	Engine speed	ON / OFF — 1cycle — 0.4 2.0 sec	Disconnect the trailing coil – terminal crank engine at least 1.5 seconds, with IG "ON" code should be heard.
2	Air flow meter	ON / OFF — 0.4 0.4 0.4 2.0 sec	Disconnect air flow meter connector, turn IG "ON" code should be heard.
3	Water thermo sensor	ON / OFF	Disconnect the water thermo sensor connector, turn IG "ON" code should be heard.
4	Oxygen (O_2) sensor	ON / OFF — 2.0 2.0 sec	
5	Throttle sensor	ON / OFF — 2.0 0.4 0.4 2.0 sec	Disconnect throttle sensor connector, turn IG "ON" code should be heard.
6	Atmospheric pressure sensor	ON / OFF — 2.0 0.4 0.4 0.4 0.4 2.0 sec	Disconnect the atmospheric pressure sensor, turn IG "ON" code should be heard.

Year – 1985
Model – 626
Engine – 2.0L (122 cid) 4 cyl
Engine Code – FE

ECM TROUBLE CODES

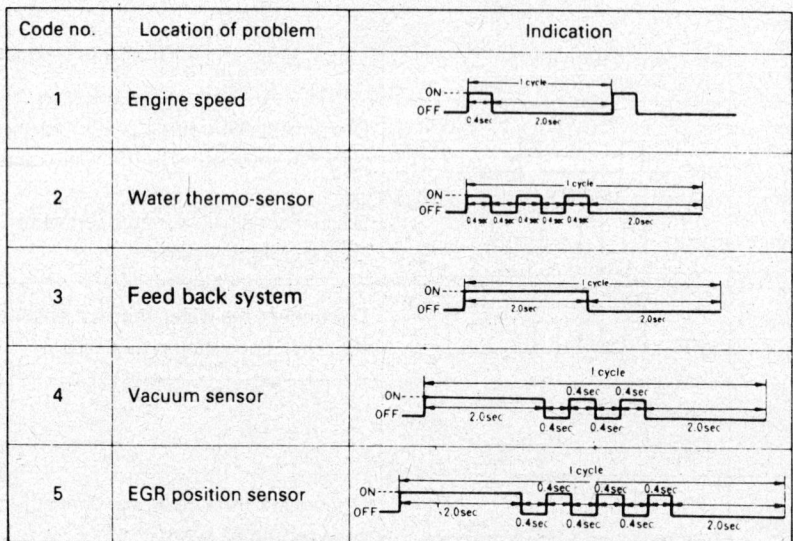

Code no.	Location of problem	Indication
1	Engine speed	
2	Water thermo-sensor	
3	Feed back system	
4	Vacuum sensor	
5	EGR position sensor	

Year – 1985
Model – RX-7
Engine – 1.3L (80 cid) Rotary
Engine Code – 13B

ECM TROUBLE CODES

Code No.	Location of problem	Indication	Checking procedure
1	Engine speed	ON / OFF — 1 cycle — 0.4 2.0 sec	Disconnect the trailing coil – terminal crank engine at least 1.5 seconds, with IG "ON" code should be heard.
2	Air flow meter	ON / OFF — 0.4 0.4 0.4 2.0 sec	Disconnect air flow meter connector, turn IG "ON" code should be heard.
3	Water thermo sensor	ON / OFF	Disconnect the water thermo sensor connector, turn IG "ON" code should be heard.
4	Oxygen (O$_2$) sensor	ON / OFF — 2.0 2.0 sec	
5	Throttle sensor	ON / OFF — 2.0 0.4 0.4 2.0 sec	Disconnect throttle sensor connector, turn IG "ON" code should be heard.
6	Atmospheric pressure sensor	ON / OFF — 2.0 0.4 0.4 0.4 0.4 sec	Disconnect the atmospheric pressure sensor, turn IG "ON" code should be heard.

Year – 1986
Model – 323
Engine – 1.6L (97 cid) EGI 4 cyl
Engine Code – B6

ECM TROUBLE CODES

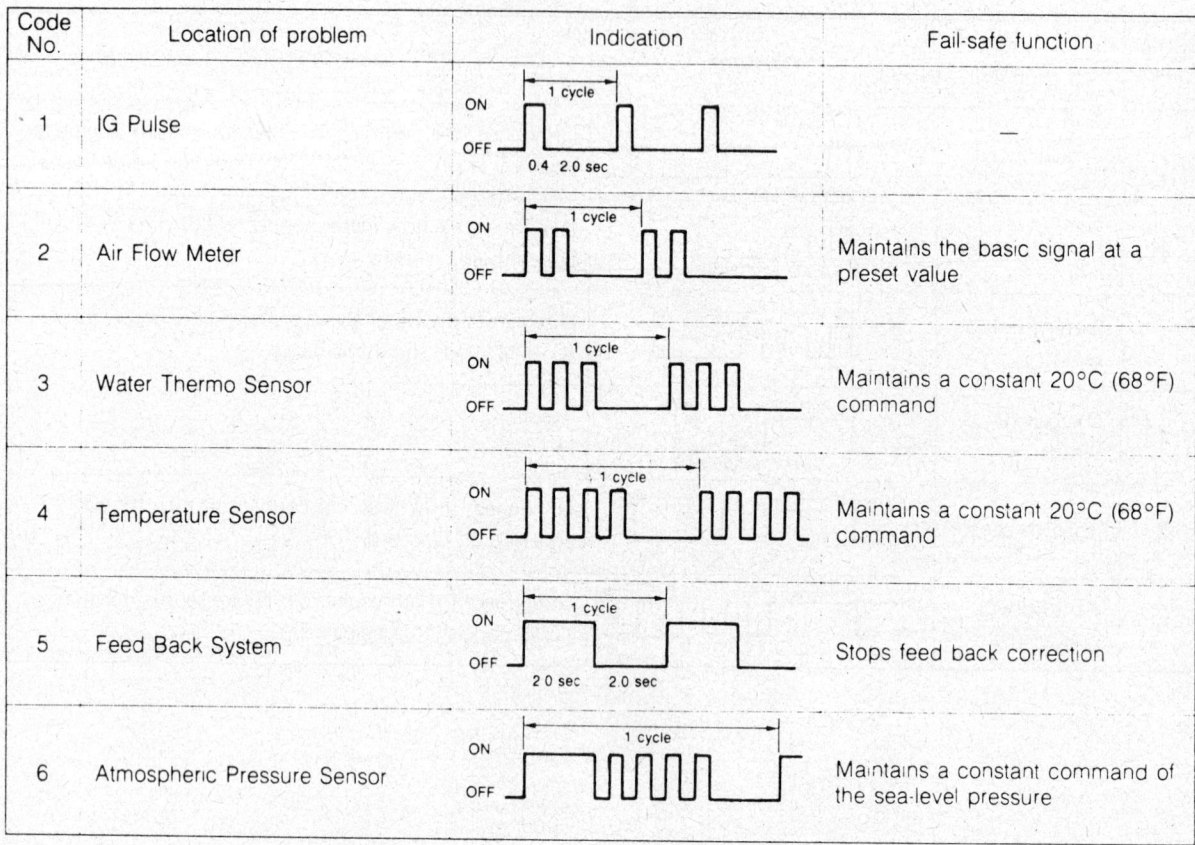

Code No.	Location of problem	Indication	Fail-safe function
1	IG Pulse		—
2	Air Flow Meter		Maintains the basic signal at a preset value
3	Water Thermo Sensor		Maintains a constant 20°C (68°F) command
4	Temperature Sensor		Maintains a constant 20°C (68°F) command
5	Feed Back System		Stops feed back correction
6	Atmospheric Pressure Sensor		Maintains a constant command of the sea-level pressure

Year—1986
Model—626
Engine—2.0L (122 cid) 4 cyl
Engine Code— FE

ECM TROUBLE CODES

Code Number	Location of problem	Buzzer	Fail-safe function
1	IG Pulse	← 1 cycle → 0 4 s 2 0 s	—
2	Air Flow Meter	← 1 cycle → 0 4 s 2 0 s	Maintains the basic signal at a preset value.
3	Water Thermo Sensor	← 1 cycle → 0 4 s 6 s 2 0 s	Maintains a constant 35°C(95°F) command.
4	Intake Air Temperature Sensor	← 1 cycle → 2 0 s 2 4 s 2 0 s	Maintains a constant 20°C(68°F) command.
5	Feedback System	← 1 cycle → 2 0 s 2 0 s	Dose not take in the feed-back.
6	Throttle Sensor	← 1 cycle → 2 0 s 0 8 s 2 0 s	Maintains a constant command opened the throttle valve fully
9	Atomspheric Pressure Sensor	← 1 cycle → 2 0 s 2 4 s 2 0 s	Maintains a constant command of the sea level pressure

MAZDA
DIAGNOSTIC CODE DATA

Year — 1986
Model — 626
Engine — 2.0L (122 cid) Turbo 4 cyl
Engine Code — FE

ECM TROUBLE CODES

Code Number	Location of problem	Buzzer	Fail-safe function
1	IG Pulse	1 cycle / 0 4 s 2 0 s	—
2	Air Flow Meter	1 cycle / 0 4 s 2 0 s	Maintains the basic signal at a preset value.
3	Water Thermo Sensor	1 cycle / 0 4 s 6 s 2 0 s	Maintains a constant 35°C(95°F) command.
4	Intake Air Temperature Sensor	1 cycle / 2 0 s 2 4 s 2 0 s	Maintains a constant 20°C(68°F) command.
5	Feedback System	1 cycle / 2 0 s 2 0 s	Dose not take in the feed-back.
6	Throttle Sensor	1 cycle / 2 0 s 0 8 s 2 0 s	Maintains a constant command opened the throttle valve fully
9	Atomspheric Pressure Sensor	1 cycle / 2 0 s 2 4 s 2 0 s	Maintains a constant command of the sea level pressure

Year — 1986
Model — RX-7
Engine — 1.3L (80 cid) EGI Rotary
Engine Code — 13B

ECM TROUBLE CODES

Code	Explanation
1	Crank angle sensor
2	Air Flow Meter (AFM) — maintains the basic signal at a present value
3	Water temperature sensor — maintains a constant 176°F (80°C) command
4	Intake Air Temperature (IAT) sensor — Air Flow Meter (AFM) — maintains a constant 68°F (20°C) command
5	Oxygen sensor — stops the feedback correction
6	Throttle sensor — maintains a constant 100% (approx. 18°) command
7	Boost sensor — maintains a constant 3.78 in. Hg (− 96mm Hg) command
9	Atmospheric Pressure Sensor (APS) — maintains a constant command of sea level pressure
12	Coil with igniter (trailing side) — stops the operation of ignition system (only trailing side)
15	Intake air temperature sensor (dynamic chamber) — maintains a constant 68°F (20°C) command

Year — 1987
Model — 323
Engine — 1.6L (97 cid) EGI 4 cyl
Engine Code — B6

ECM TROUBLE CODES

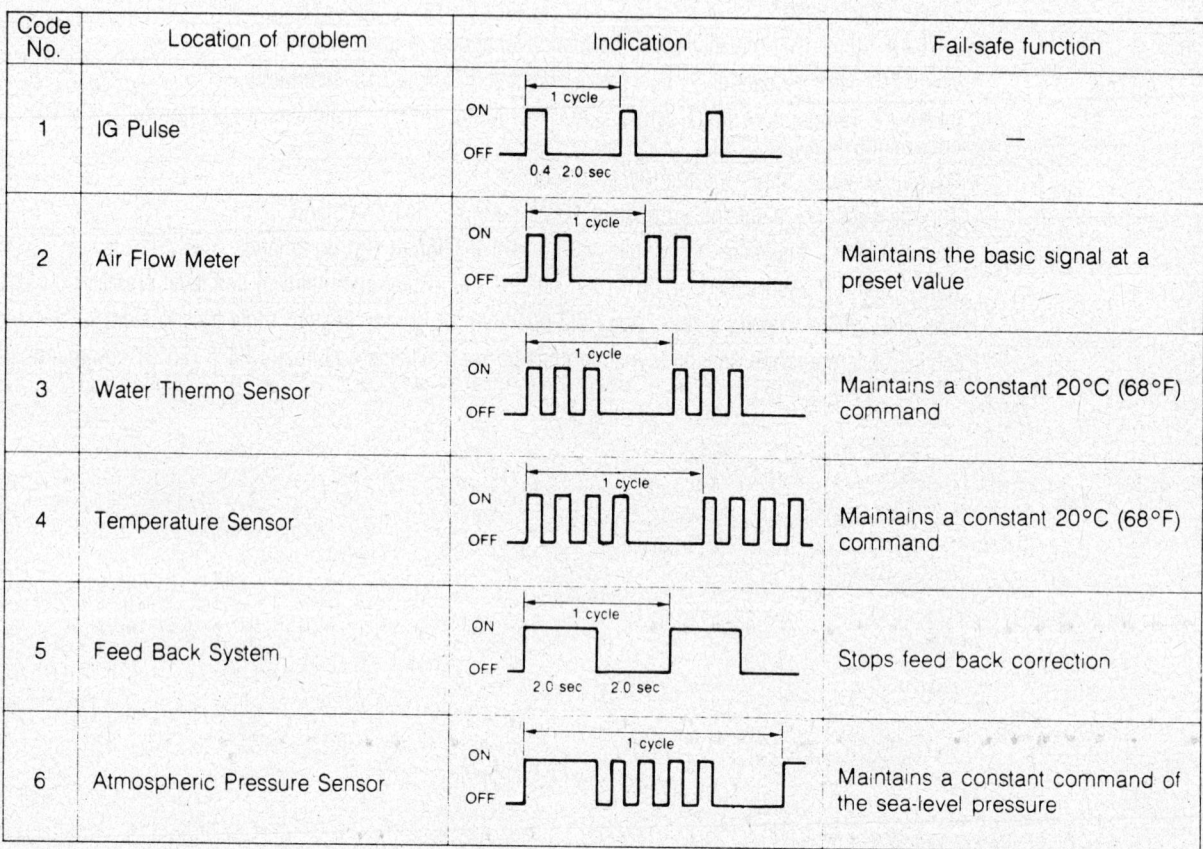

Code No.	Location of problem	Indication	Fail-safe function
1	IG Pulse	ON / OFF — 1 cycle, 0.4 2.0 sec	—
2	Air Flow Meter	ON / OFF — 1 cycle	Maintains the basic signal at a preset value
3	Water Thermo Sensor	ON / OFF — 1 cycle	Maintains a constant 20°C (68°F) command
4	Temperature Sensor	ON / OFF — 1 cycle	Maintains a constant 20°C (68°F) command
5	Feed Back System	ON / OFF — 1 cycle, 2.0 sec 2.0 sec	Stops feed back correction
6	Atmospheric Pressure Sensor	ON / OFF — 1 cycle	Maintains a constant command of the sea-level pressure

Year — 1987
Model — 626
Engine — 2.0L (122 cid) 4 cyl
Engine Code — FE

ECM TROUBLE CODES

Code No.	Location of problem	Buzzer	Fail-safe function
1	IG Pulse	1 cycle / 0.4 s 2.0 s	—
2	Air Flow Meter	1 cycle / 0.4 s 0.8 s 2.0 s	Maintains the basic signal at a preset value.
3	Water Thermo Sensor	1 cycle / 0.4 s 1.6 s 2.0 s	Maintains a constant 35°C(95°F) command.
4	Intake Air Temperature Sensor	1 cycle / 2.0 s 2.4 s 2.0 s	Maintains a constant 20°C(68°F) command.
5	Feedback system	1 cycle / 2.0 s 2.0 s	Does not take in the feedback correction
6	Throttle Sensor	1 cycle / 2.0 s 0.8 s 2.0 s	Maintains a constant command opened the throttle valve fully
8	EGR Position Sensor	1 cycle / 2.0 s 2.4 s 2.0 s	Cuts off EGR
9	Atomspheric Pressure Sensor	1 cycle / 2.0 s 3.2 s 2.0 s	Maintains a constant command of the sea level pressure
22	No.1 cylinder sensor	1 cycle / 0.4 s 2.0 s	Injects fuel at the same time (1 time/2 revolutions)

Year — 1987
Model — 626
Engine — 2.0L (122 cid) Turbo 4 cyl
Engine Code — FE

ECM TROUBLE CODES

Code No.	Location of problem	Buzzer	Fail-safe function
1	IG Pulse	← 1 cycle → / 0.4 s 2.0 s	—
2	Air Flow Meter	← 1 cycle → / 0.4 s 0.8 s 2.0 s	Maintains the basic signal at a preset value.
3	Water Thermo Sensor	← 1 cycle → / 0.4 s 1.6 s 2.0 s	Maintains a constant 35°C(95°F) command.
4	Intake Air Temperature Sensor	← 1 cycle → / 2.0 s 2.4 s 2.0 s	Maintains a constant 20°C(68°F) command.
5	Feedback system	← 1 cycle → / 2.0 s 2.0 s	Does not take in the feedback correction
6	Throttle Sensor	← 1 cycle → / 2.0 s 0.8 s 2.0 s	Maintains a constant command opened the throttle valve fully
8	EGR Position Sensor	← 1 cycle → / 2.0 s 2.4 s 2.0 s	Cuts off EGR
9	Atomspheric Pressure Sensor	← 1 cycle → / 2.0 s 3.2 s 2.0 s	Maintains a constant command of the sea level pressure
22	No.1 cylinder sensor	← 1 cycle → / 0.4 s 2.0 s	Injects fuel at the same time (1 time/2 revolutions)

Year — 1987
Model — RX-7
Engine — 1.3L (80 cid) EGI Rotary
Engine Code — 13B

ECM TROUBLE CODES

Code	Explanation
1	Crank angle sensor
2	Air Flow Meter (AFM) — maintains the basic signal at a present value
3	Water temperature sensor — maintains a constant 176°F (80°C) command
4	Intake Air Temperature (IAT) sensor — Air Flow Meter (AFM) — maintains a constant 68°F (20°C) command
5	Oxygen sensor — stops the feedback correction
6	Throttle sensor — maintains a constant 100% (approx. 18°) command
7	Boost sensor — maintains a constant 3.78 in. Hg (−96mm Hg) command
9	Atmospheric Pressure Sensor (APS) — maintains a constant command of sea level pressure
12	Coil with igniter (trailing side) — stops the operation of ignition system (only trailing side)
15	Intake air temperature sensor (dynamic chamber) — maintains a constant 68°F (20°C) command

Year—1987
Model—RX-7
Engine—1.3L (80 cid) Turbo 4 cyl
Engine Code—13B

ECM TROUBLE CODES

Code	Explanation
1	Crank angle sensor
2	Air Flow Meter (AFM)—maintains the basic signal at a present value
3	Water temperature sensor—maintains a constant 176°F (80°C) command
4	Intake Air Temperature (IAT) sensor—Air Flow Meter (AFM)—maintains a constant 68°F (20°C) command
5	Oxygen sensor—stops the feedback correction
6	Throttle sensor—maintains a constant 100% (approx. 18°) command
7	Pressure sensor—maintains a constant 7.78 in. Hg command
9	Atmospheric Pressure Sensor (APS)—maintains a constant command of sea level pressure
12	Coil with igniter (trailing side)—stops the operation of ignition system (only trailing side)
15	Intake air temperature sensor (intake air pipe)—maintains a constant 68°F (20°C) command

Year — 1988
Model — 323 SOHC
Engine — 1.6L (97 cid) EGI 4 cyl
Engine Code — B6

ECM TROUBLE CODES

Code	Explanation
01	Ignition pulse (igniter) — broken wire, short circuit
08	Air flow meter — broken wire, short circuit — basic fuel injection amount fixed as for 2 driving modes 1) idle switch: ON, 2) idle switch: OFF
09	Water thermosensor — broken wire, short circuit — coolant temperature input fixed at 176°F (80°C) for Idle Speed Control (ISC) at 68°F (20°C) for fuel injection
10	Intake air thermosensor (air flow meter) — broken wire, short circuit — intake air temperature input fixed at 68°F (20°C)
14	Atmospheric pressure sensor — broken wire, short circuit — atmospheric pressure input fixed at 29.9 in. Hg (760mm Hg)
15	Oxygen sensor — sensor output continues less than 0.55V 120 sec. after engine starts (1500 rpm) — feedback system operating cancelled
17	Feedback system — oxygen sensor output not changed 20 sec. after engine exceeds 1500 rpm — feedback operation cancelled
25	Solenoid valve for pressure regulator control (if equipped)
26	Solenoid valve for vacuum switch valve
27	Solenoid valve for No. 2 purge control
34	Solenoid valve for idle speed control valve

Year — 1988
Model — 323 DOHC
Engine — 1.6L (97 cid) EGI 4 cyl
Engine Code — B6

ECM TROUBLE CODES

Code	Explanation
01	Ignition pulse (igniter) — broken wire, short circuit
08	Air flow meter — broken wire, short circuit — basic fuel injection amount fixed as for 2 driving modes 1) idle switch: ON, 2) idle switch: OFF
09	Water thermosensor — broken wire, short circuit — coolant temperature input fixed at 176°F (80°C) for Idle Speed Control (ISC) at 68°F (20°C) for fuel injection
10	Intake air thermosensor (air flow meter) — broken wire, short circuit — intake air temperature input fixed at 68°F (20°C)
14	Atmospheric pressure sensor — broken wire, short circuit — atmospheric pressure input fixed at 29.9 in. Hg (760mm Hg)
15	Oxygen sensor — sensor output continues less than 0.55V 120 sec. after engine starts (1500 rpm) — feedback system operating cancelled
17	Feedback system — oxygen sensor output not changed 20 sec. after engine exceeds 1500 rpm — feedback operation cancelled
25	Solenoid valve for pressure regulator control (if equipped)
26	Solenoid valve for vacuum switch valve
27	Solenoid valve for No. 2 purge control
34	Solenoid valve for idle speed control valve

Year – 1988
Model – 626 (Non-Turbo)
Engine – 2.1L (133 cid) EGI 4 cyl
Engine Code – F2

ECM TROUBLE CODES

Code	Explanation
01	Ignition pulse – no ignition signal
08	Air flow meter – open or short circuit – maintains basic signal at preset value
09	Water thermosensor – open or short circuit – maintains constant command – 95°F (35°C) for EGI – 122°F (50°C) for Idle Speed Control (ISC) control use
10	Intake air thermosensor (air flow meter) – open or short circuit – maintains constant 68°F (20°C) command
12	Throttle sensor – open or short circuit – maintains constant command of throttle valve fully open
14	Atmospheric pressure sensor – open or short circuit – maintains constant command of sea level pressure
15	Oxygen sensor – sensor output continues less than 0.55V 120 sec. after engine starts (1500 rpm) – cancels EGI feedback operation
17	Feedback system – sensor output not changed 20 sec. after engine exceeds 1500 rpm – cancels EGI feedback operation
25	Solenoid valve (pressure regulator) – open or short circuit
26	Solenoid valve (purge control)
28	Solenoid valve – Exhaust Gas Recirculation (EGR)
34	Solenoid valve – idle speed control valve

Year — 1988
Model — 626 (Turbo)
Engine — 2.1L (133 cid) EGI 4 cyl
Engine Code — F2

ECM TROUBLE CODES

Code	Explanation
01	Ignition pulse — no ignition signal
02	Distributor signal — no distributor signal from crank angle sensor
03	G_1 signal — no G_1 signal — neither G_1 nor G_2 signal — engine stopped
04	G_2 signal — no G_2 signal — neither G_1 nor G_2 signal — engine stopped
05	Knock sensor and knock control unit — open or short circuit — retards ignition timing 6° in heavy load condition — waste gate opens earlier
08	Air flow meter — open or short circuit — maintains basic signal at preset value
09	Water thermosensor — open or short circuit — maintains constant command — 95°F (35°C) for EGI — 122°F (50°C) for Idle Speed Control (ISC) control use
10	Intake air thermosensor (air flow meter) — open or short circuit — maintains constant 68°F (20°C) command
12	Throttle sensor — open or short circuit — maintains constant command of throttle valve fully open
14	Atmospheric pressure sensor — open or short circuit — maintains constant command of sea level pressure
15	Oxygen sensor — sensor output continues less than 0.55V 120 sec. after engine starts (1500 rpm) — cancels EGI feedback operation
16	Exhaust Gas Recirculation (EGR) position sensor — open or short circuit — sensor output does not match target value (incorrect output) — cuts off Exhaust Gas Recirculation (EGR)
17	Feedback system — sensor output not changed 20 sec. after engine exceeds 1500 rpm — cancels EGI feedback operation
25	Solenoid valve (pressure regulator)
26	Solenoid valve (purge control)
28	Solenoid valve — Exhaust Gas Recirculation (EGR) vacuum
29	Solenoid valve — Exhaust Gas Recirculation (EGR) vent
34	Solenoid valve — idle speed control valve
42	Solenoid valve (wastegate)

Year — 1988
Model — MX6 (Non-Turbo)
Engine — 2.1L (133 cid) EGI 4 cyl
Engine Code — F2

ECM TROUBLE CODES

Code	Explanation
01	Ignition pulse — no ignition signal
08	Air flow meter — open or short circuit — maintains basic signal at preset value
09	Water thermosensor — open or short circuit — maintains constant command — 95°F (35°C) for EGI — 122°F (50°C) for Idle Speed Control (ISC) control use
10	Intake air thermosensor (air flow meter) — open or short circuit — maintains constant 68°F (20°C) command
12	Throttle sensor — open or short circuit — maintains constant command of throttle valve fully open
14	Atmospheric pressure sensor — open or short circuit — maintains constant command of sea level pressure
15	Oxygen sensor — sensor output continues less than 0.55V 120 sec. after engine starts (1500 rpm) — cancels EGI feedback operation
17	Feedback system — sensor output not changed 20 sec. after engine exceeds 1500 rpm — cancels EGI feedback operation
25	Solenoid valve (pressure regulator) — open or short circuit
26	Solenoid valve (purge control)
28	Solenoid valve — Exhaust Gas Recirculation (EGR)
34	Solenoid valve (idle speed control valve)

Year—1988
Model—MX6 (Turbo)
Engine—2.1L (133 cid) EGI 4 cyl
Engine Code—F2

ECM TROUBLE CODES

Code	Explanation
01	Ignition pulse—no ignition signal
02	Distributor signal—no distributor signal from crank angle sensor
03	G_1 signal—no G_1 signal—neither G_1 nor G_2 signal—engine stopped
04	G_2 signal—no G_2 signal—neither G_1 nor G_2 signal—engine stopped
05	Knock sensor and knock control unit—open or short circuit—retards ignition timing 6° in heavy load condition—wastegate opens earlier
08	Air flow meter—open or short circuit—maintains basic signal at preset value
09	Water thermosensor—open or short circuit—maintains constant command—95°F (35°C) for EGI—122°F (50°C) for Idle Speed Control (ISC) control use
10	Intake air thermosensor (air flow meter)—open or short circuit—maintains constant 68°F (20°C) command
12	Throttle sensor—open or short circuit—maintains constant command of throttle valve fully open
14	Atmospheric pressure sensor—open or short circuit—maintains constant command of sea level pressure
15	Oxygen sensor—sensor output continues less than 0.55V 120 sec. after engine starts (1500 rpm)—cancels EGI feedback operation
16	Exhaust Gas Recirculation (EGR) position sensor—open or short circuit—sensor output does not match target value (incorrect output)—cuts off Exhaust Gas Recirculation (EGR)
17	Feedback system—sensor output not changed 20 sec. after engine exceeds 1500 rpm—cancels EGI feedback operation
25	Solenoid valve (pressure regulator)
26	Solenoid valve (purge control)
28	Solenoid valve—Exhaust Gas Recirculation (EGR) vacuum
29	Solenoid valve—Exhaust Gas Recirculation (EGR) vent
34	Solenoid valve (idle speed control valve)
42	Solenoid valve (wastegate)

Year — 1988
Model — 929
Engine — 2.9L (180 cid) V6
Engine Code — JE

ECM TROUBLE CODES

Code	Explanation
01	Ignition pulse (igniter, ingition coil) — broken wire, short circuit
02	Distributor (Ne signal) — distributor signal not input for 1.5 sec. during cranking
03	Distributor (G_1 signal) — broken wire, short circuit
04	G_2 signal — no G_2 signal — broken wire, short circuit
08	Air flow meter — broken wire, short circuit — basic fuel injection amount fixed as for 2 driving modes 1) idle switch ON, 2) idle switch OFF
09	Water thermosensor — broken wire, short circuit — intake air temp input fixed at 176°F (80°C)
10	Intake air thermosensor (air flow meter) — broken wire, short circuit — intake air temp input fixed at 68°F (20°C)
12	Throttle sensor — broken wire, short circuit — throttle valve opening angle signal input fixed at full open
14	Atmospheric pressure sensor — broken wire, short circuit — atmospheric pressure input fixed at 760mm Hg (29.9 in Hg)
15	Oxygen sensor — sensor output below 0.55V 120 sec. after engine at above (1500 rpm) — feedback system cancelled (for EGI)
16	Exhaust Gas Recirculation (EGR) position sensor — broken wire, short circuit — sensor output does not match target value (incorrect output) — Exhaust Gas Recirculation (EGR) position signal input fixed at full closed
17	Feedback system — oxygen sensor output not change at 0.55V 60 sec. after engine at above 1500 rpm — feedback system cancelled (for EGI)
25	Solenoid valve (pressure regulator control)
26	Solenoid valve (No. 2 purge control)
27	Solenoid valve (No. 1 purge control)
28	Solenoid valve — Exhaust Gas Recirculation (EGR) vacuum side
29	Solenoid valve — Exhaust Gas Recirculation (EGR) vent side
34	Idle speed control valve — Idle Speed Control (ISC) valve
40	Solenoid valve (triple induction control system) and oxygen sensor relay
41	Solenoid valve — variable resonance induction system

Year — 1988
Model — RX-7
Engine — 1.3L (80 cid) EGI Rotary
Engine Code — 13B

ECM TROUBLE CODES

Code	Explanation
01	Crank angle sensor
02	Air flow meter — maintains basic signal at preset value
03	Water thermosensor — maintains constant 176°F (80°C) command
04	Intake air temperature sensor (air flow meter) — maintains constant 68°F (20°C) command
05	Oxygen sensor — stops feedback correction
06	Throttle sensor — maintains constant 100% (approx. 18°) command
07	Boost sensor — maintains constant 3.78 in. Hg (−96mm Hg) command
09	Atmospheric pressure sensor — maintains constant command of sea level pressure
12	Coil with igniter (trailing side) — stops operation of ignition system (only trailing side)
15	Intake air temperature sensor (dynamic chamber) — maintains constant 68°F (20°C) command

Year — 1988
Model — RX-7 (Turbo)
Engine — 1.3L (80 cid) EGI Rotary
Engine Code — 13B

ECM TROUBLE CODES

Code	Explanation
01	Crank angle sensor
02	Air flow meter — maintains basic signal at preset value
03	Water thermosensor — maintains constant 176°F (80°C) command
04	Intake air temperature sensor (air flow meter) — maintains constant 68°F (20°C) command
05	Oxygen sensor — stops feedback correction
06	Throttle sensor — maintains constant 100% (approx. 18°) command
07	Boost sensor — maintains constant 3.82 psi (26.3 kPa) command
09	Atmospheric pressure sensor — maintains constant command of sea level pressure
12	Coil with igniter (trailing side) — stops operation of ignition system (only trailing side)
15	Intake air temperature sensor (intake sir pipe) — maintains constant 68°F (20°C) command

Year — 1989
Model — 323 SOHC
Engine — 1.6L (97 cid) EGI 4 cyl
Engine Code — B6

ECM TROUBLE CODES

Code	Explanation
01	Ignition pulse (igniter) — broken wire, short circuit
08	Air flow meter — broken wire, short circuit — basic fuel injection amount fixed as for 2 driving modes 1) idle switch: ON, 2) idle switch: OFF
09	Water thermosensor — broken wire, short circuit — coolant temp. input fixed at 176°F (80°C) for ISC at 68°F (20°C) for fuel injection
10	Intake air thermo sensor (air flow meter) — broken wire, short circuit — intake air temp. input fixed at 68°F (20°C)
14	Atmospheric pressure sensor — broken wire, short circuit — atmospheric pressure input fixed at 29.9 in. Hg (760mm Hg)
15	Oxygen sensor — sensor output continues less than 0.55V 120 sec. after engine starts (1500 rpm) — feedback system operating cancelled
17	Feedback system — oxygen sensor output not changed 30 sec. after engine exceeds 1500 rpm — feedback operation cancelled
26	Solenoid valve (No. 1 purge control) — broken wire, short circuit
27	Solenoid valve (No. 2 purge control) — broken wire, short circuit
34	Solenoid valve (idle speed control valve) — broken wire, short circuit

Year — 1989
Model — 323 DOHC
Engine — 1.6L (97 cid) EGI 4 cyl
Engine Code — B6

ECM TROUBLE CODES

Code	Explanation
01	Ignition pulse — no ignition signal
03	Distributor (G signal) — no G signal
08	Air flow meter — broken wire, short circuit — basic fuel injection amount fixed as for 2 driving modes 1) idle switch: ON, 2) idle switch: OFF
09	Water thermosensor — broken wire, short circuit — coolant temp. input fixed at 176°F (80°C) for ISC, at 140°F (60°C) for fuel injection
10	Intake air thermosensor (air flow meter) — broken wire, short circuit — intake air temp. input fixed at 68°F (20°C)
12	Throttle sensor — broken wire, short circuit — throttle valve opening angle signal input fixed at full open
14	Atmospheric pressure sensor — broken wire, short circuit — atmospheric pressure input fixed at 29.9 in. Hg (760mm Hg)
15	Oxygen sensor — sensor output continues less than 0.55V 120 sec. after engine starts (1500 rpm) — feedback system operation canceled
17	Feedback system — oxygen sensor output not changed 30 sec. after engine exceeds 1500 rpm — feedback system operation canceled
25	Solenoid valve (pressure regulator control) — broken wire, short circuit
26	Solenoid valve (No. 1 purge control) — broken wire, short circuit
27	Solenoid valve (No. 2 purge control) — broken wire, short circuit
34	Solenoid valve (idle speed control valve) — broken wire, short circuit

Year — 1989
Model — 626
Engine — 2.1L (133 cid) EGI 4 cyl
Engine Code — F2

ECM TROUBLE CODES

Code	Explanation
01	Ignition pulse — no ignition signal
08	Air flow meter — open or short circuit — maintains basic signal at preset value
09	Water thermosensor — open or short circuit — maintains constant command — 95°F (35°C) for EGI — 122°F (50°C) for ISC control use
10	Intake air thermosensor (air flow meter) — open or short circuit — maintains constant 68°F (20°C) command
12	Throttle sensor — open or short circuit — maintains constant command of throttle valve fully open
14	Atmospheric pressure sensor — open or short circuit — maintains constant command of sea level pressure
15	Oxygen sensor — sensor output continues less than 0.55V 120 sec. after engine starts (1500 rpm) — cancels EGI feedback operation
17	Feedback system — oxygen sensor output not changed 20 sec. after engine exceeds 1500 rpm — cancels EGI feedback operation
25	Solenoid valve (pressure regulator) — open or short circuit
26	Solenoid valve (purge control) — open or short circuit
28	Solenoid valve (EGR) — open or short circuit
34	Solenoid valve (idle speed control) — open or short circuit

Year — 1989
Model — 626 Turbo
Engine — 2.1L (133 cid) EGI 4 cyl
Engine Code — F2

ECM TROUBLE CODES

Code	Explanation
01	Ignition pulse — no ignition signal
02	Ne signal — no Ne signal from crank angle sensor
03	G_1 signal — no G_1 signal — neither G_1 or G_2 signal: engine stopped
04	G_2 signal — no G_2 signal — neither G_1 or G_2 signal: engine stopped
05	Knock sensor and kock control unit — open or short circuit — retards ignition timing 6 degrees in heavy — load condition — waste gate opens earlier
08	Air flow meter — open or short circuit — maintains basic signal at preset value
09	Water thermosensor — open or short circuit — maintains constant command — 95°F (35°C) for EGI — 122°F (50°C) for ISC control use
10	Intake air thermosensor (air flow meter) — open or short circuit — maintains constant 68°F (20°C) command
12	Throttle sensor — open or short circuit — maintains constant command of throttle valve fully open
14	Atmospheric pressure sensor — open or short circuit — maintains constant command of sea level pressure
15	Oxygen sensor — sensor output continues less than 0.55V 120 sec. after engine starts (1500 rpm) — cancels EGI feedback operation
16	Exhaust Gas Recirculation (EGR) position — open or short circuit — sensor output does not match target value (incorrect output) — cuts off EGR
17	Feedback system — sensor output not changed 20 sec. after engine exceeds 1500 rpm — cancels EGI feedback operation
25	Solenoid valve (pressure regulator) — open or short circuit
26	Solenoid valve (purge control) — open or short circuit
28	Solenoid valve — Exhaust Gas Recirculation (EGR) vacuum — open or short circuit
29	Solenoid valve — Exhaust Gas Recirculation (EGR) vent — open or short circuit
34	Solenoid valve (idle speed control) — open or short circuit
42	Solenoid valve (waste gate) — open or short circuit

Year — 1989
Model — MX6
Engine — 2.1L (133 cid) EGI 4 cyl
Engine Code — F2

ECM TROUBLE CODES

Code	Explanation
01	Ignition pulse — no ignition signal
08	Air flow meter — open or short circuit — maintains basic signal at preset value
09	Water thermosensor — open or short circuit — maintains constant command — 95°F (35°C) for EGI — 122°F (50°C) for ISC control use
10	Intake air thermosensor (air flow meter) — open or short circuit — maintains constant 68°F (20°C) command
12	Throttle sensor — open or short circuit — maintains constant command of throttle valve fully open
14	Atmospheric pressure sensor — open or short circuit — maintains constant command of sea level pressure
15	Oxygen sensor — sensor output continues less than 0.55V 120 sec. after engine starts (1500 rpm) — cancels EGI feedback operation
17	Feedback system — oxygen sensor output not changed 20 sec. after engine exceeds 1500 rpm — cancels EGI feedback operation
25	Solenoid valve (pressure regulator) — open or short circuit
26	Solenoid valve (purge control) — open or short circuit
28	Solenoid valve — Exhaust Gas Recirculation (EGR) — open or short circuit
34	Solenoid valve (idle speed control) — open or short circuit

Year – 1989
Model – MX6 Turbo
Engine – 2.1L (133 cid) EGI 4 cyl
Engine Code – F2

ECM TROUBLE CODES

Code	Explanation
01	Ignition pulse – no ignition signal
02	Ne signal – no Ne signal from crank angle sensor
03	G_1 signal – no G_1 signal – neither G_1 or G_2 signal: engine stopped
04	G_2 signal – no G_2 signal – neither G_1 or G_2 signal: engine stopped
05	Knock sensor and kock control unit – open or short circuit – retards ignition timing 6 degrees in heavy – load condition – waste gate opens earlier
08	Air flow meter – open or short circuit – maintains basic signal at preset value
09	Water thermosensor – open or short circuit – maintains constant command – 95°F (35°C) for EGI – 122°F (50°C) for ISC control use
10	Intake air thermosensor (air flow meter) – open or short circuit – maintains constant 68°F (20°C) command
12	Throttle sensor – open or short circuit – maintains constant command of throttle valve fully open
14	Atmospheric pressure sensor – open or short circuit – maintains constant command of sea level pressure
15	Oxygen sensor – sensor output continues less than 0.55V 120 sec. after engine starts (1500 rpm) – cancels EGI feedback operation
16	Exhaust Gas Recirculation (EGR) position – open or short circuit – sensor output does not match target value (incorrect output) – cuts off EGR
17	Feedback system – sensor output not changed 20 sec. after engine exceeds 1500 rpm – cancels EGI feedback operation
25	Solenoid valve (pressure regulator) – open or short circuit
26	Solenoid valve (purge control) – open or short circuit
28	Solenoid valve – Exhaust Gas Recirculation (EGR) vacuum – open or short circuit
29	Solenoid valve – Exhaust Gas Recirculation (EGR) vent – open or short circuit
34	Solenoid valve (idle speed control) – open or short circuit
42	Solenoid valve (waste gate) – open or short circuit

Year — 1989
Model — RX7
Engine — 1.3L (80 cid) EGI Rotary
Engine Code — 13B

ECM TROUBLE CODES

Code	Explanation
01	Ignition coil (trailing side) — malfunction of spark plug broken wire, short circuit — trailing — side ignition pulse cut
02	Crank angle sensor (Ne signal) — broken wire, short circuit — fuel injection and ignition cut
03	Crank angle sensor (G signal) — broken wire, short circuit — fuel injection and ignition cut
08	Air Flow Meter (AFM) — broken wire, short circuit — basic fuel injection amount and ignition timing fixed
09	Water thermosensor — broken wire, short circuit — coolant temp. input fixed at 176°F (80°C)
10	Intake air thermosensor (AFM) — broken wire, short circuit — intake air temp. fixed at 68°F (20°C)
11	Intake air thermosensor (Engine) — broken wire, short circuit — intake air temp. fixed at 68°F (20°C)
12	Throttle sensor (Full range) — broken wire, short circuit — throttle valve opening angle input signal fixed at 20% open
13	Pressure sensor (Intake manifold pressure) — broken wire, short circuit — intake manifold pressure input signal fixed at 29.9 in. Hg (760mm Hg)
14	Atmospheric pressure sensor (ATP) — malfunctioning Electronic Control Unit (ECU) — atmospheric pressure input signal fixed at 29.9 in. Hg (760mm Hg)
15	Oxygen sensor — oxygen sensor output remains below 0.55V 80 sec. after F/B system operation beginning — feedback system canceled (for EGI)
17	Feedback system — oxygen sensor output remains 0.55V 10 sec. after F/B system operation beginning — feedback system canceled (for EGI)
18	Throttle sensor (narrow range) — broken wire, short circuit — throttle valve opening angle input signal fixed at full open
20	Metering Oil Pump (MOP) position sensor — broken wire, short circuit — MOP fixed smallest open basic fuel injection amount and ignition timing fixed
25	Solenoid valve — Pressure Regulator Control (PRC)
26	Step motor — metering oil pump
27	Metering oil pump (MPO) — malfunctioning MOP, step motors, broken wire, short circuit, or malfunctioning Electronic Control Unit (ECU) — MOP fixed smallest open basic fuel injection amount and ignition timing fixed
30	Split air solenoid valve
31	Solenoid valve — relief
32	Solenoid valve — switch
33	Port air solenoid valve
34	Solenoid valve — Bypass Air Control (BAC)
37	Metering Oil Pump (MOP) — malfunction MOP, step motors, broken wire, short circuit, malfunctioning Electronic Control Unit (ECU), alternator or battery — basic fuel injection amount and ignition timing fixed
38	Solenoid valve — Accelerated Warm-up System (AWS)
40	Auxiliary port valve
41	Solenoid valve — Variable Dynamic Effect Intake (VDI) control
51	Fuel pump resistor relay
71	Injector — front secondary
73	Injector — rear secondary

Year — 1989
Model — RX7 Turbo
Engine — 1.3L (80 cid) EGI Rotary
Engine Code — 13B

ECM TROUBLE CODES

Code	Explanation
01	Ignition coil (trailing side) — malfunction of spark plug broken wire, short circuit — trailing — side ignition pulse cut
02	Crank angle sensor (Ne signal) — broken wire, short circuit — fuel injection and ignition cut
03	Crank angle sensor (G signal) — broken wire, short circuit — fuel injection and ignition cut
08	Air Flow Meter (AFM) — broken wire, short circuit — basic fuel injection amount and ignition timing fixed
09	Water thermosensor — broken wire, short circuit — coolant temp. input fixed at 176°F (80°C)
10	Intake air thermosensor (AFM) — broken wire, short circuit — intake air temp. fixed at 68°F (20°C)
11	Intake air thermosensor (Engine) — broken wire, short circuit — intake air temp. fixed at 68°F (20°C)
12	Throttle sensor (Full range) — broken wire, short circuit — throttle valve opening angle input signal fixed at 20% open
13	Pressure sensor (Intake manifold pressure) — broken wire, short circuit — intake manifold pressure input signal fixed at 29.9 in. Hg (760mm Hg)
14	Atmospheric pressure sensor (ATP) — malfunctioning Electronic Control Unit (ECU) — atmospheric pressure input signal fixed at 29.9 in. Hg (760mm Hg)
15	Oxygen sensor — oxygen sensor output remains below 0.55V 80 sec. after F/B system operation beginning — feedback system canceled (for EGI)
17	Feedback system — oxygen sensor output remains 0.55V 10 sec. after F/B system operation beginning — feedback system canceled (for EGI)
18	Throttle sensor (narrow range) — broken wire, short circuit — throttle valve opening angle input signal fixed at full open
20	Metering Oil Pump (MOP) position sensor — broken wire, short circuit — MOP fixed smallest open basic fuel injection amount and ignition timing fixed
25	Solenoid valve — Pressure Regulator Control (PRC)
26	Step motor — metering oil pump
27	Metering Oil Pump (MPO) — malfunctioning MOP, step motors, broken wire, short circuit or malfunctioning Electronic Control Unit (ECU) — MOP fixed smallest open basic fuel injection amount and ignition timing fixed
30	Split air solenoid valve
31	Solenoid valve — relief
32	Solenoid valve — switch
33	Port air solenoid valve
34	Solenoid valve — Bypass Air Control (BAC)
37	Metering Oil Pump (MOP) — malfunction MOP, step motors, broken wire, short circuit, malfunctioning Electronic Control Unit (ECU), alternator or battery — basic fuel injection amount and ignition timing fixed
38	Solenoid valve — Accelerated Warm-up System (AWS) — and Air Supply Valve — ASV
42	Duty solenoid — turbo boost pressure control
51	Fuel pump resistor relay
71	Injector — front secondary
73	Injector — rear secondary

MAZDA TRUCKS

Year – 1986
Model – B2000 Pick-Up
Engine – 2.0L (122 cid) 4 cyl
Engine Code – FE

ECM TROUBLE CODES

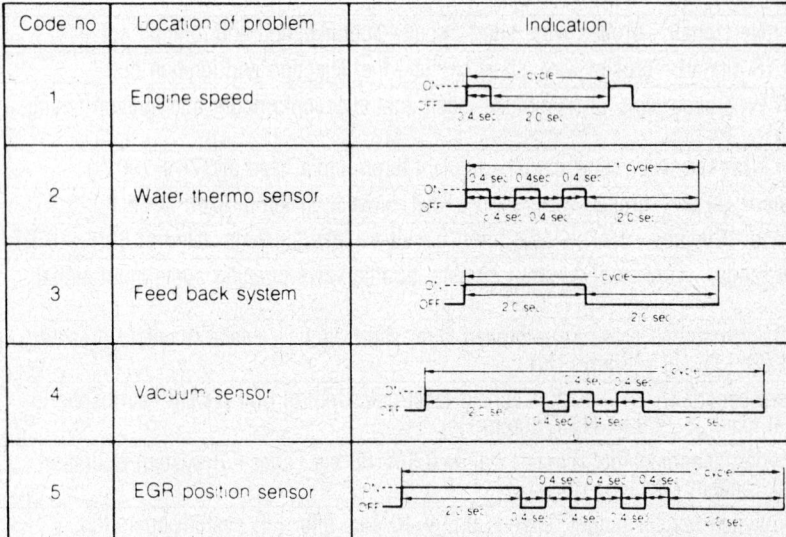

Code no	Location of problem	Indication
1	Engine speed	
2	Water thermo sensor	
3	Feed back system	
4	Vacuum sensor	
5	EGR position sensor	

Note 1: If there is trouble in 2 or more places, the indication will be for the lower code number first.

Note 2: Even if the problem is corrected during indication, 1 cycle will be indicated.

Note 3: If, after a malfunction has occured the IG key is switched OFF, the malfunction indicator for the feed back system will not be displayed on the checker.

Year – 1987
Model – B2200 Pick-Up
Engine – 2.1L (133 cid) 4 cyl
Engine Code – F2

ECM TROUBLE CODES

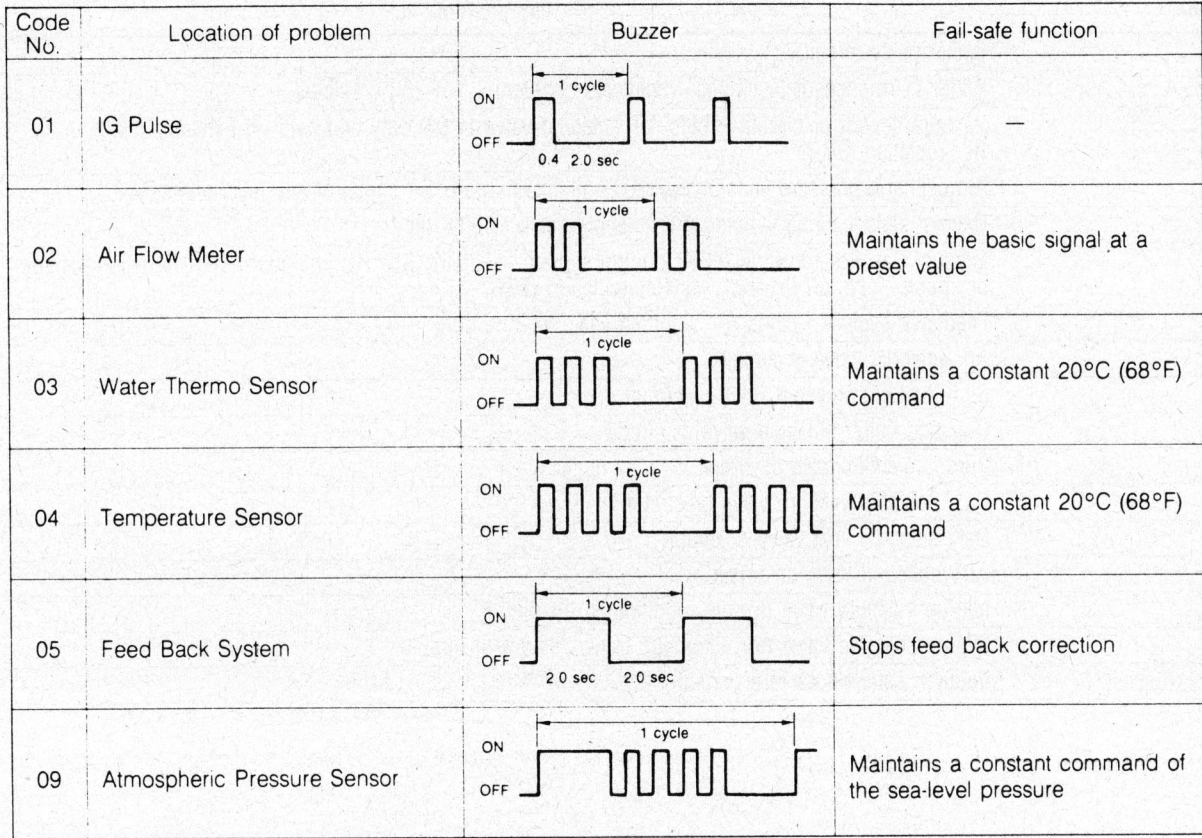

Code No.	Location of problem	Buzzer	Fail-safe function
01	IG Pulse	1 cycle — ON/OFF — 0.4 2.0 sec	–
02	Air Flow Meter	1 cycle — ON/OFF	Maintains the basic signal at a preset value
03	Water Thermo Sensor	1 cycle — ON/OFF	Maintains a constant 20°C (68°F) command
04	Temperature Sensor	1 cycle — ON/OFF	Maintains a constant 20°C (68°F) command
05	Feed Back System	1 cycle — ON/OFF — 2.0 sec 2.0 sec	Stops feed back correction
09	Atmospheric Pressure Sensor	1 cycle — ON/OFF	Maintains a constant command of the sea-level pressure

Year – 1988
Model – B2200 Pick-Up
Engine – 2.1L (133 cid) 4 cyl
Engine Code – F2

ECM TROUBLE CODES

Code	Explanation
01	Igniter pulse circuit
09	Water thermosensor or circuit—maintains constant 176°F (80°C) signal
13	Vacuum sensor or circuit—holds A/F solenoid valve to 0% duty and cuts off Exhaust Gas Recirculation (EGR)
14	Atmospheric pressure sensor or circuit—maintains constant signal of sea level pressure
15	Oxygen sensor circuit—holds A/F solenoid valve to 20% duty
16	Exhaust Gas Recirculation (EGR) control system—Exhaust Gas Recirculation (EGR) position sensor or circuit—cuts off Exhaust Gas Recirculation (EGR)
17	Feedback system—holds A/F solenoid valve to 30% duty
18	A/F solenoid valve or circuit
22	Slow fuel cut solenoid valve or circuit
23	Coasting richer solenoid valve or circuit
26	Purge solenoid valve or circuit
28	Duty solenoid vacuum valve or circuit
29	Duty solenoid vent valve or circuit
30	ACV solenoid valve or circuit
34	Idle-up solenoid valve (for air conditioning) or circuit
35	Idle-up solenoid valve (for automatic transmission) or circuit
45	Vacuum solenoid valve or circuit

Year — 1989
Model — B2200 Pick-Up
Engine — 2.1L (133 cid) 4 cyl
Engine Code — F2

ECM TROUBLE CODES

Code	Explanation
01	Igniter pulse circuit
09	Water thermosensor or circuit — maintains constant 176°F (80°C) signal
13	Vacuum sensor or circuit — holds A/F solenoid valve to 0% duty and cuts off Exhaust Gas Recirculation (EGR)
14	Atmospheric pressure sensor or circuit — maintains constant signal of sea level pressure
15	Oxygen sensor circuit — holds A/F solenoid valve to 20% duty
16	Exhaust Gas Recirculation (EGR) control system — Exhaust Gas Recirculation (EGR) position sensor or circuit — cuts off Exhaust Gas Recirculation (EGR)
17	Feedback system — holds A/F solenoid valve to 30% duty
18	A/F solenoid valve or circuit
22	Slow fuel cut solenoid valve or circuit
23	Coasting richer solenoid valve or circuit
26	Purge solenoid valve or circuit
28	Duty solenoid vacuum valve or circuit
29	Duty solenoid vent valve or circuit
30	ACV solenoid valve or circuit
34	Idle-up solenoid valve (for air conditioning) or circuit
35	Idle-up solenoid valve (for automatic transmission) or circuit
45	Vacuum solenoid valve or circuit

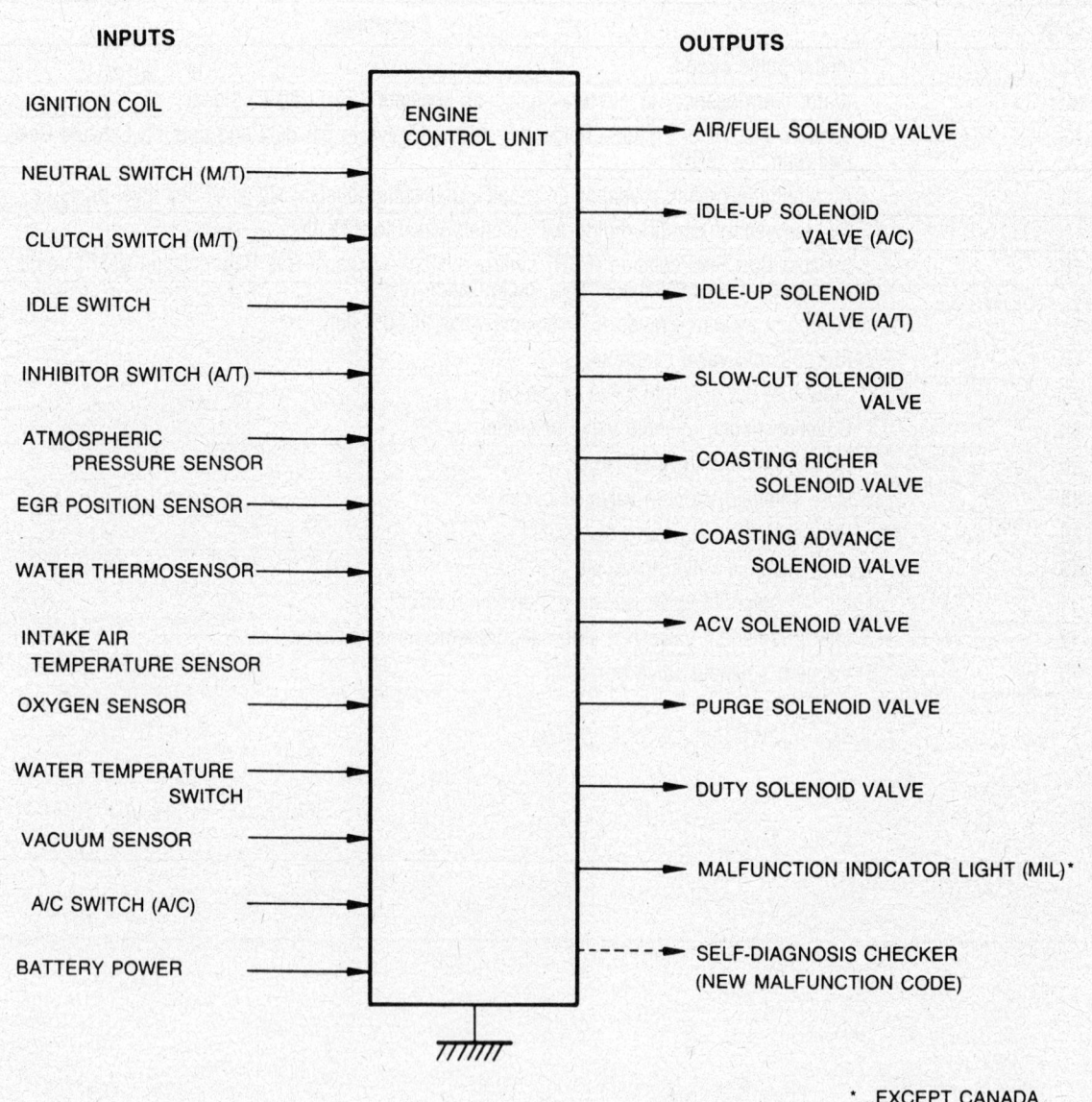

INPUTS

IGNITION COIL

NEUTRAL SWITCH (M/T)

CLUTCH SWITCH (M/T)

IDLE SWITCH

INHIBITOR SWITCH (A/T)

ATMOSPHERIC PRESSURE SENSOR

EGR POSITION SENSOR

WATER THERMOSENSOR

INTAKE AIR TEMPERATURE SENSOR

OXYGEN SENSOR

WATER TEMPERATURE SWITCH

VACUUM SENSOR

A/C SWITCH (A/C)

BATTERY POWER

ENGINE CONTROL UNIT

OUTPUTS

AIR/FUEL SOLENOID VALVE

IDLE-UP SOLENOID VALVE (A/C)

IDLE-UP SOLENOID VALVE (A/T)

SLOW-CUT SOLENOID VALVE

COASTING RICHER SOLENOID VALVE

COASTING ADVANCE SOLENOID VALVE

ACV SOLENOID VALVE

PURGE SOLENOID VALVE

DUTY SOLENOID VALVE

MALFUNCTION INDICATOR LIGHT (MIL)*

SELF-DIAGNOSIS CHECKER (NEW MALFUNCTION CODE)

*...EXCEPT CANADA

ECM operating conditions sensed and systems controlled

INDEX

MERCEDES-BENZ

CIS-E Fuel Injection System

SELF-DIAGNOSTIC SYSTEM

Description

Mercedes-Benz uses an electronically controlled Bosch K-Jetronic style Continuous Injection System (CIS-E) on all models. The input signals from various sensors and switches are continuously monitored by the Electronic Control Unit (ECU). In the event of an abnormal signal, such as a short or open circuit, the ECU will automatically revert to a Fixed Operating Mode (FOM).

While operating at normal temperature, if there is a sudden change is a sensor or circuit signal, the ECU will compare this momentary change with the normal signal value in memory. The ECU will recognize the abrupt change as an open or short and will revert to FOM for continued engine operation.

The control unit does not recognize gradual changes as malfunctions and will continue to operate as if all signals are normal.

Various components of the CIS-E system are checked by the control unit. Malfunctions resulting from interruptions or failure of any of the CIS components are indicated by the Check Engine lamp and simultaneously stored in the CIS-E memory.

The diagnosis of the feedback system is obtained through on-off ratio percentages transmitted by the lambda (oxygen sensor) measuring circuit. These ON/OFF ratio percentages can be obtained by the Mercedes or Bosch ON/OFF ratio tester through X11 round diagnostic connector.

Some vehicles use the X92 on board test connection with a pushbutton and LED located on the engine compartment firewall. When the button is pressed with the ignition switch turned **ON** the LED will begin flashing the fault codes. An impulse code reader can be attached to the X92 and codes can be obtained and cleared through this impulse reader.

After a code has been displayed, press the button to move on to the next malfunction. After all fault codes have been displayed, the CIS-E control unit switches over to the ON/OFF ratio readout.

Entering Diagnostic Mode

The following procedures are for California or other vehicles equipped with self-diagnostic capability. Make certain to record all codes as received.

IMPULSE DISPLAY READOUT

NOTE: This system used on California only 1988/Federal and California 1989 models.

Vehicles that use an on board test connection with a pushbutton and LED located on the engine compartment firewall can display codes by the LED flashing. Connecting an approved impulse reader can serve the same purpose as the LED and pushbutton.

When pressing the pushbutton for 2–4 seconds with the ignition **ON** and engine **OFF**, the LED will begin impulse code display. The malfunction is indicated by the number of LED blink impulses. After completion of the impulse readout the LED remains **ON**. By pressing the button again for 2–4 seconds a further malfunction is indicated. If no malfunction is detected, the CIS-E control unit switches over to the ON/OFF ratio readout.

After the malfunction has been corrected the CIS-E control memory must be erased to clear the stored fault code.

ON/OFF RATIO TESTING

A Bosch type ON/OFF ratio tester must be connected to the diagnostic connector. After performing the above impulse readout, if equipped, the CIS-E control will switch over to the ratio readout.

The ON/OFF ratio tester will only read 0 percent or 85 percent with the "Check Engine" lamp **ON**, if the CIS-E is not in ratio readout mode. If this happens, press the button on the X92 connector again for 2–4 seconds, record codes from LED and repeat until LED blinks once. Press the button again for 2–4 seconds to program the CIS-E control unit to read ON/OFF ratios. The LED should remain lit.

NOTE: When performing ON/OFF ratio testing, the idle speed value may deviate from the average value by more than 10 percent.

Follow the appropriate diagnostic charts to repair impulse and ON/OFF ratio faults. Clear all codes and retest for additional faults. If all fault memory is clear and lambda system feedback is approximately 50 percent at idle, the system is operating properly. The ON/OFF ratio varying constantly indicates the CIS-E unit is adjusting fuel mixture in response to the oxygen sensor signal.

Clearing Diagnostic Memory

The fault codes must be cleared 1 code at a time, by activating the impulse LED or by using the impulse reader. If no number is displayed, the last code has been cleared. If the impulse LED or impulse reader displays a code 1, the system memory does not contain any fault codes.

NOTE: The CIS-E control memory will be also be cleared if either of the following is disconnected: CIS-E control unit, overvoltage protection relay or the battery. If the battery is disconnected, the radio, radio security system, seat, climate control and clock memories will all be lost.

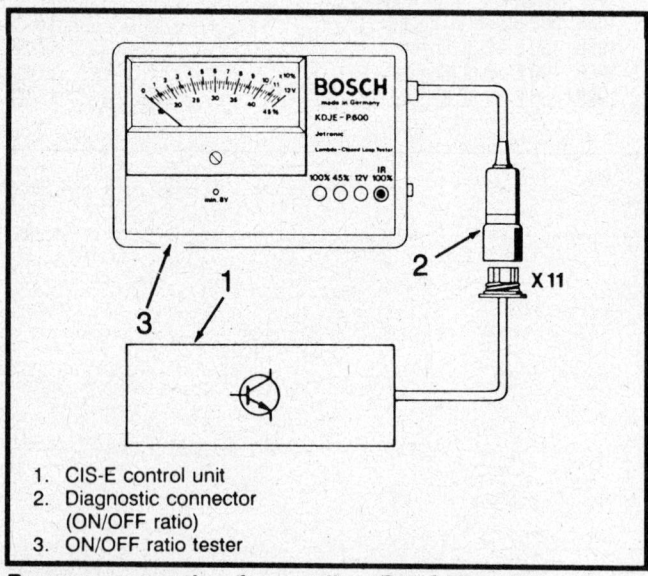

1. CIS-E control unit
2. Diagnostic connector (ON/OFF ratio)
3. ON/OFF ratio tester

Proper connection for reading ON/OFF ratio percentages

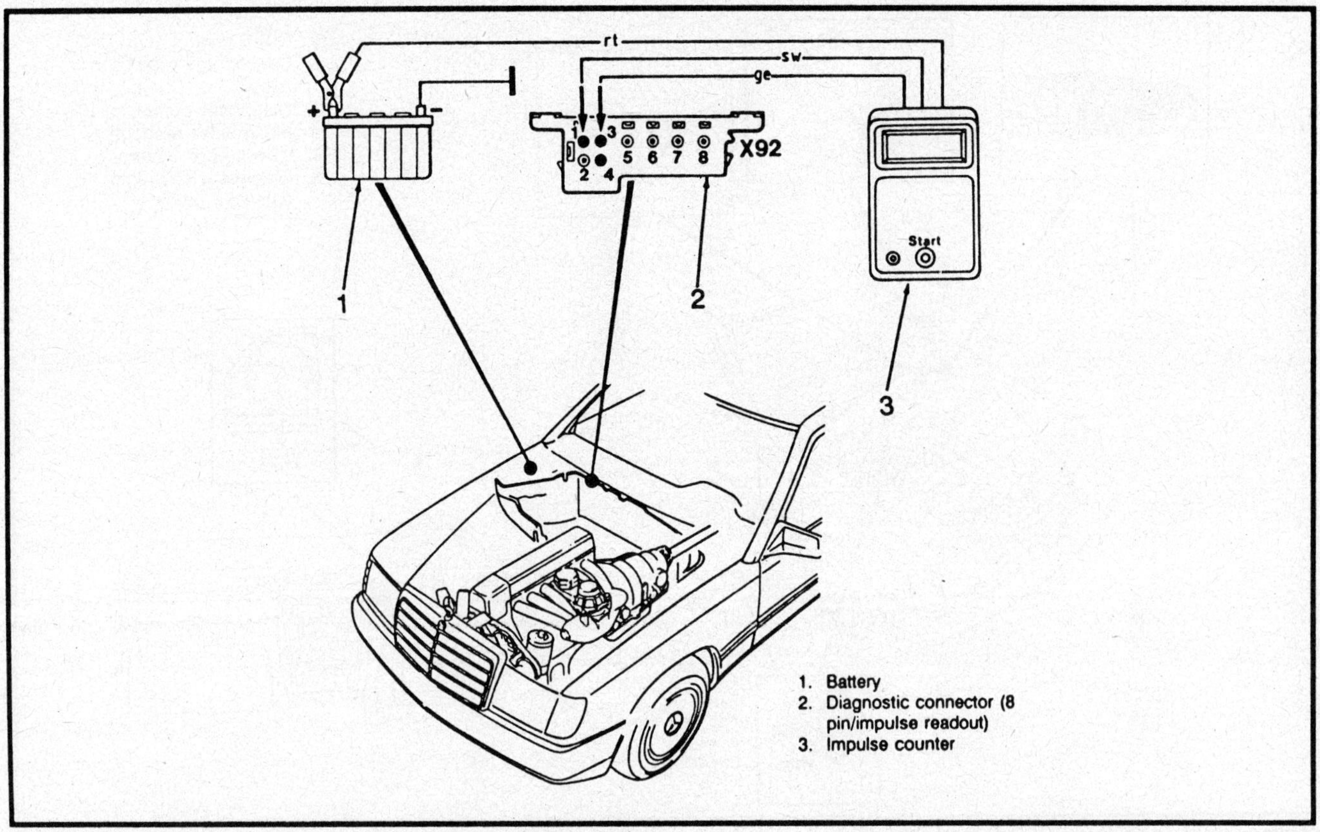
rt
sw
ge
X92
Start
1
2
3
1. Battery
2. Diagnostic connector (8 pin/impulse readout)
3. Impulse counter

Proper connection for reading impulse readout codes

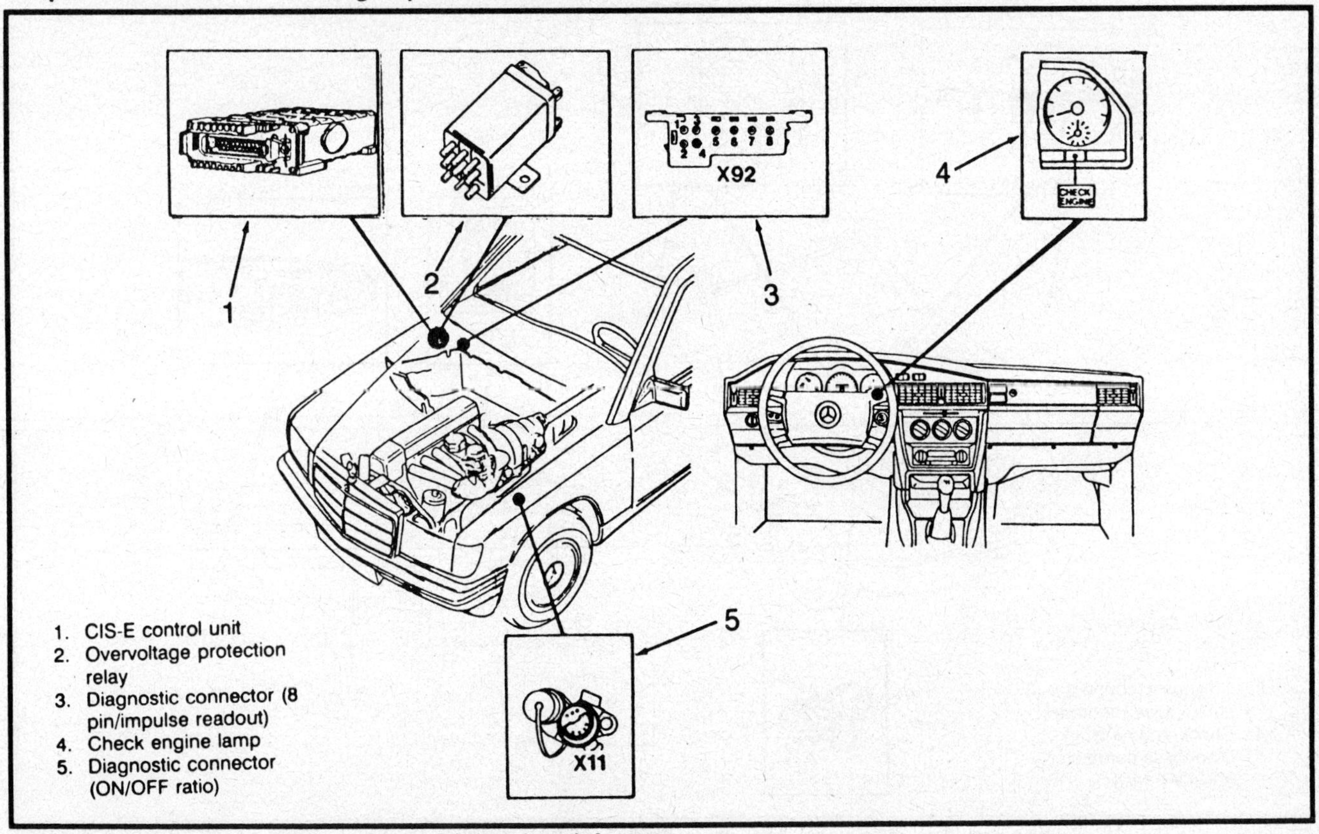
X92
CHECK ENGINE
X11
1
2
3
4
5
1. CIS-E control unit
2. Overvoltage protection relay
3. Diagnostic connector (8 pin/impulse readout)
4. Check engine lamp
5. Diagnostic connector (ON/OFF ratio)

Component location—190 series vehicles (model 201)

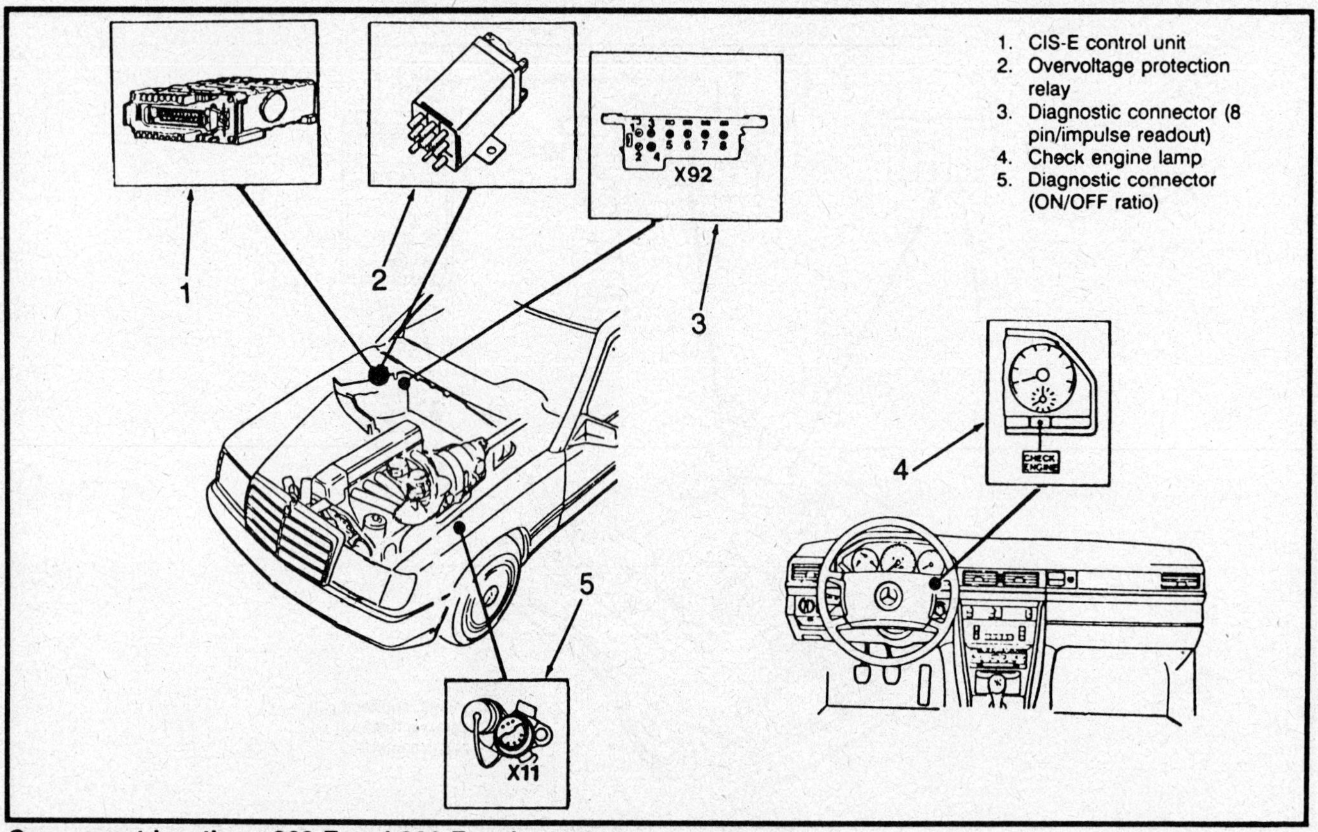

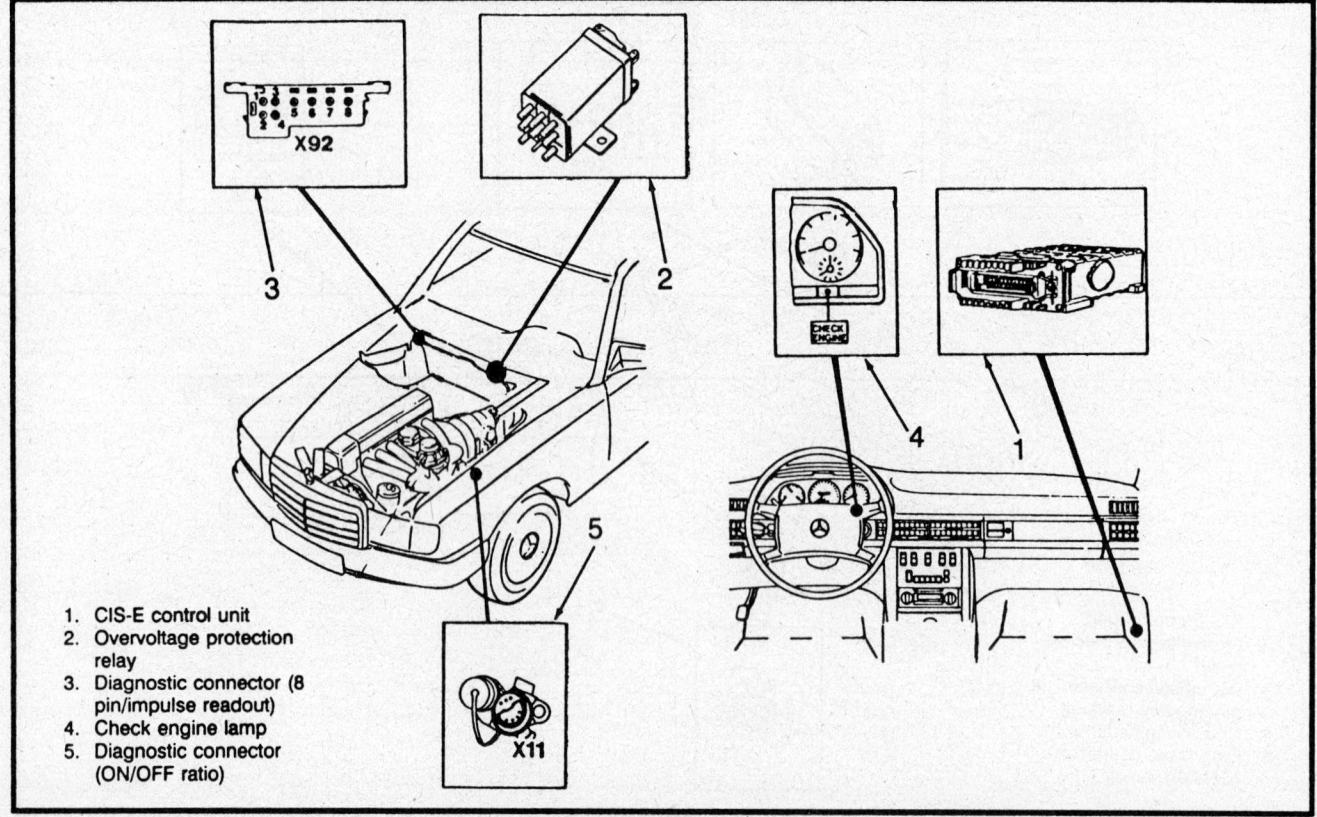

1. CIS-E control unit
2. Overvoltage protection relay
3. Diagnostic connector (8 pin/impulse readout)
4. Check engine lamp
5. Diagnostic connector (ON/OFF ratio)
X92
X11
CHECK ENGINE

Component location – 260 E and 300 E series vehicles (model 124)

X92
X11
CHECK ENGINE
1. CIS-E control unit
2. Overvoltage protection relay
3. Diagnostic connector (8 pin/impulse readout)
4. Check engine lamp
5. Diagnostic connector (ON/OFF ratio)

Component location – 300 SE, 300 SEL, 420 SEL, 560 SEL and 560 SEC vehicles (model 126)

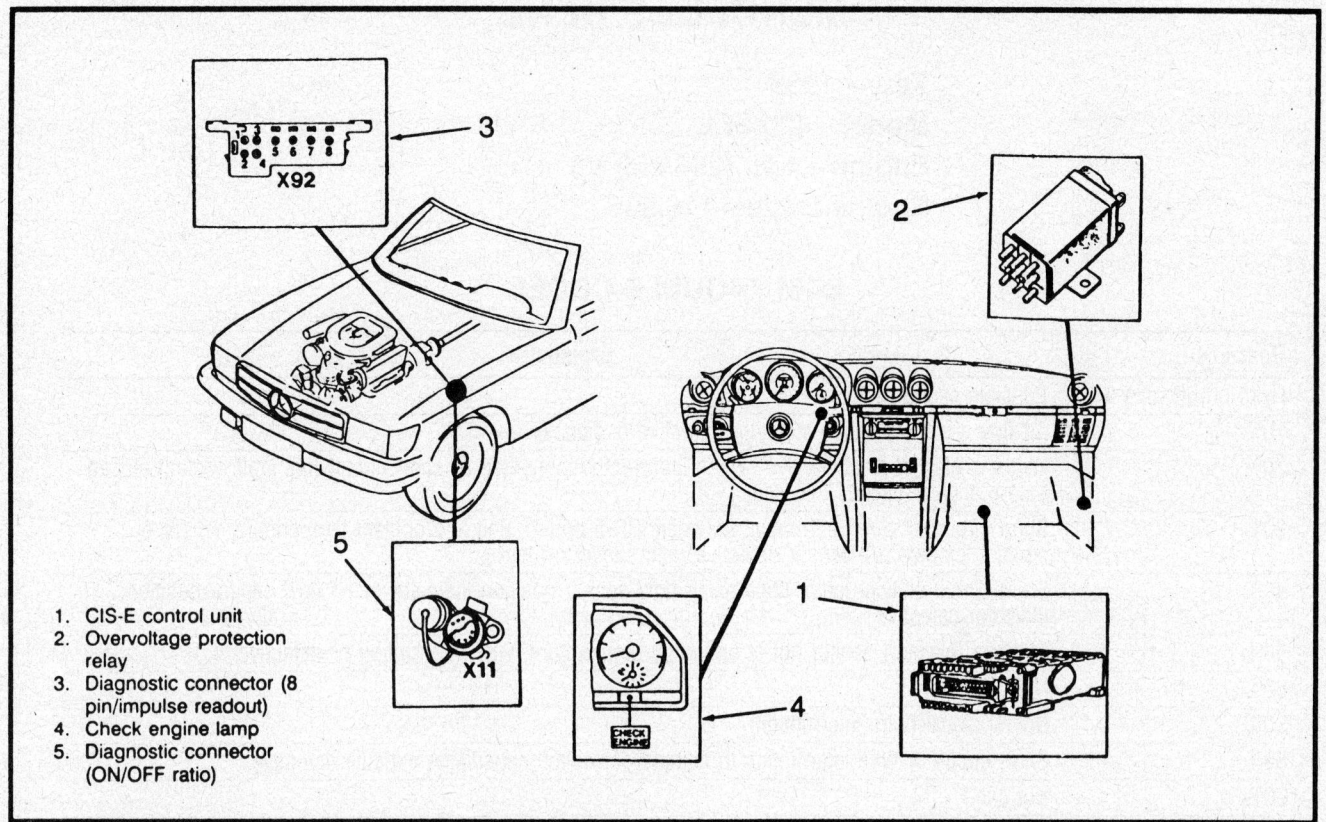

1. CIS-E control unit
2. Overvoltage protection relay
3. Diagnostic connector (8 pin/impulse readout)
4. Check engine lamp
5. Diagnostic connector (ON/OFF ratio)

Component location—560 SL vehicles (model 107)

MERCEDES BENZ

Year – 1986
Model – 420 SEL
Engine – 4.2L (256 cid) V8
Engine Code – 116.965

ECM TROUBLE CODES

Percent	Explanation
Fixed on-off ratio %	Possible cause of failure
10%	Air flow sensor position indicator defective or polarity reversed
20%	Wires in plug of throttle valve switch incorrectly connected or short circuit (full load contact closed before engine reaches full load)
30%	Short circuit or wire interruption between CIS-E control unit and coolant temperature sensor or coolant temperature sensor defective (idle speed too high)
40%	Short circuit or wire interruption to air flow sensor position indicator or air flow sensor position indicator defective
50%	Lambda (oxygen) sensor not at operating temperature, wire interruption or defective
60%	Not used
70%	No TD signal (wire interruption)
80%	Short circuit or wire interruption to altitude correction capsule or capsule defective
90%	Not used
100%	Overvoltage protection relay defect (idle speed too high, approx. 1800 rpm). Air/fuel mixture too lean, oxygen sensor defective (short circuit to ground). CIS-E control unit or on-off ration defective. No power to EHA
Reading oscillates	No malfunction within the circuit of the monitored signals. On-off ratio reading indicated

Year – 1986
Model – 560 SEL
Engine – 5.6L (338 cid) V8
Engine Code – 117.968

ECM TROUBLE CODES

Percent	Explanation
Fixed on-off ratio %	Possible cause of failure
10%	Air flow sensor position indicator defective or polarity reversed
20%	Wires in plug of throttle valve switch incorrectly connected or short circuit (full load contact closed before engine reaches full load)
30%	Short circuit or wire interruption between CIS-E control unit and coolant temperature sensor or coolant temperature sensor defective (idle speed too high)
40%	Short circuit or wire interruption to air flow sensor position indicator or air flow sensor position indicator defective
50%	Lambda (oxygen) sensor not at operating temperature, wire interruption or defective
60%	Not used
70%	No TD signal (wire interruption)
80%	Short circuit or wire interruption to altitude correction capsule or capsule defective
90%	Not used
100%	Overvoltage protection relay defect (idle speed too high, approx. 1800 rpm). Air/fuel mixture too lean, oxygen sensor defective (short circuit to ground). CIS-E control unit or on-off ration defective. No power to EHA
Reading oscillates	No malfunction within the circuit of the monitored signals. On-off ratio reading indicated

Year – 1986
Model – 560 SEC
Engine – 5.6L (338 cid) V8
Engine Code – 117.968

ECM TROUBLE CODES

Percent	Explanation
Fixed on-off ratio %	Possible cause of failure
10%	Air flow sensor position indicator defective or polarity reversed
20%	Wires in plug of throttle valve switch incorrectly connected or short circuit (full load contact closed before engine reaches full load)
30%	Short circuit or wire interruption between CIS-E control unit and coolant temperature sensor or coolant temperature sensor defective (idle speed too high)
40%	Short circuit or wire interruption to air flow sensor position indicator or air flow sensor position indicator defective
50%	Lambda (oxygen) sensor not at operating temperature, wire interruption or defective
60%	Not used
70%	No TD signal (wire interruption)
80%	Short circuit or wire interruption to altitude correction capsule or capsule defective
90%	Not used
100%	Overvoltage protection relay defect (idle speed too high, approx. 1800 rpm). Air/fuel mixture too lean, oxygen sensor defective (short circuit to ground). CIS-E control unit or on-off ration defective. No power to EHA
Reading oscillates	No malfunction within the circuit of the monitored signals. On-off ratio reading indicated

Year – 1986
Model – 560 SL
Engine – 5.6L (338 cid) V8
Engine Code – 117.967

ECM TROUBLE CODES

Percent	Explanation
Fixed on-off ratio %	Possible cause of failure
10%	Air flow sensor position indicator defective or polarity reversed
20%	Wires in plug of throttle valve switch incorrectly connected or short circuit (full load contact closed before engine reaches full load)
30%	Short circuit or wire interruption between CIS-E control unit and coolant temperature sensor or coolant temperature sensor defective (idle speed too high)
40%	Short circuit or wire interruption to air flow sensor position indicator or air flow sensor position indicator defective
50%	Lambda (oxygen) sensor not at operating temperature, wire interruption or defective
60%	Not used
70%	No TD signal (wire interruption)
80%	Short circuit or wire interruption to altitude correction capsule or capsule defective
90%	Not used
100%	Overvoltage protection relay defect (idle speed too high, approx. 1800 rpm). Air/fuel mixture too lean, oxygen sensor defective (short circuit to ground). CIS-E control unit or on-off ration defective. No power to EHA
Reading oscillates	No malfunction within the circuit of the monitored signals. On-off ratio reading indicated

Year – 1987
Model – 190 E
Engine – 2.3L (140 cid) 4 cyl
Engine Code – 102.985

ECM TROUBLE CODES

Percent	Explanation
Fixed on-off ratio	Possible cause of failure
0%	CIS-E control unit receives no voltage or is defective. Circuit to diagositc socket, terminal 3 open or on-off ratio tester defective. Air/fuel mixture too rich. Lambda (oxygen) sensor signal voltage is above 12V
10%	Air flow sensor position indicator defective or polarity reversed. Approximately 2000 rpm. Wires in plyg of throttle valve switch incorrectly connected or short circuit (full load contact closed before engine reaches full load)
20%	Full load contact polarity reversed or defective. Reading at 20% only with activated microswitch
30%	Short or open circuit between CIS-E control unit and coolant temperature sensor or coolant temperature sensor defective
40%	Short or open circuit to air flow sensor position indicator or air flow sensor position indicator defective. Increased idle rpm
50%	Oxygen sensor not at operating temperature, open circuit or defective
60%	Not used
70%	No TD signal (open circuit) at CIS-E control unit
80%	Short or open circuit to altitude correction capsule or capsule defective
90%	Not used
100%	Air/fuel mixture too lean, oxygen sensor defective (short circuit to ground). CIS-E control unit or on-off ratio tester defective. Defective overvoltage protection relay, no voltage supply. Increased idle rpm
Reading oscillates	No malfunction within the circuit of the monitored signals. On-off ratio reading indicated

Year — 1987
Model — 190 E
Engine — 2.6L (159 cid) 6 cyl
Engine Code — 103.942

ECM TROUBLE CODES

Percent	Explanation
Fixed on-off ratio	Possible cause of failure
0%	CIS-E control unit receives no voltage or is defective. Circuit to diagnositc socket, terminal 3 open or on-off ratio tester defective. Air/fuel mixture too rich. Lambda (oxygen) sensor signal voltage is above 12V
10%	Air flow sensor position indicator defective or polarity reversed. Approximately 2000 rpm. Wires in plyg of throttle valve switch incorrectly connected or short circuit (full load contact closed before engine reaches full load)
20%	Full load contact polarity reversed or defective. Reading at 20% only with activated microswitch
30%	Short or open circuit between CIS-E control unit and coolant temperature sensor or coolant temperature sensor defective
40%	Short or open circuit to air flow sensor position indicator or air flow sensor position indicator defective. Increased idle rpm
50%	Oxygen sensor not at operating temperature, open circuit or defective
60%	Not used
70%	No TD signal (open circuit) at CIS-E control unit
80%	Short or open circuit to altitude correction capsule or capsule defective
90%	Not used
100%	Air/fuel mixture too lean, oxygen sensor defective (short circuit to ground). CIS-E control unit or on-off ratio tester defective. Defective overvoltage protection relay, no voltage supply. Increased idle rpm
Reading oscillates	No malfunction within the circuit of the monitored signals. On-off ratio reading indicated

Year – 1987
Model – 260 E
Engine – 2.6L (159 cid) 6 cyl
Engine Code – 103.940

ECM TROUBLE CODES

Percent	Explanation
Fixed on-off ratio	Possible cause of failure
0%	CIS-E control unit receives no voltage or is defective. Circuit to diagnositc socket, terminal 3 open or on-off ratio tester defective. Air/fuel mixture too rich. Lambda (oxygen) sensor signal voltage is above 12V
10%	Air flow sensor position indicator defective or polarity reversed. Approximately 2000 rpm. Wires in plyg of throttle valve switch incorrectly connected or short circuit (full load contact closed before engine reaches full load)
20%	Full load contact polarity reversed or defective. Reading at 20% only with activated microswitch
30%	Short or open circuit between CIS-E control unit and coolant temperature sensor or coolant temperature sensor defective
40%	Short or open circuit to air flow sensor position indicator or air flow sensor position indicator defective. Increased idle rpm
50%	Oxygen sensor not at operating temperature, open circuit or defective
60%	Not used
70%	No TD signal (open circuit) at CIS-E control unit
80%	Short or open circuit to altitude correction capsule or capsule defective
90%	Not used
100%	Air/fuel mixture too lean, oxygen sensor defective (short circuit to ground). CIS-E control unit or on-off ratio tester defective. Defective overvoltage protection relay, no voltage supply. Increased idle rpm
Reading oscillates	No malfunction within the circuit of the monitored signals. On-off ratio reading indicated

Year — 1987
Model — 420 SEL
Engine — 4.2L (256 cid) V8
Engine Code — 116.965

ECM TROUBLE CODES

Percent	Explanation
Fixed on-off ratio %	Possible cause of failure
10%	Air flow sensor position indicator defective or polarity reversed
20%	Wires in plug of throttle valve switch incorrectly connected or short circuit (full load contact closed before engine reaches full load)
30%	Short circuit or wire interruption between CIS-E control unit and coolant temperature sensor or coolant temperature sensor defective (idle speed too high)
40%	Short circuit or wire interruption to air flow sensor position indicator or air flow sensor position indicator defective
50%	Lambda (oxygen) sensor not at operating temperature, wire interruption or defective
60%	Not used
70%	No TD signal (wire interruption)
80%	Short circuit or wire interruption to altitude correction capsule or capsule defective
90%	Not used
100%	Overvoltage protection relay defect (idle speed too high, approx. 1800 rpm). Air/fuel mixture too lean, oxygen sensor defective (short circuit to ground). CIS-E control unit or on-off ration defective. No power to EHA
Reading oscillates	No malfunction within the circuit of the monitored signals. On-off ratio reading indicated

Year — 1987
Model — 560 SEL
Engine — 5.6L (338 cid) V8
Engine Code — 117.968

ECM TROUBLE CODES

Percent	Explanation
Fixed on-off ratio %	Possible cause of failure
10%	Air flow sensor position indicator defective or polarity reversed
20%	Wires in plug of throttle valve switch incorrectly connected or short circuit (full load contact closed before engine reaches full load)
30%	Short circuit or wire interruption between CIS-E control unit and coolant temperature sensor or coolant temperature sensor defective (idle speed too high)
40%	Short circuit or wire interruption to air flow sensor position indicator or air flow sensor position indicator defective
50%	Lambda (oxygen) sensor not at operating temperature, wire interruption or defective
60%	Not used
70%	No TD signal (wire interruption)
80%	Short circuit or wire interruption to altitude correction capsule or capsule defective
90%	Not used
100%	Overvoltage protection relay defect (idle speed too high, approx. 1800 rpm). Air/fuel mixture too lean, oxygen sensor defective (short circuit to ground). CIS-E control unit or on-off ration defective. No power to EHA
Reading oscillates	No malfunction within the circuit of the monitored signals. On-off ratio reading indicated

Year—1987
Model—560 SEC
Engine—5.6L (338 cid) V8
Engine Code—117.968

ECM TROUBLE CODES

Percent	Explanation
Fixed on-off ratio %	Possible cause of failure
10%	Air flow sensor position indicator defective or polarity reversed
20%	Wires in plug of throttle valve switch incorrectly connected or short circuit (full load contact closed before engine reaches full load)
30%	Short circuit or wire interruption between CIS-E control unit and coolant temperature sensor or coolant temperature sensor defective (idle speed too high)
40%	Short circuit or wire interruption to air flow sensor position indicator or air flow sensor position indicator defective
50%	Lambda (oxygen) sensor not at operating temperature, wire interruption or defective
60%	Not used
70%	No TD signal (wire interruption)
80%	Short circuit or wire interruption to altitude correction capsule or capsule defective
90%	Not used
100%	Overvoltage protection relay defect (idle speed too high, approx. 1800 rpm). Air/fuel mixture too lean, oxygen sensor defective (short circuit to ground). CIS-E control unit or on-off ration defective. No power to EHA
Reading oscillates	No malfunction within the circuit of the monitored signals. On-off ratio reading indicated

Year – 1987
Model – 560 SL
Engine – 5.6L (338 cid) V8
Engine Code – 117.967

ECM TROUBLE CODES

Percent	Explanation
Fixed on-off ratio %	Possible cause of failure
10%	Air flow sensor position indicator defective or polarity reversed
20%	Wires in plug of throttle valve switch incorrectly connected or short circuit (full load contact closed before engine reaches full load)
30%	Short circuit or wire interruption between CIS-E control unit and coolant temperature sensor or coolant temperature sensor defective (idle speed too high)
40%	Short circuit or wire interruption to air flow sensor position indicator or air flow sensor position indicator defective
50%	Lambda (oxygen) sensor not at operating temperature, wire interruption or defective
60%	Not used
70%	No TD signal (wire interruption)
80%	Short circuit or wire interruption to altitude correction capsule or capsule defective
90%	Not used
100%	Overvoltage protection relay defect (idle speed too high, approx. 1800 rpm). Air/fuel mixture too lean, oxygen sensor defective (short circuit to ground). CIS-E control unit or on-off ration defective. No power to EHA
Reading oscillates	No malfunction within the circuit of the monitored signals. On-off ratio reading indicated

Year – 1988
Model – 190 E 2.3
Engine – 2.3L (140 cid) 4 cyl
Engine Code – 102.985

ECM TROUBLE CODES

Percent	Explanation
Fixed on-off ratio %	Possible cause of failure
10%	Air flow sensor position indicator defective or polarity reversed
20%	Wires in plug of throttle valve switch incorrectly connected or short circuit (full load contact closed before engine reaches full load)
30%	Short circuit or wire interruption between CIS-E control unit and coolant temperature sensor or coolant temperature sensor defective (idle speed too high)
40%	Short circuit or wire interruption to air flow sensor position indicator or air flow sensor position indicator defective
50%	Lambda (oxygen) sensor not at operating temperature, wire interruption or defective
60%	Not used
70%	No TD signal (wire interruption)
80%	Short circuit or wire interruption to altitude correction capsule or capsule defective
90%	Not used
100%	Overvoltage protection relay defect (idle speed too high, approx. 1800 rpm). Air/fuel mixture too lean, oxygen sensor defective (short circuit to ground). CIS-E control unit or on-off ration defective. No power to EHA
Reading oscillates	No malfunction within the circuit of the monitored signals. On-off ratio reading indicated

Year – 1988
Model – 190 E 2.6
Engine – 2.6L (159 cid) 6 cyl
Engine Code – 103.942

ECM TROUBLE CODES

Percent	Explanation
Fixed on-off ratio %	Possible cause of failure
10%	Air flow sensor position indicator defective or polarity reversed
20%	Wires in plug of throttle valve switch incorrectly connected or short circuit (full load contact closed before engine reaches full load)
30%	Short circuit or wire interruption between CIS-E control unit and coolant temperature sensor or coolant temperature sensor defective (idle speed too high)
40%	Short circuit or wire interruption to air flow sensor position indicator or air flow sensor position indicator defective
50%	Lambda (oxygen) sensor not at operating temperature, wire interruption or defective
60%	Not used
70%	No TD signal (wire interruption)
80%	Short circuit or wire interruption to altitude correction capsule or capsule defective
90%	Not used
100%	Overvoltage protection relay defect (idle speed too high, approx. 1800 rpm). Air/fuel mixture too lean, oxygen sensor defective (short circuit to ground). CIS-E control unit or on-off ration defective. No power to EHA
Reading oscillates	No malfunction within the circuit of the monitored signals. On-off ratio reading indicated

Year — 1988
Model — 260 E
Engine — 2.6L (159 cid) 6 cyl
Engine Code — 103.940

ECM TROUBLE CODES

Percent	Explanation
Fixed on-off ratio %	Possible cause of failure
10%	Air flow sensor position indicator defective or polarity reversed
20%	Wires in plug of throttle valve switch incorrectly connected or short circuit (full load contact closed before engine reaches full load)
30%	Short circuit or wire interruption between CIS-E control unit and coolant temperature sensor or coolant temperature sensor defective (idle speed too high)
40%	Short circuit or wire interruption to air flow sensor position indicator or air flow sensor position indicator defective
50%	Lambda (oxygen) sensor not at operating temperature, wire interruption or defective
60%	Not used
70%	No TD signal (wire interruption)
80%	Short circuit or wire interruption to altitude correction capsule or capsule defective
90%	Not used
100%	Overvoltage protection relay defect (idle speed too high, approx. 1800 rpm). Air/fuel mixture too lean, oxygen sensor defective (short circuit to ground). CIS-E control unit or on-off ration defective. No power to EHA
Reading oscillates	No malfunction within the circuit of the monitored signals. On-off ratio reading indicated

Year – 1988
Model – 300 E
Engine – 3.0L (181 cid) 6 cyl
Engine Code – 102.983

ECM TROUBLE CODES

Code	Explanation
1	No system malfunction
2	Throttle valve switch
3	Coolant temperature sensor
4	Air flow sensor position indicator
5	Oxygen sensor
6	Not used
7	TD-signal
8	Altitude correction capsule
9	Electrohydraulic actuator (EHA)
10	Throttle valve switch

Year – 1988
Model – 300 CE
Engine – 3.0L (181 cid) 6 cyl
Engine Code – 103.983

ECM TROUBLE CODES

Percent	Explanation
Fixed on-off ratio	Possible cause of failure
0%	CIS-E control unit receives no voltage or is defective. Circuit to diagnositc socket, terminal 3 open or on-off ratio tester defective. Air/fuel mixture too rich. Lambda (oxygen) sensor signal voltage is above 12V
10%	Air flow sensor position indicator defective or polarity reversed. Approximately 2000 rpm. Wires in plyg of throttle valve switch incorrectly connected or short circuit (full load contact closed before engine reaches full load)
20%	Full load contact polarity reversed or defective. Reading at 20% only with activated microswitch
30%	Short or open circuit between CIS-E control unit and coolant temperature sensor or coolant temperature sensor defective
40%	Short or open circuit to air flow sensor position indicator or air flow sensor position indicator defective. Increased idle rpm
50%	Oxygen sensor not at operating temperature, open circuit or defective
60%	Not used
70%	No TD signal (open circuit) at CIS-E control unit
80%	Short or open circuit to altitude correction capsule or capsule defective
90%	Not used
100%	Air/fuel mixture too lean, oxygen sensor defective (short circuit to ground). CIS-E control unit or on-off ratio tester defective. Defective overvoltage protection relay, no voltage supply. Increased idle rpm
Reading oscillates	No malfunction within the circuit of the monitored signals. On-off ratio reading indicated

Year — 1988
Model — 300 TE
Engine — 3.0L (181 cid) 6 cyl
Engine Code — 103.983

ECM TROUBLE CODES

Percent	Explanation
Fixed on-off ratio	Possible cause of failure
0%	CIS-E control unit receives no voltage or is defective. Circuit to diagnositc socket, terminal 3 open or on-off ratio tester defective. Air/fuel mixture too rich. Lambda (oxygen) sensor signal voltage is above 12V
10%	Air flow sensor position indicator defective or polarity reversed. Approximately 2000 rpm. Wires in plyg of throttle valve switch incorrectly connected or short circuit (full load contact closed before engine reaches full load)
20%	Full load contact polarity reversed or defective. Reading at 20% only with activated microswitch
30%	Short or open circuit between CIS-E control unit and coolant temperature sensor or coolant temperature sensor defective
40%	Short or open circuit to air flow sensor position indicator or air flow sensor position indicator defective. Increased idle rpm
50%	Oxygen sensor not at operating temperature, open circuit or defective
60%	Not used
70%	No TD signal (open circuit) at CIS-E control unit
80%	Short or open circuit to altitude correction capsule or capsule defective
90%	Not used
100%	Air/fuel mixture too lean, oxygen sensor defective (short circuit to ground). CIS-E control unit or on-off ratio tester defective. Defective overvoltage protection relay, no voltage supply. Increased idle rpm
Reading oscillates	No malfunction within the circuit of the monitored signals. On-off ratio reading indicated

Year – 1988
Model – 300 SE
Engine – 3.0L (181 cid) 6 cyl
Engine Code – 103.981

ECM TROUBLE CODES

Percent	Explanation
Fixed on-off ratio	Possible cause of failure
0%	CIS-E control unit receives no voltage or is defective. Circuit to diagnositc socket, terminal 3 open or on-off ratio tester defective. Air/fuel mixture too rich. Lambda (oxygen) sensor signal voltage is above 12V
10%	Air flow sensor position indicator defective or polarity reversed. Approximately 2000 rpm. Wires in plyg of throttle valve switch incorrectly connected or short circuit (full load contact closed before engine reaches full load)
20%	Full load contact polarity reversed or defective. Reading at 20% only with activated microswitch
30%	Short or open circuit between CIS-E control unit and coolant temperature sensor or coolant temperature sensor defective
40%	Short or open circuit to air flow sensor position indicator or air flow sensor position indicator defective. Increased idle rpm
50%	Oxygen sensor not at operating temperature, open circuit or defective
60%	Not used
70%	No TD signal (open circuit) at CIS-E control unit
80%	Short or open circuit to altitude correction capsule or capsule defective
90%	Not used
100%	Air/fuel mixture too lean, oxygen sensor defective (short circuit to ground). CIS-E control unit or on-off ratio tester defective. Defective overvoltage protection relay, no voltage supply. Increased idle rpm
Reading oscillates	No malfunction within the circuit of the monitored signals. On-off ratio reading indicated

Year — 1988
Model — 300 SEL
Engine — 3.0L (181 cid) 6 cyl
Engine Code — 103.981

ECM TROUBLE CODES

Percent	Explanation
Fixed on-off ratio	Possible cause of failure
0%	CIS-E control unit receives no voltage or is defective. Circuit to diagnositc socket, terminal 3 open or on-off ratio tester defective. Air/fuel mixture too rich. Lambda (oxygen) sensor signal voltage is above 12V
10%	Air flow sensor position indicator defective or polarity reversed. Approximately 2000 rpm. Wires in plyg of throttle valve switch incorrectly connected or short circuit (full load contact closed before engine reaches full load)
20%	Full load contact polarity reversed or defective. Reading at 20% only with activated microswitch
30%	Short or open circuit between CIS-E control unit and coolant temperature sensor or coolant temperature sensor defective
40%	Short or open circuit to air flow sensor position indicator or air flow sensor position indicator defective. Increased idle rpm
50%	Oxygen sensor not at operating temperature, open circuit or defective
60%	Not used
70%	No TD signal (open circuit) at CIS-E control unit
80%	Short or open circuit to altitude correction capsule or capsule defective
90%	Not used
100%	Air/fuel mixture too lean, oxygen sensor defective (short circuit to ground). CIS-E control unit or on-off ratio tester defective. Defective overvoltage protection relay, no voltage supply. Increased idle rpm
Reading oscillates	No malfunction within the circuit of the monitored signals. On-off ratio reading indicated

Year — 1988
Model — 420 SEL
Engine — 4.2L (256 cid) V8
Engine Code — 116.965

ECM TROUBLE CODES

Percent	Explanation
Fixed on-off ratio	Possible cause of failure
0%	CIS-E control unit receives no voltage or is defective. Circuit to diagnositc socket, terminal 3 open or on-off ratio tester defective. Air/fuel mixture too rich. Lambda (oxygen) sensor signal voltage is above 12V
10%	Air flow sensor position indicator defective or polarity reversed. Approximately 2000 rpm. Wires in plyg of throttle valve switch incorrectly connected or short circuit (full load contact closed before engine reaches full load)
20%	Full load contact polarity reversed or defective. Reading at 20% only with activated microswitch
30%	Short or open circuit between CIS-E control unit and coolant temperature sensor or coolant temperature sensor defective
40%	Short or open circuit to air flow sensor position indicator or air flow sensor position indicator defective. Increased idle rpm
50%	Oxygen sensor not at operating temperature, open circuit or defective
60%	Not used
70%	No TD signal (open circuit) at CIS-E control unit
80%	Short or open circuit to altitude correction capsule or capsule defective
90%	Not used
100%	Air/fuel mixture too lean, oxygen sensor defective (short circuit to ground). CIS-E control unit or on-off ratio tester defective. Defective overvoltage protection relay, no voltage supply. Increased idle rpm
Reading oscillates	No malfunction within the circuit of the monitored signals. On-off ratio reading indicated

Year — 1988
Model — 560 SEL
Engine — 5.6L (338 cid) V8
Engine Code — 117.968

ECM TROUBLE CODES

Percent	Explanation
Fixed on-off ratio	Possible cause of failure
0%	CIS-E control unit receives no voltage or is defective. Circuit to diagnositc socket, terminal 3 open or on-off ratio tester defective. Air/fuel mixture too rich. Lambda (oxygen) sensor signal voltage is above 12V
10%	Air flow sensor position indicator defective or polarity reversed. Approximately 2000 rpm. Wires in plyg of throttle valve switch incorrectly connected or short circuit (full load contact closed before engine reaches full load)
20%	Full load contact polarity reversed or defective. Reading at 20% only with activated microswitch
30%	Short or open circuit between CIS-E control unit and coolant temperature sensor or coolant temperature sensor defective
40%	Short or open circuit to air flow sensor position indicator or air flow sensor position indicator defective. Increased idle rpm
50%	Oxygen sensor not at operating temperature, open circuit or defective
60%	Not used
70%	No TD signal (open circuit) at CIS-E control unit
80%	Short or open circuit to altitude correction capsule or capsule defective
90%	Not used
100%	Air/fuel mixture too lean, oxygen sensor defective (short circuit to ground). CIS-E control unit or on-off ratio tester defective. Defective overvoltage protection relay, no voltage supply. Increased idle rpm
Reading oscillates	No malfunction within the circuit of the monitored signals. On-off ratio reading indicated

Year – 1988
Model – 560 SEC
Engine – 5.6L (338 cid) V8
Engine Code – 117.968

ECM TROUBLE CODES

Percent	Explanation
Fixed on-off ratio	Possible cause of failure
0%	CIS-E control unit receives no voltage or is defective. Circuit to diagnositc socket, terminal 3 open or on-off ratio tester defective. Air/fuel mixture too rich. Lambda (oxygen) sensor signal voltage is above 12V
10%	Air flow sensor position indicator defective or polarity reversed. Approximately 2000 rpm. Wires in plyg of throttle valve switch incorrectly connected or short circuit (full load contact closed before engine reaches full load)
20%	Full load contact polarity reversed or defective. Reading at 20% only with activated microswitch
30%	Short or open circuit between CIS-E control unit and coolant temperature sensor or coolant temperature sensor defective
40%	Short or open circuit to air flow sensor position indicator or air flow sensor position indicator defective. Increased idle rpm
50%	Oxygen sensor not at operating temperature, open circuit or defective
60%	Not used
70%	No TD signal (open circuit) at CIS-E control unit
80%	Short or open circuit to altitude correction capsule or capsule defective
90%	Not used
100%	Air/fuel mixture too lean, oxygen sensor defective (short circuit to ground). CIS-E control unit or on-off ratio tester defective. Defective overvoltage protection relay, no voltage supply. Increased idle rpm
Reading oscillates	No malfunction within the circuit of the monitored signals. On-off ratio reading indicated

Year — 1988
Model — 560 SL
Engine — 5.6L (338 cid) V8
Engine Code — 117.967

ECM TROUBLE CODES

Percent	Explanation
Fixed on-off ratio	Possible cause of failure
0%	CIS-E control unit receives no voltage or is defective. Circuit to diagnositc socket, terminal 3 open or on-off ratio tester defective. Air/fuel mixture too rich. Lambda (oxygen) sensor signal voltage is above 12V
10%	Air flow sensor position indicator defective or polarity reversed. Approximately 2000 rpm. Wires in plyg of throttle valve switch incorrectly connected or short circuit (full load contact closed before engine reaches full load)
20%	Full load contact polarity reversed or defective. Reading at 20% only with activated microswitch
30%	Short or open circuit between CIS-E control unit and coolant temperature sensor or coolant temperature sensor defective
40%	Short or open circuit to air flow sensor position indicator or air flow sensor position indicator defective. Increased idle rpm
50%	Oxygen sensor not at operating temperature, open circuit or defective
60%	Not used
70%	No TD signal (open circuit) at CIS-E control unit
80%	Short or open circuit to altitude correction capsule or capsule defective
90%	Not used
100%	Air/fuel mixture too lean, oxygen sensor defective (short circuit to ground). CIS-E control unit or on-off ratio tester defective. Defective overvoltage protection relay, no voltage supply. Increased idle rpm
Reading oscillates	No malfunction within the circuit of the monitored signals. On-off ratio reading indicated

Year — 1988
Model — 190 E
Engine — 2.3L (140 cid) 4 cyl
Engine Code — 102.985

ECM TROUBLE CODES

Code	Explanation
1	No system malfunction
2	Throttle valve switch
3	Coolant temperature sensor
4	Air flow sensor position indicator
5	Oxygen sensor
6	Not used
7	TD-signal
8	Altitude correction capsule
9	Electrohydraulic actuator (EHA)
10	Throttle valve switch idle speed contact

Year — 1988
Model — 190 E
Engine — 2.6L (159 cid) 6 cyl
Engine Code — 103.942

ECM TROUBLE CODES

Code	Explanation
1	No system malfunction
2	Throttle valve switch
3	Coolant temperature sensor
4	Air flow sensor position indicator
5	Oxygen sensor
6	Not used
7	TD-signal
8	Altitude correction capsule
9	Electrohydraulic actuator (EHA)
10	Throttle valve switch idle speed contact

Year — 1988
Model — 260 E
Engine — 2.6L (159 cid) 6 cyl
Engine Code — 103.940

ECM TROUBLE CODES

Code	Explanation
1	No system malfunction
2	Throttle valve switch
3	Coolant temperature sensor
4	Air flow sensor position indicator
5	Oxygen sensor
6	Not used
7	TD-signal
8	Altitude correction capsule
9	Electrohydraulic actuator (EHA)
10	Throttle valve switch idle speed contact

Year—1988
Model—300 E
Engine—3.0L (181 cid) 6 cyl
Engine Code—103.983

ECM TROUBLE CODES

Code	Explanation
1	No system malfunction
2	Throttle valve switch
3	Coolant temperature sensor
4	Air flow sensor position indicator
5	Oxygen sensor
6	Not used
7	TD-signal
8	Altitude correction capsule
9	Electrohydraulic actuator (EHA)
10	Throttle valve switch idle speed contact

Year—1988
Model—300 CE
Engine—3.0L (181 cid) 6 cyl
Engine Code—103.983

ECM TROUBLE CODES

Code	Explanation
1	No system malfunction
2	Throttle valve switch
3	Coolant temperature sensor
4	Air flow sensor position indicator
5	Oxygen sensor
6	Not used
7	TD-signal
8	Altitude correction capsule
9	Electrohydraulic actuator (EHA)
10	Throttle valve switch idle speed contact

Year – 1988
Model – 300 TE
Engine – 3.0L (181 cid) 6 cyl
Engine Code – 103.983

ECM TROUBLE CODES

Code	Explanation
1	No system malfunction
2	Throttle valve switch
3	Coolant temperature sensor
4	Air flow sensor position indicator
5	Oxygen sensor
6	Not used
7	TD-signal
8	Altitude correction capsule
9	Electrohydraulic actuator (EHA)
10	Throttle valve switch idle speed contact

Year – 1988
Model – 300 SE
Engine – 3.0L (181 cid) 6 cyl
Engine Code – 103.981

ECM TROUBLE CODES

Code	Explanation
1	No system malfunction
2	Throttle valve switch
3	Coolant temperature sensor
4	Air flow sensor position indicator
5	Oxygen sensor
6	Not used
7	TD-signal
8	Altitude correction capsule
9	Electrohydraulic actuator (EHA)
10	Throttle valve switch idle speed contact

Year — 1988
Model — 300 SEL
Engine — 3.0L (181 cid) 6 cyl
Engine Code — 103.981

ECM TROUBLE CODES

Code	Explanation
1	No system malfunction
2	Throttle valve switch
3	Coolant temperature sensor
4	Air flow sensor position indicator
5	Oxygen sensor
6	Not used
7	TD-signal
8	Altitude correction capsule
9	Electrohydraulic actuator (EHA)
10	Throttle valve switch idle speed contact

Year — 1988
Model — 420 SEL
Engine — 4.2L (256 cid) V8
Engine Code — 116.965

ECM TROUBLE CODES

Code	Explanation
1	No system malfunction
2	Throttle valve switch
3	Coolant temperature sensor
4	Air flow sensor position indicator
5	Oxygen sensor
6	Not used
7	TD-signal
8	Altitude correction capsule
9	Electrohydraulic actuator (EHA)
10	Throttle valve switch idle speed contact
11	Not used
12	Exhaust gas recirculation

Year—1988
Model—560 SEL
Engine—5.6L (338 cid) V8
Engine Code—117.968

ECM TROUBLE CODES

Code	Explanation
1	No system malfunction
2	Throttle valve switch
3	Coolant temperature sensor
4	Air flow sensor position indicator
5	Oxygen sensor
6	Not used
7	TD-signal
8	Altitude correction capsule
9	Electrohydraulic actuator (EHA)
10	Throttle valve switch idle speed contact
11	Not used
12	Exhaust gas recirculation

Year—1988
Model—560 SEC
Engine—5.6L (338 cid) V8
Engine Code—117.968

ECM TROUBLE CODES

Code	Explanation
1	No system malfunction
2	Throttle valve switch
3	Coolant temperature sensor
4	Air flow sensor position indicator
5	Oxygen sensor
6	Not used
7	TD-signal
8	Altitude correction capsule
9	Electrohydraulic actuator (EHA)
10	Throttle valve switch idle speed contact
11	Not used
12	Exhaust gas recirculation

Year — 1988
Model — 560 SL
Engine — 5.6L (338 cid) V8
Engine Code — 117.967

ECM TROUBLE CODES

Code	Explanation
1	No system malfunction
2	Throttle valve switch
3	Coolant temperature sensor
4	Air flow sensor position indicator
5	Oxygen sensor
6	Not used
7	TD-signal
8	Altitude correction capsule
9	Electrohydraulic actuator (EHA)
10	Throttle valve switch idle speed contact
11	Not used
12	Exhaust gas recirculation

Year – 1989
Model – 190 E 2.6
Engine – 2.6L (159 cid) 6 cyl
Engine Code – 103.942

ECM TROUBLE CODES

Percent	Explanation
Fixed on-off ratio %	Possible cause of failure
10%	Air flow sensor position indicator defective or polarity reversed
20%	Wires in plug of throttle valve switch incorrectly connected or short circuit (full load contact closed before engine reaches full load)
30%	Short circuit or wire interruption between CIS-E control unit and coolant temperature sensor or coolant temperature sensor defective (idle speed too high)
40%	Short circuit or wire interruption to air flow sensor position indicator or air flow sensor position indicator defective
50%	Lambda (oxygen) sensor not at operating temperature, wire interruption or defective
60%	Not used
70%	No TD signal (wire interruption)
80%	Short circuit or wire interruption to altitude correction capsule or capsule defective
90%	Not used
100%	Overvoltage protection relay defect (idle speed too high, approx. 1800 rpm). Air/fuel mixture too lean, oxygen sensor defective (short circuit to ground). CIS-E control unit or on-off ration defective. No power to EHA
Reading oscillates	No malfunction within the circuit of the monitored signals. On-off ratio reading indicated

Year – 1989
Model – 260 E
Engine – 2.6L (159 cid) 6 cyl
Engine Code – 103.940

ECM TROUBLE CODES

Percent	Explanation
Fixed on-off ratio %	Possible cause of failure
10%	Air flow sensor position indicator defective or polarity reversed
20%	Wires in plug of throttle valve switch incorrectly connected or short circuit (full load contact closed before engine reaches full load)
30%	Short circuit or wire interruption between CIS-E control unit and coolant temperature sensor or coolant temperature sensor defective (idle speed too high)
40%	Short circuit or wire interruption to air flow sensor position indicator or air flow sensor position indicator defective
50%	Lambda (oxygen) sensor not at operating temperature, wire interruption or defective
60%	Not used
70%	No TD signal (wire interruption)
80%	Short circuit or wire interruption to altitude correction capsule or capsule defective
90%	Not used
100%	Overvoltage protection relay defect (idle speed too high, approx. 1800 rpm). Air/fuel mixture too lean, oxygen sensor defective (short circuit to ground). CIS-E control unit or on-off ration defective. No power to EHA
Reading oscillates	No malfunction within the circuit of the monitored signals. On-off ratio reading indicated

Year – 1989
Model – 300 E
Engine – 3.0L (181 cid) 6 cyl
Engine Code – 103.983

ECM TROUBLE CODES

Code	Explanation
1	No system malfunction
2	Throttle valve switch
3	Coolant temperature sensor
4	Air flow sensor position indicator
5	Oxygen sensor
6	Not used
7	TD-signal
8	Altitude correction capsule
9	Electrohydraulic actuator (EHA)
10	Throttle valve switch

Year – 1989
Model – 300 CE
Engine – 3.0L (181 cid) 6 cyl
Engine Code – 103.983

ECM TROUBLE CODES

Percent	Explanation
Fixed on-off ratio	Possible cause of failure
0%	CIS-E control unit receives no voltage or is defective. Circuit to diagnositc socket, terminal 3 open or on-off ratio tester defective. Air/fuel mixture too rich. Lambda (oxygen) sensor signal voltage is above 12V
10%	Air flow sensor position indicator defective or polarity reversed. Approximately 2000 rpm. Wires in plyg of throttle valve switch incorrectly connected or short circuit (full load contact closed before engine reaches full load)
20%	Full load contact polarity reversed or defective. Reading at 20% only with activated microswitch
30%	Short or open circuit between CIS-E control unit and coolant temperature sensor or coolant temperature sensor defective
40%	Short or open circuit to air flow sensor position indicator or air flow sensor position indicator defective. Increased idle rpm
50%	Oxygen sensor not at operating temperature, open circuit or defective
60%	Not used
70%	No TD signal (open circuit) at CIS-E control unit
80%	Short or open circuit to altitude correction capsule or capsule defective
90%	Not used
100%	Air/fuel mixture too lean, oxygen sensor defective (short circuit to ground). CIS-E control unit or on-off ratio tester defective. Defective overvoltage protection relay, no voltage supply. Increased idle rpm
Reading oscillates	No malfunction within the circuit of the monitored signals. On-off ratio reading indicated

Year — 1989
Model — 300 TE
Engine — 3.0L (181 cid) 6 cyl
Engine Code — 103.983

ECM TROUBLE CODES

Percent	Explanation
Fixed on-off ratio	Possible cause of failure
0%	CIS-E control unit receives no voltage or is defective. Circuit to diagnositc socket, terminal 3 open or on-off ratio tester defective. Air/fuel mixture too rich. Lambda (oxygen) sensor signal voltage is above 12V
10%	Air flow sensor position indicator defective or polarity reversed. Approximately 2000 rpm. Wires in plyg of throttle valve switch incorrectly connected or short circuit (full load contact closed before engine reaches full load)
20%	Full load contact polarity reversed or defective. Reading at 20% only with activated microswitch
30%	Short or open circuit between CIS-E control unit and coolant temperature sensor or coolant temperature sensor defective
40%	Short or open circuit to air flow sensor position indicator or air flow sensor position indicator defective. Increased idle rpm
50%	Oxygen sensor not at operating temperature, open circuit or defective
60%	Not used
70%	No TD signal (open circuit) at CIS-E control unit
80%	Short or open circuit to altitude correction capsule or capsule defective
90%	Not used
100%	Air/fuel mixture too lean, oxygen sensor defective (short circuit to ground). CIS-E control unit or on-off ratio tester defective. Defective overvoltage protection relay, no voltage supply. Increased idle rpm
Reading oscillates	No malfunction within the circuit of the monitored signals. On-off ratio reading indicated

Year — 1989
Model — 300 SE
Engine — 3.0L (181 cid) 6 cyl
Engine Code — 103.981

ECM TROUBLE CODES

Percent	Explanation
Fixed on-off ratio	Possible cause of failure
0%	CIS-E control unit receives no voltage or is defective. Circuit to diagnositc socket, terminal 3 open or on-off ratio tester defective. Air/fuel mixture too rich. Lambda (oxygen) sensor signal voltage is above 12V
10%	Air flow sensor position indicator defective or polarity reversed. Approximately 2000 rpm. Wires in plyg of throttle valve switch incorrectly connected or short circuit (full load contact closed before engine reaches full load)
20%	Full load contact polarity reversed or defective. Reading at 20% only with activated microswitch
30%	Short or open circuit between CIS-E control unit and coolant temperature sensor or coolant temperature sensor defective
40%	Short or open circuit to air flow sensor position indicator or air flow sensor position indicator defective. Increased idle rpm
50%	Oxygen sensor not at operating temperature, open circuit or defective
60%	Not used
70%	No TD signal (open circuit) at CIS-E control unit
80%	Short or open circuit to altitude correction capsule or capsule defective
90%	Not used
100%	Air/fuel mixture too lean, oxygen sensor defective (short circuit to ground). CIS-E control unit or on-off ratio tester defective. Defective overvoltage protection relay, no voltage supply. Increased idle rpm
Reading oscillates	No malfunction within the circuit of the monitored signals. On-off ratio reading indicated

Year – 1989
Model – 300 SEL
Engine – 3.0L (181 cid) 6 cyl
Engine Code – 103.981

ECM TROUBLE CODES

Percent	Explanation
Fixed on-off ratio	Possible cause of failure
0%	CIS-E control unit receives no voltage or is defective. Circuit to diagnositc socket, terminal 3 open or on-off ratio tester defective. Air/fuel mixture too rich. Lambda (oxygen) sensor signal voltage is above 12V
10%	Air flow sensor position indicator defective or polarity reversed. Approximately 2000 rpm. Wires in plyg of throttle valve switch incorrectly connected or short circuit (full load contact closed before engine reaches full load)
20%	Full load contact polarity reversed or defective. Reading at 20% only with activated microswitch
30%	Short or open circuit between CIS-E control unit and coolant temperature sensor or coolant temperature sensor defective
40%	Short or open circuit to air flow sensor position indicator or air flow sensor position indicator defective. Increased idle rpm
50%	Oxygen sensor not at operating temperature, open circuit or defective
60%	Not used
70%	No TD signal (open circuit) at CIS-E control unit
80%	Short or open circuit to altitude correction capsule or capsule defective
90%	Not used
100%	Air/fuel mixture too lean, oxygen sensor defective (short circuit to ground). CIS-E control unit or on-off ratio tester defective. Defective overvoltage protection relay, no voltage supply. Increased idle rpm
Reading oscillates	No malfunction within the circuit of the monitored signals. On-off ratio reading indicated

Year — 1989
Model — 420 SEL
Engine — 4.2L (256 cid) V8
Engine Code — 116.965

ECM TROUBLE CODES

Percent	Explanation
Fixed on-off ratio	Possible cause of failure
0%	CIS-E control unit receives no voltage or is defective. Circuit to diagnositc socket, terminal 3 open or on-off ratio tester defective. Air/fuel mixture too rich. Lambda (oxygen) sensor signal voltage is above 12V
10%	Air flow sensor position indicator defective or polarity reversed. Approximately 2000 rpm. Wires in plyg of throttle valve switch incorrectly connected or short circuit (full load contact closed before engine reaches full load)
20%	Full load contact polarity reversed or defective. Reading at 20% only with activated microswitch
30%	Short or open circuit between CIS-E control unit and coolant temperature sensor or coolant temperature sensor defective
40%	Short or open circuit to air flow sensor position indicator or air flow sensor position indicator defective. Increased idle rpm
50%	Oxygen sensor not at operating temperature, open circuit or defective
60%	Not used
70%	No TD signal (open circuit) at CIS-E control unit
80%	Short or open circuit to altitude correction capsule or capsule defective
90%	Not used
100%	Air/fuel mixture too lean, oxygen sensor defective (short circuit to ground). CIS-E control unit or on-off ratio tester defective. Defective overvoltage protection relay, no voltage supply. Increased idle rpm
Reading oscillates	No malfunction within the circuit of the monitored signals. On-off ratio reading indicated

Year — 1989
Model — 560 SEL
Engine — 5.6L (338 cid) V8
Engine Code — 117.968

ECM TROUBLE CODES

Percent	Explanation
Fixed on-off ratio	Possible cause of failure
0%	CIS-E control unit receives no voltage or is defective. Circuit to diagnositc socket, terminal 3 open or on-off ratio tester defective. Air/fuel mixture too rich. Lambda (oxygen) sensor signal voltage is above 12V
10%	Air flow sensor position indicator defective or polarity reversed. Approximately 2000 rpm. Wires in plyg of throttle valve switch incorrectly connected or short circuit (full load contact closed before engine reaches full load)
20%	Full load contact polarity reversed or defective. Reading at 20% only with activated microswitch
30%	Short or open circuit between CIS-E control unit and coolant temperature sensor or coolant temperature sensor defective
40%	Short or open circuit to air flow sensor position indicator or air flow sensor position indicator defective. Increased idle rpm
50%	Oxygen sensor not at operating temperature, open circuit or defective
60%	Not used
70%	No TD signal (open circuit) at CIS-E control unit
80%	Short or open circuit to altitude correction capsule or capsule defective
90%	Not used
100%	Air/fuel mixture too lean, oxygen sensor defective (short circuit to ground). CIS-E control unit or on-off ratio tester defective. Defective overvoltage protection relay, no voltage supply. Increased idle rpm
Reading oscillates	No malfunction within the circuit of the monitored signals. On-off ratio reading indicated

Year — 1989
Model — 560 SEC
Engine — 5.6L (338 cid) V8
Engine Code — 117.968

ECM TROUBLE CODES

Percent	Explanation
Fixed on-off ratio	Possible cause of failure
0%	CIS-E control unit receives no voltage or is defective. Circuit to diagnositc socket, terminal 3 open or on-off ratio tester defective. Air/fuel mixture too rich. Lambda (oxygen) sensor signal voltage is above 12V
10%	Air flow sensor position indicator defective or polarity reversed. Approximately 2000 rpm. Wires in plyg of throttle valve switch incorrectly connected or short circuit (full load contact closed before engine reaches full load)
20%	Full load contact polarity reversed or defective. Reading at 20% only with activated microswitch
30%	Short or open circuit between CIS-E control unit and coolant temperature sensor or coolant temperature sensor defective
40%	Short or open circuit to air flow sensor position indicator or air flow sensor position indicator defective. Increased idle rpm
50%	Oxygen sensor not at operating temperature, open circuit or defective
60%	Not used
70%	No TD signal (open circuit) at CIS-E control unit
80%	Short or open circuit to altitude correction capsule or capsule defective
90%	Not used
100%	Air/fuel mixture too lean, oxygen sensor defective (short circuit to ground). CIS-E control unit or on-off ratio tester defective. Defective overvoltage protection relay, no voltage supply. Increased idle rpm
Reading oscillates	No malfunction within the circuit of the monitored signals. On-off ratio reading indicated

Year – 1989
Model – 560 SL
Engine – 5.6L (338 cid) V8
Engine Code – 117.967

ECM TROUBLE CODES

Percent	Explanation
Fixed on-off ratio	Possible cause of failure
0%	CIS-E control unit receives no voltage or is defective. Circuit to diagnositc socket, terminal 3 open or on-off ratio tester defective. Air/fuel mixture too rich. Lambda (oxygen) sensor signal voltage is above 12V
10%	Air flow sensor position indicator defective or polarity reversed. Approximately 2000 rpm. Wires in plyg of throttle valve switch incorrectly connected or short circuit (full load contact closed before engine reaches full load)
20%	Full load contact polarity reversed or defective. Reading at 20% only with activated microswitch
30%	Short or open circuit between CIS-E control unit and coolant temperature sensor or coolant temperature sensor defective
40%	Short or open circuit to air flow sensor position indicator or air flow sensor position indicator defective. Increased idle rpm
50%	Oxygen sensor not at operating temperature, open circuit or defective
60%	Not used
70%	No TD signal (open circuit) at CIS-E control unit
80%	Short or open circuit to altitude correction capsule or capsule defective
90%	Not used
100%	Air/fuel mixture too lean, oxygen sensor defective (short circuit to ground). CIS-E control unit or on-off ratio tester defective. Defective overvoltage protection relay, no voltage supply. Increased idle rpm
Reading oscillates	No malfunction within the circuit of the monitored signals. On-off ratio reading indicated

Year – 1989
Model – 190 E
Engine – 2.6L (159 cid) 6 cyl
Engine Code – 103.942

ECM TROUBLE CODES

Code	Explanation
1	No system malfunction
2	Throttle valve switch
3	Coolant temperature sensor
4	Air flow sensor position indicator
5	Oxygen sensor
6	Not used
7	TD-signal
8	Altitude correction capsule
9	Electrohydraulic actuator (EHA)
10	Throttle valve switch idle speed contact

Year — 1989
Model — 260 E
Engine — 2.6L (159 cid) 6 cyl
Engine Code — 103.940

ECM TROUBLE CODES

Code	Explanation
1	No system malfunction
2	Throttle valve switch
3	Coolant temperature sensor
4	Air flow sensor position indicator
5	Oxygen sensor
6	Not used
7	TD-signal
8	Altitude correction capsule
9	Electrohydraulic actuator (EHA)
10	Throttle valve switch idle speed contact

Year — 1989
Model — 300 E
Engine — 3.0L (181 cid) 6 cyl
Engine Code — 103.983

ECM TROUBLE CODES

Code	Explanation
1	No system malfunction
2	Throttle valve switch
3	Coolant temperature sensor
4	Air flow sensor position indicator
5	Oxygen sensor
6	Not used
7	TD-signal
8	Altitude correction capsule
9	Electrohydraulic actuator (EHA)
10	Throttle valve switch idle speed contact

Year — 1989
Model — 300 CE
Engine — 3.0L (181 cid) 6 cyl
Engine Code — 103.983

ECM TROUBLE CODES

Code	Explanation
1	No system malfunction
2	Throttle valve switch
3	Coolant temperature sensor
4	Air flow sensor position indicator
5	Oxygen sensor
6	Not used
7	TD-signal
8	Altitude correction capsule
9	Electrohydraulic actuator (EHA)
10	Throttle valve switch idle speed contact

Year — 1989
Model — 300 TE
Engine — 3.0L (181 cid) 6 cyl
Engine Code — 103.983

ECM TROUBLE CODES

Code	Explanation
1	No system malfunction
2	Throttle valve switch
3	Coolant temperature sensor
4	Air flow sensor position indicator
5	Oxygen sensor
6	Not used
7	TD-signal
8	Altitude correction capsule
9	Electrohydraulic actuator (EHA)
10	Throttle valve switch idle speed contact

Year — 1989
Model — 300 SE
Engine — 3.0L (181 cid) 6 cyl
Engine Code — 103.981

ECM TROUBLE CODES

Code	Explanation
1	No system malfunction
2	Throttle valve switch
3	Coolant temperature sensor
4	Air flow sensor position indicator
5	Oxygen sensor
6	Not used
7	TD-signal
8	Altitude correction capsule
9	Electrohydraulic actuator (EHA)
10	Throttle valve switch idle speed contact

Year — 1989
Model — 300 SEL
Engine — 3.0L (181 cid) 6 cyl
Engine Code — 103.981

ECM TROUBLE CODES

Code	Explanation
1	No system malfunction
2	Throttle valve switch
3	Coolant temperature sensor
4	Air flow sensor position indicator
5	Oxygen sensor
6	Not used
7	TD-signal
8	Altitude correction capsule
9	Electrohydraulic actuator (EHA)
10	Throttle valve switch idle speed contact

Year — 1989
Model — 420 SEL
Engine — 4.2L (256 cid) V8
Engine Code — 116.965

ECM TROUBLE CODES

Code	Explanation
1	No system malfunction
2	Throttle valve switch
3	Coolant temperature sensor
4	Air flow sensor position indicator
5	Oxygen sensor
6	Not used
7	TD-signal
8	Altitude correction capsule
9	Electrohydraulic actuator (EHA)
10	Throttle valve switch idle speed contact
11	Not used
12	Exhaust gas recirculation

Year — 1989
Model — 560 SEL
Engine — 5.6L (338 cid) V8
Engine Code — 117.968

ECM TROUBLE CODES

Code	Explanation
1	No system malfunction
2	Throttle valve switch
3	Coolant temperature sensor
4	Air flow sensor position indicator
5	Oxygen sensor
6	Not used
7	TD-signal
8	Altitude correction capsule
9	Electrohydraulic actuator (EHA)
10	Throttle valve switch idle speed contact
11	Not used
12	Exhaust gas recirculation

Year – 1989
Model – 560 SEC
Engine – 5.6L (338 cid) V8
Engine Code – 117.968

ECM TROUBLE CODES

Code	Explanation
1	No system malfunction
2	Throttle valve switch
3	Coolant temperature sensor
4	Air flow sensor position indicator
5	Oxygen sensor
6	Not used
7	TD-signal
8	Altitude correction capsule
9	Electrohydraulic actuator (EHA)
10	Throttle valve switch idle speed contact
11	Not used
12	Exhaust gas recirculation

Year – 1989
Model – 560 SL
Engine – 5.6L (338 cid) V8
Engine Code – 117.967

ECM TROUBLE CODES

Code	Explanation
1	No system malfunction
2	Throttle valve switch
3	Coolant temperature sensor
4	Air flow sensor position indicator
5	Oxygen sensor
6	Not used
7	TD-signal
8	Altitude correction capsule
9	Electrohydraulic actuator (EHA)
10	Throttle valve switch idle speed contact
11	Not used
12	Exhaust gas recirculation

Mitsubishi

INDEX

MITSUBISHI

Electronic Control Injection (ECI) and Multi-Port Fuel Injection (MPI) Systems

SELF-DIAGNOSTIC SYSTEM

Description

Many fuel injected engines (ECI or MPI) contain a self-diagnosis system. The Electronic Control Unit (ECU) monitors voltage signals from various engine sensors. When the ECU detects an abnormal condition, it records the condition as a trouble code, which corresponds to a particular sensor. An abnormal condition could be a voltage signal out of normal operating parameters, no voltage signal (indicating an open circuit) or an excessive voltage signal (indicating a shorted or grounded circuit). The trouble codes can be read either by using the manufacturer's ECI/MPI tester with adapters or an analog voltmeter. On earlier systems, the codes can only be read using the ECI/MPI tester. The ECI/MPI tester or voltmeter is connected to the diagnostic connector. The location of the diagnostic connector varies depending upon model and year.

Diagnostic Connector Location

Cordia/Tredia 1984—Self-diagnostics accessible only with ECI/MPI tester.
Cordia/Tredia 1985–88—Self-diagnostics accessible with ECI/MPI tester or analog voltmeter. Connector located in engine compartment on right side of firewall, branched from main harness.
Galant 1985–88—Self-diagnostics accessible with ECI/MPI tester or analog voltmeter. Connector located behind glove box.
Galant 1989—Self-diagnostics accessible with ECI/MPI tester or analog voltmeter. Connector located under dash on right side.
Mirage 1985–86—Self-diagnostics accessible only with ECI/MPI tester
Mirage 1987–88—Self-diagnostics accessible with ECI/MPI tester or analog voltmeter. Connector located in engine compartment on left side or firewall, branched from main harness.
Mirage 1989—Self-diagnostics accessible with ECI/MPI tester or analog voltmeter. Connector located under dash on right side.
Sigma 1989—Self-diagnostics accessible with ECI/MPI tester or analog voltmeter. Connector located behind glove box.
Starion 1985–86—Self-diagnostics accessible only with ECI/MPI tester.
Starion 1987–89—Self-diagnostics accessible with ECI/MPI tester or analog voltmeter. Connector located behind glove box.
Montero 1989—Self-diagnostics accessible with ECI/MPI tester or analog voltmeter. Connector located behind glove box.
Van/Wagon 1987–89—Self-diagnostics accessible with ECI/MPI tester or analog voltmeter. Connector located under dash on left side above fuse panel.

Entering Diagnostic Mode
ANALOG VOLTMETER

1. Turn the ignition switch **OFF**.
2. Connect analog voltmeter to correct diagnostic connector terminals.

NOTE: When connecting the analog voltmeter, be sure to observe proper polarity; otherwise, damage may occur to the Electronic Control Unit (ECU).

3. Turn ignition switch **ON**. Codes stored in ECU memory will be displayed in ascending order. The order in which the codes are displayed does not indicate the order in which the malfunction(s) occurred.

ECI/MPI TESTER

Refer to manufacturer's manual regarding diagnosis with this tester.

Types of Code Displays
NUMERICAL CODE DISPLAY

This type of display is used on systems with both 1 and 2-digit code numbers. Counting the number of sweeps of the pointer determines the trouble code. The sweep duration is 1.5 seconds for each multiple of 10 digit; 0.5 seconds for each unit digit. The multiple of 10 digits are displayed first, separated by 0.5 second pauses, there will be a 2 second pause and then the unit digits will be displayed also separated by 0.5 second pauses.

BINARY CODE DISPLAY

NOTE: The binary code display is used on the 1986–87 Galant and the 1987–88 Van/Wagon.

With this type of display, each code consists of 5 segments. The duration of each segment is 2.0 seconds. The value of each segment is either "0" or "1". The value is determined by measuring the duration of the pointer sweep within each 2.0 second segment. A segment with a sweep duration of 0.5 seconds is given a value of "0". A segment with a sweep duration of 1.5 seconds is given a value of "1". The series totaling five "0's" and "1's" corresponds to the trouble code. For example: the series 0 0 1 0 0 corresponds to trouble Code 4 (refer to Binary Trouble Code Chart). The trouble code display sequence begins with a steady 3.0 second sweep, followed by the five 2.0 second segments indicating the trouble code and another steady 3.0 second sweep before the next code.

Clearing Diagnostic Memory

Because the ECU draws its power directly from the battery, the trouble codes stored in the ECU memory will not be erased by turning the ignition switch **OFF**. The memory may be cleared by removing the negative battery cable or by disconnecting the ECU connector for not less than 15 seconds. Insure that the ignition switch is **OFF** before disconnecting either the negative battery cable or the ECU connector.

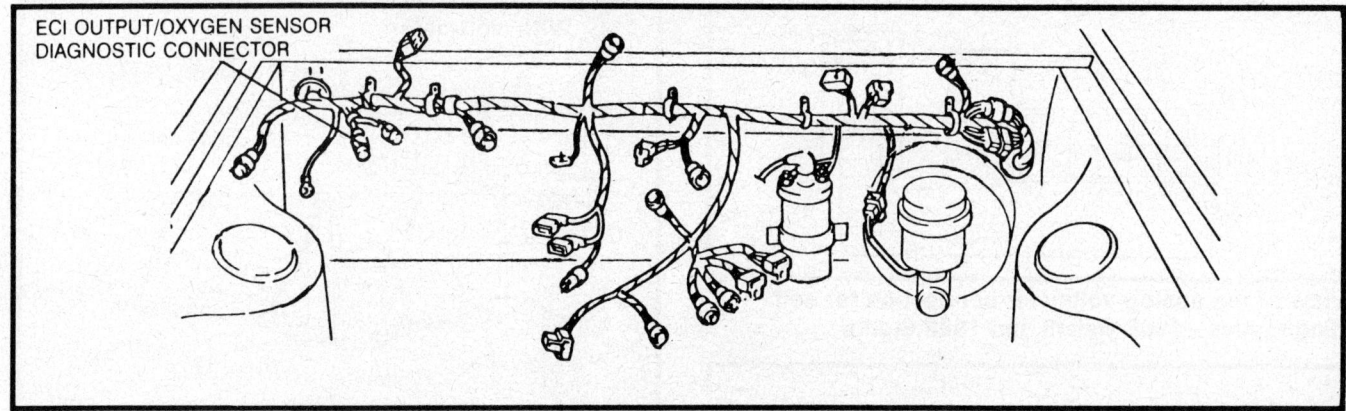

Location of the self-diagnostic connector – 1985–88 Cordia/Tredia

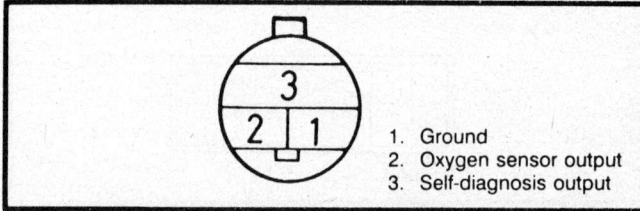

1. Ground
2. Oxygen sensor output
3. Self-diagnosis output

View of the ECI output/oxygen sensor diagnostic connector plug pin position – 1985–88 Cordia/Tredia

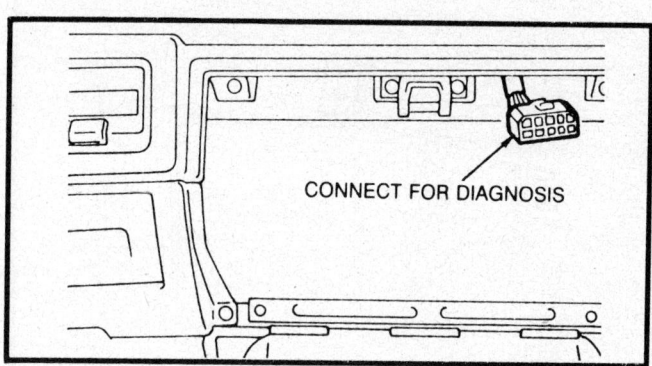

Location of the self-diagnostic connector – 1985–86 Galant

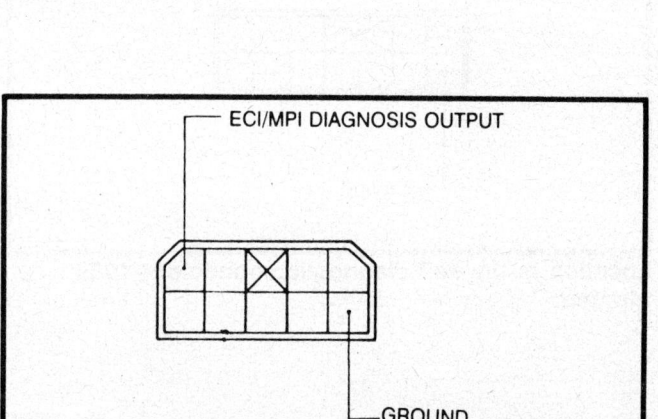

View of the self-diagnostic connector plug pin position – 1985–86 Galant

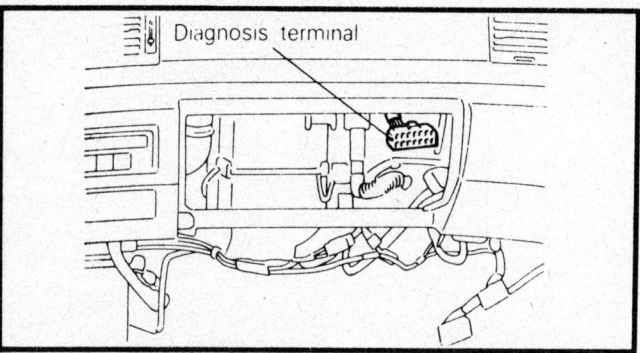

Location of the self-diagnostic connector – 1987 Galant

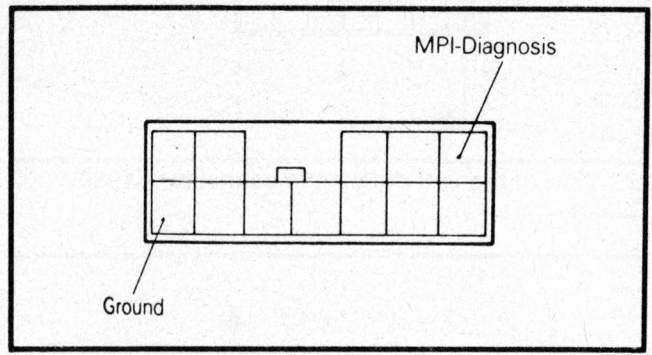

View of the self-diagnostic connector plug pin position – 1987 Galant

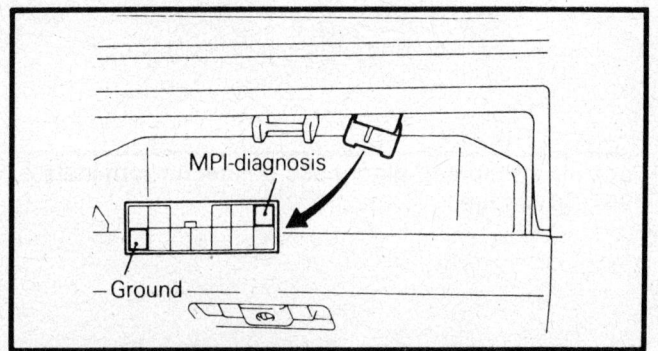

Location of the self-diagnostic connector – 1988 Galant and 1989 Sigma

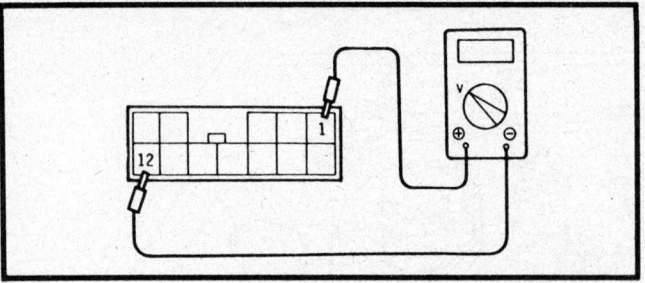

View of the analog voltmeter connection for self-diagnostics – 1988 Galant and 1989 Sigma

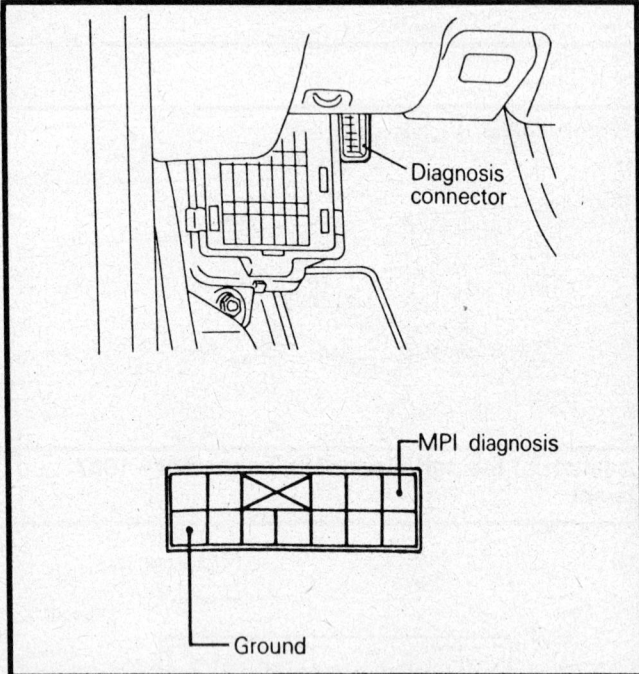

Location of the self-diagnostic connector – 1989 Galant

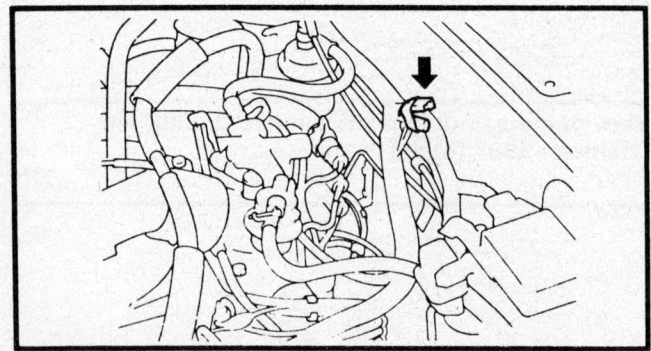

Location of the self-diagnostic connector terminals – 1987–88 Mirage

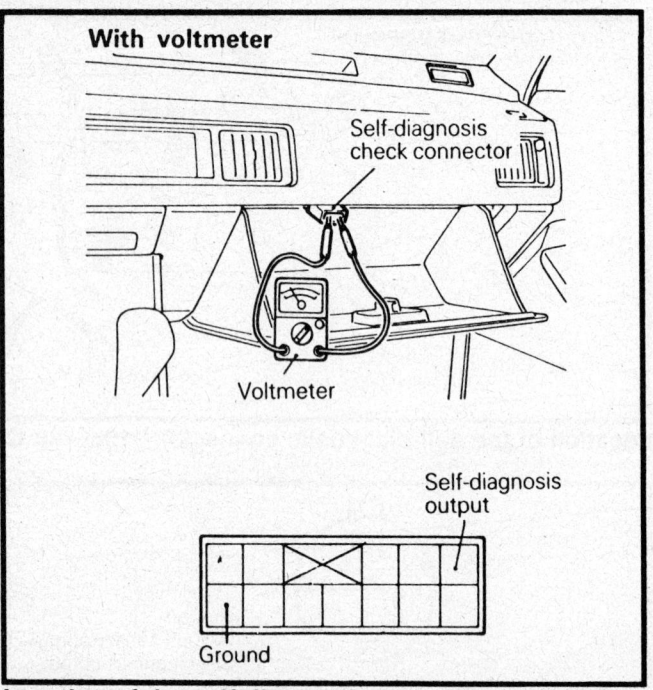

Location of the self-diagnostic connector – 1987–89 Starion

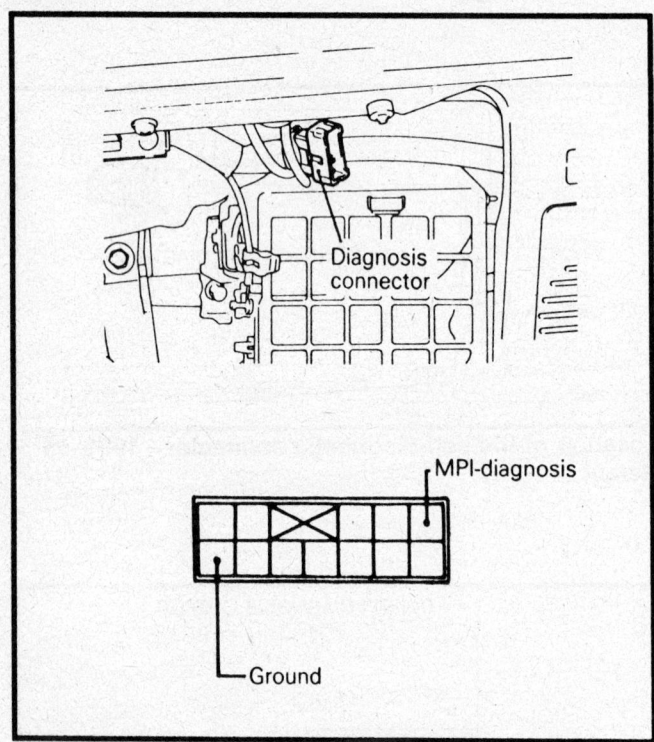

Location of the self-diagnostic connector – 1989 Montero

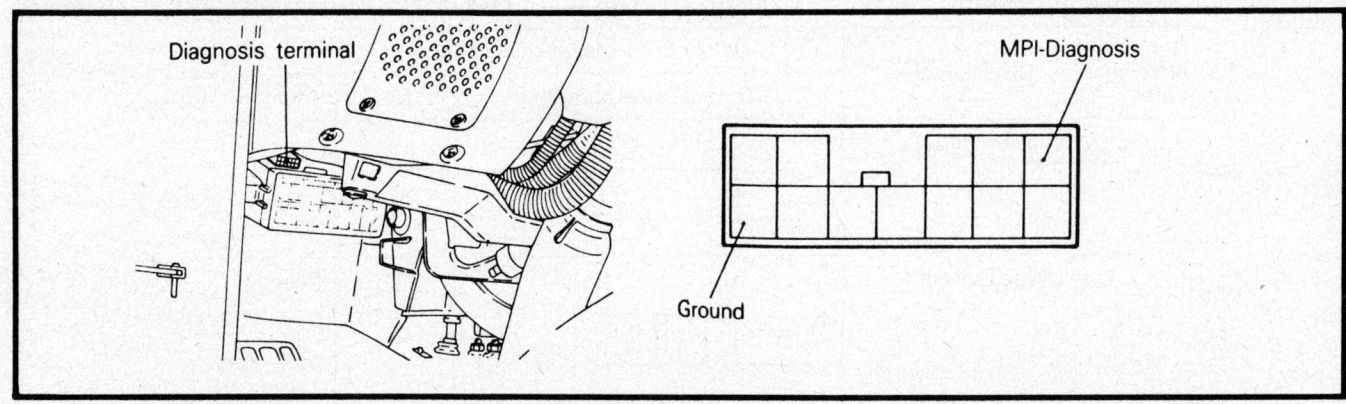

Location of the self-diagnostic connector – 1989 Van/ Wagon

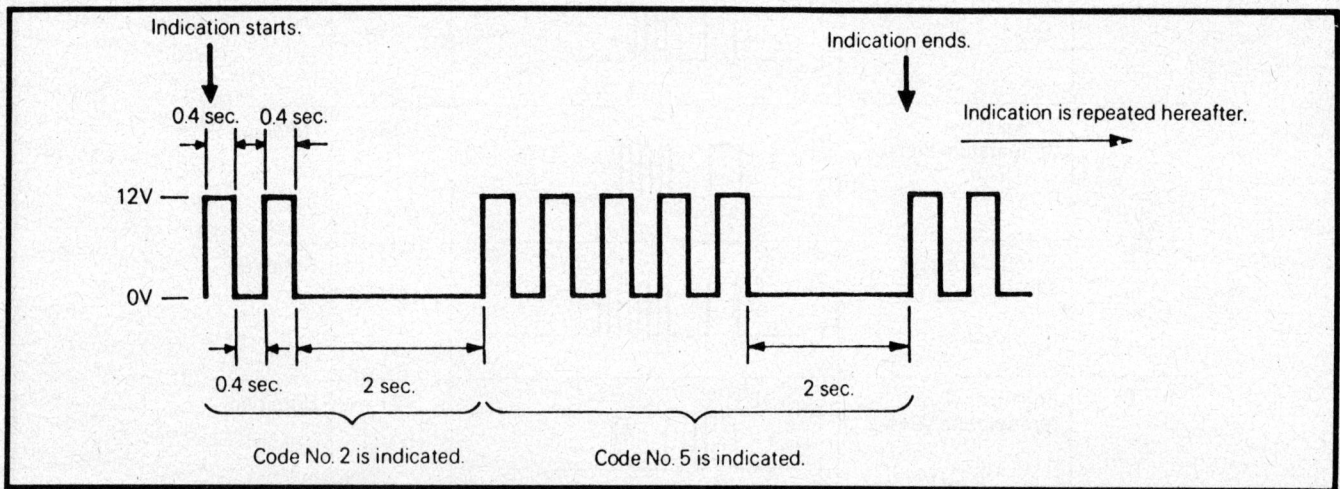

Example of the single-digit code signal pattern

Output preference order	Diagnosis item	Malfunction code		
		Output signal pattern	No.	Memory
1	Engine control unit	H ⎍ L	–	–
2	Oxygen sensor	H L	11	Retained
3	Air flow sensor	H L	12	Retained
4	Intake air temperature sensor	H L	13	Retained
5	Throttle position sensor	H L	14	Retained
6	Engine coolant temperature sensor	H L	21	Retained

Example of the 2-digit code signal pattern

MITSUBISHI

Year — 1984
Model — Starion
Engine — 2.6L (156 cid) Turbo 4 cyl
Engine Code — G54B

ECM TROUBLE CODES

Code	Explanation
1	Oxygen sensor and computer
2	Ignition pulse
3	Air Flow Sensor (AFS)
4	Pressure sensor
5	Throttle Position Sensor (TPS)
6	Idle Speed Control (ISC) motor position switch
7	Coolant Temperature Sensor (CTS)
8	Vehicle Speed Sensor (VSS)

Year — 1984
Model — Cordia
Engine — 1.8L (110 cid) 4 cyl
Engine Code — G62B

ECM TROUBLE CODES

Code	Explanation
1	Oxygen sensor and computer
2	Ignition pulse
3	Air Flow Sensor (AFS)
4	Pressure sensor
5	Throttle Position Sensor (TPS)
6	Idle Speed Control (ISC) motor position switch
7	Coolant Temperature Sensor (CTS)
8	Vehicle Speed Sensor (VSS)

Year – 1984
Model – Cordia
Engine – 2.0L (122 cid) 4 cyl
Engine Code – G63B

ECM TROUBLE CODES

Code	Explanation
1	Oxygen sensor and computer
2	Ignition pulse
3	Air Flow Sensor (AFS)
4	Pressure sensor
5	Throttle Position Sensor (TPS)
6	Idle Speed Control (ISC) motor position switch
7	Coolant Temperature Sensor (CTS)
8	Vehicle Speed Sensor (VSS)

Year — 1984
Model — Tredia
Engine — 2.0L (122 cid) 4 cyl
Engine Code — G63B

ECM TROUBLE CODES

Code	Explanation
1	Oxygen sensor and computer
2	Ignition pulse
3	Air Flow Sensor (AFS)
4	Pressure sensor
5	Throttle Position Sensor (TPS)
6	Idle Speed Control (ISC) motor position switch
7	Coolant Temperature Sensor (CTS)
8	Vehicle Speed Sensor (VSS)

Year — 1985
Model — Starion
Engine — 2.6L (156 cid) Turbo 4 cyl
Engine Code — G54B

ECM TROUBLE CODES

Code	Explanation
1	Oxygen sensorr
2	Ignition signal
3	Air Flow Sensor (AFS)
4	Pressure sensor
5	Throttle Position Sensor (TPS)
6	Idle Speed Control (ISC) motor position switch
7	Coolant Temperature Sensor (CTS)

Year — 1985
Model — Cordia
Engine — 1.8L (110 cid) 4 cyl
Engine Code — G62B

ECM TROUBLE CODES

Code	Explanation
1	Oxygen sensor and computer
2	Ignition pulse
3	Air Flow Sensor (AFS)
4	Pressure sensor
5	Throttle Position Sensor (TPS)
6	Idle Speed Control (ISC) motor position switch
7	Coolant Temperature Sensor (CTS)

Year – 1985
Model – Cordia
Engine – 2.0L (122 cid) 4 cyl
Engine Code – G63B

ECM TROUBLE CODES

Code	Explanation
1	Oxygen sensor and computer
2	Ignition pulse
3	Air Flow Sensor (AFS)
4	Pressure sensor
5	Throttle Position Sensor (TPS)
6	Idle Speed Control (ISC) motor position switch
7	Coolant Temperature Sensor (CTS)

Year – 1985
Model – Tredia
Engine – 1.8L (110 cid) 4 cyl
Engine Code – G62B

ECM TROUBLE CODES

Code	Explanation
1	Oxygen sensor and computer
2	Ignition pulse
3	Air Flow Sensor (AFS)
4	Pressure sensor
5	Throttle Position Sensor (TPS)
6	Idle Speed Control (ISC) motor position switch
7	Coolant Temperature Sensor (CTS)

Year – 1985
Model – Tredia
Engine – 2.0L (122 cid) 4 cyl
Engine Code – G63B

ECM TROUBLE CODES

Code	Explanation
1	Oxygen sensor and computer
2	Ignition pulse
3	Air Flow Sensor (AFS)
4	Pressure sensor
5	Throttle Position Sensor (TPS)
6	Idle Speed Control (ISC) motor position switch
7	Coolant Temperature Sensor (CTS)

Year – 1985
Model – Galant
Engine – 2.4L (143 cid) 4 cyl
Engine Code – G64B

ECM TROUBLE CODES

Code	Explanation
1	Oxygen sensor
2	Ignition pulse
3	Air Flow Sensor (AFS)
4	Atmospheric pressure sensor
5	Throttle Position Sensor (TPS)
6	Idle Speed Control (ISC) motor position switch
7	Coolant Temperature Sensor (CTS)

Year — 1985
Model — Mirage
Engine — 1.5L (90 cid) 4 cyl
Engine Code — G15B

ECM TROUBLE CODES

Code	Explanation
1	Oxygen sensor
2	Ignition pulse
3	Air Flow Sensor (AFS)
4	Pressure sensor
5	Throttle Position Sensor (TPS)
6	Idle Speed Control (ISC) motor position switch
7	Coolant Temperature Sensor (CTS)

Year — 1985
Model — Mirage
Engine — 1.6L (97 cid) 4 cyl
Engine Code — G32B

ECM TROUBLE CODES

Code	Explanation
1	Oxygen sensor
2	Ignition pulse
3	Air Flow Sensor (AFS)
4	Pressure sensor
5	Throttle Position Sensor (TPS)
6	Idle Speed Control (ISC) motor position switch
7	Coolant Temperature Sensor (CTS)

Year — 1986
Model — Starion
Engine — 2.6L (156 cid) Turbo 4 cyl
Engine Code — G54B

ECM TROUBLE CODES

Code	Explanation
1	Oxygen sensor and computer
2	Ignition pulse
3	Air Flow Sensor (AFS)
4	Pressure sensor
5	Throttle Position Sensor (TPS)
6	Idle Speed Control (ISC) motor position switch
7	Coolant Temperature Sensor (CTS)

Year — 1986
Model — Cordia
Engine — 1.8L (110 cid) 4 cyl
Engine Code — G62B

ECM TROUBLE CODES

Code	Explanation
1	Oxygen sensor and computer
2	Ignition pulse
3	Air Flow Sensor (AFS)
4	Pressure sensor
5	Throttle Position Sensor (TPS)
6	Idle Speed Control (ISC) motor position switch
7	Coolant Temperature Sensor (CTS)

Year – 1986
Model – Cordia
Engine – 2.0L (122 cid) 4 cyl
Engine Code – G63B

ECM TROUBLE CODES

Code	Explanation
1	Oxygen sensor and computer
2	Ignition pulse
3	Air Flow Sensor (AFS)
4	Pressure sensor
5	Throttle Position Sensor (TPS)
6	Idle Speed Control (ISC) motor position switch
7	Coolant Temperature Sensor (CTS)

Year – 1986
Model – Tredia
Engine – 1.8L (110 cid) 4 cyl
Engine Code – G62B

ECM TROUBLE CODES

Code	Explanation
1	Oxygen sensor and computer
2	Ignition pulse
3	Air Flow Sensor (AFS)
4	Pressure sensor
5	Throttle Position Sensor (TPS)
6	Idle Speed Control (ISC) motor position switch
7	Coolant Temperature Sensor (CTS)

Year – 1986
Model – Tredia
Engine – 2.0L (122 cid) 4 cyl
Engine Code – G63B

ECM TROUBLE CODES

Code	Explanation
1	Oxygen sensor and computer
2	Ignition pulse
3	Air Flow Sensor (AFS)
4	Pressure sensor
5	Throttle Position Sensor (TPS)
6	Idle Speed Control (ISC) motor position switch
7	Coolant Temperature Sensor (CTS)

Year – 1986
Model – Galant
Engine – 2.4L (143 cid) 4 cyl
Engine Code – G64B

ECM TROUBLE CODES

Code	Explanation
H/L 0 0 0 0 0	Normal
H/L 1 0 0 0 0	Oxygen sensor
H/L 0 1 0 0 0	Crank angle sensor
H/L 1 1 0 0 0	Air Flow Sensor (AFS)
H/L 0 0 1 0 0	Atmospheric pressure sensor
H/L 1 0 1 0 0	Throttle Position Sensor (TPS)
H/L 0 1 1 0 0	Motor Position Sensor (MPS)
H/L 1 1 1 0 0	Coolant temperature sensor
H/L 0 0 0 1 0	Number 1 cylinder Top Dead Center (TDC) sensor

Year — 1986
Model — Mirage
Engine — 1.5L (90 cid) 4 cyl
Engine Code — G15B

ECM TROUBLE CODES

Code	Explanation
1	Oxygen sensor
2	Ignition pulse
3	Air Flow Sensor (AFS)
4	Pressure sensor
5	Throttle Position Sensor (TPS)
6	Idle Speed Control (ISC) motor position switch
7	Coolant Temperature Sensor (CTS)

Year — 1986
Model — Mirage
Engine — 1.6L (97 cid) 4 cyl
Engine Code — G32B

ECM TROUBLE CODES

Code	Explanation
1	Oxygen sensor
2	Ignition pulse
3	Air Flow Sensor (AFS)
4	Pressure sensor
5	Throttle Position Sensor (TPS)
6	Idle Speed Control (ISC) motor position switch
7	Coolant Temperature Sensor (CTS)

Year — 1987
Model — Starion
Engine — 2.6L (156 cid) Turbo 4 cyl
Engine Code — G54B

ECM TROUBLE CODES

Code	Explanation
1	Oxygen sensor and computer
2	Ignition pulse
3	Air Flow Sensor (AFS)
5	Throttle Position Sensor (TPS)
6	Idle Speed Control (ISC) motor position switch
7	Coolant Temperature Sensor (CTS)

Year — 1987
Model — Cordia
Engine — 1.8L (110 cid) 4 cyl
Engine Code — G62B

ECM TROUBLE CODES

Code	Explanation
1	Oxygen sensor and computer
2	Ignition pulse
3	Air Flow Sensor (AFS)
4	Pressure sensor
5	Throttle Position Sensor (TPS)
6	Idle Speed Control (ISC) motor position switch
7	Coolant Temperature Sensor (CTS)

Year — 1987
Model — Cordia
Engine — 2.0L (122 cid) 4 cyl
Engine Code — G63B

ECM TROUBLE CODES

Code	Explanation
1	Oxygen sensor and computer
2	Ignition pulse
3	Air Flow Sensor (AFS)
4	Pressure sensor
5	Throttle Position Sensor (TPS)
6	Idle Speed Control (ISC) motor position switch
7	Coolant Temperature Sensor (CTS)

Year — 1987
Model — Tredia
Engine — 1.8L (110 cid) 4 cyl
Engine Code — G62B

ECM TROUBLE CODES

Code	Explanation
1	Oxygen sensor and computer
2	Ignition pulse
3	Air Flow Sensor (AFS)
4	Pressure sensor
5	Throttle Position Sensor (TPS)
6	Idle Speed Control (ISC) motor position switch
7	Coolant Temperature Sensor (CTS)

Year — 1987
Model — Tredia
Engine — 2.0L (122 cid) 4 cyl
Engine Code — G63B

ECM TROUBLE CODES

Code	Explanation
1	Oxygen sensor and computer
2	Ignition pulse
3	Air Flow Sensor (AFS)
4	Pressure sensor
5	Throttle Position Sensor (TPS)
6	Idle Speed Control (ISC) motor position switch
7	Coolant Temperature Sensor (CTS)

Year — 1987
Model — Galant
Engine — 2.4L (143 cid) 4 cyl
Engine Code — G64B

ECM TROUBLE CODES

Code	Explanation
H ⬛☐☐☐☐☐ L 0 0 0 0 0	Normal
H ⬛⬛☐☐☐☐ L 1 0 0 0 0	Oxygen sensor
H ⬛☐⬛☐☐☐ L 0 1 0 0 0	Crank angle sensor
H ⬛⬛⬛☐☐☐ L 1 1 0 0 0	Air Flow Sensor (AFS)
H ⬛☐☐⬛☐☐ L 0 0 1 0 0	Atmospheric pressure sensor
H ⬛⬛☐⬛☐☐ L 1 0 1 0 0	Throttle Position Sensor (TPS)
H ⬛☐⬛⬛☐☐ L 0 1 1 0 0	Motor Position Sensor (MPS)
H ⬛⬛⬛⬛☐☐ L 1 1 1 0 0	Coolant temperature sensor
H ⬛☐☐☐⬛☐ L 0 0 0 1 0	Number 1 cylinder Top Dead Center (TDC) sensor

Year — 1987
Model — Mirage
Engine — 1.5L (90 cid) 4 cyl
Engine Code — G15B

ECM TROUBLE CODES

Code	Explanation
1	Oxygen sensor
2	Ignition pulse
3	Air Flow Sensor (AFS)
4	Pressure sensor
5	Throttle Position Sensor (TPS)
6	Idle Speed Control (ISC) motor position switch
7	Coolant Temperature Sensor (CTS)

Year — 1987
Model — Mirage
Engine — 1.6L (97 cid) 4 cyl
Engine Code — G32B

ECM TROUBLE CODES

Code	Explanation
1	Oxygen sensor
2	Ignition pulse
3	Air Flow Sensor (AFS)
5	Throttle Position Sensor (TPS)
6	Idle Speed Control (ISC) motor position switch
7	Coolant Temperature Sensor (CTS)

Year — 1988
Model — Starion
Engine — 2.6L (156 cid) Turbo 4 cyl
Engine Code — G54B

ECM TROUBLE CODES

Code	Explanation
1	Oxygen sensor and computer
2	Ignition pulse
3	Air Flow Sensor (AFS)
5	Throttle Position Sensor (TPS)
6	Idle Speed Control (ISC) motor position switch
7	Coolant Temperature Sensor (CTS)

Year — 1988
Model — Cordia
Engine — 1.8L (110 cid) 4 cyl
Engine Code — G62B

ECM TROUBLE CODES

Code	Explanation
1	Oxygen sensor and computer
2	Ignition pulse
3	Air Flow Sensor (AFS)
4	Pressure sensor
5	Throttle Position Sensor (TPS)
6	Idle Speed Control (ISC) motor position switch
7	Coolant Temperature Sensor (CTS)

Year — 1988
Model — Cordia
Engine — 2.0L (122 cid) 4 cyl
Engine Code — G63B

ECM TROUBLE CODES

Code	Explanation
1	Oxygen sensor and computer
2	Ignition pulse
3	Air Flow Sensor (AFS)
4	Pressure sensor
5	Throttle Position Sensor (TPS)
6	Idle Speed Control (ISC) motor position switch
7	Coolant Temperature Sensor (CTS)

Year — 1988
Model — Tredia
Engine — 1.8L (110 cid) 4 cyl
Engine Code — G62B

ECM TROUBLE CODES

Code	Explanation
1	Oxygen sensor and computer
2	Ignition pulse
3	Air Flow Sensor (AFS)
4	Pressure sensor
5	Throttle Position Sensor (TPS)
6	Idle Speed Control (ISC) motor position switch
7	Coolant Temperature Sensor (CTS)

Year — 1988
Model — Tredia
Engine — 2.0L (122 cid) 4 cyl
Engine Code — G63B

ECM TROUBLE CODES

Code	Explanation
1	Oxygen sensor and computer
2	Ignition pulse
3	Air Flow Sensor (AFS)
4	Pressure sensor
5	Throttle Position Sensor (TPS)
6	Idle Speed Control (ISC) motor position switch
7	Coolant Temperature Sensor (CTS)

Year — 1988
Model — Galant
Engine — 3.0L (181 cid) V6
Engine Code — 6G72

ECM TROUBLE CODES

Code	Explanation
	Computer
11	Oxygen sensor
12	Air Flow Sensor (AFS)
13	Intake Air Temperature Sensor (ATS)
14	Throttle Position Sensor (TPS)
21	Coolant Temperature Sensor (CTS)
22	Crank Angle Sensor (CAS)
23	Number 1 cylinder TDC sensor
24	Vehicle Speed Sensor (VSS) — reed switch
25	Barometric pressure sensor
41	Injector
42	Fuel pump
43	Exhaust Gas Recirculation (EGR)
	Normal state

Year – 1988
Model – Mirage
Engine – 1.5L (90 cid) 4 cyl
Engine Code – G15B

ECM TROUBLE CODES

Code	Explanation
1	Oxygen sensor
2	Ignition pulse
3	Air Flow Sensor (AFS)
4	Pressure sensor
5	Throttle Position Sensor (TPS)
6	Idle Speed Control (ISC) motor position switch
7	Coolant Temperature Sensor (CTS)

Year – 1988
Model – Mirage
Engine – 1.6L (97 cid) 4 cyl
Engine Code – G32B

ECM TROUBLE CODES

Code	Explanation
1	Oxygen sensor
2	Ignition pulse
3	Air Flow Sensor (AFS)
5	Throttle Position Sensor (TPS)
6	Idle Speed Control (ISC) motor position switch
7	Coolant Temperature Sensor (CTS)

Year – 1989
Model – Starion
Engine – 2.6L (156 cid) Turbo 4 cyl
Engine Code – G54B

ECM TROUBLE CODES

Code	Explanation
1	Oxygen sensor and computer
2	Ignition pulse
3	Air Flow Sensor (AFS)
5	Throttle Position Sensor (TPS)
6	Idle Speed Control (ISC) motor position switch
7	Coolant Temperature Sensor (CTS)

Year – 1989
Model – Galant
Engine – 2.0L (122 cid) SOHC 4 cyl
Engine Code – 4G63

ECM TROUBLE CODES

Code	Explanation
	Computer
11	Oxygen sensor
12	Air Flow Sensor (AFS)
13	Intake Air Temperature Sensor (ATS)
14	Throttle Position Sensor (TPS)
15	Motor Position Sensor (MPS)
21	Coolant Temperature Sensor (CTS)
22	Crank Angle Sensor (CAS)
23	Number 1 cylinder TDC sensor
24	Vehicle Speed Sensor (VSS) – reed switch
25	Barometric pressure sensor
41	Injector
42	Fuel pump
43	Exhaust Gas Recirculation (EGR)
	Normal state

Year – 1989
Model – Galant
Engine – 2.0L (122 cid) DOHC 4 cyl
Engine Code – 4G63

ECM TROUBLE CODES

Code	Explanation
	Computer
11	Oxygen sensor
12	Air Flow Sensor (AFS)
13	Intake Air Temperature Sensor (ATS)
14	Throttle Position Sensor (TPS)
21	Coolant Temperature Sensor (CTS)
22	Crank Angle Sensor (CAS)
23	Number 1 cylinder TDC sensor
24	Vehicle Speed Sensor (VSS) – reed switch
25	Barometric pressure sensor
41	Injector
42	Fuel pump
43	Exhaust Gas Recirculation (EGR)
44	Ignition coil
	Normal state

Year – 1989
Model – Mirage
Engine – 1.5L (96 cid) SOHC 4 cyl
Engine Code – 4G15

ECM TROUBLE CODES

Code	Explanation
11	Oxygen sensor
12	Air Flow Sensor (AFS)
13	Intake Air Temperature Sensor (ATS)
14	Throttle Position Sensor (TPS)
15	Motor Position Sensor (MPS)
21	Engine Coolant Temperature Sensor (CTS)
22	Crank Angle Sensor (CAS)
23	Number 1 cylinder TDC sensor
24	Vehicle Speed Sensor (VSS) – reed switch
25	Barometric pressure sensor
41	Injector
42	Fuel pump
43	Exhaust Gas Recirculation (EGR)

Year — 1989
Model — Mirage
Engine — 1.6L (98 cid) DOHC 4 cyl
Engine Code — 4G61

ECM TROUBLE CODES

Code	Explanation
11	Oxygen sensor
12	Air Flow Sensor (AFS)
13	Intake Air Temperature Sensor (ATS)
14	Throttle Position Sensor (TPS)
21	Engine Coolant Temperature Sensor (CTS)
22	Crank Angle Sensor (CAS)
23	Number 1 cylinder TDC sensor
24	Vehicle Speed Sensor (VSS) — reed switch
25	Barometric pressure sensor
31	Detonation sensor
41	Injector
42	Fuel pump
43	Exhaust Gas Recirculation (EGR)
44	Ignition coil

Year — 1989
Model — Sigma
Engine — 3.0L (181 cid) V6
Engine Code — 6G72

ECM TROUBLE CODES

Code	Explanation
11	Oxygen sensor
12	Air Flow Sensor (AFS)
13	Intake Air Temperature Sensor (ATS)
14	Throttle Position Sensor (TPS)
21	Engine Coolant Temperature Sensor (CTS)
22	Crank Angle Sensor (CAS)
23	Number 1 cylinder TDC sensor
24	Vehicle Speed Sensor (VSS) — reed switch
25	Barometric pressure sensor
41	Injector
42	Fuel pump
43	Exhaust Gas Recirculation (EGR)

MITSUBISHI

Year — 1987
Model — Van
Engine — 2.4L (143 cid) 4 cyl
Engine Code — G64B

ECM TROUBLE CODES

Code	Explanation
H L 0 0 0 0 0	Normal
H L 1 0 0 0 0	Oxygen sensor
H L 0 1 0 0 0	Crank angle sensor
H L 1 1 0 0 0	Air Flow Sensor (AFS)
H L 0 0 1 0 0	Atmospheric pressure sensor
H L 1 0 1 0 0	Throttle Position Sensor (TPS)
H L 0 1 1 0 0	Motor Position Sensor (MPS)
H L 1 1 1 0 0	Coolant temperature sensor
H L 0 0 0 1 0	Number 1 cylinder Top Dead Center (TDC) sensor

Year – 1988
Model – Van
Engine – 2.4L (143 cid) 4 cyl
Engine Code – G64B

ECM TROUBLE CODES

Code	Explanation
H / L 0 0 0 0 0	Normal
H / L 1 0 0 0 0	Oxygen sensor
H / L 0 1 0 0 0	Crank angle sensor
H / L 1 1 0 0 0	Air Flow Sensor (AFS)
H / L 0 0 1 0 0	Atmospheric pressure sensor
H / L 1 0 1 0 0	Throttle Position Sensor (TPS)
H / L 0 1 1 0 0	Motor Position Sensor (MPS)
H / L 1 1 1 0 0	Coolant temperature sensor
H / L 0 0 0 1 0	Number 1 cylinder Top Dead Center (TDC) sensor

Year – 1989
Model – Montero
Engine – 3.0L (181 cid) V6
Engine Code – 6G72

ECM TROUBLE CODES

Code	Explanation
11	Oxygen sensor
12	Air Flow Sensor (AFS)
13	Intake Air Temperature Sensor (ATS)
14	Throttle Position Sensor (TPS)
21	Engine Coolant Temperature Sensor (CTS)
22	Crank Angle Sensor (CAS)
23	Number 1 cylinder TDC sensor
24	Vehicle Speed Sensor (VSS) – reed switch
25	Barometric pressure sensor (BARO)
41	Injector
42	Fuel pump
43	Exhaust Gas Recirculation (EGR)

Year — 1989
Model — Van
Engine — 2.4L (143 cid) 4 cyl
Engine Code — 4G64

ECM TROUBLE CODES

Code	Explanation
11	Oxygen sensor
12	Air Flow Sensor (AFS)
13	Intake Air Temperature Sensor (ATS)
14	Throttle Position Sensor
15	Motor Position Sensor (MPS)
21	Engine Coolant Temperature Sensor (CTS)
22	Crank Angle Sensor (CAS)
23	Number 1 cylinder Top Dead Center (TDC) sensor
24	Vehicle Speed Sensor (VSS) — reed switch
25	Barometric pressure sensor (BARO)
41	Injector
42	Fuel pump
43	Exhaust Gas Recirculation (EGR)

Nissan/ Datsun

INDEX

NISSAN

Electronic Concentrated Control System (ECCS)

SELF-DIAGNOSTIC SYSTEM

Description

Many Nissan models have a self-diagnosis function as part of the Electronic Concentrated Control System (ECCS). The self-diagnostic system is useful in diagnosing malfunctions in major sensors, actuators and wire harnesses based on the status of the input signals received by the EFI/ECCS control unit.

The self-diagnostic function monitors the input signals whenever power is furnished to the ECU. When an abnormality is detected, the ECU stores the information in memory. The results are displayed only when the diagnostic mode selector, located on the side of the control unit, is turned **ON**. When activated, the malfunction is indicated by flashing a red and green Light Emitting Diode (LED) attached to the Electronic Control Unit (ECU). The flashes indicate a 2-digit code which identifies the malfunctioning part(s) group. The red LED flashes first, followed by the green LED. The red LED refers to the code's multiple of 10-digit and the green LED refers to the single digit. For example, when the red LED flashes once and the green LED flashes twice this means that code number 12, showing the air flow meter signal, is malfunctioning.

The self-diagnostic system is provided with functions which display malfunctions being checked currently as well as those stored in the memory. In this sense, it is very effective in determining an "intermittent" malfunction. For this reason, it is important not to clear the ECU memory before beginning diagnosis of the system. When the codes have been noted and/or repairs made, the memory can be cleared following specified steps.

If the system goes unserviced, codes will remain stored in the ECU memory until the starter has been operated 50 times; the codes will then be cancelled automatically. If the malfunction which has been stored in memory occurs again, before the starter has been operated 50 times, the 2nd occurrence will replace the previous one. The new code will be stored in memory until the starter has been operated 50 times more.

MODEL	YEAR					
	84	85	86	87	88	89
200 SX	A	A	A	A	A	
240 SX						B
300 ZX	B	B	B	B	B	B
MAXIMA	D	D	D	D	D	E
PULSAR NX				D	D	D
SENTRA				D	D	D
STANZA	A	A	A	D	D	D
(MODEL D21) PATHFINDER/TRUCK			D	D	D	D
TRUCK (MODEL 720)		C	C			
VAN				F	F	

ECU LOCATION		
A — BEHIND	LEFT FRONT KICK PANEL
B — BEHIND	RIGHT FRONT KICK PANEL
C — UNDER	DRIVER'S SEAT
D — UNDER	PASSENGER'S SEAT
E — UNDER	CENTER CONSOLE
F — BEHIND	SIDE TRIM PANEL BEHIND DRIVER'S SEAT
SPACE BLANK:	MODEL NOT IN PRODUCTION OR DOES NOT HAVE SELF-DIAGNOSTICS

Location of the ECU by model – 1984–89 Nissan

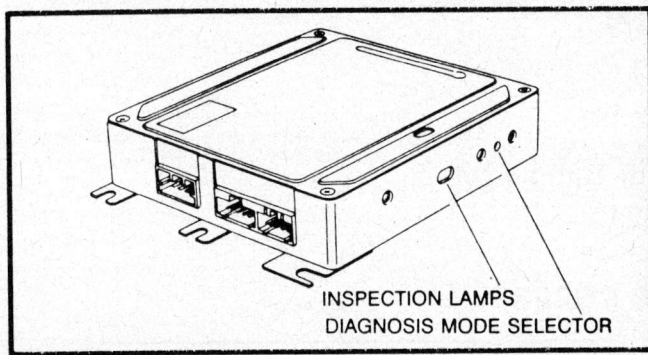

View of a typical ECU

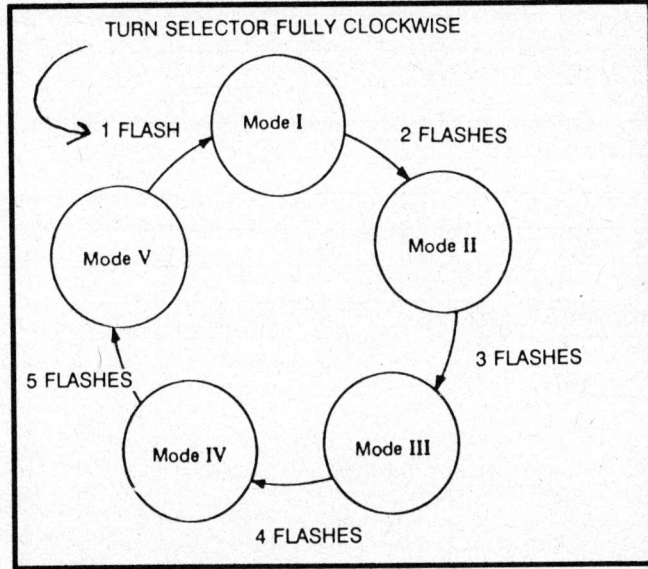

ECU mode sequence

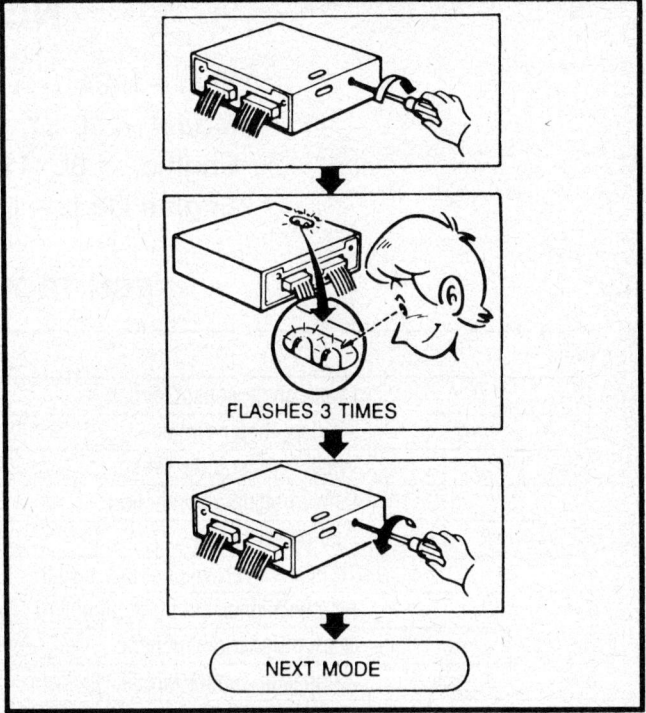

Switching modes on the ECU

On earlier systems, the ECU has only the self-diagnostic mode. Later systems use 5 modes in the self-diagnosis system.
1. Mixture ratio feedback control monitor A
2. Mixture ratio feedback control monitor B
3. Self-diagnosis—Mode 3 is the same as the "Self-diagnosis" function of earlier systems.
4. Switches ON/OFF diagnosis
5. Real time diagnosis

Entering Diagnostic Mode
EXCEPT 5 MODE SYSTEM

Refer to "Chilton's Professional Electronic Engine Controls Manual" for the correct procedure.

5 MODE SYSTEM
1. Turn ignition switch **ON**.
2. Turn the diagnostic mode selector, on the ECU, fully clockwise and wait for the LED's to flash.
3. Count the number of flashes. After the LED's have flashed 3 times, indicating Mode III, immediately turn diagnostic mode selector fully counterclockwise.

NOTE: The procedures for reading the codes stored in the ECU memory vary by model and year.

Clearing Diagnostic Memory
EARLY MODELS

Disconnect the negative battery cable or ECU harness connector for at least 15 seconds.

LATER MODELS

Turn the diagnosis mode selector clockwise to Mode 4, count 4 flashes and turn mode selector counterclockwise.

NOTE: If the selector remains in the clockwise position, the ECU will continue to cycle through the 5 Modes. In this position, the memory will not be erased.

NISSAN

Year — 1984
Model — 200 SX
Engine — 1.8L (110 cid) Turbo 4 cyl
Engine Code — CA18ET

ECM TROUBLE CODES

Code	Explanation
11	Crank angle sensor circuit
12	Air flow meter circuit
13	Water temperature sensor
21	Ignition signal malfunction
22	Fuel pump circuit
23	Throttle valve switch — idle switch
31	Air conditioner circuit malfunction
32	Starter signal malfucntion
34	Detonation sensor circuit
44	Electronic Fuel Injection (EFI)/Electronic Concentrated Control System (ECCS) is operating properly

Year — 1984
Model — 200 SX
Engine — 2.0L (120 cid) EFI 4 cyl
Engine Code — CA20E

ECM TROUBLE CODES

Code	Explanation
12	Air flow meter circuit
13	Water temperature sensor
21	Ignition signal malfunction
22	Fuel pump circuit
23	Throttle valve switch — idle switch
24	Transmission switch
31	Air conditioner circuit malfunction
32	Starter signal malfucntion
41	Air temperature sensor
44	Electronic Fuel Injection (EFI)/Electronic Concentrated Control System (ECCS) is operating properly

Year – 1984
Model – 300 ZX
Engine – 3.0L (181 cid) PFI V6
Engine Code – VG30E

ECM TROUBLE CODES

Code	Explanation
11	Crank angle sensor circuit
12	Air flow meter circuit
13	Cylinder head temperature sensor
21	Ignition signal malfunction
22	Fuel pump circuit malfunction
23	Throttle valve switch – idle switch
31	Air conditioner circuit malfunction
32	Starter signal malfucntion
41	Air temperature sensor
44	Electronic Fuel Injection (EFI)/Electronic Concentrated Control System (ECCS) is operating properly

Year — 1984
Model — 300 ZX
Engine — 3.0L (181 cid) Turbo V6
Engine Code — VG30ET

ECM TROUBLE CODES

Code	Explanation
11	Crank angle sensor circuit
12	Air flow meter circuit
13	Cylinder head temperature sensor
14	Vehicle speed sensor circuit
21	Ignition signal malfunction
22	Fuel pump circuit malfunction
23	Throttle valve switch — idle switch
24	Neutral/Park switch
31	Air conditioner system malfunction
32	Starter signal malfucntion
34	Detonation sensor circuit
41	Fuel temperature sensor
44	Electronic Fuel Injection (EFI)/Electronic Concentrated Control System (ECCS) is operating properly

Year — 1985
Model — Stanza
Engine — 2.0L (120 cid) EFI 4 cyl
Engine Code — CA20E

ECM TROUBLE CODES

Code	Explanation
12	Air flow meter circuit
13	Water temperature sensor circuit
21	Ignition signal malfunction
22	Fuel pump circuit
23	Throttle valve switch — idle switch
24	T/M switch (Top O.D.) circuit
31	F.I.C.D. system malfunction
32	Starter signal malfucntion
41	Air temperature sensor
44	Electronic Fuel Injection (EFI)/Electronic Concentrated Control System (ECCS) is operating properly

Year — 1985
Model — 200 SX
Engine — 1.8L (110 cid) Turbo 4 cyl
Engine Code — CA18ET

ECM TROUBLE CODES

Code	Explanation
11	Crank angle sensor circuit
12	Air flow meter circuit
13	Water temperature sensor
21	Ignition signal malfunction
22	Fuel pump circuit
23	Throttle valve switch — idle switch
31	F.I.C.D. system malfunction
32	Starter signal malfucntion
34	Detonation sensor circuit
44	Electronic Fuel Injection (EFI)/Electronic Concentrated Control System (ECCS) is operating properly

Year – 1985
Model – 200 SX
Engine – 2.0L (120 cid) EFI 4 cyl
Engine Code – CA20E

ECM TROUBLE CODES

Code	Explanation
12	Air flow meter circuit
13	Water temperature sensor
21	Ignition signal malfunction
22	Fuel pump circuit
23	Throttle valve switch – idle switch
24	Transmission switch circuit
31	F.I.C.D. system malfunction
32	Starter signal malfucntion
41	Air temperature sensor circuit
44	Electronic Fuel Injection (EFI)/Electronic Concentrated Control System (ECCS) is operating properly

Year — 1985
Model — Maxima
Engine — 3.0L (181 cid) PFI V6
Engine Code — VG30E

ECM TROUBLE CODES

Code	Explanation
11	Crank angle sensor circuit
12	Air flow meter circuit
13	Cylinder head temperature sensor
21	Ignition signal malfunction
22	Fuel pump circuit
23	Throttle valve switch — idle switch
31	Load signal system malfunction
32	Starter signal malfucntion
41	Not used — disregard if displayed
44	Electronic Fuel Injection (EFI)/Electronic Concentrated Control System (ECCS) is operating properly

Year—1985
Model—300 ZX
Engine—3.0L (181 cid) PFI V6
Engine Code—VG30E

ECM TROUBLE CODES

Code	Explanation
11	Crank angle sensor circuit
12	Air flow meter circuit
13	Cylinder head temperature sensor
21	Ignition signal malfunction
23	Throttle valve switch—idle switch
31	Air conditioner system malfunction
32	Starter signal malfucntion
41	Fuel temperature sensor
44	Electronic Fuel Injection (EFI)/Electronic Concentrated Control System (ECCS) is operating properly

Year — 1985
Model — 300 ZX
Engine — 3.0L (181 cid) Turbo V6
Engine Code — VG30ET

ECM TROUBLE CODES

Code	Explanation
11	Crank angle sensor circuit
12	Air flow meter circuit
13	Cylinder head temperature sensor
14	Vehicle speed sensor circuit
21	Ignition signal malfunction
23	Throttle valve switch — idle switch
24	Neutral/Park switch
31	Air conditioner system malfunction
32	Starter signal malfucntion
34	Detonation sensor circuit
41	Fuel temperature sensor
44	Electronic Fuel Injection (EFI)/Electronic Concentrated Control System (ECCS) is operating properly

Year — 1986
Model — Stanza Wagon
Engine — 2.0L (120 cid) EFI 4 cyl
Engine Code — CA20E

ECM TROUBLE CODES

Code	Explanation
12	Air flow meter circuit
13	Water temperature sensor
21	Ignition signal malfunction
22	Fuel pump circuit
23	Throttle valve switch — idle switch
31	Idle control system malfunction
32	Starter signal malfucntion
41	Air temperature sensor
44	Electronic Fuel Injection (EFI)/Electronic Concentrated Control System (ECCS) is operating properly

Year — 1986
Model — 200 SX
Engine — 2.0L (120 cid) EFI 4 cyl
Engine Code — CA20E

ECM TROUBLE CODES

Code	Explanation
12	Air flow meter circuit
13	Water temperature sensor
21	Ignition signal malfunction
22	Fuel pump circuit
23	Throttle valve switch — idle switch
24	Transmission switch circuit
31	F.I.C.D. system malfunction
32	Starter signal malfucntion
41	Air temperature sensor circuit
44	Electronic Fuel Injection (EFI)/Electronic Concentrated Control System (ECCS) is operating properly

Year – 1986
Model – 200 SX
Engine – 1.8L (110 cid) Turbo 4 cyl
Engine Code – CA18ET

ECM TROUBLE CODES

Code	Explanation
11	Crank angle sensor circuit
12	Air flow meter circuit
13	Water temperature sensor
21	Ignition signal malfunction
22	Fuel pump circuit
23	Throttle valve switch – idle switch
31	F.I.C.D. system malfunction
32	Starter signal malfucntion
34	Detonation sensor circuit
44	Electronic Fuel Injection (EFI)/Electronic Concentrated Control System (ECCS) is operating properly

Year – 1986
Model – Maxima
Engine – 3.0L (181 cid) PFI V6
Engine Code – VG30E

ECM TROUBLE CODES

Code	Explanation
11	Crank angle sensor circuit
12	Air flow meter circuit
13	Cylinder temperature sensor
21	Ignition signal malfunction
22	Fuel pump circuit
23	Throttle valve switch – idle switch
31	Load signal circuit malfunction
32	Starter signal malfucntion
41	Fuel temperature sensor
44	Electronic Fuel Injection (EFI)/Electronic Concentrated Control System (ECCS) is operating properly

Year — 1986
Model — 300 ZX
Engine — 3.0L (181 cid) PFI V6
Engine Code — VG30E

ECM TROUBLE CODES

Code	Explanation
11	Crank angle sensor circuit
12	Air flow meter circuit
13	Cylinder head temperature sensor
21	Ignition signal malfunction
22	Fuel pump circuit
23	Throttle valve switch — idle switch
31	Load signal circuit malfunction
32	Starter signal malfucntion
41	Fuel temperature sensor
44	Electronic Fuel Injection (EFI)/Electronic Concentrated Control System (ECCS) is operating properly

Year — 1986
Model — 300 ZX
Engine — 3.0L (181 cid) Turbo V6
Engine Code — VG30ET

ECM TROUBLE CODES

Code	Explanation
11	Crank angle sensor circuit
12	Air flow meter circuit
13	Cylinder head temperature sensor
14	Vehicle speed sensor circuit
21	Ignition signal malfunction
22	Fuel pump circuit
23	Throttle valve switch — idle switch
24	Neutral/Park switch
31	Load signal circuit malfunction
32	Starter signal malfucntion
34	Detonation sensor circuit
41	Fuel temperature sensor
44	Electronic Fuel Injection (EFI)/Electronic Concentrated Control System (ECCS) is operating properly

Year — 1986
Model — Maxima
Engine — 3.0L (181 cid) PFI V6
Engine Code — VG30E

ECM TROUBLE CODES

Code	Explanation
12	Air flow meter circuit
13	Water temperature sensor
21	Ignition signal malfunction
22	Fuel pump circuit
23	Throttle valve switch — idle switch
24	Transmission switch
31	Air conditioner circuit malfunction
32	Starter signal malfucntion
41	Air temperature sensor
44	Electronic Fuel Injection (EFI)/Electronic Concentrated Control System (ECCS) is operating properly

Year — 1987
Model — Sentra
Engine — 1.6L (97 cid) TBI 4 cyl
Engine Code — E16i

ECM TROUBLE CODES

Code	Explanation
11	Crank angle sensor circuit
12	Air flow meter circuit
13	Water temperature sensor circuit
14	Vehicle speed sensor circuit
15	Mixture ratio feedback control slips out
21	Ignition signal missing in primary coil
23	Idle switch circuit
25	Idle speed control slips out
31	Electronic Control Unit (ECU)
33	Exhaust gas sensor circuit
43	Throttle sensor circuit
55	No malfunctioning in the above circuits

Year – 1987
Model – Pulsar NX
Engine – 1.6L (97 cid) TBI 4 cyl
Engine Code – E16i

ECM TROUBLE CODES

Code	Explanation
11	Crank angle sensor circuit
12	Air flow meter circuit
13	Water temperature sensor circuit
21	Ignition signal missing in primary coil
22	Idle speed control slips out
33	Exhaust gas sensor circuit
41	Air temperature sensor circuit
42	Throttle sensor circuit
43	Mixture ratio feedback control slips out
44	No malfunctioning in the above circuits

Year – 1987
Model – Pulsar NX
Engine – 1.6L (97 cid) PFI 4 cyl
Engine Code – CA16DE

ECM TROUBLE CODES

Code	Explanation
11	Crank angle sensor circuit
12	Air flow meter circuit
13	Water temperature sensor circuit
21	Ignition signal
34	Detonation sensor
44	No malfunctioning in the above circuits

Year — 1987
Model — Stanza Wagon
Engine — 2.0L (120 cid) PFI 4 cyl
Engine Code — CA20E

ECM TROUBLE CODES

Code	Explanation
11	Crank angle sensor circuit
12	Air flow meter circuit
13	Water temperature sensor circuit
21	Ignition signal missing in primary coil
22	Fuel pump circuit
41	Air temperature sensor circuit
44	No malfunctioning in the above circuits

Year—1987
Model—200 SX
Engine—1.8L (110 cid) Turbo 4 cyl
Engine Code—CA18ET

ECM TROUBLE CODES

Code	Explanation
11	Crank angle sensor circuit
12	Air flow meter circuit
13	Water temperature sensor circuit
21	Ignition signal missing in primary coil
22	Fuel pump
23	Throttle valve switch
31	Air Conditioner switch
32	Start signal
34	Detonation sensor
44	No malfunctioning in the above circuits

Year – 1987
Model – 200 SX
Engine – 2.0L (120 cid) PFI 4 cyl
Engine Code – CA20E

ECM TROUBLE CODES

Code	Explanation
11	Crank angle sensor circuit
12	Air flow meter circuit
13	Water temperature sensor circuit
21	Ignition signal missing in primary coil
22	Fuel pump circuit
41	Air temperature sensor circuit
44	No malfunctioning in the above circuits

Year — 1987
Model — 200 SX
Engine — 3.0L (181 cid) PFI V6
Engine Code — VG30E

ECM TROUBLE CODES

Code	Explanation
11	Crank angle sensor circuit
12	Air flow meter circuit
13	Cylinder head temperature sensor circuit
21	Ignition signal missing in primary coil
22	Fuel pump circuit
41	Fuel temperature sensor circuit
44	No malfunctioning in the above circuits

Year — 1987
Model — Maxima
Engine — 3.0L (181 cid) PFI V6
Engine Code — VG30E

ECM TROUBLE CODES

Code	Explanation
11	Crank angle sensor circuit
12	Air flow meter circuit
13	Cylinder head temperature sensor circuit
21	Ignition signal missing in primary coil
22	Fuel pump circuit
41	Fuel temperature sensor circuit
44	No malfunctioning in the above circuits

Year— 1987
Model— 300 ZX
Engine— 3.0L (181 cid) PFI V6
Engine Code— VG30E

ECM TROUBLE CODES

Code	Explanation
11	Crank angle sensor circuit
12	Air flow meter circuit
13	Cylinder head temperature sensor circuit
21	Ignition signal missing in primary coil
22	Fuel pump circuit
41	Fuel temperature sensor circuit
44	No malfunctioning in the above circuits

Year – 1987
Model – 300 ZX
Engine – 3.0L (181 cid) Turbo V6
Engine Code – VG30ET

ECM TROUBLE CODES

Code	Explanation
11	Crank angle sensor circuit
12	Air flow meter circuit
13	Cylinder head temperature sensor circuit
21	Ignition signal missing in primary coil
22	Fuel pump circuit
34	Detonation sensor circuit
41	Fuel temperature sensor circuit
44	No malfunctioning in the above circuits

Year – 1988
Model – Sentra
Engine – 1.6L (97 cid) TBI 4 cyl
Engine Code – E16i

ECM TROUBLE CODES

Code	Explanation
11	Crank angle sensor circuit
12	Air flow meter circuit
13	Water temperature sensor circuit
14	Vehicle speed sensor circuit
15	Mixture ratio feedback control slips out
21	Ignition signal missing in primary coil
23	Idle switch circuit
25	Idle speed control slips out
31	Electronic Control Unit (ECU)
33	Exhaust gas sensor circuit
43	Throttle sensor circuit
55	No malfunctioning in the above circuits

Year – 1988
Model – Sentra
Engine – 1.6L (97 cid) TBI 4 cyl
Engine Code – E16i

ECM TROUBLE CODES

Code	Explanation
11	Crank angle sensor circuit
12	Air flow meter circuit
13	Water temperature sensor circuit
14	Vehicle speed sensor circuit
15	Mixture ratio feedback control slips out
21	Ignition signal missing in primary coil
23	Idle switch circuit
25	Idle speed control slips out
31	Electronic Control Unit (ECU)
33	Exhaust gas sensor circuit
43	Throttle sensor circuit
55	No malfunctioning in the above circuits

Year – 1988
Model – Pulsar NX
Engine – 1.8L (110 cid) EFI 4 cyl
Engine Code – CA18DE

ECM TROUBLE CODES

Code	Explanation
11	Crank angle sensor circuit
12	Air flow meter circuit
13	Water temperature sensor circuit
14	Vehicle speed sensor circuit
21	Ignition signal circuit
23	Idle switch circuit
31	Electronic Control Unit (ECU)
32	Exhaust Gas Recirculation (EGR) function
33	Exhaust gas sensor circuit
34	Detonation sensor circuit
35	Exhaust gas temperature sensor circuit
43	Throttle sensor
45	Injector lead
55	No malfunctioning in the above circuits

Year – 1988
Model – Pulsar NX
Engine – 1.6L (97 cid) TBI 4 cyl
Engine Code – E16i

ECM TROUBLE CODES

Code	Explanation
11	Crank angle sensor circuit
12	Air flow meter circuit
13	Water temperature sensor circuit
14	Vehicle speed sensor circuit
15	Mixture ratio feedback control slips out
21	Ignition signal missing in primary coil
23	Idle switch circuit
25	Idle speed control slips out
31	Electronic Control Unit (ECU)
33	Exhaust gas sensor circuit
43	Throttle sensor circuit
41	Fuel temperature sensor circuit
55	No malfunctioning in the above circuits

Year — 1988
Model — Stanza Wagon
Engine — 2.0L (120 cid) EFI 4 cyl
Engine Code — CA20E

ECM TROUBLE CODES

Code	Explanation
11	Crank angle sensor circuit
12	Air flow meter circuit
13	Water temperature sensor circuit
14	Vehicle speed sensor circuit
21	Ignition signal missing in primary coil
22	Fuel pump circuit
23	Idle switch circuit
24	Full switch circuit
31	Electronic Control Unit (ECU)
33	Exhaust gas sensor circuit
41	Air temperature sensor circuit
55	No malfunctioning in the above circuits

Year — 1988
Model — 200 SX
Engine — 1.8L (110 cid) Turbo 4 cyl
Engine Code — CA18ET

ECM TROUBLE CODES

Code	Explanation
11	Crank angle sensor circuit
12	Air flow meter circuit
13	Water temperature sensor circuit
21	Ignition signal missing in primary coil
22	Fuel pump circuit
34	Detonation sensor
44	No malfunctioning in the above circuits

Year — 1988
Model — 200 SX
Engine — 2.0L (120 cid) ECCS 4 cyl
Engine Code — CA20E

ECM TROUBLE CODES

Code	Explanation
11	Crank angle sensor circuit
12	Air flow meter circuit
13	Water temperature sensor circuit
14	Vehicle speed sensor circuit
21	Ignition signal missing in primary coil
22	Fuel pump circuit
23	Idle switch circuit
24	Full switch circuit
31	Electronic Control Unit (ECU)
33	Exhaust gas sensor circuit
41	Air temperature sensor circuit
55	No malfunctioning in the above circuits

Year – 1988
Model – 200 SX
Engine – 3.0L (181 cid) ECCS V6
Engine Code – VG30E

ECM TROUBLE CODES

Code	Explanation
11	Crank angle sensor circuit
12	Air flow meter circuit
13	Cylinder head temperature sensor circuit
14	Vehicle speed sensor circuit
21	Ignition signal missing in primary coil
22	Fuel pump circuit
23	Idle switch circuit
31	Electronic Control Unit (ECU)
33	Exhaust gas sensor circuit
42	Fuel temperature sensor circuit
55	No malfunctioning in the above circuits

Year – 1988
Model – Maxima
Engine – 3.0L (181 cid) ECCS V6
Engine Code – VG30E

ECM TROUBLE CODES

Code	Explanation
11	Crank angle sensor circuit
12	Air flow meter circuit
13	Cylinder head temperature sensor circuit
14	Vehicle speed sensor circuit
21	Ignition signal missing in primary coil
22	Fuel pump circuit
23	Idle switch circuit
31	Electronic Control Unit (ECU)
33	Exhaust gas sensor circuit
42	Fuel temperature sensor circuit
55	No malfunctioning in the above circuits

Year – 1988
Model – 300 ZX
Engine – 3.0L (181 cid) Turbo V6
Engine Code – VG30ET

ECM TROUBLE CODES

Code	Explanation
11	Crank angle sensor circuit
12	Air flow meter circuit
13	Cylinder head temperature sensor circuit
14	Vehicle speed sensor circuit
21	Ignition signal missing in primary coil
22	Fuel pump circuit
23	Idle switch circuit
31	Electronic Control Unit (ECU)
32	Exhaust Gas Recirculation (EGR) function
33	Exhaust gas sensor circuit
34	Detonation sensor circuit
35	Exhaust gas temperature circuit
42	Fuel temperature sensor circuit
43	Throttle sensor circuit
45	Injector leak
55	No malfunctioning in the above circuits

Year – 1988
Model – 300 ZX
Engine – 3.0L (181 cid) ECCS V6
Engine Code – VG30E

ECM TROUBLE CODES

Code	Explanation
11	Crank angle sensor circuit
12	Air flow meter circuit
13	Cylinder head temperature sensor circuit
14	Vehicle speed sensor circuit
21	Ignition signal missing in primary coil
22	Fuel pump circuit
23	Idle switch circuit
31	Electronic Control Unit (ECU)
32	Exhaust Gas Recirculation (EGR) function
33	Exhaust gas sensor circuit
35	Exhaust gas temperature circuit
42	Fuel temperature sensor circuit
43	Throttle sensor circuit
45	Injector leak
55	No malfunctioning in the above circuits

Year – 1989
Model – Sentra
Engine – 1.6L (97 cid) TBI 4 cyl
Engine Code – GA16i

ECM TROUBLE CODES

Code	Explanation
11	Crank angle sensor circuit
12	Air flow meter circuit
13	Water temperature sensor circuit
14	Vehicle speed sensor circuit
21	Ignition signal missing in primary coil
23	Idle switch circuit
25	Auxiliary Air Control (AAC) valve
31	Electronic Control Unit (ECU)
32	Exhaust Gas Recirculation (EGR) function
33	Exhaust gas sensor circuit
35	Exhaust gas temperature circuit
43	Throttle sensor circuit
45	Injector leak
55	No malfunctioning in the above circuits

Year – 1989
Model – Pulsar NX Coupe
Engine – 1.6L (97 cid) TBI 4 cyl
Engine Code – GA16i

ECM TROUBLE CODES

Code	Explanation
11	Crank angle sensor circuit
12	Air flow meter circuit
13	Water temperature sensor circuit
14	Vehicle speed sensor circuit
21	Ignition signal missing in primary coil
23	Idle switch circuit
25	Auxiliary Air Control (AAC) valve
31	Electronic Control Unit (ECU)
32	Exhaust Gas Recirculation (EGR) function
33	Exhaust gas sensor circuit
35	Exhaust gas temperature circuit
43	Throttle sensor circuit
45	Injector leak
55	No malfunctioning in the above circuits

Year – 1989
Model – Pulsar NX Coupe
Engine – 1.8L (110 cid) ECCS 4 cyl
Engine Code – CA18DE

ECM TROUBLE CODES

Code	Explanation
11	Crank angle sensor circuit
12	Air flow meter circuit
13	Water temperature sensor circuit
14	Vehicle speed sensor circuit
21	Ignition signal circuit
23	Idle switch circuit
31	Electronic Control Unit (ECU)
32	Exhaust Gas Recirculation (EGR) function
33	Exhaust gas sensor circuit
34	Detonation sensor circuit
35	Exhaust gas temperature sensor circuit
43	Throttle sensor circuit
45	Injector leak
55	No malfunctioning in the above circuits

Year — 1989
Model — 240 SX
Engine — 2.4L (146 cid) ECCS 4 cyl
Engine Code — KA24E

ECM TROUBLE CODES

Code	Explanation
11	Crank angle sensor circuit
12	Air flow meter circuit
13	Engine temperature sensor circuit
14	Vehicle speed sensor circuit
21	Ignition signal missing in primary coil
31	Electronic Control Unit (ECU)
32	Exhaust Gas Recirculation (EGR) function
33	Exhaust gas sensor circuit
35	Exhaust gas temperature sensor circuit
43	Throttle sensor circuit
45	Injector leak
55	No malfunctioning in the above circuits

Year — 1989
Model — Maxima
Engine — 3.0L (181 cid) ECCS V6
Engine Code — VG30E

ECM TROUBLE CODES

Code	Explanation
11	Crank angle sensor circuit
12	Air flow meter circuit
13	Engine temperature sensor circuit
14	Vehicle speed sensor circuit
21	Ignition signal missing in primary coil
22	Fuel pump circuit
31	Electronic Control Unit (ECU)
32	Exhaust Gas Recirculation (EGR) function
33	Exhaust gas sensor circuit
34	Detonation sensor circuit
35	Exhaust gas temperature sensor circuit
43	Throttle sensor circuit
45	Injector leak
55	No malfunctioning in the above circuits

Year — 1989
Model — Maxima
Engine — 3.0L (181 cid) PFI V6
Engine Code — VG30E

ECM TROUBLE CODES

Code	Explanation
11	Crank angle sensor circuit
12	Air flow meter circuit
13	Engine temperature sensor circuit
14	Vehicle speed sensor circuit
21	Ignition signal missing in primary coil
31	Electronic Control Unit (ECU)
32	Exhaust Gas Recirculation (EGR) function
33	Exhaust gas sensor circuit
35	Exhaust gas temperature sensor circuit
43	Throttle sensor circuit
45	Injector leak
55	No malfunctioning in the above circuits

Year – 1989
Model – 300 ZX
Engine – 3.0L (181 cid) ECCS V6
Engine Code – VG30E

ECM TROUBLE CODES

Code	Explanation
11	Crank angle sensor circuit
12	Air flow meter circuit
13	Cylinder head temperature sensor circuit
14	Vehicle speed sensor circuit
21	Ignition signal missing in primary coil
22	Fuel pump circuit
23	Idle switch circuit
31	Electronic Control Unit (ECU)
32	Exhaust Gas Recirculation (EGR) function
33	Exhaust gas sensor circuit
35	Exhaust gas temperature sensor circuit
42	Fuel temperature sensor circuit
43	Throttle sensor circuit
45	Injector leak
55	No malfunctioning in the above circuits

Year — 1989
Model — 300 ZX
Engine — 3.0L (181 cid) Turbo V6
Engine Code — VG30ET

ECM TROUBLE CODES

Code	Explanation
11	Crank angle sensor circuit
12	Air flow meter circuit
13	Cylinder head temperature sensor circuit
14	Vehicle speed sensor circuit
21	Ignition signal missing in primary coil
22	Fuel pump circuit
23	Idle switch circuit
31	Electronic Control Unit (ECU)
32	Exhaust Gas Recirculation (EGR) function
33	Exhaust gas sensor circuit
34	Detonation sensor circuit
35	Exhaust gas temperature sensor circuit
42	Fuel temperature sensor circuit
43	Throttle sensor circuit
45	Injector leak
55	No malfunctioning in the above circuits

NISSAN   TRUCKS

Year — 1986
Model — Pick-Up D21 Series
Engine — 2.4L (146 cid) EFI 4 cyl
Engine Code — Z24i

ECM TROUBLE CODES

Code	Explanation
11	Crank angle sensor circuit
12	Air flow meter circuit
13	Water temperature sensor
21	Ignition signal malfunction
23	Idle switch
24	Neutral and clutch inhibitor switch
32	Starter signal malfucntion
42	Throttle sensor
43	Injector
44	Electronic Fuel Injection (EFI)/Electronic Concentrated Control System (ECCS) is operating properly

Year — 1986
Model — Pick-Up D21 Series
Engine — 3.0L (181 cid) EFI V6
Engine Code — VG30i

ECM TROUBLE CODES

Code	Explanation
11	Crank angle sensor circuit
12	Air flow meter circuit
13	Cylinder head temperature sensor
21	Ignition signal malfunction
24	Neutral and clutch inhibitor switch
31	Load switch circuit malfunction
32	Starter signal malfucntion
33	Exhaust gas sensor
42	Throttle sensor
43	Injector
44	Electronic Fuel Injection (EFI)/Electronic Concentrated Control System (ECCS) is operating properly

Year — 1987
Model — Van
Engine — 2.4L (146 cid) TBI 4 cyl
Engine Code — Z24i

ECM TROUBLE CODES

Code	Explanation
11	Crank angle sensor circuit
12	Air flow meter circuit
13	Water temperature sensor circuit
21	Ignition signal missing in primary coil
33	Exhaust gas sensor circuit
42	Throttle senor circuit
43	Injector circuit
44	No malfunctioning in the above circuits

Year — 1987
Model — Pick-Up (Model D21)
Engine — 2.4L (146 cid) TBI 4 cyl
Engine Code — Z24i

ECM TROUBLE CODES

Code	Explanation
11	Crank angle sensor circuit
12	Air flow meter circuit
13	Cylinder head/water temperature sensor circuit
21	Ignition signal missing in primary coil
42	Throttle sensor circuit
43	Injector circuit
44	No malfunctioning in the above circuits

Year – 1987
Model – Pathfinder (Model D21)
Engine – 2.4L (146 cid) TBI 4 cyl
Engine Code – Z24i

ECM TROUBLE CODES

Code	Explanation
11	Crank angle sensor circuit
12	Air flow meter circuit
13	Cylinder head/water temperature sensor circuit
21	Ignition signal missing in primary coil
42	Throttle sensor circuit
43	Injector circuit
44	No malfunctioning in the above circuits

Year — 1987
Model — Pick-Up (Model D21)
Engine — 3.0L (181 cid) TBI V6
Engine Code — VG30i

ECM TROUBLE CODES

Code	Explanation
11	Crank angle sensor circuit
12	Air flow meter circuit
13	Cylinder head/water temperature sensor circuit
21	Ignition signal missing in primary coil
33	Exhaust gas sensor circuit
42	Throttle sensor circuit
43	Injector circuit
44	No malfunctioning in the above circuits

Year — 1987
Model — Pathfinder (Model D21)
Engine — 3.0L (181 cid) TBI V6
Engine Code — VG30i

ECM TROUBLE CODES

Code	Explanation
11	Crank angle sensor circuit
12	Air flow meter circuit
13	Cylinder head/water temperature sensor circuit
21	Ignition signal missing in primary coil
33	Exhaust gas sensor circuit
42	Throttle sensor circuit
43	Injector circuit
44	No malfunctioning in the above circuits

Year — 1988
Model — Van (Model C22)
Engine — 2.4L (146 cid) ECCS 4 cyl
Engine Code — Z24i

ECM TROUBLE CODES

Code	Explanation
11	Crank angle sensor circuit
12	Air flow meter circuit
13	Water temperature sensor circuit
14	Vehicle speed sensor circuit
21	Ignition signal missing in primary coil
31	Electronic Control Unit (ECU)
32	Exhaust Gas Recirculation (EGR) function
33	Exhaust gas sensor circuit
35	Exhaust gas temperature sensor circuit
43	Throttle sensor circuit
45	Injector leak
51	Injector circuit
55	No malfunctioning in the above circuits

Year – 1988
Model – Pick-Up (Model D21)
Engine – 2.4L (146 cid) TBI 4 cyl
Engine Code – Z24i

ECM TROUBLE CODES

Code	Explanation
11	Crank angle sensor circuit
12	Air flow meter circuit
13	Cylinder head/water temperature sensor circuit
21	Ignition signal missing in primary coil
31	Electronic Control Unit (ECU)
32	Exhaust Gas Recirculation (EGR) function
33	Exhaust gas sensor circuit
35	Exhaust gas temperature sensor circuit
43	Throttle sensor circuit
45	Injector leak
51	Injector
55	No malfunctioning in the above circuits

Year — 1988
Model — Pathfinder (Model D21)
Engine — 2.4L (146 cid) TBI 4 cyl
Engine Code — Z24i

ECM TROUBLE CODES

Code	Explanation
11	Crank angle sensor circuit
12	Air flow meter circuit
13	Cylinder head/water temperature sensor circuit
21	Ignition signal missing in primary coil
31	Electronic Control Unit (ECU)
32	Exhaust Gas Recirculation (EGR) function
33	Exhaust gas sensor circuit
35	Exhaust gas temperature sensor circuit
43	Throttle sensor circuit
45	Injector leak
51	Injector
55	No malfunctioning in the above circuits

Year — 1988
Model — Pick-Up (Model D21)
Engine — 3.0L (181 cid) TBI V6
Engine Code — VG30i

ECM TROUBLE CODES

Code	Explanation
11	Crank angle sensor circuit
12	Air flow meter circuit
13	Cylinder head/water temperature sensor circuit
14	Vehicle speed sensor circuit
21	Ignition signal missing in primary coil
31	Electronic Control Unit (ECU)
32	Exhaust Gas Recirculation (EGR) function
33	Exhaust gas sensor circuit
35	Exhaust gas temperature sensor circuit
43	Throttle sensor circuit
45	Injector leak
51	Injector
55	No malfunctioning in the above circuits

Year — 1988
Model — Pathfinder (Model D21)
Engine — 3.0L (181 cid) TBI V6
Engine Code — VG30i

ECM TROUBLE CODES

Code	Explanation
11	Crank angle sensor circuit
12	Air flow meter circuit
13	Cylinder head/water temperature sensor circuit
14	Vehicle speed sensor circuit
21	Ignition signal missing in primary coil
31	Electronic Control Unit (ECU)
32	Exhaust Gas Recirculation (EGR) function
33	Exhaust gas sensor circuit
35	Exhaust gas temperature sensor circuit
43	Throttle sensor circuit
45	Injector leak
51	Injector
55	No malfunctioning in the above circuits

Year – 1989
Model – Van
Engine – 2.4L (146 cid) TBI 4 cyl
Engine Code – Z24i

ECM TROUBLE CODES

Code	Explanation
11	Crank angle sensor circuit
12	Air flow meter circuit
13	Water temperature sensor circuit
14	Vehicle speed sensor circuit
21	Ignition signal missing in primary coil
31	Electronic Control Unit (ECU)
32	Exhaust Gas Recirculation (EGR) function
33	Exhaust gas sensor circuit
35	Exhaust gas temperature sensor circuit
43	Throttle sensor circuit
45	Injector leak
51	Injector circuit
55	No malfunctioning in the above circuits

Year — 1989
Model — Pick-Up (4WD)
Engine — 2.4L (146 cid) TBI 4 cyl
Engine Code — Z24i

ECM TROUBLE CODES

Code	Explanation
11	Crank angle sensor circuit
12	Air flow meter circuit
13	Cylinder head/water temperature sensor circuit
21	Ignition signal missing in primary coil
31	Electronic Control Unit (ECU)
32	Exhaust Gas Recirculation (EGR) function
33	Exhaust gas sensor circuit
35	Exhaust gas temperature sensor circuit
43	Throttle sensor circuit
45	Injector leak
55	No malfunctioning in the above circuits

Year – 1989
Model – Pathfinder (4WD)
Engine – 2.4L (146 cid) TBI 4 cyl
Engine Code – Z24i

ECM TROUBLE CODES

Code	Explanation
11	Crank angle sensor circuit
12	Air flow meter circuit
13	Cylinder head/water temperature sensor circuit
21	Ignition signal missing in primary coil
31	Electronic Control Unit (ECU)
32	Exhaust Gas Recirculation (EGR) function
33	Exhaust gas sensor circuit
35	Exhaust gas temperature sensor circuit
43	Throttle sensor circuit
45	Injector leak
55	No malfunctioning in the above circuits

Year — 1989
Model — Pick-Up (4WD)
Engine — 3.0L (181 cid) TBI V6
Engine Code — VG30i

ECM TROUBLE CODES

Code	Explanation
11	Crank angle sensor circuit
12	Air flow meter circuit
13	Cylinder head/water temperature sensor circuit
21	Ignition signal missing in primary coil
31	Electronic Control Unit (ECU)
32	Exhaust Gas Recirculation (EGR) function
33	Exhaust gas sensor circuit
35	Exhaust gas temperature sensor circuit
43	Throttle sensor circuit
45	Injector leak
51	Injector
55	No malfunctioning in the above circuits

Year — 1989
Model — Pathfinder (4WD)
Engine — 3.0L (181 cid) TBI V6
Engine Code — VG30i

ECM TROUBLE CODES

Code	Explanation
11	Crank angle sensor circuit
12	Air flow meter circuit
13	Cylinder head/water temperature sensor circuit
21	Ignition signal missing in primary coil
31	Electronic Control Unit (ECU)
32	Exhaust Gas Recirculation (EGR) function
33	Exhaust gas sensor circuit
35	Exhaust gas temperature sensor circuit
43	Throttle sensor circuit
45	Injector leak
51	Injector
55	No malfunctioning in the above circuits

INDEX

PEUGEOT

Electronic Cartographic Ignition and M1.3 Motronic Ignition Systems

SELF-DIAGNOSTIC SYSTEM

Description

ELECTRONIC CARTOGRAPHIC IGNITION SYSTEM

Peugeot uses the R. Bosch EZ 200K and EZ 115K electronic cartographic ignition with detonation sensor, which provides an optimal advance calculation. It consists of the following:

A Hall Effect impulse generator distributor

An electronic cartographic ignition control unit with detonation detection

A detonation sensor

A detonation indicator LED

An amplifier module

An ignition coil

A potentiometer and microswitch

The ignition Electronic Control Unit (ECU) incorporates a microprocessor associated with a memory. Several advance points is programmed into the ECU to provide the optimum engine performance at the limit of engine knock (detonation).

An auto-diagnostic feature is incorporated into the ignition ECU, which enables it to identify some of the faults which may occur in the system during operation. An indicator LED in the lower left corner of the instrument cluster alert the driver of any existing faults.

M1.3 MOTRONIC IGNITION SYSTEM

The Motronic M1.3 system is designed to optimize the fuel injection and ignition control systems. In order to accomplished this, both the fuel injection system and ignition control have been regrouped into a single ECU and called Motronic.

Some engine management systems incorporate a simplified Motronic M1.3. This system is designed with no detonation sensing feature nor any electronic idle regulation electrovalve. Instead, an auxiliary air device is used.

Operation

An indicator LED in the instrument cluster monitors the proper operation of the ignition system. Under normal operation, with the key **ON** and the engine **OFF**, the LED will be ON. Under normal operation, with the engine running, the LED should be OFF.

NOTE: Occasional sporadic flashes of the LED with no inconvenience may be notice. This condition is normal.

Under abnormal operation, with the engine running, constant blinking of the LED will be noticed. The number of blinks, from 1–6, will determine the origin of the fault. The frequency of these blinks will be proportional to the engines rpm.

As a safety measure, as soon as a fault in the system is detected, the system will automatically post a retard to the spark advance (−20 to −22 degrees). This retard will be noticed by a lack of power and performance of the engine.

Entering Diagnostic Mode

ELECTRONIC CARTOGRAPHIC IGNITION SYSTEM

This is done through the indicator in the lower left corner of the

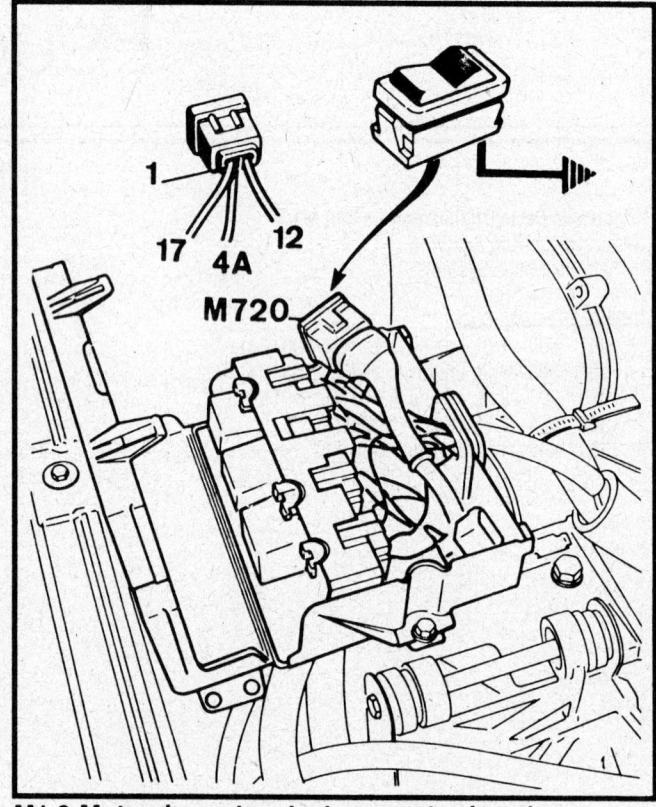

M1.3 Motronic system-test connector location

instrument cluster (orange LED). The number of blinks from the indicator determine which component presents the fault.

The speed of the blink cycles will relate directly to engine rpm. Therefore, it is imperative to make the determination of the diagnostic cycle at idle by counting the number of blinks.

M1.3 MOTRONIC IGNITION SYSTEM

1. Connect jumper switch part No. 91.42 (jumper with switch) to pin 1 of the 2-pin green connector and ground.
2. The check engine lamp on the instrument cluster will flash the defective code(s).
   a. The first set of flashes = tenths digits.
   b. The second set of flashes = unit digits.
3. Turn the key **ON**, then depress the switch for 3 seconds (indicator ON).
4. When the switch is release, the following will be noted:
   a. The check engine lamp will blink once = 1 (tenth).
   b. The check engine lamp remains OFF for 1–5 seconds.
   c. The check engine lamp blinks twice = 2 (unit). Thus, Code 12 is indicated.

NOTE: Code 12 indicates the beginning of test.

5. Wait for the check engine lamp to turn ON.
6. To proceed with test, depress the switch for 3 seconds (indicator ON).
7. When the switch is release:
   a. The check engine lamp will blinks 5 times (for example) = 5 (tenth).

b. The check engine lamp OFF for 1–5 seconds.
c. The check engine lamp blinks 4 times = 4 (unit). Thus, Code 54 is indicated.
d. Wait for the check engine lamp to come ON.
To proceed to a new test, repeat Steps 6 and 7. If several faults are detected, they will be displayed after each test.

NOTE: Code 11 indicates the end of test.

Clearing Diagnostic Memory
M1.3 MOTRONIC IGNITION SYSTEM
After performing repairs on the defective fault codes, the memory must be cleared. Proceed as follows:
1. Turn the key **ON**.
2. Perform a test up to Code 11.
3. After Code 11 is indicated, depress the switch for more than 10 seconds. The check engine lamp should be ON.

PEUGEOT

Year—1987
Model—505
Engine—2.2L (131 cid) 4 cyl
Engine Code—N9T/N9TE/N9TEA

ECM TROUBLE CODES

Code	Explanation
1	Continued detonation—Maximum correction reached
2	Battery voltage is under 10.5 volts
3	Detonation correction circuit in the ignition ECU defective
4	Erroneous signal received from detonation sensor—check for engine speed above 3200 rpm
5	Signal from potentiometer is greater the 4.3 volts
6A	Connections and wiring between ignition ECU and potentiometer defective
6B	Microswitch open—advance at full load. Microswitch closed—advance at idle. No load signal emanating from the injection ECU

PEUGEOT

Year — 1988
Model — 505
Engine — 2.2L (131 cid) 4 cyl
Engine Code — N9T/N9TE/N9TEA

ECM TROUBLE CODES

Code	Explanation
1	Continued detonation — Maximum correction reached
2	Battery voltage is under 10.5 volts
3	Detonation correction circuit in the ignition ECU defective
4	Erroneous signal received from detonation sensor — check for engine speed above 3200 rpm
5	Signal from potentiometer is greater the 4.3 volts
6A	Connections and wiring between ignition ECU and potentiometer defective
6B	Microswitch open — advance at full load. Microswitch closed — advance at idle. No load signal emanating from the injection ECU

Year – 1989
Model – 505
Engine – 2.2L (131 cid) 4 cyl
Engine Code – N9T/N9TE/N9TEA

ECM TROUBLE CODES

Code	Explanation
1	Continued detonation – Maximum correction reached
2	Battery voltage is under 10.5 volts
3	Detonation correction circuit in the ignition ECU defective
4	Erroneous signal received from detonation sensor – check for engine speed above 3200 rpm
5	Signal from potentiometer is greater the 4.3 volts
6A	Connections and wiring between ignition ECU and potentiometer defective
6B	Microswitch open – advance at full load. Microswitch closed – advance at idle. No load signal emanating from the injection ECU

Year – 1989
Model – 405
Engine – 1.9L (116 cid) 4 cyl
Engine Code – XU9J2

ECM TROUBLE CODES

Code	Explanation
11	End of test sequence
12	Beginning of test sequence
13	Air temperature sensor
14	Injection NTC sensor
15	Fuel pump(s) relay
21	Throttle switch (idle position)
22	Electronic Control Unit (ECU)
31	Self correction richness regulation function
32	Self correction richness regualtion function
33	Airflow sensor
34	Canister purge electrovalve
35	Throttle switch unit (full load position)
41	Engine rpm sensor
42	Injectors
51	Self correction richness regulation function
52	Self correction richness regulation function
53	Battery voltage
54	Electronic Control Unit (ECU)

Year — 1989
Model — 405
Engine — 1.9L (116 cid) 4 cyl
Engine Code — XU9J4

ECM TROUBLE CODES

Code	Explanation
11	End of test sequence
12	Beginning of test sequence
13	Air temperature sensor
14	Injection NTC sensor
15	Fuel pump(s) relay
21	Throttle switch (idle position)
22	Idle regulation electrovalve
31	Self correction richness regulation function
32	Self correction richness regualtion function
33	Airflow sensor
34	Canister purge electrovalve
35	Throttle switch unit (full load position)
42	Injectors
43	Detonation correction regulation (at maximum)
44	Detonation sensor
51	Self correction richness regulation function
52	Self correction richness regulation function
53	Battery voltage
54	Electronic Control Unit (ECU)

INDEX

PORSCHE

Electronic Fuel Injection System

SELF-DIAGNOSTIC SYSTEM

Description

Beginning 1989, LH/EZK control unit is capable of self-diagnosis. The 928 S4 vehicles are equipped with a 19-pin diagnostic plug, located under the right side radio booster cover.

911 Carrera 4 is equipped with a diagnostic socket located underneath a cover in the passenger's footwell.

A special developed diagnostic tester, tool No. 9268, is used to read out the fault codes, test certain components and control signals of the fuel and ignition system.

For 1989, Porsche introduced a new tester (Bosch KTS 301), which also has a 19-pin connecting plug and is protected against incorrect contacting.

If diagnosis is performed on vehicles beginning 1989, with tester 9268 as in the past, an adapter lead is required. Also, the meaning of the second digit of the 4-digit flashing code has been changed.

If a No. 1 is displayed in the 2nd digit, it indicates that there had been a fault during the last operation of the vehicle. If a No. 2 is displayed in the 2nd digit, there had been no fault existing during the last operation of the vehicle.

NOTE: Do not disconnect the battery or the DME control unit connector before diagnosis, as the memory will be erased.

Entering Diagnostic Mode

1. Locate the diagnosis socket on the retaining plate of the EZK control unit.
2. Turn the ignition switch **OFF** and connect the tester (tool No. 9268 or equivalent).
3. With the tester connected, the display should be as shown. If not, the tester terminals and/or the power supply to the diagnosis socket.
4. Turn the ignition switch **ON** and press the green key until the clear symbol is displayed.

NOTE: The diagnosis sequence for the LH control unit takes place first, followed by that of the EZK control unit.

5. If a fault code is displayed, make a note of it.
6. Press the green key again to advance to the next fault code. This must be repeated until 1000 appears on the display.
7. If no additional codes exist, the following display should appear.
8. Press the green key until the clear symbol appears on the display.

Clearing Diagnostic Memory

If the display on the tester being used indicates no additional codes, press the green key until the clear symbol appears on the display. This shows that the diagnosis on the DME control unit has been terminated.

Tester – initial display

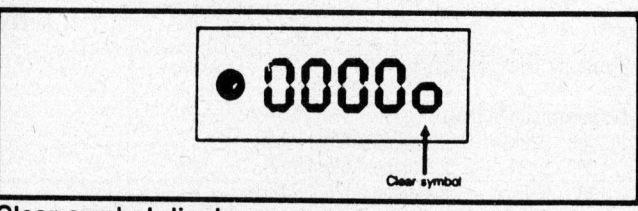

Clear symbol display

No additional code display symbol

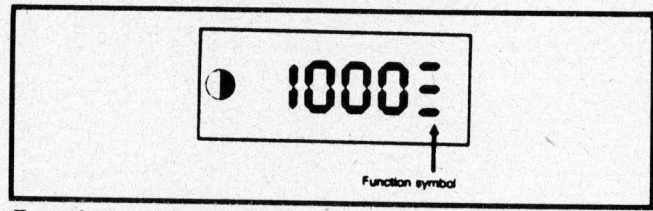

Function symbol display

Resetting Diagnostic Memory

The error memory of the EZK control unit and the LH control unit must be reset separately.

NOTE: Once the error diagnosis has been terminated for both control units, the tester will display error code 1000 for the LH control unit or error code 2000 for the EZK control unit.

To reset the error memory, proceed as follows:
1. Press the yellow key repeatedly until the function symbol appears on the display.
2. Press the green key until the clear signal appears on the display.
3. The error memory has been reset when the LED goes out and the function display changes to 0000.
4. After resetting the memory, road-test the vehicle for at least 6 minutes. AT the end of the road-test, run the engine for approximately 60 seconds without operating the throttle valve.
5. Recheck the error memory.

PORSCHE

Year — 1988
Model — 928 S4
Engine — 5.0L (302 cid) V8
Engine Code — M28/41/428

ECM TROUBLE CODES

Code	Explanation
1500	No fault
1000	Output terminated
1111	Supply voltage too low/high
1112	Idle contact
1113	Fuel load contact
1114	Engine temperature sensor
1121	Air-flow sensor
1122	Rotary idle controller
1123	Lambda control detects too rich a mixture
1124	Lambda control detects too lean a mixture
1125	Lambda probe

Year – 1988
Model – 928 S4
Engine – 5.0L (302 cid) V8
Engine Code – M28/41/42

ECM TROUBLE CODES

Code	Explanation
2500	No fault
2000	Output terminated
2112	Idle contact
2113	Full load contact
2114	Engine temperature sensor
2115	Idle/full load contact
2121	Load signal from the LH control unit
2126	Transmission safeguard switch
2131	Knock sensor I
2132	Knock sensor II
2133	Knock control in the control unit
2134	Hall generator signal
2141	EZK control unit

Year — 1988
Model — 928 S4
Engine — 5.0L (302 cid) V8
Engine Code — M28/41/42

ECM TROUBLE CODES

Code	Explanation
1311	Injection valves
1321	Rotary idle controller
1322	Solenoid valve — tank bleeding
1323	Resonance flap
1331	Speed signal from EZK to LH control unit
1332	Idle contact
1333	Full load contact
1334	Air conditioning control to the LH control unit terminal 15
1335	Air conditioning control to the LH control unit terminal 14
1336	Idle speed reduction for vehicles with automatic transmission

Year — 1989
Model — 928 S4
Engine — 5.0L (302 cid) V8
Engine Code — M28/41/428

ECM TROUBLE CODES

Code	Explanation
1500	No fault
1000	Output terminated
1111	Supply voltage too low/high
1112	Idle contact
1113	Fuel load contact
1114	Engine temperature sensor
1121	Air-flow sensor
1122	Rotary idle controller
1123	Lambda control detects too rich a mixture
1124	Lambda control detects too lean a mixture
1125	Lambda probe

Year – 1989
Model – 928 S4
Engine – 5.0L (302 cid) V8
Engine Code – M28/41/42

ECM TROUBLE CODES

Code	Explanation
2500	No fault
2000	Output terminated
2112	Idle contact
2113	Full load contact
2114	Engine temperature sensor
2115	Idle/full load contact
2121	Load signal from the LH control unit
2126	Transmission safeguard switch
2131	Knock sensor I
2132	Knock sensor II
2133	Knock control in the control unit
2134	Hall generator signal
2141	EZK control unit

Year — 1989
Model — 928 S4
Engine — 5.0L (302 cid) V8
Engine Code — M28/41/42

ECM TROUBLE CODES

Code	Explanation
1311	Injection valves
1321	Rotary idle controller
1322	Solenoid valve — tank bleeding
1323	Resonance flap
1331	Speed signal from EZK to LH control unit
1332	Idle contact
1333	Full load contact
1334	Air — conditioning control to the LH control unit terminal 15
1335	Air — conditioning control to the LH control unit terminal 14
1336	Idle speed reduction for vehicles with automatic transmission

Year — 1989
Model — 911 Carrera 4
Engine — 3.6L (220 cid) V6
Engine Code — 62

ECM TROUBLE CODES

Code	Explanation
1000	End of output
1500	No faults stored
1111	Power supply too low or high
1112	Idle speed contact
1113	Full load contact
1114	Engine temperature sensor — NTC II
1121	Air flow sensor
1123	Oxygen sensor control recognizes too rich or too lean mixture
1124	Oxygen sensor signal not correct
1125	Intake air temperatue sensor — NTC I
1131	Knock sensor I
1132	Knock sensor II
1133	Knock regulation in control unit
1134	Hall sender signal
1141	DME control unit
1151	Fuel injector — cylinder No. 1
1152	Fuel injector — cylinder No. 2
1153	Fuel injector — cylinder No. 3
1154	Fuel injector — cylinder No. 4
1155	Fuel injector — cylinder No. 5
1156	Fuel injector — cylinder No. 6

INDEX

SAAB

Bosch LH-Jetronic Fuel Injection System

NOTE: The following information pertains to 1986–89 vehicles.

SELF-DIAGNOSTIC SYSTEM

Description

The Saab 900 and 9000 are both equipped with the Bosch type LH-Jetronic fuel injection system. The most important component is the new type of air flowmeter that measures the mass flow of the air instead of its volume, as in conventional fuel injection systems. This allows oxygen in the air, which is critical to the combustion process, to be measured more accurately. The engine, therefore, is insensitive to variations in the ambient air temperature and pressure, such as those occurring when the vehicle is traveling at varying altitudes.

The LH-Jetronic system incorporates an emergency system, known as the Limp Home function. If a malfunction is detected, the Limp Home feature in the Electronic Control Unit (ECU) is actuated, enabling the vehicle to continue its journey with somewhat diminished performance. If the vehicle is operated in the Limp Home mode, the "Check Engine" lamp on the vehicle's display panel will turn ON. An integrated fault-diagnosis system makes trouble-shooting easier and improved fault diagnosis.

The Saab LH-system tester No. 8394223 has been developed for servicing and fault diagnosis work on the LH-fuel injection system. The tester, along with itself, consists of a power supply lead, a test lead incorporating a 2-way connector and a pressure sensor with magnetic base. The tester uses 2 versions of the test lead, 1 with a 25-pin connector (LH 2.2) and the other with a 35-pin connector (LH 2.4).

The tester is equipped with an automatic program for diagnosing faults, either permanent or intermittent, while the vehicle is operating. Faults detected are then stored in the memory for recall after the vehicle is road-tested.

Entering Diagnostic Mode

1. Insert the power supply lead between the door and body where there is a break in the seal, then run it under the back of the hood on the left hand side.
2. First connect the power supply lead to the tester, then connect the lead clips to the battery.

NOTE: Always clean the battery terminals to ensure the lead clips make good contact.

3. Remove the cover on the left side over the space behind the false bulkhead panel.
4. Remove the ABS-system ECU and bracket, if equipped.
5. Remove the LH-system ECU connector. Connect the test lead between the LH-system ECU and the vehicle's wiring loom. Fit a couple of ties around the connector and ECU to hold them tightly together.

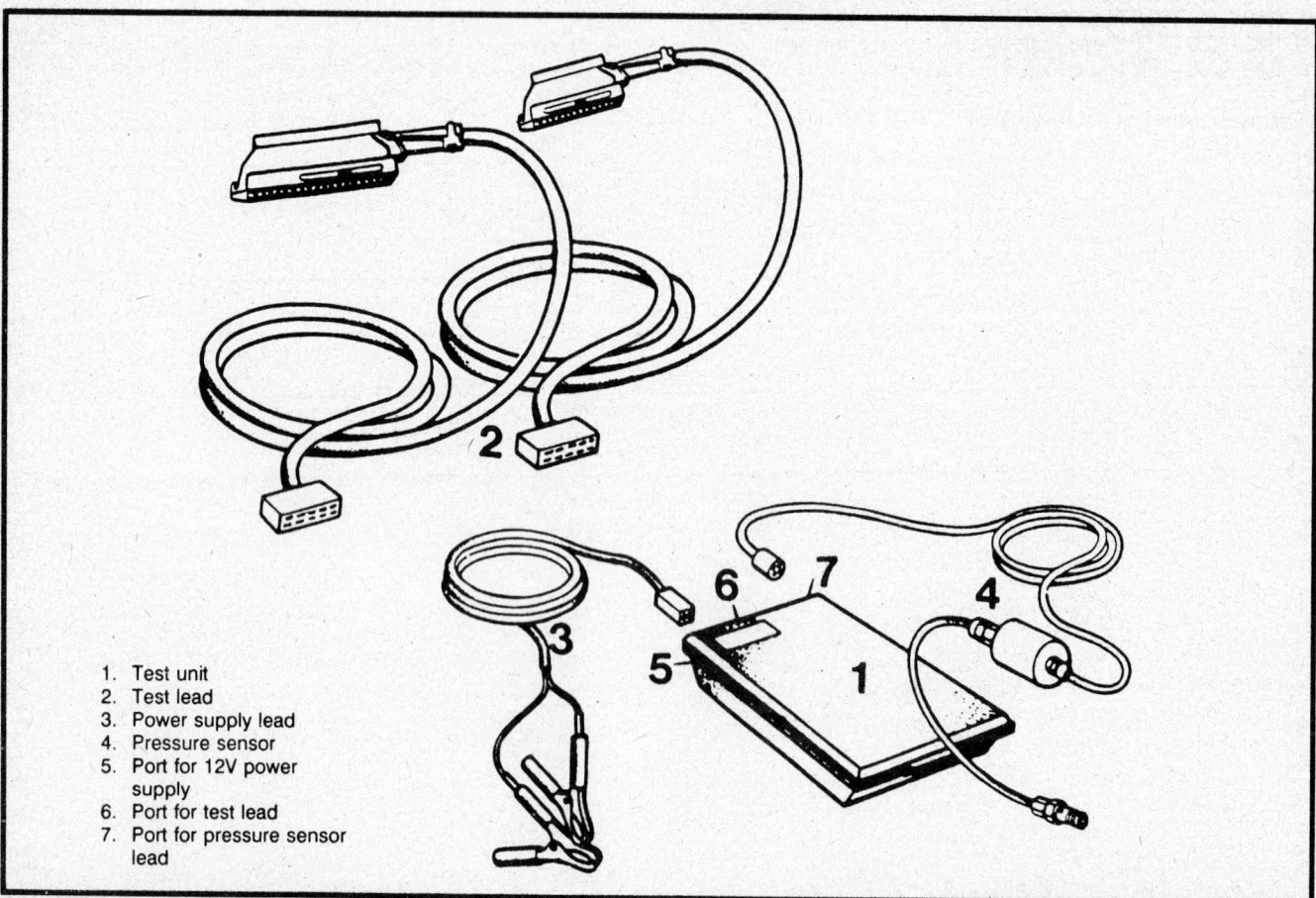

1. Test unit
2. Test lead
3. Power supply lead
4. Pressure sensor
5. Port for 12V power supply
6. Port for test lead
7. Port for pressure sensor lead

Saab LH-system tester and connectors

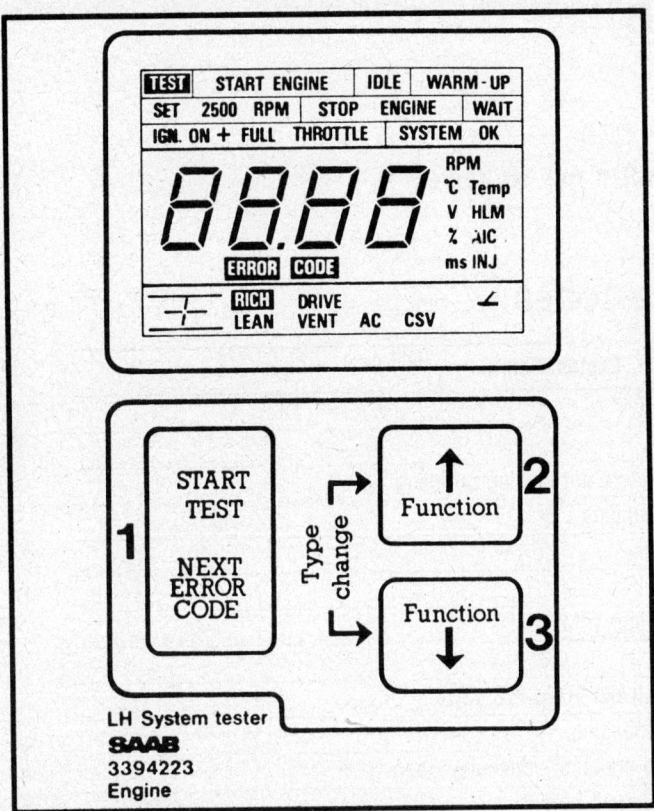

Saab LH-system tester control panel

The tester is designed to perform 3 basic functions:
Monitor Mode
Test Mode
Fuel Mode

START MODE

The tester will automatically switch to the start mode once the lead clips are connected to the battery.

If at any time the operation in progress must be interrupted, simultaneously press all 3 control buttons. This cause the tester to revert to the starting point.

MONITOR MODE

The monitor mode can be selected either by switching on the ignition or (if the ignition is off) by pressing the start test button when ''MON'' appears on the display.

When in the monitor mode, the tester is used to manually control parameter and functional checks.

TEST MODE

Test mode can only be selected from the monitor mode. Once the LH-system version has been selected, the test mode can be activated. Press the start test button to select the test mode. ''TEST'' will now appear on the display.

In the test mode, the program instructs by way of prompts in the upper part of the display.

FUEL MODE

To select the fuel mode, the ignition must be **OFF**. Initially, ''MON'' will be displayed on the tester for approximately 5 seconds. During this time, if required, the monitor mode can be selected. If none of the tester buttons is activated, ''FUEL'' will appear on the display for approximately 2 seconds. To activate the fuel mode, press the start button when ''FUEL'' is displayed.

When the tester is in the fuel mode, the following checks can be performed:
Fuel pump delivery flow
Fuel pressure and fuel-pressure regulator
Residual pressure
Fuel pump delivery pressure
Delivery flow from injectors

Clearing Diagnostic Memory

After completing the test, reset the tester to the start mode by pressing all 3 buttons simultaneously.

SAAB

Year – 1985
Model – 900 (With LH 2.2)
Engine – 2.0L (121 cid) 4 cyl 16 valve
Engine Code – VIN D

ECM TROUBLE CODES

Code	Explanation
E001	No ignition pulse
E002	No signal from temperature sensor
E003	Throttle Position Sensor (TPS) – idling contacts not closing on idling
E005	Electronic Control Unit (ECU) pin 5 not grounding
E006	Air Mass Meter (AMM) not grounding
E007	No signal from Air Mass Meter (AMM)
E008	No filament burn-off function – Air Mass Meter (AMM)
E009	No power to system relay
E010	No signal from Electronic Control Unit (ECU) pin 10 to AIC valve
E011	Electronic Control Unit (ECU) pin 11 not grounding
E012	Throttle Position Sensor (TPS) – full throttle contacts constantly open
E014	Air Mass Meter (AMM) – break in CO – adjusting circuit
E017	Fuel pump relay – control circuit faulty
E018	No power at +15 supply terminal
E020	Faulty signal from Lambda sensor
E021	System relay control circuit faulty
E023	No signal from AIC valve
E025	Electronic Control Unit (ECU) pin 25 not grounding
E101	Starter motor revolutions too low
E102	Shorting in temperature sensor circuit
E103	Throttle Position Sensor (TPS) – idling contacts not opening on increase from idling to 2500 rpm
E107	Low signal from Air Mass Meter (AMM)
E108	Filament burn-off function constantly actuated – Air Mass Meter (AMM)
E109	Low voltage from system relay
E112	Throttle Position Sensor (TPS) – full load contacts constantly closed
E207	High signal from Air Mass Meter (AMM)
E213	Continuous pulses to injectors
E320	DI/APC system Electronic Control Unit (ECU) – Pre-ignition signal constantly actuated

Year — 1985
Model — 900 (With LH 2.2)
Engine — 2.0L (121 cid) Turbo 4 cyl 16 valve
Engine Code — VIN L

ECM TROUBLE CODES

Code	Explanation
E001	No ignition pulse
E002	No signal from temperature sensor
E003	Throttle Position Sensor (TPS) — idling contacts not closing on idling
E005	Electronic Control Unit (ECU) pin 5 not grounding
E006	Air Mass Meter (AMM) not grounding
E007	No signal from Air Mass Meter (AMM)
E008	No filament burn-off function — Air Mass Meter (AMM)
E009	No power to system relay
E010	No signal from Electronic Control Unit (ECU) pin 10 to AIC valve
E011	Electronic Control Unit (ECU) pin 11 not grounding
E012	Throttle Position Sensor (TPS) — full throttle contacts constantly open
E014	Air Mass Meter (AMM) — break in CO — adjusting circuit
E017	Fuel pump relay — control circuit faulty
E018	No power at +15 supply terminal
E020	Faulty signal from Lambda sensor
E021	System relay control circuit faulty
E023	No signal from AIC valve
E025	Electronic Control Unit (ECU) pin 25 not grounding
E101	Starter motor revolutions too low
E102	Shorting in temperature sensor circuit
E103	Throttle Position Sensor (TPS) — idling contacts not opening on increase from idling to 2500 rpm
E107	Low signal from Air Mass Meter (AMM)
E108	Filament burn-off function constantly actuated — Air Mass Meter (AMM)
E109	Low voltage from system relay
E112	Throttle Position Sensor (TPS) — full load contacts constantly closed
E207	High signal from Air Mass Meter (AMM)
E213	Continuous pulses to injectors
E320	DI/APC system Electronic Control Unit (ECU) — Pre-ignition signal constantly actuated

Year – 1986
Model – 900 (With LH 2.2)
Engine – 2.0L (121 cid) 4 cyl 16 valve
Engine Code – VIN D

ECM TROUBLE CODES

Code	Explanation
E001	No ignition pulse
E002	No signal from temperature sensor
E003	Throttle Position Sensor (TPS) – idling contacts not closing on idling
E005	Electronic Control Unit (ECU) pin 5 not grounding
E006	Air Mass Meter (AMM) not grounding
E007	No signal from Air Mass Meter (AMM)
E008	No filament burn-off function – Air Mass Meter (AMM)
E009	No power to system relay
E010	No signal from Electronic Control Unit (ECU) pin 10 to AIC valve
E011	Electronic Control Unit (ECU) pin 11 not grounding
E012	Throttle Position Sensor (TPS) – full throttle contacts constantly open
E014	Air Mass Meter (AMM) – break in CO – adjusting circuit
E017	Fuel pump relay – control circuit faulty
E018	No power at +15 supply terminal
E020	Faulty signal from Lambda sensor
E021	System relay control circuit faulty
E023	No signal from AIC valve
E025	Electronic Control Unit (ECU) pin 25 not grounding
E101	Starter motor revolutions too low
E102	Shorting in temperature sensor circuit
E103	Throttle Position Sensor (TPS) – idling contacts not opening on increase from idling to 2500 rpm
E107	Low signal from Air Mass Meter (AMM)
E108	Filament burn-off function constantly actuated – Air Mass Meter (AMM)
E109	Low voltage from system relay
E112	Throttle Position Sensor (TPS) – full load contacts constantly closed
E207	High signal from Air Mass Meter (AMM)
E213	Continuous pulses to injectors
E320	DI/APC system Electronic Control Unit (ECU) – Pre-ignition signal constantly actuated

Year – 1986
Model – 900 (With LH 2.2)
Engine – 2.0L (121 cid) Turbo 4 cyl 16 valve

Engine Code – VIN L

ECM TROUBLE CODES

Code	Explanation
E001	No ignition pulse
E002	No signal from temperature sensor
E003	Throttle Position Sensor (TPS) – idling contacts not closing on idling
E005	Electronic Control Unit (ECU) pin 5 not grounding
E006	Air Mass Meter (AMM) not grounding
E007	No signal from Air Mass Meter (AMM)
E008	No filament burn-off function – Air Mass Meter (AMM)
E009	No power to system relay
E010	No signal from Electronic Control Unit (ECU) pin 10 to AIC valve
E011	Electronic Control Unit (ECU) pin 11 not grounding
E012	Throttle Position Sensor (TPS) – full throttle contacts constantly open
E014	Air Mass Meter (AMM) – break in CO – adjusting circuit
E017	Fuel pump relay – control circuit faulty
E018	No power at +15 supply terminal
E020	Faulty signal from Lambda sensor
E021	System relay control circuit faulty
E023	No signal from AIC valve
E025	Electronic Control Unit (ECU) pin 25 not grounding
E101	Starter motor revolutions too low
E102	Shorting in temperature sensor circuit
E103	Throttle Position Sensor (TPS) – idling contacts not opening on increase from idling to 2500 rpm
E107	Low signal from Air Mass Meter (AMM)
E108	Filament burn-off function constantly actuated – Air Mass Meter (AMM)
E109	Low voltage from system relay
E112	Throttle Position Sensor (TPS) – full load contacts constantly closed
E207	High signal from Air Mass Meter (AMM)
E213	Continuous pulses to injectors
E320	DI/APC system Electronic Control Unit (ECU) – Pre-ignition signal constantly actuated

Year — 1986
Model — 9000 (With LH 2.2)
Engine — 2.0L (121 cid) 4 cyl 16 valve
Engine Code — VIN D

ECM TROUBLE CODES

Code	Explanation
E001	No ignition pulse
E002	No signal from temperature sensor
E003	Throttle Position Sensor (TPS) — idling contacts not closing on idling
E005	Electronic Control Unit (ECU) pin 5 not grounding
E006	Air Mass Meter (AMM) not grounding
E007	No signal from Air Mass Meter (AMM)
E008	No filament burn-off function — Air Mass Meter (AMM)
E009	No power to system relay
E010	No signal from Electronic Control Unit (ECU) pin 10 to AIC valve
E011	Electronic Control Unit (ECU) pin 11 not grounding
E012	Throttle Position Sensor (TPS) — full throttle contacts constantly open
E014	Air Mass Meter (AMM) — break in CO — adjusting circuit
E017	Fuel pump relay — control circuit faulty
E018	No power at +15 supply terminal
E020	Faulty signal from Lambda sensor
E021	System relay control circuit faulty
E023	No signal from AIC valve
E025	Electronic Control Unit (ECU) pin 25 not grounding
E101	Starter motor revolutions too low
E102	Shorting in temperature sensor circuit
E103	Throttle Position Sensor (TPS) — idling contacts not opening on increase from idling to 2500 rpm
E107	Low signal from Air Mass Meter (AMM)
E108	Filament burn-off function constantly actuated — Air Mass Meter (AMM)
E109	Low voltage from system relay
E112	Throttle Position Sensor (TPS) — full load contacts constantly closed
E207	High signal from Air Mass Meter (AMM)
E213	Continuous pulses to injectors
E320	DI/APC system Electronic Control Unit (ECU) — Pre-ignition signal constantly actuated

Year – 1986
Model – 9000 (With LH 2.2)
Engine – 2.0L (121 cid) Turbo 4 cyl 16 valve
Engine Code – VIN L

ECM TROUBLE CODES

Code	Explanation
E001	No ignition pulse
E002	No signal from temperature sensor
E003	Throttle Position Sensor (TPS) – idling contacts not closing on idling
E005	Electronic Control Unit (ECU) pin 5 not grounding
E006	Air Mass Meter (AMM) not grounding
E007	No signal from Air Mass Meter (AMM)
E008	No filament burn-off function – Air Mass Meter (AMM)
E009	No power to system relay
E010	No signal from Electronic Control Unit (ECU) pin 10 to AIC valve
E011	Electronic Control Unit (ECU) pin 11 not grounding
E012	Throttle Position Sensor (TPS) – full throttle contacts constantly open
E014	Air Mass Meter (AMM) – break in CO – adjusting circuit
E017	Fuel pump relay – control circuit faulty
E018	No power at + 15 supply terminal
E020	Faulty signal from Lambda sensor
E021	System relay control circuit faulty
E023	No signal from AIC valve
E025	Electronic Control Unit (ECU) pin 25 not grounding
E101	Starter motor revolutions too low
E102	Shorting in temperature sensor circuit
E103	Throttle Position Sensor (TPS) – idling contacts not opening on increase from idling to 2500 rpm
E107	Low signal from Air Mass Meter (AMM)
E108	Filament burn-off function constantly actuated – Air Mass Meter (AMM)
E109	Low voltage from system relay
E112	Throttle Position Sensor (TPS) – full load contacts constantly closed
E207	High signal from Air Mass Meter (AMM)
E213	Continuous pulses to injectors
E320	DI/APC system Electronic Control Unit (ECU) – Pre-ignition signal constantly actuated

Year – 1987
Model – 900 (With LH 2.2)
Engine – 2.0L (121 cid) 4 cyl 16 valve
Engine Code – VIN D

ECM TROUBLE CODES

Code	Explanation
E001	No ignition pulse
E002	No signal from temperature sensor
E003	Throttle Position Sensor (TPS) – idling contacts not closing on idling
E005	Electronic Control Unit (ECU) pin 5 not grounding
E006	Air Mass Meter (AMM) not grounding
E007	No signal from Air Mass Meter (AMM)
E008	No filament burn-off function – Air Mass Meter (AMM)
E009	No power to system relay
E010	No signal from Electronic Control Unit (ECU) pin 10 to AIC valve
E011	Electronic Control Unit (ECU) pin 11 not grounding
E012	Throttle Position Sensor (TPS) – full throttle contacts constantly open
E014	Air Mass Meter (AMM) – break in CO – adjusting circuit
E017	Fuel pump relay – control circuit faulty
E018	No power at + 15 supply terminal
E020	Faulty signal from Lambda sensor
E021	System relay control circuit faulty
E023	No signal from AIC valve
E025	Electronic Control Unit (ECU) pin 25 not grounding
E101	Starter motor revolutions too low
E102	Shorting in temperature sensor circuit
E103	Throttle Position Sensor (TPS) – idling contacts not opening on increase from idling to 2500 rpm
E107	Low signal from Air Mass Meter (AMM)
E108	Filament burn-off function constantly actuated – Air Mass Meter (AMM)
E109	Low voltage from system relay
E112	Throttle Position Sensor (TPS) – full load contacts constantly closed
E207	High signal from Air Mass Meter (AMM)
E213	Continuous pulses to injectors
E320	DI/APC system Electronic Control Unit (ECU) – Pre-ignition signal constantly actuated

Year — 1987
Model — 900 (With LH 2.2)
Engine — 2.0L (121 cid) Turbo 4 cyl 16 valve
Engine Code — VIN L

ECM TROUBLE CODES

Code	Explanation
E001	No ignition pulse
E002	No signal from temperature sensor
E003	Throttle Position Sensor (TPS) — idling contacts not closing on idling
E005	Electronic Control Unit (ECU) pin 5 not grounding
E006	Air Mass Meter (AMM) not grounding
E007	No signal from Air Mass Meter (AMM)
E008	No filament burn-off function — Air Mass Meter (AMM)
E009	No power to system relay
E010	No signal from Electronic Control Unit (ECU) pin 10 to AIC valve
E011	Electronic Control Unit (ECU) pin 11 not grounding
E012	Throttle Position Sensor (TPS) — full throttle contacts constantly open
E014	Air Mass Meter (AMM) — break in CO — adjusting circuit
E017	Fuel pump relay — control circuit faulty
E018	No power at +15 supply terminal
E020	Faulty signal from Lambda sensor
E021	System relay control circuit faulty
E023	No signal from AIC valve
E025	Electronic Control Unit (ECU) pin 25 not grounding
E101	Starter motor revolutions too low
E102	Shorting in temperature sensor circuit
E103	Throttle Position Sensor (TPS) — idling contacts not opening on increase from idling to 2500 rpm
E107	Low signal from Air Mass Meter (AMM)
E108	Filament burn-off function constantly actuated — Air Mass Meter (AMM)
E109	Low voltage from system relay
E112	Throttle Position Sensor (TPS) — full load contacts constantly closed
E207	High signal from Air Mass Meter (AMM)
E213	Continuous pulses to injectors
E320	DI/APC system Electronic Control Unit (ECU) — Pre-ignition signal constantly actuated

Year — 1987
Model — 9000 (With LH 2.2)
Engine — 2.0L (121 cid) 4 cyl 16 valve
Engine Code — VIN D

ECM TROUBLE CODES

Code	Explanation
E001	No ignition pulse
E002	No signal from temperature sensor
E003	Throttle Position Sensor (TPS) — idling contacts not closing on idling
E005	Electronic Control Unit (ECU) pin 5 not grounding
E006	Air Mass Meter (AMM) not grounding
E007	No signal from Air Mass Meter (AMM)
E008	No filament burn-off function — Air Mass Meter (AMM)
E009	No power to system relay
E010	No signal from Electronic Control Unit (ECU) pin 10 to AIC valve
E011	Electronic Control Unit (ECU) pin 11 not grounding
E012	Throttle Position Sensor (TPS) — full throttle contacts constantly open
E014	Air Mass Meter (AMM) — break in CO — adjusting circuit
E017	Fuel pump relay — control circuit faulty
E018	No power at +15 supply terminal
E020	Faulty signal from Lambda sensor
E021	System relay control circuit faulty
E023	No signal from AIC valve
E025	Electronic Control Unit (ECU) pin 25 not grounding
E101	Starter motor revolutions too low
E102	Shorting in temperature sensor circuit
E103	Throttle Position Sensor (TPS) — idling contacts not opening on increase from idling to 2500 rpm
E107	Low signal from Air Mass Meter (AMM)
E108	Filament burn-off function constantly actuated — Air Mass Meter (AMM)
E109	Low voltage from system relay
E112	Throttle Position Sensor (TPS) — full load contacts constantly closed
E207	High signal from Air Mass Meter (AMM)
E213	Continuous pulses to injectors
E320	DI/APC system Electronic Control Unit (ECU) — Pre-ignition signal constantly actuated

Year — 1987
Model — 9000 (With LH 2.2)
Engine — 2.0L (121 cid) Turbo 4 cyl 16 valve
Engine Code — VIN L

ECM TROUBLE CODES

Code	Explanation
E001	No ignition pulse
E002	No signal from temperature sensor
E003	Throttle Position Sensor (TPS) — idling contacts not closing on idling
E005	Electronic Control Unit (ECU) pin 5 not grounding
E006	Air Mass Meter (AMM) not grounding
E007	No signal from Air Mass Meter (AMM)
E008	No filament burn-off function — Air Mass Meter (AMM)
E009	No power to system relay
E010	No signal from Electronic Control Unit (ECU) pin 10 to AIC valve
E011	Electronic Control Unit (ECU) pin 11 not grounding
E012	Throttle Position Sensor (TPS) — full throttle contacts constantly open
E014	Air Mass Meter (AMM) — break in CO — adjusting circuit
E017	Fuel pump relay — control circuit faulty
E018	No power at +15 supply terminal
E020	Faulty signal from Lambda sensor
E021	System relay control circuit faulty
E023	No signal from AIC valve
E025	Electronic Control Unit (ECU) pin 25 not grounding
E101	Starter motor revolutions too low
E102	Shorting in temperature sensor circuit
E103	Throttle Position Sensor (TPS) — idling contacts not opening on increase from idling to 2500 rpm
E107	Low signal from Air Mass Meter (AMM)
E108	Filament burn-off function constantly actuated — Air Mass Meter (AMM)
E109	Low voltage from system relay
E112	Throttle Position Sensor (TPS) — full load contacts constantly closed
E207	High signal from Air Mass Meter (AMM)
E213	Continuous pulses to injectors
E320	DI/APC system Electronic Control Unit (ECU) — Pre-ignition signal constantly actuated

Year – 1988
Model – 900 (With LH 2.2)
Engine – 2.0L (121 cid) 4 cyl 16 valve
Engine Code – VIN D

ECM TROUBLE CODES

Code	Explanation
E001	No ignition pulse
E002	No signal from temperature sensor
E003	Throttle Position Sensor (TPS) – idling contacts not closing on idling
E005	Electronic Control Unit (ECU) pin 5 not grounding
E006	Air Mass Meter (AMM) not grounding
E007	No signal from Air Mass Meter (AMM)
E008	No filament burn-off function – Air Mass Meter (AMM)
E009	No power to system relay
E010	No signal from Electronic Control Unit (ECU) pin 10 to AIC valve
E011	Electronic Control Unit (ECU) pin 11 not grounding
E012	Throttle Position Sensor (TPS) – full throttle contacts constantly open
E014	Air Mass Meter (AMM) – break in CO – adjusting circuit
E017	Fuel pump relay – control circuit faulty
E018	No power at +15 supply terminal
E020	Faulty signal from Lambda sensor
E021	System relay control circuit faulty
E023	No signal from AIC valve
E025	Electronic Control Unit (ECU) pin 25 not grounding
E101	Starter motor revolutions too low
E102	Shorting in temperature sensor circuit
E103	Throttle Position Sensor (TPS) – idling contacts not opening on increase from idling to 2500 rpm
E107	Low signal from Air Mass Meter (AMM)
E108	Filament burn-off function constantly actuated – Air Mass Meter (AMM)
E109	Low voltage from system relay
E112	Throttle Position Sensor (TPS) – full load contacts constantly closed
E207	High signal from Air Mass Meter (AMM)
E213	Continuous pulses to injectors
E320	DI/APC system Electronic Control Unit (ECU) – Pre-ignition signal constantly actuated

Year — 1988
Model — 900 (With LH 2.2)
Engine — 2.0L (121 cid) Turbo 4 cyl 16 valve

Engine Code — VIN L

ECM TROUBLE CODES

Code	Explanation
E001	No ignition pulse
E002	No signal from temperature sensor
E003	Throttle Position Sensor (TPS) — idling contacts not closing on idling
E005	Electronic Control Unit (ECU) pin 5 not grounding
E006	Air Mass Meter (AMM) not grounding
E007	No signal from Air Mass Meter (AMM)
E008	No filament burn-off function — Air Mass Meter (AMM)
E009	No power to system relay
E010	No signal from Electronic Control Unit (ECU) pin 10 to AIC valve
E011	Electronic Control Unit (ECU) pin 11 not grounding
E012	Throttle Position Sensor (TPS) — full throttle contacts constantly open
E014	Air Mass Meter (AMM) — break in CO — adjusting circuit
E017	Fuel pump relay — control circuit faulty
E018	No power at +15 supply terminal
E020	Faulty signal from Lambda sensor
E021	System relay control circuit faulty
E023	No signal from AIC valve
E025	Electronic Control Unit (ECU) pin 25 not grounding
E101	Starter motor revolutions too low
E102	Shorting in temperature sensor circuit
E103	Throttle Position Sensor (TPS) — idling contacts not opening on increase from idling to 2500 rpm
E107	Low signal from Air Mass Meter (AMM)
E108	Filament burn-off function constantly actuated — Air Mass Meter (AMM)
E109	Low voltage from system relay
E112	Throttle Position Sensor (TPS) — full load contacts constantly closed
E207	High signal from Air Mass Meter (AMM)
E213	Continuous pulses to injectors
E320	DI/APC system Electronic Control Unit (ECU) — Pre-ignition signal constantly actuated

Year — 1988
Model — 9000 (With LH 2.4)
Engine — 2.0L (121 cid) 4 cyl 16 valve
Engine Code — VIN D

ECM TROUBLE CODES

Code	Explanation
E001	No ignition pulse
E002	Throttle Position Sensor (TPS) — idling contacts not closing on idling
E003	Throttle Position Sensor (TPS) — full load contacts constantly open
E004	No battery voltage to Electronic Control Unit (ECU) memory function
E005	Electronic Control Unit (ECU) pin 5 not grounding
E006	Air Mass Meter (AMM) not grounding
E007	No signal from Air Mass Meter (AMM)
E008	No filament burn-off function — Air Mass Meter (AMM)
E009	No power to system relay
E013	No signal from temperature sensor
E017	Break in earth circuit continuity
E020	Fuel pump relay — control circuit faulty
E021	System realy control circuit faulty
E024	Faulty signal from Lambda sensor
E033	No signal to AIC valve from Electronic Control Unit (ECU) pin 3
E035	No power at +15 supply terminal
E101	Starter motor revolutions too low
E102	Throttle Position Sensor (TPS) — idling contacts not opening on increase from idling to 2500 rpm
E103	Throttle Position Sensor (TPS) — full load contacts constantly closed
E107	Low signal from Air Mass Meter (AMM)
E108	Filament burn-off function constantly actuated — Air Mass Meter (AMM)
E109	Low voltage from system relay
E113	Shorting in temperature sensor circuit
E207	High signal from Air Mass Meter (AMM)
E218	Continuous pulses to injectors
E328	Pre-ignition signal constantly earthed

Year — 1988
Model — 9000 (With LH 2.4)
Engine — 2.0L (121 cid) Turbo 4 cyl 16 valve
Engine Code — VIN L

ECM TROUBLE CODES

Code	Explanation
E001	No ignition pulse
E002	Throttle Position Sensor (TPS) — idling contacts not closing on idling
E003	Throttle Position Sensor (TPS) — full load contacts constantly open
E004	No battery voltage to Electronic Control Unit (ECU) memory function
E005	Electronic Control Unit (ECU) pin 5 not grounding
E006	Air Mass Meter (AMM) not grounding
E007	No signal from Air Mass Meter (AMM)
E008	No filament burn-off function — Air Mass Meter (AMM)
E009	No power to system relay
E013	No signal from temperature sensor
E017	Break in earth circuit continuity
E020	Fuel pump relay — control circuit faulty
E021	System realy control circuit faulty
E024	Faulty signal from Lambda sensor
E033	No signal to AIC valve from Electronic Control Unit (ECU) pin 3
E035	No power at +15 supply terminal
E101	Starter motor revolutions too low
E102	Throttle Position Sensor (TPS) — idling contacts not opening on increase from idling to 2500 rpm
E103	Throttle Position Sensor (TPS) — full load contacts constantly closed
E107	Low signal from Air Mass Meter (AMM)
E108	Filament burn-off function constantly actuated — Air Mass Meter (AMM)
E109	Low voltage from system relay
E113	Shorting in temperature sensor circuit
E207	High signal from Air Mass Meter (AMM)
E218	Continuous pulses to injectors
E328	Pre-ignition signal constantly earthed

Year — 1989
Model — 900 (With LH 2.4)
Engine — 2.0L (121 cid) 4 cyl 16 valve
Engine Code — VIN D

ECM TROUBLE CODES

Code	Explanation
E001	No ignition pulse
E002	Throttle Position Sensor (TPS) — idling contacts not closing on idling
E003	Throttle Position Sensor (TPS) — full load contacts constantly open
E004	No battery voltage to Electronic Control Unit (ECU) memory function
E005	Electronic Control Unit (ECU) pin 5 not grounding
E006	Air Mass Meter (AMM) not grounding
E007	No signal from Air Mass Meter (AMM)
E008	No filament burn-off function — Air Mass Meter (AMM)
E009	No power to system relay
E013	No signal from temperature sensor
E017	Break in earth circuit continuity
E020	Fuel pump relay — control circuit faulty
E021	System realy control circuit faulty
E024	Faulty signal from Lambda sensor
E033	No signal to AIC valve from Electronic Control Unit (ECU) pin 3
E035	No power at +15 supply terminal
E101	Starter motor revolutions too low
E102	Throttle Position Sensor (TPS) — idling contacts not opening on increase from idling to 2500 rpm
E103	Throttle Position Sensor (TPS) — full load contacts constantly closed
E107	Low signal from Air Mass Meter (AMM)
E108	Filament burn-off function constantly actuated — Air Mass Meter (AMM)
E109	Low voltage from system relay
E113	Shorting in temperature sensor circuit
E207	High signal from Air Mass Meter (AMM)
E218	Continuous pulses to injectors
E328	Pre-ignition signal constantly earthed

Year — 1989
Model — 900 (With LH 2.4)
Engine — 2.0L (121 cid) Turbo 4 cyl 16 valve
Engine Code — VIN L

ECM TROUBLE CODES

Code	Explanation
E001	No ignition pulse
E002	Throttle Position Sensor (TPS) — idling contacts not closing on idling
E003	Throttle Position Sensor (TPS) — full load contacts constantly open
E004	No battery voltage to Electronic Control Unit (ECU) memory function
E005	Electronic Control Unit (ECU) pin 5 not grounding
E006	Air Mass Meter (AMM) not grounding
E007	No signal from Air Mass Meter (AMM)
E008	No filament burn-off function — Air Mass Meter (AMM)
E009	No power to system relay
E013	No signal from temperature sensor
E017	Break in earth circuit continuity
E020	Fuel pump relay — control circuit faulty
E021	System realy control circuit faulty
E024	Faulty signal from Lambda sensor
E033	No signal to AIC valve from Electronic Control Unit (ECU) pin 3
E035	No power at +15 supply terminal
E101	Starter motor revolutions too low
E102	Throttle Position Sensor (TPS) — idling contacts not opening on increase from idling to 2500 rpm
E103	Throttle Position Sensor (TPS) — full load contacts constantly closed
E107	Low signal from Air Mass Meter (AMM)
E108	Filament burn-off function constantly actuated — Air Mass Meter (AMM)
E109	Low voltage from system relay
E113	Shorting in temperature sensor circuit
E207	High signal from Air Mass Meter (AMM)
E218	Continuous pulses to injectors
E328	Pre-ignition signal constantly earthed

Year – 1989
Model – 9000 (With LH 2.4)
Engine – 2.0L (121 cid) 4 cyl 16 valve
Engine Code – VIN D

ECM TROUBLE CODES

Code	Explanation
E001	No ignition pulse
E002	Throttle Position Sensor (TPS) – idling contacts not closing on idling
E003	Throttle Position Sensor (TPS) – full load contacts constantly open
E004	No battery voltage to Electronic Control Unit (ECU) memory function
E005	Electronic Control Unit (ECU) pin 5 not grounding
E006	Air Mass Meter (AMM) not grounding
E007	No signal from Air Mass Meter (AMM)
E008	No filament burn-off function – Air Mass Meter (AMM)
E009	No power to system relay
E013	No signal from temperature sensor
E017	Break in earth circuit continuity
E020	Fuel pump relay – control circuit faulty
E021	System realy control circuit faulty
E024	Faulty signal from Lambda sensor
E033	No signal to AIC valve from Electronic Control Unit (ECU) pin 3
E035	No power at +15 supply terminal
E101	Starter motor revolutions too low
E102	Throttle Position Sensor (TPS) – idling contacts not opening on increase from idling to 2500 rpm
E103	Throttle Position Sensor (TPS) – full load contacts constantly closed
E107	Low signal from Air Mass Meter (AMM)
E108	Filament burn-off function constantly actuated – Air Mass Meter (AMM)
E109	Low voltage from system relay
E113	Shorting in temperature sensor circuit
E207	High signal from Air Mass Meter (AMM)
E218	Continuous pulses to injectors
E328	Pre-ignition signal constantly earthed

Year — 1989
Model — 9000 (With LH 2.4)
Engine — 2.0L (121 cid) Turbo 4 cyl 16 valve
Engine Code — VIN L

ECM TROUBLE CODES

Code	Explanation
E001	No ignition pulse
E002	Throttle Position Sensor (TPS) — idling contacts not closing on idling
E003	Throttle Position Sensor (TPS) — full load contacts constantly open
E004	No battery voltage to Electronic Control Unit (ECU) memory function
E005	Electronic Control Unit (ECU) pin 5 not grounding
E006	Air Mass Meter (AMM) not grounding
E007	No signal from Air Mass Meter (AMM)
E008	No filament burn-off function — Air Mass Meter (AMM)
E009	No power to system relay
E013	No signal from temperature sensor
E017	Break in earth circuit continuity
E020	Fuel pump relay — control circuit faulty
E021	System realy control circuit faulty
E024	Faulty signal from Lambda sensor
E033	No signal to AIC valve from Electronic Control Unit (ECU) pin 3
E035	No power at +15 supply terminal
E101	Starter motor revolutions too low
E102	Throttle Position Sensor (TPS) — idling contacts not opening on increase from idling to 2500 rpm
E103	Throttle Position Sensor (TPS) — full load contacts constantly closed
E107	Low signal from Air Mass Meter (AMM)
E108	Filament burn-off function constantly actuated — Air Mass Meter (AMM)
E109	Low voltage from system relay
E113	Shorting in temperature sensor circuit
E207	High signal from Air Mass Meter (AMM)
E218	Continuous pulses to injectors
E328	Pre-ignition signal constantly earthed

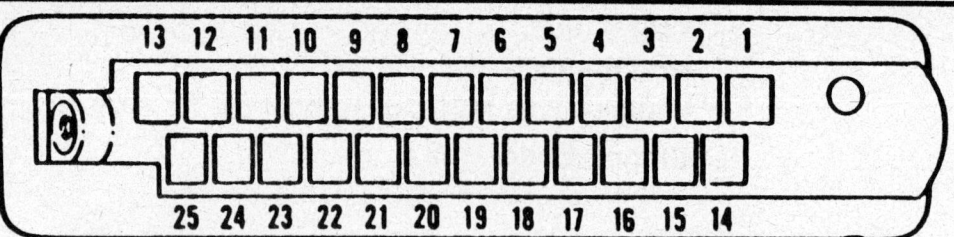

Key to ECU pins

Pin no.	Cable colour	Circuit to:	Pin no.	Cable colour	Circuit to:
1	Blue (BL)	Ignition-pulse amplifier, pin 17	13	Green/red (GN/RD)	Control signal to injectors
2	Yellow (GL)	Temperature sensor	14	White (VT)	Air mass meter pin 6
3	Grey (GR)	Throttle-position sensor, pin 1	16	Red/white (RD/VT)	AC compressor pin 9 (idling increase)
4	Orange (OR)	DRIVE-position signal (Automatics)	17	Violet (VL)	Fuel-pump relay pin 85
5	Black (SV)	Earthing point 201	18	Green/white (GN/VT)	+15 terminal on power distribution panel
6	Blue/white (BL/VT)	Air mass meter pin 2	19	Violet/white (VL/VT)	Test socket pin 2
7	Orange (OR)	Air mass meter pin 3	20	White (VT)	DI/APC-system ECU pin 26
8	Red/white (RD/VT)	Air mass meter pin 4	21	Yellow/white (GL/VT)	System relay pin 85
9	Grey/white (GR/VT)	System relay pin 87	22	Green (GN)	Test socket pin 3
10	Blue/white (BL/VT)	AIC valve pin 1	23	Yellow/red (GL/RD)	AIC valve pin 3
11	Black (SV)	Earthing point 201	24	Blue/red (BL/RD)	Tq load signal (Turbo with DI and i/S with EZK)
12	Green/red (GN/RD)	Throttle-position sensor	25	Black/white (SV/VT)	Ea rthing point 201

Electronic control unit test pin location – LH 2.2 system

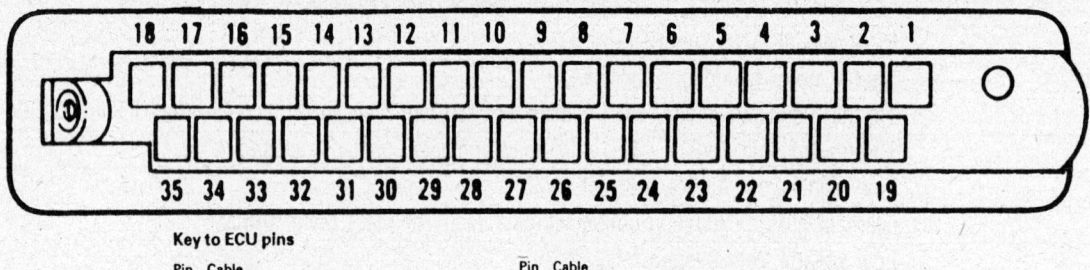

Key to ECU pins

Pin no.	Cable colour	Circuit to.	Pin no.	Cable colour	Circuit to:
1	Blue (BL)	Output module (146), pin 7	18	Green/red (GN/RD)	Injectors
2	Grey (GR)	Throttle-position sensor (203), pin 1	20	Violet (VL)	Fuel-pump relay (102) pin 85
3	Green/red (GN/RD)	Connector 75	21	Yellow/white (GL/VT)	System relay (229) pin 85
4	Red (RD)	Connector 75	22	Violet/white (VT/VT)	+15 terminal on distribution panel and test socket (code flashes) pin 2
5	Black (SV)	Earthing point (201)	24	Black (SV)	Lambda sensor
6	Blue/white (BL/VT)	Air mass meter (205), pin 2	25	Blue/red (BL/RD)	EZK-system ECU pin 8 (DI/APC-system ECU pin 36)
7	Orange (OR)	Air mass meter (205), pin 3	26	White (VT)	SHIFT-UP light (US)
8	Red/white (RD/VT)	Air mass meter (205), pin 4	27	Yellow/red (GL/RD)	Charcoal filter
9	Grey/white (GR/VT)	System relay (229), pin 87	28	White (VT)	PRE-IGN, DI/APC-system ECU pin 26
12	Blue/white (BL/VT)	Test socket (347), pin 1	29	Grey/white (GR/VT)	LH 2.4 coding
13	Yellow (GL)	Temperature sensor (202)	30 (OR)	Orange (Automatics)	Idling-increase switch (76),
14	Red/white (RD/VT)	AC relay (156), pin 9	32	Brown (BR)	Cold-start valve
15	Green/yellow (GN/GL)	Strap for cold-start valve (368)	33	Blue/white (B L/VT)	AIC valve
16	Green/red (GN/RD)	Test socket (347) pin 2	34	Green (GN)	Speed sensor pin 2
17	Black/white (SV/VT)	Test socket (204) code flashes, pin 1 Earthing point 201	35	Green/white (GN/VT)	+15 supply terminal (159)

Electronic control unit test pin location – LH 2.4 system

INDEX

SUBARU

Fuel Injection and Carburetor Control Systems

SELF-DIAGNOSTIC SYSTEM

Description

Most vehicles, except Justy, use 2 types of fuel injection systems: Multi-Point Fuel Injection (MPFI) and Single-Point Fuel Injection (SPFI); the self-diagnosis is virtually the same for both. Justy uses the Electronic Fuel-Controlled (EFC) Carburetor system.

The self-diagnosis system detects and indicates a fault in various inputs and outputs of the complex electronic control. The "Check Engine" light on the instrument panel indicates the occurrence of a fault or trouble and the Light Emitting Diode (LED) or oxygen (O_2) monitor lamp in the Electronic Control Unit (ECU) indicates a trouble code.

Further, against such a failure of sensors as may disable the drive, the fail-safe function is provided to ensure the minimal driveability.

FAIL-SAFE FUNCTION

On the fuel injected models, the part which has been judged faulty in the self-diagnosis, the Electronic Control Unit (ECU) generates the associated pseudo signal (only when convertible to electric signal) and caries out the computational processing. In this fashion, the fail-safe function is performed.

FUNCTION OF SELF-DIAGNOSIS

The self-diagnosis has 4 modes: U-check mode, Read memory mode, D-check mode and Clear memory mode. Two connectors (Read memory and Test mode) and 2 lamps (Check Engine light and oxygen monitor) are used. The connectors are for mode selection and the lamps monitor the type of problem.

READING TROUBLE CODES

The oxygen (O_2) monitor lamp flashes the code corresponding to the faulty part.

The long segment (1.2 sec., turned **ON**) indicates the tenth digit and the short segment (0.2 sec., turned **ON**) signifies the single digit.

Entering Diagnostic Mode

U-CHECK MODE

The U-check is a user-oriented mode in which only the components necessary for start-up and drive are diagnosed. On occurrence of a fault, the "Check Engine" light is turned ON to indicate that system inspection is necessary. The diagnosis of other parts which do not give significant adverse effect to start-up and drive are excluded from this mode in order to avoid unnecessary uneasiness to be taken by the user.

READ MEMORY MODE

1. Turn the ignition switch **OFF**.
2. Connect the read memory connector.
3. Turn the ignition switch **ON** with the engine **OFF**.
4. If the "Check Engine" light turns ON, trouble code(s) are present.
5. If the oxygen (O_2) monitor lamp turns ON, code(s) are being produced; confirm the trouble code(s).
6. Disconnect the read memory connector.
7. Perform the D-Check Mode.

D-CHECK MODE

1. Start the engine and warm it to normal operating temperatures.
2. Turn the ignition switch **OFF**.
3. Connect the test mode connector.
4. Turn the ignition switch ON with the engine **OFF**.
5. Make sure the "Check Engine" light turns ON; there should also be noise from the operation of the fuel pump.
6. Depress the accelerator pedal completely. Return it to ½ throttle position and hold it there for 2 seconds, then, release the pedal completely.
7. Start the engine; the "Check Engine" light should turn OFF.
8. Race the engine with the throttle fully opened.

Mode	Read memory connector	Test mode connector
U-check	DISCONNECT	DISCONNECT
Read memory	CONNECT	DISCONNECT
D-check	DISCONNECT	CONNECT
(Clear memory)	CONNECT	CONNECT

Example:

When only one part has failed:
Flashing code 12
(unit: second)

When two or more parts have failed:
Flashing codes 12 and 21
(unit: second)

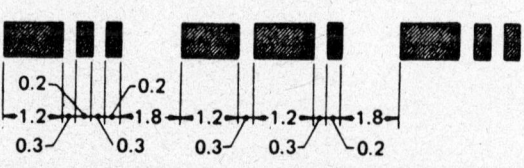

Description of the trouble codes

9. Drive the vehicle above 5 mph for at least 1 minute; warm the engine above 1500 rpm.

10. If the "Check Engine" light blinks, there are no trouble codes. If the "Check Engine" light stays ON, trouble codes are present and must be read.

Clearing Diagnostic Memory

1. Start the engine and warm it to normal operating temperatures.

2. Turn the ignition switch **OFF**.

3. Connect the test mode connector and the read memory connector.

4. Turn the ignition switch **ON** with the engine **OFF**.

5. Make sure the "Check Engine" light turns ON.

6. Depress the accelerator pedal completely. Return it to ½ throttle position and hold it there for 2 seconds, then, release the pedal completely.

7. Start the engine; the "Check Engine" light should turn OFF.

8. Race the engine with the throttle fully opened.

9. Drive the vehicle above 5 mph for at least 1 minute; warm the engine above 1500 rpm.

10. The "Check Engine" light should blink; there are no trouble codes. If the "Check Engine" light stays ON, read the trouble codes and reperform the D-check mode.

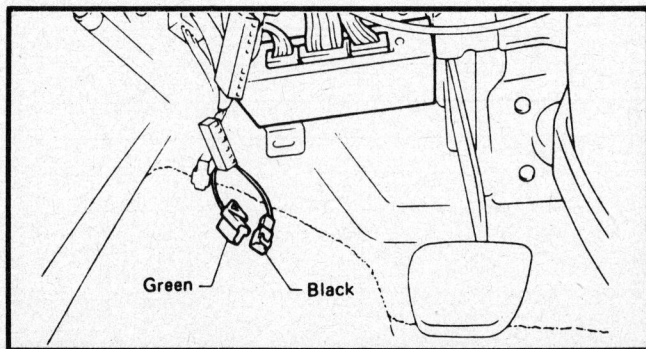

Location of Electronic Control Unit (ECU) and test connectors—Justy

11. Turn the ignition switch **OFF**.

12. Disconnect the test mode and the read memory connectors.

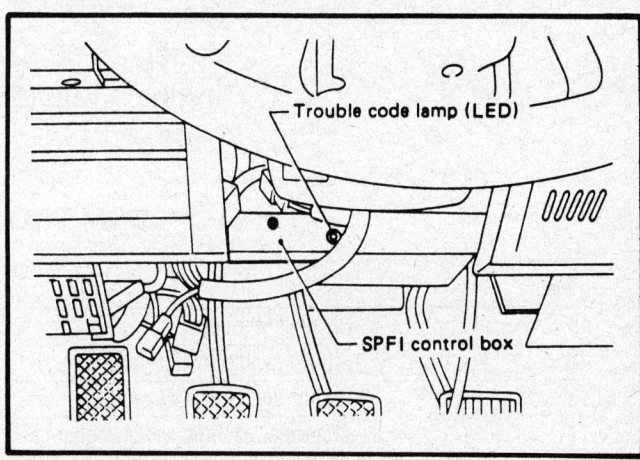

Location of Electronic Control Unit (ECU)—DL and GL models

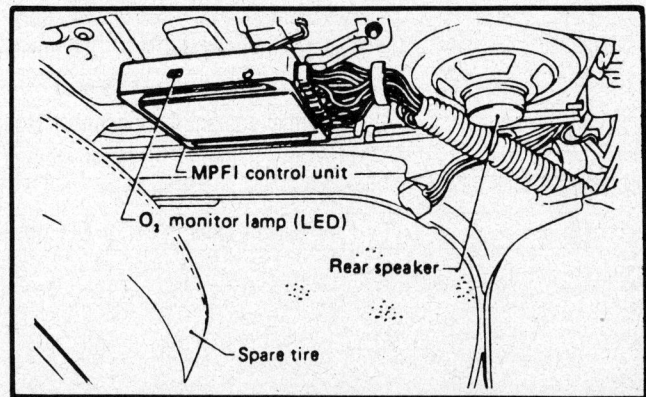

Location of Electronic Control Unit (ECU)—XT-Series

SUBARU

Year – 1984
Model – 1600 Series
Engine – 1.6L (96 cid) EGI 4 cyl
Code – VIN 2

ECM TROUBLE CODES

Code	Explanation
11	No ignition pulse
12	Starter switch in OFF mode
13	Starter switch in ON mode
14	Abnormal air flow meter signal
21	Seized air flow meter flap
22	Pressusre switch fixed in ON or OFF position
23	Idle switch fixed in ON or OFF position
24	Full switch fixed in ON or OFF position
32	Abnormal oxygen sensor signal
33	Abnormal coolant thermosensor signal
34	Abnormal aspirated air thermosensor signal
41	Open or ground in sensor
42	Fuel injector fixed in ON or OFF position

Year — 1984
Model — 1600 Series
Engine — 1.6L (96 cid) ECC 4 cyl
Code — VIN 2

ECM TROUBLE CODES

Code	Explanation
11	Ignition pulse system (NG) — engine OFF — manual transmission — Carter carburetor
12	Ignition pulse system (NG) — engine OFF — automatic transmission — Carter carburetor
13	Ignition pulse system (NG) — engine OFF — 49-state manual transmission — Hitachi carburetor
14	Ignition pulse system (NG) — engine OFF — 49-state automatic transmission — Hitachi carburetor
15	Ignition pulse system (NG) — engine OFF — manual transmission — Carter carburetor
16	Ignition pulse system (NG) — engine OFF — automatic transmission — Carter carburetor
17	Ignition pulse system (NG) — engine OFF — 49-state manual transmission — Hitachi carburetor
18	Ignition pulse system (NG) — engine OFF — 49-state automatic transmisssion — Hitachi carburetor
22	Car speed sensor system (NG) — automatic transmission in test mode only
23	Oxygen sensor system (NG)
24	Thermo sensor system (NG) — engine water temp. below 68°F (20°C)
25	Thermo sensor system (NG) — engine water temp. above 230°F (110°C)
31	Duty solenoid valve remains ON
32	Duty solenoid valve remains OFF
33	Main system in feedback system (NG) — in test mode only
34	Back-up system (NG) — back-up memory not high
35	Back-up system (NG) — back-up memory not low
42	Vacuum switch II remains ON — in test mode only
43	Vacuum switch II remains OFF — in test mode only
44	Vacuum switch I remains ON — in test mode only
45	Vacuum switch I remains OFF — in test mode only
52	Solenoid valve I remains ON
53	Solenoid valve I remains OFF
55	Auto choke power remains OFF
54	Auto choke power remains ON
62	Solenoid valve II remains ON — automatic transmission in test mode and 49-state model manual transmission (excluding 4WD) only are diagnosed
63	Solenoid valve II remains OFF — automatic transmission in test mode and 49-state model manual transmission (excluding 4WD) only are diagnosed
73	Ignition pulse system (NG) — engine OFF — California manual transmission — Hitachi carburetor
77	Ignition pulse system (NG) — engine OFF — California manual transmission — Hitachi carburetor

Year – 1984
Model – 1800 Series
Engine – 1.8L (109 cid) EGI 4 cyl
Code – VIN 5

ECM TROUBLE CODES

Code	Explanation
11	No ignition pulse
12	Starter switch in OFF mode
13	Starter switch in ON mode
14	Abnormal air flow meter signal
21	Seized air flow meter flap
22	Pressusre switch fixed in ON or OFF position
23	Idle switch fixed in ON or OFF position
24	Full switch fixed in ON or OFF position
32	Abnormal oxygen sensor signal
33	Abnormal coolant thermosensor signal
34	Abnormal aspirated air thermosensor signal
41	Open or ground in sensor
42	Fuel injector fixed in ON or OFF position

Year — 1984
Model — 1800 Series
Engine — 1.8L (109 cid) ECC 4 cyl
Code — VIN 5

ECM TROUBLE CODES

Code	Explanation
11	Ignition pulse system (NG) — engine OFF — manual transmission — Carter carburetor
12	Ignition pulse system (NG) — engine OFF — automatic transmission — Carter carburetor
13	Ignition pulse system (NG) — engine OFF — 49-state manual transmission — Hitachi carburetor
14	Ignition pulse system (NG) — engine OFF — 49-state automatic transmission — Hitachi carburetor
15	Ignition pulse system (NG) — engine OFF — manual transmission — Carter carburetor
16	Ignition pulse system (NG) — engine OFF — automatic transmission — Carter carburetor
17	Ignition pulse system (NG) — engine OFF — 49-state manual transmission — Hitachi carburetor
18	Ignition pulse system (NG) — engine OFF — 49-state automatic transmisssion — Hitachi carburetor
22	Car speed sensor system (NG) — automatic transmission in test mode only
23	Oxygen sensor system (NG)
24	Thermo sensor system (NG) — engine water temp. below 68°F (20°C)
25	Thermo sensor system (NG) — engine water temp. above 230°F (110°C)
31	Duty solenoid valve remains ON
32	Duty solenoid valve remains OFF
33	Main system in feedback system (NG) — in test mode only
34	Back-up system (NG) — back-up memory not high
35	Back-up system (NG) — back-up memory not low
42	Vacuum switch II remains ON — in test mode only
43	Vacuum switch II remains OFF — in test mode only
44	Vacuum switch I remains ON — in test mode only
45	Vacuum switch I remains OFF — in test mode only
52	Solenoid valve I remains ON
53	Solenoid valve I remains OFF
55	Auto choke power remains OFF
54	Auto choke power remains ON
62	Solenoid valve II remains ON — automatic transmission in test mode and 49-state model manual transmission (excluding 4WD) only are diagnosed
63	Solenoid valve II remains OFF — automatic transmission in test mode and 49-state model manual transmission (excluding 4WD) only are diagnosed
73	Ignition pulse system (NG) — engine OFF — California manual transmission — Hitachi carburetor
77	Ignition pulse system (NG) — engine OFF — California manual transmission — Hitachi carburetor

Year — 1984
Model — 1800 Series (GL Models)
Engine — 1.8L (109 cid) EGI 4 cyl
Code — VIN 4

ECM TROUBLE CODES

Code	Explanation
11	No ignition pulse
12	Starter switch in OFF mode
13	Starter switch in ON mode
14	Abnormal air flow meter signal
21	Seized air flow meter flap
22	Pressusre switch fixed in ON or OFF position
23	Idle switch fixed in ON or OFF position
24	Full switch fixed in ON or OFF position
32	Abnormal oxygen sensor signal
33	Abnormal coolant thermosensor signal
34	Abnormal aspirated air thermosensor signal
41	Open or ground in sensor
42	Fuel injector fixed in ON or OFF position

Year — 1984
Model — 1800 Series (GL Models)
Engine — 1.8L (109 cid) ECC 4 cyl
Code — VIN 4

ECM TROUBLE CODES

Code	Explanation
11	Ignition pulse system (NG) — engine OFF — manual transmission — Carter carburetor
12	Ignition pulse system (NG) — engine OFF — automatic transmission — Carter carburetor
13	Ignition pulse system (NG) — engine OFF — 49-state manual transmission — Hitachi carburetor
14	Ignition pulse system (NG) — engine OFF — 49-state automatic transmission — Hitachi carburetor
15	Ignition pulse system (NG) — engine OFF — manual transmission — Carter carburetor
16	Ignition pulse system (NG) — engine OFF — automatic transmission — Carter carburetor
17	Ignition pulse system (NG) — engine OFF — 49-state manual transmission — Hitachi carburetor
18	Ignition pulse system (NG) — engine OFF — 49-state automatic transmisssion — Hitachi carburetor
22	Car speed sensor system (NG) — automatic transmission in test mode only
23	Oxygen sensor system (NG)
24	Thermo sensor system (NG) — engine water temp. below 68°F (20°C)
25	Thermo sensor system (NG) — engine water temp. above 230°F (110°C)
31	Duty solenoid valve remains ON
32	Duty solenoid valve remains OFF
33	Main system in feedback system (NG) — in test mode only
34	Back-up system (NG) — back-up memory not high
35	Back-up system (NG) — back-up memory not low
42	Vacuum switch II remains ON — in test mode only
43	Vacuum switch II remains OFF — in test mode only
44	Vacuum switch I remains ON — in test mode only
45	Vacuum switch I remains OFF — in test mode only
52	Solenoid valve I remains ON
53	Solenoid valve I remains OFF
55	Auto choke power remains OFF
54	Auto choke power remains ON
62	Solenoid valve II remains ON — automatic transmission in test mode and 49-state model manual transmission (excluding 4WD) only are diagnosed
63	Solenoid valve II remains OFF — automatic transmission in test mode and 49-state model manual transmission (excluding 4WD) only are diagnosed
73	Ignition pulse system (NG) — engine OFF — California manual transmission — Hitachi carburetor
77	Ignition pulse system (NG) — engine OFF — California manual transmission — Hitachi carburetor

Year — 1985
Model — 1800 Series (2WD)
Engine — 1.8L (109 cid) MPFI 4 cyl
Engine Code — VIN 4

ECM TROUBLE CODES

Code	Explanation
11	No ignition pulse
12	Starter switch in OFF mode
13	Starter switch in ON mode
14	Abnormal air flow meter signal
21	Seized air flow meter flap
22	Pressure or vacuum switch fixed in ON or OFF position
23	Idle switch fixed in ON or OFF position
24	Wide Open Throttle (WOT) switch fixed in ON or OFF position
31	Abnormal speed sensor signal
32	Abnormal oxygen sensor signal
33	Abnormal coolant thermosensor signal
34	Abnormal aspirated air thermosensor signal
35	Exhaust Gas Recirculation (EGR) solenoid switch fixed in ON or OFF position
41	Abnormal atmospheric pressure sensor signal
42	Fuel injector fixed in ON or OFF position
43	Kickdown Low Hold (KDLH) relay fixed in ON or OFF position

Year – 1985
Model – 1800 Series (4WD)
Engine – 1.8L (109 cid) MPFI 4 cyl
Engine Code – VIN 5

ECM TROUBLE CODES

Code	Explanation
11	No ignition pulse
12	Starter switch in OFF mode
13	Starter switch in ON mode
14	Abnormal air flow meter signal
21	Seized air flow meter flap
22	Pressure or vacuum switch fixed in ON or OFF position
23	Idle switch fixed in ON or OFF position
24	Wide Open Throttle (WOT) switch fixed in ON or OFF position
31	Abnormal speed sensor signal
32	Abnormal oxygen sensor signal
33	Abnormal coolant thermosensor signal
34	Abnormal aspirated air thermosensor signal
35	Exhaust Gas Recirculation (EGR) solenoid switch fixed in ON or OFF position
41	Abnormal atmospheric pressure sensor signal
42	Fuel injector fixed in ON or OFF position
43	Kickdown Low Hold (KDLH) relay fixed in ON or OFF position

Year – 1985
Model – XT Series (2WD)
Engine – 1.8L (109 cid) MPFI 4 cyl
Engine Code – VIN 4

ECM TROUBLE CODES

Code	Explanation
11	No ignition pulse
12	Starter switch in OFF mode
13	Starter switch in ON mode
14	Abnormal air flow meter signal
21	Seized air flow meter flap
22	Pressure or vacuum switch fixed in ON or OFF position
23	Idle switch fixed in ON or OFF position
24	Wide Open Throttle (WOT) switch fixed in ON or OFF position
31	Abnormal speed sensor signal
32	Abnormal oxygen sensor signal
33	Abnormal coolant thermosensor signal
34	Abnormal aspirated air thermosensor signal
35	Exhaust Gas Recirculation (EGR) solenoid switch fixed in ON or OFF position
41	Abnormal atmospheric pressure sensor signal
42	Fuel injector fixed in ON or OFF position
43	Kickdown Low Hold (KDLH) relay fixed in ON or OFF position

Year — 1985
Model — XT Series (4WD)
Engine — 1.8L (109 cid) MPFI 4 cyl
Engine Code — VIN 7

ECM TROUBLE CODES

Code	Explanation
11	No ignition pulse
12	Starter switch in OFF mode
13	Starter switch in ON mode
14	Abnormal air flow meter signal
21	Seized air flow meter flap
22	Pressure or vacuum switch fixed in ON or OFF position
23	Idle switch fixed in ON or OFF position
24	Wide Open Throttle (WOT) switch fixed in ON or OFF position
31	Abnormal speed sensor signal
32	Abnormal oxygen sensor signal
33	Abnormal coolant thermosensor signal
34	Abnormal aspirated air thermosensor signal
35	Exhaust Gas Recirculation (EGR) solenoid switch fixed in ON or OFF position
41	Abnormal atmospheric pressure sensor signal
42	Fuel injector fixed in ON or OFF position
43	Kickdown Low Hold (KDLH) relay fixed in ON or OFF position

Year — 1986
Model — 1800 Series (2WD)
Engine — 1.8L (109 cid) MPFI 4 cyl
Engine Code — VIN 4

ECM TROUBLE CODES

Code	Explanation
11	No ignition pulse
12	Starter switch in OFF mode
13	Starter switch in ON mode
14	Abnormal air flow meter signal
21	Seized air flow meter flap
22	Pressure or vacuum switch fixed in ON or OFF position
23	Idle switch fixed in ON or OFF position
24	Wide Open Throttle (WOT) switch fixed in ON or OFF position
31	Abnormal speed sensor signal
32	Abnormal oxygen sensor signal
33	Abnormal coolant thermosensor signal
34	Abnormal aspirated air thermosensor signal
35	Exhaust Gas Recirculation (EGR) solenoid switch fixed in ON or OFF position
41	Abnormal atmospheric pressure sensor signal
42	Fuel injector fixed in ON or OFF position
43	Kickdown Low Hold (KDLH) relay fixed in ON or OFF position

Year — 1986
Model — 1800 Series (4WD)
Engine — 1.8L (109 cid) MPFI 4 cyl
Engine Code — VIN 5

ECM TROUBLE CODES

Code	Explanation
11	No ignition pulse
12	Starter switch in OFF mode
13	Starter switch in ON mode
14	Abnormal air flow meter signal
15	Pressure switch fixed in ON or OFF position
21	Seized air flow meter flap
22	Pressure or vacuum switch fixed in ON or OFF position
23	Idle switch fixed in ON or OFF position
24	Wide Open Throttle (WOT) switch fixed in ON or OFF position
31	Abnormal speed sensor signal
32	Abnormal oxygen sensor signal
33	Abnormal coolant thermosensor signal
34	Abnormal aspirated air thermosensor signal
35	Exhaust Gas Recirculation (EGR) solenoid switch fixed in ON or OFF position
41	Abnormal atmospheric pressure sensor signal
42	Fuel injector fixed in ON or OFF position
43	Kickdown Low Hold (KDLH) relay fixed in ON or OFF position

Year—1986
Model—1800 Series (2WD)
Engine—1.8L (109 cid) SPFI 4 cyl
Engine Code—VIN 4

ECM TROUBLE CODES

Code	Explanation
11	Ignition pulse
16	Crank angle sensor
17	Stater switch—indicates items which develop problems after operating in excess of 1500 rpm for a specified time. With other items, problems are indicated immediately after detection
25	Throttle sensor—idle switch—indicates items which develop problems after operating in excess of 1500 rpm for a specified time. With other items, problems are indicated immediately after detection
31	Car speed sensor—indicates items which develop problems after operating in excess of 1500 rpm for a specified time. With other items, problems are indicated immediately after detection
32	O_2 sensor—indicates items which develop problems after operating in excess of 1500 rpm for a specified time. With other items, problems are indicated immediately after detection
33	Coolant thermosensor
35	Air flow meter
42	Fuel injector
46	Neutral switch—parking switch—indicates items which develop problems after operating in excess of 1500 rpm for a specified time. With other items, problems are indicated immediately after detection
53	Fuel pump
55	Kickdown Low Hold (KDLH) control system—indicates items which develop problems after operating in excess of 1500 rpm for a specified time. With other items, problems are indicated immediately after detection
57	Canister control system—indicates items which develop problems after operating in excess of 1500 rpm for a specified time. With other items, problems are indicated immediately after detection
58	Air control valve—indicates items which develop problems after operating in excess of 1500 rpm for a specified time. With other items, problems are indicated immediately after detection
62	Exhaust Gas Recirculation (EGR) control system—indicates items which develop problems after operating in excess of 1500 rpm for a specified time. With other items, problems are indicated immediately after detection
88	Single Point Fuel Injection (SPFI) control unit-indicates items which develop problems after operating in excess of 1500 rpm for a specified time. With other items, problems are indicated immediately after detection

Year – 1986
Model – 1800 Series (4WD)
Engine – 1.8L (109 cid) SPFI 4 cyl
Engine Code – VIN 5

ECM TROUBLE CODES

Code	Explanation
11	Ignition pulse
16	Crank angle sensor
17	Stater switch – indicates items which develop problems after operating in excess of 1500 rpm for a specified time. With other items, problems are indicated immediately after detection
25	Throttle sensor – idle switch – indicates items which develop problems after operating in excess of 1500 rpm for a specified time. With other items, problems are indicated immediately after detection
31	Car speed sensor – indicates items which develop problems after operating in excess of 1500 rpm for a specified time. With other items, problems are indicated immediately after detection
32	O_2 sensor – indicates items which develop problems after operating in excess of 1500 rpm for a specified time. With other items, problems are indicated immediately after detection
33	Coolant thermosensor
35	Air flow meter
42	Fuel injector
46	Neutral switch – parking switch – indicates items which develop problems after operating in excess of 1500 rpm for a specified time. With other items, problems are indicated immediately after detection
53	Fuel pump
55	Kickdown Low Hold (KDLH) control system – indicates items which develop problems after operating in excess of 1500 rpm for a specified time. With other items, problems are indicated immediately after detection
57	Canister control system – indicates items which develop problems after operating in excess of 1500 rpm for a specified time. With other items, problems are indicated immediately after detection
58	Air control valve – indicates items which develop problems after operating in excess of 1500 rpm for a specified time. With other items, problems are indicated immediately after detection
62	Exhaust Gas Recirculation (EGR) control system – indicates items which develop problems after operating in excess of 1500 rpm for a specified time. With other items, problems are indicated immediately after detection
88	Single Point Fuel Injection (SPFI) control unit-indicates items which develop problems after operating in excess of 1500 rpm for a specified time. With other items, problems are indicated immediately after detection

Year – 1986
Model – 1800 Series (2WD)
Engine – 1.8L (109 cid) MPFI 4 cyl
Engine Code – VIN 4

ECM TROUBLE CODES

Code	Explanation
11	No ignition pulse
12	Starter switch in OFF mode
13	Starter switch in ON mode
14	Abnormal air flow meter signal
15	Pressure switch fixed in ON or OFF position
21	Seized air flow meter flap
22	Pressure or vacuum switch fixed in ON or OFF position
23	Idle switch fixed in ON or OFF position
24	Wide Open Throttle (WOT) switch fixed in ON or OFF position
31	Abnormal speed sensor signal
32	Abnormal oxygen sensor signal
33	Abnormal coolant thermosensor signal
34	Abnormal aspirated air thermosensor signal
35	Exhaust Gas Recirculation (EGR) solenoid switch fixed in ON or OFF position
41	Abnormal atmospheric pressure sensor signal
42	Fuel injector fixed in ON or OFF position
43	Kickdown Low Hold (KDLH) relay fixed in ON or OFF position

Year — 1986
Model — XT Series (4WD)
Engine — 1.8L (109 cid) MPFI 4 cyl
Engine Code — VIN 7

ECM TROUBLE CODES

Code	Explanation
11	No ignition pulse
12	Starter switch in OFF mode
13	Starter switch in ON mode
14	Abnormal air flow meter signal
15	Pressure switch fixed in ON or OFF position
21	Seized air flow meter flap
22	Pressure or vacuum switch fixed in ON or OFF position
23	Idle switch fixed in ON or OFF position
24	Wide Open Throttle (WOT) switch fixed in ON or OFF position
31	Abnormal speed sensor signal
32	Abnormal oxygen sensor signal
33	Abnormal coolant thermosensor signal
34	Abnormal aspirated air thermosensor signal
35	Exhaust Gas Recirculation (EGR) solenoid switch fixed in ON or OFF position
41	Abnormal atmospheric pressure sensor signal
42	Fuel injector fixed in ON or OFF position
43	Kickdown Low Hold (KDLH) relay fixed in ON or OFF position

Year – 1987
Model – 1800 Series (2WD)
Engine – 1.8L (109 cid) MPFI 4 cyl
Engine Code – VIN 4

ECM TROUBLE CODES

Code	Explanation
11	Crank angle sensor – no reference pulse
12	Starter switch – continuously in ON or OFF position while cranking
13	Crank angle sensor – no position pulse
14	Fuel injector – abnormal injector output
21	Water temperature sensor – open or shorted circuit
23	Air flow meter – open or shorted circuit
24	Air control valve – open or shorted circuit
31	Throttle sensor – open or shorted circuit
32	Oxygen sensor – abnormal sensor signal
33	Car-speed sensor – no signal is present during operation
34	Exhaust Gas Recirculation (EGR) solenoid valve – solenoid switch continuously in ON or OFF position
35	Purge control solenoid valve – solenoid switch continuously in ON or OFF position
42	Idle switch – abnormal idle switch signal in relation to throttle sensor output
45	Kickdown control relay – continuously in ON or OFF position
51	Neutral switch – continuously in ON position
61	Parking switch – continuously in ON position

Year — 1987
Model — 1800 Series (4WD)
Engine — 1.8L (109 cid) SPFI 4 cyl
Engine Code — VIN 5

ECM TROUBLE CODES

Code	Explanation
11	Crank angle sensor — no reference pulse
12	Starter switch — continuously in ON or OFF position while cranking
13	Crank angle sensor — no position pulse
14	Fuel injector — abnormal injector output
21	Water temperature sensor — open or shorted circuit
23	Air flow meter — open or shorted circuit
24	Air control valve — open or shorted circuit
31	Throttle sensor — open or shorted circuit
32	Oxygen sensor — abnormal sensor signal
33	Car-speed sensor — no signal is present during operation
34	Exhaust Gas Recirculation (EGR) solenoid valve — solenoid switch continuously in ON or OFF position
35	Purge control solenoid valve — solenoid switch continuously in ON or OFF position
42	Idle switch — abnormal idle switch signal in relation to throttle sensor output
45	Kickdown control relay — continuously in ON or OFF position
51	Neutral switch — continuously in ON position
61	Parking switch — continuously in ON position

Year – 1987
Model – 1800 Series (2WD)
Engine – 1.8L (109 cid) MPFI 4 cyl
Engine Code – VIN 4

ECM TROUBLE CODES

Code	Explanation
11	Crank angle sensor — no reference pulse
12	Starter switch — continuously in ON or OFF position while cranking
13	Crank angle sensor — no position pulse
14	Fuel injectors No. 1 and No. 2 — abnormal injector output
15	Fuel injectors No. 3 and No. 4 — abnormal injector output
21	Water temperature sensor — open or shorted circuit
22	Knock sensor — open or shorted circuit
23	Air flow meter — open or shorted circuit
31	Throttle sensor — open or shorted circuit
32	Oxygen sensor — abnormal sensor signal
33	Car-speed sensor — no signal is present during operation
34	Exhaust Gas Recirculation (EGR) solenoid valve — solenoid switch continuously in ON or OFF position
35	Purge control solenoid valve — solenoid switch continuously in ON or OFF position
41	System too lean
42	Idle switch — abnormal idle switch signal in relation to throttle sensor output
51	Neutral switch — continuously in ON position

Year — 1987
Model — 1800 Series (4WD)
Engine — 1.8L (109 cid) MPFI 4 cyl
Engine Code — VIN 5

ECM TROUBLE CODES

Code	Explanation
11	Crank angle sensor — no reference pulse
12	Starter switch — continuously in ON or OFF position while cranking
13	Crank angle sensor — no position pulse
14	Fuel injectors No. 1 and No. 2 — abnormal injector output
15	Fuel injectors No. 3 and No. 4 — abnormal injector output
21	Water temperature sensor — open or shorted circuit
22	Knock sensor — open or shorted circuit
23	Air flow meter — open or shorted circuit
31	Throttle sensor — open or shorted circuit
32	Oxygen sensor — abnormal sensor signal
33	Car-speed sensor — no signal is present during operation
34	Exhaust Gas Recirculation (EGR) solenoid valve — solenoid switch continuously in ON or OFF position
35	Purge control solenoid valve — solenoid switch continuously in ON or OFF position
41	System too lean
42	Idle switch — abnormal idle switch signal in relation to throttle sensor output
51	Neutral switch — continuously in ON position

Year — 1987
Model — 1800 Series (4WD) W/Air Suspension
Engine — 1.8L (109 cid) MPFI 4 cyl
Engine Code — VIN 7

ECM TROUBLE CODES

Code	Explanation
11	Crank angle sensor — no reference pulse
12	Starter switch — continuously in ON or OFF position while cranking
13	Crank angle sensor — no position pulse
14	Fuel injectors No. 1 and No. 2 — abnormal injector output
15	Fuel injectors No. 3 and No. 4 — abnormal injector output
21	Water temperature sensor — open or shorted circuit
22	Knock sensor — open or shorted circuit
23	Air flow meter — open or shorted circuit
31	Throttle sensor — open or shorted circuit
32	Oxygen sensor — abnormal sensor signal
33	Car-speed sensor — no signal is present during operation
34	Exhaust Gas Recirculation (EGR) solenoid valve — solenoid switch continuously in ON or OFF position
35	Purge control solenoid valve — solenoid switch continuously in ON or OFF position
41	System too lean
42	Idle switch — abnormal idle switch signal in relation to throttle sensor output
51	Neutral switch — continuously in ON position

Year — 1987
Model — XT Series (2WD)
Engine — 1.8L (109 cid) MPFI 4 cyl
Engine Code — VIN 4

ECM TROUBLE CODES

Code	Explanation
11	Crank angle sensor — no reference pulse
12	Starter switch — continuously in ON or OFF position while cranking
13	Crank angle sensor — no position pulse
14	Fuel injectors No. 1 and No. 2 — abnormal injector output
15	Fuel injectors No. 3 and No. 4 — abnormal injector output
21	Water temperature sensor — open or shorted circuit
22	Knock sensor — open or shorted circuit
23	Air flow meter — open or shorted circuit
31	Throttle sensor — open or shorted circuit
32	Oxygen sensor — abnormal sensor signal
33	Car-speed sensor — no signal is present during operation
34	Exhaust Gas Recirculation (EGR) solenoid valve — solenoid switch continuously in ON or OFF position
35	Purge control solenoid valve — solenoid switch continuously in ON or OFF position
41	System too lean
42	Idle switch — abnormal idle switch signal in relation to throttle sensor output
44	Duty solenoid valve (wastegate control
51	Neutral switch — continuously in ON position

Year — 1987
Model — XT Series (4WD)
Engine — 1.8L (109 cid) MPFI 4 cyl
Engine Code — VIN 7

ECM TROUBLE CODES

Code	Explanation
11	Crank angle sensor — no reference pulse
12	Starter switch — continuously in ON or OFF position while cranking
13	Crank angle sensor — no position pulse
14	Fuel injectors No. 1 and No. 2 — abnormal injector output
15	Fuel injectors No. 3 and No. 4 — abnormal injector output
21	Water temperature sensor — open or shorted circuit
22	Knock sensor — open or shorted circuit
23	Air flow meter — open or shorted circuit
31	Throttle sensor — open or shorted circuit
32	Oxygen sensor — abnormal sensor signal
33	Car-speed sensor — no signal is present during operation
34	Exhaust Gas Recirculation (EGR) solenoid valve — solenoid switch continuously in ON or OFF position
35	Purge control solenoid valve — solenoid switch continuously in ON or OFF position
41	System too lean
42	Idle switch — abnormal idle switch signal in relation to throttle sensor output
44	Duty solenoid valve (wastegate control
51	Neutral switch — continuously in ON position

Year — 1988
Model — 1800 Series (2WD)
Engine — 1.8L (109 cid) SPFI 4 cyl
Engine Code — VIN 4

ECM TROUBLE CODES

Code	Explanation
11	Crank angle sensor — no reference pulse
12	Starter switch — continuously in ON or OFF position while cranking
13	Crank angle sensor — no position pulse
14	Fuel injector — abnormal injector output
21	Water temperature sensor — open or shorted circuit
23	Air flow meter — open or shorted circuit
24	Air control valve — open or shorted circuit
31	Throttle sensor — open or shorted circuit
32	Oxygen sensor — abnormal sensor signal
33	Car-speed sensor — no signal is present during operation
34	Exhaust Gas Recirculation (EGR) solenoid valve — solenoid switch continuously in ON or OFF position or clogged EGR line (California only)
35	Purge control solenoid valve — solenoid switch continuously in ON or OFF position
42	Idle switch — abnormal idle switch signal in relation to throttle sensor output
44	Duty solenoid valve — wastegate control
45	Kickdown control relay — continuously in ON or OFF position
51	Neutral switch — continuously in ON position
55	Exhaust Gas Recirculation (EGR) gas temperature sensor — open or short circuit) — California only
61	Parking switch — continuously in ON position

Year—1988
Model—1800 Series (4WD)
Engine—1.8L (109 cid) MPFI 4 cyl
Engine Code—VIN 5

ECM TROUBLE CODES

Code	Explanation
11	Crank angle sensor—no reference pulse
12	Starter switch—continuously in ON or OFF position while cranking
13	Crank angle sensor—no position pulse
14	Fuel injectors No. 1 and No. 2—abnormal injector output
15	Fuel injectors No. 3 and No. 4—abnormal injector output
21	Water temperature sensor—open or shorted circuit
22	Knock sensor—open or shorted circuit
23	Air flow meter—open or shorted circuit
31	Throttle sensor—open or shorted circuit
32	Oxygen sensor—abnormal sensor signal
33	Car-speed sensor—no signal is present during operation
34	Exhaust Gas Recirculation (EGR) solenoid valve—solenoid switch continuously in ON or OFF position—49-states
35	Purge control solenoid valve—solenoid switch continuously in ON or OFF position
41	System too lean
42	Idle switch—abnormal idle switch signal in relation to throttle sensor output
51	Neutral switch—continuously in ON position

Year — 1988
Model — XT Series
Engine — 1.8L (109 cid) MPFI 4 cyl
Engine Code — VIN 4

ECM TROUBLE CODES

Code	Explanation
11	Crank angle sensor — no reference pulse
12	Starter switch — continuously in ON or OFF position while cranking
13	Crank angle sensor — no position pulse
14	Fuel injectors No. 1, No. 2, No. 5 and No. 6 — abnormal injector output
15	Fuel injectors No. 1, No. 2, No. 3 and No. 4 — abnormal injector output
21	Water temperature sensor — open or shorted circuit
22	Knock sensor — open or shorted circuit
23	Air flow meter — open or shorted circuit
24	Bypass air control valve — open or shorted circuit
25	Fuel injectors No. 3 and No. 4 — abnormal injector output
31	Throttle sensor — open or shorted circuit
32	Oxygen sensor — abnormal sensor signal
33	Car-speed sensor — no signal is present during operation
35	Purge control solenoid valve — solenoid switch continuously in ON or OFF position
41	System too lean
42	Idle switch — abnormal idle switch signal in relation to throttle sensor output
51	Neutral switch — no signal is present

Year — 1988
Model — Justy
Engine — 1.2L (73 cid) OHC 3 cyl
Engine Code — VIN 8

ECM TROUBLE CODES

Code	Explanation
14	Duty solenoid valve control system
15	Coasting Fuel Cut (CFC) system
21	Water temperature
22	Vacuum Line Charging (VLC) solenoid control system
23	Pressure sensor system
24	Idle-up solenoid valve control system
25	Float Chamber Ventilation (FCV) solenoid valve control system
32	Oxygen sensor system
33	Car speed sensor system
35	Purge control solenoid valve control system
52	Clutch switch system — Front Wheel Drive (FWD) model only
62	Idle-up system
63	Idle-up system

Year – 1989
Model – DL, GL 4-Door Sedan
Engine – 1.8L (109 cid) SPFI 4 cyl
Engine Code – VIN 4

ECM TROUBLE CODES

Code	Explanation
11	Crank angle sensor – no reference pulse
12	Starter switch – continuously in ON or OFF position while cranking
13	Crank angle sensor – no position pulse
14	Fuel injector – abnormal injector output
21	Water temperature sensor – open or shorted circuit
23	Air flow meter – open or shorted circuit
24	Air control valve – open or shorted circuit
31	Throttle sensor – open or shorted circuit
32	Oxygen sensor – abnormal sensor signal
33	Car-speed sensor – no signal is present during operation
34	Exhaust Gas Recirculation (EGR) solenoid valve – solenoid switch continuously in ON or OFF position or clogged EGR line (California only)
35	Purge control solenoid valve – solenoid switch continuously in ON or OFF position
42	Idle switch – abnormal idle switch signal in relation to throttle sensor output
44	Duty solenoid valve – wastegate control
45	Kickdown control relay – continuously in ON or OFF position
51	Neutral switch – continuously in ON position
55	Exhaust Gas Recirculation (EGR) gas temperature sensor – open or short circuit) – California only
61	Parking switch – continuously in ON position

Year — 1989
Model — DL, GL 4-Door Sedan
Engine — 1.8L (109 cid) SPFI 4 cyl
Engine Code — VIN 4

ECM TROUBLE CODES

Code	Explanation
11	Crank angle sensor — no reference pulse
12	Starter switch — continuously in ON or OFF position while cranking
13	Crank angle sensor — no position pulse
14	Fuel injector — abnormal injector output
21	Water temperature sensor — open or shorted circuit
23	Air flow meter — open or shorted circuit
24	Air control valve — open or shorted circuit
31	Throttle sensor — open or shorted circuit
32	Oxygen sensor — abnormal sensor signal
33	Car-speed sensor — no signal is present during operation
34	Exhaust Gas Recirculation (EGR) solenoid valve — solenoid switch continuously in ON or OFF position or clogged EGR line (California only)
35	Purge control solenoid valve — solenoid switch continuously in ON or OFF position
42	Idle switch — abnormal idle switch signal in relation to throttle sensor output
44	Duty solenoid valve — wastegate control
45	Kickdown control relay — continuously in ON or OFF position
51	Neutral switch — continuously in ON position
55	Exhaust Gas Recirculation (EGR) gas temperature sensor — open or short circuit) — California only
61	Parking switch — continuously in ON position

Year — 1989
Model — GL-10 4 Door Sedan
Engine — 1.8L (109 cid) MPFI 4 cyl
Engine Code — VIN 4

ECM TROUBLE CODES

Code	Explanation
11	Crank angle sensor — no reference pulse
12	Starter switch — continuously in ON or OFF position while cranking
13	Crank angle sensor — no position pulse
14	Fuel injectors No. 1 and No. 2 — abnormal injector output
15	Fuel injectors No. 3 and No. 4 — abnormal injector output
21	Water temperature sensor — open or shorted circuit
22	Knock sensor — open or shorted circuit
23	Air flow meter — open or shorted circuit
31	Throttle sensor — open or shorted circuit
32	Oxygen sensor — abnormal sensor signal
33	Car-speed sensor — no signal is present during operation
34	Exhaust Gas Recirculation (EGR) solenoid valve — solenoid switch continuously in ON or OFF position — 49-States
35	Purge control solenoid valve — solenoid switch continuously in ON or OFF position
41	System too lean
42	Idle switch — abnormal idle switch signal in relation to throttle sensor output
44	Duty solenoid valve — wastegate control
51	Neutral switch — continuously in ON position

Year – 1989
Model – GL 4-Door Sedan (4WD)
Engine – 1.8L (109 cid) SPFI 4 cyl
Engine Code – VIN 4

ECM TROUBLE CODES

Code	Explanation
11	Crank angle sensor – no reference pulse
12	Starter switch – continuously in ON or OFF position while cranking
13	Crank angle sensor – no position pulse
14	Fuel injector – abnormal injector output
21	Water temperature sensor – open or shorted circuit
23	Air flow meter – open or shorted circuit
24	Air control valve – open or shorted circuit
31	Throttle sensor – open or shorted circuit
32	Oxygen sensor – abnormal sensor signal
33	Car-speed sensor – no signal is present during operation
34	Exhaust Gas Recirculation (EGR) solenoid valve – solenoid switch continuously in ON or OFF position or clogged EGR line (California only)
35	Purge control solenoid valve – solenoid switch continuously in ON or OFF position
42	Idle switch – abnormal idle switch signal in relation to throttle sensor output
44	Duty solenoid valve – wastegate control
45	Kickdown control relay – continuously in ON or OFF position
51	Neutral switch – continuously in ON position
55	Exhaust Gas Recirculation (EGR) gas temperature sensor – open or short circuit) – California only
61	Parking switch – continuously in ON position

Year – 1989
Model – GL 4-Door Sedan (4WD)
Engine – 1.8L (109 cid) SPFI 4 cyl
Engine Code – VIN 5

ECM TROUBLE CODES

Code	Explanation
11	Crank angle sensor – no reference pulse
12	Starter switch – continuously in ON or OFF position while cranking
13	Crank angle sensor – no position pulse
14	Fuel injector – abnormal injector output
21	Water temperature sensor – open or shorted circuit
23	Air flow meter – open or shorted circuit
24	Air control valve – open or shorted circuit
31	Throttle sensor – open or shorted circuit
32	Oxygen sensor – abnormal sensor signal
33	Car-speed sensor – no signal is present during operation
34	Exhaust Gas Recirculation (EGR) solenoid valve – solenoid switch continuously in ON or OFF position or clogged EGR line (California only)
35	Purge control solenoid valve – solenoid switch continuously in ON or OFF position
42	Idle switch – abnormal idle switch signal in relation to throttle sensor output
44	Duty solenoid valve – wastegate control
45	Kickdown control relay – continuously in ON or OFF position
51	Neutral switch – continuously in ON position
55	Exhaust Gas Recirculation (EGR) gas temperature sensor – open or short circuit) – California only
61	Parking switch – continuously in ON position

Year — 1989
Model — GL-10 4 Door Sedan (4WD)
Engine — 1.8L (109 cid) MPFI 4 cyl
Engine Code — VIN 5

ECM TROUBLE CODES

Code	Explanation
11	Crank angle sensor — no reference pulse
12	Starter switch — continuously in ON or OFF position while cranking
13	Crank angle sensor — no position pulse
14	Fuel injectors No. 1 and No. 2 — abnormal injector output
15	Fuel injectors No. 3 and No. 4 — abnormal injector output
21	Water temperature sensor — open or shorted circuit
22	Knock sensor — open or shorted circuit
23	Air flow meter — open or shorted circuit
31	Throttle sensor — open or shorted circuit
32	Oxygen sensor — abnormal sensor signal
33	Car-speed sensor — no signal is present during operation
34	Exhaust Gas Recirculation (EGR) solenoid valve — solenoid switch continuously in ON or OFF position — 49-States
35	Purge control solenoid valve — solenoid switch continuously in ON or OFF position
41	System too lean
42	Idle switch — abnormal idle switch signal in relation to throttle sensor output
44	Duty solenoid valve — wastegate control
51	Neutral switch — continuously in ON position

Year — 1989
Model — GL-10 4 Door Sedan (4WD)
Engine — 1.8L (109 cid) MPFI 4 cyl
Engine Code — VIN 5

ECM TROUBLE CODES

Code	Explanation
11	Crank angle sensor — no reference pulse
12	Starter switch — continuously in ON or OFF position while cranking
13	Crank angle sensor — no position pulse
14	Fuel injectors No. 1 and No. 2 — abnormal injector output
15	Fuel injectors No. 3 and No. 4 — abnormal injector output
21	Water temperature sensor — open or shorted circuit
22	Knock sensor — open or shorted circuit
23	Air flow meter — open or shorted circuit
31	Throttle sensor — open or shorted circuit
32	Oxygen sensor — abnormal sensor signal
33	Car-speed sensor — no signal is present during operation
34	Exhaust Gas Recirculation (EGR) solenoid valve — solenoid switch continuously in ON or OFF position — 49-States
35	Purge control solenoid valve — solenoid switch continuously in ON or OFF position
41	System too lean
42	Idle switch — abnormal idle switch signal in relation to throttle sensor output
44	Duty solenoid valve — wastegate control
51	Neutral switch — continuously in ON position

Year — 1989
Model — RX 4 Door Sedan (4WD)
Engine — 1.8L (109 cid) MPFI 4 cyl
Engine Code — VIN 5

ECM TROUBLE CODES

Code	Explanation
11	Crank angle sensor—no reference pulse
12	Starter switch—continuously in ON or OFF position while cranking
13	Crank angle sensor—no position pulse
14	Fuel injectors No. 1 and No. 2—abnormal injector output
15	Fuel injectors No. 3 and No. 4—abnormal injector output
21	Water temperature sensor—open or shorted circuit
22	Knock sensor—open or shorted circuit
23	Air flow meter—open or shorted circuit
31	Throttle sensor—open or shorted circuit
32	Oxygen sensor—abnormal sensor signal
33	Car-speed sensor—no signal is present during operation
34	Exhaust Gas Recirculation (EGR) solenoid valve—solenoid switch continuously in ON or OFF position—49-States
35	Purge control solenoid valve—solenoid switch continuously in ON or OFF position
41	System too lean
42	Idle switch—abnormal idle switch signal in relation to throttle sensor output
44	Duty solenoid valve—wastegate control
51	Neutral switch—continuously in ON position

Year — 1989
Model — DL, GL Station Wagon
Engine — 1.8L (109 cid) SPFI 4 cyl
Engine Code — VIN 4

ECM TROUBLE CODES

Code	Explanation
11	Crank angle sensor — no reference pulse
12	Starter switch — continuously in ON or OFF position while cranking
13	Crank angle sensor — no position pulse
14	Fuel injector — abnormal injector output
21	Water temperature sensor — open or shorted circuit
23	Air flow meter — open or shorted circuit
24	Air control valve — open or shorted circuit
31	Throttle sensor — open or shorted circuit
32	Oxygen sensor — abnormal sensor signal
33	Car-speed sensor — no signal is present during operation
34	Exhaust Gas Recirculation (EGR) solenoid valve — solenoid switch continuously in ON or OFF position or clogged EGR line (California only)
35	Purge control solenoid valve — solenoid switch continuously in ON or OFF position
42	Idle switch — abnormal idle switch signal in relation to throttle sensor output
44	Duty solenoid valve — wastegate control
45	Kickdown control relay — continuously in ON or OFF position
51	Neutral switch — continuously in ON position
55	Exhaust Gas Recirculation (EGR) gas temperature sensor — open or short circuit) — California only
61	Parking switch — continuously in ON position

Year — 1989
Model — DL, GL Station Wagon
Engine — 1.8L (109 cid) SPFI 4 cyl
Engine Code — VIN 4

ECM TROUBLE CODES

Code	Explanation
11	Crank angle sensor — no reference pulse
12	Starter switch — continuously in ON or OFF position while cranking
13	Crank angle sensor — no position pulse
14	Fuel injector — abnormal injector output
21	Water temperature sensor — open or shorted circuit
23	Air flow meter — open or shorted circuit
24	Air control valve — open or shorted circuit
31	Throttle sensor — open or shorted circuit
32	Oxygen sensor — abnormal sensor signal
33	Car-speed sensor — no signal is present during operation
34	Exhaust Gas Recirculation (EGR) solenoid valve — solenoid switch continuously in ON or OFF position or clogged EGR line (California only)
35	Purge control solenoid valve — solenoid switch continuously in ON or OFF position
42	Idle switch — abnormal idle switch signal in relation to throttle sensor output
44	Duty solenoid valve — wastegate control
45	Kickdown control relay — continuously in ON or OFF position
51	Neutral switch — continuously in ON position
55	Exhaust Gas Recirculation (EGR) gas temperature sensor — open or short circuit) — California only
61	Parking switch — continuously in ON position

Year — 1989
Model — GL-10 Station Wagon
Engine — 1.8L (109 cid) SPFI 4 cyl
Engine Code — VIN 4

ECM TROUBLE CODES

Code	Explanation
11	Crank angle sensor — no reference pulse
12	Starter switch — continuously in ON or OFF position while cranking
13	Crank angle sensor — no position pulse
14	Fuel injector — abnormal injector output
21	Water temperature sensor — open or shorted circuit
23	Air flow meter — open or shorted circuit
24	Air control valve — open or shorted circuit
31	Throttle sensor — open or shorted circuit
32	Oxygen sensor — abnormal sensor signal
33	Car-speed sensor — no signal is present during operation
34	Exhaust Gas Recirculation (EGR) solenoid valve — solenoid switch continuously in ON or OFF position or clogged EGR line (California only)
35	Purge control solenoid valve — solenoid switch continuously in ON or OFF position
42	Idle switch — abnormal idle switch signal in relation to throttle sensor output
44	Duty solenoid valve — wastegate control
45	Kickdown control relay — continuously in ON or OFF position
51	Neutral switch — continuously in ON position
55	Exhaust Gas Recirculation (EGR) gas temperature sensor — open or short circuit) — California only
61	Parking switch — continuously in ON position

Year – 1989
Model – GL-10 Station Wagon
Engine – 1.8L (109 cid) MPFI 4 cyl
Engine Code – VIN 4

ECM TROUBLE CODES

Code	Explanation
11	Crank angle sensor – no reference pulse
12	Starter switch – continuously in ON or OFF position while cranking
13	Crank angle sensor – no position pulse
14	Fuel injectors No. 1 and No. 2 – abnormal injector output
15	Fuel injectors No. 3 and No. 4 – abnormal injector output
21	Water temperature sensor – open or shorted circuit
22	Knock sensor – open or shorted circuit
23	Air flow meter – open or shorted circuit
31	Throttle sensor – open or shorted circuit
32	Oxygen sensor – abnormal sensor signal
33	Car-speed sensor – no signal is present during operation
34	Exhaust Gas Recirculation (EGR) solenoid valve – solenoid switch continuously in ON or OFF position – 49-States
35	Purge control solenoid valve – solenoid switch continuously in ON or OFF position
41	System too lean
42	Idle switch – abnormal idle switch signal in relation to throttle sensor output
44	Duty solenoid valve – wastegate control
51	Neutral switch – continuously in ON position

Year — 1989
Model — DL, GL Station Wagon
Engine — 1.8L (109 cid) SPFI 4 cyl
Engine Code — VIN 4

ECM TROUBLE CODES

Code	Explanation
11	Crank angle sensor — no reference pulse
12	Starter switch — continuously in ON or OFF position while cranking
13	Crank angle sensor — no position pulse
14	Fuel injector — abnormal injector output
21	Water temperature sensor — open or shorted circuit
23	Air flow meter — open or shorted circuit
24	Air control valve — open or shorted circuit
31	Throttle sensor — open or shorted circuit
32	Oxygen sensor — abnormal sensor signal
33	Car-speed sensor — no signal is present during operation
34	Exhaust Gas Recirculation (EGR) solenoid valve — solenoid switch continuously in ON or OFF position or clogged EGR line (California only)
35	Purge control solenoid valve — solenoid switch continuously in ON or OFF position
42	Idle switch — abnormal idle switch signal in relation to throttle sensor output
44	Duty solenoid valve — wastegate control
45	Kickdown control relay — continuously in ON or OFF position
51	Neutral switch — continuously in ON position
55	Exhaust Gas Recirculation (EGR) gas temperature sensor — open or short circuit) — California only
61	Parking switch — continuously in ON position

Year – 1989
Model – GL Station Wagon
Engine – 1.8L (109 cid) SPFI 4 cyl
Engine Code – VIN 4

ECM TROUBLE CODES

Code	Explanation
11	Crank angle sensor—no reference pulse
12	Starter switch—continuously in ON or OFF position while cranking
13	Crank angle sensor—no position pulse
14	Fuel injector—abnormal injector output
21	Water temperature sensor—open or shorted circuit
23	Air flow meter—open or shorted circuit
24	Air control valve—open or shorted circuit
31	Throttle sensor—open or shorted circuit
32	Oxygen sensor—abnormal sensor signal
33	Car-speed sensor—no signal is present during operation
34	Exhaust Gas Recirculation (EGR) solenoid valve—solenoid switch continuously in ON or OFF position or clogged EGR line (California only)
35	Purge control solenoid valve—solenoid switch continuously in ON or OFF position
42	Idle switch—abnormal idle switch signal in relation to throttle sensor output
44	Duty solenoid valve—wastegate control
45	Kickdown control relay—continuously in ON or OFF position
51	Neutral switch—continuously in ON position
55	Exhaust Gas Recirculation (EGR) gas temperature sensor—open or short circuit)—California only
61	Parking switch—continuously in ON position

Year – 1989
Model – GL Station Wagon (4WD)
Engine – 1.8L (109 cid) MPFI 4 cyl
Engine Code – VIN 5

ECM TROUBLE CODES

Code	Explanation
11	Crank angle sensor – no reference pulse
12	Starter switch – continuously in ON or OFF position while cranking
13	Crank angle sensor – no position pulse
14	Fuel injectors No. 1 and No. 2 – abnormal injector output
15	Fuel injectors No. 3 and No. 4 – abnormal injector output
21	Water temperature sensor – open or shorted circuit
22	Knock sensor – open or shorted circuit
23	Air flow meter – open or shorted circuit
31	Throttle sensor – open or shorted circuit
32	Oxygen sensor – abnormal sensor signal
33	Car-speed sensor – no signal is present during operation
34	Exhaust Gas Recirculation (EGR) solenoid valve – solenoid switch continuously in ON or OFF position – 49-States
35	Purge control solenoid valve – solenoid switch continuously in ON or OFF position
41	System too lean
42	Idle switch – abnormal idle switch signal in relation to throttle sensor output
44	Duty solenoid valve – wastegate control
51	Neutral switch – continuously in ON position

Year – 1989
Model – GL-10 Station Wagon (4WD)
Engine – 1.8L (109 cid) MPFI 4 cyl
Engine Code – VIN 5

ECM TROUBLE CODES

Code	Explanation
11	Crank angle sensor – no reference pulse
12	Starter switch – continuously in ON or OFF position while cranking
13	Crank angle sensor – no position pulse
14	Fuel injectors No. 1 and No. 2 – abnormal injector output
15	Fuel injectors No. 3 and No. 4 – abnormal injector output
21	Water temperature sensor – open or shorted circuit
22	Knock sensor – open or shorted circuit
23	Air flow meter – open or shorted circuit
31	Throttle sensor – open or shorted circuit
32	Oxygen sensor – abnormal sensor signal
33	Car-speed sensor – no signal is present during operation
34	Exhaust Gas Recirculation (EGR) solenoid valve – solenoid switch continuously in ON or OFF position – 49-States
35	Purge control solenoid valve – solenoid switch continuously in ON or OFF position
41	System too lean
42	Idle switch – abnormal idle switch signal in relation to throttle sensor output
44	Duty solenoid valve – wastegate control
51	Neutral switch – continuously in ON position

Year — 1989
Model — DL, GL 3-Door
Engine — 1.8L (109 cid) SPFI 4 cyl
Engine Code — VIN 4

ECM TROUBLE CODES

Code	Explanation
11	Crank angle sensor — no reference pulse
12	Starter switch — continuously in ON or OFF position while cranking
13	Crank angle sensor — no position pulse
14	Fuel injector — abnormal injector output
21	Water temperature sensor — open or shorted circuit
23	Air flow meter — open or shorted circuit
24	Air control valve — open or shorted circuit
31	Throttle sensor — open or shorted circuit
32	Oxygen sensor — abnormal sensor signal
33	Car-speed sensor — no signal is present during operation
34	Exhaust Gas Recirculation (EGR) solenoid valve — solenoid switch continuously in ON or OFF position or clogged EGR line (California only)
35	Purge control solenoid valve — solenoid switch continuously in ON or OFF position
42	Idle switch — abnormal idle switch signal in relation to throttle sensor output
44	Duty solenoid valve — wastegate control
45	Kickdown control relay — continuously in ON or OFF position
51	Neutral switch — continuously in ON position
55	Exhaust Gas Recirculation (EGR) gas temperature sensor — open or short circuit) — California only
61	Parking switch — continuously in ON position

Year – 1989
Model – DL, GL 3-Door
Engine – 1.8L (109 cid) SPFI 4 cyl
Engine Code – VIN 4

ECM TROUBLE CODES

Code	Explanation
11	Crank angle sensor – no reference pulse
12	Starter switch – continuously in ON or OFF position while cranking
13	Crank angle sensor – no position pulse
14	Fuel injector – abnormal injector output
21	Water temperature sensor – open or shorted circuit
23	Air flow meter – open or shorted circuit
24	Air control valve – open or shorted circuit
31	Throttle sensor – open or shorted circuit
32	Oxygen sensor – abnormal sensor signal
33	Car-speed sensor – no signal is present during operation
34	Exhaust Gas Recirculation (EGR) solenoid valve – solenoid switch continuously in ON or OFF position or clogged EGR line (California only)
35	Purge control solenoid valve – solenoid switch continuously in ON or OFF position
42	Idle switch – abnormal idle switch signal in relation to throttle sensor output
44	Duty solenoid valve – wastegate control
45	Kickdown control relay – continuously in ON or OFF position
51	Neutral switch – continuously in ON position
55	Exhaust Gas Recirculation (EGR) gas temperature sensor – open or short circuit) – California only
61	Parking switch – continuously in ON position

Year – 1989
Model – GL 3-Door (4WD)
Engine – 1.8L (109 cid) SPFI 4 cyl
Engine Code – VIN 5

ECM TROUBLE CODES

Code	Explanation
11	Crank angle sensor – no reference pulse
12	Starter switch – continuously in ON or OFF position while cranking
13	Crank angle sensor – no position pulse
14	Fuel injector – abnormal injector output
21	Water temperature sensor – open or shorted circuit
23	Air flow meter – open or shorted circuit
24	Air control valve – open or shorted circuit
31	Throttle sensor – open or shorted circuit
32	Oxygen sensor – abnormal sensor signal
33	Car-speed sensor – no signal is present during operation
34	Exhaust Gas Recirculation (EGR) solenoid valve – solenoid switch continuously in ON or OFF position or clogged EGR line (California only)
35	Purge control solenoid valve – solenoid switch continuously in ON or OFF position
42	Idle switch – abnormal idle switch signal in relation to throttle sensor output
44	Duty solenoid valve – wastegate control
45	Kickdown control relay – continuously in ON or OFF position
51	Neutral switch – continuously in ON position
55	Exhaust Gas Recirculation (EGR) gas temperature sensor – open or short circuit) – California only
61	Parking switch – continuously in ON position

Year — 1989
Model — GL 3-Door (4WD)
Engine — 1.8L (109 cid) SPFI 4 cyl
Engine Code — VIN 5

ECM TROUBLE CODES

Code	Explanation
11	Crank angle sensor — no reference pulse
12	Starter switch — continuously in ON or OFF position while cranking
13	Crank angle sensor — no position pulse
14	Fuel injector — abnormal injector output
21	Water temperature sensor — open or shorted circuit
23	Air flow meter — open or shorted circuit
24	Air control valve — open or shorted circuit
31	Throttle sensor — open or shorted circuit
32	Oxygen sensor — abnormal sensor signal
33	Car-speed sensor — no signal is present during operation
34	Exhaust Gas Recirculation (EGR) solenoid valve — solenoid switch continuously in ON or OFF position or clogged EGR line (California only)
35	Purge control solenoid valve — solenoid switch continuously in ON or OFF position
42	Idle switch — abnormal idle switch signal in relation to throttle sensor output
44	Duty solenoid valve — wastegate control
45	Kickdown control relay — continuously in ON or OFF position
51	Neutral switch — continuously in ON position
55	Exhaust Gas Recirculation (EGR) gas temperature sensor — open or short circuit) — California only
61	Parking switch — continuously in ON position

Year – 1989
Model – RX 3-Door (4WD)
Engine – 1.8L (109 cid) MPFI 4 cyl
Engine Code – VIN 5

ECM TROUBLE CODES

Code	Explanation
11	Crank angle sensor – no reference pulse
12	Starter switch – continuously in ON or OFF position while cranking
13	Crank angle sensor – no position pulse
14	Fuel injectors No. 1 and No. 2 – abnormal injector output
15	Fuel injectors No. 3 and No. 4 – abnormal injector output
21	Water temperature sensor – open or shorted circuit
22	Knock sensor – open or shorted circuit
23	Air flow meter – open or shorted circuit
31	Throttle sensor – open or shorted circuit
32	Oxygen sensor – abnormal sensor signal
33	Car-speed sensor – no signal is present during operation
34	Exhaust Gas Recirculation (EGR) solenoid valve – solenoid switch continuously in ON or OFF position – 49-States
35	Purge control solenoid valve – solenoid switch continuously in ON or OFF position
41	System too lean
42	Idle switch – abnormal idle switch signal in relation to throttle sensor output
44	Duty solenoid valve – wastegate control
51	Neutral switch – continuously in ON position

Year – 1989
Model – GL, GL-10 Touring Wagon
Engine – 1.8L (109 cid) SPFI 4 cyl
Engine Code – VIN 4

ECM TROUBLE CODES

Code	Explanation
11	Crank angle sensor – no reference pulse
12	Starter switch – continuously in ON or OFF position while cranking
13	Crank angle sensor – no position pulse
14	Fuel injector – abnormal injector output
21	Water temperature sensor – open or shorted circuit
23	Air flow meter – open or shorted circuit
24	Air control valve – open or shorted circuit
31	Throttle sensor – open or shorted circuit
32	Oxygen sensor – abnormal sensor signal
33	Car-speed sensor – no signal is present during operation
34	Exhaust Gas Recirculation (EGR) solenoid valve – solenoid switch continuously in ON or OFF position or clogged EGR line (California only)
35	Purge control solenoid valve – solenoid switch continuously in ON or OFF position
42	Idle switch – abnormal idle switch signal in relation to throttle sensor output
44	Duty solenoid valve – wastegate control
45	Kickdown control relay – continuously in ON or OFF position
51	Neutral switch – continuously in ON position
55	Exhaust Gas Recirculation (EGR) gas temperature sensor – open or short circuit) – California only
61	Parking switch – continuously in ON position

Year – 1989
Model – GL Touring Wagon
Engine – 1.8L (109 cid) SPFI 4 cyl
Engine Code – VIN 4

ECM TROUBLE CODES

Code	Explanation
11	Crank angle sensor – no reference pulse
12	Starter switch – continuously in ON or OFF position while cranking
13	Crank angle sensor – no position pulse
14	Fuel injector – abnormal injector output
21	Water temperature sensor – open or shorted circuit
23	Air flow meter – open or shorted circuit
24	Air control valve – open or shorted circuit
31	Throttle sensor – open or shorted circuit
32	Oxygen sensor – abnormal sensor signal
33	Car-speed sensor – no signal is present during operation
34	Exhaust Gas Recirculation (EGR) solenoid valve – solenoid switch continuously in ON or OFF position or clogged EGR line (California only)
35	Purge control solenoid valve – solenoid switch continuously in ON or OFF position
42	Idle switch – abnormal idle switch signal in relation to throttle sensor output
44	Duty solenoid valve – wastegate control
45	Kickdown control relay – continuously in ON or OFF position
51	Neutral switch – continuously in ON position
55	Exhaust Gas Recirculation (EGR) gas temperature sensor – open or short circuit) – California only
61	Parking switch – continuously in ON position

Year – 1989
Model – GL-10 Touring Wagon
Engine – 1.8L (109 cid) MPFI 4 cyl
Engine Code – VIN 4

ECM TROUBLE CODES

Code	Explanation
11	Crank angle sensor – no reference pulse
12	Starter switch – continuously in ON or OFF position while cranking
13	Crank angle sensor – no position pulse
14	Fuel injectors No. 1 and No. 2 – abnormal injector output
15	Fuel injectors No. 3 and No. 4 – abnormal injector output
21	Water temperature sensor – open or shorted circuit
22	Knock sensor – open or shorted circuit
23	Air flow meter – open or shorted circuit
31	Throttle sensor – open or shorted circuit
32	Oxygen sensor – abnormal sensor signal
33	Car-speed sensor – no signal is present during operation
34	Exhaust Gas Recirculation (EGR) solenoid valve – solenoid switch continuously in ON or OFF position – 49-States
35	Purge control solenoid valve – solenoid switch continuously in ON or OFF position
41	System too lean
42	Idle switch – abnormal idle switch signal in relation to throttle sensor output
44	Duty solenoid valve – wastegate control
51	Neutral switch – continuously in ON position

Year – 1989
Model – XT6 (2700)
Engine – 2.7L (163 cid) MPI 6 cyl
Engine Code – VIN 8

ECM TROUBLE CODES

Code	Explanation
11	Crank angle sensor – no reference pulse
12	Starter switch – continuously in ON or OFF position while cranking
13	Crank angle sensor – no position pulse
14	Fuel injectors No. 1, No. 2, No. 5 and No. 6 – abnormal injector output
15	Fuel injectors No. 3, No. 4, No. 1 and No. 2 – abnormal injector output
21	Water temperature sensor – open or shorted circuit
22	Knock sensor – open or shorted circuit
23	Air flow meter – open or shorted circuit
24	Bypass air control valve – open or shorted circuit
25	Fuel injectors No. 3 and No. 4 – abnormal injector output
31	Throttle sensor – open or shorted circuit
32	Oxygen sensor – abnormal sensor signal
33	Car-speed sensor – no signal is present during operation
35	Purge control solenoid valve – solenoid switch continuously in ON or OFF position
41	System too lean
42	Idle switch – abnormal idle switch signal in relation to throttle sensor output
51	Neutral switch – no signal is present

Year—1989
Model—XT6 (2700) Full Time 4WD
Engine—2.7L (163 cid) MPI 6 cyl
Engine Code—VIN 9

ECM TROUBLE CODES

Code	Explanation
11	Crank angle sensor—no reference pulse
12	Starter switch—continuously in ON or OFF position while cranking
13	Crank angle sensor—no position pulse
14	Fuel injectors No. 1, No. 2, No. 5 and No. 6—abnormal injector output
15	Fuel injectors No. 3, No. 4, No. 1 and No. 2—abnormal injector output
21	Water temperature sensor—open or shorted circuit
22	Knock sensor—open or shorted circuit
23	Air flow meter—open or shorted circuit
24	Bypass air control valve—open or shorted circuit
25	Fuel injectors No. 3 and No. 4—abnormal injector output
31	Throttle sensor—open or shorted circuit
32	Oxygen sensor—abnormal sensor signal
33	Car-speed sensor—no signal is present during operation
35	Purge control solenoid valve—solenoid switch continuously in ON or OFF position
41	System too lean
42	Idle switch—abnormal idle switch signal in relation to throttle sensor output
51	Neutral switch—no signal is present

Year – 1989
Model – XT6 (2700) Full Time 4WD
Engine – 2.7L (163 cid) MPI 6 cyl
Engine Code – VIN 9

ECM TROUBLE CODES

Code	Explanation
11	Crank angle sensor – no reference pulse
12	Starter switch – continuously in ON or OFF position while cranking
13	Crank angle sensor – no position pulse
14	Fuel injectors No. 1, No. 2, No. 5 and No. 6 – abnormal injector output
15	Fuel injectors No. 3, No. 4, No. 1 and No. 2 – abnormal injector output
21	Water temperature sensor – open or shorted circuit
22	Knock sensor – open or shorted circuit
23	Air flow meter – open or shorted circuit
24	Bypass air control valve – open or shorted circuit
25	Fuel injectors No. 3 and No. 4 – abnormal injector output
31	Throttle sensor – open or shorted circuit
32	Oxygen sensor – abnormal sensor signal
33	Car-speed sensor – no signal is present during operation
35	Purge control solenoid valve – solenoid switch continuously in ON or OFF position
41	System too lean
42	Idle switch – abnormal idle switch signal in relation to throttle sensor output
51	Neutral switch – no signal is present

Year — 1989
Model — Justy DL, GL
Engine — 1.2L (73 cid) EFC 4 cyl
Engine Code — VIN 7

ECM TROUBLE CODES

Code	Explanation
14	Duty solenoid valve control system
15	Coasting Fuel Cut (CFC) system — manual transaxle only
16	Feedback system
17	Fuel pump and automatic choke
21	Thermosensor
22	Vacuum Line Charging (VLC) solenoid valve
23	Pressure sensor
24	Idle-up solenoid
25	Float Chamber Ventilation (FCV) solenoid valve
32	Oxygen sensor
33	Car-speed sensor
34	Exhaust Gas Recirculation (EGR) solenoid valve
35	CPC solenoid valve
41	Feedback system — California only
46	Radiator fan control system
52	Clutch switch — Front Wheel Drive (FWD)/manual transaxle only
53	High Altitude Compensator (HAC) solenoid valve
55	Exhaust Gas Recirculation (EGR) sensor — California only
56	Exhaust Gas Recirculation (EGR) system — California only
62	Idle-up system (1)
63	Idle-up system (2)

Year — 1989
Model — Justy GL
Engine — 1.2L (73 cid) EFC 4 cyl
Engine Code — VIN 7

ECM TROUBLE CODES

Code	Explanation
14	Duty solenoid valve control system
15	Coasting Fuel Cut (CFC) system — manual transaxle only
16	Feedback system
17	Fuel pump and automatic choke
21	Thermosensor
22	Vacuum Line Charging (VLC) solenoid valve
23	Pressure sensor
24	Idle-up solenoid
25	Float Chamber Ventilation (FCV) solenoid valve
32	Oxygen sensor
33	Car-speed sensor
34	Exhaust Gas Recirculation (EGR) solenoid valve
35	CPC solenoid valve
41	Feedback system — California only
46	Radiator fan control system
52	Clutch switch — Front Wheel Drive (FWD)/manual transaxle only
53	High Altitude Compensator (HAC) solenoid valve
55	Exhaust Gas Recirculation (EGR) sensor — California only
56	Exhaust Gas Recirculation (EGR) system — California only
62	Idle-up system (1)
63	Idle-up system (2)

Year — 1989
Model — Justy GL (4WD)
Engine — 1.2L (73 cid) EFC 4 cyl
Engine Code — VIN 8

ECM TROUBLE CODES

Code	Explanation
14	Duty solenoid valve control system
15	Coasting Fuel Cut (CFC) system—manual transaxle only
16	Feedback system
17	Fuel pump and automatic choke
21	Thermosensor
22	Vacuum Line Charging (VLC) solenoid valve
23	Pressure sensor
24	Idle-up solenoid
25	Float Chamber Ventilation (FCV) solenoid valve
32	Oxygen sensor
33	Car-speed sensor
34	Exhaust Gas Recirculation (EGR) solenoid valve
35	CPC solenoid valve
41	Feedback system—California only
46	Radiator fan control system
52	Clutch switch—Front Wheel Drive (FWD)/manual transaxle only
53	High Altitude Compensator (HAC) solenoid valve
55	Exhaust Gas Recirculation (EGR) sensor—California only
56	Exhaust Gas Recirculation (EGR) system—California only
62	Idle-up system (1)
63	Idle-up system (2)

INDEX

SUZUKI

Electronic Fuel Injection (EFI) System

SELF-DIAGNOSTIC SYSTEM

Description

The Electronic Fuel Injection (EFI) system consists of various sensors and actuators connected to the Electronic Control Module (ECM), which is located under the instrument panel on the driver's side. The ECM monitors input voltage from the sensors and controls the actuators in order to maintain optimum engine performance, maximizing fuel economy and minimizing engine emissions.

Entering Diagnostic Mode

When the ECM detects an abnormal value from one of the sensors, it energizes the "Check Engine" light and stores a trouble code in the ECM back-up memory. Since the ECM receives power directly from the battery, the code remains stored in memory even when the ignition key is turned **OFF**. When the ignition switch is turned **ON**, the "Check Engine" light turns ON until the engine is started. This serves as a "Check Engine" bulb and circuit check.

Reading Codes

Do not disconnect couplers from ECM, battery cable, ECM ground wire harness from engine or main fuse before reading the codes store in the memory; doing so will erase the trouble code memory.

The ECM memory is activated by connecting the spare fuse to the diagnosis switch terminal and turning the ignition switch **ON**. The fuse panel is located under the instrument panel, near the driver's side kick panel. The memory displays the codes in numerical order from lowest to highest. The order in which the codes are displayed does not necessarily indicate the order in which the malfunction occurred. The ECM displays each code three times, then moves on to the next code in numerical order. The entire sequence is repeated as long as the diagnosis switch terminal is grounded and ignition switch is in the **ON** position.

Clearing Diagnostic Memory

When repairs have been completed, erase the ECM back-up memory by disconnecting the negative battery cable or the ECM harness connector for 30 seconds or longer.

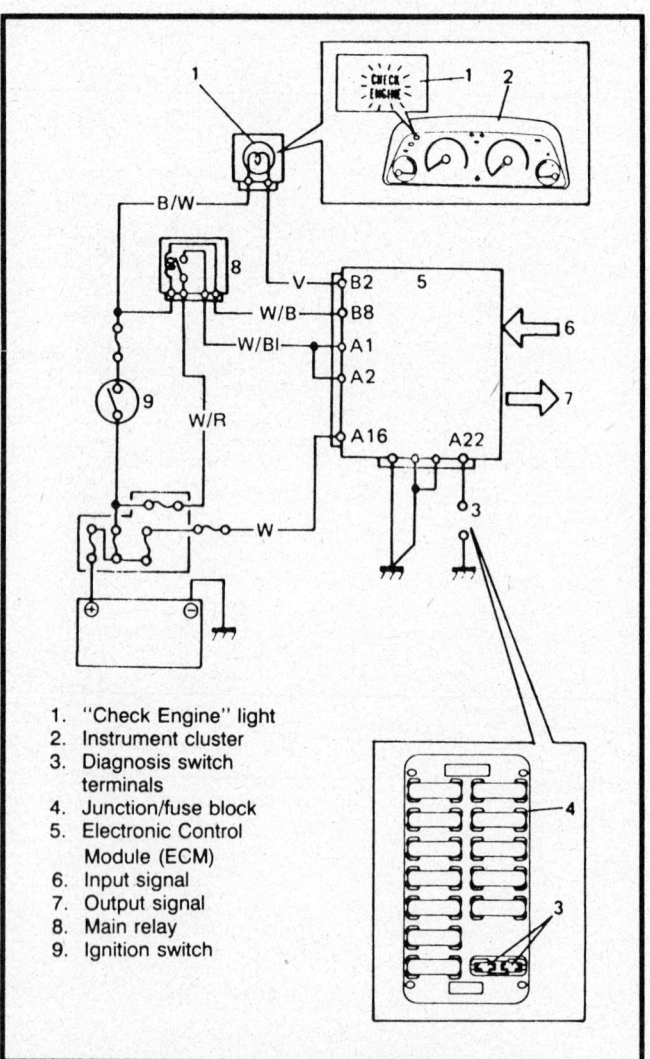

1. "Check Engine" light
2. Instrument cluster
3. Diagnosis switch terminals
4. Junction/fuse block
5. Electronic Control Module (ECM)
6. Input signal
7. Output signal
8. Main relay
9. Ignition switch

"Check Engine" light circuit – 1989 Swift

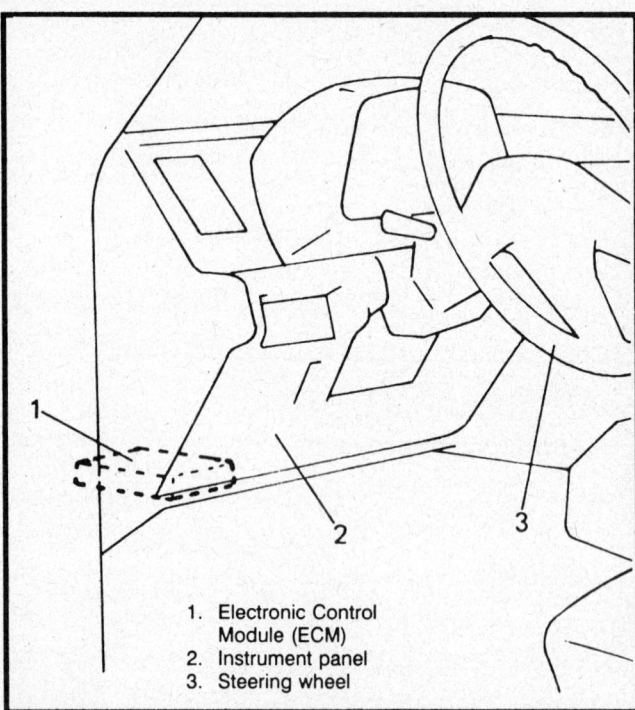

1. Electronic Control Module (ECM)
2. Instrument panel
3. Steering wheel

Electronic Control Module (ECM) location – 1989 Sidekick

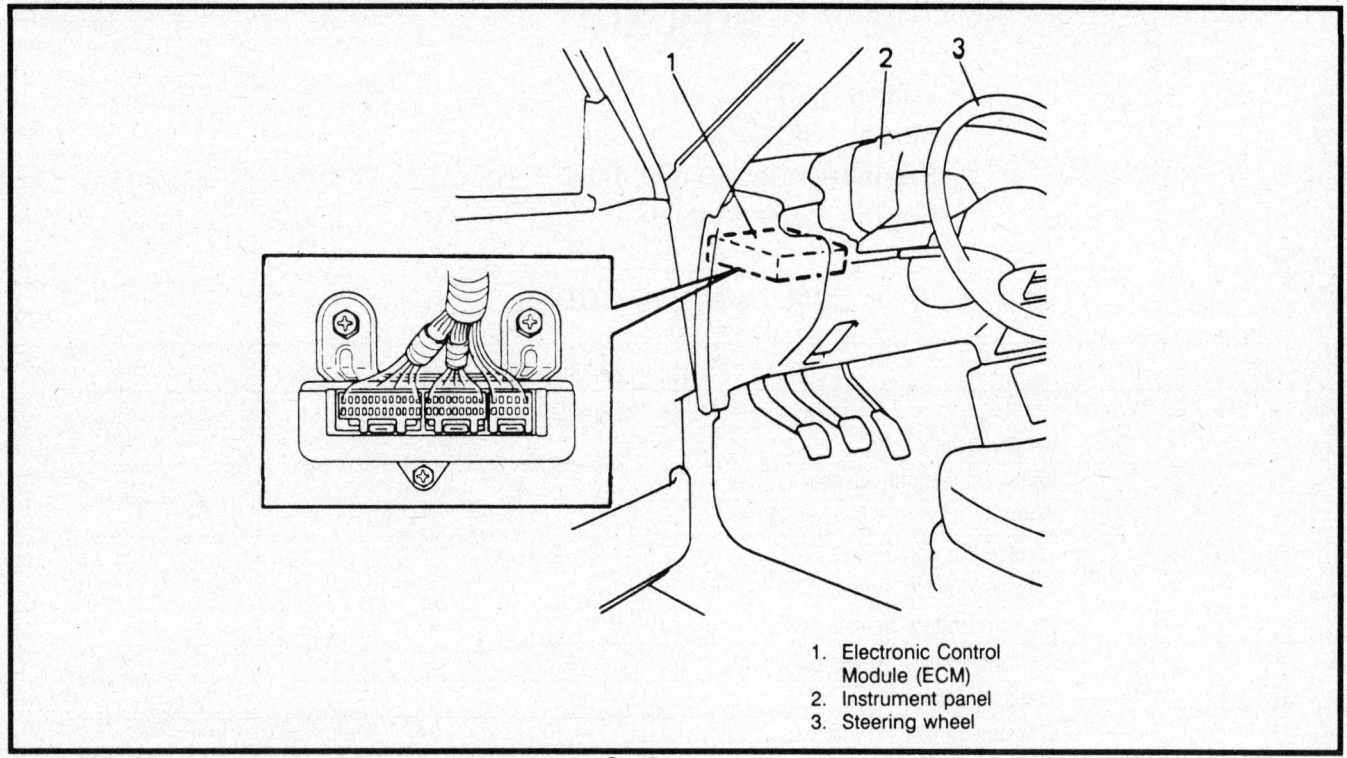

1. Electronic Control Module (ECM)
2. Instrument panel
3. Steering wheel

Electronic Control Module (ECM) location—1989 Swift

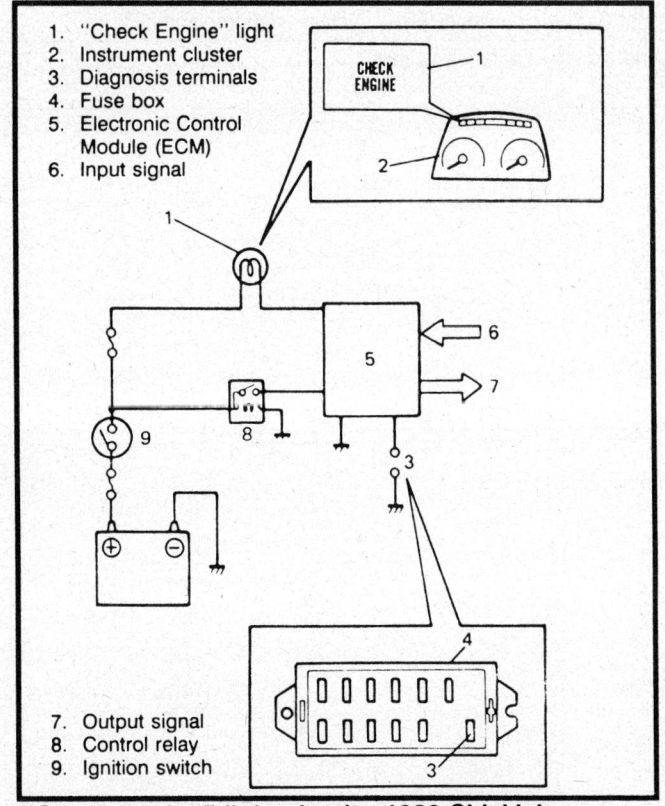

1. "Check Engine" light
2. Instrument cluster
3. Diagnosis terminals
4. Fuse box
5. Electronic Control Module (ECM)
6. Input signal

7. Output signal
8. Control relay
9. Ignition switch

"Check Engine" light circuit—1989 Sidekick

SUZUKI

Year — 1989
Model — Sidekick
Engine — 1.3L (80 cid) 4 cyl
Engine Code — VIN 5

ECM TROUBLE CODES

Code	Explanation
12	Normal
13	Oxygen sensor
14	Water Temperature Sensor (WTS)
15	Water Temperature Sensor (WTS)
21	Throttle Position Sensor (TPS)
22	Throttle Position Sensor (TPS)
23	Air Temperature Sensor (ATS)
25	Air Temperature Sensor (ATS)
31	Pressure sensor
32	Pressure sensor
41	Ignition signal
42	Lock-up signal — automatic transmission vehicle. Fifth gear switch — manual transmission vehicle
44	Idle switch of Throttle Position Sensor (TPS)
45	Idle switch of Throttle Position Sensor (TPS)
51	Exhaust Gas Recirculation (EGR) system — California vehicle
53	Ground circuit — California vehicle

Year – 1989
Model – Sidekick
Engine – 1.6L (97 cid) 4 cyl
Engine Code – VIN O

ECM TROUBLE CODES

Code	Explanation
12	Normal
13	Oxygen sensor
14	Water Temperature Sensor (WTS)
15	Water Temperature Sensor (WTS)
21	Throttle Position Sensor (TPS)
22	Throttle Position Sensor (TPS)
23	Air Temperature Sensor (ATS)
25	Air Temperature Sensor (ATS)
31	Pressure sensor
32	Pressure sensor
41	Ignition signal
42	Lock-up signal – automatic transmission vehicle. Fifth gear switch – manual transmission vehicle
44	Idle switch of Throttle Position Sensor (TPS)
45	Idle switch of Throttle Position Sensor (TPS)
51	Exhaust Gas Recirculation (EGR) system – California vehicle
53	Ground circuit – California vehicle

Year — 1989
Model — Swift
Engine — 1.6L (97 cid) DOHC 4 cyl
Engine Code — VIN U

ECM TROUBLE CODES

Code	Explanation
12	Normal
13	Oxygen sensor
14	Water Temperature Sensor (WTS)
15	Water Temperature Sensor (WTS)
21	Throttle Position Sensor (TPS)
22	Throttle Position Sensor (TPS)
24	Vehicle Speed Sensor (VSS)
33	Air Flow Sensor (AFS)
34	Air Flow Sensor (AFS)
41	Ignition signal
42	Crank Angle Sensor (CAS)
51	Exhaust Gas Recirculation (EGR) system — California vehicle
52	Fuel leakage from fuel injector — California vehicle

Year — 1989
Model — Sidekick
Engine — 1.3L (231 cid) V6
Engine Code — VIN A

ECM TROUBLE CODES

Code	Explanation
12	Normal
13	Oxygen sensor
14	Water Temperature Sensor (WTS)
15	Water Temperature Sensor (WTS)
21	Throttle Position Sensor (TPS)
22	Throttle Position Sensor (TPS)
23	Air Temperature Sensor (ATS)
25	Air Temperature Sensor (ATS)
31	Pressure sensor
32	Pressure sensor
41	Ignition signal
42	Lock-up signal — automatic transmission vehicle. Fifth gear switch — manual transmission vehicle
44	Idle switch of Throttle Position Sensor (TPS)
45	Idle switch of Throttle Position Sensor (TPS)
51	Exhaust Gas Recirculation (EGR) system — California vehicle
53	Ground circuit — California vehicle

INDEX

TOYOTA

Electronic Fuel Injection

SELF-DIAGNOSTIC SYSTEM

Description

The ECU contains a built-in self diagnosis system by which troubles with the engine signal network are detected and a "Check Engine" warning light on the instrument panel flashes code numbers. These 1 or 2 digit code number(s) vary from model-to-model. The "Check Engine" light on the instrument panel informs the driver that a malfunction has been detected. The light goes out automatically when the malfunction has been cleared.

CHECK ENGINE WARNING LIGHT CHECK

1. The check engine warning light will turn ON when the ignition switch is turned ON and the engine is not running.
2. When the engine is started, the check engine warning light should turn OFF. If the light remains ON, the diagnosis system has detected a malfunction or abnormality in the system.

SUPER MONITOR DISPLAY

1. Including "Normal" or "ENG-OK", the ECU is programmed with several diagnostic codes.
2. When more than a single code is indicated, the lowest number code will appear first. However, no other code will appear along with Code 11.
3. All detected diagnostic codes, except Code 51 and 53, will be retained in memory by the ECU from the time of detection until canceled out.
4. Once the malfunction is cleared, the "Check Engine" warning light on the instrument panel will turn OFF but the diagnostic code(s) remain stored in the ECU memory (except for Code 51 and 53).

Entering Diagnostic Mode

The diagnostic code(s) can be read by the number of blinks of the "Check Engine" warning light when the proper terminals of the check connector are short-circuited. If the vehicle is equipped with a super monitor display, the diagnostic code is indicated on the display screen. The initial conditions for entering self-diagnostics are as follows:

1. The battery voltage of the vehicle should be above 11V. The throttle valve in a fully closed position (throttle position sensor IDL points closed).
2. If equipped with an automatic transmission, place it in **P** or **N**.
3. Turn the air conditioning switch **OFF**.
4. Start the engine and allow it run to reach its normal operating temperatures.

Operation

EXCEPT SUPER MONITOR DISPLAY

Normal Mode

1. Turn the ignition switch to the **ON** position. Do not start the engine. Use a suitable jumper wire and short the terminals of the check connector.
2. Read the diagnostic code as indicated by the number of flashes of the "Check Engine" warning light.

NOTE: On some early models install an analog voltmeter to the EFI service connector. Read diagnostic codes by voltmeter needle deflection between 0V–2.5V–5V. The voltmeter needle will fluctuate between 5V and 2.5V every 0.6 seconds.

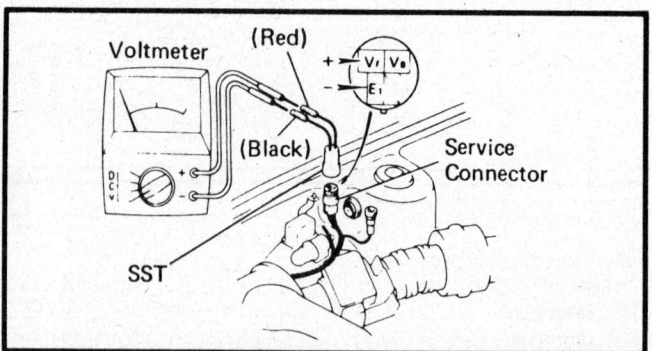

Installing analog voltmeter to EFI service connector — 1983–84 Celica Supra

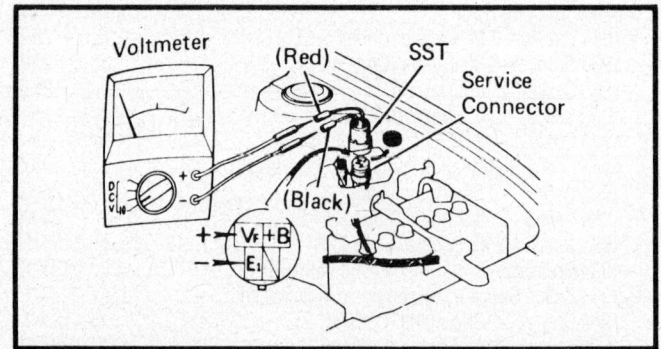

Installing analog voltmeter to EFI service connector — 1983–84 Cressida

3. If the system is operating normally (no malfunction), the light will blink once every ¼ second. On single digit code number systems the light will blink once every 3 or 4.5 seconds.
4. In the event of a malfunction, the light will blink once every ½ second (some models it may be 1, 2 or 3 seconds). The 1st number of blinks will equal the 1st digit of a 2-digit diagnostic code. After a 1.5 second pause, the 2nd number of blinks will equal the 2nd number of a 2-digit diagnostic code. If there are 2 or more codes, there will be a 2.5 second pause between each. On a single digit code number systems the light will blink a number of times equal to the malfunction code indication every 3 or 4.5 seconds.
5. After all the codes have been output, there will be a 4.5 second pause and they will be repeated as long as the terminals of the check connector are shorted.

NOTE: In event of multiple trouble codes, indication will begin from the smaller value and continue to the larger in order.

6. After the diagnosis check, remove the jumper wire from the check connector and install protective rubber cap.

Test Mode

The Cressida provides a diagnostic test mode for vehicle servicing.

1. Using a jumper wire, connect the TE2 and E1 terminals of the Toyota Diagnostic Communication Link (TDCL), then turn the ignition switch **ON** to begin the diagnostic test mode.
2. Start the engine and drive the vehicle at a speed of 10 mph or more. Simulate the conditions where the malfunction has be reported to happen.

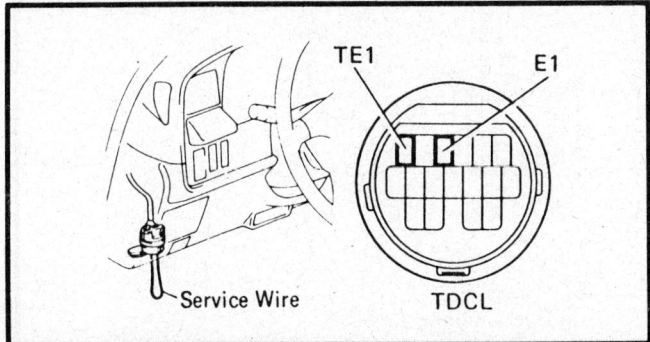

Toyota diagnostic communication link (TDCL) normal mode—late model Cressida

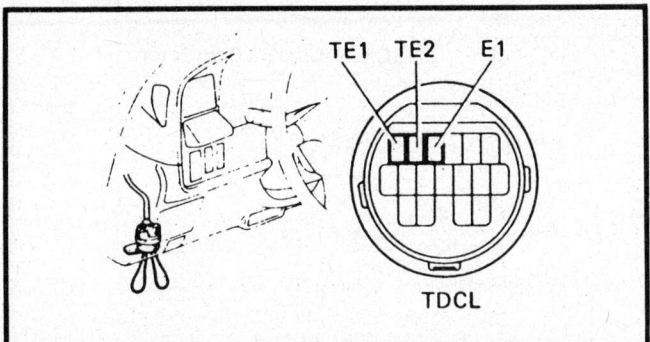

Toyota diagnostic communication link (TDCL) test mode—late model Cressida

3. Using a jumper wire, connect the TE1 and E1 terminals of the TDCL connector.

4. Read the diagnosis code as indicated by the number of engine flashes.

5. After diagnosis check remove the jumper wires.

SUPER MONITOR DISPLAY

The super monitor display system was offered as an option on some late model Toyota vehicles.

1. Turn the ignition switch **ON** but do not start the engine.

2. Simultaneously push and hold in the **SELECT** and **INPUT M** keys for at least 3 seconds. The letters **DIAG** will appear on the screen.

3. After a short pause, hold the **SET** key in for at least 3 seconds. If the system is normal (no malfunctions), **ENG-OK** will appear on the screen.

4. If there is a malfunction, the code number for it will appear on the screen. In the event of 2 or more numbers, there will be a 3 second pause between each (Example: **ENG-42**).

5. After confirmation of the diagnostic code, either turn **OFF** the ignition switch or push the super monitor display key **ON** so the time appears.

Clearing Diagnostic Memory

1. After repairing the trouble area, the diagnostic code that is retained in the ECU memory must be canceled out by removing the ECU memory fuse fuse for 30 seconds or more, depending on the ambient temperature (the lower temperature, the longer the fuse must be left out with the ignition switch **OFF**). To clear ECU memory remove the following fuse:

Camry—15A EFI fuse
Celica—15A EFI fuse

Simultaneously pushing "SELECT" and "INPUT"

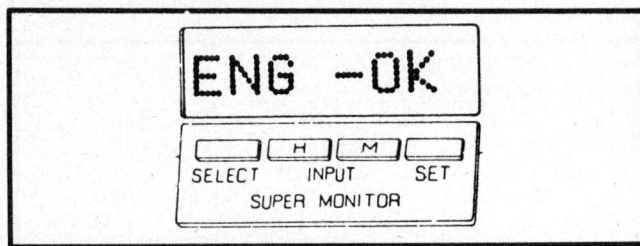

No malfunction message

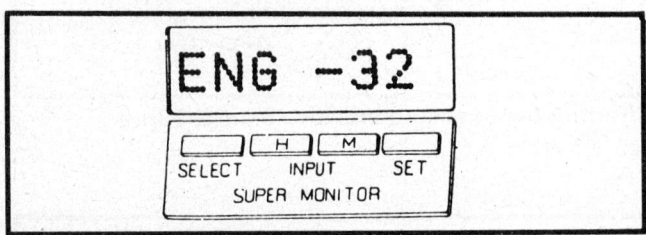

Engine Code 32 message

Corolla—15A Stop fuse
Cressida—15A or 20A EFI fuse
MR-2—7.5 AM2 fuse
Starlet—yellow fusible link
Supra—15A EFI fuse
Tercel—20A Stop fuse
Van—15A EFI fuse
Pick-Up—15A EFI fuse
4-Runner—15A EFI fuse
Land Cruiser—15A EFI fuse

NOTE: Cancellation can also be done by removing the negative battery terminal but keep in mind, when removing the negative battery cable, the other memory systems (radio, ETR, clock, etc.) will also be canceled out.

If the diagnostic code is not cancelled, it will be retained by the ECU and appear along with a new code in event of future trouble. If it is necessary to work on engine components requiring removal of the battery terminal, a check must first be made to see if a diagnostic code is detected.

2. After cancellation, perform a road test, if necessary, confirm that a normal code is now read on the "Check Engine" warning light or super monitor display.

3. If the same diagnostic code is still indicated, it indicates that the trouble area has not been repaired thoroughly.

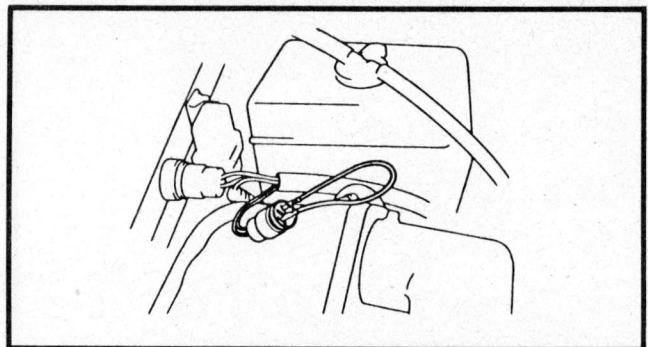

Shorting the check connector—1985 22R-E

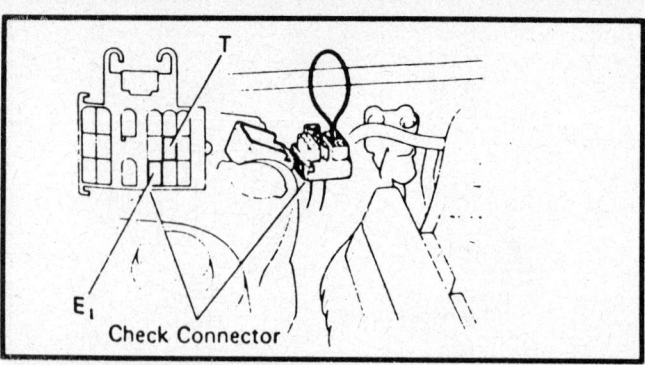

Shorting the check connector—4A-GEC, 4A-GELC and 4A-GZE engines

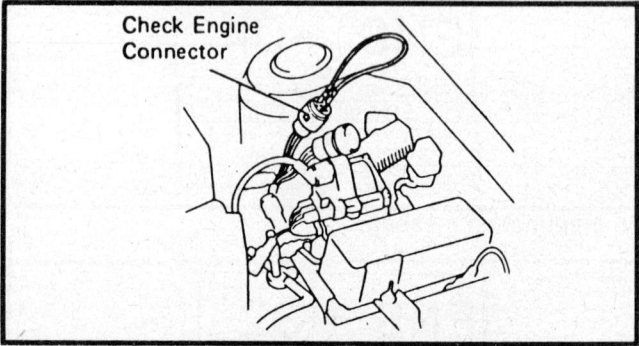

Shorting the check connector—5M-GE Supra

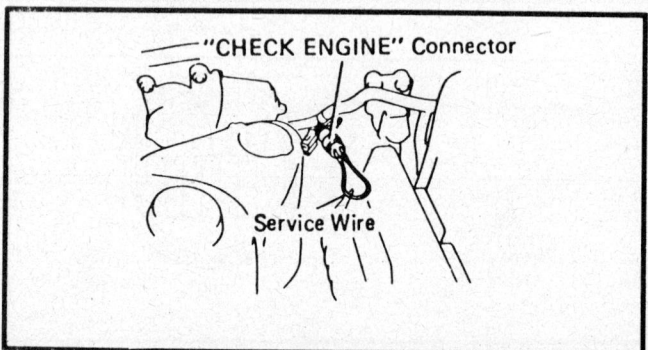

Shorting the check connector—4A-GE Corolla

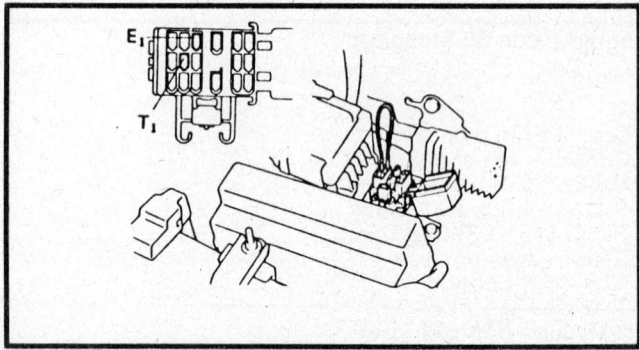

Shorting the check connector—5M-GE Cressida

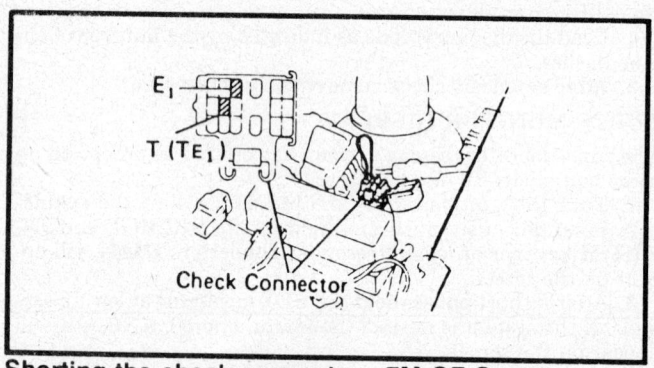

Shorting the check connector—7M-GE Supra

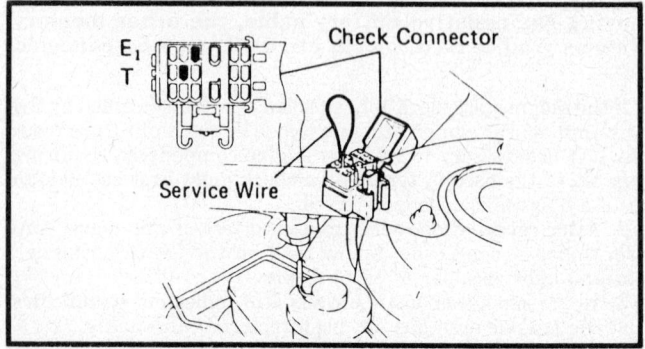

Shorting the check connector—1986 2S-E, 3S-FE, 3S-GE, 3S-GTE and 2VZ-FE engines

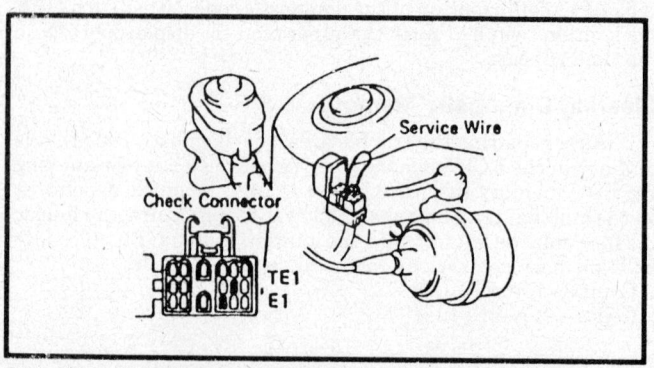

Shorting the check connector—7M-GE Cressida

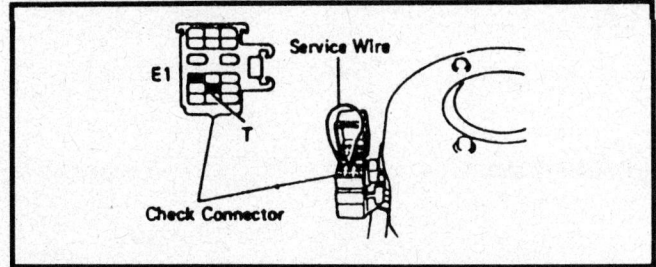

Shorting the check connector—4A-FE engine

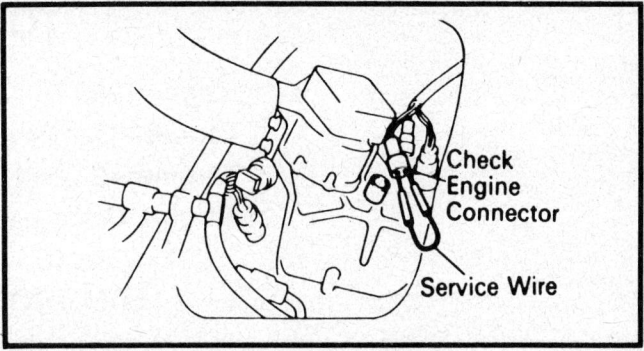

Shorting the check connector—Vans

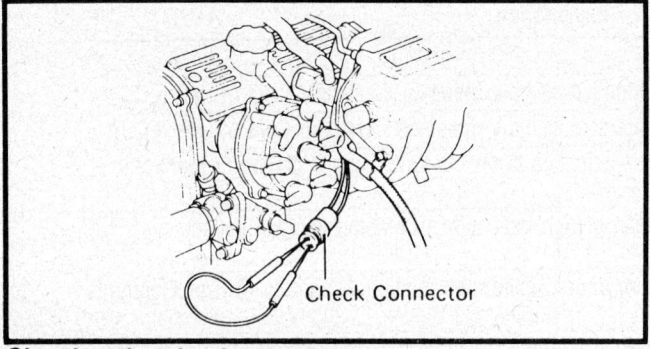

Shorting the check connector—typical location underhood

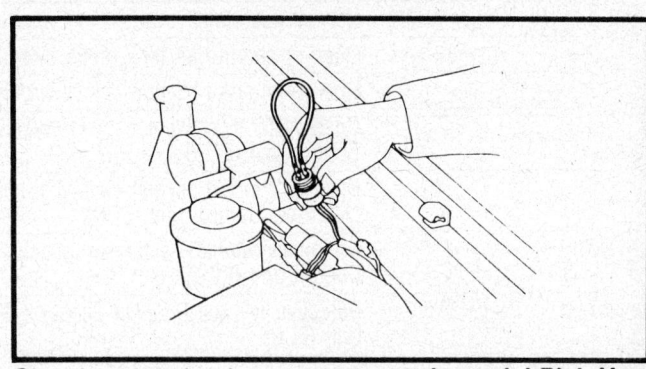

Shorting the check connector—early model Pick-Ups

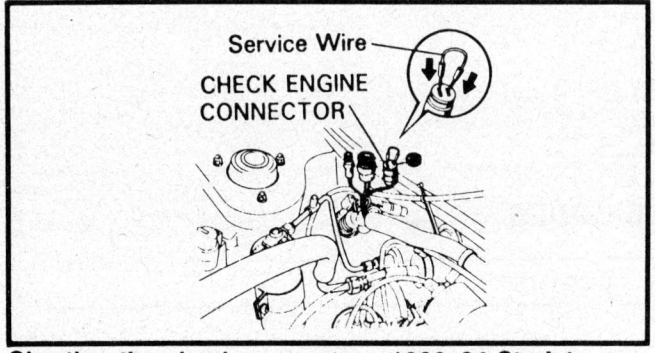

Shorting the check connector—1983–84 Starlet

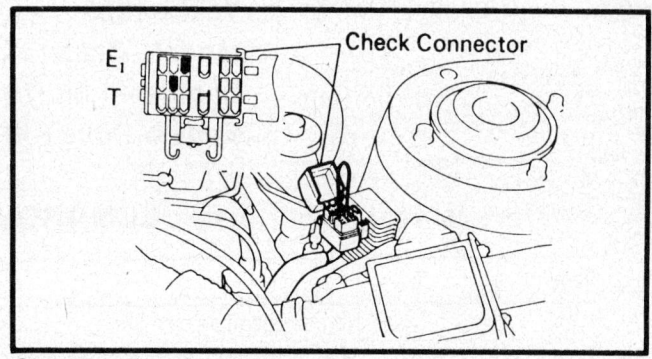

Shorting the check connector—1985–89 Camary

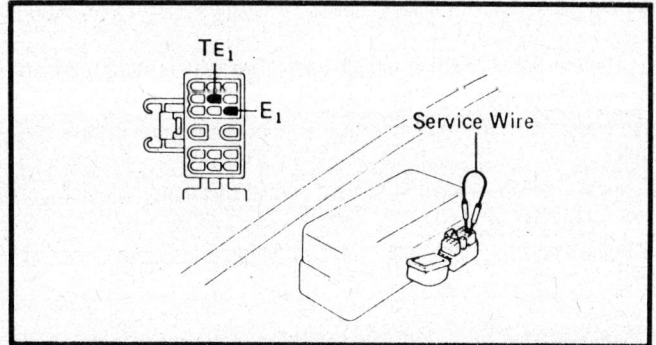

Shorting the check connector—late model Pick-Ups

TOYOTA

Year – 1983
Model – Camry
Engine – 2.0L (122 cid) EFI 4 cyl
Engine Code – 2S-E

ECM TROUBLE CODES

Code	Explanation
1	Normal operation
2	Open or shorted air flow meter circuit – defective air flow meter or Electronic Control Unit (ECU)
3	Open or shorted air flow meter circuit – defective air flow meter or Electronic Control Unit (ECU)
4	Open Water Thermo Sensor (THW) circuit – defective Water Thermo Sensor (THW) or Electronic Control Unit (ECU)
5	Open or shorted oxygen sensor circuit – lean or rich indication – defective oxygen sensor or Electronic Control Unit (ECU)
6	No ignition signal – defective ignition system circuit, Integrated Ignition Assembly (IIA) or Electronic Control Unit (ECU)
7	Defective Throttle Position Sensor (TPS) circuit, Throttle Position Sensor (TPS) or Electronic Control Unit (ECU)

Year – 1983
Model – Starlet
Engine – 1.3L (79 cid) EFI 4 cyl
Engine Code – 4K-E

ECM TROUBLE CODES

Code	Explanation
1	Normal operation
2	Open or shorted air flow meter circuit – defective air flow meter or Electronic Fuel Injection (EFI) computer
3	Open or shorted air flow meter circuit – defective air flow meter or Electronic Fuel Injection (EFI) computer
4	Open Water Thermo Sensor (THW) circuit – defective Water Thermo Sensor (THW) or Electronic Fuel Injection (EFI) computer
5	Open oxygen sensor circuit – lean indication – defective oxygen sensor or Electronic Fuel Injection (EFI) computer
6	No ignition signal – defective ignition system circuit, distributor, ignition coil and igniter or Electronic Fuel Injection (EFI) computer
7	Defective Throttle Position Sensor (TPS) circuit, Throttle Position Sensor (TPS) or Electronic Fuel Injection (EFI) computer

Year — 1983
Model — Celica
Engine — 2.4L (144 cid) EFI 4 cyl
Engine Code — 22R-E

ECM TROUBLE CODES

Code	Explanation
1	Normal operation
2	Open or shorted air flow meter circuit — defective air flow meter or Electronic Fuel Injection (EFI) computer
3	Open or shorted air flow meter circuit — defective air flow meter or Electronic Fuel Injection (EFI) computer
4	Open Water Thermo Sensor (THW) circuit — defective Water Thermo Sensor (THW) or Electronic Fuel Injection (EFI) computer
5	Open oxygen sensor circuit — lean indication — defective oxygen sensor or Electronic Fuel Injection (EFI) computer
6	No ignition signal — defective ignition system circuit, distributor, ignition coil and igniter or Electronic Fuel Injection (EFI) computer
7	Defective Throttle Position Sensor (TPS) circuit, Throttle Position Sensor (TPS) or Electronic Fuel Injection (EFI) computer

Year — 1983
Model — Celica
Engine — 2.4L (144 cid) EFI 4 cyl
Engine Code — 22R

ECM TROUBLE CODES

Code	Explanation
1	Normal operation
2	Open or shorted air flow meter circuit — defective air flow meter or Electronic Fuel Injection (EFI) computer
3	Open or shorted air flow meter circuit — defective air flow meter or Electronic Fuel Injection (EFI) computer
4	Open Water Thermo Sensor (THW) circuit — defective Water Thermo Sensor (THW) or Electronic Fuel Injection (EFI) computer
5	Open oxygen sensor circuit — lean indication — defective oxygen sensor or Electronic Fuel Injection (EFI) computer
6	No ignition signal — defective ignition system circuit, distributor, ignition coil and igniter or Electronic Fuel Injection (EFI) computer
7	Defective Throttle Position Sensor (TPS) circuit, Throttle Position Sensor (TPS) or Electronic Fuel Injection (EFI) computer

Year — 1983
Model — Cressida
Engine — 2.8L (168 cid) EFI V6
Engine Code — 5M-GE

ECM TROUBLE CODES

Code	Voltage Pattern	Diagnosis System	Diagnostic light "CHECK ENGINE"
—		This appears when none of the other codes (11 thru 51) are identified.	No indication
11		ECU power source (+B)	No indication
12		RPM signal (crank angle pulse)	ON
13		RPM signal (crank angle pulse)	ON
14		Ignition signal	ON
21		O₂ sensor signal	ON
22		Coolant temperature signal	ON
23		Intake air temperature signal	No indication
31		Air flow meter signal	ON
32		Air flow meter signal	ON
41		Throttle position sensor signal	No indication
42		Vehicle speed sensor signal	No indication
43		Starter signal	No indication
51		Air conditioner switch or neutral start switch signal	No indication

Year – 1983
Model – Celica Supra
Engine – 2.8L (168 cid) EFI V6
Engine Code – 5M-GE

ECM TROUBLE CODES

Code	Voltage Pattern	Diagnosis System	Diagnostic light "CHECK ENGINE"
–		This appears when none of the other codes (11 thru 51) are identified.	No indication
11		ECU power source (+B)	No indication
12		RPM signal (crank angle pulse)	ON
13		RPM signal (crank angle pulse)	ON
14		Ignition signal	ON
21		O₂ sensor signal	ON
22		Coolant temperature signal	ON
23		Intake air temperature signal	No indication
31		Air flow meter signal	ON
32		Air flow meter signal	ON
41		Throttle position sensor signal	No indication
42		Vehicle speed sensor signal	No indication
43		Starter signal	No indication
51		Air conditioner switch or neutral start switch signal	No indication

Year – 1984
Model – Camry
Engine – 2.0L (122 cid) EFI 4 cyl
Engine Code – 2S-E

ECM TROUBLE CODES

Code	Explanation
1	Normal operation
2	Open or shorted air flow meter circuit – defective air flow meter or Electronic Control Unit (ECU)
3	Open or shorted air flow meter circuit – defective air flow meter or Electronic Control Unit (ECU)
4	Open Water Thermo Sensor (THW) circuit – defective Water Thermo Sensor (THW) or Electronic Control Unit (ECU)
5	Open or shorted oxygen sensor circuit – lean or rich indication – defective oxygen sensor or Electronic Control Unit (ECU)
6	No ignition signal – defective ignition system circuit, Integrated Ignition Assembly (IIA) or Electronic Control Unit (ECU)
7	Defective Throttle Position Sensor (TPS) circuit, Throttle Position Sensor (TPS) or Electronic Control Unit (ECU)

Year – 1984
Model – Celica
Engine – 2.4L (144 cid) EFI 4 cyl
Engine Code – 22R-E

ECM TROUBLE CODES

Code	Explanation
1	Normal operation
2	Open or shorted air flow meter circuit – defective air flow meter or Electronic Fuel Injection (EFI) computer
3	Open or shorted air flow meter circuit – defective air flow meter or Electronic Fuel Injection (EFI) computer
4	Open Water Thermo Sensor (THW) circuit – defective Water Thermo Sensor (THW) or Electronic Fuel Injection (EFI) computer
5	Open oxygen sensor circuit – lean indication – defective oxygen sensor or Electronic Fuel Injection (EFI) computer
6	No ignition signal – defective ignition system circuit, distributor, ignition coil and igniter or Electronic Fuel Injection (EFI) computer
7	Defective Throttle Position Sensor (TPS) circuit, Throttle Position Sensor (TPS) or Electronic Fuel Injection (EFI) computer

Year — 1984
Model — Celica
Engine — 2.4L (144 cid) EFI 4 cyl
Engine Code — 22R

ECM TROUBLE CODES

Code	Explanation
1	Normal operation
2	Open or shorted air flow meter circuit — defective air flow meter or Electronic Fuel Injection (EFI) computer
3	Open or shorted air flow meter circuit — defective air flow meter or Electronic Fuel Injection (EFI) computer
4	Open Water Thermo Sensor (THW) circuit — defective Water Thermo Sensor (THW) or Electronic Fuel Injection (EFI) computer
5	Open oxygen sensor circuit — lean indication — defective oxygen sensor or Electronic Fuel Injection (EFI) computer
6	No ignition signal — defective ignition system circuit, distributor, ignition coil and igniter or Electronic Fuel Injection (EFI) computer
7	Defective Throttle Position Sensor (TPS) circuit, Throttle Position Sensor (TPS) or Electronic Fuel Injection (EFI) computer

Year — 1984
Model — Cressida
Engine — 2.8L (168 cid) EFI V6
Engine Code — 5M-GE

ECM TROUBLE CODES

Code	Voltage Pattern	Diagnosis System	Diagnostic light "CHECK ENGINE"
—		This appears when none of the other codes (11 thru 51) are identified.	No indication
11		ECU power source (+B)	No indication
12		RPM signal (crank angle pulse)	ON
13		RPM signal (crank angle pulse)	ON
14		Ignition signal	ON
21		Ox sensor signal	ON
22		Coolant temperature signal	ON
23		Intake air temperature signal	No indication
31		Air flow meter signal	ON
32		Air flow meter signal	ON
41		Throttle position sensor signal	No indication
42		Vehicle speed sensor signal	No indication
43		Starter signal	No indication
51		Air conditioner switch or neutral start switch signal	No indication

Year – 1984
Model – Celica Supra
Engine – 2.8L (168 cid) EFI V6
Engine Code – 5M-GE

ECM TROUBLE CODES

Code	Voltage Pattern	Diagnosis System	Diagnostic light "CHECK ENGINE"
–		This appears when none of the other codes (11 thru 51) are identified.	No indication
11		ECU power source (+B)	No indication
12		RPM signal (crank angle pulse)	ON
13		RPM signal (crank angle pulse)	ON
14		Ignition signal	ON
21		Ox sensor signal	ON
22		Coolant temperature signal	ON
23		Intake air temperature signal	No indication
31		Air flow meter signal	ON
32		Air flow meter signal	ON
41		Throttle position sensor signal	No indication
42		Vehicle speed sensor signal	No indication
43		Starter signal	No indication
51		Air conditioner switch or neutral start switch signal	No indication

Year – 1984
Model – Starlet
Engine – 1.3L (79 cid) EFI 4 cyl
Engine Code – 4K-E

ECM TROUBLE CODES

Code	Explanation
1	Normal operation
2	Open or shorted air flow meter circuit – defective air flow meter or Electronic Fuel Injection (EFI) computer
3	Open or shorted air flow meter circuit – defective air flow meter or Electronic Fuel Injection (EFI) computer
4	Open Water Thermo Sensor (THW) circuit – defective Water Thermo Sensor (THW) or Electronic Fuel Injection (EFI) computer
5	Open oxygen sensor circuit – lean indication – defective oxygen sensor or Electronic Fuel Injection (EFI) computer
6	No ignition signal – defective ignition system circuit, distributor, ignition coil and igniter or Electronic Fuel Injection (EFI) computer
7	Defective Throttle Position Sensor (TPS) circuit, Throttle Position Sensor (TPS) or Electronic Fuel Injection (EFI) computer

Year – 1985
Model – Camry
Engine – 2.0L (122 cid) EFI 4 cyl
Engine Code – 2S-E

ECM TROUBLE CODES

Code	Explanation
1	Normal operation
2	Open or shorted air flow meter circuit – defective air flow meter or Electronic Control Unit (ECU)
3	Open or shorted air flow meter circuit – defective air flow meter or Electronic Control Unit (ECU)
4	Open or shorted Water Thermo Sensor (THW) circuit – defective Water Thermo Sensor (THW) or Electronic Control Unit (ECU)
5	Open or shorted oxygen sensor circuit – lean or rich indication – defective oxygen sensor or Electronic Control Unit (ECU)
6	No ignition signal – defective ignition system circuit, Integrated Ignition Assembly (IIA) or Electronic Control Unit (ECU)
7	Defective Throttle Position Sensor (TPS) circuit, Throttle Position Sensor (TPS) or Electronic Control Unit (ECU)

Year – 1985
Model – Celica
Engine – 2.4L (144 cid) EFI 4 cyl
Engine Code – 22R

ECM TROUBLE CODES

Code	Explanation
1	Normal operation
2	Open or shorted air flow meter circuit – defective air flow meter or Electronic Control Unit (ECU)
3	No signal from igniter 4 times in succession – defective igniter or main relay circuit, igniter or Electronic Control Unit (ECU)
4	Open or shorted Water Thermo Sensor (THW) circuit – defective Water Thermo Sensor (THW) or Electronic Control Unit (ECU)
5	Open or shorted oxygen sensor circuit – lean or rich indication – defective oxygen sensor or Electronic Control Unit (ECU)
6	No engine revolution sensor (Ne) signal to Electronic Control Unit (ECU) or Ne value being over 1000 rpm in spite of no Ne signal to ECU – defective igniter circuit, igniter, distributor or Electronic Control Unit (ECU)
7	Open or shorted Throttle Position Sensor (TPS) circuit – defective Throttle Position Sensor (TPS) or Electronic Control Unit (ECU)
8	Open or shorted intake air thermo sensor circuit – defective intake air thermo sensor circuit or Electronic Control Unit (ECU)
10	No starter switch signal to Electronic Control Unit (ECU) with vehicle speed at 0 and engine speed over 800 rpm – defective speed sensor circuit, main relay circuit, igniter switch-to-starter circuit, igniter switch or Electronic Control Unit (ECU)
11	Short circuit in check connector terminal T with the air conditioning switch ON or throttle switch (IDL) point OFF – defective air conditioner switch, Throttle Position Sensor (TPS) circuit, Throttle Position Sensor (TPS) or Electronic Control Unit (ECU)
12	Knock control sensor signal has not reached judgement level in succession – defective knock control sensor circuit, knock control sensor or Electronic Control Unit (ECU)
13	Knock CPU faulty

Year — 1985
Model — Celica
Engine — 2.4L (144 cid) EFI 4 cyl
Engine Code — 22R-E

ECM TROUBLE CODES

Code	Explanation
1	Normal operation
2	Open or shorted air flow meter circuit — defective air flow meter or Electronic Control Unit (ECU)
3	No signal from igniter 4 times in succession — defective igniter or main relay circuit, igniter or Electronic Control Unit (ECU)
4	Open or shorted Water Thermo Sensor (THW) circuit — defective Water Thermo Sensor (THW) or Electronic Control Unit (ECU)
5	Open or shorted oxygen sensor circuit — lean or rich indication — defective oxygen sensor or Electronic Control Unit (ECU)
6	No engine revolution sensor (Ne) signal to Electronic Control Unit (ECU) or Ne value being over 1000 rpm in spite of no Ne signal to ECU — defective igniter circuit, igniter, distributor or Electronic Control Unit (ECU)
7	Open or shorted Throttle Position Sensor (TPS) circuit — defective Throttle Position Sensor (TPS) or Electronic Control Unit (ECU)
8	Open or shorted intake air thermo sensor circuit — defective intake air thermo sensor circuit or Electronic Control Unit (ECU)
10	No starter switch signal to Electronic Control Unit (ECU) with vehicle speed at 0 and engine speed over 800 rpm — defective speed sensor circuit, main relay circuit, igniter switch-to-starter circuit, igniter switch or Electronic Control Unit (ECU)
11	Short circuit in check connector terminal T with the air conditioning switch ON or throttle switch (IDL) point OFF — defective air conditioner switch, Throttle Position Sensor (TPS) circuit, Throttle Position Sensor (TPS) or Electronic Control Unit (ECU)
12	Knock control sensor signal has not reached judgement level in succession — defective knock control sensor circuit, knock control sensor or Electronic Control Unit (ECU)
13	Knock CPU faulty

Year – 1985
Model – Corolla
Engine – 1.6L (97 cid) EFI 4 cyl
Engine Code – 4A-C

ECM TROUBLE CODES

Code	Explanation
1	Normal operation
2	Open or shorted air flow meter circuit – defective air flow meter or Electronic Control Unit (ECU)
3	No signal from igniter 4 times in succession – defective igniter or main relay circuit, igniter or Electronic Control Unit (ECU)
4	Open or shorted Water Thermo Sensor (THW) circuit – defective Water Thermo Sensor (THW) or Electronic Control Unit (ECU)
5	Open oxygen sensor circuit – lean indication – defective oxygen sensor or Electronic Control Unit (ECU)
6	No engine revolution sensor (Ne) signal to Electronic Control Unit (ECU) within several seconds after the engine is cranked or no Ne signal to ECU within several seconds after the engine reaches 1000 rpm – defective distributor circuit, distributor, igniter, starter signal circuit or Electronic Control Unit (ECU)
7	Open or shorted Throttle Position Sensor (TPS) circuit – defective Throttle Position Sensor (TPS) or Electronic Control Unit (ECU)
8	Open or shorted intake air temperature sensor circuit – defective air thermo sensor circuit or Electronic Control Unit (ECU)
10	No starter switch signal to Electronic Control Unit (ECU) when the engine speed is over 800 rpm – defective starter relay circuit, igniter switch-to-starter circuit, igniter switch or Electronic Control Unit (ECU). This code will appear if the vehicle is push started
11	Air conditioning switch ON during diagnosis check – defective air conditioner switch or Electronic Control Unit (ECU)

Year — 1985
Model — Corolla
Engine — 1.6L (97 cid) EFI 4 cyl
Engine Code — 4A-GE

ECM TROUBLE CODES

Code	Explanation
1	Normal operation
2	Open or shorted air flow meter circuit — defective air flow meter or Electronic Control Unit (ECU)
3	No signal from igniter 4 times in succession — defective igniter or main relay circuit, igniter or Electronic Control Unit (ECU)
4	Open or shorted Water Thermo Sensor (THW) circuit — defective Water Thermo Sensor (THW) or Electronic Control Unit (ECU)
5	Open oxygen sensor circuit — lean indication — defective oxygen sensor or Electronic Control Unit (ECU)
6	No engine revolution sensor (Ne) signal to Electronic Control Unit (ECU) within several seconds after the engine is cranked or no Ne signal to ECU within several seconds after the engine reaches 1000 rpm — defective distributor circuit, distributor, igniter, starter signal circuit or Electronic Control Unit (ECU)
7	Open or shorted Throttle Position Sensor (TPS) circuit — defective Throttle Position Sensor (TPS) or Electronic Control Unit (ECU)
8	Open or shorted intake air temperature sensor circuit — defective air thermo sensor circuit or Electronic Control Unit (ECU)
10	No starter switch signal to Electronic Control Unit (ECU) when the engine speed is over 800 rpm — defective starter relay circuit, igniter switch-to-starter circuit, igniter switch or Electronic Control Unit (ECU). This code will appear if the vehicle is push started
11	Air conditioning switch ON during diagnosis check — defective air conditioner switch or Electronic Control Unit (ECU)

Year — 1985
Model — Cressida
Engine — 2.8L (168 cid) EFI V6
Engine Code — 5M-GE

ECM TROUBLE CODES

Code	Explanation
—	Normal system operation
11	Wire severence in the main relay of the Electronic Control Unit (ECU) — defective main relay circuit, main relay or ECU
12	No engine revolution sensor to Electronic Control Unit (ECU) within several seconds after engine is cranked — defective distributor circuit, distributor, starter signal circuit or Electronic Control Unit (ECU)
13	No igniter signal to Electronic Control Unit (ECU) within several seconds after engine reaches 1000 rpm — defective distributor circuit, distributor, starter signal circuit or Electronic Control Unit (ECU)
14	No signal from igniter 6 times in succession — defective igniter circuit, igniter or Electronic Control Unit (ECU)
21	Oxygen sensor gives a lean signal for several seconds even when the coolant temperature is above 122°F (50°C) and the engine is running under high load conditions above 1500 rpm — defective oxygen sensor circuit, oxygen sensor or Electronic Control Unit (ECU)
22	Open or shorted Coolant Temperature Sensor (CTS) signal circuit — defective Coolant Temperature Sensor (CTS) circuit, Coolant Temperature Sensor (CTS) or Electronic Control Unit (ECU)
23	Open or shorted intake air temperature sensor circuit — defective intake air temperature sensor circuit, intake air temperature sensor or Electronic Control Unit (ECU)
31	Open or shorted air flow meter signal circuit — defective air flow meter circuit, air flow meter or Electronic Control Unit (ECU)
32	Open or shorted air flow meter signal circuit — defective air flow meter circuit, air flow meter or Electronic Control Unit (ECU)
41	Open or shorted Throttle Position Sensor (TPS) circuit — defective TPS sensor or Electronic Control Unit (ECU)
42	No signal for over 5 seconds when vehicle is traveling under ½ mph and the engine running over 2500 rpm and the shift lever is in N or P for automatic transmissions — defective Vehicle Speed Sensor (VSS) circuit, VSS, torque converter or Electronic Control Unit (ECU)
43	No starter switch signal to Electronic Control Unit (ECU) when the engine is running over 800 rpm — defective main relay circuit, igniter switch to starter circuit, igniter switch or Electronic Control Unit (ECU)
51	Neutral start switch OFF or air conditioner switch ON during diagnostic check — defective neutral start switch, air conditioner switch or Electronic Control Unit (ECU)
52	Open or shorted knock sensor circuit — defective knock sensor or Electronic Control Unit (ECU)
53	Faulty Electronic Control Unit (ECU) or knock CPU — defective ECU

Year — 1985
Model — Celica Supra
Engine — 2.8L (168 cid) EFI V6
Engine Code — 5M-GE

ECM TROUBLE CODES

Code	Explanation
—	Normal system operation
11	Wire severence in the main relay of the Electronic Control Unit (ECU) — defective main relay circuit, main relay or ECU
12	No engine revolution sensor to Electronic Control Unit (ECU) within several seconds after engine is cranked — defective distributor circuit, distributor, starter signal circuit or Electronic Control Unit (ECU)
13	No igniter signal to Electronic Control Unit (ECU) within several seconds after engine reaches 1000 rpm — defective distributor circuit, distributor, starter signal circuit or Electronic Control Unit (ECU)
14	No signal from igniter 6 times in succession — defective igniter circuit, igniter or Electronic Control Unit (ECU)
21	Oxygen sensor gives a lean signal for several seconds even when the coolant temperature is above 122°F (50°C) and the engine is running under high load conditions above 1500 rpm — defective oxygen sensor circuit, oxygen sensor or Electronic Control Unit (ECU)
22	Open or shorted Coolant Temperature Sensor (CTS) signal circuit — defective Coolant Temperature Sensor (CTS) circuit, Coolant Temperature Sensor (CTS) or Electronic Control Unit (ECU)
23	Open or shorted intake air temperature sensor circuit — defective intake air temperature sensor circuit, intake air temperature sensor or Electronic Control Unit (ECU)
31	Open or shorted air flow meter signal circuit — defective air flow meter circuit, air flow meter or Electronic Control Unit (ECU)
32	Open or shorted air flow meter signal circuit — defective air flow meter circuit, air flow meter or Electronic Control Unit (ECU)
41	Open or shorted Throttle Position Sensor (TPS) circuit — defective TPS sensor or Electronic Control Unit (ECU)
42	No signal for over 5 seconds when vehicle is traveling under ½ mph and the engine running over 2500 rpm and the shift lever is in N or P for automatic transmissions — defective Vehicle Speed Sensor (VSS) circuit, VSS, torque converter or Electronic Control Unit (ECU)
43	No starter switch signal to Electronic Control Unit (ECU) when the engine is running over 800 rpm — defective main relay circuit, igniter switch to starter circuit, igniter switch or Electronic Control Unit (ECU)
51	Neutral start switch OFF or air conditioner switch ON during diagnostic check — defective neutral start switch, air conditioner switch or Electronic Control Unit (ECU)
52	Open or shorted knock sensor circuit — defective knock sensor or Electronic Control Unit (ECU)
53	Faulty Electronic Control Unit (ECU) or knock CPU — defective ECU

Year – 1986
Model – Camry (USA)
Engine – 2.0L (122 cid) EFI 4 cyl
Engine Code – 2S-EL

ECM TROUBLE CODES

Code	Explanation
1	Normal operation
2	Open or shorted air flow meter circuit – defective air flow meter or Electronic Control Unit (ECU)
3	No signal from igniter 4 times in succession – defective igniter or main relay circuit, igniter or Electronic Control Unit (ECU)
4	Open or shorted Water Thermo Sensor (THW) circuit – defective Water Thermo Sensor (THW) or Electronic Control Unit (ECU)
5	Open or shorted oxygen sensor circuit – lean or rich indication – defective oxygen sensor or Electronic Control Unit (ECU)
6	No engine revolution sensor (Ne) signal to Electronic Control Unit (ECU) or Ne value being over 1000 rpm in spite of no Ne signal to ECU – defective distributor circuit, igniter, distributor, starter signal circuit or Electronic Control Unit (ECU)
7	Open or shorted Throttle Position Sensor (TPS) circuit – defective Throttle Position Sensor (TPS) or Electronic Control Unit (ECU)
8	Open or shorted intake air thermo sensor circuit – defective air temperature sensor circuit or Electronic Control Unit (ECU)
9	Signal informing Electronic Control Unit (ECU) that vehicle stopped had been input to ECU for 8 seconds with the engine running between 2400–5000 rpm
10	No starter switch signal to Electronic Control Unit (ECU) with the vehicle stopped and the engine speed over 800 rpm – defective speed sensor circuit, igniter switch-to-starter circuit, igniter switch or Electronic Control Unit (ECU)
11	Air conditioning switch ON, idle switch OFF or shift position in any position other than P or N range during diagnosis check – defective air conditioner switch, Throttle Position Sensor (TPS) circuit, TPS, neutral start switch or Electronic Control Unit (ECU)

Year — 1986
Model — Camry (Canada)
Engine — 2.0L (122 cid) EFI 4 cyl
Engine Code — 2S-EL

ECM TROUBLE CODES

Code	Explanation
1	Normal operation
2	Open or shorted air flow meter circuit — defective air flow meter or Electronic Control Unit (ECU)
3	Open or shorted air flow meter circuit — defective air flow meter or Electronic Control Unit (ECU)
4	Open or shorted Water Thermo Sensor (THW) circuit — defective Water Thermo Sensor (THW) or Electronic Control Unit (ECU)
6	No ignition signal — defective ignition system circuit, distributor, ignition coil, igniter or Electronic Control Unit (ECU)
7	Defective Throttle Position Sensor (TPS) circuit, TPS or Electronic Control Unit (ECU)

Year — 1986
Model — Celica
Engine — 2.0L (122 cid) EFI 4 cyl
Engine Code — 2S-E

ECM TROUBLE CODES

Code	Explanation
1	Normal operation
2	Open or shorted air flow meter circuit — defective air flow meter or Electronic Control Unit (ECU)
3	No signal from igniter 4 times in succession — defective igniter or main relay circuit, igniter or Electronic Control Unit (ECU)
4	Open or shorted Water Thermo Sensor (THW) circuit — defective Water Thermo Sensor (THW) or Electronic Control Unit (ECU)
5	Open or shorted oxygen sensor circuit — lean or rich indication — defective oxygen sensor or Electronic Control Unit (ECU)
6	No engine revolution sensor (Ne) signal to Electronic Control Unit (ECU) or Ne value being over 1000 rpm in spite of no Ne signal to ECU — defective distributor circuit, igniter, distributor, starter signal circuit or Electronic Control Unit (ECU)
7	Open or shorted Throttle Position Sensor (TPS) circuit — defective Throttle Position Sensor (TPS) or Electronic Control Unit (ECU)
8	Open or shorted intake air thermo sensor circuit — defective air temperature sensor circuit or Electronic Control Unit (ECU)
9	Signal informing Electronic Control Unit (ECU) that vehicle stopped had been input to ECU for 8 seconds with the engine running between 2400–5000 rpm
10	No starter switch signal to Electronic Control Unit (ECU) with the vehicle stopped and the engine speed over 800 rpm — defective speed sensor circuit, igniter switch-to-starter circuit, igniter switch or Electronic Control Unit (ECU)
11	Air conditioning switch ON, idle switch OFF or shift position in any position other than P or N range during diagnosis check — defective air conditioner switch, Throttle Position Sensor (TPS) circuit, TPS, neutral start switch or Electronic Control Unit (ECU)

Year — 1986
Model — Celica
Engine — 2.0L (122 cid) EFI 4 cyl
Engine Code — 3S-GE

ECM TROUBLE CODES

Code	Explanation
—	Normal system operation
11	Wire severence in the main relay of the Electronic Control Unit (ECU) — defective main relay circuit, main relay or ECU
12	No engine revolution sensor to Electronic Control Unit (ECU) within several seconds after engine is cranked — defective distributor circuit, distributor, starter signal circuit or Electronic Control Unit (ECU)
13	No igniter signal to Electronic Control Unit (ECU) within several seconds after engine reaches 1000 rpm — defective distributor circuit, distributor, starter signal circuit or Electronic Control Unit (ECU)
14	No signal from igniter 6 times in succession — defective igniter circuit, igniter or Electronic Control Unit (ECU)
21	Oxygen sensor gives a lean signal for several seconds even when the coolant temperature is above 122°F (50°C) and the engine is running under high load conditions above 1500 rpm — defective oxygen sensor circuit, oxygen sensor or Electronic Control Unit (ECU)
22	Open or shorted Coolant Temperature Sensor (CTS) signal circuit — defective Coolant Temperature Sensor (CTS) circuit, Coolant Temperature Sensor (CTS) or Electronic Control Unit (ECU)
23	Open or shorted intake air temperature sensor circuit — defective intake air temperature sensor circuit, intake air temperature sensor or Electronic Control Unit (ECU)
31	Open or shorted air flow meter signal circuit — defective air flow meter circuit, air flow meter or Electronic Control Unit (ECU)
32	Open or shorted air flow meter signal circuit — defective air flow meter circuit, air flow meter or Electronic Control Unit (ECU)
41	Open or shorted Throttle Position Sensor (TPS) circuit — defective TPS sensor or Electronic Control Unit (ECU)
42	No signal for over 5 seconds when vehicle is stopped and the engine running between 1500–6000 rpm — defective Vehicle Speed Sensor (VSS) circuit, VSS or Electronic Control Unit (ECU)
43	No starter switch signal to Electronic Control Unit (ECU) when the engine is running over 800 rpm — defective main relay circuit, igniter switch to starter circuit, igniter switch or Electronic Control Unit (ECU)
51	Air conditioner switch ON, idle switch OFF or shift position other than P or N range during diagnosis check — defective neutral start switch, air conditioner switch, Throttle Position Sensor (TPS) circuit, TPS or Electronic Control Unit (ECU)

Year — 1986
Model — Cressida
Engine — 2.8L (168 cid) EFI V6
Engine Code — 5M-GE

ECM TROUBLE CODES

Code	Explanation
—	Normal system operation
11	Wire severence in the main relay of the Electronic Control Unit (ECU) — defective main relay circuit, main relay or ECU
12	No engine revolution sensor to Electronic Control Unit (ECU) within several seconds after engine is cranked — defective distributor circuit, distributor, starter signal circuit or Electronic Control Unit (ECU)
13	No igniter signal to Electronic Control Unit (ECU) within several seconds after engine reaches 1000 rpm — defective distributor circuit, distributor, starter signal circuit or Electronic Control Unit (ECU)
14	No signal from igniter 6 times in succession — defective igniter circuit, igniter or Electronic Control Unit (ECU)
21	Oxygen sensor gives a lean signal for several seconds even when the coolant temperature is above 122°F (50°C) and the engine is running under high load conditions above 1500 rpm — defective oxygen sensor circuit, oxygen sensor or Electronic Control Unit (ECU)
22	Open or shorted Coolant Temperature Sensor (CTS) signal circuit — defective Coolant Temperature Sensor (CTS) circuit, Coolant Temperature Sensor (CTS) or Electronic Control Unit (ECU)
23	Open or shorted intake air temperature sensor circuit — defective intake air temperature sensor circuit, intake air temperature sensor or Electronic Control Unit (ECU)
31	Open or shorted air flow meter signal circuit — defective air flow meter circuit, air flow meter or Electronic Control Unit (ECU)
32	Open or shorted air flow meter signal circuit — defective air flow meter circuit, air flow meter or Electronic Control Unit (ECU)
41	Open or shorted Throttle Position Sensor (TPS) circuit — defective TPS sensor or Electronic Control Unit (ECU)
42	No signal for over 5 seconds when vehicle is traveling under ½ mph and the engine running over 2500 rpm and the shift lever is in N or P for automatic transmissions — defective Vehicle Speed Sensor (VSS) circuit, VSS, torque converter or Electronic Control Unit (ECU)
43	No starter switch signal to Electronic Control Unit (ECU) when the engine is running over 800 rpm — defective main relay circuit, igniter switch to starter circuit, igniter switch or Electronic Control Unit (ECU)
51	Neutral start switch OFF or air conditioner switch ON during diagnostic check — defective neutral start switch, air conditioner switch or Electronic Control Unit (ECU)
52	Open or shorted knock sensor circuit — defective knock sensor or Electronic Control Unit (ECU)
53	Faulty Electronic Control Unit (ECU) or knock CPU — defective ECU

Year – 1986
Model – MR2
Engine – 1.6L (97 cid) EFI 4 cyl
Engine Code – 4A-GE

ECM TROUBLE CODES

Code	Explanation
1	Normal operation
2	Open or shorted air flow meter circuit – defective air flow meter or Electronic Control Unit (ECU)
3	No signal from igniter 4 times in succession – defective igniter or main relay circuit, igniter or Electronic Control Unit (ECU)
4	Open or shorted Water Thermo Sensor (THW) circuit – defective Water Thermo Sensor (THW) or Electronic Control Unit (ECU)
5	Open or shorted oxygen sensor circuit – lean or rich indication – defective oxygen sensor or Electronic Control Unit (ECU)
6	No engine revolution sensor (Ne) signal to Electronic Control Unit (ECU) or Ne value being over 1000 rpm in spite of no Ne signal to ECU – defective distributor circuit, igniter, distributor, starter signal circuit or Electronic Control Unit (ECU)
7	Open or shorted Throttle Position Sensor (TPS) circuit – defective Throttle Position Sensor (TPS) or Electronic Control Unit (ECU)
8	Open or shorted intake air thermo sensor circuit – defective air temperature sensor circuit or Electronic Control Unit (ECU)
10	No starter switch signal to Electronic Control Unit (ECU) with the vehicle stopped and the engine speed over 800 rpm – defective speed sensor circuit, igniter switch-to-starter circuit, igniter switch or Electronic Control Unit (ECU)
11	Air conditioning switch ON, idle switch OFF or shift position in D range for automatic transmissions, during diagnosis check – defective air conditioner switch, idle switch, neutral start switch or Electronic Control Unit (ECU)

Year — 1986
Model — Celica Supra
Engine — 2.0L (122 cid) EFI 4 cyl
Engine Code — 2S-E

ECM TROUBLE CODES

Code	Explanation
—	Normal system operation
11	Wire severence in the main relay of the Electronic Control Unit (ECU) — defective main relay circuit, main relay or ECU
12	No engine revolution sensor to Electronic Control Unit (ECU) within several seconds after engine is cranked — defective distributor circuit, distributor, starter signal circuit or Electronic Control Unit (ECU)
13	No igniter signal to Electronic Control Unit (ECU) within several seconds after engine reaches 1000 rpm — defective distributor circuit, distributor, starter signal circuit or Electronic Control Unit (ECU)
14	No signal from igniter 6 times in succession — defective igniter circuit, igniter or Electronic Control Unit (ECU)
21	Oxygen sensor gives a lean signal for several seconds even when the coolant temperature is above 122°F (50°C) and the engine is running under high load conditions above 1500 rpm — defective oxygen sensor circuit, oxygen sensor or Electronic Control Unit (ECU)
22	Open or shorted Coolant Temperature Sensor (CTS) signal circuit — defective Coolant Temperature Sensor (CTS) circuit, Coolant Temperature Sensor (CTS) or Electronic Control Unit (ECU)
23	Open or shorted intake air temperature sensor circuit — defective intake air temperature sensor circuit, intake air temperature sensor or Electronic Control Unit (ECU)
31	Open or shorted air flow meter signal circuit — defective air flow meter circuit, air flow meter or Electronic Control Unit (ECU)
32	Open or shorted air flow meter signal circuit — defective air flow meter circuit, air flow meter or Electronic Control Unit (ECU)
41	Open or shorted Throttle Position Sensor (TPS) circuit — defective TPS sensor or Electronic Control Unit (ECU)
42	No signal for over 5 seconds when vehicle is traveling under ½ mph and the engine running over 2500 rpm and the shift lever is in N or P for automatic transmissions — defective Vehicle Speed Sensor (VSS) circuit, VSS, torque converter or Electronic Control Unit (ECU)
43	No starter switch signal to Electronic Control Unit (ECU) when the engine is running over 800 rpm — defective main relay circuit, igniter switch to starter circuit, igniter switch or Electronic Control Unit (ECU)
51	Neutral start switch OFF or air conditioner switch ON during diagnostic check — defective neutral start switch, air conditioner switch or Electronic Control Unit (ECU)
52	Open or shorted knock sensor circuit — defective knock sensor or Electronic Control Unit (ECU)
53	Faulty Electronic Control Unit (ECU) or knock CPU — defective ECU

Year — 1986
Model — Celica Supra
Engine — 2.0L (122 cid) EFI 4 cyl
Engine Code — 3S-GE

ECM TROUBLE CODES

Code	Explanation
—	Normal system operation
11	Wire severence in the main relay of the Electronic Control Unit (ECU) — defective main relay circuit, main relay or ECU
12	No engine revolution sensor to Electronic Control Unit (ECU) within several seconds after engine is cranked — defective distributor circuit, distributor, starter signal circuit or Electronic Control Unit (ECU)
13	No igniter signal to Electronic Control Unit (ECU) within several seconds after engine reaches 1000 rpm — defective distributor circuit, distributor, starter signal circuit or Electronic Control Unit (ECU)
14	No signal from igniter 6 times in succession — defective igniter circuit, igniter or Electronic Control Unit (ECU)
21	Oxygen sensor gives a lean signal for several seconds even when the coolant temperature is above 122°F (50°C) and the engine is running under high load conditions above 1500 rpm — defective oxygen sensor circuit, oxygen sensor or Electronic Control Unit (ECU)
22	Open or shorted Coolant Temperature Sensor (CTS) signal circuit — defective Coolant Temperature Sensor (CTS) circuit, Coolant Temperature Sensor (CTS) or Electronic Control Unit (ECU)
23	Open or shorted intake air temperature sensor circuit — defective intake air temperature sensor circuit, intake air temperature sensor or Electronic Control Unit (ECU)
31	Open or shorted air flow meter signal circuit — defective air flow meter circuit, air flow meter or Electronic Control Unit (ECU)
32	Open or shorted air flow meter signal circuit — defective air flow meter circuit, air flow meter or Electronic Control Unit (ECU)
41	Open or shorted Throttle Position Sensor (TPS) circuit — defective TPS sensor or Electronic Control Unit (ECU)
42	No signal for over 5 seconds when vehicle is traveling under ½ mph and the engine running over 2500 rpm and the shift lever is in N or P for automatic transmissions — defective Vehicle Speed Sensor (VSS) circuit, VSS, torque converter or Electronic Control Unit (ECU)
43	No starter switch signal to Electronic Control Unit (ECU) when the engine is running over 800 rpm — defective main relay circuit, igniter switch to starter circuit, igniter switch or Electronic Control Unit (ECU)
51	Neutral start switch OFF or air conditioner switch ON during diagnostic check — defective neutral start switch, air conditioner switch or Electronic Control Unit (ECU)
52	Open or shorted knock sensor circuit — defective knock sensor or Electronic Control Unit (ECU)
53	Faulty Electronic Control Unit (ECU) or knock CPU — defective ECU

Year – 1987
Model – Camry
Engine – 2.0L (122 cid) EFI 4 cyl
Engine Code – 3S-FE

ECM TROUBLE CODES

Code	Explanation
—	Normal system operation
11	Wire severence in the main relay of the Electronic Control Unit (ECU) – defective main relay circuit, main relay or ECU
12	No engine revolution sensor to Electronic Control Unit (ECU) within several seconds after engine is cranked – defective distributor circuit, distributor, starter signal circuit or Electronic Control Unit (ECU)
13	No igniter signal to Electronic Control Unit (ECU) within several seconds after engine reaches 1000 rpm – defective distributor circuit, distributor, starter signal circuit or Electronic Control Unit (ECU)
14	No signal from igniter 4–5 times in succession – defective igniter circuit, igniter or Electronic Control Unit (ECU)
21	Oxygen sensor gives a lean signal for several seconds even when the coolant temperature is above 122°F (50°C) and the engine is running under high load conditions above 1500 rpm – defective oxygen sensor circuit, oxygen sensor or Electronic Control Unit (ECU)
22	Open or shorted Coolant Temperature Sensor (CTS) signal circuit – defective Coolant Temperature Sensor (CTS) circuit, Coolant Temperature Sensor (CTS) or Electronic Control Unit (ECU)
24	Open or shorted intake air temperature sensor circuit – defective intake air temperature sensor circuit, intake air temperature sensor or Electronic Control Unit (ECU)
31	Open or shorted air flow meter signal circuit – defective air flow meter circuit, air flow meter or Electronic Control Unit (ECU)
32	Open or shorted air flow meter signal circuit – defective air flow meter circuit, air flow meter or Electronic Control Unit (ECU)
41	Open or shorted Throttle Position Sensor (TPS) circuit – defective TPS sensor or Electronic Control Unit (ECU)
42	No signal for over 5 seconds when vehicle is stopped and the engine running between 2500–5500 rpm – defective Vehicle Speed Sensor (VSS) circuit, VSS or Electronic Control Unit (ECU)
43	No starter switch signal to Electronic Control Unit (ECU) when the engine is running over 800 rpm – defective main relay circuit, igniter switch to starter circuit, igniter switch or Electronic Control Unit (ECU)
51	Air conditioner switch ON, idle switch OFF or shift position other than P or N range during diagnosis check – defective neutral start switch, air conditioner switch, Throttle Position Sensor (TPS) circuit, TPS or Electronic Control Unit (ECU)

Year — 1987
Model — Celica
Engine — 2.0L (122 cid) EFI 4 cyl
Engine Code — 3S-FE

ECM TROUBLE CODES

Code	Explanation
—	Normal system operation
11	Wire severence in the main relay of the Electronic Control Unit (ECU) — defective main relay circuit, main relay or ECU
12	No engine revolution sensor to Electronic Control Unit (ECU) within several seconds after engine is cranked — defective distributor circuit, distributor, starter signal circuit or Electronic Control Unit (ECU)
13	No igniter signal to Electronic Control Unit (ECU) within several seconds after engine reaches 1000 rpm — defective distributor circuit, distributor, starter signal circuit or Electronic Control Unit (ECU)
14	No signal from igniter 4–11 times in succession — defective igniter circuit, igniter or Electronic Control Unit (ECU)
21	Oxygen sensor gives a lean signal for several seconds even when the coolant temperature is above 122°F (50°C) and the engine is running under high load conditions above 1500 rpm — defective oxygen sensor circuit, oxygen sensor or Electronic Control Unit (ECU)
22	Open or shorted Coolant Temperature Sensor (CTS) signal circuit — defective Coolant Temperature Sensor (CTS) circuit, Coolant Temperature Sensor (CTS) or Electronic Control Unit (ECU)
24	Open or shorted intake air temperature sensor circuit — defective intake air temperature sensor circuit, intake air temperature sensor or Electronic Control Unit (ECU)
31	Open or shorted air flow meter signal circuit — defective air flow meter circuit, air flow meter or Electronic Control Unit (ECU)
32	Open or shorted air flow meter signal circuit — defective air flow meter circuit, air flow meter or Electronic Control Unit (ECU)
41	Open or shorted Throttle Position Sensor (TPS) circuit — defective TPS sensor or Electronic Control Unit (ECU)
42	No signal for over 5 seconds when vehicle is stopped and the engine running between 2500–5500 rpm — defective Vehicle Speed Sensor (VSS) circuit, VSS or Electronic Control Unit (ECU)
43	No starter switch signal to Electronic Control Unit (ECU) when the engine is running over 800 rpm — defective main relay circuit, igniter switch to starter circuit, igniter switch or Electronic Control Unit (ECU)
51	Air conditioner switch ON, idle switch OFF or shift position other than P or N range during diagnosis check — defective neutral start switch, air conditioner switch, Throttle Position Sensor (TPS) circuit, TPS or Electronic Control Unit (ECU)

Year — 1987
Model — Celica
Engine — 2.0L (122 cid) EFI 4 cyl
Engine Code — 3S-GE

ECM TROUBLE CODES

Code	Explanation
—	Normal system operation
11	Wire severence in the main relay of the Electronic Control Unit (ECU) — defective main relay circuit, main relay or ECU
12	No engine revolution sensor to Electronic Control Unit (ECU) within several seconds after engine is cranked — defective distributor circuit, distributor, starter signal circuit or Electronic Control Unit (ECU)
13	No igniter signal to Electronic Control Unit (ECU) within several seconds after engine reaches 1000 rpm — defective distributor circuit, distributor, starter signal circuit or Electronic Control Unit (ECU)
14	No signal from igniter 8–11 times in succession — defective igniter circuit, igniter or Electronic Control Unit (ECU)
21	Oxygen sensor gives a lean signal for several seconds even when the coolant temperature is above 122°F (50°C) and the engine is running under high load conditions above 1500 rpm — defective oxygen sensor circuit, oxygen sensor or Electronic Control Unit (ECU)
22	Open or shorted Coolant Temperature Sensor (CTS) signal circuit — defective Coolant Temperature Sensor (CTS) circuit, Coolant Temperature Sensor (CTS) or Electronic Control Unit (ECU)
24	Open or shorted intake air temperature sensor circuit — defective intake air temperature sensor circuit, intake air temperature sensor or Electronic Control Unit (ECU)
31	Open or shorted air flow meter signal circuit — defective air flow meter circuit, air flow meter or Electronic Control Unit (ECU)
32	Open or shorted air flow meter signal circuit — defective air flow meter circuit, air flow meter or Electronic Control Unit (ECU)
41	Open or shorted Throttle Position Sensor (TPS) circuit — defective TPS sensor or Electronic Control Unit (ECU)
42	No signal for over 5 seconds when vehicle is stopped and the engine running between 2500–6000 rpm — defective Vehicle Speed Sensor (VSS) circuit, VSS or Electronic Control Unit (ECU)
43	No starter switch signal to Electronic Control Unit (ECU) when the engine is running over 800 rpm — defective main relay circuit, igniter switch to starter circuit, igniter switch or Electronic Control Unit (ECU)
51	Air conditioner switch ON, idle switch OFF or shift position other than P or N range during diagnosis check — defective neutral start switch, air conditioner switch, Throttle Position Sensor (TPS) circuit, TPS or Electronic Control Unit (ECU)

Year — 1987
Model — Corolla
Engine — 1.6L (97 cid) EFI 4 cyl
Engine Code — 4A-LC

ECM TROUBLE CODES

Code	Explanation
1	Normal operation
2	Open or shorted air flow meter circuit — defective air flow meter or Electronic Control Unit (ECU)
3	No signal from igniter 4 times in succession — defective igniter or main relay circuit, igniter or Electronic Control Unit (ECU)
4	Open or shorted Water Thermo Sensor (THW) circuit — defective Water Thermo Sensor (THW) or Electronic Control Unit (ECU)
5	Open or shorted oxygen sensor circuit — lean or rich indication — defective oxygen sensor or Electronic Control Unit (ECU)
6	No engine revolution sensor (Ne) signal to Electronic Control Unit (ECU) or Ne value being over 1000 rpm in spite of no Ne signal to ECU — defective distributor circuit, igniter, distributor, starter signal circuit or Electronic Control Unit (ECU)
7	Open or shorted Throttle Position Sensor (TPS) circuit — defective Throttle Position Sensor (TPS) or Electronic Control Unit (ECU)
8	Open or shorted intake air thermo sensor circuit — defective air temperature sensor circuit or Electronic Control Unit (ECU)
10	No starter switch signal to Electronic Control Unit (ECU) with the vehicle stopped and the engine speed over 800 rpm — defective speed sensor circuit, igniter switch-to-starter circuit, igniter switch or Electronic Control Unit (ECU)
11	Air conditioning switch ON, idle switch OFF or shift position in D range for automatic transmissions, during diagnosis check — defective air conditioner switch, idle switch, neutral start switch or Electronic Control Unit (ECU)

Year — 1987
Model — Corolla
Engine — 1.6L (97 cid) EFI 4 cyl
Engine Code — 4A-GEC

ECM TROUBLE CODES

Code	Explanation
1	Normal operation
2	Open or shorted air flow meter circuit—defective air flow meter or Electronic Control Unit (ECU)
3	No signal from igniter 4 times in succession—defective igniter or main relay circuit, igniter or Electronic Control Unit (ECU)
4	Open or shorted Water Thermo Sensor (THW) circuit—defective Water Thermo Sensor (THW) or Electronic Control Unit (ECU)
5	Open or shorted oxygen sensor circuit—lean or rich indication—defective oxygen sensor or Electronic Control Unit (ECU)
6	No engine revolution sensor (Ne) signal to Electronic Control Unit (ECU) or Ne value being over 1000 rpm in spite of no Ne signal to ECU—defective distributor circuit, igniter, distributor, starter signal circuit or Electronic Control Unit (ECU)
7	Open or shorted Throttle Position Sensor (TPS) circuit—defective Throttle Position Sensor (TPS) or Electronic Control Unit (ECU)
8	Open or shorted intake air thermo sensor circuit—defective air temperature sensor circuit or Electronic Control Unit (ECU)
10	No starter switch signal to Electronic Control Unit (ECU) with the vehicle stopped and the engine speed over 800 rpm—defective speed sensor circuit, igniter switch-to-starter circuit, igniter switch or Electronic Control Unit (ECU)
11	Air conditioning switch ON, idle switch OFF or shift position in D range for automatic transmissions, during diagnosis check—defective air conditioner switch, idle switch, neutral start switch or Electronic Control Unit (ECU)

Year – 1987
Model – Corolla
Engine – 1.6L (97 cid) EFI 4 cyl
Engine Code – 4A-GELC

ECM TROUBLE CODES

Code	Explanation
1	Normal operation
2	Open or shorted air flow meter circuit — defective air flow meter or Electronic Control Unit (ECU)
3	No signal from igniter 4 times in succession — defective igniter or main relay circuit, igniter or Electronic Control Unit (ECU)
4	Open or shorted Water Thermo Sensor (THW) circuit — defective Water Thermo Sensor (THW) or Electronic Control Unit (ECU)
5	Open or shorted oxygen sensor circuit — lean or rich indication — defective oxygen sensor or Electronic Control Unit (ECU)
6	No engine revolution sensor (Ne) signal to Electronic Control Unit (ECU) or Ne value being over 1000 rpm in spite of no Ne signal to ECU — defective distributor circuit, igniter, distributor, starter signal circuit or Electronic Control Unit (ECU)
7	Open or shorted Throttle Position Sensor (TPS) circuit — defective Throttle Position Sensor (TPS) or Electronic Control Unit (ECU)
8	Open or shorted intake air thermo sensor circuit — defective air temperature sensor circuit or Electronic Control Unit (ECU)
10	No starter switch signal to Electronic Control Unit (ECU) with the vehicle stopped and the engine speed over 800 rpm — defective speed sensor circuit, igniter switch-to-starter circuit, igniter switch or Electronic Control Unit (ECU)
11	Air conditioning switch ON, idle switch OFF or shift position in D range for automatic transmissions, during diagnosis check — defective air conditioner switch, idle switch, neutral start switch or Electronic Control Unit (ECU)

Year — 1987
Model — Cressida
Engine — 2.8L (168 cid) EFI V6
Engine Code — 5M-GE

ECM TROUBLE CODES

Code	Explanation
—	Normal system operation
11	Wire severence in the main relay of the Electronic Control Unit (ECU) — defective main relay circuit, main relay or ECU
12	No engine revolution sensor to Electronic Control Unit (ECU) within several seconds after engine is cranked — defective distributor circuit, distributor, starter signal circuit or Electronic Control Unit (ECU)
13	No igniter signal to Electronic Control Unit (ECU) within several seconds after engine reaches 1000 rpm — defective distributor circuit, distributor, starter signal circuit or Electronic Control Unit (ECU)
14	No signal from igniter 6 times in succession — defective igniter circuit, igniter or Electronic Control Unit (ECU)
21	Oxygen sensor gives a lean signal for several seconds even when the coolant temperature is above 122°F (50°C) and the engine is running under high load conditions above 1500 rpm — defective oxygen sensor circuit, oxygen sensor or Electronic Control Unit (ECU)
22	Open or shorted Coolant Temperature Sensor (CTS) signal circuit — defective Coolant Temperature Sensor (CTS) circuit, Coolant Temperature Sensor (CTS) or Electronic Control Unit (ECU)
23	Open or shorted intake air temperature sensor circuit — defective intake air temperature sensor circuit, intake air temperature sensor or Electronic Control Unit (ECU)
31	Open or shorted air flow meter signal circuit — defective air flow meter circuit, air flow meter or Electronic Control Unit (ECU)
32	Open or shorted air flow meter signal circuit — defective air flow meter circuit, air flow meter or Electronic Control Unit (ECU)
41	Open or shorted Throttle Position Sensor (TPS) circuit — defective TPS sensor or Electronic Control Unit (ECU)
42	No signal for over 5 seconds when vehicle is traveling under ½ mph and the engine running over 2500 rpm and the shift lever is in N or P for automatic transmissions — defective Vehicle Speed Sensor (VSS) circuit, VSS, torque converter or Electronic Control Unit (ECU)
43	No starter switch signal to Electronic Control Unit (ECU) when the engine is running over 800 rpm — defective main relay circuit, igniter switch to starter circuit, igniter switch or Electronic Control Unit (ECU)
51	Neutral start switch OFF or air conditioner switch ON during diagnostic check — defective neutral start switch, air conditioner switch or Electronic Control Unit (ECU)
52	Open or shorted knock sensor circuit — defective knock sensor or Electronic Control Unit (ECU)
53	Faulty Electronic Control Unit (ECU) or knock CPU — defective ECU

Year – 1987
Model – MR2
Engine – 1.6L (97 cid) EFI 4 cyl
Engine Code – 4A-GE

ECM TROUBLE CODES

Code	Explanation
1	Normal operation
2	Open or shorted air flow meter circuit – defective air flow meter or Electronic Control Unit (ECU)
3	No signal from igniter 4 times in succession – defective igniter or main relay circuit, igniter or Electronic Control Unit (ECU)
4	Open or shorted Water Thermo Sensor (THW) circuit – defective Water Thermo Sensor (THW) or Electronic Control Unit (ECU)
5	Open or shorted oxygen sensor circuit – lean or rich indication – defective oxygen sensor or Electronic Control Unit (ECU)
6	No engine revolution sensor (Ne) signal to Electronic Control Unit (ECU) or Ne value being over 1000 rpm in spite of no Ne signal to ECU – defective distributor circuit, igniter, distributor, starter signal circuit or Electronic Control Unit (ECU)
7	Open or shorted Throttle Position Sensor (TPS) circuit – defective Throttle Position Sensor (TPS) or Electronic Control Unit (ECU)
8	Open or shorted intake air thermo sensor circuit – defective air temperature sensor circuit or Electronic Control Unit (ECU)
10	No starter switch signal to Electronic Control Unit (ECU) with the vehicle stopped and the engine speed over 800 rpm – defective speed sensor circuit, igniter switch-to-starter circuit, igniter switch or Electronic Control Unit (ECU)
11	Air conditioning switch ON, idle switch OFF or shift position in D range for automatic transmissions, during diagnosis check – defective air conditioner switch, idle switch, neutral start switch or Electronic Control Unit (ECU)

Year — 1987
Model — MR2
Engine — 1.6L (97 cid) EFI 4 cyl
Engine Code — 4A-GZE

ECM TROUBLE CODES

Code	Explanation
1	Normal operation
2	Open or shorted air flow meter circuit — defective air flow meter or Electronic Control Unit (ECU)
3	No signal from igniter 4 times in succession — defective igniter or main relay circuit, igniter or Electronic Control Unit (ECU)
4	Open or shorted Water Thermo Sensor (THW) circuit — defective Water Thermo Sensor (THW) or Electronic Control Unit (ECU)
5	Open or shorted oxygen sensor circuit — lean or rich indication — defective oxygen sensor or Electronic Control Unit (ECU)
6	No engine revolution sensor (Ne) signal to Electronic Control Unit (ECU) or Ne value being over 1000 rpm in spite of no Ne signal to ECU — defective distributor circuit, igniter, distributor, starter signal circuit or Electronic Control Unit (ECU)
7	Open or shorted Throttle Position Sensor (TPS) circuit — defective Throttle Position Sensor (TPS) or Electronic Control Unit (ECU)
8	Open or shorted intake air thermo sensor circuit — defective air temperature sensor circuit or Electronic Control Unit (ECU)
10	No starter switch signal to Electronic Control Unit (ECU) with the vehicle stopped and the engine speed over 800 rpm — defective speed sensor circuit, igniter switch-to-starter circuit, igniter switch or Electronic Control Unit (ECU)
11	Air conditioning switch ON, idle switch OFF or shift position in D range for automatic transmissions, during diagnosis check — defective air conditioner switch, idle switch, neutral start switch or Electronic Control Unit (ECU)

Year – 1987
Model – Supra
Engine – 3.0L (180 cid) EFI V6
Engine Code – 7M-GE

ECM TROUBLE CODES

Code	Explanation
—	Normal system operation
11	Wire severence in the main relay of the Electronic Control Unit (ECU) — defective main relay circuit, main relay or ECU
12	No engine revolution sensor to Electronic Control Unit (ECU) within several seconds after engine is cranked — defective distributor circuit, distributor, starter signal circuit or Electronic Control Unit (ECU)
13	No igniter signal to Electronic Control Unit (ECU) within several seconds after engine reaches 1000 rpm — defective distributor circuit, distributor, starter signal circuit or Electronic Control Unit (ECU)
14	No signal from igniter 6 times in succession — defective igniter circuit, igniter or Electronic Control Unit (ECU)
21	Open or shorted oxygen sensor circuit — defective oxygen sensor circuit, oxygen sensor or Electronic Control Unit (ECU)
22	Open or shorted Coolant Temperature Sensor (CTS) signal circuit — defective Coolant Temperature Sensor (CTS) circuit, Coolant Temperature Sensor (CTS) or Electronic Control Unit (ECU)
24	Open or shorted intake air temperature sensor circuit — defective intake air temperature sensor circuit, intake air temperature sensor or Electronic Control Unit (ECU)
31	Open or shorted when the idle points are closed — defective air flow meter circuit, air flow meter or Electronic Control Unit (ECU)
32	Open or shorted air flow meter signal circuit — defective air flow meter circuit, air flow meter or Electronic Control Unit (ECU)
41	Open or shorted Throttle Position Sensor (TPS) circuit — defective TPS sensor or Electronic Control Unit (ECU)
42	Open or shorted Vehicle Speed Sensor (VSS) circuit — defective VSS circuit, VSS or Electronic Control Unit (ECU)
43	No starter switch signal to Electronic Control Unit (ECU) when the engine is running over 800 rpm — defective main relay circuit, igniter switch to starter circuit, igniter switch or Electronic Control Unit (ECU)
51	Air conditioner switch ON or idle switch OFF or shift positions other than P or N range during diagnostic check — defective neutral start switch, Throttle Position Sensor (TPS) circuit, TPS, air conditioner switch or Electronic Control Unit (ECU)
52	Open or shorted knock sensor circuit — defective knock sensor or Electronic Control Unit (ECU)
53	Faulty Electronic Control Unit (ECU) or knock CPU — defective ECU

Year – 1987
Model – Supra
Engine – 3.0L (180 cid) EFI V6
Engine Code – 7M-GTE

ECM TROUBLE CODES

Code	Explanation
–	Normal system operation
11	Wire severence in the main relay of the Electronic Control Unit (ECU) – defective main relay circuit, main relay or ECU
12	No engine revolution sensor to Electronic Control Unit (ECU) within several seconds after engine is cranked – defective distributor circuit, distributor, starter signal circuit or Electronic Control Unit (ECU)
13	No igniter signal to Electronic Control Unit (ECU) within several seconds after engine reaches 1000 rpm – defective distributor circuit, distributor, starter signal circuit or Electronic Control Unit (ECU)
14	No signal from igniter 6 times in succession – defective igniter circuit, igniter or Electronic Control Unit (ECU)
21	Open or shorted oxygen sensor circuit – defective oxygen sensor circuit, oxygen sensor or Electronic Control Unit (ECU)
22	Open or shorted Coolant Temperature Sensor (CTS) signal circuit – defective Coolant Temperature Sensor (CTS) circuit, Coolant Temperature Sensor (CTS) or Electronic Control Unit (ECU)
24	Open or shorted intake air temperature sensor circuit – defective intake air temperature sensor circuit, intake air temperature sensor or Electronic Control Unit (ECU)
31	Open or shorted air flow meter signal circuit – defective air flow meter circuit, air flow meter or Electronic Control Unit (ECU)
32	Open or shorted circuit in the High Altitude Compensation (HAC) sensor signal – defective HAC sensor circuit, HAC sensor or Electronic Control Unit (ECU)
34	Abnormal turbocharger pressure – defective turbocharger, air flow meter or Electronic Control Unit (ECU)
41	Open or shorted Throttle Position Sensor (TPS) circuit – defective TPS sensor or Electronic Control Unit (ECU)
42	Open or shorted Vehicle Speed Sensor (VSS) circuit – defective VSS circuit, VSS or Electronic Control Unit (ECU)
43	No starter switch signal to Electronic Control Unit (ECU) when the engine is running over 800 rpm – defective main relay circuit, igniter switch to starter circuit, igniter switch or Electronic Control Unit (ECU)
51	Air conditioner switch ON or idle switch OFF or shift positions other than P or N range during diagnostic check – defective neutral start switch, Throttle Position Sensor (TPS) circuit, TPS, air conditioner switch or Electronic Control Unit (ECU)
52	Open or shorted knock sensor circuit – defective knock sensor or Electronic Control Unit (ECU)
53	Faulty Electronic Control Unit (ECU) or knock CPU – defective ECU

Year – 1988
Model – Camry
Engine – 2.0L (122 cid) EFI 4 cyl
Engine Code – 3S-FE

ECM TROUBLE CODES

Code	Explanation
—	Normal system operation
11	Wire severence in the main relay of the Electronic Control Unit (ECU) – defective main relay circuit, main relay, ignition switch, ignition switch circuit or ECU
12	No engine revolution sensor to Electronic Control Unit (ECU) within several seconds after engine is cranked – defective distributor circuit, distributor, starter signal circuit or Electronic Control Unit (ECU)
13	No igniter signal to Electronic Control Unit (ECU) within several seconds after engine reaches 1000 rpm – defective distributor circuit, distributor or Electronic Control Unit (ECU)
14	No signal from igniter 4–5 times in succession – defective igniter circuit, igniter or Electronic Control Unit (ECU)
21	Oxygen sensor gives a lean signal for several seconds even when the coolant temperature is above 122°F (50°C) and the engine is running under high load conditions above 1500 rpm – defective oxygen sensor circuit, oxygen sensor or Electronic Control Unit (ECU)
22	Open or shorted Coolant Temperature Sensor (CTS) signal circuit – defective Coolant Temperature Sensor (CTS) circuit, Coolant Temperature Sensor (CTS) or Electronic Control Unit (ECU)
24	Open or shorted intake air temperature sensor circuit – defective intake air temperature sensor circuit, intake air temperature sensor or Electronic Control Unit (ECU)
31	Open or shorted air flow meter signal circuit – defective air flow meter circuit, air flow meter or Electronic Control Unit (ECU)
32	Open or shorted air flow meter signal circuit – defective air flow meter circuit, air flow meter or Electronic Control Unit (ECU)
41	If equipped with ECT, open or shorted Throttle Position Sensor (TPS) circuit. If not equipped with ECT, Throttle Position Sensor (TPS) and PSW signals being output simultaneously for several seconds – defective TPS circuit, TPS sensor or Electronic Control Unit (ECU)
42	No signal for over 5 seconds when vehicle is stopped and the engine running between 2500–5500 rpm and the coolant temperature is below 176°F (80°C), except when racing the engine – defective Vehicle Speed Sensor (VSS) circuit, VSS or Electronic Control Unit (ECU)
43	No starter switch signal to Electronic Control Unit (ECU) when the engine is running over 800 rpm – defective igniter switch circuit, igniter switch or Electronic Control Unit (ECU)
51	Air conditioner switch ON, idle switch OFF or automatic transmission shift position other than P or N range during diagnosis check – defective neutral start switch, neutral start switch circuit, air conditioner switch circuit, air conditioner amplifire, Throttle Position Sensor (TPS) circuit, TPS or accelerator pedal and cable

Year — 1988
Model — Camry All-Trac 4WD
Engine — 2.0L (122 cid) EFI 4 cyl
Engine Code — 3S-FE

ECM TROUBLE CODES

Code	Explanation
—	Normal system operation
11	Wire severance, however slight in the Electronic Control Unit (ECU) — defective ignition switch circuit, ignition switch, main relay circuit, main relay or ECU
12	No engine revolution sensor to Electronic Control Unit (ECU) within several seconds after engine is cranked — defective distributor circuit, distributor, starter signal circuit or Electronic Control Unit (ECU)
13	No igniter signal to Electronic Control Unit (ECU) within several seconds after engine reaches 1000 rpm — defective distributor circuit, distributor or Electronic Control Unit (ECU)
14	No signal from igniter to ECU 4–5 times in succession — defective igniter circuit, igniter or Electronic Control Unit (ECU)
21	Deterioration of oxygen sensor — defective oxygen sensor circuit, oxygen sensor or Electronic Control Unit (ECU)
22	Open or shorted Water Temperature Sensor (THW) signal circuit — defective THW circuit, THW or Electronic Control Unit (ECU)
24	Open or shorted intake air temperature sensor circuit — defective intake air temperature sensor circuit, intake air temperature sensor or Electronic Control Unit (ECU)
25	Air/fuel ratio lean malfunction — defective air flow meter, injector circuit, injector, fuel line pressure, oxygen sensor circuit, oxygen sensor, ignition system, water temperature sensor or Electronic Control Unit (ECU)
26	Air/fuel ratio rich malfunction — defective injector circuit, injector, fuel line pressure, air flow meter, cold start injector, water temperature sensor or Electronic Control Unit (ECU)
31	Open or shorted air flow meter signal circuit — defective air flow meter circuit, air flow meter or Electronic Control Unit (ECU)
32	Open or shorted air flow meter signal circuit — defective air flow meter circuit, air flow meter or Electronic Control Unit (ECU)
41	Throttle position sensor (IDL) and PSW signals being output simultaneously for several seconds — defective TPS circuit, TPS sensor or Electronic Control Unit (ECU)
42	No signal for several seconds when vehicle is stopped and the engine running between 2500–5500 rpm and the coolant temperature is below 176°F (80°C), except when racing the engine — defective Vehicle Speed Sensor (VSS) circuit, VSS or Electronic Control Unit (ECU)
43	No starter switch signal to Electronic Control Unit (ECU) when the engine is running over 800 rpm — defective ignition switch circuit, ignition switch or Electronic Control Unit (ECU)
51	No Throttle Position Sensor (TPS) signal or air conditioner signal to Electronic Control Unit (ECU), with the check terminals E1 and T shorted — defective air conditioning switch circuit, air conditioning amplifire, Throttle Position Sensor (TPS) circuit, TPS, acceleration pedal and cable
71	Exhaust Gas Recirculation (EGR) gas temperature below predetermined level during EGR operation — defective EGR valve, EGR hose, EGR sensor circuit, EGR sensor, Vacuum Switching Valve (BVSV) for EGR, BVSV for EGR circuit or Electronic Control Unit (ECU) — California only

Year — 1988
Model — Celica
Engine — 2.0L (122 cid) EFI 4 cyl
Engine Code — 3S-GE

ECM TROUBLE CODES

Code	Explanation
—	Normal system operation
11	Momentary interruption in the power supply to the Electronic Control Unit (ECU) — defective ignition switch circuit, ignition switch, main relay circuit, main relay or ECU
12	No engine revolution sensor to Electronic Control Unit (ECU) within several seconds after engine is cranked — defective distributor circuit, distributor, starter signal circuit or Electronic Control Unit (ECU)
13	No igniter signal to Electronic Control Unit (ECU) within several seconds after engine reaches 1000 rpm — defective distributor circuit, distributor or Electronic Control Unit (ECU)
14	No signal from igniter to ECU 8–11 times in succession — defective igniter circuit, igniter and ignition coil or Electronic Control Unit (ECU)
21	Open or shorted oxygen sensor heater and/or deterioration of oxygen sensor — defective oxygen sensor circuit, oxygen sensor, oxygen sensor heater or Electronic Control Unit (ECU)
22	Open or shorted Water Temperature Sensor (THW) signal circuit — defective THW circuit, THW or Electronic Control Unit (ECU)
24	Open or shorted intake air temperature sensor circuit — defective intake air temperature sensor circuit, intake air temperature sensor or Electronic Control Unit (ECU)
25	Air/fuel ratio lean malfunction — defective intake air system, air flow meter, injector circuit, injector, fuel line pressure, oxygen sensor circuits, oxygen sensors, ignition system or Electronic Control Unit (ECU)
26	Air/fuel ratio rich malfunction — defective injector circuits, injector, fuel line pressure, air flow meter, cold start injector or Electronic Control Unit (ECU)
31	Open or shorted air flow meter signal circuit — defective air flow meter circuit, air flow meter or Electronic Control Unit (ECU)
32	Open or shorted air flow meter signal circuit — defective air flow meter circuit, air flow meter or Electronic Control Unit (ECU)
41	Open or shorted Throttle Position Sensor (TPS) circuit — defective TPS sensor or Electronic Control Unit (ECU)
42	No signal for 5 seconds when vehicle is stopped and the engine running between 2500–6000 rpm and the coolant temperature is below 176°F (80°C), except when racing the engine — defective Vehicle Speed Sensor (VSS) circuit, VSS or Electronic Control Unit (ECU)
43	No starter switch signal to Electronic Control Unit (ECU) when the engine is running over 800 rpm — defective ignition switch circuit, ignition switch or Electronic Control Unit (ECU)
51	No Throttle Position Sensor (TPS) signal, neutral start switch signal or air conditioner signal to Electronic Control Unit (ECU), with the check terminals E1 and TE1 shorted — defective neutral start switch, air conditioning switch circuit, air conditioning amplifire, Throttle Position Sensor (TPS) circuit, TPS, acceleration pedal and cable or Electronic Control Unit (ECU)
71	Exhaust Gas Recirculation (EGR) gas temperature below predetermined level during EGR operation — defective EGR valve, EGR hose, EGR sensor circuit, EGR sensor, Vacuum Switching Valve (VSV) for EGR, VSV for EGR circuit or Electronic Control Unit (ECU) — California only

Year – 1988
Model – Celica
Engine – 2.0L (122 cid) EFI 4 cyl
Engine Code – 3S-FE

ECM TROUBLE CODES

Code	Explanation
–	Normal system operation
11	Momentary interruption in the power supply to the Electronic Control Unit (ECU) – defective ignition switch circuit, ignition switch, main relay circuit, main relay or ECU
12	No engine revolution sensor to Electronic Control Unit (ECU) within several seconds after engine is cranked – defective distributor circuit, distributor, starter signal circuit or Electronic Control Unit (ECU)
13	No igniter signal to Electronic Control Unit (ECU) within several seconds after engine reaches 1000 rpm – defective distributor circuit, distributor or Electronic Control Unit (ECU)
14	No signal from igniter to ECU 4–5 times in succession – defective igniter circuit, igniter and ignition coil or Electronic Control Unit (ECU)
21	Open or shorted oxygen sensor heater – lean indication – defective oxygen sensor circuit, oxygen sensor, oxygen sensor heater or Electronic Control Unit (ECU)
22	Open or shorted Water Temperature Sensor (THW) signal circuit – defective THW circuit, THW or Electronic Control Unit (ECU)
24	Open or shorted intake air temperature sensor circuit – defective intake air temperature sensor circuit, intake air temperature sensor or Electronic Control Unit (ECU)
31	Open or shorted air flow meter signal circuit – defective air flow meter circuit, air flow meter or Electronic Control Unit (ECU)
32	Open or shorted air flow meter signal circuit – defective air flow meter circuit, air flow meter or Electronic Control Unit (ECU)
41	Throttle position sensor (IDL) and PSW signals being output simultaneously for several seconds – defective TPS sensor or Electronic Control Unit (ECU)
42	No signal for 5 seconds when vehicle is stopped and the engine running between 2500–5500 rpm and the coolant temperature is below 176°F (80°C), except when racing the engine – defective Vehicle Speed Sensor (VSS) circuit, VSS or Electronic Control Unit (ECU)
43	No starter switch signal to Electronic Control Unit (ECU) when the engine is running over 800 rpm – defective ignition switch circuit, ignition switch or Electronic Control Unit (ECU)
51	No Throttle Position Sensor (TPS) signal, neutral start switch signal or air conditioner signal to Electronic Control Unit (ECU), with the check terminals E1 and TE1 shorted – defective neutral start switch, air conditioning switch circuit, air conditioning amplifire, Throttle Position Sensor (TPS) circuit, TPS, acceleration pedal and cable or Electronic Control Unit (ECU)

Year — 1988
Model — Corolla
Engine — 1.6L (97 cid) EFI 4 cyl
Engine Code — 4A-LC

ECM TROUBLE CODES

Code	Explanation
—	Normal system operation
12	No engine revolution sensor to Electronic Control Unit (ECU) within several seconds after engine is cranked or when the engine is run between 500–4000 rpm — defective distributor circuit, distributor, starter signal circuit, igniter circuit, igniter or Electronic Control Unit (ECU)
13	No igniter signal to Electronic Control Unit (ECU) within several seconds after engine reaches 1500 rpm — defective distributor circuit, distributor or Electronic Control Unit (ECU)
14	No signal from igniter to ECU 4 times in succession — defective igniter circuit, igniter or Electronic Control Unit (ECU)
21	Open or shorted oxygen sensor heater and/or deterioration of oxygen sensor — defective oxygen sensor circuit, oxygen sensor, oxygen sensor heater or Electronic Control Unit (ECU)
22	Open or shorted Water Temperature Sensor (THW) signal circuit — defective THW circuit, THW or Electronic Control Unit (ECU)
24	Open or shorted intake air temperature sensor circuit — defective intake air temperature sensor circuit, intake air temperature sensor or Electronic Control Unit (ECU)
25	Air/fuel ratio lean malfunction — defective intake air system, air flow meter, injector circuit, injector, fuel line pressure, oxygen sensor circuits, oxygen sensors, ignition system or Electronic Control Unit (ECU)
26	Air/fuel ratio rich malfunction — defective injector circuits, injector, fuel line pressure, air flow meter, cold start injector or Electronic Control Unit (ECU)
31	Shorted air flow meter signal circuit — defective air flow meter circuit, air flow meter or Electronic Control Unit (ECU)
41	Open or shorted Throttle Position Sensor (TPS) circuit — defective TPS sensor or Electronic Control Unit (ECU)
42	No signal for 8 seconds when vehicle is stopped and the engine running above 2800 rpm — defective Vehicle Speed Sensor (VSS) circuit, VSS or Electronic Control Unit (ECU)
43	No starter switch signal to Electronic Control Unit (ECU) when the engine is running over 800 rpm — defective main relay circuit, ignition switch, starter signal circuit or Electronic Control Unit (ECU)
51	Air conditioning switch ON, idle switch OFF or automatic transmission shift position other than P or N range, during diagnosis check — defective air conditioning switch, air conditioning switch circuit, air conditioning amplifire, Throttle Position Sensor (TPS) circuit, TPS or Electronic Control Unit (ECU)
71	Exhaust Gas Recirculation (EGR) gas temperature below predetermined level during EGR operation — defective EGR valve, EGR hose, EGR sensor circuit, EGR sensor, Vacuum Switching Valve (VSV) for EGR, VSV for EGR circuit or Electronic Control Unit (ECU) — California only

Year — 1988
Model — Corolla
Engine — 1.6L (97 cid) EFI 4 cyl
Engine Code — 4A-GEC

ECM TROUBLE CODES

Code	Explanation
—	Normal system operation
12	No engine revolution sensor to Electronic Control Unit (ECU) within several seconds after engine is cranked or when the engine is run between 500–4000 rpm — defective distributor circuit, distributor, starter signal circuit, igniter circuit, igniter or Electronic Control Unit (ECU)
13	No igniter signal to Electronic Control Unit (ECU) within several seconds after engine reaches 1500 rpm — defective distributor circuit, distributor or Electronic Control Unit (ECU)
14	No signal from igniter to ECU 4 times in succession — defective igniter circuit, igniter or Electronic Control Unit (ECU)
21	Open or shorted oxygen sensor heater and/or deterioration of oxygen sensor — defective oxygen sensor circuit, oxygen sensor, oxygen sensor heater or Electronic Control Unit (ECU)
22	Open or shorted Water Temperature Sensor (THW) signal circuit — defective THW circuit, THW or Electronic Control Unit (ECU)
24	Open or shorted intake air temperature sensor circuit — defective intake air temperature sensor circuit, intake air temperature sensor or Electronic Control Unit (ECU)
25	Air/fuel ratio lean malfunction — defective intake air system, air flow meter, injector circuit, injector, fuel line pressure, oxygen sensor circuits, oxygen sensors, ignition system or Electronic Control Unit (ECU)
26	Air/fuel ratio rich malfunction — defective injector circuits, injector, fuel line pressure, air flow meter, cold start injector or Electronic Control Unit (ECU)
31	Shorted air flow meter signal circuit — defective air flow meter circuit, air flow meter or Electronic Control Unit (ECU)
41	Open or shorted Throttle Position Sensor (TPS) circuit — defective TPS sensor or Electronic Control Unit (ECU)
42	No signal for 8 seconds when vehicle is stopped and the engine running above 2800 rpm — defective Vehicle Speed Sensor (VSS) circuit, VSS or Electronic Control Unit (ECU)
43	No starter switch signal to Electronic Control Unit (ECU) when the engine is running over 800 rpm — defective main relay circuit, ignition switch, starter signal circuit or Electronic Control Unit (ECU)
51	Air conditioning switch ON, idle switch OFF or automatic transmission shift position other than P or N range, during diagnosis check — defective air conditioning switch, air conditioning switch circuit, air conditioning amplifire, Throttle Position Sensor (TPS) circuit, TPS or Electronic Control Unit (ECU)
71	Exhaust Gas Recirculation (EGR) gas temperature below predetermined level during EGR operation — defective EGR valve, EGR hose, EGR sensor circuit, EGR sensor, Vacuum Switching Valve (VSV) for EGR, VSV for EGR circuit or Electronic Control Unit (ECU) — California only

Year – 1988
Model – Corolla
Engine – 1.6L (97 cid) EFI 4 cyl
Engine Code – 4A-GELC

ECM TROUBLE CODES

Code	Explanation
—	Normal system operation
12	No engine revolution sensor to Electronic Control Unit (ECU) within several seconds after engine is cranked or when the engine is run between 500–4000 rpm – defective distributor circuit, distributor, starter signal circuit, igniter circuit, igniter or Electronic Control Unit (ECU)
13	No igniter signal to Electronic Control Unit (ECU) within several seconds after engine reaches 1500 rpm – defective distributor circuit, distributor or Electronic Control Unit (ECU)
14	No signal from igniter to ECU 4 times in succession – defective igniter circuit, igniter or Electronic Control Unit (ECU)
21	Open or shorted oxygen sensor heater and/or deterioration of oxygen sensor – defective oxygen sensor circuit, oxygen sensor, oxygen sensor heater or Electronic Control Unit (ECU)
22	Open or shorted Water Temperature Sensor (THW) signal circuit – defective THW circuit, THW or Electronic Control Unit (ECU)
24	Open or shorted intake air temperature sensor circuit – defective intake air temperature sensor circuit, intake air temperature sensor or Electronic Control Unit (ECU)
25	Air/fuel ratio lean malfunction – defective intake air system, air flow meter, injector circuit, injector, fuel line pressure, oxygen sensor circuits, oxygen sensors, ignition system or Electronic Control Unit (ECU)
26	Air/fuel ratio rich malfunction – defective injector circuits, injector, fuel line pressure, air flow meter, cold start injector or Electronic Control Unit (ECU)
31	Shorted air flow meter signal circuit – defective air flow meter circuit, air flow meter or Electronic Control Unit (ECU)
41	Open or shorted Throttle Position Sensor (TPS) circuit – defective TPS sensor or Electronic Control Unit (ECU)
42	No signal for 8 seconds when vehicle is stopped and the engine running above 2800 rpm – defective Vehicle Speed Sensor (VSS) circuit, VSS or Electronic Control Unit (ECU)
43	No starter switch signal to Electronic Control Unit (ECU) when the engine is running over 800 rpm – defective main relay circuit, ignition switch, starter signal circuit or Electronic Control Unit (ECU)
51	Air conditioning switch ON, idle switch OFF or automatic transmission shift position other than P or N range, during diagnosis check – defective air conditioning switch, air conditioning switch circuit, air conditioning amplifire, Throttle Position Sensor (TPS) circuit, TPS or Electronic Control Unit (ECU)
71	Exhaust Gas Recirculation (EGR) gas temperature below predetermined level during EGR operation – defective EGR valve, EGR hose, EGR sensor circuit, EGR sensor, Vacuum Switching Valve (VSV) for EGR, VSV for EGR circuit or Electronic Control Unit (ECU) – California only

Year — 1988
Model — Cressida
Engine — 2.8L (168 cid) EFI V6
Engine Code — 5M-GE

ECM TROUBLE CODES

Code	Explanation
—	Normal system operation
11	Wire severence in the main relay of the Electronic Control Unit (ECU) — defective main relay circuit, main relay or ECU
12	No engine revolution sensor to Electronic Control Unit (ECU) within several seconds after engine is cranked — defective distributor circuit, distributor, starter signal circuit or Electronic Control Unit (ECU)
13	No igniter signal to Electronic Control Unit (ECU) within several seconds after engine reaches 1000 rpm — defective distributor circuit, distributor, starter signal circuit or Electronic Control Unit (ECU)
14	No signal from igniter 6 times in succession — defective igniter circuit, igniter or Electronic Control Unit (ECU)
21	Oxygen sensor gives a lean signal for several seconds even when the coolant temperature is above 122°F (50°C) and the engine is running under high load conditions above 1500 rpm — defective oxygen sensor circuit, oxygen sensor or Electronic Control Unit (ECU)
22	Open or shorted Coolant Temperature Sensor (CTS) signal circuit — defective Coolant Temperature Sensor (CTS) circuit, Coolant Temperature Sensor (CTS) or Electronic Control Unit (ECU)
23	Open or shorted intake air temperature sensor circuit — defective intake air temperature sensor circuit, intake air temperature sensor or Electronic Control Unit (ECU)
31	Open or shorted air flow meter signal circuit — defective air flow meter circuit, air flow meter or Electronic Control Unit (ECU)
32	Open or shorted air flow meter signal circuit — defective air flow meter circuit, air flow meter or Electronic Control Unit (ECU)
41	Open or shorted Throttle Position Sensor (TPS) circuit — defective TPS sensor or Electronic Control Unit (ECU)
42	No signal for over 5 seconds when vehicle is traveling under ½ mph and the engine running over 2500 rpm and the shift lever is in N or P for automatic transmissions — defective Vehicle Speed Sensor (VSS) circuit, VSS, torque converter or Electronic Control Unit (ECU)
43	No starter switch signal to Electronic Control Unit (ECU) when the engine is running over 800 rpm — defective main relay circuit, igniter switch to starter circuit, igniter switch or Electronic Control Unit (ECU)
51	Neutral start switch OFF or air conditioner switch ON during diagnostic check — defective neutral start switch, air conditioner switch or Electronic Control Unit (ECU)
52	Open or shorted knock sensor circuit — defective knock sensor or Electronic Control Unit (ECU)
53	Faulty Electronic Control Unit (ECU) or knock CPU — defective ECU

Year — 1988
Model — MR2
Engine — 1.6L (97 cid) EFI 4 cyl
Engine Code — 4A-GE

ECM TROUBLE CODES

Code	Explanation
—	Normal system operation
12	No engine revolution sensor to Electronic Control Unit (ECU) within several seconds after engine is cranked or when the engine is run between 500–4000 rpm — defective distributor circuit, distributor, starter signal circuit, igniter circuit, igniter or Electronic Control Unit (ECU)
13	No igniter signal to Electronic Control Unit (ECU) within several seconds after engine reaches 1500 rpm — defective distributor circuit, distributor or Electronic Control Unit (ECU)
14	No signal from igniter to ECU 4 times in succession — defective igniter circuit, igniter or Electronic Control Unit (ECU)
21	Open or shorted oxygen sensor heater and/or deterioration of oxygen sensor — defective oxygen sensor circuit, oxygen sensor, oxygen sensor heater or Electronic Control Unit (ECU)
22	Open or shorted Water Temperature Sensor (THW) signal circuit — defective THW circuit, THW or Electronic Control Unit (ECU)
24	Open or shorted intake air temperature sensor circuit — defective intake air temperature sensor circuit, intake air temperature sensor or Electronic Control Unit (ECU)
25	Air/fuel ratio lean malfunction — defective intake air system, air flow meter, injector circuit, injector, fuel line pressure, oxygen sensor circuits, oxygen sensors, ignition system or Electronic Control Unit (ECU)
26	Air/fuel ratio rich malfunction — defective injector circuits, injector, fuel line pressure, air flow meter, cold start injector or Electronic Control Unit (ECU)
31	Shorted air flow meter signal circuit — defective air flow meter circuit, air flow meter or Electronic Control Unit (ECU)
41	Open or shorted Throttle Position Sensor (TPS) circuit — defective TPS sensor or Electronic Control Unit (ECU)
42	No signal for 5 seconds when vehicle is stopped and the engine running above 2500 rpm — defective Vehicle Speed Sensor (VSS) circuit, VSS or Electronic Control Unit (ECU)
43	No starter switch signal to Electronic Control Unit (ECU) when the engine is running over 800 rpm — defective main relay circuit, ignition switch, starter signal circuit or Electronic Control Unit (ECU)
51	Air conditioning switch ON, idle switch OFF or automatic transmission shift position other than P or N range, during diagnosis check — defective air conditioning switch, air conditioning switch circuit, air conditioning amplifire, Throttle Position Sensor (TPS) circuit, TPS or Electronic Control Unit (ECU)
71	Exhaust Gas Recirculation (EGR) gas temperature below predetermined level during EGR operation — defective EGR valve, EGR hose, EGR sensor circuit, EGR sensor, Vacuum Switching Valve (VSV) for EGR, VSV for EGR circuit or Electronic Control Unit (ECU) — California only

Year – 1988
Model – MR2
Engine – 1.6L (97 cid) EFI 4 cyl
Engine Code – 4A-GZE

ECM TROUBLE CODES

Code	Explanation
—	Normal system operation
11	Momentary interruption in power supply to Electronic Control Unit (ECU) – defective ignition switch circuit, ignition switch, main relay circuit, main relay or ECU
12	No engine revolution sensor to Electronic Control Unit (ECU) within several seconds after engine is cranked or when the engine is run between 500–4000 rpm – defective distributor circuit, distributor, starter signal circuit, igniter circuit, igniter or Electronic Control Unit (ECU)
13	No igniter signal to Electronic Control Unit (ECU) within several seconds after engine reaches 1000 rpm – defective distributor circuit, distributor or Electronic Control Unit (ECU)
14	No signal from igniter to ECU 8–11 times in succession – defective igniter circuit, igniter and ignition coil or Electronic Control Unit (ECU)
21	Open or shorted oxygen sensor heater and/or deterioration of oxygen sensor – defective oxygen sensor circuit, oxygen sensor, oxygen sensor heater or Electronic Control Unit (ECU)
22	Open or shorted Water Temperature Sensor (THW) signal circuit – defective THW circuit, THW or Electronic Control Unit (ECU)
24	Open or shorted intake air temperature sensor circuit – defective intake air temperature sensor circuit, intake air temperature sensor or Electronic Control Unit (ECU)
25	Air/fuel ratio lean malfunction – defective intake air system, air flow meter, injector circuit, injector, fuel line pressure, oxygen sensor circuits, oxygen sensors, ignition system or Electronic Control Unit (ECU)
26	Air/fuel ratio rich malfunction – defective injector circuits, injector, fuel line pressure, air flow meter, cold start injector or Electronic Control Unit (ECU)
31	Open or shorted air flow meter signal circuit – defective air flow meter circuit, air flow meter or Electronic Control Unit (ECU)
32	Open or shorted air flow meter signal – defective air flow meter circuit, air flow meter or Electronic Control Unit (ECU)
41	Open or shorted Throttle Position Sensor (TPS) circuit – defective TPS sensor or TPS sensor circuit
42	No signal for 8 seconds when vehicle is stopped and the engine running between 2300–5000 rpm and the coolant temperature is below 176°F (80°C), except when racing the engine – defective Vehicle Speed Sensor (VSS) circuit, VSS or Electronic Control Unit (ECU)
43	No starter switch signal to Electronic Control Unit (ECU) until the engine speed reaches 800 rpm with the vehicle stopped – defective igniter switch, igniter switch circuit or Electronic Control Unit (ECU)
51	Air conditioning switch ON, idle switch OFF or automatic transmission shift position other than P or N range, during diagnosis check – defective air conditioning switch, air conditioning switch circuit, air conditioning amplifire, Throttle Position Sensor (TPS) circuit, TPS or Electronic Control Unit (ECU)
52	Open or shorted knock sensor signal circuit – defective knock sensor circuit, knock sensor or Electronic Control Unit (ECU)
53	Knock control in Electronic Control Unit (ECU) faulty – defective ECU
71	Exhaust Gas Recirculation (EGR) gas temperature below predetermined level during EGR operation – defective EGR valve, EGR hose, EGR sensor circuit, EGR sensor, Vacuum Switching Valve (VSV) for EGR, VSV for EGR circuit or Electronic Control Unit (ECU) – California only

Year – 1988
Model – Supra
Engine – 3.0L (180 cid) EFI 6 cyl
Engine Code – 7M-GE

ECM TROUBLE CODES

Code	Explanation
—	Normal system operation
11	Momentary interruption in the power supply to the Electronic Control Unit (ECU) – defective ignition switch circuit, ignition switch, main relay circuit, main relay or ECU
12	No engine revolution sensor to Electronic Control Unit (ECU) within several seconds after engine is cranked – defective distributor circuit, distributor, starter signal circuit or Electronic Control Unit (ECU)
13	No igniter signal to Electronic Control Unit (ECU) within several seconds after engine reaches 1000 rpm – defective distributor circuit, distributor or Electronic Control Unit (ECU)
14	No signal from igniter to ECU 6–8 times in succession – defective igniter circuit, igniter and ignition coil or Electronic Control Unit (ECU)
21	Deterioration of oxygen sensor – defective oxygen sensor circuit, oxygen sensor or Electronic Control Unit (ECU)
22	Open or shorted Water Temperature Sensor (THW) signal circuit – defective THW circuit, THW or Electronic Control Unit (ECU)
24	Open or shorted intake air temperature sensor circuit – defective intake air temperature sensor circuit, intake air temperature sensor or Electronic Control Unit (ECU)
25	Air/fuel ratio lean malfunction – defective intake air system, air flow meter, injector circuit, injector, fuel line pressure, oxygen sensor circuits, oxygen sensors, ignition system or Electronic Control Unit (ECU)
26	Air/fuel ratio rich malfunction – defective injector circuits, injector, fuel line pressure, air flow meter, cold start injector or Electronic Control Unit (ECU)
27	Open or shorted sub-oxygen sensor heater circuit or signal – defective sub-oxygen sensor circuit, sub-oxygen sensor, sub-oxygen sensor heater or Electronic Control Unit (ECU)
31	Open or shorted air flow meter signal circuit – defective air flow meter circuit, air flow meter or Electronic Control Unit (ECU)
32	Open or shorted air flow meter signal circuit – defective air flow meter circuit, air flow meter or Electronic Control Unit (ECU)
41	Open or shorted Throttle Position Sensor (TPS) circuit – defective TPS sensor or Electronic Control Unit (ECU)
42	No signal for over 5 seconds when vehicle is stopped and the engine running between 2500–4500 rpm and the coolant temperature is below 176°F (80°C), except when racing the engine – defective Vehicle Speed Sensor (VSS) circuit, VSS or Electronic Control Unit (ECU)
43	No starter switch signal to Electronic Control Unit (ECU) when the engine is running over 800 rpm – defective ignition switch circuit, ignition switch or Electronic Control Unit (ECU)
51	No Throttle Position Sensor (TPS) signal, neutral start switch signal or air conditioner signal to Electronic Control Unit (ECU), with the check terminals E1 and TE1 shorted – defective neutral start switch, air conditioner switch, air conditioning switch circuit, air conditioning amplifire, Throttle Position Sensor (TPS) circuit, TPS, acceleration pedal and cable or Electronic Control Unit (ECU)
52	Open or shorted knock sensor signal circuit – defective knock sensor circuit, knock sensor or Electronic Control Unit (ECU)
53	Knock control in Electronic Control Unit (ECU) faulty – defective ECU
71	Exhaust Gas Recirculation (EGR) gas temperature below predetermined level during EGR operation – defective EGR valve, EGR hose, EGR sensor circuit, EGR sensor, Vacuum Switching Valve (VSV) for EGR, VSV for EGR circuit or Electronic Control Unit (ECU) – California only

Year – 1988
Model – Supra
Engine – 3.0L (180 cid) EFI 6 cyl
Engine Code – 7M-GTE

ECM TROUBLE CODES

Code	Explanation
–	Normal system operation
11	Momentary interruption in the power supply to the Electronic Control Unit (ECU) – defective ignition switch circuit, ignition switch, main relay circuit, main relay or ECU
12	No engine revolution sensor to Electronic Control Unit (ECU) within several seconds after engine is cranked – defective distributor circuit, distributor, starter signal circuit or Electronic Control Unit (ECU)
13	No igniter signal to Electronic Control Unit (ECU) within several seconds after engine reaches 1000 rpm – defective distributor circuit, distributor or Electronic Control Unit (ECU)
14	No signal from igniter to ECU 6–8 times in succession – defective igniter circuit, igniter and ignition coil or Electronic Control Unit (ECU)
21	Deterioration of oxygen sensor – defective oxygen sensor circuit, oxygen sensor or Electronic Control Unit (ECU)
22	Open or shorted Water Temperature Sensor (THW) signal circuit – defective THW circuit, THW or Electronic Control Unit (ECU)
24	Open or shorted intake air temperature sensor circuit – defective intake air temperature sensor circuit, intake air temperature sensor or Electronic Control Unit (ECU)
31	Open or shorted air flow meter signal circuit – defective air flow meter circuit, air flow meter or Electronic Control Unit (ECU)
32	Open or shorted High Altitude Compensator (HAC) sensor circuit – defective HAC circuit, HAC sensor or Electronic Control Unit (ECU)
34	Abnormal turbocharger pressure or air flow meter signal – defective turbocharger, air flow meter, intercooler system or Electronic Control Unit (ECU)
41	Open or shorted Throttle Position Sensor (TPS) circuit – defective TPS sensor or Electronic Control Unit (ECU)
42	No signal for over 5 seconds when vehicle is stopped and the engine running between 2500–4500 rpm and the coolant temperature is below 176°F (80°C), except when racing the engine – defective Vehicle Speed Sensor (VSS) circuit, VSS or Electronic Control Unit (ECU)
43	No starter switch signal to Electronic Control Unit (ECU) when the engine is running over 800 rpm – defective ignition switch circuit, ignition switch or Electronic Control Unit (ECU)
51	No Throttle Position Sensor (TPS) signal, neutral start switch signal or air conditioner signal to Electronic Control Unit (ECU), with the check terminals E1 and TE1 shorted – defective neutral start switch, air conditioner switch, air conditioning switch circuit, air conditioning amplifire, Throttle Position Sensor (TPS) circuit, TPS, acceleration pedal and cable or Electronic Control Unit (ECU)
52	Open or shorted knock sensor signal circuit – defective knock sensor circuit, knock sensor or Electronic Control Unit (ECU)
53	Knock control in Electronic Control Unit (ECU) faulty – defective ECU
71	Exhaust Gas Recirculation (EGR) gas temperature below predetermined level during EGR operation – defective EGR valve, EGR hose, EGR sensor circuit, EGR sensor, Vacuum Switching Valve (VSV) for EGR, VSV for EGR circuit or Electronic Control Unit (ECU) – California only

Year — 1989
Model — Camry
Engine — 2.0L (122 cid) EFI 4 cyl
Engine Code — 3S-FE

ECM TROUBLE CODES

Code	Explanation
—	Normal system operation
11	Wire severence in the main relay of the Electronic Control Unit (ECU) — defective main relay circuit, main relay, ignition switch, ignition switch circuit or ECU
12	No engine revolution sensor to Electronic Control Unit (ECU) within several seconds after engine is cranked — defective distributor circuit, distributor, starter signal circuit or Electronic Control Unit (ECU)
13	No igniter signal to Electronic Control Unit (ECU) within several seconds after engine reaches 1000 rpm — defective distributor circuit, distributor or Electronic Control Unit (ECU)
14	No signal from igniter 4–5 times in succession — defective igniter circuit, igniter or Electronic Control Unit (ECU)
21	Oxygen sensor gives a lean signal for several seconds even when the coolant temperature is above 122°F (50°C) and the engine is running under high load conditions above 1500 rpm — defective oxygen sensor circuit, oxygen sensor or Electronic Control Unit (ECU)
22	Open or shorted Coolant Temperature Sensor (CTS) signal circuit — defective Coolant Temperature Sensor (CTS) circuit, Coolant Temperature Sensor (CTS) or Electronic Control Unit (ECU)
24	Open or shorted intake air temperature sensor circuit — defective intake air temperature sensor circuit, intake air temperature sensor or Electronic Control Unit (ECU)
31	Open or shorted air flow meter signal circuit — defective air flow meter circuit, air flow meter or Electronic Control Unit (ECU)
32	Open or shorted air flow meter signal circuit — defective air flow meter circuit, air flow meter or Electronic Control Unit (ECU)
41	If equipped with ECT, open or shorted Throttle Position Sensor (TPS) circuit. If not equipped with ECT, Throttle Position Sensor (TPS) and PSW signals being output simultaneously for several seconds — defective TPS circuit, TPS sensor or Electronic Control Unit (ECU)
42	No signal for several seconds when vehicle is stopped and the engine running between 2500–5500 rpm and the coolant temperature is below 176°F (80°C), except when racing the engine — defective Vehicle Speed Sensor (VSS) circuit, VSS or Electronic Control Unit (ECU)
43	No starter switch signal to Electronic Control Unit (ECU) when the engine is running over 800 rpm — defective igniter switch circuit, igniter switch or Electronic Control Unit (ECU)
51	No throttle switch (IDL) signal or air conditioner signal to the Electronic Control Unit (ECU) with the check terminals TE1 and E1 connected — defective air conditioner switch circuit, air conditioner amplifire, Throttle Position Sensor (TPS) circuit, TPS or accelerator pedal and cable

Year – 1989
Model – Camry
Engine – 2.5L (151 cid) EFI V6
Engine Code – 2VZ-FE

ECM TROUBLE CODES

Code	Explanation
–	Normal system operation
11	Momentary interruption in the power supply to the Electronic Control Unit (ECU) – defective ignition switch circuit, ignition switch, main relay circuit, main relay or ECU
12	No engine revolution sensor to Electronic Control Unit (ECU) within 2 seconds after engine is cranked – defective distributor circuit, distributor, starter signal circuit or Electronic Control Unit (ECU)
13	No igniter signal to Electronic Control Unit (ECU) within several seconds after engine reaches 1000 rpm – defective distributor circuit, distributor or Electronic Control Unit (ECU)
14	No signal from igniter to ECU 6–8 times in succession – defective igniter circuit, igniter and ignition coil or Electronic Control Unit (ECU)
21	Open or shorted oxygen sensor heater and/or deterioration of oxygen sensor – defective oxygen sensor circuit, oxygen sensor, oxygen sensor heater or Electronic Control Unit (ECU)
22	Open or shorted Water Temperature Sensor (THW) signal circuit – defective THW circuit, THW or Electronic Control Unit (ECU)
24	Open or shorted intake air temperature sensor circuit – defective intake air temperature sensor circuit, intake air temperature sensor or Electronic Control Unit (ECU)
25	Air/fuel ratio lean malfunction – defective intake air system, air flow meter, injector circuit, injector, fuel line pressure, oxygen sensor circuits, oxygen sensors, ignition system or Electronic Control Unit (ECU)
26	Air/fuel ratio rich malfunction – defective injector circuits, injector, fuel line pressure, air flow meter, cold start injector or Electronic Control Unit (ECU)
27	Open or shorted sub-oxygen sensor signal circuit – defective sub-oxygen sensor circuit, sub-oxygen sensor or Electronic Control Unit (ECU) – California only
31	Open or shorted air flow meter signal circuit – defective air flow meter circuit, air flow meter or Electronic Control Unit (ECU)
32	Open or shorted air flow meter signal circuit – defective air flow meter circuit, air flow meter or Electronic Control Unit (ECU)
41	Open or shorted Throttle Position Sensor (TPS) circuit – defective TPS sensor or Electronic Control Unit (ECU)
42	No signal for 8 seconds when vehicle is stopped and the engine running between 2500–4500 rpm and the coolant temperature is below 176°F (80°C), except when racing the engine – defective No. 1 Vehicle Speed Sensor (VSS) circuit, No. 1 VSS or Electronic Control Unit (ECU)
43	No starter switch signal to Electronic Control Unit (ECU) when the engine is running over 800 rpm – defective ignition switch circuit, ignition switch or Electronic Control Unit (ECU)
51	No throttle switch (IDL) signal, neutral start switch signal or air conditioner signal to Electronic Control Unit (ECU), with the check terminals E1 and TE1 shorted – defective neutral start switch, air conditioning switch circuit, air conditioning amplifire, Throttle Position Sensor (TPS) circuit, TPS, acceleration pedal and cable or Electronic Control Unit (ECU)
71	Exhaust Gas Recirculation (EGR) gas temperature below predetermined level during EGR operation – defective EGR valve, EGR hose, EGR sensor circuit, EGR sensor, Vacuum Switching Valve (VSV) for EGR, VSV for EGR circuit or Electronic Control Unit (ECU) – California only

Year — 1989
Model — Celica
Engine — 2.0L (122 cid) EFI 4 cyl
Engine Code — 3S-GE

ECM TROUBLE CODES

Code	Explanation
—	Normal system operation
11	Momentary interruption in the power supply to the Electronic Control Unit (ECU) — defective ignition switch circuit, ignition switch, main relay circuit, main relay or ECU
12	No engine revolution sensor to Electronic Control Unit (ECU) within several seconds after engine is cranked — defective distributor circuit, distributor, starter signal circuit or Electronic Control Unit (ECU)
13	No igniter signal to Electronic Control Unit (ECU) within several seconds after engine reaches 1000 rpm — defective distributor circuit, distributor or Electronic Control Unit (ECU)
14	No signal from igniter to ECU 8–11 times in succession — defective igniter circuit, igniter and ignition coil or Electronic Control Unit (ECU)
21	Open or shorted oxygen sensor heater and/or deterioration of oxygen sensor — defective oxygen sensor circuit, oxygen sensor, oxygen sensor heater or Electronic Control Unit (ECU)
22	Open or shorted Water Temperature Sensor (THW) signal circuit — defective THW circuit, THW or Electronic Control Unit (ECU)
24	Open or shorted intake air temperature sensor circuit — defective intake air temperature sensor circuit, intake air temperature sensor or Electronic Control Unit (ECU)
25	Air/fuel ratio lean malfunction — defective intake air system, air flow meter, injector circuit, injector, fuel line pressure, oxygen sensor circuits, oxygen sensors, ignition system or Electronic Control Unit (ECU)
26	Air/fuel ratio rich malfunction — defective injector circuits, injector, fuel line pressure, air flow meter, cold start injector or Electronic Control Unit (ECU)
31	Open or shorted air flow meter signal circuit — defective air flow meter circuit, air flow meter or Electronic Control Unit (ECU)
32	Open or shorted air flow meter signal circuit — defective air flow meter circuit, air flow meter or Electronic Control Unit (ECU)
41	Open or shorted Throttle Position Sensor (TPS) circuit — defective TPS sensor or Electronic Control Unit (ECU)
42	No signal for 8 seconds when vehicle is stopped and the engine running between 2500–6000 rpm and the coolant temperature is below 176°F (80°C), except when racing the engine — defective Vehicle Speed Sensor (VSS) circuit, VSS or Electronic Control Unit (ECU)
43	No starter switch signal to Electronic Control Unit (ECU) when the engine is running over 800 rpm — defective ignition switch circuit, ignition switch or Electronic Control Unit (ECU)
51	No throttle switch (IDL) signal or air conditioner signal to Electronic Control Unit (ECU), with the check terminals E1 and T shorted — defective neutral start switch, air conditioning switch circuit, air conditioning amplifire, Throttle Position Sensor (TPS) circuit, TPS, acceleration pedal and cable or Electronic Control Unit (ECU)
71	Exhaust Gas Recirculation (EGR) gas temperature below predetermined level during EGR operation — defective EGR valve, EGR hose, EGR sensor circuit, EGR sensor, Vacuum Switching Valve (VSV) for EGR, VSV for EGR circuit or Electronic Control Unit (ECU) — California only

Year — 1989
Model — Celica
Engine — 2.0L (122 cid) EFI 4 cyl
Engine Code — 3S-GTE

ECM TROUBLE CODES

Code	Explanation
—	Normal system operation
11	Momentary interruption in the power supply to the Electronic Control Unit (ECU) — defective ignition switch circuit, ignition switch, main relay circuit, main relay or ECU
12	No engine revolution sensor to Electronic Control Unit (ECU) within several seconds after engine is cranked — defective distributor circuit, distributor, starter signal circuit or Electronic Control Unit (ECU)
13	No igniter signal to Electronic Control Unit (ECU) within several seconds after engine reaches 1000 rpm — defective distributor circuit, distributor or Electronic Control Unit (ECU)
14	No signal from igniter to ECU 8–11 times in succession — defective igniter circuit, igniter and ignition coil or Electronic Control Unit (ECU)
21	Open or shorted oxygen sensor heater and/or deterioration of oxygen sensor — defective oxygen sensor circuit, oxygen sensor, oxygen sensor heater or Electronic Control Unit (ECU)
22	Open or shorted Water Temperature Sensor (THW) signal circuit — defective THW circuit, THW or Electronic Control Unit (ECU)
24	Open or shorted intake air temperature sensor circuit — defective intake air temperature sensor circuit, intake air temperature sensor or Electronic Control Unit (ECU)
25	Air/fuel ratio lean malfunction — defective intake air system, air flow meter, injector circuit, injector, fuel line pressure, oxygen sensor circuits, oxygen sensors, ignition system or Electronic Control Unit (ECU)
26	Air/fuel ratio rich malfunction — defective injector circuits, injector, fuel line pressure, air flow meter, cold start injector or Electronic Control Unit (ECU)
31	Open or shorted air flow meter signal circuit — defective air flow meter circuit, air flow meter or Electronic Control Unit (ECU)
32	Open or shorted air flow meter signal circuit — defective air flow meter circuit, air flow meter or Electronic Control Unit (ECU)
34	When the fuel cut-off due to high turbocharging pressure is occured — defective turbocharger, turbocharging pressure sensor or Electronic Control Unit (ECU)
35	Open or shorted turbocharging sensor pressure (PIM) circuit — defective turbocharging pressure sensor or Electronic Control Unit (ECU)
41	Open or shorted Throttle Position Sensor (TPS) circuit — defective TPS sensor or Electronic Control Unit (ECU)
42	No signal for 8 seconds when vehicle is stopped and the engine running between 2500–6000 rpm and the coolant temperature is below 176°F (80°C), except when racing the engine — defective Vehicle Speed Sensor (VSS) circuit, VSS or Electronic Control Unit (ECU)
43	No starter switch signal to Electronic Control Unit (ECU) when the engine is running over 800 rpm — defective ignition switch circuit, ignition switch or Electronic Control Unit (ECU)
51	No throttle switch (IDL) signal or air conditioner signal to Electronic Control Unit (ECU), with the check terminals E1 and T shorted — defective neutral start switch, air conditioning switch circuit, air conditioning amplifire, Throttle Position Sensor (TPS) circuit, TPS, acceleration pedal and cable or Electronic Control Unit (ECU)
52	Open or shorted knock sensor signal circuit — defective knock sensor or Electronic Control Unit (ECU)
53	Knock control in ECU faulty — defective Electronic Control Unit (ECU)
54	When intercooler's coolant level is lower than standard or water pump is locked or open — defective intercooler water pump, coolant level sensor, intercooler ECU or Electronic Control Unit (ECU)
71	Exhaust Gas Recirculation (EGR) gas temperature below predetermined level during EGR operation — defective EGR valve, EGR hose, EGR sensor circuit, EGR sensor, Vacuum Switching Valve (VSV) for EGR, VSV for EGR circuit or Electronic Control Unit (ECU) — California only

Year – 1989
Model – Corolla
Engine – 1.6L (97 cid) 4 cyl
Engine Code – 4A-F

ECM TROUBLE CODES

Code	Explanation
–	Normal system operation
12	No engine revolution sensor to Electronic Control Unit (ECU) within several seconds after engine is cranked – defective ignition coil circuit, ignition coil igniter circuit, igniter or Electronic Control Unit (ECU)
21	Deterioration of oxygen sensor – defective oxygen sensor circuit, oxygen sensor, oxygen sensor heater or Electronic Control Unit (ECU)
22	Open or shorted Water Temperature Sensor (THW) signal circuit – defective No. 1 and No. 2 THW circuit, No. 1 and No. 2 THW switches or Electronic Control Unit (ECU)
25	Air/fuel ratio lean malfunction – defective oxygen sensor circuit, oxygen sensor, EBCV circuit, EBCV or Electronic Control Unit (ECU)
26	Air/fuel ratio rich malfunction – defective EBCV always closed or a clogged hose, open EBCV circuit or Electronic Control Unit (ECU)
31	Open or shorted vacuum switch circuits – defective No. 1 or No. 2 vacuum switches or Electronic Control Unit (ECU)
41	Open or shorted Throttle Switch (THS) circuit – defective THS switch or Electronic Control Unit (ECU)
71	Exhaust Gas Recirculation (EGR) malfunction – EGR valve normally closed or a clogged hose or open EGR gas temperature sensor circuit – defective EGR valve, EGR vacuum modulator, EGR hose, EGR sensor circuit, EGR sensor or Electronic Control Unit (ECU)
72	Open Fuel Cut Solenoid (FCS) circuit – defective fuel cut solenoid or Electronic Control Unit (ECU)

Year — 1989
Model — Corolla
Engine — 1.6L (97 cid) 4 cyl
Engine Code — 4A-FE

ECM TROUBLE CODES

Code	Explanation
—	Normal system operation
11	Momentary interruption in the power supply to the Electronic Control Unit (ECU) — defective ignition switch circuit, ignition switch, main relay circuit, main relay or ECU
12	No distributor signal to Electronic Control Unit (ECU) within 2 seconds after engine is cranked — defective distributor circuit, distributor, starter signal circuit, igniter circuit, igniter or Electronic Control Unit (ECU)
13	No igniter signal to Electronic Control Unit (ECU) within several seconds after engine reaches 1000 rpm — defective distributor circuit, distributor or Electronic Control Unit (ECU)
14	No signal from igniter to ECU 4 times in succession — defective igniter circuit, igniter and ignition coil or Electronic Control Unit (ECU)
21	Deterioration of oxygen sensor — defective oxygen sensor circuit, oxygen sensor or Electronic Control Unit (ECU)
22	Open or shorted Water Temperature Sensor (THW) signal circuit — defective THW circuit, THW or Electronic Control Unit (ECU)
24	Open or shorted intake air temperature sensor circuit — defective intake air temperature sensor circuit, intake air temperature sensor or Electronic Control Unit (ECU)
25	Air/fuel ratio lean malfunction — defective injector circuit, injector, fuel line pressure, oxygen sensor circuit, oxygen sensor, air leak, vacuum sensor, ignition system or Electronic Control Unit (ECU)
26	Air/fuel ratio rich malfunction — defective injector circuit, injector, fuel line pressure, vacuum sensor, oxygen sensor circuit, cold start injector or Electronic Control Unit (ECU)
31	Open or shorted intake manifold pressure (PIM) signal — defective vacuum sensor circuit, vacuum sensor or Electronic Control Unit (ECU)
41	The throttle switch (IDL) and PSW signals are output simultaneously for several seconds — defective Throttle Position Sensor (TPS) sensor circuit, TPS or Electronic Control Unit (ECU)
42	No signal for 8 seconds when vehicle is stopped and the engine running between 2300–5500 rpm and the coolant temperature is below 176°F (80°C), except when racing the engine — defective Vehicle Speed Sensor (VSS) circuit, VSS or Electronic Control Unit (ECU)
43	No starter switch signal to Electronic Control Unit (ECU) until the engine speed reaches 800 rpm — defective ignition switch circuit, ignition switch or Electronic Control Unit (ECU)
51	No throttle switch (IDL) signal, neutral start switch signal or air conditioner signal to Electronic Control Unit (ECU), with the check terminals E1 and T shorted — defective air conditioning switch, air conditioning switch circuit, air conditioning amplifire, Throttle Position Sensor (TPS) circuit, TPS or Electronic Control Unit (ECU)

Year — 1989
Model — Corolla
Engine — 1.6L (97 cid) 4 cyl
Engine Code — 4A-GE

ECM TROUBLE CODES

Code	Explanation
—	Normal system operation
12	No distributor signal to Electronic Control Unit (ECU) within 2 seconds after engine is cranked or when the engine speed is between 500–4000 rpm — defective distributor circuit, distributor, starter signal circuit, igniter circuit, igniter or Electronic Control Unit (ECU)
13	No igniter signal to Electronic Control Unit (ECU) when the engine speed is above 1500 rpm — defective distributor circuit, distributor or Electronic Control Unit (ECU)
14	No signal from igniter to ECU 4 times in succession — defective igniter circuit, igniter or Electronic Control Unit (ECU)
21	Open or shorted oxygen sensor heater circuit and/or deterioration of oxygen sensor — defective oxygen sensor circuit, oxygen sensor, oxygen heater sensor or Electronic Control Unit (ECU)
22	Open or shorted Water Temperature Sensor (THW) signal circuit — defective THW circuit, THW or Electronic Control Unit (ECU)
24	Open or shorted intake air temperature sensor circuit — defective intake air temperature sensor circuit, intake air temperature sensor or Electronic Control Unit (ECU)
25	Air/fuel ratio lean malfunction — defective injector circuit, injector, fuel line pressure, oxygen sensor circuit, oxygen sensor, air leak, vacuum sensor, ignition system or Electronic Control Unit (ECU)
26	Air/fuel ratio rich malfunction — defective injector circuit, injector, fuel line pressure, vacuum sensor, oxygen sensor circuit, cold start injector or Electronic Control Unit (ECU)
27	Open or shorted sub-oxygen sensor circuit — defective sub-oxygen sensor circuit, sub-oxygen sensor or Electronic Control Unit (ECU) — California only
31	Open or shorted air flow meter signal — defective air flow meter circuit, air flow meter or Electronic Control Unit (ECU)
41	Open or shorted throttle position sensor (VTA) circuit — defective Throttle Position Sensor (TPS) sensor circuit, TPS or Electronic Control Unit (ECU)
42	No signal for 8 seconds when the engine running above 2800 rpm — defective Vehicle Speed Sensor (VSS) circuit, VSS or Electronic Control Unit (ECU)
43	No starter switch signal to Electronic Control Unit (ECU) until the engine speed reaches 800 rpm — defective ignition switch circuit, main relay circuit, starter signal circuit or Electronic Control Unit (ECU)
51	Air conditioner switch ON, idle switch OFF during diagnosis check — defective air conditioning switch, air conditioning switch circuit, air conditioning amplifire, Throttle Position Sensor (TPS) circuit, TPS or Electronic Control Unit (ECU)
71	Exhaust Gas Recirculation (EGR) gas temperature below predetermined level during EGR operation — defective EGR valve, EGR hose, EGR sensor circuit, EGR sensor, Vacuum Switching Valve (VSV) for EGR, VSV for EGR circuit or Electronic Control Unit (ECU) — California only

Year — 1989
Model — Cressida
Engine — 3.0L (180 cid) EFI 6 cyl
Engine Code — 7M-GE

ECM TROUBLE CODES

Code	Explanation
—	Normal system operation
11	Momentary interruption in the power supply to the Electronic Control Unit (ECU) — defective ignition switch circuit, ignition switch, main relay circuit, main relay or ECU
12	No engine revolution sensor to Electronic Control Unit (ECU) within 2 seconds after engine is cranked — defective distributor circuit, distributor, starter signal circuit or Electronic Control Unit (ECU)
13	No igniter signal to Electronic Control Unit (ECU) within several seconds after engine reaches 1000 rpm — defective distributor circuit, distributor or Electronic Control Unit (ECU)
14	No signal from igniter to ECU 6–8 times in succession — defective igniter circuit, igniter and ignition coil or Electronic Control Unit (ECU)
16	ECT control program faulty — defective Electronic Control Unit (ECU)
21	Deterioration of oxygen sensor — defective oxygen sensor circuit, oxygen sensor or Electronic Control Unit (ECU)
22	Open or shorted Water Temperature Sensor (THW) signal circuit — defective THW circuit, THW or Electronic Control Unit (ECU)
24	Open or shorted intake air temperature sensor circuit — defective intake air temperature sensor circuit, intake air temperature sensor or Electronic Control Unit (ECU)
25	Air/fuel ratio lean malfunction — defective intake air system, air flow meter, injector circuit, injector, fuel line pressure, oxygen sensor circuits, oxygen sensors, ignition system or Electronic Control Unit (ECU)
26	Air/fuel ratio rich malfunction — defective injector circuits, injector, fuel line pressure, air flow meter, cold start injector or Electronic Control Unit (ECU)
27	Open or shorted sub-oxygen sensor heater circuit or signal — defective sub-oxygen sensor circuit, sub-oxygen sensor, sub-oxygen sensor heater or Electronic Control Unit (ECU)
31	Open or shorted air flow meter signal circuit — defective air flow meter circuit, air flow meter or Electronic Control Unit (ECU)
32	Open or shorted air flow meter signal circuit — defective air flow meter circuit, air flow meter or Electronic Control Unit (ECU)
41	Open or shorted Throttle Position Sensor (TPS) circuit — defective TPS sensor or Electronic Control Unit (ECU)
42	No signal for over 8 seconds when the engine speed is above 2500 rpm and the neutral start switch is OFF — defective No. 1 Vehicle Speed Sensor (VSS) circuit, No. 1 VSS or Electronic Control Unit (ECU)
43	No starter switch signal to Electronic Control Unit (ECU) when the engine is running over 400 rpm — defective ignition switch circuit, ignition switch or Electronic Control Unit (ECU)
51	No throttle switch (IDL) signal, neutral start switch signal or air conditioner signal to Electronic Control Unit (ECU), during the diagnosis check test mode — defective neutral start switch, air conditioner switch, air conditioning switch circuit, air conditioning amplifire, Throttle Position Sensor (TPS) circuit, TPS, acceleration pedal and cable or Electronic Control Unit (ECU)
52	Open or shorted knock sensor signal circuit — defective knock sensor circuit, knock sensor or Electronic Control Unit (ECU)
53	Knock control in Electronic Control Unit (ECU) faulty — defective ECU
71	Exhaust Gas Recirculation (EGR) gas temperature below predetermined level during EGR operation — defective EGR valve, EGR hose, EGR sensor circuit, EGR sensor, Vacuum Switching Valve (VSV) for EGR, VSV for EGR circuit or Electronic Control Unit (ECU) — California only

Year – 1989
Model – Supra
Engine – 3.0L (180 cid) EFI 6 cyl
Engine Code – 7M-GE

ECM TROUBLE CODES

Code	Explanation
–	Normal system operation
11	Momentary interruption in the power supply to the Electronic Control Unit (ECU) – defective ignition switch circuit, ignition switch, main relay circuit, main relay or ECU
12	No engine revolution sensor to Electronic Control Unit (ECU) within 2 seconds after engine is cranked – defective distributor cam position sensor circuit, distributor cam position sensor, starter signal circuit or Electronic Control Unit (ECU)
13	No igniter signal to Electronic Control Unit (ECU) within several seconds after engine reaches 1000 rpm – defective distributor cam position sensor circuit, distributor cam position sensor or Electronic Control Unit (ECU)
14	No signal from igniter to ECU 6–8 times in succession – defective igniter circuit, igniter and ignition coil or Electronic Control Unit (ECU)
21	Deterioration of oxygen sensor – defective oxygen sensor circuit, oxygen sensor or Electronic Control Unit (ECU)
22	Open or shorted Water Temperature Sensor (THW) signal circuit – defective THW circuit, THW or Electronic Control Unit (ECU)
24	Open or shorted intake air temperature sensor circuit – defective intake air temperature sensor circuit, intake air temperature sensor or Electronic Control Unit (ECU)
25	Air/fuel ratio lean malfunction – defective intake air system, air flow meter, injector circuit, injector, fuel line pressure, oxygen sensor circuits, oxygen sensors, ignition system or Electronic Control Unit (ECU)
26	Air/fuel ratio rich malfunction – defective injector circuits, injector, fuel line pressure, air flow meter, cold start injector or Electronic Control Unit (ECU)
27	Open or shorted sub-oxygen sensor heater circuit or signal – defective sub-oxygen sensor circuit, sub-oxygen sensor, sub-oxygen sensor heater or Electronic Control Unit (ECU) – California only
31	Open or shorted air flow meter signal circuit – defective air flow meter circuit, air flow meter or Electronic Control Unit (ECU)
32	Open or shorted air flow meter signal circuit – defective air flow meter circuit, air flow meter or Electronic Control Unit (ECU)
41	Open or shorted Throttle Position Sensor (TPS) circuit – defective TPS sensor or Electronic Control Unit (ECU)
42	No signal for over 8 seconds when the engine speed is between 2500–4500 rpm, the coolant temperature is below 176°F (80°C) and the neutral start switch is OFF – defective Vehicle Speed Sensor (VSS) circuit, VSS or Electronic Control Unit (ECU)
43	No starter switch signal to Electronic Control Unit (ECU) when the engine is running over 800 rpm – defective ignition switch circuit, ignition switch or Electronic Control Unit (ECU)
51	No throttle switch (IDL) signal, neutral start switch signal or air conditioner signal to Electronic Control Unit (ECU), during the diagnosis check test mode – defective neutral start switch, air conditioner switch, air conditioning switch circuit, air conditioning amplifire, Throttle Position Sensor (TPS) circuit, TPS, acceleration pedal and cable or Electronic Control Unit (ECU)
52	Open or shorted knock sensor signal circuit – defective knock sensor circuit, knock sensor or Electronic Control Unit (ECU)
53	Knock control in Electronic Control Unit (ECU) faulty – defective ECU
71	Exhaust Gas Recirculation (EGR) gas temperature below predetermined level during EGR operation – defective EGR valve, EGR hose, EGR sensor circuit, EGR sensor, Vacuum Switching Valve (VSV) for EGR, VSV for EGR circuit or Electronic Control Unit (ECU) – California only

Year – 1989
Model – Supra
Engine – 3.0L (180 cid) EFI 6 cyl
Engine Code – 7M-GTE

ECM TROUBLE CODES

Code	Explanation
–	Normal system operation
11	Momentary interruption in the power supply to the Electronic Control Unit (ECU) – defective ignition switch circuit, ignition switch, main relay circuit, main relay or ECU
12	No engine revolution sensor to Electronic Control Unit (ECU) within several seconds after engine is cranked – defective distributor cam position sensor circuit, distributor cam position sensor, starter signal circuit or Electronic Control Unit (ECU)
13	No igniter signal to Electronic Control Unit (ECU) within several seconds after engine reaches 1000 rpm – defective distributor cam position sensor circuit, distributor cam position sensor or Electronic Control Unit (ECU)
14	No signal from igniter to ECU 6–8 times in succession – defective igniter circuit, igniter and ignition coil or Electronic Control Unit (ECU)
21	Deterioration of oxygen sensor – defective oxygen sensor circuit, oxygen sensor or Electronic Control Unit (ECU)
22	Open or shorted Water Temperature Sensor (THW) signal circuit – defective THW circuit, THW or Electronic Control Unit (ECU)
24	Open or shorted intake air temperature sensor circuit – defective intake air temperature sensor circuit, intake air temperature sensor or Electronic Control Unit (ECU)
31	Open or shorted air flow meter signal circuit – defective air flow meter circuit, air flow meter or Electronic Control Unit (ECU)
32	Open or shorted High Altitude Compensator (HAC) sensor circuit – defective HAC circuit, HAC sensor or Electronic Control Unit (ECU)
34	Abnormal turbocharger pressure or air flow meter signal – defective turbocharger, air flow meter, intercooler system or Electronic Control Unit (ECU)
41	Open or shorted Throttle Position Sensor (TPS) circuit – defective TPS sensor or Electronic Control Unit (ECU)
42	No signal for over 5 seconds when vehicle is stopped and the engine running between 4000 rpm and the coolant temperature is below 176°F (80°C), except when racing the engine – defective Vehicle Speed Sensor (VSS) circuit, VSS or Electronic Control Unit (ECU)
43	No starter switch signal to Electronic Control Unit (ECU) when the engine is running over 800 rpm – defective ignition switch circuit, ignition switch or Electronic Control Unit (ECU)
51	No Throttle Position Sensor (TPS) signal, neutral start switch signal or air conditioner signal to Electronic Control Unit (ECU), with the check terminals E1 and TE1 shorted – defective neutral start switch, air conditioner switch, air conditioning switch circuit, air conditioning amplifire, Throttle Position Sensor (TPS) circuit, TPS, acceleration pedal and cable or Electronic Control Unit (ECU)
52	Open or shorted knock sensor signal circuit – defective knock sensor circuit, knock sensor or Electronic Control Unit (ECU)
53	Knock control in Electronic Control Unit (ECU) faulty – defective ECU
71	Exhaust Gas Recirculation (EGR) gas temperature below predetermined level during EGR operation – defective EGR valve, EGR hose, EGR sensor circuit, EGR sensor, Vacuum Switching Valve (VSV) for EGR, VSV for EGR circuit or Electronic Control Unit (ECU) – California only

Year – 1989
Model – MR2
Engine – 1.6L (97 cid) 4 cyl
Engine Code – 4A-GE

ECM TROUBLE CODES

Code	Explanation
—	Normal system operation
12	No distributor signal to Electronic Control Unit (ECU) within 2 seconds after engine is cranked or when the engine speed is between 500 – 4000 rpm – defective distributor circuit, distributor, starter signal circuit, igniter circuit, igniter or Electronic Control Unit (ECU)
13	No igniter signal to Electronic Control Unit (ECU) when the engine speed is above 1500 rpm – defective distributor circuit, distributor or Electronic Control Unit (ECU)
14	No signal from igniter to ECU 4 times in succession – defective igniter circuit, igniter or Electronic Control Unit (ECU)
21	Open or shorted oxygen sensor heater circuit and/or deterioration of oxygen sensor – defective oxygen sensor circuit, oxygen sensor, oxygen heater sensor or Electronic Control Unit (ECU)
22	Open or shorted Water Temperature Sensor (THW) signal circuit – defective THW circuit, THW or Electronic Control Unit (ECU)
24	Open or shorted intake air temperature sensor circuit – defective intake air temperature sensor circuit, intake air temperature sensor or Electronic Control Unit (ECU)
25	Air/fuel ratio lean malfunction – defective injector circuit, injector, fuel line pressure, oxygen sensor circuit, oxygen sensor, air leak, vacuum sensor, ignition system or Electronic Control Unit (ECU)
26	Air/fuel ratio rich malfunction – defective injector circuit, injector, fuel line pressure, vacuum sensor, oxygen sensor circuit, cold start injector or Electronic Control Unit (ECU)
31	Open or shorted air flow meter signal – defective air flow meter circuit, air flow meter or Electronic Control Unit (ECU)
41	Open or shorted throttle position sensor (VTA) circuit – defective Throttle Position Sensor (TPS) sensor circuit, TPS or Electronic Control Unit (ECU)
42	No signal for 8 seconds when the engine running between 2500–5500 rpm – defective Vehicle Speed Sensor (VSS) circuit, VSS or Electronic Control Unit (ECU)
43	No starter switch signal to Electronic Control Unit (ECU) until the engine speed reaches 800 rpm – defective ignition switch circuit, main relay circuit, starter signal circuit or Electronic Control Unit (ECU)
51	Air conditioner switch ON, idle switch OFF or automatic transmission shift position other than P or N range, during diagnosis check – defective air conditioning switch, air conditioning switch circuit, air conditioning amplifire, Throttle Position Sensor (TPS) circuit, TPS or Electronic Control Unit (ECU)
71	Exhaust Gas Recirculation (EGR) gas temperature below predetermined level during EGR operation – defective EGR valve, EGR hose, EGR sensor circuit, EGR sensor, Vacuum Switching Valve (VSV) for EGR, VSV for EGR circuit or Electronic Control Unit (ECU) – California only

Year – 1989
Model – MR2
Engine – 1.6L (97 cid) EFI 4 cyl
Engine Code – 4A-GZE

ECM TROUBLE CODES

Code	Explanation
—	Normal system operation
11	Momentary interruption in power supply to Electronic Control Unit (ECU) – defective ignition switch circuit, ignition switch, main relay circuit, main relay or ECU
12	No engine revolution sensor to Electronic Control Unit (ECU) within several seconds after engine is cranked or when the engine is run between 500–4000 rpm – defective distributor circuit, distributor, starter signal circuit, igniter circuit, igniter or Electronic Control Unit (ECU)
13	No igniter signal to Electronic Control Unit (ECU) within several seconds after engine reaches 1000 rpm – defective distributor circuit, distributor or Electronic Control Unit (ECU)
14	No signal from igniter to ECU 8–11 times in succession – defective igniter circuit, igniter and ignition coil or Electronic Control Unit (ECU)
21	Open or shorted oxygen sensor heater and/or deterioration of oxygen sensor – defective oxygen sensor circuit, oxygen sensor, oxygen sensor heater or Electronic Control Unit (ECU)
22	Open or shorted Water Temperature Sensor (THW) signal circuit – defective THW circuit, THW or Electronic Control Unit (ECU)
24	Open or shorted intake air temperature sensor circuit – defective intake air temperature sensor circuit, intake air temperature sensor or Electronic Control Unit (ECU)
25	Air/fuel ratio lean malfunction – defective intake air system, air flow meter, injector circuit, injector, fuel line pressure, oxygen sensor circuits, oxygen sensors, ignition system or Electronic Control Unit (ECU)
26	Air/fuel ratio rich malfunction – defective injector circuits, injector, fuel line pressure, air flow meter, cold start injector or Electronic Control Unit (ECU)
31	Open or shorted air flow meter signal circuit – defective air flow meter circuit, air flow meter or Electronic Control Unit (ECU)
32	Open or shorted air flow meter signal – defective air flow meter circuit, air flow meter or Electronic Control Unit (ECU)
41	Open or shorted Throttle Position Sensor (TPS) circuit – defective TPS sensor or TPS sensor circuit
42	No signal for 8 seconds when vehicle is stopped and the engine running between 2300–5000 rpm and the coolant temperature is below 176°F (80°C), except when racing the engine – defective Vehicle Speed Sensor (VSS) circuit, VSS or Electronic Control Unit (ECU)
43	No starter switch signal to Electronic Control Unit (ECU) until the engine speed reaches 800 rpm with the vehicle stopped – defective igniter switch, igniter switch circuit or Electronic Control Unit (ECU)
51	Air conditioning switch ON, idle switch OFF or automatic transmission shift position other than P or N range, during diagnosis check – defective air conditioning switch, air conditioning switch circuit, air conditioning amplifire, Throttle Position Sensor (TPS) circuit, TPS or Electronic Control Unit (ECU)
52	Open or shorted knock sensor signal circuit – defective knock sensor circuit, knock sensor or Electronic Control Unit (ECU)
53	Knock control in Electronic Control Unit (ECU) faulty – defective ECU
71	Exhaust Gas Recirculation (EGR) gas temperature below predetermined level during EGR operation – defective EGR valve, EGR hose, EGR sensor circuit, EGR sensor, Vacuum Switching Valve (VSV) for EGR, VSV for EGR circuit or Electronic Control Unit (ECU) – California only

TOYOTA TRUCKS

Year – 1984
Model – Van
Engine – 2.0L (122 cid) EFI 4 cyl
Engine Code – 3Y-EC

ECM TROUBLE CODES

Code	Explanation
1	Normal operation
2	Open or shorted air flow meter circuit – defective air flow meter or Electronic Control Unit (ECU)
3	Open or shorted air flow meter circuit – defective air flow meter or Electronic Control Unit (ECU)
4	Open Water Thermo Sensor (THW) circuit – defective Water Thermo Sensor (THW) or Electronic Control Unit (ECU)
5	Open or shorted oxygen sensor circuit – lean or rich indication – defective oxygen sensor or Electronic Control Unit (ECU)
6	No ignition signal – defective ignition system circuit, Integrated Ignition Assembly (IIA) or Electronic Control Unit (ECU)
7	Defective Throttle Position Sensor (TPS) circuit, Throttle Position Sensor (TPS) or Electronic Control Unit (ECU)

Year – 1984
Model – Pick-Up
Engine – 2.4L (144 cid) EFI 4 cyl
Engine Code – 22R-E

ECM TROUBLE CODES

Code	Explanation
1	Normal operation
2	Open or shorted air flow meter circuit – defective air flow meter or Electronic Fuel Injection (EFI) computer
3	Open or shorted air flow meter circuit – defective air flow meter or Electronic Fuel Injection (EFI) computer
4	Open Water Thermo Sensor (THW) circuit – defective Water Thermo Sensor (THW) or Electronic Fuel Injection (EFI) computer
5	Open oxygen sensor circuit – lean indication – defective oxygen sensor or Electronic Fuel Injection (EFI) computer
6	No ignition signal – defective ignition system circuit, distributor, ignition coil and igniter or Electronic Fuel Injection (EFI) computer
7	Defective Throttle Position Sensor (TPS) circuit, Throttle Position Sensor (TPS) or Electronic Fuel Injection (EFI) computer

Year — 1985
Model — Van
Engine — 2.0L (122 cid) EFI 4 cyl
Engine Code — 3Y-EC

ECM TROUBLE CODES

Code	Explanation
1	Normal operation
2	Open or shorted air flow meter circuit — defective air flow meter or Electronic Control Unit (ECU)
3	Open or shorted air flow meter circuit — defective air flow meter or Electronic Control Unit (ECU)
4	Open Water Thermo Sensor (THW) circuit — defective Water Thermo Sensor (THW) or Electronic Control Unit (ECU)
5	Open or shorted oxygen sensor circuit — lean or rich indication — defective oxygen sensor or Electronic Control Unit (ECU)
6	No ignition signal — defective ignition system circuit, Integrated Ignition Assembly (IIA) or Electronic Control Unit (ECU)
7	Defective Throttle Position Sensor (TPS) circuit, Throttle Position Sensor (TPS) or Electronic Control Unit (ECU)

Year — 1985
Model — Pick-Up
Engine — 2.4L (144 cid) EFI 4 cyl
Engine Code — 22R-E

ECM TROUBLE CODES

Code	Explanation
1	Normal operation
2	Open or shorted air flow meter circuit — defective air flow meter or Electronic Control Unit (ECU)
3	No signal from igniter 4 times in succession — defective igniter or main relay circuit, igniter or Electronic Control Unit (ECU)
4	Open or shorted Water Thermo Sensor (THW) circuit — defective Water Thermo Sensor (THW) or Electronic Control Unit (ECU)
5	Open or shorted oxygen sensor circuit — lean or rich indication — defective oxygen sensor or Electronic Control Unit (ECU)
6	No engine revolution sensor (Ne) signal to Electronic Control Unit (ECU) or Ne value being over 1000 rpm in spite of no Ne signal to ECU — defective igniter circuit, igniter, distributor or Electronic Control Unit (ECU)
7	Open or shorted Throttle Position Sensor (TPS) circuit — defective Throttle Position Sensor (TPS) or Electronic Control Unit (ECU)
8	Open or shorted intake air thermo sensor circuit — defective intake air thermo sensor circuit or Electronic Control Unit (ECU)
10	No starter switch signal to Electronic Control Unit (ECU) with vehicle speed at 0 and engine speed over 800 rpm — defective speed sensor circuit, main relay circuit, igniter switch-to-starter circuit, igniter switch or Electronic Control Unit (ECU)
11	Short circuit in check connector terminal T with the air conditioning switch ON or throttle switch (IDL) point OFF — defective air conditioner switch, Throttle Position Sensor (TPS) circuit, Throttle Position Sensor (TPS) or Electronic Control Unit (ECU)
12	Knock control sensor signal has not reached judgement level in succession — defective knock control sensor circuit, knock control sensor or Electronic Control Unit (ECU)
13	Knock CPU faulty

Year — 1985
Model — 4Runner
Engine — 2.4L (144 cid) EFI 4 cyl
Engine Code — 22R-E

ECM TROUBLE CODES

Code	Explanation
1	Normal operation
2	Open or shorted air flow meter circuit — defective air flow meter or Electronic Control Unit (ECU)
3	No signal from igniter 4 times in succession — defective igniter or main relay circuit, igniter or Electronic Control Unit (ECU)
4	Open or shorted Water Thermo Sensor (THW) circuit — defective Water Thermo Sensor (THW) or Electronic Control Unit (ECU)
5	Open or shorted oxygen sensor circuit — lean or rich indication — defective oxygen sensor or Electronic Control Unit (ECU)
6	No engine revolution sensor (Ne) signal to Electronic Control Unit (ECU) or Ne value being over 1000 rpm in spite of no Ne signal to ECU — defective igniter circuit, igniter, distributor or Electronic Control Unit (ECU)
7	Open or shorted Throttle Position Sensor (TPS) circuit — defective Throttle Position Sensor (TPS) or Electronic Control Unit (ECU)
8	Open or shorted intake air thermo sensor circuit — defective intake air thermo sensor circuit or Electronic Control Unit (ECU)
10	No starter switch signal to Electronic Control Unit (ECU) with vehicle speed at 0 and engine speed over 800 rpm — defective speed sensor circuit, main relay circuit, igniter switch-to-starter circuit, igniter switch or Electronic Control Unit (ECU)
11	Short circuit in check connector terminal T with the air conditioning switch ON or throttle switch (IDL) point OFF — defective air conditioner switch, Throttle Position Sensor (TPS) circuit, Throttle Position Sensor (TPS) or Electronic Control Unit (ECU)
12	Knock control sensor signal has not reached judgement level in succession — defective knock control sensor circuit, knock control sensor or Electronic Control Unit (ECU)
13	Knock CPU faulty

Year — 1985
Model — Pick-Up
Engine — 2.4L (144 cid) EFI 4 cyl
Engine Code — 22R-TE

ECM TROUBLE CODES

Code	Explanation
1	Normal operation
2	Open or shorted air flow meter circuit — defective air flow meter or Electronic Control Unit (ECU)
3	No signal from igniter 4 times in succession — defective igniter or main relay circuit, igniter or Electronic Control Unit (ECU)
4	Open or shorted Water Thermo Sensor (THW) circuit — defective Water Thermo Sensor (THW) or Electronic Control Unit (ECU)
5	Open or shorted oxygen sensor circuit — lean or rich indication — defective oxygen sensor or Electronic Control Unit (ECU)
6	No engine revolution sensor (Ne) signal to Electronic Control Unit (ECU) or Ne value being over 1000 rpm in spite of no Ne signal to ECU — defective igniter circuit, igniter, distributor or Electronic Control Unit (ECU)
7	Open or shorted Throttle Position Sensor (TPS) circuit — defective Throttle Position Sensor (TPS) or Electronic Control Unit (ECU)
8	Open or shorted intake air thermo sensor circuit — defective intake air thermo sensor circuit or Electronic Control Unit (ECU)
10	No starter switch signal to Electronic Control Unit (ECU) with vehicle speed at 0 and engine speed over 800 rpm — defective speed sensor circuit, main relay circuit, igniter switch-to-starter circuit, igniter switch or Electronic Control Unit (ECU)
11	Short circuit in check connector terminal T with the air conditioning switch ON or throttle switch (IDL) point OFF — defective air conditioner switch, Throttle Position Sensor (TPS) circuit, Throttle Position Sensor (TPS) or Electronic Control Unit (ECU)
12	Knock control sensor signal has not reached judgement level in succession — defective knock control sensor circuit, knock control sensor or Electronic Control Unit (ECU)
13	Knock CPU faulty

Year — 1985
Model — 4Runner
Engine — 2.4L (144 cid) EFI 4 cyl
Engine Code — 22R-TE

ECM TROUBLE CODES

Code	Explanation
1	Normal operation
2	Open or shorted air flow meter circuit — defective air flow meter or Electronic Control Unit (ECU)
3	No signal from igniter 4 times in succession — defective igniter or main relay circuit, igniter or Electronic Control Unit (ECU)
4	Open or shorted Water Thermo Sensor (THW) circuit — defective Water Thermo Sensor (THW) or Electronic Control Unit (ECU)
5	Open or shorted oxygen sensor circuit — lean or rich indication — defective oxygen sensor or Electronic Control Unit (ECU)
6	No engine revolution sensor (Ne) signal to Electronic Control Unit (ECU) or Ne value being over 1000 rpm in spite of no Ne signal to ECU — defective igniter circuit, igniter, distributor or Electronic Control Unit (ECU)
7	Open or shorted Throttle Position Sensor (TPS) circuit — defective Throttle Position Sensor (TPS) or Electronic Control Unit (ECU)
8	Open or shorted intake air thermo sensor circuit — defective intake air thermo sensor circuit or Electronic Control Unit (ECU)
10	No starter switch signal to Electronic Control Unit (ECU) with vehicle speed at 0 and engine speed over 800 rpm — defective speed sensor circuit, main relay circuit, igniter switch-to-starter circuit, igniter switch or Electronic Control Unit (ECU)
11	Short circuit in check connector terminal T with the air conditioning switch ON or throttle switch (IDL) point OFF — defective air conditioner switch, Throttle Position Sensor (TPS) circuit, Throttle Position Sensor (TPS) or Electronic Control Unit (ECU)
12	Knock control sensor signal has not reached judgement level in succession — defective knock control sensor circuit, knock control sensor or Electronic Control Unit (ECU)
13	Knock CPU faulty

Year — 1986
Model — Van
Engine — 2.2L (136 cid) EFI 4 cyl
Engine Code — 4Y-EC

ECM TROUBLE CODES

Code	Explanation
1	Normal operation
2	Open or shorted air flow meter circuit — defective air flow meter or Electronic Control Unit (ECU)
3	No signal from igniter 4 times in succession — defective igniter or main relay circuit, igniter or Electronic Control Unit (ECU)
4	Open or shorted Water Thermo Sensor (THW) circuit — defective Water Thermo Sensor (THW) or Electronic Control Unit (ECU)
5	Open or shorted oxygen sensor circuit — lean or rich indication — defective oxygen sensor or Electronic Control Unit (ECU)
6	No engine revolution sensor (Ne) signal to Electronic Control Unit (ECU) or Ne value being over 1500 rpm in spite of no Ne signal to ECU — defective distributor circuit, igniter, distributor, starter signal circuit or Electronic Control Unit (ECU)
7	Open or shorted Throttle Position Sensor (TPS) circuit — defective Throttle Position Sensor (TPS) or Electronic Control Unit (ECU)
8	Open or shorted intake air thermo sensor circuit — defective air temperature sensor circuit or Electronic Control Unit (ECU)
9	Signal informing Electronic Control Unit (ECU) that vehicle stopped had been input to ECU for 8 seconds with the engine running over 2800 rpm
10	No starter switch signal to Electronic Control Unit (ECU) with the vehicle stopped and the engine speed over 800 rpm — defective speed sensor circuit, igniter switch-to-starter circuit, igniter switch or Electronic Control Unit (ECU)
11	Air conditioning switch ON, idle switch OFF or shift position in any position other than P or N range during diagnosis check — defective air conditioner switch, Throttle Position Sensor (TPS) circuit, TPS, neutral start switch or Electronic Control Unit (ECU)

Year — 1986
Model — Pick-Up
Engine — 2.4L (144 cid) EFI 4 cyl
Engine Code — 22R-E

ECM TROUBLE CODES

Code	Explanation
1	Normal operation
2	Open or shorted air flow meter circuit — defective air flow meter or Electronic Control Unit (ECU)
3	No signal from igniter 4 times in succession — defective igniter or main relay circuit, igniter or Electronic Control Unit (ECU)
4	Open or shorted Water Thermo Sensor (THW) circuit — defective Water Thermo Sensor (THW) or Electronic Control Unit (ECU)
5	Open or shorted oxygen sensor circuit — lean or rich indication — defective oxygen sensor or Electronic Control Unit (ECU)
6	No engine revolution sensor (Ne) signal to Electronic Control Unit (ECU) or Ne value being over 1000 rpm in spite of no Ne signal to ECU — defective igniter circuit, igniter, distributor or Electronic Control Unit (ECU)
7	Open or shorted Throttle Position Sensor (TPS) circuit — defective Throttle Position Sensor (TPS) or Electronic Control Unit (ECU)
8	Open or shorted intake air thermo sensor circuit — defective intake air thermo sensor circuit or Electronic Control Unit (ECU)
10	No starter switch signal to Electronic Control Unit (ECU) with vehicle speed at 0 and engine speed over 800 rpm — defective speed sensor circuit, main relay circuit, igniter switch-to-starter circuit, igniter switch or Electronic Control Unit (ECU)
11	Throttle switch (IDL) point in the Throttle Position Sensor (TPS) is OFF during diagnostic check — defective Throttle Position Sensor (TPS) circuit, Throttle Position Sensor (TPS) or Electronic Control Unit (ECU)
12	Knock control sensor signal has not reached judgement level in succession — defective knock control sensor circuit, knock control sensor or Electronic Control Unit (ECU)
13	Knock CPU faulty — defective Electronic Control Unit (ECU)

Year – 1986
Model – 4Runner
Engine – 2.4L (144 cid) EFI 4 cyl
Engine Code – 22R-E

ECM TROUBLE CODES

Code	Explanation
1	Normal operation
2	Open or shorted air flow meter circuit – defective air flow meter or Electronic Control Unit (ECU)
3	No signal from igniter 4 times in succession – defective igniter or main relay circuit, igniter or Electronic Control Unit (ECU)
4	Open or shorted Water Thermo Sensor (THW) circuit – defective Water Thermo Sensor (THW) or Electronic Control Unit (ECU)
5	Open or shorted oxygen sensor circuit – lean or rich indication – defective oxygen sensor or Electronic Control Unit (ECU)
6	No engine revolution sensor (Ne) signal to Electronic Control Unit (ECU) or Ne value being over 1000 rpm in spite of no Ne signal to ECU – defective igniter circuit, igniter, distributor or Electronic Control Unit (ECU)
7	Open or shorted Throttle Position Sensor (TPS) circuit – defective Throttle Position Sensor (TPS) or Electronic Control Unit (ECU)
8	Open or shorted intake air thermo sensor circuit – defective intake air thermo sensor circuit or Electronic Control Unit (ECU)
10	No starter switch signal to Electronic Control Unit (ECU) with vehicle speed at 0 and engine speed over 800 rpm – defective speed sensor circuit, main relay circuit, igniter switch-to-starter circuit, igniter switch or Electronic Control Unit (ECU)
11	Throttle switch (IDL) point in the Throttle Position Sensor (TPS) is OFF during diagnostic check – defective Throttle Position Sensor (TPS) circuit, Throttle Position Sensor (TPS) or Electronic Control Unit (ECU)
12	Knock control sensor signal has not reached judgement level in succession – defective knock control sensor circuit, knock control sensor or Electronic Control Unit (ECU)
13	Knock CPU faulty – defective Electronic Control Unit (ECU)

Year — 1986
Model — Pick-Up
Engine — 2.4L (144 cid) EFI 4 cyl
Engine Code — 22R-TE

ECM TROUBLE CODES

Code	Explanation
1	Normal operation
2	Open or shorted air flow meter circuit — defective air flow meter or Electronic Control Unit (ECU)
3	No signal from igniter 4 times in succession — defective igniter or main relay circuit, igniter or Electronic Control Unit (ECU)
4	Open or shorted Water Thermo Sensor (THW) circuit — defective Water Thermo Sensor (THW) or Electronic Control Unit (ECU)
5	Open or shorted oxygen sensor circuit — lean or rich indication — defective oxygen sensor or Electronic Control Unit (ECU)
6	No engine revolution sensor (Ne) signal to Electronic Control Unit (ECU) or Ne value being over 1000 rpm in spite of no Ne signal to ECU — defective igniter circuit, igniter, distributor or Electronic Control Unit (ECU)
7	Open or shorted Throttle Position Sensor (TPS) circuit — defective Throttle Position Sensor (TPS) or Electronic Control Unit (ECU)
8	Open or shorted intake air thermo sensor circuit — defective intake air thermo sensor circuit or Electronic Control Unit (ECU)
10	No starter switch signal to Electronic Control Unit (ECU) with vehicle speed at 0 and engine speed over 800 rpm — defective speed sensor circuit, main relay circuit, igniter switch-to-starter circuit, igniter switch or Electronic Control Unit (ECU)
11	Throttle switch (IDL) point in the Throttle Position Sensor (TPS) is OFF during diagnostic check — defective Throttle Position Sensor (TPS) circuit, Throttle Position Sensor (TPS) or Electronic Control Unit (ECU)
12	Knock control sensor signal has not reached judgement level in succession — defective knock control sensor circuit, knock control sensor or Electronic Control Unit (ECU)
13	Knock CPU faulty — defective Electronic Control Unit (ECU)
14	The turbocharger pressure is abnormal — defective turbocharger, air flow meter or Electronic Control Unit (ECU)

Year — 1986
Model — 4Runner
Engine — 2.4L (144 cid) EFI 4 cyl
Engine Code — 22R-TE

ECM TROUBLE CODES

Code	Explanation
1	Normal operation
2	Open or shorted air flow meter circuit — defective air flow meter or Electronic Control Unit (ECU)
3	No signal from igniter 4 times in succession — defective igniter or main relay circuit, igniter or Electronic Control Unit (ECU)
4	Open or shorted Water Thermo Sensor (THW) circuit — defective Water Thermo Sensor (THW) or Electronic Control Unit (ECU)
5	Open or shorted oxygen sensor circuit — lean or rich indication — defective oxygen sensor or Electronic Control Unit (ECU)
6	No engine revolution sensor (Ne) signal to Electronic Control Unit (ECU) or Ne value being over 1000 rpm in spite of no Ne signal to ECU — defective igniter circuit, igniter, distributor or Electronic Control Unit (ECU)
7	Open or shorted Throttle Position Sensor (TPS) circuit — defective Throttle Position Sensor (TPS) or Electronic Control Unit (ECU)
8	Open or shorted intake air thermo sensor circuit — defective intake air thermo sensor circuit or Electronic Control Unit (ECU)
10	No starter switch signal to Electronic Control Unit (ECU) with vehicle speed at 0 and engine speed over 800 rpm — defective speed sensor circuit, main relay circuit, igniter switch-to-starter circuit, igniter switch or Electronic Control Unit (ECU)
11	Throttle switch (IDL) point in the Throttle Position Sensor (TPS) is OFF during diagnostic check — defective Throttle Position Sensor (TPS) circuit, Throttle Position Sensor (TPS) or Electronic Control Unit (ECU)
12	Knock control sensor signal has not reached judgement level in succession — defective knock control sensor circuit, knock control sensor or Electronic Control Unit (ECU)
13	Knock CPU faulty — defective Electronic Control Unit (ECU)
14	The turbocharger pressure is abnormal — defective turbocharger, air flow meter or Electronic Control Unit (ECU)

Year — 1987
Model — Van
Engine — 2.2L (136 cid) EFI 4 cyl
Engine Code — 4Y-EC

ECM TROUBLE CODES

Code	Explanation
1	Normal operation
2	Open or shorted air flow meter circuit — defective air flow meter or Electronic Control Unit (ECU)
3	No signal from igniter 4 times in succession — defective igniter or main relay circuit, igniter or Electronic Control Unit (ECU)
4	Open or shorted Water Thermo Sensor (THW) circuit — defective Water Thermo Sensor (THW) or Electronic Control Unit (ECU)
5	Open or shorted oxygen sensor circuit — lean or rich indication — defective oxygen sensor or Electronic Control Unit (ECU)
6	No engine revolution sensor (Ne) signal to Electronic Control Unit (ECU) or Ne value being over 1500 rpm in spite of no Ne signal to ECU — defective distributor circuit, igniter, distributor, starter signal circuit or Electronic Control Unit (ECU)
7	Open or shorted Throttle Position Sensor (TPS) circuit — defective Throttle Position Sensor (TPS) or Electronic Control Unit (ECU)
8	Open or shorted intake air thermo sensor circuit — defective air temperature sensor circuit or Electronic Control Unit (ECU)
9	Signal informing Electronic Control Unit (ECU) that vehicle stopped had been input to ECU for 8 seconds with the engine running over 2800 rpm
10	No starter switch signal to Electronic Control Unit (ECU) with the vehicle stopped and the engine speed over 800 rpm — defective speed sensor circuit, igniter switch-to-starter circuit, igniter switch or Electronic Control Unit (ECU)
11	Air conditioning switch ON and idle switch OFF — defective air conditioner switch, Throttle Position Sensor (TPS) circuit, TPS, neutral start switch or Electronic Control Unit (ECU)

Year — 1987
Model — Pick-Up
Engine — 2.4L (144 cid) EFI 4 cyl
Engine Code — 22R-E

ECM TROUBLE CODES

Code	Explanation
1	Normal operation
2	Open or shorted air flow meter circuit — defective air flow meter or Electronic Control Unit (ECU)
3	No signal from igniter 4 times in succession — defective igniter or main relay circuit, igniter or Electronic Control Unit (ECU)
4	Open or shorted Water Thermo Sensor (THW) circuit — defective Water Thermo Sensor (THW) or Electronic Control Unit (ECU)
5	Open or shorted oxygen sensor circuit — lean or rich indication — defective oxygen sensor or Electronic Control Unit (ECU)
6	No engine revolution sensor (Ne) signal to Electronic Control Unit (ECU) or Ne value being over 1000 rpm in spite of no Ne signal to ECU — defective igniter circuit, igniter, distributor or Electronic Control Unit (ECU)
7	Open or shorted Throttle Position Sensor (TPS) circuit — defective Throttle Position Sensor (TPS) or Electronic Control Unit (ECU)
8	Open or shorted intake air thermo sensor circuit — defective intake air thermo sensor circuit or Electronic Control Unit (ECU)
10	No starter switch signal to Electronic Control Unit (ECU) with vehicle speed at 0 and engine speed over 800 rpm — defective speed sensor circuit, main relay circuit, igniter switch-to-starter circuit, igniter switch or Electronic Control Unit (ECU)
11	Neutral start switch ON or throttle switch (IDL) point in the Throttle Position Sensor (TPS) is OFF during diagnostic check — defective Throttle Position Sensor (TPS) circuit, Throttle Position Sensor (TPS), neutral start switch or Electronic Control Unit (ECU)
12	Knock control sensor signal has not reached judgement level in succession — defective knock control sensor circuit, knock control sensor or Electronic Control Unit (ECU)
13	Knock CPU faulty — defective Electronic Control Unit (ECU)

Year — 1987
Model — 4Runner
Engine — 2.4L (144 cid) EFI 4 cyl
Engine Code — 22R-E

ECM TROUBLE CODES

Code	Explanation
1	Normal operation
2	Open or shorted air flow meter circuit — defective air flow meter or Electronic Control Unit (ECU)
3	No signal from igniter 4 times in succession — defective igniter or main relay circuit, igniter or Electronic Control Unit (ECU)
4	Open or shorted Water Thermo Sensor (THW) circuit — defective Water Thermo Sensor (THW) or Electronic Control Unit (ECU)
5	Open or shorted oxygen sensor circuit — lean or rich indication — defective oxygen sensor or Electronic Control Unit (ECU)
6	No engine revolution sensor (Ne) signal to Electronic Control Unit (ECU) or Ne value being over 1000 rpm in spite of no Ne signal to ECU — defective igniter circuit, igniter, distributor or Electronic Control Unit (ECU)
7	Open or shorted Throttle Position Sensor (TPS) circuit — defective Throttle Position Sensor (TPS) or Electronic Control Unit (ECU)
8	Open or shorted intake air thermo sensor circuit — defective intake air thermo sensor circuit or Electronic Control Unit (ECU)
10	No starter switch signal to Electronic Control Unit (ECU) with vehicle speed at 0 and engine speed over 800 rpm — defective speed sensor circuit, main relay circuit, igniter switch-to-starter circuit, igniter switch or Electronic Control Unit (ECU)
11	Neutral start switch ON or throttle switch (IDL) point in the Throttle Position Sensor (TPS) is OFF during diagnostic check — defective Throttle Position Sensor (TPS) circuit, Throttle Position Sensor (TPS), neutral start switch or Electronic Control Unit (ECU)
12	Knock control sensor signal has not reached judgement level in succession — defective knock control sensor circuit, knock control sensor or Electronic Control Unit (ECU)
13	Knock CPU faulty — defective Electronic Control Unit (ECU)

Year — 1987
Model — Pick-Up
Engine — 2.4L (144 cid) EFI 4 cyl
Engine Code — 22R-TE

ECM TROUBLE CODES

Code	Explanation
1	Normal operation
2	Open or shorted air flow meter circuit — defective air flow meter or Electronic Control Unit (ECU)
3	No signal from igniter 4 times in succession — defective igniter or main relay circuit, igniter or Electronic Control Unit (ECU)
4	Open or shorted Water Thermo Sensor (THW) circuit — defective Water Thermo Sensor (THW) or Electronic Control Unit (ECU)
5	Open or shorted oxygen sensor circuit — lean or rich indication — defective oxygen sensor or Electronic Control Unit (ECU)
6	No engine revolution sensor (Ne) signal to Electronic Control Unit (ECU) or Ne value being over 1000 rpm in spite of no Ne signal to ECU — defective igniter circuit, igniter, distributor or Electronic Control Unit (ECU)
7	Open or shorted Throttle Position Sensor (TPS) circuit — defective Throttle Position Sensor (TPS) or Electronic Control Unit (ECU)
8	Open or shorted intake air thermo sensor circuit — defective intake air thermo sensor circuit or Electronic Control Unit (ECU)
10	No starter switch signal to Electronic Control Unit (ECU) with vehicle speed at 0 and engine speed over 800 rpm — defective speed sensor circuit, main relay circuit, igniter switch-to-starter circuit, igniter switch or Electronic Control Unit (ECU)
11	Throttle switch (IDL) point in the Throttle Position Sensor (TPS) is OFF during diagnostic check — defective Throttle Position Sensor (TPS) circuit, Throttle Position Sensor (TPS) or Electronic Control Unit (ECU)
12	Knock control sensor signal has not reached judgement level in succession — defective knock control sensor circuit, knock control sensor or Electronic Control Unit (ECU)
13	Knock CPU faulty — defective Electronic Control Unit (ECU)
14	The turbocharger pressure is abnormal — defective turbocharger, air flow meter or Electronic Control Unit (ECU)

Year — 1987
Model — 4Runner
Engine — 2.4L (144 cid) EFI 4 cyl
Engine Code — 22R-TE

ECM TROUBLE CODES

Code	Explanation
1	Normal operation
2	Open or shorted air flow meter circuit — defective air flow meter or Electronic Control Unit (ECU)
3	No signal from igniter 4 times in succession — defective igniter or main relay circuit, igniter or Electronic Control Unit (ECU)
4	Open or shorted Water Thermo Sensor (THW) circuit — defective Water Thermo Sensor (THW) or Electronic Control Unit (ECU)
5	Open or shorted oxygen sensor circuit — lean or rich indication — defective oxygen sensor or Electronic Control Unit (ECU)
6	No engine revolution sensor (Ne) signal to Electronic Control Unit (ECU) or Ne value being over 1000 rpm in spite of no Ne signal to ECU — defective igniter circuit, igniter, distributor or Electronic Control Unit (ECU)
7	Open or shorted Throttle Position Sensor (TPS) circuit — defective Throttle Position Sensor (TPS) or Electronic Control Unit (ECU)
8	Open or shorted intake air thermo sensor circuit — defective intake air thermo sensor circuit or Electronic Control Unit (ECU)
10	No starter switch signal to Electronic Control Unit (ECU) with vehicle speed at 0 and engine speed over 800 rpm — defective speed sensor circuit, main relay circuit, igniter switch-to-starter circuit, igniter switch or Electronic Control Unit (ECU)
11	Throttle switch (IDL) point in the Throttle Position Sensor (TPS) is OFF during diagnostic check — defective Throttle Position Sensor (TPS) circuit, Throttle Position Sensor (TPS) or Electronic Control Unit (ECU)
12	Knock control sensor signal has not reached judgement level in succession — defective knock control sensor circuit, knock control sensor or Electronic Control Unit (ECU)
13	Knock CPU faulty — defective Electronic Control Unit (ECU)
14	The turbocharger pressure is abnormal — defective turbocharger, air flow meter or Electronic Control Unit (ECU)

Year – 1987
Model – Land Cruiser
Engine – 4.2L (258 cid) EFI 6 cyl
Engine Code – 2F

ECM TROUBLE CODES

Code	Explanation
—	Normal system operation
11	Momentary interruption in the power supply to the Electronic Control Unit (ECU) – defective ignition switch circuit, ignition switch, main relay circuit, main relay or ECU
12	No engine revolution sensor to Electronic Control Unit (ECU) within several seconds after engine is cranked – defective distributor circuit, distributor, starter signal circuit or Electronic Control Unit (ECU)
13	No igniter signal to Electronic Control Unit (ECU) within several seconds after engine reaches 1000 rpm – defective distributor circuit, distributor or Electronic Control Unit (ECU)
14	No signal from igniter to ECU 6–8 times in succession – defective igniter circuit, igniter and ignition coil or Electronic Control Unit (ECU)
21	Open or shorted No. 1 oxygen sensor heater circuit or deterioration of oxygen sensor – defective oxygen sensor circuit, oxygen sensor, oxygen sensor heater or Electronic Control Unit (ECU)
22	Open or shorted Water Temperature Sensor (THW) signal circuit – defective THW circuit, THW or Electronic Control Unit (ECU)
24	Open or shorted intake air temperature sensor circuit – defective intake air temperature sensor circuit, intake air temperature sensor or Electronic Control Unit (ECU)
25	Air/fuel ratio lean malfunction – defective intake air system, air flow meter, injector circuit, injector, fuel line pressure, oxygen sensor circuits, oxygen sensors, ignition system or Electronic Control Unit (ECU)
26	Air/fuel ratio rich malfunction – defective injector circuits, injector, fuel line pressure, air flow meter, cold start injector or Electronic Control Unit (ECU)
28	Open or shorted No. 2 oxygen sensor heater circuit or deterioration of oxygen sensor – defective oxygen sensor circuit, oxygen sensor, oxygen sensor heater or Electronic Control Unit (ECU)
31	Open or shorted air flow meter signal circuit – defective air flow meter circuit, air flow meter or Electronic Control Unit (ECU)
32	Open or shorted air flow meter signal circuit – defective air flow meter circuit, air flow meter or Electronic Control Unit (ECU)
35	Open circuit in the High Altitude Compensation (HAC) sensor signal – defective or Electronic Control Unit (ECU)
41	Open or shorted Throttle Position Sensor (TPS) circuit – defective TPS sensor or Electronic Control Unit (ECU)
42	No signal for over 8 seconds when vehicle is stopped and the engine running between 2000–5000 rpm and the coolant temperature is below 176°F (80°C), except when racing the engine – defective Vehicle Speed Sensor (VSS) circuit, VSS or Electronic Control Unit (ECU)
43	No starter switch signal to Electronic Control Unit (ECU) when the engine is running over 800 rpm – defective ignition switch circuit, ignition switch or Electronic Control Unit (ECU)
51	No Throttle Position Sensor (TPS) signal, neutral start switch signal or air conditioner signal to Electronic Control Unit (ECU), with the check terminals E1 and TE1 shorted – defective neutral start switch, air conditioner switch, air conditioning switch circuit, air conditioning amplifire, Throttle Position Sensor (TPS) circuit, TPS, acceleration pedal and cable or Electronic Control Unit (ECU)
71	Exhaust Gas Recirculation (EGR) gas temperature below predetermined level during EGR operation – defective EGR valve, EGR hose, EGR sensor circuit, EGR sensor, Vacuum Switching Valve (VSV) for EGR, VSV for EGR circuit or Electronic Control Unit (ECU) – California only

Year – 1988
Model – Van
Engine – 2.2L (136 cid) EFI 4 cyl
Engine Code – 4Y-EC

ECM TROUBLE CODES

Code	Explanation
—	Normal system operation
12	No distributor to Electronic Control Unit (ECU) within several seconds after engine is cranked—defective distributor circuit, distributor, igniter circuit, igniter or Electronic Control Unit (ECU)
13	No igniter signal to Electronic Control Unit (ECU) within several seconds after engine reaches 1500 rpm—defective distributor circuit, distributor, igniter circuit, igniter or Electronic Control Unit (ECU)
14	No signal from igniter to ECU 4–5 times in succession—defective igniter circuit, igniter and coil or Electronic Control Unit (ECU)
21	Open or shorted oxygen sensor heater and/or deterioration of oxygen sensor—defective oxygen sensor circuit, oxygen sensor, oxygen sensor heater or Electronic Control Unit (ECU)
22	Open or shorted Water Temperature Sensor (THW) signal circuit—defective THW circuit, THW or Electronic Control Unit (ECU)
24	Open or shorted intake air temperature sensor circuit—defective intake air temperature sensor circuit, intake air temperature sensor or Electronic Control Unit (ECU)
25	Air/fuel ratio lean malfunction—defective air flow meter, injector circuit, injector, fuel line pressure, oxygen sensor circuit, oxygen sensor, ignition system, water temperature sensor or Electronic Control Unit (ECU)
26	Air/fuel ratio rich malfunction—defective injector circuit, injector, fuel line pressure, air flow meter, cold start injector, water temperature sensor or Electronic Control Unit (ECU)
27	Open or shorted sub-oxygen sensor circuit—defective sub-oxygen sensor circuit, sub-oxygen sensor or Electronic Control Unit (ECU)
31	Open or shorted air flow meter signal circuit—defective air flow meter circuit, air flow meter or Electronic Control Unit (ECU)
41	Throttle position sensor (IDL) and PSW signals being output simultaneously for several seconds—defective TPS circuit, TPS sensor or Electronic Control Unit (ECU)
42	No signal for 8 seconds when vehicle is stopped and the engine running between 1500–5000 rpm and the coolant temperature is below 176°F (80°C), except when racing the engine—defective Vehicle Speed Sensor (VSS) circuit, VSS or Electronic Control Unit (ECU)
43	No starter switch signal to Electronic Control Unit (ECU) when the engine is running over 800 rpm—defective ignition switch circuit, ignition switch or Electronic Control Unit (ECU)
51	No Throttle position sensor (IDL) signal, neutral start switch or air conditioner signal to Electronic Control Unit (ECU), with the check terminals E1 and T shorted—defective air conditioning switch circuit, air conditioning amplifire, Throttle Position Sensor (TPS) circuit, TPS, neutral start switch accelerator pedal and cable
71	Exhaust Gas Recirculation (EGR) gas temperature below predetermined level during EGR operation—defective EGR valve, EGR hose, EGR sensor circuit, EGR sensor, Vacuum Switching Valve (VSV) for EGR, VSV for EGR circuit or Electronic Control Unit (ECU)—California only

Year — 1988
Model — Pick-Up
Engine — 2.4L (144 cid) EFI 4 cyl
Engine Code — 22R-E

ECM TROUBLE CODES

Code	Explanation
—	Normal system operation
12	No distributor to Electronic Control Unit (ECU) within 2 seconds after engine is cranked — defective distributor circuit, distributor, igniter circuit, igniter, starter signal circuit or Electronic Control Unit (ECU)
13	No igniter signal to Electronic Control Unit (ECU) within several seconds after engine reaches 1500 rpm — defective distributor circuit, distributor, igniter circuit, igniter or Electronic Control Unit (ECU)
14	No signal from igniter to ECU 4–5 times in succession — defective igniter circuit, igniter and coil or Electronic Control Unit (ECU)
21	Open or shorted oxygen sensor heater and/or deterioration of oxygen sensor — defective oxygen sensor circuit, oxygen sensor, oxygen sensor heater or Electronic Control Unit (ECU)
22	Open or shorted Water Temperature Sensor (THW) signal circuit — defective THW circuit, THW or Electronic Control Unit (ECU)
24	Open or shorted intake air temperature sensor circuit — defective intake air temperature sensor circuit, intake air temperature sensor or Electronic Control Unit (ECU)
25	Air/fuel ratio lean malfunction — defective air flow meter, injector circuit, injector, fuel line pressure, oxygen sensor circuit, oxygen sensor, ignition system, water temperature sensor or Electronic Control Unit (ECU)
26	Air/fuel ratio rich malfunction — defective injector circuit, injector, fuel line pressure, air flow meter, cold start injector, water temperature sensor or Electronic Control Unit (ECU)
31	Open or shorted air flow meter signal circuit — defective air flow meter circuit or air flow meter
35	Open High Altitude Compensator (HAC) circuit — defective HAC sensor circuit, HAC sensor or Electronic Control Unit (ECU)
41	Open or shorted throttle position sensor (IDL) circuit — defective TPS circuit or TPS sensor
42	No signal for 5 seconds when vehicle is stopped and the engine running above 2500 rpm — defective Vehicle Speed Sensor (VSS) circuit, VSS or Electronic Control Unit (ECU)
43	No starter switch signal to Electronic Control Unit (ECU) when the engine is running over 800 rpm — defective ignition switch circuit, ignition switch or Electronic Control Unit (ECU)
51	No Throttle position sensor (IDL) signal, neutral start switch or air conditioner signal to Electronic Control Unit (ECU), with the check terminals E1 and T shorted — defective air conditioning switch circuit, air conditioning amplifire, Throttle Position Sensor (TPS) circuit, TPS, neutral start switch accelerator pedal and cable
52	Open or shorted knock sensor signal circuit — defective knock sensor circuit, knock sensor or Electronic Control Unit (ECU)
53	Knock control in Electronic Control Unit (ECU) faulty — defective ECU
71	Exhaust Gas Recirculation (EGR) gas temperature below predetermined level during EGR operation — defective EGR valve, EGR hose, EGR sensor circuit, EGR sensor, Vacuum Switching Valve (VSV) for EGR, VSV for EGR circuit or Electronic Control Unit (ECU) — California only

Year – 1988
Model – 4Runner
Engine – 2.4L (144 cid) EFI 4 cyl
Engine Code – 22R-E

ECM TROUBLE CODES

Code	Explanation
—	Normal system operation
12	No distributor to Electronic Control Unit (ECU) within 2 seconds after engine is cranked – defective distributor circuit, distributor, igniter circuit, igniter, starter signal circuit or Electronic Control Unit (ECU)
13	No igniter signal to Electronic Control Unit (ECU) within several seconds after engine reaches 1500 rpm – defective distributor circuit, distributor, igniter circuit, igniter or Electronic Control Unit (ECU)
14	No signal from igniter to ECU 4–5 times in succession – defective igniter circuit, igniter and coil or Electronic Control Unit (ECU)
21	Open or shorted oxygen sensor heater and/or deterioration of oxygen sensor – defective oxygen sensor circuit, oxygen sensor, oxygen sensor heater or Electronic Control Unit (ECU)
22	Open or shorted Water Temperature Sensor (THW) signal circuit – defective THW circuit, THW or Electronic Control Unit (ECU)
24	Open or shorted intake air temperature sensor circuit – defective intake air temperature sensor circuit, intake air temperature sensor or Electronic Control Unit (ECU)
25	Air/fuel ratio lean malfunction – defective air flow meter, injector circuit, injector, fuel line pressure, oxygen sensor circuit, oxygen sensor, ignition system, water temperature sensor or Electronic Control Unit (ECU)
26	Air/fuel ratio rich malfunction – defective injector circuit, injector, fuel line pressure, air flow meter, cold start injector, water temperature sensor or Electronic Control Unit (ECU)
31	Open or shorted air flow meter signal circuit – defective air flow meter circuit or air flow meter
35	Open High Altitude Compensator (HAC) circuit – defective HAC sensor circuit, HAC sensor or Electronic Control Unit (ECU)
41	Open or shorted throttle position sensor (IDL) circuit – defective TPS circuit or TPS sensor
42	No signal for 5 seconds when vehicle is stopped and the engine running above 2500 rpm – defective Vehicle Speed Sensor (VSS) circuit, VSS or Electronic Control Unit (ECU)
43	No starter switch signal to Electronic Control Unit (ECU) when the engine is running over 800 rpm – defective ignition switch circuit, ignition switch or Electronic Control Unit (ECU)
51	No Throttle position sensor (IDL) signal, neutral start switch or air conditioner signal to Electronic Control Unit (ECU), with the check terminals E1 and T shorted – defective air conditioning switch circuit, air conditioning amplifire, Throttle Position Sensor (TPS) circuit, TPS, neutral start switch accelerator pedal and cable
52	Open or shorted knock sensor signal circuit – defective knock sensor circuit, knock sensor or Electronic Control Unit (ECU)
53	Knock control in Electronic Control Unit (ECU) faulty – defective ECU
71	Exhaust Gas Recirculation (EGR) gas temperature below predetermined level during EGR operation – defective EGR valve, EGR hose, EGR sensor circuit, EGR sensor, Vacuum Switching Valve (VSV) for EGR, VSV for EGR circuit or Electronic Control Unit (ECU) – California only

Year – 1988
Model – Pick-Up
Engine – 2.4L (144 cid) EFI 4 cyl
Engine Code – 22R-TE

ECM TROUBLE CODES

Code	Explanation
1	Normal operation
2	Open or shorted air flow meter circuit – defective air flow meter
3	No signal from igniter 4–5 times in succession – defective igniter circuit, igniter or Electronic Control Unit (ECU)
4	Open or shorted Water Thermo Sensor (THW) circuit – defective Water Thermo Sensor (THW) or Electronic Control Unit (ECU)
5	Open or shorted oxygen sensor circuit – defective oxygen sensor or Electronic Control Unit (ECU)
6	No distributor (Ne) signal to Electronic Control Unit (ECU) when engine speed is above 1000 rpm – defective igniter circuit, igniter, distributor or Electronic Control Unit (ECU)
7	Open or shorted Throttle Position Sensor (TPS) circuit – defective Throttle Position Sensor (TPS)
8	Open or shorted intake air thermo sensor circuit – defective intake air thermo sensor circuit or Electronic Control Unit (ECU)
10	No starter switch signal to Electronic Control Unit (ECU) with vehicle speed at 0 and engine speed over 800 rpm – defective igniter switch circuit, igniter switch or Electronic Control Unit (ECU)
11	Air conditioning switch ON, neutral start switch OFF, throttle switch (IDL) OFF during diagnostic check – defective Throttle Position Sensor (TPS) circuit, TPS, air conditioning switch, air conditioning amplifier or Electronic Control Unit (ECU)
12	Open or shorted knock sensor signal – defective knock control sensor circuit, knock control sensor or Electronic Control Unit (ECU)
13	Knock control ECU faulty – defective Electronic Control Unit (ECU)
14	The turbocharger pressure is abnormal – defective turbocharger, air flow meter or Electronic Control Unit (ECU)

Year – 1988
Model – Land Cruiser
Engine – 4.2L (258 cid) EFI 6 cyl
Engine Code – 2F

ECM TROUBLE CODES

Code	Explanation
—	Normal system operation
11	Momentary interruption in the power supply to the Electronic Control Unit (ECU) – defective ignition switch circuit, ignition switch, main relay circuit, main relay or ECU
12	No engine revolution sensor to Electronic Control Unit (ECU) within several seconds after engine is cranked – defective distributor circuit, distributor, starter signal circuit or Electronic Control Unit (ECU)
13	No igniter signal to Electronic Control Unit (ECU) within several seconds after engine reaches 1000 rpm – defective distributor circuit, distributor or Electronic Control Unit (ECU)
14	No signal from igniter to ECU 6–8 times in succession – defective igniter circuit, igniter and ignition coil or Electronic Control Unit (ECU)
21	Open or shorted No. 1 oxygen sensor heater circuit or deterioration of oxygen sensor – defective oxygen sensor circuit, oxygen sensor, oxygen sensor heater or Electronic Control Unit (ECU)
22	Open or shorted Water Temperature Sensor (THW) signal circuit – defective THW circuit, THW or Electronic Control Unit (ECU)
24	Open or shorted intake air temperature sensor circuit – defective intake air temperature sensor circuit, intake air temperature sensor or Electronic Control Unit (ECU)
25	Air/fuel ratio lean malfunction – defective intake air system, air flow meter, injector circuit, injector, fuel line pressure, oxygen sensor circuits, oxygen sensors, ignition system or Electronic Control Unit (ECU)
26	Air/fuel ratio rich malfunction – defective injector circuits, injector, fuel line pressure, air flow meter, cold start injector or Electronic Control Unit (ECU)
28	Open or shorted No. 2 oxygen sensor heater circuit or deterioration of oxygen sensor – defective oxygen sensor circuit, oxygen sensor, oxygen sensor heater or Electronic Control Unit (ECU)
31	Open or shorted air flow meter signal circuit – defective air flow meter circuit, air flow meter or Electronic Control Unit (ECU)
32	Open or shorted air flow meter signal circuit – defective air flow meter circuit, air flow meter or Electronic Control Unit (ECU)
35	Open circuit in the High Altitude Compensation (HAC) sensor signal – defective or Electronic Control Unit (ECU)
41	Open or shorted Throttle Position Sensor (TPS) circuit – defective TPS sensor or Electronic Control Unit (ECU)
42	No signal for over 8 seconds when vehicle is stopped and the engine running between 2000–5000 rpm and the coolant temperature is below 176°F (80°C), except when racing the engine – defective Vehicle Speed Sensor (VSS) circuit, VSS or Electronic Control Unit (ECU)
43	No starter switch signal to Electronic Control Unit (ECU) when the engine is running over 800 rpm – defective ignition switch circuit, ignition switch or Electronic Control Unit (ECU)
51	No Throttle Position Sensor (TPS) signal, neutral start switch signal or air conditioner signal to Electronic Control Unit (ECU), with the check terminals E1 and TE1 shorted – defective neutral start switch, air conditioner switch, air conditioning switch circuit, air conditioning amplifire, Throttle Position Sensor (TPS) circuit, TPS, acceleration pedal and cable or Electronic Control Unit (ECU)
71	Exhaust Gas Recirculation (EGR) gas temperature below predetermined level during EGR operation – defective EGR valve, EGR hose, EGR sensor circuit, EGR sensor, Vacuum Switching Valve (VSV) for EGR, VSV for EGR circuit or Electronic Control Unit (ECU) – California only

Year – 1989
Model – Van
Engine – 2.2L (136 cid) EFI 4 cyl
Engine Code – 4Y-E

ECM TROUBLE CODES

Code	Explanation
–	Normal system operation
12	No distributor to Electronic Control Unit (ECU) within several seconds after engine is cranked – defective distributor circuit, distributor, igniter circuit, igniter or Electronic Control Unit (ECU)
13	No igniter signal to Electronic Control Unit (ECU) within several seconds after engine reaches 1500 rpm – defective distributor circuit, distributor, igniter circuit, igniter or Electronic Control Unit (ECU)
14	No signal from igniter to ECU 4–5 times in succession – defective igniter circuit, igniter and coil or Electronic Control Unit (ECU)
21	Open or shorted oxygen sensor heater and/or deterioration of oxygen sensor – defective oxygen sensor circuit, oxygen sensor, oxygen sensor heater or Electronic Control Unit (ECU)
22	Open or shorted Water Temperature Sensor (THW) signal circuit – defective THW circuit, THW or Electronic Control Unit (ECU)
24	Open or shorted intake air temperature sensor circuit – defective intake air temperature sensor circuit, intake air temperature sensor or Electronic Control Unit (ECU)
25	Air/fuel ratio lean malfunction – defective air flow meter, injector circuit, injector, fuel line pressure, oxygen sensor circuit, oxygen sensor, ignition system, water temperature sensor or Electronic Control Unit (ECU)
26	Air/fuel ratio rich malfunction – defective injector circuit, injector, fuel line pressure, air flow meter, cold start injector, water temperature sensor or Electronic Control Unit (ECU)
27	Open or shorted sub-oxygen sensor circuit – defective sub-oxygen sensor circuit, sub-oxygen sensor or Electronic Control Unit (ECU)
31	Open or shorted air flow meter signal circuit – defective air flow meter circuit, air flow meter or Electronic Control Unit (ECU)
41	Throttle position sensor (IDL) and PSW signals being output simultaneously for several seconds – defective TPS circuit, TPS sensor or Electronic Control Unit (ECU)
42	No signal for 8 seconds when vehicle is stopped and the engine running between 1500–5000 rpm and the coolant temperature is below 176°F (80°C), except when racing the engine – defective Vehicle Speed Sensor (VSS) circuit, VSS or Electronic Control Unit (ECU)
43	No starter switch signal to Electronic Control Unit (ECU) when the engine is running over 800 rpm – defective ignition switch circuit, ignition switch or Electronic Control Unit (ECU)
51	No Throttle position sensor (IDL) signal, neutral start switch or air conditioner signal to Electronic Control Unit (ECU), with the check terminals E1 and T shorted – defective air conditioning switch circuit, air conditioning amplifire, Throttle Position Sensor (TPS) circuit, TPS, neutral start switch accelerator pedal and cable
71	Exhaust Gas Recirculation (EGR) gas temperature below predetermined level during EGR operation – defective EGR valve, EGR hose, EGR sensor circuit, EGR sensor, Vacuum Switching Valve (VSV) for EGR, VSV for EGR circuit or Electronic Control Unit (ECU) – California only

Year – 1989
Model – Pick-Up
Engine – 2.4L (144 cid) 4 cyl
Engine Code – 22R

ECM TROUBLE CODES

Code	Explanation
—	Normal system operation
12	No signal to Electronic Control Unit (ECU) within several seconds after engine is cranked – defective ignition coil circuit, ignition coil, igniter circuit, igniter, starter signal circuit or Electronic Control Unit (ECU)
21	Deterioration of oxygen sensor – defective oxygen sensor circuit, oxygen sensor or Electronic Control Unit (ECU)
22	Open or shorted Water Temperature Sensor (THW) signal circuit – defective THW circuit, THW or Electronic Control Unit (ECU)
25	Air/fuel ratio lean malfunction – defective oxygen sensor circuit, oxygen sensor, EBCV and/or EACV circuit, EBCV and/or EACV or Electronic Control Unit (ECU)
26	Air/fuel ratio rich malfunction – defective EBCV and/or EACV circuit, EBCV and/or EACV, EBCV hose or Electronic Control Unit (ECU)
31	Open or shorted vacuum switches signal circuit – defective No. 1, No. 2 or No. 3 vacuum switches circuit, No. 1, No. 2 or No. 3 vacuum switches or Exhaust Gas Recirculation (EGR)
42	Open or shorted Vehicle Speed Sensor (VSS) signal circuit – defective Vehicle Speed Sensor (VSS) circuit, VSS or Electronic Control Unit (ECU)
71	Exhaust Gas Recirculation (EGR) gas temperature below predetermined level during EGR operation – defective EGR valve, EGR hose, EGR gas temperature sensor circuit, EGR gas temperature sensor, EGR vacuum modulator or Electronic Control Unit (ECU)
72	Open Fuel Cut Solenoid (FCS) signal circuit – defective FCS circuit, FCS or Electronic Control Unit (ECU)

Year – 1989
Model – Pick-Up
Engine – 2.4L (144 cid) EFI 4 cyl
Engine Code – 22R-E

ECM TROUBLE CODES

Code	Explanation
–	Normal system operation
12	No distributor to Electronic Control Unit (ECU) within 2 seconds after engine is cranked – defective distributor circuit, distributor, igniter circuit, igniter, starter signal circuit or Electronic Control Unit (ECU)
13	No igniter signal to Electronic Control Unit (ECU) when the engine speed is above 1500 rpm – defective distributor circuit, distributor, igniter circuit, igniter or Electronic Control Unit (ECU)
14	No signal from igniter to ECU 4–5 times in succession – defective igniter circuit, igniter and coil or Electronic Control Unit (ECU)
21	Open or shorted main oxygen sensor heater and/or deterioration of main oxygen sensor – defective oxygen sensor circuit, oxygen sensor, oxygen sensor heater or Electronic Control Unit (ECU)
22	Open or shorted Water Temperature Sensor (THW) signal circuit – defective THW circuit, THW or Electronic Control Unit (ECU)
24	Open or shorted intake air temperature sensor circuit – defective intake air temperature sensor circuit, intake air temperature sensor or Electronic Control Unit (ECU)
25	Air/fuel ratio lean malfunction – defective air flow meter, injector circuit, injector, fuel line pressure, oxygen sensor circuit, oxygen sensor, air intake system or Electronic Control Unit (ECU)
26	Air/fuel ratio rich malfunction – defective injector circuit, injector, fuel line pressure, air flow meter, cold start injector, oxygen sensor circuit, oxygen sensor or Electronic Control Unit (ECU)
27	Open or shorted sub-oxygen sensor heater circuit and/or detrioration of sub-oxygen sensor – defective sub-oxygen sensor circuit, sub-oxygen sensor, sub-oxygen sensor heater or Electronic Control Unit (ECU) – California only
31	Open or shorted air flow meter signal circuit – defective air flow meter circuit or air flow meter
41	Open or shorted throttle position sensor (IDL) circuit – defective Throttle Position Sensor (TPS) circuit or TPS sensor
42	No signal for 5 seconds when vehicle is stopped and the engine running above 2500 rpm – defective Vehicle Speed Sensor (VSS) circuit, VSS or Electronic Control Unit (ECU)
43	No starter switch signal to Electronic Control Unit (ECU) when the engine is running over 800 rpm – defective ignition switch circuit, ignition switch or Electronic Control Unit (ECU)
51	No Throttle position sensor (IDL) signal, neutral start switch or air conditioner signal to Electronic Control Unit (ECU), with the check terminals E1 and TE1 shorted – defective air conditioning switch circuit, air conditioning amplifire, Throttle Position Sensor (TPS) circuit, TPS, neutral start switch or Electronic Control Unit (ECU)
52	Open or shorted knock sensor signal circuit – defective knock sensor circuit, knock sensor or Electronic Control Unit (ECU)
53	Knock control in Electronic Control Unit (ECU) faulty – defective ECU
71	Exhaust Gas Recirculation (EGR) gas temperature below predetermined level during EGR operation – defective EGR valve, EGR hose, EGR sensor circuit, EGR sensor, Vacuum Switching Valve (VSV) for EGR, VSV for EGR circuit or Electronic Control Unit (ECU) – California only

Year – 1989
Model – 4Runner
Engine – 2.4L (144 cid) EFI 4 cyl
Engine Code – 22R-E

ECM TROUBLE CODES

Code	Explanation
–	Normal system operation
12	No distributor to Electronic Control Unit (ECU) within 2 seconds after engine is cranked – defective distributor circuit, distributor, igniter circuit, igniter, starter signal circuit or Electronic Control Unit (ECU)
13	No igniter signal to Electronic Control Unit (ECU) when the engine speed is above 1500 rpm – defective distributor circuit, distributor, igniter circuit, igniter or Electronic Control Unit (ECU)
14	No signal from igniter to ECU 4–5 times in succession – defective igniter circuit, igniter and coil or Electronic Control Unit (ECU)
21	Open or shorted main oxygen sensor heater and/or deterioration of main oxygen sensor – defective oxygen sensor circuit, oxygen sensor, oxygen sensor heater or Electronic Control Unit (ECU)
22	Open or shorted Water Temperature Sensor (THW) signal circuit – defective THW circuit, THW or Electronic Control Unit (ECU)
24	Open or shorted intake air temperature sensor circuit – defective intake air temperature sensor circuit, intake air temperature sensor or Electronic Control Unit (ECU)
25	Air/fuel ratio lean malfunction – defective air flow meter, injector circuit, injector, fuel line pressure, oxygen sensor circuit, oxygen sensor, air intake system or Electronic Control Unit (ECU)
26	Air/fuel ratio rich malfunction – defective injector circuit, injector, fuel line pressure, air flow meter, cold start injector, oxygen sensor circuit, oxygen sensor or Electronic Control Unit (ECU)
31	Open or shorted air flow meter signal circuit – defective air flow meter circuit or air flow meter
41	Open or shorted throttle position sensor (IDL) circuit – defective Throttle Position Sensor (TPS) circuit or TPS sensor
42	No signal for 5 seconds when vehicle is stopped and the engine running above 2500 rpm – defective Vehicle Speed Sensor (VSS) circuit, VSS or Electronic Control Unit (ECU)
43	No starter switch signal to Electronic Control Unit (ECU) when the engine is running over 800 rpm – defective ignition switch circuit, ignition switch or Electronic Control Unit (ECU)
51	No Throttle position sensor (IDL) signal, neutral start switch or air conditioner signal to Electronic Control Unit (ECU), with the check terminals E1 and TE1 shorted – defective air conditioning switch circuit, air conditioning amplifire, Throttle Position Sensor (TPS) circuit, TPS, neutral start switch or Electronic Control Unit (ECU)
52	Open or shorted knock sensor signal circuit – defective knock sensor circuit, knock sensor or Electronic Control Unit (ECU)
53	Knock control in Electronic Control Unit (ECU) faulty – defective ECU
71	Exhaust Gas Recirculation (EGR) gas temperature below predetermined level during EGR operation – defective EGR valve, EGR hose, EGR sensor circuit, EGR sensor, Vacuum Switching Valve (VSV) for EGR, VSV for EGR circuit or Electronic Control Unit (ECU) – California only

Year – 1989
Model – Pick-Up
Engine – 3.0L (180 cid) EFI V6
Engine Code – 3VZ-E

ECM TROUBLE CODES

Code	Explanation
—	Normal system operation
11	Momentary interruption in the power supply to the Electronic Control Unit (ECU) – defective ignition circuit, ignition switch, main relay circuit, main relay or ECU
12	No distributor to Electronic Control Unit (ECU) within 2 seconds after engine is cranked – defective distributor circuit, distributor, starter signal circuit or Electronic Control Unit (ECU)
13	No igniter signal to Electronic Control Unit (ECU) when the engine speed is above 1000 rpm – defective distributor circuit, distributor or Electronic Control Unit (ECU)
14	No signal from distributor to ECU 6–8 times in succession – defective igniter circuit or igniter and coil
21	Open or shorted oxygen sensor heater and/or deterioration of oxygen sensor – defective oxygen sensor circuit, oxygen sensor, oxygen sensor heater or Electronic Control Unit (ECU)
22	Open or shorted Water Temperature Sensor (THW) signal circuit – defective THW circuit, THW or Electronic Control Unit (ECU)
24	Open or shorted intake air temperature sensor circuit – defective intake air temperature sensor circuit, intake air temperature sensor or Electronic Control Unit (ECU)
25	Air/fuel ratio lean malfunction – defective air flow meter, injector circuit, injector, fuel line pressure, oxygen sensor circuit, oxygen sensor, ignition system, water temperature sensor or Electronic Control Unit (ECU)
26	Air/fuel ratio rich malfunction – defective injector circuit, injector, fuel line pressure, air flow meter, cold start injector, oxygen sensor circuit, oxygen sensor or Electronic Control Unit (ECU)
31	Open or shorted air flow meter signal circuit – defective air flow meter circuit, air flow meter or Electronic Control Unit (ECU)
32	Open or shorted air flow meter signal circuit – defective air flow meter circuit, air flow meter or Electronic Control Unit (ECU)
35	Open High Altitude Compensator (HAC) sensor signal circuit – defective Electronic Control Unit (ECU) – cab and chassis only
41	Open or shorted throttle position sensor (IDL) circuit – defective Throttle Position Sensor (TPS) circuit, TPS sensor or Electronic Control Unit (ECU)
42	No signal for 8 seconds when vehicle is stopped and the engine is 1500–4000 rpm and the coolant temperature is above 176°F (80°C), except when racing the engine – defective Vehicle Speed Sensor (VSS) circuit, VSS or Electronic Control Unit (ECU)
43	No starter switch signal to Electronic Control Unit (ECU) when the engine is running over 800 rpm – defective ignition switch circuit, ignition switch or Electronic Control Unit (ECU)
51	Air conditioning switch ON and idle switch OFF, during diagnosis check – defective air conditioning switch circuit, air conditioning amplifire, Throttle Position Sensor (TPS) circuit, TPS or Electronic Control Unit (ECU)
52	Open or shorted knock sensor signal circuit – defective knock sensor circuit, knock sensor or Electronic Control Unit (ECU)
53	Knock control in Electronic Control Unit (ECU) faulty – defective ECU
71	Exhaust Gas Recirculation (EGR) gas temperature below predetermined level during EGR operation – defective EGR valve, EGR hose, EGR sensor circuit, EGR sensor, Vacuum Switching Valve (VSV) for EGR, VSV for EGR circuit or Electronic Control Unit (ECU) – California only

Year — 1989
Model — 4Runner
Engine — 3.0L (180 cid) EFI V6
Engine Code — 3VZ-E

ECM TROUBLE CODES

Code	Explanation
—	Normal system operation
11	Momentary interruption in the power supply to the Electronic Control Unit (ECU) — defective ignition circuit, ignition switch, main relay circuit, main relay or ECU
12	No distributor to Electronic Control Unit (ECU) within 2 seconds after engine is cranked — defective distributor circuit, distributor, starter signal circuit or Electronic Control Unit (ECU)
13	No igniter signal to Electronic Control Unit (ECU) when the engine speed is above 1000 rpm — defective distributor circuit, distributor or Electronic Control Unit (ECU)
14	No signal from distributor to ECU 6–8 times in succession — defective igniter circuit or igniter and coil
21	Open or shorted oxygen sensor heater and/or deterioration of oxygen sensor — defective oxygen sensor circuit, oxygen sensor, oxygen sensor heater or Electronic Control Unit (ECU)
22	Open or shorted Water Temperature Sensor (THW) signal circuit — defective THW circuit, THW or Electronic Control Unit (ECU)
24	Open or shorted intake air temperature sensor circuit — defective intake air temperature sensor circuit, intake air temperature sensor or Electronic Control Unit (ECU)
25	Air/fuel ratio lean malfunction — defective air flow meter, injector circuit, injector, fuel line pressure, oxygen sensor circuit, oxygen sensor, ignition system, water temperature sensor or Electronic Control Unit (ECU)
26	Air/fuel ratio rich malfunction — defective injector circuit, injector, fuel line pressure, air flow meter, cold start injector, oxygen sensor circuit, oxygen sensor or Electronic Control Unit (ECU)
31	Open or shorted air flow meter signal circuit — defective air flow meter circuit, air flow meter or Electronic Control Unit (ECU)
32	Open or shorted air flow meter signal circuit — defective air flow meter circuit, air flow meter or Electronic Control Unit (ECU)
41	Open or shorted throttle position sensor (IDL) circuit — defective Throttle Position Sensor (TPS) circuit, TPS sensor or Electronic Control Unit (ECU)
42	No signal for 8 seconds when vehicle is stopped and the engine is 1500–4000 rpm and the coolant temperature is above 176°F (80°C), except when racing the engine — defective Vehicle Speed Sensor (VSS) circuit, VSS or Electronic Control Unit (ECU)
43	No starter switch signal to Electronic Control Unit (ECU) when the engine is running over 800 rpm — defective ignition switch circuit, ignition switch or Electronic Control Unit (ECU)
51	Air conditioning switch ON and idle switch OFF, during diagnosis check — defective air conditioning switch circuit, air conditioning amplifire, Throttle Position Sensor (TPS) circuit, TPS or Electronic Control Unit (ECU)
52	Open or shorted knock sensor signal circuit — defective knock sensor circuit, knock sensor or Electronic Control Unit (ECU)
53	Knock control in Electronic Control Unit (ECU) faulty — defective ECU
71	Exhaust Gas Recirculation (EGR) gas temperature below predetermined level during EGR operation — defective EGR valve, EGR hose, EGR sensor circuit, EGR sensor, Vacuum Switching Valve (VSV) for EGR, VSV for EGR circuit or Electronic Control Unit (ECU) — California only

Year — 1989
Model — Land Cruiser
Engine — 4.2L (258 cid) EFI 6 cyl
Engine Code — 3F-E

ECM TROUBLE CODES

Code	Explanation
—	Normal system operation
11	Momentary interruption in the power supply to the Electronic Control Unit (ECU) — defective ignition switch circuit, ignition switch, main relay circuit, main relay or ECU
12	No engine revolution sensor to Electronic Control Unit (ECU) within several seconds after engine is cranked — defective distributor circuit, distributor, starter signal circuit or Electronic Control Unit (ECU)
13	No igniter signal to Electronic Control Unit (ECU) within several seconds after engine reaches 1000 rpm — defective distributor circuit, distributor or Electronic Control Unit (ECU)
14	No signal from igniter to ECU 6–8 times in succession — defective igniter circuit, igniter and ignition coil or Electronic Control Unit (ECU)
21	Open or shorted No. 1 oxygen sensor heater circuit or deterioration of oxygen sensor — defective oxygen sensor circuit, oxygen sensor, oxygen sensor heater or Electronic Control Unit (ECU)
22	Open or shorted Water Temperature Sensor (THW) signal circuit — defective THW circuit, THW or Electronic Control Unit (ECU)
24	Open or shorted intake air temperature sensor circuit — defective intake air temperature sensor circuit, intake air temperature sensor or Electronic Control Unit (ECU)
25	Air/fuel ratio lean malfunction — defective intake air system, air flow meter, injector circuit, injector, fuel line pressure, oxygen sensor circuits, oxygen sensors, ignition system or Electronic Control Unit (ECU)
26	Air/fuel ratio rich malfunction — defective injector circuits, injector, fuel line pressure, air flow meter, cold start injector or Electronic Control Unit (ECU)
28	Open or shorted No. 2 oxygen sensor heater circuit or deterioration of oxygen sensor — defective oxygen sensor circuit, oxygen sensor, oxygen sensor heater or Electronic Control Unit (ECU)
31	Open or shorted air flow meter signal circuit — defective air flow meter circuit, air flow meter or Electronic Control Unit (ECU)
32	Open or shorted air flow meter signal circuit — defective air flow meter circuit, air flow meter or Electronic Control Unit (ECU)
35	Open circuit in the High Altitude Compensation (HAC) sensor signal — defective or Electronic Control Unit (ECU)
41	Open or shorted Throttle Position Sensor (TPS) circuit — defective TPS sensor or Electronic Control Unit (ECU)
42	No signal for over 8 seconds when vehicle is stopped and the engine running between 2000–5000 rpm and the coolant temperature is below 176°F (80°C), except when racing the engine — defective Vehicle Speed Sensor (VSS) circuit, VSS or Electronic Control Unit (ECU)
43	No starter switch signal to Electronic Control Unit (ECU) when the engine is running over 800 rpm — defective ignition switch circuit, ignition switch or Electronic Control Unit (ECU)
51	No Throttle Position Sensor (TPS) signal, neutral start switch signal or air conditioner signal to Electronic Control Unit (ECU), with the check terminals E1 and TE1 shorted — defective neutral start switch, air conditioner switch, air conditioning switch circuit, air conditioning amplifire, Throttle Position Sensor (TPS) circuit, TPS, acceleration pedal and cable or Electronic Control Unit (ECU)
71	Exhaust Gas Recirculation (EGR) gas temperature below predetermined level during EGR operation — defective EGR valve, EGR hose, EGR sensor circuit, EGR sensor, Vacuum Switching Valve (VSV) for EGR, VSV for EGR circuit or Electronic Control Unit (ECU) — California only

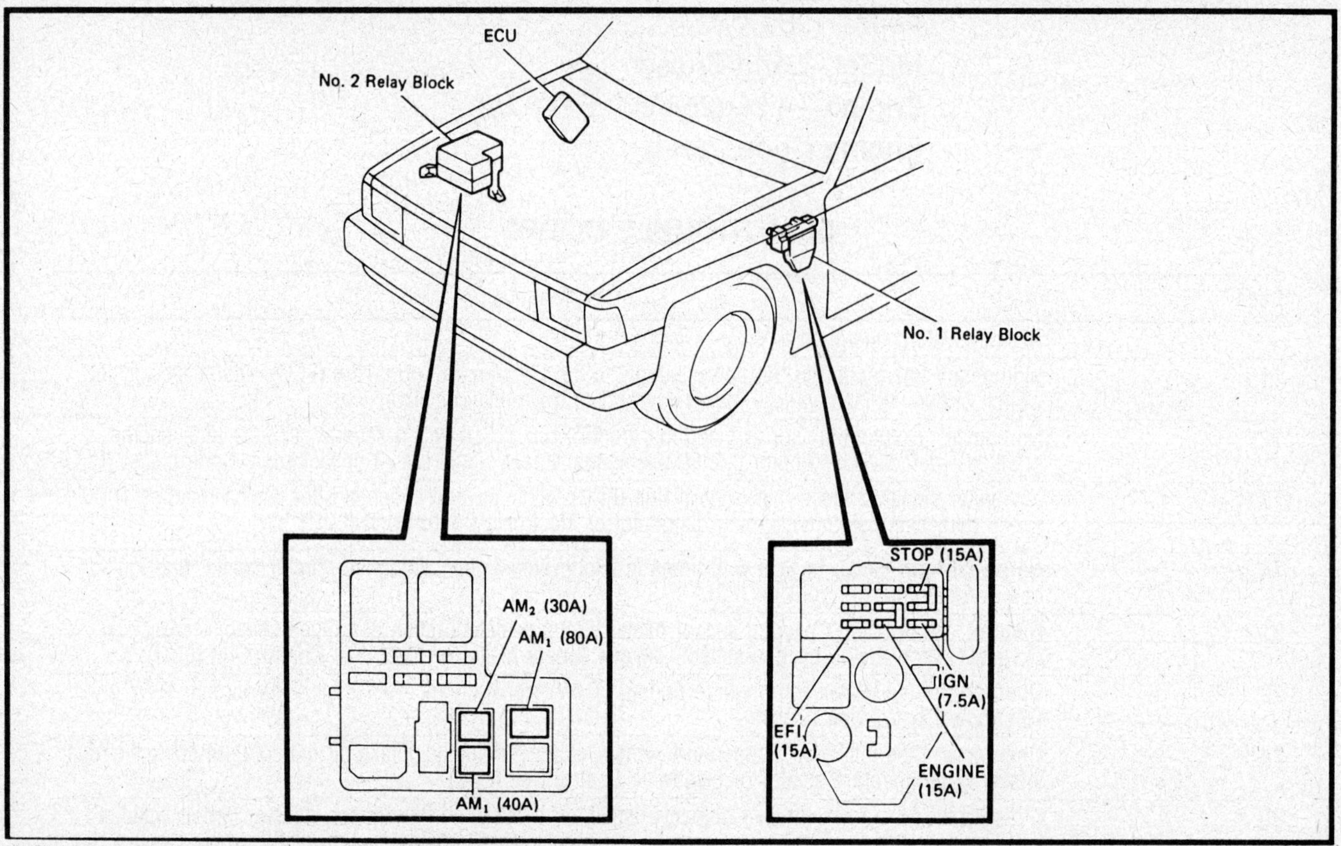

ECU and relay block location—1989 Toyota 4Runner

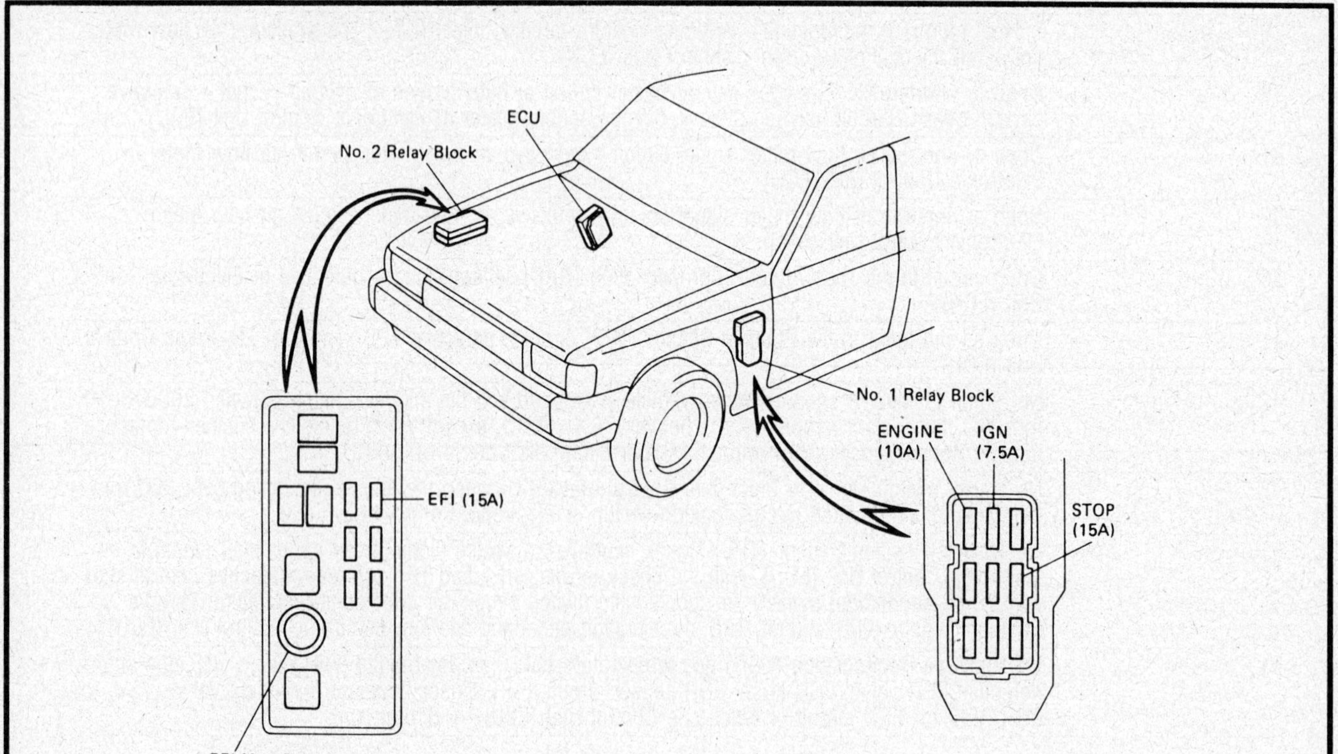

ECU and relay block location—1989 Toyota truck

Volkswagen 26

INDEX

VOLKSWAGEN

CIS-E Motronic System

SELF-DIAGNOSTIC SYSTEM

Description

The CIS-E Motronic system utilizes a self diagnosis system which in conjunction with the VAG 1551 diagnostic tester, the system can be accurately diagnosed. If a malfunction in the injection system should occur within a monitored sensor or related component, a trouble code will be stored in the fault memory of the control unit.

Faults related to emissions and safety are stored in permanent memory which must be erased after faults have been eliminated or repaired. Additional faults that can be recognized by the control unit are stored in a temporary fault memory. These faults are retained in memory when the ignition is switched **OFF**, but are automatically erased when the engine is restarted.

Entering Diagnostic Mode

To enter the self diagnostic system, the following must first be checked:

   a. Check fuses 15, 18 and 21—must check good.
   b. Turn the air conditioning switch **OFF**.
   c. Check the engine ground connection, at the ignition distributor.

NOTE: Keep in mind that a part of the memory is erased when the engine is restarted. It is important to follow the test sequence precisely so all faults are recognized during fault recall.

Operation

1. Road test the vehicle for at least 5 minutes. During the road test, the following must take place:
   a. The coolant temperature must reach 176°F (80°C) minimum.
   b. The engine speed must exceed 3000 rpm.
   c. The accelerator pedal must be fully depressed at least once.
2. After road testing, allow the engine to idle for at least 2 minutes before turning it **OFF**.
3. Restart the engine. If the engine will not start:
   a. Operate the starter for 6 seconds.
   b. Turn the ignition switch **OFF**.
4. Connect diagnostic tester VAG 1551 with adapter cable VAG 1551/1.
5. Connect the black test lead of tester VAG 1551 to the vehicles black diagnostic connector, No. 1.
6. Connect the white test lead of tester VAG 1551 to the vehicles white diagnostic connector, No. 2.

NOTE: The blue test lead of tester VAG 1551 is not needed in this check.

7. If the tester display shows:
   "VAG—SELF DIAGNOSIS HELP"
   "1—Rapid transmission" (flashing alternately)
   "2—Flash code output" (flashing alternately)
8. Turn VAG 1551 printer on by pressing the print button, the indicator lamp in the button will turn ON.
9. Turn the ignition switch **ON** and press button 1; this button selects the Rapid Data Transmission mode.
10. The display will then show:
   "Rapid data transmission HELP"
   "Input address word XX"

11. Press buttons **0** and **1**. With 01 address words "**Engine Electronics**" are input.
12. The display will show:
   "Rapid data transmission Q"
   "01 Engine Electronics"
13. Acknowledge input by pressing the **Q** button. The control unit identification will appear on the display, for example:
   "893907404 F ENGINE"
   "coding 00"
14. The following display will appear:
   "Control unit does not respond!"
   "HELP"
15. Press the **HELP** button. A list of possible fault causes will print.
16. The system is entered and ready for diagnosis.

Clearing Diagnostic Memory

NOTE: The fault memory must first be recalled before it can be canceled.

1. After the elimination of possible fault causes, re-input and acknowledge the address word 01 for "**Engine electronics**".
2. Press the "♦" (right arrow button).
3. The following display will appear:
   "Rapid data transmission HELP"
   "Input address word XX"
4. Press 0 and 2 buttons.
5. With the 02 address, function fault memory recall is selected.
6. The following display will appear:
   "Rapid data transmission"
   "02 fault memory recall"
7. Acknowledge by pressing the **Q** button. The number of stored faults or "No faults registered" is displayed.
8. Press the "♦" (right arrow button).
9. Stored faults are displayed and printed consecutively. The fault memory is now recalled and prepared for clearing.
10. When the last fault has been displayed on the print out, press the "♦" (right arrow) button.
11. The following display will appear:
   "Rapid Data Transmission HELP"
   "Select Function XX"
12. Press the 0 and **5** buttons.
13. The following display will appear:
   "Rapid Data Transmission Q"
   "05 cancel fault memory"
14. Acknowledge by pressing the **Q** button.
15. The following display will appear:
   "Faults were not recalled from fault memory."

NOTE: If the ignition is switched OFF or the engine is run between fault memory recall and fault memory clearing stages, the fault memory is not canceled.

16. If the fault memory has be successfully cleared, the following display will appear:
   "Rapid Data Transmission"
   "Fault memory is canceled"

Digifant II System

SELF-DIAGNOSTIC SYSTEM

Description

The Digifant II system is equipped with an erasable permanent memory which stores and displays any faults that affect the performance of the vehicles fuel, ignition and emission systems.

The faults will thus appear by the an illuminated indicator lamp, located on the instrument panel. When the ignition is switched **ON**, the lamp labeled "Check" must turn ON momentarily; this is an indication that the lamp is functioning.

Should a fault be detected and stored in the control unit, the fault lamp will illuminate within 1 minute. When the fault memory is activated the lamp will flash a series of flashes in code form.

A flash code consists of 4 flash impulse groups (with a maximum of 4 flash impulses per group). Between each impulse group there is a 2.5 second pause; the lamp is OFF. The fault code is constructed by adding the individual flash impulses within each impulse group which will result in a number from 1–4.

Example:
Group 1 – flashes 2 times and pauses for 2.5 seconds
Group 2 – flashes 3 times and pauses for 2.5 seconds
Group 3 – flashes 4 times and pauses for 2.5 seconds
Group 4 – flashes 2 times and pauses for 2.5 seconds
The fault code 0000 indicates **End of Fault Sequence** and is displayed in a series of 2.5 second flashes ON and OFF.

Entering Diagnostic Mode

1. Road test the vehicle for at least 10 minutes. During the road test, the following must take place:
   a. The coolant temperature must reach 176°F (80°C) minimum.
   b. The engine speed must exceed 3000 rpm.
   c. The accelerator pedal must be fully depressed at least once.
2. After road testing, allow the engine to idle for at least 2 minutes before turning **OFF**.

3. Turn the ignition switch **ON** but do not start.
4. Depress the rocker switch for at least 4 seconds; the indicator lamp will begin to flash.
5. Depress the rocker switch again for at least 4 seconds; if a fault code has been stored by the control unit, it will be displayed in sequence.
6. If the fault lamp does not turn ON and the rocker switch is depressed, flash **Code 4444** – No Faults in memory, will be shown.

NOTE: Do not depress the rocker switch during the warning lamp pauses, otherwise the control unit will not switch to the next stored fault.

Clearing Diagnostic Memory

After the elimination of fault causes are corrected or repaired it is necessary to clear all fault codes.

1. With the ignition switch **OFF**, press and hold down the rocker switch.
2. Turn the ignition switch **ON**.
3. Continue depressing the rocker switch for about 5 seconds.
4. Turn the ignition switch **OFF**; codes should be cleared at this point.
5. Road test the vehicle for a minimum of 10 minutes.
6. If a fault warning is displayed again, perform the following:
   a. Reactivate the fault memory
   b. Display and record all stored fault codes
   c. Verify existence of faults and correct if necessary
   d. Clear the fault memory
   e. Road test the vehicle for a minimum of 10 minutes.

VOLKSWAGEN

Year – 1990
Model – Passat
Engine – 2.0L (121 cid) 4 cyl
Engine Code – 9A

ECM TROUBLE CODES

Code	Explanation
1111	Defective control unit
1231	Speed sender – no signal
2112	Ignition reference sensor – no signal
2113	Hall sender – no signal
2121	Idle switch – short ground to circuit
2141	Knock sensor 1 – maximum control limit exceeded
2142	Knock sensor 1 – no signal
2144	Knock sensor 11 – no signal
2231	Idle speed regulation adaption limit undercut or exceeded
2232	Airflow sensor – open/short circuit to ground
2312	Coolant Temperature Sensor (CTS) – short circuit to ground – open/short circuit to positive
2341	Oxygen sensor control limit exceeded
2342	Oxygen sensor (heated) no signal – lean adjustment limit of mixture control unit exceeded – rich adjustment limit of mixture control unit exceeded
2411	Exhaust Gas Recirculation (EGR) system short circuit to ground – EGR system false signal
4431	Idle stabilizer valve – open/short circuit to ground – short circuit to positive
4444	No fault registered

Year – 1990
Model – Jetta
Engine – 2.0L (121 cid) 4 cyl
Engine Code – 9A

ECM TROUBLE CODES

Code	Explanation
1111	Defective control unit
1231	Speed sender – no signal
2112	Ignition reference sensor – no signal
2113	Hall sender – no signal
2121	Idle switch – short ground to circuit
2141	Knock sensor 1 – maximum control limit exceeded
2142	Knock sensor 1 – no signal
2144	Knock sensor 11 – no signal
2231	Idle speed regulation adaption limit undercut or exceeded
2232	Airflow sensor – open/short circuit to ground
2312	Coolant Temperature Sensor (CTS) – short circuit to ground – open/short circuit to positive
2341	Oxygen sensor control limit exceeded
2342	Oxygen sensor (heated) no signal – lean adjustment limit of mixture control unit exceeded – rich adjustment limit of mixture control unit exceeded
2411	Exhaust Gas Recirculation (EGR) system short circuit to ground – EGR system false signal
4431	Idle stabilizer valve – open/short circuit to ground – short circuit to positive
4444	No fault registered

Year – 1990
Model – GTI
Engine – 2.0L (121 cid) 4 cyl
Engine Code – 9A

ECM TROUBLE CODES

Code	Explanation
1111	Defective control unit
1231	Speed sender – no signal
2112	Ignition reference sensor – no signal
2113	Hall sender – no signal
2121	Idle switch – short ground to circuit
2141	Knock sensor 1 – maximum control limit exceeded
2142	Knock sensor 1 – no signal
2144	Knock sensor 11 – no signal
2231	Idle speed regulation adaption limit undercut or exceeded
2232	Airflow sensor – open/short circuit to ground
2312	Coolant Temperature Sensor (CTS) – short circuit to ground – open/short circuit to positive
2341	Oxygen sensor control limit exceeded
2342	Oxygen sensor (heated) no signal – lean adjustment limit of mixture control unit exceeded – rich adjustment limit of mixture control unit exceeded
2411	Exhaust Gas Recirculation (EGR) system short circuit to ground – EGR system false signal
4431	Idle stabilizer valve – open/short circuit to ground – short circuit to positive
4444	No fault registered

Year – 1990
Model – Jetta
Engine – 1.8L (109 cid) 4 cyl
Engine Code – RV, PF

ECM TROUBLE CODES

Code	Explanation
2312	Coolant Temperature Sensor (CTS)
2322	Intake Air Temperature (IAT) sensor
2232	Air flow sensor potentiometer
2142	Knock sensor
2342	Oxygen sensor
4444	No fault in memory

Year – 1990
Model – GTI
Engine – 1.8L (109 cid) 4 cyl
Engine Code – RV, PF

ECM TROUBLE CODES

Code	Explanation
2312	Coolant Temperature Sensor (CTS)
2322	Intake Air Temperature (IAT) Sensor
2232	Air flow sensor potentiometer
2142	Knock sensor
2342	Oxygen sensor
4444	No fault in memory

Year – 1990
Model – Golf
Engine – 1.8L (109 cid) 4 cyl
Engine Code – RV, PF

ECM TROUBLE CODES

Code	Explanation
2312	Coolant Temperature Sensor (CTS)
2322	Intake Air Temperature (IAT) sensor
2232	Air flow sensor potentiometer
2142	Knock sensor
2342	Oxygen sensor
4444	No fault in memory

Year – 1990
Model – Cabriolet
Engine – 1.8L (109 cid) 4 cyl
Engine Code – RV, PF

ECM TROUBLE CODES

Code	Explanation
2312	Coolant Temperature Sensor (CTS)
2322	Intake Air Temperature (IAT) sensor
2232	Air flow sensor potentiometer
2142	Knock sensor
2342	Oxygen sensor
4444	No fault in memory

INDEX

VOLVO

LH-Jetronic and Regina Fuel Injections Systems

SELF-DIAGNOSTICS SYSTEM

Description

SYSTEM OPERATION

The LH-Jetronic and Regina Fuel Injection Systems used on 1988–90 Volvo 240 and 740 models, incorporates a built-in self-diagnostic system and a functions testing system. It is located behind the left spring strut tower in the engine compartment. The diagnostic system uses socket No. 2 for the fuel system.

There are 18 different fault codes in the diagnostic system and the system is capable of storing up to 3 system faults. When the engine is running, the fuel system control unit continuously checks the following functions:

    Control units internal functions
    Lambda-sond and Lambda settings
    Coolant temperature sensor
    Air mass meter (LH-Jetronic)
    Air temperature sensor (Regina)
    Battery voltage
    Pressure sensor (Regina)
    Throttle shutter
    Ignition settings and engine rpm (through the ignition system control unit) .
    Speedometer and knock indicator
    Idle speed air valve and injectors
    Any faults in these functions are stored in the diagnostic system memory.

SYSTEM FAULT TRACING

The fuel system incorporates a built-in fault tracing system. It is mounted in the control unit and consists of 3 different control functions. One is to read fault codes stored in the memory and 2 for continuous testing of the components in the system.

Communication with the diagnostic system is through the diagnostic socket. The socket is located behind the left spring strut tower in the engine compartment. The diagnostic socket consists of a button, a diode light and a selector cable. When fault tracing the fuel system, the selector cable is placed in socket No. 2 of the 6 available. Pressing the button once, 2 or 3 times chooses the desired fault tracing control function.

Faults stored in the memory are read through a series of flashes from the diagnostic socket diode light. All fault codes have 3 numbers, capable of ranging from 1 through 9. The fuel system codes range only between 1 and 4. The fault codes are read from the series of flashes delivered by the diode. The codes all have 3 numbers, each code requires 3 series of uninterrupted flashes, with a 3 second interval between each series of flashes to make the codes easy to read.

Control Function 1

By pressing the diagnostic socket button once, the diagnostic system carries out continuous checks of the fuel system during engine operation. Any system fault is stored in the diagnostic systems memory as a fault code. The system can identify and store 17 different fault codes and also a code to indicate that the fuel system contains no faults. When the engine stops, the fault codes can be read counting the flashes at the diagnostic socket diode.

Control Function 2

This function tests the various fuel system breakers. As each 1 is activated, functions information is provided by the diagnostic socket diode in the form of series flashes. This function test is generally used after repairs have been made, to ensure that certain controls are connected and operating correctly.

Control Function 3

This test is performed with the engine **OFF**. It test the adjustment functions of the control system. This test consists of initiating a functions cycle, whereby the diagnostic system activates certain control components. Determine if the component is operating correctly by placing a hand on the component or by listening for a click which occurs when the component is activated.

Entering Diagnostic Mode

1. Open diagnostic socket cover and install selector cable into socket No. 2.
2. Turn ignition to the **ON** position.
3. Enter control system 1 by pressing the button once. Hold the button for at least 1 second but not more than 3.
4. Watch the diode light and count the number of flashes in the 3 flash series indicating a fault code. The flash series are separated by 3 second intervals. Note the fault codes.

NOTE: If there are no fault codes in the diagnostic unit, the diode will flash 1-1-1 and the fuel system is operating correctly. Proceed to control function 2 and control function 3, if necessary.

Clearing Diagnostic Memory

When all the fault codes have been read and corrected, the diagnostic system memory can be erased as follows:
1. Turn ignition switch to the **ON** position.
2. Read fault codes again.
3. Press and hold diagnostic socket button for approximately 5 seconds. Release button. After 3 seconds, the diode light should light.
4. While the diode light is lit, press button again for approximately 5 seconds and release the button. The diode light should turn OFF; the memory is cleared.

NOTE: To ensure that the memory has been erased, press button again for 1 second but not more than 3 seconds. The diode light should flash 1-1-1, indicating that the fuel system is operating properly.

VOLVO

Year – 1989
Model – 240
Engine – 2.3L (140 cid) 4 cyl
Engine Code – B230F

ECM TROUBLE CODES

Code	Explanation
111	No faults
112	Fault in control unit
113	Fault in injector (Break in lead, clogged etc.)
121	Signal to/from air mass meter is faulty
123	Signal to/from coolant temperature sensor, possible grounding short
131	Ignition system rpm signal missing
132	Battery potential too low or too high
133	Throttle switch; idle setting faulty, possible grounding short
142	Fault in control unit. Engine runs with safety retarded timing (about 10°)
143	Knock sensor faulty. Engine runs with safety retarded timing (about 10 °)
144	Load signal absent (from fuel system control unit). Control unit selects full-load ignition
212	Lambda-sond missing or is faulty
213	Throttle switch; full load setting faulty, possibly grounding short
214	Engine speed sensor faulty
223	Signal missing to/from idle valve
224	Coolant temperature sensor. Warm engine signal, i.e. control unit assumes 60°C engine temperature
231	Self-adjusting Lambda-sond not operating
232	Self-adjusting Lamda-sond not operating
233	Idle valve closed, possibly leaking air
234	Throttle switch for wiring faulty. Engine runs with safety retarded timing
311	Signal missing from speedometer
312	Signal missing from knock related fuel enrichment
322	Burn-off cleaning of hot wire in air mass meter not operating

Year – 1989
Model – 740
Engine – 2.3L (140 cid) 4 cyl
Engine Code – B230F

ECM TROUBLE CODES

Code	Explanation
111	No faults
112	Fault in control unit
113	Fault in injector (Break in lead, clogged etc.)
121	Signal to/from air mass meter is faulty
122	Signal missing or is faulty to/from air temperature sensor
123	Signal to/from coolant temperature sensor, possible grounding short
132	Battery potential too low or too high
133	Throttle switch; idle setting faulty, possible grounding short
142	Fault in control unit. Engine runs with safety retarded timing (about 10°)
143	Knock sensor faulty. Engine runs with safety retarded timing (about 10 °)
144	Load signal absent (from fuel system control unit). Control unit selects full-load ignition
212	Lambda-sond missing or is faulty
213	Throttle switch; full load setting faulty, possibly grounding short
214	Engine speed sensor faulty
221	Lamda-sond not operating
222	Fault in system relay
223	Signal missing to/from idle valve
224	Coolant temperature sensor. Warm engine signal, i.e. control unit assumes 60°C engine temperature
231	Self-adjusting Lambda-sond not operating
232	Self-adjusting Lambda-sond not operating
233	Idle valve closed, possibly leaking air
234	Throttle switch for wiring faulty. Engine runs with safety retarded timing – California only
311	Signal missing from speedometer
312	Signal missing from knock related fuel enrichment

Year – 1989
Model – 740
Engine – 2.3L (140 cid) 4 cyl
Engine Code – B204

ECM TROUBLE CODES

Code	Explanation
111	No faults
112	Fault in control unit
113	Fault in injector (Break in lead, clogged etc.)
121	Signal to/from air mass meter is faulty
122	Signal missing or is faulty to/from air temperature sensor
123	Signal to/from coolant temperature sensor, possible grounding short
132	Battery potential too low or too high
133	Throttle switch; idle setting faulty, possible grounding short
212	Lambda-sond missing or is faulty
213	Throttle switch; full load setting faulty, possibly grounding short
221	Lamda-sond not operating
222	Fault in system relay
223	Signal missing to/from idle valve
231	Self-adjusting Lambda-sond not operating
232	Self-adjusting Lambda-sond not operating
233	Idle valve closed, possibly leaking air
311	Signal missing from speedometer
321	Signal missing or is faulty to/from cold start valve

Year — 1989
Model — 740
Engine — 2.3L (140 cid) 4 cyl
Engine Code — B234

ECM TROUBLE CODES

Code	Explanation
111	No faults
112	Fault in control unit
113	Fault in injector (Break in lead, clogged etc.)
121	Signal to/from air mass meter is faulty
122	Signal missing or is faulty to/from air temperature sensor
123	Signal to/from coolant temperature sensor, possible grounding short
132	Battery potential too low or too high
133	Throttle switch; idle setting faulty, possible grounding short
144	Load signal absent (from fuel system control unit). Control unit selects full-load ignition
212	Lambda-sond missing or is faulty
213	Throttle switch; full load setting faulty, possibly grounding short
221	Lamda-sond not operating
222	Fault in system relay
223	Signal missing to/from idle valve
231	Self-adjusting Lambda-sond not operating
232	Self-adjusting Lambda-sond not operating
233	Idle valve closed, possibly leaking air
311	Signal missing from speedometer
321	Signal missing or is faulty to/from cold start valve

Basic Electricity

28

INDEX

FUNDAMENTALS OF ELECTRICITY

A good understanding of basic electrical theory and how circuits work is necessary to successfully perform the service and testing outlined in this manual. Therefore, this section should be read before attempting any diagnosis and repair.

All matter is made up of tiny particles called molecules. Each molecule is made up of two or more atoms. Atoms may be divided into even smaller particles called protons, neutrons and electrons. These particles are the same in all matter and differences in materials (hard or soft, conductive or non-conductive) occur only because of the number and arrangement of these particles. In other words, the protons, neutrons and electrons in a drop of water are the same as those in an ounce of lead, there are just more of them (arranged differently) in a lead molecule than in a water molecule. Protons and neutrons packed together form the nucleus of the atom, while electrons orbit around the nucleus much the same way as the planets of the solar system orbit around the sun.

The proton is a small positive natural charge of electricity, while the neutron has no electrical charge. The electron carries a negative charge equal to the positive charge of the proton. Every electrically neutral atom contains the same number of protons and electrons, the exact number of which determines the element. The only difference between a conductor and an insulator is that a conductor possesses free electrons in large quantities, while an insulator has only a few. An element must have very few free electrons to be a good insulator and vice-versa. When we speak of electricity, we're talking about these free electrons.

In a conductor, the movement of the free electrons is hindered by collisions with the adjoining atoms of the element (matter). This hindrance to movement is called **RESISTANCE** and it varies with different materials and temperatures. As temperature increases, the movement of the free electrons increases, causing more frequent collisions and therefore increasing resistance to the movement of the electrons. The number of collisions (resistance) also increases with the number of electrons flowing (current). Current is defined as the movement of electrons through a conductor such as a wire. In a conductor (such as copper) electrons can be caused to leave their atoms and move to other atoms. This flow is continuous in that every time an atom gives up an electron, it collects another one to take its place. This movement of electrons is called electric current and is measured in amperes. When 6.28 billion, billion electrons pass a certain point in the circuit in one second, the amount of current flow is called 1 ampere.

The force or pressure which causes electrons to flow in any conductor (such as a wire) is called **VOLTAGE**. It is measured in volts and is similar to the pressure that causes water to flow in a pipe. Voltage is the difference in electrical pressure measured between 2 different points in a circuit. In a 12 volt system, for example, the force measured between the two battery posts is 12 volts. Two important concepts are voltage potential and polarity. Voltage potential is the amount of voltage or electrical pressure at a certain point in the circuit with respect to another point. For example, if the voltage potential at one post of the 12 volt battery is 0, the voltage potential at the other post is 12 volts with respect to the first post. One post of the battery is said to be positive (+); the other post is negative (−) and the conventional direction of current flow is from positive to negative in an electrical circuit. It should be noted that the electron flow in the wire is opposite the current flow. In other words, when the circuit is energized, the current flows from positive to negative, but the electrons actually move from negative to positive. The voltage or pressure needed to produce a current flow in a circuit must be greater than the resistance present in the circuit. In other words, if the voltage drop across the resistance is greater than or equal to the voltage input, the voltage potential will be

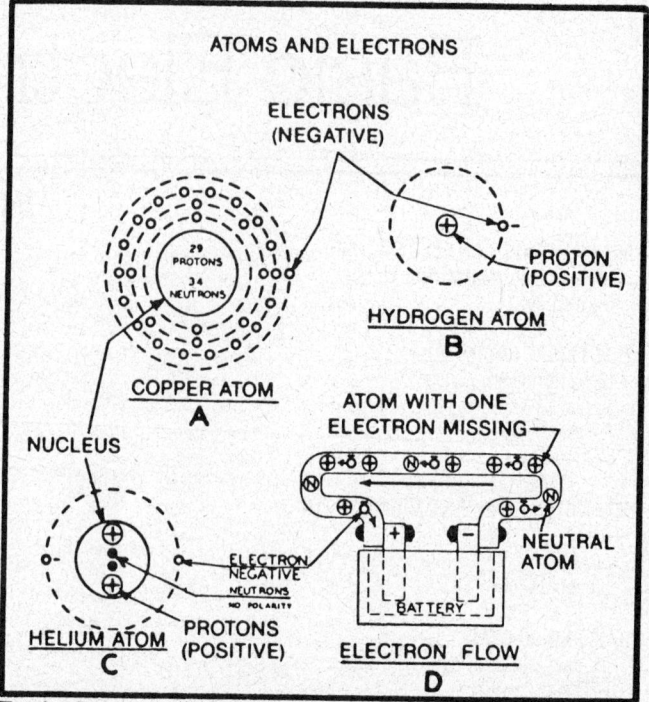

Typical atoms of copper (A), hydrogen (B) and helium (C). Electron flow in battery circuit (D)

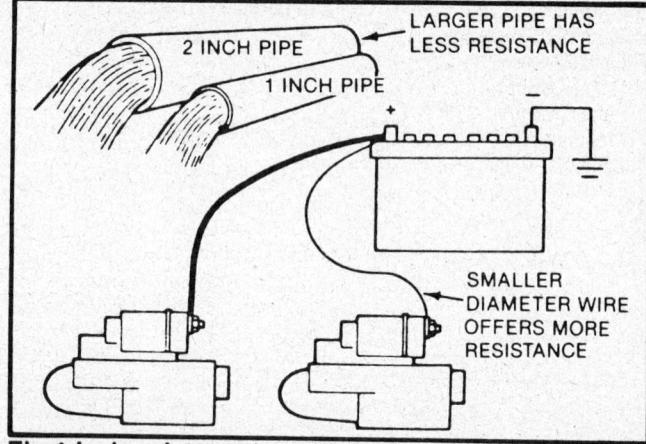

Electrical resistance can be compared to water flow through a pipe. The smaller the wire (pipe), the more resistance to the flow of electrons (water)

zero — no voltage will flow through the circuit. Resistance to the flow of electrons is measured in ohms. One volt will cause 1 ampere to flow through a resistance of 1 ohm.

Units Of Electrical Measurement

There are 3 fundamental characteristics of a direct-current electrical circuit: volts, amperes and ohms.

VOLTAGE in a circuit controls the intensity with which the loads in the circuit operate. The brightness of a lamp, the heat of an electrical defroster, the speed of a motor are all directly proportional to the voltage, if the resistance in the circuit and/or mechanical load on electric motors remains constant. Voltage available from the battery is constant (normally 12 volts), but as it operates the various loads in the circuit, voltage decreases (drops).

AMPERE is the unit of measurement of current in an electrical circuit. One ampere is the quantity of current that will flow through a resistance of 1 ohm at a pressure of 1 volt. The amount of current that flows in a circuit is controlled by the voltage and the resistance in the circuit. Current flow is directly proportional to resistance. Thus, as voltage is increased or decreased, current is increased or decreased accordingly. Current is decreased as resistance is increased. However, current is also increased as resistance is decreased. With little or no resistance in a circuit, current is high.

OHM is the unit of measurement of resistance, represented by the Greek letter Omega (Ω). One ohm is the resistance of a conductor through which a current of one ampere will flow at a pressure of one volt. Electrical resistance can be measured on an instrument called an ohmmeter. The loads (electrical devices) are the primary resistances in a circuit. Loads such as lamps, solenoids and electric heaters have a resistance that is essentially fixed; at a normal fixed voltage, they will draw a fixed current. Motors, on the other hand, do not have a fixed resistance. Increasing the mechanical load on a motor (such as might be caused by a misadjusted track in a power window system) will decrease the motor speed. The drop in motor rpm has the effect of reducing the internal resistance of the motor because the current draw of the motor varies directly with the mechanical load on the motor, although its actual resistance is unchanged. Thus, as the motor load increases, the current draw of the motor increases, and may increase up to the point where the motor stalls (cannot move the mechanical load).

Circuits are designed with the total resistance of the circuit taken into account. Troubles can arise when unwanted resistances enter into a circuit. If corrosion, dirt, grease, or any other contaminant occurs in places like switches, connectors and grounds, or if loose connections occur, resistances will develop in these areas. These resistances act like additional loads in the circuit and cause problems.

OHM'S LAW

Ohm's law is a statement of the relationship between the 3 fundamental characteristics of an electrical circuit. These rules apply to direct current (DC) only.

Ohm's law provides a means to make an accurate circuit analysis without actually seeing the circuit. If, for example, one wanted to check the condition of the rotor winding in a alternator whose specifications indicate that the field (rotor) current draw is normally 2.5 amperes at 12 volts, simply connect the rotor to a 12 volt battery and measure the current with an ammeter. If it measures about 2.5 amperes, the rotor winding can be assumed good.

An ohmmeter can be used to test components that have been removed from the vehicle in much the same manner as an ammeter. Since the voltage and the current of the rotor windings used as an earlier example are known, the resistance can be calculated using Ohms law. The formula would be ohms equals volts divided by amperes.

If the rotor resistance measures about 4.8 ohms when checked with an ohmmeter, the winding can be assumed good. By plugging in different specifications, additional circuit information can be determined such as current draw, etc.

Electrical Circuits

An electrical circuit must start from a source of electrical supply and return to that source through a continuous path. Circuits are designed to handle a certain maximum current flow. The

$$I = \frac{E}{R} \quad \text{or} \quad \text{AMPERES} = \frac{\text{VOLTS}}{\text{OHMS}}$$

$$R = \frac{E}{I} \quad \text{or} \quad \text{OHMS} = \frac{\text{VOLTS}}{\text{AMPERES}}$$

$$E = I \times R \quad \text{or} \quad \text{VOLTS} = \text{AMPERES} \times \text{OHMS}$$

Ohms Law is the basis for all electrical measurements. By simply plugging in two values, the third can be calculated using the illustrated formula.

$$R = \frac{E}{I} \quad \text{Where:} \quad E = 12 \text{ volts}$$
$$I = 2.5 \text{ amperes}$$
$$R = \frac{12 \text{ volts}}{2.5 \text{ amps}} = 4.8 \text{ ohms}$$

An example of calculating resistance (R) when the voltage (E) and amperage (I) is known.

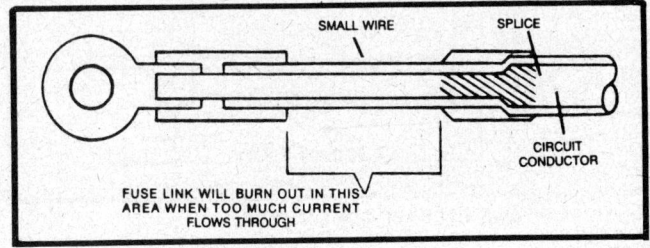

Typical fusible link wire

maximum allowable current flow is designed higher than the normal current requirements of all the loads in the circuit. Wire size, connections, insulation, etc., are designed to prevent undesirable voltage drop, overheating of conductors, arcing of contacts and other adverse effects. If the safe maximum current flow level is exceeded, damage to the circuit components will result; it is this condition that circuit protection devices are designed to prevent.

Protection devices are fuses, fusible links or circuit breakers designed to open or break the circuit quickly whenever an overload, such as a short circuit, occurs. By opening the circuit quickly, the circuit protection device prevents damage to the wiring, battery and other circuit components. Fuses and fusible links are designed to carry a preset maximum amount of current and to melt when that maximum is exceeded, while circuit breakers merely break the connection and may be manually reset. The maximum amperage rating of each fuse is marked on the fuse body and all contain a see-through portion that shows the break in the fuse element when blown. Fusible link maximum amperage rating is indicated by gauge or thickness of the wire. Never replace a blown fuse or fusible link with one of a higher amperage rating.

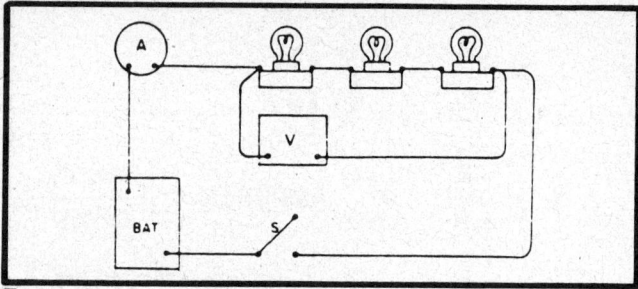

Example of a series circuit

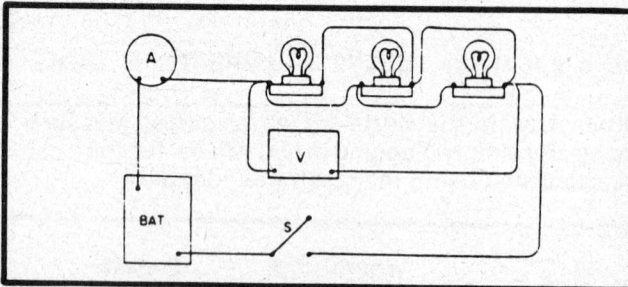

Example of a parallel circuit

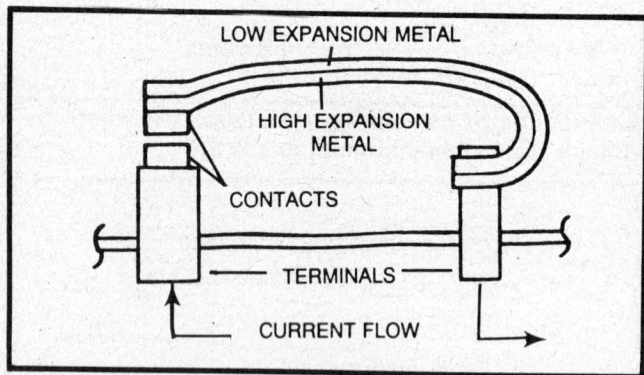

Typical circuit breaker construction

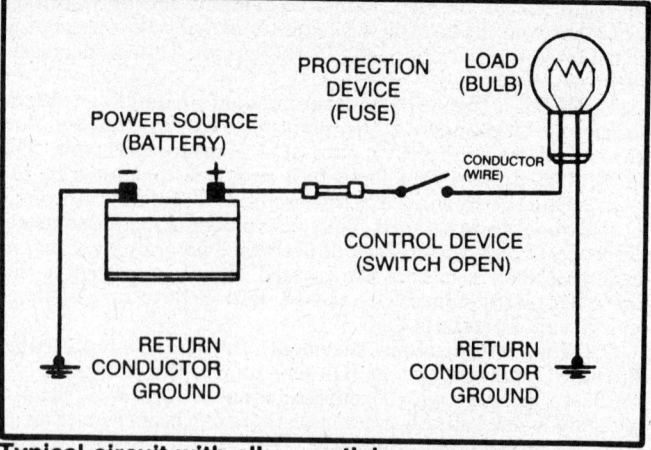

Typical circuit with all essential components

CAUTION

Resistance wires, like fusible links, are also spliced into conductors in some areas. Do not make the mistake of replacing a fusible link with a resistance wire. Resistance wires are longer than fusible links and are stamped "RESISTOR-DO NOT CUT OR SPLICE."

Circuit breakers consist of 2 strips of metal which have different coefficients of expansion. As an overload or current flows through the bimetallic strip, the high-expansion metal will elongate due to heat and break the contact. With the circuit open, the bimetal strip cools and shrinks, drawing the strip down until contact is re-established and current flows once again. In actual operation, the contact is broken very quickly if the overload is continuous and the circuit will be repeatedly broken and remade until the source of the overload is corrected.

The self-resetting type of circuit breaker is the one most generally used in automotive electrical systems. On manually reset circuit breakers, a button will pop up on the circuit breaker case. This button must be pushed in to reset the circuit breaker and restore power to the circuit. Always repair the source of the overload before resetting a circuit breaker or replacing a fuse or fusible link. When searching for overloads, keep in mind that the circuit protection devices protect only against overloads between the protection device and ground.

There are 2 basic types of circuit; Series and Parallel. In a series circuit, all of the elements are connected in chain fashion with the same amount of current passing through each element or load. No matter where an ammeter is connected in a series circuit, it will always read the same. The most important fact to remember about a series circuit is that the sum of the voltages across each element equals the source voltage. The total resistance of a series circuit is equal to the sum of the individual resistances within each element of the circuit. Using ohms law, one can determine the voltage drop across each element in the circuit. If the total resistance and source voltage is known, the amount of current can be calculated. Once the amount of current (amperes) is known, values can be substituted in the Ohms law formula to calculate the voltage drop across each individual element in the series circuit. The individual voltage drops must add up to the same value as the source voltage.

A parallel circuit, unlike a series circuit, contains 2 or more branches, each branch a separate path independent of the others. The total current draw from the voltage source is the sum of all the currents drawn by each branch. Each branch of a parallel circuit can be analyzed separately. The individual branches can be either simple circuits, series circuits or combinations of series-parallel circuits. Ohms law applies to parallel circuits just as it applies to series circuits, by considering each branch independently of the others. The most important thing to remember is that the voltage across each branch is the same as the source voltage. The current in any branch is that voltage divided by the resistance of the branch. A practical method of determining the resistance of a parallel circuit is to divide the product of the 2 resistances by the sum of 2 resistances at a time. Amperes through a parallel circuit is the sum of the amperes through the separate branches. Voltage across a parallel circuit is the same as the voltage across each branch.

By measuring the voltage drops the resistance of each element within the circuit is being measured. The greater the voltage drop, the greater the resistance. Voltage drop measurements are a common way of checking circuit resistances in automotive electrical systems. When part of a circuit develops excessive resistance (due to a bad connection) the element will show a higher than normal voltage drop. Normally, automotive wiring is selected to limit voltage drops to a few tenths of a volt. In parallel circuits, the total resistance is less than the sum of the individual resistances; because the current has 2 paths to take, the total resistance is lower.

Magnetism and Electromagnets

Electricity and magnetism are very closely associated because when electric current passes through a wire, a magnetic field is created around the wire. When a wire carrying electric current

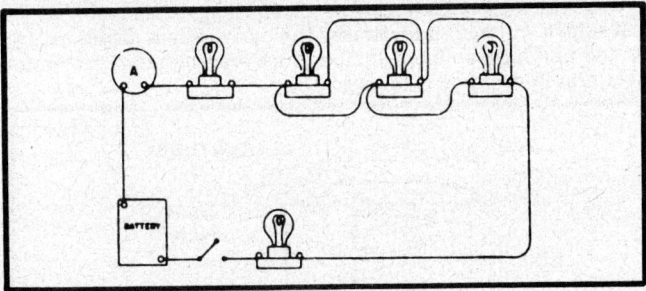
Example of a series-parallel circuit

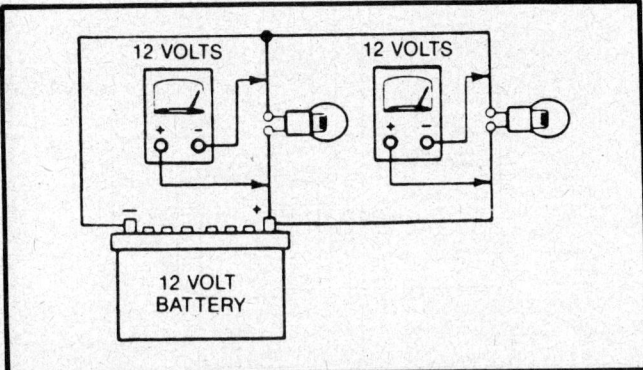
Voltage drop in a parallel circuit. Voltage drop across each lamp is 12 volts

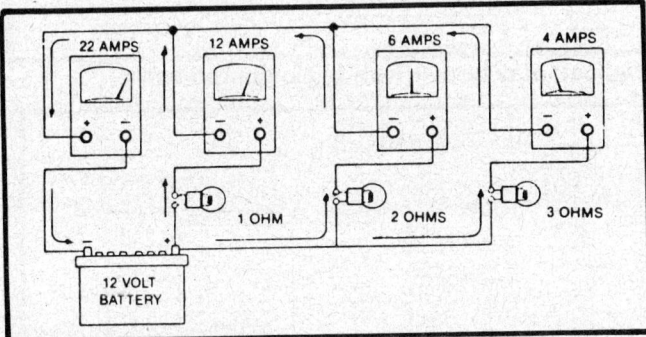
Total current in parallel circuit: 4 + 6 + 12 = 22 amps

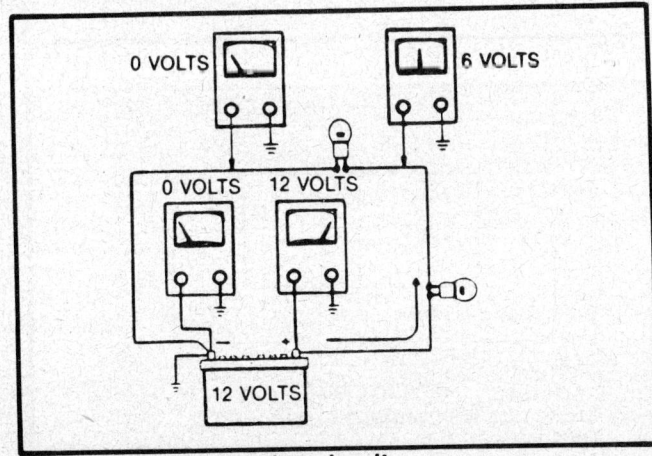
Voltage drop in a series circuit

ELECTRO-MAGNETS

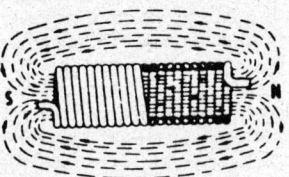

FORCE FIELD SURROUNDING A CURRENT CARRYING COIL
(WITHOUT IRON CORE)
ALL FORCE LINES ARE COMPLETE LOOPS

FORCE FIELD WITH SOFT IRON CORE
NOTE CONCENTRATION OF LINES IN IRON CORE

Magnetic field surrounding an electromagnet

MAGNETISM & PERMANENT MAGNETS

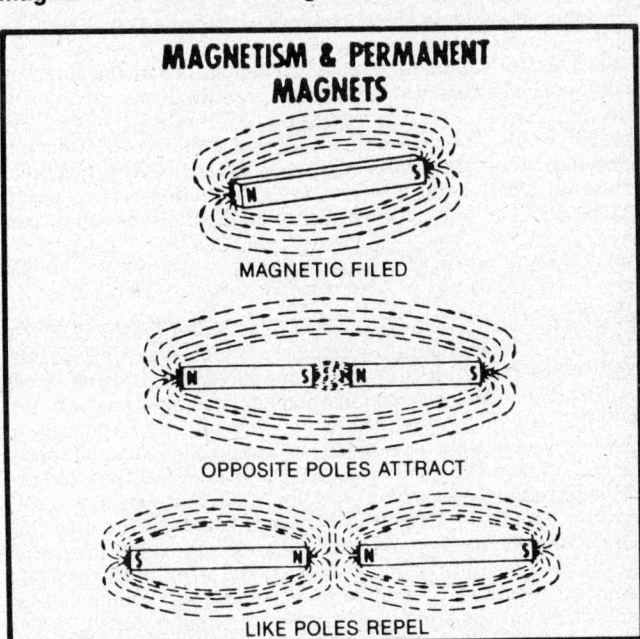

MAGNETIC FILED

OPPOSITE POLES ATTRACT

LIKE POLES REPEL

Magnetic field surrounding a bar magnet

is wound into a coil, a magnetic field with North and South poles is created just like in a bar magnet. If an iron core is placed within the coil, the magnetic field becomes stronger because iron conducts magnetic lines much easier than air. This arrangement is called an electromagnet and is the basic principle behind the operation of such components as relays, buzzers and solenoids.

A relay is basically just a remote-controlled switch that uses a small amount of current to control the flow of a large amount of current. The simplest relay contains an electromagnetic coil in series with a voltage source (battery) and a switch. A movable armature made of some magnetic material pivots at one end and is held a small distance away from the electromagnet by a spring or the spring steel of the armature itself. A contact point, made of a good conductor, is attached to the free end of the armature with another contact point a small distance away. When the relay is switched on (energized), the magnetic field created by the current flow attracts the armature, bending it until the contact points meet, closing a circuit and allowing current to flow in the second circuit through the relay to the load the circuit operates. When the relay is switched off (de-energized), the armature springs back and opens the contact points, cutting off the current flow in the secondary, or controlled, circuit. Relays can be designed to be either open or closed when energized, depending on the type of circuit control a manufacturer requires.

A buzzer is similar to a relay, but its internal connections are different. When the switch is closed, the current flows through the normally closed contacts and energizes the coil. When the coil core becomes magnetized, it bends the armature down and breaks the circuit. As soon as the circuit is broken, the spring-loaded armature remakes the circuit and again energizes the coil. This cycle repeats rapidly to cause the buzzing sound.

A solenoid is constructed like a relay, except that its core is allowed to move, providing mechanical motion that can be used to actuate mechanical linkage to operate a door or trunk lock or control any other mechanical function. When the switch is closed, the coil is energized and the movable core is drawn into the coil. When the switch is opened, the coil is de-energized and spring pressure returns the core to its original position.

Basic Solid State

The term "solid state" refers to devices utilizing transistors, diodes and other components which are made from materials known as semiconductors. A semiconductor is a material that is neither a good insulator nor a good conductor; principally silicon and germanium. The semiconductor material is specially treated to give it certain qualities that enhance its function, therefore becoming either P-type (positive) or N-type (negative) material. Most semiconductors are constructed of silicon and can be designed to function either as an insulator or conductor.

DIODES

The simplest semiconductor function is that of the diode or rectifier (the 2 terms mean the same thing). A diode will pass current in one direction only, like a one-way valve, because it has low resistance in one direction and high resistance on the other. Whether the diode conducts or not depends on the polarity of the voltage applied to it. A diode has 2 electrodes, an anode and a cathode. When the anode receives positive (+) voltage and the cathode receives negative (−) voltage, current can flow easily through the diode. When the voltage is reversed, the diode becomes non-conducting and only allows a very slight amount of current to flow in the circuit. Because the semiconductor is not a perfect insulator, a small amount of reverse current leakage will occur, but the amount is usually too small to consider. The application of voltage to maintain the current flow described is called "forward bias."

A light-emitting diode (LED) is made of a particular type of crystal that glows when current is passed through it. LED's are used in display faces of many digital or electronic instrument clusters. LED's are usually arranged to display numbers (digital readout), but can be used to illuminate a variety of electronic graphic displays.

Like any other electrical device, diodes have certain ratings that must be observed and should not be exceeded. The forward current rating (or bias) indicates how much current can safely pass through the diode without causing damage or destroying it. Forward current rating is usually given in either amperes or milliamperes. The voltage drop across a diode remains constant regardless of the current flowing through it. Small diodes designed to carry low amounts of current need no special provision for dissipating the heat generated in any electrical device, but large current carrying diodes are usually mounted on heat sinks

to keep the internal temperature from rising to the point where the silicon will melt and destroy the diode. When diodes are operated in a high ambient temperature environment, they must be de-rated to prevent failure.

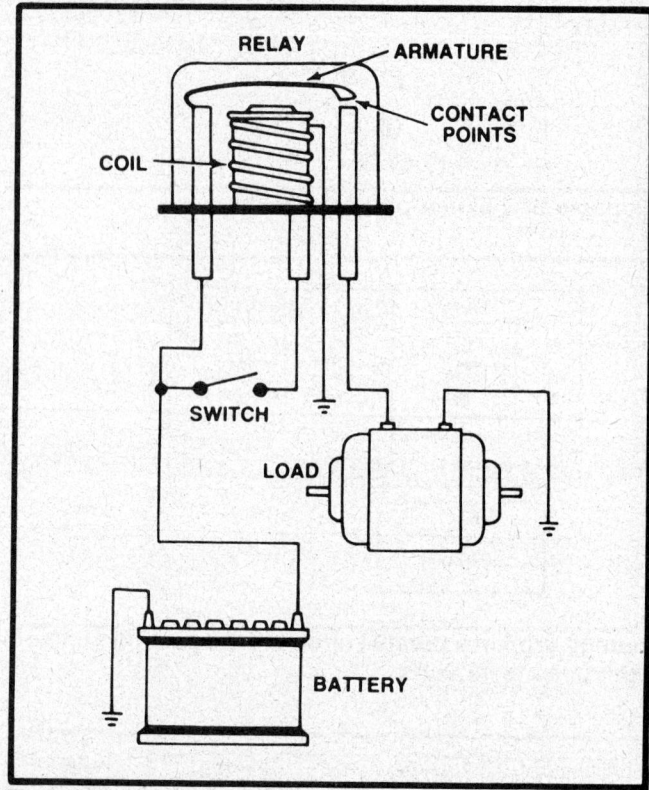

Typical relay circuit with basic components

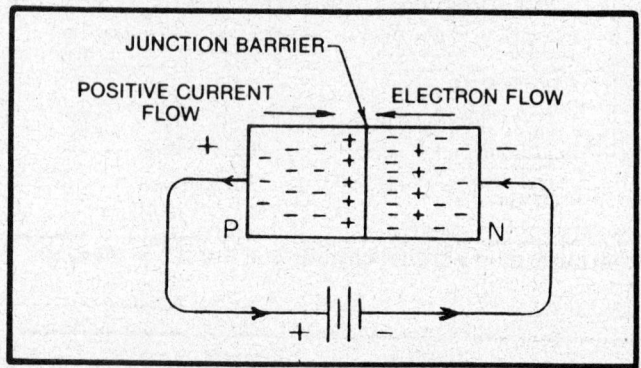

Diode with forward bias

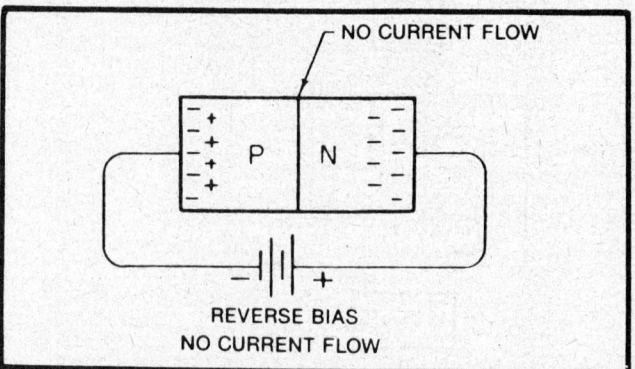

Diode with reverse bias

Another diode specification is its peak inverse voltage rating. This value is the maximum amount of voltage the diode can safely handle when operating in the blocking mode. This value can be anywhere from 50–1000 volts, depending on the diode. If voltage amount is exceeded, it will damage the diode just as too much forward current will. Most semiconductor failures are caused by excessive voltage or internal heat.

One can test a diode with a small battery and a lamp with the same voltage rating. With this arrangement one can find a bad diode and determine the polarity of a good one. A diode can fail and cause either a short or open circuit, but in either case it fails to function as a diode. Testing is simply a matter of connecting the test bulb first in one direction and then the other and making sure that current flows in one direction only. If the diode is shorted, the test bulb will remain on no matter how the light is connected.

TRANSISTORS

The transistor is an electrical device used to control voltage within a circuit. A transistor can be considered a "controllable diode" in that, in addition to passing or blocking current, the transistor can control the amount of current passing through it. Simple transistors are composed of 3 pieces of semiconductor material, P and N type, joined together and enclosed in a container. If 2 sections of P material and 1 section of N material are used, it is known as a PNP transistor; if the reverse is true, then it is known as an NPN transistor. The 2 types cannot be interchanged.

Most modern transistors are made from silicon (earlier transistors were made from germanium) and contain 3 elements; the emitter, the collector and the base. In addition to passing or blocking current, the transistor can control the amount of current passing through it and because of this can function as an amplifier or a switch. The collector and emitter form the main current-carrying circuit of the transistor. The amount of current that flows through the collector-emitter junction is controlled by the amount of current in the base circuit. Only a small amount of base-emitter current is necessary to control a large amount of collector-emitter current (the amplifier effect). In automotive applications, however, the transistor is used primarily as a switch.

When no current flows in the base-emitter junction, the collector-emitter circuit has a high resistance, like to open contacts of a relay. Almost no current flows through the circuit and transistor is considered OFF. By bypassing a small amount of current into the base circuit, the resistance is low, allowing current to flow through the circuit and turning the transistor ON. This condition is known as "saturation" and is reached when the base current reaches the maximum value designed into the transistor that allows current to flow. Depending on various factors, the transistor can turn on and off (go from cutoff to saturation) in less than one millionth of a second.

Much of what was said about ratings for diodes applies to transistors, since they are constructed of the same materials. When transistors are required to handle relatively high currents, such as in voltage regulators or ignition systems, they are generally mounted on heat sinks in the same manner as diodes. They can be damaged or destroyed in the same manner if their voltage ratings are exceeded. A transistor can be checked for proper operation by measuring the resistance with an ohmmeter between the base-emitter terminals and then between the base-collector terminals. The forward resistance should be small, while the reverse resistance should be large. Compare the readings with those from a known good transistor. As a final check, measure the forward and reverse resistance between the collector and emitter terminals.

INTEGRATED CIRCUITS

The integrated circuit (IC) is an extremely sophisticated solid

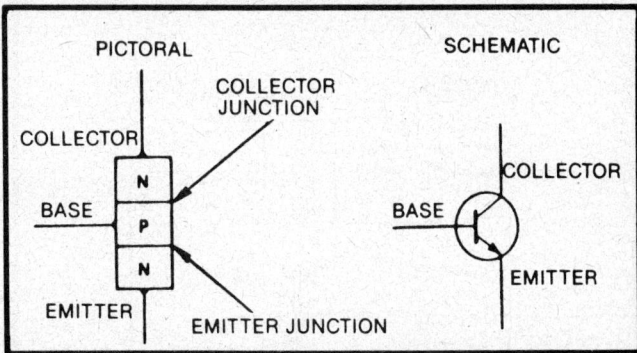

NPN transistor illustrations (pictorial and schematic)

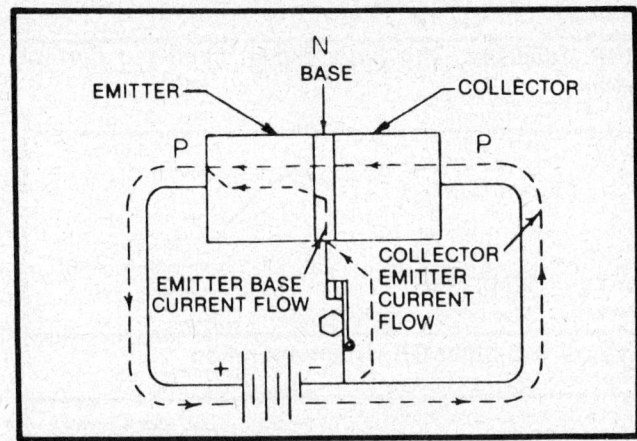

PNP transistor with base switch closed (base emitter and collector emitter current flow)

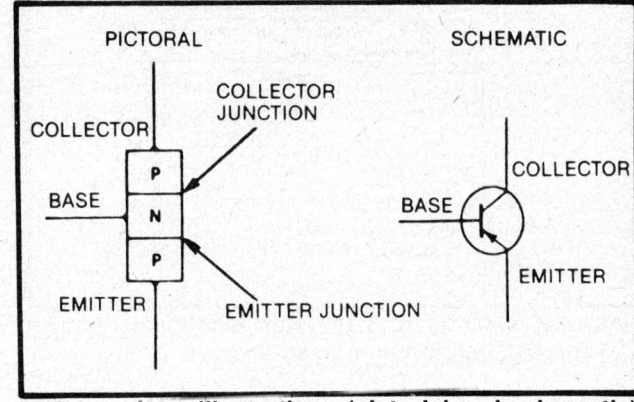

PNP transistor illustrations (pictorial and schematic)

state device that consists of a silicone wafer (or chip) which has been doped, insulated and etched many times so that it contains an entire electrical circuit with transistors, diodes, conductors and capacitors miniaturized within each tiny chip. Integrated circuits are often referred to as "computers on a chip" and are largely responsible for the current boom in electronic control technology.

Microprocessors, Computers and Logic Systems

Mechanical or electromechanical control devices lack the precision necessary to meet the requirements of modern control standards. They do not have the ability to respond to a variety of

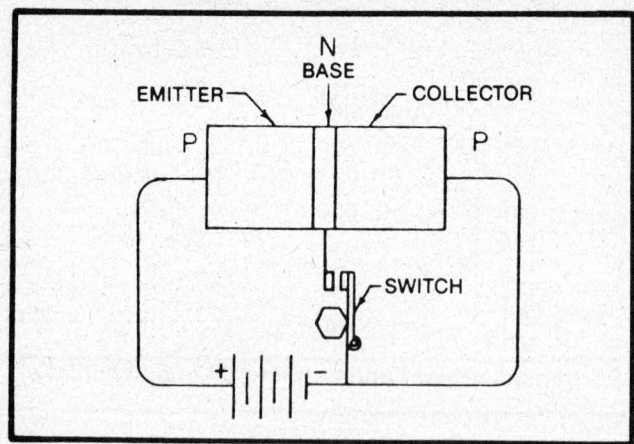

PNP transistor with base switch open (no current flow)

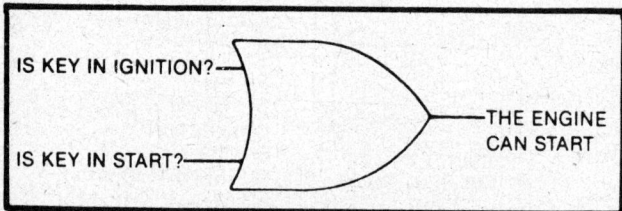

Typical two-input OR circuit operation

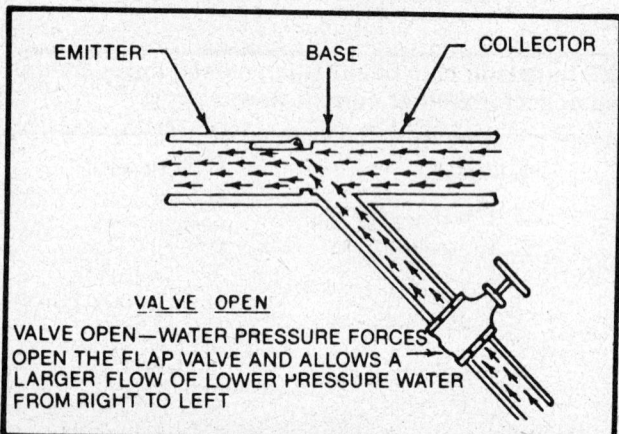

Hydraulic analogy to transistor function is shown with the base circuit energized

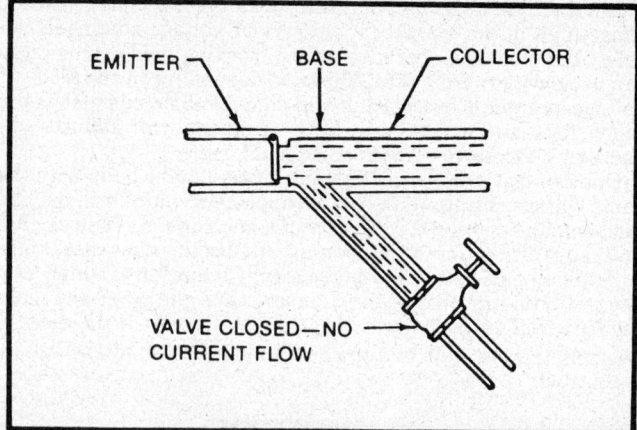

Hydraulic analogy to transistor function is shown with the base circuit shut off

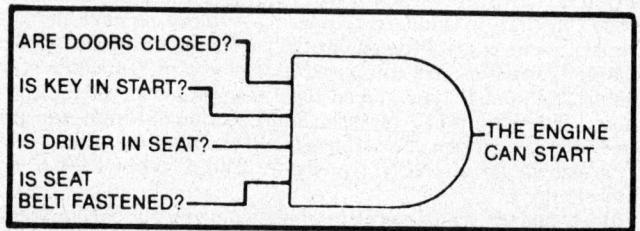

Multiple input AND operation in a typical automotive starting circuit

input conditions common to antilock brakes, climate control and electronic suspension operation. To meet these requirements, manufacturers have gone to solid state logic systems and microprocessors to control the basic functions of suspension, brake and temperature control, as well as other systems and accessories.

One of the more vital roles of microprocessor-based systems is their ability to perform logic functions and make decisions. Logic designers use a shorthand notation to indicate whether a voltage is present in a circuit (the number 1) or not present (the number 0). Their systems are designed to respond in different ways depending on the output signal (or the lack of it) from various control devices.

There are 3 basic logic functions or "gates" used to construct a microprocessor control system: the AND gate, the OR gate or the NOT gate. Stated simply, the AND gate works when voltage is present in 2 or more circuits which then energize a third (A

and B energize C). The OR gate works when voltage is present at either circuit A or circuit B which then energizes circuit C. The NOT function is performed by a solid state device called an "inverter" which reverses the input from a circuit so that, if voltage is going in, no voltage comes out and vice versa. With these three basic building blocks, a logic designer can create complex systems easily. In actual use, a logic or decision making system may employ many logic gates and receive inputs from a number of sources (sensors), but for the most part, all utilize the basic logic gates discussed above.

Stripped to its bare essentials, a computerized decision-making system is made up of three subsystems:
  a. Input devices (sensors or switches)
  b. Logic circuits (computer control unit)
  c. Output devices (actuators or controls)

The input devices are usually nothing more than switches or sensors that provide a voltage signal to the control unit logic circuits that is read as a 1 or 0 (on or off) by the logic circuits. The output devices are anything from a warning light to solenoid-operated valves, motors, linkage, etc. In most cases, the logic circuits themselves lack sufficient output power to operate these devices directly. Instead, they operate some intermediate device such as a relay or power transistor which in turn operates the appropriate device or control. Many problems diagnosed as computer failures are really the result of a malfunctioning intermediate device like a relay. This must be kept in mind whenever troubleshooting any microprocessor-based control system.

The logic systems discussed above are called "hardware" systems, because they consist only of the physical electronic components (gates, resistors, transistors, etc.). Hardware systems do not contain a program and are designed to perform specific or "dedicated" functions which cannot readily be changed. For many simple automotive control requirements, such dedicated logic systems are perfectly adequate. When more complex logic functions are required, or where it may be desirable to alter these functions (e.g. from one model vehicle to another) a true computer system is used. A computer can be programmed through its software to perform many different functions and, if that program is stored on a separate integrated circuit chip called a ROM (Read Only Memory), it can be easily changed simply by plugging in a different ROM with the desired program. Most on-board automotive computers are designed with this capability. The on-board computer method of engine control offers the manufacturer a flexible method of responding to data from a variety of input devices and of controlling an equally large variety of output controls. The computer response can be changed quickly and easily by simply modifying its software program.

The microprocessor is the heart of the microcomputer. It is the thinking part of the computer system through which all the data from the various sensors passes. Within the microprocessor, data is acted upon, compared, manipulated or stored for future use. A microprocessor is not necessarily a microcomputer, but the differences between the 2 are becoming very minor. Originally, a microprocessor was a major part of a microcomputer, but nowadays microprocessors are being called "single-chip microcomputers". They contain all the essential elements to make them behave as a computer, including the most important ingredient–the program.

All computers require a program. In a general purpose computer, the program can be easily changed to allow different tasks to be performed. In a "dedicated" computer, such as most on-board automotive computers, the program isn't quite so easily altered. These automotive computers are designed to perform one or several specific tasks, such as maintaining the passenger compartment temperature at a specific, predetermined level. A program is what makes a computer smart; without a program a computer can do absolutely nothing. The term "software" refers to the computer's program that makes the hardware preform the function needed.

The software program is simply a listing in sequential order of the steps or commands necessary to make a computer perform the desired task. Before the computer can do anything at all, the program must be fed into it by one of several possible methods. A computer can never be "smarter" than the person programming it, but it is a lot faster. Although it cannot perform any calculation or operation that the programmer himself cannot perform, its processing time is measured in millionths of a second.

Because a computer is limited to performing only those operations (instructions) programmed into its memory, the program must be broken down into a large number of very simple steps. Two different programmers can come up with 2 different programs, since there is usually more than one way to perform any task or solve a problem. In any computer, however, there is only so much memory space available, so an overly long or inefficient program may not fit into the memory. In addition to performing arithmetic functions (such as with a trip computer), a computer can also store data, look up data in a table and perform the logic functions previously discussed. A Random Access Memory (RAM) allows the computer to store bits of data temporarily while waiting to be acted upon by the program. It may also be used to store output data that is to be sent to an output device. Whatever data is stored in a RAM is lost when power is removed from the system by turning **OFF** the ignition key, for example.

Computers have another type of memory called a Read Only Memory (ROM) which is permanent. This memory is not lost when the power is removed from the system. Most programs for automotive computers are stored on a ROM memory chip. Data is usually in the form of a look-up table that saves computing time and program steps. For example, a computer designed to control the amount of distributor advance can have this information stored in a table. The information that determines distributor advance (engine rpm, manifold vacuum and temperature) is coded to produce the correct amount of distributor advance over a wide range of engine operating conditions. Instead of the computer computing the required advance, it simply looks it up in a pre-programmed table. However, not all electronic control functions can be handled in this manner; some must be

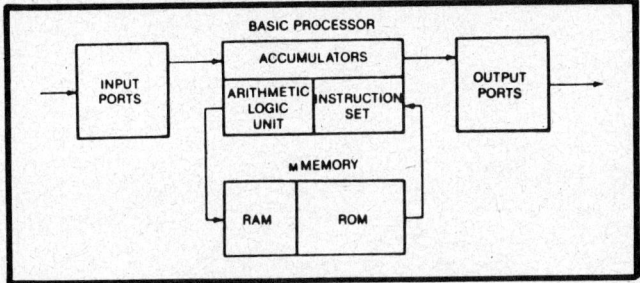

Schematic of typical microprocessor based on-board computer showing essential components

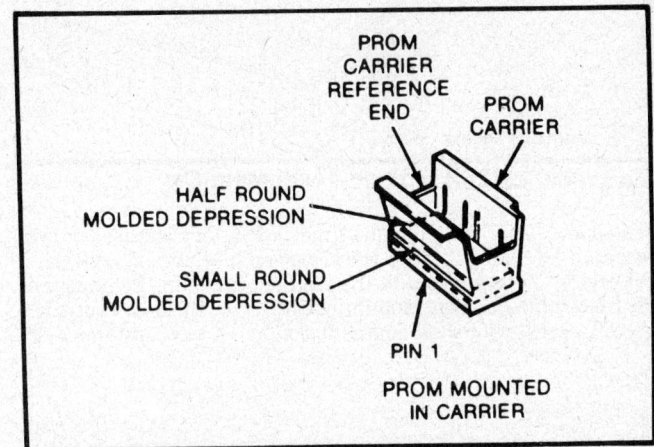

Typical PROM showing carrier refernce markings

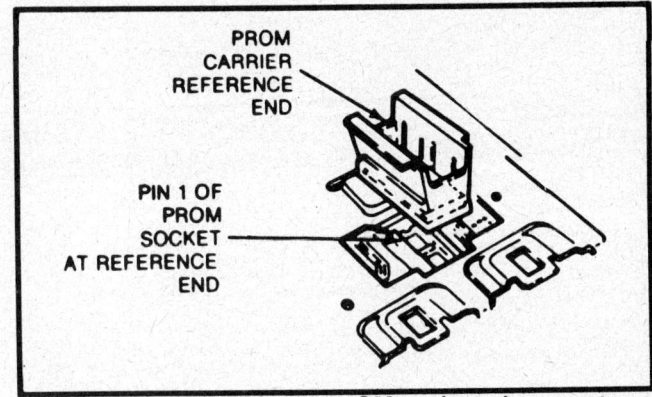

Installation of PROM unit in GM on-board computer

computed. On an antilock brake system, for example, the computer must measure the rotation of each separate wheel and then calculate how much brake pressure to apply in order to prevent one wheel from locking up and causing a loss of control.

There are several ways of programming a ROM, but once programmed the ROM cannot be changed. If the ROM is made on the same chip that contains the microprocessor, the whole computer must be altered if a program change is needed. For this reason, a ROM is usually placed on a separate chip. Another type of memory is the Programmable Read Only Memory (PROM) that has the program "burned in" with the appropriate programming machine. Like the ROM, once a PROM has been programmed, it cannot be changed. The advantage of the PROM is that it can be produced in small quantities economically, since it is manufactured with a blank memory. Program changes for various vehicles can be made readily. There is still another type of memory called an EPROM (Erasable PROM) which can be

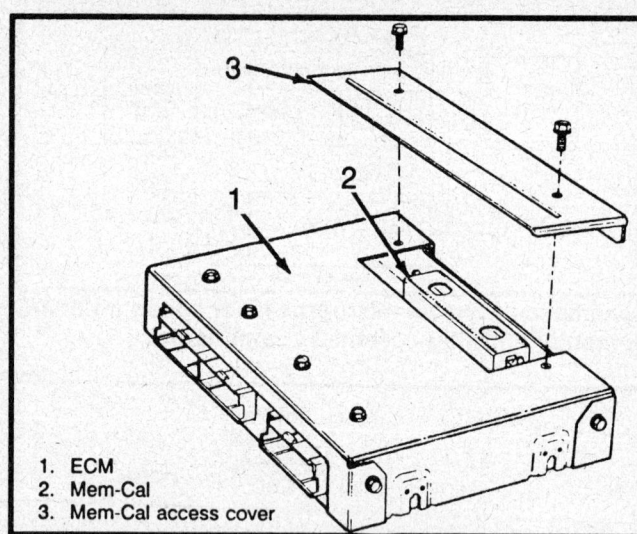

1. ECM
2. Mem-Cal
3. Mem-Cal access cover

Electronic control module—with Mem-Cal

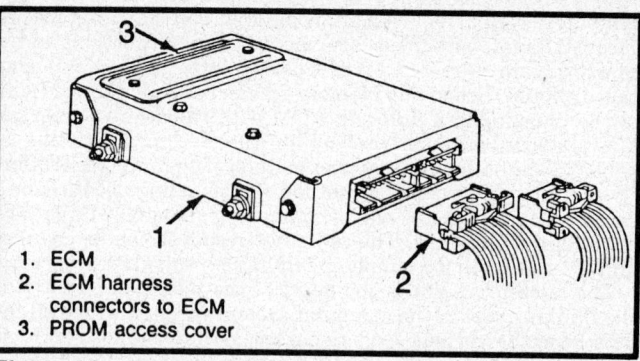

1. ECM
2. ECM harness connectors to ECM
3. PROM access cover

Electronic control module—with PROM and CalPak

erased and programmed many times. EPROM's are used only in research and development work, not on production vehicles.

General Motors refers to the engine controlling computer as an Electronic Control Module (ECM). The ECM contains the PROM necessary for all engine functions, it also contains a de-

vice called a CalPak. This allows the fuel delivery function should other parts of the ECM become damaged. It has an access door in the ECM, like the PROM has. There is a third type control module used in some ECMs called a Mem-Cal. The Mem-Cal contains the function of PROM, CalPak and Electronic Spark Control (EST) module. Like the PROM, it contains the calibrations needed for a specific vehicle, as well as the back-up fuel control circuitry required if the rest of the ECM should become damaged and the spark control. An ECM containing a PROM and CalPak can be identified by the 2 connector harnesses, while the ECM containing the Mem-Cal has 3 connector harnesses attached to it.

AAC – Auxiliary Air Control Valve

AAV – Anti Afterburning Valve

A/C – Air Conditioning

ACC – Air Conditioner Clutch Compressor

ACT – Air Charge Temperature sensor

ACV – Air Control Valve

AI – Air Injection

AIC – Automatic Idling Control valve

AIR GAP – The distance or space between the reluctor tooth and pick up coil.

AIR SENSOR – An air cone with a floating plate which measures air flow and determines plunger position on K-Jetronic type systems.

AIS – Automatic Idle Speed motor

AIS – Air Injection System

AIV – Air Injection Valve

AFS – Air Flow Sensor

A/F – Air/Fuel Ratio

AFC – Air Flow Controlled fuel injection

AMMETER – An electrical meter used to measure current flow (amperes) in an electrical circuit. Ammeter should be connected in series and current flowing in the circuit to be checked.

AMPERE (AMP) – The unit current flow is measured in Amperage equals the voltage divided by the resistance.

ARMATURE – See Reluctor for definition

ATS – Air Temperature Sensor

A/T – Automatic Transmission

APC – Automatic Performance Control

AUXILIARY AIR REGULATOR – A rotary gate valve which stabilizes idle speed during engine warm-up.

AWG – American Wire Gauge system

BAC – Bypass Air Control system

BAR – Unit of pressure measurement (1 bar is approximately 14.5 psi)

BID – Breakerless Inductive Discharge ignition system

BP – Barometric Pressure

BPA – Bypass Air Valve

BPCSV – Bypass Control Solenoid Valve

BTDC – Before Top Dead Center

CALIBRATION ASSEMBLY – A memory module that plugs into an on-board computer and contains instructions for engine operation.

CANISTER – a container in an emission control system that contains charcoal to trap fuel vapors from the fuel system.

CANP – Canister Purge solenoid that opens the fuel vapor canister line to the intake manifold when energized.

CAPACITOR – A device which stores an electrical charge

CATALYST – Special metals such as platinum and palladium that are contained within a catalytic converter. The catalyst contacts the hot exhaust gases and promotes more complete combustion of unburned hydrocarbons and reduction of carbon monoxide.

CC – Catalytic Converter

CCO – Converter Clutch Override

CFC – Coasting Fuel Cut

CHM – Cold Mixture Heater

CIS – Continuous Injection System, Bosch K-Jetronic type system

CIS-III – Electronic Continuous Injection System, Bosch L or LH- Jetronic type system

CIS-E – Electronic Continuous Injection System, Bosch L or LH- Jetronic type system

CO – Carbon monoxide

CONTROL PRESSURE – The lower chamber pressure, which is controlled by the EHA, to control mixture, warm up and deceleration air/fuel ratio.

CP – Crankshaft Position sensor

CPU – Central Processing Unit

CONDUCTOR – Any material through which an electrical current can be transmitted easily.

CONTINUITY – Continuous or complete circuit. The type of circuit that can be checked with an ohmmeter.

CYL SENSOR – Crankshaft Angle Sensor

DAMPING RESTRICTION – Bore of small cross section in the fuel distributor of the K-Jetronic type system. It dampens sensor plate movement in the air flow sensor during high load and low rpm conditions.

DI – Direct Ignition system, each spark plug has its own ignition coil

DIELECTRIC SILICONE COMPOUND – Non-conducting silicone grease applied to spark plug wire boots, rotors and connectors to prevent arcing and moisture from entering a connector.

DIFFERENTIAL PRESSURE – The difference in pressure between the upper and lower chambers of a CIS fuel distributor.

DIFFERENTIAL PRESSURE REGULATOR – An electronically controlled valve which regulates the fuel flow to the lower chamber of the CIS fuel distributor.

DIODE – An electrical devise that will allow current to flow in one direction only

DME – Digital motor electronics; a single control unit for both fuel injection and ignition control.

DSV – Deceleration Solenoid Valve

EACV – Electronic Air Control Valve

ECCS – Electronic Concentrated Control System

ECI – Electronic Control Injection

ECIT – Electronic Control Ignition Timing

ECM – Electronic Control Module

ECS – Emission Control System

ECT – Engine Coolant Temperature sensor

ECT – Electronic Controlled Transmission

ECU – Electronic Control Unit

EEC – Evaporative Emission Control

EFC – Electronic Fuel Control

EFE – Early Fuel Evaporation

EFI – Electronic Fuel Injection

EGI – Electronic Gasoline Injection

EGO – Exhaust Gas Oxygen sensor

EGR – Exhaust Gas Recirculation

EGRC – EGR Control solenoid

EGRV – EGR Vent solenoid

EHA – Electrohydraulic actuator, same as differential pressure regulator.

EICV – Electronic Idle Control Valve

EIS – Electronic Ignition System which uses a reluctor and a pick up coil along with a module to replace the ignition points and condenser.

EIS – Electronic Injection System

ELECTRONIC CONTROL UNIT (ECU) – On board computer module, used to control ignition, fuel or other engine functions.

ELECTROHYDRAULIC ACTUATOR (EHA) – An electronically controlled valve which regulates the fuel flow to the lower chamber of the CIS fuel distributor.

ELCD – Evaporative Loss Control Device

E/L – Electrical Load control unit

EMR – Emissions Maintenance Reminder

EMW – Emission Maintenance Warning

ESA – Electronic Spark Advance

ESC – Electronic Spark Control

ESS – Engine Speed Sensor

EVP – EGR Valve Position sensor

EZK – Elektrische Zundkontrolle, electronically controlled ignition

FCS – Fuel Control Solenoid

FCV – Float Chamber Ventilation system

FICB – Fast Idle Cam Breaker

FOM – Fix operating Mode, limp-in mode

FUEL ACCUMULATOR – Diaphragm unit which helps maintain residual fuel pressure for hot starting on CIS type fuel systems.

FUEL DISTRIBUTOR – The component which feeds fuel to the individual engine cylinders corresponding to the air flow rate metered by the air flow sensor on CIS systems.

GND or GRD – Ground or negative (–)

HAI – Hot Air Intake

HALL EFFECT PICK-UP ASSEMBLY – Used to input a signal to the electronic control unit. The system operates on the Hall Effect principle whereby a magnetic field is blocked from the pick-up by a rotating shutter assembly.

HC – Hydrocarbons. Any compound composed of hydrogen and carbon, such as petroleum products, that is considered a pollutant.

HCV – Exhaust Heat Control Valve

HEGO – Heat Exhaust Gas Oxygen sensor

HIC – Hot Idle Compensation

HT – High Tension

IAS – Inlet Air Solenoid

IC – Integrated Circuit

IDLE AIR STABILIZATION VALVE – Electronically controlled valve used to maintain idle speed at a predetermined level.

IG – Ignition

IGNITER – Term used by Japanese automotive and ignition manufacturers for the electronic control unit or module.

IGNITION COIL – Step-up transformer consisting of a primary and a secondary winding with an iron core. As the current flows in the primary winding stops, the magnetic field collapses across the secondary winding inducing the high secondary voltage. The coil may be oil filled or of an epoxy type design.

IMS – Inferred Mileage Sensor

INDUCTION – A means of transferring electrical energy in the form of a magnetic field. Principle used in the ignition coil to increase voltage.

INFINITY – An ohmmeter reading which indicates an open circuit in which no current will flow.

INJECTION VALVE – Same as injector

INJECTOR – a solenoid or pressure-operated fuel delivery valve used for fuel injection systems

INTERGRATED CIRCUIT (IC) – Electronic micro-circuit consisting of a semi-conductor components or elements made using thick-flim or thin-flim technology. Elements are located on a small chip made of a semi-conducting material, greatly reducing the size of the electronic control unit and allowing it to be incorporated within the distributor.

IMA Sensor – Idle Mixture Adjuster Sensor

I/O – Input/Output, for computer data transmission

ISC – Idle Speed Control device

ITS – Idle Tracking Switch. An input device that sends a signal to the control module to indicate throttle position

JSV – Jet Mixture Solenoid Valve

KDLH – Kick-Down Low Hold

KS – Knock Sensor. An input device that responds to spark knock caused by excessively advanced ignition timing

K-JETRONIC – Fuel induction by means of CIS fuel injection dependent upon the measurement of air intake by a mechanical air flow sensor.

LED – Light Emitting Diode

LOS – Limited Operation Strategy

L-JETRONIC – A CIS-E fuel injection system dependent upon the measurement of air intake by an vane type electrical air flow meter and air temperature sensor. The L stands for air flow.

LH-JETRONIC – A CIS-E fuel injection system dependent upon the measurement of air intake by a hot wire type mass air flow sensor. The LH stand for air flow and hot wire sensor.

MAF – Mass Airflow sensor. A device used to measure the amount of intake air entering the engine on some fuel injection systems

MAP – Manifold Air Pressure sensor

MAS – Mixture Adjust Screw

M/C – Mixture Control

MCT – Manifold Charge Temperature sensor

MCSV – Mixture Control Solenoid Valve

MCV – Mixture Control Valve

MICROPROCESSORS – A miniature computer on a silicone chip

MIL – Malfunction Indicator Light

MODULE – Electronic control unit, amplifier or igniter of solid state or integrated design which controls the current flow in the ignition primary circuit based on input from the pick-up coil. When the module opens the primary circuit, the high secondary voltage is induced in the coil.

MPFI – Multi-Point Fuel Injection

MPS – Motor Position Sensor

MS – Millisecond

M/T – Manual Transmission

NDS – Neutral/Drive Switch

NGS – Neutral Gear Switch

NTS – Negative Temperature Coefficient Resistor

NOx – Nitrous Oxide. A compound formed during the engine combustion process when oxygen in the air combines with nitrogen to form photochemical smog.

OCC – Output Cycling Check

OHM – the electrical unit of resistance to current flow

OHMMETER – the electrical meter used to measure the resistance in ohms. Self-powered and must be connected to a voltage free circuit or damage to the ohmmeter will result.

OXYGEN SENSOR – used with the feedback system to sense the presence of oxygen in the exhaust gas and signal the computer which can reference the voltage signal to an air/fuel ratio.

OVCV – Outer Vent Control Valve

PA SENSOR – Atmospheric Pressure Sensor

PCV – Positive Crankcase Ventilation

PGM-FI – Programmed Fuel Injection system

PGM-IG – Programmed Ignition system

PHENOMENA – Basis of symptoms

PICK-UP COIL – inputs signal to the electronic control unit to open the primary circuit. Consists of a fine wire coil mounted around a permanent magnet. As the reluctor's ferrous tooth passes through the magnetic field an alternating current is produced, signaling the electronic control unit. Can operate on the principle of metal detecting, magnetic induction or Hall Effect. Is also referred to as a stator or sensor.

PIP – Profile Ignition Pickup

POTENTIOMETER – a variable resistor used to change a voltage signal

PRC – Pressure Regulator Control solenoid

PRE-PUMP – In-tank fuel pump

PRIMARY CIRCUIT – is the low voltage side of the ignition system which consists of the ignition switch, ballast resistor or resistance wire, bypass, coil, electronic control unit and pick-up coil as well as the connecting wires and harnesses.

PSPS – Power Steering Pressure Switch

PTC HEATER – Positive Temperature Coefficient Heater

PULSE GENERATOR – also called a pulse signal generator. Term used by Japanese and German automotive and ignition manufacturers to describe the pick-up and reluctor assembly. Generates an electrical pulse which triggers the electronic control unit or igniter.

PULSE WIDTH – the amount of time the control unit energizes the fuel injectors to spray fuel into the intake manifold, usually measured in millisecond.s

PVS – Ported Vacuum Switch. A temperature-activated switch that changes vacuum connections when the coolant temperature changes.

RAD – Radiator Temperature Switch

RAM – Random Access Memory

RELAY – a switching device operated by a low-current circuit which controls the opening and closing of another circuit of higher current capacity.

RELUCTOR – Also called an armature or trigger wheel. Ferrous metal piece attached to the distributor shaft. Made up of teeth of which the number are the same as the number of engine cylinders. As the reluctor teeth pass through the pick-up magnetic field an alternating current is generated in the pick-up coil.

RESISTANCE – The opposition to the flow of current through a circuit or electrical device, and is measured in ohms. Resistance is equal to the voltage divided by the amperage.

RESIDUAL PRESSURE – Pressure remaining in the fuel system after the engine has be shut off.

ROM – Read Only Memory

RXD – Receive data line

SAS – Speed Adjusting Screw

SCSV – Slow Cut Solenoid Valve

SECONDARY – The high voltage side of the ignition system, usually above 20,000 volts. The secondary includes the ignition coil, coil wire, distributor cap and rotor, spark plug wires and spark plug.

SENSOR – Also called the pick-up coil or stator. See pick-up coil for definition.

SENSOR PLATE – A round plate bolted to the air flow sensor lever which floats in the stream of intake air on the CIS type systems.

SHUTTER – also called the vane. Used in a Hall Effect distributor to block the magnetic field from the Hall Effect pick-up. The shutter is attached to the rotor and is grounded to the distributor shaft.

SOLENOID – A wire coil with a movable core which changes position by means of electromagnetism when current flows through the coil.

SPARK DURATION – The length of time measured in milliseconds($\frac{1}{1000}$th second) the spark is established across the spark plug gap.

SPFI – Single Point Fuel Injection

SPOUT – Spark Output

STATOR – another name for a pick-coil. See pick-up coil for definition

SWITCHING TRANSISTOR – Used in some electronic ignition systems, it acts as a switch for high current in response to a low voltage signal applied to the base terminal.

SYSTEM PRESSURE – Fuel pressure in the CIS fuel distributor controlled by the pressure regulator.

TA SENSOR – Intake Air Temperature Sensor

TAB – Thermactor Air Bypass solenoid

TAD – Thermactor Air Diverter Solenoid

TAS – Throttle Adjust Screw

TCA – Thermostat Controlled Air Cleaner

TCP – Temperature Compensated Accelerator Pump

TDC – Top Dead Center

THERMO-TIME SWITCH – A switch which interupts the electrical circuit of the cold start injector based on temperature and time.

THERMISTOR – A device that changes its resistance with temperature.

TK or TKS – Throttle Kicker Solenoid. An actuator moves the throttle linkage to increase idle rpm

TPI – Tuned Port Injection

TP or TPS – Throttle Position Sensor

TRANSFER PUMP – Fuel pump located in the fuel tank, usually used with a 2 pump system.

TRANSISTOR – A semi-conductor component which can be actuated by a small voltage to perform an electrical switching function

TRIGGER WHEEL – See Reluctor for definition

TVSV – Thermostatic Vacuum Switching Valve

TW SENSOR – Coolant Temperature Sensor

TWC – Three-way catalyst, sometimes referred to as a dual catalytic converter. Combines 2 catalytic converters in one shell to control emissions of NOx, HC and CO.

TWSV – Three Way Solenoid Valve

TXD – Transmitted data line

VAF – Vane Airflow Meter

VAT – Vane Air Temperature

VB VOLTAGE – Battery Voltage

VCM – Vehicle Condition Monitor

VCV – Vacuum Control Valve

VECI – Vehicle Emission Control Information label

VF VOLTAGE – Battery Voltage

VIS – Variable Induction System

VM – Vane Meter

VLC – Vacuum Sensor and Vacuum Line Charging solenoid valve

VOLT – The unit of electrical pressure or electromotive force

VOLTAGE DROP – The difference in voltage between one point in a circuit and another, usually across a resistance. Voltage drop is measured in parallel with current flowing in the circuit.

VOLTMETER – An electrical meter used to measure voltage in a circuit. Voltmeters must be connected in parallel across the load or circuit.

VREF – The reference voltage or power supplied by the computer control unit to some sensors regulated at a specific voltage.

VSV – Vacuum Switching Valve

VTV – Vacuum Transmitting Valve

VVC – Variable Voltage Choke

WOT – Wide Open Throttle switch

Mechanics' Data **30**

SI METRIC TABLES

The following tables are given in SI (International System) metric units. SI units replace both customary (English) and the older gavimetric units. The use of SI units as a new worldwide standard was set by the International Committee of Weights and Measures in 1960. SI has since been adopted by most countries as their national standard.

These tables are general conversion tables which will allow you to convert customary units, which appear in the text, into SI units.

The following are a list of SI units and the customary units, used in this book, which they replace:

To measure:	Use SI units:	Which replace (customary units):
mass	kilograms (kg)	pounds (lbs)
temperature	Celsius (°C)	Fahrenheit (°F)
length	millimeters (mm)	inches (in.)
force	newtons (N)	pounds force (lbs)
capacities	liters (l)	pints/quarts/gallons (pts/qts/gals)
torque	newton-meters (N·m)	foot pounds (ft lbs)
pressure	kilopascals (kPa)	pounds per square inch (psi)
volume	cubic centimeters (cm')	cubic inches (cu in.)
power	kilowatts (kW)	horsepower (hp)

If you have had any prior experience with the metric system, you may have noticed units in this chart which are not familiar to you. This is because, in some cases, SI units differ from the older gravimetric units which they replace. For example, newtons (N) replace kilograms (kg) as a force unit, kilopascals (kPa) replace atmospheres or bars as a unit of pressure, and, although the units are the same, the name Celsius replaces centigrade for temperature measurement.

If you are not using the SI tables, have a look at them anyway; you will be seeing a lot more of them in the future.

ENGLISH TO METRIC CONVERSION: MASS (WEIGHT)

Current mass measurement is expressed in pounds and ounces (lbs. & ozs.). The metric unit of mass (or weight) is the kilogram (kg). Even although this table does not show conversion of masses (weights) larger than 15 lbs, it is easy to calculate larger units by following the data immediately below.

To convert ounces (oz.) to grams (g): multiply th number of ozs. by 28
To convert grams (g) to ounces (oz.): multiply the number of grams by .035

To convert pounds (lbs.) to kilograms (kg): multiply the number of lbs. by .45
To convert kilograms (kg) to pounds (lbs.): multiply the number of kilograms by 2.2

lbs	kg	lbs	kg	oz	kg	oz	kg
0.1	0.04	0.9	0.41	0.1	0.003	0.9	0.024
0.2	0.09	1	0.4	0.2	0.005	1	0.03
0.3	0.14	2	0.9	0.3	0.008	2	0.06
0.4	0.18	3	1.4	0.4	0.011	3	0.08
0.5	0.23	4	1.8	0.5	0.014	4	0.11
0.6	0.27	5	2.3	0.6	0.017	5	0.14
0.7	0.32	10	4.5	0.7	0.020	10	0.28
0.8	0.36	15	6.8	0.8	0.023	15	0.42

ENGLISH TO METRIC CONVERSION: TEMPERATURE

To convert Fahrenheit (°F) to Celsius (°C): take number of °F and subtract 32; multiply result by 5; divide result by 9

To convert Celsius (°C) to Fahrenheit (°F): take number of °C and multiply by 9; divide result by 5; add 32 to total

Fahrenheit (F)		Celsius (C)		Fahrenheit (F)		Celsius (C)		Fahrenheit (F)		Celsius (C)	
°F	°C	°C	°F	°F	°C	°C	°F	°F	°C	°C	°F
−40	−40	−38	−36.4	80	26.7	18	64.4	215	101.7	80	176
−35	−37.2	−36	−32.8	85	29.4	20	68	220	104.4	85	185
−30	−34.4	−34	−29.2	90	32.2	22	71.6	225	107.2	90	194
−25	−31.7	−32	−25.6	95	35.0	24	75.2	230	110.0	95	202
−20	−28.9	−30	−22	100	37.8	26	78.8	235	112.8	100	212
−15	−26.1	−28	−18.4	105	40.6	28	82.4	240	115.6	105	221
−10	−23.3	−26	−14.8	1'0	43.3	30	86	245	118.3	110	230
−5	−20.6	−24	−11.2	115	46.1	32	89.6	250	121.1	115	239
0	−17.8	−22	−7.6	120	48.9	34	93.2	255	123.9	120	248
1	−17.2	−20	−4	125	51.7	36	96.8	260	126.6	125	257
2	−16.7	−18	−0.4	130	54.4	38	100.4	265	129.4	130	266
3	−16.1	−16	3.2	135	57.2	40	104	270	132.2	135	275
4	−15.6	−14	6.8	140	60.0	42	107.6	275	135.0	140	284
5	−15.0	−12	10.4	145	62.8	44	112.2	280	137.8	145	293
10	−12.2	−10	14	150	65.6	46	114.8	285	140.6	150	302
15	−9.4	−8	17.6	155	68.3	48	118.4	290	143.3	155	311
20	−6.7	−6	21.2	160	71.1	50	122	295	146.1	160	320
25	−3.9	−4	24.8	165	73.9	52	125.6	300	148.9	165	329
30	−1.1	−2	28.4	170	76.7	54	129.2	305	151.7	170	338
35	1.7	0	32	175	79.4	56	132.8	310	154.4	175	347
40	4.4	2	35.6	180	82.2	58	136.4	315	157.2	180	356
45	7.2	4	39.2	185	85.0	60	140	320	160.0	185	365
50	10.0	6	42.8	190	87.8	62	143.6	325	162.8	190	374
55	12.8	8	46.4	195	90.6	64	147.2	330	165.6	195	383
60	15.6	10	50	200	93.3	66	150.8	335	168.3	200	392
65	18.3	12	53.6	205	96.1	68	154.4	340	171.1	205	401
70	21.1	14	57.2	210	98.9	70	158	345	173.9	210	410
75	23.9	16	60.8	212	100.0	75	167	350	176.7	215	414

ENGLISH TO METRIC CONVERSION: LENGTH

To convert inches (ins.) to millimeters (mm): multiply number of inches by 25.4

To convert millimeters (mm) to inches (ins.): multiply number of millimeters by .04

Inches	Decimals	Milli-meters	Inches to millimeters inches	mm	Inches	Decimals	Milli-meters	Inches to millimeters inches	mm
1/64	0.051625	0.3969	0.0001	0.00254	33/64	0.515625	13.0969	0.6	15.24
1/32	0.03125	0.7937	0.0002	0.00508	17/32	0.53125	13.4937	0.7	17.78
3/64	0.046875	1.1906	0.0003	0.00762	35/64	0.546875	13.8906	0.8	20.32
1/16	0.0625	1.5875	0.0004	0.01016	9/16	0.5625	14.2875	0.9	22.86
5/64	0.078125	1.9844	0.0005	0.01270	37/64	0.578125	14.6844	1	25.4
3/32	0.09375	2.3812	0.0006	0.01524	19/32	0.59375	15.0812	2	50.8
7/64	0.109375	2.7781	0.0007	0.01778	39/64	0.609375	15.4781	3	76.2
1/8	0.125	3.1750	0.0008	0.02032	5/8	0.625	15.8750	4	101.6
9/64	0.140625	3.5719	0.0009	0.02286	41/64	0.640625	16.2719	5	127.0
5/32	0.15625	3.9687	0.001	0.0254	21/32	0.65625	16.6687	6	152.4
11/64	0.171875	4.3656	0.002	0.0508	43/64	0.671875	17.0656	7	177.8
3/16	0.1875	4.7625	0.003	0.0762	11/16	0.6875	17.4625	8	203.2
13/64	0.203125	5.1594	0.004	0.1016	45/64	0.703125	17.8594	9	228.6
7/32	0.21875	5.5562	0.005	0.1270	23/32	0.71875	18.2562	10	254.0
15/64	0.234375	5.9531	0.006	0.1524	47/64	0.734375	18.6531	11	279.4
1/4	0.25	6.3500	0.007	0.1778	3/4	0.75	19.0500	12	304.8
17/64	0.265625	6.7469	0.008	0.2032	49/64	0.765625	19.4469	13	330.2
9/32	0.28125	7.1437	0.009	0.2286	25/32	0.78125	19.8437	14	355.6
19/64	0.296875	7.5406	0.01	0.254	51/64	0.796875	20.2406	15	381.0
5/16	0.3125	7.9375	0.02	0.508	13/16	0.8125	20.6375	16	406.4
21/64	0.328125	8.3344	0.03	0.762	53/64	0.828125	21.0344	17	431.8
11/32	0.34375	8.7312	0.04	1.016	27/32	0.84375	21.4312	18	457.2
23/64	0.359375	9.1281	0.05	1.270	55/64	0.859375	21.8281	19	482.6
3/8	0.375	9.5250	0.06	1.524	7/8	0.875	22.2250	20	508.0
25/64	0.390625	9.9219	0.07	1.778	57/64	0.890625	22.6219	21	533.4
13/32	0.40625	10.3187	0.08	2.032	29/32	0.90625	23.0187	22	558.8
27/64	0.421875	10.7156	0.09	2.286	59/64	0.921875	23.4156	23	584.2
7/16	0.4375	11.1125	0.1	2.54	15/16	0.9375	23.8125	24	609.6
29/64	0.453125	11.5094	0.2	5.08	61/64	0.953125	24.2094	25	635.0
15/32	0.46875	11.9062	0.3	7.62	31/32	0.96875	24.6062	26	660.4
31/64	0.484375	12.3031	0.4	10.16	63/64	0.984375	25.0031	27	690.6
1/2	0.5	12.7000	0.5	12.70					

ENGLISH TO METRIC CONVERSION: TORQUE

To convert foot-pounds (ft. lbs.) to Newton-meters: multiply the number of ft. lbs. by 1.3

To convert inch-pounds (in. lbs.) to Newton-meters: multiply the number of in. lbs. by .11

in lbs	N·m	in lbs	N·m	in lbs	N·m	in lbs	N·m	in lbs	N·m
0.1	0.01	1	0.11	10	1.13	19	2.15	28	3.16
0.2	0.02	2	0.23	11	1.24	20	2.26	29	3.28
0.3	0.03	3	0.34	12	1.36	21	2.37	30	3.39
0.4	0.04	4	0.45	13	1.47	22	2.49	31	3.50
0.5	0.06	5	0.56	14	1.58	23	2.60	32	3.62
0.6	0.07	6	0.68	15	1.70	24	2.71	33	3.73
0.7	0.08	7	0.78	16	1.81	25	2.82	34	3.84
0.8	0.09	8	0.90	17	1.92	26	2.94	35	3.95
0.9	0.10	9	1.02	18	2.03	27	3.05	36	4.0/

ENGLISH TO METRIC CONVERSION: TORQUE

Torque is now expressed as either foot-pounds (ft./lbs.) or inch-pounds (in./lbs.). The metric measurement unit for torque is the Newton-meter (Nm). This unit—the Nm—will be used for all SI metric torque references, both the present ft./lbs. and in./lbs.

ft lbs	N-m	ft lbs	N-m	ft lbs	N-m	ft lbs	N-m
0.1	0.1	33	44.7	74	100.3	115	155.9
0.2	0.3	34	46.1	75	101.7	116	157.3
0.3	0.4	35	47.4	76	103.0	117	158.6
0.4	0.5	36	48.8	77	104.4	118	160.0
0.5	0.7	37	50.7	78	105.8	119	161.3
0.6	0.8	38	51.5	79	107.1	120	162.7
0.7	1.0	39	52.9	80	108.5	121	164.0
0.8	1.1	40	54.2	81	109.8	122	165.4
0.9	1.2	41	55.6	82	111.2	123	166.8
1	1.3	42	56.9	83	112.5	124	168.1
2	2.7	43	58.3	84	113.9	125	169.5
3	4.1	44	59.7	85	115.2	126	170.8
4	5.4	45	61.0	86	116.6	127	172.2
5	6.8	46	62.4	87	118.0	128	173.5
6	8.1	47	63.7	88	119.3	129	174.9
7	9.5	48	65.1	89	120.7	130	176.2
8	10.8	49	66.4	90	122.0	131	177.6
9	12.2	50	67.8	91	123.4	132	179.0
10	13.6	51	69.2	92	124.7	133	180.3
11	14.9	52	70.5	93	126.1	134	181.7
12	16.3	53	71.9	94	127.4	135	183.0
13	17.6	54	73.2	95	128.8	136	184.4
14	18.9	55	74.6	96	130.2	137	185.7
15	20.3	56	75.9	97	131.5	138	187.1
16	21.7	57	77.3	98	132.9	139	188.5
17	23.0	58	78.6	99	134.2	140	189.8
18	24.4	59	80.0	100	135.6	141	191.2
19	25.8	60	81.4	101	136.9	142	192.5
20	27.1	61	82.7	102	138.3	143	193.9
21	28.5	62	84.1	103	139.6	144	195.2
22	29.8	63	85.4	104	141.0	145	196.6
23	31.2	64	86.8	105	142.4	146	198.0
24	32.5	65	88.1	106	143.7	147	199.3
25	33.9	66	89.5	107	145.1	148	200.7
26	35.2	67	90.8	108	146.4	149	202.0
27	36.6	68	92.2	109	147.8	150	203.4
28	38.0	69	93.6	110	149.1	151	204.7
29	39.3	70	94.9	111	150.5	152	206.1
30	40.7	71	96.3	112	151.8	153	207.4
31	42.0	72	97.6	113	153.2	154	208.8
32	43.4	73	99.0	114	154.6	155	210.2

ENGLISH TO METRIC CONVERSION: FORCE

Force is presently measured in pounds (lbs.). This type of measurement is used to measure spring pressure, specifically how many pounds it takes to compress a spring. Our present force unit (the pound) will be replaced in SI metric measurements by the Newton (N). This term will eventually see use in specifications for electric motor brush spring pressures, valve spring pressures, etc.

To convert pounds (lbs.) to Newton (N): multiply the number of lbs. by 4.45

lbs	N	lbs	N	lbs	N	oz	N
0.01	0.04	21	93.4	59	262.4	1	0.3
0.02	0.09	22	97.9	60	266.9	2	0.6
0.03	0.13	23	102.3	61	271.3	3	0.8
0.04	0.18	24	106.8	62	275.8	4	1.1
0.05	0.22	25	111.2	63	280.2	5	1.4
0.06	0.27	26	115.6	64	284.6	6	1.7
0.07	0.31	27	120.1	65	289.1	7	2.0
0.08	0.36	28	124.6	66	293.6	8	2.2
0.09	0.40	29	129.0	67	298.0	9	2.5
0.1	0.4	30	133.4	68	302.5	10	2.8
0.2	0.9	31	137.9	69	306.9	11	3.1
0.3	1.3	32	142.3	70	311.4	12	3.3
0.4	1.8	33	146.8	71	315.8	13	3.6
0.5	2.2	34	151.2	72	320.3	14	3.9
0.6	2.7	35	155.7	73	324.7	15	4.2
0.7	3.1	36	160.1	74	329.2	16	4.4
0.8	3.6	37	164.6	75	333.6	17	4.7
0.9	4.0	38	169.0	76	338.1	18	5.0
1	4.4	39	173.5	77	342.5	19	5.3
2	8.9	40	177.9	78	347.0	20	5.6
3	13.4	41	182.4	79	351.4	21	5.8
4	17.8	42	186.8	80	355.9	22	6.1
5	22.2	43	191.3	81	360.3	23	6.4
6	26.7	44	195.7	82	364.8	24	6.7
7	31.1	45	200.2	83	369.2	25	7.0
8	35.6	46	204.6	84	373.6	26	7.2
9	40.0	47	209.1	85	378.1	27	7.5
10	44.5	48	213.5	86	382.6	28	7.8
11	48.9	49	218.0	87	387.0	29	8.1
12	53.4	50	224.4	88	391.4	30	8.3
13	57.8	51	226.9	89	395.9	31	8.6
14	62.3	52	231.3	90	400.3	32	8.9
15	66.7	53	235.8	91	404.8	33	9.2
16	71.2	54	240.2	92	409.2	34	9.4
17	75.6	55	244.6	93	413.7	35	9.7
18	80.1	56	249.1	94	418.1	36	10.0
19	84.5	57	253.6	95	422.6	37	10.3
20	89.0	58	258.0	96	427.0	38	10.6

ENGLISH TO METRIC CONVERSION: PRESSURE

The basic unit of pressure measurement used today is expressed as pounds per square inch (psi). The metric unit for psi will be the kilopascal (kPa). This will apply to either fluid pressure or air pressure, and will be frequently seen in tire pressure readings, oil pressure specifications, fuel pump pressure, etc.

To convert pounds per square inch (psi) to kilopascals (kPa): multiply the number of psi by 6.89

Psi	kPa	Psi	kPa	Psi	kPa	Psi	kPa
0.1	0.7	37	255.1	82	565.4	127	875.6
0.2	1.4	38	262.0	83	572.3	128	882.5
0.3	2.1	39	268.9	84	579.2	129	889.4
0.4	2.8	40	275.8	85	586.0	130	896.3
0.5	3.4	41	282.7	86	592.9	131	903.2
0.6	4.1	42	289.6	87	599.8	132	910.1
0.7	4.8	43	296.5	88	606.7	133	917.0
0.8	5.5	44	303.4	89	613.6	134	923.9
0.9	6.2	45	310.3	90	620.5	135	930.8
1	6.9	46	317.2	91	627.4	136	937.7
2	13.8	47	324.0	92	634.3	137	944.6
3	20.7	48	331.0	93	641.2	138	951.5
4	27.6	49	337.8	94	648.1	139	958.4
5	34.5	50	344.7	95	655.0	140	965.2
6	41.4	51	351.6	96	661.9	141	972.2
7	48.3	52	358.5	97	668.8	142	979.0
8	55.2	53	365.4	98	675.7	143	985.9
9	62.1	54	372.3	99	682.6	144	992.8
10	69.0	55	379.2	100	689.5	145	999.7
11	75.8	56	386.1	101	696.4	146	1006.6
12	82.7	57	393.0	102	703.3	147	1013.5
13	89.6	58	399.9	103	710.2	148	1020.4
14	96.5	59	406.8	104	717.0	149	1027.3
15	103.4	60	413.7	105	723.9	150	1034.2
16	110.3	61	420.6	106	730.8	151	1041.1
17	117.2	62	427.5	107	737.7	152	1048.0
18	124.1	63	434.4	108	744.6	153	1054.9
19	131.0	64	441.3	109	751.5	154	1061.8
20	137.9	65	448.2	110	758.4	155	1068.7
21	144.8	66	455.0	111	765.3	156	1075.6
22	151.7	67	461.9	112	772.2	157	1082.5
23	158.6	68	468.8	113	779.1	158	1089.4
24	165.5	69	475.7	114	786.0	159	1096.3
25	172.4	70	482.6	115	792.9	160	1103.2
26	179.3	71	489.5	116	799.8	161	1110.0
27	186.2	72	496.4	117	806.7	162	1116.9
28	193.0	73	503.3	118	813.6	163	1123.8
29	200.0	74	510.2	119	820.5	164	1130.7
30	206.8	75	517.1	120	827.4	165	1137.6
31	213.7	76	524.0	121	834.3	166	1144.5
32	220.6	77	530.9	122	841.2	167	1151.4
33	227.5	78	537.8	123	848.0	168	1158.3
34	234.4	79	544.7	124	854.9	169	1165.2
35	241.3	80	551.6	125	861.8	170	1172.1
36	248.2	81	558.5	126	868.7	171	1179.0

ENGLISH TO METRIC CONVERSION: PRESSURE

The basic unit of pressure measurement used today is expressed as pounds per square inch (psi). The metric unit for psi will be the kilopascal (kPa). This will apply to either fluid pressure or air pressure, and will be frequently seen in tire pressure readings, oil pressure specifications, fuel pump pressure, etc.

To convert pounds per square inch (psi) to kilopascals (kPa): multiply the number of psi by 6.89

Psi	kPa	Psi	kPa	Psi	kPa	Psi	kPa
172	1185.9	216	1489.3	260	1792.6	304	2096.0
173	1192.8	217	1496.2	261	1799.5	305	2102.9
174	1199.7	218	1503.1	262	1806.4	306	2109.8
175	1206.6	219	1510.0	263	1813.3	307	2116.7
176	1213.5	220	1516.8	264	1820.2	308	2123.6
177	1220.4	221	1523.7	265	1827.1	309	2130.5
178	1227.3	222	1530.6	266	1834.0	310	2137.4
179	1234.2	223	1537.5	267	1840.9	311	2144.3
180	1241.0	224	1544.4	268	1847.8	312	2151.2
181	1247.9	225	1551.3	269	1854.7	313	2158.1
182	1254.8	226	1558.2	270	1861.6	314	2164.9
183	1261.7	227	1565.1	271	1868.5	315	2171.8
184	1268.6	228	1572.0	272	1875.4	316	2178.7
185	1275.5	229	1578.9	273	1882.3	317	2185.6
186	1282.4	230	1585.8	274	1889.2	318	2192.5
187	1289.3	231	1592.7	275	1896.1	319	2199.4
188	1296.2	232	1599.6	276	1903.0	320	2206.3
189	1303.1	233	1606.5	277	1909.8	321	2213.2
190	1310.0	234	1613.4	278	1916.7	322	2220.1
191	1316.9	235	1620.3	279	1923.6	323	2227.0
192	1323.8	236	1627.2	280	1930.5	324	2233.9
193	1330.7	237	1634.1	281	1937.4	325	2240.8
194	1337.6	238	1641.0	282	1944.3	326	2247.7
195	1344.5	239	1647.8	283	1951.2	327	2254.6
196	1351.4	240	1654.7	284	1958.1	328	2261.5
197	1358.3	241	1661.6	285	1965.0	329	2268.4
198	1365.2	242	1668.5	286	1971.9	330	2275.3
199	1372.0	243	1675.4	287	1978.8	331	2282.2
200	1378.9	244	1682.3	288	1985.7	332	2289.1
201	1385.8	245	1689.2	289	1992.6	333	2295.9
202	1392.7	246	1696.1	290	1999.5	334	2302.8
203	1399.6	247	1703.0	291	2006.4	335	2309.7
204	1406.5	248	1709.9	292	2013.3	336	2316.6
205	1413.4	249	1716.8	293	2020.2	337	2323.5
206	1420.3	250	1723.7	294	2027.1	338	2330.4
207	1427.2	251	1730.6	295	2034.0	339	2337.3
208	1434.1	252	1737.5	296	2040.8	240	2344.2
209	1441.0	253	1744.4	297	2047.7	341	2351.1
210	1447.9	254	1751.3	298	2054.6	342	2358.0
211	1454.8	255	1758.2	299	2061.5	343	2364.9
212	1461.7	256	1765.1	300	2068.4	344	2371.8
213	1468.7	257	1772.0	301	2075.3	345	2378.7
214	1475.5	258	1778.8	302	2082.2	346	2385.6
215	1482.4	259	1785.7	303	2089.1	347	2392.5

ENGLISH TO METRIC CONVERSION: LIQUID CAPACITY

Liquid or fluid capacity is presently expressed as pints, quarts or gallons, or a combination of all of these. In the metric system the liter (l) will become the basic unit. Fractions of a liter would be expressed as deciliters, centiliters, or most frequently (and commonly) as milliliters.

To convert pints (pts.) to liters (l): multiply the number of pints by .47
To convert liters (l) to pints (pts.): multiply the number of liters by 2.1
To convert quarts (qts.) to liters (l): multiply the number of quarts by .95

To convert liters (l) to quarts (qts.): multiply the number of liters by 1.06
To convert gallons (gals.) to liters (l): multiply the number of gallons by 3.8
To convert liters (l) to gallons (gals.): multiply the number of liters by .26

gals	liters	qts	liters	pts	liters
0.1	0.38	0.1	0.10	0.1	0.05
0.2	0.76	0.2	0.19	0.2	0.10
0.3	1.1	0.3	0.28	0.3	0.14
0.4	1.5	0.4	0.38	0.4	0.19
0.5	1.9	0.5	0.47	0.5	0.24
0.6	2.3	0.6	0.57	0.6	0.28
0.7	2.6	0.7	0.66	0.7	0.33
0.8	3.0	0.8	0.76	0.8	0.38
0.9	3.4	0.9	0.85	0.9	0.43
1	3.8	1	1.0	1	0.5
2	7.6	2	1.9	2	1.0
3	11.4	3	2.8	3	1.4
4	15.1	4	3.8	4	1.9
5	18.9	5	4.7	5	2.4
6	22.7	6	5.7	6	2.8
7	26.5	7	6.6	7	3.3
8	30.3	8	7.6	8	3.8
9	34.1	9	8.5	9	4.3
10	37.8	10	9.5	10	4.7
11	41.6	11	10.4	11	5.2
12	45.4	12	11.4	12	5.7
13	49.2	13	12.3	13	6.2
14	53.0	14	13.2	14	6.6
15	56.8	15	14.2	15	7.1
16	60.6	16	15.1	16	7.6
17	64.3	17	16.1	17	8.0
18	68.1	18	17.0	18	8.5
19	71.9	19	18.0	19	9.0
20	75.7	20	18.9	20	9.5
21	79.5	21	19.9	21	9.9
22	83.2	22	20.8	22	10.4
23	87.0	23	21.8	23	10.9
24	90.8	24	22.7	24	11.4
25	94.6	25	23.6	25	11.8
26	98.4	26	24.6	26	12.3
27	102.2	27	25.5	27	12.8
28	106.0	28	26.5	28	13.2
29	110.0	29	27.4	29	13.7
30	113.5	30	28.4	30	14.2